THE SHOW JUMPING ASSOCIATION BRITISH

AMATEUR GYMNASTIC ASSOCIATION

THE IRISH FOOTBALL ASSOCIATION LIMITED

AMATEUR SWIMMING ASSOCIATION

ROYAL YACHTING ASSOCIATION

WOMEN'S AMATEUR ROWING ASSOCI- ATION

ENGLISH TABLE TENNIS ASSOCIATION

THE FOOTBALL ASSOCIATION OF WALES LIMITED

ALL ENGLAND WOMEN'S HOCKEY ASSOCIATION

THE SQUASH RACKETS ASSOCI- ATION

NATIONAL ROLLER HOCKEY ASSOCIATION

GORAU·CHWARAE·CYD·CHWARAE

"LOOK FORWARD"
THE NATIONAL SMALL-BORE RIFLE ASSOCIATION

THE ROYAL AUTOMOBILE CLUB

THE BRITISH AMATEUR WRESTLING ASSOCIATION

AMATEUR BASKETBALL ASSOCIATION

NATIONAL RIFLE ASSOCIATION

BRITISH WATER SKI FEDERATION

THE GRAND NATIONAL ARCHERY SOCIETY

Encyclopædia of SPORT
Encyclopædia of SPORT
Encyclopædia of SPORT
Encyclopædia of SPORT
Encyclopædia of SPORT
Encyclopædia of SPORT
Encyclopædia of SPORT

Encyclo-paedia

of

SPORT

Edited by *Charles Harvey*

SAMPSON LOW, MARSTON AND CO. LTD.

CONT

Encyclopædia of

SPORT

SPORT

Golf

Encyclopædia of SPORT

Lawn Tennis

Compiled by

LANCE TINGAY

Lawn Tennis Correspondent of "The Daily Telegraph"

Motor Cycling

Compiled by

R. R. HOLLIDAY

Editor of "Motor Cycling"

Motor Racing

Compiled by

W. BODDY

Editor of "Motor Sport"

Netball

Compiled by

MISS E. L. SANDERS

Hon. Secretary of the All-England Netball Association

Olympic Games

Compiled by

NORRIS McWHIRTER

Athletics Correspondent of "The Star", "Observer" and B.B.C. Commentator

Pigeon Racing

Compiled by

S. W. E. BISHOP

Editor of "Pigeon Racing News"

Polo

Compiled by

BRIG. J. R. C. GANNON, C.B.E., M.V.O.

Hon. Secretary of the Hurlingham Polo Association

Rackets

Compiled by

CAPT. H. F. LAYMAN, D.S.O., R.N.

Hon. Treasurer Tennis and Rackets Association

Rifle Shooting

Compiled by

R. A. DALLEN

Chief Clerk to the National Rifle Association

Rifle Shooting, Small-Bore

Compiled by

A. J. PALMER

Secretary of The National Small-Bore Rifle Association

Roller Skating

Compiled by

HOWARD BASS

Editor of "Skater and Skier"

7

Table Tennis

Acknowledgments

Assistant Editors:

M. D. Dempsey, B.A., M. D. Carter, B.A., F. M. Hayes, C. M. Shanks, R. A. Orr, R. A. Wellings.

Caricatures by SPARK of the London "*Evening News*"

Jacket illustrated by W. H. Wiggins and C. Johnstone; colour badges by J. Lewsley and Edgar Sears.

Special thanks are due to the SPORT AND GENERAL PRESS AGENCY LTD., who kindly supplied many of the photographs reproduced in this book.

Badges and Crests of Football League Clubs

(A representative selection of famous Football League and Scottish League Clubs)

Aberdeen

Airdrieonians

Arbroath

Arsenal

Aston Villa

Barnsley

Berwick Rangers

Birmingham City

Blackburn Rovers
(Supporters Club)

Blackpool

Bolton Wanderers

Bournemouth and Boscombe

Bradford City

Bristol City

Bristol Rovers

Burnley

Bury

Cardiff City

Charlton Athletic

Chelsea

Coventry City

Crystal Palace

Derby County

Dumbarton

Dundee

Dundee United

Dumfermline Athletic

Everton

Falkirk

Fulham

Aldershot Town

Grimsby Town

Halifax Town

Hartlepools United

Heart of Midlothian

Huddersfield Town

Hull City

Ipswich Town

Kilmarnock

Leeds United

Leicester City

Leyton Orient

Lincoln City

Liverpool

Luton Town

Manchester City

Manchester United

Morton

Newcastle United

Norwich City

Notts County

Nottingham Forest

Partick Thistle

Plymouth Argyle

Portsmouth

Preston North End

Queen of the South

Rochdale

Rotherham United

St. Johnstone

Sheffield United

Sheffield Wednesday

Shrewsbury Town

Southampton

Southend United

Stockport County

Stoke City

Stranraer

Sunderland

Swansea Town

Third Lanark

T.U.A.F.C
Torquay United

Tottenham Hotspur

Tranmere Rovers

Watford

West Bromwich Albion

West Ham United

Wolverhampton Wanderers

Wrexham

The Badges of the County Cricket Clubs

Derbyshire

Essex

Glamorgan

Gloucestershire

Hampshire

Kent

Lancashire

Leicestershire

Middlesex

Northamptonshire

Nottinghamshire

Somerset

Surrey

Sussex

Warwickshire

Worcestershire

Yorkshire

Badges of Famous Rugby Union Clubs

Birkenhead Park

Swansea

Waterloo

Edinburgh Academical

Plymouth Albion

Bridgend

Blackheath

Leicester

London Scottish

Aldershot Services

Headingley

Glamorgan Wanderers

Bective Rangers

Aberavon

Stewart's College F.P.

Bridgwater & Albion

Northampton

Manchester

Coventry

Clontarf

London Irish

Saracens

Pontypridd

Camborne

Cardiff

Penzance & Newlyn

Garryowen

Hawick

Wasps

Barnstaple

Sale   London Welsh   Devonport Services   Edinburgh Wanderers   Somerset Constabulary

Old Millhillians   Gala   Wanderers   Newport   Newbridge Wanderers

Pontypool   Metropolitan Police   Richmond   St. Mary's Hospital   Neath

Burgees of Yacht Clubs

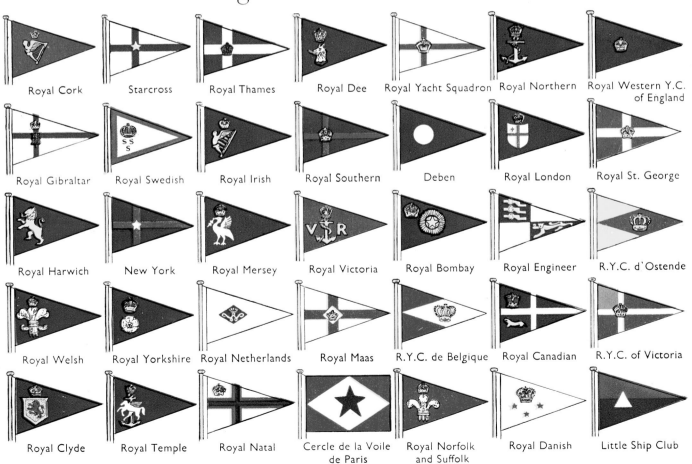

Royal Cork   Starcross   Royal Thames   Royal Dee   Royal Yacht Squadron   Royal Northern   Royal Western Y.C. of England

Royal Gibraltar   Royal Swedish   Royal Irish   Royal Southern   Deben   Royal London   Royal St. George

Royal Harwich   New York   Royal Mersey   Royal Victoria   Royal Bombay   Royal Engineer   R.Y.C. d'Ostende

Royal Welsh   Royal Yorkshire   Royal Netherlands   Royal Maas   R.Y.C. de Belgique   Royal Canadian   R.Y.C. of Victoria

Royal Clyde   Royal Temple   Royal Natal   Cercle de la Voile de Paris   Royal Norfolk and Suffolk   Royal Danish   Little Ship Club

Famous Rugby League Club Badges

Batley

Hunslet

Huddersfield

Hull Kingston Rovers

Salford

Leigh

Bramley

Castleford

Liverpool City

Keighley

Widnes

Featherstone Rovers

Hull

Rochdale Hornets

Wakefield Trinity

Warrington

Dewsbury

Amateur Boxing Club Badges

Manco

Fitzroy Lodge

Maple Leaf, Bootle

Southampton

West Ham

St. Mary's, Chatham

Norwich Lads' Club

Hove

Slough Centre

Golden Gloves

H.M.S. Ganges

Yeovil

Lynn

Woking

King's Lynn Friars

Cowes Medina

Vauxhall Motors

Badges of Famous Swimming, Diving and Water Polo Clubs

English Schools
Swimming Association

Metropolitan D.S.

Stockport S.C.

Otter S.C.

Wallasey S.C.

Motherwell S. and W.P.C.

Mermaid S.C.

Heston S.C.

Weston-super-Mare S.C.

York City S.C.

Polytechnic S. and W.P.C.

Birkenhead S.C.

Robert Gordon's College

Hampstead Ladies S.C.

Bradford Dolphin S.C.

South Manchester S.C.

Croydon Ladies S.C.

Hyde Seal S.C.

Coventry S.C.

Famous Speedway Club Badges

Oxford

Wimbledon

Poole

Norwich

Belle Vue

Coventry

Leicester

Swindon

Famous Athletic Club Badges

Belgrave H.

Tipton H.

Southgate H.

Salford H. and A.C.

Thames Valley H.

Oxford University A.C.

Finchley H.

Manchester A. and C.C.

Mitcham A.C.

Hermes C.

Hercules A.C.

Birchfield H.

Sparkhill H.

Sheffield United H. and A.C.

Small Heath H.

Liverpool H.

Polytechnic H.

Walton A.C.

Cambridge University A.C.

Herne Hill H.

Achilles Club

Ilford A.C.

Essex Beagles

Elswick H.

Ice Hockey Club Badges

Wembley Lions

Brighton Tigers

Nottingham Panthers

Paisley Pirates

Angling

Compiled by **Jack Thorndike**
Editor: Angling Times

FISHING IN ENGLAND AND WALES

Statutory close seasons for fishing in England and Wales are (all dates inclusive):

Salmon—November 1st to January 31st.

Trout—October 1st to last day of February.

Coarse fish—March 15th to June 15th.

In the case of salmon and trout, these vary tremendously, from River Board to River Board, and anglers are recommended to check with the Board concerned before fishing.

There are also variations in the coarse-fish close season, notably the Yorkshire Ouse area, in which it is from March 1st to May 31st, and the East Suffolk and Norfolk areas, in which there are breaks in the close season of four days at Easter and three days at Whitsun.

It should be noted that the possession of a River Board licence does not automatically entitle the holder to fish. It only entitles him to use a rod and line for the purpose of fishing in the area covered by the licence.

Although some waters are termed "free", and as such can be fished by an angler with only a River Board licence, most waters are owned by somebody, and permission must be obtained before fishing. Some associations and individuals owning water do allow visiting anglers to fish, either for nothing or on purchase of day, weekly or season tickets.

ENGLISH AND WELSH RIVER BOARDS
(As at 1st January, 1959)

Abbreviations: S.—Salmon. S.T.—Sea trout. T.—Trout. C.—Coarse fish. s.—Season. y.—Year. m.—Month. w.—Week. d.—Day. f.—Fortnight

The Avon and Dorset River Board:
Rostherne, 3, St. Stephen's Road, Bournemouth, Hampshire. *Clerk:* Mr. D. W. Treadgold. *Fisheries Officer:* Mr. J. Brayshaw. S., £3 s., £2 m., £1 w.; 7/6 d.; T., 15/- s., 7/6 m., 3/6 w.: C., 2/6 (no charge for juniors).

Bristol Avon River Board:
18, Bennett Street, Bath, Somerset. *Clerk:* Mr. G. M. Yates. *Fisheries Officer:* Mr. D. E. Tucker. S., 15/- s.; T., 3/6 s., 2/- m., 1/- d.; C., 1/- (6d. for juniors).

Cheshire River Board:
County Hall, Chester. *Clerk:* Mr. H. Carswell. *Fisheries Officer:* Mr. J. K. Willis. No licences required.

Cornwall River Board:
St. Johns, Western Road, Launceston, Cornwall. *Clerk:* Mr. R. G. Davey. *Pollution Officer:* Mr. W. Shaw. S., S.T. & T., £3 s., 30/- f., 10/- d.; T., 15/- s., 10/- f., 2/- d.

Cumberland River Board:
River Board House, London Road, Carlisle. Cumberland. *Clerk:* Mr. R. Birkett. *Pollution Officer:* Mr. A. J. Collins. Licence duties vary according to district.

Devon River Board:
The Castle, Exeter, Devon. *Clerk:* Mr. H. G. Godsall. *Fisheries Officer:* Mr. T. R. James. S. & T. Licence duties vary according to rivers. (Apply to Finance Officer, 3 Southernhay West, Exeter).

Dee and Clwyd River Board:
45, Nicholas Street, Chester. *Clerk:* Mr. G. A. Wright. *Fisheries Officer:* Mr. D. J. Iremonger. S. & T. Licence duties vary according to district.

East Suffolk and Norfolk River Board:
The Cedars, Albemarle Road, Norwich. *Clerk:* Mr. S. Vincent Ellis. *Fisheries Officer:* Mr. E. Quinton Bitton. S.T., £1 y.; C., 3/- y., 1/- d.; T., 6/- y.

East Sussex River Board:
1, Upper Lake, Battle, Sussex. *Clerk:* Mr. R. W. Fovargue. S. & S.T., 10/- s.; T., 5/- s.; C., 2/- s. (1/- for juniors).

[Angling Times

The Rev. E. C. Alston, who lives in Ireland, holder of the rudd record with a fish of 4 lb. 8 oz. (inset) captured in Norfolk in 1933

ANGLING QUIZ

1. Give another name for a ruffe.

★

2. Eels go where to spawn?

★

3. What angler, in the same year, and at the same place, caught two record fish—fish that still stand as records?

★

4. Name four tributaries of the Thames.

★

5. The adipose fin is only found on five fish common in Britain. What fish are they?

★

6. Tests carried out have shown that pike can move at a certain speed through water, although only in short bursts. What speed?

★

7. What is meant by "tailing a fish"?

★

8. Where are the Rivers Onny and Inny?

★

9. Which fish is sometimes called the "doctor fish" and why?

★

10. How many barbules has (a) a gudgeon, (b) a barbel, (c) a stone loach?

FRESHWATER FISH RECORDS

Recognised by the British Record (Rod-caught) Fish Committee. (As at 1st August, 1959)

Name of fish	lb.	oz.	dr.	
Barbel (*Barbus barbus*)	14	6	–	T. Wheeler, Thames, Molesey, 1888.
	14	6	–	H. D. Tryon, Hampshire Avon, 1934.
	14	6	–	F. W. Wallis, Hampshire Avon, 1937.
Bleak (*Alburnus alburnus*)		3	4	J. Oliver, Thames, Kingston, 1958.
Bream, common (*Abramis brama*)	13	8	–	E. G. Costin, Chiddingstone Castle Lake, 1945.
Bream, silver (*Blicca bjoernka*)	4	8	–	C. R. Rhind, Tortworth Lake, Gloucester, 1923.
Carp (*Cyprinus carpio*)	44	–	–	R. Walker, Redmire Pool, Herefordshire, 1952.
Chub (*Squalius cephalus*)	10	8	–	Dr. J. A. Cameron, River Annan, 1955.
Crucian carp (*Carassius carassius*)	4	11	–	H. C. Hinson, Broadwater Pond, Godalming, 1938
Dace (*Leuciscus leuciscus*)	1	8	5	R. W. Humphrey, Hampshire Avon Tributary, 1932.
Eel (*Anguilla anguilla*)	8	8	–	C. Mitchell, Bitteswell Lake, 1922.
Grayling (*Thymallus thymallus*)	7	2	–	J. Stewart, River Melgum, 1949.
Gudgeon (*Gobio gobio*)		4	4	G. Cedric, Thames, Datchet, 1933.
		4	4	W. R. Bostock, Hoggs Pond, Shipley, 1935.
		4	4	J. D. Lewtin, River Soar, 1950.
Perch (*Perca fluviatilis*)	5	15	6	P. Clark, Suffolk Stour, 1949.
Pike, English (*Esox lucius*)	37	8	–	C. Warwick, Hampshire Avon, 1944.
Pike, Scottish (*Esox lucius*)	47	11	–	T. Morgan, Loch Lomond, 1945.
Roach (*Rutilus rutilus*)	3	14	–	W. Penney, Lambeth Reservoir, Molesey, 1938.
Rudd (*Scardinius erythrophthalmus*)	4	8	–	Rev. E. C. Alston, Mere, near Thetford, Norfolk, 1933.
Sea trout (*Salmo trutta*)	22	8	–	S. R. Dwight, River Frome, 1946.
Salmon (*Salmo salar*)	64	–	–	Miss G. W. Ballantyne, River Tay, 1922.
Tench (*Tinca tinca*)	8	8	–	M. Foode, Leicester Canal, 1950.
Trout, rainbow (*Salmo irideus*)	8	8	–	Lt. Col. J. Creagh Scott, Blagdon, 1924.
Trout, brown (*Salmo trutta*)	OPEN			

English and Welsh River Boards — contd.

Essex River Board:
Rivers House, 129 Springfield Road, Chelmsford, Essex. *Clerk:* Mr. W. J. S. Bew. *Fisheries Officer:* Mr. H. Fish. S., T. & C., 5/- s.; C., 2/- s.

Glamorgan River Board:
"Tremains House", Coychurch Road, Bridgend, Glamorgan. *Clerk:* Mr. W. E. Wright. *Fisheries Officer:* Mr. A. H. Williams. S., S.T. & T., 7/6 s. (juniors, 3/6 s.); C., 2/6 s.

Great Ouse River Board:
Elmhurst, Brooklands Avenue, Cambridge. *Clerk:* Mr. K. M. Roddis. *Fisheries Officer:* Mr. N. Mackenzie. T. & C., 3/- y.

Gwynedd River Board:
Highfield, Caernarvon. *Clerk:* Mr. M. G. Crewe. *Fisheries Officer:* Mr. A. H. Jones. S. & T. Licence duties vary according to district. C. No licence required.

Hampshire River Board:
The Castle, Winchester, Hampshire. *Clerk:* Mr. G. A. Wheatley. *Fisheries Officer:* Mr. S. L. Wright. S., £3 s., £2 m., £1 w. (half price for certain rivers); T., 15/- s., 7/6 m., 3/- w.; C. No licence required.

Hull and East Yorkshire River Board:
37 North Bar Within, Beverley, Yorkshire. *Clerk:* Mr. G. Ellison. *Fisheries Officer:* Mr. J. H. Kirby. S. & S.T., 5/- y.; T. & C., 5/- y., 1/- w.; C., 2/- y.

Kent River Board:
River Board House, London Road, Maidstone. *Clerk:* Mr. A. G. Stirk. *Fisheries Officer:* Mr. W. F. Lester. T. & C., 7/6 s., 1/- d.; C., 3/- s. (1/- for juniors).

Lancashire River Board:
48 West Cliff, Preston, Lancashire. *Clerk:* Mr. H. Holmes. *Fisheries Officer:* Mr. L. Stewart, 18a, St. John Street, Lancaster. S. Licence duties according to district. S.T., 35/- s., 15/- w.; T., 15/- s., 5/- w.; C., 5/- s. (2/6 for juniors).

Lee Conservancy Catchment Board:
Brettenham House, Lancaster Place, Strand, London W.C.2. *Clerk:* Mr. J. L. Spiller. No licence required.

Lincolnshire River Board:
50 Wide Bargate, Boston, Lincolnshire. *Clerk:* Mr. G. E. Phillippo. *Fisheries Officer:* Mr. G. A. Farrow. S. & S.T., 10/- y.; T. & C., 6/- y., 3/- w.; C., 3/- y., 1/6 d. (no licence required for juniors).

Mersey River Board:
Liverpool Road, Great Sankey, Warrington, Lancashire. *Clerk:* Mr. A. H. Jolliffe. No licence required.

Nene River Board:
North Street, Oundle, Nr. Peterborough, Northamptonshire. *Clerk:* Mr. D. S. Akroyd. *Fisheries Officer:* Mr. R. G. Toms. T. & C., 5/- y., 1/6 w.

Northumberland and Tyneside River Board:
"Dunira", Osborne Road, Newcastle-upon-Tyne, 2. *Clerk:* Mr. N. H. Thomas. *Fisheries Officer:* Mr. G. Common. S. & S.T., £2 10s. 0d. (£1 10s. 0d. Tyne area) s., £1 w.; T., 10/- (juniors 5/-) s., 5/- w.; C. No licence required.

Severn River Board:
Portland House, Church Street, Great Malvern, Worcestershire. *Clerk:* Mr. J. V. Morley. *Fisheries Officer:* Mr. Llewellyn Jones. S. (for Vyrnwy, Banwy) £2 2s. 0d. s. Elsewhere £3 3s. 0d.; T. & C., 4/- s.

Somerset River Board:
The Watergate, West Quay, Bridgwater, Som. *Clerk:* Mr. T. J. M. Barrington. *Fisheries Officer:* Mr. L. Gill. T., 5/- s., 2/6 m. (juniors 3/6 s.); C., 2/- s., 1/- m. (juniors 6d. s.).

South West Wales River Board:
Penyfai House, Llanelly, Carmarthenshire. *Clerk:* Mr. E. A. Griffiths. S., £3 3s. 0d. s., £1 1s. 0d. w.; T. & S.T., £1 s., 7/6 w.; T., 10/- s.

Thames Conservancy:
2/3 Norfolk Street, Strand, London, W.C.2. *Secretary:* Mr. G. E. Walker. No licence required. Weir permits £1 per season.

Trent River Board:
P.O. Box No. 74, 206, Derby Road, Nottingham. *Clerk:* Mr. J. Hirst. *Fisheries Officer:* Mr. Inglis Spicer. S. & S.T., 10/- s.; T. & C., 1/6 s. (6d. Sat. to Tue.). (Juniors under 14 free.)

Usk River Board:
The Croft, Goldcroft Common, Caerleon, Mon. *Clerk:* Mr. W. J. R. Howells. *Fisheries Officer:* Mr. R. Haworth-Booth. S., £5 15s. 0d. s., £3 15s. 0d. June 1 to end of season, £2 m., £1 w.; T., 10/- s., 5/- w. Reservoirs, ponds and streams only 5/- s.

Wear and Tees River Board:
Greencroft East, 158 Coniscliffe Road, Darlington, Co. Durham. *Clerk:* Mr. J. A. Laven. *Fisheries Officer:* Mr. M. Gibson. S., £1 s.; T. & C., 5/- s., 1/- w. (juniors 2/6 s.).

Welland River Board:
11, Market Place, Spalding, Lincolnshire. *Clerk:* Mr. R. W. Hastings. *Fisheries Officer:* Mr. L. G. Wiles. T., 7/6 y.; C., 3/- y., 1/- d.

West Sussex River Board:
County Hall, Chichester, Sussex. *Clerk:* Mr. W. C. Hayward. No licence required.

Wye River Board:
Wilson's Chambers, Commercial Street, Hereford. *Fisheries Officer:* Mr. C. Milward. S., £5 s., £1 10s. w., 10/- d. (Wye above Llanwrthwl Bridge or tributary above Builth Bridge, £2. 10s. s.); T., 7/6 s., 2/6 w.; C., 3/6 s. (juniors 1/- s.).

Yorkshire Ouse River Board:
21 Park Square South, Leeds, 1. Yorkshire. *Clerk:* Mr. A. W. Wood. *Fisheries Officer:* Mr. M. L. Parry. S. & S.T., 5/- s. (Esk tributaries and waters to the north of Esk, £1 10s. s.); T., 2/6 s., 1/- w.; C., 1/- s.

ANGLING QUIZ

1. Give two alternative names for a Greater Spotted Dogfish.

*

2. At what stages is a salmon (*a*) a grilse, (*b*) a kelt, (*c*) a smolt.

*

3. Although basking shark are fairly common off our coast, they are never caught on rod and line. Why?

*

4. What is a burbot?

*

5. Where is Mousehole and what connection has it with angling?

*

6. What are the following: Lady of the Lake, Rolt's Witch, Tailey Tail?

*

7. What is an alevin?

*

8. How many species of wrasse are met with in British waters and name three?

*

9. In Wales sea trout are often called . . . ?

10. What did the record carp weigh?

QUIZ ANSWERS

1. Bull Huss, Nurse Hound. 2. (a) When it has returned to fresh water after spending ONE winter in the sea. (b) When it has spawned and is in the process of returning to the sea. (c) When it begins its first journey to the sea. 3. Because the basking shark lives on plankton, unlike any other shark, and will not therefore take an angler's bait. 4. A freshwater fish of the cod family, found only in certain rivers flowing into the North Sea. 5. Mousehole is a fishing station near Penzance, famous for mackerel and pollack fishing. 6. They are all artificial trout flies. 7. A fish of any species at the stage between hatching and consumption of its yolk-sac. 8. Seven. Ballan, Rainbow, Cuckoo, Corkwing, Gold-Sinny, Scale-Rayed, Rock Cook (or Small Mouth). 9. Sewin. 10. 44 lb. Captured by Richard Walker in 1952 from a lake in Herefordshire. It can be seen at the London Zoo.

[Angling Times
Bill Hughes, individual winner of the 1958 National Angling Championship

---

NATIONAL FEDERATION OF ANGLERS' CHAMPIONSHIP

A dash indicates that no record is available

Year	Place	Winners	No. of Teams	Weight lb.	oz.	dr.	Total Weight lb.	oz.	dr.
1906	Thames, Pangbourne	Boston Assn.	7	17	8	4	48	4	0
1907	Witham, Kirkstead	Sheffield Amal. A.A.	—	21	12	12			
1908	North Level Drain, Tydd	Sheffield & Dist. Assn	13	18	6	0	69	10	0
1909	The Dyke, Newark	Leeds Amal. A.A.	—	7	5	4			
1910	Derwent, Hutton's Ambo.	Leeds Amal. A.A.	—	5	8	12			
1911	Severn, Kempsey	Sheffield Amal. A.A.	19	53	6	0	355	10	4
1912	Great Ouse, Ely	Boston Assn.	25	9	0		—		
1913	Dee, Chester	Nottingham Assn.	22	2	15	0			
1914	Trent, Willington	Leeds Amal. A.A.	20	20	14	8	200	11	8
1915–18	No contests								
1919	Ancholme, Brigg	Boston Assn.	24	20	0	8	—		
1920	Weaver, Hartford	County Palatine	—	12	4	0	—		
1921	Trent, Burton Joyce	Derby Assn.	—	10	1	0	68	11	4
1922	Witham, Kirkstead	Lincoln Assn.	—	10	5	12	117	4	8
1923	Soar, Kegworth	County Palatine	—	18	11	0	280	0	12
1924	Glen, Pinchbeck	Castleford & D. Assn.	—	28	0	8	507	8	12
1925	Severn, Worcester	Long Eaton Federation	46	5	10	8	91	14	1
1926	Yorkshire Ouse, Naburn	Lincoln A.A.	—	23	11	9	371	10	10
1927	Middle Level Drain, King's Lynn	Grimsby & District	—	44	5	12	680	13	12
1928	Severn, Tewkesbury	Leeds & Dist. Amal.	44	13	2	13½	217	4	13½
1929	Witham, Kirkstead	Boston Assn.	44	50	4	0	591	9	12
1930	Soar, Kegworth	Sheffield Amal.	51	43	10	0	1,017	9	8
1931	South Forty Foot	Hull Amalgamated	48	27	9	8	521	9	8
1932	Soar, Kegworth	Loughboro Soar A.S.	47	24	15	0	698	8	12
1933	Great Ouse, Olney	Sheffield & Dist. A.A.	48	33	6	4	596	6	0
1934	Thames, Abingdon	Sheffield Amal. A.A.	54	14	3	11	280	7	4
1935	Witham, Kirkstead	Lincoln A.A.	50	43	13	2	898	6	13
1936	Thurne, Potter Heigham	Lincoln A.A.	53	74	5	15	1,564	9	14
1937	Gloucester Canal	Groves & Whitnall A.A.	56	23	15	6	464	9	6
1938	Great Ouse, Harrold	Hull & Dist. Amal. A.A.	62	38	12	7	758	0	9
1939–44	No contests								
1945	Trent, Newark	Worksop & Dist. A.A.	57	72	2	5	1,903	14	1
1946	Witham, Langrick	Hull & Dist. Amal. A.A.	66	57	0	12	1,956	3	0
1947	Witham, Kirkstead	Worksop & Dist. A.A.	70	57	8	4	1,706	11	12
1948	Huntspill, Somerset	Leeds Amal. A.A.	72	23	14	4	539	7	0
1949	Thurne, Potter Heigham	Leeds Amal. A.A.	77	49	3	4	1,684	6	8
1950	Nene, Peterborough	Peterborough A.A.	81	62	5	12	1,652	9	4
1951	Witham, Kirkstead	Doncaster & Dist. A.A.	82	63	5	0	1,637	4	2
1952	Severn, Bridgnorth	Leeds & Dist. A.S.A.	88	135	5	0	3,889	3	1
1953	Nene, Peterborough	Lincoln A.A.	92	72	5	0	2,358	11	1
1954	Trent, Gunthorpe	Hull A.P.S.	98	68	13	4	1,927	9	0
1955	Huntspill, Somerset	Sheffield Amal. A.A.	99	136	15	4	4,036	0	0
1956	Witham, Kirkstead	Coventry A.A.	94	84	4	4	2,255	10	0
1957	Severn, Bridgnorth	Nottingham A.A.	96	20	8	1	537	6	3
1958	Welland, Spalding	Coventry A.A.	98	59	15	4	1,105	0	0
1959	Nene, Peterborough	Bedford, A.C.	100	86	1	4	—		

N.F.A. INDIVIDUAL CHAMPIONS

Year	Name of Angler	Team	lb.	oz.	dr.
1906	F. Beales	Boston Association	4	11	0
1907	A. Croft	Sheffield A.A.A.	7	1	8
1908	J. Mason	Sheffield and District	12	2	0
1909	J. H. R. Bazley	Leeds A.A.A.	2	2	8
1910	A. Blackman	Hull Amalgamated	2	13	0
1911	W. Lowe	Sheffield A.A.A.	13	4	0
1912	G. Beales	Boston Association	6	11	12
1913	W. Gough	Nottingham Association	11	14	8
1914	A. Sharratt	Derby Association	6	15	12
1915–18	No contests				
1919	T. Hill	Derby Association	7	7	0
1920	R. Barlow	Hull Amalgamated	3	1	0
1921	J. Wakefield	Derby Association	6	2	12
1922	B. Hobday	Lincoln Association	3	5	8
1923	J. W. Couldwell	Sheffield A.A.A.	5	15	8
1924	W. T. Wilcocks	London A.A.	21	8	8
1925	G. Allen	Provincial A.A.	3	8	12
1926	A. Fletcher	Boston A.A.	7	1	0
1927	J. H. R. Bazley	Leeds A.A.A.	16	5	8
1928	W. Tetley	Leeds A.A.A.	3	13	3
1929	J. Sykes	Boston Association	10	15	0
1930	C. Muddimer	Leicester A.S.	15	6	0
1931	W. Daddy	Hull Amalgamated	18	9	8
1932	H. Sallis	Long Eaton	5	9	4
1933	E. Dabill	Sheffield A.A.	13	15	9
1934	H. Smith	Sheffield Amalgamated	4	14	4
1935	H. A. Kellett	Doncaster and District	18	6	15
1936	A. E. Bryant	Buckingham and District	35	1	0
1937	H. Jones	County Palatine A.A.	9	9	8
1938	G. Bright	Bristol and West of England A.A.	21	13	8
1939–44	No contests				
1945	M. T. Cotterell	Worksop and District	16	1	7
1946	G. Laybourne	York and District A.A.	12	12	8
1947	W. Edwards	Rotherham A.A.	9	4	8
1948	W. Thompson	Leeds A.A.A.	14	9	12
1949	R. Woodhall	Whitmore Reans C.A.A.	15	6	8
1950	W. Rockley	Peterborough A.A.	15	4	0
1951	S. Buxton	Doncaster and District	20	13	4
1952	H. Seed	Leeds and District A.S.A.	33	5	4
1953	N. Hazelwood	Cambridge Albion	27	14	0
1954	R. Lye	Notts. Federation	15	1	12
1955	J. Carr	Sheffield Amalgamated	68	2	4
1956	R. Lusby	Lincoln A.A.	25	8	0
1957	H. Storey	Nottingham A.A.	7	12	20
1958	W. Hughes	Northern A.A.	24	3	
1959	L. A. Sharp	Bedford A.C.	57	8	8

FISHING IN SCOTLAND

Rivers and lochs in Scotland, famous for their salmon and trout fishing, are not administered by River Boards as in England and Wales, although District Boards do exist for the administration and conservation of most salmon rivers. No licences are issued but permission to fish must be obtained from riparian owners.

A great deal of the salmon fishing is preserved, but many hotels do possess water for guests to fish. Trout fishing rights are frequently held by angling associations, from which visitors can obtain permits.

While Scotland is famed for its game fishing, there are facilities for coarse fishing in many parts of the country. There are many waters containing large numbers of pike, perch, grayling and chub.

The annual close season for trout in Scotland is from October 7th to March 14th, both dates inclusive. The close season for salmon varies widely from river to river, the closing date being as early as October 1st in some rivers and as late as December 1st in others. The opening date on some rivers is as early as January 10th and on other rivers as late as April 14th. Visiting anglers are advised to make local enquiries.

For further information on fishing in Scotland contact: *Scottish Tourist Board, 2 Rutland Place, West End, Edinburgh 1.*

[Angling Times

Bill Penny (*centre*), captor of the record roach of 3 lb. 14 oz. from Lambeth Reservoir in 1938, is seen in the company of two famous anglers and authors of angling books, Bernard Venables (*left*) and Richard Walker.

SEA FISH RECORDS

Recognised by the British Record (Rod-caught) Fish Committee. (As at 1st August, 1959.)

Name of fish	lb.	oz.	dr.	
Angler-fish (*Lophius piscatorius*)	61	8	–	R. Bishop, Isle of Wight, 1955.
Bass (*Morone labrax*)	18	2	–	F. C. Borley, Felixstowe Beach, 1943.
Bream, black (*Spondyliosoma cantharus*)	6	5	–	M. Browne, Menai Straits, 1935.
Bream, red (*Pagellus centrodontus*)	7	8	–	A. F. Bell, Fowey, 1925.
Brill (*Scophthalmus rhombus*)	16	–	–	C. H. Fisher, Isle of Man, 1950.
Bull huss (*Scyliorhinus stellaris*)	21	3	–	J. Holmes, Looe, 1955.
(Greater spotted dogfish, nurse hound)				
Coalfish (*Gadus virens*)	23	8	–	H. Millais, Land's End, 1921.
(Saithe)				
Cod (*Gadus callarias*)	32	–	–	S. G. Hook, Lowestoft, 1945.
Conger (*Conger conger*)	84	–	–	H. A. Kelly, Dungeness, 1933.
Dab (*Limanda limanda*)	2	9	8	M. L. Watts, Port Talbot, 1936.
Dogfish, lesser spotted (*Scyliorhinus caniculus*)	14	–	8	P. Tarrant, East Solent, 1955.
(Rough hound)			8	
Dogfish, spur (*Squalus acanthias*)	12	12	–	A. C. Helyer, Eastbourne, 1955.
Flounder (*Platichthys flesus*)	5	11	–	A. G. L. Cobbledick, Fowey, 1956.
Garfish (*Belone belone*)	2	9	4	F. T. Goffir, Coverack, 1935.
Gurnard (*Trigla lucerna*)	11	7	–	C. W. King, Wallasey, 1952.
(Tubfish, yellow gurnard)				
Haddock (*Gadus aeglifinus*)	7	10	8	J. G. Mackay, Belfast Lough, 1957.
Hake (*Merluccius merluccius*)	17	8	–	Mrs. J. T. Ashby, Penzance, 1911.
John Dory (*Zeus faber*)	8	8	–	J. F. Vallin, Mevagissey, 1922.
Ling (*Molva molva*)	45	–	–	H. C. Nicholl, Penzance, 1912.
Mackerel (*Scomber scombrus*)	4	–	8	Flt.-Lt. P. Porter, Isle of Man, 1952.
Monkfish (*Squatina squatina*)	62	–	–	S. Morris, Littlehampton, 1919.
Mullet, grey (*Mugil chelo*)	10	1	–	P.O. P. C. Libby, Portland, 1952.
Plaice (*Pleuronectes platessa*)	7	5	6	C. H. Riggs, Teign Estuary, 1949.
Pollack (*Gadus pollachius*)	23	8	–	G. Bartholomew, Newquay, 1957.
Pouting (*Gadus luscus*)	4	10	–	H. B. Dare, Coverack, 1935.
Ray, blonde (*Raia brachyura*)	27	13	–	W. Bellamy, Dartmouth, 1958.
Ray, thornback (*Raia clavata*)	38	–	–	J. Patterson, Rustington, 1935.
Rockling, three-bearded (*Onos tricirratus*)	2	–	–	E. Curl, Dartmouth, 1959.
Scad (*Trachurus trachurus*)	3	3	–	J. B. Thornton, Deal, 1934.
Shad, thwaite (*Alosa finta*)	3	2	–	T. Hayward, Deal, 1949.
	3	2	–	S. Jenkins, Torbay, 1954.
Shark, blue (*Carcharinus glaucus*)	180	–	–	H. Whiddett, Looe, 1955.
Shark, mako (*Isurus oxyrhinchus*)	352	–	–	Mrs. H. Eathorne, Looe, 1955.
Shark, porbeagle (*Lamna cornubica*)	271	–	–	Mrs. H. Eathorne, Looe, 1957.
Shark, thresher (*Alopias vulpes*)	280	–	–	H. A. Kelly, Dungeness, 1933.
Skate, common (*Raia batis*)	200	–	–	A. H. Bowker, Isle of Man, 1925.
Sole (*Solea solea*)	4	–	–	M. Stinton, Clevedon Pier, 1943.
Sting-ray (*Trygon pastinaca*)	59	–	–	J. M. Buckley, Clacton, 1952.
Tope (*Eugaleus galeus*) Female	73	3	–	L. Andrews, Hayling Island, 1949.
Tunny (*Thurnus thynnus*)	851	–	–	L. Mitchell Henry, Whitby, 1933.
Turbot (*Scophthalmus maximus*)	27	14	–	F. S. Stenning, Salcombe, 1907.
Weaver, greater (*Trachinus draco*)	2	4	–	P. Ainslie, Brighton, 1927.
Whiting (*Gadus merlangus*)	6	–	–	E. H. Tame, Loch Shieldaig, 1940.
Wrasse, ballan (*Labrus bergylta*)	12	12	–	F. A. Mitchell-Hedges, Looe, 1912.

ANGLING QUIZ

1. Is a skate a flat fish?

★

2. Name three predatory coarse fish.

★

3. What is a Brown Turkey?

★

4. On what rivers do the following towns stand: (a) Sheffield, (b) Lincoln, (c) Peterborough, (d) Salisbury?

★

5. Name two fish that are barred from weighing-in under National Angling Championship rules.

★

6. What is a zander?

★

7. What do these initials stand for—A.C.A., N.F.A., N.F.S.A. and B.C.A.?

★

8. On which of the following rivers would you not need a River Board fishing licence: Severn, Great Ouse, Thames, Trent and Mersey?

★

9. Where is the caudal fin on a fish?

★

10. In what counties do the following rivers rise: (a) Thames, (b) Severn, (c) Welland, (d) Trent?

QUIZ ANSWERS

1. No, a skate is classified as a round fish. 2. Pike, perch, eel. 3. A salmon fly. 4. (a) Don, (b) Witham, (c) Nene, (d) Avon. 5. Eels, salmon, sea trout and trout. 6. A zander, otherwise known as a pike-perch, was at first thought to be a hybrid—a cross between a pike and perch. It is in fact a separate species and is found in only a few waters in Great Britain, having been introduced from Europe. 7. Anglers' Co-operative Association, National Federation of Anglers, National Federation of Sea Anglers, British Casting Association. 8. The Thames and Mersey. 9. The caudal fin is the tail fin. 10. (a) Gloucestershire, (b) Montgomeryshire, (c) Northamptonshire, (d) Staffordshire.

FISHING IN EIRE

No licences are needed to fish for brown trout or coarse fish in the Irish Republic; and while there is no coarse fish close season, brown-trout fishing is prohibited before February 15th.

There are seventeen Boards of Fishery Conservators, which between them are responsible for the administration and conservation of fishing in 23 districts.

Salmon and sea-trout licences are issued by these Boards at £3 a district. For each additional district the angler wishes to fish after purchasing his licence, a further 10s. is charged.

Angling has now become one of Ireland's foremost tourist attractions, and within recent years great progress has been made in opening up new waters—particularly for the trout and coarse fishermen. Sea fishing, too, has been "discovered", and on the south and west coasts, particularly, many new centres have been developed.

Further information can be obtained from the *Irish Tourist Board, 71 Regent Street, London, W.1.*

FISHING IN NORTHERN IRELAND

Northern Ireland, like the Republic of Ireland, is becoming a popular angling holiday centre, and, as in the Republic, there are no licences issued for coarse fishing, and there is no close season for coarse fish.

Brown-trout licences cost 10s. a season, and combined salmon and sea-trout licences 30s. This applies in all areas except the Foyle Fisheries District, where salmon licences cost £2. The close seasons for salmon, sea trout and brown trout vary considerably throughout the four Fishery Districts into which Ulster is split for the purpose of administration.

Sea fishing is popular off the Northern Irish coast. This and the fine coarse fishing annually attract many angling visitors.

For further information write: *Northern Ireland Tourist Board, 10 Royal Avenue, Belfast.*

Archery

Compiled by: **C. B. Edwards**

Secretary: The Grand National Archery Society

ARCHERY QUIZ

1. Why is Roger Ascham sometimes called the Father of Modern Archery?

★

2. What connection has the phrase "play fast and loose" with archery?

★

3. Who has won most world archery titles?

★

4. What is the world record Flight Shot?

★

5. What is a "fistmele"?

★

6. What is a "crysal"?

QUIZ ANSWERS

1. Roger Ascham, sometime tutor to Edward VI and Elizabeth I, in his book *Toxophilus*, 1544, wrote—"Standing, nocking, drawing, holding, loosing, done as they should be done, make fair shooting." These five points as taught by him are still the foundation of good style in shooting. 2. Henry VIII, when granting a charter to the Honourable Artillery Company in 1537, ordained that a member would not be held responsible for shooting anyone accidentally during practice provided he called out "faste" before shooting. One who loosed his arrow too quickly after giving the warning was an unreliable fellow said to play fast and loose. Nowadays, a cry of "fast" instantly stops all shooting. 3. Mde. Kurkowska (Poland): 1933, '34, '36, '39, and '47. Hans Deutgen (Sweden): 1947, '48, '49, and '50. 4. In 1798 at Constantinople the Sultan Selim is reported to have shot an arrow 972 yards, the distance being measured in the presence of the British Ambassador. The modern world record was set up in 1958 by Norman Richards (U.S.A.) at 842 yds. 1 ft. 6 in. 5. The breadth of fist and extended thumb, used by an archer to check bracing height (distance between bow and string). 6. A transverse crack in the belly of a wooden bow, due to the fibres being constantly compressed.

ARCHERY

The governing body for the sport in the United Kingdom is the Grand National Archery Society, which, in 1861, grew out of a self-elected committee, which, in turn, had originated at a gathering of archers at York in 1844 to organise the first Grand National Archery Meeting. In the first instance the Society was, however, concerned with little more than the drawing up of rules for and the holding of an annual Championship Meeting. Other societies of a regional character were formed from time to time to organise Championship Meetings for their own areas: the Leamington & Midland Counties Meeting in 1854; the Grand Western Archery Society in 1861; the Northern Counties Archery Meeting in 1880; and in 1903 the Southern Counties Archery Meeting, which took the place of an open tournament which had been held at the Crystal Palace annually since 1859.

In 1950, with the mutual consent and co-operation of the existing regional bodies, the G.N.A.S. was officially constituted as the national governing body to which clubs are affiliated through their respective Regional Societies. Four new Regional Societies were formed [to cover the rest of the United Kingdom, with the exception of Scotland where the Scottish Archery Association has remained an independent body. The Regional Societies are self-governing in all local affairs and have the power to form County Associations in their respective areas.

The executive body of the G.N.A.S. is the National Council, consisting of a President and four Vice-Presidents elected by a General Meeting of the Society, one member appointed by the Royal Toxophilite Society, and two members from and appointed by each of the eight Regional Societies, together with up to four members who may be co-opted by the Council itself.

The success of the Society's efforts under its new constitution may be measured by the fact that the number of associated clubs grew from 85 in 1950 to 547 in 1958.

Under the Society's classification scheme all members are eligible to classify as Master Bowmen, to whom a special badge is presented, or as Class I, II, or III Archers. There is also an extremely comprehensive handicapping system, by which every archer can measure his or her progress, and which can even be used to make competition between the sexes reasonably fair. At major tournaments, besides the open prizes, there are often additional prizes for handicapped scores or for archers of the same class or handicap group. The Society will also loan to an associated club one of its Handicap Improvement Challenge Medals to be held for one year by the club's member achieving the greatest improvement in his or her handicap figure during the previous season, but perhaps the most coveted award is the Six-Gold Badge given by the Society for a "perfect end" of six arrows in the Gold.

Enquiries for the location of Archery Clubs may be addressed to the appropriate Regional Society:

Grand Western Archery Society
(*Gloucester to Cornwall*)
Capt. (S) L. J. Graham, R.N.,
Bryants, West Hatch,
Taunton.

Northern Counties Archery Society
(*Cheshire northwards*)
Mr. F. Wells,
Highland Manor, Scotland Lane,
Horsforth,
Yorks.

Southern Counties Archery Society
(All S.E. England including Norfolk Oxon, Hants)
Mr. A. R. Harvey,
Silvertrees, Knowle Grove,
Virginia Water, Surrey.

East Midlands Archery Society
(*Derby, Lincs, Northants etc.*)
Mr. P. Bush,
65 Wilford Road,
Nottingham.

West Midlands Archery Association
Mrs. V. L. Almond,
24 Prospect Road, Moseley,
Birmingham 13.

North Wales Archery Society
Mr. J. W. Till,
Silverdale, Aston Hill,
Hawarden, nr. Chester.

South Wales Archery Association
Mr. D. Whiteman,
5 Tudor Road,
Newport, Mon.

Ulster Archery Association
Mr. W. G. Greenlees,
17 Prospect Street,
Belfast.

Scottish Archery Association (*not affiliated to G.N.A.S.*)
Mr. R. Pollock McKell,
41 Hunter Crescent, Troon,
Ayrshire.

THE GRAND NATIONAL ARCHERY MEETING, 1958

The Grand National Archery Meeting in 1958, or, to give the tournament its full title, the 105th Meeting of the Archers of the United Kingdom, was held in the grounds of Worcester College, Oxford, on July 2nd and 3rd.

Ladies

		Hits	Score	Golds
1st Score	Mrs. J. C. Reynolds (*Rosyth*)	279	1,641	43
2nd Score	Miss J. E. Heywood (*Bolton*)	276	1,636	51
3rd Score	Mrs. R. Tems (*Leicester*)	274	1,616	49

Gentlemen

		Hits	Score	Golds
1st Score	Mr. R. D. Matthews (*Leamington*)	287	1,933	77
2nd Score	Mr. R. W. Goghan (*Ruislip*)	275	1,561	39
3rd Score	Mr. D. J. Dalton (*Kidderminster*)	270	1,544	42

County Teams (four archers)

Ladies: Lancashire 6,053, Warwickshire 5,922, Berkshire 5,648.
Gentlemen: Warwickshire 6,039, Lancashire 5,482, Hampshire 5,076.

Ladies shot two Hereford Rounds each consisting of six dozen arrows at 80 yards, four dozen at 60 yards and two dozen at 50 yards. Gentlemen shot two York Rounds each consisting of six dozen arrows at 100 yards, four dozen at 80 yards, and two dozen at 60 yards.

The York Round, so-named after the first meeting at York in 1844, comprises the same distances as those set up by George Prince of Wales in 1792 for shooting by the Toxophilite Society of which he was patron. However, the targets used for the "Prince's Distances" were 4 feet in diameter at 100 yards, 3 feet at 80 yards, and 2 feet at 60 yards, whereas for the York Round, and all other rounds, the 4-foot target is used throughout. The target is divided into five rings of equal width—Gold, at the centre, scoring 9 points, Red 7, Blue 5, Black 3, and White 1 point. The Hereford Round was instituted in 1894 at a tournament for ladies only, held at Hereford.]

20

NATIONAL CHAMPIONS SINCE 1844

In the following list of National Champions, the ladies shot various rounds until 1851, when four dozen at 60 yards and two dozen at 50 yards were shot each day. This round became known as the National Round and was used every year until 1947, after which the Hereford Round was adopted. Up to 1948 all shooting was in two directions with targets at each end of the ground, three arrows being shot in turn from each end. From 1949 all shooting has been with six arrows in one direction only. At the first meeting a single round only was shot, but on all other occasions a Double Round.

		Lady		Gentleman	
1844	York	(none)		Rev. J. Higginson	221
1845	York	Miss Thelwall	186	Mr. P. Muir	537
1846	York	(none)		Mr. Hubback	519
1847	Derby	Miss Wylde	245	Mr. P. Muir	631
1848	Derby	Miss J. Barrow	167	Mr. E. Maitland	581
1849	Derby	Miss Temple	189	Mr. H. A. Ford	702
1850	Edinburgh	Mrs. Calvert	161	Mr. H. A. Ford	899
1851	Leamington	Miss Villiers	504	Mr. H. A. Ford	861
1852	Leamington	Miss Brindley	336	Mr. H. A. Ford	788
1853	Leamington	Mrs. Horniblow	365	Mr. H. A. Ford	934
1854	Shrewsbury	Mrs. Davison	489	Mr. H. A. Ford	1,074
1855	Shrewsbury	Mrs. Davison	491	Mr. H. A. Ford	809
1856	Cheltenham	Mrs. Horniblow	487	Mr. H. A. Ford	985
1857	Cheltenham	Miss H. Chetwynd	636	Mr. H. A. Ford	1,251

This score by Horace Ford has stood ever since as the British record for a Double York Round shot in two directions at any Open Meeting. It should be noted also that it was shot with a traditional long-bow and wooden arrows.

		Lady		Gentleman	
1858	Exeter	Mrs. Horniblow	457	Mr. H. A. Ford	1,076
1859	Exeter	Miss Turner	630	Mr. H. A. Ford	951
1860	Bath	Mrs. E. Lister	550	Mr. G. Edwards	886
1861	Liverpool	Mrs. Atkinson	575	Mr. G. Edwards	745
1862	Worcester	Mrs. Horniblow	660	Mr. G. Edwards	902
1863	Oxford	Mrs. Horniblow	478	Mr. P. Muir	845
1864	Alexandra Palace	Miss Betham	693	Mr. G. Edwards	897
1865	Clifton	Miss Betham	606	Mr. E. A. Holmes	788
1866	Norwich	Miss Betham	662	Mr. G. Edwards	900
1867	Brighton	Mrs. E. Lister	696	Mr. H. A. Ford	1,037
1868	Hereford	Miss Betham	672	Mr. W. Rimington	807
1869	Birmingham	Mrs. Horniblow	629	Mr. W. Rimington	909
1870	Bath	Mrs. Horniblow	700	Mr. E. A. Holmes	807
1871	Cheltenham	Mrs. Horniblow	746	Capt. C. H. Fisher	955
1872	Cheltenham	Mrs. Horniblow	660	Capt. C. H. Fisher	771
1873	Leamington	Mrs. Horniblow	764	Major C. H. Fisher	898
1874	Winchester	Mrs. Pond	644	Major C. H. Fisher	873
1875	Richmond	Miss Hollins	693	Mr. G. E. S. Fryer	876
1876	Sandown Park	Mrs. W. Butt	752	Mr. H. H. Palairet	773
1877	Doncaster	Mrs. W. Butt	676	Mr. W. Rimington	703
1878	Tunbridge Wells	Mrs. Marshall	693	Mr. H. H. Palairet	932
1879	Cheltenham	Mrs. Marshall	708	Mr. R. Walters	729
1880	Shrewsbury	Mrs. Horniblow	593	Mr. H. H. Palairet	897
1881	Sutton Coldfield	Miss Legh	763	Mr. H. H. Palairet	849
1882	Leamington	Mrs. Piers Legh	750	Mr. H. H. Palairet	885
1883	Cheltenham	Mrs. Piers Legh	712	Mr. H. H. Palairet	869
1884	Windsor	Mrs. Piers Legh	701	Mr. C. E. Nesham	902
1885	Malvern	Mrs. Piers Legh	749	Mr. C. E. Nesham	917
1886	Bath	Miss Legh	726	Mr. C. E. Nesham	1,022
1887	Cheltenham	Miss Legh	773	Major C. H. Fisher	849
1888	York	Miss Legh	732	Mr. C. E. Nesham	820
1889	Oxford	Miss Legh	690	Mr. Gregson	832
1890	Southampton	Miss Legh	798	Mr. C. E. Nesham	921
1891	Worcester	Miss Legh	798	Mr. F. L. Govett	818
1892	Eastbourne	Miss Legh	804	Mr. G. E. S. Fryer	850
1893	York	Mrs. C. Bowly	779	Mr. Gregson	656
1894	Cheltenham	Mrs. C. Bowly	823	Mr. Eyre Hussey	787
1895	Hurlingham	Miss Legh	790	Mr. G. E. S. Fryer	872
1896	Bournemouth	Miss B. Oakeley	559	Mr. G. E. S. Fryer	815
1897	Malvern	Mrs. C. Bowly	711	Mr. G. E. S. Fryer	719
1898	Oxford	Miss Legh	825	Mr. Perry Keene	868
1899	Brighton	Miss Legh	767	Mr. Eyre Hussey	848
1900	Edgbaston	Miss Legh	658	Mr. R. Brooks-King	804
1901	Cheltenham	Mrs. C. Bowley	645	Mr. Eyre Hussey	758
1902	Clifton	Miss Legh	813	Mr. R. Brooks-King	767
1903	Edinburgh	Miss Legh	802	Mr. R. Brooks-King	767
1904	Malvern	Miss Legh	841	Mr. J. Penrose	814
1905	Southampton	Miss Legh	807	Mr. J. H. Bridges	838
1906	Oxford	Miss Legh	779	Mr. R. Brooks-King	779
1907	York	Miss Legh	809	Mr. H. P. Nesham	865
1908	Oxford	Miss Legh	798	Mr. R. Brooks-King	870
1909	Malvern	Miss Legh	789	Mr. W. Dod	891
1910	Clifton	Mrs. Wadsworth	753	Mr. R. Brooks-King	889
1911	Brighton	Miss Q. Newall	803	Mr. W. Dod	885
1912	Cheltenham	Miss Q. Newall	716	Mr. R. Brooks-King	829
1913	Edgbaston	Miss Legh	703	Mr. R. Brooks-King	857
1914	Cambridge	Mrs. S. H. Armitage	723	Mr. H. P. Nesham	787
1919	Malvern	Miss Hyde	579	Mr. T. H. L. Sainsbury	636
1920	Bath	Mrs. R. Sandford	697	Mr. C. K. Philips	809
1921	Cheltenham	Mrs. R. Sandford	607	Mr. W. Andrew	614
1922	Oxford	Miss Legh	584	Maj. G. A. E. Chapman	738
1923	Cambridge	Mrs. Bodham-Whetham	523	Mr. R. Brooks-King	688
1924	Oxford	Mrs. Shillito	580	Mr. W. Andrew	880
1925	Oxford	Miss N. E. Wallace	615	Maj. J. J. B. Farley	717
1926	Oxford	Miss N. E. Wallace	717	Mr. H. A. Cox	783
1927	Oxford	Miss V. M. Rushton	749	Mr. H. A. Cox	873
1928	Oxford	Mrs. Atkinson	683	Mr. H. A. Cox	810
1929	Oxford	Miss V. M. Rushton	747	Mr. H. A. Cox	728
1930	Oxford	Mrs. R. Sandford	727	Maj. F. S. Williams-Thomas	721
1931	Oxford	Mrs. Atkinson	664	Maj. F. S. Williams-Thomas	977
1932	Oxford	Mrs. R. Sandford	663	Maj. F. S. Williams-Thomas	782
1933	Oxford	Mrs. C. W. Nettleton	638	Maj. F. S. Williams-Thomas	922
1934	Oxford	Miss V. M. Rushton	666	Mr. J. H. Davey	885
1935	Oxford	Mrs. Atkinson	647	Mr. H. A. Cox	812
1936	Oxford	Miss Browett	624	Mr. J. H. Davey	927

Until about this date long-bows, mainly of yew, and wooden arrows had been exclusively used, but from then onwards steel bows, and also, after about 1946, composite bows constructed of various laminations of woods, "plastics", and fibre-glass, began to come into use together with metal arrows, generally of aluminium alloy.

1937	Oxford	Mrs. Bates	705	Gp. Capt. A. Shekleton	991
1938	Oxford	Mrs. Lindner	644	Rev. D. Lloyd Wilson	1,030
1939	Oxford	Mrs. C. W. Nettleton	666	Capt. A. H. Mole	1,234
1946	Oxford	Mrs. Macquoid	625	Mr. C. B. Edwards	1,006
1947	Oxford	Mrs. de Wharton Burr	1,277	Mr. C. Downing	1,124
1948	Oxford	Mrs. de Wharton Burr	1,169	Mr. F. L. Bilson	1,143
1949	Oxford	Miss B. J. Waterhouse	1,454	Mr. H. A. Hooker	1,299
1950	Oxford	Mrs. G. Arthur	1,236	Mr. R. J. Beal	1,376
1951	Oxford	Mrs. M. Felix	1,182	Mr. J. B. Arch	1,360
1952	Oxford	Mrs. T. C. Morgan	1,428	Mr. W. Bickerstaff	1,322
1953	Oxford (100th)	Miss A. B. Dennett	1,357	Mr. T. C. Morgan	1,586
1954	Oxford	Mrs. J. K. Flower	1,564	Mr. J. B. Collyer	1,677
1955	Oxford	Mrs. J. K. Flower	1,653	Mr. H. A. Oram	1,426
1956	Oxford	Miss J. Warner	1,698	Mr. G. Brown	1,532
1957	Oxford	Mrs. J. K. Flower	1,641	Mr. R. D. Matthews	1,633
1958	Oxford	Mrs. J. C. Reynolds	1,641	Mr. R. D. Matthews	1,933
1959	Oxford	Mrs. L. Fowler	1,745	Mr. R. Hall	1,731

ARCHERY QUIZ

1. When was the bow last used in battle on British soil?

★

2. What is the origin of the phrase "to keep tabs on" a thing, meaning to keep an eye on it?

★

3. What were Finsbury Fields?

★

4. How many archers were there at the battle of Crecy in 1346?

R. D. Matthews

QUIZ ANSWERS

1. Probably in a clan battle, Macintosh versus Macdonald, in 1688, but certainly in some battles of the Civil War around 1644. 2. A "tab" of tough leather is worn as protection on the fingers drawing the string. An archer with his tab on is alert and ready to shoot. 3. The practice grounds of the H.A.C. and other bodies for several centuries until 1791, stretching, when in full use, roughly from Moorgate to Highbury and containing nearly 200 marks for shooting at rovers. One of the marks is preserved by the H.A.C. at Armoury House. 4. 5,200 archers with 2,300 men-at-arms, faced the French army of 120,000, including 15,000 Genoese crossbowmen.

BRITISH NATIONAL RECORDS

Records are recognised only in respect of scores made at meetings organised by the G.N.A.S. or a Regional Society, or at certain County and Club Open Meetings approved by the National Council.

Ladies

Hereford Round (72 arrows at 80 yards, 48 at 60, 24 at 50)
Single	1956	Miss J. Warner	942
Double	1956	Miss J. Warner	1,817

Albion Round (36 arrows each at 80, 60, and 50 yards)
Single	1957	Mrs. W. J. E. Miles	722

Long Western (48 arrows each at 80 and 60 yards)
Single	1959	Mrs. J. F. Lyne	580

Western (48 arrows each at 60 and 50 yards)
Single	1955	Mrs. B. S. Douthwaite	665

FITA Round (Fédération Internationale de Tir à l'Arc)
(36 arrows each at 70 and 60 metres. 4-foot target. 36 arrows each at 50 and 30 metres. 80 cm. target. 10-zone targets, scoring 1 to 10.)
Single	1956	Miss J. Warner	992
Double	1956	Miss J. Warner	1,945

Gentlemen

York Round (72 arrows at 100 yards, 48 at 80, 24 at 60)
Single	1958	Mr. R. D. Matthews	991
Double	1958	Mr. R. D. Matthews	1,933

Hereford Round (as ladies)
Single	1956	Mr. G. Brown	927

St. George's Round (36 arrows each at 100, 80, and 60 yards)
Single	1956	Mr. R. F. Laker	638

Albion Round (as ladies)
Single	1954	Mr. J. B. Collyer	813

Long Western (as ladies)
Single	1958	Mr. R. D. Matthews	690

Western Round (as ladies)
Single	1958	Mr. R. P. Bishop	740

FITA Round (36 arrows each at 90, 70, 50, and 30 metres. Targets as for ladies.)
Single	1958	Mr. P. R. J. Blair	1,031
Double	1958	Mr. R. D. Matthews	2,045

Flight Shooting (shooting for distance only)
1955	Mr. J. Flinton	490 yds. and 3 in.
1959	Mrs. G. E. Oldfield	357 yds. 2 ft. 1 in.

Association Football

Compiled by **Bernard Joy**
Football Correspondent of the Evening Standard

A CENTURY OF ORGANIZED FOOTBALL

1846. The rules codified for the first time—at Cambridge University.
1857. Sheffield, the oldest club, founded.
1862. Notts County, the oldest League club, founded.
1863. The Football Association formed.
1866. The first representative match, London v. Sheffield.
1867. Queen's Park, the oldest Scottish club, founded.
1871. The F.A. Challenge Cup started.

SOCCER QUIZ

1. Which club has won the League Championship the greatest number of times?

★

2. Which club has won the Cup the greatest number of times?

★

3. And the Amateur Cup?

★

4. Who scored the greatest number of goals in a senior match at Wembley (above)?

★

5. Who scored for both sides in a Wembley Final?

★

6. Which club secured the greatest number of points in winning the First Division?

★

7. And the Second Division?

QUIZ ANSWERS

1. Arsenal—7. 2. Aston Villa—7. 3. Bishop Auckland—10. 4. D. Wilshaw—4 for England v. Scotland, 1955. 5. A. Turner for Charlton v. Derby, 1946. 6. Arsenal—66 in 1930–1. 7. Spurs—70 in 1919–20.

F.A. Cup   F.A. Amateur Cup   World Cup

1872. The first official international, England v. Scotland. (All the Scottish players were from Queen's Park.)
1873. The Scottish F.A. formed. Scottish Cup started.
1874. Shinguards introduced.
1875. The crossbar introduced instead of tape.
1875. Queen's Park conceded the first goal (to Vale of Leven) since they began in 1867.
1876. The Football Association of Wales formed.
1876. The first international between Scotland and Wales.
1879. The first international between England and Wales.
1879. Cliftonville, the oldest Irish club, founded.
1880. The Irish F.A. formed. The Irish Cup started.
1882. The first conference among the four home associations.
1882. The first international between England and Ireland.
1882. The first international between Wales and Ireland.
1883. Scotland played Ireland for the first time, and so the Home International Tournament was started.
1885. Professionalism legalised.
1886. Caps awarded for the first time for internationals.

1887. The first floodlit game in Sheffield.
1888. The Football League formed with 12 members.
1889. Preston won the Cup without conceding a goal, and the League without being beaten.
1890. The Irish League formed.
1891. The Scottish League formed.
1891. Goal nets used for the first time in the North–South match.
1891. The penalty kick introduced at the wish of the Irish F.A.
1892. Inter-League games began.
1892. The Second Division of the Football League formed.
1893. The F.A. Amateur Cup started.
1893. The Referees' Association formed.
1894. The Southern League formed.
1894. Corinthians supplied all eleven players for England against Wales at Wrexham.
1895. The F.A. Cup stolen from a Birmingham shop.
1895. The two-handed throw legalised.
1897. Aston Villa won the Cup and League.
1898. The Players' Union formed.
1898. Promotion and relegation introduced.
1898–9. During this season Rangers won every match in the Scottish League.
1902. Women's football banned by the F.A.
1903. Bury obtained the record F.A. Cup Final win by beating Derby 6–0. They did not concede a goal in the competition.
1904. The Federation of International Football Associations formed.
1905. The first £1,000 transfer—A. Common from Sunderland to Middlesbrough.

1912. United Kingdom won the Olympic Games in Stockholm. It was the last time they were successful.
1914. King George V became the first monarch to attend the Cup Final.
1919. The Football League increased to 44 clubs.
1920. The Third Division (Southern Section) formed.
1921. Northern Section added to the Third Division.
1922. The Second Division of the Scottish League formed.
1923. The first F.A. Cup Final at Wembley Stadium.
1925. The Offside Rule altered from three to two defenders in front of goal.
1926. Huddersfield completed the hat-trick of winning the First Division for the third time in a row.
1927. Cardiff beat Arsenal at Wembley and so took the Cup out of England for the only time.
1928. Britain left F.I.F.A.
1928. The first £10,000 transfer—D. Jack from Bolton to Arsenal.

David Jack   Dixie Dean

1928. Dixie Dean set up a League scoring record with 60 goals for Everton. He scored 22 goals in other games.
1928. The first radio commentary on a Cup Final.
1928. J. McGrory (Celtic) set up a Scottish First Division record with eight goals in a match.
1929. England's full international side beaten by a foreign side for the first time—by Spain 4–3 in Madrid.
1929. A. Geldard became the youngest player in the Football League by playing for Bradford at 15½.
1929–30. Brentford won all home games in the Third South—the only club to do so with a 21-match programme.
1930. Floodlit football forbidden by the F.A.
1930. The World Cup started. Uruguay won the trophy in Montevideo.

Some of the Bolton players watch the police clear the field before the first Wembley Cup Final in 1923

1931. West Bromwich won the Cup and promotion from the Second Division in the same season.

1933. Everton completed the hat-trick of winning the Second Division, First Division and Cup in successive seasons.

1934. Italy won the World Cup in Italy.

1934. S. F. Rous appointed Secretary of the F.A. in succession to Sir Frederick Wall.

1935. The two referees system tried in the Amateur and Professional trial matches.

1935. Arsenal equalled Huddersfield's record of a First Division hat-trick.

1946. The Bolton disaster. Thirty-three spectators were killed and hundreds injured during the Bolton–Stoke cup-tie.

1947. Great Britain beat Rest of Europe 6–1 at Hampden Park.

1947. Doncaster created a Football League record by obtaining 72 points in the Third North.

1949. S. F. Rous knighted.

1949. Former professional footballers permitted to take a place on the F.A. Council.

1949. Rangers performed the unique hat-trick of winning the Scottish League Cup, League and Cup in the same season.

1953. England beaten at home for the first time by a foreign side—by Hungary 6–3.

1954. Germany won the World Cup in Switzerland. England were beaten by Uruguay.

1955. The European Cup launched.

1955. The first floodlit F.A. Cup-tie—between Kidderminster and Brierley Hill.

1955. The Duke of Edinburgh became President of the F.A.

1955. Floodlighting used for the first time in a full England International—England v. Spain at Wembley.

1957. A. Hardaker became Secretary of the Football League in succession to F. Howarth.

1957. Bishop Auckland won the Amateur Cup for the third year in succession and 10 times in all.

1957. Aston Villa won the F.A. Cup for the record seventh time.

1957. J. Charles transferred from Leeds to Juventus (Turin) for £65,000 of which he received £10,000.

1958. Manchester United air disaster at Munich. Eight players, three officials and nine reporters were killed.

Da Rui (France), the Rest of Europe's goalkeeper, punches clear from Great Britain's forwards. Great Britain won 6–1. (1947)

1936. J. Payne (Luton) set up a Football League record by scoring 10 goals in a match.

1936. An F.A. report condemning Pools Football betting.

1936. Charlton completed a record jump by being promoted from the Third and Second Divisions in successive seasons.

1936. Great Britain re-entered the Olympic Games and were beaten by Poland in the second round.

1937. A crowd record for Britain set up when 149,547 watched the Scotland–England match at Hampden Park.

1938. Italy won the World Cup in France.

1939. Numbering of players introduced into the Football League.

1946. Britain rejoined F.I.F.A.

1950. The Football League extended from 88 to 92 clubs.

1950. England entered the World Cup for the first time and were beaten in the Qualifying Round in Brazil. Uruguay won the Cup.

1951. The use of the white ball legalised.

1952. N. Lofthouse (Bolton) set up a representative record with six goals for the Football League v. League of Ireland.

1953. 100,000 spectators attended the F.A. Amateur Cup Final between Pegasus and Harwich at Wembley.

1953. Arsenal won the League Championship for the record seventh time.

1953. England drew 4–4 with Rest of the World at Wembley.

John Charles　　Billy Wright

1958. Sunderland, the last club to maintain continuous membership of the First Division, relegated to the Second.

1958. All four British Associations reached the final stages of the World Cup in Sweden. Brazil won the Cup.

1958. The North and South Sections abolished and a Third and Fourth Division established.

1958. A record fee for British football of £45,000 paid by Manchester United for A. Quixall of Sheffield Wednesday.

1959. W. Wright (Wolves) obtained his hundredth cap when captaining England against Scotland at Wembley.

1959. The Football and Scottish Leagues accepted money from Football Pools of at least £300,000 a year.

HOW THE GAME IS ORGANISED

The Football Association was founded in October 1863. It consists of eighty-one affiliated associations, including the counties and the Services, and is run by the F.A. Council which is elected from the divisional representatives. The Council includes eight Football League representatives who often have a powerful say in policy decisions.

The F.A. is the governing body, being responsible for the laws of the game, and the administration of them. Various sub-committees deal with branches of activities, like Challenge Cup, Amateur Cup, Youth Cup, International, Referees, Instructional and Disciplinary.

The International Committee consists of four sections—senior, intermediate (Under-23), youth and amateur. They arrange matches and select teams. Walter Winterbottom, who is also the coaching director, acts as England's team manager. In recent years control of the amateurs has

Wright, Dickinson and Ramsey watch England goalkeeper Merrick leap into action to save from the Hungary forwards. Hungary won 6–3 to become the first foreign side to beat England at home. (1953)

SOCCER QUIZ

1. Who play on the following grounds—The Den, The Hawthorns, Brunton Park, Bramall Lane, Firhill Park, Molineux, Ashton Gate?

⭑

2. Who has the greatest number of Cup-winners' medals?

⭑

3. Which club won all its home games in a season in the Football League?

⭑

4. Which Scottish club won every League game in one season?

⭑

5. Which Scottish club was unbeaten for seven years?

⭑

6. Name the First Division sides which have not played in a Cup Final?

⭑

7. Which present Third Division sides have won the F.A. Cup?

QUIZ ANSWERS

1. Millwall, West Bromwich, Carlisle, Sheffield United, Partick Thistle, Wolves and Bristol City. 2. Lord Kinnaird, C. H. R. Woolaston, J. Forrest. 3. Brentford in 1929–30. 4. Rangers in 1898–9. 5. Queen's Park. 6. Fulham and Leeds 7. Bury, Barnsley and Bradford City.

How the game is organised—contd.

passed to Norman Creek, a former amateur international who is now on the F.A. staff.

The Council meets approximately every six weeks. To obtain a decision on a matter of urgency there is a Consultative Committee consisting of Arthur Drewry, who is also President of F.I.F.A., Sir Leslie Bowker, and Joe Richards, who is President of the Football League.

The F.A. liaise with other sporting bodies, notably the Central Council of Physical Recreation, the Olympic Association and the Playing Fields Association. They co-ordinate with the Commonwealth and the Services. They take part in a joint council with the Football League and the Players Union. Of the latter body, the chairman is Jimmy Hill, the Fulham inside right, and the secretary is Cliff Lloyd.

All Leagues, (except those outside the F.A., like Sunday Football), have to have F.A. permission and their rules must have F.A. approval.

The most important League is the Football League, which was founded in 1888 by 12 clubs. It now consists of 92 clubs divided into four Divisions. All the full and Under-23 international players during the last generation have been drawn from the League. It has also provided all the Cup finalists since 1902.

The Football Combination, Central League and Midland League are largely made up of reserve teams of Football League members. The biggest independent League is the Southern, which was formed in 1894. For season 1959–60 it incorporated eight Kent League clubs and split up into two Divisions, with promotion and relegation between them. The amateur teams within the F.A. far outnumber the

Sir Stanley Rous   Arthur Drewry   Joe Richards   Jimmy Hill

professionals. The main amateur Leagues are in the South, the most important being the Isthmian and Athenian.

There are nearly 3,000 clubs, catering for over 40,000 players, in organised Sunday football, mainly in London, Manchester, Birmingham and Liverpool. In 1955 the F.A. lifted its ban on Sunday footballers, but made no attempt to organise Sunday football.

The system in England is paralleled in the other home countries. The F.A.s are responsible for administration, discipline, rules and internationals. The Scottish and Irish Leagues are powerful bodies, but the Welsh League is of secondary importance because the leading Welsh clubs, Cardiff, Swansea, Newport and Wrexham, are members of the Football League.

The international body, Federation Internationale de Football Association (F.I.F.A.) was founded in Paris in 1904. It now comprises over 80 countries and organises the World Cup, which is held every four years. England did not join F.I.F.A. until 1906 and the other home countries followed four years later. The home countries withdrew in 1919, when enemy nations were invited to join, rejoined in 1924, and withdrew again in 1928 over the question of broken-time payment to amateurs. They entered F.I.F.A. once more in 1946.

Secretaries:

Football Association: Sir Stanley Rous, C.B.E., J.P.
Scottish Football Association: W. P. Allan.
Irish Football Association: W. J. Drennan.
Welsh Football Association: H. Powell.
Football League: A. Hardaker.
Scottish Football League: J. F. Denovan.
Irish Football League: H. J. Long.

The transfer spiral

£50,000
£46,000 M. CHARLES
£45,000 A. QUIXALL
£34,500 J. SEWELL
£40,000
£30,000 T. FORD
£26,000 E. QUIGLEY
£30,000
£20,000 T. LAWTON
£14,000 B. JONES
£20,000
£10,890 D. JACK
£10,000
£5,000 S. PUDDEFOOT
£1,000 A. COMMON

1910   1920   1930   1940   1950   1960

TRANSFERS

The transfer fee milestones are:

1905. The first £1,000—A. Common, Sunderland to Middlesbrough.
1922. The first £5,000—S. Puddefoot, West Ham to Falkirk.
1928. The first £10,000 (actually, £10,890)—D. Jack, Bolton to Arsenal.
1938. The pre-war record (£14,000)—B. Jones, Wolves to Arsenal.
1947. The first £20,000—T. Lawton, Chelsea to Notts County.
1949. The first £25,000 (actually £26,000) —E. Quigley, Sheffield Wed. to Preston.
1950. The first £30,000—T. Ford, Aston Villa to Sunderland.
1951. The first £35,000—J. Sewell, Notts County to Sheffield Wed.
1958. The first £45,000—A. Quixall, Sheffield Wed. to Manchester United.

Other record transfer fees are:

Concerning a British club—£65,000, J. Charles, Leeds to Juventus of Italy in 1957.
For a winger—£35,000, C. Jones, Swansea to Tottenham in 1958.
For a half-back—£30,000, D. Blanchflower, Aston Villa to Tottenham in 1954. And D. Mackay, Hearts to Tottenham in 1959.
For a goalkeeper—£23,000, H. Gregg, Doncaster to Manchester United in 1957.
By a Scottish club to an English one— £17,500, W. Steel, Derby to Dundee, 1950.

The record aggregate for transfer moves was set up in 1958 when Don Revie was transferred from Sunderland to Leeds. His previous clubs were Leicester, Hull and Manchester City and the total fees involved were £83,000.

The next highest is £69,000 for Trevor Ford of Swansea, Aston Villa, Sunderland, Cardiff and Eindhoven (Holland).

Andy Graver was involved in three moves within a year up to November 1955 costing just over £50,000 altogether. He went from Lincoln to Leicester, back again six months later, and then on to Stoke.

The most expensive team fielded was that of Tottenham in the 1959–60 season It included 8 players costing £182,000 in fees.

The practice of paying a transfer fee for a player's registration grew up among the clubs and was frowned upon by the authorities at first. Originally the registration was valid only for a season, but now the player is retained as long as the club offers him the minimum wage. The system was upheld in law in 1912, when Aston Villa won a test case brought against them by L. Kingaby.

No player can be transferred without his consent. The League has the power to intervene in transfers, for example by reducing the fee a club may have put on a player.

Since 1958 players transferred at the club's request can receive a sum of £300. They are also entitled to a share of benefit, not exceeding £150 for each year of service. They also receive a £20 signing-on fee.

Players transferred after March 16 must have permission from the League before taking part in a League game during the rest of the season. A player cannot play for two clubs in the same season in the F.A. Cup. He must be with a club a fortnight to be eligible for the Cup.

Bryn Jones   Trevor Ford   Tommy Lawton   Cliff Jones   Harry Gregg

WAGES

The Football League is the only League with a maximum rate of pay. Outside Scotland, however, it is rare to find a British player earning more from non-League football than he would in the League.

The first maximum wage was fixed in 1901 at £4 a week. Between the two wars it rose to £8 a week in the season and £6 a week during the summer. The last alteration was in 1958, when the rates were fixed as follows: 17-year-old £10 in the season and £9 in the summer; 18-year-old £12 10*s.* and £11; 19-year-old £15 and £13; 20 and over £20 and £17.

The minimum wages were fixed as: 17-year-old £5 and £5; 18-year-old £6 and £6; 19-year-old £7 and £7; 20 and over £8 and £8.

A player who is regarded as a first-team man can be paid the top money even if under 20. Permission must be obtained from the League. A service player is paid £1 a week as a retainer and £6 a match.

There are extra earnings. The television fee is £2 a man and £3 is paid for games other than League or Cup fixtures. The signing-on fee is £20. The match bonus is £4 a win and £2 a draw, except for the later rounds of the Cup, which are: 3rd, £5 and £2 10*s.*; 4th, £6 and £3; 5th, £8 and £4; 6th, £10 and £5; semi-final £20 and £10 and final £25 and £12 10*s.*

Talent money for success in the League is distributed as follows. First and Second Divisions: first, £1,100; second, £880; third, £660; fourth, £440; fifth, £220.

Third Division: first, £550; second, £440; third, £330; fourth, £220.

Fourth Division: first, £330; second, £220; third, £110; fourth, £55.

Talent money in the Cup is: winners, £1,100; runners-up, £880; defeated semi-finalists, £660; defeated clubs in sixth round, £440; defeated clubs in fifth round, £220.

Benefits can be paid up to £750 for five years' continuous service with the same club. A benefit of £1,000 can be paid for a further spell of five years with the same club.

The fee for an international match, originally £10, was raised to £50 in 1953.

Eight per cent of a player's earnings are paid to him tax free on his retirement from the game. The money is raised by a levy of four per cent on all Cup and League games.

REFEREEING

In an attempt to stamp out "gamesmanship", the Football Association, after consultations with the Football League, issued instructions in September 1958 giving wider authority to referees. The F.A.'s letter, which was placed on all dressing-room notice boards and printed in programmes, said "The Council . . . is seriously concerned about the increase of certain minor infringements of law and unsportsmanlike acts of so-called 'gamesmanship' which bring the game of association football into disrepute."

The following rulings were then listed:

1. Appealing. Players are forbidden to make any form of appeal to the referee or linesmen.

2. Acts of "gamesmanship". Unfair acts designed to waste time and delay play will be viewed seriously as ungentlemanly conduct. A player committing an offence such as standing on or near the ball to delay the taking of a free kick will be cautioned. If such an act is repeated by any member of the team, then the offending player may be sent off the field.

3. Injured players. They should be treated off the field whenever possible.

4. Referee's decisions. Club officials, managers, trainers, coaches and players are not to speak to the referee or linesmen about the referee's decisions.

Two months later the rulings were amended so that a captain could make a dignified and orderly appeal to the referee.

Without the slightest doubt, the authorisation stopped the unsporting practices and massed protests to a referee which had done considerable harm to the game. At the same time, many responsible managers were alarmed at the increased power given to referees and they felt that a drive was now necessary to improve the standard of refereeing so that less questionable decisions would be given.

FOOTBALL LEAGUE REFEREES

K. Aston, Ilford.
J. Bellwood, Cleckheaton.
P. Brandwood, Kidderminster.
J. Brooks, London.
L. Callaghan, Merthyr Tydfil, Glam.
R. Callaghan, Rochdale.
J. Carr, Sheffield.
W. Clements, West Bromwich.
F. Collinge, Rochdale.
K. Collinge, Altrincham.
J. Cook, Upton.
J. Cooke, Waterbeach.
T. Cooper, Bolton.
F. Cowen, Manchester.
E. Crawford, Doncaster.
W. Crossley, Lancaster.
K. Dagnall, Bolton.
T. Dawes, Norwich.
C. Dennis, Merstham, Surrey.
M. Dixon, York.
A. Ellis, Halifax.
J. Finney, Hereford.
F. Gerrard, Preston.
H. Hackney, Barnsley.
L. Hamer, Horwich, Nr. Bolton.
A. Hawcroft, Rotherham.
H. Hemingway, Pontefract.
A. Holland, Barnsley.
H. Horner, Coventry.
N. Hough, Macclesfield.
L. Howarth, Beverley.
D. Howell, Perry Barr, Birmingham.
K. Howley, Middlesbrough.
J. Hunt, Emsworth.
H. Husband, London.
E. Jennings, Stourbridge.
A. Jobling, Morecambe.
R. Jordan, Leicester Forest East.
J. Kelly, Eccleston.
C. Kingston, Newport.
R. Langdale, Darlington.
R. Leafe, Nottingham.
A. Luty, Leeds.
R. Mann, Worcester.
D. Martin, Scunthorpe.
G. McCabe, Sheffield.
M. McCoy, Doncaster.
J. McLoughlin, Manchester.
J. Mitchell, Whiston, nr. Prescot.
A. Moore, Lowestoft.
A. Murdoch, Sheffield.
J. Parkinson, Blackburn.
L. Peake, Rotherham.
J. Pickles, Stockport.
J. Powell, Rotherham.
G. Pullin, Bristol.
R. Reddaway, Kettering.
T. Reynolds, South Stanley.
P. Rhodes, Dringhouses.
A. Robottom, Walsall.
C. Rogers, London.
I. Rosekilly, Uxbridge.
R. Ryalls, Walkley, Sheffield.
C. Sant, Crewe.
J. Seddon, Southport.
J. Sherlock, Sheffield.
D. Smith, Stonehouse.
R. Smith, Newport.
A. Sparling, Grimsby.
K. Stokes, Newark.
F. Stringer, Liverpool.
W. Surtees, Langley Park.
J. Taylor, Wolverhampton.
G. Thorpe, Swindon.
L. Tirebuck, Halifax.
K. Tuck, Chesterfield.
R. Warnke, Coventry.
H. Webb, Leeds.
J. Williams, Woodthorpe.
R. Windle, Chesterfield.
C. Woan, Kensington.
S. Yates, Bristol.

FOOTBALL LEAGUE 1ST DIVISION CHAMPIONS

1888–89	Preston North End
1889–90	Preston North End
1890–91	Everton
1891–92	Sunderland
1892–93	Sunderland
1893–94	Aston Villa
1894–95	Sunderland
1895–96	Aston Villa
1896–97	Aston Villa
1897–98	Sheffield United
1898–99	Aston Villa
1899–1900	Aston Villa
1900–01	Liverpool
1901–02	Sunderland
1902–03	Sheffield Wednesday
1903–04	Sheffield Wednesday
1904–05	Newcastle United
1905–06	Liverpool
1906–07	Newcastle United
1907–08	Manchester United
1908–09	Newcastle United
1909–10	Aston Villa
1910–11	Manchester United
1911–12	Blackburn Rovers
1912–13	Sunderland
1913–14	Blackburn Rovers
1914–15	Everton
1919–20	West Bromwich Albion
1920–21	Burnley
1921–22	Liverpool
1922–23	Liverpool
1923–24	Huddersfield Town
1924–25	Huddersfield Town
1925–26	Huddersfield Town
1926–27	Newcastle United
1927–28	Everton
1928–29	Sheffield Wednesday
1929–30	Sheffield Wednesday
1930–31	Arsenal
1931–32	Everton
1932–33	Arsenal
1933–34	Arsenal
1934–35	Arsenal
1935–36	Sunderland
1936–37	Manchester City
1937–38	Arsenal
1938–39	Everton
1946–47	Liverpool
1947–48	Arsenal
1948–49	Portsmouth
1949–50	*Portsmouth
1950–51	Tottenham Hotspur
1951–52	Manchester United
1952–53	*Arsenal
1953–54	Wolverhampton Wanderers
1954–55	Chelsea
1955–56	Manchester United
1956–57	Manchester United
1957–58	Wolverhampton Wanderers
1958–59	Wolverhampton Wanderers

* *Won on goal average.*

GREAT NAMES IN SOCCER

JOE BAMBRICK (Chelsea). By scoring six goals—a double hat-trick—for Ireland against Wales in Belfast in 1930 centre forward Joe Bambrick set up a record which still stands for full internationals. He was then with Linfield and the feat brought English scouts after him. He did not move until Christmas Eve 1934, when he joined Chelsea and immediately helped them to six points over the Christmas holidays. He retained his scoring touch and twice had four goals for Chelsea, before moving on to Walsall in 1939.

E. C. BAMBRIDGE (The Swifts). A dashing and fearless outside left, E. C. Bambridge—"Bam"—played 18 times for England between 1879 and 1887. He helped to found the Corinthians in 1882 and was secretary of the club in the 1920s. During a match in 1881 he handled to prevent the ball entering the goal and the F.A. introduced a rule allowing the referee to award a goal under such circumstances. He played in the days when hacking was permitted and he returned to The Swifts after breaking a leg to play in a County Cup Final with a shinguard outside one leg. He revealed after the match that the guard was on the uninjured leg.

BILLY BASSETT (West Bromwich). The finest outside right before the twentieth century was William Isaiah Bassett. He played 16 times for England between 1889 and 1896 and helped in the momentous rise of West Bromwich, who played in five Finals from 1886 to 1895. He was only 5 feet 5½ inches tall, but was very fast and had the trick of pushing the ball past a back and running outside the touchline before coming back into play. As a result he was at his best on big grounds like Crystal Palace and the Oval. He was chairman when West Bromwich reached the Final in 1931.

CLIFF BASTIN (Arsenal). The 33 goals Cliff Bastin scored for Arsenal from the left wing in season 1932–3 still stands as a record for a winger in First Division football. He was part of the great Arsenal side of the 1930s and gained all the honours of the game before he was 21. He signed as a professional for Exeter when 17 and was transferred to Arsenal for £2,000 a few weeks afterwards, in June 1929. Originally an inside forward, Arsenal converted him to an outside left and he struck up a fine understanding with Alex James. Ice-cool for one so young, he took penalties for Arsenal when 17. He later reverted to inside forward—he played for England there, as well as on the wing—and also succeeded at wing half. Deafness interfered with his career and he retired in 1946, when 34, to take a public house in native Devon.

STEVE BLOOMER (Derby). Slight in physique and palefaced, Steve Bloomer did not look like a footballer. But he scored 352 goals in League football between 1892 and 1914 and with 28 goals from 23 internationals he set up an England record which lasted for 49 years until beaten by Nat Lofthouse. He began with Derby Swifts and was signed by the County for a starting wage of 7s. 6d. a week. In 1906 he was transferred to Middlesbrough and returned to Derby to help them to promotion from the Second Division in season 1911–12. The secret of his shooting was that he did not require a long back swing. He invariably kept the ball low and frequently baffled goalkeepers by a sudden change of feet.

DAVE BOWEN (Northampton). When the son of Tom Whittaker, the late Arsenal manager, was stationed with the R.A.F. in the Midlands he r commended a Northampton player, Dave Bowen. It was a happy action for the player, club and Wales. Bowen, then an outside left, was converted to a left half, and became a permanent member of the first team, and captain of Wales. He was born in Maesteg, attended a rugby-playing grammar school and played soccer, the game he loved, with a Boys' Club. He moved to Arsenal in 1950 and gained his first cap for Wales five years later. He joined Northampton as player-manager in 1959.

ERIC BROOK (Manchester City). One of the fiercest shots in pre-war football belonged to Eric Brook. His position according to the programme was outside-left, but he often popped up in the middle to rescue his side with dramatic goals. His first club was Barnsley and he moved to Manchester City, together with Fred Tilson, in 1929. He played in the 1933 and 1934 Cup Finals, being on the winning side in the latter. He would have won more than 19 caps for England —scoring 10 goals—but for the competition of Cliff Bastin. He was unmistakable on the field, being very fair-haired and having a stocky build more suitable to a wing half.

CHARLIE BUCHAN (Sunderland and Arsenal). Tall, willowy and exceptionally good at heading, Charlie Buchan was the finest inside forward of his day. He was born in Plumstead, played as an amateur for Arsenal—their ground was then in Plumstead—and signed as a professional for Leyton. He was transferred to Sunderland in 1911 when 18½ for the then startling fee of £1,000. At Sunderland he struck such a fine understanding with Cuggy and Mordue on the wing that opponents dubbed them the "infernal triangle". Herbert Chapman brought him back to Arsenal in 1925 for the strangest fee. Sunderland received £2,000 down and £100 for every goal in his first season. He scored 19. He played in the 1927 Final and left Arsenal for newspaper work in 1928.

RON BURGESS (Tottenham). Ron Burgess learnt his football kicking a ball about on the slagheaps above the River Ebbw in South Wales. He became a miner before Tottenham invited him to join their ground staff just before the war. He was then an inside forward and he did not develop into a great player until he changed to left half. Dark, wiry, aggressive, he was a veritable dynamo and inspired by his example. He became an automatic choice for Wales and captained Spurs when they won the Second and First Division Championships in successive seasons, 1949–51. He was left half for Great Britain against the Rest of Europe in 1947. He became team manager of Swansea in 1954, and after four years left them to become coach, and later manager, of Watford.

SOCCER QUIZ

1. Which Football League club won the Amateur Cup?

★

2. Has extra time been played in an Amateur Final at Wembley?

★

3. Has a replay been required for an Amateur Final at Wembley?

★

4. What is the biggest attendance at an Amateur Cup Final?

QUIZ ANSWERS

1. Middlesbrough, in 1895 and 1898. 2. Yes, in 1952. 3. Yes, in 1954 and 1956. 4. 100,000 in 1953.

INTERNATIONAL MATCHES

ENGLAND v. SCOTLAND

	England	Scotland
1872 Glasgow	0	0
1873 Kennington Oval	4	2
1874 Glasgow	1	2
1875 Kennington Oval	2	2
1876 Glasgow	0	3
1877 Kennington Oval	1	3
1878 Glasgow	2	7
1879 Kennington Oval	5	4
1880 Glasgow	4	5
1881 Kennington Oval	1	6
1882 Glasgow	1	5
1883 Sheffield	2	3
1884 Kennington Oval	0	1
1885 Kennington Oval	1	1
1886 Glasgow	1	1
1887 Blackburn	2	3
1888 Glasgow	5	0
1889 Kennington Oval	2	3
1890 Glasgow	1	1
1891 Blackburn	2	1
1892 Glasgow	4	0
1893 Richmond	5	2
1894 Glasgow	2	2
1895 Everton	3	0
1896 Glasgow	1	2
1897 Crystal Palace	1	2
1898 Glasgow	3	1
1899 Birmingham	2	1
1900 Glasgow	1	4
1901 Crystal Palace	2	2
1902 Birmingham	2	2
1903 Sheffield	1	2
1904 Glasgow	1	0
1905 Crystal Palace	1	0
1906 Glasgow	1	2
1907 Newcastle	1	1
1908 Glasgow	1	1
1909 Crystal Palace	2	0
1910 Glasgow	0	2
1911 Everton	1	1
1912 Glasgow	1	1
1913 Chelsea	1	0
1914 Glasgow	1	3
1920 Sheffield	5	4
1921 Glasgow	0	3
1922 Aston Villa	0	1
1923 Glasgow	2	2
1924 Wembley	1	1
1925 Glasgow	0	2
1926 Manchester	0	1
1927 Glasgow	2	1
1928 Wembley	1	5
1929 Glasgow	0	1
1930 Wembley	5	2
1931 Glasgow	0	2
1932 Wembley	3	0
1933 Glasgow	1	2
1934 Wembley	3	0
1935 Glasgow	0	2
1936 Wembley	1	1
1937 Glasgow	1	3
1938 Wembley	0	1
1939 Glasgow	2	1
1947 Wembley	1	1
1948 Glasgow	2	0
1949 Wembley	1	3
1950 Glasgow	1	0
1951 Wembley	2	3
1952 Glasgow	2	1
1953 Wembley	2	2
1954 Glasgow	4	2
1955 Wembley	7	2
1956 Glasgow	1	1
1957 Wembley	2	1
1958 Glasgow	4	0
1959 Wembley	1	0

ENGLAND v. WALES

	England	Wales
1879 Kennington Oval	2	1
1880 Wrexham	3	2
1881 Blackburn	0	1
1882 Wrexham	3	5
1883 Kennington Oval	5	0
1884 Wrexham	4	0
1885 Blackburn	1	1
1886 Wrexham	3	1
1887 Kennington Oval	4	0
1888 Crewe	5	1
1889 Stoke-on-Trent	4	1
1890 Wrexham	3	1
1891 Sunderland	4	1
1892 Wrexham	2	0
1893 Stoke	6	0
1894 Wrexham	5	1
1895 Queen's Club, Kensington	1	1
1896 Cardiff	9	1
1897 Sheffield	4	0
1898 Wrexham	3	0
1899 Bristol	4	1
1900 Cardiff	1	1
1901 Newcastle	6	0
1902 Wrexham	0	0
1903 Portsmouth	2	1
1904 Wrexham	2	2
1905 Liverpool	3	1
1906 Cardiff	1	0
1907 Fulham	1	1
1908 Wrexham	7	1
1909 Nottingham	2	0
1910 Cardiff	1	0
1911 Millwall	3	0
1912 Wrexham	2	0
1913 Bristol	4	3
1914 Cardiff	2	0
1920 Highbury	1	2
1921 Cardiff	0	0
1922 Liverpool	1	0
1923 Cardiff	2	2
1924 Blackburn	1	2
1925 Swansea	2	1
1926 Selhurst	1	3
1927 Wrexham	3	3
1927 Burnley	1	2
1928 Swansea	3	2
1929 Chelsea	6	0
1930 Wrexham	4	0
1931 Liverpool	3	1
1932 Wrexham	0	0
1933 Newcastle	1	2
1934 Cardiff	4	0
1936 Wolverhampton	1	2
1936 Cardiff	1	2
1937 Middlesbrough	2	1
1938 Cardiff	2	4
1946 Manchester	3	0
1947 Cardiff	3	0
1948 Aston Villa	1	0
1949 Cardiff	4	1
1950 Sunderland	4	2
1951 Cardiff	1	1
1952 Wembley	5	2
1953 Cardiff	4	1
1954 Wembley	3	2
1955 Cardiff	1	2
1956 Wembley	3	1
1957 Cardiff	4	0
1958 Aston Villa	2	2

ENGLAND v. IRELAND

	England	Ireland
1882 Belfast	13	0
1883 Liverpool	7	0
1884 Belfast	8	1
1885 Manchester	4	0
1886 Belfast	6	1
1887 Sheffield	7	0
1888 Belfast	5	1
1889 Everton	6	1
1890 Belfast	9	1
1891 Wolverhampton	6	1
1892 Belfast	2	0
1893 Birmingham	6	1
1894 Belfast	2	2
1895 Derby	9	0
1896 Belfast	2	0
1897 Nottingham	6	0
1898 Belfast	3	2
1899 Sunderland	13	2
1900 Dublin	2	0
1901 Southampton	3	0
1902 Belfast	1	0
1903 Wolverhampton	4	0
1904 Belfast	3	1
1905 Middlesbrough	1	1
1906 Belfast	5	0
1907 Everton	1	0
1908 Belfast	3	1
1909 Bradford	4	0
1910 Belfast	1	1
1911 Derby	2	1
1912 Dublin	6	1
1913 Belfast	1	2
1914 Middlesbrough	0	3
1919 Belfast	1	1
1920 Sunderland	2	0
1921 Belfast	1	1
1922 West Bromwich	2	0
1923 Belfast	1	2
1924 Everton	3	1
1925 Belfast	0	0
1926 Liverpool	3	3
1927 Belfast	0	2
1928 Everton	2	1
1929 Belfast	3	0
1930 Sheffield	5	1
1931 Belfast	6	2
1932 Blackpool	1	0
1933 Belfast	3	0
1935 Everton	2	1
1935 Belfast	3	1
1936 Stoke	3	1
1937 Belfast	5	1
1938 Manchester	7	0
1946 Belfast	7	2
1947 Everton	2	2
1948 Belfast	6	2
1949 Manchester	9	2
1950 Belfast	4	1
1951 Aston Villa	2	0
1952 Belfast	2	2
1953 Liverpool	3	1
1954 Belfast	2	0
1955 Wembley	3	0
1956 Belfast	1	1
1957 Wembley	2	3
1958 Belfast	3	3

ENGLAND v. ARGENTINA

	England	Argentina
1951 Wembley	2	1
1953 Buenos Aires	abandoned	

ENGLAND v. AUSTRIA

	England	Austria
1930 Vienna	0	0
1932 Chelsea	4	3
1936 Vienna	1	2
1951 Wembley	2	2
1952 Vienna	3	2
1958 Sweden (World Cup)	2	2

ENGLAND v. BELGIUM

	England	Belgium
1921 Brussels	2	0
1923 Highbury	6	1
1923 Antwerp	2	2
1924 West Bromwich	4	0
1926 Antwerp	5	3
1927 Brussels	9	1
1928 Antwerp	3	1
1929 Brussels	5	1
1931 Brussels	4	1
1936 Brussels	2	3
1947 Brussels	5	2
1950 Brussels	4	1
1952 Wembley	5	0
1954 Basle	4	4

ENGLAND v. BOHEMIA

	England	Bohemia
1908 Prague	4	0

ENGLAND v. BRAZIL

	England	Brazil
1956 Wembley	4	2
1958 Sweden (World Cup)	0	0
1959 Rio de Janeiro	0	2

ENGLAND v. BULGARIA

	England	Bulgaria
1957 Sofia	1	2

ENGLAND v. CHILE

	England	Chile
1950 Rio de Janeiro	2	0
1953 Santiago	2	1

ENGLAND v. CZECHOSLOVAKIA

	England	Czecho-slovakia
1934 Prague	1	2
1937 Tottenham	5	4

ENGLAND v. DENMARK

	England	Denmark
1948 Copenhagen	0	0
1955 Copenhagen	5	1
1956 Wolverhampton	5	2
1957 Copenhagen	4	1

ENGLAND v. F.I.F.A.

	England	F.I.F.A.
1938 Highbury	3	0
1953 Wembley	4	4

ENGLAND v. FINLAND

	England	Finland
1937 Helsinki	8	0
1956 Helsinki	5	1

ENGLAND v. FRANCE

	England	France
1923 Paris	4	1
1924 Paris	3	1
1925 Paris	3	2
1927 Paris	6	0
1928 Paris	5	1
1929 Paris	4	1
1931 Paris	2	5
1933 Tottenham	4	1
1938 Paris	4	2
1947 Highbury	3	0
1949 Paris	3	1
1951 Highbury	2	2
1955 Paris	0	1
1957 Wembley	4	0

ENGLAND v. GERMANY

	England	Germany
1930 Berlin	3	3
1935 Tottenham	3	0
1938 Berlin	6	3
1954 Wembley	3	1
1956 Berlin	3	1

ENGLAND v. HOLLAND

	England	Holland
1935 Amsterdam	1	0
1946 Huddersfield	8	2

ENGLAND v. HUNGARY

	England	Hungary
1934 Budapest	1	2
1936 Highbury	6	2
1953 Wembley	3	6
1954 Budapest	1	7

ENGLAND v. IRISH REPUBLIC

	England	Irish Republic
1946 Dublin	1	0
1949 Everton	0	2
1957 Wembley	5	1
1957 Dublin	1	1

ENGLAND v. ITALY

	England	Italy
1933 Rome	1	1
1934 Highbury	3	2
1939 Milan	2	2
1948 Turin	4	0
1949 Tottenham	2	0
1952 Florence	1	1
1958 Wembley	2	2

ENGLAND v. LUXEMBOURG

	England	Luxembourg
1927 Luxembourg	5	2

ENGLAND v. MEXICO

	England	Mexico
1959 Mexico City	1	2

ENGLAND v. NORWAY

	England	Norway
1937 Oslo	6	0
1938 Newcastle	4	0
1949 Oslo	4	1

ENGLAND v. PERU

	England	Peru
1959 Lima	1	4

ENGLAND v. PORTUGAL

	England	Portugal
1947 Lisbon	10	0
1950 Lisbon	5	3
1951 Everton	5	2
1955 Lisbon	1	3
1958 Wembley	2	1

SOCCER QUIZ

1. When was the League extended to 92 clubs?

*

2. When was the Third Division started?

*

3. And the Fourth?

*

4. And the Second?

*

5. When was the Final made an all-ticket match?

*

6. What was the first defeat abroad of the full England side?

*

7. What was the first defeat at home by a foreign side?

QUIZ ANSWERS

1. 1950. 2. 1922. 3. 1958. 4. 1892. 5. 1924. 6. By Spain in 1929. 7. By Hungary in 1953.

ENGLAND v. RUMANIA

	England	Rumania
1939 Bucharest	2	0

ENGLAND v. RUSSIA

	England	Russia
1958 Moscow	1	1
1958 Sweden (World Cup)	2	2
1958 Sweden (World Cup)	0	1
1958 Wembley	5	0

ENGLAND v. SPAIN

	England	Spain
1929 Madrid	3	4
1931 Highbury	7	1
1950 Rio de Janeiro	0	1
1955 Madrid	1	1
1955 Wembley	4	1

ENGLAND v. SWEDEN

	England	Sweden
1923 Stockholm	4	2
1923 Stockholm	3	1
1937 Stockholm	4	0
1947 Highbury	4	2
1949 Stockholm	1	3
1956 Stockholm	0	0

ENGLAND v. SWITZERLAND

	England	Switzerland
1933 Berne	4	0
1938 Zurich	1	2
1947 Zurich	0	1
1948 Highbury	6	0
1952 Zurich	3	0
1954 Berne	2	0

ENGLAND v. URUGUAY

	England	Uruguay
1953 Montevideo	1	2
1954 Basle	2	4

ENGLAND v. U.S.A.

	England	U.S.A.
1950 Belo Horizonte (Brazil)	0	1
1953 New York	6	3
1959 Los Angeles	8	1

ENGLAND v. YUGOSLAVIA

	England	Yugoslavia
1939 Belgrade	1	2
1950 Highbury	2	2
1954 Belgrade	0	1
1956 Wembley	3	0
1958 Belgrade	0	5

GREAT BRITAIN v. REST OF EUROPE (F.I.F.A.)

	G.B.	Rest of E.
1947 Glasgow	6	1
1955 Belfast	1	4

POST-WAR INTERNATIONAL APPEARANCES

Abbreviations: A—Argentina; Aus—Austria; B—Belgium; Braz—Brazil; C—Chile; Cz—Czechoslovakia; D—Denmark; E—England; EG—East Germany; FIFA—Federation of International Football Associations; Fin—Finland; F—France; G—Germany; H—Holland; Hun—Hungary; I—Ireland; Is—Israel; It—Italy; J—Jutland; L—Luxemburg; M—Mexico; N—Norway; P—Paraguay; Peru; Pol—Poland; Port—Portugal; R—Russia; S—Scotland; Sp—Spain; Swd—Sweden; Switz—Switzerland; U—Uruguay; U.S.—United States of America; W—Wales; Y—Yugoslavia.

ENGLAND

A'COURT, A. (5) (Liverpool) 1957–8 v. I, Braz, Aus, R; 1958–9 v. W.

ALLEN, R. (5) (W.B.A.) 1951–2 v. Switz; 1953–4 v. S, Y; 1954–5 v. W, G.

ARMFIELD, J. (4) (Blackpool) 1958–9 v. Braz, Peru, M, U.S.

ARMSTRONG, K. (1) (Chelsea) 1954–5 v. S.

ASTALL, G. (2) (Birmingham) 1955–6 v. Fin, G.

ASTON, J. (17) (Manchester Utd) 1948–9 v. W, S, D, Switz, Swd, N, F; 1949–50 v. W, I, S, Eire, It, Port, B, C, U.S.; 1950 v. I.

Roy Bentley

Ron Clayton

Jimmy Dickinson

ATYEO, J. (6) (Bristol City) 1955–6 v. Sp, Braz, Swd, Eire, D, Eire.

BAILY, E. (9) (Tottenham) 1949–50 v. Sp; 1950–1 v. I, W, Y; 1951–2 v. W, Aus (2), Switz; 1952–3 v. I.

BANKS, T. (6) (Bolton) 1957–8 v. R, R, Braz, Aus, R; 1958–9 v. I.

BARLOW, R. (1) (W.B.A.) 1954–5 v. I.

BARRASS, M. (3) (Bolton) 1951–2 v. W, I; 1952–3 v. S.

BAYNHAM, R. (3) (Luton) 1955–6 v. D, I, Sp.

BENTLEY, R. (12) (Chelsea) 1948–9 v. Swd; 1949–50 v. S, Port, B, C, U.S; 1952–3 v. W, B; 1954–5 v. W, G, Sp, Port.

BERRY, J. (4) (Manchester Utd) 1952–3 v. A, C, U; 1955–6 v. Swd.

BLUNSTONE, F. (5) (Chelsea) 1954–5 v. W, S, F, Port; 1956–7 v. W.

BRABROOK, P. (2) (Chelsea) 1957–8 v. R; 1958–9 v. I.

BRADFORD, G. (1) (Bristol Rovers) 1955–6 v. D.

BRADLEY, W. (2) (Manchester Utd) 1958–9 v. I, U.S.

BROADIS, I. (14) (Manchester City) 1951–2 v. Aus, S, Switz; 1952–3 v. A, C, U, U.S; (Newcastle) 1953–4 v. S, Y, Hun, B, Switz, U.

BROADBENT, P. (6) (Wolves) 1957–8 v. R; 1958–9 v. W, I, S, It, Braz.

BROOKS, J. (3) (Tottenham) 1956–7 v. W, Y, D.

BYRNE, R. (33) (Manchester Utd) 1953–4 v. S, Y, H, B, Switz, U; 1954–5 v. I, W, G, S, F, Sp, Port; 1955–6 v. D, W, I, Sp, S, Braz, Swd, Fin, G; 1956–7 v. W, Y, D, S, Eire, D, Eire; 1957–8 v. W, I, F.

CARTER, H. (7) (Derby) 1946–7 v. I, W, S, Eire, H, F, Switz.

CHARLTON, R. (12) (Manchester Utd) 1957–8 v. S, Port; 1958–9 v. W, I, R, S, It, Braz, Peru, M, U.S.

CHILTON, A. (2) (Manchester Utd) 1950–1 v. I; 1951–2 v. F.

CLAMP, E. (4) (Wolves) 1957–8 v. R, R, Braz, Aus.

CLAPTON, D. (1) (Arsenal) 1958–9 v. W.

CLARKE, H. (1) (Tottenham) 1953–4 v. S.

CLAYTON, R. (30) (Blackburn) 1955–6 v. I, Sp, Braz, Swd, Fin, G; 1956–7 v. I, W, Y, D, S, Eire, D, Eire; 1957–8 v. W, I, F, S, Port, Y, R; 1958–9 v. W, I, R, S, It, Braz, Peru, M, U.S.

COCKBURN, H. (13) (Manchester Utd) 1946–7 v. I, W, Eire; 1947–8 v. S, It; 1948–9 v. I, S, D, Switz, Swd; 1950–1 v. A, Port; 1951–2 v. F.

COMPTON, L. (2) (Arsenal) 1950–1 v. W, Y.

DEELEY, N. (2) (Wolves) 1958–9 v. Braz, Peru.

DICKINSON, J. (48) (Portsmouth) 1948–9 v. N, F; 1949–50 v. W, S, Eire, Port, B, C, U.S, Sp; 1950–1 v. I, W, Y, 1951–2 v. W, I, Aus (2), S, It, Switz; 1952–3 v. I, W, B, S, A, C, U, U.S; 1953–4 v. W, FIFA, I, Hun (2), S, Y, B, Switz, U; 1954–5 v. Sp, Port; 1955–6 v. D, W, I, Sp, S; 1956–7 v. W, Y, D.

DITCHBURN, E. (6) (Tottenham) 1948–9 v. Switz, Swd; 1952–3 v. U.S; 1956–7 v. W, Y, D.

DOUGLAS, B. (12) (Blackburn) 1957–8 v. W, I, F, S, Port, Y, R, R, Braz, Aus; 1958–9 v. R, S.

ECKERSLEY, W. (17) (Blackburn) 1949–50 v. Sp; 1950–1 v. Y, S, A, Port; 1951–2 v. Aus (2), Switz; 1952–3 v. I, A, C, U, U.S; 1953–4 v. W, FIFA, I, Hun.

EDWARDS, D. (18) (Manchester Utd) 1954–5 v. S, F, Sp, Port; 1955–6 v. S, Braz, Swd, Fin, G; 1956–7 v. I, D, S, Eire, D, Eire; 1957–8 v. W, I, F.

ELLERINGTON, W. (2) (Southampton) 1948–9 v. N, F.

ELLIOTT, W. H. (5) (Burnley) 1951–2 v. It, Aus; 1952–3 v. I, W, B.

FINNEY, T. (76) (Preston) 1946–7 v. I, W, Eire, H, F, Port; 1947–8 v. W, I, S, B, Swd, It; 1948–9 v. I, W, S, Swd, N, F; 1949–50 v. W, I, S, Eire, It, Port, B, C, U.S, Sp; 1950–1 v. W, S, A, Port; 1951–2 v. F, W, I, S, It, Aus, Switz; 1952–3 v. I, W, B, S, A, C, U, U.S; 1953–4 v. D, S, Y, Hun, B, Switz, U; 1954–5 v. G; 1955–6 v. D, W, I, Sp, S; 1956–7 v. W, Y, D, S, Eire, D, Eire; 1957–8 v. W, F, S, Port, Y, R, R; 1958–9 v. I, R.

FLOWERS, R. (7) (Wolves) 1954–5 v. F. 1958–9 v. W, S, It, Braz, Peru, U.S.

FOULKES, W. (1) (Manchester Utd) 1954–5 v. I.

FRANKLIN, N. (27) (Stoke) 1946–7 v. I, W, S, Eire, H, F, Switz, Port; 1947–8 v. W, I, S, B, Swd, It; 1948–9 v. I, W, S, D, Switz, Swd, N, F; 1949–50 v. W, I, S, Eire, It.

FROGGATT, J. (13) (Portsmouth) 1949–50 v. It; 1950–1 v. S; 1951–2 v. Aus (2), S, It, Switz; 1952–3 v. I, W, B, S, U.S.

FROGGATT, R. (4) (Sheffield Wed) 1952–3 v. W, B, S, U.S.

GRAINGER, C. (7) (Sheffield Utd) 1955–6 v. Braz, Swd, Fin, G; 1956–7 v. I, W, (Sunderland) S.

GREAVES, J. (3) (Chelsea) 1958–9 v. Peru, M, U.S.

HAGAN, J. (1) (Sheffield Utd) 1948–9 v. D.

HAINES, J. (1) (W.B.A.) 1948–9 v. Switz.

HALL, J. (17) (Birmingham) 1955–6 v. D, W, I, Sp, S, Braz, Swd, Fin, G; 1956–7 v. I, W, Y, D, S, Eire, D, Eire.

HANCOCKS, J. (3) (Wolves) 1948–9 v. Switz; 1949–50 v. W; 1950–1 v. Y.

HARDWICK, G. (13) (Middlesbrough) 1946–7 v. I, W, S, Eire, H, F, Switz, Port; 1947–8 v. W, I, S, B, Swd.

HARRIS, P. (2) (Portsmouth) 1949–50 v. Eire; 1953–4 v. Hun.

HASSALL, H. (5) (Huddersfield) 1950–1 v. S, A, Port; 1951–2 v. F; (Bolton) 1953–4 v. I.

HAYNES, J. (32) (Fulham) 1954–5 v. I; 1955–6 v. I, Sp, S, Braz, Swd, Fin, G; 1956–7 v. W, Y, Eire, D, Eire; 1957–8 v. W, I, F, S, Port, Y, R, R, Braz, Aus, R; 1958–9 v. W, I, R, S, It, Braz, Peru, M, U.S.

HODGKINSON, A. (4) (Sheffield Utd) 1956–7 v. S, Eire, D; Eire.

HOLDEN, D. (5) (Bolton) 1958–9 v. S, It, Braz, Peru, M.

HOPKINSON, E. (12) (Bolton) 1957–8 v. W, I, F, S, Port, Y; 1958–9 v. S, It, Braz, Peru, M, U.S.

HOWE, D. (19) (W.B.A.) 1957–8 v. W, I, F, S, Port, Y, R, R, Braz, Aus; 1958–9 v. W, I, R, S, It, Braz, Peru, M, U.S.

HOWE, J. (3) (Derby) 1947–8 v. It; 1948–9 v. I, S.

HUGHES, L. (3) (Liverpool) 1949–50 v. C, U.S, Sp.

JEZZARD, B. (2) (Fulham) 1953–4 v. Hun; 1955–6 v. I.

JOHNSTON, H. (10) (Blackpool) 1946–7 v. S, H; 1950–1 v. S; 1952–3 v. A, C, U, U.S; 1953–4 v. W, I, Hun.

JONES, W. H. (2) (Liverpool) 1949–50 v. Port, B.

KEVAN, D. (13) (W.B.A.) 1956–7 v. S; 1957–8 v. W, I, S, Port, Y, R, R, Braz, Aus, R; 1958–9 v. M, U.S.

LANGLEY, J. (3) (Fulham) 1957–8 v. S, Port, Y.

LANGTON, R. (11) (Blackburn) 1946–7 v. I, W, Eire, H, F, Switz; 1947–8 v. Swd; 1948–9 v. D; (Bolton) 1949–50 v. S; 1950–1 v. I.

LAWTON, T. (15) (Chelsea) 1946–7 v. I, W, S, Eire, H, F, Switz, Port; 1947–8 v. W, I, (Notts County) S, B, Swd, It; 1948–9 v. D.

LEE, J. (1) (Derby) 1950–1 v. I.

LOFTHOUSE, N. (32) (Bolton) 1950–1 v. Y; 1951–2 v. W, I, Aus (2), S, It, Switz; 1952–3 v. I, W, B, S, A, C, U, U.S; 1953–4 v. W, FIFA, I, B, U; 1954–5 v. I, S, F, Sp, Port; 1955–6 v. D, W, Sp, S; 1958–9 v. W, R.

SOCCER QUIZ

1. What six things must a referee take on to the field?

*

2. Can there be a square pitch?

*

3. When and where was the F.A. Cup stolen?

*

4. What was Dixie Dean's record total of goals?

*

5. What was his highest total for one season?

*

6. Which clubs won the Second and First Division titles in successive seasons?

*

7. What is the greatest number of clubs from the same county to finish in the leading places in the First Division?

QUIZ ANSWERS

1. A whistle, coin, watch, ball, note-book, pencil. 2. No. The laws says the pitch must be rectangular. 3. In Birmingham in 1895. 4. 451. 5. 82, including 60 in the League. 6. Liverpool, Everton and Spurs. 7. 5, when Everton, Oldham, Blackburn, Burnley and Manchester City were the top 5 in 1914–15.

Henry Cockburn

Jackie Milburn

Nat Lofthouse

27

SOCCER QUIZ

1. What is the highest fee ever paid within the Football League? And for whom?

*

2. Who were the Cup giant-killers in these years—1937, 1948, 1954, 1959?

*

3. What is the longest period of service by a player with one Football League club?

*

4. Who was the last amateur to win a full England cap?

*

5. When was the offside rule changed?

*

6. When was the first Wembley Final?

*

7. Which teams took part?

QUIZ ANSWERS

1. £45,000, Albert Quixall. 2. Millwall, Colchester, Port Vale, Norwich. 3. 24 years 3 months—E. Sagar (Everton). 4. B. Joy, 1936 v. Belgium. 5. 1925. 6. 1923. 7. Bolton and West Ham.

Post-War Internationals—(contd.)

LOWE, E. (3) (Aston V) 1946–7 v. F, Switz, Port.
McDONALD, C. (8) (Burnley) 1957–8 v. R, R, Braz, Aus, R; 1958–9 v. I, W, R.
MANNION, W. (26) (Middlesbrough) 1946–7 v. I, W, S, Eire, H, F, Switz, Port; 1947–8 v. W, I, B, Swd, It; 1948–9 v. N, F; 1949–50 v. S, Eire, Port, B, C, U.S; 1950–1 v. W, Y, S; 1951–2 v. F.
MATTHEWS, R. (5) (Coventry) 1955–6 v. S, Braz, Swd, G; 1956–7 v. I (Chelsea).
MATTHEWS, S (37) (Stoke) 1946–7 v. S, (Blackpool) Switz, Port; 1947–8 v. W, I, S, B, It; 1948–9 v. I, W, S, D, Switz; 1949–50 v. Sp; 1950–1 v. W, Braz; 1956–7 v. I, W, Y, D, S, Eire, D.
McGARRY, W. (4) (Huddersfield) 1953–4 v. Switz, U; 1955–6 v. D, W.
McGUINNESS, W. (2) (Manchester Utd) 1958–9 v. I, M.
MEADOWS, J. (2) (Manchester City) 1954–5 v. Switz, U.
MEDLEY, L. (6) (Tottenham) 1950–1 v. W, Y; 1951–2 v. F, W, I, Aus.
MERRICK, G. (23) (Birmingham) 1951–2 v. I, Aus (2), S, It, Switz; 1952–3 v. I, W, B, S, A, C, U; 1953–4 v. W, FIFA, I, Hun (2), S, Y, B, Switz, U.
METCALFE, V. (2) (Huddersfield) 1950–1 v. A, Port.
MILBURN, J. (13) (Newcastle) 1948–9 v. I, W, S, Switz; 1949–50 v. W, Port, B, Sp; 1950–1 v. W, A, Port; 1951–2 v. F; 1955–6 v. D.
MILTON, C. A. (1) (Arsenal) 1951–2 v. Aus.
MORRIS, J. (3) (Derby) 1948–9 v. N, F; 1949–50 v. Eire.
MORTENSEN, S. (25) (Blackpool) 1946–7 v. Port; 1947–8 v. W, I, S, B, Swd, It; 1948–9 v. I, W, S, Swd, N; 1949–50 v. W, I, S, It, Port, B, C, U.S; 1950–1 v. S, A; 1953–4 v. FIFA, Hun.
MOZLEY, B. (3) (Derby) 1949–50 v. W, I, Eire.
MULLEN, J. (12) (Wolves) 1946–7 v. S; 1948–9 v. N, F; 1949–50 v. B, C, U.S; 1953–4 v. W, FIFA, I, S, Y, Switz.
NICHOLLS, J. (2) (W.B.A.) 1953–4 v. S, Y.

NICHOLSON, W. (1) (Tottenham) 1950–1 v. Port.
OWEN, S. (3) (Luton) 1953–4 v. Y, H, B.
PEARSON, S. (8) (Manchester Utd) 1947–8 v. S; 1948–9 v. I, S; 1949–50 v. I, It; 1950–1 v. Port; 1951–2 v. S, It.
PEGG, D. (1) (Manchester Utd) 1956–7 v. Eire.
PERRY, W. (3) (Blackpool) 1955–6 v. I, Sp, S.
PHILLIPS, L. (3) (Portsmouth) 1951–2 v. I; 1954–5 v. W, G.
PILKINGTON, B. (1) (Burnley) 1954–5 v. I.
PYE, J. (1) (Wolves) 1949–50 v. Eire.
QUIXALL, A. (5) (Sheffield Wed) 1953–4 v. W, FIFA, I; 1954–5 v. Sp, Port.
RAMSEY, A. (32) (Southampton) 1948–9 v. Switz; (Tottenham) 1949–50 v. S, It, Port, B, C, U.S, Sp; 1950–1 v. I, W, Y, S, A, Port; 1951–2 v. F, W, I, Aus (2), S, It, Switz; 1952–3 v. I, W, B, S, A, C, U; 1953–4 v. FIFA, Hun.
REVIE, D. (6) (Manchester City) 1954–5 v. I, S, F; 1955–6 v. D, W; 1956–7 v. I.

RICKABY, S. (1) (W.B.A.) 1953–4 v. I.
ROBB, G. (1) (Tottenham) 1953–4 v. F, R, R, Braz, Aus.
ROBSON, R. (5) (W.B.A.) 1957–8 v. F, R, R, Braz, Aus.
ROWLEY, J. (6) (Manchester Utd) 1948–9 v. Switz, Swd, F; 1949–50 v. It; 1951–2 v. S.
SCOTT, L. (17) (Arsenal) 1946–7 v. I, W, S, Eire, H, F, Switz, Port; 1947–8 v. W, I, S, B, Swd, It; 1948–9 v. I, W, D.
SEWELL, J. (6) (Sheffield Wed) 1951–2 v. I, Aus, Switz; 1952–3 v. I; 1953–4 v. Hun (2).
SHACKLETON, L. (5) (Sunderland) 1948–9 v. W, D; 1949–50 v. W; 1954–5 v. W, G.
SHAW, G. (4) (Sheffield Utd.) 1958–9 v. W, R, S, It.
SHIMWELL, E. (1) (Blackpool) 1948–9 v. Swd.
SILLETT, P. (3) (Chelsea) 1954–5 v. F, Sp, Port.
SLATER, W. (11) (Wolves) 1954–5 v. W, G; 1957–8 v. S, Port, Y, R, R, Braz, Aus, R; 1958–9 v. R.
SMITH, L. (6) (Arsenal) 1950–1 v. W; 1951–2 v. W, I; 1952–3 v. W, B, S.
STANIFORTH, R. (8) (Huddersfield) 1953–4 v. S, Y, Hun, B, Switz, U; 1954–5 v. W, G.
STRETEN, B. (1) (Luton) 1949–50 v. I.
SWIFT, F. (19) (Manchester City) 1946–7 v. I, W, S, Eire, H, F, Switz, Port; 1947–8 v. W, I, S, B, Swd, It; 1948–9 v. I, W, S, D, N.
TAYLOR, E. (1) (Blackpool) 1953–4 v. Hun.
TAYLOR, J. (2) (Fulham) 1950–1 v. A, Port.
TAYLOR, P. (3) (Liverpool) 1947–8 v. W, I, Swd.
TAYLOR, T. (16) (Manchester Utd) 1952–3 v. A, C, U; 1953–4 v. B, Switz; 1955–6 v. S, Braz, Swd, Fin, G; 1956–7 v. I, D, Eire, D, Eire; 1957–8 v. W, I, F.
THOMPSON, T. (2) (Aston V) 1951–2 v. W (Preston); 1956–7 v. S.
UFTON, D. (1) (Charlton) 1953–4 v. FIFA.
WARD, T. (2) (Derby) 1947–8 v. B; 1948–9 v. W.
WATSON, W. (4) (Sunderland) 1949–50 v. It; 1950–1 v. W, Y.
WHEELER, J. (1) (Bolton) 1954–5 v. I.
WILLIAMS, B. (24) (Wolves) 1948–9 v. F; 1949–50 v. W, S, Eire, It, Port, B, C, U.S, Sp; 1950–1 v. W, Y, S, A, Port; 1951–2 v. F, W; 1954–5 v. G, S, F, Sp, Port; 1955–6 v. W.
WILLIS, A. (1) (Tottenham) 1951–2 v. F.

WILSHAW, D. (12) (Wolves) 1953–4 v. W, Switz, U; 1954–5 v. S, F, Sp, Port; 1955–6 v. W, I, Fin, G; 1956–7 v. I.
WOOD, R. (3) (Manchester Utd) 1954–5 v. I, W; 1955–6 v. Fin.
WRIGHT, W. (105) (Wolves) 1946–7 v. I, W, S, Eire, H, F, Switz, Port; 1947–8 v. W, I, S, B, Swd, It; 1948–9 v. W, I, S, D, Switz, Swd, N, F; 1949–50 v. W, I, S, Eire, H, Port, B, C, U.S, Sp; 1950–1 v. I, S, A; 1951–2 v. F, W, I, Aus (2), S, It, Switz; 1952–3 v. I, W, B, S, A, C, U, S; 1953–4 v. W, FIFA, I, Hun (2), S, Y, B, Switz, U; 1954–5 v. I, W, G, S, F, Sp, Port; 1955–6 v. D, W, I, Sp, S, Braz, Swd, Fin, G; 1956–7 v. I, W, Y, D, S, Eire, D, Eire; 1957–8 v. W, I, F, S, Port, Y, R, R, Braz, Aus, R; 1958–9 v. W, I, R, S, It, Braz, Peru, M, U.S.

SCOTLAND

AIRD, J. (4) (Burnley) 1953–4 v. N (2), Aus, U.
AITKEN, G. (8) (East Fife) 1948–9 v. E, F; 1949–50 v. I, W, Switz; (Sunderland) 1952–3 v. W, I; 1953–4 v. E.

Bobby Evans   Willie Woodburn   Billy Liddell

ANDERSON, J. (1) (Leicester) 1953–4 v. Fin.
AULD, R. (3) (Celtic) 1958–9 v. J, H, Port.
BAIRD, D. (1) (Partick Thistle) 1958–9 v. J.
BAIRD, H. (8) (Airdrieonians) 1955–6 v. Aus; (Rangers) 1956–7 v. Y, Sp, Switz, G, Sp; 1957–8 v. I, F.
BAULD, W. (3) (Hearts) 1949–50 v. E, Switz, Port.
BLACK, I. (1) (Southampton) 1947–8 v. E.
BLAIR, J. (1) (Blackpool) 1946–7 v. W.
BRENNAN, F. (7) (Newcastle) 1946–7 v. W, I; 1952–3 v. W, I, E; 1953–4 v. I, E.
BROWN, B. (4) (Dundee) 1957–8 v. F; 1958–9 v. I, W, E.
BROWN, A. (14) (East Fife) 1949–50 v. Switz, Port, F; (Blackpool) 1951–2 v. U.S, D, Swd; 1952–3 v. W; 1953–4 v. W, E, N (2), Fin, Aus, U.
BROWN, H. (3) (Partick Thistle) 1946–7 v. W, B, L.
BROWN, R. (3) (Rangers) 1946–7 v. I; 1948–9 v. I; 1951–2 v. E.
BUCKLEY, P. (3) (Aberdeen) 1953–4 v. N; 1954–5 v. W, I.
CALDOW, E. (13) (Rangers) 1956–7 v. E, Sp, Switz, G, Sp; 1957–8 v. I, Switz, W, H, Pol, Y, P, F; 1958–9 v. I, W, E, G, H, Port.
CAMPBELL, R. (3) (Chelsea) 1949–50 v. Switz, Port, F.
CAMPBELL, W. (7) (Morton) 1946–7 v. I, B, L; 1947–8 v. E, B, Switz, F.
COLLINS, R. (28) (Celtic) 1950–1 v. W, I, Aus; 1954–5 v. Y, Aus, H; 1955–6 v. I, W; 1956–7 v. W, E, Sp, Switz, G, Sp; 1957–8 v. I, Switz, W, H, Pol, Y, P, F; 1958–9 v. I, W, E, G, H, Port.
COMBE, R. (3) (Hibernian) 1947–8 v. E, B, Switz.
CONN, A. (1) (Hearts) 1955–6 v. Aus.
COWAN, J. (25) (Morton) 1947–8 v. B, Switz, F; 1948–9 v. W, E, F; 1949–50 v. I, W, E, Switz, Port, F; 1950–1 v. W, I, Aus (2), E, D, F, B; 1951–2 v. I, W, U.S, D, Swd; 1952–3 v. W, I, E; 1953–4 v. W, I, W, E.
COWIE, D. (20) (Dundee) 1952–3 v. E, Swd; 1953–4 v. I, W, N, Fin, Aus, U; 1954–5 v. W, I, Aus, Hun; 1955–6 v. W, Aus; 1956–7 v. I; 1957–8 v. Hun, Pol, Y, P.
COX, S. (25) (Rangers) 1947–8 v. F; 1948–9 v. E, F; 1949–50 v. I, W, E, Switz, Port, F; 1950–1 v. I, W, E, D, F, B, Aus; 1951–2 v. I, W, U.S, D, Swd; 1952–3 v. W, I, E; 1953–4 v. I, W, E.
CULLEN, M. (1) (Luton) 1955–6 v. Aus.

CUMMING, J. (4) (Hearts) 1954–5 v. Hun, E, Port, Y.
CUNNINGHAM, W. (8) (Preston) 1953–4 v. N (2), Fin, Aus, U; 1954–5 v. W, Hun, E.
DAVIDSON, J. (8) (Partick Thistle) 1953–4 v. N (2), Aus, U; 1954–5 v. W, I, Hun, E.
DELANEY, J. (4) (Manchester Utd) 1946–7 v. E; 1947–8 v. I, W, E.
DICK, J. (1) (West Ham) 1958–9 v. E.
DOCHERTY, T. (25) (Preston) 1951–2 v. W; 1952–3 v. E, Swd; 1953–4 v. N (2), Aus, U; 1954–5 v. W, Hun (2), E, Aus; 1956–7 v. Y, E, Sp, Switz, G, Sp; 1957–8 v. I, Switz, W, E; 1958–9 v. I, W, E.
DOUGALL, C. (1) (Birmingham) 1946–7 v. W.
DOUGAN, R. (1) (Hearts) 1949–50 v. Switz.
DUNCAN, D. (3) (East Fife) 1947–8 v. B, Switz, F.
DUNCANSON, J. (1) (Rangers) 1946–7 v. I.
EVANS, R. (41) (Celtic) 1948–9 v. W, I, E, F; 1949–50 v. I, W, Switz, Port; 1950–1 v. Aus, E; 1951–2 v. I; 1952–3 v. Swd; 1953–4 v. I, W, E, N, Fin; 1954–5 v. I, Port, Y, Aus, Hun; 1955–6 v. I, W, E, Aus; 1956–7 v. G, Sp; 1957–8 v. I, Switz, W, E, Hun, Pol, Y, P, F; 1958–9 v. E, G, H, Port.
EWING, T. (2) (Partick Thistle) 1957–8 v. W, E.
FARM, G. (10) (Blackpool) 1952–3 v. W, I, E, Swd; (1953–4 v. I, W, E; 1958–9 v. G, H, Port.
FERNIE, W. (11) (Celtic) 1953–4 v. Fin, Aus, U; 1954–5 v. W, I; 1956–7 v. Y, W, E; 1957–8 v. Switz, W, P.
FLAVELL, R. (2) (Airdrie) 1946–7 v. B, L.
FLEMING, C. (1) (East Fife) 1953–4 v. I.
FORBES, A. (14) (Sheffield Utd) 1946–7 v. E, B, L; 1947–8 v. I, W; (Arsenal) 1949–50 v. E, Port, F; 1950–1 v. W, I, Aus; 1951–2 v. W, D, Swd.
FORREST, J. (1) (Motherwell) 1957–8 v. E.
FRASER, W. (2) (Sunderland) 1954–5 v. D, I.
GARDINER (1) (Motherwell) 1957–8 v. W.
GEMMELL, T. (2) (St. Mirren) 1954–5 v. Port, Y.
GLEN (2) (Aberdeen) 1955–6 v. I, E.
GOVAN, J. (6) (Hibernian) 1947–8 v. W, E, B, Switz, F; 1948–9 v. I, W.
GRANT, J. (2) (Hibernian) 1958–9 v. I, W.
HADDOCK, H. (6) (Clyde) 1954–5 v. Hun (2), E, Port, Y; 1957–8 v. W.
HAMILTON, G. (5) (Aberdeen) 1946–7 v. I; 1950–1 v. B, Aus; 1953–4 v. N (2).
HAUGHNEY, M. (1) (Celtic) 1953–4 v. E.
HENDERSON, J. (7) (Portsmouth) 1952–3 v. Swd; 1953–4 v. I, E, N; 1955–6 v. W; 1958–9 (Arsenal) v. I, W.
HERD, D. (3) (Arsenal) 1958–9 v. I, W, E.
HERD, G. (1) (Clyde) 1957–8 v. E.
HEWIE, J. (16) (Charlton) 1955–6 v. E, Aus; 1956–7 v. I, W, E, Sp, Switz, G, Sp; 1957–8 v. W, Pol, Y, F; 1958–9 v. I, W, H, Port.
HOULISTON, W. (3) (Queen of the South) 1948–9 v. I, E, F.
HOWIE, H. (1) (Hibernian) 1948–9 v. W.
HUMPHRIES, W. (1) (Motherwell) 1951–2 v. Swd.
HUSBAND, I. (1) (Partick) 1946–7 v. W.
IMLACH, S. (4) (Notts Forest) 1957–8 v. H, Pol, Y, F.
JOHNSTONE, L. (2) (Clyde) 1947–8 v. B, Switz.
JOHNSTONE, R. (17) (Hibernian) 1950–1 v. E, D, F; 1951–2 v. I, E; 1952–3 v. E, Swd; 1953–4 v. W, E, N, Fin; 1954–5 v. I, Hun, (Manchester City) E; 1955–6 v. I, W, E.
KELLY, H. (1) (Blackpool) 1951–2 v. U.S.
KELLY, J. (2) (Barnsley) 1948–9 v. W, I.
KERR, A. (3) (Partick) 1954–5 v. Aus, H; 1958–9 v. J.
LAW, D. (5) (Huddersfield) 1958–9 v. I, W, J, H, Port.
LEGGAT, G. (12) (Aberdeen) 1955–6 v. E; 1956–7 v. W; 1957–8 v. I, H, Pol, Y, P; 1958–9 v. W, E, G, H.
LIDDELL, W. (28) (Liverpool) 1946–7 v. W, I; 1947–8 v. I, W, E; 1949–50 v. W, E, Port, F; 1950–1 v. W, I, Aus, E; 1951–2 v. I, W, E, U.S, D, Swd; 1952–3 v. W, I, E; 1953–4 v. E; 1954–5 v. Port, Y, Aus, Hun; 1955–6 v. I.
LITTLE, A. (1) (Rangers) 1952–3 v. Swd.
LINWOOD, A. (1) (Clyde) 1949–50 v. W.
LOGIE, J. (1) (Arsenal) 1952–3 v. I.
LONG, H. (1) (Clyde) 1946–7 v. I.

28

MACAULAY, A. (7) (Brentford) 1946-7 v. E; (Arsenal) 1947-8 v. I, W, E, B, Switz, F.
MACKAY, D. (6) (Hearts) 1956-7 v. Sp; 1957-8 v. F; 1958-9 v. I, W, E, G.
MARTIN, F. (6) (Aberdeen) 1953-4 v. N (2), Aus, U; 1954-5 v. N, E.
MASON, J. (7) (Third Lanark) 1948-9 v. W, I, E; 1949-50 v. I; 1950-1 v. I, B, Aus.
MATHERS, D. (1) (Partick) 1953-4 v. Fin.
McCANN, A. (1) (Motherwell) 1958-9 v. G.
McCOLL, I. (14) (Rangers) 1949-50 v. E, F; 1950-1 v. W, I, B; 1956-7 v. Y, I, W, E, Sp, Switz, G; 1957-8 v. I, E.
MacDONALD, J. (2) (Sunderland) 1955-6 v. I, W.
McFARLANE, W. (1) (Hearts) 1946-7 v. L.
McGUGAN, J. (1) (St. Mirren) 1958-9 v. J.
McKAY, D. (5) (Celtic) 1958-9 v. E, G, J, H, Port.
McKENZIE, J. (9) (Partick Thistle) 1953-4 v. W, E, N, Fin, Aus, U; 1954-5 v. W, E; 1955-6 v. Aus.
McLAREN, A. (4) (Preston) 1946-7 v. E, B, L; 1947-8 v. W.
McMILLAN, I. (5) (Airdrieonians) 1951-2 v. E, U.S, D; 1954-5 v. E; 1955-6 v. E.
McNAUGHT, W. (5) (Raith Rovers) 1950-1 v. W, I, Aus; 1951-2 v. E; 1954-5 v. I.
McPHAIL, J. (5) (Celtic) 1949-50 v. W; 1950-1 v. W, I, Aus; 1953-4 v. I.
MILLER, W. (6) (Celtic) 1946-7 v. W, E, B, L; 1947-8 v. I, W.
MITCHELL, R. (2) (Newcastle) 1950-1 v. D, F.
MOCHAN, N. (3) (Celtic) 1953-4 v. N, Aus, U.
MOIR, W. (1) (Bolton) 1949-50 v. E.
MORRIS, H. (1) (East Fife) 1949-50 v. I.
MUDIE, J. (17) (Blackpool) 1956-7 v. Y, I, W, E, Sp, Switz, G, Sp; 1957-8 v. I, Switz, W, E, Hun, Pol, Y, P, F.
MURRAY, J. (5) (Hearts) 1957-8 v. E, Hun, Pol, Y, F.
ORMOND, W. (6) (Hibernian) 1953-4 v. E, N, Fin, Aus, U; 1958-9 v. E.
ORR, T. (2) (Morton) 1951-2 v. I, W.
PARKER, A. (15) (Falkirk) 1954-5 v. Port, Y, Aus; 1955-6 v. I, W, E, Aus; 1956-7 v. Y, I, W; 1957-8 v. I, Switz, W, E, P.
PATON, A. (2) (Motherwell) 1951-2 v. D, Swd.
PEARSON, T. (2) (Newcastle) 1946-7 v. E, B.

SHAW, J. (4) (Rangers) 1946-7 v. E, B, L; 1947-8 v. I.
SLATER, R. (1) (Falkirk) 1958-9 v. J.
SMITH, G. (18) (Hibernian) 1946-7 v. I, E; 1947-8 v. W, B, Switz, F; 1951-2 v. E, U.S; 1954-5 v. Port, Y, Aus, H; 1955-6 v. I, W; 1956-7 v. E, Sp, Switz, Sp.
SMITH, W. (3) (Celtic) 1958-9 v. J, H, Port.
STEEL, W. (30) (Morton) 1946-7 v. E, B, L; (Derby) 1947-8 v. I, W, E, F; 1948-9 v. W, I, E; 1949-50 v. I, W, E, Switz, Port, F, (Dundee); 1950-1 v. W, I, Aus (2), E, D, F, B; 1951-2 v. W; 1952-3 v. W, I, E, Swd.
STEPHEN, J. (2) (Bradford) 1946-7 v. W; 1947-8 v. W.
ST. JOHN, I. (1) (Motherwell) 1958-9 v. G.
STEVENSON, W. (1) (Rangers) 1958-9 v. J.
TELFER, W. (1) (St. Mirren) 1953-4 v. W.
THORNTON, W. (7) (Rangers) 1946-7 v. W, I; 1947-8 v. I, E; 1948-9 v. F; 1951-2 v. D, Swd.
TONER, W. (2) (Kilmarnock) 1958-9 v. I, W.
TURNBULL, E. (8) (Hibernian) 1947-8 v. B, Switz; 1950-1 v. Aus; 1957-8 v. H, Pol, Y, P, F.
WADDELL, W. (17) (Rangers) 1946-7 v. W; 1948-9 v. W, I, E, F; 1949-50 v. I, E; 1950-1 v. E, D, F, B, Aus; 1951-2 v. I, W; 1953-4 v. I; 1954-5 v. W, I.
WARDHAUGH, J. (2) (Hearts) 1954-5 v. Hun; 1956-7 v. I.
WATSON, J. (2) (Motherwell) 1947-8 v. I; 1953-4 v. I.
WEIR, A. (1) (Motherwell) 1958-9 v. G.
WHITE, J. (4) (Falkirk) 1958-9 v. G, J, H, Port.
WILSON, A. (1) (Portsmouth) 1953-4 v. Fin.
WOODBURN, W. (24) (Rangers) 1946-7 v. E, B, L; 1947-8 v. I, W; 1948-9 v. W, I, E, F; 1949-50 v. I, W, E, Port, F; 1950-1 v. W, I, Aus (2), E, D, F, B; 1951-2 v. I, W, E, U.S.
WRIGHT, T. (3) (Sunderland) 1952-3 v. W, I, E.
YORSTON, H. (1) (Aberdeen) 1954-5 v. W.
YOUNG, G. (53) (Rangers) 1946-7 v. I, E, B, L; 1947-8 v. I, E, B, Switz, F; 1948-9 v. W, I, E, F; 1949-50 v. I, W, E, Switz, Port, F; 1950-1 v. W, I, Aus (2), E, D, F, B; 1951-2 v. I, W, E, U.S, D, Swd; 1952-3 v. W, I, E, Swd; 1953-4 v. I, W; 1954-5 v. W, I, Port, Y; 1955-6 v. I, W, E, Aus; 1956-7 v. Y, I, W, E, Sp, Switz.

Jack Kelsey

Alf Sherwood

Roy Paul

BLANCHFLOWER, D. (34) (Barnsley) 1949-50 v. S, W; 1950-1 v. E, S, F; (Aston V) 1951-2 v. W; 1952-3 v. E, S, F, W; 1953-4 v. S, E, W; 1954-5 v. E, S, (Tottenham) W; 1955-6 v. S, E, W; 1956-7 v. E, S, D, W, It, Port; 1957-8 v. S, E, It, W, Cz, A, Cz, F; 1958-9 v. Sp, S, E, W.
BOWLER, G. (3) (Hull) 1949-50 v. S, E, W.
BRENNAN, R. (5) (Luton) 1948-9 v. W; (Birmingham) 1949-50 v. S, E, W; (Fulham) 1950-1 v. E.
CAMPBELL, J. (2) (Fulham) 1950-1 v. E, S, W.
CAREY, J. (7) (Manchester Utd) 1946-7 v. E, S, W; 1947-8 v. E; 1948-9 v. E, S, W.
CASEY, T. (12) (Newcastle) 1954-5 v. W; 1955-6 v. W; 1956-7 v. E, S, D, W, It, Port; 1957-8 v. G, F; 1958-9 v. Sp, E.
COCHRANE, D. (10) (Leeds) 1946-7 v. E, S, W; 1947-8 v. S, E, W; 1948-9 v. S, W; 1949-50 v. S, E.
COYLE, F. (4) (Coleraine) 1955-6 v. S, E; 1956-7 v. D; (Notts Forest) 1957-8 v. A.
CUNNINGHAM, W. (24) (St. Mirren) 1950-1 v. W; 1952-3 v. E; 1953-4 v. S; 1954-5 v. S; 1955-6 v. S, E, W, (Leicester); 1956-7 v. E, S, D, W, It, Port; 1957-8 v. S, It, W, Cz, A, G, Cz, F; 1958-9 v. S, E, W.
CROSSAN, E. (3) (Blackburn) 1949-50 v. S; 1950-1 v. E; 1954-5 v. W.
CUSH, W. (19) (Glenavon) 1950-1 v. E, S; 1953 4 v. S, E; 1956-7 v. D, W, It, Port; 1957-8 v. It, (Leeds) W, Cz, A, G, Cz, F; 1958-9 v. Sp, E, S, W.
D'ARCY, S. (5) (Chelsea) 1951-2 v. W; 1952-3 v. E, (Brentford) S, F, W.
DICKSON, (1) (Linfield) 1956-7 v. S.
DICKSON, W. (12) (Chelsea) 1950-1 v. W, F; 1951-2 v. S, E, W; 1952-3 v. E, S, F, W; (Arsenal) 1953-4 v. E, W; 1954-5 v. E.
DOHERTY, P. (6) (Derby) 1946-7 v. E (Huddersfield) W; 1947-8 v. E, W; 1948-9 v. S; 1950-1 v. S.
DOUGAN, D. (1) (Portsmouth) 1957-8 v. Cz.
DOUGLAS, S. (1) (Belfast Celtic) 1946-7 v. E.
EGLINTON, T. (6) (Everton) 1946-7 v. S, W; 1947-8 v. S, E, W; 1948-9 v. E.
FARRELL, P. (7) (Everton) 1946-7 v. S, W; 1947-8 v. S, E, W; 1948-9 v. E, W.
FEENEY, J. (2) (Linfield) 1946-7 v. E; (Swansea) 1949-50 v. E.
FERRIS, R. (3) (Birmingham) 1949-50 v. S; 1950-1 v. E; 1951-2 v. S.
FORDE, J. (1) (Ards) 1958-9 v. Sp.
GALLOGLY, C. (2) (Huddersfield) 1950-1 v. E, S.
GORMAN, W. (4) (Brentford) 1946-7 v. E, S, W; 1947-8 v. W.
GRAHAM, R. (13) (Doncaster) 1950-1 v. W, F; 1951-2 v. S, E, W; 1952-3 v. S, F; 1953-4 v. E, W; 1954-5 v. S, W; 1955-6 v. E; 1958-9 v. E.
GREGG, H. (15) (Doncaster) 1953-4 v. W; 1956-7 v. S, E, S, D, W, It, Port; 1957-8 v. E, (Manchester Utd) W, Cz, A, G, Cz, F; 1958-9 v. E, W.
HILL, J. (1) (Norwich) 1958-9 v. W.
HINTON, E. (7) (Fulham) 1946-7 v. S, W; 1947-8 v. S, E, W; (Millwall) 1950-1 v. W, F.
HUGHES, W. (1) (Bolton) 1950-1 v. W.
JONES, J. (4) (Glenavon) 1955-6 v. W; 1956-7 v. E, S, W.
KEANE, J. (1) (Swansea) 1948-9 v. E.
KEITH, R. (11) (Newcastle) 1957-8 v. E, W, Cz, A, G, Cz, F; 1958-9 v. Sp, S, E, W.

KELLY, H. (4) (Fulham) 1949-50 v. E, W; (Southampton) 1950-1 v. E, S.
KELLY, P. (1) (Barnsley) 1949-50 v. S.
LOCKHART, N. (8) (Linfield) 1946-7 v. E; (Coventry) 1949-50 v. W, Port; 1951-2 v. E; (Aston V) 1953-4 v. S, E; 1954-5 v. W; 1955-6 v. W.
MARTIN, C. (6) (Glentoran) 1946-7 v. S; (Leeds) 1947-8 v. S, E, W; (Aston V) 1948-9 v. E; 1949-50 v. W.
McADAMS, W. (5) (Manchester City) 1953-4 v. W; 1954-5 v. S; 1956-7 v. E, S; 1957-8 v. S.
McALINDEN, J. (2) (Portsmouth) 1946-7 v. E; (Southend) 1948-9 v. E.
McCABE, J. (6) (Leeds) 1948-9 v. S, W; 1949-50 v. S; 1950-1 v. W; 1952-3 v. W; 1953-4 v. S.
McCAVANA, T. (3) (Coleraine) 1954-5 v. S; 1955-6 v. S, E.
McCLEARY, J. (1) (Cliftonville) 1954-5 v. W.
McCOURT, F. (6) (Manchester City) 1951-2 v. W; 1952-3 v. E, S, F, W.
McCRORY, S. (1) (Southend) 1957-8 v. W.
McGARRY, J. K. (3) (Cliftonville) 1950-1 v. S, W, F.
McILROY, J. (34) (Burnley) 1951-2 v. S, E, W; 1952-3 v. S, E; 1953-4 v. S, E, W; 1954-5 v. S, E, W; 1955-6 v. S, E, W; 1956-7 v. E, S, D, W, It, Port; 1957-8 v. S, E, It, W, Cz, A, G, Cz, F; 1958-9 v. Sp, S, E, W.
McKENNA, J. (7) (Huddersfield) 1949-50 v. S, E, W; 1950-1 v. E, S, F; 1951-2 v. E.

SOCCER QUIZ

1. How many F.A. Cups have there been?

*

2. Who played for Ireland at both soccer and rugby since the war?

*

3. Who played for both England and Wales in soccer internationals?

*

4. Name three footballers who left England for Italian football since the war.

*

5. Are caps awarded for Under-23 internationals?

*

6. How much is the bonus for a win in the Football League?

*

7. How much in the Scottish League?

QUIZ ANSWERS

1. Three. 2. The brothers Kevin and Michael Flanagan. 3. R. E. Evans (Sheffield United). 4. These four did—T. Sloan (Arsenal), E. Firmani (Charlton), J. Charles (Leeds) and T. Marchi (Spurs). 5. No. 6. £4. 7. There is no maximum.

Jimmy McIlroy

Peter McParland

Alf McMichael

REDPATH, W. (9) (Motherwell) 1948-9 v. W, I; 1950-1 v. E, D, F, B Aus; 1951-2 v. I, W.
REILLY, L. (38) (Hibernian) 1948-9 v. W, E, F; 1949-50 v. I, W, Switz, F; 1950-1 v. W, E, D, F, B Aus; 1951-2 v. I, W, E, U.S, D, Swd; 1952-3 v. W, I, E, Swd; 1953-4 v. W; 1954-5 v. Hun (2), E, Port, Y, Aus; 1955-6 v. I, W, E, Aus; 1956-7 v. I, Switz.
RING, T. (12) (Clyde) 1952-3 v. Swd; 1954-5 v. W, I, Hun, E; 1956-7 v. E, Sp, Switz, G, Sp; 1957-8 v. I, Switz.
ROBERTSON, A. (5) (Clyde) 1954-5 v. Port, Aus, Hun; 1957-8 v. Switz, P.
RUTHERFORD, E. (1) (Rangers) 1947-8 v. F.
SCOTT, A. (7) (Rangers) 1956-7 v. Y, I, G; 1957-8 v. Switz, W; 1958-9 v. Y, Port.
SCOULAR, J. (9) (Portsmouth) 1950-1 v. D, F, Aus; 1951-2 v. E, U.S, D, Swd; 1952-3 v. W, I.
SHAW, D. (8) (Hibernian) 1946-7 v. W, I; 1947-8 v. E, B, Switz, F; 1948-9 v. W, I.

YOUNGER, T. (24) (Hibernian) 1954-5 v. Port, Y, Aus, Hun; 1955-6 v. I, W, E, Aus; (Liverpool) 1956-7 v. Y, I, N, E, Sp, Switz, G, Sp; 1957-8 v. I, Switz, W, E, Hun, Pol, W, P.

IRELAND

AHERNE, T. (4) (Belfast Celtic) 1946-7 v. E; 1947-8 v. S; 1948-9 v. W; (Luton) 1949-50 v. W.
BINGHAM, W. (36) (Sunderland) 1950-1 v. F; 1951-2 v. S, E, W; 1952-3 v. S, F, W; 1953-4 v. S, E, W; 1954-5 v. E, S, W; 1955-6 v. S, E, W; 1956-7 v. E, S, D, W, It, Port; 1957-8 v. S, E, It, W, Cz, A, G, Cz, F; (Luton) 1958-9 v. Sp, S, E, W.
BLANCHFLOWER, J. (11) (Manchester Utd) 1953-4 v. W; 1954-5 v. E, S; 1955-6 v. S, W; 1956-7 v. E, S, D; 1957-8 v. S, E, It.

SOCCER QUIZ

1. Who scored the first goal at Wembley? (below)

*

2. Where were the Finals staged immediately before Wembley?

*

3. Which parson scored in a Cup Final?

*

4. Who was the first Footballer of the Year? (above)

*

5. Who won the Footballer of the Year award twice?

*

6. What is the record Cup Final score?

*

7. Two of these clubs were not among the original twelve members of the Football League — Accrington, Sunderland, Notts County, Everton, Nottingham Forest, Sheffield Wednesday, Stoke. Name the two clubs.

QUIZ ANSWERS

1. D. Jack for Bolton. 2. Stamford Bridge. 3. Rev. K. R. G. Hunt for Wolves in 1908. 4. S. Matthews. 5. T. Finney. 6. 6-0, Bury v. Derby, 1903. 7. Sunderland and Sheffield Wednesday.

Post-War Internationals—*(contd.)*

McMICHAEL, A. (36) (Newcastle) 1949-50 v. S, E; 1950-1 v. S, E, F; 1951-2 v. S, E, W; 1952-3 v. E, S, F, W; 1953-4 v. E, S, W; 1954-5 v. E, W; 1955-6 v. W; 1956-7 v. E, S, D, W, It, Port; 1957-8 v. E, S, It, W, Cz, A, G, Cz; 1958-9 v. Sp, S, W.

McMORRAN, E. (15) (Belfast Celtic) 1946-7 v. E; (Barnsley) 1950-1 v. E, S, W; 1951-2 v. S, E, W; 1952-3 v. E, S, F; (Doncaster) W; 1953-4 v. E; 1955-6 v. W; 1956-7 v. It, Port.

McPARLAND, P. (22) (Aston V) 1953-4 v. W; 1954-5 v. E, S; 1955-6 v. S, E; 1956-7 v. E, S, D, W; 1957-8 v. E, It, W, Cz, A, G, Cz, F; 1958-9 v. Sp, S, E, W.

MONTGOMERY, F. (1) (Coleraine) 1954-5 v. E.

MOORE, C. (1) (Glentoran) 1948-9 v. W.

O'DRISCOLL, J. (3) (Swansea) 1948-9 v. E, S, W.

PEACOCK, R. (21) (Celtic) 1951-2 v. S; 1952-3 v. F; 1953-4 v. W; 1954-5 v. E, S; 1955-6 v. S, E; 1956-7 v. W, It, Port; 1957-8 v. E, It, W, Cz, A, G, Cz; 1958-9 v. S, E, W.

RUSSELL, A. (1) (Linfield) 1946-7 v. E.

RYAN, R. (1) (W.B.A.) 1949-50 v. W.

SCOTT, J. (2) (Grimsby) 1957-8 v. Cz, F.

SHIELDS, J. (1) (Southampton) 1956-7 v. S.

SIMPSON, W. (8) (Rangers) 1950-1 v. W, F; 1953-4 v. S, E; 1954-5 v. E; 1956-7 v. It, Port; 1957-8 v. S, E, It, W; 1958-9 v. S.

SLOAN, W. (1) (Arsenal) 1946-7 v. W.

SMYTH, S. (9) (Wolves) 1947-8 v. S, E, W; 1948-9 v. S, E; 1949-50 v. S, E, W; (Stoke) 1951-2 v. E.

SMYTH, W. (4) (Distillery) 1948-9 v. E, S; 1953-4 v. E.

STEVENSON, A. (3) (Everton) 1946-7 v. S, W; 1947-8 v. S.

TULLY, C. (10) (Celtic) 1948-9 v. E; 1949-50 v. E; 1951-2 v. S; 1952-3 v. E, S, F, W; 1953-4 v. S; 1955-6 v. E; 1958-9 v. Sp.

UPRICHARD, N. (15) (Swindon) 1951-2 v. S, E, W; 1952-3 v. E, S, (Portsmouth) F, W; 1954-5 v. E, S, W; 1955-6 v. S, E, W; 1957-8 v. S, It, Cz; 1958-9 v. Sp, S.

VERNON, J. (17) (Belfast Celtic) 1946-7 v E, S, (W.B.A.) W; 1947-8 v. S, E, W; 1948-9 v. S, E, W; 1949-50 v. S, E, W; 1950-1 v. E, S, W, F; 1951-2 v. S, E, W.

WALKER, J. (1) (Doncaster) 1954-5 v. W.

WALSH, D. (9) (W.B.A.) 1946-7 v. S, W; 1947-8 v. S, E; 1948-9 v. E, S, W; 1949-50 v. W.

WALSH, W. (5) (Manchester City) 1947-8 v. S, E, W; 1948-9 v. E, S.

WALES

ALLCHURCH, I. (37) (Swansea) 1950-1 v. E, I, Port, Switz; 1951-2 v. E, S, I; 1952-3 v. E, I, F, Y; 1953-4 v. E, S, I, Aus; 1954-5 v. Y, S, E, I; 1955-6 v. E, S, Aus, I; 1956-7 v. E; 1957-8 v. Is, Is, I, Hun, M, Swd, Hun, Braz; (Newcastle) 1958-9 v. E, S, I.

ALLCHURCH, L. (7) (Swansea) 1954-5 v. I; 1955-6 v. Aus; 1957-8 v. EG, S, Is, I; 1958-9 v. E.

ALLEN, B. (2) (Coventry) 1950-1 v. S, E.

BAKER, C. (Cardiff) 1957-8 v. M.

BAKER, W. (1) (Cardiff) 1947-8 v. I.

BARNES, W. (21) (Arsenal) 1947-8 v. E, S, I; 1948-9 v. S, E, I; 1949-50 v. S, E, I, B; 1950-1 v. S, E, I, Port; 1951-2 v. E, S, I; 1953-4 v. E, S; 1954-5 v. Y, S.

BOWEN, D. (19) (Arsenal) 1954-5 v. Y, S; 1956-7 v. I, Cz, EG; 1957-8 v. EG, E, S, Is, Is, I, H, M, Swd, Hun, Braz; 1958-9 v. E, S, I.

BURGESS, R. (31) (Tottenham) 1946-7 v. E, S, I; 1947-8 v. E, S; 1948-9 v. S, E, I, Port, B, Switz; 1949-50 v. S, E, I, B; 1950-1 v. S, I, Port, Switz; 1951-2 v. E, S, I; 1952-3 v. S, E, I, F, Y; 1953-4 v. E, S, I, Aus.

CHARLES, J. (29) (Leeds) 1949-50 v. I; 1950-1 v. Switz; 1952-3 v. I, F, Y; 1953-4 v. E, S, I, Aus; 1954-5 v. S, E, I; 1955-6 v. E, S, Aus, I; 1956-7 v. S, E, I; (Juventus) Cz, EG, Cz; 1957-8 v. Is, Is, Hun, M, Swd, Hun.

CHARLES, M. (21) (Swansea) 1954-5 v. I; 1955-6 v. E, S, Aus; 1956-7 v. E, I, Cz, EG, Cz; 1957-8 v. EG, E, S, Is, Is, Hun, M, Swd, Hun, Braz; 1958-9 v. E, S.

CLARKE, R. (21) (Manchester City) 1948-9 v. E; 1949-50 v. S, I, B; 1950-1 v. S, E, I, Port, Switz; 1951-2 v. E, S, I; 1952-3 v. S, E; 1953-4 v. E, S; 1955-6 v. I.

CROWE, V. (2) (Aston Villa) 1958-9 v. E, I.

DANIEL, R. (20) (Arsenal) 1950-1 v. E, I, Port; 1951-2 v. E, S, I; 1952-3 v. S, E, I, F, Y; (Sunderland) 1953-4 v. E, S, I; 1954-5 v. E, I; 1956-7 v. E, S, I, Cz.

DAVIES, R. (6) (Newcastle) 1952-3 v. S, E, I; 1953-4 v. E, S; 1957-8 v. EG, E.

EDWARDS, G. (12) (Birmingham) 1946-7 v. S, E, I; 1947-8 v. E, S, I; (Cardiff) 1948-9 v. I, Port, B, Switz; 1949-50 v. E, S, I.

EDWARDS, T. (2) (Charlton) 1956-7 v. I, EG.

FORD, T. (37) (Swansea) 1946-7 v. S, (Aston V) I; 1947-8 v. S, I; 1948-9 v. S, E, I, Port, B, Switz; 1949-50 v. E, S, I, B; 1950-1 v. S, (Sunderland) E, I, Port, Switz; 1951-2 v. E, S, I; 1952-3 v. S, E, I, F, Y; (Cardiff) 1953-4 v. Aus; 1954-5 v. Y, S, E, I; 1955-6 v. E, S, Aus, I; 1956-7 v. S.

FOULKES, W. (10) (Newcastle) 1951-2 v. E, S, I; 1952-3 v. S, E, F, Y; 1953-4 v. E, S, I.

GRIFFITHS, H. (1) (Swansea) 1952-3 v. I.

GRIFFITHS, M. (11) (Leicester) 1946-7 v. I; 1948-9 v. Port, B; 1949-50 v. E, S, B; 1950-1 v. E, I, Port, Switz; 1953-4 v. Aus.

HARRINGTON, A. (7) (Cardiff) 1955-6 v. I; 1956-7 v. S, E; 1957-8 v. S, Is, Is, I.

HARRIS, W. (6) (Middlesbrough) 1953-4 v. Aus; 1956-7 v. EG, Cz; 1957-8 v. EG, E, S.

HEWITT, R. (5) (Cardiff) 1957-8 v. Is, I, Swd, Hun, Braz.

HOPKINS, M. (20) (Tottenham) 1955-6 v. I; 1956-7 v. S, E, I, Cz, EG, Cz; 1957-8 v. EG, E, S, Is, Is, I, Hun, M, Swd, Hun, Braz; 1958-9 v. E, S.

HOWELLS, R. (2) (Cardiff) 1953-4 v. E, S.

HUGHES, I. (4) (Luton) 1950-1 v. E, I, Port, Switz.

HUGHES, W. (3) (Birmingham) 1946-7 v. S, E, I.

HUGHES, W. A. (5) (Blackburn) 1948-9 v. I, E, I, Port, B, Switz.

HUMPHREYS, J. (1) (Everton) 1946-7 v. I.

JONES, B. (4) (Arsenal) 1946-7 v. S, I; 1947-8 v. E; 1948-9 v. S.

JONES, C. (23) (Swansea) 1953-4 v. Aus; 1955-6 v. E, S, Aus, I; 1956-7 v. S, I, Cz, EG, Cz; 1957-8 v. EG, E, S, Is, Is, (Tottenham) I, Hun, M, Swd, Hun, Braz; 1958-9 v. I.

JONES, E. (4) (Swansea) 1946-7 v. S, E; (Tottenham) 1949-50 v. S.

JONES, K. (1) (Aston V) 1949-50 v. S.

JONES, T. G. (13) (Everton) 1946-7 v. S, E; 1947-8 v. S, I; 1948-9 v. E, I, Port, B; 1949-50 v. E, S, B.

KELSEY, J. (27) (Arsenal) 1953-4 v. I, Aus; 1954-5 v. Y, S, I; 1955-6 v. E, S, Aus, I; 1956-7 v. S, E, I, Cz, EG, Cz; 1957-8 v. E, S, Is, Is, I, Hun, M, Swd, Hun, Braz; 1958-9 v. E, S.

KING, J. (1) (Swansea) 1954-5 v. E.

KINSEY, N. (7) (Norwich) 1950-1 v. I, Port, Switz; 1951-2 v. S; (Birmingham) 1953-4 v. I; 1955-6 v. E, S.

LAMBERT, R. (5) (Liverpool) 1946-7, v. S; 1947-8 v. E; 1948-9 v. Port, B, Switz.

LEVER, A. (1) (Leicester) 1952-3 v. S.

LOWRIE, G. (5) (Coventry) 1947-8 v. E, S, I; 1948-9 v. Port, B.

LUCAS, W. (7) (Swansea) 1948-9 v. S, I, Port, B, Switz; 1949-50 v. E; 1950-1 v. E.

MEDWIN, T. (21) (Swansea) 1952-3 v. I, F, Y; (Tottenham) 1956-7 v. S, E, I, Cz, EG, Cz; 1957-8 v. S, E, Is, Is, I, Hun, M, Hun, Braz; 1958-9 v. E, S, I.

MORRIS, W. (4) (Burnley) 1946-7 v. I; 1948-9 v. E; 1951-2 v. S, I.

PALMER, D. (3) (Swansea) 1956-7 v. Cz; 1957-8 v. EG, E.

PARRY, J. (1) (Swansea) 1950-1 v. S.

PAUL, R. (32) (Swansea) 1948-9 v. E, I, Port, Switz; 1949-50 v. E, S, I, B; (Manchester City) 1950-1 v. S, E, I; Port, Switz; 1951-2 v. E, S, I; 1952-3 v. S, E, I, F, Y; 1953-4 v. E, S, I; 1954-5 v. E, S, I; 1955-6 v. E, S, Aus, I.

POWELL, A. (8) (Leeds) 1946-7 v. S, E; 1947-8 v. E, S, I; (Everton) 1948-9 v. I; 1949-50 v. B; (Birmingham) 1950-1 v. S.

POWELL, I. (8) (Queen's Park Rangers) 1946-7 v. E; 1947-8 v. E, S, I; 1948-9 v. B; (Aston V) 1949-50 v. S, B; 1950-1 v. S.

ROUSE, V. (1) (Crystal Palace) 1958-9 v. I.

ROWLEY, A. (1) (Tranmere R.) 1958-9 v. I.

REED, W. (2) (Ipswich) 1954-5 v. Y, S.

REES, W. (3) (Cardiff) 1948-9 v. I, Switz; (Tottenham) 1949-50 v. I.

RICHARDS, S. (1) (Cardiff) 1946-7 v. E.

SCRINE, F. (2) (Swansea) 1949-50 v. E, I.

SHERWOOD, A. (41) (Cardiff) 1946-7 v. E, I; 1947-8 v. S, I; 1948-9 v. S, E, I, Port, B, Switz; 1949-50 v. E, S, I, B; 1950-1 v. S, E, I, Port, Switz; 1951-2 v. E, S, I; 1952-3 v. S, E, I, F, Y; 1953-4 v. E, S, I, Aus; 1954-5 v. S, E, I; 1955-6 v. E, S, Aus, I; (Newport) 1956-7 v. S, E.

EDWARDS, T. (2) (Charlton) 1956-7 v. I, EG.

SHORTT, W. (11) (Plymouth) 1946-7 v. I; 1949-50 v. I, B; 1951-2 v. E, S, I; 1952-3 v. S, E, I, Y.

SIDLOW, C. (7) (Liverpool) 1946-7 v. S, E; 1947-8 v. E, S, I; 1948-9 v. S; 1949-50 v. E.

STANSFIELD, F. (1) (Cardiff) 1948-9 v. S.

STITFALL, R. (2) (Cardiff) 1952-3 v. E; 1956-7 v. Cz.

SULLIVAN, D. (15) (Cardiff) 1952-3 v. I, F, Y; 1953-4 v. I; 1954-5 v. E, I; 1956-7 v. S, E; 1957-8 v. I, Hun, Swd, Hun, Braz; 1958-9 v. S, E.

TAPSCOTT, D. (14) (Arsenal) 1953-4 v. Aus; 1954-5 v. Y, S, E, I; 1955-6 v. E, S, Aus, I; 1956-7 v. I, Cz, EG; 1958-9 v. E, I.

THOMAS, D. (2) (Swansea) 1956-7 v. Cz; 1957-8 v. EG.

THOMAS, S. (4) (Fulham) 1947-8 v. E, S, I; 1948-9 v. S.

VEARNCOMBE, G. (1) (Cardiff) 1957-8 v. EG.

VERNON, R. (9) (Blackburn) 1956-7 v. I, Cz, EG, Cz; 1957-8 v. EG, E, S, Swd; 1958-9 v. S.

WARD, D. (1) (Bristol Rovers) 1958-9 v. E.

WEBSTER, C. (4) (Manchester Utd) 1956-7 v. Cz; 1957-8 v. Hun, M, Braz.

WILLIAMS, G. (1) (Cardiff) 1950-1 v. Switz.

WILLIAMS, H. (4) (Newport) 1948-9 v. I, Switz; (Leeds) 1949-50 v. I; 1950-1 v. S.

WILLIAMS, S. (17) (W.B.A.) 1953-4 v. Aus; 1954-5 v. E, I; 1955-6 v. E; 1957-8 v. E, S, Is, Is, I, Hun, M, Swd, Hun, Braz; 1958-9 v. E, S, I.

WITCOMB, D. (3) (W.B.A.) 1946-7 v. S, E; (Sheffield Wed) v. I.

WOOSNAM, P. (2) (West Ham) 1958-9 v. E, S.

UNDER-23 INTERNATIONALS

ENGLAND

ITALY 3
ENGLAND 0

at Bologna, 20th January, 1954.

Team: R. Wood (Manchester United); P. Gunter (Portsmouth), S. Ellis (Charlton Athletic); J. Whitefoot (Manchester United), W. Dodgin (Arsenal), D. Edwards (Manchester United); A. Finney (Sheffield Wednesday), P. Broadbent (Wolverhampton Wanderers), S. Leary (Charlton Athletic), J. Nicholls (West Bromwich Albion), F. Blunstone (Chelsea).

ENGLAND 5
(Hooper 2, Ayre 1, Atyeo 1, Blunstone 1)
ITALY 1

at Stamford Bridge, 19th January 1955.

Team: R. Matthews (Coventry City); W. Foulkes (Manchester United), P. Sillett (Chelsea); R. Flowers (Wolverhampton Wanderers), T. Smith (Birmingham City), D. Edwards (Manchester United); H. Hooper (West Ham United), J. Atyeo (Bristol City), R. Ayre (Charlton Athletic), J. Haynes (Fulham), F. Blunstone (Chelsea).

SCOTLAND 0
ENGLAND 6
(Blunstone 1, Atyeo 1, Edwards 3, Haynes 1)

at Shawfield (Glasgow), 8th February, 1955.

Team: R. Matthews (Coventry City); W. Foulkes (Manchester United), P. Sillett (Chelsea); R. Flowers (Wolverhampton Wanderers), T. Smith (Birmingham City), D. Edwards (Manchester United); H. Hooper (West Ham United), J. Atyeo (Bristol City), R. Ayre (Charlton Athletic), J. Haynes (Fulham), F. Blunstone (Chelsea). S. Anderson (Sunderland), substitute for Ayre.

ENGLAND 5
(Stokes 2, Haynes 2, Robson 1)
DENMARK 1

at Portsmouth, 28th September, 1955

Team: R. Matthews (Coventry City); P. Sillett (Chelsea), G. Shaw (Sheffield United); S. Anderson (Sunderland), T. Smith (Birmingham City), R. Clayton (Blackburn Rovers); A. Kaye (Barnsley), R. Robson (Fulham), A Stokes (Tottenham Hotspur), J. Haynes (Fulham), F. Blunstone (Chelsea).

ENGLAND 3
(Haynes 2, Harris 1)
SCOTLAND 1
at Hillsborough (Sheffield), 8th February, 1956.
Team: R. Matthews (Coventry City); D. Howe (West Bromwich Albion), M. Norman (Tottenham Hotspur); R. Clayton (Blackburn City), T. Smith (Birmingham City), D. Edwards (Manchester United); A. Finney (Sheffield Wednesday), A. Quixall (Sheffield Wednesday), J. Harris (Everton), J. Haynes (Fulham), D. Pegg (Manchester United).

DENMARK 0
ENGLAND 3
(Blunstone 1, Bloomfield 1, Hitchens 1)
at Copenhagen, 26th September, 1956.
Team: A. Hodgkinson (Sheffield United); J. Armfield (Blackpool), G. Shaw (Sheffield United); R. Clayton (Blackburn Rovers), T. Smith (Birmingham City), R. Neal (Lincoln City); B. Douglas (Blackburn Rovers), J. Bloomfield (Arsenal), G. Hitchens (Cardiff City), A. Jeffrey (Doncaster Rovers), F. Blunstone (Chelsea).

ENGLAND 0
FRANCE 0
at Ashton Gate (Bristol), 17th October, 1956.
Team: A. Hodgkinson (Sheffield United); D. Howe (West Bromwich Albion), G. Shaw (Sheffield United); S. Anderson (Sunderland), T. Smith (Birmingham City), R. Neal (Lincoln City); B. Douglas (Blackburn Rovers), A. Jeffrey (Doncaster Rovers), V. Groves (Arsenal), A. Cheesebrough (Burnley), A. A'Court (Liverpool). C. Booth (Wolverhampton Wanderers), substitute for Jeffrey.

SCOTLAND 1
ENGLAND 1
(Dyson 1)
at Ibrox Park (Glasgow), 26th February, 1957.
Team: A. Hodgkinson (Sheffield United); D. Howe (West Bromwich), G. Shaw (Sheffield United); R. Clayton (Blackburn City), R. Neal (Lincoln City); A. Finney (Sheffield Wednesday), J. Haynes (Fulham), B. Clough (Middlesbrough), J. Dyson (Manchester City), D. Pegg (Manchester United).

BULGARIA 2
ENGLAND 1
(Clough 1)
at Sofia, 19th May, 1957.
Team: E. Hopkinson (Bolton Wanderers), J. Armfield (Blackpool), G. Shaw (Sheffield United); S. Anderson (Sunderland), T. Smith (Birmingham City), R. Neal (Birmingham City); B. Douglas (Blackburn Rovers), J. Bloomfield (Arsenal), B. Clough (Middlesbrough), D. Kevan (West Bromwich Albion), A. A'Court (Liverpool).

RUMANIA 0
ENGLAND 1
(Haynes 1)
at Bucharest, 26th May, 1957.
Team: E. Hopkinson (Bolton Wanderers); J. Armfield (Blackpool), M. Norman (Tottenham Hotspur); R. Clayton (Birmingham City), T. Smith (Birmingham City), D. Edwards (Manchester United); B. Douglas (Blackburn Rovers), D. Stevens (Bolton Wanderers), D. Kevan (West Bromwich Albion), J. Haynes (Fulham), D. Pegg (Manchester United).

CZECHOSLOVAKIA 0
ENGLAND 2
(Edwards 2)
at Bratislava, 30th May, 1957.
Team: E. Hopkinson (Bolton Wanderers); J. Armfield (Blackpool), M. Norman (Tottenham Hotspur); R. Clayton (Birmingham City), D. Edwards (Manchester United), B. Douglas (Blackburn Rovers), D. Stevens (Bolton Wanderers), D. Kevan (West Bromwich Albion), J. Haynes (Fulham), A. A'Court (Liverpool).

ENGLAND 6
(Greaves 2, Haynes 2, A'Court 1, Brabrook 1)
BULGARIA 2
at Stamford Bridge, 25th September, 1957.
Team: E. Hopkinson (Bolton Wanderers); D. Howe (West Bromwich Albion), G. Harris (Wolverhampton Wanderers); M. Setters (West Bromwich Albion), T. Smith (Birmingham City), S. Crowther (Aston Villa); P. Brabrook (Chelsea), J. Greaves (Chelsea), D. Kevan (West Bromwich Albion), J. Haynes (Fulham), A. A'Court (Liverpool).

ENGLAND 3
(Greaves 2, Curry 1)
RUMANIA 2
at Wembley, 16th October, 1957.
Team: A. Hodgkinson (Sheffield United); J. Armfield (Blackpool), G. Harris (Wolverhampton Wanderers); M. Setters (West Bromwich Albion), T. Smith (Birmingham City), S. Crowther (Aston Villa); P. Brabrook (Chelsea), J. Greaves (Chelsea), B. Curry (Newcastle), R. Parry (Bolton Wanderers), A. A'Court (Liverpool).

ENGLAND 3
(Murray 1, Greaves 1, Hayes 1)
SCOTLAND 1
at Goodison Park, 16th January, 1958.
Team: E. Hopkinson (Bolton Wanderers); D. Howe (West Bromwich Albion), G. Harris (Wolverhampton Wanderers); M. Setters (West Bromwich Albion), T. Smith (Birmingham City), S. Crowther (Aston Villa); P. Brabrook (Chelsea), J. Greaves (Chelsea), J. Murray (Wolverhampton Wanderers), J. Hayes (Manchester City), A. A'Court (Liverpool).

WALES 2
ENGLAND 1
(Clough)
at Wrexham, 23rd April, 1958.
Team: A. Hodgkinson (Sheffield United); D. Howe (West Bromwich Albion), G. Harris (Wolverhampton Wanderers); M. Setters (West Bromwich Albion), T. Smith (Birmingham City), J. Iley (Tottenham Hotspur); H. Riley (Leicester), J. Hayes (Manchester City), B. Clough (Middlesbrough), J. Greaves (Chelsea), A. A'Court (Liverpool).

ENGLAND 4
(Charlton 3, Greaves 1)
POLAND 1
at Hillsborough, Sheffield, 24th September, 1958. 38,525.
Team: Hodgkinson (Sheffield United); Armfield (Blackpool), Allen (Stoke); Setters (West Bromwich), Scott (Chelsea), McGuinness (Manchester United); Brabrook (Chelsea), Greaves (Chelsea), Baker (Hibs), Charlton (Manchester United), Scanlon (Manchester United).

ENGLAND 3
(Charlton 2, Greaves 1)
CZECHOSLOVAKIA 0
at Carrow Road, Norwich, 15th October, 1959. 38,000.
Team: Hodgkinson (Sheffield United); Armfield (Blackpool), Allen (Stoke); Setters (West Bromwich), Scott (Chelsea), McGuinness (Manchester United); Brabrook (Chelsea), Greaves (Chelsea), Baker (Hibs), Charlton (Manchester United), Scanlon (Manchester United).

FRANCE 1
ENGLAND 1
(Murray 1)
at Lyons, France, 18th March, 1959.
Team: Hopkinson (Bolton); Armfield (Blackpool), Allen (Stoke); Setters (West Bromwich), Scott (Chelsea), McGuinness (Manchester United); Scanlon (Manchester United), Greaves (Chelsea), Murray (Wolves), Charlton (Manchester United), Parry (Bolton).

ENGLAND 3
(Parry 1, Pointer 2)
ITALY 0
at Milan, 7th May, 1959. 75,000.
Team: Macedo (Fulham); Armfield (Blackpool), Allen (Stoke); Setters (West Bromwich), Smith (Birmingham), Kay (Sheffield Wednesday); Brabrook (Chelsea), Greaves (Chelsea), Pointer (Burnley), Parry (Bolton), Scanlon (Manchester United).

ENGLAND 2
(Kay 1, Robson 1)
GERMANY 2
at Bochum, Germany, 10th May, 1959.
Team: Macedo (Fulham); Angus (Burnley), Allen (Stoke); Setters (West Bromwich), Pacey (Luton), Kay (Sheffield Wednesday); Brabrook (Chelsea), Robson (Burnley), Dobing (Blackburn), Parry (Bolton), Scanlon (Manchester United).

INTER-LEAGUE GAMES

ENGLAND v. SCOTLAND

Played 56; England won 31; Scotland 15; drawn 10.

Year	Venue	England	Scotland
1892	Bolton	2	2
1893	Glasgow	4	3
1894	Liverpool	1	1
1895	Glasgow	4	1
1896	Liverpool	5	1
1897	Glasgow	0	3
1898	Birmingham	1	2
1899	Glasgow	4	1
1900	London	2	2
1901	Glasgow	2	6
1902	Newcastle	6	3
1903	Manchester	3	0
1904	Manchester	2	1
1905	Glasgow	3	2
1906	London	6	2
1907	Glasgow	0	0
1908	Birmingham	2	3
1909	Glasgow	2	3
1910	Blackburn	2	3
1911	Glasgow	1	1
1912	Middlesbrough	2	0
1913	Glasgow	4	1
1914	Burnley	2	2
1915	Glasgow	4	1
1916–18	Not played		
1919	Birmingham	3	1
1919	Glasgow	2	3
1920	Glasgow	4	0
1921	Highbury	1	0
1922	Glasgow	3	0
1923	Newcastle	2	1
1924	Glasgow	1	1
1925	Everton	4	3
1926	Glasgow	2	0
1927	Leicester	2	2
1928	Glasgow	6	2
1929	Birmingham	2	1
1930	Glasgow	1	7
1931	Tottenham	7	3
1932	Glasgow	3	0
1933	Manchester	3	2
1934	Glasgow	2	2
1935	Stamford Bridge	2	2
1936	Glasgow	2	0
1937	Everton	2	0
1938	Glasgow	0	3
1939	Wolverhampton	2	2
1940–46	Not played		
1947	Glasgow	3	1
1948	Newcastle	1	3
1949	Glasgow	3	0
1950	Middlesbrough	3	1
1951	Glasgow	2	0
1952	Sheffield	0	1
1953	Glasgow	0	0
1954	Stamford Bridge	4	0
1955	Glasgow	2	3
1956	Sheffield	4	2
1957	Glasgow	2	1
1958	Newcastle	4	1
1959	Glasgow	1	1

ENGLAND v. IRELAND

Played 52, England won 45; Ireland 3; drawn 4.

Year	Venue	England	Ireland
1894	Belfast	4	2
1895	Not played		
1896	Stoke	2	0
1897	Belfast	2	0
1898	Manchester	8	1
1899	Belfast	5	1
1900	Bolton	3	1
1901	Belfast	4	2
1902	Woolwich	9	0
1903	Belfast	3	2
1904	Bradford	2	1
1905	Belfast	2	0
1906	Manchester	4	0
1907	Belfast	6	0
1908	Sunderland	6	3
1909	Belfast	5	0
1910	Oldham	8	1
1911	Belfast	6	2
1912	Liverpool	2	0
1913	Belfast	0	0
1914	Belfast	2	1
1915	West Bromwich		
1916–19	Not played		
1920	Liverpool	2	2
1921	Not played		
1922	Belfast	1	0
1923	Bolton	5	2
1924	Belfast	9	2
1925	Belfast	5	0
1926	Liverpool	5	1
1927	Belfast	6	1
1928	Newcastle	9	1
1929	Belfast	5	2
1930	Everton	5	2
1931	Belfast	2	0
1932	Blackpool	4	1
1933	Belfast	5	2
1934	Preston	4	0
1935	Belfast	6	1
1936	Blackpool	2	3
1937	Belfast	2	2
1938	Blackpool	3	0
1939	Belfast	8	2
1940–46	Not played		
1947	Everton	4	2
1948	Belfast	4	3
1949	Liverpool	5	1
1950	Belfast	3	1
1951	Blackpool	6	3
1952	Belfast	9	1
1953	Wolverhampton	7	0
1954	Belfast	5	2
1955	Liverpool	4	2
1956	Belfast	3	5
1957	Newcastle	2	2
1958	Belfast	4	5
1959	Liverpool	5	2

SOCCER QUIZ

1. What are the fewest number of defeats for a programme of at least 42 matches in the Third Division South?

*

2. And the Third North?

*

3. What are the fewest number of defeats for a programme of at least 38 matches in the Scottish First Division?

*

4. And the Scottish Second Division, for at least 34 matches?

*

5. Have Eire ever defeated England in England?

*

6. How many countries are there in F.I.F.A.?

*

7. When was F.I.F.A. formed?

QUIZ ANSWERS

1. 4 by Plymouth 1929–30 and Southampton 1921–2. 2. 3 by Port Vale 1953–4, Doncaster 1946–7 and Wolves 1923–4. 3. 1 by Hearts in 1957–8, Rangers 1928–9 and 1920–1, and Celtic 1916–17. 4. 2 by Cowdenbeath 1938–9 and Raith 1937–8. 5. Yes, in 1949. 6. Over 80. 7. 1904.

SCOTLAND v. IRELAND

Played 52, Scotland won 47; Ireland 5.

		Scotland	Ireland
1893	Belfast	2	3
1895	Belfast	4	1
1896	Glasgow	3	2
1897	Belfast	2	0
1898	Dundee	5	1
1899	Belfast	1	3
1900	Edinburgh	6	0
1901	Belfast	2	1
1902	Dundee	3	0
1903	Belfast	0	1
1904	Paisley	3	1
1905–8	Not played		
1909	Belfast	2	1
1910	Glasgow	2	0
1911	Belfast	3	1
1912	Glasgow	3	0
1913	Belfast	3	1
1914	Glasgow	2	1
1915	Belfast	2	1
1916–19	Not played		
1920	Belfast	2	0
1921	Glasgow	3	0
1922	Glasgow	3	0
1923	Glasgow	3	0
1924	Belfast	1	0
1925	Edinburgh	3	0
1926	Belfast	7	3
1927	Edinburgh	5	2
1928	Belfast	2	1
1929	Glasgow	8	2
1930	Belfast	4	1
1931	Glasgow	5	0
1932	Belfast	2	1
1933	Glasgow	4	3
1934	Belfast	0	1
1935	Glasgow	3	2
1936	Belfast	3	2
1937	Glasgow	5	2
1938	Belfast	3	2
1939	Glasgow	6	1
1939*	Belfast	3	1
1940–46	Not played		
1947	Belfast	7	4
1948	Glasgow	3	0
1949	Belfast	1	0
1950	Belfast	8	1
1951	Belfast	4	0
1952	Glasgow	3	0
1953	Belfast	5	1
1954	Glasgow	4	0
1955	Belfast	5	1
1956	Glasgow	3	0
1957	Belfast	7	1
1958	Glasgow	7	0
1959	Belfast	5	0

* Played in season 1939-40 prior to the outbreak of war.

SOCCER QUIZ

1. Where are the F.A. offices?

*

2. Where are the Football League offices?

*

3. Who holds the highest individual score for one match in the First Division?

*

4. For the Second Division?

*

5. For the Third South?

*

6. For the Third North?

*

7. For the Scottish First Division?

QUIZ ANSWERS

1. Lancaster Gate, London. 2. Preston. 3. 7 by E. Drake, Arsenal v. Aston Villa in 1935, and J. Ross, Preston v. Stoke 1888. 4. 7 by N. Coleman, Stoke v. Lincoln 1957, and T. Briggs, Blackburn v. Bristol Rovers 1955. 5. 10 by J. Payne, Luton v. Bristol Rovers 1936. 6. 9 by R. Bell, Tranmere v. Oldham 1935. 7. 8 by J. McGrory, Celtic v. Dunfermline 1928.

Kingstonian

Sutton

Vauxhall Motors

Leytonstone

Winchester City

ENGLAND v. LEAGUE OF IRELAND (EIRE)

		England	Eire
1947	Dublin	3	1
1948	Preston	4	0
1949	Dublin	5	0
1950	Wolverhampton	7	0
1951	Dublin	1	0
1952	Liverpool	9	1
1953	Dublin	1	0
1954	Manchester	9	1
1955	Dublin	6	0
1956	Everton	5	1
1957	Dublin	3	3
1958	Leeds	3	1
1959	Dublin	0	0

AMATEUR INTERNATIONAL MATCHES

ENGLAND v. IRELAND

		England	Ireland
1906	Dublin	2	1
1907	Tottenham	6	1
1908	Dublin	5	1
1909	Leeds	4	4
1910	Belfast	2	3
1911	Huddersfield	2	0
1912	Belfast	2	3
1913	Belfast	2	0
1919	Derby	5	0
1920	Belfast	4	0
1921	Leicester	4	1
1922	Preston	4	0
1923	Crystal Palace	3	0
1924	Belfast	3	2
1925	Maidstone	6	4
1926	Belfast	3	0
1927	Blackpool	1	1
1928	Belfast	2	0
1929	Crystal Palace	7	2
1930	Belfast	1	3
1931	York	3	2
1933	Belfast	3	4
1934	Ilford	4	0
1935	Belfast	4	2
1936	Blackpool	5	0
1937	Belfast	1	5
1938	Leicester	1	0
1939	Belfast	1	0
1947	Southport	3	1
1948	Belfast	5	0
1949	Norwich	0	1
1950	Belfast	3	1
1951	Coventry	6	3
1952	Belfast	3	1
1953	Lincoln	4	1
1953	Coleraine	1	2
1954	Selhurst Park	5	0
1955	Belfast	4	1
1956	Bromley	5	2
1957	Belfast	3	0
1958	Bournemouth	6	2

ENGLAND v. WALES

		England	Wales
1908	Stockport	1	0
1909	Aberdare	5	2
1910	Huddersfield	6	0
1911	Newtown	5	1
1912	Bishop Auckland	3	0
1913	Llandudno	3	1
1914	Plymouth	9	1
1920	Merthyr	9	1
1921	Wolverhampton	0	2
1922	Swansea	7	0
1923	Middlesbrough	4	4
1924	Llandudno	2	1
1925	Plymouth	2	1
1926	Wrexham	2	1
1927	Reading	2	0
1928	Cardiff	2	1
1929	Brighton	1	1
1930	Aberystwyth	2	1
1931	Bournemouth	5	0
1932	Swansea	3	1
1933	Torquay	1	0
1934	Bangor	5	3
1935	Wimbledon	6	1
1936	Portmadoc	7	3

1937	Portsmouth	9	1
1938	Rhyl	8	2
1939	Cheltenham	5	2
1947	Dulwich	2	2
1947	Newport	4	1
1948	Bangor	7	2
1948	Shrewsbury	3	4
1949	Swindon	4	1
1949	Llanelly	3	1
1950	Bangor	3	0
1951	Leicester	4	1
1952	Bangor	4	3
1953	Highbury	3	1
1954	Newport	2	0
1955	Bournemouth	3	2
1956	Swansea	1	5
1957	Peterborough	5	0
1957	Bangor	5	0
1958	Shrewsbury	0	2

ENGLAND v. SCOTLAND

		England	Scotland
1926	Leicester	1	4
1928	Glasgow	2	3
1929	Leeds	3	1
1930	Glasgow	0	1
1931	Chelsea	2	1
1932	Glasgow	1	3
1933	Dulwich	1	0
1934	Glasgow	2	3
1935	Dulwich	2	1
1936	Inverness	0	1
1937	Dulwich	0	1
1938	Glasgow	5	2
1939	Dulwich	8	3
1949	Glasgow	2	3
1950	Hull	0	3
1951	Glasgow	3	2
1952	Wembley	1	2
1953	Glasgow	1	0
1954	Wembley	1	4
1955	Glasgow	3	3
1956	Wembley	4	2
1957	Glasgow	0	3
1958	Wembley	2	3
1959	Dumfries	1	1

SCOTLAND v. IRELAND

		Scotland	Ireland
1930	Londonderry	3	0
1931	Aberdeen	2	0
1932	Belfast	0	4
1933	Glasgow	6	0
1934	Belfast	1	4
1935	Glasgow	2	3
1936	Belfast	5	3
1937	Glasgow	3	0
1938	Belfast	1	2
1939	Glasgow	1	1
1949	Belfast	2	2
1950	Aberdeen	2	5
1951	Londonderry	1	0
1952	Glasgow	2	1
1953	Belfast	0	1
1954	Kilmarnock	0	0
1955	Cliftonville	1	2
1956	Kilmarnock	1	3
1957	Newtownards	1	4
1958	Airdrie	1	3
1959	Coleraine	0	0

SCOTLAND v. WALES

		Scotland	Wales
1930	Glasgow	1	0
1931	Swansea	2	1
1932	Edinburgh	1	5
1933	Bangor	0	0
1934	Greenock	4	0
1935	Aberystwyth	5	2
1936	Dumfries	1	0
1937	Bangor	2	0
1950	Dumfries	1	0
1951	Ebbw Vale	1	0
1952	Inverness	3	2
1953	Wrexham	1	0
1954	Ayr	0	0
1955	Bangor	5	0
1956	Glasgow	2	2
1957	Newtown	1	1
1958	Dumfries	3	0
1959	Aberystwyth	3	1

IRELAND v. WALES

		Ireland	Wales
1954	Belfast	3	2
1955	Llanidloes	2	1
1956	Cliftonville	2	1
1957	Ebbw Vale	1	1
1958	Coleraine	3	1
1959	Llandudno	4	3

F.A. AMATEUR CUP WINNERS

1894	Old Carth	2	Casuals	1
1895	Middlesbro'	2	Old Carth	1
1896	Bishop Auck.	1	R.A. (P'tsm'th)	0
1897	Old Carth	4	Stockton	1
	(After 1–1 draw)			
1898	Middlesbro'	2	Uxbridge	1
1899	Stockton	1	Harwich and	
			Parkeston	0
1900	Bishop Auck.	5	Lowestoft T.	1
1901	Crook T.	3	King's Lynn	0
	(After 1–1 draw)			
1902	Old Malver's	5	Bishop Auck.	1
1903	Stockton	1	Oxford City	0
	(After 0–0 draw)			
1904	Sheffield	3	Ealing	1
1905	W. Hartlepool	3	Clapton	2
1906	Oxford City	3	Bishop Auck.	0
1907	Clapton	2	Stockton	1
1908	Dpt. Bn. R.E.	2	Stockton	1
1909	Clapton	6	Eston United	0
1910	R.M.L.I.			
	(Gosport)	2	South Bank	1
1911	Bromley	1	Bishop Auck.	0
1912	Stockton	1	Eston United	0
	(After 0–0 draw)			
1913	South Bank	1	Oxford City	0
	(After 1–1 draw)			
1914	Bishop Auck.	1	N. Nomads	0
1915	Clapton	1	Bishop Auck.	0
1920	Dulwich Ham.	1	Tufnell Park	0
	(During extra time)			
1921	Bishop Auck.	4	Swindon Vic.	2
1922	Bishop Auck.	5	South Bank	2
	(During extra time)			
1923	London			
	Caledonians	2	Evesham Town	1
	(During extra time)			
1924	Clapton	3	Erith & Bel.	0
1925	Clapton	2	Southall	1
1926	N. Nomads	7	Stockton	1
1927	Leyton	3	Barking Town	1
1928	Leyton	3	Cockfield	2
1929	Ilford	3	Leyton	1
1930	Ilford	5	B'm'th Gas. A.	1
1931	Wycombe W.	1	Hayes	0
1932	Dulwich Ham.	7	Marine (Liverpool)	1
1933	Kingstonian	4	Stockton	1
	(After 1–1 draw)			
1934	Dulwich Ham.	2	Leyton	1
1935	Bishop Auck.	2	Wimbledon	1
	(After 0–0 draw)			
1936	Casuals	2	Ilford	0
	(After 1–1 draw)			
1937	Dulwich Ham.	2	Leyton	0
1938	Bromley	1	Erith & Bel.	0
1939	Bishop Auck.	3	Willington	0
	(During extra time)			
1946	Barnet	3	Bishop Auck.	2
1947	Leytonstone	2	Wimbledon	1
1948	Leytonstone	1	Barnet	0
1949	Bromley	1	Romford	0
1950	Willington	4	Bishop Auck.	0
1951	Pegasus	2	Bishop Auck.	1
1952	Walthamstow	2	Leyton	1
	(During extra time)			
1953	Pegasus	6	Harwich and	
			Parkeston	0
1954	Crook Town	1	Bishop Auck.	0
	(After two 2–2 draws)			
1955	Bishop Auck.	2	Hendon	0
1956	Bishop Auck.	4	Corinthian-C.	1
	(After 1–1 draw)			
1957	Bishop Auck.	3	Wycombe W.	1
1958	Woking	3	Ilford	0
1959	Crook Town	3	Barnet	2

Ilford

Corinthian Casuals

Bishop Auckland

Pegasus

Finchley

GREAT NAMES IN SOCCER

GEORGE CAMSELL (Middlesbrough). George Camsell was unlucky to be a contemporary of Dixie Dean, so that his appearances in the England side at centre forward were limited to nine, between 1929 and 1936. Strongly built, he was hard to shake off the ball and was a prolific scorer. He established a League record by scoring 59 goals in season 1926-7, when Middlesbrough ran away with the Second Division Championship, although injuries made him miss five League matches. The record was beaten by Dean in the following season. Camsell was a one-club man. He is now their coach and centre forward Brian Clough has benefited in particular.

JOHNNY CAREY (Manchester United). Johnny Carey is possibly the most versatile footballer the game has produced. He played for United in every position except outside left—he was goalkeeper when Jack Crompton was taken ill on the morning of a match—and for Ireland in seven positions. He came from Home Farm, Dublin, as an inside forward in 1938 and settled down at right back in the great United side just after the war. As captain, he issued the instructions "Keep playing football" which rallied United when they were twice behind Blackpool in the 1948 Final. In addition to playing for Eire and Ireland, he captained the Rest of Europe against Great Britain in 1947. He turned with equal success to management when he finished as a player, first with Blackburn, whom he steered to promotion, and then with Everton.

RAICH CARTER (Sunderland and Derby). Sunderland bred and born, Raich Carter had the distinction of captaining Sunderland on the only occasion when they won the Cup—in 1937. He entered League football when 17, but a quick rise to honours was delayed by inconsistency. He conquered his weakness and settled down to be one of the greatest inside forwards England has produced. He scored goals as well as made them and had an almost disdainful air when beating opponents. He gained another Cup medal with Derby in 1946 and would have gained many more England caps than 13 in an international career lasting from 1934 to 1947, but for the war. As player-manager and now with silver-grey hair he steered Hull to promotion from the Third North in 1949 and subsequently had a spell as manager of Leeds.

JOHN CHARLES (Leeds and Juventus). The fee of £65,000 Juventus of Italy paid Leeds for John Charles in April 1957 is a record for British football. Of the sum he received £10,000 as a signing-on fee. In his first season in Italy he topped the goalscorers with 29 goals and earned the title "Il Campione Preferito"—Footballer of the Year. The English nickname "Gentle Giant" also stuck to him as "Il Gigante Buono". Charles was discovered in Swansea by a Leeds scout and signed by Major Frank Buckley, a famous maker of stars. He played for Wales when 17 and brought his caps up to 27 when he appeared in the World Cup matches in Sweden.

ALF COMMON (Middlesbrough). The first £1,000 transfer fee was paid by Middlesbrough for Alf Common, the Sunderland and England inside forward. It was labelled in newspapers at the time as "a truly sensational transaction". It was in 1905, when the maximum wage was £208 a year. The size of the fee caused clubs to introduce a transfer limit of £350, but the restriction lasted only three months. Common's first club was Sheffield United, with whom he took part in the 1901 Final. He was equally at home at centre forward and this is the position he occupied when he went to

Arsenal, who were then in Plumstead. He was a natural humorist and fond of dressing-room pranks.

WARNEY CRESSWELL (Everton). A wonderful sense of position made Warney Cresswell one of the outstanding full backs in the Football League's history. Composed, elegant and fair of hair, he strolled through a game because he anticipated so well the ball's direction. He made brilliant use of the ball, too. He began with South Shields, moved to Sunderland and reached his peak with Everton. He won England recognition during 1923-30, while serving all three clubs. He was left back for Everton in the three seasons 1931-33 when Everton won in succession the Second Division, the First Division and the Cup. He obtained 16 caps for England during 1927-33. He now runs a public house in Chester.

JIMMY DELANEY (Celtic and Manchester United). Because he was so susceptible to injuries in his early career, Jimmy Delaney was suspected of being brittle-boned. But he went on to win a Scottish Cup medal with Celtic in 1937 and an F.A. Cup medal with Manchester United in 1948. He capped that feat by winning an Irish Cup medal with Derry City in 1954, when they beat Glentoran

Stan Cullis

George Camsell

Dixie Dean

the 1933 Final and had a big part in the 3-0 victory over Manchester City. By this time his nickname among his colleagues had changed from "Iceberg" to "Grandad".

BOB CROMPTON (Blackburn). Bob Crompton's record of 34 appearances in the Home International Tournament from 1902 to 1914 stood for 44 years until beaten by Billy Wright. He was probably the finest right back England produced. His solid build was made even more impressive by a heavy, waxed moustache and he was consistency itself. He was quiet off the field and an outstanding captain on it. He gained a League Championship medal with Blackburn, whom he later managed, but Cup success eluded him.

STAN CULLIS (Wolverhampton). Stan Cullis was the finest centre half during the decade 1936 to 1946 because he retained an attacking flair when centre halves were concentrating on being third backs. He captained Wolves when 18 and took over the captaincy of England in Rumania in 1939 at the age of 21. Even in international football he did not hesitate to leave the middle in order to dribble upfield. With Cliff Britton and Joe Mercer he completed a half-back line which is one of the strongest chosen by England. He retired just after the war when 32 to become manager of Wolves and as a perfectionist in fitness, discipline and performance he drove the club to gain honours which he failed to win as a player. Under his management Wolves won the Cup in 1949 and the League Championship for the first time in their history in 1954. They won the League again in 1958 and 1959.

DIXIE DEAN (Everton). Before the last match of season 1927-8 Dixie Dean needed three goals to beat the record League total for a season of 59. He obtained them, too, despite being faced by mighty Arsenal. He also holds the record for gross total of League goals—379. A six-footer, magnificently built and with curly black hair, he was the finest header of a ball seen in football and he obtained about half his goals with headers. He made openings with his head, too. Born in Birkenhead, he began with Tranmere and found fame with Everton. He scored over 100 goals in

at the third attempt. Dashing and fearless, he was at his best on the wing, either flank, and he also played in the other forward positions. He represented Scotland at centre forward and outside right.

JIMMY DICKINSON (Portsmouth). Jimmy Dickinson is quiet and unassuming, both on and off the field, yet his total of 48 appearances for England is passed only by Wright, Finney and Matthews. A most reliable wing half, sturdily built and a good club man, he gained League Championship medals when Portsmouth won the title in successive seasons, 1949-50. He won his first England cap in 1949. *(contd. on p. 35, col. 3)*

(contd. on p. 35, col. 3)

SOCCER QUIZ

1. Which was the first match televised?

*

2. The first Cup Final televised?

*

3. For whom was the first four-figure fee paid?

*

4. The first £10,000?

*

5. The first £20,000?

*

6. The first £30,000?

*

7. Have the United States defeated England at soccer?

QUIZ ANSWERS

1. Arsenal v. Preston, Charity Shield Final of 1938. 2. 1946. 3. A. Common in 1905. 4. D. Jack in 1928. 5. T. Lawton in 1947. 6. T. Ford in 1950. 7. Yes, in the World Cup in 1950.

F.A. CHARITY SHIELD

In 1908 the Football Association set up the Charity Shield for an annual match between two teams selected by the Association, the proceeds to be devoted to charity. The first match at Stamford Bridge was between the League Champions, Manchester United, and the Champions of the Southern League, Queen's Park Rangers. United won 4-0 after a 1-1 draw. After four such games between the two Champions, the F.A. had a series of games between professionals and amateurs.

Since 1930 the custom has been to pair the League Champions and the F.A. Cup holders. An exception was in 1950, when a trial match was held between England's World Cup team and the Canadian touring side. Of the 19 games between the Champions and Cup winners, the Champions won on 16 occasions.

Arsenal have won the trophy the greatest number of times—seven. They have also twice been beaten contestants. The Shield match between Arsenal and Preston at Highbury in 1938 was the first senior match televised.

F.A. CHARITY SHIELD RESULTS

Season	Team	Score	Team	Score
1908-09	Manchester United (after drawn game 1-1)	4	Queen's Park Rangers	0
1909-10	Newcastle United	2	Northampton Town	0
1910-11	Brighton & Hove Albion	1	Aston Villa	0
1911-12	Manchester United	8	Swindon Town	4
1912-13	Blackburn Rovers	2	Queen's Park Rangers	1
1913-14	Professionals	7	Amateurs	2
1919-20	West Bromwich Albion	2	Tottenham Hotspur	0
1920-1	Tottenham Hotspur	2	Burnley	0
1921-2	Huddersfield Town	1	Liverpool	0
1922-3	No match			
1923-4	Professionals	2	Amateurs	0
1924-5	Professionals	3	Amateurs	1
1925-6	Amateurs	6	Professionals	1
1926-7	Amateurs	6	Professionals	3
1927-8	Cardiff City	2	Corinthians	1
1928-9	Everton	2	Blackburn Rovers	1
1929-30	Professionals	3	Amateurs	0
1930-1	Arsenal	2	Sheffield Wednesday	1
1931-2	Arsenal	1	West Bromwich Albion	0
1932-3	Everton	5	Newcastle United	3
1933-4	Arsenal	3	Everton	0
1934-5	Arsenal	4	Manchester City	0
1935-6	Sheffield Wednesday	1	Arsenal	0
1936-7	Sunderland	2	Arsenal	1
1937-8	Manchester City	2	Sunderland	0
1938-9	Arsenal	2	Preston North End	1
1948-9	Arsenal	4	Manchester United	3
1949-50	Portsmouth	1	Wolverhampton Wanderers	1
1950-1	World Cup XI	4	Canadian Tourists	2
1951-2	Tottenham Hotspur	2	Newcastle United	1
1952-3	Manchester United	4	Newcastle United	2
1953-4	Arsenal	3	Blackpool	1
1954-5	Wolverhampton Wanderers	4	West Bromwich Albion	4
1955-6	Chelsea	3	Newcastle United	0
1956-7	Manchester United	1	Manchester City	0
1957-8	Manchester United	4	Aston Villa	0
1958-9	Bolton	4	Wolverhampton Wanderers	1

33

Bromley

Romford

Saltaire

Clapton

Wycombe Wanderers

FOOTBALL LEAGUE CLUB DIRECTORY

FIRST DIVISION

The original League was formed in 1888 with 12 clubs. It was extended to 14 clubs in 1891, to 16 in 1892, to 18 in 1898, to 20 in 1905 and to 22 in 1919.

In Famous Internationals Ireland refers to Northern Ireland and Eire.

ARSENAL. *Ground:* Arsenal Stadium, Highbury. *Founded:* 1886. *Manager:* G. Swindin. *Colours:* Red shirts with white sleeves and collars; white shorts. *Nickname:* Gunners. *Ground Record:* 73,295. *Famous Internationals:* ENGLAND—D. Clapton, L. Smith, L. Scott, L. Compton, E. Hapgood, G. Male, C. Bastin, J. Crayston, W. Copping, F. Moss, E. Drake, D. Jack, J. Hulme, A. Ducat, J. Coleman, J. Ashcroft; SCOTLAND—T. Docherty, D. Herd, J. Henderson, J. Logie, A. Forbes, A. Macaulay, A. James, W. Harper, J. Sharp, R. Templeton; IRELAND—J. Haverty, W. Dickson, K. O'Flanagan, W. Sloan, J. Kennedy; WALES—D. Bowen, J. Kelsey, D. Tapscott, W. Barnes, B. Jones, L. Jones, C. Jones, R. Cumner, R. John, D. Lewis, C. Jenkyns. *League History:* First Division, 1904–13, 1919–. Second Division, 1893–1904, 1913–19. *League Honours:* First Division Champions, 1930–1, 1932–3, 1933–4, 1934–5, 1937–8, 1947–8, 1952–3. First Division Runners-up, 1925–6, 1931–2. *Cup Honours:* Winners, 1930, 1936, 1950. Runners-up, 1927, 1932, 1952. *Records:* Equalled Huddersfield Town's record of winning League Championship in three successive seasons (1932–5). Won League Championship seven times. Greatest number of points in the First Division—66 points in 1930–1.

SOCCER QUIZ

1. In what year was the World Cup first staged?

*

2. Where is the next World Cup to be staged?

*

3. Has Britain staged the World Cup?

*

4. Which Scottish club won the Cup, League and League Cup in the same season?

*

5. Which Scottish club won everything they competed for in the same season?

*

6. What is the longest unbeaten run in the Football League?

QUIZ ANSWERS

1. 1930. 2. Chile. 3. No. 4. Rangers in 1948–9. 5. Rangers (twice) and Celtic (before the League Cup was started). 6. 30 games by Burnley in 1920–1.

BIRMINGHAM CITY. *Ground:* St. Andrew's, Birmingham. *Founded:* 1875. *Manager:* P. Beasley. *Colours:* Royal blue shirts with white collars; white shorts. *Nickname:* Blues. *Ground Record:* 66,844. *Famous Internationals:* ENGLAND—J. Hall, G. Merrick, G. Astall, H. Hibbs, J. Bradford, T. Grosvenor, D. Tremelling, W. Corbett, C. Charsley; SCOTLAND—N. Dougall, J. Crosbie; IRELAND—R. Brennan, R. Ferris, J. Brown; WALES—A Powell, W. Hughes, N. Kinsey, G. Edwards, D. Dearson, D. Richards, C. Jones, S. Morris, C. Jenkins. *League History:* First Division, 1894–6, 1901–2, 1903–8, 1921–39, 1948–50, 1955–. Second Division, 1892–4, 1896–1901, 1902–3, 1908–21, 1939–48, 1950–5. *League Honours:* Second Division Champions, 1892–3, 1920–1, 1947–8, 1954–5. *Cup Honours:* Runners-up, 1931, 1956. *Records:* Second Division Champions 4 times.

BLACKBURN ROVERS. *Ground:* Ewood Park, Blackburn. *Founded:* 1874. *Manager:* D. Duncan. *Colours:* Blue and white halved shirts; white shorts. *Nickname:* Blue and Whites. *Ground Record:* 61,783. *Famous Internationals:* ENGLAND—R. Clayton, B. Douglas, W. Eckersley, R. Langton, A. Cunliffe, S. Puddefoot, A. Rigby, H. Healless, E. Harper, D. Shea, R. Crompton, J. Forrest, T. Booth, A. Houlker, W. Townley; SCOTLAND—J. Hutton, J. McKay, W. Aitkenhead; IRELAND—E. Crossan, M. McGrath, D. Rollo; WALES—R. Vernon, W. Hughes, W. Davies, R. Evans. *League History:* Original League, 1888–92. First Division, 1892–1936, 1939–48, 1958–. Second Division, 1936–9, 1948–58. *League Honours,* League Champions, 1911–12, 1913–14. Second Division Champions, 1938–9. *Cup Honours:* Winners, 1884, 1885, 1886, 1890, 1891, 1928. Runners-up, 1882. *Records:* Three F.A. Cup wins in succession, 1884–6.

BLACKPOOL. *Ground:* Bloomfield Road, Blackpool. *Founded:* 1887. *Manager:* R. Suart. *Colours:* Tangerine shirts with white collars; white shorts. *Nickname:* Seasiders or Tangerines. *Ground Record:* 38,098. *Famous Internationals:* ENGLAND—J. Armfield, S. Matthews, E. Taylor, S. Mortensen, W. Perry, E. Shimwell, T. Garrett, H. Johnston, J. Hampson, H. Bedford; SCOTLAND—J. Mudie, G. Farm, H. Kelly, A. Brown, J. Blair, F. O'Donnell, A. Munro; IRELAND—P. Doherty, S. Jones; WALES—F. Griffiths. *League History:* First Division, 1930–3, 1937–. Second Division, 1896–9, when failed to gain re-election; re-elected following season; 1900–30, 1933–7. *League Honours:* First Division Runners-up, 1955–6. Second Division Champions, 1929–30. *Cup Honours:* Winners, 1953. Runners-up, 1948, 1951. *Records:* 125 goals against in 1930–1—highest for First Division.

BOLTON WANDERERS. *Ground:* Burnden Park, Bolton. *Founded:* 1874. *Manager:* W. Ridding. *Colours:* White shirts; blue shorts. *Nickname:* Trotters. *Ground Record:* 69,912. *Famous Internationals:* ENGLAND—N. Lofthouse, D. Holden, T. Banks, E. Hopkinson, H. Hassall, M. Barrass, R. Langton, R. Westwood, D. Jack, G. Eastham, J. Smith, J. Seddon, R. Pym, H. Nuttall, A. Shepherd, J. Fitchett, J. Sutcliffe; SCOTLAND—W. Moir, W. Cook, W. White; IRELAND—W. Hughes; WALES—J. Roberts, E. Vizard, W. Jennings, D. Jones. *League History:* Original League, 1888–92. First Division, 1892–9, 1900–3, 1905–8, 1909–10, 1911–33, 1935–. Second Division, 1899–1900, 1903–5, 1908–9, 1910–11, 1933–5. *League Honours:* Second Division Champions, 1908–9. *Cup Honours:* Winners, 1923, 1926, 1929, 1958. Runners-up, 1894, 1904, 1953.

BURNLEY. *Ground:* Turf Moor, Burnley. *Founded:* 1881. *Manager:* H. Potts. *Colours:* Claret and light blue shirts; white shorts. *Nickname:* Turfites. *Ground Record:* 54,775. *Famous Internationals:* ENGLAND—C. McDonald, B. Pilkington, W. Elliott, L. Page, R. Kelly, J. Bruton, J. Hill, J. Dawson, G. Waterfield, J. Crabtree, B. Freeman, W. Watson; SCOTLAND—J. Aird; IRELAND—J. McIlroy, A. McCluggage, H. Flack, T. Morrison. *League History:* Original League, 1888–92. First Division, 1892–7, 1898–1900, 1913–30, 1947–. Second Division, 1897–8, 1900–13, 1930–47. *League Honours:* League Champions, 1920–1. Runners-up, 1919–20. Second Division Champions, 1897–8. *Cup Honours:* Winners, 1914. Runners-up, 1947. *Records:* 30 successive League games without defeat (Sept. 1920–March 1921).

CHELSEA. *Ground:* Stamford Bridge, Fulham. *Founded:* 1905. *Manager:* E. Drake. *Colours:* Royal blue shirts with white collars; white shorts. *Nickname:* Pensioners. *Ground Record:* 82,905. *Famous Internationals:* ENGLAND—J. Greaves, P. Brabrook, F. Blunstone, P. Sillett, R. Bentley, T. Lawton, K. Armstrong, V. Woodley, R. Spence, G. Mills, P. O'Dowd, B. Howard Baker, T. Meehan, J. Cock, J. Harrow, V. Woodward, G. Hilsdon; SCOTLAND—R. Campbell, A. Jackson, T. Law, H. Gallacher, J. Cameron; IRELAND—W. Dickson, S. D'Arcy, J. Bambrick, T. Priestley, S. Irving, W. Mitchell, J. Kirwan; WALES—T. Hewitt. *League History:* First Division, 1907–10, 1912–24, 1930. Second Division, 1905–7, 1910–12, 1924–30. *League Honours:* First Division Champions, 1954–5. *Cup Honours:* Runners-up, 1915.

EVERTON. *Ground:* Goodison Park, Liverpool. *Founded:* 1878. *Manager:* J. Carey. *Colours:* Royal blue shirts; white shorts. *Nickname:* Toffees. *Ground Record:* 78,599. *Famous Internationals:* ENGLAND—J. Mercer, C. Britton, T. Lawton, W. Boyes, E. Sagar, A. Gelderd, J. Cunliffe, S. Chedgzoy, W. Cresswell, W. Dean, T. White, J. Sharp, E. Chadwick, W. Balmer, H. Hardman, H. Makepeace; SCOTLAND—R. Collins, T. Gillick, J. Dunn, N. McBain, J. Bell, J. Robertson; IRELAND—P. Farrell, T. Eglinton, J. O'Neill, D. Donovan, A. Stevenson, W. Cook, J. Coulter, R. Irvine, W. Lacey, J. Sheriden; WALES—T. Jones, A. Powell, T. Griffiths, B. Williams, S. Davies, L. Roose, C. Parry, S. Arridge. *League History:* Original League, 1888–92. First Division, 1892–1930, 1931–51, 1954–. Second Division, 1930–1, 1951–4. *League Honours:* First Division Champions, 1890–1, 1914–15, 1927–8, 1931–2, 1938–9. First Division Runners-up, 1889–90, 1894–5, 1901–2, 1904–5, 1908–9, 1911–12. Second Division Champions, 1930–1. *Cup Honours:* Winners, 1906, 1933. Runners-up, 1893, 1897, 1907. *Records:* Won the Second and First Division Championships and the Cup in successive seasons 1930–3.

FULHAM. *Ground:* Craven Cottage, Fulham. *Founded:* 1880. *Manager:* B. Jezzard. *Colours:* White shirts; black shorts. *Nickname:* Cottagers. *Ground Record:* 49,335. *Famous Internationals:* ENGLAND—J. Haynes, J. Langley, B. Jezzard, J. Taylor, J. Arnold, A. Barratt, L. Oliver, F. Osborne; SCOTLAND—G. Leggat, J. Sharp; IRELAND—R. Lawler, J. Campbell, H. Kelly, R. Brennan, E. Hinton, A. Steele; WALES—W. Richards. *League History:* First Division, 1949–52, 1959–. Second Division, 1907–28, 1932–49, 1952–59. Third Division (South), 1928–32. *League Honours:* Second Division Champions, 1948–9.

LEEDS UNITED. *Ground:* Elland Road, Leeds. *Founded:* 1904. *Manager:* J. Taylor. *Colours:* Blue shirts with gold collar; white shorts. *Nickname:* Peacocks. *Ground Record:* 56,796. *Famous Internationals:* ENGLAND—W. Edwards, B. Sproston, W. Copping, W. Furness, E. Hart, J. Stephenson; IRELAND—W. Cush, D. Cochrane, C. Martin, J. Twoomey, R. Browne, J. Moran, W. Scott; WALES—J. Charles, H. Williams, A. Powell. *League History:* First Division, 1924–7, 1928–31, 1932–47, 1956–. Second Division, 1905–15; resigned 1919; re-elected Second Division 1920; 1920–4, 1927–8, 1931–2, 1947–56. *League Honours:* Second Division Champions, 1923–4.

LEICESTER CITY. *Ground:* Filbert Street, Leicester. *Founded:* 1884. *Manager:* M. Gillies. *Colours:* Royal blue shirts with white collars; white shorts. *Nickname:* Filberts. *Ground Record:* 47,298. *Famous Internationals:* ENGLAND—S. Smith, H. Adcock, S. Bishop, E. Hine, R. Osborne, H. Bailey SCOTLAND—J. Anderson, J. Duncan, J. Paterson, A. Aitken; IRELAND—W. Cunningham, T. Godwin, M. O'Brien; WALES—M. Griffiths, A. Lever, T. Mills, D. Jones. *League History:* First Division, 1908–9, 1925–35, 1937–9, 1954–5, 1957–. Second Division, 1894–1908, 1909–25, 1935–7, 1939–54, 1955–7. *League Honours:* First Division Runners-up, 1928–9. Second Division Champions, 1924–5, 1936–7, 1953–4, 1956–7. *Cup Honours:* Runners-up, 1949.

LUTON TOWN. *Ground:* Kenilworth Road, Luton. *Founded:* 1885. *Manager:* S. Owen. *Colours:* White shirts; black shorts. *Nickname:* Hatters, Strawplaiters. *Ground Record:* 30,069. *Famous Internationals:* ENGLAND—S. Owen, R. Baynham, B. Streten, J. Payne, E. Simms SCOTLAND—A. Brown, M. Cullen; IRELAND—W. Bingham, G. Cummins, S. Dunne, T. Aherne, A. Mathieson; WALES—I. Hughes. *League History:* First Division, 1955–. Second Division, 1897–1900, when failed to gain re-election; afterwards Southern League, 1900–20; 1937–55. Third Division, 1920–1. Third Division (South), 1921–37. *Cup honours:* Runners-up, 1959.

MANCHESTER CITY. *Ground:* Maine Road, Manchester. *Founded:* 1880. *Manager:* L. McDowall. *Colours:* Sky blue shirts; white shorts. *Nickname:* Citizens. *Ground Record:* 84,569. *Famous Internationals:* ENGLAND—D. Revie, J. Meadows, F. Swift, I. Broadis, E. Brook, S. Barkas, S. Cowan, J. Bray, C. Tilson, B. Sproston, J. Mitchell, M. Woosnam, F. Booth; SCOTLAND—R. Johnstone, M. Busby, J. McMullan, J. McLuckie, G. Livingstone; IRELAND—W. McAdams, W. Walsh, F. McCourt, P. Doherty, M. Hamill, K. McCullough, J. Mulligan; WALES—R. Paul, R. Clarke, A. Gray, W. Meredith, G. Wynn, E. Hughes, W. Jones, H. Morris. *League History:* First Division, 1899–1902, 1903–9, 1910–26, 1928–38, 1947–50, 1951–. Second Division, 1894–9, 1902–3, 1909–10, 1926–8, 1938–47, 1950–1. *League Honours:* First Division Champions, 1936–7. First Division Runners-up, 1903–4, 1920–1. Second Division Champions, 1898–9, 1902–3, 1909–10, 1927–8, 1946–7. *Cup Honours:* Winners, 1904, 1934, 1956. Runners-up, 1926, 1933, 1955. *Records:* Five Second Division championships. Their ground record is the biggest outside a Final.

MANCHESTER UNITED. *Ground:* Old Trafford, Manchester. *Founded:* 1885. *Manager:* M. Busby. *Colours:* Red shirts; white shorts. *Ground Record:* 76,962. *Famous Internationals:* ENGLAND—R. Charlton, W. Bradley, T. Taylor, R. Byrne, D. Edwards, D. Pegg, J. Berry, R. Wood, W. Foulkes, J. Rowley, A. Chilton, H. Cockburn, J. Aston, J. Spence, J. Silcock, C. Roberts, H. Halse; SCOTLAND—J. Delaney, N. McBain, A. Bell; IRELAND—W. Whelan, J. Blanchflower, J. Carey, T. Breen, W. McMillen, D Lyner, M. Hamill; WALES—C. Webster, W. Meredith, S. Bennion, T. Jones, R. Williams, E. Doughty, J. Davies. *League History:* First Division, 1892–4, 1906–22, 1925–31, 1936–7, 1938–. Second Division, 1894–1906, 1922–5, 1931–6, 1937–8. *League Honours:* First Division Champions, 1907–8, 1910–11, 1951–2, 1955–6, 1956–7. First Division Runners-up, 1946–7, 1947–8, 1948–9, 1950–1, 1958–9. *Cup Honours:* Winners, 1909, 1948. Runners-up, 1957, 1958.

NEWCASTLE. *Ground:* St. James's Park, Newcastle-upon-Tyne. *Founded:* 1882. *Manager:* C. Mitten. *Colours:* Black and white striped shirts; black shorts. *Nickname:* Magpies. *Ground Record:* 68,386. *Famous Internationals:* ENGLAND—J. Milburn, I. Broadis, S. Weaver, J. Richardson, J. Hill, F. Hundspeth, D. Fairhurst, C. Spencer, T. Urwin, C. Veitch, J. Rutherford, A. Shepherd, A. Gosnell, J. Stewart; SCOTLAND—R. Mitchell, F. Brennan, T. Pearson, N. Harris, H. Gallacher, J. Boyd, W. Low, P. McWilliam, R. McColl, J. Howie, R. Templeton, A. Aitken; IRELAND—A. McMichael, D. Keith, T. Casey, W. McCracken; WALES—R. Davies, W. Foulkes, G. Lowrie, R. Williams. *League History:* First Division, 1898–1934, 1948–. Second Division, 1893–8, 1934–48. *League Honours:* First Division Champions, 1904–5, 1906–7, 1908–9, 1926–7. *Cup Honours:* Winners, 1910, 1924, 1932, 1951, 1952, 1955. Runners-up, 1905, 1906, 1908, 1911. *Records:* Most appearances in the Cup Final—10.

NOTTINGHAM FOREST. *Ground:* City Ground, Nottingham. *Founded:* 1865. *Manager:* W. Walker. *Colours:* Red shirts, white shorts. *Nickname:* Foresters. *Ground Record:* 47,654. *Famous Internationals:* ENGLAND—T. Graham, H. Jones, A. Ironmonger, T. Lindley, S. Widdowson, A. Goodyer, J. Sands; SCOTLAND—S. Imlach; IRELAND—F. Coyle, J. Chambers, D. Martin, J. Hanna; WALES—C. Jones, A. Green, A. Morris. *League History:* First Division, 1892–1906, 1907–11, 1922–5, 1957–. Second Division, 1906–7, 1911–22, 1925–49, 1951–7. Third Division (South), 1949–51. *League Honours:* Second Division Champions, 1906–7, 1921–2. *Cup Honours:* Winners, 1898, 1959. *Records:* Highest points total in Third South—70 in 1950–1 (shared).

PRESTON NORTH END. *Ground:* Deepdale, Preston. *Founded:* 1880. *Manager:* C. Britton. *Colours:* White shirts; blue shorts. *Nickname:* Old Invincibles, Lily-Whites. *Ground Record:* 42,684. *Famous Internationals:* ENGLAND—T. Finney, T. Thompson, J. McCall, H. Holdcroft, W. Roberts, J. Goodall, F. Dewhurst, R. Bond; SCOTLAND—T. Docherty, W. Cunningham, A. McLaren, A. Beattie, R. Beattie, F. O'Donnell, J. Dougall, W. Shankly, T. Smith, G. Mutch, A. James; IRELAND—F. O'Farrell, J. McKnight; WALES—W. John, S. Davies, R. Mills-Roberts. *League History:* Original League, 1888–92. First Division, 1892–1901, 1904–12, 1913–14, 1915–25, 1934–49, 1951–. Second Division, 1901–4, 1912–13, 1914–15, 1925–34, 1949–51. *League Honours:* First Division Champions, 1888–9, 1889–90. First Division Runners-up, 1890–1, 1891–2, 1892–3, 1905–6, 1952–3, 1957–8. Second Division Champions, 1903–4, 1912–13, 1950–1. *Cup Honours:* Winners, 1889, 1938. Runners-up, 1888, 1922, 1937, 1954. *Records:* Won Cup and League 1888–9, the Cup without conceding a goal and the League without being beaten. Fourteen consecutive League wins—season 1950–1.

SHEFFIELD WEDNESDAY. *Ground:* Hillsborough, Sheffield. *Founded:* 1866. *Manager:* H. Catterick. *Colours:* Blue and white striped shirts; black shorts. *Nickname:* Owls. *Ground Record:* 72,841. *Famous Internationals:* ENGLAND—A. Quixall, J. Sewell, R. Froggatt, J. Robinson, E. Catlin, R. Starling, E. Blenkinsop, A. Strange, G. Wilson, T. Leach, W. Marsden, E. Rimmer, J. Brown, F. Spiksley, F. Bradshaw, T. Brittleton; SCOTLAND—J. Blair, A. Wilson, J. Lyall; IRELAND—E. Gannon, W. Cowdy, P. O'Connell; WALES—D. Witcomb, H. Hanford, R. Williams. *League History:* First Division, 1892–9, 1900–20, 1926–37, 1950–1, 1952–5, 1956–8, 1959–. Second Division, 1899–1900, 1920–6, 1937–50, 1951–2, 1955–6, 1958–9. *League Honours:* First Division Champions, 1902–3, 1903–4, 1928–9, 1929–30. Second Division Champions, 1899–1900, 1925–6, 1951–2, 1955–6, 1958–9. *Cup Honours:* Winners, 1896, 1907, 1935. Runners-up, 1890.

TOTTENHAM HOTSPUR. *Ground:* White Hart Lane, Tottenham. *Founded:* 1882. *Manager:* W. Nicholson. *Colours:* White shirts; blue shorts. *Nickname:* Spurs. *Ground Record:* 75,038. *Famous Internationals:* ENGLAND—J. Brooks, E. Ditchburn, G. Robb, A. Ramsey, W. Nicholson, A. Willis, E. Bailey, L. Medley, G. Hunt, A. Rowe, W. Hall, J. Dimmock, A. Grimsdell, J. Seed, F. Osborne, T. Clay, H. Bliss, V. Woodward, F. Walden; SCOTLAND—D. MacKay, A. Brown; IRELAND—D. Blanchflower, R. Rowley, J. Kirwan; WALES—C. Jones, T. Medwin, M. Hopkins, R. Burgess, W. Rees, W. Evans, E. O'Callaghan, W. Whatley, E. Hughes. *League History:* First Division, 1909–15, 1920–8, 1933–5, 1950–. Second Division, 1908–9, 1915–20, 1928–33, 1935–50. *League Honours:* First Division Champions, 1950–1. First Division Runners-up, 1921–2, 1951–2, 1956–7. Second Division Champions, 1919–20, 1949–50. *Cup Honours:* Winners, 1901, 1921. *Records:* Equalled record by winning League championship of Second and First Division in successive seasons (1949–51). 1919–20, 70 points—highest total in the Second Division.

WEST BROMWICH ALBION. *Ground:* The Hawthorns, West Bromwich. *Founded:* 1879. *Manager:* G. Clarke. *Colours:* Navy blue and white striped shirts; white shorts. *Nickname:* Throstles or Baggies. *Ground Record:* 64,815. *Famous Internationals:* ENGLAND — D. Howe, D. Kevan, R. Robson, R. Allen, R. Barlow, J. Nicholls, S. Rickaby, W. G. Richardson, E. Sandford, T. Magee, W. Boyes, J. Carter, G. Shaw, J. Pennington, W. Bassett, H. Hadley, A. Aldridge; SCOTLAND—A. McNab; IRELAND—R. Ryan, J. Vernon, D. Walsh; WALES—S. Williams, D. Witcomb, J. Murphy, W. Robbins, H. Foulkes; ENGLAND AND IRELAND—J. Reynolds. *League History:* Original League, 1888–92. First Division, 1892–1901, 1902–4, 1911–27, 1931–8, 1949–. Second Division, 1901–2, 1904–11, 1927–31, 1938–49. *League Honours:* First Division Champions, 1919–20. First Division Runners-up, 1924–5, 1953–4. Second Division Champions, 1901–2, 1910–11. *Cup Honours:* Winners, 1888, 1892, 1931, 1954. Runners-up, 1886, 1887, 1895, 1912, 1935. *Records:* Won the Cup and promotion from the Second Division in the same season, 1930–1.

WEST HAM UNITED. *Ground:* Upton Park, London. *Founded:* 1900. *Manager:* E. Fenton. *Colours:* Claret shirts with sky blue sleeves; white shorts. *Nickname:* Hammers. *Ground Record:* 44, 810. *Famous Internationals:* ENGLAND—L. Goulden, J. Barrett, V. Watson, A. Hufton, J. Tresadern, J. Morton, J. Ruffell, G. Webb; SCOTLAND—J. Dick; IRELAND—N. Cantwell, F. O'Farrell, T. Moroney, D. McGowan; WALES—P. Woosnam, W. James, R. Richards, W. Jones. *League History:* First Division, 1923–32, 1958–. Second Division, 1919–23, 1932–58. *League Honours:* Second Division champions, 1957–8. *Cup Honours:* Runners-up, 1923.

WOLVERHAMPTON WANDERERS. *Ground:* Molineux Grounds, Wolverhampton. *Founded:* 1877. *Manager:* S. Cullis. *Colours:* Gold shirts; black shorts. *Nickname:* Wolves. *Ground Record:* 61,315. *Famous Internationals:* ENGLAND—W. Wright, P. Broadbent, N. Deeley, R. Flowers, W. Slater, E. Clamp, D. Wilshaw, B. Williams, J. Pye, J. Mullen, J. Hancocks, S. Cullis, T. Galley, W. Morris, Rev. K. Hunt, J. Brodie, W. Wooldridge; IRELAND—S. Smyth, D. Martin, W. Halligan; WALES—C. Sidlow, C. Phillips, B. Jones, D. Richards, J. Bowdler, E. Peers. *League History:* Original League, 1888–92. First Division, 1892–1906, 1932–. Second Division, 1906–23, 1924–32. Third Division (North), 1923–4. *League Honours:* First Division Champions, 1953–4, 1957–8, 1958–9. First Division Runners-up, 1937–8, 1938–9, 1949–50, 1954–5. Second Division Runners-up, 1931–2. *Cup Honours:* Winners, 1893, 1908, 1949. Runners-up, 1889, 1896, 1921, 1939. *Records:* Only club to have been League Champions of 3 divisions.

GREAT NAMES IN SOCCER

JIMMY DIMMOCK (Tottenham). In the opinion of Arthur Rowe, the former Tottenham manager, Jimmy Dimmock, the Spurs outside left from 1919 to 1931, is the finest outside left he has seen. He was clever to the point of being cheeky, fast and a good finisher. Yet he gained only three caps for England. About the time Spurs won the Cup in 1901 Dimmock was born a mile away from White Hart Lane. Twenty years later he brought the Cup to Tottenham again by scoring the only goal of the 1921 Final against Wolves at Stamford Bridge. He formed a magnificent wing with Bert Bliss and Arthur Grimsdell. After scoring 112 goals for Spurs he moved on to the now-defunct Thames and finished his career with them.

PETER DOHERTY (Manchester City). The finest inside forward produced by Ireland is Peter Doherty, the flame-haired footballer, who saw service with Glentoran, Blackpool, Manchester City, Derby, Huddersfield and Doncaster. A former bus conductor, he played for Ireland during the 16 years from 1934. He combined a strategic sense to tireless energy so effectively that he was able to turn his trickery to match-winning ends. He gained a League Championship medal with Manchester City and a Cup Medal in 1946 with Derby, when he and Raich Carter made up the finest inside forward partnership that Wembley has seen. He proved to be as able a manager as a player, first with Doncaster and then with Bristol City. He is also an inspiring team manager of Ireland and one of the reasons for their international successes recently.

ANDY DUCAT (Arsenal and Aston Villa). One of the 14 men who have played for England at both football and cricket is Andy Ducat. He represented England at football six times from 1909 to 1920 and played cricket against the Australians in 1921. Arsenal brought him from Southend as a centre forward and converted him into a right half. Although solidly built, he was very light on his feet and excelled at construction. In 1909–10, when 23, he was capped in all three home internationals. Arsenal had to sell him to Aston Villa in 1911 for £1,500 in order to keep solvent and although he broke a leg in his first season, he quickly established himself again. He won a Cup medal with Villa in 1920, before being transferred to Fulham.

DALLY DUNCAN (Derby). Dally Duncan missed the train for Hull's Cup semi-final against Arsenal at Leeds in 1930. Yet he was the least perturbed of the team when he arrived in time for the kick-off on a later train. It was typical of him. He was cool, unhurried and unflurried on the field. He was the first choice outside left for Scotland in the six seasons up to the war and tackled an international as coolly as a practice game. Born in Aberdeen, he found fame in England, first with Hull and then with Derby, for whom he played in the 1946 Final. He became player-manager of Luton, went on to serve the club ably as manager and moved to Blackburn in 1958.

JIMMY DUNNE (Sheffield United and Arsenal). Brilliant in the air and quick at shooting near goal, Jimmy Dunne scored nearly 150 goals for Sheffield United. Arsenal came after him to solve their centre-forward problem and he signed for them one Saturday morning in 1933, dashed to London by the first train and took part in Arsenal's 6–0 victory over Middlesbrough the same afternoon. Born in Dublin, Dunne began with Shamrock Rovers. After being transferred to Southampton from Arsenal, he went back to Dublin to coach Bohemians. He died suddenly of a heart attack a few years ago. His son Tommy—also fair-haired—has represented the League of Ireland at right half.

DUNCAN EDWARDS (Manchester United). The greatest loss to British football caused by the Manchester United air crash in February 1958 was the death of Duncan Edwards. He was the youngest man to represent England, being 18½ when left half against Scotland in April 1955. He captained England schoolboys and graduated through the Youth and Under-23 teams to the full international side. Massively built, he moved with grace and speed, and had an unusual tactical sense for one so young. He also played at centre forward, centre half, and any position for which he was chosen. He won two Championship medals with United, took part in the 1957 Final and represented England 18 times.

BOBBY EVANS (Celtic). Wherever the fray is thickest you can find Bobby Evans, the red-haired Celtic defender. The harder the pressure, the better he likes it. Although only 5 ft. 6 in., and 10 st. 10 lb., he tackles twice his weight and wins heading duels against men six inches taller. Born in Glasgow, he joined Celtic from St. Anthony's in 1944 and won his first cap for Scotland five years later. His best position is wing half, but when George Young retired in 1957, he moved to centre half in the national side with considerable success. A back injury handicapped him in 1958.

TOM FINNEY (Preston). Tom Finney grew up under the shadow of Stanley Matthews, the greatest outside right of the generation, and came through to stamp his own greatness on current football. In internationals he switched to the left wing when Matthews was playing, and became the best outside left England had for years. In 1956 Preston tried him at centre forward and he did so well that he was capped in that position as well. With 30 goals he equals the goal-scoring record for England. Born not far from Deepdale, he joined the ground staff after leaving school and gained a first team place in the war years. Preston is his only club, despite having a fabulous offer to enter Italian football in 1952. His 74 appearances for England are surpassed only by Billy Wright.

(*contd. on p. 39, col. 2*)

Jimmy Dimmock Tom Finney Andy Ducat

SOCCER QUIZ

1. Which was the first Cup Final broadcast?

★

2. Which was the first League match broadcast?

3. Can a goal be scored direct from a corner kick?

★

4. Can you be offside from a corner kick?

QUIZ ANSWERS

1. That of 1927. 2. Arsenal v. Sheffield United of 1927. 3. Yes. 4. No.

SOCCER QUIZ

1. For how many places in the First Division is talent money awarded?

★

2. How much can be paid to a player transferred at his club's request?

★

3. What is the signing-on fee in the Football League?

★

4. What is the maximum weekly wage in the Football League?

★

5. And in Scotland?

★

6. Where was the biggest crowd ever to watch a football match?

★

7. How big was it?

QUIZ ANSWERS

1. The first five. 2. £300. 3. £20. 4. £20 in the season, £17 in the summer. 5. There is no maximum. 6. Rio de Janeiro, Brazil. 7. 200,000 for the 1950 World Cup Final.

Club Directory—(*contd.*)

SECOND DIVISION

It was formed in 1892 with 12 clubs. It was extended to 15 in 1893, to 16 in 1894, to 18 in 1898, to 20 in 1905 and to 22 in 1919.

ASTON VILLA. *Ground:* Villa Park, Birmingham. *Founded:* 1874. *Manager:* J. Mercer. *Colours:* Claret and light blue shirts; white shorts. *Nickname:* Villains. *Ground Record:* 76,588. *Famous Internationals:* ENGLAND—E. Lowe, T. Thompson, F. Broome, E. Houghton, F. Moss, R. Starling, W. Walker, W. Kirton, F. Barson, A. Dorrell, T. Gardner, T. Mort, T. Waring, R. York, A. Ducat, S. Hardy, H. Hampton, J. Crabtree, H. Spencer, S. Smith, C. Athersmith, J. Bache, J. Devey, W. Brawn; SCOTLAND—G. Cummings, A. Massie, J. Gibson, J. Cowen, T. Niblo; IRELAND—P. McParland, P. Saward, D. Blanchflower, N. Lockhart, C. Martin; WALES—V. Crowe, T. Ford, K. Jones, I. Powell, G. Edwards, D. Astley, T. Griffiths, C. Phillips, R. Evans, W. Evans. *League History:* Original League, 1888–92. First Division, 1892, 1936, 1938–59. Second Division, 1936–8, 1959–. *League Honours:* First Division Champions, 1893–4, 1895–6, 1896–7, 1898–9, 1899–1900, 1909–10. First Division Runners-up, 1888–9, 1902–3, 1907–8, 1910–11, 1912–13, 1913–14, 1930–1, 1932–3. Second Division Champions, 1937–8. *Cup Honours:* Winners, 1887, 1895, 1897, 1905, 1913, 1920, 1957. Runners-up, 1892, 1924. *Records:* Seven F.A. Cup wins. League and Cup double (shared) 1896–7. Highest First Division total of goals—128 in 1930–1.

BRIGHTON AND HOVE ALBION. *Ground:* Goldstone Ground, Hove. *Founded:* 1900. *Manager:* W. Lane. *Colours:* Blue and white striped shirts; white shorts. *Nickname:* Shrimps. *Ground Record:* 36,747. *Famous Internationals:* ENGLAND—T. Cook; IRELAND—J. Hopkins, C. Webb, J. Doran; WALES—J. Jenkins. *League History:* Second Division, 1958–. Third Division, 1920–1. Third Division (South), 1921–58. Re-elected, 1948.

BRISTOL CITY. *Ground:* Ashton Gate, Bristol. *Founded:* 1894. *Manager:* P. Doherty. *Colours:* Red shirts with white collars; white shorts. *Nickname:* Robins. *Ground Record:* 43,335. *Famous Internationals:* ENGLAND—J. Atyeo, W. Wedlock, J. Cottle; IRELAND—D. Curtis, R. Buckle; WALES—R. Matthews, B. Williams. *League History:* First Division, 1906–11. Second Division, 1901–6, 1911–22, 1923–4, 1927–32, 1955–. Third Division (South), 1922–3, 1924–7, 1932–55. *League Honours:* First Division Runners-up, 1906–7. Second Division Champions, 1905–6. *Cup Honours:* Runners-up, 1909. *Records:* 14 consecutive League wins—season 1905–6 (shared). Highest points in Third South —70 in 1954–5 (shared).

BRISTOL ROVERS. *Ground:* Eastville Stadium, Bristol. *Founded:* 1883. *Manager:* B. Tann. *Colours:* Blue and white quartered shirts; white shorts. *Nickname:* Pirates. *Ground Record:* 35,972. *Famous Internationals:* ENGLAND— G. Bradford; IRELAND — M. O'Mahoney; WALES—D. Ward, J. Lewis. *League History:* Second Division, 1953–. Third Division, 1920–21. Third Division (South), 1921–53. Re-elected, 1939.

CARDIFF CITY. *Ground:* Ninian Park, Cardiff. *Founded:* 1899. *Manager:* W. Jones. *Colours:* Royal blue shirts; white shorts. *Nickname:* Bluebirds. *Ground Record:* 61,079. *Famous Internationals:* SCOTLAND—J. Nelson, J. Blair; IRELAND—S. Irving, T. Sloan, T. Watson, T. Farquharson; WALES—D. Tapscott, D. Sullivan, G. Vearncombe, R. Stitfall, A. Sherwood, T. Ford, A. Harrington, R. Howells, R. Hewitt, W. Rees, S. Richards, G. Edwards, G. Baker, F. Keenor, L. Davies, J. Lewis, J. Nicholls, W. Robbins, L. Jones, J. Evans, L. Evans, G. Latham. *League History:* First Division, 1921–9, 1952–7. Second Division, 1920–1, 1929–31, 1947–52, 1957–. Third Division (South), 1931–47. Re-elected, 1934. *League Honours:* First Division runners-up, 1923–4. *Cup Honours:* Winners, 1927. Runners-up 1925. *Records:* Only club to take the Cup out of England.

CHARLTON ATHLETIC. *Ground:* The Valley, Charlton. *Founded:* 1906. *Manager:* J. Trotter. *Colours:* Red shirts with white collars; white shorts. *Nickname:* Haddicks or Robins. *Ground Record:* 75,031. *Famous Internationals:* ENGLAND—D. Ufton, D. Welsh, H. Hobbis, G. Armitage, J. Miller; SCOTLAND—J. Hewie; IRELAND—A. Steele; WALES—T. Edwards, D. Astley, G. Green, H. Turner. *League History:* First Division, 1936–57. Second Division, 1929–33, 1935–6, 1957–. Third Division (South), 1921–9, 1933–5. Re-elected, 1926. *League Honours:* First Division Runners-up, 1936–7. *Cup Honours:* Winners, 1947. Runners-up, 1946. *Records:* 1935–6 rose from Third Division to First Division in successive seasons.

DERBY COUNTY. *Ground:* Baseball Ground, Derby. *Founded:* 1884. *Manager:* H. Storer. *Colours:* White shirts; black shorts. *Nickname:* Rams. *Ground Record:* 38,384. *Famous Internationals:* ENGLAND—H. Carter, J. Morris, T. Ward, J. Howe, B. Mozley, J. Barker, R. Dix, S. Crooks, T. Cooper, J. Bowers, E. Keen, A. Quantrill, H. Storer, S. Bloomer, J. Goodall, F. Buckley, B. Spilsby, B. Warren; SCOTLAND—W. Steel, D. Duncan, D. McCulloch, C. Napier, H. Gallacher; IRELAND—P. Doherty, M. O'Brien, J. Mercer, W. Halligan; WALES—D. Astley, C. Morris. *League History:* Original League, 1888–92. First Division, 1892–1907, 1912–14, 1915–21, 1926–53. Second Division, 1907–12, 1914–15, 1921–6, 1953–5, 1957–. Third Division (North), 1955–7. *League Honours:* First Division Runners-up, 1895–6, 1929–30, 1935–6. Second Division Champions, 1911–12, 1914–15. *Cup Honours:* Winners, 1946. Runners-up, 1898, 1899, 1903.

HUDDERSFIELD TOWN. *Ground:* Leeds Road, Huddersfield. *Founded:* 1908. *Manager:* W. Shankly. *Colours:* Blue and white striped shirts; white shorts. *Ground Record:* 67,037. *Famous Internationals:* ENGLAND—W. McGarry, R. Staniforth, V. Metcalfe, H. Hassall, A. Beasley, A. Young, K. Willingham, S. Wadsworth, R. Kelly, C. Stephenson, W. Smith, G. Brown, F. Bullock, A. Campbell, H. Turner; SCOTLAND—D. Law, J. Watson, A. Jackson, D. Steele; IRELAND—P. Doherty, J. McKenna, W. Hayes, L. Cumming, J. McAuley; WALES—W. Lewis, D. Evans, C. Morris. *League History:* First Division, 1920–52, 1953–6. Second Division, 1910–20, 1952–3, 1956–. *League Honours:* First Division Champions, 1923–4, 1924–5, 1925–6. First Division Runners-up, 1926–7, 1927–8, 1933–4. *Cup Honours:* Winners, 1922. Runners-up, 1920, 1928, 1930, 1938. *Records:* First Division Championship hat-trick (1923–6) —shared.

HULL CITY. *Ground:* Boothferry Park, Hull. *Founded:* 1904. *Manager:* R. Brocklebank. *Colours:* Amber shirts; black shorts. *Nickname:* Tigers. *Ground Record:* 55,019. *Famous Internationals:* ENGLAND—D. Mercer; SCOTLAND—M. Gilhooley; IRELAND—G. Bowler, M. O'Brien, D. McKinney, W. Gowdy, P. O'Connell. *League History:* Second Division, 1905–30, 1933–6, 1949–56, 1959–. Third Division (North), 1930–3, 1936–49, 1956–8. New Third Division, 1958–9. *League honours:* Third Division champions 1958–9.

IPSWICH TOWN. *Ground:* Portman Road, Ipswich. *Founded:* 1880. *Manager:* A. Ramsey. *Colours:* Royal blue shirts with white sleeves and collars; white shorts. *Ground Record:* 28,194. *Famous Internationals:* WALES—W. Reed. *League History:* Second Division, 1954–5, 1957–. Third Division (South), 1938–54, 1955–7.

LEYTON ORIENT. *Ground:* Leyton Stadium, Leyton. *Founded:* 1881. *Acting Manager:* L. Gore. *Colours:* Royal blue shirts; white shorts. *Nickname:* O's. *Ground Record:* 31,000. *Famous Internationals:* ENGLAND—J. Townrow, O. Williams; WALES—P. Woosnam, T. Evans, T. Mills, E. Morley. *League History:* Second Division, 1905–29, 1956–. Third Division (South), 1929–56.

LINCOLN CITY. *Ground:* Sincil Bank, Lincoln. *Founded:* 1883. *Manager:* W. Anderson. *Colours:* Red and white striped shirts; black shorts. *Nickname:* Imps. *Ground Record:* 23,146. *Famous Internationals:* WALES—D. Pugh. *League History:* Second Division, 1892–1908, when failed to gain re-election; re-elected following season; 1909–11, when failed to gain re-election; re-elected following season; 1912–20, when failed to gain re-election; 1932–4, 1948–9, 1952–. Third Division (North), 1921–32, 1934–48, 1949–52.

LIVERPOOL. *Ground:* Anfield Road, Liverpool. *Founded:* 1892. *Manager:* P. Taylor. *Colours:* Red shirts with white facings; white shorts. *Nickname:* Reds. *Ground Record:* 61,905. *Famous Internationals:* ENGLAND—A. A'Court, P. Taylor, L. Hughes, W. Jones, T. Bromilow, T. Lucas, G. Hodgson, H. Chambers, H. Bradshaw, S. Hardy, J. Parkinson; SCOTLAND—T. Younger, W. Liddell, D. McKinlay, J. McNab, T. Miller, K. Campbell, A. Raisbeck, W. Dunlop; IRELAND—E. Scott, W. Lacey; WALES—R. Lambert, C. Sidlow, E. Parry, R. Matthews, G. Latham, M. Parry, R. Morris. *League History:* First Division, 1894–5, 1896–1904, 1905–54. Second Division, 1893–4, 1895–6, 1904–5, 1954–. *League Honours:* First Division Champions, 1900–1, 1905–6, 1921–2, 1922–3, 1946–7. First Division Runners-up, 1898–9, 1909–10. Second Division Champions, 1893–4, 1895–6, 1904–5. *Cup Honours:* Runners-up, 1914, 1950. *Records:* Champions of Second and First Divisions in successive seasons 1904–6 (shared).

MIDDLESBROUGH. *Ground:* Ayresome Park, Middlesbrough. *Founded:* 1876. *Manager:* R. Dennison. *Colours:* Red shirts with white collars; white shorts. *Nickname:* Ironsides. *Ground Record:* 53,596. *Famous Internationals:* ENGLAND—W. Mannion, G. Hardwick, R. Birkett, G. Camsell, M. Fenton, W. Pease, M. Webster, J. Carr, G. Elliott, J. Peacock, A. Common, S. Bloomer, R. Williamson; SCOTLAND—R. Baxter, J. Marshall, A. Wilson, S. Davidson, D. Cumming, W. Bruce, A. Aitken, A. Brown; IRELAND—A. Fitzsimmons, J. Hartnell, J. Desmond, J. Miller; WALES—W. Harris, T. Griffiths, F. Warren, R. Atherton. *League History:* First Division, 1902–24, 1927–8, 1929–54. Second Division, 1899–1902, 1924–7, 1928–9, 1954–. *League Honours:* Second Division Champions, 1926–7, 1928–9. *Records:* Won Amateur Cup twice (1895 and 1898). 122 goals for in 1926–7, highest total recorded in the Second Division.

PLYMOUTH ARGYLE. *Ground:* Home Park, Plymouth. *Founded:* 1886. *Manager:* J. Rowley. *Colours:* Green shirts with black collars and cuffs; white shorts. *Nickname:* Pilgrims. *Ground Record:* 43,596. *Famous Internationals:* WALES—W. Shortt, M. Russell, W. Pullen. *League History:* Second Division, 1930–50, 1952–6, 1959–. Third Division, 1920–1. Third Division (South), 1921–30, 1950–2, 1956–8. New Third Division, 1958–9. *Records:* Second in Third South for six successive seasons (1921–7).

PORTSMOUTH. *Ground:* Fratton Park, Portsmouth *Founded:* 1898. *Manager:* F. Cox. *Colours:* Royal blue shirts; white shorts. *Nickname:* Pompey. *Ground Record:* 51,385. *Famous Internationals:* ENGLAND—J. Dickinson, J. Froggatt, P. Harris, L. Phillips, J. Allen, F. Worrall, J. Smith, A. Knight, D. Cunliffe; SCOTLAND—J. Henderson, J. Scoular, A. Wilson, J. Easson; IRELAND—N. Uprichard, D. Dougan, T. Casey, J. McAlinden, J. Mackie, R. Irvine, J. Reilly; WALES—F. Cook. *League History:* First Division, 1927–59. Second Division, 1924–7, 1959–. Third Division, 1920–1. Third Division (South), 1921–4. *League Honours:* First Division Champions, 1948–9, 1949–50. *Cup Honours:* Winners, 1939. Runners-up, 1929, 1934.

ROTHERHAM UNITED. *Ground:* Millmoor, Rotherham. *Founded:* 1884. *Manager:* T. Johnston. *Colours:* Red shirts with white sleeves and collars; white shorts. *Nickname:* Merry Millers. *Ground Record:* 25,000. *Famous Internationals:* WALES—S. Davies, H. Millership. *League History:* Second Division, 1893–6, when failed to gain re-election; re-elected in 1919; 1919–23, 1951–. Third Division (North), 1923–51.

SCUNTHORPE UNITED. *Ground:* Old Show Ground, Scunthorpe. *Founded:* 1912. *Manager:* Frank Soo. *Colours:* Claret and sky-blue shirts; white shorts. *Ground Record:* 23,735. *League History:* Second Division, 1958–. Third Division (North), 1950–8.

SHEFFIELD UNITED. *Ground:* Bramall Lane, Sheffield. *Founded:* 1889. *Manager:* J. Harris. *Colours:* Red and white striped shirts; black shorts. *Nickname:* Blades. *Ground Record:* 68,287. *Famous Internationals:* ENGLAND—G. Shaw, A. Hodgkinson, C. Grainger, J. Hagan, R. Barclay, G. Green, F. Tunstall, H. Lipsham, R. Benson, A. Common, H. Hardinge, W. Foulke, E. Needham; SCOTLAND—A. Forbes; IRELAND—A. Ringstead, J. Dunne, W. Gillespie; WALES—W. John, T. Jones. ENGLAND AND WALES—R. Evans. *League History:* First Division, 1893–1934, 1939–49, 1953–6. Second Division, 1892–3, 1934–9, 1949–53, 1956–. *League Honours:* First Division Champions, 1897–8. First Division Runners-up, 1896–7, 1899–1900. Second Division Champions, 1952–3. *Cup Honours:* Winners, 1899, 1902, 1915, 1925. Runners-up, 1901, 1936.

STOKE CITY. *Ground:* Victoria Ground, Stoke-on-Trent. *Founded:* 1863. *Manager:* F. Taylor. *Colours:* Red and white striped shirts; white shorts. *Nickname:* Potters. *Ground Record:* 51,380. *Famous Internationals:* ENGLAND—N. Franklin, S. Matthews, F. Steele, J. Johnson, J. Schofield, A. Underwood, W. Rowley; SCOTLAND—T. Hyslop, W. Maxwell; IRELAND—S. Smyth, J. Sheridan; WALES—W. John, J. T. Jones, S. Meredith, L. Davies. *League History:* Original League, 1888–90, when failed to gain re-election; re-elected following season; 1891–2. First Division, 1892–1907, 1922–3, 1933–53. Second Division, 1907–8, when resigned; re-elected after war; 1919–22, 1923–6,

927-33, 1953–. Third Division (North), 926-7. *League Honours:* Second Division Champions, 1932-3.

UNDERLAND. *Ground:* Roker Park, underland. *Founded:* 1879. *Manager:* .. Brown. *Colours:* Red and white triped shirts; black shorts. *Nickname:* okerites. *Ground Record:* 75,118. *Famous Internationals:* ENGLAND—L. hackleton, W. Watson, H. Carter, . Gurney, W. Cresswell, A. McInroy, . Buchan, F. Cuggy, J. Mordue, T. orteous, P. Bach; SCOTLAND—W. raser, J. McDonald, G. Aitken, T. Vright, P. Gallacher, A. Hastings, W. Clunas, J. Connor, J. Doig, A. McCombie, C. Thompson; IRELAND—V. Bingham, R. Buckle; WALES—T. ord, R. Daniel, L. Roose. *League History:* Original League, 1890-2. First Division, 1892–1958. Second Division, 958–. *League Honours:* First Division Champions, 1891–2, 1892–3, 1894–5, 901–2, 1912–13, 1935–6. First Division Runners-up, 1893–4, 1897–8, 1900–1, 922–3, 1934–5. *Cup Honours:* Winners, 937. Runners-up, 1913. *Records:* Held the longest period of membership n the First Division.

SWANSEA TOWN. *Ground:* Vetch Field, Swansea. *Founded:* 1911. *Manager:* T. Morris. *Colours:* White shirts; white shorts. *Nickname:* Swans. *Ground Record:* 29,708. *Famous Internationals:* IRELAND—T. Feeney, T. Keane, J. O'Driscoll, J. Blair; WALES—M. Charles, D. Palmer, I. Allchurch, L. Allchurch, T. Medwin, F. Scrine, J. King, W. Lucas, T. Ford, J. Griffiths, C. Jones, W. Jones, W. John, D. Lewis, E. Morley, W. Davies, J. Fowler. *League History:* Second Division, 1925–47, 1949–. Third Division, 1920–1. Third Division (South), 1921–5, 1947–9.

THIRD DIVISION

It was formed in 1920 by absorbing the First Division of the Southern League. It consisted of 22 clubs. In the following season it was made into the Third Division, South, and 20 clubs made up the Third Division, North. In 1923 the Northern section was increased to 22 clubs. In 1950 both sections were increased to 24 clubs. In 1958 the new Third Division was formed with the top twelve clubs from each of the old South and North sections.

ACCRINGTON STANLEY. *Ground:* Peel Park, Accrington. *Founded:* 1886. *Manager:* H. Bodle. *Colours:* Red shirts with white sleeves; white shorts. *Ground Record:* 17,634. *Famous Internationals:* ENGLAND—G. Howarth. *League History:* Original League, 1888–92. First Division, 1892–3; resigned 1893. Third Division (North), 1921–58. New Third Division, 1958–. Re-elected, 1927, 1938, 1939, 1951, 1953.

BARNSLEY. *Ground:* Oakwell, Barnsley. *Founded:* 1887. *Manager:* T. Ward. *Colours:* Red shirts; white shorts. *Nickname:* Colliers. *Ground Record:* 40,255. *Famous Internationals:* ENGLAND—G. Utley; SCOTLAND—J. Kelly, J. McCann; IRELAND—E. McMorran, D. Blanchflower, P. Kelly; WALES—A. Richards. *League History:* Second Division, 1898–1932, 1934–8, 1939–53, 1955–9. Third Division, 1959–. Third Division (North), 1932–4, 1938–9, 1953–5. *Cup Honours:* Winners, 1912. Runners-up, 1910.

BOURNEMOUTH AND BOSCOMBE ATHLETIC. *Ground:* Dean Court, Bournemouth. *Founded:* 1890. *Manager:* D. Welsh. *Colours:* Red shirts with white sleeves; white shorts. *Nickname:* Cherries. *Ground Record:* 28,799. *Famous Internationals:* IRELAND—T. Godwin. *League History:* Third Division (South), 1923–58. New Third Division, 1958–. Re-elected, 1924.

BRADFORD CITY. *Ground:* Valley Parade, Bradford. *Founded:* 1903. *Manager:* P. Jackson. *Colours:* Claret shirts with amber V-neck and cuffs; white shorts. *Nickname:* Paraders. *Ground Record:* 39,416. *Famous Internationals:* ENGLAND—R. Bond, E. Lintott, J. Conlin; IRELAND—S. Russell, D. McKinney, H. Hampton, L. Bookman, F. Thompson; WALES—J. Roberts. *League History:* First Division, 1908–22. Second Division, 1903–8, 1922–7, 1929–37. Third Division (North), 1927–9, 1937–58. New Third Division, 1958–. Re-elected, 1949. *League Honours:* Second Division Champions, 1907–8. *Cup Honours:* Winners, 1911. *Records:* First holders of the present F.A. Cup. Highest total of goals in the Third North —128 in 1928–9.

BRENTFORD. *Ground:* Griffin Park, Brentford. *Founded:* 1888. *Manager:* M. MacDonald. *Colours:* Red and white striped shirts; black shorts. *Nickname:* Bees. *Ground Record:* 39,626. *Famous Internationals:* ENGLAND—L. Smith, W. Scott; SCOTLAND—A. Macaulay, D. McCulloch, R. Reid, D. McKenzie; IRELAND—S. D'Arcy, W. Gorman, M. Connor; WALES—D. Hopkins, L. Boulter, D. Richards. *League History:* First Division, 1935–47. Second Division, 1933–5, 1947–54. Third Division, 1920–21. Third Division (South), 1921–33, 1954–8. New Third Division, 1958–. Re-elected, 1921, 1925. *League Honours:* Second Division Champions, 1934–5. *Records:* Won all 21 home League games 1929–30.

BURY. *Ground:* Gigg Lane, Bury. *Founded:* 1885. *Manager:* D. Russell. *Colours:* White shirts; navy blue shorts. *Nickname:* Shakers. *Ground Record:* 34,386. *Famous Internationals:* ENGLAND—N. Bullock, J. Ball, C. Sagar, W. Hibbert; SCOTLAND—T. Bradshaw; IRELAND—J. Chambers, J. Walker. *League History:* First Division, 1895–1912, 1924–9. Second Division, 1894–5, 1912–24, 1929–57. Third Division (North), 1957–8. New Third Division, 1958–. *League Honours:* Second Division Champions, 1894–5. *Cup Honours:* Winners, 1900, 1903. *Records:* Highest Cup Final score —6–0 v. Derby 1903. Won Cup without conceding a goal 1903.

CHESTERFIELD. *Ground:* Recreation Ground, Chesterfield. *Founded:* 1866. *Manager:* D. Livingstone. *Colours:* Royal blue shirts; white shorts. *Nickname:* Spireites. *Ground Record:* 30,968. *Famous Internationals:* IRELAND—W. McMillen, D. Milligan. *League History:* Second Division, 1899–1909, when failed to gain re-election; 1931–3, 1936–51. Third Division (North), 1921–31, 1933–6, 1951–8. New Third Division, 1958–.

COLCHESTER UNITED. *Ground:* Layer Road, Colchester. *Founded:* 1937. *Manager:* B. Fenton. *Colours:* Blue and white striped shirts; white shorts. *Ground Record:* 19,072. *League History:* Third Division (South), 1950–8. New Third Division, 1958–. Re-elected, 1954, 1955.

COVENTRY CITY. *Ground:* Highfield Road, Coventry. *Founded:* 1883. *Manager:* W. Frith. *Colours:* Blue and white striped shirts; white shorts. *Nickname:* Bantams. *Ground Record:* 44,930. *Famous Internationals:* ENGLAND—R. Matthews; IRELAND—N. Lockhart, J. Brown; WALES—G. Lowrie, B. Allen, L. Jones, R. Evans. *League History:* Second Division, 1919–25, 1936–52. Third Division (North), 1925–6. Third Division (South), 1926–36, 1952–8. New Third Division 1959–. Fourth Division, 1958–9.

GRIMSBY TOWN. *Ground:* Blundell Park, Cleethorpes. *Founded:* 1878. *Manager:* *Colours:* Black and white striped shirts; black shorts. *Nickname:* Mariners. *Ground Record:* 31,653. *Famous Internationals:* ENGLAND—G. Tweedy, H. Betmead, J. Bestall; IRELAND—J. Scott, J. Coulter, W. Andrews; WALES—P. Glover, D. Collier. *League History:* First Division, 1901–3, 1929–32, 1934–48. Second Division, 1892–1901, 1903–10, when failed to gain re-election; re-elected 1911; 1911–20, 1926–9, 1932–4, 1948–51, 1956–9. Third Division, 1920–1, 1959–. Third Division (North), 1921–6, 1951–6. Re-elected, 1955. *League Honours:* Second Division Champions, 1900–1, 1933–4. *Records:* The only club to play in the Third North and Third South as well as the top two Divisions.

HALIFAX TOWN. *Ground:* Shay Ground, Halifax. *Founded:* 1911. *Manager:* H. Hooper. *Colours:* Royal blue shirts with white V-neck; white shorts. *Ground Record:* 36,995. *League History:* Third Division (North), 1921–58. New Third Division, 1958–. Re-elected, 1930, 1947, 1948, 1950, 1954.

MANSFIELD TOWN. *Ground:* Field Mill, Mansfield. *Founded:* 1905. *Manager:* S. Weaver. *Colours:* White shirts; black shorts. *Nickname:* Stags. *Ground Record:* 24,479. *League History:* Third Division (South), 1931–2, 1937–47. Third Division (North), 1932–7, 1947–58. New Third Division, 1958–. Re-elected, 1947.

NEWPORT COUNTY. *Ground:* Somerton Park, Newport. *Founded:* 1911. *Manager:* W. Lucas. *Colours:* Amber shirts with black collars; black shorts. *Nickname:* Ironsides. *Ground Record:* 24,268. *Famous Internationals:* WALES—A. Sherwood, H. Williams, F. Cook, R. Pugh, A. Waddell. *League History:* Second Division, 1939–47. Third Division, 1920–1. Third Division (South), 1921–31, when failed to gain re-election; re-elected following season; 1932–9, 1947–58. New Third Division, 1958–. Re-elected, 1923, 1933, 1935, 1936, 1950.

NORWICH CITY. *Ground:* Carrow Road, Norwich. *Founded:* 1905. *Manager:* A. Macaulay. *Colours:* Yellow shirts with green collars and cuffs; black shorts. *Nickname:* Canaries. *Ground Record:* 43,129. *Famous Internationals:* IRELAND—J. Gavin, J. Hill, O. Madden; WALES—N. Kinsey. *League History:* Second Division, 1934–9. Third Division, 1920–1. Third Division (South), 1921–34, 1939–58. New Third Division, 1958–. Re-elected, 1931, 1947, 1948, 1957.

PORT VALE. *Ground:* Vale Park, Burslem. *Founded:* 1876. *Manager:* N. Low. *Colours:* Black and amber striped shirts; black shorts. *Nickname:* Valiants. *Ground Record:* 44,000. *Famous Internationals:* WALES—E. Peers. *League History:* Second Division, 1892–6, when failed to gain re-election; re-elected 1898; 1898–1907, when failed to gain re-election; took over fixtures of Leeds club on latter's temporary retirement 1919–20; thereafter in Second Division on their own right till 1929; 1930–6, 1954–7. Third Division (North), 1929–30, 1936–8, 1952–4. Third Division (South), 1938–52, 1957–8. New Third Division, 1959–. Fourth Division, 1958–9. *League Honours:* Fourth Division Champions 1958–9. *Cup Honours:* Reached semi-final as Third North club in 1954.

QUEEN'S PARK RANGERS. *Ground:* Ellerslie Road, Shepherd's Bush. *Founded:* 1885. *Manager:* A. Stock. *Colours:* White shirts with royal blue collars and cuffs; royal blue shorts. *Nickname:* R's. *Ground Record:* 30,564. *Famous Internationals:* ENGLAND—E. Lintott; IRELAND—M. O'Brien; WALES—I. Powell, W. Greer, N. Murphy. *League History:* Second Division, 1948–52. Third Division, 1920–1. Third Division (South), 1921–48, 1952–8. New Third Division 1958–.

READING. *Ground:* Elm Park, Reading. *Founded:* 1871. *Manager:* H. Johnston. *Colours:* Blue and white hooped shirts; white shorts. *Nickname:* Biscuitmen. *Ground Record:* 33,042. *Famous Internationals:* ENGLAND—H. Smith; IRELAND—W. McConnell, H. Davey; WALES—D. Evans, J. Davies. *League History:* Second Division, 1926–31. Third Division, 1920–1. Third Division (South), 1921–6, 1931–58. New Third Division, 1958–.

SHREWSBURY TOWN. *Ground:* Gay Meadow, Shrewsbury. *Founded:* 1886. *Manager:* A. Rowley. *Colours:* Blue shirts with white V-neck and cuffs; white shorts. *Ground Record:* 18,197. *Famous Internationals:* WALES—A. Bostock, J. Bowdler. *League History:* Third Division (North), 1950–1. Third Division (South), 1951–8. Fourth Division, 1958–. Re-elected, 1953.

SOUTHAMPTON. *Ground:* The Dell, Southampton. *Founded:* 1885. *Manager:* E. Bates. *Colours:* Red and white striped shirts; black shorts. *Nickname:* Saints. *Ground Record:* 30,586. *Famous Internationals:* ENGLAND—A. Ramsey, W. Ellerington, T. Parker, F. Titmuss, W. Rawlings, C. B. Fry, A. Chadwick; SCOTLAND—I. Black, J. Robertson; IRELAND—J. Shields, H. Kelly, R. Rowley; WALES—A. Hodgkinson. *League History:* Second Division, 1922–53. Third Division, 1920–1. Third Division (South), 1921–2, 1953–8. New Third Division, 1958–. *Cup Honours:* Runners-up, 1900, 1902.

SOUTHEND UNITED. *Ground:* Roots Hall, Southend-on-Sea. *Founded:* 1906. *Manager:* E. Perry. *Colours:* Blue shirts with white collars; white shorts. *Nickname:* Shrimpers. *Ground Record:* 29,500. *Famous Internationals:* IRELAND—S. McCrory, J. McAlinden; WALES—J. Evans, W. Jones. *League History:* Third Division, 1920–1. Third Division (South), 1921–58. New Third Division, 1958–. Re-elected, 1922, 1935.

SWINDON TOWN. *Ground:* County Ground, Swindon. *Founded:* 1881. *Manager:* B. Head. *Colours:* Red shirts with white edging; white shorts. *Nickname:* Moonrakers or Robins. *Ground Record:* 28,400. *Famous Internationals:* ENGLAND—H. Fleming; SCOTLAND—J. Walker; IRELAND—N. Uprichard; WALES—A. Morris. *League History:* Third Division, 1920–1. Third Division (South), 1921–58. New Third Division 1958–. Re-elected, 1933, 1956, 1957.

TRANMERE ROVERS. *Ground:* Prenton Park, Birkenhead. *Founded:* 1883. *Manager:* P. Farrell. *Colours:* Royal blue shirts; white shorts. *Ground Record:* 22,217. *Famous Internationals:* IRELAND—W. Sloan, J. Brown; WALES—K. Rowley, A. Gray, A. Rowlands. *League History:* Second Division, 1938–9. Third Division (North), 1921–38, 1939–58. New Third Division, 1958–. Re-elected, 1957.

WREXHAM. *Ground:* Racecourse Ground, Wrexham. *Founded:* 1873. *Manager:* J. Love. *Colours:* Red shirts with white facings; white shorts. *Ground Record:* 33,160. *Famous Internationals:* WALES—G. Poland, G. Godding, T. Mathias, W. Ellis, T. Bamford, L. Williams, G. Wynn, W. Lea, W. Blew, S. Griffiths, S. Glascodine, H. Trainer, J. Trainer, O. Davies, L. Davies. *League History:* Third Division (North), 1921–58. New Third Division, 1958–. *Records:* Oldest club in Wales. Greatest number of internationals for Wales—56.

YORK CITY. *Ground:* Bootham Crescent, York. *Founded:* 1903. *Manager:* S. Bartram. *Colours:* Red shirts; white shorts. *Ground Record:* 28,123. *League History:* Third Division (North), 1929–58. New Third Division, 1959–. Fourth Division, 1958–9. Re-elected, 1950. *Cup Honours:* Reached semi-final as Third North club 1955.

SOCCER QUIZ

1. Name the club which dropped from the First Division to the Third in successive seasons.

★

2. Has a Scottish Cup-tie been played in England?

★

3. Which is the oldest Scottish club?

★

4. And the oldest Football League club?

QUIZ ANSWERS

1. Bradford in 1920–2. 2. Yes, at Berwick, between Berwick Rangers and Ayr in 1929. 3. Queen's Park (1867). 4. Notts County (1862).

SOCCER QUIZ

1. Which club secured the greatest number of points in winning the Third Division South?

*

2. And the Third North?

*

3. Who obtained the greatest number of caps for England?

*

4. For Scotland? *(above)*

*

5. For Ireland?

*

6. For Wales? *(above)*

*

7. Which club spent the most seasons in the First Division?

QUIZ ANSWERS

1. Bristol City—70 in 1954–5, and Nottingham Forest—70 in 1950–1. 2. Doncaster—72 in 1946–7. 3. W. Wright (Wolves)—105. 4. G. Young (Glasgow Rangers)—50. 5. W. Bingham (Sunderland and Luton)—36. 6. W. Meredith (Manchester City and United)—48. 7. Aston Villa—60 seasons.

Club Directory—*(contd.)*

FOURTH DIVISION

It was formed in 1958 with the bottom twelve clubs from each of the old Third South and Third North sections.

ALDERSHOT. *Ground:* Recreation Ground, Aldershot. *Founded:* 1927. *Manager:* D. Smith. *Colours:* Red shirts with blue sleeves; white shorts. *Nickname:* Shots or Soldiers. *Ground Record:* 15,611. *League History:* Third Division (South), 1932–58. Fourth Division, 1958–. Re-elected, 1937, 1949.

BARROW. *Ground:* Holker Street, Barrow in Furness. *Founded:* 1901. *Manager:* *Colours:* Blue shirts; white shorts. *Ground Record:* 16,073. *Famous Internationals:* IRELAND—W. Miller. *League History:* Third Division (North), 1921–58. Fourth Division, 1958. Re-elected, 1924, 1926, 1927, 1930, 1938.

BRADFORD. *Ground:* Park Avenue, Bradford. *Founded:* 1907. *Manager:* W. Galbraith. *Colours:* Green and white striped shirts; white shorts. *Nickname:* Avenue. *Ground Record:* 32,810. *Famous Internationals:* ENGLAND—R. Turnbull; SCOTLAND—J. Stephen; IRELAND—J. Elwood, J. McCandless, A. McCluggage; WALES—R. Matthews, J. Parris. *League History:* First Division, 1914–21. Second Division, 1908–14, 1921–2, 1928–50. Third Division (North), 1922–8, 1950–8. Fourth Division, 1958–. Re-elected, 1956. *Records:* Relegated from First to Third Division in successive seasons 1920–2.

CARLISLE UNITED. *Ground:* Brunton Park, Carlisle. *Founded:* 1903. *Manager:* A. Beattie. *Colours:* Royal blue shirts; white shorts. *Nickname:* Cumbrians. *Ground Record:* 27,500. *League History:* Third Division (North), 1928–58. Fourth Division, 1958–. Re-elected, 1935.

CHESTER. *Ground:* Sealand Road Stadium, Chester. *Founded:* 1884. *Manager:* S. Pearson. *Colours:* Blue and white striped shirts; black shorts. *Ground Record:* 20,500. *Famous Internationals:* WALES—A. Gray, W. Matthews, W. Lewis, S. Jones. *League History:* Third Division (North), 1931–58. Fourth Division, 1958–. Re-elected, 1954, 1955.

CREWE ALEXANDRA. *Ground:* Gresty Road, Crewe. *Founded:* 1876. *Manager:* H. Ware. *Colours:* Red shirts; white shorts. *Nickname:* Railwaymen. *Ground Record:* 17,883. *Famous Internationals:* ENGLAND—J. Pearson, L. Hales; WALES—F. Keenor, R. Roberts, W. Bell, T. Owen, W. Lewis. *League History:* Second Division, 1892–6, when failed to gain re-election. Third Division (North), 1921–58. Fourth Division, 1958–. Re-elected, 1956, 1957, 1958.

CRYSTAL PALACE. *Ground:* Selhurst Park, South Norwood. *Founded:* 1905. *Manager:* G. Smith. *Colours:* White shirts with claret and blue facings; black shorts. *Nickname:* Glaziers. *Ground Record:* 41,000. *Famous Internationals:* ENGLAND—J. Alderson; H. Coleclough; IRELAND—R. McCracken; WALES—V. Rouse, J. Jones, W. Davies, J. Williams. *League History:* Second Division, 1921–5. Third Division, 1920–1. Third Division (South), 1925–58. Fourth Division, 1958–. Re-elected, 1949, 1951, 1956.

DARLINGTON. *Ground:* Feethams Ground, Darlington. *Founded:* 1882. *Manager:* R. Duckworth. *Colours:* White shirts; black shorts. *Nickname:* Quakers. *Ground Record:* 19,184. *League History:* Second Division, 1925–7. Third Division (North), 1921–5, 1927–58. Fourth Division, 1958–. Re-elected, 1933, 1937, 1952.

DONCASTER ROVERS. *Ground:* Belle Vue, Doncaster. *Founded:* 1879. *Manager:* J. Crayston. *Colours:* Red shirts with white facings; white shorts. *Ground Record:* 37,149. *Famous Internationals:* IRELAND—L. Graham, H. Gregg, E. McMorran, W. Walker, J. Lawlor, P. McConnell; WALES—E. Perry. *League History:* Second Division, 1901–3, when failed to gain re-election; re-elected following season; 1904–5, when failed to gain re-election; 1935–7, 1947–8, 1950–8. Third Division (North), 1923–35, 1937–47, 1948–50. New Third Division, 1958–9. Fourth Division, 1959–. *Records:* Highest points in season for any League club—72 points in 1946–7.

EXETER CITY. *Ground:* St. James's Park, Exeter. *Founded:* 1906. *Manager:* F. Broome. *Colours:* Red shirts with white collars; white shorts. *Nickname:* Grecians. *Ground Record:* 20,984. *League History:* Third Division, 1920–1. Third Division (South), 1921–58. Fourth Division, 1958–. Re-elected, 1922, 1929, 1936, 1937, 1952, 1958.

GATESHEAD. *Ground:* Redheugh Park, Gateshead. *Founded:* 1899. *Manager:* R. Batty. *Colours:* White shirts; black shorts. *Nickname:* Laides. *Ground Record:* 20,752. *Famous Internationals:* ENGLAND—W. Cresswell. *League History:* Second Division, 1919–28. Third Division (North), 1928–58. Fourth Division, 1958–. Re-elected, 1937.

GILLINGHAM. *Ground:* Priestfield Stadium, Gillingham. *Founded:* 1893. *Manager:* H. Barratt. *Colours:* Blue shirts with white collars; white shorts. *Ground Record:* 23,002. *Famous Internationals:* ENGLAND—F. Fox. *League History:* Third Division, 1920–1. Third Division (South), 1921–38, when failed to gain re-election; re-elected 1950; 1950–8. Fourth Division, 1958–.

HARTLEPOOLS UNITED. *Ground:* Victoria Ground, West Hartlepool. *Founded:* 1908. *Manager:* R. Middleton. *Colours:* Blue and white striped shirts; black shorts. *Nickname:* Pools. *Ground Record:* 17,300. *League History:* Third Division (North), 1921–58. Fourth Division, 1958–. Re-elected, 1924, 1939.

MILLWALL. *Ground:* The Den, New Cross. *Founded:* 1885. *Manager:* R. Smith. *Colours:* Royal blue shirts with white collars; white shorts. *Nickname:* Lions. *Ground Record:* 48,327. *Famous Internationals:* ENGLAND—J. Smith, L. Graham, J. Fort, H. Banks; IRELAND—C. Hurley, E. Hinton, T. Brolly; WALES—J. Davies, W. Davis, A. Watkins. *League History:* Second Division, 1928–34, 1938–48. Third Division, 1920–1. Third Division (South), 1921–8, 1934–8, 1948–58. Fourth Division, 1958–. Re-elected, 1950, 1958. *Cup Honours:* First Third Division side to reach the F.A. Cup semi-final (1937). *Records:* 127 goals in 1927–8, the highest total for one season in the Third South.

NORTHAMPTON TOWN. *Ground:* County Ground, Northampton. *Founded:* 1897. *Manager:* D. Bowen. *Colours:* Claret shirts with white collars; white shorts. *Nickname:* Cobblers. *Ground Record:* 22,644. *Famous Internationals:* WALES—W. Williams, E. Davies. *League History:* Third Division, 1920–1. Third Division (South), 1921–58. Fourth Division, 1958–.

NOTTS COUNTY. *Ground:* Meadow Lane, Nottingham. *Founded:* 1862. *Manager:* F. Hill. *Colours:* Black and white striped shirts; black shorts. *Nickname:* Lambs. *Ground Record:* 49,000. *Famous Internationals:* ENGLAND—T. Lawton, W. Ashurst, H. Daft, A. Dobson, C. Dobson, H. Morley, E. Greenhalgh, W. Gunn, H. Morse, A. Shilton; IRELAND—E. Gannon; WALES—E. Lawrence, W. Davies, A. Green. *League History:* Original League, 1888–92. First Division, 1892–3, 1897–1913, 1914–20, 1923–6. Second Division, 1893–7, 1913–14, 1920–23, 1926–30, 1931–5, 1950–8. Third Division (South), 1930–1, 1935–50. New Third Division, 1958–9. Fourth Division, 1959–. *League Honours:* Second Division Championship, 1896–7, 1913–14, 1922–3. *Cup Honours:* Winners, 1894. Runners-up, 1891. *Records:* The oldest Football League club.

OLDHAM ATHLETIC. *Ground:* Boundary Park, Oldham. *Founded:* 1899. *Manager:* N. Dodgin. *Colours:* Blue and white striped shirts; white shorts. *Nickname:* Latics. *Ground Record:* 47,671. *Famous Internationals:* ENGLAND—J. Hacking, H. Moffat, G. Woodger; SCOTLAND—D. Wilson; IRELAND—T. Davis, L. Cumming; WALES—A. Gray, D. Davies, E. Jones. *League History:* First Division, 1910–23. Second Division, 1907–10, 1923–35, 1953–4. Third Division (North), 1935–53, 1954–8. Fourth Division, 1958–. *League Honours:* First Division Runners-up, 1914–15.

ROCHDALE. *Ground:* Willbutts Lane, Rochdale. *Founded:* 1900. *Manager:* J. Marshall. *Colours:* Black and white striped shirts; black shorts. *Nickname:* Vallians. *Ground Record:* 24,231. *League History:* Third Division (North), 1921–58. New Third Division, 1958–9. Fourth Division, 1959–. Re-elected, 1931, 1932, 1934.

SOUTHPORT. *Ground:* Haig Avenue, Southport. *Founded:* 1881. *Manager:* W. Fielding. *Colours:* Old gold shirts with black collar and cuffs; black shorts. *Nickname:* Sandgrounders. *Ground Record:* 20,010. *Famous Internationals:* IRELAND—P. McConnell; WALES—G. Lathom. *League History:* Third Division (North), 1921–58. Fourth Division, 1958–. Re-elected, 1935, 1936, 1946, 1949, 1958.

STOCKPORT COUNTY. *Ground:* Edgeley Park, Stockport. *Founded:* 1883. *Manager:* W. Moir. *Colours:* White shirts; black shorts. *Nickname:* Hatters. *Ground Record:* 27,833. *Famous Internationals:* ENGLAND—H. Hardy. *League History:* Second Division, 1900–4, when failed to gain re-election; re-elected following season; 1905–21, 1922–6, 1937–8. Third Division (North), 1921–2, 1926–37, 1938–58. New Third Division, 1958–9. Fourth Division, 1959–.

TORQUAY UNITED. *Ground:* Plainmoor, Torquay. *Founded:* 1898. *Manager:* E. Webber. *Colours:* Gold shirts with royal blue sleeves and collars; black shorts. *Ground Record:* 21,908. *League History:* Third Division (South), 1927–58. Fourth Division, 1958–. Re-elected, 1928.

WALSALL. *Ground:* Fellows Park, Walsall. *Founded:* 1868. *Manager:* W. Moore. *Colours:* Red shirts with white collars; white shorts. *Nickname:* Saddlers. *Ground Record:* 21,811. *Famous Internationals:* ENGLAND—A. Jones; IRELAND—W. Taggart; WALES—W. John. *League History:* Second Division, 1892–5, when failed to gain re-election; re-elected following season; 1896–1901, when failed to gain re-election. Third Division (North), 1921–8, 1931–6. Third Division (South), 1928–31, 1936–58. Fourth Division, 1958–. Re-elected, 1926, 1938, 1939, 1952, 1953, 1954, 1955. *Records:* Re-elected seven times.

WATFORD. *Ground:* Vicarage Road, Watford. *Founded:* 1898. *Manager:* R. Burgess. *Colours:* Blue shirts; white shorts. *Nickname:* Brewers. *Ground Record:* 32,384. *Famous Internationals:* WALES—F. Hoddinott. *League History:* Third Division, 1920–1. Third Division (South), 1921–58. Fourth Division, 1958–. Re-elected, 1927, 1951.

WORKINGTON TOWN. *Ground:* Borough Park, Workington. *Founded:* 1884. *Manager:* J. Harvey. *Colours:* Red shirts; white shorts. *Nickname:* Reds. *Ground Record:* 19,200. *League History:* Third Division (North), 1951–8. Fourth Division, 1958–. Re-elected, 1952, 1953.

PROMOTION AND RELEGATION

Automatic promotion and relegation did not come into operation until 1899. Until then, from 1892–3, the first season of the Second Division, promotion and relegation were decided by a series of test matches among the bottom clubs of the First Division and the top clubs of the Second.

The results of this interim period were:

1892–3	Sheffield United and Darwen promoted. Notts County and Accrington relegated.
1893–4	Liverpool and Small Heath promoted. Newton Heath and Darwen relegated.
1894–5	Bury promoted. Liverpool relegated.
1895–6	Liverpool promoted. Small Heath relegated.
1896–7	Notts County promoted. Burnley relegated.
1897–8	Stoke and Burnley promoted. As the League was extended, Blackburn and Newcastle also taken into the First Division.

In 1919–20, when the First Division was extended to 22 clubs, Chelsea, the bottom club before the 1914–18 war, were re-elected. Tottenham were relegated and Arsenal, who had finished sixth in the Second Division in 1914–15, were elected in their place.

RELEGATED CLUBS

FROM FIRST DIVISION

1898–9 Bolton W. and Sheffield Wed.
1899–1900 Burnley and Glossop

orkshire Amateurs | Hitchin Town | Barnet | Dulwich Hamlet | Tooting & Mitcham

00–1 Preston North End and West Bromwich
01–2 Small Heath and Manchester C.
02–3 Grimsby T. and Bolton W.
03–4 Liverpool and W.B.A.
04–5 League extended. Bury and Notts County, two bottom clubs in First Division, re-elected
905–6 Notts F. and Wolves
906–7 Derby Co. and Stoke
907–8 Bolton W. and Birmingham
908–9 Man. C. and Leicester Fosse
909–10 Bolton W. and Chelsea
910–11 Bristol C. and Nottingham F.
911–12 Preston North End and Bury
912–13 Notts C. and Woolwich Arsenal
913–14 Preston N.E. and Derby Co.
914–15 Tottenham H. and Chelsea
919–20 Notts Co. and Sheffield Wed.
920–1 Derby Co. and Bradford
921–2 Bradford C. and Manchester U.
922–3 Stoke and Oldham Athletic
923–4 Chelsea and Middlesbrough
924–5 Preston N.E. and Notts F.
925–6 Manchester C. and Notts Co.
926–7 Leeds United and W.B.A.
1927–8 Tottenham H. and Middlesbrough
1928–9 Bury and Cardiff C.
1929–30 Burnley and Everton
1930–1 Leeds U. and Manchester U.
1931–2 Grimsby T. and West Ham U.
1932–3 Bolton W. and Blackpool
1933–4 Newcastle U. and Sheffield U.
1934–5 Leicester C. and Tottenham H.
1935–6 Aston Villa and Blackburn R.
1936–7 Manchester U. and Sheffield W.
1937–8 Manchester C. and W.B.A.
1938–9 Birmingham and Leicester C.
1946–7 Brentford and Leeds U.
1947–8 Blackburn R. and Grimsby T.
1948–9 Preston N.E. and Sheffield U.
1949–50 Manchester C. and Birmingham
1950–1 Sheffield W. and Everton
1951–2 Huddersfield T. and Fulham
1952–3 Stoke C. and Derby Co.
1953–4 Middlesbrough and Liverpool
1954–5 Leicester C. and Sheffield Wed.
1955–6 Huddersfield T. and Sheffield U.
1956–7 Charlton A. and Cardiff C.
1957–8 Sheffield W. and Sunderland
1958–9 Portsmouth and Aston Villa

FROM SECOND DIVISION

1920–1 Stockport Co.
1921–2 Bradford and Bristol C.
1922–3 Rotherham C. and Wolverhampton Wan.
1923–4 Nelson and Bristol C.
1924–5 Crystal Palace and Coventry C.
1925–6 Stoke C. and Stockport Co.
1926–7 Darlington and Bradford C.
1927–8 Fulham and South Shields
1928–9 Port Vale and Clapton Orient
1929–30 Hull C. and Notts Co.
1930–1 Reading and Cardiff C.
1931–2 Barnsley and Bristol C.
1932–3 Chesterfield and Charlton A.
1933–4 Millwall and Lincoln C.
1934–5 Oldham Athletic and Notts Co.
1935–6 Port Vale and Hull C.
1936–7 Doncaster R. and Bradford C.
1937–8 Barnsley and Stockport Co.
1938–9 Norwich C. and Tranmere R.
1946–7 Swansea T. and Newport C.
1947–8 Doncaster R. and Millwall
1948–9 Notts F. and Lincoln C.
1949–50 Plymouth A. and Bradford
1950–1 Grimsby T. and Chesterfield
1951–2 Coventry C. and Q.P.R.
1952–3 Southampton and Barnsley
1953–4 Brentford and Oldham A.
1954–5 Ipswich T. and Derby Co.
1955–6 Plymouth Argyle and Hull C.
1956–7 Port Vale and Bury
1957–8 Doncaster R. and Notts Co.
1958–9 Barnsley and Grimsby

FROM THIRD DIVISION

1958–9 Rochdale, Notts County, Doncaster R. and Stockport County

GREAT NAMES IN SOCCER

TREVOR FORD (Aston Villa and Sunderland). A fiery, provocative figure, Trevor Ford cost £69,000 in transfer fees for his moves from Swansea to Aston Villa, to Sunderland and then to Cardiff. Included was £30,000 paid in 1950 by Sunderland. It was the first £30,000 fee. Dark and sinewy, Ford was a dashing opportunist and many a goal-keeper felt the impact of his sturdy shoulders. He was at his best in the red shirt of Wales, especially against England at Ninian Park. He played nearly 30 times for Wales.

NEIL FRANKLIN (Stoke). Neil Franklin was one of the pillars on which England were building the 1950 World Cup side when he departed without warning for Bogota in Colombia. Colombia was then outside F.I.F.A. and players could move there without a transfer fee being paid. Franklin did not realise the quick fortune he had expected and when he returned home his career with both England and Stoke was over. He was transferred to Hull and then to Stockport. Stylish and polished rather than forceful, he was England's first choice at centre half for 27 internationals immediately after the war.

HUGHIE GALLACHER (Newcastle and Chelsea). Although only 5 feet 5 inches tall, Hughie Gallacher was perhaps the greatest centre forward of all time. He had skilful feet to match his quicksilver brain. He climbed amazingly well to beat taller men in the air and was supreme when the ball was on the ground. His weakness was a fiery temperament and opponents played on it by trying to rile him on the field. He scored 386 goals and represented Scotland 19 times in a career which started with Airdrie. He was transferred in 1925 for £6,500 to Newcastle, where he soon became the idol of Tyneside. One season he refused a Scottish cap against England in order to help Newcastle to fight against relegation. He moved to Chelsea in 1930 and then on to Derby, Notts County, Grimsby and Gateshead.

JIMMY GIBSON (Aston Villa). Tall and slim, Jimmy Gibson was surprisingly neat in his footwork and beautifully balanced. He was one of the Scottish team who gained the title "Wembley Wizards" for their overwhelming victory over England in 1928, and he was no less graceful than the tiny forwards he played behind. He was first capped in 1926 when with Partick Thistle. He moved to Aston Villa to make up a half-back line of six-footers with Tate and Talbot. This middle line was largely responsible for making Villa the chief challengers to Arsenal in the 1930s. Gibson played eight times for Scotland between 1926 and 1930.

BILLY GILLESPIE (Sheffield United). But for the First World War Billy Gillespie would have won far more than the 25 caps he obtained for Ireland. His international career began in 1913 and lasted 18 years altogether. Serious in face and outlook, he was a master strategist at inside left, a maker of goals rather than a scorer. At Sheffield United he made up a formidable left wing with Fred Tunstall, an England international. He became bald prematurely and his shining forehead was always in evidence where most needed. He captained United when they defeated Cardiff in the 1925 Cup Final.

HARRY GREGG (Manchester United). Within twelve months up to November 1958 the following things happened to Harry Gregg, the Ireland international goalkeeper. 1. He was transferred from Doncaster to Manchester United for £23,000—a record fee for a goalkeeper. 2. He was one of the survivors of the Manchester air disaster and returned to the wreckage to rescue injured colleagues. 3. He was a key man in the rebuilding of United. 4. He was knocked out in the Cup Final when Lofthouse scored the second goal. 5. He was acclaimed the "best goalkeeper in the world" in the World Cup in Sweden. 6. He was dropped by Ireland because he would not fly to Madrid for the international against Spain. Gregg had been first choice for Ireland since 1954.

ARTHUR GRIMSDELL (Tottenham Hotspur). One of the greatest captains the game has produced was Arthur Grimsdell of Spurs. Apart from being a dominant and aggressive left half, he sized up an opening quickly and concentrated play on opponents' weaknesses. He signed for Spurs in 1912 and played a vital part in 1919–20 when the club won promotion from the Second Division with the record number of 70 points. He took over the captaincy and led Spurs to seven seasons of solid achievements, including winning the Cup in 1921.

WILLIE HALL (Tottenham Hotspur). The career of Spurs inside right Willie Hall was cut tragically short by a disease which eventually cost him both his legs.

Neil Franklin

Trevor Ford

Hughie Gallacher

Solid, fair-haired and cheerful, he was signed from Notts County, for whom he had been a professional for two years, in 1932 to succeed George Greenfield, who was out of action because of a broken leg. He gained the first of his ten England caps a year later. In November 1938, partnered by Stanley Matthews, he set up an England scoring record with five successive goals against Ireland.

EDDIE HAPGOOD (Arsenal). Bristol Rovers turned down Eddie Hapgood, then a milkman in the city, because he was small and lightly built. He joined Southern League club Kettering and went to Arsenal when 19 in 1926 to become one of the finest left-backs of all time. He timed the tackle perfectly, had the ball control of an inside forward, was quick in recovery and had an astute positional sense. He made the first of his 30 appearances for England in 1934, and went on to be an inspiring captain of both club and country. He was a vital factor in Arsenal's rise to the top in the 1930s. He won five League Championship medals and took part in three Cup Finals.

SAM HARDY (Aston Villa). Among the greatest England goalkeepers of all time is Sam Hardy. Yet he was hardly noticed on the field, because he was as unspectacular in goal as he was quiet and modest off the field. His judgement was so good that he was invariably in position when the shot was made. He first made his name with Liverpoool, whom he assisted to the Championships of the Second and First Divisions in successive seasons, 1904–6. After being transferred to Aston Villa he took part in the 1913 and 1920 Cup Finals. Villa won both without conceding a goal.

JOHNNY HAYNES (Fulham). Johnny Haynes is one of the few modern inside forwards to stand comparison with great players of the past like Alex James and Raich Carter. He excels at distribution, being particularly accurate with the through pass, and is also a good finisher He joined the Fulham office staff straight from school in North London, despite tempting offers from Arsenal and Spurs. He was one of the first to graduate through the international stages—schoolboy, youth, Under-23, "B" and full cap. He made his first full international appearance against Ireland in 1954.

Eddie Hapgood

Johnny Haynes

Harry Gregg

SOCCER QUIZ

1. What was Scotland's first defeat by a foreign team?

★

2. When did England first compete in the World Cup?

★

3. When did all four home countries reach the Final stages of the World Cup?

★

4. Who are the World Cup holders?

★

5. Which countries won the World Cup twice?

QUIZ ANSWERS

1. By Austria in Vienna in 1932. 2. 1950. 3. 1958. 4. Brazil. 5. Uruguay and Italy.

SOCCER QUIZ

1. Which club jumped from the Third Division to the First in successive seasons?

★

2. Which was the first British club to enter the European Cup?

★

3. Which club won the Second Division, First Division and Cup in successive seasons?

★

4. Which is the only club from outside England to win the Cup?

★

5. Which club won the Scottish Cup the greatest number of times?

★

6. Have Ireland won the International Championship outright?

★

7. Have Wales?

QUIZ ANSWERS

1. Charlton in 1934–6. 2. Hibernian. 3. Everton. 4. Cardiff in 1927. 5. Celtic, 17 times. 6. Yes, in 1913–14. 7. Yes, on seven occasions.

GREAT NAMES IN SOCCER

HARRY HIBBS (Birmingham). At one time during the 1920s Birmingham had three goalkeepers who had gained representative honours for England—Dan Tremelling, Ken Tewkesbury and Harry Hibbs. The greatest was Hibbs. His sense of positioning was so good that he gave the impression that forwards were shooting straight at him. On the short side for a goalkeeper, he was safe rather than spectacular and his qualities were most marked when he played for England against a Continental side which included a showy keeper. He played 26 times for England between 1930 and 1936 and was in the Birmingham side defeated by West Bromwich in the 1931 Final.

SAM IRVING (Cardiff and Chelsea). Sam Irving was an Irishman, but he made his reputation with Dundee (Scotland), Cardiff (Wales) and Chelsea (England). He was a stylish and polished player, excelling in ball distribution. He gained the first of his 20 caps in 1922 when with Dundee. After being transferred to Cardiff he won a Cup winners' medal when Cardiff beat Arsenal in the 1927 Final. Cardiff defeated Chelsea in their progress to the Final and Irving played so well that Chelsea secured his services the following season. He was an inside right with Cardiff and Chelsea changed him to a right half.

DAVID JACK (Bolton and Arsenal). The first five-figure fee—the actual figure was £10,890—was paid in 1928 by Arsenal for David Jack, the Bolton inside right. He was 29 at the time, one of the outstanding players of the day and an automatic choice for England. He scored the first goal at Wembley for Bolton in the 1923 Final against West Ham. He also played in the 1926 Final for Bolton and for Arsenal in the 1930 and 1932 Finals. He scored one of the most memorable goals for Arsenal against Aston Villa in 1931. He went past five defenders from the halfway line by use of a body swerve and touched the ball only four times in the run before dribbling past the goalkeeper. He had spells as manager of Southend and Middlesbrough. He died in 1958.

Jimmy McGrory

Joe McCall

Peter McWilliam

ALEX JACKSON (Huddersfield and Chelsea). One of the finest strokes of business by Herbert Chapman was to sign for Huddersfield Alex Jackson, Aberdeen's Scottish international outside right. Dashing and handsome, Jackson was nicknamed the "Gay Cavalier" for his goalscoring raids along the right wing. He went to Huddersfield in 1925, when they had won the League title two years running and he helped them to complete the hat-trick. He scored three goals when the Wembley Wizards trounced England in 1928, chiefly by means of his favourite habit of coming in to meet the centres from the left. Soon after being on the losing side in the 1930 Final he was transferred to Chelsea for £8,500. He was past his best, however, and gradually drifted out of football, after trying to find a niche in France and non-League soccer.

ALEX JAMES (Arsenal). The most effective player Arsenal ever had was Alex James, because he was the linkman between defence and attack when Arsenal swept to the top of the soccer world in the 1930's. He joined Arsenal from Preston in 1929 for £9,000. He had a reputation as a goalscorer. Herbert Chapman made him into a goalmaker, and James dropped back near the defence to send long passes through to raiding forwards. His tactics were perhaps the main reason for Arsenal's run of successes in the next six years—

Alex James

Fred Keenor

Bob John

four League Championships and three Final appearances. His worth to Arsenal and his influence on football are not measured by the four Scottish caps he obtained while with the London club. A lovable personality, noticeable for the baggy pants he wore, he was Arsenal's coach until his death in 1953.

BOB JOHN (Arsenal). Arsenal's most consistent footballer was Bob John. He played 421 League games for them—a club record. He also played in 50 Cup ties, including three Finals. His best position was left half, but he also appeared at inside left and was outside left in the 1932 Final, scoring Arsenal's only goal. Born in Caerphilly, he signed for Arsenal in 1922 in the face of competition from Cardiff and within six months he won the first of 16 caps for Wales. There was nothing showy about his play and he performed his tasks quietly and efficiently. After serving Arsenal for 16 years, during which period he won three Championship medals, he moved to West Ham and finally returned to Cardiff as trainer.

BRYN JONES (Arsenal). During intermittent service with Aberaman, Southend and Glenavon, Bryn Jones gave little indication that he was going to blossom out with Wolves into one of the finest inside forwards of the day. Arsenal decided that he was the man to succeed Alex James and had to pay Wolves £14,000 for him in 1938. The fee exceeded the previous best by £3,000 and remained a record for nine years. A dark-haired and darting forward, Jones had delightful ball control, but the ballyhoo attached to being the costliest footballer prevented him settling down before the war. He gave his best service to Arsenal immediately after the war, when he was still good enough to be a regular choice for Wales.

FRED KEENOR (Cardiff). Fred Keenor collected the F.A. Cup on the only occasion it has been taken out of England. He captained Cardiff when they defeated Arsenal at Wembley in 1927. Sturdy and as hard as nails, he never knew when he was beaten and was an inspiring skipper. A schoolboy international, he joined Cardiff in 1913 when 20 as a centre half. That was the position he occupied in the 1925 Final against Sheffield United, and he was right half two years later. He also played in both positions for Wales, for whom he won 16 caps. He was in the Wales team which defeated England in 1920 for the first time in nearly 40 years.

BOB KELLY (Burnley). A sinuous dribble and a flashing shot made Bob Kelly one of England's outstanding forwards just after the First World War. He appeared in all forward positions, but was most effective at inside right. He joined Burnley in 1913 and helped them in the record League run of 30 matches without defeat from September 1920 to March 1921. After winning 11 caps with Burnley he moved to Sunderland for the then-startling fee of £6,500. It was in 1925 and he was 30 years old. He moved to Huddersfield two years later and was on the losing side in the 1928 and 1930 Finals. He managed Carlisle and Stockport, whom he led to promotion from the Third Division in 1937, before coaching in Portugal, Switzerland and the Channel Islands.

LORD KINNAIRD (The Wanderers and Old Etonians). Lord Kinnaird took part in nine Cup Finals for The Wanderers and Old Etonians, and was on the winning side on five occasions. His first appearance was in 1873, the second year of the Cup. He was then a half-back and wore the kit fashionable at the time—long flannel trousers, a flannel shirt and a cricket cap. Those were the days when hacking was permitted and the shoulder charge encouraged, and Kinnaird, his red beard waving in the breeze, was conspicuous where the fray was thickest. In 1882, when Old Etonians beat Blackburn Rovers at the Oval, he was so delighted that he stood on his head in front of the pavilion. He became President of the F.A. and was presented with the F.A. Cup in 1910 to mark his 21 years as President.

TOMMY LAWTON (Everton and Notts County). Tommy Lawton signed as a professional for Burnley on his 17th birthday in 1936 and four days later he scored a hat-trick against Spurs in a League game. Strongly built, excellent in the air and a powerful shot, he was one of the most prolific scorers the game has known. He obtained 570 goals in three seasons with Castle Hill School, Bolton, and had approaching 500 in first-class soccer. Everton bought him as Dean's successor in 1937; he moved to Chelsea in 1945 and then on to Notts County for the first £20,000 fee. After helping County into the Second Division, he assisted Brentford, Arsenal and Kettering. The war limited his full international appearances to 17.

JOE McCALL (Preston). The fashion of champagne as a half-time tonic in a Cup tie was started by Joe McCall, the Preston centre half and captain, in the semi-final against Spurs in 1922. He waved aside lemons and tea and called for champagne when Preston were a goal down. Preston went out to win, but lost in the Final to Huddersfield through a disputed penalty goal. Undoubtedly the best centre half Preston have had, McCall was born in Wrea Green, a few miles from the Scottish border, and played five times for England between 1913 and 1920.

BILL McCRACKEN (Newcastle). The change in the offside rule of 1925, which reduced the number of defenders in front of goal from three to two, was due in large measure to Bill McCracken, Newcastle's Irish international right back. He perfected tactics for throwing forwards offside by a sudden move upfield, with the result that the whistle was blowing almost constantly. He was unruffled by the irritation of either opponents or crowd. He first made his name with Distillery and was obtained by Newcastle to become an essential factor in their all-conquering team of 1905 to 1911. He had an international career stretching from 1902 to 1924. Shrewd and plausible, he had a successful run as manager of Hull, Millwall and Aldershot, before becoming the Southern scout for Newcastle.

JIMMY McGRORY (Celtic). Scotland's most prolific scorer is Jimmy McGrory, Celtic's centre forward from 1922 to 1938. He had 550 goals in all games in first-class football and created a Scottish League record with 410 goals. Although short and sturdy, he obtained a high proportion of his goals with his head. He had a remarkable turn of speed which enabled him to turn a breakaway from mid-field into a shot at goal. He won every honour in the game while with Celtic—League Championship medals, a Cup winners' medal and seven caps for his country. He made a success of the unenviable task of taking over as Celtic's manager from Willie Maley, who had been over 50 years with the club.

JIMMY McMULLAN (Manchester City). Jimmy McMullan is an uncle of Matt Busby and, like Busby, he was a stylish Scottish international wing half. As he was small, he liked the ball to be kept on the ground, as it was when Scotland beat England 5–1 at Wembley in 1928. He played on 15 other occasions for his country. After starting with Partick during the 1914–18 war, he was transferred to Manchester City in 1925. A few months later City were the losing side in the Cup Final and relegated to the Second Division in the same season. His play inspired the club to win promotion in 1928 and to return to Wembley, as winners this time, in 1933. He was manager of Oldham, Aston Villa, Notts County and Sheffield Wednesday, before leaving the game in 1942 to take employment in a steelworks in Sheffield.

PETER McWILLIAM (Newcastle). A great footballer who goes on to become an even greater manager is a rarity. One is Peter McWilliam, a distinguished left half of Newcastle and Scotland, who stamped his ideas on Spurs and Middlesbrough. He was an artistic player in the Newcastle side which won three League titles and took part in five Cup Finals between 1905 and 1911. As manager of Spurs from 1913 onwards he impressed his methods on men like Seed, Grimsdell, Dimmock and Osborne, with the result that Spurs won the Cup in 1921 after they had romped away with the Second Division title with a record total of 70 points in the previous season. He was equally successful with Middlesbrough before returning to Spurs in 1938.

SCOTTISH LEAGUE CLUB DIRECTORY

FIRST DIVISION

ABERDEEN. *Ground:* Pittodrie Park, Aberdeen. *Founded:* 1903. *Manager:* D. Shaw. *Colours:* Red shirts; white shorts. *Nickname:* Dons. *Ground Record:* 45,300. *Famous Internationals:* SCOTLAND—G. Leggat, A. Glen, H. Yorston, F. Martin, P. Buckley, G. Hamilton, W. Mills, M. Armstrong, F. Hill, B. Yorston, A. Cheyne, A. Jackson, J. Hutton; IRELAND—J. Moore, E. Fallon, C. O'Hagan. *League History:* First Division, 1903–. *League Honours:* First Division Champions, 1954–5. First Division Runners-up, 1910–11, 1936–7, 1955–6. *Cup Honours:* Winners, 1947. Runners-up, 1937, 1953, 1954, 1959. League Cup Winners, 1946, 1956.

AIRDRIEONIANS. *Ground:* Broomfield Park, Airdrie. *Founded:* 1898. *Manager:* W. Steel. *Colours:* White shirts with red diamond; white shorts. *Ground Record:* 28,000. *Famous Internationals:* SCOTLAND—J. McMillan, J. Crapnell, R. McPhail, R. Bennie, H. Gallacher, W. Russell, J. Reid, J. O'Rourke, M. Scott, R. Scott, J. Connor; IRELAND—A. Snape, S. Young. *League History:* First Division, 1903–36, 1947–8, 1955–. Second Division, 1902–3, 1936–47, 1948–55. *League Honours:* First Division Runners-up, 1922–3, 1923–4, 1924–5, 1925–6. Second Division Champions, 1902–3, 1954–5. *Cup Honours:* Winners, 1924.

ARBROATH. *Ground:* Gayfield Park, Arbroath. *Founded:* 1878. *Director-in-charge:* H. Nelson. *Colours:* Maroon shirts; white shorts. *Ground Record:* 12,800. *Current Internationals:* SCOTLAND—J. Doig. *League History:* First Division, 1935–39, 1959–. Second Division, 1902–35, 1939–59. *Records:* 36–0 defeat of Bon Accord in a Scottish Cup tie in 1885 is a record for all senior matches in the British Isles.

AYR UNITED. *Ground:* Somerset Park, Ayr. *Founded:* 1910. *Manager:* J. Cox. *Colours:* White shirts; black shorts. *Ground Record:* 23,220. *Current Internationals:* SCOTLAND—R. Hepburn, M. McCloy, J. Smith, J. Hogg, J. Crosbie, J. Logan. *League History:* First Division, 1913–25, 1928–36, 1937–8, 1956–7, 1959–. Second Division, 1910–13, 1925–8, 1936–7, 1938–56, 1957–9. *League Honours:* Second Division Champions, 1927–8, 1936–7, 1958–9.

CELTIC. *Ground:* Celtic Park, Glasgow. *Founded:* 1888. *Manager:* J. McGrory. *Colours:* Green and white hooped shirts; white shorts. *Ground Record:* 92,600. *Famous Internationals:* SCOTLAND—R. Evans, D. McKay, W. Fernie, R. Collins, M. Haughney, J. McPhail, W. Miller, J. Delaney, C. Napier, J. McGorry, W. McStay, A. McLean, J. Quinn, A. McNair, J. McMenemy, A. Bennett, W. Maley, J. Campbell, J. Hay, J. Kelly; IRELAND—R. Peacock, C. Tully, E. McMorran, D. Martin, P. Gallagher, J. Mahood, H. Nicholl. *League History:* First Division, 1888–. *League Honours:* First Division Champions, 1892–3, 1893–4, 1895–6, 1897–8, 1904–5, 1905–6, 1906–7, 1907–8, 1908–9, 1909–10, 1913–14, 1914–15, 1915–16, 1916–17, 1918–19, 1921–2, 1925–6, 1935–6, 1937–8, 1953–4. First Division Runners-up, 1894–5, 1899–1900, 1900–1, 1901–2, 1911–12, 1912–13, 1917–18, 1919–20, 1920–1, 1927–8, 1928–9, 1930–1, 1934–5, 1938–9, 1954–5. *Cup Honours:* Winners, 1892, 1899, 1900, 1904, 1907, 1908, 1911, 1912, 1914, 1923, 1925, 1927, 1931, 1933, 1937, 1951, 1954. Runners-up, 1889, 1893, 1894, 1901, 1902, 1926, 1928, 1955, 1956. League Cup Winners, 1957, 1958. *Records:* 17 Cup wins; 27 Cup Final appearances; 63 matches without League defeat, November 1915 to April 1917; League and Cup double 1906–7, 1907–8, 1913–14, 1953–4; 1907–8, won everything competed for.

CLYDE. *Ground:* Shawfield Park, Glasgow. *Founded:* 1877. *Manager:* J. Haddow. *Colours:* Red shirts with white collars; white shorts. *Nickname:* Bully Wees. *Ground Record:* 52,000. *Famous Internationals:* SCOTLAND—G. Herd, H. Haddock, T. Ring, H. Long, J. Brown, D. Blair, W. Walker; IRELAND—E. Weir, J. McGrillen. *League History:* First Division, 1891–3, 1894–1900, 1905–24, 1926–51, 1952–6, 1957–. Second Division, 1893–4, 1900–5, 1924–6, 1951–2, 1956–7. *League Honours:* Second Division Champions, 1904–5, 1951–2, 1956–7. *Cup Honours:* Winners, 1939, 1955, 1958. Runners-up, 1910, 1912, 1949. *Records:* 64 points in season 1956–7, the highest total for the Second Division.

Bobby Collins

Billy Steel

Hughie Gallacher

DUNDEE. *Ground:* Dens Park, Dundee. *Founded:* 1893. *Manager:* R. Shankly. *Colours:* Dark blue shirts; white shorts. *Nickname:* Blues. *Ground Record:* 43,024. *Famous Internationals:* SCOTLAND—W. Brown, D. Cowie, W. Steel, J. Gilmour, C. McNab, A. Troup, D. Thomson, J. Fraser, J. Sharp, A. McFarlane, A. Keillor; IRELAND—S. Irving. *League History:* First Division, 1893–1917, 1919–37, 1947–. Second Division, 1917–19, 1937–47. *League Honours:* First Division Runners-up, 1902–3, 1906–7, 1908–9, 1948–9. Second Division Champions, 1946–7. *Cup Honours:* Winners, 1910. Runners-up, 1925, 1952. League Cup Winners, 1952, 1953.

DUNFERMLINE. *Ground:* East End Park, Dunfermline. *Founded:* 1907. *Manager:* W. Dickson. *Colours:* Black and white striped shirts; white shorts. *Ground Record:* 25,000. *Famous Internationals:* SCOTLAND—A. Wilson. *League History:* First Division, 1926–8, 1934–7, 1955–7, 1958–. Second Division, 1921–6, 1928–34, 1937–55, 1957–8. *League Honours:* Second Division Champions, 1925–6.

Graham Leggat

Billy Liddell

Willie Ormond

HEART OF MIDLOTHIAN. *Ground:* Tynecastle Park, Edinburgh. *Founded:* 1873. *Manager:* T. Walker. *Colours:* Maroon shirts; white shorts. *Ground Record:* 53,490. *Famous Internationals:* SCOTLAND—J. Grant, D. Mackay, W. Ormond, J. Murray, J. Cumming, J. Wardhaugh, W. Bauld, J. Dykes, D. McCulloch, A. Massie, T. Walker, A. Munro, J. Johnstone, J. Harkness, A. Anderson, R. Mercer, C. Thomson, R. Walker, G. Hogg, I. Begbie; IRELAND—J. Reid. *League History:* First Division, 1890–. *League Honours:* First Division Champions, 1894–5, 1896–7, 1957–8. First Division Runners-up, 1893–4, 1898–9, 1903–4, 1905–6, 1914–15, 1937–8, 1953–4, 1956–7, 1958–9. *Cup Honours:* Winners, 1891, 1896, 1901, 1906, 1956. *Runners-up,* 1903, 1907. League Cup Winners, 1955. *Records:* 132 goals in season 1957–8, the highest total for the First Division.

HIBERNIAN. *Ground:* Easter Road, Edinburgh. *Founded:* 1875. *Manager:* H. Shaw. *Colours:* Green shirts with white sleeves; white shorts. *Nickname:* Hibs. *Ground Record:* 65,850. *Famous Internationals:* SCOTLAND—J. Grant, G. Smith, T. Younger, R. Johnstone, L. Reilly, W. Ormond, H. Howie, J. Govan, D. Shaw, J. Dunn, W. Harper, A. Grey, H. Rennie, W. Groves; IRELAND—P. Farrell, W. Gowdy, J. Jones; WALES—R. Atherton. *League History:* First Division, 1890–1931, 1933–. Second Division, 1931–3. *League Honours:* First Division Champions, 1902–3, 1947–8, 1950–1, 1951–2. First Division Runners-up, 1896–7, 1946–7, 1949–50, 1952–3. Second Division Champions, 1932–3. *Cup Honours:* Winners, 1887, 1902. Runners-up, 1896, 1914, 1923, 1924, 1947, 1958.

KILMARNOCK. *Ground:* Rugby Park, Kilmarnock. *Founded:* 1869. *Manager:* W. Waddell. *Colours:* Blue and white hooped shirts; white shorts. *Nickname:* Killies. *Ground Record:* 32,745. *Famous Internationals:* SCOTLAND—W. Toner, T. Smith, J. Nibloe, R. Templeton, J. Mitchell, W. Agnew, R. Findlay, J. English; IRELAND—D. Lyner. *League History:* First Division, 1899–1947, 1954–. Second Division, 1893–9, 1947–54. *League Honours:* Second Division Champions, 1898–9. *Cup Honours:* Winners, 1920, 1929. Runners-up, 1898, 1932, 1938, 1957.

MOTHERWELL. *Ground:* Fir Park, Motherwell. *Founded:* 1895. *Manager:* B. Ancell. *Colours:* Claret and amber shirts; white shorts. *Ground Record:* 36,750. *Famous Internationals:* SCOTLAND—A. McCann, J. White, A. Weir, W. Gardiner, J. Forrest, W. Redpath, J. Watson, J. McMenemy, W. McFadyen, W. Telfer, A. Craig, J. Blair, G. Stevenson, G. Robertson; IRELAND—J. Murray. *League History:* First Division, 1904–53, 1954–. Second Division, 1953–4. *League Honours:* First Division Champions, 1931–2. First Division Runners-up, 1926–7, 1929–30, 1932–3, 1933–4. Second Division Runners-up, 1953–4. *Cup Honours:* Winners, 1952. Runners-up 1931, 1933, 1939, 1951. League Cup Winners, 1951.

PARTICK THISTLE. *Ground:* Firhill Park, Glasgow. *Founded:* 1876. *Manager:* W. Thornton. *Colours:* Red and yellow hooped shirts; white shorts. *Nickname:* Jags. *Ground Record:* 54,728. *Famous Internationals:* SCOTLAND—T. Ewing, J. Davidson, J. McKenzie, H. Brown, J. Husband, A. McSpadyen, J. Jackson, G. Cummings, J. Gibson, J. McMullan, J. Harris, K. Campbell, W. Paul. *League History:* First Division, 1897–9, 1900–1, 1902–. Second Division, 1896–7, 1899–1900, 1901–2. *League Honours:* Second Division Champions, 1896–7, 1899–1900. *Cup Honours:* Winners, 1921. Runners-up, 1930.

RAITH ROVERS. *Ground:* Starks Park, Kirkcaldy. *Founded:* 1883. *Manager:* R. Herdman. *Colours:* Navy blue shirts; white shorts. *Ground Record:* 32,000. *Famous Internationals:* SCOTLAND—W. McNaught, D. Morris, W. Collier, H. Anderson. *League History:* First Division, 1908–26, 1927–9, 1938–9, 1949–. Second Division, 1902–8, 1926–7, 1929–38, 1939–49. *League Honours:* Second Division Champions, 1907–8, 1937–8, 1948–9. *Cup Honours:* Runners-up, 1913. *Records:* 142 goals in season 1937–8, the highest total for the Second Division.

RANGERS. *Ground:* Ibrox Park, Glasgow. *Founded:* 1873. *Manager:* W. Scott-Symon. *Colours:* Royal blue shirts; white shorts. *Nickname:* Light Blues. *Ground Record:* 118,567. *Famous Internationals:* SCOTLAND—E. Caldow, S. Baird, G. Young, I. McColl, W. Waddell, W. Woodburn, S. Cox, W. Thornton, R. Brown, J. Dawson, J. Simpson, J. Smith, G. Brown, W. Meiklejohn, J. Marshall, A. Morton, A. Archibald, T. Cairns, T. Craig, A. Cunningham, R. McPhail, T. Muirhead, W. Reid, J. Robertson, J. Drummond, R. Hamilton, A. Smith, N. Smith, N. Gibson, R. Gillespie; IRELAND—W. Simpson, A. Stevenson, S. English, B. Manderson, W. McCandless, A. Craig. *League History:* First Division, 1890–. *League Honours:* First Division Champions, 1890–1 (shared), 1898–9, 1899–1900, 1900–1, 1901–2, 1910–11, 1911–12, 1912–13, 1917–18, 1919–20, 1920–1, 1922–3, 1923–4, 1924–5, 1926–7, 1927–8, 1928–9, 1929–30, 1930–1, 1932–3, 1933–4, 1934–5, 1936–7, 1938–9, 1946–7, 1948–9, 1949–50, 1952–3, 1955–6, 1956–7, 1958–9. First Division Runners-up, 1892–3, 1895–6, 1897–8, 1904–5, 1913–14, 1915–16, 1918–19, 1921–2, 1931–2, 1935–6, 1947–8, 1950–1, 1951–2, 1957–8. *Cup Honours:* Winners, 1894, 1897, 1898, 1903, 1928, 1930, 1932, 1934, 1935, 1936, 1948, 1949, 1950, 1953. Runners-up, 1877, 1899, 1904, 1905, 1921, 1922, 1929.

(Contd. on p. 42, col. 1)

SOCCER QUIZ

1. Who won the Cup and League in the same season?

★

2. Which Scottish clubs did the same feat in Scotland?

★

3. Who scored a hat-trick in a Wembley Final? *(above)*

★

4. Has one club ever supplied the entire England team?

★

5. Has the same feat been performed in Scotland?

★

6. Who is the longest-serving English manager?

★

7. What is the size of the goal?

QUIZ ANSWERS

1. Aston Villa and Preston. 2. Rangers and Celtic. 3. S. Mortensen, Blackpool v. Bolton in 1953. 4. Corinthians v. Wales in 1894. 5. Yes, by Queen's Park against England in 1872. 6. W. Walker (Nottingham Forest). 7. 8 yards wide and 8 feet high.

Scottish First Division—(*contd.*)

League Cup Winners, 1947, 1949. *Records:* 30 league Championship wins; League and Cup double in 1927–8, 1929–30, 1933–4, 1934–5, 1948–9, 1949–50, 1952–3; won all League matches (18) in 1898–9; hold a majority of victories over every other club; 1929–30 and 1933–4, won everything competed for; 76 points in 1920–1, the highest total for the First Division; in 1948–9 won the League, Cup and League-Cup.

STIRLING ALBION. *Ground:* Annfield Park, Stirling. *Founded:* 1945. *Director-in-charge:* T. Fergusson. *Colours:* Red and white hooped shirts; white shorts. *Ground Record:* 25,600. *League History:* First Division, 1949–50, 1951–2, 1953–6, 1958–. Second Division, 1947–9, 1950–1, 1952–3, 1956–8. *League Honours:* Second Division Champions, 1952–3, 1957–8. *Records:* 6 points in 1954–5, the lowest total for the First Division.

ST. MIRREN. *Ground:* St. Mirren Park, Paisley. *Founded:* 1877. *Manager:* W. Reid. *Colours:* Black and white striped shirts; black shorts. *Nickname:* Saints. *Ground Record:* 47,428. *Famous Internationals:* SCOTLAND—W. Telfer, G. Walker, J. Miller, J. Howieson, W. Summers, J. Hamilton, C. Pringle, D. Crawford, J. Cameron, J. Dunlop, A. Brown; IRELAND—W. Cunningham, W. O'Hagan. *League History:* First Division, 1890–1935, 1936–. Second Division, 1935–6. *Cup Honours:* Winners, 1926, 1959. Runners-up, 1908, 1934.

THIRD LANARK. *Ground:* Cathkin Park, Glasgow. *Founded:* 1872. *Manager:* B. Shankly. *Colours:* Scarlet shirts; white shorts. *Nickname:* Warriors. *Ground Record:* 45,335. *Famous Internationals:* SCOTLAND—J. Mason, J. Carabine, N. Dewar, J. Brownlie, J. Cross, T. Sloan, J. Simpson, J. Gillespie, W. Blair, J. Auld, J. Hunter. *League History:* First Division, 1890–1925, 1928–9, 1931–4, 1935–53, 1957–. Second Division, 1925–8, 1929–31, 1934–5, 1953–7. *League Honours:* First Division Champions, 1903–4. Second Division Champions, 1930–1, 1934–5. *Cup Honours:* Winners, 1889, 1905. Runners-up, 1876, 1878, 1906, 1936.

SCOTTISH CUP WINNERS

1873–4	Queen's Park	2	Clydesdale	0
1874–5	Queen's Park	3	Renton	0
1875–6	Queen's Park	2	Third Lanark	0
	(After a draw 1–1)			
1876–7	Vale of Leven	3	Rangers	2
	(After two draws 0–0, 1–1)			
1877–8	Vale of Leven	1	Third Lanark	0
1878–9	Vale of Leven awarded Cup, Rangers failing to appear at Hampden (after a draw 1–1)			
1879–80	Queen's Park	3	Thornliebank	0
1880–1	Queen's Park	3	Dumbarton	1
	(After protested game, 2–1 for Queen's Park)			
1881–2	Queen's Park	4	Dumbarton	1
	(After draw 2–2)			
1882–3	Dumbarton	2	Vale of Leven	1
	(After draw 2–2)			
1883–4	Queen's Park awarded Cup, Vale of Leven failing to appear.			
1884–5	Renton	3	Vale of Leven	1
	(After draw 0–0)			
1885–6	Queen's Park	3	Renton	1
1886–7	Hibernian	2	Dumbarton	1
1887–8	Renton	6	Cambuslang	1
1888–9	Third Lanark	2	Celtic	1
	(After replay ordered by S.F.A.)			
1889–90	Queen's Park	2	Vale of Leven	1
	(After draw 1–1)			
1890–1	Hearts	1	Dumbarton	0
1891–2	Celtic	5	Queen's Park	1
	(After protested game)			
1892–3	Queen's Park	2	Celtic	1
1893–4	Rangers	3	Celtic	1
1894–5	St. Bernard's	2	Renton	1
1895–6	Hearts	3	Hibernian	1
1896–7	Rangers	5	Dumbarton	1
1897–8	Rangers	2	Kilmarnock	0
1898–9	Celtic	2	Rangers	0
1899–1900	Celtic	4	Queen's Park	3
1900–1	Hearts	4	Celtic	3
1901–2	Hibernian	1	Celtic	0
1902–3	Rangers	2	Hearts	0
	(After two draws 1–1, 0–0)			
1903–4	Celtic	3	Rangers	2
1904–5	Third Lanark	3	Rangers	1
	(After draw 0–0)			
1905–6	Hearts	1	Third Lanark	0
1906–7	Celtic	3	Hearts	0
1907–8	Celtic	5	St. Mirren	1
1908–9	Owing to riot, the Cup was withheld after two drawn games—Celtic 2, Rangers 2; Celtic 1, Rangers 1 (Hampden).			
1909–10	Dundee	2	Clyde	1
	(After two draws 2–2, 0–0)			
1910–11	Celtic	2	Hamilton	0
	(After draw 0–0)			
1911–12	Celtic	2	Clyde	0
1912–13	Falkirk	2	Raith Rovers	0
1913–14	Celtic	4	Hibernian	1
	(After draw 0–0)			
1914–19	No competition			
1919–20	Kilmarnock	3	Albion Rov.	2
1920–1	Partick Th.	1	Rangers	0
1921–2	Morton	1	Rangers	0
1922–3	Celtic	1	Hibernian	0
1923–4	Airdrie	2	Hibernian	0
1924–5	Celtic	2	Dundee	1
1925–6	St. Mirren	2	Celtic	0
1926–7	Celtic	3	East Fife	1
1927–8	Rangers	4	Celtic	0
1928–9	Kilmarnock	2	Rangers	0
1929–30	Rangers	2	Partick Th.	1
	(After draw 0–0)			
1930–1	Celtic	4	Motherwell	2
	(After draw 2–2)			
1931–2	Rangers	3	Kilmarnock	0
	(After draw 1–1)			
1932–3	Celtic	1	Motherwell	0
1933–4	Rangers	5	St. Mirren	0
1934–5	Rangers	2	Hamilton	1
1935–6	Rangers	1	T. Lanark	0
1936–7	Celtic	2	Aberdeen	1
1937–8	East Fife	4	Kilmarnock	2
	(After draw 1–1, and after extra time in replay)			
1938–9	Clyde	4	Motherwell	0
1939–46	No competition			
1946–7	Aberdeen	2	Hibernian	1
1947–8	Rangers	1	Morton	0
	(After draw 1–1, after extra time, and after extra time in replay)			
1948–9	Rangers	4	Clyde	1
1949–50	Rangers	3	East Fife	0
1950–1	Celtic	1	Motherwell	0
1951–2	Motherwell	4	Dundee	0
1952–3	Rangers	1	Aberdeen	0
	(After draw 1–1)			
1953–4	Celtic	2	Aberdeen	1
1954–5	Clyde	1	Celtic	0
	(After draw 1–1)			
1955–6	Hearts	3	Celtic	1
1956–7	Falkirk	2	Kilmarnock	1
	(After draw 1–1 and extra time in replay)			
1957–8	Clyde	1	Hibernian	0
1958–9	St. Mirren	3	Aberdeen	1

SCOTTISH LEAGUE CUP WINNERS

1945–6	Aberdeen	3	Rangers	2
1946–7	Rangers	4	Aberdeen	0
1947–8	East Fife	4	Falkirk	1
	(After draw 1–1 after extra time)			
1948–9	Rangers	2	Raith Rovers	0
1949–50	East Fife	3	Dunfermline	0
1950–1	Motherwell	3	Hibernian	0
1951–2	Dundee	3	Rangers	2
1952–3	Dundee	2	Kilmarnock	0
1953–4	East Fife	3	Partick Th.	2
1954–5	Hearts	4	Motherwell	2
1955–6	Aberdeen	2	St. Mirren	1
1956–7	Celtic	3	Partick Th.	0
	(After draw 0–0)			
1957–8	Celtic	7	Rangers	1
1958–9	Hearts	5	Partick Th.	1

SCOTTISH SUMMARIES

Scottish Cup Wins
17—Celtic, 14—Rangers, 10—Queen's Park, 5—Hearts, 3—Clyde, 2—Falkirk, Hibernian, Kilmarnock, Renton, St. Mirren, Third Lanark, Vale of Leven, 1—Aberdeen, Airdrie, Dumbarton, Dundee, East Fife, Morton, Motherwell, Partick Thistle, St. Bernard's.

Scottish Cup Final Appearances
27—Celtic, 22—Rangers, 12—Queen's Park, 8—Hibernian, 7—Hearts, 6—Clyde, Dumbarton, Kilmarnock, Third Lanark, 5—Aberdeen, Motherwell, Renton, Vale of Leven, 4—St. Mirren, 3—Dundee, East Fife, 2—Falkirk, Hamilton, Morton, Partick Thistle, 1—Airdrie, Albion Rovers, Cambuslang, Clydesdale, Raith, St. Bernard's, Thornliebank.

Scottish League Titles
31—Rangers, 20—Celtic, 4—Hibernian, 3—Hearts, 1—Aberdeen, Motherwell, Third Lanark.

Scottish League-Cup Wins
3—East Fife, 2—Aberdeen, Celtic, Hearts, Dundee, Rangers, 1—Motherwell.

Wilf Mannion

Stanley Matthews

Joe Mercer

GREAT NAMES IN SOCCER

WILF MANNION (Middlesbrough). An elusive body swerve, bewildering ability with the ball and speed to use an opening made Wilf Mannion an outstanding inside forward immediately after the Second World War. Yet his career was far from smooth. At one time he refused to re-sign for Middlesbrough, once he was suspended by them and in 1955 he was banned by the League after refusing to amplify allegations he made in a newspaper on illegal payments. As a result he drifted into non-League football with Poole and Cambridge United before taking over a public house in Stevenage. Born in 1918, he was in Middlesbrough's League side when 17 and played 25 times for England.

STANLEY MATTHEWS (Stoke and Blackpool). Stanley Matthews is the most famous player and the biggest box-office draw that the game has known. He was a prodigy as a schoolboy international—his position then was centre half—signed for Stoke, his local club, when he was 17, and was still playing in first-class football in 1959 at the age of 44. A tantalising body swerve, a devastating burst off the mark and superb ball control made him the nightmare of left backs for a generation. He played the first of his 84 internationals for England—the total includes war-time appearances—in 1934, and his last in May 1957 in the World Cup preliminary against Denmark. The fee of £11,500, which Blackpool paid Stoke for him in 1947, ranks as one of the biggest bargains in football. He took part in three Finals for Blackpool, was Footballer of the Year in 1948 and was awarded the C.B.E. in 1957.

JOE MERCER (Everton and Arsenal). A biting tackle, despite a pair of spindly legs, and shrewd reading of the game made Joe Mercer an outstanding wing half. He used his qualities to be a successful manager with Sheffield United and Aston Villa. He joined Everton in 1932 from Ellesmere Port as a 17-year-old, gained a League Championship medal in 1938–9 and established himself with Britton and Cullis in England's all-conquering half-back line of the war. A knee injury seemed to have ended his career but he moved to Arsenal in 1946 for £7,000 and his captaincy was a vital factor in Arsenal's two League titles and two Final appearances in the next seven years. His playing career was ended in 1954 when he broke a leg while playing at Highbury.

BILLY MEREDITH (Manchester City and Manchester United). Billy Meredith did not look like a footballer; he had bony, bow-legs and always played with a toothpick in his mouth. Yet he was the greatest outside right the game has produced, next to Stanley Matthews. He was a goal-scorer as well as a goal-maker, and obtained 470 goals in 1,568 games for the two Manchester clubs and Wales. Born in Chirk, a few hundred yards inside Wales, he played 50 times for the principality between 1895 and 1920. He played 19 times altogether against England and it was not until the last one, in 1920, that he was on the winning side. He first made his reputation with Manchester City, and United obtained him for a mere £150 in 1908, when his career seemed almost over. He was transferred back to City and took part in an F.A. Cup tie against Brighton in 1924 when in his 50th year. Among the 61 medals he won were two for League Championships and two for winning the Cup. Yet the one he treasured most was awarded him at Chirk School for dribbling.

SOCCER QUIZ

1. Who holds the highest individual score for one match in the Scottish Second Division?

★

2. For the F.A. Cup? *(above)*

★

3. For the Scottish Cup?

★

4. For the Amateur Cup?

★

5. What is the minimum admission charge for Football League matches?

★

6. What was it before the war?

★

7. How much entertainment tax is paid?

QUIZ ANSWERS

1. 8 by J. Calder, Morton v. Raith 1936; J. Dyet, King's Park v. Forfar in 1930; and O. McNally, Arthurlie v. Armadale 1927. 2. 6 by R. Rooke, Fulham v. Bury in 1939, and G. Hilsdon, Chelsea v. Worksop in 1908. 3. 13 by J. Petrie, Arbroath v. Bon Accord 1885. 4. 7 by W. H. Minter, St. Albans v. Dulwich Hamlet in 1922. (St. Albans lost 8–7). 5. 2s. 6. 1s. 7. None. It was abolished in 1957.

STAN MORTENSEN (Blackpool). A fortnight after a war-time bomber crash which necessitated 12 stitches in a head wound Stanley Mortensen was playing football again. He had head pains and sleepless nights for years after the crash, but they did not prevent him winning honours for Blackpool and England. As quick as lightning, dashing and courageous, he made a wonderful foil to the artistry of his wing partner Stan Matthews. He played 25 times for England, took part in three Cup Finals—he scored in every round of the 1947–8 competition—and obtained a winners' medal in 1953. He moved to Hull in 1955, and had a spell with Southport before joining Southern League side Bath in 1958.

Stan Mortensen

Albert Quixall

Alf Ramsey

Don Revie

Jack Rowley

ALAN MORTON (Rangers). "Wee Blue Devil" was the nickname opponents gave outside left Alan Morton for his exploits in the blue shirts of Rangers and Scotland. Although only 5 feet 4½ inches, and 9½ stones, his ball control was so good that he tormented defences. He scored 115 goals in 495 games for Rangers but he is best remembered for the openings he made for others. It was said that he could put a centre from the wing on to a sixpence in the goalmouth. Born in Partick, he was educated at Airdrie Academy and joined Queen's Park, for whom he won an amateur cap in 1920. He represented Scotland in 30 full internationals, including 11 against England, from 1920 to 1932. He invariably wore an umbrella and bowler at an away game. He forgot to do so once—and Rangers lost. He is now a director of Rangers.

KEVIN O'FLANAGAN (Arsenal). In 1946, Kevin O'Flanagan represented Ireland against France at rugby, Ireland against Scotland at soccer the following Saturday and would have played for Ireland against England at rugby on the third Saturday if he had not missed the boat to Dublin. He was a first-class performer at golf and tennis, could run the 100 yards in evens and was a champion high jumper. He joined Arsenal in 1946 when working in a practice in London and his infectious enthusiasm made him a more than useful forward, particularly in the wing positions. He would undoubtedly have made a big name for himself had he been able to devote more time to the sport. He had a spell with Brentford before returning to Dublin.

ALBERT QUIXALL (Sheffield Wednesday and Manchester United). Golden-haired Albert Quixall became the "golden boy" of British football when he was transferred from Sheffield Wednesday to Manchester United for £45,000 in September 1958. The fee beats the previous record by £10,000 which was paid by Wednesday for Jackie Sewell. Neat and progressive, Quixall brings imagination and determination into his game, and United manager Matt Busby decided that he was one of the men on whom to build the new United. Born in Sheffield, Quixall gained schoolboy honours and played for Wednesday's League side when 17. He gained his first cap for England at the age of 20.

ALF RAMSEY (Tottenham Hotspur). The nickname "The General" was given to Alf Ramsey by his Spurs colleagues for his cool and studied play at right back. The constructive moves he started were a feature of Spurs' play during 1949–51, when they won the Second and First Division titles in successive seasons. He stamped his style, too, on the England team, for whom he played 31 times. Born in Dagenham in 1922, he was first spotted in Sunday football. He joined Southampton during the war and gained international honours with them before being transferred to Spurs in 1949 for £20,000. He was a sure penalty taker and scored important goals for England at Wembley against Argentina, Austria and the Rest of the World. He turned with success to management in 1956 with Ipswich.

LAURIE REILLY (Hibernian). On the small side for a centre forward—he was 5 feet 7 inches tall—Laurie Reilly was one of the most dangerous of his day. In the 1952–3 season he scored 50 goals for Hibernian, who finished runners-up to Rangers after twice winning the League title. Quick and tenacious, he invariably shone in internationals against England. He joined Hibs when 16 in 1943 and continued for some time his job as a painter before becoming a full-time professional. He won over 30 caps

for Scotland before a knee injury curtailed his career in season 1957–8.

DON REVIE (Manchester City and Leeds). By being transferred to Leeds in November 1958 for £14,000 Don Revie brought the total of fees paid for him to the record sum of £83,000. His first move was in 1949 to Hull from Leicester, where he had built up a reputation as a skilful and intelligent inside forward. Two years later he went to Manchester City, where he started the deep-lying centre-forward style which bears his name. He was on the losing side in the 1955 Cup Final and went back to Wembley a year later to obtain a winners' medal. In 1955, too, he was elected Footballer of the Year. Before joining Leeds he had two years with Sunderland, but his artistry failed to prevent Sunderland dropping out of the First Division for the first time.

HERBIE ROBERTS (Arsenal). The first stopper centre half was Herbie Roberts of Arsenal. Tall, red-haired, excellent in the air and phlegmatic in temperament, he joined Arsenal in 1926 as a wing half from Oswestry, where he had worked as a gunsmith, for a mere £200. Herbert Chapman made him into a centre half, with instructions to concentrate on defence, police the middle, and refuse to go upfield. Roberts performed the role so successfully that he was a key figure during the seven years from 1929 to 1936, when the League Championship was won four times and the Final reached on three occasions. The new style was as unpopular with the selectors as it was with opponents and Roberts played only once for England.

DICK ROOSE (Stoke and Sunderland). Although a doctor, Leigh Richmond (Dick) Roose was not fussy about the cleanliness of the shirt he wore under the goalkeeper's jersey and refused to have it washed in case it brought bad luck. He played for clubs wherever his practice took him—Aberystwyth, London Welsh, Stoke, Everton, Sunderland, Aston Villa and Arsenal. He played 23 times for Wales between 1899 and 1911. Once when Wales were reduced to ten men he refused to draw a man out of the attack and went out of goal to play back and goalkeeper. When play was at the other end of the field he used to sit with his back to a goalpost and chat with the spectators.

JACK ROWLEY (Manchester United). Although Jack Rowley, the Manchester United sharp-shooter, played in only six internationals for England he occupied all five forward positions except outside right. There was not much finesse about his play and he worked with directness and opportunism. He had a very fierce shot, especially in the left foot, and was well suited to round off the brilliant United attack just after the war. He scored twice in the 1948 Final and contributed 30 goals when United won the League title in 1951–2. He joined United for a bargain fee of just over four figures in 1938 and would have gained more honours if the war had not intervened. His brother Arthur was an equally prolific scorer for Fulham and Leicester. Rowley left United to become manager of Plymouth.

ELISHA SCOTT (Liverpool). Elisha Scott kept goal 31 times for Ireland—all in the Home International Tournament —in 15 years up to 1936 and the total remained a record until broken by Danny Blanchflower in 1958. Scott succeeded Sam Hardy at Liverpool and was strangely like him. He positioned well, was modest and quiet, had a sturdy build. There was nothing of the showman about him, although at times he defied the might of England almost single-handed. He went back to Ireland to play for Belfast Celtic and then became their manager. *(Contd. on p. 45, col. 1)*

OLYMPIC GAMES

Association football first appeared in the Olympic Games of 1900 in Paris, the second of the modern Olympiads. It was staged as a demonstration, Upton Park defeating France by 4–0.

Football made its real entry eight years later, when the Games were held at the White City, London. Since then football has appeared in every Olympiad with the exception of 1932 (Los Angeles), when there was a dispute over the payment of expenses by the South American countries.

Great Britain first entered under the name "United Kingdom" and won the title in 1908 and 1912. They withdrew after the 1920 Games owing to broken-time payments by some of the opponents, and did not compete again until 1936.

RESULTS

1908, London. 6 entries, including France A and B.

United Kingdom 2   Denmark 0

United Kingdom: H. Bailey; W. Corbett, H. Smith; R. Hawkes, K. Hunt, F. Chapman; A. Berry, V. Woodward, H. Stapley, C. Purnell, H. Hardman.

1912, Stockholm. 11 entries.

United Kingdom 4   Denmark 2

United Kingdom: R. Brebner; T. Burn, A. Knight; H. Littlewort, E. Hanney, J. Dines; A. Berry, V. Woodward, H. Walden, G. Hoare, I. Sharpe.

1920, Antwerp. 14 entries.

Belgium 2   Czechoslovakia 0

United Kingdom eliminated in the first round by Norway, 3–1.

1924, Paris. 22 entries.

Uruguay 3   Switzerland 0

1928, Amsterdam. 17 entries.

Uruguay 2   Argentina 1
(after 1–1)

1936, Berlin. 16 entries.

Italy 2   Austria 1
(after extra time)

Great Britain eliminated in the second round by Poland 5–4, after beating China 2–0.

1948, London. 18 entries.

Sweden 3   Yugoslavia 1

Great Britain defeated Holland 4–3 and France 1–0 to reach the semi-final, where they went down to Yugoslavia by 3–1. In the play-off for third place Denmark beat Great Britain 5–3.

1952, Helsinki. 25 entries.

Hungary 2   Yugoslavia 0

Great Britain were beaten in the preliminary round by Luxembourg by 5–3 (after extra time).

1956, Melbourne. 11 entries.

U.S.S.R. 1   Yugoslavia 0

Great Britain—the name was retained, even though only Englishmen took part —were defeated by Bulgaria (0–2 in Sofia and 3–3 at Wembley) in the eliminating competition. As several countries withdrew owing to the expense, however, Great Britain were invited to make up the numbers in Melbourne. After beating Thailand 9–0, Great Britain met Bulgaria again in the second round and were defeated 6–1.

(Contd. on p. 45, col. 1)

SOCCER QUIZ

1. When did Scotland first take part in the final stages of the World Cup?

★

2. Who took part in the greatest number of Home International games for Scotland?

★

3. How many Wembley Finals needed a replay?

★

4. Who won English, Scottish and Irish Cup-winners' medals? *(above)*

★

5. Have any Scottish clubs competed in the F.A. Cup?

★

6. Name the England right back who held the world long-jump record.

★

7. And the England goalkeeper who held the high-jump record.

QUIZ ANSWERS

1. 1954. 2. A. Morton (Rangers)—30. 3. None. 4. J. Delaney for Manchester United, Celtic and Derry City. 5. Yes. They include Rangers and Queen's Park. 6. C. B. Fry. 7. B. Howard Baker.

Kevin O'Flanagan

SOCCER QUIZ

1. What was the last occasion when a club side provided England with the half-back line?

★

2. Which club has provided most players to any one of the four Home countries?

★

3. How many times has Ireland won in England?

★

4. When and where?

★

5. When was the last victory by Wales over England?

★

6. When was the last time Wales beat England in England?

★

7. When was the last Scottish win over England at Hampden Park?

QUIZ ANSWERS

1. Wolves in the 1958 World Cup—W. Slater, W. Wright, E. Clamp. 2. Wrexham—56, to Wales. 3. Twice. 4. Middlesbrough in 1914 and Wembley in 1957. 5. In 1955 in Cardiff. 6. 1936. 7. 1937.

England and Scotland, who are recognised as the two most powerful home countries, failed to qualify in their groups. Wales and Ireland reached the quarter-finals before being beaten.

1958 Competition, Sweden. 46 entries.
Final: **Brazil 5 Sweden 2**

England tied with Russia in their group which also included Brazil and Austria. They had three points, obtained from drawing with all three opponents. By drawing with Brazil they were the only nation to avoid defeat from the eventual winners. In a play-off Russia defeated England by 1–0. Scotland finished bottom of their group with one point. Ireland were equal second with Czechoslovakia in their group, which also included Germany and Argentina. Ireland beat Czechoslovakia 2–1 in the play-off. Wales also had to have a deciding match with Hungary, and won 2–1. Sweden and Mexico were also in Wales's group. In the quarter-finals Brazil beat Wales 1–0 (their narrowest victory) and Ireland, who were badly hit by injuries, lost to France 4–0.

1930 Competition, Uruguay. 13 entries.
Final: **Uruguay 4 Argentina 2**

1934 Competition, Italy. 29 entries.
Final: **Italy 2 Czechoslovakia 1**
(after extra time)

1938 Competition, France. 25 entries.
Final: **Italy 4 Hungary 2**

1950 Competition, Brazil. 32 entries.
Final: **Uruguay 2 Brazil 1**

In the group competition England defeated Chile 2–1, but in the next match came the shock of shocks, a defeat by U.S.A. by 1–0. In the third game Spain beat England 1–0 and so England failed to qualify. The final in Rio created a world record for attendance and receipts. There were 200,000 spectators, who paid £125,000.

The World Cup Final of 1954. Morlock scores Germany's first goal in their 3–2 win over Hungary

1957–8	Ballymena U. 2	Linfield	0	
1956–7	Glenavon	2	Derry C.	0
1955–6	Distillery	1	Glentoran	0
	(after 2–2 and 1–1)			
1954–5	Dundela	3	Glenavon	0
1953–4	Derry C.	1	Glenavon	0
	(after 2–2 and 0–0)			
1952–3	Linfield	5	Coleraine	0
1951–2	Ards	1	Glentoran	0
1950–1	Glentoran	3	Ballymena U.	1
1949–50	Linfield	2	Distillery	1
1948–9	Derry C.	3	Glentoran	1
1947–8	Linfield	3	Coleraine	0
1946–7	Belfast Celtic 1	Glentoran	0	
1945–6	Linfield	3	Distillery	0

IRISH LEAGUE—WINNERS AND RUNNERS-UP

		Pts.		Pts.
1958–9	Linfield	34	Glenavon	31
1957–8	Ards	36	Glenavon	34
1956–7	Glenavon	35	Linfield	34
1955–6	Linfield	40	Glenavon	29

Season 1957–8 was marred by the Munich air disaster, when the plane bringing the United team back from their tie against Red Star in Belgrade crashed at Munich. United had looked like challenging successfully the monopoly of Real Madrid, but, crippled by the disaster, they went out in the next round (the semi-final) to Milano. Real Madrid completed a hat-trick of wins by defeating Milano in Brussels.

By season 1958–9 all the British clubs were anxious to "climb on the band wagon". Hearts, Ards, and Drumcondra entered as well as Wolves. Manchester United were invited out of sympathy for the previous season. United accepted, the League objected and the Football Association upheld the League. The British clubs made a poor showing, all being dismissed in the first round. Madrid won the trophy yet again.

1955–6. 18 entries.

Real Madrid 4 Rheims 3
in Paris

Chelsea withdrew and Hibernian were defeated by Rheims in the semi-final.

1956–7. 18 entries.

Real Madrid 2 Fiorentina 0
in Madrid

Manchester United defeated Anderlecht (Belgium), Borussia, Dortmund (Germany) and Bilbao (Spain) to reach the semi-final. There were eliminated by Real Madrid, losing 3–1 in Madrid and drawing 2–2 at Old Trafford. Glasgow Rangers lost to Nice (France) in the first round in a play-off in Paris. Both won their home games 2–1 and Nice won the third meeting 3–1.

1957–8. 22 entries.

Real Madrid 3 Milano 2
in Brussels

Manchester United defeated Shamrock Rovers, Dukla (Czechoslovakia) and Red Star (Yugoslavia) before the air crash at Munich on returning from Belgrade. The semi-final against Milano was postponed until May. Then United beat Milano 2–1 at Old Trafford, but went down 4–0 in the return. Milano had already accounted for Glasgow Rangers, who beat St. Etienne (France) in the first round.

1958–9.

Real Madrid 2 Stade de Rheims 0
in Stuttgart

Cliff Bastin

George Hardwick

Raich Carter

Ivor Allchurch

Noel Cantwell

WORLD CUP

The World Cup is the most important international soccer tournament. After discussions for over eight years, it was decided in 1929 to launch the competition. The main instigator was Jules Rimet, a Frenchman who had been President of F.I.F.A. since its inception in 1904. He presented a gold trophy and the Cup is sometimes called the Jules Rimet Cup.

As Uruguay, who were the Olympic title holders at the time, were celebrating the centenary of their independence, they were allowed to hold the first competition, which was in 1930. It is held every four years, and there was a break from 1938 to 1950 because of the war. The trophy was invariably won by a country of the same hemisphere as that in which the games were played until Brazil won in Sweden in 1958. The 1962 Cup is to be held in Chile.

The four Home Associations, who were outside F.I.F.A. until 1946, entered for the first time in 1950. The Home International Tournament was used as the means of finding two qualifiers for the final stages. England won, but so Scotland, who finished second, refused to go. Four years later both England and Scotland took part in the tournament in Switzerland. Neither distinguished themselves, although England did better than in 1950.

British soccer sailed triumphantly through the eliminating stages in 1958. The four countries were kept apart and grouped with continental nations. All four qualified for Sweden. There,

1954 Competition, Switzerland. 35 entries.
Final: **Germany 3 Hungary 2**

England qualified for the quarter-finals at the expense of Switzerland and Belgium. In the quarter-finals they were beaten 4–2 by the holders Uruguay. Scotland failed to score a goal in their two group games, losing 1–0 to Austria and 7–0 to Uruguay.

F.A. OF IRELAND CUP—FINALS

1958–9	St. Patrick's A 2	Waterford	1	
	(after 2–2)			
1957–8	Dundalk	1	Shamrock R.	0
1956–7	Drumcondra	2	Shamrock R.	0
1955–6	Shamrock R.	3	Cork A.	2
1954–5	Shamrock R.	1	Drumcondra	0
1953–4	Drumcondra	1	St. Patrick's A.	0
1952–3	Cork A.	2	Evergreen U.	1
	(after 2–2)			
1951–2	Dundalk	3	Cork A.	0
	(after 1–1)			
1950–1	Cork A.	1	Shelbourne	0
	(after 1–1)			
1949–50	Transports	3	Cork A.	1
	(after 2–2 and 3–3)			
1948–9	Dundalk	3	Shelbourne	0
1947–8	Shamrock R.	2	Drumcondra	1
1946–7	Cork U.	2	Bohemians	0
	(after 2–2)			
1945–6	Drumcondra	2	Shamrock R.	1

IRISH CUP—FINALS

1958–9	Glenavon	2	Ballymena U.	0
	(after 1–1)			

1954–5	Linfield	36	Glenavon	36
	(Linfield won the play-off for the Championship 2–0)			
1953–4	Linfield	36	Glentoran	35
1952–3	Glentoran	33	Linfield	31
1951–2	Glenavon	37	Glentoran	27
1950–1	Glentoran	38	Linfield	34
1949–50	Linfield	38	Glentoran	38
	(Linfield won the play-off for the Championship 2–0)			
1948–9	Linfield	36	Belfast Cel.	31
1947–8	Belfast Cel.	39	Linfield	35
1946–7	Belfast Cel.	44	Glentoran	42
1945–6	No contest.			

EUROPEAN CUP

The European Cup was started in 1955 for the League Champions of the European countries. It was formed by the European Football Federation which had itself come into being three years before. As the Football League Champions of 1954–5, Chelsea were invited to take part. They accepted, were drawn against Djurgarden of Sweden and then withdrew under pressure from the Football League. Hibernian took part and reached the semi-final before being beaten by Rheims.

Despite Chelsea's action the competition was an immense success. In the following season Manchester United entered, in the face of opposition from the League, and profited from the tremendous popularity which the new Cup had aroused. United reached the semi-final stage, where they were beaten by Real Madrid, who thus won the Cup for the second year running.

FOOTBALL ASSOCIATION YOUTH CUP

	Winner	Runner-up
1952–3	Manchester U.	Wolves
1953–4	Manchester U.	Wolves
1954–5	Manchester U.	W.B.A.
1955–6	Manchester U.	Chesterfield
1956–7	Manchester U.	West Ham
1957–8	Wolves	Chelsea
1958–9	Blackburn	West Ham

GREAT NAMES IN SOCCER

JIMMY SEED (Tottenham and Sheffield Wednesday). Because the effects of gassing in the First World War seemed to end his career, Sunderland gave Jimmy Seed a free transfer. He went to Mid-Rhondda in South Wales, then to Spurs, and finally to Sheffield Wednesday with a reputation as a brilliant inside forward and an excellent captain. He joined Wednesday in 1928 when the club looked doomed to relegation and Spurs were in a safe position. He inspired Wednesday to climb clear and it was Spurs who went down. He then led Sheffield to two Championship triumphs. He had 23 years as manager of Charlton. He steered them from the Third to the First Division in successive seasons, 1934–6, then, with practically the same team, they finished second in the First Division. Charlton won the Cup in 1947 and when Seed left the club in 1956 he had made a profit of £115,000 on transfer deals. He became Millwall's manager in 1958.

LEN SHACKLETON (Newcastle and Sunderland). Impish, unpredictable, tantalising—that was inside forward Len Shackleton,. sometimes dubbed "the clown prince of soccer". To him football was an entertainment and he set out to give spectators full value for their money with brilliant tricks of ball control and shrewd mastery of the game. He won only six caps for England, because he made it clear that he did not like Authority, football or otherwise. He joined the Arsenal groundstaff as a frail lad of 16 in 1938, went back to his home in Bradford when war broke out and became a professional for Bradford.

Len Shackleton

Joe Smith

Frank Swift

Newcastle paid £13,000 for him in 1946 and he scored six goals in his first match. He moved to Sunderland for £20,050 in 1948 and retired nine years later owing to an injured ankle.

BILL SHANKLY (Preston). Close-cropped hair, a biting tackle and a deliberate push of the ball with the inside of the foot were the distinguishing marks of Bill Shankly, the Preston right half. His qualities made him an essential base for the brilliance of Tom Finney on the right wing in front of him; and when he left Preston, Tommy Docherty, who was almost a replica, was brought from Celtic in his stead. Shankly joined Preston before the war and played five times for Scotland up to 1939. He was in the Preston Cup-winning side of 1938. After the war he helped Preston to return to the First Division in 1950–1. He did so well as manager of Carlisle that he took over at Huddersfield in succession to his former Preston and Scotland colleague, Andy Beattie.

G. O. SMITH (Corinthians). It is a sign of greatness in an occupation to be known by initials. Such was G. O. Smith of Corinthians. He was the finest centre forward of his day—the 1890s—and perhaps the greatest of all time. Wonderful balance was the reason for his dribbling and swerving powers. He rarely headed the ball because he kept it on the ground, both in dribbling and in shooting. Adept at positioning, he made as many goals for his colleagues as he scored himself. He obtained 115 goals for Corinthians in 131 matches and played 20 times for England between 1893 and 1901.

JOE SMITH (Bolton). As Bolton filed on to the Wembley pitch for the first Cup Final there, after it had been invaded by the crowd, one of the players said to skipper Joe Smith "I wouldn't like to take a penalty out there". The reply was "You won't get a chance—I'm taking the penalties." Smith was forth-

right and supremely confident. He scored in that Final—the second goal—and won another winners' medal with Bolton three years later in 1926. The secret of his powerful shooting from inside left was practice he had when a boy in Dudley Port kicking a ball made of tightly packed rags. The 38 goals he scored for Bolton in 1920–1 stood as a First Division record until broken by Dixie Dean seven years later. He would have won more than five caps for England if the 1914–18 war had not cut across his career. He was successful as a manager, first with Reading and then with Blackpool, whom he steered to three Finals.

BILLY STEEL (Derby and Dundee). The record transfer fee of £23,000 by a Scottish club to an English one was paid by Dundee for the Derby County inside left Billy Steel. It was in 1950. Three years previously he had set up a record for English football when Derby paid Morton £15,500 for him. Yet he was comparatively unknown a few months before moving to Derby. He was put in Scotland's team against England in 1947 and did so well that he was inside left for Great Britain against the Rest of Europe a month later. 5 feet 6 tall, he was lightning quick, both at shooting and sizing up an opening. After playing 30 times for Scotland he emigrated to the United States in 1958 and assisted the Los Angeles Danes.

FRANK SWIFT (Manchester City). At the end of the 1934 Final, in which Manchester City beat Portsmouth, Frank Swift, the City goalkeeper, collapsed in a faint. He was 19 and the nervous strain of the second half, during which City recovered from being a goal

down, was too much for him. Massive, likeable, with exceptional height and reach, Swift served City for 15 years and it needed a man of the stature of Bert Trautmann to take over adequately from him. But for a tendency to showmanship, Swift might have been the greatest goalkeeper of all time. As it was, he represented England 19 times after the war, and was captain on two occasions. He was killed in the Manchester United air crash, when he travelled with the party as a journalist.

BOBBY TEMPLETON (Newcastle). Wayward and irresponsible, Bobby Templeton never fully realised the tremendous possibilities in his superb ball control and tactical genius. Yet Peter McWilliam, with whom he played at Newcastle, named him as the best outside left of his playing experience. He won the first of his 11 caps for Scotland when with Aston Villa and was transferred to Newcastle in 1902. After two years he moved on to Arsenal, then struggling to keep solvent at their ground in Woolwich. He found his best form when he moved back to Scotland in 1908 to assist Kilmarnock.

COLIN VEITCH (Newcastle). In 1903 Newcastle were doing so badly that the chairman asked Colin Veitch to give a hand in team selection. The result was the birth of one of the finest teams of all time—the Newcastle side which reached the Final five times and won the League title on three occasions from 1904 to 1911. In the first four of those Finals Veitch played in different positions—inside left, centre forward, centre half and right half. The Finals were played at Crystal Palace and the only one won was in 1909 in a replay at Everton against Barnsley. The supreme ease with which he mastered the ball was the reason for his versatility and he read a game so well that he was an outstanding captain. He represented England four times.

(Contd. on p. 47 col. 3)

Tommy Taylor scores Manchester United's only goal in the 1957 Cup Final: Aston Villa won 2–1

F.A. Challenge Cup Finals

1871–2 WANDERERS 1
(Betts)
ROYAL ENGINEERS 0

WANDERERS: C. W. Alcock, E. E. Bowen, A. G. Bonsor, M. P. Betts, T. C. Hooman, W. P. Crake, E. Lubbock, A. C. Thompson, R. C. de Welch, C. H. R. Wollaston, R. W. S. Vidal.

ROYAL ENGINEERS: Capt. Marindin Capt. Merriman, Lt. Addison, Lt. Cresswell, Lt. Mitchell, Lt. Renny-Tailyour, Lt. Rich, Lt. Goodwyn, Lt. Muirhead, Lt. Cotter, Lt. Boyle. *Referee:* A. Stair (Upton Park).

1872–3 WANDERERS 2
(Kinnaird, Wollaston)
OXFORD UNIVERSITY 0

WANDERERS: A. F. Kinnaird, R. C. de Welch, L. S. Howell (*back*), E. E. Bowen, C. H. R. Wollaston, R. K. Kingsford, A. G. Bonsor, W. S. Kenyon-Slaney, C. M. Thompson, J. R. Sturgis, Rev. H. H. Stewart.

OXFORD UNIVERSITY: A. Kirke-Smith, A. J. Leach (*goal*), C. C. Mackarness (*back*), F. H. Birley (*half-back*), G. H. Longman, F. C. Maddison, H. B. Dixon, W. B. Paton, R. W. S. Vidal, W. E. Sumner, C. J. Ottaway. *Referee:* A. Stair (Upton Park).

1873–4 OXFORD UNIVERSITY 2
(Mackarness, Patton)
ROYAL ENGINEERS 0

OXFORD UNIVERSITY: C. J. Ottaway (*capt.*), C. E. B. Nepean, C. C. Mackarness, F. H. Birley, R. H. Benson, F. S. Green, F. B. Chappel-Maddison, W. S. Rawson, F. J. Patton, Rev. A. H. Johnson, R. W. S. Vidal.

ROYAL ENGINEERS: Major Marindin (*capt.*), Capt. Merriman, Lt. G. W. Addison, Lt. G. C. Onslow, Lt. H. G. Oliver, Lt. T. Digby, Lt. H. W. Renny-Tailyour, Lt. H. E. Rawson, Lt. J. E. Blackman, Lt. A. K. Wood, Lt. P. G. von Donop. *Referee:* A. Stair (Upton Park).

1874–5 ROYAL ENGINEERS 2
OLD ETONIANS 0
(After 1–1 draw, goalscorers not known)

ROYAL ENGINEERS: Capt. Merriman, Lt. G. H. Sim, Lt. G. Onslow, Lt. R. M. Ruck, Lt. P. G. von Donop, Lt. C. K. Wood, Lt. H. E. Rawson, Lt. R. H. Stafford, Capt. H. W. Renny-Tailyour, Lt. Mein, Lt. C. Wingfield Stratford.

OLD ETONIANS: Capt. E. H. Drummond Moray, M. Farrer, E. Lubbock, F. H. Wilson, Hon. A. F. Kinnaird, J. H. Stronge, F. J. Patton, C. E. Farmer, A. G. Bonsor, A. Lubbock, T. Hammond. (C. J. Ottaway, W. S. Kenyon-Slaney, R. H. Benson and A. C. Thompson took part in the first match in the place of A. Lubbock, T. Hammond, M. Farrer and Capt. E. H. Drummond Moray.) *Referee:* C. W. Alcock (Wanderers).

1875–6 WANDERERS 3
(Hughes 2, Wollaston)
OLD ETONIANS 0
(After 0–0 draw)

WANDERERS: W. D. O. Greig, A. H. Stratford, W. Lindsay, F.B. C. Maddison, F. H. Birley, C. H. R. Wollaston, H. Heron, F. Heron, J. H. Edwards, J. Kenrick, T. B. Hughes. (W. D. Cleeg played in goal in first match in place of W. D. O. Greig).

OLD ETONIANS: Q. Hogg, E. Lubbock, Hon. E. Lyttleton, M. G. Faner, Hon. A. F. Kinnaird, J. H. Stronge, W. S. Kenyon-Slaney, Hon. A. Lyttleton, J. R. Sturgis, A. G. Bonsor, H. P. Allene. (C. Meysey, A. C. Thompson and J. E. C. Welldon took part in the first match in place of J. H. Stronge, M. G. Faner, and E. Lubbock.) *Referee:* W. S. Rawson (Oxford University).

1876–7 WANDERERS 2
OXFORD UNIVERSITY 0
(Scorers not known)

WANDERERS: Hon. A. F. Kinnaird, W. Lindsay, A. H. Stratford, F. H. Birley, C. A. Denton, F. T. Green, H. Heron, T. B. Hughes, J. Kenrick, H. Wace, C. H. R. Wollaston.

OXFORD UNIVERSITY: E. H. Alington, J. Bain, O. R. Dunell, J. H. Savory, A. H. Tod, E. W. Waddington, P. H. Fernandez, A. F. Hills, H. S. Otter, E. H. Parry, W. S. Rawson. *Referee:* S. H. Wright (Marlow).

1877–8 WANDERERS 3
ROYAL ENGINEERS 1
(Scorers not known)

WANDERERS: J. Kirkpatrick, A. H. Stratford, W. Lindsay, Hon. A. F. Kinnaird, F. T. Green, C. H. R. Wollaston, H. Heron, J. G. Wylie, H. Wace, C. A. Denton, J. Kenrick.

ROYAL ENGINEERS: L. B. Friend, J. H. Cowan, W. J. Morris, C. B. Mayne, F. C. Heath, C. E. Haynes, M. Lindsay, R. B. Hedley, F. G. Bond, H. H. Barnet, O. E. Ruck. *Referee:* S. R. Bastard (Upton Park).

SOCCER QUIZ

The winning Preston North End Cup team of 1889

1878–9 OLD ETONIANS 1
Scorer not known)
CLAPHAM ROVERS 0

OLD ETONIANS: J. P. Hawtrey, E. Christian, L. Bury, Hon. A. F. Kinnaird, E. Lubbock, C. J. Clerke, N. Pares, H. C. Goodhart, H. Whitfield, J. B. T. Chevallier, H. Beaufoy. *Referee:* C. W. Alcock (Wanderers).

1879–80 CLAPHAM ROVERS 1
(Lloyd-Jones)
OXFORD UNIVERSITY 0

CLAPHAM ROVERS: R. H. Birkett, R. A. Ogilvie, E. Field, A. Weston, N. C. Bailey, H. Brougham, A. J. Stanley, F. Barry, F. J. Sparks, C. A. Lloyd-Jones, E. A. Ram.
OXFORD UNIVERSITY: P. C. Parr, C. W. Wilson, C. J. S. King, F. A. H. Phillips, B. Rogers, R. T. Heygate, G. B. Childs, J. Eyre, F. D. Crowdy, E. H. Hill, J. B. Lubbock. *Referee:* Major Marindin (R.E.).

1880–1 OLD CARTHUSIANS 3
(Scorers not known)
OLD ETONIANS 0

OLD CARTHUSIANS: L. F. Gillett, W. H. Norris, E. G. Colvin, J. F. M. Prinsep, A. J. Vintcent, W. E. Hansell, L. M. Richards, W. R. Page, E. G. Wynyard, E. H. Parry, A. H. Tod.
OLD ETONIANS: J. F. P. Rawlinson, C. W. Foley, C. H. French, Hon. A. F. Kinnaird, R. B. Farrer, J. B. T. Chevallier, W. J. Anderson, H. C. Goodhart, R. H. Macaulay, H. Whitfield, P. C. Novelli. *Referee:* W. Peirce Dix (Sheffield).

1881–2 OLD ETONIANS 1
(Anderson)
BLACKBURN ROVERS 0

OLD ETONIANS: J. F. P. Rawlinson, T. H. French, P. J. de Paravicini, Hon. A. F. Kinnaird, C. W. Foyle, P. C. Novelli, A. T. B. Dunn, R. H. Macaulay, H. C. Goodhart, W. J. Anderson, J. B. T. Chevallier.
BLACKBURN ROVERS: R. Howarth, H. McIntyre, F. Suter, H. Sharples, F. W. Hargreaves, J. Duckworth, J. Douglas, T. Strachan, J. Brown, G. Avery, J. Hargreaves. *Referee:* J. C. Clegg (Sheffield).

1882–3 BLACKBURN OLYMPIC 2
(Matthews, Costley)
OLD ETONIANS 1
(Goodhart)

BLACKBURN OLYMPIC: T. Hacking, J. T. Ward, S. A. Warburton, T. Gibson, W. Astley, J. Hunter, T. Dewhurst, A. Matthews, G. Wilson, J. Costley, J. Yates.
OLD ETONIANS: J. F. P. Rawlinson, T. H. French, P. J. de Paravicini, Hon. A. F. Kinnaird, C. W. Foley, J. B. T. Chevallier, W. J. Anderson, R. H. Macaulay, H. C. Goodhart, A. T. B. Dunn, H. W. Bainbridge. *Referee:* C. Crump (Wolverhampton).

1883–4 BLACKBURN ROVERS 2
(Brown, Forrest)
QUEEN'S PARK, GLASGOW 1
(Christie)

BLACKBURN ROVERS: H. J. Arthur; J. Beverley, F. Suter; H. McIntyre, J. H. Forrest; J. M. Lofthouse, J. Douglas, J. Brown, J. Inglis, J. Sowerbutts, J. Hargreaves.
QUEEN'S PARK: G. Gillespie; W. Arnott, J. MacDonald; C. Campbell, J. J. Gow; W. Anderson, W. W. Watt, Dr. Smith, W. Harrower, D. S. Allan, R. M. Christie. *Referee:* Major Marindin (R.E.).

1884–5 BLACKBURN ROVERS 2
(Brown, Forrest)
QUEEN'S PARK, GLASGOW 0

BLACKBURN ROVERS: H. Arthur, R. G. Turner, F. Suter; G. Haworth, H. McIntyre, J. H. Forrest; J. M. Lofthouse, J. Douglas, J. Brown, H. Fecitt, J. Sowerbutts.
QUEEN'S PARK: G. Gillespie; W. Arnott, W. MacLeod; C. Campbell, J. MacDonald, A. Hamilton; W. Anderson, W. Sellar, W. Gray, N. McWhannel, D. S. Allan. *Referee:* Major Marindin (R.E.).

1885–6 BLACKBURN ROVERS 2
(Brown, Sowerbutts)
WEST BROMWICH ALBION 0
(After 0–0 draw)

BLACKBURN ROVERS: H. J. Arthur; Turner, Suter; Douglas, McIntyre, Forrest; Walton, Strachan, Brown, Fecitt, J. Sowerbutts. (Heyes played in the first match at the Oval, but Walton took part in the replay.)
WEST BROMWICH ALBION: Roberts; H. Green, H. Bell; Horton, Perry, Timmons; Woodhall, T. Green, Bayliss, Loach, G. Bell. *Referee:* Major Marindin (R.E.).

1886–7 ASTON VILLA 2
(Hunter, Hodgetts)
WEST BROMWICH ALBION 0

ASTON VILLA: Warner; Coulton, Simmonds; Yates, Dawson, Burton; Davis, Brown, Hunter, Vaughton, Hodgetts.
WEST BROMWICH ALBION: Roberts; H. Green, Aldridge; Horton, Perry, Timmins; Woodhall, T. Green, Bayliss, Paddock, Pearson. *Referee:* Major Marindin (R.E.).

1887–8 WEST BROMWICH ALBION 2
(Woodhall, Bayliss)
PRESTON NORTH END 1
(Dewhurst)

WEST BROMWICH ALBION: Roberts; Aldridge, Green; Horton, Perry, Timmins; Bassett, Woodhall, Bayliss, Wilson, Pearson.
PRESTON NORTH END: Dr. R. H. Mills-Roberts; Howarth, N. J. Ross; Holmes, Russell, Graham; Gordon, J. Ross, J. Goodall, F. Dewhurst, Drummond. *Referee:* Major Marindin (R.E.).

1888–9 PRESTON NORTH END 3
(Gordon, Goodall, Thompson)
WOLVERHAMPTON 0

PRESTON NORTH END: Dr. R. H. Mills-Roberts; Howarth, Holmes; Drummond, Russell, Graham; Gordon, J. Ross, J. Goodall, F. Dewhurst, Thompson.
WOLVERHAMPTON WANDERERS: Baynton, Baugh, Mason; Fletcher, Allen, Lowder; Hunter, Wykes, Broodie, Wood, Knight. *Referee:* Major Marindin (R.E.).

1889–90 BLACKBURN ROVERS 6
(Townley 3, Lofthouse, Southwood (John), Walton)
SHEFFIELD WEDNESDAY 1
(Mumford)

BLACKBURN ROVERS: J. K. Horne; Southwood (James), Forbes; Barton, Dewar, Forrest; Lofthouse, Campbell, Southwood (John), Walton, Townley.
SHEFFIELD WEDNESDAY: Smith (J.); Brayshaw, H. Morley; Dungworth, Betts, Waller; Ingram, Woodhouse, Bennett, Mumford, Cawley. *Referee:* Major Marindin (R.E.).

1890–1 BLACKBURN ROVERS 3
(Southwood, Townley, Dewar)
NOTTS COUNTY 1
(Oswald)

BLACKBURN ROVERS: Pennington; Brandon, Forbes; Barton, Dewar, Forrest; Lofthouse, Walton, Southwood (John), Hall, Townley.
NOTTS COUNTY: Thraves; Ferguson, Hendry; Osborne, Calderhead, Shelton; A. McGregor, McInnes, Oswald, Locker, H. B. Daft. *Referee:* C. J. Hughes (Northwich).

1892–3 WOLVERHAMPTON WANDERERS 1
(Allen)
EVERTON 0

WOLVERHAMPTON WANDERERS: Rose; Baugh, Swift; Malpass, Allen, Kinsey; R. Topham, Wykes, Butcher, Wood, Griffin.
EVERTON: Williams; Howarth, Kelso; Stewart, Holt, Boyle; Latta, Gordon, Maxwell, Chadwick, Milward. *Referee:* C. J. Hughes (Northwich).

1893–4 NOTTS COUNTY 4
(Logan 3, Watson)
BOLTON WANDERERS 1
(Bentley)

NOTTS COUNTY: Toone; Harper, Hendry; Bramley, Calderhead, Shelton; Watson, Donnelly, Logan, Bruce, H. B. Daft.
BOLTON WANDERERS: Sutcliffe; Somerville, Jones; Gardiner, Patton, Hughes; Dickinson, Wilson, Tannahill, Bentley, Cassidy. *Referee:* C. J. Hughes (Northwich).

1894–5 ASTON VILLA 1
(Devey)
WEST BROMWICH ALBION 0

ASTON VILLA: Wilkes; Spencer, Welford; Reynolds, Cowan (James), Russell; Athersmith, Chatt, Devey, Hodgetts, Smith (S.).
WEST BROMWICH ALBION: Reader; Williams, Horton; Taggart, Higgins, T. Perry; Bassett, McLeod, Richards, Hutchinson, Banks. *Referee:* J. Lewis (Blackburn).

1895–6 SHEFFIELD WEDNESDAY 2
(Spiksley 2)
WOLVERHAMPTON WANDERERS 1
(Black)

SHEFFIELD WEDNESDAY: Massey; Earp, Langley; H. Brandon, Crawshaw, Petrie; Brash, Brady, L. Bell, Davis, Spiksley.
WOLVERHAMPTON WANDERERS: Tennant; Baugh, Dunn; Owen, Malpass, Griffiths; Tonks, Henderson, Beats, Wood, Black. *Referee:* Lieut. W. Simpson (Army).

1896–7 ASTON VILLA 3
(Campbell, Wheldon, Crabtree)
EVERTON 2
(Bell, Boyle)

ASTON VILLA: Whitehouse; Spencer, Evans; Reynolds, Cowan (Jas.), Crabtree; Athersmith, Devey (J.), Campbell, Wheldon, Cowan (John).
EVERTON: Menham; Meecham, Storrier; Boyle, Holt, Stewart; Taylor, Bell, Hartley, Chadwick, Milward. *Referee:* J. Lewis (Blackburn).

Dean scoring Everton's second goal in the 1933 Cup Final against Manchester City.

1891–2 WEST BROMWICH ALBION 3
(Nicholls, Geddes, Reynolds)
ASTON VILLA 0

WEST BROMWICH ALBION: Reader; Nicholson, McCulloch; Reynolds, Perry, Groves; Bassett, McLeod, Nicholls, Pearson, Geddes.
ASTON VILLA: Warner; Evans, Cox; Devey (D.), Cowan, Baird; Athersmith, Devey (J.), Dickson, Campbell, Hodgetts. *Referee:* J. C. Clegg (Sheffield).

1897–8 NOTTINGHAM FOREST 3
(Capes 2, McPherson)
DERBY COUNTY 1
(Bloomer)

NOTTINGHAM FOREST: Allsop; Ritchie, Scott; Forman (Frank), McPherson, Wragg; McInnes, Richards, Benbow, Capes, Spouncer.
DERBY COUNTY: Fryer; Methven, Leiper; Cox, Goodall (A.), Turner; Goodall (J.), Bloomer, Boag, Stevenson, McQueen. *Referee:* J. Lewis (Blackburn).

46

1898–9 SHEFFIELD UNITED 4
(Bennett, Beers, Almond, Priest)
DERBY COUNTY 1
(Boag)

SHEFFIELD UNITED: Foulke; Thickett, Boyle; Johnson, Morren, Needham; Bennett, Beers, Hedley, Almond, Priest.
DERBY COUNTY: Fryer; Methven, Staley, Cox, Paterson, May; Arkesden, Bloomer, Boag, McDonald, Allen. *Referee:* A. Scragg (Crewe).

1899–1900 BURY 4
(McLuckie 2, Wood, Plant)
SOUTHAMPTON 0

BURY: Thompson; Darrock, Davidson; Pray, Leeming, Ross; Richards, Wood, McLuckie, Sagar, Plant.
SOUTHAMPTON: Robinson; Meehan, Durber; Meston, Chadwick, Petrie; Turner, Yates, Farrell, Wood, Milward. *Referee:* A. Kingscott (Derby).

1900–1 TOTTENHAM HOTSPUR 3
(Cameron, Smith, Brown)
SHEFFIELD UNITED 1
(Priest)
(After 2–2 draw)

TOTTENHAM HOTSPUR: Clawley; Erentz, Tait; Morris, Hughes, Jones; Smith, Cameron, Brown, Copeland, Kirwan.
SHEFFIELD UNITED: Foulke; Thickett, Boyle; Johnson, Morren, Needham; Bennett, Field, Hedley, Priest, Lipsham. *Referee:* A. Kingscott (Derby).

1901–2 SHEFFIELD UNITED 2
(Hedley, Barnes)
SOUTHAMPTON 1
(Brown)
(After 1–1 draw)

SHEFFIELD UNITED: Foulke; Thickett, Boyle; Needham, Wilkinson, Johnson; Barnes, Common, Hedley, Priest, Tipsham. (Bennett was injured in the first match and Barnes took his place in the replay.)
SOUTHAMPTON: Robinson; C. B. Fry, Molyneux; Meston, Bowman, Lee; A. Turner, Wood, Brown, Chadwick, J. Turner. *Referee:* T. Kirkham (Burslem).

1902–3 BURY 6
(Ross, Sagar, Leeming 2, Wood, Plant)
DERBY COUNTY 0

BURY: Monteith; Lindsay, McEwen; Johnson, Thorpe, Ross; Richards, Wood, Sagar, Leeming, Plant.
DERBY COUNTY: Fryer; Methven, Morris, Warren, Goodall (A.), May; Warrington, York, Boag, Richards, Davis. *Referee:* J. Adams (Birmingham).

1903–4 MANCHESTER CITY 1
(Meredith)
BOLTON WANDERERS 0

MANCHESTER CITY: Hillman McMahon, Burgess; Frost, Hynds, S. B. Ashworth; Meredith, Livingstone, Gillespie, Turnbull (A.), Booth.
BOLTON WANDERERS: D. Davies; Brown, Struthers; Clifford, Greenhalgh, Freebairn; Stokes, Marsh, Yenson, White, Taylor. *Referee:* A. J. Barker (Hanley).

1904–5 ASTON VILLA 2
(Hampton 2)
NEWCASTLE UNITED 0

ASTON VILLA: George; Spencer, Miles; Pearson, Leake, Windmill; Brawn, Garratty, Hampton, Bache, Hall.
NEWCASTLE UNITED: Lawrence; McCombie, Carr; Gardner, Aitken, McWilliam; Rutherford, Howie, Appleyard, Veitch, Gosnell. *Referee:* P. R. Harrower (London).

1905–6 EVERTON 1
(Young)
NEWCASTLE UNITED 0

EVERTON: Scott; Balmer (W.), Crelly; Makepeace, Taylor, Abbott; Sharp, Bolton, Young, Settle, H. P. Hardman.
NEWCASTLE UNITED: Lawrence; McCombie, Carr; Gardner, Aitken, McWilliam; Rutherford, Howie, Veitch, Orr, Gosnell. *Referee:* F. Kirkham (Preston).

West Bromwich Albion winger, Boyes, scores the equaliser in 1935 Final against Sheffield Wednesday.

1906–7 SHEFFIELD WEDNESDAY 2
(Stewart, Simpson)
EVERTON 1
(Sharp)

SHEFFIELD WEDNESDAY: Lyall; Layton, Burton; Brittleton, Crawshaw, Bartlett; Chapman, Bradshaw, Wilson, Stewart, Simpson.
EVERTON: Scott; Balmer (W.), Balmer (R.); Makepeace, Taylor, Abbott; Sharp, Bolton, Young, Settle, H. P. Hardman. *Referee:* N. Whittaker (London).

1907–8 WOLVERHAMPTON WANDERERS 3
(Rev. K. Hunt, Hedley, Harrison)
NEWCASTLE UNITED 1
(Howie)

WOLVERHAMPTON WANDERERS: Lunn; Jones, Collins; K. R. G. Hunt, Wooldridge, Bishop; Harrison, Shelton, Hedley, Radford, Pedley.
NEWCASTLE UNITED: Lawrence; McCracken, Pudan; Gardner, Veitch, McWilliam; Rutherford, Howie, Appleyard, Speedie, Wilson. *Referee:* T. P. Campbell (Blackburn).

1908–9 MANCHESTER UNITED 1
(Turnbull (A.))
BRISTOL CITY 0

MANCHESTER UNITED: Moger; Stacey, Hayes; Duckworth, Roberts, Bell; Meredith, Halse, Turnbull (J.), Turnbull (A.), Wall.
BRISTOL CITY: Clay; Annan, Cottle; Hanlin, Wedlock, Spear; Staniforth, Hardy, Gilligan, Burton, Hilton. *Referee:* J. Mason (Burslem).

1909–10 NEWCASTLE UNITED 2
(Shepherd 2, 1 pen.)
BARNSLEY 0
(After 1–1 draw)

NEWCASTLE UNITED: Lawrence; McCracken, Carr; Veitch, Low, McWilliam; Rutherford, Howie, Shepherd, Higgins, Wilson. (Whitson was injured in first match and Carr took his place in the replay.)
BARNSLEY: Mearns; Downs, Ness; Glendinning, Boyle, Utley; Bartrop, Gadsby, Lillycrop, Tufnell, Forman. *Referee:* J. T. Ibbotson (Derby).

1910–11 BRADFORD CITY 1
(Spiers)
NEWCASTLE UNITED 0
(After 0–0 draw)

BRADFORD CITY: Mellors; Campbell, Taylor; Robinson, Torrance, McDonald; Logan, Spiers, O'Rourke, Devine, Thompson. (Gildea played centre-half in the first match.)
NEWCASTLE UNITED: Lawrence; McCracken, Whitson; Veitch, Low, Willis; Rutherford, Jobey, Stewart, Higgins, Wilson. *Referee:* J. H. Pearson (Crewe).

1911–12 BARNSLEY 1
(Tufnell)
WEST BROMWICH ALBION 0

BARNSLEY: Cooper; Downs, Taylor; Glendinning, Bratley, Utley; Bartrop, Tufnell, Lillycrop, Travers, Moore.
WEST BROMWICH ALBION: Pearson; Cook, Pennington; Baddeley, Buck, McNeal; Jephcott, Wright, Pailor, Bowser, Shearman. *Referee:* J. R. Schumacher (London).

1912–13 ASTON VILLA 1
(Barber)
SUNDERLAND 0

ASTON VILLA: Hardy; Lyons, Weston, Barber, Harrop, Leach; Wallace, Halse, Hampton, Shepherson (C.), Bache.
SUNDERLAND: Butler; Gladwin, Ness; Cuggy, Thomson, Low; Mordue, Buchan, Richardson, Holley, Martin. *Referee:* A. Adams (Nottingham).

(Contd. on p. 48, col. 1)

SOCCER QUIZ

1. What happens to the proceeds of the pre-season practice matches in England?

★

2. And in Scotland?

★

3. Which clubs won the Scottish Cup three times in succession?

★

4. Which club won it four times in a row?

★

5. How long is the season in England?

★

6. And in Scotland?

QUIZ ANSWERS

1. They go to charity. 2. The same. 3. Queen's Park (twice), Vale of Leven and Rangers (twice). 4. No club has done it. 5. It includes two Saturdays in August and one in May. 6. It starts on the 2nd Saturday in August and finishes at the end of April.

G. O. Smith   Billy Walker   George Young

GREAT NAMES IN SOCCER

BILLY WALKER (Aston Villa). Billy Walker had an angular, awkward build which was deceptive. He moved with surprising speed, had deft ball control and was very dangerous in the air. He was originally a centre forward, and this was the position he occupied when Aston Villa won the Cup in 1920. He was even more effective when he moved to inside left. A former miner in the Black Country, he served Aston Villa for nearly 15 years and played 18 times for England between 1922 and 1933. After becoming manager of Sheffield Wednesday and helping them to win the Cup in 1935, he moved outside the League to Chelmsford. The grounding here was one of the reasons why he became the League's longest serving manager with Nottingham Forest, whom he joined before the war. He also steered them to winning the Cup—in 1959.

A. M. and P. M. WALTERS (Corinthians). The Corinthians were formed in 1882 in order to improve the teamwork of the England side. Two of the stalwarts they soon developed into full internationals were the Walters brothers, A. M. (Arthur) and P. M. (Percy). They formed a full-back partnership which served England on nine occasions. They went to Charterhouse School and were on opposite sides in the 1885 Varsity match. A few months afterwards they were capped together against Ireland. They were strongly built, charged fearlessly and kicked a good length. In 1890 a younger brother died as a result of an accident while playing in London and the brothers gave up the game at the request of their mother.

VIVIAN WOODWARD (Spurs and Chelsea). In 1915, when Chelsea reached the Cup Final, Vivian Woodward, their amateur international centre forward, obtained leave of absence from the Army to see the match. Chelsea asked him to play, but he refused, saying "Bob Thomson helped Chelsea to reach the Final. He must play in it." The

gesture was typical of Woodward. He was as great a sportsman as he was a footballer. He played 60 times for England in the early 1900s in full and amateur internationals, and once scored six goals against Holland at Stamford Bridge. He relied on artistry and accuracy rather than speed and power, held the attack well together and was an able dribbler. He left Spurs for Chelsea in 1909 and became a Spurs director when he finished playing. He died in 1954 at the age of 74.

BILLY WRIGHT (Wolverhampton Wanderers). By playing against Scotland at Wembley in April 1959, Billy Wright brought his number of appearances for England to the phenomenal total of 100. He was dropped once since the Second World War and missed another two games owing to injury. He was originally a right half and moved to centre half during the 1954 World Cup. He became England's captain against Ireland in 1948, when he was 24. He captained Wolves when they won the Cup in 1949 and led them to winning the League title in 1953–4, 1957–8 and 1958–9. Yet a few months after he joined Wolves as a 15-year-old boy the club nearly sent him home because they feared he was not good enough. He brought the total of caps up to 105 by playing in the American tour and then retired in August 1959.

GEORGE YOUNG (Rangers). George Young holds the record of having captained Scotland for six successive times against England. He also played more times for Scotland than any other player—50 appearances altogether. Like his great rival Wright, he changed his position to centre half, in his case from right back. Heavily built, he was commanding in the air and surprisingly neat in footwork. He joined Rangers from Kirkintilloch Rob Roy in 1941 and Rangers was his only senior club. With them he won six League Championship medals and four Cup-winning medals. He retired in 1957 when 35 to take over several business interests in Glasgow.

47

SOCCER QUIZ

1. Has England ever defeated Russia?

★

2. Or Brazil?

★

3. Who holds the balance of wins in the England-Yugoslavia meetings?

★

4. And in the Scotland-Yugoslavia meetings?

★

5. And the Scotland-Austria meetings?

★

6. Which club won the Amateur Cup three times in succession?

★

7. Has Pegasus won the Amateur Cup?

QUIZ ANSWERS

1. Yes, by 5–0 in 1958. 2. Yes, by 4–2 in 1956. 3. Yugoslavia, three to one, with one drawn. 4. Scotland, one win, two draws and no defeats. 5. Austria, four wins, one defeat and three draws. 6. Bishop Auckland. 7. On two occasions, 1951 and 1953.

1913–14 BURNLEY 1
(Freeman)
LIVERPOOL 0

BURNLEY: Sewell; Bamford, Taylor; Halley, Boyle, Watson; Nesbit, Lindley, Freeman, Hodgson, Mosscrop.

LIVERPOOL: Campbell; Longworth, Pursell; Fairfoul, Ferguson, McKinlay; Sheldon, Metcalf, Miller, Lacey, Nicholl. *Referee:* H. S. Bamlett (Gateshead).

1914–15 SHEFFIELD UNITED 3
(Simmons, Fazackerley, Kitchen)
CHELSEA 0

SHEFFIELD UNITED: Gough; Cook, English; Sturgess, Brelsford, Utley; Simmons, Fazackerley, Kitchen, Masterman, Evans.

CHELSEA: Molyneux; Bettridge, Harrow; Taylor, Logan, Walker; Ford, Halse, Thomson, Croal, McNeil. *Referee:* H. H. Taylor (Altrincham).

1919–20 ASTON VILLA 1
(Kirton)
HUDDERSFIELD TOWN 0

ASTON VILLA: Hardy; Smart, Weston; Ducat, Barson, Moss; Wallace, Kirton, Walker, Stephenson (C.), Dorrell.

HUDDERSFIELD TOWN: Mutch; Wood, Bullock; Slade, Wilson, Watson; Richardson, Mann, Taylor, Swan, Islip. *Referee:* J. T. Howcroft (Bolton).

1920–1 TOTTENHAM HOTSPUR 1
(Dimmock)
WOLVERHAMPTON WANDERERS 0

TOTTENHAM HOTSPUR: Hunter; Clay, M'Donald; Smith, Walters, Grimsdell; Banks, Seed, Cantrell, Bliss, Dimmock.

WOLVERHAMPTON WANDERERS: George; Woodward, Marshall; Gregory, Hodnett, Riley; Lea, Burrill, Edmonds, Potts, Brooks. *Referee:* J. Davies (Rainhill).

1921–2 HUDDERSFIELD TOWN 1
(Smith, pen.)
PRESTON NORTH END 0

HUDDERSFIELD TOWN: Mutch; Wood, Wadsworth; Slade, Wilson, Watson; Richardson, Mann, Islip, Stephenson, Smith (W. H.).

PRESTON NORTH END: J. F. Mitchell; Hamilton, Doolan; Duxbury, McCall, Williamson; Rawlings, Jefferis, Roberts, Woodhouse, Quinn. *Referee:* J. W. D. Fowler (Sunderland).

Bolton versus West Ham, 1923.

1922–3 BOLTON WANDERERS 2
(Jack, Smith (J.R.))
WEST HAM UNITED 0

BOLTON WANDERERS: Pym; Haworth, Finney, Nuttall, Seddon, Jennings; Butler, Jack, Smith (J.R.), Smith (J.), Vizard.

WEST HAM UNITED: Hufton; Henderson, Young; Bishop, Kay, Tresadern; Richards, Brown, Watson (V.), Moore, Ruffell. *Referee:* D. H. Asson (West Bromwich).

1923–4 NEWCASTLE UNITED 2
(Harris, Seymour)
ASTON VILLA 0

NEWCASTLE UNITED: Bradley; Hampson, Hudspeth; Mooney, Spencer, Gibson; Low, Cowan, Harris, M'Donald, Seymour.

ASTON VILLA: Jackson; Smart, Mort; Moss, Dr. V. E. Milne, Blackburn; York, Kirton, Capewell, Walker, Dorrell. *Referee:* W. E. Russell (Swindon).

1924–5 SHEFFIELD UNITED 1
(Tunstall)
CARDIFF CITY 0

SHEFFIELD UNITED: Sutcliffe; Cook, Milton; Pantling, King, Green; Mercer, Boyle, Johnson, Gillespie, Tunstall.

CARDIFF CITY: Farquharson; Nelson, Blair; Wake, Keenor, Hardy; Davies (W.), Gill, Nicholson, Beadles, Evans (J.). *Referee:* G. N. Watson (Nottingham).

1925–6 BOLTON WANDERERS 1
(Jack)
MANCHESTER CITY 0

BOLTON WANDERERS: Pym; Haworth, Greenhalgh; Nuttall, Seddon, Jennings; Butler, Jack, Smith (J.R.), Smith (J.), Vizard.

MANCHESTER CITY: Goodchild; Cookson, McCloy; Pringle, Cowan, McMullan; Austin, Browell, Roberts, Johnson, Hicks. *Referee:* J. Baker (Crewe).

1926–7 CARDIFF CITY 1
(Ferguson)
ARSENAL 0

CARDIFF CITY: Farquharson; Nelson, Watson; Keenor, Sloan, Hardy; Curtis, Irving, Ferguson, Davies (L.), M'Lachlan.

ARSENAL: Lewis; Parker, Kennedy; Baker, Butler, John; Hulme, Buchan, Brain, Blyth, Hoar. *Referee:* W. F. Bunnell (Preston).

1927–8 BLACKBURN ROVERS 3
(Roscamp 2, M'Lean)
HUDDERSFIELD TOWN 1
(Jackson)

BLACKBURN ROVERS: Crawford; Hutton, Jones; Healless, Rankin, Campbell; Thornewell, Puddefoot, Roscamp, M'Lean, Rigby.

HUDDERSFIELD TOWN: Mercer; Goodall, Barkas; Redfern, Wilson, Steele; Jackson (A.), Kelly, Brown, Stephenson, Smith (W.H.). *Referee:* T. G. Bryan (Willenhall).

1928–9 BOLTON WANDERERS 2
(Butler, Blackmore)
PORTSMOUTH 0

BOLTON WANDERERS: Pym; Haworth, Finney; Kean, Seddon, Nuttall; Butler, M'Clelland, Blackmore, Gibson, Cook.

PORTSMOUTH: Gilfillan; Mackie, Bell; Nichol, McIlwaine, Thackeray; Forward, Smith (J.), Weddle, Watson, Cook (F.). *Referee:* A. Josephs (South Shields).

1929–30 ARSENAL 2
(James, Lambert)
HUDDERSFIELD TOWN 0

ARSENAL: Preedy; Parker, Hapgood; Baker, Seddon, John; Hulme, Jack, Lambert, James, Bastin.

HUDDERSFIELD TOWN: Turner; Goodall, Spence; Naylor, Wilson, Campbell; Jackson (A.), Kelly, Davies, Raw, Smith (W.H.). *Referee:* T. Crew (Leicester).

1930–1 WEST BROMWICH ALBION 2
(Richardson (W. G.) 2)
BIRMINGHAM CITY 1
(Bradford)

WEST BROMWICH ALBION: Pearson; Shaw, Trentham; Magee, Richardson (W.), Edwards; Glidden, Carter, Richardson (W.G.), Sandford, Wood.

BIRMINGHAM CITY: Hibbs; Liddell, Barkas; Cringan, Morrall, Leslie; Briggs, Crosbie, Bradford, Gregg, Curtis. *Referee:* A. H. Kingscott (Long Eaton).

1931–2 NEWCASTLE UNITED 2
(Allen 2)
ARSENAL 1
(John)

NEWCASTLE UNITED: McInroy; Nelson, Fairhurst; McKenzie, Davidson, Weaver; Boyd, Richardson, Allen, McMenemy, Lang.

ARSENAL: Moss; Parker, Hapgood; Jones (C.), Roberts, Male; Hulme, Jack, Lambert, Bastin, John. *Referee:* W. P. Harper (Stourbridge).

1932–3 EVERTON 3
(Stein, Dean, Dunn)
MANCHESTER CITY 0

EVERTON: Sagar; Cook, Cresswe'l; Britton, White, Thomson; Geldard, Dunn, Dean, Johnson, Stein.

MANCHESTER CITY: Langford; Cann, Dale; Busby, Cowan, Bray; Toseland, Marshall, Herd, McMullan, Brook. *Referee:* E. Wood (Sheffield).

1933–4 MANCHESTER CITY 2
(Tilson 2)
PORTSMOUTH 1
(Rutherford)

MANCHESTER CITY: Swift; Barnett, Dale; Busby, Cowan, Bray; Toseland, Marshall, Tilson, Herd, Brook.

PORTSMOUTH: Gilfillan; Mackie, Smith (W.); Nichol, Allen, Thackeray; Worrall, Smith (J.), Weddle, Easson, Rutherford. *Referee:* S. F. Rous (Herts).

1934–5 SHEFFIELD WEDNESDAY 4
(Rimmer 2, Palethorpe, Hooper)
WEST BROMWICH ALBION 2
(Boyes, Sandford)

SHEFFIELD WEDNESDAY: Brown; Nibloe, Catlin; Sharp, Millership, Burrows; Hooper, Surtees, Palethorpe, Starling, Rimmer.

WEST BROMWICH ALBION: Pearson; Shaw, Trentham; Murphy, Richardson (W.), Edwards; Glidden, Carter, Richardson (W. G.), Sandford, Boyes. *Referee:* A. E. Fogg (Bolton).

1935–6 ARSENAL 1
(Drake)
SHEFFIELD UNITED 0

ARSENAL: Wilson; Male, Hapgood; Crayston, Roberts, Copping; Hulme, Bowden, Drake, James, Bastin.

SHEFFIELD UNITED: Smith; Hooper, Wilkinson; Jackson, Johnson, McPherson; Barton, Barclay, Dodds, Pickering, Williams. *Referee:* H. Nattrass (New Seaham).

The five members of Arsenal's Cup-winning team of 1936 who played for England against Ireland. Left to right: Copping, Bastin, Hapgood, Drake and Male.

1936–7 SUNDERLAND 3
(Gurney, Carter, Burbanks)
PRESTON NORTH END 1
(O'Donnell)

SUNDERLAND: Mapson; Gorman, Hall; Thomson, Johnson, McNab; Duns, Carter, Gurney, Gallacher, Burbanks.

PRESTON NORTH END: Burns; Gallimore, Beattie (A.); Shankley, Tremelling, Milne; Dougal, Beresford, O'Donnell (F.), Fagan, O'Donnell (H.). *Referee:* R. G. Rudd (Kenton).

Glidden, the West Bromwich Albion captain, leads his players off the field after the 1931 Cup Final.

48

Peter Doherty

Ted Drake

Johnny Carey

1937–8 PRESTON NORTH END 1
(Mutch, pen.)
HUDDERSFIELD TOWN 0

PRESTON NORTH END: Holdcroft; Galli-more, Beattie (A.); Shankly, Smith, Batey; Whatmough, Mutch, Maxwell, Beattie (R.), O'Donnell (H.).
HUDDERSFIELD TOWN: Hesford; Craig, Mountford; Willingham, Young, Boot; Hulme, Isaac, McFadyen, Barclay, Beasley. Referee: A. J. Jewell (London).

1938–9 PORTSMOUTH 4
(Parker 2, Barlow, Anderson)
WOLVERHAMPTON WANDERERS 1
(Dorsett)

PORTSMOUTH: Walker; Morgan, Roch-ford; Guthrie, Rowe, Wharton; Worrall, McAlinden, Anderson, Barlow, Parker.
WOLVERHAMPTON WANDERERS: Scott, Morris, Taylor; Galley, Cullis, Gardiner; Burton, McIntosh, Westcott, Dorsett, Maguire. Referee: T. Thompson (Leming-ton-on-Tyne).

1945–6 DERBY COUNTY 4
(Turner (H.) o.g., Doherty, Stamps 2)
CHARLTON ATHLETIC 1
(Turner (H.))

DERBY COUNTY: Woodley; Nicholas, Howe; Bullions, Leuty, Musson; Har-rison, Carter, Stamps, Doherty, Duncan.
CHARLTON ATHLETIC: Bartram; Phipps, Shreeve; Turner (H.), Oakes, Johnson; Fell, Brown, Turner (A. A.), Welsh, Duffy. Referee: E. D. Smith (White-haven).

1946–7 CHARLTON ATHLETIC 1
(Duffy)
BURNLEY 0

CHARLTON ATHLETIC: Bartram; Croker, Shreeve; Johnson, Phipps, Whittaker; Hurst, Dawson, Robinson (W.), Welsh, Duffy.
BURNLEY: Strong; Woodruff, Mather; Attwell, Brown, Bray; Chew, Morris, Harrison, Potts, F. P. Kippax. Referee: J. M. Wiltshire (Sherborne).

1947–8 MANCHESTER UNITED 4
(Rowley 2, Pearson, Anderson)
BLACKPOOL 2
(Shimwell, pen., Mortensen)

MANCHESTER UNITED: Crompton; Carey, Aston; Anderson, Chilton, Cockburn; Delaney, Morris, Rowley, Pearson, Mitten.
BLACKPOOL: Robinson; Shimwell, Cross-land; Johnston, Hayward, Kelly; Mat-thews, Munro, Mortensen, Dick, Rickett. Referee: C. J. Barrick (Northampton).

1948–9 WOLVERHAMPTON WAN-DERERS 3
(Pye 2, Smyth)
LEICESTER CITY 1
(Griffiths)

WOLVERHAMPTON WANDERERS: Williams; Pritchard, Springthorpe; Crook (W.), Shorthouse, Wright; Hancocks, Smyth, Pye, Dunn, Mullen.
LEICESTER CITY: Bradley; Jelly, Scott; Harrison (W.), Plummer, King; Griffiths, Lee, Harrison (J.), Chisholm, Adam. Referee: R. A. Mortimer (West Riding).

1949–50 ARSENAL 2
(Lewis 2)
LIVERPOOL 0

ARSENAL: Swindin; Scott, Barnes; Forbes, Compton (L.), Mercer; Cox, Logie, Goring, Lewis, Compton (D.).
LIVERPOOL: Sidlow; Lambert, Spicer; Taylor, Hughes, Jones; Payne, Baron, Stubbins, Fagan, Liddell. Referee: H. Pearce (Luton).

1950–1 NEWCASTLE UNITED 2
(Milburn 2)
BLACKPOOL 0

NEWCASTLE UNITED: Fairbrother; Cowell, Corbett; Harvey, Brennan, Crowe; Walker, Taylor, Milburn, Robledo (G.), Mitchell.
BLACKPOOL: Farm; Shimwell, Garrett; Johnston, Hayward, Kelly; Matthews, Mudie, Mortensen, W. J. Slater, Perry. Referee: W. Ling (Cambridge).

1951–2 NEWCASTLE UNITED 1
(Robledo (G.))
ARSENAL 0

NEWCASTLE UNITED: Simpson; Cowell, McMichael; Harvey, Brennan, Robledo (E.); Walker, Foulkes, Milburn, Robledo (G.), Mitchell.
ARSENAL: Swindin; Barnes, Smith (L.); Forbes, Daniel, Mercer; Cox, Logie, Holton, Lishman, Roper. Referee: A. E. Ellis (Halifax).

1952–3 BLACKPOOL 4
(Mortensen 3, Perry)
BOLTON WANDERERS 3
(Lofthouse, Moir, Bell)

BLACKPOOL: Farm; Shimwell, Garrett; Fenton, Johnston, Robinson; Matthews, Taylor, Mortensen, Mudie, Perry.
BOLTON WANDERERS: Hanson: Ball, Banks (R.); Wheeler, Barrass, Bell; Holden, Moir, Lofthouse, Hassall, Langton. Referee: B. M. Griffiths (Newport, Mon.).

1953–4 WEST BROMWICH ALBION 3
(Allen 2, 1 pen., Griffin)
PRESTON NORTH END 2
(Morrison, Wayman)

WEST BROMWICH ALBION: Sanders; Kennedy, Millard; Dudley, Dugdale, Barlow; Griffin, Ryan, Allen, Nicholls, Lee.
PRESTON NORTH END: Thompson; Cun-ningham, Walton; Docherty, Marston, Forbes; Finney, Foster, Wayman, Baxter, Morrison. Referee: A. W. Luty (Leeds).

1954–5 NEWCASTLE UNITED 3
(Milburn, Mitchell, Hannah)
MANCHESTER CITY 1
(Johnstone)

NEWCASTLE UNITED: Simpson; Cowell, Batty; Scoular, Stokoe, Casey; White, Milburn, Keeble, Hannah, Mitchell.
MANCHESTER CITY: Trautmann; Meadows, Little; Barnes, Ewing, Paul; Spurdle, Hayes, Revie, Johnstone, Fagan. Referee: R. J. Leafe (Nottingham).

1955–6 MANCHESTER CITY 3
(Hayes, Dyson, Johnstone)
BIRMINGHAM CITY 1
(Kinsey)

MANCHESTER CITY: Trautmann; Leivers, Little; Barnes, Ewing, Paul; Johnstone, Hayes, Revie, Dyson, Clarke.

BIRMINGHAM CITY: Merrick; Hall, Green; Newman, Smith, Boyd; Astall, Kinsey, Brown, Murphy, Govan. Referee: A. Bond (London).

1956–7 ASTON VILLA 2
(McParland 2)
MANCHESTER UNITED 1
(Taylor)

ASTON VILLA: Sims; Lynn, Aldis; Crow-ther, Dugdale, Saward; Smith, Sewell, Myerscough, Dixon, McParland.
MANCHESTER UNITED: Wood; Foulkes, Byrne; Colman, Blanchflower, Edwards; Berry, Whelan, Taylor, Charlton, Pegg. Referee: F. B. Coultas (Hull).

1957–8 BOLTON WANDERERS 2
(Lofthouse 2)
MANCHESTER UNITED 0

BOLTON WANDERERS: Hopkinson; Hartle, Banks; Hennin, Higgins, Edwards; Birch, Stevens, Lofthouse, Parry, Holden.
MANCHESTER UNITED: Gregg; Foulkes, Greaves; Goodwin, Cope, Crowther; Dawson, Taylor, Charlton, Violett, Webster. Referee: J. V. Sherlock (Sheffield).

1958–9 NOTTINGHAM FOREST 2
(Dwight, Wilson)
LUTON TOWN 1
(Pacey)

NOTTINGHAM FOREST: Thomson; Whare, McDonald; Whitefoot, McKinlay, Bur-kitt; Dwight, Quigley, Wilson, Gray, Imlach.
LUTON TOWN: Baynham; McNally, Hawkes; Groves, Owen, Pacey; Bing-ham, Brown, Morton, Cummins, Gregory. Referee: J. Clough (Bolton).

FOOTBALLER OF THE YEAR

Selected by the Football Writers every year since season 1947–8. The award is a silver statuette.

1947–8.	Stanley Matthews (Blackpool)
1948–9.	Johnny Carey (Manchester United)
1949–50.	Joe Mercer (Arsenal)
1950–1.	Harry Johnston (Blackpool)
1951–2.	Billy Wright (Wolverhampton Wanderers)
1952–3.	Nat Lofthouse (Bolton)
1953–4.	Tom Finney (Preston)
1954–5.	Don Revie (Manchester City)
1955–6.	Bert Trautmann (Manchester City)
1956–7.	Tom Finney (Preston)
1957–8.	Danny Blanchflower (Tottenham Hotspur)
1958–9.	Syd Owen (Luton Town)

VENUES OF THE F.A. CUP FINALS

The Oval, London. 1872 and 1874 to 1892.
Lillie Bridge, London. 1873.
Fallowfield, Manchester. 1893.
Goodison Park, Everton. 1894.
Crystal Palace, London. 1895 to 1914.
Old Trafford, Manchester. 1915.
Stamford Bridge, London. 1920 to 1922.
Wembley Stadium, London. 1923 onwards.

MOST F.A. CUP WINS

Seven times—Aston Villa. Six times—Blackburn Rovers and Newcastle United. Five times—The Wanderers.

MOST F.A. CUP FINAL APPEARANCES

Ten times—Newcastle United. Nine times—Aston Villa and West Bromwich Albion. Seven times—Blackburn Rovers, Bolton Wanderers, Wolverhampton Wanderers.

MOST WINNERS' MEDALS

Five—James Forrest (Blackburn Rovers), Lord Kinnaird (three with The Wan-derers and two with Old Etonians) and C. H. R. Wollaston (The Wanderers).

MOST WEMBLEY APPEARANCES

Clubs. Six by Arsenal (three won), five by Newcastle (all won), by Bolton (four won) and Manchester City (two won).

Players. Five by J. Hulme (four for Arsenal, one for Huddersfield). Four by D. Jack (two for Bolton, two for Arsenal).

Winners' Medals. R. Pym, R. Haworth, H. Nuttall, J. Seddon, and J. Butler played in the successful Bolton sides of 1923, 1926 and 1929. J. Milburn, R. Cowell and R. Mitchell were in the Newcastle winning sides of 1951, 1952 and 1955. D. Jack obtained two winners' medals with Bolton and one with Arsenal.

Moir, on ground, scores Bolton's second goal in the 1953 Cup Final.

Wally Barnes   Jack Fairbrother   Nat Lofthouse

49

OVERSEAS FOOTBALL

ARGENTINA.

Although football is very commercialised in Argentina, most of the players have outside occupations. International goalkeeper Julio Mussimessi, for example, is a singer and has recorded folklore songs. The drain of talent to Europe, particularly Italy, has been intense, and over 100 players—nine full international teams—have gone since the war. The most famous clubs are River Plate and Racing Club. Both are in Buenos Aires and have stadia holding over 100,000 people.

The best known player is Angel Labruna, the Argentinian Stanley Matthews. He played in first-class football when over 40 and has been with River Plate over 25 years. He was named Sportsman of the Year in preference even to racing-car ace Fangio.

Argentina's captain is Pedro Dellancha, who has been with Boca Juniors since he was 15. He plays left back and is nicknamed "Don Pedro" because of the way he calls to his colleagues.

AUSTRIA.

In the 1930s Austria had the most powerful side on the Continent and it was proudly called the "wunderteam". Since then Austria have declined, although their polished football and novel defensive ideas make them a difficult side to beat. Vienna, the home of clubs like Rapide, Austria and Vienna, dominates Austrian football.

Their captain Gerhard Hanappi has played for Austria 70 times and has twice represented F.I.F.A. A tousle-haired blond, he is an architect for a Viennese engineering firm. He is very versatile and is at home in most positions on the field.

BRAZIL.

Although the Brazilian F.A. was not founded until 1914, the game is easily the most popular in Brazil and the quality of play is such that Brazil worthily won the World Cup in 1958. The world's largest stadium is in Rio de Janeiro. It held 200,000 for the 1950 World Cup Final and the receipts were £125,000. Brazil beat England here 2–0 in 1959. There are two main football centres—Rio and Sao Paulo. In the former centre the chief clubs are Vasco da Gama and Botafogo.

All the Brazilian players are known by nicknames, or by their Christian name. That is just as well, because the full name of their 1958 World Cup star is Waldira Pereira. He is known as Didi. He is most skilful with the ball and pops up disconcertingly in a dangerous position near goal. He merits the nickname, "the Black Cobra".

Unlike many of his colleagues, captain Nilton Santos is quiet and relaxed, even on the field. Although he is a full back he has the ball control of an inside forward. He joined Botafogo when he was 20, in 1948.

FRANCE.

The balance of power in French football has swung away from Paris to the provinces. Racing Club, who began an annual series with Arsenal in the 1930s, are no longer the strongest club and the League and Cup usually go to a provincial club like Rheims, St. Etienne and Lille.

Rheims paid the French record fee of £30,000 for Roger Piantoni, the Nancy inside forward. Because he is short in stature and slightly-built, defences often under-estimate him, but he is a goal-scorer, as well as a goalmaker.

By scoring 13 goals in the World Cup in Sweden, Juste Fontaine, the Rheims centre forward, not only created a Cup record, but also helped France to take third place. He is very quick off the mark and a deadly finisher.

GERMANY.

The resilience of German football is clearly shown by the fact that they won the World Cup in 1954, six years after organised football had restarted. They were fourth in the 1958 series. Since the war Germany has been handicapped by having to limit selection to the Western half and the most powerful clubs are there, mainly in the industrial centres. They include Rot-Weiss Essen, who are so named because of their red and white colours, Stuttgart Kickers, Schalke and Kaiserlautern. There is only part-time professionalism in Germany.

The German counterpart to the late Duncan Edwards is left half Horst Szymaniak, 23-year-old son of a Polish miner in the Ruhr. He is broad-shouldered, tireless and tackles strongly.

Hero of the 1954 World Cup triumph was outside right Helmut Rahn. Fast and fearless, he cuts in to score many goals. He was also so effective in the 1958 series that he was named one of the best wingers in Sweden.

HUNGARY.

In 1953 Hungary became the first foreign country to defeat England in England. They were then undoubtedly the finest side in the world, and were unlucky to lose the 1954 World Cup Final to Germany. After the Hungarian revolution in 1956 the great side broke up and Hungary became a pathetic shadow of their former glory. The chief clubs are Honved (the Army side) and Red Banner. Both toured England in 1954.

Three of Hungary's world-class footballers went abroad—Ferenc Puskas, the tubby brains of the attack, to Spain; Sandor Kocsis, the elusive and graceful inside right, to Switzerland; and Zoltan Czibor, the dashing outside left, to Italy.

Two of the great side remaining are Jozsef Bozsik and Nandor Hidegkuti. Bozsik is an M.P. for a district in Budapest. He is a skilful and intelligent right half. Hidegkuti was the man who demoralised the England defence in 1953 by playing the retreating centre forward game. He got near enough goal, too, to score three times.

ITALY.

Italy has easily the most commercialised football in the world and stars are obtained from abroad to keep up the standard. The cost of importing them does not matter and Juventus paid £65,000 for John Charles of Leeds and Wales. The home products have suffered as a result and in 1958 Italy failed for the first time to qualify for the final stages of the World Cup. The two Milan clubs, Juventus and Milano, are the greatest rivals in Italy. Not far behind them in standard is Roma.

The most talented home player is Giampiero Boniperti, who played for the Rest of Europe against England in 1953. He has played in all forward positions and at wing half, and has won all the honours in the game.

Roma signed Jose Mazzola, Brazil's centre forward, for £80,000 after the 1958 World Cup. Mazzola is so nicknamed after one of Italy's greatest forwards, whom he resembles in style. He combines craft with forcefulness near goal.

U.S.S.R.

No tours by foreign clubs in Britain have created as much interest as those of Dynamo and Spartak of Russia. Dynamo first came in 1945 and were unbeaten in four matches which included encounters with Cardiff and Glasgow Rangers. Spartak came in 1954 and Dynamo paid their second visit a year later. Football teams in Russia are bound up with factories and trades unions. An exception is Spartak, which is a club in the broader sense. Other well-known teams are Red Army, Locomotive, Torpedo and Kiev Dynamo. Officially Russian players are amateurs and U.S.S.R. won the Olympic title in Melbourne in 1956.

Russia's captain is Igor Netto, a tall fair-haired wing half. He is an Honoured Master of Sport, like most of the top-flight sportsmen. He has masterly ball-control and prefers the attacking side of his game.

In goal is Lev Yashin, nicknamed "the Black Octopus" because he wears an all-black kit. Tall and willowy, he has an enormous reach and does not hesitate to leave the penalty area if he can cut off a pass. He plays for Dynamo.

SPAIN.

The outstanding club side of Europe is Real (Royal) Madrid of Spain. They won the European Cup for the first four years of its inception. They play in the Chamartin Stadium, which holds 120,000 spectators in three huge tiers, built steeply up from the pitch. They import players from abroad in order to maintain the standard, and the quality of the national side is below that of Real. Barcelona used to offer the chief rivalry to Madrid as the country's soccer centre, but the biggest challenge nowadays comes from the north-west, where the rainy weather and heavy grounds have produced an English-style game. The best club here is Bilbao.

Real's oustanding player is centre forward Alfredo di Stefano. He is probably the highest-paid footballer in the world. An uncanny control of the ball makes him very hard to tackle and he is a shrewd general. He was born in Argentina and started with River Plate. After a spell in Bogota he was transferred to Barcelona and later to Real. He is nicknamed "the White Arrow".

Stefano was Europe's Footballer of the Year in 1957 and he was succeeded in 1958 by his clubmate Raymond Kopa. Kopa is a Frenchman of Polish extraction and he was the most brilliant forward in the 1958 World Cup. He is at his best at centre forward and plays on the right wing for Real. Although on the small side, he is strongly built.

SWEDEN.

The drain of leading players to professionalism abroad, especially Italy, lowered the standard of football in Sweden. They brought several professionals back to reach the Final of the World Cup in Sweden. Owing to the severe winter, football is virtually a summer game and the big centres are in the milder areas of the south. The leading club is A.I.K. of Stockholm. One supporter is so keen that he named his four children with Christian names beginning with the initials A, I and K. A little further north is Norrkoping, which produced the four Nordahl brothers. Three of them played against England in 1949. Well in the hunt for the championship every year is Malmo from the southern tip.

Their outstanding player in the World Cup was dashing fair-haired outside right Kurt Hamrin. He was released by Juventus of Italy and has since been transferred to Fiorentina. Confident to the point of cheekiness, he has the ability to score goals as well as to disrupt defences.

URUGUAY.

Uruguay may not have a big population but they have won the World Cup twice, in 1930 and 1950. They also won the Olympic title twice. One of the sensational results of the 1958 Cup preliminaries was the elimination of Uruguay by Paraguay by 5–0. Paraguay failed to live up to expectations in Sweden. The chief centre for football in Uruguay is Montevideo and there are only 14 first-class teams.

After the 1954 World Cup their fine inside forward Juan Schiaffino was transferred to Milan of Italy. A graceful and subtle player, he is not strongly made and has to rely on skill. That he has in abundance. He was reported to receive £30,000 himself out of the transfer. By a curious twist of the rules made by the Italians, Schiaffino played for Italy. After three international games he was declared an Italian citizen.

YUGOSLAVIA.

Football clubs in Yugoslavia were re-formed after the war and bear names honouring war organisations, like Red Star and Partisan. Despite the small size, Yugoslavia are one of the most powerful sides in the world and won the silver medals at the last three Olympic Games. In the five meetings with England they won three and lost two. They defeated England 5–0 in Belgrade in 1958.

Goalkeeper Vladimir Beara is a former ballet dancer and, as might be expected, is acrobatic and spectacular. He represented the Rest of the World against England in 1953. He has played for Yugoslavia over 60 times and his club is Red Star of Belgrade.

Inside forward Dragoslav Sekularac—also Red Star—is only 20 and has a big future. He is of Serbian extraction, small in stature and has closely-cropped dark hair.

Helmut Rahn (Germany) — Ferenc Puskas (Hungary) — Alfredo di Stefano (Spain) — Kurt Hamrin (Sweden) — Vladimir Beara (Yugoslavia)

SOCCER QUIZ

1. When did the British countries rejoin F.I.F.A.?

★

2. When was extra time needed in a Wembley Final?

★

3. Which was the last Second Division club to win the Cup?

★

4. Which was the last Second Division club in the Final?

★

5. What are the greatest number of consecutive ties without defeat?

★

6. Which English club made the most draws in a season?

QUIZ ANSWERS

1 1946. 2. 1947, 1946 and 1938. 3. West Bromwich in 1931. 4. Leicester in 1949. 5. 24 by Blackburn Rovers in 1883–6. 6. Plymouth, 21 in 1920–1.

Compiled by **Norris McWhirter**

Athletics Correspondent: The Observer
and B.B.C. Television Commentator

Athletics

A BRIEF HISTORY

Track and field athletics originated in Greece with the ancient Olympic Games, whose earliest origins go back to the thirteenth century B.C.

The earliest individual name of an Olympic athlete which has come down to us is that of Coroebas, who won a foot race in July 776 B.C. The races were run over a distance of one *stade* (192 metres), hence the modern word stadium.

The only measurement of a field event which has survived is a long jump of 23 ft. 1½ ins. by Chionis of Sparta made in c. 656 B.C.

With the abolition of the Olympic Games by Emperor Theodosius in his Milan edict of A.D. 393, athletics suffered centuries of neglect.

The sports revival was cradled in England and meetings as early as c. 1810 are known to have taken place at the Royal Military Academy, Sandhurst.

Athletics began at Cambridge in 1857 and at Oxford in 1860. The Amateur Athletic Association was founded in 1880 and the International Amateur Athletic Federation (I.A.A.F.) was formed in 1913 and now has 89 affiliated countries.

E. L. Page (*far right*) wins the 100 yds. A.A.A. Championships, Stamford Bridge, 1931

PROGRESSIVE WORLD RECORDS

100 YARDS—MEN

Time	Name	Country	Date	Place
9.6	D. J. KELLY	U.S.A.	23.6.1906	Spokane, Wash., U.S.A.
9.6	H. P. DREW	U.S.A.	28.3.1914	Berkeley, Cal., U.S.A.
9.6	C. W. PADDOCK	U.S.A.	26.3.1921	Berkeley, Cal., U.S.A.
9.6	C. W. PADDOCK	U.S.A.	23.4.1921	Redlands, Cal., U.S.A.
9.6	C. W. PADDOCK	U.S.A.	18.6.1921	Pasadena, Cal., U.S.A.
9.6	C. W. PADDOCK	U.S.A.	4.7.1921	Pasadena, Cal., U.S.A.
9.6	C. H. COAFFEE	Canada	12.8.1922	Hamilton, Canada
9.6	C. W. PADDOCK	U.S.A.	6.9.1924	Los Angeles, Cal., U.S.A.
9.6	C. W. PADDOCK	U.S.A.	15.5.1926	Los Angeles, Cal., U.S.A.
9.6	DE HART HUBBARD	U.S.A.	5.6.1926	Cincinnati, Ohio, U.S.A.
9.6	C. BOWMAN	U.S.A.	2.7.1927	Lincoln, Neb., U.S.A.
9.5	T. E. TOLAN	U.S.A.	25.5.1929	Evanston, Ill., U.S.A.
9.4	F. C. WYKOFF	U.S.A.	10.5.1930	Los Angeles, Cal., U.S.A.
9.4*	D. J. JOUBERT	S. Africa	16.5.1931	Grahamstown, S. Africa
9.4	J. C. OWENS	U.S.A.	25.5.1935	Ann Arbor, Mich., U.S.A.
9.4	J. C. OWENS	U.S.A.	20.6.1936	Chicago, Ill., U.S.A.
9.4	C. H. JEFFREY	U.S.A.	16.3.1940	Long Beach, Cal., U.S.A.
9.4	M. E. PATTON	U.S.A.	24.5.1947	Los Angeles, Cal., U.S.A.
9.3	M. E. PATTON	U.S.A.	15.5.1948	Fresno, Cal., U.S.A.
9.3*	H. D. HOGAN	Australia	13.3.1954	Sydney, Australia
9.3	J. J. GOLLIDAY	U.S.A.	14.5.1955	Evanston, Ill., U.S.A.
9.3	L. KING	U.S.A.	12.5.1956	Fresno, Cal., U.S.A.
9.3	D. W. SIME	U.S.A.	19.5.1956	Raleigh, N. Car., U.S.A.
9.3	D. W. SIME	U.S.A.	9.6.1956	Sanger, Cal., U.S.A.
9.3	D. W. SIME	U.S.A.	18.5.1957	Raleigh, N. Car., U.S.A.
9.3	B. J. MORROW	U.S.A.	14.6.1957	Austin, Texas, U.S.A.
9.3	R. NORTON	U.S.A.	12.4.1958	San Jose, Cal., U.S.A.

* Made on a grass track.

100 METRES WORLD RECORDS—MEN

Time	Name	Country	Date	Place
10.6	D. F. LIPPINCOTT	U.S.A.	6.7.1912	Stockholm, Sweden
10.6	J. V. SCHOLZ	U.S.A.	6.9.1920	Stockholm, Sweden
10.4	C. W. PADDOCK	U.S.A.	23.4.1921	Redlands, Cal., U.S.A.
10.4	T. E. TOLAN	U.S.A.	8.8.1929	Stockholm, Sweden
10.4	T. E. TOLAN	U.S.A.	25.9.1929	Copenhagen, Denmark
10.3	P. WILLIAMS	Canada	9.8.1930	Toronto, Canada
10.3	T. E. TOLAN	U.S.A.	1.8.1932	Los Angeles, Cal., U.S.A.
10.3	R. H. METCALFE	U.S.A.	12.8.1933	Budapest, Hungary
10.3	E. PEACOCK	U.S.A.	6.8.1934	Oslo, Norway
10.3	C. D. BERGER	Netherlands	26.8.1934	Amsterdam, Netherlands
10.3	R. H. METCALFE	U.S.A.	15.9.1934	Osaka, Japan
10.3	R. H. METCALFE	U.S.A.	23.9.1934	Dairen, Manchuria
10.3	R. YOSHIOKA	Japan	15.6.1935	Tokyo, Japan
10.2	J. C. OWENS	U.S.A.	20.6.1936	Chicago, Ill., U.S.A.
10.2	H. DAVIS	U.S.A.	6.6.1941	Compton, Cal., U.S.A.
10.2	L. B. LA BEACH	Panama	15.5.1948	Fresno, Cal., U.S.A.
10.2	N. H. EWELL	U.S.A.	9.7.1948	Evanston, Ill., U.S.A.
10.2	E. McD. BAILEY	G.B. and N.I.	25.8.1951	Belgrade, Yugoslavia
10.2	H. FUTTERER	Germany	31.10.1954	Yokohama, Japan
10.2	B. J. MORROW	U.S.A.	19.5.1956	Houston, Texas, U.S.A.
10.2	I. J. MURCHISON	U.S.A.	1.6.1956	Compton, Cal., U.S.A.
10.2	B. J. MORROW	U.S.A.	22.6.1956	Bakersfield, Cal., U.S.A.
10.2	I. J. MURCHISON	U.S.A.	29.6.1956	Los Angeles, Cal., U.S.A.
10.2	B. J. MORROW	U.S.A.	29.6.1956	Los Angeles, Cal., U.S.A.
10.1	W. J. WILLIAMS	U.S.A.	3.8.1956	Berlin, Germany
10.1	I. J. MURCHISON	U.S.A.	4.8.1956	Berlin, Germany
10.1	L. KING	U.S.A.	20.10.1956	Ontario, Cal., U.S.A.
10.1	L. KING	U.S.A.	27.10.1956	Santa Ana, Cal., U.S.A.

200 METRES WORLD RECORDS—MEN

Time	Name	Country	Date	Place
21.6	A. HAHN	U.S.A.	31.8.1904	St. Louis, Mo., U.S.A.
20.8	C. W. PADDOCK	U.S.A.	26.3.1921	Berkeley, Cal., U.S.A.
20.8	C. W. PADDOCK	U.S.A.	6.9.1924	Los Angeles, Cal., U.S.A.
20.6	R. A. LOCKE	U.S.A.	1.5.1926	Lincoln, Neb., U.S.A.
20.6	R. H. METCALFE	U.S.A.	12.8.1933	Budapest, Hungary
20.3	J. C. OWENS	U.S.A.	25.5.1935	Ann Arbor, Mich., U.S.A.
20.2	M. E. PATTON	U.S.A.	7.5.1949	Los Angeles, Cal., U.S.A.
20.1	D. W. SIME	U.S.A.	11.5.1956	Durham, N. Car., U.S.A.
20.0	D. W. SIME	U.S.A.	9.6.1956	Sanger, Cal., U.S.A.

ATHLETICS QUIZ

1. Which athlete has won the record number of A.A.A. Championships? (*below*)

2. Who was the first man to beat 190 feet with a discus throw?

★

3. Name the Olympic decathlon champion who was subsequently disqualified for professionalism?

★

4. Name the only man to have won an Olympic track title on a walk-over.

QUIZ ANSWERS

1. E. McDonald Bailey (Trinidad) with fourteen 100 and 220 yards titles and two relay titles between 1946 and 1953. 2. S. G. Iness (U.S.A.) in Nebraska in 1953. 3. James Thorpe (U.S.A.), winner of the 1912 Olympic decathlon. 4. Lt. Wyndham Halswelle in the 1908 Olympic 400 metres.

Gordon Pirie (*left*)
M. Szabo (*Hungary*) (*right*)

Roger Bannister running the first under 4 minute mile.

J. E. Lovelock   S. Jungwirth (Czech.)   Ron Delany (Eire)

880 YARDS WORLD RECORDS—MEN

Time	Name	Country	Date	Place
1:52.5	J. E. MEREDITH	U.S.A.	8.7.1912	Stockholm, Sweden
1:52.2	J. E. MEREDITH	U.S.A.	13.5.1916	Philadelphia, Pa., U.S.A.
1:51.6	O. PELTZER	Germany	3.7.1926	London, England
1:50.9	B. EASTMAN	U.S.A.	4.6.1932	San Francisco, U.S.A.
1:49.8	B. EASTMAN	U.S.A.	16.6.1934	Princeton, N.J., U.S.A.
1:49.6	E. ROBINSON	U.S.A.	11.7.1937	Randall's Is., N.Y., U.S.A.
1:49.2	S. C. WOODERSON	G.B. and N.I.	20.8.1938	Motspur Pk., Surrey, England
1:49.2	M. G. WHITFIELD	U.S.A.	19.8.1950	Berea, Ohio, U.S.A.
1:48.6	M. G. WHITFIELD	U.S.A.	17.7.1953	Turku, Finland
1:48.6	N. G. NIELSEN	Denmark	30.9.1954	Copenhagen, Denmark
1:47.5	L. V. SPURRIER	U.S.A.	26.3.1955	Berkeley, Cal., U.S.A.
1:46.8	T. W. COURTNEY	U.S.A.	24.5.1957	Los Angeles, Cal., U.S.A.

1,000 METRES WORLD RECORDS—MEN

Time	Name	Country	Date	Place
2:32.3	G. MICKLER	Germany	22.6.1913	Hanover, Germany
2:29.1	A. BOLIN	Sweden	22.9.1918	Stockholm, Sweden
2:28.6	S. LUNDGREN	Sweden	12.9.1922	Stockholm, Sweden
2:26.8	S. MARTIN	France	30.9.1926	Paris, France
2:25.8	O. PELTZER	Germany	18.9.1927	Paris, France
2:23.6	J. LADOUMEGUE	France	19.10.1930	Paris, France
2:21.5	R. HARBIG	Germany	24.5.1941	Dresden, Germany
2:21.4	O. R. GUSTAFSSEN	Sweden	4.9.1946	Boras, Sweden
2:21.4	M. HANSENNE	France	27.8.1948	Gothenburg, Sweden
2:21.3	O. W. ABERG	Sweden	10.8.1952	Copenhagen, Denmark
2:21.2	S. JUNGWIRTH	Czecho-slovakia	27.10.1952	Stará Boleslav, Czechoslovakia
2:20.8	M. G. WHITFIELD	U.S.A.	16.8.1953	Eskilstuna, Sweden
2:20.4	A. BOYSEN	Norway	17.9.1953	Oslo, Norway
2:19.5	A. BOYSEN	Norway	18.8.1954	Gavle, Sweden
2:19.0	A. BOYSEN	Norway	30.8.1955	Gothenburg, Sweden
2:19.0	I. ROZSAVÖLGYI	Hungary	21.9.1955	Tata, Hungary
2:18.1	D. WAERN	Sweden	19.9.1958	Turku, Finland

220 YARDS WORLD RECORDS—MEN

Time	Name	Country	Date	Place
21.2	B. J. WEFERS	U.S.A.	13.6.1896	Travers Is., N.Y., U.S.A.
21.2	R. C. CRAIG	U.S.A.	28.5.1910	Philadelphia, Pa., U.S.A.
21.2	D. F. LIPPINCOTT	U.S.A.	31.5.1913	Cambridge, Mass., U.S.A.
21.2	H. P. DREW	U.S.A.	28.2.1914	Claremont, Cal., U.S.A.
21.2*	W. R. APPLEGARTH	G.B. and N.I.	4.7.1914	London, England
21.2	G. PARKER	U.S.A.	2.10.1914	Fresno, Cal., U.S.A.
20.8	C. W. PADDOCK	U.S.A.	26.3.1921	Berkeley, Cal., U.S.A.
20.8	C. W. PADDOCK	U.S.A.	6.9.1924	Los Angeles, Cal., U.S.A.
20.6	R. A. LOCKE	U.S.A.	1.5.1926	Lincoln, Neb., U.S.A.
20.3	J. C. OWENS	U.S.A.	25.5.1935	Ann Arbor, Mich., U.S.A.
20.2	M. E. PATTON	U.S.A.	7.5.1949	Los Angeles, Cal., U.S.A.
20.1	D. W. SIME	U.S.A.	11.5.1956	Durham, N. Car., U.S.A.
20.0	D. W. SIME	U.S.A.	9.6.1956	Sanger, Cal., U.S.A.

* Made round a turn, banked track.

1,500 METRES WORLD RECORDS—MEN

Time	Name	Country	Date	Place
3:55.8	A. R. KIVIAT	U.S.A.	8.6.1912	Cambridge, Mass., U.S.A.
3:54.7	J. ZANDER	Sweden	5.8.1917	Stockholm, Sweden
3:52.6	P. NURMI	Finland	19.6.1924	Helsinki, Finland
3:51.0	O. PELTZER	Germany	11.9.1926	Charlottenburg, Germany
3:49.2	J. LADOUMEGUE	France	5.10.1930	Paris, France
3:49.0	L. BECCALI	Italy	9.9.1933	Turin, Italy
3:49.0	L. BECCALI	Italy	17.9.1933	Milan, Italy
3:48.8	W. R. BONTHRON	U.S.A.	30.6.1934	Milwaukee, Wis., U.S.A.
3:47.8	J. E. LOVELOCK	N. Zealand	6.8.1936	Berlin, Germany
3:47.6	G. HÄGG	Sweden	10.8.1941	Stockholm, Sweden
3:45.8	G. HÄGG	Sweden	17.7.1942	Stockholm, Sweden
3:45.0	A. ANDERSSON	Sweden	17.8.1943	Gothenburg, Sweden
3:43.0	L. STRAND	Sweden	16.7.1947	Malmö, Sweden
3:43.0	W. LUEG	Germany	29.6.1952	Berlin, Germany
3:42.8	W. SANTEE	U.S.A.	4.6.1954	Compton, Cal., U.S.A.
3:41.8	J. M. LANDY	Australia	21.6.1954	Turku, Finland
3:40.8	S. IHAROS	Hungary	28.7.1955	Helsinki, Finland
3:40.8	L. TABORI	Hungary	6.9.1955	Oslo, Norway
3:40.8	N. G. NIELSEN	Denmark	6.9.1955	Oslo, Norway
3:40.6	I. ROZSAVÖLGYI	Hungary	3.8.1956	Tata, Hungary
3:40.2	O. SALSOLA	Finland	11.7.1957	Turku, Finland
3:40.2	O. SALONEN	Finland	11.7.1957	Turku, Finland
3:38.1	S. JUNGWIRTH	Czecho-slovakia	12.7.1957	Stará Boleslav, Czechoslovakia

400 METRES WORLD RECORDS—MEN

Time	Name	Country	Date	Place
48.2	C. D. REIDPATH	U.S.A.	13.7.1912	Stockholm, Sweden
47.4*	J. E. MEREDITH	U.S.A.	27.5.1916	Cambridge, Mass., U.S.A.
47.0	E. SPENCER	U.S.A.	12.5.1928	Palo Alto, Cal., U.S.A.
46.4	B. B. EASTMAN	U.S.A.	26.3.1932	Stanford, Cal., U.S.A.
46.2	W. A. CARR	U.S.A.	5.8.1932	Los Angeles, Cal., U.S.A.
46.1	A. F. WILLIAMS	U.S.A.	19.6.1936	Chicago, Ill., U.S.A.
46.0	R. HARBIG	Germany	12.8.1939	Frankfurt am Main, Germany
46.0	G. KLEMMER	U.S.A.	29.6.1941	Philadelphia, Pa., U.S.A.
46.0*	H. H. McKENLEY	Jamaica	5.6.1948	Berkeley, Cal., U.S.A.
45.9	H. H. McKENLEY	Jamaica	2.7.1948	Milwaukee, U.S.A.
45.8	V. G. RHODEN	Jamaica	22.8.1950	Eskilstuna, Sweden
45.4	L. W. JONES	U.S.A.	18.3.1955	Mexico City, Mexico
45.2	L. W. JONES	U.S.A.	30.6.1956	Los Angeles, Cal., U.S.A.

* Ran 440 yards (402.34 metres).

440 YARDS WORLD RECORDS—MEN

Time	Name	Country	Date	Place
47.8	M. W. LONG	U.S.A.	29.9.1900	Guttenburg, N.J., U.S.A.
47.4	J. E. MEREDITH	U.S.A.	27.5.1916	Cambridge, Mass., U.S.A.
47.4	B. B. EASTMAN	U.S.A.	16.5.1931	Palo Alto, Cal., U.S.A.
47.4	V. E. WILLIAMS	U.S.A.	30.5.1931	Philadelphia, Pa., U.S.A.
46.4	B. B. EASTMAN	U.S.A.	26.3.1932	Stanford, Cal., U.S.A.
46.4	G. KLEMMER	U.S.A.	31.5.1941	Berkeley, Cal., U.S.A.
46.3	H. H. McKENLEY	Jamaica	28.6.1947	Berkeley, Cal., U.S.A.
46.0	H. H. McKENLEY	Jamaica	5.6.1948	Berkeley, Cal., U.S.A.
45.8	J. G. LEA	U.S.A.	26.5.1956	Modesto, Cal., U.S.A.
45.8	G. A. DAVIS	U.S.A.	24.5.1958	Lafayette, Indiana, U.S.A.
45.7	G. A. DAVIS	U.S.A.	14.6.1958	Berkeley, Cal., U.S.A.

1 MILE WORLD RECORDS—MEN

Time	Name	Country	Date	Place
4:14.4	J. P. JONES	U.S.A.	31.5.1913	Cambridge, Mass., U.S.A.
4:12.6	N. S. TABER	U.S.A.	16.7.1915	Cambridge, Mass., U.S.A.
4:10.4	P. NURMI	Finland	23.8.1923	Stockholm, Sweden
4:09.2	J. LADOUMEGUE	France	4.10.1931	Paris, France
4:07.6	J. E. LOVELOCK	N. Zealand	15.7.1933	Princeton, N.J., U.S.A.
4:06.8	G. CUNNINGHAM	U.S.A.	16.6.1934	Princeton, N.J., U.S.A.
4:06.4	S. C. WOODERSON	G.B. and N.I.	28.8.1937	Motspur Pk., Surrey, England
4:06.2	G. HÄGG	Sweden	1.7.1942	Gothenburg, Sweden
4:06.2	A. ANDERSSON	Sweden	10.7.1942	Stockholm, Sweden
4:04.6	G. HÄGG	Sweden	4.9.1942	Stockholm, Sweden
4:02.6	A. ANDERSSON	Sweden	1.7.1943	Gothenburg, Sweden
4:01.6	A. ANDERSSON	Sweden	18.7.1944	Malmö, Sweden
4:01.4	G. HÄGG	Sweden	17.7.1945	Malmö, Sweden
3:59.4	R. G. BANNISTER	G.B. and N.I.	6.5.1954	Oxford, England
3:58.0	J. M. LANDY	Australia	21.6.1954	Turku, Finland
3:57.2	G. D. IBBOTSON	G.B. and N.I.	19.7.1957	London, England
3:54.5	H. J. ELLIOTT	Australia	6.8.1958	Dublin, Eire

800 METRES WORLD RECORDS—MEN

Time	Name	Country	Date	Place
1:51.9	J. E. MEREDITH	U.S.A.	8.7.1912	Stockholm, Sweden
1:51.6	O. PELTZER	Germany	3.7.1926	London, England
1:50.6	S. MARTIN	France	14.7.1928	Paris, France
1:49.8	T. HAMPSON	G.B. and N.I.	2.8.1932	Los Angeles, Cal., U.S.A.
1:49.8	B. B. EASTMAN	U.S.A.	16.6.1934	Princeton, N.J., U.S.A.
1:49.7	G. CUNNINGHAM	U.S.A.	20.8.1936	Stockholm, Sweden
1:49.6	E. ROBINSON	U.S.A.	11.7.1937	Randall's Is., N.Y., U.S.A.
1:48.4	S. C. WOODERSON	G.B. and N.I.	20.8.1938	Motspur Pk., Surrey, England
1:46.6	R. HARBIG	Germany	15.7.1939	Milan, Italy
1:45.7	R. MOENS	Belgium	3.8.1955	Oslo, Norway

ATHLETICS QUIZ

1. How many times do a marathon runner's feet hit the ground in the course of a race?

    *

2. What do the initials I.A.A.F. stand for, and when was it founded?

3. What was the distance of the longest race ever recorded in athletic history?

QUIZ ANSWERS

1. About 27,500 times. 2. International Amateur Athletic Federation, founded in 1913. 3. 3,610 miles from New York to Los Angeles, March 21st–June 16th, 1929.

Emil Zatopek

Sydney Wooderson

Herb Elliott

2,000 METRES WORLD RECORDS—MEN

Time	Name	Country	Date	Place
5:30.4	J. ZANDER	Sweden	16.6.1918	Stockholm, Sweden
5:26.3	P. NURMI	Finland	4.9.1922	Tampere, Finland
5:26.0	E. WIDE	Sweden	11.6.1925	Stockholm, Sweden
5:24.6	P. NURMI	Finland	18.6.1927	Kuopio, Finland
5:23.4	P. BORG	Finland	9.8.1927	Viipuri, Finland
5:21.8	J. LADOUMEGUE	France	2.7.1931	Paris, France
5:20.4	M. SZABO	Hungary	4.10.1936	Budapest, Hungary
5:18.4	H. JONSSON	Sweden	2.7.1937	Stockholm, Sweden
5:16.8	A. J. SAN ROMANI	U.S.A.	26.8.1937	Helsinki, Finland
5:16.4	G. HÄGG	Sweden	21.7.1942	Malmö, Sweden
5:11.8	G. HÄGG	Sweden	23.8.1942	Östersund, Sweden
5:07.0	G. E. G. REIFF	Belgium	29.9.1948	Brussels, Belgium
5:02.2	I. ROZSAVÖLGYI	Hungary	2.10.1955	Budapest, Hungary

3,000 METRES WORLD RECORDS—MEN

Time	Name	Country	Date	Place
8:36.8	H. KOLEHMAINEN	Finland	12.7.1912	Stockholm, Sweden
8:33.2	J. ZANDER	Sweden	7.8.1918	Stockholm, Sweden
8:28.6	P. NURMI	Finland	27.8.1922	Turku, Finland
8:27.6	E. WIDE	Sweden	7.6.1925	Halmstad, Sweden
8:25.4	P. NURMI	Finland	24.5.1926	Berlin, Germany
8:20.4	P. NURMI	Finland	13.7.1926	Stockholm, Sweden
8:18.8	J. KUSOCINSKI	Poland	19.6.1932	Antwerp, Belgium
8:18.4	H. NIELSEN	Denmark	24.7.1934	Stockholm, Sweden
8:14.8	G. HÖCKERT	Finland	16.9.1936	Stockholm, Sweden
8:09.0	H. KÄLARNE	Sweden	14.8.1940	Stockholm, Sweden
8:01.2	G. HÄGG	Sweden	28.8.1942	Stockholm, Sweden
7:58.8	G. E. G. REIFF	Belgium	12.8.1949	Gävle, Sweden
7:55.6	S. IHAROS	Hungary	14.5.1955	Budapest
7:55.6	D. A. G. PIRIE	G.B. and N.I.	22.6.1956	Trondheim, Norway
7:52.8	D. A. G. PIRIE	G.B. and N.I.	4.9.1956	Malmö, Sweden

2 MILES WORLD RECORDS—MEN

Time	Name	Country	Date	Place
9:09.6	A. E. SHRUBB	G.B. and N.I.	11.6.1904	Glasgow, Scotland
9:01.4	E. WIDE	Sweden	12.9.1926	Charlottenburg, Germany
8:59.6	P. NURMI	Finland	24.7.1931	Helsinki, Finland
8:58.4	D. R. LASH	U.S.A.	13.6.1936	Princeton, N.J., U.S.A.
8:57.4	G. HÖCKERT	Finland	24.9.1936	Stockholm, Sweden
8:56.0	M. SZABO	Hungary	30.9.1937	Budapest, Hungary
8:53.2	T. A. MAKI	Finland	7.7.1939	Helsinki, Finland
8:47.8	G. HÄGG	Sweden	3.7.1942	Stockholm, Sweden
8:46.4	G. HÄGG	Sweden	25.6.1944	Östersund, Sweden
8:42.8	G. HÄGG	Sweden	4.8.1944	Stockholm, Sweden
8:40.4	G. E. G. REIFF	Belgium	26.8.1952	Paris, France
8:33.4	S. IHAROS	Hungary	30.5.1955	London, England
8:32.0	A. G. THOMAS	Australia	7.8.1958	Dublin, Eire

Diane Leather   S. Iharos   Valerie Ball-Winn

3 MILES WORLD RECORDS—MEN

Time	Name	Country	Date	Place
14:17.6	A. E. SHRUBB	G.B. and N.I.	21.5.1903	London, England
14:11.2	P. NURMI	Finland	24.8.1923	Stockholm, Sweden
13:50.6	L. A. LEHTINEN	Finland	19.6.1932	Helsinki, Finland
13:42.4	T. A. MÄKI	Finland	16.6.1939	Helsinki, Finland
13:35.4	G. HÄGG	Sweden	11.9.1942	Stockholm, Sweden
13:32.4	G. HÄGG	Sweden	20.9.1942	Gothenburg, Sweden
13:32.2	F. GREEN	G.B. and N.I.	10.7.1954	London, England
13:32.2	C. J. CHATAWAY	G.B. and N.I.	10.7.1954	London, England
13:27.4	V. P. KUTS	U.S.S.R.	29.8.1954	Berne, Switzerland
13:27.0	V. P. KUTS	U.S.S.R.	13.10.1954	London, England
13:26.4	V. P. KUTS	U.S.S.R.	23.10.1954	Prague, Czechoslovakia
13:23.2	C. J. CHATAWAY	G.B. and N.I.	30.7.1955	London, England
13:14.2	S. IHAROS	Hungary	23.10.1955	Budapest, Hungary
13:10.8	A. G. THOMAS	Australia	9.7.1958	Dublin, Eire

5,000 METRES WORLD RECORDS—MEN

Time	Name	Country	Date	Place
14:36.6	H. KOLEHMAINEN	Finland	10.7.1912	Stockholm, Sweden
14:35.4	P. NURMI	Finland	12.9.1922	Stockholm, Sweden
14:28.2	P. NURMI	Finland	19.6.1924	Helsinki, Finland
14:17.0	L. LEHTINEN	Finland	19.6.1932	Helsinki, Finland
14:08.8	T. A. MÄKI	Finland	16.6.1939	Helsinki, Finland
13:58.2	G HÄGG	Sweden	20.9.1942	Gothenburg, Sweden
13:57.2	E. ZATOPEK	Czechoslovakia	30.5.1954	Paris, France
13:56.6	V. P. KUTS	U.S.S.R.	29.8.1954	Berne, Switzerland
13:51.6	C. J. CHATAWAY	G.B. and N.I.	13.10.1954	London, England
13:51.2	V. P. KUTS	U.S.S.R.	23.10.1954	Prague, Czecho-slovakia
13:50.8	S. IHAROS	Hungary	10.9.1955	Budapest, Hungary
13:46.8	V. P. KUTS	U.S.S.R.	18.9.1955	Belgrade, Yugoslavia
13:40.6	S. IHAROS	Hungary	23.10.1955	Budapest, Hungary
13:36.8	D. A. G. PIRIE	G.B. and N.I.	19.6.1956	Bergen, Norway
13:35.0	V. P. KUTS	U.S.S.R.	13.10.1957	Rome, Italy

Thelma Hopkins

6 MILES WORLD RECORDS—MEN

Time	Name	Country	Date	Plac
29:59.4	A. E. SHRUBB	G.B. and N.I.	5.11.1904	Glasgow, Scotland
29:36.4	P. NURMI	Finland	9.6.1930	London, England
29:08.4	I. SALMINEN	Finland	18.7.1937	Kouvola, Finland
28:55.6	T. A. MÄKI	Finland	17.9.1939	Helsinki, Finland
28:38.6	V. A. HEINO	Finland	25.8.1944	Helsinki, Finland
28:30.8	V. A. HEINO	Finland	1.9.1949	Kouvola, Finland
28:19.4	D. A. G. PIRIE	G.B. and N.I.	10.7.1953	London, England
28:08.4	E. ZATOPEK	Czechoslovakia	1.11.1953	Stará Boleslav, Czechoslovakia
27:59.2	E. ZATOPEK	Czechoslovakia	1.6.1954	Brussels, Belgium
27:54.0	D. J. STEPHENS	Australia	25.1.1956	Melbourne, Australia
27:43.8	S. IHAROS	Hungary	15.7.1956	Budapest, Hungary

10,000 METRES WORLD RECORDS—MEN

Time	Name	Country	Date	Place
30:58.8	J. BOUIN	France	16.11.1911	Paris, France
30:40.2	P. NURMI	Finland	22.6.1921	Stockholm, Sweden
30:35.4	V. RITOLA	Finland	25.5.1924	Helsinki, Finland
30:23.2	V. RITOLA	Finland	6.7.1924	Paris, France
30:06.2	P. NURMI	Finland	31.8.1924	Kuopi, Finland
30:05.6	I. SALMINEN	Finland	18.7.1937	Kuovola, Finland
30:02.0	T. A. MÄKI	Finland	29.9.1938	Tampere, Finland
29:52.6	T. A. MÄKI	Finland	17.9.1939	Helsinki, Finland
29:35.4	V. A. HEINO	Finland	25.8.1944	Helsinki, Finland
29:28.2	E. ZATOPEK	Czechoslovakia	11.6.1949	Ostrava, Czechoslovakia
29:27.2	V. A. HEINO	Finland	1.9.1949	Kouvola, Finland
29:21.2	E. ZATOPEK	Czechoslovakia	22.10.1949	Ostrava, Czechoslovakia
29:02.6	E. ZATOPEK	Czechoslovakia	4.8.1950	Turku, Finland
29:01.6	E. ZATOPEK	Czechoslovakia	1.11.1953	Stará Boleslav, Czechoslovakia
28:54.2	E. ZATOPEK	Czechoslovakia	1.6.1954	Brussels, Belgium
28:42.8	S. IHAROS	Hungary	15.7.1956	Budapest, Hungary
28:30.4	V. P. KUTS	U.S.S.R.	11.9.1956	Moscow, U.S.S.R.

10 MILES WORLD RECORDS—MEN

Time	Name	Country	Date	Place
50:40.6	A. E. SHRUBB	G.B. and N.I.	5.11.1904	Glasgow, Scotland
50:15.0	P. NURMI	Finland	7.10.1928	Berlin, Germany
49:41.6	V. A. HEINO	Finland	30.9.1945	Turku, Finland
49:22.2	V. A. HEINO	Finland	14.9.1946	Helsinki, Finland
46:12.0	E. ZATOPEK	Czechoslovakia	29.9.1951	Stará Boleslav, Czechoslovakia

1 HOUR RUNNING WORLD RECORDS—MEN

Mls.	Yds.	Name	Country	Date	Place
11	1,137	A. E. SHRUBB	G.B. and N.I.	5.11.1904	Glasgow, Scotland
11	1,442	J. BOUIN	France	6.7.1913	Stockholm, Sweden
11	1,648	P. NURMI	Finland	7.10.1928	Berlin, Germany
12	29	V. A. HEINO	Finland	30.9.1945	Turku, Finland
12	269	E. ZATOPEK	Czechoslovakia	15.9.1951	Prague, Czechoslovakia
12	809	E. ZATOPEK	Czechoslovakia	29.9.1951	Stará Boleslav, Czechoslovakia

ATHLETICS QUIZ

1. Where were organised amateur athletics first recorded in England?

★

2. What is the fastest time ever recorded for a 100 yards with a flying start?

QUIZ ANSWERS

1. At the Royal Military College, Sandhurst, about 1810. 2. 8.3 secs. in 1949 by Melvin Patton (U.S.A.) and in 1956 by Bobby-Joe Morrow (U.S.A.).

20,000 METRES WORLD RECORDS—MEN

Time	Name	Country	Date	Place
1:7:40.2	T. KOLEHMAINEN	Finland	18.5.1913	Helsinki, Finland
1:7:11.2	A. O. STENROOS	Finland	9.9.1923	Helsinki, Finland
1:7:07.2	V. KYRÖNEN	Finland	31.8.1924	Hamina, Finland
1:6:29.0	V. J. SIPILA	Finland	19.6.1925	Stockholm, Sweden
1:4:38.4	P. NURMI	Finland	13.9.1930	Stockholm, Sweden
1:4:00.2	J. C. ZABALA	Argentine	19.4.1936	Munich, Germany
1:3:01.2	A. CSAPLAR	Hungary	26.10.1941	Budapest, Hungary
1:2:40.0	V. A. HEINO	Finland	22.9.1949	Turku, Finland
1:1:15.8	E. ZATOPEK	Czechoslovakia	15.9.1951	Prague, Czechoslovakia
59:51.8	E. ZATOPEK	Czechoslovakia	29.9.1951	Stará Boleslav, Czechoslovakia

15 MILES WORLD RECORDS—MEN

Time	Name	Country	Date	Place
1:20:04.4	F. APPLEBY	G.B. and N.I.	21.7.1902	London, England
1:19:48.6	E. J. TAMILA	Finland	29.8.1937	Joensuu, Finland
1:18:48.0	M. HIETANEN	Finland	20.8.1947	Kuopio, Finland
1:17:28.6	M. HIETANEN	Finland	23.5.1948	Gamlakarleby, Finland
1:16:26.4	E. ZATOPEK	Czechoslovakia	26.10.1952	Stará Boleslav, Czechoslovakia
1:14:01.0	E. ZATOPEK	Czechoslovakia	29.10.1955	Celakovice, Czechoslovkaia

25,000 METRES WORLD RECORDS—MEN

Time	Name	Country	Date	Place
1:26:29.6	H. KOLEHMAINEN	Finland	10.10.1920	Tampere, Finland
1:25:19.6	H. KOLEHMAINEN	Finland	22.6.1922	Tampere, Finland
1:24:24.0	M. MARTTELIN	Finland	16.9.1928	Tampere, Finland
1:23:45.8	E. HARPER	G.B. and N.I.	25.8.1929	Berlin, Germany
1:22:28.6	M. MARTTELIN	Finland	14.9.1930	Viipuri, Finland
1:21:27.0	E. J. TAMILA	Finland	3.9.1939	Joensuu, Finland
1:20:14.0	M. HIETANEN	Finland	23.5.1948	Gamlakarleby, Finland
1:19:11.8	E. ZATOPEK	Czechoslovakia	26.10.1952	Stará Boleslav, Czechoslovakia
1:17:34.0	A. IVANOV	U.S.S.R.	27.9.1955	Moscow, U.S.S.R.
1:16:36.4	E. ZATOPEK	Czechoslovakia	29.10.1955	Celakovice, Czechoslovakia

30,000 METRES WORLD RECORDS—MEN

Time	Name	Country	Date	Place
1:48:06.2	A. O. STENROOS	Finland	26.9.1915	Helsinki, Finland
1:47:13.4	T. KOLEHMAINEN	Finland	1.10.1922	Viipuri, Finland
1:46:11.6	A. O. STENROOS	Finland	31.8.1924	Viipuri, Finland
1:43:07.8	V. SIPILA	Finland	16.9.1928	Tampere, Finland
1:42:30.4	J. C. ZABALA	Argentine	10.10.1931	Vienna, Austria
1:40:57.6	J. RIBAS	Argentine	27.5.1932	Buenos Aires, Argentine
1:40:49.8	M. HIETANEN	Finland	28.9.1947	Jyvaskyla, Finland
1:40:46.4	M. HIETANEN	Finland	20.6.1948	Jyvaskyla, Finland
1:39:14.6	F. K. VANIN	U.S.S.R.	1.11.1949	Tbilisi, U.S.S.R.
1:38:54.0	J. Z. MASKATCHENOV	U.S.S.R.	3.10.1951	Moscow, U.S.S.R.
1:35:23.8	E. ZATOPEK	Czechoslovakia	26.10.1952	Stará Boleslav, Czechoslovakia
1:35:03.6	A. VISKARI	Finland	21.10.1956	Lappeenranta, Finland
1:35:01.0	A. IVANOV	U.S.S.R.	6.6.1957	Moscow, U.S.S.R.

3,000 METRES STEEPLECHASE WORLD RECORDS—MEN

Time	Name	Country	Date	Place
8:49.6	S. ROZSNYOI	Hungary	28.8.1954	Berne, Switzerland
8:47.8	P. KARVONEN	Finland	1.7.1955	Helsinki, Finland
8:45.4	P. KARVONEN	Finland	15.7.1955	Oslo, Norway
8:45.4	V. VLASENKO	U.S.S.R.	18.8.1955	Moscow, U.S.S.R.
8:41.2	J. CHROMIK	Poland	31.8.1955	Brno, Czechoslovakia
8:40.2	J. CHROMIK	Poland	11.9.1955	Budapest, Hungary
8:39.8	S. RZHISHCHIN	U.S.S.R.	14.8.1956	Moscow, U.S.S.R.
8:35.6	S. ROZSNYOI	Hungary	16.9.1956	Budapest, Hungary
8:35.6	S. RZHISHCHIN	U.S.S.R.	21.6.1958	Tallin, U.S.S.R.
8:32.0	J. CHROMIK	Poland	2.8.1958	Warsaw, Poland

H. Armitage   Marjorie Jackson   Betty Cuthbert

120 YARDS HURDLES WORLD RECORDS—MEN

Time	Name	Country	Date	Place
15.0*	F. C. SMITHSON	U.S.A.	25.7.1908	London, England
14.4	E. J. THOMSON	Canada	29.5.1920	Philadelphia, Pa., U.S.A.
14.4*	E. WENNSTRÖM	Sweden	25.8.1929	Stockholm, Sweden
14.4	S. E. ANDERSON	U.S.A.	23.8.1930	Pittsburg, Pa., U.S.A.
14.2	P. M. BEARD	U.S.A.	4.7.1931	Lincoln, Neb., U.S.A.
14.2*	P. M. BEARD	U.S.A.	6.8.1934	Oslo, Norway
14.2	T. MOORE	U.S.A.	11.5.1935	Fresno, Cal., U.S.A.
14.2	P. F. COPE	U.S.A.	15.6.1935	Los Angeles, Cal., U.S.A.
14.2	R. M. STALEY	U.S.A.	15.6.1935	Los Angeles, Cal., U.S.A.
14.2*	A. MOREAU	U.S.A.	2.8.1935	Oslo, Norway
14.1*	F. G. TOWNS	U.S.A.	19.6.1936	Chicago, Ill., U.S.A.
14.1*	F. G. TOWNS	U.S.A.	6.8.1936	Berlin, Germany
13.7	F. G. TOWNS	U.S.A.	27.8.1936	Oslo, Norway
13.7*	F. WOLCOTT	U.S.A.	29.6.1941	Philadelphia, Pa., U.S.A.
13.6	W. H. DILLARD	U.S.A.	17.4.1948	Kansas, U.S.A.
13.5	R. H. ATTLESEY	U.S.A.	13.5.1950	Fresno, Cal., U.S.A.
13.5*	R. H. ATTLESEY	U.S.A.	10.7.1950	Helsinki, Finland
13.5	J. DAVIS	U.S.A.	9.6.1956	Sanger, Cal., U.S.A.
13.4*	J. DAVIS	U.S.A.	22.6.1956	Bakersfield, Cal., U.S.A.
13.4	M. G. CAMPBELL	U.S.A.	31.5.1957	Compton, Cal., U.S.A.

* Made over 110 metres (120.30 yds.).

110 METRES HURDLES WORLD RECORDS—MEN

Time	Name	Country	Date	Place
15.0	F. C. SMITHSON	U.S.A.	25.7.1908	London, England
14.8	E. J. THOMSON	Canada	18.8.1920	Antwerp, Belgium
14.8	S. PETTERSSON	Sweden	18.9.1927	Stockholm, Sweden
14.6	G. C. WEIGHTMAN-SMITH	S. Africa	13.7.1928	Amsterdam, Netherlands
14.4	E. WENNSTRÖM	Sweden	25.8.1929	Stockholm, Sweden
14.4	B. SJÖSTEDT	Finland	29.8.1931	Helsinki, Finland
14.4	P. M. BEARD	U.S.A.	23.6.1932	Cambridge, Mass., U.S.A.
14.4	J. KELLER	U.S.A.	16.7.1932	Palo Alto, Cal., U.S.A.
14.4	G. J. SALING	U.S.A.	2.8.1932	Los Angeles, Cal., U.S.A.
14.4	J. MORRISS	U.S.A.	12.8.1933	Budapest, Hungary
14.4	J. MORRISS	U.S.A.	8.9.1933	Turin, Italy
14.3	P. M. BEARD	U.S.A.	26.7.1934	Stockholm, Sweden
14.2	P. M. BEARD	U.S.A.	6.8.1934	Oslo, Norway
14.2	A. MOREAU	U.S.A.	2.8.1935	Oslo, Norway
14.1	F. G. TOWNS	U.S.A.	19.6.1936	Chicago, Ill., U.S.A.
14.1	F. G. TOWNS	U.S.A.	6.8.1936	Berlin, Germany
13.7	F. G. TOWNS	U.S.A.	27.8.1936	Oslo, Norway
13.7	F. WOLCOTT	U.S.A.	29.6.1941	Philadelphia, Pa., U.S.A.
13.6	R. H. ATTLESEY	U.S.A.	24.6.1950	College Park, Maryland, U.S.A.
13.5	R. H. ATTLESEY	U.S.A.	10.7.1950	Helsinki, Finland
13.4	J. DAVIS	U.S.A.	22.6.1956	Bakersfield, Cal., U.S.A.

200 METRES HURDLES WORLD RECORDS—MEN

Time	Name	Country	Date	Place
24.6	H. L. HILLMAN	U.S.A.	1.10.1904	Travers Is., N.Y., U.S.A.
23.0*	C. R. BROOKINS	U.S.A.	17.5.1924	Ames, Iowa, U.S.A.
23.0*	N. PAUL	U.S.A.	6.5.1933	Los Angeles, Cal., U.S.A.
22.6*	J. C. OWENS	U.S.A.	25.5.1935	Ann Arbor, Mich., U.S.A.
22.3†	F. WOLCOTT	U.S.A.	8.6.1940	Princeton, N.J., U.S.A.
22.3*	W. H. DILLARD	U.S.A.	21.6.1947	Salt Lake City, U.S.A.
22.2*	D. SIME	U.S.A.	5.5.1956	Durham, N. Car., U.S.A.
22.2*	A. ROBINSON	U.S.A.	15.6.1957	Austin, Texas, U.S.A.
22.1*	E. GILBERT	U.S.A.	17.5.1958	Raleigh, N. Car., U.S.A.

* Made in 220 yds. (201.17 m.) race.
† Made in a 220 yds. (201.17 m.) race but separately timed.

220 YARDS HURDLES WORLD RECORDS—MEN

Time	Name	Country	Date	Place
23.6	A. C. KRAENZLEIN	U.S.A.	28.5.1898	New York City, U.S.A.
23.6	J. I. WENDELL	U.S.A.	31.5.1913	Cambridge, Mass., U.S.A.
23.6	R. SIMPSON	U.S.A.	27.5.1916	Columbia, Mo., U.S.A.
23.2	C. R. BROOKINS	U.S.A.	2.6.1923	Mason City, Iowa, U.S.A.
23.0	C. R. BROOKINS	U.S.A.	17.5.1924	Ames, Iowa, U.S.A.
23.0	N. PAUL	U.S.A.	6.5.1933	Los Angeles, Cal., U.S.A.
22.6	J. C. OWENS	U.S.A.	25.5.1935	Ann Arbor, Mich., U.S.A.
22.5	F. WOLCOTT	U.S.A.	8.6.1940	Princeton, N.J., U.S.A.
22.5	W. H. DILLARD	U.S.A.	8.6.1946	Delaware, Ohio, U.S.A.
22.3	W. H. DILLARD	U.S.A.	21.6.1947	Salt Lake City, Utah, U.S.A.
22.2	D. W. SIME	U.S.A.	5.5.1956	Durham, N. Car., U.S.A.
22.2	A. ROBINSON	U.S.A.	15.6.1957	Austin, Texas, U.S.A.
22.1	E. GILBERT	U.S.A.	17.5.1958	Raleigh, N. Car., U.S.A.

ATHLETICS QUIZ

1. Have the measurements of any performances from the ancient Olympic Games survived?

★

2. Which woman athlete has won most W.A.A.A. titles?

★

3. Name the Olympic race in which all the competitors ran one lap too many.

QUIZ ANSWERS

1. Yes. Chionis of Sparta, long jump 23 ft. 1½ ins. in circa 656 B.C. 2. Nellie Halstead with 11. 3. The 1932 Steeplechase at Los Angeles.

McDonald Bailey (right) and B. Shenton (Polytechnic Harriers)

54

400 METRES HURDLES WORLD RECORDS—MEN

Time	Name	Country	Date	Place
55.0	C. J. BACON	U.S.A.	22.7.1908	London, England
54.0	F. F. LOOMIS	U.S.A.	16.8.1920	Antwerp, Belgium
53.8	S. PETTERSSON	Sweden	4.10.1925	Paris, France
52.0	F. M. TAYLOR	U.S.A.	4.7.1928	Philadelphia, Pa., U.S.A.
52.0	G. F. HARDIN	U.S.A.	1.8.1932	Los Angeles, Cal., U.S.A.
51.8	G. F. HARDIN	U.S.A.	30.6.1934	Milwaukee, Wis., U.S.A.
50.6	G. F. HARDIN	U.S.A.	26.7.1934	Stockholm, Sweden
50.4	Y. N. LITUYEV	U.S.S.R.	20.9.1953	Budapest, Hungary
49.5	G. A. DAVIS	U.S.A.	29.6.1956	Los Angeles, Cal., U.S.A.
49.2	G. A. DAVIS	U.S.A.	6.8.1958	Budapest, Hungary

440 YARDS HURDLES WORLD RECORDS—MEN

Time	Name	Country	Date	Place
56.8	G. R. L. ANDERSON	G.B. and N.I.	16.7.1910	London, England
54.2	J. K. NORTON	U.S.A.	26.6.1920	Pasadena, Cal., U.S.A.
54.2	LORD BURGHLEY*	G.B. and N.I.	2.7.1927	London, England
52.6	J. A. GIBSON	U.S.A.	2.7.1927	Lincoln, Neb., U.S.A.
52.2	R. B. COCHRAN	U.S.A.	25.4.1942	Des Moines, Iowa, U.S.A.
52.2	R. F. AULT	U.S.A.	31.8.1949	Oslo, Norway
51.9	A. FILIPUT	Italy	8.10.1950	Milan, Italy
51.9	C. H. MOORE	U.S.A.	4.8.1952	London, England
51.6	C. H. MOORE	U.S.A.	9.8.1952	London, England
51.3	Y. N. LITUYEV	U.S.S.R.	13.10.1954	London, England
50.7	G. C. POTGIETER	S. Africa	20.4.1957	Queenstown, S. Africa
50.5	J. CULBREATH	U.S.A.	9.8.1957	Oslo, Norway
49.9	G. A. DAVIS	U.S.A.	20.6.1958	Bakersfield, Cal., U.S.A.
49.7	G. C. POTGIETER	S. Africa	22.7.1958	Cardiff, Wales

* Now the Marquess of Exeter.

T. Courtney (U.S.A.) G. D. Ibbotson H. Dillard (U.S.A.) L. Tabori

HIGH JUMP WORLD RECORDS—MEN

Ft.	Ins.	Name	Country	Date	Place
6	7	G. L. HORINE	U.S.A.	18.5.1912	Stanford, Cal., U.S.A.
6	7¼	E. BEESON	U.S.A.	2.5.1914	Berkeley, Cal., U.S.A.
6	8¼	H. M. OSBORN	U.S.A.	27.5.1924	Urbana, Ill., U.S.A.
6	8⅝	W. MARTY	U.S.A.	13.5.1933	Fresno, Cal., U.S.A.
6	9¼	W. MARTY	U.S.A.	28.4.1934	Palo Alto, Cal., U.S.A.
6	9¾	C. C. JOHNSON	U.S.A.	12.7.1936	New York, N.Y., U.S.A.
6	9¾	D. D. ALBRITTON	U.S.A.	12.7.1936	New York, N.Y., U.S.A.
6	10⅜	M. WALKER	U.S.A.	12.8.1937	Malmö, Sweden
6	11	L. STEERS	U.S.A.	17.6.1941	Los Angeles, Cal., U.S.A.
6	11¼	W. F. DAVIS	U.S.A.	27.6.1953	Dayton, Ohio, U.S.A.
7	0½	C. E. DUMAS	U.S.A.	29.6.1956	Los Angeles, Cal., U.S.A.
7	1	Y. N. STEPANOV	U.S.S.R.	13.7.1957	Leningrad, U.S.S.R.

POLE VAULT WORLD RECORDS—MEN

Ft.	Ins.	Name	Country	Date	Place
13	2¼	M. S. WRIGHT	U.S.A.	8.6.1912	Cambridge, Mass., U.S.A.
13	5	F. K. FOSS	U.S.A.	20.8.1920	Antwerp, Belgium
13	6¼	C. HOFF	Norway	3.9.1922	Copenhagen, Denmark
13	9¾	C. HOFF	Norway	22.7.1923	Copenhagen, Denmark
13	10¼	C. HOFF	Norway	13.8.1925	Oslo, Norway
13	11¼	C. HOFF	Norway	27.9.1925	Turku, Finland
14	0	S. W. CARR	U.S.A.	27.5.1927	Philadelphia, Pa., U.S.A.
14	1½	L. BARNES	U.S.A.	28.4.1928	Fresno, Cal., U.S.A.
14	4⅜	W. N. GRABER	U.S.A.	16.7.1932	Palo Alto, Cal., U.S.A.
14	5¼	K. S. BROWN	U.S.A.	1.6.1935	Boston, Mass., U.S.A.
14	6¼	G. VAROFF	U.S.A.	4.7.1936	Princeton, N.J., U.S.A.
14	11	W. H. SEFTON	U.S.A.	29.5.1937	Los Angeles, Cal., U.S.A.
14	11	E. MEADOWS	U.S.A.	29.5.1937	Los Angeles, Cal., U.S.A.
15	1¼	C. A. WARMERDAM	U.S.A.	29.6.1940	Fresno, Cal., U.S.A.
15	5¾	C. A. WARMERDAM	U.S.A.	6.6.1941	Compton, Cal., U.S.A.
15	7¾	C. A. WARMERDAM	U.S.A.	23.5.1942	Modesto, Cal., U.S.A.
15	8¼	R. A. GUTOWSKI	U.S.A.	27.4.1957	Palo Alto, Cal., U.S.A.

LONG JUMP WORLD RECORDS—MEN

Ft.	Ins.	Name	Country	Date	Place
24	11½	P. O'CONNOR	G.B. & N.I.	5.8.1901	Dublin, Ireland
25	3	E. O. GOURDIN	U.S.A.	23.7.1921	Cambridge, Mass., U.S.A.
25	5¼	R. LE GENDRE	U.S.A.	7.7.1924	Paris, France
25	10⅞	DE HART HUBBARD	U.S.A.	13.6.1925	Chicago, Ill., U.S.A.
25	11¼	E. B. HAMM	U.S.A.	7.7.1928	Cambridge, Mass., U.S.A.
26	0½	S. CATOR	Haiti	9.9.1928	Paris, France
26	2¼	C. NAMBU	Japan	27.10.1931	Tokyo, Japan
26	8¼	J. C. OWENS	U.S.A.	25.5.1935	Ann Arbor, Mich., U.S.A.

HOP, STEP AND JUMP WORLD RECORDS—MEN

Ft.	Ins.	Name	Country	Date	Place
50	11	D. F. AHEARN	U.S.A.	31.7.1909	Boston, Mass., U.S.A.
50	11¼	A. W. WINTER	Australia	12.7.1924	Paris, France
51	1⅜	M. ODA	Japan	27.10.1931	Tokyo, Japan

Ft.	Ins.	Name	Country	Date	Place
51	7	C. NAMBU	Japan	4.8.1932	Los Angeles, Cal., U.S.A.
51	9¾	J. P. METCALFE	Australia	14.12.1935	Sydney, Australia
52	5½	N. TAJIMA	Japan	6.8.1936	Berlin, Germany
52	5¼	A. F. DA SILVA	Brazil	3.12.1950	Sao Paulo, Brazil
52	6¼	A. F. DA SILVA	Brazil	30.9.1951	Rio de Janeiro, Brazil
52	10¼	A. F. DA SILVA	Brazil	23.7.1952	Helsinki, Finland
53	2¼	A. F. DA SILVA	Brazil	23.7.1952	Helsinki, Finland
53	2¼	L. SHCHERBAKOV	U.S.S.R.	19.7.1953	Moscow, U.S.S.R.
54	3¼	A. F. DA SILVA	Brazil	16.3.1955	Mexico City, Mexico
54	5	O. RYAKHOVSKIY	U.S.S.R.	28.7.1958	Moscow, U.S.S.R.

PUTTING THE SHOT WORLD RECORDS—MEN

Ft.	Ins.	Name	Country	Date	Place
51	0	R. W. ROSE	U.S.A.	21.8.1909	San Francisco, U.S.A.
51	9¾	E. HIRSCHFELD	Germany	6.5.1928	Breslau, Germany
52	0½	J. KUCK	U.S.A.	29.7.1928	Amsterdam, Netherlands
52	7½	E. HIRSCHFELD	Germany	26.8.1928	Bochum, Germany
52	7½	F. DOUDA	Czecho-slovakia	4.10.1931	Brno, Czechoslovakia
52	7½	Z. HELJASZ	Poland	29.6.1932	Poznan, Poland
52	10½	L. J. SEXTON	U.S.A.	27.8.1932	Freeport, N.Y., U.S.A.
53	1¼	F. DOUDA	Czecho-slovakia	24.9.1932	Prague, Czechoslovakia
54	1	J. C. LYMAN	U.S.A.	21.4.1934	Palo Alto, Cal., U.S.A.
55	1¼	J. TORRANCE	U.S.A.	24.4.1934	Des Moines, Iowa, U.S.A.
55	5	J. TORRANCE	U.S.A.	30.6.1934	Milwaukee, Wis., U.S.A.
57	1	J. TORRANCE	U.S.A.	5.8.1934	Oslo, Norway
58	0¼	C. E. FONVILLE	U.S.A.	17.4.1948	Lawrence, Kansas, U.S.A.
58	4½	J. E. FUCHS	U.S.A.	28.7.1949	Oslo, Norway
58	5¼	J. E. FUCHS	U.S.A.	29.4.1950	Los Angeles, U.S.A.
58	8½	J. E. FUCHS	U.S.A.	20.8.1950	Visby, Sweden
58	10½	J. E. FUCHS	U.S.A.	22.8.1950	Eskilstuna, Sweden
59	0¾	W. P. O'BRIEN	U.S.A.	9.5.1953	Fresno, Cal., U.S.A.
59	2¼	W. P. O'BRIEN	U.S.A.	5.6.1953	Compton, Cal., U.S.A.
60	5¼	W. P. O'BRIEN	U.S.A.	8.5.1954	Los Angeles, Cal., U.S.A.
60	5¾	W. P. O'BRIEN	U.S.A.	21.5.1954	Los Angeles, Cal., U.S.A.
60	10	W. P. O'BRIEN	U.S.A.	11.6.1954	Los Angeles, Cal., U.S.A.
61	1	W. P. O'BRIEN	U.S.A.	5.5.1956	Salt Lake City, Utah, U.S.A.
61	4	W. P. O'BRIEN	U.S.A.	15.6.1956	Los Angeles, Cal., U.S.A.
62	6¼	W. P. O'BRIEN	U.S.A.	3.9.1956	Eugene, Oregon, U.S.A.
63	2	W. P. O'BRIEN	U.S.A.	1.11.1956	Los Angeles, Cal., U.S.A.

THROWING THE DISCUS WORLD RECORDS—MEN

Ft.	Ins.	Name	Country	Date	Place
156	1⅜	J. H. DUNCAN	U.S.A.	2.6.1912	Celtic Park, N.Y., U.S.A.
156	2¼	T. J. LIEB	U.S.A.	14.9.1924	Chicago, Ill., U.S.A.
157	1⅜	G. HARTRANFT	U.S.A.	2.5.1925	San Francisco, Cal., U.S.A.
158	1¼	C. L. HOUSER	U.S.A.	3.4.1926	Palo Alto, Cal., U.S.A.
167	5⅞	E. C. W. KRENZ	U.S.A.	17.5.1930	Palo Alto, Cal., U.S.A.
169	8⅝	P. B. JESSUP	U.S.A.	23.8.1930	Pittsburg, Penn., U.S.A.
171	11½	H. ANDERSSON	Sweden	25.8.1934	Oslo, Norway
174	2½	W. SCHRÖDER	Germany	28.4.1935	Magdeburg, Germany
174	8¼	A. HARRIS	U.S.A.	20.6.1941	Palo Alto, Cal., U.S.A.
175	0	A. CONSOLINI	Italy	26.10.1941	Milan, Italy
177	11	A. CONSOLINI	Italy	14.4.1946	Helsinki, Finland
180	2¼	R. E. FITCH	U.S.A.	8.6.1946	Minneapolis, Minn., U.S.A.
181	6	A. CONSOLINI	Italy	10.10.1948	Milan, Italy
185	2¼	F. E. GORDIEN	U.S.A.	9.7.1949	Lisbon, Portugal
186	11	F. E. GORDIEN	U.S.A.	14.8.1949	Hameenlinna, Finland
190	0½	S. G. INESS	U.S.A.	20.6.1953	Lincoln, Neb., U.S.A.
190	7½	F. E. GORDIEN	U.S.A.	11.7.1953	Pasadena, Cal., U.S.A.
194	6	F. E. GORDIEN	U.S.A.	22.8.1953	Pasadena, Cal., U.S.A.

M. E. Hiscox D. W. Sime (U.S.A.)  N. Otkalenko (U.S.S.R.)

ATHLETICS QUIZ

1. Who was the first man to run exactly 4 minutes for the mile?

★

2. Name the last track on which athletes ran clockwise.

★

3. Who was the first man to beat 50 feet with the 16-lb. shot?

QUIZ ANSWERS

1. George Derek Ibbotson (G.B.) at White City stadium, London, on 3rd September 1958. 2. Fenners, at Cambridge, which was closed in June 1959. 3. Ralph Rose (U.S.A.) in California in 1909.

THROWING THE HAMMER WORLD RECORDS—MEN

Ft.	Ins.	Name	Country	Date	Place
189	6½	P. RYAN	U.S.A.	17.8.1913	New York, U.S.A.
193	6⅞	E. BLASK	Germany	27.8.1938	Stockholm, Sweden
193	7½	I. NÉMETH	Hungary	14.7.1948	Tata, Hungary
195	5	I. NÉMETH	Hungary	4.9.1949	Katowice, Poland
196	5½	I. NÉMETH	Hungary	16.5.1950	Budapest, Hungary
197	11½	J. CSERMAK	Hungary	24.7.1952	Helsinki, Finland
200	11	S. STRANDLI	Norway	14.9.1952	Oslo, Norway
204	7	S. STRANDLI	Norway	5.9.1953	Oslo, Norway
207	9½	M. P. KRIVONOSOV	U.S.S.R.	29.8.1954	Berne, Switzerland
210	1½	S. NYENASHEV	U.S.S.R.	12.12.1954	Baku, U.S.S.R.
211	0½	M. P. KRIVONOSOV	U.S.S.R.	4.8.1955	Warsaw, Poland
211	8	M. P. KRIVONOSOV	U.S.S.R.	19.9.1955	Belgrade, Yugoslavia
216	0½	M. P. KRIVONOSOV	U.S.S.R.	25.4.1956	Nalchik, U.S.S.R.
217	9	M. P. KRIVONOSOV	U.S.S.R.	8.7.1956	Minsk, U.S.S.R.
220	10	M. P. KRIVONOSOV	U.S.S.R.	22.10.1956	Tashkent, U.S.S.R.
224	10½	H. V. CONNOLLY	U.S.A.	2.11.1956	Los Angeles, Cal., U.S.A.
225	4	H. V. CONNOLLY	U.S.A.	20.6.1958	Bakersfield, Cal., U.S.A.

THROWING THE JAVELIN WORLD RECORDS—MEN

Ft.	Ins.	Name	Country	Date	Place
204	5½	E. V. LEMMING	Sweden	19.9.1912	Stockholm, Sweden
216	10⅜	J. MYYRA	Finland	24.8.1919	Stockholm, Sweden
218	6⅞	G. LINDSTRÖM	Sweden	12.10.1924	Eksjo, Sweden
229	3⅛	E. PENTTILA	Finland	8.10.1927	Viipuri, Finland
232	11⅝	E. LUNDQVIST	Sweden	15.8.1928	Stockholm, Sweden
234	9¾	M. H. JARVINEN	Finland	8.8.1930	Viipuri, Finland
235	2⅞	M. H. JARVINEN	Finland	17.8.1930	Tampere, Finland
235	9⅞	M. H. JARVINEN	Finland	31.8.1930	Vaasa, Finland
239	3¼	M. H. JARVINEN	Finland	14.9.1930	Viipuri, Finland
242	10¼	M. H. JARVINEN	Finland	27.6.1932	Turku, Finland
243	8⅜	M. H. JARVINEN	Finland	25.5.1933	Mikkeli, Finland
244	9⅜	M. H. JARVINEN	Finland	7.6.1933	Vaasa, Finland
249	8	M. H. JARVINEN	Finland	15.6.1933	Helsinki, Finland
251	6	M. H. JARVINEN	Finland	7.9.1934	Turin, Italy
253	4½	M. H. JARVINEN	Finland	18.6.1936	Helsinki, Finland
255	5¾	Y. NIKKANEN	Finland	25.8.1938	Karhula, Finland
258	2	Y. NIKKANEN	Finland	16.10.1938	Kotka, Finland
263	10	F. HELD	U.S.A.	8.8.1953	Pasadena, Cal., U.S.A.
268	2½	F. HELD	U.S.A.	21.5.1955	Modesto, Cal., U.S.A.
274	1½	S. N. NIKKINEN	Finland	24.6.1956	Kuhmoinen, Finland
274	5½	J. SIDLO	Poland	30.6.1956	Milan, Italy
281	2	E. DANIELSEN	Norway	26.11.1956	Melbourne, Australia

G. C. Potgieter

DECATHLON WORLD RECORDS—MEN

Points Tables Prior to 1934	1934	1952	Name	Country	Date	Place
7,481.69	6,450		A. KLUMBERG	Esthonia	16/17.9.1922	Helsinki, Finland
7,710.775	6,877		H. M. OSBORN	U.S.A.	11/12.7.1924	Paris, France
7,820.93	6,889		P. YRJOLÄ	Finland	17/18.7.1926	Viipuri, Finland
7,995.19	7,053		P. YRJOLÄ	Finland	16/17.7.1927	Helsinki, Finland
8,053.29	7,071		P. YRJOLÄ	Finland	3/4.8.1928	Amsterdam, Netherlands
8,255.475	7,378		A. JARVINEN	Finland	19/20.7.1930	Viipuri, Finland
8,462.235	7,396	6,588	J. A. B. BAUSCH	U.S.A.	5/6.8.1932	Los Angeles, Cal., U.S.A.
8,467.62	7,432	6,635	H. H. SIEVERT	Germany	22/23.7.1933	Hamburg, Germany
8,790.46	7,824	7,135	H. H. SIEVERT	Germany	7/8.7.1934	Hamburg, Germany
	7,900	7,310	G. E. MORRIS	U.S.A.	7/8.8.1936	Berlin, Germany
	8,042	7,444	R. B. MATHIAS	U.S.A.	29/30.6.1950	Tulare, U.S.A.
		7,887	R. B. MATHIAS	U.S.A.	25/26.7.1952	Helsinki, Finland
		7,985	R. L. JOHNSON	U.S.A.	10/11.6.1955	Kingsburg, Cal., U.S.A.
		8,014	V. KUZNETSOV	U.S.S.R.	17/18.5.1958	Krasnodar, U.S.S.R.
		8,302	R. L. JOHNSON	U.S.A.	27/28.7.1958	Moscow, U.S.S.R.

60 METRES WORLD RECORDS—WOMEN

Time	Name	Country	Date	Place
7.3	S. WALASIEWICZOWNA-OLSEN	Poland	24.9.1933	Lemberg, Poland

100 YARDS WORLD RECORDS—WOMEN

Time	Name	Country	Date	Place
11.0	B. BURKE	S. Africa	20.4.1935	Pretoria, S. Africa
11.0	F. E. KOEN	Netherlands	19.6.1938	Amsterdam, Netherlands
11.0	D. LUMLEY	N. Zealand	11.3.1939	Auckland, N. Zealand
11.0	D. J. NORMAN	Australia	18.3.1939	Morrinsville, N. Zealand
10.8	F. E. BLANKERS-KOEN	Netherlands	18.5.1944	Amsterdam, Netherlands
10.8	M. JACKSON-NELSON	Australia	4.1.1950	Adelaide, Australia
10.8	M. JACKSON-NELSON	Australia	4.2.1950	Auckland, New Zealand
10.7	M. JACKSON-NELSON	Australia	31.3.1950	Newcastle, Australia
10.4	M. JACKSON-NELSON	Australia	8.3.1952	Sydney, Australia
10.4	B. CUTHBERT	Australia	1.3.1958	Sydney, Australia
10.3	M. J. MATHEWS-WILLARD	Australia	20.3.1958	Sydney, Australia

100 METRES WORLD RECORDS—WOMEN

Time	Name	Country	Date	Place
11.7	S. WALASIEWICZOWNA-OLSEN	Poland	26.8.1934	Warsaw, Poland
11.6	S. WALASIEWICZOWNA-OLSEN	Poland	1.8.1937	Berlin, Germany
11.5	F. E. BLANKERS-KOEN	Netherlands	13.6.1948	Amsterdam, Netherlands
11.5	M. JACKSON-NELSON	Australia	21.7.1952	Helsinki, Finland
11.4	M. JACKSON-NELSON	Australia	4.10.1952	Gifu, Japan
11.3	S. B. STRICKLAND-DE LA HUNTY	Australia	4.8.1955	Warsaw, Poland

200 METRES WORLD RECORDS—WOMEN

Time	Name	Country	Date	Place
23.6	S. WALASIEWICZOWNA-OLSEN	Poland	15.8.1935	Warsaw, Poland
23.6	M. JACKSON-NELSON	Australia	25.7.1952	Helsinki, Finland
23.4	M. JACKSON-NELSON	Australia	25.7.1952	Helsinki, Finland
23.2	B. CUTHBERT	Australia	16.9.1956	Sydney, N.S.W., Australia

220 YARDS WORLD RECORDS—WOMEN

Time	Name	Country	Date	Place
24.3	S. WALASIEWICZOWNA-OLSEN	Poland	9.6.1935	Cleveland, Ohio, U.S.A.
24.3	M. JACKSON-NELSON	Australia	9.2.1950	Auckland, New Zealand
24.2	F. E. BLANKERS-KOEN	Netherlands	29.6.1950	Brescia, Italy
24.0	M. JACKSON-NELSON	Australia	5.8.1954	Vancouver, Canada
23.6	M. L. ITKINA	U.S.S.R.	22.7.1956	Kiev, U.S.S.R.
23.6	B. CUTHBERT	Australia	18.1.1958	Perth, W. Australia
23.5	B. CUTHBERT	Australia	8.3.1958	Sydney, N.S.W., Australia
23.4	M. J. MATHEWS-WILLARD	Australia	22.3.1958	Sydney, N.S.W., Australia

White City 1954.
Chris Chataway winning the 5,000 metres from V. Kuts of Moscow, one of the greatest races of his career. He broke the world record by 5 seconds with a time of 13 mins. 51.6 secs.

ATHLETICS QUIZ

1. What is the international limit of assisting wind strength for a record to be allowed?

★

2. In what year was the A.A.A. founded?

★

3. Who was (*a*) the first man, (*b*) the first woman to high jump 6 feet?

QUIZ ANSWERS

1. 4.47 m.p.h. directly behind the runner. This allows a quartering wind of 6.32 m.p.h. 2. April 24, 1880 with the Hon. Brian Wise in the chair at the Randolph Hotel, Oxford. 3. (*a*) The Hon. Marshall Jones Brooks at Marston near Oxford on March 17, 1876. (*b*) Mlle. Iolande Balas (Rumania) at Bucharest on October 18, 1958.

400 METRES WORLD RECORDS—WOMEN

Time	Name	Country	Date	Place
57.0	M. J. MATHEWS-WILLARD	Australia	6.1.1957	Sydney, N.S.W., Australia
57.0	M. A. M. CHAMBERLAIN	N. Zealand	16.2.1957	Christchurch, New Zealand
56.3	N. I. BOYLE	Australia	24.2.1957	Sydney, N.S.W., Australia
55.2	P. A. SOLOPOVA-LAZAREVA	U.S.S.R.	10.5.1957	Moscow, U.S.S.R.
54.0	M. L. ITKINA	U.S.S.R.	8.6.1957	Minsk, U.S.S.R.
53.6	M. L. ITKINA	U.S.S.R.	6.7.1957	Moscow, U.S.S.R.

Records at this distance only recognised from 4.12.56.

440 YARDS WORLD RECORDS—WOMEN

Time	Name	Country	Date	Place
57.0	M. J. MATHEWS-WILLARD	Australia	6.1.1957	Sydney, N.S.W., Australia
57.0	M. A. M. CHAMBERLAIN	N. Zealand	16.2.1957	Christchurch, New Zealand
56.3	N. I. BOYLE	Australia	24.2.1957	Sydney N.S.W., Australia
56.1	M. A. M. CHAMBERLAIN	N. Zealand	8.3.1958	Christchurch, New Zealand
55.6	M. E. HISCOX	G.B. and N.I.	2.8.1958	London, England

Records at this distance only recognised from 4.12.56.

800 METRES WORLD RECORDS—WOMEN

Time	Name	Country	Date	Place
2:16.8	L. BATSCHAUER-RADKE	Germany	2.8.1928	Amsterdam, Netherlands
2:15.9	A. LARSSON-HEDLUND	Sweden	28.8.1944	Stockholm, Sweden
2:14.8	A. LARSSON-HEDLUND	Sweden	19.8.1945	Halsingborg, Sweden
2:13.8	A. LARSSON-HEDLUND	Sweden	30.8.1945	Stockholm, Sweden
2:13.0	Y. M. VASILJEVA	U.S.S.R.	17.7.1950	Moscow, U.S.S.R.
2:12.2	V. A. POMOGAYEVA	U.S.S.R.	26.7.1951	Moscow, U.S.S.R.
2:12.0	N. G. PLETNYEVA	U.S.S.R.	26.8.1951	Minsk, U.S.S.R.
2:08.5	N. G. PLETNYEVA	U.S.S.R.	15.6.1952	Kiev, U.S.S.R.
2:07.3	N. G. PLETNYEVA-OTKALENKO	U.S.S.R.	27.8.1953	Moscow, U.S.S.R.
2:06.6	N. G. PLETNYEVA-OTKALENKO	U.S.S.R.	16.9.1954	Kiev, U.S.S.R.
2:05.0	N. G. PLETNYEVA-OTKALENKO	U.S.S.R.	24.9.1955	Zagreb, Yugoslavia

880 YARDS WORLD RECORDS—WOMEN

Time	Name	Country	Date	Place
2:26.6	M. LINES	G.B. and N.I.	30.8.1922	London, England
2:17.4	O. M. HALL	G.B. and N.I.	25.7.1936	Birmingham, England
2:15.6	A. LARSSON-HEDLUND	Sweden	5.9.1945	Stockholm, Sweden
2:14.5	V. M. BALL-WINN	G.B. and N.I.	17.9.1952	London, England
2:12.6	U. JUREWITZ-DONATH	Germany	19.8.1953	Budapest, Hungary
2:11.6	A. KAZI	Hungary	29.5.1954	Budapest, Hungary
2:09.0	D. S. LEATHER	G.B. and N.I.	19.6.1954	London, England
2:08.4	N. G. PLETNYEVA-OTKALENKO	U.S.S.R.	18.7.1954	Moscow, U.S.S.R.
2:06.6	N. G. PLETNYEVA-OTKALENKO	U.S.S.R.	10.6.1956	Moscow, U.S.S.R.

80 METRES HURDLES WORLD RECORDS—WOMEN

Time	Name	Country	Date	Place
11.6	R. ENGELHARDT	Germany	11.8.1934	London, England
11.6	T. VALLA	Italy	5.8.1936	Berlin, Germany
11.6	B. BURKE	S. Africa	1.8.1937	Berlin, Germany
11.6	L. GELIUS	Germany	30.7.1938	Breslau, Germany
11.3	C. TESTONI	Italy	23.7.1939	Garmisch-Partenkirchen, Germany
11.3	C. TESTONI	Italy	13.8.1939	Dresden, Germany
11.3	F. E. BLANKERS-KOEN	Netherlands	20.9.1942	Amsterdam, Netherlands
11.0	F. E. BLANKERS-KOEN	Netherlands	20.6.1948	Amsterdam, Netherlands
11.0	S. B. STRICKLAND-DE LA HUNTY	Australia	23.7.1952	Helsinki, Finland
10.9	S. B. STRICKLAND-DE LA HUNTY	Australia	24.7.1952	Helsinki, Finland
10.9	M. GOLUBNICHAYA	U.S.S.R.	3.8.1954	Kiev, U.S.S.R.
10.8	G. YERMOLENKO-GRINWALD	U.S.S.R.	5.7.1955	Leningrad, U.S.S.R.
10.6	Z. GASTL-COPP	Germany	29.7.1956	Frechen, Germany

HIGH JUMP WORLD RECORDS—WOMEN

Ft.	Ins.	Name	Country	Date	Place
5	5	J. M. SHILEY	U.S.A.	7.8.1932	Los Angeles, Cal., U.S.A.
5	5	M. DIDRIKSON	U.S.A.	7.8.1936	Los Angeles, Cal., U.S.A.
5	5¼	D. J. B. ODAM-TYLER	G.B. and N.I.	29.5.1939	Brentwood, England
5	7¼	F. E. BLANKERS-KOEN	Netherlands	30.5.1943	Amsterdam, Netherlands
5	7½	S. ALEXANDER-LERWILL	G.B. and N.I.	7.7.1951	London, England
5	8	A. C. G. CHUDINA	U.S.S.R.	22.5.1954	Kiev, U.S.S.R.
5	8½	T. E. HOPKINS	G.B. and N.I.	5.5.1956	Belfast, N. Ireland
5	8¾	I. BALAS	Roumania	14.7.1956	Bucharest, Roumania
5	9¼	M. McDANIEL	U.S.A.	1.12.1956	Melbourne, Australia
5	9¼	I. BALAS	Roumania	13.10.1957	Bucharest, Roumania
5	9½	CHENG FENG JUNG	China	17.11.1957	Peking, China
5	10	I. BALAS	Roumania	7.6.1958	Bucharest, Roumania
5	10¾	I. BALAS	Roumania	22.6.1958	Cluj, Roumania
5	11¼	I. BALAS	Roumania	31.7.1958	Poiana Stalin, Roumania
5	11½	I. BALAS	Roumania	4.10.1958	Bucharest, Roumania
6	0	I. BALAS	Roumania	18.10.1958	Bucharest, Roumania

LONG JUMP WORLD RECORDS—WOMEN

Ft.	Ins.	Name	Country	Date	Place
19	7½	H. HITOMI	Japan	20.5.1928	Osaka, Japan
20	0¾	C. SCHULZ	Germany	30.7.1939	Berlin, Germany
20	6	F. E. BLANKERS-KOEN	Netherlands	19.9.1943	Leiden, Netherlands
20	7½	Y. W. WILLIAMS-CORLETT	N. Zealand	20.2.1954	Gisborne, N. Zealand
20	7½	G. M. VINOGRADOVA-POPOVA	U.S.S.R.	11.9.1955	Moscow, U.S.S.R.
20	8¼	G. M. VINOGRADOVA-POPOVA	U.S.S.R.	18.11.1955	Tbilisi, U.S.S.R.
20	10	E. DUNSKA-KRZESINSKA	Poland	20.8.1956	Budapest, Hungary
20	10	E. DUNSKA-KRZESINSKA	Poland	27.11.1956	Melbourne, Australia

PUTTING THE SHOT WORLD RECORDS—WOMEN

Ft.	Ins.	Name	Country	Date	Place
31	4¾	H. KOPPL	Austria	20.6.1926	Vienna, Austria
47	2⅛	G. MAUERMAYER	Germany	15.7.1934	Warsaw, Poland
47	10¼	T. N. SEVRJUKOVA	U.S.S.R.	4.8.1948	Moscow, U.S.S.R.
48	9	K. A. TOCHENOVA	U.S.S.R.	30.10.1949	Tbilisi, U.S.S.R.
49	3¼	A. S. ANDREYEVA	U.S.S.R.	9.11.1950	Ploesti, Roumania
50	1½	G. I. ZYBINA	U.S.S.R.	26.7.1952	Helsinki, Finland
50	5	G. I. ZYBINA	U.S.S.R.	20.9.1952	Frunze, U.S.S.R.
50	7	G. I. ZYBINA	U.S.S.R.	1.10.1952	Frunze, U.S.S.R.
53	1¾	G. I. ZYBINA	U.S.S.R.	9.10.1953	Malmö, Sweden
53	4¾	G. I. ZYBINA	U.S.S.R.	14.9.1954	Kiev, U.S.S.R.
53	5¼	G. I. ZYBINA	U.S.S.R.	5.9.1955	Leningrad, U.S.S.R.
54	8¼	G. I. ZYBINA	U.S.S.R.	15.11.1955	Tbilisi, U.S.S.R.
54	11¾	G. I. ZYBINA	U.S.S.R.	13.10.1956	Tashkent, U.S.S.R.

THROWING THE DISCUS WORLD RECORDS—WOMEN

Ft.	Ins.	Name	Country	Date	Place
158	6	G. MAUERMAYER	Germany	11.7.1936	Dresden, Germany
174	8½	N. DUMBADZE-DJATSKOV	U.S.S.R.	8.8.1948	Moscow, U.S.S.R.
175	1	N. DUMBADZE-DJATSKOV	U.S.S.R.	27.5.1951	Goru, U.S.S.R.
175	10½	N. ROMASHKOVA-PONOMARYEVA	U.S.S.R.	9.8.1952	Odessa, U.S.S.R.
187	1½	N. DUMBADZE-DJATSKOV	U.S.S.R.	18.10.1952	Tbilisi, U.S.S.R.

THROWING THE JAVELIN WORLD RECORDS—WOMEN

ft.	in.	Name	Country	Date	Place
153	4¾	N. GINDELE	U.S.A.	18.6.1932	Chicago, Ill. U.S.A.
154	11¾	A. STEINHEUER	Germany	21.6.1942	Frankfurt, Germany
158	2	H. BAUMA	Austria	29.6.1947	Vienna, Austria
159	6½	H. BAUMA	Austria	12.9.1948	Vienna, Austria
162	8	N. V. SMIRNITSKAYA-DYATLOVA	U.S.S.R.	25.7.1949	Moscow, U.S.S.R.
175	2½	N. V. SMIRNITSKAYA-DYATLOVA	U.S.S.R.	5.8.1949	Moscow, U.S.S.R.
175	8½	N. E. KONJAYEVA-SAMOILOVA	U.S.S.R.	5.2.1954	Leningrad, U.S.S.R.
180	9½	N. E. KONJAYEVA-SAMOILOVA	U.S.S.R.	22.5.1954	Kiev, U.S.S.R.
182	0	N. E. KONJAYEVA-SAMOILOVA	U.S.S.R.	6.8.1954	Kiev, U.S.S.R.
182	10	D. INGROVA-ZATOPKOVA	Czechoslovakia	1.6.1958	Prague, Czechoslovakia
188	4	A. WOJTASZEK-PAZERA	Australia	24.7.1958	Cardiff, Wales
188	7½	B. ZALAGAITITE	U.S.S.R.	30.10.1958	Tbilisi, U.S.S.R.

PENTATHLON WORLD RECORDS—WOMEN

Points	Tables 1954	Name	Country	Date	Place
377		G. MAUERMAYER	Germany	9/11.8.1934	London, England
418	3921	G. MAUERMAYER	Germany	16/17.7.1938	Stuttgart, Germany
	4692	F. E. BLANKERS-KOEN	Netherlands	15/16.9.1951	Amsterdam, Netherlands
	4704	A. C. G. CHUDINA	U.S.S.R.	8/9.8.1953	Bucharest, Roumania
	4747	N. MARTYNENKO-VINOGRADOVA	U.S.S.R.	6/7.7.1955	Leningrad, U.S.S.R.
	4750	A. C. G. CHUDINA	U.S.S.R.	6/7.9.1955	Moscow, U.S.S.R.
	4767	N. MARTYNENKO-VINOGRADOVA	U.S.S.R.	11/12.8.1956	Moscow, U.S.S.R.
	4846	G. P. DOLSHENKOVA-BYSTROVA	U.S.S.R.	15/16.10.1957	Odessa, U.S.S.R.

ATHLETICS QUIZ

1. In what year was the marathon internationally standardized at 26 miles 385 yards?

★

2. How many barriers are negotiated in a 3,000 metres steeplechase?

★

3. What is the world's professional record for a mile?

QUIZ ANSWERS

1. 1924. 2. Thirty-five (including the water jump 7 times). 3. 4 mins. 7.0 secs. by Michael Glen (Scotland) at Keswick, Cumberland, on 1st August 1955.

D

ATHLETICS QUIZ

1. Who has run the most miles inside 4 minutes?

★

2. What is the furthest distance ever run in 24 hours, and who did it?

QUIZ ANSWERS

1. As at August 1959, Herbert James Elliott (Australia) with 11. 2. The 159 miles 562 yards by Walter H. Hayward (South Africa) at Motspur Park on November 20-21, 1953.

Mal Whitfield

Paavo Nurmi

Progressive World Records—contd.

4×100 METRES RELAY WORLD RECORDS (MEN)

Time sec.	Team and Names	Date	Place
42.3	GERMAN NATIONAL TEAM (K. Halt, M. Hermann, E. Kern, R. Rau)	8.7.1912	Stockholm, Sweden
42.2	U.S.A. NATIONAL TEAM (J. V. Scholz, L. C. Murchison, M. M. Kirksey, C. W. Paddock)	22.8.1920	Antwerp, Belgium
42.0	G.B. & N.I. NATIONAL TEAM (H. M. Abrahams, W. Rangeley, L. C. Royle, W. P. Nichol)	12.7.1924	Paris, France
42.0	DUTCH NATIONAL TEAM (J. Boot, H. A. Broos, J. C. de Vries, M. van den Berghe)	12.7.1924	Paris, France
41.0	U.S.A. NATIONAL TEAM (L. A. Clarke, F. Hussey, J. A. le Coney, L. C. Murchison)	13.7.1924	Paris, France
41.0	NEWARK A.C., U.S.A. (C. Bowman, J. Currie, J. Pappas, H. H. Cumming)	4.7.1927	Lincoln, U.S.A.
41.0	SPORTS CLUB EINTRACHT, GERMANY (E. Geerling, F. W. Wichmann, A. Metzner, H. Salz)	10.6.1928	Halle, Germany
40.8	GERMAN NATIONAL TEAM (A. Jonath, R. Corts, H. Houben, H. Körnig)	2.9.1928	Berlin, Germany
40.8	SPORTS CLUB, CHARLOTTENBURG, GERMANY (H. Körnig, W. Grosser, A. Natan, A. Schloske)	22.7.1929	Breslau, Germany
40.8	UNIVERSITY OF SOUTHERN CALIFORNIA, U.S.A. (R. Delby, M. Maurer, M. Guyer, F. C. Wykoff)	9.5.1931	Fresno, Cal., U.S.A.
40.0	U.S.A. NATIONAL TEAM (R. A. Kiesel, E. Toppino, H. M. Dyer, F. C. Wykoff)	7.8.1932	Los Angeles, Cal., U.S.A.
39.8	U.S.A. NATIONAL TEAM (J. C. Owens, R. H. Metcalfe, F. Draper, F. C. Wykoff)	9.8.1936	Berlin, Germany
39.5	U.S.A. NATIONAL TEAM (I. J. Murchison, L. King, W. T. Baker, B-J. Morrow)	1.12.1956	Melbourne, Australia
39.5	GERMAN NATIONAL TEAM (M. Steinbach, M. Lauer, H. Fütterer, M. Germar)	29.8.1958	Cologne, Germany

4×110 YARDS RELAY WORLD RECORDS (MEN)

Time sec.	Team and Names	Date	Place
42.8	U.S.A. NATIONAL TEAM (S. G. Landers, F. S. Davis, W. C. Haymond, E. Smith)	7.6.1919	Philadelphia, Pa., U.S.A.
42.4	NEW YORK A.C., U.S.A. (B. J. Wefers, Jr., F. K. Lovejoy, H. Ray, E. Farrell)	5.7.1921	Pasadena, Cal., U.S.A.
42.4	UNIVERSITY OF ILLINOIS, U.S.A. (P. C. Sweet, H. T. Evans, S. M. Hughes, R. B. Ayres)	28.4.1923	Des Moines, Iowa, U.S.A.
42.0	UNIVERSITY OF CALIFORNIA, U.S.A. (B. Taylor, R. Lee, E. House, K. Lloyd)	16.5.1925	Los Angeles, Cal., U.S.A.
41.0	NEWARK A.C., U.S.A. (C. Bowman, J. Currie, J. Pappas, H. H. Cumming)	4.7.1927	Lincoln, Neb., U.S.A.
40.8	UNIVERSITY OF SOUTHERN CALIFORNIA, U.S.A. (R. Delby, M. Maurer, M. Guyer, F. C. Wykoff)	9.5.1931	Fresno, Cal., U.S.A.
40.5	UNIVERSITY OF SOUTHERN CALIFORNIA, U.S.A. (L. La Fond, W. C. Anderson, P. Jordan, A. C. Talley)	14.5.1938	Fresno, Cal., U.S.A.
40.5	TEXAS UNIVERSITY, U.S.A. (F. D. Smith, J. Prewit, A. Frieden, C. Thomas)	22.5.1954	Los Angeles, Cal., U.S.A.
40.2	TEXAS UNIVERSITY, U.S.A. (F. D. Smith, A. Frieden, J. Prewit, R. Whilden)	21.5.1955	Modesto, Cal., U.S.A.
39.9	UNIVERSITY OF TEXAS TEAM (W. Wilson, S. E. Southern, H. Gainey, B. Whilden)	20.4.1957	Kansas, U.S.A.
39.9	ABILENE CHRISTIAN COLLEGE, U.S.A. (W. Griggs, B. Woodhouse, J. Segrest, B-J. Morrow)	11.5.1957	Fresno, Cal., U.S.A.

4×200 METRES RELAY WORLD RECORDS (MEN)

Time min. sec.	Team and Names	Date	Place
1:36.0	A.I.K., STOCKHOLM, SWEDEN (A. Ljung, I. Pettersson, M. Almqvist, H. Hakansson)	13.9.1908	Stockholm, Sweden
1:27.8*	UNIVERSITY OF PENNSYLVANIA, U.S.A. (S. G. Landers, F. S. Davis, W. C. Haymond, E. Smith)	7.6.1919	Philadelphia, Pa., U.S.A.
1:27.4*	NEW YORK A.C., U.S.A. (B. J. Wefers Jr., F. K. Lovejoy, H. Ray, E. Farrell)	5.7.1921	Pasadena, Cal., U.S.A.
1:25.8*	UNIVERSITY OF SOUTHERN CALIFORNIA, U.S.A. (E. House, M. Smith, C. E. Borah, J. Lewis)	14.5.1927	Los Angeles, Cal., U.S.A.
1:25.0*	STANFORD UNIVERSITY, U.S.A. (J. A. P. Kneubuhl, S. J. Hiserman, R. Malott, J. Weiershauser)	15.5.1937	Fresno, Cal., U.S.A.
1:24.4*	UNIVERSITY OF SOUTHERN CALIFORNIA, U.S.A. (M. E. Patton, R. Frazier, G. Pasquali, N. Stocks)	14.5.1949	Fresno, Cal., U.S.A.
1:24.0*	UNIVERSITY OF SOUTHERN CALIFORNIA, U.S.A. (M. E. Patton, R. Frazier, G. Pasquali, N. Stocks)	20.5.1949	Los Angeles, Cal., U.S.A.
1:24.0	ABILENE CHRISTIAN COLLEGE, U.S.A. (B. Woodhouse, J. Segrest, D. Condor, B-J. Morrow)	26.5.1956	Modesto, Cal., U.S.A.
1:23.8*	U.S.A. NATIONAL TEAM (L. King, A. W. Stanfield, W. T. Baker, B-J. Morrow)	5.12.1956	Sydney, N.S.W., Australia
1:22.7*	UNIVERSITY OF TEXAS (W. Wilson, S. E. Southern, H. Gainey, B. Whilden)	5.4.1957	Austin, Texas, U.S.A.

made over 4 x 220 yards (201.17 m.)

PROGRESSIVE UNITED KINGDOM BEST PERFORMANCES

y=mark made at longer English distance.
e=place-time estimated by interval.
m=mark made at longer metric distance.

100 YARDS

Time	Name	Date
9.5	P. F. RADFORD	25 April '59
9.6	P. F. RADFORD	16 Aug. '58
9.6	P. F. RADFORD	14 June '58
9.7	C. B. HOLMES	5 Feb. '38
9.7	A. G. K. BROWN	4 June '37
9.7	E. H. LIDDELL	7 July '23
9.8	W. R. APPLEGARTH	20 June '14
9.8	W. R. APPLEGARTH	2 Aug. '13
9.8	V. H. d'ARCY	'11

100 METRES

Time	Name	Date
10.3	P. F. RADFORD	13 Sept. '58
10.3	E. R. SANDSTROM	19 Aug. '56
10.4	A. W. SWEENEY	3 July '37
10.5	W. R. RANGELEY	15 Sept. '35
10.6	J. E. LONDON	30 July '28
10.6	H. M. ABRAHAMS	7 July '24
10.6	H. M. ABRAHAMS	7 July '24
10.6	H. M. ABRAHAMS	6 July '24
10.6	W. R. APPLEGARTH	5 Aug. '14

200 METRES (turn)

Time	Name	Date
20.8	P. F. RADFORD	14 Sept. '58
21.0	D. H. SEGAL	28 Aug. '58
21.0	D. H. SEGAL	22 Aug. '58
21.2y	D. H. SEGAL	11 July '58
21.2	B. SHENTON	14 Sept. '57
21.2	B. SHENTON	27 July '56
21.2	G. S. ELLIS	29 Aug. '54
21.2y	C. B. HOLMES	10 Feb. '38
21.2y	A. W. SWEENEY	14 Sept. '35
21.2y	W. R. APPLEGARTH	4 July '14
21.6	W. R. APPLEGARTH	20 June '14
21.6y	W. R. APPLEGARTH	5 July '13
21.8y	W. R. APPLEGARTH	21 Sept. '12
21.8y	C. G. WOOD	25 June '87

220 YARDS (turn)

Time	Name	Date
21.0	P. F. RADFORD	4 Oct. '58
21.2	D. H. SEGAL	11 July '58
21.2	C. B. HOLMES	10 Feb. '38
21.2	A. W. SWEENEY	14 Sept. '35
21.2	W. R. APPLEGARTH	4 July '14
21.6	W. R. APPLEGARTH	5 July '13
21.8	W. R. APPLEGARTH	21 Sept. '12
21.8	C. G. WOOD	25 June '87

400 METRES

Time	Name	Date
46.3	J. D. WRIGHTON	23 Aug. '58
46.7	A. G. K. BROWN	7 Aug. '36
47.3	A. G. K. BROWN	7 Aug. '36
47.6	E. H. LIDDELL	11 July '24
48.0	G. M. BUTLER	11 July '24
48.4	W. HALSWELLE	22 July '08
48.4y	W. HALSWELLE	1 July '08
48.5y	E. C. BREDIN	22 June '95
48.5y	H. C. L-TINDALL	29 June '89

440 YARDS

Time	Name	Date
46.8	E. J. SAMPSON	22 July '58
47.2	J. E. SALISBURY	12 July '58
47.3	J. D. WRIGHTON	21 June '58
47.5	J. E. SALISBURY	14 June '58
47.5	F. P. HIGGINS	21 May '56
47.6	A. G. K. BROWN	1 Aug. '38
47.7	A. G. K. BROWN	10 July '37
48.0	G. L. RAMPLING	7 Aug. '34
48.4	W. HALSWELLE	1 July '08
48.5	E. C. BREDIN	22 June '95
48.5	H. C. L-TINDALL	29 June '89
49.8	C. G. WOOD	3 July '86

800 METRES

Time	Name	Date
1:46.6	D. J. N. JOHNSON	9 Aug. '57
1:46.9	D. J. N. JOHNSON	31 July '57
1:47.4	D. J. N. JOHNSON	28 July '54
1:48.4	S. C. WOODERSON	20 Aug. '38
1:49.7	T. HAMPSON	2 Aug. '32
1:51.2	D. G. A. LOWE	19 Aug. '28
1:52.0ey	D. G. A. LOWE	7 July '26
1:52.4	D. G. A. LOWE	8 July '24
1:53.4	A. G. HILL	17 Aug. '20
1:54.4y	F. J. K. CROSS	9 Mar. '88

880 YARDS

Time	Name	Date
1:47.8	B. S. HEWSON	14 June '58
1:48.5	D. J. N. JOHNSON	20 July '57
1:48.6	B. S. HEWSON	13 Aug. '55
1:48.7	D. J. N. JOHNSON	1 Aug. '55
1:49.2	S. C. WOODERSON	20 Aug. '38
1:50.9	S. C. WOODERSON	1 Aug. '38
1:52.0e	D. G. A. LOWE	7 July '26
1:54.4	F. J. K. CROSS	9 Mar. '88

1,500 METRES

Time	Name	Date
3:41.1	B. S. HEWSON	22 Aug. '58
*3:41.9	G. D. IBBOTSON	19 July '57
*3:42.2	R. G. BANNISTER	7 Aug. '54
*3:43.0	R. G. BANNISTER	6 May '54
*3:44.8	R. G. BANNISTER	27 June '53
3:46.0	R. G. BANNISTER	26 July '52
3:48.0	G. W. NANKEVILLE	27 Aug. '50
*3:48.4	S. C. WOODERSON	9 Sept. '45
3:48.7	S. C. WOODERSON	15 Sept. '38
3:49.0	S. C. WOODERSON	6 Aug. '38
*3:50.3	S. C. WOODERSON	28 Aug. '37
3:51.0	S. C. WOODERSON	25 July '37
3:51.4	F. CORNES	6 Aug. '36

Time	Name	Date
3:52.6	J. F. CORNES	6 Aug. '32
3:55.0	R. H. THOMAS	2 Aug. '31
3:55.6	H. B. STALLARD	10 July '24
3:56.8	A. N. S. JACKSON	10 July '12
3:59.8	H. A. WILSON	30 May '08

* Denotes made in course of a mile event.

ONE MILE

Time	Name	Date
3:57.2	G. D. IBBOTSON	19 July '57
3:58.4	G. D. IBBOTSON	15 June '57
3:58.8	R. G. BANNISTER	7 Aug. '54
3:59.4	R. G. BANNISTER	6 May '54
4:02.0	R. G. BANNISTER	27 June '53
4:03.6	R. G. BANNISTER	2 May '53
4:04.2	S. C. WOODERSON	9 Sept. '45
4:06.4	S. C. WOODERSON	28 Aug. '37
4:10.8	S. C. WOODERSON	20 June '36
4:12.0	R. GRAHAM	20 Aug. '35
4:12.7	S. C. WOODERSON	3 Aug. '35
4:13.4	R. H. THOMAS	25 May '31
4:13.8	A. G. HILL	2 July '21
4:16.8	A. G. HILL	9 Aug. '19
4:16.8	J. BINKS	5 July '02
4:17.0	F. E. BACON	6 July '95
4:18.4	W. G. GEORGE	21 June '84

TWO MILES

Time	Name	Date
8:34.8	K. WOOD	30 May '55
8:41.0	C. J. CHATAWAY	7 June '54
8:47.4	D. A. G. PIRIE	30 Sept. '53
8:47.8	D. A. G. PIRIE	9 Sept. '53
8:49.6	C. J. CHATAWAY	25 May '53
8:55.6	C. J. CHATAWAY	12 June '52
9:03.4	C. A. J. EMERY	25 July '39
9:07.6	C. A. J. EMERY	27 Aug. '38
9:09.6	A. SHRUBB	11 June '04
9:17.0	A. SHRUBB	12 Sept. '03
9:17.4	W. G. GEORGE	26 Apr. '84

THREE MILES

Time	Name	Date
13:20.8	G. D. IBBOTSON	13 July '57
13:23.2	C. J. CHATAWAY	30 July '55
13:27.2	C. J. CHATAWAY	13 Oct. '54
13:32.2	F. GREEN	10 July '54
13:32.2	C. J. CHATAWAY	10 July '54
*13:34.0	D. A. G. PIRIE	29 Aug. '53
13:36.4	D. A. G. PIRIE	1 Aug. '53
13:41.8	D. A. G. PIRIE	20 June '53
13:44.8	D. A. G. PIRIE	31 May '52
13:53.2	S. C. WOODERSON	20 July '46
*14:02.0	P. D. H. WARD	4 Sept. '37
14:15.8	P. D. H. WARD	11 July '36
14:17.6	A. SHRUBB	21 May '03
14:24.0	S. THOMAS	22 Oct. '92

* Mark made in course of a 5,000 metre race.

5,000 METRES

Time	Name	Date
13:36.8	D. A. G. PIRIE	19 June '56
13:51.6	C. J. CHATAWAY	13 Oct. '54
14:02.6	D. A. G. PIRIE	29 Aug. '53
14:08.6	S. C. WOODERSON	23 Aug. '46
14:31.6	P. D. H. WARD	4 Sept. '37
14:42.0	P. D. H. WARD	23 Aug. '37
14:48.2	P. D. H. WARD	24 July '37
14:54.8	T. EVENSON	30 Aug. '31

SIX MILES

Time	Name	Date
28:05.0	S. E. ELDON	28 June '58
28:13.6	K. L. NORRIS	13 July '56
28:19.4	D. A. G. PIRIE	10 July '53
28:47.4	D. A. G. PIRIE	18 Apr. '53
28:55.6	D. A. G. PIRIE	20 June '52
29:13.8	W. HESKETH	6 Aug. '51
29:32.0	D. A. G. PIRIE	13 July '51
29:43.2	F. E. AARON	17 June '50
29:45.0	J. A. BURNS	10 July '36
29:51.4	W. E. EATON	13 Apr. '36
29:59.4	A. SHRUBB	5 Nov. '04
30:17.8	S. THOMAS	22 Oct. '92

10,000 METRES

Time	Name	Date
29:02.8	S. E. ELDON	19 Aug. '58
29:06.4	G. KNIGHT	7 Sept. '57
29:17.2	D. A. G. PIRIE	4 July '56
29:17.2	D. A. G. PIRIE	3 Sept. '53
29:51.8	F. D. SANDO	20 July '52
30:31.6	F. E. AARON	23 Aug. '50
30:58.2	J. A. BURNS	2 Aug. '36
31:02.4	A. SHRUBB	5 Nov. '04

HIGH HURDLES

Time	Name	Date
14.3	P. B. HILDRETH	12 May '59
14.3m	P. B. HILDRETH	14 Sept. '58
14.3m	P. B. HILDRETH	28 Aug. '58
14.3m	P. B. HILDRETH	26 Aug. '58
14.3m	P. B. HILDRETH	14 Sept. '57
14.3	F. J. PARKER	30 July '55
14.3m	D. O. FINLAY	4 Sept. '38
14.4m	D. O. FINLAY	5 Aug. '36
14.5	MARQUESS OF EXETER	9 June '30
14.8	MARQUESS OF EXETER	11 June '27
15.1	F. R. GABY	3 July '26
15.2	F. R. GABY	18 July '25
15.2	F. R. GABY	7 June '23
15.2	G. R. L. ANDERSON	11 May '12
15.6	K. POWELL	22 Mar. '07
15.8	G. B. SHAW	6 July '95
16.0	W. R. POLLOCK	8 Apr. '84
16.0	A. B. LODER	7 Apr. '76
16.0	C. N. JACKSON	Mar. '67
16.0	C. N. JACKSON	15 Nov. '66

4×220 YARDS RELAY WORLD RECORDS (MEN)

Time min. sec.	Team and Names	Date	Place
1:27.8	U.S.A. NATIONAL TEAM (S. G. Landers, F. S. Davis, W. C. Haymond, E. Smith)	7.6.1919	Philadelphia, Pa., U.S.A.
1:27.4	NEW YORK A.C., U.S.A. (B. J. Wefers Jr., F. K. Lovejoy, H. Ray, E. Farrell)	5.7.1921	Pasadena, Cal., U.S.A.
1:25.8	UNIVERSITY OF SOUTHERN CALIFORNIA, U.S.A. (E. House, H. Smith, C. E. Borah, W. Lewis)	14.5.1927	Los Angeles, Cal., U.S.A.
1:25.0	STANFORD UNIVERSITY, U.S.A. (J. A. P. Kneubuhl, S. J. Hiserman, R. Malott, J. Weiershauser)	15.5.1937	Fresno, Cal., U.S.A.
1:24.4	UNIVERSITY OF SOUTHERN CALIFORNIA, U.S.A. (M. E. Patton, R. Frazier, G. Pasquali, N. Stocks)	14.5.1949	Fresno, Cal., U.S.A.
1:24.0	UNIVERSITY OF SOUTHERN CALIFORNIA, U.S.A. (M. E. Patton, R. Frazier, G. Pasquali, N. Stocks)	20.5.1949	Los Angeles, Cal., U.S.A.
1:23.8	U.S.A. NATIONAL TEAM (L. King, A. W. Stanfield, W. T. Baker, B.-J. Morrow)	5.12.1956	Sydney, N.S.W., Australia
1:22.7	UNIVERSITY OF TEXAS TEAM (W. Wilson, S. E. Southern, H. Gainey, B. Whilden)	5.4.1957	Austin, Texas, U.S.A.

4×400 METRES RELAY WORLD RECORDS (MEN)

Time min. sec.	Team and Names	Date	Place
3:18.2	U.S.A. NATIONAL TEAM (H. Schaaf, M. W. Sheppard, H. Gissing, J. M. Rosenberger)	4.9.1911	Celtic Park, N.Y., U.S.A.
3:16.6	U.S.A. NATIONAL TEAM (M. W. Sheppard, C. D. Reidpath, J. E. Meredith, F. J. Lindberg)	15.7.1912	Stockholm, Sweden
3:16.0	U.S.A. NATIONAL TEAM (C. S. Cochrane, A. B. Helffrich, J. O. McDonald, W. E. Stevenson)	13.7.1924	Paris, France
3:14.2	U.S.A. NATIONAL TEAM (G. Baird, E. Spencer, F. P. Alderman, R. J. Barbuti)	5.8.1928	Amsterdam, Netherlands
3:13.4*	U.S.A. NATIONAL TEAM (G. Baird, F. M. Taylor, R. J. Barbuti, E. Spencer)	11.8.1928	London, England
3:12.6*	STANFORD UNIVERSITY, U.S.A. (M. Shove, A. A. Hables, L. T. Hables, B. B. Eastman)	8.5.1931	Fresno, Cal., U.S.A.
3:08.2	U.S.A. NATIONAL TEAM (I. Fuqua, E. A. Ablowich, K. D. Warner, W. A. Carr)	7.8.1932	Los Angeles, Cal., U.S.A.
3:03.9	JAMAICAN NATIONAL TEAM (A. S. Wint, L. A. Laing, H. H. McKenley, V. G. Rhoden)	27.7.1952	Helsinki, Finland

* Made over 4 x 440 yards (402.34 m.)

4×440 YARDS RELAY WORLD RECORDS (MEN)

Time mins. sec.	Team and Names	Date	Place
3:18.2	U.S.A. NATIONAL TEAM (H. Schaaf, M. W. Sheppard, H. Gissing, J. M. Rosenberger)	4.9.1911	Celtic Park, N.Y., U.S.A.
3:18.0	UNIVERSITY OF PENNSYLVANIA, U.S.A. (F. C. Kaufman, J. Lockwood, D. F. Lippincott, J. E. Meredith)	24.4.1915	Philadelphia, Pa., U.S.A.
3:13.4	U.S.A. NATIONAL TEAM (G. Baird, F. M. Taylor, R. Barbuti, E. Spencer)	11.8.1928	London, England
3:12.6	STANFORD UNIVERSITY, U.S.A. (M. B. Shore, A. A. Hables, L. I. Hables, B. B. Eastman)	8.5.1931	Fresno, Cal., U.S.A.
3:11.6	UNIVERSITY OF CALIFORNIA, U.S.A. (E. Johnson, J. Cassin, R. H. Smallwood, A. L. Fitch)	16.5.1936	Fresno, Cal., U.S.A.
3:10.5	STANFORD UNIVERSITY, U.S.A. (C. Shaw, E. Clark, C. Williamson, C. H. Jeffrey)	13.4.1940	Palo, Alto, Cal., U.S.A.
3:09.4	UNIVERSITY OF CALIFORNIA, U.S.A. (J. L. Reese, F. A. Froom, C. F. Barnes, G. Klemmer)	17.6.1941	Los Angeles, Cal., U.S.A.
3:08.8	U.S.A. NATIONAL TEAM (E. G. Cole, J. W. Mashburn, R. Pearman, M. G. Whitfield)	9.8.1952	London, England
3:07.3	U.S.A. NATIONAL TEAM (C. L. Jenkins, L. V. Spurrier, T. W. Courtney, L. W. Jones)	1.11.1956	Los Angeles, Cal., U.S.A.

H. M. Abrahams

Gunder Hägg

ATHLETICS QUIZ

Who was the first marathon runner to average over 11 m.p.h.?

QUIZ ANSWER

James Henry Peters (G.B.) in the Windsor to Chiswick marathon in June 1952, covered in 2 hrs. 20 mins. 42.2 secs. (average 11.24 m.p.h.).

4×800 METRES RELAY WORLD RECORDS (MEN)

Time min. sec.	Team and Names	Date	Place
8:01.0	S.C. TEUTONIA, BERLIN, GERMANY (R. Schmidt, Isermann, H. Walpert, H. Bocher)	3.9.1927	Berlin, Germany
7:41.4	BOSTON A.A., U.S.A. (S. H. Martin, C. Sansone, C. Welch, L. Hahn)	6.7.1926	Philadelphia, Pa., U.S.A.
7:35.8	U.S.A. NATIONAL TEAM (C. C. Hornbostel, R. C. Young, H. C. Williamson, J. Woodruff)	15.8.1936	London, England
7:30.4	GERMAN NATIONAL TEAM (H. Seibert, H. Grau, L. Kaindl, R. Harbig)	23.8.1941	Brunswick, Germany
7:29.0	SWEDISH NATIONAL TEAM (T. Stein, O. Linden, S. Lindgard, L. Strand)	13.9.1946	Stockholm, Sweden
7:28.0	U.D.A. CZECHOSLOVAKIA (D. Cikel, A. Stizinek, L. Liska, S. Jungwirth)	29.7.1953	Stará Boleslav, Czechoslovakia
7:26.8	SOVIET ARMY TEAM, U.S.S.R. (O. Ageev, S. Sukhanov, G. Modoj, G. Ivakin)	25.7.1954	Kiev, U.S.S.R.
7:26.4	U.S.S.R. NATIONAL TEAM (G. Ivakin, O. Ageev, G. Modoj, E. Sokolov)	1.8.1955	Riga, Latvia
7:15.8	BELGIAN NATIONAL TEAM (A. Ballieux, A. Langenus, E. Leva, R. Moens)	8.8.1956	Brussels, Belgium

220 YARDS LOW HURDLES

Time	Name	Date
23.7	P. A. L. VINE	15 July '55
24.0m	F. J. PARKER	5 June '51
24.0	S. BROOKS	13 Feb. '51
24.2	S. BROOKS	6 June '50
24.3e	MARQUESS OF EXETER	13 June '30
24.6m	MARQUESS OF EXETER	18 Sept. '27
24.7	MARQUESS OF EXETER	9 July '27
24.8	MARQUESS OF EXETER	21 Mar. '25

Straightaway marks:

23.3	P. B. HILDRETH	27 Aug. '55
24.7	MARQUESS OF EXETER	18 July '25

400 METRES HURDLES

51.1	T. S. FARRELL	23 Aug. '57
51.5	H. KANE	13 Oct. '54
52.2	MARQUESS OF EXETER	1 Aug. '32
53.4	MARQUESS OF EXETER	30 July '28
54.0	T. C. LIVINGSTONE-LEARMONTH	29 July '28
54.0y	MARQUESS OF EXETER	7 July '28

440 YARDS HURDLES

51.6	C. E. GOUDGE	4 Aug. '58
51.8	H. KANE	13 Oct. '54
52.7	H. WHITTLE	11 July '53
52.7	D. K. GRACIE	9 Aug. '52
53.2	A. W. SCOTT	4 Aug. '52
53.3	H. WHITTLE	21 June '52
53.4	H. WHITTLE	1 Aug. '49
53.7	H. WHITTLE	6 June '49
53.8	MARQUESS OF EXETER	5 July '30
54.0	MARQUESS OF EXETER	7 July '28
54.2	MARQUESS OF EXETER	2 July '27
55.0	MARQUESS OF EXETER	3 July '26
56.8	G. R. L. ANDERSON	16 July '10
57.2	G. B. SHAW	12 Aug. '91

3,000 METRES STEEPLECHASE

8:41.2	C. W. BRASHER	29 Nov. '56
8:44.2	J. I. DISLEY	11 Sept. '55
8:51.8	J. I. DISLEY	25 July '52
8:59.4	J. I. DISLEY	23 July '52
9:11.6	J. I. DISLEY	26 Sept. '51
9:18.4	J. I. DISLEY	28 June '50
9:18.8	T. EVENSON	1 Aug. '32
9:27.4	T. EVENSON	2 Aug. '31
9:40.2	H. W. TOWNSEND	28 July '29
9:57.6*	J. E. WEBSTER	6 Aug. '27
10:00.8	P. HODGE	20 Aug. '20

* 8 laps steeplechase in excess of 3,000 metres (1 mile, 1,520.8 yards).

HIGH JUMP

ft. ins.	Name	Date
6 8½	C. W. FAIRBROTHER	5 Sept. '59
6 8	C. W. FAIRBROTHER	1 Aug. '59
6 7½	P. WELLS	11 Dec. '54
6 7¼	A. S. PATERSON	2 Aug. '47
6 6¾	A. S. PATERSON	7 July '46
6 5¾	A. S. PATERSON	8 June '46
6 5	A. S. PATERSON	15 May '46
6 5	B. H. BAKER	25 June '21
6 3½	B. H. BAKER	4 Sept. '20
6 3½	B. H. BAKER	3 July '20
6 2¼	M. J. BROOKS	7 Apr. '76
6 0¾	M. J. BROOKS	17 Mar. '76

ATHLETICS QUIZ

1. In his world record 400 metres of 45.2 secs., in what time did Lou Jones (U.S.A.) pass through the halfway mark?

★

2. How long did Roger Moens take to cover the first lap of his world record 800 metres in Oslo?

★

3. What is the irreducible minimum reaction time for any sprinter to the gun?

QUIZ ANSWERS

1. 21.3 secs. 2. 52.0 secs. to finish in 1 min. 45.7 secs. 3. 0.37 secs. is the fastest that a sprinter could break contact with his starting blocks.

Valerie Ball-Winn    Diane Leather    Fanny Blankers-Koen    Betty Cuthbert

Progressive World Records—*contd.*

4×880 YARDS RELAY WORLD RECORDS (MEN)

Time min. sec.	Team and Names	Date	Place
7:53.0	U.S.A. NATIONAL TEAM (F. M. Riley, J. Bromflow, M. W. Sheppard, A. R. Kiviat)	5.9.1910	Celtic, Park, N.Y., U.S.A.
7:50.4	OXFORD AND CAMBRIDGE UNIVERSITIES, G.B. & N.I. (W. G. Tatham, H. B. Stallard, W. R. Milligan, B. G. d'U. Rudd)	1.5.1920	Philadelphia, Pa., U.S.A.
7:49.4	UNIVERSITY OF PENNSYLVANIA, U.S.A. (J. E. Meredith, J. Holden, E. W. McMullen, L. A. Brown)	29.4.1922	Philadelphia, Pa., U.S.A.
7:47.6	BOSTON COLLEGE, U.S.A. (W. T. McKillop, P. J. Mahoney, T. T. Cavanaugh, L. R. Welch)	26.4.1924	Philadelphia, Pa., U.S.A.
7:42.0	GEORGETOWN UNIVERSITY, U.S.A. (E. Swinburne, J. Holden, W. Sullivan, G. Marsters)	25.4.1925	Philadelphia, Pa., U.S.A.
7:41.4	BOSTON A.A., U.S.A. (S. H. Martin, C. Sansone, L. R. Welch, L. Hahn)	6.7.1926	Philadelphia, Pa., U.S.A.
7:35.8	U.S.A. NATIONAL TEAM (C. C. Hornbostel, R. C. Young, H. W. Williamson, J. Y. Woodruff)	15.8.1936	London, England
7:34.5	UNIVERSITY OF SOUTHERN CALIFORNIA, U.S.A. (J. L. Reese, G. Klemmer, D. Peter, C. F. Barnes)	24.5.1941	Los Angeles, Cal., U.S.A.
7:30.6	G.B. & N.I. NATIONAL TEAM (G. W. Nankeville, A. Webster, F. Evans, H. J. Parlett)	26.9.1951	London, England
7:29.2	U.S.A. NATIONAL TEAM (W. Ashenfelter, R. Pearman, J. B. Barnes, M. G. Whitfield)	4.8.1952	London, England
7:27.3	FORDHAM UNIVERSITY, U.S.A. (T. Foley, F. Tarsney, W. Persichetty, T. W. Courtney)	21.5.1954	Los Angeles, Cal., U.S.A.
7:23.0	U.S.A. NATIONAL TEAM (J. D. Walters, L. V. Spurrier, A. M. Sowell, T. W. Courtney)	5.12.1956	Sydney, N.S.W., Australia
7:22.8	OCCIDENTAL COLLEGE, U.S.A. (T. S. White, D. A. Reisbord, L. G. Wray, T. D. Hadley)	24.5.1957	Los Angeles, Cal., U.S.A.

4×1,500 METRES RELAY WORLD RECORDS (MEN)

Time min. sec.	Team and Names	Date	Place
16:40.2	I.K. GÖTA, STOCKHOLM, SWEDEN (G. Petersson, J. Lindblom, R. Falk, S. Lundgren)	12.8.1919	Stockholm, Sweden
16:37.0	I.F. LINNÉA, STOCKHOLM, SWEDEN, (H. Adamsson, Gösta Fosselius, Gunnar Fosselius, E. Wide)	2.8.1925	Norrköping, Sweden
16:26.2	TURUN URHEILULIITTO, ABO, FINLAND (N. Koivunalho, E. Katz, F. Liewendahl, P. Nurmi)	12.7.1926	Stockholm, Sweden
16:11.4	TURUN URHEILULIITTO, ABO, FINLAND (F. Liewendahl, E. Katz, N. Koivunalho, P. Nurmi)	17.7.1926	Viipuri, Finland
15:55.6	ENGLISH NATIONAL TEAM (A. A. Harris, H. W. Hedges, J. F. Cornes, R. H. Thomas)	30.8.1931	Cologne, Germany
15:54.8	FINNISH NATIONAL TEAM (P. Salovaara, M. Salovaara, T. Sarkama, N. Hartikaa)	17.9.1939	Gothenburg, Sweden
15:42.0	BRANDKARENS, I. K. STOCKHOLM, SWEDEN (B. Jansson, H. Karlén, H. Kälarne, B. Hellström)	3.8.1941	Gothenburg, Sweden
15:38.6	MALMO ALLM. IF. SWEDEN (G. Jakobson, S. Stridsberg, L. Strand, G. Hägg)	29.7.1945	Norrköping, Sweden
15:34.6	GEFLE IDROTTSFORENING, SWEDEN (I. Bengtsson, G. Bergqvist, O. W. Aberg, H. Eriksson)	27.7.1947	Karlsbad, Sweden
15:30.2	GEFLE IDROTTSFORENING, SWEDEN (O. W. Aberg, I. Bengtsson, G. Bergqvist, H. Eriksson)	3.7.1949	Gävle, Sweden
15:29.2	HUNGARIAN NATIONAL TEAM (S. Garay, E. Béres, I. Rózsavölgyi, S. Iharos)	23.9.1953	Budapest, Hungary
15:27.2	G.B. & N.I. NATIONAL TEAM (R. H. Dunkley, D. C. Law, D. A. G. Pirie, G. W. Nankeville)	23.9.1953	London, England
15:21.2	BUDAPEST HONVED SPORT EGYESULET (L. Tábori, I. Rózsavölgyi, F. Mikes, S. Iharos)	14.7.1954	Budapest, Hungary
15:14.8	BUDAPEST HONVED SPORT EGYESULET (F. Mikes, L. Tábori, I. Rózsavölgyi, S. Iharos)	29.9.1955	Budapest, Hungary
15:11.4	EAST GERMAN TEAM (S. Valentin, H. Reinnagel, S. Herrmann, K. Richtzenhain)	9.8.1958	Poznan, Poland

4×1 MILE RELAY WORLD RECORDS (MEN)

Time min. sec.	Team and Names	Date	Place
17:51.2	U.S.A. NATIONAL TEAM (H. F. Mahoney, E. T. Marceau, J. Powers, O. Hedlund)	17.6.1913	Easton, Pa., U.S.A.
17:51.2	U.S.A. NATIONAL TEAM (G. Taylor, J. Hoffmire, V. Windnagle, D. Potter)	29.4.1916	Philadelphia, Pa., U.S.A.
17:45.0	UNIVERSITY OF ILLINOIS, U.S.A. (H. Yates, B. Patterson, G. McGinnis, R. Wharton)	29.4.1922	Des Moines, Iowa, U.S.A.
17:21.4	ILLINOIS A.C., U.S.A. (E. E. Krogh, R. Buker, R. B. Watson, J. W. Ray)	23.6.1923	Chicago, Ill., U.S.A.
17:17.2	U.S.A. NATIONAL TEAM (C. C. Hornbostel, E. G. Venzke, A. J. San Romani, G. Cunningham)	15.8.1936	London, England
17:16.2	INDIANA UNIVERSITY, U.S.A. (M. Truitt, J. Smith, T. Deckard, D. R. Lash)	24.4.1937	Philadelphia, Pa., U.S.A.
17:02.8	BRANDKARENS IDROTTSKLUBB, STOCKHOLM, SWEDEN (B. Jansson, H. Kárlen, H. Kälarne, B. Hellström)	15.8.1941	Stockholm, Sweden
16:55.8	GEFLE IDROTTSFORENING, SWEDEN (R. Wallgren, I. Bengtsson, O. W. Aberg, H. Ericsson)	27.8.1948	Gothenburg, Sweden
16:42.8	GEFLE IDROTTS FORENING, SWEDEN (I. Bengtsson, G. Bergqvist, O. W. Aberg, H. Ericsson)	5.8.1949	Stockholm, Sweden
16:41.0	G.B. & N.I. NATIONAL TEAM (C. J. Chataway, G. W. Nankeville, D. C. Seaman, R. G. Bannister)	1.8.1953	London, England

Time min. sec.	Team and Names	Date	Place
16:30.6	ENGLISH NATIONAL TEAM, (M. T. Blagrove, P. R. Clark, D. G. Ibbotson, B. S. Hewson)	27.9.1958	London, England
†16:25.6	AUSTRALIAN NATIONAL TEAM (D. Wilson, A. G. Thomas, J. Murray, H. J. Elliott)	22.3.1959	Melbourne, Australia
	† not yet ratified		

POLE VAULT

ft. ins.	Name	Date
14 1¼	G. M. ELLIOTT	30 Sept. '59
14 1¼	G. M. ELLIOTT	12 Sept. '59
14 1¼	G. M. ELLIOTT	27 Aug. '58
14 1¼	G. M. ELLIOTT	3 July '57
14 1¼	G. M. ELLIOTT	28 Aug. '54
14 0¼	G. M. ELLIOTT	12 June '54
13 9¾	G. M. ELLIOTT	4 Aug. '53
13 9	G. M. ELLIOTT	23 July '53
13 8	G. M. ELLIOTT	13 June '53
13 7¾	G. M. ELLIOTT	23 Aug. '52
13 6	G. M. ELLIOTT	9 Aug. '52
13 6	G. M. ELLIOTT	5 July '52
13 6	G. M. ELLIOTT	7 June '52
13 6	G. M. ELLIOTT	31 May '52
13 6	G. M. ELLIOTT	14 May '52
13 6	N. G. A. GREGOR	30 June '51
13 1¾	F. R. WEBSTER	5 Aug. '36
12 9½	F. R. WEBSTER	16 July '36
12 9	F. R. WEBSTER	11 July '36
12 8	F. R. WEBSTER	4 July '36
12 7½	L. T. BOND	2 Aug. '31
12 6½	L. T. BOND	13 June '30
12 4¾	L. T. BOND	3 May '30
12 1¼	L. T. BOND	3 May '30
11 10¼	L. T. BOND	23 June '28
11 9	R. D. DICKINSON	4 July '91

4×100 METRES RELAY WORLD RECORDS (WOMEN)

Time secs.	Team and Names	Date	Place
46.4	GERMAN NATIONAL TEAM (E. Albus, K. Krauss, M. Dollinger, I. Dorffeldt)	8.8.1936	Berlin, Germany
46.1	AUSTRALIAN NATIONAL TEAM (S. B. Strickland, de la Hunty, V. Johnson, W. Cripps, M. Jackson)	27.7.1952	Helsinki, Finland
45.9	U.S.A. NATIONAL TEAM (A. M. Faggs, B. Jones, J. Morreau, C. Hardy)	27.7.1952	Helsinki, Finland
45.9	GERMAN NATIONAL TEAM (U. Knabe, M. Domagalla-Sander, H. Erny-Klein, M. Petersen)	27.7.1952	Helsinki, Finland
45.6	U.S.S.R. NATIONAL TEAM (V. Kalashnikova-Krepkina, Z. Safronova, N. Dvalishvili-Khnikina, I. R. Turova-Boshkareya)	20.9.1953	Budapest, Hungary
45.6	U.S.S.R. NATIONAL TEAM (G. Vinogradova-Popova, M. L. Itkina, Z. Safronova, L. Polinichenko)	11.9.1955	Moscow, U.S.S.R.
45.2	U.S.S.R. NATIONAL TEAM (V. Kalashnikova-Krepkina, O. Kosholeva, M. L. Itkina, I. R. Turova-Boshkareya)	27.7.1956	Kiev, U.S.S.R.
45.1	GERMAN NATIONAL TEAM (E. Fisch, G. Köhler-Birkemeyer, C. Seliger-Stubnick, B. Mayer)	30.9.1956	Dresden, Germany
44.9	AUSTRALIAN NATIONAL TEAM (S. B. Strickland, de la Hunty, N. C. Croker-Fleming, F. Mellor, B. Cuthbert)	1.12.1956	Melbourne, Australia
44.9	GERMAN NATIONAL TEAM (G. Köhler, B. Mayer, M. Sander, C. Seeliger Stubnick)	1.12.1956	Melbourne, Australia
44.5	AUSTRALIAN NATIONAL TEAM (S. B. Strickland, de la Hunty, N. C. Croker-Fleming, F. Mellor, B. Cuthbert)	1.12.1956	Melbourne, Australia

LONG JUMP

	Name	Date
24 10¼	A. R. CRUTTENDEN	5 Dec. '56
24 8¼	K. S. D. WILMSHURST	5 Aug. '54
24 3	K. S. D. WILMSHURST	26 June '54
24 2½	H. M. ABRAHAMS	7 June '24
23 9½	H. M. ABRAHAMS	31 May '24
23 8½	H. M. ABRAHAMS	7 July '23
23 7½	H. M. ABRAHAMS	24 Mar. '23
23 6½	C. B. FRY	5 Mar. '93
23 5	C. B. FRY	8 Apr. '92
23 0½	J. W. PARSONS	30 June '83
22 10½	E. J. DAVIES	27 Mar. '74

4×110 YARDS RELAY WORLD RECORDS (WOMEN)

	Team and Names	Date	Place
49.8	G.B. & N.I. NATIONAL TEAM (F. Haynes, D. E. Scouler, R. Thompson, E. Edwards)	29.8.1926	Gothenburg, Sweden
48.8	NETHERLANDS NATIONAL TEAM (F. E. Blankers-Koen, J. Adema, N. Timmer, G. J. M. Koudys)	18.5.1944	Amsterdam, Netherlands
47.4	NETHERLANDS NATIONAL TEAM (X. S. de Jongh, N. Timmer, G. J. M. Koudys, F. E. Blankers-Koen)	25.7.1948	Ryswyk, Netherlands
47.3	SOUTH AFRICAN NATIONAL TEAM (F. C. Wills, S. Black, E. Maskell, D. L. E. Hasenfager-Robb)	10.4.1950	Kimberley, S. Africa
46.9	SOUTH AFRICAN NATIONAL TEAM (F. C. Wills, S. Black, D. L. E. Hasenjager-Robb, E. Maskell)	26.3.1951	Pretoria, S. Africa
46.9	AUSTRALIAN NATIONAL TEAM (S. B. Strickland, de la Hunty, M. Jackson-Nelson, W. Cripps-Dennis, V. Johnson)	5.7.1952	London, England
46.3	AUSTRALIAN NATIONAL TEAM (S. B. de la Hunty, V. Johnson, W. Cripps-Dennis, M. Jackson)	4.8.1952	London, England
45.8	D.D.R. EAST GERMAN TEAM (G. Hanning, C. Seeliger-Stubnick, G. Köhler-Birchemeyer, B. Mayer)	29.7.1956	Rostock, E. Germany
45.6	AUSTRALIAN NATIONAL TEAM (S. B. Strickland, de la Hunty, N. W. Croker-Fleming, F. Mellor, B. Cuthbert)	5.12.1956	Sydney, N.S.W., Australia
45.3	ENGLISH NATIONAL TEAM (H. J. Armitage-Young, J. F. Foulds-Paul, D. Hyman, V. M. Weston)	26.7.1958	Cardiff, Wales

SHOT PUTT

	Name	Date
61 0	A. ROWE	14 Aug. '59
60 0	A. ROWE	14 Aug. '59
58 11	A. ROWE	13 Sept. '58
58 11	A. ROWE	3 Sept. '58
58 5½	A. ROWE	28 Aug. '58
58 4	A. ROWE	23 Aug. '58
58 0	A. ROWE	16 Aug. '58
57 8	A. ROWE	24 July '58
56 9	A. ROWE	11 July '58
55 7	A. ROWE	24 July '57
55 6	W. B. L. PALMER	10 Oct. '56
55 2	J. A. SAVIDGE	8 May '54
54 9½	J. A. SAVIDGE	23 Aug. '52
54 9¼	J. A. SAVIDGE	4 May '52
54 5	J. A. SAVIDGE	2 June '51
51 11½	J. A. SAVIDGE	13 May '50
51 4½	J. A. SAVIDGE	26 Nov. '49
48 10½	J. A. SAVIDGE	23 July '49
48 9	R. L. HOWLAND	23 Sept. '35
46 0	R. L. HOWLAND	13 June '29
45 8½	T. KIRKWOOD	26 Sept. '06

4×200 METRES RELAY WORLD RECORDS (WOMEN)

Time min. sec.	Team and Names	Date	Place
1:45.8	GERMAN NATIONAL TEAM (R. Engelhard, Feldmann, G. Wittmann, Gericke)	26.6.1932	Neurossen, Germany
1:45.3	GERMAN NATIONAL TEAM (E. Albus, I. Dorffeldt, D. Voigt, A. Müller)	19.6.1938	Cottbus, Germany
1:41.0	NETHERLANDS NATIONAL TEAM (L. Sluyters, F. E. Blankers-Koen, N. Timmer, G. J. M. Koudys)	27.8.1944	Hilversum, Netherlands
1:40.6	DYNAMO CLUB, U.S.S.R. (S. R. Malshina, A. G. Chudina, Z. Duhovitch, Y. I. Sechenova)	12.7.1950	Moscow, U.S.S.R.
1:39.7	U.S.S.R. NATIONAL TEAM (N. Khnykina, Y. I. Sechenova, Z. Safronova, S. R. Malshina)	27.9.1951	Bucharest, Roumania
1:39.7	SOUTHERN COUNTIES W.A.A.A., G.B. & N.I. (A. E. Johnson, J. F. Foulds-Paul, S. Hampton-Pirie, S. Cheeseman-Disley)	17.9.1952	London, England
1:36.4	U.S.S.R. NATIONAL TEAM (F. Calajnicova, V. Kazenteva, Z. Safronova, N. Dvalijvili-Khnykina)	9.8.1953	Budapest, Hungary
1:36.4	D.D.R. EAST GERMAN TEAM (G. Henning, C. Seeliger-Birchemeyer, G. Köhler-Birchemeyer, B. Mayer)	29.7.1956	Rostock, E. Germany
1:36.3	AUSTRALIAN NATIONAL TEAM (M. J. Matthews, N. C. Croker-Fleming, F. Mellor, B. Cuthbert)	5.12.1956	Sydney, N.S.W., Australia

DISCUS THROW

	Name	Date
178 11	G. E. CARR	21 May '58
178 0½	M. PHARAOH	27 Nov. '56
174 0½	M. PHARAOH	21 July '56
169 11	M. PHARAOH	15 Sept. '55
166 9	M. PHARAOH	9 July '55
165 8½	M. PHARAOH	2 June '54
163 0½	M. PHARAOH	6 May '54
162 5½	M. PHARAOH	20 June '53
161 1	M. PHARAOH	20 June '53
155 3½	J. A. SAVIDGE	9 May '53
155 3	H. I. DUGUID	12 May '51
154 6½	J. A. SAVIDGE	3 May '50
153 8	D. YOUNG	25 June '38
142 10½	D. R. BELL	1 June '36
140 0	D. R. BELL	2 June '34
135 6¾	K. H. PRIDIE	13 June '31

4×220 YARDS RELAY WORLD RECORDS (WOMEN)

	Team and Names	Date	Place
1:43.9	SPARTAN L.A.C., G.B. & N.I. (V. Robins, B. Turner, J. F. Foulds-Paul, S. Cheeseman-Disley)	17.7.1951	London, England
1:43.4	SPARTAN L.A.C., G.B. & N.I. (J. F. Foulds-Paul, V. Robins, V. M. Ball-Winn, S. Cheeseman-Disley)	19.9.1951	Motspur Park, England
1:41.4	WOMEN'S A.A.A., G.B. & N.I. (S. Cheeseman-Disley, B. Foster, M. Brian, D. G. Hall)	16.9.1951	London, England
1:40.0	U.S.A. NATIONAL TEAM. (A. M. Faggs, D. Dwyer, J. Morreau, C. Hardy)	4.8.1952	London, England
1:39.9	G.B. & N.I. NATIONAL TEAM (A. Pashley, J. Newboult, S. Hampton-Pirie, A. E. Johnson)	30.9.1953	London, England
1:36.4	D.D.R. EAST GERMAN TEAM (G. Henning, C. Seeliger-Stubnick, G. Köhler-Birchemeyer, B. Meyer)	29.7.1956	Rostock, E. Germany
1:36.3	AUSTRALIAN NATIONAL TEAM (M. J. Mathews-Willard, N. C. Croker-Fleming, F. Mellor, B. Cuthbert)	5.12.1956	Sydney, N.S.W., Australia

---

ATHLETICS QUIZ

Which male athlete has won most Olympic Gold medals?

★

QUIZ ANSWER

Ray Ewry (U.S.A.) with 8 between 1900 and 1908.

3×800 METRES RELAY WORLD RECORDS (WOMEN)

Time min. sec.	Team and Names	Date	Place
7:37.4	V.f.B. BRESLAU, GERMANY (Nitschke, Schniechen, Radke)	6.8.1933	Breslau, Germany
7:32.0	GRUPPO SPORTIVO VENCHI UNICA DE TURIN (C. Balbo, G. Giorda, L. Bulzacchi)	29.6.1937	Turin, Italy
7:22.6	FRENCH NATIONAL TEAM (M. Fize, T. Lucas, G. Vincent)	16.7.1939	Monaco
7:15.8	FRENCH NATIONAL TEAM (P. Delepine, M. Loubet, J. Dufour)	3.10.1943	Paris, France
7:07.8	SOUTHERN COUNTIES TEAM, G.B. & N.I. (D. Born, E. D. Garrett, V. M. Ball)	6.8.1949	London, England
6:53.8	U.S.S.R. NATIONAL TEAM (G. Zhiljcova, K. Dmitruk, Y. M. Vasiljeva)	28.10.1949	Tbilisi, U.S.S.R.
6:49.6	U.S.S.R. NATIONAL TEAM (L. Sokolova, N, Kabysh-Solotova, Y. M. Vasiljeva)	24.7.1950	Moscow, U.S.S.R.
6:33.2	U.S.S.R. NATIONAL TEAM (N. Chernoshchok, D. Barahovich-Kozlova, N. G. Pletyneva-Otkalenko)	19.9.1953	Budapest, Hungary
6:27.6	U.S.S.R. NATIONAL TEAM (N. G. Pletyneva-Otkalenko, L. Lysenko-Schevzova, A. Galdina-Lapshina)	11.9.1955	Moscow, U.S.S.R.
6:27.4	UKRAINIAN S.S.R. TEAM (L. Yanvayera, D. Barahovich-Kozlova, L. Lysenko-Schevzova)	9.9.1958	Kiev, U.S.S.R.

3×880 YARDS RELAY WORLD RECORDS (WOMEN)

Time min. sec.	Team and Names	Date	Place
7:07.8	SOUTHERN COUNTIES TEAM, G.B. & N.I. (D. Born, E. D. Garrett, V. M. Ball)	6.8.1949	London, England
7:00.6	ILFORD A.C., G.B. & N.I. (B. Critchley, J. F. Dryden, P. E. M. Green)	28.6.1952	Ilford, England
6:49.0	G.B. & N.I. NATIONAL TEAM (N. R. Smalley, D. S. Leather, M. C. Slemon)	3.8.1953	London, England
6:46.0	G.B. & N.I. NATIONAL TEAM (D. S. Leather, I. E. A. Oliver, N. R. Smalley)	17.7.1954	London, England
6:36.2	HUNGARIAN NATIONAL TEAM (A. Bleha-Bácskai, A. Oros, A. Kazi)	21.7.1954	Tata, Hungary

A.A.A. CHAMPIONSHIPS

The A.A.A. Championships have been held every year since 1880 except for the ten war years 1915–18 and 1940–45.

The Championships have been held at 14 venues. From 1880 to 1905 they were held in London, the Midlands and the North in strict rotation. From 1909 to 1931 they were held at Stamford Bridge, London, since when they have always been held at the White City Stadium, London.

Several championships, notably the 10 miles, Marathon, Relays and Decathlon have sometimes been held separately from the main Championship meeting.

A.A.A. CHAMPIONS

100 YARDS

Date	Name	Club	Sec.
1880	W. P. PHILLIPS	(London A.C.)	10.2
1881	W. P. PHILLIPS	(London A.C.)	10.2
1882	W. P. PHILLIPS	(London A.C.)	10.2
1883	J. M. COWIE	(London A.C.)	10.2
1884	J. M. COWIE	(London A.C.)	10.2
1885	J. M. COWIE	(London A.C.)	10.2
1886	A. WHARTON	(Darlington Coll. F.C.)	10.0
1887	A. WHARTON	(Darlington Coll. F.C.)	10.1
1888	F. WESTING	(U.S.A.)	10.2
1889	E. H. PELLING	(London A.C.)	10.4
1890	N. D. MORGAN	(Ireland)	10.4
1891	L. H. CARY	(U.S.A.)	10.2
1892	C. A. BRADLEY	(Huddersfield C. & A.C.)	10.2
1893	C. A. BRADLEY	(Huddersfield C. & A.C.)	10.0
1894	C. A. BRADLEY	(Huddersfield C. & A.C.)	10.2
1895	C. A. BRADLEY	(Huddersfield C. & A.C.)	10.0
1896	N. D. MORGAN	(Ireland)	10.4
1897	J. H. PALMER	(Essex Beagles)	10.8
1898	F. W. COOPER	(Bradford A. & F.C.)	10.0
1899	R. W. WADSLEY	(Highgate H.)	10.2
1900	A. F. DUFFY	(U.S.A.)	10.0
1901	A. F. DUFFY	(U.S.A.)	10.0
1902	A. F. DUFFY	(U.S.A.)	10.0
1903	A. F. DUFFY	(U.S.A.)	10.0
1904	J. W. MORTON	(South London H.)	10.0
1905	J. W. MORTON	(South London H.)	10.2
1906	J. W. MORTON	(South London H.)	10.4
1907	J. W. MORTON	(South London H.)	10.8
1908	R. KERR	(Canada)	10.0
1909	R. E. WALKER	(South Africa)	10.0
1910	F. L. RAMSDELL	(U.S.A.)	10.2
1911	F. L. RAMSDELL	(U.S.A.)	10.4
1912	G. H. PATCHING	(South Africa)	9.8

(*Contd. opposite*)

ATHLETICS QUIZ

1. What is the world's best recorded performance for 100 yards in a 3-legged race?

★

2. Of the 60 medals distributed for the 100, 200, 400 and 800 metres in the last 5 Olympic Games, how many have been won by coloured athletes?

★

QUIZ ANSWER

1. 11.0 secs. by Henry L. Hillman and Lawson Robertson at Brooklyn, N.Y., on April 24th, 1909. 2. 34.

HAMMER THROW

Ft.	Ins.	Name	Date
213	1	M. J. ELLIS	4 June '59
211	9¾	M. J. ELLIS	15 Sept. '57
210	11½	M. J. ELLIS	6 Sept. '57
206	3¼	M. J. ELLIS	6 Sept. '57
205	9	M. J. ELLIS	23 Aug. '57
199	10	M. J. ELLIS	19 July '57
197	9	M. J. ELLIS	12 July '57
195	7	P. C. ALLDAY	2 Sept. '56
192	6	E. C. K. DOUGLAS	28 Apr. '55
188	5	E. C. K. DOUGLAS	25 Sept. '54
185	3	E. C. K. DOUGLAS	11 Sept. '54
183	9½	D. McD. M. CLARK	4 Mar. '50
180	0½	D. McD. M. CLARK	21 Feb. '50
178	8¼	D. McD. M. CLARK	13 Sept. '47
173	1⅛	M. C. NOKES	29 July '23
172	0¼	M. C. NOKES	16 June '23
166	9½	T. R. NICHOLSON	19 Aug. '08
162	8	T. R. NICHOLSON	'08

JAVELIN THROW

Ft.	Ins.	Name	Date
246	7	C. G. SMITH	14 Sept. '57
238	3	C. G. SMITH	3 Aug. '57
236	7	P. S. CULLEN	13 July '57
232	11	C. G. SMITH	13 July '57
230	0	C. G. SMITH	13 July '57
229	2	C. G. SMITH	13 July '57
228	6	P. S. CULLEN	10 July '57
224	9½	P. S. CULLEN	6 Aug. '56
223	1	P. S. CULLEN	27 Aug. '55
222	5	R. D. W. MILLER	5 Aug. '54
221	11½	R. D. W. MILLER	28 June '52
216	1	M. J. DENLEY	21 June '52
214	7½	M. J. DENLEY	29 May '52
210	9½	M. J. W. DALRYMPLE	6 June '48
204	8½	D. W. JACOBS	'45
202	2¾	J. A. McD. McKILLOP	1 July '39
194	2	S. WILSON	17 July '37
191	7¼	W. A. LAND	29 June '35
187	0	E. R. TURNER	9 July '32

Jesse Owens   Chris Brasher   Roger Bannister

Date	Name	Club	Sec.
1913	W. R. APPLEGARTH	(Polytechnic H.)	10.0
1914	W. R. APPLEGARTH	(Polytechnic H.)	10.0
1919	W. A. HILL	(Surrey A.C.)	10.0
1920	H. F. V. EDWARD	(Polytechnic H.)	10.0
1921	H. F. V. EDWARD	(Polytechnic H.)	10.2
1922	H. F. V. EDWARD	(Polytechnic H.)	10.0
1923	E. H. LIDDELL	(Scotland)	9.7
1924	H. M. ABRAHAMS	(Achilles C.)	9.9
1925	L. MURCHISON	(U.S.A.)	9.9
1926	R. CORTS	(Germany)	10.0
1927	H. KÖRNIG	(Germany)	10.1
1928	W. B. LEGG	(South Africa)	9.9
1929	J. E. LONDON	(Polytechnic H.)	10.0
1930	C. BERGER	(Netherlands)	9.9
1931	E. L. PAGE	(Blackheath H.)	10.0
1932	F. P. REID	(Atlanta Club)	9.9
1933	G. T. SAUNDERS	(Polytechnic H.)	9.9
1934	J. SIR	(Hungary)	9.9
1935	A. W. SWEENEY	(Milocarian A.C.)	10.2
1936	M. B. OSENDARP	(Netherlands)	9.8
1937	C. B. HOLMES	(Manchester Univ. A.C.)	9.9
1938	M. B. OSENDARP	(Netherlands)	9.8
1939	A. W. SWEENEY	(Milocarian A.C.)	9.9
1946	E. McD. BAILEY	(Polytechnic H.)	9.8
1947	E. McD. BAILEY	(Polytechnic H.)	9.7
1948	J. F. TRELOAR	(Australia)	9.8
1949	E. McD. BAILEY	(Polytechnic H.)	9.7
1950	E. McD. BAILEY	(Polytechnic H.)	9.9
1951	E. McD. BAILEY	(Polytechnic H.)	9.6
1952	E. McD. BAILEY	(Polytechnic H.)	9.6
1953	E. McD. BAILEY	(Polytechnic H.)	9.8
1954	G. S. ELLIS	(London A.C.)	9.9
1955	E. R. SANDSTROM	(R.A.F.)	10.0
1956	J. R. C. YOUNG	(Bishop Vesey's G.S.)	9.9
1957	K. J. BOX	(Liverpool H. & A.C.)	10.0
1958	J. S. O. OMAGBEMI	(Nigeria)	9.9
1959	P. F. RADFORD	(Birchfield H.)	9.7

220 YARDS

Date	Name	Club	Sec.
1902	R. W. WADSLEY	(Highgate H.)	22.4
1903	G. F. BREWILL	(Loughborough Corinthians A.F.C.)	23.0
1904	C. H. JUPP	(London A.C.)	22.8
1905	H. A. HYMAN	(U.S.A.)	22.4
1906	C. H. JUPP	(London A.C.)	22.6
1907	J. P. GEORGE	(Liverpool H.)	22.8
1908	R. KERR	(Canada)	22.4
1909	N. J. CARTMELL	(U.S.A.)	22.0
1910	F. L. RAMSDELL	(U.S.A.)	22.4
1911	F. L. RAMSDELL	(U.S.A.)	22.2

Date	Name	Club	Sec.
1912	W. R. APPLEGARTH	(Polytechnic H.)	22.0
1913	W. R. APPLEGARTH	(Polytechnic H.)	21.6
1914	W. R. APPLEGARTH	(Polytechnic H.)	21.2
1919	W. A. HILL	(Surrey A.C.)	22.6
1920	H. F. V. EDWARD	(Polytechnic H.)	21.6
1921	H. F. V. EDWARD	(Polytechnic H.)	22.2
1922	H. F. V. EDWARD	(Polytechnic H.)	22.0
1923	E. H. LIDDELL	(Scotland)	21.6
1924	H. P. KINSMAN	(South Africa)	21.7
1925	L. MURCHISON	(U.S.A.)	21.6
1926	G. M. BUTLER	(Achilles Club)	21.9
1927	H. HOUBEN	(Germany)	21.8
1928	F. W. WICHMANN	(Germany)	21.7
1929	J. A. T. HANLON	(Polytechnic H.)	21.9
1930	S. E. ENGLEHART	(York H.)	22.0
1931	R. MURDOCH	(Glasgow Univ. A.C.)	22.5
1932	F. P. REID	(Scotland)	22.0
1933	C. BERGER	(Netherlands)	22.0
1934	R. MURDOCH	(Glasgow Univ. A.C.)	22.1
1935	M. B. OSENDARP	(Netherlands)	22.2
1936	A. W. SWEENEY	(Milorcarian A.C.)	21.9
1937	A. W. SWEENEY	(Milorcarian A.C.)	21.9
1938	W. VAN BEVEREN	(Netherlands)	22.1
1939	C. B. HOLMES	(Bolton United H.)	21.9
1946	E. McD. BAILEY	(Polytechnic H.)	22.3
1947	E. McD. BAILEY	(Polytechnic H.)	21.7
1948	A. McCORQUODALE	(London A.C.)	22.2
1949	E. McD. BAILEY	(Polytechnic H.)	21.7
1950	E. McD. BAILEY	(Polytechnic H.)	21.8
1951	E. McD. BAILEY	(Polytechnic H.)	21.4
1952	E. McD. BAILEY	(Polytechnic H.)	21.4
1953	H. C. L. TINDALL	(Polytechnic H.)	21.4
1954	B. SHENTON	(Polytechnic H.)	21.5
1955	G. S. ELLIS	(London A.C.)	22.0
1956	B. SHENTON	(Polytechnic H.)	21.8
1957	D. H. SEGAL	(Thames Valley H.)	21.9
1958	D. H. SEGAL	(Thames Valley H.)	21.4
1959	D. H. JONES	(Woodford Green A.C.)	21.7

440 YARDS

Date	Name	Club	Sec.
1880	M. SHEARMAN	(Oxford Univ. A.C.)	52.2
1881	L. E. MYERS	(U.S.A.)	48.6
1882	H. R. BALL	(London A.C.)	50.2
1883	J. M. COWIE	(London A.C.)	51.0
1884	J. M. COWIE	(London A.C.)	50.4
1885	L. E. MYERS	(U.S.A.)	52.4
1886	C. G. WOOD	(Blackheath H.)	49.8
1887	C. G. WOOD	(Blackheath H.)	51.0
1888	H. C. L. TINDALL	(London A.C.)	51.4
1889	H. C. L. TINDALL	(London A.C.)	48.5
1890	T. L. NICHOLAS	(Monmouth F.C.)	51.8
1891	M. REMINGTON	(U.S.A.)	51.0
1892	C. DICKENSON	(Ireland)	50.4
1893	E. C. BREDIN	(London A.C.)	49.2
1894	E. C. BREDIN	(London A.C.)	50.0
1895	W. FITZHERBERT	(Cambridge Univ. A.C.)	49.6
1896	J. C. MEREDITH	(Ireland)	52.0
1897	S. ELLIOTT	(Goldsmiths' Institute A.C.)	53.2
1898	W. FITZHERBERT	(Cambridge Univ. A.C.)	50.0
1898	R. W. WADSLEY	(Highgate H.)	54.6
1900	M. W. LONG	(U.S.A.)	49.8
1901	R. W. WADSLEY	(Highgate H.)	49.8
1902	G. W WHITE	(Northampton Rodley H.)	50.2
1903	C. McLACHLAN	(Herne Hill H.)	52.2
1904	R. L. WATSON	(Scotland)	51.8
1905	W. HALSWELLE	(Scotland)	50.8
1906	W. HALSWELLE	(Scotland)	48.8
1907	E. H. MONTAGUE	(South London H.)	52.6
1908	W. HALSWELLE	(Scotland)	49.4
1909	A. PATTERSON	(Salford H.)	51.2
1910	L. J. DE B. REED	(South London H.)	51.0
1911	F. J. HALBAUS	(Canada)	50.8
1912	C. N. SEEDHOUSE	(Blackheath H.)	49.8
1913	G. NICOL	(Polytechnic H.)	49.4
1914	C. N. SEEDHOUSE	(Blackheath H.)	50.0
1919	G. M. BUTLER	(Cambridge Univ. A.C.)	49.2
1920	B. G. D'U. RUDD	(Achilles Club)	49.2
1921	R. A. LINDSAY	(Blackheath H.)	50.4
1922	H. F. V. EDWARD	(Polytechnic H.)	50.4
1923	W. E. STEVENSON	(Achilles C. and U.S.A.)	49.6
1924	E. H. LIDDELL	(Edinburgh Univ. A.C.)	49.6
1925	H. B. STALLARD	(Achilles Club)	50.0
1926	J. W. J. RINKEL	(Achilles Club)	49.8
1927	D. G. A. LOWE	(Achilles Club)	48.8
1928	D. G. A. LOWE	(Achilles Club)	50.0
1929	J. A. T. HANLON	(Polytechnic H.)	49.1
1930	K. C. BRANGWIN	(South London H.)	49.8
1931	G. L. RAMPLING	(Milocarian A.C.)	48.6
1932	C. H. STONELEY	(Milocarian A.C.)	48.6
1933	F. F. WOLFF	(London A.C.)	49.8
1934	G. L. RAMPLING	(Milocarian A.C.)	49.0
1935	W. ROBERTS	(Salford H.)	49.6
1936	A. G. K. BROWN	(Achilles Club)	49.0
1937	W. ROBERTS	(Salford H.)	48.6
1938	A. G. K. BROWN	(Achilles Club)	48.2
1939	A. PENNINGTON	(Achilles Club)	49.2
1946	A. S. WINT	(Polytechnic H.)	48.8
1947	J. P. REARDON	(Ireland)	48.3
1948	M. J. CUROTTA	(Australia)	48.2
1949	D. C. PUGH	(South London H.)	48.5
1950	L. C. LEWIS	(Walton A.C.)	48.2
1951	D. C. PUGH	(South London H.)	47.9
1952	A. S. WINT	(Polytechnic H.)	48.1
1953	P. G. FRYER	(London A.C.)	48.9
1954	P. G. FRYER	(London A.C.)	48.4
1955	P. G. FRYER	(London A.C.)	47.7
1956	M. K. V. WHEELER	(Bournemouth)	47.7
1957	F. P. HIGGINS	(Southgate H.)	47.6
1958	J. E. SALISBURY	(Birchfield H.)	47.2
1959	J. D. WRIGHTON	(Southgate H.)	47.5

Sydney Wooderson   Jim Peters   Marquess of Exeter

880 YARDS

Date	Name	Club	Min.	Sec.
1880	S. K. HOLMAN	(London A.C.)	2	00.4
1881	S. H. BAKER	(London A.C.)	2	02.2
1882	W. G. GEORGE	(Moseley H.)	1	58.2
1883	W. BIRKETT	(London A.C.)	1	58.0
1884	W. G. GEORGE	(Moseley H.)	2	02.2
1885	L. E. MYERS	(U.S.A.)	2	01.0
1886	E. D. ROBINSON	(South London H.)	1	59.0
1887	F. J. K. CROSS	(Oxford Univ. A.C.)	1	59.0
1888	A. G. LE MAITRE	(Oxford Univ. A.C.)	2	00.2
1889	H. C. L. TINDALL	(London A.C.)	1	56.4
1890	T. T. PITMAN	(London A.C.)	1	58.4
1891	W. J. HOLMES	(North Lonsdale H.)	2	00.8
1892	W. J. HOLMES	(North Lonsdale H.)	2	00.0
1893	E. C. BREDIN	(London A.C.)	1	55.25
1894	E. C. BREDIN	(London A.C.)	1	56.8
1895	E. C. BREDIN	(London A.C.)	1	55.8
1896	A. W. DE C. KING	(London A.C.)	2	01.4
1897	A. E. RELF	(Finchley H.)	1	56.2
1898	A. E. TYSOE	(Salford H.)	1	58.6
1899	A. E. TYSOE	(Salford H.)	1	58.6
1900	A. E. TYSOE	(Salford H.)	1	57.8
1901	J. R. CLEAVE	(Oxford Univ. A.C.)	1	59.6
1902	A. B. MANNING	(Swansea A.C.)	1	59.8
1903	B. J. BLUNDEN	(Blackheath H.)	1	58.8
1904	H. W. WORKMAN	(Cambridge Univ. A.C.)	1	59.4
1905	B. J. BLUNDEN	(Blackheath H.)	2	02.0
1906	A. ASTLEY	(Salford H.)	1	57.8
1907	I. F. FAIRBAIRN-CRAWFORD	(Scotland)	1	59.6
1908	T. H. JUST	(Cambridge Univ. A.C.)	1	58.2
1909	H. BRAUN	(Germany)	1	57.6
1910	J. M. HILL	(Queen's Park H.)	2	01.4
1911	H. BRAUN	(Germany)	1	59.8
1912	H. BRAUN	(Germany)	1	58.2
1913	E. WIDE	(Sweden)	2	00.6
1914	H. BAKER	(U.S.A.)	1	54.4
1919	A. G. HILL	(Polytechnic H.)	1	55.2
1920	B. G. D'U. RUDD	(Achilles Club)	1	55.8
1921	E. D. MOUNTAIN	(Cambridge Univ. A.C.)	1	56.8
1922	E. D. MOUNTAIN	(Cambridge Univ. A.C.)	1	55.6
1923	C. R. GRIFFITHS	(Surrey A.C.)	1	56.6
1924	H. B. STALLARD	(Achilles Club)	1	54.6
1925	C. R. GRIFFITHS	(Surrey A.C.)	1	57.2
1926	O. PELTZER	(Germany)	1	51.6
1927	D. G. A. LOWE	(Achilles Club)	1	54.6
1928	D. G. A. LOWE	(Achilles Club)	1	56.6
1929	C. ELLIS	(Birchfield H.)	1	54.6
1930	T. HAMPSON	(Achilles Club)	1	53.2
1931	T. HAMPSON	(Achilles Club)	1	54.8
1932	T. HAMPSON	(Achilles Club)	1	56.4
1933	C. WHITEHEAD	(Salford H.)	1	54.0
1934	J. A. COOPER	(C.A. Vandervell H.)	1	56.6
1935	J. C. STOTHARD	(Achilles Club)	1	53.3
1936	J. V. POWELL	(London A.C.)	1	54.7
1937	A. J. COLLYER	(Watford H.)	1	53.3
1938	A. J. COLLYER	(Watford H.)	1	53.7
1939	A. G. K. BROWN	(Achilles Club)	1	55.1
1946	A. S. WINT	(Polytechnic H.)	1	54.8
1947	C. T. WHITE	(Lincoln Wellington A.C.)	1	53.8
1948	H. J. PARLETT	(Dorking St. Paul's A.C.)	1	52.2
1949	H. J. PARLETT	(Dorking St. Paul's A.C.)	1	53.7
1950	A. S. WINT	(Polytechnic H.)	1	51.6
1951	A. S. WINT	(Polytechnic H.)	1	49.6
1952	R. G. BANNISTER	(Achilles Club)	1	51.5
1953	B. S. HEWSON	(Mitcham A.C.)	1	54.2
1954	B. S. HEWSON	(Mitcham A.C.)	1	52.2
1955	D. J. N. JOHNSON	(Woodford Green A.C.)	1	51.4
1956	M. A. RAWSON	(Birchfield H.)	1	51.3
1957	R. DELANY	(Eire)	1	49.6
1958	B. S. HEWSON	(Mitcham A.C.)	1	48.3
1959	B. S. HEWSON	(Mitcham A.C.)	1	52.0

ATHLETICS QUIZ

1. What is the record number of Olympic medals won by a woman athlete?

*

2. Name the "Immortal Loser" who was disqualified after reaching the Olympic stadium in 1908.

3. Who was the first woman to run a mile under 5 minutes?

QUIZ ANSWERS

1. Shirley Barbara Strickland Delahunty (Australia) with 3 gold, 1 silver and 3 bronze, making 7. 2. Dorando Pietre, the Italian marathon runner. 3. Diane Susan Leather (now Mrs. Charles) (G.B.).

ONE MILE

Date	Name	Club	Min.	Sec.
1880	W. G. GEORGE	(Moseley H.)	4	28.6
1881	B. R. WISE	(Oxford U.A.C.)	4	24.4
1882	W. G. GEORGE	(Moseley H.)	4	32.8
1883	W. SNOOK	(Moseley H.)	4	25.8
1884	W. G. GEORGE	(Moseley H.)	4	18.4
1885	W. SNOOK	(Moseley H.)	4	44.0
1886	T. B. NALDER	(Knowle C.C. Bristol)	4	25.8
1887	F. J. K. CROSS	(Oxford U.A.C.)	4	25.4
1888	T. P. CONNEFF	(U.S.A.)	4	31.6
1889	J. KIBBLEWHITE	(Essex Beagles)	4	29.8
1890	J. KIBBLEWHITE	(Essex Beagles)	4	23.2
1891	J. KIBBLEWHITE	(Essex Beagles)	4	28.6
1892	H. WADE	(London A.C.)	4	19.2
1893	F. E. BACON	(Reading A.C.)	4	22.2
1894	F. E. BACON	(Reading A.C.)	4	25.8
1895	F. E. BACON	(Reading A.C.)	4	17.0
1896	B. LAWFORD	(South London H.)	4	31.4
1897	A. E. TYSOE	(Salford H.)	4	27.0
1898	H. WELSH	(Watson's College A.C.)	4	17.2
1899	H. WELSH	(Watson's College A.C.)	4	25.0
1900	C. BENNETT	(Finchley H.)	4	28.2
1901	F. G. COCKSHOTT	(Cambridge U.A.C.)	4	21.4
1902	J. BINKS	(Unity A.C.)	4	16.8
1903	A. SHRUBB	(South London H.)	4	24.0
1904	A. SHRUBB	(South London H.)	4	22.0
1905	G. BUTTERFIELD	(Darlington H.)	4	25.2
1906	G. BUTTERFIELD	(Darlington H.)	4	18.4
1907	G. BUTTERFIELD	(Darlington H.)	4	22.4
1908	H. A. WILSON	(Hallamshire H.)	4	20.2
1909	E. OWEN	(Broughton H. and A.C.)	4	23.0
1910	E. R. VOIGHT	(Manchester A.C.)	4	26.2
1911	D. F. McNICOL	(Polytechnic H.)	4	22.2
1912	E. OWEN	(Broughton H. & A.C.)	4	21.4
1913	J. ZANDER	(Sweden)	4	25.8
1914	G. W. HUTSON	(Surrey A.C.)	4	22.0
1919	A. G. HILL	(Polytechnic H.)	4	21.2
1920	A. BURTIN	(France)	4	23.0
1921	A. G. HILL	(Polytechnic H.)	4	13.8
1922	D. McPHEE	(West of Scotland H.)	4	27.4
1923	H. B. STALLARD	(Achilles Club)	4	21.6
1924	W. R. SEAGROVE	(Achilles Club)	4	21.2
1925	B. MACDONALD	(Birchfield H.)	4	18.0
1926	G. BARATON	(France)	4	17.4
1927	C. ELLIS	(Birchfield H.)	4	17.0
1928	C. ELLIS	(Birchfield H.)	4	20.8
1929	C. ELLIS	(Birchfield H.)	4	22.0
1930	R. H. THOMAS	(Royal Air Force)	4	15.2
1931	R. H. THOMAS	(Royal Air Force)	4	16.4
1932	J. F. CORNES	(Achilles Club)	4	14.2
1933	R. H. THOMAS	(Surrey A.C.)	4	14.2
1934	J. E. LOVELOCK	(Achilles C. and New Zealand)	4	26.6
1935	S. C. WOODERSON	(Blackheath H.)	4	17.2
1936	S. C. WOODERSON	(Blackheath H.)	4	15.0
1937	S. C. WOODERSON	(Blackheath H.)	4	12.2
1938	S. C. WOODERSON	(Blackheath H.)	4	13.4
1939	S. C. WOODERSON	(Blackheath H.)	4	11.8
1946	D. G. WILSON	(Polytechnic H.)	4	17.4
1947	S. GARAY	(Hungary)	4	10.6
1948	G. W. NANKEVILLE	(Old Woking A.C.)	4	14.2
1949	G. W. NANKEVILLE	(Walton A.C.)	4	08.8
1950	G. W. NANKEVILLE	(Walton A.C.)	4	12.2
1951	R. G. BANNISTER	(Achilles Club)	4	07.8
1952	G. W. NANKEVILLE	(Walton A.C.)	4	09.8
1953	R. G. BANNISTER	(Achilles Club)	4	05.2
1954	R. G. BANNISTER	(Achilles Club)	4	07.6
1955	B. S. HEWSON	(Mitcham A.C.)	4	05.4
1956	K. WOOD	(Sheffield Utd.)	4	06.8
1957	B. S. HEWSON	(Mitcham A.C.)	4	06.7
1958	G. EVERETT	(Shettleston H.)	4	06.4
1959	K. WOOD	(Sheffield Utd.)	4	08.1

Herb Elliott

Chris Chataway

Emil Zatopek

FOUR MILES

Date	Name	Club	Min.	Sec.
1880	W. G. GEORGE	(Moseley H.)	20	45.8
1881	G. M. NEHAN	(Blackheath H.)	20	26.2
1882	W. G. GEORGE	(Moseley H.)	Ran over	
1883	W. SNOOK	(Moseley H.)	20	37.0
1884	W. G. GEORGE	(Moseley H.)	20	12.8
1885	W. SNOOK	(Moseley H.)	21	51.8
1886	C. ROGERS	(Southampton H.)	21	01.8
1887	E. C. CARTER	(New York A.C.)	21	10.0
1888	E. W. PARRY	(Salford H.)	20	22.2
1889	S. THOMAS	(Ranelagh H.)	20	31.8
1890	J. KIBBLEWHITE	(Essex Beagles)	20	16.4
1891	W. H. MORTON	(Salford H.)	20	53.6
1892	J. KIBBLEWHITE	(Essex Beagles)	19	50.6
1893	C. PEARCE	(Birchfield H.)	20	12.6
1894	F. E. BACON	(Reading A.C.)	19	48.8
1895	H. A. MUNRO	(London A.C.)	19	49.4
1896	H. HARRISON	(Manchester H.)	20	27.4
1897	C. BENNETT	(Finchley H.)	20	52.6
1898	C. BENNETT	(Finchley H.)	20	14.4
1899	C. BENNETT	(Finchley H.)	20	49.6
1900	J. T. RIMMER	(Southport H.)	20	11.0
1901	A. SHRUBB	(South London H.)	20	01.8
1902	A. SHRUBB	(South London H.)	20	01.4
1903	A. SHRUBB	(South London H.)	20	06.0
1904	A. SHRUBB	(South London H.)	19	56.8
1905	J. SMITH	(Bradford A.C.)	21	08.8
1906	F. H. HULFORD	(Birchfield H.)	20	27.4
1907	A. DUNCAN	(Salford H.)	19	51.4
1908	E. R. VOIGHT	(Manchester A.C.)	19	47.4
1909	E. R. VOIGHT	(Manchester A.C.)	19	57.6
1910	A. G. HILL	(Polytechnic H.)	20	00.6
1911	H. KOLEHMAINEN	(Finland)	20	03.6
1912	G. W. HUTSON	(Surrey A.C.)	20	10.8
1913	G. W. HUTSON	(Surrey A.C.)	19	32.0
1914	G. W. HUTSON	(Surrey A.C.)	19	41.4
1919	E. BACKMAN	(Sweden)	19	56.4
1920	C. E. BLEWITT	(Birchfield H.)	20	10.8
1921	W. MONK	(Birchfield H.)	19	59.2
1922	P. J. NURMI	(Finland)	19	52.2
1923	C. E. BLEWITT	(Birchfield H.)	19	56.6
1924	W. M. COTTERELL	(R.C. Signals)	19	45.6
1925	C. E. BLEWITT	(Birchfield H.)	19	54.6
1926	J. E. WEBSTER	(Birchfield H.)	19	49.6
1927	B. OHRN	(Sweden)	19	40.8
1928	W. BEAVERS	(York H.)	19	41.6
1929	W. BEAVERS	(York H.)	19	49.4
1930	L. VIRTANEN	(Finland)	19	36.2
1931	J. A. BURNS	(Elswick H.)	19	49.4

Event discontinued in favour of championships over 3 and 6 miles.

THREE MILES

Date	Name	Club	Min.	Sec.
1932	W. J. BEAVERS	(York H.)	14	23.2
1933	L. LEHTINEN	(Finland)	14	09.2
1934	J. KUSOCINSKI	(Poland)	14	13.6
1935	A. V. REEVE	(Polytechnic H.)	14	38.0
1936	P. D. WARD	(Achilles Club)	14	15.8
1937	P. D. WARD	(Achilles Club)	14	19.8
1938	C. A. J. EMERY	(Achilles Club)	14	21.0
1939	C. A. J. EMERY	(Achilles Club)	14	08.0
1946	S. C. WOODERSON	(Blackheath H.)	13	53.2
1947	J. LATASTER	(Holland)	14	20.0
1948	W. SLYKHUIS	(Holland)	14	07.0
1949	J. J. BARRY	(Eire)	14	11.0
1950	L. THEYS	(Belgium)	14	09.0
1951	W. R. BECKETT	(Hythe A.C.)	14	02.6
1952	C. J. CHATAWAY	(Walton A.C.)	13	59.6
1953	D. A. G. PIRIE	(South London H.)	13	43.4
1954	F. GREEN	(Birchfield H.)	13	32.2
1955	C. J. CHATAWAY	(Achilles Club)	13	33.6
1956	G. D. IBBOTSON	(Royal Air Force)	13	32.6
1957	G. D. IBBOTSON	(South London H.)	13	20.8
1958	S. E. ELDON	(Windsor & Eton H.)	13	22.4
1959	M. B. S. TULLOH	(Portsmouth A.C.)	13	31.2

SIX MILES

Date	Name	Club	Min.	Sec.
1932	J. H. POTTS	(Saltwell H.)	30	23.2
1933	J. T. HOLDEN	(Tipton H.)	30	32.2
1934	J. T. HOLDEN	(Tipton H.)	30	43.8
1935	J. T. HOLDEN	(Tipton H.)	30	50.6
1936	J. NOJI	(Poland)	29	43.4
1937	J. KELEN	(Hungary)	30	07.8
1938	G. BEVIACQUA	(Italy)	30	06.6
1939	S. O. A. PALMER	(Mitcham A.C.)	30	06.4
1946	J. H. PETERS	(Essex Beagles)	30	50.4
1947	A. H. CHIVERS	(Reading A.C.)	30	31.4
1948	S. E. W. COX	(Southgate H.)	30	08.4
1949	V. LILLAKAS	(Polytechnic H.)	30	15.0
1950	F. E. AARON	(Leeds St. Mark's H.)	29	33.6
1951	D. A. G. PIRIE	(South London H.)	29	32.0
1952	D. A. G. PIRIE	(South London H.)	28	55.6
1953	D. A. G. PIRIE	(South London H.)	28	19.4
1954	P. B. DRIVER	(South London H.)	28	34.8
1955	K. L. NORRIS	(Thames Valley H.)	29	00.6
1956	K. L. NORRIS	(Thames Valley H.)	28	13.6
1957	G. KNIGHT	(Essex Beagles)	28	50.4
1958	S. E. ELDON	(Windsor and Eton A.C.)	28	05.0
1959	S. E. ELDON	(Windsor and Eton A.C.)	28	12.4

ATHLETICS QUIZ

1. What is (a) the shortest and (b) the longest track distance for which world records are officially recognised?

2. What time for 1,500 metres is of equal merit to a 4-minute mile?

QUIZ ANSWERS

1. (a) 60 metres for women; (b) 50,000 metres (31 miles 120 yards) track walk.
2. 3 mins. 41.6 secs.

TEN MILES

Date	Name	Club	Min.	Sec.
1880	C. H. MASON	(London A.C.)	56	07.0
1881	G. A. DUNNING	(Clapton Beagles)	54	34.0
1882	W. G. GEORGE	(Moseley H.)	54	41.0
1883	W. SNOOK	(Moseley H.)	57	41.0
1884	W. G. GEORGE	(Moseley H.)	54	02.0
1885	W. SNOOK	(Moseley H.)	53	25.2
1886	W. H. COAD	(South London H.)	55	44.2
1887	E. C. CARTER	(Queen's Park H.)	55	09.0
1888	E. W. PARRY	(Salford H.)	53	43.4

64

Date	Name	Club	Min.	Sec.
1889	S. THOMAS	(Ranelagh H.)	51	31.4
1890	J. KIBBLEWHITE	(Essex Beagles)	53	49.0
1891	W. H. MORTON	(Salford H.)	52	33.8
1892	S. THOMAS	(Ranelagh H.)	53	25.2
1893	S. THOMAS	(Ranelagh H.)	52	41.4
1894	S. THOMAS	(Ranelagh H.)	51	37.0
1895	F. E. BACON	(Reading A.C.)	52	43.8
1896	G. CROSSLAND	(Salford H.)	52	05.0
1897	A. E. TYSOE	(Salford H.)	55	59.6
1898	S. J. ROBINSON	(Northampton C.A.C.)	53	12.0
1899	C. BENNETT	(Finchley H.)	54	18.4
1900	S. J. ROBINSON	(Northampton C.A.C.)	53	14.4
1901	A. SHRUBB	(South London H.)	53	32.0
1902	A. SHRUBB	(South London H.)	52	25.4
1903	A. SHRUBB	(South London H.)	51	55.8
1904	A. SHRUBB	(South London H.)	54	30.4
1905	A. ALDRIDGE	(Highgate H.)	51	49.0
1906	A. ALDRIDGE	(Highgate H.)	54	07.2
1907	A. UNDERWOOD	(Birchfield H.)	54	03.0
1908	A. DUNCAN	(Salford H.)	53	40.4
1909	A. E. WOOD	(Essex Beagles)	52	40.0
1910	F. O'NEILL	(Ireland)	52	41.4
1911	W. SCOTT	(Broughton H. & A.C.)	52	26.4
1912	W. SCOTT	(Broughton H. & A.C.)	52	35.0
1913	E. GLOVER	(Hallamshire H.)	51	56.8
1914	T. FENNAH	(Crewe H.)	53	33.4
1919	C. E. BLEWITT	(Birchfield H.)	53	45.6
1920	C. T. CLIBBON	(Birchfield H.)	53	53.4
1921	H. BRITTON	(Derby & County C. & A.C.)	54	58.2
1922	H. BRITTON	(Derby & County C. & A.C.)	53	24.2
1923	E. HARPER	(Hallamshire H.)	53	34.6
1924	H. BRITTON	(Derby & County C. & A.C.)	52	48.8
1925	J. E. WEBSTER	(Birchfield H.)	52	32.6
1926	E. HARPER	(Hallamshire H.)	52	04.0
1927	E. HARPER	(Hallamshire H.)	52	21.2
1928	J. E. WEBSTER	(Birchfield H.)	52	16.2
1929	E. HARPER	(Hallamshire H.)	52	15.8
1930	J. W. WINFIELD	(Derby & County C. & A.C.)	53	05.4
1931	J. W. WINFIELD	(Derby & County C. & A.C.)	54	34.4
1932	J. F. WOOD	(Heriot's A.C.)	52	00.2
1933	G. W. BAILEY	(Salford H.)	50	51.0
1934	J. T. HOLDEN	(Tipton H.)	52	21.4
1935	F. MARSLAND	(Manchester H.)	54	38.6
1936	W. E. EATON	(Salford H.)	50	30.8
1937	R. WALKER	(Wakefield Trinity H.)	52	33.8
1938	R. V. DRAPER	(Hinckley Tech. Coll.)	52	40.6
1939	J. CHAPELLE	(Belgium)	51	55.0
1947	J. H. PETERS	(Essex Beagles)	53	21.0
1958	F. NORRIS	(Bolton United H.)	49	39.0
1959	F. NORRIS	(Bolton United H.)	48	32.4

MARATHON (26 miles 385 yards)

Date	Name	Club	Hr.	Min.	Sec.
1925	S. FERRIS	(R.A.F. (Uxbridge))	2	35	58.2
1926	S. FERRIS	(R.A.F. (Uxbridge))	2	42	24.2
1927	S. FERRIS	(R.A.F. (Uxbridge))	2	40	32.2
1928	H. W. PAYNE	(Woodford Green A.C.)	2	34	34.0
1929	H. W. PAYNE	(Woodford Green A.C.)	2	30	57.6
1930	D. McLEOD WRIGHT	(Maryhill H.)	2	38	29.4
1931	D. McLEOD WRIGHT	(Maryhill H.)	2	49	54.2
1932	D. McNAB ROBERTSON	(Maryhill H.)	2	34	32.6
1933	D. McNAB ROBERTSON	(Maryhill H.)	2	43	13.6
1934	D. McNAB ROBERTSON	(Maryhill H.)	2	41	55.0
1935	A. J. NORRIS	(Polytechnic H.)	3	2	57.8
1936	D. McNAB ROBERTSON	(Maryhill H.)	2	35	2.4
1937	D. McNAB ROBERTSON	(Maryhill H.)	2	37	19.2
1938	J. W. BEMAN	(Birchfield H.)	2	36	39.6
1939	D. McNAB ROBERTSON	(Maryhill H.)	2	35	37.0
1946	S. S. YARROW	(Polytechnic H.)	2	43	14.4
1947	J. T. HOLDEN	(Tipton H.)	2	33	20.2
1948	J. T. HOLDEN	(Tipton H.)	2	36	44.6
1949	J. T. HOLDEN	(Tipton H.)	2	34	10.6
1950	J. T. HOLDEN	(Tipton H.)	2	31	03.4
1951	J. H. PETERS	(Essex Beagles)	2	31	42.4
1952	J. H. PETERS	(Essex Beagles)	2	20	42.2
1953	J. H. PETERS	(Essex Beagles)	2	22	29.0
1954	J. H. PETERS	(Essex Beagles)	2	17	39.4
1955	R. W. McMINNIS	(R.A.F. & Sutton H. & A.C.)	2	39	35.0
1956	H. J. HICKS	(Hampstead H.)	2	26	15.0
1957	E. KIRKUP	(Rotherham A.C.)	2	22	27.8
1958	C. K. KEMBALL	(Wolverhampton H)	2	22	27.4
1959	J. C. FLEMING-SMITH	(Rotherham H. & A.C.)	2	30	11.6

120 YARDS HURDLES

Date	Name	Club	Sec.
1880	G. P. C. LAWRENCE	(Oxford U.A.C.)	16.4
1881	G. P. C. LAWRENCE	(Oxford U.A.C.)	16.2
1882	S. PALMER	(Cambridge U.A.C.)	16.6
1883	S. PALMER	(Cambridge U.A.C.)	
	W. R. POLLOCK	(Cambridge U.A.C.)	
1884	C. W. GOWTHORPE	(Notts. Forest F.C.)	16.6
1885	C. F. DAFT	(Notts. Forest F.C.)	16.6
1886	C. F. DAFT	(Notts. Forest F.C.)	16.0
1887	J. LE FLEMING	(Cambridge U.A.C.)	16.2
1888	S. JOYCE	(Cambridge U.A.C.)	16.0
1889	C. W. HAWARD	(London A.C.)	16.4
1890	C. F. DAFT	(Notts. Forest F.C.)	16.8
1891	D. D. BULGER	(Ireland)	16.6
1892	D. D. BULGER	(Ireland)	16.0
1893	G. B. SHAW	(New Zealand & London A.C.)	16.4
1894	G. B. SHAW	(New Zealand & London A.C.)	16.6
1895	G. B. SHAW	(New Zealand & London A.C.)	15.8
1896	G. B. SHAW	(New Zealand & London A.C.)	15.6
1897	A. TRAFFORD	(Birmingham A.C.)	17.4
1898	H. R. PARKES	(Oxford U.A.C.)	16.4
1899	W. G. PAGET-TOMLINSON	(Cambridge U.A.C.)	16.4
1900	A. C. KRAENZLEIN	(U.S.A.)	15.4
1901	A. C. KRAENZLEIN	(U.S.A.)	15.6
1902	G. W. SMITH	(New Zealand)	16.0
1903	G. R. GARNIER	(Oxford U.A.C.)	15.8
1904	R. S. STRONACH	(Scotland)	16.0

Date	Name	Club	Sec.
1905	R. S. STRONACH	(Scotland)	16.8
1906	R. S. STRONACH	(Scotland)	16.6
1907	O. GROENINGS	(Polytechnic H.)	16.8
1908	V. DUNCKER	(South Africa)	16.2
1909	A. H. HEALEY	(Blackheath H.)	15.8
1910	G. R. L. ANDERSON	(Oxford U.A.C.)	16.0
1911	P. R. O'R. PHILIPS	(Cambridge U.A.C.)	16.2
1912	G. R. L. ANDERSON	(Oxford U.A.C.)	15.6
1913	G. H. GRAY	(Salford H.)	16.0
1914	G. H. GRAY	(Salford H.)	15.8
1919	H. E. WILSON	(New Zealand)	15.8
1920	G. A. TROWBRIDGE	(U.S.A.)	15.4
1921	H. BERNARD	(France)	15.8
1922	F. R. GABY	(Polytechnic H.)	15.6
1923	F. R. GABY	(Polytechnic H.)	15.2
1924	S. J. M. ATKINSON	(South Africa)	15.1
1925	F. R. GABY	(Polytechnic H.)	15.2
1926	F. R. GABY	(Polytechnic H.)	15.1
1927	F. R. GABY	(Polytechnic H.)	14.9
1928	S. J. M. ATKINSON	(South Africa)	14.7
1929	LORD BURGHLEY	(Achilles Club)	15.4
1930	LORD BURGHLEY	(Achilles Club)	15.2
1931	LORD BURGHLEY	(Achilles Club)	14.8
1932	D. O. FINLAY	(Royal Air Force)	14.9
1933	D. O. FINLAY	(Royal Air Force)	15.0
1934	D. O. FINLAY	(Royal Air Force)	14.8
1935	D. O. FINLAY	(Royal Air Force)	15.0
1936	D. O. FINLAY	(Royal Air Force)	14.6
1937	D. O. FINLAY	(Royal Air Force)	14.5
1938	D. O. FINLAY	(Royal Air Force)	14.4
1939	R. J. BRASSER	(Netherlands)	14.7
1946	P. BRAEKMAN	(Belgium)	14.9
1947	P. BRAEKMAN	(Belgium)	14.9
1948	J. R. BIRRELL	(Barrow G.S.)	15.1
1949	D. O. FINLAY	(Royal Air Force)	14.6
1950	P. B. HILDRETH	(Polytechnic H.)	15.2
1951	F. J. PARKER	(South London H.)	14.8
1952	R. H. WEINBERG	(Australia)	14.4
1953	P. B. HILDRETH	(Polytechnic H.)	14.6
1954	F. J. PARKER	(South London H.)	14.7
1955	F. J. PARKER	(South London H.)	14.6
1956	P. B. HILDRETH	(Polytechnic H.)	14.5
1957	E. F. KINSELLA	(Eire)	14.7
1958	K. St. H. A. GARDNER	(Jamaica)	14.1
1959	V. C. MATTHEWS	(London A.C.)	14.5

220 YARDS HURDLES

Date	Name	Club	Sec.
1952	P. B. HILDRETH	(Polytechnic H.)	24.6
1953	H. WHITTLE	(Reading A.C.)	24.2
1954	P. B. HILDRETH	(Polytechnic H.)	24.6
1955	P. A. L. VINE	(Achilles Club)	23.7
1956	P. A. L. VINE	(Achilles Club)	24.5
1957	J. R. A. SCOTT-OLDFIELD	(Achilles Club)	24.2
1958	K. S. D. WILMSHURST	(Walton A.C.)	24.3
1959	J. METCALF	(Achilles Club)	23.8

440 YARDS HURDLES

Date	Name	Club	Sec.
1914	J. C. ENGLISH	(Manchester A.C.)	59.8
1919	G. H. GRAY	(Salford H.)	59.8
1920	E. W. WHELLER	(Surrey A.C.)	57.4
1921	C. A. CHRISTIERNSSON	(Sweden)	55.4
1922	W. S. KENT-HUGHES	(Achilles Club)	59.0
1923	L. H. PHILLIPS	(Southend H.)	58.0
1924	W. G. TATHAM	(Achilles Club)	57.6
1925	I. H. RILEY	(U.S.A.)	57.8
1926	LORD BURGHLEY	(Achilles Club)	55.0
1927	LORD BURGHLEY	(Achilles Club)	54.2
1928	LORD BURGHLEY	(Achilles Club)	54.0
1929	L. FACELLI	(Italy)	53.4
1930	LORD BURGHLEY	(Achilles Club)	53.8
1931	L. FACELLI	(Italy)	54.6
1932	LORD BURGHLEY	(Achilles Club)	54.4
1933	L. FACELLI	(Italy)	55.6
1934	R. K. BROWN	(Achilles Club)	55.4
1935	F. A. R. HUNTER	(London A.C.)	55.3
1936	J. SHEFFIELD	(Milocarian A.C.)	55.6
1937	J. BOSMANS	(Belgium)	55.0
1938	J. BOSMANS	(Belgium)	54.1
1939	J. BOSMANS	(Belgium)	54.9
1946	D. R. EDE	(Epsom & Ewell H.)	57.0
1947	H. WHITTLE	(Reading A.C.)	55.0
1948	H. WHITTLE	(Reading A.C.)	54.9
1949	H. WHITTLE	(Reading A.C.)	54.9
1950	H. WHITTLE	(Reading A.C.)	55.2
1951	H. WHITTLE	(Reading A.C.)	54.2
1952	H. WHITTLE	(Reading A.C.)	53.3
1953	H. WHITTLE	(Reading A.C.)	52.7
1954	H. KANE	(London, A.C.)	53.4
1955	R. D. SHAW	(Achilles Club)	52.2
1956	I. SAVEL	(Rumania)	52.2
1957	T. S. FARRELL	(Liverpool H. & A.C.)	52.1
1958	D. F. LEAN	(Australia)	51.2
1959	C. E. GOUDGE	(Bolton United H. & A.C.)	52.7

ATHLETICS QUIZ

1. Who has walked the greatest distance in an hour, and how far?

★

2. What is the time advantage in running a 220 yards straight instead of round a 180° bend?

3. Who is regarded as the fastest starting sprinter of all time?

★

QUIZ ANSWERS

1. G. Panichkin (U.S.S.R.) on May 9, 1959, with 8 miles 1,294 yards. 2. It varies from runner to runner, but averages out at about 0.4 secs. 3. Takayoshi Yoshioka (Japan), the 1932 100-metre Olympic finalist.

STEEPLECHASE

Courses were not standardised until 1913. From 1913 to 1953 it was over a distance of two miles.

Date	Name	Club	Min.	Sec.
1880	J. CONCANNON	(Widnes F.C.)		—
1881	J. OGDEN	(Birchfield H.)		—
1882	T. CRELLIN	(Liverpool A.C.)		—
1883	T. THORNTON	(Birchfield H.)		—
1884	W. SNOOK	(Moseley H.)		—
1885	W. SNOOK	(Moseley H.)		—
1886	M. A. HARRISON	(Spartan H.)		—
1887	M. A. HARRISON	(Spartan H.)		—
1888	J. C. COPE	(Birchfield H.)		—
1889	T. WHITE	(Spartan H.)		—
1890	E. W. PARRY	(Salford H.)		—
1891	E. W. PARRY	(Salford H.)		—
1892	W. H. SMITH	(Birchfield H.)		—
1893	G. MARTIN	(Essex Beagles)		—
1894	A. B. GEORGE	(Liverpool H.)		—
1895	E. J. WILKINS	(London A.C.)		—
1896	S. J. ROBINSON	(Northampton C.A.C.)		—
1897	G. H. LEE	(Polytechnic H.)		—
1898	G. W. ORTON	(U.S.A.)		—
1899	W. STOKES	(Birchfield H.)		—
1900	S. J. ROBINSON	(Northampton C.A.C.)		—
1901	S. J. ROBINSON	(Northampton C.A.C.)		—
1902	G. MARTIN	(Essex Beagles)		—
1903	S. J. ROBINSON	(Northampton C.A.C.)		—
1904	A. RUSSELL	(Walsall H. and A.C.)		—
1905	A. RUSSELL	(Walsall H. and A.C.)		—
1906	A. RUSSELL	(Walsall H. and A.C.)		—
1907	J. C. ENGLISH	(Manchester A.C.)		—
1908	R. NOAKES	(Sparkhill H.)		—
1909	R. NOAKES	(Sparkhill H.)		—
1910	J. C. ENGLISH	(Manchester A.C.)		—
1911	R. NOAKES	(Sparkhill H.)		—
1912	S. FROST	(Sparkhill H.)		—
1913	C. H. RUFFELL	(Highgate H.)	11	03.6
1914	S. FROST	(Sparkhill H.)	11	10.6
1919	P. HODGE	(Surrey A.C.)	11	53.6
1920	P. HODGE	(Surrey A.C.)	11	22.8
1921	P. HODGE	(Surrey A.C.)	10	57.2
1922	P. NURMI	(Finland)	11	11.2
1923	P. HODGE	(Surrey A.C.)	11	13.6
1924	C. E. BLEWITT	(Birchfield H.)	11	02.0
1925	J. E. WEBSTER	(Birchfield H.)	11	01.4
1926	J. E. WEBSTER	(Birchfield H.)	10	34.2
1927	J. E. WEBSTER	(Birchfield H.)	11	06.0
1928	J. E. WEBSTER	(Birchfield H.)	10	44.8
1929	E. H. OLIVER	(Reading A.C.)	10	53.2
1930	G. W. BAILEY	(Salford H.)	10	55.4
1931	T. EVENSON	(Salford H.)	10	36.4
1932	T. EVENSON	(Salford H.)	10	13.8
1933	V. ISO-HOLLO	(Finland)	10	06.6
1934	S. G. SCARSBROOK	(Surrey A.C.)	10	48.4
1935	G. W. BAILEY	(Salford H.)	10	20.4
1936	T. EVENSON	(Manchester A.C.)	10	24.8
1937	W. C. WYLIE	(Darlington H.)	10	27.0
1938	J. H. POTTS	(Saltwell H.)	10	39.2
1939	J. CHAPELLE	(Belgium)	10	22.4
1946	M. VAN DE WATTYNE	(Belgium)	10	27.6
1947	H. HIRES	(Hungary)	10	39.3
1948	T. P. E. CURRY	(Achilles Club)	10	31.8
1949	F. T. HOLT	(Liverpool Pembroke A. and C.C.)	10	29.0
1950	P. SEGEDIN	(Jugoslavia)	10	02.4
1951	P. SEGEDIN	(Jugoslavia)	9	58.6
1952	J. I. DISLEY	(London A.C.)	9	44.0
1953	E. G. ELLIS	(Thames Valley H.)	10	02.8

3,000 METRES STEEPLECHASE

Date	Name	Club	Min.	Sec.
1954	K. E. JOHNSON	(Leicester College of Art and Technology)	9	00.8
1955	J. I. DISLEY	(London A.C.)	8	56.6
1956	E. SHIRLEY	(Finchley H.)	8	51.6
1957	J. I. DISLEY	(London A.C.)	8	56.8
1958	E. SHIRLEY	(Finchley H.)	8	51.0
1959	M. HERRIOTT	(Sparkhill H.)	8	52.8

HIGH JUMP

Date	Name	Club	ft.	in.
1880	J. W. PARSONS	(Scotland)	5	9¾
1881	P. DAVIN	(Ireland)	6	0½
1882	R. F. HOUGHTON	(Newport F.C.)	5	7¼
1883	J. W. PARSONS	(Scotland)	6	0¼
1884	T. RAY	(Ulverston A.C.)	5	7
1885	P. J. KELLY	(Ireland)	5	11
1886	G. W. ROWDON	(Teignmouth F.C.)	5	11½
1887	G. W. ROWDON	(Teignmouth F.C.)		
	W. B. PAGE	(U.S.A.)	6	0
1888	G. W. ROWDON	(Teignmouth F.C.)	5	8
1889	T. JENNINGS	(Cambridge U.A.C.)	5	8½
1890	C. W. HAWARD	(London A.C.)	5	8½
1891	T. JENNINGS	(Cambridge U.A.C.)	5	9½
1892	A. WATKINSON	(Hull Gymnastic Society)	5	8½
1893	J. M. RYAN	(Ireland)	6	2½
1894	R. WILLIAMS	(London A.C.)	5	9¼
1895	J. M. RYAN	(Ireland)	5	11½
1896	M. O'BRIEN	(Ireland)	5	11
1897	C. E. H. LEGGATT	(London A.C.)	5	9
1898	P. LEAHY	(Ireland)	5	11⅝
1899	P. LEAHY	(Ireland)	5	10¼
1900	I. K. BAXTER	(U.S.A.)	6	2
1901	I. K. BAXTER	(U.S.A.)	5	11
1902	S. S. JONES	(U.S.A.)	6	3
1903	P. O'CONNOR	(Ireland)	5	8
		No other competitor		
1904	P. O'CONNOR	(Ireland)		
	R. G. MURRAY	(Scotland)	5	9½
	J. B. MILNE	(Scotland)		
1905	C. LEAHY	(Ireland)	5	10¼
1906	C. LEAHY	(Ireland)	6	0
1907	C. LEAHY	(Ireland)	6	0
1908	C. LEAHY	(Ireland)	5	11
1909	J. H. BANKS	(Sparkhill H.)	5	9
1910	B. H. BAKER	(Liverpool H. and A.C.)	5	8½
1911	R. PASEMANN	(Germany)	6	0
1912	B. H. BAKER	(Liverpool H. and A.C.)	6	0
1913	B. H. BAKER	(Liverpool H. and A.C.)	6	0
1914	W. M. OLER	(U.S.A.)	6	2½
1919	B. H. BAKER	(Liverpool H.)	5	11
1920	B. H. BAKER	(Liverpool H.)	6	3¾
1921	B. H. BAKER	(Northern Counties A.A.)	6	2¼
1922	P. LEWDEN	(France)	5	11
1923	P. LEWDEN	(France)	6	4
1924	L. STANLEY	(Dublin Police A.C.)	6	1½
1925	H. M. OSBORN	(U.S.A.)	6	4
1926	C. T. VAN GEYZEL	(Achilles Club)	6	1
1927	H. ADOLFSSON	(Sweden)	6	0
1928	C. MENARD	(France)	6	3
1929	C. KESMARKI	(Hungary)	6	3
1930	C. E. S. GORDON	(Achilles Club)	6	1
1931	A. J. GRAY	(Polytechnic H.)	6	0
1932	W. A. LAND	(Army Athletic Assoc.)	6	1
1933	M. BODOSI	(Hungary)	6	3
1934	M. BODOSI	(Hungary)	6	3
1935	S. R. WEST	(Polytechnic H.)	6	3
1936	J. P. METCALFE	(Australia)	6	1
1937	J. L. NEWMAN	(London A.C.)	6	2
1938	R. O'RAFFERTY	(Eire)	6	1
1939	J. L. NEWMAN	(Lloyds Bank A.C.)	6	2
1946	A. S. PATERSON	(Victoria Park A.A.C.)	6	2
1947	PRINCE A. F. ADEDOYIN	(Queen's University, Belfast)	6	4
1948	J. A. WINTER	(Australia)	6	4
1949	A. S. PATERSON	(Victoria Park A.A.C.)	6	4
1950	A. S. PATERSON	(Victoria Park A.A.C.)	6	4
1951	R. C. PAVITT	(Polytechnic H.)	6	5
1952	R. C. PAVITT	(Polytechnic H.)	6	4
1953	D. R. J. COX	(Eton Manor A.C.)	6	3
1954	B. M. P. O'REILLY	(A.A.U. Eire and Donore H.)	6	5
1955	W. PIPER	(Glasgow Police A.A.)	6	3
1956	O. SOETER	(Rumania)	6	4
1957	O. OKUWOBI	(Cambridge H.)	6	5
1958	P. ETOLU	(Uganda)	6	8
1959	C. W. FAIRBROTHER	(Victoria Pk. A.A.C.)	6	7

POLE VAULT

Date	Name	Club	ft.	in.
1880	E. A. STRACHAN	(Royal Inniskilling Fusiliers)	10	4
1881	T. RAY	(Ulverston A.C.)	11	3
1882	T. RAY	(Ulverston A.C.)	10	6
1883	H. J. COBBOLD	(Felixstowe C.C.)	9	6
1884	T. RAY	(Ulverston A.C.)	10	4
1885	T. RAY	(Ulverston A.C.)	10	0
1886	T. RAY	(Ulverston A.C.)	10	11½
1887	T. RAY	(Ulverston A.C.)	11	1
1888	E. L. STONES	(Ulverston A.C.)		
	T. RAY	(Ulverston A.C.)	11	0½
1889	E. L. STONES	(Ulverston A.C.)	11	1¾
1890	R. D. DICKINSON	(Windermere)	11	0
1891	R. WATSON	(Bardsea)	11	3
1892	R. WATSON	(Bardsea)		
	R. D. DICKINSON	(Windermere)	11	0
1893	R. D. DICKINSON	(Windermere)	11	2
1894	R. D. DICKINSON	(Windermere)	10	11
1895	R. D. DICKINSON	(Windermere)	10	0
1896	R. E. FORESHAW	(Ulverston F.C.)	10	0
1897	J. POOLE	(Windermere)	9	10½
1898	J. POOLE	(Windermere)	10	3
1899	E. C. PRITCHARD	(Kidderminster)	9	1
1900	B. JOHNSON	(U.S.A.)	11	4
1901	I. K. BAXTER	(U.S.A.)		
	W. H. HODGSON	(Milnthorpe)	9	10
1902	F. J. KAUSER	(Hungary)	10	8
1903	S. MORRISS	(German Gymnastic Society)	8	6
1904	A. PUYSEIGUR	(France)	10	6
1905	F. GONDER	(France)	10	2
1906	A. E. A. HARRAGIN	(Trinidad)	10	4
1907	B. SODERSTROM	(Sweden)	10	6
1908	E. B. ARCHIBALD	(Canada)	12	0
1909	A. E. FLAXMAN	(London A.C.)	9	7½
1910	K. DE SZATHMARY	(Hungary)	11	7½
1911	R. PASEMANN	(Germany)	12	0
1912	A. O. CONQUEST	(Herne Hill H.)	9	6½
1913	C. GILLE	(Sweden)	12	1
1914	R. SJOBERG	(Sweden)	11	2
1919	G. HOGSTROM	(Sweden)	11	0
1920	A. FRANQUENELLE	(France)	10	6
1921	E. RYDBERG	(Sweden)	12	2¾
1922	C. HOFF	(Norway)	12	0
1923	P. LEWDEN	(France)		No other competitor
1924	D. J. R. SUMNER	(Achilles Club)	10	3
1925	P. W. JONES	(U.S.A.)	11	6
1926	F. J. KELLEY	(U.S.A. & Hampshire A.A.A.)	12	0
1927	H. LINDBLAD	(Sweden)	12	6
1928	F. J. KELLEY	(U.S.A. & Hampshire A.A.A.)	12	7

ATHLETICS QUIZ

1. Who was the first man to high jump 7 feet?

★

2. Which country has won most Olympic medals in women's events?

★

3. What is the fastest recorded wind-assisted 100 yards?

QUIZ ANSWERS

1. Excluding professional performances unsubjected to independent scrutiny, Charles E. Dumas (U.S.A.) at Los Angeles in July 1956. 2. U.S.A. with 11. 3. 9.1 secs. first by M. E. Patton (U.S.A.) at Los Angeles on May 7th, 1949.

Date	Name	Club	ft.	in.
1929	H. FORD	(Achilles Club)	11	9
1930	H. LINDBLAD	(Sweden)		
	A. VAN DE ZEE	(Holland)	12	0
1931	H. LINDBLAD	(Sweden)		
	A. VAN DE ZEE	(Holland)	12	6
1932	P. B. B. OGILVIE	(Achilles Club)	12	0
1933	D. INNOCENTI	(Italy)	12	6
1934	F. PHILLIPSON	(Salford H.)	12	3
1935	K. BROWN	(U.S.A.)	13	10
1936	F. R. WEBSTER	(Achilles Club)	12	9
1937	J. H. DODD	(Hull H.)	12	0
1938	M. ROMEO	(Italy)	13	0
1939	F. R. WEBSTER	(Achilles Club)	12	3
1946	C. LAMOREE	(Holland)	12	10
1947	Z. ZITVAY	(Hungary)	12	6
1948	F. R. WEBSTER	(Achilles Club)	12	3
1949	P. G. HARWOOD	(U.S.A.)	12	6
1950	R. STJERNILD	(Denmark)	12	6
1951	T. BRYNGEIRSSON	(Iceland)	13	3
1952	G. M. ELLIOTT	(Woodford Green A.C.)	13	0
1953	G. M. ELLIOTT	(Woodford Green A.C.)	13	6
1954	T. HOMONNAY	(Hungary)	14	0
1955	G. M. ELLIOTT	(Woodford Green A.C.)	13	6
1956	I. WARD	(Bury A.C.)	13	0
1957	I. WARD	(Bury A.C.)	13	5
1958	M. D. RICHARDS	(New Zealand)	13	6
1959	A. DITTA	(Pakistan)	13	6

LONG JUMP

1880	C. L. LOCKTON	(London A.C.)	22	2
1881	P. DAVIN	(Ireland)	22	11
1882	T. M. MALONE	(Ireland)	21	9½
1883	J. W. PARSONS	(Scotland)	23	0¼
1884	E. HORWOOD	(Blackheath H.)	21	9
1885	J. PURCELL	(Ireland)	21	10½
1886	J. PURCELL	(Ireland)	22	4
1887	F. B. ROBERTS	(Cambridge U.A.C.)	22	4
1888	A. A. JORDAN	(U.S.A.)	21	8¾
1889	D. D. BULGER	(Ireland)	21	6
1890	R. G. HOGARTH	(United Hospitals' A.C.)	20	0
1891	D. D. BULGER	(Ireland)		
	M. W. FORD	(U.S.A.)	20	4
1892	D. D. BULGER	(Ireland)	21	4½
1893	T. M. DONOVAN	(Ireland)	21	11
1894	T. M. DONOVAN	(Ireland)	20	8
1895	W. J. OAKLEY	(Oxford U.A.C.)	21	6½
1896	C. E. H. LEGGATT	(London A.C.)	23	0¾
1897	C. E. H. LEGGATT	(London A.C.)	21	4
1898	W. J. M. NEWBURN	(Ireland)	23	7
1899	W. J. M. NEWBURN	(Ireland)	22	2
1900	A. C. KRAENZLEIN	(U.S.A.)	22	10¼
1901	P. O'CONNOR	(Ireland)	23	8½
1902	P. O'CONNOR	(Ireland)	23	7½
1903	P. O'CONNOR	(Ireland)	22	9½
1904	P. O'CONNOR	(Ireland)	23	2½
1905	P. O'CONNOR	(Ireland)	23	9½
1906	P. O'CONNOR	(Ireland)	23	5½
1907	D. MURRAY	(Ireland)	22	0
1908	W. H. BLEADEN	(Oxford U.A.C.)	22	3½
1909	T. J. AHEARNE	(Ireland)	22	4¼
1910	P. KIRWAN	(Ireland)	22	0¾
1911	P. KIRWAN	(Ireland)	23	5½
1912	P. KIRWAN	(Ireland)	23	2½
1913	S. S. ABRAHAMS	(London A.C.)	22	6
1914	P. C. KINGSFORD	(London A.C.)	23	3¼
1919	W. BJORNEMAN	(Sweden)	23	6¾
1920	D. B. LOURIE	(U.S.A.)	22	4
1921	H. C. TAYLOR	(U.S.A.)	22	1
1922	C. HOFF	(Norway)	23	3
1923	H. M. ABRAHAMS	(Achilles Club)	23	8¾
1924	H. M. ABRAHAMS	(Achilles Club)	22	8½
1925	R. ST. J. HONNER	(London A.C.)	23	11½
1926	R. ST. J. HONNER	(London A.C.)	23	8
1927	R. DOBERMANN	(Germany)	23	11¾
1928	H. DE BOER	(Netherlands)	24	2¼
1929	H. J. COHEN	(Achilles Club)	22	7
1930	O. HALLBERG	(Sweden)	24	2
1931	H. DE BOER	(Netherlands)	23	8
1932	R. M. EVANS	(South Africa)	23	2
1933	L. BALOGH	(Hungary)	23	2¼
1934	R. PAUL	(France)	23	1
1935	R. PAUL	(France)	23	10¾
1936	G. T. TRAYNOR	(Thames Valley H.)	23	2¼
1937	L. LONG	(Germany)	24	6¾
1938	A. MAFFEI	(Italy)	24	8
1939	W. E. N. BREACH	(Reading A.C.)	23	8
1946	D. C. V. WATTS	(Polytechnic H.)	23	4
1947	H. WHITTLE	(Reading A.C.)	23	9½
1948	T. BRUCE	(Australia)	23	9½
1949	H. WHITTLE	(Reading A.C.)	23	5¾
1950	H. E. ASKEW	(Achilles Club)	23	2¼
1951	S. O. WILLIAMS	(Glasgow U.A.C.)	23	1½
1952	S. O. WILLIAMS	(Nigeria and Polytechnic H.)	24	0¼
1953	K. A. B. OLOWU	(Nigeria and Polytechnic H.)	23	5½
1954	O. FOLDESSY	(Hungary)	24	6½
1955	K. A. B. OLOWU	(Nigeria and Polytechnic H.)	24	2
1956	A. R. CRUTTENDEN	(Polytechnic H.)	23	9½
1957	A. R. CRUTTENDEN	(Polytechnic H.)	23	10
1958	K. A. B. OLOWU	(Nigeria and Polytechnic H.)	23	10½
1959	D. J. WHYTE	(Dundee Hawkhill)	23	9

HOP, STEP AND JUMP

Date	Name	Club	ft.	in.
1914	I. SAHLIN	(Sweden)	46	0¼
1920	C. E. LIVELY	(Sparkhill H.)	43	3½
1921	F. JANSSON	(Sweden)	46	6¾
1922	V. TUULOS	(Finland)	46	9¾
1923	J. ODDE	(Polytechnic H.)	46	4½
1924	J. HIGGINSON	(Preston H.)	45	11
1925	E. SOMFAI	(Hungary)	46	10½
1926	J. HIGGINSON	(Preston H.)	45	6
1927	W. PETERS	(Netherlands)	50	9
1928	W. PETERS	(Netherlands)	48	11
1929	W. PETERS	(Netherlands)	46	8
1930	W. PETERS	(Netherlands)	49	6¾
1931	J. BLANKERS	(Netherlands)	46	7¾
1932	A. J. GRAY	(Polytechnic H.)	45	4
1933	J. BLANKERS	(Netherlands)	48	2½
1934	E. BOYCE	(North Belfast H.)	47	8¾
1935	W. PETERS	(Netherlands)	46	10½
1936	J. P. METCALFE	(Australia)	49	5½
1937	W. PETERS	(Netherlands)	47	0
1938	E. BOYCE	(North Belfast H.)	46	1½
1939	J. PALAMIOTIS	(Greece)	49	3¾
1946	D. C. V. WATTS	(Polytechnic H.)	46	10½
1947	D. C. V. WATTS	(Polytechnic H.)	46	9
1948	G. G. AVERY	(Australia)	46	5
1949	H. VAN EGMOND	(Netherlands)	47	0
1950	S. E. CROSS	(Birchfield H.)	46	9½
1951	S. E. CROSS	(Small Heath H.)	47	0
1952	W. BURGARD	(Saarland)	47	10½
1953	K. S. D. WILMSHURST	(Walton A.C.)	47	1½
1954	K. S. D. WILMSHURST	(Walton A.C.)	48	9½
1955	K. S. D. WILMSHURST	(Walton A.C.)	49	9½
1956	K. S. D. WILMSHURST	(Walton A.C.)	49	9
1957	K. S. D. WILMSHURST	(Walton A.C.)	48	9
1958	D. S. NORRIS	(New Zealand)	51	4
1959	J. E. C. WHALL	(Blackheath H.)	49	2¾

W. H. Dillard John Landy Vladimir Kuts

PUTTING THE WEIGHT

Date	Name	Club	ft.	in.
1880	W. Y. WINTHROP	(London A.C.)	37	3
1881	M. DAVIN	(Ireland)	39	6½
1882	G. ROSS	(Patricroft)	42	4
1883	O. HARTE	(Ireland)	41	1
1884	O. HARTE	(Ireland)	39	10
1885	D. J. MACKINNON	(Scotland)	43	0½
1886	J. S. MITCHELL	(Ireland)	38	1
1887	J. S. MITCHELL	(Ireland)	39	1½
1888	G. R. GRAY	(U.S.A.)	43	7
1889	W. J. M. BARRY	(Ireland)		
	R. A. GREEN	(Manchester A.C.)	39	8
1890	R. A. GREEN	(Manchester A.C.)	37	8
1891	W. J. M. BARRY	(Ireland)	40	8
1892	W. J. M. BARRY	(Ireland)	42	10½
1893	D. HORGAN	(Ireland)	42	9
1894	D. HORGAN	(Ireland)	42	4
1895	D. HORGAN	(Ireland)	44	3½
1896	D. HORGAN	(Ireland)	43	5½
1897	D. HORGAN	(Ireland)	45	4
1898	D. HORGAN	(Ireland)	45	0
1899	D. HORGAN	(Ireland)	46	0½
1900	R. SHELDON	(U.S.A.)	45	10½
1901	W. W. COE	(U.S.A. and London A.C.)	45	5½
1902	W. W. COE	(U.S.A. and London A.C.)	42	10½
1903	T. R. NICOLSON	(Scotland)	40	7½
1904	D. HORGAN	(Ireland)	45	2
1905	D. HORGAN	(Ireland)	44	5½
1906	T. KIRKWOOD	(Scotland)	45	4½
1907	T. KIRKWOOD	(Scotland)	44	2
1908	D. HORGAN	(Ireland)	44	7
1909	D. HORGAN	(Ireland)	44	1
1910	D. HORGAN	(Ireland)	42	9
1911	J. BARRETT	(Ireland)	43	5
1912	D. HORGAN	(Ireland)	44	10
1913	E. NILSSON	(Sweden)	47	4½
1914	A. R. TAIPALE	(Finland)	44	7½
1919	B. JANSSON	(Sweden)	42	7
1920	R. PAOLI	(France)	43	10
1921	B. JANSSON	(Sweden)	46	2½
1922	V. PÖRHÖLA	(Finland)	47	10
1923	J. BARRETT	(Gaelic A.A.)	39	2½
1924	R. S. WOODS	(Achilles Club)	43	10
1925	H. H. SCHWARZE	(U.S.A.)	47	3
1926	R. S. WOODS	(Achilles Club)	44	11
1927	G. BRECHENMACHER	(Germany)	46	6½
1928	E. DUHOUR	(France)	47	5
1929	J. DARANYI	(Hungary)	46	7
1930	J. NOEL	(France)	45	2

ATHLETICS QUIZ

1. What 100 yard time is the equivalent of the world 100 metre record of 10.1 secs.?

2. Who has run the greatest distance in 1 hour?

QUIZ ANSWERS

1. 9.3 secs. 2. 12 miles 809 yards by Col. Emil Zatopek (Czechoslovakia) on September 29th, 1951.

Date	Name	Club	ft.	in.
1931	J. DARANYI	(Hungary)	49	11½
1932	H. B. HART	(South Africa)	48	5½
1933	Z. HELJASZ	(Poland)	51	8¼
1934	Z. HELJASZ	(Poland)	48	10¼
1935	A. G. J. DE BRUYN	(Netherlands)	48	9¾
1936	A. G. J. DE BRUYN	(Netherlands)	46	2½
1937	H. WOELLKE	(Germany)	50	6
1938	C. PROFETI	(Italy)	46	1¾
1939	A. G. J. DE BRUYN	(Netherlands)	48	6¼
1946	A. G. J. DE BRUYN	(Netherlands)	43	8
1947	D. GUINEY	(Clonliffe H.)	47	6¼
1948	D. GUINEY	(Clonliffe H.)	47	3½
1949	J. A. GILES	(Southgate H.)	46	4½
1950	P. SARCEVIC	(Jugoslavia)	49	11½
1951	G. HUSEBY	(Iceland)	52	0¾
1952	J. A. SAVIDGE	(R.N.A.C. (South))	54	1¾
1953	J. A. SAVIDGE	(R.N.A.C. (South))	53	0½
1954	J. A. SAVIDGE	(R.N.A.C. (South))	51	0
1955	W. B. L. PALMER	(Achilles Club)	49	7
1956	W. B. L. PALMER	(Achilles Club)	54	2
1957	A. ROWE	(Doncaster P.W.A.C.)	53	9
1958	A. ROWE	(Doncaster P.W.A.C.)	56	9
1959	A. ROWE	(Doncaster P.W.A.C.)	58	10¾

THROWING THE 56 lb. WEIGHT

1920	W. W. COE	(U.S.A. & Achilles Club)	23	8

THROWING THE DISCUS

1914	A. R. TAIPALE	(Finland)	144	6¼
1920	P. QUINN	(Dublin Police A.C.)	123	5¼
1921	O. ZALLHAGEN	(Sweden)	134	6½
1922	V. NITTYMAN	(Finland)	136	7
1923	G. T. MITCHELL	(University of London A.C.)	110	3
1924	P. J. BERMINGHAM	(Dublin Police A.C.)	135	1
1925	P. J. BERMINGHAM	(Dublin Police A.C.)	138	7½
1926	P. J. BERMINGHAM	(Dublin Police A.C.)	142	4
1927	K. MARVALITS	(Hungary)	145	8½
1928	E. PAULUS	(Germany)	147	0
1929	H. STENERUD	(Norway)	142	10
1930	J. NOEL	(France)	146	6
1931	E. MADARASZ	(Hungary)	141	4¾
1932	P. J. BERMINGHAM	(Dublin Garda A.C.)	139	2¾
1933	E. MADARASZ	(Hungary)	144	11¼
1934	P. J. BERMINGHAM	(Irish Free State)	135	4¾
1935	H. ANDERSSON	(Sweden)	169	11¾
1936	B. L. PRENDERGAST	(St. Mary's Hospital A.C.)	141	5
1937	N. SYLLAS	(Greece)	161	4
1938	A. CONSOLINI	(Italy)	143	0¾
1939	N. SYLLAS	(Greece)	161	1¾
1946	R. J. BRASSER	(Netherlands)	142	11¾
1947	R. J. BRASSER	(Netherlands)	143	7
1948	C. CLANCY	(Donore H.)	138	6
1949	F. KLICS	(Hungary)	156	4½
1950	R. KINTZIGER	(Belgium)	153	4
1951	G. TOSI	(Italy)	175	9½
1952	M. PHARAOH	(Manchester University A.C.)	146	8
1953	M. PHARAOH	(Christie Club and Walton A.C.)	156	4
1954	F. KLICS	(Hungary)	168	5
1955	M. PHARAOH	(Walton A.C.)	156	7
1956	M. PHARAOH	(Walton A.C.)	164	1
1957	M. R. LINDSAY	(Queens Park H.)	166	6
1958	S. J. DU PLESSIS	(S. Africa)	171	4
1959	M. R. LINDSAY	(Queens Park H.)	175	7½

THROWING THE HAMMER

1880	W. LAWRENCE	(Oxford U.A.C.)	96	0
1881	M. DAVIN	(Ireland)	98	10
1882	E. BADDELEY	(Cambridge U.A.C.)	96	4
1883	J. GRUER	(Scotland)	101	2½
1884	O. HARTE	(Ireland)	83	5
1885	W. J. M. BARRY	(Ireland)	108	10
1886	J. S. MITCHELL	(Ireland)	110	4
1887	J. S. MITCHELL	(Ireland)	124	0½
1888	J. S. MITCHELL	(Ireland)	124	8
1889	W. J. M. BARRY	(Ireland)	130	0
1890	R. LINDSAY	(New Zealand)	102	2
1891	C. A. J. QUECKBERNER	(U.S.A.)	129	10¼
1892	W. J. M. BARRY	(Ireland)	133	3
1893	D. CAREY	(Ireland)	123	4½
1894	W. J. M. BARRY	(Ireland)	126	8½
1895	W. J. M. BARRY	(Ireland)	132	11½
1896	J. J. FLANAGAN	(Ireland and U.S.A.)	131	11
1897	T. F. KIELY	(Ireland)	142	5
1898	T. F. KIELY	(Ireland)	140	1
1899	T. F. KIELY	(Ireland)	136	4½
1900	J. J. FLANAGAN	(Ireland and U.S.A.)	163	4
1901	T. F. KIELY	(Ireland)	148	6½
1902	T. F. KIELY	(Ireland)	142	9
1903	T. R. NICOLSON	(Scotland)	142	7
1904	T. R. NICOLSON	(Scotland)	157	5½
1905	T. R. NICOLSON	(Scotland)	155	10½
1906	H. A. LEEKE	(Cambridge U.A.C.)	123	1
1907	T. R. NICOLSON	(Scotland)	158	9
1908	S. P. GILLIS	(U.S.A.)	164	5⅜
1909	T. R. NICOLSON	(Scotland)	164	8
1910	A. E. FLAXMAN	(London A.C.)	117	5½
1911	G. E. PUTNAM	(U.S.A. and Oxford U.A.C.)	147	7½
1912	T. R. NICOLSON	(Scotland)	162	2¼
1913	C. J. LINDH	(Sweden)	155	7½
1914	C. J. LINDH	(Sweden)	163	3½
1919	E. MIDTGAARD	(Denmark)	144	4

June Foulds-Paul   Peter Radford   Sylvia Cheeseman-Disley

Date	Name	Club	ft.	in.
1920	T. SPEERS	(U.S.A.)	140	5½
1921	C. J. LINDH	(Sweden)	161	11¼
1922	C. J. LINDH	(Sweden)	172	3½
1923	M. C. NOKES	(Achilles Club)	161	4½
1924	M. C. NOKES	(Achilles Club)	167	8½
1925	M. C. NOKES	(Achilles Club)	151	0½
1926	M. C. NOKES	(Achilles Club)	159	6
1927	O. SKOLD	(Sweden)	165	0
1928	W. BRITTON	(Cavan A.C.)	152	11
1929	W. BRITTON	(Cavan A.C.)	156	2
1930	O. SKOLD	(Sweden)	167	9
1931	O. SKOLD	(Sweden)	168	6
1932	G. WALSH	(Dublin Garda A.C.)	141	7½
1933	W. BRITTON	(Cavan A.C.)	147	6½
1934	P. O. CALLAGHAN	(Irish Free State)	168	8¾
1935	F. WARNGARD	(Sweden)	146	2¾
1936	N. H. DRAKE	(Sutton-in-Ashfield H.)	151	9
1937	K. HEIN	(Germany)	183	3
1938	B. HEALION	(Eire)	172	1½
1939	B. HEALION	(Eire)	161	8½
1946	J. H. HOUTZAGER	(Netherlands)	159	0½
1947	I. NÉMETH	(Hungary)	174	11¾
1948	N. H. DRAKE	(Blackpool Fylde H.)	161	6½
1949	I. NÉMETH	(Hungary)	182	5½
1950	D. McD. M. CLARK	(Royal Ulster Constabulary)	178	4½
1951	T. TADDIA	(Italy)	177	2½
1952	D. McD. M. CLARK	(Royal Ulster Constabulary)	173	11½
1953	D. W. J. ANTHONY	(Watford H.)	174	8
1954	J. CSERMAK	(Hungary)	194	11
1955	E. C. K. DOUGLAS	(Field Events Club)	185	5
1956	P. C. ALLDAY	(London A.C.)	187	11
1957	M. J. ELLIS	(Thames Valley H.)	197	9
1958	M. J. ELLIS	(Thames Valley H.)	203	2
1959	M. J. ELLIS	(Thames Valley H.)	201	0½

THROWING THE JAVELIN

1914	M. KOCZAN	(Hungary)	195	11
1920	F. L. MURRAY	(U.S.A.)	149	9
1921	G. LINDSTRÖM	(Sweden)	205	0
1922	P. JOHANSSON	(Finland)	200	5
1923	J. DALRYMPLE	(Bedford and County A.C.)	148	9½
1924	E. G. SUTHERLAND	(South Africa)	173	11
1925	B. SZEPES	(Hungary)	176	11
1926	O. SUNDE	(Norway)	201	3
1927	B. SZEPES	(Hungary)	212	7½
1928	S. A. LAY	(New Zealand)	222	9
1929	B. SZEPES	(Hungary)	218	10
1930	A. DOMINUTTI	(Italy)	202	1
1931	O. SUNDE	(Norway)	199	4½
1932	O. JURGIS	(Latvia)	211	8
1933	W. P. ABELL	(Derby and County A.C.)	169	1½
1934	C. G. BOWEN	(Lancs. Fusiliers A.C.)	169	9¼
1935	L. ATTERWALL	(Sweden)	215	6¾
1936	J. F. VAN DER POLL	(Holland)	189	2
1937	S. WILSON	(Birchfield H.)	194	2
1938	R. E. M. BLAKEWAY	(Achilles Club and S. Africa)	197	1¼
1939	J. A. McD. McKILLOP	(Milocarian A.C.)	186	7
1946	N. B. LUTKEVELD	(Netherlands)	185	8½
1947	J. STENDZENIEKS	(Latvian D.P.)	210	7½
1948	J. STENDZENIEKS	(Lincoln Wellington A.C.)	218	9
1949	A. F. HIGNELL	(Achilles Club)	184	9½
1950	M. J. DENLEY	(Thames Valley H.)	192	0½
1951	A. METTEUCCI	(Italy)	200	5
1952	M. J. DENLEY	(Thames Valley H.)	216	1
1953	M. J. DENLEY	(Thames Valley H.)	208	7
1954	M. MORRELL	(Wirrall A.C.)	198	0
1955	D. ZAMFIR	(Rumania)	222	9
1956	P. S. CULLEN	(Rotherham H. and A.C.)	214	2
1957	P. S. CULLEN	(Rotherham H. and A.C.)	236	7
1958	C. G. SMITH	(Thames Valley H.)	218	1
1959	C. G. SMITH	(Thames Valley H.)	229	4½

DECATHLON

From 1937 to 1950 the 1934 Tables were in use

Date	Name	Club	Points
1928	H. B. HART	(South Africa)	6,016
1937	J. MIGGINS	(Ireland)	4,647
1938	T. L. LANGTON-LOCKTON	(Achilles Club)	5,513
1947	H. J. MOESGAARD-KJELDSEN	(Denmark)	5,965
1948	H. J. MOESGAARD-KJELDSEN	(Denmark)	5,794
1949	H. J. MOESGAARD-KJELDSEN	(Denmark)	6,138
1950	H. WHITTLE	(Reading A.C.)	6,087
1951	L. PINDER	(Doncaster P.W.A.C.)	5,089
1952	L. PINDER	(Doncaster P.W.A.C.)	5,504
1953	L. PINDER	(Doncaster P.W.A.C.)	5,321
1954	L. PINDER	(Doncaster P.W.A.C.)	5,415
1955	M. DODDS	(R.A.F.)	4,690
1956	A. G. BROWN	(Rhodesia)	4,934
1957	H. L. WILLIAMS	(R.A.F.)	5,370
1958	C. J. ANDREWS	(Army A.A.)	5,113
1959	C. J. ANDREWS	(Army A.A.)	5,517

ATHLETICS QUIZ

1. What European 800 metre record was set in the U.S.A.?

2. Which country has won most Olympic gold medals?

*

QUIZ ANSWERS

1. Tom Hampson's (G.B.) 1 min. 49.8 secs. at Los Angeles, 2nd August 1932.
2. U.S.A. with 171.

A. A. A. JUNIOR CHAMPIONS

100 YARDS

Date	Name	Club	Sec.
1931	W. P. HEATH	(Notts. A.C.)	10.3
1932	J. S. K. GLOVER	(Wallasley A.C.)	10.4
1933	C. R. CHALK	(S. London H.)	10.3
1934	A. PENNINGTON	(Berkhamsted School)	10.3
1935	W. R. LOADER	(South Shields H.)	10.1
1936	K. J. RICHARDSON	(Bedford Mod. Sch.)	10.2
1937	A. W. ELSTRON	(Middlesbro' H.)	10.2
1938	R. J. B. ROACH	(Palmer's Sch.)	10.1
1939	A. WATT	(Shettleston H.)	10.0
1946	W. J. FERGUSON	(Notts. A.C.)	10.6
1947	W. N. JONES	(Llanelly Grammar Sch.)	10.2
1948	N. SCOTT	(Blackpool and Fylde H.)	10.2
1949	N. SCOTT	(Blackpool and Fylde H.)	10.0
1950	A. W. LILLINGTON	(Elswick H.)	10.0
1951	K. T. SCOTT	(Swindon)	10.3
1952	A. DUNBAR	(Stranraer H.)	10.6
1953	H. A. MORRISON	(Cambridge H.)	10.7
1954	J. A. N. RAILTON	(Pembroke H. and A.C.)	9.9
1955	E. KEATING	(George Heriot's S.)	10.0
1956	J. R. C. YOUNG	(Bishop Vesey's G.S.)	9.9
1957	A. MEAKIN	(Blackpool and Fylde A.C.)	10.1
1958	D. H. JONES	(Southend-on-Sea A.C.)	10.0
1959	R. NICHOLSON	(Heaton H.)	9.9

220 YARDS

Date	Name	Club	Sec.
1931	W. P. HEATH	(Notts. A.C.)	23.7
1932	No Race		
1933	C. F. CHALK	(South London H.)	23.2
1934	A. PENNINGTON	(Berkhamsted Sch.)	22.9
1935	D. S. HIGGINS	(Chiswick County Sch.)	22.8
1936	E. G. FORSYTH	(Polytechnic H.)	23.2
1937	J. F. LOCKWOOD	(Queen Elizabeth's G.S., Barnet)	22.6
1938	C. O. HOLLAND	(Short's A.C.)	23.6
1939	R. R. KIRK	(Old Farnhamians)	23.1
1946	W. J. FERGUSON	(Notts A.C.)	23.4
1947	A. Y. MONAHAN	(Renfrew Y.M.C.A.)	23.0
1948	A. D. SEXTON	(Belgrave H.)	22.9
1949	A. D. SEXTON	(Belgrave H.)	22.1
1950	G. S. ELLIS	(Keswick G.S.)	22.4
1951	G. S. ELLIS	(Keswick G.S.)	21.9
1952	J. L. BOOTH	(Notts A.C.)	22.9
1953	D. PULSFORD	(Rhymney G.S.)	22.9
1954	M. J. RUDDY	(Polytechnic H.)	21.9
1955	I. R. SMITH	(Dulwich College)	22.5
1956	J. R. C. YOUNG	(Bishop Vesey's G.S.)	22.6
1957	R. I. BRIGHTWELL	(Shrewsbury T.C.)	22.5
1958	M. C. SMITH	(Bingley H.)	22.2
1959	M. G. HILDERY	(Victoria Pk. A.A.C.)	22.2

440 YARDS

Date	Name	Club	Sec.
1931	J. W. ANDERSON	(Middlesbro' H.)	51.3
1932	G. N. BLAKE	(Univ. London A.C.)	52.4
1933	R. D. L. WELLS	(Maidstone H.)	52.8
1934	G. E. NICHOLLS	(Polytechnic H.)	52.6
1935	R. G. R. CHANDLER	(Cambridge H.)	52.2
1936	R. G. R. CHANDLER	(Cambridge H.)	51.0
1937	E. G. FORSYTH	(Polytechnic H.)	52.5
1938	L. H. HATT	(North London H.)	52.2
1939	M. W. PIKE	(Ibis A.C.)	50.8
1946	G. U. CHESTER	(Daniel Stewarts Coll.)	51.5
1947	A. G. BANNISTER	(Manchester A.C.)	51.7
1948	M. M. T. PAXTON	(Millfield S.)	51.0
1949	M. T. WRIGHT	(Appleby-Frodingham A.C.)	51.1
1950	D. J. N. JOHNSON	(Fairbairn and Mansfield)	48.8
1951	D. J. N. JOHNSON	(Fairbairn and Mansfield)	49.1
1952	K. C. CHAMBERS	(Ilford A.C.)	50.3
1953	W. J. WARMINGTON	(C. of Oxford S.)	51.0
1954	H. R. SMITH	(Halesowen T.C.)	50.1
1955	H. R. SMITH	(Halesowen H. and A.C.)	50.8
1956	D. H. JONES	(Holywell H.)	51.2
1957	J. B. HOLT	(Manchester G.S.)	49.5
1958	H. M. YARDLEY	(Ald. Newton's S.)	51.3
1959	B. JACKSON	(Lozells H.)	48.7

880 YARDS

Date	Name	Club	Min.	Sec.
1931	A. C. J. POOLE	(Colfe's G.S.)	2	7
1932	B. JENKINS	(Luton United H.)	2	2.4
1933	C. H. OADES	(Southgate and W.G.A.A.)	2	4.2
1934	C. H. OADES	(Southgate H.)	2	1.4
1935	C. H. OADES	(Southgate H.)	2	2.6
1936	M. G. ELIOT	(Royal Military Coll.)	1	58.8
1937	R. G. H. BROWN	(Portsmouth H.)	2	4.7
1938	A. J. SMITH	(Southgate H.)	2	0.1
1939	R. L. B. SARBUTT	(Ilford A.C.)	2	0.1
1946	D. PICKLES	(Airdale H.)	2	2
1947	B. GOLDIE	(B.T.H. Rugby)	2	8
1948	P. L. RICHARDS	(Seaford Coll.)	2	2.4
1949	A. J. PERRY	(Polytechnic H.)	1	57.2
1950	A. G. BUNNER	(Liverpool H. and A.C.)	2	4.2
1951	B. S. HEWSON	(Mitcham A.C.)	1	55.3
1952	B. S. HEWSON	(Mitcham A.C.)	1	55.6
1953	R. D. HENDERSON	(Elswick H.)	1	57.7
1954	R. A. BEAUMONT	(Shaftesbury H.)	1	58.7
1955	R. A. BEAUMONT	(Shaftesbury H.)	1	56.7
1956	D. A. F. HAITH	(Thames Valley H.)	1	57.6
1957	B. S. LINKE	(Sutton and Cheam H.)	1	57.1
1958	B. C. SAVORY	(C. of London S.)	1	55.2
1959	A. J. HARRIS	(Mitcham A.C.)	1	54.3

ONE MILE

Date	Name	Club	Min.	Sec.
1931	A. E. WOODLEY	(Colfe's G.S.)	4	36.6
1932	D. SAMUEL	(Watford H.)	4	32.6
1933	C. C. JACKSON	(King Edward Sch., Chelmsford)	4	39.6
1934	A. LITTLER	(Leigh H.)	4	39
1935	W. MOORCROFT	(Lincoln Wellington A.C.)	4	31.4
1936	A. G. R. NOBLE	(Royal Military Coll.)	4	29.6
1937	V. W. G. FOSTER	(London A.C.)	4	30.6
1938	J. TIMMINS	(Tipton H.)	4	33.8
1939	R. GOODBODY	(Surrey A.C.)	4	25
1946	D. R. BURFITT	(Belgrave H.)	4	23.2
1947	E. G. ELLIS	(Thames Valley H.)	4	32.6
1948	E. G. ELLIS	(Thames Valley H.)	4	29.6
1949	E. G. ELLIS	(Thames Valley H.)	4	28.8
1950	D. C. SEAMAN	(London A.C.)	4	29.0
1951	D. M. HUMPHREY	(Horsham Blue Star H.)	4	19.2
1952	J. L. HENDRY	(Elgin Academy)	4	21.2
1953	R. DUNKLEY	(Shaftesbury H.)	4	25.9
1954	R. DUNKLEY	(Shaftesbury H.)	4	15.6
1955	A. A. COCKING	(Bramley and Dist. H.)	4	23.2
1956	S. R. LANGRIDGE	(South London H.)	4	18.4
1957	W. C. CORNELL	(Chelmsford A.C.)	4	15.5
1958	P. McC. MONTAGUE	(Manchester and Dist. L.C.H.)	4	25.5
1959	R. T. JONES	(Hampstead H.)	4	10.0

4 X 110 YARDS RELAY

Date	Club	Sec.
1931	Polytechnic H.	46.4
1932	Polytechnic H.	45.6
1933	South London H.	46.0
1934	Cambridge H.	45.6
1935	Polytechnic H.	45.7
1936	R.A.F., Halton	46.4
1937	Southgate H.	46.0
1938	Portsmouth A.C.	45.9
1939	R.A.F., Halton	44.8
1946	Merchant Taylors, Crosby	45.5
1947	Polytechnic H.	45.2
1948	Cambridge H.	44.9
1949	Cambridge H.	44.6
1950	Portsmouth A.C.	44.1
1951	Mitcham A.C.	44.6
1952	Mitcham A.C.	44.8
1953	Polytechnic H.	43.9
1954	Liverpool Pembroke A. and C.C.	44.0
1955	Victoria Park A.A.C.	43.8
1956	Blackheath H.	43.8
1957	Polytechnic H.	43.5
1958	Coventry Godiva H.	43.9
1959	Shettleston H.	43.7

Gordon Pirie

120 YARDS HURDLES

Date	Name	Club	Sec.
1931	F. C. KINGDON	(Woodford Green A.C.)	16.0
1932	J. N. OWEN	(R.A.F., Halton)	15.9
1933	B. C. LEDEBOER	(Imperial Service Coll.)	15.8
1934	M. L. H. CARTER	(Polytechnic H.)	15.9
1935	D. S. LOCK	(Roundhay Sch. Leeds)	15.9
1936	T. L. LOCKTON	(London A.C.)	15.9
1937	D. A. WILKINSON	(King's Sch., Canterbury)	15.5
1938	H. W. J. HEARN	(Southgate H.)	15.4
1939	A. B. P. CHADBURN	(Eastbourne Coll.)	15.6
1946	J. HODGKINSON	(W. Bridgford G.S.)	17.0
1947	J. R. BIRRELL	(Barrow G.S.)	15.9
1948	J. R. BIRRELL	(Barrow G.S.)	15.1
1949	D. R. KAY	(Blackpool and Fylde H.)	15.4
1950	G. F. PARR	(Polytechnic H.)	15.7
1951	R. D. SHAW	(Manchester G.S.)	14.7
1952	H. KANE	(Grafton A.C.)	15.4
1953	V. C. MATTHEWS	(London A.C.)	14.9
1954	R. A. SUTTON	(Polytechnic H.)	15.2
1955	R. A. WOODLAND	(Hercules A.C.)	15.5
1956	R. A. WOODLAND	(Hercules A.C.)	14.8
1957	M. C. STOKELEY	(South London H.)	14.6
1958	S. S. TARRANT	(St. Lawrence C.)	14.9
1959	P. SUNDERLAND	(Darlington H.)	14.9

220 YARDS HURDLES

Date	Name	Club	Sec.
1951	J. B. DUFFY	(Polytechnic H.)	23.3
1952	H. KANE	(Grafton A.C.)	23.3
1953	H. EDWARDS	(Bellahouston H.)	24.0
1954	W. B. THOMPSON	(Worksop College)	23.5
1955	A. HANNAH	(Preston Lodge S.)	23.4
1956	M. C. STOKELEY	(South London H.)	24.0
1957	M. C. STOKELEY	(South London H.)	23.4
1958	J. SAMS	(Fulham A.A.C.)	23.1
1959	O. H. BAGGOTT	(Kingston A.C.)	22.7

STEEPLECHASE

(Over ¾ mile 1931 to 1939; over 1 mile 1956 and 1957; now run over 1,500 metres)

Date	Name	Club	Min.	Sec.
1931	R. H. HAINSWORTH	(R.A. Lister R. and S.C.)	3	55.4
1932	R. H. HAINSWORTH	(R.A. Lister R. and S.C.)	3	44.6
1933	T. PRESTON JONES	(St. Gregory's S.)	3	51.0
1934	E. J. NANKIVELL	(Southgate H.)	3	59.0
1935	H. DYALL	(Wanstead C.H.S.)	3	48.4
1936	H. DYALL	(Southgate H.)	3	42.0
1937	A. J. SMITH	(Southgate H.)	4	1.6
1938	A. J. SMITH	(Southgate H.)	4	46.6
1939	P. R. K. BURLEY	(Blackheath H.)	3	33.6
1956	B. HALL	(Manchester and Dist. L.C.H.)	4	50.4
1957	M. HERRIOTT	(Sparkhill H.)	4	50.5
1958	M. HERRIOTT	(Sparkhill H.)	4	20.7
1959	A. J. YATES	(S. London H.)	4	23.0

ATHLETICS QUIZ

On which of his six trials did Jesse Owens make his world long jump record of 26 ft. 8¼ ins.?

QUIZ ANSWER
His first and only jump

ONE MILE WALK

Date	Name	Club	Min.	Sec.
1947	K. HARDING		7	38.2
1948	E. SHARP	(London Vidarians W.C.)	7	22.6
1949	D. BOTT	(Sheffield United H.)	7	06.0
1950	N. R. READ	(Steyning A.C.)	7	04.8
1951	J. LOWTHER	(St. Julians H.S.)	6	59.2
1952	G. H. LEWIS	(Univ. Coll. Aberystwyth)	6	53.6
1953	G. HOWELL	(Ferndale G.S.)	6	49.9
1954	G. HOWELL	(University College, London)	6	54.0
1955	J. W. EDGINGTON	(Coventry Godiva H.)	7	13.4
1956	M. S. SHANNON	(Newport H.S.)	7	07.4
1957	M. S. SHANNON	(Newport H.S.)	6	55.3
1958	D. C. READ	(Steyning A.C.)	6	57.8
1959	P. MARLOW	(Southend A.C.)	7	05.4

HIGH JUMP

Date	Name	Club	ft.	in.
1931	L. G. TOVELL	(Lowestoft A.C.)	5	7
1932	F. R. FORD	(Univ. London A.C.)	5	7
	H. L. TATE	(Bedford Mod. Sch.)	5	7
1933	B. C. LEDEBOER	(Imperial Service Coll.)	5	10
1934	E. E. BREWSTER	(Southend and C.H.)	5	9
1935	J. L. NEWMAN	(London A.C.)	5	11
1936	J. V. H. GECKS	(Slough Sec. Sch.)	5	8
1937	P. L. TANCRED	(Queensland, Australia)	5	10
1938	M. A. C. DOWLING	(Bradfield Coll.)	5	8
1939	J. T. RUMBLE	(Ilford A.C.)	5	10
1946	A. S. PATERSON	(Victoria Park A.A.C.)	6	2½
1947	P. WELLS	(Old Elizabethans A.C.)	6	0
1948	G. M. ELLIOTT	(Wanstead C.H.S.)	5	8
1949	N. P. KANE	("Q" A.C.)	5	10
1950	N. D. FINCH	(Bangor Univ.)	5	10
1951	T. J. REYNOLDS	(Q.E.G.S., Wakefield)	6	0
1952	T. J. REYNOLDS	(Q.E.G.S., Wakefield)	6	1
1953	A. P. J. S. ORTON	(Shaftesbury H.)	5	10
1954	J. BILLINGTON	(St. Albans S.)	6	0
1955	M. F. THATCHER	(R.A.F., Halton)	5	11
1956	D. WILSON	(Hercules A.C.)	5	10
1957	A. R. HOUSTON	(Victoria Park A.A.C.)	6	1
1958	G. A. MILLER	(Hermes Club)	6	0
1959	A. J. DAVIES	(Hampstead H.)	6	4¼

POLE VAULT

Date	Name	Club	ft.	in.
1931	L. G. TOVELL	(Lowestoft A.C.)	10	0
	G. L. EDWARDS	(Ponders End A.C.)	10	0
1932	F. R. WEBSTER	(London A.C.)	11	0
1933	F. R. WEBSTER	(London A.C.)	11	0
1934	H. CHALK	(Fed. London Deaf C.)	9	3
1935	F. BUCK	(R.A.F.)	9	9
	C. J. ASPINALL	(North Herts A.C.)	9	9
1936	C. J. ASPINALL	(Southgate H.)	10	3
1937	L. I. HAMILTON	(Plymton G.S.)	9	0
1938	A. M. ROBINSON	(Bloxham Sch.)	10	0
1939	A. M. ROBINSON	(Achilles Club)	11	2½
1946	R. FERRIS	(Plympton G.S.)	10	0
1947	R. PETITJEAN	(St. Bedes)	10	6
1948	G. M. ELLIOTT	(Wanstead C.H.S.)	10	0
1949	W. PIPER	(Kilmarnock H.)	11	0
1950	A. HANLON	(Shettleston H.)	11	0
1951	G. E. BROAD	(Herne Hill H.)	12	0
1952	G. E. BROAD	(Herne Hill H.)	11	6
1953	G. M. SCHMIDT	(John Fisher S.)	11	6
1954	M. E. NUGENT	(John Fisher S.)	11	9
1955	M. E. NUGENT	(John Fisher S.)	11	6
1956	A. J. F. PITT	(Kelly College)	11	9
1957	D. A. BARNARD	(John Fisher S.)	11	9
1958	D. A. BARNARD	(John Fisher S.)	12	1
1959	R. ADDIS	(Coventry Godiva H.)	12	0

LONG JUMP

Date	Name	Club	ft.	in.
1931	L. G. BUTLER	(Cambridge H.)	21	2¼
1932	C. A. SHURMER	(Herne Hill H.)	20	9
1933	D. C. HIGHAM	(Old Gaytonians)	20	8¼
1934	W. E. N. BREACH	(Reading A.C.)	22	6¾
1935	J. S. TATE	(Bedford Mod. Sch.)	21	1
1936	G. PICKTHALL	(Royal Liberty Sch.)	20	9¼
1937	L. R. WISE	(Enfield A.C.)	21	8¾
1938	J. E. WRIGHT	(Birchfield H.)	21	2
1939	A. WATT	(Shettleston H.)	22	3
1946	V. R. TINDALE	(Wallasey G.S.)	20	8
1947	W. N. JONES	(Llanelly G.S.)	19	8¼
1948	D. G. HULYER	(Cambridge T.A.C.)	21	2½
1949	R. A. SLEIGH	(Sutton and Cheam H.)	22	0½
1950	L. BARTON	(Pembroke H. and A.C.)	21	11
1951	G. E. BROAD	(Herne Hill H.)	23	0½
1952	G. E. BROAD	(Herne Hill H.)	22	2¾
1953	J. C. BROWN	(South London H.)	21	1½
1954	D. J. HADLER	(Cambridge H.)	22	4
1955	J. B. WOOLLEY	(Grove Park G.S.)	22	4
1956	J. R. MELVILLE	(Coventry Godiva H.)	22	3
1957	D. W. CHURCHILL	(Bedford and County A.C.)	21	6
1958	D. J. WHYTE	(Dundee Hawkhill H.)	23	4
1959	L. BIRCHALL	(Norwich R.M.I.)	22	4¼

ATHLETICS QUIZ

1. What is the weight of a discus?

*

2. Name the five events of a women's pentathlon?

3. What pressure is required to topple a 3 ft. 6 ins. hurdle?

QUIZ ANSWERS

1. A man's discus weighs 4 lb. 6.6 oz. 2. 200 metres, 80 metre hurdles, high jump, long jump and shot-putt. 3. 28 lb.

HOP, STEP AND JUMP

Date	Name	Club	ft.	in.
1950	D. J. ASHURST	(A.A.S., Beadley)	42	10½
1951	K. C. CHAMBERS	(Ilford A.C.)	44	3½
1952	A. REEVE	(Wirral A.C.)	45	11¾
1953	W. G. DAWES	(Q.E.G.S., Wakefield)	44	9½
1954	J. T. DARLINGTON	(Birchfield H.)	44	5½
1955	I. A. MITCHELL	(Peterborough A.C.)	43	0
1956	A. D. EVANS	(Cowbridge G.S.)	45	0
1957	F. J. ALSOP	(Hornchurch H.)	46	5
1958	J. WELFORD	(Woodford Green A.C.)	43	3
1959	D. C. A. STEPHENS	(Castleford G.S.)	46	3¾

PUTTING THE WEIGHT

1931	C. J. REIDY	(King Edward VI Sch.)	38	6½
1932	H. L. TATE	(Bedford Mod. Sch.)	38	10
1933	L. REAVELL CARTER	(Reading Univ.)	45	8
1934	D. H. S. NEILSON	(Bedford Mod. Sch.)	41	8
1935	H. PIETARU	(Stade Français)	50	6
1936	L. HAAS-GOERZ	(Bryanston Sch.)	42	1½
1937	M. G. HEATH	(Royal Mil. Acad.)	43	0¾
1938	A. ROSENBERG	(King's Coll. Sch.)	42	7
1939	A. F. JOHNSTON	(Eastbourne Coll.)	48	5
1946	A. J. S. TOPHAM-STEEL	(Wirrall A.C.)	41	3¼
1947	J. BANES	(London A.C.)	45	7½
1948	B. W. DODD	(St. Albans C.S.)	42	8½
1949	A. G. I. WOOD	(Pocklington S.)	51	4
1950	D. R. CHAPPELL	(Leeds Univ. A.C.)	45	9½
1951	J. M. HUTCHISON	(Polytechnic H.)	46	1
1952	K. L. JONES	(Merioneth Sec. Sch. A.A.)	48	4¾
1953	G. A. CARR	(Wanstead C.H.S.)	49	10
1954	J. P. JONES	(Belgrave H.)	53	1
1955	D. R. HARRISON	(Bath and County A.C.)	51	0
1956	M. R. LINDSAY	(Queen's Park H.)	55	4
1957	M. R. LINDSAY	(Queen's Park H.)	59	11
1958	J. R. DAVIES	(Llanelly G.S.)	53	10
1959	J. R. DAVIES	(Llanelly G.S.)	53	2

THROWING THE DISCUS

1931	H. EASTWOOD	(Old Bedford Mod.)	115	3½
1932	F. R. WEBSTER	(London A.C.)	108	4½
1933	F. R. WEBSTER	(London A.C.)	115	4
1934	N. C. DOWNIE	(Polytechnic H.)	131	11½
1935	J. F. K. KLEIN	(Stade Malherbe)	146	6¾
1936	P. G. DAWSON	(Holborn Est. G.C.)	123	7
1937	J. D. LINAKER	(London A.C.)	132	8
1938	D. C. J. BURGES	(Mitcham A.C.)	132	7
1939	M. A. C. DOWLING	(London A.C.)	135	10
1946	A. L. SADLER		132	5
1947	B. W. DODD	(St. Albans C.S.)	118	10
1948	B. W. DODD	(St. Albans C.S.)	145	5½
1949	M. PHARAOH	(Manchester G.S.)	151	7½
1950	P. ATKINSON	(Preston Manor C.S.)	133	8½
1951	R. D. SHAW	(Manchester G.S.)	137	5
1952	J. SAMPSON	(Kent A.C.)	143	0
1953	G. A. CARR	(Wanstead C.H.S.)	155	7
1954	G. A. CARR	(Wanstead C.H.S.)	166	4
1955	J. A. PULLINGER	(Gosport A.C.)	149	11
1956	M. R. LINDSAY	(Queen's Park H.)	182	0
1957	M. R. LINDSAY	(Queen's Park H.)	176	10
1958	J. W. SHELDRICK	(Newmarket H.)	170	0
1959	J. E. WEIGHTMAN	(Ilford A.C.)	153	11

Jack Holden   G. W. Nankeville   Jack E. Lovelock

HAMMER THROW

Date	Name	Club	ft.	in.
1951	I. S. BAIN	(Fettes Coll.)	143	11
1952	I. S. BAIN	(Fettes Coll.)	156	4½
1953	M. MARTIN	(John Fisher Sch.)	168	7½
1954	M. J. ELLIS	(Thames Valley H.)	181	8
1955	M. J. ELLIS	(Thames Valley H.)	190	10
1956	P. A. RITCHIE	(City London Sch.)	172	9
1957	P. C. NEWTON	(John Fisher Sch.)	173	4
1958	P. C. NEWTON	(Queen's Park H.)	176	7
1959	D. G. MITCHELL	(Eton Manor A.C.)	177	11½

THROWING THE JAVELIN

1931	G. L. EDWARDS	(Ponders End A.C.)	149	9
1932	J. C. HEATH	(Birchfield H.)	177	8
1933	E. H. FINNERON	(Belgrave H.)	176	0
1934	J. A. McD. MACKILLOP	(Queen's Own Cameron Highlanders)	173	9
1935	J. F. K. KLEIN	(Stade Malherbe)	191	0
1936	F. D. ADAMS	(Birchfield H.)	184	8½
1937	R. E. EVANS	(Southgate H.)	155	2
1938	R. E. EVANS	(Southgate H.)	160	2½
1939	M. J. W. DALRYMPLE	(Birchfield H.)	160	9
1946	R. G. B. WILLIAMS	(Birkenhead Sch.)	185	10
1947	J. SWASLAND	(Polytechnic H.)	181	6
1948	G. A. BELL	(George Heriot's S.)	168	6½
1949	M. J. DENLEY	(Thames Valley H.)	200	0½

Date	Name	Club	ft.	in.
1950	M. E. MORRELL	(Wirral A.C.)	176	0½
1951	M. HARRADINE	(Thames Valley H.)	201	1½
1952	J. McDONALD	(Margate W.T.C.)	186	2
1953	C. G. SMITH	(Thames Valley H.)	201	3½
1954	M. J. LANNING	(Thames Valley H.)	182	10
1955	B. D. WHITAKER	(Derby and County A.C.)..	199	5
1956	A. J. FARMER	(London A.C.)	211	0
1957	G. E. BUCKNELL	(Bishop Stortford C.)	201	0
1958	J. P. ANDREWS	(Norwich and Norfolk A.C.)	211	3
1959	J. V. McSORLEY	(Thames Valley H.)	205	9½

A COMPLETE COMPILATION OF UNDER-4-MINUTE MILES

Time			Date
3:59.4	R. G. BANNISTER (*Great Britain*)	Oxford	6.5.54
3:57.9	J. M. LANDY (*Australia*)	Turku, Finland	21.6.54
3:58.8	R. G. BANNISTER (*Great Britain*)	Vancouver	7.8.54
3:59.6	J. M. LANDY (*Australia*)	Vancouver	7.8.54
3:59.0	L. TABORI (*Hungary*)	London	28.5.55
3:59.8	C. J. CHATAWAY (*Great Britain*)	London	28.5.55
3:59.8	B. S. HEWSON (*Great Britain*)	London	28.5.55
3:58.6	J. M. LANDY (*Australia*)	Melbourne	28.1.56
3:58.6	J. M. LANDY (*Australia*)	Melbourne	7.4.56
3:58.6	J. J. BAILEY (*Australia*)	Los Angeles	5.5.56
3:58.7	J. M. LANDY (*Australia*)	Los Angeles	5.5.56
3:59.1	J. M. LANDY (*Australia*)	Fresno, U.S.A.	12.5.56
3:59.0	R. DELANY (*Republic of Ireland*)	Compton, U.S.A.	1.6.56
3:59.1	N. G. NIELSEN (*Denmark*)	Compton, U.S.A.	1.6.56
3:59.4	G. D. IBBOTSON (*Great Britain*)	London	6.8.56
3:59.0	I. ROZSAVOLGYI (*Hungary*)	Budapest	26.8.56
3:58.9	M. G. LINCOLN (*Australia*)	Melbourne	23.3.57
3:58.7	D. W. BOWDEN (*U.S.A.*)	Stockton, U.S.A.	1.6.57
3:58.4	G. D. IBBOTSON (*Great Britain*)	Glasgow	15.6.57
3:57.2	G. D. IBBOTSON (*Great Britain*)	London	19.7.57
3:58.8	R. DELANY (*Republic of Ireland*)	London	19.7.57
3:59.1	S. JUNGWIRTH (*Czechoslovakia*)	London	19.7.57
3:59.3	K. WOOD (*Great Britain*)	London	19.7.57
3:59.3	D. WAERN (*Sweden*)	Stockholm	19.7.57
3:59.7	D. WAERN (*Sweden*)	Malmo, Sweden	6.8.57
3:58.7	G. D. IBBOTSON (*Great Britain*)	Naantali, Finland	7.8.57
3:59.1	O. VUORISALO (*Finland*)	Naantali, Finland	7.8.57
3:59.6	D. WAERN (*Sweden*)	Goteborg, Sweden	26.8.57
3:58.5	D. WAERN (*Sweden*)	Malmo, Sweden	4.9.57
3:58.9	R. MOENS (*Belgium*)	Malmo, Sweden	4.9.57
3:59.9	H. J. ELLIOTT (*Australia*)	Melbourne	25.1.58
3:58.7	H. J. ELLIOTT (*Australia*)	Melbourne	30.1.58
3:59.0	M. G. LINCOLN (*Australia*)	Melbourne	30.1.58
3:59.6	H. J. ELLIOTT (*Australia*)	Perth	15.2.58
3:59.6	M. G. LINCOLN (*Australia*)	Perth	15.2.58
3:57.8	H. J. ELLIOTT (*Australia*)	Los Angeles	16.5.58
3:58.1	H. J. ELLIOTT (*Australia*)	Compton, U.S.A.	6.6.58
3:57.9	H. J. ELLIOTT (*Australia*)	Bakersfield	21.6.58
3:58.5	M. G. LINCOLN (*Australia*)	Bakersfield	21.6.58
3:59.0	H. J. ELLIOTT (*Australia*)	Cardiff	26.7.58
3:54.5	H. J. ELLIOTT (*Australia*)	Dublin	6.8.58
3:55.9	M. G. LINCOLN (*Australia*)	Dublin	6.8.58
3:57.5	R. DELANY (*Republic of Ireland*)	Dublin	6.8.58
3:57.5	M. G. HALBERG (*New Zealand*)	Dublin	6.8.58
3:58.6	A. G. THOMAS (*Australia*)	Dublin	6.8.58
3:58.0	H. J. ELLIOTT (*Australia*)	Malmo, Sweden	29.8.58
3:55.4	H. J. ELLIOTT (*Australia*)	London	3.9.58
3:58.9	B. S. HEWSON (*Great Britain*)	London	3.9.58
3:59.7	Z. ORYWAL (*Poland*)	London	3.9.58
3:58.9	H. J. ELLIOTT (*Australia*)	Brisbane	14.3.59
3:56.5	S. VALENTIN (*E. Germany*)	Potsdam	28.5.59
3:59.2	D. WAERN (*Sweden*)	Vasteras	12.8.59

W.A.A.A. CHAMPIONSHIPS

Date	Name	Club	Sec.
60 METRES			
1935	A. WADE	(Essex Ladies)	8.0
1936	B. LOCK	(Hercules A.C.)	7.6
1937	B. LOCK	(Hercules A.C.)	7.8
1938	B. LOCK	(Mitcham A.C.)	7.6
1939	B. LOCK	(Mitcham A.C.)	7.6
1946	I. STRETTON	(Bolton United)	8.1
1947	I. ROYCE	(Bolton United)	7.9
1948	D. BATTER	(London Olympiades)	9.1
1949	D. BATTER	(London Olympiades)	7.7
1950	Q. SHIVAS	(Aberdeen Univ.)	7.8
100 YARDS			
1923	M. LINES	(London Olympiades)	12.0
1924	E. W. EDWARDS	(London Olympiades)	11.4
1925	R. E. THOMPSON	(Manor Pk.)	11.8
1926	F. C. HAYNES	(London Olympiades)	12.0
1927	E. W. EDWARDS	(London Olympiades)	11.4
1928	M. A. GUNN-CORNELL	(Mitcham A.C.)	11.6
1929	I. K. WALKER	(Cambridge H.)	11.4
1930	E. M. HISCOCK-WILSON	(London Olympiades)	11.4
1931	N. HALSTEAD	(Bury A.C.)	11.4
1932	E. JOHNSON	(Bolton United)	11.0
100 METRES			
1933	E. M. HISCOCK-WILSON	(London Olympiades)	12.2
1934	E. M. HISCOCK-WILSON	(London Olympiades)	12.2
1935	E. M. HISCOCK-WILSON	(London Olympiades)	12.2
1936	B. BURKE	(Mitcham A.C.)	12.8
1937	W. S. JEFFREY-JORDAN	(Birchfield H.)	12.2
1938	B. LOCK	(Mitcham A.C.)	12.2
1939	B. LOCK	(Mitcham A.C.)	12.4
1945	W. S. JEFFERY-JORDAN	(Birchfield H.)	12.8
1946	M. A. J. GARDNER-DYSON	(Oxford L.A.C.)	12.6
1947	W. S. JEFFREY-JORDAN	(Birmingham)	12.1
1948	W. S. JEFFREY-JORDAN	(Birchfield H.)	12.6
1949	S. CHEESEMAN-DISLEY	(Spartan L.A.C.)	12.1
1950	J. F. FOULDS-PAUL	(Spartan L.A.C.)	12.6
1951	J. F. FOULDS-PAUL	(Spartan L.A.C.)	12.3
100 YARDS			
1952	H. J. ARMITAGE-YOUNG	(Longwood H.)	10.9
1953	A. PASHLEY	(Gt. Yarmouth A.C.)	11.0

Date	Name	Club	Sec.
1954	A. PASHLEY	(Gt. Yarmouth A.C.)	11.1
1955	S. M. FRANCIS	(Manchester Univ.)	10.8
1956	J. F. FOULDS-PAUL	(Spartan L.A.C.)	10.6
1957	H. J. ARMITAGE-YOUNG	(Longwood H.)	10.9
1958	V. M. WESTON	(Selsonia L.A.C.)	10.6
1959	D. HYMAN	(Hickleton Main Y.C.)	10.8
220 YARDS			
1922	M. LINES	(London Olympiades)	26.8
1923	E. W. EDWARDS	(London Olympiades)	27.0
1924	E. W. EDWARDS	(London Olympiades)	26.2
1925	V. PALMER	(Middlesex L.A.C.)	26.8
1926	V. PALMER	(Middlesex L.A.C.)	26.8
1927	E. W. EDWARDS	(London Olympiades)	25.8
1928	K. HITOMI	Japan	26.2
1929	W. WELDON	(Manor Pk.)	26.4
1930	N. HALSTEAD	(Bury A.C.)	25.2
1931	N. HALSTEAD	(Bury A.C.)	25.5
1932	N. HALSTEAD	(Bury A.C.)	25.6
200 METRES			
1933	E. M. HISCOCK-WILSON	(London Olympiades)	25.8
1934	N. HALSTEAD	(Radcliffe)	25.6
1935	E. M. HISCOCK-WILSON	(London Olympiades)	25.3
1936	B. BURKE	(Mitcham A.C.)	25.2
1937	L. CHALMERS	(Portsmouth A.C.)	24.9
1938	D. S. SAUNDERS	(Spartan L.A.C.)	25.0
1939	L. CHALMERS	(Portsmouth A.C.)	25.6
1945	W. S. JEFFREY-JORDAN	(Birchfield H.)	26.7
1946	S. CHEESEMAN-DISLEY	(Spartan L.A.C.)	25.7
1947	S. CHEESEMAN-DISLEY	(Spartan L.A.C.)	25.0
1948	S. CHEESEMAN-DISLEY	(Spartan L.A.C.)	25.7
1949	S. CHEESEMAN-DISLEY	(Spartan L.A.C.)	25.4
1950	D. G. MANLEY-HALL	(Essex Ladies)	25.2
1951	S. CHEESEMAN-DISLEY	(Spartan L.A.C.)	25.0
220 YARDS			
1952	S. CHEESEMAN-DISLEY	(Spartan L.A.C.)	25.0
1953	A. E. JOHNSON	(Cambridge H.)	25.0
1954	A. E. JOHNSON	(Cambridge H.)	25.1
1955	J. E. SCRIVENS	(Selsonia L.A.C.)	24.9
1956	J. F. FOULDS-PAUL	(Spartan L.A.C.)	23.8
1957	H. J. ARMITAGE-YOUNG	(Longwood H.)	24.2
1958	H. J. ARMITAGE-YOUNG	(Longwood H.)	24.5
1959	D. HYMAN	(Hickleton Main Y.C.)	24.5
440 YARDS			
1923	M. LINES	(London Olympiades)	62.4
1924	V. PALMER	(Middlesex L.A.C.)	65.0
1925	V. PALMER	(Middlesex L.A.C.)	61.4
1926	V. PALMER	(Middlesex L.A.C.)	61.8
1927	D. PROCTOR	(Middlesex L.A.C.)	62.4
1928	F. C. HAYNES	(London Olympiades)	60.8
1929	M. KING	(Kent)	59.2
1930	E. E. WRIGHT	(Cambridge H.)	59.8
1931	N. HALSTEAD	(Bury A.C.)	58.8
1932	N. HALSTEAD	(Bury A.C.)	56.8
400 METRES			
1933	N. HALSTEAD	(Radcliffe)	58.8
1934	V. BRANCH	(London Olympiades)	60.0
1935	O. M. HALL	(G.E.C. Magnet Club)	61.9
1936	O. M. HALL	(G.E.C. Magnet Club)	58.6
1937	N. HALSTEAD	(Radcliffe)	60.1
1938	O. M. HALL	(G.E.C. Magnet Club)	60.0
1939	L. CHALMERS	(Portsmouth A.C.)	59.5
440 YARDS			
1945	W. S. JEFFREY-JORDAN	(Birchfield H.)	61.8
400 METRES			
1946	M. WALKER	(Spartan L.A.C.)	59.3
1947	J. UPTON	(Spartan L.A.C.)	61.6
1948	V. M. BALL-WINN	(Spartan L.A.C.)	60.8
1949	V. M. BALL-WINN	(Spartan L.A.C.)	59.4
1950	V. M. BALL-WINN	(Spartan L.A.C.)	57.5
1951	V. M. BALL-WINN	(Spartan L.A.C.)	58.2
440 YARDS			
1952	V. M. BALL-WINN	(Spartan L.A.C.)	59.3
1953	V. M. BALL-WINN	(Spartan L.A.C.)	57.6
1954	G. GOLDSBOROUGH-JACKSON	(David Brown A.C.)	57.1
1955	J. E. RUFF	(Basingstoke A.C.)	56.9
1956	J. E. RUFF	(Basingstoke A.C.)	56.5
1957	J. E. RUFF	(Basingstoke A.C.)	56.4
1958	S. HAMPTON-PIRIE	(Phoenix L.A.C.)	56.4
1959	M. J. PICKERELL	(Watford H.)	55.9

ATHLETICS QUIZ

What is the fastest time in which anyone has run 440 yards on a straight track?

(opposite)

★

QUIZ ANSWER

45.0 secs. by H. H. McKINLEY (Jamaica) at Long Branch, N.J., on August 23rd, 1947.

880 YARDS

1923	E. F. TRICKEY	(London Olympiades)	2:40.2
1924	E. F. TRICKEY	(London Olympiades)	2:24.0
1925	E. F. TRICKEY	(London Olympiades)	2:26.6
1926	E. F. TRICKEY	(London Olympiades)	2:28.0
1927	E. F. TRICKEY	(London Olympiades)	2:32.4
1928	J. BARBER	(Luton)	2:27.6
1929	V. STREATER	(Middlesex L.A.C.)	2:25.8
1930	G. A. LUNN	(Birchfield H.)	2:18.2
1931	G. A. LUNN	(Birchfield H.)	2:22.4
1932	G. A. LUNN	(Birchfield H.)	2:20.4

800 METRES

1933	R. CHRISTMAS	(London Olympiades)	2:23.0
1934	G. A. LUNN	(Birchfield H.)	2:18.3
1935	N. HALSTEAD	(Radcliffe)	2:15.6
1936	O. M. HALL	(G.E.C. Magnet Club)	2:20.2
1937	G. A. LUNN	(Birchfield H.)	2:18.5
1938	N. HALSTEAD	(Bolton United)	2:20.4
1939	O. M. HALL	(G.E.C. Magnet Club)	2:21.0

880 YARDS

1945	P. RICHARDS	(Birmingham)	2:26.7

800 METRES

1946	P. RICHARDS	(Birmingham)	2:21.0
1947	N. BATSON	(Small Heath)	2:23.1
1948	N. BATSON	(Small Heath)	2:20.3
1949	H. SPEARS	(Middlesex L.A.C.)	2:19.4
1950	M. K. HUME	(Essex Ladies)	2:20.5
1951	N. BATSON	(Small Heath)	2:18.4

880 YARDS

1952	M. TAYLOR	(Birchfield H.)	2:17.5
1953	I. E. A. OLIVER	(Gosforth H. and A.C.)	2:15.0
1954	D. S. LEATHER	(Birchfield H.)	2:09.0
1955	D. S. LEATHER	(Birchfield H.)	2:09.7
1956	P. E. M. GREEN-PERKINS	(Ilford L.A.C.)	2:13.2
1957	D. S. LEATHER	(Birchfield H.)	2:09.4
1958	J. W. JORDAN	(Spartan L.A.C.)	2:13.3
1959	J. W. JORDAN	(Spartan L.A.C.)	2:09.5

ONE MILE

1936	G. A. LUNN	(Birchfield H.)	5:23.0
1937	G. A. LUNN	(Birchfield H.)	5:17.0
1938	D. HARRIS	(Birchfield H.)	5:29.4
1939	E. FORSTER	(Civil Service A.C.)	5:15.3
1945	P. M. SANDALL	(Birchfield H.)	5:40.2
1946	B. E. HARRIS	(Birchfield H.)	5:33.6
1947	N. BATSON	(Small Heath)	5:37.6
1948	N. BATSON	(Small Heath)	5:31.8
1949	E. D. GARRITT	(Ilford L.A.C.)	5:20.0
1950	M. J. HEATH	(Small Heath)	5:25.8
1951	H. NEEDHAM	(Cambridge H.)	5:23.4
1952	I. E. A. OLIVER	(Gosforth H. and A.C.)	5:11.0
1953	E. HARDING-VIVIAN	(London Olympiades)	5:09.8
1954	P. E. M. GREEN-PERKINS	(Ilford A.C.)	5:09.6
1955	P. E. M. GREEN-PERKINS	(Ilford A.C.)	5:05.2
1956	D. S. LEATHER	(Birchfield H.)	5:01.0
1957	D. S. LEATHER	(Birchfield H.)	4:55.3
1958	M. A. BONNANO-SMITH	(Highgate H.)	5:02.6
1959	J. S. BRIGGS	(Selsonia L.A.C.)	5:02.2

TRACK WALK

ONE MILE

1945	J. RIDDINGTON	(London Trams)	8:42.8

1,600 METRES

1946	D. MANN	(Birchfield H.)	8:38.6
1947	J. D. RIDDINGTON	(Birchfield H.)	8:36.4
1948	M. J. HEATH	(Small Heath)	8:17.8
1949	M. J. HEATH	(Small Heath)	8:25.0
1950	M. J. HEATH	(Small Heath)	8:17.0
1951	M. J. HEATH	(Small Heath)	7:50.0

ONE MILE

1952	B. E. M. DAY-RANDLE	(Birmingham)	7:58.2
1953	B. E. M. DAY-RANDLE	(Birchfield H.)	7:48.2
1954	B. E. M. DAY-RANDLE	(Birchfield H.)	7:38.4
1955	B. E. M. DAY-RANDLE	(Birchfield H.)	7:59.4
1956	D. WILLIAMS	(Birchfield H.)	7:47.6
1957	D. WILLIAMS	(Birchfield H.)	8:08.4
1958	B. FRANKLIN	(Birchfield H.)	8:09.4

ONE AND A HALF MILES

1959	B. A. FRANKLIN	(Birchfield H.)	12:56.4

80 METRES HURDLES

1945	L. HANCOCK	(Birmingham)	13.6
1946	B. CROWTHER	(Middlesex L.A.C.)	12.8
1947	M. A. J. GARDNER-DYSON	(Oxford L.A.C.)	11.5
1948	M. A. J. GARDNER-DYSON	(Oxford L.A.C.)	12.0
1949	J. C. DESFORGES-PICKERING	(Essex L.A.C.)	11.9
1950	M. A. J. GARDNER-DYSON	(Oxford L.A.C.)	11.6
1951	M. A. J. GARDNER-DYSON	(Oxford L.A.C.)	11.7
1952	J. C. DESFORGES-PICKERING	(Essex L.A.C.)	11.4
1953	J. C. DESFORGES-PICKERING	(Essex L.A.C.)	11.5
1954	J. C. DESFORGES-PICKERING	(Essex L.A.C.)	11.4
1955	S. M. FRANCIS	(Manchester Univ.)	11.3
1955	P. G. SEABORNE-ELLIOTT	(Essex Ladies)	11.1
1957	T. E. HOPKINS	(Queen's Univ.)	11.4
1958	C. L. QUINTON	(Birchfield H.)	10.9
1959	M. D. BIGNALL	(London Olympiades)	11.3

HIGH JUMP (*Post War*)

			ft.	in.
1945	D. K. GARDNER	(Middlesex Ladies A.C.)	5	0
1946	D. K. GARDNER	(Middlesex Ladies A.C.)	5	1
1947	G. E. YOUNG	(Bournemouth)	5	1
1948	D. J. B. ODAM-TYLER	(Mitcham A.C.)	5	4
1949	D. J. B. ODAM-TYLER	(Mitcham A.C.)	5	3
1950	S. ALEXANDER-LERWILL	(Spartan Ladies A.C.)	5	4
1951	S. ALEXANDER-LERWILL	(Spartan Ladies A.C.)	5	7⅝
1952	D. J. B. ODAM-TYLER	(Mitcham A.C.)	5	5
1953	S. ALEXANDER-LERWILL	(Spartan Ladies A.C.)	5	5
1954	S. ALEXANDER-LERWILL	(Spartan Ladies A.C.)	5	4
1955	T. E. HOPKINS	(Queen's Univ., Belfast)	5	5
1956	D. J. B. ODAM-TYLER	(Mitcham A.C.)	5	3
1957	T. E. HOPKINS	(Queen's Univ., Belfast)	5	5
1958	M. D. BIGNALL	(London Olympiades A.C.)	5	5
1959	N. ZWIER	(Netherlands)	5	5

LONG JUMP (*Post War*)

			ft.	in.
1945	K. DUFFY	(Selsonia L.A.C.)	15	7½
1946	E. M. RABY-DAVIES	(Middlesex Ladies A.C.)	16	7
1947	K. DUFFY	(Selsonia L.A.C.)	17	3½
1948	J. C. SHEPHERD	(Essex Ladies A.C.)	18	8½
1949	M. ERSKINE	(Birmingham)	17	7½
1950	M. ERSKINE	(Birmingham)	17	10¾
1951	D. J. B. ODAM-TYLER	(Mitcham A.C.)	18	3¾
1952	S. CRAWLEY	(Spartan L.A.C.)	18	5
1953	J. C. DESFORGES-PICKERING	(Essex L.A.C.)	18	10¾
1954	J. C. DESFORGES-PICKERING	(Essex L.A.C.)	19	1½
1955	T. E. HOPKINS	(Queen's Univ., Belfast)	18	11
1956	S. H. HOSKIN	(Spartan L.A.C.)	18	6½
1957	C. M. COPS-PERSIGHETTI	(Southend A.C.)	19	3¼
1958	S. H. HOSKIN	(Spartan L.A.C.)	19	6¾
1959	M. D. BIGNALL	(London Olympiades A.C.)	19	9¾

PUTTING THE SHOT (*Post War*)

			ft.	in.
1945	K. DYER	(Mitcham A.C.)	30	9¾
1946	K. DYER	(Mitcham A.C.)	33	5¼
1947	B. A. REID-SHERGOLD	(Mitcham A.C.)	36	2¼
1948	B. A. REID-SHERGOLD	(Mitcham A.C.)	40	5¾
1949	B. A. REID-SHERGOLD	(Mitcham A.C.)	40	6⅛
1950	J. LINSELL	(Essex L.A.C.)	36	3¾
1951	B. A. REID-SHERGOLD	(Mitcham A.C.)	38	8
1952	J. LINSELL	(Essex L.A.C.)	39	8½
1953	J. LINSELL	(Essex L.A.C.)	39	9
1954	S. FARMER-ALLDAY	(Spartan L.A.C.)	41	1
1955	J. PAGE-COOK	(London Olympiades A.C.)	39	0½
1956	S. FARMER-ALLDAY	(Spartan L.A.C.)	43	11¼
1957	J. PAGE-COOK	(London Olympiades A.C.)	41	4¼
1958	S. FARMER-ALLDAY	(Spartan L.A.C.)	46	5
1959	S. FARMER-ALLDAY	(Spartan L.A.C.)	43	3½

THROWING THE DISCUS (*Post War*)

			ft.	in.
1945	K. DYER	(Mitcham A.C.)	99	8
1946	M. O. LASBREY	(Spartan L.A.C.)	93	0½
1947	M. LUCAS-BIRTWHISTLE	(Epsom and Ewell H.)	119	5
1948	B. A. REID-SHERGOLD	(Mitcham A.C.)	120	6
1949	B. A. REID-SHERGOLD	(Mitcham A.C.)	121	3½
1950	J. M. SMITH	(Middlesex L.A.C.)	108	4¾
1951	B. A. REID-SHERGOLD	(Mitcham A.C.)	130	10¼
1952	S. FARMER-ALLDAY	(Brighton L.A.C.)	129	0½
1953	S. FARMER-ALLDAY	(Brighton L.A.C.)	131	3
1954	M. GIRI	(Phoenix L.A.C.)	129	4
1955	M. GIRI	(Phoenix L.A.C.)	136	9
1956	S. FARMER-ALLDAY	(Spartan L.A.C.)	154	3
1957	S. NEEDHAM	(Spartan L.A.C.)	131	11½
1958	S. FARMER-ALLDAY	(Spartan L.A.C.)	156	6
1959	S. FARMER-ALLDAY	(Spartan L.A.C.)	148	4

THROWING THE JAVELIN (*Post War*)

(Both hands aggregate)

			ft.	in.
1945	G. M. CLARK	(Birchfield H.)	104	1
1946	M. O. LASBREY	(Spartan L.A.C.)	113	0
1947	M. TAIBLOVA	(Epsom and Ewell H).	103	4
1948	B. A. REID-SHERGOLD	(Mitcham A.C.)	102	0½
1949	E. J. ALLEN	(Unattached)	103	9
1950	D. COATES	(Oxford L.A.C.)	128	1¾
1951	D. COATES	(Oxford L.A.C.)	124	9½
1952	D. COATES	(Oxford L.A.C.)	148	7½
1953	A. M. COLLINS	(London Olympiades A.C.)	119	11½
1954	A. J. DUKES	(Cambridge H.)	129	9
1955	D. COATES	(Oxford L.A.C.)	137	1
1956	D. ORPHALL	(Spartan L.A.C.)	133	11
1957	A. M. WILLIAMS	(Blue Coat A.C.)	132	0
1958	A. M. WILLIAMS	(Blue Coat A.C.)	142	8
1959	S. PLATT	(London Olympiades)	160	10½

CROSS COUNTRY (*Post War*)

1946	Birchfield H.	P. SANDALL (Birchfield)
1947	Birchfield H.	R. M. WRIGHT (St. Greg.)
1948	Birchfield H.	I. KIBBLER (Birchfield)
1949	Birchfield H.	E. JOHNSON (Airedale)
1950	Birchfield H.	A. GIBSON (North Shields)
1951	Ilford L.A.C.	P. E. M. GREEN-PERKINS (Ilford)
1952	Ilford L.A.C.	P. E. M. GREEN-PERKINS (Ilford)
1953	Birchfield H.	D. S. LEATHER (Birchfield)
1954	Birchfield H.	D. S. LEATHER (Birchfield)
1955	Ilford L.A.C.	D. S. LEATHER (Birchfield H.)
1956	Ilford L.A.C.	D. S. LEATHER (Birchfield H.)
1957	Ilford L.A.C.	J. BRIDGLAND (Southampton)
1958	Highgate H.	R. ASHBY (Coventry Godiva)
1959	London Olympiades A.C.	J. BYATT (Hampstead H.)

ATHLETICS QUIZ

What is the world's best recorded performance for running 100 yards backwards?

QUIZ ANSWER

13.2 secs. by Bill Robinson (U.S.A.)

★

Compiled by H. A. E. Scheele
Secretary: The International Badminton Federation

Badminton

BADMINTON QUIZ

1. Why is the trophy for the International Badminton Championship called the Thomas Cup?

★

2. Miss Heather Ward won the ladies' singles at the 1959 All-England Championships. When did an English player last win a singles title at that tournament?

★

3. Most of the All-England singles champions have been English. What other countries' players have won those titles, and how often?

★

4. The competitions for the Thomas Cup and Uber Cup are played off in four geographical zones (American, Asian, Australasian and European) for the prelimi-nary rounds. Must a country take part in its natural zone?

★

5. What is the authority responsible for organising the Thomas Cup and Uber Cup contests?

QUIZ ANSWERS

1. Because it was presented by Sir George Thomas, one of the game's most famous players of the past and President of the International Badminton Federation. 2. In 1938, before Miss Ward was actually born. 3. In the men's singles, Ireland (J. F. Devlin and G. S. B. Mack) 7; Malaya Wong Peng Soon and E. B. Choong) 7; Denmark (T. Madsen, C. Jepsen, J. Skaarup and E. Kops) 4; U.S.A. (D. G. Freeman) 1; Indonesia (Tan Joe Hok) 1. In the ladies' singles, Denmark (Misses Ussing, Thorndahl, Jacobsen and Mrs. Ahm) 7; U.S.A. (Misses J. Devlin and Varner) 5; and Canada (Mrs. Walton) 1. 4. No. The restriction is where the ties shall be played. India once played in the American Zone of the Thomas Cup, and Indonesia in the Australasian Zone. In the Uber Cup contest of 1959–60 both Indonesia and Thailand entered in the Australasian Zone. 5. The International Badminton Federation, to which are affiliated the national organisations of 37 countries.

ALL ENGLAND CHAMPIONSHIPS

(Unless otherwise stated, all winners are English players. Figures in parentheses refer to married names listed on page 74.)

	Men's Singles	Ladies' Singles
1899	*No Competition*	*No Competition*
1900	S. H. Smith	Miss E. Thomson (1)
1901	Capt. H. W. Davies	Miss E. Thomson (1)
1902	Ralph Watling	Miss M. Lucas (21)
1903	Ralph Watling	Miss E. Thomson (1)
1904	H. N. Marrett	Miss E. Thomson (1)*
1905	H. N. Marrett	Miss M. Lucas
1906	N. Wood	Miss E. Thomson (1)
1907	N. Wood	Miss M. Lucas
1908	H. N. Marrett	Miss M. Lucas
1909	F. Chesterton	Miss M. Lucas*
1910	F. Chesterton	Miss M. Lucas
1911	G. A. Sautter	Miss M. Larminie (3)
1912	F. Chesterton	Mrs. R. C. Tragett
1913	G. A. Sautter	Miss L. C. Radeglia
1914	G. A. Sautter	Miss L. C. Radeglia
1915–19	*No Competition*	*No Competition*
1920	Sir G. A. Thomas, Bart.	Miss K. McKane (3)
1921	Sir G. A. Thomas, Bart.	Miss K. McKane (3)
1922	Sir G. A. Thomas, Bart.*	Miss K. McKane (3)*
1923	Sir G. A. Thomas, Bart.	Miss L. C. Radeglia
1924	G. S. B. Mack (Ireland)	Miss K. McKane (3)
1925	J. F. Devlin (Ireland)	Mrs. A. D. Stocks
1926	J. F. Devlin (Ireland)	Mrs. F. G. Barrett
1927	J. F. Devlin (Ireland)*	Mrs. F. G. Barrett
1928	J. F. Devlin (Ireland)	Mrs. R. C. Tragett
1929	J. F. Devlin (Ireland)	Mrs. F. G. Barrett
1930	D. C. Hume	Mrs. F. G. Barrett*
1931	J. F. Devlin (Ireland)	Mrs. F. G. Barrett
1932	R. C. F. Nichols	Miss L. M. Kingsbury (4)
1933	R. M. White	Miss A. Woodroffe (5)
1934	R. C. F. Nichols	Miss L. M. Kingsbury (4)
1935	R. M. White	Mrs. H. S. Uber
1936	R. C. F. Nichols	Miss T. Kingsbury (16)
1937	R. C. F. Nichols*	Miss T. Kingsbury (16)
1938	R. C. F. Nichols	Miss D. M. C. Young (17)
1939	Tage Madsen (Denmark)	Mrs. W. R. Walton, Jr. (Canada)
1940–46	*No Competition*	*No Competition*
1947	Conny Jepsen (Sweden)	Miss Marie Ussing (25) (Denmark)
1948	Jorn Skaarup (Denmark)	Miss Kirsten Thorndahl (24) (Denmark)
1949	D. G. Freeman (U.S.A.)	Miss A. Schiott Jacobsen (Denmark)
1950	Wong Peng Soon (Malaya)	Mrs. Tonny Ahm (Denmark)
1951	Wong Peng Soon (Malaya)	Miss A. Schiott Jacobsen (Denmark)
1952	Wong Peng Soon (Malaya)*	Mrs. Tonny Ahm (Denmark)
1953	E. B. Choong (Malaya)	Miss Marie Ussing (26) (Denmark)
1954	E. B. Choong (Malaya)	Miss J. Devlin (U.S.A.)
1955	Wong Peng Soon (Malaya)	Miss M. Varner (U.S.A.)
1956	E. B. Choong (Malaya)	Miss M. Varner (U.S.A.)
1957	E. B. Choong (Malaya)*	Miss J. Devlin (U.S.A.)
1958	E. Kops (Denmark)	Miss J. Devlin (U.S.A.)
1959	Tan Joe Hok (Indonesia)	Miss H. M. Ward

* Trophy won outright.

THE INTERNATIONAL BADMINTON CHAMPIONSHIP
(Thomas Cup)

Season	Competing Nations	Challenge Round Result	Venue
1948–49	10	*Malaya *beat* Denmark, 8–1	Preston
1951–52	11	Malaya *beat* U.S.A., 7–2	Singapore
1954–55	20	Malaya *beat* Denmark, 8–1	Singapore
1957–58	18	Indonesia *beat* Malaya, 6–3	Singapore

*Final tie.

THE LADIES' INTERNATIONAL BADMINTON CHAMPIONSHIP
(Uber Cup)

Season	Competing Nations	Challenge Round Result	Venue
1956–57	11	*U.S.A. *beat* Denmark, 6–1	Lytham

* Final tie.

SUMMARY OF INTERNATIONAL MATCH RESULTS
(to September, 1959)

ENGLAND

	Played	Fixtures Won	Lost	Matches Won	Lost
Thomas Cup:					
v. Denmark	3	0	3	2	25
v. France	3	3	0	27	0
v. Germany	1	1	0	9	0
v. Ireland	1	1	0	8	1
v. Scotland	2	2	0	14	4
v. Sweden	1	0	1	2	7
Uber Cup:					
v. Denmark	1	0	1	2	5
Other Matches:					
v. Denmark	10	2	8	18	48
v. Ireland	45	45	0	313	81
v. Malaya	2	0	2	0	16
v. Scotland	30	30	0	244	26
v. South Africa	14	10	4	87	51
v. Sweden	9	5	4	25	38
v. Wales	5	5	0	45	0
v. Ireland, Scotland & Wales Combined	2	2	0	14	4
	129	106	23	810	306

IRELAND

	Played	Fixtures Won	Lost	Matches Won	Lost
Thomas Cup:					
v. Denmark	3	0	3	2	25
v. England	1	0	1	1	8
v. Scotland	1	1	0	6	3
Uber Cup:					
v. Denmark	1	0	1	1	6
v. Scotland	1	1	0	5	2
v. Sweden	1	1	0	6	1
Other Matches:					
v. Denmark	1	0	1	1	6
v. England	45	0	45	81	313
v. Malaya	1	0	1	0	10
v. Scotland	36	27	9	197	121
v. Sweden	3	1	2	8	15
v. Wales	11	11	0	84	11
	105	42	63	392	521

SCOTLAND

	Played	Fixtures Won	Lost	Matches Won	Lost
Thomas Cup:					
v. England	2	0	2	4	14
v. Ireland	1	0	1	3	6
v. Sweden	1	0	1	0	9
Uber Cup:					
v. Ireland	1	0	1	2	5
Other Matches:					
v. Denmark	1	0	1	0	7
v. England	30	0	30	26	244
v. Ireland	36	9	27	121	197
v. Sweden	3	2	1	11	10
v. U.S.A.	1	0	1	0	9
v. Wales	10	10	0	75	15
	86	21	65	242	516

WALES

	Played	Fixtures Won	Lost	Matches Won	Lost
Thomas Cup:					
v. Denmark	1	0	1	0	9
Other Matches:					
v. Denmark	5	1	4	10	21
v. England	5	0	5	0	45
v. Ireland	11	0	11	11	84
v. Scotland	10	0	10	15	75
	32	1	31	36	234

E

BADMINTON QUIZ

1. The Laws of Badminton impose certain restrictions with regard to the position of the server. Must the shuttle, at the moment of impact, also be within the restricted area?

*

2. What is the height of the net at the posts? And at the centre of the court?

*

3. How many shuttles will be required to balance a one-pound weight?

*

4. How many feathers are there in a shuttle?

*

5. What is considered to be the minimum height of a hall for first-class play?

*

6. If the shuttle is caught in or on the net during a rally, after having passed over the net, what is the decision?

*

7. In doubles, which partner should serve first, and which receive first at the commencement of the second game?

*

8. If a side has rejected the right to "set" a game at 13-all, may they, or their opponents, elect to "set" if the score later reaches 14-all?

*

9. What restrictions are there on the size of a racket?

*

10. If, on winning the toss before a match, you elect to commence play at one particular end, does your opponent have to serve first?

Men's Doubles

1899	D. Oakes and S. M. Massey
1900	H. L. Mellersh and F. S. Collier
1901	H. L. Mellersh and F. S. Collier
1902	H. L. Mellersh and F. S. Collier*
1903	S. M. Massey and E. L. Huson
1904	A. D. Prebble and H. N. Marrett
1905	C. T. J. Barnes and S. M. Massey
1906	H. N. Marrett and G. A. Thomas
1907	A. D. Prebble and N. Wood
1908	H. N. Marrett and G. A. Thomas
1909	F. Chesterton and A. D. Prebble
1910	H. N. Marrett and G. A. Thomas
1911	P. D. Fitton and E. Hawthorn
1912	Dr. H. N. Marrett and G. A. Thomas*
1913	F. Chesterton and G. A. Thomas
1914	F. Chesterton and G. A. Thomas
1915–19	*No Competition*
1920	A. F. Engelbach and R. du Roveray
1921	Sir G. A. Thomas, Bt., and F. Hodge
1922	J. F. Devlin (Ireland) and G. A. Sautter
1923	J. F. Devlin and G. S. B. Mack (Ireland)
1924	Sir G. A. Thomas, Bt., and F. Hodge
1925	H. S. Uber and A. K. Jones
1926	J. F. Devlin and G. S. B. Mack (Ireland)
1927	J. F. Devlin and G. S. B. Mack (Ireland)
1928	Sir G. A. Thomas, Bt., and F. Hodge
1929	J. F. Devlin and G. S. B. Mack (Ireland)*
1930	J. F. Devlin and G. S. B. Mack (Ireland)
1931	J. F. Devlin and G. S. B. Mack (Ireland)
1932	D. C. Hume and R. M. White
1933	D. C. Hume and R. M. White
1934	D. C. Hume and R. M. White*
1935	D. C. Hume and R. M. White
1936	L. Nichols and R. C. F. Nichols
1937	L. Nichols and R. C. F. Nichols
1938	L. Nichols and R. C. F. Nichols*
1939	T. H. Boyle and J. L. Rankin (Ireland)
1940–46	*No Competition*
1947	Tage Madsen and Poul Holm (Denmark)
1948	Preben Dabelsteen and Borge Frederiksen (Denmark)
1949	Ooi Teik Hock and Teoh Seng Khoon (Malaya)
1950	Preben Dabelsteen and Jorn Skaarup (Denmark)
1951	E. L. Choong and E. B. Choong (Malaya)
1952	E. L. Choong and E. B. Choong (Malaya)
1953	E. L. Choong and E. B. Choong (Malaya)*
1954	Ooi Teik Hock and Ong Poh Lim (Malaya)
1955	Finn Kobbero and J. Hammergaard Hansen (Denmark)
1956	Finn Kobbero and J. Hammergaard Hansen (Denmark)
1957	J. C. Alston (U.S.A.) and H. A. Heah (Malaya)
1958	E. Kops and P. E. Nielsen (Denmark)
1959	Teh Kew San and Lim Say Hup (Malaya)

Trophy won outright.

Ladies' Doubles

1899	Miss M. Lucas and Miss Graeme
1900	Miss M. Lucas and Miss Graeme
1901	Miss St. John and Miss E. M. Moseley (⁶)
1902	Miss M. Lucas and Miss E. Thomson (¹)
1903	Miss M. C. Hardy (⁷) and Miss D. K. Douglass (⁸)
1904	Miss M. Lucas and Miss E. Thomson (¹)
1905	Miss M. Lucas and Miss E. Thomson (¹)
1906	Miss M. Lucas and Miss E. Thomson (¹)*
1907	Miss M. Lucas and Miss G. L. Murray
1908	Miss M. Lucas and Miss G. L. Murray
1909	Miss M. Lucas and Miss G. L. Murray*
1910	Miss M. Lucas and Miss M. K. Bateman (¹⁴)
1911	Miss A. Gowenlock and Miss D. Cundall (⁹)
1912	Miss A. Gowenlock and Miss D. Cundall (⁹)
1913	Miss H. Hogarth and Miss M. K. Bateman (¹⁴)
1914	Mrs. R. C. Tragett and Miss E. G. Peterson
1915–19	*No Competition*
1920	Miss L. C. Radeglia and Miss V. Elton
1921	Miss K. McKane (³) and Miss M. McKane (¹⁰)
1922	Mrs. R. C. Tragett and Miss H. Hogarth
1923	Mrs. R. C. Tragett and Miss H. Hogarth
1924	Mrs. A. D. Stocks and Miss K. McKane (³)
1925	Mrs. R. C. Tragett and Miss H. Hogarth
1926	Mrs. A. M. Head and Miss V. Elton
1927	Mrs. R. C. Tragett and Miss H. Hogarth*
1928	Mrs. F. G. Barrett and Miss V. Elton
1929	Mrs. F. G. Barrett and Miss V. Elton
1930	Mrs. F. G. Barrett and Miss V. Elton*
1931	Mrs. H. S. Uber and Mrs. R. J. Horsley
1932	Mrs. F. G. Barrett and Miss L. M. Kingsbury (⁴)
1933	Miss T. Kingsbury (¹⁶) and Miss M. Bell (¹¹)
1934	Miss T. Kingsbury (¹⁶) and Mrs. M. Henderson
1935	Miss T. Kingsbury (¹⁶) and Mrs. M. Henderson*
1936	Miss T. Kingsbury (¹⁶) and Mrs. M. Henderson
1937	Mrs. H. S. Uber and Miss D. Doveton
1938	Mrs. H. S. Uber and Miss D. Doveton
1939	Mrs. R. Dalsgard and Miss T. Olsen (¹⁹) (Denmark)
1940–46	*No Competition*
1947	Miss K. Thorndahl (²⁴) and Miss T. Olsen (¹⁹) (Denmark)
1948	Miss K. Thorndahl (²⁴) and Mrs. G. Ahm (Denmark)
1949	Mrs. H. S. Uber and Miss Q. M. Allen (²⁰)
1950	Miss K. Thorndahl (²⁴) and Mrs. G. Ahm (Denmark)
1951	Miss K. Thorndahl (²⁴) and Mrs. G. Ahm (Denmark)*
1952	Miss A. Jacobsen and Mrs. G. Ahm (Denmark)
1953	Miss I. L. Cooley (²³) and Miss J. R. White (²²)
1954	Miss S. Devlin and Miss J. Devlin (U.S.A.)
1955	Miss I. L. Cooley (²³) and Miss J. R. White (²²)
1956	Miss S. Devlin and Miss J. Devlin (U.S.A.)
1957	Mrs. A. Hammergaard Hansen and Mrs. K. Granlund (Denmark)
1958	Miss M. Varner (U.S.A.) and Miss H. M. Ward
1959	Mrs. W. C. E. Rogers and Mrs. E. J. Timperley

Trophy won outright.

Mixed Doubles

1899	D. Oakes and Miss St. John
1900	D. Oakes and Miss St. John
1901	F. S. Collier and Miss E. M. Stawell-Brown (¹²)
1902	L. U. Ransford and Miss E. M. Moseley (⁶)
1903	G. A. Thomas and Miss E. Thomson (¹)
1904	H. N. Marrett and Miss D. K. Douglass (⁸)
1905	H. N. Marrett and Miss H. Hogarth
1906	G. A. Thomas and Miss E. Thomson (¹)
1907	G. A. Thomas and Miss G. L. Murray
1908	Norman Wood and Miss M. Lucas
1909	A. D. Prebble and Miss D. Boothby (¹³)
1910	G. A. Sautter and Miss D. Cundall (⁹)
1911	G. A. Thomas and Miss M. Larminie (²)
1912	E. Hawthorn and Miss H. Hogarth
1913	G. A. Sautter and Miss M. E. Mayston (¹⁵)
1914	G. A. Thomas and Miss H. Hogarth
1915–19	*No Competition*
1920	Sir G. A. Thomas, Bt., and Miss H. Hogarth
1921	Sir G. A. Thomas, Bt., and Miss H. Hogarth*
1922	Sir G. A. Thomas, Bt., and Miss H. Hogarth
1923	G. S. B. Mack (Ireland) and Mrs. R. C. Tragett
1924	J. F. Devlin (Ireland) and Miss K. McKane (³)
1925	J. F. Devlin (Ireland) and Miss K. McKane (³)
1926	J. F. Devlin (Ireland) and Miss E. G. Peterson
1927	J. F. Devlin (Ireland) and Miss E. G. Peterson
1928	A. E. Harbot and Mrs. R. C. Tragett
1929	J. F. Devlin (Ireland) and Mrs. R. J. Horsley
1930	H. S. Uber and Mrs. H. S. Uber
1931	H. S. Uber and Mrs. H. S. Uber
1932	H. S. Uber and Mrs. H. S. Uber*
1933	D. C. Hume and Mrs. H. S. Uber
1934	D. C. Hume and Mrs. H. S. Uber
1935	D. C. Hume and Mrs. H. S. Uber*
1936	D. C. Hume and Mrs. H. S. Uber
1937	I. Maconachie (Ireland) and Miss T. Kingsbury (¹⁶)
1938	R. M. White and Mrs. H. S. Uber
1939	R. C. F. Nichols and Miss B. M. Staples (¹⁸)
1940–46	*No Competition*
1947	P. Holm and Miss T. Olsen (¹⁹) (Denmark)
1948	J. Skaarup and Miss K. Thorndahl (²⁴) (Denmark)
1949	Clinton Stephens and Mrs. Stephens (U.S.A.)
1950	P. Holm and Mrs. G. Ahm (Denmark)
1951	P. Holm and Mrs. G. Ahm (Denmark)
1952	P. Holm and Mrs. G. Ahm (Denmark)*
1953	E. L. Choong (Malaya) and Miss J. R. White (²²)
1954	J. R. Best and Miss I. L. Cooley (²³)
1955	F. Kobbero and Miss K. Thorndahl (²⁴) (Denmark)
1956	A. D. Jordan and Mrs. E. J. Timperley
1957	F. Kobbero and Mrs. K. Granlund (Denmark)
1958	A. D. Jordan and Mrs. E. J. Timperley
1959	P. E. Nielsen and Mrs. I. B. Hansen (Denmark)

Trophy won outright.

(¹)	Mrs. D. R. Larcombe	(¹⁴)	Mrs. Flaxman
(²)	Mrs. R. C. Tragett	(¹⁵)	Mrs. Walker
(³)	Mrs. L. A. Godfree	(¹⁶)	Mrs. C. W. Welcome
(⁴)	Mrs. H. Middlemost	(¹⁷)	Mrs. J. Warrington
(⁵)	Mrs. R. J. Teague	(¹⁸)	Mrs. J. B. Shearlaw
(⁶)	Mrs. Allen	(¹⁹)	Mrs. G. Ahm
(⁷)	Mrs. Lionel Smith	(²⁰)	Mrs. F. G. Webber
(⁸)	Mrs. Lambert Chambers	(²¹)	Mrs. King Adams
(⁹)	Mrs. B. L. Bisgood	(²²)	Mrs. E. J. Timperley
(¹⁰)	Mrs. A. D. Stocks	(²³)	Mrs. W. C. E. Rogers
(¹¹)	Mrs. M. Henderson	(²⁴)	Mrs. P. Granlund
(¹²)	Mrs. Hemsted	(²⁵)	Mrs. A. Nylen
(¹³)	Mrs. A. C. Geen		

QUIZ ANSWERS

1. No. Except that a service must be delivered underhand, the only restrictions concern the feet of the player. It is quite permissible for a player's arm and racket to extend beyond the confines of the service court. 2. 5 feet 1 inch at the posts, and 5 feet exactly at the centre. 3. Almost exactly 90! The Laws of Badminton stipulate that a shuttle shall weigh between 73 and 85 grains. 7,000 grains equal a pound, avoirdupois, so that a 78-grain shuttle (the most commonly used in Europe) weighs just about one-ninetieth of a pound. 4. Sixteen. The laws stipulate from 14 to 16, though 16 is the more normal. 5. 25 feet is recommended by the Badminton Association of England, though many halls have a greater height. 6. It is a "let". 7. In both cases, either partner; though play must start from and to the right half-court. 8. Yes, either can do so if they have gained the right of option in the normal way. 9. None at all, and a player may hold one in each hand if he should want to. 10. No. He then has the right to choose whether to serve first himself, or to receive the service.

MOST INTERNATIONAL APPEARANCES

HISTORY

The game of badminton owes its origin to Badminton Hall in Gloucestershire, the seat of the Duke of Beaufort, where it was first played at an unknown date during the sixties of the last century. For many years it remained an unorganised pastime, though a set of laws was drawn up in India in the eighties. Proper organisation came in 1893 with the establishment of the Badminton Association, which thus became the ruling body. In 1934 there was founded the International Badminton Federation, which is able, 25 years later, to boast of 37 affiliated national organisations, and the original governing body altered its name to the Badminton Association of England.

The All-England Championships, acknowledged throughout the world as the leading tournament, were instituted in 1899, and 1902–03 saw the first international fixture when England and Ireland clashed at Dublin. The I.B.F. (International Badminton Federation) instituted the International Badminton Championship for the Thomas Cup in 1948, and the Ladies' International Badminton Championship for the Uber Cup in 1956. Both these competitions are held triennially, with concluding ties taking place in the country of the holder.

IMPORTANT RESULTS OF 1958-59
International Matches

England beat Scotland at Leicester, 9–0; beat Ireland at Cork, 9–0; lost to Denmark at Eastbourne, 0–7; beat Sweden at Cheltenham, 4–3.

Scotland beat Ireland at Edinburgh, 7–2; beat Wales at Barry, 9–0.

All-England Championship Finals
at Wembley

Men's Singles—Tan Joe Hok (Indonesia) beat F. A. Sonneville (Indonesia), 15–8, 10–15, 15–3.

Ladies' Singles—Miss H. M. Ward (England) beat Miss J. M. Devlin (U.S.A.), 11–7, 3–11, 11–4.

Men's Doubles—Lim Say Hup and Teh Kew San (Malaya) beat H. Borch and J. Hammergaard Hansen (Denmark), 15–2, 15–10.

Ladies' Doubles—Mrs. W. C. E. Rogers and Mrs. E. J. Timperley (England) beat Miss S. F. Devlin and Miss J. M. Devlin (U.S.A.), 11–15, 15–10, 15–11.

Mixed Doubles—P. E. Nielsen and Mrs. I. B. Hansen (Denmark) beat J. Hammergaard Hansen and Mrs. K. Granlund (Denmark), 14–17, 15–7, 15–3.

Irish Open Championships
at Cork

Men's Singles—C. T. Coates beat H. T. Findlay, 15–11, 6–15, 15–10.

Ladies' Singles—Miss H. M. Ward beat Mrs. W. C. E. Rogers, 11–8.

Men's Doubles—A. D. Jordan and R. J. Lockwood beat H. T. Findlay and P. J. Waddell, 12–15, 17–14, 15–4.

Ladies' Doubles—Mrs. W. C. E. Rogers and Mrs. E. J. Timperley beat Miss H. M. Ward and Miss B. J. Carpenter, 15–6, 15–7.

Mixed Doubles—A. D. Jordan and Mrs. E. J. Timperley beat R. J. Lockwood and Mrs. W. C. E. Rogers, 15–10, 15–7.

(All finalists were English players.)

Scottish Open Championships
at Edinburgh

Men's Singles—R. S. McCoig beat J. P. Doyle (Ireland), 15–9, 15–2.

Ladies' Singles—Miss W. Tyre beat Miss C. E. Dunglison, 12–10, 11–1.

Men's Doubles—A. W. Horden and D. Ross beat G. Henderson and R. C. McCormack (Ireland), 13–15, 15–4, 15–4.

Ladies' Doubles—Miss W. Tyre and Miss M. A. McIntosh beat Miss C. E. Dunglison and Mrs. J. H. Gordon, 17–14, 15–4.

Mixed Doubles—R. S. McCoig and Miss W. Tyre beat A. W. Horden and Miss C. E. Dunglison, 15–6, 9–15, 18–17.

(All finalists were Scottish except where mentioned.)

Inter-County Championship Final
Surrey beat Cheshire at Wimbledon, 12–3.

QUIZ ANSWERS

1. Denmark was the first country to beat England. It was in April, 1948, in Copenhagen, that England suffered her first international defeat. 2. Mrs. Barrett, Miss T. Kingsbury and Miss K. Thorndahl were all left-handed. All the men champions have been right-handers. 3. Misses Leonie and Thelma Kingsbury. The former subsequently played for South Africa when she was Mrs. Middlemost, and the latter for U.S.A. when she was Mrs. Welcome. 4. G. A. Sautter was a Swiss, though all his badminton was played in England which he represented. C. Stephens was an American. I. C. Maconachie was an Irishman though resident in England. Ong Poh Lim, though a Malayan international, was a native of Sarawak, a British colony on the island of Borneo; he did not move to Singapore until he was grown up. Miss Judy Devlin, though regarded as an American player, was of British nationality; she was born in Canada of Irish and English parents. 5. Two couples: Mr. and Mrs. H. S. Uber and Mr. and Mrs. E. J. Timperley. The former also won the All-England mixed doubles championship three times.

BADMINTON QUIZ

1. England played her first international match in 1902–03. What country was the first to defeat England, and when?

*

2. Have there been any left-handed All-England singles champions? Who were they?

*

3. Two well-known sisters, both All-England champions and English internationals, also, after marriage, played for other countries. Who were they, and for what countries did they play?

*

4. What nationality were the following All-England champions: G. A. Sautter, C. Stephens, I. C. Maconachie, Ong Poh Lim, Miss Judy Devlin?

*

5. Have any married couples played for England in the same fixture? Who were they?

Compiled by Norris McWhirter
Athletics Correspondent: The Observer and B.B.C. Television Commentator

Baseball

BASEBALL HISTORY

Baseball is a totally North American derivative of the English game of cricket (first recorded in the U.S. in 1747) and the now little played English game of rounders. The game evolved early in the last century. Haphazard versions of the so-called Town Ball Game grew up in Boston, New York and Philadelphia during the period 1820 to 1833. The earliest book outlining the game was *The Book of Sports* by R. Carver published in Boston, Mass., in 1834. The various local rules were not codified until September 23, 1845, by Alexander Joy Cartwright of New York City.

The earliest match on record under the codified rules was played in Hoboken, New Jersey, on June 19, 1846, when the "New York Nine" defeated Cartwright's Knickerbocker Club 23 to 1 in four "hands" or innings. In its infancy the game was essentially amateur though as early as 1858 New York City and Brooklyn players demanded and received a percentage of the admission receipts. The earliest fully professional side were the Red Stockings of Cincinnati, whose ten-man team averaged $850 per man in their first season of 1869.

The World Series between the champions of two major professional leagues, the National League and the American League, was inaugurated in 1903. On July 27th, 1959, the formation of a third league, the Continental League, was announced.

BASEBALL WORLD CHAMPIONSHIPS
A.L.—American League   N.L.—National League

	Winners		Losers	
1903	Boston, A.L.	5	Pittsburgh, N.L.	3
1904	New York, N.L. refused to play Boston, A.L.			
1905	New York, N.L.	4	Philadelphia, A.L.	1
1906	Chicago, A.L.	4	Chicago, N.L.	2
1907*	Chicago, N.L.	4	Detroit, A.L.	0
1908	Chicago, N.L.	4	Detroit, A.L.	1
1909	Pittsburgh, N.L.	4	Detroit, A.L.	3
1910	Philadelphia, A.L.	4	Chicago, N.L.	1
1911	Philadelphia, A.L.	4	New York, N.L.	2
1912*	Boston, A.L.	4	New York, N.L.	3
1913	Philadelphia, A.L.	4	New York, N.L.	1
1914	Boston, N.L.	4	Philadelphia, A.L.	0
1915	Boston, A.L.	4	Philadelphia, N.L.	1
1916	Boston, A.L.	4	Brooklyn, N.L.	1
1917	Chicago, A.L.	4	New York, N.L.	2
1918	Boston, A.L.	4	Chicago, N.L.	2
1919	Cincinnati, N.L.	5	Chicago, A.L.	3
1920	Cleveland, A.L.	5	Brooklyn, N.L.	2
1921	New York, N.L.	5	New York, A.L.	3
1922*	New York, N.L.	4	New York, A.L.	0
1923	New York, A.L.	4	New York, N.L.	2
1924	Washington, A.L.	4	New York, N.L.	3
1925	Pittsburgh, N.L.	4	Washington, A.L.	3
1926	St. Louis, N.L.	4	New York, A.L.	3
1927	New York, A.L.	4	Pittsburgh, N.L.	0
1928	New York, A.L.	4	St. Louis, N.L.	0
1929	Philadelphia, A.L.	4	Chicago, N.L.	1
1930	Philadelphia, A.L.	4	St. Louis, N.L.	2
1931	St. Louis, N.L.	4	Philadelphia, A.L.	3
1932	New York, A.L.	4	Chicago, N.L.	0
1933	New York, N.L.	4	Washington, A.L.	1
1934	St. Louis, N.L.	4	Detroit, A.L.	3
1935	Detroit, A.L.	4	Chicago, N.L.	2
1936	New York, A.L.	4	New York, N.L.	2
1937	New York, A.L.	4	New York, N.L.	1
1938	New York, A.L.	4	Chicago, N.L.	0
1939	New York, A.L.	4	Cincinnati, N.L.	0
1940	Cincinnati, N.L.	4	Detroit, A.L.	3
1941	New York, A.L.	4	Brooklyn, N.L.	1
1942	St. Louis, N.L.	4	New York, A.L.	1
1943	New York, A.L.	4	St. Louis, N.L.	1
1944	St. Louis, N.L.	4	St. Louis, A.L.	2
1945	Detroit, A.L.	4	Chicago, N.L.	3
1946	St. Louis, N.L.	4	Boston, A.L.	3
1947	New York, A.L.	4	Brooklyn, N.L.	3
1948	Cleveland, A.L.	4	Boston, N.L.	2
1949	New York, A.L.	4	Brooklyn, N.L.	1
1950	New York, A.L.	4	Philadelphia, N.L.	0
1951	New York, A.L.	4	New York, N.L.	2
1952	New York, A.L.	4	Brooklyn, N.L.	3
1953†	New York, A.L.	4	Brooklyn, N.L.	2
1954	New York, N.L.	4	Cleveland, A.L.	0
1955	Brooklyn, N.L.	4	New York, A.L.	3
1956	New York, A.L.	4	Brooklyn, N.L.	3
1957	Milwaukee, N.L.	4	New York, A.L.	3
1958	New York, A.L.	4	Milwaukee, N.L.	3

* One tied game. † First major league club to win five world championships in succession.

BASEBALL QUIZ

1. Which has been hit further—a cricket ball or a baseball?

*

QUIZ ANSWERS

1. A baseball—565 ft. by Mickey Mantle (New York Yankees) in a home run at the Griffith Stadium, Washington D.C., on April 17th, 1953. The cricket record is 525 ft. by the Rev. W. Fellows in 1856.

Basketball

Compiled by **K. K. Mitchell**

Hon. Secretary:
Amateur Basketball Association

INTERNATIONAL BASKETBALL

International Basketball is controlled by the International Basketball Federation. It was formed in 1932 and now has 71 independent member national federations. F.I.B.A. is responsible for drawing up the International Rules, which is normally done on the occasion of the Olympic Games. F.I.B.A. also sponsors several international tournaments. The results of the chief three are set out below.

WORLD CHAMPIONS

Date	Venue	Champion	Runner-up
1950	Buenos Aires	Argentine	U.S.A.
1954	Rio de Janeiro	U.S.A.	Chile
1959	Santiago, Chile	Brazil	U.S.A.

OLYMPIC CHAMPIONS

1936	Berlin	U.S.A.	Canada
1948	London	U.S.A.	France
1952	Helsinki	U.S.A.	U.S.S.R.
1956	Melbourne	U.S.A.	U.S.S.R.
1960	Rome		

EUROPEAN CHAMPIONS

1935	Geneva	Latvia	Spain
1937	Riga	Lithuania	Italy
1939	Kaunas	Lithuania	Latvia
1946	Geneva	Czechoslovakia	Italy
1947	Prague	U.S.S.R.	Czechoslovakia
1949	Cairo	Egypt	France
1951	Paris	U.S.S.R.	Czechoslovakia
1953	Moscow	U.S.S.R.	Hungary
1955	Budapest	Hungary	Czechoslovakia
1957	Sofia	U.S.S.R.	Bulgaria
1959	Istanbul	U.S.S.R.	Czechoslovakia

RESULTS OF COUPE D'EUROPE 1958

Countries	Venue	Result
Greece v. Roumania	Athens	60–63 (31–32)
Roumania v. Greece	Bucharest	75–72 (38–35)
Jugoslavia v. Turkey	Ljubljana	86–45 (38–22)
Turkey v. Jugoslavia	Istanbul	67–74 (41–38)
Bulgaria v. Syria	Sofia	84–58 (35–25)
Syria v. Bulgaria	Alep	43–73 (28–42)
Jugoslavia v. Bulgaria	Ljubljana	64–80 (33–39)
Bulgaria v. Jugoslavia	Sofia	81–80 (37–43)
Roumania v. Israel	Bucharest	84–65 (38–37)
Israel v. Roumania	Tel Aviv	61–63 (25–35)
Switzerland v. Czechoslovakia	Geneva	54–84 (20–47)
Austria v. Hungary	Vienna	55–83 (26–40)
Hungary v. Austria	Budapest	108–43 (54–26)
Italy v. Pays Bas	Milan	115–47 (45–23)
Pays Bas v. Italy	Amsterdam	42–90 (18–38)

Triangular Tournament		
Italy v. Czechoslovakia	Milan	65–47 (39–19)
Czechoslovakia v. Hungary		52–61 (14–28)
Italy v. Hungary		80–72 (41–36)
U.S.S.R. v. Germany	Riga	85–56 (46–27)
West Germany v. U.S.S.R.	Berlin	56–91 (26–44)
Finland v. Poland	Helsinki	64–62 (34–33)
Poland v. Finland	Varsovia	71–67 (36–38)
Belgium v. Luxembourg	Brussels	82–43 (35–22)
Luxembourg v. Belgium	Ettelbruck	36–63 (14–34)
Belgium v. France	Brussels	80–51 (35–27)
France v. Belgium	Villeurbanne	93–76 (42–43)
Portugal v. Spain	Lisbon	51–68 (33–42)
Spain v. Portugal	Madrid	86–40 (38–21)
Quarter Finals		
Poland v. U.S.S.R.	Varsovia	63–61 (31–36)
U.S.S.R. v. Poland	Riga	93–59 (40–26)
Spain v. Belgium	Madrid	78–59 (35–28)
Belgium v. Spain	Brussels	57–43 (29–22)
Roumania v. Bulgaria	Bucharest	64–73 (27–37)
Bulgaria v. Roumania	Sofia	77–78 (38–33)
Hungary v. Italy		95–85 (50–42)
Semi-Finals		
Hungary v. Bulgaria	Budapest	87–89 (42–33)
Bulgaria v. Hungary	Sofia	76–64 (39–27)
U.S.S.R. v. Spain	Riga	2–0
Spain v. U.S.S.R.	Madrid	0–2
Final		
U.S.S.R. v. Bulgaria	Riga	86–81 (52–36)
Bulgaria v. U.S.S.R.	Sofia	71–84 (31–39)

Winners—U.S.S.R. represented by Sportklub, Riga.
Runners-up—Bulgaria represented by Akademik, Sofia.

BASKETBALL QUIZ

1. Who are the Harlem Globetrotters?

★

2. Are the international rules for men and women the same?

★

3. When was the last occasion that England took part in the European Basketball Championships?

★

4. How long is allowed for:
(i) a time-out?
(ii) a substitution?
(ii) a free throw at the basket?
(iv) a throw in from out of bounds?

(v) the replacement of an injured player?

★

5. How many officials are required to control the game?

★

6. How long:
(i) does a game last?
(ii) is the interval between halves?

QUIZ ANSWERS

1. A professional team who tours the world playing demonstration games. They claim to be the world champions. Nearly 2,000,000 watch their games annually. 2. Yes. 3. 1955 in Budapest. 4. (i) 1 min. (ii) 30 secs. (iii) 10 secs. (iv) 5 secs. (v) 1 min. 5. Two officials—referee and umpire, who are assisted by two table officials, the scorer and time-keeper. 6. (i) 20 mins. actual play each way. (ii) 10 mins.

INTERNATIONAL MATCHES PLAYED BY ENGLAND

Date	Venue	Countries	Result
1938	Berlin	Germany v. England	—
1946	Geneva	England v. Holland	—
,,	,,	England v. France	—
,,	,,	England v. Luxembourg	—
,,	,,	England v. Poland	—
,,	Glasgow	Scotland v. England	—
1947	Glasgow	Scotland v. England	—
1948	Turin	Italy v. England	62–18
,,	London	England v. Brazil	11–76
,,	,,	England v. Uruguay	17–69
,,	,,	England v. Canada	24–44
,,	,,	England v. Hungary	23–60
,,	,,	England v. Italy	28–49
,,	,,	England v. Eire	46–21
,,	,,	England v. China	25–54
,,	,,	England v. Egypt	18–50
1951	Glasgow	Scotland v. England	—
1952	Wembley	England v. Scotland	39–29
1953	Wembley	England v. Wales	45–19
,,	,,	England v. Ireland	54–21
,,	Pwllheli	England v. Ireland	51–29
,,	,,	Wales v. England	27–62
1954	Dublin	Ireland v. England	26–30
,,	Glasgow	Scotland v. England	50–57
1955	Budapest	England v. France	50–97
,,	,,	England v. Poland	44–140
,,	,,	England v. Jugoslavia	53–98
,,	,,	England v. Austria	48–69
,,	,,	England v. Switzerland	50–67
,,	,,	England v. Finland	60–94
,,	,,	England v. Sweden	59–53
,,	,,	England v. Austria	51–48
,,	,,	England v. France	55–103
,,	,,	England v. Turkey	54–77
,,	Luxembourg	England v. Belgium	26–61
,,	,,	England v. France	36–61
,,	,,	Luxembourg v. England	41–61
1955	Ruislip	England v Scotland	36–37
1956	Aldershot	England v. Spain	53–55
,,	Kirkcaldy	Scotland v. England	47–43
1957	Boulogne	France v. England	53–44
,,	Moscow	England v. Czechoslovakia	48–96
,,	,,	England v. Bulgaria	46–101
,,	,,	England v. Belgium	56–80
,,	,,	England v. Egypt	57–90
,,	,,	England v. Tunis	58–32
,,	,,	England v. China	52–89
,,	,,	England v. Switzerland	60–66
,,	,,	England v. Finland	47–85
1958	London	England v. Belgium	44–90
1958	Heyst	Belgium v. England	57–21
1959	Leeds	England v. Scotland (Juniors)	34–64

ENGLAND INTERNATIONALS

The following players have represented England in the period 1953–57.

Name	Club	No. of Appearances
Agnelli, U.	London Central Y.M.C.A.	2
Bluck, D.	R.A.E., Farnborough	2
Bruce, A.	Polytechnic	13
Byrne, W.	Manchester Y.M.C.A.	8
Cladingboel, A.	Polytechnic	6
Cook, G. R.	London Central Y.M.C.A.	15
Fearn, R.	London Central Y.M.C.A.	17
Fyles, D.	Nottingham Y.M.C.A.	6
Gold, J.	Polytechnic	3
Hoy, A.	London Central Y.M.C.A.	13
Hughes, M.	R.A.E., Farnborough	1
Keogh, T.	Royal Air Force	7
Ledbrook, K.	Polytechnic	11
Legg, R.	Dolobran	10
McMeekan, S.	Dolobran	2
Osborne, S.	Polytechnic	5
Povey, G.	Nottingham Y.M.C.A.	2
Rix, R.	Eastbury	7
Roblou, M.	Polytechnic	13
Smith, M.	Eastbury	8
Sowden, W.	Army	2
Stappard, E.	Royal Air Force	1
Taylor, J.	Army	1
Tillot, A.	Polytechnic	7
Webb, R.	Polytechnic	9
Wedge, C.	Polytechnic	15
Wilkinson, D.	London Central Y.M.C.A.	18

THE AMATEUR BASKETBALL ASSOCIATION NATIONAL CHAMPIONSHIPS

Date	Venue		Results
1936	Birmingham	Hoylake Y.M.C.A. bt. London Polytechnic	32–21
1937	Liverpool	Hoylake Y.M.C.A. bt. Latter Day Saints London	23–17
1938	Wembley	Catford Saints bt. Rochdale Greys	61–47
1939	London	Catford Saints bt. Rochdale Greys	53–41
1940	London	Birmingham Athletic Institute bt. London Central Y.M.C.A.	35–30
1941–46	No competition		
1950	Nottingham	Latter Day Saints London bt. U.S.A.F. Burtonwood	34–33
1951	Nottingham	Dolobran bt. Polytechnic	34–33
1952	Wembley	Polytechnic bt. Dolobran	40–29
1953	Manchester	Polytechnic bt. Dolobran	55–46
1954	Birmingham	Polytechnic bt. Nottingham Y.M.C.A.	98–53
1955	London	Polytechnic bt. Dolobran	58–54
1956	No competition		
1957	London	Central Y.M.C.A. bt. Polytechnic	63–51
1958	London	Central Y.M.C.A. bt. East Ham	
1959	Leicester	Aspley Old Boys bt. Dolobran	58–39

Junior

Date	Venue		Results
1938	Birmingham	Ton Pentre bt. London Polytechnic	12–6
1939	Birmingham	Ton Pentre bt. Birmingham Y.M.C.A.	38–27
1940	Pontypridd	Ton Pentre bt. Wreckin Boys' Club	45–14
1941–45	No competition		
1946	Birmingham	Ton Pentre bt. Eastbury	31–29
1947	Birmingham	1. Smethwick, 2. Ton Pentre, 3. Eastbury. Triangular tournament	
1950	Nottingham	Eastbury bt. Ton Pentre	
1951	Brighton	Quinton School bt. Pear Tree Youth Club	
1952	Wembley	Quinton School bt. Eastbury	42–28
1953	Manchester	Bournville bt. Quinton School	46–40
1954	Birmingham	Florence Institute Liverpool bt. Eastbury	50–48
1955	R.A.F. Cosford	Eastbury bt. Florence Institute	
1956	R.A.F. Cosford	Eastbury bt. Rose Lane Old Boys	38–33
1957	No competition		
1958	R.A.F. Cosford	Rose Lane Old Boys bt. Downer G.S.	
1959	Leicester	Downer G.S. bt. R.A.F. Cosford (Apprentices)	81–60

Open

Date	Venue		Results
1951	Brighton	U.S.A.F. Lakenheath bt. Latter Day Saints London	41–29
1952	Wembley	U.S.A.F. Lakenheath bt. U.S.A.F. Ruislip	
1953	Bath	Manchester Y.M.C.A. bt. Eastbury	55–51
1954	London	Polytechnic bt. Central Y.M.C.A.	71–47
1955	London	U.S. Navy bt. Polytechnic	64–60
1956	London	Oxford University bt. Hoddesdon	75–59
1957	No competition		

Inter-Area Tournament

Date	Venue		Results
1948	Birmingham	South-East bt. West Midland	
1949	Birmingham	South-East bt. West Midland	
1950	Birmingham	South-East bt. West Midland	
1951–54	No competition		
1955	R.A.F. Cosford	West Midland bt. North-West	51–36
1956	R.A.F. Cosford	East Midland bt. West Midland	54–33

Intermediate

Date	Venue		Results
1956	R.A.F. Cosford	Derby Technical College bt. Polytechnic	54–28
1957	R.A.F. Cosford	Whitemore T.C. bt. Aspley Old Boys	
1958	R.A.F. Cosford	Watford Technical College bt. Nottingham Dodgers	
1959	Leicester	R.A.F. Chessington bt. Pegasus (Birkenhead)	63–45

NATIONAL CHAMPIONSHIPS, 1958–59

JUNIOR

1st Round

Venue		Results
Hanwell	Downer G.S. bt. Bournville Y.C.	55–14
Hanwell	Wellington Avenue bt. Bayswater Wednesday	45–42
Leicester	R.A.F. Cosford App. bt. Eastbury	41–39
Leicester	Kings Norton Grammar bt. North Oxford Swallows	34–32
Derby	Rose Lane Old Boys bt. Internal Combustion	63–23
Derby	Rolls Royce App. bt. Derby Youth	34–28
Watford	R.A.F. Locking App. bt. Shaftesbury Club	55–38
Watford	Dolobran bt. H.M.S. Collingwood	45–28

Quarter Finals

Venue		Results
Hanwell	Downer G.S. bt. Wellington Avenue	52–38
Cosford	R.A.F. Cosford App. bt. R.A.F. Locking App.	62–41
Cosford	Rolls Royce App. bt. Kings Norton Grammar	44–25
Cosford	Rose Lane Old Boys bt. Dolobran	53–23

Semi-Finals

		Results
	Downer G.S. bt. Rolls Royce	67–38
	R.A.F. Cosford bt. Rose Lane Old Boys	2–0 (default)

Final

		Results
	Downer G.S. bt. R.A.F. Cosford App.	81–60

INTERMEDIATE

1st. Round

Venue		Results
Hanwell	R.A.F. Chessington bt. R.C.A.F. Langer	84–36
Hanwell	Central Y.M.C.A. bt. Watford Tech. College	62–24
Cosford	Stechford bt. Birmingham Hornets	37–20
Cosford	Ada Road Y.C. bt. Stoke	52–45
Derby	Pegasus bt. Internal Combustion	45–35
Chatham	Iroquois bt. R.A.F. Abingdon	43–22

Quarter Finals

Venue		Results
Leicester	Pegasus bt. Stechford	
Halton	R.A.F. Chessington bt. Ada Road Y.C.	57–41
Halton	Central Y.M.C.A. bt. Rolls Royce App.	59–30
Aldershot	Viking Sports bt. Iroquois	34–28

Semi-Finals

		Results
	R.A.F. Chessington bt. Central Y.M.C.A.	68–65
	Pegasus bt. Oxford City	2–0 (default)

Final

		Results
	R.A.F. Chessington bt. Pegasus	63–45

SENIOR

1st Round

Venue		Results
Aldershot	East Ham bt. Manchester Y.M.C.A.	2–0
Aldershot	Aspley Old Boys bt. Barnhurst Blue Stars	76–36
Rolls Royce	Nottingham Dodgers bt. Dartford Black Aces	69–38
Rolls Royce	Manchester University bt. Leeds University	53–32
Cosford	Derby Youth bt. Birmingham Y.M.C.A.	2–0
Cosford	Birmingham Athletic Inst. bt. Oxford City	2–0
Halton	R.A.F. Locking bt. Polytechnic	54–47
Halton	Birmingham Dolobran bt. R.A.E. Eagles	37–36

Quarter Finals

Venue		Results
Leicester	Nottingham Dodgers bt. Derby Youth	68–46
Leicester	Aspley Old Boys bt. Polytechnic	65–54
Cosford	Dolobran bt. East Ham	38–36
Cosford	Birmingham Ath. Inst. bt. Manchester University	41–29

Semi-Finals

		Results
	Aspley Old Boys bt. Birmingham Ath. Inst.	70–47
	Dolobran bt. Nottingham Dodgers	59–57

Final

		Results
	Aspley Old Boys bt. Dolobran	58–39

BASKETBALL QUIZ

1. How many players are there in a team?

★

2. What happens if there is a tie at full time?

★

3. Where and when was basketball first played?

★

4. How many personal fouls disqualify a player?

★

5. What is the height of the ring?

★

6. What are the average dimensions of a basketball court?

★

7. How many points for:
   (i) a field goal?
   (ii) a free throw?

8. What is the origin of the word basketball?

★

9. If the final whistle sounds as the ball is on its way to the basket, is the goal counted if made?

QUIZ ANSWERS

1. Five. A team is allowed a further seven substitutes. 2. If the score is a tie at the expiration of the second half, play shall be continued for an extra period of 5 minutes or as many such periods of 5 minutes as may be necessary to break the tie. Before the first extra period the teams shall toss for baskets and shall change baskets at the beginning of each additional extra period. An intermission of 2 minutes shall be allowed before each extra period. At the beginning of each extra period, the ball shall be put in play at the centre. 3. In 1891 at the Y.M.C.A., Springfield, Mass., U.S.A. 4. Five. 5. 10 feet from the ground. 6. 85 feet x 46 feet. 7. (i) 2. (ii) I. 8. Dr. Naismith, who invented the game, used peach baskets suspended at each end of the gym. The object was to get the ball into the basket. 9. The basket counts.

Billiards

Compiled by Richard Holt
Editor: The Billiard Player

THE DERIVATION OF BILLIARDS

The game of billiards, in, more or less, its present form, dates roughly back to the early nineteenth century. Edwin (Jonathan) Kentfield (top break 149) was the first accredited champion; next came John Roberts senior (top break 346) whose son, John Roberts junior, the "great" John Roberts, dominated the game till about 1904. In 1870 the Professional Championship was established. Thence, up to about 1938, there have been, roughly, three "golden eras" of the game:

1. 1870–1905, with Roberts jun., W. Cook, J. Bennett, W. Mitchell, W. J. Peall; and others less prominent.
2. 1906–1920, in which C. Dawson, H. W. Stevenson, E. Diggle, C. Harverson, M. Inman and T. Reece were protagonists.
3. 1921–1939, during which the leading lights were Willie Smith, Claude Falkiner, Tom Newman, Joe Davis, Clark Mc-Conachy and Walter Lindrum, with Melbourne Inman and Tom Reece overlapping from the second period, and Sidney Smith, Kingsley Kennerley, Sidney Lee and John Barrie being prominent in the 1947–51 period, after which date professional billiards gave way to snooker so far as championships were concerned. (See Records.) The only break of note made in a professional championship since the war was 714, by John Barrie, in 1950. Billiards championship play is now confined to the amateur sphere.

PRESENT WORLD RECORDS

(Breaks)

PROFESSIONAL

*Walter Lindrum (*Australia*) 4,137 (1932)
†Joe Davis (*England*) 1,784 (1936)
(English record under present rules.)
‡Willie Smith (*England*) 2,743 (1928)
(All-round break.)
Ruth Harrison (*England*) 197 (1937)
(Women's Prof.)

* *Lindrum's great break of 4,137 took 175 minutes. Details: Jan. 19th, afternoon session 701 (30 mins.), evening session 2,450 (105 mins.); Jan 20th, afternoon session 986 (40 mins.).*
† *Davis's break was made under the present Baulk-line rule.*
‡ *Willie Smith's break was made without "Nursery" or "Close" cannon play, and is considered to be the finest break composed of all-round billiards, i.e. without sequences of such cannons. Lindrum's and Davis's breaks included "Nurseries".*

AMATEUR

Robert Marshall (*Australia*) 702 (1953)
(Made in Australian Championship)

"Nursery" or "Close" Cannons

PROFESSIONAL

Walter Lindrum 529, consecutive (1933)

AMATEUR

Sydney Lee 103, consecutive (1934)
(For average and aggregate records see under names of players.)

RECORD BREAKS IN PRINCIPAL AMATEUR CHAMPIONSHIPS

World Amateur Billiards Championship
T. Cleary (Australia) 682 (1954)
English Amateur Billiards Championship
K. Kennerley 549 (1937)
Australian Amateur Championship
R. Marshall 702 (1953)
Indian Amateur Championship
W. Jones (Bombay) 452 (1958)
Scottish Amateur Billiards Championship
J. Bates 323 (1954)
Welsh Amateur Billiards Championship
T. G. Morse 211 (1947)

TYPES OF PLAY THROUGH-OUT BILLIARDS HISTORY

PROFESSIONAL

1870-1900. All-round play (i.e., losing hazards or in-offs, winning hazards or pots, and cannons), the "Spot" stroke (unrestricted potting of the red ball into the top pockets) predominating. The "Spot" stroke was barred in 1898.
1900-1926. All-round play, with sequences of losing hazards off red (unrestricted) and top-of-the-table play (sequences of potting red into the top pockets, alternating with cannons) as leading features. In general, the red losing hazard played a main role, though the top professionals favoured top-of-the-table play.
1926-1951 (in which year professional competitive play practically ceased) top-of-the-table play and "Nursery" cannons (sequences of close cannons round the cushions) were the main methods of scoring. Losing hazards were restricted to 25 in 1926.

AMATEUR

To 1926, unrestricted red-ball play (losing hazards) was the principal scoring means. After 1926, when red-ball play was restricted to 25 consecutive losing hazards (or pots), all-round play, with top-of-the-table play by the most expert amateurs, constituted the main scoring force. Very few amateurs have been, and are, skilled at "Nursery" cannons, and then only to a limited extent.

IMPORTANT RULE ALTERATIONS

"Spot" stroke barred in 1898.
"Push" stroke barred in 1898.
Losing hazards limited to 25 in 1926; 1930, limited to 15 in Amateur Championship. 1959, reversion from 1960 to 25 (championships included).
Consecutive direct cannons were limited to 25 in 1926, and 35 in 1927–8.
The Baulk-line rule was passed in 1932 (modified later) with a view to restricting "Nursery" cannon play. The present rule requires that the player cross the Baulk-line by a particular stroke which scores one or more of the last 20 points of each 200 points (professional) and at least once in each 400 points scored in the break (amateur). This mainly affected professional play, as 400 breaks are infrequent in amateur play.

DEFINITIONS

All-round play. Scoring sequence composed of losing hazards (in-offs), winning hazards (pots) and ordinary cannon play.
"Nursery" or "Close" cannons. Sequences of cannons with the three balls close together, the player taking them along the cushion by gentle strokes.
"Push" stroke. A stroke in which the cue remains on the cue-ball when the latter contacts the first object-ball.
"Spot" stroke. Potting the red ball off its Spot continuously.
Top-of-the-table play. Sequences of cannons and pots at the top end, only the top pockets being used.
"Anchor" or *"Cradle" cannon*, *"Pendulum" cannon,* and *"Jam" cannon* are cannons made with two balls in a fixed position, each stroke being the same.
"Jump Shot". A stroke causing the cue ball to jump over an intervening ball. Banned in 1958 (both games).

QUIZ ANSWERS

1. Not officially defined, but usually from 4½ to 5 ounces. 2. The trophy to be presented by Burroughes & Watts Ltd., to the first amateur to make a thousand-break on a standard table. (Robert Marshall's break of 702 is the amateur record. (See Amateur Achievements, p. 80.) 3. Eight (many believe it to be 6). 4. It is a relic of the days when it was permissible to play a stroke with the butt end of the cue. 5. Five.

BILLIARDS QUIZ

1. What is the weight of a billiard ball?

★

2. What billiards trophy has not yet been won, though it has been possible to win it for some years?

★

3. How many legs has a full-size billiard table?

★

4. What is the reason for the bevel at the butt end of a cue?

★

5. How many slates has a full-size billiard table?

WORLD PROFESSIONAL BILLIARDS CHAMPIONSHIP

Year	Winner	Runner-up	Scores
1870	W. Cook	*John Roberts sen.*	1,200–1,083
1870	John Roberts jun.	*W. Cook*	1,000–522
1870	John Roberts jun.	*A. Bowles*	1,000–759
1871	John Roberts jun.	*J. Bennett*	1,000–905
1871	W. Cook	*John Roberts jun.*	1,000–637
1871	W. Cook	*John Roberts jun.*	1,000–799
1872	W. Cook	*John Roberts jun.*	1,000–985
1874	W. Cook	*John Roberts jun.*	1,000–784
1875	John Roberts jun.	*W. Cook*	1,000–784
1875	John Roberts jun.	*W. Cook*	1,000–837
1877	John Roberts jun.	*W. Cook*	1,000–865
1880	J. Bennett	*W. Cook*	1,000–779
1881	J. Bennett	*T. Taylor*	1,000–949
1885	John Roberts jun.	*W. Cook*	1,000–910
1885	John Roberts jun.	*J. Bennett*	3,000–2,908
1889	Charles Dawson	*J. North*	3,000–1,360
1900	Charles Dawson	*H. W. Stevenson*	9,000–4,715
1901	H. W. Stevenson	*Charles Dawson*	9,000–6,775
1901	Charles Dawson	*H. W. Stevenson*	9,000–6,406
1901	No contest. H. W. Stevenson declared Champion		9,000–5,796
1903	Charles Dawson	*H. W. Stevenson*	9,000–8,700
1908	No contest. Melbourne Inman declared Champion		
1909	Melbourne Inman	*A. E. Williams*	9,000–7,662
1909	No contest. H. W. Stevenson declared Champion		
1910	H. W. Stevenson	*Melbourne Inman*	13,370–13,212
	(Match abandoned)		
1910	H. W. Stevenson	*Melbourne Inman*	18,000–16,907
1911	H. W. Stevenson	*Melbourne Inman*	18,000–16,914
1912	Melbourne Inman	*Tom Reece*	18,000–9,675
1913	Melbourne Inman	*Tom Reece*	18,000–16,627
1914	Melbourne Inman	*Tom Reece*	18,000–12,826
1919	Melbourne Inman	*H. W. Stevenson*	16,000–9,468
1920	Willie Smith	*Claude Falkiner*	16,000–14,500
1921	Tom Newman	*Tom Reece*	16,000–10,744
1922	Tom Newman	*Claude Falkiner*	16,000–15,167
1923	Willie Smith	*Tom Newman*	16,000–15,180
1924	Tom Newman	*Tom Reece*	16,000–14,845
1925	Tom Newman	*Tom Reece*	16,000–10,092
1926	Tom Newman	*Joe Davis*	16,000–9,505
1927	Tom Newman	*Joe Davis*	16,000–14,763
1928	Joe Davis	*Tom Newman*	16,000–14,874
1929	Joe Davis	*Tom Newman*	18,000–17,219
1930	Joe Davis	*Tom Newman*	20,198–20,117
1931	No contest		
1932	Joe Davis	*Clark McConachy*	25,161–19,259
1933	Walter Lindrum	*Joe Davis*	21,815–21,121
1934	Walter Lindrum	*Joe Davis*	23,553–22,678
1951	Clark McConachy	*John Barrie*	9,294–6,428

No contest between 1934 and 1951 (last time of holding)

PROFESSIONAL UNITED KINGDOM BILLIARDS CHAMPIONSHIP

Year	Winner	Runner-up	Scores
1934	Joe Davis	*Tom Newman*	18,745–18,309
1935	Joe Davis	*Tom Newman*	21,733–19,910
1936	Joe Davis	*Tom Newman*	21,710–19,791
1937	Joe Davis	*Tom Newman*	22,601–18,321
1938	Joe Davis	*Tom Newman*	20,933–19,542
1939	Joe Davis	*Tom Newman*	21,601–18,321
1940–46	No contests		
1947	Joe Davis	*John Barrie*	Walk-over
1948	Sidney Smith	*John Barrie*	7,002–6,428
1949	No contest		
1950	John Barrie	*Kingsley Kennerley*	9,046–5,069
1951	Fred Davis	*Kingsley Kennerley*	8,120–6,011
1952–59	No contests		

BILLIARDS QUIZ

1. What test can be made to judge the feasibility of applying the billiard iron to a table?

★

2. When was the first governing body for the control of billiards formed?

★

3. What is the room space needed for a full-size table?

★

4. What is a line ball, and what test can be applied to establish the fact?

5. Which famous players were born (a) at Whitwell, Derbyshire; (b) at Chesterfield, Derbyshire?

★

6. How many ivory balls could be made from an elephant's tusk?

QUIZ ANSWERS

1. Try it on a newspaper; if it scorches the paper it is too hot. Or hold palm of the hand within a couple of inches or so of the face of the iron, and if it is just bearable the iron may be used with safety. 2. 1885; the Billiards Association, which was amalgamated with the Control Club (1909) in 1919. Present title: Billiards Association and Control Council, or "B.A. & C.C." 3. 22 ft. by 16 ft. 4. A ball resting exactly on the baulk line and not playable. Place a coin each side of the ball. 5. (a) Joe Davis, (b) Fred Davis. 6. Five.

PROFESSIONAL RECORDS AND ACHIEVEMENTS (BILLIARDS)

W.R.=World Record; P.R.=Personal Record. (All achievements in England unless otherwise stated.)

WALTER LINDRUM (Australia)

Breaks: 4,137 (1932), W.R., P.R; 3,905 in 185 min. (1930); 3,262 in 123 min. (1929). In Australia: 3,361 (1940); 3,735 and 3,360 (1941); 3,612 in 146 min. (1942); 3,737 and 3,752 (1944), consecutive visits. Also 29 breaks of over 2,000 but under 3,000; 711 over 1,000 but under 2,000 in his career.

Aggregates: 1 day's play (4 hours) 4,815 (1930), W.R.; 1 session (2 hours) 2,664 (1930), W.R.; 2 weeks' play (48 hours) 36,256 (1930), W.R.; 674 per hour during 42 hours (1929).

Averages: 1 session (2 hours) 2,664 (1930), W.R.; 2-week match 262 (1930).

"Nursery" Cannons: 529 consecutive cannons (break of 1,058: 2⅛ times round the table) in 1933, W.R.

Fast Scoring: 100 in 46 sec. (1941), in Australia; 1,011 in 30 min. (1930); 663 in 15 min. (1930); 346 in 8 min. (1934), Australia. Also 100 in 27.5 sec. (reported from Australia but not confirmed).

In two visits to England, 1929-30 and 1930-31, Lindrum made 134 thousand-breaks. In 1930 he made breaks of 1,925 and 1,228 on the same day. He visited England four times: 1929, 1930, 1931 and 1933. The last time he played in England was May 28th, 1933.

JOE DAVIS (England)

Breaks: 2,052 (1930), P.R.; 2,002 (1935); 2,500 (1927) by "Pendulum" cannon stroke (see "Specialized or Repetitive Strokes"); 1,784 (1936), English record under present Baulk-line rule, P.R.; 182 "Nursery" cannons, just over once round table, being break of 364, P.R.; has made 87 thousand-breaks; immediately after "sitting out" Lindrum's break of 4,137 (1932) Davis made a break of 1,247.

CLARK McCONACHY (New Zealand)

Breaks: 1,943 (1932), P.R., 1,927 (1934), in Australia; 1,739 (1930); first player to make a thousand-break in consecutive visits: 1,368 and 1,196 (1929).

"Nursery" Cannons: 466 consecutive cannons (second only to Lindrum's 529, q.v.), 13 times along top cushion (1932); P.R.; 297 consecutive cannons (1932).

TOM NEWMAN (England)

Breaks: 1,827 (1931), P.R.; 1,814 (1930); 1,370 (1924), ivory ball record. Ivory balls were discontinued about 1926-8, being replaced by composition balls, though these and other makes, bonzaline, vitalite, etc., had been used many years previously. In 1923 Newman made breaks of 542, 705, 850, 0 (a miss) and 529 in succession. In season 1930-1 he made 30 thousand-breaks. In 1928 he made 656, 548, 501, and 509 in one day's play.

WILLIE SMITH (England)

Breaks: 2,743 (1928); considered by some to be the finest break ever made, as it did not include any "Nursery" cannons, which mode of scoring figured prominently in the play of Walter Lindrum, Joe Davis, Tom Newman, Clark McConachy, etc., and was made purely by all-round play. Had these players, however, excluded "Nursery" cannons, it is conceivable they would have equalled or surpassed this figure, particularly Lindrum. Also 2,030 (1929), in Australia; 7 breaks of 1,000 or over in a week's play (1932); 96 500 and over (1926). At 63, Smith scored 1,754 (av. 79) in a day's play, v. J. Barrie, in the U.K. Championship (1950).

Specialized Strokes. These include the types of cannon, such as the "Anchor" or "Cradle" cannon, the "Pendulum" cannon, the "Spot" stroke, and the "Push" stroke (both the latter being barred in 1898). Breaks by these strokes consisted of one stroke repeated any number of times. Cannon play on such lines was restricted in 1907 ("Cradle" or "Anchor") and 1927 ("Pendulum"); "Nursery" or "Close" cannons are not repetitive strokes; each stroke mentioned below are normal, unless otherwise stated. Red-ball breaks by losing hazards (in-offs) were normal billiards, though restricted in 1926 to 25 consecutive in-offs; red-ball breaks by unlimited potting of the red off its spot ("Spot" stroke) were barred in 1898 by a rule transferring the red to the centre Spot after being potted twice in succession.

Other Outstanding Professionals, Breaks, etc.

JOHN ROBERTS JUN. (1847-1919), the W. G. Grace of billiards. Roberts dominated billiards for over 30 years. 1,392 (1894; "Spot" stroke "Push" included). P.R.; 1,117 (1894; "Spot" barred, "Push" included); 821 (1905) at 58 years of age.

W. J. PEALL (1854-1952), the "Spot Stroke King". 3,304 (3,174 red-ball pots, one run of 400 consecutive) in 1890; average of 325 for 49 visits (1890); 8 other breaks, including "Spot" stroke, over 2,000; scored 1,000 in 44 min.

W. COOK 42,746 (made by "Anchor" cannon; highest official break ever made) in 1907.

W. MITCHELL 6 thousand-breaks ("Spot" stroke), highest 1,839 (613 consecutive "Spots", 1883); made first thousand-break in public, 1,055 (350 "Spots"), at Black Horse Hotel, Rathbone Place, London, in 1882.

C. DAWSON 823 (1899), P.R.; 1,848 (613 consecutive "Spots") in 1890; 933 ("Spot" barred, "Push" included) in 1893; 23,769 (1907), by "Anchor" cannon.

E. DIGGLE 985 ("Spot" barred) in 1895; 791 (1902). In making this break, first player to keep opponent from table for a whole session since abolition of "Spot" and "Push" strokes in 1898.

G. GRAY (Australia) visited England 1910-11, when he compiled 23 thousand-breaks, highest 2,916 (1911), with red-ball in-offs as basis; 1,620 off red ball, P.R.; 289 middle-pocket in-offs consecutively (red ball).

M. INMAN 950 (1924), P.R.; 894 (1913), ivories.

T. REECE 901 (1916), ivories, P.R.; 872 (1920), ivories; 499,135 unfinished, by "Anchor" cannon; break refused official recognition, as press and public not present during whole of break which took 5 weeks (85 hours 49 min.: 1907); 1,151 (1927), P.R., by "Pendulum" cannon (Championship), also 6,000- and 3,000-odd by same stroke; 675 and 618 (1913) same session.

H. W. STEVENSON (famous as stylist) 1,016 (1921), P.R., being first "Spot"-barred thousand-break; 919 (1913), ivories; 802 (1905); 788 (1904).

C. FALKINER 1,130 (1924), P.R.; 1,001 (1924), in Australia; 230 "Nursery" cannons (1924); 985 (1924), in Australia; 625 in 25 min. (1919).

WORLD AMATEUR BILLIARDS CHAMPIONSHIP

	Winner	Runner-up	Venue
1926	J. Earlham (England)	G. Shailer (Australia)	London
1927	A. Prior (South Africa)	H. Coles (Wales)	London
1929	L. Hayes (Australia)	A. Prior (South Africa)	London
1931	S. Lee (England)	S. Lee (England)	Johannesburg
1933	L. Steeples (England)	T. Jones (Wales)	Sydney
1935	H. Coles (Wales)	J. McGhie (Scotland)	London
1936	R. Marshall (Australia)	A. Prior (South Africa)	London
1938	R. Marshall (Australia)	K. Kennerley (England)	Johannesburg
1951	R. Marshall (Australia)	F. Edwards (England)	Melbourne
1952	A. L. Driffield (England)	R. Marshall (Australia)	London
1954	T. Cleary (Australia)	R. Marshall (Australia)	Calcutta
1958	W. Jones (India)	A. L. Driffield (England)	Sydney
			Calcutta

1926-38: entitled British Empire Championship.

BREAKS

682, Tom Cleary (1954), record; also 501, W. Jones (1958); 499, A. L. Driffield (1958); 472, K. Kennerley (1938); 470, L. Steeples (1931); 461 (unfinished), L. Steeples (1931); 433, S. Lee (1931); 427 (1938), 423 (1951) and 417 (1951), R. Marshall.

AVERAGES

Session (2 hours): 112.0, L. Steeples (1931), record; also 109.9, A. L. Driffield (1958); 109.6, R. Marshall (1938).

Match: 79.9, A. L. Driffield (1958), record; also 67.8, R. Marshall (1951).

Aggregate in 1 session: 1,864, R. Marshall, (1939), record.

Centuries in 1 session: 7, Robert Marshall (1938), record (amateur); 6, A. L. Driffield (1952).

ENGLISH AMATEUR BILLIARDS CHAMPIONSHIP

	Winner	Runner-up	Scores
1888	H. A. Lonsdale	J. Tither	500-356
1888	A. P. Gaskell	H. A. Lonsdale	1,500-1,349
1889	A. P. Gaskell declared champion		
1889	A. P. Gaskell	E. W. Alabone	1,500-1,278
1890	A. P. Gaskell	S. H. Fry	1,500-1,395
1890	A. P. Gaskell	N. Defries	1,500-1,395
1890	W. D. Courtney	A. P. Gaskell	1,500-1,141
1891	W. D. Courtney	A. P. Gaskell	1,500-971
1891	A. P. Gaskell	W. D. Courtney	1,500-1,188
1892	A. R. Wisdom	"Osbourne"	1,500-1,094
1892	S. S. Christey	S. H. Fry	1,500-928
1893	A. R. Wisdom	Mr. Buxton	1,500-852
1893	S. H. Fry	A. R. Wisdom	1,500-1,239
1893	A. H. Vahid	S. S. Christey	1,500-1,395
1894	H. Mitchell	A. Vinson	1,500-1,464
1894	W. T. Maughan	H. Mitchell	1,500-1,202
1896	S. H. Fry	W. T. Maughan	1,500-1,430
1899	A. R. Wisdom	S. H. Fry	1,500-1,297
1900	S. H. Fry	A. R. Wisdom	1,500-1,428
1901	S. S. Christey	W. S. Jones	1,500-1,305
1902	A. W. T. Good	S. S. Christey	2,000-1,689
1902	A. W. T. Good	A. J. Browne	2,000-1,669
1903	A. R. Wisdom	A. W. T. Good	2,000-1,783
1903	S. S. Christey	G. A. V. Diehl	2,000-1,314
1904	W. A. Lovejoy	A. W. T. Good	2,000-1,733
1905	A. W. T. Good	G. Heginbottom	2,000-1,739
1906	E. C. Breed	A. W. T. Good	2,000-1,620
1907	H. C. Virr	J. Nugent	2,000-1,896
1908	H. C. Virr	G. Heginbottom	2,000-1,841
1909	Major Fleming	H. C. Virr	2,000-1,501
1910	H. A. Lonsdale	Major Fleming	2,000-1,882
1911	H. C. Virr	Major Fleming	3,000-2,716
1912	H. C. Virr	Major Fleming	3,000-2,993
1913	H. C. Virr	J. Nugent	3,000-1,956
1914	H. C. Virr	J. Nugent	3,000-1,962
1915	A. W. T. Good	G. Heginbottom	2,000-1,444
1916	S. H. Fry	G. Heginbottom	2,000-1,417
1917	J. Graham-Symes	S. H. Fry	2,000-1,540
1918	J. Graham-Symes	"Osbourne"	2,000-1,121
1919	S. H. Fry	J. Graham-Symes	2,000-1,729
1920	S. H. Fry	W. B. Marshall	3,000-2,488
1921	S. H. Fry	J. Graham-Symes	3,000-2,591
1922	J. Graham-Symes	W. P. McLeod	3,000-2,661
1923	W. P. McLeod	J. Graham-Symes	3,000-2,867
1924	W. P. McLeod	J. Graham-Symes	3,000-2,862
1925	S. H. Fry	W. B. Marshall	3,000-2,778
1926	J. Earlham	C. M. Helyer	3,000-1,751
1927	L. Steeples	H. F. E. Coles	3,000-2,449
1928	A. Wardle	A. W. T. Good	3,000-2,189
1929	H. F. E. Coles	S. Lee	3,000-2,215
1930	L. Steeples	H. F. E. Coles	3,000-2,462
1931	S. Lee	M. A. Boggin	3,793-3,134
1932	S. Lee	F. Edwards	4,674-3,508
1933	S. Lee	H. F. E. Coles	4,458-3,237
1934	S. Lee	F. Edwards	3,929-3,509
1935	H. F. E. Coles	M. A. Boggin	3,707-3,272
1936	J. Thompson	J. H. Beetham	3,149
1937	K. Kennerley	J. Thompson	4,703-3,633
1938	K. Kennerley	J. Thompson	4,714-3,925
1939	K. Kennerley	A. Spencer	4,423-3,264
1940	K. Kennerley	A. Spencer	3,931-3,749
1941-45	No contests		
1946	M. Showman	J. H. Beetham	3,077-2,593
1947	J. Thompson	A. Hibbert	4,104-3,185
1948	J. Thompson	H. G. Terry	*5,202-2,816

English Amateur Billiards Championship—contd.

	Winner	Runner-up	Scores
1949	F. Edwards	J. Tregoning	4,813–3,297
1950	F. Edwards	J. Tregoning	4,968–3,385
1951	F. Edwards	J. Tregoning	5,015–3,791
1952	A. L. Driffield	J. H. Beetham	2,894–2,793
1953	A. L. Driffield	F. Edwards	4,136–3,016
1954	A. L. Driffield	F. Edwards	4,165–3,030
1955	F. Edwards	A. Nolan	4,194–3,206
1956	F. Edwards	A. L. Driffield	3,395–3,327
1957	A. L. Driffield	F. Edwards	4,464–2,894
1958	A. L. Driffield	J. T. Wright	4,483–2,587
1959	A. L. Driffield	J. H. Beetham	3,803–2,792

* Record aggregate for Final.

Record Break: K. Kennerley 549 (1937). Also J. H. Beetham 481, unfinished (1959); A. Nolan 461 (1955); A. L. Driffield 444 (1951); F. Edwards 438 (1955). All in Competition Proper.

Highest Session Average: A. Nolan 103.3 (1955).

Highest Session Aggregate: F. Edwards 1,279 (1953).

Highest 2-Session Average: F. Edwards 2,383 (1956).

Highest Match Average: A. L. Driffield 51.3 (1958).

6 century-breaks in 1 session: F. Edwards (1953).

AUSTRALIAN AMATEUR BILLIARDS CHAMPIONSHIP

	Winner	Runner-up
1920	J. R. Hooper	—
1921	G. B. Shailer	—
1922	G. B. Shailer	—
1923	G. B. Shailer	—
1924	E. Eccles	—
1925	G. B. Shailer	—
1926	L. W. Hayes	—
1927	L. W. Hayes	—
1928	L. W. Hayes	—
1929	A. H. Hearndon	—
1930	S. Ryan	—
1931	H. L. Goldsmith	—
1932	A. Sakzewski	—
1933	L. W. Hayes	—
1934	L. W. Hayes	—
1935	L. W. Hayes	Tom Cleary
1936	R. Marshall	A. G. Bull
1937	R. Marshall	Tom Cleary
1938	R. Marshall	Tom Cleary
1939	R. Marshall	A. Sakzewski
1940–45	No contests	
1946	R. Marshall	J. Harris
1947	Tom Cleary	A. G. Bull
1948	R. Marshall	Tom Cleary
1949	R. Marshall	Tom Cleary
1950	Tom Cleary	R. Marshall
1951	R. Marshall	J. Harris
1952	R. Marshall	J. Long
1953	R. Marshall	Tom Cleary
1954	R. Marshall	Tom Cleary
1955	R. Marshall	Tom Cleary
1956	J. Long	O. Pitman
1957	R. Marshall	O. Pitman
1958	Tom Cleary	

Record Break: R. Marshall 702 (1953). Also R. Marshall 596 (1957), 589, unfinished (1951), 540 and 500 (1948), 498 (1952), 464 and 419 in 1 sess. (1950); T. Cleary 435 (1947), 408 (1954), 413 (1948). R. Marshall; other breaks of 400-odd.

Highest Session Average: R. Marshall 110.77 (1951).

Highest Match Average: R. Marshall 70.1 (1957).

Highest 1-Session Aggregate: R. Marshall.

Highest 2-Session Aggregate: R. Marshall 3,189 (1952). Also R. Marshall 3,144 (1950); T. Cleary 3,185 (1950).

Centuries in 1 session: R. Marshall 6; T. Cleary 6 (1950).

SCOTTISH AMATEUR CHAMPIONSHIP (BILLIARDS)

POST-WAR PERIOD

	Winner	Runner-up
1946	J. Levey	R. McKendrick
1947	A. Ramage	G. Aitken
1948	W. Ramage	A. Ramage
1949	W. Ramage	A. Ramage
1950	A. Ramage	W. Ramage
1951	W. Ramage	G. Jardine
1952	J. Murray	R. Gillon
1953	J. Bates	W. Ramage
1954	J. Bates	J. Murray
1955	W. Ramage	A. Ramage
1956	W. Ramage	A. Ramage
1957	W. Ramage	M. Morrin
1958	W. Ramage	P. Spence
1959	W. Ramage	W. Taylor

Record Break: J. Bates 323 (1954). *Session Average:* J. Bates 66 (1954). *5 100 Breaks in 1 Session:* J. Bates. (1954) (twice), in Open and in West v East.

INDIAN AMATEUR BILLIARDS CHAMPIONSHIP

	Winner	Runner-up
1931	M. M. Begg	—
1932	P. K. Deb	—
1933	Major Meade	—
1934	Mg. Ba Sin	—
1935	P. K. Deb	—
1936	P. K. Deb	—
1937	M. M. Begg	—
1938	P. K. Deb	—
1939	P. K. Deb	—
1940	S. H. Lyth	—
1941	V. R. Freer	—
1942	V. R. Freer	—
1943–45	No contests	
1946	Chandra Hirjee	C. C. James
1947	Chandra Hirjee	T. A. Selvaraj
1948	V. R. Freer	P. K. Deb
1949	T. A. Selvaraj	Wilson Jones
1950	Wilson Jones	T. A. Selvaraj
1951	Wilson Jones	T. A. Selvaraj
1952	Wilson Jones	Chandra Hirjee
1953	A. L. Driffield	W. Ramage
1954	Wilson Jones	Chandra Hirjee
1955	Wilson Jones	Chandra Hirjee
1956	Chandra Hirjee	Wilson Jones
1957	Wilson Jones	Chandra Hirjee
1958	Chandra Hirjee	Wilson Jones
1959	T. Cleary	Wilson Jones

Record Break: W. Jones 452 (1958). Also W. Jones 399 (1954), 342 (1951); T. Cleary 373 (1951); C. Hirjee 337 (1957).

Highest Session Average: A. L. Driffield 55.05 (1953); C. Hirjee 54.6 (1957); W. Jones 42.3 (1957).

Highest Match Average: C. Hirjee 45.1 (1957); A. L. Driffield 35.73 (1953); W. Jones 32.3 (1958).

Centuries in 1 session: 6, A. L. Driffield (1952), Indian record.

N.B. A. L. Driffield & W. Ramage, in India for AM. World Championship (1953). T. Cleary (1959).

WELSH AMATEUR CHAMPIONSHIP

POST-WAR PERIOD

	BILLIARDS	SNOOKER
	Winner	Winner
1947	T. C. Morse	T. Jones
1948	J. Tregoning	R. Smith
1949	I. Edwards	A. J. Ford
1950	W. Pierce	R. Reardon
1951	W. Pierce	R. Reardon
1952	J. Tregoning	R. Reardon
1953	B. Sainsbury	R. Reardon
1954	R. Smith	R. Reardon
1955	J. Tregoning	R. Reardon
1956	J. Ford	C. Wilson
1957	R. Smith	R. D. Meredith
1958	R. W. Oriel	A. Kemp
1959	J. Ford	J. R. Price

Record Break (Billiards): T. G. Morse 211 (1947).

EMPIRE TOURNAMENT

	Winner	Runner-up
1931	W. Lindrum	T. Newman

"GOLD CUP" TOURNAMENTS

	Winner	Runner-up
1933	T. Newman "News of the World"	C. McConachy
1935	T. Newman "Daily Mail" (Sealed Handicap)	W. Smith
1936	M. Inman "Daily Mail" (Sealed Handicap)	S. Smith

BILLIARDS AMATEUR CHAMPIONSHIPS: EIRE, ALL-IRELAND AND NORTHERN IRELAND

Winners from 1952

	EIRE	ALL-IRELAND	NORTHERN IRELAND
1952	M. Nolan	M. Nolan	R. Taylor
1953	D. Turley	D. Turley	W. Sanlon
1954	M. Nolan	W. Sanlon	W. Sanlon
1955	M. Nolan	D. Turley	D. Turley
1956	M. Nolan	M. Nolan	J. Stevenson
1957	M. Nolan	W. Sanlon	W. Sanlon
1958	W. Dennison	W. Dennison	W. Hanna
1959	No official contest	No official contest	W. Hanna

WOMEN'S CHAMPIONSHIPS

PROFESSIONAL

	Winner
1931	Joyce Gardner
1932	Joyce Gardner
1933	Joyce Gardner
1934	Ruth Harrison
1935	Joyce Gardner
1936	Joyce Gardner
1937	Joyce Gardner
1938	Joyce Gardner
1939	Ruth Harrison
1940	Thelma Carpenter
1941–47	No contests
1948	Thelma Carpenter
1949	Thelma Carpenter
1950	Thelma Carpenter
1951–59	No contests.

AMATEUR

1931	Ruth Harrison
1932	Thelma Carpenter
1933	Thelma Carpenter
1934	Thelma Carpenter
1935	Vera Seals
1936	Vera Seals
1937	Grace Philips
1938	Mrs. McDougall
1939	Mrs. McDougall
1940–47	No contests
1948	Sadie Isaacs
1949	E. Morland-Smith
1950	M. Keeton
1951	Helen Futo
1952	No contest
1953	E. Morland-Smith
1954	E. Morland-Smith
1955	Helen Futo
1956	Maureen Barrett
1957	Maureen Barrett
1958	Maureen Barrett
1959	E. Morland-Smith

AMATEUR RECORDS AND ACHIEVEMENTS (BILLIARDS)

W.R.=World Record ; P.R.=Personal Record ; A.C.=Australian Championship ; W.C.=World Championship ; E.C.=English Championship ; I.C.=Indian Championship.

ROBERT MARSHALL
(all in Australia)

Breaks: 702 (1953), W.R., P.R.; also 589 unfinished (1951), 553 (1946), 596 (1957), 540 (1948), all in A.C.; several breaks o 400 and over. *Aggregates:* one 2-hour session 1,864 (1938, W.C.), W.R. P.R.; two 2-hour sessions 3,189 (1952), W.R.; also 3,144 (1950, A.C.), W.R., P.R. *Averages:* 110.77, 1 session (1951, A.C.), P.R.; 109.64, 1 session (1938, W.C.); 70, match (1957, A.C.), W.R., P.R. In 1950 Marshall made breaks of 464 and 419 in the same session (A.C., W.R., P.R.).

TOM CLEARY
(in Australia & India)

Breaks: 682 (1954, W.C.), W.C. record, P.R.; also 435 (1957, A.C.), 408 (1954, A.C.), 431 (1958, W.C., India), 432 (1950, A.C.). *Aggregate:* 3,185, 2 sessions (1950, A.C.), P.R. *Averages:* 93.6, 1 session (1958, W.C., India), P.R.

WILSON JONES
(made in India)

Breaks: 501 (1958, W.C.), P.R.; 452 (1958, I.C.), Indian record; 438 (1958, W.C.). *Averages:* 67.8, 1 session (1958, W.C.), P.R.

A. L. DRIFFIELD (England)

Breaks: 499 (1958, W.C., India), P.R.; 444 (1951, E.C.); 470 and 435 (1958, W.C., India); 365 and 277, consecutive visits (1958, E.C.); 203, 207 and 209, consecutive visits (1958, W.C., India). *Averages:* 109.9, 1 session (1958, W.C., India), P.R.; 79.9, match (1958, W.C., India), W.C. record, W.R., 51.3, match (1958, E.C.), E.C. record.

BILLIARDS QUIZ

1. What is the weight of a full-size billiard table?

*

2. What professional made a break of 56 consecutive winning hazards (pots) into the two middle pockets and the two top pockets from the pyramid spot?

*

3. May an amateur play for a declared wager or staked bet without losing his amateur status?

*

4. What is the ideal speed for a billiard table?

*

5. Which amateur won the Amateur Billiards Championship 32 years after he had won it for the first time?

*

6. What year was the first English book on billiards written, and who wrote it?

QUIZ ANSWERS

1. From 25 to 30 cwt., according to thickness of slates and type of wood. 2. E. Diggle; the billiard Spot was occupied by the object white, the present rule re spotting of red not then being in existence. 3. No, but he may back himself. 4. From 4½ to 5 lengths (i.e., a ball forcibly hit with the cue would travel that distance before coming to a stop). 5. S. H. Fry; first win 1893, last win 1925 (6 wins in between). 6. 1801; E. White (A Treatise on English Billiards).

FRANK EDWARDS (England)

Breaks: 438 (1955, E.C.), P.R.; 343 (1951, W.C., England); 6 century-breaks, 1 session (1953, E.C.), E.C. record. *Aggregates:* 1 session record 1,279 (1953, E.C.), P.R.; 2 session record 2,383 (1956, E.C.), P.R.; break of 152 in 4 min. 40 sec. (1947).

HERBERT BEETHAM (England)

Break: 481 unfinished (1959, E.C.), second highest E.C., P.R.; four times runner-up E.C.

ALFRED NOLAN (England)

Break: 461 (1955, E.C.), third highest E.C., P.R. *Average:* 103.3, 1 session (1955 E.C.), E.C. record, P.R. Nolan, in 1955, performed the outstanding feat of becoming runner-up in both amateur championships (billiards and snooker). This had been done before the war but amateur snooker was then much less advanced. He won the snooker championship in 1950.

L. STEEPLES (England)

Break: 461 unfinished (1931, W.C., P.R., Australia). *Average:* 112, 1 session (1931, W.C.), W.C. record, W.R.

SIDNEY LEE (England)

Break: 433 (1931, W.C., Australia). 103 close cannons, consecutive (1934).

Compiled by **Howard Bass**
Editor: The Skater and Skier

Bobsleigh

THE ORIGINS OF BOBSLEIGH

The sport of sliding down natural or artificial ice slopes on hand-sleighs fitted with runners, generally called tobogganing in Europe and coasting in North America, has been popular for centuries wherever suitable climatic conditions permit.

The earliest form of American sleds are thought to have been originated by Indians. Until 1886 the Swiss *schlittli*, a small-scale copy of the ancient horse sledge, was in common competitive use. In 1887 the American clipper sled—built low, with long, pointed sides and round steel rods for runners—was introduced in international events by L. P. Child. The rider lies flat upon it (the *ventre-à-terre* position) and steers with his feet, wearing spiked shoes to assist braking.

The modern bobsleigh or "double runner" consists of two toboggans joined together and steered by ropes, a wheel or cross-bar. They are constructed to seat in an upright position from four to ten persons.

The world administration of competitive bobsleighing is now controlled by the International Federation of Bobsleigh and Tobogganing and the sport has become particularly popular in the Engadine winter resorts of Switzerland. The first regular toboggan races were organised in Switzerland during the late nineteenth century by John Addington Symonds, who inaugurated an annual open competition for a challenge trophy on an ideal natural course from Davos to Klosters.

Colin Mitchell

Permanent artificial runs were later constructed, the most famous being the Cresta Run at St. Moritz, built in 1884. Fitted with an electrical timing apparatus, it is 1,320 yards long, with steeply banked curves including a notably hazardous bend called the Horse Shoe. The total drop from start to finish is just over 500 feet and the average gradient is 1 in 7.7. The "Grand National" championships have been contested here annually since 1885, the winner's time being the shortest aggregate of three heats.

There is a widely held misconception that the St. Moritz bobsleigh course for four-man and two-man bobs is the same as the Cresta Run, but in fact it runs roughly parallel with it, being a separate track of solid ice one and a half miles long, with a drop of 400 feet, and it has fourteen bends including a very tricky hairpin called Sunny Corner in addition to the Horse Shoe turn. Speeds in excess of seventy miles per hour have sometimes been attained and the highest average speeds for the whole course are near fifty miles per hour.

Bobsleigh won a place in the 1924 Winter Olympic Games at Chamonix, when the only event, four-man bob, was won by Switzerland, with Great Britain second and Belgium third.

An Olympic event for one-man skeleton toboggans was added in 1928 and 1948, the only two occasions when it has been included. Nino Bibbia (Italy),

who became most famous in this event, won in 1948. Two-man and four-man bobs have been otherwise the recognised Olympic events. Four-man bob-sleds weigh around 500 lb. and two-man "boblets" some 300 lb.

A special bobsleigh run, built to Olympic requirements for the 1932 Games, is situated on Mt. Van Hoevenberg in the Adirondaks, just outside the village of Lake Placid, N.Y. Approximately one and a half miles in length, it has twenty-eight bends. U.S.A. won both the two-man and the four-man Olympic events there in 1932.

Eighteen teams from nine nations entered the 1952 Olympic two-man bob event in Oslo, Germany's Andreas Ostler and Lorenz Nieberl being victorious. These two, together with Friedrich Khun and Franz Kemser, also won for Germany the four-man event.

In 1956, at Cortina d'Ampezzo, Italians on their home ground took the first two places in the two-man bob and were runners-up to Switzerland in the four-man event.

The sport is especially popular in eastern Canada, where there have been built a five-track chute at Mt. Royal, Montreal, and a three-track chute at Dufferin Terrace, Quebec. In Norway courses more than three miles long exist in the Oslo area.

From Great Britain, where the British Bobsleigh Association controls the sport's national administration, the emergence of very successful post-war performers perhaps reflects the fact that, although bob-sledding calls for considerable skill and daring, it is possible to reach world class after relatively little overseas preparation, compared with the years of training and experience necessary to become a top-class skier.

Major Hubert Martineau has been a leading administrative figure as president of the British and St. Moritz Bobsleigh Clubs, St. Moritz to bobsleigh being as Lord's is to cricket.

The R.A.F. Winter Sports Association has particularly encouraged training facilities, which enabled Flt. Lt. Colin Mitchell to be one of the most prominent individual performers of the 1959 season, when he won the Cresta Run Grand National as well as the world championship, also the Curzon Cup and Morgan Cup events. Britain's No. 1 four-man team also commanded much respect, finishing fourth in the world event, with Henry Taylor (driver), Anthony Nash, Michael Davidson and Robin Dixon. A second British team comprised Lord Suffolk, Rory Cochran-Dyer, Andrew Hedges and Robert Cooper.

Bibliography: *Winter Sports* (The *Skater and Skier*) magazine.

BOBSLEIGH 1959

WORLD CHAMPIONSHIPS

(*St. Moritz, February* 5, 6, 8 *and* 15)
Individual:
1. C. Mitchell   (Great Britain)
2. R. Kuderli   (Switzerland)
3. N. Bibbia   (Italy)
2-man bob:
1. Italy   (E. Monti and R. Alvera)
4-man bob:
1. U.S.A.†   (A. Tyler, G. Sheffield, P. Vooris and T. Butler)
2. Italy   (Driver, S. Zardini)
3. Germany   (Driver, F. Schelle)
(† *included mile track record, 1m. 17.4s.*)

CRESTA RUN GRAND NATIONAL

(*St. Moritz, February* 16)
1. C. Mitchell*   (Great Britain)
2. C. Fischbacher   (Switzerland)
3. S. Eccles   (Great Britain)
(* *3-course total time, 169.2 secs., beat record*)

SWISS OPEN CHAMPIONSHIP

(*St. Moritz, February* 22)
1. N. Bibbia   (Italy)
2. R. Kuderli   (Switzerland)
3. K. Taskent   (Turkey)

BOTT CUP (Handicap)

(*St. Moritz, February* 18)
1. V. Emery   (Canada)
2. C. Nater   (Switzerland)

CURZON CUP

(*St. Moritz, February* 1)
1. C. Mitchell   (Great Britain)
2. R. Kuderli   (Switzerland)
3. N. Bibbia   (Italy)

BARON OERTZEN CUP (Handicap)

(*St. Moritz, February* 9)
1. G. Corelle   (U.S.A.)
2. C. Mitchell   (Great Britain)

MORGAN CUP

(*St. Moritz, February* 11)
1. C. Mitchell   (Great Britain)
2. S. Eccles   (Great Britain)
3. P. Bridgman   (Great Britain)

BOBLET DERBY (2-men bobs)

(*St. Moritz, February* 1)
1. A. Tyler and T. Butler   (U.S.A.)

MARTINEAU CUP (4-men bobs)

(*St. Moritz, February* 10)
1. Germany   (Driver, F. Schelle)
2. Italy   (Driver, S. Zardini)
3. U.S.A.   (Driver, A. Tyler)

OLYMPIC CHAMPIONS

Year	Event	Winner	Venue
1924	4-man bob:	Switzerland	Chamonix
1928	5-man-bob:	U.S.A.	St. Moritz
	Skeleton:	U.S.A.	
1932	2-man bob:	U.S.A.	Lake Placid
	4-man bob:	U.S.A.	
1936	2-man bob:	U.S.A.	Garmisch-Partenkirchen
	4-man bob:	Switzerland	
1948	2-man bob:	Switzerland	St. Moritz
	4-man bob:	U.S.A.	
	Skeleton:	U.S.A.	
1952	2-man bob:	Germany	Oslo
	4-man bob:	Germany	
1956	2-man bob:	Italy	Cortina d'Ampezzo
	4-man bob:	Switzerland	

A British team hurtle round a banked bend on the St. Moritz bobsleigh course.

BOBSLEIGH QUIZ

1. Who won the bobsleigh "Grand National" in 1959?

∗

2. Where is the Cresta Run?

∗

3. What is the approximate weight of a four-man bob-sled?

∗

4. Which nation won the 1959 world championship for two-man bobs?

∗

5. When was the first Olympic bobsleigh race held?

∗

6. How long is the Cresta Run course?

QUIZ ANSWERS

1. Colin Mitchell (Great Britain). 2. St. Moritz, in Switzerland. 3. 500 pounds. 4. Italy. 5. 1924 at Chamonix. 6. 1,320 yards.

A general view of the scene as a competitor starts off down the famous Cresta Run at St. Moritz.

Bowls

Compiled by E. Sussum
Secretary: English Bowling Association

BOWLS QUIZ

1. What are the minimum and maximum widths of a rink?

*

2. What is the largest circumference of a bowl?

*

3. A bowl after delivery is dead if it comes to rest within a certain distance of the front of the mat. What is the distance?

*

4. If it becomes necessary to measure the length of a jack, from where is the measurement made?

*

5. If at the commencement of a game the mat, by mistake, is placed in a wrong position and the first bowl is delivered, can the mat be afterwards moved to what should have been its right position?

*

6. Can a player in a competition or match play on the green on the day of the competition or match before play commences?

*

7. If the jack is driven to the side boundary of the rink and not wholly beyond its limits can it be played to on either hand?

*

8. What is the minimum distance the jack can be played to?

*

9. When must a "toucher" be marked?

*

10. If a game is stopped by reason of weather, what is the position when the game is resumed?

QUIZ ANSWERS

1. 19 ft.; 21 ft. 2. 16½ ins. 3. 15 yds. 4 From the front of the mat. 5. No. 6. No. 7. Yes. 8. 25 yds. 9. Before the delivery of the succeeding bowl. 10. With the scores as they were when the game was stopped. An end commenced but not completed shall be declared null.

ENGLISH BOWLING ASSOCIATION

The Association was founded in 1903.

Dr. W. G. Grace, the famous cricketer, was elected the first president in the presence of 31 club representatives. Previously there were many clubs and separate associations.

The main idea in forming the Association was to have an authority which could act and speak for England.

The objects of the Association were, amongst others, to promote, foster and safeguard the amateur level-green game of bowls for men in England, and to establish in every county a single association with a view to the effective organization of the game.

The Association grew very rapidly and is still growing, as the following figures will show:

Year	Counties	Clubs
1903	Association formed	
1904	24	44
1923	29	730
1933	29	1,346
1938	30	1,719
1958	34	2,418

The affairs of the English Bowling Association are conducted by a Council consisting of the President, Senior Vice-President, Junior Vice-President, the Retiring President (for a period of three years after he has passed the Chair), Hon. Treasurer and Secretary, Members elected by the respective County Associations and the Indoor Section, and the Honorary Members—a total membership of 126.

The Council meet twice a year in January and October and the Annual General Meeting of the Association is held in December.

The Council elect annually a General Purposes Committee and an International Selection Committee.

The General Purposes Committee, besides conducting the ordinary business of the Association, appoint a number of sub-committees for various matters.

The Association publishes annually a Year Book.

The Association is a member of the International Bowling Board which consists of members representative of the National Associations of England, Ireland, Scotland, Wales, Australia, Canada, New Zealand, South Africa and the United States of America.

The brothers N. and P. Richards and team-mate T. Dodge from Rookery Suffolk, winners of the 1954 Triples Championship.

Percy Baker, three times winner of the Single-Handed Championship, sends a wood down the green.

SINGLE-HANDED CHAMPIONSHIP

The winner holds for one year the Sir Thomas Lipton Cup, and receives from the Association a gold medal.

	Winners	Runners-up
1905	J. G. Carruthers (*Muswell Hill, Middx.*)	James Telford (*Newcastle West End, Northumberland*)
1906	C. L. Cummings (*Sunderland, Durham*)	A. Taylor (*Finsbury Park, Middx.*)
1907	J. S. Emmerson (*Edenside, Carlisle, Cumberland*)	H. W. Gibson (*Leicester*)
1908	R. Knights (*Hero of Switzerland, Surrey*)	M. Turner (*Carlisle Subscription, Cumberland*)
1909	J. W. Dick (*Gosforth, Northumberland*)	Harry Childs (*Reading, Berks*)
1910	F. Shatford (*Kettering, Northants*)	J. Dauncey (*Victoria, Somerset*)
1911	J. J. Postlethwaite (*Carlisle Courtfield, Cumberland*)	J. Work (*Tunbridge Wells Grove, Kent*)
1912	W. J. Jones (*Crouch Hill, Middx.*)	G. E. Edmondson (*Holme Head, Carlisle, Cumberland*)
1913	C. Gibb (*Sunderland, Durham*)	J. G. Carruthers (*Muswell Hill, Middx.*)
1914	D. Irvine Watson (*Malden, Surrey*)	W. Dean (*Balham, Surrey*)
1915–18	Not played during war period	
1919	E. E. Moore (*Bellingham, Kent*)	E. Dean (*Bournemouth, Hants*)
1920	A. E. Godsall (*Forest Hill, Kent*)	W. F. Hamilton (*Summerhill, Newcastle, Northumberland*)

Year	Winner	Runner-up
1921	A. F. Warner (*Belmont, Surrey*)	J. Harwood (*Preston, Sussex*)
1922	W. F. Hamilton (*Hexham, Northumberland*)	C. G. Roach (*Plymouth Hoe, Devon*)
1923	W. F. Wade (*Hinckley, Leicester*)	G. Sainsbury (*Wendover & Chiltern Hill, Bucks*)
1924	R. Hodge (*Torrington, Devon*)	E. C. Redman (*Banister Park, Hants*)
1925	H. P. Webber (*Plymouth, Devon*)	W. Jennings (*Taunton Deane, Somerset*)
1926	R. Jack (*Plymouth, Devon*)	A. P. Poingdestre (*Bromley, Kent*)
1927	T. Tickle (*Park Institute, Reading, Berks*)	E. C. Redman (*Banister Park, Hants*)
1928	G. Wright (*Southern Railway, Eastleigh, Hants*)	W. Barlow (*Bellingham, Kent*)
1929	Capt. R. G. Colquhoun (*Bromley, Kent*)	E. F. Gudgeon (*Preston, Brighton, Sussex*)
1930	W. F. Wade (*Hinckley, Leicester*)	H. P. Webber (*Plymouth, Devon*)
1931	E. P. Topp (*Ryde, Isle of Wight*)	H. Duggan (*Gloucester*)
1932	E. P. Baker (*Poole Park, Dorset*)	E. W. Fortune (*St. George's, Bristol, Somerset*)
1933	J. M. McKinlay (*Paddington, Middx.*)	Percy Guy (*Shanklin, Isle of Wight*)
1934	A. K. Cochrane (*Southampton, Hants*)	M. D. Burdon (*Dunelm, Durham*)
1935	W. Linton (*Smith's Docks, Yorks*)	J. E. Gallagher (*Cowes, I.O.W.*)
1936	G. D. Goodson (*Chesham, Bucks*)	A. W. Knowling, Jnr. (*Worthing, Sussex*)
1937	W. Prentice (*Redcar, Zetland, Yorks*)	H. P. Webber (*Torbay C. Club, Devon*)
1938	K. I. Cross (*Cosham, Hants*)	H. Cook (*Tynemouth, Northumberland*)
1939	J. J. Laws (*Summerhill, Northumberland*)	A. R. Allen (*Oxford*)
1940–44	Not played during war period	
1945	A. A. Keech (*Bootham, Yorks*)	J. W. Robison (*Henleaze, Gloucester*)
1946	E. P. Baker (*Poole Park, Dorset*)	E. Newton (*Windsor & Eton, Berks*)
1947	P. P. Mercer (*Worthing, Sussex*)	J. Thompson (*North Shields, Northumberland*)
1948	E. Newton (*Windsor & Eton, Berks*)	E. W. Fortune (*Bristol Greenbank, Gloucester*)
1949	A. R. Allen (*Oxford City & County, Oxford*)	A. Collins (*West Ealing, Middx.*)
1950	J. Thompson (*N. Shields West End, Northumberland*)	L. Whitworth (*New Herrington, Durham*)
1951	A. Pikesley (*St. Albans, Herts*)	S. Jackson (*Luton Town, Beds*)
1952	E. P. Baker (*Poole Park, Dorset*)	A. R. Allen (*Oxford City & County, Oxford*)
1953	R. G. W. Cramp (*Clay Hall, Essex*)	F. Watts (*Rugby, Warwick*)
1954	J. W. Griffiths (*Wallsend Boro', Northumberland*)	G. F. Ham (*Stroud, Glos*)
1955	E. P. Baker (*Poole Park, Dorset*)	J. W. Fletcher (*York Co-op, Yorks*)
1956	N. C. Butler (*Windsor and Eton, Berks*)	C. J. Webber (*Rock Park, Barnstaple, Devon*)
1957	N. King (*Parliament Hill, Middx.*)	F. I. Smith (*Hatfield, Herts*)
1958	H. Powell (*Farnborough B.L., Hants*)	F. Crockford (*Bembridge, Isle of Wight*)
1959	K. Coulson (*Croydon, Surrey*)	T. Fleming (*Middlesbrough, Yorks*)

Only two players have won the Championship more than once:
W. F. Wade (*Hinckley, Leicestershire*) in 1923 and 1930.
E. P. Baker (*Poole Park, Dorset*) in 1932, 1946 and 1952.

PAIRS CHAMPIONSHIP

The winners hold for one year the Sir Thomas Dewar Cup, and each player receives from the Association a gold medal.

	Winners	Runners-up
1912	Clarence Park (*Somerset*)	Malden (*Surrey*)
1913	Forest Hill (*Kent*)	Southend-on-Sea (*Essex*)
1914	Bristol (*Somerset*)	Hexham-on-Tyne (*Northumberland*)
1915–18	Not played during war period	
1919	Beach Hill (*Beds*)	Metropolitan Special Constabulary, Y Div. (*Middx.*)
1920	Taunton (*Somerset*)	Crouch Hill (*Middx.*)
1921	Preston (*Sussex*)	Abbey Park (*Leicester*)
1922	Roker Park (*Durham*)	East Oxford (*Oxford*)
1923	Gosforth (*Northumberland*)	Exeter City (*Devon*)
1924	Taunton (*Somerset*)	Bradford-on-Avon (*Wilts*)
1925	Abbey Park (*Leicester*)	Banister Park (*Hants*)
1926	Poole Park (*Dorset*)	Park Institute (*Berks*)
1927	Poole Park (*Dorset*)	Faversham (*Kent*)
1928	Wellingborough (*Northants*)	Downhills (*Middx.*)
1929	Carlisle Subscription (*Cumberland*)	Salisbury (*Wilts*)
1930	Frome Selwood (*Somerset*)	Carlisle Subscription (*Cumberland*)
1931	St. George's (*Somerset*)	Tally-Ho (*Warwick*)
1932	Wellingborough (*Northants*)	Faversham (*Kent*)
1933	Callenders (*Kent*)	Richmond Park (*Hants*)
1934	Callenders (*Kent*)	Park Institute (*Berks*)
1935	Saltburn-by-Sea (*Yorks*)	Blackheath & Greenwich (*Kent*)
1936	White Rock, Hastings (*Sussex*)	Bloomfield, Bath (*Somerset*)
1937	Worthing (*Sussex*)	Bristol St. Andrews (*Gloucester*)
1938	Worthing (*Sussex*)	Harrogate (*Yorks*)
1939	Durham City (*Durham*)	Summerhill (*Northumberland*)
1940–44	Not played during war period	
1945	Bellingham (*Kent*)	Abington (*Northants*)
1946	Penzance (*Cornwall*)	Swindon (*Wilts*)
1947	County Ground (*Worcester*)	Chippenham B.C. (*Wilts*)
1948	Tiverton Boro (*Devon*)	Bootham (*Yorks*)
1949	Darlington R.A. (*Durham*)	Marlow (*Bucks*)
1950	Poole Park (*Dorset*)	Edenside (*Cumberland*)
1951	South Oxford (*Oxford*)	Torquay (*Devon*)
1952	Torquay (*Devon*)	Collingwood (*Northumberland*)
1953	Bootham (*Yorks*)	Poole Park (*Dorset*)
1954	Dean and Chapter (*Durham*)	Trowbridge Town (*Wilts*)
1955	Worthing (*Sussex*)	Croydon (*Surrey*)
1956	Darlington East Park (*Durham*)	Chippenham Town (*Wilts*)
1957	Worthing (*Sussex*)	Banbury Boro (*Oxon*)
1958	Mid-Surrey (*Surrey*)	Lenton Unionists (*Notts*)
1959	Paddington (*Middx.*)	Clevedon (*Somerset*)

BOWLS QUIZ

1. If a bowl whilst in motion or at rest on the green be interfered with or displaced by one of the players, who has the power to decide what shall happen?

★

2. If a jack has been played into the ditch, can it be operated on by a bowl from the green?

3. When the jack is dead is the end counted as a played end even though all the bowls have been played?

★

4. What happens when the jack is damaged?

QUIZ ANSWERS

1. The opposing skip. 2. Yes, if the bowl is a "toucher". 3. No. 4. Another jack is substituted and the end played anew in the same direction.

TRIPLES CHAMPIONSHIP

The winners hold for one year the George Burrows Cup and the three members of the winning team each receive from the Association a gold medal.

	Winners	Runners-up
1945	Penzance (*Cornwall*)	Parsons Green (*Middx.*)
1946	Saltburn (*Yorkshire*)	Magdalen Park (*Surrey*)
1947	Redhill (*Surrey*)	Worthing (*Sussex*)
1948	Faversham (*Kent*)	Torbay Country (*Devon*)
1949	Worthing Pavilion (*Sussex*)	Three Spires (*Warwick*)
1950	Hereford (*Hereford*)	Rushden Town (*Northants*)
1951	North Oxford (*Oxford*)	Century (*Middx.*)
1952	Reading (*Berks*)	New Herrington (*Durham*)
1953	Darlington Woodland (*Durham*)	Abington (*Northants*)
1954	Rookery (*Suffolk*)	Tiverton Boro' (*Devon*)
1955	Southbourne (*Hants*)	Evesham (*Worcs*)
1956	Avenue, Leamington (*Warwickshire*)	Swindon North End (*Wilts*)
1957	Redbourn (*Lincs*)	Crouch Hill (*Middx.*)
1958	Blackpool (*Lancs*)	Townsend St. Albans (*Herts*)
1959	Hatfield (*Herts*)	Bannister Park (*Hants*)

SINGLE RINK CHAMPIONSHIP

The winners hold for one year the Wood Australian Cup and the four members of the winning team each receive from the Association a gold medal.

	Winners	Runners-up
1905	Carlisle Subscription (*Cumberland*)	Bounds Green (*Middx.*)
1906	Newcastle West End (*Northumberland*)	Upper Clapton (*Middx.*)
1907	Carlisle West End (*Cumberland*)	Forest Hill (*Kent*)
1908	Carlisle Edenside (*Cumberland*)	Upper Clapton (*Middx*)
1909	Wellingborough (*Northants*)	Newcastle West End (*Northumberland*)
1910	Victoria (*Somerset*)	Carlisle Subscription (*Cumberland*)
1911	Banbury (*Oxford*)	Reading (*Berks*)
1912	Wellingborough (*Northants*)	Paddington (*Middx.*)
1913	Dulwich (*Surrey*)	Bellingham (*Kent*)
1914	Reading (*Berks*)	Gillingham (*Kent*)
1915–18	Not played during war period	
1919	Belgrave (*Leicester*)	Dulwich (*Surrey*)
1920	Sunderland (*Durham*)	South Oxford (*Oxford*)
1921	Belgrave (*Northumberland*)	Wellingborough (*Northants*)
1922	Belgrave (*Leicester*)	Darlington East Park (*Durham*)
1923	Alnwick (*Northumberland*)	Central Park (*Essex*)
1924	Southend-on-Sea (*Essex*)	Summerhill (*Northumberland*)
1925	Belgrave (*Northumberland*)	Prospect Park (*Berks*)
1926	Preston (*Sussex*)	Newbury (*Berks*)
1927	Margate (*Kent*)	Harrow (*Middx.*)
1928	Luton Town (*Beds*)	Alnwick (*Northumberland*)
1929	Basingstoke Town (*Hants*)	Frome Selwood Printing Works (*Somerset*)
1930	Lammas (*Middx.*)	St. Albans (*Herts*)
1931	Kingston Canbury (*Surrey*)	Ryde (*Isle of Wight*)
1932	Atherley (*Hants*)	Sidney Gardens (*Somerset*)
1933	Southsea Waverley (*Hants*)	Torbay Country Club (*Devon*)
1934	Worthing (*Sussex*)	Southbourne (*Hants*)
1935	Sunderland (*Durham*)	Avenue, Leamington Spa (*Warwick*)
1936	Boscombe Cliff (*Hants*)	Parsons Green (*Middx.*)
1937	Sheen Common (*Surrey*)	Hinckley (*Leicester*)
1938	Paddington (*Middx.*)	Siddick (*Cumberland and West*)
1939	High Wycombe (*Bucks*)	Bedford Boro' (*Beds*)
1940–44	Not played during war period	
1945	Ilford (*Essex*)	Faversham (*Kent*)
1946	Faversham (*Kent*)	Marlboro' Ipswich (*Suffolk*)
1947	Redhill (*Surrey*)	South Oxford (*Oxford*)
1948	Oxford City & County (*Oxford*)	Gloucester Wagon Works (*Gloucester*)
1949	Skefko (*Beds*)	Stockton United (*Durham*)
1950	Richmond Park (*Hants*)	Eltham (*Kent*)
1951	Oxford City & County (*Oxford*)	Motspur Park (*Surrey*)
1952	Prospect Park (*Berks*)	Fleming Park, Eastleigh (*Hants*)
1953	Poole Park (*Dorset*)	Moordown (*Hants*)
1954	Belgrave (*Leicester*)	Abington (*Northants*)
1955	Wootton Basset (*Wilts*)	Eldon Grove (*Durham*)
1956	Fleet United (*Hants*)	Rookery (*Suffolk*)
1957	Clevedon (*Somerset*)	Wokingham (*Berks*)
1958	Morton (*Cumberland*)	Livesey Memorial (*Kent*)
1959	Princes Risborough (*Bucks*)	Penlee (*Cornwall*)

BOWLS QUIZ

1. On the resumption of an unfinished game on another day is a trial end allowed?

★

2. If the jack is improperly thrown for the second time in any end, where should the mat be placed?

★

3. If a player, after having been warned by the umpire for foot faulting, again infringes the law, what happens to the bowl he has just delivered?

4. If a "toucher" coming to rest in a ditch is not marked, is it a live or dead bowl?

★

5. If a "toucher" rebounds from the bank to the rink is it still in play?

★

QUIZ ANSWERS

1. Yes. 2. Back edge of mat one yard from the ditch. 3. Bowl is stopped and removed to the bank. 4. Dead. 5. Yes

A. R. Allen   A. W. Knowling   Harold Shapland   Norman King

COUNTY STATISTICS, 1958

These statistics show the number of clubs in the Association and the number of players who entered for the competitions in 1958 leading up to the National Championships.

COMPETITION ENTRIES—OFFICIAL RETURNS

County	Clubs	Singles	Pairs	Triples	Rinks	Entries	Players
BEDS	50	170	215	123	107	615	1,397
BERKS	45	295	250	156	106	807	1,687
BUCKS	50	204	210	125	92	631	1,367
CAMBS	44	211	195	128	111	645	1,429
CORNWALL	40	157	101	71	63	392	824
CUMB.	52	123	101	62	58	344	743
DERBY	13	38	47	29	31	145	343
DEVON	93	352	237	126	99	814	1,600
DORSET	25	140	108	55	42	345	689
DURHAM	97	214	238	127	113	692	1,523
ESSEX	179	577	503	275	182	1,537	3,136
GLOS	58	275	244	136	97	752	1,559
HANTS	88	452	356	183	124	1,115	2,209
HEREFORD	13	39	42	22	18	121	261
HERTS	72	334	306	174	133	947	2,000
ISLE OF WIGHT	12	66	67	33	30	196	419
KENT	212	864	917	500	335	2,616	5,538
LANCS	6	32	19	11	6	68	127
LEICS	70	365	354	205	166	1,090	2,352
LINCS	31	139	126	88	65	418	915
MIDDLESEX	240	734	649	346	244	1,973	4,046
NORFOLK	29	221	187	109	92	609	1,290
NORTHANTS	63	216	221	143	115	695	1,547
NORTHUMBERLAND	60	317	238	143	114	612	1,678
NOTTS	63	262	209	149	110	730	1,567
OXON	39	245	212	134	95	686	1,451
SOMERSET	63	327	328	173	137	965	2,050
SUFFOLK	52	265	267	174	113	819	1,773
SURREY	245	593	666	386	269	1,914	4,159
SUSSEX	118	329	238	118	75	760	1,459
WARWICKS	51	263	234	146	119	762	1,645
WILTS	43	210	202	113	95	620	1,333
WORCS	32	150	150	87	72	459	999
YORKS	70	228	179	111	79	579	1,235
	2,418	9,407	8,616	4,961	3,707	26,691	56,350

	Total Clubs	Total Players in Competitions		Total Clubs	Total Players in Competitions
1927	966	12,485	1945	1,710	28,428
1928	1,048	14,037	1946	1,805	37,590
1929	1,143	15,218	1947	1,882	41,611
1930	1,216	16,875	1948	1,952	43,141
1931	1,261	16,676	1949	2,026	47,108
1932	1,300	17,043	1950	2,117	49,096
1933	1,346	17,754	1951	2,210	51,367
1934	1,402	18,556	1952	2,246	54,220
1935	1,487	19,846	1953	2,319	55,442
1936	1,556	20,609	1954	2,350	54,709
1937	1,639	21,655	1955	2,375	56,044
1938	1,718	22,697	1956	2,399	55,968
1939	1,815	23,384	1957	2,400	55,233
1940–44 War period.			1958	2,418	56,350

INTERNATIONAL MATCHES

Matches are played each year between teams of five rinks a side representing England, Scotland, Ireland and Wales.

The matches are played in each of the countries in turn and each country plays one game against the other three countries.

The matches began in 1903 and were first played in London.

		Winners	Second	Third	Fourth
1903	London	England	Scotland	Ireland	Wales
1904	Glasgow	Scotland	England	Ireland	Wales
1905	Cardiff	Ireland	Scotland	England	Wales
1906	Belfast	England	Scotland	Wales	Ireland
1907	Newcastle	Scotland	Ireland	England	Wales
1908	Edinburgh	Scotland	Wales	England	Ireland
1909	Cardiff	Scotland	Wales	England	Ireland
1910	Belfast	Scotland	Ireland	England	Wales
1911	London	England	Wales	Scotland	Ireland
1912	Glasgow	Scotland	Ireland	England	Wales
1913	Cardiff	Scotland	Wales	Ireland	England
1914	Belfast	Scotland	Ireland	Wales	England
1915–18	Not played owing to war.				
1919	Carlisle	Scotland	England	Wales	Ireland
1920	Glasgow	Wales	England	Scotland	Ireland
1921	Cardiff	Scotland	Wales	England	Ireland
1922	Larne	Scotland	Ireland	Wales	England
1923	London	Scotland	England	Wales	Ireland
1924	Glasgow	England	Scotland	Ireland	Wales
1925	Llandrindod Wells	Wales	England	Scotland	Ireland
1926	Belfast	England	Ireland	Scotland	Wales
1927	Southampton	England	Scotland	Wales	Ireland
1928	Glasgow	Scotland	England	Ireland	Wales
1929	Llandrindod Wells	England	Wales	Scotland	Ireland
1930	Dublin	Wales	Scotland	England	Ireland
1931	Westcliff-on-Sea	Wales	Scotland	England	Ireland
1932	Glasgow	Scotland	England	Wales	Ireland
1933	Cardiff	Wales	England	Scotland	Ireland
1934	Belfast	Wales	Scotland	England	Ireland
1935	Weston-super-Mare	England	Wales	England	Ireland
1936	Glasgow	Scotland	Ireland	England	Wales
1937	Llandrindod Wells	Wales	England	Ireland	Scotland
1938	Larne	Wales	Ireland	Scotland	England
1939	London	England	Wales	Scotland	Ireland
1940–45	Not played owing to the War.				
1946	Glasgow	Wales	Scotland	England	Ireland
1947	Newport	England	Wales	Scotland	Ireland
1948	Bangor	Wales	Scotland	England	Ireland
1949	Brighton	England	Wales	Scotland	Ireland
1950	Glasgow	Scotland	Wales	England	Ireland
1951	Swansea	Ireland	England	Scotland	Wales
1952	Dublin	Scotland	Ireland	Wales	England
1953	Brighton	Scotland	Wales	England	Ireland
1954	Glasgow	England	Scotland	Wales	Ireland
1955	Cardiff	England	Wales	Ireland	Scotland
1956	Belfast	England	Ireland	Wales	Scotland
1957	Bournemouth	Wales	Scotland	England	Ireland
1958	Glasgow	England	Wales	Scotland	Ireland
1959	Cardiff	England	Scotland	Ireland	Wales

Scotland has won the Championship 19 times, England 15, Wales 11 and Ireland 2.

INTER-COUNTY CHAMPIONSHIP— MIDDLETON CUP

Games are played each year between teams from each county and the winning county holds the Middleton Cup for one year.

Each member of the winning team and runners-up receive from the Association a medal.

The games began in 1911, and the following are the results from that year.

	Winners	Runners-up
1911	Middlesex	Surrey
1912	Kent	Devon
1913	Middlesex	Sussex
1914	Surrey	Essex
1915–18	War period	
1919	Bedfordshire	Devon
1920	Surrey	Essex
1921	Surrey	Devon
1922	Bedfordshire	Berks
1923	Surrey	Kent
1924	Surrey	Middlesex
1925	Middlesex	Kent
1926	Northumberland	Essex
1927	Surrey	Cumberland and Westmorland
1928	Surrey	Devon
1929	Kent	Northumberland
1930	Northumberland	Essex
1931	Surrey	Isle of Wight
1932	Northamptonshire	Surrey
1933	Surrey	Hampshire
1934	Northamptonshire	Hampshire
1935	Hampshire	Northamptonshire
1936	Gloucestershire	Surrey
1937	Surrey	Hampshire
1938	Dorset	Durham
1939	Surrey	Northumberland
1940–44	Not played during war period	
1945	Northumberland	Hampshire
1946	Yorkshire	Sussex
1947	Yorkshire	Devon
1948	Devon	Gloucestershire
1949	Devon	Surrey
1950	Devon	Surrey
1951	Northumberland	Middlesex
1952	Middlesex	Surrey
1953	Yorkshire	Surrey
1954	Middlesex	Nottinghamshire
1955	Surrey	Somerset
1956	Sussex	Yorkshire
1957	Surrey	Northamptonshire
1958	Surrey	Buckinghamshire
1959	Devonshire	Northumberland

It will be observed that Surrey have won the Championship 14 times and have been runners-up 7 times.

Boxing

Compiled by **Jack Wilson**
Editor, Boxing News

HOW THE TITLES HAVE CHANGED HANDS

Boxing, as we know it today, is less than eighty years old. The first heavyweight title contest, fought with gloves, took place in 1892 and the fashion of using a covering for the fists has remained with us ever since. The rules that govern the sport, the Queensberry Rules, came into force around 1867, and the present rules, somewhat modified, have as their basis the twelve laws laid down by the Marquis of Queensberry.

The Queensberry Rules superseded the London Prize Ring Rules which governed bare-knuckle contests between 1838 and the advent of the noble marquis. Before the London Prize Ring Rules came into force all fights for prize-money were under Broughton's Rules. These latter regulations were the brain-child of John Broughton, known as the "Father of the English School of Boxing". Broughton taught the Noble Art, was Champion of England and is buried in Westminster Abbey.

The weight class which exists today did not apply in the last century. Quite often a welterweight (ten stone seven) would challenge a man two, three and sometimes four stone heavier. With the arrival of boxing gloves, matches were made with men at equal weight and eight classes were eventually made, from flyweight (eight stone) to heavyweight (over twelve stone seven pounds).

KEY: PTS—points; KO—knock-out; RET—retired; RSF—referee stopped fight; DISQ—disqualified; W—won; number attached to each result=round in which contest finished.

WEIGHTS AT WHICH TITLES ARE CONTESTED

Fly	8 stone and under
Bantam	8 stone 6 pounds and under
Feather	9 stone and under
Light	9 stone 9 pounds and under
Welter	10 stone 7 pounds and under
Middle	11 stone 6 pounds and under
Light-heavy	12 stone 7 pounds and under
Heavy	Any weight

Bob Fitzsimmons

HEAVYWEIGHT DIVISION

7.9.1892	James J. Corbett	W KO 21	John L. Sullivan, New Orleans
17.3.97	Bob Fitzsimmons	W KO 14	James J. Corbett, Carson City
9.6.99	James J. Jeffries	W KO 11	Bob Fitzsimmons, Coney Island

Jeffries successfully defended his title against Tom Sharkey, Corbett (twice), Fitzsimmons, Gus Ruhlin and Jack Munroe before he retired undefeated in 1904.

3.7.05	Marvin Hart	W RSF 12	Jack Root, Reno
23.2.06	Tommy Burns	W PTS 20	Marvin Hart, Los Angeles

Burns successfully defended against Jim Flynn, Philadelphia Jack O'Brien (twice), Bill Squires (three times), Gunner Moir, Jack Palmer, Jem Roche, Jewey Smith and Bill Lang.

26.12.08	Jack Johnson	W RSF 14	Tommy Burns, Sydney

Johnson became the first coloured fighter to win the World's title and reigned for nearly seven years. During this time he defended against Stanley Ketchel, Jim Jeffries (attempting a come-back), Jim Flynn, Andre Spoul and Frank Moran.

5.4.15	Jess Willard	W KO 26	Jack Johnson, Havana
4.7.19	Jack Dempsey	W KO 3	Jess Willard, Toledo

Dempsey successfully defended against Billy Miske, Bill Brennan, Georges Carpentier, Tom Gibbons and Luis Firpo.

23.9.26	Gene Tunney	W PTS 10	Jack Dempsey, Philadelphia

Tunney kept his title against Dempsey in a return contest and beat Tom Heeney before retiring undefeated.

12.6.30	Max Schmeling	W DISQ 4	Jack Sharkey, New York

Schmeling defended against Young Stribling.

Jack Dempsey

Gene Tunney

Georges Carpentier

GREAT NAMES IN BOXING

JOHN L. SULLIVAN (1858–1918). Last of the bare-knuckle heavyweight champions. Christened the "Boston Strong Boy", Sullivan was Irish-American and operated between 1878 and 1905. A boastful lion of a man, he is nevertheless revered in boxing memory. Sullivan's last fight under London Prize Ring rules was with Jake Kilrain whom he beat after 75 rounds. Lost his World title to James J. Corbett in 1892.

"GENTLEMAN" JAMES J. CORBETT (1866–1933). "Gentleman Jim" Corbett was the first World's heavyweight champion under Marquis of Queensbury rules. A former bank clerk, Corbett brought the science of self-defence back into boxing. Came into prominence when he held Peter Jackson to a draw over 61 rounds in 1891. Lost title to Bob Fitzsimmons in 1897. Made come-backs in 1900 and 1903 but was beaten each time by Jim Jeffries.

ROBERT L. FITZSIMMONS (1862–1917). Born in Helston, Cornwall, Bob Fitzsimmons is the only British-born fighter to win the World's heavyweight title. "Fitz" won immortal fame as the only boxer to win the three heaviest titles. He won the middleweight title in 1891, the heavyweight crown in 1897, and the light-heavyweight title in 1903, yet Bob never weighed much more than middleweight. He boxed until he was 52. Called a boxing "freak" due to his appearance, Fitzsimmons was long in leg and arms, freckled, knock-kneed and bony, yet he could hit like a mule, and is generally recognised as the "father" of the solar-plexus punch.

Jack Johnson

JACK JOHNSON (1878–1946). First coloured boxer to win the World's heavyweight title, Johnson is recognised as probably the greatest defensive master in the division. Defeated Tommy Burns for the title in Sydney, Australia, in 1908 and held the title until Jess Willard knocked him out in the twenty-sixth round in 1915. Lost three times in 90 contests. Born in very humble circumstances, Johnson worked in the cotton fields and horse-racing stables. Commenced boxing in 1899 and was top of the tree for almost twenty years. Killed in an automobile accident in North Carolina in 1946.

JACK DEMPSEY (1895–   ). Known as the "Manassa Mauler", Jack Dempsey is perhaps the most popular of all heavyweight champions. He had colour and won the distinction of being the first man to attract a million-dollar gate to the box-office. Won the title from Jess Willard in 1919 and lost it to Gene Tunney in 1926. Retired in 1932, but had three contests in 1940. Is the proprietor of the Jack Dempsey Restaurant in New York City, and still active as boxing and wrestling referee.

BOXING QUIZ

1. What famous Irish boxer won a World's title in Dublin, on St. Patrick's Night?

★

2. A world champion lost his first fight ever in 1959, who was he?

★

3. Who was the Brockton Blockbuster? (*above*.)

★

4. Where are the Amateur Boxing Association championships held?

★

5. How many Irishmen hold British titles?

★

6. Who are the most famous brothers in British amateur boxing?

★

7. Who was the Ambling Alp and who took his title from him?

★

8. Which country produced the most European professional champions in 1958?

★

9. Who was the first man to beat Gene Tunney?

★

10. What disability singled out Mario D'Agata from his fellow boxers?

QUIZ ANSWERS

1. Mike McTigue. 2. Pascual Perez. 3. Rocky Marciano. 4. Wembley Pool and Sports Arena, Middlesex. 5. One. Freddie Gilroy, bantam champion. 6. Harry and Fred Mallin. They each won the A.B.A. middleweight title five years in succession. 7. Primo Carnera. Max Baer. 8. Italy. They produced the champions at four weights, viz. bantam, feather, light and welterweight. 9. Harry Greb. 10. He was the first deaf-mute to win a World championship.

BOXING QUIZ

1. Who was the tallest man to win the World heavyweight title and who was the heaviest?

★

2. Who was the famous French boxer killed in an air crash in 1949?

★

3. What is the lightweight limit in (a) amateur boxing, (b) professional boxing, in this country?

★

4. How does a British boxer win a Lonsdale Belt outright?

★

5. Who was the Michigan Assassin and how did he die?

★

6. How many coloured men have won the World heavyweight title?

★

7. How many heavyweight champions of the world retired undefeated?

★

8. Who was the Brown Bomber?

★

9. How many times did Jack Dempsey and Gene Tunney meet in the ring?

★

10. How many fathers and sons have won the same title in British ring history this century? (One pair shown above.)

QUIZ ANSWERS

1. Tallest was Jess Willard at 6 ft. 6¼ in. Heaviest was Primo Carnera at 19 stone 1 pound. 2. Former World middleweight champion Marcel Cerdan. 3. (a) 9 stone 7 pounds, (b) 9 stone 9 pounds. 4. A Lonsdale Belt becomes the property of a man who wins three championship contests at one weight. They do not necessarily have to be consecutive. 5. Stanley Ketchel. He was shot to death. 6. Five. Jack Johnson, Joe Louis, Ezzard Charles, Jersey Joe Walcott and Floyd Patterson. 7. Two. Gene Tunney and Rocky Marciano. (Jim Jeffries and Joe Louis retired undefeated but made disastrous comebacks.) 8. Joe Louis. 9. Twice. Gene Tunney won each time. 10. Two. Jim "Spider" Kelly and his son Billy "Spider" Kelly won the featherweight title; Jack London and his son Brian London won the heavyweight crown.

HENRY ARMSTRONG (1912–   ). "Homicide Hank" is the only man in the ring's history to hold three World titles, at different weights, *at the same time*. Armstrong won the featherweight title in 1936 and the welter and lightweight titles, in that order, in 1938. In addition Armstrong challenged for the middleweight crown and drew with Ceferino Garcia in 1940. Henry commenced boxing in 1931 and retired in 1945. In 1951 he was ordained a minister in the Baptist Church.

Henry Armstrong

JOE GANS (1874–1910). One of the greatest lightweights ever. A brilliant boxer and often known as the "Old Master". Boxed from 1891 to 1909. Won the lightweight title twice and is remembered for his three bouts with Battling Nelson, the "Durable Dane", which covered some 81 rounds.

Freddie Welsh

OSCAR BATTLING NELSON (1882–1954). Whenever fight fans discuss gameness and durability, the name of Battling Nelson, the "Durable Dane", is always brought up as the yardstick by which all fighters are measured. Far from outstanding as a boxer, Nelson made up for this with his amazing courage and fighting instincts. He was always prepared to fight to a finish and won his battles when his rivals had reached the end of their tether. Won the lightweight title in 1905 and again in 1908 and lost the crown to Ad Wolgast in 1910 in one of the fiercest fights on record.

FREDDIE WELSH (1886–1927). A Welshman, born Frederick Hall Thomas, Freddie Welsh was an outstanding lightweight who held World, European, British Empire and British titles. First outright winner of a Lonsdale Belt, Welsh had more bouts in America than he did in Britain. Won the World's title (British version) in 1912, but gained world-wide recognition when he defeated Willie Ritchie, in London, in 1914. Lost his title to Benny Leonard in 1917.

BENNY LEONARD (1896–1947). Held the lightweight title from 1917 until 1924 when he retired. Made a come-back as a welterweight in 1931 and had considerable success until he was knocked out by Jimmy McLarnin, when he called it a day. Served in two world wars and became one of New York's leading ring officials. Collapsed and died while refereeing a bout in New York.

Date	Winner	Result		Opponent, Venue
21.6.32	Jack Sharkey	W PTS	15	Max Schmeling, Long Island
29.6.33	Primo Carnera	W KO	6	Jack Sharkey, Long Island

Carnera, the Italian giant, who weighed eighteen stone or more, defended against Paulino Uzcuden and Tommy Loughran.

14.6.34	Max Baer	W KO	11	Primo Carnera, Long Island
13.6.35	James J. Braddock	W PTS	15	Max Baer, Long Island
22.6.37	Joe Louis	W KO	8	James J. Braddock, Chicago

Joe Louis (the Brown Bomber) made more title defences than any other heavyweight in the history of the division. Between the years 1937 and 1948, when he retired, Louis beat Tommy Farr, Nathan Mann, Harry Thomas, Max Schmeling, John Henry Lewis, Jack Roper, Tony Galento, Bob Pastor, Arturo Godoy (twice), Johnny Paychek, Al McCoy, Red Burman, Gus Dorazio, Abe Simon (twice), Tony Musto, Buddy Baer (twice), Billy Conn (twice), Tami Mauriello, Lou Nova and Jersey Joe Walcott (twice).

| 22.6.49 | Ezzard Charles | W PTS | 15 | Jersey Joe Walcott, Chicago |

Charles made eight successful defences, against: Gus Lesnevich, Pat Valentino, Freddie Beshore, Joe Louis (making a come-back), Nick Barone, Lee Oma, Jersey Joe Walcott and Joey Maxim.

| 18.7.51 | Jersey Joe Walcott | W KO | 7 | Ezzard Charles, Pittsburgh |

Walcott again defeated Charles in a return match.

| 23.9.52 | Rocky Marciano | W KO | 13 | Jersey Joe Walcott, Philadelphia |

Marciano remained undefeated throughout his career until he retired in 1956. He beat, in turn, Jersey Joe Walcott, for the second time, Roland LaStarza, Ezzard Charles (twice), Don Cockell and Archie Moore.

30.11.56	Floyd Patterson	W KO	5	Archie Moore, Chicago
29.7.57	Floyd Patterson	W RSF	10	Tommy Jackson, New York
22.8.57	Floyd Patterson	W KO	6	Pete Rademacher, Seattle
18.8.58	Floyd Patterson	W RET	12	Roy Harris, Los Angeles
1.5.59	Floyd Patterson	W KO	11	Brian London, Indianapolis
26.6.59	Ingemar Johansson	W RSF	3	Floyd Patterson, New York

Left: James J. Braddock. *Above:* Max Schmeling, Joe Louis. *Below:* Max Baer, Ingemar Johansson.

LIGHT-HEAVYWEIGHT DIVISION

| 22.4.03 | Jack Root | W PTS | 10 | Kid McCoy, Detroit |

This was the first official match at a new weight. Both McCoy (a former middleweight champion) and Root had outgrown middleweight and yet they were too light to tackle heavyweights. Lou Houseman, a Chicago sportswriter and boxing promoter-cum-manager, hit upon the idea of making a match at a new weight, midway between middle (limit eleven stone six pounds) and heavyweight (more than twelve stone seven pounds). He also managed Root.

4.7.03	George Gardner	W KO	12	Jack Root, Fort Erie
25.11.03	Bob Fitzsimmons	W PTS	20	George Gardner, San Francisco
20.12.05	Philadelphia Jack O'Brien	W KO	13	Bob Fitzsimmons, San Francisco

Fitzsimmons, who never scaled much more than a middleweight, won the middles title in 1891, the heavyweight crown in 1897 and was 41 when he won the light-heavyweight title. Born in Cornwall, Fitz is the only man to have won the three heaviest weight titles.

| 28.11.06 | Phil. Jack O'Brien | DREW | 20 | Tommy Burns, Los Angeles |

As Burns was reigning heavyweight champ and O'Brien holder of the light-heavy title and the match was made at the cruiser poundage, both titles were at stake. A draw left each man champion at their respective weights.

| 8.5.07 | Tommy Burns | W PTS | 20 | Phil. Jack O'Brien, Los Angeles |
| 28.4.14 | Jack Dillon | W PTS | 10 | Al Norton, Kansas City |

Dillon claimed the title when Burns elected to let the championship slide into obscurity. Following his victory over Norton, Dillon beat Battling Levinsky and Tim O'Neill.

| 24.10.16 | Battling Levinsky | W PTS | 12 | Jack Dillon, Boston |
| 12.10.20 | Georges Carpentier | W KO | 4 | Battling Levinsky, New York |

Carpentier defeated Ted (Kid) Lewis in London.

| 24.9.22 | Battling Siki | W KO | 6 | Georges Carpentier, Paris |

This was the notorious bout which ended when the referee announced that Siki was disqualified 'for tripping', after the coloured man had overwhelmed the Pride of France and left him an unconscious heap in the middle of the canvas in the sixth round. Pandemonium broke out in the crowd and after half an hour the judges rescinded the referee's decision and Siki was announced the new champion, on a knock-out.

| 17.3.23 | Mike McTigue | W PTS | 20 | Battling Siki, Dublin |

Siki, an over-rated fighter, asked for trouble when he elected to defend his title against an Irishman, in Dublin, on St. Patrick's Night during the heart of the Irish Rebellion.

| 31.5.25 | Paul Berlanbach | W PTS | 15 | Mike McTigue, New York |

Berlanbach successfully defended against Jimmy Slattery, Jack Delaney and Young Stribling.

| 16.7.26 | Jack Delaney | W PTS | 15 | Paul Berlanbach, Brooklyn |

Len Harvey v. Jock McAvoy 1939   Freddie Mills v. Gus Lesnevich 1948

Light-Heavyweight Division—contd.

7.10.27	Tommy Loughran	W PTS 15	Mike McTigue, New York	

Loughran got his chance when Delaney relinquished the crown to campaign against the leading heavyweights. The handsome Philadelphian defended his title six times in less than two years, against Jimmy Slattery, Leo Lomski, Pete Latzo (twice), Mickey Walker (the middleweight titleholder of that period) and James J. Braddock, before deciding to try his luck among the heavies.

10.2.30	Jimmy Slattery	W PTS 15	Lou Scozza, Buffalo
25.6.30	Maxie Rosenbloom	W PTS 15	Jimmy Slattery, New York

'Slapsie Maxie', later to become well known as a stooge-cum-comedian, on stage, screen and T.V., held the crown for more than three years and defended against Abe Bain, Jimmy Slattery, Lou Scozza, Al Stillman, Ad Heuser, Bob Goodwin, Mickey Walker and Joe Knight.

16.11.34	Bob Olin	W PTS 15	Maxie Rosenbloom, New York
31.10.35	John Henry Lewis	W PTS 15	Bob Olin, St. Louis

Lewis kept his laurels in face of challenges from Jock McAvoy, Len Harvey, Bob Olin, Emilo Martinez and Al Gainer. He was forced to give up the title through failing eyesight.

28.11.38	Tiger Jack Fox	W PTS 15	Al Gainer, New York
3.2.39	Melio Bettina	W RSF 9	Tiger Jack Fox, New York
10.7.39	Len Harvey	W PTS 15	Jock McAvoy, London

Britain refused to recognise the men put up in America as successors to John Henry Lewis. Both Harvey and McAvoy had given Lewis a run for his money and the British pairing won support in many parts of the globe. Throughout the war years and until Mills met Lesnevich in 1946, there were two claimants to the title.

13.7.39	Billy Conn	W PTS 15	Melio Bettina, Pittsburgh

Conn twice outpointed Lesnevich over fifteen rounds in defence of his crown.

13.1.41	Anton Christoforidis	W PTS 15	Melio Bettina, Cleveland
22.5.41	Gus Lesnevich	W PTS 15	Anton Christoforidis, New York

Lesnevich twice outpointed Tami Mauriello in title defences.

20.6.42	Freddie Mills	W KO 2	Len Harvey, London
14.5.46	Gus Lesnevich	W RSF 10	Freddie Mills, London

Lesnevich twice beat Billy Fox in title defences.

26.7.48	Freddie Mills	W PTS 15	Gus Lesnevich, London
24.1.50	Joey Maxim	W KO 10	Freddie Mills, London

Maxim successfully defended against Bob Murphy and Ray Robinson. 'Sugar Ray', welterweight champion from 1946 to 1950, was reigning middleweight champion when he challenged Maxim, but was overcome by the excessive heat and retired after thirteen rounds.

Archie Moore v. Yolande Pompey 1956

17.12.52	Archie Moore	W PTS 15	Joey Maxim, St. Louis
24.6.53	Archie Moore	W PTS 15	Joey Maxim, Ogden
27.1.54	Archie Moore	W PTS 15	Joey Maxim, Miami
11.8.54	Archie Moore	W RSF 14	Harold Johnson, New York
22.6.55	Archie Moore	W KO 3	Carl 'Bobo' Olson, New York
5.6.56	Archie Moore	W RSF 10	Yolande Pompey, London
20.9.57	Archie Moore	W RSF 7	Tony Anthony, Los Angeles
10.12.58	Archie Moore	W KO 11	Yvon Durelle, Montreal
12.8.59	Archie Moore	W KO 3	Yvon Durelle, Montreal

The phenomenal Moore is not only the World's longest reigning champion (six years) but also the oldest champion. On his licence Moore's birthday is given as December 13, 1916, but his mother says he is at least three years older than this.

JOE LOUIS (1914–). The "Brown Bomber" started boxing in 1934, won the World's heavyweight title in 1937 and held it until 1948—against 25 challengers —when he retired undefeated. Made a come-back in 1950 and was beaten by Ezzard Charles in a title bout. Challenged Rocky Marciano for the title in the following year and was stopped in eight rounds. A great boxer with a great punch in both hands, Louis is classed by many critics as the greatest heavyweight of all time.

GEORGES CARPENTIER (1894–). The "Idol of France", Georges Carpentier is recognised as the greatest French boxer of all time. Started boxing at the age of fourteen and won every French and European title from welterweight to heavyweight. Lost to Dempsey for the World's heavyweight crown; won the light-heavyweight title by defeating Battling Levinsky in 1920 and lost it to Battling Siki in 1922; lost to Frank Klaus and Billy Papke in World middleweight title bouts. One of the "household names" in boxing, Carpentier now runs a dressmaking shop in Paris with his wife.

ARCHIE MOORE (1916–). Present-day light-heavyweight champion of the world, Moore has held the title since 1952. His mother says he is three years older than the age given on his licence, which makes the phenomenal Moore something like 46. Boxed for a great number of years before he won recognition. A terrific puncher and wonderful craftsman, Moore has an uncanny knack of shedding something like a stone and a half for his cruiser title defences. When Rocky Marciano retired in 1956, Moore, who was Marciano's last title challenger, met Floyd Patterson for the vacant title and was knocked out in the fifth round.

Ted (Kid) Lewis

TED (KID) LEWIS (1894–). Born in the East End of London, Ted Lewis is one of the greats of British and World rings. Lewis won the World's welterweight title during the First World War and held European titles at feather, welter and middleweight. In addition Lewis won the British featherweight crown (1913), welterweight title (1920–4) and middleweight titles between 1920 and 1923. Started boxing in 1910 and boxed until 1929. Lewis boxed at every weight from bantam to heavy. Engaged in more than 400 contests.

RAY ROBINSON (1920–). The fabulous "Sugar Ray", real name Walker Smith, was World's welterweight champion from 1946 to 1950, and middleweight champion, on and off, from 1951 to the present day. A great amateur boxer, Ray turned professional in 1940. A graceful, scintillating fighter, Robinson is publicity conscious and travels around with a large and varied entourage. The vast moneys he has earned in the ring have been sensibly invested in real estate and industry. "Sugar Ray" lost his middleweight title to Randy Turpin in London in 1951 and re-won it in New York two months later. Robinson also re-won the crown after losing it to Gene Fullmer and Carmen Basilio. Retired in 1952 to take up a dancing career on the stage, but came back, with obvious results, in 1955.

Sugar Ray Robinson v. Randolph Turpin 1951

BOXING QUIZ

1. How many British titles did Len Harvey win?

★

2. Did Edward Govier win a British or a World championship?

★

3. Where will the next Olympic Games be held?

★

4. What nationality was Dave Sands?

★

5. How many times did Ezzard Charles and Jersey Joe Walcott meet in World title contests?

★

6. What famous Liverpool middleweight boxed for the Danish title?

★

7. Which weight-class in boxing was created last?

★

8. Who is the youngest World champion at present?

★

9. How many present-day World champions won an Olympic Gold Medal?

★

10. Who was the first prominent boxer to use gumshields and who originated them?

QUIZ ANSWERS

1. Three. Heavy, light-heavy and middleweight. 2. He won both. Edward Govier was Terry Allen of Islington. 3. Rome. 4. Australian. 5. Four. 6. Martin Hansen. He was born in Liverpool, but spent most of his boxing life in Denmark before returning to this country a few years ago. 7. Flyweight. Created in England around 1910. 8. Joe Becerra (Mexico) World bantamweight champion, born in 1936. 9. One. Pascual Perez. 10. Ted (Kid) Lewis. They were the invention of London dentist Jack Marks, in 1902.

GEORGE DIXON (1870–1909). Born in Nova Scotia, Dixon was one of the greatest fighters in ring history. Won both bantam and featherweight titles and fought for twenty years. Nicknamed "Little Chocolate", Dixon was amazingly clever and a hard puncher. Was a great favourite at the old National Sporting Club in London, where he met, among others, Spike Robson, Pedlar Palmer, Ben Jordan, Digger Stanley and Will Curley. Held a World's title for more than ten years.

TERRY McGOVERN (1880–1918). Known as "Terrible Terry", McGovern won both bantam and featherweight World titles and won nine title bouts by a knockout. Lost his featherweight crown to Young Corbett in 1901. The Irish-American later boxed as a lightweight, but retired in 1908.

Jim Driscoll

JIM DRISCOLL (1881–1925). Born in Cardiff, "Peerless Jim" Driscoll was perhaps the finest exponent of the straight left that the Game has ever known. When he died from pneumonia in January, 1925, the streets of Cardiff were lined with mourners. Driscoll fought the then reigning champion, Abe Attell, a ten-rounds no-decision bout in 1909, won the newspaper decision and claimed the World's title. Held the British featherweight title from 1906 until 1913, and also won the European crown.

WILLIE PEP (1922–   ). Commenced boxing in 1940 and retired in 1959. Won the World's featherweight title for the first time in 1942, lost it to Sandy Saddler in 1948, but re-won the crown in 1949 before finally losing his laurels in 1950. Won more than 200 contests. Born William Papaleo.

HOGAN BASSEY (1932–   ). Born in Calabar, Nigeria, Bassey learned his trade in British rings and won the World's featherweight title in 1957. Started boxing in 1949 in Nigeria, came to Britain in 1952 and is based at Liverpool. Won the Empire title in 1955. Awarded an M.B.E. in the 1958 New Year Honours List.

MIDDLEWEIGHT DIVISION

30.8.1884 Jack Dempsey   W KO 22   George Fulljames, Toronto
Dempsey (The Nonpareil) retained his title against Jack Fogarty, George LaBlanche, and Johnny Reagan.

27.8.1889 George LaBlanche   W KO 32   Jack Dempsey, San Francisco
Dempsey retained his title because LaBlanche used the pivot punch which was subsequently declared illegal.

18.2.1890 Jack Dempsey   W 28   Australian Bill McCarthy, San Francisco

14.1.1891 Bob Fitzsimmons   W KO 13   Jack Dempsey, New Orleans
When Fitzsimmons went after the big fellows and left the middleweight title open there were several claimants to the crown including Kid McCoy and Tommy Ryan, both of whom had won the welterweight championship.

18.6.1898 Tommy Ryan   W KO 14   Tommy West, New York
Ryan defended against Jack Bonner, Frank Craig, Tommy West, Kid Carter and Johnny Gorman.

4.7.1907 Stanley Ketchel   DREW 20   Joe Thomas, Marysville

2.9.07 Stanley Ketchel   W KO 32   Joe Thomas, San Francisco
Ketchel, known as the Michigan Assassin, and one of the toughest fighters ever to lace on a glove, retained his title against Joe Thomas on two further occasions, and against Mike Twin Sullivan (twice), Billy Papke and Hugo Kelly.

7.9.08 Billy Papke   W KO 12   Stanley Ketchel, Los Angeles

26.11.08 Stanley Ketchel   W KO 11   Billy Papke, San Francisco
Ketchel gave Papke yet another chance to take the title away but Ketchel proved the master. Towards the end of 1909 he challenged Jack Johnson for the heavyweight crown and was knocked out in the twelfth round after putting Johnson on the canvas. Ketchel came to a sticky end when he was shot dead in 1910.

19.3.10 Billy Papke   W KO 3   Willie Lewis, Paris

11.2.11 Johnny Thompson   W PTS 20   Billy Papke, Sydney

8.6.11 Billy Papke   W KO 9   Jim Sullivan, London

22.2.12 Frank Mantell   W PTS 20   Billy Papke, Sacramento
After Ketchel's death there were several claimants to the middleweight title. Among those who won and defended the 'title' around the same time were Mantell, Papke, Frank Klaus, Pat O'Keefe, George Chip, Al McCoy, Jeff Smith, Les Darcy, Mike O'Dowd, Johnny Wilson and Jock Malone. Then Harry Greb appeared on the scene and soon won world-wide recognition.

Marcel Cerdan   **Tony Zale**   **Jimmy McLarnin**

31.8.23 Harry Greb   W PTS 15   Johnny Wilson, New York
Greb retained his laurels against Bryan Downey, Johnny Wilson, Fay Keiser, Ted Moore, Mickey Walker and Tony Marulla.

26.2.26 Tiger Flowers   W PTS 15   Harry Greb, New York
Flowers defeated Greb again in the same year.

3.12.26 Mickey Walker   W PTS 10   Tiger Flowers, Chicago
Walker (the Toy Bulldog) defended against Tommy Milligan, Ace Hudkins (twice) and Willie Oster, before relinquishing the crown to campaign in the light-heavyweight class.

25.8.31 Gorilla Jones   W PTS 10   Tiger Flowers, Milwaukee
Jones kept his title by defeating Oddone Piazza and Young Terry.

11.6.32 Marcel Thil   W DISQ 11   Gorilla Jones, Paris
Thil defended against Len Harvey in London.

11.11.32 Ben Jeby   W PTS 15   Chuck Devlin, New York
Jeby gained recognition by the New York Commission. Thil was recognised in Europe and parts of America and another titleholder, or rather an old one, Gorilla Jones, claimed the title once more when he beat Sammy Slaughter in 1933. For the next nine years the middleweight title was in constant dispute by Jeby, Thil and the men who beat them under championship conditions, viz. Lou Brouillard, Vince Dundee, Teddy Yarosz, Ed Risko, Freddie Steele, Fred Apostoli, Al Hostak, Solly Kreiger, Ceferino Garcia, Ken Overlin, Tony Zale and Billy Soose. When Zale opposed Georgie Abrams in 1941 he at last won full world support.

28.11.41 Tony Zale   W PTS 15   Georgie Abrams, New York
Zale successfully defended against Rocky Graziano.

16.7.47 Rocky Graziano   W KO 6   Tony Zale, Chicago

10.6.48 Tony Zale   W KO 3   Rocky Graziano, Newark

21.9.48 Marcel Cerdan   W RSF 12   Tony Zale, Jersey City

16.6.49 Jake LaMotta   W RET 10   Marcel Cerdan, Detroit
Cerdan was killed in an air-crash in the Azores in October 1949 while on the way back to New York to meet LaMotta in a return contest. LaMotta retained his title against Tiberio Mitri and Laurent Dauthuille.

14.2.51 Ray Robinson   W RSF 13   Jake LaMotta, Chicago

10.7.51 Randolph Turpin   W PTS 15   Ray Robinson, London

12.9.51 Ray Robinson   W RSF 10   Randolph Turpin, New York
Robinson, who held the welterweight title from 1946 until 1950, beat Carl 'Bobo' Olson and Rocky Graziano in title defences, and then announced retirement in 1952 after challenging for the cruiserweight crown.

9.6.53 Randolph Turpin   W PTS 15   Charles Humez, London
Recognised only in Britain and France.

21.10.53 Carl 'Bobo' Olson   W PTS 15   Randolph Turpin, New York
Olson retained title against Kid Gavilan, Rocky Castellani and Pierre Langlois.

9.12.55 Ray Robinson   W KO 2   Carl 'Bobo' Olson, Chicago
After an extensive tour on the stages of the world, where he shone as a dancer, Robinson proved the old adage that they never come back to be wrong. He beat Olson again in 1956.

2.1.57 Gene Fullmer   W PTS 15   Ray Robinson, New York

1.5.57 Ray Robinson   W KO 5   Gene Fullmer, Chicago

23.9.57 Carmen Basilio   W PTS 15   Ray Robinson, New York

25.3.58 Ray Robinson   W PTS 15   Carmen Basilio, Chicago
Robinson fully earned the title 'Fabulous' when he won the middleweight title for the fifth time at the age of 38. He also proved that Chicago was his lucky city. The N.B.A. of America took Robinson's title away from him in May, 1959, for failing to defend the championship in the given period.

WELTERWEIGHT DIVISION

14.12.1892 'Mysterious' Billy Smith W KO 14 Danny Needham, San Francisco
Smith retained title against Tom Williams.

26.7.94 Tommy Ryan W PTS 20 Myst. Billy Smith, Minneapolis
Ryan drew with Smith in a return bout.

2.3.96 Kid McCoy W PTS 15 Tommy Ryan, Long Island

14.4.98 Myst. Billy Smith DREW 25 Joe Walcott, Bridgeport
Smith retained title against Matty Matthews, Charles McKeever, Joe Walcott, Billy Edwards, Kid Lavigne, drew with McKeever and then beat McKeever again in their third meeting.

15.1.1900 Rube Ferns W DISQ 21 Myst. Billy Smith, Buffalo

16.10.00 Matty Matthews W PTS 15 Rube Ferns, Detroit
Matthews successfully defended against Tom Couhig.

24.5.01 Rube Ferns W KO 10 Matty Matthews, Toronto
Ferns retained title against Frank Erne.

18.12.01 Joe Walcott W KO 5 Rube Ferns, Fort Erie
Walcott retained title against Tommy West.

30.4.04 Dixie Kid W DISQ 20 Joe Walcott, San Francisco
Dixie Kid drew with Walcott in a return contest, then outgrew the class and Walcott re-claimed title.

16.10.06 Billy 'Honey' Mellody W PTS 15 Joe Walcott, Chelsea (U.S.A.)

23.4.07 Mike Twin Sullivan W PTS 20 'Honey' Mellody, Los Angeles
Sullivan became a middleweight and for several years there were many claimants to the title including Harry Lewis, Dixie Kid, Waldemar Holberg, Tom McCormick, Matt Wells, Mike Glover, Jack Britton, Ted (Kid) Lewis and Jimmy Clabby.

25.6.17 Ted (Kid) Lewis W PTS 20 Jack Britton, Dayton
Lewis defended against Johnny Griffiths, Albert Badoud, Johnny Tillman and Benny Leonard.

17.3.19 Jack Britton W KO 9 Ted (Kid) Lewis, Canton
Britton retained his crown against Johnny Griffiths, Lou Bogash, Ted (Kid) Lewis, Dave Shade and Benny Leonard. Britton and Ted Lewis met twenty times in all, eleven times in no-decision bouts.

1.2.22 Mickey Walker W PTS 15 Jack Britton, New York
Walker retained his title against Pete Latzo, Lew Tendler, Bobby Barrett and Dave Shade.

20.5.26 Pete Latzo W PTS 10 Mickey Walker, Scranton
Latzo defended against Willie Harmon and George Levine.

3.6.27 Joe Dundee W PTS 15 Pete Latzo, New York
Dundee held his title against Hilario Martinez.

30.8.28 Young Jack Thompson W RSF 2 Joe Dundee, Chicago

25.3.29 Jackie Fields W PTS 10 Young Jack Thompson, Chicago
Fields held the title against Joe Dundee.

9.5.30 Young Jack Thompson W PTS 15 Jackie Fields, Detroit

5.9.30 Tommy Freeman W PTS 15 Young Jack Thompson, Cleveland
Freeman defended against Pete August, Eddie Murdock, Duke Trammel, Al (Kid) Kober, and Alfredo Gaona.

14. 4.31 Young Jack Thompson W KO 12 Tommy Freeman, Cleveland

23.10.31 Lou Brouillard W PTS 15 Young Jack Thompson, Boston

28.1.32 Jackie Fields W PTS 10 Lou Brouillard, Chicago

22.2.33 Young Corbett III W PTS 10 Jackie Fields, San Francisco

29.5.33 Jimmy McLarnin W KO 1 Young Corbett III, Los Angeles

28.5.34 Barney Ross W PTS 15 Jimmy McLarnin, New York

17.9.34 Jimmy McLarnin W PTS 15 Barney Ross, New York

28.5.35 Barney Ross W PTS 15 Jimmy McLarnin, New York
Ross defended against Izzy Jannazzo and Ceferino Garcia.

31.5.38 Henry Armstrong W PTS 15 Barney Ross, New York
Armstrong was featherweight champion of the world when he annexed the welter crown from Ross. Three months later he was to win the lightweight title and make history as the only man to hold three world titles at one and the same time. As welter champion, Armstrong defended against Ceferino Garcia, Al Manfredo (twice), Baby Arizmendi, Bobby Pacho (twice), Lew Feldman, Davey Day, Ernie Roderick, Howard Scott, Ritchie Fontaine, Jimmy Garrison (twice), Joe Ghnouly, Pedro Montanez, Paul Junior (twice), Ralph Zanelli, Lew Jenkins and Phil Furr.

4.10.40 Fritzie Zivic W PTS 15 Henry Armstrong, New York
Zivic drew with Lew Jenkins in a title defence, and beat Armstrong again.

Ray Robinson   Kid Gavilan   Carmen Basilio

29.7.41 Freddie Red Cochrane W PTS 15 Fritzie Zivic, Newark
Cochrane enlisted in the U.S. Navy and the title was not contested for more than four years.

1.2.46 Marty Servo W KO 4 Freddie Red Cochrane, New York
Servo retired in 1947.

20.12.46 Ray Robinson W PTS 15 Tommy Bell, New York
Robinson defended against Jimmy Doyle, Chuck Taylor, Bernard Docusen, Kid Gavilan and Charlie Fusari.

14.3.51 Johnny Bratton W PTS 15 Charlie Fusari, Chicago

18.5.51 Kid Gavilan W PTS 15 Johnny Bratton, New York
Gavilan defended against Billy Graham (twice), Bobby Dykes, Gil Turner, Chuck Davey, Carmen Basilio and Johnny Bratton.

20.10.54 Johnny Saxton W PTS 15 Kid Gavilan, Philadelphia.

1.4.55 Tony DeMarco W RSF 14 Johnny Saxton, Boston

10.6.55 Carmen Basilio W RSF 12 Tony DeMarco, Syracuse
Basilio defeated DeMarco in a return contest.

14.3.56 Johnny Saxton W PTS 15 Carmen Basilio, Chicago

12.9.56 Carmen Basilio W RSF 9 Johnny Saxton, Syracuse
Basilio defeated Saxton again in 1957 and then won the middleweight title from Ray Robinson and relinquished the welter crown.

6.6.58 Virgil Akins W RSF 4 Vince Martinez, St. Louis

5.12.58 Don Jordan W PTS 15 Virgil Akins, Los Angeles

24.4.59 Don Jordan W PTS 15 Virgil Akins, St. Louis

11.7.59 Don Jordan W PTS 15 Denny Moyer, Portland

PANAMA AL BROWN (1902–1951). Born Alphonse Theo Brown in Panama, Brown won the World's bantam title in 1929 and held the crown until 1935. Tall for a featherweight, he was nearly six feet. Brown defended his title against all-comers and was successful on twelve occasions in keeping his title. He out-pointed British champion Johnny King at Manchester in 1933. Brown boxed from 1922 until 1944.

Manuel Ortiz

MANUEL ORTIZ (1917–). Born in California of Mexican descent, Ortiz was champion of the bantamweight division from 1942 until 1950. He made twenty-one successful defences of his crown. Lost to Harold Dade in 1947, but re-won the crown within ten weeks. Finally lost his title to South African Vic Toweel, at Johannesburg, in 1950. Was beaten by British featherweight champion Ronnie Clayton while still World's bantam champ.

JIMMY CARRUTHERS (1929–). Australian-born Carruthers took part in only nineteen contests between 1950 and 1954. He won every bout and defeated Vic Toweel for the World's bantam crown in 1952. Retained his title against Toweel in a return and defended against Pappy Gault and Chamrern Songkitrat before retiring undefeated. Now runs a hotel in Australia.

Jimmy Wilde

JIMMY WILDE (1892–). The "Mighty Atom" never weighed much more than 7 stone 7 pounds, yet he flattened men a stone or more heavier. His punching had wonderful timing and Wilde won most of his contests inside the distance. Won the World's flyweight title in 1916 and held the honours until 1923. Like Fitzsimmons, Wilde looked a freak in the ring. Of boyish appearance, he was small, skinny and pale-faced. But when he hit he had the power of a donkey's hind legs in his arms.

BENNY LYNCH (1913–1946). World's flyweight champion 1935 to 1937. Died a tragic death at the age of thirty-three, due to his love for the contents of a bottle. Started boxing at the age of eight. Won the British title in 1935. Lost his World's title on the scales when he was due to defend against Jackie Jurich of America. Contracted to be under 8 stone, Lynch weighed-in on the day of the fight at 8 stone 6 pounds 8 ounces. A great boxer, a tragic figure, Lynch left a host of memories and was sadly missed.

BOXING QUIZ

1. Who is the General Secretary of the British Boxing Board of Control and what was he previous to this appointment?

*

2. What former World champion was reputed to have run errands, when a boy, for renowned gangster Al Capone? (*above.*)

*

3. What have these famous ex-boxers in common—Tommy Farr, Freddie Mills and Ernie Jarvis?

4. Can you name two sets of boxing twins, active in this country in the professional ranks?

*

5. Promoter Jack Solomons managed a former British lightweight champion. Can you name the boxer? (*above.*)

*

6. Who was the Canadian heavyweight who beat Primo Carnera in this country? He was managed by present-day promoter, Harry Levene.

QUIZ ANSWERS

1. Mr. E. J. (Teddy) Waltham, former Star referee and Waltham Cross welterweight. 2. Barney Ross, former World light- and welterweight champion. 3. They are present-day boxing journalists. 4. The Coopers (Henry and Jim) and the Howards (Johnny and Alan). 5. Eric Boon. 6. Larry Gains.

LIGHTWEIGHT DIVISION

Arthur Chambers of England and Jack McAuliffe of America laid claim to the World's lightweight title between the years 1872 and 1892.

1.6.1894 George (Kid) Lavigne W KO 17 Dick Burge, London
Lavigne defeated against Jack Everhardt, Kid McPartland, Eddie Connolly, Joe Walcott, Jack Daly, Frank Erne and Tom Tracey.

3.7.1899 Frank Erne W PTS 20 George (Kid) Lavigne, Buffalo
Erne drew with Jack O'Brien and defeated Joe Gans in title contests.

12.5.02 Joe Gans W KO 1 Frank Erne, Fort Erie
Gans defeated Gus Gardner in a title defence. Another claimant about this time was Jimmy Britt, who defeated Frank Erne and Jabez White before losing to Battling Nelson. Meantime Gans defeated Steve Crosby and Jimmy Britt in title bouts that carried an official label.

3.9.06 Joe Gans W DISQ 42 Battling Nelson, Goldfield
Gans successfully defended against Jimmy Britt, George Memsic, Spike Robson, and Rudy Unholz.

4.7.08 Battling Nelson W KO 17 Joe Gans, San Francisco
Nelson defeated Gans again and also Dick Hyland and Jack Clifford in title defences.

22.2.10 Ad Wolgast W KO 40 Battling Nelson, Port Richmond
Wolgast successfully defended against George Memsic, Antonio La Grave, One-Round Hogan, Frankie Burns, Owen Moran and Mexican Joe Rivers.

Benny Leonard

Jimmy Carter

Joe Brown

28.11.12 Willie Ritchie W DISQ 16 Ad Wolgast, Daly City
Ritchie retained his title against Joe Rivers and Tommy Murphy. In Britain at this time, Freddie Welsh gained recognition as World's champion when he defeated Hughie Mehegan, and a meeting between Ritchie and Welsh was a 'natural'.

7.7.14 Freddie Welsh W PTS 20 Willie Ritchie, London
Welsh retained his title against Ad Wolgast and Charlie White.

28.5.17 Benny Leonard W KO 9 Freddie Welsh, New York
Leonard retained his title against Johnny Kilbane, Charlie White, Joe Welling, Richie Mitchell, Rocky Kansas (thrice) and Lew Tendler (twice). Leonard retired undefeated in 1925, but made a come-back in 1931 as a welterweight.

3.7.25 Jimmy Goodrich W KO 2 Stanislaus Loayza, Long Island
Goodrich won a lightweight tournament organised by the New York Commission and became recognised as champion.

7.12.25 Rocky Kansas W PTS 15 Jimmy Goodrich, New York

3.7.26 Sammy Mandell W PTS 10 Rocky Kansas, Chicago
Mandell retained his title against Jimmy McLarnin and Tony Canzoneri.

17.7.30 Al Singer W KO 1 Sammy Mandell, New York

14.11.30 Tony Canzoneri W KO 1 Al Singer, New York
Canzoneri retained his title against Jack (Kid) Berg (twice), Cecil Payne, Kid Chocolate and Billy Petrolle.

23.6.33 Barney Ross W PTS 10 Tony Canzoneri, Chicago
Ross beat Canzoneri in a return title contest.

10.5.35 Tony Canzoneri W PTS 15 Lou Ambers, New York
Canzoneri defeated Al Roth in a title defence.

3.9.36 Lou Ambers W PTS 15 Tony Canzoneri, New York
Ambers defeated Canzoneri in a return, also Pedro Montanez.

17.8.38 Henry Armstrong W PTS 15 Lou Ambers, New York

22.8.39 Lou Ambers W PTS 15 Henry Armstrong, New York

10.5.40 Lew Jenkins W KO 3 Lou Ambers, New York
Jenkins successfully defended against Pete Lello. Another claimant to the title at this time was Sammy Angott, on the strength of a win over Davey Day in 1940.

19.12.41 Sammy Angott W PTS 15 Lew Jenkins, New York
Angott defended against Allie Stolz. Now yet another claimant appeared on the scene in the figure of Beau Jack, who won recognition in New York State for his victory against Tippy Larkin. Slugger White also claimed the title.

21.5.43 Bob Montgomery W PTS 15 Beau Jack, New York

27.10.43 Sammy Angott W PTS 15 Slugger White, Los Angeles

19.11.43 Beau Jack W PTS 15 Bob Montgomery, New York

3.3.44 Bob Montgomery W PTS 15 Beau Jack, New York

8.3.44 Juan Zurita W PTS 15 Sammy Angott, Hollywood

18.4.45 Ike Williams W KO 2 Juan Zurita, Mexico City
The National Boxing Association of America recognised Williams, while New York Commission upheld Montgomery's claims. Williams defended his title against Enrique Bolanos and Ronnie James; Montgomery beat Allie Stolz and Wesley Mouzon.

4.8.47 Ike Williams W KO 6 Bob Montgomery, Philadelphia
Now undisputed World lightweight titleholder, Williams retained his crown against Enrique Bolanos (twice), Beau Jack, Jesse Flores and Freddie Dawson.

25.5.51 Jimmy Carter W RSF 14 Ike Williams, New York
Carter retained his title against Art Aragon and Lauro Salas.

14.5.52 Lauro Salas W PTS 15 Jimmy Carter, Los Angeles

15.10.52 Jimmy Carter W PTS 15 Lauro Salas, Chicago
Carter retained his title against Tommy Collins, George Araujo and Armand Savoie.

5.3.54 Paddy DeMarco W PTS 15 Jimmy Carter, New York

17.11.54 Jimmy Carter W RSF 15 Paddy DeMarco, San Francisco

29.6.55 Wallace (Bud) Smith W PTS 15 Jimmy Carter, Boston
Smith retained his title in a return bout with Carter.

24.8.56 Joe Brown W PTS 15 Wallace (Bud) Smith, New Orleans

13.2.57 Joe Brown W RSF 10 Wallace (Bud) Smith, Miami

19.6.57 Joe Brown W RSF 15 Orlando Zulueta, Denver

4.12.57 Joe Brown W RSF 11 Joe Lopes, Chicago

7.5.58 Joe Brown W RSF 8 Ralph Dupas, Houston

23.7.58 Joe Brown W PTS 15 Kenny Lane, Houston

11.2.59 Joe Brown W PTS 15 Johnny Busso, Houston

3.6.59 Joe Brown W RSF 8 Pavlo Rosi, Washington

AMATEUR BOXING ASSOCIATION CHAMPIONS SINCE 1881

HEAVYWEIGHT

1881	R. Frost-Smith	1919 H. Brown
1882	H. Dearsley	1920 R. Rawson
1883	H. Dearsley	1921 R. Rawson
1884	H. Dearsley	1922 T. Evans
1885	W. West	1923 E. Eagan
1886	A. Diamond	1924 A. Clifton
1887	E. White	1925 Lt. D. Lister
1888	W. King	1926 T. Petersen
1889	A. Bowman	1927 Lt. C. Capper
1890	J. Steers	1928 J. O'Driscoll
1891	V. Barker	1929 H. Floyd
1892	J. Steers	1930 V. Stuart
1893	J. Steers	1931 M. Flanaghan
1894	H. King	1932 V. Stuart
1895	Capt. W. Edgeworth Johnstone	1933 C. O'Grady
		1934 H. Floyd
		1935 H. Floyd
1896	Capt. W. Edgeworth Johnstone	1936 V. Stuart
		1937 V. Stuart
		1938 G. Preston
1897	G. Townsend	1939 A. Porter
1898	G. Townsend	1940–1943
1899	F. Parks	No Competition
1900	W. Dees	1944 M. Hart
1901	F. Parks	1945 D. Scott
1902	F. Parks	1946 H. Floyd
1903	E. Dickson	1947 G. Scriven
1904	A. Horner	1948 J. Gardner
1905	F. Parks	1949 A. Worrall
1906	F. Parks	1950 P. Toch
1907	H. Brewer	1951 A. Halsey
1908	S. Evans	1952 E. Hearn
1909	C. Brown	1953 J. Erskine
1910	F. Storbeck	1954 B. Harper
1911	W. Hazell	1955 D. Rowe
1912	R. Smith	1956 D. Rent
1913	R. Smith	1957 D. Thomas
1914	E. Chandler	1958 D. Thomas
1915–1918		1959 D. Thomas
No Competition		

LIGHT-HEAVYWEIGHT

1920	H. Franks	1939 B. Woodcock
1921	L. Collett	1940–1943
1922	H. Mitchell	No Competition
1923	H. Mitchell	1944 E. Shackleton
1924	H. Mitchell	1945 A. Watson
1925	H. Mitchell	1946 J. Taylor
1926	D. McCorkindale	1947 A. Watson
		1948 D. Scott
1927	A. Jackson	1949 Declared no
1928	A. Jackson	contest
1929	J. Goyder	1950 P. Messervy
1930	J. Murphy	1951 G. Walker
1931	J. Petersen	1952 H. Cooper
1932	J. Goyder	1953 H. Cooper
1933	G. Brennan	1954 A. Madigan
1934	G. Brennan	1955 D. Rent
1935	R. Hearns	1956 D. Mooney
1936	J. Magill	1957 T. Green
1937	J. Wilby	1958 J. Leeming
1938	A. Brown	1959 J. Ould

MIDDLEWEIGHT

1881	T. Bellhouse	1921 H. Mallin
1882	A. Curnick	1922 H. Mallin
1883	A. Curnick	1923 H. Mallin
1884	W. Brown	1924 J. Elliott
1885	M. Salmon	1925 J. Elliott
1886	W. King	1926 F. Crawley
1887	R. Hair	1927 F. Crawley
1888	R. Hair	1928 F. Mallin
1889	G. Sykes	1929 F. Mallin
1890	J. Hoare	1930 F. Mallin
1891	J. Steers	1931 F. Mallin
1892	J. Steers	1932 F. Mallin
1893	J. Steers	1933 A. Shawyer
1894	W. Sykes	1934 J. Magill
1895	G. Townsend	1935 J. Magill
1896	W. Ross	1936 A. Harrington
1897	W. Dees	1937 M. Dennis
1898	G. Townsend	1938 H. Tiller
1899	R. Warnes	1939 H. Davies
1900	E. Mann	1940–1943
1901	R. Warnes	No Competition
1902	E. Mann	1944 J. Hockley
1903	R. Warnes	1945 R. Parker
1904	E. Mann	1946 R. Turpin
1905	J. Douglas	1947 R. Agland
1906	A. Murdock	1948 J. Wright
1907	R. Warnes	1949 S. Lewis
1908	W. Child	1950 P. Longo
1909	W. Child	1951 E. Ludlam
1910	R. Warnes	1952 T. Gooding
1911	W. Child	1953 R. Barton
1912	E. Chandler	1954 K. Phillips
1913	W. Bradley	1955 F. Hope
1914	H. Brown	1956 R. Redrup
1915–1918		1957 P. Burke
No Competition		1958 P. Hill
1919	H. Mallin	1959 F. Elderfield
1920	H. Mallin	

LIGHT-MIDDLEWEIGHT

1951 A. Lay	1956 J. McCormack
1952 B. Foster	
1953 B. Wells	1957 J. Cunningham
1954 B. Wells	
1955 B. Foster	1958 S. Pearson
	1959 S. Pearson

WELTERWEIGHT

1920 F. Whitbread	1939 R. Thomas
1921 A. Ireland	*1940–1943*
1922 E. White	*No Competition*
1923 P. Green	1944 H. Hall
1924 P. O'Hanrahan	1945 R. Turpin
1925 P. O'Hanrahan	1946 J. Ryan
1926 B. Marshall	1947 J. Ryan
	1948 M. Shacklady
1927 H. Dunn	1949 A. Buxton
1928 H. Bone	1950 T. Ratcliffe
1929 T. Wigmore	1951 J. Maloney
1930 F. Brooman	1952 J. Maloney
1931 J. Barry	1953 L. Morgan
1932 D. McCleave	1954 N. Gargano
1933 P. Peters	1955 N. Gargano
1934 D. McCleave	1956 N. Gargano
1935 D. Lynch	1957 R. Warnes
1936 W. Pack	1958 B. Nancurvis
1937 D. Lynch	1959 J. McGrail
1938 C. Webster	

LIGHT-WELTERWEIGHT

1951 W. Conner	1956 D. Stone
1952 P. Waterman	1957 D. Stone
1953 D. Hughes	1958 R. Kane
1954 G. Martin	1959 R. Kane
1955 F. McQuillan	

CHAMPIONSHIP WEIGHTS
(Amateurs)

Flyweight	8 st. and under
Bantam	8 st. 7 lb. and under
Feather	9 st. and under
Light	9 st. 7 lb. and under
Light-welter	10 st. and under
Welter	10 st. 8 lb. and under
Light-middle	11 st. 2 lb. and under
Middle	11 st. 11 lb. and under
Light-heavy	12 st. 10 lb. and under
Heavyweight	Any weight

LIGHTWEIGHT

1881 F. Hobday	1921 G. Shorter
1882 A. Bettinson	1922 G. Renouf
1883 A. Diamond	1923 G. Shorter
1884 A. Diamond	1924 W. White
1885 A. Diamond	1925 Signaller Viney
1886 G. Roberts	
1887 J. Hair	1926 T. Slater
1888 A. Newton	1927 W. Hunt
1889 W. Neale	1928 F. Webster
1890 A. Newton	1929 W. Hunt
1891 E. Dettmer	1930 J. Waples
1892 E. Dettmer	1931 D. McCleave
1893 W. Campbell	1932 F. Meacham
1894 W. Campbell	1933 H. Mizler
1895 A. Randall	1934 J. Rolland
1896 A. Vanderhout	1935 F. Frost
	1936 F. Simpson
1897 A. Vanderhout	1937 A. Danahar
	1938 T. McGrath
1898 H. Marks	1939 H. Groves
1899 H. Brewer	*1940–1943*
1900 G. Humphries	*No Competition*
1901 A. Warner	1944 W. Thompson
1902 A. Warner	
1903 H. Fergus	1945 J. Williamson
1904 M. Wells	1946 E. Thomas
1905 M. Wells	1947 C. Morrissey
1906 M. Wells	1948 R. Cooper
1907 M. Wells	1949 A. Smith
1908 H. Holmes	1950 R. Latham
1909 F. Grace	1951 R. Hinson
1910 T. Tees	1952 F. Reardon
1911 A. Spenceley	1953 D. Hinson
1912 R. Marriott	1954 G. Whelan
1913 R. Grace	1955 S. Coffey
1914 R. Marriott	1956 R. McTaggart
1915–1918	1957 J. Kidd
No Competition	1958 R. McTaggart
1919 F. Grace	1959 P. Warwick
1920 F. Grace	

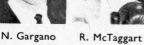

N. Gargano   R. McTaggart

FEATHERWEIGHT DIVISION

Dal Hawkins was the first recognised champion at featherweight, but the weight then was between 8 stone 6 pounds and 8 stone 10 pounds, as against the present-day 9 stone limit. After Hawkins came Ike Weir and Australian Billy Murphy. The latter was beaten by Young Griffo.

6.9.1892   George Dixon   W KO   8   Jack Skelly, New Orleans

Dixon, who also held the bantamweight crown, is said to have participated in 800-odd fights, including many in vaudeville shows where he took on all-comers. He defended his featherweight laurels against Eddie Pierce, Solly Smith, Young Griffo, Johnny Griffin, Martin Flaherty and Tommy White.

27.11.1896   Frank Erne   W PTS 20   George Dixon, New York

7.4.1897   George Dixon   W PTS 25   Frank Erne, New York

Dixon made further title defences against Johnny Griffin, Eddie Santry and Dal Hawkins.

4.10.1897   Solly Smith   W PTS 20   George Dixon, San Francisco

Dixon continued to defend his title and accounted for Eddie Santry, Dave Sullivan, Oscar Gardner, Young Pluto, Kid Broad, Joe Berstein, Tommy White, Will Curley and Eddie Lenny.

In the meantime, Solly Smith defeated Billy O'Donnell, drew with Tommy White and lost to Dan Sullivan. Ben Jordan beat Dixon in New York in 1898 and defended his 'title' against Harry Greenfield in London and then lost to Eddie Santry in New York.

Battling Battalino   Sandy Saddler   Willie Pep

9.1.1900   Terry McGovern   W KO   8   George Dixon, New York

McGovern won the title although the weight for the above match was made at 8 stone 6 pounds. McGovern retained his title in defences against Eddie Santry, Oscar Gardner, (twice) Joe Berstein, Tommy White and Aurelio Herrera.

28.11.01   Young Corbett III   W KO   2   Terry McGovern, Hartford

Neither Corbett nor McGovern could make 9 stone after this and Abe Attell laid claim to the title.

1.2.04   Abe Attell   W KO   4   Harry Forbes, St. Louis

Attell defended against Johnnie Reagan.

13.10.04   Tommy Sullivan   W KO   5   Abe Attell, St. Louis

Sullivan defended against Eddie Toy, but Attell still claimed the title. Abe drew with Kid Goodman, Kid Herman and Owen Moran (twice) and defeated Harry Baker (twice), Jimmy Walsh, Kid Solomon, Freddie Weeks and Tommy Sullivan. When Jim Driscoll drew with Attell in a no-decision contest in New York in 1909, he was given the 'newspaper decision' and laid claim to the crown.

26.3.09   Abe Attell   W KO   8   Frankie White, Dayton

Attell retained his title against Harry Forbes.

22.2.12   Johnny Kilbane   W PTS 20   Abe Attell, Vernon

Kilbane drew with Jimmy Walsh in a title contest. Meantime Driscoll accounted for Jean Poesy in London, and drew with Owen Moran. Kilbane continued to put his title at stake. He boxed Tommy Dixon in a no-decision bout, drew with Johnny Dundee, defeated George Chaney and Alvie Miller. There were also other claimants in Tommy Noble and Johnny Dundee.

2.6.23   Eugene Criqui   W KO   6   Johnny Kilbane, New York

26.7.23   Johnny Dundee   W PTS 15   Eugene Criqui, New York

Dundee relinquished title in 1924.

2.1.25   Louis (Kid) Kaplan   W KO   9   Danny Kramer, New York

Kaplan defended against Babe Herman (twice) and Bobby Garcia. Honey Boy Finnegan laid claim to title in 1926 when he defeated Chick Suggs.

19.9.27   Benny Bass   W PTS 10   Red Chapman, Philadelphia

Tony Canzoneri claimed title when he beat Johnny Dundee in 1927.

10.2.27   Tony Canzoneri   W PTS 15   Benny Bass, New York

28.9.28   Andrew Routis   W PTS 15   Tony Canzoneri, New York

Routis defended against Buster Brown.

23.9.29   Battling Battalino   W PTS 15   Andrew Routis, Hartford

Battalino defended his title against Ignacio Fernandez, Kid Chocolate, Fidel La Barba, Bobby Brady, Freddie Miller (twice) and Earl Mastro. He relinquished title in 1932.

26.5.32   Tommy Paul   W PTS 10   Johnny Pena, Detroit

4.8.32   Kid Chocolate   W PTS 10   Eddie Shea, Chicago

Paul was recognised by the National Boxing Association; Kid Chocolate by the New York State Athletic Commission. Paul lost to Lew Feldman, who in turn lost to Chocolate. The last named defeated Fidel La Barba and Seaman Tommy Watson. Another claimant was Baby Arizmenti. He defeated Tommy Paul.

13.1.33   Freddie Miller   W PTS 10   Tommy Paul, Chicago

24.2.33   Freddie Miller   W PTS 10   Baby Arizmenti, Los Angeles

Miller defeated Speedy Dado, Jack Sharkey, Nel Tarleton (twice), Jose Girones, Vernon Cormier, Johnny Pena and Petey Sarron. Throughout the following years and until 1946, there was more than one featherweight title claimant. They were: Mike Belloise, Petey Sarron, Henry Armstrong, Joey Archibald, Leo Rodak, Jimmy Perrin, Petey Scalzo, Harry Jeffra, Ritchie Lemos, Chalky Wright, Jackie Wilson, Willie Pep, Jackie Callura, Phil Terranova, Sal Bartola.

20.11.42   Willie Pep   W PTS 15   Chalky Wright, New York

Pep defended against Sal Bartola, Chalky Wright and Phil Terranova.

7.6.46   Willie Pep   W KO   12   Sal Bartola, New York

Pep made further defences against Jock Leslie and Humberto Sierra.

29.10.48   Sandy Saddler   W KO   4   Willie Pep, New York

11.2.49   Willie Pep   W PTS 15   Sandy Saddler, New York

Pep successfully defended his crown against Eddie Compo, Charlie Riley and Ray Famechon.

8.9.50   Sandy Saddler   W RET 8   Willie Pep, New York

Saddler retained his crown against Pep, Teddy Davis and Flash Elorde. The title was held in abeyance when Saddler joined the U.S. Army in 1952. He retired in 1957.

24.6.57   Hogan Bassey   W RSF 10   Cherif Hamia, Paris

1.4.58   Hogan Bassey   W KO   3   Ricardo Moreno, Los Angeles

18.3.59   Davey Moore   W RET 13   Hogan Bassey, Los Angeles

19.8.59   Davey Moore   W RET 10   Hogan Bassey, Los Angeles

BOXING QUIZ

1. In the history of the World heavyweight championship only one contest has ended in a disqualification. Can you name the bout and the result?

★

2. Who did Freddie Mills win the World light-heavyweight title from and to whom did he lose it?

★

3. Who was the last British heavyweight to win the European title?

★

4. Which was the shortest World heavyweight title fight?

★

5. Who was "Peerless Jim"? Was it Jimmy Wilde, Jimmy Braddock, Jim Driscoll or Jim Jeffries?

★

6. Can you name the present-day boxing manager of Terry Spinks?

★

7. Between the wars it was permissible for a Commonwealth boxer to fight for British titles. Can you name an overseas boxer who won the heavyweight title?

★

8. Only once in the history of the World heavyweight championship has the title been contested by two non-Americans. Can you name the contest?

★

9. A Dutch boxer won the European lightweight title in 1931 and boxed for the European welterweight title in 1955. Can you name him?

★

10. Floyd Patterson has been defeated only twice since he turned professional in 1952. Can you name his conquerors?

QUIZ ANSWERS

1. Max Schmeling v. Jack Sharkey. Schmeling won in the fourth. 2. Gus Lesnevich, Joey Maxim. 3. Jack Gardner. 4. Tommy Burns knocked out Jem Roche in 1 min. 28 secs., 1908. 5. Jim Driscoll. 6. Sammy McCarthy, former British featherweight champion. 7. Ben Foord of South Africa. 8. Primo Carnera (Italy) v. Paulino Uzcuden (Spain). 9. Bep van Klaveren. 10. Joey Maxim and Ingemar Johansson.

BOXING QUIZ

1. Three former World champions visited England on the occasion of the final show in Harringay Arena. Who were they?

★

2. What famous British fight manager defeated Georges Carpentier?

★

3. Name three British champions who boxed southpaw.

★

4. How old must you be before you can box for a British title?

5. Who is the famous British heavyweight champion who used to "beat the gong" in the introduction to all Rank Organisation films? (*above*)

★

6. Can a referee stop a professional contest even though both men have never been off their feet?

★

7. Name the birthplace of Bob Fitzsimmons.

★

8. Name the boxing brothers of Bellingham.

★

9. Did film actor Victor McGlaglan ever fight Jack Johnson?

QUIZ ANSWERS

1. Maxie Baer, Gus Lesnevich and Henry Armstrong. 2. Ted Broadribb, who boxed under the name of "Young Snowball". 3. Any three from the following will do: Jackie Paterson, Freddie Gilroy, John Kelly, Joe Lucy, Wally Thom. 4. Twenty-one. 5. Bombardier Billy Wells. 6. Yes. He can stop a contest for one of the following reasons: (*a*) to save a man unnecessary punishment, (*b*) because one man is so far ahead on points that his opponent is outclassed, (*c*) he can stop a contest and disqualify a man for a foul blow or misconduct. 7. Helston, Cornwall. 8. Henry and Jim Cooper. (Jim's real name is George Cooper.) 9. Yes. Johnson won a six-rounder in Vancouver in 1909.

FEATHERWEIGHT

1881 T. Hill
1882 T. Hill
1883 T. Hill
1884 E. Hutchings
1885 J. Pennill
1886 T. McNeill
1887 J. Pennill
1888 J. Taylor
1889 T. McNeill
1890 G. Belsey
1891 F. Curtis
1892 F. Curtis
1893 T. Davidson
1894 R. Gunn
1895 R. Gunn
1896 R. Gunn
1897 N. Smith
1898 P. Lunn
1899 J. Scholes
1900 R. Lee
1901 C. Clarke
1902 C. Clarke
1903 J. Godfrey
1904 C. Morris
1905 H. Holmes
1906 A. Miner
1907 C. Morris
1908 T. Ringer
1909 A. Lambert
1910 C. Houghton
1911 H. Bowers
1912 G. Baker
1913 G. Baker
1914 G. Baker
1915–1918
No Competition
1919 G. Baker
1920 J. Fleming
1921 G. Baker
1922 E. Swash
1923 E. Swash
1924 A. Beavis
1925 A. Beavis
1926 R. Minshull
1927 F. Webster
1928 F. Meachem
1929 F. Meachem
1930 J. Duffield
1931 B. Caplan
1932 H. Mizler
1933 J. Walters
1934 J. Treadaway
1935 E. Ryan
1936 J. Treadaway
1937 A. Harper
1938 C. Gallie
1939 C. Gallie
1940–1943
No Competition
1944 D. Sullivan
1945 J. Carter
1946 P. Brander
1947 S. Evans
1948 P. Brander
1949 H. Gilliland
1950 P. Brander
1951 J. Travers
1952 P. Lewis
1953 P. Lewis
1954 D. Charnley
1955 T. Nicholls
1956 T. Nicholls
1957 M. Collins
1958 M. Collins
1959 G. Judge

BANTAMWEIGHT

1884 A. Woodward
1885 A. Woodward
1886 T. Ilsey
1887 T. Ilsey
1888 H. Oakman
1889 H. Brown
1890 J. Rowe
1891 E. Moore
1892 F. Godbold
1893 E. Watson
1894 P. Jones
1895 P. Jones
1896 P. Jones
1897 C. Lamb
1898 F. Herring
1899 A. Avent
1900 J. Freeman
1901 W. Morgan
1902 A. Miner
1903 H. Perry
1904 H. Perry
1905 W. Webb
1906 T. Ringer
1907 E. Adams
1908 H. Thomas
1909 J. Condon
1910 W. Webb
1911 W. Allen
1912 W. Allen
1913 A. Wye
1914 W. Allen
1915–1918
No Competition
1919 W. Allen
1920 G. McKenzie
1921 L. Tarrant
1922 W. Goulding
1923 A. Smith
1924 L. Tarrant
1925 A. Goom
1926 F. Webster
1927 E. Warwick
1928 J. Garland
1929 F. Bennett
1930 H. Mizler
1931 F. Bennett
1932 J. Treadaway
1933 G. Johnston
1934 A. Barnes
1935 L. Case
1936 A. Barnes
1937 A. Barnes
1938 J. Pottinger
1939 R. Watson
1940–1943
No Competition
1944 R. Bissell
1945 P. Brander
1946 C. Squire
1947 D. O'Sullivan
1948 T. Proffitt
1949 T. Miller
1950 K. Lawrence
1951 T. Nicholls
1952 T. Nicholls
1953 J. Smillie
1954 J. Smillie
1955 G. Dormer
1956 O. Reilly
1957 J. Morrissey
1958 H. Winstone
1959 D. Weller

T. Nicholls

T. Spinks

FLYWEIGHT

1920 H. Groves
1921 W. Cuthbert-son
1922 L. Tarrant
1923 E. Warwick
1924 E. Warwick
1925 E. Warwick
1926 J. Hill
1927 J. Rolland
1928 C. Taylor
1929 T. Pardoe
1930 T. Pardoe
1931 T. Pardoe
1932 T. Pardoe
1933 T. Pardoe
1934 P. Palmer
1935 G. Fayaud
1936 G. Fayaud
1937 P. O'Donaghue
1938 A. Russell
1939 D. McKay
1940–1943
No Competition
1944 J. Clinton
1945 J. Bryce
1946 R. Gallagher
1947 J. Clinton
1948 H. Carpenter
1949 H. Riley
1950 A. Jones
1951 G. John
1952 D. Dower
1953 R. Currie
1954 R. Currie
1955 D. Lloyd
1956 T. Spinks
1957 R. Davies
1958 J. Brown
1959 M. Gushlow

BANTAMWEIGHT DIVISION

The champions of the bantamweight class really started with George Dixon who came to London to defeat Nunc Wallace, although the weight stipulated for this match was 8 stone. Earlier Tommy Kelly claimed the title—at 7 stone 7 pounds—there being no flyweight class then in existence.

27.6.1890 George Dixon W RSF 18 Nunc Wallace, London
Dixon retained his title against Johnny Murphy, Cal McCarthy and Abe Willis, before relinquishing crown. Billy Plimmer and Jimmy Barry claimed title.
9.5.1892 Billy Plimmer W 10 Tommy Kelly, Coney Island
Plimmer drew with Johnny Murphy; beat George Corfield.
15.9.1894 Jimmy Barry W KO 28 Caspar Leon, Lamont
Barry defeated Jack Madden, Walter Croot and drew twice with Caspar Leon.
25.11.1895 Pedlar Palmer W RSF 14 Billy Plimmer, London
Palmer defended against Johnny Murphy, Ernie Stanton, Dave Sullivan, Billy Plimmer and Billy Rotchford.
12.9.1899 Terry McGovern W KO 1 Pedlar Palmer, New York
McGovern defeated Harry Forbes and relinquished title. Harry Harris defeated Palmer in London and claimed title.
2.4.01 Harry Forbes W PTS 15 Caspar Leon, Memphis
Forbes defended against Dan Dougherty, Tommy Feltz, Frankie Neil and Andrew Tokell.
13.8·03 Frankie Neil W KO 2 Harry Forbes, San Francisco
Neil retained his title against Billy De Coursey, Johnny Reagan and Harry Forbes. Digger Stanley drew with Jimmy Walsh in London in 1904 and defeated Ike Bradley in Liverpool in 1906 and gained some recognition.

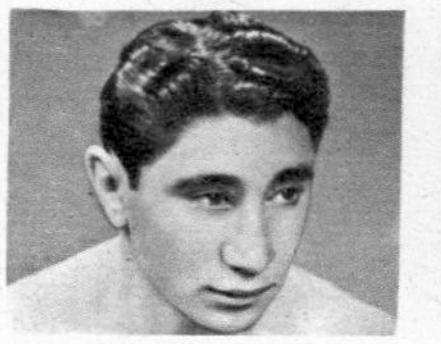
Vic Toweel

Jimmy Carruthers

Al Brown

17.10.04 Joe Bowker W PTS 20 Frankie Neil, London
29.3.05 Jimmy Walsh W KO 6 Monte Attell, Philadelphia
Walsh claimed title.
20.10.05 Jimmy Walsh W PTS 15 Digger Stanley, Chelsea
Walsh moved up into the featherweight division.
8.1.08 Johnny Coulon W PTS 10 Kid Murphy, Peoria
Coulon retained the title until 1914 when he was beaten by Kid Williams. He defended against Kid Murphy (twice), Cooney Kelly, Earl Denning (twice) Jim Kenrick (twice), Frankie Conley (twice), Harry Forbes and Frankie Burns. Meantime Digger Stanley defended his 'title' and Frankie Conley, Charles Ledoux, Eddie Campi and Kid Williams claimed the bantamweight laurels.
9.6.14 Kid Williams W KO 3 Johnny Coulon, Los Angeles
Williams retained title against Kid Herman, Eddie Campi, Jimmy Taylor, Frankie Burns and Pete Herman.
9.1.17 Pete Herman W PTS 20 Kid Williams, New Orleans
Herman defended against Frankie Burns.
22.12.20 Joe Lynch W PTS 15 Pete Herman, New York
25.7.21 Pete Herman W PTS 15 Joe Lynch, New York
23.9.21 Johnny Buff W PTS 15 Pete Herman, New York
Buff retained title against Johnny Sharkey.
10.7.22 Joe Lynch W KO 14 Johnny Buff, New York
Lynch retained title against Midget Smith.
21.3.24 Abe Goldstein W PTS 15 Joe Lynch, New York
Goldstein retained title against Charles Ledoux and Tommy Ryan.
19.12.24 Eddie Martin W PTS 15 Abe Goldstein, New York
30.3.25 Charlie Rosenburg W PTS 15 Eddie Martin, New York
Rosenburg defended against George Butch and Eddie Shea. Matched with Bushy Graham, Rosenburg failed to make the weight and forfeited the title. Bud Taylor claimed the title and was recognised by the N.B.A.
26.3.27 Bud Taylor DREW 10 Tony Canzoneri, Chicago
24.6.27 Bud Taylor W PTS 10 Tony Canzoneri, Chicago
Teddy Baldock claimed title when he defeated Archie Bell in London. Taylor vacated N.B.A. crown, and two title claimants emerged in Willie Smith, who beat Baldock, and Bushy Graham, who defeated Izzy Schwartz.
18.6.29 Al Brown W PTS 15 Vidal Gregorio, New York
Al Brown held the title for almost six years and defended against Knud Larson, Eugene Huat (twice), Nick Bensa, Pete Sanstol, Kid Francis (twice), Emile Pladner, Dom Bernasconi, Johnny King, Young Perez (twice).
1.6.35 Baltazar Sangchilli W PTS 15 Al Brown, Valencia
Sixto Escobar gained N.B.A. recognition as titleholder when he defeated Baby Casanova in 1934 and until 1940 there was more than one claimant to the title. These included Lou Salica, Tony Marino and Harry Jeffra.
24.9.40 Lou Salica W PTS 15 Georgie Pace, New York
Salica successfully defended against Small Montana, Tommy Forte (twice) and Lou Transparenti.
7.8.42 Manuel Ortiz W PTS 12 Lou Salica, Hollywood
Except for a period of two months, Ortiz held the crown for six and a half years. He retained the title against Kenny Lindsay (twice), George Freitas, Lou Salica, Lupe Cordoza, Joe Robleto (twice), Leonardo Lopez, Benny Goldberg, Ernesto Aguilar, Tony Olivera, Louis Costello (thrice) and Jackie Jurich.
6.1.47 Harold Dade W PTS 15 Manuel Ortiz, San Francisco
11.3.47 Manuel Ortiz W PTS 15 Harold Dade, Los Angeles
Ortiz defended against David Young, Tirso Del Rosario, Memo Valero and Dado Marino in further title contests.
31.5.50 Vic Toweel W PTS 15 Manuel Ortiz, Johannesburg
Toweel retained his title against Danny O'Sullivan, Luis Romero and Peter Keenan.
15.11.52 Jimmy Carruthers W KO 1 Vic Toweel, Johannesburg
Carruthers, who retired undefeated, retained his title against Vic Toweel, Pappy Gault and Chamrern Songkitrat.
19.9.54 Robert Cohen W PTS 15 Chamrern Songkitrat, Bangkok
Cohen retained his title when he drew with Willie Toweel. Raton Macias was recognised by the N.B.A. when he defeated Songkitrat.
29.6.56 Mario D'Agata W RET 6 Robert Cohen, Rome
1.4.57 Alphonse Halimi W PTS 15 Mario D'Agata, Paris
6.11.57 Alphonse Halimi W PTS 15 Raton Macias, Los Angeles
9.7.59 Jose Becerra W KO 8 Alphonse Halimi, Los Angeles

Rinty Monaghan

Jackie Paterson

Terry Allen

FLYWEIGHT DIVISION

The flyweight class was created in 1909 and given official recognition by the National Sporting Club in London. The first international contest at the weight—8 stone—took place in Paris.

11.4.13	Sid Smith	W PTS 20	Eugene Criqui, Paris
2.6.13	Bill Ladbury	W KO 11	Sid Smith, London
26.1.14	Percy Jones	W PTS 20	Bill Ladbury, London

Jones defended against Eugene Criqui.

15.5.14	Joe Symonds	W KO 18	Percy Jones, Plymouth

Symonds retained his title against Tancy Lee.

14.2.16	Jimmy Wilde	W KO 12	Joe Symonds, London

Jimmy Wilde, perhaps the greatest of all flyweights, christened 'The Ghost with a hammer in his hands' by bantam champion Pedlar Palmer, due to his terrific hitting power from a frail body, defended his title against Johnny Rosner, Tancy Lee, Johnny Hughes, Young Zulu Kid and George Clark, and held the title for more than seven years.

18.6.23	Pancho Villa	W KO 7	Jimmy Wilde, New York

Villa remained champion for two years and died in 1925 from blood poisoning caused by an infected tooth. American champion Frankie Genaro claimed the crown.

22.8.25	Fidel La Barba	W PTS 10	Frankie Genaro, Los Angeles

La Barba defended title against Elky Clark, then retired.

16.12.27	Izzy Schwartz	W PTS 10	Newsboy Brown, New York

Schwartz defended against Routier Parra, Frisco Grande, Frenchie Belanger. Meanwhile the title had other claimants in Johnny Hill, Frenchie Belanger, Frankie Genaro, Emile Pladner, Young Perez, and Willie La Morte.

16.5.30	Midget Wolgast	W KO 6	Willie La Morte, New York
10.6.30	Frankie Genaro	W PTS 10	Frenchie Belanger, Toronto

Genaro defended against Willie La Morte, Midget Wolgast, Victor Ferrand, Jackie Harmon and Valentin Angelmann.

27.10.31	Young Perez	W KO 2	Frankie Genaro, Paris
31.10.32	Jackie Brown	W RSF 13	Young Perez, Manchester

Brown defended his title against Valentin Angelmann (thrice) and Ginger Foran.

9.9.35	Benny Lynch	W RET 2	Jackie Brown, Manchester

Lynch defended against Pat Palmer, Small Montana (who claimed the title at one time) and Peter Kane. Matched with Jackie Jurich, Lynch came to the weigh-in half a stone overweight and forfeited the title. He died in 1946.

22.9.38	Peter Kane	W PTS 15	Jackie Jurich, Liverpool
19.6.43	Jackie Paterson	W KO 1	Peter Kane, Glasgow

Paterson defended against Joe Curran, then concentrated on the bantamweight division.

20.10.47	Rinty Monaghan	W PTS 15	Dado Marino, London

Monaghan defended against Jackie Paterson, Maurice Sandeyron, and Terry Allen. He retired undefeated champion.

25.4.50	Terry Allen	W PTS 15	Honore Pratesi, London
1.8.50	Dado Marino	W PTS 15	Terry Allen, Honolulu

Marino retained his crown in a return with Allen.

Yoshio Shirai v. Dado Marino 1952

19.5.52	Yoshio Shirai	W PTS 15	Dado Marino, Tokyo

Shirai, first Japanese to win a World's boxing title, retained his title against Dado Marino, Tanny Campo, Terry Allen and Leo Espinosa.

26.11.54	Pascual Perez	W PTS 15	Yoshio Shirai, Tokyo
30.5.55	Pascual Perez	W KO 5	Yoshio Shirai, Tokyo
11.1.56	Pascual Perez	W PTS 15	Leo Espinosa, Buenos Aires
30.6.56	Pascual Perez	W RET 11	Oscar Suarez, Montevideo
30.3.57	Pascual Perez	W KO 1	Dai Dower, Buenos Aires
7.12.57	Pascual Perez	W KO 2	Young Martin, Buenos Aires
19.4.58	Pascual Perez	W PTS 15	Ramon Arias, Caracas
15.12.58	Pascual Perez	W PTS 15	Dommy Ursua, Manila
10.8.59	Pascual Perez	W PTS 15	Kenji Yonecura, Tokyo

BOXING QUIZ

1. Can a professional boxer manage his own affairs?

★

2. What is the minimum time allowed by the British Boxing Board of Control for a professional contest?

★

3. Is a "knockout" official?

★

4. Who were: (a) the Livermore Larruper, (b) the Leamington Licker, and (c) the Coffee Cooler?

★

5. Where is Madison Square Garden?

★

6. What nationality was Tommy Burns and what was his correct name?

★

7. No World cruiserweight champion has gone on to win the World heavyweight crown. True or false?

★

8. Two contestants deliver blows at the same time, both fall to the canvas and both fail to get up inside ten seconds. Who is the winner?

★

9. What was the relationship between J. Williamson, A.B.A. lightweight champion in 1945, and Frank Johnson, British lightweight champion 1952 and 1955–6?

★

10. What fantastic feat was performed by H. Floyd in 1946?

QUIZ ANSWERS

1. Yes. 2. Twelve minutes. 3. No. There is no such thing as a "knockout". A boxer counted out of a contest cannot score any further points, thus his opponent wins a hypothetical maximum for each uncompleted round and must be the winner. 4. (a) Max Baer, (b) Randy Turpin, (c) Frank Craig. 5. New York City. 6. Canadian. Noah Brusso. 7. True. Bob Fitzsimmons won both titles, but was successful in the heavyweight division first. 8. Providing the incident does not happen in the first round, the referee will award the contest to the boxer who was ahead on points at the time of the double knockout. 9. They were brothers. Williamson boxed under the name of Jackie Braddock when he turned professional. 10. He won the A.B.A. title at heavyweight for the fourth time, BUT his fourth win took place seventeen years after his initial success.

BRITISH CHAMPIONS SINCE 1890

HEAVYWEIGHT DIVISION

7.2.1890	Charlie Mitchell	W RSF 3	Jem Mace, Edinburgh
27.7.1891	Ted Pritchard	W 3	Jem Smith, London
10.5.1895	Jem Smith	W 2	Ted Pritchard, London
27.1.1896	Dan Creedon	W KO 2	Jem Smith, London
19.2.1897	George Crisp	W 5	Jem Smith, Newcastle
2.5.03	Jack Palmer	W KO 12	Ben Taylor, Newcastle
29.10.06	Gunner Moir	W DISQ 9	Jack Palmer, London
19.4.09	Iron Hague	W KO 1	Gunner Moir, London
24.4.11	Bombardier Billy Wells	W KO 6	Iron Hague, London
27.2.19	Joe Beckett	W KO 5	Bomb. Billy Wells, London
26.5.19	Frank Goddard	W KO 10	Jack Curphey, London
17.6.19	Joe Beckett	W KO 2	Frank Goddard, London
21.11.23	Frank Goddard	W DISQ 2	Jack Bloomfield, London
18.3.26	Phil Scott	W KO 3	Frank Goddard, London
16.11.31	Reggie Meen	W PTS 15	Charlie Smith, Leicester
12.7.32	Jack Petersen	W KO 2	Reggie Meen, London
30.11.33	Len Harvey	W PTS 15	Jack Petersen, London
4.6.34	Jack Petersen	W RSF 12	Len Harvey, London
17.8.36	Ben Foord	W RSF 3	Jack Petersen, Leicester
15.3.37	Tommy Farr	W PTS 15	Ben Foord, London
1.12.38	Len Harvey	W DISQ 4	Eddie Phillips, London
15.9.44	Jack London	W PTS 15	Freddie Mills, Manchester
17.7.45	Bruce Woodcock	W KO 6	Jack London, London
14.11.50	Jack Gardner	W RET 11	Bruce Woodcock, London
11.3.52	Johnny Williams	W PTS 15	Jack Gardner, London
12.5.53	Don Cockell	W PTS 15	Johnny Williams, London
27.8.56	Joe Erskine	W PTS 15	Johnny Williams, Cardiff
3.6.58	Brian London	W KO 8	Joe Erskine, London
12.1.59	Henry Cooper	W PTS 15	Brian London, London

Bombardier Billy Wells and Jack Petersen won Lonsdale Belts outright in this division.

Bruce Woodcock v. Jack London 1945

Don Cockell v. Johnny Williams 1952

BOXING QUIZ

1. Which active boxer has won most fights inside the distance?

*

2. Who is Gerardo Gonzalez?

*

3. How many boxers have won TWO Lonsdale Belts outright?

*

4. Who came first — Jack Dempsey (the Nonpareil) or Jack Dempsey (the Manassa Mauler)?

*

5. What is the scheduled distance of British title bouts?

*

6. Can a man from Cork win (a) a British title, (b) an A.B.A. title?

*

7. Did Danny O'Sullivan box for a World title; if so, against whom and where?

*

8. Five post-war British heavyweight champions have one other thing in common —what is it?

*

9. What are the names of Randy Turpin's brothers and what titles did they win?

*

10. Who was Slapsie Maxie and why was he so called?

QUIZ ANSWERS

1. Archie Moore. When he beat Yvon Durelle last December, Moore chalked up his 128th inside-the-distance victory, beating the previous best, 127, held by Young Stribling. 2. Kid Gavilan, former welterweight champion of the World. 3. Three. Nel Tarleton, Ronnie Clayton and Peter Keenan. 4. The Nonpareil. 5. Fifteen rounds, three minutes each round. 6. (a) No. (b) Yes. (See qualification explanation in answers to questions Nos. 26 and 27.) 7. Yes. He boxed Vic Toweel in Johannesburg. 8. Woodcock, Gardner, Erskine, London and Cooper also won A.B.A. titles. (Woodcock and Cooper were amateur light-heavyweight champions.) 9. Dick and Jackie Turpin. Dick was British and British Empire middleweight champion. Jackie did not box for a title. 10. Maxie Rosenbloom. He won the nickname for his habit of hitting with the inside of the glove (slapping).

Jock McAvoy

Ernie Roderick

Pat McAteer

29.3.20	Tom Gummer	W RSF 14	Jim Sullivan, London
28.3.21	Gus Platts	W KO 6	Tom Gummer, Sheffield
31.5.21	Johnny Basham	W PTS 20	Gus Platts, London
27.6.21	Ted (Kid) Lewis	W PTS 20	Jack Bloomfield, London
15.2.23	Roland Todd	W PTS 20	Ted (Kid) Lewis, London
12.7.26	Tommy Milligan	W RSF 14	George West, London
16.2.27	Frank Moody	W PTS 15	Roland Todd, London
14.3.28	Alex Ireland	W DISQ 9	Tommy Milligan, Edinburgh
6.8.28	Frank Moody	W KO 1	Tommy Milligan, Glasgow
17.9.28	Alex Ireland	W PTS 15	Frank Moody, Edinburgh
16.5.29	Len Harvey	W KO 7	Alex Ireland, London
10.4.33	Jock McAvoy	W PTS 15	Len Harvey, Manchester
29.5.45	Ernie Roderick	W PTS 15	Vince Hawkins, London
28.10.46	Vince Hawkins	W PTS 15	Ernie Roderick, London
28.6.48	Dick Turpin	W PTS 15	Vince Hawkins, Birmingham
24.4.50	Albert Finch	W PTS 15	Dick Turpin, Nottingham
17.10.50	Randolph Turpin	W KO 5	Albert Finch, London
14.9.54	Johnny Sullivan	W KO 1	Gordon Hazell, London
16.6.55	Pat McAteer	W DISQ 9	Johnny Sullivan, Liverpool
30.9.58	Terry Downes	W RSF 13	Phil Edwards, London

Pat O'Keefe, Len Harvey, Jock McAvoy and Pat McAteer won Lonsdale Belts outright in this division.

WELTERWEIGHT DIVISION

2.1.03	Pat O'Keefe	W 3	Jack Kingsland, London
21.5.06	Charlie Knock	W RSF 17	Curley Watson, London
17.12.06	Curley Watson	W RSF 10	Charlie Knock, London
25.3.07	Andrew Jeptha	W KO 4	Curley Watson, London
8.8.07	Joe White	W PTS 15	Andrew Jeptha, Merthyr
18.11.07	Curley Watson	W PTS 15	Andrew Jeptha, London
21.5.08	Joe White	W PTS 20	Curley Watson, Liverpool
13.3.09	Curley Watson	W RSF 6	Jack Goldswain, London
22.5.09	Jack Goldswain	W RSF 6	Curley Watson, London
11.6.09	Curley Watson	W RET 6	Jack Goldswain, London
21.3.10	Young Joseph	W DISQ 11	Jack Goldswain, London
23.1.11	Arthur Evernden	W DISQ 3	Young Joseph, London
11.4.12	Johnny Summers	W PTS 20	Young Joseph, Liverpool
14.12.14	Johnny Basham	W KO 9	Johnny Summers, London
9.6.20	Ted (Kid) Lewis	W KO 9	Johnny Basham, London
26.11.24	Tommy Milligan	W PTS 20	Ted (Kid) Lewis, Edinburgh
8.10.25	Hamilton Johnny Brown	W PTS 20	Harry Mason, London
19.11.25	Harry Mason	W PTS 20	Hamilton Johnny Brown, London
31.5.26	Jack Hood	W PTS 20	Harry Mason, London
11.6.34	Harry Mason	W DISQ 14	Len (Tiger) Smith, Birmingham
17.12.34	Pat Butler	W PTS 15	Harry Mason, Leicester
23.4.36	Dave McCleave	W PTS 15	Chuck Parker, London
2.6.36	Jake Kilrain	W KO 8	Dave McCleave, Glasgow
23.3.39	Ernie Roderick	W KO 7	Jake Kilrain, Liverpool
8.11.48	Henry Hall	W PTS 15	Ernie Roderick, London
14.11.49	Eddie Thomas	W PTS 15	Henry Hall, London
16.10.51	Wally Thom	W PTS 15	Eddie Thomas, London
24.7.52	Cliff Curvis	W KO 9	Wally Thom, Liverpool
24.9.53	Wally Thom	W PTS 15	Peter Fallon, Liverpool
5.6.56	Peter Waterman	W RET 5	Wally Thom, London
15.7.58	Tommy Molloy	W PTS 15	Jimmy Newman, London

Johnny Basham, Jack Hood, Ernie Roderick and Wally Thom won Lonsdale Belts outright in this division.

Kid Berg

Randolph Turpin

Joe Lucy

Tommy Farr

Len Harvey

Ron Barton

British Champions—cont.

LIGHT-HEAVYWEIGHT DIVISION

9.3.14	Dick Smith	W PTS 20	Dennis Haugh, London
10.10.16	Harry Reeve	W PTS 20	Dick Smith, London
25.2.18	Dick Smith	W PTS 20	Joe Beckett, London
28.4.19	Boy McCormick	W DISQ 11	Harold Rolph, London
1.5.22	Jack Bloomfield	W RSF 9	Harry Drake, London
9.3.25	Tom Berry	W PTS 20	Sid Pape, London
25.4.27	Gipsy Daniels	W PTS 20	Tom Berry, London
27.11.27	Frank Moody	W PTS 20	Ted Moore, London
25.11.29	Harry Crossley	W PTS 15	Frank Moody, London
23.5.32	Jack Petersen	W PTS 15	Harry Crossley, London
13.6.33	Len Harvey	W PTS 15	Eddie Phillips, London
4.2.35	Eddie Phillips	W PTS 15	Tommy Farr, Mountain Ash
27.4.37	Jock McAvoy	W KO 14	Eddie Phillips, Wembley
7.4.38	Len Harvey	W PTS 15	Jock McAvoy, London
20.6.42	Freddie Mills	W KO 2	Len Harvey, London
17.10.50	Don Cockell	W KO 14	Mark Hart, London
10.6.52	Randolph Turpin	W RSF 11	Don Cockell, London
26.3.53	Dennis Powell	W RET 11	George Walker, Liverpool
26.10.53	Alex Buxton	W RSF 10	Dennis Powell, Nottingham
26.4.55	Randolph Turpin	W KO 2	Alex Buxton, London
13.3.56	Ron Barton	W RET 8	Albert Finch, London
26.11.56	Randolph Turpin	W RSF 5	Alex Buxton, Leicester

Title now vacant.

Dick Smith and Randolph Turpin won Lonsdale Belts outright in this division.

MIDDLEWEIGHT DIVISION

April 1882	Charlie Mitchell claimed title.		
8.2.1890	Toff Wall	W PTS 12	Chesterfield Goode, London
12.3.1891	Ted Pritchard	W KO 3	Jack Burke, London
25.2.1898	Anthony Diamond	W PTS 12	Dido Plumb, Birmingham
19.3.06	Pat O'Keefe	W PTS 15	Mike Crawley, London
23.5.06	Tom Thomas	W PTS 15	Pat O'Keefe, London
14.11.10	Jim Sullivan	W PTS 20	Tom Thomas, London
10.5.12	Jack Harrison	W PTS 20	Private McEnroy, London
23.2.14	Pat O'Keefe	W PTS 20	Harry Reeve, London
22.5.16	Bandsman Blake	W PTS 20	Pat O'Keefe, London
28.1.18	Pat O'Keefe	W KO 2	Bandsman Blake, London
11.3.20	Ted (Kid) Lewis	W KO 4	Johnny Bee, London

LIGHTWEIGHT DIVISION

25.5.1891	Dick Burge	W DISQ 11	Jem Carney, London
31.5.1897	Tom Causer	W DISQ 7	Dick Burge, London
8.10.1897	Dick Burge	W KO 1	Tom Causer, London
20.11.1899	Jabez White	W KO 8	Harry Greenfield, London
23.4.06	Jack Goldswain	W PTS 20	Jabez White, London
23.11.08	Johnny Summers	W RSF 14	Jack Goldswain, London
8.11.09	Freddie Welsh	W PTS 20	Johnny Summers, London
27.2.11	Matt Wells	W PTS 20	Freddie Welsh, London
11.11.12	Freddie Welsh	W PTS 20	Matt Wells, London
23.6.19	Bob Marriott	W DISQ 10	Johnny Summers, London
11.4.21	Ernie Rice	W KO 7	Ben Callicott, London
18.9.22	Seaman James Hall	W PTS 20	Ernie Rice, Liverpool

17.5.23	Harry Mason	W DISQ 13	Seaman James Hall, London
24.11.24	Ernie Izzard	W PTS 20	Jack Kirk, London
22.6.25	Harry Mason	W PTS 20	Ernie Izzard, London
17.9.28	Sam Steward	W KO 12	Ernie Rice, London
2.5.29	Fred Webster	W PTS 15	Sam Steward, London
21.5.30	Al Foreman	W KO 1	Fred Webster, London
11.8.32	Johnny Cuthbert	W RSF 10	Jim Hunter, Glasgow
18.1.34	Harry Mizler	W PTS 15	Johnny Cuthbert, London
29.10.34	Jack (Kid) Berg	W RSF 10	Harry Mizler, London
24.4.36	Jimmy Walsh	W RSF 9	Jack (Kid) Berg, Liverpool
23.6.38	Dave Crowley	W PTS 15	Jimmy Walsh, Liverpool
15.12.38	Eric Boon	W KO 13	Dave Crowley, London
12.8.44	Ronnie James	W KO 10	Eric Boon, Cardiff
16.10.47	Billy Thompson	W RSF 3	Stan Hawthorne, Liverpool
28.8.51	Tommy McGovern	W KO 1	Billy Thompson, London
25.7.52	Frank Johnson	W PTS 15	Tommy McGovern, Manchester
29.9.53	Joe Lucy	W PTS 15	Tommy McGovern, London
26.4.55	Frank Johnson	W PTS 15	Joe Lucy, London
13.4.56	Joe Lucy	W RSF 8	Frank Johnson, Manchester
9.4.57	Dave Charnley	W PTS 15	Joe Lucy, London

Freddie Welsh, Eric Boon, Billy Thompson and Joe Lucy won Lonsdale Belts outright in this division.

Eric Boon v. Dave Crowley 1938

FEATHERWEIGHT DIVISION

29.4.1895	Fred Johnson	W KO 4	Charlie Beading, Newcastle
11.1.1897	Harry Greenfield	W KO 13	Fred Johnson, London
22.2.1897	Ben Jordan	W KO 13	Fred Johnson, London
3.5.1897	Harry Greenfield	W KO 8	Larry Barnes, Birmingham
29.11.1897	Ben Jordan	W KO 19	Tommy White, London
21.1.01	Jack Roberts	W KO 7	Wilf Curley, London
20.10.02	Ben Jordan	W KO 5	Jack Roberts, London
30.3.05	Joe Bowker	W KO 12	Pedlar Palmer, London
29.1.06	Johnny Summers	W PTS 20	Spike Robson, London
28.5.06	Jim Driscoll	W PTS 15	Joe Bowker, London
1.10.06	Johnny Summers	W PTS 20	Boss Edwards, London
17.12.06	Spike Robson	W DISQ 4	Johnny Summers, London
1.6.07	Jim Driscoll	W KO 17	Joe Bowker, London
6.10.13	Ted (Kid) Lewis	W RSF 17	Alec Lambert, London
31.5.15	Llew Edwards	W DISQ 10	Owen Moran, London
4.6.17	Charlie Hardcastle	W KO 1	Alf Wye, London
5.11.17	Tancy Lee	W KO 4	Charlie Hardcastle, London
26.1.20	Mike Honeyman	W PTS 20	Billy Marchant, London
31.10.21	Joe Fox	W PTS 20	Mike Honeyman, London
2.6.24	George McKenzie	W PTS 20	Harry Leach, London
30.3.25	Johnny Curley	W PTS 20	George McKenzie, London
24.1.27	Johnny Cuthbert	W PTS 20	Johnny Curley, London
12.3.28	Harry Corbett	W PTS 20	Johnny Cuthbert, London
16.5.29	Johnny Cuthbert	W PTS 15	Harry Corbett, London
1.10.31	Nel Tarleton	W PTS 15	Johnny Cuthbert, Liverpool
10.11.32	Seaman Tommy Watson	W PTS 15	Nel Tarleton, Liverpool
26.7.34	Nel Tarleton	W PTS 15	Seaman Tommy Watson, Liverpool
24.9.36	Johnny McGrory	W PTS 15	Nel Tarleton, Liverpool
23.11.38	'Spider' Jim Kelly	W PTS 15	Benny Caplan, Belfast
28.6.39	Johnny Cusick	W RSF 12	'Spider' Jim Kelly, Belfast
1.2.40	Nel Tarleton	W PTS 15	Johnny Cusick, Liverpool
11.9.47	Ronnie Clayton	W PTS 15	Al Phillips, Liverpool
1.6.54	Sammy McCarthy	W RET 8	Ronnie Clayton, London
22.1.55	'Spider' Billy Kelly	W PTS 15	Sammy McCarthy, Belfast
4.2.56	Charlie Hill	W RSF 15	'Spider' Billy Kelly, Belfast
13.4.59	Bobby Neill	W KO 9	Charlie Hill, Nottingham

Jim Driscoll, Tancy Lee, Johnny Cuthbert and Charlie Hill won a Lonsdale Belt outright; Nel Tarleton and Ronnie Clayton won TWO Lonsdale Belts outright, in this division.

BANTAMWEIGHT DIVISION

2.4.1891	Billy Plimmer	W RET 15	Jem Stevens, London
25.11.1895	Pedlar Palmer	W DISQ 14	Billy Plimmer, London
12.11.1900	Harry Ware	W PTS 20	Pedlar Palmer, London
1901	Andrew Tokell	W PTS 20	Harry Ware,
15.12.02	Joe Bowker	W KO 8	Joe Bowker, London
17.10.10	Digger Stanley	W PTS 20	Harry Ware, London
2.6.13	Bill Beynon	W PTS 20	Digger Stanley, London
31.10.13	Digger Stanley	W PTS 20	Bill Beynon, London
20.4.14	Curley Walker	W DISQ 13	Digger Stanley, London
22.11.15	Joe Fox	W RSF 16	Jimmy Berry, London
25.11.18	Tommy Noble	W PTS 20	Joe Symonds, London
30.6.19	Walter Ross	W RSF 13	Tommy Noble, London
23.2.20	Jim Higgins	W RSF 13	Harold Jones, London
26.6.22	Tommy Harrison	W KO 13	Jim Higgins, Liverpool
26.2.23	Bugler Harry Lake	W PTS 20	Tommy Harrison, London

26.11.23	Johnny Brown	W PTS 20	Bugler Harry Lake, London
4.6.28	Kid Pattenden	W KO 12	Kid Nicholson, London
29.8.28	Teddy Baldock	W RSF 2	Johnny Brown, London
25.11.28	Kid Pattenden	W RSF 12	Johnny Brown, London
16.5.29	Teddy Baldock	W PTS 15	Kid Pattenden, London
21.12.31	Dick Corbett	W PTS 15	Johnny King, Manchester
10.10.32	Johnny King	W PTS 15	Dick Corbett, Manchester
12.2.34	Dick Corbett	W PTS 15	Johnny King, Manchester
27.5.35	Johnny King	W PTS 15	Len Hampston, Leeds
10.2.47	Jackie Paterson	W KO 7	Johnny King, Manchester
24.3.49	Stan Rowan	W PTS 15	Jackie Paterson, Liverpool
13.12.49	Danny O'Sullivan	W RET 9	Teddy Gardner, London
9.5.51	Peter Keenan	W KO 6	Danny O'Sullivan, Glasgow
3.10.53	John Kelly	W PTS 15	Peter Keenan, Belfast
21.9.54	Peter Keenan	W KO 6	John Kelly, Paisley
10.1.59	Freddie Gilroy	W RSF 11	Peter Keenan, Belfast

Digger Stanley, Joe Fox, Jim Higgins, Johnny Brown and Johnny King won Lonsdale Belts outright; Peter Keenan won TWO Lonsdale Belts outright, in this division.

Nel Tarleton

Charlie Hill

Dai Dower

FLYWEIGHT DIVISION

4.12.11	Sid Smith	W PTS 20	Joe Wilson, London
2.6.13	Bill Ladbury	W KO 11	Sid Smith, London
26.1.14	Percy Jones	W PTS 20	Bill Ladbury, London
15.5.14	Joe Symonds	W KO 18	Percy Jones, Plymouth
26.11.14	Jimmy Wilde	W PTS 15	Joe Symonds, London
25.1.15	Tancy Lee	W RSF 17	Jimmy Wilde, London
18.10.15	Joe Symonds	W RSF 16	Tancy Lee, London
14.2.16	Jimmy Wilde	W RSF 12	Joe Symonds, London
31.3.24	Elky Clark	W RSF 20	Kid Kelly, London
23.5.27	Johnny Hill	W RSF 14	Alf Barber, London
13.10.29	Jackie Brown	W KO 3	Bert Kirby, Birmingham
3.3.30	Bert Kirby	W KO 3	Jackie Brown, London
2.2.31	Jackie Brown	W PTS 15	Bert Kirby, Manchester
9.9.35	Benny Lynch	W RET 2	Jackie Brown, Manchester
30.9.39	Jackie Paterson	W KO 13	Paddy Ryan, Glasgow
23.3.48	Rinty Monaghan	W KO 7	Jackie Paterson, Belfast
11.6.51	Terry Allen	W PTS 15	Vic Herman, Leicester
17.3.52	Teddy Gardner	W PTS 15	Terry Allen, Newcastle
21.10.52	Terry Allen	W RSF 6	Eric Marsden, London
7.2.55	Dai Dower	W PTS 15	Eric Marsden, London
31.7.57	Frankie Jones	W KO 11	Len Reece, Porthcawl

Jimmy Wilde, Jackie Brown, Jackie Paterson and Terry Allen won Lonsdale Belts outright in this division.

OLYMPIC GAMES CHAMPIONS

1904—St. Louis, U.S.A.

Heavy: Sam Berger (U.S.). *Middle:* Charles Mayer (U.S.). *Welter:* Al Young (U.S.). *Light:* H. J. Spangler (U.S.). *Feather:* O. L. Kirk (U.S.). *Bantam:* O. L. Kirk (U.S.). *Fly:* G. V. Finnegan (U.S.).

1908—London

Heavy: A. L. Oldham (Britain). *Middle:* J. W. H. T. Douglas (Britain). *Light:* F. Grace (Britain). *Feather:* R. K. Gunn (Britain). *Bantam:* H. Thomas (Britain).

1920—Antwerp

Heavy: R. R. Rawson (Britain). *Light-heavy:* E. Eagan (U.S.). *Middle:* H. W. Mallin (Britain). *Welter:* T. Schneider (Canada). *Light:* S. Mossberg (U.S.). *Feather:* R. Fritsch (France). *Bantam:* C. Walker (S. Africa). *Fly:* F. Genaro (U.S.).

1924—Paris

Heavy: O. Von Perat (Norway). *Light-heavy:* H. J. Mitchell (Britain). *Middle:* H. W. Mallin (Britain). *Welter:* J. Delarge (Belgium). *Light:* H. Nielson (Denmark). *Feather:* J. Fields (U.S.). *Bantam:* W. Smith (S. Africa). *Fly:* F. La Barba (U.S.).

1928—Amsterdam

Heavy: A. Rodriguez Jurado (Argentina). *Light-heavy:* V. Avendano (Argentina). *Middle:* P. Toscani (Italy). *Welter:* E. Morgan (New Zealand). *Light:* C. Orlando (Italy). *Feather:* L. Van Klaveran (Holland). *Bantam:* V. Tamagnini (Italy). *Fly:* A. Kossis (Hungary).

1932—Los Angeles

Heavy: S. A. Lovell (Argentina). *Light-heavy:* D. E. Carstens (S. Africa). *Middle:* C. Barth (U.S.) *Welter:* E. Flynn (U.S.). *Light:* L. Stevens (S. Africa). *Feather:* C. A. Robledo (Argentina). *Bantam:* H. Gwynne (Canada). *Fly:* S. Enekes (Hungary).

1936—Berlin

Heavy: H. Runge (Germany). *Light-heavy:* R. Michelot (France). *Middle:* J. Despeaux (France). *Welter:* S. Suvie (Finland). *Light:* I. Harangi (Hungary). *Feather:* O. Casanovas (Argentina). *Bantam:* U. Sergo (Italy). *Fly:* W. Kaiser (Germany).

1948—London

Heavy: R. Iglesis (Argentina). *Light-heavy:* G. Hunter (S. Africa). *Middle:* L. Papp (Hungary). *Welter:* J. Torma (Czechoslovakia). *Light:* G. Dreyer (S. Africa). *Feather:* E. Formenti (Italy). *Bantam:* T. Csik (Hungary). *Fly:* P. Perez (Argentina).

1952—Helsinki

Heavy: E. Sanders (U.S.). *Light-heavy:* N. Lee (U.S.). *Middle:* F. Patterson (U.S.). *Light-middle:* L. Papp (Hungary). *Welter:* Z. Zygmunt Chychia (Poland). *Light-welter:* C. Adkins (U.S.). *Light:* A. Bolognesi (Italy). *Feather:* J. Zachara (Czechoslovakia). *Bantam:* P. Hamalainnen (Finland). *Fly:* N. Brooks (U.S.).

1956—Melbourne

Heavy: P. Rademacher (U.S.). *Light-heavy:* J. Boyd (U.S.). *Middle:* Schatkov (Russia). *Light-middle:* L. Papp (Hungary). *Welter:* N. Linca (Rumania). *Light-welter:* V. Jengibarian (Russia). *Welter:* R. McTaggart (Britain). *Feather:* V. Safronov (Russia). *Bantam:* W. Behrendt (Germany). *Fly:* T. Spinks (Britain).

Pascual Perez   **Floyd Patterson**

Bridge

Compiled by **Mrs. A. L. Fleming**

Secretary: English Bridge Union

BRIDGE QUIZ

1. Which Cabinet Minister captained Great Britain in 1951?

★

2. Which British winner of the European Championship is also known for his novels, adapted for radio and television plays?

★

3. Which British winner of the European Championship is now better known as a leader of fashion?

★

4. Which English international and county bridge player played regularly for the same county at cricket?

★

5. Why is Crockford's Club so called?

★

6. Who said "I heard it last night at Crockford's, one always hears things there four and twenty hours before other places"?

★

QUIZ ANSWERS

1. The Rt. Hon. Iain MacLeod, M.P., European Championship at Venice 1951.
2. The late S. J. Simon (Copenhagen 1948), who in collaboration with Caryl Brahms wrote *Titania has a Mother, Don't Mr. Disraeli, Trottie True,* etc. 3. Edward Rayne (Copenhagen 1948, Paris 1949). 4. R. D. F. Bland (Notts). Bridge v. Scotland 1950. Cricket 1929, 1930 and 1931. 5. After the famous gambler William Crockford (1775-1845), who started in life as a fishmonger's assistant and later is reputed to have become a millionaire. 6. Benjamin Disraeli in *Sybil.*

NOTES ON ADMINISTRATION

of Competitive Bridge in England

Chairman: R. F. Corwen (Yorkshire)
Secretary: Mrs. A. L. Fleming, 12 Frant Road, Tunbridge Wells, Kent. *Hon. Tournament Secretary:* G. Fell. *Hon. Treasurer:* H. Collins.

The English Bridge Union is the governing body of competitive bridge in England. It is comprised of twenty-four county or regional associations. Delegates from the associations (in proportion to the number of members) attend council meetings held quarterly in London. Committees are elected from the council members to administer all the aspects of the competitive game. A Spring Congress is held in the North and an Autumn Congress in the South of England. Other congresses are held by individual associations but have to be licensed by the E.B.U. The English Bridge Union is a member, with the other home countries, of the British Bridge League, which runs the British Open Championship (Gold Cup), the British Women's Championship (Lady Milne Cup) and the British Mixed Pairs Championship (Portland Cup). The British Bridge League selects the teams to represent Great Britain in the European Championships annually and runs the Camrose Trophy for the home countries international.

Among the competitions run by the E.B.U. are the Crockford's Cup (open teams of four), the Whitelaw Cup (women's teams of four) and the Hubert Phillips Bowl (mixed teams of four).

BRITISH CHAMPIONSHIPS

GOLD CUP—OPEN TEAMS OF FOUR

1959 J. Lazarus (*Capt.*), B. H. Franks, S. Blaser, I. M. Morris, F. Farrington
1958 N. Gardener (*Capt.*), N. Squire, A. Rose, J. Nunes, A. Dormer, D. Rimington
1957 Dr. S. Lee (*Capt.*), S. Booker, Mrs. F. Gordon, C. Rodrigue, L. Tarlo
1956 J. T. Reese (*Capt.*), B. Schapiro, K. Konstam, L. Dodds, P. Juan, A. Meredith
1955 R. Preston (*Capt.*), R. Swimer, J. Nunes, P. Topley
1954 L. Tarlo (*Capt.*), H. Franklin, N. Gardener, A. Rose, N. Squire.
1953 J. T. Reese (*Capt.*), B. Schapiro, H. Leist, A. Meredith, S. Booker, Dr. S. Lee
1952 J. T. Reese (*Capt.*), B. Schapiro, A. Meredith, H. Leist, Dr. S. Lee, S. Booker
1951 L. Tarlo (*Capt.*), N. Gardener, L. Baron, A. Rose
1950 J. T. Reese (*Capt.*), B. Schapiro, A. Meredith, H. Leist, Mrs. A. L. Fleming, Dr. S. Lee

LADY MILNE CUP—WOMEN'S TEAMS OF FOUR

1959 Mrs. A. L. Fleming (*Capt.*), Mrs. F. Gordon, Mrs. A. Gardner, Mrs. H. Rye
1958 Mrs. A. L. Fleming (*Capt.*), Mrs. F. Gordon, Mrs. R. F. Corwen, Mrs. R. Oldroyd
1957 Mrs. J. Craig (*Capt.*), Miss Evans, Mrs. Goodall, Mrs. Evins
1956 Mrs. A. L. Ellsworth, Mrs. K. Alexander, Mrs. A. Reid, Mrs. A. J. Carlisle, Mrs. Benjamin, Mrs. W. Davidson
1955 Mrs. MacDonnell, Miss D. Coen, Mrs. B. Gordon, Mrs. N. Gardener
1954 Mrs. MacDonnell, Miss D. Coen, Mrs. M. Lester, Mrs. B. Gordon
1953 Mrs. A. L. Fleming (*Capt.*), Mrs. F. Gordon, Mrs. R. Markus, Miss D. Pearson, Lady Rhodes
1952 Mrs. P. Williams (*Capt.*), Mrs. R. Evans, Mrs. N. Gardener, Mrs. M. Lester, Miss Shanahan
1951 Mrs. A. L. Fleming (*Capt.*), Mrs. F. Gordon, Mrs. R. Markus, Lady Rhodes, Miss D. Pearson
1950 Mrs. T. G. Porteous, Mrs. W. Davidson, Mrs. A. Irvine, Miss E. Donaldson

PORTLAND CLUB CUP—MIXED PAIRS

1959 Mrs. R. Markus, M. Wolach
1958 Mrs. F. Gordon, C. Rodrigue
1957 Mr. and Mrs. A. E. Brookes
1956 Miss Shanahan, M. Harrison-Gray

ENGLISH CHAMPIONSHIPS

CROCKFORD'S CUP—OPEN TEAMS OF FOUR

1959 C. Griffiths (*Capt.*), P. Richardson, E. J. Spurway, P. F. Spurway
1958 J. Lazarus (*Capt.*), B. H. Franks, S. Blaser, I. M. Morris, F. Farrington, W. Wong
1957 R. Preston (*Capt.*), R. Swimer, A. Rose, N. Gardener, N. Squire
1956 R. Preston (*Capt.*), R. Swimer, A. Rose, N. Gardener, N. Squire
1955 J. Pavlides (*Capt.*), S. Booker, L. Bradley, L. Dodds, Dr. S. Lee
1954 L. Tarlo (*Capt.*), H. Franklin, N. Gardener, A. Rose, R. Preston, R. Swimer
1953 Dr. P. Browne, V. Gerard, I. P. Gibb, A. Wolfeld
1952 L. Ellison (*Capt.*), J. Tarlo, J. Sharples, R. Sharples
1951 J. Pavlides (*Capt.*), B. Oliner, L. Dodds, E. P. C. Cotter, S. Merkin, E. Rayne
1950 Mrs. A. L. Fleming (*Capt.*), E. B. Parker, K. Konstam, G. Mathieson, J. T. Reese, B. Schapiro

WHITELAW CUP—WOMEN'S TEAMS OF FOUR

1959 Mrs. A. L. Fleming (*Capt.*), Mrs. F. Gordon, Mrs. J. M. Moss, Miss D. Pearson, Mrs. A. Gardner, Mrs. H. Rye
1958 Mrs. A. L. Fleming (*Capt.*), Mrs. F. Gordon, Mrs. R. F. Corwen, Mrs. R. Oldroyd
1957 Mrs. J. Craig (*Capt.*), Miss Evans, Mrs. Goodall, Mrs. Evins
1956 Mrs. R. Markus (*Capt.*), Lady Rhodes, Mrs. F. Gordon, Mrs. P. M. Williams, Miss D. Shanahan; Mrs. G. Durran
1955 Mrs. MacDonnell (*Capt.*), Miss D. Coen, Mrs. P. Gardener, Mrs. B. Gordon
1954 Mrs. MacDonnell (*Capt.*), Miss D. Coen, Mrs. M. Lester, Mrs. E. M. Summers
1953 Mrs. A. L. Fleming (*Capt.*), Mrs. F. Gordon, Mrs. R. Markus, Miss D. Pearson, Lady Rhodes
1952 Mrs. P. Williams (*Capt.*), Mrs. M. Lester, Mrs. R. Evans, Mrs. N. Gardener, Miss Shanahan
1951 Mrs. A. L. Fleming (*Capt.*), Mrs. F. Gordon, Mrs. R. Markus, Miss D. Pearson, Lady Rhodes
1950 Mrs. T. S. Crisford (*Capt.*), Mrs. Carr, Mrs. M. Davies, Mrs. Preedy, Mrs. Le Couteur, Mrs. Gardener

HUBERT PHILLIPS BOWL—MIXED TEAMS OF FOUR

1959 Mrs. F. Gordon (*Capt.*), S. Booker, Dr. S. Lee, G. F. Mathieson
1958 J. Hochwald (*Capt.*), Mrs. E. Dick, E. C. Milnes, C. Vickerman
1957 Miss Shanahan (*Capt.*), M. Harrison-Gray, J. Sharples, R. Sharples
1956 Mrs. G. Durran (*Capt.*), G. Durran, Mrs. K. Richard, Dr. K. Richard, A. Grossman, E. Rosenfelder
1955 Mrs. R. Markus (*Capt.*), Lady Rhodes, L. Dodds, Dr. S. Lee, J. Pavlides, B. Schapiro
1954 Mrs. P. Williams (*Capt.*), F. Emmett, Mrs. N. Gardener, N. Gardener, J. Pearlstone
1953 Mrs. R. Markus (*Capt.*), E. P. C. Cotter, Dr. S. Lee, J. Pavlides, Lady Rhodes, B. Schapiro
1952 G. Fell (*Capt.*), Mrs. R. F. Corwen, H. Franklin, F. Farrington, Mrs. A. Kremer
1951 L. Ellison, Miss Shanahan, J. Sharples, R. Sharples

NATIONAL PAIRS CHAMPIONSHIP

1959 Dr. M. Rockfelt, R. Swimer
1958 J. Lazarus, B. H. Franks
1957 D. Myers, R. Myers
1956 Miss Shanahan, M. Harrison-Gray
1955 Mrs. Van Rees, N. L. Hughes
1954 J. Tarlo, J. Sharples
1953 F. North, C. Hunt
1952 N. Gardener, L. Tarlo
1951 A. Meredith, J. T. Reese
1950 H. Franklin, G. Fell

NORTH OF ENGLAND PAIRS CHAMPIONSHIP

1959 J. Ingham, J. Miezis
1958 J. Lazarus, B. H. Franks
1957 J. Lazarus, B. H. Franks
1956 J. Lazarus, B. H. Franks
1955 S. Denby, M. Goldstone
1954 Mr. and Mrs. H. Ford
1953 A. J. Preston, B. P. Topley
1952 C. E. Phillips, A. P. Driver
1951 J. Brown, J. M. Woodhouse

MIDLANDS PAIRS CHAMPIONSHIP

1959 E. J. Spurway, D. F. Spurway
1958 W. Lee, J. S. Daniel
1957 E. J. and D. F. Spurway
1956 E. Foster, A. Smith
1955 Mrs. Van Rees, N. L. Hughes
1954 R. D. F. and R. F. Bland
1953 W. Morley Burry, P. Richardson
1952 A. G. Bonner, Mrs. W. Morley Burry
1951 C. L. Haddon, J. H. C. Godfrey

SOUTH OF ENGLAND PAIRS CHAMPIONSHIP

1959 M. J. Flint, R. A. Priday
1958 Mrs. A. L. Fleming, N. S. L. Smart
1957 Miss Shanahan, M. Harrison-Gray
1956 Miss Shanahan, M. Harrison-Gray

1955 Mrs. A. L. Fleming, N. S. L. Smart
1954 G. Burrows, L. F. Jones
1953 Mr. and Mrs. J. W. Waller
1952 G. C. H. Fox, Mrs. D. Shammon
1951 H. Ingram, Mrs. Hurner
1950 Mr. and Mrs. H. R. Evans

MASTERS PAIRS

1959 J. T. Reese, B. Schapiro
1958 R. Preston, R. Swimer
1957 M. Wolach, Mrs. R. Markus
1956 J. T. Reese, B. Schapiro
1955 K. Konstam, L. Dodds
1954 J. T. Reese, B. Schapiro
1953 N. Gardener, A. Meredith
1952 L. Tarlo, H. Franklin
1951 R. Preston, R. Swimer
1950 J. Sharples, R. Sharples

TOLLEMACHE CUP COUNTY TEAM OF EIGHT

1959 London
1958 Middlesex
1957 Middlesex
1956 North-Western
1955 North-Western
1954 Middlesex
1953 London

PACHABO CUP COUNTY TEAM OF FOUR

1959 Sussex
1958 Surrey and Yorkshire
1957 Yorkshire
1956 Yorkshire
1955 Leicester
1954 Surrey

RIXI MARKUS CUP WOMEN'S INDIVIDUAL

1959 Mrs. R. Markus
1958 Mrs. T. Symons
1957 Mrs. R. Markus
1956 Mrs. I. Golding
1955 Mrs. G. Thompson
1954 Miss L. Raynor
1953 Mrs. R. Markus
1952 Mrs. R. Markus

EUROPEAN CHAMPIONSHIP OPEN

1948 Great Britain: M. Harrison-Gray (*Capt.*), L. Dodds, K. Konstam, E. Rayne, J. T. Reese, B. Schapiro, S. J. Simon
1949 Great Britain: M. Harrison-Gray (*Capt.*), L. Dodds, K. Konstam, E. Rayne, J. T. Reese, B. Schapiro, A. Meredith
1950 Great Britain: M. Harrison-Gray (*Capt.*), L. Dodds, N. Gardener, K. Konstam, J. C. H. Marx, L. Tarlo
1951 Italy
1952 Sweden
1953 France
1954 Great Britain: R. F. Corwen (*non-playing capt.*), L. Dodds, K. Konstam, A. Meredith, J. Pavlides, J. T. Reese, B. Schapiro

1955 France
1956 Italy
1957 Italy
1958 Italy
1959 Italy

Great Britain won the World Championship in January 1955 in New York, (the 1954 team).

EUROPEAN CHAMPIONSHIP WOMEN

1948 Denmark
1949 Denmark
1950 Great Britain: Col. Walshe (*non-playing capt.*), Mrs. Crisford, Mrs. Carr, Mrs. R. Evans, Mrs. F. Gordon, Mrs. N. Renshaw, Mrs. P. M. Williams
1951 Great Britain: Dr. S. Lee (*non-playing capt.*), Mrs. R. Evans, Mrs. A. L. Fleming, Mrs. F. Gordon, Mrs. Markus, Lady Rhodes, Mrs. P. M. Williams
1952 Great Britain: E. Kempson (*non-playing capt.*), Mrs. R. Evans, Mrs. A. L. Fleming, Mrs. F. Gordon, Mrs. Markus, Lady Rhodes, Mrs. P. M. Williams
1953 France
1954 France
1955 Denmark
1956 France
1957 Denmark
1958 Denmark
1959 Great Britain

BRITISH REPRESENTATIVES IN EUROPEAN CHAMPIONSHIPS

The following players have represented Great Britain in the European Open Championships since the War:
L. W. Dodds, Mrs. A. L. Fleming, H. Franklin, N. Gardener, M. Harrison-Gray, K. Konstam, J. C. H. Marx, A. Meredith, J. Pavlides, E. Rayne, J. T. Reese, M. Rockfelt, A. Rose, B. Schapiro, J. Sharples, R. Sharples, S. J. Simon, L. P. P. F. Swinnerton-Dyer, J. Tarlo, L. Tarlo, A. F. Truscott, R. d'Unienville, B. H. Franks, J. Lazarus.

The following players have represented Great Britain in the Women's European Championship since the War:
Mrs. Carr, Miss D. Coen, Mrs. V. Cooper, Mrs. R. F. Corwen, Mrs. T. S. Crisford, Mrs. A. L. Della Porta, Mrs. R. Evans, Mrs. A. L. Fleming, Mrs. N. Gardener, Mrs. B. Gordon, Mrs. F. Gordon, Mrs. A. Hardie, Mrs. M. Lester, Mrs. L. Litante, Mrs. M. MacDonnell, Mrs. R. Markus, Mrs. R. Oldroyd, Miss D. Pearson, Mrs. H. Renshaw, Lady Rhodes, Miss D. Shanahan, Mrs. S. J. Simon, Mrs. M. Van Rees, Mrs. M. Whittaker, Mrs. P. M. Williams, Mrs. M. Edwards, Mrs. G. E. Higginson.

Compiled by J. W. Dudderidge
Hon. Secretary, The British Canoe Union

Canoeing

HOW IT ALL BEGAN
Primitive origins

Canoes are ancient craft and have been in use in all parts of the world from time immemorial, and although no one definition will cover every type, it is true to say that a canoe is a boat usually pointed at both ends and propelled by a crew facing forward and using a paddle not attached to the boat, or sailed under easily dismountable spars and sails. Native canoes, although in wide variety, fit into three classes:

a. Dug-out canoes carved from a trunk of a tree and found mostly on tropical rivers and coasts.
b. Bark canoes, of which the best known is the birch bark of the North American Indian.
c. Kayaks, skin-covered decked craft paddled by means of a double-ended paddle, of which the best known is the hunting kayak of the Eskimo.

Primitive peoples use their craft for transport, hunting and other essential purposes, and explorers have found their importance in traversing tropical forest and the lake and forest country of northern Canada.

Foundation of Canoeing as a modern sport

The sport of CANOEING is only about one hundred years old, and dates back to 1865 when a certain John MacGregor had designed and built a boat of oak and cedar which he named "Rob Roy". It was clinker built, decked like a kayak, and paddled by means of a double-ended paddle. In this kayak or canoe John MacGregor made extended voyages on the rivers and lakes of Europe, and on his return wrote books and lectured on his travels. This led other adventurous young men to become interested, and more canoes were built, all called "Rob Roy Canoes", after the name of the prototype. These young men persuaded MacGregor to form a club to foster this new sport, and in 1866, at a meeting in Richmond, "The Canoe Club" was formed, "To improve canoes, promote canoeing and unite canoeists". MacGregor was its first Captain and retained that office until his death in 1891. In 1867 the Prince of Wales became Commodore of the Canoe Club, holding that office until his accession to the throne in 1901. In 1873 a Royal Warrant was issued commanding that the Canoe Club should henceforth be styled the Royal Canoe Club. This ancient club, the first to be formed in the world, prospers to this day, active in every branch of the sport and with a clubhouse on the Thames at Teddington. The Royal Canoe Club grew rapidly and soon branch clubs were established at Oxford, Cambridge, on the Mersey, the Humber and the Clyde. Competitive sport soon developed and the first regatta for Rob Roy canoes was held on the Thames in 1867. Very soon special racing canoes were being designed, not unlike the modern racing kayak, and before long a four-man Rob Roy was built and became very popular. This was the ancestor of the Kayak Fours of today.

Modification of the Rob Roy Canoe for Sailing

MacGregor carried simple sailing gear on his voyages in order to make use of favourable winds, and soon the sailing enthusiasts began to modify their canoes to make them sail better. This led to the evolution of the true sailing canoe, and from this point the sailing and paddling branches of the sport followed different lines of development.

Canoeing spreads abroad

MacGregor and other members of the Canoe Club travelled widely in their craft, introducing the sport to many regions. Students attending foreign universities, government officials posted overseas, business men and others took their canoes with them to their new homes, and soon the seeds of the sport had been sown in America and many of the countries of Europe. Canoe clubs

CANOEING QUIZ

I. What is the Hasler Trophy?

*

2. At what season is the Devizes to Westminster Race held, how long is it and how many portages are involved?

*

3. In the field of international paddling racing, whose name stands out above all others? To which country does he belong?

QUIZ ANSWERS

1. The Hasler Trophy is "for Long Distance Racing between Clubs in Annual Competition under the B.C.U." and was presented by Lloyds Underwriters to commemorate the Raid up the Gironde River in December 1942 by 10 Royal Marines led by Lt.-Col. H. G. Hasler, D.S.O., O.B.E., R.M. in five two-man canoes to destroy enemy shipping in Bordeaux. There were only two survivors. 2. During the Easter weekend. The distance is 125 miles and there are about 77 portages. 3. Gert Fredriksson of Sweden with 5 Olympic Gold Medals plus three World Championships and many international honours gained since the renewal of competition in 1948.

sprang up, and in 1880 the American Canoe Association was formed, followed by the British Canoe Association in 1887. Soon after the turn of the century national associations were formed in Germany, Sweden and several other countries.

Following the First World War there was a rapid growth in interest in canoeing and in 1924 the International Canoe Federation was formed to provide an international authority for competitive sport and for the exchange of touring information. The old British Canoe Association after many years' activity became moribund and in 1933 a new association was formed. In 1936 the British Canoe Union took over as the national canoeing authority for Great Britain.

In 1946 at a Congress held in Stockholm, the International Canoe Federation was revived and one of its first duties was to authorise the British Canoe Union to organise the 1948 Olympic Games Canoe Regatta at Henley.

Administration of Canoeing

The British Canoe Union (B.C.U.) is primarily an association of clubs with provision for individual membership, and its objects are to foster the interests of canoeists, promote canoeing in all its forms, assist members in pursuit of their sport at home and abroad, and arrange mutual exchange of privileges amongst the clubs and with overseas associations. The B.C.U. is governed by a Council elected at the annual general meeting, and this is assisted by technical sub-committees controlling the various branches of activity, Racing, Slalom and Touring.

The International Canoe Federation (I.C.F.) is a federation of national associations and exists to formulate rules for international competition, establish a clearing house for touring information, take responsibility for the organisation of world championships and, in every way open to it, serve the wider interests of the sport.

The I.C.F. is governed by the biennial Congress to which member federations may send a delegate. This Congress elects a Board of Management and also sub-committees to handle the three main branches of activity, Racing, Slalom and Touring. The first World Canoeing Championships were staged in 1933 at Prague, and so successful were they that three years later the sport of canoe racing was admitted to the programme of the Olympic Games in Berlin, where Britain made its international debut.

The introduction of Canoe Slalom

Slalom is a term used in ski-ing to denote a competition involving the negotiation of a course marked by poles on a hillside. The term has been adopted by canoeists to describe a similar competition on fast-moving, broken water. The competitor negotiates a serpentine course marked by poles hung from wires stretched across the river. The course is so laid that the competitor has to use great technical skill and strength if he is to follow it without incurring penalties for touching the obstacles. In 1937 the sport was brought to Britain by an Austrian canoeist, Franz Schulhof, and two years later he organised the first British National Slalom on the River Dee near Llangollen.

WINNERS OF THE DEVIZES TO WESTMINSTER CANOE RACE SINCE ITS INSTITUTION

		h.	m.	s.
1950	R. Webb—H. Ross Richmond C.C.	34	52	0
1951	O. Dansie—R. Dry S.A.S. Regt. T.A.	24	7	0
1952	H. Ross—M. Wilkins Richmond C.C.	24	51	0
1953	J. Junior—E. G. Marchant S.A.S. Regt. T.A.	30	47	0
1954	D. Mitchell—S. Syrad Royal Marines C.C.	28	13	0
1955	D. Mitchell—S. Syrad Royal Marines C.C.	25	32	15
1956	G. R. Howe—J. P. Clarke Royal Marines C.C.	28	32	0
1957	B. D. White—K. Aston Royal Marines C.C.	25	28	15
1958	C. Edmunds—G. Howe Royal Marines C.C.	24	27	0
1959	S. L. Syrad—T. Shenton Royal Marines C.C.	23	17	15 (Record)

WINNERS OF BRITISH OPEN CHAMPIONSHIPS PADDLING RACING 1936–1958

(Key to boat classes: F.1=Single Folding Canoe; F.2=Pair Folding Canoe; K.1=Single Rigid Kayak; K.2=Pair Rigid Kayak; K.4=Four-man Rigid Kayak; C.1=Single Canadian Canoe; C.2=Pair Canadian Canoe.) No F.1 or F.2 after 1938.

Year	Class	1,000 metres	10,000 metres
1936	F.1	G. W. Lawton	G. W. Lawton
	F.2	A. R. Brearley–J. W. Dudderidge	A. R. Brearley–G. W. Lawton
	C.1	G. W. Lawton	No contest
1937	F.1	G. W. Lawton	G. W. Lawton
	F.2	A. R. Brearley–J. W. Dudderidge	A. R. Brearley–J. W. Dudderidge
	C1.	R. C. Bending	No contest
1938	F.1	No contest	A. W. J. Simmons
	C.1	B. H. Champion	No contest
	C.2	B. H. Champion–R. C. Bending	
	K.1	A. W. J. Simmons	G. W. Lawton
	K.2	G. W. Lawton–A. W. J. Simmons	No contest
1939	C.1	G. W. Lawton	,, ,,
	C.2	G. W. Lawton–W. C. Wilkinson	,, ,,
	K.1	A. W. J. Simmons	A. W. J. Simmons
	K.2	A. R. Brearley–J. Harris	No contest
1947	C.1	G. W. Lawton	,, ,,
	K.1	N. W. Dobson	N. W. Dobson
	K.2	G. W. Lawton–A. W. J. Simmons	,, ,,
1948	C.1	H. E. Maidment	,, ,,
	C.2	J. M. D. Symonds–H. van Zwanenberg	,, ,,
	K.1	N. W. Dobson	,, ,,
	K.2	A. W. J. Simmons–J. H. Henderson	,, ,,
	K.1	(Women, 500 metres) J. Richards	,, ,,
1949	C.1	G. H. Marchand	A. W. J. Simmons
	K.1	A. W. J. Simmons	
	K.2	A. W. J. Simmons–J. H. Henderson	A.W.J.Simmons–J. H. Henderson
	K.1	(500 metres) Men–A. W. J. Simmons	Women–J. Richards
	K.2	(500 metres) Men–A. Todd–R. Webb	Women–No contest
1950	C.1	G. H. Marchand	G. H. Marchand
	K.1	A. W. J. Simmons	A. W. J. Simmons
	K.2	No contest	A. W. J. Simmons–C. E. Farnham
	K.1	(500 metres) Men–A. W. J. Simmons	Women–J. Farnham
	K.1	Relay 4 x 500 metres	Canoe Camping Club

		500 metres	1,000 metres	10,000 metres
1951	C.1	No contest	G. H. Marchand	No contest
	K.1	W. Young	R. Prout	G. Colyer
	K.2	F. Prout–R. Prout	F. Prout–R. Prout	No contest
	K.4	1,000 metres. R. Prout, F. Prout, G. Chambers, G. Vandersteen		
	K.1	Women J. Webb		
	K.2	Women J. Webb–A. Jenkin		
	K.1	Relay 4 x 500 metres Richmond Canoe Club		
1952	C.1	G. Marchand unchallenged at all distances until he retired in 1954. No contests held but represented G.B. in Olympics 1952.		
	K.1	G. Colyer	R. J. Parker	G. Colyer
	K.2	F. Prout–R. Prout	R. J. Parker–S. Speel	R. J. Parker–S. Speel
	K.4	(1,000 metres) Richmond Canoe Club		
	K.1	Relay 4 x 500 metres Richmond Canoe Club		
	K.1	Women J. Farnham		
	K.2	Women S. Ascott–B. Milbourne		
1953	K.1	G. Colyer	G. Colyer	G. Colyer
	K.2	F. Prout–R. Prout	F. Prout–R. Prout	F. Prout–R. Prout
	K.4	(1,000 metres) Royal Canoe Club		
	K.1	Relay 4 x 500 metres Royal Canoe Club		
	K.1	Women P. Moody		
	K.2	Women P. Moody–M. White		
1954	K.1	J. White	G. Colyer	R. J. Parker
	K.2	M. Knight–G. Palmer	F. Prout–R. Prout	F. Prout–R. Prout
	K.1	Relay 4 x 500 metres Richmond Canoe Club		
	K.1	Women P. Moody		
	K.2	Women P. Moody–S. Andrews		
1955	K.1	R. C. Blick	B. Bullivant	B. Bullivant
	K.2	B. Bullivant– R. C. Blick	B. Bullivant– R. C. Blick	R. J. Parker– G. Colyer
	K.1	Relay 4 x 500 metres Royal Canoe Club		
	K.1	Women P. Moody		
	K.2	Women P. Moody– S. Andrews		
1956	K.1	B. Bullivant	B. Bullivant	B. Bullivant
	K.2	B. Bullivant–R. C. Blick unchallenged at all three distances.		
	K.1	Women P. Moody		
	K.2	Women P. Moody– E. Sheridan		
1957	K.1	No contest	No contest	B. Bullivant

1958 COMPETITION RESULTS NATIONAL CHAMPIONSHIPS

Seniors

C.1	1,000 METRES	J. Shambrook
C.2	1,000 METRES	J. Shambrook–A. Hubbard
K.1	500 METRES	R. Rhodes
	1,000 METRES	E. Szorenyi
	10,000 METRES	R. C. Blick
K.2	500 METRES, 1,000 METRES and 10,000 METRES	E. Szorenyi–F. Wagner
K.4	1,000 METRES	E. Szorenyi, F. Wagner, R. C. Blick, E. W. Emes
K.4	10,000 METRES	E. Szorenyi, F. Wagner, R. C. Blick, G. Konyi
K.1	RELAY 4 x 500 METRES	Birmingham Canoe Club
K.1	WOMEN, 500 METRES	M. Satchell
K.2	WOMEN, 500 METRES	M. Chandler–P. Ayris

Juniors

K.1	500 METRES and 1,000 METRES	R. Lowery
K.1	10,000 METRES	G. Konyi
K.2	500 METRES, 1,000 METRES and 10,000 METRES	G. Konyi–R. James
K.4	1,000 METRES	R. James, D. J. Woolley, J. Harris, R. W. Emes
K.4	10,000 METRES	R. James, D. J. Woolley, M. Powell, J. Harris
NCK.1	1,000 METRES	I. Clark
NCK.2	1,000 METRES	D. J. Woolley

LIST OF WINNERS OF BRITISH OPEN CHAMPIONSHIPS SLALOM 1939–1959 (Class F.1)

Year	Venue	Men	Women
1939	R. Dee (Trevor Rocks)	J. Harris (Birmingham C.C.)	—
1940	R. Teme (Ludlow Weir)	H. Renold (Manchester C.C.)	
1948	R. Dee (Tymaen Island)	D. Taylor (Royal C.C.)	
1949	Cancelled through drought		
1950	R. Eden (Armathwaite)	M. Smith (Tay C.C.)	E. E. McLellan (C.C.C.)
1951	R. Usk (Llangynidr)	J. McLean (Tay C.C.)	Mrs. McLean (Tay C.C.)
1952	R. Usk (Builth Wells)	D. Campbell (Tay C.C.)	K. Tootill (C.C.C.)
1953	R. Eden (Armathwaite)	P. Farrant (Chalfont C.C.)	S. Andrews (C.C.C.)
1954	R. Thames (Marsh Weir)	K. White (Manchester C.C.)	M. Farrant (Chalfont C.C.)
1955	R. Tees (Barnard Castle)	D. Campbell (Tay C.C.)	H. Meakin (Lakeland C.C.)
1956	R. Eden (Armathwaite)	W. H. Horsman (Chalfont C.C.)	H. Meakin (Lakeland C.C.)
1957	R. Tyne (Hexham)	J. McLean (Tay C.C.)	H. Goodman (Lakeland)
1958	R. Tay (Thistle Brig)	I. Carmichael (Twickenham C.C.)	No contest
1959	R. Thames (Marsh Weir)	I. Carmichael (Twickenham C.C.)	No contest

LIST OF WINNERS OF WORLD CHAMPIONSHIPS IN SLALOM 1949–1959

Year Venue	F.1 (Men)	F.1 (Women)	C.1 (Men)	C.2 (Men)	C.2 (Mixed)
1949 GENEVA					
INDIVIDUAL	Eiterer (Austria)	Pillwein (Austria)	d'Alencon (France)	Duboille–Rousseau (Fr.)	—
TEAM EVENT	Switzerland	Austria	France	France	
1951 STEYR					
INDIVIDUAL	Fruehwirth (Austria)	Pertlwieser (Austria)	Dussuet (Switzerland)	Neveu–Paris (France)	—
TEAM EVENT	Austria	Austria	Czechoslovakia	France	
1953 MERANO					
INDIVIDUAL	Kirschbaum (West Germany)	Schwingl (Austria)	Dussuet (Switzerland)	Engler–Dussuet (Switzerland)	—
TEAM EVENT	Austria	Czechoslovakia	Czechoslovakia	France	
1955 TACEN					
INDIVIDUAL	Holzbauer (West Germany)	Bisinger (West Germany)	Jirasek (Czechoslovakia)	Neveu–Paris (France)	Martanova–Pecka (Czech.)
TEAM EVENT	West Germany	East Germany	Czechoslovakia	Czechoslovakia	
1957 AUGSBURG					
INDIVIDUAL	Vogt (West Germany)	Magnus (East Germany)	Schubert (East Germany)	Friedrich–Kleinert (East Germany)	Schmidt–Glockner (East Germany)
TEAM EVENT	East Germany	East Germany	West Germany	Czechoslovakia	
1959 GENEVA					
INDIVIDUAL	Farrant (Great Britain)	Ubaniak (West Germany)	Jirasek (Czechoslovakia)	Friedrich–Kleinert (East Germany)	Behrend–Merkel (East Germany)
TEAM EVENT	East Germany	East Germany	Czechoslovakia	East Germany	

WORLD CHAMPIONSHIPS IN CANOE RACING 1936–1950—LIST OF CHAMPIONS

Class	1936 Berlin (Olympic Games)	1938 Vaxholm	1948 Henley (Olympic Games)	1950 Copenhagen
10,000 METRES				
F.1 MEN	Hradetzky (Aus.)	Bogren (Swe.)	—	—
F.2 MEN	Johansson–Bladstroem (Sweden)	Helstrand–Helsvik (Sweden)	—	—
K.1 MEN	Krebs (Austria)	Widmark (Sweden)	Fredriksson (Sweden)	Stromberg (Finland)
K.2 MEN	Wevers–Landen (Germany)	Johansson–Berndtsson (Sweden)	Akerlund–Wetterstroem (Sweden)	Akerlund–Wetterstroem (Sweden)
C.1 MEN	—	—	Capek (Czechoslavakia)	Boutigny (France)
C.2 MEN	Mottl–Skrdlant (Czechoslovakia)	Karlik–Brzak (Czechoslovakia)	Macknowski–Lysak (U.S.A.)	Brzak–Kudrna (Czechoslovakia)
1,000 METRES				
K.1 MEN	Hradetzky (Austria)	Widmark (Sweden)	Fredriksson (Sweden)	Fredriksson (Sweden)
K.2 MEN	Kainz–Dorfner (Austria)	Triebe–Eberle (Germany)	Berglund–Klingstroem (Sweden)	Glasser–Hedberg (Sweden)
K.4 MEN	—	Kube–Bruggeman Gebruder–Strahtman (Germany)	Berglund–Klingstroem–Akerlund–Wetterstroem (Sweden)	Pihl–Eriksson–Pettersson–Haeppling (Sweden)
C.1 MEN	Amyot (Canada)	Newmuller (Germany)	Holecek (Czechoslovakia)	Holecek (Czechoslovakia)
C.2 MEN	Syrovatka–Brzak (Czechoslovakia)	Proissl–Weinstabl (Germany)	Brzak–Kudrna (Czechoslovakia)	Brzak–Kudrna (Czechoslovakia)
500 METRES				
K.1 MEN	—	—	Fredriksson (Sweden)	Kobberup (Denmark)
K.2 MEN	—	—	Axelsson–Christensen (Finland)	Glasser–Hedberg (Sweden)
K.1 WOMEN	—	Kalka (Finland)	Hoff (Denmark)	Saimo (Finland)
K.2 WOMEN	—	Pavlisova–Zvolankova (Czechoslovakia)	Hoff–Svendsen (Denmark)	Saimo–Gronholm (Finland)
10,000 METRES				
K.4 1950	Andersson–Gustavsson–Johansson–Andersson (Sweden)			

WORLD CHAMPIONSHIPS IN CANOE RACING 1952–1958—LISTS OF CHAMPIONS

Class	1952 Helsinki (Olympic Games)	1954 Macon	1956 Ballarat (Olympic Games)	1958 Prague
10,000 METRES				
K.1 MEN	Stromberg (Finland)	Hatlacsky (Hungary)	Fredriksson (Sweden)	Stromberg (Finland)
K.2 MEN	Wires–Heitanen (Finland)	Raub–Wiedermann (Austria)	Uranyi–Fabian (Hungary)	Uranyi–Fabian (Hungary)
K.4 MEN	—	Pihl–Frick–Heurlin–Anderson (Sweden)	—	Scheuer–Lietz–Schmidt–Kleine (West Germany)
C.1 MEN	Havens (U.S.A.)	Vokner (Czechoslovakia)	Rottman (Rumania)	Bukharin (U.S.S.R.)
C.2 MEN	Turlier–Laudet (France)	Wieland–Halmai (Hungary)	Kharin–Botev (U.S.S.R.)	Oschenkov–Silaev (U.S.S.R.)
1,000 METRES				
K.1 MEN	Fredriksson (Sweden)	Fredriksson (Sweden)	Fredriksson (Sweden)	Briel (West Germany)
K.2 MEN	Wires–Hietanen (Finland)	Meszaros–Meszaros (Hungary)	Scheuer–Miltenberger (Germany)	van der Moere–Verbrugghe (Belgium)
K.4 MEN	—	Vagyosky–Kovacs–Nagy–Szigetti (Hungary)	—	Scheuer–Lietz–Schmidt–Kleine (West Germany)
C.1 MEN	Holecek (Czechoslovakia)	Parti (Hungary)	Rottman (Rumania)	Bukharin (U.S.S.R.)
C.2 MEN	Rasch–Haunstoft (Denmark)	Liebhart–Lulla (Austria)	Dumitru–Ismailciuc (Rumania)	Ismailciuc–Alexe (Rumania)
500 METRES				
K.1 MEN	—	Fredriksson (Sweden)	—	Kaplaniak (Poland)
K.2 MEN	—	Steinhauer–Miltenberger (West Germany)	—	Kaplaniak–Zielinski (Poland)
K.1 WOMEN	Saimo (Finland)	Zenz (Sarre)	Dementieva (U.S.S.R.)	Kislova (U.S.S.R.)
K.2 WOMEN	—	Punter–Banfalvi (Hungary)	—	Shubina–Gruzintseva (U.S.S.R.)

K.1 RELAY 4 x 500 METRES 1948 Sweden. 1950 Sweden. 1954 Sweden. 1958 West Germany

CANOEING QUIZ

1. What is the name of the international canoe sailing trophy for which a challenge has been made by a British team this year?

*

2. A protest was made at the 1948 Olympic Canoe Regatta at the use by certain teams of "crooked" canoes. What were these crooked canoes and why were they the cause of a protest?

*

3. Who holds the record for a solo crossing of the English Channel by canoe?

QUIZ ANSWERS

1. The New York Canoe Club International Cup instituted 1884. 2. The "crooked" canoes were Canadian canoes built on curved keel giving them a tendency to turn in the direction of the curve. When paddled solo the curve in the keel would cancel the turning effect of the stroke and the canoe would run straight with little or no steering. This would be a great advantage to the paddler and lead to unfair competition with canoes on straight keels needing constant steering correction by the paddle. The protest was not allowed since the curve in the keel was not specifically forbidden in the Rules, but in subsequent amendments to the Rules it was laid down that canoes must be built symmetrical along the fore and aft line. 3. A. R. Waterhouse who made an officially timed crossing from St. Margarets Bay to Cap Blanc Nez in 1953 taking 4 hours 8 mins.

SOME DATA ON CRAFT AND COURSES USED IN RACING AND SLALOM

1. Racing canoes and kayaks

	Max. length cms.	Min. beam cms.	Min. width kgs.
K.1	520	51	12
K.2	650	55	18
K.4	1,100	60	30
C.1	520	75	20
C.2	650	75	20

2. Slalom canoes and kayaks

	Min. length cms.	Min. beam cms.
F.1	400	60
C.1	400	80
C.2	458	80

F.1 must be truly folding and collapsible

3. Wildwater racing canoes and kayaks

	Max. length cms.	Min. length cms.	Min. beam cms.
F.1	450	400	60
R.1	450	400	60
C.1	430	400	80
C.2	500	458	80

R.1 is a rigid kayak (not collapsible)
Classes: F.1 Men, F.1 Women; R.1 Men; C.1 Men; C.2 Men; C.2 Mixed.

4. Rules
In Slalom the order of finishing is based on the sum of the time in seconds and the penalty points imposed.
In Wildwater Racing the finishing order is based on time.
In Combined Events (Slalom and Wildwater Race) each part is run according to its respective rules and a formula is used to combine the results to obtain a final order.

Chess

Compiled by **A. F. Stammwitz**

Hon. Secretary: The British Chess Federation

THE BRITISH CHESS FEDERATION

The British Chess Federation is responsible for the organisation of the game at national level. Subsidiary tournaments and competitions are organised by the unions—Midlands, South, North, Welsh and West—who are directly represented on the Federation by nominated delegates. The affiliated counties arrange their own tournaments and leagues with all the affiliated clubs directly represented, and in turn the affiliated clubs organise their own internal tournaments. All adult players who compete in organised events have to be registered as members of the Federation, their union and county, whilst the registration of junior players is optional, unless they wish to compete in senior events for which registration is obligatory. The B.C.F. is represented on F.I.D.E. (the International Chess Federation) by a delegate appointed by the Council. F.I.D.E. is responsible for the organisation of international individual and team competitions, which include the World Championship and a biennial team tournament, and also for all matters concerning the laws of the game.

In addition to the delegates from the unions, other subsidiary organisations are directly represented on the Federation as non-territorial units. These include the British Chess Problem Society, British Correspondence Chess Association, British Ladies' Chess Association, British Universities Chess Association and Chess Education Society.

CHESS QUIZ

1. Who has been British champion most times?

★

2. Which organisation is responsible for the laws of the game?

★

3. How many times has H. Golembek been the B.C.F. champion?

★

4. Which county has won the B.C.F. County Championship most times?

QUIZ ANSWERS

1. H. E. Atkins, nine times. 2. Federation Internationale des Echecl (F.I.D.E.), while the B.C.F. itself issues from time to time rules for play in tournaments. 3. Three, 1947, 1949, 1955. 4. Middlesex, 19 times.

The Federation invites players to become individual members, who receive certain voting and other rights and who are represented on both the Council and Executive Committee on a basis as laid down in the constitution. By such means additional income is obtained to enable the Federation to carry out a very detailed programme of events.

Any player who is a British subject can play in a qualifying competition that enables him to play in the British Championship. Each year the B.C.F. organises its own congress which takes place in various parts of the country during August. In addition to the national championships at all levels—Men, Ladies, Boys under 18 and under 15, and Girls under 18—other tournaments for all grades of players are open for entry to any registered player. Although Scotland has its own national organisation, which is directly affiliated to F.I.D.E., Scottish players can be nominated for entry to the Men's Championship on an agreed scale and their entry to all the other tournaments is open without any restriction.

During recent years a special effort has been made to organise the game for juniors on an ever-increasing scale and all the unions and the majority of their affiliated counties appoint a junior organiser whose particular responsibilities are devoted to the organisation of junior events throughout the country, and one junior congress held annually in Liverpool regularly attracts over a thousand entries every Easter. It is by such means that the B.C.F. hopes to improve the general standard of the game throughout the country.

The secretary of the B.C.F. receives a considerable mail that consists of enquiries from potential players, and a brief summary arising from these may be of help to those interested in joining clubs or participating in events organised for their benefit:

(a) Any player wishing to join a club should address his enquiry to the B.C.F. Secretary, 5 Clifford Road, Hounslow West, Mdx., or phone Hounslow 3000.

(b) Any player interested in playing postal chess should contact one of the two large correspondence organisations: The B.C.C.A., 9 The Vale, Muswell Hill, London N.10, or Postal Chess, "Chess", Sutton Coldfield, Warwicks.

(c) The following competitions are open to individuals and clubs:

The British Championship—closing date 1st October in each year.
The National Club Championship—teams of 6 a side; closing date 31st October.
The National Works Championship—teams of 6 a side; closing date 31st October.
B.C.F. Annual Congress—open to any player; closing date 30th June.

Competitions are contested on a regional basis to facilitate travelling. Entry forms and further particulars can be obtained from the B.C.F. Secretary.

(d) Two monthly chess magazines are published regularly. Specimen copies can be obtained from the editors as follows: The British Chess Magazine, 20 Chestnut Road, West Norwood, London, S.E.27, or "Chess", Sutton Coldfield, Warwicks. The Federation publishes a bi-monthly news-letter which contains results of both national and regional tournaments, the subscription being 4/6 p.a., to commence with the issue of the first number. A specimen copy can be obtained from the B.C.F. Publicity Officer, 39 Balmoral Terrace, Gosforth, Newcastle-on-Tyne.

(e) The Federation issues a Year Book which contains full details of the activities of the Federation and its affiliated organisations, together with results and a complete directory of affiliated clubs, giving the addresses of their head quarters, their days of meeting, and names and addresses of their secretaries. Copies can be obtained from the B.C.F. Secretary, price 3/6 post paid.

(f) The categories of individual membership of the Federation are as follows:

Vice-Presidents (Individual and Corporate) .... £5/5/- p.a.
Full Members (Individual and Corporate) .... £2/2/- p.a.
Associate Members ....10/- p.a.
Life Members ....£10 down or ten annual payments of £1.

Details, together with a 16-page leaflet setting out the advantages of individual membership, can be obtained on application to the B.C.F. Secretary.

(g) The laws of the game were completely revised in 1953 and a copy of the English translation can be obtained from the B.C.F. Secretary, price 1/3 post paid. The B.C.F. tournament rules, which are widely used by congresses and clubs for their own individual tournaments, can be obtained from the same source on receipt of a stamped addressed envelope. These rules have been completely revised to bring them into line with the last edition of the laws and came into operation early this year.

(h) There is a uniform age limit for junior competitions—thus under 18 means that a player must be under that age on the 1st September in the year prior to the event. Competitions—both team and individual at national, union and county level—are organised under the jurisdiction of the B.C.F., and in addition a National Schools Tournament, open on a handicap basis to any school in England, Scotland and Wales, can be entered. The B.C.F. Secretary will always be pleased to supply details.

In the international field the Federation enters for many officially sponsored events, including both the Men's and Women's World Championships. Owing to its limited income the Federation is forced to confine its activities mainly to such events, although it receives many invitations to play matches against other countries. It also now receives invitations to send players to compete in many junior events in which the age limit is often as high as under 21 on the day of the tournament. Again its limited income restricts these activities; but on two occasions in recent years teams have been sent to Holland, and the B.C.F. is normally represented in such events as the Junior World Championship and the Students' World Championship.

In recent months the B.B.C. has at last recognised the increasing importance of the game to the community by the inauguration of a series of 24 weekly programmes on Network Three, and the response to these by the listening public has resulted in a spate of correspondence in which the main enquiries have been dealt with above.

The Federation, in conjunction with the unions, prepares an annual Grading List of all the leading players. This is issued at the end of December and is applicable to all games played during the previous three years, up to and including the national championships in the previous August.

Whilst the administration of the Federation is carried out under the jurisdiction of the Executive Committee who meet quarterly, the main day-to-day work is carried out by the officers, with the help and assistance of three standing sub-committees, which are respectively responsible for Development, Tournament and Match, and Junior activities. Volunteers to assist in this purely honorary work are always welcome. Work in connection with the registration of players is carried out by a Records Secretary, whilst the adjudication of unfinished games is organised through a Panel Secretary, with the help and assistance of duly elected professional players for a fee paid by the unsuccessful claimants.

The names and addresses of secretaries of other organisations affiliated to the Federation are as follows:

Unions:
Southern—J. J. Lauder, 37 Dora Road, Wimbledon, London, S.W. 19.
Midlands—G. H. Simmons, 75 Ferry Road, Scunthorpe, Lincs.
Northern—B. L. Wilkinson, 45 Park Road, Chorley, Lancs.
Western—A. E. Giles, 18 Grosvenor Road, Swindon, Wilts.
Welsh—G. C. Rollings, Kingston Chambers, Church Place, Neath, Glamorgan.

British Correspondence Chess Association:
W. S. J. Lampard, "Ommaroo', Hamesmoor Way, Mychett, Aldershot.

British Chess Problem Society:
G. W. Chandler, 46 Worcester Road, Sutton, Surrey.

British Ladies Chess Association:
Miss M. Henniker-Heaton, 607 Kensington Close, Wrights Lane, London, W.8.

British Universities Chess Association:
R. Fletcher, Selwyn College, Cambridge.

Chess Education Society:
S. Morrison, 31 Chatsworth Way, West Norwood, London, S.E.27.

The following is a summary of the principal international and national events which have taken place over the past year, together with details of the year-by-year winners of the national championships. It is felt appropriate that certain events in which British players have participated abroad should be excluded owing to lack of space, and it has also been found necessary to exclude the results of various international congresses which have taken place in this country. For the record, however, entry to these congresses is open to any player and the B.C.F. Secretary will be pleased to supply details of these, which take place at Christmas, Easter, Whitsun and during August and September.

WORLD CHAMPIONS

The Men's Championship is open to entry from all countries affiliated to F.I.D.E. and is competed for by a series of qualifying tournaments extending over a three-year period. 1959 will see the conclusion of a cycle when the Candidates' Tournament will be held in September. The players who have qualified to compete in this tournament, the winner of which will challenge Botvinnik (U.S.S.R.) for his title, are Keres, Petroshan, Smyslov and Tal (U.S.S.R.); Benko (stateless); Gligoric (Yugoslavia); Olafsson (Iceland); and Fischer (U.S.A.). At the age of fifteen Fischer, by qualifying for this tournament, automatically earned himself the title of Grand Master.

The first recognised World Champion was Wilhelm Steinitz, who held the title from 1866 to 1894, when he was succeeded by Emanuel Lasker, who similarly held the title for the considerable period of 27 years. Subsequent holders of the title were:

1921 J. R. Capablanca
1927 A. A. Alekhine
1935 M. Euwe
1937 A. A. Alekhine (d. 1946).

With the death of Alekhine the championship was decided upon a more competitive basis, with arrangements for the qualifying tournaments being amended from time to time, and the title has been held up to date as follows:

1948 M. Botvinnik
1957 V. Smyslov
1958 M. Botvinnik.

One of the conditions agreed to is that in the event of the champion losing his title he can challenge his successor to another match in the following year.

Thus although Smyslov gained the supreme crown from Botvinnik in 1957 he held the title for the shortest period on record so far, as in their return match Botvinnik easily turned the tables on his younger opponent.

The list of champions truly illustrates the international character of the game. Steinitz was born in Prague, Lasker in Berlin, Capablanca in Havana, and Alekhine in Moscow, but he spent the major part of his chess life in Western Europe; Dr. Euwe was born in Amsterdam and is still playing the game, whilst both Botvinnik and Smyslov were born in the U.S.S.R.

The World Ladies' Championship is played on similar lines, one of the British representatives—Mrs. Elaine Pritchard—having qualified for the Candidates' Tournament, which takes place this year in Bulgaria.

INTERNATIONAL TEAM TOURNAMENT 1958

Played at the Deutches Museum from 1st to 23rd October 1958

After a series of shocks and counter-shocks the B.C.F. team succeeded in qualifying for the top section in the Final Tournament, in which, unfortunately, the team failed to do full justice to itself. To finish eleventh out of the 36 competing nations, above both Hungary and Holland, was, however, quite an achievement. Details of scores are as follows:

THE PRELIMINARIES—FINAL TABLES

Section A

	U	*B*	*Au*	*H*	*D*	*Fr*	*It*	*PR*	*Ird*	*Ttl.*
1 U.S.S.R.	—	3½	2½	2½	3	4	4	3½	4	27
2 Bulgaria	½	—	3	1½	2	4	4	3½	4	21½
3 Austria	1½	1	—	2	2½	2½	4	3½	4	21
4 Holland	1½	2½	2	—	1½	3	3	3	4	20½
5 Denmark	1	2	1½	2½	—	1½	1½	2½	4	16½
6 France	0	0	1½	1	2½	—	2	3½	4	14½
7 Italy	0	½	0	1	2½	2	—	3½	1½	11
8 Puerto Rico	½	½	½	1	1½	½	½	—	3	8
9 Ireland	0	½	0	0	0	0	2½	1	—	4

Section B

	Sp	*US*	*WG*	*F*	*Ic*	*Is*	*N*	*SA*	*Ir*	*Ttl.*
1 Spain	—	2	2½	3	2½	3	3½	3½	3½	23½
2 U.S.A.	2	—	1½	3½	3	3	3	3½	3½	23
3 West Germany	1½	2½	—	2	3	1½	4	4	3½	22
4 Finland	1	½	2	—	2	3	2½	1½	3	15½
5 Iceland	1½	1	1	2	—	2½	2	2	3½	15½
6 Israel	1	1	2½	1	1½	—	2	3	3	15
7 Norway	½	1	0	1½	2	2	—	2½	2	11½
8 South Africa	½	½	0	2½	2	1	1½	—	2½	10½
9 Iran	½	½	½	1	½	1	2	1½	—	7½

Section C

	A	*EG*	*E*	*Hu*	*Po*	*C*	*Ph*	*Sc*	*L*	*Ttl.*
1 Argentina	—	2½	1½	2½	2	3	3½	4	4	23
2 East Germany	1½	—	3	2	2½	3	2½	2½	4	21
3 England (B.C.F.)	2½	1	—	1½	3	2	3	3	4	20
4 Hungary	1½	2	2½	—	2½	1	3½	3½	3	19½
5 Poland	2	1½	1	1½	—	2	3½	3½	4	19
6 Colombia	1	1	2	3	2	—	1½	2½	3½	16½
7 Philippines	½	1½	1	½	½	2½	—	2	4	12½
8 Scotland	0	1½	1	½	½	1½	2	—	3	10
9 Lebanon	0	0	0	1	0	½	0	1	—	2½

Section D

	Cz	*Y*	*Sw*	*C*	*Sd*	*B*	*P*	*T*	*G*	*Ttl.*
1 Czechoslovakia	—	2	3	2	2½	4	3½	4	4	25
2 Yugoslavia	2	—	2	4	2½	2½	3½	4	3½	24
3 Switzerland	1	2	—	1½	2½	4	3½	4	1½	20
4 Canada	2	0	2½	—	2½	3	2	3½	3½	19
5 Sweden	1½	1½	1½	1½	—	3½	4	2	3	18½
6 Belgium	0	1½	0	1	½	—	2½	2½	2½	10½
7 Portugal	½	½	½	2	0	1½	—	2	3	10
8 Tunisia	0	0	0	½	2	1½	2	—	3½	9½
9 Greece	0	½	2½	½	1	1½	1	½	—	7½

CHAMPIONSHIP SECTION

	U	*Y*	*A*	*US*	*Cz*	*EG*	*WG*	*Sw*	*Sp*	*B*	*E*	*Au*	*Ttl.*
1 U.S.S.R.	—	2	2	2	3½	4	2½	3½	3½	3½	4	4	34½
2 Yugoslavia	2	—	2½	2½	3	3½	2½	3½	2½	2½	2½	2	29
3 Argentina	2	1½	—	2	2	3	3	2½	3	2	2½	2	25½
4 U.S.A.	2	1½	2	—	2	2	2½	2½	2½	2	3	2	24
5 Czechoslovakia	½	1	2	2	—	2½	1½	3	2	2½	3	2	22
6 East Germany	0	½	1	2	1½	—	3½	2½	1½	3	2½	4	22
7 West Germany	1½	1½	1	1½	2½	½	—	3	3½	2	2½	2½	22
8 Switzerland	½	½	1½	1½	1	1½	1	—	3	2½	2½	3½	19
9 Spain	½	1½	1	1½	2	2½	½	1	—	2	2½	2½	17½
10 Bulgaria	½	1½	2	2	1½	1	2	1½	2	—	1½	1½	17
11 England (B.C.F.)	0	1½	1½	1	1	1½	1½	1½	1½	2½	—	2½	16
12 Austria	0	2	2	2	2	0	1½	½	1½	2½	1½	—	15½

Group B: 1. Hungary 31; 2. Holland 28½; 3. Canada 24½; 4. Colombia 24½; 5. Israel 23½; 6. Denmark 23; 7. Poland 22½; 8. Sweden 21; 9. Finland 19; 10. Iceland 18; 11. France 15; 12. Belgium 13½.

Group C

	N	*Ph*	*SA*	*It*	*Sc*	*G*	*P*	*Ir*	*PR*	*Ird*	*T*	*L*	*Ttl.*
1 Norway	—	1½	2	3	3	3	2½	2	3	2½	4	3½	30
2 Philippines	2½	—	2	2	3	2	3	2	4	3½	3	2½	29½
3 South Africa	2	2	—	2	2	2	3	2½	2½	4	3½	2½	28
4 Italy	1	2	2	—	2½	1½	1½	3	3	2½	4	3½	26½
5 Scotland	1	1	2	1½	—	2	2½	2½	3½	4	2	3½	25½
6 Greece	1	2	2	2½	2	—	2½	2½	2½	2	3	3	25
7 Portugal	1½	1	1	2½	1½	1½	—	2½	2	2½	3½	3½	23
8 Iran	2	2	1½	1	1½	1½	1½	—	3	1	3	2	20
9 Puerto Rico	1	0	1½	1	½	1½	2	1	—	2½	1½	2	14½
10 Ireland	1½	½	0	1½	0	2	1½	3	1½	—	1	2	14½
11 Tunisia	0	1	½	0	2	1	½	1	2½	3	—	2½	14
12 Lebanon	½	1½	1½	½	½	1	½	2	2	2	1½	—	13½

CHESS QUIZ

1. What title are awarded to players who qualify by performances in international events?

★

2. What title is awarded to players who qualify by performances in England?

★

3. Which competitions are the postal play equivalent of the Counties Championships?

4. Which players have won the B.C.F. Individual Correspondence Championships most times?

★

QUIZ ANSWERS

1. International Master, International Judge, International Judge for Correspondence Chess. 2. British Master. 3. Ward-Higgs and Sinclair Cup Tournaments. 4. F. Parr and Dr. R. C. Macdonald, four times.

THIRD INTERNATIONAL DEAF AND DUMB TOURNAMENT

This was played at the Royal Hotel, Woburn Place, London, from May 17th to 24th under the auspices of the International Committee of Silent Chess for teams of four.

The entries were England, Finland, Germany, Holland, Hungary, Poland, Spain and Yugoslavia and was won by the combined East and West German team, who won five and drew its other two matches. The Polish team had a similar score, but the issue was decided on the respective games scores, which were as follows:

	E-WG	*Po*	*Sp*	*Y*	*Hu*	*H*	*GB*	*F*	*Games*	*Pts.*
1 East-West Germany	—	2½	3	2	3	2	3½	2½	18½	6
2 Poland	1½	—	3	2½	2½	2	3	4	18½	5½
3 Spain	1	1	—	1	3	3	4	3	16	4
4 Yugoslavia	2	1½	3	—	0	4	2	3½	16	4
5 Hungary	1	1½	1	4	—	2	2½	2½	14½	3½
6 Holland	2	2	1	0	2	—	2½	2½	12	3½
7 Great Britain	½	1	0	2	1½	1½	—	2	8½	1
8 Finland	1½	0	1	½	1½	1½	2	—	8	½

B.C.F. CONGRESSES AND NATIONAL CHAMPIONS

	Venue	*British Champion*	*British Lady Champion*
1904	Hastings	W. E. Napier	Miss K. B. Finn
1905	Southport	H. E. Atkins	Miss K. B. Finn
1906	Shrewsbury	H. E. Atkins	Mrs. Herring
1907	Crystal Palace	H. E. Atkins	Mrs. Herring
1908	Tunbridge Wells	H. E. Atkins	Mrs. A. L. Curling
1909	Scarborough	H. E. Atkins	Mrs. D. L. Anderson
1910	Oxford	H. E. Atkins	Mrs. Houlding
1911	Glasgow	H. E. Atkins	Mrs. Houlding
1912	Richmond	R. C. Griffiths	Mrs. D. L. Anderson
1913	Cheltenham	F. D. Yates	Mrs. Moseley
1914	Chester	F. D. Yates	Mrs. Houlding
1915–18	No Congress	No Contest	No Contest
1919	Hastings	No Contest	Mrs. S. J. Holloway
1920	Edinburgh	R. H. V. Scott	Mrs. Agnes Stevenson
1921	Malvern	F. D. Yates	Mrs. D. L. Anderson
1922	London	No Contest	Miss E. C. Price
1923	Southsea	Sir G. A. Thomas, Bt.	Miss E. C. Price
1924	Southport	H. E. Atkins	Miss E. C. Price
1925	Stratford-on-Avon	H. E. Atkins	Mrs. A. Stevenson
1926	Edinburgh	F. D. Yates	Mrs. A. Stevenson
1927	London	No Contest	No Contest
1928	Tenby	F. D. Yates	Miss E. C. Price
1929	Ramsgate	Mir Sultan Khan	Miss D. M. Gilchrist
1930	Scarborough	No Contest	Mrs. A. Stevenson
1931	Worcester	F. D. Yates	Mrs. R. P. Michell Mrs. T. H. Wheelwright
1932	London	Mir Sultan Khan	Mrs. R. P. Michell
1933	Folkestone	Mir Sultan Khan (Special Tournament at Hastings)	Miss Fatima
1934	Chester	Sir G. A. Thomas, Bt.	Miss D. M. Gilchrist
1935	Yarmouth	W. Winter	Mrs. R. P. Michell
1936	Nottingham	W. Winter (Special Tournament at Bournemouth)	Mrs. S. J. Holloway
1937	Blackpool	W. A. Fairhurst	Miss R. M. Dew
1938	Brighton	C. H. O'D. Alexander	Miss Musgrave
1939	Bournemouth	No Contest	Miss E. Saunders
1940–45	No Congress	No Contest	No Contest
1946	Nottingham	R. F. Combe	Miss Saunders
1947	Harrogate	H. Golombek	Miss E. Tranmer
1948	London	R. J. Broadbent	Miss E. C. Price
1949	Felixstowe	H. Golombek	Miss E. Tranmer
1950	Buxton	R. J. Broadbent	Mrs. R. M. Bruce
1951	Swansea	E. Klein	Mrs. R. M. Bruce
1952	Chester	R. G. Wade	No Contest
1953	Hastings	D. A. Yanofsky	Miss E. Tranmer
1954	Nottingham	L. W. Barden and A. Phillips	Mrs. R. M. Bruce
1955	Aberystwyth	H. Golombek	Miss J. F. Doulton and Mrs. R. M. Bruce
1956	Blackpool	C. H. O'D. Alexander	Mrs. E. Pritchard
1957	Plymouth	Dr. S. Fazekas	Capt. P. A. Sunnucks
1958	Leamington	J. Penrose	Capt. P. A. Sunnucks
1959	York*		Mrs. R. M. Bruce

*H. Golombek, M. J. Haygarth, J. Penrose (tie). To be played off in November.

The results of the National Junior Championships, which have been included in the Congress programme since 1954, are given in the section devoted to junior activities.

B.C.F. COUNTY AND INDIVIDUAL CORRESPONDENCE CHAMPIONS

	Counties Championship	*Individual Correspondence Champions*	*Counties Correspondence Championship*
1908	Middlesex	—	—
1909	Middlesex	—	—
1910	Middlesex	—	—
1911	Surrey	—	—
1912	Kent	—	—
1913	Middlesex	—	—
1914	Middlesex	—	—
1915–19	No Contest	—	—
1920	Surrey	—	—
1921	Yorkshire	Rev. F. E. Hammond	—
1922	Lancashire	J. H. Blake	Cornwall
1923	Lancashire	W. A. Hooper	Kent
1924	Surrey	W. H. Gunston	West of Scotland
1925	Middlesex	Thorold Gosset	Lancashire
1926	Lancashire	Dr. R. C. Macdonald	Lancashire
1927	Middlesex	Dr. R. C. Macdonald	Somerset
1928	Middlesex	W. H. Gunston	Middlesex and Surrey (*eq.*)
1929	Surrey	J. E. West	Middlesex
1930	Lancashire	Dr. R. C. Macdonald	Middlesex
1931	Middlesex	W. H. Whicher	Middlesex
1932	Middlesex	T. H. Tylor	Yorkshire
1933	Lancashire	T. H. Tylor	Cambridgeshire
1934	Middlesex	T. H. Tylor	Lancashire
1935	Lancashire	G. S. A. Wheatcroft	Lancashire and Surrey (*eq.*)
1936	Middlesex	W. L. Roche	Cambridge and Middlesex (*eq.*)
1937	Middlesex	Dr. R. C. Macdonald	Middlesex
1938	Lancashire	F. A. Richardson and E. A. Ellison	Yorkshire
1939	No Contest	H. A. Marshall	Yorkshire
1940	No Contest	W. L. Roche	Berkshire
1941	No Contest	J. Wolstenholme	Lancashire
1942	No Contest	W. R. Morry	Lancashire
1943	No Contest	R. W. Bonham	Yorkshire
1944	No Contest	D. V. Hooper	Surrey
1945	No Contest	B. H. Wood	Warwickshire
1946	Lancashire	G. Wood	Lancashire
1947	Middlesex	R. W. Bonham J. Cairncross	Lancashire
1948	Lancashire	F. Parr G. Wood	Sussex
1949	Middlesex	H. Israel F. Parr	Cheshire
1950	Middlesex	F. Parr	Lancashire
1951	Oxfordshire	R. W. Bonham E. Brown	Essex
1952	Oxfordshire	A. Hallmark	Essex
1953	Middlesex	H. G. Rhodes	Middlesex
1954	Surrey	J. A. Fuller	Middlesex
1955	Middlesex	J. A. Fuller	Gloucestershire
1956	Middlesex	F. Parr	Hampshire
1957	Warwickshire	S. C. Davey	Lancashire
1958	Essex	P. J. Oakley	Suffolk
1959	Lancashire	S. Milan	Yorkshire

B.C.F. PLAYERS' PANEL

This panel was formed to assist clubs to arrange displays with a minimum of trouble and expense. The fees payable to recognised professional players are £4 4*s.* 0*d.* for a lecture or £4 4*s.* 0*d.* plus expenses for a simultaneous display for up to 20 boards, with an additional amount of £1 1*s.* 0*d.* for each additional 10 boards or part thereof. For details write to H. O. Bidgood, 78 Downie Road, Bilbrook, Nr. Wolverhampton.

NATIONAL CLUB CHAMPIONSHIP

The final of the 1957–58 competition resulted as follows:

LEICESTERSHIRE		CAMBRIDGE UNIVERSITY	
1. P. N. Wallis	1	1. J. D. Taylor	0
2. W. Tabakiernik	0	2. M. F. Collins	1
3. P. D. Sanderson	½	3. M. Davis	½
4. V. J. A. Russ	0	4. K. W. Lloyd	1
5. R. Starosolsky	*0	5. D. T. A. Lamport	*1
6. P. E. Collier	1	6. G. B. Hardingham	0
	2½		3½

Cambridge University won on board count
* Adjudicated.

CHESS QUIZ

1. Which county has won the County and District Correspondence Championships most times?

★

2. In what year was the British Chess Federation founded?

★

3. Who has been British Lady Champion most times?

4. How many International Masters are at present resident in U.K.?

★

QUIZ ANSWERS

1. Middlesex, eight times. 2. 1906. 3. Miss E. C. Price, five times. 4. Six. C. H. O'D. Alexander, W. A. Fairhurst, Dr. S. Fazekas, H. Golombek, Sir George Thomas, R. G. Wade.

COUNTIES CHAMPIONSHIP

The detailed score of the final, played in London on 5th July 1958, was as follows:

ESSEX		YORKSHIRE	
1. Dr. S. Fazekas	½	1. P. C. Gibbs	½
2. J. Penrose	½	2. M. Haygarth	½
3. P. H. Clarke	1	3. J. H. Beaty	0
4. H. I. Woolverton	1	4. A. M. Hallmark	0
5. J. B. Hawson	0	5. R. B. Edwards	1
6. R. Payne	*1	6. B. Petkevich	*0
7. Dr. B. Sturgeon	0	7. N. Littlewood	1
8. A. J. Morrell	0	8. K. Beaumont	1
9. J. Grieshaber	1	9. E. G. Berg	0
10. P. C. Doye	1	10. J. E. Povey	0
11. J. V. Skilleter	½	11. I. Goldberg	½
12. K. E. Stanley	0	12. W. C. Evans	1
13. L. A. J. Glyde	½	13. S. Wilkinson	½
14. J. M. Soesan	*1	14. R. W. Ives	*0
15. V. Tornofsky	0	15. J. M. Myers	1
16. P. W. Haddock	1	16. M. E. Binks	0
17. J. R. Cooke	½	17. M. A. Haigh	½
18. P. W. Hempson	½	18. H. Boothroyd	½
19. M. R. Porter	1	19. O. Hardy	0
20. S. Wilkinson	0	20. C. G. Addingley	1
	11		9

Essex had white on the even-numbered boards.
* Adjudicated.

NATIONAL WORKS CHAMPIONSHIP

The final of the 1957–58 competition resulted as follows:

E.M.I., HAYES		APPLEBY-FRODINGHAM, SCUNTHORPE	
1. R. Speirs	½	1. L. B. Pawson	½
2. J. Guthrie	1	2. G. H. Simmons	0
3. R. L. Barnett	1	3. J. T. Jarvis	0
4. G. C. Hitches	½	4. P. B. Peart	½
5. A. Cramb	0	5. A. W. Mullard	1
6. R. Soundy	0	6. E. C. Robinson	1
	3		3

E.M.I. won on the board count.

OXFORD v. CAMBRIDGE

In the annual Varsity match, which was played at the R.A.C. on 21st March, the scores were as follows:

OXFORD		CAMBRIDGE	
1. T. M. Bailey	1	1. M. E. Davis	0
2. A. S. Hollis	0	2. K. M. Lloyd	1
3. A. Hall	0	3. R. C. Kennedy	1
4. R. Hollinghurst	0	4. R. Fletcher	1
5. M. Lipton	½	5. J. Meade	½
6. D. R. Walker	1	6. J. Hinden	0
7. R. Busby	1	7. D. B. Pennycuick	0
	3½		3½

Cumulative score of matches to date—Oxford 38½, Cambridge 38½.

ENGLAND v. SCOTLAND

The second of a recent biennial series of matches was played at the R.A.C. on April 21st and resulted in an overwhelming victory for the home country by 6½–1½. Detailed scores:

ENGLAND		SCOTLAND	
1. Dr. S. Fazekas	1	1. Dr. J. M. Aitken	0
2. J. Penrose	½	2. W. A. Fairhurst	½
3. P. H. Clarke	1	3. P. B. Anderson	0
4. L. W. Barden	½	4. M. Fallone	½
5. C. H. O'D. Alexander	1	5. G. Dickson	0
6. B. Cafferty	½	6. N. MacLeod	½
7. J. A. Fuller	1	7. N. A. Perkins	0
8. B. J. Moore	1	8. Dr. R. C. Nairn	0
	6½		1½

JUNIOR EVENTS
NATIONAL CHAMPIONSHIPS

Under 18, Boys'—D. J. Mabbs (Harrow).
Under 15, Boys'—M. J. Neave (London) and M. A. Stevenson (Wolverhampton).
Under 18, Girls'—Sheila Corbyn (Birmingham).

JUNIOR COUNTIES CHAMPIONSHIP

This tournament is played under the Jamboree System which enables a series of team matches to be played at the same time by a system of cross-pairings between members of the five counties who compete annually in the final. The championship was won by Middlesex for the third time. Since the inception of the competition Warwickshire have also won the championship a similar number of times and Gloucestershire have won it once. The winners who go forward to this stage are the Junior Team Champions of their respective unions.

NATIONAL SCHOOLS TOURNAMENT

This tournament was inaugurated in 1958 with 241 competing schools, each of whom played in a zonal tournament. The 16 finalists were then required to play a further two rounds to reduce the number of entrants to four schools. The semi-finals and final were played over a period of two days at a hotel in London. In the final Calday Grange Grammar School of Wirral, Cheshire, beat Varndean Grammar School of Hove. The semi-finalists in the 1959 competition are Calday Grange, William Ellis (London), Glyn Grammar (Epsom) and Queen Elizabeth's (Barnet).

Compiled by **Jane Pontifex**

Secretary: Combined Training Committee,
The British Horse Society

Combined Training

INTRODUCTION

Combined Training is a comprehensive test of horse and rider. The horse must be fit, supple and obedient, possessing stamina and speed; the rider must be able to train and condition his horse in order to produce its best performance; both must have spirit and courage and a mutual confidence and understanding.

The principal Combined Training competition is known as the Three-Day Event, in which the same horse and rider undergo three distinct tests on three consecutive days:

DRESSAGE—a series of exercises to test the horse's training and obedience, marked by a panel of judges.
SPEED, ENDURANCE & CROSS-COUNTRY—a 13- to 25-mile route, partly along roads and tracks, partly over a steeplechase course and partly across country with fixed, natural obstacles, to be completed within a stipulated time, penalties being incurred for falls and disobedience at the obstacles.
JUMPING—a jumping test in an arena.

Of these, the exacting test on the second day is the most important. The dressage test is to show that the horse has acquired the requisite standard of training and obedience, while the jumping test is simply to prove that, despite the great demands made upon him, he is fit and supple enough to continue in service.

The Three-Day Event was first included as an Olympic event in 1912, as an all-round test and competition for chargers, hence its original name, "The Military". Since then it has been opened to civilians but the form of the competition has remained virtually the same.

Olympic and International Three-Day Events are controlled by the Fédération Equestre Internationale, but the British Horse Society, as National Federation affiliated to the F.E.I., is the governing body in this country.

After the 1948 Olympic Games in London, the Duke of Beaufort, Vice-Patron of the British Horse Society, invited the Society to organise a Three-Day Event on his land at Badminton. The Badminton Horse Trials became an annual event and is the prime factor in the growth of the sport of Combined Training in Great Britain. Interest in the sport gradually increased, among both competitors and spectators, the standard rose each year and, in 1953, Badminton was appointed the first European Championships (held in a different country each year, under the auspices of the F.E.I.). In 1953, another Three-Day Event was started at Harewood, in Yorkshire, by gracious permission of H.R.H. The Princess Royal. The interest taken by H.M. The Queen has been a great encouragement; in 1955 Her Majesty allowed the European Championships to be held in Windsor Great Park; in 1956 her horse, Countryman, was in the British team which won the Olympic Gold Medal at Stockholm.

In order to prepare horses and riders for the two major annual events, the British Horse Society instituted similar competitions on a smaller scale, known as Horse Trials, of which about 20 are now organised up and down the country each year. These, like the Three-Day Events, comprise Dressage, Cross-Country and Jumping tests, but the cross-country course is much shorter and the whole competition can be completed in one day.

There are three classes in Horse Trials: Preliminary, Intermediate and Open. Thus a competitor may proceed by carefully-planned stages from his first simple competition as a novice to a full-scale Three-Day Event, where he may come to the notice of the selectors for international trial.

HORSE TRIALS QUIZ

1. Who were the members of the British team which won the Olympic Gold Medal at Stockholm in 1956?

*

2. Who was the first lady rider ever to win a Three-Day Event?

*

3. Has any rider ever won the Badminton Horse Trials three years in succession?

*

4. Are ladies eligible to compete in International Three-Day Events?

*

5. Is there any weight restriction in a Three-Day Event?

*

6. Is there a minimum height for horses competing in official Horse Trials?

*

7. What is the penalty for falls of horse or rider outside the penalty zones at Cross-Country obstacles?

*

8. Does it matter how often a rider falls during the Speed, Endurance and Cross-Country test?

*

9. Can a horse be eliminated purely on grounds of unfitness once a Three-Day Event is in progress?

*

10. In the event of a tie for first place in a Three-Day Event, what decides the winner?

*

11. Does elimination from one of the tests in a Three-Day Event or Horse Trial entail elimination from the whole competition?

*

12. How many competitors make up a team in an International Three-Day Event, and how is the team classification reached?

OLYMPIC THREE-DAY EVENT WINNERS

	INDIVIDUAL	TEAM
1912 (*Stockholm*)	Lt. Nordlander (Sweden) on LADY ARTIST	Sweden
1920 (*Antwerp*)	Count Moerner (Sweden) on GERMANIA	Sweden
1924 (*Paris*)	Lt. Voort van Zijp (Holland) on SILVER PIECE	Holland
1928 (*Amsterdam*)	Lt. de Mortanges (Holland) on MARCROIX	Holland
1932 (*Los Angeles*)	Lt. de Mortanges (Holland) on MARCROIX	U.S.A.
1936 (*Berlin*)	Capt. Stubbendorff (Germany) on NURMI	Germany
1948 (*London*)	Capt. B. M. Chevallier (France) on AIGLONNE	U.S.A.
1952 (*Helsinki*)	Capt. H. von Blixen-Finecke (Sweden) on JUBAL	Sweden
1956 (*Stockholm*)	P. Kastenman (Sweden) on ILLUSTER	G.B.

EUROPEAN CHAMPIONSHIP WINNERS

	INDIVIDUAL	TEAM
1953 (*Badminton*)	Major A. L. Rook (G.B.) on STARLIGHT	G.B.
1954 (*Bâle*)	A. E. Hill (G.B.) on CRISPIN	G.B.
1955 (*Windsor*)	Major F. W. C. Weldon (G.B.) on KILBARRY	G.B.
1957 (*Copenhagen*)	Miss S. M. Willcox (G.B.) on HIGH AND MIGHTY	G.B.
1959 (*Harewood*)	Major H. Schwarzenbach (Switzerland) on BURN TROUT	Germany

BADMINTON THREE-DAY EVENT WINNERS

1949 J. Shedden on GOLDEN WILLOW
1950 Capt. J. A. Collings on REMUS
1951 Capt. H. Schwarzenbach (Switzerland) on VAE VICTIS
1952 Capt. M. A. Q. Darley on EMILY LITTLE
1953 Major A. L. Rook on STARLIGHT
1954 Miss M. Hough on BAMBI
1956 Lt.-Col. F. W. C. Weldon on KILBARRY
1957 Miss S. M. Willcox on HIGH AND MIGHTY
1958 Miss S. M. Willcox on HIGH AND MIGHTY
1959 Mrs. J. Waddington (née Willcox) on AIRS AND GRACES

HAREWOOD THREE-DAY EVENT WINNERS

1953 Miss V. I. Machin Goodall on NEPTUNE
1954 Miss P. Molteno on CARMENA
1955 Lt.-Col. F. W. C. Weldon on KILBARRY
1956 Miss S. M. Willcox on HIGH AND MIGHTY
1957 I. H. Dudgeon (Ireland) on CHARLEVILLE
1958 O. Pohlmann (Germany) on POLARFUCHS
1959 Major H. Schwarzenbach (Switzerland) on BURN TROUT

QUIZ ANSWERS

1. Lt.-Col. F. W. C. Weldon on Kilbarry, Major A. L. Rook on Wild Venture, Mr. A. E. Hill on Countryman. 2. Miss V. I. Machin Goodall, who won at Harewood in 1953, riding Neptune. 3. Yes. Mrs. J. Waddington (née Sheila Willcox) won in 1957 and 1958, riding High and Mighty, and in 1959, riding Airs and Graces. 4. Ladies are eligible to compete in all International Three-Day Events except at the Olympic Games. 5. Yes. A minimum weight of 75 kg. (165 lb.) must be carried in the Speed, Endurance and Cross-Country test and in the Jumping test at all International Three-Day Events. 6. Yes. 15 hands. 7. None. 8. No, but if a *horse* falls more than three times in either the Steeplechase or the Cross-Country phase it is eliminated. 9. Yes. A horse which is unfit, exhausted or lame may be eliminated by the Ground Jury at any stage in the competition. 10. The winner is the competitor who completed the Cross-Country phase in the fastest time. If this time is equal, then the fastest time in the Steeplechase phase is taken into account. 11. Yes. 12. Teams consist of four competitors, but at the final team classification only the marks of the three best are taken into account. Teams of three competitors are also admitted, in which case the marks of all three are considered for the final classification.

Coursing

Compiled by Leo C. Wilson
Editor: Greyhound Express and Coursing News

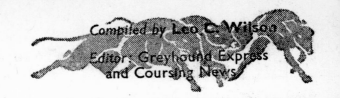

INTRODUCTION

Coursing is one of the oldest sports known and hunting with greyhound-like dogs goes back about 4,000 years. The National Coursing Club, which controls the sport in England, was formed in 1858 but the first Waterloo Cup was held in 1836. Up to 1857 the Waterloo Cup was for 32 dogs but since 1857 it has been for 64 dogs. The first Waterloo Cup in 1836 was an 8-dog stake and the next year a 16-dog stake. It became a 32-dog stake in 1838.

In Ireland coursing comes under the same control as greyhound racing, i.e., by the Irish Coursing Club which is government controlled and the tracks have a close season during the coursing season.

WATERLOO CUP WINNERS

Year		Winner
1836	(8 dogs)	Milanie
	Runner Up	Unicus
1837	(16 dogs)	Fly
	Runner Up	Dr. Fop
1838	(32 dogs)	Bugle
	Runner Up	Risk
1839		Empress
	Runner Up	Brenda
1840		Earwig
	Runner Up	Emperor
1841		Bloomsbury
	Runner Up	Saddler
1842		Priam
	Runner Up	Barrier
1843		Major
	Runner Up	Solon
1844		Speculation
	Runner Up	Dressmaker
1845		Titania
	Runner Up	Sherwood
1846		Harlequin
	Runner Up	Oliver Twist
1847		Senate
	Runner Up	Flirt
1848		Shade
	Runner Up	Smut
1849		Magician
	Runner Up	Forward
1850		Cerito
	Runner Up	Neville
1851		Hughie Graham
	Runner Up	Staymaker
1852		Cerito
	Runner Up	Larriston
1853		Cerito
	Runner Up	Movement
1854		Sackcloth
	Runner Up	Larriston
1855		Judge
	Runner Up	Scotland Yet
1856		Protest
	Runner Up	Judge
1857	(64 dogs)	King Lear
	Runner Up	Sunbeam
1858		Neville
	Runner Up	Deacon
1859		Clive
	Runner Up	Selby
1860		Maid of the Mill
	Runner Up	Sampler
1861		Canaradzo
	Runner Up	Sea Rock
1862		Roaring Meg
	Runner Up	Bowfell
1863		Chloe
	Runner Up	Rebe
1864		King Death
	Runner Up	Rebe
1865		Meg
	Runner Up	King Tom
1866		Brigadier
	Runner Up	Fieldfare
1867		Lobelia
	Runner Up	Royal Seal
1868		Master M'Grath
	Runner Up	Cock Robin
1869		Master M'Grath
	Runner Up	Bab at the Bowster
1870		Sea Cove
	Runner Up	Bendimere
1871		Master M'Grath
	Runner Up	Pretender
1872		Bed of Stone
	Runner Up	Peasant Boy
1873		Muriel
	Runner Up	Peasant Boy
1874		Magnano
	Runner Up	Surprise
1875		Honeymoon
	Runner Up	Corby Castle
1876		Donald
	Runner Up	Lord Glendyne
1877		Coomassie
	Runner Up	Braw Lass
1878		Coomassie
	Runner Up	Zazel
1879		Misterton
	Runner Up	Commerce
1880		Honeywood
	Runner Up	Plunger
1881		Princess Dagmar
	Runner Up	Bishop
1882		Snowflight
	Runner Up	Hornpipe
1883		Wild Mint
	Runner Up	Snowflight
1884		Mineral Water
	Runner Up	Greentick
1885	Divided	Bit of Fashion / Miss Glendyne
1886		Miss Glendyne
	Runner Up	Penelope II
1887	Divided	Greater Scot / Hershel
1888		Burnaby
	Runner Up	Duke MacPherson
1889	Divided	Fullerton / Troughend
1890		Fullerton
	Runner Up	Downpour
1891		Fullerton
	Runner Up	Faster and Faster
1892		Fullerton
	Runner Up	Fitz Fife
1893		Character
	Runner Up	Button Park
1894		Texture
	Runner Up	Falconer
1895		Thoughtless Beauty
	Runner Up	Fortuna Favente
1896		Fabulous Fortune
	Runner Up	Wolf Hill
1897		Gallant
	Runner Up	Five by Tricks
1898		Wild Night
	Runner Up	Lang Syne
1899		Black Fury
	Runner Up	Lapal
1900		Fearless Footsteps
	Runner Up	Lavishly Clothed
1901		Fearless Footsteps
	Runner Up	Cleughbrae
1902		Farndon Ferry
	Runner Up	Wartnaby
1903		Father Flint
	Runner Up	Paracelsus
1904		Homfray
	Runner Up	Minchmuir
1905		Pistol II
	Runner Up	Prince Plausible
1906		Hoprend
	Runner Up	Dividend Deferred
1907		Long Span
	Runner Up	Glenbridge
1908		Hallow Eve
	Runner Up	Silhouette
1909		Dendraspis
	Runner Up	Such a Sell
1910		Heavy Weapon
		Full Steam withdrawn in decider
1911		Jabberwock
	Runner Up	Silk and Scarlet
1912		Tide Time
	Runner Up	Adversary
1913		Hung Well
	Runner Up	Huldee
1914		Dilwyn
	Runner Up	Leucoryx
1915		Winning Number
	Runner Up	Happy Challenge
1916		Harmonicon
	Runner Up	Hopsack
1917-18-19	Cup not held	
1920		Fighting Force
	Runner Up	Honeyman
1921		Shortcoming
	Runner Up	Jassiona
1922		Guard's Brigade
	Runner Up	Beaded Bob
1923		Latto
	Runner Up	Hidden Screw
1924		Cushey Job
	Runner Up	Whitechapel
1925		Pentonville
	Runner Up	Lawman
1926		Jovial Judge
	Runner Up	Running Rein
1927		Golden Seal
	Runner Up	Demetrius
1928		White Collar
	Runner Up	Hastings
1929		Golden Surprise
	Runner Up	Bassoon
1930		Church Street
	Runner Up	Winspear
1931		Conversion
	Runner Up	Had Again
1932		Ben Tinto
	Runner Up	Get Off
1933		Genial Nobleman
	Runner Up	Sold Again
1934		Bryn Truthful
	Runner Up	Rustling Reed
1935		Dee Rock
	Runner Up	Jocker's Resort
1936		Hand Grenade
	Runner Up	Rotten Row
1937		Rotten Row
	Runner Up	Mellow Outlook
1938		Perambulate
	Runner Up	Rotten Row
1939		Delightful Devon
	Runner Up	Dutton Rock
1940		Dee Flint
	Runner Up	Chancellor
1941		Swinging Light
	Runner Up	Stanbridge Selerity
1942		Swinging Light
	Runner Up	Shy Bess
1943		Countryman
	Runner Up	String
1944		Dutton Swordfish
	Runner Up	Jazz Record
1945		Bryn Tritoma
	Runner Up	Joint Command
1946		Maesydd Michael
	Runner Up	Job's Comfort
1947		Constable
	Runner Up	Western Water
1948		Noted Sunlight
	Runner Up	Lady of the Lamp
1949		Life Line
	Runner Up	Roving Minstrel
1950		Roving Minstrel
	Runner Up	Scorpion
1951		Peter's Poet
	Runner Up	Lily of Laguna
1952		Dew Whaler
	Runner Up	Bus Conductor
1953		Holystone Lifelong
	Runner Up	Sucker
1954		Cotton King
	Runner Up	Mayo Post
1955		Full Pete
	Runner Up	Eton Graduate
1956		Magical Lore
	Runner Up	Eternity Ring
1957		Old Kentucky Minstrel
	Runner Up	Dustcoat
1958		Holystone Elf
	Runner Up	Caer Pilot
1959		Mutual Friend
	Runner Up	Lindon Calypso

COURSING QUIZ

1. Which greyhounds (if any) achieved the hat trick in the Waterloo Cup?

★

2. Which was the smallest greyhound to win the Waterloo Cup?

★

3. Is it true that bulldogs were crossed with greyhounds to improve their courage?

★

4. What is park coursing?

★

5. When were coursing rules first drawn up?

★

6. Is a course won by the greyhound which kills the hare?

★

7. What noteworthy break with tradition is associated with Capt. Brice.

★

8. Can track greyhounds take part in coursing meetings without special preparation?

QUIZ ANSWERS

1. Only Fullerton won 3 Waterloo Cups in succession (in fact he won 4 in succession, including the divided win of 1889). Master M'Grath won the Cup 3 times but he missed a year, being beaten in the 1st round. 2. Coomassie, at 44 lbs., was the lightest Waterloo Cup winner on record. 3. Yes. Lord Orford carried out this experiment in the middle of the 18th century. 4. Coursing on an enclosed ground where the hare escapes into an artificial "sough" at the end of the field. This is illegal in England, but is carried out in Ireland. 5. The first comprehensive rules were drawn up in the time of Charles I but they were based on rules drawn up in A.D. 200. 6. Not necessarily. Points are scored for each piece of work and the dog which kills may not have scored any points until the hare is driven into his jaws. 7. He was the first and only Waterloo Cup judge to officiate other than on horseback. This was when, owing to a broken leg, he could not ride and the committee preferred that he should judge from an elevated platform than that they should find another judge. 8. Yes, though most track greyhounds competing at coursing meetings do have extra work and exercise of a different character.

Cricket

Compiled by **Roy Webber**

B.B.C. and *News Chronicle*
Cricket Statistician

A reference to the Prince of Wales playing "creag" appears in the Royal Household Accounts of King Edward I, and it is possible that this is the first reference to the game of cricket, but there can be no definite proof of this. There is no doubt, however, that cricket was played at the Free School of Guildford around the middle of the sixteenth century. There is not much data available covering cricket in the seventeenth century, but it is certain that the period between 1650 and 1700 saw a considerable advance in the popularity of the game.

The evolution of the cricket bat, 1748–1948

The first eleven-a-side match of which there is documentary evidence took place in Sussex in 1697, but it is recorded that sailors played a match near Aleppo, Antioch, in 1676. The first inter-county match, between Kent and London, took place at Lamb's Conduit Fields in 1719.

Laws of Cricket

The earliest known Laws of Cricket are dated 1744, but there is little doubt that this was really a revision of previous laws which have remained lost. Over the years many amendments have been made to the laws, but there have been very few complete revisions—in effect recasting of the existing laws at the time.

The first revision by the M.C.C., then only a year old, took place in 1788, but the next half-century was a period of continual slight change and in 1835 a complete revision was undertaken and a new code of laws published. Again, half-a-century later, in 1884, came another complete revision, while as recently as 1947 came the fourth complete revision of the laws.

Lord's and the M.C.C.

Thomas Lord, a Yorkshireman, backed by the Earl of Winchelsea and the Duke of Richmond, opened the first of the three Lord's grounds in 1787, on the site where Dorset Square now stands. The formation of the Marylebone Cricket Club took place at the same time and within a year of its formation had taken on the responsibilities of law-makers and controllers of the game.

Lord's first move—to North Bank—was made in October 1808, although the first ground was not actually vacated until 1810. But the new situation was short-lived, as in 1813 the ground was needed for development, and in 1814 Lord opened his third, and last, ground at St. John's Wood: the present ground where so much history has been made.

The first Eton v. Harrow match, in which the poet Lord Byron appeared for Harrow, took place at Lord's in 1805, the first Gentlemen v. Players match in 1806 and the first University match between Oxford and Cambridge in 1827. For many years they were the three main matches of the season, but the start of tours and the natural next step of Test cricket meant that these three historical matches lost a great deal of their glamour.

The All-England Eleven

Cricket spread its wings during the first half of the nineteenth century. In the early years cricket had been confined mainly to Hampshire, Sussex and Kent, but as the years passed the game moved north and Yorkshire and Nottinghamshire were soon playing a part in the growth of county cricket.

In 1846 William Clarke, a Nottinghamshire bowler who had been responsible for the opening of the Trent Bridge cricket ground, started the All-England Eleven, composed of the best cricketers of the day. They toured the country playing matches wherever a team could be found to oppose them. XI's, XIV's, XVI's, XVIII's and XXII's came alike to the professionals, but all was not happy under the surface and in the 1850's there were splinter movements away from Clarke's original team. But the gospel had been spread and the way was clear for county cricket to start on an organised basis.

Cricket Tours

Surrey had planned to play a series of matches in Paris in 1789, but the start of the French Revolution prevented the trip being more than an idea. Seventy years were to pass before the first team of cricket tourists left England, and then, in September 1859, under the captaincy of George Parr, twelve cricketers left for a short tour of Canada and the United States.

Once Australia heard about this they felt it was their turn next, and Messrs. Spiers and Pond sent an agent to London to arrange a tour as soon as possible. In 1861–62 the first English team toured Australia, the first of a series of trips over the intervening century.

England have always been leading missionaries in the spreading of cricket and over the next few years maiden tours were undertaken to South Africa (in 1888–89), West Indies (in 1894–95), New Zealand (in 1902–03 for a full-scale tour, although some teams to Australia had also played odd matches in New Zealand), India (1926–27), and Argentine (1911–12). In addition English teams have toured Holland, Denmark, Portugal, Egypt, Kenya—to name only a few countries.

Poster for the Eton-Harrow match of 1836

CRICKET QUIZ

1. Which was the shortest first-class match?

★

2. Which Test batsman spread one innings over four playing days?

★

3. What is the highest individual innings which has been followed by defeat for his side?

★

4. Which player is the only batsman to have hit five sixes off consecutive balls in first-class cricket?

★

5. Which batsmen share the record of scoring ten fifties in consecutive innings in first-class cricket?

★

6. Which batsman scored an innings of 122 while his partners scored only 9 runs in a match at Lord's?

★

QUIZ ANSWERS

1. The Middlesex v. Somerset match at Lord's in 1899 was completed in just over three hours' play. Middlesex scored 86, dismissed Somerset for totals of 35 and 44, winning by an innings and seven runs. 2. I. D. Craig (36), playing for Australia v. England at Manchester in 1956, started his innings on Friday evening and was dismissed after lunch on Tuesday. C. C. McDonald also batted for the four days, but his innings was interrupted by a retirement for injury. 3. P. A. Perrin scored 343 not out for Essex at Chesterfield in 1904, but Derbyshire won by nine wickets. 4. A. W. Wellard (Somerset)—off F. E. Woolley at Wells in 1936 and off T. R. Armstrong at Wells in 1938. 5. E. Tyldesley (Lancashire) in 1926 and D. G. Bradman (Australia) in 1947–48 and 1948. 6. F. R. Brown for Gentlemen v. Players in 1950.

George Parr's team en route for N. America in 1859

CRICKET QUIZ

1. Which batsmen scored a century in their only match in first-class cricket?

★

2. Which batsman scored a century in the first match in which he played in each of the different countries in which he played?

3. Who is the only batsman to score a double-century in each innings of a first-class match? (*above*)

★

4. Who has scored the most centuries in consecutive innings in first-class cricket?

★

5. What is the record aggregate of runs by one batsman in a first-class season in England?

★

6. What is the highest score made by a "last man in", a number 11 batsman?

★

7. What is the highest aggregate of runs scored in a month by one batsman?

★

8. What is the highest batting average recorded in an English season?

QUIZ ANSWERS

1. Five batsmen—N. Callaway for New South Wales in 1914–15, S. C. Wootton for Victoria in 1923–24, H. Grangel for Victoria in 1935–36, M. N. Harbottle for Army in 1938 and J. R. Gill for Ireland in 1948. 2. A. R. Morris of New South Wales—148 and 111 v. Queensland at Sydney in 1940–41, 138 v. Worcestershire in 1948 in his first match in England, 153 v. Natal at Durban in 1949–50 in his first match in South Africa and 157 v. Jamaica at Kingston in 1954–55 in his first match in the West Indies. 3. A. E. Fagg scored 244 and 202 not out for Kent v. Essex at Colchester in 1938. 4. C. B. Fry in 1901 and D. G. Bradman in 1938–39 have both scored six consecutive centuries. 5. D. C. S. Compton scored 3,816 runs (average 90.85) in 1947. 6. T. P. B. Smith, playing for Essex v. Derbyshire at Chesterfield in 1947, scored 163 and shared in a last wicket stand of 218 with F. H. Vigar. 7. L. Hutton scored 1,294 runs (average 92.42) in June 1949. 8. D. G. Bradman scored 2,429 runs with an average of 115.66 in 1938.

Once tours had started abroad, the way was clear for overseas teams to come to England and in 1868 a team of Australian aborigines, under Charles Lawrence's managership, played a long series of matches in England. The first Australian team came to England in 1878, the South Africans followed in 1894, West Indies in 1900, India in 1911, New Zealand in 1927 and South America in 1932.

But before Test cricket could start, in 1876–77, the County Championship had started in England.

The County Cricket Championship

The first-class cricket counties had played a kind of unofficial championship in the 1860s, but it was obviously very rough and ready, and in the winter of 1872–73 the counties held a series of meetings and from them emerged the rules of county cricket qualification. Thus the way was clear to start a proper competition in 1873; but although this is the year which has always been regarded as the first year of the competition, it was not officially recognised by the M.C.C. and the counties themselves until 1890.

Charles Absolom   J. T. Tyldesley

Nine counties competed in the first season (1873)—Derbyshire, Gloucestershire, Kent, Lancashire, Middlesex, Nottinghamshire, Surrey, Sussex and Yorkshire. Derbyshire dropped out after 1887, but the 1890s saw the competition almost double in size. Somerset were added in 1891, Derbyshire returned and Essex, Hampshire, Leicestershire, and Warwickshire entered for the first time in 1895 and Worcestershire were added in 1899. This brought the competing counties to fifteen, and this century Northamptonshire (in 1905) and Glamorgan (in 1921) have been the only new additions. Devon (in 1949) made an application to be granted first-class status, but this was refused by the County Cricket Advisory Committee.

The rules of county qualification have changed greatly over the years, but the basic requirements of birth or residence still hold good, apart from the provision made for "special registration" of a player for one county when he is not required by the county for whom he is qualified.

The methods of deciding the Championship have been changed frequently and there have been

---

James Lillywhite's team which toured Australia in 1876–77

altogether 16 different ways of winning points. From 1873 to 1886 the smallest number of lost matches decided the order, but that was obviously unfair and for the years 1887 to 1889 a win counted one point and a draw half-a-point. From 1890 to 1909 the number of points gained was decided by deducting losses from wins, but in 1910 the result was decided by the percentage of matches won to matches played (perhaps the best system of all). In 1911 first innings points were awarded for the first time; and although the points value was changed on occasion, it was not until the start of bonus points for faster scoring on first innings in 1957 that a real change was made in the method of allocating points.

As the table of Championships shows, the title moved freely between north and south up to the 1914–18 war, but between the wars the two wins by Middlesex (in 1920 and 1921) were the only challenge to northern supremacy.

Test Cricket

The first match on level terms between England and Australian teams took place at Melbourne in March 1877, Australia winning by 45 runs after Charles Bannerman had opened the match by scoring the first Test century (165 retired hurt). The 1878 Australian team to England did not play a Test match, but two years later the first Test was played in England at the Oval, England winning by five wickets after W. G. Grace had scored the first century (152) for his country.

Australia defeated England by the narrow margin of seven runs at the Oval in August 1882, and on the following day the *Sporting Times* published their now famous obituary of English cricket. A few months later the Hon. Ivo Bligh (later Earl Darnley) captained the England team which won the second and third Tests of a rubber in Australia and was presented, by some Australian ladies, with a little urn containing the ashes of a burnt stump—and so started the story of the Ashes.

England's first Test match against South Africa was played in 1888–89, and Australia first met South Africa in 1902–03, but it was not until 1928 that a fourth country entered the field of Test cricket. West Indies were granted Test-match status for their 1928 tour to England, New Zealand just over a year later (in 1929–30) when they were hosts to an M.C.C. team, India in 1932 and Pakistan as recently as 1952–53.

Whether in fact the early Test matches were really considered as such at the time is doubtful, and the term "Test match" does not seem to have been used before 1894–95. Certainly most of the early English teams that visited Australia were far below the full strength of English cricket, while there is no doubt at all that the Test matches between England and South Africa between 1888–89 and 1898–99 were not regarded as even of first-class status at the time they were played. Over-indulgent statisticians included most of these matches in Test records, and nearly a century later their status is safe by tradition alone.

The urn and bag of "The Ashes"

Administration of Cricket

The leading cricket club in England in the middle of the eighteenth century was Hambledon, but it lost its power in the 1780s and in 1792 the players had their last match. A few years earlier, in 1787, the Marylebone Cricket Club was formed and as they were the leading club socially they took over the position as controllers and law-makers of the game. Within a year of their formation they were responsible for a complete revision of the laws of the game, and they have held the highest position in world cricket ever since.

County cricket in the early years was played on a very happy-go-lucky basis, and it was not until 1836 that Sussex, the oldest of the county clubs, was formed. Most counties were slow to follow this start, and it is interesting to see the table of formation of county clubs by date (the earliest formation date is given, not that of a later reforming):

1836—Sussex.
1843—Northamptonshire.
1845—Surrey.
1859—Kent and Nottinghamshire.
1863—Hampshire, Warwickshire and Yorkshire.
1864—Essex, Lancashire and Middlesex.
1865—Worcestershire.
1870—Derbyshire and Gloucestershire.
1873—Leicestershire.
1875—Somerset.
1888—Glamorgan.

Until the 1872–73 meeting of the county clubs and the laying down of rules of county qualification there were no rules for county cricket of any kind, and for years after that date it was due to the members of the press that the County Championship table was compiled and the title of County Champion awarded. At a meeting in December 1889 the county secretaries officially recognised the competition and laid down rules for the awarding of points, and both this meeting and that of the county captains which followed a few years later were held annually and decided the problems connected with county cricket. The Advisory County Cricket Committee which took their place, and now deals with county cricket in every aspect, was formed by the M.C.C. in 1904. Rule 3 of the constitution states that "All resolutions passed by this committee shall be submitted to the M.C.C. Committee for confirmation", so that the ruling body position of the M.C.C. is confirmed over that of the Advisory County Cricket Committee.

In the early years of Test cricket in England the county committee of the ground staging the Test match was responsible for the selection of the England team. As far as overseas tours were concerned, they were all privately organised and had no official status at all. This was, obviously, an undesirable state of affairs and in 1898, due to the exertions of Lord Hawke, the Board of Control for Test Matches in England was formed. This Board is responsible for the

organisation and administration of all matters connected with Test and trial matches in England, but delegates the authority for the selection of the actual England teams to a Selection Committee. This committee is usually composed of five: a chairman, three members and the captain of the England team. As far as overseas tours are concerned, the M.C.C. took over the responsibility for official touring teams in 1903–04, with a visit to Australia, and have been the controlling body ever since.

With the spread of cricket in the first decade of this century it was decided to hold a joint meeting of the M.C.C., the Australian Board of Control and the South African Cricket Association at Lord's in 1909—this was the first Imperial Cricket Conference. This body is now

concerned with the approval of the interchange of official tours, the qualification rules for Test players and other matters of common interest. In 1947, for the first time, they laid down definite rules for the classification of first-class matches (in earlier years this matter had been left to the interested statistician and historian).

All members of the Imperial Cricket Conference meet in Test cricket—England, Australia and South Africa, the original members in 1909, were joined by West Indies, New Zealand and India in 1926 and Pakistan in 1952.

Other countries which have central ruling cricket bodies, but do not play first-class cricket, are Canada, Ceylon, Denmark, Fiji, Holland, Malaya and a combined body representing Kenya, Tanganyika and Uganda.

GREAT NAMES IN CRICKET

This selection does not include cricketers currently playing

ROBERT ABEL (Surrey). Born in South London 30/11/1857, died at his home near the Oval 10/12/1936, aged 79. One of the shortest players in first-class cricket, his fine batting as opening batsman made him a valued member of the Surrey team for many years. He appeared for the county from 1881 to 1904, but did not mature until 1886 and in his last two seasons was troubled with failing eyesight. He played in 13 Tests for England, and toured Australia in 1887–88 and 1891–92 and South Africa in 1888–89. His full career figures were 32,621 runs (av. 35.53), 74 centuries and 255 wickets (av. 24.17). His best score of 357 not out was made against Somerset at the Oval in 1899, when he carried his bat through an innings of 811—still the greatest number of runs seen added by one batsman during his innings. He was at his best between 1895 and 1902, when he never failed to pass the 2,000 runs mark, with a best of 3,309 runs (av. 55.15) in 1901. It is interesting to note that he appeared in no fewer than 41 first-class matches in 1902—more than any modern first-class cricketer is required to do.

Indies in 1929–30 and 1934–35 and to India in 1950–51 as captain of the Commonwealth team. His career aggregate was 37,254 runs (av. 43.56), 102 centuries, and 1,113 dismissals (698 ct., 415 st.).

SYDNEY F. BARNES (Warwickshire, Lancashire and Staffordshire). Born at Smethwick 19/4/1876. Has strong claims to the title of the greatest bowler of all—a right-arm bowler of above medium-pace who could move or spin the ball either way and was a master of accuracy and length. Oddly enough, he spent most of his career playing Minor County cricket for Staffordshire and League cricket for various teams, with the result that much of his first-class cricket was in representative matches. He played for Warwickshire in 1895 and 1896, for Lancashire from 1899 to 1903 and, after missing three seasons, returned in 1907 and continued in odd matches until 1930. His final bag of wickets was 719 (av. 17.09), with a best of 131 wickets (av. 17.85) in 1903. He toured Australia in 1901–02, 1907–08, and 1911–12 and took

Robert Abel

L. E. G. Ames

B. J. T. Bosanquet

LESLIE E. G. AMES (Kent). Born at Elham 3/12/1905. Few would decline Ames' claim to be the finest wicket-keeping batsman the world has seen. On three occasions he completed the wicket-keeper's double of 1,000 runs and 100 dismissals in a season (in 1928, 1929 and 1932), and only J. T. Murray of Middlesex (in 1957) has equalled this feat. Ames' total of 127 dismissals (79 ct., 48 st.) in 1929 remains a record. His first match was in 1926, but recurrent back trouble caused his retirement in 1951 (he had virtually given up wicket-keeping in 1939). Between 1929–30 and 1938–39 he played in 47 Tests for England, and was first appointed as an England Test selector in 1950. He scored 1,000 runs in a season 17 times and hit a best score of 295 v. Gloucestershire at Folkestone in 1933. One of the few cricket tourists to have been virtually everywhere—to Australia and New Zealand in 1928–29, 1932–33 and 1936–37, to South Africa in 1938–39, to West

104 wickets (av. 10.74) on the 1913–14 South African tour. He played in only 27 Tests for England, but took 189 wickets (av. 16.43), including a record of 49 wickets (av. 10.93) in four Tests of the 1913–14 rubber against South Africa. At Johannesburg he took 17 for 159 in the match, which remained a record for Tests until J. C. Laker took 19 at Manchester in 1956.

B. J. T. BOSANQUET (Middlesex). Born at Enfield 13/10/1877, died in Surrey 12/10/1936, aged 58. A fine all-round cricketer who was educated at Eton and Oxford University, he will be chiefly remembered as the inventor of the googly. He played first-class cricket from 1898 to 1919, but rarely bowled after 1905. He won two Test matches for England, taking 6 for 51 v. Australia at Sydney in 1903–04 and 8 for 107 v. Australia at Nottingham in 1905, but only appeared in seven Tests altogether. He played quite a lot of cricket over a

(Contd. on p. 113 col. 3)

short span of years, and visited North America in 1898, 1899 and 1901, West Indies in 1901–02, New Zealand and Australia in 1902–03 and Australia in 1903–04. The best of his 21 centuries was 214 for Rest of England v. Yorkshire at the Oval in 1908, while he twice took nine wickets in an innings—9 for 31 for Oxford U. v. Sussex at Oxford in 1900 and 9 for 107 for M.C.C. v. South Africans at Lord's in 1904.

CRICKET QUIZ

1. In which year was the first University match between Oxford and Cambridge played?

★

2. Which batsman scored a century in each of the three University matches in which he played? (*above*)

★

3. Which players enjoyed the largest benefits (*a*) before 1914, (*b*) between the wars, (*c*) since the 1939–45 war?

★

4. Which batsman scored a century without hitting a single boundary?

★

5. Only one bowler has taken 100 wickets in an Australian first-class season. Who is he?

★

6. What is the longest recorded throw of a cricket ball?

★

7. What are the three lowest individual innings scores that have not yet been recorded?

★

8. Who is the youngest player to appear in first-class cricket?

QUIZ ANSWERS

1. 1827; the match at Lord's was drawn. 2. M. J. K. Smith of Oxford—201 not out in 1954, 104 in 1955 and 117 in 1956. 3. (a) £3,703 by G. H. Hirst of Yorkshire in 1904, (b) £4,016 by R. Kilner of Yorkshire in 1925, (c) £14,000 by C. Washbrook of Lancashire in 1948. 4. W. M. Woodfull (118) for Australians v. Surrey at the Oval in 1926—Woodfull's only four was his last scoring stroke. 5. C. T. B. Turner took 106 wickets (average 13) in 1887–88. 6. 140 yards 2 feet by R. Percival on the Durham Sands Racecourse in 1884. 7. No batsman has yet scored 289, 298, 307. 8. C. C. Dacre was aged only 14 when he played for Auckland v. Wellington at Auckland in 1914–15.

CRICKET QUIZ

1. Who is the oldest player to appear in first-class cricket?

★

2. How many pairs of twin brothers have appeared in first-class cricket?

★

3. What is the highest number of runs seen added by one batsman in an innings in first-class cricket?

★

4. Which was the longest match in first-class cricket?

★

5. Which batsmen have scored a century before lunch on the first day of a Test match?

★

6. Which Australian batsman was dismissed five times in the nineties in Test matches against England?

★

7. Which batsman played the first ball he received into the stumps without removing a bail and went on to score a Test century?

★

8. What is the highest score made by a "night-watchman" batsman in Test cricket?

QUIZ ANSWERS

1. Raja Maharaj Singh, at the age of 72, captained the Bombay Governor's XI v. Commonwealth at Bombay in 1950–51. 2. Four—A. V. and E. A. Bedser of Surrey, J. S. and W. H. Denton of Northamptonshire, A. D. E. and A. E. S. Rippon of Somerset, F. G. and W. H. Stephens of Warwickshire. 3. 811 by R. Abel (357 not out) for Surrey v. Somerset at the Oval in 1899. Abel carried his bat through the innings. 4. The South Africa v. England Test at Durban in 1938–39, lasted for ten days, and was then left drawn. 5. V. T. Trumper at Manchester in 1902, C. G. Macartney at Leeds in 1926 and D. G. Bradman at Leeds in 1930, all for Australia v. England. 6. C. Hill—96 in 1897–98, 99, 98 and 97 in consecutive innings in 1901–02 and 98 in 1911–12. 7. F. E. Woolley, playing for England v. South Africa at Johannesburg in 1922–23, played the first ball he received, from A. E. Hall, into his stumps, but went on to score 115 not out. 8. 98 by H. Larwood, for England v. Australia at Sydney in 1932–33.

Alfred Shaw   V. T. Trumper   F. E. Woolley

TEST CRICKET—RESULTS AND SCORES OF ALL MATCHES

ENGLAND v. AUSTRALIA

Venue and Result	England 1st Inns	England 2nd Inns	Australia 1st Inns	Australia 2nd Inns
1876-77 in Australia				
Melbourne—Australia 45 runs	196	108	245	104
Melbourne—England 4 wkts	261	122–6	122	259
1878-79 in Australia				
Melbourne—Australia 10 wkts	113	160	256	19–0
1880 in England				
Oval—England 5 wkts	420	57–5	149	327

The M.C.C. team in Australia, 1911–12

1881-82 in Australia				
Melbourne—Drawn	294	308	320	127–3
Sydney—Australia 5 wkts	133	232	197	169–5
Sydney—Australia 6 wkts	188	134	260	66–4
Melbourne—Drawn	309	234–2	300	—
1882 in England				
Oval—Australia 7 runs	101	77	63	122
1882-83 in Australia				
Melbourne—Australia 9 wkts	177	169	291	58–1
Melbourne—England Inns & 27 runs	294	—	114	153
Sydney—England 69 runs	247	123	218	83
Sydney—Australia 4 wkts	263	197	262	199–6
1884 in England				
Manchester—Drawn	95	180–9	182	—
Lord's—England Inns & 5 runs	379	—	229	145
Oval—Drawn	346	85–2	551	—
1884-85 in Australia				
Adelaide—England 8 wkts	369	67–2	243	191
Melbourne—England 10 wkts	401	7–0	279	126
Sydney—Australia 6 runs	133	207	181	165
Sydney—Australia 8 wkts	269	77	309	38–2
Melbourne—England Inns & 98 runs	386	—	163	125

1886 in England				
Manchester—England 4 wkts	223	107–6	205	123
Lord's—England Inns & 106 runs	353	—	121	126
Oval—England Inns & 217 runs	434	—	68	149
1886-87 in Australia				
Sydney—England 13 runs	45	184	119	97
Sydney—England 71 runs	151	154	84	150
1887-88 in Australia				
Sydney—England 126 runs	113	137	42	82
1888 in England				
Lord's—Australia 61 runs	53	62	116	60
Oval—England Inns & 137 runs	317	—	80	100
Manchester—England Inns & 21 runs	172	—	81	70
1890 in England				
Lord's—England 7 wkts	173	137–3	132	176
Oval—England 2 wkts	100	95–8	92	102
Manchester—Abandoned	—	—	—	—
1891-92 in Australia				
Melbourne—Australia 54 runs	264	158	240	236
Sydney—Australia 72 runs	307	157	145	391
Adelaide—England Inns & 230 runs	499	—	100	169
1893 in England				
Lord's—Drawn	334	234–8d	269	—
Oval—England Inns & 43 runs	483	—	91	349
Manchester—Drawn	243	118–4	204	236
1894-95 in Australia				
Sydney—England 10 runs	325	437	586	166
Melbourne—England 94 runs	75	475	123	333
Adelaide—Australia 382 runs	124	143	238	411
Sydney—Australia 6 runs	65	72	284	—
Melbourne—England 6 wkts	385	298–4	414	267
1896 in England				
Lord's—England 6 wkts	292	111–4	53	347
Manchester—Australia 3 wkts	231	305	412	125–7
Oval—England 66 runs	145	84	119	44
1897-98 in Australia				
Sydney—England 9 wkts	551	96–1	237	408
Melbourne—Australia Inns & 55 runs	315	150	520	—
Adelaide—Australia Inns & 13 runs	278	282	573	—
Melbourne—Australia 8 wkts	174	263	323	115–2
Sydney—Australia 6 wkts	335	178	239	276–4
1899 in England				
Nottingham—Drawn	193	155–7	252	230–8d
Lord's—Australia 10 wkts	206	240	421	28–0
Leeds—Drawn	220	19–0	172	224
Manchester—Drawn	372	94–3	196	346–7d
Oval—Drawn	576	—	352	254–5
1901-02 in Australia				
Sydney—England Inns & 124 runs	464	—	168	172
Melbourne—Australia 229 runs	61	175	112	353
Adelaide—Australia 4 wkts	388	247	321	315–6
Sydney—Australia 7 wkts	317	99	299	121–3
Melbourne—Australia 32 runs	189	178	144	255
1902 in England				
Birmingham—Drawn	376–9d	—	36	46–2
Lord's—Drawn	102–2	—	—	—
Sheffield—Australia 143 runs	145	195	194	289
Manchester—Australia 3 runs	262	120	299	86
Oval—England 1 wkt	183	263–9	324	121
1903-04 in Australia				
Sydney—England 5 wkts	577	194–5	285	485
Melbourne—England 185 runs	315	103	122	111
Adelaide—Australia 216 runs	245	278	388	351
Sydney—England 157 runs	249	210	131	171
Melbourne—Australia 218 runs	61	101	247	133
1905 in England				
Nottingham—England 213 runs	196	426–5d	221	188
Lord's—Drawn	282	151–5	181	—
Leeds—Drawn	301	295–5d	195	224–7
Manchester—England Inns & 80 runs	446	—	197	169
Oval—Drawn	430	261–6d	363	124–4
1907-08 in Australia				
Sydney—Australia 2 wkts	273	300	300	275–8
Melbourne—England 1 wkt	382	282–9	266	397
Adelaide—Australia 245 runs	363	183	285	506
Melbourne—Australia 308 runs	105	186	214	385
Sydney—Australia 49 runs	281	229	137	422
1909 in England				
Birmingham—England 10 wkts	121	105–0	74	151
Lord's—Australia 9 runs	269	121	350	41–1
Leeds—Australia 126 runs	182	87	188	207
Manchester—Drawn	119	108–3	147	279–9d
Oval—Drawn	352	104–3	325	339–5d

108

1911-12 in Australia

Sydney—Australia 146 runs	318	291	447	308
Melbourne—England 8 wkts	265	219–2	184	299
Adelaide—England 7 wkts	501	112–3	133	476
Melbourne—England Inns & 225 runs ..	589	—	191	173
Sydney—England 70 runs	324	214	176	292

1912 in England

Lord's—Drawn	310–7d	—	282–7	—
Manchester—Drawn	203	—	14–0	—
Oval—England 244 runs	245	175	111	65

1920-21 in Australia

Sydney—Australia 377 runs	190	281	267	581
Melbourne—Australia Inns & 91 runs ..	251	157	499	—
Adelaide—Australia 119 runs	447	370	354	582
Melbourne—Australia 8 wkts	284	315	389	211–2
Sydney—Australia 9 wkts	204	280	392	93–1

1921 in England

Nottingham—Australia 10 wkts	112	147	232	30–0
Lord's—Australia 8 wkts	187	283	342	131–2
Leeds—Australia 219 runs	259	202	407	273–7d
Manchester—Drawn	362–4d	44–1	175	—
Oval—Drawn	403–8d	244–2	389	—

1924-25 in Australia

Sydney—Australia 193 runs	298	411	450	452
Melbourne—Australia 81 runs	479	290	600	250
Adelaide—Australia 11 runs	365	363	489	250
Melbourne—England Inns & 29 runs ..	548	—	269	250
Sydney—Australia 307 runs	167	146	295	325

1926 in England

Nottingham—Drawn	32–0	—	—	—
Lord's—Drawn	475–3d	—	383	194–5
Leeds—Drawn	294	254–3	494	—
Manchester—Drawn	305–5	—	335	—
Oval—England 289 runs	280	436	302	125

1934 in England

Nottingham—Australia 238 runs	268	141	374	273–8d
Lord's—England Inns & 38 runs	440	—	284	118
Manchester—Drawn	627–9d	123–0d	491	66–1
Leeds—Drawn	200	229–6	584	—
Oval—Australia 562 runs	321	145	701	327

1936-37 in Australia

Brisbane—England 322 runs	358	256	234	58
Sydney—England Inns & 22 runs	426–6d	—	80	324
Melbourne—Australia 365 runs	76–9d	323	200–9d	564
Adelaide—Australia 148 runs	330	243	288	433
Melbourne—Australia Inns & 200 runs ..	239	165	604	—

1938 in England

Nottingham—Drawn	658–8d	—	411	427–6
Lord's—Drawn	494	242–8d	422	204–6
Manchester—Abandoned	—	—	—	—
Leeds—Australia 5 wkts	223	123	242	107–5
Oval—England Inns & 579 runs	903–7d	—	201	123

1946-47 in Australia

Brisbane—Australia Inns & 332 runs ..	141	172	645	—
Sydney—Australia Inns & 33 runs ..	255	371	659–8d	—
Melbourne—Drawn	351	310–7	365	536
Adelaide—Drawn	460	340–8d	487	215–1
Sydney—Australia 5 wkts	280	186	253	214–5

1948 in England

Nottingham—Australia 8 wkts	165	441	509	98–2
Lord's—Australia 409 runs	215	186	350	460–7d
Manchester—Drawn	363	174–3d	221	92–1
Leeds—Australia 7 wkts	496	365–8d	458	404–3
Oval—Australia Inns & 149 runs ..	52	188	389	—

1950-51 in Australia

Brisbane—Australia 70 runs	68–7d	122	228	32–7d
Melbourne—Australia 28 runs	197	150	194	181
Sydney—Australia Inns & 13 runs ..	290	123	426	—
Adelaide—Australia 274 runs	272	228	371	403–8d
Melbourne—England 8 wkts	320	95–2	217	197

A. E. Trott

D. C. S. Compton

W. Bardsley

R. R. Lindwall

D. Tallon

1928-29 in Australia

Brisbane—England 675 runs	521	342–8d	122	66
Sydney—England 8 wkts..............	636	16–2	253	397
Melbourne—England 3 wkts	417	332–7	397	351
Adelaide—England 12 runs...........	334	383	369	336
Melbourne—Australia 5 wkts	519	257	491	287–5

1930 in England

Nottingham—England 93 runs	270	302	144	335
Lord's—Australia 7 wkts..............	425	375	729–6d	72–3
Leeds—Drawn	391	95–3	566	—
Manchester—Drawn	251–8	—	345	—
Oval—Australia Inns & 39 runs	405	251	695	—

1932-33 in Australia

Sydney—England 10 wkts	524	1–0	360	164
Melbourne—Australia 111 runs	169	139	228	191
Adelaide—England 338 runs	341	412	222	193
Brisbane—England 6 wkts	356	162–4	340	175
Sydney—England 8 wkts..........	454	168–2	435	182

C. Washbrook

T. E. Bailey

A. R. Morris

CRICKET QUIZ

1. Which county fielded a complete team of "foreigners", not one of whom had been born within the county borders, against the 1948 Australian team?

★

2. Which batsman holds the record for the slowest fifty in first-class cricket?

★

3. Which batsman holds the record for the slowest century in first-class cricket?

★

4. Which batsman holds the record for the slowest double-century in first-class cricket?

★

5. What is the oldest age to which a first-class cricketer has lived (as far as reliable records can prove)?

★

6. What is the longest time that a first-class county has been without a single victory?

★

7. What is the best performance by a bowler before lunch on the first day of a first-class match?

★

8. Which player captained both a successful England team and a County Championship team in the same season?

QUIZ ANSWERS

1. Warwickshire. 2. T. E. Bailey, 50 in 361 minutes for England v. Australia at Brisbane in 1958–59. 3. D. J. McGlew, 100 in 545 minutes for South Africa v. Australia at Durban in 1957–58. 4. S. G. Barnes, 200 in 570 minutes for Australia v. England at Sydney in 1946–47. 5. 98 by Herbert Jenner, G. C. Attfield and F. A. Mackinnon. 6. Northamptonshire did not win a single match between May 1935 and May 1939. 7. W. R. Hammond took 9 for 23 for Gloucestershire v. Worcestershire at Cheltenham in 1928. 8. P. B. H. May led England to rubber victories against West Indies in 1957 and New Zealand in 1958, Surrey being County Champions each season.

CRICKET QUIZ

1. What is the record innings total in all first-class cricket?

★

2. What is the record innings total for a County Championship match?

★

3. What is the highest innings total ever recorded in a second innings by a first-class team?

★

4. What is the highest total recorded in the fourth innings of a first-class match?

★

5. Who recorded the first century in all cricket?

★

6. What is the record individual innings at Lord's?

★

7. Who has scored the most double-centuries in first-class cricket?

★

8. Which batsmen scored a century in each innings of their debut match in first-class cricket?

QUIZ ANSWERS

1. Victoria scored 1,107 against New South Wales at Melbourne in 1926–27. In the return match at Sydney, four weeks later, New South Wales dismissed Victoria for a total of 35 all out. 2. Yorkshire totalled 887 against Warwickshire at Birmingham in 1896. 3. New South Wales totalled 770 in their second innings against South Australia at Adelaide in 1920–21; they had totalled 304 in their first innings. 4. England scored 654 for five wickets against South Africa at Durban in 1938–39 after being set to get 696 runs for victory. 5. John Small, sen., playing for Hambledon against Surrey at Hambledon in 1775, scored 136—the first recorded century. 6. J. B. Hobbs scored 316 not out for Surrey against Middlesex in 1926. 7. D. G. Bradman with 37 is the leader, but W. R. Hammond with 36 is a close runner-up. 8. A. R. Morris (148 and 111) for New South Wales v. Queensland at Sydney in 1940–41 and N. J. Contractor (152 and 102 not out) for Gujerat v. Baroda at Baroda in 1952–53. Both batsmen, oddly enough, were left-handed.

C. T. B. Turner

H. Larwood

H. J. Tayfield

England v. Australia (contd.)

	1st Inns	2nd Inns	1st Inns	2nd Inns
1953 in England				
Nottingham—Drawn	144	120–1	249	123
Lord's—Drawn	372	282–7	346	368
Manchester—Drawn	276		318	35–8
Leeds—Drawn	167	275	266	147–4
Oval—England 8 wkts	306	132–2	275	162
1954–55 in Australia				
Brisbane—Australia Inns & 154 runs	190	257	601–8d	
Sydney—England 38 runs	154	296	228	184
Melbourne—England 128 runs	191	279	231	111
Adelaide—England 5 wkts	341	97–5	323	111
Sydney—Drawn	371–7d	—	221	118–6
1956 in England				
Nottingham—Drawn	217–8d	188–3d	148	120–3
Lord's—Australia 185 runs	171	186	285	257
Leeds—England Inns & 42 runs	325	—	143	140
Manchester—England Inns & 170 runs	459	—	84	205
Oval—Drawn	247	182–3d	202	27–5
1958–59 in Australia				
Brisbane—Australia 8 wkts	134	198	186	147–2
Melbourne—Australia 8 wkts	259	87	308	42–2
Sydney—Drawn	219	287–7d	357	54–2
Adelaide—Australia 10 wkts	240	270	476	36–0
Melbourne—Australia 9 wkts	205	214	351	70–1

R. Benaud

P. B. H. May

D. V. P. Wright

ENGLAND v. SOUTH AFRICA

	England		South Africa	
	1st Inns	2nd Inns	1st Inns	2nd Inns
1888–89 in South Africa				
Port Elizabeth—England 8 wkts	148	67–2	84	129
Cape Town—England Inns & 202 runs	292	—	47	43
1891–92 in South Africa				
Cape Town—England Inns & 189 runs	369	—	97	83
1895–96 in South Africa				
Port Elizabeth—England 288 runs	185	226	93	30
Johannesburg—England Inns & 197 runs	482	—	151	134
Cape Town—England Inns & 33 runs	265	—	115	117
1898–99 in South Africa				
Johannesburg—England 32 runs	145	237	251	99
Cape Town—England 210 runs	92	330	177	35
1905–06 in South Africa				
Johannesburg—South Africa 1 wkt	184	190	91	287–9
Johannesburg—South Africa 9 wkts	148	160	277	33–1
Johannesburg—South Africa 243 runs	295	196	385	349–5d
Cape Town—England 4 wkts	198	160–6	218	138
Cape Town—South Africa Inns & 16 runs	187	130	333	—
1907 in England				
Lord's—Drawn	428		140	185–3
Leeds—England 53 runs	76	162	110	75
Oval—Drawn	295	138	178	159–5
1909–10 in South Africa				
Johannesburg—South Africa 19 runs	310	224	208	345
Durban—South Africa 95 runs	199	252	199	347
Johannesburg—England 3 wkts	322	221–7	305	237
Cape Town—South Africa 4 wkts	203	178	207	175–6
Cape Town—England 9 wkts	417	16–1	103	327
1912 in England				
Lord's—England Inns & 62 runs	337	—	58	217
Leeds—England 174 runs	242	238	147	159
Oval—England 10 wkts	176	14–0	95	93
1913–14 in South Africa				
Durban—England Inns & 157 runs	450	—	182	111
Johannesburg—England Inns & 12 runs	403	—	160	231
Johannesburg—England 91 runs	238	308	151	304
Durban—Drawn	163	154–5	170	305–9d
Port Elizabeth—England 10 wkts	411	11–0	193	228
1922–23 in South Africa				
Johannesburg—South Africa 168 runs	182	218	148	420
Cape Town—England 1 wkt	183	173–9	113	242
Durban—Drawn	428	11–1	368	—
Johannesburg—Drawn	244	376–6d	295	247–4
Durban—England 109 runs	281	241	179	234
1924 in England				
Birmingham—England Inns & 18 runs	438	—	30	390
Lord's—England Inns & 18 runs	531–2d	—	273	240
Leeds—England 9 wkts	396	60–1	132	323
Manchester—Drawn	—		116–4	—
Oval—Drawn	421–8		342	—
1927–28 in South Africa				
Johannesburg—England 10 wkts	313	57–0	196	170
Cape Town—England 87 runs	133	428	250	224
Durban—Drawn	430	132–2	246	464–8d
Johannesburg—South Africa 4 wkts	265	215	328	156–6
Durban—South Africa 8 wkts	282	118	332–7d	69–2
1929 in England				
Birmingham—Drawn	245	308–4d	250	171–1
Lord's—Drawn	302	312–8d	322	90–5
Leeds—England 5 wkts	328	186–5	236	275
Manchester—England Inns & 32 runs	427–7d	—	130	265
Oval—Drawn	258	264–1	492–8d	—
1930–31 in South Africa				
Johannesburg—South Africa 28 runs	193	211	126	306
Cape Town—Drawn	350	252	513–8d	—
Durban—Drawn	223–1d		177	145–8
Johannesburg—Drawn	442	169–9d	295	280–7
Durban—Drawn	230	72–4	252	219–7d
1935 in England				
Nottingham—Drawn	384–7d		220	17–1
Lord's—South Africa 157 runs	198	151	228	278–7d
Leeds—Drawn	216	294–7d	171	194–5
Manchester—Drawn	357	231–6d	318	169–2
Oval—Drawn	534–6d	—	476	287–6
1938–39 in South Africa				
Johannesburg—Drawn	422	291–4d	390	108–1
Cape Town—Drawn	559–9d	—	286	201–2
Durban—England Inns & 13 runs	469–4d	—	103	353
Johannesburg—Drawn	215	203–4	349–8d	—
Durban—Drawn	316	654–5	530	481
1947 in England				
Nottingham—Drawn	208	551	533	166–1
Lord's—England 10 wkts	554–8d	26–0	327	252
Manchester—England 7 wkts	478	130–3	339	267
Leeds—England 10 wkts	317–7d	47–0	175	184
Oval—Drawn	427	325–6d	302	423–7
1948–49 in South Africa				
Durban—England 2 wkts	253	128–8	161	219
Johannesburg—Drawn	608	—	315	270–2
Cape Town—Drawn	308	276–3	356	142–4
Johannesburg—Drawn	379	253–7d	257–9d	194–4
Port Elizabeth—England 3 wkts	395	174–7	379	187–3d
1951 in England				
Nottingham—South Africa 71 runs	419–9d	114	483–9d	121
Lord's—England 10 wkts	311	16–0	115	211
Manchester—England 9 wkts	211	142–1	158	191
Leeds—Drawn	505	—	538	87–0
Oval—England 4 wkts	194	164–6	202	154
1955 in England				
Nottingham—England Inns & 5 runs	334	—	181	148
Lord's—England 71 runs	133	353	304	111
Manchester—South Africa 3 wkts	284	381	521–8d	145–7
Leeds—South Africa 224 runs	191	256	171	500
Oval—England 92 runs	151	204	112	151
1956–57 in South Africa				
Johannesburg—England 131 runs	268	150	215	72
Cape Town—England 312 runs	369	220–6d	205	72
Durban—Drawn	218	254	283	142–6
Johannesburg—South Africa 17 runs	251	214	340	142
Port Elizabeth—South Africa 58 runs	110	130	164	134

T. Hayward and J. B. Hobbs

H. Sutcliffe and L. Hutton

ENGLAND v. WEST INDIES

	England 1st Inns	England 2nd Inns	West Indies 1st Inns	West Indies 2nd Inns
1928 in England				
Lord's—England Inns & 58 runs	401	—	177	166
Manchester—England Inns & 30 runs ..	351	—	206	115
Oval—England Inns & 71 runs	438	—	238	129
1929-30 in West Indies				
Barbados—Drawn	467	167–3	369	384
Trinidad—England 167 runs	208	425–8d	254	212
Georgetown—West Indies 289 runs	145	327	471	290
Kingston—Drawn	849	272–9d	286	408–5
1933 in England				
Lord's—England Inns & 27 runs	296	—	97	172
Manchester—Drawn	374	—	375	225
Oval—England Inns & 17 runs	312	—	100	195
1934-35 in West Indies				
Barbados—England 4 wkts	81–7d	75–6	102	51–6d
Trinidad—West Indies 217 runs	258	107	302	280–6d
Georgetown—Drawn	226	160–6d	184	104–5
Kingston—West Indies Inns & 161 runs	271	103	535–7d	—
1939 in England				
Lord's—England 8 wkts	404–5d	100–2	277	225
Manchester—Drawn	164–7d	128–6d	133	43–4
Oval—Drawn	352	366–3	498	—
1947-48 in West Indies				
Barbados—Drawn	253	86–4	296	351–9d
Trinidad—Drawn	362	275	497	72–3
Georgetown—West Indies 7 wkts	111	263	297–8d	78–3
Kingston—West Indies 10 wkts	227	336	490	76–0
1950 in England				
Manchester—England 202 runs	312	288	215	183
Lord's—West Indies 326 runs.........	151	274	326	425–6d
Nottingham—West Indies 10 wkts	223	436	558	103–0
Oval—West Indies Inns & 56 runs	344	103	503	—
1953-54 in West Indies				
Kingston—West Indies 140 runs	170	316	417	209–6d
Barbados—West Indies 181 runs	181	313	383	292–2d
Georgetown—England 9 wkts..........	435	75–1	251	256
Trinidad—Drawn	537	98–3	681–8d	212–4d
Kingston—England 9 wkts	414	72–1	139	346
1957 in England				
Birmingham—Drawn	186	583–4d	474	72–7
Lord's—England Inns & 36 runs	424	—	127	261
Nottingham—Drawn	619–6d	64–1	372	367
Leeds—England Inns & 5 runs	279	—	142	132
Oval—England Inns & 237 runs	412	—	89	86

ENGLAND v. NEW ZEALAND

	England 1st Inns	England 2nd Inns	New Zealand 1st Inns	New Zealand 2nd Inns
1929-30 in New Zealand				
Christchurch—England 8 wkts	181	66–2	112	131
Wellington—Drawn	320	107–4	440	164–4d
Auckland—Drawn	330–4d	—	96–1	—
Auckland—Drawn	540	22–3	387	—
1931 in England				
Lord's—Drawn	454	146–5	224	469–9d
Oval—England Inns & 26 runs	416–4d	—	193	197
Manchester—Drawn	224–3	—	—	—
1932-33 in New Zealand				
Christchurch—Drawn	560–8d	—	223	35–0
Auckland—Drawn	548–7d	—	158	16–0
1937 in England				
Lord's—Drawn	424	226–4d	295	175–8
Manchester—England 130 runs	358–9d	187	281	134
Oval—Drawn	254–7d	31–1	249	187
1946-47 in New Zealand				
Christchurch—Drawn	265–7d	—	345–9d	—
1949 in England				
Leeds—Drawn	372	267–4d	341	195–2
Lord's—Drawn	313–9d	306–5	484	—
Manchester—Drawn	440–9d	—	293	348–7
Oval—Drawn	482	—	345	308–9d
1950-51 in New Zealand				
Christchurch—Drawn	550	—	417–8d	46–3
Wellington—England 6 wkts	227	91–4	125	189
1954-55 in New Zealand				
Dunedin—England 8 wkts	209–8d	49–2	125	132
Auckland—England Inns & 20 runs ..	246	—	200	26
1958 in England				
Birmingham—England 205 runs........	221	215–6d	94	137
Lord's—England Inns & 148 runs ..	269	—	47	74
Leeds—England Inns & 71 runs	267–2d	—	67	129
Manchester—England Inns & 13 runs ..	365–9d	—	267	85
Oval—Drawn	219–9d	—	161	91–3
1958-59 in New Zealand				
Christchurch—England Inns & 99 runs..	374	—	142	133
Auckland—Drawn	311–7	—	181	—

ENGLAND v. INDIA

	England 1st Inns	England 2nd Inns	India 1st Inns	India 2nd Inns
1932 in England				
Lord's—England 158 runs	259	275–8d	189	187
1933-34 in India				
Bombay—England 9 wkts	438	40–1	219	258
Calcutta—Drawn	403	7–2	247	237
Madras—England 202 runs	335	261–7d	145	249
1936 in England				
Lord's—England 9 wkts	134	108–1	147	93
Manchester—Drawn	571–8d	—	203	390–5
Oval—England 9 wkts...............	471–8d	64–1	222	312
1946 in England				
Lord's—England 10 wkts	428	48–0	200	275
Manchester—Drawn	294	153–5d	170	152–9
Oval—Drawn	95–3	—	331	—
1951-52 in India				
New Delhi—Drawn	203	368–6	418–6d	—
Bombay—Drawn	456	55–2	485–9d	208
Calcutta—Drawn	342	252–5d	344	103–0
Kanpur—England 8 wkts	203	76–2	121	157
Madras—India Inns & 8 runs	266	183	457–9d	—
1952 in England				
Leeds—England 7 wkts	334	128–3	293	165
Lord's—England 8 wkts	537	79–2	235	378
Manchester—England Inns & 207 runs	347–9d	—	58	82
Oval—Drawn	326–6d	—	98	—
1959 in England				
Nottingham—England Inns & 59 runs ..	422	—	206	157
Lords—England 8 wkts	226	108–2	168	165
Leeds—England Inns & 173 runs	483–8d	—	161	149
Manchester—England 171 runs	490	265–8d	208	376
Oval—England Inns & 27 runs	361	—	140	194

ENGLAND v. PAKISTAN

	England 1st Inns	England 2nd Inns	Pakistan 1st Inns	Pakistan 2nd Inns
1954 in England				
Lord's—Drawn	117–9d	—	87	121–3
Nottingham—England Inns & 129 runs	558–6d	—	157	272
Manchester—Drawn	359–8d	—	90	25–4
Oval—Pakistan 24 runs	130	143	133	164

P. Roy

K. S. Ranjitsinhji

E. D. Weekes

CRICKET QUIZ

1. What is the lowest aggregate of runs scored in a completed first-class match?

★

2. What is the most devastating victory in a first-class match?

★

3. What is the highest individual score in a first-class match in England?

★

4. A batsman is given six runs for a hit which clears the playing area without first touching the ground, but when did that ruling come into effect?

★

5. What is or was the Lawrence Trophy?

★

6. Who was the first batsman to score a century before lunch on the first day of the match?

★

7. Which batsman scored 2,000 runs in a season the most times in consecutive seasons?

★

8. Which batsmen have scored 14 or more centuries in a season in England?

QUIZ ANSWERS

1. 105 runs—by M.C.C. (33 and 19) v. Australians (41 and 12 for 1 wicket) at Lord's in 1878. 2. Victoria (1,059 all out) defeated Tasmania by an innings and 666 runs at Melbourne in 1922–23. 3. 424 by A. C. MacLaren for Lancashire v. Somerset at Taunton in 1895. 4. 1910—before that only hits right out of the ground earned six runs. 5. Awarded by Sir Walter Lawrence for the fastest century of the season, it lasted from 1934 to 1939, but was not continued after the war. 6. H. H. Massie (206) in his first match in England for the Australians v. Oxford U. at Oxford in 1882. 7. H. Sutcliffe (Yorkshire)—14 times, 1922 to 1935. 8. D. C. S. Compton 18 in 1947, J. B. Hobbs 16 in 1925, W. R. Hammond 15 in 1938 and H. Sutcliffe 14 in 1932.

CRICKET QUIZ

1. What do the initials M.C.C. stand for?

★

2. Which University Blues later turned cricket professionals?

★

3. Which batsmen hold the record for the highest scores for the Gentlemen and Players in the annual match between the two sides?

★

4. Which batsman started three consecutive tours to England with a double-century each time?

★

5. Which Test team had the experience of losing four wickets before a run had been scored in the innings?

★

6. What is the record in all first-class cricket for the most wickets down before a run had been scored?

★

7. What is the lowest innings total in first-class cricket to include (*a*) an individual innings of 50, (*b*) a century, (*c*) a double-century, and (*d*) a triple-century?

8. Which two public schoolboys were selected to tour with an official M.C.C. touring team within a few weeks of leaving school?

QUIZ ANSWERS

1. Marylebone Cricket Club (in Australia, of course, they also stand for Melbourne C.C.). 2. P. A. Gibb and A. B. D. Parsons, both of Cambridge. 3. C. B. Fry scored 232 not out for Gentlemen at Lord's in 1903 and J. B. Hobbs scored 266 not out for Players at Scarborough in 1925. 4. D. G. Bradman (Australians) with 236 in 1930, 206 in 1934 and 258 in 1938, all at Worcester. 5. India, at Leeds in 1952, lost four second innings wickets for 0 runs. 6. M.C.C. lost seven wickets for 0 runs v. Surrey at Lord's in 1872, the eighth wicket fell at 2, the ninth at 8 and the total was 16. 7. (a) S. Nazir Ali scored 52 in Indians' total of 66 v. Yorkshire at Harrogate in 1932, (b) F. E. Woolley scored 103 not out in Kent's total of 144 v. Warwickshire at Folkestone in 1931, (c) W. H. Ponsford scored 214 in Victoria's total of 315 v. New South Wales at Adelaide in 1926–27, and (d) V. S. Hazare scored 309 in Rest's total of 387 v. Hindus at Bombay in 1943–44. 8. J. N. Crawford of Repton with the 1905–06 team to South Africa and N. C. Tufnell of Eton with the 1906–07 team to New Zealand.

M. A. Noble

W. Woodfull

C. L. McCool

	Australia 1st Inns	Australia 2nd Inns	South Africa 1st Inns	South Africa 2nd Inns
Melbourne—South Africa 82 runs	243	290	227	388
Sydney—Australia Inns & 38 runs	443	—	173	232
Adelaide—Drawn	530	233–3d	387	177–6
Melbourne—Australia 6 wkts	520	209	435	297–4
1957-58 in South Africa				
Johannesburg—Drawn	368	162–3	470–9d	201
Cape Town—Australia Inns & 141 runs	449	—	209	99
Durban—Drawn	163	292–7	384	—
Johannesburg—Australia 10 wkts	401	1–0	203	198
Port Elizabeth—Australia 8 wkts	291	68–2	214	144

AUSTRALIA v. WEST INDIES

	Australia 1st Inns	Australia 2nd Inns	West Indies 1st Inns	West Indies 2nd Inns
1930-31 in Australia				
Adelaide—Australia 10 wkts	376	172–0	296	249
Sydney—Australia Inns & 172 runs	369	—	107	90
Brisbane—Australia Inns & 217 runs	558	—	193	148
Melbourne—Australia Inns & 122 runs	328–8d	—	99	107
Sydney—West Indies 30 runs	224	220	350–6d	124–5d
1951-52 in Australia				
Brisbane—Australia 3 wkts	226	236–7	216	245
Sydney—Australia 7 wkts	517	137–3	362	290
Adelaide—West Indies 6 wkts	82	255	105	233–4
Melbourne—Australia 1 wkt	216	260–9	272	203
Sydney—Australia 202 runs	116	377	78	213
1954-55 in West Indies				
Kingston—Australia 9 wkts	515–9d	20–1	259	275
Trinidad—Drawn	600–9d	—	382	273–4
Georgetown—Australia 8 wkts	257	133–2	182	207
Barbados—Drawn	668	249	510	234–6
Kingston—Australia Inns & 82 runs	758–8d	—	357	319

AUSTRALIA v. NEW ZEALAND

	Australia 1st Inns	Australia 2nd Inns	New Zealand 1st Inns	New Zealand 2nd Inns
1945-46 in New Zealand				
Wellington—Australia Inns & 103 runs	199–8d	—	42	54

AUSTRALIA v. INDIA

	Australia 1st Inns	Australia 2nd Inns	India 1st Inns	India 2nd Inns
1947-48 in Australia				
Brisbane—Australia Inns & 226 runs	382–8d	—	58	98
Sydney—Drawn	107	—	188	61–7
Melbourne—Australia 233 runs	394	255–4d	291–9d	125
Adelaide—Australia Inns & 16 runs	674	—	381	277
Melbourne—Australia Inns & 177 runs	575–8d	—	331	67
1956-57 in India				
Madras—Australia Inns & 5 runs	319	—	161	153
Bombay—Drawn	523–7d	—	251	250–5
Calcutta—Australia 94 runs	177	189–9d	136	136

AUSTRALIA v. PAKISTAN

	Australia 1st Inns	Australia 2nd Inns	Pakistan 1st Inns	Pakistan 2nd Inns
1956-57 in Pakistan				
Karachi—Pakistan 9 wkts	80	187	199	69–1

SOUTH AFRICA v. NEW ZEALAND

	South Africa 1st Inns	South Africa 2nd Inns	New Zealand 1st Inns	New Zealand 2nd Inns
1931-32 in New Zealand				
Christchurch—South Africa Inns & 12 runs	451	—	293	146
Wellington—South Africa 8 wkts	410	150–2	364	193
1952-53 in New Zealand				
Wellington—South Africa Inns & 180 runs	524–8d	—	172	172
Auckland—Drawn	377	200–5d	245	31–2
1953-54 in South Africa				
Durban—South Africa Inns & 58 runs	437–9d	—	230	149
Johannesburg—South Africa 132 runs	271	148	187	100
Cape Town—Drawn	326	159–3	505	—
Johannesburg—South Africa 9 wkts	243	25–1	79	188
Port Elizabeth—South Africa 5 wkts	237	215–5	226	222

WEST INDIES v. NEW ZEALAND

	West Indies 1st Inns	West Indies 2nd Inns	New Zealand 1st Inns	New Zealand 2nd Inns
1951-52 in New Zealand				
Christchurch—West Indies 5 wkts	287	142–5	236	189
Auckland—Drawn	546–6d	—	160	17–1
1955-56 in New Zealand				
Dunedin—West Indies Inns & 71 runs	353	—	74	208
Christchurch—West Indies Inns & 64 runs	386	—	158	164
Wellington—West Indies 9 wkts	404	13–1	208	208
Auckland—New Zealand 190 runs	145	77	255	157–9d

W. J. O'Reilly

F. R. Spofforth

G. R. Langley

AUSTRALIA v. SOUTH AFRICA

	Australia 1st Inns	Australia 2nd Inns	South Africa 1st Inns	South Africa 2nd Inns
1902-03 in South Africa				
Johannesburg—Drawn	296	372–7d	454	101–4
Johannesburg—Australia 159 runs	175	309	240	85
Cape Town—Australia 10 wkts	252	59–0	85	225
1910-11 in Australia				
Sydney—Australia Inns & 114 runs	528	—	174	240
Melbourne—Australia 89 runs	348	327	506	80
Adelaide—South Africa 38 runs	465	339	482	360
Melbourne—Australia 530 runs	328	578	205	171
Sydney—Australia 7 wkts	364	198–3	160	401
1912 in England				
Manchester—Australia Inns & 88 runs	448	—	265	95
Lord's—Australia 10 wkts	390	48–0	263	173
Nottingham—Drawn	219	—	329	—
1921-22 in South Africa				
Durban—Drawn	299	324–7d	232	184–7
Johannesburg—Drawn	450	7–0	243	472–8d
Cape Town—Australia 10 wkts	396	1–0	180	216
1931-32 in Australia				
Brisbane—Australia Inns & 163 runs	450	—	170	117
Sydney—Australia Inns & 155 runs	469	—	153	161
Melbourne—Australia 169 runs	198	554	358	225
Adelaide—Australia 10 wkts	513	73–0	308	274
Melbourne—Australia Inns & 72 runs	153	—	36	45
1935-36 in South Africa				
Durban—Australia 9 wkts	429	102–1	248	282
Johannesburg—Drawn	250	274–2	157	491
Cape Town—Australia Inns & 78 runs	362–8d	—	102	182
Johannesburg—Australia Inns & 184 runs	439	—	157	98
Durban—Australia Inns & 6 runs	455	—	222	227
1949-50 in South Africa				
Johannesburg—Australia Inns & 85 runs	413	—	137	191
Cape Town—Australia 8 wkts	526–7d	87–2	278	333
Durban—Australia 5 wkts	75	336–5	311	99
Johannesburg—Drawn	465–8d	259–2	352	—
Port Elizabeth—Australia Inns & 259 runs	549–7d	—	158	132
1952-53 in Australia				
Brisbane—Australia 96 runs	280	277	221	240

WEST INDIES v. INDIA

	West Indies		India	
1948-49 in India	1st Inns	2nd Inns	1st Inns	2nd Inns
New Delhi—Drawn	631	—	454	220–6
Bombay—Drawn	629–6d	—	273	333–3
Calcutta—Drawn	366	336–9d	272	325–3
Madras—West Indies Inns & 193 runs ..	582	—	245	144
Bombay—Drawn	286	267	193	355–8
1952-53 in West Indies				
Trinidad—Drawn	438	142–0	417	294
Barbados—West Indies 142 runs	296	228	253	129
Trinidad—Drawn	315	192–2	279	362–7d
Georgetown—Drawn	364	—	262	190–5
Kingston—Drawn	576	92–4	312	444
1958-59 in India				
Bombay—Drawn	227	323–4d	152	289–5
Kanpur—West Indies 203 runs	222	443–7d	222	240
Calcutta—West Indies Inns & 336 runs..	614–5d	—	124	154
Madras—West Indies 295 runs	500	168–5d	222	151
New Delhi—Drawn	644–8d	—	415	275

W. A. Johnston

J. R. Reid

P. R. Umrigar

WEST INDIES v. PAKISTAN

	West Indies		Pakistan	
1957-58 in West Indies	1st Inns	2nd Inns	1st Inns	2nd Inns
Barbados—Drawn	579–9d	28–0	106	657–8d
Trinidad—West Indies 120 runs	325	312	282	235
Kingston—West Indies Inns & 174 runs..	790–3d	—	328	288
Georgetown—West Indies 8 wkts	410	317–2	408	318
Trinidad—Pakistan Inns & 1 run	268	227	496	—
1958-59 in Pakistan				
Karachi—Pakistan 10 wkts	146	245	304	88–0
Dacca—Pakistan 41 runs	76	172	145	144
Third Test—West Indies Inns & 156 runs	469	—	209	104

NEW ZEALAND v. INDIA

	New Zealand		India	
1955-56 in India	1st Inns	2nd Inns	1st Inns	2nd Inns
Hyderabad—Drawn	326	212–2	498–4d	—
Bombay—India Inns & 27 runs	258	136	421–8d	—
New Delhi—Drawn	450–2d	112–1	531–7d	—
Calcutta—Drawn	336	74–6	132	438–7d
Madras—India Inns & 109 runs	209	219	537–3d	—

NEW ZEALAND v. PAKISTAN

	New Zealand		Pakistan	
1955-56 in Pakistan	1st Inns	2nd Inns	1st Inns	2nd Inns
Karachi—Pakistan Inns & 1 run	164	124	289	—
Lahore—Pakistan 4 wkts.............	348	328	561	117–6
Dacca—Drawn	70	69–6	195–6d	—

INDIA v. PAKISTAN

	India		Pakistan	
1952-53 in India	1st Inns	2nd Inns	1st Inns	2nd Inns
New Delhi—India Inns & 70 runs	372	—	150	152
Lucknow—Pakistan Inns & 43 runs ..	106	182	331	—
Bombay—India 10 wkts	387–4d	45–0	186	242
Madras—Drawn	175–6	—	344	—
Calcutta—Drawn	397	28–0	257	236–7d
1954-55 in Pakistan				
Dacca—Drawn	148	147–2	257	158
Bahawalpur—Drawn	235	209–5	312–9d	—
Lahore—Drawn	251	74–2	328	136–5d
Peshawar—Drawn	245	23–1	188	182
Karachi—Drawn	145	69–2	162	241–5d

PLAYING RECORD BY EACH COUNTRY

	Played	Won	Drawn	Lost	First Test Played
England	358	145	110	103	1876–77
Australia	242	119	55	68	1876–77
South Africa	137	27	41	69	1888–89
West Indies	79	25	25	29	1928
New Zealand...............	52	1	24	27	1929–30
India	62	5	30	27	1932
Pakistan	26	8	11	7	1952–53
Total	956	330	296	330	

GREAT NAMES IN CRICKET

SIR DONALD G. BRADMAN (New South Wales and South Australia). Born at Cootamundra (N.S.W.) 27/8/1908. Undoubtedly the greatest run-scoring machine the world has ever seen, although his limitations on damaged wickets prevent him ranking with J. B. Hobbs as the best batsman ever. Bradman started with a century (118) against South Australia in his first innings in first-class cricket and continued with an average of one century in every third visit to the wicket until his retirement. He played for New South Wales from 1927–28 to 1933–34, transferring to South Australia in 1935–36 and retiring in 1948–49. His full career record was 28,067 runs (av. 95.14) in 338 innings, 117 of which were centuries. He reached 200 on 37 occasions and passed the 300 mark six times—his 452 not out v. Queensland at Sydney in 1929–30 stood as a world record for 29 years until Hanif Mohammed scored 499 in 1958–59. He twice passed 300 in Test cricket at Leeds—334 in 1930 (309 of them on the first day of the match) and 304 in 1934. Space does not permit a full list of Bradman's records, but he scored six consecutive centuries in 1938–39, four consecutive centuries in 1931–32 and three consecutive centuries in 1929–30, 1933–34, 1934, 1935–36, 1938, 1946–47, 1947–48 and 1948. He played 52 Tests for Australia, 24 of them as captain, and scored 6,996 runs (av. 99.94, including 29 centuries—a 4 instead of a duck in his last Test innings at the Oval in 1948 would have given him an average of 100.00 in Tests. Since his retirement he has alternated as a Test selector and a journalist. He was knighted in the 1949 New Year's Honours List.

Sir D. G. Bradman (T. G. Evans wicket-keeping)

GEORGE BROWN (Hampshire). Born at Cowley 6/10/1887. One of the "big four" of Hampshire cricket—Kennedy, Mead and Newman are the others. Brown was a strong left-handed batsman who often opened the innings, a right-arm bowler and a wicket-keeper good enough to play for England in seven Test matches in 1921 and 1922–23. His career covered the years 1908 to 1933 and he ended with career figures of 25,650 runs (av. 26.71), 37 centuries, 640 dismissals (565 ct., 75 st.), and 626 wickets (av. 29.81). He toured South Africa in 1922–23, West Indies in 1910–11 and 1931–32 and India in 1926–27. He scored 1,000 runs in a season eleven times and hit a best score of 232 not out v. Yorkshire at Leeds in 1920.

A. P. F. CHAPMAN (Kent). Born at Reading 3/9/1900. A tall left-handed batsman with powerful strokes and a brilliant close field. Educated at Uppingham, he gained his Blue at Cambridge and played in the 1920, 1921 and 1922 University matches. He first played for Berkshire, but joined Kent in 1924 and captained the county from 1931 to 1936. He retired after 1939, but had made only odd appearances since 1936. He is best remembered as an England captain—he was leader of the team which regained the Ashes at the Oval in 1926 and successfully defended them in Australia in 1928–29. He captained England 17 times, and, after winning his first nine matches in succession, failed to win one of his last eight matches. Is the only player to have scored centuries at Lord's in the University match, for Gentlemen v. Players and for England (M. P. Donnelly has paralleled this feat with a century for New Zealand). The best of his 27 centuries was 260 v. Lancashire at Maidstone in 1927.

(Contd. on p. 115 col. 1)

CRICKET QUIZ

1. Which batsman has recorded the highest percentage of a complete innings total? (*above*)

★

2. What is the highest number of runs added to the score by one batsman while the other batsman did not score a single run?

★

3. What are the earliest dates that batsmen have completed (*a*) 1,000 runs, (*b*) 2,000 runs, (*c*) 3,000 runs, in an English season?

★

4. What is the fastest fifty scored by a batsman in first-class cricket?

★

5. What is the fastest century scored by a batsman in first-class cricket?

★

6. What is the fastest double-century scored by a batsman in first-class cricket?

★

7. What is the fastest triple-century scored by a batsman in first-class cricket?

★

8. What is the greatest number of runs scored off a six-ball over?

QUIZ ANSWERS

1. V. S. Hazare scored 309 in a total of 387 for Rest v. Hindus at Bombay in 1943–44—79% of the total. 2. G. L. Jessop scored 66 runs out of 66 added for Gloucestershire v. Sussex at Bristol in 1901. 3. (a) May 27th by D. G. Bradman in 1938, (b) July 5th by T. Hayward in 1906, (c) August 20th by T. Hayward in 1906. 4. C. I. J. Smith reached 50 in 11 minutes for Middlesex v. Gloucestershire at Bristol in 1938. 5. P. G. H. Fender reached 100 in 35 minutes for Surrey v. Northamptonshire at Northampton in 1920. 6. G. L. Jessop reached 200 not out in 120 minutes for Gloucestershire v. Sussex at Hove in 1903. 7. D. C. S. Compton scored 300 in 181 minutes for M.C.C. v. North-Eastern Transvaal at Benoni in 1948–49. 8. C. Smart scored 32 runs (664664) off an over by G. Hill when playing for Glamorgan v. Hampshire at Cardiff in 1935. E. Alletson scored 34 runs off an over by E. H. Killick for Nottinghamshire v. Sussex at Hove in 1911, but the over included two no-balls.

SOME IMPORTANT CRICKET RECORDS
HIGHEST INNINGS TOTALS

1107	Victoria v. New South Wales (Melbourne)	1926–27
1059	Victoria v. Tasmania (Melbourne)	1922–23
918	New South Wales v. South Australia (Sydney)	1900–01
912–8d	Holkar v. Mysore (Indore)	1938
903–7d	England v. Australia (Oval)	1938
887	Yorkshire v. Warwickshire (Birmingham)	1896
849	England v. West Indies (Kingston)	1929–30

LOWEST INNINGS TOTALS

12	Oxford University v. M.C.C. (Oxford)	1877
12	Northamptonshire v. Gloucestershire (Gloucester)	1907
13	Auckland v. Canterbury (Auckland)	1877–78
13	Nottinghamshire v. Yorkshire (Nottingham)	1901

HIGHEST INDIVIDUAL INNINGS

499	Hanif Mohammed—Karachi v. Bahawalpur (Karachi)	1958–59
452*	D. G. Bradman—New South Wales v. Queensland (Sydney)	1929–30
443*	B. B. Nimbalkar—Maharashtra v. Western India States (Poona)	1948–49
437	W. H. Ponsford—Victoria v. Queensland (Melbourne)	1927–28
429	W. H. Ponsford—Victoria v. Tasmania (Melbourne)	1922–23
424	A. C. MacLaren—Lancashire v. Somerset (Taunton)	1895
385	B. Sutcliffe—Otago v. Canterbury (Christchurch)	1952–53
383	C. W. Gregory—New South Wales v. Queensland (Brisbane)	1906–07
369	D. G. Bradman—South Australia v. Tasmania (Adelaide)	1935–36
365*	C. Hill—South Australia v. New South Wales (Adelaide)	1900–01
365*	G. Sobers—West Indies v. Pakistan (Kingston)	1957–58
364	L. Hutton—England v. Australia (Oval)	1938
359*	V. M. Merchant—Bombay v. Maharashtra (Bombay)	1943–44
357*	R. Abel—Surrey v. Somerset (Oval)	1899
357	D. G. Bradman—South Australia v. Victoria (Melbourne)	1935–36
355	B. Sutcliffe—Otago v. Auckland (Dunedin)	1949–50
352	W. H. Ponsford—Victoria v. New South Wales (Melbourne)	1926–27

* Not out.

Hanif Mohammed   A. E. Fagg   G. Sobers

CRICKET QUIZ

1. Which bowler has achieved the record number of hat-tricks?

★

2. Only one bowler has achieved the feat of all ten wickets in an innings and seventeen wickets in a match on the same day in first-class cricket. Who is he?

★

3. What is the record number of wickets taken by one bowler in a first-class match?

★

4. What is the record distance for a bail to travel when a batsman has been clean bowled in a first-class match?

★

5. What is the greatest number of balls bowled by one bowler without conceding a run in first-class cricket?

★

6. What is the earliest dates that bowlers have completed (a) 100 wickets, (b) 200 wickets, (c) 300 wickets, in an English season?

★

7. What is the longest spell of bowling by one bowler in a first-class match?

★

8. Which cricketers have completed doubles of (a) 2,000 runs and 200 wickets, (b) 3,000 runs and 100 wickets, in a first-class season in England?

QUIZ ANSWERS

1. D. V. P. Wright of Kent with seven between 1937 and 1949. 2. C. Blythe took 17 for 48 (10 for 30 and 7 for 18) for Kent v. Northamptonshire at Northampton in 1907. 3. J. C. Laker took 19 for 90 (9 for 37 and 10 for 53) for England v. Australia at Manchester in 1956. 4. R. D. Burrows sent the bail 67 yards 6 inches when bowling W. Huddleston, for Worcestershire v. Lancashire at Manchester in 1911. 5. 137 balls by H. J. Tayfield for South Africa v. England at Durban in 1956–57. Tayfield ended the first innings with 119 balls (14 maidens) without conceding a run and then started the second innings with two maidens before conceding a two off the third ball of his third over. 6. (a) June 12th by J. T. Hearne in 1896 and C. W. L. Parker in 1931, (b) July 27th by A. P. Freeman in 1928, (c) September 14th by A. P. Freeman in 1928. 7. 66 consecutive six-ball overs by J. Iremonger for Nottinghamshire v. Hampshire at Southampton in 1914. 8. (a) G. H. Hirst of Yorkshire in 1906, (b) J. H. Parks of Sussex in 1937.

England v. Australia, Old Trafford, 1956. K. Mackay is caught Oakman bowled Laker, during Laker's 19-wicket rout of the Australians.

RECORD PARTNERSHIP FOR EACH WICKET

1st.	555	P. Holmes & H. Sutcliffe—Yorkshire v. Essex (Leyton)	1932
2nd.	455	B. B. Nimbalkar & K. V. Bhandarkar—Maharashtra v. Western India States (Poona)	1948–49
3rd.	445	W. N. Carson & P. E. Whitelaw—Auckland v. Otago (Dunedin)	1936–37
4th.	577	Gul Mahomed & V. S. Hazare—Baroda v. Holkar (Baroda)	1946–47
5th.	405	S. G. Barnes & D. G. Bradman—Australia v. England (Sydney)	1946–47
6th.	487*	G. Headley & C. C. Passailaigue—Jamaica v. Lord Tennyson's XI (Kingston)	1931–32
7th.	347	D. Atkinson & C. C. Depeiza—West Indies v. Australia (Barbados)	1954–55
8th.	433	V. T. Trumper & A. Sims—Australians v. Canterbury (Christchurch)	1913–14
9th.	283	J. Chapman & A. R. Warren—Derbyshire v. Warwickshire (Blackwell)	1910
10th.	307	A. F. Kippax & J. E. H. Hooker—New South Wales v. Victoria (Melbourne)	1928–29

HIGHEST AGGREGATES OF RUNS IN A SEASON

	Season	Inns.	N.O.	Runs	H.S.	Avge.	100s
D. C. S. Compton	1947	50	8	3816	246	90.85	18
W. J. Edrich	1947	52	8	3539	267*	80.43	12
T. Hayward	1906	61	8	3518	219	66.37	13
L. Hutton	1949	56	6	3429	269*	68.58	12
F. E. Woolley	1928	59	4	3352	198	60.94	12

* Not out.

HIGHEST AGGREGATES OF WICKETS IN A SEASON

	Season	Overs	Mdns.	Runs	Wkts.	Avge.
A. P. Freeman	1928	1976.1	423	5489	304	18.05
A. P. Freeman	1933	2039	651	4549	298	15.26
T. Richardson	1895	1691.1	463	4170	290	14.37
C. T. B. Turner	1888	2427.1	1127	3307	283	11.68

H. Sutcliffe   S. G. Barnes   L. E. G. Ames

MISCELLANEOUS

J. C. Laker took nineteen wickets (9 for 37 and 10 for 53) in the match for England v. Australia at Manchester in 1956—the only occasion on which a bowler has taken more than seventeen wickets in a first-class match.

M. J. Stewart, playing for Surrey v. Northamptonshire at Northampton in 1957, held seven catches in an innings—the first fielder to hold more than six.

W. R. Hammond (78 in 1928) and M. J. Stewart (77 in 1957) have held the most catches in one season.

D. C. S. Compton holds the record for most centuries in one season with 18 in 1947. The next-best are: 16 by J. B. Hobbs in 1925, 15 by W. R. Hammond in 1938 and 14 by H. Sutcliffe in 1932.

Two batsmen have scored six centuries in consecutive innings in first-class cricket—C. B. Fry in 1901 and D. G. Bradman in Australia in 1938–39.

A. E. Fagg is the only batsman to have scored a double-century in each innings of a first-class match—244 and 202 not out for Kent v. Essex at Colchester in 1938.

The two highest aggregates of runs in a first-class match are: 2,376 for 38 wickets by Bombay and Maharashtra at Poona in 1948–49 and 2,078 for 40 wickets by Bombay and Halkar at Bombay in 1944–45. The record for Test cricket is 1,981 runs for 35 wickets by England and South Africa at Durban in 1938–39. The record in England is 1723 for 31 wickets by England and Australia at Leeds in 1948.

L. E. G. Ames dismissed 127 batsmen (79 caught and 48 stumped) in the 1929 season: a record for wicket-keepers. The other 'keepers to have dismissed more than 100 batsman in one season are F. H. Huish, G. Duckworth, H. Yarnold and J. T. Murray.

GREAT NAMES IN CRICKET

LEARY N. CONSTANTINE (Trinidad). Born at Port of Spain, Trinidad, 21/9/1902. A brilliant all-rounder—hard-hitting batsman, really fast bowler and brilliant field anywhere. He made his debut in first-class cricket in 1921–22 and made a final appearance for the Dominions XI at Lord's in 1945. He toured England in 1923, 1928 and 1939, and assisted the 1933 West Indies team in a few matches, and also visited Australia in 1930–31. His figures in 18 Test matches were 641 runs (av. 19.42) and 58 wickets (av. 30.10): a case where statistics do not truly reflect a man's ability or the pleasure which he gave to thousands. His full career figures were 4,451 runs (av. 24.32), 5 centuries and 424 wickets (av. 20.60). Two of his centuries were scored inside an hour and his average rate of run-scoring was second only to that of G. L. Jessop. His

L. N. Constantine

best score was 133 for Trinidad v. Barbados in Trinidad in 1928–29 and his best bowling 8 for 38 v. Barbados in Barbados in 1923–24. In 1929 he became a League cricketer with the avowed intention of becoming a lawyer: an ambition which he ultimately realised.

MARTIN P. DONNELLY (Wellington and Warwickshire). Born at Ngaruawahia 17/10/1917. A graceful left-handed batsman, who has strong claims to be regarded as the finest batsman from New Zealand; his early retirement from the game was a severe blow to his country's Test hopes. After only one first-class match at home, he was selected for the 1937 New Zealand team to tour England and played in all three Test matches that summer. Before any further progress could be made the war intervened and Donnelly served in the Army before going up to Oxford University, where he gained a Blue and played in the 1946 and 1947 University matches. After one match for Middlesex in 1946 he joined Warwickshire and stayed with them until 1950, when he moved to Australia and retired from first-class cricket. In 1949 he joined the New Zealand team on their arrival in England and was a tower of strength to their batting, scoring 2,287 runs (av. 61.81), including a fine inning of 206 v. England at Lord's. His final career aggregate was 9,210 runs (av. 47.72) and 23 centuries.

PERCY G. H. FENDER (Sussex and Surrey). Born at Balham 22/8/1892. A tall, spectacled all-rounder—aggressive right-handed batsman, leg-break and googly bowler and smart slip field. He played for Sussex from 1910 to 1913, but then joined Surrey in 1914. A brilliant captain, he was handicapped by a moderate Surrey bowling attack, or he would have taken the County Championship to the Oval sometime between 1920 and 1931, his years of office. His main claim to immortality is that he hit the fastest century in the history of first-class cricket, in 35 minutes v. Northamptonshire at Northampton in 1920 (113 not out in 42 minutes altogether). Scored 1,000 runs in a season nine times and completed the double six times, with a best season in 1923, when he totalled 1,427 runs (av. 29.12) and 178 wickets (av. 19.98). He played 13 times for England between 1920–21 and 1929, but never captained his country—probably the best captain to miss the honour. He toured Australia in 1920–21, South Africa in 1922–23 and Jamaica in 1926–27. A good goalkeeper, he played for Casuals, Corinthians and Fulham.

A. P. FREEMAN (Kent). Born at Lewisham 17/5/1889. A leg-spin and googly bowler whose career total of 3,776 wickets (av. 18.42) is second only to that of W. Rhodes. His career for Kent spanned the years between 1914 and 1936, and he took 100 wickets in a season seventeen times. His record year was 1928, when he took 304 wickets (av. 18.05), and he followed with 267 (av. 18.27) in 1929, 275 (av. 16.84) in 1930, 276 (av. 15.60) in 1931, 253 (av. 16.39) in 1932, 298 (av. 15.26) in 1933, 205 (av. 23.18) in 1934 and 212 (av. 21.51) in 1935—truly a remarkable record of consistency. He took all ten wickets in an innings three times—v. Lancashire at Maidstone in 1929, v. Essex at Southend in 1930 and v. Lancashire at Manchester in 1931. He twice took seventeen wickets in a match and achieved three hat-tricks. He toured Australia and New Zealand in 1922–23, Australia in 1924–25 and 1928–29 and South Africa in 1927–28, and

C. B. Fry

totalled 12 Tests for England, but it is as a county cricket bowler that he gained his real fame.

CHARLES BURGESS FRY (Sussex and Hampshire). Born at Croydon 25/4/1872, died at Hampstead 7/9/1956, aged 84. Educated at Repton, he went on to Oxford University and a career of accomplishment without equal. In addition to being a fine attractive batsman at cricket, he played for England v. Ireland at soccer in 1901 and for Southampton in the 1902 F.A. Cup final, gained a Blue for athletics and held the long-jump record of 23 feet 5 inches from 1892 to 1913, was a fine rugger player and just missed his Blue in 1894–95 (an injured thigh caused him to miss the University match after he had played in all the season's fixtures), was a master at Charterhouse before turning to journalism and spent the greater part of his life with H.M.S. Mercury before his retirement (from 1908 to 1950). He

M. P. Donnelly   P. G. H. Fender   W. G. Grace

tried several times to become a member of Parliament but was unsuccessful in this direction, although he was offered and rejected the Kingdom of Albania. He played one match for Surrey in 1891 (against Warwickshire) and made his debut in first-class cricket in 1892. He played regularly for Sussex from 1894 to 1908, but joined Hampshire in 1909 and made occasional appearances until

1921. His various activities restricted his cricket overseas, but he went to South Africa in 1895–96 and his last first-class match was played at Bombay in 1921–22. He played in 26 Tests for England, and was captain in the 1912 Triangular Tournament. A useful right-arm medium-pace bowler, he was called on numerous occasions for "throwing" and was one of the bowlers who came under the ban in 1900. His career figures were 30,886 runs (av. 50.21), 94 centuries and 166 wickets (av. 29.34). He shares with D. G. Bradman the record of six centuries in consecutive innings in first-class cricket (Fry did this in 1901, Bradman in 1938–39).

WILLIAM GILBERT GRACE (Gloucestershire). Born at Downend (Bristol) 18/8/1848, died at Eltham (Kent) 23/10/1915, aged 67. He played his first match for West Gloucestershire one day after his ninth birthday, scoring 3 not out, and made his debut in first-class cricket in 1865. By the time he played his last first-class match in 1908 he had seen the game grow in stature from club cricket with occasional big matches to a game of international repute. He started a long list of first-class cricket records, being the first to score a double-century, the first to get two centuries in a match, the first to pass 300, the first to score three consecutive centuries (in 1871) the first to score 2,000 runs in a season (2,739 in 1871), the first to complete the cricketer's double of 1,000 runs and 100 wickets (in 1873) and the first batsman to score 100 centuries in first-class cricket (in 1895). Undoubtedly the best batsman of his generation, a slow-medium bowler and fine field close to the wicket, his career figures of 54,896 runs, 2,876 wickets and 871 catches may never be surpassed. He toured Australia in 1873–74 and 1891–92, appeared in 22 Tests for England between 1880 and 1899, being captain 13 times. It has been estimated that in all matches in which he played he totalled about 80,000 runs and took 7,000 wickets.

CLARENCE VICTOR GRIMMETT (Wellington and South Australia). Born in New Zealand 25/12/1892. One of the great leg-break and googly bowlers, he started his career in New Zealand in 1911–12 and did not gain fame until he moved to Australia and played for South Australia, having a few matches for Victoria en route. He gained a place in Australia's team for the first time v. England at Sydney in 1924–25 and, by taking eleven wickets, rose to the front rank. He then played regularly for Australia until 1935–36, by which time he had set up a new record for Test cricket with 216 wickets (av. 24.21). He toured England in 1926,

1930 and 1934, and might well have come again with the 1938 team but for the inclusion of two other fine spin bowlers in W. J. O'Reilly and L. O'B. Fleetwood-Smith. He finally retired in 1940–41, by which time he had taken 1,424 wickets (av. 22.19) in first-class cricket—figures that few overseas bowlers can hope to exceed.

(Contd. on p. 117 col. 1)

CRICKET QUIZ

1. Which fielding captain appealed against the light in Test cricket and had his appeal upheld?

★

2. Which father and son were both appointed Test captains?

★

3. Which three brothers all appeared in the same Test match?

★

4. Which player holds the record for most consecutive appearances in Test cricket? *(above)*

★

5. Which Test captain later became a Hollywood film star?

★

6. Only one player appeared in first-class cricket before the First World War and after the Second World War. Who was he?

★

7. G. Headley, West Indies leading batsman before the war, was not born in the West Indies. Where was he born?

★

8. Only one cricketer has enjoyed the following distinctions: (*a*) England Test cap, (*b*) Member of county winning County Championship, (*c*) F.A. Cup winners' medal, (*d*) League Championship medal, (*e*) England cap at soccer. Who is he?

QUIZ ANSWERS

1. H. F. Wade, for South Africa v. Australia at Johannesburg in 1935–36. 2. F. T. Mann for England v. South Africa in 1922–23 and F. G. Mann for England v. South Africa in 1948–49 and v. New Zealand in 1949. 3. The three brothers Grace (E. M., W. G. and G. F.) all played for England v. Australia at the Oval in 1880. The three brothers Hearne all played in the Cape Town Test of 1891–92, A. and G. G. for England and F. for South Africa. 4. F. E. Woolley played 52 consecutive Test matches for England between 1909 and 1926. 5. C. A. Smith, later Sir Aubrey, who captained England v. South Africa in 1888–89. 6. W. H. Ashdown of Kent. 7. Panama. 8. H. Makepeace of Lancashire.

CRICKET QUIZ

1. Which bowler holds the record for taking the most wickets in one month in first-class cricket?

★

2. Only three English counties have not yet entered a team in either the County Championship or the Minor County Championship—which are they?

★

3. How many seasons, since the extension of the first-class fixture list in 1894, have failed to provide at least one double of 1,000 runs and 100 wickets?

★

4. Who is the only player to achieve the double of 1,000 runs and 100 wickets in his debut season in first-class cricket? (above)

★

5. Which was the first match to be played on a turf wicket in South Africa?

★

6. Which bowler was no-balled for bowling a lob without informing the batsman and umpire of his change of delivery?

★

7. Which county was dismissed for a first innings total of 15 and followed-on but won the match by 155 runs?

★

8. Which batsman in first-class cricket was credited with five runs as one of his strokes was stopped with a cap by a fielder?

QUIZ ANSWERS

1. C. L. Townsend took 94 wickets for Gloucestershire in August 1895. 2. Huntingdonshire, Rutland and Westmoreland. 3. Two—1951 and 1958. 4. D. B. Close (Yorkshire) in 1949. 5. The Currie Cup match between Natal and Border at Durban in 1926–27. 6. H. Verity, for Yorkshire v. Surrey at the Oval in 1933. F. Chester was the umpire. 7. Hampshire, against Warwickshire at Birmingham in 1922. 8. A. Melville, for Sussex v. Gloucestershire at Cheltenham in 1932. T. W. Goddard was the fielder.

R. Subba Row

T. W. Graveney

M. C. Cowdrey

D. B. Carr

A. C. D. Ingleby-Mackenzie

FIRST-CLASS COUNTY CRICKET CLUB DIRECTORY

DERBYSHIRE

Formed: 1870. *Colours:* Chocolate, amber and pale blue. *Badge:* Rose and crown. *County Championship:* 1873 to 1887, re-entered 1895. *Champions:* 1874, 1936. *Secretary:* W. T. Taylor, 18 St. James's Street, Derby. *Captain in 1958 and 1959:* D. B. Carr. *County grounds:* Burton-on-Trent, Buxton, Chesterfield, Derby, Ilkeston.

ESSEX

Formed: 1864–65, dissolved in 1866 and re-formed in 1876 and 1886. *Colours:* Blue, gold and red. *Badge:* Three scimitars with word "Essex" underneath. *Promoted to first-class status:* 1894 (1895 in Championship). *Best final position in Championship:* Third in 1897. *Secretary:* T. E. Bailey, 60 London Road, Chelmsford. *Captain in 1958 and 1959:* D. J. Insole. *County grounds:* Brentwood, Chelmsford, Clacton, Colchester, Ilford, Leyton, Romford, Southend, Westcliff.

GLAMORGAN

Formed: 1888–89. *Colours:* Blue and gold. *Badge:* Gold daffodil. *Promoted to first-class status:* 1921. *Champions:* 1948. *Secretary:* W. Wooller, 6 High Street, Cardiff. *Captain in 1958 and 1959:* W. Wooller. *County grounds:* Cardiff, Ebbw Vale, Llanelly, Neath, Newport, Pontypridd, Swansea.

GLOUCESTERSHIRE

Formed: 1870. *Colours:* Blue, gold, brown, sky-blue, green and red. *Badge:* Coat of arms of the City and County of Bristol. *County Championship:* Original member in 1873. *Champions:* 1876, 1877. *Joint Champions:* 1873, 1880. *Secretary:* C. H. G. Thomas, County Ground, Bishopston, Bristol, 7. *Captain in 1958:* G. M. Emmett. *Captain in 1959:* T. W. Graveney. *County grounds:* Bristol, Cheltenham, Gloucester, Stroud.

HAMPSHIRE

Formed: 1863. *Colours:* Blue, gold and white. *Badge:* Tudor rose and crown. *Promoted to first-class status:* 1895. *Best final position in Championship:* Runners-up in 1958. *Secretary:* E. D. R. Eagar, County Cricket Ground, Northlands Road, Southampton. *Captain in 1958 and 1959:* A. C. D. Ingleby-Mackenzie. *County grounds:* Bournemouth, Cowes, Portsmouth, Southampton.

KENT

Formed: 1859, re-formed 1870. *Colours:* Red and white. *Badge:* White horse on a red background. *County Championship:* Original member in 1873. *Champions:* 1906, 1909, 1910, 1913. *Secretary:* N. Christopherson, St. Lawrence Ground, Canterbury. *Captain in 1958 and 1959:* M. C. Cowdrey. *County grounds:* Blackheath, Canterbury, Dartford, Dover, Folkestone, Gillingham, Gravesend, Maidstone, Tunbridge Wells.

LANCASHIRE

Formed: 1864. *Colours:* Red, green and blue. *Badge:* Red rose. *County Championship:* Original member in 1873. *Champions:* 1881, 1897, 1904, 1926, 1927, 1928, 1930, 1934. *Joint Champions:* 1875, 1879, 1882, 1889, 1950. *Secretary:* C. G. Howard, Old Trafford, Manchester, 16. *Captain in 1958 and 1959:* C. Washbrook. *County grounds:* Blackpool, Liverpool, Manchester, Southport.

LEICESTERSHIRE

Formed: 1873. *Colours:* Scarlet and dark green. *Badge:* Running fox (gold) on green background. *Promoted to first-class status:* 1894 (1895 in Championship). *Best final position in Championship:* Third in 1953. *Secretary:* R. A. Diment, Spencer Chambers, 4 Market Place, Leicester. *Captain in 1958 and 1959:* W. Watson. *County grounds:* Ashby-de-la-Zouch, Coalville, Hinckley, Leicester, Loughborough.

MIDDLESEX

Formed: 1864. *Colours:* Blue. *Badge:* Three seaxes. *County Championship:* Original member in 1873. *Champions:* 1878 1903, 1920, 1921, 1947. *Joint Champions:* 1949. *Secretary:* F. G. Mann, Lord's Cricket Ground, St. John's Wood, N.W.8. *Captain in 1958 and 1959:* J. J. Warr. *County ground:* Lord's. Hornsey allocated a match in 1959.

D. J. Insole   M. F. Tremlett   W. Watson

NORTHAMPTONSHIRE

Formed: 1843, re-formed 1878. *Colours:* Maroon. *Badge:* Tudor rose. *Promoted to first-class status:* 1905. *Best final position in Championship:* Runners up in 1912 and 1957. *Secretary:* K. Turner, County Cricket Ground, Wantage Road, Northampton. *Captain in 1958 and 1959:* R. Subba Row. *County grounds:* Kettering, Northampton, Peterborough, Rushden, Wellingborough.

NOTTINGHAMSHIRE

Formed: 1859. *Colours:* Green and gold. *Badge:* County badge of Nottinghamshire. *County Championship:* Original member in 1875. *Champions:* 1883, 1884, 1885, 1886, 1907, 1929. *Joint Champions:* 1873, 1875, 1879, 1880, 1882, 1889. *Secretary:* R. M. Poulton, County Cricket Ground, Trent Bridge, Nottingham. *Captain in 1958 and 1959:* R. T. Simpson. *County ground:* Nottingham.

SOMERSET

Formed: 1875, reorganised 1885. *Colours:* Black, white and maroon. *Badge:* Wessex dragon. *Promoted to first-class status:* 1891. *Best final position in Championship:* Third in 1892 and 1958. *Secretary:* R. Robinson, County Cricket Ground, St. James's Street, Taunton. *Captain in 1958 and 1959:* M. F. Tremlett. *County grounds:* Bath, Frome, Glastonbury, Taunton, Weston-super-mare, Yeovil.

SURREY

Formed: 1845. *Colours:* Chocolate. *Badge:* Prince of Wales' feathers. *County Championship:* Original member in 1873. *Champions:* 1887, 1888, 1890, 1891, 1892, 1894, 1895, 1899, 1914, 1952, 1953, 1954, 1955, 1956, 1957, 1958. *Joint Champions:* 1889, 1950. *Secretary:* B. O. Babb, Kennington Oval, London, S.E.11. *Captain in 1958 and 1959:* P. B. H. May. *County grounds:* Guildford, Kennington Oval.

SUSSEX

Formed: 1836, re-formed 1839 and 1857. *Colours:* Dark blue, light blue and gold. *Badge:* County arms of six martlets (in shape of inverted pyramid). *County Championship:* Original member in 1873. *Joint Champions:* 1875. *Runners-up:* 1902, 1903, 1932, 1933, 1934, 1953. *Secretary:* Lt.-Col. G. S. Grimston, County Cricket Ground, Eaton Road, Hove, 3. *Captain in 1958 and 1959:* R. G. Marlar. ⸱*County grounds:* Eastbourne, Hastings, Hove, Worthing.

WARWICKSHIRE

Formed: 1863–64, re-formed 1882. *Colours:* Blue, yellow and white. *Badge:* Bear and ragged staff. *Promoted to first-class status:* 1894 (1895 in Championship). *Champions:* 1911, 1951. *Secretary:* L. T. Deakins, County Cricket Ground, Edgbaston, Birmingham, 5. *Captain in 1958 and 1959:* M. J. K. Smith. *County grounds:* Birmingham, Coventry.

WORCESTERSHIRE

Formed: 1865. *Colours:* Dark green and black. *Badge:* Shield, *argent* bearing *fess* between three *pears sable. Promoted to first-class status:* 1899. *Best final position in Championship:* Joint runners-up in 1907, Third in 1949. *Secretary:* J. Lister, County Cricket Ground, New Road, Worcester. *Captain in 1958:* P. E. Richardson. *Captain in 1959:* D. Kenyon. *County grounds:* Dudley, Kidderminster, Stourbridge, Worcester.

YORKSHIRE

Formed: 1863. *Colours:* Oxford blue, Cambridge blue and gold. *Badge:* White rose. *County Championship:* Original member in 1873. *Champions:* 1893, 1896, 1898, 1900, 1901, 1902, 1905, 1908, 1912, 1919, 1922, 1923, 1924, 1925, 1931, 1932, 1933, 1935, 1937, 1938, 1939, 1946 (22 times). *Joint-Champions:* 1949. *Secretary:* J. H. Nash, Old Bank Chambers, Park Row, Leeds, 1. *Captain in 1958 and 1959:* J. R. Burnet. *County grounds:* Bradford, Harrogate, Hull, Leeds, Middlesbrough, Scarborough, Sheffield.

CHAMPION COUNTY AND RUNNER-UP EACH SEASON

(† Championship, or runners-up position, shared.)

CHAMPIONS	RUNNERS-UP	CHAMPIONS	RUNNERS-UP
1873 Glos. and Notts. †		1911 Warwicks.	Kent
1874 Derby.	Glos.	1912 Yorks.	Northants.
1875 Lancs., Notts. and Sussex †		1913 Kent	Yorks.
		1914 Surrey	Middlesex
1876 Glos.	Middlesex	1919 Yorks.	Kent
1877 Glos.	Derby	1920 Middlesex	Lancs.
1878 Middlesex	Glos.	1921 Middlesex	Surrey
1879 Lancs. and Notts. †		1922 Yorks.	Notts.
1880 Glos. and Notts. †		1923 Yorks.	Notts.
1881 Lancs.	Glos.	1924 Yorks.	Middlesex
1882 Lancs. and Notts. †		1925 Yorks.	Surrey
1883 Notts.	Middlesex and Yorks. †	1926 Lancs.	Yorks.
		1927 Lancs.	Notts.
1884 Notts.	Middlesex	1928 Lancs.	Kent
1885 Notts.	Yorks.	1929 Notts.	Lancs. and Yorks. †
1886 Notts.	Surrey		
1887 Surrey	Lancs.	1930 Lancs.	Glos.
1888 Surrey	Kent and Yorks.†	1931 Yorks.	Glos.
1889 Lancs., Notts. and Surrey †		1932 Yorks.	Sussex
		1933 Yorks.	Sussex
1890 Surrey	Lancs.	1934 Lancs.	Sussex
1891 Surrey	Lancs.	1935 Yorks.	Derby
1892 Surrey	Notts.	1936 Derby.	Middlesex
1893 Yorks.	Lancs.	1937 Yorks.	Middlesex
1894 Surrey	Yorks.	1938 Yorks.	Middlesex
1895 Surrey	Lancs.	1939 Yorks.	Middlesex
1896 Yorks.	Lancs.	1946 Yorks.	Middlesex
1897 Lancs.	Surrey	1947 Middlesex	Glos.
1898 Yorks.	Middlesex	1948 Glamorgan	Surrey
1899 Surrey	Middlesex	1949 Middlesex and Yorks. †	
1900 Yorks.	Lancs.	1950 Lancs. and Surrey †	
1901 Yorks.	Middlesex		
1902 Yorks.	Sussex	1951 Warwicks.	Yorks.
1903 Middlesex	Sussex	1952 Surrey	Yorks.
1904 Lancs.	Yorks.	1953 Surrey	Sussex
1905 Yorks.	Lancs.	1954 Surrey	Yorks.
1906 Kent	Yorks.	1955 Surrey	Yorks.
1907 Notts.	Worcs. and Yorks. †	1956 Surrey	Lancs.
		1957 Surrey	Northants.
1908 Yorks.	Kent	1958 Surrey	Hampshire
1909 Kent	Lancs.	1959 Yorks	Glos.
1910 Kent	Surrey		

CHAMPION MINOR COUNTY AND RUNNER-UP

(†Championship, or runners-up position, shared. In most seasons the title has been decided by a challenge match between teams finishing first and second in the table.)

CHAMPIONS	RUNNERS-UP	CHAMPIONS	RUNNERS-UP
1895 Durham, Norfolk and Worcestershire †		1925 Buckingham	Northumberland
		1926 Durham	Oxfordshire
1896 Worcestershire	Buckingham	1927 Staffordshire	Notts II
1897 Worcestershire	Glamorgan	1928 Berkshire	Lancashire II
1898 Worcestershire	Berkshire and Northants †	1929 Oxfordshire	Buckingham
		1930 Durham	Surrey II
1899 Northants and Buckingham †		1931 Leicestershire II	Surrey II
1900 Glamorgan, Durham and Northants†		1932 Buckingham	Berkshire
		1933 Title held in abeyance.	
1901 Durham	Surrey II	1934 Lancashire II	Surrey II
1902 Wiltshire	Surrey II	1935 Middlesex II	Hertfordshire
1903 Northants	Durham	1936 Hertfordshire	Norfolk
1904 Northants	Wiltshire	1937 Lancashire II	Surrey II
1905 Norfolk	Monmouthshire	1938 Buckingham	Lancashire II
1906 Staffordshire	Devon	1939 Surrey II	Lancashire II
1907 Lancashire II	Glamorgan	1946 Suffolk	Buckingham
1908 Staffordshire	Glamorgan	1947 Yorkshire II	Surrey II
1909 Wiltshire	Glamorgan	1948 Lancashire II	Bedfordshire
1910 Norfolk	Berkshire	1949 Lancashire II	Oxfordshire
1911 Staffordshire	Surrey II	1950 Surrey II	Bedfordshire
1912 Title held in abeyance.		1951 Kent II	Lancashire II
1913 Norfolk	Glamorgan	1952 Buckingham	Kent II
1914 Competition not finished owing to war.		1953 Berkshire	Buckingham
		1954 Surrey II	Buckingham & Notts II †
1920 Staffordshire	Berkshire and Kent II †	1955 Surrey II	Northumberland
		1956 Kent II	Northumberland
1921 Staffordshire	Berkshire	1957 Yorkshire II	Warwickshire II
1922 Buckingham	Norfolk	1958 Yorkshire II	Oxfordshire
1923 Buckingham	Surrey II	1959 Warwickshire II	Lancashire II
1924 Berkshire	Northumberland		

GREAT NAMES IN CRICKET

GEORGE GUNN (Nottinghamshire). Born at Hucknall 13/6/1879, died in Sussex 28/6/1958, aged 79. Perhaps the greatest batsman against fast bowling ever: he had the habit of walking down the pitch towards the bowler and turning the length of the ball into something suitable for himself. He played for his county from 1902 to 1932, and totalled 35,190 runs (av. 35.90), including 62 centuries. He played in 15 Test matches for England, scoring 119 v. Australia at Sydney in 1907-08 on his debut in that class of cricket. He was the leading light of a cricketing family, of whom William and John preceded him and his son, G.V., came later. In 1931 he and his son scored centuries in the same innings v. Warwickshire, the only time that father and son have achieved that unique record. Having promised to score a century on his fiftieth birthday, Gunn scored 164 not out in 5¼ hours v. Worcestershire at Worcester and redeemed his promise.

WALTER R. HAMMOND (Gloucestershire). Born at Dover 19/6/1903. The majesty of his right-handed batting is apt to obscure the fact that he was also a very fine right-arm medium-pace bowler and a slip field whose exceptionally safe hands held a total of 819 catches in first-class cricket. His first county appearance was in 1920; he turned amateur in 1937, captained his county in 1939 and 1946 and retired at the end of the 1946–47 M.C.C. tour to Australia and New Zealand (he reappeared for odd matches in 1950 and 1951). Between 1927–28 and 1946–47 he played 85 Test matches for England, the last 20 of them as captain, and totalled 7,249 runs (av. 58.45), 22 centuries, 83 wickets (av. 37.79) and 110 catches: an all-round feat without equal in Test cricket. His best Test score was 336 not out in only 5¼ hours v. New Zealand at Auckland in 1932–33: at that time a Test record. He missed the whole of the 1926 season owing to illness, when he would almost certainly have been able to gain his first cap against Australia. He went on nine overseas tours: to Australia and New Zealand in 1928–29, 1932–33, 1936–37 and 1946–47, to South Africa in 1927–28, 1930–31 and 1938–39 and West Indies in 1925–26 and 1934–35. He scored two centuries in the same match seven times: a record for first-class cricket. He also holds the fielding records: 78 catches in the 1928 season and 10 catches in a match v. Surrey at Cheltenham in the same season. His 36 double-centuries in first-class cricket have only been exceeded by D. G. Bradman (with 37). Scored 1,000 runs in a season 17 times in England and 5 times on overseas tours. His final career aggregates were 50,493 runs (av. 56.10), 167 centuries, 732 wickets (av. 30.58) and 819 catches.

TOM HAYWARD (Surrey). Born at Cambridge 29/3/1871, died at Cambridge 19/7/1939, aged 68. Stylish, with a grand array of strokes, Hayward was a Surrey regular from 1893 to 1914. Right-handed opening batsman and right-arm off-break bowler, Hayward totalled 43,551 runs (av. 41.80) including 104 centuries, and 481 wickets, (av. 22.95) in first-class cricket. In 1906 he set the then seasonal record by scoring 3,518 runs (av. 66.37) and 13 centuries. He achieved the double in 1897 with 1,368 runs and 114 wickets, but later concentrated on his batting. He scored 1,999 runs (av. 34.45) in 35 Test matches, touring Australia in 1897–98, 1901–02 and 1903–04 and South Africa in 1895–96. His best score in first-class cricket was 315 not out v. Lancashire at the Oval in 1898, and he three times scored two centuries in a match (twice within six days in 1906—144 not out and 100 v. Nottinghamshire at Nottingham and 143 and 125 v. Leicestershire at Leicester). Hayward completed 1,000 runs before the end of May in 1900, but was assisted by some runs scored in April.

A. LINDSAY HASSETT (Victoria). Born at Geelong 28/8/1913. Technically sound, his right-handed batting served his country well in the immediate years after the retirement of D. G. Bradman. A charming companion, with a puckish sense of humour, he made his debut in first-class cricket in 1932–33 and retired after his testimonial match (he received £5,503) in 1953–54. He played in 43 Tests for Australia, captaining his country 24 times, and toured England in 1938, 1948 and 1953, and South Africa in 1949–50. He played cricket in England, India, Australia and New Zealand within the space of six months in 1945–46. He totalled 16,890 runs (av. 58.24), and his 59 centuries ranks only second to D. G. Bradman for an overseas player. He served in the A.I.F. during the war and captained the Australian Services team in the unofficial Tests against England in 1945. His best score was 232 v. M.C.C. at Melbourne in 1950–51.

W. R. Hammond (top) and Lindsay Hassett

CRICKET QUIZ

1. Which captain of a touring team to England scored only two runs in first-class matches on the tour?

★

2. There are only two first-class counties for which no bowler has yet taken ten wickets in an innings: which are they?

★

3. Which were the nine original counties in the County Championship?

★

4. In which years did the other eight counties enter the Championship?

★

5. Which professional captains have taken their team to the County Championship?

★

6. What is the highest number of innings played by one batsman in a season?

★

7. Who is the only cricketer to have played in Test cricket for England v. Australia and for Australia v. England?

★

8. How many Test matches have been abandoned without a ball being bowled, and which were they?

QUIZ ANSWERS

1. Maharajah of Porbandar, captain of the 1932 Indian team. 2. Hampshire and Worcestershire. 3. Derbyshire, Gloucestershire, Kent, Lancashire, Middlesex, Nottinghamshire, Surrey, Sussex and Yorkshire. 4. Somerset in 1891, Essex, Hampsh re, Leicestershire, Warwickshire in 1895, Worcestershire in 1899, Northamptonshire in 1905 and Glamorgan in 1921. 5. A. Shaw of Nottinghamshire in 1883, 1884, 1885 and 1886 and H. E. Dollery of Warwickshire in 1951. 6. 70 by A. H. H. Gilligan (Sussex) in 1923. 7. W. E. Midwinter—for Australia in 1876–77, 1882–83, 1884 and 1886–87, and for England in 1881–82. 8. Both between England and Australia at Manchester, 1890 and 1938.

CRICKET QUIZ

1. Which batsman scored four consecutive centuries in one week of first-class cricket?

*

2. Which England Test captain was clean bowled first ball in each innings of his first match in first-class cricket?

*

3. Name at least three players who never registered "a pair of spectacles" in first-class cricket?

*

4. How many century stands for the first wicket did J. B. Hobbs share in during his career in first-class cricket, and who were his leading partners in these stands?

*

5. What is the longest distance from hit to pitch that a batsman has hit a cricket ball?

*

6. Which batsman hit a ball over the top of the present Lord's pavilion and which bowler was involved?

*

7. Which cricketer spent six consecutive winters on cricket tours?

*

8. Which cricketer was selected for three official Test-playing tours, although he had played only two first-class matches prior to his original selection?

QUIZ ANSWERS

1. T. Hayward of Surrey, 144 not out and 100 v. Nottinghamshire at Nottingham and 143 and 125 v. Leicestershire at Leicester in 1906. 2. J. W. H. T. Douglas was "bowled Hirst 0" in each innings for Essex v. Yorkshire at Leyton in 1901. 3. W. G. Grace, K. S. Ranjitsinhji, H. Sutcliffe, D. G. Bradman and D. C. S. Compton are among those who never registered a "double-duck". 4. 166—66 with A. Sandham, 40 with T. Hayward, 26 with H. Sutcliffe and 13 with W. Rhodes. 5. 175 yards by Rev. W. Fellows, while at practice at Christchurch ground, Oxford, in 1856. 6. A. E. Trott hit M. A. Noble, when playing for Middlesex v. Australians in 1899. 7. W. E. Astill (Leicestershire) —to South Africa in 1924–25, to West Indies in 1925–26, to India in 1926–27, to South Africa in 1927–28, to Jamaica in 1928–29 and to West Indies in 1929–30. 8. A. F. Rae, after only two matches for Jamaica in 1946–47, was selected for the West Indies teams to India in 1948–49, England in 1950 and Australia and New Zealand in 1951–52.

YOUNG CRICKETERS OF THE YEAR

At the end of each season the members of the Cricket Writers' Club select by ballot the player who they consider to be the best young cricketer of that season. The award, a suitable trophy, is presented to the player at the clubs' annual dinner. The winner each season since the institution of the trophy in 1950 has been as follows:

1950	R. Tattersall (Lancashire)
1951	P. B. H. May (Surrey)
1952	F. S. Trueman (Yorkshire)
1953	M. C. Cowdrey (Kent)
1954	P. J. Loader (Surrey)
1955	K. F. Barrington (Surrey)
1956	B. Taylor (Essex)
1957	M. J. Stewart (Surrey)
1958	A. C. D. Ingleby-Mackenzie (Hampshire)

R. Tattersall   F. S. Trueman   P. J. Loader

THE "COUNTY" CUPS

The most recent awards for first-class cricketers in England are the "County" cups, instituted in 1954. They are awarded annually for the fastest century, the best bowling performance on figures, the fielder taking the most catches, the wicket-keeper dismissing the most batsmen and a special award for the best performance of the season. The Visitor's Award was instituted in 1958. The winners each year, together with details of their performances, have been:

BATTING—FASTEST CENTURY
1954	G. M. Emmett (84 mins.) for Gloucestershire v. Somerset at Taunton.
1955	Ray Smith (73 mins.) for Essex v. Northamptonshire at Wellingborough.
1956	A. C. Walton (61 mins.) for Oxford U. v. Sussex at Oxford.
1957	R. E. Marshall (66 mins.) for Hampshire v. Kent at Southampton.
1958	A. C. D. Ingleby-Mackenzie (61 mins.) for Hampshire v. Somerset at Bournemouth.
1959	J. M. Parks (61 mins.) for Sussex v. Lancashire at Manchester.

BOWLING—BEST FIGURES IN AN INNINGS
1954	J. H. Wardle (9 for 25) for Yorkshire v. Lancashire at Manchester.
1955	J. Flavell (9 for 30) for Worcestershire v. Kent at Dover.
1956	J. C. Laker (10 for 53 and 9 for 37) for England v. Australia at Manchester.
1957	D. J. Halfyard (9 for 39) for Kent v. Glamorgan at Neath.
1958	P. J. Loader (9 for 17) for Surrey v. Warwickshire at the Oval.
1959	J. D. Bannister (10 for 41) for Warwickshire v. Com. Services at Birmingham

FIELDING—MOST CATCHES IN A SEASON
1954	44 by C. A. Milton (Gloucestershire)
1955	69 by John Langridge (Sussex)
1956	60 by C. A. Milton (Gloucestershire)
1957	75 by M. J. Stewart (Surrey)
1958	61 by M. J. Stewart (Surrey)
1959	64 by P. M. Walker (Glamorgan)

C. A. Milton   H. W. Stephenson   D. Shackleton

WICKET-KEEPING—MOST VICTIMS IN A SEASON
1954	86 (50 ct., 36 st.) by H. W. Stephenson (Somerset)
1955	85 (65 ct., 20 st.) by A. J. McIntyre (Surrey)
1956	77 (63 ct., 14 st.) by J. T. Murray (Middlesex)
1957	94 (79 ct., 15 st.) by J. T. Murray (Middlesex)
1958	81 (74 ct., 7 st.) by J. T. Murray (Middlesex)
1959	91 (85 ct., 6 st.) by J. M. Parks (Sussex)

SPECIAL AWARD FOR BEST PERFORMANCE OF SEASON
1954	Fazal Mahmood, for taking 12 wickets for 99 runs in fourth Test for Pakistan v. England at the Oval, when Pakistan won by 24 runs.
1955	South African cricket team, for their cricket during the season.
1956	Surrey and their captain, Stuart Surridge, on their record performance in winning the County Championship for five consecutive seasons.
1957	P. B. H. May and M. C. Cowdrey, for sharing in a fourth wicket stand of 411 for England v. West Indies at Birmingham, the highest partnership ever made for England.
1958	D. Shackleton, whose 165 wickets played such a large part in the Hampshire challenge to Surrey's supremacy in the Championship (Hampshire finished runners-up, their best-ever final position).
1959	M. J. K. Smith, Warwickshire captain, the first batsman to pass the 3,000 runs aggregate for ten years.

VISITOR'S AWARD
| 1958 | J. R. Reid of New Zealand (captain of the touring team). |
| 1959 | A. A. Baig of India—century (112) on Test debut at Manchester. |

Note. Performances in festival matches are not included in the figures when calculating the award. Also the Champion County v. The Rest matches were excluded in 1956 and 1957 and games outside England and Wales are also banned.

GREAT NAMES IN CRICKET

GEORGE HEADLEY (Jamaica). Born at Panama 30/5/1909. A brilliant right-handed batsman who before the war was his country's main batting power. He made his first-class debut in 1927–28 and startled the world in his Test debut rubber against England in 1929–30 by scoring four centuries—176 in his first match, 112 and 114 in his third, and 223 in his fourth. He toured Australia in 1930–31 and came to England in 1933 and 1939, scoring 107 and 106 in the Lord's Test match on the second tour. He played in 22 Tests for West Indies, being a regular choice in 19 Tests before the war, and played v. England once in 1947–48 and once in 1953–54 and v. India once in 1948–49 after the war. His best score was 344 not out for Jamaica v. Hon. L. H. Tennyson's XI at Kingston in 1931–32, when he added 487 with C. C. Passailague in an unfinished stand for the sixth wicket. He played a considerable amount of League cricket in England and his son made his debut for Worcestershire in 1958.

E. "Patsy" Hendren

ELIAS "PATSY" HENDREN (Middlesex). Born at Chiswick 5/2/1889. Probably the best hooker of fast bowling the game has seen, Hendren's career covered the years from 1907 to 1938 and brought him a total of 57,611 runs (av. 50.81), including 170 centuries. He started slowly, but by 1911 he had reached 1,000 runs in a season for the first time and after the war he was a "first-choice" for England for many years. He scored 3,525 runs (av. 47.63), including 7 centuries, between 1920–21 and 1934–35 in 51 Tests for England. He toured Australia in 1920–21, 1924–25 and 1928–29, South Africa in 1930–31 and West Indies in 1929–30 and 1934–35. On the 1929–30 tour he scored 1,765 runs (av. 135.76) and set a record for West Indian cricket that may never be equalled. The best of his 22 double-centuries was 301 not out v. Worcestershire at Dudley in 1933. As outside left with Manchester City and Brentford, Hendren was good enough to gain a "Victory" cap for England just after the 1914–18 war.

GEORGE H. HIRST (Yorkshire). Born at Kirkheaton 7/9/1871, died at Huddersfield 10/5/1954, aged 82. One of the great all-rounders—right-handed batsman and left-arm medium-fast bowler—who was the first of the real seam bowlers. Between 1891 and 1929 he totalled 36,323 runs (av. 34.13), including 60 centuries, and 2,739 wickets (av. 18.72). He actually retired after 1921, but returned for one match in the 1929 Scarborough Festival at the age of 58. He achieved the double of 1,000 runs and 100 wickets in 14 seasons between 1896 and 1913, the last 11 of them in succession. Against Somerset at Bath in 1906 he achieved the unique feat of a century in each innings (111 and 117 not out) and took five wickets in each innings of the match. In that season he also achieved the unique double of 2,385 runs (av. 45.86) and 208 wickets (av. 16.50)—that season's double was completed on 28th June, still a record for the feat. He played in 24 Tests for England, and toured Australia in 1897–98 and 1903–04—he also played in two matches in India in 1921–22. His best score of 341 v. Leicestershire at Leicester in 1905 is still a county record.

SIR JOHN BERRY HOBBS (Surrey). Born at Cambridge 16/12/1882. No one has ever seriously opposed the view that Hobbs was the greatest batsman on all wickets that has graced the game of cricket. After a few matches for Cambridgeshire he offered his services to Essex, and that county, to their permanent chagrin, turned him down. Consequently he turned to Surrey and between 1905 and 1934 scored 61,237 runs (av. 50.65), including 197 centuries, to set up two records that may well stand for ever. It is not generally realised that Hobbs was 40 when he scored his 100th century, yet went on to score 97 more centuries at an age when most present-day first-class cricketers have retired to a slippered ease. He played in 61 Tests for England between 1907–08 and 1930, scoring 5,410 runs (av. 56.94), including 15 centuries, and over a long period of years was first-choice as opening batsman. Hobbs was fortunate in finding several fine batsmen with whom to open the innings—T. Hayward and A. Sandham for Surrey and W. Rhodes and H. Sutcliffe for England were his main

often been attacked for his defensive, or canny, approach to cricket, but has the perfect answer in the results and success which he attained.

HON. F. S. JACKSON (Yorkshire). Born at Chapel Allerton, Leeds, 21/11/1870, died in London 9/3/1947, aged 76. A stylish right-handed batsman, right-arm fast-medium bowler and brilliant field, he was educated at Harrow and Cambridge University. He will always be remembered for his captaincy in 1905, when he led England to victory against Australia, headed both the batting and bowling averages and won all five tosses of the rubber. Oddly enough, his opposite number, J. Darling, the Australian captain, was born on exactly the same day as Jackson. Between 1890 and 1907 Jackson totalled 15,824 runs (av. 34.03), including 31 centuries, and 770 wickets (av. 20.33). He could not find time to go on an official overseas tour, his only tour being a minor one to India in 1892–93. After service in the Boer War and the 1914–18 war, Jackson entered Parliament and was later appointed

His final career aggregates were 26,698 runs (av. 32.63), 53 centuries and 873 wickets (av. 22.79). On 14 occasions he scored 1,000 runs in a season and completed the double by also taking 100 wickets in 1897 and 1900.

HAROLD LARWOOD (Nottinghamshire). Born at Nuncargate 14/11/1904. A great fast bowler who played in 21 Tests for England between 1926 and 1932–33 and was a central figure in the body-line controversy of 1932–33. On that tour his speed was too much for the Australian batsmen and he took 33 wickets in the five Tests, but he suffered an injury to a foot and his effectiveness was reduced in later years. His career lasted from 1924 to 1938 and he took 1,427 wickets (av. 17.51), with a best of 162 wickets (av. 12.86) in 1932 when he finished top of the seasonal bowling averages. He achieved two hat-tricks and his best bowling figures were 9 for 41 v. Kent at Nottingham in 1931. He has now made his home in Australia, where he toured with successful M.C.C. teams in 1928–29 and 1932–33.

1. Which cricketer appeared for the Gentlemen at Lord's while still at school?

★

2. Which cricketer holds the record of scoring centuries in the University match at Lord's, the Gentlemen v. Players match at Lord's and for England in a Test match at Lord's?

★

3. When were first innings points introduced for County Championship matches?

★

4. Who was President of the M.C.C. for the longest term?

★

5. Who was a member of the England Test Selection Committee for nine consecutive seasons?

★

6. Not all of the University matches between Oxford and Cambridge have been played at Lord's. When and where were the exceptions played?

★

7. Which batsmen have scored 1,000 runs in the month of May?

George Headley   J. B. Hobbs   L. Hutton   Gilbert Jessop   Philip Mead

partners—and it is surprising to note that no fewer than 166 century first-wicket stands were included in his 1,315 innings in first-class cricket. Hobbs made five trips to Australia, in 1907–08, 1911–12, 1920–21, 1924–25 and 1928–29, and in addition toured South Africa in 1909–10 and 1913–14. His 316 not out for Surrey v. Middlesex in 1926 is a record for Lord's and his 266 not out for the Players at Scarborough in 1925 is still the record for the whole series of Gentlemen v. Players matches. His 16 centuries in the 1925 season has only been beaten by Compton's 18 in 1947. It was in 1925 that Hobbs first equalled and then beat W. G. Grace's record of 126 centuries in the same match against Somerset at Taunton. Hobbs finished as the leading batsman of the season several times, but in 1920 he was also at the top of the season's bowling averages. Hobbs was knighted in the 1953 Coronation Honours List.

SIR LEONARD HUTTON (Yorkshire). Born at Fulneck, Pudsey, 23/6/1916. The third in a line of distinguished England opening batsmen whose careers stretch back over a period of 90 years—W. G. Grace (1865–1908), J. B. Hobbs (1905–1934) and L. Hutton (1934–1957). He started his first-class career with a duck in 1934, and three years later collected a duck in his first Test match, but by the time he played his last match had scored 40,051 runs (av. 55.54), including 129 centuries. His best score of 364 v. Australia at the Oval in 1938, which lasted for 800 minutes, was a record in Test cricket for size and length, but both these records were taken from him in the winter of 1957–58. He played in 79 Tests for England, scoring 6,971 runs (av. 56.67) and was the first modern professional to be appointed England captain—he skippered his country from 1952 to 1954–55, not only regaining the Ashes in 1953 but successfully defending them in 1954–55. He toured Australia and New Zealand in 1946–47, 1950–51 and 1954–55, South Africa in 1938–39 and 1948–49, West Indies in 1947–48 and 1953–54, and Jamaica with Yorkshire in 1935–36. He suffered a severe injury to his left arm while in the Army during the war and all his post-war cricket was played under this handicap. He has

Governor of Bombay, but his service to cricket continued—in 1921 he was President of the M.C.C., in 1934 chairman of the England Test selectors, and in 1943 presided over the special committee appointed by the M.C.C. to prepare the way for the resumption of first-class cricket.

DOUGLAS R. JARDINE (Surrey). Born at Bombay 23/10/1900, died at Montreux 18/6/1958, aged 57. Educated at Winchester, he gained a Blue at Oxford and played in the 1920, 1921 and 1923 University matches. A wonderfully correct and academic batsman, he scored 14,821 runs (av. 46.90), including 35 centuries, in first-class cricket between 1920 and 1948—he played only rare matches after 1933–34. His best score was 214 for M.C.C. v. Tasmania at Launceston in 1928–29, after having opened the tour with three successive centuries. It is as a captain, however, that he will be chiefly remembered. Between 1931 and 1933–34 he led England in 15 Test matches, losing only one, and regaining the Ashes from Australia in the historic body-line rubber of 1932–33. The feelings against these tactics were such that Jardine virtually dropped out of first-class cricket a year later.

GILBERT L. JESSOP (Gloucestershire). Born at Cheltenham 19/5/1874, died at Dorchester 11/5/1955, aged 80. A truly great all-rounder, he was a very hard-hitting right-handed batsman, a fast right-arm bowler and a brilliant field in the covers. Throughout his career he scored his runs at about 80 an hour, and only four of his 53 centuries were scored at less than a run-a-minute. He scored his highest innings of 286 in only 175 minutes v. Sussex at Hove in 1903, and only once batted for more than three hours although he scored five double-centuries. On eleven occasions he completed his century within an hour of starting his innings. He made his debut in 1894, gained a Blue at Cambridge and played in the 1896, 1897, 1898 and 1899 University matches, played in 18 Test matches for England between 1899 and 1912 and captained his county from 1900 to 1911. He toured Australia in 1901–02.

MAURICE LEYLAND (Yorkshire). Born at Harrogate 20/7/1900. A fine left-handed batsman, who revelled in a crisis, fast outfield and more than useful slow left-arm bowler. He played for Yorkshire from 1920 to 1946 and ended his first-class career in 1948 with a career record of 33,660 runs (av. 40.50), 80 centuries and 466 wickets (av. 29.29). He was perhaps at his best in 1934, when he scored three Test centuries against Australia—109 at Lord's, 153 at Manchester and 110 at the Oval—but in his final Test match, v. Australia at the Oval in 1938, he scored an innings of 187 and put England well on the way to a record total with a second-wicket stand of 382 with L. Hutton. He played in 41 Test matches for England, totalling 2,764 runs (av. 46.06), including 9 centuries, and toured Australia and New Zealand in 1928–29, 1932–33 and 1936–37, South Africa in 1930–31, West Indies in 1934–35, Jamaica with Yorkshire in 1935–36 and visited India in 1926–27 on a coaching engagement and played against the M.C.C. His best score was 263 v. Essex at Hull in 1936, and he achieved the hat-trick v. Surrey at Sheffield in 1935.

1. G. T. S. Stevens in 1919, while still at University College School. 2. A. P. F. Chapman (Kent)—102 not out for Cambridge in 1922, 160 in 1922 and 108 in 1926 for Gentlemen and 121 for England v. Australia in 1930. 3. In 1911. 4. S. Christopherson was appointed in 1939 and held the office right through the war, his successor being appointed in 1946, seven years later. 5. P. A. Perrin (Essex) from 1931 to 1939. 6. On the Magdalen Ground at Oxford in 1829, at Bullingdon Green at Oxford in 1843, on the Magdalen ground again in 1846 and 1848, and at Cowley Marsh at Oxford in 1850. 7. W. G. Grace in 1895, W. R. Hammond in 1927 and C. Hallows in 1928.

D. R. Jardine   Maurice Leyland   A. C. MacLaren

ARCHIBALD C. MACLAREN (Lancashire). Born at Manchester 1/12/1871, died 17/11/1944, aged 72. Captain of England in 22 Test matches between 1897–98 and 1909, he is regarded as one of the best captains the game has known (he won only 4 of the 22 matches, however, and one would have thought that success was a major attribute of captaincy). His career spanned the years between 1890 and 1922–23, and he completed an unusual feat by scoring

108 v. Sussex at Hove in his first innings in first-class cricket and 200 not out v. New Zealand XI at Wellington in his last. In 1895 he scored 424 v. Somerset at Taunton, a county record that may never be surpassed. He played altogether in 35 Tests for England, and toured Australia in 1894–95, 1897–98 and 1901–02, Australia and New Zealand in 1922–23, North America in 1899 and South America in 1911–12. Managed 1924–25 English team to South Africa.

K. R. Miller   A. D. Nourse   W. H. Ponsford

CRICKET QUIZ

1. Which cricketers were known under the following nicknames: (a) Smith, (b) Croucher, (c) Lol, (d) Tiger, (e) Dodger?

★

2. Which Australian made eight consecutive tours to England?

★

3. Which player made three tours to Australia, playing in eleven Tests, but never played against Australia in England?

★

4. Which is the only country to win a Test match on their first tour of England?

★

5. Name the only players who have been captain of two consecutive M.C.C. touring teams?

★

6. When did Middlesex C.C.C. make Lord's their headquarters?

★

7. Which first-class county has had at least one stand of 200 for each of the ten wickets?

★

8. Which are the seven grounds on which Test cricket has been played in England?

QUIZ ANSWERS

1. (a) K. S. Ranjitsinhji, (b) G. L. Jessop, (c) H. Larwood, (d) E. J. Smith, (e) W. W. Whysall. 2. J. McC. Blackham, wicket-keeper with the first Australian team in 1878, came again in 1880, 1882, 1884, 1886, 1888, 1890, and was captain on his eighth visit in 1893. 3. W. Voce (Nottinghamshire). 4. Pakistan in 1954, by 24 runs at the Oval. 5. P. F. Warner to Australia 1903–04 and South Africa 1905–06, J. W. H. T. Douglas to South Africa 1913–14 and Australia 1920–21, D. R. Jardine to Australia and New Zealand 1932–33 and India 1933–34, W. R. Hammond to South Africa 1938–39 and Australia and New Zealand 1946–47, L. Hutton to West Indies 1953–54 and Australia and New Zealand 1954–55, P. B. H. May to South Africa 1956–57 and Australia and New Zealand 1958–59. 6. In 1877. 7. Essex. 8. Birmingham, Nottingham, Lord's, Leeds, Manchester, the Oval and Sheffield (the last named v. Australia in 1902).

GREAT NAMES IN CRICKET

CHARLES PHILIP MEAD (Hampshire). Born at Battersea 9/3/1887, died at Bournemouth 26/3/1958, aged 71. One of the greatest batsmen in cricket history, only three batsmen—J. B. Hobbs, F. E. Woolley and E. Hendren—have passed his 55,060 runs in first-class cricket, and only Hobbs (197) and Hendren (170) have bettered his 153 centuries. In county cricket he was the heaviest scorer, as no batsman has surpassed the 48,892 runs (av. 48.84) that Mead scored for Hampshire. He first applied to join Surrey, but that county declined his services—one of the biggest blunders of all time. Mead then turned to Hampshire, played one match in 1905, became qualified in 1906, and scored over 1,000 runs each season until he retired after the 1936 summer. He toured Australia in 1911–12 and 1928–29, South Africa in 1913–14 and 1922–23 and Jamaica in 1927–28. A fine slip field, he held 668 catches (627 for Hampshire) and as a slow left-arm bowler took 277 wickets (av. 34.70). He played in only 17 Tests for England, but in Mead's day Tests were not as plentiful as they are now. He played for Suffolk from 1937 to 1939, but as the years passed he began to lose his sight and for some years before his death was totally blind. One unique record held by Mead is that of sharing in at least one century stand for each of the ten wickets for his county.

KEITH ROSS MILLER (Victoria and New South Wales). Born at Melbourne 28/11/1919. It would not be an exaggeration to claim Miller as the greatest all-rounder in cricket history—a glorious stroke-player when in the mood, he could also play an innings of studied defence at need; a fast bowler feared by most batsmen, who had the ability to bowl almost every type of ball; and a fielder close to the wicket who held some miraculous catches. He played first-class cricket from 1937–38 to 1956–57, totalling 14,019 runs (av. 48.50), and 40 centuries, and 493 wickets (av. 22.27). He played in 55 of Australia's first 57 post-war Tests, with a total of 2,958 runs (av. 36.97), 7 centuries, 38 catches and 170 wickets (av. 22.97)—figures in excess of all other Test cricketers. He was one of the most travelled of cricketers—touring England in 1948, 1953 and 1956, South Africa in 1949–50, West Indies in 1954–55, New Zealand in 1945–46, India in 1945–46 and Pakistan in 1956–57. He scored 181 for Victoria v. Tasmania at Melbourne in his first match in first-class cricket in 1937–38 and hit the best score of his career with 262 not out v. Combined Services at Kingston on the 1953 English tour. He served in the R.A.A.F. during the war and was a member of the Australian Services team which played in England in 1945—his 185 in 165 minutes for Dominions XI v. England XI at Lord's is still remembered by those fortunate enough to see it.

A. DUDLEY NOURSE (Natal). Born at Durban 12/11/1910—son of A. Dave Nourse, who played for South Africa from 1902–03 to 1924. An aggressive right-handed batsman, he scored 12,472 runs (av. 51.53), including 41 centuries, in his career which spanned the years from 1931–32 to 1952–53. He played in 34 Tests for South Africa, the last 15 as captain, scoring 2,960 runs (av. 53.81), with a best score of 231 v. Australia at Johannesburg in 1935–36. He toured England in 1935, 1947 and 1951—the last time as captain. Early on that tour he suffered a fracture of his left thumb and batted in all five Tests with the break pinned. He scored 208 in 550 minutes in

the first Test at Nottingham, but the buffeting his thumb received virtually meant his early retirement from first-class cricket. His best score in all first-class cricket was 260 not out v. Transvaal at Johannesburg in 1936–37.

CHARLES W. L. PARKER (Gloucestershire). Born at Prestbury 14/10/1884. A fine slow left-arm bowler who made his first-class debut in 1903 and played for his county from 1905 to 1935. Before the 1914–18 war he was second-string spinner to G. Dennett, but between 1920 and 1935 he took over 100 wickets every season and ended with a career aggregate of 3,278 wickets (av. 19.47), with 222 wickets (av. 14.91) in 1925 as his best return. He achieved the then record of six hat-tricks in his career, including one in each innings of the match v. Middlesex at Bristol in 1924, took all ten wickets in an innings (for 79 runs) v. Somerset at Bristol in 1921 and seventeen wickets in the match (for 56 runs) v. Essex at Gloucester in 1925. Surprisingly, Parker played only once for England, v. Australia at Manchester in 1921, and his only tour was to South Africa in 1924–25 with Hon. L. H. Tennyson's team.

WILLIAM H. PONSFORD (Victoria). Born at North Calton, Melbourne, 19/10/1900. Before the arrival of Bradman, Ponsford was easily the most prolific run-scorer in the game, and he is

still the only batsman to have twice scored over 400. He hit 429 v. Tasmania at Melbourne in 1922–23, and five years later (in 1927–28) broke his own record with 437 v. Queensland at Melbourne. Like most Australians his career was short, but he scored 13,819 runs (av. 65.18) between 1920–21 and 1934–35. He appeared in 29 Test matches for Australia, scoring 2,122 runs (av. 48.22), with a best score of 266 v. England at the Oval in 1934. He toured England in 1926, 1930 and 1934 and New Zealand in 1927–28. Several batsmen have scored 1,000 runs in a month's cricket, but no one can equal Ponsford's record of scoring 1,146 runs (av. 229.20) in the month of December 1927.

EDWARD POOLEY (Surrey). Born at Richmond 13/2/1838, died at Lambeth 18/7/1907, aged 69. A wicket-keeper of the highest class, he joined the Surrey staff in 1862, played for Middlesex in 1864 and then started his first-class career with Surrey in 1865. He dismissed twelve batsmen (8 ct., 4 st.) in the match v. Sussex at the Oval in 1868: still a record, although equalled by D. Tallon in 1938–39. He went to Australia and New Zealand in 1876–77, but was languishing in prison in New Zealand at a time when he should have been playing for England v. Australia in the first two Test matches played.

(Contd. on p. 124 col. 4)

TEST CRICKETERS SINCE THE WAR

Abbreviations: Eng—England, Aust—Australia, SA—South Africa, WI—West Indies, NZ—New Zealand, Ind—India, Pak—Pakistan. Total number of Tests shown in brackets after the name—where two figures are shown, i.e. (3–25), it means that the player has appeared in 3 Tests since the war, but in a total of 25 altogether, including pre-war appearances.

England

ALLEN, G. O. (3–25)—3 v. WI 1947–48.
ANDREW, K. V. (1)—1 v. Aust 1954–55.
APPLEYARD, R. (9)—1 v. Pak 1954, 4 v. Aust and 2 v. NZ 1954–55, 1 v. SA 1955, 1 v. Aust 1956.
BAILEY, T. E. (61)—4 v. NZ 1949, 2 v. WI 1950, 4 v. Aust and 2 v. NZ 1950–51, 2 v. SA 1951, 5 v. Aust 1953, 5 v. WI 1953–54, 3 v. Pak 1954, 5 v. Aust and 2 v. NZ 1954–55, 5 v. SA 1955, 4 v. Aust 1956, 5 v. SA 1956–57, 4 v. WI 1957, 4 v. NZ 1958, 5 v. Aust 1958–59.

CLOSE, D. B. (6)—1 v. NZ 1949, 1 v. Aust 1950–51, 1 v. SA 1955, 2 v. WI 1957, 1 v. Ind 1959.
COMPTON, D. C. S. (70–78)—3 v. Ind 1946, 5 v. Aust and 1 v. NZ 1946–47, 5 v. SA 1947, 5 v. Aust 1948, 5 v. SA 1948–49, 4 v. NZ 1949, 1 v. WI 1950, 4 v. Aust and 2 v. NZ 1950–51, 4 v. SA 1951, 2 v. Ind 1952, 5 v. Aust 1953, 5 v. WI 1953–54, 4 v. Pak 1954, 5 v. Aust 1954–55, 5 v. SA 1955, 1 v. Aust 1956, 5 v. WI 1956–57.
COOK, C. (1)—1 v. SA 1947.
COPSON, W. H. (1–3)—1 v. SA 1947.
COWDREY, M. C. (39)—5 v. Aust and 2 v. NZ 1954–5, 1 v. SA 1955, 5 v.

F. R. Brown   K. F. Barrington   E. R. Dexter

BARNETT, C. J. (4–20)—3 v. SA 1947, 1 v. Aust 1948.
BARRINGTON, K. F. (7)—2 v. SA 1955, 5 v. Ind 1959.
BEDSER, A. V. (51)—3 v. Ind 1946, 5 v. Aust and 1 v. NZ 1946–47, 2 v. SA 1947, 5 v. Aust 1948, 5 v. SA 1948–49, 2 v. NZ 1949, 3 v. WI 1950, 5 v. Aust and 2 v. NZ 1950–51, 4 v. SA 1951, 4 v. Ind 1952, 5 v. Aust 1953, 2 v. Pak 1954, 1 v. Aust 1954–55, 1 v. SA 1955.
BERRY, R. (2)—2 v. WI 1950.
BOWES, W. E. (1–15)—1 v. Ind 1946.
BRENNAN, D. V. (2)—2 v. SA 1951.
BROOKES, D. (1)—1 v. WI 1947–48.
BROWN, F. R. (16–22)—2 v. NZ 1949, 1 v. WI 1950, 5 v. Aust and 2 v. NZ 1950–51, 5 v. SA 1951, 1 v. Aust 1953.
BUTLER, H. J. (2)—1 v. SA 1947, 1 v. WI 1947–48.
CARR, D. B. (2)—2 v. Ind 1951–52.

Aust 1956, 5 v. SA 1956–57, 5 v. WI 1957, 4 v. NZ 1958, 5 v. Aust and 2 v. NZ 1958–59, 5 v. Ind 1959.
COXON, A. (1)—1 v. Aust 1948.
CRANSTON, K. (8)—3 v. SA 1947, 4 v. WI 1947–48, 1 v. Aust 1948.
CRAPP, J. F. (7)—3 v. Aust 1948, 4 v. SA 1948–49.
DEWES, J. G. (5)—1 v. Aust 1948, 2 v. WI 1950, 2 v. Aust 1950–51.
DEXTER, E. R. (7)—1 v. NZ 1958, 2 v. Aust and 2 v. NZ 1958–59, 2 v. Ind 1959.
DOGGART, G. H. G. (2)—2 v. WI 1950.
DOLLERY, H. E. (4)—1 v. SA 1947, 2 v. Aust 1950, 1 v. WI 1950.
EDRICH, W. J. (30–39)—1 v. Ind 1946, 5 v. Aust and 1 v. NZ 1946–47, 5 v. SA 1947, 5 v. Aust 1948, 4 v. NZ 1949, 2 v. WI 1950, 3 v. Aust 1953, 1 v. Pak 1954, 4 v. Aust 1954–55.
EMMETT, G. M. (1)—1 v. Aust 1948.

T. E. Bailey   A. V. Bedser   D. C. S. Compton

CRICKET QUIZ

1. What is the highest number of runs conceded by one bowler in a first-class match?

2. What is the highest number of runs conceded by one bowler in an innings in a first-class match?

3. Which player scored a century in his first match and took a wicket with his first ball in first-class cricket?

4. Which players completed the double of 1,000 runs and 100 wickets for more than one county?

5. Which two batsmen, apart from the first season in which they appeared, never failed to pass the 1,000 runs aggregate in every season of their career?

6. Which batsman holds the record of sharing in a century stand for each of the ten wickets for his county?

7. Who were the Sheffield Shield, Currie Cup, Plunket Shield and Ranji Trophy named after?

8. Which cricketer played for both Oxford and Cambridge Universities?

QUIZ ANSWERS

1. 428 runs by C. S. Nayudu (6 for 153 and 5 for 275) for Holkar v. Bombay at Bombay in 1944–45. 2. 362 runs off 64 eight-ball overs, by A. A. Mailey for New South Wales v. Victoria at Melbourne in 1926–27. 3. F. W. Stocks (Nottinghamshire). 4. V. W. C. Jupp for Sussex in 1920 and 1921 and Northamptonshire eight times between 1925 and 1933. F. R. Brown for Surrey in 1932 and for Northamptonshire in 1949 and 1952. 5. F. E. Woolley of Kent, 28 times from 1907 to 1938 (debut in 1906), and C. P. Mead of Hampshire, 27 times from 1906 to 1936 (debut in 1905). 6. C. P. Mead of Hampshire. Both W. R. Hammond and W. Rhodes achieved this in all first-class cricket, but not for their counties only. 7. Lord Sheffield (who took the 1891–92 England team to Australia), Sir Donald Currie (ship-owner), Lord Plunket (Governor-General of New Zealand in 1906–07), K. S. Ranjitsinhji. 8. G. S. Seaton, for Cambridge in 1946 and for Oxford in 1957.

EVANS, T. G. (91)—1 v. Ind 1946, 4 v. Aust and 1 v. NZ 1946–47, 5 v. SA 1947, 4 v. WI 1947–48, 5 v. Aust 1948, 3 v. SA 1948–49, 4 v. NZ 1949, 3 v. WI 1950, 5 v. Aust and 2 v. NZ 1950–51, 3 v. SA 1951, 4 v. Ind 1952, 5 v. Aust 1953, 4 v. WI 1953–54, 4 v. Pak 1954, 4 v. Aust and 2 v. NZ 1954–55, 3 v. SA 1955, 5 v. Aust 1956, 5 v. SA 1956–57, 5 v. WI 1957, 5 v. NZ 1958, 3 v. Aust 1958–59, 2 v. Ind 1959.
FISHLOCK, L. B. (2–4)—1 v. Ind 1946, 1 v. Aust 1946–47.
GIBB, P. A. (3–8)—2 v. Ind 1946, 1 v. Aust 1946–47.
GLADWIN, C. (8)—2 v. SA 1947, 5 v. SA 1948–49, 1 v. NZ 1949.
GOVER, A. R. (1–4)—1 v. Ind 1946.
GRAVENEY, T. W. (48)—1 v. SA 1951, 4 v. Ind 1951–52, 4 v. Ind 1952, 5 v. Aust 1953, 5 v. WI 1953–54, 3 v. Pak 1954, 2 v. Aust and 2 v. NZ 1954–55, 5 v. SA 1955, 2 v. Aust 1956, 4 v. WI 1957, 4 v. NZ 1958, 5 v. Aust and 2 v. NZ 1958–59.
GREENHOUGH, T. (3)—3 v. Ind 1959.
GRIFFITH, S. C. (3)—1 v. WI 1947–48, 2 v. SA 1948–49.
HAMMOND, W. R. (8–85)—3 v. Ind 1946, 4 v. Aust and 1 v. NZ 1946–47.
HARDSTAFF, J. jun. (7–23)—2 v. Ind 1946, 1 v. Aust 1946–47, 3 v. WI 1947–48, 1 v. Aust 1948.
HILTON, M. J. (4)—1 v. WI 1950, 1 v. SA 1951, 2 v. Ind 1951–52.
HOLLIES, W. E. (10–13)—3 v. SA 1947, 1 v. Aust 1948, 4 v. NZ 1949, 2 v. WI 1950.
HORTON, M. J. (2)—2 v. Ind 1959.
HOWARD, N. D. (4)—4 v. Ind 1951–52.
HOWORTH, R. (5)—1 v. SA 1947, 4 v. WI 1947–48.
HUTTON, L. (66–79)—3 v. Ind 1946, 5 v. Aust 1946–47, 5 v. SA 1947, 2 v. WI 1947–48, 4 v. Aust 1948, 5 v. SA 1948–49, 4 v. NZ 1949, 3 v. WI 1950, 5 v. Aust and 2 v. NZ 1950–51, 5 v. SA 1951, 4 v. Ind 1952, 5 v. Aust 1953, 5 v. WI 1953–54, 3 v. Pak 1954, 5 v. Aust and 2 v. NZ 1954–55.
IKIN, J. T. (18)—2 v. Ind 1946, 5 v. Aust and 1 v. NZ 1946–47, 4 v. WI 1947–48, 3 v. SA 1951, 2 v. Ind 1952, 1 v. SA 1955.
ILLINGWORTH, R. (3)—1 v. NZ 1958, 2 v. Ind 1959.
INSOLE, D. J. (9)—1 v. WI 1950, 1 v. SA 1955, 1 v. Aust 1956, 5 v. SA 1956–57, 1 v. WI 1957.
JACKSON, H. L. (1)—1 v. NZ 1949.
JENKINS, R. O. (9)—5 v. SA 1948–49, 2 v. WI 1950, 2 v. Ind 1952.
KENYON, D. (8)—3 v. Ind 1951–52, 2 v. Aust 1953, 3 v. SA 1955.
LAKER, J. C. (46)—4 v. WI 1947–48, 3 v. Aust 1948, 1 v. NZ 1949, 1 v. WI 1950, 2 v. SA 1951, 4 v. Ind 1952, 3 v. Aust 1953, 4 v. WI 1953–54, 1 v. Pak 1954, 1 v. SA 1955, 5 v. Aust 1956, 5 v. SA 1956–57, 4 v. WI 1957, 4 v. NZ 1958, 4 v. Aust 1958–59.
LANGRIDGE, James (1–8)—1 v. Ind 1946.
LEADBEATER, E. (2)—2 v. Ind 1951–52.
LOADER, P. J. (13)—1 v. Pak 1954, 1 v. SA 1955, 4 v. SA 1956–57, 2 v. WI 1957, 3 v. NZ 1958, 2 v. Aust 1958–59.
LOCK, G. A. R. (31)—2 v. Ind 1952, 2 v. Aust 1953, 5 v. WI 1953–54, 3 v. SA 1955, 4 v. Aust 1956, 1 v. SA 1956–57, 3 v. WI 1957, 5 v. NZ 1958, 4 v. Aust and 2 v. NZ 1958–59.
LOWSON, F. A. (7)—2 v. SA 1951, 4 v. Ind 1951–52, 1 v. SA 1955.
MANN, F. G. (7)—5 v. SA 1948–49, 2 v. NZ 1949.
MARTIN, J. W. (1)—1 v. SA 1947.
MAY, P. B. H. (59)—2 v. SA 1951, 4 v. Ind 1952, 2 v. Aust 1953, 5 v. WI 1953–54, 4 v. Pak 1954, 5 v. Aust and 2 v. NZ 1954–55, 5 v. SA 1955,

5 v. Aust 1956, 5 v. SA 1956–57, 5 v. WI 1957, 5 v. NZ 1958, 5 v. Aust and 2 v. NZ 1958–59, 3 v. Ind 1959.
McCONNON, J. E. (2)—2 v. Pak 1954.
McINTYRE, A. J. (3)—1 v. WI 1950, 1 v. Aust 1950–51, 1 v. SA 1955.
MILTON, C. A. (6)—2 v. NZ 1958, 2 v. Aust 1958–59, 2 v. Ind 1959.
MORTIMORE, J. (5)—1 v. Aust and 2 v. NZ 1958–59, 2 v. Ind 1959.
MOSS, A. E. (5)—1 v. WI 1953–54, 1 v. Aust 1956, 3 v. Ind 1959.
OAKMAN, A. S. M. (2)—2 v. Aust 1956, 2 v. Ind 1959.
PALMER, C. H. (1)—1 v. WI 1953–54.
PARKHOUSE, W. G. A. (7)—2 v. WI 1950, 2 v. Aust and 1 v. NZ 1950–51, 2 v. Ind. 1959.
PARKS, J. M. (1)—1 v. Pak 1954.
PLACE, W. (3)—3 v. WI 1947–48.
POLLARD, R. (4)—1 v. Ind 1946, 1 v. Aust 1946–47, 2 v. Aust 1948.
POOLE, C. J. (3)—3 v. Ind 1951–52.
POPE, G. H. (1)—1 v. SA 1947.
PULLAR, G. (3)—3 v. Ind 1959.
RHODES, H. J. (2)—2 v. Ind 1959.
RICHARDSON, D. W. (1)—1 v. WI 1957.
RICHARDSON, P. E. (25)—5 v. Aust 1956, 5 v. SA 1956–57, 5 v. WI 1957, 4 v. NZ 1958, 4 v. Aust and 2 v. NZ 1958–59.
RIDGWAY, F. (5)—5 v. Ind 1951–52.
ROBERTSON, J. D. (11)—1 v. SA 1947, 4 v. WI 1947–48, 1 v. NZ 1949, 5 v. Ind 1951–52.
SHACKLETON, D. (3)—1 v. WI 1950, 1 v. SA 1951, 1 v. Ind 1951–52.
SHEPPARD, D. S. (12)—1 v. WI 1950, 2 v. Aust and 1 v. NZ 1950–51, 2 v. Ind 1952, 2 v. Pak 1954, 2 v. Aust 1956, 2 v. WI 1957.
SIMPSON, R. T. (27)—1 v. SA 1948–49, 2 v. NZ 1949, 3 v. WI 1950, 5 v. Aust and 2 v. NZ 1950–51, 3 v. SA 1951, 2 v. Ind 1952, 3 v. Aust 1953, 3 v. Pak 1954, 1 v. Aust and 2 v. NZ 1954–55.
SMAILES, T. F. (1)—1 v. Ind 1946.
SMITH, D. V. (3)—3 v. WI 1957.
SMITH, M. J. K. (5)—3 v. NZ 1958, 2 v. Ind 1959.
SMITH, T. P. B. (4)—1 v. Ind 1946, 2 v. Aust and 1 v. NZ 1946–47.
SMITHSON, G. A. (2)—2 v. WI 1947–48.
SPOONER, R. T. (7)—5 v. Ind 1951–52, 1 v. WI 1953–54, 1 v. SA 1955.
STATHAM, J. B. (47)—1 v. NZ 1950–51, 2 v. SA 1951, 5 v. Ind 1951–52, 1 v. Aust 1953, 4 v. WI 1953–54, 4 v. Pak 1954, 5 v. Aust and 2 v. NZ 1954–55, 4 v. SA 1955, 3 v. Aust 1956, 4 v. SA 1956–57, 3 v. WI 1957, 2 v. NZ 1958, 4 v. Aust 1958–59, 3 v. Ind 1959.
SUBBA ROW, R. (2)—1 v. NZ 1958, 1 v. Ind 1959.
SWETMAN, R. (7)—2 v. Aust and 2 v. NZ 1958–59, 3 v. Ind 1959.
TATTERSALL, R. (16)—2 v. Aust and 2 v. NZ 1950–51, 5 v. SA 1951, 5 v. Ind 1951–52, 1 v. Aust 1953, 1 v. Pak 1954.
TAYLOR, K. (2)—2 v. Ind 1959.
TITMUS, F. J. (2)—2 v. SA 1955.
TREMLETT, M. F. (3)—3 v. WI 1947–48.
TRUEMAN, F. S. (31)—4 v. Ind 1952, 1 v. Aust 1953, 3 v. WI 1953–54, 1 v. SA 1955, 2 v. Aust 1956, 5 v. WI 1957, 5 v. NZ 1958, 3 v. Aust and 2 v. NZ 1958–59, 5 v. Ind 1959.
TYSON, F. H. (17)—1 v. Pak 1954, 5 v. Aust and 2 v. NZ 1954–55, 1 v. SA 1955, 1 v. Aust 1956, 2 v. SA 1956–57, 2 v. Aust and 2 v. NZ 1958–59.
VOCE, W. (3–27)—1 v. Ind 1946, 2 v. Aust 1946–47.
WARDLE, J. H. (28)—1 v. WI 1947–48, 1 v. WI 1950, 3 v. SA 1951, 3 v. Aust 1953, 2 v. WI 1953–54, 4 v. Pak 1954, 4 v. Aust and 2 v. NZ 1954–55, 3 v. SA 1955, 1 v. Aust 1956, 4 v. SA 1956–57, 1 v. WI 1957.

WARR, J. J. (2)—2 v. Aust 1950–51.
WASHBROOK, C. (36–37)—3 v. Ind 1946–47, 5 v. Aust and 1 v. NZ 1946–47, 5 v. SA 1947, 4 v. Aust 1948, 5 v. SA 1948–49, 2 v. NZ 1949, 2 v. WI 1950, 5 v. Aust and 1 v. NZ 1950–51, 3 v. Aust 1956.
WATKINS, A. J. (15)—1 v. Aust 1948, 5 v. SA 1948–49, 1 v. NZ 1949, 5 v. Ind 1951–52, 3 v. Ind 1952.
WATSON, W. (23)—5 v. SA 1951, 1 v. Ind 1952, 3 v. Aust 1953, 5 v. WI 1953–54, 1 v. SA 1955, 2 v. Aust 1956, 2 v. NZ 1958, 2 v. Aust and 2 v. NZ 1958–59.
WHARTON, W. (1)—1 v. NZ 1949.
WRIGHT, D. V. P. (25–34)—2 v. Ind 1946, 5 v. Aust and 1 v. NZ 1946–47, 5 v. SA 1947, 1 v Aust 1948, 3 v. SA 1948–49, 1 v. NZ 1949, 1 v. WI 1950, 5 v. Aust and 2 v. NZ 1950–51.
YARDLEY, N. W. D. (19–20)—5 v. Aust and 1 v. NZ 1946–47, 5 v. SA 1947, 5 v. Aust 1948, 3 v. WI 1950.
YOUNG, J. A. (8)—1 v. SA 1947, 3 v. Aust 1948, 2 v. SA 1948–49, 2 v. NZ 1949.

W. J. Edrich   R. T. Simpson   D. G. Bradman

Australia

ARCHER, K. M. (5)—3 v. Eng 1950–51, 2 v. WI 1951–52.
ARCHER, R. G. (19)—1 v. SA 1952–53, 3 v. Eng 1953, 4 v. Eng 1954–55, 5 v. WI 1954–55, 5 v. Eng 1956, 1 v. Pak 1956–57.
BARNES, S. G. (12–13)—1 v. NZ 1945–46, 4 v. Eng 1946–47, 3 v. Ind 1947–48, 4 v. Eng 1948.
BENAUD, R. (37)—1 v. WI 1951–52, 4 v. SA 1952–53, 3 v. Eng 1953, 5 v. Eng 1954–55, 5 v. WI 1954–55, 5 v. Eng 1956, 1 v. Pak and 3 v. Ind

1956–57, 5 v. SA 1957–58, 5 v. Eng 1958–59.
BRADMAN, D. G. (15–52)—5 v. Eng 1946–47, 5 v. Ind 1947–48, 5 v. Eng 1948.
BROWN, W. A. (6–22)—4 v. NZ 1945–46, 3 v. Ind 1947–48, 2 v. Eng 1948.
BURGE, P. (10)—1 v. Eng 1954–55, 1 v. WI 1954–55, 3 v. Eng 1956, 3 v. Ind 1956–57, 1 v. SA 1957–58, 1 v. Eng 1958–59.
BURKE, J. W. (24)—2 v. Eng 1950–51, 1 v. WI 1951–52, 2 v. Eng 1954–55, 5 v. Eng 1956, 1 v. Pak and 3 v. Ind 1956–57, 5 v. SA 1957–58, 5 v. Eng 1958–59.
CRAIG, I. D. (11)—1 v. SA 1952–53, 2 v. Eng 1956, 1 v. Pak and 2 v. Ind 1956–57, 5 v. SA 1957–58.
CRAWFORD, P. (4)—1 v. Eng 1956, 3 v. Ind 1956–57.
DAVIDSON, A. K. (22)—5 v. Eng 1953, 3 v. Eng 1954–55, 2 v. Eng 1956, 1 v. Pak and 1 v. Ind 1956–57, 5 v. SA 1957–58, 5 v. Eng 1958–59.
DE COURCY, J. H. (3)—3 v. Eng 1953.
DOOLAND, B. (3)—2 v. Eng 1946–47, 1 v. Ind 1947–48.
FAVELL, L. (8)—4 v. Eng 1954–55, 4 v. WI 1954–55, 2 v. Eng 1958–59.
FREER, F. W. (1)—1 v. Eng 1946–47.
GAUNT, R. (1)—1 v. SA 1957–58.
GROUT, A. W. (10)—5 v. SA 1957–58, 5 v. Eng 1958–59.
HAMENCE, R. A. (3)—1 v. Eng 1946–47, 2 v. Ind 1947–48.
HARVEY, M. (1)—1 v. Eng 1946–47.
HARVEY, R. N. (57)—2 v. Ind 1947–48, 2 v. Eng 1948, 5 v. SA 1949–50, 5 v. Eng 1950–51, 5 v. WI 1951–52, 5 v. SA 1952–53, 5 v. Eng 1953, 5 v. Eng 1954–55, 5 v. WI 1954–55, 5 v. Eng 1956, 1 v. Pak and 3 v. Ind 1956–57, 4 v. SA 1957–58, 5 v. Eng 1958–59.

G

CRICKET QUIZ

1. Only two players have gained international honours for England at both cricket and soccer since 1945: who are they?

*

2. Which county captain has enjoyed the longest tenure of office?

*

3. In the first known laws of cricket four balls were allowed to the over. In which years have subsequent changes been made?

*

4. What is the shortest innings played in first-class cricket?

*

5. What is the lowest task set a defeated side in a first-class match?

*

6. Which batsman scored two centuries on the same day in first-class cricket?

7. Which batsman scored a century in each innings of a first-class match, carrying his bat through both completed innings of the game?

*

8. Which batsman scored 474 runs in seven consecutive innings before being dismissed?

QUIZ ANSWERS

1. W. Watson and C. A. Milton. 2. W. G. Grace captained Gloucestershire from 1871 to 1899—his appointment was terminated in the middle of the 1899 season. 3. Increased to five balls in 1889 and six balls in 1900. The eight-ball over was experimented with in 1939. 4. Lancashire declared their second innings closed after only one ball had been bowled against Nottinghamshire at Liverpool in 1956. 5. Border were left to score 42 runs for victory in their Currie Cup match against Eastern Province at East London in 1946–47, but were all out for 34 and lost the match by seven runs. 6. K. S. Ranjitsinhji, playing for Sussex v. Yorkshire at Hove in 1896, scored 100 in the first innings and 125 not out in the follow-on on the last day of the match. 7. C. J. B. Wood (107 not out and 117 not out) for Leicestershire v. Yorkshire at Bradford in 1911. 8. W. G. Quaife (Warwickshire) in 1898—60, 117, 157, 24, 52, 61 and 3 (all innings but the 3 were not out).

W. R. Endean

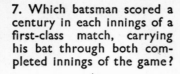

A. R. Morris

N. B. F. Mann

R. N. Harvey

I. W. Johnson

K. R. Miller

HASSETT, A. L. (39–43)—1 v. NZ 1945–46, 5 v. Eng 1946–47, 4 v. Ind 1947–48, 5 v. Eng 1948, 5 v. SA 1949–50, 5 v. Eng 1950–51, 4 v. WI 1951–52, 5 v. SA 1952–53, 5 v. Eng 1953.

HILL, J. C. (3)—2 v. Eng 1953, 1 v. WI 1954–55.

HOLE, G. B. (18)—1 v. Eng 1950–51, 5 v. WI 1951–52, 4 v. SA 1952–53, 5 v. Eng 1953, 3 v. Eng 1954–55.

IVERSON, J. (5)—5 v. Eng 1950–51.

JOHNSON, I. W. (45)—1 v. NZ 1945–46, 4 v. Eng 1946–47, 4 v. Ind 1947–48, 4 v. Eng 1948, 5 v. SA 1949–50, 5 v. Eng 1950–51, 4 v. WI 1951–52, 1 v. SA 1952–53, 4 v. Eng 1954–55, 5 v. WI 1954–55, 5 v. Eng 1956, 1 v. Pak and 2 v. Ind 1956–57.

JOHNSON, J. (1)—1 v. Ind 1947–48.

JOHNSTON, W. A. (40)—4 v. Ind 1947–48, 5 v. Eng 1948, 5 v. SA 1949–50, 5 v. Eng 1950–51, 5 v. WI 1951–52, 5 v. SA 1952–53, 3 v. Eng 1953, 4 v. Eng 1954–55, 4 v. WI 1954–55.

KLINE, L. (7)—5 v. SA 1957–58, 2 v. Eng 1958–59.

LANGLEY, G. R. (26)—5 v. WI 1951–52, 5 v. SA 1952–53, 4 v. Eng 1953, 2 v. Eng 1954–55, 4 v. WI 1954–55, 3 v. Eng 1956, 1 v. Pak and 2 v. Ind 1956–57.

LINDWALL, R. R. (57)—1 v. NZ 1945–46, 4 v. Eng 1946–47, 5 v. Ind 1947–48, 5 v. Eng 1948, 4 v. SA 1949–50, 5 v. Eng 1950–51, 5 v. WI 1951–52, 4 v. SA 1952–53, 5 v. Eng 1953, 4 v. Eng 1954–55, 5 v. WI 1954–55, 4 v. Eng 1956, 1 v. Pak and 3 v. Ind 1956–57, 2 v. Eng 1958–59.

LOXTON, S. J. E. (12)—1 v. Ind 1947–48, 3 v. Eng 1948, 5 v. SA 1949–50, 3 v. Eng 1950–51.

MACKAY, K. (16)—3 v. Eng 1956, 3 v. Ind 1956–57, 5 v. SA 1957–58, 5 v. Eng 1958–59.

MADDOCKS, L. (7)—3 v. Eng 1954–55, 1 v. WI 1954–55, 2 v. Eng 1956, 1 v. Ind 1956–57.

McCOOL, C. L. (14)—1 v. NZ 1945–46, 5 v. Eng 1946–47, 3 v. Ind 1947–48, 5 v. SA 1949–50.

McDONALD, C. C. (31)—1 v. WI 1951–52, 5 v. SA 1952–53, 2 v. Eng 1954–55, 5 v. WI 1954–55, 2 v. Eng 1956, 1 v. Pak and 2 v. Ind 1956–57, 5 v. SA 1957–58, 5 v. Eng 1958–59.

MECKIFF, I. (8)—4 v. SA 1957–58, 4 v. Eng 1958–59.

MEULEMAN, K. (1)—1 v. NZ 1945–46.

MILLER, K. R. (55)—1 v. NZ 1945–46, 5 v. Eng 1946–47, 5 v. Ind 1947–48, 5 v. Eng 1948, 5 v. SA 1949–50, 5 v. Eng 1950–51, 5 v. WI 1951–52, 4 v. SA 1952–53, 5 v. Eng 1953, 4 v. Eng 1954–55, 5 v. WI 1954–55, 5 v. Eng 1956, 1 v. Pak 1956–57.

MORONEY, J. A. R. (7)—5 v. SA 1949–50, 1 v. Eng 1950–51, 1 v. WI 1951–52.

MORRIS, A. R. (46)—5 v. Eng 1946–47, 4 v. Ind 1947–48, 5 v. Eng 1948, 5 v. SA 1949–50, 5 v. Eng 1950–51, 4 v. WI 1951–52, 5 v. SA 1952–53, 5 v. Eng 1953, 4 v. Eng 1954–55, 4 v. WI 1954–55.

NOBLET, G. J. (3)—1 v. SA 1949–50, 1 v. WI 1951–52, 1 v. SA 1952–53.

O'NEILL, N. (5)—5 v. Eng 1958–59.

O'REILLY, W. J. (1–27)—1 v. NZ 1945–46.

RING, D. T. (13)—1 v. Ind 1947–48, 1 v. Eng 1948, 5 v. WI 1951–52, 5 v. SA 1952–53, 1 v. Eng 1953.

RORKE, G. (2)—2 v. Eng 1958–59.

RUTHERFORD, J. (1)—1 v. Ind 1956–57.

SAGGERS, R. A. (6)—1 v. Eng 1948, 5 v. SA 1949–50.

SIMPSON, R. (6)—5 v. SA 1957–58, 1 v. Eng 1958–59.

SLATER, K. (1)—1 v. Eng 1958–59.

TALLON, D. (21)—1 v. NZ 1945–46, 5 v. Eng 1946–47, 5 v. Ind 1947–48, 4 v. Eng 1948, 5 v. Eng 1950–51, 1 v. Eng 1953.

THOMS, G. (1)—1 v. WI 1951–52.

TOSHACK, E. R. H. (12)—1 v. NZ 1945–46, 5 v. Eng 1946–47, 2 v. Ind 1947–48, 4 v. Eng 1948.

TRIBE, G. (3)—3 v. Eng 1946–47.

WATSON, W. (4)—1 v. Eng 1954–55, 3 v. WI 1954–55.

WILSON, J. (1)—1 v. Ind 1956–57.

South Africa

ADCOCK, N. A. T. (19)—5 v. NZ 1953–54, 4 v. Eng 1955, 5 v. Eng 1956–57, 5 v. Aust 1957–58.

BEGBIE, D. W. (5)—3 v. Eng 1948–49, 2 v. Aust 1949–50.

BURGER, C. G. (2)—2 v. Aust 1957–58.

CARLSTEIN, P. (1)—1 v. Aust 1957–58.

CHEETHAM, J. E. (24)—1 v. Eng 1948–49, 3 v. Aust 1949–50, 5 v. Eng 1951, 5 v. Aust and 2 v. NZ 1952–53, 5 v. NZ 1953–54, 3 v. Eng 1955.

CHUBB, G. W. A. (5)—5 v. Eng 1951.

DAWSON, O. C. (9)—5 v. Eng 1947, 4 v. Eng 1948–49.

DRAPER, R. G. (2)—2 v. Aust 1949–50.

DUCKWORTH, C. A. R. (2)—2 v. Eng 1956–57.

DYER, D. V. (3)—3 v. Eng 1947.

ENDEAN, W. R. (28)—1 v. Eng 1951, 5 v. Aust and 2 v. NZ 1952–53, 5 v. NZ 1953–54, 5 v. Eng 1955, 5 v. Eng 1956–57, 5 v. Aust 1957–58.

FULLER, E. R. H. (7)—2 v. Aust and 2 v. NZ 1952–53, 2 v. Eng 1955, 1 v. Aust 1957–58.

FULLERTON, G. M. (7)—2 v. Eng 1947, 2 v. Aust 1949–50, 3 v. Eng 1951.

FUNSTON, K. J. (18)—5 v. Aust and 2 v. NZ 1952–53, 3 v. NZ 1953–54, 3 v. Eng 1956–57, 5 v. Aust 1957–58.

GODDARD, T. L. (15)—5 v. Eng 1955, 5 v. Eng 1956–57, 5 v. Aust 1957–58.

HANLEY, M. A. (1)—1 v. Eng 1948–49.

HARRIS, T. A. (3)—2 v. Eng 1947, 1 v. Eng 1948–49.

HEINE, P. S. (13)—4 v. Eng 1955, 5 v. Eng 1956–57, 4 v. Aust 1957–58.

IRONSIDE, D. E. J. (3)—3 v. NZ 1953–54.

KEITH, H. J. (8)—1 v. Aust 1952–53, 4 v. Eng 1955, 3 v. Eng 1956–57.

LINDSAY, J. D. (3)—3 v. Eng 1947.

MANN, N. B. F. (19)—5 v. Eng 1947, 5 v. Eng 1948–49, 5 v. Aust 1949–50, 4 v. Eng 1951.

MANSELL, P. N. F. (13)—2 v. Eng 1951, 5 v. Aust and 2 v. NZ 1952–53, 4 v. Eng 1955.

MARKHAM, L. A. (1)—1 v. Eng 1948–49.

McCARTHY, C. N. (15)—5 v. Eng 1948–49, 5 v. Aust 1949–50, 5 v. Eng 1951.

McGLEW, D. J. (24)—2 v. Eng 1951, 4 v. Aust and 2 v. NZ 1952–53, 5 v. NZ 1953–54, 5 v. Eng 1955, 1 v. Eng 1956–57, 5 v. Aust 1957–58.

McLEAN, R. A. (28)—3 v. Eng 1951, 5 v. Aust and 2 v. NZ 1952–53, 4 v. NZ 1953–54, 5 v. Eng 1955, 5 v. Eng 1956–57, 4 v. Aust 1957–58.

MELLE, M. G. (7)—2 v. Aust 1949–50, 1 v. Eng 1951, 4 v. Aust 1952–53.

MELVILLE, A. (6–11)—5 v. Eng 1947, 1 v. Eng 1948–49.

MITCHELL, B. (10–42)—5 v. Eng 1947, 5 v. Eng 1948–49.

MURRAY, A. R. A. (10)—4 v. Aust and 2 v. NZ 1952–53, 4 v. NZ 1953–54.

NEL, J. D. (6)—5 v. Aust 1949–50, 1 v. Aust 1957–58.

NOURSE, A. D. jun. (20–34)—5 v. Eng 1947, 5 v. Aust 1949–50, 5 v. Eng 1951.

PITHEY, A. T. (3)—3 v. Eng 1956–57.

PLIMSOLL, J. B. (1)—1 v. Eng 1947.

ROWAN, A. M. B. (15)—5 v. Eng 1947, 5 v. Eng 1948–49, 5 v. Eng 1951.

ROWAN, E. A. B. (14–26)—5 v. Eng 1948–49, 5 v. Aust 1949–50, 5 v. Eng 1951.

SMITH, V. I. (9)—4 v. Eng 1947, 3 v. Aust 1949–50, 1 v. Eng 1955, 1 v. Aust 1957–58.

TAYFIELD, H. J. (32)—5 v. Aust 1949–50, 5 v. Aust and 2 v. NZ 1952–53, 5 v. NZ 1953–54, 5 v. Eng 1955, 5 v. Eng 1956–57, 5 v. Aust 1957–58.

TAYLOR, A. I. (1)—1 v. Eng 1956–57.

TUCKETT, L. (9)—5 v. Eng 1947, 4 v. Eng 1948–49.

VAN RYNEVELD, C. B. (19)—5 v. Eng 1951, 5 v. NZ 1953–54, 5 v. Eng 1956–57, 4 v. Aust 1957–58.

VILJOEN, K. J. (7–27)—5 v. Eng 1947, 2 v. Eng 1948–49.

WADE, W. W. (8–11)—5 v. Eng 1948–49, 3 v. Aust 1949–50.

WAITE, J. H. B. (31)—4 v. Eng 1951, 5 v. Aust and 2 v. NZ 1952–53, 5 v. NZ 1953–54, 5 v. Eng 1955, 5 v. Eng 1956–57, 5 v. Aust 1957–58.

WATKINS, J. C. (15)—3 v. Aust 1949–50, 5 v. Aust and 2 v. NZ 1952–53, 3 v. NZ 1953–54, 2 v. Eng 1956–57.

WESTCOTT, R. J. (5)—3 v. NZ 1953–54, 2 v. Aust 1957–58.

WINSLOW, P. L. (5)—2 v. Aust 1949–50, 3 v. Eng 1955.

WYNNE, O. E. (6)—3 v. Eng 1948–49, 3 v. Aust 1949–50.

West Indies

ALEXANDER, F. C. M. (15)—2 v. Eng 1957, 5 v. Pak 1957–58, 5 v. Ind and 3 v. Pak 1958–59.

ASGARALI, N. (2)—2 v. Eng 1957.

ATKINSON, D. (22)—4 v. Ind 1948–49, 2 v. Aust and 1 v. NZ 1951–52, 4 v. Eng 1953–54, 4 v. Aust 1954–55, 4 v. NZ 1955–56, 2 v. Eng 1957, 1 v. Pak 1957–58.

D. J. McGlew

A. D. Nourse

R. E. Marshall

ATKINSON, E. (8)—3 v. Pak 1957–58, 3 v. Ind and 2 v. Pak 1958–59.
BINNS, A. P. (5)—1 v. Ind 1952–53, 1 v. Aust 1954–55, 3 v. NZ 1955–56.
BUTCHER, B. F. (8)—5 v. Ind and 3 v. Pak 1958–59.
BUTLER, L. (1)—1 v. Aust 1954–55.
BYNOE, R. (1)—1 v. Pak 1958–59.
CAMERON, F. J. (5)—5 v. Ind 1948–49.
CAREW, G. (3–4)—2 v. Eng 1947–48, 1 v. Ind 1948–49.
CHRISTIANI, R. J. (22)—4 v. Eng 1947–48, 5 v. Ind 1948–49, 4 v. Eng 1950, 5 v. Aust and 1 v. NZ 1951–52, 2 v. Ind 1952–53, 1 v. Eng 1953–54.
DEPEIZA, C. (5)—3 v. Aust 1954–55, 2 v. NZ 1955–56.
DEWDNEY, T. (9)—2 v. Aust 1954–55, 3 v. NZ 1955–56, 1 v. Eng 1957, 3 v. Pak 1957–58.
FERGUSON, W. (8)—4 v. Eng 1947–48, 3 v. Ind 1948–49, 1 v. Eng 1953–54.
FREDERICK, M. (1)—1 v. Eng 1953–54.
FURLONGE, H. (3)—1 v. Aust 1954–55, 2 v. NZ 1955–56.
GANTEAUME, A. G. (1)—1 v. Eng 1947–48.
GASKIN, B. M. (2)—2 v. Eng 1947–48.

K. T. Ramadhin

GIBBS, G. (1)—1 v. Aust 1954–55.
GIBBS, L. (8)—4 v. Pak 1957–58, 1 v. Ind and 3 v. Pak 1958–59.
GILCHRIST, R. (13)—4 v. Eng 1957, 5 v. Pak 1957–58, 4 v. Ind 1958–59.
GODDARD, J. D. C. (27)—4 v. Eng 1947–48, 5 v. Ind 1948–49, 4 v. Eng 1950, 4 v. Aust and 2 v. NZ 1951–52, 3 v. NZ 1955–56, 5 v. Eng 1957.
GOMEZ, G. E. (27–29)—4 v. Eng 1947–48, 5 v. Ind 1948–49, 4 v. Eng 1950, 5 v. Aust and 1 v. NZ 1951–52, 4 v. Ind 1952–53, 4 v. Eng 1953–54.
GUILLEN, S. C. (5)—3 v. Aust and 2 v. NZ 1951–52.
HALL, W. (8)—5 v. Ind and 3 v. Pak 1958–59.
HEADLEY, G. (3–22)—1 v. Eng 1947–48, 1 v. Ind 1948–49, 1 v. Eng 1953–54.
HOLT, J. K. (17)—5 v. Eng 1953–54, 5 v. Aust 1954–55, 5 v. Ind and 2 v. Pak 1958–59.
JOHNSON, H. H. (3)—1 v. Eng 1947–48, 2 v. Eng 1950.
JONES, P. E. (9)—1 v. Eng 1947–48, 5 v. Ind 1948–49, 2 v. Eng 1950, 1 v. Aust 1951–52.
KANHAI, R. (18)—5 v. Eng 1957, 5 v. Pak 1957–58, 5 v. Ind and 3 v. Pak 1958–59.
HUNTE, C. C. (11)—5 v. Pak 1957–58, 5 v. Ind and 1 v. Pak 1958–59.
KENTISH, E. S. M. (2)—1 v. Eng 1947–48, 1 v. Eng 1953–54.
KING, F. (14)—5 v. Ind 1952–53, 3 v. Eng 1953–54, 4 v. Aust 1954–55, 2 v. NZ 1955–56.
LEGALL, R. (4)—4 v. Ind 1952–53.
MADRAY, I. (2)—2 v. Pak 1957–58.
MARSHALL, N. (1)—1 v. Aust 1954–55.
MARSHALL, R. E. (4)—2 v. Aust and 2 v. NZ 1951–52.
McMORRIS, E. (1)—1 v. Pak 1957–58.
McWATT, C. A. (6)—5 v. Eng 1953–54, 1 v. Aust 1954–55.
MILLER, R. (1)—1 v. Ind 1952–53.
PAIRAUDEAU, B. H. (13)—4 v. Ind 1952–53, 5 v. Eng 1953–54, 4 v. NZ 1955–56, 2 v. Eng 1957.
PIERRE, L. R. (1)—1 v. Eng 1947–48.
RAE, A. F. (15)—5 v. Ind 1948–49, 4 v. Eng 1950, 3 v. Aust and 1 v. NZ 1951–52, 2 v. Ind 1952–53.
RAMADHIN, K. T. (37)—4 v. Eng 1950, 5 v. Aust and 2 v. NZ 1951–52, 4 v. Ind 1952–53, 5 v. Eng 1953–54, 4 v. Aust 1954–55, 4 v. NZ 1955–56, 5 v. Eng 1957, 2 v. Ind and 2 v. Pak 1958–59.

RICKARD, K. (2)—1 v. Eng 1947–48, 1 v. Aust 1951–52.
ROBERTS, A. (1)—1 v. NZ 1955–56.
SCOTT, A. P. H. (1)—1 v. Ind 1952–53.
SMITH, O. G. (26)—4 v. Aust 1954–55, 4 v. NZ 1955–56, 5 v. Eng 1957, 5 v. Pak 1957–58, 5 v. Ind and 3 v. Pak 1958–59.
SOBERS, G. (27)—1 v. Eng 1953–54, 4 v. Aust 1954–55, 4 v. NZ 1955–56, 5 v. Eng 1957, 5 v. Pak 1957–58, 5 v. Ind and 3 v. Pak 1958–59.
SOLOMON, J. (7)—4 v. Ind and 3 v. Pak 1958–59.
SOLOMON, J. (4)—4 v. Ind 1958–59.
STOLLMEYER, J. B. (29–32)—2 v. Eng 1947–48, 4 v. Ind 1948–49, 4 v. Eng 1950, 5 v. Aust and 2 v. NZ 1951–52, 4 v. Ind 1952–53, 5 v. Eng 1953–54, 2 v. Aust 1954–55.
TAYLOR, J. (3)—1 v. Eng 1957–58, 1 v. Ind and 1 v. Pak 1958–59.
TRIM, J. (4)—1 v. Eng 1947–48, 2 v. Ind 1948–49, 1 v. Aust 1951–52.
VALENTINE, A. L. (29)—4 v. Eng 1950, 5 v. Aust and 2 v. NZ 1951–52, 5 v. Ind 1952–53, 3 v. Eng 1953–54, 3 v. Aust 1954–55, 4 v. NZ 1955–56, 2 v. Eng 1957, 1 v. Pak 1957–58.

C. L. Walcott

WALCOTT, C. L. (42)—4 v. Eng 1947–48, 5 v. Ind 1948–49, 4 v. Eng 1950, 3 v. Aust and 2 v. NZ 1951–52, 5 v. Ind 1952–53, 5 v. Eng 1953–54, 5 v. Aust 1954–55, 5 v. Eng 1957, 4 v. Pak 1957–58.
WEEKES, E. D. (48)—4 v. Eng 1947–48, 5 v. Ind 1948–49, 4 v. Eng 1950, 5 v. Aust and 2 v. NZ 1951–52, 5 v. Ind 1952–53, 4 v. Eng 1953–54, 5 v. Aust 1954–55, 5 v. NZ 1955–56, 5 v. Eng 1957, 5 v. Pak 1957–58.
WIGHT, L. (1)—1 v. Ind 1952–53.
WILLIAMS, E. A. V. (3–4)—3 v. Eng 1947–48.
WORRELL, F. M. (32)—3 v. Eng 1947–48, 4 v. Eng 1950, 5 v. Aust and 2 v. NZ 1951–52, 5 v. Ind 1952–53, 4 v. Eng 1953–54, 4 v. Aust 1954–55, 5 v. Eng 1957.

J. B. Stollmeyer

CRICKET QUIZ

1. Only two cricketers have played in Test cricket in England, Australia, South Africa, West Indies, New Zealand, India and Pakistan: who are they?

*

2. Which county cricketer was allocated a Test match against Australia as a benefit match?

*

3. Which batsman scored a century and shared in an opening stand of 173 in his only innings in Test cricket?

*

4. Which country appointed a different captain for each Test match of one rubber?

*

5. Which Test captain led his side to victory in each of the first nine matches in which he held the appointment?

6. Which public schoolboy gained an England Test cap, but could not gain a regular place in his school team?

*

7. Which bowler opened his Test career by sending down eight maiden overs before conceding his first run in the ninth over?

QUIZ ANSWERS

1. I. W. Johnson and R. R. Lindwall of Australia. 2. J. M. Read of Surrey was given the Oval Test match in 1893 as his benefit game. 3. A. G. Ganteaume (112) for West Indies v. England at Trinidad in 1947–48. 4. West Indies in 1929–30—E. L. G. Hoad in the first Test at Barbados, M. I. Grell in the second Test at Trinidad, M. P. Fernandes in the third Test at Georgetown and R. K. Nunes in the fourth Test at Kingston. 5. A. P. F. Chapman—v. Australia at the Oval in 1926, all three Tests v. West Indies in 1928, the first four Tests v. Australia in 1928–29 and the first Test at Nottingham v. Australia in 1930. 6. H. D. Read, of Winchester, played for England v. South Africa at the Oval in 1935, but could not get into the 1919 school team. 7. N. B. F. Mann for South Africa v. England at Nottingham in 1947.

BURKE, C. C. (1)—1 v. Aust 1945–46.
BURTT, T. B. (10)—1 v. Eng 1946–47, 4 v. Eng 1949, 2 v. Eng 1950–51, 2 v. WI 1951–52, 1 v. SA 1952–53.
BUTTERFIELD, L. A. (1)—1 v. Aust 1945–46.
CAVE, H. B. (19)—4 v. Eng 1949, 2 v. Eng 1954–55, 3 v. Pak and 5 v. Ind 1955–56, 3 v. WI 1955–56, 2 v. Eng 1958.
CHAPPLE, M. E. (8)—1 v. SA 1952–53, 5 v. SA 1953–54, 1 v. Eng 1954–55, 1 v. WI 1955–56.
CLEVERLEY, D. C. (1–2)—1 v. Aust 1945–46.
COLQUHOUN, I. A. (2)—2 v. Eng 1954–55.
COWIE, J. A. (6–9)—1 v. Aust 1945–46, 1 v. Eng 1946–47, 4 v. Eng 1949.
CRESSWELL, G. F. (3)—1 v. Eng 1949, 2 v. Eng 1950–51.
D'ARCY, J. W. (5)—5 v. Eng 1958.
DEMPSTER, E. W. (5)—1 v. SA 1952–53, 4 v. SA 1953–54.
DONNELLY, M. P. (4–7)—4 v. Eng 1949.
EMERY, R. W. G. (2)—2 v. WI 1951–52.

E. D. Weekes

A. R. MacGibbon

F. M. Worrell

New Zealand

ALABASTER, J. C. (8)—1 v. Pak and 4 v. Ind 1955–56, 1 v. WI 1955–56, 2 v. Eng 1958.
ANDERSON, W. M. (1)—1 v. Aust 1945–46.
BARBER, R. T. (1)—1 v. WI 1955–56.
BEARD, D. D. (4)—2 v. WI 1951–52, 2 v. WI 1955–56.
BECK, J. E. F. (8)—4 v. SA 1953–54, 4 v. WI 1955–56.
BELL, W. (2)—2 v. SA 1953–54.
BLAIR, R. W. (14)—2 v. SA 1952–53, 4 v. SA 1953–54, 1 v. Eng 1954–55, 2 v. WI 1955–56, 3 v. Eng 1958, 2 v. Eng 1958–59.
BOLTON, B. A. (2)—2 v. Eng 1958–59.

FISHER, F. E. (1)—1 v. SA 1952–53.
GUILLEN, S. C. (3)—3 v. WI 1955–56.
GUY, J. W. (10)—1 v. Pak and 5 v. Ind 1955–56, 2 v. WI 1955–56, 2 v. Eng 1958–59.
HADLEE, W. A. (8–11)—1 v. Aust 1945–46, 1 v. Eng 1946–47, 4 v. Eng 1949, 2 v. Eng 1950–51.
HARFORD, N. S. (8)—2 v. Pak and 2 v. Ind 1955–56, 4 v. Eng 1958.
HARRIS, P. G. Z. (3)—2 v. Pak and 1 v. Ind 1955–56.
HARRIS, R. M. (2)—2 v. Eng 1958–59.
HAYES, J. A. (15)—2 v. Eng 1950–51, 2 v. WI 1951–52, 1 v. Eng 1954–55, 1 v. Pak and 5 v. Ind 1955–56, 4 v. Eng 1958.
HOUGH, K. W. (2)—2 v. Eng 1958–59.

LEGGAT, I. B. (1)—1 v. SA 1953–54.
LEGGAT, J. G. (9)—1 v. WI 1951–52, 1 v. SA 1952–53, 1 v. Eng 1954–55, 2 v. Pak and 3 v. Ind 1955–56, 1 v. WI 1955–56.
LISSETTE, A. F. (2)—2 v. WI 1955–56.
MacGIBBON, A. R. (26)—2 v. Eng 1950–51, 1 v. SA 1952–53, 5 v. SA 1953–54, 2 v. Eng 1954–55, 3 v. Pak and 5 v. Ind 1955–56, 3 v. WI 1955–56, 5 v. Eng 1958.
McGREGOR, S. N. (15)—2 v. Eng 1954–55, 3 v. Pak and 4 v. Ind 1955–56, 5 v. WI 1955–56, 1 v. Eng 1958–59.
McMAHON, T. G. (5)—1 v. Pak and 3 v. Ind 1955–56, 1 v. WI 1955–56.
McRAE, D. A. N. (1)—1 v. Aust 1945–46.
MEALE, T. (2)—2 v. Eng 1958.
MEULI, E. M. (1)—1 v. SA 1952–53.
MILLER, L. S. M. (13)—2 v. SA 1952–53, 4 v. SA 1953–54, 3 v. WI 1955–56, 4 v. Eng 1958.
MOIR, A. M. (17)—2 v. Eng 1950–51, 2 v. WI 1951–52, 1 v. SA 1952–53, 2 v. Eng 1954–55, 3 v. Pak and 2 v. Ind 1955–56, 1 v. WI 1955–56, 2 v. Eng 1958, 2 v. Eng 1958–59.
MOONEY, F. L. H. (14)—3 v. Eng 1949, 2 v. Eng 1950–51, 3 v. WI 1951–52, 2 v. SA 1952–53, 5 v. SA 1953–54.
OVERTON, G. W. F. (3)—3 v. SA 1953–54.
PETRIE, E. C. (11)—2 v. Pak and 2 v. Ind 1955–56, 5 v. Eng 1958, 2 v. Eng 1958–59.
POORE, M. B. (14)—1 v. SA 1952–53, 5 v. SA 1953–54, 1 v. Eng 1954–55, 3 v. Pak and 4 v. Ind 1955–56.
PLAYLE, W. R. (5)—5 v. Eng 1958.
RABONE, G. O. (12)—4 v. Eng 1949, 2 v. WI 1951–52, 1 v. SA 1952–53, 3 v. SA 1953–54, 2 v. Eng 1954–55.
REID, J. R. (34)—2 v. Eng 1949, 2 v. Eng 1950–51, 2 v. WI 1951–52, 2 v. SA 1952–53, 5 v. SA 1953–54, 2 v. Eng 1954–55, 3 v. Pak and 5 v. Ind 1955–56, 4 v. WI 1955–56, 5 v. Eng 1958, 2 v. Eng 1958–59.
ROWE, C. G. (1)—1 v. Aust 1945–46.
SCOTT, R. H. (1)—1 v. Eng 1946–47.
SCOTT, V. J. (10)—1 v. Aust 1945–46, 1 v. Eng 1946–47, 4 v. Eng 1949, 2 v. Eng 1950–51, 2 v. Eng 1951–52.
SINCLAIR, I. M. (2)—2 v. WI 1955–56.
SMITH, F. B. (4)—1 v. Eng 1946–47, 2 v. Eng 1949, 1 v. WI 1951–52.
SNEDDEN, C. A. (1)—1 v. Eng 1946–47.
SPARLING, J. T. (5)—3 v. Eng 1958, 2 v. Eng 1958–59.
SUTCLIFFE, B. (34)—1 v. Eng 1946–47, 4 v. Eng 1949, 2 v. Eng 1950–51, 2 v. WI 1951–52, 2 v. SA 1952–53, 5 v. SA 1953–54, 2 v. Eng 1954–55, 3 v. Pak and 5 v. Ind 1955–56, 2 v. WI 1955–56, 4 v. Eng 1958, 2 v. Eng 1958–59.

CRICKET QUIZ

1. Lord's Cricket Ground has had three different sites: where were they and in which years were the moves made?

★

2. Which was the first county to organise a county club on a proper basis?

★

3. When and where did the M.C.C. play their first match outside the United Kingdom?

★

4. When and where did a father and son bat against the bowling of a father and son in a first-class match?

★

5. Which was the first cricket match to be the subject of a radio programme?

★

6. Which bowler hit the stumps five times with five consecutive balls in a first-class match? *(above)*

★

7. Who are the oldest players to have appeared regularly in first-class cricket?

★

8. What is the longest gap between a player's appearances in first-class cricket?

QUIZ ANSWERS

1. The first Lord's ground (where Dorset Square stands today) lasted from 1787 to 1810, the second (at North Bank) from 1809 to 1813, and the third, the present site, was opened in 1814. 2. Sussex in 1836. 3. At Paris in April 1867. 4. At Derby in 1922, W. G. and B. W. Quaife of Warwickshire batting against the bowling of W. and R. Bestwick of Derbyshire. 5. An eye-witness report of the Essex v. New Zealanders match at Leyton was broadcast in 1927. 6. C. W. L. Parker, for Gloucestershire v. Yorkshire at Bristol in 1922; the second ball was a no-ball. 7. J. H. King of Leicestershire (in 1925) and W. G. Quaife of Warwickshire (in 1927) were both aged 56 in their last full season. 8. 32 years—Rev. R. H. Moss, an Oxford Blue, played one match for the M.C.C. in 1893, but did not appear in first-class cricket again until 1925, when he played once for Worcestershire.

L. Amarnath

V. S. Hazare

V. Mankad

TAYLOR, D. D. (3)—1 v. Eng 1946-47, 2 v. WI 1955-56.
TINDILL, E. W. (2-5)—1 v. Aust 1945-46, 1 v. Eng 1946-47.
WALLACE, W. M. (10-13)—1 v. Aust 1945-46, 1 v. Eng 1946-47, 4 v. Eng 1949, 2 v. Eng 1950-51, 2 v. SA 1952-53.
WATT, L. A. (1)—1 v. Eng 1954-55.

India

ADHIKARI, H. R. (21)—5 v. Aust 1947-48, 5 v. WI 1948-49, 3 v. Eng 1951-52, 3 v. Eng 1952, 2 v. Pak 1952-53, 2 v. Aust 1956-57, 1 v. WI 1958-59.
AMARNATH, L. (21-24)—3 v. Eng 1946, 5 v. Aust 1947-48, 5 v. WI 1948-49, 3 v. Eng 1951-52, 5 v. Pak 1952-53.
AMIR ELAHI (1)—1 v. Aust 1947-48.
APTE, A. L. (1)—1 v. Eng 1959.
APTE, M. L. (7)—2 v. Pak 1952-53, 5 v. WI 1952-53.
BAIG, A. A. (2)—2 v. Eng 1959.
BANERJEE, S. (1)—1 v. WI 1948-49.
BANERJEE, S. N. (1)—1 v. WI 1948-49.
BHANDARI, P. (3)—1 v. Pak 1954-55, 1 v. NZ 1955-56, 1 v. Aust 1956-57.
BORDE, C. G. (8)—4 v. WI 1958-59, 4 v. Eng 1959.
CHOWDHURY, N. R. (2)—1 v. WI 1948-49, 1 v. Eng 1951-52.
CONTRACTOR, N. J. (14)—4 v. NZ 1955-56, 1 v. Aust 1956-57, 5 v. WI 1958-59, 4 v. Eng 1959.
DANI, H. T. (1)—1 v. Pak 1952-53.
DESAI, R. (6)—1 v. WI 1958-59, 5 v. Eng 1959.
DIVECHA, R. V. (5)—2 v. Eng 1951-52, 2 v. Eng 1952, 1 v. Pak 1952-53.
GADKARI, C. V. (6)—3 v. WI 1952-53, 3 v. Pak 1954-55.
GAEKWAD, D. K. (10)—1 v. Eng 1952, 2 v. Pak 1952-53, 2 v. WI 1952-53, 1 v. WI 1958-59, 4 v. Eng 1959.
GAEKWAD, H. G. (1)—1 v. Pak 1952-53.
GHORPADE, J. M. (8)—2 v. WI 1952-53, 1 v. NZ 1955-56, 1 v. Aust 1956-57, 1 v. WI 1958-59, 3 v. Eng 1959.
GHULAM AHMED (22)—3 v. WI 1948-49, 2 v. Eng 1951-52, 4 v. Eng 1952, 4 v. Pak 1952-53, 4 v. Pak 1954-55, 1 v. NZ 1955-56, 2 v. Aust 1956-57, 1 v. WI 1958-59.
GOPINATH, C. D. (7)—3 v. Eng 1951-52, 1 v. Eng 1952, 1 v. Pak 1952-53, 2 v. Pak 1954-55.
GUARD, G. (1)—1 v. WI 1958-59.
GUL MOHAMED (8)—1 v. Eng 1946, 5 v. Aust 1947-48, 2 v. Pak 1952-53.
GUPTE, S. P. (31)—1 v. Eng 1951-52, 2 v. Pak 1952-53, 5 v. WI 1952-53, 5 v. Pak 1954-55, 5 v. NZ 1955-56, 3 v. Aust 1956-57, 5 v. WI 1958-59, 5 v. Eng 1959.
HARDIKAR, M. S. (2)—2 v. WI 1958-59.
HAZARE, V. S. (30)—3 v. Eng 1946, 5 v. Aust 1947-48, 5 v. WI 1948-49, 5 v. Eng 1951-52, 4 v. Eng 1952, 3 v. Pak 1952-53, 5 v. WI 1952-53.
HINDLEKAR, D. D. (3-4)—3 v. Eng 1946.
IBRAHIM, K. C. (4)—4 v. WI 1948-49.
IRANI, J. K. (2)—2 v. Aust 1947-48.
JAISIMHA, M. L. (1)—1 v. Eng 1959.
JOSHI, P. G. (10)—2 v. Eng 1951-52, 1 v. Pak 1952-53, 3 v. WI 1952-53, 1 v. WI 1958-59, 3 v. Eng 1959.
KARDAR, A. H. (3)—3 v. Eng 1946.
KENNY, R. B. (1)—1 v. WI 1958-59.
KISHENCHAND, G. (5)—4 v. Aust 1947-48, 1 v. Pak 1952-53.
KRIPAL SINGH, A. G. (8)—4 v. NZ 1955-56, 2 v. Aust 1956-57, 1 v. WI 1958-59, 1 v. Eng 1959.
MAKA, E. S. (2)—1 v. Pak 1952-53, 1 v. WI 1952-53.
MANJREKAR, V. L. (32)—2 v. Eng 1951-52, 4 v. Eng 1952, 3 v. Pak 1952-53, 4 v. WI 1952-53, 5 v. Pak 1954-55, 5 v. NZ 1955-56, 3 v. Aust 1956-57, 4 v. WI 1958-59, 2 v. Eng 1959.
MANKAD, V. (44)—3 v. Eng 1946, 5 v. Aust 1947-48, 5 v. WI 1948-49, 5 v. Eng 1951-52, 3 v. Eng 1952, 4 v. Pak 1952-53, 5 v. WI 1952-53, 5 v. Pak 1954-55, 4 v. NZ 1955-56, 3 v. Aust 1956-57, 2 v. WI 1958-59.
MANTRI, M. K. (4)—1 v. Eng 1951-52, 2 v. Eng 1952, 1 v. Pak 1954-55.
MEHRA, V. (2)—2 v. NZ 1955-56.
MERCHANT, V. M. (4—10)—3 v. Eng 1946, 1 v. Eng 1951-52.
MODI, R. S. (10)—3 v. Eng 1946, 5 v. WI 1948-49, 1 v. Eng 1951-52, 1 v. Pak 1952-53.
MUSHTAQ ALI (6-11)—2 v. Eng 1946, 3 v. WI 1948-49, 1 v. Eng 1951-52.
NADKARNI, R. G. (6)—1 v. NZ 1955-56, 1 v. WI 1958-59, 4 v. Eng 1959.
NAYUDU, C. S. (7-11)—2 v. Eng 1946, 4 v. Aust 1947-48, 1 v. Eng 1951-52.
NYALCHAND (1)—1 v. Pak 1952-53.
PATANKAR, C. T. (1)—1 v. NZ 1955-56.
PATAUDI, Nawab of (3)—3 v. Eng 1946. (Also played 3 Tests for England pre-war.)
PATEL, J. S. (4)—1 v. Pak 1954-55, 1 v. NZ 1955-56, 2 v. Aust 1956-57.
PATIL, S. R. (1)—1 v. NZ 1955-56.
PHADKAR, D. G. (31)—4 v. Aust 1947-48, 4 v. WI 1948-49, 4 v. Eng 1951-52, 4 v. Eng 1952, 2 v. Pak 1952-53, 4 v. WI 1952-53, 3 v. Pak 1954-55, 4 v. NZ 1955-56, 1 v. Aust 1956-57, 1 v. WI 1958-59.
PUNJABI, P. L. (5)—5 v. Pak 1954-55.
RAI SINGH (1)—1 v. Aust 1947-48.
RAJINDERNATH (1)—1 v. Pak 1952-53.
RAMCHAND, G. S. (28)—4 v. Eng 1952, 3 v. Pak 1952-53, 5 v. WI 1952-53, 5 v. Pak 1954-55, 5 v. NZ 1955-56, 3 v. Aust 1956-57, 3 v. WI 1958-59.
RANGACHARI, C. R. (4)—2 v. Aust 1947-48, 2 v. WI 1948-49.
RANGNEKAR, K. M. (3)—3 v. Aust 1947-48.
RANJANE, V. (1)—1 v. WI 1958-59.
REGE, M. R. (1)—1 v. WI 1948-49.
ROY, P. (37)—5 v. Eng 1951-52, 4 v. Eng 1952, 3 v. Pak 1952-53, 4 v. WI 1952-53, 5 v. Pak 1954-55, 3 v. NZ 1955-56, 3 v. Aust 1956-57, 5 v. WI 1958-59, 5 v. Eng 1959.
SARWATE, C. T. (9)—1 v. Eng 1946, 5 v. Aust 1947-48, 2 v. WI 1948-49, 1 v. Eng 1951-52.
SEN, P. (14)—3 v. Aust 1947-48, 5 v. WI 1948-49, 2 v. Eng 1951-52, 2 v. Eng 1952, 2 v. Pak 1952-53.
SENGUPTA, A. K. (1)—1 v. WI 1958-59.
SHINDE, S. G. (7)—1 v. Eng 1946, 1 v. WI 1948-49, 3 v. Eng 1951-52, 2 v. Eng 1952.
SHODHAN, D. H. (3)—1 v. Pak 1952-53, 2 v. WI 1952-53.
SOHONI, S. W. (4)—2 v. Eng 1946, 1 v. Aust 1947-48, 1 v. Eng 1951-52.
SUNDERRAM, G. (2)—2 v. NZ 1955-56.
SURENDRA NATH (7)—2 v. WI 1958-59, 5 v. Eng 1959.
SWAMY, N. V. (1)—1 v. NZ 1955-56.
TAMHANE, N. S. (18)—5 v. Pak 1954-55, 4 v. NZ 1955-56, 3 v. Aust 1956-57, 4 v. WI 1958-59, 2 v. Eng 1959.
TARAPORE, K. K. (1)—1 v. WI 1948-49.
UMRIGAR, P. R. (42)—1 v. WI 1948-49, 5 v. Eng 1951-52, 4 v. Eng 1952, 5 v. Pak 1952-53, 5 v. WI 1952-53, 5 v. Pak 1954-55, 5 v. NZ 1955-56, 3 v. Aust 1956-57, 5 v. WI 1958-59, 4 v. Eng 1959.

1952-53, 4 v. WI 1952-53, 5 v. Pak 1954-55, 5 v. NZ 1955-56, 3 v. Aust 1956-57, 4 v. WI 1958-59, 2 v. Eng 1959.

Pakistan

AGHA SAADAT ALI (1)—1 v. NZ 1955-56.
ALIMUDDIN (18)—3 v. Eng 1954, 5 v. Ind 1954-55, 3 v. NZ 1955-56, 1 v. Aust 1956-57, 5 v. WI 1957-58, 1 v. WI 1958-59.
AMIR ELAHI (5)—5 v. Ind 1952-53.
ANTAO D'SOUZA (1)—1 v. WI 1958-59.
ANWAR HUSSAIN (4)—4 v. Ind 1952-53.
FAZAL MAHMOOD (24)—5 v. Ind 1952-53, 4 v. Eng 1954, 4 v. Ind 1954-55, 2 v. NZ 1955-56, 1 v. Aust 1956-57, 5 v. WI 1957-58, 3 v. WI 1958-59.
GHAZALI, M. E. Z. (2)—2 v. Eng 1954.
GUL MAHOMED (1)—1 v. Aust 1956-57.
HANIF MOHAMMED (24)—5 v. Ind 1952-53, 4 v. Eng 1954, 5 v. Ind 1954-55, 3 v. NZ 1955-56, 1 v. Aust 1956-57, 5 v. WI 1957-58, 1 v. WI 1958-59.
HASEEB AHSAN (4)—3 v. WI 1957-58, 1 v. WI 1958-59.
IJAZ BUTT (3)—3 v. WI 1958-59.
IMTIAZ AHMED (26)—5 v. Ind 1952-53, 4 v. Eng 1954, 5 v. Ind 1954-55, 3 v. NZ 1955-56, 1 v. Aust 1956-57, 5 v. WI 1957-58, 3 v. WI 1958-59.
ISRAR ALI (2)—2 v. Ind 1952-53.
KARDAR, A. H. (23)—5 v. Ind 1952-53, 4 v. Eng 1954, 5 v. Ind 1954-55, 3 v. NZ 1955-56, 1 v. Aust 1956-57, 5 v. WI 1957-58.
KHALID HASSAN (1)—1 v. Eng 1954.
KHALID WAZIR (2)—2 v. Eng 1954.
KHAN MOHAMMED (13)—1 v. Ind 1952-53, 2 v. Eng 1954, 4 v. Ind 1954-55, 3 v. NZ 1955-56, 1 v. Aust 1956-57, 2 v. WI 1957-58.
MAHMOOD HUSSAIN (18)—4 v. Ind 1952-53, 2 v. Eng 1954, 5 v. Ind 1954-55, 1 v. NZ 1955-56, 3 v. WI 1957-58, 3 v. WI 1958-59.
MAQSOOD AHMED (16)—5 v. Ind 1952-53, 4 v. Eng 1954, 5 v. Ind 1954-55, 2 v. NZ 1955-56.
MIRAN BUX (2)—2 v. Ind 1954-55.
MOHAMMED ASLAM (1)—1 v. Eng 1954.
MUSHTAQ MOHAMMED (1)—1 v. WI 1958-59.
NASIMUL GHANI (8)—5 v. WI 1957-58, 3 v. WI 1958-59.
NAZAR MOHAMMED (5)—5 v. Ind 1952-53.
REHMAN, S. F. (1)—1 v. WI 1957-58.
SAEED AHMED (8)—5 v. WI 1957-58, 3 v. WI 1958-59.
SHUJAUDDIN (14)—3 v. Eng 1954, 5 v. Ind 1954-55, 3 v. NZ 1955-56, 3 v. WI 1958-59.
WALLIS MATHIAS (10)—1 v. NZ 1955-56, 1 v. Aust 1956-57, 5 v. WI 1957-58, 3 v. WI 1958-59.
WAQAR HASSAN (20)—5 v. Ind 1952-53, 4 v. Eng 1954, 5 v. Ind 1954-55, 3 v. NZ 1955-56, 1 v. Aust 1956-57, 1 v. WI 1957-58, 1 v. WI 1958-59.
WAZIR MOHAMMED (19)—1 v. Ind 1952-53, 2 v. Eng 1954, 5 v. Ind 1954-55, 2 v. NZ 1955-56, 1 v. Aust 1956-57, 5 v. WI 1957-58, 3 v. WI 1958-59.
ZULFIQAR AHMED (9)—3 v. Ind 1952-53, 2 v. Eng 1954, 3 v. NZ 1955-56, 1 v. Aust 1956-57.

GREAT NAMES IN CRICKET

K. S. RANJITSINHJI (Sussex). Born at Sarodar, Kathiawar, 10/9/1872, died at Delhi 2/4/1933, aged 60. A brilliant batsman with a fine array of strokes, his greatest shot was the leg glance—a stroke which he can be said to have perfected. Educated in India, he came to England and was awarded his cricket Blue at Cambridge in 1893. He first played for Sussex in 1895, scoring 150 v. M.C.C. at Lord's in his first match, and assisted them regularly until 1904. He succeeded as the Maharaja of Nawanagar in 1906, and his future cricket was restricted to 1908 and 1912, with two matches in 1920 when he played under the handicap of blindness in one eye, the result of a shooting accident. Ranji went to Australia in 1897-98 and North America in 1899, but never played in a first-class cricket match in India. He captained Sussex from 1899 to 1903 and appeared in 15 Test matches for England. One unique record he holds is that of scoring two centuries on the same day—100 and 125 not out for Sussex v. Yorkshire at Hove on 22nd August 1896.

Ranji was the first batsman to score more than 3,000 in a season—3,159 runs (av. 63.18) in 1899 and 3,065 runs (av. 87.57) in 1900. His best score was 285 not out v. Somerset at Taunton in 1901, and altogether in first-class cricket his figures were 24,692 runs (av. 56.37), 72 centuries and 133 wickets (av. 34.59).

TOM RICHARDSON (Surrey and Somerset). Born at Byfleet 11/8/1870, died at St. Jean d'Arvey 2/7/1912, aged 41. A fine fast bowler, who played for Surrey from 1892 to 1904 and ended his career with a match for Somerset v. Australians in 1905. He jumped to the front immediately and took 1,005 wickets in the four seasons 1894 to 1897, with 290 (av. 14.37) as his best record. He toured Australia in 1894–95 and 1897–98 and took 88 wickets (av. 25.22) in 14 consecutive Test matches against Australia between 1893 and 1897–98. He achieved three hat-tricks for Surrey and took all ten wickets in an innings (at a cost of 45 runs) v. Essex at the Oval in 1894.

WILFRED RHODES (Yorkshire). Born at Kirkheaton 29/10/1877. The leading wicket-taker in first-class cricket with 4,187 (av. 16.71) during a career which spanned the years from 1898 to 1930. A slow left-arm spinner of immaculate length, he was a right-handed batsman who started at No. 11 and rose to open the innings for England with J. B. Hobbs. As a batsman he scored 39,802 runs (av. 30.83), including 58 centuries. He played in 58 Tests for England, totalling 2,325 runs (av. 30.19), 2 centuries and 127 wickets (av. 26.96). He holds the record of sixteen doubles of 1,000 runs and 100 wickets, including two runs of seven in consecutive seasons (from 1903 to 1909 and from 1914 to 1924). After five years' absence from the Test team he was recalled for the historic Oval Test against Australia in 1926 and made his last bow in Test cricket with four Tests v. West Indies on the 1929–30 tour. He also toured Australia in 1903–04, 1907–08, 1911–12 and 1920–21, South Africa in 1909–10 and 1913–14 and played in India in 1921–22 and 1926–27. His best score was 267 not out v. Leicestershire at Leeds in 1921, while as a bowler he took nine wickets in an innings three times and achieved the hat-trick v. Derbyshire at Derby in 1920.

T. Richardson

W. Rhodes

A. Sandham

ANDREW SANDHAM (Surrey). Born at Streatham 6/7/1890. A really fine right-handed opening batsman who was unlucky in that his best years coincided with those of J. B. Hobbs and H. Sutcliffe, and so missed the Test honours that should have come to him. He played in 14 Test matches between 1921 and 1929–30, with a best score of 325 v. West Indies at Kingston in his last Test match. A motoring accident a few months later caused him to miss the 1930–31 Tests against South Africa, and with them the chance of succeeding Hobbs as England's opening bat. These two had 66 century stands for Surrey's first wicket, and in his career (1911 to 1937–38) Sandham scored 41,284 runs (av. 44.82), including 107 centuries. He toured Australia in 1924–25, South Africa in 1922–23 and 1930–31, West Indies in 1929–30, India in 1926–27, Jamaica in 1928–29 and South America in 1937–38.

ALFRED SHAW (Nottinghamshire). Born at Burton Joyce 29/8/1842, died at Gedling 16/1/1907, aged 64. The most accurate bowler of all time, with the ability to turn the ball either way, Shaw actually bowled more overs during his career than he conceded runs. He played for Nottinghamshire from 1864 to 1887 and ended with a few matches for Sussex between 1894 and 1897. He played in seven of the first eight Test matches against Australia, and toured Australia in 1876–77, 1881–82, 1884–85, 1886–87 and 1887–88, and was manager of Lord Sheffield's team to Australia in 1891–92. He had his best season in 1878 with 196 wickets (av. 10.63), and achieved the hat-trick three times—in each innings of the match v. Gloucestershire at Nottingham in 1884, when he also took three wickets in four balls in another spell. He took all ten wickets in an innings (at a cost of 73 runs) for M.C.C. v. North at Lord's in 1874. Perhaps his greatest performance was to take 7 wickets at a cost of only 7 runs in 41.2 four-ball overs for his county v. M.C.C. at Lord's in 1875.

ARTHUR SHREWSBURY (Nottinghamshire). Born at Nottingham 11/4/1856, died by his own hand at Gedling 19/5/1903, aged 47. One of the great batsmen of last century, he was the counterpart of W. G. Grace for the professionals and was head and shoulders above the other county batsmen. He played for his county from 1875 to 1902, but his health then broke down and it was obvious that his cricket career was over. He played for England in 23 Tests and captained them seven times in 1884–85 and 1886–87—the next professional captain for England was L. Hutton in 1952. He hit 59 centuries in first-class cricket, ten of them over 200, with a best of 267 v. Middlesex at Nottingham in 1887 and again v. Sussex at Nottingham in 1890. He batted 10½ hours when hitting his 267 in 1887—at that time a record long innings, and still only once surpassed in England (by L. Hutton with 364 in 800 minutes v. Australia at the Oval in 1938).

C. I. JAMES SMITH (Middlesex). Born at Corsham, Wiltshire, 25/8/1906. A tall fast bowler and hard-hitting right-handed batsman whose really fine hostile pace bowling has had to take second place to his feats as a hitter. Smith appeared in first-class cricket from 1930 to 1939, but started in Minor County Cricket with his native county and was not qualified for Middlesex until 1934. He played five times for England: all four Tests on the 1934–35 tour of the West Indies and once v. New Zealand in 1937. His fastest knock was to reach 50 in only 11 minutes when scoring 66 (in only 18 minutes) v. Gloucestershire at Bristol in 1938. He needed only eleven scoring strokes to reach fifty, his full strokes being 2–4–4–6–1–6–6–6–1–6–2–6–6–2–2–6, the three sixes in consecutive balls being hit off R. A. Sinfield. In the same season he hit 69 in 20 minutes v. Sussex at Lord's. In 1935 he scored 50 with twelve scoring strokes against Kent at Maidstone—the first 49 runs were scored off three consecutive overs from A. P. Freeman and a single to complete the fifty off C. S. Marriott after only 14 minutes' batting.

HERBERT SUTCLIFFE (Yorkshire). Born at Pudsey 24/11/1894. With Jack Hobbs formed the best-known and most successful opening partnership in first-class cricket—they were responsible for 15 century stands for the first wicket in 38 starts for England in Test cricket, their average stand being no less than 87. Sutcliffe was the only player to appear regularly in first-class cricket between 1919 and 1939, but retired after one match in 1945. He scored 1,839 runs (average 44.85) in his first season in 1919, and never failed to score 1,000 runs a season, ending with an aggregate of

A. Shrewsbury

M. W. Tate

H. Sutcliffe

50,135 runs (average 52.00), including 149 centuries. He appeared in 54 Test matches for England between 1924 and 1935, and was appointed a Test selector in 1959. His best score was 313 v. Essex at Leyton in 1932, when he shared with P. Holmes in a first-wicket stand of 555: still a world record. His batting average of 96.96 for 3,006 runs in 1931 is the best ever by an English batsman (only D. G. Bradman and W. A. Johnston have bettered this average). He toured Australia in 1924–25, 1928–29 and 1932–33, and South Africa in 1927–28.

MAURICE W. TATE (Sussex). Born at Brighton 29/4/1895, died at Wadhurst 18/5/1956, aged 61. Son of F. W. Tate, who also played for Sussex and England. After some years as an aggressive right-handed batsman and useful slow off-break bowler, Tate turned to fast-medium-pace bowling, with a devastating swing and speed off the pitch, and for a decade was regarded as the most dangerous bowler in the game. Tate played for Sussex from 1912 to 1937, scored 1,000 runs in a season eleven times, took 100 wickets thirteen times and achieved the double eight times. In addition he totalled 1,193 runs and 116 wickets on the 1926–27 M.C.C. tour to India—the only time that the double has been achieved in an overseas season. In addition to that tour Tate went to Australia in 1924–25, 1928–29 and 1932–33, to South Africa in 1930–31 and New Zealand in 1932–33. In 39 Tests between 1924 and 1935 Tate took 155 wickets (av. 26.10), including a wicket at Birmingham in 1924 with the very first ball he bowled in Tests. His career aggregates were 21,698 runs (av. 25.02), 23 centuries, and 2,783 wickets (av. 18.16).

VICTOR T. TRUMPER (New South Wales). Born at Sydney 2/11/1877, died at Sydney 28/6/1915, aged 37. Perhaps the best batsman that has ever been produced by Australia, as he was in the first rank as a batsman on a damaged pitch—something to which few Australian batsmen have had a claim. His career stretched from 1894–95 to 1913–14, during which he scored 16,909 runs (av. 44.86), including 42 centuries. He played in 48 consecutive Test matches between 1899 and 1911–12, totalling 3,163 runs (av. 39.04), including 8 centuries, but did not come to England in 1912 because of the dispute between the leading Australian cricketers and the Board of Control. Trumper toured England in 1899, 1902, 1905, and 1909, South Africa in 1902–03 and New Zealand in 1904–05 and 1913–14. His best score was 300 not out v. Sussex at Hove in 1899, but his fastest was 293 in three hours v. Canterbury at Christchurch in 1913–14—on that occasion he and A. Sims added 411 for the eighth wicket in the same time, setting up the still-standing world record for that wicket.

HEDLEY VERITY (Yorkshire). Born at Headingley, Leeds, 18/5/1905, died when a prisoner of war in Italy 31/7/1943, as a result of wounds received in action at Catania, aged 38. One of the great slow left-arm spinners, Verity was 25 before he played in first-class cricket, and ten short years later his career was over. He took 1,956 wickets (av. 14.87), and passed the 100 wickets mark in nine seasons (1931 to 1939) with a best of 216 wickets (av. 13.18) in 1936. He twice took all ten wickets in an innings, 10 for 36 v. Warwickshire at Leeds in 1931 and 10 for 10 v. Nottinghamshire at Leeds in 1932,

CRICKET QUIZ

1. What is the lowest number of runs scored in one day's play in a first-class match?

*

2. What is the record partnership for any wicket in first-class cricket?

*

3. Which batsman has shared in two wicket partnerships of over 500 in first-class cricket?

4. Which bowler has taken the highest number of wickets in a first-class season in England? (*above*)

5. Only five bowlers have taken 250 wickets or more in a first-class season—who are they?

*

6. A. E. Trott achieved a unique feat for Middlesex in his benefit match v. Somerset at Lord's in 1907—what was it?

*

7. Which players were involved in a hat-trick of stumpings?

QUIZ ANSWERS

1. 95 by Australia (80 all out) and Pakistan (15 for 2 wickets) on the first day of the Test match at Karachi in 1956–57. 2. 577 for the fourth wicket by Gul Mahomed and V. S. Hazare for Holkar v. Baroda at Baroda in 1946–47. 3. F. M. Worrell—502 (unparted) with J. D. C. Goddard for the fourth wicket for Barbados v. Trinidad at Barbados in 1943–44, and 574 (unparted) with C. L. Walcott for Barbados v. Trinidad at Trinidad in 1945–46. 4. A. P. Freeman (Kent) took 304 wickets (average 18.05) in 1928. 5. A. P. Freeman six times, W. Rhodes and T. Richardson twice each, J. T. Hearne and C. T. B. Turner once each. 6. In the second innings of the match he first took four wickets with consecutive balls and later performed the hat-trick. 7. W. H. Brain the wicket-keeper, C. L. Townsend the bowler, for Gloucestershire v. Somerset at Cheltenham in 1893.

CRICKET QUIZ

1. Which player never scored a run in first-class cricket although he played in five matches and had nine innings?

*

2. Has a one-legged player ever appeared in county cricket?

*

3. Who were the first three professionals to be appointed county captain in modern first-class cricket?

*

4. Which first-class county has provided the most players for England Test teams?

*

5. Which Champion Counties beat the Rest of England in the years in which this fixture was played?

QUIZ ANSWERS

1. S. Clark, a wicket-keeper with Somerset in 1930. 2. A. D. Denton, who had lost a leg in the First World War, played two games for Northamptonshire in 1919. 3. W. E. Astill of Leicestershire in 1935, L. G. Berry of Leicestershire in 1946 and H. E. Dollery of Warwickshire in 1948. 4. Yorkshire—R. Illingworth (v. New Zealand at Manchester in 1958) was the 50th. 5. Yorkshire in 1905 and 1935, Middlesex in 1947 and Surrey in 1957.

GREAT NAMES IN CRICKET

and took nine wickets in an innings seven times. He took 17 for 91 in the match v. Essex at Leyton in 1933. Possibly his greatest performance was when he took 15 wickets for 104 runs for England v. Australia at Lord's in 1934, his 14 wickets on the third day hurrying Australia to an innings defeat. In 40 Test matches for England he took 144 wickets (av. 24.37).

SIR PELHAM F. WARNER (Middlesex). Born at Port of Spain, Trinidad, 2/10/1873. The elder statesman of cricket, he was educated at Rugby and Oxford University. His first visit to Lord's was in May 1887, when he could have had little idea that his life would be so bound up with the ground. He made his debut

Sir P. F. Warner

n first-class cricket in 1894 and retired as captain of Middlesex at the end of 1920, when he had skippered the county to the Championship, but did not make his final first-class appearance until 1929. He played in only 15 Tests for England, but captained the M.C.C. teams to Australia in 1903–04 and South Africa in 1905–06. On the first tour he regained the Ashes after Australia had won four consecutive rubbers. Knighted in 1937 for his services to cricket, he acted as Secretary of the M.C.C. during the Second World War and held the office of President of the M.C.C. in 1950. One of the most travelled of cricket tourists, he went to Australia in 1903–04 and 1911–12 (on the second tour he was taken ill after playing in only one match), to South Africa in 1898–99 and 1905–06, West Indies in 1896–97, New Zealand in 1902–03, North America in 1897 and 1898 and South America

in"1926–27. His career totals were 29,028 runs (average 36.28), including 60 centuries, with a best of 244 for Rest of England v. Warwickshire at the Oval in 1911. On numerous occasions he served as an England Test selector—in 1905, 1911, 1926, 1931, 1932 and from 1935 to 1938.

JOHN WISDEN (Sussex). Born at Brighton 5/9/1826, died in London 5/4/1884, aged 57. His career with Sussex covered the years from 1845 to 1863, but he also held several engagements elsewhere. Undoubtedly his greatest claim to fame is the little yellow books which bear his name and will celebrate their centenary in 1964, but he was also the founder of the sports outfitters and a fine cricketer. Described as a "hard hitter" as a batsman, he started as a pace bowler, but reduced his speed in the 1850s. Playing for the North v. South at Lord's in 1850 he took all ten

F. E. Woolley

second innings wickets without assistance from the field, all ten batsmen being clean bowled. This feat is still unequalled in first-class cricket. Wisden visited North America in 1859, on the first-ever cricket tour, but his career was over before cricket really began to gather momentum in the 1860s.

FRANK E. WOOLLEY (Kent). Born at Tonbridge 27/5/1887. One of the really great all-round cricketers—an elegant left-handed batsman with powerful strokes, fine slow left-arm spinner and safe catch in the slips—as his career record of 58,969 runs (av. 40.75), 145 centuries, 2,068 wickets (av. 19.85) and 913 catches testifies. One can take heart from his experiences in his first match in

first-class cricket against Lancashire at Manchester in 1906—he collected a duck, dropped two catches and was hit for 103 runs while taking only one wicket. That disastrous start was the beginning of a brilliant career in which he played in 64 Test matches for England, the record number of 52 of them in succession between 1909 and 1926. He toured Australia in 1911–12, 1920–21 and 1924–25, South Africa in 1909–10, 1913–14 and 1922–23 and Australia and New Zealand in 1929–30. His best score of 305 not out for M.C.C. v Tasmania at Hobart in 1911–12 lasted for only 210 minutes of aggressive hitting. He had the odd experience of hitting 3,352 runs (av. 61.03) in 1928, yet being omitted from the M.C.C. team to visit Australia in the following winter.

E. "Patsy" Hendren

DOUGLAS V. P. WRIGHT (Kent). Born at Sidcup 21/8/1914. A leg-break and googly bowler, rather faster than normal for his type, who on his day was almost unplayable, but whose 'in-and-out' form made him somewhat of an enigma. He played for Kent from 1932 to 1957, and totalled 2,056 wickets (av. 23.98). He toured Australia and New Zealand in 1946–47 and 1950–51 and South Africa in 1938–39 and 1948–49, and played in 34 Tests for England with a total of 108 wickets (av. 39.11). He holds the record of seven hat-tricks in first-class cricket and had best bowling figures of 9 for 47 v. Gloucestershire at Bristol in 1939 and 9 for 51 v. Leicestershire at Maidstone in 1949. Although a professional, he captained Kent from August 1953 to the end of the 1956 season, and was granted two benefits —£5,254 in 1950 and £3,601 in 1957.

Croquet

Compiled by **S. S. Townsend** of the Croquet Association

CROQUET QUIZ

1. A ball reaches the playing side of its hoop by going through from the non-playing side, leaving an edge between the uprights. Can the hoop be run?

*

2. A moving ball, after running its hoop, is interfered with by a playful dog. Has the striker any redress?

*

3. May a player remove the top section of the peg?

QUIZ ANSWERS

1. Yes, if the ball cannot be touched by a straight edge on the non-playing side. 2. Yes. The stroke may be played again but the point scored cannot be claimed if this course is chosen. 3. Yes. Whenever it interferes with his stance or swing, or for a jump shot.

THE CROQUET ASSOCIATION

The official organisation which encourages and controls the game of Croquet in all its aspects is the Croquet Association which was formed in 1896 and has as its president Sir Compton Mackenzie. The Association controls the laws of the game and the regulations for tournaments and is available to give any assistance required by Croquet clubs, which are about fifty registered with the Association. The management of the affairs of the Association is vested in a council consisting of twenty-four members.

Associates, who pay an annual subscription of 30s., receive free the official magazine *Croquet*, which is published seven times a year and contains topical news of the game, tournament programmes, results, etc.

The Open Championship dates

back to 1867. Other historical highlights are the change from the "Balls in Sequence" game to the "Either Ball" game prior to World War I, the revised setting of the court with one peg instead of two, and the introduction of the lift-shot principle in "A" Opens in 1928. The size of hoops varied considerably in the early years of the game but became the present standard width of 3¾ inches by 1914.

An International Trophy is competed for periodically between

England, New Zealand and Australia. Of the six contests which have taken place since 1925, England have won three, Australia two and New Zealand one. The last contest took place in 1956 when a team from New Zealand visited England and was beaten in a series of five test matches. Negotiations are in progress regarding a possible visit of a team from this country to Australia and New Zealand in 1962–3. No visiting team has as yet won the Trophy.

Northern Lawn Tennis and Croquet Club

Roehampton Club

Information on any aspect of Croquet can be obtained from the Secretary, The Croquet Association, The Hurlingham Club, S.W.6.

THE CROQUET CHAMPIONSHIP

1867 Walter Jones Whitmore
1868 W. H. Peel
1869 G. C. Joad
1870 W. H. Peel
1871 W. H. Peel
1872 C. Black
1873 J. D. Heath
1874 J. D. Heath
1875 R. Gray
1876 Colonel Busk
1877 B. C. Evelegh
1878 A. H. Spong
1879 C. B. Evelegh
1880 A. H. Spong
1881 A. H. Spong
1882 A. H. Spong
1883–1896 No Competition
1897 C. E. Willis
1898 Rev. C. Powell
1899 B. C. Evelegh
1900 J. E. Austin
1901 R. N. Roper
1902 C. Corbally
1903 C. Corbally
1904 R. C. J. Beaton
1905 Miss L. Gower
1906 C. Corbally
1907 R. C. J. Beaton
1908 C. Corbally
1909 G. Ashmore
1910 C. L. O'Callaghan
1911 Edgar Whitaker
1912 C. L. O'Callaghan
1913 C. Corbally
1914 P. D. Mathews
1915–1918 No Competition
1919 P. D. Mathews
1920 P. D. Mathews
1921 Capt. C. L. O'Callaghan
1922 C. E. Pepper
1923 Capt. H. W. J. Snell
1924 D. L. G. Joseph
1925 Miss D. D. Steel
1926 Ben C. Apps
1927 P. D. Mathews
1928 Capt. K. H. Coxe
1929 Lt.-Col. W. B. Du Pre
1930 Ben C. Apps
1931 Ben C. Apps
1932 H. O. Hicks
1933 Miss D. D. Steel
1934 Lt.-Col. W. B. Du Pre
1935 Miss D. D. Steel
1936 Miss D. D. Steel
1937 C. F. Colman
1938 D. J. V. Hamilton-Miller
1939 H. O. Hicks
1940–45 No Competition
1946 D. J. V. Hamilton-Miller
1947 H. O. Hicks
1948 H. O. Hicks
1949 H. O. Hicks
1950 H. O. Hicks
1951 G. L. Reckitt
1952 H. O. Hicks
1953 J. W. Solomon
1954 A. G. F. Ross (N.Z.)
1955 E. P. C. Cotter
1956 J. W. Solomon
1957 Dr. W. R. D. Wiggins
1958 E. P. C. Cotter
1959 J. W. Solomon

THE MEN'S CHAMPIONSHIP

1925 C. R. Elwes
1926 C. Corbally
1927 Lt.-Col. W. B. Du Pre
1928 B. G. Klein
1929 Ben C. Apps
1930 H. O. Hicks
1931 Ben C. Apps
1932 H. O. Hicks
1933 Lt.-Col. W. B. Du Pre
1934 J. N. Lovett
1935 Maurice B. Reckitt
1936 Lt.-Col. W. B. Du Pre
1937 J. A. McMordie
1938 C. F. Colman
1939 R. Tingey
1940–1945 No Competition
1946 Maurice B. Reckitt
1947 E. L. Ward Petley
1948 H. O. Hicks
1949 H. O. Hicks
1950 H. O. Hicks
1951 J. W. Solomon
1952 E. P. C. Cotter
1953 J. W. Solomon

1954 E. P. C. Cotter
1955 H. O. Hicks
1956 H. O. Hicks
1957 Dr. W. R. D. Wiggins
1958 J. W. Solomon
1959 J. W. Solomon

THE WOMEN'S CHAMPIONSHIP

1869 Mrs. Joad
1870 Miss Walter
1871 Mrs. Walsh
1872 Mrs. Walsh
1873 Mrs. Walsh
1874 Miss Williamson
1875 Mrs. Hallowes
1876 Miss K. Philbrick
1877 Miss K. Philbrick
1878 Miss Walsh
1879 Miss Walsh
1880 Miss Walsh
1881 Miss K. Philbrick
1882 Miss K. Philbrick
1883–1896 No Competition
1897 Miss M. Drummond
1898 Miss O. Henry
1899 Miss L. Gower
1900 Miss L. Gower
1901 Miss L. Gower
1902 Miss M. Glyn
1903 Miss N. E. Coote
1904 Miss V. Rowley
1905 Miss N. E. Coote
1906 Mrs. J. Preston
1907 Miss E. M. Bramwell
1908 Miss E. M. Bramwell
1909 Miss N. J. Beausire
1910 Miss B. Willis
1911 Miss Elsie Reid
1912 Miss Ella D. B. Simeon
1913 Lady Julian Parr
1914 Miss E. M. Bramwell
1915–1918 No Competition
1919 Miss D. D. Steel
1920 Mrs. W. H. Hope
1921 Miss N. S. L. Gilchrist
1922 Miss D. D. Steel
1923 Mrs. C. W. C. Strickland
1924 Miss Mona Bryan
1925 Miss D. D. Steel
1926 Miss D. D. Steel
1927 Miss D. D. Steel
1928 Mrs. R. C. J. Beaton
1929 Miss D. D. Steel
1930 Miss D. D. Steel
1931 Mrs. A. C. Ionides
1932 Miss D. D. Steel
1933 Miss D. D. Steel
1934 Miss D. D. Steel
1935 Miss D. D. Steel
1936 Miss D. D. Steel
1937 Miss D. D. Steel
1938 Miss D. D. Steel
1939 Miss D. D. Steel
1940–1945 No Competition
1946 Mrs. B. H. Wiggins
1947 Mrs. G. F. H. Elvey
1948 Mrs. G. F. H. Elvey
1949 Miss D. A. Lintern
1950 Miss M. Claughton (N.Z.)
1951 Miss D. A. Lintern
1952 Mrs. E. Rotherham
1953 Mrs. E. Rotherham
1954 Miss D. A. Lintern
1955 Mrs. E. Rotherham
1956 Mrs. W. H. Kirk (N.Z.)
1957 Miss D. A. Lintern
1958 Miss D. A. Lintern
1959 Mrs. E. Rotherham

PRESIDENT'S CUP

1934 Miss D. D. Steel, 13 *Games*
1935 Lt.-Col. W. B. Du Pre, 13 *Games*
(After a tie with D. J. V. Hamilton-Miller)
1936 Mrs. L. C. Apps, 13 *Games*
1937 Miss D. D. Steel, 13 *Games*
1938 C. F. Colman, 14 *Games*
(After a tie with R. Tingey)
1939–1945 No Competition
1946 D. J. V. Hamilton-Miller, 10 *Games*
(After a tie with E. L. Ward Petley)
1947 H. O. Hicks, 11 *Games*
1948 H. O. Hicks, 11 *Games*
1949 E. P. C. Cotter, 13 *Games*
1950 E. P. C. Cotter, 12 *Games*
1951 H. O. Hicks, 11 *Games*
1952 E. P. C. Cotter, 11 *Games*
(After a tie with J. W. Solomon)
1953 E. P. C. Cotter, 12 *Games*
(After a tie with J. W. Solomon)
1954 H. O. Hicks, 14 *Games*
1955 J. W. Solomon, 12 *Games*
1956 E. P. C. Cotter, 15 *Games*
(After a tie with J. W. Solomon)
1957 J. W. Solomon, 13 *Games*
1958 J. W. Solomon, 11 *Games*
1959 J. W. Solomon, 13 *Games*

THE DOUBLES CHAMPIONSHIP

1924 T. Dickson and Miss D. D. Steel
1925 P. D. Mathews and Trevor Williams
1926 Col. C. E. Wilson and Mrs. R. C. J. Beaton
1927 Miss D. D. Steel and Mrs. H. de la Mothe
1928 Miss D. D. Steel and Mrs. H. de la Mothe
1929 B. G. Klein and C. S. Wentworth Reeve
1930 Lt.-Col. W. B. Du Pre and Miss D. D. Steel
1931 Lt.-Col. W. B. Du Pre and Miss D. D. Steel
1932 Col. C. E. Wilson and W. Windsor Richards
1933 B. G. Klein and Maurice B. Reckitt
1934 B. G. Klein and Maurice B. Reckitt
1935 H. Reginald Poulter and E. L. Ward Petley
1936 Rev. G. F. H. Elvey and Mrs. G. F. H. Elvey
1937 The Lord Tollemache and Sir Gerald Burke
1938 C. F. Colman and Mrs. R. C. J. Beaton
1939 R. Tingey and Capt. K. H. Coxe
1940–1945 No Competition
1946 Maurice B. Reckitt and Miss D. A. Lintern
1947 R. Tingey and Col. J. G. Clarke
1948 H. O. Hicks and D. J. V. Hamilton-Miller
1949 H. O. Hicks and D. J. V. Hamilton-Miller
1950 G. L. Reckitt and M. B. Reckitt
1951 H. O. Hicks and D. J. V. Hamilton-Miller
1952 H. O. Hicks and Dr. W. R. D. Wiggins
1953 H. O. Hicks and Dr. W. R. D. Wiggins
1954 E. P. C. Cotter and J. W. Solomon
1955 E. P. C. Cotter and J. W. Solomon
1956 Major G. F. Stone and L. Kirk-Greene
1957 H. O. Hicks and Dr. W. R. D. Wiggins
1958 E. P. C. Cotter and J. W. Solomon
1959 E. P. C. Cotter and J. W. Solomon

THE MIXED DOUBLES CHAMPIONSHIP

1899 B. C. Evelegh and Miss M. Drummond
1900 R. N. Roper and Miss J. M. Cowie
1901 R. N. Roper and Miss J. M. Cowie
1902 G. H. Woolston and Miss V. Rowley
1903 C. Corbally and Miss L. Gower
1904 R. C. J. Beaton and Miss L. Gower
1905 H. Corbally and Miss N. E. Coote
1906 R. C. J. Beaton and Mrs. R. C. J. Beaton (Miss L. Gower)
1907 R. C. J. Beaton and Mrs. R. C. J. Beaton
1908 Talbot J. Considine and Miss N. E. Coote
1909 C. L. O'Callaghan and Miss H. Johnson-Houghton
1910 C. L. O'Callaghan and Miss H. Johnson-Houghton
1911 C. Corbally and Miss N. Barlow
1912 C. L. O'Callaghan and Mrs. G. G. Lockett (Miss H. Johnson-Houghton)
1913 H. Corbally and Miss Elsie Reid
1914 C. L. O'Callaghan and Mrs. G. G. Lockett
1915–1918 No Competition
1919 Claude F. Barry and Mrs. W. H. Hope
1920 R. C. J. Beaton and Mrs. R. C. J. Beaton
1921 Capt. C. L. O'Callaghan and Miss E. M. Bramwell
1922 Major R. G. O'Callaghan and Miss N. S. L. Gilchrist
1923 Lord Tollemache and Miss D. D. Steel
1924 D. L. G. Joseph and Miss Winifred Heap
1925 R. Leetham Jones and Miss M. K. Haslam
1926 Ben C. Apps and Mrs. C. W. C. Strickland
1927 Ben C. Apps and Mrs. C. W. C. Strickland
1928 D. L. G. Joseph and Miss Winifred Heap
1929 Lt.-Col. W. B. Du Pre and Mrs. R. C. J. Beaton
1930 E. Trevor Hardman and Mrs. T. H. F. Clarkson
1931 H. O. Hicks and Mrs. F. H. White
1932 Lt.-Col. W. B. Du Pre and Miss D. D. Steel
1933 Trevor Williams and Mrs. A. C. Ionides
1934 Lt.-Col. W. B. Du Pre and Miss D. D. Steel
1935 Lt.-Col. W. B. Du Pre and Miss D. D. Steel
1936 Lt.-Col. W. B. Du Pre and Miss D. D. Steel
1937 Maurice B. Reckitt and Mrs. L. C. Apps
1938 Lt.-Col. W. B. Du Pre and Mrs. R. C. J. Beaton
1939 E. L. Ward Petley and Miss D. D. Steel
1940–1945 No Competition
1946 Maurice B. Reckitt and Miss D. A. Lintern
1947 E. L. Ward Petley and Miss D. D. Steel
1948 M. B. Reckitt and Miss D. A. Lintern
1949 A. D. Heenan (N.Z.) and Mrs. E. D. Kingsford
1950 H. O. Hicks and Mrs. E. Rotherham
1951 E. P. C. Cotter and Mrs. G. J. Turketine
1952 M. B. Reckitt and Miss D. A. Lintern
1953 Dr. W. R. D. Wiggins and Mrs. E. Rotherham
1954 J. W. Solomon and Mrs. N. Oddie
1955 H. O. Hicks and Mrs. E. Rotherham
1956 G. Rowling and Mrs. T. McKenzie-Smartt (N.Z.)
1957 E. P. C. Cotter and Mrs. E. Rotherham
1958 M. B. Reckitt and Miss D. A. Lintern
1959 Dr. W. R. D. Wiggins and Mrs. E. Rotherham

CROQUET QUIZ

1. Blue pegs out Black which rebounds off the peg causing Blue to come in contact with the striker's mallet. Is this a foul?

*

2. A player takes off from a ball and while watching its course allows the croqueted ball while still moving to hit his foot. Is this a foul?

*

3. A player takes off from a ball and watches its course. The player then moves forward to continue the turn and kicks the croqueted ball which had come to rest. Is this a foul?

*

4. Can a bisque be taken after a foul?

QUIZ ANSWERS

1. No. Blue must be replaced where in the striker's opinion it would have come to rest. 2. Yes. 3. No, the stroke was finished. It is an inadvertence. The ball kicked must be replaced and the turn continues. 4. Yes.

CROQUET QUIZ

1. Blue takes off from Black and in doing so hits Yellow and goes off the court. Does Blue's turn cease?

*

2. Where is baulk line B?

*

3. In what circumstances can a player have a turn without going on to the court?

QUIZ ANSWERS

1. No. Blue was in hand after hitting Yellow. 2. The yard line from the middle of the north boundary to the third corner spot. 3. By announcing his intention to leave the balls as they lie.

THE INTER-COUNTY CHAMPIONSHIP

1897 Berkshire	1932 Middlesex
1898 Berkshire	1933 Surrey
1899 Berkshire	1934 Surrey
1900 Berkshire	1935 Surrey
1908 Hertfordshire	1936 Bedford
1909 Kent	1937 Middlesex
1910 Kent	1938 Hampshire
1911 Middlesex	1939 Middlesex
1912 Kent	1940–1945 No competition
1913 Middlesex	
1914 Middlesex	
1915–1919 No competition	1946 Bedford
	1947 Bedford and Hunts
1920 Middlesex	1948 Surrey
1921 Middlesex	1949 Middlesex
1922 Surrey	1950 Surrey
1923 Surrey (after a tie with Bedford)	1951 Middlesex
	1952 Middlesex
1924 Hampshire	1953 Surrey
1925 Surrey	1954 Surrey
1926 Surrey	1955 Surrey
1927 Middlesex	1956 Hants and Dorset
1928 Surrey	1957 Surrey
1929 Hampshire	1958 Middlesex
1930 Surrey	1959 Middlesex
1931 Irish Counties	

THE LADIES' FIELD CUP

1911 Mrs. R. C. J. Beaton, 7 *Games* (After a tie with Mrs. W. P. Blood and Miss N. E. Coote)
1912 Miss D. M. Standring, 8 *Games*
1913 Mrs. W. P. Blood, 7 *Games* (After a tie with Miss E. D. B. Simeon)

1914 Miss D. D. Steel, 14 *Games*
1915–1918 No competition
1919 Miss D. D. Steel, 16 *Games*
1920 Miss D. D. Steel, 17 *Games*
1921 Miss N. S. L. Gilchrist, 14 *Games*
1922 Mrs. R. C. J. Beaton, 16 *Games*
1923 Mrs. A. C. Ionides, 14 *Games* (After a tie with Miss Evelyn Steel)
1924 Miss Mona Bryan, 14 *Games*
1925 Miss Mona Bryan, 14 *Games*
1926 Miss J. Retallack, 9 *Games*
1927 Miss Mona Bryan, 12 *Games*
1928 Mrs. Edmund Reeve, 9 *Games* (After a tie with Miss Mona Bryan, Miss J. Retallack, and Miss Ella D. B. Simeon)
1929 Mrs. Edmund Reeve, 11 *Games*
1930 Miss Winifred Heap, 11 *Games*
1931 Mrs. Edmund Reeve, 11 Games
1932 Miss D. D. Steel, 12 *Games*
1933 Mrs. A. C. Ionides, 14 *Games*
1934 Miss J. Retallack, 13 *Games*
1935 Mrs. L. C. Apps, 14 *Games*
1936 Mrs. L. C. Apps, 15 *Games*
1937 Mrs. L. C. Apps, 15 *Games*
1938 Mrs. T. H. F. Clarkson, 14 *Games*
1939 Miss D. A. Lintern, 13 *Games*
1940–1945 No competition
1946 Miss D. A. Lintern, 11 *Games*
1947 Mrs. G. F. H. Elvey, 11 *Games*
1948 Mrs. E. Reeve, 10 *Games*
1949 Miss D. A. Lintern, 12 *Games*
1950 Miss D. A. Lintern, 11 *Games*
1951 Miss D. A. Lintern, 9 *Games* (After a tie with Mrs. W. Longman)
1952 Miss D. A. Lintern, 13 *Games*
1953 Miss D. A. Lintern, 8 *Games* (After a tie with Mrs. E. Rotherham)
1954 Miss D. A. Lintern, 13 *Games*

1955 Mrs. E. Rotherham, 13 *Games* (After a tie with Miss D. A. Lintern)
1956 Mrs. E. Rotherham, 13 *Games*
1957 Mrs. E. Rotherham, 12 *Games*
1958 Mrs. W. Longman, 11 *Games*
1959 Miss E. J. Warwick, 11 *Games*

ALL ENGLAND HANDICAP

1923 J. P. Hubbard (4½)
1924 C. B. Hubbard (0)
1925 F. P. B. Caffyn (5)
1926 Mrs. C. E. Boote (3½)
1927 J. N. Lovett (5½)
1928 C. F. Colman (0)
1929 Dr. W. D. Wiggins (11)
1930 Rev. H. B. W. Denison (*3)
1931 Lady Gurney Dixon (9)
1932 G. C. Branthwaite (2)
1933 H. Reginald Poulter (−1½)
1934 Mrs. C. Ravenhill (5)
1935 Miss M. J. Daldy (3½)
1936 Lt.-Col. J. H. S. Murray (2)
1937 E. A. Philpots (8)
1938 Miss M. E. Norman (6½)
1939–1945 No competition
1946 Miss M. E. Norman (3½)
1947 Mrs. Eustace Rotherham (−1)
1948 E. P. C. Cotter (−2)
1949 Miss G. Forbes-Cowan (8)
1950 G. W. Solomon (7)
1951 Dr. B. R. Sandiford (4)
1952 Miss D. A. Lintern (−2½)
1953 Major J. H. Dibley, M.C. (2)
1954 S. S. Townsend (1½)
1955 W. P. Ormerod (1½)
1956 D. E. Buckland (2½)
1957 J. A. Hollweg (1)
1958 G. E. W. Hitchcock (3½)
1959 N. F. Blackwood (5½)

Cross-Country and Walking

Compiled by
Norris McWhirter

Athletics Correspondent: The Observer
and B.B.C. Television Commentator

INTRODUCTION

Cross-Country racing originated as a winter pursuit for oarsmen among the Thames Rowing Club in 1867. The first recorded English Cross-Country Championship was at Roehampton in 1877. International Cross-Country was inaugurated with a race between England and France on March 20th, 1898, at Ville D'Avray, outside Paris. Hamilton Park Racecourse in Scotland was the scene of the first International Cross-Country Championship on March 28th, 1903. The original teams participating were England, Ireland, Scotland and Wales. In 1907 the French came in but did not win their first team success until 1922. The Belgians made the contest six-sided in 1924, while in 1929 the Spaniards, Italians, Swiss and Luxembourgers all sent teams to the championship staged at Vincennes, Paris. The Netherlands sent their first team in 1950, and in 1953 Jugoslavia became the eleventh country to take part.

ROAD RACING QUIZ

1. What is the mountain racing record up Great Britain's highest mountain, Ben Nevis?

*

2. What is the official record for running 100 miles from London to Bath?

*

3. How many athletes have won the International Cross-Country race at their first attempt?

*

4. What is the greatest winning margin recorded in the International Cross-Country Race?

QUIZ ANSWERS

1. 1 hr. 46 mins. 8 secs. by David Spencer from Barrow-in-Furness on September 6, 1958. 2. 12 hrs. 18 mins. 16.0 secs. by R. F. Hopcroft (Thames Valley Harriers) on October 25, 1958. 3. 14, of whom S. E. Eldon (1958) was the only Englishman since the war. 4. J. T. Holden (England) won in 1934 at Ayr by 56 secs.—nearly 400 yards.

THE INTERNATIONAL CROSS-COUNTRY CHAMPIONSHIP

Date	Individual Winner	Winning Time	Team Winner	Venue
1903	A. Shrubb (E)	46:22	England	Hamilton
1904	A. Shrubb (E)	47:58	England	St. Helens
1905	A. Aldridge (E)	40:20	England	Dublin
1906	C. J. Straw (E)	57:32	England	Newport
1907	A. Underwood (E)	54:26	England	Scotstoun
1908	A. J. Robertson (E)	50:26	England	Paris
1909	A. E. Wood (E)	58:03	England	Derby
1910	A. E. Wood (E)	54:02	England	Belfast
1911	J. Bouin (F)	54:07	England	Newport
1912	J. Bouin (F)	51:46	England	Edinburgh
1913	J. Bouin (F)	51:52	England	Paris
1914	A. H. Nicholls (E)	60:23	England	Chesham
1920	J. Wilson (S)	55:06	England	Belfast
1921	W. Freeman (E)	56:53	England	Newport
1922	J. Guillemot (F)	63:59	France	Glasgow
1923	C. E. Blewitt (E)	58:11	France	Paris
1924	W. M. Cotterell (E)	55:35	England	Newcastle-on-Tyne
1925	J. E. Webster (E)	56:55	England	Dublin
1926	E. Harper (E)	44:17	France	Brussels
1927	L. Payne (E)	51:40	France	Newport
1928	H. Eckersley (E)	52:34	France	Ayr
1929	W. M. Cotterell (E)	42:46	France	Paris
1930	T. Evenson (E)	53:49	England	Leamington Spa
1931	T. F. Smythe (I)	48:52	England	Dublin
1932	T. Evenson (E)	50:51	England	Brussels
1933	J. T. Holden (E)	53:40	England	Newport
1934	J. T. Holden (E)	50:28	England	Ayr
1935	J. T. Holden (E)	47:52	England	Paris
1936	W. E. Eaton (E)	47:38	England	Blackpool
1937	J. C. Flockhart (S)	49:50	England	Brussels
1938	C. A. J. Emery (E)	49:57	England	Belfast
1939	J. T. Holden (E)	47:23	France	Cardiff
1946	R. Pujazon (F)	51:51	France	Ayr
1947	R. Pujazon (F)	50:26	France	Paris
1948	J. Doms (B)	54:05	Belgium	Reading
1949	A. Mimoun (F)	47:50	France	Dublin
1950	L. Thys (B)	45:42	France	Brussels
1951	G. B. Saunders (E)	54:07	England	Newport
1952	A. Mimoun (F)	48:19	France	Hamilton
1953	F. Mihalic (Jugoslav.)	47:53	England	Paris

Date	Individual Winner	Winning Time	Team Winner	Venue
1954	A. Mimoun (F)	47:51	England	Birmingham
1955	F. D. Sando (E)	46:09	England	San Sebastian
1956	A. Mimoun (F)	45:18	France	Belfast
1957	F. D. Sando (E)	45:58	Belgium	Waregem
1958	S. E. Eldon (E)	46:29	England	Cardiff
1959	F. Norris (E)	42:44	England	Lisbon

ENGLISH CROSS-COUNTRY CHAMPIONS

Date	Individual Champion	Team Champion
1877	P. H. Stenning (Thames H. & H.)	Thames H. & H.
1878	P. H. Stenning (Thames H. & H.)	Spartan H.
1879	P. H. Stenning (Thames H. & H.)	Thames H. & H.
1880	P. H. Stenning (Thames H. & H.)	Birchfield H.
1881	G. A. Dunning (Clapton B.)	Moseley H.
1882	W. G. George (Moseley H.)	Moseley H.
1883	G. A. Dunning (Clapton B.)	Moseley H.
1884	W. G. George (Moseley H.)	Moseley H.
1885	W. Snook (Birchfield H.)	Liverpool H.
1886	J. E. Hickman (Godiva H.)	Birchfield H.
1887	J. E. Hickman (Godiva H.)	Birchfield H.
1888	E. W. Parry (Salford H.)	Birchfield H.
1889	E. W. Parry (Salford H.)	Salford H.
1890	E. W. Parry (Salford H.)	Salford H.
1891	J. Kibblewhite (Spartan H.)	Birchfield H.
1892	H. A. Heath (South London H.)	*Birchfield H.
1893	H. A. Heath (South London H.)	*Essex Beagles
1894	G. Crossland (Salford H.)	Essex Beagles
1895	S. Cottrill (Thames Valley H.)	Salford H.
1896	G. Crossland (Manchester H.)	Birchfield H.
1897	S. J. Robinson (Northampton and C.A.C.)	Salford H.
1898	S. J. Robinson (Northampton & C.A.C.)	*Salford H.
1899	C. Bennett (Finchley H.)	*Manchester H.
1900	C. Bennett (Finchley H.)	Salford H.
1901	A. Shrubb (South London H.)	Highgate H.
1902	A. Shrubb (South London H.)	Finchley H.
1903	A. Shrubb (South London H.)	Essex Beagles
1904	A. Shrubb (South London H.)	Highgate H.
1905	A. Aldridge (Highgate H.)	Birchfield H.
1906	C. Straw (Sutton H. & A.C.)	Highgate H.
1907	G. Pearse (Highgate H.)	Highgate H.
1908	A. J. Robertson (Birchfield H.)	Sutton H. & A.C.
1909	J. Murphy (Hallamshire H.)	Birchfield H.
1910	F. C. Neaves (Surrey A.C.)	Hallamshire H.
1911	F. N. Hibbins (Thrapston H. & A.C.)	Birchfield H.
1912	F. N. Hibbins (Thrapston H. & A.C.)	Hallamshire H.
1913	E. Glover (Hallamshire H.)	Hallamshire H.
1914	C. H. Ruffell (Highgate H.)	Birchfield H.
1920	J. Guillemot (France)	Surrey A.C.
1921	W. Freeman (Birchfield H.)	Birchfield H.
1922	J. Guillemot (France)	Birchfield H.
1923	C. E. Blewitt (Birchfield H.)	Birchfield H.
1924	Cpl. W. M. Cotterell (Royal Corps of Signals)	Birchfield H.
1925	Cpl. W. M. Cotterell (Royal Corps of Signals)	Birchfield H.
1926	J. E. Webster (Birchfield H.)	Birchfield H.
1927	E. Harper (Hallamshire H.)	Hallamshire H.
1928	J. E. Webster (Birchfield H.)	Birchfield H.
1929	E. Harper (Hallamshire H.)	Birchfield H.
1930	W. B. Howard (Kettering Town H.)	Birchfield H.
1931	J. H. Potts (Saltwell H.)	Birchfield H.
1932	J. A. Burns (Elswick H.)	Birchfield H.
1933	T. Evenson (Salford H.)	Birchfield H.
1934	S. Dodd (Wirrall A.C.)	Birchfield H.
1935	F. Close (Reading A.C.)	Belgrave H.
1936	J. H. Potts (Saltwell H.)	Birchfield H.
1937	H. B. Clark (York H.)	Birchfield H.
1938	J. T. Holden (Tipton H.)	Mitcham A.C.
1939	J. T. Holden (Tipton H.)	Belgrave H.
1946	J. T. Holden (Tipton H.)	Belgrave H.
1947	A. A. Robertson (Reading A.C.)	Sutton H.
1948	S. C. Wooderson (Blackheath H.)	Belgrave H.
1949	F. E. Aaron (Leeds St. Mark's H.)	Sutton H.
1950	F. E. Aaron (Leeds St. Mark's H.)	Sutton H.
1951	F. E. Aaron (Leeds St. Mark's H.)	Sutton H.
1952	W. Hesketh (Manchester A. & C.C.)	Victoria Park A.A.C. (Scotland)
1953	D. A. G. Pirie (South London H.)	Birchfield H.
1954	D. A. G. Pirie (South London H.)	Bolton United H.
1955	D. A. G. Pirie (South London H.)	South London H.
1956	K. L. Norris (Thames Valley H.)	Sheffield United H. & A.C.
1957	F. D. Sando (Aylesford P.M.A.C.)	South London H.
1958	A. F. Perkins (Ilford A.C.)	South London H.
1959	F. Norris (Bolton United H.)	Sheffield United H. & A.C.

* Tie for first place.

TWENTY MILES WALKING CHAMPIONSHIP

	Individual	Team	h. m. s.
1908	H. V. L. Ross (Tooting A.C.)	Surrey W.C.	2 56:32.0
1909	S. C. A. Schofield (Surrey W.C.)	Surrey W.C.	2 56:48.4
1910	H. V. L. Ross (Tooting A.C.)	Surrey W.C.	2 53:45.4
1911	T. Payne (Middlesex W.C.)	Middlesex W.C.	2 50:30.0
1912	H. V. L. Ross (Middlesex W.C.)	Surrey W.C.	2 51:21.4
1913	H. V. L. Ross (Uxbridge & West Middlesex A.C.)	Surrey W.C.	2 50:37.4
1914	H. V. L. Ross (Uxbridge & West Middlesex A.C.)	Surrey W.C.	2 49:53.4
1920	H. V. L. Ross (Herne Hill H.)	Herne Hill H.	2 57:59.6
1921	W. Hehir (Surrey A.C.)	Herne Hill H.	2 58:56.4
1922	W. Hehir (Surrey A.C.)	Surrey W.C.	2 50:12.0
1923	F. Poynton (Leicester W.C.)	Surrey W.C.	2 51:25.0
1924	F. Poynton (Leicester W.C.)	Belgrave H.	2 47:17.5
1925	F. Poynton (Leicester W.C.)	Belgrave H.	2 48:17.4
1927	T. Lloyd Johnson (Surrey A.C.)	Surrey A.C.	2 55:53.0

CROSS-COUNTRY QUIZ

1. Name the two individual cross-country runners who have four times won the International Cross-Country race (instituted 1903)?

★

2. What other distinction do these two great runners share?

★

3. What is the greatest number of cross-country internationals ever won?

★

4. Which has been the most successful cross-country club in the English championship?

QUIZ ANSWERS

1. Jack Holden (England) 1933, 1934, 1935 and 1939, and Alain Mimoun (France) in 1949, 1952, 1954 and 1956. 2. Both were marathon champions. Holden won the European title in 1950 and Mimoun in the 1956 Olympics. 3. Fourteen by D. Phillips of Wales, 1922–37, and E. Thomas of Wales, 1931–45. 4. Birchfield Harriers with 27 wins and 1 tie between 1880 and 1953.

	Individual	Team	h. m. s.
1928	L. Stewart (London Vidarians)	Belgrave H.	2 50:20.6
1929	A. E. Plumb (North London H.)	Belgrave H.	2 50:18.0
1930	A. E. Plumb (North London H.)	Birmingham W.C.	2 46:30.4
1931	T. Lloyd Johnson (Leicester W.C.)	Derby W.C.	2 52:41.0
1932	A. E. Plumb (North London H.)	Derby W.C.	2 43:38.6
1933	A. H. G. Pope (Woodford Green A.C.)	Surrey W.C.	2 48:38.0
1934	T. Lloyd Johnson (Leicester W.C.)	Surrey W.C.	2 49:58.0
1935	J. Medlicott (Birmingham W.C.)	Surrey W.C.	2 47:46.0
1936	H. A. Hake (Surrey W.C.)	Surrey W.C.	2 47:23.0
1937	S. A. Fletcher (Derbyshire S.C.)	{ Leicester W.C. / Surrey W.C. }	2 47:54.0
1938	J. Hopkins (Lancashire W.C.)	Belgrave H.	2 49:10.0
1939	H. H. Whitlock (Metropolitan W.C.)	Belgrave H.	2 51:03.0
1946	H. J. Forbes (Birmingham W.C.)	Leicester W.C.	2 50:43.0
1947	H. J. Forbes (Birmingham W.C.)	Surrey W.C.	2 47:40.0
1948	G. B. R. Whitlock (Metropolitan W.C.)	Surrey W.C.	2 52:07.0
1949	L. Allen (Sheffield United H. & A.C.)	Sheffield United H & A.C.	2 51:18.0
1950	L. Allen (Sheffield United H. & A.C.)	Woodford Green A.C.	2 52:16.0
1951	L. Allen (Sheffield United H. & A.C.)	Woodford Green A.C.	2 51:52.0
1952	J. W. Proctor (Sheffield United H. & A.C.)	Belgrave H.	2 52:07.0
1953	R. F. Goodall (Woodford Green A.C.)	Woodford Green A.C.	2 50:40.0
1954	L. Allen (Sheffield United H. & A.C.)	Belgrave H.	2 47:48.0
1955	G. W. Coleman (Highgate H.)	Belgrave H.	2 40:08.0
1956	R. Hardy (Sheffield United H. & A.C.)	Sheffield United H. & A.C.	2 38:27.0
1957	E. W. Hall (Belgrave H.)	Belgrave H.	2 45:12.0
1958	L. Allen (Sheffield United H. & A.C.)	Metropolitan W.C.	2 43:21.0

FIFTY KILOMETRES WALKING CHAMPIONSHIP

1930	T. W. Green (Belgrave H.)	—	4 35:36.0
1931	T. Lloyd Johnson (Leicester W.C.)	—	4 55:48.0
1932	F. Pretti (Italy)	Birmingham W.C.	4 41:54.0
1933	H. H. Whitlock (Metropolitan W.C.)	Birmingham W.C.	4 39:00.0
1934	T. Lloyd Johnson (Leicester W.C.)	Belgrave H.	4 36:30.0
1935	H. H. Whitlock (Metropolitan W.C.)	Belgrave H.	4 39:08.0
1936	H. H. Whitlock (Metropolitan W.C.)	Belgrave H.	4 30:38.0
1937	H. H. Whitlock (Metropolitan W.C.)	Metropolitan W.C.	4 38:43.0
1938	H. H. Whitlock (Metropolitan W.C.)	Belgrave H.	4 43:01.2
1939	H. H. Whitlock (Metropolitan W.C.)	Metropolitan W.C.	4 40:43.0
1946	C. Megnin (Highgate H.)	Leicester W.C.	4 53:25.0
1947	H. J. Forbes (Birmingham W.C.)	Surrey W.C.	4 40:06.0
1948	G. B. R. Whitlock (Metropolitan W.C.)	Surrey W.C.	4 35:35.0
1949	T. Lloyd Johnson (Leicester W.C.)	Surrey W.C.	4 51:50.0
1950	J. W. Proctor (Sheffield U.H.)	Woodford Green A.C.	4 43:04.0
1951	D. Tunbridge (Highgate H.)	Belgrave H.	4 45:34.0
1952	D. Tunbridge (Highgate H.)	Woodford Green A.C.	4 38:02.0
1953	F. G. Baily (Polytechnic H.)	Polytechnic H.	4 46:10.0
1954	J. Ljunggren (Sweden)	Belgrave H.	4 32:47.0
1955	A. Johnson (Sheffield U.H.)	Polytechnic H.	4 31:32.0
1956	D. J. Thompson (Metropolitan W.C.)	Belgrave H.	4 24:39.0
1957	D. J. Thompson (Metropolitan W.C.)	Belgrave H.	4 41:48.0
1958	D. J. Thompson (Metropolitan W.C.)	Belgrave H.	4 21:50.0
1959	D. T. Thompson (Metropolitan W.C.)	Metropolitan W.C.	4 12:19.0

A.A.A. CHAMPIONS

2 MILES WALK

			m. s.
1901	G. Deyermond	(Ireland)	14 17.4
1902	W. J. Sturgess	(Polytechnic H.)	14 46.6
1903	E. J. Negus	(Northampton)	14 44.4
1904	G. E. Larner	(Brighton & County H.)	13 57.6
1905	G. E. Larner	(Brighton & County H.)	13 50
1906	A. T. Yeomans	(Swansea A. and C.C.)	14 20.4
1907	H. Harrison	(North Shields Walking C.)	14 01.8
1908	G. E. Larner	(Brighton & County H.)	13 58.4
1909	E. J. Webb	(Herne Hill H.)	13 56.4
1910	E. J. Webb	(Herne Hill H.)	13 54.4
1911	H. V. L. Ross	(Herne Hill H.)	13 55.4
1912	R. Bridge	(Lancashire Walking C.)	13 55.4
1913	R. Bridge	(Lancashire Walking C.)	13 51.8
1914	R. Bridge	(Lancashire Walking C.)	13 57.2
1919	R. Bridge	(Lancashire Walking C.)	14 18.4

ROAD RACING QUIZ

1. Who holds the London to Brighton running record?

*

2. How does this record compare with the walking record over the same route?

QUIZ ANSWERS

1. Gerald Walsh (South Africa) with 5 hrs. 26 mins. 20 secs. on September 28, 1957. 2. D. J. Thompson (Metropolitan Walking Club) returned 7 hrs. 35 mins 12.0 secs. two weeks before.

			m. s.
1936	Y. W. Stone	(Polytechnic H.)	53 21.2
1937	J. Mikaelsson	Sweden	50 19.2
1938	J. Mikaelsson	Sweden	51 48.2
1939	H. W. Churcher	(Belgrave H.)	52 37
1946	L. Hindmar	Sweden	52 30
1947	H. G. Churcher	(Belgrave H.)	52 48.4
1948	H. G. Churcher	(Belgrave H.)	52 23.8
1949	H. G. Churcher	(Belgrave H.)	52 41.8
1950	R. Hardy	(Sheffield United H.)	50 11.6
1951	R. Hardy	(Sheffield United H.)	51 14.6
1952	R. Hardy	(Sheffield United H. & A.C.)	50 05.6
1953	R. Hardy	(Sheffield United H. & A.C.)	51 47
1954	G. W. Coleman	(Highgate Harriers)	51 22.8
1955	R. Hardy	(Sheffield Harriers & A.C.)	53 04.6
1956	G. W. Coleman	(Highgate Harriers)	50 19.0
1957	S. F. Vickers	(Belgrave H.)	51 34.4
1958	S. F. Vickers	(Belgrave H.)	51 10.2

A.A.A. Champions—contd.

			m. s.
1920	C. S. Dowson	(Queen's Park H.)	14 32
1921	J. F. Evans	(Metropolitan Police A.A.)	14 40.2
1922	U. Frigerio	Italy	14 30
1923	G. H. Watts	(Surrey W.C.)	14 24
1924	G. R. Goodwin	(Surrey W.C.)	14 11.2
1925	G. R. Goodwin	(Surrey W.C.)	14 07.4
1926	W. N. Cowley	(Surrey A.C.)	14 32.4
1927	A. H. G. Pope	(Woodford Green A.C.)	14 21.6
1928	A. H. G. Pope	(Woodford Green A.C.)	14 04.8
1929	A. H. G. Pope	(Woodford Green A.C.)	13 57.6
1930	C. W. Hyde	(Enfield A.C.)	13 56.4
1931	A. H. G. Pope	(Woodford Green A.C.)	13 52.6
1932	A. A. Cooper	(Woodford Green A.C.)	13 44.6
1933	A. A. Cooper	(Woodford Green A.C.)	13 39.8
1934	A. A. Cooper	(Woodford Green A.C.)	13 41
1935	A. A. Cooper	(Woodford Green A.C.)	13 46.6
1936	A. A. Cooper	(Woodford Green A.C.)	13 50
1937	A. A. Cooper	(Woodford Green A.C.)	13 58.2
1938	A. A. Cooper	(Woodford Green A.C.)	14 02.2
1939	H. G. Churcher	(Belgrave H.)	13 50
1946	L. Hindmar	Sweden	13 59
1947	L. Hindmar	Sweden	13 54.4
1948	H. G. Churcher	(Belgrave H.)	13 49.3
1949	K. A. Borjesson	Sweden	14 06.6
1950	R. Hardy	(Sheffield United H.)	13 46.8
1951	R. Hardy	(Sheffield United H. & A.C.)	13 43.2
1952	R. Hardy	(Sheffield United H. & A.C.)	13 27.8
1953	G. W. Coleman	(Highgate Harriers)	14 02.2
1954	G. W. Coleman	(Highgate H.)	13 52.0
1955	G. W. Coleman	(Highgate H.)	14 01.0
1956	R. F. Goodall	(Woodford Green A.C.)	14 20.8
1957	S. F. Vickers	(Belgrave H.)	14 05.6
1958	S. F. Vickers	(Belgrave H.)	13 38.4
1959	K. T. Matthews	(R. Sutton Coldfield)	13 19.4

A.A.A. TRACK WALKING CHAMPIONS

4 MILES WALK

			m. s.
1894	H. Curtis	(Highgate H.)	30 05.8
1895	W. J. Sturgess	(Polytechnic H.)	30 17.4
1896	W. J. Sturgess	(Polytechnic H.)	28 57.6
1897	W. J. Sturgess	(Polytechnic H.)	28 24.8
1898	W. J. Sturgess	(Polytechnic H.)	29 10
1899	W. J. Sturgess	(Polytechnic H.)	29 20.6
1900	W. J. Sturgess	(Polytechnic H.)	30 20.8

7 MILES WALK

			m. s.
1880	G. P. Beckley	(London A.C.)	56 40
1881	J. W. Raby	(Elland)	54 48.2
		No other competitor finished	
1882	H. Whyatt	(Notts. Forest F.C.)	55 56.2
1883	H. Whyatt	(Notts. Forest F.C.)	59 15
1884	W. H. Meek	(U.S.A.)	54 27
1885	J. Jervis	(Liverpool H.)	56 10.6
1886	J. H. Jullis	(Finchley H.)	56 30.2
1887	C. W. V. Clarke	(Southampton A.C.)	56 59.8
1888	C. W. V. Clarke	(Southampton A.C.)	57 08.6
1889	W. Wheeler	(Southampton A.C.)	56 29.4
1890	H. Curtis	(Highgate H.)	52 28.4
1891	H. Curtis	(Highgate H.)	54 00.2
1892	H. Curtis	(Highgate H.)	55 56.2
1893	H. Curtis	(Highgate H.)	56 37.2
1894-1900	This event was discontinued.		
1901	J. Butler	(Polytechnic H.)	54 37
1902	W. J. Sturgess	(Polytechnic H.)	52 49.4
1903	J. Butler	(Polytechnic H.)	56 17.2
1904	G. E. Larner	(Brighton & County H.)	52 57.4
1905	G. E. Larner	(Brighton & County H.)	52 34
1906	F. T. Carter	(Queen's Park H.)	53 20.2
1907	F. B. Thompson	(London, A.C.)	52 46.6
1908	E. J. Webb	(Herne Hill H.)	53 2.6
1909	E. J. Webb	(Herne Hill H.)	52 37
1910	E. J. Webb	(Herne Hill H.)	51 37
1911	G. E. Larner	(Polytechnic H.)	52 8
1912	R. Bridge	(Lancashire Walking C.)	52 45.6
1913	R. Bridge	(Lancashire Walking C.)	52 8.4
	H. V. L. Ross	(Herne Hill H.)	52 8.4
1914	R. Bridge	(Lancashire Walking C.)	52 32
1919	W. Hehir	(Surrey A.C.)	53 23.6
1920	C. S. Dowson	(Queen's Park H.)	53 50
1921	H. V. L. Ross	(Herne Hill H.)	55 48.6
1922	G. H. Watts	(Surrey W.C.)	53 24.2
1923	G. H. Watts	(Surrey W.C.)	54 35.4
1924	G. R. Goodwin	(Surrey W.C.)	52 0.6
1925	G. H. Watts	(Surrey W.C.)	52 53.8
1926	G. R. Goodwin	(Surrey A.C.)	53 56
1927	W. N. Cowley	(Enfield A.C.)	56 46.4
1928	C. W. Hyde	(Enfield A.C.)	55 46.2
1929	C. W. Hyde	(Enfield A.C.)	53 38.6
1930	C. W. Hyde	(Enfield A.C.)	53 32.4
1931	U. Frigerio	Italy	54 09.0
1932	A. H. G. Pope	(Woodford Green A.C.)	51 25.6
1933	L. F. Johnson	(Enfield A.C.)	53 1.6
1934	L. F. Johnson	(Enfield A.C.)	52 10.2
1935	H. A. Hake	(Surrey W.C.)	53 48

WORLD RECORDS†

3,000 METRES WALK—MEN*

min. secs.				
12:53.8	G. Rasmussen	Denmark	7.7.1918	Copenhagen, Denmark
12:38.2	A. A. Cooper	G.B. & N.I.	20.7.1935	London, England
12:36.0	C. Jonning	Sweden	23.8.1936	Mjolby, Sweden
12:34.2	J. F. Mikaelsson	Sweden	13.7.1937	Copenhagen, Denmark
12:23.8	E. H. Bruun	Norway	23.9.1937	Oslo, Norway
12:19.0	J. F. Mikaelsson	Sweden	5.9.1942	Malmö, Sweden
12:10.4	G. H. W. Hardmo	Sweden	25.8.1943	Orebro, Sweden
12:02.2	G. H. W. Hardmo	Sweden	8.9.1943	Stockholm, Sweden
11:59.8	G. H. W. Hardmo	Sweden	22.7.1944	Uppsala, Sweden
11:56.0	G. H. W. Hardmo	Sweden	21.8.1945	Tibro, Sweden
11:51.8	G. H. W. Hardmo	Sweden	1.9.1945	Malmö, Sweden

2 MILES WALK—MEN

13:11.4	G. E. Larner	G.B. & N.I.	13.7.1904	Manchester, England
13:09.8	G. H. W. Hardmo	Sweden	18.6.1943	Vasteras, Sweden
13:05.2	G. H. W. Hardmo	Sweden	26.9.1943	Orebro, Sweden
13:00.8	G. H. W. Hardmo	Sweden	28.6.1944	Stockholm, Sweden
13:00.0	G. H. W. Hardmo	Sweden	17.7.1944	Malmö, Sweden
12:54.0	G. H. W. Hardmo	Sweden	19.7.1945	Landskrona, Sweden
12:45.0	G. H. W. Hardmo	Sweden	1.9.1945	Malmö, Sweden

5,000 METRES WALK—MEN

24:35.8	T. Bildt	Sweden	30.7.1911	Stockholm, Sweden
21:59.8	G. Rasmussen	Denmark	6.7.1918	Copenhagen, Denmark
21:59.0	A. T. Schwab	Switzerland	30.5.1931	Riga, Latvia
21:52.4	A. A. Cooper	G.B. & N.I.	14.9.1935	London, England
21:49.2	J. F. Mikaelsson	Sweden	13.9.1936	Kristinehamn, Sweden
21:42.0	E. H. Bruun	Norway	16.6.1937	Oslo, Norway
21:14.0	J. F. Mikaelsson	Sweden	13.7.1937	Copenhagen, Denmark
21:02.8	E. H. Bruun	Norway	26.9.1937	Oslo, Norway
20:55.8	J. F. Mikaelsson	Sweden	5.9.1942	Malmö, Sweden
20:31.6	G. H. W. Hardmo	Sweden	4.9.1943	Malmö, Sweden
20:26.8	G. H. W. Hardmo	Sweden	31.7.1945	Kumla, Sweden

5 MILES WALK—MEN

35:43.4	H. G. Churcher	G.B. & N.I.	5.6.1948	Motspur Park, England
35:33.0	H. G. Churcher	G.B. & N.I.	16.6.1949	London, England
35:24.0	R. G. Hardy	G.B. & N.I.	4.8.1951	London, England
35:15.0	R. G. Hardy	G.B. & N.I.	31.5.1952	London, England
35:00.0	J. Dolezal	Czechoslovakia	4.5.1955	Tabor, Czechoslovakia
34:32.8	J. Dolezal	Czechoslovakia	15.10.1955	Manchester, England

10,000 METRES WALK—MEN

46:28.3	G. H. Goulding	Canada	11.7.1912	Toronto, Canada
45:26.4	G. Rasmussen	Denmark	18.8.1918	Copenhagen, Denmark
44:42.4	A. H. G. Pope	G.B. & N.I.	31.8.1932	London, England
43:52.0	E. H. Bruun	Norway	25.6.1937	Oslo, Norway
43:25.2	E. H. Bruun	Norway	26.9.1937	Oslo, Norway
43:21.4	G. H. W. Hardmo	Sweden	29.8.1943	Vaxjo, Sweden
42:47.8	G. H. W. Hardmo	Sweden	19.9.1943	Mariestad, Sweden
42:39.6	G. H. W. Hardmo	Sweden	9.9.1945	Kumla, Sweden
42:18.3	G. Panichkin	U.S.S.R.	7.5.1958	Stalinabad, U.S.S.R.
41:35.0*	G. Panichkin	U.S.S.R.	15.9.1959	Krasnodar, U.S.S.R.

7 MILES WALK—MEN

50:50.8	G. E. Larner	G.B. & N.I.	30.9.1905	London, England
50:40.8	G. H. Goulding	Canada	23.10.1915	New York, U.S.A.
50:28.8	A. H. G. Pope	G.B. & N.I.	31.8.1932	London, England
50:19.2	J. F. Mikaelsson	Sweden	3.4.1937	London, England
49:59.2	G. H. W. Hardmo	Sweden	13.9.1942	Kumla, Sweden
49:21.2	J. F. Mikaelsson	Sweden	27.9.1942	Kristinehamn, Sweden
49:04.6	G. H. W. Hardmo	Sweden	10.9.1944	Kumla, Sweden
48:53.6	G. H. W. Hardmo	Sweden	1.10.1944	Orebro, Sweden
48:36.4	J. F. Mikaelsson	Sweden	1.9.1945	Stockholm, Sweden
48:15.2	G. H. W. Hardmo	Sweden	9.9.1945	Kumla, Sweden

WALKING 1 HOUR—MEN

Mls.	Yds.				
8	438	G. E. Larner	G.B. & N.I.	30.9.1905	London, England
8	474	A. H. G. Pope	G.B. & N.I.	31.8.1932	London, England
8	535	F. Schwab	Switzerland	9.8.1941	Berlin, Germany
8	744	J. F. Mikaelsson	Sweden	5.10.1941	Kumla, Sweden
8	785	G. H. W. Hardmo	Sweden	8.10.1944	Arvika, Sweden
8	1,025	J. F. Mikaelsson	Sweden	1.9.1945	Stockholm, Sweden
8	1,294	G. Panichkin	U.S.S.R.	9.5.1958	Stalinabad, U.S.S.R.

15,000 METRES WALK—MEN

1h. 9:04.8	A. T. Schwab	Switzerland	20.6.1935	Oslo, Norway
1h. 8:28.0	D. Paraschivescu	Roumania	20.3.1949	Bucarest, Roumania
1h. 8:08.0	B. Junk	U.S.S.R.	11.9.1951	Kkarkov, U.S.S.R.
1h. 7:54.0	J. Dolezal	Czecho-slovakia	1.11.1953	Stará Boleslav, Czechoslovakia

1h. 5:59.6	J. Dolezal	Czechoslovakia	30.4.1954	Stará Boleslav, Czechoslovakia
1h. 5:45.8	L. Spirin	U.S.S.R.	7.5.1957	Moscow, U.S.S.R.
1h. 5:18.0	L. Spirin	U.S.S.R.	24.9.1957	Dnepropetrovsk, U.S.S.R.

10 MILES WALK—MEN

1h. 15:57.4	G. E. Larner	G.B. & N.I.	17.7.1908	London, England
1h. 14:30.6	F. J. Redman	G.B. & N.I.	26.5.1934	London, England
1h. 13:59.4	J. F. Mikaelsson	Sweden	2.9.1939	Sundbyberg, Sweden
1h. 13:03.8	J. F. Mikaelsson	Sweden	30.8.1942	Soderhamn, Sweden
1h. 11:58.0	C. H. W. Hardmo	Sweden	8.10.1944	Arvika, Sweden
1h. 10:55.8	J. F. Mikaelsson	Sweden	23.8.1945	Stockholm, Sweden
1h. 10:45.8	J. Dolezal	Czechoslovakia	30.4.1954	Stará Boleslav, Czechoslovakia

20,000 METRES WALK—MEN

1h. 39:22.0	N. Peterson	Denmark	30.6.1918	Copenhagen, Denmark
1h. 39:20.4	A. Valente	Italy	2.12.1926	Bologna, Italy
1h. 38:53.2	A. Callegari	Italy	26.12.1926	Milan, Italy
1h. 37:42.2	D. Pavesi	Italy	23.10.1927	Milan, Italy
1h. 36:34.4	A. Valente	Italy	25.10.1930	Genoa, Italy
1h. 34:26.0	J. Dalinsh	Latvia	1.6.1933	Riga, Latvia
1h. 32:28.4	J. F. Mikaelsson	Sweden	12.7.1942	Vaxjo, Sweden
1h. 30:26.4	J. Dolezal	Czechoslovakia	1.11.1953	Stará Boleslav, Czechoslovakia
1h. 30:02.8	V. Golubnichiy	U.S.S.R.	2.10.1955	Kiev, U.S.S.R.
1h. 28:45.2	L. Spirin	U.S.S.R.	13.6.1956	Kiev, U.S.S.R.
1h. 27:58.2	M. Lavrov	U.S.S.R.	13.8.1956	Moscow, U.S.S.R.
1h. 27:38.6	G. Panichkin	U.S.S.R.	9.5.1958	Stalinabad, U.S.S.R.
1h. 27:05.0	V. Golubrichiy	U.S.S.R.	23.9.1958	Simfyeropd, U.S.S.R.
1h. 26:31.2*	V. Golubrichiy	U.S.S.R.	15.9.1959	Krasnodar, U.S.S.R.

WALKING 2 HOURS—MEN

Miles	Yards				
15	128	H. V. L. Ross	G.B. & N.I.	20.5.1911	Liverpool, England
15	147	A. Valente	Italy	28.9.1930	Paris, France
15	768	J. Dalinsh	Latvia	1.6.1933	Riga, Latvia
15	1,228	E. Bruun	Norway	8.10.1939	Kristinehamn, Sweden
15	1,521	O. Andersson	Sweden	15.9.1941	Stockholm, Sweden
15	1,591	J. Dolezal	Czechoslovakia	12.10.1952	Prague, Czechoslovakia
15	1,707	J. Dolezal	Czechoslovakia	14.5.1955	Stará Boleslav, Czechoslovakia
16	126	A. Vedjakov	U.S.S.R.	7.10.1955	Moscow, U.S.S.R.
16	403	E. J. Allsopp	Australia	22.9.1956	Melbourne, Australia

30,000 METRES WALK—MEN

2h. 37:18.2	H. Muller	Germany	11.9.1921	Munich, Germany
2h. 30:33.6	H. Schmidt	Germany	27.4.1941	Hamburg, Germany
2h. 28:57.4	H. Olsson	Sweden	15.8.1943	Boras, Sweden
2h. 27:46.6	S. Laszlo	Hungary	18.5.1952	Budapest, Hungary
2h. 27:42.0	J. Ljunggren	Sweden	3.8.1952	Varnamo, Sweden
2h. 21:38.6	J. Dolezal	Czechoslovakia	12.10.1952	Prague, Czechoslovakia
2h. 20:40.2	A. Vedjakov	U.S.S.R.	7.10.1955	Moscow, U.S.S.R.
2h. 19:43.0	A. Vedjakov	U.S.S.R.	23.8.1958	Moscow, U.S.S.R.

20 MILES WALK—MEN

2h. 47:52.0	T. Griffiths	G.B. & N.I.	30.12.1870	London, England
2h. 43:38.0	A. E. Plumb	G.B. & N.I.	7.5.1932	Birmingham, England
2h. 41:07.0	H. Olsson	Sweden	15.8.1943	Boras, Sweden
2h. 39:22.8	J. Ljunggren	Sweden	3.8.1952	Varnamo, Sweden
2h. 33:09.4	J. Dolezal	Czechoslovakia	14.5.1954	Stará Boleslav, Czechoslovakia
2h. 31:33.0	A. Vedjakov	U.S.S.R.	23.8.1958	Moscow, U.S.S.R.

30 MILES WALK—MEN

4h. 29:31.8	H. H. Whitlock	G.B. & N.I.	5.10.1935	London, England
4h. 24:54.2	F. Cornet	France	11.10.1942	Paris, France
4h. 21:38.2	J. Ljunggren	Sweden	29.7.1951	Gislaved, Sweden
4h. 21:12.6	A. Roka	Hungary	1.6.1952	Budapest, Hungary
4h. 21:11.0	J. Ljunggren	Sweden	8.8.1953	Fristad, Sweden
4h. 20:10.6	A. Roka	Hungary	30.10.1955	Budapest, Hungary
4h. 16:14.8	M. Skront	Czechoslovakia	30.4.1956	Krnov, Czechoslovakia
4h. 12:03.4	L. Moc	Czechoslovakia	21.6.1956	Prague, Czechoslovakia
4h. 07:11.0	S. A. Lobastov	U.S.S.R.	23.8.1958	Moscow, U.S.S.R.

50,000 METRES WALK—MEN

4h. 34:03.3	P. Sievert	Germany	5.10.1924	Munich, Germany
4h. 32:52.0	J. Ljunggren	Sweden	29.7.1951	Gislaved, Sweden
4h. 31:21.6	A. Roka	Hungary	1.6.1952	Budapest, Hungary
4h. 29:58.0	J. Ljunggren	Sweden	8.8.1953	Fristad, Sweden
4h. 27:28.4	L. Moc	Czechoslovakia	13.10.1955	Znojme, Czechoslovakia
4h. 26:05.2	M. Skront	Czechoslovakia	30.4.1956	Krnov, Czechoslovakia
4h. 21:07.0	L. Moc	Czechoslovakia	21.6.1956	Prague, Czechoslovakia
4h. 16:08.6	S. A. Lobastov	U.S.S.R.	28.8.1958	Moscow, U.S.S.R.

† At the I.A.A.F. Congress of August 1958 it was decided that records at distances below 20,000 metres (12m. 752yds.) would no longer be recognised.
* Unratified as at Oct. 1, 1959.

ROAD RACING QUIZ

1. Which is the oldest of the official British track walking records, and who holds it?

*

2. Road walkers who achieve 100 miles or over in 24 hrs. are elected to the "Centurion Club". What is the fastest time this distance has been walked?

QUIZ ANSWERS

1. The 3 and 4 mile records set up in Brighton by G. E. Larner on August 19, 1905. 2. 17 hrs. 35 mins. 40.0 secs. by T. W. Richardson at Bradford on September 18-19, 1936.

Compiled by **H. White**
Hon. Secretary: British Crown Green Amateur Bowling Association

Crown Green Bowls

THE STORY OF CROWN GREEN BOWLS

It has been claimed in authoritative circles that the number of actual participants in the game of bowls exceeds the number of players in any other sport.

It would, however, be difficult to draw accurate comparisons between the numbers engaged in the crown green game and the flat green or rink game, but the combined totals are believed to number well into seven figures.

The crown green game is regarded as being confined almost entirely to the North and Midlands, but in some of these areas the activities of the bowling fraternity are such that the predominance of the game is unmistakable.

As might be expected in such a wide field, there are varying types of competitions which cater for both the team bowler and the ambitious individualist, but while the popularity of some of the individual tournaments cannot be disputed, by far the greater majority of competitive bowlers have engagements with their clubs which occupy them in team play for most of the season.

The principal authority governing amateur crown green bowls, the British Crown Green Amateur Bowling Association, in addition to its controlling capacity, organises the inter-county championship tournament in which nine counties compete.

The tournament is divided into two sections, Northern and Southern, and the winners of the two sections play off in the championship final, the winners receiving the Crosfield Cup, while the runners-up hold the consolation trophy, the Lewis Cup.

Since the inauguration of the championship tournament in 1908, a year after the British Crown Green Association was founded, the Northern counties have almost completely dominated the situation, with Lancashire as the outstanding county.

The success of the County Palatine in the 1959 tournament brought their total of Crosfield Cup wins to twenty, and their eighth since the competition was re-introduced in 1946, after a lapse of six years during the Second World War.

Lancashire's nearest rivals are Cheshire with twelve championship wins to their credit, while Yorkshire come next in line with nine successes.

Staffordshire are the only county at present in the Southern section to have gained championship honours; they have won the Crosfield Cup three times, but their last success dates back to 1938, their two previous wins being in 1929 and 1932.

It is believed, however, that a Staffordshire player holds the record for the number of appearances in county championship games. George Howells, the veteran Staffordshire bowler, known throughout the crown green world, recently made his hundredth appearance for Staffordshire, and in a match played in his honour, one of the sides was fittingly selected by another centurion in a different field of sport, Billy Wright, the former Wolves and England captain.

Staffordshire can also boast of having provided the first winner of the British Crown Green Individual Championship Tournament in E. Peers.

This competition, which is regarded as the highlight of amateur crown green bowls, was instituted by the British Crown Green Amateur Bowling Association in 1910, and is now the main feature of the bowling calendar.

The event is a regular August Bank Holiday Monday fixture, and is held in each county in turn in accordance with an agreed rota.

The sixty-four contestants qualify by virtue of having reached the quarter-finals of their respective county merit competitions.

The county in which the event happens to be staged have eight representatives, and the remaining eight counties each get seven

131

BOWLS QUIZ

1. What is the regulation size of a bowling green?

★

2. What is the minimum distance that a bowl can be played and count?

★

3. Is there a regulation size or weight of jack or bowl?

★

4. Is a player compelled to tell his opponent with what bias he has played?

QUIZ ANSWERS

1. There is no stipulation as to the size of a bowling green, but the laws of the game state that it shall be deemed "not a mark" if the jack comes to rest less than 21 yards from the footer, the measurement to be taken from the centre of the footer to the centre of the jack. The most popular size of a bowling green is in the region of 40 yards square. 2. The rule, amended in 1959, states: A bowl must be played at least three yards from the footer to count. The rule was amended to remove all doubt as to the position when both the opponent's bowls had been played off the green. 3. Standard jacks must be of two full bias and weigh not less than twenty ounces, and not more than twenty-three ounces. The minimum diameter that is permitted in accordance with rule is 3¾ in., and the maximum 3⅞ in. 4. The leader of the jack, having given his opponent (in accordance with rule) an opportunity of seeing his delivery, shall not be compelled to tell his opponent with what bias he has bowled the jack.

---

places; the lowest scorer in each of the eight quarter-finals being omitted.

As in the inter-county team championship, Lancashire head the list of winners in the individual tournament, but the successes registered by Red Rose representatives in this event have not been so pronounced as in the former.

Of the forty-four British Individual Championships so far, twelve have been won by Lancashire players, Cheshire come close behind with eleven winners, Staffordshire have provided seven champions and Yorkshire six; while Shropshire are credited with having had three title-holders. Warwickshire and Worcestershire, a combined force, and North Wales, each have had two successes and Derbyshire one.

It is worthy of note that George Howells, previously referred to, is numbered among Staffordshire's seven former champions.

The outstanding performance in this tournament, however, is undoubtedly the triple win of Lancashire's Joe Gleave, the famous Warrington bowler. He won the title in 1923, 1928 and 1934, and now, in 1959, although in his seventies, Gleave still figures prominently in competitive bowls.

Probably two of the most noted "Open Handicaps" in the North are the two Blackpool tournaments, the "Talbot" and the "Waterloo." Each event is limited to an entry of 1,024, with play taking place each week-day for approximately six weeks to determine the eight competitors to contest the grand finals in October.

INTER-COUNTY CHAMPIONSHIP

	Winners	Runners-up
1908	Lancashire	Yorkshire
1909	Lancashire	Yorkshire
1910	Cheshire	Yorkshire
1911	Cheshire	Yorkshire
1912	Lancashire	Yorkshire
1913	Cheshire	Staffordshire
1914	Lancashire	Yorkshire
1915	Cheshire	Lancashire
1916	Lancashire	Cheshire
1919	Lancashire	Yorkshire
1920	Cheshire	Lancashire
1921	Cheshire	Yorkshire
1922	Lancashire	Cheshire
1923	Yorkshire	Lancashire & Cheshire (tied)
1924	Cheshire	Lancashire
1925	Yorkshire	Warwick & Worcester
1926	Lancashire	Warwick & Worcester
1927	Yorkshire	Staffordshire
1928	Lancashire	Staffordshire
1929	Staffordshire	Warwick & Worcester
1930	Yorkshire	Staffordshire
1931	Yorkshire	Staffordshire
1932	Staffordshire	Yorkshire
1933	Lancashire	Staffordshire
1934	Lancashire	Warwick & Worcester
1935	Lancashire	Staffordshire
1936	Yorkshire	Staffordshire
1937	Yorkshire	Staffordshire
1938	Staffordshire	Cheshire
1939	Cheshire	Warwick & Worcester
1940–45	No contest	
1946	Cheshire	Staffordshire
1947	Lancashire	Staffordshire
1948	Lancashire	Staffordshire
1949	Yorkshire	Warwick & Worcester
1950	Cheshire	Staffordshire
1951	Lancashire	Warwick & Worcester
1952	Lancashire	Staffordshire
1953	Cheshire	Warwick & Worcester
1954	Lancashire	Shropshire
1955	Cheshire	Warwick & Worcester
1956	Lancashire	Warwick & Worcester
1957	Yorkshire	Shropshire
1958	Lancashire	Staffordshire
1959	Lancashire	North Wales

BRITISH CROWN GREEN INDIVIDUAL CHAMPIONSHIP

Winners

1910 E. Peers, Staffordshire
1911 J. Stead, Yorkshire
1912 T. Dale, Cheshire
1913 J. Chester, Cheshire
1914 A. Robinson, Staffordshire
1915 J. Charnock, Lancashire
1916 S. Sackville, Lancashire
1917 J. Gough, Staffordshire
1918 T. B. Burgess, Cheshire
1919 J. Charnock, Lancashire
1920 W. Twist, Lancashire
1921 F. Dickinson, Yorkshire
1922 John Gleave, Lancashire
1923 Joe Gleave, Lancashire
1924 E. Blackledge, Lancashire
1925 F. Bentley, Lancashire
1926 A. Booth, Yorkshire
1927 P. Ainscough, Cheshire
1928 Joe Gleave, Lancashire
1929 J. Gough, Staffordshire
1930 G. A. Fielding, Yorkshire
1931 J. Fort, Yorkshire
1932 C. Garside, Derbyshire
1933 J. Eyes, Cheshire
1934 Joe Gleave, Lancashire
1935 J. W. Pickering, Shropshire
1936 G. Howells, Staffordshire
1937 W. Garrard, Cheshire
1938 J. Davies, Cheshire
1939 W. H. Garside, Cheshire
1940–45 No contest

1946	B. Longbottom, Yorkshire	1953	W. Slater, Staffordshire
1947	H. King, Lancashire	1954	N. Norris, Cheshire
1948	R. G. Meyrick, Shropshire	1955	H. Burgess, Cheshire
1949	A. Bebbington, Cheshire	1956	E. Fish, Shropshire
1950	J. Barnsley, Warwick & Worcester	1957	N. Hardman, Lancashire
1951	J. Pilling, Lancashire	1958	C. Littlehales, North Wales
1952	A. A. Shore, Warwick & Worcester	1959	E. Ashton, North Wales

THE "TALBOT" BOWLING HANDICAP

Year	Winners	Runners-up
1882	Thomas Hart	T. Barron
1883	W. Parker	J. Green
1884	R. Barlow & J. Butler (divided)	
1885	T. Carter	T. Wilson
1886	J. Rothwell	H. Brocklebank
1887	T. Salisbury	H. Baines
1888	D. Greenhalgh	W. Bromilow
1889	J. Bowden	J. Hilton
1890	D. Greenhalgh	W. H. Law
1891	H. Rutter	H. Brocklebank
1892	Wm. Balmer	J. Seddon
1893	John Peace	D. Greenhalgh
1894	Thos. Berry	W. Hopwood
1895	Gerard Hart	A. Sugden
1896	R. Mather	Ed. Barton
1897	Thos. Meadows	I. Rothwell
1898	Thos. Hayes	C. Hudson
1899	John Peace	J. Aspinall
1900	Ed. Barton	G. Beatty
1901	James Platt	H. Fairhurst
1902	James Ward	H. Dootson
1903	W. Fairhurst	E. Wolstenholme
1904	C. Farrington	Eli Yates
1905	M. Sharples	G. Beatty
1906	W. Taylor	G. Hart
1907	J. Bagot	J. Cross
1908	S. Massey	T. Barlow
1909	W. H. Law	R. Mawdesley
1910	R. Hart	L. Banks
1911	F. Threlfall	T. Meadows
1912	Rd. Birchall	John Wilson
1913	H. Southern	T. Hilton
1914	J. Bromilow	Joe Ward
1915	T. Richardson	T. Roscoe
1916	R. Johnson	R. Cowburn
1917	G. F. Hampson	W. Simms
1918	Eli Yates	H. Waddicor
1919	Ed. Whiteside	W. Finch
1920	L. Banks	D. Jacks
1921	F. Threlfall	L. Appleton
1922	W. Finch	W. A. Smith
1923	J. Farnworth	F. Whitehead
1924	Tom Rose	J. Leach
1925	Jack Cox	T. Lowe
1926	G. Beswick	J. Winstanley
1927	T. Monks	J. Barlow
1928	G. Beswick	F. Wolstencroft
1929	W. R. Hardy	R. Pendlebury
1930	H. Walkden	T. Suttie
1931	R. Pendlebury	T. Edwards
1932	Jas. Heyes	T. Monks
1933	T. Turner	R. Turner
1934	H. Hardman	G. Leach
1935	H. Bury	T. Kenyon
1936	W. Grace	P. Flynn
1937	G. Lomax	J. Hart
1938	W. Molyneux	J. Ball
1939	(Abandoned)	
1940	W. J. Wilcock	G. Butterworth
At No. 3 Hotel		
1941	J. Edmondson	T. Moore
At Raikes Hotel		
1942	Geo. Croker	R. Spencer
1943	F. Gillett	R. Singleton
1944	W. Ashton	J. Clegg
1945	J. Jolly	L. McGuirk
1946	A. Raby	J. Wilcock
1947	R. Thomas	H. Whittaker
1948	J. H. Hill	W. Molyneux
1949	J. Molyneux	E. Cleaver
1950	J. Wolstencroft	T. Smith
1951	W. Parr	F. Thomas
At Talbot Hotel		
1952	J. Timmins	R. Collier
1953	J. Molyneux	F. Hill
1954	H. Wallwork	S. Casson
1955	W. Simm	J. Cunliffe
1956	J. Rothwell	R. Peat
1957	J. E. Ball	W. Lacey
1958	R. Mercer	W. E. Dabbs

THE "WATERLOO" BOWLING HANDICAP

1907	John Rothwell	T. Richardson
1908	Geo. Beatty	James Southern
1909	Tom Meadows	W. H. Andrews
1910	No handicap	
1911	John Peace	F. Walmsley
1912	Thos. Lowe	C. Farrington
1913	Gerard Hart	R. Hart
1914	John Rothwell	F. Percival
1915	W. Fairhurst	W. Simms
1916	J. Parkinson	E. Hall
1917	Geo. Barnes	H. Hemingway
1918	W. Simms	J. Pimblett
1919	Len Moss	T. Richardson

132

Year	Winners		Runners-up
1920	E. Whiteside		
1921	J. Bagot		D. Brown
1922	W. A. Smith		Walter Guest
1923	J. Martin		Geo. Barnes
1924	Rowland Hill		Geo. Barnes
1925	Jack Cox		R. Banks
1926	T. Roscoe		T. Whittle
1927	H. Waddecar		T. Cornwell
1928	T. Whittle		Seth Mason
1929	Chas. Halpin		J. Meadows
1930	J. Chadwick		J. Hart
1931	A. Gleave		W. Park
1932	T. E. Booth		W. Grace
1933	A. Ogden		T. Davies
1934	W. Derbyshire		R. Thomas
1935	C. Roberts		W. Hargreaves
1936	H. Yates		R. Thomas
1937	A. King		F. Wolstencroft
1938	J. W. Whitter		T. Suttie
			D. Jacks

Year	Winner	Runner-up
1939	(Abandoned)	
1940	H. Holden	J. Swithenbank
1941	W. J. Wilcock	W. Finch
1942	T. Bimson	J. Ormond
1943	S. Ivell	J. Stevenson
1944	T. Tinker	T. Richardson
1945	W. Grace	D. Aryton
1946	C. Parkinson	T. Bimson
1947	W. Dalton	R. Robinson
1948	A. E. Ringrose	W. Darbyshire
1949	J. Egan	J. Lawton
1950	H. Finch	W. Green
1951	J. Waterhouse	T. Bimson
1952	L. Thompson	W. Worthington
1953	B. Kelly	H. Tabener
1954	B. Kelly	A. Holden
1955	J. Heyes	G. Bromley
1956	J. Sumner	H. Pennington
1957	W. Lacy	T. Bimson
1958	F. Salisbury	W. Carter

Compiled by Howard Bass
Editor: The Skater and Skier

Curling

Although the sport is believed by some historians to have originated in Holland some four hundred years ago, curling has certainly been most popular in Scotland, the centre of its development since the early seventeenth century. The international legislative body, the Royal Caledonian Curling Club, was formed in 1838 as the Grand Caledonian Curling Club, the title of "Royal" being granted four years later after the game had been demonstrated to Queen Victoria and Prince Albert on the polished floor of the drawing room in the Palace of Scone. The Prince Consort, who was then presented with a pair of curling stones, consented to become patron of the club and was succeeded in this office by subsequent British monarchs.

The game in many ways resembles bowls, with the basic difference that whinstone or granite stones on ice instead of wooden balls on turf are the main implements used. The rules provide that these disc-shaped curling stones with smoothly curved edges shall not exceed 44 pounds in weight or 36 inches in circumference, nor must they be of less height than one-eighth of the circumference. The two flat sides or soles of each well-polished stone are designed so that one is more suitable for use on hard ice and the other on soft ice. Modern stones are named after the districts in which they are quarried, some of the best known being Ailsa Craigs, Burnocks, Carsphairn Reds and Crawfordjohns. Each stone is fitted at the top with a detachable metal handle, with which it is propelled along a marked channel of ice, known as the rink, towards a fixed point called the tee, round which a circle of seven feet radius is drawn. As in bowls, there is a tee at either end, 38 yards apart.

Each side, also termed a rink, comprises four players, who each use two stones and play them alternately with his opponent. Each stone is played from a point known as the "hack" or "crampit" on a line called the foot-score (four yards behind each tee). A stone not clearing the "hog-score," a line seven yards from the tee, is called a "hog" and removed from the rink. When all sixteen stones have been played, each stone lying nearer the tee than an opposing stone scores a point and, after the scores are counted, the game proceeds from the opposite end and so on until an agreed number of "ends" or "heads" have been completed under the jurisdiction of an umpire.

In a crouching position the player swings his stone backwards, regulating the power of his shot according to the extent of swing and subsequent follow-through movement. As he "soles" the stone on to the ice, the bias or "curl" is achieved by the manner and extent of its being twisted at the moment of delivery. An inward twist of the handle imparts a swerve to the left, an outward twist a swerve to the right, so that the stone actually rotates on its journey to the tee and accordingly curls to the right or left as it finally slows to a stop.

Each side is directed by a captain, known as the "skip," from the tee end of the rink, one of his team temporarily taking over this responsible task while the skip plays his own stones. Under the skip's directions the ice may be swept with special brooms in front of a moving stone, without touching it, from the middle of the rink to the tee. This sweeping, usually called "sooping," forms an important part of the game and provides much excitement as two sweepers frantically steer the rotating stone by diligently and feverishly polishing the ice just ahead in order to adjust its speed or direction.

Sooping, in certain conditions, will take a stone an extra five or six yards. Without sooping, its progress would be slowed down by ice dust or, if outdoors, by snow flakes.

To the uninitiated the game as a spectacle may at first look uninteresting and the sooping somewhat amusing, but once it has been played the skill of curling holds for most an ever-increasing fascination and is played by young and old alike.

The technique of delivering the stone and the moment of releasing it and the process of positioning the stones around the tee ("building up the head") are tasks calling for much subtlety and tactical planning which constantly intrigue the enthusiast.

Often called "the roaring game" because of the sound made by the stones as they speed towards the tee, curling has claimed a keen following among women and a Ladies Challenge Trophy is annually contested in Scotland, where the sport is practised regularly at ten indoor, artificially refrigerated rinks.

Outside Scotland, the game has developed especially in Canada, the Strathcona Cup matches between Scotland and Canada being a regular highlight of the fixture list. The Royal Caledonian Curling Club has affiliated members in Australia, Canada, China, France, New Zealand, Sweden, Switzerland and U.S.A.

The sport flourishes on many outdoor ice rinks at Swiss winter sports resorts, where special rinks are used exclusively by the local curling clubs and not for other ice sports. Competitions or "bonspiels" (matches between several clubs) often attract a considerable spectator following.

Curling has been slow to capture interest in England, partly due to much precious ice time being monopolised by skaters, but the game has won a marked support now at Manchester and Richmond.

No particular clothing is specified beyond the fact that the footwear, usually rubber soled and of material to give suitable warmth, must not have spikes or other contrivance which may break or damage the surface of the ice.

Bibliography: Annuals of the Royal Caledonian Curling Club, *Winter Sports* (The Skater and Skier) magazine.

STRATHCONA CUP WINNERS

Year		Year	
1903	Canada	1926*	Scotland
1909*	Canada	1938	Canada
1912	Canada	1949	Canada
1921*	Scotland	1950*	Scotland
1923	Canada	1957	Canada

(* Matches played in Scotland; the remainder in Canada)

CURLING QUIZ

1. How many players are there in a side?

★

2. What is a team captain usually called?

★

3. Name the trophy regularly contested between Canada and Scotland.

★

4. What is the maximum weight of a stone permitted?

★

5. When is a stone called a "hog"?

★

6. Name the sport's internationally recognised administrative authority.

QUIZ ANSWERS

1. Four. 2. The "skip". 3. Strathcona Cup. 4. 44 pounds. 5. When it stops more than seven yards short of the tee. 6. The Royal Caledonian Curling Club.

Cycling

Compiled by **H. H. England**

Consulting Editor: Cycling and Mopeds

CYCLING QUIZ

1. Who holds the record of world titles?

★

2. Which of these three has the unique distinction?

★

3. Who had the longest period of world championship racing?

★

4. Which sprinters have won a hat trick, or more, of world championships?

★

5. Recall any other hat tricks in the world series?

★

6. How many world titles have been won by Britain?

QUIZ ANSWERS

1. Leon Meredith of Britain (seven amateur paced 100 km. titles), T. Ellegaard of Denmark (seven professional sprints) and Scherens of Belgium (seven professional sprints). 2. Jeff Scherens, who won six of his titles in a row (1932-37). 3. Arie Van Vliet of Holland whose record ran from 1934 to 1957. In the amateur series he was second in 1934 and 1935, and won in 1936. He was second in the professional series in 1937, won in 1938; 3rd in 1946; won in 1948; 3rd in 1949; won in 1950; won again in 1953; second in 1954; 3rd in 1955 and second in 1957. 4. (Amateur) W. J. Bailey, England, 1909-11; (Professional) T. Ellegaard, Denmark, 1901-3; P. Moeskops, Holland, 1921-24; L. Michard, France, 1927-30; J. Scherens, 1932-37; Reg Harris, 1949-51. 5. (Pro. pursuit) Messina, Italy, 1954-56; (Motor-paced pro. 100 kms.) G. Parent, France, 1909-11; A. Verschueren, Belgium 1952-54; (Paced amateur 100 kms.) Leon Meredith, 1907-9. 6. Thirty-one. (Professional sprint) Reg Harris, 1949-51 and 1954; (Amateur sprint) T. Summersgill, 1899; A. L. Reed, 1903; J. S. Benyon, 1905; V. L. Johnson, 1908; W. J. Bailey, 1909-11 and 1913; H. T. Johnson, 1922; Reg Harris, 1947; Cyril Peacock 1954. (Amateur pursuit) Norman Sheil, 1955 and 1958; (Motor-paced pro. 100 kms.) J. Michael, 1895; A. A. Chase, 1896; W. Stocks, 1897; R. Palmer, 1898. (Paced, amateur, 100 kms.) E. Gould, 1897; A. J. Cherry, 1898; Leon Meredith, 1904, 1905, 1907, 1908, 1909, 1911 and 1913. (Road, amateur) David Marsh, 1922.

Jeff Scherens (Belgium)

Cyril Peacock

Reg Harris

INTRODUCTION

The most sensational performance in modern cycling prowess was achieved in 1956 by Ray Booty of Nottingham in the Bath Road 100-miles Competition event when, riding a bicycle alone and unpaced 50 miles out and 50 miles back, he broke the four-hour barrier to clock 3 hrs. 58 mins. 28 secs.

In cycling parlance a speed of 20 m.p.h. was referred to as "evens", but 25 m.p.h. has become the modern "evens". The out-and-home 25-miles distance was first ridden within the hour in 1939 and two hours for 50 miles was broken in 1947. But the top test of a time trialist, a lone rider in a timed competition, riding out-and-home, is 100 miles. Below that distance speed is everything, and above that distance— 12- and 24-hour competitions— the ability to stay the course, stamina, is the emphasis. At the testing century distance the victor must have his speed at knife-edge and that speed must be maintained over two 50-mile sections of unequal gradient, pedalling with the breeze one way and not losing rhythm when facing the wind in the other direction. Booty's four-hour ride had never been done before and has not been equalled, or indeed neared, since.

The 20 m.p.h. "evens" record at 100 miles out-and-home was put up in 1910, so that it required 46 years to take an hour off the record time.

A notable breaking of the 20 m.p.h. standard also occurred in 1956 in the 24-hours time-trial competition when Dennis White topped 484 miles in a stupendous unpaced ride in the Wessex area. Again in 1958 he repeated the same performance in the same event, adding a few yards and amassing 484¾ miles in his twice-round-the-clock ride.

The out-and-home nature of these rides has been emphasized and the significance of this is

There was a series of world title races for amateurs over 100 kilometres paced from 1893 to 1914 and in 1959. Of the twenty-two world champions, nine were British. E. Gould, 1897; A. J. Cherry, 1898 and Leon Meredith 1904, 1905, 1907, 1908, 1909, 1911 and 1913.

CHAMPIONS OF THE WORLD (ROAD)

Year	Venue	Distance Kms.	Amateur	Distance Kms.	Professional
1921	Copenhagen	190	SKOLD, S.	—	—
1922	Liverpool	161	MARSH, E.	—	—
1923	Zurich	160	FERRARIO, I.	—	—
1924	Paris	180	LEDUCQ, F.	—	—
1925	Amsterdam	188	HOEVENAARS, B.	—	—
1926	Turin	183	DAYEN, F.	—	—
1927	Adenau-Nurburg	184	AERTS, B.	184	BINDA, I.
1928	Budapest	200	GRANDI, I.	200	RONSSE, B.
1929	Zurich	200	BERTOLAZZI, I.	200	RONSSE, B.
1930	Liege	193	MARTANO, I.	210	BINDA, I.
1931	Copenhagen	170	HANSEN, D.	170	GUERRA, I.
1932	Rome	138	MARTANO, I.	206	BINDA, I.
1933	Paris	125	EGLI, SW.	250	SPEICHER, F.
1934	Leipzig	113	PELLENAERS, H.	226	KAERS, B.
1935	Floreffe	162	MANCINI, I.	216	AERTS, B.
1936	Berne	140	BUCHWALDER, SW.	218	MAGNE, F.
1937	Copenhagen	204	LEONI, I.	258	MEULENBERG, B.
1938	Valkenburg	185	KNECHT, SW.	267	KINT, B.
	1939-1945 Championships suspended				
1946	Zurich	200	AUBRY, F.	270	KNECHT, SW.
1947	Reims	164	FERRARI, I.	274	MIDDLEKAMP, H.
1948	Valkenburg	185	SNELL, SW.	267	SCHOTTE, B.
1949	Copenhagen	194	FARNHOF, H.	290	VAN STEENBERGHEN, B.
1950	Moorslede	175	HOUBIN, A.	284	SCHOTTE, B.
1951	Varese	172	CHIDINI, I.	295	KUBLER, SW.
1952	Luxemburg	175	CIANCOLA, I.	280	MULLER, G.
1953	Schweiz	180	FILIPPI, I.	270	COPPI, I.
1954	Solingen	150	VAN CAUTER, B.	240	BOBET, F.
1955	Rome	190	RANUCCI, I.	294	OCKERS, B.
1956	Ballerup	195	MAHN, H.	285	VAN STEENBERGHEN, B.
1957	Waregem	190	PROOST, B.	285	VAN STEENBERGHEN, B.
1958	Reims	176	SCHUR, E.G.	275	BALDINI, I.
1959	Zandvoort	188	SCHUR, E.G.	292	DARRIGADE, F.

CHAMPIONS OF THE WORLD (WOMEN)

Year	Venue	Amateur Sprint	Amateur Pursuit	Distance Kms.	Amateur Road
1958	Paris/Reims	ERMOLAEVA, R.	KOTCHETOVA, R.	59	JACOBS, L.
1959	Liege	ERMOLAEVA, R.	BURTON, E.	70	REYNDERS, B.

A=Australia, B=Belgium, D=Denmark, E=England, E.G.=East Germany, F=France, G=Germany, H=Holland, I=Italy, IRE=Ireland, L=Luxembourg, R=Russia, Sp=Spain, S=Sweden, SW=Switzerland, U.S.A.=United States of America.

made clear when we turn from the "competition" rides to the "straightaway" bests of the R.R.A. (Road Records Association) list. The same 100-miler, Ray Booty, also holds the R.R.A. 100-miles record with a time of 3 hrs. 28 mins. 40 secs. The one-way ride, all the way, was worth half-an-hour in a distance of 100 miles.

Just as moving air plays its important part in slowing a cyclist if it faces him, so too must distinction be made between paced and unpaced riding. A race in line, all riders starting together, provides pacing opportunities; and in cycle sprinting on the track, if a top-grade rider had to take the lead at speed from the gun with a much poorer performer "on his wheel" the big chance is that the man who had had the benefit of shelter all the way would "come out" on the last straight for the line and defeat his tiring pace-maker. That is why cycle "sprinting" starts slowly, each man manœuvring for the rear position or awaiting a chance to jump to a lead without providing shelter for his opponent. To those who understand sprint

tactics, these manœuvring preambles are most thrilling and as exciting as the race of speed proper. But because uninformed public opinion has demanded that "sprinting" should live up to its name, the world body introduced the pursuit championships in 1946 wherein two riders, one on each side of the track, pursue each other unpaced and alone for 4,000 metres (amateur) and 5,000 metres (professional) and the first to cross his own line at the end (or to catch his opponent) is declared the winner.

Motor-pacing provides a veritable high-speed acrobatic performance, with the cyclist using a small front wheel to get nearer his pace and riding a very big-geared machine. When speeds began to exceed 60 m.p.h. earlier in the century, and riders were getting killed, the world controlling organization decided to put the "roller" (a spinnable tube on a rod held by struts behind the motorcycle) farther back so that the rider obtained less shelter and thus speeds were reduced. It will be noted in the

CHAMPIONS OF THE WORLD (TRACK)

Year	Venue	Amateur Sprint	Professional Sprint	100 Kilometres Motor Paced	Amateur Pursuit	Professional Pursuit
1893	Chicago	ZIMMERMAN, U.S.A.	—	—	—	—
1894	Antwerp	LEHR, G.	—	—	—	—
1895	Cologne	EDEN, H.	PROTIN, B.	MICHAEL, E.	—	—
1896	Copenhagen	REYNOLDS, IRE.	BOURRILON, F.	CHASE, E.	—	—
1897	Glasgow	SCHRADER, D.	AREND, G.	STOCKS, E.	—	—
1898	Vienna	ALBERT, G.	BANKER, U.S.A.	PALMER, E.	—	—
1899	Montreal	SUMMERSGILL, E.	TAYLOR, U.S.A.	GIBSON, U.S.A.	—	—
1900	Paris	DIDIER-NAUTS, B.	JACQUELIN, F.	HURET, F.	—	—
1901	Berlin	MAITROT, F.	ELLEGAARD, D.	ROBL, G.	—	—
1902	Rome	PIARD, F.	ELLEGAARD, D.	ROBL, G.	—	—
1903	Copenhagen	REED, E.	ELLEGAARD, D.	DICKENTMANN, H.	—	—
1904	London	HURLEY, U.S.A.	LAWSON, U.S.A.	WALTHOUR, U.S.A.	—	—
1905	Antwerp	BENYON, E.	POULAIN, F.	WALTHOUR, U.S.A.	—	—
1906	Geneva	VERRI, I.	ELLEGAARD, D.	DARRAGON, F.	—	—
1907	Paris	DEVOISSOUX, F.	FRIOL, F.	DARRAGON, F.	—	—
1908	Berlin	JOHNSON, E.	ELLEGAARD, D.	RYSER, SW.	—	—
1909	Copenhagen	BAILEY, E.	ELLEGAARD, D.	PARENT, F.	—	—
1910	Brussels	BAILEY, E.	FRIOL, F.	PARENT, F.	—	—
1911	Rome	BAILEY, E.	ELLEGAARD, D.	PARENT, F.	—	—
1912	Newark	McDONALD, U.S.A.	KRAMER, U.S.A.	WILEY, U.S.A.	—	—
1913	Berlin	BAILEY, E.	RUTT, G.	GUIGNARD, F.	—	—
			1914–1919 Championships Suspended			
1920	Antwerp	PEETERS, H.	SPEARS, A.	SERES, F.	—	—
1921	Copenhagen	ANDERSEN, D.	MOESKOPS, H.	LINART, B.	—	—
1922	Paris	JOHNSON, E.	MOESKOPS, H.	VANDERSTUYFT, B.	—	—
1923	Zurich	MICHARD, F.	MOESKOPS, H.	SUTER, SW.	—	—
1924	Paris	MICHARD, F.	MOESKOPS, H.	LINART, B.	—	—
1925	Amsterdam	MEYER, H.	KAUFMANN, SW.	GRASSIN, F.	—	—
1926	Milan	MARTINETTI, I.	MOESKOPS, H.	LINART, B.	—	—
1927	Cologne	ENGEL, G.	MICHARD, F.	LINART, B.	—	—
1928	Budapest	HANSEN, D.	MICHARD, F.	SAWALL, G.	—	—
1929	Zurich	MAZAIRAC, H.	MICHARD, F.	PAILLARD, F.	—	—
1930	Brussels	GERARDIN, F.	MICHARD, F.	MOLLER, G.	—	—
1931	Copenhagen	HARDER, D.	HANSEN, D.	SAWALL, G.	—	—
1932	Rome	RICHTER, G.	SCHERENS, B.	PAILLARD, F.	—	—
1933	Paris	VAN EGMONT, H.	SCHERENS, B.	LACQUEHAY, F.	—	—
1934	Leipzig	POLA, I.	SCHERENS, B.	METZE, G.	—	—
1935	Brussels	MERKENS, G.	SCHERENS, B.	LACQUEHAY, F.	—	—
1936	Zurich	VAN VLIET, H.	SCHERENS, B.	RAYNAUD, F.	—	—
1937	Copenhagen	VAN DE VYVER, H.	SCHERENS, B.	LOHMANN, G.	—	—
1938	Amsterdam	VAN DE VYVER, H.	VAN VLIET, H.	METZE, G.	—	—
1939	Milan	DERKSEN, H.	—	—	—	—
			1940–1945 Championships Suspended			
1946	Zurich	PLATTNER, SW.	DERKSEN, H.	FROSIO, I.	RIOLAND, F.	PETERS, H.
1947	Paris	HARRIS, E.	SCHERENS, B.	LESUEUR, F.	BENFENATI, I.	COPPI, I.
1948	Amsterdam	GHELLA, I.	VAN VLIET, H.	LAMBOLEY, F.	MESSINA, I.	SCHULTE, H.
1949	Copenhagen	PATTERSON, A.	HARRIS, E.	FROSIO, I.	ANDERSEN, D.	COPPI, I.
1950	Liege	VERDEUN, F.	HARRIS, E.	LESUEUR, F.	PATTERSON, A.	BEVILAQUA, I.
1951	Milan	SACCHI, I.	HARRIS, E.	PRONK, H.	DE ROSSI, I.	BEVILAQUA, I.
1952	Paris	SACCHI, I.	PLATTNER, SW.	VERSCHUEREN, B.	VAN HEUSDEN, H.	PATTERSON, A.
1953	Zurich	MORETTINI, I.	VAN VLIET, H.	VERSCHUEREN, B.	MESSINA, I.	PATTERSON, A.
1954	Cologne	PEACOCK, E.	HARRIS, E.	VERSCHUEREN, B.	FAGGIN, I.	MESSINA, I.
1955	Milan	OGNA, I.	MASPES, I.	TIMONER, Sp.	SHEIL, E.	MESSINA, I.
1956	Copenhagen	ROUSSEAU, F.	MASPES, I.	FRENCH, A.	BALDINI, I.	MESSINA, I.
1957	Liege	ROUSSEAU, F.	DERKSEN, H.	DE PAEPE, B.	SIMONIGH, I.	RIVIERE, F.
1958	Paris	GASPARELLA, I.	ROUSSEAU, F.	BUCHER, SW.	SHEIL, E.	RIVIERE, F.
1959	Amsterdam	GASPARELLA, I.	MASPES, I.	TIMONER, Sp.	ALTIG, G.	RIVIERE, F.

---

world record table that with this restricted pace the hour record, outdoors, stands at 58 miles 737 yards. With unrestricted pace (roller close up to motorcycle) the unofficial record, fully authenticated, stands at 76 miles 504 yards. Over short distances, a speed exceeding 109 m.p.h. has been attained.

The "human-paced" table in the British Track record list refers to tandem-pacing.

The distinctions in road racing and record breaking have to some degree been indicated. Unpaced road racing, an essentially British sport, is called time trialing. A hundred or more riders take part in an event. They are started individually at minute intervals and each rides alone and unpaced. The courses are arranged so that the riders go out about halfway and return again to the start or near it. The record times are designated as competition rides or "out-and-home" and the sport is controlled by the Road Time Trials Council (R.T.T.C.).

The R.R.A. (Road Records Association) observes and hallmarks single unpaced time trials (not done in competition) and most of the scheduled distances and courses are straightaway performances, with the exception of the London to Bath and Back, London to Brighton and Back and the London to Portsmouth and Back records. As examples of the place-to-place performances on the R.R.A. books I have selected the classic course for historic record: the Land's End to John o' Groats.

A sport of growing interest in this country is the massed-start road game. The riders, as the title indicates, start in line and the first man at the finish is the winner. The greatest and most gruelling race in the world, the Tour de France, is listed since its inception. It started in 1903 as a six-stage race (six daily massed-start races with the riders' times aggregated to indicate the fastest) and has increased in length to last year's 24 stages.

The Tour of Britain is an imitation of the French classic and has gradually established itself in this country, although cycle racing in Britain is not the No. 1 sport that it is in France, Belgium, Italy and other Continental countries.

Although not currently a world champion, and now on the retired list, the greatest name in British cycling today is Reg Harris, who was amateur sprint champion of the world in 1947 and who in 1949, in his first year as a professional, was the first cyclist ever to become a world pro. champion at his first attempt. That great position he maintained for three years running in 1950 and 1951, and he was the world professional sprint champion again in 1954.

Harris, a self-made racing man, ended a long spell during which Britain was in the doldrums of world cycling. We had to look back 40 years to that other notable British sprinter, W. J. ("Bill") Bailey, who took the amateur world titles in 1909, 1910, 1911 and 1913.

Harris's example set other ambitions aiming at top-place honours and it was not unnatural for our British skill in the time-trial field to show ability at the pursuit match. Norman Sheil of Liverpool was the world amateur pursuit champion in 1955 and he again won that title in 1958. Another British sprinter, Cyril Peacock, topped the world honours list as an amateur in 1954, so that in that year this country headed the sprinting of the world, both amateur (Peacock) and professional (Harris).

The women of Britain have played a unique part in developing world interest in their cycling prowess. During recent years they have strongly urged a plea for the recognition of women's cycle racing with the Union Cycliste Internationale, the body for world cycle sport, and they succeeded in getting women's records on the U.C.I. books in 1955 with their own names in the lists. Now the Russian girls dominate the record table, with one outstanding Luxembourg girl, Elsy Jacobs.

The women's world titles were conceded, again at the instigation of the British women delegates, only last year, and here again the honours were shared by Russia and Luxembourg. In 1959, however, the brilliant girl, Beryl Burton of Morley, Yorkshire, has won the world's pursuit title.

CYCLING QUIZ

1. What is the greatest distance ridden in 24 hours behind pace and who accomplished it?

★

2. A good bet: That a motorist cannot maintain a speed on the road twice as fast as a cyclist for the same distance?

★

3. Who was the great long-distance record breaker in the history of cycling sport?

★

4. There are 21 record distances on the Women's Road Records Association books. Which professional lady has broken all 21 and still holds them all?

★

5. Who was famous as walker, cyclist and swimmer?

★

6. What is the unrestricted motor-paced record for one hour and who holds it?

QUIZ ANSWERS

1. 860 miles 367 yards by Hurbert Opperman in 1932 in Australia. 2. Cycling road performance: 50 miles in 1 hr. 39 min. 42 secs. (30 m.p.h.); 100 miles in 3-28-40 (28¾ m.p.h.); 24 hours to cover 484¼ miles (over 20 m.p.h.). 3. G. P. Mills, broke 19 national records. He broke six records from Land's End to John o' Groats on four types of cycle. Won the first Bordeaux-Paris race in 1891 by over an hour. He rode three 24-hour races in one week! At the age of 18 between July and October of 1886 he rode twice from Land's End to John o' Groats and three 24-hour events! 4. Eileen Sheridan. 5. Monty Holbein. From foot road race winner he turned to cycling and broke 32 national records. He was the first in 1889 to ride 20 miles in the hour on the road. After breaking his leg in 1897 he turned to swimming and got within 500 yds. of swimming the Channel when the tide turned. At 75 years of age he swam the Thames from Richmond to London Bridge. 6. Leon Vanderstuyft, a Belgian, rode behind an Anzani motor cycle at Montlhéry, near Paris, in 1928, a distance of 76 miles 504 yards in one hour.

CYCLING QUIZ

1. Which sporting body first laid down an amateur definition?

★

2. Who was the first cyclist to ride 20 miles in the hour?

★

3. Who was the first cyclist to ride over 60 miles in one hour, behind big motors?

★

4. What sensational cycling record was achieved in America in 1899.

QUIZ ANSWERS

1. The National Cyclists' Union in 1878. The N.C.U. Amateur Championships date from that year. 2. H. L. Cortis in 1882. He was riding a high bicycle or "Penny Farthing". The ride took place at the Crystal Palace track. 3. Englishman A. E. Wills, the "Putney Midget", at Munich in 1908. He covered 60½ miles. 4. Charles ("Mile-a-Minute") Murphy rode on a path laid between the railway lines and was paced by a train to clock 57⅘ secs. for one mile.

Ray Booty

OLYMPIC GAMES WINNERS

CYCLING

1896 (Greece)
2 kms. P. Masson (France)
10 kms. P. Masson (France)
333.3 m. P. Masson (France)
12 hrs. A. Schmall (Austria)
100 kms. paced L. Flameng (France)
Road Race. A. Constantinides (Greece)

1900 (France)
1,000 m. Taillendier (France)

1904 (U.S.A.)
No cycling events.

1908 (Britain)
603.4 m. V. L. Johnson (Britain)
1,000 m. Void, time limit exceeded
5 kms. B. Jones (Britain)
20 kms. C. B. Kingsbury (Britain)
100 kms. C. H. Bartlett (Britain)
2 kms. Tandem. M. Schilles and A. Auffray (France)
Team Pursuit. Great Britain

1912 (Sweden)
No track events were held, there being no suitable track.
Road Race. G. R. Lewis (South Africa)

1916
No Olympic Games held owing to First World War.

1920 (Belgium)
1,000 m. M. Peeters (Holland)
2 kms. Tandem. H. E. Ryan and T. Lance (Britain)
50 kms. H. Georges (Belgium)
Team Pursuit. Italy
Road Race. E. H. Stenquist (Sweden)

1924 (France)
1,000 m. L. Michard (France)
2 kms. Tandem. J. Cugnot and L. Choury (France)
50 kms. J. Willems (Holland)
Team Pursuit. Italy
Road Race. A. Blanchonnet (France)

1928 (Denmark)
1,000 m. R. Beaufrand (France)
2 kms. Tandem. Van Dyk and B. Leene (Holland)
1,000 m. Time Trial. W. Falck Hansen (Denmark)
Team Pursuit. Italy
Road Race. H. Hansen (Denmark)

1932 (U.S.A.)
1,000 m. J. Van Egmond (Holland)
2 kms. Tandem. M. Perrin and L. Chaillot (France)
1,000 m. Time Trial. E. L. Gray (Aus.)
Team Pursuit. Italy
Road Race. A. Pavesi (Italy)

1936 (Germany)
1,000 m. Sprint. T. Merkens (Germany)
2,000 m. Tandem. D. Ihbe & C. Lorenz (Germany)
1,000 m. Time Trial. A. Van Vliet (Holland)
4,000 m. Team Pursuit. France
Road Race. R. Charpentier (France)

1948 (Britain)
1,000 m. Sprint. M. Ghella (Italy)
2,000 m. Tandem. F. Teruzzi and R. Perona (Italy)
1,000 m. Time Trial. J. Dupont (France)
4,000 m. Team Pursuit. France
Road Race. J. Beyaert (France)

1952 (Finland)
1,000 m. Sprint. E. Sacchi (Italy)
2,000 m. Tandem. R. Mockridge and L. Cox (Australia)
1,000 m. Time Trial. R. Mockridge (Australia)
4,000 m. Team Pursuit. Italy
Road Race. A. Noyelle (Belgium)

1956 (Australia)
1,000 m. Sprint. M. Rousseau (France)
2,000 m. Tandem. I. Browne and A. Marchant (Australia)
1,000 m. Time Trial. L. Faggin (Italy)
4,000 m. Team Pursuit. Italy
Road Race. E. Baldini (Italy)

BRITISH EMPIRE GAMES WINNERS

CYCLING

1934 (Manchester)
1,000 yds. Sprint. E. W. Higgins (England)
10 miles. R. McLeod (Canada)
1,000 m. Time Trial. D. Gray (Australia)

1938 (Sydney)
1,000 m. Time Trial. D. Gray (Australia)
10 miles. W. W. Maxfield (England)
1,000 m. Time Trial. R. Porter (Australia)
Road Race. H. Binnerman (S. Africa)

1950 (Auckland)
1,000 yds. Sprint. R. Mockridge (Australia)
10 miles. W. Heseltine (Australia)
1,000 m. Time Trial. R. Mockridge (Australia)
Road Race. H. Sutherland (Australia)

1954 (Vancouver)
1,000 m. Sprint. C. F. Peacock (England)
10 miles. L. Cocks (Australia)
1,000 m. Time Trial. R. Ploog (Australia)
J. Swift (S. Africa) Tie
4,000 m. Individual Pursuit. N. Sheil (England)
Road Race. E. G. Thompson (England)

1958 (Cardiff)
1,000 m. Sprint. R. Ploog (Australia)
10 miles. I. Browne (Australia)
1,000 m. Time Trial. N. Tong (England)
4,000 m. Individual Pursuit. N. Sheil (England)
Road Race. R. C. Booty (England)

CHIEF BRITISH TRACK RECORDS

UNPACED AMATEUR BICYCLE, MEN

Class	Rider, track and year	Record h.	m.	s.
¼ mile f.s.	C. F. Peacock, H.H., 1953			24.4
½ mile f.s.	C. F. Peacock, H.H., 1953			53.9
1 mile f.s.	F. W. Southall, H.H., 1927		1	59.8
¼ mile s.s.	V. L. Johnson, H.H., 1909			28
½ mile s.s.	A. Danson, F., 1955			57.2
1 mile s.s.	E. V. Mills, H.H., 1937		2	1.2
5 miles s.s.	N. Sheil, F., 1957		10	52.8
10 miles s.s.	N. Sheil, F., 1957		22	4.2
25 miles s.s.	N. Sheil, F., 1957		55	59.8
1 km. s.s.	K. J. Harrison, F., 1956		1	12.2
3 km. s.s.	Not applicable		—	
4 km. s.s.	M. J. Gambrill, H.H., 1957		5	12.2
		m.		yds.
1 hour s.s.	N. Sheil, F., 1957	26		1,398

UNPACED AMATEUR TANDEM BICYCLE, MEN

Class	Rider, track and year	Record h.	m.	s.
¼ mile f.s.	R. H. Harris and A. Bannister, H.H., 1948			23.2
½ mile f.s.	M. G. Southall and C. H. Hallerback, H.H., 1930			48.8
1 mile f.s.	E. V. Mills and W. G. Paul, H.H., 1937		1	43.8
¼ mile s.s.	J. E. Sibbit and E. H. Chambers, H.H., 1928			27.4
½ mile s.s.	J. E. Sibbit and E. H. Chambers, H.H., 1928			51.8
1 mile s.s.	E. V. Mills and W. G. Paul, H.H., 1937		1	48.6
5 miles s.s.	M. J. and C. R. Gambrill, H.H., 1958		9	48.8
10 miles s.s.	R. W. Buchan and D. G. Hill, H.H., 1955		20	3.6
1 km. s.s.	Not applicable		—	
3 km. s.s.	Not applicable		—	
4 km. s.s.	Not applicable		—	
		m.		yds.
1 hour s.s.	E. V. Mills and W. G. Paul, H.H., 1936	30		793

UNPACED AMATEUR BICYCLE, WOMEN

Class	Rider, track and year	Record h.	m.	s.
¼ mile f.s.	Mrs. J. Dunn, H.H., 1958			29.2
½ mile f.s.	Mrs. B. Tingey, H.H., 1958		1	5.2
1 mile f.s.	Miss S. Ball, H.H., 1958		2	15.2
¼ mile s.s.	Mrs. J. Dunn, H.H., 1958			33
½ mile s.s.	Mrs. B. Tingey, H.H., 1958		1	5.4
1 mile s.s.	Miss S. Ball, H.H., 1958		2	18
5 miles s.s.	Miss M. Robinson, F., 1958		12	15.6
10 miles s.s.	Miss M. Robinson, F., 1958		24	54.2
25 miles s.s.	Miss M. Robinson, F., 1958	1	2	41
1 km. s.s.	Mrs. B. Tingey, H.H., 1958		1	23.6
3 km. s.s.	Miss S. Ball, H.H., 1958		4	19.3
4 km. s.s.	Mrs. D. M. Franks, H.H., 1956		5	55.7
		m.		yds.
1 hour s.s.	Miss M. Robinson, F., 1958	23		1,708

UNPACED PROFESSIONAL BICYCLE, MEN

Class	Rider, track and year	Record h.	m.	s.
¼ mile f.s.	R. H. Harris, P., 1953			24
½ mile f.s.	R. H. Harris, H.H., 1952			51
1 mile f.s.	S. Patterson, H.H., 1952		1	57.6
¼ mile s.s.	R. H. Harris, F., 1951			27.7
½ mile s.s.	R. H. Harris, F., 1952			55
1 mile s.s.	W. J. Bailey, H.H., 1938		2	5.6
1 km. s.s.	R. H. Harris, F., 1950		1	11.2
3 km. s.s.	Not applicable		—	
		m.		yds.
1 hour s.s.	H. H. Hill, P., 1939	26		1,003

HUMAN PACED AMATEUR BICYCLE, MEN

Class	Rider, track and year	Record h.	m.	s.
¼ mile f.s.	J. A. Dennis, H.H., 1950			23
½ mile f.s.	W. E. Gimber, H.H., 1951			48.5
1 mile f.s.	H. W. Payne, C.P., 1898		1	39.4
¼ mile s.s.	S. T. Cozens, H.H., 1929			28
½ mile s.s.	L. C. Hart, H.H., 1948			54.8
1 mile s.s.	F. W. Southall, H.H., 1931		1	47.6
5 miles s.s.	F. W. Southall, H.H., 1929		9	12
10 miles s.s.	F. W. Southall, H.H., 1929		18	42.8
25 miles s.s.	F. W. Southall, H.H., 1929		47	4.8
50 miles s.s.	D. Fleming, H.H., 1953	1	36	42.2
100 miles s.s.	F. W. Southall, H.H., 1930	3	29	58
		m.		yds.
1 hour s.s.	F. W. Southall, H.H., 1929	31		1,457
6 hours s.s.	R. T. Spanton, H.H., 1955	162		883
12 hours s.s.	D. A. Marsh, H.H., 1955	307		108
24 hours s.s.	J. E. Holdsworth, H.H., 1930	534		1,500

HUMAN PACED AMATEUR BICYCLE, WOMEN

Class	Rider, track and year	Record h.	m.	s.
¼ mile f.s.	Mrs. J. Dunn, H.H., 1958			27.4
½ mile f.s.	Mrs. J. Dunn, H.H., 1958			56.5
1 mile f.s.	Miss J. Dean, H.H., 1948		2	0.2
¼ mile s.s.	Mrs. M. Maitland, C., 1955			32.2
½ mile s.s.	Miss D. M. Stockwell, H.H., 1950		1	2.2
1 mile s.s.	Miss D. M. Stockwell, H.H., 1950		1	59.2
5 miles s.s.	Miss J. Dean, H.H., 1948		10	16.4

HUMAN PACED PROFESSIONAL BICYCLE, MEN

Class	Rider, track and year	Record h.	m.	s.
¼ mile s.s.	J. Green, C.P., 1899			27.4
½ mile s.s.	J. Green, C.P., 1899			51.2
1 mile s.s.	J. Green, C.P., 1899		1	40.4
		m.		yds.
1 hour s.s.	D. Bedwell, H.H., 1952	31		1,560

MOTOR PACED PROFESSIONAL BICYCLE, MEN

Class	Rider, track and year					Record	
						h. m.	s.
1 mile f.s.	A. Constant, H.H., 1933	..	..	..	..	1 18.2	
1 mile s.s.	H. Grant, H.H., 1933	..	..	..	..	1 35.8	
5 miles s.s.	A. Fournier, F., 1949	..	..	..	..	7 0.4	
10 miles s.s.	A. Fournier, F., 1949	..	..	..	..	13 46.8	
25 miles s.s.	W. Summers, H.H., 1947	..	..	..	..	35 29.2	
50 miles s.s.	W. Summers, H.H., 1947	..	..	..	..	1 13 13.6	

MOTOR PACED AMATEUR BICYCLE, MEN

Class	Rider, track and year					Record	
Class "A"						h. m.	s.
¼ mile f.s.	F. H. Wyld, H.H., 1927	..	..	..	..	19.6	
½ mile f.s.	F. H. Wyld, H.H., 1927	..	..	..	..	39.8	
1 mile f.s.	H. Grant, H.H., 1929	..	..	..	..	1 17.6	
1 mile s.s.	H. Grant, H.H., 1929	..	..	..	..	1 29.8	
5 miles s.s.	F. H. Wyld, H.H., 1927	..	..	..	..	7 6.8	
10 miles s.s.	H. Oxley, H.H., 1935	..	..	..	..	14 28.4	
25 miles s.s.	H. Oxley, H.H., 1938	..	..	..	..	35 50	
50 miles s.s.	L. Meredith, P., 1903	..	..	..	..	1 25 24.4	
100 miles s.s.	L. Meredith, P., 1903	..	..	..	..	2 58 12.8	
						m.	yds.
1 hour	H. Oxley, H.H., 1938	..	..	..	..	41	1,634

H.H.—Herne Hill. C.P.—Crystal Palace. P.—Paddington. F.—Fallowfield.
C.—Cannock. B.—Butts, Coventry. f.s.—flying start; s.s.—standing start.

CHIEF TRACK RECORDS OF THE WORLD

PROFESSIONAL

Class	Holder and Nation		Place	Year	Record	
S.S.:					h. m.	s.
(Outdoor)						
1 km.	Harris (G.B.)	..	Milan	1952	1	8.6
5 km.	Faggin (It.)	..	Milan	1958	6	6.4
10 km.	Riviere (Fr.)	..	Milan	1958	12	22.8
20 km.	Riviere (Fr.)	..	Milan	1958	24	50.6
100 km.	De Benedetti (It.)	..	Milan	1942	2 20	44.8
					m.	yds.
1 hour	Riviere (Fr.)	..	Milan	1958	29	739
(Indoor)					h. m.	s.
1 km.	Harris (G.B.)	..	Zurich	1957	1	8.0
5 km.	Strehler (Switz.)	..	Zurich	1956	6	9.4
10 km.	Riviere (Fr.)	..	Paris	1958	12	26.8
20 km.			*	*	*	
100 km.			*	*	*	
1 hr.			*	*	*	
F.S.:						
(Outdoor)						
200 m.	Van Vliet (H.)	..	Ord.	1955		11.0
500 m.	Morettini (It.)	..	Milan	1955		28.8
1 km.	Morettini (It.)	..	Milan	1956	1	3.6
(Indoor)						
200 m.	Plattner (Switz.)	..	Zurich	1956		11.0
500 m.	Plattner (Switz.)	..	Zurich	1956		28.6
1 km.	Von Buren (Switz.)	..	Zurich	1956	1	1.6
M.P.:						
(Outdoor)					h. m.	s.
100 km.†	Lohmann (Ger.)	..	Wup.	1955	1 3	40.0
					m.	yds.
1 hr.†	Lohmann (Ger.)	..	Wup.	1955	58	737
					h. m.	s.
100 km.**	Damasse (Fr.)	..	Mon.	1955	1 33	26.2
					m.	yds.
1 hr.**	Damasse (Fr.)	..	Mon.	1956	44	261
(Indoor)					h. m.	s.
100 km.†	Lohmuller (Switz.)	..	St. Et.	1952	1 29	37.2
					m.	yds.
1 hr.†	Solente (Fr.)	..	Paris	1955	46	637
1 hr.**	Browaeys (Fr.)	..	Paris	1950	39	1,558
100 km.**			*	*	*	

AMATEUR

Class	Holder and Nation		Place	Year	Record	
S.S.:					h. m.	s.
(Outdoor)						
1 km.	Faggin (It.)	..	Milan	1956	1	9.2
5 km.	Faggin (It.)	..	Milan	1956	6	15.4
10 km.	Baldini (It.)	..	Milan	1956	12	37.6
20 km.	Baldini (It.)	..	Milan	1956	25	20.0
100 km.	Zucchetti (It.)	..	Milan	1956	2 25	58.6
					m.	yds.
1 hour	Baldini (It.)	..	Milan	1956	28	1,456
(Indoor)					h. m.	s.
1 km.	Gaignard (Fr.)	..	Paris	1954	1	10.2
5 km.	Schweizer (Switz.)	..	Zurich	1956	6	14.2
10 km.	Simic (Austria)	..	Zurich	1957	12	52.2
20 km.	Ruegg (Switz.)	..	Zurich	1958	26	15.2
100 km.			*	*	*	
					m.	yds.
1 hr.	Ruegg (Switz.)	..	Zurich	1958	28	575
F.S.:						
(Outdoor)					h. m.	s.
200 m.	Ploog (Australia)	..	Mel.	1956		11.2
500 m.	Gasparella (It.)	..	Milan	1955		29.8
1 km.	Chiesa (It.)	..	Milan	1955	1	3.8
(Indoor)						
200 m.	Pesenti (It.)	..	Milan	1957		11.5
500 m.	Pesenti (It.)	..	Milan	1957		29.4
1 km.	Gassner (Switz.)	..	Zurich	1957	1	4.2

WOMEN

Class	Holder and Nation		Place	Year	Record	
S.S.:					h. m.	s.
(Outdoor)						
1 km.	Brovina (U.S.S.R.)	..	Irk.	1955	1	17.9
5 km.	Sadovaya (U.S.S.R.)	..	Irk.	1955	7	3.3
10 km.	Jacobs (Lux.)	..	Milan	1958	14	27
20 km.	Jacobs (Lux.)	..	Milan	1958	29	2.6
100 km.	Tumentseva (U.S.S.R.)	..	Irk.	1958	2 46	27.2

Class	Holder and Nation	Place	Year	Record	
				m.	yds.
1 hour	Jacobs (Lux.)	Milan	1958	25	1,207
1 km.	*	*	*	*	
5 km.	*	*	*	*	
10 km.	*	*	*	*	
20 km.	*	*	*	*	
100 km.	*	*	*	*	
1 hr.	*	*	*	*	
F.S.:					
(Outdoor)				h. m.	s.
200 m.	Rozouvaeva (U.S.S.R.)	Irk.	1955		12.3
500 m.	Rozouvaeva (U.S.S.R.)	Irk.	1955		32.8
1 km.	Brovina (U.S.S.R.)	Irk.	1955	1	12.9
(Indoor)					
200 m.	*	*	*	*	
500 m.	*	*	*	*	
1 km.	*	*	*	*	

*To be established. †Large Motors. **Commercial Motors.
Ord.—Ordrup. Mon.—Montlhery. Wup.—Wuppertal. St. Et.—St. Etienne.
Irk.—Irkoutsk. Mel.—Melbourne.
S.S.—Standing Start. F.S.—Flying Start. M.P.—Motor paced.

Eileen Sheridan   Mrs. Bobbie Tingey   Daisy Franks

CYCLING QUIZ

1. Henri Desgrange, the cyclist who established the first unpaced hour record at 21 miles 1,674 yards in 1893 was famous for another great enterprise. What was it?

2. What freak attempts have been made to increase the hour record distances?

3. Where was the first cycle race held and who won it?

4. What is the fastest speed ever done on a bicycle?

5. Who is the oldest living British Champion?

6. At the end of the 1920s the Wyld family of Derby were noted champions. Why were they so successful on the Derby track?

7. Are British championships open to the world?

8. Who holds all the current women's road championships in time trial sport?

9. One would expect the "Ordinary" bicycle to be the one we see ridden on the streets today. Why is this not so?

QUIZ ANSWERS

1. He established the Tour de France in 1903. 2. Berthet, who broke the hour record (unpaced) in 1907, and twice in 1913, built a torpedo-shaped enclosure on his bicycle in which, at the age of 47, he claimed to have covered 31 miles in the hour. A lying-down cycle called a "Velocar" on which leg thrust was helped by a back rest, was ridden by a cyclist named Faure in 1934 to cover 28 miles in the hour, when the orthodox cycle record stood at 27 miles 1,450 yards. 3. It was decided at the Parc de St. Cloud, Paris, in 1868 (on May 31), and won by an Englishman, James Moore. It was over 2 kms. and raced on the original Michaux Velocepedes (which when they came to England that year were called Bone-shakers). The date of this race is important as there was a cycle race the following day, June 1, at the Welsh Harp, Hendon, London. 4. 109.12 m.p.h. by José Meiffret, in 1951. His gear was 275 inches. 5. A. J. Watson, 5 miles champion in 1893 and still living at Hastings. (He was also the one and five miles champion in 1895.) 6. Properly made cycle track bankings are slightly convex. The Derby track is a saucer: concave. Thus the Wyld brothers would take turns at leading a race. Rivals behind could not pass to the front easily because the track shape was too fast at the top steep slope to overtake a Wyld at speed and too slow on the inner flat section. The angles of the riders to the track surface meant that shoulders touched if the passing was close. 7. No, but they were until 1935 when Toni Merkens of Germany was the sprint champion of England. 8. Beryl Burton is 25 miles, 50 miles and 100 miles champion for 1959. 9. The bicycle of the early days was the high machine with the big front driving wheel. When the low-down safety bicycle was coming into use the high-bicycle riders were scathing about its appearance and referred to the safety riders as "Cads on Castors". So the high machine was the normal Ordinary bicycle and the safety was the innovation. Old-timers do not like the Old Ordinary Bicycle referred to as a "Penny Farthing".

CYCLING QUIZ

1. When was the cycle recognized as a "Carriage" in law?

*

2. Which was the first cycling road out of London?

*

3. What is the earliest Bicycle Club, still extant?

*

4. Where was the first cycling hill climb?

*

5. Where was the pneumatic tyre first seen on the race track?

*

6. Where and when did ladies' cycling bloomers come into public prominence?

QUIZ ANSWERS

1. In 1888, the Local Government Act expressly declared a cycle to be "a carriage". Before then a cyclist was faced with having to know, and abide by, the different regulations appertaining to cyclists in each county. 2. The Ripley Road, as it was then called, because the pioneer riders rode out to the "Anchor" at Ripley where the Dibble family made them welcome. In Ripley Church there is a memorial window to the Misses Dibbles installed by their cycling friends. 3. The Pickwick Bicycle Club founded in 1870, the year that Charles Dickens died. 4. It was ridden on Boneshakers in 1869 on a hill near Fountains Abbey, Yorks. 5. William Hume raced one of the first Dunlop 2 in. pneumatic-tyred bicycles in 1889 at Queen's College Sports, Belfast. There, Hume, a mediocre rider, won all four races against such rivals as the du Cros family. 6. Lady Harberton stopped for a meal at the "Hautboy", Ockham, in 1898 and was refused service in the coffee-room, because of her dress. The Cyclists' Touring Club sued the innkeeper on Lady Harberton's behalf but lost the case as she had not been refused food but only a certain room was barred to her.

NATIONAL CYCLING CHAMPIONS (TRACK)

("Penny Farthing" bicycles and tricycles only were the current mounts until 1888; the modern Safety bicycle championships were introduced in 1889)

1878
2 miles, Hon. Ion K. Falconer; 25 miles, A. A. Wier.

Miles	1879	1880	1881
1	H. L. Cortis	C. E. Liles	G. Lacy Hillier
5	H. L. Cortis	H. L. Cortis	G. Lacy Hillier
25	H. L. Cortis	H. L. Cortis	G. Lacy Hillier
50	H. L. Cortis	H. L. Cortis	G. Lacy Hillier

Miles	1882	1883	1884
1	F. Moore	H. W. Gaskell	H. A. Speechley
5	J. S. Whatton	F. Sutton	R. Chambers
25	F. Moore	C. E. Liles	R. H. English
50	Hon. Ion K. Falconer	H. F. Wilson	F. R. Fry
1 Tricycle		C. E. Liles	C. E. Liles
5 Tricycle	C. E. Liles		C. E. Liles
10 Tricycle	—	C. E. Liles	C. E. Liles
25 Tricycle		C. E. Liles	C. E. Liles

Miles	1885	1886	1887
1	Sanders Sellers	P. Furnivall	W. A. Ilston
5	M. V. J. Webber	P. Furnivall	W. A. Ilston
25	R. H. English	J. E. Fenlon	W. A. Ilston
50	R. H. English	J. E. Fenlon	J. H. Adams
1 Tricycle	P. Furnivall	P. Furnivall	E. Kiderlen
5 Tricycle	L. Cripps	F. W. Allard	R. J. Mecredy
25 Tricycle	G. Gatehouse	R. J. Mecredy	F. J. Osmond

Miles	1888		Miles	1889
1	H. Synyer		1	August Lehr
5	H. Synyer		5	H. Synyer
25	J. H. Adams		25	F. J. Osmond
50	F. P. Wood		50	J. H. Adams
1 Tricycle	S. F. Edge		1 Safety	F. T. Fletcher
5 Tricycle	F. J. Osmond		25 Safety	F. T. Fletcher
25 Tricycle	F. P. Wood		50 Safety	J. H. Adams
			1 Tricycle	H. H. Sansom
			5 Tricycle	H. H. Sansom
			25 Tricycle	W. G. H. Bransom

Miles	1890
1	F. J. Osmond
5	F. J. Osmond
25	F. J. Osmond
50	F. J. Osmond
1 Safety	R. J. Mecredy
5 Safety	R. J. Mecredy
25 Safety	R. J. Mecredy
50 Safety	R. J. Mecredy
1 Tricycle	K. N. Stadnicki
5 Tricycle	H. H. Sansom
25 Tricycle	L. Stroud

Miles	1891	1892	1893
1	J. H. Adams	J. H. Adams	"Penny Farthing" championships discontinued
5	U. L. Lambley	J. H. Adams	
25	J. H. Adams	J. H. Adams	
50	J. H. Adams	J. H. Adams	
1 Safety	P. W. Schelt-Beduin	A. A. Zimmerman	W. C. Sanger
5 Safety	A. W. Harris	A. A. Zimmerman	A. J. Watson
25 Safety	F. J. Osmond	R. L. Ede	J. Stocks
50 Safety	F. J. Osmond	A. A. Zimmerman	L. Stroud
1 Tricycle	P. W. Schelt-Beduin	W. Tischbein	F. Bramson
5 Tricycle	W. G. H. Bransom		
25 Tricycle	L. Stroud		
10 Tricycle	—	F. Bramson	F. Bramson

Miles	1894	1895	Miles	1896
1 Safety	C. J. Peterson	A. J. Watson	¼	A. Macpherson
5 Safety	J. Green	A. J. Watson	1	P. W. Brown
25 Safety	J. Green	E. Scott	5	M. Djakoft
50 Safety	J. Green	C. G. Ridgway	25	M. Djakoft
1 Tricycle	J. W. Rowley	G. Gatehouse	50	W. H. Bardsley
10 Tricycle	J. W. Rowley	A. F. Illsley		Tricycle Championships Discontinued

Miles	1897	1898	1899
¼	J. A. Metcalf	T. Summersgill	P. Albert
1	T. Summersgill	W. A. Edmonds	P. Albert
5	E. H. Ainsworth	A. S. Ingham	A. S. Ingram
25	W. P. Fawcett	H. W. Payne	H. W. Payne
50	A. J. Cherry	H. Chinn	G. F. Payne
2 Tandem	—	{ F. Burnand { E. J. Callaghan	{ A. S. Ingram { R. Janson

Miles	1900	1901	1902
¼	A. S. Ingram	A. S. Ingram	A. S. Ingram
1	W. A. Edmonds	C. Pease	A. L. Reed
5	A. S. Ingram	C. Pease	H. W. Payne
25	W. S. Ramsey	R. Reynolds	B. Andrews
50	H. W. Payne	W. B. Dudden	L. Meredith

Miles	1903	1904	1905
¼	A. S. Ingram	J. S. Benyon	E. Payne
1	Declared Void	A. L. Reed	E. Payne
5	A. L. Reed	L. Meredith	L. Meredith
25	L. Meredith	A. E. Wills	A. E. Wills
50	W. J. Pett	L. Meredith	W. J. Pett

Miles	1906	1907	1908
¼	E. Payne	G. C. Anderson	V. L. Johnson
1	E. Payne	E. Payne	C. B. Kingsbury
5	W. A. Edmonds	C. B. Kingsbury	B. Jones
25	H. Crowther	S. C. Robertson	L. Meredith
50	W. J. Pett	L. Meredith	C. H. Bartlett
1 Tandem	{ J. Mathews { A. Rushen	{ H. T. Johnson { F. G. Hamlin	{ W. H. T. Isaacs { C. Brooks

Miles	1909	1910	1911
¼	C. B. Kingsbury	W. J. Bailey	V. L. Johnson
1	W. J. Bailey	V. L. Johnson	V. L. Johnson
5	W. J. Bailey	B. Jones	V. L. Johnson
25	J. Harvey	C. B. Kingsbury	C. B. Kingsbury
50	C. H. Bartlett	C. A. Denny	C. B. Kingsbury
1 Tandem	{ H. T. Johnson { F. G. Hamlin	{ H. T. Johnson { F. G. Hamlin	{ H. H. Lee { C. A. Alden

Miles	1912	1913	1914
¼	V. L. Johnson	W. J. Bailey	W. A. Ormston
1	W. J. Bailey	W. J. Bailey	W. A. Ormston
5	F. Boor	R. L. Player	W. A. Ormston
25	R. L. Player	H. E. Ryan	Not held because of the War.
50	C. B. Kingsbury	C. A. Alden	
1 Tandem	{ E. F. Ryan { W. T. Dunn	{ A. White { C. White	

		Miles	1919	1920
1915–1918 Championships Suspended		¼	H. E. Ryan	A. White
		1	H. E. Ryan	A. White
		5	H. E. Ryan	A. White
		25	S. Wagstaff	A. White
		50	W. G. Stewart	W. R. Smith
	1 Tandem		Not held	{ H. H. Lee { W. A. Ormston

Miles	1921	1922	1923
¼	A. White	G. Owen	A. White
1	G. Owen	G. Owen	H. E. Fuller
5	A. White	J. E. Sibbit	H. H. Lee
25	W. H. Genders	A. White	A. White
50	S. Scott	S. Scott	S. G. Owen
1 Tandem	{ H. E. Ryan { T. Harvey	{ H. E. Ryan { T. Harvey	{ H. H. Lee { C. A. Alden

Miles	1924	Miles	1925	1926
¼	H. E. Fuller	¼	J. E. Sibbit	A. Theaker
1	G. Owen	1	C. A. Alden	A. Theaker
5	A. White	5	A. White	F. H. Wyld
25	A. White	25	L. A. Wyld	A. Theaker
50	F. H. Wyld	50 Tandem paced	F. H. Wyld	H. Grant
1 Tandem	{ J. E. Sibbit { A. White	1 Tandem	{ C. A. Alden { F. H. Habberfield	{ A. Theaker { A. White
		2 Team pursuit	—	Derby R.C.C.

Miles	1927	1928	1929
¼	J. E. Sibbit	F. H. Wyld	S. T. Cozens
1	H. Pryor	F. H. Wyld	F. H. Wyld
5	A. Theaker	F. H. Wyld	F. H. Wyld
25	A. Theaker	F. H. Wyld	J. E. Sibbit
50 Tandem-paced	F. H. Wyld	H. Grant	F. H. Wyld
1 Tandem	{ F. H. Habberfield { A. R. M. Harbour	{ E. H. Chambers { J. E. Sibbit	{ E. H. Chambers { J. E. Sibbit
2 Team pursuit	Derby R.C.C.	Derby R.C.C.	Norwood Paragon C.C.

The ¼, 1 and 5 miles championships were discontinued and replaced by the 1,000 yards sprint.

	1930	1931	1932
1,000 yds.	S. T. Cozens	J. E. Sibbit	J. E. Sibbit
25	D. S. Horn	C. W. Horn	D. S. Horn
50 Tandem-paced	F. W. Southall	H. Grant	F. W. Southall
1 Tandem	{ E. H. Chambers { J. E. Sibbit	{ E. W. Higgins { J. E. Sibbit	{ D. S. Horn { J. E. Sibbit
2 Team pursuit	Norwood Paragon C.C.	Belle Vue C.C.	Belle Vue C.C.
1 Grass	—	—	D. S. Horn
5 Grass	—	—	D. S. Horn

	1933	1934	1935
1,000 yds.	F. Dusika	T. Merkens	T. Merkens
25	D. S. Horn	D. S. Horn	D. S. Horn
50 Tandem-paced	F. W. Southall	F. G. Frost	F. G. Frost
1 Tandem	A. G. Sier / R. Meller	Race declared void	D. S. Horn / E. W. Higgins
2 Team pursuit	Poole Wh. C. & A.C.	Rover R.C.C.	Marlboro A. C.
1 Grass	C. W. Horn	E. H. Chambers	J. H. Tipping
5 Grass	D. S. Horn	D. S. Horn	B. J. Donnelly

	1936	1937	1938
1,000 yds.	C. B. Helps	C. W. Horn	D. S. Horn
25	J. Holland	W. W. Maxfield	W. W. Maxfield
50 Tandem-paced	E. V. Mills	E. V. Mills	R. W. Shand
1 Tandem	J. E. Sibbit / E. H. Chambers	J. E. Sibbit / E. H. Chambers	R. Meller / F. W. Tickler
2 Team pursuit	Belle Vue C.C.	Catford C.C.	Belle Vue C.C.
1 Grass	D. S. Horn	—	—
5 Grass	T. Blick	F. E. Pollington	G. A. Newberry
½ Grass	—	M. Schofield	W. W. Maxfield

	1939
1,000 yds.	W. W. Maxfield
25	G. H. Fleming
50 Tandem-paced	G. H. Fleming
1 Tandem	G. N. Burgess / L. R. Pond
½ Grass	J. R. Henderson
5 Grass	B. Hughes
2 Team pursuit	Not completed

1940–43
Championships suspended

	1944	1945
1,000 yds.	R. H. Harris	R. H. Harris
¼	R. H. Harris	R. H. Harris
5	R. H. Harris	L. R. Pond
5 Grass	T. C. Godwin	T. C. Godwin
25	—	T. C. Godwin
½ Grass	—	R. H. Harris
1 Grass	—	R. Waters

	1946	1947	1948
1,000 yds.	R. H. Harris	R. H. Harris	A. Bannister
25	T. C. Godwin	R. Waters	R. A. Geldard
50 Tandem-paced	G. H. Fleming	A. W. Butler	A. W. Butler
1 Tandem	S. V. Harrison / J. Hampshire	A. Bannister / R. H. Harris	A. Bannister / R. H. Harris
½ Grass	E. Ilott	W. Lane	D. E. Guy
5 Grass	T. C. Godwin	R. Waters	J. Atkinson
4,000 metres Individual pursuit	—	C. G. Marriner	C. Cartwright / C. G. Marriner } Tie
4,000 metres Team pursuit	Belle Vue C.C.	Manchester Whs.	S. Paragon C.C.

Oscar Plattner (Switzerland)

Tommy Godwin

Alan Bannister

	1949	1950	1951
1,000 yds.	A. Bannister	A. Bannister	C. Bardsley
25	R. A. Geldard	R. A. Geldard	W. B. Box
50 Tandem-paced	R. Waters	R. Waters	R. Waters
1 Tandem	A. Bannister / L. Jackson	A. Bannister / L. Jackson	A. Bannister / L. Jackson
4,000 metres Individual pursuit	T. C. Godwin	C. Cartwright	D. Keeler
4,000 metres Team pursuit	Rover R.C.C.	Norwood Paragon C.C.	E. Mid. Clarion
½ Grass	P. Brotherton	B. Barnes	R. Kitchenham
5 Grass	L. Wilson	R. Waters	W. E. Jones

	1952	1953	1954
1,000 metres	C. Peacock	C. Peacock	C. Peacock
500 metres junior	C. Wiles	M. Hasler	K. Barton
10	—	M. Ward	D. Burgess
25	W. E. Jones	—	
50 Tandem-paced	Not run	D. J. Fleming	B. C. Pusey
1,000 metres Tandem	A. Bannister / L. Wilson	P. Brotherton / E. G. Thompson	M. Ward / J. Crebbin
4,000 metres Individual pursuit	G. K. Bentley	K. H. Mitchell	N. Sheil
4,000 metres Team pursuit	E. Mid. Clarion	Norwood Paragon C.C.	Void
½ Grass	M. Ward	J. D. Tighe	M. Ward
5 Grass	K. J. Harrison	B. Sandy	B. Sandy

	1955	1956	1957
1,000 metres	L. Binch	L. Binch	L. Binch
500 metres Junior	R. Springett	B. Wiles	T. Millard
10	E. G. Thompson	D. Burgess	N. Sheil
50 Tandem-paced	R. Waters	R. Waters	M. Gambrill
4,000 metres Individual pursuit	N. Sheil	M. Gambrill	R. Sefton
1,000 metres Tandem	M. Ward / J. Crebbin	P. Brotherton / E. G. Thompson	D. Handley / W. Towers
4,000 metres Team pursuit	Polytechnic C.C.	Norwood Paragon C.C.	Polytechnic C.C.
½ Grass	E. G. Thompson	R. Swinnerton	N. Tong
5 Grass	B. Sandy	R. Webster	K. J. Harrison

	1958	1959
1,000 metres	L. Binch	L. Binch
500 metres Junior	A. Millard	—
10	J. Geddes	D. Skene
50 Tandem-paced	R. Sefton	—
4,000 metres Individual pursuit	T. Simpson	N. Sheil
1,000 metres Tandem	D. Handley / P. Carter	D. Handley / P. Carter
4,000 metres Team pursuit	Melling Wh. "A"	Clarence Wh.
½ Grass	A. Birkett	K. Barton
5 Grass	B. Hawkridge	—

CYCLING QUIZ

1. What is the amateur unpaced world record for one hour and who holds it?

*

2. Do you know the brief history of the Olympic Games?

*

3. What is the greatest distance ever ridden on a bicycle in one year?

*

4. Who holds the women's record for a year's cycling?

QUIZ ANSWERS

1. E. Baldini, Italy, at Vel Vigorelli, Milan, broke the world's hour record, beating professional Anquetil, in 1956, when Baldini was an amateur. He covered 28 miles 1,458 yards. 2. Their first inception in Greece was in 850 B.C. They became a regular promotion from 776 B.C. They were revived into the present modern series in 1896 by a Frenchman, Baron Coubertin. 3. Tommy Godwin amassed a total of 75,065 miles during 1939. He went on to cover 100,000 miles in 499 days. 4. Mrs. "Billy" Dovey covered 29,604 miles during 1938 between her morning and evening household chores.

NATIONAL CYCLING CHAMPIONS (ROAD)

1938	J. Holmes
1939	J. Fancourt
1940–43	Championships suspended
1944	R. K. Braddick
1945	J. A. O'Driscoll
1946	E. A. Clements
1947	A. Taylor
1948	R. J. Maitland
1949	A. D. Newman
1950	G. W. Thomas
1951	P. Procter
1952	G. J. Vines
1953	*Senior:* E. C. Gerrard; *Junior:* H. Reynolds
1954	*Senior:* B. J. King; *Junior:* D. Smith
1955	*Senior:* B. J. King; *Junior:* D. W. Tarr
1956	*Senior:* A. Jackson; *Junior:* S. Praill
1957	*Senior:* A. S. Brittain; *Junior:* A. Engers
1958	*Senior:* W. Seggar; *Junior:* J. Goodrum

All unquoted distances are in miles.

Penny Farthing championships discontinued from 1893.

Tricycle championships discontinued from 1896.

Massed-start road championships started 1945.

4,000 metres team pursuit championships started 1946.

4,000 metres individual pursuit championships started 1947.

Women's championships created 1947.

Junior sprint title created 1952.

Metric distances for sprint and tandem events came in 1952.

Women's individual pursuit reduced to 3,000 metres 1952.

Metric distance for women's sprint came in 1952.

25 miles changed to 10 miles in 1953.

Junior massed-start title added 1953.

NATIONAL CYCLING CHAMPIONS (WOMEN)

	1947	1948	1949
550 yds.	D. Hobbs	A. Hunnisett	D. M. Stockwell
½ grass	M. Martin	M. E. Brown	M. E. Brown

	1950	1951	1952
550 yds.	D. M. Stockwell	D. M. Stockwell	E. Newman (500 metres)
½ grass	P. Byrne	I. Hoult	M. Beevers
4,000 metres Individual pursuit	—	D. M. Farrell	D. M. Franks (3,000 metres)

	1953	1954	1955
500 metres	M. Beevers	M. R. Flasby	J. Bell
½ grass	M. Beevers	D. Grayson	P. Hodson
3,000 metres Individual pursuit	D. M. Franks	D. M. Franks	G. Tiley

	1956	1957	1958	1959
500 metres	B. Cannell	J. Dunn	J. Dunn	J. Dunn
½ grass	B. Cannell	B. Cannell	P. Hodson	—
3,000 metres Individual pursuit	D. M. Franks	S. Ball	S. Ball	—
Road	—	S. Mayers	J. Poole	D. Johnson

CYCLING QUIZ

1. Who invented the pneumatic tyre?

*

2. Who broke all four tricycle records, 50 and 100 miles and 12 and 24 hours, on both road and track?

*

3. Where should one carry one's luggage when cycling?

*

4. R. Booty was the first man to ride 100 miles out-and-home inside four hours in 1956. Who first rode 100 miles inside five hours?

*

5. What was the cushion tyre and did it precede the pneumatic?

QUIZ ANSWERS

1. R. W. Thomson, in 1845. A laminated tyre for use on carriages. There were then no cycles to take it up. This patent was unknown to J. B. Dunlop, who invented, and applied to cycles, a pneumatic tyre in 1888. 2. F. T. Bidlake, one of the greatest cyclists in the history of the game. As well as an outstanding tricyclist he was timekeeper, journalist and North Road Cycling Club president. 3. Never on the body. Let the cycle carry the weight. The usual container is a saddle bag fixed to the rear of the saddle. 4. Leon Meredith rode 100 miles in 4 hours 52 min. 52 sec. in 1910. 5. No, it was a reply to the pneumatic tyre. It was a non-inflated rubber tyre with a hole through the middle.

NATIONAL ROAD CHAMPIONS (TIME TRIALS)
(Under the Rules and Regulations of the Road Time Trials Council)

25 MILES

Year	Champion	Champion Team
1944	J. SIMPSON, Barnsley R.C.	Dukinfield C.C.
1945	C. CARTWRIGHT, Manchester Clarion	Calleva R.C.
1946	B. B. FRANCIS, Solihull C.C.	Solihull C.C.
1947	R. FIRTH, Altrincham Ravens	Altrincham Ravens
1948	C. CARTWRIGHT, Manchester Wh.	Kingston R. C.C.
1949	G. F. FELL, Becontree Wh.	Becontree Wh.
1950	G. F. FELL, Becontree Wh.	Solihull C.C.
1951	R. INMAN, Mercury R.C.	Mercury R.C.
1952	S. F. HIGGINSON, Halesowen A. and C.C.	Halesowen A. and C.C.
1953	S. F. HIGGINSON, Halesowen A. and C.C.	Halesowen A. and C.C.
1954	S. F. HIGGINSON, Halesowen A. and C.C.	Halesowen A. and C.C.
1955	G. IAN, Mansfield Victoria	Norwood Paragon C.C.
1956	M. J. GAMBRILL, Clarence Wh.	Crescent Wh.
1957	N. L. SHEIL, Molyneux R.C.	Clarence Wh.
1958	M. WARD, Haverhill Wh.	Clarence Wh.
1959	G. IAN, Nottingham Wh.	Nottingham Wh.

50 MILES

Year	Champion	Champion Team
1944	A. C. HARDING, Middlesex R.C.	Yorkshire R.C.
1945	J. SIMPSON, Barnsley R.C.	Calleva R.C.
1946	A. E. DERBYSHIRE, Calleva R.C.	Yorkshire R.C.
1947	G. FLEMING, Belle Vue C.C.	Solihull C.C.
1948	R. FIRTH, Altrincham Ravens	Medway Wh.
1949	J. SIMPSON, Midland C. and A.C.	Medway Wh.
1950	W. FOWLER, Tees-side Clarion C. and A.C.	Brentwood R.C.
1951	G. K. BENTLEY, Bec C.C.	Brentwood R.C.
1952	G. K. BENTLEY, Bec C.C.	Medway Wh.
1953	P. H. JACKSON, Dixie Wh.	Manchester Clarion C. and A.C.
1954	V. A. GIBBONS, Brentwood R.C.	Mercury C.C.
1955	V. A. GIBBONS, Brentwood R.C.	Willesden C.C.
1956	M. WARD, Haverhill Wh.	Willesden C.C.
1957	R. JOWERS, Twickenham C.C.	Crescent Wh.
1958	M. WARD, Haverhill Wh.	Crescent Wh.
1959	M. WARD, Haverhill Wh.	

100 MILES

Year	Champion	Champion Team
1944	A. C. HARDING, Middlesex R.C.	Altrincham Ravens
1945	B. L. SMITH, Yorkshire R.C.	Yorkshire R.C.
1946	A. E. G. DERBYSHIRE, Calleva R.C.	Calleva R.C.
1947	R. FIRTH, Altrincham Ravens	Yorkshire R.C.
1948	J. MUMBERSON, Northumbrian R.C.	Yorkshire R.C.
1949	S. HASLAM, Lancashire R.C.	Medway Wh.
1950	K. H. JOY, Medway Wh.	Norwood Paragon C.C.
1951	L. V. WILLMOTT, Midland C. and A.C.	Concorde R.C.C.
1952	K. R. WHITMARSH, Southampton Wh.	Medway Wh.
1953	E. BRITTEN, Yorkshire R.C.	Yorkshire R.C.
1954	V. A. GIBBONS, Brentwood R.C.	Yorkshire R.C.
1955	R. C. BOOTY, Ericsson Wh.	Midland Clarion C. and A.C.
1956	R. C. BOOTY, Ericsson Wh.	Colchester Rovers
1957	R. C. BOOTY, Army C.U.	Midland Clarion C. and A.C.
1958	R. C. BOOTY, Army C.U.	Midland Clarion C. and A.C.
1959	R. C. BOOTY, Ericsson Wh.	Ericsson Wh.

12 HOURS

Year	Champion	Champion Team
1944	A. E. G. DERBYSHIRE, Calleva R.C.	Altrincham Calleva } Tie
1945	D. H. HEPPLETSON, Yorkshire R.C.	Calleva R.C.
1946	A. E. G. DERBYSHIRE, Calleva R.C.	Altrincham Ravens
1947	A. E. G. DERBYSHIRE, Calleva R.C.	Middlesex R.C.
1948	A. N. HAMMOND, Cheshire R.C.	Cheshire Roads Club
1949	B. J. BROWN, Norwood Paragon C.C.	Norwood Paragon C.C.
1950	K. H. JOY, Medway Wh.	Norwood Paragon C.C.
1951	K. H. JOY, Medway Wh.	Kentish Wh.
1952	G. A. T. LAWS, Catford C.C.	Kentish Wh.
1953	B. W. APPLEBY, Kentish Wh.	Kentish Wh.
1954	R. C. BOOTY, Ericsson Wh.	Mercury C.C.
1955	R. C. BOOTY, Ericsson Wh.	Rutland C.C.
1956	R. C. BOOTY, Ericsson Wh.	Midland Clarion C. and A.C.
1957	R. C. BOOTY, Army C.U.	Middlesex R.C.
1958	R. C. BOOTY, Army C.U.	Middlesex R.C.
1959	P. BESWICK, Manchester Vic.	

24 HOURS

Year	Champion	Champion Team
1948	G. H. BASHAM, Wessex R.C.	Luton Wh.
1949	S. E. HARVEY, Addiscombe C.C.	Solihull C.C.
1950	S. M. BUTLER, Norwood Paragon C.C.	Addiscombe C.C.
1951	G. ANDREWS, Addiscombe C.C.	Addiscombe C.C.
1952	E. MUNDY, Addiscombe C.C.	Addiscombe C.C.
1953	P. E. A. CARTER, South Lancs. R.C.	South Lancs. R.C.
1954	S. THOMPSON, Rutland C.C.	Addiscombe C.C.
1955	K. PRICE, Cardiff 100-miles R.C.	Rutland C.C.
1956	F. BURRELL, Middlesex R.C.	Rutland C.C.
1957	J. LEVERSIDGE, Rutland C.C.	Rutland C.C.
1958	D. H. WHITE, Swindon Wh.	Rutland C.C.
1959	R. COUKHAM, Rutland C.C.	

HILL CLIMB

Year	Champion	Champion Team
1944	F. H. WORTHEN, Manchester Clar.	Manchester Clar.
1945	R. J. MAITLAND, Solihull C.C.	Solihull C.C.
1946	V. CLARK, Manchester Clar.	Manchester Clar.
1947	V. CLARK, Coventry C.C.	Manchester Clar.
1948	V. CLARK, Coventry C.C.	Coventry C.C.
1949	R. J. MAITLAND, Concorde R.C.C.	Concorde R.C.C.
1950	R. STRINGWELL, Bramley Wh.	Concorde R.C.C.
1951	R. STRINGWELL, Bramley Wh.	Huddersfield R.C.
1952	R. ROBINSON, Huddersfield R.C.	Huddersfield R.C.
1953	R. KEIGHLEY, Shipley R.C.	Bramley Wh.
1954	W. L. INGMAN, Norwood Paragon C.C.	Bramley Wh.
1955	E. WILSON, Rossendale R.C.	Bramley Wh.
1956	W. L. INGMAN, Norwood Paragon C.C.	Bramley Wh.
1957	E. WILSON, Rossendale R.C.	Bramley Wh.
1958	P. J. GRAHAM, West Pennine R.C.	Bramley Wh.

LADIES' 25 MILES

Year	Champion	Champion Team
1944	S. RIMMINGTON, Chesterfield Spire	29th Wheelers
1945	E. SHERIDAN, Coventry R.C.	Pyramid R.C.
1946	S. M. FARRELL, Rickmansworth	Pyramid R.C.
1947	S. M. FARRELL, Yiewsley R.C.	Yiewsley R.C.
1948	J. J. DEAN, Apollo C.C.	Meersbrook C.C.
1949	S. M. FARRELL, Yiewsley R.C.	Coventry C.C.
1950	E. M. HORTON, Coventry R.C.	Coventry R.C.
1951	C. BROWN, South Shields Victoria C.C.	Apollo C.C.
1952	C. BROWN, South Shields Victoria C.C.	Coventry C.C.
1953	J. HARRIS, Apollo C.C.	Hull Thursday R.C.
1954	D. M. HACKNEY, Mephisto C.C.	Liverpool Grosvenor C.C.
1955	M. J. ROBINSON, Manx Viking Wh.	Silchester C.C.
1956	M. J. ROBINSON, Manx Viking Wh.	Silchester C.C.
1957	M. J. ROBINSON, Manx Viking Wh.	Silchester C.C.
1958	B. BURTON, Morley C.C.	Silchester C.C.
1959	B. BURTON, Morley C.C.	

LADIES' 50 MILES

Year	Champion	Champion Team
1948	S. M. FARRELL, Yiewsley R.C.	Meersbrook C.C.
1949	J. GREGORY, Nottingham Wh.	Coventry R.C.
1950	E. SHERIDAN, Coventry R.C.	Coventry R.C.
1951	D. M. STOCKWELL, Apollo C.C.	Apollo C.C.
1952	J. HARRISS, Apollo C.C.	Coventry C.C.
1953	C. BROWN, South Shields Victoria C.C.	Apollo C.C.
1954	D. M. HACKNEY, Mephisto C.C.	Addiscombe C.C.
1955	D. M. FRANKS, Apollo C.C.	Addiscombe C.C.
1956	I. MILES, Scala Wh.	Silchester C.C.
1957	I. MILES, Scala Wh.	Tees-side Clarion C. and A.C.
1958	B. BURTON, Morley C.C.	Southampton Wh.
1959	B. BURTON, Morley C.C.	

LADIES' 100 MILES

Year	Champion	Champion Team
1950	E. SHERIDAN, Coventry C.C.	Rosslyn Ladies' C.C.
1951	D. M. STOCKWELL, Apollo C.C.	Apollo C.C.
1952	J. HARRIS, Apollo C.C.	Apollo C.C.
1953	D. M. FRANKS, Apollo C.C.	Apollo C.C.
1954	J. G. SUTHERLAND, Mussleburgh R.C.	Addiscombe C.C.
1955	F. M. DAWSON, Tees-side R.C.	Addiscombe C.C.
1956	I. MILES, Scala Wh.	Addiscombe C.C.
1957	R. CLARKE, Leicestershire R.C.	Tees-side Clarion C. and A.C.
1958	B. BURTON, Morley C.C.	Morley C.C.
1959	B. BURTON, Morley C.C.	

WOMEN'S ROAD RECORDS (W.R.R.A)
(Standing on the books at September, 1959)

In February 1946 the Women's R.R.A. separated amateur and professional records. It was also decided to make the amateur performances retrospective so that previous amateur "bests" could be recorded.

Type of Machine	Amateur or Professional	Holder	Time		
			h.	m.	s.
25 Miles					
Bicycle	A	MISS J. DEAN	1	3	29
Bicycle	P	MRS. E. SHERIDAN	1	3	58
Tandem	A	MRS. D. FRANKS and MRS. J. POOLE		57	36
Tricycle	A	MRS. D. TUFFNELL	1	16	34
Tricycle	P	MRS. L. DOVEY	1	21	49
50 Miles					
Bicycle	A	MRS. A. BRIERCLIFFE	1	59	14
Bicycle	P	MRS. E. SHERIDAN	1	55	0
Tandem	A	MRS. C. WATTS and MRS. D. GRIST	1	55	34
Tricycle	A	MRS. D. TUFFNELL	2	35	4
Tricycle	P	MRS. L. DOVEY	2	26	17

Type of Machine	Amateur or Professional	Holder	Time h.	m.	s.
		100 Miles			
Bicycle	A	Miss M. Wilson	4	31	8
Bicycle	P	Mrs. E. Sheridan	4	16	1
Tandem	A	Mrs. C. Watts and Mrs. D. Grist	3	57	11
Tricycle	A	Mrs. D. Tuffnell	5	27	43
Tricycle	P	Mrs. L. Dovey	5	35	57
		1,000 Miles	*d.*	*h.*	*m.*
Bicycle	A	Mrs. W. Wrightson	3	15	53
Bicycle	P	Mrs. E. Sheridan	3	1	0
		12 Hours		*Miles*	
Bicycle	A	Mrs. E. Atkins		234¾	
Bicycle	P	Mrs. E. Sheridan		250½	
Tandem	A	Mrs. J. Terry and Miss A. Bendall		241½	
		24 Hours			
Bicycle	A	Mrs. E. Atkins		422	
Bicycle	P	Mrs. E. Sheridan		446¼	
		London to York	*h.*	*m.*	*s.*
Bicycle	A	Mrs. E. Atkins	9	56	20
Bicycle	P	Mrs. E. Sheridan	9	5	20
Tandem	A	Misses A. Caley and M. Callagher	10	43	0
		London to Birmingham			
Bicycle	A	Mrs. E. Sheridan	5	22	0
Bicycle	P	Mrs. E. Sheridan	5	19	35
Tandem	A	Misses T. M. Biggs and J. Springall	5	14	0
		London to Bath and Back			
Bicycle	A	Mrs. E. Atkins	11	11	34
Bicycle	P	Mrs. E. Sheridan	10	41	22
Tandem	A	Mrs. J. Terry and Miss A. Bendall	10	16	35
		London to Brighton and Back			
Bicycle	A	Mrs. D. M. Franks	4	59	50
Bicycle	P	Mrs. E. Sheridan	5	2	11
Tandem	A	Mrs. C. Watts and Mrs. D. Grist	4	36	6

Type of Machine	Amateur or Professional	Holder	Time h.	m.	s.
		London to Portsmouth and Back			
Bicycle	A	Miss D. R. Stratford	7	18	25
Bicycle	P	Mrs. E. Sheridan	6	56	40
		Land's End to London			
Bicycle	A	Mrs. E. Atkins	17	13	31
Bicycle	P	Mrs. E. Sheridan	14	36	18
		London to Liverpool			
Bicycle	A	Mrs. F. Uren	11	53	0
Bicycle	P	Mrs. E. Sheridan	9	39	0
		Edinburgh to Glasgow and Back			
Bicycle	A	Mrs. E. Atkins	4	38	56
Bicycle	P	Mrs. E. Sheridan	4	18	30
		Liverpool to Edinburgh			
Bicycle	A	Mrs. E. Atkins	11	20	40
Bicycle	P	Mrs. E. Sheridan	10	8	20
		Land's End to John o' Groats	*d.*	*h.*	*m.*
Bicycle	A	Mrs. E. Atkins	2	18	4
Bicycle	P	Mrs. E. Sheridan	2	11	7
		London to Oxford and Back	*h.*	*m.*	*s.*
Bicycle	A	Mrs. E. Sheridan	5	27	19
Bicycle	P	Mrs. E. Sheridan	5	26	10
Tandem	A	Miss J. Terry and Miss A. Bendell	5	0	22
		London to Edinburgh			
Bicycle	A	Mrs. E. Atkins	21	37	0
Bicycle	P	Mrs. E. Sheridan	20	11	35
		London to Holyhead			
Bicycle	A	Mrs. E. Atkins	13	31	57
Bicycle	P	Mrs. E. Sheridan	13	20	11
		Edinburgh to York			
Bicycle	A	Mrs. E. Atkins	10	40	24
Bicycle	P	Mrs. E. Sheridan	9	22	30
		London to Great Yarmouth			
Bicycle	A	Mrs. E. Atkins	6	1	46
Bicycle	P	Mrs. E. Sheridan	6	28	7

The women's R.R.A. recognises bicycle, tandem and tricycle records at all these distances, times and place-to-place records. There are twenty-one records for each of the three types now awaiting attempts on the W.R.R.A. books.

CYCLING QUIZ

1. How did the Union Cycliste Internationale come into being?

★

2. Who was the first man in this country to ride 25 miles in the hour in out-and-home competition?

★

3. When was 50 miles first ridden in competition inside two hours and who by?

★

4. What is the gear of a cycle?

★

5. Why is a racing cyclist's saddle board hard?

QUIZ ANSWERS

1. Early in the 1890's an international cycle racing organization was founded by Britain in which England, Scotland, Ireland and Wales had separate representation. Soon the other European countries complained that Britain had too great an influence in world cycling affairs and so, leaving Britain out of the foundation plans, the U.C.I. came into being in 1900 and this country had to apply for membership at a later date with only a one-country voice. 2. In 1939 Ralph Dougherty won the Solihull "25" with a record ride of 59 minutes 29 seconds to be the first man in competition to ride the distance inside one hour. 3. G. H. Fleming, Belle Vue C.C., rode 50 miles out-and-home in 1 hr. 59 min. 14 sec. in 1947. 4. The Old High bicycle (called, today, the Penny Farthing) was directly driven with cranks solidly fixed to the big front wheel. The gear was the diameter of this driving wheel and a long-legged man could ride a bigger gear (wheel) than a short-legged man. $3\frac{1}{7}$ (pi) times his gear was the distance travelled by one complete revolution of the pedals. The gear of a modern bicycle is similarly related to distance travelled with one pedal turn. The formula now is to multiply the diameter in inches of the back wheel by the number of teeth on the chainwheel and divide the result by the number of teeth on the rear sprocket. 5. Economy of effort is the answer. A near-streamlined cyclist shares his weight on saddle, 'bars and pedals. His saddle positions him between the thighs rather than acts as a cushion to sit on. If muscular effort is used in distorting the saddle that effort is lost to the forward thrust.

ROAD RECORDS, COMPETITION (R.T.T.C.)

Distance	Name and Club	Date	Time or Distance
	Bicycle (Individual)		
25 miles	D. S. Evans, Acme Wh. (Rhondda)	1958	55 m. 45 s.
30 miles	R. Jowers, Twickenham C.C.	1955	1 hr. 7 m. 30 s.
50 miles	G. Ian, Nottingham Wh.	1959	1hr. 55 m. 9s.
100 miles	R. C. Booty, Ericsson Wh.	1956	3 hr. 58 m. 28 s.
12 hours	O. G. Blower, Leicestershire R.C.	1958	271.80 miles
24 hours	D. H. White, Swindon Wh.	1958	484.75 miles
	Bicycle (Team)		
25 miles	Nottingham Wh.	1959	2 hr. 52 m. 54s.
30 miles	Willesden C.C.	1954	3 hr. 32 m. 54 s.
50 miles	Crescent Wh.	1958	5 hr. 54 m. 52 s.
100 miles	Midland Clarion C. and A.C.	1958	12 hr. 43 m. 42 s.
12 hours	Leicestershire R.C.	1958	772.70 miles
24 hours	Rutland C.C.	1958	1,402.69 miles
	Tricycle		
25 miles	C. Grainger, Sparton Wh.	1958	1 hr. 2 m. 27 s.
30 miles	W. F. Johnson, Colchester Rovers C.C.	1957	1 hr. 16 m. 50 s.
50 miles	C. Grainger, Sparton Wh.	1958	2 hr. 8 m. 43 s.
100 miles	L. G. Bowerman, Charlotteville C.C.	1958	4 hr. 32 m. 46 s.
12 hours	J. F. Arnold, Middleton C.C.	1953	246.15 miles
24 hours	J. F. Arnold, Middleton C.C.	1953	457.33 miles
	Tandem		
30 miles	M. Gambrill and A. Killick Clarence Wh.	1955	1 hr. 0 m. 48 s.
50 miles	M. Gambrill and A. Killick, Clarence Wh.	1955	1 hr. 45 m. 11 s.
100 miles	K. H. Joy and P. Beardsmore, Medway Wh.	1947	3 hr. 49 m. 35 s.

WINNERS OF THE TOUR DE FRANCE

Date	Name and Country	Distance kms.	Time h.	m.	s.
1903	M. Garin, France	2,428	94	33	0
1904	H. Cornet, France	2,388	96	5	55
1905	L. Trousselier, France	2,975	110	26	58
1906	R. Pottier, France	4,637	173	0	7
1907	L. Petit-Breton, France	4,488	158	54	5
1908	L. Petit-Breton, France	4,488	147	50	7
1909	F. Faber, Luxembourg	4,497	157	1	22
1910	O. Lapize, France	4,700	162	41	30
1911	G. Garrigou, France	5,544	195	37	0
1912	O. Defraye, Belgium	5,229	190	30	28
1913	Ph. Thys, Belgium	5,387	197	54	0
1914	Ph. Thys, Belgium	5,414	200	28	48
	1915–1918 suspended				
1919	F. Lambot, Belgium	5,560	231	7	15
1920	Ph. Thys, Belgium	5,503	228	36	13
1921	L. Scieur, Belgium	5,484	221	50	26
1922	F. Lambot, Belgium	5,375	222	8	6
1923	H. Pelissier, France	5,386	222	15	30
1924	O. Bottecchia, Italy	5,427	226	18	21
1925	O. Bottecchia, Italy	5,430	219	10	18
1926	L. Buysse, Belgium	5,475	238	44	25
1927	N. Frantz, Luxembourg	5,321	198	16	42
1928	N. Frantz, Luxembourg	5,377	192	48	58
1929	M. Dewaele, Belgium	5,286	186	39	16
1930	A. Leducq, France	4,818	172	12	16
1931	A. Magne, France	5,095	177	10	3
1932	A. Leducq, France	4,502	154	11	49
1933	G. Speicher, France	4,395	147	59	37
1934	A. Magne, France	4,363	147	13	58
1935	R. Maes, Belgium	4,302	141	32	39
1936	S. Maes, Belgium	4,442	142	47	32
1937	R. Lapebie, France	4,415	138	58	31
1938	G. Bartali, Italy	4,694	148	29	12
1939	S. Maes, Belgium	4,224	132	3	17
	1940–1946 suspended				
1947	J. Robic, France	4,640	144	22	7
1948	G. Bartali, Italy	4,922	147	20	51
1949	Fausto Coppi, Italy	4,775	149	42	50
1950	F. Kubler, Switzerland	4,808	145	36	56
1951	H. Koblet, Switzerland	4,697	142	20	14
1952	Fausto Coppi, Italy	4,807	151	57	20
1953	L. Bobet, France	4,479	129	25	55
1954	L. Bobet, France	4,855	140	6	5
1955	L. Bobet, France	4,495	130	29	26
1956	R. Walkowiak, France	4,528	124	1	16
1957	J. Anquetil, France	4,686	135	44	42
1958	C. Gaul, Luxembourg	4,320	117	2	37
1959	F. Bahamontes, Spain	—	123	46	45

CYCLING QUIZ

1. When, and by whom, was the modern safety bicycle invented?

*

2. Who invented the bicycle?

*

3. When did cycling start as an established movement?

QUIZ ANSWERS

1. The first safety bicycle with a diamond frame almost like the modern machine in shape was invented by J. K. Starley in 1885. He was the nephew of James Starley, the Father of the Cycle Industry. 2. It is claimed by Britain that the bicycle driven with the feet on treadles was invented by Kirkpatrick Macmillan at Courthill in Dumfriesshire, Scotland, in 1839. He fitted treadle-driven levers to rear-wheel cranks to a Hobby-horse. 3. Macmillan's invention was forgotten and had no vogue. In 1861 Michaux in Paris fitted cranks and pedals to the front wheel of a Hobby-horse. Samples crossed to England and a sewing-machine company started making them in 1869 in Coventry where the cycle industry was established.

LONDON TO BRIGHTON & BACK

(104½ miles)

		h.	m.	s.
	Paced			
1892	R. C. Nesbitt (Penny Farthing)	7	42	50
1890	F. W. Shorland	7	19	0
1890	S. F. Edge	7	2	50
1890	C. A. Smith	6	52	10
1892	S. F. Edge	6	51	7
1892	E. Dance	6	49	1
1893	S. F. Edge	6	13	48
1893	A. E. Knight	6	10	29
1893	C. A. Smith	6	6	46
1893	S. F. Edge	5	52	30
1894	E. Dance	5	52	18
1894	C. G. Wridgway	5	35	32
1895	A. A. Chase	5	34	58
1896	C. G. Wridgway	5	22	33
1897	W. J. Neason	5	19	39
1897	R. Palmer	5	9	45
1897	W. J. Neason	5	6	42
	Unpaced			
1898	E. J. Steel	6	23	55
1899	H. Green	5	50	23
1902	H. Green	5	30	22
1905	R. Shirley	5	22	5
1906	H. Green	5	20	22
1906	R. Shirley	5	15	29
1909	H. Green	5	12	14
1912	F. H. Grubb	5	9	41
1926	A. R. M. Harbour	5	7	35
1926	C. Marshall	5	6	46
1927	F. W. Southall	4	53	20
1935	E. Milliken	4	49	23
1935	E. Milliken	4	39	25
1935	F. W. Southall	4	38	27
1949	P. Beardsmore	4	36	8
1949	K. H. Joy	4	34	13
1950	A. R. J. Hill	4	32	19
1953	K. H. Joy	4	25	33

F. W. Southall　　Norman Shiel　　Louison Bobet (France)

ROAD RECORDS, NATIONAL (R.R.A.)

(Standing on the books at September 1, 1959)

Note. P=Paced

"Ordinary" bicycle refers to the old high bicycle; the "Safety" is the modern type.

Type of Machine	*Date*	*Holder*		*Time* h.	m.	s.
		50 Miles				
Ordinary Bicycle	1891	*S. C. Houghton*	(P)	2	45	55
Safety Bicycle	1939	*H. Earnshaw*		1	39	42
Tandem Bicycle	1954	*L. J. Blackhurst and A. Griffiths*		1	35	45
Tricycle	1936	*A. Watson*		2	0	40
Tandem Tricycle	1954	*A. Crimes and J. F. Arnold*		1	49	55
		100 Miles				
Ordinary Bicycle	1891	*J. F. Walsh*	(P)	6	22	15
Safety Bicycle	1956	*R. C. Booty*		3	28	40
Tandem Bicycle	1955	*L. J. Blackhurst and A. Griffiths*		3	33	49
Tricycle	1958	*D. Duffield*		4	31	52
Tandem Tricycle	1954	*A. Crimes and J. F. Arnold*		3	46	30
		1,000 Miles				
Safety Bicycle	1956	*A. Render*		2	16	50
Tandem Bicycle	1952	*S. F. Cowsill and A. E. Denton*		3	7	41
Tricycle	1958	*A. Crimes*		2	21	37
Tandem Tricycle	1954	*A. Crimes and J. F. Arnold*		2	13	59

Type of Machine	*Date*	*Holder*		*Miles*
		12 Hours		
Ordinary Bicycle	1891	*J. F. Walsh*	(P)	175½
Safety Bicycle	1939	*H. Earnshaw*		276½
Tandem Bicycle	1935	*E. W. Milliken and W. F. Stuart*		274¾
Tricycle	1955	*D. Duffield*		230¾
Tandem Tricycle	1954	*A. Crimes and J. F. Arnold*		257¾
		24 Hours		
Ordinary Bicycle	1891	*J. F. Walsh*	(P)	312
Safety Bicycle	1954	*K. H. Joy*		475¾
Tandem Bicycle	1959	*J. A. Bailey and J. Forrest*		*487¾
Tricycle	1952	*J. F. Arnold*		428½
Tandem Tricycle	1954	*A. Crimes and J. F. Arnold*		466¼

Type of Machine	*Date*	*Holder*		*Time* h.	m.	s.
		London to York				
Safety Bicycle	1939	*H. Earnshaw*		8	23	0
Tandem Bicycle	1950	*R. Needle and L. C. Young*		8	0	0
Tricycle	1938	*S. W. Parker*		10	24	0
Tandem Tricycle	1953	*A. S. Fowler and R. D. Cook*		9	9	0
		York to Edinburgh				
Safety Bicycle	1953	*K. H. Joy*		8	32	0
Tandem Bicycle	1937	*C. Heppleston and E. J. Atherton*		8	23	0
Tricycle	1953	*C. E. Green*		10	28	0
Tandem Tricycle	1956	*E. Tweddell and C. Sandham*		9	38	0
		London to Liverpool				
Safety Bicycle	1954	*K. H. Joy*		7	56	0
Tandem Bicycle	1956	*L. J. Blackhurst and A. Griffiths*		8	4	0
Tricycle	1952	*J. F. Arnold*		9	50	0
Tandem Tricycle	1953	*A. Crimes and J. F. Arnold*		8	19	0
		Liverpool to Edinburgh				
Safety Bicycle	1954	*K. J. Joy*		9	6	0
Tandem Bicycle	1955	*L. Heald and A. Tyson*		9	21	0
Tricycle	1958	*G. Tait*		10	54	0
Tandem Tricycle	1953	*A. Crimes and J. F. Arnold*		9	4	0
		London to Edinburgh				
Safety Bicycle	1939	*C. Heppleston*		18	57	0
Tandem Bicycle	1950	*R. C. Smith and A. E. Collins*		19	4	0
Tricycle	1949	*E. Tweddell*		24	11	0
Tandem Tricycle	1956	*E. Tweddell and C. Sandham*		21	16	0
		Land's End to John o'Groats		d.	h.	m.
Ordinary Bicycle	1886	*G. P. Mills*	(P)	5	1	45
Safety Bicycle	1958	*R. F. Randall*		2	1	58
Tandem Bicycle	1952	*S. F. Cowsill and A. E. Denton*		2	8	47
Tricycle	1893	*G. P. Mills*	(P)	3	16	47
Tricycle	1957	*A. Crimes*		2	12	37
Tandem Tricycle	1954	*A. Crimes and J. F. Arnold*		2	4	26
		Land's End to London		h.	m.	s.
Safety Bicycle	1954	*R. J. Maitland*		12	34	0
Tandem Bicycle	1955	*R. T. and F. L. Powney*		13	27	0
Tricycle	1959	*R. N. West*		15	25	31
Tandem Tricycle	1952	*E. G. E. Widdows and J. M. P. Robinson*		16	12	0
		London to Bath and Back				
Ordinary Bicycle	1891	*R. C. Nesbitt*	(P)	15	40	34
Safety Bicycle	1953	*K. H. Joy*		9	36	23
Tandem Bicycle	1935	*E. Milliken and H. Opperman*		8	55	34
Tricycle	1956	*A. R. Chamberlain*		11	33	26
Tandem Tricycle	1953	*E. Tweddell and J. W. Stott*		10	34	55
		London to Brighton and Back				
Ordinary Bicycle	1892	*R. C. Nesbitt*	(P)	7	42	50
Safety Bicycle	1953	*K. H. Joy*		4	25	33
Tandem Bicycle	1935	*E. Milliken and W. F. Stuart*		4	9	43
Tricycle	1955	*J. Mortimer*		5	0	53
Tandem Tricycle	1955	*A. O. Wingrave and R. H. Oldridge*		4	46	56
		London to Portsmouth and Back				
Safety Bicycle	1953	*K. H. Joy*		6	12	0
Tandem Bicycle	1955	*G. R. Winkworth and P. T. Warhurst*		6	1	7
Tricycle	1957	*D. A. Wright*		7	1	38
Tandem Tricycle	1955	*R. Lake and V. G. Knibbs*		6	36	43
		London to Pembroke				
Safety Bicycle	1953	*K. H. Joy*		10	22	0
Tandem Bicycle	1955	*G. R. Winkworth and P. T. Warhurst*		10	44	0
Tricycle	1958	*D. A. Wright*		13	28	0
Tandem Tricycle	1951	*E. T. Tweddell and J. W. Stott*		12	58	0
		London to Cardiff				
Bicycle	1959	*C. M. Caton*		7	2	0

*Subject to confirmation.

THE WORLD'S UNPACED HOUR RECORD

Date	*Distance miles*	*yards*	*Holder*	*Track*
1893	21	1,674	†H. Desgrange (France)	Paris-Buffalo
1894	23	1,320	*J. Dubois (France)	Paris-Buffalo
1897	24	676	*M. Van Den Eynde (Belgium)	Paris-Municip.
1898	25	600	*W. W. Hamilton (America)	Denver, Colorado
1905	25	961	*Petit-Breton (France)	Paris-Buffalo
1907	25	1,410	†M. Berthet (France)	Paris-Buffalo
1912	26	308	*Oscar Egg (Switzerland)	Paris-Buffalo
1913	26	509	*R. Weise (Germany)	Berlin-Zehl
1913	26	984	*M. Berthet (France)	Paris-Buffalo
1913	27	81	*Oscar Egg (Switzerland)	Paris-Buffalo
1913	27	356	*M. Berthet (France)	Paris-Buffalo
1914	27	871	*Oscar Egg (Switzerland)	Paris-Buffalo
1933	27	1,450	*M. Richard (France)	Saint-Trond
1935	28	33	*G. Olmo (Italy)	Vel Vigorelli, Milan
1936	28	368	*M. Richard (France)	Vel Vigorelli, Milan
1937	28	545	*F. Slaats (Holland)	Vel Vigorelli, Milan
1937	28	851	*M. Archambaud (France)	Vel Vigorelli, Milan
1942	28	885	*Fausto Coppi (Italy)	Vel Vigorelli, Milan
1956	28	1,201	*J. Anquetil (France)	Vel Vigorelli, Milan
1956	28	1,458	†E. Baldini (Italy)	Vel Vigorelli, Milan
1957	29	276	*R. Riviere (France)	Vel Vigorelli, Milan
1958	29	739	*R. Riviere (France)	Vel Vigorelli, Milan

* Professional.　　† Amateur.

Year	Winner	Distance miles	Time h.	m.	s.
1951	IAN STEEL, Glasgow	1,403	63	9	53
1952	KEN RUSSELL, Bradford	1,470	61	26	49
1953	G. W. THOMAS, Britain	1,624	70	3	44
1954	E. TAMBURLINI, France	1,433	60	12	15
1955	A. HEWSON, Sheffield Aspirant	963	42	10	8
1956	No race				
1957	No race				
1958	R. DURLACHER, Austria	1,316	59	53	59
1959	W. BRADLEY, England	—	61	30	36

NATIONAL COMPETITION TIME TRIALS RECORDS (WOMEN)

Individual Bicycle

Distance miles	Holder	Year	Time h.	m.	s.
10	S. M. Ball, West Kent R.C.	1956		25	5
25	B Burton, Morley C.C.	1959	1	1	27
30	N. K. Jarvis, Gravesend C.C.	1956	1	17	44
50	B. Burton, Morley C.C.	1959	2	6	38
100	B. Burton, Morley C.C.	1959	4	20	4
12 hours	C. M. Watts, Addiscombe C.C.	1954		*Miles* 237.91	

Team

Distance miles	Holder	Year	Time h.	m.	s.
10	Southampton Wh.	1955	1	20	5
25	Apollo C.C.	1951	3	16	56
30	Apollo C.C.	1951	4	10	8
50	Morley C.C.	1959	6	41	31
100	Apollo C.C.	1953	14	1	25
12 hours	Addiscombe C.C.	1954		*Miles* 675.10	

LAND'S END TO JOHN O' GROATS

(Recent routes used about 870 miles)

PENNY FARTHING

		Days	Hrs.	Mins.
1885	J. LENNOX	6	16	7
1886	G. P. MILLS	5	1	45

SAFETY

		Days	Hrs.	Mins.
1891	G. P. MILLS	4	11	17
1892	T. A. EDGE	4	0	40
1892	L. FLETCHER	3	23	55
1894	R. H. CARLISLE	3	14	15
1894	G. P. MILLS	3	5	49

The above records were paced

Unpaced

		Days	Hrs.	Mins.
1903	C. J. MATHER	5	5	12
1904	F. W. WESLEY	4	7	25
1905	G. A. OLLEY	3	20	15
1907	T. PECK	3	12	53
1907	W. WELSH	3	8	4
1908	G. A. OLLEY	3	5	20
1908	T. PECK	2	22	42
1908	H. GREEN	2	19	50
1929	J. W. ROSSITER	2	13	22
1934	H. OPPERMAN	2	9	1
1937	S. H. FERRIS	2	6	33
1958	D. KEELER	2	3	9
1958	R. F. RANDALL	2	1	58

CYCLING QUIZ

How was the differential gear now used in almost every car first invented?

QUIZ ANSWER

James Starley had developed his Salvo tricycle into a side-by-side two-seater. Testing it near Coventry with his son William, it was found that on an incline the young man pushed his side of the machine ahead of his father's side and upset the steering. James went back to the works, invented a differential gear which transmitted the drive to both wheels even though their speeds varied, and travelled to London on the Monday following to patent it! (1877).

Compiled by **Norris McWhirter**

Athletics Correspondent: The Observer and B.B.C. Television Commentator

Darts

INTRODUCTION

The throwing of small darts at a board, divided into numbered sectors of differing scoring value, is predominantly an English game. It is centred competitively on the public house, inn and club, rather than in the home. A reasonable estimate of the total number of players, ranging from true devotees to occasional performers, is about 6,000,000 in the British Isles. About one million are registered players, being members of the 7,000 or so darts clubs.

There are reports from Tudor times of "dartes" being thrown at a marked board or quintain. This was a natural refinement on the warlike pastime of throwing javelins and "dartes" for sheer distance. Dart throwing in its original competitive form did not suffer the prohibition of many of the sports of the Middle Ages, because it was regarded as a military activity and therefore useful to the authorities.

It is recorded that the luckless Anne Boleyn, mother of Queen Elizabeth, presented her husband Henry VIII with "darts of Biscayan fashion richly ornamented". It is later chronicled that the Pilgrim Fathers took darts on board the *Mayflower* in 1620.

The specification of the boards used vary slightly in different parts of the country, but the rules used in the major competitions are as follows: The board is circular, being made of elm, or, more expensively, of bristle. It is divided by thin wires into 20 equal sectors numbered from 1 to 20 in value. A small bull's eye has an inner ring valued at 50 points and an outer circle worth 25 points. There is also a narrow inner ring and a narrow outer ring, which forms the outer edge of the scoring circle, that trebles and doubles the score respectively. The centre of the board is usually 5 ft. 8 in. from the ground—a height very close to the national average for a male in England and Wales.

Throwing of the darts is free-style, and in fact a wide variety of minor differences of technique exist. The darts themselves have a metal, often brass, body or a wooden body, weighted with lead inserts, and the tail is flighted with materials ranging from feathers to fins made of plastics. Keen players go to great pains to select darts that suit their style and habitually carry their own darts to all competitions.

The throwing distance varies between 8 feet and 9 feet. Women players—and there are about 400 clubs exclusively for them—and children throw from the nearest permissible distance, while men usually elect whether to have their feet behind a mark at 8 ft. 6 in. or 9 feet. It should be noted, however, that in the Individual Championship organised by the *News of the World* the throwing distance is only 8 feet.

"NEWS OF THE WORLD" ENGLAND AND WALES INDIVIDUAL DARTS CHAMPIONSHIP

	Winners		Runners-up	
1948	Harry Leadbetter	*Windle Labour Club, St. Helens, Lancs.*	T. Small	*South Durham Steel & Iron Social Club, West Hartlepool, Co. Durham.*
1949	Jackie Boyce	*Social Club, New Southgate, Middlesex.*	S. Outten	*Doctor Johnson, Barkingside, Essex.*
1950	Dixie Newbury	*The Albert, Hitchen, Herts.*	R. Ridley	*King Edward Hotel, Newcastle-upon-Tyne.*
1951	Harry Perryman	*H.O. Social Club, Greenford, Middlesex.*	L. Runchman	*Feathers Inn, Felixstowe, Suffolk.*
1952	Tommy Gibbons	*Ivanhoe W. M. Club, Conisbrough, Yorks.*	J. Wallace	*British Legion, Low Seaton, Workington Cumb.*
1953	Jimmy Carr	*Red Lion Hotel, Dipton Co. Durham.*	E. Greatbatch	*Horse Vaults Hotel, Pontefract, Yorks.*
1954	Oliver James	*Ex-Servicemen's Club Onllwyn, Glam.*	J. Bell	*Sun Inn, Waltham Abbey, Essex.*
1955	Tom Reddington	*New Inn, Stonebroom, Derbys.*	J. Bell	*Sun Inn, Waltham Abbey, Essex.*
1956	Trevor Peachey	*Black Fox Inn, Thurston, Suffolk.*	L. Campbell	*Boot Inn, Dinas, Glam.*
1957	Alwyn Mullins	*Traveller's Rest Hotel, Tickhill, Yorks.*	L. Baker	*Corporation Hotel, Cardiff, Glam.*
1958	Tommy Gibbons	*Ivanhoe W.M. Club, Conisbrough, Yorks.*	E. Moss	*Railway Tavern, Harleston, Norfolk.*
1959	Albert Welsh	*Horden Hotel, Horden Colliery, Seaham, Co. Durham.*	F. Whitebread	*White Rose Hotel, Rossington, Nr. Doncaster.*

The form that a game can take is of infinite variety. The most usual is "301 up". This involves starting with any "double" and then subtracting the score gained from 301, until the winner reaches nought but with the proviso that he must also end on a "double". The darts are thrown in groups of three in turn by the competitors. This popular form of game is varied from 201 up to 1,001 up according to the time available. Another popular game is to race "round the clock" either in singles or, to make the task more exacting, in "doubles" or even "trebles". Perhaps the best-known of all darts players, Jim Pike, went round the clock in "doubles" throwing from 9 feet and retrieving his own darts, in 3 mins. 30 secs. at King John's Head, Blackfriars, London, in 1937. By reducing the throwing distance to arm's length, Pike in 1944 at Newmarket lowered this time to 14.5 secs. There are many other forms of game; many of them are, however, peculiar to a locality. Darts is a game more than most others with a slang of its own, but here again much of it is only heard in a particular county or area.

The game of darts has been spread by British influence to many parts of the world, notably by the Armed Services in the two world wars, but it rarely survives for long amongst the local people after the departure of a garrison or other services unit.

The major annual competitions are run by national Sunday newspapers. *The People* organise a team championship for the Lonsdale Trophy, while the *News of the World* run an individual championship on a district basis. For this latter annual event there are about 500,000 starters. Such is the interest that in 1939 at the Agricultural Hall, Islington, London, a record crowd of 17,000 watched the final rounds.

DARTS QUIZ

1. What is the lowest number of throws to achieve 1,001 up (straight start)?

*

2. Has this ever been achieved in competition?

QUIZ ANSWERS

1. 17 throws. 2. No. It needs 15 treble 20's, a treble 17 and a 50.

Fencing

Compiled by **C-L. de Beaumont**
President: Amateur Fencing Association

FENCING QUIZ

1. In what year was (a) the European Championships at all weapons first held, and where; (b) the title of this event changed to World Championship?

*

2. What is the Prince Rainier Cup? When was it first competed for, and who were the first winners?

*

3. What was the first governing body for fencing in Great Britain, and by whom was it founded?

*

4. Has any fencer ever won both an amateur and a professional world fencing championship? If so, name him and state with which weapon.

*

5. Give the dates of the first British amateur championships and name winners at: (a) Ladies' Foil; (b) Men's Foil; (c) Epée; (d) Sabre.

*

6. In a competition is a fencer allowed to start a bout with one hand and finish it with the other?

*

7. What is a period of fencing time?

*

8. Is there a penalty for intentionally forcing a corps à corps (without violence) at (a) Foil, (b) Epée, (c) Sabre?

*

9. If the time limit for a bout expires and a further hit is required to decide the winner, do the fencers recommence (a) in the positions they occupy at that moment on the piste, or (b) in the centre of the piste?

*

10. Can a fencer ever score a hit when he has both feet off the piste?

NOTES ON FENCING

Fencing is an art with a long and fascinating history and its roots in the traditions of chivalry.

Swords existed long before the dawn of history, and throughout the centuries much attention was devoted to their development and the study of methods of using them.

Fencing today, while preserving much of its romantic background and traditional courtesies, is a very modern and athletic sport practised increasingly throughout the world.

The swords in use today, the foil, the épée and the sabre, each with its own technique, have evolved from the ancient weapons and the basic movements, and many of the fencing terms in current use have been used by generations of swordsmen for centuries.

In Britain a revival of interest in fencing began in the mid-nineteenth century and this led to the foundation in 1902 of the Amateur Fencing Association which is the governing body for the sport in Great Britain and Northern Ireland.

The sport of the few before the First World War, fencing became more popular between the wars but was mainly confined to London and a few provincial towns. By 1939 the Association had 109 affiliated clubs and two sections, or area organizations, outside London.

The last war disrupted this progress and by 1945 only 51 clubs remained active. Since then there has been a dramatic increase in interest in fencing throughout the United Kingdom and fencing is now practised by persons of every class and calling.

By 1959 the Association included some 400 clubs besides a large number of evening institute classes, and fourteen sections now cover every part of the country.

This increase in numbers has been matched by an equal advance in technical standard

due, in great measure, to the success of the Association's national coaching scheme.

Today British fencers have reached the first flight in international competition, especially at foil and épée. Miss Gillian Sheen was the first British fencer to win an Olympic gold medal in 1956, while Mr. H. W. F. Hoskyns won the World Epée Championship in 1958.

INDIVIDUAL CHAMPIONS

The Olympic Games

	Ladies' Foil	Men's Foil	Epée	Sabre
1896	—	E. Gravelotte (Fr.)		J. Giorgiades (Gr.)
1900	—	C. Costa (Fr.)	R. Fonst (Cuba)	G. de la Falaise (Fr.)
1904	—	R. Fonst (Cuba)	R. Fonst (Cuba)	M. de Diaz (Cuba)
1906	—	M. Dillon-Kavanagh (Fr.)	G. de la Falaise (Fr.)	J. Giorgiades (Gr.)
1908	—	—	M. Alibert (Fr.)	J. Fuchs (Hun.)
1912	—	N. Nadi (It.)	P. Anspach (Belg.)	J. Fuchs (Hun.)
1920	—	N. Nadi (It.)	A. Massard (Fr.)	N. Nadi (It.)
1924	E.O. Osiier (Den.)	R. Ducret (Fr.)	C. Delporte (Belg.)	A. Posta (Hun.)
1928	H. Mayer (Ger.)	L. Gaudin (Fr.)	L. Gaudin (Fr.)	E. Tersztiansky (Hun.)
1932	E. Preiss (Aus.)	G. Marzi (It.)	G. C. Cornaggia (It.)	G. Piller (Hun.)
1936	I. Elek (Hun.)	G. Gaudini (It.)	F. Riccardi (It.)	A. Kabos (Hun.)
1948	I. Elek (Hun.)	J. Buhan (Fr.)	L. Cantone (It.)	A. Gerevich (Hun.)
1952	I. Camber (It.)	C. d'Oriola (Fr.)	E. Mangiarotti (It.)	P. Kovacs (Hun.)
1956	G. M. Sheen (G.B.)	C. d'Oriola (Fr.)	C. Pavesi (It.)	R. Karpati (Hun.)

Civil Service Fencing Union

Epée Club

London Fencing Club

The World Championships
(Called European Championships until 1936)

	Ladies' Foil	Men's Foil	Epée	Sabre
1921	—	—	L. Gaudin (Fr.)	A. de Jong (Hol.)
1922	—	—	R. Heide (Nor.)	A. de Jong (Hol.)
1923	—	—	W. Brouwer (Hol.)	J. Garay (Hun.)
1925	—	G. Chiavacci (It.)	G. Tainturier (Fr.)	A. Gombos (Hun.)
1926	—	O. Puliti (It.)	G. Buchard (Fr.)	A. Gombos (Hun.)
1927	—	O. Puliti (It.)	P. Cattiau (Fr.)	J. Glyckais (Hun.)
1929	H. Mayer (Ger.)	O. Puliti (It.)	P. Cattiau (Fr.)	G. Piller (Hun.)
1930	J. Addams (Belg.)	G. Gaudini (It.)	P. Cattiau (Fr.)	G. Piller (Hun.)
1931	H. Mayer (Ger.)	E. Lemoine (Fr.)	G. Buchard (Fr.)	G. Piller (Hun.)
1933	G. Neligan (G.B.)	G. Guaragna (It.)	G. Buchard (Fr.)	A. Kabos (Hun.)
1934	I. Elek (Hun.)	G. Gaudini (It.)	P. Dunay (Hun.)	A. Kabos (Hun.)
1935	I. Elek (Hun.)		H. Drakenberg (Sweden)	A. Gerevich (Hun.)
1937	H. Mayer (Ger.)	G. Marzi (It.)	B. Schmetz (Fr.)	P. Kovacs (Hun.)
1938	M. Sediva (Czech.)	G. Guaragna (It.)	M. Pécheux (Fr.)	A. Montano (It.)
1947	E. Muller-Preiss (Aus.)	C. d'Oriola (Fr.)	A. Artigas (Fr.)	A. Montano (It.)
1949	E. Muller-Preiss (Aus.)	C. d'Oriola (Fr.)	D. Mangiarotti (It.)	G. Daré (It.)
1950	E. Muller-Priess (Aus.) and R. Garilhe (Fr.)	R. Nostini (It.)	M. Luchow (Den.)	J. Levavasseur (Fr.)
1951	I. Elek (Hun.)	M. di Rosa (It.)	E. Mangiarotti (It.)	A. Gerevich (Hun.)
1953	I. Camber (It.)	C. d'Oriola (Fr.)	J. Sakovicz (Hun.)	P. Kovacs (Hun.)
1954	K. Lachmann (Den.)	C. d'Oriola (Fr.)	E. Mangiarotti (It.)	R. Karpati (Hun.)
1955	L. Domolki (Hun.)	J. Gyurica (Hun.)	G. Anglesio (It.)	A. Gerevich (Hun.)
1957	A. Zabelina (U.S.S.R.)	M. Fulop (Hun.)	A. Mouyal (Fr.)	J. Pawlowski (Pol.)
1958	V. Kisseleva (U.S.S.R.)	G. Bergamini (It.)	H. W. F. Hoskyns (G.B.)	I. Rylskyi (U.S.S.R.)
1959	E. Efimoua (U.S.S.R.)	A. Jay (G.B.)	B. Khabarov (U.S.S.R.)	R. Karpati (Hun.)

The British Empire and Commonwealth Games

	Ladies' Foil	Men's Foil	Epée	Sabre
1950	M. A. Glen Haig (Eng.)	R. R. C. Paul (Eng.)	C-L. de Beaumont (Eng.)	A. G. Pilbrow (Eng.)
1954	M. A. Glen Haig (Eng.)	R. R. C. Paul (Eng.)	I. Lund (Aust.)	M. J. Amberg (Eng.)
1958	G. M. Sheen (Eng.)	R. R. V. Paul (Eng.)	H. W. F. Hoskyns (Eng.)	H. W. F. Hoskyns (Eng.)

THE AMATEUR CHAMPIONS OF GREAT BRITAIN

	Ladies' Foil	Men's Foil	Epée	Sabre
1898	—	H. Turner		W. Edgworth-Johnstone
1899	—	B. C. Praed	—	T. P. Hobbins
1900	—	T. P. Hobbins		W. Edgworth-Johnstone
1901	—	H. Evan James		T. P. Hobbins
1902	—	J. Jenkinson	—	T. P. Hobbins
1903	—	J. Jenkinson		H. Evan James
1904	—	J. Jenkinson		C. A. Wilson
1905	—	R. Montgomerie	E. Seligman	C. A. Wilson
1906	—	E. Seligman	R. Montgomerie	C. A. Wilson
1907	M. Hall	E. Seligman	E. Seligman	F. E. B. Feilmann
1908	M. Hall	R. Montgomerie	C. L. Daniell	W. W. Marsh
1909	C. E. Martin-Edmunds	R. Montgomerie	R. Montgomerie	W. W. Marsh
1910	J. Johnstone	R. Montgomerie	E. M. Amphlett	A. Ridley Martin
1911	G. Daniell	E. M. Amphlett	J. P. Blake	W. Hammond
1912	G. Daniell	P. G. Doyne	R. Montgomerie	C. van der Byl
1913	A. B. Walker	G. R. Alexander	G. G. M. Vereker	A. Ridley Martin
1914	A. B. Walker	R. M. P. Willoughby	R. Montgomerie	W. Hammond
1920	C. A. Walker	P. G. Doyne	M. D. V. Holt	C. A. Kershaw
1921	G. Daniell	R. Sutton	H. F. S. Huntington	W. Hammond
1922	M. Hall	R. Sutton	G. M. Burt	A. H. Corble
1923	G. M. Davis	E. Stenson Cooke	M. D. V. Holt	E. Seligman
1924	G. Daniell	F. G. Sherriff	C. H. Biscoe	E. Seligman
1925	G. M. Davis	F. G. Sherriff	C. B. Notley	C. A. Kershaw
1926	G. M. Davis	S. R. Bousfield	Hon. I. D. Campbell-Gray	C. A. Kershaw
1927	M. Freeman	A. D. Pearce	C. B. Notley	A. H. Corble
1928	M. M. Butler	J. Emrys Lloyd	B. Childs	G. L. G. Harry
1929	M. Freeman	J. Evan James	L. V. Fildes	R. B. Campbell
1930	M. M. Butler	J. Emrys Lloyd	Hon. I. D. Campbell-Gray	O. G. Trinder
1931	M. M. Butler	J. Emrys Lloyd	B. Childs	O. G. Trinder
1932	M. M. Butler	J. Emrys Lloyd	Hon. I. D. Campbell-Gray	A. G. Pilbrow
1933	J. Guinness	J. Emrys Lloyd	A. E. Pelling	O. G. Trinder
1934	G. Neligan	H. D. H. Bartlett	A. E. Pelling	O. G. Trinder
1935	G. Neligan	H. D. H. Bartlett	Hon. I. D. Campbell-Gray	A. G. Pilbrow
1936	G. Neligan	C. R. Hammersley	C.-L. de Beaumont	R. E. Brook
1937	G. Neligan	J. Emrys Lloyd	C.-L. de Beaumont	R. F. Tredgold
1938	J. Penn Hughes	J. Emrys Lloyd	C.-L. de Beaumont	A. G. Pilbrow
1939	E. C. Arbuthnott	H. Cooke	T. E. Beddard	R. F. Tredgold
1947	E. C. Arbuthnott	R. R. C. Paul	P. C. Dix	R. F. Tredgold
1948	M. A. Glen Haig	A. R. Smith	R. Parfitt	R. F. Tredgold
1949	G. M. Sheen	R. R. C. Paul	P. C. Dix	R. F. Tredgold
1950	M. A. Glen Haig	R. R. C. Paul	R. Parfitt	A. G. Pilbrow
1951	G. M. Sheen	H. Cooke	A. E. Pelling	P. M. Turquet
1952	G. M. Sheen	U. L. Wendon	A. L. N. Jay	O. B. Porebski
1953	G. M. Sheen	R. R. V. Paul	C.-L. de Beaumont	O. B. Porebski
1954	G. M. Sheen	J. E. Fethers	P. A. Greenhalgh	A. R. Cooperman
1955	G. M. Sheen	R. R. V. Paul	R. A. Harrison	R. F. Tredgold
1956	G. M. Sheen	R. R. C. Paul	H. W. F. Hoskyns	O. B. Porebski
1957	G. M. Sheen	R. R. V. Paul	H. W. F. Hoskyns	M. J. Amberg
1958	G. M. Sheen	R. R. V. Paul	H. W. F. Hoskyns	M. J. Amberg
1959	M. Stafford	H. W. F. Hoskyns	A. L. N. Jay	M. J. Amberg

Ladies' Cercle d'Escrime

Birmingham F.C.

A.F.A. Leaders Club

FENCING QUIZ

1. In what year was the Amateur Fencing Association founded? Name the first President.

*

2. What is the international governing body for fencing called, and when was it founded?

*

3. Name the British fencer who has won the Amateur Championship at foil, epée and sabre.

*

4. Name (with date) the first British fencer to win: (a) a European title; (b) a world title; (c) an Olympic title.

*

5. Name the fencer who has won most British amateur championships at: (a) Ladies' Foil; (b) Men's Foil; (c) Epée; (d) Sabre.

*

6. Name (with date) the eminent Prime Minister who won a Public Schools Foil Championship.

*

7. In what year was the electrical judging apparatus first used in a European or World or Olympic championship at (a) Foil, (b) Epée?

*

8. Name (with date) the first British fencer to win the Amateur Championship in three successive years at: (a) Ladies' Foil; (b) Men's Foil; (c) Epée; (d) Sabre.

*

9. Has any fencer won the World Championship or Olympic Games at all three weapons?

*

10. When was fencing first included in the British Empire Games, and where held? Name the winners of the four individual events.

QUIZ ANSWERS

1. 1902: Captain Alfred Hutton. 2. Fédération Internationale d'Escrime: 1913. 3. Edgar Seligman. 4. (a) 1933 Miss G. Neligan; (b) 1958 H. W. F. Hoskyns; (c) 1956 Miss G. Sheen. 5. (a) Miss G. Sheen (9); (b) J. Emrys Lloyd (7); (c) R. Montgomerie (5); (d) Dr. R. F. Tredgold (6). 6. Sir Winston Churchill, 1892. 7. (a) 1955; (b) 1933. 8. (a) Miss M. M. Butler 1930-1-2; (b) J. Jenkinson 1902-3-4; (c) C-L. de Beaumont 1936-7-8; (d) C. A. Wilson 1904-5-6. 9. No. 10. 1950: Auckland, N.Z. Ladies' Foil: Mrs. M. A. Glen Haig (England). Men's Foil: René Paul (England). Epée: C-L. de Beaumont (England). Sabre: A. G. Pilbrow (England).

The Sabre Club

The Scottish Fencing Club

INDIVIDUAL INTERNATIONAL COMPETITIONS HELD IN GREAT BRITAIN

	Ladies' Foil	Men's Foil	Epée	Sabre
1913	Miss A. B. Walker	—	—	—
1920	Miss J. Johnstone	—	—	—
1921	Miss G. Daniell	—	—	—
1922	Miss G. M. Davis	—	—	—
1923	Miss G. M. Davis	—	—	—
1924	Mrs. H. Freeman	—	—	—
1925	Miss G. Daniell	—	—	—
1926	Miss G. Daniell	—	—	—
1927	Fr. H. Mayer	—	—	—
1928	Fro. M. Holst	—	V. Clayton Morris	—
1929	Miss M. M. Butler	—	L. V. Fildes	—
1930	Fr. H. Mayer	—	C.-L. de Beaumont	—
1931	Miss M. M. Butler	—	C.-L. de Beaumont	—
1932	Miss G. Neligan	—	C.-L. de Beaumont	—
1933	Miss J. Guinness	—	T. E. Beddard	—
1934	Miss G. Neligan	—	C.-L. de Beaumont	—
1935	Fr. E. Preiss	—	C.-L. de Beaumont	—

	Ladies' Foil	Men's Foil	Epée	Sabre
1936	Mlle J. Addams	—	F. Soille	—
1937	Fro. G. Olsen	J. Emrys Lloyd	E. S. Bruneau	—
1938	Mlle J. Addams	F. Stark	C.-L. de Beaumont	—
1939		T. Praem		
1947	Fro. K. Lachmann	H. Cooke	T. E. Beddard	R. F. Tredgold
1948	Fro. K. Lachmann	A. R. Smith	M. D. McCready	J. Erdelyi
1949	Fro. K. Lachmann	H. Cooke	P. C. Dix	O. B. Porebski
1950	Miss G. Sheen	R. R. C. Paul	C. D. Grose Hodge	R. F. Tredgold
1951	Fro. K. Lachmann	R. R. C. Paul	R. R. C. Paul	R. J. G. Anderson
1952	Fro. K. Lachmann	R. R. C. Paul	C. Nigon	R. J. G. Anderson
1953	Mrs. M. Glen-Haig	Prof. R. Crosnier	A. L. N. Jay	M. J. Amberg
1954	Miss G. Sheen	R. R. C. Paul	H. W. F. Hoskyns	O. B. Porebski
1955	Fro. K. Lachmann	R. R. V. Paul	A. L. N. Jay	A. Gerevich
1956	Mrs. M. Glen-Haig	A. Verhalle	A. L. N. Jay	E. M. Verebes
1957	Miss G. Sheen	A. L. N. Jay	A. L. N. Jay	E. M. Verebes
1958	Frau I. Keydel	R. R. V. Paul	H. W. F. Hoskyns	M. J. Amberg
1959	Miss G. Sheen	H. W. F. Hoskyns	H. W. F. Hoskyns	D. D. Stringer

145

Fives, Eton

Compiled by Gordon Stringer
and P. C. Curtis
Secretary: Eton Fives Association

HISTORY

The design of an Eton Fives court is based on the location of the first playing area, namely a natural court outside the Chapel at Eton formed by the Chapel wall, a flying buttress on the left and another wall on the right. In the early part of the nineteenth century boys played a game resembling the present game at this spot whilst awaiting roll call, and by 1840 it had become sufficiently popular for the then Headmaster, Dr. Hawtrey, to instigate the building, on a more suitable site, of the first Eton Fives courts—incorporating the characteristics of the Chapel court. The game continued to flourish at Eton to such an extent that many more courts were added in subsequent years, but it was not until after 1870 that the game spread to other schools. As far as is known, Harrow was the second school to build courts. Charterhouse, Highgate and Westminster also adopted the game shortly afterwards, and in later years courts were built at many other schools, largely due to the enthusiasm of Old Etonian schoolmasters joining the staff.

Several years elapsed before the game really prospered at schools other than Eton, and the first record of an inter-school fixture was in 1885 when Eton challenged Harrow to a one-pair match. Eton won easily but the match stimulated interest and the standard gradually improved at the other schools so that by the time of the First World War there was a considerable number of inter-school matches.

ETON FIVES QUIZ

1. Which one-handed player was said to have been able to do more with one hand than many could do with two?

*

2. Which is regarded as the best handbook on Eton Fives?

*

3. At which school is Eton Fives compulsory?

*

QUIZ ANSWERS

1. This was said of the late G. H. C. Lewis (Old Citizens) in *Squash Rackets and Fives*. 2. From the Lonsdale Library, *Rackets, Squash Rackets, Tennis, Fives and Badminton* with the Eton Fives article written by David Egerton. 3. Shrewsbury School.

The regulating body for the game is the Eton Fives Association, which is primarily responsible for promoting and maintaining general interest in the game. In addition, the Association organises championships and competitions including the Amateur Championship for the Kinnaird Cup and the Public Schools Competition, arranges facilities for the playing of the game and, from time to time, regulates and publishes the laws of the game.

The Amateur Championship is a knock-out competition which, since the Second World War, has been played over an extended period—the first round starting in November and the final normally taking place in April. The average entry, restricted to Old Boys of schools or Old Boy clubs affiliated to the Association, has been about thirty pairs, and matches have to be played on courts approved by the Committee (mostly within a sixty-mile radius of London). In recent years, the semi-finals and final have usually been played on the courts at Eton College or Ludgrove School, Wokingham; in the case of the latter, due to the hospitality of the Headmaster, Mr. A. T. Barber, himself twice winner of the competition and Chairman of Committee since 1950.

Before the Second World War the Public Schools Competition was played at Queen's Club and was organised on a handicap basis. The Club's courts were, however, bombed during the war and, in spite of protracted negotiations between the Club and the Association, it was not possible to reach agreement on the provision of finance for rebuilding and subsequent upkeep. As a result, since the war the competition has, thanks to the kindness of the Governors and Headmaster, been held during the Easter holidays on the courts of Highgate School.

A further competition, the Queen's Club Competition, was started in 1932 as a knock-out competition between teams from the various Old Boys' clubs but this has lapsed since the destruction of the courts at Queen's. Many of the Old Boys' clubs now have full fixture lists during the main Eton Fives season (September to April), playing friendly matches against other Old Boys' clubs, schools and Oxford and Cambridge Universities.

The Laws

As with most games, the laws of Eton Fives in the early years were based on oral tradition and it was not until 1877 that they were first codified by A. C. Ainger. Even then, individual rules were variously interpreted by different schools and the first authoritative set of laws was published by the Eton Fives Association in 1931. These were last amended in 1950.

Location of Courts

Before the Second World War London was generally regarded as the main centre of the game due largely to the popularity of the Queen's Club courts and also to the fact that it was mainly at the schools in and around London that the game of Eton Fives was most popular. Since the war, however, the membership of the Association has gradually increased and the game has become increasingly popular at schools all over England. There are now over 30 Public and Grammar schools which play the game regularly as well as about 12 Preparatory schools. In addition to the schools, there are both College and University courts at Oxford and Cambridge, where the game has been credited with half-blue status, and a court at the Liverpool Racquet Club. Again, before the war both the London Hospital and St. Mary's Hospital, Sidcup, played the game on their own courts but, as in the case of Queen's, the courts suffered bomb damage and have not since been rebuilt.

Eton Fives Abroad

The game was first introduced on the Continent largely through the efforts of Mr. E. Gordon Spencer, a master at Zuoz College, Switzerland, in 1924, when three open-air courts were built. In the thirties, a team from the Association visited Zuoz and in subsequent years the College has sent a team to this country to play various Public schools. Since the war, the game at Zuoz has remained popular helped by an annual visit from the Old Citizens who for several years have arranged a Continental tour. In 1957, Highgate School also sent a team to Switzerland to play Zuoz College, who, in their turn, have sent pairs to this country to compete in the Public Schools Competition.

Other courts on the Continent include one built in the middle fifties at Wellenburg Castle, near Augsburg, Germany, by Prince Fugger, an Old Boy of Zuoz. The Old Citizens have, for the past few years, been invited to play on this court. There is also a court at Salzburg in Austria on the premises of the Hotel Mönchstein, once the residence of the Veicht family who introduced the game in the twenties. There are also courts at the Institut Montana at Zugerberg bei Zug, near Zurich, and four courts were built in the late twenties at the Alpine College at Arvey bei Villars near Bex.

In Australia, too, the game of Eton Fives forms part of the sporting activities of the Geelong Grammar School. In this case, a revival of interest in the game followed an exchange visit a few years ago by Mr. M. L. Charlesworth, the master in charge of Fives at Shrewsbury School.

Finally, it should be mentioned that the game has for many years been played in the Northern Region of Nigeria where several schools have their own courts. The present Prime Minister of the Northern Region is himself a keen supporter of the game, and it is interesting to note that one of the winning pair in this year's Public Schools Competition first played Fives in this part of the world.

The Association's main problems are firstly to find a suitable replacement for the court at Queen's Club, which before the war was regarded as the Headquarters of the game, and secondly to make sure that the game is not prevented from expanding due to any difficulties over the supply of suitable balls.

Kinnaird Cup

1926	R. G. de Quetteville and R. A. Redhead (Etonians)
1927	No competition
1928	R. G. de Quetteville and R. A. Redhead (Etonians)
1929	K. C. Gandar Dower and G. R. McConnell (Harrovians)
1930	A. H. Fabian and C. A. Aguirre (Cholmeleians)
1931	W. M. Welch and H. G. de Gray Warter (Harrovians)
1932	K. C. Gandar Dower and G. R. McConnell (Harrovians)
1933	W. M. Welch and H. G. de Gray Warter (Harrovians)
1934	D. M. Backhouse and A. T. Barber (Salopians)
1935	J. M. Peterson and C. E. W. Sheepshanks (Salopian, Etonian)
1936	D. M. Backhouse and A. T. Barber (Salopians)
1937	A. H. Fabian and J. K. G. Webb (Cholmeleians)
1938	J. M. Peterson and C. E. W. Sheepshanks (Salopian, Etonian)
1939	A. H. Fabian and J. K. G. Webb (Cholmeleians)
1940–47	No competition
1948	A. H. Fabian and J. K. G. Webb (Cholmeleians)
1949	A. J. Wreford-Brown and T. R. Garnett (Carthusians)
1950	J. M. Peterson and C. E. W. Sheepshanks (Salopian, Etonian)
1951	P. B. H. May and J. W. H. May (Carthusians)
1952	P. B. H. May and J. W. H. May (Carthusians)
1953	P. B. H. May and J. W. H. May (Carthusians)
1954	A. R. Kittermaster and A. R. B. Moulsdale (Salopians)
1955	A. R. Kittermaster and A. R. B. Moulsdale (Salopians)
1956	A. R. Kittermaster and A. R. B. Moulsdale (Salopians)
1957	P. C. Curtis and J. W. Biggs (Reptonian, Olavian)
1958	A. Hughes and A. J. G. Campbell (Edwardians)
1959	D. J. S. Guilford and M. J. Shortland-Jones (Harrovians)

PRESENT MEMBERSHIP OF ETON FIVES ASSOCIATION

(a) Schools

Aldenham School
Berkhamsted School
Charterhouse
City of London School
Cranleigh School
Emanuel School
Eton College
Harrow School
Highgate School
King Edward's School, Birmingham
King Edward's Five Ways School, Birmingham
Lancing College
Marlborough College
Mill Hill School
Oakham School
Queen Elizabeth's School, Barnet
Repton School
Rydal School
St. Olave's Grammar School
Shrewsbury School
Uppingham School
Westminster School

Hon. Members

Geelong Grammar School
Zuoz College

(b) Clubs

Jesters
Cambridge University
Oxford University
Old Aldenhamians
Old Carthusians
Old Chigwellians
Old Cholmeleians
Old Citizens
Old Edwardians
Old Etonians
Old Harrovians
Old Olavians
Old Reptonians
Old Salopians
Old Uppinghamians
Old Westminsters

COMPETITION WINNERS
Public Schools

1929	Harrow
1930	Harrow
1931	Harrow
1932	Uppingham
1933	Harrow
1934	Charterhouse
1935	Eton
1936	Harrow
1937	Eton
1938	Shrewsbury
1939	Shrewsbury
1940–48	No competition
1949	Charterhouse
1950	Charterhouse
1951	Eton
1952	Eton
1953	King Edward's, Birmingham
1954	Aldenham
1955	Aldenham
1956	Eton
1957	Aldenham
1958	Highgate
1959	Aldenham

Compiled by **R. A. Colville**

Hon. Secretary:
Rugby Fives Association

Fives, Rugby

HISTORICAL NOTES

Fives in its modern form dates back to about 1850, when we hear of it as a game for schoolboys. After 1870 inter-school matches began to find favour. It is noteworthy that a full match was held to consist of two meetings of the rival teams, one match on both the "home" and "away" courts. The total points of the two matches would decide the result. In those days there was no such concept as the standard court and it was customary for the home side to win regularly. Courts differed in size, height of the board and number of walls.

Before 1920 few men played unless they were in the teaching profession, but after that date all the big London schools that played Rugby Fives ran Old Boys sides that had extensive fixture lists.

The name of Edgar Cyriax is one that will always be associated with the game. For over 35 years he remained undefeated and continued to play for long after his initial defeat. It is to Dr. Cyriax that the Rugby Fives Association owes much. For long he wished to impart some degree of uniformity to the game not only with regard to the rules but also to the actual dimensions of the court. The Association was founded in 1928 and its objects were "to act as a control authority, to formulate, alter, and add to the rules governing the game of Rugby Fives". After drawing up the rules of the game it drew up the measurements of the standard court which were approved in 1931.

The first Open Fives competition for doubles play was inaugurated by Dr. Cyriax in 1926 and was known as the Cyriax Cup. Up to 1933 it was a competition between pairs representing individual clubs. In 1934 the name was changed to the Amateur Doubles Championship and the cup was competed for by individual pairs not entered by any particular club. It continues as such today.

In 1928 J. F. Burnet started the Jesters' Club which was then purely a Rugby Fives club with a roving commission. Apart from the forty or fifty matches played every season, which did much to increase interest in the game, the Jesters inaugurated two annual championships, one for public schools and the other for individual singles play. After they had been firmly established both these events were handed over to the Association. The Public Schools Singles and Doubles started in 1930 and were played on the courts of the Bank of England; they later took the form of two competitions run simultaneously. The first Open Singles Championship was held in 1932 on the courts of St. Paul's School.

The public schools and the universities are the strongholds of the game today. Although Fives has been alive at the schools for some 75 years or more, its recognition as a sport at the universities, and particularly at Oxford and Cambridge, is of much more recent date. It was not until 1925 that the first match was played between these two universities; since then the fixture has been an annual one with the exception of the war years.

Regional championships are also held in the North of England and Scotland. The North of England was first held in 1936 and took the form of a doubles championship. In 1953 after a break of several years the championship was restarted as both a singles and doubles event and is held at Durham. The Scottish Singles and Doubles Championships were started in 1950 and are competed for annually in Edinburgh.

In 1929 the Marchant Cup was awarded for annual competition between the London grammar schools. In 1959 a West of England Schools Tournament was held in Bristol for the first time.

OXFORD v. CAMBRIDGE

The university match between Oxford and Cambridge was first played in 1925. Of the matches to date Cambridge have won twenty-three and Oxford five. Oxford's five victories were in 1928, 1935, 1949, 1955 and 1957. There was no match during the war years 1940–45.

AMATEUR DOUBLES CHAMPIONSHIP

CYRIAX CUP

1926	Gonville and Caius College, Cambridge
1930	Alleyn Old Boys
1931	Alleyn Old Boys
1932	Alleyn Old Boys
1933	Alleyn Old Boys
1934	H. A. Oundjian and K. R. R. Readhead
1935	H. A. Oundjian and V. E. Oundjian
1936	F. K. Truman and J. Battersby
1937	E. Ll. Bailey and C. L. E. Mitchell
1938	H. A. Oundjian and V. E. Oundjian
1939	E. Ll. Bailey and C. L. E. Mitchell
1940–46	No competition
1947	E. R. Conradi and L. A. B. Pilkington
1948	C. T. Reichwald and W. A. Gluck
1949	B. M. W. Trapnell and E. S. Isaacs
1950	A. D. R. Dawes and J. R. Nicol
1951	A. D. R. Dawes and E. R. Conradi
1952	E. Ll. Bailey and J. F. Pretlove
1953	B. M. W. Trapnell and J. G. Rogers
1954	J. F. Pretlove and R. Birmingham
1955	R. Birmingham and H. R. Smith
1956	J. F. Pretlove and D. R. W. Silk
1957	J. F. Pretlove and D. R. W. Silk
1958	J. F. Pretlove and D. R. W. Silk
1959	J. F. Pretlove and D. R. W. Silk

AMATEUR SINGLES CHAMPIONSHIP

JESTERS' CLUB CUP

1932	K. C. Gandar-Dower
1933	P. A. Malt
1934	P. A. Malt
1935	P. A. Malt
1936	J. G. W. Davies
1937	J. G. W. Davies
1938	J. Armitage
1939	J. G. W. Davies
1940–47	No competition
1948	R. J. Knight
1949	B. M. W. Trapnell
1950	A. D. R. Dawes
1951	A. D. R. Dawes
1952	A. D. R. Dawes
1953	J. F. Pretlove
1954	R. Birmingham
1955	J. F. Pretlove
1956	J. F. Pretlove
1957	H. R. Smith
1958	J. F. Pretlove
1959	J. N. H. Smith

NORTH OF ENGLAND CHAMPIONSHIPS

Doubles

1936	C. L. E. Mitchell and J. W. Dowlen
1937	D. J. Hill and J. J. A. Newman
1938	J. S. Brearley and C. G. Morley
1939	J. S. Brearley and C. G. Morley
1940–46	No competition
1946	E. R. Conradi and F. M. Wilson
1950	J. Darlington and J. G. Johnston

FULLER CUP

1953	D. A. Sheard and F. J. Unsworth
1954	A. W. Seddon and E. H. Miller
1955	F. J. Unsworth and G. Van Lottum
1956	A. C. Dracup and D. T. Sparrow
1957	D. E. Gardner and P. J. W. Grender
1958	D. E. Gardner and F. R. Fisher

Singles

FERENS TROPHY

1953	G. P. M. Cuthbertson
1954	A. I. F. Mackenzie
1955	A. I. F. Mackenzie
1956	J. N. H. Smith
1957	D. E. Gardner
1958	J. N. H. Smith

QUIZ ANSWERS

1. Length, 28 ft. Breadth, 18 feet. 2. Walls, black. Floor, red. Door in middle of back wall. 3. 2 ft. 6 in. 4. Diameter 1 7/16 ins. Weight 1.34 oz. 5. Oundle, 11 times.

SCOTTISH CHAMPION-SHIPS

Doubles

SCOTTISH DOUBLES CUP

1950	B. Jackman and M. Rothera
1951	B. Jackman and M. Rothera
1952	B. Jackman and D. A. Sheard
1953	V. Latham and F. J. Unsworth
1954	J. A. Dand and D. A. Sheard
1955	V. Latham and F. J. Unsworth
1956	D. T. Sparrow and A. C. Dracup
1957	D. E. Gardner and P. J. W. Grender
1958	D. E. Gardner and P. J. W. Grender
1959	D. E. Gardner and S. Holt

Singles

CUTHBERTSON QUAICH

1950	J. G. Johnston
1951	D. V. Thomas
1952	J. A. Forsyth
1953	G. P. M. Cuthbertson
1954	J. A. Forsyth
1955	J. N. H. Smith
1956	M. C. Leslie
1957	D. E. Gardner
1958	D. E. Gardner
1959	D. E. Gardner

FIVES QUIZ

I. What are the length and breadth of a standard court?

★

2. What are the colours of the walls and floor of a standard court and where should the door be?

★

3. What is the height of the top of the board in a standard court?

★

4. What is the approximate diameter and weight of a Rugby Fives ball?

★

5. Which school has won the Schools Doubles Competition the greatest number of times?

LONDON GRAMMAR SCHOOLS' COMPETITION

MARCHANT CUP

1929	*Strand*
1930	*Sir Walter St. John's*
1931	*Henry Thornton*
1932	*Henry Thornton*
1933	*Sir Walter St. John's*
1934	*Sir Walter St. John's*
1935	*Henry Thornton*
1936	*Henry Thornton*
1937	*Henry Thornton*
1938	*St. Marylebone*
1939–48	No competition
1949	*St. Marylebone*
1950	*St. Marylebone*
1951	*Sloane*
1952	*Wandsworth*
1953	*Wandsworth*
1954	*Sloane*
1955	*Hackney Downs*
1956	*Hackney Downs*
1957	*Sir Walter St. John's*
1958	*Sir Walter St. John's*

SCHOOLS' SINGLES COMPETITION

JESTERS' CUP

1930	R. de W. K. Winlaw (*Winchester*)
1931	R. de W. K. Winlaw (*Winchester*)
1932	H. A. Oundjian (*St. Paul's*)
1933	R. J. Knight (*Dulwich*)
1934	R. J. Knight (*Dulwich*)
1935	J. M. Reichwald (*Oundle*)
1936	J. D. G. Craib (*Eastbourne*)
1937	G. H. M. Riddell (*Alleyn's*)
1938	E. R. Conradi (*Oundle*)
1939	J. H. Gray (*Sutton Valence*)
1940–45	No competition
1946	J. A. Holroyd (*Oundle*)
1947	J. A. Holroyd (*Oundle*)
1948	A. D. R. Dawes (*Bedford*)
1949	A. D. R. Dawes (*Bedford*)
1950	J. F. Pretlove (*Alleyn's*)
1951	J. F. Pretlove (*Alleyn's*)
1952	M. P. Skliros (*Oundle*)
1953	D. T. Sparrow (*Denstone*)
1954	R. G. Freebairn (*Oundle*)
1955	D. Smith (*Sedbergh*)
1956	D. Smith (*Sedbergh*)
1957	R. F. Dorey (*Alleyn's*)
1958	E. Marsh (*St. Dunstan's*)
1959	J. T. Watkinson (*Bristol G.S.*)

SCHOOLS' DOUBLES COMPETITION

MAPPIN CUP

1930	*St. Paul's School* (J. G. Richards and G. C. Shneerson)
1931	*Winchester College* (R. de W. K. Winlaw and H. J. H. Lamb)
1932	*St. Paul's School* (K. R. R. Readhead and H. A. Oundjian)
1933	*Dulwich College* (B. C. Gough and R. J. Knight)
1934	*Tonbridge School* (D. A. S. Day and W. G. Popple)
1935	*Oundle School* (J. M. Reichwald and J. C. Pearson)
1936	*Oundle School* (J. H. L. Brittain and P. S. Cowen)
1937	*Oundle School* (P. B. Nicholls and E. R. Conradi)
1938	*Oundle School* (E. R. Conradi and H. J. Hague)
1939	*Oundle School* (D. J. Forbes and C. T. Reichwald)
1940–45	No competition
1946	*Oundle School* (J. A. Holroyd and G. Muller)
1947	*Oundle School* (J. A. Holroyd and J. F. Warburg)
1948	*Oundle School* (M. T. Swan and C. J. Swan)
1949	*Oundle School* (J. R. Nicol and S. M. Pickard)
1950	*Denstone College* (S. D. Hignell and W. G. Tobias)
1951	*Alleyn's School* (J. F. Pretlove and J. S. T. Fletcher)
1952	*Oundle School* (M. P. Skliros and P. Granger)
1953	*Denstone College* (D. T. Sparrow and A. C. Dracup)
1954	*Oundle School* (J. F. Granger and R. G. Freebairn)
1955	*Whitgift School* (J. D. Ewart and I. R. M. Anderson)
1956	*Denstone College* (R. S. D. Jones and N. H. Wood)
1957	*St. Dunstan's College* (E. Marsh and D. S. Clift)
1958	*St. Dunstan's College* (E. Marsh and D. S. Clift)
1959	*Blundells* (C. J. McLachlan and R. W. White)

Gaelic Football & Hurling

Compiled by **Colman O'Higgins**

THE GAELIC ATHLETIC ASSOCIATION

The Gaelic Athletic Association is the controlling body in Ireland for hurling and Gaelic football.

Hurling is an ancient game which is often referred to in the early Gaelic classics. Setanta, or, as he is better known, Cú Chulainn, one of the great figures of Ireland's sagas, played hurling on the plains of Ulster. The game is played on a rather large pitch—160 yards by 90 yards is the usual area. There are fifteen players a side—a goalkeeper, six backs, two midfield, and six forwards. The scoring posts are seven yards apart and sixteen feet high. At eight feet from the ground there is a crossbar; a goal (three points) is scored when the ball is driven under the bar; a point is scored when the ball passes between the posts and above the bar. The duration of play is sixty minutes—two half-hour periods with a ten-minute interval. The game starts with all backs in position; the midfield players and forwards line up with crossed hurleys at centre and the referee throws the ball in fast and low between them.

The hurling ball is made with a core of cork and woollen thread rolled firmly, covered with white chrome leather. It weighs about four ounces and is nine inches in circumference. The hurley (called a caman in Irish) is three feet long and made of specially selected root of ash which carries a natural bend for the striking part (or boss), which is about two-and-a-half inches wide, and with it the ball can be hit accurately, both on the sod and over-head—this being one of the distinguishing characteristics of hurling, making for speed and brilliancy.

The hurling ball is resilient and can be hit long distances—a score direct from a midfield drive being always possible. All tripping, hacking, charging from behind is prohibited; the ball may be caught in the air but must only be lifted from the ground with the hurley and not the hand. Speed, skill, judgment, teamship, accuracy—these are vital attributes of a good hurler. Courage, tenacity in tackling and stamina are all essentials. The skill with which the flying ball is hit is a source of wonder to those seeing the game for the first time.

Championships in all grades are played in Ireland each year, on a county basis. Inter-county, inter-province and All-Ireland semi-finals and finals all attract capacity gates.

Gaelic Football, like hurling,

is played in every county in Ireland and by Irishmen who have emigrated to Great Britain, the United States, Argentina, Canada, Australia and Africa. It is a fast strenuous team game, played fifteen aside—i.e. a goalman, two lines of defenders, two centre-field men, and two lines of forwards. A round, leather-covered ball which weighs 13–15 ounces is used. The players aim at driving the ball under the cross-bar and into the goal-net, thereby scoring a goal. A goal equals three points. A point may be scored by driving the ball over the cross-bar between the two upright posts.

The Gaelic Athletic Association

Duration of game is sixty minutes—thirty minutes in each half, with a ten-minute interval. The ball is carried by hand-to-toe movement or fisted or kicked ahead. Possession may be gained in the air. Charging of player in possession is prohibited, either from front or behind, and the player in possession of the ball cannot charge another player. A player cannot carry the ball over three steps, and he can hop the ball only once while in possession.

When a defender crosses his own line a free kick of 50 yards is awarded against him, or when any player crosses the side-line a free kick is awarded to his opponent from the exact spot and from this kick a score can result directly.

Dimensions of playing pitch are 160 yards long by 90–100 yards wide. The field is usually of a green sod.

During play three substitutes are allowed for injured players, but when extra time is played three more substitutes are allowed on.

Players are purely amateurs. Competitions are numerous, so there is no closed season.

ALL-IRELAND HURLING CHAMPIONS

1887 Tiobrad Arann (Durlas Éile)
1888 *Unfinished due to U.S.A. "invasion"*
1889 Ath Cliath (C. J. Kickhams)
1890 Corcaigh (Acadh Bolg)
1891 Ciarraidhe (Baile Dubh)
1892 Corcaigh (Redmonds)
1893 Corcaigh (Carraig Dhubh)
1894 Corcaigh (Carraig Dhubh)
1895 Tiobrad Arann (Tobar na nDeor)
1896 Tiobrad Arann (Tobar na nDeor)
1897 Luimneach (Cill Fhionáin)
1898 Tiobrad Arann (Tobar na nDeor)
1899 Tiobrad Arann (Magh Cairce)
1900 Tiobrad Arann (Buirgheas Luigheach)
1901 Lonndain (London Irish)
1902 Corcaigh (Dun Guairne)
1903 Corcaigh (Carraig Dhubh)
1904 Cill Chainnigh (Tulach Ruadhan)
1905 Cill Chainnigh (Erin's Own)
1906 Tiobrad Arann (Durlas Eile)
1907 Cill Chainnigh (Tulach Ruadhan)
1908 Tiobrad Arann (Durlas Eile)
1909 Cill Chainnigh (Móin Chuinn)
1910 Loch Garman (Caisleán an Droichid)
1911 Cill Chainnigh
1912 Cill Chainnigh
1913 Cill Chainnigh
1914 An Clár
1915 Laois
1916 Tiobrad Arann
1917 Ath Cliath
1918 Luimneach
1919 Corcaigh
1920 Ath Cliath
1921 Luimneach
1922 Cill Chainnigh
1923 Gaillimh
1924 Ath Cliath
1925 Tiobrad Arann
1926 Corcaigh
1927 Ath Cliath
1928–9 Corcaigh
1930 Tiobrad Arann
1931 Corcaigh
1932 Cill Chainnigh
1933 Cill Chainnigh
1934 Luimneach
1935 Cill Chainnigh
1936 Luimneach
1937 Tiobrad Arann
1938 Ath Cliath
1939 Cill Chainnigh
1940 Luimneach
1941–2 Corcaigh
1943 Corcaigh
1944 Corcaigh
1945 Tiobrad Arann
1946 Corcaigh
1947 Cill Chainnigh
1948 Port Láirge
1949 Tiobrad Arann
1950 Tiobrad Arann
1951 Tiobrad Arann
1952 Corcaigh
1953 Corcaigh
1954 Corcaigh
1955 Loch Garman
1956 Loch Garman
1957 Cill Chainnigh
1958 Tiobrad Arann

ALL-IRELAND FOOTBALL CHAMPIONS

1887 Luimneach (Commercials)
1888 *Unfinished due to U.S.A. "invasion"*
1889 Tiobrad Arann (Bóthar Ruadh)
1890 Corcaigh (Mainistir na Corann)
1891 Ath Cliath (Young Irelands)
1892 Ath Cliath (Young Irelands)
1893 Loch Garman (Young Irelands)
1894 Ath Cliath (Young Irelands)
1895 Tiobrad Arann (Arravale Rovers)
1896 Luimneach (Commercials)
1897 Ath Cliath (C. J. Kickhams)
1898 Ath Cliath (Geraldines)
1899 Ath Cliath (Geraldines)
1900 Tiobrad Arann (Clonmel Shamrocks)
1901 Ath Cliath (Isles of the Sea)
1902 Ath Cliath (Bray Emmets)
1903 Ciarraidhe (John Mitchells, Tralee)
1904 Ciarraidhe (John Mitchells, Tralee)
1905 Cill Dara
1906 Ath Cliath (Kickhams)
1907 Ath Cliath (Kickhams)
1908 Ath Cliath (Geraldines)
1909 Ciarraidhe (Mitchells)
1910 Lughbhaidh
1911 Corcaigh (Lees)
1912 Lughbhaidh (Tredaghs)
1913 Ciarraidhe
1914 Ciarraidhe
1915 Loch Garman
1916 Loch Garman
1917 Loch Garman
1918 Loch Garman
1919 Cill Dara
1920 Tiobrad Arann
1921 Ath Cliath
1922 Ath Cliath
1923 Ath Cliath
1924 Ciarraidhe
1925 Gaillimh
1926 Ciarraidhe
1927 Cill Dara
1928 Cill Dara
1929 Ciarraidhe
1930 Ciarraidhe
1931 Ciarraidhe
1932 Ciarraidhe
1933 Cabhán
1934 Gaillimh
1935 Cabhán
1936 Muigheo
1937 Ciarraidhe
1938 Gaillimh
1939 Ciarraidhe
1940 Ciarraidhe
1941 Ciarraidhe
1942 Ath Cliath
1943 Ros Comáin
1944 Ros Comáin
1945 Corcaigh
1946 Ciarraidhe
1947 Cabhán
1948 Cabhán
1949 An Mhidhe
1950 Muigheo
1951 Muigheo
1952 An Cabhán
1953 Ciarraidhe
1954 An Mhidhe
1955 Ciarraidhe
1956 Gaillimh
1957 Lughbhaidh
1958 Ath Cliath

148

Compiled by **P. H. Whitaker**

Assistant Editor: The Shooting Times

Game Shooting

GAME SHOOTING RECORDS

In this modern day and age the game shooting field is not rich in records. Once upon a time, in the days of the great estates with hand-rearing of game at its zenith and the "battue" type of covert shoot a sign of prosperity and a mark of prestige, things were very different. Game of all sorts was more plentiful than it is nowadays and with the large estates vieing with each other for supremacy in shooting renown, the size of the bag was a matter of major importance and keen competition. Three-quarters of a century ago J. M. Walsh, who wrote under the famous pen-name of "Stonehenge", reflected the atmosphere of the heydays of covert shooting in the following paragraph.

"The pheasant, grouse or partridge shooter is more voracious and the quality of his sport is too often measured by the weight of the game bag. I confess that, in my humble opinion, this thirst for blood, or, as the phrenologist would say, destructiveness, is destructive often of true sport. The bag is considered too much; and to get game (in a sportsmanlike manner if possible, but at all events to get it) is too often the desire of the gentlemen in shooting costume; still, such is now the prevailing taste, and if you wish to gratify your friends with a day's shooting, your only certain plan of affording them that gratification is to show them plenty of game."

Although there are, even now, "a few gentlemen in shooting costume" to whom the making of a sizeable bag by fair and, sometimes, not so fair means, is the be-all and end-all of shooting enjoyment, the greater majority of present-day shots share the opinion that the value of their sport is to be measured not so much by the amount of game hanging in the larder, but by the circumstances under which it was obtained. And although critics may shout "sour grapes" and point out that the comparative scarcity of game and lack of time, money and opportunity today lend false emphasis to this argument, the fact remains that never since the last World War has shooting had a stronger following bent on recapturing, as far as possible, the olden, golden days. In this they are largely helped by modern methods of game rearing and preservation, much simpler and more effective than those practised by their predecessors, which have been, perforce, evolved in the face of progressive and more destructive means of agriculture, building expansion, an increased population and the like, but while big bags are still by no means out of the question, the accent now is rather on conservation and controlled shooting, and perpetuating all species of game birds for the benefit of succeeding generations.

Moreover, it should be remembered that shooting today, when more gun and game licences are being issued annually than ever before, is no longer the perquisite of the wealthy landowner, but a sport whose practitioners are drawn mostly from the ranks of farmers, syndicates comprising members from all walks of life, and those who find their enjoyment inexpensively and modestly on the foreshores of these islands or by permission of sympathetic landowners and tenants.

Big bags are not to be condemned out of hand, however. If circumstances and the stock of birds warrant there is no reason why they should not be made. Cases in point in this connection, referred to below, are the existing record bags of partridges and pigeon. In the former case the achievement made no difference to the stock at Rothwell, even in a decade which has seen a sorry decline in partridges almost everywhere . . . (at the time of publication Mr. Nickerson reports 1959 prospects as the best since the year in which he established his record) while in the latter, it is to be hoped that the pigeon record will be exceeded often, for woodpigeon constitute a major pest of agriculture. These are bag records which may be beaten in the not so distant future. Other records of this nature are likely to stand for a long time yet, and some of the major ones as listed in Hugh S. Gladstone's "Record Bags" are included in the summary below.

RECORD GAME BAGS MADE IN THE BRITISH ISLES

GROUSE. 2,929 shot on August 12th, 1915, on the Littledale and Abbeystead beat, Lancs., by eight guns: The Earl of Sefton; the Hon. J. Ward; the Hon. H. Stonor; Mr. E. de C. Oakley; Major the Hon. J. Dawnay; Capt. the Hon. T. Fitzherbert; Capt. the Hon. H. Bridgeman and Major the Hon. E. Beaumont.

PARTRIDGES. 2,119 shot October 3rd, 1952, at Rothwell, Lincs., by six guns: Messrs. Joseph Nickerson; F. R. Davy; R. F. Dennis; P. K. Dennis; L. Lamyman; S. Nickerson.

PHEASANTS. 3,937 shot at Hall Barn, Beaconsfield, on December 18th, 1913, by seven guns: H. M. King George V; The Prince of Wales; Lord Charles Fitzmaurice; Lord Ilchester; Lord Dalhousie; Lord Herbert Vane-Tempest and the Hon. H. Stonor.

WOODCOCK. 228 shot at Ashford, Co. Galway, by six guns: the Earl of Bandon; the Don O'Connor; the Hon. E. O'Brien; Mr. Percy La Touche; Mr. Beecher and Major C. P. R. Coote.

HARES. 1,215 shot on December 19th, 1877, at Holkham, Norfolk, by eleven guns.

SNIPE. 1,108 shot between October 25th and November 3rd, 1906, by Lord Elphinstone and Mr. J. D. Cobbold on the Inner Hebridean island of Tiree.

PIGEON. 470 shot on Monday, August 1st, 1955, by Mr. R. Hampton.)

RABBITS. 6,943 shot on October 7th, 1898, at Blenheim in Oxfordshire, by five guns: The Duke of Marlborough; Prince Victor Duleep Singh; Prince Frederick Duleep Singh; Sir Robert Gresley and Mr. Stephen Wombwell.

BLACKGAME. The record is probably 252 shot in about 1860 on Cannock Chase in Staffordshire.

CAPERCAILLIE. 69 shot on November 4th, 1910, at Dunkeld, Perthshire, by seven guns: the Duke of Atholl; the Marquis of Tullibardine; Lord George Murray; Colonel Ruggles Brise; Count Clary; Capt. Moray and Capt. Wentworth.

WILDFOWL. Record bags of duck and geese are generally somewhat in doubt, but perhaps the most notable is the bag of 704 brent geese made about 1860 on the Dengie Flats in the River Blackwater, Essex, by thirty-two punt-gunners under the command of Colonel Russell. Including the later pick-up, it is reasonable to suppose that the total reached 1,000. On this occasion all the punt-guns were fired simultaneously.

SHOOTING SEASONS

(All dates inclusive)

GROUSE
August 12th—December 10th

PARTRIDGE
September 1st—February 1st

(Contd. on p. 150, col. I)

QUIZ ANSWERS

1. "This licence expires on the 31st July." 2. Under this system, partridge eggs as they are laid are taken up and incubated under a sitting hen, being replaced in the nests by sham eggs. Subsequently the real eggs, when chipped, are returned, and the sham eggs taken away. 3. To increase the supply of edible heather and thereby a greater stock of birds. As much early spring feed as possible is the aim. 4. Pheasant and partridge eggs 24 days: duck 28 days: grouse 21–22 days. 5. Punt-guns are restricted to a barrel which has an internal diameter at the muzzle of not more than 1¾ inches. 6. (a) Old birds' primaries are rounder and blunter. Young birds' are pointed and sharper. (b) The medium wing coverts of cock birds have a longitudinal pale buff stripe running down the shaft and on each side of the shaft the feathers are mottled grey or brown. The hen has the same pale buff stripe on these feathers, but they are barred with buff and dark brown, not mottled. 7. There are two features of Skeet which differ essentially from Down-the-Line. The rigid rule is "gun down" (i.e. not ready at the shoulder) and the shooter may neither "call for" nor "address" his bird. Skeet offers a variety of shots at many angles from a high and a low trap house, very similar to those met in the field. Down the line is essentially a specialised, competitive sport, and only one trap is used. The old method of gauging the bore of a shotgun was by the number of identical spherical balls exactly fitting the bore that went to the pound. Thus, in the case of the 12-bore there were 12; the 20-bore took 20 and so on.

GAME SHOOTING QUIZ

1. What is printed in red across the top of a gun licence?

★

2. What, briefly, is the Euston system?

★

3. Why do grouse-moor keepers burn heather?

★

4. What is the incubation period of the eggs of pheasants, duck, partridges and grouse?

★

5. What limitation did the Protection of Birds Act, 1954, impose upon the users of punt-guns?

★

6. By looking at the wings of a partridge, how can you differentiate between (a) young and old; (b) cock and hen?

★

7. What is the difference between "skeet" and "down-the-line" shooting?

★

8. Why is a 12-bore so called?

PHEASANT
October 1st—February 1st

PTARMIGAN
August 12th—December 10th
(*Scotland only*)

BLACKGAME
August 20th—December 10th

CAPERCAILLIE
October 1st—January 31st

SNIPE
August 12th—January 31st

WOODCOCK
October 1st—January 31st
(*Scotland Sept. 1st-Jan. 31st*)

HARES
No close season, but Hares may not be sold or offered for sale during the months March to July, both months inclusive.

It is illegal in England and Wales to shoot Grouse, Blackgame, Partridges, or Pheasants, on Sundays or Christmas Day. Although not game, a game licence is required for Snipe and Woodcock.

WILD GEESE, DUCK & WADERS

In or over any area below high water mark of ordinary Spring Tides
September 1st—February 20th
Elsewhere
September 1st—January 31st
Waders may be shot only
September 1st—January 31st

Wildfowl that may be shot during the season are as follows:

Wild Duck: Common Pochard, Gadwall, Mallard, Pintail, Goldeneye, Garganey, Common Scoter, Scaup, Velvet Scoter, Long-Tailed Duck, Shoveller, Teal, Tufted Duck, Widgeon.

Geese: Bean Goose, Canada Goose, Pinkfooted Goose, Whitefronted Goose, Greylag Goose.

Waders: Curlew, Whimbrel, Redshank, Bar-Tailed Godwit, Golden Plover, Grey Plover.

Wildfowlers are advised to make enquiries of their local council if there are any local orders in force restricting the season for any particular birds.

CLAY PIGEON SHOOTING

The most outstanding clay pigeon shooter in Great Britain since World War II is Joseph Wheater of Hull, Yorkshire.

Aged 40, he has won over 100 championships of various kinds, and he has proved himself to be the best "all-rounder" ever known in this country. His performances include:

Skeet: Winner of the British Open Skeet Championship (1949, 1951, 1953, 1954, 1958 and 1959).

First in Great Britain to score 100-straight at Skeet.

Down-the-line: Winner of the English Open D.T.L. Championship (1955, 1956) and British Open D.T.L. Championship (1956, 1958).

High Gun, International Team Match (1952, 1957).

In 1952, first to score 100-straight, single barrel; and 200 straight (double barrel), in 1959.

Double-Rise: Winner of English Open Double-Rise Championship (1956, 1957, 1958).

Olympic Trench: Represented Great Britain at Olympic Games, Melbourne, 1956.

Won Coupe des Nations in France in 1958.

Won German Championship and European Championship in 1959, beating the Olympic Champion (Rossini) and fellow countryman (Fear) in shoot-off in the latter event.

Won Czechoslovakian Grand Prix at Berno, Sept. 1959, scoring 198 ex 200.

Sporting: Winner of British Open Sporting Championship (1954, 1956).

In 1957 reduced time for killing 1,000 clays to 42 mins. 22.5 secs. at Bedford Gun Club.

General: Winner of the C.P.S.A.'s Coronation Cup six times since 1953 for best all-round performance at national championships.

GAME SHOOTING QUIZ

1. What is the easiest way of distinguishing between a great, common and jack snipe?

*

2. What is the difference between cast-off in a shotgun and cast-on? *

3. What do the abbreviations B.F.S.S. and W.A.G.B.I. stand for?

*

4. Why was July 31, 1958, a significant date for gamekeepers?

*

5. How does the preparation of snipe and woodcock for cooking differ from that of a teal?

6. Is it necessary to hold a game licence before you may shoot snipe and woodcock on the foreshore?

*

7. Who is the patron saint of field sports?

*

8. What is the difference between a boxlock gun and a sidelock?

QUIZ ANSWERS

1. By the relative sizes in conjunction with a count of the tail feathers. The great snipe has 16; the common 14; and the jack 12. 2. If a gunstock is cast-off, it is bent to the right. If cast-on, to the left. 3. The British Field Sports Society and The Wildfowlers' Association of Great Britain and Ireland. The addresses of their relative secretaries are: 51 Victoria St., London S.W.1: and 19 Castle St., Liverpool 2. 4. On that date the gin trap became illegal in England and Wales. It is now also illegal in Scotland, except for the trapping of foxes and otters. 5. Snipe and woodcock are cooked without being eviscerated. 6. Yes. A game licence must be taken out before you may shoot snipe or woodcock anywhere. 7. St. Hubert. 8. Sidelocks of hammerless guns are fixed behind the action body and let into the side of the gun. Boxlocks are fitted into the body of the gun's action.

Gliding

Compiled by Mrs. J. R. Bonham
Former Secretary: The British Gliding Association

HISTORY

The very first gliding was done by Otto Lilienthal in 1895, who hovered for only a few seconds. He was followed by Orville Wright in 1911, who achieved 9¾ minutes. Nine years later, in 1921, Wolfgang Klemperer beat the previous record with a flight of 15 minutes, and in 1922 A. Martens first soared for 1 hour and F. H. Hentzen for 3 hours. Max Kegel climbed in a thunderstorm in 1926, and in 1928 Robert Kronfeld came on the scene and discovered it was possible to soar other than to the windward slopes of hills. In 1929 he set up an altitude record of 8,494 ft. and soared a distance of over 93 miles.

It was on the 4th December 1929 at the Comedy Restaurant in Panton Street that the British Gliding Association, which is the controlling body for the sport in the United Kingdom, was formed. **The Association has continued its steady growth throughout the last thirty years until there are today**

38 Civilian Gliding Clubs with a total membership of over 5,000 active pilots who operate approximately 252 gliders. In 1958 these pilots flew a total of 30,165 miles on soaring flights involving 21,536 hours and 135,074 launches. In 1955 H.R.H. The Duke of Edinburgh graciously consented to become the Patron of the Association, and in 1957 he opened at the Lasham Gliding Centre in Hampshire one of the largest gliding meetings ever held in the world. Over 70 gliders competed on that occasion.

GLIDING QUIZ

1. What is the governing body for gliding in the U.K. and when was it formed?

*

2. Who made the first British soaring flight?

*

3. What is the greatest height ever to have been attained in a glider?

*

4. Who has been British National Gliding Champion most times?

*

5. Where and when was the first National Glider Aerobatic Championship held and who is current champion?

*

6. What aerobatics can normally be performed by British Gliders?

*

7. What is the approximate wingspan of a high performance glider?

*

8. What is a bunge launch?

*

9. What is a total energy variometer?

*

10. How much training does a pilot need before he can fly solo in a glider; are there any age limits?

QUIZ ANSWERS

1. The British Gliding Association formed in 1929. 2. E. C. Gordon England on the 27th June, 1909, who rose about 40 ft. over Amberley Mount and remained airborne for 58 seconds. 3. 42,100 ft. (World Absolute Altitude Record). 4. Philip Wills, four times. 5. The London Gliding Club, Dunstable in September 1958, when David Ince became Champion. 6. Loop, stall turns, tight turns and spins. 7. 60 ft. 8. The launching of a glider by catapult from the top of a hill. 9. An instrument which tells the pilot whether he is flying through rising or falling air. 10. About 40/50 flights in a two-seater trainer each lasting 2-5 minutes are required before solo. You may not fly solo under the age of 16. There is no upper age limit.

Statistics

27,296 pilots in the United Kingdom have obtained a Certificate with an "A" Endorsement.

808 pilots in the United Kingdom have obtained a Certificate with the Silver "C".

46 pilots in the United Kingdom have obtained a Certificate with the Gold "C".

Only one pilot, Commander H. C. N. Goodhart, has added 3 Diamonds to his Gold "C", although 46 pilots have one or two Diamonds to their credit.

THE HISTORY OF UNITED KINGDOM DISTANCE AND HEIGHT RECORDS IN SINGLE SEATER GLIDERS 1932–59

	Distance miles	Gain of Height feet
1932	13	
1933	19	1,750
1934	95	3,800
1936	104	4,514
		8,323
1938	{ 120	10,180
	{ 209	
1939		{ 10,350
		{ 14,170
1946		15,247
1949	233	
1950		19,120
1951	257	
1955		21,000
1957		26,500
1958	{ 295	
	{ 315	
1959	360	

British National Gliding Champions

1939	C. Nicholson
1948	P. A. Wills
1949	P. A. Wills
1950	P. A. Wills
1951	R. C. Forbes
1953	G. H. Stephenson
1955	P. A. Wills
1957	A. J. Deane-Drummond
1959	G. H. Stephenson

Proficiency Certificates

No pilots' licences are required to glide in this country, but the British Gliding Association issues a Proficiency Certificate with various endorsements to suitably qualified pilots. The qualifications for these are as follows and each endorsement entitles the holder to wear a different badge:

"A" Endorsement is awarded when a pilot has carried out one solo flight in a glider and made a normal landing.
Badge: One white gull on blue.

"B" Endorsement is awarded when a pilot has carried out a minimum of three solo flights and has demonstrated his ability to turn in both directions and make normal landings.
Badge: Two white gulls on blue.

"C" Endorsement is awarded when a pilot has carried out a soaring flight for a continuous period of at least five minutes.
Badge: Three white gulls on blue.

International Silver "C" Badge and Endorsement is awarded when a pilot has made the following flights:
a. A flight of not less than 5 hours
b. Flown a distance of not less than 50 kms. (31.07 miles)
c. Reached a height of not less than 1,000 m. (3,281 ft.).
Badge: Three white gulls on blue surrounded by a silver wreath.

International Gold "C" Badge and Endorsement is awarded when a pilot has made the following flights:
a. A distance of not less than 300 kms. (186.42 miles)
b. A flight with a gain of height of not less than 3,000 m. (9,843 ft.).
Badge: Three white gulls on blue surrounded by a gold wreath.

Diamonds may also be added to the gold badge for each of the following flights:
a. A distance of not less than 500 kms. (310.7 miles)
b. A flight to a goal declared in advance by the pilot, of not less than 300 kms. (186.42 miles)
c. A gain of height of not less than 5,000 m. (16,404 ft.).

British Pilots who have become World Champions

P. A. Wills	1952–54 Single Seater Champion
H. C. N. Goodhart } F. Foster }	1956–58 Two Seater Champions

First Pilot to cross the Channel
G. H. Stephenson 1939

The First National Aerobatic Champions
1958 D. H. G. Ince
1959 Flt. Lt. B. B. Sharman

UNITED KINGDOM RECORDS

Distance: H. C. N. Goodhart. From Lasham, Hampshire, to Portmoak, Scotland, on the 10th May 1959. 360 miles.

Gain of Height: J. S. Williamson. From Lasham, Hampshire, on the 19th July 1957. 26,300 ft.

Absolute Altitude: J. S. Williamson. From Lasham, Hampshire, on the 19th July 1957. 28,500 ft.

Out and Return: A. J. Deane-Drummond. From Lasham, Hampshire, to Kidderminster, Worcestershire, and return to Lasham on the 1st June 1957. 197 miles.

Goal Flight: H. C. N. Goodhart. From Lasham, Hampshire, to Portmoak, Scotland, on the 10th May 1959. 360 miles.

100 Km. Triangle Speed: Frank Foster. From Dunstable on the 23rd June 1957 at a speed of 46.3 m.p.h.

200 Km. Triangle Speed: A. J. Deane-Drummond. From Lasham on the 2nd June 1957 at a speed of 38 m.p.h.

300 Km. Triangle Speed: H. C. N. Goodhart. From Lasham on the 25th June 1957 at a speed of 41.2 m.p.h.

WORLD CHAMPIONSHIPS

Dates, Locations and Winning Countries of World Championships

Year	Location	Winner
1938	Germany	Germany
1948	Switzerland	Sweden
1950	Sweden	Sweden
1952	Spain	Great Britain and Spain
1954	Great Britain	France and Yugoslavia
1956	France	U.S.A. and Great Britain
1958	Poland	Germany and Poland
1960	Germany	

*Where two winning countries are given the second country is the winner of the two-seater or standard class.

INTERNATIONAL GLIDING RECORDS

SINGLE-SEAT GLIDERS:

Distance in a Straight Line: Richard H. Johnson (U.S.A.) in a Ross-Johnson sailplane, from Odessa, Texas, to Salina, Kansas, August 5, 1951 .... 535.17 miles

Distance to Fixed Goal: Commandant René Fonteilles (France) in a Breguet 901, from Troyes-Barberey to Dax, May 13, 1956   421.05 miles

Distance to Fixed Goal and return to Point of Departure: Vladislav Zejda (Czechoslovakia) in VT-100 Demant, from Vrchlabi to Trencin Hrad and back, May 30, 1957... 321.91 miles

Height: William S. Ivans Jr. (U.S.A.) in a Schweizer S.G.S. 1-23, at Bishop, California, December 30, 1950 .... 42,100 ft.

Gain of Height: Karl Bauer (Germany). In a Weihe, at Dettingen-Teck, Germany, June 20, 1959 .... 31,711 ft.

Speed over 100-km. Triangular Course: Richard Schreder (U.S.A.) in an H-P-8, in Texas, August 11, 1959 (unratified)............. 65 m.p.h.

Speed over 200-km. Triangular Course: Richard Schreder (U.S.A.) in an H-P-8, in Texas, August 6, 1959 (unratified)............. 67 m.p.h.

Speed over 300-km. Triangular Course: Richard Schreder (U.S.A.) in an H-P-8, in Texas, August 7, 1959 (unratified)............. 59 m.p.h.

MULTI-SEAT GLIDERS:

Distance in a Straight Line: Victor Iltchenko (Russia) and Grigory Petchnikov in an A-10 sailplane, from Kountsevo, Moscow, to Ilovlia, Stalingrad, May 26, 1953 ...... 515.625 miles

Distance to Fixed Goal: Jerzy Popiel (Poland) and Adolf Siemaszkiewicz in Zuraw II sailplane, from Lublin to Hrubieszow, July 20, 1953 .... 336.35 miles

Distance to Fixed Goal and Return to Point of Departure: Evert Dommisse (South Africa) and Samuel J. Barker in a Kranich II sailplane, from Keetmanshoop to Mariental and back, February 9, 1952 ...... 270.92 miles

Height: Laurence E. Edgar (U.S.A.) and H. E. Klieforth, in a Pratt-Read sailplane, at Bishop, California, March 19, 1952 ..... 44,255 ft.

Gain of Height: Laurence E. Edgar (U.S.A.) and H. E. Klieforth, in a Pratt-Read sailplane, at Bishop, California, March 19, 1952 .... 34,425 ft.

Speed over 100-km. Triangular Course: Harland C. Ross (U.S.A.) and Horace E. Jensen in Ross R-6 sailplane, Odessa (Texas)–intersection of routes 115 and 128–intersection of route 51 and a closed road–Odessa, August 14, 1958 .... 54.377 m.p.h.

Speed over 200-km. Triangular Course: Harland C. Ross (U.S.A.) and Horace E. Jensen in Ross R-6 sailplane, Odessa (Texas)–Wink (Texas)–Eunice (New Mexico)–Odessa, August 12, 1958 .... 50.548 m.p.h.

Speed over 300-km. Triangular Course: Harland C. Ross (U.S.A.) and Paul E. Wilson in Ross R-6 sailplane, Odessa (Texas)–Wink (Texas)–Eunice (New Mexico)–Lamesa (Texas)–Odessa, August 13, 1958 ...... 51.169 m.p.h.

GLIDING QUIZ

1. What are the motifs on the official gliding tie?

*

2. What is the name of the International organisation responsible for gliding and where does it have its offices?

*

3. What is a standing wave, when does it occur and where can the most famous one be found?

*

4. What famous broadcaster and ornithologist is also a keen glider pilot?

*

5. Do glider pilots wear parachutes?

*

6. What are the methods by which gliders may be launched?

*

7. What basic instruments are carried in most gliders?

*

8. What gliders were flown by the winning British pilots in the 1952 and 1956 World Championships?

*

9. What are the main controls fitted to gliders and what are their functions?

*

10. One of the subsidiary controls fitted to modern gliders are airbrakes. What is their function?

*

QUIZ ANSWERS

1. Silver stripes with small silver gliders on navy blue background. 2. The Federation Aeronautique International with offices in Paris. 3. A standing wave is a more or less stationary form of upcurrent discovered by the glider pilot. It occurs when a torrent of stable air blows down a line of hills or range of mountains. In the right conditions the crest of each layer of wave is marked by a lens-shaped cloud called a lenticular cloud, which is stationary in relation to the ground. The most famous wave is to be found at Bishop in the lee of the Sierra Nevada mountains in California, U.S.A. 4. Peter Scott who flies with the Bristol Gliding Club at Nympsfield in Gloucester. 5. Yes, when going on cross-country flights. 6. Winchtow, auto-tow, aero-tow or bungey. 7. Airspeed indicator, altimeter and variometer. 8. The Slingsby Sky and Eagle. 9. (a) The control column or stick which operates the ailerons and elevators; (b) the rudder bar on which the pilot rests his feet and operates the rudder; (c) the launching cable release knob. 10. By opening the airbrakes, which are situated in the wings of a glider, the pilot can vary the angle of glide of the aircraft.

Golf

Compiled by **Tom Scott**
Editor: Golf Illustrated

Since golf first came to Britain and was played on the links at Musselburgh in Scotland the game has seen many landmarks.

There was the day in 1860 at Prestwick when eight professionals gathered to play in the first competition for the Open Championship Belt and a first prize of a few shillings. The winner was Willie Park. Park was to win the Championship several times, but soon the competition was dominated by the two Morrises, Tom Sen. and Tom Jun. Between them they won eight times, and had it not been for young Tommy's early death the total would have been greater.

In 1958, ninety-eight years after the first event, the Open Championship was won by the Australian Peter Thomson for the fourth time, and the first prize was one thousand pounds.

In its early years the Open Championship was organised by the Prestwick Club, but since 1872 it has been under the sponsorship of the Royal and Ancient Club of St. Andrews, whose first rules of the game have been accepted by golfers everywhere. The Amateur Championship is also under the same auspices, although, like the Open Championship, it too was a private venture, the first competition taking place at the Hoylake Club in Cheshire and the winner being Mr. A. F. McFie. The present holder is D. W. Beaman.

OPEN CHAMPIONSHIP

The Belt

Year	Winner	Venue	Score
1860	W. Park, Musselburgh	Prestwick	174
1861	Tom Morris, sen., Prestwick	Prestwick	163
1862	Tom Morris, sen., Prestwick	Prestwick	163
1863	W. Park, Musselburgh	Prestwick	168
1864	Tom Morris, sen., Prestwick	Prestwick	167
1865	A. Strath, St. Andrews	Prestwick	162
1866	W. Park, Musselburgh	Prestwick	169
1867	Tom Morris, sen., St. Andrews	Prestwick	170
1868	Tom Morris, jun., St. Andrews	Prestwick	157
1869	Tom Morris, jun., St. Andrews	Prestwick	154
1870	Tom Morris, jun., St. Andrews	Prestwick	149

The Cup

Year	Winner	Venue	Score
1872	Tom Morris, jun., St. Andrews	Prestwick	166
1873	Tom Kidd, St. Andrews	St. Andrews	179
1874	Mungo Park, Musselburgh	Musselburgh	159
1875	Willie Park, Musselburgh	Prestwick	166
1876	Bob Martin, St. Andrews	St. Andrews	176
1877	Jamie Anderson, St. Andrews	Musselburgh	160
1878	Jamie Anderson, St. Andrews	Prestwick	157
1879	Jamie Anderson, St. Andrews	St. Andrews	170
1880	Bob Ferguson, Musselburgh	Musselburgh	162
1881	Bob Ferguson, Musselburgh	Prestwick	170
1882	Bob Ferguson, Musselburgh	St. Andrews	171
1883	W. Fernie, Dumfries	Musselburgh	159
1884	Jack Simpson, Carnoustie	Prestwick	160
1885	Bob Martin, St. Andrews	St. Andrews	171
1886	D. Brown, Musselburgh	Musselburgh	157
1887	W. Park, jun., Musselburgh	Prestwick	161
1888	Jack Burns, Warwick	St. Andrews	171
1889	W. Park, jun., Musselburgh	Musselburgh	155
1890	Mr. John Ball, Royal Liverpool	Prestwick	164
1891	Hugh Kirkaldy, St. Andrews	St. Andrews	166

After 1891 the competition was extended to seventy-two holes

Year	Winner	Venue	Score
1892	Mr. H. H. Hilton, Royal Liverpool	Muirfield	305
1893	W. Auchterlonie, St. Andrews	Prestwick	322
1894	J. H. Taylor, Winchester	Sandwich	326
1895	J. H. Taylor, Winchester	St. Andrews	322
1896	H. Vardon, Ganton	Muirfield	316
1897	Mr. H. H. Hilton, Royal Liverpool	Hoylake	314
1898	H. Vardon, Ganton	Prestwick	307
1899	H. Vardon, Ganton	Sandwich	310
1900	J. H. Taylor, Mid-Surrey	St. Andrews	309
1901	James Braid Romford	Muirfield	309
1902	Alex Herd, Huddersfield	Hoylake	307
1903	H. Vardon, Totteridge	Prestwick	300
1904	Jack White, Sunningdale	Sandwich	296
1905	James Braid, Walton Heath	St. Andrews	318
1906	James Braid, Walton Heath	Muirfield	300
1907	Arnaud Massy, La Boulie	Hoylake	312
1908	James Braid, Walton Heath	Prestwick	291
1909	J. H. Taylor, Mid-Surrey	Deal	295
1910	James Braid, Walton Heath	St. Andrews	299
1911	Harry Vardon, Totteridge	Sandwich	303
1912	E. Ray, Oxhey	Muirfield	295
1913	J. H. Taylor, Mid-Surrey	Hoylake	304
1914	Harry Vardon, Totteridge	Prestwick	306
1915–19	No Championship owing to World War I		
1920	George Duncan, Hanger Hill	Deal	303
1921	Jock Hutchison, Glenview, Chicago	St. Andrews	296
1922	Walter Hagen, Detroit (U.S.A.)	Sandwich	300
1923	A. G. Havers, Coombe Hill	Troon	295
1924	Walter Hagen, Detroit (U.S.A.)	Hoylake	301

GOLF QUIZ
THE OPEN

1. What is its full title?

 ★

2. Who won in 1926, 1936, 1946, 1956?

 ★

3. When was Sunningdale used for the Open?

 ★

4. When was the Open last played in Wales?

 ★

5. Who was the last amateur to be Open Champion?

 ★

6. Who asked for consistency in the height of the flagsticks, and where?

 ★

7. In which Open were balls holed without being struck?

8. How many times has Dai Rees been Open Champion?

 ★

9. What prevented Harry Bradshaw from winning the 1949 Open?

 ★

10. Who decided against competing for the Open title when he knew Ben Hogan had entered?

QUIZ ANSWERS

1. The Open Golf Championship. 2. Bobby Jones, Alf Padgham, Sam Snead, Peter Thomson. 3. In 1926, when regional qualifying rounds were played. 4. Never. 5. Bobby Jones. 6. Ben Hogan at Carnoustie in 1953. 7. At Sandwich in 1938 when the gale was so violent it blew some balls in from the lip of the hole. 8. Never. 9. His ball lodged in a broken beer bottle, which he would have been justified in removing. 10. Ed Oliver.

Year	Winner	Venue	Score
1925	Jim Barnes, U.S.A.	Prestwick	300
1926	Mr. R. T. Jones, U.S.A.	Royal Lytham & St. Annes	291
1927	Mr. R. T. Jones, U.S.A.	St. Andrews	285
1928	Walter Hagen, U.S.A.	Sandwich	292
1929	Walter Hagen, U.S.A.	Muirfield	292
1930	Mr. R. T. Jones, U.S.A.	Hoylake	291
1931	T. D. Armour, U.S.A.	Carnoustie	296
1932	G. Sarazen, U.S.A.	Prince's Sandwich	283
1933	D. Shute, U.S.A.	St. Andrews	292
1934	T. H. Cotton, Waterloo, Belgium	Sandwich	283
1935	A. Perry, Leatherhead	Muirfield	283
1936	A. H. Padgham, Sundridge Park	Hoylake	287
1937	T. H. Cotton, Ashridge	Carnoustie	290
1938	R. A. Whitcombe, Parkstone	Sandwich	295
1939	R. Burton, Sale	St. Andrews	290
1940–45	No Championship owing to World War II		
1946	S. Snead, U.S.A.	St. Andrews	290
1947	F. Daly, Balmoral	Hoylake	293
1948	T. H. Cotton, Royal Mid-Surrey	Muirfield	284
1949	A. D. Locke, South Africa	Sandwich	283
1950	A. D. Locke, South Africa	Troon	279
1951	M. Faulkner, Unattached	Portrush	285
1952	A. D. Locke, South Africa	Royal Lytham	287
1953	Ben Hogan, U.S.A.	Carnoustie	282
1954	P. W. Thomson, Australia	Royal Birkdale	283
1955	P. W. Thomson, Australia	St. Andrews	281
1956	P. W. Thomson, Australia	Hoylake	286
1957	A. D. Locke, South Africa	St. Andrews	279
1958	P. W. Thomson, Australia	Royal Lytham	278
1959	G. J. Player, South Africa	Muirfield	284

AMATEUR CHAMPIONSHIP

Year	Winner	Runner-up	Venue	By
1885	A. F. Macfie	H. G. Hutchinson	Hoylake	7 and 6
1886	H. G. Hutchinson	Henry Lamb	St. Andrews	7 and 6
1887	H. G. Hutchinson	John Ball	Hoylake	1 hole
1888	John Ball	J. E. Laidlay	Prestwick	5 and 4
1889	J. E. Laidlay	L. M. B. Melville	St. Andrews	2 and 1
1890	John Ball	J. E. Laidlay	Hoylake	4 and 3
1891	J. E. Laidlay	H. H. Hilton	St. Andrews	20th hole
1892	John Ball	H. H. Hilton	Sandwich	3 and 1
1893	Peter Anderson	J. E. Laidlay	Prestwick	1 hole
1894	John Ball	S. M. Fergusson	Hoylake	1 hole
1895	J. M. B. Melville	John Ball	St. Andrews	19th hole
1896	F. G. Tait	H. H. Hilton	Sandwich	8 and 7

Thirty-six holes played on and after this date.

Year	Winner	Runner-up	Venue	By
1897	A. J. T. Allan	James Robb	Muirfield	4 and 2
1898	F. G. Tait	S. M. Fergusson	Hoylake	7 and 5
1899	John Ball	F. G. Tait	Prestwick	37th hole
1900	H. H. Hilton	James Robb	Sandwich	8 and 7
1901	H. H. Hilton	J. L. Low	St. Andrews	1 hole
1902	C. Hutchings	S. H. Fry	Hoylake	1 hole
1903	R. Maxwell	H. G. Hutchinson	Muirfield	7 and 5
1904	W. J. Travis	Ed. Blackwell	Sandwich	4 and 3
1905	A. G. Barry	Hon. O. Scott	Prestwick	3 and 2
1906	James Robb	C. C. Lingen	Hoylake	4 and 3

Bobby Locke

Peter Thomson

Year	Winner	Runner-up	Venue	Margin
1947	W. P. Turnesa	R. D. Chapman	Carnoustie	3 and 2
1948	F. R. Stranahan	C. Stowe	Sandwich	5 and 4
1949	S. M. M'Cready	W. P. Turnesa	Portmarnock	2 and 1
1950	F. R. Stranahan	R. D. Chapman	St. Andrews	8 and 6
1951	R. D. Chapman	C. R. Coe	Porthcawl	5 and 4
1952	E. H. Ward	F. R. Stranahan	Prestwick	6 and 5
1953	J. B. Carr	E. Harvie Ward	Hoylake	2 holes
1954	D. W. Bachli	W. C. Campbell	Muirfield	2 and 1
1955	J. W. Conrad	A. Slater	Royal Lytham St. Annes	3 and 2
1956	J. C. Beharrell	L. G. Taylor	Troon	5 and 4
1957	R. Reid Jack	H. B. Ridgley	Formby	2 and 1

In 1956 and 1957 the Quarter Finals, Semi-Finals and Final were played over 36 holes.

Year	Winner	Runner-up	Venue	Margin
1958	J. B. Carr	A. Thirlwell	St. Andrews	3 and 2
1959	D. Beman	W. Hyndman	Sandwich	3 and 2

Year	Winner	Runner-up	Venue	Margin
1907	John Ball	C. A. Palmer	St. Andrews	6 and 4
1908	E. A. Lassen	H. E. Taylor	Sandwich	7 and 6
1909	R. Maxwell	Capt. C. K. Hutchison	Muirfield	1 hole
1910	John Ball	C. Aylmer	Hoylake	10 and 9
1911	H. H. Hilton	E. A. Lassen	Prestwick	4 and 3
1912	John Ball	Abe Mitchell	Westward Ho!	38th hole
1913	H. H. Hilton	R. Harris	St. Andrews	6 and 5
1914	J. L. C. Jenkins	C. O. Hezlet	Sandwich	3 and 2
1915–19	No Championship owing to World War I			
1920	C. J. H. Tolley	R. A. Gardner	Muirfield	37th hole
1921	W. I. Hunter	A. J. Graham	Hoylake	12 and 11
1922	E. W. E. Holderness	J. Caven	Prestwick	1 hole
1923	R. H. Wethered	R. Harris	Deal	7 and 6
1924	E. W. E. Holderness	E. F. Storey	St. Andrews	3 and 2
1925	Robert Harris	K. F. Fradgley	Westward Ho!	13 and 12
1926	Jesse Sweetser	A. F. Simpson	Muirfield	6 and 5
1927	Dr. W. Tweddell	D. E. Landale	Hoylake	7 and 6
1928	T. P. Perkins	R. H. Wethered	Prestwick	6 and 4
1929	C. J. H. Tolley	J. N. Smith	Sandwich	4 and 3
1930	R. T. Jones	R. H. Wethered	St. Andrews	7 and 6
1931	E. Martin Smith	J. D. Forest	Westward Ho!	1 hole
1932	J. De Forest	E. W. Fiddian	Muirfield	3 and 1
1933	Hon. M. Scott	T. A. Bourn	Hoylake	4 and 3
1934	W. Lawson Little	J. Wallace	Prestwick	14 and 13
1935	W. Lawson Little	Dr. W. Tweddell	Royal Lytham and St. Annes	1 hole
1936	H. Thomson	J. Ferrier	St. Andrews	2 holes
1937	R. Sweeny, jun.	L. O. Munn	Sandwich	3 and 2
1938	C. R. Yates	R. C. Ewing	Troon	3 and 2
1939	A. T. Kyle	A. A. Duncan	Hoylake	2 and 1
1940–45	Suspended during World War II			
1946	J. Bruen	R. Sweeny	Birkdale	4 and 3

ENGLISH AMATEUR CHAMPIONSHIP

Year	Winner	Runner-up	Venue	Margin
1925	T. F. Ellison	S. Robinson	Hoylake	1 hole
1926	T. F. Ellison	Sq. Lead. C. H. Hayward	Walton Heath	6 and 4
1927	T. P. Perkins	J. B. Beddard	Little Aston	2 and 1
1928	J. A. Stout	T. P. Perkins	Royal Lytham and St. Annes	3 and 2
1929	W. Sutton	E. B. Tipping	Gosforth	3 and 2
1930	T. A. Bourn	C. E. Hardman	Burnham	3 and 2
1931	L. G. Crawley	W. Sutton	Hunstanton	1 hole
1932	E. W. Fiddian	A. S. Bradshaw	Royal St. George's	1 hole
1933	J. Woollam	T. A. Bourn	Ganton	4 and 3
1934	S. Lunt	L. G. Crawley	Formby	37th hole
1935	J. Woollam	E. W. Fiddian	Hollinwell	2 and 1
1936	H. G. Bentley	J. D. A. Langley	Deal	5 and 4
1937	J. J. Pennink	L. G. Crawley	Saunton	6 and 5
1938	J. J. Pennink	S. E. Banks	Moortown	2 and 1
1939	A. L. Bentley	W. Sutton	Birkdale	5 and 4
1946	I. R. Patey	K. Thom	Royal Mid-Surrey	5 and 4
1947	G. H. Micklem	C. Stowe	Ganton	1 hole
1948	A. G. B. Helm	H. J. R. Roberts	Little Aston	2 and 1
1949	R. J. White	C. Stowe	Formby	5 and 4
1950	J. D. A. Langley	I. R. Patey	Deal	1 hole
1951	G. P. Roberts	H. Bennett	Hunstanton	39th hole
1952	E. Millward	I. J. Shorrock	Burnham and Berrow	2 holes
1953	G. H. Micklem	R. J. White	Royal Birkdale	2 and 1
1954	A. Thirlwell	H. G. Bentley	Royal St. George's	2 and 1
1955	A. Thirlwell	M. Burgess	Ganton	7 and 6
1956	G. B. Wolstenholme	H. Bennett	Royal Lytham and St. Annes	1 hole
1957	A. Walker	G. Whitehead	Royal Liverpool	4 and 3
1958	D. Sewell	D. Proctor	Walton Heath	8 and 7
1959	G. B. Wolstenholme	M. Bonallack	Formby	1 hole

Harry Vardon

T. D. Armour

"Bobby" Jones

Cyril Tolley

Gerald Micklem

G. P. Roberts

GOLF QUIZ

THE AMATEURS

1. With what professions do you associate G. P. Roberts; Gerald Micklem; Ronnie White; Tony Duncan?

★

2. Which teen-ager has won an Open Amateur Championship since World War II?

★

3. When may amateurs receive payment for giving lessons?

★

4. From whom may they accept travelling expenses when playing as individuals and not in a team?

★

5. Which British amateur took lessons from Ben Hogan?

★

6. How many times has Britain won the Walker Cup?

★

7. When did a limerick prove costly to a firm of confectioners?

★

8. Who became a professional for non-professional reasons?

★

9. Which of the following have been amateurs: Fred Daly; Ugo Grappasonni; Cary Middlecoff; Arthur Lees?

★

10. Who was the Open Amateur Champion throughout World War II?

ANSWERS TO QUIZ

1. Teaching, stockbroking, the law, the army. 2. John Beharrell. 3. When instruction is part of the sports curriculum at an educational establishment which employs them. 4. From anyone on whom, in normal circumstances, they are financially dependent. 5. Philip Scrutton. 6. Once. 7. When a well-known golfer sued Fry's for reflecting on his amateur status by using his name in an advertisement. 8. Frank Stranahan. 9. Only Middlecoff. 10. A. T. Kyle, who won in 1939.

John Beharrell, who won the Amateur Championship at Troon in 1956 when 18

GOLF QUIZ

COURSES

1. How many are there at Troon?

*

2. Which courses are adjacent to the Dormy Hotel; the Greenbrier Hotel; Kew Gardens; the stationmaster's garden?

*

3. Which is the most northerly "Royal" club in Britain?

*

4. Which big city would you travel to for a game at El Sereno; Espinho; Templenewsam; Riversdale?

*

5. Where in Southern England does one 18-hole course enclose another?

*

6. Which course used to be dreaded for its furrowed bunkers?

*

7. Which English club is 350 years old?

*

8. How many courses are there in Yugoslavia?

*

9. Which course dyed its lakes blue?

*

10. Which popular English city is without a course?

ANSWERS TO QUIZ

1. Two. 2. Ferndown, White Sulphur Springs, Royal Mid-Surrey, the Old Course at St. Andrew's. 3. Royal Dornoch. 4. Los Angeles, Oporto, Leeds, Melbourne. 5. At the Royal Mid-Surrey. 6. Oakmont, Pennsylvania. 7. Royal Blackheath. 8. One—Brioni. 9. Augusta National, Georgia. 10. Salford.

SCOTTISH AMATEUR CHAMPIONSHIP

Year	Winner	Runner-up	Venue	Margin
1922	J. Wilson	E. Blackwell	St. Andrews	19th hole
1923	T. M. Burrell	Dr. A. R. McCallum	Troon	1 hole
1924	W. W. Mackenzie	W. Tulloch	Aberdeen	3 and 2
1925	J. T. Dobson	W. W. Mackenzie	Muirfield	3 and 2
1926	W. J. Guild	S. O. Shepherd	Leven	2 and 1
1927	A. Jamieson, Jr.	Rev. D. S. Rutherford	Gailes	22nd hole
1928	W. W. Mackenzie	W. E. Dodds	Muirfield	5 and 3
1929	J. T. Bookless	J. E. Dawson	Aberdeen	5 and 4
1930	K. Greig	T. Wallace	Carnoustie	9 and 8
1931	J. Wilson	A. Jamieson, Jr.	Prestwick	2 and 1
1932	J. McLean	K. Greig	Dunbar	5 and 4
1933	J. McLean	K. C. Forbes	Aberdeen	6 and 4
1934	J. McLean	W. Campbell	Western Gailes	3 and 1
1935	H. Thomson	J. McLean	St. Andrews	2 and 1
1936	E. D. Hamilton	R. Neill	Carnoustie	1 hole
1937	H. McInally	K. G. Patrick	Barassie	6 and 5
1938	E. D. Hamilton	R. Rutherford	Muirfield	4 and 2
1939	H. McInally	H. Thomson	Prestwick	6 and 5
1946	E. C. Brown	R. Rutherford	Carnoustie	3 and 2
1947	H. McInally	J. Pressley	Western Gailes	10 and 8
1948	A. S. Flockhart	G. N. Taylor	Royal Aberdeen	7 and 6
1949	R. Wight	H. McInally	Muirfield	1 hole
1950	W. C. Gibson	D. A. Blair	Prestwick	2 and 1
1951	J. M. Dykes	J. C. Wilson	St. Andrews	4 and 2
1952	F. G. Dewar	J. C. Wilson	Carnoustie	4 and 3
1953	D. A. Blair	J. W. McKay	Western Gailes	3 and 1
1954	J. W. Draper	W. G. H. Gray	Nairn	4 and 3
1955	R. Reid Jack	A. C. Miller	Muirfield	2 and 1
1956	Dr. F. Deighton	A. MacGregor	Troon	8 and 7
1957	J. S. Montgomerie	J. Burnside	Aberdeen	2 and 1
1958	W. D. Smith	I. Harris	Prestwick	6 and 5
1959	Dr. F. W. G. Deighton	R. M. K. Murray	St. Andrews	6 and 5

WELSH AMATEUR NATIVE CHAMPIONSHIP

Instituted 1895. Finalists since 1930.

Year	Winner	Runner-up	Venue	By
1930	H. R. Howell	D. R. Lewis	Tenby	2 and 1
1931	H. R. Howell	W. G. Morgan	Aberdovey	7 and 6
1932	H. R. Howell	H. E. Davies	Ashburnham	7 and 6
1933	J. L. Black	A. A. Duncan	Porthcawl	2 and 1
1934	S. B. Roberts	G. S. Noon	Prestatyn	4 and 3
1935	R. Chapman	G. S. Noon	Tenby	1 hole
1936	R. M. de Lloyd	G. Wallis	Aberdovey	2 and 1
1937	D. H. Lewis	R. Glossop	Porthcawl	2 holes
1938	A. A. Duncan	S. B. Roberts	Rhyl	2 and 1
1946	J. V. Moody	A. Marshman	Porthcawl	9 and 8
1947	S. B. Roberts	G. Breen Turner	Harlech	8 and 7
1948	A. A. Duncan	S. B. Roberts	Porthcawl	2 and 1
1949	A. D. Evans	Mervyn A. Jones	Aberdovey	2 and 1
1950	J. L. Morgan	D. J. Bonnell	Southerndown	9 and 7
1951	J. L. Morgan	W. I. Tucker	Harlech	3 and 2
1952	A. A. Duncan	J. L. Morgan	Ashburnham	4 and 3
1953	S. B. Roberts	D. Pearson	Prestatyn	5 and 4

1954	A. A. Duncan	K. Thomas	Tenby	6 and 5
1955	T. J. Davies	P. Dunn	Harlech	at 38th
1956	A. Lockley	W. I. Tucker	Southerndown	2 and 1
1957	E. S. Mills	H. Griffiths	Harlech	2 and 1
1958	H. Squirrell	A. D. Lake	Conway	4 and 3
1959	H. Squirrell	N. Rees	Porthcawl	8 and 7

ENGLISH WOMEN'S CHAMPIONSHIP

Instituted 1912. Finalists since 1930

Year	Winner	Runner-up	Venue	Margin
1930	Miss E. Wilson	Mrs. R. O. Porter	Aldeburgh	12 and 11
1931	Miss W. Morgan	Miss M. Gourlay	Ganton	3 and 1
1932	Miss D. Fishwick	Miss B. Brown	Royal Ashdown Forest	5 and 4
1933	Miss D. Pearson	Miss M. Johnson	Westward Ho!	5 and 3
1934	Miss P. Wade	Miss M. Johnson	Seacroft	4 and 3
1935	Mrs. M. Garon	Miss E. Corlett	Birkdale	38th hole
1936	Miss W. Morgan	Miss P. Wade	Hayling	2 and 1
1937	Miss W. Morgan	Miss M. Fyshe	St. Enodoc	4 and 2
1938	Miss E. Corlett	Miss J. Winn	Aldeburgh	2 and 1
1947	Miss M. Wallis	Miss E. Price	Ganton	3 and 1
1948	Miss Frances Stephens	Mrs. Zara Bolton	Hayling	1 hole
1949	Mrs. A. C. Critchley	Lady Katherine Cairns	Burnham	3 and 2
1950	Hon. Mrs. A. Gee	Miss Pamela Davies	Sheringham	8 and 6
1951	Miss J. Bisgood	Mrs. A. Keiller	St. Annes Old Links	2 and 1
1952	Miss Pamela Davies	Miss Jacqueline Gordon	Westward Ho!	6 and 5
1953	Miss J. Bisgood	Miss J. McIntyre	Prince's Sandwich	6 and 5
1954	Miss Frances Stephens	Miss E. Price	Woodhall Spa	37th hole
1955	Mrs. R. Smith (née Frances Stephens)	Miss E. Price	Moortown	4 and 3
1956	Miss Bridget Jackson	Mrs. Ruth Ferguson	Hunstanton	2 and 1
1957	Miss J. Bisgood	Miss M. Nichol	Queen's Park, Bournemouth	10 and 8
1958	Mrs. M. F. Bonallack	Miss B. Jackson	Formby	3 and 2
1959	Miss R. Porter	Mrs. F. Smith	Aldeburgh	5 and 4

Mrs. R. Smith

Miss J. Bisgood

Miss Pam Barton

SCOTTISH WOMEN'S CHAMPIONSHIP

Instituted 1903. Finalists since 1930.

Year	Winner	Runner-up	Venue	Margin
1930	Mrs. A. M. Holm	Miss Doris Park	Turnberry	1 hole
1931	Miss J. McCulloch	Miss Doris Park	Gullane	19th hole
1932	Mrs. A. M. Holm	Mrs. G. Coates	Cruden Bay	23rd hole
1933	Miss M. J. Couper	Mrs. A. M. Holm	Turnberry	22nd hole
1934	Miss N. Baird	Miss J. Anderson	North Berwick	1 hole
1935	Miss M. Robertson Durham	Miss N. Baird	Lossiemouth	20th hole
1936	Miss D. Park	Miss P. R. Montgomery	Turnberry	19th hole
1937	Mrs. A. M. Holm	Mrs. I. Bowhill	Gleneagles	3 and 2
1938	Miss J. Anderson	Mrs. A. M. Holm	Nairn	2 holes
1939	Miss J. Anderson	Miss C. M. Park	Turnberry	19th hole
1947	Miss J. Donald	Miss J. Kerr	Elie	5 and 3
1948	Mrs. A. M. Holm	Mrs. C. Falconer	Gleneagles	5 and 4
1949	Miss J. Donald	Mrs. A. M. Holm	Troon	6 and 5
1950	Mrs. A. M. Holm	Mrs. E. C. Beddows	St. Andrews	6 and 5
1951	Mrs. G. Valentine	Miss M. C. Paterson	Nairn	3 and 2
1952	Miss J. Donald	Mrs. R. T. Peel	Gullane	13 and 11
1953	Mrs. G. Valentine	Miss J. Donald	Carnoustie	8 and 7
1954	Mrs. R. T. Peel	Mrs. G. Valentine	Turnberry	7 and 6
1955	Mrs. G. Valentine	Miss N. Couper	North Berwick	8 and 6
1956	Mrs. G. Valentine	Mrs. A. M. Holm	Dornoch	8 and 7
1957	Miss M. Speir	Mrs. A. M. Holm	Troon	7 and 5
1958	Miss D. Sommerville	Miss J. Robertson	Elie	1 hole
1959	Miss J. Robertson	Miss B. McCorkindale	Nairn	6 and 5

WELSH WOMEN'S CHAMPIONSHIP

Instituted 1905. Finalists since 1930.

Year	Winner	Runner-up	Venue	Margin
1930	Miss M. J. Jeffreys	Mrs. Rieben	Llandudno	2 holes
1931	Miss M. J. Jeffreys	Miss B. Pyman	Southerndown	4 and 2
1932	Miss I. Rieben	Miss M. J. Jeffreys	Aberdovey	2 and 1
1933	Miss M. Jeffreys	Mrs. Bridge	Porthcawl	2 and 1
1934	Miss I. Rieben	Miss M. J. Jeffreys	Harlech	3 and 2
1935	Owing to snowstorm play had to be abandoned in third round—venue Tenby.			
1936	Mrs. Rieben	Miss M. Thompson	Prestatyn	2 and 1
1937	Mrs. G. S. Emery	Dr. P. Whittaker	Porthcawl	10 and 9
1938	Miss B. Pyman	Mrs. G. S. Emery	Llandudno	1 hole
1939	Mrs. B. Burrell	Miss H. Reynolds	Swansea	2 and 1
1947	Miss M. Barron	Miss E. Jones	Prestatyn	1 hole
1948	Mrs. N. Seely	Miss M. Barron	Prestatyn	12 and 11
1949	Miss S. Bryan-Smith	Mrs. E. D. Brown	Newport	3 and 2
1950	Dr. Garfield Evans	Miss N. Cook	Porthcawl	2 and 1
1951	Mrs. E. Bromley Davenport	Miss N. Cook	Harlech	1 hole
1952	Miss E. Lever	Miss P. Roberts	Southerndown	6 and 5
1953	Miss Nancy Cook	Miss Elsie Lever	Llandudno	3 and 2
1954	Miss Nancy Cook	Mrs. E. D. Brown	Tenby	1 hole
1955	Miss Nancy Cook	Miss P. Roberts	Holyhead	2 holes
1956	Miss R. Roberts	Miss Barron	Royal Porthcawl	2 and 1
1957	Miss M. Barron	Miss P. Roberts	Harlech	6 and 4
1958	Mrs. M. Wright (Miss N. Cook)	Miss P. Roberts	Newport	1 hole
1959	Miss P. Roberts	Miss A. Gwyther	Caernarvonshire	6 and 4

IRISH AMATEUR OPEN CHAMPIONSHIP
Instituted 1892. Finalists since 1930.

Year	Winner	Runner-up	Venue	Margin
1930	W. Sutton	D. A. Fiddian	Portmarnock	4 and 3
1931	E. McRuvie	D. E. B. Soulby	Newcastle	7 and 5
1932	J. McLean	J. C. Brown	Dollymount	9 and 8
1933	J. McLean	E. Fiddian	Newcastle	3 and 2
1934	H. Thomson	H. G. Bentley	Portmarnock	3 and 2
1935	H. Thomson	J. McLean	Portrush	5 and 4
1936	J. C. Brown	Dr. W. M. O'Sullivan	Portmarnock	39th hole
1937	J. Fitzsimmons	R. A. McKinna	Dollymount	4 and 3
1938	J. Bruen, jun.	J. R. Mahon	Newcastle	9 and 8
1946	J. B. Carr	A. T. Kyle	Portrush	3 and 1
1947	J. Burke	J. B. Carr	Dollymount	1 hole
1948	R. C. Ewing	J. B. Carr	Newcastle	1 hole
1949	Dr. W. M. O'Sullivan	B. J. Scannell	Killarney	2 holes
1950	J. B. Carr	R. C. Ewing	Rosses Point	40th hole
1951	R. C. Ewing	J. B. Carr	Portmarnock	2 and 1
1952	N. V. Drew	C. Beamish	Portrush	5 and 4
1953	N. V. Drew	W. M. O'Sullivan	Killarney	3 and 2
1954	J. B. Carr	C. Ewing	Dollymount	6 and 4
1955	J. Fitzgibbon	W. Hulme	Newcastle	1 hole
1956	J. B. Carr	Dr. J. R. Mahon	Portmarnock	1 hole
1957	I. Balmforth	W. Meharg	Royal Portrush	37th hole
1958	T. Craddock	Stroke Play	Dollymount	294
1959	J. Duncan	Stroke Play	Newcastle	313

IRISH AMATEUR CLOSE CHAMPIONSHIP
Instituted 1893. Finalists since 1930.

Year	Winner	Runner-up	Venue	Margin
1930	J. Burke	F. P. McConnell	Lahinch	6 and 5
1931	J. Burke	F. P. McConnell	Rosses Point	6 and 4
1932	J. Burke	M. Crowley	Portrush	6 and 4
1933	J. Burke	G. T. McMullan	Cork	3 and 2
1934	J. C. Brown	Roy McConnell	Rosslare	6 and 5
1935	Roy McConnell	J. Burke	Galway	2 and 1
1936	J. Burke	Roy McConnell	Castlerock	7 and 6
1937	J. Bruen, jun.	J. Burke	Ballybunion	3 and 2
1938	J. Bruen, jun.	R. Simcox	Rathfarnham Castle	3 and 2
1939	G. H. Owens	R. M. McConnell	Rosses Point	6 and 5
1940	J. Burke	W. M. O'Sullivan	Dollymount	4 and 3
1946	J. Burke	R. C. Ewing	Dollymount	2 and 1
1947	J. Burke	J. Fitzsimmons	Lahinch	2 holes
1948	R. C. Ewing	B. J. Scannell	Royal Portrush	3 and 2
1949	J. Carroll	T. P. Murphy	Galway	4 and 3
1950	B. Herlihy	B. C. McManus	Baltray	4 and 3
1951	M. Power	J. B. Carr	Cork	3 and 2
1952	T. W. Egan	J. C. Brown	Royal Belfast	41st hole
1953	J. Malone	M. Power	Rosses Point	2 and 1
1954	J. B. Carr	I. Forsythe	Carlow	4 and 3
1955	Dr. James Mahon	G. Crosbie	Lahinch	3 and 2
1956	A. G. H. Love	G. Crosbie	Malone	37th hole
1957	J. B. Carr	G. Crosbie	Galway	2 holes
1958	C. Ewing	G. Young	Ballybunion	5 and 3
1959	T. Craddock	J. B. Carr	Portmarnock	38th hole

IRISH WOMEN'S CHAMPIONSHIP
Instituted 1894. Finalists since 1930.

Year	Winner	Runner-up	Venue	Margin
1930	Mrs. J. B. Walker	Mrs. J. F. Jameson	Portmarnock	2 and 1
1931	Miss E. C. Pentony	Mrs. J. H. Todd	Rosses Point	2 and 1
1932	Miss B. Latchford	Miss D. Ferguson	Ballybunion	7 and 5
1933	Miss E. C. Pentony	Miss F. Blake	Newcastle	3 and 2
1934	Mrs. P. Sherlock Fletcher	Mrs. J. B. Walker	Portmarnock	3 and 2
1935	Miss D. Ferguson	Miss E. Ellis	Rosapenna	2 and 1
1936	Miss C. Tiernan	Miss S. Moore	Ballybunion	7 and 6
1937	Mrs. H. V. Glendinning	Miss E. L. Kidd	Portrush	37th hole
1938	Mrs. J. Beck	Miss B. Jackson	Portmarnock	5 and 4
1939	Miss C. MacGeagh	Miss E. Gildea	Bundoran	1 hole
1946	Miss P. Garvey	Mrs. V. Reddan	Lahinch	39th hole
1947	Miss P. Garvey	Miss C. Smye	Portrush	5 and 4
1948	Miss P. Garvey	Mrs. Val Reddan	Rosslare	9 and 7
1949	Miss C. Smye	Mrs. J. Beck	Baltray	9 and 7
1950	Miss P. Garvey	Mrs. T. Marks	Rosses Point	6 and 4
1951	Miss P. Garvey	Miss D. Forster	Ballybunion	12 and 10
1952	Miss D. M. Forster	Mrs. P. G. McCann	Newcastle	3 and 2
1953	Miss P. Garvey	Mrs. Hegarty	Rosslare	8 and 7
1954	Miss P. Garvey	Mrs. H. V. Glendinning	Portmarnock	13 and 12
1955	Miss P. Garvey	Miss A. O'Donohoe	Rosses Point	10 and 9
1956	Miss P. O'Sullivan	Mrs. J. F. Hegarty	Killarney	14 and 12
1957	Miss P. Garvey	Mrs. K. McCann	Portrush	2 and 1
1958	Miss P. Garvey	Mrs. Z. Fallon	Carlow	7 and 6
1959	Miss P. Garvey	Miss H. Colhoun	Lahinch	12 and 10

EUROPEAN AMATEUR CHAMPIONSHIPS, 1958

Date	Country	Course	Event	Result	
Mar. 2–9	Portugal	Estoril	Portuguese Amateur	M. Easby (G.B.) bt. Carlos de Vilhena (P.)	8/7
May 4–6	Spain	Madrid	Spanish Amateur	Luis Rezola (Sp.) bt. J. A. Andreu (Sp.)	3/2
May 25–27	Austria	Vienna	Austrian Amateur	O. Dillier (Ch.) bt. E. Lacinik (Ger.)	1 up
June 11–14	France	Deauville	French Amateur	H. de Lamaze (Fr.) bt. Tim Holland (U.S.A.)	4/3
July 4–6	Holland	Eindhoven	Dutch Amateur	D. W. Frame (G.B.) bt. J. Moerman (B.)	3/2

RYDER CUP
Instituted 1927

1927 U.S.A. 9 matches, Great Britain 2 matches; 1 match halved. At Worcester, Mass.

1929 Great Britain 6 matches, U.S.A. 4 matches; 2 matches halved. At Moortown, Leeds.

1931 U.S.A. 9 matches, Great Britain 3 matches. At Scioto, Columbus, Ohio.

1933 Great Britain 6 matches, U.S.A. 5 matches; 1 match halved. At Southport and Ainsdale Course, Southport.

1935 U.S.A. 8 matches, Great Britain 2 matches; 2 matches halved. At Ridgewood, New Jersey.

1937 U.S.A. 7 matches, Great Britain 3 matches; 2 matches halved.

1939 No contest owing to World War II

1947 U.S.A. 11 matches, Great Britain 1 match. At Portland, Oregon.

1949 U.S.A. 7 matches, Great Britain 5 matches. At Ganton, Scarborough.

1951 U.S.A. 9 matches, Great Britain 2 matches; 1 match halved. At Pinehurst, North Carolina.

1953 U.S.A. 6 matches, Great Britain 5 matches; 1 match halved. At Wentworth, Surrey.

1955 U.S.A. 8 matches, Great Britain 4 matches. At Palm Springs.

1957 Great Britain 7 matches, U.S.A. 4 matches; 1 match halved. At Lindrick, Sheffield.

Bobby Jones and Laurie Ayton go round the Royal and Ancient at the Eisenhower Cup 1958

WALKER CUP
Instituted 1922

1922 U.S.A. 8 matches, Great Britain 4 matches. At National Links, Long Island.

1923 U.S.A. 6 matches, Great Britain 5 matches. One match halved. At St. Andrews.

1924 U.S.A. 9 matches, Great Britain 3 matches. At Garden City, New York.

1926 U.S.A. 6 matches, Great Britain 5 matches. At St. Andrews.

1928 U.S.A. 11 matches, Great Britain 1 match. At Chicago Golf Club, Wheaton, U.S.A.

1930 U.S.A. 10 matches, Great Britain 2 matches. At Royal St. George's, Sandwich.

1932 U.S.A. 8 matches, Great Britain 1 match. One match halved. At Brooklyn, Mass.

1934 U.S.A. 9 matches, Great Britain 2 matches. One match halved. At St. Andrews.

1936 U.S.A. 9 matches, Great Britain 0 matches. Three matches halved. At Pine Valley.

1938 Great Britain 7 matches, U.S.A. 4 matches. One match halved. At St. Andrews.

1947 Great Britain 8 matches, U.S.A. 4 matches. At. St. Andrews.

1949 U.S.A. 10 matches, Great Britain 2 matches. At Winged Foot, New York.

1951 U.S.A. 6 matches, Great Britain 3 matches. Three matches halved. At Birkdale, Lancashire.

1953 U.S.A. 9 matches, Great Britain 3 matches. At Marion, Massachusetts.

1955 U.S.A. 10 matches, Great Britain 2 matches. At St. Andrews.

1957 U.S.A. 8 matches, Great Britain 3 matches. One match halved. At Minikahda.

1959 U.S.A. 9 matches, Great Britain 3 matches. At Muirfield.

Lloyd Mangrum and the Ryder Cup

GOLF QUIZ
THE RYDER CUP

1. Who are the only father and son to have played in the series?

★

2. What have Eric Green and Ken Bousfield in common?

★

3. Which Ryder Cup match was cancelled?

★

4. How many Yorkshire clubs have staged the match?

★

5. What was Samuel Ryder's profession?

★

6. Why was the Lindrick course shortened for the 1957 match?

★

7. Which Ryder Cup player abandoned professional golf?

★

8. From which of the following clubs have players been chosen: Pasadena; Huddersfield; Sandy Lodge; Agua Caliente; Wallasey; Barton-on-Sea; Grand Rapids; Sutton Coldfield?

★

9. Who attributed British defeats to the "laziness" of British professionals?

★

10. What advantage have British teams had since the war?

ANSWERS TO QUIZ

1. Percy and Peter Alliss. 2. In 1947 and 1955 respectively they both travelled as far as the Pacific Coast without playing in the match. 3. The 1939 one, because of war. 4. Three—Moortown, Ganton, Lindrick. 5. Seed-merchant. 6. A neighbouring landowner refused the use of one of the tees, which was on her property. 7. Syd Easterbrook. 8. All except Barton-on-Sea. 9. Walter Hagen. 10. The help of players from Eire.

Ken Bousfield

"Babe" Zaharias with the Ladies' Amateur Open Golf Cup

European Amateur Championships 1958—contd.

Date	Country	Course	Event	Result
July 12–14	Luxembourg	Royal Luxembourg	Luxembourg Amateur	Maj.-Gen. Timberlake (U.S.A.) bt. Dr. G. Vandeweghe (U.S.A.) at 37th
July 18–20	Belgium	Spa	Belgian Amateur	R. Taylor (S.A.) bt. G. Nash (U.S.A.) 7/6
July 21–24	Germany	Krefeld	German Amateur	R. Taylor (S.A.) bt. B. Verwey (S.A.) 3/1
Aug. 20–24	Sweden	Tylosand	Scandinavian Amateur	G. Carlander (S.) bt. M. N. Ferguson (G.B.) 7/6
Aug. 27–31	Switzerland	Crans-s-Sierre	Swiss Amateur	Capt. Francis Francis (G.B.) bt. O. Barras (Ch.) 3/1
Sept. 27–30	Italy	Villa D'Este	Italian Amateur	H. de Lamaze (Fr.) bt. J. Moerman (B.) 2/1

P.–Portugal; Sp.–Spain; Ch.–Switzerland; Ger.–Germany; Fr.–France; B.–Belgium; S.A.–South Africa; S.–Sweden.

GOLF QUIZ
THE RULES

1. Between tee and putting surface what part of the course is not defined as "through the green"?

＊

2. When is a green "through the green"?

＊

3. Can you improve the surface of a bunker before playing a second shot out of it?

＊

4. Is an insect on your ball a loose impediment?

＊

5. Can there be two markers for a card?

＊

6. What substances are forbidden in the manufacture of tees?

＊

7. If you are hopeful enough to ask advice from your opponent do you break the rules?

＊

8. What is the penalty for playing out of turn in a stroke competition?

＊

9. When can you finger the line of your putt without penalty?

＊

10. If your opponent is mistaken in the number of strokes he tells you he has played, how can he escape losing the hole?

ANSWERS TO QUIZ

1. Any hazard. 2. When it is not the green of the hole being played. 3. Yes, if you don't disturb the lie of the ball, or improve its position. 4. No. 5. Yes. 6. None. 7. Yes. 8. None. 9. When picking up loose impediments. 10. By correcting himself before you play your next shot.

EUROPEAN OPEN CHAMPIONSHIPS, 1958

Date	Country	Course	Event	Result
July 8–10	Belgium	Royal Belgique	Belgian Open	(1) K. Bousfield (G.B.) 271 (2) A. Cerda (Arg.) 274
July 13–15	France	St. Germain	French Open	(1) F. Van Donck (B.) 276 Play off: F. Van Donck 137 H. Henning 141
July 19–20	Holland	Zandvoort	Dutch Open	(1) D. Thomas (G.B.) 277 (2) A. Cerda (Arg.) 280
July 25–29	Germany	Krefeld	German Open	(1) F. De Luca (Arg.) 275
Sept. 3–5	Switzerland	Crans-s-Sierre	Swiss Open	(1) K. Bousfield (G.B.) 272
Sept. 6–7	Sweden	Lund	Scandinavian Open	Pros: (1) H. Karlson (S.) 311 (2) C. Poulsen (D.) 312
Oct. 10–12	Italy	Varese	Italian Open	(1) P. Alliss (G.B.) 282
Oct. 17–19	Spain	Madrid	Spanish Open	(1) P. Alliss (G.B.) 268
Oct. 26–28	Portugal	Estoril	Portuguese Open	(1) P. Alliss (G.B.) 264

Arg.–Argentina; B.–Belgium; S.–Sweden; D.–Denmark.

G. P. Roberts

R. J. White

N. Quigley

H. Weetman

A. A. Duncan

AMERICAN OPEN CHAMPIONSHIP

Instituted 1894. Winners since 1913.

Year	Winner	Venue	Score
1913	Mr. F. Ouimet, Woodland (after a tie with H. Vardon and E. Ray)	Brookline, Mass.	304
1914	Walter Hagen, Rochester	Blue Island	297
1915	Mr. J. D. Travers, Montclair	Baltusrol	290
1916	Mr. Charles Evans, Edgewater	Minikahda	286
1919	Walter Hagen, Rochester	Brae Burn	301
1920	E. Ray, Oxhey	Inverness	295
1921	Jim Barnes, Pelham	Washington	289
1922	G. Sarazen, Titusville	Glencoe	288
1923	Mr. R. T. Jones, Atlanta	Inwood, L.I.	296
1924	Cyril Walker, Englewood	Oakland Hills	297
1925	Wm. MacFarlane, Oak Ridge	Worcester	291
1926	Mr. R. T. Jones, Atlanta	Scioto	293
1927	T. D. Armour, Congressional	Oakmont	301
1928	J. Farrell, Quaker Ridge	Olympia Fields	294
1929	Mr. R. T. Jones, Atlanta	Winged Foot, New York	294
1930	Mr. R. T. Jones, Atlanta	Interlachen	287
1931	B. Burke, Round Hill	Toledo	292
1932	G. Sarazen, Lakeville	Flushing, L.I.	286
1933	Mr. J. Goodman, Omaha	Glenview, Ill.	287
1934	O. Dutra, Brentwood Heights	Merion	293
1935	S. Parks, South Hills	Oakmont	299
1936	T. Manero, Greensboro	Baltusrol	282
1937	R. Guldahl, Beverley Hills	Oakland Hills	281
1938	R. Guldahl, Madison	Cherry Hills	284
1939	Byron Nelson, Reading, Pa.	Philadelphia	284
1940	W. Lawson Little	Canterbury, Ohio	287
1941	Craig Wood, Winged Foot	Fort Worth, Texas	284
1946	Lloyd Mangrum	Canterbury	284
1947	Lew Worsnam, Oakmont	St. Louis	282
1948	Ben Hogan, Hershey, Pa.	Los Angeles	276
1949	Dr. Cary Middlecoff, Memphis	Medinah, Ill.	286
1950	Ben Hogan, Hershey, Pa.	Merion, Pa.	287
1951	Ben Hogan, Hershey, Pa.	Oakland Hills, Mich.	287
1952	Julius Boros, Southern Pines, N.C.	Dallas, Texas	281
1953	Ben Hogan, Hershey, Pa.	Oakmont	283
1954	Ed. Furgol, Clayton, Mo.	Baltusrol	284
1955	J. Fleck, Davenport, Iowa	San Francisco	287
1956	Dr. Cary Middlecoff, Dallas	Oakhills	281
1957	Dick Mayer, Florida	Inverness	282
1958	Tommy Bolt, Port Paradise	Southern Hills	283
1959	Billy Casper, Apple Valley	Winged Foot, New York	282

WORPLESDON MIXED FOURSOMES

Instituted 1921. Finals since 1930.

1930 Miss M. Gourlay and Major C. O. Hezlet beat Miss Diana Esmond and R. H. Wethered, 5 and 4.
1931 Miss J. Wethered and Hon. M. Scott beat Miss Doris Park and Stuart Forsyth, 4 and 3.
1932 Miss J. Wethered and R. H. Oppenheimer beat Miss A. Regnart and Commander Johnstone, 8 and 7.
1933 Miss J. Wethered and B. Darwin beat Mrs. P. Garon and A. McNair, 8 and 7.
1934 Miss M. Gourlay and T. A. Torrance beat Miss K. Garnham and E. N. Layton, 6 and 5.
1935 Miss G. Craddock Hartopp and J. Craddock Hartopp beat Miss J. Hamilton and S. Forsyth, 2 and 1.
1936 Miss J. Wethered and Hon. T. Coke beat Miss D. Wilkins and C. J. Anderson, 3 and 2.
1937 Mrs. Heppel and L. G. Crawley beat Miss K. Garnham and A. S. G. Thompson, 5 and 4.
1938 Mrs. M. Garon and E. F. Storey beat Miss W. Morgan and K. A. Morrice, 6 and 5.
1946 Miss J. Gordon and A. A. Duncan beat Miss J. Pemberton and H. Longhurst, 4 and 3.
1947 Miss J. Gordon and A. A. Duncan beat Mrs. Beck and John B. Beck, 8 and 7.
1948 Miss W. Morgan and E. F. Storey beat Lady Heathcoat-Amory and Sir John Heathcoat-Amory, 5 and 4.
1949 Miss F. Stephens and L. G. Crawley beat Mrs. A. C. Critchley and C. J. H. Tolley, 4 and 3.
1950 Miss F. Stephens and L. G. Crawley beat Miss E. Johnston and P. J. MacDonald, 6 and 5.
1951 Mrs. A. C. Barclay and G. Evans beat Mrs. R. T. Peel and G. W. Mackie, by 1 hole.
1952 Mrs. R. T. Peel and G. W. Mackie beat Miss Frances Stephens and W. A. Slark, by 3 and 2.
1953 Miss J. Gordon and G. Knipe beat Mrs. A. Spearman and J. C. E. Atkins, by 1 hole.
1954 Miss F. Stephens and W. A. Slark beat Miss J. McIntyre and P. F. Scrutton, by 2 holes.
1955 Miss P. Garvey and P. F. Scrutton beat Mrs. A. van Oss and G. Duncan, 2 and 1.
1956 Mrs. L. Abrahams and Major W. D. Henderson beat Mlle. O. Semelaigne and G. H. Micklem, 3 and 1.
1957 Mrs. B. Singleton and W. D. Smith beat Miss J. Gordon and H. B. Ridgley, 5 and 4.
1958 Mr. and Mrs. M. F. Bonallack beat Mrs. B. Singleton and W. D. Smith, 4 and 3.

JOY CUP MATCH

Great Britain v. Europe

(Professionals)

1954 Saint Cloud: Gt. Britain, 10 matches; Europe, 4 matches; 1 match halved.
1955 Royal Lytham and St. Annes: Gt. Britain, 9 matches; Europe, 6 matches.
1956 Antwerp: Gt. Britain, 9 matches; Europe, 2 matches; 1 match halved.
1957 Not held.
1958 Madrid: Gt. Britain, 9 matches; Europe, 5 matches; 1 match halved.

1958 JOY CUP

(Played at Madrid)

Great Britain 9½ Matches — *Rest of Europe 5½ Matches*

FOURSOMES

Great Britain		Rest of Europe	
P. Alliss (Parkstone) and J. R. M. Jacobs (Sandy Lodge)	0	S. Miguel (Spain) and J. B. Ado (France), 3 and 2	1
H. Weetman (Selsdon Park) and B. J. Hunt (Hartsbourne C.C.), 6 and 5	1	A. Angelini (Italy) and D. Swaelens (Belgium)	0
D. J. Rees (South Herts) and K. Bousfield (Coombe Hill)	0	A. Casera (Italy) and R. Cotton (France), 2 holes	1
H. Bradshaw (Portmarnock) and C. O'Connor (Bundoran), 1 hole	1	F. van Donck (Belgium) and J. Garaialde (France)	0
E. C. Brown (Buchanan Castle) and R. P. Mills (Pinner Hill), 2 and 1	1	A. Miguel (Spain) and C. Celles (Spain)	0
	3		2

SINGLES

Great Britain		Rest of Europe	
H. Weetman	0	K. Sota, 8 and 7	1
J. R. M. Jacobs, 2 and 1	1	A. Casera	0
K. Bousfield, 8 and 7	1	R. Cotton	0
B. J. Hunt, 6 and 5	1	S. Miguel	0
P. Mills, 3 and 2	1	J. B. Ado	0
D. J. Rees, 5 and 4	1	D. Swaelens	0
C. O'Connor	0	F. van Donck, 4 and 3	1
H. Bradshaw	½	J. Garaialde	½
E. Brown, 1 hole	1	A. Angelini	0
P. Alliss	0	A. Miguel, 2 and 1	1
	6½		3½

CURTIS CUP

Year	GREAT BRITAIN	U.S.A.	Venue
1930	8	6	*Sunningdale*
1932	3½	5½	*Wentworth*
1934	2½	6½	*Chevy Chase*
1936	4½	4½	*Gleneagles*
1938	3½	5½	*Essex County Club*
1948	2½	6½	*Birkdale*
1950	1½	7½	*Buffalo*
1952	5	4	*Muirfield*
1954	3½	6	*Merion*
1956	5	4	*Prince's, Sandwich*
1958	4½	4½	*Brae Burn*

Lloyd Mangrum

Miss P. Garvey

Gary Player

GOLF QUIZ

THE LADIES

1. How many Curtis Cup matches has Britain won?

★

2. Who later became Mrs. Heathcoat-Amory (*above*); Lady Critchley; Mrs. Henry Cotton; Madame Rene Lacoste; Mrs. Herbert Morrison?

★

3. When did a Canadian win the Ladies' Championship?

★

4. What handicap range is covered by the Bronze Division?

★

5. Who hit a 200-yard drive at the first attempt?

★

6. Who partnered Norman Sutton when they won the Penfold Ladies' and Professionals' event?

★

7. What is the age limit for the Girls' Championship?

★

8. Which lady golfer is considered by Bobby Jones to be among the world's best three of either sex?

★

9. Who was awarded a M.B.E. in the New Year Honours List of 1959?

★

10. When would a lady play off the men's tee?

ANSWERS TO QUIZ

1. Two. 2. Joyce Wethered, Diana Fishwick, Mrs. M. I. E. Moss, Mlle Simone Thion de la Chaume, Edith Meadowcroft. 3. In 1953—Marlene Stewart. 4. 19 to 36. 5. Babe Zaharias. 6. The Hon. Mrs. Adrian Gee. 7. 19 on the last day of the event. 8. Joyce Wethered. 9. Mrs. George Valentine. 10. In a mixed foursome, when her partner's drive finished within the limits of the teeing ground or out of bounds.

GOLF QUIZ
WHAT THE MAN SAID

Who was responsible for the following remarks (or something like them):

1. "Hang it all, man, you're spoiling everything!"

★

2. "If the PGA sue me, I'll sue them—right down to the porter."

★

3. "I never wanted to be a millionaire—I just wanted to live like one."

★

4. "Give me an opponent who keeps his left arm straight."

★

5. "If he doesn't win it this time I'll put him to work."

★

6. "Of course, in presenting this Cup I'm quite impartial—but I must say I'm pleased we've won."

★

7. "If they took a fork to their mouths the way they take the club back they'd starve to death."

★

8. "I've so much strength in my right hand I could kill a man with it."

★

9. "A weak left hand? That's all right—I take cheques with the other one."

★

10. "I'm interested in the modern—not the Ancient."

ANSWERS TO QUIZ

1. A steward at the Ryder Cup match at Southport when a spectator put his foot in a bunker. 2. Jimmy Demaret, during a dispute about his appearance in a Mexican event. 3. Walter Hagen. 4. Harry Vardon. 5. Frank Stranahan's father. 6. The Prince of Wales in 1933 when presenting the Ryder Cup. 7. Sam Snead, speaking of certain golfers. 8. Harry Bradshaw. 9. Bobby Locke in America. 10. Ed Furgol at St. Andrew's.

Frank Stranahan

Walter Hagen

U.S.A. PROFESSIONAL GOLFERS' ASSOCIATION CHAMPIONSHIP

Instituted 1916. Finalists since 1930.

Year	Winner	Runner-up	Venue	By
1930	T. D. Armour	G. Sarazen	Fresh Meadow	1 hole
1931	T. Creavy	D. Shute	Wannamoisett	2 and 1
1932	O. Dutra	F. Walsh	St. Paul's, Minnesota	4 and 3
1933	G. Sarazen	W. Goggin	Milwaukee	5 and 4
1934	P. Runyan	Craig Wood	Buffalo	38th hole
1935	J. Revlta	T. D. Armour	Oklahoma	5 and 4
1936	D. Shute	J. Thompson	Pinehurst	3 and 2
1937	D. Shute	H. McSnaden	Pittsburg	37th hole
1938	P. Runyan	S. Snead	Shawnee	8 and 7
1939	H. Picard	B. Nelson	Pomonok	37th hole
1940	Byron Nelson	Sam Snead	Hershey, Pa.	1 hole
1941	Vic Ghezzi	Byron Nelson	Denver, Colo.	38th hole
1942	Sam Snead	Jim Turneas	Atlantic City	2 and 1
1943	No Championship			
1944	Bob Hamilton	Byron Nelson	Spokane, Wash.	1 hole
1945	Byron Nelson	Sam Byrd	Dayton, Ohio	4 and 3
1946	Ben Hogan	Ed Oliver	Portland	6 and 4
1947	Jim Ferrier	Chick Harbert	Detroit	2 and 1
1948	Ben Hogan	Mike Turneas	Norwood Hills	7 and 6
1949	Sam Snead	Johnny Palmer	Richmond, Va.	3 and 2
1950	Chandler Harper	Henry Williams	Scioto, Ohio	4 and 3
1952	Jim Turnesa	Chick Harbert	Big Spring, Louisville	1 hole
1953	Walter Burkemo	Felice Lorza	Birmingham, Michigan	2 and 1
1954	Chick Harbert	Walter Burkemo	St. Paul's, Minnesota	4 and 3
1955	D. Ford	C. Middlecoff	Detroit	4 and 3
1956	J. Burk	T. Kroll	Boston	3 and 2
1957	L. Hebert	D. Finsterwald	Miami Valley, Dayton	3 and 1

Championship decided by stroke-play in 1958.

| 1958 | D. Finsterwald | B. Casper | Havertown, Pen. | 276 |
| 1959 | B. Rosburg | J. Barber } D. Sanders } | Minneapolis | 277 |

"News of the World" Match Play Championship: Peter Thomson in 1954; right, Dai Rees in 1955

"NEWS OF THE WORLD" MATCH PLAY CHAMPIONSHIP

Year	Winner	Runner-up	Semi-finalists		Venue
1903	J. Braid	E. Ray	J. H. Taylor	G. Coburn	Sunningdale
1904	J. H. Taylor	A. Toogood	J. Hepburn	A. Herd	Mid-Surrey
1905	J. Braid	T. Vardon	R. Jones	A. Mitchell	Walton Heath
1906	A. Herd	C. Mayo	G. Duncan	R. Jones	Hollinwell
1907	J. Braid	J. H. Taylor	E. Ray	H. Vardon	Sunningdale
1908	J. H. Taylor	F. Robson	C. Mayo	J. G. Sherlock	Mid-Surrey
1909	T. Ball	A. Herd	H. Vardon	J. Hepburn	Walton Heath
1910	J. G. Sherlock	G. Duncan	Bannister	C. Hughes	Sunningdale
1911	J. Braid	E. Ray	Williamson	H. Vardon	Walton Heath
1912	H. Vardon	E. Ray	Wilson	H. Cawsey	Sunningdale
1913	G. Duncan	J. Braid	Wilson	W. Watt	Walton Heath
1919	A. Mitchell	G. Duncan	Rainford	F. Robson	Walton Heath
1920	A. Mitchell	Josh Taylor	B. Seymour	L. Holland	Mid-Surrey
1921	B. Seymour	J. Gaudin	E. Ray	C. Wingate	Oxhey
1922	G. Gadd	F. Leach	E. R. Whitcombe	C. Johns	Sunningdale
1923	R. G. Wilson	T. Renouf	A. Mitchell	T. Williamson	Walton Heath
1924	E. R. Whitcombe	G. Gadd	A. Herd	T. Barber	St. George's Hill
1925	A. Compston	G. Gadd	G. Duncan	L. Holland	Moor Park
1926	A. Herd	J. Bloxham	Wilson	W. H. Ball	Mid-Surrey
1927	A. Compston	J. Braid	Williamson	E. R. Whitcombe	Walton Heath
1928	C. A. Whitcombe	T. H. Cotton	J. J. Taylor	H. C. Jolly	Stoke Poges
1929	A. Mitchell	P. Rodgers	A. Compston	A. Beck	Wentworth
1930	C. A. Whitcombe	T. H. Cotton	A. Mitchell	S. Easterbrook	Oxhey
1931	A. H. Padgham	M. Seymour	C. H. Ward	C. W. Thomson	Royal Mid-Surrey
1932	T. H. Cotton	A. Perry	A. J. Lacey	J. H. Jolly	Moor Park
1933	P. Alliss	M. Seymour	E. R. Whitcombe	A. Compston	Purley Downs
1934	J. J. Busson	C. A. Whitcombe	A. Chevalier	R. A. Whitcombe	Walton Heath
1935	A. H. Padgham	P. Alliss	R. Burton	R. A. Whitcombe	Royal Mid-Surrey
1936	D. J. Rees	E. R. Whitcombe	P. Alliss	J. J. Taylor	Oxhey
1937	P. Alliss	J. Adams	D. Curtis	C. A. Whitcombe	Stoke Poges
1938	D. J. Rees	E. E. Whitcombe	A. G. Havers	L. Ayton, jun.	Walton Heath
1940	T. H. Cotton	A. H. Padgham	R. G. French	A. J. Lacey	Royal Mid-Surrey
1945	R. W. Horne	P. Alliss	R. A. Knight	T. E. Odams	Walton Heath
1946	T. H. Cotton	J. Adams	A. D. Locke	R. Burton	Hoylake
1947	F. Daly	J. van Donck	C. H. Ward	T. H. Cotton	St. Anne's
1948	F. Daly	L. Ayton	S. L. King	C. H. Ward	Birkdale
1949	D. J. Rees	T. H. Cotton	S. L. King	L. Mangrum	Walton Heath
1950	D. J. Rees	F. Jowle	K. Bousfield	T. H. Cotton	Carnoustie
1951	H. Weetman	J. Adams	A. S. Waters	S. L. King	Hoylake
1952	F. Daly	F. van Donck	J. Panton	G. Johnson	Walton Heath
1953	M. Faulkner	D. J. Rees	J. R. M. Jacobs	F. Daly	Ganton
1954	P. Thomson	F. Jowle	N. Sutton		St. Andrews
1955	K. Bousfield	E. C. Brown	A. Lees	F. Jowle	Walton Heath
1956	J. Panton	H. Weetman	K. Bousfield	R. P. Mills	Hoylake
1957	C. O'Connor	T. B. Haliburton	H. Bradshaw	E. C. Brown	Turnberry
1958	H. Weetman	B. J. Hunt	C. O'Connor	A. Fox	Walton Heath
1959	D. Snell	H. Weetman	D. Thomas	N. Sutton	R. Birkdale

158

Ben Hogan in the
1956 Canada Cup

H. Bradshaw
1958 Canada Cup Winner

CANADA CUP TOURNAMENT

Year	Winners	Venue	Score
1953	Argentina (A. Cerda and R. de Vicenzo)	Toronto	287
1954	Australia (P. Thomson and K. Nagle)	Laval-sur-le-Lac	556
1955	United States (C. Harbert and Ed Furgol)	Washington	560
1956	America (Ben Hogan and Sam Snead)	Wentworth	567
1957	Japan (Torakichi Nakamura and Koichi Ono)	Tokyo	557
1958	Ireland (H. Bradshaw and C. O'Connor)	Mexico City	579

1958 CANADA CUP

(Played at Mexico City)

FINAL PLACINGS

579—**Ireland** (H. Bradshaw, 70, 70, 76, 70 —286; C. O'Connor, 73, 73, 74, 73—293).

582—**Spain** (A. Miguel, 72, 73, 71, 70—286; S. Miguel, 76, 75, 73, 72—296).

584—**South Africa** (H. R. Henning, 80, 68, 74, 71—293; G. J. Player, 74, 72, 74, 71—291).

588—**Scotland** (E. C. Brown, 72, 72, 70, 75—289; J. Panton, 73, 77, 74, 75—299).

Australia (K. Nagle, 72, 73, 80, 74—299; F. Phillips, 70, 77, 72, 70—289).

593—**England** (P. Alliss, 73, 73, 76, 74—296; B. J. Hunt, 71, 76, 76, 74—297).

594—**Argentina** (F. de Luca, 74, 77, 79, 72—302; L. Ruiz, 70, 74, 77, 71—292).

595—**Wales** (D. J. Rees, 76, 74, 74, 77—301; D. C. Thomas, 77, 73, 73, 71—294).

601—**Venezuela** (M. Bernardez, 82, 71, 72, 73—298; T. Perez, 75, 74, 80, 74—303).

603—**Colombia** (P. Molina, 80, 75, 85, 75—315; M. Sala; 69, 74, 74, 71—288).

Belgium (D. Swaelens, 82, 80, 76, 78—316; F. van Donck, 70, 72, 71, 74—287).

604—**Italy** (A. Angelini, 75, 76, 75, 71—297; A. Casera, 76, 81, 70, 80—307).

China (Shieh Yung-Yo, 78, 74, 80, 79—311; Chen Ching-Po, 72, 73, 72, 76—293).

605—**Brazil** (L. Rapisarda, 72, 76, 70, 78—296; M. Gonzales, 74, 82, 79, 74—309).

606—**Philippines** (B. Arda, 75, 74, 73, 78—300; C. Tugot, 73, 78, 75, 80—306).

607—**Japan** (T. Nakamura, 76, 73, 75 77—301; K. Ono, 75, 76, 74, 81—306)

New Zealand (F. Buckler, 79, 73, 78, 75 —305; E. Southerden, 76, 76, 73, 77—302).

608—**Canada** (A. Balding, 76, 81, 77, 80 —314; H. Martell, 74, 73, 77, 70—294).

611—**Chile** (L. Calderon, 81, 78, 76, 74—309; E. Orellana, 74, 74, 79, 75—302).

617—**Mexico** (J. Gonzales, 84, 73, 82, 74 —313; J. Neri, 80, 76, 72, 76—304).

619—**Germany** (F. Becker, 79, 82, 78, 74 —313; G. Bessner, 77, 73, 79, 77—306).

Peru (E. Dunezat, 80, 82, 74, 81—317; A. Tibbles, 75, 77, 74, 77—303).

622—**Switzerland** (J. Bonvin, 75, 76, 80, 77—308; O. Schopner, 83, 78, 78, 75—314).

626—**Denmark** (H. Kristensen, 78, 79, 75, 82—314; C. Poulsen, 78, 76, 80, 73—312).

628—**Sweden** (H. Karlssen, 81, 77, 77, 78 —313; A. Wekell, 80, 80, 77, 78—315).

633—**France** (J. Garaialde, 77, 72, 76, 81 —306; J. B. Ado, 80, 84, 81, 82—327).

641—**United Arab Republic** (Naaman Aly, 83, 81, 81—326; Mohamed Said Moussa, 81, 79, 81, 74—315).

659—**Korea** (Bok Man Kin, 87, 81, 82, 87—337; Myon Chul Park, 78, 84, 83, 77—322).

667—**Portugal** (H. Paulino, 84, 89, 83, 81 —337; F. Silva, 84, 79, 82, 85—330).

COMMONWEALTH

LADIES' CHAMPIONSHIPS 1958

AUSTRALIA—Miss M. Masters
CANADA—Mrs. M. Stewart Streit
NEW ZEALAND—Miss N. Campbell
SOUTH AFRICA—Mrs. R. Easton

MEN'S CHAMPIONSHIPS 1958

AUSTRALIA
Open—Gary Player
Amateur—K. Hartley

CANADA
Open—Wes Ellis, Jr.
Amateur—B. Castator

NEW ZEALAND
Open—K. Nagle
Amateur—W. J. Godfrey

SOUTH AFRICA
Open—Mr. A. A. Stewart
Amateur—J. R. Boyd

DUNLOP MASTERS' TOURNAMENT

Year	Winner	Venue	Score
1946	A. D. Locke / J. Adams	Stoneham	286
1947	A. Lees	Little Aston	286
1948	N. Von Nida	Sunningdale	272
1949	C. H. Ward	St. Andrews	290
1950	D. J. Rees	Hoylake	281
1951	M. Faulkner	Wentworth	281
1952	H. Weetman	Mere	281
1953	H. Bradshaw	Sunningdale	272
1954	A. D. Locke	Prince's, Sandwich	291
1955	H. Bradshaw	Little Aston	277
1956	C. O'Connor	Prestwick	277
1957	E. C. Brown	Hollinwell	275
1958	H. Weetman	Little Aston	276

BRITISH WOMEN'S CHAMPIONSHIP

Year	Winner	Runner-up	Venue	By
1893	Lady Margaret Scott	Miss Issette Pearson	St. Anne's	7 and 5
1894	Lady Margaret Scott	Miss Issette Pearson	Littlestone	3 and 2
1895	Lady Margaret Scott	Miss E. Lythgoe	Portrush	5 and 4
1896	Miss Pascoe	Miss L. Thomson	Hoylake	3 and 2
1897	Miss E. C. Orr	Miss Orr	Gullane	4 and 3
1898	Miss L. Thomson	Miss E. C. Neville	Yarmouth	7 and 5
1899	Miss M. Hezlet	Miss Magill	Newcastle, Co. Down	2 and 1
1900	Miss Adair	Miss I. Neville	Westward Ho!	6 and 5
1901	Miss Graham	Miss R. Adair	Aberdovey	3 and 1
1902	Miss M. Hezlet	Miss E. Neville	Deal	19th hole
1903	Miss Adair	Miss F. Walker-Leigh	Portrush	4 and 3
1904	Miss L. Dod	Miss M. Hezlet	Troon	1 hole
1905	Miss B. Thompson	Miss M. E. Stuart	Cromer	3 and 2
1906	Mrs. Kennion	Miss B. Thompson	Burnham	4 and 3
1907	Miss M. Hezlet	Miss F. Hezlet	Newcastle, Co. Down	2 and 1
1908	Miss M. Titterton	Miss D. Campbell	St. Andrews	19th hole
1909	Miss D. Campbell	Miss F. Hezlet	Birkdale	4 and 3
1910	Miss Grant Suttie	Miss L. Moore	Westward Ho!	6 and 4
1911	Miss D. Campbell	Miss V. Hezlet	Portrush	3 and 2
1912	Miss G. Ravenscroft	Miss S. Temple	Turnberry	3 and 2
	Final played over 36 holes after 1912			
1913	Miss M. Dodd	Miss Chubb	St. Anne's	8 and 6
1914	Miss C. Leitch	Miss G. Ravenscroft	Hunstanton	2 and 1
1915–18	No Championship owing to World War I			
1919	No Championship at Burnham in October, owing to Railway Strike.			
1920	Miss C. Leitch	Miss Molly Griffiths	Newcastle, Co. Down	7 and 6
1921	Miss C. Leitch	Miss J. Wethered	Turnberry	4 and 3
1922	Miss J. Wethered	Miss C. Leitch	Prince's, Sandwich	9 and 7
1923	Miss D. Chambers	Mrs. A. Macbeth	Burnham, Somerset	2 holes
1924	Miss J. Wethered	Mrs. Cautley	Portrush	7 and 6
1925	Miss J. Wethered	Miss C. Leitch	Troon	37th hole
1926	Miss C. Leitch	Mrs. M. Garon	Harlech	8 and 7
1927	Mlle Thion de la Chaume	Miss D. Pearson	Newcastle, Co. Down	5 and 4
1928	Mlle Nanette Le Blan	Miss S. Marshall	Hunstanton	3 and 2
1929	Miss J. Wethered	Miss G. Collett	St. Andrews	3 and 1
1930	Miss D. Fishwick	Miss G. Collett	Formby	4 and 3
1931	Miss E. Wilson	Miss W. Morgan	Portmarnock	7 and 6
1932	Miss E. Wilson	Miss C. P. R. Montgomery	Saunton	7 and 6
1933	Miss E. Wilson	Miss D. Plumpton	Gleneagles	5 and 4
1934	Mrs. A. M. Holm	Miss P. Barton	Royal Porthcawl	6 and 5
1935	Miss W. Morgan	Miss P. Barton	Newcastle, Co. Down	3 and 2
1936	Miss P. Barton	Miss B. Newell	Southport and Ainsdale	5 and 3
1937	Miss J. Anderson	Miss D. Park	Turnberry	6 and 4
1938	Mrs. A. M. Holm	Miss E. Corlett	Burnham	4 and 3
1939	Miss P. Barton	Mrs. T. Marks	Portrush	2 and 1
1946	Mrs. G. W. Hetherington	Miss P. Garvey	Hunstanton	1 hole
1947	Mrs. George Zaharias	Miss J. Gordon	Gullane	5 and 4
1948	Miss Louise Suggs	Miss J. Donald	Royal Lytham	1 hole
1949	Miss Frances Stephens	Mrs. Val Reddan	Harlech	5 and 4
1950	Viscomtesse de Saint Sauveur	Mrs. G. Valentine	Newcastle, Co. Down	3 and 2
1951	Mrs. P. G. MacCann	Miss Frances Stephens	Broadstone	4 and 3
1952	Miss Moira Paterson	Miss Frances Stephens	Troon	38th hole
1953	Miss Marlene Stewart	Miss P. Garvey	Porthcawl	7 and 6
1954	Miss Frances Stephens	Miss E. Price	Ganton	4 and 3
1955	Mrs. G. Valentine	Miss B. Romack	Portrush	7 and 6
1956	Miss Margaret Smith	Miss Mary P. Janssen	Sunningdale	8 and 7
1957	Miss P. Garvey	Mrs. G. Valentine	Troon	4 and 3
1958	Mrs. G. Valentine	Miss E. Price	Hunstanton	1 hole
1959	Miss E. Price	Miss B. McCorkindale	Caernarvonshire	6 and 4

P.G.A. NATIONAL CLOSE CHAMPIONSHIP

Originated 1955

Year	Winner	Club	Venue	Score
1955	K. Bousfield	Coombe Hill	Pannal	277
1956	C. H. Ward	Little Aston	Maesdu	282
	(After a tie with E. C. Brown. Tie scores, Ward 139, Brown 141.)			
1957	Peter Alliss	Parkstone	Maesdu	286
1958	H. Bradshaw	Portmarnock	Llandudno	287
1959	D. J. Rees	South Herts.	Ashburnham	283

GOLF QUIZ

A RAGBAG

1. Who beat who 18 and 17?

★

2. Why was the centre-shafted putter legalized in Britain?

★

3. Where is world golf information concentrated in the United States?

★

4. Who is odd man out among: Bernard Hunt; Sebastian Miguel; John Burton; Jim Turnesa; Peter Thomson; Trevor Wilkes?

★

5. Who was the first Australian golfer to become world-famous?

★

6. Who, according to Gene Sarazen, is "the slowest player in the entire world"?

ANSWERS TO QUIZ

1. Archie Compston beat Walter Hagen by this margin in 1929. 2. Because the fact that many American golfers preferred the orthodox kind proved that it gave the player no particular advantage. 3. Golf House, New York City. 4. Peter Thomson is the only one without an eminent golfing brother. 5. Joe Kirkwood. 6. Tommy Armour.

GOLF QUIZ
THE SCRIBES

1. Who wrote *Down the Fairway*; *Green Fairways*; *The Murder on the Links*?

*

2. Who is the golf correspondent of the *Daily Mail*; *The Field*; the *Scotsman*; the *Daily Express*?

*

3. For whom was Ted Ray a constant inspiration?

*

4. Whose book of instruction recommended the very short putt as the first lesson?

*

5. Which golf correspondent had a film-star daughter?

*

6. When was Bernard Darwin born—1883, 1901, 1895, 1876?

*

7. How many of the following have been the subject of biographies: Pam Barton; Abe Mitchell; Bobby Locke; Cyril Tolley; Flory van Donck?

*

8. Who wrote a tutor only after years of persuasion?

*

9. Who was the Oldest Member?

*

10. Which of the following have written golf stories or poems: Ring Lardner; Damon Runyon; John Betjeman; Ogden Nash?

*

ANSWERS TO QUIZ

1. O. B. Keeler and Bobby Jones; Louis Stanley; Agatha Christie. 2. Frank Pennink, Leonard Crawley, Frank Moran, Ronald Heager. 3. Tom Webster, the cartoonist. 4. Lloyd Mangrum's. 5. Grantland Rice. Florence Rice was his daughter. 6. 1876. 7. Only Bobby Locke. 8. Tommy Armour. 9. A P. G. Wodehouse character. 10. All except Damon Runyon.

L. G. Crawley   P. F. Scrutton   N. Sutton

EISENHOWER CUP SCORES
First meeting October 1958 at St. Andrews

Australia	918	Bermuda	985
United States	918	Germany	998
Great Britain and Ireland	919	Kenya	998
New Zealand	921	Netherlands	1,005
Argentina	940	Japan	1,006
Canada	945	Brazil	1,009
South Africa	945	Venezuela	1,015
France	949	Finland	1,017
Sweden	957	Malaya	1,029
Italy	963	Norway	1,040
Belgium	964	China	1,049
Philippines	970	Portugal	1,049
Spain	974	Austria	1,071
India	981	Iceland	1,084
Switzerland	981		

LEADING INDIVIDUALS

301 B. W. Devlin (*Australia*) 81, 73, 74, 73
    R. Jack (*Britain*) 72, 77, 74, 78
    W. Hyndman (*U.S.*) 79, 77, 73, 72
305 C. R. Coe (*U.S.*) 74, 77, 76, 78
    R. J. Charles (*New Zealand*) 74, 74, 76, 81

Other leading placings:
307 H. de Lamaze (*France*)

308 L. Silverio (*Philippines*)
310 R. F. Stevens (*Australia*); A. Walker (*South Africa*); P. A. Toogood (*Australia*); G. B. Wolstenholme (*Britain*)
312 E. J. McDougall (*New Zealand*)
313 G. Carlander (*Sweden*); W. J. Patton (*U.S.*); A. H. Perowne (*Britain*).

AMERICAN MASTERS' TOURNAMENT
Venue—Augusta National Golf Course, Augusta, Georgia.

Year	Winner	Score	Year	Winner	Score
1934	Horton Smith	284	1949	Sam Snead	282
1935	Gene Sarazen	282	1950	Jimmy Demaret	283
1936	Horton Smith	285	1951	Ben Hogan	280
1937	Byron Nelson	283	1952	Sam Snead	286
1938	Henry Picard	285	1953	Ben Hogan	274
1939	Ralph Guldahl	279	1954	Sam Snead	289
1940	Jimmy Demaret	280	1955	Cary Middlecoff	279
1941	Craig Wood	280	1956	Jackie Burke	289
1942	Byron Nelson	280	1957	Doug Ford	283
1946	Herman Keiser	282	1958	Arnold Palmer	284
1947	Jimmy Demaret	281	1959	Art Wall	284
1948	Claude Harmon	279			

AMERICAN AMATEUR CHAMPIONSHIP
Instituted 1893

Year	Winner	Runner-up	Venue	Margin
1893	W. G. Lawrence	C. B. Macdonald	Newport, R.I.	4 and 3
1894	L. B. Stoddart	C. B. Macdonald	St. Andrews	5 and 4
1895	C. B. Macdonald	C. Sands	Newport, R.I.	12 and 11
1896	H. J. Whigham	J. G. Thorp	Shinnecock	8 and 7
1897	H. J. Whigham	W. R. Betts	Wheaton, Ill.	8 and 6
1898	F. S. Douglas	W. B. Smith	Morris County	5 and 3
1899	H. M. Harriman	F. S. Douglas	Onwentsia	3 and 2
1900	W. J. Travis	F. S. Douglas	Garden City	2 holes
1901	W. J. Travis	W. E. Egan	Atlantic City	5 and 4
1902	Louis N. James	E. M. Byers	Glen View	4 and 3
1903	W. J. Travis	E. M. Byers	Nassau	5 and 4
1904	H. Chandler Egan	F. Herreschoff	Baltusrol	8 and 6
1905	H. Chandler Egan	D. E. Sawyer	Wheaton, Ill.	6 and 5
1906	E. M. Byers	Geo. S. Lyon	Englewood	2 holes
1907	Jerome D. Travers	Arch. Graham	Cleveland	6 and 5
1908	Jerome D. Travers	Max H. Behr	Midlothian, Ill.	8 and 7
1909	R. Gardner	H. C. Egan	Wheaton, Ill.	4 and 3
1910	W. C. Fownes, jun.	W. K. Wood	Brookline	4 and 3
1911	H. H. Hilton	F. Herreschoff	Apawamis	37th hole
1912	Jerome D. Travers	Charles Evans	Wheaton, Ill.	7 and 6
1913	Jerome D. Travers	J. G. Anderson	Garden City	5 and 4
1914	F. Ouimet	J. D. Travers	Vermont	6 and 5
1915	R. A. Gardner	J. G. Anderson	Detroit	5 and 4
1916	Chas. Evans	R. A. Gardner	Merion	4 and 3
1919	S. D. Herron	R. T. Jones, jun.	Oakmont	5 and 4
1920	C. Evans	F. Ouimet	Engineers Club	7 and 6
1921	J. Guildford	Robert Gardner	St. Louis, Clayton	7 and 6
1922	J. Sweetser	Chas. Evans	Brookline	3 and 2
1923	Max Marston	Jesse Sweetser	Flossmoor	38th hole
1924	R. T. Jones, jun.	G. von Elm	Merion	9 and 8
1925	R. T. Jones, jun.	W. Gunn	Oakmont	8 and 7
1926	Geo. Von Elm	R. T. Jones, jun.	Baltusrol	2 and 1
1927	R. T. Jones, jun.	C. Evans	Minikahda	8 and 7
1928	R. T. Jones, jun.	T. P. Perkins	Brae Burn	10 and 9
1929	H. R. Johnston	Dr. O. F. Willing	Del Monte	4 and 3
1930	R. T. Jones, jun.	E. V. Homans	Merion	8 and 7
1931	F. Ouimet	J. Westland	Beverley	6 and 5
1932	C. R. Somerville	J. Goodman	Baltimore	2 and 1
1933	G. T. Dunlap	M. R. Marston	Kenwood	6 and 5
1934	W. Lawson Little	D. Goldman	Brookline	8 and 7
1935	W. Lawson Little	W. Emery	Cleveland	4 and 2
1936	J. Fischer	J. McLean	Garden City	37th hole
1937	J. Goodman	R. Billows	Portland	2 holes
1938	W. P. Turnesa	B. P. Abbott	Oakmont	8 and 7
1939	M. H. Ward	R. Billows	Glenview	7 and 5
1940	R. D. Chapman	W. B. McCullough	Winged Foot	11 and 9
1941	M. H. Ward	B. P. Abbott	Omaha	4 and 3
1942–45	No Championship			
1946	S. E. Bishop	S. Quick	Baltusrol	37th hole
1947	R. H. Riegel	J. Dawson	Pebble Beach	2 and 1
1948	W. P. Turnesa	R. Billows	Memphis	2 and 1
1949	C. R. Coe	Rufus King	Oak Hill	11 and 10
1950	S. Urzetta	F. R. Stranahan	Minneapolis	39th hole
1951	W. J. Maxwell	J. Gagliardi	Saucon Valley, Pa.	4 and 3
1952	J. Westland	A. Mengert	Seattle	3 and 2
1953	G. Littler	D. Morey	Oklahoma	1 hole
1954	A. Palmer	R. Sweeney	Detroit	1 hole
1955	J. Harvie Ward	W. Hyndman	Richmond, Va.	9 and 8
1956	J. Harvie Ward	C. Kocsis	Lake Forest	5 and 4
1957	H. Robbins	Dr. F. Taylor	Brookline	5 and 4
1958	C. R. Coe	T. Aaron	Olympic, San Francisco	5 and 4

AMERICAN WOMEN'S CHAMPIONSHIP
Instituted 1895. Finalists since 1930.

Year	Winner	Runner-up	Venue	Score
1930	Miss Glenna Collett	Miss V. Van Wie	Los Angeles	2 and 1
1931	Miss H. Hicks	Mrs. G. C. Vare	Buffalo	2 and 1
1932	Miss V. Van Wie	Mrs. G. C. Vare	Peabody	10 and 8
1933	Miss V. Van Wie	Miss H. Hicks	Exmoor	4 and 3
1934	Miss V. Van Wie	Miss T. Traung	Whitemarsh Valley	2 and 1
1935	Mrs. G. C. Vare	Miss P. Berg	Interlachen	3 and 2
1936	Miss Pam Barton	Mrs. M. O. Crews	Canoe Brook	4 and 3
1937	Mrs. J. A. Page	Miss P. Berg	Memphis City	7 and 6
1938	Miss P. Berg	Mrs. J. A. Page	Westmoreland	6 and 5
1939	Miss B. Jameson	Miss D. Kirby	Wee Burn	3 and 2
1940	Miss B. Jameson	Miss J. Cochran	Pebble Beach	6 and 5
1941	Mrs. H. Newell	Miss H. Sigel	Brookline	5 and 3
1942–1945	No Championship			
1946	Mrs. G. Zaharias	Mrs. C. Sherman	Southern Hills, Tulsa	11 and 9
1947	Miss L. Suggs	Miss D. Kirby	Detroit	2 holes
1948	Miss Grace Lenczyk	Miss Helen Sigel	Pebble Beach	4 and 3
1949	Mrs. Mark A. Porter	Miss D. Kielty	Merion	3 and 2
1950	Miss Beverly Hanson	Miss Mae Murray	Atlanta	6 and 4
1951	Miss Dorothy Kirby	Miss Claire Doran	St. Paul, Minn.	2 and 1
1952	Mrs. J. Pung	Miss S. McFedters	Long Beach, Calif.	2 and 1
1953	Miss M. L. Faulk	Miss P. Riley	Rhode Island	3 and 2
1954	Miss B. Romack	Miss M. Wright	Pittsburgh	4 and 2
1955	Miss Pat Lesser	Miss J. Nelson	Charlotte	7 and 6
1956	Miss Marlene Stewart	Miss J. Gunderson	Indianapolis	2 and 1
1957	Miss J. Gunderson	Mrs. A. C. Johnstone	Del Paso	8 and 6
1958	Miss A. Quast	Miss B. Romack	Wee Burn	3 and 2
1959	Miss B. McIntire	Miss J. Goodwin	Washington	4 and 3

Compiled by Leo C. Wilson

Editor: Greyhound Express and Coursing News

Greyhound Racing

INTRODUCTION

Although greyhound racing in its present form started in England in 1926 at Manchester, the first race after an artificial hare took place at the Welsh Harp, Hendon, in 1876. This was really artificial coursing and the races were over 400 yards straight.

Greyhound racing on a circular greyhound track was patented in America fourteen years later but modern greyhound racing only received its start in 1923 in Oklahoma. The sport in England is controlled mainly by the National Greyhound Racing Society which has 65 member tracks, and there are a number of smaller racecourses outside that control.

In Ireland the sport is under the control of the Irish Coursing Club. Greyhounds registered with the National Coursing Club or the Irish Coursing Club are eligible to race under N.G.R.C. rules provided they have also an N.G.R.C. registration certificate.

The N.G.R.C. runs a very efficient security force and has an excellent identification system which has proved so effective that a similar method is now employed at horseracing.

Although greyhound racing has not recently reached the heights of popularity it enjoyed in the boom period which followed the war years, it maintains a solid and sound following which does not vary much year by year so far as attendances are concerned. In the past year attendance figures have again been steady and the turnover on the tote has tended to rise slightly.

GRAND NATIONAL WINNERS
(525 yds. hurdles. White City)

		Secs.
1927	Bonzo	31.42
1928	Cormorant	31.16
1929	Levator	31.09
1930	Stylish Cutlet	30.94
1931	Rule the Roost	32.17
1932	Long Hop	31.44
1933	Scapegoat	31.20
1934	Lemonition	30.84
1935	Quarter Day	30.76
1936	Kilganny Bridge	30.70
1937	Flying Wedge	30.61
1938	Juvenile Classic	30.35
1939	Valiant Bob	30.50
1940	Juvenile Classic	30.23
1946	Barry from Limerick	30.61
1947	Baytown Pigeon	30.67
1948	Joves Reason	30.37
1949	Blossom of Annagura	30.20
1950	Blossom of Annagura	29.38
1951	XPDNC	29.80
1952	Whistling Laddie	30.13
1953	Denver Berwick	30.26
1954	Prince Lawrence	30.29
1955	Barrowside	29.43
1956	Blue Sand	29.70
1957	Tanyard Tulip	29.85
1958	Fodda Champion	30.20
1959	Prince Poppit	30.10

GREYHOUND DERBY WINNERS
(525 yds. White City)

1927 *Mr. E. Baxter's* Bd.D. Entry Badge (T5) *J. Harmon* (W. City) F1–4 29.01*
1928 *Mrs. M. Stokes'* Bd.D. Boher Ash (T1) *T. Johnstone* (Edinburgh) 5–1 30.48
1929 *Mr. A. H. Williams'* Bd.D. Mick the Miller (T4) *P. Horan* (Dublin) F4–7 29.96†
1930 *Mrs. A. H. Kempton's* Bd.D. Mick the Miller (T1) *S. Orton* (Wimbledon) F4–9 30.24
1931 *Messrs. H. Hammond & J. J. Flemming's* F.D. Seldom Led (T4) *W. Green* (West Ham) 7–2 30.04†
1932 *Mr. S. Johnson's* Bd.D. Wild Woolley (T6) *J. Rimmer* (Belle Vue) 5–2 29.72
1933 *Mrs. W. A. Evershed's* Bd.D. Future Cutlet (T3) *A. Probert* (Wembley) 6–1 29.80
1934 *Mr. F. Brook's* Bk.W.D. Davesland (T4) *J. Harvey* (Harringay) 3–1 29.81
1935 *Mr. J. Lockhart Mummery's* R.F.B. Greta Ranee (T3) *A. Jonas* (W. City) 4–1 30.18
1936 *Mrs. M. Yates'* Bd.D. Fine Jubilee (T3) *Mrs. M. Yates* (Private) F10–11 29.48
1937 *Mrs. R. H. Dent's* Bd.D. Wattle Bark (T6) *J. Syder* (Wembley) 5–1 29.26
1938 *Mr. J. Walsh's* Bd.D. Lone Keel (T3) *S. Wright* (Private) 9–4 29.62
1939 *Mr. J. Harty's* R.F.D. Highland Rum (T6) *P. Fortune* (Wimbledon) JF2–1 29.35
1940 *Mr. O. G. Leach's* R.F.D. G. R. Archduke (T1) *C. Ashley* (Harringay) 100–7 29.66‡
1945 *Mrs. F. Stow & Mr. A. Vivian's* Bd.D. Ballyhennessy Seal (T1) *S. Martin* (Wimbledon) F1–1 29.56
1946 *Mr. D. T. Stewart's* Bd.D. Mondays News (T3) *F. Farey* (Private) 5–1 29.24
1947 *Mr. F. Trevillion's* Bd.D. Trevs Perfection (T2) *F. Trevillion* (Private) 4–1 28.95
1948 *Mr. W. P. O'Kane's* Bd.D. Priceless Border (T1) *L. Reynolds* (Wembley) F1–2 28.78
1949 *Mr. W. J. Reid's* F.B. Narrogar Ann (T2) *L. Reynolds* (Wembley) 5–1 28.95
1950 *Mr. T. Nicholl's* Bd.D. Ballymac Ball (T4) *S. Martin* (Wimbledon) 7–2 28.72
1951 *Mr. A. N. Dupont's* W.Bd.D. Ballylanigan Tanist (T1) *L. Reynolds* (Wembley) 11–4 28.62
1952 *Mr. H. E. Gocher's* Bd.D. Endless Gossip (T6) *L. Reynolds* (Wembley) F1–1 28.50
1953 *Mr. D. Fitzgerald's* Bd.D. Daws Dancer (T5) *P. McEvoy* (Private) 10–1 29.20
1954 *Mr. T. H. Watford's* Bd.D. Pauls Fun (T2) *L. Reynolds* (Wembley) F8–15 28.84
1955 *Mr. & Mrs. F. Johnson's* Bk.W.D. Rushton Mack (T2) *F. Johnson* (Private) 5–1 28.97
1956 *Mr. J. McAllister's* F.D. Dunmore King (T3) *P. McEvoy* (Clapton) 7–2 29.22
1957 *Messrs. Hill & Frost's* Bk.D. Ford Spartan (T1) *D. Hannafin* (Wimbledon) F1–1 28.84
1958 *Mr. A. Burnett's* Bd.D. Pigalle Wonder (T1) *J. P. Syder* (Wembley) F4–5 28.65
1959 *Mr. Noel Purvis'* Bd. D. Mile Bush Pride (T4) *J. Harvey* (Wembley) F1–1 28.76

* Over 500 yds. † Rerun. ‡ Run at Harringay.

ST. LEGER WINNERS
(700 yds. Wembley)

1928	Burletta	41.91
1929	Loughnagare	42.76
1930	Maidens Boy	41.48
1931	Mick the Miller	41.31
1932	Fret Not	41.35
1933	The Daw	41.24
1934	Bosham	41.17
1935	Satans Baby	40.95
1936	Ataxy	40.39
1937	Grosvenor Bob	41.13
1938	Gretas Rosary	40.82
1939	Gayhunter	41.79
1945	Robeen Printer	40.03
1946	Bohernagraga Boy	39.92
1947	Dante II	39.70
1948	Street After Midnight	40.40
1949	Lovely Rio	40.77
1950	Fawn Mack	40.56
1951	Black Mire	40.19
1952	Funny Worker	40.50
1953	Magourna Reject	39.88
1954	Pancho Villa	40.99
1955	Title Role	40.78
1956	Jakfigaralt	40.50
1957	Duke of Alva	39.97
1958	Barry's Prince	40.01
1959	Wincot Clifford	40.25

CESAREWITCH WINNERS
(600 yds. West Ham)

1928	Dicks Son	34.25
1929	Five of Hearts	34.82
1930	Mick the Miller	34.11
1931	Future Cutlet	34.03
1932	Future Cutlet	34.11
1933	Elsell	34.22
1934	Brilliant Bob	33.80
1935	Grand Flight II	33.97
1936	Ataxy	*31.24
1937	Jesmond Cutlet	34.56
1938	Ballyjoker	34.02
1945	Hurry Kitty	*31.26
1946	Col Skookum	*31.28
1947	Red Tan	*31.30
1948	Local Interprize	*30.88
1949	Drumgoon Boy	*30.53

1950	Quare Customer	*30.80
1951	Prionsa Luath	33.77
1952	Shaggy Swank	34.03
1953	Magourna Reject	33.24
1954	Matchlock	33.03
1955	Gulf of Darien	32.99
1956	Coming Champion	33.03
1957	Scoutbush	33.05
1958	Pigalle Wonder } dh Rylane Pleasure	33.06

* 550 yards.

GOLD COLLAR WINNERS
(440 yds. Catford)

1933	Wild Woolley	26.63
1934	Davesland	*32.70
1935	Bosham	*32.84
1936	Fine Jubilee	26.00
1937	Avion Ballerina	25.87
1938	Junior Classic	25.77
1939	Grosvenor Ferdinand	25.92
1940	Cash Balance	25.74
1945	Ballyhennessy Seal	25.45
1946	King Silver	25.88
1947	Trevs Perfection	25.52
1948	Local Interprize	25.71
1949	Local Interprize	25.88
1950	Islandeady	26.07
1951	Loyal Accomplice	25.63
1952	Hectic Birthday	25.41
1953	Mushera Silver	25.70
1954	Ardskeagh Ville	25.86
1955	Firgrove Slipper	26.35
1956	Ponsford	25.69
1957	Silent Worship	25.50
1958	Five Up	25.43
1959	Dunstown Warrior	25.77

* 540 yards.

LAURELS WINNERS
(500 yds. Wimbledon)

1930	Kilbrean Boy	29.20
1931	Future Cutlet	28.52
1932	Beef Cutlet	28.47
1933	Wild Woolley	28.80
1934	Brilliant Bob	28.46
1935	Kitshine	29.05

1936	Top O' The Carlow Road	28.30
1937	Ballyhennessy Sandhills	28.25
1938	Ballyhennessy Sandhills	28.50
1939	Musical Duke	28.42
1940	April Burglar	28.56
1945	Burhill Moon	28.42
1946	Shannon Shore	28.26
1947	Rimmells Black	28.77
1948	Good Worker	28.49
1949	Ballymac Ball	28.61
1950	Ballymac Ball	28.19
1951	Ballylanigan Tanist	28.37
1952	Endless Gossip	27.96
1953	Polonius	28.04
1954	Coolkill Chieftain	28.05
1955	Duet Leader	28.25
1956	Duet Leader	28.13
1957	Ford Spartan	27.89
1958	Granthamian	28.57
1959	Mighty Hassan	28.01

SCURRY WINNERS
(400 yds. Clapton)

1928	Cruseline Boy	24.91
1929	Loose Card	24.13
1930	Barlock	24.19
1931	Brave Enough	23.62
1932	Experts Boast	23.61
1933	Creamery Border	23.31
1934	Brilliant Bob	23.47
1935	Jacks Joke	23.15
1936	Mitzvah	23.29
1937	Hexham Bridge	23.37
1938	Orlucks Best	23.24
1939	Silver Wire	23.53
1945	Country Life	23.50
1946	Mischievous Manhattan	23.40
1947	Rimmells Black	23.11
1948	Local Interprize	23.04
1949	Burndennet Brook	23.48
1950	Gortnagory	23.47
1951	Defence Leader	22.99
1952	Monachdy Girlie	23.08
1953	Rolling Mike	22.77
1954	Demon King	22.84
1955	Chance Me Paddy	22.85
1956	Belingas Customer	22.82
1957	Lisbrook Chieftain	23.09
1958	Beware Champ	22.71
1959	Gorey Airways	29.95

I*

Aberdeen

Distance	Dog	Time (sec.)	Date recorded
400 yds.	Old Cappyricks	23.30	1941
400 yds.	Stirabout Stick	23.30	1950

Bradford

310 yds.	Oola Rattler	17.20	1945
440 yds.	W.W.W.	25.24	1934
500 yds.	Cheerful Comedy	28.08	1947
650 yds.	Rona	37.29	1949
700 yds.	Peartree Man	40.90	1938
730 yds.	Silkshine	44.45	1937
860 yds.	Well Schooled	52.25	1938
*500 yds.	Ball of Valse	28.34	1958

Brighton

500 yds.	Happy Prince	28.42	1955
525 yds.	Trabolgan Star	29.11	1950
565 yds.	Quare Customer	31.25	1950
750 yds.	Drastic O'Leer	42.60	1950
780 yds.	Stoneyhill Gift	45.77	1951
*500 yds.	Jumping Pole (pt)	28.68	1958

Bristol (Eastville)

500 yds.	Wincot Clifford (pt)	28.06	1958
700 yds.	Shaggy Lass	40.61	1948
938 yds.	Courtland Ben (pt)	55.88	1958
*500 yds.	Red Nuxer	29.21	1945

Bristol (Knowle)

525 yds.	Hello Deeps (pt)	29.99	1956
550 yds.	Neat Wager (pt)	31.54	1957
700 yds.	Night Willow (pt)	40.85	1957

Catford

440 yds.	Rusty Chain (pt)	25.26	1956
600 yds.	Paracelsus (pt)	35.19	1956
810 yds.	Tia Tina (pt)	48.48	1958
970 yds.	Budget Surplus (pt)	58.87	1958
1180 yds.	Brissies Rose	73.13	1954
*440 yds.	Minorkas Glass (pt)	26.04	1956
*600 yds.	Ollys Playboy (pt)	36.26	1958

Charlton

415 yds.	The Gifts Champion (pt)	23.71	1958
600 yds.	Kilcaskin Kern (pt)	34.55	1958
776 yds.	Churchtown Ben (pt)	46.22	1958
*415 yds.	Tanyard Tulip (pt)	24.62	1957

Clapton

400 yds.	Beware Champ (pt)	22.53	1958
550 yds.	Prince Chancer (pt)	31.76	1954
575 yds.	Dark Rose (pt)	33.14	1957
760 yds.	Jockey Club (pt)	44.54	1956
*400 yds.	Fodda Champion (pt)	23.18	1957
*550 yds.	Fodda Champion (pt)	32.55	1957
*575 yds.	Prince Lawrence	34.67	1954

Coventry

525 yds.	Step Inside (pt)	29.23	1954
700 yds.	Perfect Peter II	40.56	1950
750 yds.	Model Dasher	43.65	1945
*525 yds.	Bewitching Batchelor (pt)	30.21	1956

Crayford

285 yds.	Snow White Brown (pt)	16.43	1954
490 yds.	Coming Captain (pt)	28.21	1954
520 yds.	Gortaleen (pt)	29.95	1954
700 yds.	Churchtown Ben (pt)	41.80	1958

Dagenham

460 yds.	Yankee Touch	26.20	1950
550 yds.	Cheerful Host (pt)	31.72	1955
650 yds.	Blackburn Mad	37.45	1951
840 yds.	Hyport (pt)	49.30	1958
1030 yds.	Pigalle (pt)	61.84	1956
*460 yds.	Flashy Paddy	26.81	1951
*550 yds.	Overleigh Hotspur (pt)	32.84	1956

Darnall, Sheffield

475 yds.	Cheerful Catapult	26.56	1957
530 yds.	Very Hot	29.90	1956
650 yds.	Very Hot	36.87	1956

Derby

460 yds.	Special Intention	26.00	1950
650 yds.	Glencoy Regent	37.07	1950
270 yds.	Cheerful Cricket	15.21	1957

Edinburgh (Powderhall)

440 yds.	Hellcat Spartan (pt)	25.06	1957
500 yds.	Pigalle Wonder (pt)	27.97	1958
500 yds.	Rushton Mac	27.81	1954
500 yds.	Just Fame (pt)	27.81	1958
700 yds.	Blue Falcon II (pt)	40.66	1958
880 yds.	Caledonian Olga (pt)	52.19	1958
940 yds.	Grimsby Coastguard (pt)	57.25	1955
*500 yds.	Fodda Champion (pt)	28.87	1958
*500 yds. (chase)	Temple Mercury (pt)	29.77	1958

Gloucester

500 yds.	Magourna Reject (pt)	28.09	1953
650 yds.	Bundle of Fun	37.25	1948
700 yds.	Whiddy Rates (pt)	40.30	1958
*500 yds.	Latest Story (pt)	29.06	1958

Hackney Wick

340 yds.	Midnight Curate (pt)	18.80	1953
500 yds.	Galtee Cleo (pt)	27.75	1954
550 yds.	Manhattan Man (pt)	30.74	1958
*340 yds.	Vintners Cup (pt)	19.48	1956
*550 yds.	Minnies Commandant (pt)	31.60	1958

Hall Green

500 yds.	Rushton Spot	27.94	1954
700 yds.	Brooklands Hunter (pt)	40.10	1958
937 yds.	Tarry Oh No (pt)	56.10	1956
*500 yds.	Spotless O'Leer (pt)	29.09	1956
	Fodda Champion (pt)	29.09	1957
*700 yds.	Border Rambler	42.30	1939

Harringay

500 yds.	Demotic Mack	28.46	1938
525 yds.	Pigalle Wonder (pt)	29.03	1958
700 yds.	Noreview King (pt)	40.24	1958
880 yds.	Tugwell	52.64	1936
963 yds.	Budget Surplus (pt)	56.76	1957
*500 yds.	Kilganny Bridge	29.53	1936
*500 yds.	Blue Sand (pt)	29.81	1956
†525 yds.	Fodda Champion (pt)	30.36	1957
*700 yds.	Misty Bridge (pt)	41.61	1958

Glasgow (White City)

320 yds.	Ballydowney Captain	17.44	1954
530 yds.	Loughane Gold	29.49	1957
550 yds.	Loughane Gold	30.44	1958
590 yds.	Hay Box	33.14	1958

Hendon

475 yds.	Prince Chancer (pt)	27.18	1954
650 yds.	Bushy Mac (pt)	38.19	1957
823 yds.	Roving Ways (pt)	49.68	1957
*475 yds.	Harwin Boyerler (pt)	28.26	1956

Hull

500 yds.	Coolmine Jack	28.24	1956
700 yds.	Joan Burette	41.10	1952

Kings Heath

282 yds.	Maesydd Melampus	15.48	1955
480 yds.	Silent Worship	26.39	1957
495 yds.	Go Doggie Go	27.31	1957
500 yds.	Town Bells	27.91	1953
700 yds.	The Cure	40.19	1956
*480 yds.	Step Inside	27.49	1956

Leeds

325 yds.	Hepicoleum	17.95	1947
512 yds.	Cheerful Comedy	28.75	1947
743 yds.	Paddy the Gag	43.48	1948
700 yds.	Autumn Mist	40.44	1954
500 yds.	Dancing Sheik	28.13	1958

Leicester

525 yds.	Pargo (pt)	29.26	1954

Middlesbrough

288 yds.	Blue Dusty	16.61	1957
306 yds. (handicap)	Sandy's Peach	17.61	1956
500 yds.	Cold and Frisky	28.88	1957
518 yds. (handicap)	Blue Dusty	29.70	1956

Manchester (Belle Vue)

500 yds.	Rushton Spot	27.73	1954
700 yds.	Oozoo	40.17	1951
934 yds.	Western Stream	55.30	1951
*500 yds.	Baytown Dean	29.18	1955
*700 yds.	Grouncil	43.91	1933
*500 yds. (chase)	Novelty Cast	30.06	1958

Manchester (Salford)

300 yds.	Baytown Code	17.31	1957
450 yds.	Trust No Man	26.87	1952
*518 yds.	Rush St.	30.94	1955
518 yds.	Ace Kid	29.25	1957
700 yds.	English Warrior	42.38	1934

GREYHOUND QUIZ

1. What deduction is made from tote bets?

★

2. If there is fighting in a race is the race void?

★

3. Is it true or false that the photo-finish camera favours the dog nearest the camera?

★

4. How are greyhounds started consistently?

★

5. Is the G.R.A. the controlling body of greyhound racing?

6. What part does the National Greyhound Racing Society play?

★

QUIZ ANSWERS

1. 16%. Ten per cent is tax and six per cent expenses. 2. No. Under the recently changed rules of the N.G.R.C. results are first past the post except in unusual circumstances like mechanical breakdown or outside interference. 3. No. The camera is so constructed that the first part of the first dog over the line is registered on the film regardless of its position on the track. 4. By means of a trip switch placed in a pre-determined position relative to the trap and operated by the hare as it passes the trap. 5. No. The Greyhound Racing Association is the name of the largest promoting company owning tracks all over the country but the controlling body is the National Greyhound Racing Club. 6. It looks after the business interests of the tracks under N.G.R.C. control.

MANCHESTER (White City)			
Distance	*Dog*	*Time (sec.)*	*Date recorded*
500 yds.	Baytown Dagger	28.04	1955
525 yds.	Ballypatrick	29.39	1958
700 yds.	Registered Cash	40.42	1955
725 yds.	Blackberry Rambler	42.16	1956
949 yds.	Naytown Dentist	56.40	1955
*525 yds.	Stoney Ley II	30.38	1958

NEWCASTLE-UPON-TYNE (Brough Park)

500 yds.	Malanna Must	28.03	1958
525 yds.	Imperial Town	29.27	1958
700 yds.	Gulf of Darien	40.21	1955

NEWCASTLE (Gosforth)

440 yds. (handicap)	Eridash	26.09	1958
600 yds. (handicap)	Tinks Papa	35.97	1958

NEW CROSS

415 yds.	Home Luck (*pt*)	23.48	1954
550 yds.	Prince Norroy	32.26	1941
600 yds.	Gambling Dick	34.95	1951
770 yds.	Gallant Maid (*pt*)	46.12	1958
*415 yds.	Vintners Cup (*pt*)	24.16	1957
*600 yds.	Mazel Tov (*pt*)	36.22	1958

NEWPORT

450 yds.	Antarctica	25.29	1958

NORWICH (Boundary Park)

300 yds.	Anxious Night	17.04	1956
500 yds.	Rimmells Black	28.40	1946

NOTTINGHAM

362 yds.	Cheerful Catapult	19.90	1958
525 yds.	Lancewood Pal	29.32	1957

OXFORD

500 yds.	Kensington Perfection (*pt*)	28.25	1954
715 yds.	Come Up First	40.72	1947

PARK ROYAL

400 yds.	Montego Bay (*pt*)	22.04	1953
550 yds.	Waltzers Choice (*pt*)	31.11	1953
*400 yds.	Vintners Cup (*pt*)	22.76	1957
*550 yds.	Chic Chic	33.45	1936

PERRY BARR

300 yds.	Malt Hasty	16.74	1957
340 yds.	Fearless Champion	18.91	1958
500 yds.	Blackburn Blue	28.30	1950
525 yds.	Dancing Sheik	29.49	1958
550 yds.	Go Doggie Go	31.01	1957
700 yds.	Wolf Wild	40.43	1953
755 yds.	Lancewood Olly	43.89	1958
*340 yds.	Twinkle Champion	19.98	1958
*525 yds.	Surely Tadie	31.39	1958

PORTSMOUTH

470 yds.	White Olly	27.07	1957
655 yds.	Shaggy Lass	38.34	1946
*470 yds.	Tuathal Teachmar	28.29	1938

RAMSGATE

440 yds.	Just Subtle	25.62	1950
460 yds.	Our Dan	26.89	1956
500 yds.	Moymett Cottage (*pt*)	28.70	1958
600 yds.	Crissies Tanist	35.31	1947
700 yds.	Keystone	41.46	1947
*500 yds.	Blossom of Annagura	29.76	1951

READING

340 yds.	Lough Legend (*pt*)	18.88	1954
400 yds.	Tickled Pink (*pt*)	25.70	1957
500 yds.	Nutgrove Mick (*pt*)	28.31	1956
525 yds.	Clopook Dasher (*pt*)	29.45	1954
600 yds.	Clonmore Darcel	33.62	1952
700 yds.	Jocular Nero (*pt*)	40.05	1957
775 yds.	Bourneen Tusk (*pt*)	44.84	1954
908 yds.	Cool Magourna (*pt*)	53.77	1958
*340 yds.	Outlaw O'Leer (*pt*)	19.57	1954
*460 yds.	Highwood Samson (*pt*)	26.50	1958
*500 yds.	Mina Digger (*pt*)	28.68	1955
*525 yds.	Connors Company (*pt*)	30.80	1938

ROCHESTER

525 yds.	Stretton Duke (*pt*)	29.99	1957
700 yds.	Able Champion	41.58	1954

ROMFORD

265 yds.	Haverbrack Ling (*pt*)	15.47	1957
460 yds.	Kitty D.	25.83	1951
650 yds.	Highway Tim (*pt*)	36.78	1958
840 yds.	Kilcaskin Katherine (*pt*)	48.86	1958
1030 yds.	Raydens Rebel (*pt*)	62.37	1957
*460 yds.	Vintners Cup (*pt*)	26.19	1957
*650 yds.	Devil Again (*pt*)	41.06	1955

SLOUGH

275 yds.	Oola Rattler	15.51	1946
475 yds.	Tax Diablo (*pt*)	26.74	1955
675 yds.	Silver Man (*pt*)	39.00	1956
875 yds.	Fairy Loup	54.91	1934
*475 yds.	Cadet Captain	27.69	1946

SOUTHAMPTON

440 yds.	Ideal Monday (*pt*)	25.08	1953
600 yds.	Millbrook	35.11	1946
635 yds.	Tubrid Champion (*pt*)	37.23	1956

SOUTHEND

300 yds.	Tickled Pink (*pt*)	16.65	1958
500 yds.	Red Wind	27.78	1949
525 yds.	Harry Ivan	29.46	1950
700 yds.	Drastic O'Lear	39.91	1950
*500 yds.	Sprightly Peter	28.72	1949
*525 yds.	O Alaha (*pt*)	30.31	1948
*700 yds.	Flying Wedge	41.98	1937

SOUTH SHIELDS

395 yds.	Diamond Glory	23.34	1936
400 yds.	Terry's Monach	23.41	1946
410 yds.	Proud Seal	23.61	1951
540 yds.	Joyful Holidays	32.51	1935
565 yds.	Clementine	34.54	1933
575 yds.	Sandy's Double	33.50	1951

STAMFORD BRIDGE

500 yds.	Haslet of Selsdon (*pt*)	27.46	1956
700 yds.	Dark Rose (*pt*)	39.44	1957
934 yds.	Hyport (*pt*)	54.26	1958
*500 yds.	Highwood Samson (*pt*)	28.39	1958
*700 yds.	Vitae Via Virtus (*pt*)	41.29	1958

WALTHAMSTOW

300 yds.	Marsh Harrier (*pt*)	16.90	1953
500 yds.	Malanna Must (*pt*)	27.98	1958
525 yds.	Duet Leader (*pt*)	29.24	1956
700 yds.	Shy Champion (*pt*)	40.08	1957
936 yds.	Pigalle (*pt*)	55.63	1956
*500 yds.	Cooleen Flyer (*pt*)	29.32	1951
*525 yds.	Flintex Major (*pt*)	30.60	1950

WANDSWORTH

440 yds.	Town Prince (*pt*)	25.22	1958
600 yds.	Fly Red II (*pt*)	34.98	1958
825 yds.	Rapid Progress II (*pt*)	49.22	1958
*440 yds.	Vintners Cup (*pt*)	26.08	1957
*600 yds.	Fodda Champion (*pt*)	35.81	1958

WEMBLEY

525 yds.	Pigalle Wonder (*pt*)	28.78	1958
700 yds.	Highwood Sovereign (*pt*)	39.64	1957
990 yds.	Cool Magourna (*pt*)	58.19	1958
*525 yds.	Tanyard Tulip (*pt*)	30.09	1956
†525 yds.	History Book (*pt*)	30.73	1958
*700 yds.	Sammy Light (*pt*)	41.12	1958

† Over six hurdles.

WEST HAM

350 yds.	Foolish Billy (*pt*)	19.14	1952
400 yds.	Cooks Sandhills	21.91	1942
400 yds.	Wireless Time	21.91	1942
525 yds.	Coolkill Chieftain (*pt*)	28.65	1954
550 yds.	Calhoon (*pt*)	30.43	1957
600 yds.	Gulf of Darien (*pt*)	32.92	1956
700 yds.	Jocular Nero (*pt*)	39.04	1957
*550 yds.	Fodda Champion (*pt*)	30.62	1957

WHITE CITY

500 yds.	Outside Left (*pt*)	27.55	1958
525 yds.	Pigalle Wonder (*pt*)	28.44	1958
550 yds.	Clara Prince (*pt*)	30.16	1957
725 yds.	Happy Jamnie (*pt*)	40.85	1958
800 yds.	Jockey Club (*pt*)	45.30	1956
1025 yds.	Rimmels Pearl (*pt*)	59.75	1954
*550 yds.	Barrowside (*pt*)	31.35	1955
	Spotless O'Leer (*pt*)	31.35	1955
†550 yds.	Fodda Champion (*pt*)	31.18	1957
*725 yds.	Mad Trust (*pt*)	43.98	1954

† Over seven hurdles.

WILLENHALL

400 yds.	Five Up	22.77	1957
565 yds.	The Lunatic	32.87	1956
575 yds.	Barnabrow	34.02	1938
740 yds.	Ballyherwick	44.21	1957
*400 yds.	Cranagh Tom	24.45	1938

WIMBLEDON

275 yds.	Tickled Pink (*pt*)	15.42	1957
500 yds.	Coolkill Chieftain	27.67	1954
700 yds.	Hurry Cleo (*pt*)	39.58	1958
725 yds.	Rapid Choice (*pt*)	41.36	1951
940 yds.	Budget Surplus (*pt*)	55.05	1958
1140 yds.	Cool Magourna (*pt*)	68.17	1958
*500 yds.	Fodda Champion (*pt*)	28.83	1958
*550 yds.	Vintners Cup (*pt*)	28.87	1957

WOLVERHAMPTON

300 yds.	Belingas Fancy	16.90	1952
475 yds.	Coynes Castle	27.14	1946
500 yds.	Intrepid Bachelor	28.23	1955
525 yds.	Intrepid Bachelor	29.49	1955
700 yds.	Rimmells Pearl	40.41	1953
*525 yds.	Coast Raider	30.60	1957

* Hurdles.   *pt* photo timed.

GREYHOUND QUIZ

1. Which greyhound holds the record for a winning sequence?

★

2. Which dog came nearest to breaking that record?

★

3. Has any greyhound won the Greyhound Derby 3 times?

★

QUIZ ANSWERS

1. Mick the Miller with 19 races without defeat. 2. Ballynennan Moon would have had 24 consecutive wins but was beaten a short head in one of these races. 3. No, but if the rules had been as they are now Mick the Miller would have done so because he was first past the post in his third Derby but the race was re-run.

163

IRISH RECORD HOLDERS

CELTIC PARK

Distance	Dog	Time (secs.)
375 yds.	Hilarious Champion	20.16
525 yds.	Nimble Star (hand timed)	28.90
525 yds.	True Picture (ray timed)	28.97
550 yds.	Mazurka	30.98
600 yds.	Ashley Park Boy	33.45
*375 yds.	Neidins Carnero	21.46
*525 yds.	Nicotina	31.05
*550 yds.	Neidins Beautiful	32.70
*600 yds.	Another Circle	36.28

CLONES

325 yds.	Flying Heart	18.34
	Landslide	18.34
500 yds.	Follum Flash	28.95
525 yds.	Formal Hope	30.09
550 yds.	Cooladrummon	31.65
*525 yds.	Hello Guy	31.65

CLONMEL

300 yds.	Handsome Prince	16.70
310 yds.	Cormacs Blackie	17.55
	Orinoco River	17.55
330 yds.	Brilliant Tulip	18.30
500 yds.	Huberts Pet	28.30
525 yds.	The Grand Fire	29.40
550 yds.	Captain the Killer	31.25
700 yds.	Tanyard Tan	40.95
*500 yds.	Knockdrina Ranger	29.95
*525 yds.	Fair King	31.00

CORK

300 yds.	Garrys Rebel	16.70
310 yds.	Odd Crest	17.20
500 yds.	Prince of Bermuda	27.95
525 yds.	Kilcaskin Kern	29.45
550 yds.	Spanish Lad	31.00
700 yds.	Muskerry Cream	40.85
740 yds.	Kilmurry Gift	44.30
*525 yds.	Tanyard Slow	30.50

DERRY

300 yds.	Alt Lad	16.78
440 yds.	Figert Daisy	25.11
500 yds.	Pauls Express	28.40
525 yds.	Prionsa Luath	29.67
600 yds.	Mad Glen	34.35

DUNDALK

325 yds.	Mourne Return	17.85
500 yds.	Pointers Prince	28.80
525 yds.	Skipit Quick	30.15
550 yds.	Fine Arrow	31.65
*325 yds.	Bellafinniffy	19.35
	Cloneen War Lord	19.35
*525 yds.	Coastal Cruise	31.86

DUNGANNON

325 yds.	Big Champ	17.91
500 yds.	Tit For Tat	28.24
525 yds.	Coolkill	29.87
550 yds.	Coolkill	31.49

DUNMORE

435 yds.	Mushera Sherry	23.60
500 yds.	Strong Mutton	28.51
525 yds.	Coolkill Hero	29.02
550 yds.	Firgrove Seignor	30.99
600 yds.	Craigs Look	33.95
*435 yds.	Carstown Boy	24.94
*500 yds.	Half Rose	29.76
*525 yds.	Curries Ferry	30.78

ENNISCORTHY

325 yds.	No Play	18.05
500 yds.	Precious Princess	28.70
525 yds.	Colonel Payne	29.90
550 yds.	Larkins Flight	31.30
*325 yds.	Palm Sonny	18.55
*525 yds.	You Drop Out	31.40
	One For The Road	31.40
	Flying Cleritas	31.40

GALWAY

325 yds.	Palm Tree	18.14
330 yds.	Carra Dee	18.60
500 yds.	Golden Victory	28.82
525 yds.	Sean Suaire	29.87
550 yds.	Erris Rebel	31.30
600 yds.	Farmhill Prince	35.05
*325 yds.	Lavally Roe	19.00
*330 yds.	Hailsham Playboy	19.80
*525 yds.	Golsto	30.55
*550 yds.	Gormans Fancy	32.90

HAROLDS CROSS

325 yds.	Ballinclea Dancer	18.30
350 yds.	Sky Patrol	19.20
500 yds.	Shaggy Lad	27.97
525 yds.	Balrath Flute	29.38
550 yds.	Coolkill Hero	31.02
575 yds.	That Won't Do	32.90
	Camaghey Lad	32.90
580 yds.	Dee Diabolo	33.35
600 yds.	Mad Astley	33.80
750 yds.	Soaring Leary	45.30
*350 yds.	Printer	20.36
*500 yds.	Inly	30.08
*525 yds.	General Kildare	30.72
*580 yds.	Druze	34.73

KILKENNY

300 yds.	Give Here	16.60
	Kilcomney Mistress	16.60
	Palm Tree	16.60
500 yds.	Gala Friend	28.70
525 yds.	Fourth of July	29.30
550 yds.	Clever Shaggy	31.55
	Dashing Wildwood	31.55
	Lingo	31.55
	Gentle Patsy	31.55
	Rose Of Slievenamon	31.55
*300 yds.	Singing Border	17.35
*525 yds.	An Gorm Lady	30.40

LIMERICK

300 yds.	Brook Prancer	16.69
525 yds.	Hurry Up Judy	29.85
550 yds.	Prince of Bermuda	30.56
600 yds.	Nancys Laurel	34.70
700 yds.	Speir Bhean	40.80
*525 yds.	Jerrys Dreamer	30.65

LONGFORD

330 yds.	Cooleney Twister	18.58
525 yds.	Cooleney Twister	29.98
550 yds.	Jubeau	31.40
*330 yds.	Drumreel Flash	19.70
*525 yds.	Fort William Pagan	31.40

MULLINGAR

325 yds.	Tender Cutlet	18.45
330 yds.	Fair Warrior	18.90
	Counts Lawyer	18.90
360 yds.	Clonmeen Garden	20.01
525 yds.	Dancing Jock	30.11
550 yds.	Dromore Printer	31.60
600 yds.	Ballet Festival	34.16
*360 yds.	Quiet Sergeant	21.05
*525 yds.	Greville Boy	31.06

NAVAN

350 yds.	Ougham Boreen	19.15
525 yds.	Aughavadden Tommie	29.35
550 yds.	Sarsfield Castle	31.20
	Fine Arrow	31.20
600 yds.	Star Witness	34.10

NEWBRIDGE

310 yds.	Brooklyn Orchard	17.82
350 yds.	P for Poor	19.88
525 yds.	Dusty Curragh	29.92
550 yds.	Calverstown Flower	31.89
600 yds.	Red Palmer	35.30
	Kilcar Darkie	35.30
*350 yds.	Chestnut Bridge	21.08
	Jigger Lee	21.08
*525 yds.	Gun Rattler	31.18

SHELBOURNE PARK

360 yds.	Kilbelin Battleship	19.80
525 yds.	Prince of Bermuda	28.98
550 yds.	Drumman Rambler	31.18
600 yds.	Galloping Home	33.95
	Castlemore	33.95
*525 yds.	Yobistrap	30.94
*550 yds.	Kyleside	32.60
*600 yds.	Old Son	35.82

THURLES

330 yds.	Hopalong Bob	18.20
360 yds.	Lisboney Grosvenor	20.20
525 yds.	Footless	29.75
600 yds.	Spanish Figtree	34.15
*330 yds.	Lucky Cleo	18.90
*360 yds.	Gambling Charlie	21.10
	Lord Fergus	21.10
*525 yds.	Ollys Playboy	30.70
*550 yds.	Golsto	31.60

TRALEE

315 yds.	Lomond Laddie	17.45
	Ballyard Dick	17.45
500 yds.	Sugar Prince	28.55
525 yds.	Brookville Tom	29.65
550 yds.	Another High Jack	31.10
	Footless	31.10
600 yds.	Glittering Smack	33.65
*525 yds.	Mushera Foreman	31.30

WATERFORD

310 yds.	Lough Legend	17.35
500 yds.	Knockeven Princess	28.90
525 yds.	Quare Customer	29.80
*525 yds.	Cosy Bar	30.60
*310 yds.	Dance It Sammy	18.15
	Fitzs Palm	18.15
*300 yds.	Cloghala Twinkle	29.65

YOUGHAL

325 yds.	Golden Sail	17.95
	Cahermore Jewel	17.95
350 yds.	Joyful Bob	19.65
500 yds.	Tillie O'Leer	28.90
525 yds.	Duchess Kitty	29.95
550 yds.	Castletown Express	31.50
	Yankee Sergeant	31.50

* Hurdles.

GREYHOUND QUIZ

1. How are greyhound track licensed?

*

2. How many meetings a year are tracks allowed by law?

*

3. Which trainer has won the Greyhound Derby most times?

*

4. What is his chief ambition?

*

5. If a dog's weight varies by 2 lb. from one race to another is it allowed to run?

*

QUIZ ANSWERS

1. By the local authority, Borough or County, according to the location of the track. 2. 108 on 104 appointed days. Most tracks hold double meetings on Bank Holidays. 3. Leslie Reynolds of Wembley. 4. To win the Waterloo Cup like his brother, Lewis Reynolds. 5. Yes. The weight variation must be more than 2 lbs. for it to be withdrawn.

Gymnastics

Compiled by Norris McWhirter

Athletics Correspondent: The Observer and B.B.C. Television Commentator

A BRIEF HISTORY

Gymnastics involving bodily exercises and disciplines were originally developed by the Greeks in the seventh century B.C., and were a prominent part of the ancient Olympic programme. With the deterioration of the Olympic movement into gladiatorial spectacles, competitive gymnastics virtually died out until a revival at the end of the eighteenth century.

Gymnastics were included among the original nine sports of the revived Olympic Games of 1896 in Athens. The events were, parallel bars (individual and team), horizontal bar (individual and team), pommelled horse, rings, vaulting horse and a rope climb. In 1900 there was a combined competition which comprised also a high jump, pole vault, long jump and tug-of-war.

The Americans in 1904 again revised the programme which was, as at Athens, dominated by the Germans.

The team competition at the London Olympics of 1908 involved large teams of over fifty gymnasts performing a heptathlon.

In Stockholm in 1912 the Swedes again won the competition, and the Italian, Alberto Braglia, retained his individual title. In 1924 the Swedish system was dropped from the programme and the original disciplines of 1896 were largely restored. At Los Angeles in 1932 the Americans inserted tumbling and Indian club swinging, but these were taken out by the Germans in Berlin in 1936, where women's events were first included.

The programme has at last become stabilised in the three post World War II celebrations with parallel bars, horizontal bar, pommelled horse, rings, vaulting horse, and free-standing exercises.

The Olympic champions are as follows:

OLYMPIC RESULTS
(MEN)
Combined Competitions
(Individual)

1900	S. Sandras (France)	
1904	Max Emmerich (U.S.A.) (triathlon)	
1904	Julius Lenhardt (U.S.A.) (hexathlon)	
1904	Anton Heida (U.S.A.) (7 apparatus)	
1904	Adolf Spinnler (Germany) (combined)	
1908	Alberto Braglia (Italy) (heptathlon)	
1912	Alberto Braglia (Italy)	
1920	Giorgio Zampori (Italy) (7 apparatus)	
1924	Leon Stukelj (Yugoslavia)	
1928	Georges Miez (Switzerland)	
1932	Romeo Neri (Italy)	
1932	István Pelle (Hungary) (calisthenics)	
1936	Alfred Schwarzmann (Germany)	
1948	Veikkö Huhtanen (Finland)	
1952	Viktor Tchukarin (U.S.S.R.)	
1956	Viktor Tchukarin (U.S.S.R.)	

Combined Competitions
(Team)

1904	U.S.A. I
1908	Sweden (team heptathlon)
1912	Sweden (Swedish System)

1912 Italy (prescribed apparatus)
1912 Norway (optional apparatus)
1920 Sweden (Swedish System)
1920 Italy (European System)
1920 Denmark (optional apparatus)
1924 Italy
1928 Switzerland
1932 Italy
1932 U.S.A. (Calisthenics)
1936 Germany
1948 Finland
1952 U.S.S.R.
1956 U.S.S.R.

Indian Clubs

1904 E. A. Hennig (U.S.A.)
1932 George Roth (U.S.A.)

Parallel Bars

1896 Alfred Flatow (Germany)
1904 George Eyser (U.S.A.)
1924 August Güttinger (Switzerland)
1928 Ladislav Vácha (Czechoslovakia)
1932 Romeo Neri (Italy)
1936 Konrad Frey (Germany)
1948 Michael Reusch (Switzerland)
1952 Hans Eugster (Switzerland)
1956 Viktor Tchukarin (U.S.S.R.)

Horizontal Bar

1896 Hermann Weingartner (Germany)
1904 {Anton Heida (U.S.A.)
      {E. A. Hennig (U.S.A.)
1924 Leon Stukelj (Czechoslovakia)
1928 Georges Miez (Switzerland)
1932 Dallas Bixler (U.S.A.)
1936 Aleksanteri Saarvala (Finland)
1948 Josef Stalder (Switzerland)
1952 Jack Günthard (Switzerland)
1956 T. Ono (Japan)

Pommelled Horse

1896 Louis Zutter (Switzerland)
1904 Anton Heida (U.S.A.)
1924 Josef Wilhelm (Switzerland)
1928 Hermann Hänggi (Switzerland)

1936 Konrad Frey (Germany)
1948 Paavo Aaltonen (Finland)
1952 Viktor Tchukarin (U.S.S.R.)
1956 Viktor Tchukarin (U.S.S.R.)

Rings

1896 Jean Mitropulos (Greece)
1904 Hermann Glass (U.S.A.)
1924 Franco Martino (Italy)
1928 Leon Stukelj (Yugoslavia)
1932 George Gulack (U.S.A.)
1936 Alois Hudec (Czechoslovakia)
1948 Karl Frei (Switzerland)
1952 Grant Shaginyan (U.S.S.R.)
1956 A. Azarian (U.S.S.R.)

Vaulting Horse

1896 Karl Schumann (Germany)
1904 Anton Heida (U.S.A.)
1924 Frank Kriz (U.S.A.) (lengthwise)
     A. Séguin (France) (sideways)
1928 Eugen Mack (Switzerland)
1932 Savino Guglielmetti (Italy)
       (lengthwise)
     István Pelle (Hungary) (sideways)
1936 Karl Schwarzmann (Germany)
1948 Paavo Aaltonen (Finland)
1952 Viktor Tchukarin (U.S.S.R.)
1956 {H. Bantz (Germany)
      {V. Muratov (U.S.S.R.)

Rope Climb

1896 Nicolaos Andriakopulos (Greece)
1904 George Eyser (U.S.A.)
1924 Bedrich Supcik (Czechoslovakia)
1932 Raymond Bass (U.S.A.)

Tumbling

1932 Rowland Wolfe (U.S.A.)

Free Standing Exercises

1936 Georges Miez (Switzerland)
1948 Ferenc Pataki (Hungary)
1952 Karl Thoresson (Sweden)
1956 V. Muratov (U.S.S.R.)

OLYMPIC RESULTS (WOMEN)

Combined (Team)

1928 Netherlands
1936 Germany
1948 Czechoslovakia
1952 U.S.S.R.
1956 U.S.S.R.

Combined (Individual)

1952 Maria Gorokhovskaya (U.S.S.R.)
1956 L. Latynina (U.S.S.R.)

Team Drill

1952 Sweden
1956 Hungary

Parallel Bars

1952 Margit Korondi (Hungary)
1956 Agnes Keleti (Hungary)

Vaulting Horse

1952 Yekaterina Kalunchuk (U.S.S.R.)
1956 L. Latynina (U.S.S.R.)

Floor Exercises

1952 Agnes Keleti (Hungary)
1956 {L. Latynina (U.S.S.R.)
      {Agnes Keleti (Hungary)

Beam

1952 Nina Bocharova (U.S.S.R.)
1956 Agnes Keleti (Hungary)

GYMNASTICS QUIZ

1. Where is the world's largest gymnasium?

*

2. What is the record for climbing a 20 ft. rope (hands alone)?

*

3. Who has been the most successful of all Olympic gymnasts?

*

4. What is the height of the greatest backward somersault ever recorded?

*

5. Who holds the feminine world record for repetitions in one-handed chinning the bar?

*

QUIZ ANSWERS

1. The Payne Whitney Gymnasium at Yale University at Newhaven, Connecticut, U.S.A., completed in 1932 at the cost of $18 million. 2. 2.8 secs. by Don Perry, U.S.A., at the University of Illinois on April 3, 1954. 3. Viktor Tchoukarine, U.S.S.R., with 5 gold, 3 silver (1 shared) and 1 bronze medal. 4. 7 ft. 6 ins. (one-footed take-off) by Dick Browning (U.S.A.) at Santa Barbara, California, in April 1954. 5. The 7 stone Lillian Lietzel (U.S.A.) with 17 left hand and 27 right hand.

Compiled by Norris McWhirter
Athletics Correspondent: The Observer and B.B.C. Television Commentator

Highland Games

HIGHLAND GAMES

The Highland Games of Scotland are of no great antiquity, and had their origin at Inverness and Braemar probably no earlier than 1824. This coincided with the period of the visit to Edinburgh in 1822 of King George IV (1820–1830), which touched off the great "Highland Cult" and the wearing of numerous tartans.

The early meetings were both crude and of very limited scope. With the arrival of Queen Victoria as the tenant of Balmoral Castle in 1848 Highland Games suddenly blossomed forth. The traditional programme of today began to take shape with the Braemar Gatherings on Deeside about the mid 1850's. The events comprised:

1. **Professional Athletics** (handicap races, running high leap, running flat leap, putting the stone (heavy and light), and throwing the shafted hammer and the 56 lb. weight for height. (Record 16 ft. 11¼ in. by P. Donovan, Feb. 20, 1914.) Later (after 1880) pole vaulting, "hop, step and leap", putting the iron 16 lb. shot, and relay racing were often added as professionalism lost ground to the amateur sport.
2. **Caber Tossing.** The earliest mention of the event was in July 1862. The word caber comes from the Gaelic *Cabar* =pole or spar. The greatest caber-tossing feat was the tossing of the 21-foot-long 230 lb. Braemar Caber in September 1951 at Braemar by George Clark. It had defied all previous comers, but has since been tossed three times by Sandy Grey.
3. **Highland Dancing in Costume.** The repertoire now includes reels, Strathspeys, the Highland Fling and Sword Dancing for adults, boys, girls and children.
4. **Piping Contests.** These are both for individuals and bands. Drumming contests are now sometimes added.
5. **Wrestling.** The Cumberland and catch as catch can are put on in preference to freestyle or Greco-Roman contests.
6. **Cycling.** With the advent of cycle racing in 1868, these events become increasingly usual with both handicap and pursuit races.
7. **Ben Running.** Local mountain races regularly feature in a number of gatherings.

The most famous traditional Highland Games staged annually are the Northern Meeting at Inverness, the Braemar Gathering on Deeside, the Oban Games and the Cowal Games. Since the war there have been annual "Highland Games" at Murrayfield, Edinburgh, with imported world-class amateur athletes and 5-a-side football. A similar Anglo-Scots promotion at the White City Stadium in London entitled "Caledonian Games" featured also Sheep Trials and the drum, pipe and fife bands of Scottish regiments. "Highland Games" continue to be staged in Canada, particularly British Columbia, Australia and New Zealand.

165

Hockey

Compiled by **David Wiggins**
Hockey Reporter

HOCKEY QUIZ

1. Easter appears to be a time of feverish activity. Is there special significance in the names chosen for the clubs engaged?

★

2. Does mixed hockey receive much support?

QUIZ ANSWERS

1. Clubs often play at festivals or on Sundays under a pseudonym and most are Saturday clubs in disguise. Others, including Ghosts, Tramps and Bacchanalians, were formed purely for festivals or tours and are expected to field teams of at least county strength. This admixture of players adds further to a game noted for its sociability. 2. Mixed hockey is not recognised by the Hockey Association or the All-England Women's Hockey Association. It is fairly widely played on Sundays and festive occasions, but is usually regarded as a hazardous sport and frowned upon by the majority of hockey enthusiasts of both sexes.

A BRIEF HISTORY

Man's natural inclination to hit a ball faster than he can run or harder than he can kick easily finds expression in hockey. The present-day game, skilfully played throughout the world and nowhere better than in India, has been evolved in the past 100 years from rough-and-tumble slogging matches with few rules and no administration. In that time, too, pitches have improved out of all recognition.

Although Blackheath's date of birth is obscure, records of the club exist after 1860 and they were responsible for drawing up the first set of rules as we know them today. The Hockey Association was founded in 1886, and for 15 years rapid expansion took place, the modern administrative framework emerged and regular county, divisional, and international fixtures commenced. Sticks became lighter and speed and skill replaced brute force.

The popularity of the game soon spread and the Northern Counties H.A. was formed in 1888, two years later playing the South for the first time. Oxford also first played Cambridge in the Inter-Varsity match that year, and by now alterations and additions to the rules were becoming frequent.

In 1892 the most far-reaching rule was passed, and one still jealously guarded today. It ensured that hockey remained the most widely-played purely amateur game in England: "no affiliated associations and no club belonging to the H.A. . . . and no player or member of any such club shall institute or take part in any hockey challenge cup or prize competition".

In 1894 reverse-stick play was permitted and the first men's international match between England and Ireland took place at Richmond. France became England's first Continental opponents in 1907, but it was not until 1950, when Holland won 3-0 at Amsterdam, that England suffered defeat by any European country.

Since then the record against foreign opposition has been indifferent, and although the game here grows in popularity and clubs and players increase annually, standards overseas have consistently improved. Great Britain entered for the three post-war Olympic Games tournaments, but India have comfortably remained champions since 1924.

Meanwhile in world hockey the English women's team continues to be pre-eminent. The game is well taught in the schools, and the available talent carefully watched in county and territorial matches to produce fine English sides. Tours and tournaments take place in all parts of the world, and national standards have progressed greatly since Ireland provided the first opposition in 1896. At Wembley in 1959 50,000 spectators saw England beat South Africa, and although such crowds watch hockey only once a year the game gives enjoyment to an ever-growing number of players each weekend in winter, and also nowadays on many summer evenings. It is refreshing still to find a sport catering essentially for the club player and with no cups, medals or financial rewards as inducement.

MEN'S INTERNATIONAL MATCH SUMMARY
Including season 1958-1959

	Played	Won		Drawn	Goals	
England v. Ireland	53	England 35	Ireland 11	7	England 149	Ireland 72
England v. Wales	50	England 49	Wales 0	1	England 270	Wales 44
England v. Scotland	45	England 36	Scotland 3	6	England 182	Scotland 44
England v. France	22	England 21	France 0	1	England 149	France 13
England v. Germany	4	England 1	Germany 1	2	England 12	Germany 7
England v. Holland	8	England 3	Holland 4	1	England 17	Holland 14
England v. Belgium	6	England 4	Belgium 1	1	England 18	Belgium 8
England v. Denmark	1	England 1	Denmark 0	0	England 5	Denmark 0
England v. S. Africa	5	England 1	S. Africa 1	3	England 9	S. Africa 9
England v. Kenya	1	England 1	Kenya 0	0	England 6	Kenya 4

SCHOOLS

	Played	Won		Drawn	Goals	
England v. Ireland	2	England 0	Ireland 1	1	England 2,	Ireland 3

N. F. Borrett

D. J. Carnill

J. A. Cockett

INTERNATIONAL MATCHES (MEN)
BRITISH HOCKEY BOARD (Instituted 1948)

Year	Place		Goals		Goals
1948	†At Park Royal	Great Britain 0		Switzerland	0
	†At Sudbury	Great Britain 8		Afghanistan	0
	†At Chiswick	Great Britain 11		U.S.A.	0
	†At Wembley	Great Britain 2		Pakistan	0
	†At Wembley	India 4		Great Britain	0
	At Amsterdam	Holland 4		Great Britain	1
	At Amsterdam	Great Britain 6		France	0
1952	At Amsterdam	Great Britain 5		Holland	4
	†At Helsinki	Great Britain 1		Belgium	0
	†At Helsinki	Great Britain 2		Pakistan	1
	†At Helsinki	India 3		Great Britain	1
1953	At Bristol	Great Britain 2		Belgium	2
1954	At Amsterdam	Great Britain 3		Holland	1
	At Brussels	Great Britain 5		France	0
	At Brussels	Great Britain 4		Switzerland	0
	At Brussels	Belgium 1		Great Britain	0
	At Brussels	Great Britain 1		Holland	1
1955	At Dunfermline	Holland 2		Great Britain	1
1956	At Newport (Mon.)	Great Britain 4		Germany	2
1957	†At Melbourne	Great Britain 2		Malaya	2
	†At Melbourne	Great Britain 1		Kenya	1
	†At Melbourne	Great Britain 2		Australia	1
	†At Melbourne	Great Britain 1		Australia	0
	†At Melbourne	Pakistan 3		Great Britain	2
	†At Melbourne	Germany 3		Great Britain	1
1959	At Hove	Great Britain 0		Belgium	1

† Olympic Games.

Played 26: Great Britain won 13; lost 8; drawn 5. Goals: for 66; against 36.

ENGLAND v. IRELAND
(Instituted 1895)

Year	Place	Winner	Score
1895	At Richmond	England	5-0
1896	At Dublin	England	1-0
1897	At Wimbledon	England	8-3
1898	At Dublin	Drawn	1-1
1899	At Richmond	England	3-1
1900	At Belfast	England	2-1
1901	At Surbiton	England	4-2
1902	At Dublin	England	2-0
1903	At Surbiton	England	1-0
1904	At Dublin	Ireland	3-2
1905	At Surbiton	England	4-1
1906	At Dublin	England	2-1
1907	At Bromley	England	5-0
1908	At Dublin	England	4-0
1909	At Dublin	England	8-0
1910	At Kensington	England	4-1
1911	At Dublin	Drawn	2-2
1912	At Beckenham	England	10-3
1913	At Dublin	England	1-0
1914	At Bournville	Drawn	2-2
1915-19	(No matches)		
1920	At Dublin	Ireland	3-2
1921	At Beckenham	Drawn	1-1
1922	At Dublin	England	3-2
1923	At Edgbaston	England	4-1
1924	At Dublin	Ireland	3-2
1925	At Edgbaston	England	4-2
1926	At Belfast	England	2-1
1927	At Liverpool	England	6-1
1928	At Belfast	Ireland	3-2
1929	At Folkestone	England	3-0
1930	At Dublin	Ireland	2-1
1931	At Edgbaston	England	5-3
1932	At Dublin	England	3-0
1933	At Beckenham	Ireland	2-0
1934	At Belfast	England	2-1
1935	At Bristol	England	4-0
1936	At Dublin	England	3-1
1937	At The Oval	Ireland	1-0
1938	At Belfast	Ireland	3-0
1939	At Birmingham	Ireland	1-0
1940-46	(No matches)		
1947	At Dublin	Ireland	2-1
1948	At Manchester	Drawn	2-2
1949	At Dublin	Ireland	3-2
1950	At Birmingham	England	3-2
1951	At Dublin	Drawn	1-1
1952	At Park Royal	England	5-1
1953	At Dublin	England	3-1
1954	At Blackpool	England	3-2
1955	At Dublin	England	3-2
1956	At Birmingham	England	4-1
1957	At Dublin	Drawn	0-0
1958	At Hove	England	2-1
1959	At Belfast	England	2-1

ENGLAND v. WALES
(Instituted 1898)

Year	Place	Winner	Score
1898	At Kersal, Man.	England	7-0
1899	At Newport	England	3-0
1900	At Kersal	England	10-0
1901	At Swansea	England	4-0
1902	At Kersal	England	7-0
1903	At Llandudno	England	6-3

1904	At Bath	England	4–1
1905	At Newport	England	6–0
1906	At Manchester	England	13–2
1907	At Llandudno	England	6–0
1908	At Bath	England	4–2
1909	At Swansea	England	6–0
1910	At Cambridge	England	9–0
1911	At Llandudno	England	7–0
1912	At Huddersfield	England	6–3
1913	At Whitchurch	England	3–0
1914	At West-s-Mare	England	6–2
1915–19	(No matches)		
1920	At Barry	England	8–1
1921	At Liverpool	England	5–1
1922	At Cardiff	England	8–0
1923	At Bristol	England	5–1
1924	At Ruthin	England	11–2
1925	At Merton Abbey	England	10–4
1926	At Abergavenny	England	4–0
1927	At Nottingham	England	2–0
1928	At Rhyl	England	9–0
1929	At Bristol	England	4–2
1930	At Whitchurch	England	2–0
1931	At Beckenham	England	5–3
1932	At Gobowen	England	7–2
1933	At Edgbaston	England	1–0
1934	At Penarth	Drawn	2–2
1935	At Great Crosby	England	6–2
1936	At Rhyl	England	4–1
1937	At Bristol	England	6–0
1938	At Cardiff	England	5–0
1939	At The Oval	England	4–1
1940–46	(No matches)		
1947	At Hawarden	England	3–1
1948	At Bristol	England	6–2
1949	At Abergavenny	England	7–0
1950	At Bournemouth	England	4–0
1951	At Hawarden	England	4–1
1952	At Bristol	England	5–0
1953	At Newport	England	4–2
1954	At Reading	England	6–2
1955	At Shotton	England	3–0
1956	At Guildford	England	2–0
1957	At Abergavenny	England	1–0
1958	At Bristol	England	5–1
1959	At Wrexham	England	5–0

ENGLAND v. SCOTLAND

(Instituted 1903)

1903	At Birmingham	England	5–0
1904	At Glasgow	Drawn	2–2
1905	At Surbiton	England	9–0
1906	At Glasgow	England	3–0
1907	At Birmingham	England	3–0
1908	At Edinburgh	England	3–1
1909	At Manchester	England	5–2
1910	At Aberdeen	England	3–0
1911	At Bristol	England	5–0
1912	At Edinburgh	Scotland	2–1
1913	At Beckenham	England	5–0
1914	At Glasgow	England	5–1
1915–19	(No matches)		
1920	At Birmingham	England	8–1
1921	At St. Andrews	England	8–0
1922	At Edgbaston	England	8–1
1923	At Aberdeen	England	9–1
1924	At Manchester	England	3–1
1925	At Perth	England	4–2
1926	At Bristol	England	3–2
1927	At Aberdeen	Scotland	4–3
1928	At Edgbaston	England	5–1
1929	At Glasgow	Scotland	3–0
1930	At Manchester	England	4–0
1931	At Perth	England	2–1
1932	At Brooklands	England	9–1
1933	At Peebles	Drawn	1–1
1934	At Beckenham	England	7–2
1935	At Edinburgh	England	2–1
1936	At Luton	England	2–0
1937	At St. Andrews	England	5–1
1938	At Liverpool	England	7–0
1939	At Paisley	England	1–0
1940–46	(No matches)		
1947	At Luton	England	1–0
1948	At Inverness	Drawn	1–1
1949	At Scarborough	Drawn	0–0
1950	At Aberdeen	England	5–2
1951	At Port Sunlight	England	4–2
1952	At Glasgow	England	7–0
1953	At Guildford	Drawn	3–3
1954	At Dundee	England	5–1
1955	At Norwich	England	5–3
1956	At Edinburgh	England	7–0
1957	At Leeds	England	1–0
1958	At Grangemouth	England	2–0
1959	At Sunderland	Drawn	1–1

ENGLAND v. FRANCE

(Instituted 1907)

1907	At Beckenham	England	14–0
1908	At Paris	Drawn	2–2
1909	At Acton	England	9–1
1910	At Paris	England	6–3
1911	At Folkestone	England	4–0
1912	At Paris	England	9–1
1913	At Cambridge	England	14–0
1914	At Paris	England	6–0
1915–21	(No matches)		
1922	At Beckenham	England	16–0
1923	At Paris	England	2–1
1924	At Folkestone	England	9–0
1925	At Paris	England	5–2
1926	At Folkestone	England	9–0
1927	At Paris	England	6–2
1928	At Folkestone	England	12–0
1929	At Le Touquet	England	8–1
1932	At Folkestone	England	5–1
1937	At Paris	England	2–0
1947	At Folkestone	England	2–1
1951	At Teddington	England	5–0
1952	At Boulogne	England	2–0
1957	At Eastbourne	England	2–0

ENGLAND v. GERMANY

(First official game 1913)

1913	At Beckenham	England	9–1
1931	At Hamburg	Drawn	1–1
1936	At Edgbaston	Drawn	2–2
1957	At Nottingham	Germany	3–0

ENGLAND v. HOLLAND

(First official game 1930)

1930	At Scarborough	England	9–1
1935	At Amsterdam	England	2–1
1939	At Luton	England	3–0
1950	At Amsterdam	Holland	3–0
1951	At Twickenham	Holland	3–2
1953	At Nottingham	Drawn	1–1
1955	At Amsterdam	Holland	3–0
1959	At Hurlingham	Holland	2–0

ENGLAND v. BELGIUM

(First official game 1933)

1933	At Brussels	England	3–1
1938	At Worthing	England	7–1
1948	At Brussels	Drawn	2–2
1951	At Twickenham	Belgium	1–0
1955	At Bournemouth	England	3–2
1956	At Brussels	England	3–1

ENGLAND v. DENMARK

(First official game 1954)

1954	At Folkestone	England	5–0

ENGLAND v. S. AFRICA

(Instituted 1957)

1957	At Reading	S. Africa	2–1
1958	At Port Elizabeth	Drawn	2–2
1958	At Durban	England	3–2
1958	At Johannesburg	Drawn	1–1
1958	At Salisbury	Drawn	2–2

ENGLAND v. KENYA

(Instituted 1958)

1958	At Nairobi	England	6–4

ENGLAND SCHOOLS v. IRELAND

1958	At Dublin	Drawn	1–1
1959	At Park Royal	Ireland	2–1

INTER-DIVISIONALS

NORTH v. SOUTH

(Instituted 1890)

1890	South	6–0	1906	South	7–2
1891	South	5–0	1907	South	4–2
1892	South	4–2	1908	South	4–1
1893	South	4–2	1909	South	6–2
1894	Drawn	2–2	1910	North	3–2
1895	South	3–2	1911	North	2–1
1896	South	4–2	1913	South	5–0
1897	South	1–0	1914	South	4–3
1898	South	4–2	1921	South	4–0
1899	South	3–2	1923	South	2–1
1900	North	2–0	1925	South	6–2
1901	North	4–1	1927	South	2–1
1902	South	5–0	1929	Drawn	2–2
1903	South	9–0	1932	South	14–0
1904	South	6–3	1935	South	1–0
1905	South	4–2	1937	South	5–3

1939	Brooklands	South	3–1
1949	Worthing	South	3–0
1951	Crosby	South	5–3
1954	Folkestone	North	3–2
1956	Liverpool	South	4–0
1959	Guildford	South	5–4

Played 38 South won 31 North 5 Drawn 2 Goals: South 152 North 61

MIDLANDS v. NORTH

(Instituted 1895)

1895	Sale	North	5–1
1896	Edgbaston	North	4–2
1897	Kersal	North	1–0
1898	Edgbaston	North	3–2
1899	Kersal	North	3–2
1900	Wolverhampton	North	3–2
1901	Kersal	Drawn	2–2
1902	Olton	Midlands	4–0
1903	Manchester	North	3–1
1904	Olton	Midlands	2–1
1905	Olton	North	2–1
1906	Derby	Midlands	4–1
1907	Darlington	Midlands	5–1
1908	Birmingham	Midlands	4–3
1909	Scarborough	Midlands	5–1
1910	Derby	North	3–2
1911	Crosby	Midlands	3–2
1912	Nottingham	Drawn	5–5
1914	Manchester	Midlands	6–5
1920	Manchester	North	5–1
1922	Nottingham	North	8–1
1924	Sheffield	North	6–2
1926	Walsall	North	3–1
1928	Warrington	Midlands	6–4
1930	Crosby	North	4–2
1933	Crosby	North	3–2
1938	Nottingham	North	2–1
1948	Nottingham	Midlands	5–4
1953	Northampton	Midlands	3–0
1957	Manchester	Midlands	2–0
1958	Northampton	North	4–1

Played 31 North won 17 Midlands 12 Drawn 2 Goals: North 91 Midlands 80

NORTH v. WEST

(Instituted 1905)

1905	Tewkesbury	North	4–2
1906	Bowdon	North	2–1
1907	Cheltenham	North	3–2
1908	Manchester	North	8–2
1909	Cheltenham	North	2–1
1910	Manchester	North	2–1
1911	Cheltenham	North	5–0
1913	Brooklands	North	6–1
1921	Derby	West	3–1
1923	Nottingham	North	8–0
1927	Sheffield	North	6–3
1929	Cheltenham	West	5–2
1931	Northwich	West	6–2
1934	Cheltenham	North	3–1
1936	Warrington	North	3–2
1948	Crosby	North	2–1
1950	Hereford	West	3–2
1953	Manchester	North	4–2
1955	Hereford	West	3–1

Played 19 North won 14 West 5 Drawn 0 Goals: North 65 West 39

MIDLANDS v. SOUTH

(Instituted 1897)

1897	Surbiton	South	5–1
1898	Erdington	Midlands	1–0
1900	Richmond	Midlands	2–0
1901	Edgbaston	Midlands	2–1
1902	Surbiton	Drawn	2–2
1903	Coventry	South	3–2
1904	Bromley	South	2–0
1905	Erdington	South	3–2
1906	Bromley	South	5–1
1907	Edgbaston	South	2–1
1908	Bromley	South	1–0
1909	Bournville	Drawn	1–1
1910	Beckenham	Midlands	3–2
1911	Bournville	Midlands	3–2
1912	Bromley	South	4–1
1914	Northampton	South	4–1
1920	Beckenham	South	4–2
1921	Edgbaston	Drawn	3–3
1923	Surbiton	South	3–0
1925	Northampton	Drawn	2–2
1927	Kent House	South	3–2
1929	Leicester	South	3–0
1931	Reading	South	4–0
1933	Wellesbourne	South	8–0
1934	Oxford	Drawn	3–3
1936	Teddington	Midlands	5–4
1939	Coventry	South	4–1
1948	Slough	South	3–1
1950	Nottingham	South	6–2
1953	Kent House	South	2–1
1955	Edgbaston	South	8–1
1958	Slough	South	5–0

Played 32 South won 21 Midlands 6 Drawn 5 Goals: South 102 Midlands 46

MIDLANDS v. WEST

(Instituted 1895)

1895	Cheltenham	West	1–0
1896	Chester Road	Midlands	4–3
1897	Cheltenham	Midlands	3–2
1898	Wolverhampton	Midlands	2–1
1899	Bristol	West	4–0
1900	Erdington	Midlands	3–0
1901	Weston-s-Mare	Midlands	4–2
1902	Erdington	Midlands	7–0
1903	Weston-s-Mare	West	2–1
1904	Pershore	Midlands	3–2
1905	Bath	Midlands	2–0
1906	Bromsgrove	Midlands	9–1
1907	Taunton	Midlands	6–0
1908	Worcester	Midlands	3–2
1909	Bristol	Midlands	3–0
1910	Hampton-in-A	Drawn	2–2
1911	Weston-s-Mare	Drawn	2–2
1912	Wolverhampton	Midlands	2–1
1913	Bristol	Midlands	10–2
1914	Edgbaston	Midlands	5–1
1922	Bristol	West	4–2
1924	Leamington	Midlands	5–3
1926	Weston-s-Mare	Midlands	3–1
1928	Nottingham	West	3–1
1930	Evesham	Drawn	3–3
1932	Marlborough C.	West	3–0
1935	Evesham	Drawn	3–3
1937	Cheltenham	Midlands	5–1
1949	Evesham	Midlands	3–1
1954	Coventry	Drawn	1–1
1956	Gloucester	West	2–1
1959	Leamington	Midlands	3–1

Played 32 Midlands won 20 West 7 Drawn 5 Goals: Midlands 101 West 54

WEST v. SOUTH

(Instituted 1901)

1901	Teddington	West	4–2
1902	Bristol	South	4–3
1903	Surbiton	South	4–1
1904	Weston-s-Mare	Drawn	2–2
1905	Surbiton	South	7–0
1906	Cheltenham	South	3–0
1907	Bromley	South	13–0
1908	Bristol	West	4–3
1909	Oxford	South	3–1
1910	Exeter	South	2–1
1911	Oxford	Drawn	2–2
1913	Bristol	South	2–0
1922	Oxford	South	9–2
1924	Weston-s-Mare	South	4–0
1926	Reading	South	3–1
1928	Weston-s-Mare	South	7–4
1930	Weston-s-Mare	West	3–2
1933	Hove	South	6–3
1936	Newton Abbott	West	2–0
1938	Purley	Drawn	2–2
1947	Hereford	West	3–0
1950	Reading	Drawn	2–2
1952	Canford School	South	5–1
1957	New Beckenham	South	2–1

Played 24 South won 15 West 5 Drawn 4 Goals: South 88 West 42

HOCKEY QUIZ

1. What clubs are affiliated direct to Divisional Associations and not to counties?

★

2. Name the date of publication of the first issue of *Hockey News*.

★

3. When and for what purpose was the British Hockey Board formed?

★

4. State when the County Championship was instituted and name the winners to date.

★

5. When and where was the striking circle first introduced into hockey?

★

6. What games of similar derivation to hockey are still played in (*a*) Ireland; (*b*) Scotland; (*c*) Wales?

QUIZ ANSWERS

1. Oxford University to the South. Cambridge University to the East. Occidentals to the West. 2. September 1951. 3. In 1948 England, Scotland and Wales formed the British Hockey Board as an essential preliminary to entering a team representing Great Britain in the Olympic Games. The Board is now responsible for raising, entering and managing British teams in such events or for tours undertaken by the three countries and Northern Ireland jointly. 4. 1957–58 Season. Lincolnshire defeated Warwickshire in 1958, and Middlesex beat Gloucestershire in the 1959 final. 5. By Teddington Hockey Club at Bushey Park in 1876. 6. (*a*) Hurling; (*b*) Shinty; (*c*) Bandy.

EAST v. WEST
(Instituted 1909)

Year	Venue	Winner	Score
1909	St. Albans	East	3–0
1910	Weston-s-Mare	West	4–3
1911	Cambridge	East	4–1
1912	Bristol	East	3–0
1913	Cambridge	East	10–2
1914	Cheltenham	East	6–2
1921	Bristol	East	4–0
1923	Cambridge	East	6–1
1925	Cheltenham	East	5–4
1927	Bedford	East	6–2
1929	Weston-s-Mare	East	5–3
1931	Weston-s-Mare	East	1–0
1934	Luton	West	3–0
1938	Bristol	West	5–2
1948	Exeter	West	3–1
1952	Watford	West	4–3
1953	Swindon	East	3–0
1957	Broxbourne	Drawn	0–0
1958	Innsworth	Drawn	1–1

Played 19 East won 12 West 5
Drawn 2 Goals: East 68 West 37

EAST v. MIDLANDS
(Instituted 1909)

Year	Venue	Winner	Score
1909	Coventry	Midlands	6–1
1910	Cambridge	Midlands	6–3
1911	Leicester	Midlands	3–1
1912	Bedford	East	4–1
1913	Birmingham	East	4–0
1920	Edgbaston	Midlands	5–2
1921	Cambridge	East	6–1
1923	Birmingham	East	4–1
1925	Lincoln	Drawn	2–2
1927	Coventry	East	4–2
1929	Bedford	Drawn	4–4
1932	Nottingham	East	4–1
1935	Gainsborough	Drawn	2–2
1937	Cheddleton	Midlands	4–3
1939	Norwich	East	2–1
1950	Chelmsford	Midlands	3–2
1952	Leicester	Midlands	6–4
1955	Lincoln	East	5–1
1957	Edgbaston	Drawn	3–3

Played 19 East won 8 Midlands 7
Drawn 4 Goals: East 60 Midlands 54

EAST v. NORTH
(Instituted 1909)

Year	Venue	Winner	Score
1909	Cambridge	East	5–2
1910	Newcastle	East	4–2
1911	Ipswich	Drawn	1–1
1912	Brooklands	East	2–1
1914	Cambridge	East	8–4
1922	Cambridge	East	4–3
1924	Bowdon	North	7–2
1926	Loughton	East	3–2
1928	Brooklands	East	5–1
1931	Bedford	East	4–2
1934	Doncaster	North	3–2
1936	Norwich	East	2–0
1938	Warrington	North	8–0
1947	Watford	North	5–0
1949	Sheffield	East	2–1
1951	Lincoln	Drawn	1–1
	(Abandoned)		
1954	Newcastle	Drawn	0–0

Played 16 East won 10 North 4
Drawn 2 Goals: East 44 North 42

SOUTH v. EAST
(Instituted 1909)

Year	Venue	Winner	Score
1909	Beckenham	South	5–2
1910	St. Albans	South	4–3
1911	Beckenham	South	4–2
1913	Broxbourne	East	3–2
1920	Cambridge	South	3–2
1922	Beckenham	South	4–1
1924	Cambridge	South	6–2
1926	Bromley	East	5–3
1928	Luton	Drawn	2–2
1930	Folkestone	Drawn	1–1
1932	Skegness	South	5–2
1935	Beckenham	East	2–1
1947	Southgate	East	3–1
1949	Norwich	South	6–1
1951	Folkestone	Drawn	1–1
1953	Felixstowe	South	5–0
1959	Cambridge	South	4–1

Played 17 South won 10 East 4
Drawn 3 Goals: South 57 East 33

WOMEN'S INTERNATIONAL MATCH SUMMARY
Including Season 1958-1959

	Played	Won		Drawn	Goals	
England v. Ireland	52	England 45	Ireland 4	3	England 260	Ireland 59
England v. Scotland	47	England 44	Scotland 2	1	England 231	Scotland 50
England v. Wales	32	England 32	Wales 0	0	England 276	Wales 23
England v. France	2	England 2	France 0	0	England 33	France 0
England v. S. Africa	3	England 3	S. Africa 0	0	England 28	S. Africa 2
England v. Australia	2	England 1	Australia 0	1	England 9	Australia 1
England v. Denmark	1	England 1	Denmark 0	0	England 10	Denmark 0
England v. Germany	2	England 2	Germany 0	0	England 11	Germany 4
England v. Holland	5	England 5	Holland 0	0	England 18	Holland 0
England v. U.S.A.	3	England 3	U.S.A. 0	0	England 30	U.S.A. 2
England v. Belgium	3	England 3	Belgium 0	0	England 25	Belgium 1

WOMEN'S INTERNATIONAL MATCH RESULTS

ENGLAND v. IRELAND

Year	Result	E.	I.
1896	Ireland	0	2
1897	Draw	0	0
1898	England	1	0
1899	England	3	1
1900	England	2	1
1901	England	3	1
1902	Ireland	1	5
1903	England	7	1
1904	England	1	0
1905	England	3	1
1906	England	2	0
1907	England	7	3
1908	Ireland	2	4
1909	England	4	0
1910	England	6	1
1911	England	4	3
1912	England	8	0
1913	England	9	0
1914	England	7	2
1920	England	16	2
1921	England	8	1
1922	England	11	0
1923	England	3	0
1924	England	5	1
1925	England	11	1
1926	England	10	1
1927	England	8	0
1928	England	11	0
1929	England	2	1
1930	England	3	2
1931	England	6	1
1932	England	9	0
1933	England	4	1
1934	England	7	3
1935	England	6	2
1936	England	3	1
1937	England	5	0
1938	England	9	2
1939	England	3	0
1947	Draw	0	0
1948	England	5	1
1949	England	3	0
1950	Ireland	3	5
1951	England	6	1
1952	England	1	0
1953	England	5	2
1954	England	5	0
1955	England	8	0
1956	England	2	1
1957	England	2	0
1958	Draw	2	2
1959	England	8	2

ENGLAND v. SCOTLAND

Year	Result	E.	S.
1902	England	4	0
1903	England	11	0
1904	England	7	2
1905	Draw	1	1
1906	England	4	1
1907	England	2	1
1908	England	5	1
1909	Scotland	1	4
1910	England	6	0
1911	England	3	1
1912	England	4	1
1913	England	6	1
1914	England	6	0
1920	England	6	1
1921	England	11	0
1922	England	4	0
1923	England	13	0
1924	England	6	1
1925	England	7	2
1926	England	1	0
1927	England	5	0
1928	England	6	1
1929	England	4	1
1930	England	8	0
1931	England	8	0
1932	England	5	0
1933	Scotland	1	2
1934	England	3	1
1935	England	5	1
1936	England	1	0
1937	England	3	0
1938	England	4	1
1939	England	4	3
1946	England	4	3
1947	England	4	1
1948	England	5	0
1949	England	3	2
1950	England	6	2
1951	England	8	1
1952	England	9	2
1953	England	5	1
1954	England	5	2
1955	England	7	5
1956	England	5	3
1957	England	3	1
1958	England	5	2
1959	England	7	0

ENGLAND v. WALES

Year	Result	E.	W.
1900	England	13	0
1901	England	13	0
1902	England	15	0
1924	England	13	0
1925	England	8	0
1926	England	20	0
1927	England	11	1
1928	England	5	1
1929	England	2	0
1930	England	8	0
1931	England	10	0
1932	England	6	1
1933	England	6	3
1934	England	6	2
1935	England	2	1
1936	England	10	2
1937	England	10	2
1938	England	11	0
1939	England	8	1
1947	England	8	0
1948	England	7	1
1949	England	13	1
1950	England	11	1
1951	England	10	2
1952	England	12	2
1953	England	6	1
1954	England	10	1
1955	England	6	0
1956	England	6	0
1957	England	6	0
1958	England	5	1
1959	England	6	1

ENGLAND v. FRANCE

Year	Result	E.	F.
1923	England	23	0
1924	England	10	0

ENGLAND v. SOUTH AFRICA

Year	Result	E.	S.A.
1927	England	11	0
1936	England	13	1
1959	England	4	1

ENGLAND v. AUSTRALIA

Year	Result	E.	A.
1931	England	8	0
1959	Draw	1	1

ENGLAND v. DENMARK

Year	Result	E.	D.
1933	England	10	0

ENGLAND v. GERMANY

Year	Result	E.	G.
1935	England	6	4
1937	England	5	0

ENGLAND v. HOLLAND

Year	Result	E.	H.
1938	England	8	0
1950	England	1	0
1955	England	4	1
1956	England	4	0
1957	England	1	0

ENGLAND v. U.S.A.

Year	Result	E.	U.S.A.
1924	England	17	1
1933	England	7	1
1956	England	6	0

ENGLAND v. BELGIUM

Year	Result	E.	B.
1952	England	2	1
1953	England	11	0
1954	England	12	0

HOCKEY QUIZ

1. Name the patron of the Hockey Association.

2. Name a hockey personality who has (a) played for his country; (b) umpired an international match; (c) played cricket for his county.

3. Who is the Hon. Secretary and Treasurer of the International Hockey Board?

4. Name the managers of the Great Britain Olympic XIs at (a) Helsinki; (b) Melbourne.

5. Who is the national coach to the Hockey Association?

6. Name the outstanding England players in post-war hockey.

7. The above players are all defenders. Has the supply of high-class forwards been as good?

8. Are the prospects for the future any brighter?

9. Women's hockey now attracts a crowd of 50,000 to their international match at Wembley. Will the men ever do this?

QUIZ ANSWERS

1. H.M. Queen Elizabeth II. 2. C. T. A. Wilkinson. 3. M. G. Cowlishaw. 4. (a) R. Y. Fison; (b) E. S. Hoare. 5. S. D. Dickins. 6. D. J. Carnill, J. A. Cockett and A. J. B. Robinson, between them, have gained 122 caps since the war. All three are, or were, players of the highest class and have also appeared in two Olympic Games hockey tournaments. 7. N. F. Borrett with 30 caps and J. V. Conroy (28) are outstanding post-war forwards of different eras. England's poor record against overseas opposition is largely attributable on the field to a lack of high-class forwards and weaknesses near goal. Very few stick players have emerged; and while, it is easier to defend than to attack, too few goals have been scored to give sound defences a fair chance. 8. Training programmes, the coaching of coaches, an instructional film and a general awareness of our international shortcomings are all healthy signs. Though a careful eye is kept on schoolboy players and the popularity of hockey continues to increase, it is hard for such a purely amateur sport with its consequent shortage of funds to make quick progress. 9. Very unlikely. Hockey is only a minor sport for men and Wembley is largely filled by schoolgirls. If a national ground in London was obtained and home internationals always played there on dates fixed well in advance, then 5,000 to 10,000 should be attending regularly. At present hockey's great attraction is always as a sport to be played and the success of the Easter festivals epitomizes this.

COMBINED SERVICES
(Instituted 1920)

Year	Place		Goals		Goals
1921	Wimbledon	South	8	Army & R.A.F.	0
1921	Bristol	Royal Navy	4	The West	3
1922	Birmingham	Com. Services	1	Midlands	1
1922	Bromley	South	5	Com. Services	0
1923	Portsmouth	Com. Services	4	West	4
1923	Sheffield	Com. Services	2	The North	2
1924	Bedford	East	3	Com. Services	0
1924	Bristol	Com. Services	6	West	2
1924	Portsmouth	Com. Services	1	South	1
1925	Roehampton	Com. Services	3	Midlands	3
1926	Chatham	North	4	Com. Services	0
1926	Teddington	Com. Services	3	South	2
1927	Bristol	Com. Services	2	West	0
1927	Birmingham	Midlands	2	Com. Services	1
1928	Hove	South	3	Com. Services	1
1928	York	Com. Services	3	North	1
1929	Aldershot	Com. Services	0	Midlands	1
1929	Portsmouth	Com. Services	1	West	0
1930	Grimsby	East	4	Com. Services	2
1930	Uxbridge	Com. Services	7	North	2
1931	Aldershot	Com. Services	3	South	2
1931	Nottingham	Midlands	2	Com. Services	2
1932	Portsmouth	West	7	Com. Services	1
1932	Leeds University	Com. Services	4	North	2
1933	Luton	East	6	Com. Services	2
1933	Uxbridge	North	3	Com. Services	2
1934	Nottingham	Midlands	2	Com. Services	2
1934	Aldershot	Com. Services	1	South	1
1935	Hereford	West	5	Com. Services	3
1935	Chatham	North	2	Com. Services	0
1936	Uxbridge	Com. Services	5	East	2
1936	Leicester	Com. Services	2	Midlands	2
1937	Aldershot	West	6	Com. Services	0
1937	Lytham	North	3	Com. Services	1
1938	Portsmouth	Com. Services	2	Midlands	2
1938	Folkestone	South	5	Com. Services	2
1939		Com. Services	3	West	2
1939	Brentwood	East	3	Com. Services	1
1947	Portsmouth	Midlands	4	Com. Services	2
1948	St. Albans	Com. Services	3	East	1
1948	Portsmouth	Com. Services	1	South	0
1949	Uxbridge	Midlands	3	Com. Services	1
1949	Swindon	West	4	Com. Services	1
1950	Manchester	Com. Services	3	North	3
1950	Aldershot	Com. Services	3	East	2
1951	Olton	Midlands	5	Com. Services	1
1951	Portsmouth	Com. Services	4	West	3
1952	Halton	Com. Services	4	North	1
1952	Slough	Com. Services	7	South	1
1953	Peterborough	East	3	Com. Services	3
1953	Aldershot	Com. Services	4	South	0
1954	Weston-s-Mare	Com. Services	6	West	1
1954	Eastney	Com. Services	3	Midlands	1
1955	Uxbridge	Com. Services	2	East	0
1956	Edgbaston	Com. Services	3	Midlands	0
1957	Worthing	South	1	Com. Services	0
1957	Chatham	Com. Services	5	North	0
1958	Colchester	East	5	Com. Services	1
1958	Uxbridge	South	7	Com. Services	1
1959	Weston-s-Mare	Com. Services	1	West	0
1959	Chatham	Com. Services	6	Midlands	4

Played 61. Com. Services won 25 Lost 25 Drawn 11. Goals: Com. Services 145 Other Divisions 156

OXFORD UNIVERSITY v. CAMBRIDGE UNIVERSITY
(Instituted 1890)

Year	Place	Winners	Score
1890	Oxford	Oxford	2–1
1891	Queen's Club	Oxford	3–2
1892	Queen's Club	Drawn	2–2
1893	Richmond	Oxford	3–1
1894	Richmond	Drawn	1–1
1895	Richmond	Drawn	3–3
1896	Richmond	Cambridge	3–1
1897	Richmond	Cambridge	4–0
1898	Richmond	Cambridge	4–0
1899	Richmond	Cambridge	5–2
1900	Richmond	Cambridge	3–2
1901	Richmond	Cambridge	4–1
1902	Richmond	Oxford	3–2
1903	Surbiton	Oxford	3–0
1904	Surbiton	Oxford	1–0
1905	Surbiton	Oxford	3–1
1906	Surbiton	Cambridge	4–1
1907	Bromley	Cambridge	3–2
1908	Bromley	Cambridge	3–1
1909	Beckenham	Oxford	6–3
1910	Beckenham	Oxford	5–4
1911	Beckenham	Cambridge	4–1
1912	Beckenham	Oxford	3–1
1913	Beckenham	Cambridge	7–2
1914	Beckenham	Oxford	2–1
1920	Beckenham	Oxford	3–1
1921	Beckenham	Cambridge	4–1
1922	Beckenham	Cambridge	3–2
1923	Beckenham	Cambridge	4–1
1924	Beckenham	Oxford	3–0
1925	Beckenham	Oxford	3–2
1926	Beckenham	Cambridge	3–2
1927	Beckenham	Cambridge	4–1
1928	Beckenham	Cambridge	5–1
1929	Beckenham	Cambridge	3–1
1930	Beckenham	Drawn	2–2
1931	Beckenham	Oxford	3–2
1932	Beckenham	Drawn	1–1
1933	Beckenham	Cambridge	2–0
1934	Beckenham	Cambridge	4–1
1935	Beckenham	Drawn	0–0
1936	Beckenham	Drawn	1–1
1937	Beckenham	Oxford	3–0
1938	Beckenham	Drawn	1–1
1939	Beckenham	Cambridge	3–2
1946	Beckenham	Drawn	3–3
1947	Beckenham	Cambridge	3–0
1948	Beckenham	Cambridge	2–0
1949	Beckenham	Oxford	3–1
1950	Beckenham	Cambridge	1–0
1951	Beckenham	Oxford	4–0
1952	Beckenham	Cambridge	6–3
1953	Beckenham	Oxford	5–2
1954	Beckenham	Oxford	3–1
1955	Beckenham	Cambridge	2–1
1956	Beckenham	Cambridge	2–0
1957	Beckenham	Drawn	0–0
1958	Edgbaston	Oxford	5–1
1959	Edgbaston	Drawn	0–0

Played 59. Cambridge won 27; Oxford 21; drawn 11. Goals: Cambridge 135; Oxford 112.

D. D. Archer

A. J. B. Robinson

D. S. Milford

ENGLISH POST-WAR INTERNATIONAL PLAYERS

Names	Matches played		Names	Matches played
ABELL, T. G.	5		HINDLE, J.	14
ADLARD, R. E.	4		HOLMES, E.	6
AITKEN, J. B.	8		HUDSON, A. J.	2
ARCHER, D. D.	24		HUDSON, G.	3
ARGYLE, R. M.	3		HUGHES, C. H.	3
AUSTEN, P. B.	12		ISSITT, R.	2
BAYLIS, G. A.	7		IVENS, J. F. B.	14
BELLERBY, J. D.	1		JONES, W. H. R.	3
BERRILL, H. M.	2		KEY, C. J.	1
BORRETT, N. F.	30		KITTRELL, M. R.	11
BROOKS-HILL, F.	3		LEDGER, P. K.	6
BUNNELL, J. K.	5		MAPLES, J. S.	6
BUTTON, E. N.	5		MIDGLEY, R. K.	3
CAMPBELL, I. P.	4		MILLER, D. R.	3
CARNILL, D. J.	41		NEILL, J. W.	8
CLARE, P. A.	1		NORRIS, R. O. A.	17
CLARKE, I. M.	5		NUNN, A. S.	2
COCKETT, J. A.			NUTTALL, R. H.	4
CONROY, J. V.	37		OSBORNE, L. W. A.	1
COOKE, D. W.	28		PEAKE, J. M.	4
DANN, A. J.	4		PITT, W. A.	4
DAREWSKI, B. R.	9		PORTER, T. R.	5
DAVIS, F. H. V.	4		REYNOLDS, F. O.	12
DAY, D. M.	22		RIDDINGTON, G. M.	2
DICKINS, S. D.	14		ROBINSON, A. J. B.	44
DODDS, R. L.	3		ROWAN, Sir Leslie, K.C.B., C.V.O.	31
DOUGHTY, M. O. H.	5		SCHAD, R. C.	4
EADES, P. F.	8		SELF, F. G.	4
ELLERTON, G. H.	4		SELLEY, W. T.	4
EVANS, J. B.	1		SMITH, P. D. R.	25
EWING GAY, W. A. H.	18		SMITH, R. D.	19
FLETCHER, R. A.	10		STOCKS, J. C. G.	5
FORSTER, N. M.	22		STROVER, J. A.	14
GALE, P. M. H. P.	15		STUDD, C. A.	2
GREENE, W. O.	1		THOMPSON, C. J.	1
GROVE, R.	12		TURNER, M. L.	1
HEIDEN, C. G.	2		WALFORD, D.	3
			WALFORD, M. M.	17
			WESTON, D. B. S.	3
			WHITBREAD, P.	11
			WILMAN, D.	4
			WOOTTON, J. C.	4
			WOOTTON, W. A.	6
			WYATT, C. E. N.	30

HOCKEY QUIZ

1. Has an umpire the power to stop (conclude) a match before full time?

*

2. Can a game of hockey be played under International Hockey Board rules with a red cricket ball?

*

3. What is the weight of a hockey stick?

*

4. What is the maximum legal length of a stick?

*

5. What happens if a penalty bully is awarded and the offending player is so incapacitated that he cannot defend it?

*

6. What provision is made in the rules if both umpires whistle simultaneously, and award free hits in opposite directions?

*

7. State the award when a shot inside the circle is going wide, strikes the umpire and is deflected into goal.

8. State the minimum size of a hockey pitch.

*

9. When is a goal scored without the ball crossing the goal line?

*

10. When was (a) the radius of the striking circle increased to 16 yards; (b) the 16-yard hit introduced as a rule?

*

11. When does a 25 yard bully now take place?

*

12. A player in an offside position in the opponents' half of the field sees a pass coming towards him from his own defence. Should he be penalized if he comes back into his own half to collect it?

QUIZ ANSWERS

1. No. It is the captains' decision. 2. Yes. Rule 6 (c) says a ball of any description may be used as agreed by the captains. 3. Not to exceed 28 oz., not less than 12 oz. 4. None. 5. Any other player on his side may deputise. 6. None. A bully would be the expected outcome. 7. A goal. 8. 100 yards by 55 yards. 9. By the defender committing an offence at a penalty bully. 10. (a) 1950; (b) 1958. 11. After a successfully defended penalty bully. 12. Yes.

Horse Racing

Compiled by
A. I. C. W. Stubbs,
Solon of the Sporting Life

A BRIEF HISTORY OF RACING

Racing goes back a long way. It is recorded that the earliest race in this country took place about A.D. 210 at Netherby in Yorkshire. Roman Emperor Septimus Alexander was responsible.

It was not until many years later, in the reign of Richard I, that horse racing became fashionable. In King Henry II's reign they raced where the famous Smithfield meat market is now situated.

In the year 1377 the Prince of Wales, who afterwards became King Richard II, raced against the Earl of Arundel. In those days racing consisted mostly of matches between the nobles.

Chester is the oldest racecourse. The Roodee was opened in 1540 during the reign of King Henry VIII. Racing took place around 1574 at Croydon and on Salisbury Plain. Queen Elizabeth was a frequent attender.

During the reign of James I there were courses at Enfield and Garterley. There was no prize money and winners received golden and silver bells. James I had studs at Tutbury, Hampton Court, Eltham and Cole Park.

RACING QUIZ

1. How many classic winners did Fred Archer ride?

★

2. Name Sir Gordon Richards last mount in public?

★

3. How many times did Golden Miller run in the Grand National?

★

4. Name the horse who finished second three times in the Cambridgeshire.

★

5. When was the first meeting held at Gatwick?

★

6. Who was the lightest jockey ever to ride in public?

QUIZ ANSWERS

1. Twenty-one. 2,000 guineas (4 times), 1,000 guineas (twice), Derby (5 times), Oaks, (4 times), St. Leger (6 times). 2. Loundon, third in the Eclipse Stakes at Sandown on July 10th 1954. 3. Five. In 1933 (fell), 1934 (won), 1935 (unseated rider), 1936 (fell), 1937 (refused). 4. Bendigo, second in 1884, 1885, 1887. 5. 1891. 6. Kitchener. His weight was 3 stone 7 lb. when he won the Chester Cup in 1844. It is reported that four years earlier, at Ascot, he weighed only 2 stone 1 lb.

By now racing was taking a firm hold and meetings were being held at Newmarket, Doncaster, Liverpool, York and Lincoln.

Only when Charles I came to the throne were different prizes instituted. The Newmarket Gold Cup first took place in 1634. In 1640 the first racing took place at Hyde Park.

Betting with wagers of £1,000 and more, and cups taking the place of the bells all showed that horse racing was becoming increasingly more popular. Races up to six miles were run and weights varied between ten and seventeen stone.

Council of State under the Commonwealth prohibited racing in 1654. But it was restored when Charles II came to the throne.

It was the Merry Monarch who decreed that Newmarket should be the headquarters of racing. In June 1711 Queen Anne founded Royal Ascot. Epsom was opened in 1730.

The Jockey Club was formed in 1750. Steeplechasing first took place in Ireland around 1752. Cheltenham had its first meeting in 1833, while Liverpool was founded three years later.

The blame must be attached to Mr. Pedley for present-day shouting of odds. He was heard to shout "6–4 the field" at Newmarket in 1842. This same Mr. Pedley won the Derby of 1847 with Cossack, by Hetman Platoff, and ridden by S. Templeman.

The Derby had been going some time by then, having been instituted in 1780, the first race going to Sir Charles Bunbury's Diomed, by Florizel. The St. Leger, first run in 1776, is the oldest of the five classics.

Racing colours worn by jockeys were made compulsory in 1762. The first official Judge was appointed in 1772. The first handicap event, the Oatlands Stakes, was run at Ascot in 1791.

The Racing Calendar was first published in 1773 and the first volume of the *General Stud Book* appeared eighteen years later.

The Darley Arabian, the Byerley Turk and the Godolphin Arabian or Barb. were imported into this country during the 17th and 18th centuries and thoroughbreds the world over are traced back in direct male line to one of these three.

In 1885 Admiral Rous was appointed Handicapper to the Jockey Club and to this day his Scale of Weight for Age is used. The National Hunt Committee was formed in 1866.

Sandown Park was founded in 1875, Kempton in 1878, Hurst Park, 1891 and Newbury held its first meeting in 1905.

Racing under Jockey Club Rules is controlled by three men, the Stewards of the Jockey Club. The present Stewards are Lord Irwin, the Duke of Roxburghe and Major-General Sir Randle Feilden. They see that the rules of the Jockey Club are carried out. They grant licences to racecourses, trainers and jockeys, draw up the fixture list, and have the power to exclude at their discretion any person from all or any places under their control.

Each meeting has three stewards and it is their duty to see the rules are enforced.

Sir Gordon Richards   Douglas Smith   Steve Donoghue

CHAMPION JOCKEYS (FLAT)

Year		Races won	Year		Races won
1840	E. Flatman	50	1899	S. Loates	160
1841	E. Flatman	68	1900	L. Reiff	143
1942	E. Flatman	42	1901	O. Madden	130
1843	E. Flatman	60	1902	W. Lane	170
1844	E. Flatman	64	1903	O. Madden	154
1845	E. Flatman	81	1904	O. Madden	161
1846	E. Flatman	81	1905	E. Wheatley	124
1847	E. Flatman	89	1906	W. Higgs	149
1848	E. Flatman	104	1907	W. Higgs	146
1849	E. Flatman	94	1908	D. Maher	139
1850	E. Flatman	88	1909	F. Wootton	165
1851	E. Flatman	78	1910	F. Wootton	137
1852	E. Flatman	92	1911	F. Wootton	187
1853	J. Wells	86	1912	F. Wootton	118
1854	J. Wells	82	1913	D. Maher	115
1855	G. Fordham	70	1914	S. Donoghue	129
1856	G. Fordham	108	1915	S. Donoghue	62
1857	G. Fordham	84	1916	S. Donoghue	43
1858	G. Fordham	91	1917	S. Donoghue	42
1859	G. Fordham	118	1918	S. Donoghue	66
1860	G. Fordham	146	1919	S. Donoghue	129
1861	G. Fordham	106	1920	S. Donoghue	143
1862	G. Fordham	166	1921	S. Donoghue	141
1863	G. Fordham	103	1922	S. Donoghue	102
1864	J. Grimshaw	164	1923	S. Donoghue	89
1865	G. Fordham	142	1923	E. C. Elliott	89
1866	S. Kenyon	123	1924	E. C. Elliott	106
1867	G. Fordham	143	1925	G. Richards	118
1868	G. Fordham	110	1926	T. Weston	95
1869	G. Fordham	95	1927	G. Richards	164
1870	W. Gray	76	1928	G. Richards	148
1870	C. Maidment	76	1929	G. Richards	135
1871	G. Fordham	86	1930	F. Fox	129
1871	C. Maidment	86	1931	G. Richards	145
1872	T. Cannon	87	1932	G. Richards	190
1873	H. Constable	110	1933	G. Richards	259
1874	F. Archer	147	1934	G. Richards	212
1875	F. Archer	172	1935	G. Richards	210
1876	F. Archer	207	1936	G. Richards	177
1877	F. Archer	218	1937	G. Richards	214
1878	F. Archer	229	1938	G. Richards	206
1879	F. Archer	197	1939	G. Richards	155
1880	F. Archer	120	1940	G. Richards	68
1881	F. Archer	220	1941	H. Wragg	71
1882	F. Archer	210	1942	G. Richards	67
1883	F. Archer	232	1943	G. Richards	65
1884	F. Archer	241	1944	G. Richards	88
1885	F. Archer	246	1945	G. Richards	104
1886	F. Archer	170	1946	G. Richards	212
1887	C. Wood	151	1947	G. Richards	269
1888	F. Barrett	108	1948	G. Richards	224
1889	T. Loates	167	1949	G. Richards	261
1890	T. Loates	147	1950	G. Richards	201
1891	M. Cannon	137	1951	G. Richards	227
1892	M. Cannon	182	1952	G. Richards	231
1893	T. Loates	222	1953	G. Richards	191
1894	M. Cannon	167	1954	D. Smith	129
1895	M. Cannon	184	1955	D. Smith	168
1896	M. Cannon	164	1956	D. Smith	155
1897	M. Cannon	145	1957	A. Breasley	173
1898	O. Madden	161	1958	D. Smith	165

LEADING OWNERS ON THE FLAT

Year	Owner	Winning Horses	Races Won	Value £	s.
1882	Mr. Lefevre	—	—	15,687	5
1883	Mr. Lefevre	—	—	20,563	15
1884	Mr. J. Hammond	—	—	12,379	5
1885	Mr. R. Peck	—	—	22,195	10
1886	Duke of Westminster	—	18	24,430	5
1887	Mr. Abington	—	47	20,124	8
1888	Duke of Portland	—	19	26,811	10
1889	Duke of Portland	—	33	73,858	10
1890	Duke of Portland	—	14	25,203	0
1891	Mr. N. Fenwick	—	15	20,519	0
1892	Baron De Hirsch	—	22	33,383	0
1893	Mr. H. McCalmont	—	30	25,431	0
1894	Mr. H. McCalmont	—	16	37,674	0
1895	Mr. L. de Rothschild	—	41	20,749	0
1896	Mr. L. de Rothschild	—	54	46,766	2
1897	Mr. J. Gubbins	—	8	22,739	0
1898	Mr. L. de Rothschild	—	53	30,267	10
1899	Duke of Westminster (the late)		16	43,965	0
1900	H.R.H. The Prince of Wales	3	9	29,585	10
1901	Sir G. Blundell Maple	24	58	21,370	0
1902	Mr. R. S. Sievier	5	10	23,686	0
1903	Sir James Miller	8	15	24,768	0
1904	Sir James Miller	14	25	28,923	0
1905	Col. W. Hall Walker	6	18	23,687	0
1906	Lord Derby (late)	20	44	32,926	0
1907	Col. W. Hall Walker	7	13	17,910	0
1908	Mr. J. B. Joel	10	19	26,246	0
1909	Mr. "Fairie"	6	23	37,719	0
1910	Mr. "Fairie"	7	17	35,352	0
1911	Lord Derby	11	30	42,781	0
1912	Mr. T. Pilkington	2	5	20,822	0
1913	Mr. J. B. Joel	17	31	25,430	0
1914	Mr. J. B. Joel	11	22	30,724	0
1915	Mr. L. Neumann	7	7	13,546	0
1916	Mr. E. Hutton	14	22	13,764	0
1917	Mr. "Fairie"	3	10	11,751	0
1918	Lady James Douglas	2	5	14,735	0
1919	Lord Glanely	10	45	30,514	0
1920	Sir Robert Jardine	15	29	19,385	0

Year	Owner	Winning Horses	Races Won	Value £	s.
1921	Mr. S. B. Joel	21	37	33,048	10
1922	Lord Woolavington	9	21	32,090	0
1923	Lord Derby	13	29	40,388	0
1924	H.H. Aga Khan	11	19	44,367	0
1925	Lord Astor	8	20	35,723	0
1926	Lord Woolavington	6	15	47,256	0
1927	Lord Derby	18	37	40,355	0
1928	Lord Derby	23	45	65,603	0
1929	H.H. Aga Khan	20	35	39,886	0
1930	H.H. Aga Khan	16	23	46,259	0
1931	Mr. J. A. Dewar	10	15	39,034	10
1932	H.H. Aga Khan	14	28	57,778	5
1933	Lord Derby	11	16	27,559	10
1934	H.H. Aga Khan	18	45	64,897	15
1935	H.H. Aga Khan	13	23	49,201	0
1936	Lord Astor	9	19	38,131	0
1937	H.H. Aga Khan	17	30	30,655	10
1938	Lord Derby	24	50	34,434	0
1939	Lord Rosebery	6	14	38,464	15
1940	Lord Rothermere	2	5	6,868	15
1941	Lord Glanely	9	21	8,762	0
1942	His Majesty	5	10	10,535	15
1943	Miss D. Paget	16	26	13,145	15
1944	H.H. Aga Khan	13	23	13,985	0
1945	Lord Derby	13	26	25,067	0
1946	H.H. Aga Khan	18	33	24,118	0
1947	H.H. Aga Khan	16	28	44,020	0
1948	H.H. Aga Khan	17	28	46,393	0
1949	H.H. Aga Khan	19	39	68,916	9
1950	M.M. Boussac	10	11	57,044	4
1951	M.M. Boussac	12	17	39,339	19
1952	H.H. Aga Khan	14	29	92,518	13
1953	Sir Victor Sassoon	23	39	58,579	7
1954	Her Majesty	10	19	40,993	18
1955	Lady Zia Wernher	2	6	46,345	0
1956	Major L. B. Holliday	21	43	39,327	0
1957	Her Majesty	16	30	62,211	0
1958	Mr. J. McShain	2	6	63,264	0

LEADING SIRES

Year	Sire	Value £	s.
1883	Hermit	30,801	0
1884	Hermit	29,236	0
1885	Hermit	30,121	0
1886	Bend Or	22,803	0
1887	Hampton	31,779	0
1888	Galopin	30,156	10
1889	Galopin	43,516	13
1890	St. Simon	32,799	12
1891	St. Simon	26,890	15
1892	St. Simon	55,995	0
1893	St. Simon	36,369	0
1894	St. Simon	42,092	0
1895	St. Simon	30,485	0
1896	St. Simon	59,728	0
1897	Kendall	28,746	0
1898	Galopin	21,699	0
1899	Orme	46,643	0
1900	St. Simon	58,625	0
1901	St. Simon	28,671	15
1902	Persimmon	36,810	0
1903	St. Frusquin	26,526	0
1904	Gallinule	30,105	10
1905	Isinglass	24,642	0
1906	Persimmon	21,737	0
1907	Gallinule	23,383	10
1908	Persimmon	24,484	15
1909	Cyllene	35,550	0
1910	Cyllene	38,001	10
1911	Sundridge	33,284	0
1912	Persimmon	21,993	0
1913	Desmond	30,973	10
1914	Polymelus	29,607	0
1915	Polymelus	17,738	0
1916	Polymelus	16,081	0
1917	Bayardo	12,337	0
1918	Bayardo	15,650	0
1919	The Tetrarch	27,976	10
1920	Polymelus	39,704	0
1921	Polymelus	34,307	0
1922	Lemberg	32,988	10
1923	Swynford	37,897	0
1924	Son-in-Law	32,476	0
1925	Phalaris	41,475	0
1926	Hurry On	59,109	0
1927	Buchan	45,918	0
1928	Phalaris	46,393	0
1929	Tetratema	53,025	15
1930	Son-in-Law	44,754	18
1931	Pharos	43,922	1
1932	Gainsborough	34,789	11
1933	Gainsborough	38,138	16
1934	Blandford	75,706	10
1935	Blandford	57,538	6
1936	Fairway	57,931	10
1937	Solario	52,888	15
1938	Blandford	31,840	2
1939	Fairway	53,441	0
1940	Hyperion	13,407	10
1941	Hyperion	22,699	15
1942	Hyperion	13,801	0
1943	Fairway	12,133	15
1944	Fairway	15,704	8
1945	Hyperion	39,727	0
1946	Hyperion	52,960	15
1947	Nearco	42,554	0
1948	Big Game	40,690	0
1949	Nearco	52,545	13
1950	Fair Trial	37,887	0
1951	Nasrullah	44,664	3
1952	Tehran	84,177	0
1953	Chanteur II	57,164	0
1954	*Hyperion	46,894	17
1955	*Alycidon	54,954	6
1956	*Court Martial	49,238	0
1957	*Court Martial	58,307	0
1958	Mossborough	66,471	0

*Including winners in Ireland.

LEADING TRAINERS (FLAT)

Year	Trainer	Winning Horses	Races Won	Value £	s.
1896	A. Hayhoe	17	39	43,642	0
1897	R. Marsh	26	39	33,531	0
1898	R. Marsh	27	60	34,239	0
1899	J. Porter	26	42	56,546	0
1900	R. Marsh	20	31	43,321	10
1901	J. Huggins	16	42	29,142	0
1902	R. S. Sievier	5	10	23,686	0
1903	G. Blackwell	14	24	34,135	0
1904	P. P. Gilpin	17	44	35,694	0
1905	W. T. Robinson	26	52	34,466	0
1906	Hon. G. Lambton	22	46	34,068	15
1907	A. Taylor	17	31	24,708	10
1908	C. Morton	12	20	26,431	0
1909	A. Taylor	25	49	47,825	0
1910	A. Taylor	24	47	52,364	0
1911	Hon. G. Lambton	23	48	49,769	0
1912	Hon. G. Lambton	29	55	22,884	0
1913	R. Wootton	31	66	28,284	0
1914	A. Taylor	19	39	52,052	0
1915	C. Peck	7	13	15,299	0
1916	R. Dawson	21	32	16,386	0
1917	A. Taylor	15	25	17,924	0
1918	A. Taylor	14	33	36,629	0
1919	A. Taylor	23	41	33,208	0
1920	A. Taylor	27	47	35,907	0
1921	A. Taylor	28	51	48,280	10
1922	A. Taylor	24	55	52,059	10
1923	A. Taylor	25	46	49,190	0
1924	R. C. Dawson	18	26	48,857	0
1925	A. Taylor	25	51	56,570	0
1926	F. Darling	24	48	63,408	0
1927	Frank Butters	26	54	57,468	0

Year	Trainer	Winning Horses	Races Won	Value £	s.
1928	Frank Butters	27	50	67,539	0
1929	R. C. Dawson	35	58	74,754	0
1930	H. S. Persse	26	46	49,487	0
1931	J. Lawson	34	69	93,899	10
1932	Frank Butters	34	62	72,436	10
1933	F. Darling	32	64	44,276	15
1934	Frank Butters	33	79	88,844	5
1935	Frank Butters	29	48	59,687	15
1936	J. Lawson	32	49	61,773	5
1937	C. Boyd-Rochfort	26	43	61,212	15
1938	C. Boyd-Rochfort	29	44	51,350	5
1939	J. L. Jarvis	20	34	56,219	5
1940	F. Darling	15	25	16,166	10
1941	F. Darling	18	37	19,025	15
1942	F. Darling	11	20	12,843	5
1943	W. Nightingall	18	29	13,833	15
1944	Frank Butters	18	34	17,585	0
1945	W. Earl	21	41	29,557	0
1946	Frank Butters	31	60	56,140	0
1947	F. Darling	26	56	65,313	0
1948	C. F. N. Murless	33	63	66,542	0
1949	Frank Butters	20	42	71,721	0
1950	C. H. Semblat (France)	10	11	57,044	0
1951	J. L. Jarvis	37	62	56,397	8
1952	M. Marsh	15	30	92,093	0
1953	J. L. Jarvis	39	60	71,546	11
1954	C. Boyd-Rochfort	25	39	65,326	5
1955	C. Boyd-Rochfort	24	38	74,424	0
1956	C. F. Elsey	45	83	61,621	0
1957	C. F. N. Murless	32	48	116,898	0
1958	C. Boyd-Rochfort	24	37	84,186	0

RACING COLOURS OF SOME LEADING OWNERS

Her Majesty The Queen	Purple, gold braid, scarlet sleeves, black velvet cap with gold fringe
Lord Astor	Light blue, pink sash and cap
Sir Alfred Butt	Yellow, graduated blue hoops, blue cap
Lord Carnarvon	Scarlet, blue collar, white cap
Sir William Cooke	Purple, scarlet sleeves and cap
Lord Derby	Black, white cap
Mrs. J. A. Dewar	White, tartan cross
Lord Ellesmere	Red, white sleeves, black cap
Lord Howard de Walden	Apricot
Mr. Jack Hylton	Black, jazz hoops and armlets, white cap
Mr. H. J. Joel	Black, scarlet cap
The Aly Khan	Green and chocolate hoops, chocolate cap
Lt.-Col. Giles Loder	Yellow, dark blue sleeves, black cap
Sir Malcolm McAlpine	McAlpine tartan, gold cap
Major Dermot McCalmont	Light blue and scarlet (quartered) white cap
Mrs. R. Macdonald-Buchanan	White, black hoop and armlets, red cap with gold tassel
Mr. Clifford Nicholson	Grey, scarlet sleeves, collar, braid and cap
Duke of Norfolk	Sky blue, sky blue and gold quartered cap
Duchess of Norfolk	Sky blue and scarlet check, sky blue sleeves, scarlet cap
Sir Eric Ohlson	White, blue striped sleeves and hoop on cap
Miss Dorothy Paget	Blue, yellow hoop on body and sleeves, yellow cap with blue hoop
Mrs. John Rogerson	Navy blue, pink and green sash, hooped cap
Lord Rosebery	Primrose and rose hoops, rose top
Mrs. James A. de Rothschild	Dark blue, yellow chevrons and cap
Lord Sefton	White, primrose sleeves, black cap
Sir Humphrey de Trafford	Scarlet and white (quartered)
Lady Zia Wernher	Green and yellow (halved), yellow cap
Mr. J. H. Whitney	Pink, black and white striped sleeves, white cap
Lord Willoughby de Broke	Yellow, chocolate hooped sleeves, chocolate cap
Lord Zetland	White, red spots, red cap
Queen Elizabeth the Queen Mother	Blue, buff stripes, blue sleeves, black cap, gold tassel
H.R.H. The Princess Royal	Royal blue, red hooped sleeves, black cap
Major L. B. Holliday	White maroon cap and armlets, maroon cap
Mr. Stanhope Joel	Green and pink stripes, pink cap
Mr. H. L. Cottrill	Cerise and black stripes, quartered cap
Mr. Stavros Niarchos	Dark blue, light blue cross-belts, white cap
Mr. Arpad Plesch	Light blue, scarlet spots
Mr. Phil Bull	Cerise, white circle
Mr. J. S. Gerber	Silver grey, blue cross back and front, pale green sleeves, red cap
Sir Winston Churchill	Pink, chocolate sleeves and cap
Lord Irwin	Light blue, chocolate sleeves, hooped cap

RACING QUIZ

1. When was the Derby last run on a Thursday?

★

2. When did the Grand National first become a handicap race?

★

3. What is the highest amount ever reached at the subsequent auction following a selling race?

★

4. Name the highest steeple-chase jump at Liverpool?

QUIZ ANSWERS

1. 1837. 2. 1843. 3. 6,800 gns., when Fair Reward was bought in at York on August 18th, 1959. 4. The Open Ditch at Aintree is 5 ft. 2 in. high, 3 ft. 9 in. wide, ditch on the take-off side 6 ft. wide, guard rail in front of ditch 1 ft. 6 in. in height.

SCALE OF WEIGHT FOR AGE (Flat)

Table compiled in 1873 by Admiral Rous

		Mar./Apr.	May	June	July	Aug.	Sept.	Oct.	Nov.
5 F.	TWO YRS.	6 0	6 2	6 7	6 10	7 2	7 7	7 9	7 12
	THREE YRS.	8 4	8 3	8 5	8 7	8 9	8 12	8 12	8 13
	FOUR YRS.	9 4	9 0	9 0	9 0	9 0	9 0	9 0	9 0
	FIVE, SIX and AGED	9 5	9 0	9 0	9 0	9 0	9 0	9 0	9 0
6 F.	TWO YRS.	—	6 4	6 7	6 11	7 0	7 6	7 9	7 13
	THREE YRS.	8 5	8 6	8 8	8 10	8 12	9 0	9 2	9 3
	FOUR YRS.	9 7	9 7	9 7	9 7	9 7	9 7	9 7	9 7
	FIVE, SIX and AGED	9 9	9 8	9 7	9 7	9 7	9 7	9 7	9 7
1 M.	TWO YRS.	—	—	—	—	—	6 7	6 9	6 12
	THREE YRS.	7 8	7 11	7 13	8 2	8 4	8 6	8 7	8 8
	FOUR YRS.	9 0	9 0	9 0	9 0	9 0	9 0	9 0	9 0
	FIVE, SIX and AGED	9 4	9 3	9 2	9 0	9 0	9 0	9 0	9 0
1½ M.	TWO YRS.	—	—	—	—	—	6 0	6 4	6 7
	THREE YRS.	7 7	7 9	7 11	7 13	8 1	8 3	8 5	8 7
	FOUR YRS.	9 0	9 0	9 0	9 0	9 0	9 0	9 0	9 0
	FIVE, SIX and AGED	9 5	9 4	9 3	9 2	9 1	9 0	9 0	9 0
2 M.	TWO YRS.	—	—	—	—	—	6 0	6 2	6 2
	THREE YRS.	7 8	7 11	7 12	8 0	8 3	8 4	8 5	8 5
	FOUR YRS.	9 4	9 4	9 4	9 4	9 4	9 4	9 4	9 4
	FIVE, SIX and AGED	9 10	9 9	9 8	9 7	9 6	9 5	9 4	9 4
3 M.	THREE YRS.	7 1	7 4	7 5	7 7	7 9	7 11	7 13	7 13
	FOUR YRS.	9 0	9 0	9 0	9 0	9 0	9 0	9 0	9 0
	FIVE YRS.	9 8	9 7	9 6	9 5	9 5	9 4	9 3	9 3
	SIX and AGED	9 10	9 8	9 7	9 6	9 5	9 4	9 3	9 3

To calculate weight in terms of distance, count one length the equal of 3 lb. A head and a neck equal 1 lb.

BEST TIMES FOR COURSES

The following times represent the best over the various distances and courses from March 20, 1922, according to those returned in the *Sporting Chronicle Racing Up-to-Date*. Reproduced by kind permission of the *Sporting Chronicle*. * Denotes best time since 1945.

NEWMARKET

Course	*Distance*	*Time*	*Age & Weight*	*Going*	*Horse*	*Date*
Rous	5f.	57⅘	8 7	Firm	Mumtaz Mahal	May 16, 1923
Chesterfield	5f.	58⅘	9 0	Firm	Linklater	May 15, 1941
Chesterfield	5f.	58⅘	8 8	Hard	Happy Morn	June 6, 1944
T.Y.O.	5f. 134y	1/6⅗	8 11	Good	Gay Angela	Oct. 2, 1923
Last 5f. of Ab. M.	5f.	58⅕	9 7	Hard	Blenheim	Oct. 2, 1929
New T.Y.O.	5f. 140y	1/6⅘	8 3	Good	Helofajest	July 13, 1922
Bretby Stakes	6f.	1/10⅗	6 6	Hard	Sun Gem	May 15, 1928
Bretby Stakes	6f.	1/10⅗	8 2	Firm	Run Honey	Oct. 1, 1948
Peel	6f.	1/12⅖	9 2	Hard	Linby	May 3, 1923
Last 6f. of Ab. M.	6f.	1/13	8 0	Good	Quinine	Oct. 29, 1929
Last 6f. of B.M.	6f.	1/10⅘	8 9	Hard	Arausio	July 16, 1924
Exeter	6f.	1/9⅘	9 10	Firm	Bellacose	July 4, 1935
Dewhurst Stks.	7f.	1/24	7 5	Firm	Lutestring	Oct. 16, 1929
Beaufort	7f.	1/23	7 12	Hard	Paravant	July 17, 1928
Last 7f. of B.M.	7f.	1/23⅖	7 3	Firm	Ti-Chin	June 17, 1944
Rowley Mile	1m.	1/35⅕	9 0	Hard	My Babu	April 28, 1948
Rowley Mile	1m.	1/35⅘	9 7	Firm	Palais Royal II	Oct. 16, 1929
Abingdon Mile	1m.	1/38⅖	8 9	Firm	Fair Reproach	Sept. 28, 1948
Abingdon Mile	1m.	1/38⅗	8 0	Firm	Black Cloud	Sept. 29, 1953
Ditch Mile	1m.	1/37⅕	8 9	Firm	Faris II	April 6, 1938
Bunbury Mile	1m.	1/37⅕	9 7	Hard	Pink Flower	June 6, 1944
New C'mbr'dshire	1m. 1f.	1/49⅗	7 11	Good	Disarmament	Oct. 28, 1931
Across the Flat	1m. 2f.	2/0	9 0	Firm	Top Gallant	May 16, 1923
Last 1¼m. Suffolk Course	1m. 2f.	2/2⅖	9 7	Firm	Borealis	May 2, 1944
Ellesmere Stks.	1m. 3f.	2/13⅖	7 7	Firm	Brush Off	June 16, 1944
Suffolk Stks.	1½m.	2/25⅘	9 0	Hard	Persian Gulf	June 6, 1944
Last 1½m. Cesarewitch	1½m.	†2/23	8 12	Firm	Bastard	Oct. 18, 1929
Last 1¾m. Cesarewitch	1¾m.	2/56.19	8 11	Firm	Buckhound	Oct. 1, 1953
Last 2m. Cesarewitch	2m.	3/27.27	8 12	Firm	Chantry	Sept. 29, 1953
Two Middle Miles of B.C.	2m.	3/29	9 2	Hard	Corbridge	May 4, 1923
Summer	2m. 24y	3/7⅗	9 4	Firm	Persian Gulf	June 16, 1944
Cesarewitch	2¼m.	3/41⅖	7 6	Firm	West Wicklow	Oct. 16, 1929

† Distance record

NEWMARKET—Electrically Recorded

Rous	5f.	57.83	2–8–11	Good	Wilna	Oct. 31, 1952
Chesterfield	5f.	59.22	3–8–10	Good	Lady Midge	July 6, 1956
Bretby Stakes	6f.	1/11.14	4–8–1	Firm	Light Harvest	May 16, 1956
Last 6f. of B.M.	6f.	1/11.77	3–8–10	Good	Matador	July 7, 1956
Dewhurst Stakes	7f.	1/25.05	2–8–9	Good	Sunset	Oct. 31, 1952
Last 7f. of B.M.	7f.	1/25.65	3–8–12	Firm	My Smokey	Aug. 6 1955
Rowley Mile	1m.	1/36.46	5–9–8	Firm	My Smokey	May 16, 1957
Bunbury Mile	1m	1/38.90	3–8–2	Good	Sundry	July 14, 1954
New C'mbr'dshire	1m. 1f.	1/50.66	3–7–11	Good	Devonshire Lass	Oct. 31, 1952
Across the Flat	1m 2f.	2/4.54	3–9–0	Firm	Pirate King	May 16, 1957
Across the Flat	1m. 2f.	2/4.54	3–9–0	Firm	Acropolis	May 11, 1955
Last 1¼m. of Suffolk Course	1m. 2f.	2/7.76	6–8–3	Good	Mid View	July 1, 1953
Suffolk Stakes	1½m.	2/31.02	3–7–10	Good	Dormello	July 7, 1956
Last 1½m. of Cesarewitch	1½m.	2/32.00	4–7–1	Firm	Bronzamazon	Sept. 30, 1953
Last 1¾m. of Cesarewitch	1¾m.	2/56.19	4–8–11	Firm	Buckhound	Oct. 1, 1953
Last 1m. 6f. 171y. of Summer Course	1m. 6f. 171y.	3/9.18	9–7–12	Firm	Anglo-Iranian	July 3, 1959
Last 2m. of Cesarewitch	2m.	3/27.27	4–8–12	Firm	Chantry	Sept. 29, 1953
Cesarewitch	2¼m.	3/53.42	7–8–3	Good	French Design	Oct. 13, 1954

ALEXANDRA PARK

Distance	*Time*	*Weight*	*Going*	*Horse*	*Date*
5f.	59⅗	8 9	Firm	V.3	July 1, 1930
†1m.	1/43⅖	8 8	Hard	Miss Twinthorne	Sept. 14, 1929
1¼m.	2/⅘	9 0	Firm	Paddy	July 3, 1926
1m. 5f.	2/46⅗	6 13	Firm	Top "C"	Sept. 28, 1959

† 1m. 150yds. (now 1m. 160yds.)

ASCOT

The following represent the best over the various distances since course alterations 1955

5f.	1/0.82	8 10	Firm	Chris	June 19, 1959
6f.	1/13.78	8 10	Firm	Dionisio	June 21, 1957
7f.	1/28.76	8 3	Good	Faith Healer	June 18, 1958
1m. (str.)	1/40.64	7 10	Firm	Baron's Folly	June 18, 1957
1m. (O. crse.)	1/40.97	7 12	Firm	Meldon	June 21, 1957
1½m.	2/30.18	9 1	Firm	Eric	June 21, 1957
2m.	3/26.89	8 5	Firm	Owen Glendower	June 20, 1959
2½m.	4/21.77	6 8	Firm	Bonhomie	June 18, 1957
2m. 6f. 34yds.	4/57.35	8 0	Good	Birthday Present	July 18, 1958

AYR

5f.	58	9 7	Good	British Lion	Sept. 14, 1949
6f.	1/10.60	7 13	Firm	Charbon	Sept. 16, 1959
1m.	1/36	7 1	Good	The Squire	Sept. 15, 1949
1m.	1/36	7 13	Firm	Sufi	Sept. 16, 1959
1¼m.	2/5⅕	7 4	Firm	Cleeve	June 3, 1939
1m. 3f.	2/13⅖	8 3	Good	Spahee	Sept. 15, 1948
* 1m. 7f.	3/13⅕	7 9	Firm	Brumfield	June 14, 1952

BATH

5f.	1/1⅕	7 10	Good	Donum	May 30, 1934
5f. 170yds.	1/11⅗	8 10	Firm	Nero's Saga	July 16, 1959
6f.	1/13⅗	9 4	Good	Copacabana	July 14, 1932
6f.	1/13⅖	9 4	Good	Scarlet Fly	July 14, 1932
7f.	1/27⅗	8 1	Firm	Golden Judge	Sept. 9, 1959
1m.	1/41⅗	8 8	Firm	Daneway	Aug. 29, 1959
1¼m.	2/10⅗	6 8	Good	Shahid	April 15, 1948
† 1½m.	2/42⅕	6 10	Firm	Hardly	Sept. 10, 1959

† 1m. 4f. 200yds.

BEVERLEY

6f.	1/1⅕	8 4	Good	Short Cut	June 11, 1936
1m.	1/38⅖	7 3	Hard	Brawby Lad	Aug. 31, 1949
1¼m.	2/3⅘	7 5	Good	Cecil's Choice	Aug. 27, 1953
1m. 5f.	2/45⅖	6 13	Good	Procne	May 29, 1946

BIRMINGHAM

5f.	58	8 12	Firm	Ondine	May 17, 1948
6f.	1/9⅕	8 2	Good	Tosh	April 3, 1934
7f.	1/25⅖	6 7	Good	Phi-Phi	Oct. 30, 1922
1m.	1/35⅕	8 11	Good	Diobrook	April 3, 1934
1¼m.	2/2⅖	9 8	Firm	Silver Gate	July 31, 1950
1½m.	2/29⅗	9 1	Firm	Highlander	Aug. 2, 1928
1m. 5f.	2/44⅕	9 7	Hard	Philantrope	Sept. 1, 1952
2m.	3/26.83	7 9	Firm	Game Rights	April 23, 1957

BOGSIDE

5f.	59⅗	8 4	Firm	Semperatus	July 22, 1949
6f.	1/10⅗	9 0	Firm	Red Ranger	June 7, 1952
1m.	1/37⅘	8 5	Good	Kwei Hill	June 6, 1959
1¼m.	2/4	8 3	Good	Gentle Lily	Sept. 18, 1937
1½m.	2/31⅕	7 8	Good	Why Tell	April 25, 1952

BRIGHTON

Distance	Time	Weight	Going	Horse	Date
† 5f.	1/0⅗	8 2	Good	Unlikely	Aug. 4, 1931
† 5f.	1/0⅗	9 0	Firm	Hidden Valley	June 11, 1947
6f.	§1/6⅕	8 11	Good	Broken Tendril	Aug. 6, 1929
7f.	1/21	8 4	Hard	Canardeau	Aug. 25, 1955
7f.	1/21	8 7	Firm	Mullin	Aug. 27, 1959
7f.	1/21	7 12	Firm	Offspring	Aug. 27, 1959
1m.	§1/32	7 7	Firm	Mopsus	June 22, 1939
1¼m.	1/58⅗	8 7	Hard	Fione Buidhe	June 29, 1953
1½m.	2/29⅘	8 9	Hard	Old Pretender	Aug. 6, 1935
1½m.	2/29⅘	9 7	Good	Manati	Aug. 30, 1956

† 5f. 66yds. § Distance record.

CARLISLE

5f.	1/0⅗	7 8	Hard	Dignitary	July 3, 1953
6f.	1/14⅕	8 3	Hard	Telephone Boy	June 29, 1949
1m.	1/40⅕	7 7	Good	Bone	July 1, 1936
1m.	1/40⅕	7 11	Firm	Norcrest	July 5, 1957
1¼m.	2/8⅗	8 7	Hard	Marula	July 3, 1953
1½m.	2/29⅘	7 6	Firm	Cannebiere	July 4, 1957

CATTERICK BRIDGE

5f.	58⅗	8 6	Firm	Granville Greta	July 23, 1959
7f.	1/24⅖	6 11	Firm	Hartley Fare	Aug. 1, 1952
1½m.	2/31	8 9	Good	Friar's Belle	Oct. 13, 1933
* 1m. 5f. 140yds.	2/53	7 2	Firm	Ray Westwood	Aug. 2, 1952

CHEPSTOW

5f.	58⅕	7 13	Hard	Thoroughwort	June 28, 1949
6f.	1/8⅘	7 11	Firm	Precipitant	Aug. 1, 1955
7f.	1/21⅕	7 3	Firm	Cintrist	July 3, 1954
1m.	1/32⅗	8 8	Hard	Alizarene	June 28, 1949
1¼m.	2/6⅕	9 5	Good	Sculptor	June 10, 1957
1½m.	2/34⅗	9 0	Hard	Ox and Ass	July 13, 1928

CHESTER

5f.	1/0⅕	7 9	Firm	Inverbroom	May 7, 1958
6f.	1/4⅘	10 10	Firm	Canfield	May 10, 1928
7f.	1/26⅘	8 3	Firm	Sapor	May 10, 1928
7f. 118yds.	1/33⅕	8 13	Good	Cock of the North	May 7, 1953
1¼m.	2/6⅗	8 3	Firm	His Reverence	May 9, 1935
1½m.	2/33⅗	8 7	Good	Neapolitan	May 9, 1946
* 1m. 5f. 75yds.	2/51⅘	8 0	Good	Empire Honey	May 5, 1953
1m. 6f. 75yds.	3/4⅗	8 11	Good	Wyandank	May 7, 1953

Danny Maher

T. Weston

A. Breasley

DONCASTER

5f.	57⅗	8 8	Firm	Sir Gatric	Sept. 10, 1959
5f. 152 yds.	1/5⅗	8 12	Good	Rosemary's Pet	Sept. 13, 1934
6f.	1/10⅕	7 9	Good	Ryecroft	May 16, 1959
7f.	1/22⅗	8 5	Firm	Harpist	Sept. 14, 1928
1m.	1/36⅕	8 0	Firm	Lovestone	Sept. 12, 1958
1¼m.	2/9	8 5	Firm	Ringmaster	June 1, 1934
1m. 3f.	2/17⅕	8 5	Good	Pampered Love	July 24, 1948
1½m.	2/31	7 4	Good	Nevermore	Sept. 9, 1926
1m. 6f. 132yds.	3/1⅗	9 0	Hard	Windsor Lad	Sept. 12, 1934
1m. 6f. 132yds.	3/1⅗	9 0	Good	Coronach	Sept. 8, 1926

EDINBURGH

5f.	58⅗	8 10	Firm	Baroda	Sept. 20, 1949
7f.	1/27⅗	8 13	Good	Turton Fair	July 5, 1948
7f.	1/27⅗	7 4	Good	Ring of Fortune	April 20, 1953
1m.	1/39⅕	9 7	Firm	Signalman	Sept. 20, 1949
1m.	1/39⅕	7 2	Firm	Glenythan	Sept. 16, 1952
* 1m. 3f.	2/19⅘	8 7	Firm	Sunnyray	Sept. 19, 1949
1½m.	2/33	8 2	Good	Bibi Mah	Sept. 15, 1958
* 1m. 7f.	3/10⅕	8 0	Good	Cunningham	Sept. 21, 1953

EPSOM

5f.	†54⅗	7 5	Hard	Devineress	June 2, 1933
6f.	1/7⅗	8 11	Hard	Golly-Eyes	May 30, 1922
7f.	1/20⅗	8 2	Good	Poetaster	April 24, 1928
*1m. 110yds.	1/41⅗	7 9	Firm	Arletta	June 5, 1956
1¼m.	2/4	8 13	Hard	Sans Changer	June 7, 1929
1½m.	2/33	9 6	Firm	Apelle	June 7, 1928
2m. 2f.	3/54	6 8	Firm	Gay Ballad	April 23, 1957

† Distance record.

FOLKESTONE

5f.	59⅕	8 0	Firm	Nero's Saga	June 22, 1959
6f.	1/10⅘	7 12	Hard	Beladorius	July 3, 1951
1¼m.	2/4	8 2	Firm	Port of Call	Sept. 3, 1937
1½m.	2/35⅕	8 5	Good	Candelabra	July 23, 1956
1m. 7f. 100yds.	3/10	7 4	Hard	Don's Fancy	July 3, 1951
2m. 100yds.	3/35	8 12	Good	Cheyne	July 21, 1953

RACING QUIZ

1. Why is the Silver Ring so named?

★

2. What does the term "bored" mean?

★

3. What does the term "claiming the seven" mean?

★

4. What does the term "bar shouting" mean?

★

5. What is an amateur race?

★

6. Name the slang term for an amateur race.

QUIZ ANSWERS

1. Because silver rather than notes is generally used for betting. 2. When a horse is pushed off a straight course in running by another horse. 3. An apprentice claiming the 7 lb. allowance which is deducted from a horse's weight. 4. When a race is virtually decided before the winning post is reached. 5. When a race is confirmed to gentlemen riders. 6. It is known as "Bumpers".

GOODWOOD

Distance	Time	Weight	Going	Horse	Date
5f.	58	8 3	Firm	Democratic	July 27, 1955
6f.	1/11⅗	8 9	Firm	Gunboat	July 30, 1937
6f.	1/11⅗	8 11	Firm	King Bruce	July 26, 1955
1m.	1/39⅗	7 8	Firm	Rocky Royale	July 30, 1959
1¼m.	2/7	9 7	Firm	Finalist	July 30, 1937
1m. 3f. 200yds.	2/35⅗	7 8	Firm	Grey Magic	July 28, 1955
1½m.	2/54⅗	8 12	Firm	Quorn II	July 28, 1937
1m. 6f.	3/4⅗	8 5	Good	Almeria	July 30, 1957
* 2m. 3f.	4/12⅗	8 7	Firm	French Design	July 27, 1955
2m. 5f.	4/42	9 2	Firm	Fearless Fox	July 29, 1937

HAMILTON PARK

5f.	59⅕	9 3	Firm	Anton	June 20, 1959
6f.	1/11⅕	8 10	Firm	Dignitary	July 16, 1955
† 1m.	1/45⅕	7 8	Good	Chance View	July 13, 1956
* 1m. 3f.	2/23⅕	8 6	Good	Shall Cross	Sept. 26, 1949
1½m.	2/36⅕	9 0	Hard	Las Vegas	Aug. 30, 1947
* 1m. 5f.	2/43⅘	8 5	Good	Royal Pact	Aug. 26, 1949

HAYDOCK PARK

5f.	59⅗	7 9	Firm	Zuccarino	Sept. 19, 1959
6f.	1/11⅘	9 3	Firm	Brassie	Oct. 7, 1933
7f.	1/24⅗	8 3	Firm	Lucky Sarah	Oct. 7, 1933
1m.	1/37⅗	6 11	Good	Prince Yaky	July 2, 1954
1⅛m.	2/3⅗	7 6	Firm	King's Glen	July 4, 1959
1½m.	2/27⅗	8 12	Firm	Courier	July 8, 1950
2m.	3/30⅗	9 2	Good	Atlas	May 18, 1957

HURST PARK

5f.	59⅕	8 1	Good	Autonomy	May 22, 1956
6f.	1/11⅗	7 10	Firm	Astrol	May 19, 1959
7f.	1/20	9 0	Good	First Edition	May 25, 1926
1m.	1/39⅗	9 3	Good	Soldier Song	Aug. 19, 1922
1¼m.	2/3⅗	8 0	Good	Lauzun	Aug. 19, 1922
1½m.	2/40	7 7	Fairly good	Monsieur	July 25, 1925
* 1m. 5f. 40yds.	2/49⅗	7 9	Firm	Mosstrooper of Chantry	Sept. 5, 1959
1m. 6f. 66yds.	3/0⅘	8 1	Firm	Governor	May 18, 1948
1m. 7f. 66yds.	3/15⅗	8 7	Firm	Compound Fracture	June 10, 1930
2m.	3/24⅕	7 13	Good	Mizzen Mast	July 22, 1922

KEMPTON PARK

5f.	57⅘	8 11	Good	Fair Reward	Sept. 18, 1959
6f.	1/10⅗	8 10	Good	Zabara	Sept. 22, 1951
7f.	1/25	8 8	Firm	Nero's Love	July 22, 1959
1m. (Rd.)	1/38⅘	7 0	Good	Bright Silk	July 25, 1956
1m. (Jub.)	1/39⅗	8 5	Firm	Rococo	June 3, 1947
1¼m.	2/1⅗	8 3	Firm	Someo	Mar. 27, 1948
* 1m. 3f.	2/18⅕	9 2	Good	Tintinnabulum	July 26, 1956
1½m.	2/29	7 11	Good	Ainess	Oct. 9, 1925
2m.	3/23⅗	7 6	Good	Incredule	July 26, 1956

LANARK

5f.	1/0⅗	8 12	Firm	Wallace's Tower	July 20, 1956
7f.	1/24⅗	7 4	Good	Mutineer	May 1, 1954
1m.	1/39	7 5	Good	Sunny Turk	July 23, 1952
1m.	1/39	7 2	Good	Gay Trio	July 17, 1957
1¼m.	2/4⅘	8 5	Firm	Devancer	July 21, 1949
1½m.	2/31⅘	8 11	Firm	No Comment	Sept. 5, 1959

LEICESTER

5f.	59	8 10	Good	Whimsical Walker	Sept. 21, 1953
6f.	1/11⅕	9 10	Good	Beladorius	Sept. 21, 1953
6f.	1/11⅕	8 5	Firm	Fazeley Fair	June 14, 1958
7f.	1/24⅕	8 2	Good	Identical	Sept. 21, 1953
1m.	1/35	7 5	Fairly good	Primrose League	July 19, 1926
1¼m.	2/5⅗	9 3	Hard	Good Deal	July 23, 1935
1½m.	2/26⅗	8 4	Firm	Roi des Aulnes	July 22, 1929

LEWES

5f.	55⅗	8 10	Firm	Scarlet Pimpernel	June 8, 1953
1m.	1/35⅗	8 5	Firm	Sandblast	Aug. 6, 1926
1¼m.	2/3	6 12	Good	Waterwitch	Aug. 5, 1922
1½m.	2/31⅘	7 11	Firm	British Quota	Aug. 7, 1937

LINCOLN

5f.	59⅗	9 0	Good	Palazzoli	Sept. 5, 1957
6f.	1/10⅕	8 9	Good	Kety	Sept. 17, 1948
7f.	1/22⅘	8 7	Firm	Royal Parentage	June 10, 1959
1m. (str.)	1/36⅗	8 2	Hard	Guitarist	Sept. 23, 1959
1m. (rd.)	1/37⅕	8 9	Good	Trespass	July 23, 1949
1¼m.	2/1⅘	8 7	Firm	Philodrendron	June 11, 1959
1½m.	2/31⅗	9 0	Hard	Tuckernuck	Aug. 31, 1955
2m.	3/24⅗	9 0	Firm	The Master Cutler	Sept. 4, 1952

RACING QUIZ

1. When was the Oaks first run and who won?

★

2. State the racing colours of Major L. B. Holliday.

★

3. In the 1932 St. Leger the late Aga Khan owned 1st, 2nd, 4th and 5th. Name them.

★

4. What was the highest weight carried by a horse in the Grand National?

5. In what year did 66 runners compete for the Grand National? This is a record for any event under National Hunt rules.

★

6. Which horse collapsed a few yards from the post with the race at his mercy in the 1956 Grand National?

QUIZ ANSWERS

1. Bridget in 1779. 2. White, maroon cap and armlets. 3. 1st Firdaussi, 2nd Dastur, 4th Udaipur, 5th Taj Kasra. 4. Lottery carried 13 st. 4 lb., in 1841. 5. 1929. 6. The Queen Mother's Devon Loch.

E. C. Elliott W. Johnstone Lester Piggo

Best Times for Courses—*contd.*

LINGFIELD PARK

Distance	*Time*	*Weight*	*Going*	*Horse*	*Date*
5f.	57	7 8	Hard	Hazel Bridge	Oct. 6, 1949
5f.	57	8 6	Firm	Kingham Vale	June 13, 1952
6f.	1/8⅗	8 9	Good	Mr. Tinkle	Oct. 20, 1924
7f	1/19	8 5	Hard	Spartan Fare	Oct. 5, 1949
7f. 140yds.	1/28	6 9	Hard	Lancashire Lassie	Aug. 25, 1950
1m.	1/33	8 8	Hard	Blue Pete	July 11, 1924
1¼m.	2/5⅘	8 3	Hard	Stuart	Aug. 12, 1949
1½m.	2/32	7 8	Hard	Chapeau	July 11, 1924
2m.	3/25⅕	7 10	Good	Nonchalant	Oct. 6, 1926

LIVERPOOL

5f.	59⅗	9 7	Good	Gold Bridge	July 19, 1933
6f.	1/12⅘	7 12	Firm	Popalongabit	July 3, 1957
1m.	1/38⅗	7 11	Good	Gleamer	July 22, 1936
1¼m.	2/3⅘	9 1	Good	Fair Copy	July 22, 1938
1m. 2f. 170yds.	2/14	8 4	Firm	His Reverence	July 26, 1935
1½m.	2/34	8 3	Good	Norseman	July 26, 1923
1m. 5f.	2/47	8 13	Good	Voluntary	June 27, 1946
* 1m. 6f.	3/4⅗	9 4	Good	Gallant Scot	Nov. 7, 1947
2m.	3/34⅘	7 12	Good	Miraculous Atom	Nov. 8, 1947

MANCHESTER

5f.	57⅘	7 3	Good	Games	June 4, 1936
6f.	1/7⅗	8 10	Good	Her Eminence	Sept. 2, 1933
1m.	1/36⅕	7 2	Good	Tapestry II	Sept. 1, 1933
1¼m.	2/2⅘	7 8	Good	Castle Donnington	June 5, 1952
1½m.	2/27⅘	8 1	Firm	Robber Chief	June 9, 1933
2m.	3/19⅘	8 9	Hard	Chivalrous	June 8, 1922
2m. 3f. 75yds.	4/7.69	8 10	Firm	Alexis	Sept. 5, 1959

NEWBURY

5f.	59	8 12	Good	Minstrel's Gallery	June 18, 1955
6f.	1/11⅕	9 0	Good	Oubliette	May 11, 1940
7f.	1/23⅗	8 4	Firm	Artist's Prince	June 10, 1937
7f. 60yds.	1/26⅘	7 1	Firm	Bucktail	June 25, 1959
1m.	1/37⅕	7 11	Good	Hills of Devon	Aug. 17, 1951
1m.	1/37⅕	7 8	Good	Desideria	June 18, 1955
1m.	1/37⅕	8 12	Firm	Pappagena	Aug. 12, 1955
1¼m.	2/2	7 6	Firm	Osman Pasha	June 13, 1934
1½m.	2/26⅘	9 0	Firm	Columcille	Sept. 23, 1938
2m.	3/27	8 10	Firm	Flighty Frances	Oct. 3, 1953

NEWCASTLE

5f.	58⅗	9 0	Firm	Weensland	June 21, 1951
6f.	1/12	8 8	Firm	Bellisle	June 25, 1959
7f.	1/24⅗	7 12	Firm	Leros	Aug. 7, 1950
1m.	1/37	7 5	Soft	Duncooler	June 20, 1933
1¼m.	2/8⅖	7 12	Good	Mixed Blessing	Sept. 24, 1939
1½m.	2/33⅘	8 7	Firm	Fernlehurst	April 18, 1938
2m.	3/21⅘	7 10	Firm	Carpathus	June 27, 1923

NOTTINGHAM

5f.	59⅕	7 8	Firm	Witness Box	Aug. 10, 1959
6f.	1/12	8 0	Firm	Seven Dials	July 4, 1938
6f.	1/12	8 11	Firm	Live Spirit	Aug. 9, 1955
7f.	1/24⅗	8 8	Firm	Rough	June 8, 1953
1m.	1/36⅘	7 13	Hard	Somali	Oct. 4, 1949
1¼m.	2/4	7 9	Hard	Tewkesbury	Aug. 13, 1935
1¼m.	2/4	7 12	Firm	Sweet Legend	July 8, 1935
1½m.	2/37[illegible]	9 3	Good	Mandelieu	Oct. 5, 1926
2m.	3/24	8 10	Good	Green Fire	Oct. 4, 1926

PONTEFRACT

5f.	1/1	7 3	Firm	Young Vigorous	June 23, 1951
6f.	1/11⅖	8 5	Firm	Cardington Star	June 22, 1951
1m.	1/38⅘	9 3	Firm	Layalpur	Oct. 5, 1945
1¼m.	2/10	7 12	Hard	Good Sport	Aug. 7, 1944
1½m.	2/35⅗	7 10	Firm	Little Pip	June 3, 1944

REDCAR

5f.	59	8 12	Good	Blackwell	July 27, 1949
6f.	1/9	8 4	Firm	Flying William	May 2, 1958
7f.	1/22⅗	7 8	Firm	Rub-a-Dub	May 25, 1953
1m.	1/36⅕	9 7	Good	Saint Andrews II	Aug. 14, 1939
1¼m.	2/2⅖	7 8	Firm	Tale of Two Cities	May 21, 1956
1½m.	2/30⅗	7 5	Firm	Family Affair	May 2, 1958

RIPON

5f.	58⅗	7 4	Good	Pearly Chase	Aug. 26, 1950
6f.	1/11⅗	7 11	Firm	Roman Vale	Aug. 5, 1957
1m.	1/38⅘	7 3	Firm	Daily Bread	May 6, 1938
1¼m.	2/5	7 12	Hard	Tangram	April 30, 1954
1½m.	2/28	7 12	Hard	Royal Avenue	Sept. 11, 1937
2m.	3/26⅕	9 10	Hard	Alexis	Aug. 22, 1959

SALISBURY

Distance	*Time*	*Weight*	*Going*	*Horse*	*Date*
5f.	1/0⅕	9 4	Hard	Divot	July 10, 1934
6f.	1/14⅕	9 3	Good	Tangle	May 17, 1950
7f.	1/28⅗	7 3	Good	Eunuch	Aug. 23, 1950
1m.	1/42⅗	7 11	Firm	Dark Knight	May 9, 1942
1¼m.	2/11	9 9	Firm	Kar	July 10, 1923
1½m.	2/35	7 1	Firm	Dark Fox	July 9, 1924
2m.	3/15	10 2	Good	Polazel	July 8, 1924

SANDOWN PARK

5f.	59⅖	7 12	Good	Organic	April 27, 1928
7f.	1/28	8 8	Firm	Nero's Love	June 13, 1959
1m.	1/41⅘	8 12	Firm	St. Peter	June 24, 1949
1m.	1/41⅘	9 0	Firm	Petersfield	April 27, 1957
1¼m.	2/6⅘	9 7	Firm	King Salmon	July 20, 1934
* 1m. 5½f.	2/58	8 4	Firm	Kilbi	April 27, 1957
2m.	3/33	9 8	Firm	Induna	June 12, 1959

STOCKTON

5f.	57⅖	9 9	Hard	Dante	May 29, 1944
6f.	1/10⅗	8 11	Hard	Bell Agnes	May 29, 1943
7f.	1/23	7 4	Hard	Mellanthus	June 26, 1943
1m.	1/36	7 13	Firm	Papana	July 14, 1945
1¼m.	2/3⅘	7 7	Firm	Newland Well	Aug, 20, 1949
1¼m.	2/3⅘	6 0	Firm	Torch Singer	Oct. 10, 1953
1½m.	2/30⅕	9 2	Good	Baystar	Aug. 19, 1936

THIRSK

5f.	58⅖	8 0	Firm	Keepatwoatwo	Aug. 6, 1949
5f.	58⅖	7 7	Good	Gold Finder	July 19, 1952
6f.	1/8⅘	8 2	Firm	Second Helping	Sept. 29, 1933
7f.	1/24⅗	7 12	Firm	Mentone	May 29, 1959
1m.	1/38⅖	8 8	Good	Liscloon	May 2, 1936
1½m.	2/33⅖	7 13	Firm	Merry Maid	Aug. 9, 1935
2m.	3/23⅗	8 1	Hard	Royal Pact	June 10, 1950

WARWICK

5f.	58	8 11	Hard	Flying Phoenix	Sept. 18, 1928
6f.	1/12⅖	7 9	Firm	Gold Spinner	May 16, 1959
7f.	1/24⅘	6 8	Firm	Dancing Idol	July 30, 1955
7f.	1/24⅘	7 12	Firm	Blackshore	May 19, 1956
7f.	1/24⅘	8 8	Firm	Cintrist	May 16, 1959
1m.	1/37⅕	7 12	Firm	Blackshore	Oct. 10, 1955
1m.	1/37⅕	6 13	Hard	Harvest Moon	Sept. 7, 1959
1¼m.	2/3	8 3	Good	Kings Oven	April 9, 1929
2m.	3/22⅗	7 11	Firm	Siren Light	Aug. 12, 1950

WINDSOR

5f.	59	7 0	Hard	Vaincu	Aug. 16, 1935
5f.	59	8 12	Hard	Constantia	July 6, 1951
6f.	1/10⅖	7 11	Good	White Spot	Aug. 14, 1926
1m.	1/40⅖	8 11	Good	Chanter	May 10, 1946
1m. 111yds.	1/47⅘	8 10	Firm	Pam's Brother	May 27, 1953
1¼m.	2/7⅘	8 6	Soft	My Adventure	Nov. 5, 1948
1½m.	2/32⅕	7 11	Hard	Zucchero	July 7, 1951

WOLVERHAMPTON

5f.	58⅖	9 8	Firm	Gold Spinner	Aug. 4, 1959
5f. 190yds.	1/8⅖	9 11	Good	Edmundo	May 13, 1957
6f.	1/10⅕	8 12	Firm	Time Keeper	Aug. 18, 1936
7f.	1/24⅘	8 10	Good	Sea Artist	April 13, 1954
1m.	1/37	8 0	Good	Fair Cop	Aug. 17, 1936
1¼m.	2/9⅖	8 11	Good	Duet	Aug. 17, 1926
1½m.	2/32⅕	8 3	Hard	Parting Shot	July 1, 1952

WORCESTER

5f.	58⅘	9 7	Firm	Eastern Imp	April 29, 1957
6f.	1/12	9 2	Firm	Golden Light	Aug. 22, 1959
1m.	1/38⅖	8 0	Firm	Refund	June 13, 1955
1m.	1/38⅖	7 12	Firm	Timepiece	June 13, 1953
1¼m.	2/6	7 3	Hard	El Monte	July 16, 1951
1¼m.	2/6	7 1	Firm	Illuminant	Aug. 20, 1935

YARMOUTH

5f.	1/0	9 0	Good	Golden Fox	June 8, 1938
6f.	1/10⅕	9 3	Hard	Herridge	June 1, 1939
6f.	1/10⅕	7 12	Good	Riccordo	June 9, 1956
7f.	1/22⅗	7 7	Firm	Brother Victor	July 9, 1959
1m.	1/34⅘	8 8	Hard	Calf Love	June 1, 1939
1¼m.	2/5	7 10	Good	Starlight Serenade	July 7, 1954
1¾m.	2/59⅕	9 0	Firm	Sunflash	Aug. 5, 1959

YORK

5f.	57	8 12	Hard	Gold Bridge	Aug. 28, 1934
6f.	1/10⅕	7 13	Good	Live Spirit	May 21, 1953
1m.	1/35⅗	8 12	Good	Rising Flame	Aug. 23, 1951
1¼m.	2/0⅗	8 8	Firm	Read-Admiral	May 29, 1930
1m. 2½f.	2/9	7 6	Firm	Chino	May 26, 1959
1½m.	2/27⅗	8 4	Good	Teresina	Aug. 30, 1923
2m.	†3/21⅗	7 6	Firm	Blue Pennant	May 23, 1946

‡Valerius's time, 3/12⅘ (May 20, 1936), is cancelled from records.

EFFECT OF DRAW

Course		Best Numbers
ALEXANDRA PARK	(Right-hand)	High for sprints
ASCOT	(Right-hand)	Doubtful advantage
AYR	(Left-hand)	Low for sprints. In heavy going high
BATH	(Left-hand)	Low for sprints
BEVERLEY	(Right-hand)	High for 5f., 8f.
BIRMINGHAM	(Right-hand)	Low for 5f., 6f., 8f.
BOGSIDE	(Right-hand)	Low for sprints
BRIGHTON	(Left-hand)	Low for sprints
CARLISLE	(Right-hand)	High up to a mile
CATTERICK BRIDGE	(Left-hand)	Low for sprints
CHEPSTOW	(Left-hand)	High up to a mile
CHESTER	(Left-hand)	Low numbers are best for all distances
DONCASTER	(Left-hand)	Low on round course. High for 5f., 6f., 7f., 8f.
EDINBURGH	(Right-hand)	High up to a mile
EPSOM	(Left-hand)	Low. Derby Course, middle numbers are best
FOLKESTONE	(Right-hand)	Low numbers for 5f., 6f.
GOODWOOD	(Right-hand)	High for 5f., 6f.
HAMILTON PARK	(Right-hand)	Middle numbers
HAYDOCK	(Left-hand)	Low from 6f. to 8f. No advantage over 5f.
HURST PARK	(Right-hand)	Low for sprints
KEMPTON PARK	(Right-hand)	High for Jubilee Course. No advantage on Straight Course
LANARK	(Right-hand)	Low for 5f. High for 7f. and 8f.
LEICESTER	(Right-hand)	5f. to 8f. no advantage. Low in heavy going
LEWES	(Right-hand)	High up to a mile

Course		Best Numbers
LINCOLN	(Left-hand)	No advantage over 5f. High numbers 6f., 7f., 8f. (straight)
LINGFIELD	(Left-hand)	High for sprints. Low in heavy going
LIVERPOOL	(Left-hand)	High for 5f. Low for 6f. and 8f.
MANCHESTER	(Right-hand)	Low 5f., 6f. High for a mile
NEWBURY	(Left-hand)	High 5f., 6f. Low over 7f. 60 yds.
NEWCASTLE	(Left-hand)	No advantage
NEWMARKET Rowley Mile July Course		Over the mile course and upwards high numbers have an advantage
NOTTINGHAM	(Left-hand)	No advantage
PONTEFRACT	(Left-hand)	Low for sprints
REDCAR	(Left-hand)	No advantage
RIPON	(Right-hand)	Low for sprints. High over a mile
SALISBURY	(Right-hand)	High for sprints
SANDOWN	(Right-hand)	Low over 5f. High for 7f. and a mile
STOCKTON	(Left-hand)	Low from 5f. to a mile
THIRSK	(Left-hand)	High for 5f., 6f. Low for 7f. and a mile
WARWICK	(Left-hand)	Low for 5f., 7f., and a mile
WINDSOR	(Right-hand)	High numbers for 5f. and 6f.
WOLVERHAMPTON	(Left-hand)	High for 5f., 6f. Low for 7f. and a mile
WORCESTER	(Left-hand)	Low from 5f. to a mile
YARMOUTH	(Left-hand)	High for 5f., 6f., and a mile
YORK	(Left-hand)	No advantage for 5f., 6f. Heavy going high.

2,000 GUINEAS

Run at Newmarket's First Spring Meeting, over the Rowley Mile. It is the first of the season's classic events. First run in 1809, it is for three-year-old colts and fillies.

Year		Horse	Jockey	Starting Price
1809	1	Wizard	W. Clift	5-4 on
	2	Robin		6-1
	3	Fair Star		7-1
1810	1	Hephestion	F. Buckle	5-1
	2	The Dandy		7-1
	3	B. c. brother to Sir David		—
1811	1	Trophonius	S. Barnard	5-2
	2	Barrosa		6-1
	3	Magnus		
1812	1	Cwrw	S. Chifney	7-1
	2	Cato		9-2
	3	Octavius		4-1
1813	1	Smolensko	H. Miller	7-4
	2	Music		
	3	Phosphor		5-1 & 6-1
1814	1	Olive	W. Arnold	5-1
	2	Ch. c. by Haphazard (only two placed)		7-4
1815	1	Tigris	W. Arnold	7-4
	2	Castanet (only two placed)		—
1816	1	Nectar	W. Arnold	5-2
	2	Milton (only two placed)		3-1
1817	1	Manfred	W. Wheatley	4-1
	2	Sylvanus		7-4
	3	Havock		—
1818	1	Interpreter	W. Clift	7-4 to 5-4
	2	Secundus		—
	3	Picardoon		
1819	1	Antar	E. Edwards	4-1
	2	B. c. by Robens		6-5
	3	Euphrates		3-1
1820	1	Pindarrie	F. Buckle	evens
	2	Ch. c. by Soothsayer		7-2
	3	Hoo Poe		5-1
1821	1	Reginald	F. Buckle	11-10
	2	Ch. c. by Cardinal York		3-1
	3	Incantator		—
1822	1	Pastille	F. Buckle	6-4 on
	2	Midsummer		—
	3	B. c. by Marmion		—
1823	1	Nicolo	W. Wheatley	5-1
	2	Talisman		7-2
	(Only two placed)			
1824	1	Schahriar	W. Wheatley	10-1
	2	Tiara		2-1
	3	Conviction		4-1
1825	1	Enamel	J. Robinson	7-4
	2	B. c. brother to Addy		4-1
	3	Bolero		—
1826	1	Dervise	J. B. Day	7-2
	2	Hobgoblin		—
	3	Black Swan		6-1
1827	1	Turcoman	F. Buckle	5-1
	2	Chrysalis		7-4
	3	Grampus		11-8
1828	1	Cadland	J. Robinson	5-2
	2	Lepanto (Late Sharpset)		8-1
	(Only two placed)			
1829	1	Patron	F. Boyce	8-1 on
	2	Kean		—
	(Only two ran)			
1830	1	Augustus	P. Conolly	7-4 on
	2	Br. c. by Godolphin		—
	(Only two ran)			
1831	1	Riddlesworth	J. Robinson	5-1 on
	2	Sarpedon		—
	3	Bohemian		—
1832	1	Archibald	Pavis	7-4 & 2-1
	2	B. c. by Woful		4-1
	(Only two placed)			

Year		Horse	Jockey	Starting Price
1833	1	Clearwell	J. Robinson	5-4
	2	Sir Robert		5-1
	(Only two placed)			
1834	1	Glencoe	J. Robinson	6-1
	2	Flatterer		7-2
	3	Bentley		11-4
1835	1	Ibrahim	J. Robinson	7-1 on
	2	Paulus		—
	3	Stockport		—
1836	1	Bay Middleton	J. Robinson	6-4 on
	2	Elis		5-2
	3	Ch. c. brother to May-Day		
1837	1	Achmet	E. Edwards	6-4 on
	2	Mustee		10-1
	3	Troilus		4-1
1838	1	Grey Momus	J. B. Day	4-1
	2	Saintfoin		5-2
	3	Bamboo		6-4
1839	1	The Corsair	Wakefield	10-1
	2	Caesar		7-1 on
	3	Pether		
1840	1	Crucifix	J. B. Day	11-8 on
	2	Confederate		7-2
	3	Angelo		6-1
1841	1	Ralph	J. B. Day	5-2
	2	Joachim		12-1
	3	Mustapha		
1842	1	Meteor	W. Scott	6-4
	2	Wiseacre		7-1
	3	Misdeal		3-1
1843	1	Cotherstone	W. Scott	3-1 on
	2	Cornopean	S. Rogers	—
	3	Mallard	E. Flatman	
1844	1	The Ugly Buck	J. Day, jun.	7-2 on
	2	The Devil to Pay	S. Rogers	—
	3	Joe Lovell	F. Butler	
1845	1	Idas	E. Flatman	6-5 on
	2	Worthless	J. Day jun.	—
	3	Winchelsea	J. Howlett	7-2
1846	1	Sir Tatton Sykes (late Tibthorpe)	W. Scott	5-1
	2	Tom Tulloch	F. Butler	13-8 on
	3	St. Demetri	S. Mann	—
1847	1	Conyngham	J. Robinson	4-1
	2	Planet	E. Flatman	5-4
	(Only two placed)			
1848	1	Flatcatcher	J. Robinson	4-1
	2	Glendower	E. Flatman	7-4
	3	Blaze	F. Butler	6-4
1849	1	Nunnykirk	F. Butler	6-5 on
	2	Honeycomb	E. Robinson	10-1
	3	Vatican	Templeman	4-1
1850	1	Pitsford	A. Day	5-2
	2	The Bee-Hunter	Templeman	2-1
	3	Hardinge	E. Flatman	3-1
1851	1	Hernandez	E. Flatman	5-1
	2	Mountain Deer	Templeman	2-1
	3	Glenhawk	Dockeray	10-1
1852	1	Stockwell	Norman	10-1
	2	Homebrewed	E. Flatman	5-2
	3	Filius	A. Day	3-1
1853	1	West Australian	F. Butler	6-4 on
	2	Sittingbourne	Pettit	15-1
	3	Barbatus	E. Flatman	7-1
1854	1	The Hermit	A. Day	12-1
	2	Middlesex	Charlton	—
	(Only two placed)			
1855	1	Lord of the Isles	Aldcroft	5-2
	2	St. Hubert	J. Wells	7-4 on
	3	Kingstown	A. Day	100-8

G. Wilson (Nat. Hunt)

RACING QUIZ

1. Who rode Windsor Lad in the 1934 Derby? (*below*)

*

2. Can you name the jockey who rode Cameronian in the Derby of 1931? (*below*)

*

3. Name the horse who won the One Thousand Guineas in 1943.

*

4. Who was leading trainer in 1937 and 1938?

*

5. Danny Maher was Champion jockey in 1908 and 1913. In which country was he born?

*

6. How old was Fred Archer when he died?

*

7. When was the use of rattles by jockeys banned?

*

8. Has a future monarch ever won the Grand National?

*

9. What was the smallest field for the Derby?

QUIZ ANSWERS

1. Charlie Smirke. 2. Freddy Fox. 3. Herringbone. 4. C. Boyd-Rochfort. 5. He was born in Hartford, Connecticut, U.S.A., on October 29, 1881. 6. Thirty-one. He was born on January 11, 1857, and died on November 8, 1886. 7. In 1935, after J. Hickey had won on Speed On at Folkestone. 8. Yes. King Edward VII did with Ambush II, in 1900. 9. Four, in 1794.

2,000 Guineas—*contd.*

Year	*Horse*	*Jockey*	*Starting Price*
1856	1 Fazzoletto	E. Flatman	5–1
	2 Yellow Jack	S. Rogers	2–1
	3 Pitapat	J. Mann	15–1
1857	1 Vedette	J. Osborne	5–2
	2 Anton	A. Day	5–1
	3 Loyola	S. Rogers	4–1
1858	1 Fitz-Roland	J. Wells	100–6
	2 The Happy Land	G. Fordham	7–1
	3 Clydesdale	J. Goater	3–1
1859	1 The Promised Land	A. Day	Evens
	2 Cynricus	S. Rogers	100–6
	3 Crafton	J. Osborne	100–6
1860	1 The Wizard	Ashmall	20–1
	2 The Rap	J. Goates	—
	3 Traducer	E. Sharp	6–1
1861	1 Diophantus	A. Edwards	25–1
	2 Kettledrum	J. Snowden	4–1
	3 Klarikoff	G. Fordham	5–2
1862	1 The Marquis	Ashmall	5–1
	2 Caterer	T. Chaloner	7–1
	†B. c. by Stockwell	Aldcroft	5–1
	†Nottingham	J. Goater	5–1
1863	1 Macaroni	T. Chaloner	10–1
	2 Saccharometer	J. Goater	7–1
	3 King of the Vale	J. Wells	100–3
186[illegible]	1 General Peel	Aldcroft	7–2
	2 Paris	G. Fordham	4–1
	3 Historian	S. Adams	50–1
1865	1 Gladiateur	H. Grimshaw	7–1
	2 Archimedes	Aldcroft	12–1
	3 Liddington	Daley	4–1
1866	1 Lord Lyon	Thomas	7–4 on
	2 Monarch of the Glen	T. Chaloner	—
	3 Knight of the Crescent	Ashmall	—
1867	1 Vauban	G. Fordham	5–2
	2 Knight of the Garter	Custance	20–1
	3 Marksman	T. Chaloner	7–1
1868	†Moslem	T. Chaloner	100–7
	†Formosa	G. Fordham	3–1
	3 St. Ronan	Custance	12–1
	After a dead-heat with Formosa. Moslem walked over.		
1869	1 Pretender	J. Osborne	3–1
	2 Belladrum	S. Kenyon	10–1
	3 Perry Down	Butler	66–1
1870	1 Macgregor	J. Daley	100–30
	2 Normanby	Grimshaw	66–1
	3 Kingcraft	T. French	75–40
1871	1 Bothwell	J. Osborne	11–2
	2 Sterling	T. Cannon	11–2
	3 King of the Forest	Snowden	55–20
1872	1 Prince Charlie	J. Osborne	2–1
	2 Cremorne	C. Maidment	11–4
	3 Queen's Messenger	T. French	100–7
1873	1 Gang Forward	T. Chaloner	8–1
	2 Kaiser	C. Maidment	2–1
	3 Suleiman	T. Osborne	12–1
1874	1 Atlantic	F. Archer	10–1
	2 Reverberation	H. Jeffrey	100–8
	3 Ecossais	G. Fordham	5–4
1875	1 Camballo	J. Osborne	7–2
	2 Pic-Nic	G. Fordham	8–1
	3 Breechloader	Custance	100–7
1876	1 Petrarch	Luke	20–1
	2 Julius Caesar	F. Webb	100–8
	3 Kaleidescope	Morris	3–1
1877	1 Chamant	J. Goater	2–1
	2 Brown Prince	Custance	100–3
	3 Silvio	F. Archer	100–6
1878	1 Pilgrimage	T. Cannon	2–1
	2 Insulate	J. Goater	9–4
	3 Sefton	J. Osborne	10–1
1879	1 Charibert	F. Archer	25–1
	2 Cadogan	Lemaire	7–1
	3 Rayon d'Or	J. Goater	5–1
1880	1 Petronel	G. Fordham	20–1
	2 Muncaster	F. Webb	9–2
	3 The Abbot	Luke	10–1
1881	1 Peregrine	F. Webb	15–2
	2 Iroquois	Morgan	50–1
	3 Don Fulano	C. Wood	100–1
1882	1 Shotover	T. Cannon	10–1
	2 Quicklime	C. Wood	22–1
	3 Marden	R. Wyatt	100–8
1883	1 Galliard	F. Archer	9–2
	2 Goldfield	T. Cannon	10–1
	3 The Prince	C. Wood	5–1
1884	1 Scot-free (Late Donald II)	Platt	3–1
	2 St. Medard (Late Crusader II)	F. Archer	11–2
	3 Harvester	F. Webb	20–1
1885	1 Paradox	F. Archer	3–1 on
	2 Crafton	T. Cannon	200–7
	3 The Child of the Mist	C. Wood	8–1
1886	1 Ormonde	G. Barrett	7–2
	2 Minting	J. Watts	11–10
	3 Mephisto	T. Cannon	100–3
1887	1 Enterprise	T. Cannon	2–1
	2 Phil	C. Wood	10–1
	3 Eglamore	J. Fagan	6–1
1888	1 Ayrshire	J. Osborne	8–1
	2 Johnny Morgan	F. Barrett	25–1
	3 Orbit	F. Webb	100–7
1889	1 Enthusiast	T. Cannon	25–1
	2 Donovan	F. Barrett	85–20 on
	3 Pioneer	J. Watts	100–8
	1 m. $52\frac{1}{5}$ s.		
1890	1 Surefoot	Liddiard	5–4
	2 Le Nord	F. Barrett	15–2
	3 Blue-green	G. Barrett	100–6

Year	*Horse*	*Jockey*	*Starting Price*
1891	1 Common	G. Barrett	9–1
	2 Orvieto	J. Osborne	6–1
	3 Peter Flower	Rickaby	3–1
	1 m. 47 s. (*J. Porter*)		
1892	1 Bonavista	W. Robinson	10–1
	2 St. Angelo	R. Chaloner	6–1
	3 Curio	F. Webb	40–1
	1 m. 54 s. (*Jarvis*)		
1893	1 Isinglass	T. Loates	5–4 on
	2 Ravensbury	Barker	100–7
	3 Raeburn	J. Watts	10–1
	1 m. $42\frac{3}{5}$ s. (*J. Jewitt*)		
1894	1 Ladas	J. Watts	6–5 on
	2 Matchbox	M. Cannon	9–4
	3 Athlone	W. Bradford	1000–15
	1 m. $44\frac{1}{5}$ s. (*M. Dawson*)		
1895	1 Kirkconnel	J. Watts	10–1
	2 Laveno	M. Cannon	100–8
	3 Sir Visto	W. Bradford	5–1
	1 m. $42\frac{3}{5}$ s. (*J. Day*)		
1896	1 St. Frusquin	T. Loates	100–12 on
	2 Love Wisely	S. Loates	25–1
	3 Labrador	M. Cannon	100–6
	1 m. $43\frac{3}{5}$s. (*A. Hayhoe*)		
1897	1 Galtee More	C. Wood	5–4
	2 Velasquez	J. Watts	6–4
	3 Minstrel	O. Madden	50–1
	1 m. $40\frac{3}{5}$ s. (*S. Darling*)		
1898	1 Disraeli	S. Loates	100–8
	2 Wantage	T. Loates	40–1
	3 Ninus	R. Colling	100–30
	1 m. $44\frac{4}{5}$s. (*J. Dawson*)		
1899	1 Flying Fox	M. Cannon	6–5 on
	2 Caiman	Sloan	5–1
	3 Trident	T. Loates	100–14
	1 m. 43s. (*J. Porter*)		
1900	1 Diamond Jubilee	H. Jones	11–4
	2 Bonarosa	L. Reiff	50–1
	3 Sidus	T. Loates	100–1
	1 m. $43\frac{3}{5}$ s. (*R. Marsh*)		
1901	1 Handicapper	W. Halsey	33–1
	2 Doricles	K. Cannon	4–1
	3 Osboch	H. Jones	40–1
	1 m. 43 s. (*F. W. Day*)		
1902	1 Sceptre	H. Randall	4–1
	2 Pistol	J. H. Martin	50–1
	3 Ard Patrick	K. Cannon	9–2
	1 m. 39 s. (*R. S. Sievier*)		
1903	1 Rock Sand	J. H. Martin	6–4
	2 Flotsam	D. Maher	7–1
	3 Rabelais	K. Cannon	8–1
	1 m. 42 s. (*G. Blackwell*)		
1904	1 St. Amant	K. Cannon	11–4
	2 John o' Gaunt	Mr. G. Thursby	10–1
	3 Henry the First	O. Madden	8–1
	1 m. $38\frac{4}{5}$ s. (*A. Hayhoe*)		
1905	1 Vedas	H. Jones	11–2
	2 Signorino	B. Dillon	25–1
	3 Llangibby	O. Madden	4–1
	1 m. $41\frac{1}{5}$ s. (*W. Robinson*)		
1906	1 Gorgos	H. Jones	20–1
	2 Sancy	O. Madden	100–8
	3 Ramrod	W. Higgs	100–7
	1 m. $43\frac{4}{5}$ s. (*R. Marsh*)		
1907	1 Slieve Gallion	W. Higgs	11–4 on
	2 Bezonian	D. Maher	100–9
	3 Linacre	W. Halsey	100–6
	1 m. $41\frac{4}{5}$ s. (*S. Darling*)		
1908	1 Norman III	O. Madden	25–1
	2 Sir Archibald	Mr. G. Thursby	5–1
	3 White Eagle	L Hewitt	100–7
	1 m. $44\frac{3}{5}$ s. (*J. Watson*)		
1909	1 Minoru	H. Jones	4–1
	2 Phaleron	W. Earl	33–1
	3 Louviers	G. Stern	100–7
	1 m. $37\frac{4}{5}$ s. (*R. Marsh*)		
1910	1 Neil Gow	D. Maher	2–1
	2 Lemberg	B. Dillon	7–2
	3 Whisk Broom	J. H. Martin	100–7
	1 m. $40\frac{3}{5}$ s. (*P. Peck*)		
1911	1 Sunstar	G. Stern	5–1
	2 Stedfast	F. Wootton	100–9
	3 Lycaon	E. Shaw	50–1
	1 m. $37\frac{3}{5}$ s. (*C. Morton*)		
1912	1 Sweeper II	D. Maher	6–1
	2 Jaeger	Walter Griggs	100–1
	3 Hall Cross	W. Saxby	9–2
	1 m. $38\frac{2}{5}$ s. (*H. S. Persse*)		
1913	1 Louvois	J. Reiff	25–1
	2 Craganour	W. Saxby	3–1
	3 Meeting House	F. O'Neill	50–1
	1 m. $38\frac{4}{5}$ s. (*D. Waugh*)		
1914	1 Kennymore	G. Stern	2–1
	2 Corcyra	F. O'Neill	7–2
	3 Black Jester	H. Randall	20–1
	1 m. 38 s. (*Alec Taylor*)		
1915	1 Pommern	S. Donoghue	2–1
	2 Tournament	Walter Griggs	100–6
	3 The Vizier	F. Bullock	25–1
	1 m. $43\frac{4}{5}$ s. (*C. Peck*)		
1916	1 Clarissimus	J. Clark	100–7
	2 Kwang-Su	F. Templeman	10–1
	3 Nassovian	N. Spear	20–1
	1 m. $39\frac{3}{5}$ s. (*W. Waugh*)		
1917	1 Gay Crusader	S. Donoghue	9–4
	2 Magpie	O. Madden	6–1
	3 Athdara	J. Evans	25–1
	1 m. $40\frac{2}{5}$ s. (*Alec Taylor*)		
1918	1 Gainsborough	J. Childs	4–1
	2 Somme Kiss	J. H. Martin	8–1
	3 Blink	R. Colling	100–6
	1 m. $44\frac{2}{5}$ s. (*Alec Taylor*)		

2,000 Guineas—*contd.*

Year	*Horse*	*Jockey*	*Starting Price*
1919	1 The Panther	R. Cooper	10–1
	2 Buchan	V. Smyth	100–8
	3 Dominion	A. Smith	100–6
	1 m. $44\frac{3}{5}$ s (*G. Manser*)		
1920	1 Tetratema	B. Carslake	2–1
	2 Allenby	F. Slade	100–7
	3 Paragon	A. Smith	8–1
	1 m. $44\frac{3}{5}$ s. (*H. S. Persse*)		
1921	1 Craig an Eran	J. Brennan	100–6
	2 Lemonora	J. Childs	100–7
	3 Humorist	S. Donoghue	3–1
	1 m. $41\frac{3}{5}$ s. (*Alec Taylor*)		
1922	1 St Louis	G. Archibald	6–1
	2 Pondoland	F. O'Neill	5–1
	3 Captain Cuttle	V. Smyth	4–1
	1 m. $43\frac{3}{5}$ s. (*P. P. Gilpin*)		
1923	1 Ellangowan	E. C. Elliott	7–1
	2 Knockando	G. Archibald	25–1
	3 D'Orsay	R. A. Jones	50–1
	1 m. $37\frac{4}{5}$ s. (*J. L. Jarvis*)		
1924	1 Diophon	G. Hulme	11–2
	2 Bright Knight	F. Bullock	100–9
	3 Green Fire	S. Donoghue	100–8
	1 m. 39 s. (*R. Dawson*)		
1925	1 Manna	S. Donoghue	100–8
	2 St. Becan	E. C. Elliott	9–1
	3 Oojah	C. Smirke	10–1
	1 m. $39\frac{3}{5}$ s. (*F. Darling*)		
1926	1 Colorado	T. Weston	100–8
	2 Coronach	J. Childs	5–4
	3 Apple Sammy	H. Jelliss	10–1
	1 m. $43\frac{3}{5}$ s. (*Hon. G. Lambton*)		
1927	1 Adam's Apple	J. Leach	20–1
	2 Call Boy	E. C. Elliott	5–2
	3 Sickle	T. Weston	10–1
	1 m. $38\frac{3}{5}$ s. (*H. L. Cottrill*)		
1928	1 Flamingo	E. C. Elliott	5–1
	2 Royal Minstrel	H. Beasley	7–2
	3 O'Curry	P. Beasley	33–1
	1 m. $38\frac{4}{5}$ s. (*J. L. Jarvis*)		
1929	1 Mr. Jinks	H. Beasley	5–2
	2 Cragadour	H. Jelliss	4–1
	3 Gay Day	S. Donoghue	20–1
	1 m. $39\frac{4}{5}$ s. (*H. S. Persse*)		
1930	1 Diolite	F. Fox	10–1
	2 Paradine	R. Perryman	33–1
	3 Silver Flare	E. C. Elliott	25–1
	1 m. $42\frac{3}{5}$ s. (*F. Templeman*)		
1931	1 Cameronian	J. Childs	100–8
	2 Goyescas	E. C. Elliott	8–1
	3 Orpen	R. A. Jones	18–1
	1 m. $39\frac{3}{5}$ s. (*F. Darling*)		
1932	1 Orwell	R. A. Jones	Evens
	2 Dastur	M. Beary	10–1
	3 Hesperus	E. C. Elliott	25–1
	1 m. $42\frac{3}{5}$ s. (*J. Lawson*)		
1933	1 Rodosto	R. Brethes	9–1
	2 King Salmon	H. Wragg	25–1
	3 Gino	E. C. Elliott	100–6
	1 m. $40\frac{3}{5}$ s. (*H. Count, in France*)		
1934	1 Colombo	W. R. Johnstone	7–2 on
	2 Easton	C. Semblat	20–1
	3 Badruddin	F. Fox	50–1
	1 m. 40 s. (*T. Hogg*)		
1935	1 Bahram	F. Fox	7–2
	2 Theft	G. Richards	11–2
	3 Sea Bequest	E. Smith	100–7
	1 m. $41\frac{3}{5}$ s. (*Frank Butters*)		
1936	1 Pay Up	R. Dick	11–2
	2 Mahmoud	S. Donoghue	100–8
	3 Thankerton	T. Burns	40–1
	1 m. $39\frac{3}{5}$ s. (*J. Lawson*)		
1937	1 Le Ksar	C. Semblat	20–1
	2 Goya II	E. C. Elliott	7–1
	3 Mid-day Sun	T. Lowrey	25–1
	1 m. $44\frac{4}{5}$ s. (*F. Carter, in France*)		
1938	1 Pasch	G. Richards	5–2
	2 Scottish Union	B. Carslake	9–1
	3 Mirza II	H. Wragg	7–1
	1 m. $39\frac{4}{5}$ s. (*F. Darling*)		
1939	1 Blue Peter	E. Smith	5–1
	2 Admiral's Walk	H. Wragg	100–7
	3 Fairstone	M. Beary	13–2
	1 m. 40 s. (*J. L. Jarvis*)		
1940	1 Djebel	E. C. Elliott	9–4
	2 Stardust	H. Wragg	100–9
	3 Tant Mieux	G. Richards	13–2
	1 m. $42\frac{3}{5}$ s. (*A. Swann, in France*)		
1941	1 Lambert Simnel	E. C. Elliott	10–1
	2 Morogoro	H. Wragg	100–30
	3 Sun Castle	P. Beasley	100–7
	1 m. $42\frac{3}{5}$ s. (*F. Templeman*)		
	Run as "New Two Thousand Guineas" on July course.		
1942	1 Big Game	G. Richards	11–8 on
	2 Watling Street	S. Ellis	13–2
	3 Gold Nib	R. A. Jones	100–7
	1 m. $40\frac{4}{5}$ s. (*F. Darling*)		
	Run as "New Two Thousand Guineas" on July course.		
1943	1 Kingsway	S. Wragg	18–1
	2 Pink Flower	T. Lowrey	100–9
	3 Way In	C. Richards	100–9
	1 m. $37\frac{3}{5}$ s. (*J. Lawson*)		
	Run as "New Two Thousand Guineas" on July course.		
1944	1 Garden Path	H. Wragg	5–1
	2 Growing Confidence	K. Mullins	20–1
	3 Tehran	P. Gomez	50–1
	1 m. $39\frac{3}{5}$ s. (*W. Earl*)		
1945	1 Court Martial	C. Richards	13–2
	2 Dante	W. Nevett	Evens
	3 Royal Charger	R. A. Jones	40–1
	1 m. $40\frac{3}{5}$ s. (*J. Lawson*)		

Capt. C. Boyd-Rochfort

J. L. Jarvis

A. Taylor

Year	*Horse*	*Jockey*	*Starting Price*
1946	1 Happy Knight	T. Weston	28–1
	2 Khaled	R. A. Jones	100–30
	3 Radiotherapy	T. H. Carey	100–6
	1 m. $38\frac{1}{5}$ s. (*H. Jelliss*)		
1947	1 Tudor Minstrel	G. Richards	11–8
	2 Saravan	E. C. Elliott	25–1
	3 Sayajirao	E. Britt	33–1
	1 m. 37 s. (*F. Darling*)		
1948	1 My Babu	C. Smirke	2–1
	2 The Cobbler	G. Richards	100–30
	3 Pride of India	E. Britt	20–1
	1 m. $34\frac{4}{5}$ s. (*F. Armstrong*)		
1949	1 Nimbus	E. C. Elliott	10–1
	2 Abernant	G. Richards	5–4
	3 Barnes Park	W. Cook	100–1
	1 m. 38 s. (*G. S. Colling*)		
1950	1 Palestine	C. Smirke	4–1
	2 Prince Simon	W. H. Carr	3–1
	3 Masked Light	D. Smith	7–2
	1 m. $37\frac{3}{5}$ s. (*M. Marsh*)		
1951	1 Ki Ming	A. Breasley	100–8
	2 Stokes	G. Younger	33–1
	3 Malka's Boy	W. Cook	40–1
	1 m. $42\frac{3}{5}$ s. (*M. Beary*)		
1952	1 Thunderhead II	R. Poincelet	100–7
	2 King's Bench	T. Gosling	22–1
	3 Argur	E. C. Elliott	8–1
	1 m. $42\frac{1}{2}$ s. (*E. Pollet, in France*)		
1953	1 Nearula	E. Britt	2–1
	2 Bebe Grande	W. Snaith	10–1
	3 Oleandrin	R. Fawdon	20–1
	1 m. 38.26 s. (*C. F. Elsey*)		
1954	1 Darius	E. Mercer	8–1
	2 Ferriol	W. R. Johnstone	100–9
	3 Poona	C. Smirke	40–1
	1 m. 39.45 s. (*H. Wragg*)		
1955	1 Our Babu	D. Smith	13–2
	2 Tamerlane	A. Breasley	5–1
	3 Klairon	J. Deforge	28–1
	1 m. 38.83 s. (*G. T. Brooke*)		
1956	1 Gilles de Retz	F. Barlow	50–1
	2 Chantelsey	E. Britt	10–1
	3 Buisson Ardent	R. Poincelet	20–1
	1 m. 38.76 s. (*C. Jerdein*)		
1957	1 Crepello	L. Piggott	7–2
	2 Quorum	A. J. Russell	100–8
	3 Pipe of Peace	A. Breasley	100–30
	1 m. 38.24 s. (*C. F. N. Murless*)		
1958	1 Pall Mall	D. Smith	20–1
	2 Major Portion	E. Smith	5–1
	3 Nagami	J. Mercer	8–1
	1 m. 39.43 s. (*C. Boyd-Rochfort*)		
1959	1 Taboun	G. Moore	5–2
	2 Masham	D. Smith	9–2
	3 Carnoustie	L. Piggott	11–2
	1 m. 42.42 s. (*A. Head, in France*)		

RACING QUIZ

1. What does the term "Asking the odds" mean in betting?

★

2. What is a Weight for Age Race?

★

3. What is a Nursery Handicap?

★

4. When does the Nursery "season" commence?

★

5. What is the "Blower"?

★

6. Steve Donoghue was champion jockey for ten successive years. Name the years.

QUIZ ANSWERS

1. When a horse is odds on. 2. When the weights carried are fixed according to the conditions of the race. 3. A Handicap event for two-year-olds up to a mile in distance. 4. On September 1st. 5. An organisation acting as liaison agent between office bookmakers and race-course bookmakers for the transmission of commissions. 6. 1914–1923.

King of the Tudors, K. Gethin up, wins the 1954 Eclipse from Darius and Landau.

The finish of the Derby 1913, won by Mr. A. P. Cunliffe's Aboyeur, ridden by E. Piper. Craganour came in first but was disqualified.

RACING QUIZ

1. What does the term "Coup" mean?

*

2. What was The Tetrarch's nickname?

*

3. Name the horse which won the Two Thousand Guineas in 1945. He is now a very successful sire.

QUIZ ANSWERS

1. Where the connections of a horse have won a vast amount of money having previously kept the horse's capabilities a secret. 2. The Spotted Wonder. 3. Court Martial.

E. C. Elliott

R. Poincelet

Lester Piggott

WINNERS OF MORE THAN ONE 2,000 GUINEAS

JOCKEYS

NINE—J. Robinson. 1825, 1828, 1831, 1833, 1834, 1835, 1836, 1847, 1848
SIX—J. Osborne. 1857, 1869, 1871, 1872, 1875, 1888
FIVE—F. Buckle. 1810, 1820, 1821, 1822, 1827
E. C. Elliott, 1923, 1928, 1940, 1941, 1949
FOUR—J. B. Day, 1826, 1838, 1840, 1841
F. Archer, 1874, 1879, 1883, 1885
T. Cannon, 1878, 1882, 1887, 1889
H. Jones, 1900, 1905, 1906, 1909
THREE—W. Arnold, 1814, 1815, 1816
W. Wheatley, 1817, 1823, 1824
W. Scott, 1842, 1843, 1846
E. Flatman, 1845, 1851, 1856
A. Day, 1850, 1854, 1859
T. Chaloner, 1863, 1868 (dead-heat), 1873
G. Fordham, 1867, 1868 (dead-heat), 1880
S. Donoghue, 1915, 1917, 1925
G. Richards, 1938, 1942, 1947
TWO—W. Clift, 1809, 1818
E. Edwards, 1819, 1837
F. Butler, 1849, 1853
Ashmall, 1860, 1862
Aldcroft, 1855, 1864
G. Barrett, 1886, 1891
J. Watts, 1894, 1895
T. Loates, 1893, 1896
D. Maher, 1910, 1912
G. Stern, 1911, 1914
J. Childs, 1918, 1931
F. Fox, 1930, 1935
T. Weston, 1926, 1946
C. Smirke, 1948, 1950
D. Smith, 1955, 1958

OWNERS

FIVE—Duke of Grafton, 1820, 1821, 1822, 1826, 1827
Lord Jersey, 1831, 1834, 1835, 1836, 1837
FOUR—Lord Exeter, 1825, 1829, 1830, 1852
Lord Falmouth, 1874, 1879, 1883, 1916
THREE—Mr. John Bowes, 1842, 1843, 1853
Mr. Merry, 1855, 1870, 1890
Duke of Westminster, 1882, 1886, 1899
H.H. Aga Khan, 1924, 1935, 1950
Lord Astor, 1921, 1936, 1945
Fifth Lord Rosebery, 1894, 1910, 1923
TWO—Lord G. Bentinck, 1838, 1840
Mr. A. Nichol, 1849, 1860
Mr. J. Johnstone, 1869, 1871
Mr. W. S. Crawford, 1868, 1873
Count F. de Lagrange, 1865, 1877
Duke of Beaufort, 1867, 1880
Mr. Douglas Baird, 1887, 1889
Mr. Leopold de Rothschild, 1896, 1904
Major D. McCalmont, 1920, 1929
Mr. H. E. Morris, 1925, 1938
Seventeenth Lord Derby, 1926, 1944
Mr. J. A. Dewar, 1931, 1947

TRAINERS

FIVE—F. Darling, 1925, 1931, 1938, 1942, 1947
FOUR—J. Porter, 1882, 1886, 1891, 1899
Alec Taylor, 1914, 1917, 1918, 1921
J. Lawson, 1932, 1936, 1943, 1954
THREE—R. Marsh, 1900, 1906, 1909
H. S. Persse, 1912, 1920, 1929
J. L. Jarvis, 1923, 1928, 1939
TWO—J. Kent, 1838, 1840
J. Scott, 1853, 1862
J. Dawson 1876, 1892
A. Hayhoe, 1896, 1904
S. Darling, 1897, 1907
F. Templeman, 1930, 1941

T. Hyde on Prince Regent—winner of Cheltenham Gold Cup 1946.

L. McMorrow on Russian Hero, winner of Grand National 1949, taking the last fence.

1,000 GUINEAS

First run in 1814, the race, like the Two Thousand Guineas, is run over the Rowley Mile at Newmarket's First Spring Meeting Three-year-old fillies only.

Year	Horse	Jockey	Starting Price	Year	Horse	Jockey	Starting Price
1814 1	Charlotte	W. Clift	11–5	1829 1	B. f. by Godolphin	Arnull	—
2	Vestal	—	10–1	2	Green Mantle	—	6–4
3	Medora	—	5–2	3	Pauline	—	11–8 on
1815 1	Br. f. by Selim, dam by Cesario	W. Clift	3–1	1830 1	Charlotte West	J. Robinson	5–1
2	Minuet	—	2–1 on	2	Zillah	—	3–1
3	Discord	—		3	Brambilla	—	3–1
1816 1	Rhoda	S. Barnard	3–1 & 5–2	1831 1	Galantine	Conolly	10–1
2	Duenna	—		2	Lioness	—	6–1
3	Guendolen	—	5–4 & 11–8		Only two placed		
1817 1	Neva	W. Arnold	7–4	1832 1	Galata	Arnull	2–1 on
2	Clearwell Lass	—	6–1	2	Olga	—	—
3	Trictrac	—	4–1	3	Salute	—	—
1818 1	Corinne	F. Buckle	7–1	1833 1	Tarantella	Wright	2–1
2	Loo	—	5–4 & 6–4	2	Falernia	—	6–1
	Only two placed			3	Vespa	—	5–2
1819 1	Catgut	—	20–1	1834 1	May-Day	J. Day	6–1
2	Espagnolle	—	5–2 on	2	Velocity	—	—
	Only two placed			3	Amadou	—	5–2
1820 1	Rowena	F. Buckle	7–4	1835 1	Preserve	E. Flatman	3–1 on
2	Caroline	—	7–2	2	Br. f. by Bustard	—	—
3	Br. f. by Hedley	—		3	Ch. f. by Emilius	—	—
1821 1	Zeal	F. Buckle	6–4 on	1836 1	Destiny	J. Day	6–4
2	Amy	—	—	2	Toga	—	5–1
3	Breeze	—	—	3	Zenana	—	5–1
1822 1	Whizgig	F. Buckle	5–2 on	1837 1	Chapeau d'Espagne	J. Day	5–2 on
		Duke of Grafton coupled		2	Velure	—	—
2	Rosalind	—	6–1	3	Comate	—	—
3	Varnish	—		1838 1	Bacarolle	E. Edwards	4–1
1823 1	Zinc	F. Buckle	6–4 on	2	Mecca	—	7–1
2	Spermaceti	—	5–2	3	Romania	—	4–1
	Only two placed			1839 1	Cara	G. Edwards	7–4
1824 1	Cobweb	J. Robinson	5–2	2	Caenis	—	Evens & 6–5
2	Rebecca	—	11–8 on	3	Alexandrina	—	8–1
3	Milto	—	—	1840 1	Crucifix	J. Day	10–1 on
1825 1	Tontine	—	Walk over	2	Rosa Bianca	—	—
1826 1	Problem	J. Day	5–1	3	Spangle	—	—
2	Tears	—	5–1	1841 1	Potentia	J. Robinson	6–4
3	Butterfly	—	6–4 on	2	Florence	—	6–4
1827 1	Arab	F. Buckle	8–1	3	The Queen of Beauty	—	—
2	Monody	—	5–2	1842 1	Firebrand	S. Rogers	—
	Only two placed			2	Celia	—	7–4
1828 1	Zoe	J. Robinson	6–5	3	Eliza	—	7–2
2	Trampoline	—	2–1	1843 1	Extempore	S. Chifney	7–1
	Only two placed			2	Spiteful	G. Edwards	5–1
					Only two placed		

178

Year	Horse	Jockey	Starting Price
1844	1 Sorella	J. Robinson	10–1
	2 Merope	S. Mann	12–1
	3 Emerald	Sly	7–2
1845	1 Pic-nic	W. Abdale	5–2
	2 Pug	E. Flatman	2–1
	3 Heather Bell	F. Butler	7–1
1846	1 Mendicant	S. Day	Evens
	2 Mowerina	F. Butler	5–1
	3 Prussic Acid	Sly	6–1
1847	1 Clementina	E. Flatman	5–2
	2 Slander	F. Butler	5–4 on
	3 Brown Bess	J. Robinson	4–1
1848	1 Canezou	F. Butler	5–1
	2 Vexation	J. Marson	5–1
	3 Prairie Bird	Sly	7–4
1849	1 Flea	A. Day	—
	2 Clarissa	E. Flatman	3–1
	3 St. Rosalia	Chapple	—
1850	1 Ch. f. by Slane	F. Butler	6–5 on
	2 Tiff	Templeman	7–4
	Only two placed		
1851	1 Aphrodite	J. Marson	6–5 on
	2 Anspach	E. Flatman	8–1
	3 Iris	F. Butler	2–1
1852	1 Kate	A. Day	4–1
	2 Lady in Waiting	Charlton	7–1
	3 B. f. by Launcelot	W. Day	—
1853	1 Mentmore Lass	Charlton	12–1
	2 Comfit	E. Flatman	3–1
	3 Sylphine	Sly	7–4
1854	1 Virago	J. Wells	3–1 on
	2 Meteora	Templeman	7–2
	3 Honeysuckle	E. Flatman	—
1855	1 Habena	S. Rogers	Evens
	2 Capucine	Aldcroft	10–1
	3 Clotilde	J. Prince	3–1
1856	1 Manganese	J. Osborne	2–1
	2 Mincepie	A. Day	5–4 on
	3 Queen's Head	J. Wells	—
1857	1 Imperieuse	E. Flatman	100–8
	2 Tasmania	Bumby	—
	3 Pyacanora	A. Day	4–1
1858	1 Governess	Ashmall	6–1
	2 Hepatica	E. Flatman	9–4
	3 Perfection	J. Goater	3–1
1859	1 Mayonaise	G. Fordham	9–2
	2 Ariadne	A. Day	5–2 on
	3 Prelude	Withington	—
1860	1 Sagitta	Aldcroft	5–2
	2 Aurora	A. Day	10–1
	3 B. f. by Longbow	J. Wells	4–1
1861	1 Nemesis	G. Fordham	10–1
	2 Fairwater	J. Osborne	4–1
	3 Brown Duchess	L. Snowden	2–1
1862	1 Hurricane	Ashmall	11–2
	2 Bertha	A. Edwards	4–1
	3 Sappho	H. Custance	100–8
1863	1 Lady Augusta	A. Edwards	3–1
	2 Flying Fish	Roper	20–1
	3 Cadeau	Daley	25–1
1864	1 Tomato	J. Wells	10–1
	2 Breeze	Daley	100–3
	3 Tooi-tooi	Ashmall	100–8
1865	1 Siberia	G. Fordham	3–1
	2 White Duck	Ashmall	10–1
	3 La Fortune	H. Grimshaw	10–1
1866	1 Repulse	T. Cannon	2–1 on
	2 Bayonette	H. Grimshaw	6–1
	3 Mirella	T. Chaloner	—
1867	1 Achievement	H. Custance	8–1 on
	2 Soeur de Charité	C. Loates	—
	3 Mayflower	Grimshaw	—
1868	1 Formosa	G. Fordham	11–10 on
	2 Athena	T. Cannon	10–1
	3 Lady Coventry	Daley	11–4
1869	1 Scottish Queen	G. Fordham	100–8
	2 Morna	J. Adams	6–4
	3 Brigantine	T. Cannon	100–15
1870	1 Hester	J. Grimshaw	6–4
	2 Frivolity	T. Chaloner	11–2
	3 Mahonia	C. Maidment	11–2
1871	1 Hannah	C. Maidment	2–1
	2 Steppe	H. Jeffery	100–6
	3 Noblesse	T. Chaloner	4–1
1872	1 Reine	H. Parry	20–1
	2 Derelict	Huxtable	25–1
	3 Highland Fling	J. Morris	20–1
1873	1 Cecilia	J. Morris	100–3
	2 Angela	J. Osborne	7–1
	3 Windermere	J. Goater	100–3
1874	1 Apology	J. Osborne	5–2
	2 La Coureuse	G. Fordham	3–1
	3 Blanchefleur	F. Archer	10–1
1875	1 Spinaway	F. Archer	10–1
	2 Per Se	T. Cannon	5–4 on
	3 Chaplet	H. Custance	100–15
1876	1 Camelia	T. Glover	4–1
	2 Allumette	J. Morris	50–1
	3 La Seine	C. Wood	3–1
	1 m. 53½s.		
1877	1 Belphoebe	H. Jeffery	100–6
	2 Lady Ronald	H. Parey	100–3
	3 Lady Golightly	F. Archer	100–30
	1 m. 55 s.		
1878	1 Pilgrimage	T. Cannon	5–4 on
	2 Jannette	F. Archer	25–1
	3 Clementine	J. Goater	5–1
1879	1 Wheel of Fortune	F. Archer	75–40 on
	2 Abbaye	J. Goater	—
	3 Reconciliation	C. Wood	100–30

Left to right: Bruce Hobbs, Atty Persse, Michael Beary, Edgar Britt.

Finish of the Ascot Gold Cup 1939, won by E. Smith on Flyon.

Year	Horse	Jockey	Starting Price
1880	1 Elizabeth	C. Wood	9–2
	2 Versigny	F. Archer	2–1
	3 Evasion	F. Webb	5–1
	1 m. 56 s.		
1881	1 Thebais	G. Fordham	6–5 on
	2 Thora	J. Watts	100–7
	3 Bal Gal	F. Archer	9–2
1882	1 St. Marguerite	C. Wood	10–1
	2 Shotover	T. Cannon	4–1 on
	3 Nellie	G. Fordham	10–1
	1 m. 55⅗ s.		
1883	1 Hauteur	G. Fordham	9–4
	2 Malibran	J. Goater	5–1
	3 Lovely	C. Wood	100–8
	1 m. 52⅘ s.		
1884	1 Busybody	T. Cannon	85–40
	2 Queen Adelaide	F. Webb	6–1
	3 Whitelock	C. Wood	9–2
	1 m. 47 s.		
1885	1 Farewell	G. Barrett	20–1
	2 Jane	J. Goater	33–1
	3 Satchel	E. Rossiter	9–1
	1 m. 47⅘ s. (*J. Ryan*)		
1886	1 Miss Jummy	J. Watts	3–1
	2 Argo Navis	H. Arnull	25–1
	3 Jewel Song	J. Woodburn	100–9
1887	1 Reve d'Or	C. Wood	Evens
	2 Porcelain	J. Fagan	100–6
	3 Freedom	G. Barrett	3–1
	1 m. 47⅗ s.		
1888	1 Briar-root	W. Warne	100–9
	2 Seabreeze	W. Robinson	6–4
	3 Belle Mahone	J. Fagan	8–1
1889	1 Minthe	J. Woodburn	4–1
	2 Wrinkle	G. Chaloner	50–1
	3 Polka	F. Webb	50–1
1890	1 Semolina	J. Watts	2–1 on
	2 Memoir	G. Barrett	10–1
	3 Fatuité	C. Loates	100–7
1891	1 Mimi	F. Rickaby	7–1
	2 Melody	F. Webb	20–1
	3 Siphonia	T. Cannon	2–1
	1 m. 44⅕ s.		
1892	1 La Fleche	G. Barrett	2–1 on
	2 The Smew	W. Robinson	6–1
	3 Adoration	R. Chaloner	100–8
	1 m. 52⅖ s. (*J. Porter*)		
1893	1 Siffleuse (late La Belle Siffleuse)	T. Loates	33–1
	2 Dame President	J. Woodburn	3–1
	3 Tressure	A. White	100–14
	1 m. 53 s. (*J. Day*)		
1894	1 Amiable	W. Bradford	100–8
	2 Lady Minting	F. Rickaby	100–6
	3 Mecca	F. Allsopp	6–1
	1 m. 46 s. (*G. Dawson*)		
1895	1 Galeottia	F. Pratt	100–8
	2 La Sagesse	S. Loates	100–8
	3 Gas	O. Madden	20–1
	1 m. 47⅕ s. (*J. Ryan*)		
1896	1 Thais	J. Watts	5–1
	2 Santa Maura	F. Rickaby	10–1
	3 Jolly Boat	S. Loates	10–1
	1 m. 46⅕ s. (*R. Marsh*)		
1897	1 Chelandry	J. Watts	9–4
	2 Galatia	R. Colling	20–1
	3 Goletta	J. Fagan	13–8
	1 m. 42⅖ s. (*W. Walters, Jun.*)		
1898	1 Nun Nicer	S. Loates	11–2
	2 Airs and Graces	O. Madden	100–6
	3 Alt Mark	F. Rickaby	100–8
	1 m. 48⅗ s. (*W. Waugh*)		
1899	1 Sibola	J. T. Sloan	13–8
	2 Fascination	F. Pratt	20–1
	3 Musa	F. Rickaby	100–7
	1 m. 44½ s. (*J. Huggins*)		
1900	1 Winifreda	S. Loates	11–2
	2 Inquisitive	J. T. Sloan	100–7
	3 Vain Duchess	J. H. Martin	4–1
	1 m. 46 s. (*T. Jennings, Jun.*)		

RACING QUIZ

1. Name the horse which won the Derby in 1932. He was trained by Tom Walls.

★

2. Name the horse which won the Derby in 1939.

★

3. Name the year when Sansovino won the Derby.

QUIZ ANSWERS

1. April the 5th. 2. Blue Peter. 3. 1924.

Aureole holds off Vamos to win the 1954 King George VI and Queen Elizabeth Stakes.

Miss D. Paget's Golden Miller (G. Wilson up), 1935.

RACING QUIZ

1. Which horse died 21 days after winning the 1921 Derby?

★

2. When was the only dead-heat for first place in the Derby?

★

3. Three fillies have won both the Derby and the Oaks. Name them.

★

4. Steve Donoghue rode three successive Derby winners. Name the horses and year.

★

5. When was the only time an English-trained horse has failed to reach a place in the Derby?

★

6. When was the Derby first run and who won?

QUIZ ANSWERS

1. Humorist. 2. In 1884 by St. Gatien and Harvester. 3. Eleanor (1801), Blink Bonny (1857), Signorinetta (1908). 4. Humorist (1921), Captain Cuttle (1922), Papyrus (1923). 5. In 1956 (1) Lavandin (France), (2) Montaval (France), (3) Roistar (Ireland). 6. Diomed n 1780.

1,000 Guineas—*contd.*

Year		*Horse*	*Jockey*	*Starting Price*
1901	1	Aida	D. Maher	13–8
	2	Fleur d'Ete	W. Halsey	10–1
	3	Santa Brigida	J. Reiff	10–1
		1 m. $44\frac{3}{5}$ s. (*G. Blackwell*)		
1902	1	Sceptre	H. Randall	2–1 on
	2	St. Windeline	W. Lane	100–7
	3	Black Fancy	J. Childs	33–1
		1 m. $40\frac{1}{5}$ s. (*R. S. Sievier*)		
1903	1	Quintessence	H. Randall	4–1
	2	Sun-Rose	W. Halsey	20–1
	3	Skyscraper	D. Maher	9–4
		1 m. 48 s. (*J. Chandler*)		
1904	1	Pretty Polly	W. Lane	4–1 on
	2	Leucadia	H. Aylin	33–1
	3	Flamma	D. Maher	100–1
		1 m. 49 s. (*P. P. Gilpin*)		
1905	1	Cherry Lass	G. McCall	5–4
	2	Koorhaan	B. Dillon	33–1
	3	Jongleuse	H. Pipe	33–1
		1 m. $43\frac{3}{5}$ s. (*W. Robinson*)		
1906	1	Flair	B. Dillon	11–10 on
	2	Lischana	W. Higgs	20–1
	3	Paid Up	H. Randall	20–1
		1 m. $40\frac{3}{5}$ s. (*P. P. Gilpin*)		
1907	1	Witch Elm	B. Lynham	4–1
	2	Frugality	G. McCall	20–1
	3	Sixty	W. Halsey	20–1
		1 m. $42\frac{3}{5}$ s. (*W. Robinson*)		
1908	1	Rhodora	L. Lyne	100–8
	2	Bracelet	B. Lynham	5–1
	3	Ardentrive	W. Halsey	100–6
		1 m. $43\frac{4}{5}$ s. (*G. Allen*)		
1909	1	Electra	B. Dillon	9–1
	2	Princesse de Galles	H. Jones	5–2
	3	Perola	F. Wootton	3–1
		1 m. $40\frac{3}{5}$ s. (*P. P. Gilpin*)		
1910	1	Winkipop	B. Lynham	5–2
	2	Maid of Corinth	H. Jones	100–8
	3	Rosedrop	C. Trigg	20–1
		1 m. 41 s. (*W. Waugh*)		
1911	1	Atmah	F. Fox	7–1
	2	Radiancy	J. H. Martin	25–1
	3	Knockfeerna	F. O'Neill	100–8
		1 m. $35\frac{3}{5}$ s. (*F. Pratt*)		
1912	1	Tagalie	L. H. Hewitt	20–1
	2	Alope	B. Carslake	20–1
	3	Belleisle	H. Jones	7–4
		1 m. $39\frac{3}{5}$ s. (*D. Waugh*)		
1913	1	Jest	F. Rickaby Jun.	9–1
	2	Taslett	E. Wheatley	6–1
	3	Prue	D. Maher	9–1
		1 m. $40\frac{4}{5}$ s. (*C. Morton*)		
1914	1	Princess Dorrie	W. Huxley	100–9
	2	Glorvina	F. Rickaby Jun.	100–7
	3	Torchlight	G. Stern	Evens
		1 m. 42 s. (*C. Morton*)		
1915	1	Vaucluse	F. Rickaby Jun.	5–2
	2	Silver Tag	S. Donoghue	4–1
	3	Bright	F. Fox	10–1
		1 m. $40\frac{4}{5}$ s. (*F. Hartigan*)		
1916	1	Canyon	F. Rickaby Jun.	9–4
	2	Fifinella	J. Childs	11–10
	3	Salamandra	A. Whalley	10–1
		1 m. 40 s. (*Hon. G. Lambton*)		
1917	1	Diadem	F. Rickaby Jun.	6–4
	2	Sunny Jane	R. Cooper	25–1
	3	Nonpareil	A. Whalley	25–1
		1 m. 43 s. (*Hon. G. Lambton*)		
1918	1	Ferry	B. Carslake	50–1
	2	My Dear	S. Donoghue	6–4
	3	Herself	F. Fox	20–1
		1 m. $46\frac{1}{5}$ s. (*Hon. G. Lambton*)		
1919	1	Roseway	A. Whalley	2–1
	2	Britannia	F. Fox	6–1
	3	Glaciale	G. Colling	20–1
		1 m. $47\frac{3}{5}$ s. (*F. Hartigan*)		
1920	1	Cinna	Wm. Griggs	4–1
	2	Cicerole	J. Childs	100–8
	3	Valescure	Q. Preece	25–1
		1 m. $40\frac{2}{5}$ s. (*T. Waugh*)		

Year		*Horse*	*Jockey*	*Starting Price*
1921	1	Bettina	G. Bellhouse	33–1
	2	Petrea	B. Carslake	33–1
	3	Pompadour	J. Brennan	7–1
		1 m. $44\frac{3}{5}$ s. (*P. Linton*)		
1922	1	Silver Urn	B. Carslake	10–1
	2	Soubriquet	V. Smyth	100–12
	3	Golden Corn	S. Donoghue	7–4
		1 m. 40 s. (*H. S. Persse*)		
1923	1	Tranquil	E. Gardner	5–2
	2	Cos	G. Hulme	10–1
	3	Shrove	W. McLachan	100–6
		1 m. 39 s. (*Hon. G. Lambton*)		
1924	1	Plack	E. C. Elliott	8–1
	2	Mumtaz Mahal	G. Hulme	6–5
	3	Straitlace	F. O'Neill	7–2
		1 m. $39\frac{3}{5}$ s. (*J. L. Jarvis*)		
1925	1	Saucy Sue	F. Bullock	4–1 on
	2	Miss Gadabout	J. Brennan	20–1
	3	Firouze Mahal	B. Carslake	7–1
		1 m. $42\frac{1}{5}$ s. (*Alec Taylor*)		
1926	1	Pillion	R. Perryman	25–1
	2	Trilogy	F. Lane	8–1
	3	Short Story	J. Brennan	20–1
		1 m. 42 s. (*J. Watson*)		
1927	1	Cresta Run	A. Balding	10–1
	2	Book Law	H. Jelliss	13–2
	3	Endowment	J. Childs	3–1
		1 m. 38 s. (*P. P. Gilpin*)		
1928	1	Scuttle	J. Childs	15–8
	2	Jurisdiction	G. Richards	100–8
	3	Toboggan	T. Weston	11–2
		1 m. $44\frac{1}{5}$ s. (*W. Jarvis*)		
1929	1	Taj Mah	W. Sibbritt	33–1
	2	Sister Anne	J. Childs	5–2
	3	Ellanvale	E. C. Elliott	20–1
		1 m. $40\frac{2}{5}$ s. (*J. Torterolo, in France*)		
1930	1	Fair Isle	T. Weston	7–4
	2	Torchere	R. Perryman	10–1
	3	Sister Clover	J. Sirett	10–1
		1 m. 42 s. (*Frank Butters*)		
1931	1	Four Course	E. C. Elliott	100–9
	2	Lady Marjorie	G. Richards	4–1
	3	Lindos Ojos	H. Beasley	10–1
		1 m. $39\frac{4}{5}$ s. (*Fred Darling*)		
1932	1	Kandy	E. C. Elliott	33–1
	2	Thorndean	R. A. Jones	20–1
	3	Safe Return	G. Richards	100–6
		1 m. 44 s. (*F. Carter, in France*)		
1933	1	Brown Betty	J. Childs	8–1
	2	Fur Tor	R. A. Jones	100–6
	3	Myrobella	G. Richards	5–1
		1 m. $39\frac{2}{5}$ s. (*C. Boyd-Rochfort*)		
1934	1	Campanula	H. Wragg	5–2 on
	2	Light Brocade	B. Carslake	100–6
	3	Spend a Penny	R. Perryman	100–9
		1 m. 39 s. (*J. L. Jarvis*)		
1935	1	Mesa	W. R. Johnstone	8–1
	2	Hyndford Bridge	H. Wragg	20–1
	3	Caretta	G. Richards	9–4
		1 m. 43 s. (*M. P. Corbiere, in France*)		
1936	1	Tide-way	R. Perryman	100–30
	2	Feola	F. Fox	28–1
	3	Ferrybridge	G. Richards	11–4
		1 m. $41\frac{4}{5}$ s. (*C. Leader*)		
1937	1	Exhibitionist	S. Donoghue	10–1
	2	Spray	P. Beasley	100–6
	3	Gainsborough Lass	E. Smith	11–10 on
		1 m. 44 s. (*J. Lawson*)		
1938	1	Rockfel	S. Wragg	8–1
	2	Laughing Water	W. Stephenson	20–1
	3	Solar Flower	R. Perryman	20–1
		1 m. 38 s. (*O. Bell*)		
1939	1	Galatea II	R. A. Jones	6–1
	2	Aurora	R. Perryman	7–1
	3	Olein	T. Lowrey	9–2
		1 m. $38\frac{2}{5}$ s. (*J. Lawson*)		
†1940	1	Godiva	D. Marks	10–1
	2	Golden Penny	G. Richards	11–8 on
	3	Allure	M. Beary	10–1
		1 m. $40\frac{3}{5}$ s. (*W. Jarvis*)		
†1941	1	Dancing Time	R. Perryman	100–8
	2	Beausite	H. Wragg	7–1
	3	Keystone	G. Richards	11–2
		1 m. $40\frac{4}{5}$ s. (*J. Lawson*)		
†1942	1	Sun Chariot	G. Richards	Evens
	2	Perfect Peace	R. A. Jones	5–1
	3	Light of Day	S. Ellis	25–1
		1 m. $39\frac{3}{5}$ s. (*Fred Darling*)		
†1943	1	Herringbone	H. Wragg	15–2
	2	Ribbon	E. Smith	6–4
	3	Cincture	W. Nevett	100–7
		1 m. 41 s. (*W. Earl*)		
†1944	1	Picture Play	E. C. Elliott	15–2
	2	Grande Corniche	P. Evans	100–6
	3	Superior	T. Weston	100–9
		1 m. $40\frac{3}{5}$ s. (*J. Watts*)		
‡1945	1	Sun Stream	H. Wragg	5–2
	2	Blue Smoke	E. Smith	25–1
	3	Mrs. Feather	A. Wragg	4–1
		1 m. $45\frac{2}{5}$ s. (*W. Earl*)		
1946	1	Hypericum	D. Smith	100–6
	2	Neolight	G. Richards	6–4 on
	3	Iona	E. Smith	9–1
		1 m. $41\frac{3}{5}$ s. (*C. Boyd-Rochfort*)		
1947	1	Imprudence	W. R. Johnstone	4–1
	2	Rose o' Lynn	S. Smith	100–6
	3	Wise Child	T. Lowrey	20–1
		1 m. 46 s. (*J. Lieux, in France*)		
1948	1	Queenpot	G. Richards	6–1
	2	Ariostar	J. Marshall	100–6
	3	Duplicity	W. Nevett	33–1
		1 m. $41\frac{4}{5}$ s. (*C. F. N. Murless*)		

The St. Leger Stakes, at Doncaster 1936—won by Mr. W. Woodward's Boswell, ridden by P. Beasley.

Bernard Carslake

Year	Horse	Jockey	Starting Price
1949	1 Musidora	E. Britt	100–8
	2 Unknown Quantity	W. Rickaby	7–2
	3 Solar Myth	T. Gosling	100–8
	1 m. 40 s. (C. F. Elsey)		
1950	1 Camaree	W. R. Johnstone	10–1
	* Catchit	G. Littlewood	50–1
	* Tambara	G. Richards	10–1
	1 m. 37 s. (A. Lieux, in France)		
1951	1 Belle of All	G. Richards	4–1
	2 Subtle Difference	W. Rickaby	100–8
	3 Bob Run	K. Gethin	50–1
	1 m. 44¾ s. (N. Bertie)		
1952	1 Zabara	K. Gethin	7–1
	2 La Mirambule	R. Poincelet	2–1
	3 Refreshed	G. Richards	100–8
	1 m. 41 s. (V. Smyth)		
1953	1 Happy Laughter	E. Mercer	10–1
	2 Tessa Gillian	W. Rickaby	9–2
	3 Bebe Grande	W. Snaith	4–1
	1 m. 45·05 s. (J. L. Jarvis)		
1954	1 Festoon	A. Breasley	9–2
	2 Big Berry	L. Piggott	20–1
	3 Welsh Fairy	F. Durr	20–1
	1 m. 38.91 s. (N. Cannon)		
1955	1 Meld	W. H. Carr	11–2
	2 Aberlady	E. Mercer	100–1
	3 Feria	A. Breasley	6–1
	1 m. 42.16 s. (C. Boyd-Rochfort)		
1956	1 Honeylight	E. Britt	100–6
	2 Midget II	R. Poincelet	100–30
	3 Arietta	E. Hide	33–1
	1 m. 38.01 s. (C. F. Elsey)		
1957	1 Rose Royale II	C. Smirke	6–1
	2 Sensualita	J. Massard	33–1
	3 Angelet	E. Hide	4–1
	1 m. 39.15 s. (A. Head, in France)		
1958	1 Bella Paola	S. Boullenger	11–8 on
	2 Amante	J. Massard	9–1
	3 Alpine Bloom	E. Mercer	100–7
	1 m. 38.75 s. (F. Mathet, in France)		
1959	1 Petite Etoile	D. Smith	8–1
	2 Rosalba	J. Mercer	9–4
	3 Paraguana	G. Moore	5–2
	1 m. 40.36 s. (C. F. N. Murless)		

* Dead heat.
† Run over Bunbury Mile as "New 1,000 Guineas Stakes".
‡ Bunbury Mile.

WINNERS OF MORE THAN ONE 1,000 GUINEAS

JOCKEYS

SEVEN—G. Fordham, 1859, 1861, 1865, 1868, 1869, 1881, 1883

SIX—F. Buckle, 1818, 1820, 1821, 1822, 1823, 1827

FIVE—J. Robinson, 1824, 1828, 1830, 1841, 1844
J. Day, 1826, 1834, 1836, 1837, 1840

FOUR—J. Watts, 1886, 1890, 1896, 1897
E. C. Elliott, 1924, 1931, 1932, 1944
F. Rickaby, Jun., 1913, 1915, 1916, 1917

THREE—E. Flatman, 1835, 1847, 1857
C. Wood, 1880, 1882, 1887
T. Cannon, 1866, 1878, 1884
R. Perryman, 1926, 1936, 1941
H. Wragg, 1934, 1943, 1945
W. R. Johnstone, 1935, 1947, 1950
G. Richards, 1942, 1948, 1951

TWO—W. Clift, 1814, 1815
Arnull, 1829, 1832
F. Butler, 1848, 1850
A. Day, 1849, 1852
S. Rogers, 1842, 1855
Ashmall, 1858, 1862
J. Wells, 1854, 1864
J. Osborne, 1856, 1874
F. Archer, 1875, 1879
G. Barrett, 1885, 1892
S. Loates, 1898, 1900
H. Randall, 1902, 1903
B. Dillon, 1906, 1909
B. Lynham, 1907, 1910
B. Carslake, 1918, 1922
J. Childs, 1928, 1933
E. Britt, 1949, 1956
D. Smith, 1946, 1959

OWNERS

EIGHT—Duke of Grafton, 1819, 1820, 1821, 1822, 1823, 1825, 1826, 1827

SEVEN—17th Lord Derby, 1916, 1918, 1923, 1930, 1936, 1943, 1945

THREE—Lord Falmouth, 1873, 1875, 1879
Baron Rothschild, 1853, 1864, 1871
Duke of Beaufort, 1865, 1869, 1887
Mr. W. S. Crawfurd, 1859, 1881, 1882
5th Lord Rosebery, 1897, 1915, 1924

TWO—Lord Jersey, 1824, 1830
Lord G. Bentinck, 1840, 1842
Mr. C. J. Lefevre, 1872, 1883
Duke of Portland, 1890, 1894
Sir J. Blundell Maple, 1893, 1898
Mr. W. Hall Walker, 1905, 1907
Mr. J. B. Joel, 1913, 1914
Mr. W. Raphael, 1912, 1921
Sir Victor Sassoon, 1937, 1956
His Majesty King George VI, 1942, 1946

TRAINERS

FOUR—P. P. Gilpin, 1904, 1906, 1909, 1927
Hon. G. Lambton, 1916, 1917, 1918, 1923

THREE—J. L. Jarvis, 1924, 1934, 1953
J. Lawson, 1937, 1939, 1941
C. Boyd-Rochfort, 1933, 1946, 1955

TWO—J. Ryan, 1885, 1895
W. Robinson, 1905, 1907
W. Waugh, 1898, 1910
C. Morton, 1913, 1914
F. Hartigan, 1915, 1919
W. Jarvis, 1928, 1940
Fred Darling, 1931, 1942
W. Earl, 1943, 1945
C. F. Elsey, 1949, 1956
C. F. N. Murless, 1948, 1959

Winner of the Derby and Oaks 1908, Signorinetta, with jockey W. Bullock.

THE DERBY

Run at Epsom

The race was first run on May 4th, 1780. The origin of the Derby cannot be traced. It is open to both three-year-old colts and fillies. However, geldings were barred in 1904. The race is run over one mile and four furlongs.

Year	Horse	Jockey	Starting Price
1780	1 Diomed	S. Arnull	6–4
	2 Budroo	—	4–1
	3 Spitfire	—	7–1
1781	1 Young Eclipse	Hindley	10–1
	2 Crop	—	5–4
	3 Prince Orange	—	—
1782	1 Assassin	S. Arnull	5–1
	2 Sweet Robin	—	3–1
	3 Fortunio	—	10–1
1783	1 Saltram	Hindley	5–2
	2 Dungannon	—	5–1
	3 Parlington	—	10–1
1784	1 Sergeant	J. Arnull	3–1
	2 Carlo Khan	—	20–1
	3 Dancer	—	8–1
1785	1 Aimwell	Hindley	7–1
	2 Grantham	—	2–1
		(Lord Grosvenor stable coupled)	
	3 C. by Highflyer	—	—
1786	1 Noble	J. White	30–1
	2 Meteor	—	3–1
	3 Claret	—	10–1
1787	1 Sir Peter Teazle	S. Arnull	2–1
	2 Gunpowder	—	8–1
	3 Bustler	—	7–4
1788	1 Sir Thomas	W. South	6–5 on
	2 Aurelius	—	5–2
	3 Feenow	—	—
1789	1 Skyscraper	S. Chifney, Sen.	7–4 on
	2 Sir George	—	—
	3 B. c. brother to Skylark	—	—
1790	1 Rhadamanthus	J. Arnull	5–4
	2 Asparagus	—	4–1
	3 Lee Boo	—	7–1
1791	1 Eager	Stephenson	5–2
	2 Vermin	—	5–4
	3 Proteus	—	10–1
1792	1 John Bull	F. Buckle	6–4 on
	2 Speculator	—	100–1
	3 Bustard	—	5–2
1793	1 Waxy	W. Clift	12–1
	2 B. c. brother to Precipitate	—	11–10 on
	3 Triptolemus	—	—
1794	1 Daedalus	F. Buckle	6–1
	2 Highflyer	—	2–1
	3 Leon	—	5–4 on & 6–4 on
1795	1 Spread Eagle	A. Wheatley	3–1 & 5–2
	2 Caustic	—	—
	3 Pelter	—	9–1
1796	1 Didelot	J. Arnull	—
	2 Stickler	—	7–1
	3 Leviathan	—	9–2
1797	1 B. c. by Fidget	J. Singleton	10–1
	2 Esculus	—	20–1
	3 Plaistow	—	2–1

RACING QUIZ

1. State the racing colours of Her Majesty.

★

2. At what age are horses nominated for the Derby?

★

3. Has any jockey ridden the winner of the Lincolnshire Handicap and Grand National? (below)

★

4. Which horse won four classics in 1902?

5. What was the name of the King's horse brought down in the Derby of 1913 by a suffragette?

★

6. Which horse holds the record time for the Grand National?

QUIZ ANSWERS

1. Purple, gold braid, scarlet sleeves, black velvet cap with gold fringe. 2. They are entered as yearlings. 3. Yes, D. V. Dick who won the Lincolnshire on Gloaming in 1941 and the National on E.S.B. in 1956. 4. Sceptre, the 2,000 Guineas, One Thousand Guineas, Oaks and St. Leger. 5. Anmer. 6. Golden Miller, 9 m. 20¾ s.

F. Bullock

K. Gethin

D. Smith

Grand National 1933. Pelorous Jack (left) and the winner Kellsboro' Jack.

Captain Cuttle winning the Derby at Epsom 1922.

RACING QUIZ

1. Did the Derby winner Bahram ever suffer defeat?

★

2. Bayardo ran 25 times. Of these how many did he win?

★

3. Name the horse that won the Ascot Gold Cup of 1842. As a help he won 51 races out of 64.

QUIZ ANSWERS

1. No, he was unbeaten in nine races. 2. 22 races. 3. Beeswing, who also won the Newcastle Cup six years in succession.

F. B. Rees winning the Grand National 1921 on Shaun Spadah.

The Derby—contd.

Year		Horse	Jockey	Starting Price
1798	1	Sir Harry	S. Arnull	6–4 & 7–4
	2	Telegraph	—	100–3
	3	Young Spear	—	8–1
1799	1	Archduke	J. Arnull	12–1
	2	Gislebert	—	17–1
	3	B. c. brother to Spread Eagle		Evens
1800	1	Champion	W. Clift	7–4
	2	Ch. c. by Precipitate	—	4–1
	3	Ch. c. by Woodpecker	—	—
1801	1	Eleanor	Saunders	5–4
	2	B. c. by Fidget	—	—
	3	Remnant	—	7–1
1802	1	Tyrant	F. Buckle	7–1
	2	B. c. by Young Eclipse	—	11–8
	3	Orlando	—	10–1
1803	1	Ditto	W. Clift	7–2
	2	B. c. by Sir Peter	—	9–1
	3	B. c. brother to Stamford		7–4
1804	1	Hannibal	W. Arnull	5–2 & 3–1
	2	B. c. by Waxy	—	2–1
	3	Hippocampus	—	9–2
1805	1	Cardinal Beaufort	Fitzpatrick	20–1
	2	Plantagenet	—	5–2 & 3–1
	3	Goth	—	—
1806	1	Paris	J. Shepherd	5–1
	2	Trafalgar	—	6–1
	3.	Hector	—	—
1807	1	Election	J. Arnull	3–1
	2	B. c. by Sir Solomon	—	4–1
	3	Coriolanus		very high odds
1808	1	Pan	Collinson	25–1
	2	Vandyke	—	9–4
	3	Chester	—	20–1
1809	1	Pope	T. Goodison	20–1
	2	Wizard	—	11–8 on
	3	Salvator	—	10–1
1810	1	Whalebone	W. Clift	2–1
	2	The Dandy	—	8–1
	3	Eccleston	—	7–1
1811	1	Phantom	F. Buckle	5–1
	2	Magic	—	7–1
		(Only two placed)		
1812	1	Octavius	W. Arnull	7–1
	2	B. c. Gohanna	—	10–1
	3	Comus	—	3–1
1813	1	Smolensko	T. Goodison	Evens
	2	Caterpillar	—	7–1
	3	B. c. by Haphazard	—	—
1814	1	Blucher	W. Arnull	5–2
	2	Ch. c. by Haphazard	—	4–1
	3	Bourbon	—	3–1 & 7–2
1815	1	Whisker	T. Goodison	8–1
	2	Raphael	—	3–1 & 7–2
		(Only two placed)		
1816	1	Prince Leopold	W. Wheatley	20–1
	2	Nectar	—	10–6
	3	Ch. c. by Walton	—	15–1
1817	1	Azor	J. Robinson	50–1
	2	Young Wizard	—	50–1
		(Only two placed)		
1818	1	Sam	S. Chifney, Jun.	7–2
	2	Gr. c. by Sorcerer	—	—
	3	Prince Paul	—	11–5
1819	1	Tiresias	W. Clift	2–1 & 5–2
	2	Sultan	—	3–1 & 5–2
		(Only two placed)		
1820	1	Sailor	S. Chifney, Jun.	4–1 & 7–2
	2	Abjer	—	15–1
	3	Tiger	—	—
1821	1	Gustavus	S. Day	2–1
	2	Reginald	—	4–1
	3	Sir Huldibrand	—	50–1
1822	1	Moses	T. Goodison	6–1
	2	Figaro	—	—
	3	Hampden	—	3–1
1823	1	Emilius	F. Buckle	5–4 & 11–8
	2	Tancred	—	6–4 & 13–8
	3	Talisman	—	—
1824	1	Cedric	J. Robinson	9–2
	2	Osmond	—	16–1
		(Only two placed)		
1825	1	Middleton	J. Robinson	7–4
	2	Rufus	—	11–5
	3	Hogarth	—	10–1
1826	1	Lap-dog	G. Dockeray	50–1
	2	Shakspeare	—	13–1
		(Only two placed)		

Year		Horse	Jockey	Starting Price
1827	1	Mameluke	J. Robinson	9–1
	2	Glenartney	—	5–1
		(Only two placed)		
1828(a)	1	Cadland	J. Robinson	4–1
	2	The Colonel	W. Scott	7–2
		(Only two placed)		

(a) After a dead-heat with Mr. Petre's The Colonel. Evens and 5–4 on The Colonel.

Year		Horse	Jockey	Starting Price
1829	1	Frederick	Forth	40–1
	2	The Exquisite	Buckle, Jun.	—
		(Only two placed)		
1830	1	Priam	S. Day	4–1
	2	Little Red Rover	—	5–1
	3	Mahmoud	—	16–1
1831	1	Spaniel	W. Wheatley	50–1
	2	Riddlesworth	—	6–4 on
		(Only two placed)		
1832	1	St. Giles	W. Scott	3–1
	2	Perion	—	6–1
	3	Trustee	—	25–1
1833	1	Dangerous	J. Chapple	30–1
	2	Connoisseur	—	100–1
	3	Revenge	—	15–1
1834	1	Plenipotentiary	P. Conolly	9–4
	2	Shilelagh	—	11–4
	3	Glencoe	—	11–1
1835	1	Mündig	W. Scott	6–1
	2	Ascot	—	3–1
		(Only two placed)		
1836	1	Bay Middleton	J. Robinson	7–4
	2	Gladiator	—	11–1
		(Only two placed)		
1837	1	Phosphorus	G. Edwards	40–1
	2	Caravan	—	7–2
		(Only two placed)		
1838	1	Amato	J. Chapple	30–1
	2	Ion	—	13–1
	3	Grey Momus	—	5–2
1839	1	Bloomsbury	S. Templeman	25–1
	2	Deception	—	12–1
		(Only two placed)		
1840	1	Little Wonder	Macdonald	20–1
	2	Launcelot	—	9–4
		(Only two placed)		
1841	1	Coronation	P. Conolly	5–2
	2	Van Amburgh	—	12–1
		(Only two placed)		
1842	1	Attila	W. Scott	5–1
	2	Robert de Gorham	Cotton	100–1
		(Only two placed)		
1843	1	Cotherstone	W. Scott	13–8
	2	Gorhambury	Buckle	66–1
		(Only two placed)		
1844(b)	1	Orlando	E. Flatman	20–1
	2	Ionian	G. Edwards	15–1
	3	Bay Momus	F. Butler	20–1

(b) A horse falsely described as Running Rein came in first, but was subsequently disqualified, proved to be a 4-y-o colt called Maccabeus (afterwards Zanoni).

Year		Horse	Jockey	Starting Price
1845	1	The Merry Monarch	F. Bell	—
	2	Annandale	Marson	50–1
	3	Old England	S. Day	22–1
1846	1	Pyrrhus the First	S. Day	8–1
	2	Sir Tatton Sykes	W. Scott	16–1
	3	Brocardo	Holmes	25–1
1847	1	Cossack	S. Templeman	5–1
	2	War Eagle	W. Boyce	20–1
	3	Van Tromp	J. Marson	7–1
1848	1	Surplice	S. Templeman	evens
	2	Springy Jack	F. Butler	15–1
	3	Shylock	S. Mann	14–1
1849	1	The Flying Dutchman	Marlow	2–1
	2	Hotspur	Whitehouse	50–1
	3	Tadmor	E. Flatman	2–1
1850	1	Voltigeur	J. Marson	16–1
	2	Pitsford	A. Day	12–1
	3	Clincher	F. Butler	4–1
1851	1	Teddington	J. Marson	3–1
	2	Marlborough Buck	G. Whitehouse	7–2
	3	Neasham	J. Holmes	15–1
1852	1	Daniel O'Rourke	F. Butler	25–1
	2	Barbarian	Hiett	1,000–10
	3	Chief Baron Nicholson	Kitchener	40–1
1853	1	West Australian	F. Butler	6–4
	2	Sittingbourne	S. Rogers	8–1
	3	Cineas	Bumby	20–1
1854	1	Andover	A. Day	7–2
	2	King Tom	Charlton	8–1
	3	Hermit	Wells	14–1
1855	1	Wild Dayrell	R. Sherwood	evens
	2	Kingstown	A. Day	12–1
	3	Lord of the Isles	Aldcroft	7–4
1856	1	Ellington	Aldcroft	20–1
	2	Yellow Jack	Wells	15–1
	3	Cannobie	R. Sherwood	6–1
1857	1	Blink Bonny	Charlton	20–1
	2	Black Tommy	Covey	1,000–5
	3	Adamas	Wells	12–1
1858	1	Beadsman	J. Wells	10–1
	2	Toxophilite	E. Flatman	100–30
	3	The Hadji	Aldcroft	20–1
1859	1	Musjid	J. Wells	9–4
	2	Marionette	S. Rogers	22–1
	3	Trumpeter	A. Day	4–1
1860	1	Thormanby	H. Custance	4–1
	2	The Wizard	A. French	3–1
	3	Horror	T. Chaloner	25–1

Year		Horse	Jockey	Starting Price
1861	1	Kettledrum	Bullock	16–1
	2	Dundee	H. Custance	3–1
	3	Diophantus	A. Edwards	4–1
1862	1	Caractacus	J. Parsons	40–1
	2	The Marquis	Ashmall	5–2
	3	Buckstone	H. Grimshaw	100–30
1863	1	Macaroni	T. Chaloner	10–1
	2	Lord Clifden	G. Fordham	4–1
	3	Rapid Rhone	Doyle	50–1
1864	1	Blair Athol	J. Snowden	14–1
	2	General Peel	Aldcroft	9–2
	3	Scottish Chief	J. Adams	9–2
1865	1	Gladiateur	H. Grimshaw	5–2
	2	Christmas Carol	T. French	100–6
	3	Eltham	S. Adams	1,000–10
1866	1	Lord Lyon	H. Custance	6–5 on
	2	Savernake	T. French	20–1
	3	Rustic	Cannon	5–1
1867	1	Hermit	J. Daley	1,000–15
	2	Marksman	J. Grimshaw	10–1
	3	Vauban	Fordham	6–4
1868	1	Blue Gown	J. Wells	7–2
	2	King Alfred	Norman	50–1
	3	Speculum	S. Kenyon	14–1
1869	1	Pretender	J. Osborne	11–8
	2	Pero Gomez	Wells	11–2
	3	The Drummer	Morris	20–1
1870	1	Kingcraft	T. French	20–1
	2	Palmerston	T. Chaloner	100–6
	3	Muster	Maidment	—
1871	1	Favonius	T. French	9–1
	*	Albert Victor	Custance	4–1
	*	King of the Forest	Snowden	14–1
1872	1	Cremorne	C. Maidment	3–1
	2	Pell Mell	T. Chaloner	50–1
	3	Queen's Messenger	T. French	6–1
1873	1	Doncaster	F. Webb	45–1
	*	Gang Forward	T. Chaloner	9–4
	*	Kaiser	Maidment	4–1
1874	1	George Frederick	H. Custance	9–1
	2	Couronne De Fer	T. Chaloner	7–1
	3	Atlantic	T. Osborne	100–8
1875	1	Galopin	Morris	2–1
	2	Claremont	Maidment	100–7
	3	C. by Macaroni	F. Archer	100–8
1876	1	Kisber	C. Maidment	4–1
	2	Forerunner	F. Webb	100–15
	3	Julius Caesar	Cannon	40–1
1877	1	Silvio	F. Archer	100–9
	2	Glen Arthur	Dodge	50–1
	3	Rob Roy	Custance	3–1
1878	1	Sefton	H. Constable	100–12
	2	Insulaire	J. Goater	100–30
	3	Childeric	F. Archer	100–8
1879	1	Sir Bevys	G. Fordham	20–1
	2	Palmbearer	J. Osborne	100–1
	3	Visconti	Constable	60–1
1880	1	Bend Or	F. Archer	2–1
	2	Robert the Devil	Rossiter	7–1
	3	Mask	Glover	20–1
1881	1	Iroquois	F. Archer	11–2
	2	Peregrine	F. Webb	6–5
	3	Town Moor	Lemaire	33–1
1882	1	Shotover	T. Cannon	11–2
	2	Quicklime	C. Wood	6–1
	3	Sachem	F. Webb	100–8
1883	1	St. Blaise	C. Wood	5–1
	2	Highland Chief	F. Webb	100–8
	3	Galliard	F. Archer	7–2
1884	*	St. Gatien	C. Wood	100–8
	*	Harvester	S. Loates	100–7
	3	Queen Adelaide	F. Webb	5–2
1885	1	Melton	F. Archer	15–8
	2	Paradox	F. Webb	6–1
	3	Royal Hampton	Giles	10–1
1886	1	Ormonde	F. Archer	85–40 on
	2	The Bard	C. Wood	7–2
	3	St. Mirin	T. Cannon	40–1
1887	1	Merry Hampton	J. Watts	100–9
	2	The Baron	T. Cannon	5–4 on
	3	Martley	F. Barrett	10–1
1888	1	Ayrshire	F. Barrett	6–5 on
	2	Crowberry	J. Osborne	6–1
	3	Van Dieman's Land	J. Watts	20–1
1889	1	Donovan	T. Loates	11–8 on
	2	Miguel	G. Barrett	25–1
	3	El Dorado	T. Cannon	100–8
1890	1	Sainfoin	J. Watts	100–15
	2	Le Nord	F. Barrett	100–7
	3	Orwell	G. Barrett	100–1
1891	1	Common	G. Barrett	11–10 on
	2	Gouverneur	J. Woodburn	100–9
	3	Martenhurst	J. Fagan	50–1
1892	1	Sir Hugo	Allsopp	40–1
	2	La Fleche	G. Barrett	11–10
	3	Bucentaure	Chesterman	100–1
1893	1	Isinglass	T. Loates	9–4 on
	2	Ravensbury	H. Barker	25–1
	3	Raeburn	J. Watts	20–1
1894	1	Ladas	J. Watts	9–2 on
	2	Matchbox	M. Cannon	9–1
	3	Reminder	G. Chaloner	33–1
1895	1	Sir Visto	S. Loates	9–1
	2	Curzon	G. Chaloner	33–1
	3	Kilconnel	W. Bradford	100–8
1896	1	Persimmon	J. Watts	5–1
	2	St. Frusquin	T. Loates	13–8 on
	3	Earwig	F. Allsopp	33–1
1897	1	Galtee More	C. Wood	4–1 on
	2	Velasquez	J. Watts	10–1
	3	History	M. Cannon	25–1

Left to right: E. Mercer, H. Nicholson, A. Brabazon, T. E. Leader.

Supertello, ridden by Doug Smith, winning the £11,500 Ascot Gold Cup 1950.

Year		Horse	Jockey	Starting Price
1898	1	Jeddah	O. Madden	100–1
	2	Batt	M. Cannon	10–1
	3	Dunlop	F. Pratt	100–1
1899	1	Flying Fox	M. Cannon	5–2 on
	2	Damocles	S. Loates	15–1
	3	Innocence	W. Halsey	50–1
1900	1	Diamond Jubilee	H. Jones	6–4
	2	Simon Dale	M. Cannon	100–6
	3	Disguise II	J. F. Sloan	8–1
		2 m. 42 s. *(R. Marsh)*		
1901	1	Volodyovski	L. Reiff	5–2
	2	William the Third	M. Cannon	100–7
	3	Veronese	F. Rickaby	40–1
		2 m. $40\frac{4}{5}$ s. *(J. Huggins)*		
1902	1	Ard Patrick	J. H. Martin	100–14
	2	Rising Glass	G. McCall	40–1
	3	Friar Tuck	M. Cannon	100–7
		2 m. $42\frac{1}{5}$ s. *(S. Darling)*		
1903	1	Rock Sand	D. Maher	6–4 on
	2	Vinicius	G. Thompson	11–2
	3	Flotsam	Halsey	100–14
		2 m. $42\frac{4}{5}$ s. *(G. Blackwell)*		
1904	1	St. Amant	K. Cannon	5–1
	2	John o'Gaunt	Mr. G. Thursby	4–1
	3	St. Denis	Halsey	50–1
		2 m. $45\frac{3}{5}$ s. *(A. Hayhoe)*		
1905	1	Cicero	D. Maher	11–4 on
	2	Jardy	G. Stern	4–1
	3	Signorino	K. Cannon	50–1
		2 m. $39\frac{3}{5}$ s. *(P. P. Peck)*		
1906	1	Spearmint	D. Maher	6–1
	2	Picton	Mr. G. Thursby	18–1
	3	Troutbeck	J. H. Martin	33–1
		2 m. $36\frac{4}{5}$ s. *(P. Gilpin)*		
1907	1	Orby	J. Reiff	100–9
	2	Wool Winder	O. Madden	100–9
	3	Slieve Gallion	W. Higgs	13–8 on
		2 m. 44 s. *(J. Allen, in Ireland)*		
1908	1	Signorinetta	W. Bullock	100–1
	2	Primer	B. Dillon	40–1
	3	Llangwm	D. Maher	100–8
		2 m. $39\frac{4}{5}$ s. *(Chev. Ginistrelli)*		
1909	1	Minoru	H. Jones	7–2
	2	Louviers	G. Stern	9–1
	3	William the Fourth	W. Higgs	20–1
		2 m. $42\frac{2}{5}$ s. *(R. Marsh)*		
1910	1	Lemberg	B. Dillon	7–4
	2	Greenback	F. Templeman	100–8
	3	Charles O'Malley	S. Donoghue	33–1
		2 m. $35\frac{1}{5}$ s. *(Alec Taylor)*		
1911	1	Sunstar	G. Stern	13–8
	2	Stedfast	B. Lynham	100–8
	3	Royal Tender	S. Donoghue	25–1
		2 m. $36\frac{4}{5}$ s. *(C. Morton)*		
1912	1	Tagalie	J. Reiff	100–8
	2	Jaeger	Walter Griggs	8–1
	3	Tracery	G. Bellhouse	66–1
		2 m. $38\frac{4}{5}$ s. *(D. Waugh)*		
1913	1	Aboyeur	E. Piper	100–1
	2	Louvois	W. Saxby	10–1
	3	Great Sport	G. Stern	20–1
		2 m. $37\frac{3}{5}$ s. *(T. Lewis)*		
		Craganour came in first, beating Aboyeur by a head, but was disqualified.		
1914	1	Durbar II	M. MacGee	20–1
	2	Hapsburg	C. Foy	33–1
	3	Peter the Hermit	R. Watson	100–1
		2 m. $38\frac{2}{5}$ s. *(T. Murphy)*		
		Run at Newmarket.		
1915	1	Pommern	S. Donoghue	11–10
	2	Let Fly	J. Childs	10–1
	3	Rossendale	J. Clark	40–1
		2 m. $32\frac{3}{5}$ s. *(C. Peck)*		
1916	1	Fifinella	J. Childs	11–2
	2	Kwang-Su	F. Templeman	3–1
	3	Nassovian	F. O'Neill	11–2
		2 m. $36\frac{3}{5}$ s. *(R. Dawson)*		

RACING QUIZ

1. Name the horse who won the Grand National in 1884 and competed in the Derby of this season.

★

2. How many times was George Fordham champion jockey?

★

3. How many times did Fred Archer win the championship?

QUIZ ANSWERS

1. Voluptuary. 2. 14 times. 3. 13 times.

Frank Butters

Joe Lawson

RACING QUIZ

1. How many times did Golden Miller win the Cheltenham Gold Cup?

★

2. When were crash helmets made compulsory under National Hunt Rules?

★

3. When were crash helmets made compulsory under Jockey Club Rules?

★

4. When was the Totalisator first introduced?

★

5. Name the year when 58 runners (a record) started for the Lincolnshire Handicap.

★

6. Which horse set up the record time for the Derby?

QUIZ ANSWERS

1. Five times. In 1932, 1933, 1934, 1935, 1936. He also finished second in 1938. 2. 1924. 3. 1956. 4. July 2nd 1929 at Newmarket and Carlisle. 5. 1948. 6. Mahmoud, 2 m. $33\frac{4}{5}$ s. in 1936.

AVERAGE TIMES

The following times represent the average of true-run race times over the various distances and courses, brought to 12 stone. Reproduced by kind permission of the *Sporting Chronicle*.

AYR

Hurdles

2 miles	3/46 s.
$2\frac{1}{2}$ miles	5/$4\frac{4}{5}$ s.
3 miles	5/54 s.

'Chase

2 miles	3/58 s.
$2\frac{1}{2}$ miles	5/4 s.
3 miles 125 yards.	6/20 s.

BIRMINGHAM

Hurdles

2 miles	3/$54\frac{2}{5}$ s.
2 miles 5 furlongs	5/10 s.

'Chase

2 miles and a few yards	4/9 s.
$2\frac{1}{2}$ miles	5/12 s.
3 miles	6/$12\frac{2}{5}$ s.
3 miles 3 furlongs	7/8 s.
4 miles	8/$21\frac{1}{5}$ s.

Continued on next page

The Derby—*contd.*

Year		Horse	Jockey	Starting Price
1917	1	Gay Crusader	S. Donoghue	7–4
	2	Dansellon	R. Watson	7–1
	3	Dark Legend	J. Childs	100–15
		2 m. $40\frac{3}{5}$ s.	(*Alec Taylor*)	
1918	1	Gainsborough	J. Childs	13–8 on
	2	Blink	R. Collins	100–8
	3	Treclare	W. Langford	20–1
		2 m. $33\frac{1}{5}$ s.	(*Alec Taylor*)	
		Run at Epsom		
1919	1	Grand Parade	F. Templeman	33–1
	2	Buchan	J. Brennan	7–1
	3	Paper Money	S. Donoghue	8–1
		2 m. $35\frac{4}{5}$ s.	(*F. Darling*)	
1920	1	Spion Kop	F. O'Neill	100–6
	2	Archaic	G. Bellhouse	10–1
	3	Orpheus	F. Leach	50–1
		2 m. $34\frac{4}{5}$ s.	(*P. P. Gilpin*)	
1921	1	Humorist	S. Donoghue	6–1
	2	Craig an Eran	J. Brennan	5–1
	3	Lemonora	J. Childs	8–1
		2 m. $36\frac{1}{5}$ s.	(*C. Morton*)	
1922	1	Captain Cuttle	S. Donoghue	10–1
	2	Tamar	F. Bullock	10–1
	3	Craigangower	M. Beary	20–1
		2 m. $34\frac{3}{5}$ s.	(*F. Darling*)	
1923	1	Papyrus	S. Donoghue	100–15
	2	Pharos	E. Gardner	6–1
	3	Parth	A. Walker	33–1
		2 m. 38 s.	(*B. Jarvis*)	
1924	1	Sansovino	T. Weston	9–2
	2	St. Germans	F. Bullock	100–7
	3	Hurstwood	V. Smyth	20–1
		2 m. $46\frac{3}{5}$ s.	(*Hon. G. Lambton*)	
1925	1	Manna	S. Donoghue	9–1
	2	Zionist	B. Carslake	10–1
	3	The Sirdar	A. Esling	50–1
		2 m. $40\frac{3}{5}$ s.	(*F. Darling*)	
1926	1	Coronach	J. Childs	11–2
	2	Lancegaye	R. Perryman	40–1
	3	Colorado	T. Weston	2–1
		2 m. $47\frac{4}{5}$ s.	(*F. Darling*)	
1927	1	Call Boy	E. C. Elliott	4–1
	2	Hot Night	H. Wragg	9–2
	3	Shian Mor	F. Lane	22–1
		2 m. $34\frac{2}{5}$ s.	(*J. Watts*)	
1928	1	Felstead	H. Wragg	33–1
	2	Flamingo	E. C. Elliott	9–2
	3	Black Watch	C. Smirke	33–1
		2 m. $35\frac{3}{5}$ s.	(*O. Bell*)	
1929	1	Trigo	J. Marshall	33–1
	2	Walter Gay	F. Fox	100–8
	3	Brienz	R. A. Jones	50–1
		2 m. $36\frac{2}{5}$ s.	(*R. Dawson*)	
1930	1	Blenheim	H. Wragg	18–1
	2	Iliad	R. A. Jones	25–1
	3	Diolite	C. Ray	11–4
		2 m. $38\frac{1}{5}$ s.	(*R. Dawson*)	
1931	1	Cameronian	F. Fox	7–2
	2	Orpen	R. A. Jones	9–1
	3	Sandwich	H. Wragg	8–1
		2 m. $36\frac{3}{5}$ s.	(*F. Darling*)	
1932	1	April the Fifth	F. Lane	100–6
	2	Dastur	M. Beary	18–1
	3	Miracle	H. Wragg	100–9
		2 m. $43\frac{1}{5}$ s.	(*T. Walls*)	
1933	1	Hyperion	T. Weston	6–1
	2	King Salmon	H. Wragg	7–1
	3	Statesman	B. Carslake	20–1
		2 m. 34 s.	(*Hon. G. Lambton*)	
1934	1	Windsor Lad	C. Smirke	15–2
	2	Easton	G. Richards	100–9
	3	Colombo	W. R. Johnstone	11–8
		2 m. 34 s.	(*M. Marsh*)	
1935	1	Bahram	F. Fox	5–4
	2	Robin Goodfellow	T. Weston	50–1
	3	Field Trial	R. Dick	9–1
		2 m. 36 s.	(*Frank Butters*)	

The 1913 Derby. The race at Tattenham Corner showing the Suffragette outrage on Anmer, the King's horse.

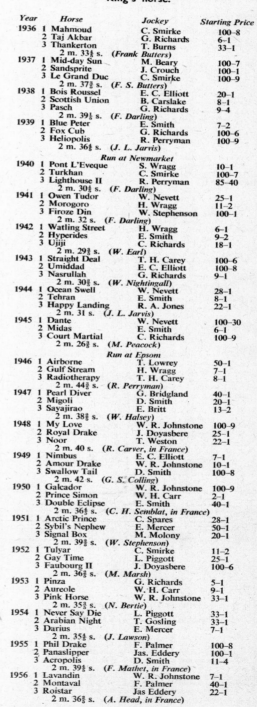

Year		Horse	Jockey	Starting Price
1936	1	Mahmoud	C. Smirke	100–8
	2	Taj Akbar	G. Richards	6–1
	3	Thankerton	T. Burns	33–1
		2 m. $33\frac{4}{5}$ s.	(*Frank Butters*)	
1937	1	Mid-day Sun	M. Beary	100–7
	2	Sandsprite	J. Crouch	100–1
	3	Le Grand Duc	C. Smirke	100–9
		2 m. $37\frac{3}{5}$ s.	(*F. S. Butters*)	
1938	1	Bois Roussel	E. C. Elliott	20–1
	2	Scottish Union	B. Carslake	8–1
	3	Pasch	G. Richards	9–4
		2 m. $39\frac{1}{5}$ s.	(*F. Darling*)	
1939	1	Blue Peter	E. Smith	7–2
	2	Fox Cub	G. Richards	100–6
	3	Heliopolis	R. Perryman	100–9
		2 m. $36\frac{4}{5}$ s.	(*J. L. Jarvis*)	
		Run at Newmarket		
1940	1	Pont L'Eveque	S. Wragg	10–1
	2	Turkhan	C. Smirke	100–7
	3	Lighthouse II	R. Perryman	85–40
		2 m. $30\frac{4}{5}$ s.	(*F. Darling*)	
1941	1	Owen Tudor	W. Nevett	25–1
	2	Morogoro	H. Wragg	11–2
	3	Firoze Din	W. Stephenson	100–1
		2 m. 32 s.	(*F. Darling*)	
1942	1	Watling Street	H. Wragg	6–1
	2	Hyperides	E. Smith	9–2
	3	Ujiji	C. Richards	18–1
		2 m. $29\frac{3}{5}$ s.	(*W. Earl*)	
1943	1	Straight Deal	T. H. Carey	100–6
	2	Umiddad	E. C. Elliott	100–8
	3	Nasrullah	G. Richards	9–1
		2 m. $30\frac{2}{5}$ s.	(*W. Nightingall*)	
1944	1	Ocean Swell	W. Nevett	28–1
	2	Tehran	E. Smith	8–1
	3	Happy Landing	R. A. Jones	22–1
		2 m. 31 s.	(*J. L. Jarvis*)	
1945	1	Dante	W. Nevett	100–30
	2	Midas	E. Smith	6–1
	3	Court Martial	C. Richards	100–9
		2 m. $26\frac{3}{5}$ s.	(*M. Peacock*)	
		Run at Epsom		
1946	1	Airborne	T. Lowrey	50–1
	2	Gulf Stream	H. Wragg	7–1
	3	Radiotherapy	T. H. Carey	8–1
		2 m. $44\frac{3}{5}$ s.	(*R. Perryman*)	
1947	1	Pearl Diver	G. Bridgland	40–1
	2	Migoli	D. Smith	20–1
	3	Sayajirao	E. Britt	13–2
		2 m. $38\frac{2}{5}$ s.	(*W. Halsey*)	
1948	1	My Love	W. R. Johnstone	100–9
	2	Royal Drake	J. Doyasbere	25–1
	3	Noor	T. Weston	22–1
		2 m. 40 s.	(*R. Carver, in France*)	
1949	1	Nimbus	E. C. Elliott	7–1
	2	Amour Drake	W. R. Johnstone	10–1
	3	Swallow Tail	D. Smith	100–8
		2 m. 42 s.	(*G. S. Colling*)	
1950	1	Galcador	W. R. Johnstone	100–9
	2	Prince Simon	W. H. Carr	2–1
	3	Double Eclipse	E. Smith	40–1
		2 m. $36\frac{4}{5}$ s.	(*C. H. Semblat, in France*)	
1951	1	Arctic Prince	C. Spares	28–1
	2	Sybil's Nephew	E. Mercer	50–1
	3	Signal Box	M. Molony	20–1
		2 m. $39\frac{2}{5}$ s.	(*W. Stephenson*)	
1952	1	Tulyar	C. Smirke	11–2
	2	Gay Time	L. Piggott	25–1
	3	Faubourg II	J. Doyasbere	100–6
		2 m. $36\frac{2}{5}$ s.	(*M. Marsh*)	
1953	1	Pinza	G. Richards	5–1
	2	Aureole	W. H. Carr	9–1
	3	Pink Horse	W. R. Johnstone	33–1
		2 m. $35\frac{3}{5}$ s.	(*N. Bertie*)	
1954	1	Never Say Die	L. Piggott	33–1
	2	Arabian Night	T. Gosling	33–1
	3	Darius	E. Mercer	7–1
		2 m. $35\frac{4}{5}$ s.	(*J. Lawson*)	
1955	1	Phil Drake	F. Palmer	100–8
	2	Panaslipper	Jas. Eddery	100–1
	3	Acropolis	D. Smith	11–4
		2 m. $39\frac{4}{5}$ s.	(*F. Mathet, in France*)	
1956	1	Lavandin	W. R. Johnstone	7–1
	2	Montaval	F. Palmer	40–1
	3	Roistar	Jas Eddery	22–1
		2 m. $36\frac{3}{5}$ s.	(*A. Head, in France*)	

Gordon Richards and Steve Donoghue, 1932.

Lord Rosebery leads in his 1939 Derby winner Blue Peter.

Prince Aly Khan and trainer Frank Butters.

The Derby—*contd.*

Year		Horse	Jockey	Starting Price
57	1	Crepello	L. Piggott	6–4
	2	Ballymoss	T. Burns	33–1
	3	Pipe of Peace	A. Breasley	100–8
		2 m. 35$\frac{3}{5}$ s. (*C. F. N. Murless*)		
58	1	Hard Ridden	C. Smirke	18–1
	2	Paddu's Point	G. W. Robinson	100–1
	3	Nagami	J. Mercer	10–1
		2 m. 41$\frac{1}{5}$ s. (*J. Rogers, in Ireland*)		
59	1	Parthia	W. H. Carr	10–1
	2	Fidalgo	J. Mercer	10–1
	3	Shantung	F. Palmer	11–2
		2 m. 36 s. (*C. Boyd-Rochfort*)		

WINNERS OF MORE THAN ONE DERBY

JOCKEYS

SIX—J. Robinson, 1817, 1824, 1825, 1827, 1828, 1836
S. Donoghue, 1915, 1917, 1921, 1922, 1923, 1925
FIVE—J. Arnull, 1784, 1790, 1796, 1799, 1807
F. Buckle, 1792, 1794, 1802, 1811, 1823
W. Clift, 1793, 1800, 1803, 1810, 1819
F. Archer 1877, 1880, 1881, 1885, 1886
FOUR—S. Arnull, 1780, 1782, 1787, 1798
T. Goodison, 1809, 1813, 1815, 1822
W. Scott, 1832, 1835, 1842, 1843
J. Watts, 1887, 1890, 1894, 1896
C. Smirke, 1934, 1936, 1952, 1958
THREE—Hindley, 1781, 1783, 1785
W. Arnull, 1804, 1812, 1814
S. Day, 1821, 1830, 1846
S. Templeman, 1839, 1847, 1848
J. Wells, 1858, 1859, 1868
H. Custance, 1860, 1866, 1874
C. Wood, 1883, 1884 (*dead-heat*), **1897**
D. Maher, 1903, 1905, 1906
J. Childs, 1916, 1918, 1926
E. C. Elliott, 1927, 1938, 1949
H. Wragg, 1928, 1930, 1942
W. Nevett, 1941, 1944, 1945
W. R. Johnstone, 1948, 1950, **1956**
TWO—W. Wheatley, 1816, 1831
S. Chifney, Jun., 1818, 1820
J. Chapple 1833, 1838
P. Conolly, 1834, 1841
J. Marson 1850, 1851
F. Butler, 1852, 1853
T. French, 1870, 1871
C. Maidment, 1872, 1876
S. Loates, 1884 (*dead-heat*), 1895
T. Loates, 1889, 1893
H. Jones, 1900, 1909
J. Reiff, 1907, 1912
T. Weston, 1924, 1933
F. Fox, 1931, 1935
L. Piggott, 1954, 1957

OWNERS

FIVE—Earl of Egremont, 1782, 1804, 1805, 1807, 1826
H. H. Aga Khan, 1930, 1935, 1936, 1948, 1952
FOUR—Mr. John Bowes, 1835, 1843, 1852, 1853
Sir Joseph Hawley, 1851, 1858, 1859, 1868
Duke of Westminster, 1880, 1882, 1886, 1899
Third Duke of Grafton, 1802, 1809, 1810, 1815
THREE—Sir Charles Bunbury, 1780, 1801, 1813
Duke of Bedford, 1789, 1791, 1797
Lord Grosvenor, 1790, 1792, 1794
Sir F. Standish, 1795, 1796, 1799
Lord Jersey, 1825, 1827, 1836
Fifth Lord Rosebery, 1894, 1895, 1905
King Edward VII, 1896, 1900 (*both when Prince of Wales*), 1909
Seventeenth Lord Derby, 1924, 1933, 1942
Sir Victor Sassoon, 1953, 1957, 1958
TWO—Mr. D. O'Kelly, 1781, 1784
Sir H. Williamson, 1803, 1808
Sir J. Shelley, 1811, 1824
Mr. Thornhill, 1818, 1820
Mr. Gratwicke, 1829, 1845
Mr. W. Ridsdale, 1832, 1839
Mr. John Gully, 1846, 1854
Mr. W. I'Anson, 1857, 1864
Mr. James Merry, 1860, 1873
Lord Falmouth, 1870, 1877
Sir F. Johnstone, 1883, 1891
Sixth Duke of Portland, 1888, 1889
Sir J. Miller, 1890, 1903
Mr. J. Gubbins, 1879, 1902
Mr. J. B. Joel, 1911, 1921
Lord Woolavington, 1922, 1926
Sixth Lord Rosebery, 1939, 1944

TRAINERS

EIGHT—F. Darling, 1919, 1922, 1925, 1926, 1931, 1938, 1940, 1941. SEVEN—J. Porter, 1868, 1882, 1883, 1886, 1890, 1891, 1899. SIX—M. Dawson, 1860, 1870, 1877, 1885, 1894, 1895. FOUR—R. MARSH, 1896, 1898, 1900, 1909. J. Hayhoe, 1871, 1876, 1879. THREE—R. Dawson, 1916, 1929, 1930. A. Taylor, 1910, 1917, 1918. TWO—J. Scott, 1852, 1853. W. I'Anson, 1857, 1864. G. Manning, 1858, 1859. T. Dawson, 1856, 1869. R. Peck, 1873, 1880. J. Jewitt 1884 (dead-heat), 1893. G. Dawson, 1888, 1889. S. Darling, 1897, 1902. Frank Butters, 1935, 1936. P. P. Gilpin, 1906, 1920. J. L. Jarvis, 1939, 1944. Hon. G. Lambton, 1924, 1933. M. Marsh, 1934, 1952. C. Morton, 1911, 1921.

K

THE OAKS

The Oaks is run over the same course and distance of the Derby. First run in 1779. The race is for three-year-old fillies.

Year		Horse	Jockey	Starting Price
1779	1	Bridget	R. Goodison	5–2
	2	Fame	—	3–1
	3	Filly by Eclipse	—	8–1
1780	1	Teetotum	R. Goodison	6–4
	2	Filly by Chymist	—	6–4
	3	Filly by Goldfinder	—	—
1781	1	Faith	R. Goodison	4–1
	2	Dido	—	—
	3	Camilla	—	—
1782	1	Ceres	Chifney, Sen.	7–4 on
	2	Countess	—	10–1
	3	Catchfly	—	6–1
1783	1	Maid of Oakes	Chifney, Sen.	4–1
	2	Filly by Mark Anthony	—	—
	3	Filly by Eclipse	—	—
1784	1	Stella	C. Hindley	20–1
	2	Lady Teagle	—	5–4
	3	Elden	—	10–1
1785	1	Trifle	J. Bird	5–1
	2	B. f. sister to Camilla	—	evens
	3	Miss Kitty	—	—
1786	1	Perdita filly by Tanden	J. Edwards	5–2
	2	Letitia	—	10–1
	3	Scota	—	8–1
1787	1	Annette	Fitzpatrick	6–4
	2	Augusta	—	4–1
	3	Filly by Alfred	—	—
1788	1	Nightshade	Fitzpatrick	2–1 on
	2	Busy	—	High odds
	3	Filly by Alfred	—	High odds
1789	1	Tag	Chifney, Sen.	5–2
	2	B. f. sister to Trifle	—	7–1
	3	Hope	—	5–2
1790	1	Hippolyta	Chifney, Sen.	6–1
	2	Misseltoe	—	3–1
	3	Filly by Giant	—	—
1791	1	Portia	J. Singleton	2–1 & 5–2
	2	Astraea	—	7–2
	3	Kezia	—	—
1792	1	Volante	C. Hindley	4–1
			5–4 Lord Clermont coupled	
	2	Trumpetta	—	3–1
	3	Filly by Highflyer	—	—
1793	1	Caelia	J. Singleton	4–1,
			5–2 Duke of Bedford coupled	
	2	Black Puss	—	3–1
	3	Rachel	—	5–1 & 6–1
1794	1	Hermione	S. Arnull	5–2
	2	Eliza	—	7–4
	3	Jessica	—	4–1
1795	1	Platina	Fitzpatrick	3–1
	2	Filly by Justice (only 2 placed)	—	5–1
1796	1	Parissot	I. Arnull	7–2
	2	Br. f. sister to Viret	—	4–1
	3	B. f. by Pot 8o's	—	—
1797	1	Nike	F. Buckle	15–8
	2	Mother Shipton	—	—
	3	Rose	—	3–1 & 7–2
1798	1	Bellissima	F. Buckle	6–4
	2	Dutchess of Limbs	—	—
	3	Lady Bull	—	6–1
1799	1	Bellina	F. Buckle	5–2
	2	Lady Jane	—	4–1
	3	St. Ann	—	11–8
1800	1	Ephemera	Fitzpatrick	9–4
	2	Wowski	—	—
	3	Miss Totteridge	—	—
1801	1	Eleanor	Saunders	7–4 & 2–1 on
	2	Ch. f. by Buzzard-Tulip	—	—
	3	B. f. by Woodpecker	—	9–2
1802	1	Scotia	F. Buckle	5–4 & 6–4
	2	Julia	—	2–1
	3	Ch. f. by Buzzard-Violet	—	5–1
1803	1	Theophania	F. Buckle	5–2
	2	Fanny	—	6–1 & 7–1
	3	Parasol	—	2–1
1804	1	Pelisse	W. Clift	5–4 on
	2	B. f. by Precipitate	—	5–1
	3	Maud	—	5–1
1805	1	Meteora	F. Buckle	7–2 & 3–1
	2	Dondona	—	2–1
	3	B. f. sister to Duxbury	—	—
1806	1	Bronze	W. Edwards	10–1
	2	Jerboa	—	4–1
	3	Rosabella	—	—
1807	1	Briseis	S. Chifney	15–1
	2	Margaret	—	7–1
	3	Pantina	—	—
1808	1	Morel	W. Clift	3–1
	2	Goosander	—	7–1
	3	Miranda	—	4–1
1809	1	Maid of Orleans	J. Moss	100–6
	2	Zaida	—	8–1
	3	Spindle	—	9–2
1810	1	Oriana	W. Peirse	4–1
	2	Pirouette	—	2–1
	3	Donna Clara	—	—
1811	1	Sorcery	S. Chifney	3–1
	2	B. f. sister to Pirouette	—	5–1
	3	B. f. by Sancho	—	—
1812	1	Manuella	W. Peirse	20–1
	2	Elizabeth	—	—
	3	B. f. Gohanna	—	—
1813	1	Music	T. Goodison	5–2
	2	Vulpecula	—	6–1
	3	Wilful	—	6–1

RACING QUIZ

1. Can an amateur rider participate in a race under Jockey Club Rules?

*

2. Name the meeting and year when the last two-year-old race over four furlongs was run.

*

3. Can you name Fred Archer's last winner?

*

4. Also his last mount.

*

5. Who was leading National Hunt jockey in 1941–42?

*

6. Who rode Arctic Prince in the 1951 Derby?

QUIZ ANSWERS

1. No. Under National Hunt Rules, however, an amateur rider can take part in a race with professional jockeys. 2. Hurst Park, in 1912. The race was won by Tosson. 3. Blanchland, at Newmarket in 1886. 4. Tommy Tittlemouse, at Lewes in the same year. 5. R. V. Smyth, who is now a trainer at Epsom. 6. C. Spares.

Average Times—*contd.*

BOGSIDE

Hurdles

2 miles .... 3/46 s.

'Chase

2 miles 125 yards. .... 4/4 s.
3 miles .... 6/8$\frac{3}{5}$ s.
3 miles 7 furlongs.......... 7/56 s.

CARLISLE

Hurdles

2 miles .... 4/8$\frac{1}{5}$ s.
3 miles 100 yards. .... 6/13$\frac{3}{5}$ s.

'Chase

2 miles .... 4/12$\frac{3}{5}$ s.

CATTERICK BRIDGE

Hurdles

2 miles .... 3/51 s.

'Chase

2 miles .... 4/5$\frac{1}{5}$ s.
3 miles 300 yards .... 6/40 s.
3$\frac{1}{2}$ miles.................... 7/28 s.

CHELTENHAM

Hurdles
(Provisional)

2 miles 100 yards .... 4/3$\frac{3}{5}$ s.

'Chase

2 miles .... 4/2 s.
About 2 miles 4 furlongs...... 5/3$\frac{1}{5}$ s.
3 miles .... 6/7 s.
3$\frac{1}{4}$ miles .... 6/37 s.
3$\frac{1}{2}$ miles .... 7/10$\frac{3}{5}$ s.
4 miles .... 8/14 s.

CHEPSTOW

Hurdles

2 miles .... 4/2 s.
2$\frac{1}{2}$ miles .... 5/0 s.
3 miles .... 6/8$\frac{2}{5}$ s.

'Chase

2 miles .... 4/10$\frac{3}{5}$ s.
2$\frac{1}{2}$ miles .... 5/7$\frac{2}{5}$ s.
3 miles .... 6/14 s.
3 miles 6 furlongs.......... 7/46 s.

DEVON AND EXETER

Hurdles

2 miles .... 4/2 s.
2$\frac{1}{2}$ miles .... 4/51 s.

'Chase

2 miles .... 4/12 s.
2 miles 3 furlongs.......... 4/53$\frac{2}{5}$ s.
3 miles .... 6/29$\frac{3}{5}$ s.

contd. next page

RACING QUIZ

1. Name the only jockey to have ridden the winner of the Grand National and the French Derby.

★

2. Name the first course to use the photo-finish camera under National Hunt Rules.

★

3. Name the first course to use the photo-finish camera for racing entirely under National Hunt Rules.

★

4. How many times did Underhand win the Northumberland Plate?

★

5. In what year were racing colours worn by jockeys made compulsory?

★

6. Only two Irish-trained horses have won the Derby. Can you name them?

QUIZ ANSWERS

1. Percy Woodland. 2. Carlisle in October 1957; it was a mixed meeting. 3. Cheltenham in January 1958. 4. Three times: 1857, 1858, 1859. 5. 1762. 6. Orby in 1907, and Hard Ridden in 1958.

Average Times—*contd.*

DONCASTER

Hurdles
(Provisional)

2 miles 133 yards	3/57 s.
2 miles 4 furlongs	4/46 s.
3 miles 40 yards	5/55 s.

'Chase
(Provisional)

2 miles 133 yards	4/5 s.
$2\frac{1}{2}$ miles	$5/1\frac{3}{5}$ s.
3 miles 105 yards	6/3 s.

FOLKESTONE

Hurdles

2 miles	$3/43\frac{2}{5}$ s.

'Chase

2 miles 50 yards	4/0 s.
3 miles	6/5 s.

FONTWELL

Hurdles

2 miles 1 furlong	$4/12\frac{2}{5}$ s.

'Chase

2 miles 2 furlongs	$4/31\frac{3}{5}$ s.
3 miles 2 furlongs	6/52 s.

HAYDOCK

Hurdles

2 miles	$3/55\frac{2}{5}$ s.

'Chase

2 miles	4/5 s.
3 miles	$6/18\frac{3}{5}$ s.
$3\frac{1}{2}$ miles	7/28 s.

HEREFORD

Hurdles

2 miles	3/58 s.

'Chase

2 miles	$4/8\frac{2}{5}$ s.
3 miles	$6/16\frac{1}{5}$ s.

contd. next page

The Oaks—*contd.*

Year		*Horse*	*Jockey*	*Starting Price*
1814	1	Medora	Barnard	10–1
	2	Vestal	—	10–1
	3	Wire	—	11–5
1815	1	Minuet	T. Goodison	3–1
	2	Mouse	—	8–1
	3	Madejda	—	—
1816	1	Landscape	S. Chifney	2–1
	2	Duenna	—	4–1
	3	Ch. f. by Selim	—	12–1
1817	1	Neva	F. Buckle	evens
	2	Amabel	—	8–1
	3	B. f. by Election	—	—
1818	1	Corinne	F. Buckle	5–2
	2	Fay	—	—
	3	Fanny	—	6–4
1819	1	Shoveler	S. Chifney	2–1
	2	Espagnolle	—	10–1
	3	Schidam	—	20–1
1820	1	Caroline	H. Edwards	8–1
	2	Rowena	—	6–4 & 7–4
	3	Bombasine	—	—
1821	1	Augusta	J. Robinson	20–11
	2	Ibla	—	5–1
	3	My Lady	—	5–2
1822	1	Pastille	H. Edwards	7–2
	2	Ch. f. by Rubens	—	12–1
		(only 2 placed)		
1823	1	Zinc	F. Buckle	evens & 6–5 on
	2	Dandizette	—	12–1
	3	B. f. by Pioneer	—	20–1
1824	1	Cobweb	J. Robinson	11–8 on
	2	Fille de Joie	—	8–1 & 9–1
		(only 2 placed)		
1825	1	Wings	S. Chifney	13–1
	2	Pastime	—	13–1
	3	Tontine	—	11–10 to 6–4 on
1826	1	Lilias	T. Lye	15–1
	2	Problem	—	5–4
		(only 2 placed)		
1827	1	Gulnare	F. Boyce	14–1
	2	Translation	—	35–1
	3	Brocard	—	7–2
1828	1	Turquoise	J. B. Day	25–1
	2	Ruby	—	—
		(only 2 placed)		
1829	1	Green Mantle	G. Dockeray	5–2
	2	Varna	F. Boyce	5–2
		(only 2 placed)		
1830	1	Variation	G. Edwards	28–1
	2	Mouche	—	9–2
	3	Jenny Vertpre	—	—
1831	1	Oxygen	J. B. Day	12–1
	2	Marmora	—	30–1
	3	Guitar	—	12–1
1832	1	Galata	P. Conolly	9–4
	2	Lady Fly	—	—
	3	Eleanor	—	16–1
1833	1	Vespa	Chapple	50–1
	2	Octave	—	14–1
	3	Revelry	—	—
1834	1	Pussy	J. B. Day	20–1
	2	Louisa	—	7–2
	3	Lady de Gros	—	—
1835	1	Queen of Trumps	T. Lye	8–1
	2	Preserve	—	2–1 on
	3	Bodice	—	14–1
1836	1	Cyprian	W. Scott	9–4
	2	Destiny	—	9–1
		(only 2 placed)		
1837	1	Miss Letty	J. Holmes	7–1
	2	Chateau d'Espagne	—	2–1
	3	Velure	—	—
1838	1	Industry	W. Scott	9–2
	2	Callisto	—	5–2
		(only 2 placed)		
1839	1	Deception	J. B. Day	13–8 on
	2	Carolina	—	9–1
	3	Louisa	—	—
1840	1	Crucifix	J. B. Day	3–1 on
	2	Welfare	—	40–1
	3	Teleta	—	50–1
1841	1	Ghuznee	W. Scott	7–4
	2	Miss Stilton	—	30–1
		(only 2 placed)		
1842	1	Our Nell	T. Lye	8–1
	2	Meal	F. Butler	20–1
		(only 2 placed)		
1843	1	Poison	F. Butler	30–1
	2	Extempore	Chifney	11–1
		(only 2 placed)		
1844	1	The Princess	F. Butler	5–1
	2	Merope	Boyce	14–1
	3	Barricade	Marson	7–1
1845	1	Refraction	H. Bell	25–1
	2	Hope	Marlow	12–1
	3	Miss Sarah	J. Holmes	30–1
1846	1	Mendicant	S. Day	9–4
	2	Laundry Maid	F. Bell	12–1
	3	Conspiracy	J. Holmes	35–1
1847	1	Miami	Templeman	9–1
	2	Clementina	E. Flatman	7–4
	3	Ellerdale	Marson	10–1
1848	1	Cymba	Templeman	7–1
	2	Attraction	J. Robinson	8–1
	3	Queen of the May	Bumby	8–1
1849	1	Lady Evelyn	F. Butler	3–1
	2	Lady Superior	J. Robinson	12–1
	3	Woodlark	A. Day	10–1
1850	1	Rhedycina	F. Butler	6–1
	2	Kathleen	A. Day	10–1
	3	Countess	S. Mann	—
1851	1	Iris	F. Butler	4–1
	2	Miserrima	Whitehouse	15–1
	3	Hesse Homburg	E. Flatman	6–1
1852	1	Songstress	F. Butler	2–1
	2	Bird on the Wing	S. Rogers	15–1
	3	Gossamer	Marson	8–1
1853	1	Catherine Hayes	Marlow	5–4
	2	Dove	S. Rogers	30–1
	3	B. f. by Don John	Pettit	40–1
1854	1	Mincemeat	Charlton	10–1
	2	Meteora	Marlow	6–4 on
	3	Bribery	E. Flatman	4–1
1855	1	Marchioness	Templeman	12–1
	2	Blooming Heather	Charlton	3–1
	3	Capucine	Bartholomew	5–1
1856	1	Mincepie	A. Day	5–2
	2	Melissa	Sly	20–1
	3	Victoria	Bartholomew	7–1
1857	1	Blink Bonny	Charlton	5–4 on
	2	Sneeze	Aldcroft	10–1
	3	Moestissima	Ashworth	12–1
1858	†	Governess	Ashmall	4–1
	†	Gildermire	Aldcroft	9–4
	3	Tunstall Maid	Charlton	9–1
		(*Dead heat for first place, Governess won the decider, Gildermire* 6–5 *on*)		
1859	1	Summerside	G. Fordham	4–1
	2	Scent	J. Mann	—
	3	Wild Rose	L. Snowden	100–6
1860	1	Butterfly	J. Snowden	10–1
	2	Avalanche	J. Wells	100–8
	3	Contadina	L. Snowden	10–1
1861	1	Brown Duchess	L. Snowden	100–7
	2	Lady Ripon	Bullock	40–1
	3	Fairwater	J. Osbourne	100–30
1862	1	Feu de Joie	T. Challoner	20–1
	2	Imperatrice	J. Snowden	20–1
	3	Hurricane	Ashmall	5–2
1863	1	Queen Bertha	Aldcroft	40–1
	2	Marigold	J. Doyle	7–1
	3	Vivid	Watkins	20–1
1864	1	Fille de l'Air	A. Edwards	6–4
	2	Breeze	J. Daley	10–1
	3	Tomato	J. Osborne	100–15
1865	1	Regalia	Norman	20–1
	2	Wild Agnes	J. Osborne	9–4
	3	Zephyr	J. Wells	100–7
1866	1	Tormentor	J. Mann	5–1
	2	Mirella	H. Covey	40–1
	3	Ischia	T. Cannon	3–1
1867	1	Hippia	J. Daley	11–1
	†	Achievement	Custance	3–1 on
	†	Romping Girl	J. Osborne	40–1
1868	1	Formosa	G. Fordham	11–8 on
	2	Lady Coventry	J. Daley	12–1
	3	Athena	T. French	—
1869	1	Brigantine	T. Cannon	7–2
	2	Morna	J. Adams	6–4
	3	Martinique	Snowden	8–1
1870	1	Gamos	G. Fordham	100–8
	2	Sunshine	Snowden	4–1
	3	Pate	T. Challoner	9–2
1871	1	Hannah	C. Maidment	6–5
	2	Noblesse	T. Cannon	20–1
	3	Hopbine	T. French	—
1872	1	Reine	G. Fordham	3–1
	2	Louise Victoria	Custance	5–2
	3	Guadaloupe	J. Snowden	30–1
1873	1	Marie Stuart	T. Cannon	2–1
	2	Wild Myrtle	T. Challoner	100–6
	3	Angela	Loates	100–8
1874	1	Apology	J. Osborne	5–2
	2	Miss Toto	G. Fordham	7–4
	3	Lady Patricia	J. Goater	5–1
1875	1	Spinaway	F. Archer	5–4
	2	Ladylove	Constable	7–4
	3	Toxophilite	T. Challoner	33–1
1876	†	Enguerrande	Hudson	4–1
	†	Camelia	Glover	5–4
	3	Merry Duchess	J. Osborne	100–3
		(*Enguerrande afterwards walked over and the stakes were divided*)		
1877	1	Placida	H. Jeffrey	2–1
	2	Belphoebe	T. Cannon	5–1
	3	Muscatel	J. Osborne	7–1
1878	1	Jannette	F. Archer	65–40
	2	Pilgrimage	T. Cannon	evens
	3	Clementine	J. Goater	100–8
1879	1	Wheel of Fortune	F. Archer	3–1 on
	2	Coromandel II	J. Osborne	100–3
	3	Adventure	C. Wood	40–1
1880	1	Jenny Howlet	J. Snowden	33–1
	2	Boonie Marden	J. Goater	20–1
	3	War Horn	C. Wood	—
1881	1	Thebais	G. Fordham	6–4 on
	2	Lucy Glitters	Morgan	100–6
	3	Myra	T. Cannon	20–1
1882	1	Geheimniss	T. Cannon	6–4 on
	2	St. Marguerite	C. Wood	11–4
	3	Nellie	G. Fordham	11–2
1883	1	Bonny Jean	J. Watts	5–1
	2	Malibran	J. Goater	20–1
	3	Ettare	Morgan	—
1884	1	Busybody	T. Cannon	105–100 on
	2	Superba	F. Archer	4–1
	3	Queen Adelaide	F. Webb	9–2
1885	1	Lonely	F. Archer	85–40
	2	St. Helena	J. Watts	9–2
	3	Cipollina	T. Cannon	200–15
1886	1	Miss Jummy	J. Watts	evens
	2	Argo Navis	T. Cannon	1,000–30
	3	Braw Lass	F. Webb	4–1
1887	1	Reve d'Or	C. Wood	11–8 on
	2	St. Helen	T. Weldon	40–1
	3	Freedom	G. Barrett	100–8

Year	Horse	Jockey	Starting Price
1888	1 Seabreeze	W. Robinson	7–4
	2 Rada	F. Webb	100–7
	3 Belle Mahone	J. Fagan	100–8
1889	1 L'Abbesse de Jouarre	J. Woodburn	20–1
	2 Minthe	F. Webb	9–4
	3 Seclusion	S. Loates	10–1
1890	1 Memoir	J. Watts	100–30
	2 Signorina	G. Barrett	evens
	3 Ponza	T. Cannon	100–8
1891	1 Mimi	F. Rickaby	7–4 on
	2 Corstorphine	J. Watts	7–2
	3 Lady Primrose	J. Osborne	50–1
1892	1 La Fleche	G. Barrett	11–8 on
	2 The Smew	J. Watts	100–6
	3 Lady Hermit	M. Cannon	100–8
1893	1 Mrs. Butterwick	J. Watts	100–7
	2 Tressure	White	6–1
	3 Cypria	Barker	100–1
1894	1 Amiable	W. Bradford	7–1
	2 Sweet Duchess	S. Chandley	20–1
	3 Sarana	F. Finlay	7–1
1895	1 La Sagesse	S. Loates	5–1
	2 Galeottia	F. Pratt	100–15
	3 Penkridge	W. Bradford	33–1
1896	1 Canterbury Pilgrim	F. Rickaby	100–8
	2 Thais	J. Watts	13–8
	3 Proposition	W. Bradford	100–7
1897	1 Limasol	W. Bradford	100–8
	2 Chelandry	J. Watts	5–2 on
	3 Fortalice	F. Finlay	40–1
1898	1 Airs and Graces	W. Bradford	100–8
	2 Nun Nicer	S. Loates	evens
	3 Cauliflower	Allsopp	33–1
1899	1 Musa	O. Madden	20–1
	2 Sibola	Sloan	7–4 on
	3 Corposant	C. Wood	40–1
1900	1 La Roche	M. Cannon	5–1
	2 Merry Gal	K. Cannon	100–7
	3 Lady Schomberg	Sloan	3–1
	2 m. 45⅕ s. (*J. Porter*)		
1901	1 Cap and Bells II	M. Henry	9–4
	2 Sabrinetta	C. Jenkins	50–1
	3 Minnie Dee	L. Reiff	10–1
	2 m. 44⅗ s. (*S. Darling*)		
1902	1 Sceptre	H. Randall	5–2
	2 Glass Jug	G. McCall	10–1
	3 Elba	D. Maher	25–1
	2 m. 46⅗ s. (*R. S. Sievier*)		
1903	1 Our Lassie	M. Cannon	6–1
	2 Hammerkop	J. H. Martin	2–1
	3 Skyscraper	D. Maher	100–7
	2 m. 44⅗ s. (*C. Morton*)		
1904	1 Pretty Polly	W. Lane	100–8 on
	2 Bitters	K. Cannon	20–1
	3 Fiancee	J. Watts	100–7
	2 m. 45⅕ s. (*P. P. Gilpin*)		
1905	1 Cherry Lass	H. Jones	5–4 on
	2 Queen of the Earth	W. Higgs	100–14
	3 Amitie	D. Maher	100–6
	2 m. 38 s. (*W. T. Robinson*)		
1906	1 Keystone II	D. Maher	5–2
	2 Gold Riach	O Madden	5–1
	3 Snow-Glory	W. Halsey	100–9
	2 m. 38⅗ s. (*G. Lambton*)		
1907	1 Glass Doll	H. Randall	25–1
	2 Laomedia	O. Madden	10–1
	3 Lady Hasty	J. Thompson	100–14
	2 m. 42 s. (*C. Morton*)		
1908	1 Signorinetta	W. Bullock	3–1
	2 Courtesy	Wm. Griggs	100–7
	3 Santeve	W. Higgs	100–7
	2 m. 42⅖ s. (*Chev. E. Ginistrelli*)		
1909	1 Perola	F. Wootton	5–1
	2 Princesse de Galles	H. Jones	11–2
	3 Verne	Walter Griggs	25–1
	2 m. 39⅘s. (*G. Davies*)		
1910	1 Rosedrop	C. Trigg	7–1
	2 Evolution	J. Thompson	25–1
	3 Pernelle	W. Higgs	25–1
	2 m. 38⅕ s. (*Alec Taylor*)		
1911	1 Cherimoya	F. Winter	25–1
	2 Tootles	S. Donoghue	7–2
	3 Hair Trigger II	F. Wootton	9–1
	2 m. 41⅗ s. (*C. Marsh*)		
1912	1 Mirska	J. Childs	33–1
	2 Equitable	F. O'Neill	33–1
	3 Bill and Coo	F. Wootton	10–1
	2 m. 43 s. (*T. Jennings*)		
1913	1 Jest	F. Rickaby, jun.	8–1
	2 Depeche	Walter Griggs	20–1
	3 Arda	W. Earl	100–8
	2 m. 37⅗ s. (*C. Morton*)		
1914	1 Princess Dorrie	W. Huxley	11–4
	2 Wassilissa	E. Huxley	100–6
	3 Torchlight	G. Stern	10–1
	2 m. 38⅕ s. (*C. Morton*)		
	Run at Newmarket as New Oaks Stakes		
1915	1 Snow Marten	Walter Griggs	20–1
	2 Bright	W. Huxley	7–1
	3 Silver Tag	S. Donoghue	11–4
	2 m. 36⅕ s. (*P. P. Gilpin*)		
1916	1 Fifinella	J. Childs	13–8 on
	2 Salamandra	A. Whalley	8–1
	3 Market Girl	S. Donoghue	20–1
	2 m. 35 s. (*R. Dawson*)		
1917	1 Sunny Jane	O. Madden	4–1
	2 Diadem	F. Rickaby	7–4
	3 Moravia	E. Wheatley	100–8
	2 m. 43⅗ s. (*Alec Taylor*)		

Year	Horse	Jockey	Starting Price
1918	1 My Dear	S. Donoghue	3–1
	† Ferry	B. Carslake	100–6
	† Silver Bullet	O. Madden	33–1
	2 m. 34⅘ s. (*Alec Taylor*)		
	(Stony Ford (J. H. Martin) came in first by a length, but was disqualified.)		
	Run at Epsom		
1919	1 Bayuda	J. Childs	100–7
	2 Roseway	S. Donoghue	7–4 on
	3 Mapledurham	G. Hulme	25–1
	2 m. 37⅕ s. (*Alec Taylor*)		
1920	1 Charlebelle	A. Whalley	7–2
	2 Cinna	Wm. Griggs	2–1
	3 Roselet	V. Smyth	25–1
	2 m. 38⅕ s. (*H. Braime*)		
1921	1 Love in Idleness	J. Childs	5–1
	2 Lady Sleipner	P. Mason	25–1
	3 Long Suit	F. Lane	10–1
	2 m. 36⅕ s. (*Alec Taylor*)		
1922	1 Pogrom	E. Gardner	5–4
	2 Soubriquet	S. Donoghue	7–2
	3 Mysia	G. Archibald	100–8
	2 m. 36⅕ s. (*Alec Taylor*)		
1923	1 Brownhylda	V. Smyth	10–1
	2 Shrove	E. C. Elliott	100–7
	3 Teresina	G. Hulme	8–1
	2 m. 37 s. (*R. Dawson*)		
1924	1 Straitlace	F. O'Neill	100–30
	2 Plack	E. C. Elliott	11–10
	3 Mink	R. A. Jones	100–7
	2 m. 47 s. (*D. Waugh*)		
1925	1 Saucy Sue	F. Bullock	100–30 on
	2 Miss Gadabout	J. Brennan	100–8
	3 Riding Light	S. Donoghue	20–1
	2 m. 38⅕ s. (*Alec Taylor*)		
1926	1 Short Story	R. A. Jones	5–1
	2 Resplendent	T. Burns	100–1
	3 Gay Bird	J. Brennan	100–8
	2 m. 43⅖ s. (*Alec Taylor*)		
1927	1 Beam	T. Weston	4–1
	2 Book Law	H. Jelliss	5–2
	3 Grande Vitesse	S. Donoghue	25–1
	2 m. 34⅗ s. (*Frank Butters*)		
1928	1 Toboggan	T. Weston	100–15
	2 Scuttle	J. Childs	evens
	3 Flegere	R. A. Jones	100–9
	2 m. 37⅖ s. (*Frank Butters*)		
1929	1 Pennycomequick	H. Jelliss	11–10
	2 Golden Silence	C. Ray	20–1
	3 Sister Anne	J. Childs	7–2
	2 m. 35⅘ s. (*J. Lawson*)		
1930	1 Rose of England	G. Richards	7–1
	2 Wedding Favour	M. Wing	33–1
	3 Micmac	C. Ray	33–1
	2 m. 39 s. (*T. Hogg*)		
1931	1 Brulette	E. C. Elliott	7–2
	2 Four Course	F. Fox	6–1
	3 Links Tor	R. A. Jones	10–1
	2 m. 39⅕ s. (*F. Carter, in France*)		
1932	1 Udaipur	M. Beary	10–1
	2 Will o' the Wisp	G. Richards	9–4
	3 Giudecca	T. Weston	10–1
	2 m. 43⅕ s. (*Franks Butters*)		
1933	1 Chatelaine	S. Wragg	25–1
	2 Solfatara	S. Donoghue	20–1
	3 Fur Tor	R. A. Jones	100–8
	2 m. 36⅘ s. (*F. Templeman*)		
1934	1 Light Brocade	B. Carslake	7–4
	2 Zelina	S. Donoghue	9–4
	3 Instantaneous	R. Dick	20–1
	2 m. 35⅕ s. (*Frank Butters*)		
1935	1 Quashed	H. Jelliss	33–1
	2 Ankaret	F. Fox	100–6
	3 Mesa	W. R. Johnstone	5–4
	2 m. 41⅗ s. (*C. Leader*)		
1936	1 Lovely Rosa	T. Weston	33–1
	2 Barrowby Gem	P. Beasley	22–1
	3 Feola	F. Fox	10–1
	2 m. 36 s. (*H. L. Cottrill*)		
1937	1 Exhibitionist	S. Donoghue	3–1
	2 Sweet Content	W. Sibbritt	33–1
	3 Sculpture	R. A. Jones	20–1
	2 m. 37 s. (*J. Lawson*)		
1938	1 Rockfel	H. Wragg	3–1
	2 Radiant	C. Smirke	100–7
	3 Solar Flower	R. Perryman	100–9
	2 m. 37⅗ s. (*O. Bell*)		
1939	1 Galatea II	R. A. Jones	11–10 on
	2 White Fox	E. C. Elliott	9–1
	3 Superbe	P. Beasley	20–1
	2 m. 40⅗ s. (*J. Lawson*)		
	Run at Newmarket as New Oaks Stakes		
1940	1 Godiva	D. Marks	7–4
	2 Silverlace II	G. Richards	100–8
	3 Valeraine	T. Weston	33–1
	2 m. 30⅗ s. (*W. Jarvis*)		
1941	1 Commotion	H. Wragg	8–1
	2 Turkana	P. Evans	100–8
	3 Dancing Time	R. Perryman	7–4 on
	2 m. 37 s. (*Fred Darling*)		
1942	1 Sun Chariot	G. Richards	4–1 on
	2 Afterthought	E. Smith	10–1
	3 Feberion	T. H. Carey	20–1
	2 m. 31⅕ s. (*Fred Darling*)		
1943	1 Why Hurry	E. C. Elliott	7–1
	2 Ribbon	E. Smith	5–2
	3 Tropical Sun	G. Richards	7–4
	2 m. 33⅕ s. (*N. Cannon*)		
1944	1 Hycilla	G. Bridgland	8–1
	2 Monsoon	P. Maher	33–1
	3 Kannabis	A. Richardson	18–1
	2 m. 30⅗s. (*C. Boyd-Rochfort*)		

RACING QUIZ

1. When was the last meeting held at Croydon?

★

2. First overseas win in the Derby went to Iroquois, in 1881. Name the country he came from?

★

3. Name the first successfull woman owner in the Derby.

★

4. With what horse did Miss Dorothy Paget win the Derby?

★

5. First overseas success in the St. Leger went to?

★

6. Jockey W. Scott rode four successive St. Leger winners. Name the years.

★

7. Name the figure paid by the Irish National Stud for Derby winner Tulyar.

QUIZ ANSWERS

1. 1890. 2. He was bred, owned and trained in America. 3. Lady Jane Douglas in 1918 with Gainsborough. 4. Straight Deal in 1943. 5. Iroquois, from America; he also won the Derby. 6. 1838, 1839, 1840, 1841. 7. £250,000.

Average Times—*contd.*

HURST

Hurdles

2 miles	3/54 s.
2 miles 4 furlongs...........	5/4 s.

'Chase

2 miles 275 yards	4/20⅗ s.
3 miles	6/6 s.
4 miles 1 furlong	8/32 s.

KELSO

Hurdles

2 miles	3/55 s.
2½ miles	5/1 s.
3 miles	6/5 s.

'Chase

2 miles	4/14 s.
2½ miles	5/19 s.
3 miles	6/20 s.

KEMPTON

Hurdles

2 miles 180 yards	4/7 s.
3 miles	6/0 s.

'Chase

2 miles	4/3 s.
2 miles 4 furlong 90 yards....	5/12⅗ s.
3 miles	6/8⅗ s.

LEICESTER

Hurdles

2 miles	3/59⅗ s.
3 miles	6/4 s.

'Chase

2 miles	4/17 s.
3 miles	6/13 s.

LINGFIELD

Hurdles

2 miles	3/58⅗ s.
2 miles 6 furlongs...........	5/43⅗ s.

'Chase

2 miles	4/10 s.
2½ miles	5/12 s.
3 miles	6/10 s.

contd. next page

RACING QUIZ

1. How many Oaks winners did Alec Taylor train.

★

2. Name E. C. Elliott's first winner since he took out a training licence after returning from France.

★

3. Explain the meaning of when a horse is cast in its box.

★

4. In what year did Gordon Richards beat Fred Archer's record of 246 winners.

★

5. Name the last gelding to run in the Derby.

★

6. When were geldings barred from competing in the Derby?

QUIZ ANSWERS

1. Eight. 1910, 1917, 1918, 1919, 1921, 1922, 1925, 1926. 2. Little Redskin, winner of the May Stakes at Newmarket on Saturday May 2nd 1959. 3. It means that he has slipped and hurt himself. 4. 1933 when he rode 259. 5. Clacquer in 1901. 6. 1904.

Average Times—*contd.*

LIVERPOOL

Hurdles

2 miles 1 furlong .... 4/9 s.
2 miles 5 furlongs........... 5/23 s.

'Chase

2 miles 4 furlongs........... 5/13 s.
2 miles 5 furlongs........... 5/$28\frac{1}{5}$ s.
2 miles 6 furlongs .... 5/$42\frac{3}{5}$ s.
2 miles $7\frac{1}{2}$ furlongs.......... 6/4 s.
4 miles 856 yards .... 9/$24\frac{3}{5}$ s.

(Mildmay Course)

2 miles .... 4/3 s.
3 miles 1 furlong 130 yards.... 6/34 s.

LUDLOW

Hurdles

2 miles 150 yards .... 4/$8\frac{3}{5}$ s.
3 miles .... 6/3 s.

'Chase

2 miles .... 4/$1\frac{3}{5}$ s.
$2\frac{1}{2}$ miles .... 5/$4\frac{2}{5}$ s.
3 miles .... 6/$5\frac{3}{5}$ s.

MANCHESTER

Hurdles

2 miles .... 3/53 s.
3 miles .... 6/$0\frac{3}{5}$ s.

'Chase

2 miles .... 4/9 s.
2 miles 4 furlongs.......... 5/$13\frac{1}{5}$ s.
3 miles .... 6/13 s.

MARKET RASEN

Hurdles

2 miles .... 4/3 s.

'Chase

2 miles 90 yards .... 4/29 s.
3 miles .... 6/32 s.

NEWBURY

Hurdles

2 miles (Provisional)......... 3/50 s.
2 miles 4 furlongs 120 yards 5/8 s.
3 miles .... 5/$58\frac{3}{5}$ s.

'Chase

2 miles 160 yards (Provisional) 4/$7\frac{3}{5}$ s.
$2\frac{1}{2}$ miles .... 5/8 s.
3 miles .... 6/$8\frac{3}{5}$ s.

Cont'd next page

The Oaks—*contd.*

Year		*Horse*	*Jockey*	*Starting Price*
1945	1	Sun Stream	H. Wragg	6–4
	2	Naishapur	D. Smith	20–1
	3	Solar Princess	G. Richards	20–1
		2 m. 30 s. (*W. Earl*)		
		Run at Epsom		
1946	1	Steady Aim	H. Wragg	7–1
	2	Iona	E. Smith	2–1
	3	Nelia	M. Beary	7–1
		2 m. 41 s. (*Frank Butters*)		
1947	1	Imprudence	W. R. Johnstone	7–4
	2	Netherton Maid	W. Rickaby	7–1
	3	Mermaid	E. Smith	6–1
		2 m. 40 s. (*L. Lieux, in France*)		
1948	1	Masaka	W. Nevett	7–1
	2	Angelola	W. H. Carr	20–1
	3	Folie II	J. Doyasbere	33–1
		2 m. $40\frac{3}{5}$ s. (*Frank Butters*)		
1949	1	Musidora	E. Britt	4–1
	2	Coronation V	E. C. Elliott	6–1
	3	Vice Versa II	W. R. Johnstone	5–1
		2 m. 40 s. (*C. F. Elsey*)		
1950	1	Asmena	W. R. Johnstone	5–1
	2	Plume II	E. C. Elliott	10–1
	3	Stella Polaris	M. Molony	100–7
		2 m. $42\frac{3}{5}$ s. (*C. H. Semblat, in France*)		
1951	1	Neasham Belle	S. Clayton	33–1
	2	Chinese Cracker	A. Breasley	10–1
	3	Belle of All	E. C. Elliott	5–1
		2 m. $41\frac{1}{5}$ s. (*G. T. Brooke*)		
1952	1	Frieze	E. Britt	100–7
	2	Zabara	K. Gethin	9–2
	3	Moon Star	W. H. Carr	9–1
		2 m. $35\frac{4}{5}$ s. (*C. F. Elsey*)		
1953	1	Ambiguity	J. Mercer	18–1
	2	Kerkeb	G. Richards	28–1
	3	Noemi	J. Massard	100–8
		2 m. $36\frac{4}{5}$ s. (*R. J. Colling*)		
1954	1	Sun Cap	W. R. Johnstone	100–8
	2	Altana	E. Mercer	8–1
	3	Philante	J. Doyasbere	20–1
		2 m. $39\frac{1}{5}$ s. (*R. Carver, in France*)		
1955	1	Meld	W. H. Carr	7–4
	2	Ark Royal	E. Mercer	8–1
	3	Reel In	A. Breasley	100–6
		2 m. $47\frac{4}{5}$ s. (*C. Boyd-Rochfort*)		
1956	1	Sicarelle	F. Palmer	3–1
	2	Janiari	S. Boullenger	100–8
	3	Yasmin	J. Massard	25–1
		2 m. 42 s. (*F. Mathet, in France*)		
1957	1	Carrozza	L. Piggott	100–8
	2	Silken Gilder	Jas Eddery	20–1
	3	Rose Royale II	J. Massard	11–10
		2 m. $37\frac{3}{5}$ s. (*C. F. N. Murless*)		
1958	1	Bella Paola	M. Garcia	6–4
	2	Mother Goose	W. H. Carr	20–1
	3	Cutter	E. Mercer	25–1
		2 m. 40 s. (*F. Mathet, in France*)		
1959	1	Petite Etoile	L. Piggott	11–2
	2	Cantelo	E. Hide	7–4
	3	Rose of Medina	E. Smith	100–8
		2 m. $35\frac{4}{5}$ s. (*C. F. N. Murless*)		

WINNERS OF MORE THAN ONE OAKS

JOCKEYS

NINE—F. Buckle, 1797, 1798, 1799, 1802, 1803, 1805, 1817, 1818, 1823

SIX—F. Butler, 1843, 1844, 1849, 1850, 1851, 1852

FIVE—S. Chifney, 1807, 1811, 1816, 1819, 1825
J. B. Day, 1828, 1831, 1834, 1839, 1840
G. Fordham, 1859, 1868, 1870, 1872, 1881

FOUR—Chifney, sen., 1782, 1783, 1789, 1790
Fitzpatrick, 1787, 1788, 1795, 1800
T. Cannon, 1869, 1873, 1882, 1884
F. Archer, 1875, 1878, 1879, 1885
J. Watts, 1883, 1886, 1890, 1893
J. Childs, 1912, 1916, 1919, 1921
H. Wragg, 1938, 1941, 1945, 1946

THREE—R. Goodison, 1779, 1780, 1781
T. Lye, 1826, 1835, 1842
W. Scott, 1836, 1838, 1841
Templeman, 1847, 1848, 1855
W. Bradford, 1894, 1897, 1898
T. Weston, 1927, 1928, 1936
W. R. Johnstone, 1947, 1950, 1954

TWO—J. Singleton, 1791, 1793
C. Hindley, 1784, 1792
W. Clift, 1804, 1808
W. Peirse, 1810, 1812
T. Goodison, 1813, 1815
H. Edwards, 1820, 1822
J. Robinson, 1821, 1824
Charlton, 1854, 1857
J. Snowden, 1860, 1880
F. Rickaby, 1891, 1896
M. Cannon, 1900, 1903
H. Randall, 1902, 1907
H. Jellis, 1929, 1935
S. Donoghue, 1918, 1937
R. A. Jones, 1926, 1939
G. Richards, 1930, 1942
E. C. Elliott, 1931, 1943
E. Britt, 1949, 1952
L. Piggott, 1957, 1959

OWNERS

EIGHT—Duke of Grafton, 1804, 1808, 1813, 1815, 1822, 1823, 1828, 1831

SIX—Lord Grosvenor, 1781, 1782, 1783, 1797, 1799, 1805

FIVE—Lord Egremont, 1788, 1789, 1795, 1800, 1820

FOUR—Lord Falmouth, 1863, 1875, 1878, 1879
Duke of Portland, 1890, 1893, 1894, 1900
Mr. J. B. Joel, 1903, 1907, 1913, 1924
Lord Astor, 1922, 1926, 1929, 1953

THREE—Duke of Bedford, 1790, 1791, 1793
Lord Exeter, 1821, 1829, 1832

TWO—Lord Clermont, 1785, 1792
Lord Derby, 1779, 1794
Sir F. Standish, 1786, 1796
Duke of Rutland, 1811, 1814
General L. Gower, 1809, 1816
Duke of Richmond, 1827, 1845
Lord Chesterfield, 1838, 1849
Mr. J. Scott, 1836, 1852
Mr. H. Hill, 1848, 1856
Baron Rothschild, 1867, 1871
16th Lord Derby, 1896, 1906
Lord Durham, 1927, 1934
17th Lord Derby, 1928, 1945
H.H. Aga Khan, 1932, 1948

TRAINERS

EIGHT—Alec Taylor, 1910, 1917, 1918, 1919, 1921, 1922, 1925, 1926

SIX—Frank Butters, 1927, 1928, 1932, 1934, 1946, 1948

FOUR—C. Morton, 1903, 1907, 1913, 1914

THREE—J. Lawson, 1929, 1937, 1939

TWO—J. Porter, 1892, 1900
G. Dawson, 1893, 1894
G. Lambton, 1896, 1906
T. Jennings, 1897, 1912
P. P. Gilpin, 1904, 1915
R. Dawson, 1916, 1923
Fred Darling, 1941, 1942
C. F. Elsey, 1949, 1952
C. Boyd-Rochfort, 1944, 1955
F. Mathet (France), 1956, 1958
C. F. N. Murless, 1957, 1959

ST. LEGER

(Run at Doncaster)

Founded three years before the Oaks, the St. Leger is the oldest of the five classics. The race was named after Lieutenant-General Anthony St. Leger.

Until 1813 the race was run over two miles; in this year the distance was changed to one mile six furlongs and 193 yards. It was again changed in 1826 to one mile six furlongs and 132 yards which has remained ever since. For three-year-old colts and fillies.

Year		*Horse*	*Jockey*	*Starting Price*
1776	1	Allabaculia	J. Singleton	2–1 on
	2	F. by Surly	—	—
	3	Orestes	—	—
1777	1	Bourbon	J. Cade	3–1
	2	Ballad Singer	—	—
	3	F. by Snap	—	—
1778	1	Hollandaise	G. Hearon	5–2
	2	C. by Wildair	—	—
	3	Trinculo	—	—
1779	1	Tommy	G. Lowry, Sen.	evens
	2	Br. f. by Tantrum	—	—
	3	Moses	—	—
1780	1	Ruler	J. Mangle	5–2
	2	Antagonist	—	6–4 on
	3	B. c. brother to Omnium	—	—
1781	1	Serina	R. Forster	—
	2	F. by Dux	—	favourite
	3	Wisdom	—	—
1782	1	Imperatrix	G. Searle	—
	2	Monk	—	evens
	3	Haphazard	—	—
1783	1	Phœnomenon	A. Hall	5–4 on
	2	Pacolet	—	—
	3	Myrtle	—	—
1784	1	Omphale	J. Kirton	—
	2	Harlequin Junior	—	—
	3	B. c. by Alfred	—	—
1785	1	Cowslip	G. Searle	favourite
	2	Matron	—	—
	3	Verjuice	—	—
1786	1	Paragon	J. Mangle	—
	2	Trojan	—	—
	3	Carlton	—	—
1787	1	Spadille	J. Mangle	2–1
	2	Edmund	—	—
	3	Prince le Boo	—	—
1788	1	Young Flora	J. Mangle	2–1
	2	Thistle	—	6–4
	3	C. by Tandem	—	—
1789	1	Pewett	J. Singleton	—
	2	Bellona	—	—
	3	Ostrich	—	—
		(Zanga came in first but was disqualified for jostling)		
1790	1	Ambidexter	G. Searle	5–1
	2	Fortitude	—	—
	3	Spanker	—	5–4 on
1791	1	Young Traveller	J. Jackson	—
	2	Huby	—	favourite
	3	Trimmer	—	—
1792	1	Tartar	J. Mangle	50–2
	2	Skypeeper	—	—
	3	Adonis	—	—
1793	1	Ninety-three	W. Peirse	15–1
	2	Foreigner	—	—
	3	Hornet	—	2–1

Year	Horse	Jockey	Starting Price
1794	1 Beningborough	J. Jackson	2–1
	2 Prior	—	7–4
	3 Brilliant	—	—
1795	1 Hambletonian	Boyes	6–4 on
	2 B. c. brother to Overton		
	3 Why Not	—	—
1796	1 Ambrosio	J. Jackson	5–4 on
	2 Cardinal	—	—
	3 Rosolio	—	—
1797	1 Lounger	J. Shepherd	High odds
	2 Stamford	--	7–4 on
	(Only two placed)		
1798	1 Symmetry	J. Jackson	4–1
	2 Barnaby	—	High odds
	3 Honeycomb	—	3–1
1799	1 Cockfighter	T. Fields	6–4 on
	2 Expectation	—	—
	3 Slap-bang	—	—
1800	1 Champion	F. Buckle	2–1
	2 Rolla	—	6–1
	3 Richmond	—	5–1
1801	1 Quiz	J. Shepherd	7–1
	2 Belleisle	—	5–1
	3 Miracle	—	4–1 & 5–1
1802	1 Orville	J. Singleton, Jun.	5–1
	2 Pipylin	—	—
	3 Sparrowhawk	—	5–2
1803	1 Remembrancer	B. Smith	5–2
	2 Macmanus	—	7–1
	3 Sir Oliver	—	3–1
1804	1 Sancho	F. Buckle	2–1
	2 Master Betty	—	3–1
	(Only two placed)		
1805	1 Staveley	J. Jackson	5–1 & 6–1
	2 Caleb Quotem	—	10–1
	3 Sir Paul	—	—
1806	1 Fyldener	T. Carr	7–4
	2 Cassio	—	—
	3 Shuttlecock	—	—
1807	1 Paulina	W. Clift	8–1
	2 Scud	—	10–1
	3 Eaton	—	5–2
1808	1 Petronius	B. Smith	20–1
	2 Clinker	—	8–1
	3 Easton	—	6–1 & 7–1
1809	1 Ashton	B. Smith	15–8
	2 Middlethorpe	—	8–1
	3 Lisette	—	25–1
1810	1 Octavian	W. Clift	12–1
	2 Recollection	—	7–2
	3 Oriana	—	11–8
1811	1 Soothsayer	B. Smith	6–1
	2 Amadis de Gaul	—	—
	3 Scamp	—	11–1
1812	1 Ottrington	R. Johnson	50–1
	2 Benedict	—	9–1
	3 Herrington	—	9–1
1813	1 Altisidora	J. Jackson	5–2
	2 Camelopard	—	6–1
	3 Tiger	—	5–1
1814	1 William	J. Shepherd	7–1
	2 Heart of Oak	—	17–1
	(Only two placed)		
1815	1 Filho da Puta	J. Jackson	evens
	2 Dinmont	—	3–1
	3 Fulford	—	10–1
1816	1 The Duchess (late Duchess of Leven)	B. Smith	12–1
	2 Captain Candid	—	20–1
	3 Rasping	—	4–1
1817	1 Ebor	R. Johnson	20–1
	2 Black Lock	—	5–4 on
	3 Restless	—	—
1818	1 Reveller	R. Johnson	7–2 & 4–1
	2 Ranter	—	20–1
	3 The Marshal	—	20–1
	3 m. 15 s.		
1819	1 Antonio	J. Nicholson	25 to 30–1
	2 Wrangler	—	7–4
	3 Archibald	—	10–1
1820	1 St. Patrick	J. Johnson	7–1
	2 Copeland	—	100–1
	3 Locksley	—	18–1
1821	1 Jack Spiggot	W. Scott	6–1
	2 Fortuna	—	30–1
	3 Coronation	—	20–1
1822	1 Theodore	J. Jackson	100–1
	2 Violet	—	40–1
	3 Professor	—	—
1823	1 Barefoot	T. Goodison	4–1
	2 Sherwood	—	20–1
	3 Comte d'Artois	—	20–1
1824	1 Jerry	B. Smith	9–1
	2 Canteen	—	15–1
	(Only two placed)		
1825	1 Memnon	W. Scott	3–1
	2 Tne Alderman	—	10–1
	(Only two placed)		
1826	1 Tarrare	G. Nelson	20–1
	2 Mulatto	—	7–1 & 8–1
	(Only two placed)		
1827	1 Matilda	J. Robinson	9–1 & 10–1
	2 Mameluke	—	5–2
	3 Laurel	—	—
1828	1 The Colonel	W. Scott	5–2 & 3–1
	2 Belinda	—	100–1
	(Only two placed)		
1829	1 Rowton	W. Scott	7–2
	2 Voltaire	—	4–1
	3 Sir Hercules	—	10–1
1830	1 Birmingham	P. Conolly	15–1
	2 Priam	S. Chifney	11–10
	3 Emancipation	—	—

Year	Horse	Jockey	Starting Price
1831	1 Chorister	J. B. Day	20–1
	2 The Saddler	—	3–1
	(Only two placed)		
1832	1 Margrave	J. Robinson	8–1
	2 Birdcatcher	—	11–1
	(Only two placed)		
1833	1 Rockingham	S. Darling	7–1
	2 Mussulman	—	6–1
	(Only two placed)		
1834	1 Touchstone	G. Calloway	40–1
	2 Bran	—	—
	3 General Chassé	—	10–1
1835	1 Queen of Trumps	T. Lye	11–8
	2 Hornsea	—	2–1
	3 Br. c. brother to Hope	—	25–1
	(Later named Sheet Anchor)		
1836	1 Elis	J. B. Day	7–2
	2 Scroggins	—	6–4
	(Only two placed)		
1837	1 Mango	S. Day, Jun.	13–2
	2 Abraham Newland	—	20–1
	(Only two placed)		
1838	1 Don John	W. Scott	13–8
	2 Ion	—	9–4
	(Only two placed)		
1839	1 Charles the Twelfth	W. Scott	6–4 on
	2 Euclid	P. Conolly	13–1
	(Only two placed)		
	(Charles the Twelfth and Euclid ran a dead-heat. In the run off Charles the Twelfth won. Betting began at 6–4 on Charles the Twelfth and finished at 6–5 on Euclid.)		
1840	1 Launcelot	W. Scott	7–4
	2 Maroon	—	4–1
	(Only two placed)		
1841	1 Satirist	W. Scott	6–1
	2 Coronation	—	2–1 on
	(Only two placed)		
1842	1 Blue Bonnet	T. Lye	8–1
	2 Sea-horse	Chapple	20–1
	(Only two placed)		
1843	1 Nutwith	J. Marson	100–6
	2 Cotherstone	F. Butler	6–4 on
	3 Prizefighter	J. Holmes	11–2
1844	1 Foig a Ballagh	H. Bell	7–2
	2 The Cure	J. Marson	5–4
	3 The Princess	F. Butler	4–1
1845	1 The Baron	F. Butler	10–1
	2 Miss Sarah	J. Holmes	5–2
	3 Pantasa	C. Marlow	10–1
1846	1 Sir Tatton Sykes	W. Scott	3–1
	2 Iago	F. Butler	10–1
	3 Brocardo	J. Holmes	3–1
1847	1 Van Tromp	J. Marson	4–1
	2 Cossack	S. Templeman	5–4 on
	3 Eryx	Marlow	12–1
1848	1 Surplice	E. Flatman	9–4
	2 Canezou	F. Butler	7–4
	3 Flatcatcher	J. Robinson	7–2
1849	1 The Flying Dutchman	Marlow	9–4 on
	2 Nunnykirk	A. Day	15–1
	3 Vatican	J. Marson	15–1
1850	1 Voltigeur	J. Marson	13–8 on
	2 Russborough	J. Robinson	20–1
	3 Bolingbroke	W. Boyce	25–1
	(Voltigeur and Russborough ran a dead-heat. In the run off Voltigeur won. Betting in deciding heat 6–4 on Voltigeur.)		
1851	1 Newminster	S. Templeman	12–1
	2 Aphrodité	J. Marson	2–1
	3 Hook'em Snivvey	J. Holmes	—
1852	1 Stockwell	J. Norman	7–4
	2 Harbinger	E. Flatman	7–1
	3 Daniel O'Rourke	F. Butler	5–2
1853	1 West Australian	F. Butler	6–4
	2 The Reiver	Marlow	7–1
	3 Rataplan	J. Wells	7–1
1854	1 Knight of St. George	Basham	11–1
	2 Ivan	Ashmall	20–1
	3 Arthur Wellesley	J. Prince	1,000–15
1855	1 Saucebox	J. Wells	40–1
	2 Rifleman	E. Flatman	evens
	3 Lady Tatton	J. Osborne	—
1856	1 Warlock	E. Flatman	12–1
	† Bonnie Scotland	J. Wells	9–1
	† Artillery	Basham	12–1
1857	1 Imperieuse	E. Flatman	100–6
	2 Commotion	Aldcroft	14–1
	3 Tournament	G. Fordham	8–1
1858	1 Sunbeam	L. Snowden	15–1
	2 The Hadji	Aldcroft	7–1
	3 Blanche of Middlebie	Withington	15–1
1859	1 Gamester	Aldcroft	20–1
	2 Defender	L. Snowdon	10–1
	3 Magnum	J. Osborne	—
1860	1 St. Albans	L. Snowden	8–1
	2 High Treason	Bullock	100–3
	3 The Wizard	Aldcroft	4–1
1861	1 Caller Ou	T. Chaloner	1,000–15
	2 Kettledrum	L. Snowden	6–4
	3 Kildonan	G. Fordham	6–1
1862	1 The Marquis	T. Chaloner	100–30
	2 Buckstone	G. Fordham	3–1
	3 Clarissimus	J. Osborne	50–1
1863	1 Lord Clifden	J. Osborne	100–30
	2 Queen Bertha	J. Wells	7–1
	3 Borealis	T. Chaloner	100–7
1864	1 Blair Athol	J. Snowden	2–1
	2 General Peel	J. Wells	3–1
	3 Camboscan	Edwards	100–6
1865	1 Gladiateur	H. Grimshaw	13–8 on
	2 Regalia	J. Osborne	9–1
	3 Archimedes	Carroll	25–1

RACING QUIZ

1. Name the oldest race for two-year-olds.

★

2. When was the last meeting held at Hampton?

★

3. Name the three Stewards of the Jockey Club?

★

4. State the racing colours of Mr. Phil Bull.

★

5. Name the jockey who at Mullingar went through the card by riding in hurdle, steeplechase and flat events.

★

6. Name the horse who won the Derby for Lord Jersey which, by the way, was his only race.

QUIZ ANSWERS

1. The July Stakes at Newmarket dating from 1786. 2. 1877. 3. Lord Irwin, the Duke of Roxburghe, and Major-General Sir Randle Feilden. 4. Cerise, white circle. 5. "Tick" Mason. 6. Middleton in 1825.

Average Times—*contd.*

NEWCASTLE

Hurdles

2 miles 60 yards .... 3/57 s.
$2\frac{1}{2}$ miles .... 4/59 s.
3 miles 10 yards .... 5/51$\frac{2}{5}$ s.

'Chase

2 miles 120 yards .... 4/11 s.
$2\frac{1}{2}$ miles .... 5/6$\frac{1}{5}$ s.
3 miles 10 yards .... 6/9 s.

NEWTON ABBOT

Hurdles

2 miles .... 3/52 s.
$2\frac{1}{2}$ miles .... 4/49 s.

'Chase

2 miles .... 4/6$\frac{2}{5}$ s.
$2\frac{1}{2}$ miles .... 5/4 s.
3 miles 1 furlong .... 6/16 s.

NOTTINGHAM

Hurdles

2 miles .... 3/50 s.
$2\frac{1}{2}$ miles .... 4/49$\frac{3}{5}$ s.
2 miles 6 furlongs .... 5/16$\frac{1}{5}$ s.

'Chase

2 miles .... 4/0$\frac{2}{5}$ s.
3 miles and a few yards .... 6/13 s.

PERTH

Hurdles

2 miles .... 3/55$\frac{2}{5}$ s.
$2\frac{1}{2}$ miles .... 4/58$\frac{1}{5}$ s.
3 miles .... 6/3$\frac{2}{5}$ s.

'Chase

2 miles .... 4/2$\frac{4}{5}$ s.
3 miles 585 yards .... 6/53 s.

PLUMPTON

Hurdles

2 miles .... 3/50 s.
3 miles .... 6/1 s.

'Chase

2 miles .... 4/6$\frac{2}{5}$ s.
2 miles 750 yards .... 5/2$\frac{1}{5}$ s.
3 miles .... 6/17 s.

SANDOWN

Hurdles

2 miles .... 3/58 s.
2 miles 5 furlongs 75 yards .... 5/19$\frac{3}{5}$ s.

'Chase

2 miles 25 yards .... 4/2 s.
2 miles 4 furlongs 5 yards...... 5/11 s.
3 miles 125 yards .... 6/19$\frac{3}{5}$ s.
3 miles 5 furlongs 25 yards.... 7/29 s.

contd. next page

RACING QUIZ

1. Name the horse which was leading at the last fence in the 1936 Grand National and ran out.

*

2. When did the last National Hunt meeting take place at Newmarket?

*

3. In what year were the 2,000 guineas and 1,000 guineas run on the same day?

*

4. How many times was Gordon Richards champion jockey?

*

5. How many times did Brown Jack win the Queen Alexandra Stakes at Ascot?

*

6. Why is the steeplechaser Bob Tailed 'un so named?

QUIZ ANSWERS

1. Davy Jones. 2. December 28th 1905. 3. At Newmarket on Friday April 29th, 1921. 4. 26 times. 5. Six successive times between 1929 and 1934. 6. His tail was broken at birth, and all he has is a short stump.

Average Times—*contd.*

SEDGEFIELD

Hurdles

2 miles .... 4/12 s.
2 miles 4 furlongs.......... 5/9⅗ s.

'Chase

2 miles .... 4/21⅗ s.
3 miles 250 yards .... 6/44 s.

SOUTHWELL

Hurdles

2 miles 80 yards .... 3/57 s.
2 miles 4 furlongs.......... 4/57 s.

'Chase

2 miles .... 4/6 s.
3 miles .... 6/14 s.

STRATFORD-ON-AVON

Hurdles

2 miles .... 3/53⅕ s.
2½ miles .... 4/53 s.

'Chase

2 miles and a few yards...... 4/7 s.
2 miles 2½ furlongs.......... 4/50 s.
3 miles .... 6/10s.
3 miles 2 furlongs.......... 6/55 s.

TAUNTON

Hurdles

2 miles .... 3/53⅗ s.
2 miles 3 furlongs.......... 4/45⅖ s.

'Chase

2 miles .... 4/3 s.
2 miles 3 furlongs.......... 4/49 s.
3 miles 1 furlong .... 6/18 s.

UTTOXETER

Hurdles

2 miles 180 yards .... 4/9 s.
2½ miles .... 4/58 s.

'Chase

2 miles 40 yards .... 4/8 s.
2½ miles .... 5/14 s.
3 miles .... 6/10 s.

WARWICK

Hurdles

2 miles .... 3/53 s.
2 miles 5 furlongs.......... 5/5 s.

'Chase

2 miles .... 4/10 s.
2½ miles .... 5/17⅗ s.
3 miles .... 6/12 s.

contd. next page

St. Leger—*contd.*

Year		*Horse*	*Jockey*	*Starting Price*
1866	1	Lord Lyon	H. Custance	7–4 on
	2	Savernake	T. Chaloner	9–2
	3	Knight of the Crescent	Norman	25–1
1867	1	Achievement	T. Chaloner	75–40
	2	The Hermit	H. Custance	5–4
	3	Julius	Daley	100–6
1868	1	Formosa	T. Chaloner	100–30
	2	Paul Jones	G. Fordham	100–15
	3	Mercury	J. Osborne	25–1
1869	1	Pero Gomez	J. Wells	3–1
	2	Martyrdom	G. Fordham	7–1
	3	George Osbaldeston	T. French	33–1
1870	1	Hawthornden	J. Grimshaw	1,000–35
	2	Kingcraft	T. French	2–1
	3	Wheat-Ear	F. Webb	10–1
1871	1	Hannah	C. Maidment	9–4
	2	Albert Victor	T. French	3–1
	3	Ringwood	T. Chaloner	10–1
1872	1	Wenlock	C. Maidment	8–1
	2	Prince Charlie	T. French	3–1
	3	Vanderdecken	T. Cannon	100–6
1873	1	Marie Stuart	T. Osborne	9–4
	2	Doncaster	F. Webb	100–30
	3	Kaiser	C. Maidment	6–4
1874	1	Apology	J. Osborne	4–1
	2	Leolinus	T. Osborne	7–1
	3	Trent	T. Cannon	5–1
1875	1	Craig Millar	T. Chaloner	7–1
	2	Balfe	T. Cannon	100–8
	3	Earl of Dartrey	J. Goater	5–1
1876	1	Patrarch	J. Goater	5–1
	2	Wild Tommy	H. Custance	100–1
	3	Julius Caesar	F. Webb	100–3
1877	1	Silvio	F. Archer	65–40
	2	Lady Golightly	Morris	4–1
	3	Manoeuvre	J. Snowden	100–6
1878	1	Jannette	F. Archer	5–2
	2	Childeric	H. Custance	10–1
	3	Master Kildare	T. Glover	100–8
1879	1	Rayon d'Or	J. Goater	3–1
	2	Ruperra	C. Wood	100–15
	3	Exeter	H. Custance	28–1
1880	1	Robert the Devil	T. Cannon	4–1
	2	Cipollato	H. Constable	100–6
	3	The Abbot	F. Webb	20–1
1881	1	Iroquois	F. Archer	2–1
	2	Geologist	T. Cannon	11–1
	3	Lucy Glitters	J. Snowden	66–1
1882	1	Dutch Oven	F. Archer	40–1
	2	Geheimniss	C. Loates	11–8 on
	3	Shotover	E. Rossiter	100–15
1883	1	Ossian	J. Watts	9–1
	2	Chislehurst	J. Osborne	100–6
	3	Highland Chief	F. Webb	5–2
1884	1	The Lambkin	J. Watts	9–1
	2	Sandiway	G. Barrett	40–1
	3	Superba	C. Wood	5–1
1885	1	Melton	F. Archer	15–8 on
	2	Isobar	C. Wood	11–1
	3	Lonely	T. Cannon	10–1
1886	1	Ormonde	F. Archer	7–1 on
	2	St. Mirin	G. Barrett	100–7
	3	Exmoor	J. Goater	100–1
1887	1	Kilwarlin	W. Robinson	4–1
	2	Merry Hampton	J. Watts	6–1
	3	Timothy	F. Barrett	100–8
1888	1	Seabreeze	W. Robinson	5–2
	2	Chillington	F. Rickaby	40–1
	3	Zanzibar	G. Barrett	20–1
1889	1	Donovan	F. Barrett	13–8 on
	2	Miguel	F. Webb	33–1
	3	Davenport	F. Rickaby	20–1
1890	1	Memoir	J. Watts	10–1
	2	Blue Green	G. Barrett	10–1
	3	Gonsalvo	J. Osborne	200–1
1891	1	Common	G. Barrett	5–4 on
	2	Reverend	J. Woodburn	11–2
	3	St. Simon of the Rock	M. Cannon	50–1
1892	1	La Fleche	J. Watts	7–2
	2	Sir Hugo	T. Weldon	10–1
	3	Watercress	J. Osborne	20–1
1893	1	Isinglass	T. Loates	95–40 on
	2	Ravensbury	M. Cannon	11–2
	3	Le Nicham	G. Barrett	33–1
1894	1	Throstle	M. Cannon	50–1
	2	Ladas	T. Loates	11–10 on
	3	Matchbox	J. Watts	2–1
1895	1	Sir Visto	S. Loates	9–4
	2	Telescope	F. Allsopp	1000–35
	3	Butterfly	W. Bradford	8–1
1896	1	Persimmon	J. Watts	11–2 on
	2	Labrador	M. Cannon	6–1
	3	Rampion	R. Moreton	200–1
1897	1	Galtee More	C. Wood	10–1 on
	2	Chelandry	M. Cannon	25–1
	3	St. Cloud II	W. Bradford	33–1
1898	1	Wildfowler	C. Wood	10–1
	2	Jeddah	J. Watts	6–5 on
	3	Bridegroom II	T. Loates	25–1
1899	1	Flying Fox	M. Cannon	7–2 on
	2	Caiman	T. Sloan	4–1
	3	Scintillant	F. Wood	300–1
1900	1	Diamond Jubilee	H. Jones	7–2 on
	2	Elopement	M. Cannon	100–7
	3	Courlan	T. Sloan	25–1
1901	1	Doricles	K. Cannon	40–1
	2	Volodyovski	L. Reiff	6–5 on
	3	Revenue	H. Jones	100–8
1902	1	Sceptre	F. W. Hardy	100–30
	2	Rising Glass	W. Halsey	9–1
	3	Friar Tuck	H. Randall	7–1
1903	1	Rock Sand	D. Maher	5–2 on
	2	William Rufus	O. Madden	100–9
	3	Mead	M. Cannon	7–1
1904	1	Pretty Polly	W. Lane	5–2 on
	2	Henry the First	O. Madden	50–1
	3	Almscliff	D. Maher	100–6
1905	1	Challacombe	O. Madden	100–6
	2	Polymelus	M. Cannon	10–1
	3	Cherry Lass	H. Jones	6–4 on
1906	1	Troutbeck	G. Stern	5–1
	2	Prince William	W. Halsey	25–1
	3	Beppo	W. Higgs	100–9
1907	1	Wool Winder	W. Halsey	11–10
	2	Baltinglass	B. Dillon	100–8
	3	Acclaim	W. Higgs	8–1
1908	1	Your Majesty	Walter Griggs	11–8
	2	White Eagle	D. Maher	100–7
	3	Santo Strato	O. Madden	100–6
1909	1	Bayardo	D. Maher	11–10 on
	2	Valens	F. Wootton	100–8
	3	Mirador	B. Dillon	40–1
1910	1	Swynford	F. Wootton	9–2
	2	Bronzino	F. Fox	20–1
	3	Lemberg	D. Maher	5–4 on
1911	1	Prince Palatine	F. O'Neill	100–30
	2	Lycaon	G. Stern	100–30
	3	King William	F. Wootton	6–4
1912	1	Tracery	G. Bellhouse	8–1
	2	Maiden Erlegh	G. Stern	100–8
	3	Hector	A. Escott	10–1
1913	1	Night Hawk	E. Wheatley	50–1
	2	White Magic	F. Wootton	33–1
	3	Seremond	N. Spear	33–1
		3 m. 3⅗ s. (*W. Robinson*)		
1914	1	Black Jester	Walter Griggs	10–1
	2	Kennymore	F. Templeman	7–2
	3	Cressingham	H. Jelliss	100–1
		3 m. 2⅗ s. (*C. Morton*)		
		Run at Newmarket as the September Stakes		
1915	1	Pommern	S. Donoghue	3–1 on
	2	Snow Marten	Walter Griggs	9–1
	3	Achtoi	C. Trigg	25–1
		2 m. 55⅗ s. (*C. Peck*)		
1916	1	Hurry On	C. Childs	11–10
	2	Clarissimus	F. Bullock	5–2
	3	Atheling	J. Childs	4–1
		2 m. 59⅗ s. (*F. Darling*)		
1917	1	Gay Crusader	S. Donoghue	11–2 on
	2	Kingston Black	T. Burns	33–1
	3	Dansellon	F. Rickaby	100–15
		2 m. 59⅗ s. (*Alec Taylor*)		
1918	1	Gainsborough	J. Childs	11–4 on
	2	My Dear	S. Donoghue	9–1
	3	Prince Chimay	O. Madden	100–14
		3 m. 4 s. (*Alec Taylor*)		
		Run at Doncaster		
1919	1	Keysoe	B. Carslake	100–8
	2	Dominion	A. Smith	7–1
	3	Buchan	J. Childs	8–1
		3 m. 6⅘ s. (*Hon. G. Lambton*)		
1920	1	Caligula	A. Smith	100–6
	2	Silvern	F. Templeman	8–1
	3	Manton	F. Lane	33–1
		3 m. 7⅗ s. (*H. Leader*)		
1921	1	Polemarch	J. Childs	50–1
	2	Franklin	E. Gardner	100–6
	3	Westward Ho	B. Carslake	8–1
		3 m. 6⅘ s. (*T. Green*)		
1922	1	Royal Lancer	R. A. Jones	33–1
	2	Silurian	E. Gardner	100–8
	3	Ceylonese	F. Bullock	25–1
		3 m. 14⅕ s. (*A. D. Sadler, Jun.*)		
1923	1	Tranquil	T. Weston	100–9
	2	Papyrus	S. Donoghue	15–8
	3	Teresina	G. Hulme	100–7
		3 m. 5 s. (*C. Morton*)		
1924	1	Salmon-Trout	B. Carslake	6–1
	2	Santorb	G. Hulme	40–1
	3	Polyphontes	W. McLachlan	100–30
		3 m. 13⅕ s. (*R. C. Dawson*)		
1925	1	Solario	J. Childs	7–2
	2	Zambo	B. Carslake	6–1
	3	Warden of the Marches	W. Wells	18–1
		3 m. 4⅗ s. (*R. Day*)		
1926	1	Coronach	J. Childs	15–8 on
	2	Caissot	B. Carslake	100–9
	3	Foliation	J. Brennan	100–7
		3 m. 1⅗ s. (*F. Darling*)		
1927	1	Book Law	H. Jelliss	7–4
	2	Hot Night	H. Wragg	4–1
	3	Son and Heir	B. Carslake	25–1
		3 m. 14⅗ s. (*Alec Taylor*)		
1928	1	Fairway	T. Weston	7–4
	2	Palais Royal II	M. Allemand	100–6
	3	Cyclonic	R. A. Jones	100–15
		3 m. 3 s. (*Frank Butters*)		
1929	1	Trigo	M. Beary	5–1
	2	Bosworth	T. Weston	9–1
	3	Horus	E. C. Elliott	25–1
		3 m. 3⅗ s. (*R. C. Dawson*)		
1930	1	Singapore	G. Richards	4–1
	2	Parenthesis	F. Fox	4–1
	3	Rustom Pasha	H. Wragg	20–1
		3 m. 9⅕ s. (*T. Hogg*)		
1931	1	Sandwich	H. Wragg	9–1
	2	Orpen	J. Childs	11–2
	3	Sir Andrew	P. Beasley	20–1
		3 m. 11⅕ s. (*J. L. Jarvis*)		
1932	1	Firdaussi	F. Fox	20–1
	2	Dastur	M. Beary	6–1
	3	Silvermere	R. Dick	33–1
		3 m. 4⅗ s. (*Frank Butters*)		

Year	Horse	Jockey	Starting Price
1933	1 Hyperion	T. Weston	6–4
	2 Felicitation	M. Beary	22–1
	3 Scarlet Tiger	B. Carslake	100–8
	3 m. 6⅘ s. *(Hon. G. Lambton)*		
1934	1 Windsor Lad	C. Smirke	9–4 on
	2 Tiberius	R. A. Jones	20–1
	3 Lo Zingaro	G. Richards	100–9
	3 m. 1⅗ s. *(M. Marsh)*		
1935	1 Bahram	C. Smirke	11–4 on
	2 Solar Ray	J. Sirett	100–6
	3 Buckleigh	H. Wragg	25–1
	3 m. 1⅘ s. *(Frank Butters)*		
1936	1 Boswell	P. Beasley	20–1
	2 Fearless Fox	E. Smith	100–6
	3 Mahmoud	C. Smirke	5–1
	3 m. 8⅕ s. *(C. Boyd-Rochfort)*		
1937	1 Chulmleigh	G. Richards	18–1
	2 Fair Copy	R. Perryman	6–1
	3 Mid-day Sun	M. Beary	3–1
	3 m. 7⅕ s. *(T. Hogg)*		
1938	1 Scottish Union	B. Carslake	7–1
	2 Challenge	E. Smith	100–8
	3 Pasch	G. Richards	6–5
	3 m. 11⅗ s. *(N. Cannon)*		
1939	Abandoned owing to outbreak of war		
	Run at Thirsk as the Yorkshire St. Leger		
1940	1 Turkhan	G. Richards	4–1
	2 Stardust	H. Wragg	9–4
	3 Hippius	E. Smith	4–1
	3 m. 32⅗ s. *(Frank Butters)*		
	Run at Manchester as New St. Leger		
1941	1 Sun Castle	G. Bridgland	10–1
	2 Chateau Larose	R. A. Jones	11–2
	3 Dancing Time	M. Beary	25–1
	3 m. 4⅗ s. *(C. Boyd-Rochfort)*		
	Run at Newmarket as New St. Leger		
1942	1 Sun Chariot	G. Richards	9–4
	2 Watling Street	H. Wragg	2–1
	3 Hyperides	E. Smith	9–2
	3 m. 8⅕ s. *(F. Darling)*		
1943	1 Herringbone	H. Wragg	100–6
	2 Ribbon	E. Smith	10–1
	3 Straight Deal	T. H. Carey	100–30
	3 m. 5⅗ s. *(W. Earl)*		
1944	1 Tehran	G. Richards	9–2
	2 Borealis	H. Wragg	11–2
	3 Ocean Swell	E. Smith	11–2
	3 m. 6⅕ s. *(Frank Butters)*		
	Run at York		
1945	1 Chamossaire	T. Lowrey	11–2
	2 Rising Light	D. Smith	9–2
	3 Stirling Castle	H. Wragg	7–1
	2 m. 56⅗ s. *(R. Perryman)*		
	Run at Doncaster		
1946	1 Airborne	T. Lowrey	3–1
	2 Murren	T. Weston	40–1
	3 Fast and Fair	C. Richards	100–9
	3 m. 10 s. *(R. Perryman)*		
1947	1 Sayajirao	E. Britt	9–2
	2 Arbar	E. C. Elliott	5–1
	3 Migoli	G. Richards	9–4
	3 m. 7⅘ s. *(F. Armstrong)*		
1948	1 Black Tarquin	E. Britt	15–2
	2 Alycidon	D. Smith	20–1
	3 Solar Slipper	E. Smith	13–2
	3 m. 8⅗ s. *(C. Boyd-Rochfort)*		
1949	1 Ridge Wood	M. Beary	100–7
	2 Dust Devil	W. R. Johnstone	40–1
	3 Lone Eagle	W. H. Carr	6–1
	3 m. 8⅕ s. *(C. F. N. Murless)*		
1950	1 Scratch II	W. R. Johnstone	9–2
	2 Vieux Manoir	J. Laumain	7–4
	3 Sanlinea	E. Smith	33–1
	3 m. 8⅘ s. *(C. H. Semblat, in France)*		
1951	1 Talma II	W. R. Johnstone	7–1
	2 Fraise du Bois II	C. Smirke	15–2
	3 Medway	D. Smith	40–1
	3 m. 13⅘ s. *(C. H. Semblat, in France)*		
1952	1 Tulyar	C. Smirke	11–10 on
	2 Kingsfold	E. Smith	66–1
	3 Alcinus	E. C. Elliott	100–6
	3 m. 7⅘ s. *(M. Marsh)*		
1953	1 Premonition	E. Smith	10–1
	2 Northern Light	G. Lequeux	5–2
	3 Aureole	W. H. Carr	5–4
	3 m. 6⅘ s. *(C. Boyd-Rochfort)*		
1954	1 Never Say Die	C. Smirke	100–30
	2 Elopement	W. Nevett	22–1
	3 Estremadur	E. Mercer	100–6
	3 m. 10⅗ s. *(J. Lawson)*		
1955	1 Meld	W. H. Carr	11–10 on
	2 Nucleus	L. Piggott	9–1
	3 Beau Prince	S. Boullenger	4–1
	3 m. 14⅗ s. *(C. Boyd-Rochfort)*		
1956	1 Cambremer	F. Palmer	8–1
	2 Hornbeam	J. Mercer	5–1
	3 French Beige	G. Littlewood	100–8
	3 m. 12⅕ s. *(G. Bridgland, in France)*		
1957	1 Ballymoss	T. P. Burns	8–1
	2 Court Harwell	A. Breasley	100–8
	3 Brioche	E. Hide	6–1
	3 m. 15⅗ s. *(M. V. O'Brien, in Ireland)*		
1958	1 Alcide	W. H. Carr	9–4 on
	2 None Nicer	S. Clayton	10–1
	3 Nagami	J. Mercer	100–8
	3 m. 6 s. *(C. Boyd-Rochfort)*		
1959	1 Cantelo	E. Hide	100–7
	2 Fidalgo	J. Mercer	8–1
	3 Pindari	L. Piggott	100–6
	3 *m.* 4⅗ *s.* *(C. F. Elsey)*		

WINNERS OF MORE THAN ONE ST. LEGER

JOCKEYS

NINE—William Scott, 1821, 1825, 1828, 1829, 1838, 1839, 1840, 1841, 1846

EIGHT—John Jackson, 1791, 1794, 1796, 1798, 1805, 1813, 1815, 1822

SIX—Fred Archer, 1877, 1878, 1881, 1882, 1885, 1886
B. Smith, 1803, 1808, 1809, 1811, 1816, 1824

FIVE—J. Mangle, 1780, 1786, 1787, 1788, 1792
T. Chaloner, 1861, 1862, 1867, 1868, 1875
J. Watts, 1883, 1884, 1890, 1892, 1896
G. Richards, 1930, 1937, 1940, 1942, 1944

FOUR—J. Childs, 1918, 1921, 1925, 1926
C. Smirke, 1934, 1935, 1952, 1954

THREE—G. Searle, 1782, 1785, 1790
J. Shepherd, 1797, 1801, 1814
R. Johnson, 1812, 1817, 1818
J. Marson, 1843, 1847, 1850
E. Flatman, 1848, 1856, 1857
B. Carslake, 1919, 1924, 1938
T. Weston, 1923, 1928, 1933

TWO—J. Singleton, 1776, 1789
F. Buckle, 1800, 1804
W. Clift, 1807, 1810
J. Robinson, 1827, 1832
J. B. Day, 1831, 1836
T. Lye, 1835, 1842
F. Butler, 1845, 1853
J. Wells, 1855, 1869
L. Snowden, 1858, 1860
J. Osborne, 1863, 1874
C. Maidment, 1871, 1872
J. Goater, 1876, 1879
W. Robinson, 1887, 1888
C. Wood, 1897, 1898
M. Cannon, 1894, 1899
D. Maher, 1903, 1909
Walter Griggs, 1908, 1914
S. Donoghue, 1915, 1917
M. Beary, 1929, 1949
H. Wragg, 1931, 1943
T. Lowrey, 1945, 1946
E. Britt, 1947, 1948
W. R. Johnstone, 1950, 1951
W. H. Carr, 1955, 1958

OWNERS

SEVEN—Lord A. Hamilton (afterwards Duke of Hamilton), 1786, 1787, 1788, 1792, 1808, 1809, 1814

SIX—17th Lord Derby, 1910, 1919, 1923, 1928, 1933, 1943
H.H. Aga Khan, 1924, 1932, 1935, 1940, 1944, 1952

FOUR—Mr. R. Watt, 1813, 1823, 1825, 1833
Hon. E. Petre, 1822, 1827, 1828, 1829

THREE—Lord Westminster, 1834, 1840, 1841
Earl Fitzwilliam, 1789, 1802, 1807
Lord Falmouth, 1877, 1878, 1882
Lord Eglinton, 1842, 1847, 1849
Duke of Westminster, 1886, 1899, 1906

TWO—Mr. Hutchinson, 1791, 1794
Mr. G. Crompton, 1797, 1801
Mr. J. Clifton, 1793, 1806
Mr. H. Mellish, 1804, 1805
Sir T. Gasgoigne, 1778, 1798
Mr. R. O. Gasgoigne, 1811, 1824
Mr. Peirse, 1817, 1818
Mr. A. Nichol, 1851, 1856
Mr. John Merry, 1858, 1873
Mr. W. I'Anson, 1861, 1864
Count F. de Lagrange, 1865, 1879
Duke of Portland, 1889, 1890
Prince of Wales (afterwards King Edward VII), 1896, 1900
Mr. J. B. Joel, 1908, 1914
Mr. "Fairie", 1909, 1917
Lord Woolavington (Mr. J. Buchanan), 1916, 1926
Lord Glanely, 1930, 1937
Mr. William Woodward, 1936, 1948
M. Marcel Boussac, 1950, 1951

TRAINERS

EIGHT—J. Scott, 1834, 1839, 1851, 1853, 1856, 1857, 1859, 1862

SIX—M. Dawson, 1877, 1878, 1882, 1884, 1885, 1895
J. Porter, 1869, 1886, 1891, 1892, 1894, 1899
C. Boyd-Rochfort, 1936, 1941, 1948, 1953, 1955, 1958

FIVE—Alec Taylor, 1905, 1909, 1917, 1918, 1927
Frank Butters, 1928, 1932, 1935, 1940, 1944

THREE—R. Marsh, 1883, 1896, 1900
J. Jewitt, 1887, 1888, 1893
C. Morton, 1908, 1914, 1923
Hon. G. Lambton, 1910, 1919, 1933
Fred Darling, 1916, 1926, 1942

TWO—W. I'Anson, 1861, 1864
J. Dover, 1866, 1867
A. Taylor, Sen., 1860, 1875
J. Dawson, 1870, 1876
T. Jennings, 1865, 1879
G. Dawson, 1889, 1890
S. Darling, 1897, 1898
R. C. Dawson, 1924, 1929
T. Hogg, 1930, 1937
M. Marsh, 1934, 1952
R. Perryman, 1945, 1946
C. H. Semblat, 1950, 1951

RACING QUIZ

1. In what year were jockeys first licensed?

★

2. In what year was the first list of members of the Jockey Club first published?

★

3. What is the maximum speed of a race-horse?

★

4. How does one ascertain the age of a horse?

★

5. Can a horse vomit?

★

6. Can an apprentice engage himself to ride without the consent of his master?

QUIZ ANSWERS

1. 1879. 2. 1835. 3. 42 miles per hour, which is 6 m.p.h. faster than a greyhound. 4. By its teeth up to the age of six, after which there is an element of doubt. 5. No. 6. No, the master is responsible for the riding arrangements.

Average Times—*contd.*

WETHERBY

Hurdles

2 miles	3/59 s.
2½ miles	5/12 s.
3 miles	6/0 s.
'Chase	
2 miles 70 yards	4/13⅗ s.
3 miles 300 yards	6/36⅘ s.
3½ miles	6/59⅗ s.

WINCANTON

Hurdles

2 miles	3/55 s.
2½ miles	5/1 s.
2 miles 6 furlongs	5/31⅕ s.
'Chase	
2 miles	4/6⅗ s.
2½ miles	5/12 s.
3 miles 1 furlong	6/35⅗ s.
3 miles 2 furlongs	6/49 s.

WINDSOR

Hurdles

2 miles 120 yards	4/7 s.
3 miles 85 yards	6/10 s.
'Chase	
2 miles	4/9⅗ s.
3 miles	6/14⅗ s.

WOLVERHAMPTON

Hurdles

2 miles	3/52 s.
3 miles	5/59 s.
'Chase	
2 miles 33 yards	4/6 s.
2 miles 4 furlongs	5/9 s.
3 miles	6/9⅗ s.

WOORE

Hurdles

2 miles 100 yards	4/1 s.
'Chase	
2 miles 50 yards	4/8 s.

WORCESTER

Hurdles

2 miles	3/51 s.
2 miles 6 furlongs	5/25⅕ s.
'Chase	
2 miles	3/59 s.
3 miles	6/2 s.

WYE

Hurdles

2 miles	3/53 s.
'Chase	
2 miles	4/3 s.
3 miles	6/14⅗ s.

RACING QUIZ

1. Name the jockey with the best riding record in the classics.

*

2. John Porter trained seven Derby winners. Name as many as you can.

*

3. When was the Lincoln and Grand National run on the same day?

*

4. State the racing colours of Miss Dorothy Paget.

*

5. When was the Northumberland Plate first run?

*

6. In how many races was Ormonde unbeaten?

QUIZ ANSWERS

1. F. Buckle, with 27 winners. 2. Blue Gown, Shotover, St. Blaise, Ormonde, Sainfoin, Common, and Flying Fox. 3. 1871. 4. Blue, yellow hoop on body and sleeves, yellow cap with blue hoop. 5. 1833. 6. 16. He was also the Triple Crown of 1886.

R. Smyth (Nat. Hunt)

T. Rimell (Nat. Hunt)

B. Marshall (Nat. Hunt)

RIDING RECORDS : THE CLASSICS

Jockey	Year of First Classic Winner	2,000 gns.	1,000 gns.	Derby	Oaks	St. Leger	Total Number of Winners
F. Buckle	1792	5	6	5	9†	2	27
J. Robinson	1817	9†	5	6†	2	2	24
F. Archer	1874	4†	2	5	4	2	21
J. Watts	1883	2	4	4	4	6	19
W. Scott	1821	3	0	4	3	5	19
J. B. Day	1826	4	5	0	5	9†	19
G. Fordham	1859	3	7†	1	5	2	16
J. Childs	1912	2	2	3*	5	0	16
F. Butler	1843	2	2	2*	4*	4*	15
S. Donoghue	1915	3	1	6*	2	2*	14
E. C. Elliott	1923	5‡	4‡	3	2‡	0	14
G. Richards	1930	3‡	3	1	2	5	14
W. Clift	1793	2	2	3	2	5‡	14
T. Cannon	1866	4	3	1	4	1	13
H. Wragg	1928	1‡	3‡	3‡	4	1	13
J. Osborne	1856	6	2	3‡	4‡	2‡	13
W. R. Johnstone	1934	1	3	3	1	2	12
T. Weston	1923	1	1	3	3	2	12
C. Smirke	1934	2	1	4	0	3	11
E. Flatman	1835	3	3	1	0	4	11
T. Chaloner	1861	3	0	0	1	3	10
E. Britt	1947	1	2	1	2	5	10
L. Piggott	1954	0	1	2	2	2	7
W. H. Carr	1955	0	1	1	1	2	5

* Includes substitute races run at Newmarket between 1915 and 1918.
† Record for the race.
‡ Includes substitute races run at Newmarket 1939–45.

WINNERS OF TWO OR MORE CLASSICS

2,000 Guineas, 1,000 Guineas, Oaks and St. Leger: Formosa (1868); Sceptre (1902).
2,000 Guineas, Derby and St. Leger: West Australian (1853); Gladiateur (1865); Lord Lyon (1866); Ormonde (1886); Common (1891); Isinglass (1893); Galtee More (1897); Flying Fox (1899); Diamond Jubilee (1900); Rock Sand (1903); Pommern (1915); Gay Crusader (1917); Gainsborough (1918); Bahram (1935).
2,000 Guineas, 1,000 Guineas and Oaks: Crucifix (1840).
2,000 Guineas and Derby: Smolensko (1813); Cadland (1828); Bay Middleton (1836); Cotherstone (1843); Macaroni (1863); Pretender (1869); Shotover (1882); Ayrshire (1888); Ladas (1894); St. Amant (1904); Minoru (1909); Sunstar (1911); Manna (1925); Cameronian (1931); Blue Peter (1939); Nimbus (1949); Crepello (1957).
2,000 Guineas and St. Leger: Sir Tatton Sykes (1846); Stockwell (1852); The Marquis (1862), Petrarch (1876).
2,000 Guineas and Oaks: Pastille (1822).
2,000 Guineas and 1,000 Guineas: Pilgrimage (1878).
1,000 Guineas and Derby: Tagalie (1912).
1,000 Guineas, Oaks and St. Leger: Hannah (1871); Apology (1874); La Flèche (1892); Pretty Polly (1904); Sun Chariot (1942); Meld (1955).

1,000 Guineas and Oaks: Neva (1817); Corinne (1818); Zinc (1823); Cobweb (1824); Galata (1832); Mendicant (1846); Governess (1858); Reine (1872); Spinaway (1875); Camelia (1876); Wheel of Fortune (1879); Thebais (1881); Busybody (1884); Miss Jummy (1886); Reve d'Or (1887); Mimi (1891); Amiable (1894); Cherry Lass (1905); Jest (1913); Princess Dorrie (1914); Saucy Sue (1925); Exhibitionist (1937); Rockfel (1938); Galatea II (1939); Godiva (1940); Sun Stream (1945); Imprudence (1947); Musidora (1949); Bella Paola (1958); Petite Étoile (1959).
1,000 Guineas and St. Leger: Imperieuse (1857); Achievement (1867); Tranquil (1923); Herringbone (1943).
Oaks and St. Leger: Queen of Trumps (1835); Marie Stuart (1873); Jannette (1878); Seabreeze (1888); Memoir (1890).
Derby and Oaks: Eleanor (1801); Blink Bonny (1857); Signorinetta (1908); Fifinella (1916).
Derby and St. Leger: Champion (1800); Surplice (1848); The Flying Dutchman (1849); Voltigeur (1850); Blair Athol (1864); Silvio (1877); Iroquois (1881); Melton (1885); Donovan (1889); Sir Visto (1895); Persimmon (1896); Coronach (1926); Trigo (1929); Hyperion (1933); Windsor Lad (1934); Airborne (1946); Tulyar (1952); Never Say Die (1954).

ASCOT GOLD CUP
2½ m. (First run 1807)

Year	Horse	Jockey	Starting Price
1939	Flyon	E. Smith	100–6
1940	No race.		
Run at Newmarket (2¼ m.)			
1941	Finis	H. Wragg	4–1
1942	Owen Tudor	G. Richards	5–2
1943	Ujiji	G. Richards	8–1
1944	Umiddad	G. Richards	5–4
Run at Ascot (2½ m.)			
1945	Ocean Swell	E. Smith	6–1
1946	Caracalla II	E. C. Elliott	9–4 on
1947	Souverain	M. Lollierou	6–4
1948	Arbar	E. C. Elliott	6–4 on
1949	Alycidon	D. Smith	5–4
1950	Supertello	D. Smith	10–1
1951	Pan II	R. Poincelet	100–8
1952	Aquino II	G. Richards	4–1
1953	Souepi	E. C. Elliott	11–2
1954	Elpenor	J. Doyasbere	100–8
1955	Botticelli	E. Camici	9–4
1956	Macip	S. Boullenger	6–1
1957	Zarathustra	L. Piggott	6–1
1958	Gladness	L. Piggott	3–1
1959	Wallaby II	F. Palmer	9–4

CAMBRIDGESHIRE STAKES
Newmarket. 1 m. 1 f. (First run 1839)

Year	Horse	Jockey	Starting Price
1945	Esquire	G. Packer	40–1
1946	Sayani	W. R. Johnstone	25–1
1947	Fairey Fulmar	T. Gosling	28–1
1948	Sterope	D. Schofield	25–1
1949	Sterope	E. C. Elliott	25–1
1950	Kelling	D. Smith	100–7
1951	Fleeting Moment	A. Breasley	28–1
1952	Richer	K. Gethin	100–6
1953	Jupiter	G. Richards	100–6
1954	Minstrel	C. Gaston	66–1
1955	Retrial	P. Robinson	18–1
1956	Loppylugs	E. Smith	100–7
1957	Stephanotis	W. H. Carr	100–6
1958	London Cry	A. Breasley	22–1

CESAREWITCH STAKES
Newmarket, 2 m. 2 f. (First run 1839)

Year	Horse	Jockey	Starting Price
1939‡	Cantatrice II	D. Smith	7–2
1940‡	Hunter's Moon IV	G. Richards	100–8
1941‡	Filator	S. Wragg	100–9
1942–44	No race.		
1945	Kerry Piper	E. Britt	25–1
1946	Monsieur l'Amiral	H. Wragg	33–1
1947	Whiteway	W. T. Evans	100–8
1948	Woodburn	E. Britt	100–9
1949	Strathspey	E. Smith	25–1
1950	Above Board	E. Smith	18–1
1951	Three Cheers	E. Mercer	17–2
1952	Flush Royal	W. Nevett	33–1
1953	Chantry	K. Gethin	4–1
1954	French Design	D. Smith	100–6
1955	Curry	P. Tulk	100–6
1956	Prelone	E. Hide	20–1
1957	Sandiacre	D. Smith	100–8
1958	Morecambe	J. Sime	15–2

‡ Summer Course (2 m. 24 yds.).

CORONATION CUP
Epsom. 1 m. 4 f. (First run 1902)

Year	Horse	Jockey	Starting Price
At Newbury			
1941	Winterhalter	D. Smith	7–2
1942	No race		
At Newmarket			
1943	Hyperides	E. Smith	7–4
1944	Persian Gulf	R. A. Jones	5–2
1945	Borealis	H. Wragg	5–2
At Epsom			
1946	Ardan	E. C. Elliott	6–5 on
1947	Chanteur II	R. Brethes	3–1 on
1948	Goyama	E. C. Elliott	5–2
1949	Beau Sabreur	W. Cook	9–4
1950	Amour Drake	R. Poincelet	15–8
1951	Tantieme	J. Doyasbere	7–2 on
1952	Nuccio	R. Poincelet	3–1
1953	Zucchero	L. Piggott	100–7
1954	Aureole	E. Smith	5–2
1955	Narrator	F. Barlow	100–30
1956	Tropique	P. Blanc	13–8
1957	Fric	J. Deforge	7–2
1958	Ballymoss	A. Breasley	evens
1959	Nagami	L. Piggott	5–4

GOODWOOD CUP
Goodwood. 2m. 5f. *(First run 1812)*

Year	Horse	Jockey	Starting Price
1939	Dubonnet	T. Lowrey	6–4
1940–45	No race		
1946	Marsyas II	E. C. Elliott	3–1 on
1947	Monsieur l'Amiral	C. Smirke	2–1 on
1948	Tenerani	E. Camici	100–30
1949	Alycidon	D. Smith	100–30 on
1950	Val Drake	R. Poincelet	4–1
1951	Pan II	R. Poincelet	6–5 on
1952	Medway	D. Smith	5–1
1953	Souepi	E. C. Elliott	2–1
1954	Blarney Stone	W. Rickaby	13–2
1955	Double Bore	T. Gosling	9–1
1956	Zarathustra	W. H. Carr	11–10 on
1957	Tenterhooks	E. Britt	2–1
1958	Gladness	L. Piggott	2–1 on
1959	Dickens	D. Smith	9–4

KING GEORGE VI AND QUEEN ELIZABETH FESTIVAL OF BRITAIN STAKES
Ascot. 1½ m.

Year	Horse	Jockey	Starting Price
1951	Supreme Court	E. C. Elliott	100–9

KING GEORGE VI AND QUEEN ELIZABETH STAKES
Ascot. 1½ m.

Year	Horse	Jockey	Starting Price
1952	Tulyar	C. Smirke	3–1
1953	Pinza	G. Richards	2–1
1954	Aureole	E. Smith	9–2
1955	Vimy	R. Poincelet	10–1
1956	Ribot	E. Camici	5–2 on
1957	Montaval	F. Palmer	20–1
1958	Ballymoss	A. Breasley	7–4
1959	Alcide	W. H. Carr	2–1

LINCOLNSHIRE HANDICAP
Lincoln. 1 mile *(First run 1853)*

Year	Horse	Jockey	Starting Price
1939	Squadron Castle	V. Mitchell	40–1
1940	Quartier-Maitre	G. Richards	7–2
1941	Gloaming	D. Dick	100–7
At Pontefract, run as "Northern Lincoln"			
1942	Cuerdley	J. Taylor	3–1
At Pontefract, run as "Substitute Lincoln"			
1943	Lady Electra	R. Colven	9–2
1944	Backbite	M. Pearson	33–1
1945	Double Harness	D. Stansfield	33–1
At Lincoln			
1946	Langton Abbot	T. Weston	7–1
1947†	Jockey Treble	E. Mercer	100–1
† Run on Round Course			
1948	Commissar	W. Rickaby	33–1
1949	Fair Judgement	E. Smith	6–1
1950	Dramatic	G. Richards	7–1
1951	Barnes Park	J. Sime	33–1
1952	Phariza	D. Forte	33–1
1953	Sailing Light	A. Roberts	100–8
1954	Nahar	J. Massard	100–7
1955	Military Court	E. Mercer	8–1
1956	Three Star II	D. W. Morris	40–1
1957	Babur	E. Hide	25–1
1958	Babur	E. Britt	25–1
1959	Marshal Pil	P. Robinson	15–2

MANCHESTER NOVEMBER HANDICAP
1 m. 4 f. *(First run 1876)*

Year	Horse	Jockey	Starting Price
1939	Tutor	E. Smith	9–2
1940	Beinn Dearg	W. Nevett	9–1
1941	Crown Colony	C. Richards	100–6
Substitute Races at Pontefact			
1942	Golden Boy	D. Smith	10–1
1943	Mad Carew	J. Sime	33–1
1944	Kerry Piper	C. Spares	25–1
1945	Oatflake	E. Britt	100–8
At Manchester			
1946	Las Vegas	H. Wragg	20–1
1947	Regret	J. Walker	66–1
1948	Sports Master	D. Greening	20–1
1949	Fidonia	W. H. Carr	40–1
1950	Coltbridge	J. Sime	100–6
1951	Good Taste	W. Nevett	28–1
1952	Summer Rain	P. Evans	100–6
1953	Torch Singer	D. Ward	40–1
1954	Abandoned		
1955	Tearaway	W. Bentley	40–1
1956	Trentham Boy	J. Gifford	100–6
1957	Chief Barker	D. W. Walker	33–1
1958	Paul Jones	J. Mercer	100–7

ROYAL HUNT CUP
Ascot 7f. 155 yds. *(First run 1843)*

Year	Horse	Jockey	Starting Price
1945	Battle Hymn	P. Maher	20–1
1946	Friars Fancy	E. Smith	15–2
1947	Master Vote	T. Sidebotham	25–1
1948	Master Vote	W. R. Johnstone	100–7
1949	Sterope	J. Caldwell	100–6
1950	Hyperbole	A. Breasley	10–1
1951	Val d'Assa	N. Sellwood	100–6
1952	Queen of Sheba	F. Barlow	100–7
1953	Choir Boy	D. Smith	100–6
1954	Chivalry	D. Forte	33–1
(Run over one mile)			
1955	Nicholas Nickleby	W. Snaith	50–1
1956	Alexander	W. H. Carr	13–2
1957	Retrial	P. Robinson	100–7
1958	Amos	P. E. Boothman	20–1
1959	Faultless Speech	G. Lewis	8–1

ECLIPSE STAKES
Sandown Park 1m. 2f. *(First run 1883)*

Year	Horse	Jockey	Starting Price
Run at Ascot			
1946	Gulf Stream	H. Wragg	13–8 on
At Sandown Park			
1947	Migoli	C. Smirke	7–2
1948	Petition	K. Gethin	8–1
1949	Djeddah	E. C. Elliott	6–4
1950	Flocon	F. Palmer	100–9
1951	Mystery IX	L. Piggott	100–8
1952	Tulyar	C. Smirke	3–1 on
1953	Argur	E. C. Elliott	100–9
1954	King of the Tudors	K. Gethin	9–2
1955	Darius	L. Piggott	11–10
1956	Tropique	P. Blanc	3–1
1957	Arctic Explorer	L. Piggott	100–30
1958	Ballymoss	A. Breasley	11–8 on
1959	Saint Crespin III	G. Moore	5–2

RACING QUIZ

1. When were saddle cloths first used?

★

2. Name the meeting where the starting gate was used for the first time.

★

3. State the racing colours of Lord Derby.

★

4. Name the jockey who was nicknamed "The Tinman".

★

5. What does the American expression "on the nose" mean?

★

6. When was the Ascot Gold Cup stolen?

QUIZ ANSWERS
1. 1923. 2. Lincoln in 1900. 3. Black, white cap. 4. Fred Archer 5. To win. 6. In 1907.

T. Molony (Nat. Hunt)

F. Winter (Nat. Hunt)

NATIONAL HUNT
The National Hunt Committee recommend the following Scale of Weight for Age:

		Age	Jan. st. lb.	Feb. st. lb.	Mar. st. lb.	Apr. st. lb.	May st. lb.	June st. lb.	Aug. st. lb.	Sept. st. lb.	Oct. st. lb.	Nov. st. lb.	Dec. st. lb.
Steeple Chases	Two miles	4 years	10 9	10 10	10 11	10 12	10 13	11 0	11 2	11 3	11 4	11 5	11 6
		5 years	11 8	11 9	11 10	11 10	11 10	11 11	11 12	11 13	12 0	12 1	12 1
		6 years and aged	12 3	12 3	12 3	12 3	12 3	12 3	12 3	12 3	12 3	12 3	12 3
	Two miles and a half	4 years	10 7	10 8	10 9	10 11	10 12	10 13	11 2	11 3	11 4	11 5	11 6
		5 years	11 8	11 8	11 9	11 10	11 10	11 11	11 11	11 12	11 13	12 0	12 1
		6 years and aged	12 3	12 3	12 3	12 3	12 3	12 3	12 3	12 3	12 3	12 3	12 3
	Three miles	4 years	10 3	10 5	10 7	10 9	10 10	10 11	11 0	11 1	11 2	11 4	11 6
		5 years	11 8	11 8	11 9	11 10	11 10	11 11	11 10	11 11	11 12	11 13	12 1
		6 years and aged	12 3	12 3	12 3	12 3	12 3	12 3	12 3	12 3	12 3	12 3	12 3
Hurdle Races	Two miles	3 years	—	—	—	—	—	—	10 7	10 9	10 11	11 0	
		4 years	11 3	11 5	11 7	11 9	11 9	11 9	11 12	11 12	11 12	11 12	11 12
		5 years	11 13	12 0	12 1	12 1	12 2	12 2	12 1	12 1	12 1	12 1	12 1
		6 years and aged	12 3	12 3	12 3	12 3	12 3	12 3	12 3	12 3	12 3	12 3	12 3

GRAND NATIONAL COURSE
DESCRIPTION OF FENCES, ETC.
Distance from the start to first fence, 471 yards. The run in, 494 yards.

1 and 17—Thorn fence (gorse), 4 ft. 6 in. high, 2 ft. 9 in. wide.

2 and 18—Thorn fence (gorse), 4 ft. 7 in. high, 3 ft. 6 in. wide.

3 and 19—Thorn fence (spruce), 5 ft. high, 3 ft. 6 in. wide, with ditch on take-off side 6 ft. wide, 2 ft. 6 in. deep, banked up to guard rail 1 ft. 6 in. high in front of ditch.

4 and 20—Thorn fence (fir), 4 ft. 10 in. high, 3 ft. wide.

5 and 21—Thorn fence (spruce), 4 ft. 11 in. high, 3 ft. 6 in. wide.

6 and 22—"Becher's Brook", a thorn fence (fir), 4 ft. 10 in. high, 3 ft. 3 in. wide, with a natural brook on far side, 5 ft. 6 in. wide.

7 and 23—Thorn fence (fir), 4 ft. 6 in. high, 3 ft. wide.

8 and 24—The "Canal turn", a thorn fence (spruce), 5 ft. high, 3 ft. 3 in. wide.

9 and 25—"Valentine's Brook", a thorn fence (fir), 5 ft. high, 3 ft. 3 in. wide, a natural brook on far side, 5 ft. 6 in. wide.

10 and 26—Thorn fence (gorse), 5 ft. high, 3 ft. wide.

11 and 27—Thorn fence (spruce), 5 ft. high, 3 ft. wide, ditch on take-off side 6 ft. wide, 2 ft. deep banked to guard rail 1 ft. 6 in. high in front of ditch.

12 and 28—Thorn fence (gorse), 5 ft. high, 3 ft. wide, ditch on far side 5 ft. 6 in. wide, 4 ft. deep.

13 and 29—Thorn fence (gorse), 4 ft. 7 in. high, 3 ft. wide.

14 and 30—Thorn fence (fir) 4 ft. 6 in. high, 3 ft. wide.

15 —The "Open Ditch", a thorn fence (spruce), 5 ft. 2 in. high, 3 ft. 9 in. wide, ditch on take-off side 6 ft. wide, 2 ft. 6 in. deep, and banked to guard rail 1 ft. 6 in. high in front of ditch.

16 —The "Water Jump", 15 ft. wide over all, with thorn fence (spruce), 2 ft. 6 in. high, 2 ft. 6 in. wide, 12 ft. 6 in. of water, 2 ft. 6 in. deep.

RACING QUIZ

1. What does Pony mean in betting?

*

2. When did Good Friday fall on Boxing Day?

*

3. Which famous jockey shot himself in a paroxysm of madness caused by typhoid fever?

*

4. Who was leading trainer on the flat in 1957 and his approximate winnings.

*

5. When was the "Trodmore" meeting supposed to have been held?

*

6. When were trainer's licences first issued?

QUIZ ANSWERS

1. £25. 2. Good Friday fell in the Thorneycroft Chase at Wolverhampton on Boxing Day, 1899. 3. Fred Archer on Nov. 8th 1886. 4. C. F. N. Murless. £116,898. 5. August 1st 1898. 6. In 1905.

CHAMPION JOCKEYS (NATIONAL HUNT)

Year	Jockey	Total
1900	Mr. H. S. Sidney	53
1901	F. Mason	58
1902	F. Mason	67
1903	P. Woodland	54
1904	F. Mason	59
1905	F. Mason	73
1906	F. Mason	58
1907	F. Mason	59
1908	P. Cowley	65
1909	R. Gordon	45
1910	E. Piggott	67
1911	W. Payne	76
1912	I. Anthony	78
1913	E. Piggott	60
1914	Mr. J. R. Anthony	60
1915	E. Piggott	44
1916	C. Hawkins	17
1917	W. Smith	15
1918	G. Duller	17
1919	Mr. H. Brown	48
1920	F. B. Rees	64
1921	F. B. Rees	65
1922	J. Anthony	78
1923	F. B. Rees	64
1924	F. B. Rees	108
1925	E. Foster	76
1925–26	T. Leader	61
1926–27	F. B. Rees	59
1927–28	W. Stott	88
1928–29	W. Stott	76
1929–30	W. Stott	77
1930–31	W. Stott	81
1931–32	W. Stott	77
1932–33	G. Wilson	61
1933–34	G. Wilson	56
1934–35	G. Wilson	73
1935–36	G. Wilson	57
1936–37	G. Wilson	45
1937–38	G. Wilson	59
1938–39	T. Rimell	61
1939–40	T. Rimell	24
1940–41	G. Wilson	22
1941–42	R. Smyth	12
1942–43	No racing	
1943–44	No racing	
1944–45	H. Nicholson	15
	T. Rimell	15
1945–46	T. Rimell	54
1946–47	J. Dowdeswell	58
1947–48	B. Marshall	66
1948–49	T. Molony	60
1949–50	T. Molony	95
1950–51	T. Molony	83
1951–52	T. Molony	99
1952–53	F. Winter	121
1953–54	R. Francis	76
1954–55	T. Molony	67
1955–56	F. Winter	74
1956–57	F. Winter	80
1957–58	F. Winter	82
1958–59	T. Brookshaw	83

Prior to 1925–26 figures were taken for the period January to December

GRAND NATIONAL

Liverpool   4 m. 856 yds.   (First run 1837)

Year	Horse	Jockey	Starting Price
	At Maghull		
1837	The Duke	Mr. Potts	—
1838	Sir Henry	T. Olliver	—
	At Liverpool		
1839	Lottery	Jem Mason	5–1
1840	Jerry	Mr. B. Bretherton	12–1
1841	Charity	Mr. Powell	14–1
1842	Gaylad	T. Olliver	7–1
1843	Vanguard	T. Olliver	12–1
1844	Discount	Crickmere	5–1
1845	Cure-All	W. G. Loft	—
1846	Pioneer	Taylor	—
1847	Matthew	D. Wynne	10–1
1848	Chandler	Capt. Little	12–1
1849	Peter Simple	T. Cunningham	20–1
1850	Abdel Kader	C. Green	
1851	Abdel Kader	T. Abbot	7–1
1852	Miss Mowbray	Mr. A. Goodman	
1853	Peter Simple	T. Olliver	9–1
1854	Bourton	Tasker	4–1
1855	Wanderer	J. Hanlon	25–1
1856	Freetrader	G. Stevens	25–1
1857	Emigrant	C. Boyce	10–1
1858	Little Charley	W. Archer	100–6
1859	Half Caste	C. Green	7–1
1860	Anatis	Mr. Thomas	7–2
1861	Jealousy	J. Kendall	5–1
1862	Huntsman	H. Lamplugh	3–1
1863	Emblem	G. Stevens	4–1
1864	Emblematic	G. Stevens	10–1
1865	Alcibiade	Capt. Coventry	100–7
1866	Salamander	Mr. A. Goodman	40–1
1867	Cortolvin	J. Page	100–6
1868	The Lamb	Mr. Edwards	10–1
1869	The Colonel	G. Stevens	13–1
1870	The Colonel	G. Stevens	4–1
1871	The Lamb	Mr. Thomas	5–1
1872	Casse Tete	J. Page	20–1
1873	Disturbance	Mr. J. M. Richardson	20–1
1874	Reugny	Mr. J. M. Richardson	5–1
1875	Pathfinder	Mr. Thomas	100–6
1876	Regal	J. Cannon	25–1
1877	Austerlitz	Mr. F. G. Hobson	15–1
1878	Shifnal	J. Jones	100–15
1879	The Liberator	Mr. G. Moore	5–1
1880	Empress	Mr. T. Beasley	8–1
1881	Woodbrook	Mr. T. Beasley	6–1
1882	Seaman	Lord Manners	10–1
1883	Zoedone	Count C. Kinsky	100–8
1884	Voluptuary	Mr. E. P. Wilson	10–1
1885	Roquefort	Mr. E. P. Wilson	100–30
1886	Old Joe	T. Skelton	25–1
1887	Gamecock	W. Daniells	20–1
1888	Playfair	Mawson	40–1
1889	Frigate	Mr. T. Beasley	8–1
1890	Ilex	A. Nightingall	4–1
1891	Come Away	Mr. H. Beasley	4–1
1892	Father O'Flynn	Capt. E. R. Owen	20–1
1893	Cloister	Dollery	9–2
1894	Why Not	A. Nightingall	5–1
1895	Wild Man From Borneo	Mr. Joseph Widger	10–1
1896	The Soarer	Mr. D. G. M. Campbell	40–1
1897	Manifesto	T. Kavanagh	6–1
1898	Drogheda	J. Gourley	25–1
1899	Manifesto	G. Williamson	5–1
1900	Ambush II	A. Anthony	4–1
1901	Grudon	A. Nightingall	9–1
1902	Shannon Lass	D. Read	20–1
1903	Drumcree	P. Woodland	13–2
1904	Moifaa	A. Birch	25–1
1905	Kirkland	F. Mason	6–1
1906	Ascetic's Silver	Hon. A. Hastings	20–1
1907	Eremon	A. Newey	8–1
1908	Rubio	H. B. Bletsoe	66–1
1909	Lutteur III	G. Parfrement	100–9
1910	Jenkinstown	R. Chadwick	100–8
1911	Glenside	Mr. J. R. Anthony	20–1
1912	Jerry M.	E. Piggott	4–1
1913	Covercoat	P. Woodland	100–9
1914	Sunloch	W. J. Smith	100–6
1915	Ally Sloper	Mr. J. R. Anthony	100–8
	At Gatwick (called The Race Course Association Chase)		
1916	Vermouth	J. Reardon	100–8
	At Gatwick (called The War National Chase)		
1917	Ballymacad	E. Driscoll	100–9
	At Gatwick		
1918	Poethlyn	E. Piggott	5–1
	At Liverpool		
1919	Poethlyn	E. Piggott	11–4
1920	Troytown	Mr. J. R. Anthony	6–1
1921	Shaun Spadah	F. B. Rees	100–9
1922	Music Hall	F. B. Rees	100–9
1923	Sergeant Murphy	Capt. G. N. Bennet	100–6
1924	Master Robert	R. Trudgill	25–1
1925	Double Chance	Major J. P. Wilson	100–9
1926	Jack Horner	W. Watkinson	25–1
1927	Sprig	T. E. Leader	8–1
1928	Tipperary Tim	Mr. W. P. Dutton	100–1
1929	Gregalach	R. Everett	100–1
1930	Shaun Goilin	T. Cullinan	100–8
1931	Grakle	R. Lyall	100–6
1932	Forbra	J. Hamey	50–1
1933	Kellsboro' Jack	D. Williams	25–1
1934	Golden Miller	G. Wilson	8–1
1935	Reynoldstown	F. C. Furlong	22–1
1936	Reynoldstown	F. T. Walwyn	10–1
1937	Royal Mail	E. Williams	100–6
1938	Battleship	B. Hobbs	40–1
1939	Workman	T. Hyde	100–8
1940	Bogskar	M. Jones	25–1
1941–45	No race		
1946	Lovely Cottage	Capt. R. Petre	25–1
1947	Caughoo	E. Dempsey	100–1
1948	Sheila's Cottage	A. P. Thompson	50–1
1949	Russian Hero	L. McMorrow	66–1
1950	Freebooter	J. Power	10–1
1951	Nickel Coin	J. A. Bullock	40–1
1952	Teal	A. P. Thompson	100–7
1953	Early Mist	B. Marshall	20–1
1954	Royal Tan	B. Marshall	8–1
1955	Quare Times	P. Taaffe	100–9
1956	E.S.B.	D. V. Dick	100–7
1957	Sundew	F. Winter	20–1
1958	Mr. What	A. R. Freeman	18–1
1959	Oxo	M. Scudamore	8–1

1839, '40, '41, '42, all starters carried the same weight of 12 stone each. In 1843 the race became a handicap.

CHELTENHAM GOLD CUP

Chase 3¼ m.   (First run 1924)

Year	Horse	Jockey	Starting Price
1924	Red Splash	F. B. Rees	5–1
1925	Ballinode	T. E. Leader	3–1
1926	Koko	J. Hamey	10–1
1927	Thrown-in	H. Grosvenor	10–1
1928	Patron Saint	F. B. Rees	7–2
1929	Easter Hero	F. B. Rees	7–4
1930	Easter Hero	T. Cullinan	11–8 on
1931	Abandoned owing to frost		
1932	Golden Miller	T. E. Leader	13–2
1933	Golden Miller	W. Stott	7–4 on
1934	Golden Miller	G. Wilson	6–5
1935	Golden Miller	G. Wilson	2–1 on
1936	Golden Miller	E. Williams	21–20
1937	Abandoned owing to snow and floods		
1938	Morse Code	D. Morgan	13–2
1939	Brendans Cottage	G. Owen	8–1
1940	Roman Hackle	E. Williams	evens
1941	Poet Prince	R. Burford	7–2
1942	Medoc II	H. Nicholson	9–2
1943	No race		
1944	No race		
1945	Red Rower	D. Jones	11–4
1946	Prince Regent	T. Hyde	7–4 on
1947	Fortina	Mr. R. Black	8–1
1948	Cottage Rake	A. Brabazon	10–1
1949	Cottage Rake	A. Brabazon	6–4 on
1950	Cottage Rake	A. Brabazon	6–5 on
1951	Silver Fame	M. Molony	6–4
1952	Mont Tremblant	D. V. Dick	8–1
1953	Knock Hard	T. Molony	11–2
1954	Four Ten	T. Cusack	100–6
1955	Gay Donald	A. Grantham	33–1
1956	Limber Hill	J. Power	11–8
1957	Linwell	M. Scudamore	100–9
1958	Kerstin	S. Hayhurst	7–1
1959	Roddy Owen	H. Beasley	5–1

CHAMPION HURDLE

Cheltenham, 2 m.   (First run 1927)

Year	Horse	Jockey	Starting Price
1927	Blaris	G. Duller	11–10
1928	Brown Jack	F. B. Rees	4–1
1929	Royal Falcon	F. B. Rees	11–2
1930	Brown Tony	T. Cullinan	7–2
1931	No race owing to frost		
1932	Insurance	T. E. Leader	5–4 on
1933	Insurance	W. Stott	11–10 on
1934	Chenango	D. Morgan	9–4 on
1935	Lion Courage	G. Wilson	100–8
1936	Victor Norman	H. Nicholson	4–1
1937	Free Fare	G. Pellerin	2–1
1938	Our Hope	Capt. R. Harding	5–1
1939	African Sister	K. Piggott	10–1
1940	Solford	S. Magee	5–2
1941	Seneca	R. Smyth	7–1
1942	Forestation	R. Smyth	10–1
1943	No race		
1944	No race		
1945	Brains Trust	T. Rimell	9–2
1946	Distel	R. J. O'Ryan	5–4 on
1947	National Spirit	D. Morgan	7–1
1948	National Spirit	R. Smyth	6–4
1949	Hatton's Grace	A. Brabazon	100–7
1950	Hatton's Grace	A. Brabazon	5–2
1951	Hatton's Grace	T. Molony	4–1
1952	Sir Ken	T. Molony	3–1
1953	Sir Ken	T. Molony	5–2 on
1954	Sir Ken	T. Molony	9–4 on
1955	Clair Soleil	F. Winter	5–2
1956	Doorknocker	H. Sprague	100–9
1957	Merry Deal	G. Underwood	28–1
1958	Bandalore	G. Slack	20–1
1959	Fare Time	F. Winter	13–2

A BRIEF HISTORY OF HUNTING

Hunting has been carried on all through the ages. In Greek, Egyptian and Roman literature there are references to hounds and the chase, and so there are on every page of English history. But few records are available to tell us when the present popular style of foxhunting started, for there were many Hunts in existence long before the first half of the 18th century, the date it is generally accepted foxhunting became an integral part of English country life.

In feudal times hounds were kept for hunting any sort of quarry—deer, hare or fox—in the royal forests and parks, and it was a sport that principally only the great nobles were privileged to enjoy. Gradually more interest was taken in breeding hounds for a specific purpose. Then staghunting enjoyed a long period of popularity. It remained the fashionable form of sport until the changing face of the countryside and conditions of life in general led to its decline in favour of foxhunting.

Which is the oldest pack of foxhounds in England is difficult to say. Claims are made for the Bilsdale Hunt, in the North Riding; the Goathland, which is said to date back to 1650; and the Sinnington, also in Yorkshire, whose first Master was the Duke of Buckingham in about 1680. It is unlikely we shall ever know to which Hunt the honour falls.

Today foxhunting, beagling and otter hunting remain the popular forms of recreation for the countryman, in spite of two world wars and the acute changes in the life of the people they brought about. With staghunting, which is still carried on to a limited extent, they could not survive, however, without the support of farmers over whose land they are conducted.

In fact, in latter years, with fewer private packs, farmers have been taking a more active part in the running and management of many Hunts, and people who enjoy foxhunting owe them a great debt for doing so.

Foxhunting has a two-fold object—to kill foxes, and to provide thrills and a healthy form of exercise for those who ride after hounds. But there is also a science in it for the countryman keenly interested in the mysteries of scent and the way hounds work on the line of the fox.

The time is long past when the sport was the prerogative of the rich. Today it has an attraction for people in all walks of life, and although, of course, there are a few of the more fashionable Hunts whose subscriptions are high compared with others, the majority continue to run with the support of people of moderate means. Naturally the costs of keeping and feeding hounds and horses in these days are high. But there is an enthusiasm for hunting that seems to overcome economic difficulties, and hundreds of people who do not ride or own a horse turn out to enjoy a day's sport following hounds on foot, by bicycle or in motor cars. They are welcomed by the Hunts, many of whom have formed supporters' clubs from this type of follower in order to encourage their interest in the sport.

HUNTING QUIZ

I. Name the outstanding doghound Show winner of modern times.

★

2. What king initiated the wearing of the velvet hunting cap?

★

3. What M.F.H. between the wars has since twice won the Derby (including New Derby)?

★

4. What Hunt was once known as "The Stars of the West"?

★

5. Give the meanings of the hunting terms: (a) "Feather"; (b) "Hit off the line"; (c) "Huic Holloa".

★

6. How many officially recognised foxhound packs are there in (a) England and Wales; (b) Scotland; (c) Ireland?

★

7. What is the controlling body of foxhunting, and who is its present chairman?

QUIZ ANSWERS

I. The Duke of Beaufort's Distaff, champion of show champions. **2.** George III. **3.** Lord Rosebery (M. F. H. Whaddon Chase) won the Derby with Blue Peter 1939, and Ocean Swell 1944. **4.** Exmoor Foxhounds when it was started under Mastership of Mr. Nicholas Snow 1869–89. **5.** (a) A hound "feathers" when he waves his stern (tail) before he is sure he is on the line to give tongue; (b) When hounds find the scent and start hunting; (c) A cheer to tell huntsman and hounds that a Holloa has been heard. **6.** (a) 200; (b) 10; (c) 30. **7.** Masters of Foxhounds Association; Lord Irwin.

FOXHOUNDS

Kennel addresses and days of meets

ALBRIGHTON. *Kennels:* Whiston Cross, Albrighton, Wolverhampton. *Tel.:* Albrighton 270. Tues., Thurs., Sat.

ALBRIGHTON WOODLAND. *Kennels:* Hurcott, Kidderminster. *Tel.:* Kidderminster 3069. Wed., Sat.

ASHFORD VALLEY. *Kennels:* The Forest, Hothfield, nr. Ashford, Kent. *Tel.:* Ashford 1248. Mon., or Wed., Sat.

ATHERSTONE. *Kennels:* Witherley, Atherstone. *Tel.:* Atherstone 3157. Wed., Fri., Sat.

AVON VALE. *Kennels:* Spye Park, Chippenham. *Tel.:* Lacock 277. Tues., Sat., occ. bye.

BADSWORTH. *Kennels:* Hillthorpe, East Hardwick, nr. Pontefract. *Tel.:* Wentbridge 325. Tues., Sat., occ. bye Thurs.

BANWELL. *Kennels:* Banwell. *Tel.:* Banwell 6. 2 days a week.

BARLOW. *Kennels:* Horsley Gate, Holmesfield, Sheffield. *Tel.:* Holmesfield 245. Mon., Thurs., occ. Sat.

BEAUFORT'S, DUKE OF. *Kennels:* Badminton, Glos. 4 days a week.

BEDALE. *Kennels:* Low Street, Northallerton. *Tel.:* Kirkby Fleetham 242. Alt. Mon., Fri., and Mon., Wed., Fri.

BELVOIR. *Kennels:* Belvoir Castle. *Tel.:* Knipton 273. Tue., Wed., Fri., Sat.

BERKELEY. *Kennels:* Berkeley, Glos. *Tel.:* Berkeley 40. 3 days a week.

BERKELEY, OLD. *Kennels:* Dodds Charity, Kimblewich, Aylesbury. *Tel.:* Stoke Mandeville 3232. Tues., Thurs., Sat., and Tues., Sat., alt.

BERKSHIRE, OLD. *Kennels:* Faringdon. *Tel.:* Faringdon 2153. Mon., Wed., Sat.

BERKS, SOUTH. *Kennels:* Purley, Reading. *Tel.:* Pangbourne 14. Wed., Sat.

BEWCASTLE. *Kennels:* Ainstable. *Tel.:* Ainstable 220. Mon., Thurs., Sat.

BICESTER AND WARDEN HILL. *Kennels:* Stratton Audley, Bicester. *Tel.:* Stratton Audley 209. Mon., Tues., Thurs., Sat.

BILSDALE. *Kennels:* Hill End Farm, Bilsdale, nr. Middlesbrough. Tues., Sat.

BISLEY. *Kennels:* Chaseley, Bisley. *Tel.:* Brookwood 3348. Sat.

BLACKMORE VALE. *Kennels:* Charlton Horethorne, nr. Sherborne. *Tel.:* Corston Denham 214. Tues., Wed., Fri., Sat.

BLANKNEY. *Kennels:* Blankney, Lincs. *Tel.:* Metheringham 250. Wed., Sat.

BLENCATHRA. *Kennels:* Gate Gyll, Threlkeld. *Tel.:* Threlkeld 219. 3 days a week.

BORDER. *Kennels:* Overacres Farm, Otterburn. *Tel.:* Otterburn 44. 5 days a fortnight.

BRAES OF DERWENT. *Kennels:* Tinkler Hill, Shotley Bridge. *Tel.:* Shotley Bridge 32. Wed., Sat.

BRAMHAM MOOR. *Kennels:* Hope Hall, Boston Spa. *Tel.:* Boston Spa 2126. Wed., Sat., alt. Mon.

BRECON. *Kennels:* Upper Dan-y-Parc, Llandefalle. Wed., Sat.

BRECON (MRS. BRANDON'S). *Kennels:* Canal Bank, Brecon. *Tel.:* Brecon 191. Wed., Sat. and byes.

BROCKLESBY. *Kennels:* Brocklesby Park. Wed., Sat.

BURGHLEY. *Kennels:* Burghley House, Stamford, Lincs. *Tel.:* Stamford 2671. Wed., Sat.

BURTON. *Kennels:* Riseholme, Lincoln. *Tel.:* Lincoln 22798. Wed., Sat., occ. bye.

CAMBRIDGESHIRE. *Kennels:* Caxton, Cambs. *Tel.:* Caxton 213. Tues., Fri.

CARMARTHENSHIRE. *Kennels:* Castell Gorfod. *Tel.:* St. Clears 210. Mon., Thurs.

CATTISTOCK. *Kennels:* Cattistock, nr. Dorchester. *Tel.:* Maiden Newton 210. 4 days a week.

CHESHIRE. *Kennels:* Sandiway, Cheshire. *Tel.:* Sandiway 3004. Mon., Wed., Sat.

CHESHIRE FOREST. *Kennels:* Littleton Old Hall, Chester. *Tel.:* Chester 35646. Tues., Thurs., Sat.

CHIDDINGFOLD AND LECONFIELD. *Kennels:* Petworth Park. *Tel.:* Petworth 2193. Mon., Wed., Sat.

CHIDDINGFOLD FARMERS'. *Kennels:* Unstead Gardens, Godalming. *Tel.:* Godalming 12. Wed., Sat.

CLEVELAND. *Kennels:* Tocketts, Guisborough. *Tel.:* Guisborough 25. 3 days a week.

CLIFTON-ON-TEME. *Kennels:* Tedstone Wafre, Bromyard. *Tel.:* Bromyard 3193. Wed., Sat., occ. bye.

COLLEGE VALLEY. *Kennels:* Langham Toll, Mindrum, Northumberland. *Tel.:* Mindrum 217. Tues., Thurs., Sat.

CONISTON. *Kennels:* Green Bank, Ambleside. *Tel.:* Ambleside 2124. 3 days a week.

CORNWALL, EAST. *Kennels:* Little Gimble, St. Clear, Liskeard. *Tel.:* Liskeard 2018. Tues., Fri.

CORNWALL, NORTH. *Kennels:* St. Breward, Bodmin. *Tel.:* St. Tudy 223. 2 days per week.

COTSWOLD. *Kennels:* Andoversford, Glos. *Tel.:* Andoversford 206. Mon., Wed., Sat., and bye.

COTSWOLD, NORTH. *Kennels:* Broadway, Worcs. *Tel.:* Broadway 2379. Mon., Wed., Sat.

COTSWOLD VALE FARMERS'. *Kennels:* Boddington Manor, Cheltenham. *Tel.:* Coombe Hill 326. Tues., Fri., occ. bye.

COTTESMORE. *Kennels:* Ashwell, Oakham. *Tel.:* Ashwell 29. Tues., Thurs., Sat.

COWDRAY. *Kennels:* Midhurst, Sussex. *Tel.:* Midhurst 113. Tues., Sat., occ. bye.

CRAVEN FARMERS'. *Kennels:* Baydon House Farm, Baydon, Wilts. *Tel.:* Aldbourne 288. Wed., Sat.

CRAWLEY AND HORSHAM. *Kennels:* West Grinstead. *Tel.:* Cowfold 275. Tues., Thurs., Sat.

CROOME. *Kennels:* Kinnersley, Severn Stoke. *Tel.:* Severn Stoke 215. Tues., Sat.

CUMBERLAND. *Kennels:* Brayton Aspatria, Cumberland. *Tel.:* Aspatria 414. Mon., Thurs.

CUMBERLAND FARMERS'. *Kennels:* Beech House, Welton, Dalston, Carlisle. *Tel.:* Raughton Head 248. Wed., Sat., and Mon. every other week.

CURRE, THE. *Kennels:* Itton, nr. Chepstow. *Tel.:* Chepstow 2354. Mon., Sat., and Tues., Fri.—alt.

DARTMOOR. *Kennels:* Ivybridge, S. Devon. *Tel.:* Ivybridge 178. Tues., Wed. or Fri., Sat.

DAVID DAVIES. *Kennels:* Llandinam, Mont. *Tel.:* Caersws 348. Sat. and byes.

DERWENT. *Kennels:* Snainton, nr. Scarborough. *Tel.:* Snainton 253. Tues., Sat.

DEVON, EAST. *Kennels:* Clyst St. Mary, Exeter. *Tel.:* Topsham 3025. Tues., Sat., alt. Thurs.

DEVON, MID. *Kennels:* Factory Cross, Chagford. *Tel.:* Chagford 2280. Tues., Sat.

DEVON, SOUTH. *Kennels:* Pulsford, Denbury, Newton Abbot. *Tel.:* Ipplepen 229. Mon., Tues., Thurs., Sat.

DORSET, SOUTH. *Kennels:* Bere Regis, Wareham. *Tel.:* Bere Regis 213. Mon., Thurs., Sat.

DULVERTON, EAST. *Kennels:* East Anstey, Tiverton. *Tel.:* Anstey Mills 229. 4 days a fortnight.

DULVERTON, WEST. *Kennels:* Court Hall, North Molton. *Tel.:* North Molton 233. Mon., Wed., Fri.

DURHAM, SOUTH. *Kennels:* Sedgefield, Stockton-on-Tees. *Tel.:* Sedgefield 229. Alt. Tues. and Wed., Sat.

EGGESFORD. *Kennels:* Wembworthy, Chulmleigh, N. Devon. *Tel.:* Chulmleigh 230. Mon., Thurs., Sat.

ENFIELD CHASE. *Kennels:* Holwell Court, Essendon, Herts. *Tel.:* Essendon 368. Tues., Sat.

ERIDGE. *Kennels:* Hamsell, Tunbridge Wells. *Tel.:* Frant 352. Wed., Sat.

ESKDALE AND ENNERDALE. *Kennels:* Sword House, Eskdale. *Tel.:* Eskdale 69. 3 days a week.

ESSEX. *Kennels:* Harlow, Essex. *Tel.:* Harlow 3248. Mon., Wed., Sat.

ESSEX AND SUFFOLK. *Kennels:* Layham, Hadleigh. *Tel.:* Hadleigh 3129. Mon., Wed., Thurs., Sat.

ESSEX, EAST. *Kennels:* Earls Colne. *Tel.:* Earls Colne 208. Tues., Thurs., Sat.

HUNTING QUIZ

1. What famous huntsman of what famous Hunt retired last season after 30 years?

*

2. Who said: "A Gen'leman should do nothin' but 'unt—it's the sport of kings, the image of war, without its guilt, and only five-and-twenty per cent of its danger"?

*

3. What is the origin of the ornamental ribbon at the back of the velvet hunting cap?

*

4. What well-known Hunt has as its uniform "blue coat, blue collar, buff facings" and who are its masters?

QUIZ ANSWERS

1. George Barker of the Quorn. 2. John Jorrocks in R. S. Surtees' *Handley Cross*. 3. It originally tied back the queue or braid of hair at the back of the head when hats were worn. Today it serves only to keep th rain from running down the wearer's neck. 4. The Duke of Beaufort's. Masters: The Duke of Beaufort and Major G. Gundry.

Foxhounds—*contd.*

ESSEX FARMERS'. *Kennels:* Althorne Lodge, Althorne, Essex. *Tel.:* Southminster 253. Sat., alt. Wed.
ESSEX UNION. *Kennels:* Billericay, Essex. *Tel.:* Billericay 108 and 1150. Tues., Thurs., Sat.
EXMOOR. *Kennels:* Balewater, Simonsbath, nr. Minehead. *Tel.:* Exford 254. 5 days a fortnight.
FARNDALE. *Kennels:* Farndale, Kirby Moorside. Tues., Sat.
FERNIE. *Kennels:* Great Bowden, Market Harborough. *Tel.:* Market Harboro' 2081. Wed., Sat.
FITZWILLIAM (MILTON). *Kennels:* Milton, Peterborough. *Tel.:* Castor 263. Mon., Wed., Sat.
FLINT AND DENBIGH. *Kennels:* Cefn, St. Asaph. *Tel.:* Trefnant 255. Tues., Sat.
FOUR BURROW. *Kennels:* St. Day. 3 days a week.
GARTH. *Kennels:* Bracknell, Berks. *Tel.:* Bracknell 100. Mon., Fri., occ. bye Sat.
GELLYGAER. *Kennels:* Summerfield Hall, Maesycwmmer. Sat., alt. Wed.
GLAISDALE. *Kennels:* The Hall, Glaisdale. *Tel.:* Glaisdale 54. Tues., Sat.
GLAMORGAN. *Kennels:* Penllyn Castle. *Tel.:* Cowbridge 228. Mon., Thurs.
GOATHLAND. *Kennels:* Alumgarth Farm, Sleights, nr. Whitby. *Tel.:* Grosmont 51. Tues., Fri.
GOGERDDAN. *Kennels:* Ffynnon Caradog. *Tel.:* Bow Street 354. Wed., Sat.
GOLDEN VALLEY. *Kennels:* Whitney-on-Wye. *Tel.:* Clifford 221. Tues., Sat.
GRAFTON. *Kennels:* Paulerspury, Towcester. *Tel.:* Paulersbury 214. Tues., Thurs., Sat.
GROVE AND RUFFORD. *Kennels:* Barnby Moor, Retford. *Tel.:* Ranskill 230. Tues., Thurs., Sat.
HALIFAX AND DISTRICT. Sat. and byes.
HAMBLEDON. *Kennels:* Droxford. *Tel.:* Droxford 2. Wed., Sat.
HAMPSHIRE (H.H.). *Kennels:* Ropley, Alresford. *Tel.:* Ropley 2106. Mon., Tues., Thurs., Sat.
HAYDON. *Kennels:* Langley Castle, Haydon Bridge. *Tel.:* Haydon Bridge 287. Wed., Sat.
HEREFORDSHIRE, NORTH. *Kennels:* Bodenham, Hereford. *Tel.:* Bodenham 238. Tues., Sat.
HEREFORDSHIRE, SOUTH. *Kennels:* Wormelow, Hereford. *Tel.:* Wormelow 319. Tues., Sat., and bye Thurs.
HERTFORDSHIRE. *Kennels:* Houghton Regis, Dunstable. *Tel.:* Dunstable 95. Mon., Wed., Sat.
HEYTHROP. *Kennels:* Chipping Norton. *Tel.:* Chipping Norton 52. Mon., Wed., Fri., Sat.
HOLDERNESS. *Kennels:* Etton, Beverley. *Tel.:* Dalton Holme 250. Tues., Sat.
HURSLEY. *Kennels:* Braishfield, Romsey. *Tel.:* Braishfield 330. Normally Tues., Fri.
HURWORTH. *Kennels:* West Rounton, Northallerton. *Tel.:* E. Harsley 213. 2 days a week.
IRFON AND TOWY. *Kennels:* Clynsaer, Cynghordy, Llandovery. Various.
ISLE OF WIGHT. *Kennels:* Catcombe, Newport, I.o.W. *Tel.:* Ghillerton 225. Wed., Sat.
KENT, EAST. *Kennels:* Elham, nr. Canterbury. *Tel.:* Elham 236. Wed., Sat.
KENT, WEST. *Kennels:* Hamptons, Shipbourne, nr. Tonbridge. *Tel.:* Plaxtol 236. 2 days a week.
LAMERTON. *Kennels:* Stowford, Lewdown, Okehampton. *Tel.:* Lewdown 300. Mon., Thurs.
LEDBURY. *Kennels:* Bromesberrow, Ledbury. *Tel.:* Bromesberrow 207. Mon., Fri., occ. Wed.
LEDBURY, NORTH. *Kennels:* Suckley, Worcester. *Tel.:* Suckley 215. Tues., Sat., occ. bye.
LEWES'S. *Kennels:* Llanayron, Ciliau Aeron, Lampeter, Cardigan. *Tel.:* Aberayron 200. Tues., Fri.
LLANDILO FARMERS'. *Kennels:* Pantyrodyn, Capel Isaac. Tues., alt. Fri., Sat.
LLANGEINOR. *Kennels:* Derwen Goppa, Coity, nr. Bridgend, Glam. Wed., Sat.
LLANGIBBY. *Kennels:* Llangibby. *Tel.:* Usk 241. Tues., Sat.
LONSDALE, NORTH. *Kennels:* Pennybridge Hall, Ulverston, Lancs. *Tel.:* Greenodd 212. 3 days a week.
LUDLOW. *Kennels:* Caynham, Ludlow. *Tel.:* Ludlow 198. Mon., Wed., Sat.
LUNESDALE. *Kennels:* New House, Orton, Westmorland. *Tel.:* Ravensworth 217. 3 days a week.
MELBREAK. *Kennels:* Miller Place, Lorton, Cockermouth. *Tel.:* Lorton 233. Mon., Thurs., Sat.
MENDIP FARMERS'. *Kennels:* Priddy, nr. Wells. *Tel.:* Priddy 271. Wed., Sat.
MEYNELL. *Kennels:* Sudbury, Derbyshire. *Tel.:* Sudbury 203. Tues., Sat., occ. bye Thurs.
MIDDLETON AND MIDDLETON EAST. *Kennels:* Birdsall, Malton. *Tel.:* North Grimston 209. Mon., Wed., Fri., Sat.
MILVAIN (PERCY). *Kennels:* Belford, Northumberland. *Tel.:* Belford 375. Tues., Thurs., Sat.; Mon. and Fri. every third week.
MONMOUTHSHIRE. *Kennels:* Gobion, Abergavenny. *Tel.:* Gobion 225. Wed., Sat., occ. Mon.
MORPETH. *Kennels:* Rivergreen, Morpeth. *Tel.:* Whalton 212. Tues., Sat. alt. Thurs.
NEW FOREST. *Kennels:* Furzey Lawn, Lyndhurst. *Tel.:* Lyndhurst 152. Tues., Sat.
NEWMARKET AND THURLOW. *Kennels:* Thurlow, Suffolk. *Tel.:* Thurlow 203. Mon., Thurs.
NORFOLK, WEST. *Kennels:* Corbetts Lodge, Necton, King's Lynn. *Tel.:* Holme Hale 341. Mon., Wed., Sat.
NORTHUMBERLAND, NORTH. *Kennels:* Slainsfield, Cornhill-on-Tweed. *Tel.:* Crookham 215. Mon., Fri., bye Wed.
NOTTS, SOUTH. *Kennels:* Epperstone, Notts. *Tel.:* Woodboro' 277. Mon., Thurs.
OAKLEY. *Kennels:* Milton Ernest, Bedford. *Tel.:* Oakley 266. Tues., Thurs., Sat.
OXFORDSHIRE, SOUTH. *Kennels:* Stadhampton, Oxon. *Tel.:* Stadhampton 239. Tues., Sat., and at least one Thurs. in each month.
PANDY. *Kennels:* Little Park, Llanvihangel-Crucorney. *Tel.:* Crucorney 278. Wed., Sat.
PEMBROKESHIRE. *Kennels:* Slade, Haverfordwest. *Tel.:* Haverfordwest 172. Wed., Sat.
PEMBROKESHIRE, SOUTH. *Kennels:* Cresselly, Kilgetty, Pem. *Tel.:* Carew 228. Wed., Sat.
PENTYRCH. *Kennels:* Pentyrch, Glam. Tues., Sat.
PERCY. *Kennels:* Canongate, Alnwick. *Tel.:* Alnwick 2047. Tues., Sat.
PERCY, WEST. *Kennels:* Callaly High Houses, Whittingham. *Tel.:* Callaly 32. Tues., Sat., occ. bye.
PLAS MACHYNLLETH. *Kennels:* Machynlleth. *Tel.:* Machynlleth 107. 3 days a week.
PORTMAN. *Kennels:* Bryanston, nr. Blandford. *Tel.:* Blandford 50. Mon., Wed., alt. Fri., Sat.
PUCKERIDGE. *Kennels:* Brent Pelham, Buntingford, Herts. *Tel.:* Brent Pelham 241. Mon., Wed., Sat.
PYTCHLEY. *Kennels:* Brixworth, Northampton. *Tel.:* Brixworth 204. Mon., Wed., Sat.
PYTCHLEY, WOODLAND. *Kennels:* Brigstock. *Tel.:* Brigstock 202. Wed., Sat.
QUORN. *Kennels:* Barrow-on-Soar, Loughborough. *Tel.:* Sileby 258. Mon., Tues., Fri., Sat.
RADNORSHIRE AND WEST HEREFORDSHIRE. *Kennels:* Titley, Kington, Hereford. *Tel.:* Kington 33. Mon., Fri.
ROMNEY MARSH. *Kennels:* Iden. *Tel.:* Iden 215. 2 days a week.
R.A. (SALISBURY PLAIN). *Kennels:* Bulford Camp, Salisbury. *Tel.:* Bulford 3171, Ext. 405. Wed., Sat.
SALTERSGATE FARMERS'. *Kennels:* Lockton, Yorks. *Tel.:* Lockton 243. 2 days a week.
SANDHURST. *Kennels:* Staff College, Camberley, Surrey. *Tel.:* Camberley 1510, Ext. 21. Wed., Sat.
SEAVINGTON. *Kennels:* Seavington St. Mary, Ilminster, Som. *Tel.:* South Petherton 479. Mon., Thurs.
SHROPSHIRE, NORTH. *Kennels:* Lee Bridge, Preston Brockhurst, Salop. *Tel.:* Lee Brockhurst 234. Wed., Sat., occ. bye.
SHROPSHIRE, SOUTH. *Kennels:* Annscroft. *Tel.:* Hanwood 255. Mon., Thurs., occ. bye Sat.
SILVERTON. *Kennels:* Drews Clieve, Stoke Hill, Exeter. *Tel.:* Stoke Cannon 216. Wed., Sat.
SINNINGTON. *Kennels:* Kirby Moorside. Mon., Thurs.
SOMERSET, WEST. *Kennels:* Bowerhayes, Carhampton, nr. Minehead. *Tel.:* Dunster 240. Wed., Sat.
SOMERSET, WEST, VALE. *Kennels:* Swang. Tues., Fri., occ. Sat.
SOUTHDOWN. *Kennels:* Ringmer, Sussex. *Tel.:* Ringmer 2. Mon., Wed., Sat.
SOUTH WOLD. *Kennels:* Belchford, Horncastle. *Tel.:* Tetford 213. Tues., Sat.
SPOONERS. *Kennels:* Mason's Gate, Whitchurch, Tavistock. *Tel.:* Tavistock 15. Wed., Sat.
STAFFORDSHIRE, NORTH. *Kennels:* Hill Chorlton, Baldwins Gate, nr. Newcastle, Staffs. *Tel.:* Whitmore 232. Wed., Sat.
STAFFORDSHIRE, SOUTH. *Kennels:* Upper Longdon, Rugeley. *Tel.:* Armitage 262. Tues., Sat.
STAINTONDALE. *Kennels:* Stainton Farm, Stainton Dale, Scarborough. *Tel.:* Cloughton 289. Tues., Fri., byes.
STEVENSTONE. *Kennels:* The Old Kennels, Torrington Station. *Tel.:* Torrington 2297. Mon., Thurs.
SUFFOLK. *Kennels:* Barton Road, Bury St. Edmunds. *Tel.:* B. St. E. 314. Tues., Sat.
SURREY, OLD, AND BURSTOW. *Kennels:* Felbridge, E. Grinstead. *Tel.:* E. Grinstead 168. Wed., Sat.
SURREY UNION. *Kennels:* Oakwood Hill, Ockley, Surrey. *Tel.:* Oakwood Hill 370. Wed., Sat.
SUSSEX, EAST. *Kennels:* Catsfield. *Tel.:* Battle 22. Tues., Sat.
TAUNTON VALE. *Kennels:* Henlade, Taunton. *Tel.:* Henlade 223. Tues., Fri., Mon., Wed., Fri.—alt.
TEDWORTH. *Kennels:* Westcourt, Burbage, Marlborough. *Tel.:* Burbage 234. Tues., Sat., occ. bye.
TEME VALLEY. *Kennels:* Knighton, Radnorshire. *Tel.:* Knighton 179. Tues., Sat.
TETCOTT. *Kennels:* Weekstone, Holsworthy. *Tel.:* Holsworthy 9. Mon., Thurs.
TETCOTT, SOUTH. *Kennels:* Tetcott, Holsworthy. *Tel.:* North Tamerton 240. Tues., Sat.
TICKHAM. *Kennels:* Wren's Hill, nr. Faversham. *Tel.* Teynham 264. Wed., Sat.
TIVERTON. *Kennels:* Hensleigh, Tiverton. *Tel.:* Tiverton 2670. Wed., Sat.
TORRINGTON FARMERS'. *Kennels:* Stevenstone, St. Giles. Wed., Sat.
TOWY AND COTHI. *Kennels:* Nantfforest, Llandovery. 6 days a fortnight.
TREDEGAR FARMERS'. *Kennels:* Tredegar Park, Bassaleg, Mon. *Tel.:* Rhiwderin 456. Mon., Thurs.
TYNEDALE. *Kennels:* Stagshaw Bank. *Tel.:* Corbridge-on-Tyne 40. Mon., Wed., Sat.
TYNE, NORTH. *Kennels:* Ealingham, Wark, Hexham. 5 days a fortnight.
ULLSWATER. *Kennels:* Grassthwaite How, Glenridding. *Tel.:* Glenridding 230. Mon., Wed., Sat.
UNITED. *Kennels:* Bishops Castle, Shropshire. *Tel.:* Bishops Castle 80. Wed., Sat.
VALE OF CLETTWR. *Kennels:* Blaenpant, Pencader. *Tel.:* Pencader 200. Mon., Thurs., occ. Sat.
V.W.H. (EARL BATHURST'S). *Kennels:* Cirencester Park. *Tel.:* Cirencester 136. Tues., Sat.
V.W.H. (CRICKLADE). *Kennels:* Meyseyhampton. Fairford, Glos. *Tel.:* Poulton 232. Tues., Thurs., Sat.
VINE. *Kennels:* Hannington, Basingstoke. *Tel.:* Kingsclere 282. Tues., Sat.
WARWICKSHIRE. *Kennels:* Kineton, Warwicks. *Tel.:* Kineton 220. Mon., Thurs., Sat., occ. bye.
WARWICKSHIRE FARMERS' (WEST). *Kennels:* Temple Grafton Court, nr. Alcester. *Tel.:* Bidford-on-Avon 2175. Mon., Thurs.
WARWICKSHIRE, NORTH. *Kennels:* Rouncil Lane, Kenilworth. *Tel.:* Kenilworth 84. Tues., Wed., Fri., Sat.
WESTERN. *Kennels:* Madron, Penzance. *Tel.:* Penzance 2667. Tues., Fri.
WEST STREET. *Kennels:* Solly Farm, Worth, nr. Deal, Kent. *Tel.:* Sandwich 2158. Tues., Sat.
WHADDON CHASE. *Kennels:* Ascott, Wing, Bucks. *Tel.:* Wing 243. Tues., Sat.
WHEATLAND. *Kennels:* Eardington, Bridgnorth. *Tel.:* Bridgnorth 2263. Wed., Sat.
WILLIAMS-WYNN'S, SIR WATKIN. *Kennels:* Wynnstay, Ruabon, Wrexham. *Tel.:* Ruabon 2296. Mon., Thurs.
WILTON. *Kennels:* Wilton, nr. Salisbury. *Tel.:* Wilton 3156. Wed., Sat.
WILTS, SOUTH AND WEST. *Kennels:* Motcombe, Shaftesbury. *Tel.:* Shaftesbury 2149. Mon., Wed., Sat.
WORCESTERSHIRE. *Kennels:* Fernhill Heath, nr. Worcester. *Tel.:* Fernhill Heath 204. 5 days a fortnight.
WYLYE VALLEY. *Kennels:* Tytherington, Warminster. *Tel.:* Sutton Veny 339. Wed., Sat.
YNYSFOR. *Kennels:* Ynysfor, Penrhyndeudraeth, Merioneth. *Tel.:* Penrhyndeudraeth 282. Sat.
YORK AND AINSTY, NORTH. *Kennels:* Copgrove Hall. *Tel.:* Copgrove 227. Wed., Sat.
YORK AND AINSTY, SOUTH. *Kennels:* Acomb, York. *Tel.:* York 78324. Tues., Sat.
ZETLAND. *Kennels:* Aldborough St. John, Richmond, Yorks. *Tel.:* Piercebridge 330. Tues., Thurs., Sat.

Scotland

BERWICKSHIRE. *Kennels:* Brieryhill, Duns, Berwicks. *Tel.:* Duns 41. Tues., Sat.
BUCCLEUCH'S, DUKE OF. *Kennels:* St. Boswells. *Tel.:* St. Boswells 3158. Mon., Wed., Thurs., Sat.
CHALLOCH. *Kennels:* Challoch, Newton-Stewart, Wigtownshire. *Tel.:* Newton-Stewart 109. One day a week.
DUMFRIESSHIRE. *Kennels:* Glenholm, Lockerbie. *Tel.:* Kettleholm 7. Tues., Sat.
EGLINTON. *Kennels:* Earlston, Kilmarnock. *Tel.:* Kilmarnock 428. Wed., Sat., alt. Mon.
FIFE. *Kennels:* Harlswynd, Ceres, Fife. *Tel.:* Ceres 232. Wed., Sat.
JED FOREST. *Kennels:* Abotrule, Bonchester Bridge, Hawick. Wed., Sat.
LANARKSHIRE AND RENFREWSHIRE. *Kennels:* Houston, Renfrewshire. *Tel.:* Bridge of Weir 22. Tues., Sat.
LAUDERDALE. *Kennels:* Trabroun, Lauder, Berwickshire. *Tel.:* Lauder 205. Tues., Fri.
LIDDESDALE. *Kennels:* Saughtree, Newcastleton. *Tel.:* Steele Road 224. 2 days a week.
LINLITHGOW AND STIRLINGSHIRE. *Kennels:* Golfhall, Corstorphine, Edinburgh 12. *Tel.:* Ratho 336. Tues., Sat., occ. Thurs.

Ireland

AVONDHU. *Kennels:* Corrinville, Fermoy. *Tel.:* Fermoy 71. Wed., Sun.
BALLYMACAD. *Kennels:* Moylough, Oldcastle. *Tel.:* Oldcastle 44. Tues., Fri.
BERMINGHAM AND NORTH GALWAY. *Kennels:* Bermingham House. Alt. Sun. and Mon.; Thurs.
BREE. *Kennels:* Newtownbarry House, Bunclody, Co. Wexford. *Tel.:* Bunclody 4. Mon., Thurs.
CARBERRY. *Kennels:* Old Military Barracks, Bandon. *Tel.:* Bandon 5. Thurs., Sun.
CARLOW. *Kennels:* Moyle, Carlow. *Tel.:* Carlow 17. Tues., Sat.
DOWN, EAST. *Kennels:* Seaforde, Co. Down. *Tel.:* Seaforde 67.

DUHALLOW. *Kennels:* Blackrock, Mallow. *Tel.:* Mallow 52. Mon., Wed., Fri., Sat.

GALWAY, COUNTY ("THE BLAZERS"). *Kennels:* Craughwell, Co. Galway. *Tel.:* Craughwell 3. 3 days a week.

GOLDEN VALE. *Kennels:* Tullamaine, Fethard. *Tel.:* Fethard 28. Thurs., and bye.

ISLAND. *Kennels:* Rockmount, Ferns. *Tel.:* Ferns 7. Tues., Thurs., Sat.

KILDARE. *Kennels:* Jigginstown, Naas. *Tel.:* Naas 44. Tues., Thurs., Sat., alt. Mon.

KILKENNY. *Kennels:* Mount Juliet, Thomastown, Co. Kilkenny. Fri.

KILKENNY, NORTH. *Kennels:* Ballyring, Freshford, Co. Kilkenny. Fri.

LEIX (QUEEN'S COUNTY). *Kennels:* Beechfield, Abbeyleix. *Tel.:* Abbeyleix 45. Wed., Sat.

LIMERICK, CO. *Kennels:* Clonshire, Adare, Co. Limerick. *Tel.:* Adare 20. Mon., Wed., Fri.

LOUTH. *Kennels:* Lissrenny, Ardee, Co. Louth. *Tel.:* Tallanstown 3. 2 days a week.

MEATH. *Kennels:* Nugentstown, Kells, Co. Meath. *Tel.:* Kells 30. Mon., Tues., Thurs., Fri.

MUSKERRY. *Kennels:* Cloghroe, Blarney, Co. Cork. *Tel.:* Blarney 85121. Wed., Sat.

ORMOND. *Kennels:* Knocknacree, Cloughjordan, Co. Tipperary. Tues., Thurs., Sat.

SCARTEEN. *Kennels:* Scarteen, Knocklong. *Tel.:* Knocklong 5. Mon., Thurs.

SOUTH UNION. *Kennels:* Furney, Carrigaline. Tues., Fri.

STRABANE. *Kennels:* Carricklee. *Tel.:* Strabane 205. Wed., Sat.

TIPPERARY. *Kennels:* Tullamaine, Fethard, Co. Tipperary. *Tel.:* Fethard 28. 4 days a week.

TIPPERARY, NORTH. *Kennels:* Derryknockane, Limerick. 3 days a fortnight —Tues., Sat.

UNITED HUNT CLUB. *Kennels:* Knockgriffen, Midleton. *Tel.:* Midleton 55. Wed., Sat.

WATERFORD. *Kennels:* Rockmount, Kilmacthomas. *Tel.:* Kilrossanty 3. Tues., Sat.

WATERFORD, WEST. *Kennels:* Bishopstown, Lismore. Wed. and Sat. (Nov. to Jan.); thereafter Tues., and Sat.

WESTMEATH. *Kennels:* Culleen, Mullingar. *Tel.:* Mullingar 252. Mon., Wed., Fri.

WEXFORD. *Kennels:* Moorfields, Ballinaboola, Wexford. *Tel.:* Ballinaboola 2. Tues., Fri.

WICKLOW. *Kennels:* Knockbawn, Inch. *Tel.:* Inch 16. Wed., Sat.

HARRIERS

England and Wales

ALDENHAM. *Kennels:* Puddephat's Farm, Markyate. *Tel.:* N. Markyate 317. Wed. or Thurs., occ. Sat.

AXE VALE. *Kennels:* Homer Lane, Seaton. *Tel.:* Seaton 339. Wed., Sat.

BOLVENTOR. *Kennels:* Fellover, St. Breward. *Tel.:* St. Tudy 232. Wed., Sat.

CAMBRIDGE FARMERS'. *Kennels:* Old Tiles, Horningsea. *Tel.:* Waterbeach 291. Tues., Sat.

COTLEY. *Kennels:* Cotley Wash, Membury, nr. Axminster. *Tel.:* South Chard 269. Wed., Sat.

CURY. *Kennels:* Mawgan, nr. Helston. *Tel.:* Manaccan 318. Tues., Sat.

DART VALE AND HALDON. *Kennels:* Lounard Mill, Week, Dartington, nr. Totnes. *Tel.:* Totnes 2010. Mon., Thurs., Sat.

DUNSTON. *Kennels:* Kenningham Hall, Mulbarton, Norwich. *Tel.:* Mulbarton 270. Tues., Fri.

EASTON. *Kennels:* Easton, Woodbridge, Suffolk. *Tel.:* Wickham Market 353. Mon., Thurs.

HATHERLEIGH. *Kennels:* Wembworthy, Chulmleigh. *Tel.:* Chulmleigh 230. 3 days a month, or by invitation.

HIGH PEAK. *Kennels:* The Shutts, Bakewell, Derbyshire. *Tel.:* Bakewell 20. Wed., Sat. occ. bye.

HOLCOMBE. *Kennels:* Kirklees, Brandlesholme, nr. Bury. *Tel.:* Tottington 85. Wed., Sat.

MINEHEAD. *Kennels:* Huntsham, Wootton Courtenay. *Tel.:* Timberscombe 376. Wed., Sat.

MODBURY. *Kennels:* Modbury. *Tel.:* Modbury 388. Tues., Fri. or Sat.

NORFOLK, NORTH. *Kennels:* Melton Constable Park, Norfolk. *Tel.:* Melton Constable 365. Tues., Thurs., Sat.

PENDLE FOREST AND CRAVEN. *Kennels:* Ellenthorpe, Gisburn, via Clitheroe. *Tel.:* Gisburn 222. Tues., Sat., bye Thurs.

ROCKWOOD. *Kennels:* Meal Hill, New Mill, nr. Huddersfield. *Tel.:* Holmfirth 21. Wed., Sat.

ROSS. *Kennels:* New House, Goodrich, Ross-on-Wye. Tues., Fri.

SENNOWE PARK. *Kennels:* Sennowe Park. Usually Tues., and Sat.

SINCLAIR'S, MR. *Kennels:* Southwoods Hall, Thirsk, Yorks. *Tel.:* Sutton (Thirsk) 206. 2 days a week.

SOUTH POOL. *Kennels:* Chillington. *Tel.:* Torcross 362. Sat.

SPARKFORD VALE. *Kennels:* Wales, Queen Carmel, nr. Yeovil. *Tel.:* Marston Magna 240. Wed., Sat.

TAUNTON VALE. *Kennels:* Blackbrook. Mon., Thurs., occ. Sat.

THANET AND HERNE. *Kennels:* Highstead Gravel Pit, Chislet, nr. Canterbury. *Tel.:* Chislet 221. Sat., occ. bye.

VALE OF LUNE. *Kennels:* Hornby, nr. Lancaster. *Tel.:* Hornby 210. Wed., Sat.

WAVENEY VALLEY. *Kennels:* Bungay Road Farm, Rumburgh, Suffolk. *Tel.:* Ilketshall 268. Sat., alt. Tues.

WESTON. *Kennels:* Webbington, Axbridge, Som. Wed., Sat.

WINDERMERE. *Kennels:* Dungeon Ghyll, Langdale, Westmorland. *Tel.:* Langdale 213. 3 days a week.

Ireland

ANTRIM, EAST. *Kennels:* Ballysavage, Templepatrick, Co. Antrim. *Tel.:* Templepatrick 316. Wed., Sat.

ANTRIM, MID. *Kennels:* Galgorm Parks, Co. Antrim. Tues., Fri.

BRAY. *Kennels:* Lehaunstown Park, Cabinteely. Wed., Sat.

CLARE, CO. *Kennels:* Ballycar, Newmarket-on-Fergus, Co. Clare. *Tel.:* Newmarket-on-Fergus 13. Mon., Thurs., and bye.

CLONMEL. *Kennels:* Heywood Road, Clonmel. Tues., Fri.

CROOM. *Kennels:* Liskennett House, Croom, Co. Limerick. Tues., occ. bye.

DERRY, SOUTH. *Kennels:* White Hill, Bellaghy. *Tel.:* Bellaghy 237. Wed., Sat.

DOWN, NORTH. *Kennels:* Islandhill Road, Comber. *Tel.:* Comber 309. Wed., Sat., occ. bye.

DUBLIN, CO., SOUTH. *Kennels:* Dundrum, Co. Dublin. Wed., Sat.

DUNGARVAN. *Kennels:* Youghal Road, Dungarvan. Sun. and byes.

FERMANAGH. *Kennels:* Lisanelly Camp, Omagh. Wed., Sat.

FINGAL. *Kennels:* Coolquay. The Ward, Co. Dublin. *Tel.:* Kilsallaghan 7. Tues., Fri.

IVEACH. *Kennels:* Tonnaghmore, Banbridge, Co. Dublin. *Tel.:* Lenaderg 250. Wed., Sat.

KILDARE, NORTH. *Kennels:* Straffan, Co. Kildare. Mon., Fri.

KILLINICK. *Kennels:* Churchtown. Mon., Thurs.

KILLULTAGH, OLD ROCK, AND CHICHESTER. *Kennels:* Dundrod, Co. Antrim. *Tel.:* Dundrod 281. Wed., Sat.

KILMOGANNY. *Kennels:* Castletown House, Carrick-on-Suir, Co. Kilkenny. *Tel.:* Carrick 30. 2 days a week.

LIMERICK. *Kennels:* Derryknockane, Limerick. Thurs., occ. bye.

LITTLEGRANGE. *Kennels:* Lisdornan, Julianstown, Co. Meath. Mon., Thurs.

LONGFORD, CO. *Kennels:* Ballinree, Edgeworthstown, Co. Longford. *Tel.:* Edgeworthstown 26. Tues., Fri.

MONKSTOWN. *Kennels:* Glen Road, Monkstown, Co. Cork. Sun., occ. bye.

NAAS. *Kennels:* New Abbey, Kilcullen, Co. Kildare. *Tel.:* Kilcullen5. Wed., Fri.

NEWRY. *Kennels:* Drumbanagher, Newry, Co. Down. *Tel.:* Poyntzpass 204. Tues., Sat.

RAKES OF MALLOW. *Kennels:* Mallow, Co. Cork. Sun., byes.

ROUTE. *Kennels:* Crossreagh, Portrush. *Tel.:* Portrush 3259. Wed., Sat.

SLIGO, CO. *Kennels:* Cloverhill House, Sligo. Wed., byes.

SLIGO, CO. (SOUTH): *Kennels:* Annaghbeg, Collooney. Fri., and alt. Tues. after Christmas.

TARA. *Kennels:* Bective House, Navan. *Tel.:* Navan 244. Mon., Thurs.

TYNAN AND ARMAGH. Wed., Sat.

STAGHOUNDS

England

DEVON AND SOMERSET. *Kennels:* Exford. *Tel.:* Exford 262. Tues., Thurs., Sat.

KENT, MID. *Kennels:* Mount Ephraim. *Tel.:* Boughton 378. Wed., Sat.

NEW FOREST BUCKHOUNDS. *Kennels:* Brockenhurst. *Tel.:* Brockenhurst 2203. Mon., Fri.

NORWICH. *Kennels:* Wacton House, Norwich. *Tel.:* Long Stratton 265. Mon., Thurs.

QUANTOCK. *Kennels:* Bagborough, Taunton. *Tel.:* Bishops Lydeard 269. Mon., Thurs.

TIVERTON. *Kennels:* Leigh Barton, Loxbeare, Tiverton. *Tel.:* Tiverton 2049. Sat., and one other day per fortnight.

Ireland

DOWN, COUNTY. *Kennels:* Rockmount, Ballykine, Ballynahinch, Co. Down. *Tel.:* Ballynahinch 235. Tues., Sat.

WARD UNION. *Kennels:* Ashbourne, Co. Neath. *Tel.:* Ashbourne 3. Tues., Sat.

FOOT HARRIERS AND BEAGLES

England and Wales

AIREDALE BEAGLES. *Kennels:* Eldwick, nr. Bingley, Yorks.

ALDERSHOT BEAGLES. *Kennels:* Oxney Farm, Bordon.

AMPLEFORTH COLLEGE BEAGLES. *Kennels:* Gilling Castle, Gilling East, Yorks.

ANGLESEY BEAGLES. *Kennels:* Llangefni, Anglesey.

BEACON BEAGLES. *Kennels:* Blackbrook, Taunton.

BERKELEY, OLD, BEAGLES. *Kennels:* Beamond End, nr. Amersham.

BLEAN BEAGLES. *Kennels:* Waterham Farm, Hernhill, Faversham.

BLEASDALE BEAGLES. *Kennels:* Killington, nr. Sedbergh.

BOLEBROKE BEAGLES. *Kennels:* Crowdleham, Kent.

BRIGHTON AND STORRINGTON FOOT BEAGLES. *Kennels:* Clappers Lane, Fulking, Poynings, Sussex.

BRITANNIA BEAGLES. *Kennels:* Britannia Royal Naval College, Dartmouth.

BUCKS, NORTH, BEAGLES. *Kennels:* Putnoe Farm, Bedford.

CASTLETON BEAGLES. *Kennels:* Red Barn, Castleton, nr. Cardiff.

CATTERICK BEAGLES. *Kennels:* White House Farm, Waitwith, Catterick Camp, Yorks.

CHESHIRE BEAGLES. *Kennels:* Dodleston, Chester.

CHILMARK BEAGLES. *Kennels:* Chilmark, nr. Salisbury.

CHRIST CHURCH AND NEW COLLEGE BEAGLES. *Kennels:* Garsington, Oxon.

CLARO BEAGLES. *Kennels:* Field House Farm, Darley, Harrogate.

CLIFTON FOOT HARRIERS. *Kennels:* Yatton, Som.

COLCHESTER GARRISON BEAGLES. *Kennels:* Berechurch Camp, Colchester.

COLNE VALLEY BEAGLES. *Kennels:* Butternab Wood, Beaumont Park, Huddersfield.

CUMBERLAND, WEST, BEAGLES. *Kennels:* Bootle.

DALGETY'S, MR., BEAGLES. *Kennels:* Gatcombe, I.O.W.

DERWENT VALLEY BEAGLES. *Kennels:* Westow Lodge, Westow, Yorks.

DUMMER BEAGLES. *Kennels:* Little Rissington Manor, nr. Cheltenham, Glos.

ECCLESFIELD BEAGLES. *Kennels:* Townsend Road, Ecclesfield, nr. Sheffield.

ESSEX, MID, BEAGLES. *Kennels:* Spurriers, Norton Heath, nr. Ingatestone.

ETON COLLEGE BEAGLES. *Kennels:* Eton College, Windsor.

FARLEY HILL BEAGLES. *Kennels:* Bensgrove Farm, Goring Heath, Oxon.

FOREST AND DISTRICT BEAGLES. *Kennels:* Long Ridge, Sutton.

GEACH'S, MR. HARRY, BEAGLES. *Kennels:* Mill House, Walesby, nr. Market Rasen, Lincs.

GLYN CELYN BEAGLES. *Kennels:* Verlands, Crickadarn, Erwood, nr. Builth Wells, Brecon.

HERTS, SOUTH, BEAGLES. *Kennels:* Church Lodge, Stagenhoe, Whitwell, Herts.

HOLME VALLEY BEAGLES. *Kennels:* Upperthong, nr. Holmfirth.

MARLBOROUGH COLLEGE BEAGLES. *Kennels:* Marlborough College, Wilts.

MEON VALLEY AND WINCHESTER BEAGLES. *Kennels:* West End House, Hambledon.

NEWCASTLE AND DISTRICT BEAGLES. *Kennels:* High Seat, Heddon-on-the-Wall.

NEW FOREST BEAGLES. *Kennels:* Bartley, Southampton.

PER ARDUA (R.A.F.) BEAGLES. *Kennels:* R.A.F. Station, Cranwell, Sleaford, Lincs.

PEVENSEY MARSH BEAGLES. *Kennels:* Highwoods Farm, Wydown, Bexhill-on-Sea.

PIPEWELL FOOT BEAGLES. *Kennels:* Pipewell, nr. Kettering.

RADLEY COLLEGE BEAGLES. *Kennels:* Radley College, nr. Abingdon, Berks.

ROCHDALE FOOT HARRIERS. *Kennels:* Sparth, Rochdale.

ROYAL AGRICULTURAL COLLEGE BEAGLES. *Kennels:* Coates, nr. Cirencester, Glos.

R.A.S.C. PIMPERNEL BEAGLES. *Kennels:* Blandford Camp, Dorset.

ROYAL ROCK BEAGLES. *Kennels:* Ledsham, nr. Chester.

SANDHURST BEAGLES. *Kennels:* Royal Military Academy, Sandhurst, Camberley.

SCHOOL OF INFANTRY BEAGLES. *Kennels:* School of Infantry, Warminster, Wilts.

SHROPSHIRE BEAGLES. *Kennels:* Grove House, Rodington, Shrewsbury.

SPROUGHTON FOOT BEAGLES. *Kennels:* Pigeon Lane, Washbrook, Ipswich.

STAFFORDSHIRE BEAGLES. *Kennels:* Newtown, nr. Walsall.

STAFFORDSHIRE, NORTH, MOORLAND BEAGLES. *Kennels:* Hemheath Farm, Trentham, Staffs.

STEWARD'S, MR., BEAGLES. *Kennels:* St. James's Street, Nottingham.

STOKE HILL BEAGLES. *Kennels:* Trumps, Aylesbeare, E. Devon.

STOKESLEY FARMERS' BEAGLES. *Kennels:* Greenhow Moor, Nunthorpe, Middlesbrough.

SURREY, WEST, AND HORSELL BEAGLES. *Kennels:* Dog Kennel Green, Ranmore, Dorking.

TEES VALLEY BEAGLES. *Kennels:* Barford Camp, Barnard Castle.

TRINITY FOOT BEAGLES. *Kennels:* Barton, Cambs.

VALE OF CLWYD BEAGLES. *Kennels:* Erw Vran, Denbigh.

WARWICKSHIRE BEAGLES. *Kennels:* Beoley, nr. Redditch.

WEARDALE BEAGLES. *Kennels:* The Dene, Stanhope, Co. Durham.

WICK AND DISTRICT BEAGLES. *Kennels:* Old Rectory, Syston, Mangotsfield, nr. Bristol.

WORCESTER PARK AND BUCKLAND BEAGLES. *Kennels:* Mugswell, Chipstead.

WYE COLLEGE BEAGLES. *Kennels:* Coldharbour, Wye, Kent.

WYE FOREST BEAGLES. *Kennels:* Hawkstone Otterhounds' Kennels, Shobdon, Hereford.

Scotland

CASTLE MILK FOOT HARRIERS. *Kennels:* Castle Milk, Lockerbie, Dumfriesshire.

ETTRICK FOREST BEAGLES. *Kennels:* Rutherford, Kelso (bitches) and Hyndhope, Ettrick, Selkirk (doghounds).

Ireland

ARMAGH AND DISTRICT BEAGLES.

CASHEL BEAGLES. Sun.

CORDUFF BEAGLES. *Kennels:* Corduff House, Lusk, Co. Dublin.

CURRAGH FOOT BEAGLES. *Kennels:* Curragh Camp, Co. Kildare.

GOLDBURN BEAGLES. *Kennels:* Main Street, Dunboyne, Co. Neath.

GOREY AND DISTRICT BEAGLES. *Kennels:* Raheenagurrin, Gorey, Co. Wexford.

HOLYCROSS BEAGLES. *Kennels:* Inch, Thurles, Co. Tipperary.

KILFEACLE BEAGLES.

MARYBOROUGH FOOT BEAGLES. *Kennels:* Laplands, Douglas, Co. Cork.

MIDLETON FOOT BEAGLES. *Kennels:* Avoncore, Midleton, Co. Cork.

RIVERSTOWN BEAGLES. *Kennels:* Riverstown, Co. Cork.

WELFORT BEAGLES. *Kennels:* Rahan Lodge, Tullamore.

HUNTING QUIZ

1. Who was known as the "Father of the Trojans" and why?

★

2. What is the average weight of: (*a*) dog-fox; (*b*) vixen; (*c*) dog-hound; (*d*) bitch?

★

3. What pre-war Olympic athlete is a present M.F.H. and with what Hunt?

★

4. What hounds are known as the "Black and Tans"?

QUIZ ANSWERS

1. Mr. John Corbet who hunted the Warwickshire (1791–1811), because he bred Trojan, one of the most famous doghounds, used for breeding. 2. (*a*) 15 lb.; (*b*) 13½ lb.; (*c*) 75 lb.; (*d*) 65 lb. 3. The Marquess of Exeter (Olympic hurdler). The Burghley Foxhounds. 4. The Scarteen in Ireland.

Ice Hockey

Compiled by Howard Bass
Editor: The Skater and Skier

ICE HOCKEY QUIZ

1. How many players from each team are allowed on the ice during play?

*

2. What are the regulation height and width of a goal?

*

3. Who was captain of Britain's victorious Olympic team in 1936?

*

4. How many periods of play are there in a match?

*

5. How long does each period last?

*

6. Who scored the most goals in the 1958 British Autumn Cup competition?

*

7. How many players may be in their own defence zone when the puck is outside that zone?

*

8. With which teams have Lou Bates and Chick Zamick been mainly associated?

*

9. When was the first European championship held and which nation won?

*

10. How much does a puck weigh?

QUIZ ANSWERS

1. Six. These normally comprise a goalminder, two defence men and three forwards. 2. Four feet high, six feet wide. 3. Carl Erhardt. 4. Three. 5. Twenty minutes' actual playing time measured by stop-watch. 6. Ike Scott (Paisley Pirates), 31 goals. 7. Three. 8. Lou Bates with Wembley Lions and Chick Zamick with Nottingham Panthers. 9. 1910. Great Britain at Les Avants. 10. About five and a half ounces.

BRITISH AUTUMN CUP
WINNERS

1946–47	Brighton Tigers
1947–48	Harringay Racers
1948–49	Wembley Monarchs
1949–50	Harringay Racers
1950–51	Brighton Tigers
1951–52	Streatham
1952–53	Harringay Racers
1953–54	Harringay Racers
1954–55	Streatham
1955–56	Nottingham Panthers
1956–57	Brighton Tigers
1957–58	Wembley Lions
1958–59	Brighton Tigers

WORLD AND EUROPEAN CHAMPIONSHIPS 1958-59

(Held concurrently: Czechoslovakia, March 5–15)

FINAL TABLE

		P.	W.	D.	L.	F.	A.	Pts.
1.	Canada	5	4	0	1	21	7	8
2.	Russia	5	4	0	1	20	10	8
3.	Czechoslovakia	5	3	0	2	23	14	6
4.	U.S.A.	5	3	0	2	22	14	6
5.	Sweden	5	1	0	4	6	21	2
6.	Finland	5	0	0	5	7	32	0

World champions: Canada. European champions: Russia.

Other nations competing (not in the first six): East Germany, Italy, Norway, Poland, Switzerland and West Germany.

BRITISH AUTUMN CUP 1958-59

(Matches played in England and Scotland: October to December)

		P.	W.	D.	L.	F.	A.	Pts.
1.	Brighton Tigers	24	15	1	8	139	120	31
2.	Murrayfield Royals	24	13	3	8	136	111	29
3.	Paisley Pirates	24	12	1	11	117	121	25
4.	Wembley Lions	24	9	2	13	121	129	20
5.	Nottingham Panthers	24	6	3	15	93	125	15

Chick Zamick

Lou Bates

Bill Glennie

LEADING AUTUMN CUP SCORERS 1958-59

		Goals	Assists	Pts.
Lemon	(Paisley Pirates)	12	44	56
Booth	(Wembley Lions)	16	38	54
Key	(Murrayfield Royals)	17	30	47
Hemmerling	(Brighton Tigers)	22	24	46
Edwards	(Brighton Tigers)	23	22	45
Domenico	(Paisley Pirates)	22	23	45
Anning	(Brighton Tigers)	29	15	44
McCaskell	(Murrayfield Royals)	27	17	44
Scott, I.	(Paisley Pirates)	31	12	43
Pachal	(Murrayfield Royals)	23	19	42
Krekelwetz, V.	(Murrayfield Royals)	22	15	37
Orris	(Brighton Tigers)	16	20	36

BRITISH LEAGUE 1958-59

(Matches played in England and Scotland: January to April)

		P.	W.	D.	L.	F.	A.	Pts.
1.	Paisley Pirates	30	17	2	11	163	126	36
2.	Wembley Lions	30	14	5	11	164	138	33
3.	Brighton Tigers	30	13	2	15	148	189	28
4.	Nottingham Panthers	30	9	5	16	124	146	23

LEADING BRITISH LEAGUE SCORERS 1958-59

		Goals	Assists	Pts.
Lemon	(Paisley Pirates)	22	55	77
Domenico	(Paisley Pirates)	35	31	66
Scott	(Paisley Pirates)	43	19	62
Hemmerling	(Brighton Tigers)	36	25	61
Pachal	(Nottingham Panthers)	29	29	58
Booth	(Wembley Lions)	12	42	54
Scott, G.	(Wembley Lions)	30	22	52
Krekelwetz, V.	(Wembley Lions)	31	19	50
Edwards	(Brighton Tigers)	20	26	46
Anning	(Brighton Tigers)	27	17	44
Pichette	(Wembley Lions)	23	21	44
Moore	(Wembley Lions)	22	22	44

ICE HOCKEY

HISTORY OF THE GAME

Now frequently described as the world's fastest team game, the ancestry of ice hockey dates as far back as the second century and its roots are deeply embedded in Canadian ice.

The foundation of the game with a recognised characteristic or identity separate from field hockey—the use of a puck as distinct from a ball—is generally recognised to stem from the first recorded "proper" game, played by Englishmen on the frozen expanse of Kingston Harbour, Ontario, in 1860.

These pioneer players were predominated by Crimean War veterans in a regiment of the Royal Canadian Rifles. Subsequently, Montreal became the central point of the game's early progress.

In the summer of 1879 W. F. Robertson, a student of Montreal's McGill University, visited England and saw field hockey matches. As a skating enthusiast he wondered how the game could be suitably adapted so that it could be played on ice. After returning to Montreal he collaborated with a fellow student, R. F. Smith, and they devised rules and regulations, adding a few original ideas to what was basically a combination of field hockey and rugby rules. A square rubber puck was used with nine players on each side.

The first recognised regular team was organised during the winter of 1880–81 and called McGill University Hockey Club. The game was introduced to Ottawa five years later by one of the original members, A. P. Low. With natural climatic encouragement the sport developed and spread rapidly across Canada, more gradually gaining a hold in the United States as more electrically refrigerated rinks came into being.

The game has flourished particularly in North America, where the most highly organised professional competitions, the National Hockey League of North America and the Stanley Cup tournament, have brought together the top teams from Canada and U.S.A. and brought worldwide fame to New York Rangers, Toronto Maple Leafs, Montreal Canadiens, Detroit Red Wings, Chicago Black Hawks, Boston Bruins and New York Americans.

The Stanley Cup was instituted in 1893 and the National League began in 1917. These senior contests retain an international as well as an inter-state element and leading matches at great arenas like Madison Square Garden, New York, and Maple Leaf Gardens, Toronto, provide very big occasions for the sport's followers.

There are hundreds of other teams,

amateur and professional, of varying grades throughout North America taking part in league tournaments which might be compared in diversity to those of association football in Britain.

The sport began to grow in Europe at the turn of the century and the world administration, the *Ligue Internationale de Hockey sur Glace*, was organised in 1908. The prime mover in this was Louis Magnus, a Frenchman — a reminder that the name "hockey" is derived from a French word, *hoquet*, meaning a shepherd's crook or curved stick.

The first European championship was won by Great Britain in 1910 at Les Avants. The world championship was instituted ten years later, with Canada the first victors. Canadian demonstration popularised the game in Great Britain sufficiently to warrant a five-team league competition in 1903. The first game in Scotland took place at Crossmyloof, Glasgow, in 1908.

During the great freeze of 1895 two future monarchs attracted further attention to the sport when they participated in a match on the lake in Buckingham Palace grounds—King Edward VII and King George V, then Prince of Wales and Duke of York.

The British Ice Hockey Association was founded in 1914. The five founder clubs were Cambridge, Manchester, Oxford, Royal Engineers and Princes. The Scottish Ice Hockey Association came into being in 1929.

Progress in Britain was accelerated by the opening of the Westminster rink in 1926, but the senior sport really started flourishing in the country after the Empire Pool, Wembley, started promoting matches in 1934. Other large arenas at Brighton, Empress Hall and Harringay joined in attractive league fixtures, with leading personalities like Lou Bates, Red Stapleford and Joe Beaton becoming great favourites.

During the last years before World War II, perhaps the sport's best seasons in Britain, an international club tournament was contested between four London clubs, Wembley Canadians, Richmond Hawks, Streatham and Wembley Lions, and six continental teams, Berlin, Français Volants, Milan, Munich, Prague and Stade Français.

In 1936 Great Britain, captained by Carl Erhardt, made ice hockey history by beating Canada to win the Olympic title—Canada's only defeat since ice hockey first gained Olympic inclusion in 1920, until Russia captured the title in 1956 at Cortina d'Ampezzo.

Since the war the sport in Britain has relied, probably more than it should, on Canadian players who have held ninety per cent of the senior team positions. With national economic conditions not conducive to building large new ice arenas, the post-war era has provided many difficulties with which the B.I.H.A. has somehow coped.

In 1954–55 an enterprising senior Anglo-Scottish tournament comprising twelve teams was tried, but the high running costs proved too much for some of the smaller rinks and now only five teams contest the season's major British competitions, the Autumn Cup and the British League—Brighton Tigers, Nottingham Panthers, Paisley Pirates, Wembley Lions and Streatham.

Among the most prominent post-war players in Britain have been Bill Glennie and Joe Shack (Harringay Racers), Gib Hutchinson, Bobby Lee, Les Anning, Fred Denny and Red Kurz (Brighton Tigers), Sonny Rost and Kenny Booth (Wembley Lions), Chick Zamick and Les Strongman (Nottingham Panthers) and Tom Lemon (Paisley Pirates).

An intermediate grade of ice hockey is played by clubs with headquarters at Ayr, Blackpool, Dundee, Durham, Falkirk, Glasgow, Kirkcaldy, Liverpool, Murrayfield, Perth, Richmond, Southampton, Streatham and Whitley Bay.

OLYMPIC CHAMPIONS

		Venue
1920	Canada	Antwerp
1924	Canada	Chamonix
1928	Canada	St. Moritz
1932	Canada	Lake Placid
1936	Great Britain	Garmisch-Partenkirchen
1948	Canada	St. Moritz
1952	Canada	Oslo
1956	Russia	Cortina d'Ampezzo

WORLD CHAMPIONS

		Venue
1920	Canada	Antwerp
1924	Canada	Chamonix
1928	Canada	St. Moritz
1930	Canada	Chamonix
1931	Canada	Krynica
1932	Canada	Berlin
1933	U.S.A.	Prague
1934	Canada	Milan
1935	Canada	Davos
1936	Great Britain	Garmisch-Partenkirchen
1937	Canada	London
1938	Canada	Prague
1939	Canada	Zürich
1947	Czechoslovakia	Prague
1948	Canada	St. Moritz
1949	Czechoslovakia	Stockholm
1950	Canada	London
1951	Canada	Paris
1952	Canada	Oslo
1953	Sweden	Zürich
1954	Russia	Stockholm
1955	Canada	Dusseldorf
1956	Russia	Cortina d'Ampezzo
1957	Sweden	Moscow
1958	Canada	Oslo
1959	Canada	Prague

EUROPEAN CHAMPIONS

		Venue
1910	Great Britain	Les Avants
1911	Bohemia	Berlin
1913	Belgium	Munich
1914	Bohemia	Berlin
1921	Sweden	Stockholm
1922	Czechoslovakia	St. Moritz
1923	Sweden	Antwerp
1924	France	Milan
1925	Czechoslovakia	Prague
1926	Switzerland	Davos
1927	Austria	Vienna
1928	Switzerland	St. Moritz
1929	Czechoslovakia	Budapest
1930	Germany	Berlin
1931	Austria	Krynica
1932	Sweden	Berlin
1933	Czechoslovakia	Prague
1934	Germany	Milan
1935	Switzerland	Davos
1936	Great Britain	Garmisch-Partenkirchen
1937	Great Britain	London
1938	Great Britain	Prague
1939	Switzerland	Basle
1947	Czechoslovakia	Prague
1948	Czechoslovakia	St. Moritz
1949	Czechoslovakia	Stockholm
1950	Switzerland	London
1951	Sweden	Paris
1952	Sweden	Oslo
1953	Sweden	Zürich
1954	Russia	Stockholm
1955	Russia	Dusseldorf
1956	Russia	Cortina d'Ampezzo
1957	Sweden	Moscow
1958	Russia	Oslo
1959	Russia	Prague

STANLEY CUP CHAMPIONS
(U.S.A. and Canada)

1893–94	Montreal A.A.A.
1894–95	Montreal Victorias
1895–96	Montreal Victorias
1896–97	Montreal Victorias
1897–98	Montreal Victorias
1898–99	Montreal Victorias
1899–1900	Montreal Shamrocks
1900–01	Winnipeg Victorias
1901–02	Montreal A.A.A.
1902–03	Ottawa Silver Seven
1903–04	Ottawa Silver Seven
1904–05	Ottawa Silver Seven
1905–06	Montreal Wanderers
1906–07	Kenora Thistles
1906–07*	Montreal Wanderers
1907–08	Montreal Wanderers
1908–09	Ottawa Senators
1909–10	Montreal Wanderers
1910–11	Ottawa Senators
1911–12	Quebec Bull Dogs
1912–13	Quebec Bull Dogs
1913–14	Toronto
1914–15	Vancouver Millionaires
1915–16	Montreal Canadiens
1916–17	Seattle Metropolitans
1917–18	Toronto Arenas
1918–19	Ottawa Senators
1919–20	Ottawa Senators
1920–21	Ottawa Senators
1921–22	Toronto St. Patricks
1922–23	Ottawa Senators
1923–24	Montreal Canadiens
1924–25	Victoria Cougars
1925–26	Montreal Maroons
1926–27	Ottawa Senators
1927–28	New York Rangers
1928–29	Boston Bruins
1929–30	Montreal Canadiens
1930–31	Montreal Canadiens
1931–32	Toronto Maple Leafs
1932–33	New York Rangers
1933–34	Chicago Black Hawks
1934–35	Montreal Maroons
1935–36	Detroit Red Wings
1936–37	Detroit Red Wings
1937–38	Chicago Black Hawks
1938–39	Boston Bruins
1939–40	New York Rangers
1940–41	Boston Bruins
1941–42	Toronto Maple Leafs
1942–43	Detroit Red Wings
1943–44	Montreal Canadiens
1944–45	Toronto Maple Leafs
1945–46	Montreal Canadiens
1946–47	Toronto Maple Leafs
1947–48	Toronto Maple Leafs
1948–49	Toronto Maple Leafs
1949–50	Detroit Red Wings
1950–51	Toronto Maple Leafs
1951–52	Detroit Red Wings
1952–53	Montreal Canadiens
1953–54	Detroit Red Wings
1954–55	Detroit Red Wings
1955–56	Montreal Canadiens
1956–57	Montreal Canadiens
1957–58	Montreal Canadiens
1958–59	Montreal Canadiens

*The cup was competed for twice in 1906–7.

Sonny Rost

Kenny Booth

Les Strongman

NATIONAL HOCKEY LEAGUE WINNERS
(U.S.A. and Canada)

1917–18	Toronto Arenas
1918–19	Montreal Canadiens
1919–20	Ottawa Senators
1920–21	Ottawa Senators
1921–22	Toronto St. Patricks
1922–23	Ottawa Senators
1923–24	Montreal Canadiens
1924–25	Montreal Canadiens
1925–26	Montreal Maroons
1926–27	Ottawa Senators
1927–28	New York Rangers
1928–29	Boston Bruins
1929–30	Montreal Canadiens
1930–31	Montreal Canadiens
1931–32	Toronto Maple Leafs
1932–33	Toronto Maple Leafs
1933–34	Detroit Red Wings
1934–35	Toronto Maple Leafs
1935–36	Detroit Red Wings
1936–37	Detroit Red Wings
1937–38	Toronto Maple Leafs
1938–39	Boston Bruins
1939–40	New York Rangers
1940–41	Boston Bruins
1941–42	New York Rangers
1942–43	Detroit Red Wings
1943–44	Montreal Canadiens
1944–45	Montreal Canadiens
1945–46	Montreal Canadiens
1946–47	Montreal Canadiens
1947–48	Toronto Maple Leafs
1948–49	Detroit Red Wings
1949–50	Detroit Red Wings
1950–51	Detroit Red Wings
1951–52	Detroit Red Wings
1952–53	Detroit Red Wings
1953–54	Detroit Red Wings
1954–55	Detroit Red Wings
1955–56	Montreal Canadiens
1956–57	Detroit Red Wings
1957–58	Montreal Canadiens
1958–59	Montreal Canadiens

ICE HOCKEY QUIZ

1. Which team has won the British Autumn Cup most times?

*

2. Who is credited with inventing the game basically as it is played today?

*

3. When may a player not take a pass from a team-mate?

*

4. Which four teams contested the British League championship in 1959?

*

5. Where and when was the first occasion on record that a puck was used in an ice hockey match?

*

6. Which seven teams annually compete in the National Hockey League of North America?

*

7. What is the diameter of a puck?

*

8. In what position did Gib Hutchinson play and primarily for which team?

*

9. Name the first proper team, formed in 1880.

*

10. When may a player enter the attacking zone without being penalised?

QUIZ ANSWERS

1. Brighton Tigers and Harringay Racers, four times each. 2. W. F. Robertson and R. F. Smith at Montreal in 1879. 3. When the team-mate is in another zone at the moment of passing. 4. Brighton Tigers, Nottingham Panthers, Paisley Pirates and Wembley Lions. 5. At Kingston Harbour, Ontario, in 1860. 6. Boston Bruins, Chicago Black Hawks, Detroit Red Wings, Montreal Canadiens, New York Americans, New York Rangers and Toronto Maple Leafs. 7. Three inches. 8. Goalminder for Brighton Tigers. 9. McGill University Hockey Club. 10. When in line with or behind the puck or puck carrier.

ICE HOCKEY QUIZ

1. Who coached Brighton Tigers in 1958–59 season?

*

2. Which famous club's home rink is called Madison Square Garden?

*

3. Name the five founder clubs of the British Ice Hockey Association.

*

4. What colour is the centre (half-way) line painted on the ice?

*

5. When was ice hockey first played at Wembley's Empire Pool?

*

6. Name the world's controlling organisation for the sport.

*

7. Can a player score direct from a kick?

*

8. Which nation won the 1956 Olympic title?

*

9. Which famous London rink ceased to function in 1958?

*

10. What team colours are used by Wembley Lions?

*

QUIZ ANSWERS

1. George Edwards. 2. New York Rangers; also New York Americans. 3. Cambridge, Manchester, Oxford Canadians, Royal Engineers and Princes. 4. Red, to distinguish from the blue defence zone lines. 5. In 1934. 6. Ligue Internationale de Hockey sur Glace. 7. No. 8. Russia, at Cortina d'Ampezzo. 9. Harringay Arena. 10. Red and white.

BRITISH (NATIONAL) LEAGUE WINNERS

1934	Grosvenor House
1935	Streatham
1936	Wembley Lions
1937	Wembley Lions
1938	Harringay Racers
1939	Harringay Greyhounds
1940	Harringay Greyhounds
1947	Brighton Tigers
1948	Brighton Tigers
1949	Harringay Racers
1950	Streatham
1951	Nottingham Panthers
1952	Wembley Lions
1953	Streatham
1954	Nottingham Panthers
1955	Harringay Racers
1956	Nottingham Panthers
1957	Wembley Lions
1958	Brighton Tigers
1959	Paisley Pirates

NOTES ON PLAY

Games are controlled by two referees, one in each half of the playing area, as in the case of field hockey umpires. A match is divided into three periods, each of twenty minutes' actual playing time, i.e. while the puck is in play, measured by an official stop watch visible to the spectators.

Six players a side are permitted on the ice at the same time, the usual line-up being a goalminder, two defence men and three forwards. Substitute players are used because of the fast tempo and much of a team's tactical skill depends on determining the right moments for alternating fresh and tired players. Leading teams normally carry at least twelve players, including a complete alternative forward trio. A goalminder is not usually changed during a match unless he is injured.

At the beginning of each period and after a goal has been scored play is commenced by a "face-off", the referee dropping the puck in the centre of the rink between the two opposing centre forwards. The puck remains in play when it hits the barrier and only becomes "dead" if hit over the barrier or when the whistle blows for an infringement, when a face-off is made, so far as possible, where a misplay originated.

A player may stop the puck with his hand, body or skate at any time, but may only push the puck forward with his skate or stick. He may kick the puck, but cannot score direct from a kick.

Goal judges, stationed behind each goal, signal when a goal has been scored by switching on a red light behind the goal concerned. The goals are six feet wide and four feet high. The puck weighs approximately five and a half ounces, is disc shaped—one inch thick and three inches in diameter—and made of solid vulcanised rubber.

The ideal size of an ice hockey rink is two hundred feet long by eighty-five feet wide, slightly rounded at each corner, with a narrow area behind each goal on which the puck can still be in play, so that players can actually skate with the puck behind the goal net.

The playing area is divided into three equal zones, known to each side as defence, neutral and attacking zones, and these are distinguished by blue lines marked on the ice. A centre line is marked in red.

Only three players are permitted in their own defence zone when the puck is outside that zone. A player may only enter his attacking zone in line with or behind the puck or puck carrier. He may not take a pass from a team-mate who is in another zone at the moment of passing.

For serious infringements a player is sent off the ice for one, two or more minutes and no substitute may take his place while he serves his suspension time in a special penalty box provided for the purpose. Offences which can be thus penalised include charging, elbowing, body-checking (pushing an opponent deliberately on to the barrier boards), high sticks and deliberately hitting out of the rink or falling on the puck (excepting the goalminder in the latter instance).

Ice hockey clothing is specially designed to suit the sport's protective requirements. Players wear knee-pads, shin-guards, hip-guards, elbow-guards and shoulder-guards, thick gauntlet gloves, long stockings which fit over the knee-pads, a special type of shorts which lace up in the front and sweaters in team colours.

The sticks, made entirely of wood, are limited to 53 inches handle and 14½ inches blade, except that of the goal-minder, who may use a heavier and wider stick, but his leg pads are restricted to 10 inches in width. The hockey skate blade is straight and narrow, with a plain pointed end in front instead of the figure skate toe-rake.

Bibliography: *Ice Hockey* ("Doc" Brodrick), *Ice Hockey* (Robert Giddens), *Let's Play Hockey* (Lynn Patrick and Leo Monahan), *This Skating Age* (Howard Bass), *The Skater and Skier* magazine.

Judo

Compiled by **A. R. Menzies**
Editor: Judo

JUDO QUIZ

1. In which year was the founder of Judo born?

*

2. Who presented the Inter-University Challenge Cup?

*

3. How many times has a Welsh University won the Inter-University Challenge Cup?

*

4. What is a judoka and a judogi?

*

5. Who, apart from the Japanese, holds the highest Judo grade?

*

QUIZ ANSWERS

1. 1860. 2. The Japan Society of Great Britain. 3. None. 4. A Judoka is a person who practises Judo and a Judogi is the outfit worn. 5. T. P. Leggett 6th Dan, a member of the Budokwai.

JUDO

Judo, as it is practised today, in this country and throughout the world, was originated by Dr. Jigoro Kano, who was born in 1860, in the province of Settsu, in Japan.

Dr. Kano moved to Tokyo in 1870, and graduated from the Imperial University in 1881. Feeling the need for greater physical activity, he attended several ju-jitsu schools and, after a scientific examination of the techniques and guiding principles of each, he welded the best into one system called Judo. In February 1882 he founded his own school, The Kodokan, which since that date has become so popular as the headquarters of world judo that a new building costing 270 million yen was opened in 1958. Some 1,000 persons, including 100 women and 100 foreigners, practise daily.

Judo was first introduced into Britain in the early part of this century by visiting exponents of the art. Many of these became very well known for their displays in the music halls of the day. Foremost amongst these was Yukio Tani, who became the first instructor to The Budokwai, the premier British Judo Club, founded in 1918 by Gunji Koizumi.

Judo in Britain owes its present-day popularity to the untiring efforts of Mr. Koizumi who, although now 80 years old, is still extremely active in the sport. In 1948 the British Judo Association was formed, and at the present time represents some 300 judo clubs, with a total membership of approximately 10,000. In the same year the European Judo Union, representing the Judo Associations of Europe, was inaugurated and officially recognised by The Kodokan.

The degree of efficiency in judo is indicated by the wearing of a coloured belt. The grades these colours denote are divided into two parts, pupil or kyu grades, and master or dan grades. Pupil grades run from 6th kyu to 1st kyu, and master grades from 1st Dan to 10th Dan, as follows:

White	6th kyu
Yellow	5th "
Orange	4th "
Green	3rd "
Blue	2nd "
Brown	1st "

Black 1st, 2nd, 3rd, 4th and 5th Dan
Red & White 6th, 7th and 8th Dan.
Red 9th and 10th Dan

although it is common for all Dan grades to wear a black belt, the coloured belts only being worn on ceremonial occasions.

In 1955 *Judo*, the National Magazine for this sport, was established, and now enjoys a world-wide reputation as the only magazine in the English language on sale to the public.

Information: For all information regarding judo in Great Britain and abroad write to:

The General Secretary, British

Risei Kano, son of Jigoro Kano and President of the Kodokan

Judo Association, 68–70 Chandos House, Palmer Street, London, S.W.1. *ABBEY* 6697.

Judo Limited, 91 Wellesley Road, Croydon, Surrey. *CROYDON* 0200.

CUP COMPETITIONS

THE BARON MATSUI INTER-CLUB CHALLENGE CUP

Presented by H.E. Baron Matsui, the Japanese Ambassador, 1927.

1928	Metropolitan Association Club
1929	The Budokwai
1930	Ealing s/c Judo Club
1931	The Budokwai
1932	Metropolitan Police
1933	Oxford University
1934	The Budokwai
1935	The Budokwai
1936	M.P.A.A. Wrestling Section
1937	Cambridge University
1938	Metropolitan Police
1939	Metropolitan Police
1950	The Budokwai
1951	G.E.C.
1952	The Budokwai
1953	No competition
1954	Tora Judokwai Coventry
1955	Swansea Judo Club
1956	East London Judo Club
1957	North London Judo Club
1958	No competition

THE INTER-UNIVERSITY CHALLENGE CUP

Presented to the Budokwai by the Japan Society, London, in memory of Yukio Tani (1881–1950) who first brought jujitsu to Europe, and who was the first instructor to the Budokwai.

1950–51	Manchester
1951–52	Leeds
1952–53	No competition
1953–54	Aberdeen
1954–55	No competition
1955–56	Leeds
1956–57	Leeds
1957–58	Leeds
1958–59	Glasgow

Kyuzo Mifune (10th Dan), reputed to be the greatest living exponent of judo

THE GOLDBERG-VASS MEMORIAL TROPHY

Instituted by the London Judo Society in 1955, in memory of two club members accidentally drowned.

1956	A. Petherbridge
1957	D. Young
1958	J. Gowland
1959	B. Burns

CHAMPIONSHIPS

BRITISH JUDO ASSOCIATION NATIONAL AREA CHAMPIONSHIPS

1956	Welsh Area
1957	London Area
1958	Midland Area
1959	Southern Area

EUROPEAN CHAMPIONSHIPS

1951	France
1952	France
1953	Holland
1954	France
1955	France
1956	No championships
1957	Great Britain
1958	Great Britain
1959	Great Britain

ALL-JAPAN CHAMPIONSHIPS

1948	Matsumoto (6th Dan)
1949	Ishikawa (6th Dan) & Kimura (7th Dan). Held jointly
1950	Ishikawa (7th Dan)
1951	Daigo (6th Dan)
1952	Yoshimatsu (6th Dan)
1953	Yoshimatsu (6th Dan)
1954	Daigo (6th Dan)
1955	Yoshimatsu (7th Dan)
1956	No championship
1957	Natsui (6th Dan)
1958	Sone (5th Dan)
1959	Inokuma (4th Dan)

TOKYO CHAMPIONSHIPS

1953	Osawa (6th Dan)
1954	Ishibashi (5th Dan)
1955	Ishibashi (5th Dan)
1956	Ikeda (5th Dan)
1957	Matsushita (4th Dan)
1958	Sone (5th Dan)
1959	Watanabe (5th Dan) & Kaminaga (5th Dan). Held jointly.

WORLD CHAMPIONSHIPS (BIENNIAL)

1956	Natsui (6th Dan)
1958	Sone (5th Dan)

Gunji Koizumi, founder of The Budokwai, has Ian Morris in difficulties on a formal demonstration

JUDO QUIZ

1. What is the name of the oldest-established Judo Club in Great Britain?

★

2. In 1948 two important Associations were founded. What were they?

★

3. In which country did Judo originate?

★

4. What was the name of the founder of Judo?

★

5. Which country has created a record in the European Championships?

★

6. Who won three major championships in 1958?

★

7. What is the name of the ruling authority in this country recognised by the Kodokan?

QUIZ ANSWERS

1. The Budokwai, London. 2. The British Judo Association and The European Judo Union. 3. Japan. 4. Jigoro Kano. 5. Great Britain by winning the European Championships three times running. 6. K. Sone, 5th Dan; he won Tokyo Championships, All Japan Championships, and World Championships, during 1958. 7. British Judo Association.

Compiled by **J. W. R. Taylor**

Assistant Compiler:
Jane's All The World's Aircraft

King's Cup

KING'S CUP AIR RACE A BRIEF HISTORY

In 1922 H. M. King George V presented a Cup to the Royal Aero Club, as the prize for a contest to encourage progress in British aircraft design. The conditions for the contest have changed throughout the years; the only permanent requirement being that the competitors and their aircraft must be British, a term which includes the Commonwealth.

The first race was won by Capt. F. L. Barnard of Instone Air Lines in a D.H.4A at a speed of 124 m.p.h., and the contest proved so popular that it became an annual event. King George V gave a new Cup each year until he died in 1936, after which one Cup was given by King Edward VIII and two by King George VI. The likelihood of war prevented the organisation of a race in 1939. There were no races during World War II and the contest was not resumed until 1949, when King George VI provided the present Cup, which is held by the winner for one year only. The only break since then has been in 1951, when the event was abandoned because of bad weather.

Whether or not the original object of the contest has been attained is doubtful. It was won in the first year by a modification of a World War I bomber design and many recent winners were designed in the 1930s, which hardly seems to indicate any steady progress in the development of aircraft entered for the King's Cup air races. But this does not necessarily detract from the excitement of the races themselves.

KING'S CUP AIR RACE RESULTS

Year	No. of Starters	Length of Course in Miles	Winner	Aircraft (Engine)	Speed m.p.h.
1922	21	810	F. L. Barnard	de Havilland D.H.4A (350 h.p. Rolls-Royce Eagle)	124
1923	15	794	F. T. Courtney	Armstrong Whitworth Siskin (325 h.p. Armstrong Siddeley Jaguar)	149
1924	10	950	Alan J. Cobham	de Havilland D.H.50 (230 h.p. Armstrong Siddeley Puma)	107
1925	14	1,608	F. L. Barnard	Armstrong Whitworth Siskin (395 h.p. Armstrong Siddeley Jaguar)	151
1926	14	1,464	H. S. Broad	de Havilland Moth (60 h.p. Cirrus I)	91
1927	16	540	W. L. Hope	de Havilland Moth (60 h.p. Cirrus I)	93
1928	36	1,097	W. L. Hope	de Havilland Moth (85 h.p. D.H. Gipsy)	101
1929	41	1,170	R. L. R. Atcherley	Gloster Grebe (385 h.p. Armstrong Siddeley Jaguar)	150
1930	88	750	Miss Winifred Brown	Avro Avian (95 h.p. Cirrus III)	103
1931	40	983	E. C. T. Edwards	Blackburn Bluebird (115 h.p. Cirrus Hermes II)	118
1932	42	1,223	W. L. Hope	D.H. Fox Moth (120 h.p. D.H. Gipsy III)	124
1933	42	831	Capt. Geoffrey de Havilland	D.H. Leopard Moth (130 h.p. D.H. Gipsy Major)	140
1934	43	801	H. M. Schofield	Monospar ST-10 (two 90 h.p. Pobjoy Niagara)	134

Year	No. of Starters	Length of Course in Miles	Winner	Aircraft (Engine)	Speed m.p.h.
1935	29	1,303	T. Rose	Miles Falcon-Six (200 h.p. D.H. Gipsy Six)	176
1936	26	1,536	C. E. Gardner	Percival Vega Gull (210 h.p. D.H. Gipsy Six)	164
1937	27	1,443	C. E. Gardner	Percival Mew Gull (210 h.p. D.H. Gipsy Six)	234
1938	19	1,102	Alex Henshaw	Percival Mew Gull (210 h.p. D.H. Gipsy Six)	236
1949	36	60	J. N. Somers	Miles Gemini (two 130 h.p. D.H. Gipsy Major)	164
1950	36	186	E. Day	Miles Hawk Trainer (130 h.p. D.H. Gipsy Major)	139
1952	12	131	C. Gregory	Taylorcraft Plus (90 h.p. Cirrus Minor)	114
1953	11	60	W. P. I. Fillingham	D.H. Chipmunk (140 h.p. D.H. Gipsy Major)	140
1954	15	68	H. Wood	Miles Messenger (145 h.p. Cirrus Major)	133
1955	15	68	P. Clifford	Percival Mew Gull (210 h.p. D.H. Gipsy Six)	213

The Miles Sparrowjet, in which F. Dunkerley won in 1957

Year	No. of Starters	Length of Course in Miles	Winner	Aircraft (Engine)	Speed m.p.h.
1956	16	68	J. H. Denyer	Auster J/1N Alpha (130 h.p. D.H. Gipsy Major)	124
1957	35	112	F. Dunkerley	Miles Sparrowjet (two 330 lb. s.t. Turbomeca Palas)	228
1958	21	79.4	J. H. Denyer	D.H. Tiger Moth (130 h.p. D.H. Gipsy Major)	118
1959	21	72	A. J. Spiller	Percival Proctor 3 (208 h.p. D.H. Gipsy Queen)	143

Lacrosse

Compiled by **G. Wilkinson**

Editor: Lacrosse News

LACROSSE QUIZ

1. Which club has won most major trophies?

*

2. Which was the first lacrosse club formed in Great Britain?

*

3. What is the minimum length of a lacrosse stick?

*

4. What is the size of a lacrosse pitch?

*

5. What is the longest recorded distance that a lacrosse ball has been thrown with a lacrosse stick?

*

6. When was the English Lacrosse Union founded?

QUIZ ANSWERS

1. Stockport: Iroquois Cup 15 times: Northern Senior Flags 16 times: Northern League 16 times. 2. Glasgow, founded 1867. 3. 3 feet. 4. There are no boundaries, but the goals are between 90 yards and 100 yards apart. There must be at least 10 yards playing area behind each goal. 5. 162 yards, 2 feet, 7½ inches by B. Quin of Ottawa. 6. 1892.

Oxford University goal-keeper and point (*dark shirts*) try to intercept a shot by a Hampstead attack player

LACROSSE

Although the actual origin of the game of lacrosse is unknown, there is no doubt that the game, in a primitive form, called "baggataway", was well established amongst the American Indians by the 17th century. Whole tribes played against each other. There were no rules, and so limbs and even life suffered.

During the 18th century, English and French troops, and settlers in North America began to take an interest. The French gave the name "La Crosse" to the stick used by the Indians because of its resemblance to a bishop's crosier.

In 1839, the first non-Indian club was formed, but it was not until 1867 that this same club, the Montreal Lacrosse Club, drew up the first set of rules for the game. Shortly afterwards it organised a convention for all interested in the sport, which was now growing in popularity in other Canadian towns. The outcome was the formation of the National Lacrosse Association of Canada—the first organisation for the control of lacrosse in its modern form.

During that same year, 1867, a party of Caughnawaga Indians played a series of games in the United Kingdom and France, and the first British club was founded in Glasgow. A rapid development of the sport around Glasgow, Liverpool and London and in Ireland took place during the next decade. The first territorial match recorded, North of England v. South of England, took place in 1877. The formation of the Northern and Southern Lacrosse Associations shortly afterwards was the logical conclusion of playing in localised areas.

Although international matches between the home countries commenced in 1875, the English Lacrosse Union was not founded until 1892. The Union, formed from the Northern and Southern Associations, assumed control over international lacrosse matters and over the Laws of Lacrosse, but the constituent associations retained responsibility for the organisation of lacrosse in their respective areas.

The laws were gradually modified so that essential outstanding features of the Indian game were retained amidst a code of behaviour designed to make the game more civilised and safe.

At the turn of the century, transatlantic tours became a regular feature. The game spread to South-West England and to South Wales, and in 1903, the first Oxford v. Cambridge match was played. The game progressed well in England, but it began to fall in standard in Scotland and Ireland until the first world war, during which all competitive lacrosse ceased.

After the war, the game was revived in England, where it has been spreading ever since, but Scotland and Ireland did not recommence to play.

Lacrosse has changed its form comparatively little over the last forty years, maintaining particularly the strong spirit of amateurism which pervades all players and administrators of the English game.

INTERNATIONAL MATCHES

The winning team is given first, not the home team.

ENGLAND v. SCOTLAND

1875	Scotland	4	England	3
1877	Scotland	1	England	1

ENGLAND v. IRELAND

1881	Ireland	7	England	4
1882	Ireland	4	England	3
1883	Ireland	12	England	6
1884	Ireland	4	England	0
1885	Ireland	6	England	0
1886	Ireland	5	England	4
1887	Ireland	10	England	1
1888	England	7	Ireland	3
1889	Ireland	5	England	4
1890	England	6	Ireland	2
1891	Ireland	12	England	0
1892	Ireland	5	England	2
1893	Ireland	6	England	3
1894	Ireland	5	England	5
1895	Ireland	9	England	2
1896	England	5	Ireland	6
1897	England	8	Ireland	1
1898	England	11	Ireland	4
1899	England	8	Ireland	1
1900	No Match			
1901	England	14	Ireland	6
1902	England	10	Ireland	6
1903	England	17	Ireland	8

(Summary: Played 22; Ireland won 12; England won 9; Drawn 1.)

ENGLAND v. WALES

1907	England	18	Wales	2
1908	England	18	Wales	4
1909	England	15	Wales	4

(Summary: Played 3; England won 3.)

U.K. v. AMERICA and CANADA

1883	Canada	12	U.K.	1
1884	U.K.	5	America	3
1884	America	2	England	0
1885	America	3	Ireland	2
1908	Canada	14	U.K.	10

(At London Olympic Games.)

1928	Canada	9	England	5

(At Amsterdam Olympic Games.)

1928	England	7	America	6

(At Amsterdam Olympic Games.)

1937	America	12	England	8
	America	10	England	5

NORTH OF ENGLAND v. SOUTH OF ENGLAND

1877	South	2	North	2
1882	North	2	South	0
1883	North	4	South	3
1884	North	9	South	2
1885	North	9	South	5
1886	South	4	North	1
1887	North	7	South	2
1888	North	12	South	1
1889	South	6	North	5
1890	North	13	South	2
1891	South	11	North	9
1892	North	6	South	1
1893	North	7	South	4

Year				
1894	North	10	South	7
1895	North	8	South	4
1896	North	10	South	1
1897	North	11	South	7
1898	North	13	South	2
1899	North	14	South	3
1900	North	6	South	4
1901	North	7	South	4
1902	South	8	North	4
1903	North	11	South	5
1904	North	4	South	3
1905	North	8	South	4
1906	North	9	South	5
1907	North	15	South	4
1908	South	9	North	9
1909	North	9	South	4
1910	North	13	South	4
1911	North	16	South	7
1912	North	16	South	7
1913	North	7	South	4
1914	North	20	South	5
1915–1920	No game			
1921	North	12	South	4
1922	North	11	South	8
1923	North	11	South	9
1924	North	19	South	6
1925	North	15	South	7
1926	North	10	South	5
1927	North	26	South	2
1928	North	13	South	5
1929	North	14	South	1
1930	North	14	South	1
1931	North	16	South	9
1932	North	22	South	1
1933	North	10	South	3
1934	North	14	South	9
1935	North	10	South	4
1936	North	19	South	8
1937	North	16	South	5
1938	North	14	South	6
1939	North	12	South	5
1940–1946	No game			
1947	North	16	South	8
1948	North	17	South	1
1949	South	9	North	9
1950	North	18	South	4
1951	North	17	South	6
1952	North	17	South	3
1953	North	17	South	4
1954	North	19	South	5
1955	North	12	South	6
1956	North	15	South	3
1957	North	12	South	1
1958	North	18	South	1
1959	North	12	South	4

(Summary: Played 66; North won 59; South won 4; Drawn 3.)

OXFORD UNIVERSITY v. CAMBRIDGE UNIVERSITY

Year				
1903	Cambridge	19	Oxford	6
1904	Cambridge	10	Oxford	4
1905	Cambridge	14	Oxford	3
1906	Cambridge	10	Oxford	3
1907	Oxford	13	Cambridge	9
1908	Oxford	10	Cambridge	5
1909	Cambridge	8	Oxford	6
1910	Cambridge	9	Oxford	6
1911	Cambridge	8	Oxford	3
1912	Oxford	9	Cambridge	4
1913	Oxford	13	Cambridge	4
1914	Oxford	15	Cambridge	1
1915–1920	No game			
1921	Oxford	13	Cambridge	2
1922	Oxford	13	Cambridge	4
1923	Oxford	18	Cambridge	3
1924	Cambridge	6	Oxford	6
1925	Oxford	10	Cambridge	4
1926	Oxford	17	Cambridge	8
1927	Oxford	7	Cambridge	6
1928	Oxford	10	Cambridge	3
1929	Oxford	15	Cambridge	2
1930	Oxford	6	Cambridge	2
1931	Oxford	10	Cambridge	3
1932	Oxford	19	Cambridge	8
1933	Oxford	16	Cambridge	3
1934	Cambridge	7	Oxford	6
1935	Cambridge	10	Oxford	6
1936	Oxford	6	Cambridge	5
1937	Oxford	5	Cambridge	5
1938	Cambridge	7	Oxford	3
1939	Cambridge	7	Oxford	5
1940–1947	No game			
1948	Cambridge	14	Oxford	3
1949	Cambridge	5	Oxford	2
1950	Cambridge	7	Oxford	3
1951	Oxford	6	Cambridge	5
1952	Cambridge	7	Oxford	3
1953	Cambridge	12	Oxford	10
1954	Cambridge	11	Oxford	6
1955	Cambridge	25	Oxford	4
1956	Cambridge	17	Oxford	2
1957	Cambridge	17	Oxford	5
1958	Oxford	8	Cambridge	4
1959	Cambridge	8	Oxford	6

(Summary: Played 43; Cambridge won 21; Oxford won 20; Drawn 2.)

THE IROQUOIS CUP WINNERS
(The English Club Championship)

Year	Winner	Year	Winner
1890	South Manchester	1927	Heaton Mersey
1895	South Manchester	1928	Stockport
1896	Surbiton	1929	Boardman
1897	Stockport	1930	Old Mancunians
1898	Stockport	1931	Oxford University
1899	Stockport	1932	Old Hulmeians
1900	Stockport	1933	South Manchester
1901	Stockport	1934	Stockport
1902	No game	1935	Mellor
1903	Stockport	1936	Mellor
1904	South Manchester	1937	Mellor
1905	Stockport	1938	Old Waconians
1906	South Manchester	1939	Old Waconians
1907	Old Hulmeians	1940–1946	No game
1908	Old Hulmeians	1947	Old Waconians
1909	South Manchester	1948	Mellor
1910	Old Hulmeians	1949	Old Hulmeians
1911	Stockport	1950	Old Hulmeians
1912	Stockport	1951	Old Waconians
1913	Stockport	1952	Old Waconians
1914	Old Hulmeians	1953	Old Waconians
1915–1920	No game	1954	Heaton Mersey
1921	Lee	1955	Old Waconians
1922	Boardman	1956	Cambridge University
1923	Stockport	1957	Old Mancunians
1924	Stockport	1958	Heaton Mersey
1925	Albert Park	1959	Heaton Mersey
1926	Stockport		

(Summary: Played 52; Stockport won 15; Old Hulmeians won 7; Old Waconians won 7.)

NORTH OF ENGLAND LEAGUE CHAMPIONSHIP WINNERS

Year	Winner	Year	Winner
1895–96	Cheetham	1926–27	Old Mancunians
1896–97	Stockport	1927–28	Old Hulmeians
1897–98	Stockport	1928–29	Stockport
1898–99	Albert Park	1929–30	Old Mancunians
1899–1900	Stockport	1930–31	Old Hulmeians
1900–01	Stockport	1931–32	Old Hulmeians
1901–02	Stockport	1932–33	Old Hulmeians
1902–03	Stockport	1933–34	Stockport
1903–04	South Manchester	1934–35	Mellor
1904–05	Heaton Mersey	1935–36	Mellor
1905–06	South Manchester	1936–37	Mellor
1906–07	South Manchester	1937–38	Boardman & Eccles
1907–08	South Manchester	1938–39	Boardman & Eccles
1908–09	Stockport	1939–1946	No competition
1909–10	South Manchester	1946–47	Old Waconians
1910–11	Stockport	1947–48	Old Waconians
1911–12	Stockport	1948–49	Old Waconians
1912–13	Old Hulmeians	1949–50	Mellor
1913–14	Old Hulmeians	1950–51	Old Hulmeians
1914–1919	No competition	1951–52	Old Hulmeians
1919–20	South Manchester	1952–53	Old Hulmeians
1920–21	South Manchester	1953–54	Heaton Mersey
1921–22	Boardman	1954–55	Old Maacunians
1922–23	Stockport	1955–56	Old Hulmeians
1923–24	Stockport	1956–57	Old Hulmeians
1924–25	Stockport	1957–58	Old Hulmeians
1925–26	Stockport	1958–59	Heaton Mersey

(Summary: Played 52; Stockport won 16; Old Hulmeians won 12.)

SOUTH OF ENGLAND LEAGUE CHAMPIONSHIP WINNERS

Year	Winner	Year	Winner
1936–37	Willoughby	1950–51	Oxford University
1937–38	Willoughby	1951–52	Purley
1938–39	Hampstead	1952–53	Purley
1939–1946	No competition	1953–54	Purley
1946–47	Hampstead	1954–55	Hampstead
1947–48	Cambridge University	1955–56	Purley
1948–49	Cambridge University	1956–57	Kenton
1949–50	Cambridge University	1957–58	Kenton
		1958–59	Kenton

(Summary: Played 16; Purley won 4; Cambridge University, Hampstead and Kenton won 3 each.)

NORTH OF ENGLAND SENIOR FLAG FINAL WINNERS

Year	Winner	Year	Winner
1885	Liverpool	1922	Boardman
1886	South Manchester	1923	Old Hulmeians
1887	Owens College	1924	South Manchester
1888	Owens College	1925	Albert Park
1889	South Manchester	1926	Stockport
1890	South Manchester	1927	Heaton Mersey
1891	South Manchester	1928	Stockport
1892	South Manchester	1929	Boardman
1893	Cheetham	1930	Old Mancunians
1894	Cheetham	1931	Stockport
1895	South Manchester	1932	Old Hulmeians
1896	Stockport	1933	South Manchester & Wythenshawe
1897	Stockport		
1898	Stockport	1934	Stockport
1899	Stockport	1935	Mellor
1900	Stockport	1936	Mellor
1901	Stockport	1937	Mellor
1902	Stockport	1938	Old Waconians
1903	Stockport	1939	Old Waconians
1904	South Manchester	1940–1946	No competition
1905	Stockport	1947	Old Waconians
1906	South Manchester	1948	Mellor
1907	Old Hulmeians	1949	Old Hulmeians
1908	Old Hulmeians	1950	Old Hulmeians
1909	South Manchester	1951	Old Waconians
1910	Old Hulmeians	1952	Old Waconians
1911	Stockport	1953	Old Waconians
1912	Stockport	1954	Heaton Mersey
1913	Stockport	1955	Old Waconians
1914	Old Hulmeians	1956	Old Hulmeians
1915–1919	No competition	1957	Old Mancunians
1920	South Manchester	1958	Heaton Mersey
1921	Boardman	1959	Heaton Mersey

(Summary: Played 63; Stockport won 16; South Manchester won 12; Old Hulmeians won 9; Old Waconians won 7.)

SOUTH OF ENGLAND SENIOR FLAG FINAL WINNERS

Year	Winner	Year	Winner
1884	London	1922	Lee
1885	Leys School	1923	Oxford University
1886	Cambridge University	1924	Hampstead
1887	Clapton	1925	Buckhurst Hill
1888	Leys School	1926	Buckhurst Hill
1889	Clapton	1927	Oxford University
1890	West London	1928	Oxford University
1891	Clapton	1929	Lee
1892	Clapton	1930	Oxford University
1893	West London	1931	Oxford University
1894	Snaresbrook	1932	Oxford University
1895	Snaresbrook	1933	Oxford University
1896	Surbiton	1934	Cambridge University
1897	West London	1935	Cambridge University
1898	Surbiton	1936	Surbiton
1899	West London	1937	Hampstead
1900	Woodford	1938	Willoughby
1901	Woodford	1939	Hampstead
1902	Woodford	1940–1946	No competition
1903	Woodford	1947	Hampstead
1904	Catford	1948	Cambridge University
1905	Surbiton	1949	Cambridge University
1906	Surbiton	1950	Cambridge University
1907	Surbiton	1951	Oxford University
1908	Surbiton	1952	Purley
1909	Catford	1953	Purley
1910	Catford	1954	Cambridge University
1911	Lee	1955	Cambridge University
1912	Lee	1956	Cambridge University
1913	Lee	1957	Cambridge University
1914	Lee	1958	Oxford University
1915–1920	No competition	1959	Cambridge University
1921	Lee		

(Summary: Played 63; Cambridge University won 11; Oxford University won 9; Lee and Surbiton won 7 each.)

LACROSSE QUIZ

1. Which is the largest lacrosse club in England?

★

2. What is the name of the first lacrosse club to be founded in the U.S.A.?

★

3. When did the current English "Laws of Lacrosse" come into force?

★

4. What was the original Indian name for "Lacrosse"?

QUIZ ANSWERS

1. The Centurion Lacrosse Club with nearly 200 members. 2. The Mohawk Club of Troy, New York, founded 1868. 3. 1st September 1958. 4. Baggataway.

An unorthodox flying defensive leap is made by an Oxford University lacrosse player during a match at Oxford

Lawn Tennis

Compiled by **Lance Tingay**

Lawn Tennis Correspondent
of the Daily Telegraph

TENNIS QUIZ

1. What is the greatest number of games played in a Davis Cup tie?

2. Who was known as "Poker Face"?

3. Who was "Big Bill"?

4. Who was "Little Bill"?

5. Who was "The Ghost"?

6. Who was "The Bounding Basque"? (*Above*.)

7. Who was the youngest men's singles champion at Wimbledon?

8. Who was the oldest men's singles champion at Wimbledon?

9. When, and between what nations, was the first Davis Cup tie?

10. What nations have won the Davis Cup?

QUIZ ANSWERS

1. 270 in the challenge round U.S.A. v. Australia at Brisbane in December 1958. 2. Miss Helen Wills, later Mrs. F. S. Moody. 3. William Tatem Tilden (U.S.A.). 4. William M. Johnston (U.S.A.). 5. H. S. Mahony, Irish winner at Wimbledon in 1896, because of his frail appearance. 6. Jean Borotra. 7. Wilfred Baddeley, who was 19 years 5 months 23 days old when he won on July 4th 1891. 8. Arthur Wentworth Gore, who was 41 years 6 months when he won for the third time in July 1909. 9. The British Isles and the United States in August 1900 at the Longwood Cricket Club, Boston. 10. Only the United States, Great Britain, France and Australia.

HISTORY

The invention of the game of lawn tennis, which is derived mainly from the very old game of tennis, or court tennis or royal tennis or real tennis as it is sometimes called, and partly from rackets and badminton, is usually attributed to Major Walter Clopton Wingfield who, in 1874, patented his game of "Sphairistike". It quickly replaced croquet as a country-house pastime. Major Wingfield's efforts undoubtedly did much to boost the new game even though his own rules were discarded almost as soon as they were made. The M.C.C. had a hand in framing the first generally accepted rules but the real codification of the game was not until the All England Croquet and Lawn Tennis Club, as it was then called, staged the first tournament in 1877. The rules they decided upon then have remained the rules of lawn tennis without basic change.

The M.C.C. gradually dropped out of the picture and the ruling body of the game became the All England Club until the formation of the Lawn Tennis Association in 1888. The United States L.T.A. was formed as early as 1881. What is now a world-wide game is governed by the International Lawn Tennis Federation, formed just before the First World War. Lawn tennis has, in fact, become the most international of all games.

Wimbledon has maintained its importance as the outstanding individual championship. The outstanding team event, however, is the contest for the Davis Cup.

THE DAVIS CUP

The history of the Davis Cup, more properly the International Lawn Tennis Championship, is one of steady growth and interest since its inception as a challenge match between the United States and Great Britain in 1900. It has always been played to the same pattern, two singles players each opposing one another, making a total of four singles, and a doubles contest. A team may accordingly consist of only two players or as many as four.

It is run on a challenge basis, the winner standing out of the next year's competition until the challengers, by playing off among themselves, have eliminated all but the qualifier for the challenge round. To make the eliminating rounds simpler zoning was introduced in 1923 and there are now three zones, the European, the American and the Eastern.

The governing body of the Davis Cup is only indirectly the International Lawn Tennis Federation. The competition is administered by a committee of Davis Cup nations.

A total of 56 nations has made challenge, though one of them, Peru, never actually put a team into court. Newcomers for the 1959 competition were Korea, Iran and Colombia. By the end of 1958 Great Britain had played 106 Davis Cup ties, the U.S.A. 119, Australia 98 and France 97. By the same time 850 ties had been played in all.

Individually the largest number of Davis Cup rubbers was, by the end of 1958, played by Baron G. Von Cramm who turned out 102 times for Germany between 1932 and 1953 in 37 ties.

Winners

In 1901 and 1910 the holder retained the trophy by default, no challenge being taken to the court. From 1915 to 1918 and from 1940 to 1945 there was no competition.

1900–02	U.S.A.
1903–04–05–06	British Isles*
1907–08–09–11	Australasia†
1912	British Isles
1913	U.S.A.
1914	Australasia
1919	Australasia
1920–21–22–23–24–25–26	U.S.A.
1927–28–29–30–31–32	France
1933–34–35–36	Great Britain
1937–38	U.S.A.
1939	Australia
1946–47–48–49	U.S.A.
1950–51–52–53	Australia
1954	U.S.A.
1955–56–57	Australia
1958	U.S.A.
1959	Australia

* Included Ireland up to 1922.
† Included New Zealand up to 1923.

G. Von Cramm

M. A. Trabert

R. L. Riggs

Challenge Round Results

1900 *Boston.* U.S.A. *bt* British Isles 3–0.
1902 *New York.* U.S.A. *bt* British Isles 3–2.
1903 *Boston.* British Isles *bt* U.S.A. 4–1.
1904 *Wimbledon.* British Isles *bt* Belgium 5–0.
1905 *Wimbledon.* British Isles *bt* U.S.A. 5–0.
1906 *Wimbledon.* British Isles *bt* U.S.A. 5–0.
1907 *Wimbledon.* Australasia *bt* British Isles 3–2.
1908 *Melbourne.* Australasia *bt* U.S.A. 3–2.
1909 *Sydney.* Australasia *bt* U.S.A. 5–0.
1911 *Christchurch,* N.Z. Australasia *bt* U.S.A. 5–0.
1912 *Melbourne.* British Isles *bt* Australasia 3–2.
1913 *Wimbledon.* U.S.A. *bt* British Isles 3–2.
1914 *New York.* Australasia *bt* U.S.A. 3–2.
1919 *Sydney.* Australasia *bt* British Isles 4–1.
1920 *Auckland,* N.Z. U.S.A. *bt* Australasia 5–0.
1921 *New York.* U.S.A. *bt* Japan 5–0.
1922 *New York.* U.S.A. *bt* Australasia 4–1.
1923 *New York.* U.S.A. *bt* Australasia 4–1.
1924 *Philadelphia.* U.S.A. *bt* Australia 5–0.
1925 *Philadelphia.* U.S.A. *bt* France 5–0.
1926 *Philadelphia.* U.S.A. *bt* France 4–1.
1927 *Philadelphia.* France *bt* U.S.A. 3–2.
1928 *Paris.* France *bt* U.S.A. 4–1.
1929 *Paris.* France *bt* U.S.A. 3–2.
1930 *Paris.* France *bt* U.S.A. 4–1.
1931 *Paris.* France *bt* Gt. Britain 3–2.
1932 *Paris.* France *bt* U.S.A. 3–2.
1933 *Paris.* Gt. Britain *bt* France 3–2.
1934 *Wimbledon.* Gt. Britain *bt* U.S.A. 4–1.
1935 *Wimbledon.* Gt. Britain *bt* U.S.A. 5–0.
1936 *Wimbledon.* Gt. Britain *bt* Australia 3–2.
1937 *Wimbledon.* U.S.A. *bt* Gt. Britain 4–1.
1938 *Philadelphia.* U.S.A. *bt* Australia 3–2.
1939 *Philadelphia.* Australia *bt* U.S.A. 3–2.
1946 *Melbourne.* U.S.A. *bt* Australia 5–0.
1947 *New York.* U.S.A. *bt* Australia 4–1.
1948 *New York.* U.S.A. *bt* Australia 5–0.
1949 *New York.* U.S.A. *bt* Australia 4–1.
1950 *New York.* Australia *bt* U.S.A. 4–1.
1951 *Sydney.* Australia *bt* U.S.A. 3–2.
1952 *Adelaide.* Australia *bt* U.S.A. 4–1.
1953 *Melbourne.* Australia *bt* U.S.A. 3–2.
1954 *Sydney.* U.S.A. *bt* Australia 3–2.
1955 *New York.* Australia *bt* U.S.A. 5–0.
1956 *Adelaide.* Australia *bt* U.S.A. 5–0.
1957 *Melbourne.* Australia *bt* U.S.A. 3–2.
1958 *Brisbane.* U.S.A. *bt* Australia 3–2.*
1959 *New York.* Australia *bt* U.S.A. 3–2.
First day. N. A. Fraser (Aus) *bt* A. Olmedo 8–6 6–8 6–4 8–6. R. Laver (Aus) *lost to* B. MacKay 5–7 4–6 1–6.
Second day. Fraser and R. Emerson (Aus) *bt* Olmedo and E. Buchholz 7–5 7–5 6–4.
Third day. Laver *lost to* Olmedo 7–9 6–4 8–10 10–12. Frazer *bt* MacKay 8–6 3–6 6–2 6–4.

*(NOTE. *The doubles match, with its total of 82 games, was the longest rubber played up to this time in the Davis Cup. Furthermore the total of 270 games for the whole tie was the greatest number played in the challenge or any other round.*

(*It is also of interest to record that 1939, when Australia beat the U.S.A. 3–2 in Philadelphia, was the only occasion the challenge round was won after the loss of the two opening matches.*)

The Penultimate Stages

The first victory of the British Isles in 1903 brought further challenges for the Davis Cup other than between Britain and the U.S.A. A play-off competition accordingly became necessary to decide the right of challenging the holders. The following are the results of the final tie before the challenge round.

1904 Belgium *bt* France 3–2
1905 U.S.A. *bt* Australasia 5–0
1906 U.S.A. *bt* Australasia 3–2
1907 Australasia *bt* U.S.A. 3–2
1908 U.S.A. *bt* British Isles 4–1
1909 U.S.A. *bt* British Isles 5–0
1910 *no contests*
1911 U.S.A. *bt* British Isles 4–1
1912 British Isles *walked over* U.S.A.
1913 U.S.A. *bt* Canada 3–0
1914 Australasia *bt* British Isles 3–0
1915–1918 *no contests*
1919 British Isles *bt* France 3–2
1920 U.S.A. *walked over* Holland
1921 Japan *bt* Australasia 4–1
1922 Australasia *bt* Spain 4–1

In 1923 the competition was divided into American and European zones, the winners playing off an inter-zone final to decide the challenger. In the following E.Z. indicates the European Zone final, A.Z. the American Zone final and I.Z.F. the Inter-Zone final.

1923 E.Z. France *bt* Spain 3–2
A.Z. Australia *bt* Japan 4–1
I.Z.F. Australia *bt* France 4–1
1924 E.Z. France *bt* Czechoslovakia 5–0
A.Z. Australia *bt* Japan 5–0
I.Z.F. Australia *bt* France 3–2
1925 E.Z. France *bt* Holland 4–0
A.Z. Australia *bt* Japan 4–1
I.Z.F. France *bt* Australia 3–1
1926 E.Z. France *bt* England 4–0
A.Z. Japan *bt* Cuba 5–0
I.Z.F. France *bt* Japan 3–2
1927 E.Z. France *bt* Denmark 3–0
A.Z. Japan *bt* Canada 3–2
I.Z.F. France *bt* Japan 3–0
1928 E.Z. Italy *bt* Czechoslovakia 3–2
I.Z.F. U.S.A. *bt* Italy 4–1
1929 E.Z. Germany *bt* Gt. Britain 3–2
A.Z. U.S.A. *bt* Cuba 5–0
I.Z.F. U.S.A. *bt* Germany 5–0
1930 E.Z. Italy *bt* Japan 3–2
A.Z. U.S.A. *bt* Mexico 5–0
I.Z.F. U.S.A. *bt* Italy 4–1
1931 E.Z. Gt. Britain *bt* Czechoslovakia 4–1
A.Z. U.S.A. *bt* Argentina 5–0
I.Z.F. Gt. Britain *bt* U.S.A. 3–2
1932 E.Z. Germany *bt* Italy 5–0
A.Z. U.S.A. *bt* Brazil 5–0
I.Z.F. U.S.A. *bt* Germany 3–2
1933 E.Z. Gt. Britain *bt* Australia 3–2
A.Z. U.S.A. *bt* Argentina 4–0
I.Z.F. Gt. Britain *bt* U.S.A. 4–1
1934 E.Z. Australia *bt* Czechoslovakia 3–2
A.Z. U.S.A. *bt* Mexico 5–0
I.Z.F. U.S.A. *bt* Australia 3–2
1935 E.Z. Germany *bt* Czechoslovakia 4–1
A.Z. U.S.A. *walked over* Brazil
I.Z.F. U.S.A. *bt* Germany 4–1
1936 E.Z. Germany *bt* Yugoslavia 3–0
A.Z. Australia *bt* U.S.A. 3–2
I.Z.F. Australia *bt* Germany 4–1
1937 E.Z. Germany *bt* Czechoslovakia 4–1
A.Z. U.S.A. *bt* Australia 5–0
I.Z.F. U.S.A. *bt* Germany 3–2
1938 E.Z. Germany *bt* Yugoslavia 3–2
A.Z. Australia *bt* Japan 3–2
I.Z.F. Australia *bt* Germany 5–0
1939 E.Z. Yugoslavia *bt* Germany 3–2
A.Z. Australia *bt* Cuba 5–0
I.Z.F. Australia *bt* Yugoslavia 4–1
1940–1945 *no contests*
1946 E.Z. Sweden *bt* Yugoslavia 3–2
A.Z. U.S.A. *bt* Mexico 5–0
I.Z.F. U.S.A. *bt* Sweden 5–0
1947 E.Z. Czechoslovakia *bt* Yugoslavia 4–0
A.Z. Australia *bt* Canada 5–0
I.Z.F. Australia *bt* Czechoslovakia 4–1
1948 E.Z. Czechoslovakia *bt* Sweden 4–1
A.Z. Australia *bt* Mexico 4–1
I.Z.F. Australia *bt* Czechoslovakia 3–2
1949 E.Z. Italy *bt* France 3–2
A.Z. Australia *bt* Mexico 5–0
I.Z.F. Australia *bt* Italy 5–0
1950 E.Z. Sweden *bt* Denmark 4–0
A.Z. Australia *bt* Mexico 4–1
I.Z.F. Australia *bt* Sweden 3–2
1951 E.Z. Sweden *bt* Germany 4–1
A.Z. U.S.A. *bt* Canada 5–0
I.Z.F. U.S.A. *bt* Sweden 5–0

W. T. Tilden, Wimbledon champion in 1920, 1921 and 1930.
Right: F. J. Perry, Wimbledon champion 1934–36.

1955 E.Z. Italy *bt* Sweden 5–0
A.Z. Australia *bt* Canada 5–0
Eas.Z. Japan *bt* Philippines 3–2
I.Z.F. Australia *bt* Japan 4–0
Australia *bt* Italy 5–0
1956 E.Z. Italy *bt* Sweden 5–0
A.Z. U.S.A. *bt* Mexico 4–1
Eas.Z. India *bt* Japan 3–2
I.Z.F. U.S.A. *bt* Italy 4–1
U.S.A. *bt* India 4–1
1957 E.Z. Belgium *bt* Italy 3–2
A.Z. U.S.A. *bt* Brazil 5–0
Eas.Z. Philippines *bt* Japan 3–2
I.Z.F. U.S.A. *bt* Philippines 5–0
U.S.A. *bt* Belgium 3–2

1958 European Zone Final: Italy *bt* Gt. Britain 4–1 at Milan.
(*Details:* N. Pietrangeli (I) *lost to* M. G. Davies 4–6 3–6 1–6; O. Sirola (I) *bt* W. A. Knight 6–3 7–5 6–3; Pietrangeli and Sirola *bt* Davies and Knight 6–3 5–7 6–4 4–6 9–7; Pietrangeli *bt* Knight 4–6 6–3 6–4 6–1; Sirola *bt* Davies 6–3 6–2 6–2.)

American Zone Final: U.S.A. *bt* Argentina 5–0 at Rye, N.Y.
(*Details:* B. MacKay (U.S.) *bt* E. Soriano 6–2 6–2 3–6 6–3; H. Richardson (U.S.) *bt* E. Morea 6–1 6–2 7–9 6–2; S. Giammalva and MacKay *bt* Morea and Soriano 6–3 6–2 6–2; Richardson *bt* Soriano 6–4 6–2 7–5; MacKay *bt* Morea 6–2 6–2 6–2.)

Eastern Zone Final: Philippines *bt* Ceylon 5–0 at Tokyo.
(*Details:* F. Ampon (P) *bt* B. Pinto 6–1 6–0 6–1; R. Deyro (P) *bt* R. Ferdinands 6–2 6–0 6–1; M. Dungo and J. Jose (P) *bt* Pinto and Ferdinands 6–1 6–0 6–4; Dungo *bt* R. Praesoody 6–2 6–3 7–5; Jose *bt* Ferdinands 6–1 6–4 6–3.)

Inter-Zone Final: Italy *bt* Philippines 5–0 at Sydney.

A. J. Mottram

R. K. Wilson

A. Olmedo

In 1952 an additional zone, the Eastern Zone, was created, necessitating two matches at the inter-zone stage. *E.Z.* indicates the European Zone, *Eas.Z.* the Eastern Zone, *A.Z.* the American Zone finals, and *I.Z.F.* the Inter-Zone finals.

1952 E.Z. Italy *bt* Belgium 3–1
A.Z. U.S.A. *bt* Canada 4–1
Eas.Z. India *walked over*
I.Z.F. Italy *bt* India 3–2
U.S.A. *bt* Italy 5–0
1953 E.Z. Belgium *bt* Denmark 3–2
A.Z. U.S.A. *bt* Canada 5–0
Eas.Z. India *walked over*
I.Z.F. Belgium *bt* India 5–0
U.S.A. *bt* Belgium 4–1
1954 E.Z. Sweden *bt* France 3–2
A.Z. U.S.A. *bt* Mexico 4–1
Eas.Z. *no challenge*
I.Z.F. U.S.A. *bt* Sweden 5–0

(*Details:* O. Sirola (I) *bt* R. Deyro 8–6 6–3 6–4; N. Pietrangeli (I) *bt* F. Ampon 6–2 6–2 7–5; Pietrangeli and Sirola *bt* M. Dungo and J. Jose 6–3 6–3 7–5; Pietrangeli *bt* Dungo 6–2 6–2 6–2; G. Merlo (I) *bt* Jose 6–2 7–5 6–1.)
U.S.A. *bt* Italy 5–0 at Perth.
(*Details:* A. Olmedo (U.S.) *bt* N. Pietrangeli 5–7 10–8 6–0 6–1; H. Richardson (U.S.) *bt* O. Sirola 6–4 6–2 7–5; Olmedo and Richardson *bt* Pietrangeli and Sirola 7–9 6–4 13–11 7–5; B. MacKay (U.S.) *bt* Pietrangeli 6–4 3–6 5–7 8–6 8–6; Olmedo *bt* Sirola 20–18 6–1 6–4.)
1959 E.Z. Italy *bt* Spain 4–1
A.Z. Australia *bt* Cuba 5–0
Eas.Z. India *bt* Philippines 4–1
Australia *bt* Italy 4–1.
I.Z.F. Australia *bt* India 4–1

Great Britain's Record in the Davis Cup

Challenge was originally made as the British Isles. From 1922 to 1928 the challenge was made as England and from 1929 onwards as Great Britain.

1900 v. U.S.A. Boston. *Lost* 0–3.
1901 v. U.S.A. *Scratched.*
1902 v. U.S.A. New York. *Lost* 2–3.
1903 v. U.S.A. Boston. *Won* 4–1.
1904 v. Belgium. Wimbledon. *Won* 5–0.
1905 v. U.S.A. Wimbledon. *Won* 5–0.
1906 v. U.S.A. Wimbledon. *Won* 5–0.
1907 v. Australasia. Wimbledon. *Lost* 2–3.
1908 v. U.S.A. Boston. *Lost* 1–4.
1909 v. U.S.A. Philadelphia. *Lost* 0–5.
1910 *Scratched.*
1911 v. U.S.A. New York. *Lost* 1–4.
1912 v. France. Folkestone. *Won* 4–1.
v. Australasia. Melbourne. *Won* 3–2.
1913 v. U.S.A. Wimbledon. *Lost* 2–3.
1914 v. Belgium. Folkestone. *Won* 5–0.
v. France. Wimbledon. *Won* 4–1.
v. Australasia. Boston. *Lost* 0–3.
1915–1918 *no contest.*
1919 v. South Africa. Eastbourne. *Won* 4–1.
v. France. Deauville. *Won* 3–2.
v. Australasia. Sydney. *Lost* 1–4.
1920 v. U.S.A. Wimbledon. *Lost* 0–5.
1921 v. Spain. Hendon. *Won* 4–1.
v. Australasia. Pittsburgh. *Lost* 2–3.
1922 v. Italy. Roehampton. *Won* 4–0.
v. Spain. *Scratched.*
1923 v. Belgium. Brussels. *Won* 3–2.
v. Spain. Manchester. *Lost* 2–3.
1924 v. Belgium. Torquay. *Won* 3–2.
v. Spain. Birmingham. *Won* 3–2.
v. South Africa. Scarborough. *Won* 4–1.
v. France. Eastbourne. *Lost* 1–4.
1925 v. Poland. Warsaw. *Won* 5–0.
v. Denmark. Copenhagen. *Won* 3–0.
v. France. Eastbourne. *Lost* 0–4.
1926 v. Poland. Harrogate. *Won* 5–0.
v. Italy. Rome. *Won* 3–2.
v. Spain. Barcelona. *Won* 4–1.
v. France. Corbourg. *Lost* 0–4.
1927 v. Sweden. Birmingham. *Won* 4–1
v. Denmark. Harrogate. *Lost* 2–3.
1928 v. Argentina. Torquay. *Won* 4–1.
v. Finland. Helsinki. *Won* 5–0.
v. Germany. Birmingham. *Won* 5–0.
v. Italy. Felixstowe. *Lost* 1–4.
1929 v. Poland. Warsaw. *Won* 5–0.
v. South Africa. Bournemouth. *Won* 5–0.
v. Hungary. Budapest. *Won* 3–2.
v. Germany. Berlin. *Lost* 2–3.
1930 v. Germany. Queen's Club. *Won* 3–2.
v. Poland. Torquay. *Won* 5–0.
v. Australia. Eastbourne. *Lost* 1–4.
1931 v. Monaco. Plymouth. *Won* 5–0.
v. Belgium. Brussels. *Won* 5–0.
v. South Africa. Eastbourne. *Won* 5–0.
v. Japan. Eastbourne. *Won* 5–0.
v. Czechoslovakia. Prague. *Won* 4–1.
v. U.S.A. Paris. *Won* 3–2.
v. France. Paris. *Lost* 2–3.
1932 v. Roumania. Torquay. *Won* 5–0.
v. Poland. Warsaw. *Won* 4–1.
v. Germany. Berlin. *Lost* 2–3.
1933 v. Spain. Barcelona. *Won* 4–1.
v. Finland. Queen's Club. *Won* 5–0.
v. Italy. Eastbourne. *Won* 4–1.

TENNIS QUIZ

1. What British men reached the singles last eight at Wimbledon between 1946 and 1958?

★

2. What British women reached the singles final at Wimbledon between 1946 and 1958?

★

3. What Englishmen have won the Australian singles title?

★

4. What post-war champions were never beaten in singles at Wimbledon?

★

5. In what years was Belgium in the Davis Cup challenge round?

★

6. Why was Cochet's 1927 Wimbledon victory so memorable?

★

7. Who won his first Wimbledon title at the age of 43? (*Above*.)

★

8. Who played 12 rubbers in the Davis Cup challenge round without defeat?

★

9. Who were the two Helens?

★

10. What is the longest set recorded in first-class play?

QUIZ ANSWERS

1. Only A. J. Mottram in 1948 and R. K. Wilson in 1958. 2. Miss Angela Buxton in 1956 and Miss Angela Mortimer in 1958. 3. F. G. Lowe, A. R. F. Kingscote, J. C. Gregory and F. J. Perry. J. C. Parke was Irish. 4. Ted Schroeder, Pauline Betz and Miss Maureen Connolly. 5. In 1904. 6. Because he lost the first two sets in the quarter-final against F. T. Hunter, the first two sets in the semi-final against W. T. Tilden and the first two sets in the final against J. Borotra who had six match points. 7. Gardnar Mulloy in taking the men's doubles with Budge Patty in 1957. 8. H. L. Doherty for Britain 1902 to 1906. 9. Helen Wills and Helen Jacobs who came from the same street in Berkeley, California, and pursued a rivalry for many years. 10. 60 games when, in May 1949 at Los Angeles, F. R. Schroeder and R. Falkenburg beat R. Gonzales and H. Stewart 36–34 3–6 4–6 6–4 19–17 after four and three-quarter hours. This total of 135 games is the longest on record.

TENNIS QUIZ

1. What is the longest recorded duration for a championship match?

★

2. When was the first international between Britain and the U.S.A.?

★

3. Who won the Wimbledon women's singles without the loss of one game in the whole event?

★

4. What finalist at Wimbledon was subsequently convicted for murder?

★

5. Who was the first overseas player to win the American women's singles championship?

★

6. What two sisters played against each other in a Wimbledon final?

★

7. What woman won an American national championship title 34 years after her first?

★

8. Who, in a national championship, won a five-set match with eighteen games running?

★

9. What is the longest known rally?

★

10. Who were the first Davis Cup players?

QUIZ ANSWERS

1. 6 hours, in the Olympic Games at Antwerp in 1920 when F. G. Lowe (G.B.) took that time to beat A. J. Zerlendi (Greece). It had to be postponed overnight and the score was 14–12 8–10 5–7 6–4 6–4. 2. In 1883. J. S. and C. M. Clark, brothers, came as a representative American side to play William and Ernest Renshaw at Wimbledon. The Renshaws won the first match 6–4 8–6 3–6 6–1 and the second 6–3 6–2 6–3. 3. Mrs. Lambert Chambers when, as defending title holder, she won the 1911 challenge round against Miss D. Boothby 6–0 6–0. 4. V. St. Leger Gould, all-comers' finalist in 1879. The crime was committed in Monte Carlo in 1907 and Gould later died on Devil's Island. 5. Molla Bjurstedt (later Mrs. Mallory) in 1915. She was then a Norwegian. 6. Maud and Lilian Watson in 1884. 7. Hazel Wightman, U.S. singles champion in 1909, U.S. indoor women's doubles champion in 1943. 8. The Chinese Kho Sin Kie when, in the men's singles quarter-final of the 1938 British Hard Court Championships at Bournemouth, he beat his compatriot W. C. Choy 4–6 4–6 6–1 6–0 6–0 after being 0–1 down in the third set. 9. Something over 300 shots when, in the 1920's, Mrs. P. Satterthwaite played Signorina Valerio at Bordighera in Italy. 10. A. W. Gore, E. D. Black and H. Roper Barrett for Britain and D. F. Davis, M. D. Whitman and H. Ward for the U.S. in 1900.

 H. E. Vines

 H. Cochet

 J. D. Budge

 F. R. Schroeder

 F. Sedgman

Davis Cup—contd.
1933 v. Czechoslovakia. Eastbourne. Won 5–0.
v. Australia. Wimbledon. Won 3–2.
v. U.S.A. Paris. Won 4–1.
v. France. Paris. Won 3–2.
1934 v. U.S.A. Wimbledon. Won 4–1.
1935 v. U.S.A. Wimbledon. Won 5–0.
1936 v. Australia. Wimbledon. Won 3–2.
1937 v. U.S.A. Wimbledon. Lost 1–4.
1938 v. Roumania. Harrogate. Won 3–2.
v. Yugoslavia. Zagreb. Lost 0–5.
1939 v. New Zealand. Brighton. Won 3–2.
v. France. Wimbledon. Won 3–2.
v. Germany. Berlin. Lost 0–5.
1940–1945 no contest.
1946 v. France. Paris. Lost 0–5.
1947 v. Poland. Warsaw. Won 3–2.
v. South Africa. Scarborough. Lost 1–4.
1948 v. India. Harrogate. Won 3–2.
v. Norway. Oslo. Won 4–1.
v. Holland. Birmingham. Won 4–1.
v. Sweden. Stockholm. Lost 1–4.
1949 v. Portugal. Lisbon. Won 5–0.
v. Czechoslovakia. Wimbledon. Lost 1–4.
1950 v. Italy. Eastbourne. Lost 2–3.
1951 v. France. Wimbledon. Won 3–2.
v. Sweden. Scarborough. Lost 0–5.
1952 v. Yugoslavia. Belgrade. Won 3–2.
v. Italy. Bologna. Lost 1–4.
1953 v. Norway. Oslo. Won 5–0.
v. Belgium. Brussels. Lost 1–4.
1954 v. Brazil. Eastbourne. Won 4–1.
v. Belgium. Scarborough. Lost 2–3.
1955 v. Austria. Vienna. Won 4–1.
v. India. Manchester. Won 3–2.
v. Italy. Birmingham. Lost 0–5.
1956 v. Yugoslavia. Belgrade. Won 5–0.
v. Chile. Bristol. Won 3–2.
v. Sweden. Stockholm. Lost 1–4.
1957 v. New Zealand. Eastbourne. Won 5–0.
v. France. Paris. Won 3–2.
v. Belgium. Brussels. Lost 2–3.
1958 v. Brazil. Eastbourne. Won 5–0.
v. Germany. Scarborough. Won 5–0.
v. France. Manchester. Won 5–0.
v. Italy. Milan. Lost 1–4.
1959 v. Luxembourg. Mondorf. Won 5–0.
v. Chile. Eastbourne. Won 3–2.
v. Spain. Barcelona. Lost 2–3.

Davis Cup Challengers

The following lists the nations that have played in the Davis Cup, the year of first entry being indicated. Peru challenged in 1933 and 1934 but never played. Germany was expelled from the competition from 1919 to 1926 and from 1946 to 1950 and Japan from 1946 to 1950. Austria was absorbed into Germany in 1938 and 1939 and Czechoslovakia in 1939.

U.S.A., British Isles (1900)
Belgium, France (1904)
Australasia, Austria (1905)
Germany, Canada, South Africa (1913)
Holland (1920)
Spain, Czechoslovakia, India, Denmark, Japan (1921)
Italy, Roumania (1922)
Switzerland, Ireland, Argentina, Hawaii (1923)
New Zealand, Hungary, Cuba, China, Mexico (1924)
Sweden, Portugal, Poland (1925)
Philippines (1926)
Greece, Yugoslavia (1927)
Chile, Finland, Norway (1928)
Monaco, Egypt (1929)
Paraguay, Uruguay (1931)
Brazil (1932)
Estonia (1934)
Luxembourg (1947)
Pakistan, Turkey (1948)
Israel (1949)
British West Indies, Ceylon (1953)
Burma (1955)
Malaya, Lebanon, Venezuela (1957)
Thailand (1958)
Korea, Iran, Colombia (1959)

THE WIGHTMAN CUP

Officially called the Ladies' International Lawn Tennis Championship, the contest for the Wightman Cup is held every year in alternate countries between the women of the United States and Great Britain. Five singles, with the two top nominated players opposed to each other, and two doubles are played in a two-day fixture. The participation of France was originally envisaged but never came about.

1923 *Forest Hills, N.Y.* U.S.A. 7-0
1924 *Wimbledon.* Gt. Britain 6-1
1925 *Forest Hills, N.Y.* Gt. Britain 4-3
1926 *Wimbledon.* U.S.A. 4-3
1927 *Forest Hills, N.Y.* U.S.A. 5-2
1928 *Wimbledon.* Gt. Britain 4-3
1929 *Forest Hills, N.Y.* U.S.A. 4-3
1930 *Wimbledon.* Gt. Britain 4-3
1931 *Forest Hills, N.Y.* U.S.A. 5-2
1932 *Wimbledon.* U.S.A. 4-3
1933 *Forest Hills, N.Y.* U.S.A. 4-3
1934 *Wimbledon.* U.S.A. 5-2
1935 *Forest Hills, N.Y.* U.S.A. 4-3
1936 *Wimbledon.* U.S.A. 4-3
1937 *Forest Hills, N.Y.* U.S.A. 6-1
1938 *Wimbledon.* U.S.A. 5-2
1939 *Forest Hills, N.Y.* U.S.A. 5-2
1940–1945 *no competition*

1946 *Wimbledon.* U.S.A. 7-0
1947 *Forest Hills, N.Y.* U.S.A. 7-0
1948 *Wimbledon.* U.S.A. 6-1
1949 *Philadelphia.* U.S.A. 7-0
1950 *Wimbledon.* U.S.A. 7-0
1951 *Chestnut Hill, Mass.* U.S.A. 6-1
1952 *Wimbledon.* U.S.A. 7-0
1953 *Rye, N.Y.* U.S.A. 7-0
1954 *Wimbledon.* U.S.A. 6-0, one unplayed
1955 *Rye, N.Y.* U.S.A. 6-1
1956 *Wimbledon.* U.S.A. 5-2
1957 *Sewickley, Pa.* U.S.A. 6-1
1958 *Wimbledon.* Gt. Britain 4-3

First day: Miss S. J. Bloomer (G.B.) *lost to* Miss A. Gibson 3–6 4–6, Miss C. C. Truman (G.B.) *bt* Mrs. D. P. Knode 6–4 6–4, Miss Bloomer and Miss Truman *bt* Mrs. Knode and Miss K. Fageros 6–2 6–3.

Second day: Miss Bloomer *lost to* Mrs. Knode 4–6 2–6, Miss Truman *bt* Miss Gibson 2–6 6–3 6–4, Miss A. S. Haydon (G.B.) *bt* Miss M. Arnold 6–3 5–7 6–3, Miss J. A. Shilcock and Miss P. E. Ward (G.B.) *lost to* Miss Gibson and Miss J. Hopps 4–6 6–3 3–6.

1959 *Sewickley, Pa.* U.S.A. 4-3

The winning Wightman Cup team of 1958. *Left to Right:* Ann Shilcock, Shirley Bloomer, Christine Truman, Mrs. Halford, non-playing captain, Ann Haydon and Pat Ward

WIMBLEDON CHAMPIONSHIPS

The Championships, the oldest and most outstanding lawn tennis tournament of the world, have always been played on grass at the All England Lawn Tennis and Croquet Club, originally in Worple Road, Wimbledon, and, since 1922, at Church Road, Wimbledon.

Men's Singles

Originally the men's singles were played on a challenge-round basis, the holder standing out and playing the winner of the all-comers' competition.

c indicates a result of the challenge-round match.

f indicates a result of the all-comers' final, the winner taking the championship on the outcome because the holder did not defend.

The challenge-round system was abolished in 1922.
Seeding of overseas players was introduced in 1924.
Full seeding was introduced in 1927.

1877 S. W. Gore *bt* W. C. Marshall 6–1 6–2 6–4
1878 *c* P. F. Hadow *bt* S. W. Gore 7–5 6–1 9–7
1879 *f* J. T. Hartley *bt* V. St. L. Gould 6–2 6–4 6–2
1880 *c* J. T. Hartley *bt* H. F. Lawford 6–0 6–2 2–6 6–3
1881 *c* W. Renshaw *bt* J. T. Hartley 6–0 6–2 6–1
1882 *c* W. Renshaw *bt* E. Renshaw 6–1 2–6 4–6 6–2 6–2
1883 *c* W. Renshaw *bt* E. Renshaw 2–6 6–3 6–3 4–6 6–3
1884 *c* W. Renshaw *bt* H. F. Lawford 6–0 6–4 9–7
1885 *c* W. Renshaw *bt* H. F. Lawford 7–5 6–2 4–6 7–5
1886 *c* W. Renshaw *bt* H. F. Lawford 6–0 5–7 6–3 6–4
1887 *f* H. F. Lawford *bt* E. Renshaw 1–6 6–3 3–6 4–6 6–4
1888 *c* E. Renshaw *bt* H. F. Lawford 6–3 7–5 6–0
1889 *c* W. Renshaw *bt* E. Renshaw 6–4 6–1 3–6 6–0
1890 *c* W. J. Hamilton *bt* W. Renshaw 6–8 6–2 3–6 6–1 6–1
1891 *f* W. Baddeley *bt* J. Pim 6–4 1–6 7–5 6–0
1892 *c* W. Baddeley *bt* J. Pim 4–6 6–3 6–3 6–2
1893 *c* J. Pim *bt* W. Baddeley 3–6 6–1 6–3 6–2

1894 c J. Pim bt W. Baddeley 10–8 6–2 8–6
1895 f W. Baddeley bt W. V. Eaves 4–6 2–6 8–6 6–2 6–3
1896 c H. S. Mahoney bt W. Baddeley 6–2 6–8 5–7 8–6 6–3
1897 c R. F. Doherty bt H. S. Mahony 6–4 6–4 6–3
1898 c R. F. Doherty bt H. L. Doherty 6–3 6–3 2–6 5–7 6–1
1899 c R. F. Doherty bt A. W. Gore 1–6 4–6 6–3 6–3 6–3
1900 c R. F. Doherty bt S. H. Smith 6–8 6–3 6–1 6–2
1901 c A. W. Gore bt R. F. Doherty 4–6 7–5 6–4 6–4
1902 c H. L. Doherty bt A. W. Gore 6–4 6–3 3–6 6–0
1903 c H. L. Doherty bt F. L. Riseley 7–5 6–3 6–0
1904 c H. L. Doherty bt F. L. Riseley 6–1 7–5 8–6
1905 c H. L. Doherty bt N. E. Brookes 8–6 6–2 6–4
1906 c H. L. Doherty bt F. L. Riseley 6–4 6–6 6–2 6–3
1907 f N. E. Brookes bt A. W. Gore 6–4 6–2 6–2
1908 f A. W. Gore bt H. Roper Barrett 6–3 6–2 4–6 3–6 6–4
1909 c A. W. Gore bt M. J. G. Ritchie 6–8 1–6 6–2 6–2 6–2
1910 c A. F. Wilding bt A. W. Gore 6–4 7–5 4–6 6–2
1911 c A. F. Wilding bt H. Roper Barrett 6–4 4–6 2–6 6–2 ret'd
1912 c A. F. Wilding bt A. W. Gore 6–4 6–4 4–6 6–4
1913 c A. F. Wilding bt M. E. McLoughlin 8–6 6–3 10–8
1914 c N. E. Brookes bt A. F. Wilding 6–4 6–4 7–5
1915–1918 no competition
1919 c G. L. Patterson bt N. E. Brookes 6–3 7–5 6–2
1920 c W. T. Tilden bt G. L. Patterson 2–6 6–3 6–2 6–4
1921 c W. T. Tilden bt B. I. C. Norton 4–6 2–6 6–1 6–0 7–5

Challenge round abolished

1922 G. L. Patterson bt R. Lycett 6–3 6–4 6–2
1923 W. M. Johnston bt F. T. Hunter 6–0 6–3 6–1
1924 J. Borotra bt R. Lacoste 6–1 3–6 6–1 3–6 6–4
1925 R. Lacoste bt J. Borotra 6–3 6–3 4–6 8–6
1926 J. Borotra bt H. O. Kinsey 8–6 6–1 6–3
1927 H. Cochet bt J. Borotra 4–6 4–6 6–3 6–4 7–5
1928 R. Lacoste bt H. Cochet 6–1 4–6 6–4 6–2
1929 H. Cochet bt J. Borotra 6–4 6–3 6–4
1930 W. T. Tilden bt W. L. Allison 6–3 9–7 6–4
1931 S. B. Wood walk-over F. X. Shields
1932 H. E. Vines bt H. W. Austen 6–4 6–2 6–0
1933 J. H. Crawford bt H. E. Vines 4–6 11–9 6–2 2–6 6–4
1934 F. J. Perry bt J. H. Crawford 6–3 6–0 7–5
1935 F. J. Perry bt G. Von Cramm 6–2 6–4 6–4
1936 F. J. Perry bt G. Von Cramm 6–1 6–1 6–0
1937 J. D. Budge bt G. Von Cramm 6–3 6–4 6–2
1938 J. D. Budge bt H. W. Austin 6–1 6–0 6–3
1939 R. L. Riggs bt E. T. Cooke 2–6 8–6 3–6 6–3 6–2
1940–1945 no competition
1946 Y. Petra bt G. E. Brown 6–2 6–4 7–9 5–7 6–4
1947 J. A. Kramer bt T. Brown 6–1 6–3 6–2
1948 R. Falkenburg bt J. E. Bromwich 7–5 0–6 6–2 3–6 7–5
1949 F. R. Schroeder bt J. Drobny 3–6 6–0 6–3 4–6 6–4
1950 J. E. Patty bt F. A. Sedgman 6–1 8–10 6–2 6–3
1951 R. Savitt bt K. McGregor 6–4 6–4 6–4
1952 F. A. Sedgman bt J. Drobny 4–6 6–2 6–3 6–2
1953 E. V. Seixas bt K. Nielsen 9–7 6–3 6–4
1954 J. Drobny bt K. R. Rosewall 13–11 4–6 6–2 9–7
1955 M. A. Trabert bt K. Nielsen 6–3 7–5 6–1
1956 L. A. Hoad bt K. R. Rosewall 6–2 4–6 7–5 6–4
1957 L. A. Hoad bt A. J. Cooper 6–2 6–1 6–2
1958 A. J. Cooper bt N. A. Fraser 3–6 6–3 6–4 13–11
1959 A. Olmedo bt R. Laver 6–4 6–3 6–4

Women's Singles

As with the men's singles c indicates a result of the challenge-round match and f indicates the result of the all-comers' final when the winner took the championship because the holder did not defend. The challenge-round system in this event was not introduced until 1886 but, as with the men's singles, was abolished in 1922. Seeding was introduced in 1927.

1884 Miss M. E. A. Watson bt Miss L. Watson 6–8 6–3 6–3
1885 Miss M. E. A. Watson bt Miss B. Bingley 6–1 7–5
1886 c Miss B. Bingley bt Miss M. E. A. Watson 6–3 6–3
1887 c Miss C. Dod bt Miss B. Bingley 6–2 6–0
1888 c Miss C. Dod bt Mrs. G. W. Hillyard 6–3 6–3
1889 f Mrs. G. W. Hillyard bt Miss L. Rice 4–6 8–6 6–4
1890 f Miss L. Rice bt Miss L. Jacks 6–4 6–1
1891 f Miss C. Dod bt Mrs. G. W. Hillyard 6–2 6–1
1892 c Miss C. Dod bt Mrs. G. W. Hillyard 6–1 6–1
1893 c Miss C. Dod bt Mrs. G. W. Hillyard 6–8 6–1 6–4
1894 f Mrs. G. W. Hillyard bt Miss L. Austin 6–1 6–1
1895 f Miss C. Cooper bt Miss H. Jackson 7–5 8–6
1896 c Miss C. Cooper bt Mrs. W. H. Pickering 6–2 6–3
1897 c Mrs. G. W. Hillyard bt Miss C. Cooper 5–7 7–5 6–2
1898 f Miss C. Cooper bt Miss L. Martin 6–4 6–4
1899 c Mrs. G. W. Hillyard bt Miss C. Cooper 6–2 6–3
1900 c Mrs. G. W. Hillyard bt Miss C. Cooper 4–6 6–4 6–4
1901 c Mrs A. Sterry bt Mrs. G. W. Hillyard 6–2 6–2
1902 c Miss M. E. Robb bt Mrs. A. Sterry 7–5 6–1, replaying after unfinished score ot 4–6 13–11
1903 c Miss D. K. Douglass bt Miss E. W. Thomson 4–6 6–4 6–2
1904 c Miss D. K. Douglass bt Mrs. A. Sterry 6–0 6–3
1905 c Miss M. Sutton bt Miss D. K. Douglass 6–3 6–4
1906 c Miss D. K. Douglass bt Miss M. Sutton 6–3 9–7
1907 c Miss M. Sutton bt Mrs. Lambert Chambers 6–1 6–4
1908 f Mrs. A. Sterry bt Miss A. M. Morton 6–4 6–4
1909 f Miss D. Boothby bt Miss A. M. Morton 6–4 4–6 8–6
1910 c Mrs. Lambert Chambers bt Miss D. Boothby 6–2 6–2
1911 c Mrs Lambert Chambers bt Miss D. Boothby 6–0 6–0
1912 f Mrs. D. R. Larcombe bt Mrs. A. Sterry 6–3 6–1
1913 f Mrs. Lambert Chambers bt Mrs. R. J. McNair 6–0 6–4
1914 c Mrs. Lambert Chambers bt Mrs. D. R. Larcombe 7–5 6–4
1915–1918 no competition
1919 c Mlle S. Lenglen bt Mrs. Lambert Chambers 10–8 4–6 9–7
1920 c Mlle S. Lenglen bt Mrs. Lambert Chambers 6–3 6–0
1921 c Mlle S. Lenglen bt Miss E. Ryan 6–2 6–0

Challenge round abolished

1922 Mlle S. Lenglen bt Mrs. F. Mallory 6–2 6–0
1923 Mlle S. Lenglen bt Miss K. McKane 6–2 6–2
1924 Miss K. McKane bt Miss H. Wills 4–6 6–4 6–4
1925 Mlle S. Lenglen bt Miss J. Fry 6–2 6–0
1926 Mrs. L. A. Godfree bt Sen. E. de Alvarez 6–2 4–6 6–3
1927 Miss H. Wills bt Sen. E. de Alvarez 6–2 6–2
1928 Miss H. Wills bt Sen. E. de Alvarez 6–2 6–3
1929 Miss H. Wills bt Miss H. Jacobs 6–1 6–2

Suzanne Lenglen

Elizabeth Ryan

Pauline Betz

Dorothy Round

Althea Gibson

Alice Marble

1930 Mrs. F. S. Moody bt Miss E. Ryan 6–2 6–2
1931 Frl. C. Aussem bt Frl. H. Krahwinkel 6–2 7–5
1932 Mrs. F. S. Moody bt Miss H. Jacobs 6–3 6–1
1933 Mrs. F. S. Moody bt Miss D. E. Round 6–4 6–8 6–3
1934 Miss D. E. Round bt Miss H. Jacobs 6–2 5–7 6–3
1935 Mrs. F. S. Moody bt Miss H. Jacobs 6–3 3–6 7–5
1936 Miss H. Jacobs bt Fru. S. Sperling 6–2 4–6 7–5
1937 Miss D. E. Round bt Panna J. Jedrzejowska 6–2 2–6 7–5
1938 Mrs. F. S. Moody bt Miss H. Jacobs 6–4 6–0
1939 Miss A. Marble bt Miss K. E. Stammers 6–2 6–0
1940–1945 no competition
1946 Miss P. M. Betz bt Miss A. L. Brough 6–2 6–4
1947 Miss M. E. Osborne bt Miss D. J. Hart 6–2 6–4
1948 Miss A. L. Brough bt Miss D. J. Hart 6–3 8–6
1949 Miss A. L. Brough bt Mrs. W. D. du Pont 10–8 1–6 10–8
1950 Miss A. L. Brough bt Mrs. W. D. du Pont 6–1 3–6 6–1
1951 Miss D. J. Hart bt Miss S. J. Fry 6–1 6–0
1952 Miss M. Connolly bt Miss A. L. Brough 7–5 6–3
1953 Miss M. Connolly bt Miss D. J. Hart 8–6 7–5
1954 Miss M. Connolly bt Miss A. L. Brough 6–2 7–5
1955 Miss A. L. Brough bt Mrs. J. Fleitz 7–5 8–6
1956 Miss S. J. Fry bt Miss A. Buxton 6–3 6–1
1957 Miss A. Gibson bt Miss D. R. Hard 6–3 6–2
1958 Miss A. Gibson bt Miss A. Mortimer 8–6 6–2
1959 Miss M. E. Bueno bt Miss D. R. Hard 6–4 6–3

TENNIS QUIZ

1. Who, since the abolition of the challenge round in 1922, has won the women's singles at Wimbledon with the loss of the least number of games?

★

2. What post-war Wimbledon final was won 6–0 6–0?

★

3. What Australian played in the Davis Cup for Britain?

★

4. What American played in the Davis Cup for Brazil?

★

5. What Peruvian played in the Davis Cup for the United States?

★

6. Who played right through the Wimbledon men's singles without losing a set?

★

7. What player has the longest span between his first and last Davis Cup match?

★

8. Who was the "Californian Comet"?

★

9. What royal monarch competed at Wimbledon?

★

10. Who competed at Wimbledon the greatest number of years?

QUIZ ANSWERS

1. Mlle Suzanne Lenglen in 1925. She lost a total of only 5 games in five rounds. 2. Women's doubles 1953 when Miss S. J. Fry and Miss D. J. Hart beat Miss M. Connolly and Miss J. Sampson. 3. Randolph Lycett in 1921 and 1923. 4. Robert Falkenburg in 1954 and 1955. 5. Alejandro Olmedo in 1958. 6. J. Donald Budge in 1938. 7. John Colin Gregory who played first for Britain in 1926 and last in 1952. 8. Maurice McLoughlin, because of his fast service. 9. The late George VI. As Duke of York in 1926 he played in the men's doubles with Sir Louis Greig. 10. Arthur Wentworth Gore. First in 1888 and last in 1927 without missing a year, 36 times in all.

TENNIS QUIZ

1. Who, at his first attempt, won all three events at Wimbledon and never played there again?

★

2. What is the oldest national women's singles championship?

★

3. What is the world's oldest lawn tennis tournament?

★

4. Who was the first overseas player to win the men's singles at Wimbledon?

★

5. Who was the first overseas player to win the women's singles at Wimbledon?

★

6. What is the largest number of games played in any match in the Wimbledon Championships?

★

7. What is the largest number of games played in a singles match in the Wimbledon Championships?

★

8. Who has won the men's singles at Wimbledon the greatest number of times?

★

9. Who has won the women's singles at Wimbledon the greatest number of times? (Above.)

★

10. Who has won the most Wimbledon Championships?

QUIZ ANSWERS

1. R. L. Riggs (U.S.) in 1939. 2. The Irish Championship, dating from 1879. The first champion was Miss M. Langrishe. 3. The Wimbledon Championships, dating from 1877. 4. N. E. Brookes, the Australian left-hander, in 1907. 5. Miss May Sutton of California in 1905. 6. 94. In 1950 in the men's doubles quarter-final J. E. Patty and M. A. Trabert beat F. A. Sedgman and K. MacGregor 6–4 31–29 7–9 6–2. 7. 93. In 1953 in the third round of the men's singles J. Drobny beat J. E. Patty 8–6 16–18 3–6 8–6 12–10 after four and a quarter hours. 8. William Renshaw. 7 times. 9. Mrs. F. S. Moody, the former Miss H. Wills. 8 times. 10. Miss Elizabeth ("Bunny") Ryan. 19 doubles titles.

Men's Doubles

From 1879 to 1883 the men's doubles championship was played at Oxford. It was played as a knock-out competition 1879 to 1885, on a challenge-round basis 1886 to 1921. For the challenge-round period from 1886 to 1921 *f* indicates a year when the holders did not defend. Seeding was introduced in 1928.

1879 L. R. Erskine and H. F. Lawford
1880–81 W. and E. Renshaw
1882 J. T. Hartley and J. T. Richardson
1883 C. W. Grinstead and C. E. Welldon
1884–85–86 W. and E. Renshaw
1887 *f* P. B. Lyon and H. W. W. Wilberforce
1888–89 W. and E. Renshaw
1890 *f* J. Pim and F. O.'Stoker
1891 H. and W. Baddeley
1892 H. S. Barlow and E. W. Lewis
1893 J. Pim and F. O. Stoker
1894–95–96 H. and W. Baddeley
1897–98–99–1900–01 H. L. and R. F. Doherty
1902 F. L. Riseley and S. H. Smith
1903–5 H. L. and R. F. Doherty
1906 F. L. Riseley and S. H. Smith

F. A. Parker and R. A. Gonzales

1907 *f* N. E. Brookes and A. F. Wilding
1908 *f* M. J. G. Ritchie and A. F. Wilding
1909 *f* H. Roper Barrett and A. W. Gore
1910 M. J. G. Ritchie and A. F. Wilding
1911 M. Decugis and A. H. Gobert
1912–13 C. P. Dixon and H. Roper Barrett
1914 N. E. Brookes and A. F. Wilding
1915–18 *no competition*
1919 P. O'Hara Wood and R. V. Thomas
1920 *f* C. S. Garland and R. N. Williams
1921 *f* R. Lycett and M. Woosnam
1922 J. O. Anderson and R. Lycett
1923 L. A. Godfree and R. Lycett
1924 F. T. Hunter and V. Richards
1925 J. Borotra and R. Lacoste
1926 J. Brugnon and H. Cochet
1927 F. T. Hunter and W. T. Tilden
1928 J. Brugnon and H. Cochet
1929–30 W. L. Allison and J. van Ryn
1931 G. M. Lott and J. van Ryn
1932–33 J. Borotra and J. Brugnon
1934 G. M. Lott and L. R. Stoefen
1935 J. H. Crawford and A. K. Quist
1936 G. P. Hughes and C. R. D. Tuckey
1937–38 J. D. Budge and C. G. Mako
1939 E. T. Cooke and R. L. Riggs
1940–1945 *no competition*
1946 T. Brown and J. A. Kramer
1947 R. Falkenburg and J. A. Kramer
1948 J. E. Bromwich and F. A. Sedgman
1949 R. A. Gonzales and F. A. Parker
1950 J. E. Bromwich and A. K. Quist
1951–52 K. McGregor and F. A. Sedgman
1953 L. A. Hoad and K. R. Rosewall
1954 R. N. Hartwig and M. G. Rose
1955 R. N. Hartwig and L. A. Hoad
1956 L. A. Hoad and K. R. Rosewall
1957 G. Mulloy and J. E. Patty
1958 S. Davidson and U. Schmidt
1959 R. Emerson and N. A. Fraser

J. E. Patty

Miss M. Connolly

Miss S. J. Fry

Women's Doubles

The women's doubles at Wimbledon was not instituted as a championship event until 1913, though from 1899 to 1907 a women's doubles tournament was held. The All England Women's Doubles Championship was played at Buxton from 1884 until 1953 when the tournament ceased. The Wimbledon tournament winners were:

1899 Mrs. G. W. Hillyard and Miss B. Steedman
1900 Mrs. W. H. Pickering and Miss M. E. Robb
1901 Mrs. G. W. Hillyard and Mrs. A. Sterry
1902 Miss A. M. Morton and Mrs. A. Sterry
1903 Miss D. K. Douglass and Mrs. W. H. Pickering
1904–05 Miss W. Longhurst and Miss E. W. Thomson
1906 Mrs. G. W. Hillyard and Miss M. Sutton
1907 Mrs. Lambert Chambers and Miss C. M. Wilson

Championship

1913 Miss D. Boothby and Mrs. R. J. McNair
1914 Miss A. M. Morton and Miss E. Ryan
1915–18 *no competition*
1919–20–21–22–23 Mlle S. Lenglen and Miss E. Ryan
1924 Mrs. G. W. Wightman and Miss H. Wills
1925 Mlle S. Lenglen and Miss E. Ryan
1926 Miss M. K. Browne and Miss E. Ryan
1927 Miss E. Ryan and Miss H. Wills
1928 Miss P. Saunders and Mrs. P. H. Watson
1929 Mrs. L. R. C. Michell and Mrs. P. H. Watson
1930 Mrs. F. S. Moody and Miss E. Ryan
1931 Miss P. E. Mudford and Mrs. D. C. Shepherd-Barron
1932 Mlle D. Metaxa and Mlle J. Sigart
1933–34 Mme R. Mathieu and Miss E. Ryan
1935–36 Miss F. James and Miss K. E. Stammers
1937 Mme R. Mathieu and Miss A. M. Yorke
1938–39 Mrs. M. Fabyan and Miss A. Marble
1940–45 *no competition*
1946 Miss A. L. Brough and Miss M. E. Osborne
1947 Miss D. J. Hart and Mrs. P. C. Todd
1948–49–50 Miss A. L. Brough and Mrs. W. D. du Pont
1951–52–53 Miss S. J. Fry and Miss D. J. Hart
1954 Miss A. L. Brough and Mrs. W. D. du Pont
1955 Miss A. Mortimer and Miss J. A. Shilcock
1956 Miss A. Gibson and Miss A. Buxton
1957 Miss A. Gibson and Miss D. R. Hard
1958 Miss M. E. Bueno and Miss A. Gibson
1959 Miss J. Arth and Miss D. R. Hard

Miss A. L. Brough

Miss A. Buxton

Mixed Doubles

The mixed doubles at Wimbledon was not instituted as a championship event until 1913 though a mixed tournament was held from 1900. The All England Mixed Doubles Championship was played in alternate years in Manchester and Liverpool from 1888 until 1938 when the title lapsed. The Wimbledon tournament winners were:

1900 H. A. Nisbet and Mrs. W. H. Pickering
1901–02 H. L. Doherty and Mrs. A. Sterry
1903–04 S. H. Smith and Miss E. W. Thomson
1905 A. W. Gore and Miss C. M. Wilson
1906 A. F. Wilding and Miss D. K. Douglass
1907 B. C. Wright and Miss M. Sutton
1908 A. F. Wilding and Mrs. Lambert Chambers
1909 H. Roper Barrett and Miss A. M. Morton
1910 S. N. Doust and Mrs. Lambert Chambers
1911 T. M. Mavrogordato and Mrs. E. G. Parton
1912 J. C. Parke and Mrs. D. R. Larcombe

Championship

1913 H. Crisp and Mrs. C. O. Tuckey
1914 J. C. Parke and Mrs. D. R. Larcombe
1915–18 *no competition*
1919 R. Lycett and Miss E. Ryan
1920 G. L. Patterson and Mlle S. Lenglen
1921 R. Lycett and Miss E. Ryan
1922 P. O'Hara Wood and Mlle S. Lenglen
1923 R. Lycett and Miss E. Ryan
1924 J. B. Gilbert and Miss K. McKane
1925 J. Borotra and Mlle S. Lenglen
1926 L. A. Godfree and Mrs. Godfree
1927 F. T. Hunter and Miss E. Ryan
1928 P. D. B. Spence and Miss E. Ryan
1929 F. T. Hunter and Miss H. Wills
1930 J. H. Crawford and Miss E. Ryan
1931 G. M. Lott and Mrs. L. A. Harper
1932 E. Maier and Miss E. Ryan
1933 G. von Cramm and Frl. H. Krahwinkel
1934 R. Miki and Miss D. E. Round
1935–36 F. J. Perry and Miss D. E. Round
1937–38 J. D. Budge and Miss A. Marble
1939 R. L. Riggs and Miss A. Marble
1940–45 *no competition*
1946 T. Brown and Miss A. L. Brough
1947–48 J. E. Bromwich and Miss A. L. Brough
1949 E. W. Sturgess and Mrs. S. P. Summers
1950 E. W. Sturgess and Miss A. L. Brough
1951–52 F. A. Sedgman and Miss D. J. Hart
1953–54–55 E. V. Seixas and Miss D. J. Hart
1956 E. V. Seixas and Miss S. J. Fry
1957 M. G. Rose and Miss D. R. Hard
1958 R. N. Howe and Miss L. Coghlan
1959 R. Laver and Miss D. R. Hard

Miss A. Mortimer

E. V. Seixas

All England Plate

Open to players defeated in the first or second round of the singles.

Men's Singles

1896 A. W. Gore
1897 H. Baddeley
1898 G. W. Hillyard
1899 W. V. Eaves
1900 G. Greville
1901 P. G. Pearson
1902 B. Hillyard
1903 A. W. Gore
1904 G. Greville
1905 W. V. Eaves
1906 G. W. Hillyard
1907 A. F. Wilding
1908 O. Kreuzer
1909 R. B. Powell
1910 A. H. Gobert
1911 A. H. Lowe
1912 F. M. Pearson
1913 F. G. Lowe
1914 C. P. Dixon
1915–1918 no competition
1919 F. R. L. Crawford
1920 F. G. Lowe
1921 J. B. Gilbert
1922 B. I. C. Norton
1923 J. Washer
1924 J. Condon
1925 B. von Kehrling
1926 J. B. Gilbert
1927 A. Gentien
1928 M. Sleem
1929 E. G. Chandler
1930 E. du Plaix
1931 V. G. Kirby
1932 H. Cochet
1933 F. H. D. Wilde
1934 H. W. Artens
1935 J. Yamagishi
1936 D. N. Jones
1937 W. Sabin
1938 D. W. Butler
1939 W. D. McNeill
1940–1945 no competition
1946 R. Abdesselam
1947 E. W. Sturgess
1948 F. H. Ampon
1949 E. H. Cochell
1950 G. L. Paish
1951 N. M. Cockburn
1952 L. Ayala
1953 G. L. Paish
1954 H. W. Stewart
1955 N. A. Fraser
1956 H. W. Stewart
1957 G. L. Forbes
1958 P. Remy
1959 J. Javorsky

Women's Singles

1933 Mlle C. Rosambert
1934–35 Signorina L. Valerio
1936 Miss F. S. Ford
1937 Miss F. James
1938 Miss D. Stevenson
1939 Mrs. R. D. McKelvie
1940–45 no competition
1946–47 Panna J. Jedrzejowska
1948 Senora H. Weiss
1949 Signora A. Bossi
1950 Miss K. L. A. Tuckey
1951 Mrs. F. J. Bartlett
1952 Mrs. B. Abbas
1953 Miss M. P. Harrison
1954 Miss R. Walsh
1955 Miss F. Muller
1956 Mrs. T. Long
1957 Miss M. Hellyer
1958 Miss S. Reynolds
1959 Mrs. C. W. Brasher

International Junior Tournament

Since 1949 the nations of the world have been invited to send outstanding junior players to watch the Wimbledon Championships. The following are the winners of the singles tournament in which they take part.

Boys' Singles

1949 S. Stockenberg (Sweden)
1950 J. A. T. Horn (Gt. Britain)
1951 J. Kupferburger (S. Africa)
1952 R. K. Wilson (Gt. Britain)
1953 W. A. Knight (Gt. Britain)
1954 R. Krishnan (India)
1955 M. P. Hann (Gt. Britain)
1956 R. Holmberg (U.S.A.)
1957 J. I. Tattersall (Gt. Britain)
1958 E. Buchholz (U.S.A.)
1959 T. Leius (U.S.S.R.)

Girls' Singles

1949 Mlle C. Mercellis (Belgium)
1950 Miss L. Cornell (Gt. Britain)
1951 Miss L. Cornell (Gt. Britain)
1952 Miss F. ten Bosch (Holland)
1953 Miss D. Kilian (S. Africa)
1954 Miss V. A. Pitt (Gt. Britain)
1955 Miss S. M. Armstrong (Gt. Britain)
1956 Miss A. S. Haydon (Gt. Britain)
1957 Miss M. Arnold (U.S.A.)
1958 Miss S. M. Moore (U.S.A.)
1959 Miss J. Cross (S. Africa)

TENNIS QUIZ

1. What national British title had an all-Chinese final?

★

2. Who were the last two Englishmen to win the Wimbledon singles?

★

3. What players have become men's singles champion of Australia, France, Wimbledon and the United States in the same year?

★

4. What players have become women's singles champion of Australia, France, Wimbledon and the United States in the same year?

★

5. Who became men's singles champion at Wimbledon at his first attempt and never saw another championship match until 48 years after?

★

6. Who, since the abolition of the challenge round in 1922, has won the Wimbledon men's singles with the loss of the least number of games? (above, right)

★

7. When did Great Britain last win the Davis Cup?

★

8. How many times was Mrs. Helen Wills Moody beaten in singles at Wimbledon?

★

9. How many times was Mlle Suzanne Lenglen beaten in singles at Wimbledon?

★

10. How many times was Mlle Suzanne Lenglen beaten in singles anywhere between 1919 and her turning professional in 1926?

QUIZ ANSWERS

1. The men's singles in the Hard Court Championships 1939, Kho Sin Kie against W. C. Choy. 2. F. J. Perry in 1934, 1935, and 1936; A. W. Gore in 1909, 1908 and 1901. 3. Only J. Donald Budge (U.S.) in 1938. 4. Only Miss Maureen Connolly (U.S.) in 1953. 5. P. F. Hadow in 1878. He was a planter in Ceylon. 6. Jack Kramer in 1947. He lost only 37 games in seven matches, including the loss of a set. 7. 1936. 8. Once only. In the final by Miss K. McKane in 1924. 9. She was never beaten. 10. Once. In the U.S. Championships at Forest Hills in 1921 when, Mrs. Molla Mallory having won the first set 6–2, Mlle Lenglen retired because of illness. She never played in America as an amateur again.

ALL ENGLAND CHAMPIONSHIPS

When Wimbledon held its first meeting in 1877 it staged the men's singles only and the title played for was the All England Championship. In 1884 both the All England Women's Singles Championship and the All England Men's Doubles Championship (the latter having begun in 1879 at Oxford) were added to the event at the All England Club. These titles still pertain but have been overshadowed by the more simple title of Wimbledon Championships. The All England Women's and Mixed Doubles titles, however, have never belonged to Wimbledon. The Women's Doubles title was started by the Buxton club at its tournament in 1885 and belonged to it until the cessation of the tournament and the extinction of the title after 1953. It was always played on a knock-out basis.

The All England Mixed Doubles title was part of the Northern Championships meeting held in alternate years in Liverpool and Manchester. This was played on a challenge-round basis until 1922, after which no more challenge rounds were played. This title became extinct after 1938.

These once-much-sought-after titles deserve preservation in the records

Women's Singles

1885 Miss G. Bracewell and Mrs. F. Watts
1886–87–88 Miss C. Dod and Miss M. Langrishe
1889–90 Miss B. Steedman and Miss M. Steedman
1891 Miss L. Marriott and Miss M. Marriott
1892 Miss H. Jackson and Miss Crofton
1893–94–95–96 Mrs. G. W. Hillyard and Miss B. Steedman
1897 Miss G. W. Hillyard and Mrs. W. H. Pickering
1898 Miss R. Dyas and Miss B. Steedman
1899 Mrs. N. Durlacher and Miss B. Steedman
1900–01–02 Mrs. W. H. Pickering and Miss M. E. Robb
1903–04 Miss D. K. Douglass and Miss E. W. Thomson
1905 Miss H. Lane and Miss C. M. Wilson
1906–07 Mrs. G. W. Hillyard and Miss C. Meyer
1908 Miss H. M. Garfit and Mrs. A. Sterry
1909 Miss H. Aitchison and Miss C. O. Tuckey
1910 Miss H. M. Garfit and Mrs. W. E. Hudleston
1911–12–13 Mrs. D. R. Larcombe and Miss W. A. Longhurst
1914–18 no competition
1919–20–21 Mrs. D. R. Larcombe and Miss E. Ryan
1922 Miss K. McKane and Mrs. G. Peacock
1923 Miss C. Beckingham and Miss E. M. Beckingham
1924 Miss A. Clayton and Miss E. D. Holman
1925 Mrs. P. Satterthwaite and Miss M. Valentine
1926 Miss D. Gordon and Mrs. G. Hawkins
1927 Miss E. A. Goldsack and Miss P. Saunders
1928 Miss B. Feltham and Miss E. Hemmant
1929 Miss J. C. Boucher and Miss M. Howes
1930 Miss M. Heeley and Miss G. Vaughton
1931 Miss J. Ingram and Miss F. K. Scott

1932 Miss J. Ingram and Miss F. K. Scott
1933 Miss J. Ingram and Miss F. K. Scott
1934 Miss J. McAlpine and Miss A. M. Yorke
1935 Mrs. C. P. Brutton and Miss A. M. Yorke
1936 Mrs. V. Burr and Miss M. Heeley
1937 Miss S. Noel and Miss J. Saunders } divided
1937 Mrs. V. Burr and Miss M. Heeley } divided
1938 Miss V. E. Scott and Miss M. Whitmarsh
1939 Miss R. Jarvis and Mrs. R. D. McKelvie
1940–45 no competition
1946 Mrs. B. Carris and Miss E. H. Harvey
1947–48–49 Miss G. C. Hoahing and Miss E. A. Middleton
1950 Mrs. D. L. Wedderburn and Miss G. E. Woodgate
1951 Miss R. F. Woodgate and Mrs. S. Van Coller
1952 Miss R. F. Woodgate and Mrs. J. M. E. Wallace } divided
1952 Miss B. Penrose and Miss D. Spiers } divided
1953 Miss K. Nevill Smith and Miss R. Walsh } divided
1953 Miss R. H. Bentley and Miss P. A. Hird } divided

Mixed Doubles

1888 E. Renshaw and Mrs. G. W. Hillyard
1889 J. C. Kay and Mrs. G. W. Hillyard
1890 J. Baldwin and Miss K. Hill
1891 J. C. Kay and Miss H. Jackson
1892 A. Dod and Miss C. Dod
1893 W. Baddeley and Mrs. G. W. Hillyard
1894–95–96–97–98 H. S. Mahony and Miss C. Cooper
1899 C. H. L. Cazalet and Miss M. E. Robb

1900 H. L. Doherty and Miss C. Cooper
1901–02 S. H. Smith and Miss L. Martin
1903 F. L. Riseley and Miss D. K. Douglass
1904–05 S. H. Smith and Miss E. W. Thomson
1906 F. L. Riseley and Miss D. K. Douglass
1907 N. E. Brookes and Mrs. G. W. Hillyard
1908 X. E. Casdagli and Mrs. A. Sterry
1909 X. E. Casdagli and Miss H. M. Garfit
1910 J. C. Parke and Miss J. F. Luard
1911 T. M. Mavrogordato and Mrs. E. G. Parton
1912–13–14 J. C. Parke and Mrs. D. R. Larcombe
1915–18 no competition
1919 F. L. Riseley and Mrs. Lambert Chambers
1920–21–22 R. Lycett and Miss E. Ryan
1923 M. Woosnam and Miss E. Ryan
1924 W. Radcliffe and Miss E. M. Beckingham
1925 M. Woosnam and Miss E. Ryan
1926 W. Radcliffe and Mrs. F. M. Strawson
1927 D. A. Hodges and Miss C. Beckingham
1928 H. C. Hopman and Miss V. B. Southam
1929–30 D. M. Greig and Miss F. M. Strawson
1931 D. A. Hodges and Mrs. P. H. Watson } divided
1931 J. S. Oliff and Miss J. McAlpine } divided
1932 H. Timmer and Miss J. McAlpine
1933 J. H. Booth and Miss E. Goldsworth
1934 V. G. Kirby and Mrs. F. M. Strawson
1935 W. Hines and Miss M. Whitmarsh
1936 J. L. Chamberlain and Mrs. F. M. Strawson
1937 A. C. Stedman and Mme R. Mathieu
1938 C. E. Malfroy and Fru S. Sperling

L*

UNITED STATES CHAMPIONSHIPS

Second in prestige only to Wimbledon, the championships of the United States have, since their inception, been held on grass, a playing surface confined to the eastern seaboard. The bulk of lawn tennis in California, which has produced so many outstanding players, is on cement but nevertheless Americans have remained faithful to the original surface for which the game was designed. The championships have been played at various places which are indicated. The major difference between the Wimbledon Championships and those of the United States is the separation in America of the singles and doubles events. The men's and women's doubles are held in Boston and the singles, together with the mixed doubles, in New York about five days later as quite distinct meetings.

Men's Singles

The challenge-round system was instituted in 1884 and abolished in 1912. For that period *c* indicates the result of a challenge-round match, *f* the result of the all-comers' final in the years the holder did not defend.

Held at the Casino, Newport, Rhode Island.
1881 R. D. Sears *bt* W. E. Glyn 6–0 6–3 6–2
1882 R. D. Sears *bt* C. M. Clark 6–1 6–4 6–0
1883 R. D. Sears *bt* J. Dwight 6–2 6–0 9–7
1884 *c* R. D. Sears *bt* H. A. Taylor 6–1 6–6 6–0 6–2
1885 *c* R. D. Sears *bt* G. M. Brinley 6–3 4–6 6–0 6–3
1886 *c* R. D. Sears *bt* R. L. Beeckman 4–6 6–1 6–3 6–4
1887 *c* R. D. Sears *bt* H. W. Slocum 6–1 6–3 6–2
1888 *f* H. W. Slocum *bt* H. A. Taylor 6–4 6–1 6–0
1889 *c* H. W. Slocum *bt* Q. A. Shaw 6–3 6–1 4–6 6–2
1890 *c* O. S. Campbell *bt* H. W. Slocum 6–2 4–6 6–3 6–1
1891 *c* O. S. Campbell *bt* C. Hobart 2–6 7–5 7–9 6–1 6–2
1892 *c* O. S. Campbell *bt* F. H. Hovey 7–5 3–6 6–3 7–5
1893 *f* R. D. Wrenn *bt* F. H. Hovey 6–4 3–6 6–4 6–4
1894 *c* R. D. Wrenn *bt* M. F. Goodbody 6–8 6–1 6–4 6–4
1895 *c* F. H. Hovey *bt* R. D. Wrenn 6–3 6–2 6–4
1896 *c* R. D. Wrenn *bt* F. H. Hovey 7–5 3–6 6–0 1–6 6–1
1897 *c* R. D. Wrenn *bt* W. V. Eaves 4–6 8–6 6–3 2–6 6–2
1898 *f* M. D. Whitman *bt* D. F. Davis 3–6 6–2 6–2 6–1
1899 *c* M. D. Whitman *bt* J. P. Paret 6–1 6–2 3–6 7–5
1900 *c* M. D. Whitman *bt* W. A. Larned 6–4 1–6 6–2 6–2
1901 *c* W. A. Larned *bt* B. C. Wright 6–2 6–8 6–4 6–4
1902 *c* W. A. Larned *bt* R. F. Doherty 4–6 6–2 6–4 8–6
1903 *c* H. L. Doherty *bt* W. A. Larned 6–0 6–3 10–8
1904 *f* H. Ward *bt* W. J. Clothier 10–8 6–4 9–7
1905 *c* B. C. Wright *bt* H. Ward 6–2 6–1 11–9
1906 *c* W. J. Clothier *bt* B. C. Wright 6–3 6–0 6–4
1907 *f* W. A. Larned *bt* R. Le Roy 6–2 6–2 6–4
1908 *c* W. A. Larned *bt* B. C. Wright 6–1 6–2 8–6
1909 *c* W. A. Larned *bt* W. J. Clothier 6–1 6–2 5–7 1–6 6–1
1910 *c* W. A. Larned *bt* T. C. Bundy 6–1 5–7 6–0 6–8 6–1
1911 *c* W. A. Larned *bt* M. E. McLoughlin 6–4 6–4 6–2
Challenge round abolished
1912 M. E. McLoughlin *bt* W. M. Johnston 3–6 2–6 6–3 6–4 6–1
1913 M. E. McLoughlin *bt* R. N. Williams 6–4 5–7 6–3 6–1
1914 R. N. Williams *bt* M. E. McLoughlin 6–3 8–6 10–8
Held at West Side Tennis Club, New York.
1915 W. M. Johnston *bt* M. E. McLoughlin 1–6 6–0 7–5 10–8
1916 R. N. Williams *bt* W. M. Johnston 4–6 6–4 0–6 6–2 6–4
1917 *patriotic tournament only.* R. L. Murray *bt* N. W. Niles 5–7 8–6 6–3 6–3
1918 R. L. Murray *bt* W. T. Tilden 6–3 6–1 7–5
1919 W. M. Johnston *bt* W. T. Tilden 6–4 6–4 6–3
1920 W. T. Tilden *bt* W. M. Johnston 6–1 1–6 7–5 5–7 6–3
Held at Germantown Cricket Club, Philadelphia
1921 W. T. Tilden *bt* Wallace F. Johnson 6–1 6–3 6–1
1922 W. T. Tilden *bt* W. M. Johnston 4–6 3–6 6–2 6–3 6–4
1923 W. T. Tilden *bt* W. M. Johnston 6–4 6–1 6–4
Played at West Side Tennis Club, Forest Hills, New York
1924 W. T. Tilden *bt* W. M. Johnston 6–1 9–7 6–2
1925 W. T. Tilden *bt* W. M. Johnston 4–6 11–9 6–3 4–6 6–3

1926 R. Lacoste *bt* J. Borotra 6–4 6–0 6–4
1927 R. Lacoste *bt* W. T. Tilden 11–9 6–3 11–9
1928 H. Cochet *bt* F. T. Hunter 4–6 6–4 3–6 7–5 6–3
1929 W. T. Tilden *bt* F. T. Hunter 3–6 6–3 4–6 6–2 6–4
1930 J. H. Doeg *bt* F. X. Shields 10–8 1–6 6–4 16–14
1931 H. E. Vines *bt* G. M. Lott 7–9 6–3 9–7 7–5
1932 H. E. Vines *bt* H. Cochet 6–4 6–4 6–4
1933 F. J. Perry *bt* J. H. Crawford 6–3 11–13 4–6 6–0 6–1
1934 F. J. Perry *bt* W. L. Allison 6–4 6–3 3–6 1–6 8–6
1935 W. L. Allison *bt* S. B. Wood 6–2 6–2 6–3
1936 F. J. Perry *bt* J. D. Budge 2–6 6–2 8–6 1–6 10–8
1937 J. D. Budge *bt* G. Von Cramm 6–1 7–9 6–1 3–6 6–1
1938 J. D. Budge *bt* C. G. Mako 6–3 6–8 6–2 6–1
1939 R. L. Riggs *bt* S. W. Van Horn 6–4 6–2 6–4
1940 D. McNeill *bt* R. L. Riggs 4–6 6–8 6–3 6–3 7–5
1941 R. L. Riggs *bt* F. Kovacs 5–7 6–1 6–3 6–3
1942 F. R. Schroeder *bt* F. Parker 8–6 7–5 3–6 4–6 6–2
1943 J. R. Hunt *bt* J. Kramer 6–3 6–8 10–8 6–0
1944 F. Parker *bt* W. F. Talbert 6–4 3–6 6–3 6–3
1945 F. Parker *bt* W. F. Talbert 14–12 6–1 6–2
1946 J. Kramer *bt* T. Brown 9–7 6–3 6–0
1947 J. Kramer *bt* F. Parker 4–6 2–6 6–1 6–0 6–3
1948 R. A. Gonzales *bt* E. W. Sturgess 6–2 6–3 14–12
1949 R. A. Gonzales *bt* F. R. Schroeder 16–18 2–6 6–1 6–2 6–4
1950 A. Larsen *bt* H. Flam 6–3 4–6 5–7 6–4 6–3
1951 F. A. Sedgman *bt* E. V. Seixas 6–4 6–1 6–1
1952 F. A. Sedgman *bt* G. Mulloy 6–1 6–2 6–3
1953 M. A. Trabert *bt* E. V. Seixas 6–3 6–2 6–3
1954 E. V. Seixas *bt* R. N. Hartwig 3–6 6–2 6–4 6–4
1955 M. A. Trabert *bt* K. R. Rosewall 9–7 6–3 6–3
1956 K. R. Rosewall *bt* L. A. Hoad 4–6 6–2 6–3 6–3
1957 M. J. Anderson *bt* A. J. Cooper 10–8 7–5 6–4
1958 A. J. Cooper *bt* M. J. Anderson 6–2 3–6 4–6 10–8 8–6
1959 N. A. Fraser *bt* A. Olmedo 6–3 5–7 6–2 6–4

E. V. Seixas   Miss A. L. Brough   K. R. Rosewall

Women's Singles

A remarkable feature of the women's singles, which has been played side by side with the men's singles at Forest Hills only from 1924 onwards, is that around the turn of the century the best of five set matches were played, resulting in some of the longest matches in which women can ever have taken part. The championship was played under the challenge-round system until 1919. For that period *c* indicates the result of a challenge-round match, *f* the outcome of the all-comers' final when the holder did not defend. Some of the early scores of the finals of this championship were unrecorded and lost. There are nine omissions of the final score.

Played at the Philadelphia Cricket Club.
1887 Miss E. Hansell *bt* Miss L. Knight
1888 *c* Miss B. L. Townsend *bt* Miss E. Hansell
1889 *c* Miss B. L. Townsend *bt* Miss L. D. Voorhees 7–5 6–2
1890 *c* Miss E. C. Roosevelt *bt* Miss B. L. Townsend
1891 *c* Miss M. E. Cahill *bt* Miss E. C. Roosevelt
1892 *c* Miss M. E. Cahill *bt* Miss E. H. Moore
1893 *f* Miss A. M. Terry *bt* Miss A. Schultz
1894 *c* Miss H. R. Helwig *bt* Miss A. M. Terry 7–5 3–6 6–0 3–6 6–3
1895 *c* Miss J. P. Atkinson *bt* Miss H. R. Helwig 6–4 6–2 6–1
1896 *c* Miss E. H. Moore *bt* Miss J. P. Atkinson 6–4 4–6 6–3 6–2
1897 *c* Miss J. P. Atkinson *bt* Miss E. H. Moore 6–3 6–3 4–6 3–6 6–3
1898 *c* Miss J. P. Atkinson *bt* Miss M. Jones 6–3 5–7 6–4 2–6 7–5
1899 *f* Miss M. Jones *bt* Miss M. Banks
1900 *f* Miss M. McAteer *bt* Miss E. Parker
1901 *c* Miss E. H. Moore *bt* Miss M. McAteer 6–4 3–6 7–5 2–6 6–2
1902 *c* Miss M. Jones *bt* Miss E. H. Moore 6–1 1–0 ret'd
1903 *c* Miss E. H. Moore *bt* Miss M. Jones 7–5 8–6
1904 *c* Miss M. Sutton *bt* Miss E. H. Moore 6–1 6–2
1905 *f* Miss E. H. Moore *bt* Miss H. Homans 6–4 5–7 6–1
1906 *f* Miss H. Homans *bt* Mrs. M. Barger-Wallach
1907 *f* Miss E. Sears *bt* Miss C. B. Neely 6–3 6–2
1908 *c* Mrs. M. Barger-Wallach *bt* Miss E. Sears 6–2 1–6 6–3
1909 *c* Miss H. Hotchkiss *bt* Mrs. M. Barger-Wallach 6–0 6–1
1910 *c* Miss H. Hotchkiss *bt* Miss L. Hammond 6–4 6–2
1911 *c* Miss H. Hotchkiss *bt* Miss M. Sutton 8–10 6–1 9–7
1912 *f* Miss M. K. Browne *bt* Miss E. Sears 6–4 6–2
1913 *c* Miss M. K. Browne *bt* Miss D. Green 6–2 7–5
1914 *c* Miss M. K. Browne *bt* Miss M. Wagner 6–2 1–6 6–1
1915 *f* Miss M. Bjurstedt *bt* Mrs. G. W. Wightman 4–6 6–2 6–0
1916 *c* Miss M. Bjurstedt *bt* Mrs. E. Raymond 6–0 6–1
1917 *patriotic tournament only.* Miss M. Bjurstedt *bt* Miss M. Vanderhoef 4–6 6–0 6–2
1918 *c* Miss M. Bjurstedt *bt* Miss E. Goss 6–4 6–3
Challenge round abolished
1919 Mrs. G. W. Wightman *bt* Miss M. Zinderstein 6–1 6–2
1920 Mrs. F. Mallory *bt* Miss M. Zinderstein 6–3 6–1
Played at West Side Tennis Club, Forest Hills, New York.
1921 Mrs. F. Mallory *bt* Miss M. K. Browne 4–6 6–4 6–2
1922 Mrs. F. Mallory *bt* Miss H. Wills 6–3 6–1
1923 Miss H. Wills *bt* Mrs. F. Mallory 6–2 6–1
1924 Miss H. Wills *bt* Mrs. F. Mallory 6–1 6–2
1925 Miss H. Wills *bt* Miss K. McKane 3–6 6–0 6–2
1926 Mrs. F. Mallory *bt* Miss E. Ryan 4–6 6–4 9–7
1927 Miss H. Wills *bt* Miss B. Nuthall 6–1 6–4
1928 Miss H. Wills *bt* Miss H. Jacobs 6–2 6–1
1929 Miss H. Wills *bt* Mrs. P. H. Watson 6–4 6–2

TENNIS QUIZ

1. How many married couples have won the mixed doubles at Wimbledon?

*

2. What is the longest set in which a woman was involved?

*

3. Who was Mary Outerbridge?

*

4. Who was Major Walter Clopton Wingfield?

*

5. What Norwegian won the singles championship of the U.S.?

*

6. On what surface is the French Championships played?

*

7. Where is the West Side Tennis Club?

*

8. Where is the Stade Roland Garros?

*

9. Where was the Rote-Weiss Club?

*

10. What championship is held at the Longwood Cricket Club?

QUIZ ANSWERS

1. One only. Mr. and Mrs. L. A. Godfree in 1926. 2. Probably 52 games. In the U.S. mixed doubles semi-final in 1948 W. F. Talbert and Mrs. W. D. du Pont beat R. Falkenburg and Miss G. Moran 27–25 5–7 6–1. 3. She introduced lawn tennis to the United States in 1874. 4. The inventor of "Sphairistike" in 1872–73. The game of lawn tennis is mainly derived from his efforts. 5. Miss Molla Bjurstedt, afterwards Mrs. Mallory. 6. "Terre battue", like the normal red English hard court. 7. At Forest Hills, Queen's, New York. 8. At Auteuil, Paris. 9. Berlin. 10. The U.S. National Doubles. It is on the outskirts of Boston.

Women's Singles—cont.

1930 Miss B. Nuthall *bt* Mrs. L. A. Harper 6–4 6–1
1931 Mrs. F. S. Moody *bt* Mrs. E. F. Whittingstall 6–4 6–1
1932 Miss H. Jacobs *bt* Miss C. A. Babcock 6–2 6–2
1933 Miss H. Jacobs *bt* Mrs. F. S. Moody 8–6 3–6 3–0 ret'd
1934 Miss H. Jacobs *bt* Miss S. H. Palfrey 6–1 6–4
1935 Miss H. Jacobs *bt* Mrs. M. Fabyan 6–1 6–4
1936 Miss A. Marble *bt* Miss H. Jacobs 4–6 6–3 6–2
1937 Sen. A. Lizana *bt* Panna J. Jedrzejowska 6–4 6–2
1938 Miss A. Marble *bt* Miss N. Wynne 6–0 6–3
1939 Miss A. Marble *bt* Miss H. Jacobs 6–0 8–10 6–4
1940 Miss A. Marble *bt* Miss H. Jacobs 6–2 6–3
1941 Mrs. E. T. Cooke *bt* Miss P. M. Betz 6–1 6–4
1942 Miss P. M. Betz *bt* Miss L. Brough 4–6 6–1 6–4
1943 Miss P. M. Betz *bt* Miss L. Brough 6–3 5–7 6–3

1944 Miss P. M. Betz *bt* Miss M. E. Osborne 6–3 8–6
1945 Miss E. T. Cooke *bt* Miss P. M. Betz 3–6 8–6 6–4
1946 Miss P. M. Betz *bt* Miss D. J. Hart 11–9 6–3
1947 Miss A. L. Brough *bt* Miss M. E. Osborne 8–6 4–6 6–1
1948 Mrs. W. D. du Pont *bt* Miss A. L. Brough 4–6 6–4 15–13
1949 Mrs. W. D. du Pont *bt* Miss D. J. Hart 6–4 6–1
1950 Mrs. W. D. du Pont *bt* Miss D. J. Hart 6–3 6–3
1951 Miss M. Connolly *bt* Miss S. J. Fry 6–3 1–6 6–4
1952 Miss M. Connolly *bt* Miss D. J. Hart 6–3 7–5
1953 Miss M. Connolly *bt* Miss D. J. Hart 6–2 6–4
1954 Miss D. J. Hart *bt* Miss A. L. Brough 6–8 6–1 8–6
1955 Miss D. J. Hart *bt* Miss P. E. Ward 6–4 6–2
1956 Miss S. J. Fry *bt* Miss A. Gibson 6–3 6–4
1957 Miss A. Gibson *bt* Miss A. L. Brough 6–3 6–2
1958 Miss A. Gibson *bt* Miss D. R. Hard 3–6 6–1 6–2
1959 Miss M. E. Bueno *bt* Miss C. C. Truman 6–1 6–4

L. A. Hoad

Men's Doubles

From 1881 to 1889 this championship was held in conjunction with the singles at Newport, R.I. In 1890 tournaments were held in the East and the West, the winners playing off to meet the standing-out champions. In 1907 the sectional tournaments were increased to three and further increased in subsequent years. The 1918 meeting was held as a play-through tournament, the challenge round revived in 1919 but abolished for good from 1920 onwards, since when the venue has been the Longwood Cricket Club, near Boston.

1881 C. M. Clark and F. W. Taylor
1882–83–84 J. Dwight and R. D. Sears
1885 J. S. Clark and R. D. Sears
1886–87 J. Dwight and R. D. Sears
1888 O. S. Campbell and V. G. Hall
1889 H. W. Slocum and H. A. Taylor
1890 V. G. Hall and C. Hobart
1891–92 O. S. Campbell and R. P. Huntingdon, Jnr.
1893–94 C. Hobart and F. H. Hovey
1895 M. G. Chase and R. D. Wrenn
1896 C. B. Neel and S. R. Neel
1897–98 G. P. Sheldon and L. E. Ware
1899–1900–01 D. F. Davis and H. Ward
1902–03 H. L. Doherty and R. F. Doherty
1904–05–06 H. Ward and B. C. Wright
1907–08–09–10 F. B. Alexander and H. H. Hackett
1911 R. D. Little and G. F. Touchard
1912–13–14 T. C. Bundy and M. E. McLoughlin

1915–16 C. J. Griffin and W. M. Johnston
1917 F. B. Alexander and H. A. Throckmorton (*patriotic tournament only*)
1918 V. Richards and W. T. Tilden
1919 N. E. Brookes and G. L. Patterson
1920 C. J. Griffin and W. M. Johnston
1921–22 V. Richards and W. T. Tilden
1923 B. I. C. Norton and W. T. Tilden
1924 H. O. Kinsey and R. G. Kinsey
1925–26 V. Richards and R. N. Williams
1927 F. T. Hunter and W. T. Tilden
1928 J. F. Hennessey and G. M. Lott
1929–30 J. H. Doeg and G. M. Lott
1931 W. L. Allison and J. van Ryn
1932 K. Gledhill and H. E. Vines
1933–34 G. M. Lott and L. R. Stoefen
1935 W. L. Allison and J. van Ryn
1936 J. D. Budge and C. G. Mako
1937 G. Von Cramm and H. Henkel

1938 J. D. Budge and C. G. Mako
1939 J. E. Bromwich and A. K. Quist
1940–41 J. A. Kramer and F. R. Schroeder
1942 G. Mulloy and W. F. Talbert
1943 J. A. Kramer and F. A. Parker
1944 R. Falkenburg and W. D. McNeill
1945–46 G. Mulloy and W. F. Talbert
1947 J. A. Kramer and F. R. Schroeder
1948 G. Mulloy and W. F. Talbert
1949 J. E. Bromwich and O. W. Sidwell
1950 J. E. Bromwich and F. A. Sedgman
1951 K. McGregor and F. A. Sedgman
1952 M. G. Rose and E. V. Seixas
1953 R. N. Hartwig and M. G. Rose
1954 E. V. Seixas and M. A. Trabert
1955 K. Kamo and A. Miyagi
1956 L. A. Hoad and K. R. Rosewall
1957 A. J. Cooper and N. A. Fraser
1958 H. Richardson and A. Olmedo
1959 R. Emerson and N. A. Fraser

Women's Doubles

This event was played from 1890 to 1920 at the Philadelphia Cricket Club, from 1921 to 1934 at Forest Hills and from 1935 onwards at the Longwood Cricket Club, Chestnut Hill, near Boston, Mass.

1890 Miss E. C. Roosevelt and Miss G. W. Roosevelt
1891 Miss M. E. Cahill and Mrs. W. Fellowes Morgan
1892 Miss M. E. Cahill and Miss A. M. McKinley
1893 Miss H. Butler and Miss A. M. Terry
1894–95 Miss J. P. Atkinson and Miss H. R. Helwig
1896 Miss J. P. Atkinson and Miss E. H. Moore
1897–98 Miss J. P. Atkinson and Miss K. Atkinson
1899 Miss J. W. Craven and Miss M. McAteer
1900 Miss H. Champlin and Miss E. Parker
1901 Miss J. P. Atkinson and Miss M. McAteer
1902 Miss J. P. Atkinson and Miss M. Jones
1903 Miss E. H. Moore and Miss C. B. Neely
1904 Miss M. Hall and Miss M. Sutton
1905 Miss H. Homand and Miss C. B. Neely
1906 Mrs. L. S. Coe and Miss D. S. Platt
1907 Miss C. B. Neely and Miss M. Weimer
1908 Miss M. Curtis and Miss E. Sears
1909–10 Miss H. Hotchkiss and Miss E. E. Roach
1911 Miss H. Hotchkiss and Miss E. Sears
1912 Miss M. K. Browne and Miss D. Green
1913–14 Miss M. K. Browne and Mrs. R. H. Williams
1915 Miss E. Sears and Mrs. G. W. Wightman
1916–17 Miss M. Bjurstedt and Miss E. Sears (1917 *patriotic tournament only*)
1918–19–20 Miss E. Goss and Miss M. Zinderstein

1921 Miss M. K. Browne and Mrs. L. Williams
1922 Mrs. J. B. Jessup and Miss H. Wills
1923 Mrs. B. C. Covell and Miss K. KcKane
1924 Mrs. G. W. Wightman and Miss H. Wills
1925 Miss M. K. Browne and Miss H. Wills
1926 Miss E. Goss and Miss E. Ryan
1927 Mrs. L. A. Godfree and Miss E. H. Harvey
1928 Mrs. G. W. Wightman and Miss H. Wills
1929 Mrs. L. R. C. Michell and Mrs. P. H. Watson
1930 Miss B. Nuthall and Miss S. H. Palfrey
1931 Miss B. Nuthall and Mrs. E. F. Whittingstall
1932 Miss H. Jacobs and Miss S. H. Palfrey
1933 Miss F. James and Miss B. Nuthall
1934 Miss H. Jacobs and Miss S. H. Palfrey
1935 Mrs. M. Fabyan and Miss H. Jacobs
1936 Miss C. Babcock and Mrs. J. van Ryn
1937–40 Mrs. M. Fabyan and Miss A. Marble
1941 Mrs. E. T. Cooke and Miss M. E. Osborne
1942–43–44–45–46–47 Miss A. L. Brough and Miss M. E. Osborne
1948–49–50 Miss A. L. Brough and Mrs. W. D. du Pont
1951–52–53–54 Miss S. J. Fry and Miss D. J. Hart
1955–56–57 Miss A. L. Brough and Mrs. W. D. du Pont
1958–59 Miss J. Arth and Miss D. R. Hard

Mixed Doubles

This event was held at the Philadelphia Cricket Club from 1892 to 1920, at the Longwood Cricket Club, Chestnut Hill, Boston from 1921 to 1941 and from 1942 onwards at the West Side Tennis Club, Forest Hills, New York, in conjunction with the singles championships.

1892 C. Hobart and Miss M. E. Cahill
1893 C. Hobart and Miss E. C. Roosevelt
1894–96 E. P. Fischer and Miss J. P. Atkinson
1897 D. L. Magruder and Miss L. Henson
1898 E. P. Fischer and Miss C. B. Neely
1899 A. L. Hoskins and Miss E. J. Rastall
1900 A. Codman and Miss M. J. Hunnewell
1901 R. D. Little and Miss M. Jones
1902 W. C. Grant and Miss E. H. Moore
1903 H. F. Allen and Miss H. Chapman
1904 W. C. Grant and Miss E. H. Moore
1905 C. Hobart and Mrs. Hobart
1906 E. B. Dewhurst and Miss S. Coffin
1907 W. F. Johnson and Miss M. Sayres
1908 N. W. Niles and Miss E. E. Rotch
1909 W. F. Johnson and Miss H. Hotchkiss
1910 J. R. Carpenter and Miss H. Hotchkiss
1911 W. F. Johnson and Miss H. Hotchkiss
1912 R. N. Williams and Miss M. K. Browne
1913–14 W. T. Tilden and Miss M. K. Browne
1915 H. C. Johnson and Mrs. G. W. Wightman
1916 W. E. Davis and Miss E. Sears
1917 I. C. Wright and Miss M. Bjurstedt (*patriotic tournament only*)
1918 I. C. Wright and Mrs. G. W. Wightman
1919 V. Richards and Miss M. Zinderstein
1920 W. F. Johnson and Mrs. G. W. Wightman
1921 W. M. Johnston and Miss M. K. Browne
1922–23 W. T. Tilden and Mrs. F. Mallory
1924 V. Richards and Miss H. Wills

1925 J. B. Hawkes and Miss K. McKane
1926 J. Borotra and Miss E. Ryan
1927 H. Cochet and Miss E. Bennett
1928 J. B. Hawkes and Miss H. Wills
1929 G. M. Lott and Miss B. Nuthall
1930 W. L. Allison and Miss E. Cross
1931 G. M. Lott and Miss B. Nuthall
1932 F. J. Perry and Miss S. H. Palfrey
1933 H. E. Vines and Miss E. Ryan
1934 G. M. Lott and Miss H. Jacobs
1935 E. Maier and Mrs. M. Fabyan
1936 C. G. Mako and Miss A. Marble
1937 J. D. Budge and Mrs. M. Fabyan
1938 J. D. Budge and Miss A. Marble
1939 H. C. Hopman and Miss A. Marble
1940 R. L. Riggs and Miss A. Marble
1941 J. A. Kramer and Mrs. E. T. Cooke
1942 F. R. Schroeder and Miss A. L. Brough
1943–44–45–46 W. F. Talbert and Miss M. E. Osborne
1947 J. E. Bromwich and Miss A. L. Brough
1948 T. Brown and Miss A. L. Brough
1949 W. Sturgess and Miss A. L. Brough
1950 K. McGregor and Mrs. W. D. du Pont
1951–52 F. A. Sedgman and Miss D. J. Hart
1953–54–55 E. V. Seixas and Miss D. J. Hart
1956 K. R. Rosewall and Mrs. W. D. du Pont
1957 K. Neilsen and Miss A. Gibson
1958–59 N. A. Fraser and Mrs. W. D. du Pont

THE FRENCH CHAMPIONSHIPS

The outstanding hard-court meeting of the world was a closed championship until 1925 when it was thrown open to players of all nationalities. In 1925 and 1927 it was played at St. Cloud and in 1926 at the Racing Club de France. Since 1928 it has been held at the Stade Roland Garros, Auteuil, all these venues being in or near Paris.

Men's Singles

1925 R. Lacoste *bt* J. Borotra 7–5 6–1 6–4	1940–45 not held. *"Tournoi de France"* won 1941–2 by B. Destremau, 1943–5 by Y. Petra.
1926 H. Cochet *bt* R. Lacoste 6–2 6–4 6–3	1946 M. Bernard *bt* J. Drobny 3–6 2–6 6–1 6–4 6–3
1927 R. Lacoste *bt* W. T. Tilden 6–4 4–6 5–7 6–3 11–9	1947 J. Asboth *bt* E. W. Sturgess 8–6 7–5 6–4
1928 H. Cochet *bt* R. Lacoste 5–7 6–3 6–1 6–3	1948 F. Parker *bt* J. Drobny 6–4 7–5 5–7 8–6
1929 R. Lacoste *bt* J. Borotra 6–3 2–6 6–0 2–6 8–6	1949 F. Parker *bt* J. E. Patty 6–3 1–6 6–1 6–4
1930 H. Cochet *bt* W. T. Tilden 3–6 8–6 6–3 6–1	1950 J. E. Patty *bt* J. Drobny 6–1 6–2 3–6 5–7 7–5
1931 J. Borotra *bt* C. Boussus 2–6 6–4 7–5 6–4	1951 J. Drobny *bt* E. W. Sturgess 6–3 6–3 6–3
1932 H. Cochet *bt* G. de Stefani 6–0 6–4 4–6 6–3	1952 J. Drobny *bt* F. A. Sedgman 6–2 6–0 3–6 6–4
1933 J. H. Crawford *bt* H. Cochet 8–6 6–1 6–3	1953 K. R. Rosewall *bt* E. V. Seixas 6–3 6–4 1–6 6–2
1934 G. Von Cramm *bt* J. H. Crawford 6–4 7–9 3–6 7–5 6–3	1954 M. A. Trabert *bt* A. Larsen 4–7 5–6 6–1
1935 F. J. Perry *bt* G. Von Cramm 6–3 3–6 6–1 6–3	1955 M. A. Trabert *bt* S. Davidson 2–6 6–1 6–4 6–2
1936 G. Von Cramm *bt* F. J. Perry 6–0 2–6 6–2 2–6 6–0	1956 L. A. Hoad *bt* S. Davidson 6–4 8–6 6–3
1937 H. Henkel *bt* H. W. Austin 6–1 6–4 6–3	1957 S. Davidson *bt* H. Flam 6–3 6–4 6–4
1938 J. D. Budge *bt* R. Menzel 6–3 6–2 6–4	1958 M. G. Rose *bt* L. Ayala 6–3 6–4 6–4
1939 W. D. McNeill *bt* R. L. Riggs 7–5 6–0 6–3	1959 N. Pietrangeli *bt* I. C. Vermaak 3–6 6–3 6–4 6–1

Women's Singles

1925 Mlle S. Lenglen *bt* Miss K. McKane 6–1 6–2	Mlle A. Weiwers, 1943 Mme S. Lafargue, 1944 Mlle R. Veber, 1945 Mme L. Dodille
1926 Mlle S. Lenglen *bt* Miss M. K. Browne 6–1 6–0	1946 Miss M. E. Osborne *bt* Miss P. M. Betz 1–6 8–6 7–5
1927 Mlle K. Bouman *bt* Mrs. G. Peacock 6–2 6–4	1947 Mrs. P. C. Todd *bt* Miss D. J. Hart 6–3 3–6 6–4
1928 Miss H. Wills *bt* Miss E. Bennett 6–1 6–2	1948 Mme N. Landry *bt* Miss S. J. Fry 6–2 0–6 6–0
1929 Miss H. Wills *bt* Mme R. Mathieu 6–3 6–4	1949 Miss W. D. du Pont *bt* Mme N. Adamson 7–5 6–2
1930 Mrs. F. S. Moody *bt* Miss H. Jacobs 6–2 6–1	1950 Miss D. J. Hart *bt* Mrs. P. C. Todd 6–4 4–6 6–2
1931 Frl C. Aussem *bt* Miss B. Nuthall 8–6 6–1	1951 Miss S. J. Fry *bt* Miss D. J. Hart 6–3 3–6 6–3
1932 Mrs. F. S. Moody *bt* Mme R. Mathieu 7–5 6–1	1952 Miss D. J. Hart *bt* Miss S. J. Fry 6–4 6–4
1933 Miss M. C. Scriven *bt* Mme R. Mathieu 6–2 4–6 6–4	1953 Miss M. Connolly *bt* Miss D. J. Hart 6–2 6–4
1934 Miss M. C. Scriven *bt* Miss H. Jacobs 7–5 4–6 6–1	1954 Miss M. Connolly *bt* Mme G. Bucaille 6–4 6–1
1935 Fru S. Sperling *bt* Mme R. Mathieu 6–2 6–1	1955 Miss A. Mortimer *bt* Miss D. P. Knode 2–6 7–5 10–8
1936 Fru S. Sperling *bt* Mme R. Mathieu 6–3 6–4	1956 Miss A. Gibson *bt* Miss A. Mortimer 6–0 12–10
1937 Fru S. Sperling *bt* Mme R. Mathieu 6–2 6–4	1957 Miss S. J. Bloomer *bt* Mrs. D. P. Knode 6–1 6–3
1938 Mme R. Mathieu *bt* Mme N. Landry 6–0 6–3	1958 Miss S. Kormoczy *bt* Miss S. J. Bloomer 6–4 1–6 6–2
1939 Mme R. Mathieu *bt* Panna J. Jedrzejowska 6–3 8–6	1959 Miss C. C. Truman *bt* Mrs. S. Kormoczy 6–4 7–5
1940–45 not held. *"Tournoi de France"* won 1941–2 by	

Men's Doubles

1925 J. Borotra and R. Lacoste	1935 J. H. Crawford and A. K. Quist	1950 W. F. Talbert and T. Trabert
1926 H. Kinsey and V. Richards	1936 M. Bernard and J. Borotra	1951–52 K. McGregor and F. A. Sedgman
1927 J. Brugnon and H. Cochet	1937 G. Von Cramm and H. Henkel	1953 L. A. Hoad and K. R. Rosewall
1928 J. Borotra and J. Brugnon	1938 B. Destremau and Y. Petra	1954–55 E. V. Seixas and T. Trabert
1929 J. Borotra and R. Lacoste	1939 C. Harris and W. D. McNeill	1956 D. W. Candy and R. M. Perry
1930 J. Brugnon and H. Cochet	1940–45 not held	1957 M. J. Anderson and A. J. Cooper
1931 G. M. Lott and J. van Ryn	1946 M. Bernard and Y. Petra	1958 A. J. Cooper and N. A. Fraser
1932 J. Brugnon and H. Cochet	1947 E. Fannin and E. W. Sturgess	1959 N. Pietrangeli and O. Sirola
1933 G. P. Hughes and F. J. Perry	1948 L. Bergelin and J. Drobny	
1934 J. Borotra and J. Brugnon	1949 R. A. Gonzales and F. A. Parker	

Women's Doubles

1925–26 Mlle S. Lenglen and Mlle D. Vlasto	1940–45 not held
1927 Miss E. L. Heine and Mrs. G. Peacock	1946–47 Miss A. L. Brough and Miss M. E. Osborne
1928 Miss E. Bennett and Mrs. P. H. Watson	1948 Miss D. J. Hart and Mrs. P. C. Todd
1929 Senorita L. de Alvarez and Mlle K. Bouman	1949 Miss A. L. Brough and Mrs. W. D. du Pont
1930 Mrs. F. S. Moody and Miss E. Ryan	1950–51–52–53 Miss S. J. Fry and Miss D. J. Hart
1931 Miss B. Nuthall and Miss E. F. Whittingstall	1954 Miss M. Connolly and Mrs. H. C. Hopman
1932 Mrs. F. S. Moody and Miss E. Ryan	1955 Mrs. J. Fleitz and Miss D. R. Hard
1933–34 Mme R. Mathieu and Miss E. Ryan	1956 Miss A. Buxton and Miss A. Gibson
1935 Miss M. C. Scriven and Miss K. E. Stammers	1957 Miss S. J. Bloomer and Miss D. R. Hard
1936–38 Mme R. Mathieu and Miss A. M. Yorke	1958 Sen. Y. Ramirez and Sen. R. M. Reyes
1939 Mme R. Mathieu and Mlle J. Jedrzejowska	1959 Miss S. Reynolds and Miss R. Shuurman

R. Lacoste	J. E. Bromwich	M. G. Rose	J. H. Crawford

Mixed Doubles

1925–26 J. Brugnon and Mlle S. Lenglen	1946 J. E. Patty and Miss P. M. Betz
1927 J. Borotra and Mme M. Bordes	1947 E. W. Sturgess and Mrs. S. P. Summers
1928–29 H. Cochet and Miss E. Bennett	1948 J. Drobny and Mrs. P. C. Todd
1930 W. T. Tilden and Frl. C. Aussem	1949 E. W. Sturgess and Mrs. S. P. Summers
1931 P. D. B. Spence and Miss B. Nuthall	1950 E. Morea and Miss B. Scofield
1932 F. J. Perry and Miss B. Nuthall	1951–52 F. A. Sedgman and Miss D. J. Hart
1933 J. H. Crawford and Miss M. C. Scriven	1953 E. V. Seixas and Miss D. J. Hart
1934 J. Borotra and Mlle C. Rosambert	1954 L. A. Hoad and Miss M. Connolly
1935 M. Bernard and Mlle L. Payot	1955 G. L. Forbes and Miss D. R. Hard
1936 M. Bernard and Miss A. M. Yorke	1956 L. Ayala and Mrs. T. Long
1937 Y. Petra and Mme R. Mathieu	1957 J. Javorsky and Mme V. Puzejova
1938 D. Mitic and Mme R. Mathieu	1958 N. Pietrangeli and Miss S. J. Bloomer
1939 E. T. Cooke and Mrs. M. Fabyan	1959 W. A. Knight and Miss Y. Ramirez
1940–45 not held	

(NOTE: *The first French championship dates from 1891 and because it was a closed championship restricted to French nationals the results up to 1924 have no international significance. It is worth indicating, however, that the fabulous Mlle Suzanne Lenglen was champion in singles, women's doubles and mixed doubles 1920–21–22 and 1923.*)

AUSTRALIAN CHAMPIONSHIPS

The oldest meeting in Australia is the State Championship of Victoria, dating from 1880. The Australian Championships, originally known as the Australasian Championships, date from the federation of the country in 1905. The meeting has always been held at different venues and has been staged in New Zealand but of latter years has alternated between Melbourne, Sydney and Adelaide.

Men's Singles

1905	R. W. Heath
1906	A. F. Wilding
1907	H. Rice
1908	F. B. Alexander
1909	A. F. Wilding
1910	R. W. Heath
1911	N. E. Brookes
1912	J. C. Parke
1913	E. F. Parker
1914	A. H. O'Hara Wood
1915	F. G. Lowe
1916–18	*no competition*
1919	A. R. F. Kingscote
1920	P. O'Hara Wood
1921	R. H. Gemmell
1922	J. O. Anderson
1923	P. O'Hara Wood
1924–25	J. O. Anderson
1926	J. B. Hawkes
1927	G. L. Patterson
1928	J. Borotra
1929	J. C. Gregory
1930	E. F. Moon
1931–32–33	J. H. Crawford
1934	F. J. Perry
1935	J. H. Crawford
1936	A. K. Quist
1937	V. B. McGrath
1938	J. D. Budge
1939	J. E. Bromwich
1940	A. K. Quist
1941–45	*no competition*
1946	J. E. Bromwich
1947	D. Pails
1948	A. K. Quist
1949–50	F. A. Sedgman
1951	R. Savitt
1952	K. McGregor
1953	K. R. Rosewall
1954	M. G. Rose
1955	K. R. Rosewall
1956	L. A. Hoad
1957–58	A. J. Cooper
1959	A. Olmedo

TENNIS QUIZ

1. On what surface is the U.S. Hard Court Championship played?

*

2. What is the King's Cup?

*

3. What is the Mitre Cup?

*

4. What is the Wightman Cup?

*

5. What is the official name for the Davis Cup?

QUIZ ANSWERS

1. Cement. 2. Team championship on covered courts played like the Davis Cup. The King of Sweden donated the trophy. 3. A competition on Davis Cup lines between the nations of South America. 4. The annual contest between women's teams of United States and Great Britain. 5. The International Lawn Tennis Championship.

Women's Singles

The early history of the women's events is obscure, even in contemporary publications. The women's singles championship of 1908 was won by Miss P. A. Stewart, of 1910 by Miss L. Addison and of 1914 by Miss P. A. Stewart again, but a complete list of champions is available only from 1922.

1922–23 Mrs. B. H. Molesworth
1924 Miss S. Lance
1925–26 Miss D. Akhurst
1927 Miss E. Boyd
1928–29–30 Miss D. Akhurst
1931–32 Mrs. C. Buttsworth
1933–34 Miss J. Hartigan
1935 Miss D. E. Round
1936 Miss J. Hartigan
1937 Miss N. Wynne
1938 Miss D. M. Bundy
1939 Mrs. V. Westacott
1940 Miss N. Wynne
1941–45 no competition
1946–47–48 Mrs. N. Bolton
1949 Miss D. J. Hart
1950 Miss A. L. Brough
1951 Miss N. Bolton
1952 Mrs. T. Long
1953 Miss M. Connolly
1954 Mrs. T. Long
1955 Miss B. Penrose
1956 Miss M. Carter
1957 Miss S. J. Fry
1958 Miss A. Mortimer
1959 Mrs. M. Reitano

Men's Doubles

1905 R. Lycett and T. Tachell
1906 R. W. Heath and A. F. Wilding
1907 W. A. Begg and H. A. Parker
1908 F. B. Alexander and A. W. Dunlop
1909 J. P. Keane and E. F. Parker
1910 A. Campbell and H. Rice
1911 R. W. Heath and R. Lycett
1912 C. P. Dixon and J. C. Parke
1913 A. H. Hedemann and E. F. Parker
1914 A. Campbell and G. L. Patterson
1915 H. Rice and C. V. Todd
1916–18 no competition
1919–20 P. O'Hara Wood and R. V. Thomas
1921 S. H. Eaton and R. H. Gemmell
1922 J. B. Hawkes and G. L. Patterson
1923 P. O'Hara Wood and F. B. St. John
1924 J. O. Anderson and N. E. Brookes
1925 P. O'Hara Wood and G. L. Patterson
1926–27 J. B. Hawkes and G. L. Patterson
1928 J. Borotra and J. Brugnon
1929–30 J. H. Crawford and H. C. Hopman
1931 C. Donohoe and R. Dunlop
1932 J. H. Crawford and E. F. Moon
1933 K. Gledhill and H. E. Vines
1934 G. P. Hughes and F. J. Perry
1935 J. H. Crawford and V. B. McGrath
1936–37 A. K. Quist and D. P. Turnbull
1938–39–40 J. E. Bromwich and A. K. Quist
1941–45 no competition
1946–47–48–49–50 J. E. Bromwich and A. K. Quist
1951–52 K. McGregor and F. A. Sedgman
1953 L. A. Hoad and K. R. Rosewall
1954 R. N. Hartwig and M. G. Rose
1955 E. V. Seixas and M. A. Trabert
1956 L. A. Hoad and K. R. Rosewall
1957 N. A. Fraser and L. A. Hoad
1958 A. J. Cooper and N. A. Fraser
1959 R. Laver and R. Mark

TENNIS QUIZ

1. Can women play in the Davis Cup?

*

2. Who has played the most Davis Cup rubbers?

*

3. When were the French Championships made open to all nationalities?

4. When did jumping while serving become legal?

*

5. What two Wimbledon champions adopted a singing career?

QUIZ ANSWERS

1. By custom and implication, no. But the rules do not specifically indicate that it must be men. 2. Baron Gottfried Von Cramm. 102 rubbers for Germany between 1932 and 1953. 3. 1925. 4. On the 1st January 1959. 5 Miss Alice Marble and Miss Althea Gibson.

J. Drobny

Kho Sin Kie

Miss D. J. Hart

Women's Doubles

1922 Miss E. F. Boyd and Miss M. Mountain
1923 Miss E. F. Boyd and Miss S. Lance
1924 Miss D. Akhurst and Miss S. Lance
1925 Miss D. Akhurst and Mrs. R. Harper
1926 Miss E. F. Boyd and Mrs. P. O'Hara Wood
1927 Miss L. Bickerton and Mrs. P. O'Hara Wood
1928 Miss D. Akhurst and Miss E. F. Boyd
1929 Miss D. Akhurst and Miss L. Bickerton
1930 Miss E. Hood and Mrs. B. H. Molesworth
1931 Miss L. Bickerton and Mrs. R. Cozens
1932 Mrs. C. Buttsworth and Mrs. J. H. Crawford
1933–34 Mrs. B. H. Molesworth and Mrs. V. Westacott
1935 Miss E. Dearman and Miss N. M. Lyle
1936–37–38–39–40 Miss T. Coyne and Miss N. Wynne
1941–45 no competition
1946 Miss M. Bevis and Miss J. Fitch
1947–48–49 Mrs. N. Bolton and Mrs. T. Long

1950 Miss A. L. Brough and Miss D. J. Hart
1951–52 Mrs. N. Bolton and Mrs. T. Long
1953 Miss M. Connolly and Miss J. Sampson
1954–55 Mrs. K. Hawton and Miss B. Penrose
1956 Mrs. K. Hawton and Mrs. T. Long
1957 Miss S. J. Fry and Miss A. Gibson
1958 Mrs. K. Hawton and Mrs. T. Long
1959 Miss S. Reynolds and Miss R. Schuurman

Mixed Doubles

1922 J. B. Hawkes and Miss E. F. Boyd
1923 H. M. Rice and Miss S. Lance
1924–25 J. Willard and Miss D. Akhurst
1926–27 J. B. Hawkes and Miss E. F. Boyd
1928 J. Borotra and Miss D. Akhurst
1929 E. F. Moon and Miss D. Akhurst
1930 H. C. Hopman and Miss N. Hall

1931–32–33 J. H. Crawford and Mrs. Crawford
1934 E. F. Moon and Miss J. Hartigan
1935 C. Boussus and Miss L. Bickerton
1936–37 H. C. Hopman and Mrs. Hopman
1938 J. E. Bromwich and Miss M. Wilson
1939 H. C. Hopman and Mrs. Hopman
1940 C. Long and Miss N. Wynne
1941–45 no competition
1946–48 C. Long and Mrs. N. Bolton
1949–50 F. A. Sedgman and Miss D. J. Hart
1951–52 G. E. Worthington and Mrs. T. Long
1953 R. N. Hartwig and Miss J. Sampson
1954 R. N. Hartwig and Mrs. T. Long
1955 G. E. Worthington and Mrs. T. Long
1956 N. A. Fraser and Miss B. Penrose
1957 M. J. Anderson and Miss F. Muller
1958 R. N. Howe and Mrs. K. Hawton
1959 R. Mark and Miss S. Reynolds

BRITISH HARD COURT CHAMPIONSHIPS

Instituted in 1924, this championship was held until 1926 at Torquay; from 1927 its venue has been the West Hants Club, Bournemouth.

Men's Singles

1924 R. Lycett bt C. van Lennep 6–1 3–6 6–4 6–3
1925 P. D. B. Spence bt C. H. Kingsley 6–4 4–6 9–7
1926 J. Brugnon bt H. W. Austin 7–5 4–6 3–6 8–6 6–3
1927 R. Lacoste bt P. D. B. Spence 6–1 6–2 6–2
1928 R. Lacoste bt P. D. B. Spence 6–2 6–2 6–2
1929 H. W. Austin bt L. Raymond 6–3 6–2 1–6 6–4
1930 H. G. N. Lee bt E. C. Peters 6–3 2–6 6–4 6–4
1931 C. Boussus bt G. P. Hughes 8–6 6–4 4–6 6–2
1932 F. J. Perry bt G. L. Rogers 4–6 7–9 6–3 6–0 6–2
1933 F. J. Perry bt H. W. Austin 2–6 7–5 7–5 6–2
1934 F. J. Perry bt J. H. Crawford 8–6 7–5 6–1
1935 F. J. Perry bt H. W. Austin 0–6 6–4 6–2 6–0
1936 F. J. Perry bt H. W. Austin 6–2 8–6 6–3
1937 H. W. Austin bt H. G. N. Lee 6–2 6–2 6–0
1938 Kho Sin Kie bt H. W. Austin 6–4 6–4 6–3
1939 Kho Sin Kie bt W. C. Choy 7–5 6–1 6–4
1940–45 no competition
1946 J. E. Harper bt D. W. Barton 7–5 6–2 6–1
1947 E. W. Sturgess bt I. Tloczynski 11–9 6–1 6–4
1948 E. W. Sturgess bt I. Tloczynski 6–2 3–6 6–1
1949 P. Masip bt H. Cochet 6–3 4–6 6–2 9–7
1950 J. Drobny bt G. E. Brown 7–5 6–0 6–4
1951 J. Drobny bt F. Ampon 6–4 6–2 6–0
1952 J. Drobny bt F. A. Sedgman 6–2 6–4 1–6 6–4
1953 E. Morea bt F. Ampon 6–3 6–2 6–1
1954 A. J. Mottram bt G. L. Paish 6–4 6–3 7–5
1955 S. Davidson bt R. Becker 11–9 6–3 6–1
1956 J. E. Patty bt H. Richardson 1–6 6–3 6–3 6–3
1957 J. Drobny bt L. A. Hoad 6–4 6–4 6–4
1958 W. A. Knight bt G. Merlo 5–7 6–0 6–2 6–3
1959 L. A. Gerrard bt W. A. Knight 3–6 2–6 6–2 7–5 9–7

Women's Singles

1924 Miss E. Ryan bt Mrs. A. E. Beamish 6–2 6–2
1925 Miss E. Ryan bt Miss J. Fry 6–2 6–2
1926 Miss J. Fry bt Mrs. P. H. Watson 6–1 7–9 6–1
1927 Miss B. Nuthall bt Miss E. R. Clarke 8–6 6–2
1928 Miss A. Goldsack bt Miss J. C. Ridley 8–6 6–4
1929 Miss E. L. Heine bt Miss J. C. Ridley 6–4 3–6 8–6
1930 Miss J. Fry bt Mrs. W. D. List 6–1 2–6 6–2
1931 Mme. R. Mathieu bt Miss M. Heeley 6–4 6–4
1932 Mme. R. Mathieu bt Miss D. E. Round 6–1 6–2
1933 Miss D. E. Round bt Miss H. Jacobs 3–6 6–2 6–3
1934 Miss D. E. Round bt Miss M. C. Scriven 6–2 2–6 8–6
1935 Miss K. E. Stammers bt Miss M. C. Scriven 6–2 6–2
1936 Miss K. E. Stammers bt Sen. A. Lizana 7–5 7–5
1937 Sen. A. Lizana bt Miss M. C. Scriven 7–5 6–3
1938 Miss M. C. Scriven bt Miss N. Wynne 7–5 6–2
1939 Miss K. E. Stammers bt Mrs. R. Ellis 6–3 6–3
1940–45 no competition
1946 Mrs. E. W. A. Bostock bt Mrs. M. Menzies 6–3 6–4
1947 Mrs. N. Bolton bt Miss P. J. Curry 7–5 6–3
1948 Mrs. B. E. Hilton bt Mrs. D. R. Bocquet 6–1 6–4
1949 Miss P. J. Curry bt Miss J. Quertier 3–6 7–5 7–5
1950 Miss P. J. Curry bt Sen. H. Weiss 8–6 8–6
1951 Miss D. J. Hart bt Mrs. J. J. Walker-Smith 6–4 8–6
1952 Miss D. J. Hart bt Miss S. J. Fry 6–4 6–3
1953 Miss D. J. Hart bt Miss S. J. Fry 6–3 4–6 6–4
1954 Miss D. J. Hart bt Mrs. A. J. Mottram 6–1 6–3
1955 Miss A. Mortimer bt Miss A. Buxton 6–1 6–1
1956 Miss A. Mortimer bt Miss J. S. Bloomer 7–5 5–7 6–1
1957 Miss S. J. Bloomer bt Miss P. E. Ward 3–6 6–2 6–3
1958 Miss S. J. Bloomer bt Miss A. S. Haydon 6–4 6–4
1959 Miss A. Mortimer bt Miss C. C. Truman 6–4 2–6 6–4

Men's Doubles

1924 F. L. Riseley and J. D. B. Wheatley
1925 H. S. L. Barclay and C. H. Kingsley
1926 G. R. O. Crole-Rees and C. G Eames
1927 J. Brugnon and R. Lacoste
1928 C. H. Kingsley and P. D. B. Spence
1929 G. R. O. Crole-Rees and C. G. Eames
1930 H. W. Austin and J. S. Olliff
1931 H. W. Austin and C. H. Kingsley
1932 J. S. Olliff and F. J. Perry
1933 J. H. Crawford and D. P. Turnbull
1934 J. H. Crawford and V. B. McGrath
1935 C. E. Malfroy and A. C. Stedman
1936 G. P. Hughes and C. R. D. Tuckey
1937 C. E. Hare and F. H. D. Wilde
1938 Kho Sin Kie and G. L. Rogers
1939 H. Billington and J. S. Olliff
1940–45 no competition
1946 J. E. Harper and C. E. Malfroy
1947 E. Fannin and E. W. Sturgess
1948 E. W. Sturgess and R. Van Meegeren
1949 J. Bartoli and P. Masip
1950 V. Cernik and J. Drobny
1951 L. Norgarb and E. W. Sturgess
1952 J. Drobny and F. A. Sedgman
1953 F. Ampon and R. Deyro
1954 K. Neilsen and T. Ulrich
1955 A. J. Mottram and G. L. Paish
1956 R. N. Howe and U. Schmidt
1957 G. L. Forbes and A. Segal
1958 M. G. Davies and R. K. Wilson
1959 G. L. Forbes and A. Segal

Women's Doubles

1924 Miss E. Ryan and Mrs. D. C. Shepherd-Barron
1925 Miss E. L. Colyer and Miss E. Ryan
1926 Miss B. Nuthall and Miss G. R. Sterry
1927 Miss M. V. Chamberlain and Mrs. C. O. Tuckey
1928 Miss B. Nuthall and Mrs. P. H. Watson
1929 Miss E. A. Goldsack and Miss J. C. Ridley
1930 Miss J. Fry and Miss E. H. Harvey
1931 Miss B. Nuthall and Miss E. Ryan
1932 Miss B. Nuthall and Mrs. E. F. Whittingstall
1933 Miss M. Heeley and Miss D. E. Round

1934 Mrs. L. A. Godfree and Miss S. Noel
1935 Mrs. J. B. Pittman and Miss A. M. Yorke
1936 Miss F. James and Miss K. E. Stammers
1937–38 Miss E. M. Dearman and Miss J. Ingram
1939 Miss J. Nicoll and Miss B. Nuthall
1940–45 *no competition*
1946 Mrs. E. W. A. Bostock and Mrs. M. Menzies
1947 Mrs. N. Bolton and Mrs. H. C. Hopman
1948 Miss B. E. Hilton and Mrs. M. Menzies
1949 Mrs. W. C. J. Halford and Mrs. B. E. Hilton

1950 Mrs. B. E. Hilton and Miss K. L. A. Tuckey
1951–52–53 Miss S. J. Fry and Miss D. J. Hart
1954 Miss D. J. Hart and Mrs. A. J. Mottram
1955 Miss S. J. Bloomer and Miss P. E. Ward
1956 Miss A. Buxton and Miss D. R. Hard
1957 Miss S. J. Bloomer and Miss D. R. Hard
1958 Miss J. A. Shilcock and Miss P. E. Ward
1959 Miss A. Mortimer and Miss P. E. Ward

Mixed Doubles

1924 R. Lycett and Miss E. Ryan
1925 P. D. B. Spence and Miss E. L. Colyer
1926 D. A. Hodges and Miss J. Fry
1927 P. D. B. Spence and Miss B. Nuthall
1928 H. Cochet and Miss E. Bennett
1929 G. P. Hughes and Miss J. Fry
1930 C. H. Kingsley and Miss J. Fry
1931 F. J. Perry and Miss M. Heeley
1932 A. Martin Legeay and Mme R. Mathieu
1933 H. G. N. Lee and Miss F. James

1934 R. Miki and Miss D. E. Round
1935 C. R. D. Tuckey and Miss M. C. Scriven
1936 F. J. Perry and Miss D. E. Round
1937 F. H. D. Wilde and Miss M. Whitmarsh
1938 C. Boussus and Miss N. Wynne
1939 C. E. Malfroy and Miss B. Nuthall
1940–45 *no competition*
1946 D. W. Butler and Mrs. E. W. A. Bostock
1947 E. W. Sturgess and Mrs. S. P. Summers
1948 E. W. Sturgess and Miss J. Quertier

1949 P. Masip and Miss J. Gannon
1950 G. E. Brown and Miss B. E. Hilton
1951 E. W. Sturgess and Miss D. J. Hart
1952–53 G. L. Paish and Miss J. Rinkel-Quertier
1954 K. Neilsen and Miss D. J. Hart
1955 R. N. Howe and Miss J. A. Shilcock
1956 R. N. Howe and Miss P. E. Ward
1957 R. N. Howe and Miss D. R. Hard
1958 W. A. Knight and Miss S. J. Bloomer
1959 W. A. Knight and Miss S. J. Bloomer

BRITISH COVERED COURT CHAMPIONSHIPS

Played on wood at Queen's Club, London. Up to 1922 the four events were played on a challenge-round basis.

Men's Singles

1885 H. F. Lawford
1886 E. L. Williams
1887–88–89–90–91 E. W. Lewis
1892 E. G. Meers
1893–94 H. S. Mahony
1895–96 E. W. Lewis
1897–98–99 W. V. Eaves
1900 A. W. Gore
1901–02–03–04–05–06 H. L. Doherty
1907 A. F. Wilding
1908 A. W. Gore
1909 M. J. G. Ritchie
1910 F. G. Lowe
1911–12 A. H. Gobert
1913 P. M. Davson

1914 M. J. G. Ritchie
1915–18 *no competition*
1919 P. M. Davson
1920–21–22 A. H. Gobert
1923 J. D. P. Wheatly
1924 P. D. B. Spence
1925 S. M. Jacob
1926 J. Borotra
1927 E. Higgs
1928–29–30–31–32–33 J. Borotra
1934 H. W. Austin
1935 J. Borotra
1936 K. Schroeder
1937 H. W. Austin
1938 J. Borotra
1939–47 *no competition*
1948–49 J. Borotra
1950 J. Drobny
1951 G. L. Paish
1952–53–54 J. Drobny
1955 W. Skonecki
1956 A. Huber
1957–58 M. G. Davies
1958–59 R. K. Wilson

Women's Singles

1890 Miss L. Jacks
1891–92–93 Miss M. Shackle
1894 Miss L. Austin
1895 Miss C. Cooper
1896–97–98–99 Miss L. Austin
1900 Miss T. Lowther
1901 Mrs. G. W. Hillyard
1902–03 Miss T. Lowther
1904 Miss D. K. Douglas
1905 Miss H. Lane
1906 Miss D. K. Douglas
1907 Miss G. Eastlake Smith
1908 Mrs. Lambert Chambers
1909 Miss D. Boothby
1910–11 Mrs. Lambert Chambers
1912 Miss E. D. Holman
1913 Mrs. Lambert Chambers
1914 Miss E. D. Holman
1915–18 *no competition*
1919 Mrs. Lambert Chambers
1920 Miss E. Ryan
1921–22 Miss E. D. Holman

1923 Mrs. R. C. Clayton
1924 Mrs. A. E. Beamish
1925 Miss J. Reid-Thomas
1926 Miss P. Saunders
1927 Miss E. Bennett
1928 Mrs. L. A. Godfree
1929 Mrs. L. R. C. Michell
1930 Miss J. C. Ridley
1931 Miss M. Heeley
1932 Miss M. C. Scriven
1933–34 Mrs. M. R. King
1935 Miss M. C. Scriven
1936 Sen. A. Lizana
1937–38 Miss M. C. Scriven
1939–47 *no competition*
1948 Miss G. C. Hoahing
1949 Miss P. J. Curry
1950 Miss J. Quertier
1951 Miss J. S. V. Partridge
1952–53–54 Miss A. Mortimer
1955 Miss J. A. Shilcock
1956 Miss A. Buxton
1957–58 Miss J. A. Shilcock
1958–59 Miss A. Mortimer

Men's Doubles

1890–91 G. W. Hillyard and H. S. Scrivenor
1892–93–94 H. S. Mahony and E. G. Meers
1895–96 W. V. Eaves and C. H. Martin
1897 G. Greville and H. A. Nisbet
1898–99–1900–01–02–03 H. L. Doherty and R. F. Doherty
1904–05 H. L. Doherty and G. W. Hillyard
1906 H. L. Doherty and R. F. Doherty
1907–08 M. J. G. Ritchie and A. F. Wilding
1909 A. W. Gore and H. Roper Barrett
1910 S. N. Doust and L. O. S. Poidevin
1911 A. H. Gobert and M. J. G. Ritchie
1912–13 S. N. Doust and A. F. Wilding
1914 P. M. Davson and T. M. Mavrogordato
1915–18 *no competition*

1919 R. W. Heath and R. Lycett
1920 A. H. Gobert and R. Lycett
1921 P. M. Davson and T. M. Mavrogordato
1922 S. N. Doust and R. Lycett
1923 A. W. Asthalter and S. N. Doust
1924–25 C. H. Kingsley and P. D. B. Spence
1926–27 G. R. O. Crole-Rees and C. G. Eames
1928 C. H. Kingsley and J. D. P. Wheatley
1929 G. R. O. Crole-Rees and C. G. Eames
1930–31 H. W. Austin and J. S. Olliff
1932 H. G. N. Lee and G. L. Tuckett
1933 V. G. Kirby and G. L. Rogers
1934 J. S. Olliff and D. Prenn
1935 D. N. Jones and D. Prenn

1936 C. E. Hare and F. H. D. Wilde
1937 D. W. Butler and F. H. D. Wilde
1938 H. Billington and J. S. Olliff
1939–47 *no competition*
1948 C. J. Hovell and C. M. Jones
1949 H. Billington and G. L. Paish
1950 H. Cochet and J. Drobny
1951–52 A. J. Mottram and G. L. Paish
1953 J. E. Barrett and D. L. M. Black
1954 J. Drobny and R. K. Wilson
1955 R. N. Howe and W. Skonecki
1956 G. L. Paish and J. A. Pickard
1957–58 M. G. Davies and R. K. Wilson
1958–59 A. R. Mills and G. L. Paish

Women's Doubles

This event was not graded as a championship event until 1935

1929 Mrs. L. R. C. Michell and Miss M. E. Dix
1930 *not held*
1931 Mrs. L. R. C. Michell and Miss E. H. Harvey
1932 Mrs. L. R. C. Michell and Miss D. E. Round
1933 Mrs. L. R. C. Michell and Miss M. C. Scriven
1934 Mrs. J. B. Pittman and Miss A. M. Yorke
1935 Mrs. J. B. Pittman and Miss A. M. Yorke
1936 Miss M. Whitmarsh and Miss A. M. Yorke
1937 Miss J. Saunders and Miss V. E. Scott
1938 Miss E. M. Dearman and Miss J. Ingram
1939–47 *no competition*

1948 Miss P. J. Curry and Miss J. Quertier
1949 Mrs. W. C. J. Halford and Miss P. A. O'Connell
1950 Mrs. R. Anderson and Miss P. J. Curry
1951 Mrs. E. W. Dawson Scott and Miss E. M. Wilford
1952 Miss H. M. Fletcher and Mrs. J. Rinkel-Quertier
1953 Mme P. Chatrier and Miss J. A. Shilcock
1954 Miss J. R. Bulleid and Miss A. Mortimer
1955–56 Miss J. A. Shilcock and Miss P. E. Ward
1957–58 Miss J. A. Shilcock and Miss P. E. Ward
1958–59 Miss A. Mortimer and Miss P. E. Ward

TENNIS QUIZ

1. Who was R. D. Sears?

*

2. Who were the "Four Musketeers"?

*

3. Who was the first overseas player to win the U.S. men's singles title?

*

4. When was the only occasion the Davis Cup challenge round was won from a deficit of 0–2?

QUIZ ANSWERS

1. First winner of the U.S. singles title.
2. Jean Borotra, Jacques Brugnon, René Lacoste and Henri Cochet of France.
3. The British H. L. Doherty in 1903.
4. In 1939 at Philadelphia when Australia beat the U.S.A.

Mixed Doubles

1898–99–1900 R. F. Doherty and Miss C. Cooper
1901 G. W. Hillyard and Mrs. Hillyard
1902–03 H. L. Doherty and Miss T. Lowther
1904 G. Greville and Mrs. Greville
1905 R. F. Doherty and Miss G. Eastlake Smith
1906 A. F. Wilding and Miss D. K. Douglass
1907–08 A. F. Wilding and Miss G. Eastlake Smith
1909 F. W. Rahe and Miss E. L. Bosworth
1910 H. Roper Barrett and Mrs. O'Neill
1911 A. F. Wilding and Mrs. Lambert Chambers
1912 A. H. Gobert and Mrs. O'Neill
1913 S. N. Doust and Mrs. Lambert Chambers
1914 E. Gwynne Evans and Miss E. D. Holman
1915–18 *no competition*
1919–20 R. Lycett and Miss E. Ryan
1921 F. M. B. Fisher and Mrs. G. Peacock
1922 R. Lycett and Mrs. K. McKane
1923 A. W. Asthalter and Mrs. H. Edgington
1924 C. G. Eames and Mrs. A. E. Beamish
1925 P. D. B. Spence and Miss E. L. Colyer

1926 S. N. Doust and Miss J. C. Ridley
1927 G. R. O. Crole-Rees and Mrs. J. Hill
1928–29 G. R. O. Crole-Rees and Mrs. L. R. C. Michell
1930 C. H. Kingsley and Miss J. C. Ridley
1931 J. S. Olliff and Miss P. G. Brazier
1932–33 J. Borotra and Miss B. Nuthall
1934–35 J. Borotra and Miss M. C. Scriven
1936 J. S. Olliff and Miss F. James
1937 K. Schroeder and Miss J. Saunders
1938 C. M. Jones and Miss E. H. Harvey
1939–47 *no competition*
1948 J. Borotra and Mrs. G. Walter
1949–50–51 G. L. Paish and Miss J. Quertier
1952 G. L. Paish and Mrs. J. Rinkel-Quertier
1953 G. Oakley and Mme P. Chatrier
1954 M. G. Davies and Miss D. Spiers
1955 W. A. Knight and Miss J. A. Shilcock
1956 G. L. Paish and Miss J. A. Shilcock
1957–58 M. G. Davies and Miss P. E. Ward
1958–59 *not held*

CHAMPIONSHIPS OF THE WORLD

Between 1913, following the founding of the International Lawn Tennis Federation, and 1923 the "Championships of the World" were held on three surfaces: grass, hard courts and wood courts. The grass court titles were held by the winners at Wimbledon.

Hard Courts

These titles, first held in 1912, were played for in Paris except 1922 when the venue was Brussels.

Men's Singles

1912 O. Froitzheim
1913–14 A. F. Wilding
1920 W. H. Laurentz
1921 W. T. Tilden
1922 W. M. Johnston

Women's Singles

1912 Mlle M. Broquedis
1913 Frl. M. Rieck
1914 Mlle S. Lenglen
1920 Miss E. D. Holman
1921–22–23 Mlle S. Lenglen

Men's Doubles

1912 O. Froitzheim and O. Kreuzer
1913 Baron Von Bissing and R. Kleinschroth
1914 M. Decugis and M. Germot
1920–21 A. H. Gobert and W. H. Laurentz
1922 J. Brugnon and H. Cochet
1923 J. Brugnon and M. Dupont

Women's Doubles

1914 Mlle S. Lenglen and Miss E. Ryan
1920 Miss E. D. Holman and Mrs. P. Satterthwaite
1921 Mme J. Golding and Mlle S. Lenglen
1922 Mlle S. Lenglen and Miss E. Ryan
1923 Mrs. A. E. Beamish and Miss K. McKane

Mixed Doubles

1912 M. Decugis and Mme P. de Borman
1913–14 M. Decugis and Miss E. Ryan
1920 W. H. Laurentz and Mme J. Golding
1921 M. Decugis and Mlle S. Lenglen
1922–23 H. Cochet and Mlle S. Lenglen

Covered Courts

These championships were held 1913 in Stockholm, 1919 Paris, 1920 Queen's Club, London, 1921 Copenhagen, 1922 St. Moritz, 1923 Barcelona.

Men's Singles

1913 A. F. Wilding
1919 A. H. Gobert
1920 F. G. Lowe
1921 W. H. Laurentz
1922–23 H. Cochet

Women's Singles

1913 Miss H. Aitchison
1919 Miss E. D. Holman
1920 Mrs. A. E. Beamish
1921 Frk Brehm
1922 Mme J. Golding
1923 Miss K. McKane

Men's Doubles

1913 M. Decugis and M. Germot
1919 A. H. Gobert and W. H. Laurentz
1920 T. M. Mavrogordato and P. M. Davson
1921 M. Germot and W. H. Laurentz
1922 J. Borotra and H. Cochet
1923 H. Cochet and J. Couiteas

Women's Doubles

1919–20 Mrs. A. E. Beamish and Miss K. McKane
1921 Frk Brehm and Frk E. Mayer
1922 Mme J. Golding and Mme Vaussard
1923 Mrs. A. E. Beamish and Miss K. McKane

Mixed Doubles

1913 M. Decugis and Mme K. Fenwick
1919 M. Decugis and Mrs. A. E. Beamish
1920 F. M. B. Fisher and Mrs. G. Peacock
1921 E. Tegner and Frk Brehm
1922 J. Borotra and Mme J. Golding
1923 W. C. Crawley and Miss K. McKane

BRITISH JUNIOR CHAMPIONSHIPS

These championships, restricted now to British players under 18 at the start of the tournament, were originally played at various venues—1908 Ventnor, 1909 Scarborough, 1910 Felixstowe, 1911 Windlesham, 1912 Ventnor, 1913 Folkestone, 1919 Ventnor, 1920 Folkestone, 1921 Surbiton, 1922 Weybridge, 1923 Beddington Park. Since 1924 they have been held on the hard courts at the All England Club, Wimbledon.

Boys' Singles

1908 C. G. Eames
1909 C. A. Caslon
1910 P. W. James
1911 H. L. de Morpurgo
1912 V. Burr
1913 B. Martyr
1914–18 no competition
1919 C. H. Weinberg
1920 C. H. Weinberg
1921 J. Weakley
1922 H. W. Austin
1923 N. H. Latchford
1924 J. S. Olliff
1925 J. S. Olliff
1926 E. R. Avory
1927 R. A. Court
1928 F. H. D. Wilde
1929 J. W. Nuthall
1930 D. G. Freshwater
1931 C. E. Hare
1932 H. D. B. Faber
1933 M. D. Deloford
1934 R. E. Mulliken
1935 H. T. Baxter
1936 H. T. Baxter
1937 G. L. Emmett
1938 D. G. Snart
1939–45 no competition
1946 A. G. Roberts
1947 A. G. Roberts
1948 J. A. T. Horn
1949 J. A. T. Horn
1950 J. Prouse
1951 R. K. Wilson
1952 W. A. Knight
1953 W. A. Knight
1954 G. E. Mudge
1955 O. S. Prenn
1956 J. I. Tattersall
1957 J. I. Tattersall
1958 H. M. Harvey
1959 J. Baker

Girls' Singles

1908 Miss L. E. Bull
1909 Miss E. M. Hirst
1910 Miss V. Fison
1911 Miss V. M. Speer
1912 Miss V. M. Speer
1913 Miss G. B. Palmer
1914–18 no competition
1919 Miss D. Bouette
1920 Miss J. W. Austin
1921 Miss J. W. Austin
1922 Miss G. R. Sterry
1923 Miss B. Corbin
1924 Miss B. Nuthall
1925 Miss B. Nuthall
1926 Miss B. Nuthall
1927 Miss N. Mackintosh
1928 Miss M. Heeley
1929 Miss M. C. Scriven
1930 Miss P. G. Brazier
1931 Miss S. K. W. Hewitt
1932 Miss J. R. Harman
1933 Miss E. N. S. Dickin
1934 Miss D. Rowe
1935 Miss V. E. Scott
1936 Miss G. C. Hoahing
1937 Miss R. Thomas
1938 Miss J. Nicoll
1939–45 no competition
1946 Miss P. Rodgers
1947 Miss N. T. Seacy
1948 Miss J. S. V. Partridge
1949 Miss L. M. Cornell
1950 Miss L. M. Cornell
1951 Miss E. M. Watson
1952 Miss V. A. Pitt
1953 Miss V. A. Pitt
1954 Miss A. S. Haydon
1955 Miss A. S. Haydon
1956 Miss C. C. Truman
1957 Miss C. C. Truman
1958 Miss C. Webb
1959 Miss R. A. Blakelock

Boys' Doubles

1921 C. E. J. Evers and J. Weakley
1922 H. G. N. Cooper and D. S. Milford
1923 H. W. Austin and M. V. Callendar
1924 M. V. Callendar and R. D. N. Pryce-Jones
1925 C. S. Higgins and J. S. Olliff
1926 J. S. Olliff and M. McL. Symington
1927 J. W. Nuthall and R. K. Tinkler
1928 J. W. Nuthall and F. H. D. Wilde
1929 J. W. Nuthall and Hon. P. Aitken
1930 M. E. Angel and W. I. Nicoll
1931 H. D. B. Faber and G. L. Mytton
1932 M. K. J. A. Dewar and C. E. Hare
1933 D. M. Bull and J. S. Nuthall
1934 J. D. Eggar and C. J. Hovell
1935 D. R. Bocquet and J. B. H. Daniel
1936 H. T. Baxter and G. L. Emmett
1937 G. L. Emmett and R. C. Nicoll
1938 D. N. Hardwick and P. E. Hare
1939–45 no competition
1946 C. W. Fox and T. R. Manderson
1947 B. G. Hawkings and A. G. Roberts
1948 C. V. Baxter and J. A. T. Horn
1949 J. A. T. Horn and G. T. Lewis
1950 J. M. Gracie and R. J. Lee
1951 W. A. Knight and R. K. Wilson
1952 W. A. Knight and R. K. Wilson
1953 W. A. Knight and R. K. Wilson
1954 R. D. Bennett and M. P. Hann
1955 M. L. Booth and D. P. Gordon
1956 C. R. Applewhaite and J. I. Tattersall
1957 C. R. Applewhaite and J. I. Tattersall
1958 W. J. King and R. Taylor
1959 J. Baker and T. J. Reynolds

Girls' Doubles

1921 Miss D. Soames and Miss G. R. Sterry
1922 Miss B. Corbin and Miss M. Lambert
1923 Miss B. Corbin and Miss M. Lambert
1924 Miss B. Nuthall and Miss S. Hartley
1925 Miss T. Lamb and Miss B. Nuthall
1926 Miss E. M. Dearman and Miss B. Nuthall
1927 Miss N. Mackintosh and Miss J. Marshall
1928 Miss B. M. Kendle and Miss A. M. Yorke
1929 Miss J. Cunningham and Miss F. K. Scott
1930 Miss Y. J. Allnatt and Miss P. Craske
1931 Miss J. Saunders and Miss K. E. Stammers
1932 Miss E. N. S. Dickin and Miss M. Whitmarsh
1933 Miss E. N. S. Dickin and Miss M. Whitmarsh
1934 Miss P. W. Hewitt and Miss E. M. Vavasour
1935 Miss P. W. Hewitt and Miss B. M. Stuart Johnson
1936 Miss A. P. Cardinall and Miss B. M. Stuart Johnson
1937 Miss B. M. Crosoer and Miss P. L. MacCorkindale
1938 Miss M. I. Harris and Miss J. Nicoll
1939–45 no competition
1946 Miss P. Rodgers and Miss P. E. Ward
1947 Miss N. T. Seacy and Miss I. S. Vallance
1948 Miss J. P. Mead and Miss S. P. Thain
1949 Miss R. J. R. Bulleid and Miss A. Mortimer
1950 Miss J. M. Petchell and Miss D. Spiers
1951 Miss V. M. Lewis and Miss M. L. Morgan
1952 Miss P. Della-Porta and Miss D. Midgley
1953 Miss P. Della-Porta and Miss D. Midgley
1954 Miss A. S. Haydon and Miss G. I. M. Hurdman
1955 Miss S. M. Armstrong and Miss A. S. Haydon
1956 Miss S. M. Armstrong and Miss A. S. Haydon
1957 Miss D. M. Catt and Miss C. C. Truman
1958 Miss C. Webb and Miss M. G. White
1959 Miss R. A. Blakelock and Miss A. E. O'Neil

Mixed Doubles

1921 H. W. Austin and Miss J. W. Austin
1922 H. W. Austin and Miss E. M. Dearman
1923 H. W. Austin and Miss E. M. Dearman
1924 C. G. Fletcher and Miss B. Nuthall }
     J. S. Olliff and Miss S. Hartley } divided
1925 not held
1926 J. W. Nuthall and Miss B. Nuthall
1927 R. J. Ritchie and Miss J. M. Ingram
1928 F. H. D. Wilde and Miss E. V. Elder
1929 D. G. Freshwater and Miss P. G. Brazier
1930 M. E. Angel and Miss Y. J. Allnatt
1931 H. D. B. Faber and Miss K. E. Stammers
1932 G. L. Mytton and Miss M. Whitmarsh
1933 N. E. Hooper and Miss E. N. S. Dickin
1934–35 not held
1936 D. R. Bocquet and Miss P. M. Seaton
1937 P. E. Hare and Miss R. Thomas
1938 R. C. Nicoll and Miss J. Nicoll
1939–45 no competition
1946 A. G. Roberts and Miss P. Rodgers
1947 A. G. Roberts and Miss R. J. R. Bulleid
1948 C. V. Baxter and Miss N. T. Seacy
1949 J. A. T. Horn and Miss P. A. Lewis
1950 D. S. Timms and Miss M. Harris
1951 R. Becker and Miss E. M. Watson
1952 W. A. Knight and Miss V. A. Pitt
1953 W. A. Knight and Miss V. A. Pitt
1954 M. P. Hann and Miss J. A. Fulton
1955 O. S. Prenn and Miss J. A. Fulton
1956 J. I. Tattersall and Miss H. J. M. Durose
1957 C. R. Applewhaite and Miss C. C. Truman
1958 G. C. Bluett and Miss C. A. Silver
1959 T. D. Phillips and Miss C. Webb

TENNIS QUIZ

1. Two grips are known as the Eastern Grip and the Western Grip. Why?

★

2. When was the first all-American men's singles final at Wimbledon?

★

3. What is the greatest number of games recorded in a first-class singles?

★

4. Who was "Little Mo"?

QUIZ ANSWERS

1. It comes from U.S. usage in the early nineteen hundreds. The Eastern players adopted the grip most suitable for grass, on which they played; while the Western players, who did not play on grass, had developed a grip more suited to a higher-bounding ball. 2. 1923, W. M. Johnston against F. T. Hunter. 3. 100. At Lyons, France, in February 1955 in the final of the covered courts tournament J. Drobny and J. E. Patty stood 21–19 8–10 21–21 when they agreed to divide. They had been on court 3 hours 40 minutes. 4. Maureen Connolly.

BRITISH JUNIOR COVERED COURT CHAMPIONSHIPS

Played at Queen's Club, London.

Boys' Singles

1956–57 M. J. Sangster
1958 J. I. Tattersall
1959 J. Baker

Girls' Singles

1956 Miss C. C. Truman
1957 Miss S. M. Armstrong
1958 Miss C. C. Truman
1959 Miss C. Webb

Boys' Doubles

1956 R. W. Dixon and M. J. Sangster
1957 M. J. Sangster and M. J. Woolven
1958 H. M. Harvey and M. J. Sangster
1959 R. B. B. Avory and J. Baker

Girls' Doubles

1956 Miss D. M. Catt and Miss C. C. Truman
1957 Miss S. M. Armstrong and Miss M. R. O'Donnell
1958 Miss D. M. Catt and Miss J. Trewby
1959 Miss J. E. Kemp and Miss J. M. Tee

In the 1959 meeting a boys' doubles match was won by R. B. B. Avory and J. Baker against W. J. King and R. Taylor by 6–4 28–26, held to be the longest set ever played among juniors.

PROFESSIONAL LAWN TENNIS

The loosely knit structure of the professional game, which has increased tremendously in importance in recent years, militates against the compilation of records. Much activity has been confined to exhibition matches. However, since 1951 the London Indoor Professional Championships have been officially sponsored by the L.T.A., and this notable meeting, on a wood court at Wembley, deserves its place in the records. So, too, does another recognised professional meeting, the Slazenger Tournament, held on grass at Scarborough 1946 to 1957 and in 1958 at Eastbourne.

London Indoor Champions

Singles

1951 R. A. Gonzales *bt* F. Segura 6–2 2–6 6–4
1952 R. A. Gonzales *bt* J. A. Kramer 3–6 3–6 6–2 6–4 7–5
1953 F. A. Sedgman *bt* R. A. Gonzales 6–1 6–2 6–2
1954–55 *not held*
1956 R. A. Gonzales *bt* F. A. Sedgman 4–6 11–9 11–9 9–7
1957 K. R. Rosewall *bt* F. Segura 1–6 6–3 6–4 6–4
1958 F. A. Sedgman *bt* M. A. Trabert 6–4 6–3 6–4
1959 M. Anderson *bt* F. Segura 4–6 6–4 3–6 6–3 8–6

Doubles

1951 R. A. Gonzales and F. Segura
1952 R. A. Gonzales and F. Segura
1953 J. D. Budge and F. A. Sedgman
1954–55 *not held*
1956 R. A. Gonzales and M. A. Trabert
1957 L. A. Hoad and K. R. Rosewall
1958 R. A. Gonzales and K. R. Rosewall
1959 L. A. Hoad and M. A. Trabert

Slazenger Tournament

Singles

1946–47 D. Maskell
1948 F. J. Perry
1949 J. A. Kramer
1950–51 F. J. Perry
1952 R. A. Gonzales
1953 F. Segura
1954 J. W. Cawthorn
1955 R. A. Gonzales
1956 J. W. Cawthorn
1957 G. Worthington
1958 K. R. Rosewall *bt* M. A. Trabert 6–0 6–2 6–8 2–6 7–5
1959 A. J. Cooper *bt* L. A. Hoad 9–11 4–6 6–1 6–4 6–0

Doubles

1946–47 T. C. Jeffrey and D. Maskell
1948 Y. Petra and K. Schroeder
1949 J. D. Budge and J. A. Kramer
1950 F. J. Perry and F. H. D. Wilde
1951 J. de Mos and K. Schroeder
1952 R. A. Gonzales and F. Segura
1953 K. McGregor and F. A. Sedgman
1954 J. W. Cawthorn and D. Tregonning
1955 R. A. Gonzales and F. Segura
1956–57 J. W. Cawthorn and G. Worthington
1958 F. Segura and M. A. Trabert *bt* L. A. Hoad and K. R. Rosewall 6–2 1–6 6–3 6–4
1959 L. A. Hoad and M. A. Trabert *bt* M. Anderson and A. J. Cooper 6–2 6–2 6–4

R. Becker   Miss C. C. Truman   W. A. Knight

OLYMPIC GAMES

Lawn tennis, with a crowded international calendar of its own, has not been an Olympic sport since 1924. The gold-medallists, however, are worthy of record.

1896 *Athens*
 Men's Singles: J. P. Boland
 Men's Doubles: J. P. Boland and F. Thraun

1900 *Paris*
 Men's Singles: H. L. Doherty
 Women's Singles: Miss C. Cooper
 Men's Doubles: H. L. and R. F. Doherty
 Mixed Doubles: R. F. Doherty and Miss C. Cooper

1904 *St. Louis*
 Men's Singles: B. C. Wright
 Men's Doubles: E. W. Leonard and B. C. Wright

1908 *Covered Courts, Queen's Club, London*
 Men's Singles: A. W. Gore
 Women's Singles: Miss G. Eastlake Smith
 Men's Doubles: A. W. Gore and H. Roper Barrett

 Grass Courts, Wimbledon.
 Men's Singles: M. J. G. Ritchie
 Women's Singles: Mrs. Lambert Chambers
 Men's Doubles: R. F. Doherty and G. W. Hillyard

1912 *Covered Courts, Stockholm*
 Men's Singles: A. H. Gobert
 Women's Singles: Mrs. F. J. Hannam
 Men's Doubles: A. H. Gobert and M. Germot
 Mixed Doubles: C. P. Dixon and Mrs. F. J. Hannam

 Hard Courts, Stockholm
 Men's Singles: C. L. Winslow
 Women's Singles: Mlle M. Broquedis
 Men's Doubles: H. A. Kitson and C. L. Winslow
 Mixed Doubles: H. Schomburgk and Frl. Koring

1920 *Hard Courts, Antwerp*
 Men's Singles: L. Raymond
 Women's Singles: Mlle S. Lenglen
 Men's Doubles: O. G. N. Turnbull and M. Woosnam
 Women's Doubles: Miss K. McKane and Mrs. R. J. McNair
 Mixed Doubles: M. Decugis and Mlle S. Lenglen

1924 *Hard Courts, Colombes, Paris*
 Men's Singles: V. Richards
 Women's Singles: Miss H. Wills
 Men's Doubles: V. Richards and F. T. Hunter
 Women's Doubles: Mrs. G. W. Wightman and Miss H. Wills
 Mixed Doubles: R. N. Williams, and Mrs. G. W. Wightman

MARRIED NAMES

In the above records the following appear under both married and single names:

Mme. N. Adamson—*Mme. N. Landry*
Mrs. R. Anderson—*Miss R. Jarvis*
Mrs. N. Bolton—*Miss N. Wynne*
Mrs. E. W. A. Bostock—*Miss J. Nicoll*
Mme. P. Chatrier—*Miss J. S. V. Partridge*
Mrs. E. T. Cooke—*Mrs. M. Fabyan—Miss S. Palfrey*
Mrs. R. Cozens—*Miss D. Akhurst*
Mrs. W. D. du Pont—*Miss M. E. Osborne*
Mrs. R. Ellis—*Sen. A. Lizana*
Mrs. M. Fabyan—*Miss S. Palfrey (Mrs. E. T. Cooke)*
Mrs. L. A. Godfree—*Miss K. McKane*
Mrs. G. Greville—*Miss L. Austin*
Mrs. W. C. J. Halford—*Miss M. Whitmarsh*
Mrs. R. Harper—*Miss S. Lance*
Mrs. G. W. Hillyard—*Miss B. Bingley*
Mrs. H. C. Hopman—*Miss N. Hall*
Mrs. Lambert Chambers—*Miss D. K. Douglass*
Mrs. D. R. Larcombe—*Miss E. W. Thomson*
Mrs. T. Long—*Miss T. Coyne*
Mrs. F. Mallory—*Miss M. Bjurstedt*
Mrs. M. Menzies—*Miss K. E. Stammers*
Mrs. L. R. C. Michell—*Miss P. Saunders*
Mrs. F. S. Moody—*Miss H. Wills*
Mrs. J. B. Pittman—*Miss E. A. Goldsack*
Mrs. E. Raymond—*Miss L. Hammond*
Mrs. M. Reitano—*Miss M. Carter*
Mrs. J. Rinkel-Quertier—*Miss J. Quertier*
Fru S. Sperling—*Frl. H. Krahwinkel*
Mrs. A. Sterry—*Miss C. Cooper*
Mrs. E. F. Whittingstall—*Miss E. Bennett*
Mrs. G. W. Wightman—*Miss H. Hotchkiss*

TENNIS QUIZ

1. Who has retained a national championship for the greatest number of years?

★

2. When was Richard Gonzales champion of Wimbledon?

★

3. What left-handers were Wimbledon men's singles champions?

QUIZ ANSWERS

1. Panna Jadwiga Jedrzejowska. She was Polish champion first in 1929 and still champion, without ever having lost that position, in 1958. 2. In 1949 when he won the men's doubles with Frank Parker. 3. Norman Brookes and Jaroslav Drobny.

Compiled by
R. R. Holliday
Editor: Motor Cycling

Motorcycling

INTRODUCTION

Although pioneer motor bicycles and tricycles were often demonstrated, and sometimes "raced", on pedal-cycle tracks around the turn of the 19th century, the first really important competitive event to be organised on British public roads for petrol vehicles, including motorcycles, was, according to Eric W. Walford's standard work "Early Days in the British Motorcycle Industry", a 1,000 Mile Trial run in the spring of 1900. It did much to convince the public of the possibilities of the internal combustion engine, but unfortunately neither of the two French-built Werner motorbicycles that were entered reached the starting line.

By 1902, however, British motorcycles were putting up good performances in such testing events as the R.A.C. Trials, and in the next year the Auto-Cycle Club (to become the Auto-Cycle Union) was founded to take control of all branches of motorcycle sport. The A.C.C. ran numerous events in both speed and reliability fields and sent teams of British riders to compete in foreign races; the Isle of Man, because of its freedom from highway restrictions on speed, was used for selection purposes.

The year 1907 was a momentous one, for not only did the A.C.C. become the "Union", but it also organised the first of the long series of I.o.M. Tourist Trophy races, the premier sporting competition in the motorcycle world. Exactly who he was and how he came to do it is not now very clear, but it was the Marquis de Mouzilly St. Mars who suggested the T.T. and he donated the Trophy. The race was originally designed for both single- and multi-cylinder machines and speed was to a large extent governed by fuel consumption regulations.

In 1911 the Junior and Senior races (for machines with engines approximating to 350 and 500 c.c.) were introduced and the Mountain Course of about 37 miles was substituted for the old "Short Course". The Senior winner's average speed was 47.60 m.p.h.: 46 years later, in 1957, the average speed over eight laps had risen to within striking distance of 100 m.p.h., 98.99 m.p.h. to be exact, and already the lap speed was over the 100 m.p.h. mark.

Other nations, of course, were also active in the road-racing field very early in the history of the sport. Unhampered by speed limits on public roads, foreign organizers were able to stage events much more easily than the British, but for many years it was British riders on British machines who dominated the principal contests, the Grands Prix. In the years between the great wars the sporting calendar crystallized into a set of *grandes épreuves*, the G.P.'s organised by Belgium, France, Germany, Holland, Italy, Ireland and Spain being the main ones. The governing body of motorcycling sport throughout the world, then called the Federation Internationale des Club Motocyclistes and now the Federation Internationale Motocliste, in those days used to accord in yearly rotation to the major races the title of European Championship. Thus if, say, the Belgian G.P. happened to be also the Championship event, then the winners of the various categories were able for that year to style themselves European Champions. After the Hitler war this rather unsatisfactory arrangement was abandoned in favour of a World Championship, riders and manufacturers gaining points according to finishing positions in a specified number of classic races each season.

In addition to the big-time events, hundreds of smaller races are run all over the world, and for many years groups of British riders have travelled the European circuits during the summer, nomad fashion, competing each weekend at different centres. This grand tour progress is known as the Continental Circus.

An important, but different, kind of race is the Manx Grand Prix, originally called the Amateur Road Race Championships, or Amateur T.T., when it was introduced in 1923 as a race for the not-so-expert riders over the T.T. course under T.T. conditions. Broadly these conditions have continued to the present day.

Another kind of racing which, over the past 30 years, has given a tremendous amount of entertainment, is the Speedway, imported from Australia to Britain in 1928, when it was first called dirt-track racing. From a rather haphazard fairground-show sort of beginning, it grew into a highly organised competition run on league lines between teams, after the fashion of Association football.

Rough-country racing is another form of speed sport that is growing more and more in popularity. It developed from grass racing and cross-country "scrambling" and was confined almost entirely to England before the last war. Post-war, under the French name of moto-cross, it spread rapidly across the Continent and today has a Championship system similar to that of road racing.

Sprints, sand races and hill climbs are not nowadays so numerous as they were, although there is a resurgence of interest in sprinting. Apart from the I.o.M., speed events in Great Britain had, after 1945, mainly to be confined to disused airfields, for the two pre-war centres of racing, the banked concrete Brooklands track and the magnificent natural road circuit at Donington in the Midlands, were war casualties. However, there is today a wide selection of good circuits, some adapted from airfields, some on private or corporation property and some specially constructed for racing.

Whilst there is an apparently never-ending supply of riders for motorcycling speed work, the number of available makes of machines specifically constructed for racing has dwindled, especially in the larger capacity sizes. However, there is an increasing interest among continental manufacturers in racing small-engined machines, and endeavours are being made by the controlling body, the F.I.M., to foster the larger models by means of Formula I racing which aims at encouraging the manufacture of production-type "sold over the counter" race machines, as distinct from expensive, specially-built factory property.

World speed record breaking, once a very active branch of motorcycling sport, has of recent years been sparsely supported. The present world's fastest motorcycle record officially recognised by the F.I.M. is held by Germany (NSU) at 211 m.p.h., but an American, riding a British-engined machine, has exceeded 214 m.p.h. In both cases these speeds were calculated on the mean of times taken over a kilometre ridden in two directions.

Motorcycling reliability trials—as old almost as the industry itself—continue to provide sport for a very large number of clubmen, not only in Britain but on the Continent, and also in America, where the trial is called an "enduro". The pattern of the British reliability trial has not altered much, although organisers are finding it increasingly difficult to devise courses that contain hills steep enough, and hazards sufficiently exacting, severely to test the reliability of the modern machine. Indeed in

MOTORCYCLING QUIZ

MISCELLANEOUS

1. Who won a T.T. while on his honeymoon?

★

2. What was an "oil-boiler"?

★

3. Who were the two English brothers who made headlines in the early days of the dirt-tracks?

★

4. When did a British machine last win the Lightweight T.T.?

★

5. Who holds the F.I.M. World Solo Motorcycle speed record?

★

6. Who, what or where, is or was, "Eppynt"?

★

7. Where is Engineers' Corner?

★

8. For what did the initials of the following famous competition machines stand: (a) N.U.T., (b) D.O.T., (c) B.A.T., (d) O.E.C.

★

9. The following countries have been represented in T.T. races by what makes of machine? (a) Spain, (b) Switzerland, (c) Sweden, (d) Holland.

★

10. Who were the two New Zealanders who broke World speed records in solo and sidecar classes with the same make of machine?

QUIZ ANSWERS

1. Bob Foster, Lightweight, 1936. 2. The oil-cooled Bradshaw engine used in several makes of T.T. machine in the 1920s. 3. Roger and Buster Frogley. 4. 1936, A. R. Foster (New Imperial). 5. Wilhelm Herz (NSU), 211 m.p.h. at Bonneville, U.S.A., 1956. 6. A race circuit now disused, situated in Wales between Brecon and Builth Wells. 7. On the Blandford, Dorset, circuit. 8. (a) Newcastle-upon-Tyne, (b) Devoid of trouble, (c) Best after test, (d) Osborne Engineering Company. 9. (a) Montesa, (b) Motosacoche, (c) Husqvarna, (d) Eysink. 10. Russel Wright (solo) and Rob Burns (sidecar): Vincent H.R.D.

217

Introduction—*contd.*

most events, except possibly the two classic long-distance contests, the International Six Days' Trial and the Scottish Six Days' Trial, it is the skill of the driver rather than the reliability of his mount that comes under test.

The phenomenal post-war growth of the motor scooter movement has so far had only slight impact on motorcycle sport generally. Scooter riders in the main seem to prefer the rally type of event; however, there is an indication, revealed especially in the quite recently introduced I.o.M. Scooter Rally, that this kind of event is likely to become highly competitive, and many believe that the Island will be instrumental in encouraging scooter owners and manufacturers to develop the sort of sporting rivalry which it did amongst the motorcyclists more than half a century ago.

MOTORCYCLING QUIZ

TOURIST TROPHY RACE

1. Who was the rider who raised the lap record to over 60, then over 70 and then over 80 m.p.h.?

*

2. Who has won the greatest number of T.T. races?

*

3. Where was the start of the first (1907) T.T. race?

*

4. Four machines entered and finished 1, 2, 3, 4. Which make?

*

5. Which make first won the Manufacturers' Team Prize?

*

6. The Jimmy Simpson (fastest lap) Trophy has only once been won by the rider of a 350 c.c. machine. Who and when?

QUIZ ANSWERS

1. J. H. (Jimmy) Simpson. 1924 (350 A.J.S.), 64.54; 1926 (500 A.J.S.), 70.43; 1931 (500 Norton), 80.82. 2. Stanley Woods—10. 3. At St. John's, close to Ballacraine, well-known landmark on the present course. 4. Mondial, 125 c.c. Lightweight Race, 1951. 5. Rover in 1913. 6. Ray Amm (Norton), 1954.

T.T. WINNERS 1907–1959

Results from the inception of the events are given in the cases of the Tourist Trophy Races, Manx Grand Prix Races and International and Scottish Six Days Trials. Others are taken back as far as 1950. Some 1959 events had not been held when these pages were sent to press.

PEEL COURSE

				m.p.h.
1907	Single Cyl. Class	C. R. Collier	Matchless	38.23
	Twin Cyl. Class	H. Rem Fowler	Norton	36.22
1908	Single Cyl. Class	J. Marshall	Triumph	40.49
	Twin Cyl. Class	H. Reed	Dot	38.59
1909	—	H. A. Collier	Matchless	49.00
1910	—	C. R. Collier	Matchless	50.63

MOUNTAIN AND CLYPSE COURSES

(Asterisk indicates Clypse Course)

Lightweight—125 c.c.

			m.p.h.
1951	W. A. C. McCandless	Mondial	74.85
1952	C. C. Sandford	M.V.	75.54
1953	R. L. Graham	M.V.	77.79
1954*	R. Hollaus	N.S.U.	69.57
1955*	C. Ubbiali	M.V.	69.67
1956*	C Ubbiali	M.V.	69.13
1957*	T. Provini	Mondial	73.69
1958*	C. Ubbiali	M.V.	72.86
1959*	T. Provini	M.V.	74.06

Lightweight—250 c.c.

1922	G. S. Davison	Levis	49.89
1923	J. A. Porter	New Gerrard	51.93
1924	E. Twemlow	New Imperial	55.44
1925	E. Twemlow	New Imperial	57.74
1926	C. W. Johnston	Cotton	60.20
1927	W. L. Handley	Rex-Acme	63.30
1928	F. A. Longman	O.K. Supreme	62.90
1929	S. A. Crabtree	Excelsior	63.87
1930	J. Guthrie	A.J.S.	64.71
1931	G. W. Walker	Rudge	68.98
1932	L. H. Davenport	New Imperial	70.48
1933	S. Gleave	Excelsior	71.59
1934	J. H. Simpson	Rudge	70.81
1935	S. Woods	Guzzi	71.56
1936	A. R. Foster	New Imperial	74.28
1937	O Tenni	Guzzi	74.72
1938	E. Kluge	D.K.W.	78.48
1939	E A. Mellors	Benelli	74.25
1947	M. Barrington	Guzzi	73.22
1948	M. Cann	Guzzi	75.17
1949	M. Barrington	Guzzi	77.96
1950	D. Ambrosini	Benelli	78.08
1951	T. L. Wood	Guzzi	81.39
1952	F. Anderson	Guzzi	83.82
1953	F. Anderson	Guzzi	84.73
1954	W. Haas	N.S.U.	90.88
1955*	W. A. Lomas	M.V.	71.37
1956*	C. Ubbiali	M.V.	67.05
1957*	C. C. Sandford	Mondial	75.80
1958*	T. Provini	M.V.	76.89
1959*	T. Provini	M.V.	77.77

Ultra Lightweight—175 c.c.

1924	J. A. Porter	New Gerrard	51.20
1925	W. L. Handley	Rex-Acme	53.45

Junior—350 c.c.

1911	P. J. Evans	Humber	41.46
1912	W. H. Bashall	Douglas	39.65
1913	H. Mason	N.U.T.	41.08
1914	E. Williams	A.J.S.	45.72
1920	C. Williams	A.J.S.	40.74
1921	E. Williams	A.J.S.	52.11
1922	T. M. Sheard	A.J.S.	54.75
1923	S. Woods	Cotton	55.73
1924	K. Twemlow	New Imperial	56.57
1925	W. L. Handley	Rex-Acme	65.02
1926	A. Bennett	Velocette	66.70
1927	F. W. Dixon	H.R.D.	67.19
1928	A. Bennett	Velocette	68.65
1929	F. G. Hicks	Velocette	69.71
1930	H. G. Tyrell Smith	Rudge	71.08
1931	P. Hunt	Norton	73.94
1932	S. Woods	Norton	77.16
1933	S. Woods	Norton	78.08
1934	J. Guthrie	Norton	79.16
1935	J. Guthrie	Norton	79.14
1936	F. L. Frith	Norton	80.14
1937	J. Guthrie	Norton	84.43
1938	S Woods	Velocette	84.08
1939	S. Woods	Velocette	83.19
1947	A. R. Foster	Velocette	80.31
1948	F. L. Frith	Velocette	81.45
1949	F. L. Frith	Velocette	83.15
1950	A. J. Bell	Norton	86.33
1951	G. E. Duke	Norton	89.90
1952	G. E. Duke	Norton	90.29
1953	W. R. Amm	Norton	90.52
1954	R. W. Coleman	A.J.S.	91.51
1955	W. A. Lomas	Guzzi	92.33
1956	T. K. Kavanagh	Guzzi	89.29
1957	R. McIntyre	Gilera	94.99
1958	J. Surtees	M.V.	93.97
1959	J. Surtees	M.V.	95.38

Formula I—350 c.c.

1959	A. King	A.J.S.	94.66

Senior—500 c.c.

1911	O. C. Godfrey	Indian	47.60
1912	F. A. Applebee	Scott	48.70
1913	H. O. Wood	Scott	48.27
1914	C. G. Pullin	Rudge	49.49
1920	T. C. de la Hay	Sunbeam	51.79
1921	H. R. Davies	A.J.S. (350 c.c.)	54.49
1922	A. Bennett	Sunbeam	58.31
1923	T. M. Sheard	Douglas	55.55
1924	A. Bennett	Norton	61.64
1925	H. R. Davies	H.R.D.	66.13
1926	S. Woods	Norton	67.54
1927	A. Bennett	Norton	68.41
1928	C. J. P. Dodson	Sunbeam	62.98
1929	C. J. P. Dodson	Sunbeam	72.05
1930	W. L. Handley	Rudge	74.24
1931	P. Hunt	Norton	77.90
1932	S. Woods	Norton	79.38
1933	S. Woods	Norton	81.04
1934	J. Guthrie	Norton	78.01
1935	S. Woods	Guzzi	84.68
1936	J. Guthrie	Norton	85.80
1937	F. L. Frith	Norton	88.21
1938	H. L. Daniell	Norton	89.11
1939	G. Meier	B.M.W.	89.38
1947	H. L. Daniell	Norton	82.81
1948	A. J. Bell	Norton	84.97
1949	H. L. Daniell	Norton	86.93
1950	G. E. Duke	Norton	92.27
1951	G. E. Duke	Norton	93.83
1952	H. R. Armstrong	Norton	92.97
1953	W. R. Amm	Norton	93.85
1954	W. R. Amm	Norton	88.12
1955	G. E. Duke	Gilera	97.93
1956	J. Surtees	M.V.	96.57
1957	R. McIntyre	Gilera	98.99
1958	J. Surtees	M.V.	98.63
1959	J. Surtees	M.V.	87.94

Formula I—500 c.c.

1959	R. McIntyre	Norton	97.77

Sidecar

1923	F. W. Dixon	Douglas	53.15
1924	G. H. Tucker	Norton	51.31
1925	L. Parker	Douglas	55.22
1954*	E. S. Oliver	Norton	68.87
1955*	W. Schneider	B.M.W.	70.01
1956*	F. Hillebrand	B.M.W.	70.03
1957*	F. Hillebrand	B.M.W.	71.89
1958*	W. Schneider	B.M.W.	73.01

Lightweight Clubman's

1947	W. McVeigh	Triumph	65.30
1948	M. V. Lockwood	Excelsior	64.93
1949	C. V. Taft	Excelsior	68.10
1950	F. Fletcher	Excelsior	66.89

Junior Clubman's

1947	D. Parkinson	Norton	70.74
1948	R. J. Hazlehurst	Velocette	70.33
1949	H. Clarke	B.S.A.	75.81
1950	B. A. Jackson	B.S.A.	74.25
1951	B. G. Purslow	B.S.A.	75.36
1952	E. Housley	B.S.A.	78.92
1953	D. T. Powell	B.S.A.	80.17
1954	P. Palmer	B.S.A.	81.83
1955*	J. Buchan	B.S.A.	68.23
1956	B. D. Codd	B.S.A.	82.02

Senior Clubman's

1947	E. E. Briggs	Norton	78.67
1948	J. D. Daniels	Vincent H.R.D.	80.51
1949	G. E. Duke	Norton	82.97
1950	P. H. Carter	Norton	75.60
1951	I. K. Arber	Norton	79.70
1952	B. J. Hargreaves	Triumph	82.45
1953	R. D. Keeler	Norton	84.14
1954	A. King	B.S.A.	85.76
1955*	W. E. Dow	B.S.A.	70.73
1956	B. D. Codd	B.S.A.	86.33

1000 c.c. Clubman's

1949	D. G. Lashmar	Vincent H.R.D.	76.30
1950	A. Phillip	Vincent H.R.D.	78.58
1953	G. P. Douglas	Vincent H.R.D.	81.54

F.I.M. ROAD RACING WORLD CHAMPIONSHIPS

		Individual	*Mfr.*
1950	125 c.c.	B. Ruffo	Mondial
	250 c.c.	D. Ambrosini	Benelli
	350 c.c.	A. R. Foster	Velocette
	500 c.c.	U. Masetti	Norton
	s/car	E. Oliver	Norton
1951	125 c.c.	C. Ubbiali	Mondial
	250 c.c.	B. Ruffo	Guzzi
	350 c.c.	G. E. Duke	Norton
	500 c.c.	G. E. Duke	Norton
	s/car	E. S. Oliver	Norton

	Individual	Mfr.
1952	125 c.c. C. C. Sandford	M.V.
	250 c.c. E. Lorenzetti	Guzzi
	350 c.c. G. E. Duke	Norton
	500 c.c. U. Masetti	Gilera
	s/car C. Smith	Norton
1953	125 c.c. W. Haas	M.V.
	250 c.c. W. Haas	NSU
	350 c.c. F. K. Anderson	Guzzi
	500 c.c. G. E. Duke	Gilera
	s/car E. S. Oliver	Norton
1954	125 c.c. R. Hollaus	
	250 c.c. W. Haas	
	350 c.c. F. K. Anderson	
	500 c.c. G. E. Duke	
	s/car W. Noll	
1955	125 c.c. C. Ubbiali	M.V.
	250 c.c. H. P. Muller	M.V.
	350 c.c. W. A. Lomas	Guzzi
	500 c.c. G. E. Duke	Gilera
	s/car W. Faust	B.M.W.
1956	125 c.c. C. Ubbiali	MV
	250 c.c. C. Ubbiali	MV
	350 c.c. W. A. Lomas	Guzzi
	500 c.c. J. Surtees	MV
	s/car W. Noll	
1957	125 c.c. T. Provini	Mondial
	250 c.c. C. C. Sandford	Mondial
	350 c.c. K. R. Campbell	Gilera
	500 c.c. L. Liberati	Gilera
	s/car F. Hillebrand	B.M.W.
1958	125 c.c. C. Ubbiali	M.V.
	250 c.c. T. Provini	M.V.
	350 c.c. J. Surtees	M.V.
	500 c.c. J. Surtees	M.V.
	s/car W. Schneider	B.M.W.
1959	125 c.c. C. Ubbiali	M.V.
	250 c.c. C. Ubbiali	M.V.
	350 c.c. J. Surtees	M.V.
	500 c.c. J. Surtees	M.V.
	s/car W. Schneider	B.M.W.

N.B. No Manufacturers' Contest in 1954.

CLASSIC ROAD RACE RESULTS
(not including I.O.M. T.T.)

Belgian Grand Prix

1950 350 c.c. A. R. Foster (*Velocette*)
500 c.c. U. Masetti (*Gilera*)
s/car E. S. Oliver (*Norton*)
1951 350 c.c. G. E. Duke (*Norton*)
500 c.c. G. E. Duke (*Norton*)
s/car E. S. Oliver (*Norton*)
1952 350 c.c. G. E. Duke (*Norton*)
500 c.c. U. Masetti (*Gilera*)
s/car E. S. Oliver (*Norton*)
1953 350 c.c. F. Anderson (*Guzzi*)
500 c.c. A. Milani (*Gilera*)
s/car E. S. Oliver (*Norton*)
1954 350 c.c. K. Kavanagh (*Guzzi*)
500 c.c. G. E. Duke (*Gilera*)
s/car E. S. Oliver (*Norton*)
1955 350 c.c. W. A. Lomas (*Guzzi*)
500 c.c. G. Colnago (*Gilera*)
s/car W. Noll (*B.M.W.*)
1956 125 c.c. C. Ubbiali (*M.V.*)
250 c.c. C. Ubbiali (*M.V.*)
350 c.c. J. Surtees (*M.V.*)
500 c.c. J. Surtees (*M.V.*)
s/car W. Noll (*B.M.W.*)
1957 125 c.c. T. Provini (*Mondial*)
250 c.c. J. Hartle (*M.V.*)
350 c.c. K. R. Campbell (*Guzzi*)
500 c.c. L. Liberati (*Gilera*)
s/car W. Schneider (*B.M.W.*)
1958 125 c.c. A. Gandossi (*Ducati*)
250 c.c. (*not run*)
350 c.c. J. Surtees (*M.V.*)
500 c.c. J. Surtees (*M.V.*)
s/car W. Schneider (*B.M.W.*)
1959 125 c.c. C. Ubbiali (*M.V.*)
350 c.c. *G. Hocking (*Norton*)
500 c.c. J. Surtees (*M.V.*)
s/car W. Schneider (*B.M.W.*)

*Formula I race.

Dutch Grand Prix

1950 125 c.c. B. Ruffo (*Mondial*)
350 c.c. A. R. Foster (*Velocette*)
500 c.c. U. Masetti (*Gilera*)
1951 125 c.c. G. Leoni (*Mondial*)
350 c.c. W. Doran (*A.J.S.*)
500 c.c. G. E. Duke (*Norton*)
1952 125 c.c. C. C. Sandford (*M.V.*)
250 c.c. E. Lorenzetti (*Guzzi*)
350 c.c. G. E. Duke (*Norton*)
500 c.c. U. Masetti (*Gilera*)
1953 125 c.c. W. Haas (*N.S.U.*)
250 c.c. W. Haas (*N.S.U.*)
350 c.c. E. Lorenzetti (*Guzzi*)
500 c.c. G. E. Duke (*Gilera*)

German Grand Prix

1952 125 c.c. W. Haas (*N.S.U.*)
250 c.c. R. Felgenheier (*D.K.W.*)
350 c.c. H. R. Armstrong (*Norton*)
500 c.c. H. R. Armstrong (*Norton*)
s/car C. Smith (*Norton*)
1953 125 c.c. C. Ubbiali (*M.V.*)
250 c.c. W. Haas (*N.S.U.*)
350 c.c. C. Bandirola (*M.V.*)
500 c.c. W. Zeller (*M.V.*)
1954 125 c.c. R. Hollaus (*N.S.U.*)
250 c.c. W. Haas (*N.S.U.*)
350 c.c. W. R. Amm (*Norton*)
500 c.c. G. E. Duke (*Gilera*)
s/car W. Noll (*B.M.W.*)
1955 125 c.c. C. Ubbiali (*M.V.*)
250 c.c. H. P. Müller (*N.S.U.*)
350 c.c. W. A. Lomas (*Guzzi*)
500 c.c. G. E. Duke (*Gilera*)
s/car W. Faust (*B.M.W.*)
1956 125 c.c. R. Ferri (*Gilera*)
250 c.c. C. Ubbiali (*M.V.*)
350 c.c. W. A. Lomas (*Guzzi*)
500 c.c. H. R. Armstrong (*Gilera*)
s/car W. Noll (*B.M.W.*)
1957 125 c.c. C. Ubbiali (*M.V.*)
250 c.c. C. Ubbiali (*M.V.*)
350 c.c. L. Liberati (*Gilera*)
500 c.c. L. Liberati (*Gilera*)
s/car F. Hillebrand (*B.M.W.*)
1958 125 c.c. C. Ubbiali (*M.V.*)
250 c.c. T. Provini (*M.V.*)
350 c.c. J. Surtees (*M.V.*)
500 c.c. J. Surtees (*M.V.*)
s/car W. Schneider (*B.M.W.*)
1959 125 c.c. C. Ubbiali (*M.V.*)
250 c.c. C. Ubbiali (*M.V.*)
350 c.c. J. Surtees (*M.V.*)
500 c.c. J. Surtees (*M.V.*)
s/car F. Camathias (*B.M.W.*)

Ulster Grand Prix

1950 125 c.c. C. Ubbiali (*Mondial*)
250 c.c. M. Cann (*Guzzi*)
350 c.c. A. R. Foster (*Velocette*)
500 c.c. G. E. Duke (*Norton*)
1951 125 c.c. W. A. C. McCandless
(*Mondia*)
250 c.c. B. Ruffo (*Guzzi*)
350 c.c. G. E. Duke (*Norton*)
500 c.c. G. E. Duke (*Norton*)
1952 125 c.c. C. C. Sandford (*M.V.*)
250 c.c. M. Cann (*Guzzi*)
350 c.c. K. T. Kavanagh (*Norton*)
500 c.c. W. A. C. McCandless
(*Gilera*)
1953 125 c.c. W. Haas (*N.S.U.*)
250 c.c. H. R. Armstrong (*N.S.U.*)
350 c.c. K. H. Mudford (*Norton*)
500 c.c. K. T. Kavanagh (*Norton*)
s/car C. Smith (*Norton*)
1954 125 c.c. R. Hollaus (*N.S.U.*)
250 c.c. W. Haas (*N.S.U.*)
350 c.c. W. R. Amm (*Norton*)
500 c.c. W. R. Amm (*Norton*)
s/car E. S. Oliver (*Norton*)
1955 250 c.c. J. Surtees (*N.S.U.*)
350 c.c. W. A. Lomas (*Guzzi*)
500 c.c. W. A. Lomas (*Guzzi*)
1956 125 c.c. C. Ubbiali (*M.V.*)
250 c.c. L. Taveri (*M.V.*)
350 c.c. W. A. Lomas (*Guzzi*)
500 c.c. J. Hartle (*Norton*)
s/car W. Noll (*B.M.W.*)
1957 125 c.c. L. Taveri (*M.V.*)
250 c.c. C. C. Sandford (*Mondial*)
350 c.c. K. R. Campbell (*Guzzi*)
500 c.c. L. Liberati (*Gilera*)

Swiss Grand Prix

1950 250 c.c. D. Ambrosini (*Benelli*)
350 c.c. R. L. Graham (*A.J.S.*)
500 c.c. R. L. Graham (*A.J.S.*)
s/car E. S. Oliver (*Norton*)
1951 250 c.c. D. Ambrosini (*Benelli*)
350 c.c. R. L. Graham (*Velocette*)
500 c.c. F. K. Anderson (*Guzzi*)
s/car (500 c.c.) E. Frigerio (*Gilera*)
s/car (750 c.c.) H. Haldemann
(*Norton*)
1952 250 c.c. F. K. Anderson (*Guzzi*)
350 c.c. G. E. Duke (*Norton*)
500 c.c. J. Brett (*A.J.S.*)
s/car Alb. Milani (*Gilera*)
1953 250 c.c. H. R. Armstrong (*N.S.U.*)
350 c.c. F. K. Anderson (*Guzzi*)
500 c.c. G. E. Duke (*Gilera*)
s/car E. S. Oliver (*Norton*)
1954 250 c.c. R. Hollaus (*N.S.U.*)
350 c.c. F. K. Anderson (*Guzzi*)
500 c.c. G. E. Duke (*Gilera*)
s/car W. Noll (*B.M.W.*)
1955 Abandoned

Italian Grand Prix

1950 125 c.c. G. Leoni (*Mondial*)
250 c.c. D. Ambrosini (*Benelli*)
350 c.c. G. E. Duke (*Norton*)
500 c.c. G. E. Duke (*Norton*)
s/car E. S. Oliver (*Norton*)
1951 125 c.c. C. Ubbiali (*Mondial*)
250 c.c. E. Lorenzetti (*Guzzi*)
350 c.c. G. E. Duke (*Norton*)
500 c.c. Alfredo Milani (*Gilera*)
s/car Alb. Milani (*Gilera*)
1952 125 c.c. E. Mendogni (*Morini*)
250 c.c. E. Lorenzetti (*Guzzi*)
350 c.c. W. R. Amm (*Norton*)
500 c.c. R. L. Graham (*M.V.*)
s/car E. Merlo (*Gilera*)
1953 125 c.c. W. Haas (*N.S.U.*)
250 c.c. E. Lorenzetti (*Guzzi*)
350 c.c. E. Lorenzetti (*Guzzi*)
500 c.c. G. E. Duke (*Gilera*)
s/car E. S. Oliver (*Norton*)
1954 125 c.c. G. Sala (*M.V.*)
250 c.c. A. F. Wheeler (*Guzzi*)
350 c.c. F. K. Anderson (*Guzzi*)
500 c.c. G. E. Duke (*Gilera*)
s/car W. Noll (*B.M.W.*)
1955 125 c.c. C. Ubbiali (*M.V.*)
250 c.c. C. Ubbiali (*M.V.*)
350 c.c. R. H. Dale (*Guzzi*)
500 c.c. U. Masetti (*M.V.*)
s/car W. Noll (*B.M.V.*)
1956 125 c.c. C. Ubbiali (*M.V.*)
250 c.c. C. Ubbiali (*M.V.*)
350 c.c. L. Liberati (*Gilera*)
500 c.c. G. E. Duke (*Gilera*)
s/car Alb. Milani (*Gilera*)
1957 125 c.c. C. Ubbiali (*M.V.*)
250 c.c. T. Provini (*Mondial*)
350 c.c. R. McG. McIntyre
(*Gilera*)
500 c.c. L. Liberati (*Gilera*)
s/car Alb. Milani (*Gilera*)
1958 125 c.c. R. Spaggiari (*Ducati*)
250 c.c. E. Mendogni (*Morini*)
350 c.c. J. Surtees (*M.V.*)
500 c.c. J. Surtees (*M.V.*)
1959 125 c.c. E. Degner (*M.Z.*)
250 c.c. C. Ubbiali (*M.V.*)
350 c.c. J. Surtees (*M.V.*)
500 c.c. J. Surtees (*M.V.*)

French Grand Prix

1951 250 c.c. B. Ruffo (*Guzzi*)
350 c.c. G. E. Duke (*Norton*)
500 c.c. Alfredo Milani (*Gilera*)
s/car E. Oliver (*Norton*)
1953 350 c.c. F. K. Anderson (*Guzzi*)
500 c.c. G. E. Duke (*Gilera*)
s/car E. S. Oliver (*Norton*)
1954 250 c.c. W. Haas (*N.S.U.*)
350 c.c. P. Monneret (*A.J.S.*)
500 c.c. P. Monneret (*Gilera*)
1955 125 c.c. C. Ubbiali (*M.V.*)
350 c.c. D. Agostini (*Guzzi*)
500 c.c. G. E. Duke (*Gilera*)
1959 350 c.c. J. Surtees (*M.V.*)
500 c.c. J. Surtees (*M.V.*)
s/car F. Scheidegger (*B.M.W.*)

Second column upper:

1954 125 c.c. R. Hollaus (*N.S.U.*)
250 c.c. W. Haas (*N.S.U.*)
350 c.c. F. K. Anderson (*Guzzi*)
500 c.c. G. E. Duke (*Gilera*)
1955 125 c.c. C. Ubbiali (*M.V.*)
250 c.c. L. Taveri (*M.V.*)
350 c.c. K. T. Kavanagh (*Guzzi*)
500 c.c. G. E. Duke (*Gilera*)
s/car W. Faust (*B.M.W.*)
1956 125 c.c. C. Ubbiali (*M.V.*)
250 c.c. C. Ubbiali (*M.V.*)
350 c.c. W. A. Lomas (*Guzzi*)
380 c.c. J. Surtees (*M.V.*)
s/car F. Hillebrand (*B.M.W.*)
1957 125 c.c. T. Provini (*Mondial*)
250 c.c. T. Provini (*Mondial*)
350 c.c. K. Campbell (*Guzzi*)
500 c.c. J. Surtees (*M.V.*)
s/car F. Hillebrand (*B.M.W.*)
1958 125 c.c. C. Ubbiali (*M.V.*)
250 c.c. T. Provini (*M.V.*)
350 c.c. J. Surtees (*M.V.*)
500 c.c. J. Surtees (*M.V.*)
s/car F. Camathias (*B.M.W.*)
1959 125 c.c. C. Ubbiali (*M.V.*)
250 c.c. C. Ubbiali (*M.V.*)
350 c.c. *R. N. Brown (*Norton*)
500 c.c. J. Surtees (*M.V.*)
s/car F. Camathias (*B.M.W.*)

*Formula I race.

Third column upper:

1958 125 c.c. C. Ubbiali (*M.V.*)
250 c.c. C. Ubbiali (*M.V.*)
350 c.c. J. Surtees (*M.V.*)
500 c.c. J. Surtees (*M.V.*)
1959 125 c.c. S. M. B. Hailwood (*Ducati*)
250 c.c. G. Hocking (*M.Z.*)
350 c.c. J. Surtees (*M.V.*)
500 c.c. J. Surtees (*M.V.*)

MOTORCYCLING QUIZ

GENERAL RACING

1. By whom are the solo and sidecar records at Brooklands held?

*

2. Which two famous riders put O.B.E. after their names?

*

3. Where are, or were, the following: (a) The Cascades, (b) Melling Crossing, (c) Cocoa Bends, (d) Railway Straight, (e) Pilgrims Rise.

*

4. What are the racing colours of the following countries: (a) Italy, (b) France, (c) Finland, (d) Holland, (e) Belgium.

*

5. Give the makes of machine which have the following alternative names: (a) Gambalunghino, (b) Featherbed, (c) Rennmax, (d) Lighthouse, (e) Porcupine.

*

6. Give the names of the racing men whose sobriquets follow: (a) Fearless, (b) Schorch, (c) Fairgoose, (d) Pip, (e) Professor.

*

7. Which is the out-of-place circuit among the following? Avus, Hockenheim, Nurburgring, Saxtorp, Solitude.

*

8. Give the surnames of the following pioneer speedway riders: (a) Cyclone Billy, (b) Broadside Vic, (c) Jerrahjerker, (d) Sprouts.

*

9. Which are the nearest large towns or cities to the following race circuits: (a) Montjuich, (b) Les Essarts, (c) Charterhall, (d) Drenthe.

*

10. What is the length of the Clypse Course, Isle of Man?

QUIZ ANSWERS

1. Both by Noel Pope (Brough Superior). 2. Freddie Frith and Geoff Duke. 3. (a) Oulton Park, (b) Aintree, (c) Burneville, Francorchamps, Belgium, (d) Brooklands, (e) Brands Hatch. 4. (a) Red, (b) Blue, (c) Black, (d) Orange, (e) Yellow. 5. (a) Guzzi, (b) Norton, (c) NSU, (d) O.K.-Supreme, (e) A.J.S. 6. (a) Bob Foster, (b) Georg Meier, (c) Fergus Anderson, (d) P. V. Harris, (e) Joe Craig. 7. All are German except Saxtorp which is in Sweden. 8. (a) Lamont, (b) Huxley, (c) Johnson, (d) Elder. 9. (a) Barcelona, Spain, (b) Rouen, France, (c) Edinburgh, (d) Groeningen, Holland. 10. 10.79 miles.

MOTORCYCLING QUIZ

TRIALS

1. What did oldtime trials riders mean by l.p.a.?

*

2. Women motorcyclists once represented Great Britain in the Silver Vase contest of the International Six Days' Trial. Who were they?

*

3. Why is the Victory Trial so called?

*

4. What is meant in the Scottish Six Days' Trial by a "star" hill?

*

5. Generally regarded as the grandfather of all one-day reliability events, the first Colmore Cup Trial was won by . . .? And when?

*

6. Which is the oldest trial in the world still being held annually?

*

7. In an observed section a rider's machine swerves right round and he continues to the finish without stopping or footing. Should he be penalized?

*

8. Who is the now well-known T.T. rider who once competed in trials with a three-wheeler equipped with two engines?

*

9. Which is the "odd man out" among the following famous veteran trials men— V. N. Brittain, A. E. Perrigo, D. K. Mansell, N. P. O. Bradley, G. B. Goodman?

QUIZ ANSWERS

1. Light pedal assistance. 2. Miss Marjorie Cottle, Miss Edyth Foley and Mrs. McLean (1927). 3. It was first run in 1919 to commemorate allied victory in the First World War. 4. One on which marks are lost at the rate of five for a stop, three for footing and one for a single foot or dab. 5. W. D. Smith (Scott) 1911. 6. The Motor Cycling Club's "London-Edinburgh" first run in 1904. 7. Yes; if the trial is run under A.C.U. rules it is stipulated that the machine must continue in a forward direction in relation to the course. 8. Frank Cope, whose B.S.A. had a separate two-stroke unit driving the rear wheel. 9. Brittain and Perrigo won open trials on solos and never competed with sidecars: the opposite was the case with Mansell and Bradley. Goodman won premier awards on both solos and sidecars.

Classic Road Race Results—contd.

Spanish Grand Prix

1951	125 c.c.	G. Leoni (Mondial)
	350 c.c.	T. L. Wood (Velocette)
	500 c.c.	U. Masetti (Gilera)
	s/car	E. S. Oliver (Norton)
1952	125 c.c.	E. Mendogni (Morini)
	500 c.c.	R. L. Graham (M.V.)
	s/car	E. S. Oliver (Norton)
1953	125 c.c.	A. A. Coppeta (M.V.)
	250 c.c.	E. Lorenzetti (Guzzi)
	500 c.c.	F. K. Anderson (345 Guzzi)
1954	125 c.c.	T. Provini (Mondial)
	350 c.c.	F. K. Anderson (Guzzi)
	500 c.c.	R. H. Dale (M.V.)
1955	125 c.c.	L. Taveri (M.V.)
	500 c.c.	H. R. Armstrong (Gilera)
	s/car	W. Faust (B.M.W.)

Swedish Grand Prix

1958	125 c.c.	A. Gandossi (Ducati)
	250 c.c.	H. Fügner (M.Z.)
	350 c.c.	G. E. Duke (Norton)
	500 c.c.	G. E. Duke (Norton)
1959	125 c.c.	T. Provini (M.V.)
	250 c.c.	G. Hocking (M.Z.)
	350 c.c.	J. Surtees (M.V.)
	500 c.c.	*R. N. Brown (Norton)

*Formula I race.

MANX GRAND PRIX
AMATEUR ROAD RACE CHAMPIONSHIPS

			m.p.h.
1923		L. Randles (Sunbeam)	52.77
1924		L. Randles (Sunbeam)	56.71
1925		H. G. Dobbs (Norton)	59.97
1926		R. D. Adams (A.J.S.)	58.46
1927		P. Hunt (Norton)	57.66
1928		P. Hunt (Norton)	67.94
	Junior	W. H. T. Meageen (Rex-Acme)	61.58
1929	Senior	E. N. Lea (Norton)	64.02
	Junior	E. N. Lea (Velocette)	65.24

MANX GRAND PRIX RACES

			m.p.h.
1930	Senior	E. R. Merrill (Rudge)	69.49
	Junior	D. J. Pirie (Velocette)	61.63
1931	Senior	J. M. Muir (Norton)	71.79
	Junior	D. J. Pirie (Velocette)	69.59
1932	Senior	N. Gledhill (Norton)	67.32
	Junior	J. H. Carr (New Imperial)	69.27
1933	Senior	H. L. Daniell (Norton)	76.98
	Junior	A. Munks (Velocette)	74.14
1934	Senior	D. J. Pirie (Norton)	79.19
	Junior	J. H. White (Norton)	75.59
	L/wt	W. D. Mitchell (Cotton)	63.49
1935	Senior	J. K. Swanston (Norton)	79.62
	Junior	F. L. Frith (Norton)	76.02
	L/wt	R. Harris (New Imperial)	68.56
1936	Senior	A. Munks (Norton)	78.88
	Junior	A. Munks (Velocette)	73.93
	L/wt	D. Parkinson (Excelsior)	65.68
1937	Senior	M. Cann (Norton)	81.65
	Junior	M. Cann (Norton)	76.23
	L/wt	D. Parkinson (Excelsior)	69.68
1938	Senior	K. Bills (Norton)	84.81
	Junior	K. Bills (Norton)	78.76
	L/wt	D. Parkinson (Excelsior)	71.05
1946	Senior	E. Lyons (Triumph)	76.73
	Junior	K. Bills (Norton)	75.78
	L/wt	L. W. Parsons (Rudge)	65.11
1947	Senior	E. E. Briggs (Norton)	78.34
	Junior	E. E. Briggs (Norton)	74.64
	L/wt	A. Munks (Guzzi)	70.63
1948	Senior	D. G. Crossley (Triumph)	80.62
	Junior	D. Parkinson (Norton)	78.19
	L/wt	R. H. Dale (Guzzi)	73.36
1949	Senior	G. E. Duke (Norton)	86.06
	Junior	W. A. C. McCandless (Norton)	81.82
1950	Senior	P. Romaine (Norton)	84.12
	Junior	D. G. Crossley (A.J.S.)	82.58
1951	Senior	D. E. Bennett (Norton)	87.05
	Junior	R. H. Sherry (A.J.S.)	82.61
1952	Senior	D. K. Farrant (Matchless)	88.65
	Junior	R. M. G. McIntyre (A.J.S.)	85.73
1953	Senior	D. Parkinson (Norton)	89.68
	Junior	F. M. Fox (Norton)	84.73
1954	Senior	G. R. Costain (Norton)	80.95
	Junior	D. Ennett (A.J.S.)	86.33
1955	Senior	G. B. Tanner (Norton)	91.38
	Junior	G. B. Tanner (Norton)	88.46
1956	Senior	J. Buchan (Norton)	90.83
	Junior	J. Buchan (Norton)	88.54
1957	Senior	W. A. Holmes (Norton)	91.43
	Junior	W. A. Holmes (Norton)	89.13
1958	Senior	E. J. Washer (Norton)	92.24
	Junior	A. Shepherd (Bancroft-A.J.S.)	89.08
	Snaefell 350 c.c.	G. Bell (Norton)	84.15
	Snaefell 500 c.c.	P. E. Richardson (Norton)	85.06
1959	Senior	E. Crooks (Norton)	94.87
	Junior	P. C. Middleton (Norton)	88.73

SCOTTISH SIX DAYS' TRIAL

From 1909 to 1927 there were no individual awards; gold medals and silver cups were awarded to all who returned a specified minimum number of marks forfeited.

Year	Winners
1928	BEST SOLO: V. C. King (Douglas). BEST SIDECAR: G. W. Shepherd (Scott).
1929	BEST OVER 350: J. Amott (Rudge). BEST OVER 350 S.C.: G. R. Butcher (Rudge).
1930	BEST OVER 350: G. B. Goodman (Norton). BEST OVER 350 S.C.: H. G. Uzzell (B.S.A.).
1931	BEST OVER 350: J. Amott (A.J.S.). BEST OVER 350 S.C.: H. S. Perrey (Ariel).
1932	BEST SOLO: R. MacGregor (Rudge). BEST SIDECAR: H. Flook (Norton).
1933	BEST SOLO: L. Heath (Ariel). BEST SIDECAR: E. A. Morris (Baughan).
1934	BEST SOLO: J. Williams (Norton). BEST SIDECAR: H. Flook (B.S.A.).
1935	BEST SOLO: R. MacGregor (Rudge). BEST SIDECAR: A. Calder (Triumph).
1936	BEST SOLO: W. T. Tiffen (Velocette). BEST SIDECAR: H. Flook (B.S.A.).
1937	BEST SOLO: J. Williams (Norton). BEST SIDECAR: H. Flook (Norton).
1938	BEST SOLO: G. F. Povey (Ariel). BEST SIDECAR: W. S. Waycott (Velocette).
1939	BEST SOLO: A. Jefferies (Triumph). BEST SIDECAR: F. H. Whittle (Panther).
1947	BEST SOLO: B. H. M. Viney (A.J.S.). BEST SIDECAR: H. R. Taylor (Ariel).
1948	BEST SOLO: B. H. M. Viney (A.J.S.). BEST SIDECAR: H. Tozer (B.S.A.).
1949	BEST SOLO: B. H. M. Viney (A.J.S.). NO SIDECARS.
1950	BEST SOLO: L. A. Ratcliffe (Matchless). BEST SIDECAR: H. Tozer (B.S.A.).
1951	BEST SOLO: G. J. Draper (B.S.A.). NO SIDECARS.
1952	BEST SOLO: J. V. Brittain (Royal Enfield). NO SIDECARS.
1953	BEST SOLO: B. H. M. Viney (A.J.S.). NO SIDECARS.
1954	BEST SOLO: L. A. Ratcliffe (Matchless). NO SIDECARS.
1955	BEST SOLO: J. V. Smith (B.S.A.). NO SIDCARS.
1956	BEST SOLO: G. L. Jackson (A.J.S.). NO SIDECARS.
1957	BEST SOLO: J. V. Brittain (Royal Enfield). NO SIDECARS.
1958	BEST SOLO: G. L. Jackson (A.J.S.). BEST SIDECAR: J. S. Oliver (B.S.A.).
1959	BEST SOLO: R. S. Peplow (Triumph). BEST SIDECAR: P. W. Roydhouse (Norton).

INTERNATIONAL SIX DAYS' TRIAL

Year	Winning Countries	Location
1920	Switzerland	France
1921–2	Switzerland	Switzerland
1923	Sweden	Scandinavia
1924	Trophy: Britain	Belgium
	Vase: Norway	
1925–8	Trophy: Britain	England
	Vase: Britain	
1929	Trophy: Britain	Central Europe
	Vase: Britain	
1930	Trophy: Italy	France & Italy
	Vase: France	
1931	Trophy: Italy	Italy
	Vase: Holland	
1932	Trophy: Britain	Italy
	Vase: Britain	
1933	Trophy: Germany	England & Wales
	Vase: Britain	
1934	Trophy: Germany	Germany
	Vase: Britain	
1935	Trophy: Germany	Germany
	Vase: Germany	
1936	Trophy: Britain	Germany
	Vase: Britain	
1937	Trophy: Britain	England & Wales
	Vase: Holland	
1938	Trophy: Britain	England & Wales
	Vase: Germany	
1939	Results annulled	Germany
1947	Trophy: Czechoslovakia	Czechoslovakia
	Vase: Czechoslovakia	
1948	Trophy: Britain	Italy
	Vase: Britain	
1949	Trophy: Britain	England & Wales
	Vase: Czechoslovakia	
1950	Trophy: Britain	England & Wales
	Vase: Britain	
1951	Trophy: Britain	Italy
	Vase: Holland	
1952	Trophy: Czechoslovakia	Austria
	Vase: Czechoslovakia	
1953	Trophy: Britain	Czechoslovakia
	Vase: Czechoslovakia	
1954	Trophy: Czechoslovakia	England & Wales
	Vase: Holland	
1955	Trophy: Germany	Czechoslovakia
	Vase: Czechoslovakia	
1956	Trophy: Germany	Germany
	Vase: Holland	
1957	Trophy: Germany	Czechoslovakia
	Vase: Czechoslovakia	
1958	Trophy: Czechoslovakia	Germany
	Vase: Czechoslovakia	
1959	Trophy: Czechoslovakia	Czechoslovakia
	Vase: Czechoslovakia	

BRITISH EXPERTS

	Solo	Sidecar
1950	W. Nicholson (B.S.A.)	H. Tozer (B.S.A.)
1951	T. U. Ellis (B.S.A.)	C. V. Kemp (Norton)
1952	J. V. Brittain (Royal Enfield)	H. Tozer (B.S.A.)
1953	J. V. Brittain (Royal Enfield)	F. Wilkins (Ariel)

1954 W. Nicholson (*B.S.A.*)   F. Darrieulat (*B.S.A.*)
1955 J. V. Smith (*B.S.A.*)   A. J. Humphries (*Norton*)
1956 J. V. Smith (*B.S.A.*)   F. Darrieulat (*B.S.A.*)
1957 J. V. Smith (*B.S.A.*)   F. Wilkins (*Ariel*)
1958 G. L. Jackson (*A.J.S.*)   F. Wilkins (*Ariel*)

NORTHERN EXPERTS

	Solo	Sidecar
1950	W. A. J. Milner (*A.J.S.*)	P. Wraith (*Ariel*)
(Run January 1951)		
1951	W. A. Lomas (*James*)	C. V. Kemp (*Norton*)
1952	T. D. Wark (*Francis Barnett*)	P. Wraith (*Ariel*)
1953	T. E. Leach (*Norton*)	F. H. Whittle (*Panther*)
1954	J. V. Brittain (*Royal Enfield*)	J. Sandford (*Ariel*)
1955	A. Shutt (*Francis-Barnett*)	S. H. Crouch (*Ariel*)
1956	Not held—petrol rationing	
1957	G. S. Blakeway (*Ariel*)	P. Wraith (*Ariel*)
1958	R. S. Peplow (*Triumph*)	P. Wraith (*Ariel*)

SOUTHERN EXPERTS

	Solo	Sidecar
1950	A. B. N. Taylor (*Matchless*)	—
1951	W. Nicholson (*B.S.A.*)	A. J. Humphries (*Norton*)
1952	W. Nicholson (*B.S.A.*)	B. T. Welch (*Ariel*)
1953	G. J. Draper (*B.S.A.*)	F. Darrieulat (*B.S.A.*)
1954	P. T. Stirland (*James*)	A. J. Humphries (*Norton*)
1955	P. T. Stirland (*Royal Enfield*)	A. J. Humphries (*Norton*)
1956	P. T. Stirland (*Royal Enfield*)	A. Pullman (*Matchless*)
1957	P. T. Stirland (*Royal Enfield*)	F. Darrieulat (*B.S.A.*)
1958	B. W. Martin (*B.S.A.*)	F. Wilkins (*Ariel*)

A.C.U. INTER-CENTRE TEAM TRIAL

Winning Centre

1950	East Midland
1951	East Midland
1952	South Eastern
1953	Midland
1954	South Eastern
1955	South Eastern
1956	South Eastern
1957	Midland
1958	Midland
1959	Midland

A.C.U. TRIALS DRIVERS' STAR

	Solo	Sidecar
1950	P. H. Alves	H. Tozer
1951	W. Nicholson	H. Tozer
1952	W. Nicholson	F. Wilkins
1953	J. V. Smith	F. Wilkins
1954	J. V. Smith	A. J. Humphries
1955	G. L. Jackson	A. J. Humphries

1956 J. V. Brittain   F. Darrieulat
1957 Cancelled through petrol rationing
1958 G. L. Jackson   F. Darrieulat

MOTO-CROSS AND SCRAMBLES
EUROPEAN MOTO-CROSS CHAMPIONSHIPS

1952	V. Leloup (Belgium—*F.N.*)
1953	A. Mingels (Belgium—*Matchless & F.N.*)
1954	A. Mingels (Belgium—*F.N.*)
1955	G. J. Draper (Great Britain—*B.S.A.*)
1956	L. R. Archer (Great Britain—*Norton*)
1957	B. Nillson (Sweden—*A.J.S.*)
1958	R. Baeton (Belgium—*F.N.*)
1959	S. Lundin (Sweden—*Monark*)

MOTO-CROSS DES NATIONS

	Winning Country	Individual
1950	Great Britain	G. J. Draper (G.B.—*B.S.A.*)
1951	Belgium	V. Leloup (Belgium—*F.N.*)
1952	Great Britain	B. G. Stonebridge (G.B.—*Matchless*)
1953	Great Britain	L. R. Archer (G.B.—*Norton*)
1954	Great Britain	B. Nilsson (Sweden—*B.S.A.*)
1955	Sweden	J. V. Smith (G.B.—*B.S.A.*)
1956	Great Britain	J. V. Smith (G.B.—*B.S.A.*)
1957	Great Britain	J. V. Smith (G.B.—*B.S.A.*)
1958	Sweden	B. Nilsson (Sweden—*Crescent*)
1959	Great Britain	D. J. Rickman (*Metisse*)

A.C.U. INTER-CENTRE TEAM SCRAMBLE

Winning Centre

1954	Midland
1955	Southern
1956	South Midland
1957	South Midland
1958	Midland
1959	Southern

EXPERTS GRAND NATIONAL

1950	B. W. Hall (*B.S.A.*)
1951	B. G. Stonebridge (*Matchless*)
1952	G. H. Ward (*A.J.S.*)
1953	G. H. Ward (*A.J.S.*)
1954	J. V. Smith (*B.S.A.*)
1955	J. V. Smith (*B.S.A.*)
1956	J. V. Smith (*B.S.A.*)
1957	G. H. Ward (*A.J.S.*)
1958	D. G. Curtis (*Matchless*)
1959	J. V. Smith (*B.S.A.*)

A.C.U. SCRAMBLES STAR

1951	G. H. Ward (*A.J.S.*)
1952	J. C. M. Avery (*B.S.A.*)
1953	G. H. Ward (*A.J.S.*)
1954	G. H. Ward (*A.J.S.*)
1955	J. V. Smith (*B.S.A.*)
1956	J. V. Smith (*B.S.A.*)
1958	D. G. Curtis (*Matchless*)

A.C.U. ROAD RACING STARS

1958	125 c.c.	S. M. B. Hailwood
	250 c.c.	S. M. B. Hailwood
	350 c.c.	S. M. B. Hailwood
	500 c.c.	A. M. Godfrey
	s/car	P. V. Harris

Compiled by **W. Boddy** Editor *Motor Sport*

Motor Racing

A BRIEF HISTORY OF MOTOR RACING

The first motor race took place in France in the year 1894, being run from Paris to Rouen and won by Count de Dion in a de Dion steam vehicle at a speed of 11.6 m.p.h. From that time onwards many great town-to-town races were held over the long straight roads of France and for each of them special cars, each more powerful than the last, were constructed for the sole purpose of attempting to win these early motor races. Although the roads of France at the turn of the century were comparatively deserted, crowds of curious spectators were wont to gather along the route and in 1903 their presence at the Paris–Madrid race resulted in so many accidents that the race was stopped at Bordeaux by order of the Government and the racing cars towed to the station behind horses.

This meant the end of the long-distance races over open public roads casually guarded by soldiers and instead races had to be organised over properly closed circuits. Some of these circuits were still of considerable length and on the Continent consisted of temporarily closed public roads. Because racing started in France their National club wielded great authority and to this day the

F.I.A. — Federation of International Automobile Clubs—in Paris sits in judgment on the rules governing the world's motor races and ratifies all record attempts, which have to be officially timed and observed by the approved National club and run over correctly surveyed courses. The F.I.A. also states under what technical rules the Grands Prix (or premier) motor races shall be run, publishing these rules after consultation with representatives of National automobile clubs.

In 1900 the Gordon Bennett Cup races were commenced, these attempting to make motor racing a contest between nations,

by having teams of cars competing from different countries, the country which produced the winning car being required to hold the race the following year. After S. F. Edge had won the Gordon Bennett Cup for Great Britain in 1902 with a Napier car we had to hold the 1903 race in Ireland, because in England it never has been possible to close public roads for motor racing.

After 1905 the Gordon Bennett races were replaced by the French Grand Prix, the first of which was won by Szisz at the wheel of a big Renault. For many years the French Grand Prix was the premier race of the world and was a contest between manufacturers

MOTOR RACING QUIZ

1. Who was the first driver to be knighted for his achievements in the field of motor sport?

★

2. Was it Stirling Moss's father or mother who took part in motoring competitions before Stirling became interested?

★

3. Who was the first British driver to win the Drivers' World Championship?

★

4. Which driver, in the pioneer days of racing, was known as the "Red Devil"?

★

5. And who, in the same period, was called "The Eternal Second" and why?

★

6. For what reason were the British Napier cars disqualifixd from the French Grand Prix race of 1908?

★

7. What make of car first officially exceeded a speed of 200 m.p.h. and how many engines did it have?

★

8. Can you name two racing cars which, after their drivers had been killed, were, respectively, buried in the sand and dropped into the sea?

★

9. Who won the first of the French Grand Prix races and in what make of car?

★

10. In what major respect did the 1924 Grand Prix Sunbeam differ from the 1923 Grand Prix Sunbeam?

QUIZ ANSWERS

1. The late Sir Henry Segrave. 2. They both did. His father raced Crouch and Fronty-Ford cars at Brooklands; Stirling's mother took part in rallies with a Marendaz Special. 3. The late Michael Hawthorn. 4. Jenatzy. 5. Giradot, on account of the number of times his cars finished in second place. 6. Because they were fitted with detachable wheels, which the regulations did not allow. 7. The twin-engined 1,000 h.p. Sunbeam driven by Segrave at Daytona Beach, U.S.A., in 1927. 8. The Thomas Special "Babs", buried at Pendine after Parry Thomas had been killed in it, and R. B. Howey's Ballot, after he was killed at Boulogne. 9. Szisz, driving a Renault. 10. The engine was supercharged.

---

rather than between nations. The leading car-producing manufacturers built special cars for this race and signed on the best drivers to drive them. In 1923 at Tours Britain won this classic race when Segrave crossed the line victorious at the wheel of a green 2-litre Sunbeam. Each country had its own racing colour, of which Britain's was green, Italy's red, France's blue and Germany's white.

Each year different rules governed the sort of racing cars which could take part in these Grand Prix races, to encourage technical progress; but as the cost of building the required special cars increased, the rules remained static over a period of years. After the First World War other countries besides France held an annual Grand Prix race and as time went on other races, for smaller cars, were held to supplement the main events. This practice is continued to-day, with Formula Two and Formula Three races, which are supplementary to the main Grand Prix races. Sports car racing is also popular. Such racing virtually originated at Le Mans in 1923 with the 24-Hour Grand Prix d'Endurance. After a British Bentley had won this very gruelling race in 1924 it caught the imagination of the English, who entered for it with avidity, Bentley and later Jaguar cars having notable successes at this twice-round-the-clock race in the Sarthe. But whereas sports cars had originally to run with road equipment such as normal windscreens, hoods, starters, etc. today, although they are required to retain some of these items, they have developed into disguised Grand Prix cars of very considerable performance.

Just before World War Two it was felt that Grand Prix racing cars were becoming dangerously fast and the F.I.A. sought to slow them down by introducing a maximum weight limit. However, Hitler, following a precedent set by Mussolini, saw in motor racing a powerful propaganda medium and gave two German firms material support in building world-beating racing cars. Thus it became possible to use expensive light alloys in the construction of the 1937–9 Auto-Union and Mercedes-Benz Grand Prix machines and the weight limit was rendered ludicrous, very large engines being possible in light-weight chassis. Speeds rose to over 180 m.p.h. down the straight portions of the road circuits and so powerful were these immediately pre-war German Grand Prix cars that not more than half a dozen drivers were available who could safely extend them. Nuvolari, who had been supreme in the preceding decade and was probably the greatest racing driver of all time, was asked to drive an Auto-Union and Dick Seaman, a young ex-undergraduate amateur driver, was invited to drive in the Mercedes-Benz team, a high honour for Britain. Seaman was killed at Spa driving for the German team.

After the war Grand Prix racing was revived with rather smaller cars, although improved road holding enabled these to set up new circuit records. Stirling Moss quickly rose to fame after entering motor racing with Formula Three 500 c.c. motor-cycle-engined cars. Last year was a proud season for Britain, because for the first time Mike Hawthorn, soon afterwards to be so tragically

---

Spa, Francorchamps, Belgium. Lap: 8·76 miles (approx.)

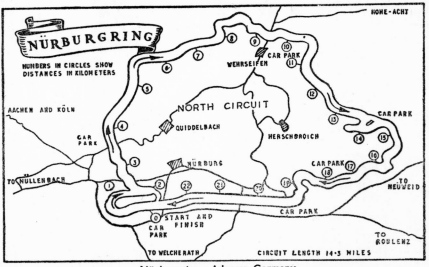

Nürburgring—Adenau, Germany

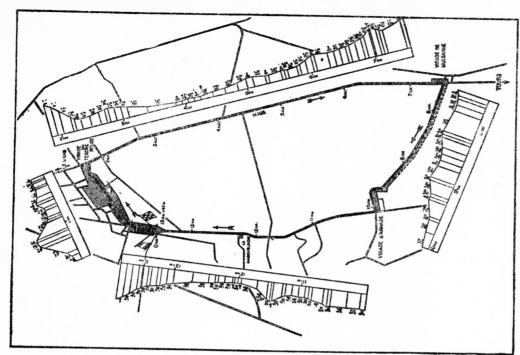

Le Mans—France. Lap: 8·68 miles.

1. Who was the financial sponsor of the E.R.A. team?

★

2. And who foots the bill for the present B.R.M.s?

★

3. In 1958 Grand Prix rules called for a change-over from alcohol to what kind of fuel?

★

4. When was the 500 Mile Race at Indianapolis Speedway in America first held?

★

5. Who won it?

★

6. Name the banked track which is situated near Paris.

★

7. When was it opened?

★

8. Name the two-engined racing car which appeared at Tripoli and Avus in 1935.

★

9. Did the famous P3 Alfa Romeo have one or two superchargers?

★

10. Who was the millionaire American who made brave attempts to win the Le Mans 24-Hour race after the war?

★

11. In what year was Brooklands Track opened for racing?

★

12. Who built it?

★

13. Give the name by which most of Malcolm Campbell's racing cars were known.

★

14. Can you describe the obvious differences between the valve gear of the pre-war and post-war competition Lago Talbot engines?

killed in a road accident, won the World Drivers' Championship for this country, driving in the Italian Ferrari team, and the Vanwall team of green cars, sponsored by millionaire industrialist Tony Vandervell, gained the Manufacturers' Championship in Grand Prix racing, the other team drivers being Tony Brooks, by profession a dental surgeon, and the late Stewart Lewis-Evans.

Apart from motor racing, it is possible to establish records for speed over a large number of distances and durations, cars being divided for this purpose into a number of engine-size classes. Such records have to be electrically-timed by approved time-keepers under the auspices of the National club, in this case the Competitions Department of the Royal Automobile Club, Pall Mall, London, S.W.

N.B.—The present Grand Prix formula calls for engines without superchargers, not exceeding a capacity of 2,500 c.c. and running on aviation petrol. From 1961 onwards the formula will change, and will call for a maximum engine size of 1,500 c.c. and a minimum chassis weight, with safety again in mind.

RESULTS OF WORLD CHAMPIONSHIP RACES 1950–1958

1950

European Grand Prix, Silverstone
1. Farina (*Alfa Romeo*) 90.95 m.p.h.
2. Fagioli (*Alfa Romeo*)
3. Parnell (*Alfa Romeo*)

Monaco Grand Prix
1. Fangio (*Alfa Romeo*) 61.66 m.p.h.
2. Ascari (*Ferrari*)
3. Chiron (*Maserati*)

Swiss Grand Prix
1. Farina (*Alfa Romeo*) 92.76 m.p.h.
2. Fagioli (*Alfa Romeo*)
3. Rosier (*Talbot*)

Belgian Grand Prix
1. Fangio (*Alfa Romeo*) 110.04 m.p.h.
2. Fagioli (*Alfa Romeo*)
3. Rosier (*Lago Talbot*)

French Grand Prix
1. Fangio (*Alfa Romeo*) 104.85 m.p.h.
2. Fagioli (*Alfa Romeo*)
3. P. Whitehead (*Ferrari*)

1951

Italian Grand Prix
1. Farina (*Alfa Romeo*) 109.7 m.p.h.
2. Serafini/Ascari (*Ferrari*)
3. Fagioli (*Alfa Romeo*)

Swiss Grand Prix
1. Fangio (*Alfa Romeo*) 89.05 m.p.h.
2. Taruffi (*Ferrari*)
3. Farina (*Alfa Romeo*)

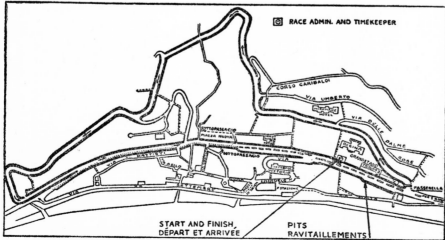

San Remo—Italy. Lap: 2·1 miles.

MOTOR RACING QUIZ

1. Who were the two runners-up to Hawthorn in the 1958 Drivers' World Championship?

Alberto Ascari

2. When was the first Targa Florio race held?

*

3. Who will hold for all time the Brooklands absolute lap record? (above centre)

*

4. Likewise, who will hold for eternity the Brooklands mountain lap record?

*

5. Under what stable name did the brothers Evans and their sister Doreen race before the war?

*

6. On which motor-cycle engine was the Vanwall Grand Prix engine based?

7. Who beat Kay Petre to the ladies lap record at Brooklands?

*

8. In which year was the first British Grand Prix held?

Stirling Moss

9. The late Mike Hawthorn had a narrow escape when he was thrown out of a car in a race at Goodwood. What car was he driving?

*

10. What did the initials E.R.A. stand for?

*

11. And B.R.M.?

*

QUIZ ANSWERS

1. Moss and Brooks. 2. 1906. 3. John Cobb in the Napier-Railton. 4. Raymond Mays with an E.R.A. 5. The Bellevue Stable. 6. Norton. 7. Gwenda Stewart. 8. 1926. 9. A B.R.M. 10. English Racing Automobile. 11. British Racing Motor.

WINNERS OF HISTORIC RACES

Year	Race	Winner	Speed
1894	Paris–Rouen	Count de Dion (De Dion steamer)	11.6 m.p.h.
1895	Bordeaux–Paris	Levassor (Panhard)	15.0 m.p.h.
1896	Paris–Marseilles–Paris	Mayade (Panhard)	15.7 m.p.h.
1897	Paris–Dieppe	Count de Dion (De Dion)	24.6 m.p.h.
1898	Paris–Amsterdam–Paris	Charron (Panhard)	26.9 m.p.h.
1899	Paris–Bordeaux	Charron (Panhard)	29.9 m.p.h.
1900	Gordon Bennett Cup	Charron (Panhard)	38.6 m.p.h.
1901	Gordon Bennett Cup	Giradot (Panhard)	37.0 m.p.h.
1902	Gordon Bennett Cup	Edge (Napier)	31.8 m.p.h.
1903	Gordon Bennett Cup	Jenatzy (Mercedes)	49.2 m.p.h.
1904	Gordon Bennett Cup	Thery (Richard-Brasier)	54.5 m.p.h.
1905	Gordon Bennett Cup	Thery (Richard-Brasier)	48.4 m.p.h.
1906	French Grand Prix	Szisz (Renault)	63.0 m.p.h.
1907	French Grand Prix	Nazzaro (Fiat)	70.5 m.p.h.
1908	French Grand Prix	Lautenschlager (Mercedes)	69.0 m.p.h.
1909	Coupe de l'Auto	Guippone (Lion-Peugeot)	47.5 m.p.h.
1910	Coupe de l'Auto	Zuccarelli (Hispano-Suiza)	56.7 m.p.h.
1911	Coupe de l'Auto	Bablot (Delage)	54.8 m.p.h.
1912	French Grand Prix	Boillot (Peugeot)	68.5 m.p.h.
1913	French Grand Prix	Boillot (Peugeot)	71.6 m.p.h.
1914	French Grand Prix	Lautenschlager (Mercedes)	65.3 m.p.h.
1921	French Grand Prix	Murphy (Duesenberg)	78.1 m.p.h.
1921	Italian Grand Prix	Goux (Ballot)	90.4 m.p.h.
1922	French Grand Prix	Nazzaro (Fiat)	79.2 m.p.h.
1922	Italian Grand Prix	Bordino (Fiat)	83.7 m.p.h.
1923	French Grand Prix	Segrave (Sunbeam)	75.3 m.p.h.
1923	Italian Grand Prix	Salamano (Fiat)	91.0 m.p.h.
1924	French Grand Prix	Campari (Alfa-Romeo)	71.0 m.p.h.
1924	Italian Grand Prix	Ascari (Alfa-Romeo)	98.8 m.p.h.
1925	French Grand Prix	Benoist/Divo (Delage)	69.7 m.p.h.
1925	Italian Grand Prix	Brilli-Peri (Alfa-Romeo)	94.7 m.p.h.
1926	French Grand Prix	Goux (Bugatti)	68.2 m.p.h.
1926	Italian Grand Prix	"Sabipa" (Bugatti)	85.8 m.p.h.
1926	German Grand Prix	Caracciola (Mercedes)	84.5 m.p.h.
1927	French Grand Prix	Benoist (Delage)	77.2 m.p.h.
1927	Italian Grand Prix	Benoist (Delage)	90.0 m.p.h.
1927	German Grand Prix	Merz (Mercedes)	63.7 m.p.h.
1928	French Grand Prix	Williams (Bugatti)	84.8 m.p.h.
1928	Italian Grand Prix	Chiron (Bugatti)	99.1 m.p.h.
1928	German Grand Prix	Caracciola/Werner (Mercedes)	64.6 m.p.h.
1929	French Grand Prix	Williams (Bugatti)	82.6 m.p.h.
1929	German Grand Prix	Williams (Bugatti)	66.8 m.p.h.
1930	French Grand Prix	Etancelin (Bugatti)	90.2 m.p.h.
1931	French Grand Prix	Chiron/Varzi (Bugatti)	78.1 m.p.h.
1931	Italian Grand Prix	Campari/Nuvolari (Alfa-Romeo)	96.1 m.p.h.
1931	German Grand Prix	Caracciola (Mercedes)	67.3 m.p.h.
1932	French Grand Prix	Nuvolari (Alfa-Romeo)	92.2 m.p.h.
1932	Italian Grand Prix	Nuvolari/Campari (Alfa-Romeo)	104.1 m.p.h.
1932	German Grand Prix	Caracciola (Mercedes)	74.1 m.p.h.
1933	French Grand Prix	Campari (Maserati)	81.5 m.p.h.
1933	Italian Grand Prix	Fagioli (Alfa-Romeo)	108.6 m.p.h.

Belgian Grand Prix
1. Farina (Alfa Romeo) 114.26 m.p.h.
2. Ascari (Ferrari)
3. Villoresi (Ferrari)

European Grand Prix, Reims
1. Fangio (Alfa Romeo) 110.97 m.p.h.
2. Ascari (Ferrari)
3. Villoresi (Ferrari)

British Grand Prix
1. Gonzalez (Ferrari) 96.11 m.p.h.
2. Fangio (Alfa Romeo)
3. Villoresi (Ferrari)

German Grand Prix
1. Ascari (Ferrari) 83.76 m.p.h.
2. Fangio (Alfa Romeo)
3. Gonzalez (Ferrari)

Italian Grand Prix
1. Ascari (Ferrari) 115.53 m.p.h.
2. Gonzalez (Ferrari)
3. Farina/Benetto (Alfa Romeo)

Spanish Grand Prix
1. Fangio (Alfa Romeo) 98.76 m.p.h.
2. Gonzalez (Ferrari)
3. Farina (Alfa Romeo)

1952

Swiss Grand Prix
1. Taruffi (Ferrari) 92.78 m.p.h.
2. Fischer (Ferrari)
3. Behra (Gordini)

European Grand Prix, Spain
1. Ascari (Ferrari) 103.13 m.p.h.
2. Farina (Ferrari)
3. Manzon (Gordini)

French Grand Prix
1. Ascari (Ferrari) 80.14 m.p.h.
2. Farina (Ferrari)
3. Taruffi (Ferrari)

British Grand Prix
1. Ascari (Ferrari) 91.43 m.p.h.
2. Taruffi (Ferrari)
3. Hawthorn (Cooper-Bristol)

German Grand Prix
1. Ascari (Ferrari) 82.7 m.p.h.
2. Farina (Ferrari)
3. Fischer (Ferrari)

Dutch Grand Prix
1. Ascari (Ferrari) 81.15 m.p.h.
2. Farina (Ferrari)
3. Villoresi (Ferrari)

Italian Grand Prix
1. Ascari (Ferrari) 109.8 m.p.h.
2. Gonzalez (Maserati)
3. Villoresi (Ferrari)

1953

Argentine Grand Prix
1. Ascari (Ferrari) 78.14 m.p.h.
2. Villoresi (Ferrari)
3. Gonzalez (Maserati)

Dutch Grand Prix
1. Ascari (Ferrari) 81.04 m.p.h.
2. Farina (Ferrari)
3. Gonzalez (Maserati)

Belgian Grand Prix
1. Ascari (Ferrari) 112.47 m.p.h.
2. Villoresi (Ferrari)
3. Marimon (Maserati)

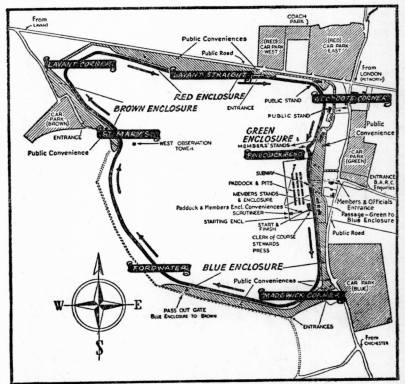

Goodwood

Year	Grand Prix	Winner	Speed
1933	German Grand Prix	Not held	
1934	French Grand Prix	Chiron (*Alfa-Romeo*)	85.0 m.p.h.
1934	Italian Grand Prix	Caracciola/Fagioli (*Mercedes-Benz*)	65.3 m.p.h.
1934	German Grand Prix	Stuck (*Auto-Union*)	76.3 m.p.h.
1935	French Grand Prix	Caracciola (*Mercedes-Benz*)	77.4 m.p.h.
1935	Italian Grand Prix	Stuck (*Auto-Union*)	85.1 m.p.h.
1935	German Grand Prix	Nuvolari (*Alfa-Romeo*)	75.2 m.p.h.
1936	French Grand Prix	Wimille/Sommer (*Bugatti*)	77.8 m.p.h.
1936	Italian Grand Prix	Rosemeyer (*Auto-Union*)	84.1 m.p.h.
1936	German Grand Prix	Rosemeyer (*Auto-Union*)	81.8 m.p.h.
1937	French Grand Prix	Chiron (*Talbot*)	82.4 m.p.h.
1937	Italian Grand Prix	Caracciola (*Mercedes-Benz*)	81.6 m.p.h.
1937	German Grand Prix	Caracciola (*Mercedes-Benz*)	82.7 m.p.h.
1938	French Grand Prix	Brauchitsch (*Mercedes-Benz*)	101.3 m.p.h.
1938	Italian Grand Prix	Nuvolari (*Auto-Union*)	96.7 m.p.h.
1938	German Grand Prix	Seaman (*Mercedes-Benz*)	80.7 m.p.h.
1939	French Grand Prix	Muller (*Auto-Union*)	105.2 m.p.h.
1939	Italian Grand Prix	Not held	
1939	German Grand Prix	Caracciola (*Mercedes-Benz*)	75.1 m.p.h.
1947	French Grand Prix	Chiron (*Talbot*)	78.1 m.p.h.
1947	Italian Grand Prix	Trossi (*Alfa-Romeo*)	70.2 m.p.h.
1947	German Grand Prix	Not held	
1948	French Grand Prix	Wimille (*Alfa-Romeo*)	102.1 m.p.h.
1948	Italian Grand Prix	Wimille (*Alfa-Romeo*)	70.3 m.p.h.
1948	German Grand Prix	Not held	
1949	French Grand Prix	Pozzi (*Delahaye*)	87.9 m.p.h.
1949	Italian Grand Prix	Ascari (*Ferrari*)	105.1 m.p.h.
1949	German Grand Prix	Not held	
1950	French Grand Prix	Fangio (*Alfa-Romeo*)	104.8 m.p.h.
1950	Italian Grand Prix	Farina (*Alfa-Romeo*)	109.6 m.p.h.
1950	German Grand Prix	Ascari (*Ferrari*)	77.6 m.p.h.
1951	French Grand Prix	Fangio/Fagioli (*Alfa-Romeo*)	110.9 m.p.h.
1951	Italian Grand Prix	Ascari (*Ferrari*)	115.4 m.p.h.
1951	German Grand Prix	Ascari (*Ferrari*)	83.7 m.p.h.
1952	French Grand Prix	Ascari (*Ferrari*)	80.1 m.p.h.
1952	Italian Grand Prix	Ascari (*Ferrari*)	109.8 m.p.h.
1952	German Grand Prix	Ascari (*Ferrari*)	82.2 m.p.h.
1953	French Grand Prix	Hawthorn (*Ferrari*)	120.5 m.p.h.
1953	Italian Grand Prix	Fangio (*Maserati*)	111.3 m.p.h.
1953	German Grand Prix	Farina (*Ferrari*)	84.0 m.p.h.
1954	French Grand Prix	Fangio (*Mercedes-Benz*)	116.6 m.p.h.
1954	Italian Grand Prix	Fangio (*Mercedes-Benz*)	112.6 m.p.h.
1954	German Grand Prix	Fangio (*Mercedes-Benz*)	83.4 m.p.h.
1955	French Grand Prix	Not held	
1955	Italian Grand Prix	Fangio (*Mercedes-Benz*)	129.2 m.p.h.
1955	German Grand Prix	Not held	
1956	French Grand Prix	Collins (*Ferrari*)	124.2 m.p.h
1956	Italian Grand Prix	Moss (*Maserati*)	130.4 m.p.h
1956	German Grand Prix	Fangio (*Ferrari*)	86.1 m.p.h
1957	French Grand Prix	Fangio (*Maserati*)	100.5 m.p.h
1957	Italian Grand Prix	Moss (*Vanwall*)	120.9 m.p.h
1957	German Grand Prix	Fangio (*Maserati*)	89.3 m.p.h
1958	French Grand Prix	Hawthorn (*Ferrari*)	125.46 m.p.h
1958	German Grand Prix	Maclaren (*Cooper*)	86.37 m.p.h
1959	Italian Grand Prix	Brooks (*Vanwall*)	121.24 m.p.h

Tazio Nuvolari   **Rudolf Caracciola**

European Grand Prix, Monaco
1. Trintignant (*Ferrari*) 65.8 m.p.h.
2. Castellotti (*Lancia*)
3. Perdisa/Behra (*Maserati*)

Belgian Grand Prix
1. Fangio (*Mercedes-Benz*) 118.84 m.p.h.
2. Moss (*Mercedes-Benz*)
3. Farina (*Ferrari*)

Dutch Grand Prix
1. Fangio (*Mercedes-Benz*) 89.62 m.p.h.
2. Moss (*Mercedes-Benz*)
3. Musso (*Maserati*)

British Grand Prix
1. Moss (*Mercedes-Benz*) 86.47 m.p.h.
2. Fangio (*Mercedes-Benz*)
3. Kling (*Mercedes-Benz*)

Italian Grand Prix
1. Fangio (*Mercedes-Benz*) 128.5 m.p.h.
2. Taruffi (*Mercedes-Benz*)
3. Castellotti (*Ferrari*)

1956

Argentine Grand Prix
1. Fangio/Musso (*Ferrari*) 79.39 m.p.h.
2. Behra (*Maserati*)
3. Hawthorn (*Maserati*)

Monaco Grand Prix
1. Moss (*Maserati*) 64.94 m.p.h.
2. Fangio/Collins (*Ferrari*)
3. Behra (*Maserati*)

Belgian Grand Prix
1. Collins (*Ferrari*) 115.43 m.p.h.
2. Frere (*Ferrari*)
3. Moss/Perdisa (*Maserati*)

French Grand Prix
1. Collins (*Ferrari*) 122.29 m.p.h.
2. Castellotti (*Ferrari*)
3. Behra (*Maserati*)

British Grand Prix
1. Fangio (*Ferrari*) 98.56 m.p.h.
2. de Portago/Collins (*Ferrari*)
3. Behra (*Maserati*)

German Grand Prix
1. Fangio (*Ferrari*) 85.86 m.p.h.
2. Moss (*Maserati*)
3. Behra (*Maserati*)

Grand Prix of Europe, Monza
1. Moss (*Maserati*) 129.73 m.p.h.
2. Collins/Fangio (*Ferrari*)
3. Flockhart (*Connaught*)

1957

Argentine Grand Prix
1. Fangio (*Maserati*) 80.62 m.p.h.
2. Behra (*Maserati*)
3. Menditeguy (*Maserati*)

MOTOR RACING QUIZ

1. In which year did Britain win the Gordon Bennett Cup and who was the driver of the victorious Napier?

★

2. In what year was the first Italian Grand Prix held?

★

3. The race was won by J. Goux. What car was he driving?

★

4. Who was the Italian mechanic who prepared the 1½-litre Delage raced so successfully by the late R. J. B. Seaman?

★

5. Can you say which driver and car first exceeded 100 m.p.h. and in which year?

★

6. And which driver and car first attained the target of 300 m.p.h.?

★

7. Who was the first driver, and in what car, to cover over 100 miles in the hour?

★

8. What was the car which was raced in 1925 with a 350 c.c. motor-cycle engine?

★

9. What racing cars were called after Rudyard Kipling's Kim?

★

10. When Basil Davenport started racing a G.N., what did he call his car?

QUIZ ANSWERS

1. 1902, S. F. Edge. 2. 1921. 3. A Ballot. 4. Giulio Ramponi. 5. Rigolly in a Gobron-Brillie in 1904. 6. The late Sir Malcolm Campbell in one of his "Bluebirds", in 1936. 7. The late Percy Lambert in a 25 h.p. Talbot at Brooklands Track, in 1913. 8. The Jappic. 9. Capt. A. Frazer-Nash's G.N.s. 10. "The Spider".

Mike Hawthorn   **Louis Chiron**   **Peter Collins**

French Grand Prix
1. Hawthorn (*Ferrari*) 113.65 m.p.h.
2. Fangio (*Maserati*)
3. Gonzalez (*Maserati*)

British Grand Prix
1. Ascari (*Ferrari*) 92.97 m.p.h.
2. Fangio (*Maserati*)
3. Farina (*Ferrari*)

German Grand Prix
1. Farina (*Ferrari*) 83.89 m.p.h.
2. Fangio (*Maserati*)
3. Hawthorn (*Ferrari*)

Swiss Grand Prix
1. Ascari (*Ferrari*) 97.17 m.p.h.
2. Farina (*Ferrari*)
3. Hawthorn (*Ferrari*)

Italian Grand Prix
1. Fangio (*Maserati*) 110.69 m.p.h.
2. Farina (*Ferrari*)
3. Villoresi (*Ferrari*)

1954

Argentine Grand Prix
1. Fangio (*Maserati*) 110.69 m.p.h.
2. Farina (*Ferrari*)
3. Gonzalez (*Ferrari*)

Belgian Grand Prix
1. Fangio (*Maserati*) 115.08 m.p.h.
2. Trintignant (*Ferrari*)
3. Moss (*Maserati*)

French Grand Prix
1. Fangio (*Mercedes-Benz*) 115.67 m.p.h.
2. Kling (*Mercedes-Benz*)
3. Manzon (*Ferrari*)

British Grand Prix
1. Gonzalez (*Ferrari*) 89.69 m.p.h.
2. Hawthorn (*Ferrari*)
3. Marimon (*Maserati*)

European Grand Prix, Nürburgring
1. Fangio (*Mercedes-Benz*) 82.77 m.p.h.
2. Hawthorn/Gonzalez (*Ferrari*)
3. Trintignant (*Ferrari*)

Swiss Grand Prix
1. Fangio (*Mercedes-Benz*) 99.17 m.p.h.
2. Gonzalez (*Ferrari*)
3. Herrmann (*Mercedes-Benz*)

Italian Grand Prix
1. Fangio (*Mercedes-Benz*) 111.99 m.p.h.
2. Hawthorn (*Ferrari*)
3. Gonzalez/Maglioli (*Ferrari*)

Spanish Grand Prix
1. Hawthorn (*Ferrari*) 98.58 m.p.h.
2. Musso (*Maserati*)
3. Fangio (*Mercedes-Benz*)

1955

Argentine Grand Prix
1. Fangio (*Mercedes-Benz*) 75.1 m.p.h.
2. Farina (*Ferrari*)
3. Maglioli-Farina/Trintignant (*Ferrari*)

Juan Fangio in a Maserati

MOTOR RACING QUIZ

1. What brake horse-power was quoted for the 1958 Vanwall which won the Formula One Manufacturers' Championship for Britain?

★

2. Which driver was the first to be credited with a lap of Brooklands Track at over 120 m.p.h.?

★

3. Who was the lady driver who drove Austin, E.R.A. and big Delage cars at Brooklands? (below)

★

4. Who designed the body on the 1959 Lister-Jaguar?

★

5. In what year was the Monte Carlo Rally first held?

QUIZ ANSWERS
1. 265 b.h.p. at 7,400 r.p.m. 2. Felice Nazzaro. 3. Kay Petre. 4. Frank Costin. 5. 1911.

Monaco Grand Prix
1. Fangio (*Maserati*) 64.73 m.p.h.
2. Brooks (*Vanwall*)
3. Gregory (*Maserati*)

French Grand Prix
9. Fangio (*Maserati*) 100.2 m.p.h.
2. Musso (*Ferrari*)
3. Collins (*Ferrari*)

Grand Prix of Europe, Aintree
1. Moss/Brooks (*Vanwall*) 86.80 m.p.h.
2. Musso (*Ferrari*)
3. Hawthorn (*Ferrari*)

German Grand Prix
1. Fangio (*Maserati*) 88.7 m.p.h.
2. Hawthorn (*Ferrari*)
3. Collins (*Ferrari*)

Pescara Grand Prix
1. Moss (*Vanwall*) 95.55 m.p.h.
2. Fangio (*Maserati*)
3. Schell (*Maserati*)

Italian Grand Prix
1. Moss (*Vanwall*) 120.28 m.p.h.
2. Fangio (*Maserati*)
3. von Trips (*Ferrari*)

1958

Argentine Grand Prix
1. Moss (*Cooper*) 83.61 m.p.h.
2. Musso (*Ferrari*)
3. Hawthorn (*Ferrari*)

Monaco Grand Prix
1. Trintignant (*Cooper*) 66.19 m.p.h.
2. Musso (*Ferrari*)
3. Collins (*Ferrari*)

Tazio Nuvolari driving an Auto Union.

Two of Sir Malcolm Campbell's famous *Bluebirds*, those of 1927 and 1933.

Tony Brooks driving a Vanwall. The Vanwall team gained the Manufacturers' Championship in Grand Prix racing in 1958

Dutch Grand Prix
1. Moss (*Vanwall*) 93.9 m.p.h.
2. Schell (*B.R.M.*)
3. Behra (*B.R.M.*)

Grand Prix of Europe, Spain
1. Brooks (*Vanwall*) 129.93 m.p.h.
2. Hawthorn (*Ferrari*)
3. Lewis-Evans (*Vanwall*)

French Grand Prix
1. Hawthorn (*Ferrari*) 125.46 m.p.h.
2. Moss (*Vanwall*)
3. von Trips (*Ferrari*)

British Grand Prix
1. Collins (*Ferrari*) 102.64 m.p.h.
2. Hawthorn (*Ferrari*)
3. Salvadori (*Cooper*)

German Grand Prix
1. Brooks (*Vanwall*) 90.35 m.p.h.
2. Salvadori (*Cooper*)
3. Trintignant (*Cooper*)

Portuguese Grand Prix
1. Moss (*Vanwall*) 105.03 m.p.h.
2. Hawthorn (*Ferrari*)
3. Lewis-Evans (*Vanwall*)

Italian Grand Prix
1. Brooks (*Vanwall*) 121.2 m.p.h.
2. Hawthorn (*Ferrari*)
3. P. Hill (*Ferrari*)

Moroccan Grand Prix
1. Moss (*Vanwall*) 116.2 m.p.h.
2. Hawthorn (*Ferrari*)
3. P. Hill (*Ferrari*)

HISTORY OF THE WORLD'S LAND SPEED RECORD

Year	Driver (Car)	Speed
1898	Chasseloup-Laubat (*Jeantaud electric*)	39.24 m.p.h.
1899	Jenatzy (*Jenatzy electric*)	41.42 m.p.h.
1899	Chausseloup-Laubat (*Jeantaud electric*)	43.69 m.p.h.
1899	Jenatzy (*Jenatzy electric*)	49.92 m.p.h.
1899	Chausseloup-Laubat (*Jeantaud electric*)	57.60 m.p.h.
1899	Jenatzy (*Jenatzy electric*)	65.79 m.p.h.
1902	Serpollet (*Serpollet steam car*)	75.06 m.p.h.
1902	Vanderbilt (*Mors*)	76.08 m.p.h.
1902	Fournier (*Mors*)	76.60 m.p.h.
1902	Augieres (*Mors*)	77.13 m.p.h.
1903	Duray (*Gobron-Brillie*)	83.47 m.p.h.
1903	Duray (*Gobron-Brillie*)	84.73 m.p.h.
1904	Ford (*Ford 999*)	91.37 m.p.h.
1904	Vanderbilt (*Mercedes*)	92.30 m.p.h.
1904	Rigolly (*Gobron-Brillie*)	103.55 m.p.h.
1904	Barras (*Darracq*)	104.52 m.p.h.
1905	Macdonald (*Napier*)	104.65 m.p.h.
1905	Hemery (*Darracq*)	109.65 m.p.h.
1906	Marriott (*Stanley steam car*)	121.57 m.p.h.
1909	Hemery (*Benz*)	125.95 m.p.h.
1910	Oldfield (*Benz*)	131.72 m.p.h.
1914	Hornsted (*Benz*)	*124.10 m.p.h.
1922	Guinness (*Sunbeam*)	133.75 m.p.h.
1924	Thomas, Rene (*Delage*)	143.31 m.p.h.
1924	Eldridge (*Fiat*)	146.01 m.p.h.
1924	Campbell (*Sunbeam*)	146.16 m.p.h.
1925	Campbell (*Sunbeam*)	150.87 m.p.h.
1926	Segrave (*Sunbeam*)	152.33 m.p.h.
1926	Thomas, J. G. P. (*Thomas Special*)	169.30 m.p.h.
1926	Thomas, J. G. P. (*Thomas Special*)	171.02 m.p.h.
1927	Campbell (*Napier-Campbell*)	174.88 m.p.h.
1927	Segrave (*Sunbeam*)	203.79 m.p.h.
1928	Campbell (*Napier-Campbell*)	206.96 m.p.h.
1928	Keech (*White-Triplex*)	207.55 m.p.h.
1929	Segrave (*Irving-Napier*)	231.44 m.p.h.
1931	Campbell (*Napier-Campbell*)	246.09 m.p.h.
1932	Campbell (*Napier-Campbell*)	253.97 m.p.h.
1933	Campbell (*Campbell Special*)	272.46 m.p.h.
1935	Campbell (*Campbell Special*)	276.82 m.p.h.
1935	Campbell (*Campbell Special*)	301.13 m.p.h.
1937	Eyston (*Thunderbolt*)	312.00 m.p.h.
1938	Eyston (*Thunderbolt*)	345.50 m.p.h.
1938	Cobb (*Railton*)	350.20 m.p.h.
1938	Eyston (*Thunderbolt*)	357.50 m.p.h.
1939	Cobb (*Railton*)	369.70 m.p.h.
1947	Cobb (*Railton*)	394.20 m.p.h.

*After 1910 records had to be timed in two directions and the mean speed taken, hence Hornsted was able to break the record with a lower speed than the previous holder's one-way speed.

WINNERS OF THE LE MANS 24-HOUR SPORTS CAR RACE

Year	Winners (Car)
1923	Lagache and Leonard (*Chenard-Walcker*)
1924	Duff and Clement (*Bentley*)
1925	de Courcelles and Rossignol (*Lorraine-Dietrich*)
1926	Bloch and Rossignol (*Lorraine-Dietrich*)
1927	Benjafield and Davis (*Bentley*)
1928	Barnato and Rubin (*Bentley*)
1929	Barnato and Birkin (*Bentley*)
1930	Barnato and Kidston (*Bentley*)
1931	Howe and Birkin (*Alfa-Romeo*)
1932	Sommer and Chinetti (*Alfa-Romeo*)
1933	Sommer and Nuvolari (*Alfa-Romeo*)
1934	Chinetti and Etancelin (*Alfa-Romeo*)
1935	Hindmarsh and Fontes (*Lagonda*)
1936	No race
1937	Wimille and Benoist (*Bugatti*)
1938	Chaubord and Tremoulet (*Delahaye*)
1939	Wimille and Veyron (*Bugatti*)
1949	Chinetti and Selsdon (*Ferrari*)
1950	Rosier and Rosier (*Talbot*)
1951	Walker and Whitehead (*Jaguar*)
1952	Lang and Riess (*Mercedes-Benz*)
1953	Hamilton and Rolt (*Jaguar*)
19 4	Gonzalez and Trintignant (*Ferrari*)
1955	Hawthorn and Bueb (*Jaguar*)
1956	Flockhart and Sanderson (*Jaguar*)
1957	Flockhart and Bueb (*Jaguar*)
1958	Hill and Gendebien (*Ferrari*)

THE WORLD CHAMPION DRIVERS

Year	Driver	Country
1950	Dr. Giuseppe Farina	Italy
1951	Juan Manual Fangio	Argentina
1952	Alberto Ascari	Italy
1953	Alberto Ascari	Italy
1954	Juan Manual Fangio	Argentina
1955	Juan Manual Fangio	Argentina
1956	Juan Manual Fangio	Argentina
1957	Juan Manual Fangio	Argentina
1958	Mike Hawthorn	Britain

Parry Thomas

J. Parry Thomas in his record breaking Thomas-Special, 1926.

John Cobb and his Railton Mobil Special.

226

SOME NOTES ON HOW TO PLAY THE GAME OF NETBALL

Netball as played today is played by seven players on a hard-surface court 100 feet long by 50 feet wide, marked clearly by lines. The court is divided into three equal parts, and has a centre spot 3 inches in diameter marked in the centre of the court, on which the player with the ball must stand at the start of the game, and after each goal scored, until the ball has left her hands.

A semi-circle with a radius of 16 feet is marked round each goalpost; these are called the shooting circles.

The goalposts, with a metal ring 15 inches in diameter, should be placed in the middle of each goal line. The ring should be 10 feet above the ground, projecting 6 inches from the supporting surface, and have a net open at both ends. The top of the post should be on a level with the ring.

The ball shall be a size 5 association football.

The players are known as:

Shooter
Attack
Attacking Centre
Centre
Defending Centre
Defence
Goalkeeper.

The shooters and attacks, together with their goalkeepers and defences, may only play in the shooting areas and up to their opponents' two-thirds line; the six centre-court players may only play in the centre court, and must not enter the shooting areas. Penalties are awarded to opponents if these rules are broken.

The game is started by the player with the ball who has won the toss, and chosen to take the first pass, standing on the centre spot until she has thrown the ball. The game is continued by throwing or bouncing the ball from player to player until the ball reaches the shooter or attack in the shooting area, who then throws the ball into and through the net to score a goal. No player may take a complete step, or run with the ball, and may not hold it for more than three seconds, neither may she touch, push or charge her opponent in any way, or knock the ball out of her opponent's hands. Various penalties are awarded for the infringement of any of these rules.

The game is played for 20 minutes each way, with an interval of not less than five minutes. The players change ends at half-time. The game may be shortened for schools or when a series of matches are played at tournaments.

There shall be two umpires who shall give decisions in half of the court. For this purpose the length of the court is divided in half.

HISTORICAL NOTES

1891 Game invented in America.
1895 Game introduced by an American, Dr. Toles, into England.
1897 Game played on grass with small ball, waste-paper baskets on broomsticks or jumping stands, with no circles or boundaries and no printed rules.
1898 Rules introduced. Court divided into three areas, a large ball introduced, and an obstruction rule.
1901 Rules published. Introduction of shooting circle, the "throw in", and non-interference of player with the ball. Posts with rings with a sleeve of net made by Slazengers.
1923 Register of clubs and leagues taken.
1926 Inaugural meeting held in London of the All England Women's Net Ball Association (later to be known as the All England Netball Association).
1932 First inter-county tournament held. This continues as an annual event today.
1949 First international matches played between England, Scotland, and Wales at Wembley.
1955 The commencement of annual international matches between England, Northern Ireland, Scotland and Wales, to be played in each country in rotation.
1956 The first overseas team (Australia) toured England, learned the game en route and ended the tour by beating England by 14 goals to 11 at Harringay Arena.
1957 The first England touring team went to South Africa and returned with an unbeaten record, having played 19 matches, including three test-matches versus South Africa.
1957 The first International Rules Board Conference was held in England, with representatives of England, Scotland, Northern Ireland, Wales, America, Australia, New Zealand, and South Africa present.
1959 Steps are in hand to form an International Federation, with a future meeting possibly in Ceylon.
1959 Return visit of a South African touring team to England.

Today the All England Netball Association has practically every county in England organised with a netball association and affiliated to it. In addition, the three women's Services, and practically all schools and sections of the national youth organisations for girls and women, are affiliated.

It has a main council representative of the whole country, with committees for all aspects of teaching, promoting and organising the game.

The West Indies, Trinidad, Ceylon, Australia, and South Africa, in particular, are in close contact with it, and many other contacts throughout the world may be linked when the Federation contemplated becomes a reality.

INTER-COUNTY TOURNAMENT WINNERS

1932	Essex	13	Kent	5
1933	None held			
1934	Essex	7	Warwickshire	3
1935	Middlesex	8	U.L.A.U.	7
1936	Essex	7	Yorkshire	5
1937	Essex	10	Middlesex	9
1938	Middlesex	16	Essex	6
1939	Civil Service	15	Middlesex	15
1945	Lancashire	12	Bedford	9
1946	Surrey	9	Northumberland	1
1947	Middlesex	13	Lancashire	3
1948	Bedford P.T. College	8	Surrey	5
1949	Surrey	12	Middlesex	6
1950	Surrey	16	Lancashire	9
1951	Surrey	13	Lancashire	9
1952	Surrey	18	Warwickshire	8
1953	Surrey	23	Middlesex	12
1954	Surrey	11	Birmingham	6
1955	Tournament abandoned			
1956	Surrey	18	Essex	10
1957	Surrey	15	Essex	12
1958	Surrey	13	Middlesex	6
1959	Surrey	10	Warwickshire	9

HOME INTERNATIONALS

1955	England	36	Scotland	5
	England	40	Wales	4
	N. Ireland	11	Scotland	22
	N. Ireland	13	Wales	10
1956	England	36	N. Ireland	1
	England	34	Scotland	1
	Wales	17	N. Ireland	15
	Wales	13	Scotland	15
	Australia	14	England	11
1957	England	28	N. Ireland	6
	England	34	Wales	5
	Wales	9	Scotland	16
	Scotland	17	N. Ireland	5
1958	England	35	N. Ireland	3
	England	32	Scotland	9
	England	33	Wales	4
1959	England	45	N. Ireland	4
	England	42	Scotland	12
	England	43	Wales	5

NETBALL QUIZ

1. Give the weight and size of a netball.

2. When was the first inter-county tournament held and which county won it?

3. Which All England Netball Association official holds the longest service record in her present office? How long has she held this office?

4. In 1947 two groups of netball players went to Europe to demonstrate netball. In which countries did they play?

5. In which year were the first international matches played, and who was England's captain?

6. Up to February 1959 how long had Surrey been County Champions?

7. "Netball operation airlift" came into force in 1953. What was this?

8. Which was the first overseas team to tour England, and what was the score when they played against England at Harringay Arena?

9. Which former England player held the world high-jump record?

10. Which counties use the following symbols in their badge—(*a*) a rose, (*b*) an eagle, (*c*) a hart, (*d*) a horse?

QUIZ ANSWERS

1. Weight between 14 and 16 ounces. Size 5 association football between 27 and 28 inches in circumference. 2. In 1932. Essex. 3. The All England Netball Association Honorary Secretary, Miss E. L. Sanders. 20 years. 4. In Czechoslovakia and in Denmark. 5. In 1949. Eva Owen of Lancashire. 6. 10 years. 7. The transporting of over 300 players and officials by air to Jersey at Easter 1953 for the Inter-County Tournament. 8. Australia in 1956. Australia 14, England 11. 9. Sheila Alexander (now Mrs. Lerwill) of Surrey. 10. (*a*) Lancashire and Yorkshire; (*b*) Northumberland; (*c*) Hertfordshire; (*d*) Wiltshire.

Olympic Games

Compiled by **Norris McWhirter**

Athletics Correspondent: The Observer
and B.B.C. Television Commentator

OLYMPIC GAMES

The Olympic Games, which were held in Ancient Greece for 12 centuries, and, according to some evidence, 17 centuries, before their termination in the year 394 A.D., were revived in modern form at Athens in 1896. Ten countries participated with a total of 59 athletes contesting the programme of 12 track and field events.

The venues of the Games since 1896 are as in the table below. It will be noted that Celebrations are numbered strictly whether or not the Games were actually held. The Games of 1916, 1940 and 1944 were cancelled owing to the two World Wars.

I	Athens	1896
II	Paris	1900
III	St. Louis	1904
†	Athens	1906
IV	London	1908
V	Stockholm	1912
VI*	Berlin	1916
VII	Antwerp	1920
VIII	Paris	1924
IX	Amsterdam	1928
X	Los Angeles	1932
XI	Berlin	1936
XII*	Tokyo, then Helsinki	1940
XIII*	London	1944
XIV	London	1948
XV	Helsinki	1952
XVI	Melbourne	1956
XVII	Rome	1960

* Cancelled due to World Wars.
† Intercalated Celebration.

Track and field athletics has always been the major Olympic sport. The traditional programme on the track is as follows: 100 metres, 200 metres (instituted 1900), 400 metres, 800 metres, 1,500 metres, 5,000 metres (instituted 1912), and 10,000 metres (instituted 1912).

The long-distance race in 1896 was over 24 miles 1,500 yards, between the site of the ancient battlefield of Marathon and the new Averoff stadium in Athens. Since then the long-distance event has always been called "The Marathon", the distance becoming in 1924 standardised at the 26 miles 385 yards first used at London in 1908.

The 4 × 100 metres and the 4 × 400 metres relay races and the decathlon were introduced at Stockholm in 1912.

The hurdling programme of 110 metres high hurdles and 400 metres intermediate hurdles became stabilised in 1908, and the steeplechase was eventually standardised at 3,000 metres in 1920.

Six of the eight standard field events, as follows, high jump, pole vault, long jump, hop, step and jump, shot putt and discus throw have always been on the programme, but the hammer throw was not held in 1896 and the javelin throw was only introduced in 1908.

Various odd events of the early celebrations, such as, for example, the 60 metres sprint, the various team races, the standing jumps and the pentathlon were all eliminated by 1928.

It was in that year at Amsterdam that five women's events were introduced as follows; 100 metres, 800 metres, 4 × 100 metres relay, high jump and discus throw. The 800 metres was immediately dropped and is not to reappear until 1960. The present programme is now of ten events, the 80 metres hurdles and javelin throw having been added in 1932, and the 200 metres, long jump and shot putt in 1948.

Jesse Owens (U.S.A.), 100 metres, 200 metres and Long Jump winner in the 1936 Games.

R. B. Mathias (U.S.A.), Decathlon winner in the 1948 and 1952 Games, throwing the discus.

Mal Whitfield (U.S.A.), twice winner of 800 metres (1948 and 1952 Games).

OLYMPICS QUIZ

1. How many hurdles are normally found in the 110 metres hurdling event?

*

2. One athletics event has been won by the U.S.A. in every modern Olympic Games. What is it?

QUIZ ANSWERS
1. 10. 2. The Pole Vault.

The opening ceremony of the 1948 Olympic Games at the crowded Wembley Stadium.

ROLL OF OLYMPIC ATHLETIC CHAMPIONS

100 Metres

1896	Thomas Burke	(U.S.A.)	12.0
1900	Francis Jarvis	(U.S.A.)	11.0
1904	Archie Hahn	(U.S.A.)	11.0
1908	Reginald Walker	(S. Africa)	10.8
1912	Ralph Craig	(U.S.A.)	10.8
1920	Charles Paddock	(U.S.A.)	10.8
1924	Harold Abrahams	(G.B.)	10.6
1928	Percy Williams	(Canada)	10.8
1932	Eddie Tolan	(U.S.A.)	10.3
1936	Jesse Owens	(U.S.A.)	*10.3
1948	Harrison Dillard	(U.S.A.)	10.3
1952	Lindy Remigino	(U.S.A.)	10.4
1956	Bobby-Joe Morrow	(U.S.A.)	10.5

* Wind assisted.

400 Metres

1896	Thomas Burke	(U.S.A.)	54.2
1900	Maxie Long	(U.S.A.)	49.4
1904	Harry Hillman	(U.S.A.)	49.2
1908	Wyndham Halswelle	(U.S.A.)	50.0
1912	Charles Reidpath	(U.S.A.)	48.2
1920	Bevil Rudd	(S. Africa)	49.6
1924	Eric Liddell	(G.B.)	47.6
1928	Raymond Barbuti	(U.S.A.)	47.8
1932	William Carr	(U.S.A.)	46.2
1936	Archie Williams	(U.S.A.)	46.5
1948	Arthur Wint	(Jamaica)	46.2
1952	George Rhoden	(Jamaica)	45.9
1956	Charlie Jenkins	(U.S.A.)	46.7

200 Metres

1896	Event not held		
1900	Walter Tewkesbury	(U.S.A.)	22.2
1904	Archie Hahn	(U.S.A.)	21.6
1908	Robert Kerr	(Canada)	22.6
1912	Ralph Craig	(U.S.A.)	21.7
1920	Allen Woodring	(U.S.A.)	22.0
1924	Jackson Scholz	(U.S.A.)	21.6
1928	Percy Williams	(Canada)	21.8
1932	Eddie Tolan	(U.S.A.)	21.2
1936	Jessie Owens	(U.S.A.)	20.7
1948	Melvin Patton	(U.S.A.)	21.1
1952	Andy Stanfield	(U.S.A.)	20.7
1956	Bobby-Joe Morrow	(U.S.A.)	20.6

800 Metres

1896	Edwin Flack	(Australia)	2:11.0
1900	Alfred Tysoe	(G.B.)	2:01.2
1904	James Lightbody	(U.S.A.)	1:56.0
1908	Melvin Sheppard	(U.S.A.)	1:52.8
1912	James Meredith	(U.S.A.)	1:51.9
1920	Albert Hill	(G.B.)	1:53.4
1924	Douglas Lowe	(G.B.)	1:52.4
1928	Douglas Lowe	(G.B.)	1:50.8
1932	Tommy Hampson	(G.B.)	1:49.8
1936	John Woodruff	(U.S.A.)	1:52.9
1948	Mal Whitfield	(U.S.A.)	1:49.2
1952	Mal Whitfield	(U.S.A.)	1:49.2
1956	Tom Courtney	(U.S.A.)	1:47.7

1,500 Metres

1896	Edwin Flack	(Australia)	4:33.2
1900	Charles Bennett	(G.B.)	4:06.2
1904	James Lightbody	(U.S.A.)	4:05.4
1908	Melvin Sheppard	(U.S.A.)	4:03.4
1912	Arnold Jackson	(G.B.)	3:56.8
1920	Albert Hill	(G.B.)	4:01.8
1924	Paavo Nurmi	(Finland)	3:53.6
1928	Harri Larva	(Finland)	3:53.2
1932	Luigi Beccali	(Italy)	3:51.2
1936	Jack Lovelock	(New Zealand)	3:47.8
1948	Henry Eriksson	(Sweden)	3:49.8
1952	Joseph Barthel	(Luxembourg)	3:45.2
1956	Ronnie Delany	(Eire)	3:41.2

5,000 Metres

1896, 1900, 1904 and 1908 event not held.

1912	Hans Kolehmainen	(Finland)	14:36.6
1920	Joseph Guillemot	(France)	14:55.6
1924	Paavo Nurmi	(Finland)	14:31.2
1928	Ville Ritola	(Finland)	14:38.0
1932	Laurie Lehtinen	(Finland)	14:30.0
1936	Gunnar Höckert	(Finland)	14:22.2
1948	Gaston Reiff	(Belgium)	14:17.6
1952	Emil Zátopek	(Czechoslovakia)	14:06.6
1956	Vladimir Kuts	(U.S.S.R.)	13:39.6

10,000 Metres

1912	Hans Kolehmainen	(Finland)	31:20.8
1920	Paavo Nurmi	(Finland)	31:45.8
1924	Ville Ritola	(Finland)	30:23.2
1928	Paavo Nurmi	(Finland)	30:18.8
1932	Janusz Kusocinski	(Poland)	30:11.4
1936	Ilmari Salminen	(Finland)	30:15.4
1948	Emil Zátopek	(Czechoslovakia)	29:59.6
1952	Emil Zátopek	(Czechoslovakia)	29:17.0
1956	Vladimir Kuts	(U.S.S.R.)	28:45.6

Marathon

1896	Spyridon Louis	(Germany)	2 58:50.0
1900	Michel Theato	(France)	2 59:45.0
1904	Thomas Hicks	(U.S.A.)	3 28:53.0
1908*	John Hayes	(U.S.A.)	2 55:18.4
1912	Kenneth McArthur	(S. Africa)	2 36:54.6
1920	Hans Kolehmainen	(Finland)	2 32:35.8
1924	Albin Stenroos	(Finland)	2 41:22.6
1928	El Ouafi	(France)	2 32:57.0
1932	Juan Zabala	(Argentina)	2 31:36.0
1936	Kitei Son	(Japan)	2 29:19.2
1948	Delfo Cabrera	(Argentina)	2 34:51.6
1952	Emil Zátopek	(Czechoslovakia)	2 23:03.2
1956	Alain Mimoun	(France)	2 25:00.0

* Dorando Pietri (Italy) finished first but was disqualified.

Long Jump

			ft.	in.
1896	Ellery Clark	(U.S.A.)	20	10
1900	Alva Kraenzlein	(U.S.A.)	23	$6\frac{5}{8}$
1904	Myer Prinstein	(U.S.A.)	24	1
1908	Frank Irons	(U.S.A.)	24	$6\frac{1}{2}$
1912	Albert Gutterson	(U.S.A.)	24	$11\frac{1}{4}$
1920	William Pettersson*	(Sweden)	23	$5\frac{1}{2}$
1924	Hart de Hubbard	(U.S.A.)	24	$4\frac{7}{8}$
1928	Edward Hamm	(U.S.A.)	25	$4\frac{3}{8}$
1932	Edward Gordon	(U.S.A.)	25	$0\frac{3}{4}$
1936	Jesse Owens	(U.S.A.)	26	$5\frac{3}{8}$
1948	Willie Steele	(U.S.A.)	25	8
1952	Jerome Biffle	(U.S.A.)	24	10
1956	Gregory Bell	(U.S.A.)	25	$8\frac{1}{4}$

* Later changed his name to Björnemann.

Melbourne 1956. Final of the 5,000 metres. V. Kuts (winner) (U.S.S.R.) leading from G. Pirie (second) (G.B.), D. Ibbotson (third) (G.B.) and C. Chataway (G.B.)

Hop, Step and Jump

			ft.	in.
1896	James Connolly	(U.S.A.)	44	$11\frac{3}{4}$
1900	Myer Prinstein	(U.S.A.)	47	$5\frac{3}{4}$
1904	Myer Prinstein	(U.S.A.)	47	1
1908	Tim Ahearne	(G.B.)	48	$11\frac{1}{4}$
1912	Gustaf Lindblom	(Sweden)	48	$5\frac{1}{8}$
1920	Vilho Tuulos	(Finland)	47	$6\frac{7}{8}$
1924	Archibald Winter	(Australia)	50	$11\frac{1}{4}$
1928	Mikio Oda	(Japan)	49	$10\frac{7}{8}$
1932	Chuhei Nambu	(Japan)	51	7
1936	Naoto Tajima	(Japan)	52	$5\frac{7}{8}$
1948	Arne Ahman	(Sweden)	50	$6\frac{1}{4}$
1952	Adhemar Ferreira da Silva	(Brazil)	53	$2\frac{1}{2}$
1956	Adhemar Ferreira da Silva	(Brazil)	53	$7\frac{5}{8}$

Shot Putt

			ft.	in.
1896	Robert Garrett	(U.S.A.)	36	$9\frac{3}{4}$
1900	Richard Sheldon	(U.S.A.)	46	$3\frac{1}{8}$
1904	Ralph Rose	(U.S.A.)	48	7
1908	Ralph Rose	(U.S.A.)	46	$7\frac{1}{2}$
1912	Pat McDonald	(U.S.A.)	50	$3\frac{7}{8}$
1920	Ville Pörhölä	(Finland)	48	$1\frac{7}{8}$
1924	Clarence Houser	(U.S.A.)	49	$2\frac{1}{8}$
1928	John Kuck	(U.S.A.)	52	$0\frac{3}{4}$
1932	Leo Sexton	(U.S.A.)	52	6
1936	Hans Woellke	(Germany)	53	$1\frac{3}{4}$
1948	Wilbur Thompson	(U.S.A.)	56	2
1952	Parry O'Brien	(U.S.A.)	57	$1\frac{1}{2}$
1956	Parry O'Brien	(U.S.A.)	60	11

Discus Throw

			ft.	in.
1896	Robert Garrett	(U.S.A.)	95	$7\frac{3}{4}$
1900	Rudolf Bauer	(Hungary)	118	3
1904	Martin Sheridan	(U.S.A.)	128	$10\frac{1}{2}$
1908	Martin Sheridan	(U.S.A.)	134	2
1912	Armas Taipale	(Finland)	148	$3\frac{7}{8}$
1920	Elmer Niklander	(Finland)	146	$7\frac{1}{4}$
1924	Clarence Houser	(U.S.A.)	151	$4\frac{7}{8}$
1928	Clarence Houser	(U.S.A.)	155	3
1932	John Anderson	(U.S.A.)	162	$4\frac{7}{8}$
1936	Kenneth Carpenter	(U.S.A.)	165	$7\frac{3}{8}$
1948	Alfredo Consolini	(Italy)	173	2
1952	Sim Iness	(U.S.A.)	180	$6\frac{1}{2}$
1956	Al. Oerter	(U.S.A.)	184	$10\frac{7}{8}$

Hammer Throw

			ft.	in.
1896	Event not held			
1900	John Flanagan	(U.S.A.)	163	$1\frac{3}{4}$
1904	John Flanagan	(U.S.A.)	168	1
1908	John Flanagan	(U.S.A.)	170	$4\frac{1}{4}$
1912	Matt. McGrath	(U.S.A.)	179	$7\frac{1}{8}$
1920	Pat Ryan	(U.S.A.)	173	$5\frac{1}{2}$
1924	Frederick Tootell	(U.S.A.)	174	$10\frac{1}{4}$
1928	Pat O'Callaghan	(Eire)	168	$7\frac{1}{4}$
1932	Pat O'Callaghan	(Eire)	176	11
1936	Karl Hein	(Germany)	185	4
1948	Imre Németh	(Hungary)	183	$11\frac{1}{2}$
1952	Joszéf Csermák	(Hungary)	197	$11\frac{3}{4}$
1956	Hal. Connolly	(U.S.A.)	207	$3\frac{3}{4}$

Javelin Throw

1896, 1900 and 1904 event not held

			ft.	in.
1908	Erik Lemming	(Sweden)	179	$10\frac{1}{2}$
1912	Erik Lemming	(Sweden)	198	$11\frac{3}{8}$
1920	Jonni Myrrä	(Finland)	215	$9\frac{3}{4}$
1924	Jonni Myrrä	(Finland)	206	$6\frac{3}{4}$
1928	Erik Lundkvist	(Sweden)	218	6
1932	Matti Järvinen	(Finland)	238	7
1936	Gerhard Stöck	(Germany)	235	$8\frac{3}{8}$
1948	Tapio Rautavaara	(Finland)	228	$10\frac{7}{8}$
1952	Cy Young	(U.S.A.)	242	$0\frac{3}{4}$
1956	Egil Danielson	(Norway)	281	$2\frac{3}{8}$

Fanny Blankers-Koen (Netherlands)

H. Dillard (U.S.A.)

C. W. Brasher (G.B.)

Ronnie Delany (Eire)

George Rhoden (Jamaica), winner of the 400 metres in 1952 with a record time of 45.9 secs.

OLYMPICS QUIZ

1. Who was the runner who brought in the torch to the Stadium at the London Olympics in 1948?

★

2. What is the weight of a standard discus?

★

3. Only one male athlete has won the same individual event in three consecutive Games. Who is he?

★

4. At what age did R. Mathias (U.S.A.) win the first of his two gold medals for the Decathlon?

QUIZ ANSWERS

1. J. W. E. Mark. 2. 4 pounds 6.4 ounces. 3. John Flanagan (U.S.A.) who won the Hammer Throw in 1900, 1904 and 1908. 4. 17.

Decathlon

			Points
1912*	Hugo Wieslander	(Sweden)	7724.495
1920	Helge Lövland	(Norway)	6804.35
1924	Harold Osborn	(U.S.A.)	7710.775
1928	Paavo Yrjölä	(Finland)	8053.29
1932	James Bausch	(U.S.A.)	8463.23
1936	Glenn Morris	(U.S.A.)	7900
1948	Robert Mathias	(U.S.A.)	7139
1953	Robert Mathias	(U.S.A.)	7887
1956	Milton Campbell	(U.S.A.)	7937

* J Thorpe (U.S.A.) won with a total of 8412.955 but was subsequently disqualified for professionalism.

4 × 100 Metres Relay

1912	Great Britain	42.4
1920	United States	42.2
1924	United States	41.0
1928	United States	41.0
1932	United States	40.0
1936	United States	39.8
1948	United States	40.6
1952	United States	40.1
1956	United States	39.5

4 × 400 Metres Relay

1912	United States	3:16.6
1920	Great Britain	3:22.2
1924	United States	3:16.0
1928	United States	3:14.2
1932	United States	3:08.2
1936	Great Britain	3:09.0
1948	United States	3:10.4
1952	Jamaica	3:03.9
1956	United States	3:04.8

P. J. Nurmi, the popular Finnish runner, had the honour to bring the Torch into the stadium and light the Altar at the Helsinki Games (1952).

OLYMPIC QUIZ

In 1928 a member of the British peerage won the 400 metres hurdling event. Who was he?

QUIZ ANSWER

The Marquess of Exeter (Lord Burghley).

N. A. E. Saeys (Belgium), Throwing the Javelin finalist in the 1948 Games.

110 Metres Hurdles

1896*	Thomas Curtis	(U.S.A.)	17.6
1900	Alva Kraenzlein	(U.S.A.)	15.4
1904	Frederick Schule	(U.S.A.)	16.0
1908	Forrest Smithson	(U.S.A.)	15.0
1912	Fred Kelly	(U.S.A.)	15.1
1920	Earl Thomson	(Canada)	14.8
1924	Dan Kinsey	(U.S.A.)	15.0
1928	Sidney Atkinson	(S. Africa)	14.8
1932	George Saling	(U.S.A.)	14.6
1936	Forrest Towns	(U.S.A.)	14.2
1948	William Porter	(U.S.A.)	13.9
1952	Harrison Dillard	(U.S.A.)	13.7
1956	Lee Calhoun	(U.S.A.)	13.5

* Distance was only 100 metres over 8 instead of 10 flights.

400 Metres Hurdles

1896	Event not held		
1900	Walter Tewkesbury	(U.S.A.)	57.6
1904*	Harry Hillman	(U.S.A.)	53.0
1908	Charles Bacon	(U.S.A.)	55.0
1912	Event not held		
1920	Frank Loomis	(U.S.A.)	54.0
1924	F. Morgan Taylor	(U.S.A.)	52.6
1928	†The Marquess of Exeter	(G.B.)	53.4
1932	Robert Tisdall	(Eire)	51.8
1936	Glenn Hardin	(U.S.A.)	52.4
1948	Roy Cochran	(U.S.A.)	51.1
1952	Charlie Moore	(U.S.A.)	50.8
1956	Glenn Davis	(U.S.A.)	50.1

* Height of hurdles was only 2 ft. 6 in. instead of 3 ft. 0 in.
† Then Lord Burghley.

3,000 Metres Steeplechase

1920	Percy Hodge	(G.B.)	10:00.4
1924	Ville Ritola	(Finland)	9:33.6
1928	Toivo Loukola	(Finland)	9:21.8
1932*	Volmari-Iso-Hollo	(Finland)	10:33.4
1936	Volmari-Iso-Hollo	(Finland)	9:03.8
1948	Tore Sjöstrand	(Sweden)	9:04.6
1952	Horace Ashenfelter	(U.S.A.)	8:45.4
1956	Christopher Brasher	(G.B.)	8:41.2

* An extra lap was run due to an error, making the total distance 3,460 metres.

20,000 Metres Walk*

1956	Leonid Spirin	(U.S.S.R.)	1 31:27.0

* Not previously held.

50,000 Metres Road Walk

1932*	Tommy Green	(G.B.)	4 50:10.0
1948	John Ljunggren	(Sweden)	4 41:52.0
1952	Giuseppe Dordoni	(Italy)	4 28:07.8
1956	Norman Read	(New Zealand)	4 30:42.8

* This event was not previously held in the Games.

High Jump

1896	Ellery Clark	(U.S.A.)	5 ft. 11¼ in.
1900	Irving Baxter	(U.S.A.)	6 ft. 2¾ in.
1904	Samuel Jones	(U.S.A.)	5 ft. 11 in.
1908	Harry Porter	(U.S.A.)	6 ft. 3 in.
1912	Alma Richards	(U.S.A.)	6 ft. 4 in.
1920	Richmond Landon	(U.S.A.)	6 ft. 4⅜ in.
1924	Harold Osborn	(U.S.A.)	6 ft. 6 in.
1928	Robert King	(U.S.A.)	6 ft. 4⅜ in.
1932	Duncan McNaughton	(Canada)	6 ft. 5⅝ in.
1936	Cornelius Johnson	(U.S.A.)	6 ft. 7⅞ in.
1948	John Winter	(Australia)	6 ft. 6 in.
1952	Walter Davis	(U.S.A.)	6 ft. 8¼ in.
1956	Charles Dumas	(U.S.A.)	6 ft. 11½ in.

Pole Vault

1896	William Hoyt	(U.S.A.)	10 ft. 9¾ in.
1900	Irving Baxter	(U.S.A.)	10 ft. 9¾ in.
1904	Charles Dvorak	(U.S.A.)	11 ft. 6 in.
1908	Edward Cook / Albert Gilbert	(U.S.A.)	12 ft. 2 in.
1912	Harry Babcock	(U.S.A.)	12 ft. 11½ in.
1920	Frank Foss	(U.S.A.)	13 ft. 5 in.
1924	Lee Barnes	(U.S.A.)	12 ft. 11½ in.
1928	Sabin Carr	(U.S.A.)	13 ft. 9⅜ in.
1932	William Miller	(U.S.A.)	14 ft. 1⅞ in.
1936	Earle Meadows	(U.S.A.)	14 ft. 3¼ in.
1948	Guinn Smith	(U.S.A.)	14 ft. 1¼ in.
1952	Bob Richards	(U.S.A.)	14 ft. 11¼ in.
1956	Bob Richards	(U.S.A.)	14 ft. 11½ in.

ROLL OF OLYMPIC CHAMPIONS (WOMEN)

100 METRES

1928	Elizabeth Robinson	United States	12.2
1932	Stanislawa Walasiewiczówna	Poland	11.9
1936	Helen Stephens	United States	11.5
1948	Francina Blankers-Koen	Netherlands	11.9
1952	Marjorie Jackson	Australia	11.5
1956	Betty Cuthbert	Australia	11.5

200 METRES

1948	Francina Blankers-Koen	Netherlands	24.4
1952	Marjorie Jackson	Australia	23.7
1956	Betty Cuthbert	Australia	23.4

4 × 100 METRES RELAY

1928	Canada	48.4
1932	United States	47.0
1936	United States	46.9
1948	Netherlands	47.5
1952	United States	45.9
1956	Australia	44.5

80 METRES HURDLES

1932	Mildred Didrikson	United States	11.7
1936	Trebisonda Valla	Italy	11.7
1948	Francina Blankers-Koen	Netherlands	11.2
1952	Shirley DelaHunty	Australia	10.9
1956	Shirley DelaHunty	Australia	10.7

HIGH JUMP

1928	Ethel Catherwood	Canada	5	2½
1932	Jean Shiley	United States	5	5¼
1936	Ibolya Csák	Hungary	5	3
1948	Alice Coachman	United States	5	6⅛
1952	Esther Brand	South Africa	5	5¾
1956	Mildred McDaniel	United States	5	9¼

LONG JUMP

1948	Olga Gyarmati	Hungary	18	8¼
1952	Yvette Williams	New Zealand	20	5¾
1956	Elzbieta Dunska-Krzesinska	Poland	20	9¾

PUTTING THE WEIGHT

1948	Mícheline Ostermeyer	France	45	1½
1952	Galina Zybina	U.S.S.R.	50	1½
1956	Tamara Tishkyevich	U.S.S.R.	54	5

THROWING THE DISCUS

1928	Halina Konopacka-Matuszewska	Poland	129	11¾
1932	Lillian Copeland	United States	133	2
1936	Gisela Mauermeyer	Germany	156	3¼
1948	Micheline Ostermeyer	France	137	6½
1952	Nina Romashkova-Ponomaryeva	U.S.S.R.	168	8½
1956	Olga Fikotova-Connolly	Czechoslovakia	176	1¾

THROWING THE JAVELIN

1932	Mildred Didrikson	United States	143	4
1936	Tilly Fleischer	Germany	148	2¾
1948	Herma Bauma	Austria	149	6
1952	Dana Zátopková	Czechoslovakia	165	7
1956	Inessa Yaunzeme	U.S.S.R.	176	1¾

Melbourne, 1956. Final of the women's 80 metres hurdles. Shirley Strickland (*left*) (Australia) winning from G. Kohler (*second from right*) (Germany).

Compiled by **S. W. E. Bishop**

Editor: Pigeon Racing News

Pigeon Racing

A BRIEF HISTORY

The Racing Pigeon is not, ornithologically speaking, a pigeon but a dove (Columba Livia) which since time immemorial has been domesticated and used by man for a variety of purposes: message carrying, sacrificial rites (see the Bible) and sport. The bird's sporting ability derives from its habit of returning to its home loft, even from long distances.

Its use in sport was spasmodic, limited and casual up to the 1840's, but it was used commercially by merchants for ship to shore communications, stockbrokers and bankers for bringing latest market prices (especially from Manchester Cotton Exchange to London) and by newspapers and news agencies.

In the 1840's the electric telegraph ousted the racing pigeon as a speedy news carrier and the merchants closed their lofts and disposed of their pigeons. Thus, a vast number of well-bred and well-trained pigeons came on to the market and went cheaply to those who were interested in their use in the field of sport. Sportsmen took advantage of cheap transport offered by the new railway networks (to train and race pigeons from distant towns) and the sport began to prosper. Clubs sprang up everywhere, and in 1898 they combined to promote the National Homing Union as their legislative and governing body. Today, five Unions control the sport, namely, National H. U., North of England H. U., Scottish H. U., Welsh H. U., and Irish H. U. (Northern Ireland).

In 1898 the first "national" clubs were formed to organise "classic" open races. The National Flying Club first, followed by the North Road Championship Club, the Scottish N.F.C. and the Irish N.F.C. These clubs organised competitions that were open to all members of the respective Unions. These events have grown in popularity. In the Scottish National event members compete for about £35,000 and the National Flying Club of England offers comparative rewards.

King Edward VII became the sport's first Royal Patron when he erected pigeon racing-lofts at Sandringham, followed by George V, who presented the first "King's Cups" (one to each of the four "classic" clubs). George VI preserved the royal interest and our Gracious Queen Elizabeth presented the sport with its first "Queen's Cup" soon after her Coronation.

A fancier breeds and races his own birds. Pedigree plays an important part in the breeding, and some fanciers trace the bloodlines of their stock back over many years, some to nearly a century ago. Club members take their birds to a central collecting station (the clubhouse), where they are "race-rung" (i.e. flexible rubber rings bearing serial numbers are placed on the birds' legs), and sent in baskets to the chosen town for liberation. They are liberated en masse to fly back to their home area, where they split up and "home" to their individual lofts. The winning bird is the one which makes the highest "velocity proper", i.e. which flies home at the greatest velocity in yards per minute. At the home loft, the fancier removes the rubber ring from his race pigeon, inserts it into an Automatic (locked) Time Recording Clock and records the time of its arrival. Each loft is separately measured from the racepoint by Gt. Circle System which produces actual distance in miles and yards.

All racing pigeons are "rung" with a special metal-alloy registration (Union) ring when 6 to 7 days old; the ring is supplied by the Union and its serial index number is recorded in the Union's books so that any pigeon and owner can be traced and identified. Over one million of these rings are sold to members every year, giving an index to the large number of new pigeons raised by members annually.

Race distances usually start at 100 miles and increase during the season to long-distance flights of 500–1000 miles. In these very long races pigeons generally are capable of flying from 12 to 17 hours non-stop (without food and water). No other animal in the world is capable of such stupendous physical output in terms of work and stamina. Specialised breeding over thousands of years, intensified by modern knowledge of genetics, has produced a veritable "flying machine" which flies faster than any other bird, in level flight, and at enormous speeds. With an average speed of 40 m.p.h. pigeons have been known to negotiate distances of over 500 miles, on the day, at about 70 m.p.h.

N.F.C. RACES

		Velocity
Bordeaux		
1898	Ward	744
1899	J. W. Toft	908
1900	Shinner	1297
1901	Orchardson	891
1902	J. L. Baker	952
1911	Mitchell Bros.	990
1912	P. Brough	785
1913	E. H. Grellett	888
1914	H. T. Stratton	1073
1920	S. Theelan	901
1946	L. Gilbert	840
1947	G. E. Jarvis	935
Lerwick		
1899	King Edward VII	1307
La Roche		
1903	Eldsen	951
Marennes		
1904	Cannon	1098
1905	Matten	964
1906	Stephens	1178
1907	Jenkins	1422
1914	Deakin & Redfern	1289
Mirande		
1908	J. Wones	940
1909	W. Saunders	860
1910	Higham Bros.	739
1937	W. H. Hardcastle	922
1938	F. Marks	992
1939	G. Weller	1053
Dax		
1912	G. W. Scadden	814
Pons		
1914	J. Wones	1238
San Sebastian		
1921	W. H. Peters	493
1922	J. W. Logan	714
1923	E. A. Turner	786
1924	F. W. Marriott	862
1925	F. W. Marriott	811
1926	M. Edmunds	930
1927	W. Ashman	786
1928	R. Wright	875
1929	W. B. Reeve	1024
1930	H. F. Hoole	1246
1931	W. R. James	920
1932	R. M. Antingham	747
1933	Elliott Bros.	959
1934	V. Robinson	956
1935	Sir William Jury	1012
1936	R. Tustian	1095
1953	Barker Bros.	1014
Penzance		
1940	F. W. Marriott	1415
1941	Lambert & Son	1105
1942	Parry & Corfield	1408
1943	J. H. Long	1924
1944	R. F. Boyen	1480
1945	Sharrock Bros.	1881
Guernsey		
1948	Fearn & Son	——
Luxembourg		
1949	F. Jarvis	——
Pau		
1950	Moore & Wootton	1108
1951	Godfrey Bros.	——
1952	G. King	942
1954	Ranaboldo Bros.	989
1955	Vic Robinson	837
1956	J. W. Langstone	890
1957	Skone & Everall	1137
Bordeaux		
1958	W. Middle Weston-s-M	1106

UP NORTH COMBINE

		Velocity
Amiens		
1925	Urwin	911
1926	Whitfield Bros.	1025
1927	Dance, Harris & Smith	1082
1928	H. Brown	1108
1929	J. Paxton	1019
1930	R. Nesbit	1267
1931	J. Christie	1021
1932	J. G. Crawford	1044
Arras		
1933	Henderson	1086
1934	Jammieson Bros.	1344.7
1935	Hughes & Cummings	1569.1
1936	G. Marley	1279.1
1937	W. Laing	950.2
1938	Potts Bros.	1428.3
1939	Gammon Bros.	1223.5
Luxembourg		
1951	J. Peach	——
1952	J. Hall	970
1953	R. B. Nichols	1299
Melun		
1925	Smith & Son	1086
1926	Allen Bros.	1397
1927	Dowson	1102
1928	Lothian, Embleton &	982
	Hedley	1175
	A Wilson	1055
1929	McKee & Son	1266
1930	Ranson & Crossier	1029.31
1931	Nesbit & Ptrs.	1425
1932	Mutton & Ptrs.	1326
1933	Potts & Cairns	1266
1934	Robinson	1045.6
1935	Gray Bros.	993.5
	Carter & Clark	1090.4
1936	R. Allan	796.9
	Ellison Bros.	899.1
1937	Terry Bros.	1636.6
1938	Rowe & Rowe	1000.3
1939	T. Gibson	1129.5
Troyes		
1921	Donaldson	1268
1922	Brass & Bruce	1577
1924	Jones	1582
Nevers		
1925	W. Johnson	1319
1926	J. Ellis	834
1927	Peat Bros.	859
1928	Davidson Bros.	928
1929	Dodds & Stewart	1121
1930	Collins Bros.	1104
1931	Dryden & Cochrane	1475
1932	W. Baston	929
1933	Johnson & Brown	980
1934	Cobbledick & Wallace	1086.1
1935	Soulsby & Son	917.1
1936	A. Hallimond	1118.5
1937	J. Ward	1147.4
1938	Hayton & Son	1005.4
1939	W. Heyden	1306.7
Le Puy		
1930	Lothian & Embleton	863
1931	J. O'Neil	825
1932	Hickman & Simpson	5th day
1934	Jones	1006.3
Le Bourget		
1947	T. Pilmour	1073.3
1954	Tinkler, Son & Piggford Bros.	1078
Cormeilles		
1955	Stewart & Barkes	946
1958	W. Snowdon	——
Bourges		
1956	Heydon Bros.	1245
1957	Robinson & Ptrs.	1209
Guernsey		
1948	1st Race Hird & Graham	1053.9
	2nd Race Robson & Son	1185.5
	3rd Race M. Ward	1359.9

N.R.C.C. RACES

		Velocity
Lerwick		
1901	J. T. Hincks	815
1902	G. Pulley	1459
1903	H. Pickering	——
1904	P. Clutterbuck	995
1907	R. Mattock	660
1908	A. Braithwaite	1314
1909	A. Crawford	831
1910	Hubbard & Warren	1238
1911	D. Fitzjohn	1104
1912	Hustwaitt Bros.	469
1913	W. L. Thackray	1763
1914	P. Clutterbuck	916
1920	F. W. Marriott	441
1921	F. W. Marriott	1087
1922	C. Clark	778
1923	G. W. Gammons	619
1924	J. S. Hartridge	658
1925	Brown & Horton	731
1926	W. Westcott	1428
1927	B. J. Westcott	948
1928	A. H. Quibell	1226
1929	Brown & Horton	1207
1930	J. S. Hartridge	1279
1931	G. W. Graves	1139
1932	F. Stevenson	928
1933	Branstone, Son & Smith	849
1934	S. R. Atkins	1257
1935	J. R. Marriott	784
1936	D. Robotham & Sons	1035
1937	R. F. Towle	1390
1938	G. S. Rogers	1279
1939	Jepson Bros & Curtis	1875
Fraserburgh		
1940	North & Son	1789
1941	H.M. The King	1199
1942	W. J. Smith	794
1943	W. L. Thackray	1601
1944	A. Bush	867
Banff		
1945	Jepson Bros. & Curtis	1204
1946	Perry, Morgan & Heardman	938
1947	R. Preston	1466
1948	A. Bush	913
1949	S. Powling	1800
1950	E. Stevenson	955
1951	H.M. The King	1362
1952	V. Divit	1157
1953	H. Harding	793
1954	Mrs. H. A. Bridge	1370
1955	A. Keeble	1221
1956	H. A. Bridge	1690
1957	Marsh & Bailey	1787
1958	A. Smith Mansfield	——

S.N.F.C. RACES

		Velocity
Skibbereen		
1901	S. Taylor	——
1902	G. Hamilton	1068
Bath		
1903	G. Hamilton	627
Weymouth		
1904	J. Tennant	958
Guernsey		
1905	Wyper & Tait	929
1906	T. Chambers	844
1907	Muir Bros.	762
1948	W. Gray	——
Granville		
1908	Lindsay Bros.	919
1909	Smart Bros.	769
Rennes		
1910	W. McLean	881
1911	J. McMeekin	699
1912	T. Paton	1432
1913	A. C. Christie	760
1914	Sharp Bros.	1369
1920	Dr. W. Anderson	1098
1921	Watson Bros.	792
1922	W. Gardiner	905
1923	White & Dickson	1488
1924	J. Birrell	1142
1925	J. Browlee	891
1926	D. McInroy	1012
1927	McGinn Bros.	999
1928	F. Murdoch	1017
1929	D. Macauley	930
1930	J. Robertson	881
1931	R. Duncanson	1171
1932	Swain Bros.	1189
1933	J. Laidlaw	961
1934	Frame & Cochrane	962
1935	Casey Bros.	1231
1936	J. Russell	809
1937	J. Kirkpatrick	1559
1938	H. Park	1083
1939	Anderson Bros.	——
1950	G. Lupton	1152
1951	J. Mackay	1012
1952	J. Marshall	——
1953	Montgomery Bros.	987
1954	D. Fowler	1061
1955	J. Hodgson	1139
1956	A. Galloway	1385
1957	G. Hay	1075.990
1958	Thomson & Kean, Annan	——
Hastings		
1946	A. Paterson	——
St. Jaques		
1947	N. Campbell	——
Charleroi		
1949	G. Mitchell	1092

PIGEON RACING QUIZ

1. A hen pigeon lays two eggs which normally hatch one youngster from each. Can an egg produce twins?

★

2. Can pigeons make "milk"?

★

3. What is an "impossible" velocity?

QUIZ ANSWERS

1. Yes, provided the fancier assists the youngsters to emerge from the shell.
2. Yes, both cock and hen build up a curd of milk on their breasts commencing from the 14th day of sitting and incubation.
3. A velocity is held to be "impossible" when the speed of the bird is in excess of what is ruled to be reasonable and possible in the conditions governing the race.

Polo

Compiled by **Brigadier J. R. C. Gannon, C.B.E., M.V.O.**

Hon. Secretary: The Hurlingham Polo Association

POLO QUIZ

1. In the equipment of players and ponies, what is (*a*) compulsory and (*b*) not allowed?

★

2. When are you allowed to hook an opponent's stick?

★

3. What do you understand by the "right of way", and when may a player enter or cross it?

★

4. There are five examples of dangerous riding given in the rules. Name three of them.

★

5. What penalty would you award in the following cases: (*a*) dangerous foul in the vicinity of goal; (*b*) player hits behind his own line; (*c*) the side *fouled* fail to carry out Penalty 2 or 3 correctly?

QUIZ ANSWERS

1. (*a*) Compulsory. Player: helmet or cap *with chin strap*. Ponies: boots or bandages. (*b*) Not allowed. Player: sharp spur, buckles or studs on upper part of boots. Ponies: blinkers or shadow rolls, frost nails or screws, *but* a calkin is allowed if placed in heel of hind shoe. (Field Rules 4, 5 and supplementary Rule 3.) 2. (*a*) A player may hook an opponent's stick if he is on the same side of the opponent's pony as the ball, or in a direct line behind and his stick is neither over nor under the body or across the legs of an opponent's pony. The stick may not be hooked or struck unless the opponent is in the act of striking the ball. (Field Rule 19 (*a*).) 3. (*a*) At each moment of the game there exists a right of way, which is considered to extend ahead of the player entitled to it and in the direction he is riding. (*b*) A player may only enter or cross the right of way at such a distance that there is not the slightest risk of collision or of interfering with the stroke of the player entitled to the right of way. (Field Rule 16 (*a*) (*i*).) 4. The five examples of dangerous riding are: (*a*) Bumping at a dangerous angle. (*b*) Zigzagging in front of another player in such a way as to cause him to check his pace or risk a fall. (c) Pulling across or over a pony's legs. (*d*) Riding an opponent across the right of way. (e) Intimidation. (Field Rule 17.) 5. (*a*) (*i*) Penalty 1 (award a goal) if considered to be "in order to save a goal" *or* (*ii*) Penalty 2—free hit at the ball 30 yards from the goal line at a spot opposite the middle of the goal, *or if preferred*, from the spot where the foul occurred. (*b*) Penalty 6—a free hit at the ball from a spot 60 yards from the back line opposite where the ball crossed. (*c*) Penalty 7 (*b*)—the defenders allowed to hit in from the middle of their own goal.

THE EARLY HISTORY OF POLO

Polo is one of the oldest games; King Darius about 525 B.C., annoyed with Alexander the Great, who had withheld the tribute exacted by former Persian kings and was prepared to fight about it, sent him a polo stick (called a *Chaugān*) and ball, suggesting that the game was better suited to his youth than war. Alexander's prophetic reply was that the ball was the earth, and he was going to be the stick. Much ancient Polo history was written by the Persian poets attached to the courts of the Emperors of the Moghul dynasty. The best known was the poet Firdausi, A.D. 935–1020. In his *Shahnahmah* (The Book of Kings), 60,000 couplets in length, is a description of a game of Polo about 600 B.C. between the Persians (or Iranians) and the Turkomans at the conclusion of a war, watched by the soldiers of both armies. On its conclusion a golden couch was brought, on which the two kings sat together to signify peace had been declared and an alliance made. The French translator M. Mohl describes how King Siyoash started the game by throwing the ball into the air and then hitting it upwards "si foit avec la raquette qu'il lui fit voir de près de la lune"! This method of starting the game was called the *Tambuk* and is still used today by the players in the mountainous regions north of India from Chitrall to Leh.

Firdausi's story, though legendary, was taken from the ancient Pehlavi papers and other old fragments recording the feats of the Sassanian kings. Another Persian poet Nizam-Ud-Din (1141–1202) described how the beautiful Shirin, wife of one of the Sassanian kings, played Polo with her handmaidens against the king and his courtiers. The poet Jami, of the fifteenth century, wrote intelligently of Polo in his *Salaman and Abdul*, and in Fitzgerald's translation of Omar Khayyam comes:

"The ball no question makes of Ayes
 and Noes
But right and left as strikes the player,
 goes."

Many of these handwritten books of poems with their exquisitely coloured illustrations can be seen at the British Museum.

Slowly the game spread beyond Persia, even as far as Egypt and Constantinople. The Saracens played, and Tamerlane, that bloodthirsty warrior, ordered his commanders to play with the heads of his decapitated foes. At Isfahan the remains of stone goal posts can still be seen, three feet or so thick at the base: time has not altered the game completely, for the distance between those stone goal posts is eight yards, and the length of the ground three hundred yards, as laid down in the rules of Polo today.

Eastwards it spread to China and later Japan. The answer to its reaching these distant lands lies in the constant use of that ancient and romantic highway, the great silk road along which caravans crawled from Pekin as far as Constantinople, passing just north of the Hindu Kush through Balkh, once Alexander's capital of Bactria. It was along this route that Genghis Khan organised his galloping horse mail with its long chain of relay stables, supporting possibly the greatest mounted army in history.

Pictures at the Victoria and Albert Museum of Chinese Polo show the players in heavy rough clothes and with thick quilted saddles, suggesting that the game was not closed to kings. The ball was a very small one. Ponies were of a coarse Mongolian type, with their tails tied up to avoid catching the swing of the stick, a universal habit today. In Chamberlain's *Classical Poetry of the Japanese* is a description of a match played by the nobles, when the Mikado took strong objection to the fact that all his guards deserted their posts at the Palace to watch the game. This was about A.D. 727. The Moghul Emperors brought Polo to India. They were the patrons of the poets mentioned. The Emperor Jehangir is the centre of a picture with the players wearing decorative clothing, and the ponies, standing cloth martingales. Akbar's Prime Minister wrote a book called the *Ain-I-Akbari*, in which he exalts Akbar's skill, and states that he valued the game for teaching promptitude and decision. The dissertation ends "It is impossible to describe the excellence of this game". In a back lane of the Anarkalli bazaar at Lahore is a small monument, the grave of Sultan Kutab-Ud-Din Aibak, the builder of the Kutab Tower near Delhi who was killed playing Polo in A.D. 1206.

Polo ceased in India with the end of the Moghul dynasty till the English restarted it. But the game continued in the mountains of the north from Chitrall to Leh—in many a village—a rough and tumble game with 8 or 9 a side was often played as it still is along the village street. When we left India the Mehtar of Chitrall, at the end of a game, read aloud to assembled players extracts from Firdausi's *Shahnahmah*. Behind him on a big chenar tree was an inscription from a poem by Hafiz:

"Let others play at other things
The king of games is still the game of
 kings."

The name Polo is derived from Pulu, a Tibetan word used to describe the ball.

In the hills north-east of India in Manipur and Cachar Polo flourished. Captain Pemberton considers that the Tartar invaders between A.D. 700 and 800 brought the game with them. It became the national game. One Rajah of Manipur went to war with Cachar to recover a stolen Polo pony. The enthusiasm for the game was such that players were known to have pawned their wives to buy a pony.

By about 1850 the tea planters round Cachar were playing Polo with the local inhabitants. The country was under British administration, and, in 1859, shortly after the Mutiny, Lt. Colonel Robert Stewart, the district superintendent, held a meeting in his bungalow and the Silehar Polo Club, known as the first white man's Polo club, was formed.

The first Rules of Polo were drawn up, some a little startling to modern players such as "Spurs and whips may be freely used, but only on the rider's own horse" and "No player shall be under the influence of spirituous liquors." Visitors from Calcutta began to be interested in the game and Stewart's assistant Lt. John Shearer, R.A., took a team of the native players there with the result that the Calcutta Polo Club was formed in 1862 and is still in existence to-day. When Shearer retired as a Major General, he was known as the father of English Polo.

POLO FROM 1862 TO 1900

The game now spread rapidly. A brother of the Superintendent of Cachar, Captain G. Stewart of the Guides, started it in Cawnpore, Lahore, and the north-west frontier. Officers in northern India also began to play when on leave in Kashmir, where the game had spread south from Gilghit. The 7th Hussars and the 2nd Bn. The Rifle Brigade were playing at Umballa in 1862, and the 19th Hussars and another battalion of the Rifle Brigade at Meerut in 1864. Officers of the Punjab Frontier Force in the north-west were early starters. 1863 saw Polo started in Burma at Tonghoo.

The hill natives played on ponies of 12–2 to 13 hands: the advantage of an increasing height was first shown when the 54th Foot, considered the best team in India, marched down on relief from the north in the early seventies. The 10th Hussars, who had recently arrived at Muttra, challenged them for a match to be played at Delhi as they were passing through. The 10th, who had mounted themselves on ponies of 13 hands and over, out-galloped the 54th to win comfortably. In 1876, during the Prince of Wales' tour in India, a match between the Calcutta Polo Club and a native Manipuri team was staged during his visit to Calcutta. It ended in a draw. Many Polo players were looking on, and following discussion and under the organisation of St. Quintin of the 10th Hussars, the Indian Inter-regimental Tournament was started in 1877 at Meerut for a Challenge Cup presented by British Cavalry Officers. The 9th Lancers beat the 10th Hussars in the final—the standard height of ponies was fixed at 13–3 hands or under. The last 5-a-side big match had been played when the great John Watson, 13th Hussars, led a British Cavalry team against an Indian Cavalry team. Four a side began with this inter-regimental tournament.

The Indian Cavalry Tournament was started in 1883. Up to the end of the 1st World War there were 39 regiments; they were then reduced to 21.

The Infantry Tournament began in 1884 for a challenge cup presented by the Earl of Airlie.

By this time Polo was being played in almost every cantonment in India, and the Indian Princes were playing in their States. The Commander in Chief, Lord Roberts, who supported the game, issued an order—owing to a number of accidents—that all players must wear a Polo helmet. Later a protected cap also came into use, and it has been one of the rules of Polo for many years that a helmet or cap must be worn in every country.

It was in 1869 that the 10th Hussars thought it time to try the game in England and the first regular match was played between the 9th Lancers and the 10th Hussars with eight a side. The *Morning Post* account begins "Nearly all fashionable London journeyed from town to Hounslow on Tuesday to witness a new game called 'Hockey on Horseback' between Officers of the 9th Lancers and 10th Hussars". The game lasted an hour and a half with a ten minute interval in the middle. The 10th won by 3 goals to 2. Both regiments left soon afterwards for India.

The game caught on quickly. In 1873 a five-a-side match between the Household Cavalry and Light Cavalry was played at Lillie Bridge, a ground now covered by the houses at Earls Court. In 1875 a match between the 7th Hussars and Staffordshire was played at Manchester.

In 1872 the brothers F. and R. Herbert started the first country club in Monmouthshire. Hurlingham started Polo in 1874 and soon became the headquarters of the game. The Champion Cup was started there in 1876 and was won by the Royal Horse Guards. The Hurlingham Inter-regimental started in 1878 and was won by the 5th Lancers. The Oxford v. Cambridge match, won by Oxford, also started in 1878. Polo had reached America in the early eighties. In 1886 Hurlingham sent a team to play in the first of the series between England and America for the Westchester Cup. It was played at Newport, Rhode Island. John Watson, recently back from India, captained the team. His development of the use of the backhander surprised the Americans. Our ponies were also better schooled. England won the two matches played, by 14 goals to 2 and 10 to 4.

In Ireland the game began about 1872. In the eighties it had spread to Australia, New Zealand, South Africa, Canada, Egypt, China, the West Indies and to Malta, Gibraltar, the Gold Coast, and other individual stations where our Navy and Army held sway. In France, Spain, Russia and Germany Polo began in the nineties. Argentine, to become a leading Polo playing country, also started in the eighties, followed by Chile. All ponies played in tournaments had to be officially measured. In England 14 hands and under was changed to 14–2 in 1895. In India 13–3 and under till 1899 when it was raised to 14–1. The Champion

Cup at Hurlingham was the blue riband of England's Polo, and remained so till its end in 1939. The Hurlingham Club presented a £50 cup each year to the winning team.

The three brothers J., A.L., and A. Peat were early consistent winners for the Sussex team in 1881, 82, 83, again in 85 and then for 6 consecutive years from 1888 to 1893 when their fourth man was the Hon. F. Mildmay, father of that great Gentleman Rider Lord Mildmay of Flete. Their combination was outstanding and they were beautifully mounted. One of their ponies, "Sailor", was sold for 720 guineas, the highest price known in England up to the end of the nineteenth century.

Another team with three brothers then appeared, Lt. Colonel E. D., G. A., and C. D. Miller. They started the celebrated country club at Spring Hill, Rugby, in 1892 and won the Champion Cup in 1897, 98, and 99, 1901 and 1903.

Up to 1900 the 7th Hussars had won the Inter-regimental Tournament on five occasions and the 9th Lancers on four. Oxford had 9 victories against 11 for Cambridge. Douglas Haig played for Oxford in 1883, as well as the American T. Hitchcock who represented America for the Westchester in 1886 and was the father of the greatest American player, Tommy Hitchcock. Haig played in the winning 7th Hussars teams at Hurlingham in 1885 and 86 and again for them in the Indian Inter-regimental in 1891, and finally when commanding the 17th Lancers at Hurlingham in 1903.

Future internationals in winning Cambridge teams were: Buckmaster, Freake and Lord Wodehouse, later Lord Kimberley. And for Oxford: C. P.

Nickalls and Devereux Milburn in 1902, the great American back.

In 1885 the County Cup, for the benefit of Country clubs, was started. It was played off in districts with semi-finals and finals played at Hurlingham.

With the exception of the tournaments mentioned, the ground at Hurlingham was used for some matches and members' games. Ranelagh opened in 1878 with one ground used for members' games, till 1896, when a second ground was made. The Subalterns' Tournament, started in 1896, was first won by the 9th Lancers and the Ranelagh Open Cup in 1897 won by the Millers Rugby team.

The first rules in England were drawn up by the Monmouthshire Club in 1873. Hurlingham produced official rules in 1875.

In India by the end of the century more Polo was being played than in any other country. Ponies were cheap, grooms' wages and the cost of corn very small, and play continued all the year round. British and Indian infantry played regularly as well as the Cavalry. The Durham Light Infantry won the Indian Inter-regimental in 1896, 97 and 98 and were the best team in India, led by Captain de Lisle.

The 9th Lancers had six victories and the Queen's Bays three.

The Indian Polo Association was formed in 1891 with a committee who brought the rules up to date and controlled all tournaments. The I.P.A tournament was started as a championship. The leading Indian State teams came from Jodhpur, Patiala, Golconda and Alwar. Close touch with Polo in England was maintained, with players appearing alternatively in both countries.

POLO QUIZ

1. When did the Inter-regimental in India start?

★

2. Between 1879 and 1939 there were four families, with three brothers, playing top-class polo in the London season. Give their names.

★

3. In which year was the handicapping system of 10 goals to 0 for all players instituted in England? And in which year was the offside rule abolished?

4. In England the height of polo ponies was first limited to 14 hands. (a) In which year was it raised to 14.2 hands? (b) In which year was measurement abolished?

★

5. Which regiments won the Inter-regimental tournaments the greatest number of times (a) in England, (b) in India?

QUIZ ANSWERS

1. 1877. 2. The Peats. The Millers. The Nickalls. The four Ashton brothers from Australia. 3. Both in 1910. 4. (a) 1895, (b) 1919. 5. (a) The 17th, later 17th/21st Lancers, eleven times. (b) The 10th Royal Hussars, ten times.

INDIA

The four army tournaments which follow were all played for the last time in India in 1939. The I.P.A. Championship has recently been revived in a small way.

The Inter-Regimental Polo Tournament

Date	Place	Winners	Runners-up
1877	Meerut	9th Lancers	10th Hussars
1878	Meerut	9th Lancers	10th Hussars
1879 1880	No tournament on account of Afghan War		
1881	Ambala	10th Hussars	Rifle Brigade
1882	Ambala	10th Hussars	Rifle Brigade
1883	Ambala	9th Lancers	Rifle Brigade
1884	Ambala	9th Lancers	8th Hussars
1885	Meerut	9th Lancers	8th Hussars
1886	Ambala	8th Hussars	Carabineers
1887	Ambala	8th Hussars	Carabineers
1888	Meerut	17th Lancers	7th Hussars
1889	Meerut	17th Lancers	7th D.G.'s
1890	Ambala	5th Lancers (1st Team)	17th Lancers
1891	Ambala	7th Hussars	7th D.G.'s
1892	Ambala	Queen's Bays	7th Hussars
1893	Ambala	Queen's Bays	16th Lancers
1894	Ambala	Queen's Bays	5th Lancers
1895	Ambala	7th Hussars	18th Hussars
1896	Ambala	Durham L.I.	5th D.G.'s
1897	Meerut	Durham L.I.	16th Lancers
1898	Meerut	Durham L.I.	4th D.G.'s
1899	Meerut	4th Hussars	4th D.G.'s
1900	Meerut	3rd Rifle Bde.	4th Hussars
1901	Meerut	20th Hussars	15th Hussars
1902	Meerut	15th Hussars	4th D.G.'s
1903	Meerut	15th Hussars	10th Hussars
1904	Meerut	15th Hussars	9th Lancers
1905	Meerut	15th Hussars	9th Lancers
1906	Meerut	9th Lancers	15th Hussars
1907	Meerut	10th Hussars	15th Hussars
1908	Meerut	10th Hussars	The Carabineers
1909	Meerut	10th Hussars	1st K.D.G.'s
1910	Meerut	10th Hussars	1st K.D.G.'s
1911	Meerut	10th Hussars	1st K.D.G.'s
1912	Meerut	10th Hussars	17th Lancers
1913	Meerut	17th Lancers	1st K.D.G.'s
1914	Meerut	17th Lancers	The Inniskillings
1915–20	No tournament on account of War		
1921	Meerut	17th Cavalry	21st Lancers
1922	Meerut	C.I.H.	P.A.V.O. Cav.
1923	Meerut	15th Lancers	11th Hussars
1924	Meerut	P.A.V.O. Cav.	C.I.H.
1925	Meerut	P.A.V.O. Cav.	C.I.H.
1926	Meerut	15th Lancers	C.I.H.
1927	Meerut	C.I.H.	Probyn's Horse
1928	Meerut	P.A.V.O. Cav.	C.I.H.
1929	Meerut	C.I.H.	15th Lancers
1930	Meerut	C.I.H.	15th/19th Hussars
1931	Meerut	C.I.H.	15th Lancers
1932	Meerut	15th Lancers	15th/19th Hussars
1933	Meerut	10th R. Hussars	15th K.R. Hussars
1934	Meerut	P.A.V.O. Cav.	C.I.H.
1935	Meerut	P.A.V.O. Cav.	13th/18th Hussars
1936	Meerut	10th R. Hussars	19th K.G.O. Lancers
1937	Meerut	15th Lancers	17th/21st Lancers
1938	Meerut	17th/21st Lancers	13th/18th Royal Hussars
1939	Meerut	P.A.V.O. Cav.	17th/21st Lancers

The Indian Cavalry Tournament

Date	Place	Winners	Runners-up
1883	Ambala	12th B.C.	18th B.C.
1884	Ambala	11th B.L.	2nd C.I.H.
1885	Rawalpindi	18th B.C.	12th B.C.
1886	Ambala	18th B.L.	12th B.C.
1887	Ambala	9th B.L.	12th B.C.
1888	Sialkot	18th B.C.	12th B.C.
1889	No tournament		
1890	Ambala	9th B.L.	14th B.C.
1891	Ambala	9th B.L.	19th B.L.
1892	Ambala	14th B.L.	12th B.C.
1893	Sialkot	9th B.L.	18th B.L.
1894	Sialkot	9th B.L.	18th B.L.
1895	Ambala	18th B.L.	12th B.C.
1896	Ambala	18th B.L.	The Guides
1897	Ambala	2nd C.I.H.	17th B.C.
1898	Ambala	8th B.C.	5th B.C.
1899	Ambala	18th B.L.	8th B.C.
1900	Mean Meer	18th B.L.	17th B.C.
1901	Mean Meer	18th B.L.	2nd B.L.
1902	Mean Meer	18th B.L.	19th B.L.
1903	Ambala	19th B.L.	15th B.L.
1904	Mean Meer	11th Lancers	9th H.H.
1905	Ambala	18th T. Lancers	9th H.H.
1906	Ambala and Peshawar	The Guides	8th Cav.
1907	Ambala	26th L. Cav.	10th Lancers
1908	Ambala	4th Cav.	39th C.I.H.
1909	Ambala	39th C.I.H.	18th Lancers
1910	Ambala	39th C.I.H.	26th L. Cav.
1911	Ambala	39th C.I.H.	9th H.H.
1912	Ambala	17th Cav.	3rd S.H.
1913	Delhi	18th Lancers	17th Cav.
1914	Delhi	9th H.H.	3rd S.H.
1915–20	No tournament on account of War		
1921	Delhi	17th Cav.	28th Cav.
1922	Delhi	17th/37th Cav.	C.I.H.
1923	Lahore	C.I.H.	15th Lancers
1924	Lahore	C.I.H.	P.A.V.O. Cav.
1925	Lahore	Probyn's Horse	P.A.V.O. Cav.
1926	Lahore	15th Lancers	C.I.H.
1927	Lahore	C.I.H.	P.A.V.O. Cav.
1928	Lahore	P.A.V.O. Cav.	C.I.H.
1929	Lahore	C.I.H.	15th Lancers
1930	Lahore	19th Lancers	C.I.H.
1931	Lahore	P.A.V.O. Cav.	7th Light Cav.
1932	Lahore	2nd Lrs. (G.H.)	P.A.V.O. Cav.
1933	Lahore	Probyn's Horse	P.A.V.O. Cav.
1934	Lahore	P.A.V.O. Cav.	Probyn's Horse
1935	Lahore	Probyn's Horse	Guides Cav. F.F.
1936	Lahore	Probyn's Horse	Guides Cav. F.F.
1937	Lahore	15th Lancers	Skinner's Horse
1938	Lahore	Guides Cav. F.F.	Skinner's Horse
1939	Lahore	Guides Cav. F.F.	13th D.C.O. Lancers

The Infantry Polo Tournament

Date	Place	Winners	Runners-up
1884	Ambala	1st King's Own Scottish Borderers	No record
1885	Meerut	1st King's Own Scottish Borderers	,,
1886	Ambala	1st Duke of Wellington's Regt.	,,
1887	Ambala	1st Duke of Wellington's Regt.	,,
1888	Ambala	1st Duke of Wellington's Regt.	,,
1889	Ambala	1st King's Own Scottish Borderers	,,
1890	Ambala	2nd Royal Irish Regt.	,,
1891	Ambala	2nd West York Regt.	,,
1892	Lucknow	2nd Gloucester Regt.	,,
1893	Lucknow	2nd Gloucester Regt.	,,
1894	Lucknow	2nd Durham L.I.	,,
1895	Lucknow	2nd Durham L.I.	,,
1896	Lucknow	2nd Durham L.I.	,,

POLO QUIZ

1. Who was the distinguished soldier who played in a winning team for Oxford v. Cambridge and later for his regiment on four occasions when winning Inter-regimental tournaments in England and India?

★

2. In which year did America first win the Westchester Cup?

★

3. When did England win it back?

★

4. Who holds the Cup now?

★

5. (*a*) What were the names of the three polo clubs of the London season? (*b*) When was the last London season played?

★

6. (*a*) Name the two leading polo clubs of today. (*b*) How many grounds have they?

★

7. In which country is most polo played today?

QUIZ ANSWERS

1. Field Marshal the Earl Haig. 2. 1909. 3. 1914. 4. America last won in 1939. 5. (*a*) Hurlingham, Ranelagh, Roehampton. (*b*) In 1939. 6. (*a*) Cowdray Park, Household Brigade Club at Windsor Great Park. (*b*) Cowdray Park, 5 match grounds, 2 practice grounds; Household Brigade Club, 4 match grounds. 7. Argentina.

POLO FROM 1900 TO 1914

Both in England and India the standard of our Polo probably reached its zenith towards the end of the period between the finish of the South African war and 1914.

In 1901 Colonel C. D. Miller founded the Roehampton Club with three grounds. Ranelagh had three, and Hurlingham two. By 1914 there were 15 grounds within a radius of 10 miles from Charing Cross, including two at Wimbledon Park, two at Kingsbury, one each at Gunnersbury, Wembley and Worcester Park. Country Clubs in 1902 included Bedford County, Blackmore Vale, Bowden, Burgley Park, near Stamford, Cambridge, Catterick Bridge, Cheltenham, Chislehurst, Cirencester, Cleveland, near Middlesbrough, Cricklewood, Eden Park, Edinburgh, Hertfordshire, Holderness, near Hull, Hutton, near Romford, Kingsbury, Liverpool, the London Club at the Crystal Palace, Manchester, Market Harborough, Middlewood, North Middlesex, North Wilts, Plymouth, Rugby, South Hants, Stansted, near Bishops Stortford, St. Neots, in Cornwall, Stratford-on-Avon, Warwickshire, Wellington, Berkshire, Wirral in Cheshire, and Worcester. Cowdray Park started in 1911.

The original clubs of Monmouthshire Ludlow, Swindon, Staffordshire and Eastbourne had ceased to exist. The County Polo Association was formed to look after the interests of these County Clubs and run the County and junior County Cups tournaments. Representatives of Ranelagh, Roehampton, The County Polo Association and overseas associations attended the Council meetings of the Hurlingham Club Polo Association.

America challenged for the Westchester Cup in 1900. England won by 8 goals to 2 at Hurlingham. They came again in 1902 when England won by 2 matches to 1. English Polo received a shock in 1909 when Mr. H. P. Whitney brought over his team known as the big four (L. Waterbury, J. Waterbury, H. P. Whitney, and D. Milburn) to challenge again. They played a very fast game, frequently meeting the ball, and won both matches decisively. England quickly challenged again in 1911 and 1913, losing narrowly on both occasions. The game was not stopped in America for fouls during play, but the umpires took fractions off the score at the end of the chukka. One match England lost by 4½ goals to 3½ and another by 4½ to 4¼.

England was now being represented mostly by cavalry soldiers who had learnt their Polo in India. Captains Cheape, Hardress-Lloyd, Ritson, Noel Edwards and Lockett all played in these two matches. Then in 1914 we challenged again, and Captains Tomkinson, Cheape, Barrett and Lockett won both matches decisively to bring the cup home.

Mr. W. S. Buckmaster's celebrated old Cantabs Team was outstanding in this period in the Champion Cup, which they won in 1900, 04, 08, 10, 12, and 14. On the last four occasions his team was Major Belville No. 1, F. Freake No. 2, W. Buckmaster No. 3, and Lord Wodehouse back.

No Inter-regimental or Subalterns tournaments were played during the South African War. The 17th Lancers won the first revival in 1903 led by Col. Douglas Haig, playing brilliantly on a white Arab pony called "Akbar" that he had ridden at the battle of the Atbara. There were 18 entries in 1904 when the 17th won again before leaving for India. This tournament was still one of the features of the London season. The 12th Lancers won it in 1914, when Hucks startled the spectators by flying over the ground after the match and looping the loop twice.

America had started a handicapping system in 1891, rating their best players at 10 goals and the lowest at 0. After the South African war England and India introduced a form list of the best players, enabling secretaries to arrange tournaments limiting the number of form-list players in any team. In 1910 England and India adopted the American system of handicapping from 10 to 0 goals. Another rule taken from America in 1910 was the abolition of the off side rule, which made the game faster.

In India, with the height of ponies raised from 13–3 to 14–1 hands, the game developed rapidly. In 1907 the height was raised to 14–2. There were over 5,000 playing members of the Indian Polo Association. Soon after the South African war the Indian Princes' state teams dominated the Durbar tournament played in December 1902. It was won decisively by the Maharajah of Alwar's team, trained and led by Captain Ricketts of the 10th Bengal Lancers. They beat Jodhpur in the final easily.

India had introduced 8 chukkers or periods of 7½ minutes for the Inter-regimental and the IPA championships. Indian Cavalry and Infantry tournaments played 6 chukkers of 7½ minutes. In England at the start of the century 6 chukkas of 10 minutes were still played; soon afterwards the 8 chukka system was adopted. Polo reached a very high standard, particularly among British Cavalry Regiments. The 15th Hussars, led by the International player Capt. Barrett, won the Inter-regimental from 1902 to 1905. After the 9th Lancers victory in 1905, the 10th Hussars accomplished a fine record by winning 6 times from 1907 to 1912. Led and trained by Colonel John Vaughan for the first 3 years, their other regular players were Capts. Llewelen Palmer, W. Palmes, The Hon. A. Annesley, and W. O. Gibbs. They were all hard fought victories against the 17th Lancers led by Capt. Lockett, the King's Dragoon Guards led by our great International Capt. Leslie Cheape, and the Inniskilling Dragoons, led by Capt. Ritson. In the Delhi Durbar tournament of 1911, the British Cavalry teams were too strong for the Indian state teams. The Inniskilling Dragoons beat the K.D.G.'s in the final.

The Infantry Polo Tournament—(*contd.*)

Date	*Place*	*Winners*	*Runners-up*
1897	*Lucknow*	2nd Durham L.I.	No record
1898	No tournament		
1899	*Ambala*	1st S.W. Borderers	Royal Fus.
1900	*Meerut*	3rd Rifle Brigade	S.W. Borderers
1901	*Meerut*	3rd Rifle Brigade	1st E.S. Regt.
1902	*Meerut*	2nd Queen's Regt.	2nd/60th Rifles
1903	*Lahore*	2nd Queen's Regt.	2nd Gurkhas
1904	*Meerut*	1st Seaforth Highrs.	The Queen's Regt.
1905	*Meerut*	2nd/6th Rifles	1st Seaforth Highrs.
1906	*Lucknow*	1st Durham L.I.	The Queen's Regt.
1907	*Meerut*	2nd Rifle Brigade	1st Seaforth Highrs.
1908	*Bareilly*	The Queen's Regt.	2nd Gurkhas
1909	*Bareilly*	2nd Rifle Brigade	3rd/60th Rifles
1910	*Lucknow*	Durham L.I.	Gordon Highrs.
1911	*Bareilly*	2nd Rifle Brigade	Seaforth Highrs.
1912	*Bareilly*	1st Durham L.I.	R. Welch Fus.
1913	*Delhi*	2nd R. Welch Fus.	Northumberland Fus.
1914	*Bareilly*	2nd Gurkhas	2nd Rifle Brigade
1915–20	No tournament on account of War		
1921	*Bareilly*	2nd Seaforth Highrs.	3rd/60th Rifles
1922	*Meerut*	2nd Seaforth Highrs.	3rd/60th Rifles
1923	*Bareilly*	2nd Somerset L.I.	1st Rifle Brigade
1924	*Delhi*	1st Rifle Brigade	1st/60th Rifles
1925	*Rawalpindi*	2nd Durham L.I.	2nd Sherwood Foresters
1926	*Rawalpindi*	2nd Durham L.I.	1st/60th Rifles
1927	*Lahore*	2nd Seaforth Highrs.	9th Gurkhas
1928	*Lahore*	1st/60th Rifles	2nd Durham L.I.
1929	*Lahore*	2nd Seaforth Highrs.	1st/60th Rifles
1930	*Bareilly*	1st Royal Welch Fus.	1st/60th Rifles
1931	*Bareilly*	2nd Gurkhas	1st/60th Rifles
1932	*Bareilly*	1st Rifle Brigade	Black Watch
1933	*Bareilly*	2nd Durham L.I.	Black Watch
1934	*Bareilly*	2nd Durham L.I.	Black Watch
1935	*Bareilly*	Black Watch	2nd Durham L.I.
1936	*Bareilly*	2nd K.E.O. Gurkhas	1st Cameronians
1937	*Bareilly*	Royal Scots	52nd Light Infantry
1938	*Bareilly*	1st Cameronians	Royal Fus,
1939	*Bareilly*	2nd K.E. VII's O. Gurkhas	1st Cameronians

POLO FROM 1919 TO 1939

English Polo was hard hit by War I. No young players got started, and no ponies were trained. The clubs suffered financially. In 1919 the height measurement was abolished to come in line with America and Argentina and also because few ponies of 14–2 had been bred. India and the rest of the world followed suit. America challenged for the Westchester Cup in 1921. Play had continued there throughout the war. Capt. Cheape had been killed in action and we were in difficulties over ponies. America won the series. Tommy Hitchcock, considered by many the greatest player the world has seen, made his first appearance for America. Though we challenged in 1924, 1927, 1930, 1936 and 1939 we never won the cup back. In 1936, by arrangement, the matches were played in England at Hurlingham, when we lost the first match by 1 goal and the second by 2 goals. The rest were played at Meadowbrook. L. Lacey, Capt. Roark, G. Balding, Capt. H. Guinness, and E. Tyrrell-Martin were our best players. With the handicapping system in full use there was more Polo than ever at the three Clubs during the London season. Members' games finally passed away. In addition to the open Cups, handicap tournaments for teams of an aggregate of 17 goals and over, of 16 to 9 goals, and of 8 goals and under were organised to run through the season without clashing by the three Polo managers at Hurlingham, Ranelagh and Roehampton.

About 860 ponies were stabled at the three clubs and others privately. The handicap system helped to bring on young players.

The Champion Cup with the additional open Cups of Ranelagh and Roehampton brought many strong visiting teams from overseas in this period. In the nineties players from Argentina had begun to visit us and the English landowners there began to breed Polo ponies by bringing English thoroughbred stallions to cover their Criollo pony mares. Strong teams came over between 1900 and 1914, but did not win the Champion Cup. Argentine ponies began to be imported regularly.

In 1922 the Argentine Federation team came for the season. There was no international match as Lewis Lacey, their captain, was an Englishman who later played for England. The Miles brothers and J. Nelson completed the team. Their ponies were now outstanding in pace and quality. They won the Champion Cup and their only defeat was by the 17th/21st Lancers in the Coronation Cup.

The price of top class ponies now began to rise. In 1928 international matches between America and Argentina began. America won, and at the sale of the Argentine ponies the fabulous and record price of £4,400 was paid for M. Lacey's "Jupiter". America beat Argentina again in 1932.

In 1936, after winning the Polo at the Olympic Games, Argentina beat America, and after it the sale of their whole stud fetched over £38,000. Argentina won again when this series was last played in 1950.

In 1925 the Indian Jodhpur team came for a successful season and the American Army beat the British Army at Hurlingham. Jaipur won the Champion Cup in 1933, Aurora (U.S.A.) in 1934, Kashmir in 1935, Templeton (U.S.A.) in 1936, Goulburn with the four Ashton brothers from Australia in 1937 and the Texas Rangers (U.S.A.) in 1938.

The 17th/21st Lancers dominated the Inter-regimental at first, winning it from 1922 to 1926 and again from 1928 to 1930. The Royal Navy entered in 1936, to be beaten in a close final by the 12th Lancers.

The Duke of Gloucester played for Cambridge when they won in 1920 and the American, Mr. Sanford, in 1921. An international, Mr. John Lakin, Lord Cowdray and Lord Poole were in a winning Oxford team.

English teams had visited tournaments on the continent regularly for many years at Deauville, Le Touquet, Ostend, Frankfurt, Vienna, Budapest and Madrid. King Alfonso was a keen player.

In India the rising cost of Polo and the use of motor cars began to affect the number of players, but in 1939 there were still 130 clubs registered with the Indian Polo Association. A new 1st class tournament, the Prince of Wales tournament, was instituted in 1921. Four Indian state teams (Jodhpur, Jaipur, Kashmir and Bhopal), superbly mounted, were very high class teams. Indian Cavalry, reduced to 21 regiments from 39 on amalgamation in 1921–22, won the Inter-regimental 16 times out of the 19 times played between 1921 and 1939. Prince Albert Victor's Own Cavalry, late 21st and 23rd Cavalry won it 6 times and the Central India Horse and 15th Lancers, late 17th and 37th Cavalry 5 times each. Capt. Dening (P.A.V.O. Cavalry), Capts. Williams and George (CIH), Capts. Atkinson, Pert, and Kirkwood (15th Lancers) played for England in the Westchester Cup. In the last final to be played in 1939 the P.A.V.O. Cavalry beat the 17th/21st Lancers by 1 goal.

Polo at the Olympic Games was won by England in 1908 at Hurlingham, by Argentina in Paris in 1924, and by Argentina in Berlin in 1936. It has not been played for since.

Notable new country clubs were formed at Badminton, Dunster Castle, and Toulston, while many of the older ones had passed away.

The Subalterns' Polo Tournament

Date	Place	Winners	Runners-up
1904	Ambala	4th D.G.'s	9th Lancers
1905	Meerut	15th Hussars	3rd Hussars
1906	Ambala	9th Lancers	12th Lancers
1907	Ambala	10th Hussars	12th Lancers
1908		12th Lancers	No record
1909	Ambala	12th Lancers	1st K.D.G.'s
1910	Ambala	10th Hussars	12th Hussars
1911	Ambala	2nd Rifle Bde.	17th Lancers
1912	Meerut	10th Hussars	17th Lancers
1913	Meerut	1st K.D.G.'s	17th Lancers
1914	Meerut	17th Lancers	1st K.D.G.'s
1915–20	No tournament on account of War		
1921	Meerut	21st Lancers	17th Cavalry
1922	Meerut	11th Hussars	22nd/25th Cavalry
1923	Meerut	7th Hussars	Hodson's Horse
1924	Meerut	11th Hussars	4th Hussars
1925	Meerut	Queen's Bays	11th Hussars
1926	Meerut	12th Cavalry	Queen's Bays
1927	Meerut	4th/7th Dragoon G'ds.	4th Hussars
1928	Meerut	4th/7th Dragoon G'ds.	4th Hussars
1929	Meerut	4th Hussars	"I" Bty., R.H.A.
1930	Meerut	4th Hussars	9th Lancers
1931	Meerut	P.A.V.O. Cav.	Royals
1932	Meerut	10th R. Hussars	18th K.E.O. Cav.
1933	Meerut	The Royals	Probyn's Horse
1934	Meerut	The Royals	Probyn's Horse
1935	Meerut	10th R. Hussars	The Royals
1936	Meerut	13th/18th R. Hussars	17th/21st Lancers
1937	Meerut	17th/21st Lancers	19th K.G.O. Lancers
1938	Meerut	17th/21st Lancers	13th/18th Royal Hussars
1939	Meerut	17th/21st Lancers	16th/5th Lancers

The Indian Polo Association Championship Tournament

Date	Place	Winners	Runners-up
1900	Lucknow	Goona Freebooters	Chutter Munzul
1901	Meerut	Alwar State	H.H.M. Urjin Singh's team
1902	Meerut	Alwar State	Jodhpur Durbar
1903	No tournament		
1904	No tournament		
1905	Ambala	Wanderers	Patiala
1906	Calcutta	The Pilgrims	15th Hussars
1907	Calcutta	Rajputana Pilgrims	Calcutta "A"
1908	Calcutta	Calcutta "A"	15th Hussars
1909	Calcutta	Calcutta "A"	H.E. The Viceroy's Staff
1910	Calcutta	Calcutta	Kishengarh Durbar
1911	Calcutta	10th Hussars	Calcutta
1912	No tournament		
1913	Calcutta	17th Lancers	Kishengarh
1914	Calcutta	H.E. The Viceroy's Staff	Travellers
1915–20	No tournament on account of War		
1921	Calcutta	Jodhpur	Fox Hunters
1922	Calcutta	H.E. The Viceroy's Staff	16th/5th Lancers
1923	Calcutta	H.E. The Viceroy's Staff	Poona Horse
1924	Calcutta	Jodhpur	Cavalry School
1925	Calcutta	Scouts	Army-in-India
1926	Calcutta	Army-in-India	Pilgrims
1927	Calcutta	Bhopal	Deccan Travellers
1928	Calcutta	The Gladiators	8th K.G.O. Light Cavalry
1929	Calcutta	15th Lancers	8th K.G.O. Light Cavalry
1930	Calcutta	Jaipur Pilgrims	Bhopal Scouts
1931	Calcutta	Jodhpur	C.I.H.
1932	Calcutta	Jaipur	10th Royal Hussars
1933	Calcutta	Jaipur	Kashmir
1934	Calcutta	Jaipur	Gladiators
1935	Calcutta	Jaipur	Kashmir
1936	Calcutta	Jaipur	The Bing Boys
1937	Calcutta	Jaipur	Bhopal
1938	Calcutta	Jaipur	Guides Cavalry, F.F.
1958	Calcutta	Jaipur	
1959	Calcutta	Jaipur	

POLO FROM 1947 TO 1959

Many doubts were expressed about the revival of Polo after the long years of the 2nd Great War. In the Army the Cavalry and Artillery regiments are mechanized. The great training centres for Polo of India and Egypt were no more, grooms' wages and keep of ponies were higher than ever, and ponies were hard to find. The Ham Club, near Richmond Park, actually started first, but it was Lord Cowdray's organisation of his club in Cowdray Park that got the game going. To the three pre-war grounds were added two full sized ones and two practice grounds nearby, at Ambersham. A system of keeping ponies for hire was started, and is maintained today with 50 ponies. The number of playing members has risen to over 70.

Lord Cowdray was the pioneer in introducing Polo as a spectacle to the general public by admitting cars for ten shillings, thus producing attractive programmes and a commentator to explain the points of the game. About 14,000 spectators were present at a match in the Coronation tournament of 1953. Clubs next started at Henley, Hertfordshire, Rhinefield in the New Forest, Canford Magna, near Wimborne, Toulston in Yorkshire; Oxford and Cambridge clubs revived in 1951 as did Cheshire and Cirencester, with three grounds in 1952

and Kirtlington in 1954. An important addition was the Household Brigade Club at Windsor in 1955, with H.R.H. the Duke of Edinburgh taking an active part. Tauntonvale, Tidworth, Catterick, Harrogate, Jericho Priory, Silver Leys, and Millfield School complete the list of 20 clubs today. In 1951 an Argentine team, La Espadaña, visited England, and played a series of three matches against a Hurlingham team, won by the latter. In 1953 a Coronation Cup tournament was organised and played at Cowdray Park. Visiting teams came from America, Argentina, Chile and Spain. Argentina beat England in the final by 1 goal. Teams were limited to a total of 24 goals on handicap. In 1956 the Argentine team Los Indios, an Indian team, and a New Zealand team spent the summer with us, and two teams from Paris also came for the Cowdray Gold Cup.

Every year both Argentina and India send over individual players who play with different clubs. Rao Rajah Hanut Singh keeps ponies in England and has not missed a season since the War. The main tournaments for 1959 were The Royal Windsor Cup and Smith's Lawn Cup at Windsor in Ascot week.

The Inter-Regimental Tournament at Tidworth in early July is followed by the Subalterns' tournament. The Cowdray Gold Open Cup is in mid July. The County is followed by the tournaments

at Cowdray Park in Goodwood week. In August the Junior County Cup at Woolmers Park is followed by the Rhinefield low goal tournament in the New Forest. Oxford v. Cambridge is played at Windsor in June and the Whitbread Cup is played off through the season at different clubs. There are many local tournaments at most clubs.

The Cowdray Park Gold Cup, an open Cup for teams totalling 20 goals to 13, was won by Los Indios (Argentina) in 1956, Windsor Park in 1957 and Cowdray Park in 1958).

Owing to the absence abroad of regiments, the Inter-regimental was not revived in England till 1958 when won by the 7th Hussars. The Subalterns', also restarted in 1958, was won by the 10th Hussars. An Inter-regimental for regiments quartered in Germany was won by the 3rd Hussars 1951 to 1953, the 17th/21st Lancers 1954 to 1958, and Queen's Dragoon Guards 1959.

Cambridge have won the varsity match on 33 occasions, Oxford 30.

The governing body of Polo was renamed the Hurlingham Polo Association between the Wars. With the end of the London Polo season after the last war, the County Polo Association was amalgamated with the Hurlingham Polo Association. Soon after the revival began an English team visited Argentina. It was agreed that our remaining international players, G. Balding, Lt. Col. H. Guinness, J. Lakin, and Rao Rajah Hanut Singh, should be handi-capped at 6 and, to extend the handi-cap range, beginners were handicapped down to −1 and 2. The council of the Hurlingham Polo Association has representatives from the Royal Naval Saddle Club, the Army Saddle Club and the All Ireland Polo Association and from the following Commonwealth Associations: India, Pakistan, South Africa (45 clubs), Rhodesia (14 clubs), Kenya (14 clubs) Australia (53 clubs), New Zealand (19 clubs), Nigeria (9 clubs), Jamaica (6 clubs), Malaya (5 clubs), and Malta. Other overseas clubs without representatives are Accra, Aden, Assam, Colombo, Tangier, Somaliland and Tamale.

There is more Polo played in Argentina and other South American states than anywhere else. They have a splendid supply of ponies bred on their estancias. The game continues in France, Spain, and Italy; high-class teams enter for the tournament at Deauville, held every year in August.

In 1890 America issued their rules of Polo; though rules in different countries varied but little, their form was irregular. In 1938 Lord Louis Mountbatten, the chairman of the small Hurlingham Rules Committee, in consultation with America and other countries, drew up the inter-national Rules of Polo, so that all countries should have their rules similarly worded and numbered. These rules consist of General Rules and Field Rules, with necessary local rules to appear as supplementary rules. The rule size of a full sized Polo ground is 300 yds. in length by 200 yds. in width. If the sides are boarded the width to be 160 yds. Each goal to be 8 yds. wide. Few grounds are boarded now in England.

ENGLAND

The Subalterns' Cup

(at Ranelagh)

Winners

1896	9th Lancers
1897	Royal Horse Guards
1898	Royal Horse Guards
1899	7th Hussars
1900–3	No tournament (South African War)
1904	2nd Life Guards
1905	Royal Horse Guards
1906–7	1st Life Guards
1908	21st Lancers
1909	1st Life Guards
1910	7th Hussars
1911	9th Lancers
1912	9th Lancers
1913–14	12th Lancers
1915–16	No tournament
1920	13th Hussars
1921	1st Life Guards
1922	15th Hussars
1923	12th Lancers
1924–8	17th/21st Lancers
1929	Royal Artillery
1930	17th/21st Lancers
1931–2	Royal Scots Greys
1933	11th Hussars
1934–5	Royal Scots Greys

1936	The Royals
1937	12th Lancers
1938	The Royals
1939	The Queen's Bays
1940–57	No tournament
1958	10th Hussars (at Tidworth)
1959	The Queen's Own Hussars (at Tidworth)

The County Cup

Instituted 1885. Revived in 1951

Winners

1951	Beechwood
1952	Polo Cottage
1953	Cotswold Park
1954	Henley
1955	Polo Cottage
1956	Ancient Mariners
1957	Media Luna (Argentina)
1958	Silver Leys
1959	The Jersey Lilies

The Junior County Cup

Instituted 1905. Revived 1959

Winners

1959	The Jersey Lilies

The Cowdray Park Gold Cup

Winners

1956	Los Indios (Argentina)
1957	Windsor Park
1958	Cowdray Park
1959	Casarejo

The Royal Windsor Cup

Winners

1955	Ratanada
1956	Warren Mere
1957	Media Luna (Argentina)
1958	Windsor Park
1959	Cowdray Park

Oxford v. Cambridge

Instituted 1878

Winners

1951	Oxford
1952–54	Cambridge
1955–56	Oxford
1957	Cambridge
1958	Oxford
1959	Cambridge

POLO QUIZ

1. (a) What is the maximum duration of a chukka and how many minutes are allowed between each? (b) How does each chukka end?

*

2. What is the height limit for ponies?

*

3. How does the game commence and teams line up?

*

4. What is the size of a polo ground?

*

5. When are ends changed?

QUIZ ANSWERS

1. (a) 7½ minutes, with intervals between chukkas of 3 minutes. There is an interval of 5 minutes at half-time. (b) Except in the last chukka, which stops on the bell, each chukka stops after the bell has been rung as soon as the ball goes out or is in such a position that the umpire can stop the game without favouring either side. (General Rule 7 (a) and (d). 2. No limit. (General Rule 1.) 3. (a) Two teams line up in the middle of the ground, the umpire bowls the ball in between the opposing ranks of players. Players must remain stationary until the ball has left his hand. (Field Rule 7.) 4. A full-sized ground shall not exceed 300 yards in length by 200 yards in width, if unboarded, and 300 by 160 yards if boarded. (General Rule 2.) 5. Ends are changed after each goal, except when a goal is awarded under Penalty 1, and if at half-time no goals have been scored. (Field Rule 9.)

The Champion Cup

(at Hurlingham)

Winners

1876	Royal Horse Guards
1877	Monmouthshire tied with Tyros
1878	Monmouthshire
1879	Hurlingham
1880	Ranelagh
1881	Sussex
1882	Sussex
1883	Sussex
1884	Freebooters
1885	Sussex
1886	Freebooters
1887	Freebooters
1888–93	Sussex
1894–96	Freebooters
1897–99	Rugby
1900	Old Cantabs
1901	Rugby
1902	Freebooters
1903	Rugby
1904	Old Cantabs
1905–06	Roehampton
1907	Old Cantabs
1908	Old Cantabs
1909	Roehampton
1910	Old Cantabs
1911	Eaton
1912	Old Cantabs
1913	Quidnuncs
1914	Old Cantabs
1915–18	No tournament
1919	Freebooters
1920	Freebooters
1921	Freebooters
1922	Argentine Federation
1923	Robots
1924	Eastcott

1925	Eaton
1926	Harlequins
1927–8	Hurricanes
1929	El Gordo
1930	Hurricanes
1931	Merchiston
1932	Osmaston
1933	Jaipur
1934	Aurora (U.S.A.)
1935	Kashmir
1936	Templeton (U.S.A.)
1937	Goulburn (Australia)
1938	Texas Rangers (U.S.A.)
1939	Jaguars

Inter-Regimental Tournament

(at Hurlingham)

Winners

1878	5th Lancers
1879	5th Lancers
1880	16th Lancers
1881	16th Lancers
1882	5th Lancers
1883	7th Hussars
1884	7th Hussars
1885	7th Hussars
1886	7th Hussars
1887	9th Lancers
1888	10th Hussars
1889	9th Lancers
1890	9th Lancers
1891	9th Lancers
1892	13th Hussars
1893	10th Lancers
1894	13th Hussars
1895	13th Hussars
1896	9th Lancers
1897	Inniskillings
1898	Inniskillings
1899	7th Hussars
1900–2	No tournament (South African War)
1903	17th Lancers
1904	17th Lancers
1905	Inniskillings
1906	20th Hussars
1907	20th Hussars
1908	11th Hussars
1909	11th Hussars
1910	Royal Horse Guards
1911	4th Dragoon Guards
1912	Royal Horse Guards
1913	15th Hussars
1914	12th Lancers
1915–19	No tournament
1920	17th Lancers
1921	17th Lancers
1922	17th Lancers
1923	17th/21st Lancers
1924	17th/21st Lancers
1925	17th/21st Lancers
1926	17th/21st Lancers
1927	Royal Artillery
1928	17th/21st Lancers
1929	17th/21st Lancers
1930	17th/21st Lancers
1931	Queen's Bays
1932	Royal Artillery
1933	Royal Scots Greys
1934	7th Hussars
1935	3rd Brig. R.H.A.
1936	12th Lancers
1937	10th Hussars
1938	Royal Scots Greys
1939	10th Hussars
1940–57	No tournament
1958	7th Hussars (at Tidworth)
1959	Royal Wiltshire Yeomanry

INTERNATIONAL POLO

Great Britain v. United States— 1886–1939

WESTCHESTER CUP

1886 Won by GREAT BRITAIN (10–4, 14–2) at Newport, R.I. GREAT BRITAIN: No. 1, Capt. T. Hone; No. 2, Hon. R. Lawley; No. 3, Capt. Malcolm Little; Back, John Watson. UNITED STATES: No. 1, Winthrop K. Thorne; No. 2, R. Belmont; No. 3, Foxhall P. Keene; Back, Thomas Hitchcock.

1900 Won by GREAT BRITAIN (8–1, only one match played). GREAT BRITAIN: No. 1. Capt. The Hon. J. G. Beresford; No. 2, F. M. Freake; No. 3, W. S. Buckmaster; Back, John Watson. UNITED STATES: No. 1, W. McCreery; No. 2, F. S. MacKay; No. 3, Foxhall Keene; Back, L. McCreery.

1902 Won by GREAT BRITAIN (1–2, 6–1, 7–1) at Hurlingham. GREAT BRITAIN: No. 1, Cecil P. Nickalls; No. 2, P. W. Nickalls and F. M. Freake; No. 3, Walter Buckmaster and George A. Miller; Back, Charles D. Miller and Walter Buckmaster. UNITED STATES: No. 1, R. L. Agassiz and J. M. Waterbury, Jr.; No. 2, J. E. Cowdin and Lawrence Waterbury; No. 3, Foxhall P. Keene; Back, Lawrence Waterbury and R. L. Agassiz.

1909 Won by UNITED STATES (9–5, 8–2) at Hurlingham. UNITED STATES: No. 1, Lawrence Waterbury; No. 2, J. M. Waterbury, Jr.; No. 3, Harry Payne Whitney; Back, Devereux Milburn. GREAT BRITAIN: No. 1, Capt. Herbert H. Wilson and Harry Rich; No. 2, F. M. Freake; No. 3, P. W. Nickalls; Back, Lord Wodehouse and Capt. J. Hardress Lloyd.

1911 Won by UNITED STATES (4½–3, 4½–3½) at Meadow Brook. UNITED STATES: No. 1, Lawrence Waterbury; No. 2, J. M. Waterbury, Jr.; No. 3, Harry Payne Whitney; Back, Devereux Milburn. GREAT BRITAIN: No. 1, Capt. Leslie St. G. Cheape; No. 2, A. Noel Edwards; No. 3, Capt. J. Hardress Lloyd; Back, Capt. Herbert H. Wilson.

1913 Won by UNITED STATES (5½–3, 4½–4½) at Meadow Brook. UNITED STATES: No. 1, Lawrence Waterbury and Louis E. Stoddard; No. 2, J. M. Waterbury, Jr., and Lawrence Waterbury; No. 3, Harry Payne Whitney; Back, Devereux Milburn. GREAT BRITAIN: No. 1, Capt. Leslie St. G. Cheape; No. 2, Noel Edwards and F. M. Freake; No. 3, Capt. R. G. Ritson; Back, Capt. Vivian N. Lockett.

1914 Won by GREAT BRITAIN (8½–3, 4–2½) at Meadow Brook. GREAT BRITAIN: No. 1, Capt. H. A. Tomkinson; No. 2, Capt. Leslie St. G. Cheape; No. 3, Maj. F. W. Barrett; Back, Capt. Vivian N. Lockett. UNITED STATES: No. 1, Rene LaMontagne; No. 2, J. M. Waterbury, Jr.; No. 3, Devereux Milburn and Lawrence Waterbury; Back, Lawrence Waterbury and Devereux Milburn.

1921 Won by UNITED STATES (11–4, 10–6) at Hurlingham. UNITED STATES: No. 1, Louis E. Stoddard; No. 2, Thomas Hitchcock, Jr.; No. 3, J. Watson Webb; Back, Devereux Milburn. GREAT BRITAIN: No. 1, Lt. Col. H. A. Tomkinson; No. 2, Maj. F. W. Barrett; No. 3, Lord Wodehouse; Back, Maj. Vivian N. Lockett.

1924 Won by UNITED STATES (16–5, 14–5) at Meadow Brook. UNITED STATES: No. 1, J. Watson Webb; No. 2, Thomas Hitchcock, Jr.; No. 3, Malcolm Stevenson and Robert E. Strawbridge, Jr.; Back, Devereux Milburn. GREAT BRITAIN: No. 1, Maj. T. W. Kirkwood and Lt. Col. T. P. Melvill; No. 2, Maj. F. W. Hurndall and Maj. G. H. Phipps-Hornby; No. 3, Maj. E. G. Atkinson; Back, Lewis L. Lacey.

1927 Won by UNITED STATES (13–3, 8–5) at Meadow Brook. UNITED STATES: No. 1, J. Watson Webb; No. 2, Thomas Hitchcock, Jr.: No. 3, Malcolm Stevenson; Back, Devereux Milburn. GREAT BRITAIN: No. 1, Capt. Claude E. Pert and Capt. R. George; No. 2, Maj. Austin H. Williams and Capt. J. P. Dening; No. 3, Capt. C. T. I. Roark; Back, Maj. E. G. Atkinson.

1930 Won by UNITED STATES (10–5, 14–9) at Meadow Brook. UNITED STATES: No. 1, Eric Pedley; No. 2, Earle A. S. Hopping; No. 3, Thomas Hitchcock, Jr.; Back, Winston F. C. Guest. GREAT BRITAIN: No. 1, Gerald Balding; No. 2, Lewis L. Lacey; No. 3, Capt. C. T. I. Roark; Back, Humphrey P. Guinness.

1936 Won by UNITED STATES (10–9, 8–6) at Hurlingham. UNITED STATES: No. 1, Eric Pedley; No. 2, Michael G. Phipps; No. 3, Stewart B. Iglehart; Back, Winston F. C. Guest. GREAT BRITAIN: No. 1, Hesketh D. Hughes; No. 2, Gerald Balding; No. 3, Eric H. Tyrrell-Martin; Back, Humphrey P. Guinness.

1939 Won by UNITED STATES (11–7, 9–4) at Meadow Brook. UNITED STATES: No. 1, Michael G. Phipps; No. 2, Thomas Hitchcock, Jr.; No. 3, Stewart B. Iglehart; Back, Winston F. C. Guest. GREAT BRITAIN: No. 1, Robert Skene; No. 2, Aidan Roark; No. 3, Gerald Balding; Back, Eric H. Tyrell-Martin.

Argentina v. United States— 1928–1950

CUP DE LAS AMERICAS

1928 Won by UNITED STATES (7–6, 7–10, 13–7) at Meadow Brook. UNITED STATES: No. 1, W. A. Harriman; No. 2, Thomas Hitchcock, Jr., and E. A. S. Hopping; No. 3, Malcolm Stevenson and Thomas Hitchcock, Jr.; Back, Winston F. C. Guest. ARGENTINA: No. 1, Arturo Kenny; No. 2, J. D. Nelson; No. 3, J. B. Miles; Back, Lewis L. Lacey.

1932 Won by UNITED STATES (9–6, 7–8, 12–10) at Buenos Aires. UNITED STATES: No. 1, Michael G. Phipps; No. 2, Elmer J. Boeseke, Jr.; No. 3, Winston F. C. Guest; Back, William Post, 2nd. ARGENTINA: No. 1, Arturo Kenny; No. 2, J. D. Nelson and Martin Reynal; No. 3, Jose Reynal; Back, Manuel Andrada.

1936 Won by ARGENTINA (21–9, 8–4) at Meadow Brook. ARGENTINA: No. 1, Luis Duggan; No. 2, Roberto Cavanagh; No. 3, Andres Gazzotti; Back, Manuel Andrada. UNITED STATES: No. 1, G. H. Bostwick; No. 2, Gerald Balding; No. 3, Thomas Hitchcock, Jr.; Back, John Hay Whitney.

1950 Won by ARGENTINA (14–10, 11–7) at Buenos Aires. ARGENTINA: No. 1, Juan Cavanagh; No. 2, Roberto Cavanagh; No. 3, Enrique Alberdi; Back, Juan C. Alberdi. UNITED STATES: No. 1, Delmar Carroll; No. 2, Peter Perkins; No. 3, George K. Oliver; Back, Lewis Smith.

Mexico v. United States

GENERAL MANUEL AVILA CAMACHO CUP

1941 Won by UNITED STATES (6–5, 6–4, 12–4) at Mexico City. UNITED STATES: No. 1, Michael G. Phipps and Henry Lewis; No. 2, Cecil Smith; No. 3, Winston F. C. Guest; Back, Harry Evinger. MEXICO: No. 1, Gabriel Gracida and Eduardo Gallardo; No. 2, Jesus Grijalva and Antonio Nava; No. 3, Ramos Sesma and Juan Gracia; Back, Guillermo Cisneros and Ramos Sesma

1946 (September) Won by UNITED STATES (10–4, 11–4) at Meadow Brook. UNITED STATES: No. 1, M. G. Phipps; No. 2, Cecil Smith; No. 3, Stewart B. Iglehart; Back, Peter Perkins. MEXICO: No. 1, G. Gracida; No. 2, G. Gracida; No. 3, A. Gracida; Back, J. Gracida.

1946 (November) Won by UNITED STATES (7–0, 11–9, 5–4) at San Antonio. UNITED STATES: No. 1, Stephen Sanford; No. 2, Cecil Smith and William Barry; No. 3, Stewart B. Iglehart and Cecil Smith; Back, J. T. Mather. MEXICO: No. 1, G. Gracida and Antonio Herretia; No. 2, G. Gracida; No. 3, A. Gracida; Back, Jose Gracida.

Compiled by **Capt. H.F. Layman, D.S.O., R.N.**

Joint Hon. Treasurer: Tennis and Rackets Association

Rackets

HISTORY

The game of rackets evolved from the age-old pastime of just throwing a ball against a wall and catching it full pitch or first bounce. Later, the ball was struck with the hand, then with a solid bat and finally with a strung racket. The original "court" was any handy smooth wall and a flat piece of ground on which lines could be drawn to indicate boundaries. Since a single wall meant constant interruption of the game when retrieving the ball, it was natural for side walls and eventually a back wall to be added. Modern courts, of course, have a roof and electric lighting. In the early part of the 19th century a form of rackets was played, chiefly in taverns and in the debtors' prisons. Charles Dickens, in the *Pickwick Papers*, has described the game as played in the Fleet Prison. The game, however, was taken up by clubs, universities, schools and the Services. During the second half of the 19th century many rackets courts were built in England and in India and the game spread to the U.S.A.

EARLIER PLAYERS OF NOTE

Between 1860 and 1878 the most prominent professional players were Francis Erwood and members of the famous Gray family—Henry, William, Walter and Joseph. In 1887 began the long and highly successful reign over the World's Championship of Peter Latham, to whom is generally conceded the title of "the greatest player of all time". In 1862, for the first time, the World's Championship was held by an amateur, W. H. Hart Dyke (later Sir William Hart Dyke). Just before the turn of the century, H. K. Foster, the eldest of seven famous athletic brothers, dominated the scene by winning the Amateur Singles Championship on seven consecutive occasions and eight times in all. In the early part of the present century the World's Championship was won by an Indian, J. Jamsetjhi, the professional at Bombay Gymkhana. The title later went to the U.S.A., where it was held, between 1914 and 1935, either by Jock Soutar or by Charles Williams, both English-born. The year 1902 marked the beginning of the highly successful career in the Amateur Championships of E. M. Baerlein, a great authority on the game, who won the singles event on nine occasions, with a span of 20 years between his first and last success. After the First World War the increasing popularity of other court games, particularly squash rackets, resulted in a reduction in the amount of rackets played on the Clubs and Services courts, but the game continued to flourish at the public schools. Among the most successful amateurs between the two world wars must be mentioned H. W. Leatham and J. C. F. Simpson. The Hon. C. N. Bruce (later Lord Aberdare) was not only a very fine player but also took the greatest interest in all aspects of the game. In 1935 D. S. Milford began his four consecutive years' successful run in the Amateur Singles Championship and in 1937 beat Norbert Setzler in New York and at Queen's Club for the World's Championship. D. S. Milford was again winner of the Amateur Singles Championship in 1950 and 1951 and a finalist in 1955 when he was nearly 50 years old—a truly remarkable record. However, it must be mentioned that J. H. Pawle, a fine stylist, was successful against D. S. Milford in three consecutive finals, 1947, '48 and '49.

PRESENT-DAY PLAYERS OF NOTE

Outstanding present-day amateur players are G. W. T. Atkins, the World Champion, at present resident in the U.S.A., J. R. Thompson, M. R. Coulman and M. C. Cowdrey. Among the younger players of championship class are R. M. K. Gracey, J. M. G. Tildesley, C. J. Swallow and C. T. M. Pugh. The most consistently successful player is J. R. Thompson, who has won the Amateur Championship singles on five occasions and, in partnership with D. S. Milford, has won the doubles on ten occasions. The best professional player is James Dear, who gained the World's Championship in 1947 and withstood two subsequent challenges, until he was beaten by G. W. T. Atkins, in a close match, in 1954. A curious and, in many ways, unfortunate feature of the present time is that a top team of amateurs would almost certainly beat a top team of professionals, many of the latter having passed the peak of their form. Consequently there is now an urgent need to recruit young professionals.

WHERE THE GAME IS PLAYED

Most players in England learn the game at the public schools, some of which have more than one court. The British Championships are all played at The Queen's Club, West Kensington. There are courts at the Manchester Tennis and Racquet Club, Britannia Royal Naval College, Dartmouth, R.M.A. Sandhurst, R.E. Barracks, Chatham, and the Garrison Court at Gibraltar. There is a court in use at Cambridge but the Oxford court has not been used for many years, players from that university being generally given hospitality in the nearby Radley College court. In the U.S.A. there are courts in New York, Philadelphia, Boston, Chicago, Tuxedo and Detroit. In Canada the game is much played in a court in Montreal. In the Argentine there is a court at Hurlingham, near Buenos Aires. Since the departure of the British Services from India and Pakistan it is doubtful whether the game is much played there, though at one time there were as many as 70 courts, mostly of the open-air type.

THE PUBLIC SCHOOLS DOUBLES CHAMPIONSHIP

This is undoubtedly the most popular annual event, for which each school may enter two pairs. During play, the spectators' gallery at Queen's Club is filled by past and present members of the rival schools, parents and friends of the players and many "lights of other days". In a close match, with the marker's cry of "play" rising in a crescendo during a long rally, the excitement is often intense. This is a very difficult championship to win, especially for those schools which do not have many players. Success depends greatly upon the personality and coaching ability of the school professional. It is also a great advantage if a boy becomes good enough to play in one of his school pairs at an early age, so that he can gain experience over several seasons, particularly in the Queen's Club court. From the start of this championship in 1868, either Harrow or Eton were the winners (except for a win by Rugby in 1870) until 1888, when Charterhouse succeeded in breaking the spell. Other schools in turn achieved prominence, until now every school can claim to have registered a win or to have appeared in a final. From 1943 onwards the record of Winchester deserves special mention because in this comparatively short time they scored eight wins (including two runs of three wins in succession) and were runners-up on two occasions.

OXFORD v. CAMBRIDGE

Records of matches date from 1855 and it is most noticeable that those who represented their University often achieved prominence later on in the Amateur Championships. The University match originally consisted of one double and one single, but since 1937 the second strings have played a single, counting towards the result of the match. Also, for some years past, the second pairs have played an informal "dinner" match. Of the 90 first-string singles matches, Oxford have won 52 and Cambridge 38. In the 91 doubles matches, Oxford have been successful on 52 occasions and Cambridge on 39. Cambridge had a remarkable run of 15 consecutive victories from 1876 in the doubles. Since the University match was resumed after the wartime break, in 1947, Oxford have won the doubles ten times and Cambridge three.

ROYAL NAVY, ARMY AND ROYAL AIR FORCE

The inter-regimental doubles dates from 1892 and the Army Singles Championship from 1903. The Greenjackets have a specially good record in these events. Among outstanding players in the singles between the two world wars were S. H. Sheppard, A. J. H. Sloggett, T. O. Jameson and G. N. Scott-Chad. In 1921, S. H. Sheppard, then a Major-General, won the Army Singles Championship, and six years later, such was his remarkable fitness at the age of 57, he was able to take D. S. Milford to a fifth game in the second round of the Amateur Championship. Since World War II the most prominent Army players have been A. R. Taylor, A. D. Myrtle and M. W. Bolton. The Royal Navy Singles Championship was first held in 1919 and for the first two years was won by J. C. Leach. Others who have won on more than one occasion are H. F. H. Layman, D. E. Holland-Martin and A. P. Pellew. Present-day outstanding naval players are J. D. L. Repard, W. J. Foster, R. M., and C. N. Copeman. Until 1939 the Army and Navy Championships were played at Princes Club and thereafter at Queens Club. The Royal Air Force has some good players but as there is no R.A.F. Championship their names have not come into prominence. However, all three services are eligible for the Combined Services (Past and Present) singles and doubles competitions, which started in 1949.

THE TENNIS AND RACKETS ASSOCIATION

The governing body for the game is the Tennis and Rackets Association, c/o Barclay's Bank, 95 Victoria St., S.W.1. This association was formed in 1907, when it was known as the Tennis, Rackets and Fives Association and at one time embraced squash rackets, until the formation of separate associations. The executive committee of the Tennis and Rackets Association is composed of the reigning champions of the two games and representatives of the Services, clubs and schools. The majority of rackets players subscribe to the Association, whose honorary officers administer the funds entirely for the benefit of the games.

THE NEW POLYTHENE BALL

After the last world war, one of the Tennis and Rackets Association's biggest problems was to design an entirely new rackets ball, because manufacture of the old leather-covered ball was no longer feasible and existing stocks were getting low. Many of the professionals carried out their own experiments with different types of ball; and though these trials were useful steps towards the final solution, no really satisfactory ball emerged from them. It was then that Dr. J. C. Swallow of Imperial Chemical Industries suggested using a ball with a polythene centre. Several professionals took a hand in making up polythene-centred balls for trial, but the one finally approved and adopted was produced at Marlborough College by the school professional, W. E. J. Gordon, under the direction of Mr. J. R. Thompson. The advantage of the new ball over the old is that it keeps its shape for a long time and it can be re-covered very simply, using adhesive tape. It is now not uncommon for less than a dozen balls to be used in a long doubles match, whereas over 50 of the old type of ball would have been necessary. The new polythene ball has thus had the welcome effect of considerably cheapening the game.

RACKETS QUIZ

1. Identify these racket courts: (*a*) During the last war (*i*) used to store sugar against a siege, (*ii*) used by an officers' interview board, (*iii*) requisitioned by a government department. (*b*) Longer and wider than standard size. (*c*) The two fastest courts in the U.K. (*d*) A school's court, once in the centre of London. (*e*) A court which had a marble floor.

★

2. Name the professional (*a*) employed for 44 years at a school, (*b*) whose father and grandfather were also rackets professionals.

★

3. Name the three players to have scored the greatest number of wins in the Amateur Singles Championship.

★

4. Name three Army players who reached the final round of an Amateur Singles Championship.

★

5. When were the following events played outside London: (*a*) final of Public School Doubles, (*b*) Oxford v. Cambridge?

QUIZ ANSWERS

1. (*a*) (*i*) Garrison Court, Gibraltar. (*ii*) Britannia R.N. College, Dartmouth. (*iii*) Malvern College. (*b*) Harrow School. (*c*) Opinions differ but it is generally conceded that the courts at Manchester Tennis and Racquets Club and at Clifton College are very fast. (*d*) Westminster School. (*e*) Naval court in Malta Dockyard. 2. (*a*) Walter Hawes, an exceptionally fine coach, at Wellington College. His sons became rackets professionals at Eton and Charterhouse. (*b*) P. H. Gray at Rugby School. 3. E. M. Baerlein 9, H. K. Foster 8, D. S. Milford 7. 4. S. H. Sheppard, who won in 1906. W. C. Hedley and T. O. Jameson were runners-up in 1890 and 1924 respectively. 5. (*a*) In 1941 at Wellington College. (*b*) In 1855 at Oxford, in 1887 at Manchester.

WORLD'S RACKETS CHAMPIONSHIP

Eleven ace games played in 1838; closed court for first time in 1860

1820	Robert Mackay	London	claimed			
1825	Thomas Pittman	London	claimed			
1834	Thomas Pittman	London	resigned			
1834	John Pittman	London	claimed			
1838	John Lamb	London	*beat*	John Pittman	8–4	Belvedere Gardens, Pentonville Rd.
1846	L. C. Mitchell	Bristol	*beat*	J. C. M. Young	–	Birmingham & Bristol
1860	Francis Erwood	Woolwich	*beat*	L. C. Mitchell	–	Woolwich & Bristol
1862	Mr. W. H. Dyke	Prince's	*beat*	Francis Erwood	8–3	Woolwich & Prince's
1863	Mr. W. H. Dyke	Prince's	resigned			
1863	Henry Gray	Cambridge	claimed			
1866	Henry Gray	Camb.	resigned			
1866	William Gray	Eton	claimed			
1875	William Gray	Eton	died			
1876	H. B. Fairs	Prince's	*beat*	Joseph Gray	8–3	Prince's & Rugby
1878	H. B. Fairs	Prince's	died			
1878	Joseph Gray	Rugby	claimed			
1887	Peter Latham	Manchester	*beat*	Joseph Gray	7–4	Rugby & Manchester
1888	Peter Latham	Queen's	*beat*	Walter Gray	6–3	Queen's & Charterhouse
1892	Peter Latham	Queen's	*beat*	George Standing	5–0	Queen's & Prince's
1897	Peter Latham	Queen's	*beat*	George Standing	8–4	Queen's & New York
1901	Peter Latham	Queen's	*beat*	Gilbert Browne	5–1	Queen's & Prince's
1902	Peter Latham	Queen's	resigned			
1903	J. Jamsetjhi	Bombay	*beat*	Gilbert Browne	5–1	Queen's & Prince's
1911	Charles Williams	Harrow	*beat*	J. Jamsetjhi	5–1	Queen's & Prince's
1914	Jock Soutar	Philadelphia	*beat*	Charles Williams	6–4	Queen's & New York
1923	Jock Soutar	Phil.	*beat*	Charles Williams	7–4	Phil. & New York
1927	Jock Soutar	Phil.	*beat*	William Standing	8–1	Phil. & New York
1928	Charles Williams	Chicago	*beat*	Jock Soutar	7–3	Phil. & Chicago
1935	Charles Williams	Chicago	died			
1937	Mr. D. S. Milford	Marlborough	*beat*	Norbert Setzler	7–4	New York & Queen's
1947	James Dear	Queen's	*beat*	Kenneth Chantler	8–1	Montreal & Queen's
1948	James Dear	Queen's	*beat*	Mr. J. H. Pawle	8–4	Queen's
1951	James Dear	Queen's	*beat*	Mr. J. H. Pawle	8–2	Queen's
1954	Mr. G. W. T. Atkins	Queen's	*beat*	James Dear	6–4	Queen's

OPEN RACKETS CHAMPIONSHIP OF THE BRITISH ISLES
Sheppard Cup

1929	Mr. J. C. F. Simpson	*beat*	C. R. Read	5–1
1930	Mr. J. C. F. Simpson	*beat*	C. R. Read	5–0
1932	Lord Aberdare	*beat*	Mr. J. C. F. Simpson	8–2
1933	Mr. I. Akers-Douglas	*beat*	Lord Aberdare	4–0 retd.
1934	A. G. Cooper	*beat*	Mr. I. Akers-Douglas	7–4
1936	Mr. D. S. Milford	*beat*	A. G. Cooper	8–3
1946	James Dear	*beat*	Mr. P. Kershaw	8–1
1954	Mr. G. W. T. Atkins	*beat*	James Dear	6–4
1959	Mr. J. R. Thompson	*beat*	Mr. R. M. K. Gracey	3–1

AMATEUR RACKETS SINGLES CHAMPIONSHIP

	Winner	*Runner-up*	
1888	C. D. Buxton	E. M. Hadow	3–0
1889	E. M. Butler	C. D. Buxton	3–2
1890	P. Ashworth	Capt. W. C. Hedley	3–0
1891	H. Philipson	P. Ashworth	3–2
1892	F. Dames-Longworth	H. Philipson	3–0
1893	F. Dames-Longworth	H. K. Foster	3–1
1894	H. K. Foster	F. Dames-Longworth	3–1
1895	H. K. Foster	G. F. Vernon	3–1
1896	H. K. Foster	E. H. Miles	3–0
1897	H. K. Foster	P. Ashworth	3–2
1898	H. K. Foster	W. L. Foster	3–0
1899	H. K. Foster	E. H. Miles	3–0
1900	H. K. Foster	P. Ashworth	3–0
1901	F. Dames-Longworth	J. Howard	3–1
1902	E. H. Miles	F. Dames-Longworth	3–1
1903	E. M. Baerlein	E. H. Miles	3–2
1904	H. K. Foster	E. M. Baerlein	3–0
1905	E. M. Baerlein	E. H. Miles	3–0
1906	Maj. S. H. Sheppard	P. Ashworth	3–1
1907	E. B. Noel	B. S. Foster	3–2
1908	E. M. Baerlein	E. B. Noel	3–1
1909	E. M. Baerlein	H. Brougham	3–1
1910	E. M. Baerlein	P. Ashworth	3–0
1911	E. M. Baerlein	H. A. Denison	3–0
1912	B. S. Foster	G. G. Kershaw	3–1
1913	B. S. Foster	H. W. Leatham	3–0
1914	H. W. Leatham	E. M. Baerlein	3–2
1920	E. M. Baerlein	Hon. C. N. Bruce	3–1
1921	E. M. Baerlein	Hon. C. N. Bruce	3–0
1922	Hon. C. N. Bruce	E. M. Baerlein	3–0
1923	E. M. Baerlein	Hon. C. N. Bruce	3–1
1924	H. W. Leatham	Capt. T. O. Jameson	3–2
1925	C. C. Pell	H. W. Leatham	3–0
1926	J. C. F. Simpson	H. W. Leatham	3–2
1927	J. C. F. Simpson	Hon. C. N. Bruce	3–2
1928	J. C. F. Simpson	Hon. C. N. Bruce	3–0
1929	C. S. Crawley	H. D. Hake	3–0
1930	D. S. Milford	I. Akers-Douglas	3–0
1931	Lord Aberdare	I. Akers-Douglas	3–0
1932	I. Akers-Douglas	J. C. F. Simpson	3–1
1933	I. Akers-Douglas	C. S. Crawley	3–0
1934	I. Akers-Douglas	A. M. Hedley	3–0
1935	D. S. Milford	I. Akers-Douglas	3–1
1936	D. S. Milford	J. H. Pawle	3–1
1937	D. S. Milford	R. C. Riseley	3–0
1938	D. S. Milford	I. Akers-Douglas	3–0
1939	P. Kershaw	R. A. A. Holt	3–1
1946	J. H. Pawle	I. Akers-Douglas	3–2
1947	J. H. Pawle	D. S. Milford	3–2
1948	J. H. Pawle	D. S. Milford	3–2
1949	J. H. Pawle	D. S. Milford	3–0
1950	D. S. Milford	G. H. G. Doggart	3–0
1951	D. S. Milford	G. W. T. Atkins	3–2
1952	G. W. T. Atkins	M. C. Cowdrey	3–0
1953	G. W. T. Atkins	D. S. Milford	3–2
1954	J. R. Thompson	D. S. Milford	3–1
1955	J. R. Thompson	D. S. Milford	3–2
1956	G. W. T. Atkins	J. R. Thompson	3–1
1957	J. R. Thompson	M. R. Coulman	3–2
1958	J. R. Thompson	R. M. K. Gracey	3–0
1959	J. R. Thompson	J. M. G. Tildesley	3–2

AMATEUR RACKETS DOUBLES CHAMPIONSHIP

1890	P. Ashworth and Capt. W. C. Hedley
1891	P. Ashworth and E. L. Metcalfe
1892	E. M. Butler and M. C. Kemp
1893	F. H. Browning and H. K. Foster
1894	H. K. Foster and C. S. C. F. Ridgeway
1895	F. Dames-Longworth and F. H. Browning
1896–1897	H. K. Foster and P. Ashworth
1898	H. K. Foster and W. L. Foster
1899–1900	H. K. Foster and P. Ashworth
1901	F. Dames-Longworth and V. H. Pennell
1902	E. M. Baerlein and E. H. Miles
1903	H. K. Foster and B. S. Foster
1904–1905	E. M. Baerlein and E. H. Miles
1906	E. H. Miles and F. Dames-Longworth
1907	W. L. Foster and B. S. Foster
1908	F. Dames-Longworth and V. H. Pennell
1909	E. M. Baerlein and P. Ashworth
1910–1911	B. S. Foster and Hon. C. N. Bruce
1912	H. W. Leatham and H. A. Denison
1913	B. S. Foster and H. Brougham
1914 & 1920	E. M. Baerlein and G. G. Kershaw
1921	Hon. C. N. Bruce and H. W. Leatham
1922–1923	J. C. F. Simpson and R. C. O. Williams
1924–1927	Hon. C. N. Bruce and H. W. Leatham
1928	Hon. C. N. Bruce and A. C. Raphael
1929	J. C. F. Simpson and R. C. O. Williams
1930	Lord Aberdare and H. W. Leatham
1931	J. C. F. Simpson and C. S. Crawley
1932–1933	K. A. Wagg and I. Akers-Douglas
1934	Lord Aberdare and P. W. Kemp-Welch
1935	K. A. Wagg and I. Akers-Douglas
1936–1937	C. S. Crawley and J. C. F. Simpson
1938	D. S. Milford and P. M. Whitehouse
1939 & 1946	C. S. Crawley and J. H. Pawle
1947	R. A. A. Halt and Maj. A. R. Taylor
1948	D. S. Milford and J. R. Thompson
1949	R. A. A. Holt and Maj. A. R. Taylor
1950–1952	D. S. Milford and J. R. Thompson
1953	P. Kershaw and G. W. T. Atkins
1954–1959	D. S. Milford and J. R. Thompson

PROFESSIONAL RACKETS CHAMPIONSHIP OF THE BRITISH ISLES
Scott-Chad Cup

1931	C. R. Read	1932	A. G. Cooper	1946	J. Dear

OLD BOYS' PUBLIC SCHOOL RACKETS CHAMPIONSHIP
Noel-Bruce Cup

1929	Eton (R. C. O. Williams & I. Akers-Douglas)
1930–31	Rugby (D. S. Milford & J. C. F. Simpson)
1932	Eton (K. A. Wagg & I. Akers-Douglas)
1933–34	Rugby (D. S. Milford & J. C. F. Simpson)
1935	Winchester (N. McCaskie & J. T. Faber)
1936–38	Rugby (R. F. Lumb & P. Kershaw)
1946–53	Rugby (D. S. Milford & P. Kershaw)
1954	Tonbridge (J. R. Thompson & M. C. Cowdrey)
1955	Rugby (D. S. Milford & P. Kershaw)
1956	Tonbridge (J. R. Thompson & M. C. Cowdrey)
1957	Tonbridge (J. R. Thompson & R. M. K. Gracey)
1958	Tonbridge (J. R. Thompson & M. C. Cowdrey)
1959	Tonbridge (J. R. Thompson & R. M. K. Gracey)

PUBLIC SCHOOLS SINGLES CHAMPIONSHIP
H. K. Foster Memorial Cup

	Winner	*Runner-up*	
1955	J. M. G. Tildesley (Rugby)	R. M. K. Gracey (Tonbridge)	3–1
1956	C. J. Swallow (Charterhouse)	P. R. Chamberlain (Marlborough)	3–1
1957	P. D. Rylands (Tonbridge)	J. W. Leonard (Eton)	3–0
1958	J. W. Leonard (Eton)	D. M. Norman (Eton)	3–1
1959	J. L. Cuthbertson (Rugby)	J. W. T. Wilcox (Malvern)	3–1

RACKETS QUIZ

1. Has the Amateur Singles Championship always been won by a national of Great Britain?

*

2. Do Oxford and Cambridge award full or half blues for rackets?

QUIZ ANSWERS

1. C. C. Pell of the U.S.A. won in 1925.
2. Full blues at Oxford, half blues at Cambridge.

238

PUBLIC SCHOOLS RACKETS CHAMPIONSHIP

From 1868 *to* 1886 *played at Old Prince's Club, on site of present Hans Place.*
In 1887 *played at Lord's. In* 1888 *and onwards played at Queen's, with one exception.*

1868	Eton, C. J. Ottaway & W. F. Tritton, *beat* Cheltenham, J. J. Read & A. T. Myers	4–3
1869	Eton, C. J. Ottaway & J. P. Rodger, *beat* Rugby, S. K. Gwyer & H. W. Gardner	4–0
1870	Rugby, H. W. Gardner & T. S. Pearson, *beat* Eton, J. P. Rodger & F. C. Ricardo	4–2
1871	Harrow, G. A. Webbe & A. A. Hadow, *beat* Eton, F. C. Ricardo & A. W. Ridley	4–3
1872	Harrow, G. A. Webbe & A. A. Hadow, *beat* Eton, E. O. Wilkinson & W. W. Whitmore	4–1
1873	Harrow, P. F. Hadow & F. D. Leyland, *beat* Rugby, J. J. Barrow & J. Harding	4–0
1874	Harrow, F. D. Leyland & C. W. M. Kemp, *beat* Winchester, H. J. B. Hollings & H. R. Webbe	4–0
1875	Eton, J. Oswald & D. Lane, *beat* Winchester, H. R. Webbe & A. L. Ellis	4–1
1876	Harrow, H. E. Meek & L. K. Jarvis, *beat* Eton, Hon. I. F. W. Bligh & V. A. Butler	4–1
1877	Eton, C. A. C. Ponsonby & Hon. I. F. W. Bligh, *beat* Marlborough, G. M. Butterworth & F. M. Lucas	4–1
1878	Eton, C. A. C. Ponsonby & J. D. Cobbold, *beat* Harrow, H. F. de Paravicini & M. C. Kemp	4–0
1879	Harrow, M. C. Kemp & Hon. F. R. de Moleyns, *beat* Rugby, C. F. H. Leslie & W. G. Stutfield	4–0
1880	Harrow, M. C. Kemp & E. M. Hadow, *beat* Eton, P. St. L. Grenfell & J. C. B. Eastwood	4–2
1881	Harrow, E. M. Hadow & A. F. Kemp, *beat* Marlborough, A. W. Martyn & H. M. Leaf	4–1
1882	Eton, R. H. Pemberton & A. C. Richards, *beat* Harrow, H. E. Crawley & C. D. Buxton	4–2
1883	Harrow, H. E. Crawley & C. D. Buxton, *beat* Eton, R. H. Pemberton & H. Phillipson	4–2
1884	Harrow, E. M. Butler & C. D. Buxton, *beat* Eton, H. Phillipson & J. H. B. Noble	4–3
1885	Harrow, E. M. Butler & E. Crawley, *beat* Eton, H. Phillipson & H. W. Forster	4–3
1886	Harrow, E. Crawley & N. T. Holmes, *beat* Haileybury, J. D. Campbell & H. M. Walters	4–2
1887	Harrow, P. Ashworth & R. D. Cheales, *beat* Charterhouse, H. L. Meyer & R. Nicholson	4–1
1888	Charterhouse, E. C. Streatfield & W. Shelmerdine, *beat* Harrow, R. D. Cheales & E. W. F. Castleman	4–2
1889	Winchester, E. J. Neve & T. B. Case, *beat* Charterhouse, W. Shelmerdine & F. S. Cokayne	4–2
1890	Harrow, A. H. M. Butler & W. F. G. Wyndham, *beat* Wellington, G. J. Mordaunt & R. H. Raphael	4–3
1891	Wellington, G. J. Mordaunt & R. H. Raphael, *beat* Malvern, H. K. Foster & W. L. Foster	4–2
1892	Malvern, H. K. Foster & W. L. Foster, *beat* Harrow, B. N. Bosworth-Smith & F. G. H. Clayton	4–2
1893	Charterhouse, E. Garnett & V. H. Pennell, *beat* Eton, P. W. Cobbold & H. Harben	4–3
1894	Charterhouse, V. H. Pennell & E. Garnett, *beat* Malvern, C. J. Burnup & H. H. Marriott	4–2
1895	Harrow, J. H. Stogdon & A. S. Crawley, *beat* Clifton, R. O. de Gex & A. H. C. Kearsey	4–0
1896	Rugby, W. E. Wilson-Johnston & G. T. Hawes, *beat* Eton, H. C. B. Underdown & E. A. Biedermann	4–3
1897	Harrow, L. F. Andrewes & W. F. A. Rattigan, *beat* Winchester, E. B. Noel & R. A. Williams	4–3
1898	Harrow, W. F. A. Rattigan & L. F. Andrewes, *beat* Eton, E. M. Baerlein & J. E. Tomkinson	4–2
1899	Eton, S. MacNaghten & I. A. de la Rue, *beat* Harrow, F. B. Wilson & S. J. G. Hoare	4–1
1900	Malvern, B. S. Foster & W. H. B. Evans, *beat* Rugby, S. C. Blackwood & O. Fleischmann	4–0
1901	Marlborough, A. J. Graham & L. E. Gillett, *beat* Haileybury, S. M. Toyne & P. F. Reid	4–0
1902	Harrow, G. A. Phelips & C. Browning, *beat* Rugby, K. M. Agnew & J. V. Nesbitt	4–2
1903	Harrow, G. A. Phelips & L. M. MacLean, *beat* Rugby, K. M. Agnew & J. Powell	4–2
1904	Winchester, Hon. C. N. Bruce & E. L. Wright, *beat* Malvern, G. N. Foster & A. P. Day	4–0
1905	Eton, J. J. Astor & M. W. Bovill, *beat* Wellington, H. Brougham & T. Hone	4–1
1906	Charterhouse, C. V. L. Hooman & R. M. Garnett, *beat* Wellington, H. Brougham & E. C. Harrison	4–1
1907	Wellington, H. Brougham & E. C. Harrison, *beat* Malvern, M. K. Foster & F. T. Mann	4–1
1908	Malvern, M. K. Foster & N. J. A. Foster, *beat* Rugby, C. F. B. Simpson & C. C. Watson	4–1
1909	Charterhouse, H. A. Denison & H. W. Leatham, *beat* Eton, J. C. Craigie & V. Bulkeley-Johnson	4–1
1910	Charterhouse, H. W. Leatham & H. A. Denison, *beat* Eton, E. L. Bury & Hon. J. N. Manners	4–0
1911	Rugby, C. F. B. Simpson & W. H. Clarke, *beat* Winchester, L. de O. Tollemache & D. F. McConnel	4–3
1912	Charterhouse, G. A. Wright & C. B. Leatham, *beat* Wellington, E. G. Bartlett & W. G. Grenville Grey	4–0
1913	Wellington, E. G. Bartlett & F. G. Carnegy, *beat* Haileybury, H. D. Hake & L. F. Marson	4–0
1914	Charterhouse, L. D. B. Monier-Williams & J. H. Strachan, *beat* Wellington, E. A. Simson & C. P. Hancock	4–3
1915–18	*No Contest*	
1919	Marlborough, G. S. Butler & G. W. F. Hazelhurst, *beat* Malvern, C. G. W. Robson & N. E. Partridge	4–1
1920	Malvern, C. G. W. Robson & J. A. Deed, *beat* Eton, H. P. Guinness & R. Aird	4–1
1921	Wellington, P. N. Durlacher & L. Lees, *beat* Eton, R. Aird & H. D. Sheldon	4–1
1922	Eton, G. S. Incledon-Webber & O. C. Smith-Bingham, *beat* Radley, F. C. Dawnay & A. E. Blair	4–2
1923	Rugby, D. S. Milford & G. M. Goodbody, *beat* Radley, F. C. Dawnay & A. E. Blair	4–2
1924	Rugby, D. S. Milford & E. F. Longrigg, *beat* Eton, C. J. Child & T. A. Pilkington	4–2
1925	Harrow, A. C. Raphael & N. M. Ford, *beat* Eton, C. J. Child & T. A. Pilkington	4–3
1926	Wellington, R. C. Dobson & J. Powell, *beat* Harrow, N. M. Ford & A. M. Crawley	4–3
1927	Eton, K. A. Wagg & I. Akers-Douglas, *beat* Harrow, R. H. A. G-Calthorpe & G. L. Raphael	4–0
1928	Eton, I. Akers-Douglas & I. A. de Lyle, *beat* Winchester, P. J. Brett & W. D. Evans	4–3
1929	Winchester, N. McCaskie & R. H. Priestley, *beat* Haileybury, E. N. Evans & R. W. Bulmore	4–0
1930	Radley, P. I. Van der Gucht & W. H. Vestey, *beat* Eton, R. Grant & J. de P. Whitaker	4–1
1931	Harrow, R. Pulbrook & J. M. F. Lightly, *beat* Eton, A. M. Hedley & J. C. Atkinson-Clark	4–2
1932	Harrow, R. Pulbrook & J. H. Pawle, *beat* Rugby, R. A. Gray & R. F. Lumb	4–2
1933	Rugby, R. A. Gray & R. F. Lumb, *beat* Harrow, R. Pulbrook & J. H. Pawle	4–2
1934	Rugby, R. F. Lumb & P. Kershaw, *beat* Haileybury, W. M. Robertson & F. R. E. Malden	4–2
1935	Winchester, J. T. Faber & A. B. Kingsley, *beat* Marlborough, P. M. Whitehouse & J. D. L. Dickson	4–2
1936	Malvern, P. D. Manners & N. W. Beeson, *beat* Clifton, W. E. Brassington & S. G. Greenbury	4–0
1937	Malvern, P. D. Manners & N. W. Beeson, *beat* Tonbridge, J. R. Thompson & P. Pettman	4–3
1938	Rugby, A. Kershaw & J. D. L. Repard, *beat* Malvern, P. D. Manners & D. Chalk	4–2
1939	Rugby, J. D. L. Repard & W. H. D. Dunnett, *beat* Winchester, A. R. Taylor & H. E. W. Bowyer	4–0
1940	Haileybury, J. K. Drinkall & A. Fairbairn, *beat* Rugby, L. G. H. Hingley & P. M. Dagnall	4–1
1941	Haileybury, J. K. Drinkall & A. Fairbairn, *beat* Clifton, R. J. Potter & L. J. Waugh	4–0
1942	*No Contest*	
1943	Winchester, G. H. G. Doggart & J. B. Thursfield, *beat* Harrow, I. N. Mitchell & J. G. Hogg	4–2
1944	Winchester, H. E. Webb & G. H. J. Myrtle, *beat* Eton, A. J. H. Ward & J. R. Greenwood	4–2
1945	Winchester, H. E. Webb & G. H. J. Myrtle, *beat* Eton, J. A. R. Clench & W. H. R. Brooks	4–1
1946	Wellington, C. B. Haycraft & J. E. L. Ainslie, *beat* Harrow, G. R. Simmonds & J. A. Glynne-Percy	4–1
1947	Harrow, G. R. Simmonds & R. K. F. C. Treherne-Thomas, *beat* Eton, R. F. H. Ward & W. J. Collins	4–2
1948	Harrow, D. W. Taylor & T. A. M. Pigott, *beat* Wellington, A. H. Swift & R. L. Lees	4–3
1949	Winchester, P. M. Welsh & M. R. Coulman, *beat* Eton, I. C. de S. la Terriere & A. C. Ingleby-Mackenzie	4–3
1950	Winchester, M. R. Coulman & A. D. Myrtle, *beat* Harrow, R. L. O. Bridgeman & R. J. McAlpine	4–2
1951	Winchester, M. R. Coulman & A. D. Myrtle, *beat* Tonbridge, M. C. Cowdrey & J. F. Campbell	4–2
1952	Rugby, D. R. W. Harrison & J. G. H. Hogben, *beat* Wellington, P. de Mesquita & M. W. Bolton	4–2
1953	Winchester, R. T. C. Whatmore & D. B. D. Lowe, *beat* Radley, E. R. Dexter & I. A. K. Dipple	4–3
1954	Harrow, C. A. Strang & R. B. Bloomfield, *beat* Marlborough, N. R. C. Marr & P. R. H. Anderson	4–2
1955	Eton, C. T. M. Pugh & Lord Chelsea, *beat* Winchester, C. N. Copeman & M. M. Mitchell-Thomson	4–1
1956	Charterhouse, J. J. Carless & C. J. Swallow, *beat* Tonbridge, M. S. Connell & M. R. V. Clinch	4–2
1957	Tonbridge, M. S. Connell & P. D. Rylands, *beat* Marlborough, P. Pyemont & N. C. H. Harris	4–1
1958	Eton, J. W. Leonard & D. M. Norman, *beat* Winchester, P. J. L. Wright & Nawab of Pataudi	4–1
1959	Winchester, Nawab of Pataudi & C. E. M. Snell *beat* Eton, D. M. Norman & R. M. Bailey	4–3

SUMMARY TO 1959

School	*Professional*	*Colours*	*Winners*	*Runners-up*
Charterhouse	E. S. Hawes	Pink	9	2
Cheltenham		Cerise & Black	—	1
Clifton	G. Ferguson	Royal Blue	—	3
Eton	R. Hawes	Light Blue	13	24
Haileybury		Magenta	2	5
Harrow	F. S. Crosby	Dark Blue	25	11
Malvern	R. Hughes	Red	6	6
Marlborough	W. E. J. Gordon	Blue & White	2	5
Radley	R. J. Lay	Cerise	1	3
Rugby	P. H. Gray	Light Blue	10	9
Tonbridge	A. A. Hull	White	1	3
Wellington	J. P. Dear	Light Blue & Old Gold	6	7
Winchester	G. L. Padwick	Dark Blue	12	8
		Total Matches	87	87

Note: In this Championship, Cheltenham entered a pair regularly until 1939 but has not done so since. Westminster School occasionally entered a pair, as did the R.N. College, Dartmouth (before the age for cadet entry was raised).

RACKETS QUIZ

1. The marker throws a new ball down to the server. Can the server reject it?

★

2. A's partner misses a volley in a rally. A has wisely "backed him up" but is prevented from attempting a stroke owing to the ball hitting an opponent. Which side wins the stroke?

★

3. A player persistently balks his opponent by not giving him ample room to play his stroke. What can the referee do?

★

4. In a doubles match, can a pair change their order of serving?

★

5. In a doubles match, can a pair change their courts for receiving service?

★

6. In a strenuous single the score reaches 2 games all. Both players ask for a few minutes' rest. How long an interval can the referee allow?

★

7. By mistake, the marker calls "play" to a palpable fault on a first service. Hand-out, however, takes the service, loses the subsequent rally and then appeals to the referee for a fault. What decision should be given?

★

8. A ball, after being struck and before reaching the front wall, hits the striker's opponent. Who wins the stroke?

★

9. What does a "double" mean?

QUIZ ANSWERS

1. Not until after one good service has been delivered. (The rules for taking a new ball are under review.) 2. A let would be allowed. 3. The referee has power to award a stroke to the opponent. 4. Yes, at the beginning of a game. Also, a player serving when a game is won must continue to serve in the following game but need not serve first thereafter in that game. 5. A change can only be made when a pair is first hand-out in any game. 6. None. Play must be continuous, so far as is practical. 7. Hand-out loses the stroke as no appeal can be made if a first service is taken. 8. If the return would have been good a let is allowed, but if the return would not have been good the striker loses the stroke. 9. "Double" means the ball after it has touched the floor a second time.

Rifle Shooting

Compiled by
R. A. Dallen
Chief Clerk:
National Rifle Association

SHOOTING QUIZ

1. What is the size of targets used on (a) Short Range, (b) Long Range? And (c) what is the diameter of the largest scoring circle? (d) Is there any area on the target which does not count?

*

2. What is the longest distance achieved with a Match Rifle?

*

3. Where and when did this take place, and what was the size of the target used?

*

4. What are the colours of the targets used at Bisley for (a) Short and (b) Long Range?

*

5. What does the N.R.A. Crest consist of and what is the motto?

*

6. What are the colours of the N.R.A.?

*

7. Who was the famous artist who drew the original design of the "Running Deer" target?

*

8. What was the "Bisley Bullet"?

*

9. Who was the first Chairman of the N.R.A. and what is the competition which bears his name?

*

10. How many Challenge Trophies are competed for at the Bisley Meeting: (a) 55, (b) 110, (c) 125, (d) 140?

QUIZ ANSWERS

1. (a) Short Range 4 ft. Square, 200–300 yds.; 6 ft. square 500–600 yds.; (b) Long Range 6 ft. × 10 ft.; (c) Short Range 4 ft. Long Range 6 ft. (d) Yes, on Short Range. 2. 2,100 yards. 3. At Barry, Angus in August 1957. Size of target 10 ft. × 14 ft. 4. (a) Top half—light grey, bottom half—sand. (b) Black bull's-eye on white target. 5. Figures of an Archer and Musketryman; Sit Perpetuum. 6. Blue and Silver. 7. E. Landseer in 1864. 8. The nickname given to the train which ran between Brookwood and Bisley Camp during the Bisley Meetings. Made its last journey on 19th July, 1952. 9. Colonel The Earl of Wemyss and March (Lord Elcho). The Elcho Challenge Shield (Match Rifle). 10. (c) 125.

THE NATIONAL RIFLE ASSOCIATION

The National Rifle Association was founded in 1860 "to promote and encourage marksmanship throughout the Queen's Dominions in the interests of Defence and the permanence of the Volunteer and Auxiliary Forces, Naval, Military and Air". Incorporated by Royal Charter in 1890.

Patron—Her Majesty The Queen.

President—H.R.H. The Duke of Gloucester, K.G.

Chairman of Council—Marshal of the Royal Air Force The Lord Tedder, G.C.B.

Secretary—Captain E. K. Le Mesurier, M.V.O., R.N. (Retd.).

The affairs of the Association are administered by a Council which is elected by the members of the Association. The N.R.A. is a charitable organisation and owes its origin to a few leaders of the Volunteer movement in 1859, who concerned themselves with the future of the Volunteers and of rifle shooting in England, and formed a Committee under the Chairmanship of Earl Spencer to promote a great National Association with these objects in view. The first Bisley Meeting was held on Wimbledon Common in 1860 and continued there until 1890, in which year the N.R.A. was established in Bisley Camp, where the Annual Meeting has been held every year, with the exception of the periods of the two World Wars.

The Centenary of the Association will be celebrated in 1960.

Bisley is regarded throughout the shooting world as the "mecca" of rifle shooting, and attracts marksmen from all over Gt. Britain and overseas, who eagerly compete for the many challenge trophies and other prizes. The premier award is "Her Majesty The Queen's Prize" which consists of a gold medal, a gold badge, £250 and a signed portrait of H.M. The Queen. This prize was first competed for at Wimbledon in 1860, and up to the present year the record of Mr. Arthur G. Fulton, M.B.E., who was the winner on three occasions, viz. 1912, 1926 and 1931, remains unequalled and unbeaten. Miss Marjorie Foster, M.B.E., is likewise the only lady competitor to have won this award, which she achieved in 1930.

The Programme of the Meeting covers various types of rifle and pistol shooting and consists mainly of:

(a) Service Rifle (a)—Individual and Team—Service rifle as issued.
(b) Service Rifle (b)—Individual and Team—Service Rifle with variable sights and slings.
(c) Match Rifle—Individual and Team—Long Range, viz. 900–1,200 yds., with telescopic sights and special ammunition.
(d) Sporting Rifle—Individual—Moving targets.
(e) Sub-Machine Gun—Individual and Team—Service personnel only.
(f) Pistol — Individual and Team—Small-bore and full-bore pistols and revolvers.

The Meeting is open to members of H.M. Forces and civilians. The major events are confined to subjects of H.M. The Queen and the remainder to "All Comers".

The personnel required for Camp Administration, manning of the Butts and Firing Points, is provided by the War Office and augmented by the Royal Navy, the Royal Marines and the Royal Air Force.

RANGES AT BISLEY CAMP

Name	No. of Targets	Distances (yards)
Stickledown	50	900–1,200
Short	35	200
Century	100	100–600
Short Siberia	20	100–300
Long Siberia	24	200–600

The "Cheylesmore" Range caters for Sub-Machine gun and special Pistol events, and has automatically controlled targets. Thirty targets, from 10 to 50 yards, are provided on the Pistol Ranges. There is also the Running Deer Range for sporting rifle and .22 (Small-bore) shooting.

BISLEY CAMP

The Camp is situated in pleasant surroundings of open heathland and covers approximately 100 acres (excluding the ranges), and is within easy reach of Brookwood Railway Station, which has an excellent train service to and from Waterloo. There are numerous attractive clubhouses which are the headquarters of associations and clubs, and the venue of riflemen throughout the shooting season. The N.R.A. provides accommodation in huts and cubicles which is increased by the provision of furnished tents for the period of the Bisley fortnight.

The N.R.A. main building and offices are open to visitors and contain Honours Boards of the major competitions, types of rifles which have been used throughout its history and other features of interest. There is also the N.R.A. Pavilion which was rebuilt in 1924, and is open to visitors during the season. It is fully licensed and has a large ballroom which is ideal for dinners and functions during the winter months.

Some Overseas Rifle Associations have their clubhouses in the Camp, notably the Dominion of Canada Rifle Association and the Australian Council of State Rifle Associations.

RECORD OF RESULTS OF MAJOR COMPETITIONS, TEAM AND INDIVIDUAL, 1949–1959

(In alphabetical order. The date in brackets indicates the year in which the competition was first instituted.)

ALBERT (1862)

(*Match Rifle. 15 shots at each distance.*)

Year	Winners	Distances (yards)	Scores	H.P.S.	Rifle used
1949	Vicars, A. H., F/Lt. Late R.A.F.V.R.	900, 1,000 and 1,100	214	225	Match
1950	Webster, A. P. C., Mr., North London R.C.	,,	218	,,	,,
1951	Kinnier-Wilson, A. B., Major. Late R.A.M.C.	,,	215	,,	,,
1952	Crawford, J. A., Major. Late R. Scots	,,	217	,,	,,
1953	Culf, A. B., Mrs. English VII IClub	,,	205	,,	,,
1954	Boyd, B. D., Mr. North London R.C.	,,	219	,,	,,
1955	Copland, C. M., Canon. N.R.C. of Scotland	,,	211	,,	,,
1956	Blackhurst, J. H., Major. English VIII Club.	,,	214	,,	,,
1957	Darell-Brown, H. N., Mr. C.U.R.A.	,,	215	,,	,,
1958	Cumming, R. A., Mr. C.U.R.A.	1,000, 1,100 and 1,200	216	,,	,,
1959	Swanston, D. S., Capt. Late R.N.	,,	201	,,	,,

ALL COMERS' AGGREGATE (1884)

(*Service Rifle (b). Aggregate of Daily Telegraph, Alexandra, Times, Daily Mail, Wimbledon, Duke of Gloucester.*)

Year	Winners	Distances (yards)	Scores	H.P.S.	Rifle used
1949	Prow, N. V., Mr., South Hants R.C.	200–600	307	335	.303 Mag.
1950	French, F. S., Arm/Sgt. Late Herts Yeo.	,,	310	,,	,,
1951	Wheeler, S. F., Mr. North London R.C.	,,	311	,,	,,
1952	Hutton, F. E. P., Rear/Adml. Late R.N.	,,	310	,,	,,

		Distances	Scores	H.P.S.	Rifle used
1953	Johnson, R. E. W., Lt.-Col. Late L.R.B.	,,	306	,,	,,
1954	Robson, W., Capt. R.M.	,,	306	,,	,,
1955	Blanchette, A. H., Cpl. Canada	,,	309	,,	,,
1956	Homer, H. L., S/Ldr. R.N.Z.A.F.	,,	310	,,	,,
1957	Reynolds, E. G. B., Major. Late Suffolk Regt.	,,	313	,,	,,
1958	Tetlow, A. J., Mr. North London R.C.	,,	307	,,	,,
1959	French, F. S., Arm/Sgt. Late Herts. Yeo.	,,	311	,,	,,

ASHBURTON CHALLENGE SHIELD (1861)
(Schools only. Service Rifle (b). 7 shots at each distance. Teams of 8.)

Year	Winners	Distances (yards)	Scores	H.P.S.	Rifle used
1949	Glenalmond (Trinity College)	200–500	512	560	.303 Mag.
1950	The Leys	,,	513	,,	
1951	Allhallows	,,	511	,,	
1952	Glenalmond (Trinity College)	,,	512	,,	
1953	The Leys	,,	508	,,	
1954	Allhallows	,,	524	,,	
1955	Winchester	,,	515	,,	
1956	Blundells	,,	515	,,	
1957	Uppingham	,,	529	,,	
1958	Repton	,,	508	,,	
1959	St. Lawrence	,,	517	,,	

CHANCELLORS' CHALLENGE PLATE (1862)
(Oxford and Cambridge. Service Rifle (b). 10 Shots at each distance. Teams of 8.)

Year	Winners	Distances (yards)	Scores	H.P.S.	Rifle used
1949	Cambridge University	300, 500 and 600	1,065	1,200	.303 Mag.
1950	,, ,,	,,	1,079	,,	
1951	,, ,,	,,	1,093	,,	
1952	,, ,,	,,	1,084	,,	
1953	,, ,,	,,	1,088	,,	
1954	,, ,,	,,	1,090	,,	
1955	,, ,,	,,	1,098	,,	
1956	Oxford University	,,	1,120	,,	
1957	Cambridge University	,,	1,109	,,	
1958	,, ,,	,,	1,100	,,	
1959	,, ,,	,,	1,115	,,	

H.R.H. THE DUKE OF GLOUCESTER'S PRIZE (1936)
(Service Rifle (b). 15 shots at 600 yards.)

Year	Winners	Distances (yards)	Scores	H.P.S.	Rifle used
1949	Grist, S. H., Sgt. Late Glos. Regt.	600	74	75	.303 Mag.
1950	Laceby-Stevens, C., S/Ldr. Late R.A.F.V.R.	,,	74	,,	,,
1951	Magnay, W. H., Major. City R.C.	,,	74	,,	,,
1952	Hunt, A. C., Mr. South Hants R.C.	,,	73	,,	,,
1953	Baskett, J. P., Lt. Old Chomelians R.C.	,,	74	,,	,,
1954	Hibbert, W. H., Sgt. Late R.A.	,,	72	,,	,,
1955	Blake, N. G., Lt.-Col. North London R.C.	,,	72	,,	,,
1956	Warner, E. L., Lt. Canada	,,	75	,,	,,
1957	Prince-Cox, W. C. H., Mr. South Hants R.C.	,,	73	,,	,,
1958	English, R., Mr. City of Newcastle R.C.	,,	73	,,	,,
1959	French, F. S., Arm/Sgt. Late Herts. Yeo.	,,	74	,,	,,

ELCHO CHALLENGE SHIELD (1862)
(Match Rifle. 15 shots at each distance. Teams of 8 from England, Scotland and Ireland.)

Year	Winners	Distances (yards)	Scores	H.P.S.	Rifle used
1949	England	900, 1,000 and 1,100	1,613	1,800	Match
1950	England	,,	1,649	,,	,,
1951	England	,,	1,681	,,	,,
1952	England	,,	1,668	,,	,,
1953	Scotland	,,	1,667	,,	,,
1954	England	,,	1,651	,,	,,
1955	Scotland	,,	1,589	,,	,,
1956	England	,,	1,700	,,	,,
1957	England	1,000, 1,100 and 1,200	1,524	,,	,,
1958	England	,,	1,622	,,	,,
1959	England	,,	1,638	,,	,,

GRAND AGGREGATE (1873)
(Service Rifle (b). Major Aggregate comprising 11 competitions)

Year	Winners	Distances (yards)	Scores	H.P.S.	Rifle used
1949	Clarke, G. A. C.P.O. R.N.	200–1,000	564	615	.303 Mag.
1950	French, F. S. Arm/Sgt. Late Herts Yeo.	,,	565	,,	,,
1951	Wardle, B., Mr. City R.C.	,,	566	,,	,,
1952	Hutton, F. E. P. Rear/Adml. Late R.N.	,,	570	,,	,,
1953	Bennett, R. W.O. Late R.A.F.	,,	564	,,	,,
1954	Slocock, J. A., Mr. Chobham and District R.C.	,,	558	,,	,,
1955	Rigden, J. A., Mr. City R.C.	,,	571	,,	,,
1956	Pavey, P. A., Mr. Australia	,,	569	,,	,,
1957	Swansea, Lord. Porthcawl R.C.	,,	573	,,	,,
1958	Gilbert, V. H., Mr. North London R.C.	,,	563	,,	,,
1959	Armour, S., Major, R.M.	,,	570	,,	,,

HOPTON CHALLENGE CUP (1900)
(Match Rifle Championship. Aggregate of Match Rifle Competitions.)

Year	Winners	Distances (yards)	Scores	H.P.S.	Rifle used
1949	Fremantle, Hon. J. Lt.-Col. Eng. VIII Club	900–1,200	796	875	Match
1950	Crawford, J. A., Major. Late Royal Scots	,,	810	,,	,,
1951	Fremantle, Hon. J., Lt.-Col. Eng. VIII Club	,,	811	,,	,,
1952	Hale, A. C., Mr. Midland C.R.C.	,,	814	,,	,,
1953	Whitelock, A. T. W/Cdr. Eng. VIII Club	,,	805	,,	,,
1954	Maxwell, H. St. G., Capt. N.R.C. of Scotland	,,	654	725	,,
1955	Fremantle, Hon. J., Lt.-Col. Eng. VIII Club	,,	787	875	,,
1956	Hale, A. C., Mr. Eng. VIII Club	,,	821	,,	,,
1957	Dadd, C. V., Mr. Eng. VIII Club	,,	815	,,	,,
1958	Green, J. B., Mr. Eng. VIII Club	,,	964	1,050	,,
1959	Hutton, F. E. P., Rear-Admiral. Late R.N.	,,	950	,,	,,

INTER-SERVICES XX MATCH (1926)
(Service Rifle (b). 10 shots at each distance. Teams of 20.)

Year	Winners	Distances (yards)	Scores	H.P.S.	Rifle used
1949	Regular Army	300, 500 and 600	2,712	3,000	.303 Mag.
1950	Regular Army	,,	2,749	,,	,,
1951	Territorial Army	,,	2,751	,,	,,
1952	Regular Army	,,	2,766	,,	,,
1953	Territorial Army	,,	2,738	,,	,,
1954	Royal Marines	,,	2,711	,,	,,
1955	Territorial Army	,,	2,746	,,	,,
1956	Regular Army	,,	2,750	,,	,,
1957	Royal Navy	,,	2,783	,,	,,
1958	Territorial Army	,,	2,736	,,	,,
1959	Royal Air Force	,,	2,722	,,	,,

THE RAJAH OF KOLAPORE IMPERIAL CHALLENGE CUP (1871)
(Service Rifle (b). 10 shots at each distance. Teams of 8 from the Mother Country and Dominions.)

Year	Winners	Distances (yards)	Scores	H.P.S.	Rifle used
1949	Mother Country	300, 500 and 600	1,114	1,200	.303 Mag.
1950	Mother Country	,,	1,113	,,	
1951	Canada	,,	1,120	,,	
1952	South Africa	,,	1,123	,,	
1953	Australia	,,	1,125	,,	
1954	Mother Country	,,	1,112	,,	
1955	Mother Country	,,	1,108	,,	
1956	Mother Country	,,	1,130	,,	
1957	Mother Country	,,	1,140	,,	
1958	Mother Country	,,	1,120	,,	
1959	Mother Country	,,	1,127	,,	

MACKINNON CHALLENGE CUP (1891)
(Service Rifle (b). 10 shots at each distance. Teams of 12 from Great Britain, Ireland and Dominions.)

Year	Winners	Distances (yards)	Scores	H.P.S.	Rifle used
1949	England	900–1,000	1,036	1,200	.303 Mag.
1950	England	,,	1,044	,,	
1951	Ireland	,,	1,041	,,	
1952	Canada	,,	1,031	,,	
1953	New Zealand	,,	1,005	,,	
1954	England	,,	1,002	,,	
1955	England	,,	1,063	,,	
1956	England	,,	1,047	,,	
1957	Scotland	,,	1,044	,,	
1958	England	,,	1,029	,,	
1959	England	,,	1,002	,,	

SHOOTING QUIZ

1. Who fired the first shot at the first Meeting held at Bisley in 1890?

*

2. What was the distance?

*

3. Which type of rifle was used?

*

4. What is the outstanding landmark on the Bisley Ranges?

5. What are the dimensions of the Aiming Mark on the Bisley targets at (a) 200 yards, (b) 300 yards, (c) 500/600 yards?

*

6. What method of scoring is used on the Bisley targets?

QUIZ ANSWERS

1. H.R.H. The Princess of Wales. 2. 500 yards. 3. Lee-Metford fixed on a rest. 4. The Clock Tower, which was transferred from Wimbledon Common in 1890. 5. (a) 12″ dia. (b) 18″ dia. (c) 36″ dia. 6. Bull, counting 5; Inner, counting 4; Magpie, counting 3. Outer, counting 2·

REVOLVER GOLD BADGE (1899)

(Revolver Championship Aggregate.)

Year	Winners	Distances (yards)	Scores	H.P.S.
1949	Willott, C. C., S/Ldr. R.A.F.	10–50	788	900
1950	Kennedy, H., F/Lt. R.A.F.	,,	655	750
1951	Willott, C. C., S/Ldr. R.A.F.	,,	709	810
1952	Steele, H. A., F/Lt. R.A.F.	,,	706	,,
1953	Willott, C. C., S/Ldr. R.A.F.	,,	690	,,
1954	Willott, C. C., S/Ldr. R.A.F.	,,	547	655
1955	Viney, V. H., Capt. R.E.M.E.	,,	448	510
1956	Willott, C. C., S/Ldr. R.A.F.	,,	449	,,
1957	Clark, A. J., C.E.R.A. R.N.	,,	442	,,
1958	Willott, C. C., S/Ldr. Late R.A.F.	,,	449	,,
1959	Meaker, W., W.O. R.E.M.E.	,,	444	,,

ST. GEORGE'S CHALLENGE VASE (1862)

(Service Rifle (b). From 1957, 1st stage 15 shots at 300 yds., 2nd stage 15 shots at 600 yds., 3rd stage 15 shots at 900 yds.)

Year	Winners	Distances (yards)	Scores	H.P.S.	Rifle used
1949	White, W. H., Capt. Inf. Weapons Staff	900	71	75	.303 Mag.
1950	Richardson, G., F/Lt. Late R.A.F.	,,	73	,,	,,
1951	Magnay, W. H., Major. City R.C.	,,	71	,,	,,
1952	Ferrier, W. F., Capt. Army Cadet Force	,,	72	,,	,,
1953	Johnson, S., Lt.-Col. Canada	,,	73	,,	,,
1954	McBean, L. M., Lt.-Col. S. Rhodesia	,,	70	,,	,,
1955	Swiegers, J. U., Mr. N. Rhodesia	,,	71	,,	,,
1956	Malpas, H. E., Lt. S.A.S.C.	,,	74	,,	,,
1957	Swansea, Lord. Porthcawl R.C.	600 & 900	145	150	,,
1958	Martel, G. T., O/Cdt. C.U.O.T.C.	,,	139	,,	,,
1959	Price, W. L. V., Mr. Univ. of London R.C.		141	,,	,,

SERVICE RIFLE CHAMPIONSHIP AGGREGATE (1905)

(Service Rifle (a). Comprising 7 Competitions from 1958.)

Year	Winners	Distances (yards)	Scores	H.P.S.	Rifle used
1949	Parsons, R. M., Major. R.U.R.	100–600	463	525	.303 Mag.
1950	Lawrence, H. J., S.I. S.A.S.C.	,,	464	,,	,,
1951	Baudains, W. H., Major. R.U.R.	,,	452	,,	,,
1952	Dennis, F. W., R.S.M. Oxford and Bucks L.I.	,,	458	,,	,,
1953	Willott, C. C., S/Ldr. R.A.F.	,,	465	,,	,,
1954	Baudains, W. H., Major. R.U.R.	,,	337	375	,,
1955	Platfoot, C. G. F., Capt. R.A.S.C.	,,	326	,,	,,
1956	Marchant, M. R., Lt. R.M.	,,	326	380	,,
1957	Gillam, J. D., Q.M.S.I. S.A.S.C.	,,	330	,,	,,
1958	Mitchell, E. P. E., W.O.1. R.E.M.E.	,,	372	430	,,
1959	Carpenter, D. O., Lt. R.O.A.C.	,,	361	,,	,,

UNITED SERVICE CHALLENGE CUP (1880)

(Service Rifle (a). Standardised Service Conditions in 4 Practices. Teams of 8 from British Forces.)

Year	Winners	Distances (yards)	Scores	H.P.S.	Rifle used
1949	Royal Marines	600–100	1,350	1,600	.303 Mag.
1950	Royal Marines	,,	1,333	,,	,,
1951	Regular Army	,,	1,354	,,	,,
1952	Royal Air Force	,,	1,345	,,	,,
1953	Royal Air Force	,,	1,346	,,	,,
1954	Royal Navy	,,	1,339	,,	,,
1955	Regular Army	,,	1,367	,,	,,
1956	Regular Army	,,	1,384	,,	,,
1957	Regular Army	,,	1,330	,,	,,
1958	Regular Army	,,	1,354	,,	,,
1959	Royal Marines	,,	1,201	,,	,,

WHITEHEAD CHALLENGE CUP (1894)

(Revolver. Teams of 8 from each Service.)

Year	Winners	Distances (yards)	Scores	H.P.S.
1949	Royal Air Force	10, 20 & 50	719	960
1950	,, ,, ,,	,,	732	,,
1951	,, ,, ,,	,,	708	,,
1952	,, ,, ,,	,,	743	,,
1953	,, ,, ,,	,,	704	,,
1954	,, ,, ,,	,,	717	,,
1955	,, ,, ,,	,,	722	,,
1956	,, ,, ,,	,,	698	,,
1957	,, ,, ,,	,,	741	,,
1958	,, ,, ,,	,,	728	,,
1959	,, ,, ,,	,,	760	,,

NATIONAL CHALLENGE TROPHY (1864)

(Service Rifle (b). 7 shots at each distance. Teams of 20 from England, Scotland, Ireland and Wales.)

Year	Winners	Distances (yards)	Scores	H.P.S.	Rifle used
1949	England	200, 500 and 600	1,883	2,100	.303 Mag.
1950	England	,,	1,933	,,	,,
1951	England	,,	1,922	,,	,,
1952	Scotland	,,	1,953	,,	,,
1953	England	,,	1,954	,,	,,
1954	England	,,	1,931	,,	,,
1955	England	200 and 500	1,304	1,400	,,
1956	Scotland	200, 500, 600	1,960	2,100	,,
1957	England	,,	1,973	,,	,,
1958	England	,,	1,918	,,	,,
1959	England	,,	1,961	,,	,,

HER MAJESTY THE QUEEN'S PRIZE (from 1952)

formerly

HIS MAJESTY THE KING'S PRIZE (1901)

(Service Rifle (b). Shot in Three Stages. Second Stage—300 competitors. Third Stage 100 Competitors.)

FIRST STAGE.	Distances: 200, 500 and 600 yds. No. of Shots: 7 at each distance.
SECOND STAGE.	Distances: 300, 500 and 600 yds. No. of Shots: 10 at each distance.
THIRD STAGE.	Distances: 900 and 1,000 yds. No. of Shots: 15 at each distance.

SECOND STAGE.

Year	Winners	Distances (yards)	Scores	H.P.S.	Rifle used
1949	Fox, A. G., Mr. March R.C.	300, 500 and 600	146	150	.303 Mag.
1950	Draper, J. A., C.Q.M.S. Canada	,,	144	,,	,,
1951	Gill, H., F/Lt. R.A.F.	,,	144	,,	,,
1952	Magney, W. H., Major. City R.C.	,,	146	,,	,,
1953	Saunders, R. L., Mr. City R.C.	,,	145	,,	,,
1954	Twine, G. E., Major. Late R.A.	,,	145	,,	,,
1955	Watts, O. A., Lt.-Col. Late Suffolk Regt.	,,	146	,,	,,
1956	Bromley, A. F., Capt. Devonia R.C.	,,	142	,,	,,
1957	Adams, F., Lt.-Col. North London R.C.	,,	147	,,	,,
1958	Swansea, Lord. Porthcawl R.C.	,,	145	,,	,,
1959	Hook, M., Lt. Bank of England R.C.	,,	146	,,	,,

THIRD STAGE (Aggregate of Second and Third Stages).

Year	Winners	Distances (yards)	Scores	H.P.S.	Rifle used
1949	Brookes, E., Capt. Late R.A.S.C.	900–1,000	278	300	.303 Mag.
1950	Greig, R. D., Capt. Late Royal Scots Fus.	,,	277	,,	,,
1951	Boa, G. S., Lt. Canada	,,	285	,,	,,
1952	Kinnier Wilson, A. B., Major. Late R.A.M.C.	,,	277	,,	,,
1953	McCaw, N. W., Major. Late L.R.B.	,,	273	,,	,,
1954	Twine, G. E., Major. Late R.A.	,,	278	,,	,,
1955	Fenwick, L. R., Mr. City R.C.	,,	286	,,	,,
1956	Twine, G. E., Major. Late R.A.	,,	283	,,	,,
1957	Love, J. R. C., Mr. Kyle R.C.	,,	283	,,	,,
1958	Fulton, R. A., Major. R.A. (T.A.R.O.)	,,	281	,,	,,
1959	Mallabar, L. W., Lt. City R.C.	,,	276	,,	,,

THE "QUEEN MARY" (1911)

(Service Rifle (a). Standardised Service Conditions in 4 Practices.)

Year	Winners	Distances (yards)	Scores	H.P.S.	Rifle used
1949	Parsons, R. M., Major. Roy. Ulster Rifles	600–100	183	200	.303 Mag.
1950	Treylen, J. F., Major. Royal Marines	,,	177	,,	,,
1951	Armstrong, G. R., Q.M.S. Gren. Guards	,,	179	,,	,,
1952	Orr, R. M., C.E.A. Royal Navy	,,	177	,,	,,
1953	Willott, C. C., S/Ldr. R.A.F.	,,	184	,,	,,
1954	Baudains, W. H., Major. Roy. Ulster Rifles	,,	183	,,	,,
1955	Malpas, H. E., Lt. Small Arms School Corps	,,	183	,,	,,
1956	Johnson, M. L., Cd/Gnr. Royal Navy	,,	179	,,	,,
1957	Snelgrove, R. L., Cpl. R.C.A.F.	,,	183	,,	,,
1958	Platfoot, C. G. F., Capt. R.A.S.C.	,,	183	,,	,,
1959	Green, G. F., P.O.A.F. R.N.	,,	174	,,	,,

Compiled by A. J. Palmer
Secretary: The National Small-Bore Rifle Association

Rifle Shooting (Small-Bore)

THE NATIONAL SMALL-BORE RIFLE ASSOCIATION

Small-bore (.22 in. calibre) target shooting, started in 1901 by Field Marshal Earl Roberts as a "Civilian Army", is today a very flourishing if exacting sport. But it retains its value as a means of training in the rudiments of marksmanship.

There is no parallel to this organisation which was formed for Defence and which now attracts people from all walks of life, whose object is to place ten consecutive shots into the tiny bullseye as frequently as possible.

Shooting at printed targets, at predetermined range distances, particularly with rifles in the prone position, is a sport for people of all ages and both sexes.

Prior to 1901 there were two organisations, both struggling for existence, and called the British Rifle League and the Society of Working Men's Rifle Clubs. They combined to form the Society of Miniature Rifle Clubs, under the Presidency of Lord Roberts, who held that office until his death in 1914.

As technical design and skill advanced, so did the ability of the marksman. From light sporting rifles weighing a few pounds has developed the present precision .22 in. calibre Match rifle of today weighing up to 14 lb. fitted with micrometer adjusting rear sights and scientifically designed aperture foresights.

Side by side with the improvement of the weapons, the target-scoring rings became smaller and smaller until now the bullseye is so tiny that at 15, 20 and 25 yards ranges the scoring of shots has become a real problem. Despite this an average person, be he or she 15 or 50, can achieve a Club average of ability within six months.

Development of firearms and improved technique tended to outmode the title "Miniature" which is popularly believed to refer to the length of ranges. In the early days few ranges exceeded 25 yards in length. Therefore in 1947 the title of the parent body was changed to National Small-bore Rifle Association whilst the County Associations and Rifle Clubs changed their titles from "Miniature" to "Small-bore".

Throughout the world the .22 in. calibre weapon is now known as "small-bore", and whilst the majority of small-bore shooting in Britain is at 15, 20 and 25 yards we are yearly increasing the number of 50 and 100 yards ranges here. Abroad, and particularly in the Continent of Europe the range is fixed at 50 metres (54½ yards).

In the past there has been a vital difference between small-bore shooting in the English-speaking countries and in other countries. Until 1947, when the International Shooting Union was revived in Stockholm, the English-speaking marksmen fired in the prone position. Since Great Britain entered the 1947 World Championships, we have taken greater interest in "positional" shooting —in the standing and kneeling positions.

"Positional" shooting is an exacting form of the sport, and physical stamina plays a greater part than when shooting prone, consequently it is the younger men who excel.

Until Great Britain can introduce a new concept of small-bore shooting, training the newcomers from the start to shoot standing and kneeling, as well as prone, we will not hold our place in the forefront internationally as we have done for years past in prone-position shooting. In the 1958 World Championships, staged in Moscow, Great Britain won the team and individual prone championships at 50 metres range and was placed third, both individual and prone, in the 50 and 100 metres event.

PISTOL SHOOTING

Any rifle range which has been approved by the War Office for small-bore rifles may also be used for pistol shooting with certain minor reservations.

Consequently some four hundred Clubs in the U.K. have a pistol section. Despite the reluctance of the Police more freely to sanction personal possession of pistols, thirty-five new pistol sections were formed in 1958.

Pistol shooting internationally is divided into three sections, slow-fire, with what are known as "Free" pistols, rapid-fire with automatic weapons, and centre-fire or larger calibre weapons. Free pistols are costly and therefore scarce. The trigger pressure is very light and its mechanism is as delicate as that of a watch. The grip or stock is fashioned individually to fit the hand of the firer, and the cost ranges from £60 upwards. It is hardly surprising that free pistol shooting makes little progress in Great Britain.

Far more popular are the single-shot Webley pistols costing around £14 and automatics of American, German and French origin ranging from £16 to £35.

As with rifle shooting, so for hand-gun shooting the English-speaking countries have developed on lines of their own. In Britain club team and individual events are fired at 20 yards, and either single-shot or automatic pistols may be used. There are few club ranges which allow shooting at the other standard distance 50 yards (or metres) because a butt wall 20 ft. high is necessary. Only at Bisley is there much 50 yards or 50 metres pistol shooting.

Internationally British pistol shooters have done remarkably well considering the restrictions at home, though we have yet to capture an Olympic, World or European Championship.

Organised pistol shooting under the National Small-bore Rifle Association dates from the 1930's. Nevertheless, in the 1948 Olympic Games in London we were placed 12th from an entry of 59 in the rapid-fire, in 1952 at Helsinki we again took twelfth place from an entry of 48 in the Free Pistol event, whilst at Melbourne, Australia, in the 1956 Olympics, again for Free Pistol, one of our two entrants was tenth.

General Organisation

In using the term Rifle Club, we infer that membership is open to the General Public, probably one in two admits lady members and one in four provide pistol shooting.

Of the four thousand affiliated units which comprise the National Small-bore Rifle Association, some two and a half thousand are civilian rifle clubs. The balance is made up of almost sixty County Rifle Associations, one hundred and fifty local Rifle Associations and Leagues, a few National Associations and the rest are comprised of H.M. Forces, Cadet, Police and Industrial Clubs.

As small-bore shooting attracts all sections of the community it is not surprising that the Police have almost three hundred clubs. Dating from World War II there are still some twenty Civil Defence Rifle Clubs and 130 Home Guard Rifle Clubs. Membership in most of these H.G. Clubs is, by the way, open to the General Public, but the title is retained for sentimental reasons.

Junior units number over six hundred. They come from the Schools from the Sea Cadet Corps, the Army Cadet Force, the Air Training Corps, the Boy Scouts, Church Lads' Brigade, Boys' Brigade, etc.

POST-WAR RECORDS OF THE MORE IMPORTANT COMPETITIONS

INTERNATIONAL MATCHES

LORD DEWAR CUP

1946	United States of America	7,951
1947	United States of America	7,934
1948	United States of America	7,906
1950	Great Britain	7,930
1951	United States of America	7,953
1952	Great Britain	7,964
1953	United States of America	7,984
1954	Great Britain	7,969
1955	United States of America	7,983
1956	United States of America	7,984
1957	United States of America	7,974
1958	United States of America	7,972
	Fired on British National Targets.	
1959	Great Britain	7,742

RANDLE TROPHY

1952	United States of America	3,966
1953	United States of America	3,972
1954	United States of America	3,956
1955	United States of America	3,981
1956	United States of America	3,970
1957	United States of America	3,968
1958	United States of America	3,982

LORD WAKEFIELD MONUMENT TROPHY

1947	Great Britain	3,931
1948	Sweden	3,959
1949	Sweden	3,949
1950	Great Britain	3,960
1951	Sweden	3,977
1952	Great Britain	3,959
1953	Great Britain	3,975
1954	Sweden	3,981
1955	Great Britain	3,963
1956	Sweden	3,970
1957	Sweden	3,985
1958	Sweden	3,911

PISTOL—MAYLEIGH TROPHY

1947	United States of America	1,828
1948	United States of America	1,809
1949	United States of America	1,856
1950	Great Britain	1,728
1951	United States of America	1,875
1952	United States of America	1,820
1953	United States of America	1,845
1954	United States of America	1,813
1955	United States of America	1,830
1956	United States of America	1,838
1957	United States of America	1,837
1958	United States of America	1,842

SHOOTING QUIZ

1. Why is the Dewar Cup so frequently won by the United States of America and how did it get its name?

★

2. What is considered to be the most important honour which the small-bore rifle shooter in Britain can gain?

★

3. How are the International teams selected?

QUIZ ANSWERS

1. The late Sir Thomas Dewar, later Lord Dewar, presented the trophy for small-bore shooting in 1909. The small-bore shooters who attend Camp Perry are trained to shoot to a very much higher standard because telescope sights are an accepted accessory in the United States. 2. Undoubtedly the British Championship for the Earl Roberts Memorial Trophy which has been fired for every year since 1923. 3. For most of the post-war years the team selection has been by a process of trials which start on club ranges and by progressively eliminating numbers are reduced to probably 40 or maybe 50 for a team of 20 and half as many for a team of 10, who fire side by side in a final trial.

INDIVIDUAL CHAMPIONSHIPS—BRITISH

EARL ROBERTS MEMORIAL CUP

1946	V. H. Gilbert	Ham and Petersham	791
1947	V. H. Gilbert	Ham and Petersham	790
1948	H. S. Yeoman	Twickenham	596
1949	G. A. J. Jones	Twickenham	598
1950	H. R. Hammond	Borough of Wandsworth	598
1951	J. Hall	City of Birmingham	597
1952	W. B. Godwin	City of Birmingham	590
1953	J. E. Leggett	3rd V.B. Warwicks	599
1954	H. A. S. Bayley	Styvechale	600
1955	H. A. S. Bayley	Old Silhillians	599
1956	D. King	University of London	595
1957	D. R. V. Parish	Deepbottom Valley	598
1958	T. J. Knight	City of Birmingham (B.N. Targets)	589
1959	A. Skinner	City of Birmingham (,, ,,)	572

ROYAL SOCIETY OF ST. GEORGE

1946	V. H. Gilbert	Ham and Petersham	791
1947	V. H. Gilbert	Ham and Petersham	790
1948	H. S. Yeoman	Twickenham	596
1949	G. A. J. Jones	Twickenham	598
1950	H. R. Hammond	Borough of Wandsworth	598
1951	J. Hall	City of Birmingham	597
1952	W. B. Godwin	City of Birmingham	590
1953	J. E. Leggett	3rd V.B. Warwicks	599
1954	H. A. S. Bayley	Styvechale	600
1955	H. A. S. Bayley	Old Silhillians	599
1956	D. King	University of London	595
1957	D. R. V. Parish	Deepbottom Valley	598
1958	Miss V. M. Hills	St. Nicholas	388
1959	R. W. Edwards	East Bristol	391

SCOTTISH

EARL HAIG MEMORIAL CUP

1946	J. D. Young	Porthlethen	Edinburgh	789
1947	A. A. Smith	Glasgow Police	Perth	796
1948	A. A. Smith	Glasgow Police	Largs	784
1949	A. Leighton	Hampton	Aberdeen	791
1950	R. J. Ramsey	Irvine	Glasgow	792
1951	W. Bain	Wick Old Stagers	Montrose	596
1952	A. J. Nicoll	Perth City and County	Edinburgh	593
1953	C. R. Glen	Irvine	Glasgow	599
1954	Mrs. J. J. McKenzie	Dundee and Strathmore	Aberdeen	597
1955	T. B. Band	Perth City and County	St. Andrews	597
1956	A. A. Smith	Glasgow Police	Berwick	600
1957	Mrs. J. J. McKenzie	Dundee and Strathmore	Carnoustie	598
1958	Mrs. J. J. McKenzie	Dundee and Strathmore	Grantown-on-Spey	595
1959	W. B. Smillie	Falkirk Lord Roberts	Stirling (B.N. Targets)	583

SHOOTING QUIZ

1. Which club team do you consider to be the best in post-war years?

*

2. Are there such people as left-handers in shooting and how do they compare with the orthodox position shooters?

QUIZ ANSWERS

1. Without a doubt, the City of Birmingham Rifle Club has proved itself far more expert in winning national championships at the longer ranges, that is at 50 and 100 yards. In fact they have won the National League, which is shot over those distances, for the past eight years. At short ranges, however, honours are more widely enjoyed, though one of the most successful clubs is Lensbury and Britannic House, whose members are drawn from the oil companies and their associates in the London area. 2. As in every other activity there are left-handers and some rifle manufacturers make left-handed rifles. At national meetings special provision is made in the allocation of firing point space for left-handers. There appears to be no marked difference between the potential success or ability whether one shoots from the right or the left shoulder. A new gadget is about to be produced to enable those whose left eye is the master eye but who prefer to shoot from the right shoulder, to use their left eye for sighting and to shoot from the orthodox position. It will contain prisms which transfer the line of sight across the distance between the eyes.

NORTHERN IRELAND

1950	C. H. Craig	C.I.Y.M.S. Belfast	Glasgow	388
1951	M. Dickson, Jnr.	Co. Londonderry XB	Bisley	388
1952	Capt. R. T. Boyd	R.A.P.C. Wolverley	Bisley	390
1953	T. D. G. Ward	Omagh	Glasgow	396
1954	M. Dickson, Jnr.	Co. Londonderry XB	Bisley	398
1955	T. D. G. Ward	Omagh	Bisley	393
1956	J. Gorman	C.I.Y.M.S. Belfast	Bisley	391
1957	J. W. Cunningham	Co. Londonderry XB	Bisley	392
1958	W. A. Ward	Queen's University	Bisley (B.N. Targets)	380
1959	M. Dickson	Co. Londonderry XB	Bisley „ „	372

WELSH
"WESTERN MAIL & ECHO" CUP

1947	G. Jewell	Lockheed	Cardiff	782
1948	G. Jewell	Lockheed	„	393
1949	W. Bliss	Metropolitan Police "L" Division	„	595
1950	J. G. Ellis	Lensbury and Britannic House	„	396
1951	G. Jewell	Lockheed	„	393
1952	J. G. Ellis	Lensbury and Britannic House	Bisley	588
1953	G. Jewell	Lockheed	„	594
1954	G. Jewell	Lockheed	„	599
1955	G. Jewell	Lockheed	„	596
1956	M. E. Cox	East Worthing	„	586
1957	J. G. Ellis	Lensbury and Britannic House	„	589
1958	D. M. Goddard	Cardiff	„	385
1959	J. G. Ellis	Lensbury and Britannic House	„	370

SHORT RANGE CHAMPIONSHIPS—POSTAL
"NEWS OF THE WORLD" CUP

1946	M. Cann	Leicester and District	298
1947	C. C. Sonley	Hull	298
1948	T. J. Knight	Kynoch	300
1949	H. S. Yeoman	Twickenham	300
1950	J. W. Johnson	Borough of Wandsworth	299
1951	E. L. King	B.S.A. Redditch	300
1952	J. W. R. Newman	Beaminster	300
1953	C. J. Hyde	Salisbury	299
1954	T. B. Band	Perth City and County	300
1955	G. Watson	Sunderland	400
1956	C. J. Hyde	Salisbury	400
1957	A. E. Martin	Dartford	400
1958	C. J. Hyde	Salisbury	400
1959	M. P. Singleton	University of London	400

BRITISH WOMEN'S INDIVIDUAL CHAMPIONSHIP
W. R. A. FLOWERS TROPHY

1946	Mrs. A. B. Culf	Manchester City	295
1947	Miss H. Millar	Perth City and County	298
1948	Mrs. G. Broughton	Ham and Petersham	298
1949	Mrs. J. J. McKenzie	City of Dundee	592
1950	Mrs. W. M. Hyde	Salisbury	595
1951	Miss H. Millar	Perth City and County	595
1952	Mrs. J. J. McKenzie	City of Dundee	594
1953	Miss J. B. English	Masonic, Edinburgh	598
1954	Mrs. F. S. Norman	Mocatra	598
1955	Mrs. W. M. Hyde	Salisbury	599
1956	Mrs. J. J. McKenzie	Dundee and Strathmore	598
1957	Mrs. W. Hart	L.N.E.R. Chesterfield	599
1958	Mrs. J. J. McKenzie	Dundee and Strathmore—Grantown-on-Spey	597
1959	Mrs. J. J. McKenzie	Dundee and Strathmore—Bisley (B.N. Targets)	584

INDIVIDUAL CHAMPIONSHIPS, BRITISH—PISTOL
J. K. GALLIE MEMORIAL CUP

1951	W/Cdr. R. F. B. Guy	R.A.F. Shinfield Park	183
1952	W/O. R. V. Sperring	R.A.F.	275
1953	W/Cdr. R. F. B. Guy	R.A.F.	268
1954	Major P. C. Freeman	B.V.P.M. and N.N.P.M.	272
1955	F. Cooper	Blackburn	268
1956	W/Cdr. R. F. B. Guy	Harrogate	272
1957	P. Marchant	Worplesdon	273
1958	P. Marchant	Worplesdon	281
1959	K. Pinder	Lucas	

ARGENTINE TROPHY—RAPID FIRE

			Hits	Points
1949	C. Mylonas	City	30	275
1950	S/Ldr. C. C. Willott	R.A.F.	30	280
1951	S/Ldr. C. C. Willott	R.A.F.	30	290
1952	J. F. Chandler	Twickenham	30	280
1953	S/Ldr. C. C. Willott	R.A.F. Brampton	30	286

			Hits	Points
1954	Capt. V. H. Viney	Army Apprentices' School, Arborfield	30	285
1955	S/Ldr. L. D. Vickery	R.A.F. Brampton	30	278
1956	F/Lt. H. A. Steele	R.A.F.	30	282
1957	S/Ldr. C. C. Willott	R.A.F.	30	287
1958	E. M. Malone	N.S.R.A.	30	292
1959	F/Lt. H. A. Steele	R.A.F.	60	575

ALLIES' TROPHY—POSTAL CHAMPIONSHIP

1945	M. Bergson	Lee-Brad.	192
1946	Mrs. B. Moorshead	Twickenham	187
1947	C.S.M. W. Meaker	Bicester Garrison	187
1948	C.S.M. W. Meaker	Bicester Garrison	190
1949	K. Mitt	Cafferata	190
1950	F. Waher	Cafferata	194
1951	F. Waher	Cafferata	196
1952	P.O. I. Fenton	R.A.F. Valley	181
1953	W/Cdr. R. F. B. Guy	Harrogate	181
1954	W/Cdr. R. F. B. Guy	Harrogate	185
1955	W/Cdr. R. F. B. Guy	Harrogate	186
1956	W/Cdr. R. F. B. Guy	Harrogate	185
1957	J. W. Crocker	West Ham and District	181
1958	W. N. Parker	Hampton	181
1959	W. N. Parker	Ham and Petersham	190

COUNTY COMPETITIONS
RIFLE
QUEEN ALEXANDRA CUP

1947	Essex	2,420
1948	Middlesex	2,434
1949	Yorkshire	2,435
1950	Surrey	2,422
1951	Yorkshire	2,427
1952	Warwickshire	2,438
1953	Warwickshire	2,449
1954	Warwickshire	2,455
1955	London	2,458
1956	Warwickshire	2,456
1957	Warwickshire	2,437
1958	Sussex	2,451
1959	Kent	2,411

B.S.A. CUP

1946	Middlesex	3,941
1947	Quebec	3,960
1948	Middlesex	3,961
1949	Surrey	3,976
1950	Surrey	3,978
1951	Surrey	3,973
1952	Surrey	3,972
1953	Warwickshire	3,978
1954	London	3,987
1955	Kent	3,988
1956	Kent	3,986
1957	Wellington, N.Z.	3,987
1958	Wellington, N.Z.	3,992

COLONIAL AND CITIES
TEAM COMPETITIONS
EMPIRE CITIES MATCH

1947	London	2,964
1948	Montreal	2,970
1949	Montreal	2,962
1950	London	2,941
1951	London	2,963
1952	London	2,969
1953	London	2,979
1954	Calgary	2,975
1955	Calgary	2,973
1956	London	2,988
1957	Christchurch	2,986
1958	Christchurch	2,989

H.M. SERVICES
INTER-SERVICES SMALL-BORE MATCH

1947	Royal Air Force	7,717
1948	Royal Air Force	7,798
1949	Royal Air Force	7,886
1950	Royal Air Force	7,869
1951	Royal Air Force	7,870
1952	Royal Air Force	7,884
1953	Royal Air Force	7,906
1954	Royal Air Force	7,929
1955	Royal Air Force	7,937
1956	Royal Air Force	7,950
1957	Territorial Army	7,952
1958	Territorial Army	7,959
1959	Royal Air Force	7,946

INTER-SERVICES XXXX CADET SMALL-BORE MATCH

1952	Air Training Corps	7,477
1953	Army Cadet Force	7,555
1954	Air Training Corps	7,628
1955	Air Training Corps	7,659
1956	Air Training Corps	7,679
1957	Army Cadet Force	7,730
1958	Army Cadet Force	7,658
1959	Air Training Corps	7,639

ARMY SMALL-BORE MATCH
I.C.I. BOWL

1947	School of Infantry, H.W.W., Netheravon	1,946
1948	School of Infantry, Warminster	1,940
1949	Military Det. Experimental Est., Pendine	1,964
1950	9 Central Workshops R.E.M.E.	1,961

1951	9 Central Workshops R.E.M.E.	1,948
1952	55 Training Regt., R.A.	1,946
1953	School of Military Engineering	1,955
1954	H.Q. Northern Army Group B.A.O.R.	1,967
1955	Royal Military College of Science	1,967
1956	Royal Military College of Science	1,973
1957	Royal Military College of Science	1,973
1958	1st Bn. Seaforth Highlanders	1,968
1959	Royal Military College of Science	1,964

CADET CHAMPIONSHIP OF GREAT BRITAIN
PUNCH TROPHY

1947	42F Sqdn. A.T.C. King's Lynn	924
1948	16th Coy., 7th C. Bn., Royal Warwickshire Reg.	762
1949	470 Falkirk Sqdn. A.T.C.	960
1950	470 Falkirk Sqdn. A.T.C.	953
1951	470 Falkirk Sqdn. A.T.C.	959
1952	470 Falkirk Sqdn. A.T.C.	974
1953	470 Falkirk Sqdn. A.T.C.	948
1954	470 Falkirk Sqdn. A.T.C.	971
1955	470 Falkirk Sqdn. A.T.C.	970
1956	470 Falkirk Sqdn. A.T.C.	967
1957	470 Falkirk Sqdn. A.T.C.	975
1958	470 Falkirk Sqdn. A.T.C.	969
1959	470 Falkirk Sqdn. A.T.C.	967

BRITISH CLUB TEAM CHAMPIONSHIP (Rifle)
LONG RANGE
TWINING CUP
National League, Div. I

1946	City of Birmingham	1,967.5
1947	City of Birmingham	1,970.2
1948	Twickenham	1,981.7
1949	Twickenham	1,986.6
1950	Twickenham	1,987.9
1951	City of Birmingham	1,978.9
1952	City of Birmingham	1,990.9
1953	City of Birmingham	1,993.6
1954	City of Birmingham	1,994.6
1955	City of Birmingham	1,994.6
1956	City of Birmingham	1,994.9
1957	City of Birmingham	1,992.9
1958	City of Birmingham	1,944.0

SHORT RANGE (Teams of four)
BURROUGHES & WATTS CUP

1947	Kynoch
1948	Twickenham
1949	Twickenham
1950	Worplesdon
1951	Borough of Wandsworth
1952	Ham and Petersham
1953	Worplesdon
1954	Lensbury and Britannic House
1955	Borough of Wandsworth
1956	Wimbledon Park
1957	East Bristol
1958	Lensbury and Britannic House
1959	Salisbury

(Teams of six)
"NEWS OF THE WORLD" CUP

1946	Falkirk Lord Roberts
1947	Perth City and County
1948	Edinburgh Citizens
1949	Lensbury and Britannic House
1950	Ham and Petersham
1951	Lensbury and Britannic House
1952	Borough of Wandsworth
1953	Lensbury and Britannic House
1954	Kynoch
1955	Wimbledon Park
1956	Lensbury and Britannic House
1957	Lytham St. Annes
1958	Kynoch
1959	Lensbury and Britannic House

Compiled by
Howard Bass

Editor: The Skater and Skier

Roller Skating

THE HISTORY OF ROLLER SKATING

Although a roller skate of sorts was previously invented by a Belgian, Joseph Merlin, in 1760, the first practical four-wheel skate was introduced by an American, James L. Plympton, in 1863. The original idea was nothing beyond providing a means for ice skaters to simulate their art and practise when there was no natural ice; but possibilities of developing the sport on a separate medium soon became apparent and, in 1866, Plympton himself opened the first successful public roller rink at Newport, Rhode Island.

The subsequent American invention of the more satisfactory Richardson ball-bearing skate in 1884 was another step forward. A boom on both sides of the Atlantic reached its zenith in 1910, when nearly every town seemed to have at least one rink and every available floor space, flat roofs included, seemed to be used at the slightest excuse. Charles B. Cochran, the impresario, controlled a large rink inside the Olympia, London, at this time.

The National Skating Association of Great Britain (instituted in 1879) assumed control of roller skating in 1893 in addition to its responsibilities to ice skating. The present N.S.A. chairman, R. D. Gilbey, and vice-chairman, L. C. Seagrave, are in fact both former national champions on rollers.

As on ice there are four major variations of the competitive sport—solo figure, pair, dance and speed.

The first British figure championship was won by W. Stanton in 1910 at Maida Vale and was open to men and women until 1939, since which time separate events for each have been organised and since the war Britain's most successful individual performers have been Donald Stirling and Albert Wilson in the men's contests and Jean Phethean and Maureen Jackson in the women's, Ken Byrne and Jean Phethean being the outstanding pair.

European championships were instituted at Stuttgart in 1937 and the first world figure championships were not held until 1947 in Washington, Donald Mounce (U.S.A.) and Ursula Wehrli (Switzerland) winning the men's and women's titles respectively and Fernand Leemans and Elvire Collin (Belgium) the pairs. On the last four occasions Germany has monopolised all three honours.

In roller dancing three of the six world championships so far held have been won by British couples—Ken Byrne with Jean Phethean in 1949, Ted Ellis with Marion Mercer in 1952 and Sidney and Patricia Cooper in 1958, with Germany, in this branch, too, providing the strongest opposition.

There are today twenty-five approved N.S.A. roller dance variations, grouped below according to the respective proficiency tests in which they are included:

Preliminary: Barn dance; glide waltz.
Third Class: Promenade two-step; spreadeagle waltz; collegiate.

Intermediate Second Class: Mohawk (cutaway) waltz; drop three waltz (serpentine); fourteen-step: foxtrot.
Second Class: Morris barn dance; staircase waltz; tango; kilian; blues.
Intermediate First Class: Eight-step waltz; drop three waltz; Johnson wave waltz; rocker foxtrot; bear change edge.
First Class: Paso doble; Westminster waltz; Iceland tango; Viennese waltz; Argentine tango; quickstep.

These dances vary to some degree from those used on ice, but the internationally recognised schedule of forty-one different figures is the same on both media.

A British speed championship over one mile was instituted in 1894 and won by C. J. Wilson, but it was not held again until started on an annual basis in 1910. World championships have been organised since 1937 and are now held over four distances for men—1,000, 5,000, 10,000 and 20,000 metres. Women's events, introduced in 1953, are held over three distances—500, 5,000 and 10,000 metres.

A glance at the records confirms a complete Italian superiority in this department, the men's best times being shared by G. Venanzi, L. Faggioli and V. Pelizzari and *all* the women's monopolised by A. Vianello.

There are more than four thousand roller rinks in America today and more than a hundred British rinks are officially listed by the N.S.A. The sport is also very widely practised in Australia, Belgium, Canada, Egypt, Eire, France, Germany, Holland, Italy, New Zealand, Portugal, South Africa, Spain and Switzerland. The number of those participating in the sport throughout the world is considerably higher than the number practising some of the sports at present included in the Olympic Games schedule and this is a state of affairs which causes deep if not bitter feeling among roller skating enthusiasts.

In 1907 the N.S.A. applied to the British Olympic Council for the sport's inclusion in the IVth Olympiad, which was held in London the following year. The application failed and the sport's world governing body, the *Fédération Internationale de Roller Skating,* has continually pressed hard, but in vain, ever since for this recognition.

WORLD FIGURE AND DANCE CHAMPIONSHIPS 1958–59

(Bologna, Italy, October 24–26, 1958)

MEN'S FIGURES

1. K. Losch (Germany)
2. D. Menegotto (Italy)
3. M. Schnelldorfer (Germany)
4. F. Villagrossi (Italy)

4 competitors

LADIES' FIGURES

1. M. Kilius (Germany)
2. G. Piglia (Italy)
3. U. Kitz (Germany)
4. M. Jackson (Great Britain)
5. S. Gardiner (Great Britain)
6. R. Mazzotti (Italy)

19 competitors

PAIRS

1. W. Mensching and R. Blumenberg (Germany)
2. L. Goyvaerts and J. Van de Zande (Belgium)
3. D. Fingarle and S. Schneider (Germany)
4. C. Preston and J. Loudwell (Great Britain)
5. F. Villagrossi and P. Bolla (Italy)
6. M. Cardena and E. Echevarrieta (Spain)

7 competitors

DANCE

1. S. Cooper and P. Cooper (Great Britain)
2. P. Kwiet and R. Paucka (Germany)
3. A. Moore and R. Pearce (Great Britain)
4. H. Burkhard and E. Thal (Germany)

4 competitors

WORLD AND EUROPEAN SPEED CHAMPIONSHIPS 1958-59

(Finale Ligure, Italy, September 6–7, 1958)

MEN

1,000 metres	S. Rossi (Italy)
5,000 metres	L. Faggioli (Italy)
10,000 metres	S. Rossi (Italy)
20,000 metres	L. Lori (Italy)

LADIES

500 metres	A. Vianello (Italy)
5,000 metres	A. Vianello (Italy)
10,000 metres	M. Danisi (Italy)

BRITISH FIGURE AND DANCE CHAMPIONSHIPS 1958–59

MEN'S FIGURES

(Birch Park, Manchester, March 22, 1959)

1. A. Wilson
2. D. Smalley

2 competitors

LADIES' FIGURES

(Birch Park, Manchester, April 19, 1959)

1. M. Jackson	4. L. Maaren
2. S. Date	5. L. Sadler
3. I. Farthing	6. J. Davenport

9 competitors

PAIRS

(Herne Bay, April 4, 1959)

1. C. Preston and J. Loudwell
2. C. Smith and B. Sinclair
3. D. Sweasey and C. Sharp
4. R. Balls and J. Johns
5. B. Colclough and P. Colclough
6. G. Chase and V. Stott

6 competitors

DANCE

(Brixton, May 18, 1959)

1. S. Cooper and P. Cooper
2. A. Moore and R. Pearce
3. S. Hill and P. Holden
4. B. Colclough and P. Colclough
5. C. Smith and E. Sinclair
6. R. Gibbs and M. Churchyard

10 competitors

BRITISH SPEED CHAMPIONSHIPS 1958-59

MEN

1 mile	J. Lipyeat	3 m. 57.4 s.
Herne Bay		April 18, 1959
5 miles	L. Eason	15 m. 36.4 s.
Birmingham		February 28, 1959
½ mile	L. Eason	1 m. 42.4 s.
Leicester		December 6, 1958

LADIES

½ mile	P. Harris	1 m. 48.2 s.
Leicester		December 6, 1958
¼ mile	C. Ronaldson	1 m. 3.0s
Herne Bay		February 21, 1959

ROLLER SKATING QUIZ

1. Name the world controlling organisation in the sport.

*

2. Has a mile on rollers ever been skated in less than two and a half minutes?

*

3. Why is the salchow jump so called?

*

4. Which British champion's parents were both professional instructors?

*

5. How much should a roller hockey ball weigh?

*

6. The N.S.A. preliminary roller dance test requires a certain proficiency in each of two dances. What are they?

QUIZ ANSWERS

1. Fédération Internationale de Roller Skating (F.I.R.S.). 2. Yes; the world record is 2 minutes 22.5 seconds, set up by L. Faggioli (Italy) in 1957 at Ferrare. 3. It was originated by Ulrich Salchow of Sweden. 4. Maureen Jackson, daughter of Brian and Mary Jackson. 5. Five and a half ounces. 6. The barn dance and glide waltz.

ROLLER HOCKEY

Hockey on roller skates started developing quite rapidly at the beginning of this century and the first rules were passed in 1913 by the sport's governing body in Great Britain, now known as the National Roller Hockey Association.

The first official European championship was held at Herne Bay in 1926. This and every subsequent pre-war meeting was won by Great Britain. In 1936 the world championship was instituted and staged in conjunction with the ninth European contest at Stuttgart.

When, after the war, international hockey was resumed at Lisbon in 1947, Britain lost her supremacy to Portugal, the present holder and winner of seven post-war world championships.

In Britain the game has been particularly popular in Kent and Essex and Herne Bay has tended to become recognised to British roller hockey what Lord's is to cricket.

The duration of a match is a quarter of an hour each way. A team comprises five players—goalkeeper, back, half-back, right forward and left forward—plus one reserve who may be substituted during the course of a game.

There is no off-side and play continues in the area immediately behind the goals, as in ice hockey. When the ball leaves the playing area a free hit is awarded to the team opposing the last striker of the ball.

The ball is made of composition compressed cork, measures nine inches in circumference and weighs five and a half ounces. It is an infringement to loft the ball higher than six feet when a shot is played except when two players strike it simultaneously or when the goalkeeper does so when making a save with his hands, legs or feet.

The goalkeeper is the only player allowed to kick or handle the ball, but he may not catch it, nor must his hands or any part of his body other than his feet be in contact with the floor when making a save. High sticks, pushing, barging, body-checking, back-tackling and tripping are against the rules.

The stick, similar in shape to that used in field hockey, is flat both sides and limited to eighteen ounces in weight. Special protective clothing, other than knee-pads, is not normally worn.

Bibliography: *This Skating Age* (Howard Bass), *N.S.A. Roller Dance Skating Manual, N.S.A. Handbook, The Skater and Skier* magazine.

WORLD AND EUROPEAN ROLLER HOCKEY CHAMPIONSHIP

(Oporto, Portugal, May 24-31, 1958)

FINAL TABLE

	P	W	D	L	F	A	Pts
1. Portugal	9	8	1	0	61	7	17
2. Spain	9	6	3	0	70	13	15
3. Italy	9	7	1	1	38	10	15
4. Holland	9	6	0	3	34	37	12
5. England	9	5	0	4	46	32	10
6. Belgium	9	3	1	5	26	23	7
7. Germany	9	3	0	6	30	36	6
8. Switzerland	9	2	1	6	16	30	5
9. France	9	1	1	7	22	45	3
10. Denmark	9	0	0	9	4	114	0

WORLD ROLLER HOCKEY CHAMPIONS

		Venue			Venue
1936	Great Britain	Stuttgart	1951	Spain	Barcelona
1937	Great Britain	Herne Bay	1952	Portugal	Oporto
1938	Great Britain	Antwerp	1953	Italy	Geneva
1939	Great Britain	Montreux	1954	Spain	Barcelona
1947	Portugal	Lisbon	1955	Spain	Milan
1948	Portugal	Montreux	1956	Portugal	Oporto
1949	Portugal	Lisbon	1958	Portugal	Oporto
1950	Portugal	Milan			

ROLLER SKATING QUIZ

1. How many Olympic titles are contested in roller skating?

2. Are substitutes allowed in roller hockey?

3. Approximately how many roller rinks are there in England—twenty, thirty, fifty, or a hundred?

4. When and by whom was the four-wheel roller skate invented?

QUIZ ANSWERS

1. None. Efforts have been made for more than fifty years to gain Olympic recognition, so far without success. 2. The rules provide for one reserve player on each side, who may be substituted during a match provided the referee is notified. 3. More than a hundred. 4. In 1863 by James L. Plympton.

WORLD MEN'S FIGURE CHAMPIONS

			Venue
1947	D. Mounce	(U.S.A.)	Washington
1949	K. Peter	(Switzerland)	Barcelona
1951	F. Stein	(Germany)	Turin
1952	F. Stein	(Germany)	Dortmund
1955	F. Ningel	(Germany)	Barcelona
1956	F. Ningel	(Germany)	Barcelona
1958	K. Losch	(Germany)	Bologna

WORLD LADIES' FIGURE CHAMPIONS

			Venue
1947	U. Wehrli	(Switzerland)	Washington
1949	F. Rio	(Italy)	Barcelona
1951	F. Rio	(Italy)	Turin
1952	L. Cadenbach	(Germany)	Dortmund
1955	H. Kienzle	(Germany)	Barcelona
1956	R. Blumenberg	(Germany)	Barcelona
1958	M. Kilius	(Germany)	Bologna

WORLD PAIR CHAMPIONS

			Venue
1947	F. Leemans and E. Collin	(Belgium)	Washington
1949	K. Byrne and J. Phethean	(Great Britain)	Barcelona
1951	P. Falk and R. Baran	(Germany)	Turin
1952	G. Koch and S. Knake	(Germany)	Dortmund
1955	G. Koch and S. Knake	(Germany)	Barcelona
1956	G. Koch and S. Knake	(Germany)	Barcelona
1958	W. Mensching and R. Blumenberg	(Germany)	Bologna

WORLD DANCE CHAMPIONS

			Venue
1947	F. Ludwig and B. Gallagher	(U.S.A.)	Washington
1949	K. Byrne and J. Phethean	(Great Britain)	Barcelona
1952	E. Ellis and M. Mercer	(Great Britain)	Dortmund
1955	K. Beyer and M. Schafer	(Germany)	Barcelona
1956	G. Koch and S. Knake	(Germany)	Barcelona
1958	S. Cooper and P. Cooper	(Great Britain)	Bologna

EUROPEAN MEN'S FIGURE CHAMPIONS

			Venue
1937	F. Handel	(Ger.)	Stuttgart
1938	F. Handel	(Ger.)	Manchester
1946	F. Leemans	(Bel.)	Antwerp
1948	K. Peter	(Swit.)	San Remo
1950	L. Muller	(Ger.)	London
1954	F. Stein	(Ger.)	Karlsruhe
1957	F. Ningel	(Ger.)	Bologna

EUROPEAN LADIES' FIGURE CHAMPIONS

			Venue
1937	L. Wahl	(Ger.)	Stuttgart
1938	L. Wahl	(Ger.)	Manchester
1946	U. Wehrli	(Swit.)	Antwerp
1948	F. Rio	(Italy)	San Remo
1950	I. Fischlein	(Ger.)	London
1954	L. Cadenbach	(Ger.)	Karlsruhe
1957	R. Blumenberg	(Ger.)	Bologna

EUROPEAN PAIR CHAMPIONS

			Venue
1937	B. Walter and L. Roth	(Germany)	Stuttgart
1938	K. Waldeck and M. Lauer	(Germany)	Manchester
1946	K. Peter and G. Muller	(Switzerland)	Antwerp
1948	K. Byrne and J. Phethean	(Great Britain)	San Remo
1950	P. Falk and R. Baran	(Germany)	London
1954	G. Koch and S. Knake	(Germany)	Karlsruhe
1957	W. Mensching and R. Blumenberg	(Germany)	Bologna

EUROPEAN DANCE CHAMPIONS

			Venue
1950	K. Byrne and J. Phethean	(Great Britain)	London
1954	G. Koch and S. Knake	(Germany)	Karlsruhe
1957	M. Whelan and M. Grainger	(Great Britain)	Bologna

BRITISH MEN'S FIGURE CHAMPIONS

		Venue			Venue
1910	W. Stanton	Maida Vale	1936	H. Lidstone	Birmingham
1911	W. Stanton	Holland Park	1937	H. Lidstone	Birmingham
1912	D. Resta	Holland Park	1938	H. Lidstone	Forest Gate
1913	W. Stanton	Holland Park	1939	H. Lidstone	Birmingham
1914	W. Stanton	Holland Park	1947	D. Stirling	Alexandra Palace
1921	*Miss Lodge	Holland Park	1948	D. Stirling	Batley
1924	A. Buller	Holland Park	1949	D. Stirling	Cricklewood
1925	A. Buller	Holland Park	1950	D. Stirling	Bradford
1927	A. Buller	Holland Park	1951	D. Stirling	Bradford
1929	A. Buller	Alexandra Palace	1952	A. Wilson	Bradford
1930	R. Gilbey	Alexandra Palace	1954	A. Wilson	Manchester
1931	R. Gilbey	Alexandra Palace	1955	W. Tingle	Cricklewood
1932	L. Seagrave	Alexandra Palace	1956	A. Wilson	Brixton
1933	R. Gilbey	Forest Gate	1957	A. Wilson	Brixton
1934	R. Gilbey	Forest Gate	1958	A. Wilson	Brixton
1935	H. Lidstone	Forest Gate	1959	A. Wilson	Manchester

* The event was open to ladies before 1939.

BRITISH LADIES' FIGURE CHAMPIONS

		Venue			Venue
1939	S. Westcott	Birmingham	1953	S. Gardiner	Alexandra Palace
1946	J. Phethean	Birch Park	1954	M. Jackson	Manchester
1947	J. Phethean	Herne Bay	1955	M. Jackson	Bradford
1948	J. Phethean	Herne Bay	1956	M. Jackson	Birch Park
1949	J. Phethean	Herne Bay	1957	M. Jackson	Birmingham
1950	J. Phethean	Bradford	1958	M. Jackson	Alexandra Palace
1951	J. Phethean	Bradford	1959	M. Jackson	Birch Park
1952	J. Phethean	Bradford			

BRITISH PAIR CHAMPIONS

		Venue
1939	J. Hargreaves and R. Peel	Batley
1946	K. Byrne and J. Phethean	Alexandra Palace
1947	W. Drummond and V. Lea	Alexandra Palace
1948	K. Byrne and J. Phethean	Herne Bay
1949	K. Byrne and J. Phethean	Herne Bay
1950	K. Byrne and J. Phethean	Forest Gate
1951	K. Byrne and J. Phethean	Birmingham
1952	K. Byrne and J. Phethean	Leicester
1953	S. Hill and P. Holden	Birmingham
1954	A. Wilson and S. Anderson	Birmingham
1955	A. Wilson and S. Anderson	Manchester
1956	S. Hill and P. Holden	Birmingham
1957	S. Hill and P. Holden	Leicester
1958	C. Preston and J. Loudwell	Herne Bay
1959	C. Preston and J. Loudwell	Herne Bay

BRITISH DANCE CHAMPIONS

		Venue
1922	J. Blaver and J. Garth	Holland Park
1923	J. Blaver and J. Garth	Holland Park
1924	J. Blaver and J. Craven	Holland Park
1925	J. Blaver and G. Hogg	Holland Park
1926	J. Blaver and G. Hogg	Alexandra Palace
1927	J. Blaver and G. Hogg	Holland Park
1929	E. Clarke and M. Beesley	Alexandra Palace
1930	E. Clarke and M. Beesley	Alexandra Palace
1931	E. Clarke and M. Beesley	East Ham
1933	H. Lidstone and J. Lidstone	Cricklewood
1934	H. Lidstone and J. Lidstone	Forest Gate
1935	H. Lidstone and J. Lidstone	Forest Gate
1936	H. Lidstone and J. Lidstone	Birmingham
1937	E. Clarke and J. Lancaster	Birmingham
1938	F. Burrows and M. May	Birmingham
1939	F. Burrows and M. May	Birmingham
1946	K. Byrne and J. Phethean	Alexandra Palace
1947	E. Brodie and J. Mount	Batley
1948	K. Byrne and J. Phethean	Middlesbrough
1949	K. Byrne and J. Phethean	Forest Gate
1950	K. Byrne and J. Phethean	Leicester
1951	E. Ellis and M. Mercer	Bradford
1952	E. Ellis and M. Mercer	Bradford
1953	E. Ellis and M. Mercer	Alexandra Palace
1954	S. Hill and P. Holden	Brixton
1955	I. Tomkins and M. Warboys	Alexandra Palace
1956	M. Whelan and M. Grainger	Brixton
1957	M. Whelan and M. Grainger	Brixton
1958	S. Cooper and P. Cooper	Brixton
1959	S. Cooper and P. Cooper	Brixton

WORLD MEN'S SPEED CHAMPIONS

*On track; remainder on road

1,000 METRES

			Venue
1937	L. Fichaux	(France)	Monza
1938	L. Fichaux	(France)	Ferrare
1938	A. Garagnani	(Italy)	*Wembley
1948	L. Lazzari	(Italy)	Monfalcone

246

Year	Name	Country	Venue
1949	J. Weynen	(Belgium)	Ferrare
1949	J. Weynen	(Belgium)	*Lisbon
1951	G. Venanzi	(Italy)	Monfalcone
1953	G. Venanzi	(Italy)	Venice
1954	L. Cavallini	(Italy)	*Bari
1956	L. Cavallini	(Italy)	*Barcelona
1958	S. Rossi	(Italy)	Finale Ligure

5,000 METRES

Year	Name	Country	Venue
1938	W. Ross	(Great Britain)	*Wembley
1948	G. Venanzi	(Italy)	Monfalcone
1949	L. Lazzari	(Italy)	Ferrare
1949	M. Meeus	(Belgium)	*Lisbon
1951	G. Venanzi	(Italy)	Monfalcone
1953	G. Venanzi	(Italy)	Venice
1954	L. Lori	(Italy)	*Bari
1956	L. Cavallini	(Italy)	*Barcelona
1958	L. Faggioli	(Italy)	Finale Ligure

10,000 METRES

Year	Name	Country	Venue
1937	R. Brousteau	(France)	Monza
1938	L. Fichaux	(France)	Ferrare
1938	W. Ross	(Great Britain)	*Wembley
1948	G. Venanzi	(Italy)	Monfalcone
1949	G. Fasana	(Italy)	Ferrare
1949	A. Taeymans	(Belgium)	*Lisbon
1951	L. Lazzari	(Italy)	Monfalcone
1953	S. Rossi	(Italy)	Venice
1954	L. Lori	(Italy)	*Bari
1956	S. Rossi	(Italy)	*Barcelona
1958	S. Rossi	(Italy)	Finale Ligure

20,000 METRES

Year	Name	Country	Venue
1937	L. Fichaux	(France)	Monza
1938	L. Fichaux	(France)	Ferrare
1938	A. Cooper	(Great Britain)	*Wembley
1948	L. Lazzari	(Italy)	Monfalcone
1949	L. Lazzari	(Italy)	Ferrare
1949	M. Meeus	(Belgium)	*Lisbon
1951	L. Lazzari	(Italy)	Monfalcone
1953	G. Caroli	(Italy)	Venice
1954	L. Lori	(Italy)	*Bari
1956	S. Rossi	(Italy)	*Barcelona
1958	L. Lori	(Italy)	Finale Ligure

WORLD LADIES' SPEED CHAMPIONS

(*On track; remainder on road)

500 METRES

Year	Name	Country	Venue
1953	A. Vianello	(Italy)	Venice
1954	V. Lazzari	(Italy)	*Bari
1956	A. Vianello	(Italy)	*Barcelona
1958	A. Vianello	(Italy)	Finale Ligure

5,000 METRES

Year	Name	Country	Venue
1953	V. Lazzari	(Italy)	Venice
1954	A. Tassi	(Italy)	*Bari

10,000 METRES

Year	Name	Country	Venue
1953	A. Gobitta	(Italy)	Venice
1954	A. Vianello	(Italy)	*Bari
1956	A. Vianello	(Italy)	*Barcelona
1958	M. Danisi	(Italy)	Finale Ligure

BRITISH MEN'S SPEED CHAMPIONS

ONE MILE

1894	C. Wilson
1910	H. O'Hagan
1911	D. Swain
1912	S. Cole
1913	W. Bowley
1914	G. Clarkson
1921	T. Wilson
1922	O. Lerwill
1923	T. Wilson
1924	B. Lee
1925	B. Lee
1926	R. Symondson
1927	C. Bush
1928	C. Bush
1929	J. Reed
1930	J. Reed
1931	H. Wilkinson
1932	J. Reed
1933	J. Reed
1934	D. Howard
1935	H. Wilkinson
1936	H. Wilkinson
1937	J. Reed
1938	J. Robbins
1939	F. Lamb
1946	S. Hartigan
1947	F. Lamb
1948	A. Martin
1949	D. Hill
1950	D. Hill
1951	D. Hill
1952	D. Hill
1953	J. Whatley
1954	A. Cattee
1955	G. Wright
1956	L. Eason
1957	J. Whatley
1958	L. Woodley
1959	J. Lipyeat

FIVE MILES

L. Meredith
L. Meredith
A. Eglington
G. Clarkson
G. Clarkson
T. Wilson
T. Wilson
T. Wilson
B. Lee
B. Lee
R. Symondson
J. Spry
J. Spry
J. Reed
J. Weatherburn
E. Stumbke
J. Reed
H. Wilkinson
H. Wilkinson
H. Wilkinson
J. Reed
J. Robbins
A. Cooper
S. Hartigan
S. Hartigan
A. Martin
D. Hill
J. Reeves
J. Whatley
P. Wimble
D. Hill
R. Parsons
G. Wright
G. Stead
L. Eason
G. Wright
L. Eason

HALF MILE

B. Lee
B. Lee
R. Symondson
J. Weatherburn
J. Weatherburn
J. Reed
A. McLagan
J. Weatherburn
E. Stumbke
E. Stumbke
E. Stumbke
H. Wilkinson
P. Walters
J. Reed
D. Jackson
D. Jackson
P. Walters
G. Sanders
A. Martin
D. Brown
D. Brown
D. Brown
J. Reeves
J. Reeves
D. Hill
D. Hill
C. Applebee
L. Woodley
L. Eason

BRITISH LADIES' SPEED CHAMPIONS

HALF MILE

Year	Name	Year	Name	Year	Name
1927	H. Meakin	1936	D. Janes	1951	Y. Brod
1928	F. Arnold	1937	V. Kirby	1952	M. Stewart
1929	F. Arnold	1938	V. Kirby	1953	I. Turner
1930	E. Morgan	1939	V. Kirby	1954	O. Hoyle
1931	W. Davies	1946	V. Kirby	1955	S. Gardiner
1932	W. Davies	1947	J. Gillard	1956	P. Harris
1933	A. Webb	1948	V. Kirby	1957	P. Harris
1934	A. Webb	1949	Y. Brod	1958	P. Harris
1935	D. Janes	1950	Y. Brod	1959	P. Harris

QUARTER MILE

Year	Name	Year	Name	Year	Name
1950	Y. Brod	1954	S. Gardiner	1958	C. Ronaldson
1951	L. Ashby	1955	S. Gardiner	1959	C. Ronaldson
1952	Y. Brod	1956	P. Harris		
1953	J. Robinson	1957	P. Harris		

WORLD MEN'S SPEED RECORDS

Metres	Name	Country	h.	m.	s.	Year	Venue
500	G. Venanzi	(Italy)			46.4	1948	Udine
1,000	L. Faggioli	(Italy)		1	30.0	1957	Ferrare
1,500	L. Faggioli	(Italy)		2	12.4	1957	Ferrare
5,000	L. Faggioli	(Italy)		7	44.9	1957	Ferrare
10,000	G. Venanzi	(Italy)		16	54.5	1947	Campoformido
15,000	G. Venanzi	(Italy)		26	16.7	1947	Campoformido
20,000	V. Pelizzari	(Italy)		33	30.0	1956	Ferrare
25,000	V. Pelizzari	(Italy)		44	40.1	1956	Ferrare
30,000	V. Pelizzari	(Italy)		54	50.9	1956	Ferrare
50,000	G. Venanzi	(Italy)	1	43	53.2	1948	Udine
100,000	G. Venanzi	(Italy)	4	22	42.2	1948	Udine

Miles	Name	Country	m.	s.	Year	Venue
1/2	G. Venanzi	(Italy)		37.6	1955	Ferrare
3/4	L. Faggioli	(Italy)	1	13.6	1957	Ferrare
1	L. Faggioli	(Italy)	2	22.5	1957	Ferrare
3	L. Faggioli	(Italy)	7	28.4	1957	Ferrare
5	L. Faggioli	(Italy)	14	15.1	1957	Ferrare
10	V. Pelizzari	(Italy)	29	25.1	1956	Ferrare
15	V. Pelizzari	(Italy)	43	9.7	1956	Ferrare
20	V. Pelizzari	(Italy)	57	49.3	1956	Ferrare

WORLD LADIES' SPEED RECORDS

Metres	Name	Country	h.	m.	s.	Year	Venue
500	A. Vianello	(Italy)			49.6	1955	Ferrare
1,000	A. Vianello	(Italy)		1	42.7	1955	Ferrare
1,500	A. Vianello	(Italy)		2	38.3	1955	Ferrare
5,000	A. Vianello	(Italy)		9	20.8	1955	Ferrare
10,000	A. Vianello	(Italy)		18	55.6	1955	Ferrare
15,000	A. Vianello	(Italy)		28	45.4	1955	Ferrare
20,000	A. Vianello	(Italy)		39	30.4	1955	Ferrare
25,000	A. Vianello	(Italy)		50	7.5	1955	Ferrare
30,000	A. Vianello	(Italy)	1	0	36.5	1955	Ferrare

Miles	Name	Country	h.	m.	s.	Year	Venue
1/2	A. Vianello	(Italy)			40.6	1955	Ferrare
3/4	A. Vianello	(Italy)		1	23.4	1955	Ferrare
1	A. Vianello	(Italy)		2	50.1	1955	Ferrare
3	A. Vianello	(Italy)		9	2.0	1955	Ferrare
5	A. Vianello	(Italy)		15	11.1	1955	Ferrare
10	A. Vianello	(Italy)		31	16.2	1955	Ferrare
15	A. Vianello	(Italy)		48	16.1	1955	Ferrare
20	A. Vianello	(Italy)	1	5	18.0	1955	Ferrare

BRITISH MEN'S SPEED RECORDS

Miles	Name	m.	s.	Year	Venue
1/2	W. Davie	1	25.6	1929	Brixton
1	A. Eglington	2	48.4	1911	Olympia
2	A. Eglington	5	55.8	1911	Olympia
3	L. Goodchild	8	58.0	1956	Birmingham
4	L. Goodchild	11	58.8	1956	Birmingham
5	L. Goodchild	14	57.0	1956	Birmingham
6	O. Lerwill	18	24.0	1922	Holland Park
7	O. Lerwill	21	24.0	1922	Holland Park
8	O. Lerwill	24	29.0	1922	Holland Park
9	O. Lerwill	27	38.0	1922	Holland Park
10	O. Lerwill	30	49.0	1922	Holland Park
15	O. Lerwill	46	52.0	1922	Holland Park

BRITISH LADIES' SPEED RECORDS

Miles	Name	m.	s.	Year	Venue
1/2	P. Kirkham		46.0	1952	Birmingham
3/4	P. Kirkham	1	31.4	1952	Birmingham
1	P. Kirkham	3	4.2	1952	Birmingham
2	P. Harris	6	23.6	1956	Birmingham
3	P. Harris	9	35.0	1956	Birmingham
5	P. Harris	16	0.0	1956	Birmingham
10	P. Harris	32	18.2	1956	Birmingham
15	P. Harris	48	58.4	1956	Birmingham

ROLLER SKATING QUIZ

1. Which nation holds the greatest number of world speed records?

*

2. Who created the skating tango?

3. How many roller rinks are there in the London postal area?

QUIZ ANSWERS

1. Italy. 2. Trudi Harris and Paul Kreckow. 3. Five, at Alexandra Palace, Battersea Park, Brixton, Cricklewood and Forest Gate.

Rowing

Compiled by **R.D. Burnell**

Rowing Correspondent: The Times

ROWING QUIZ

1. One man once entered twice for the same event at Henley. How did that occur?

*

2. Two brothers once rowed against each other in the Boat Race. Who were they?

*

3. How long does it take to build a racing eight?

*

4. Who wrote: "There is nothing—absolutely nothing —half so worth doing as simply messing about in boats."

*

5. Who was the first World Professional Sculling Champion?

*

6. Which is the oldest rowing club in England?

*

7. What is the largest number of events ever contested by one man at Henley Regatta?

QUIZ ANSWERS

1. In 1866 W. B. Woodgate entered for the Silver Goblets twice, once under his own name in partnership with E. L. Corrie, and once as "Wat Bradford" with M. M. Brown. The second entry was disallowed, and led to the framing of the rule "No one shall enter twice for the same race". 2. T. B. Etherington-Smith (Oxford) and R. B. Etherington-Smith (Cambridge) 1900. 3. In 1934 the late Bossie Phelps built an eight for Oxford in 3 days 21 hours—70 hours' working time. 4. Kenneth Grahame—"The Wind in the Willows". 5. C. Campbell (Westminster) in 1831. 6. Generally accepted as Leander Club, probably founded in 1818. 7. In 1863 W. B. Woodgate entered for the Grand, Ladies', Stewards', Visitors', Goblets and Diamonds. He won the Visitors' and Goblets.

GOVERNING BODIES

Fédération Internationale des Sociétés d'Aviron (F.I.S.A.). Amateur Rowing Association. *Chairman:* G. O. Nickalls. *Hon. Sec.:* J. H. Page, O.B.E., The Tower, The Terrace, Barnes, S.W.13.

Women's Amateur Rowing Association. *Chairman:* Miss A. C. Gentry. *Hon. Sec.:* Miss H. B. Freestone, 29 Belsize Sq., N.W.3.

Scottish Amateur Rowing Association. *President:* J. N. Fenton. *Hon. Sec.:* G. A. Hunter, 7 Pitt St., Portobello, Midlothian.

International rowing is governed by F.I.S.A., which at present has its headquarters in Switzerland, and which consists of representatives of the national governing bodies of affiliated countries. F.I.S.A. organizes the Olympic and European Championship regattas.

In the United Kingdom the Scottish and Women's A.R.As are independent and self-governing; but since F.I.S.A. recognizes only one governing body for each member country, Scottish and Women's entries for F.I.S.A. international regattas are sponsored by the A.R.A., which itself consists of representatives of certain "nominating clubs"—the original founders of the Association—and of elected representatives of clubs grouped in roughly geographical areas.

EUROPEAN CHAMPIONSHIPS

For the first time, in 1958, the European Championships were held behind the so-called Iron Curtain, at Poznan, in Poland. Here they were staged, with great success and efficiency, on an artificial lagoon. For the second year in succession Germany was supreme, reaching all seven finals, and winning three of them. For this purpose East and West Germany were combined. The Eights were won by Italy, with a crew rigged in the new manner recently introduced by them, with Bow, 4, 5 and stroke on one side, and 2, 3, 6 and 7 on the other side of the boat. D. A. T. Leadley and C. G. V. Davidge, of Great Britain, defending the Pair-oar title which they won in 1957, unfortunately suffered from gastric troubles, as did certain other competitors, including the British coxed and coxswainless fours, and finished fourth.

Results

Eights: Italy 6 min. 19.5 sec., U.S.A. 6 min. 22.7 sec., U.S.S.R. 6 min. 25.6 sec., Czechoslovakia 6 min. 27.5 sec., Germany 6 min. 29.1 sec., Switzerland 6 min. 31.4 sec. *Coxswainless Fours:* Germany 7 min. 0.8 sec., Roumania 7 min. 7 sec., Czechoslovakia 7 min. 8.5 sec., Denmark 7 min. 11.4 sec., Great Britain 7 min. 12.1 sec., Poland 7 min. 17.9 sec. *Coxed Fours:* Germany 7 min. 29.3 sec., Roumania 7 min. 34.1 sec., Yugoslavia 7 min. 34.1 sec., Italy 7 min. 37.8 sec., Poland 7 min. 39.2 sec., Switzerland 7 min. 40.6 sec. *Coxswainless Pairs:* Finland 7 min. 52.4 sec., Germany 7 min. 53.8 sec., Roumania 8 min. 2.5 sec., Great Britain 8 min. 2.7 sec., U.S.S.R. 8 min. 12.6 sec., Poland 8 min. 20.7 sec. *Coxed Pairs:* Germany 8 min. 11.8 sec., Italy 8 min. 17.9 sec., Switzerland 8 min. 22.7 sec., Roumania 8 min. 23.8 sec., U.S.S.R. 8 min. 26.9 sec., Finland scratched. *Double Sculls:* U.S.S.R. 7 min. 10.7 sec., France 7 min. 13.2 sec., Germany 7 min. 16.5 sec., Switzerland 7 min. 23.8 sec., Belgium 7 min. 25.3 sec., Poland 7 min. 31.7 sec. *Single Sculls:* Australia 7 min. 58.7 sec., Germany 8 min. 6 sec., U.S.S.R. 8 min. 11 sec., Czechoslovakia 8 min. 12.6 sec., Holland 8 min. 17.6 sec., Austria 8 min. 22.1 sec.

BRITISH EMPIRE AND COMMONWEALTH GAMES

The British Empire and Commonwealth Games Regatta was held on Lake Padarn, in North Wales, in the town of Llanberis, beneath the foot of Snowdon. A splendid 2,000-metre four-lane course was laid out on the lake, with lines of floating buoys and overhead guide markers slung on cables. For most of the practice period the weather was good, but during the regatta itself a strong wind sprang up, and the course, at times, was very rough. Indeed the floating judges'-box was in danger of capsizing, shortly after it had been visited by H.R.H. The Duke of Edinburgh. Unfortunately the control centre of the public-address system was put out of action at the same time, which caused considerable inconvenience.

Attendances at this regatta were disappointingly low, due to its inaccessibility from Cardiff, the main centre of the Games, and to inadequate publicity. Nevertheless there was some first-class racing and plenty of surprises. The chief of these was the failure of the reputedly strong Canadian contingent, who seemed unable to cope with the rough conditions. Their eight, which was substantially the same as that which finished second in the 1956 Olympics in Melbourne, just won from Australia, but, though equally favoured, both their fours lost to England. As England also won the Double Sculls they were the most successful country competing at Padarn, which was quite contrary to expectations.

Results

Eights: Canada 5 min. 55.1 sec., Australia 5 min. 56.1 sec., England 6 min. 10.2 sec., Scotland 6 min. 15.5 sec. *Coxswainless Fours:* England 6 min. 34.4 sec., Canada 6 min. 38. 9 sec., Wales 6 min. 47.9 sec., Australia 7 min. 11.7 sec. *Coxed Fours:* England 6 min. 47.6 sec., Canada 6 min. 53.7 sec., Australia, New Zealand (no times). *Coxswainless Pairs:* New Zealand 7 min. 11 sec., England, Australia, Wales (no times). *Double Sculls:* England 6 min. 56.4 sec., Australia 7 min. 1.4 sec., New Zealand, Canada (no times). *Single Sculls:* Australia 7 min. 20.1 sec., New Zealand 7 min. 23.9 sec., England 7 min. 26.8 sec., South Africa 7 min. 33.3 sec.

OLYMPIC REGATTA RESULTS

	Venue	Coxed Fours	Coxless Pairs	Single Sculls	Coxed Pairs	Coxless Fours	Double Sculls	Eights
1908	*Gt. Britain	—	Gt. Britain	Gt. Britain 9.41·0	—	Gt. Britain 8.34·0	—	Gt. Britain 7.52·0
1912	Stockholm	Germany 6.59·4	—	Gt. Britain 7.47·0	—	—	—	Gt. Britain 6.15·0
1920	Antwerp	Switzerland 6.54·0	—	U.S.A. 7.35·0	Italy 7.56·0	—	U.S.A. 7.09·0	U.S.A. 6.02·6
1924	Paris	Switzerland 7.18·4	Holland 8.19·4	Gt. Britain 7.49·2	Switzerland 8.39·1	Gt. Britain 7.08·6	U.S.A. 6.34·0	U.S.A. 6.33·4
1928	Amsterdam	Italy 6.47·8	—	Australia 7.11·0	Switzerland 7.42·6	Gt. Britain 6.36·0	U.S.A. 6.41·4	U.S.A. 6.03·2
1932	Los Angeles	Germany 7.19·0	Gt. Britain 8.00·0	Australia 7.44·4	U.S.A. 8.25·8	Gt. Britain 6.58·2	U.S.A. 7.17·4	U.S.A. 6.37·6
1936	Berlin	Germany 7.16·2	Germany 8.16·1	Germany 8.21·5	Germany 8.46·9	Germany 7.01·8	Gt. Britain 7.20·8	U.S.A. 6.25·4
1948	†Gt. Britain	U.S.A. 6.50·3	Gt. Britain 7.21·1	Australia 7.24·4	Denmark 8.00·5	Italy 6.39·0	Gt. Britain 6.51·3	U.S.A. 6.56·7
1952	Finland	Czechoslovakia 7.33·4	U.S.A. 8.20·7	U.S.S.R. 8.12·8	France 8.28·6	Yugoslavia 7.16·0	Argentina 7.32·5	U.S.A. 6.25·9
1956	Ballarat	Italy 7.19·4	U.S.A. 7.55·4	U.S.S.R. 8.26·1	U.S.A. 8.26·1	Canada 7.08·8	U.S.S.R. 7.02·4	U.S.A. 6.35·2

The Olympic regattas are held over a 2,000-metre course.

* In 1908 the course was 1½ miles upstream, at Henley.

† In 1948 the course was 1,880 metres upstream, at Henley, which was considered to be equivalent to 2,000 metres in still water.

Winning British Crews

1908. *Eights:* Leander Club—A. C. Gladstone *bow*, F. S. Kelly, B. C. Johnstone, Guy Nickalls, C. D. Burnell, R. H. Sanderson, R. B. Etherington-Smith, H. C. Bucknall *stroke*, G. S. Maclagan *cox*. *Coxless Fours:* Magdalen Coll. Oxf.—C. R. Cudmore *bow*, J. A. Gillan, D. Mackinnon, J. R. Somers-Smith *stroke*. *Coxless Pairs:* J. R. K. Fenning and G. L. Thompson. *Single Sculls:* H. T. Blackstaffe.

1912. *Eights:* Leander Club—E. R. Burgess *bow*, S. E. Swann, L. G. Wormald, E. D. Horsfall, J. A. Gillan, A. S. Garton, A. G. Kirby, P. Fleming *stroke*, H. B. Wells *cox*. *Single Sculls:* W. D. Kinnear.

1924. *Coxless Fours:* Third Trinity B.C. Cam.—C. R. M. Ely *bow*, J. A. Macnabb, R. E. Morrison, T. R. B. Sanders *stroke*. *Single Sculls:* J. Beresford jun.

1928. *Coxless Fours:* First Trinity B.C. Cam.—E. V. Bevan *bow*, R. Beesley, M. H. Warriner, J. G. H. Lander *stroke*.

1932. *Coxless Fours:* R. D. George *bow*, J. Beresford jun., H. R. A. Edwards, J. C. Badcock *stroke*. *Coxless Pair-Oar:* H. R. A. Edwards and L. Clive.

1936. *Double Sculls:* J. Beresford jun. and L. F. Southwood.

1948. *Coxless Pairs-Oar:* W. G. R. M. Laurie and J. H. T. Wilson. *Double Sculls:* B. H. T. Bushnell and R. D. Burnell.

248

WINNERS OF THE EUROPEAN CHAMPIONSHIPS

	Venue	Coxed Fours	Coxless Pairs	Single Sculls	Coxed Pairs	Coxless Fours	Double Sculls	Eights
1893	Orta (Italy)	Switzerland	—	Belgium	—	—	—	France
1894	Macon	France	—	France	Belgium	—	—	France
1895	Ostend	France	—	Belgium	France	—	—	France
1896	Geneva	France	—	Switzerland	Belgium	—	—	France
1897	Pallanza	Belgium	—	Belgium	Belgium	—	—	Belgium
1898	Torino	Belgium	—	Belgium	France	—	France	Belgium
1899	Ostend	Belgium	—	France	France	—	Belgium	Belgium
1900	Paris (Courb)	Belgium	—	France	France	—	France	Belgium
1901	Zurich	Italy	—	France	France	—	France	Belgium
1902	Strasbourg	France	—	Italy	Belgium	—	Belgium	Belgium
1903	Venice	Belgium	—	France	Belgium	—	Belgium	Belgium
1904	Paris (Courb)	Belgium	—	Switzerland	France	—	France	Belgium
1905	Gand	Belgium	—	Als.-Lorr.	Belgium	—	Belgium	France
1906	Pallanza	Belgium	—	France	Italy	—	Belgium	Belgium
1907	Strasbourg	Belgium	—	France	Belgium	—	Italy	Belgium
1908	Lucerne	Italy	—	France	Belgium	—	Belgium	Belgium
1909	Juvisy	Italy	—	Italy	Italy	—	Belgium	France
1910	Ostend	Italy	—	France	Belgium	—	France	Belgium
1911	Como	Switzerland	—	Italy	Italy	—	Italy	Italy
1912	Geneva	Switzerland	—	Belgium	Switzerland	—	Italy	Switzerland
1913	Gand	Switzerland	—	Germany	France	—	France	Germany
1920	Macon	Switzerland	—	Switzerland	France	—	France	Switzerland
1921	Amsterdam	Switzerland	—	Holland	Belgium	—	Holland	Switzerland
1922	Barcelona	France	—	Switzerland	Switzerland	—	Switzerland	France
1923	Como	Switzerland	—	Switzerland	Switzerland	—	Switzerland	Italy
1924	Zurich	Holland	Switzerland	Switzerland	Holland	—	Switzerland	Holland
1925	Prague	Italy	Switzerland	Holland	Switzerland	Switzerland	France	Switzerland
1926	Lucerne	Italy	Switzerland	Switzerland	Switzerland	Switzerland	Switzerland	Holland
1927	Como	Italy	Italy	Italy	Italy	Italy	Switzerland	Italy
1929	Bydgoszcz	Italy	Italy	Holland	Italy	Italy	Switzerland	Italy
1930	Liege	Denmark	Poland	Hungary	Italy	Italy	Switzerland	U.S.A.
1931	Paris	Italy	Holland	Switzerland	France	Switzerland	Hungary	France
1932	Beograz	Italy	Switzerland	Italy	Holland	Hungary	Hungary	Yugoslavia
1933	Budapest	Italy	Hungary	Poland	Hungary	Denmark	France	Hungary
1934	Lucerne	Italy	Austria	Germany	Hungary	Germany	Switzerland	Hungary
1935	Berlin	Germany	Hungary	Poland	Italy	Switzerland	Poland	Hungary
1937	Amsterdam	Germany	Italy	Switzerland	Germany	Germany	Germany	Germany
1938	Milan	Germany	Germany	Germany	Italy	Switzerland	Italy	Italy
1947	Lucerne	France	Denmark	France	Hungary	Italy	Holland	Italy
1949	Amsterdam	Italy	Sweden	U.S.A.	Italy	Italy	Denmark	Italy
1950	Milan	Denmark	Switzerland	Denmark	Italy	Italy	Denmark	Italy
1951	Macon	Italy	Belgium	Denmark	Italy	Belgium	Switzerland	Gt. Britain
1953	Copehagen	Czecho-slovakia	Russia	Yugoslavia	France	Denmark	Switzerland	U.S.S.R.
1954	Amsterdam	U.S.S.R.	Denmark	Switzerland	Switzerland	Italy	Germany	U.S.S.R.
1955	Ghent	Arnegta	U.S.S.R.	Poland	Switzerland	Rumania	U.S.S.R.	U.S.S.R.
1956	Bled	Finland	U.S.S.R.	U.S.S.R.	Germany	Italy	U.S.S.R.	Czechoslovakia
1957	Duisburg	Germany	Gt. Britain	Australia	Germany	Germany	U.S.S.R.	Italy
1958	Poznan	Germany	Finland	Australia	Germany	Germany	U.S.S.R.	Italy
1959	Macon	Germany	Germany	U.S.S.R.	Germany	Swizerland	U.S.S.R.	Germany

WINNERS AT THE BRITISH EMPIRE AND COMMONWEALTH GAMES

	Venue	Coxed Fours	Single Sculls	Coxless Pairs	Coxless Fours	Double Sculls	Eights
1930	Canada	N. Zealand	Australia	—	England	—	England
1938	Australia	Australia	Australia	—	—	—	England
1950	N. Zealand	N. Zealand	Australia	Australia	—	Australia	Australia
1954	Canada	Australia	N. Zealand	N. Zealand	—	Australia	Canada
1958	Wales	England	Australia	N. Zealand	England	England	Canada

HENLEY ROYAL REGATTA

THE GRAND CHALLENGE CUP

The original trophy put up for competition at the first Henley Regatta in 1839. Open eight-oar event.

1839	First Trinity B.C. Cam.	8.30
1840	Leander Club	9.15
1841	Cambridge Sub. Rooms	—
1842	Cambridge Sub. Rooms	8.30
1843	Oxford Univ. B.C.	9.0
1844	Etonian Club, Oxf.	8.25
1845	Cambridge Univ. B.C.	8.30
1846	Thames Club, London	8.15
1847	Oxford Univ. B.C.	8.0
1848	Oxford Univ. B.C.	9.11
1849	Wadham Coll. Oxf.	—
1850	Oxford Univ. B.C.	R.O.
1851	Oxford Univ. B.C.	7.45
1852	Oxford Univ. B.C.	—
1853	Oxford Univ. B.C.	8.3
1854	First Trinity B.C. Cam.	8.15
1855	Cambridge Univ. B.C.	8.32
1856	Royal Chester R.C.	—
1857	London R.C.	7.55
1858	Cambridge Univ. B.C.	7.26
1859	London R.C.	7.45
1860	First Trinity B.C. Cam.	8.45
1861	First Trinity B.C. Cam.	8.10
1862	London R.C.	8.5
1863	University Coll. Oxf.	7.42
1864	Kingston R.C.	7.43
1865	Kingston R.C.	7.25
1866	Etonian Club, Oxf.	8.29
1867	Etonian Club, Oxf.	7.54
1868	London R.C.	7.20
1869	Etonian Club, Oxf.	7.28
1870	Etonian Club, Oxf.	7.18
1871	Etonian Club, Oxf.	8.5
1872	London R.C.	8.27
1873	London R.C.	7.52
1874	London R.C.	7.41
1875	Leander Club	7.19
1876	Thames R.C.	7.26
1877	London R.C.	8.2½
1878	Thames R.C.	7.42
1879	Jesus Coll. Cam.	8.39
1880	Leander Club	7.3
1881	London R.C.	7.23
1882	Exeter Coll. Oxf.	8.11
1883	London R.C.	7.51
1884	London R.C.	7.27
1885	Jesus Coll. Cam.	7.22
1886	Trinity Hall Cam.	6.53½
1887	Trinity Hall Cam.	6.56
1888	Thames R.C.	7.1
1889	Thames R.C.	7.4
1890	London R.C.	7.4½
1891	Leander Club	6.51
1892	Leander Club	7.48½
1893	Leander Club	7.12
1894	Leander Club	7.22
1895	Trinity Hall Cam.	7.30
1896	Leander Club	7.43
1897	New Coll. Oxf.	6.51
1898	Leander Club	7.13
1899	Leander Club	7.12
1900	Leander Club	7.6
1901	Leander Club	7.4½
1902	Third Trinity B.C. Cam.	7.17
1903	Leander Club	7.9
1904	Leander Club	7.20
1905	Leander Club	6.58
1906	Club Nautique de Gand, Belgium	7.9
1907	Sport Nautique de Gand, Belgium	7.31
1908	Christ Church Oxf.	7.10
1909	Royal Club Nautique de Gand, Belgium	7.8
1910	Magdalen Coll. Oxf.	7.19
1911	Magdalen Coll. Oxf.	7.2
1912	Sydney R.C., Australia	7.6
1913	Leander Club	7.11
1914	Harvard Athletic Assoc. B.C., U.S.A.	7.20
1920	Magdalen Coll. Oxf.	7.24
1921	Magdalen Coll. Oxf.	6.54
1922	Leander Club	7.36
1923	Thames R.C.	6.45
1924	Leander Club	8.3
1925	Leander Club	6.53
1926	Leander Club	6.56
1927	Thames R.C.	7.16
1928	Thames R.C.	6.56
1929	Leander Club	7.0
1930	London R.C.	6.59
1931	London R.C.	7.33
1932	Leander Club	7.19
1933	London R.C.	7.36
1934	Leander Club	6.45
1935	Pembroke Coll. Cam.	6.52
1936	F. C. Zurich R.C., Switzerland	7.25
1937	R. Wiking, Germany	7.33
1938	London R.C.	6.58
1939	Harvard Univ., U.S.A.	7.40
1940-45	No contest.	
1946	Leander Club	7.1
1947	Jesus Coll. Cam.	7.14
1948	Thames R.C.	7.2
1949	Leander Club	6.54
1950	Harvard Univ., U.S.A.	7.23
1951	Lady Margaret B.C. Cam.	7.16
1952	Leander Club	6.38
1953	Leander Club	6.49
1954	Club Krylia Sovetov, U.S.S.R.	7.16
1955	Univ. of Pennsylvania, U.S.A.	6.56
1956	Centre Sportif des Forces de l'Armée Française	7.6
1957	Cornell Univ., U.S.A.	6.53
1958	Trud Club, Leningrad, U.S.S.R.	6.40
1959	Harvard Univ., U.S.A.	6.57

ROWING QUIZ

1. Name the oarsman who has won most Henley medals.

★

2. What is an Octuple?

★

3. Name a Henley Trophy now competed for in Australia.

★

4. Two men once won five events at Henley. Who were they?

★

5. Of whom, and on what occasion, was it written:

"To keep him from the river
They've ranged stout waiters four,
And they've barred the windows firmly
And firmly locked the door"?

★

6. A Brasenose cox once jumped out of his boat at the start of a race. Why, and with what result?

★

7. Who owns the swans on the River Thames?

QUIZ ANSWERS

1. Guy Nickalls, with 23 wins. His son, G. O. Nickalls, with a total of 10, had the highest number of wins in the Grand Challenge Cup (7). 2. An eight sculler, as raced in the United States and elsewhere. Leander Club owned one prior to 1939, but for recreation only. 3. The King's Cup, presented by H. M. King George V for the 1919 Peace Regatta, won by the Australian Army crew, and now the Trophy for the Australian Inter-State Eight-Oared Championship. 4. W. H. Milman and M. Haggard, in 1848, won the Grand, Ladies', Stewards', Visitors' and Goblets. However, this only entailed five races, of which two were not contested, and one was won on a foul. 5. Fletcher Menzies, captain and stroke of the Oxford University crew, who succumbed to fever before the final of the Grand Challenge Cup in 1853. This resulted in the famous seven oar race, in which Oxford beat the Cambridge University Subscription Rooms. 6. In the Stewards' Cup in 1868, as part of a campaign for coxswainless fours. Brasenose were disqualified, but coxswainless fours were introduced in the following year. 7. The Crown, and, by licence from the Crown, the Dyers' Company, and the Vintners' Company.

PRINCESS ELIZABETH CHALLENGE CUP

Instituted in 1946. Eight-oar event for public schools in the United Kingdom.

1946	Bedford School	4.54*
1947	Bedford School	7.25
1948	Bedford School	7.20
1949	Winchester Coll.	7.11
1950	St. Paul's School	7.44
1951	Bedford School	7.27
1952	Radley Coll.	7.0
1953	St. Paul's School	7.6
1954	Winchester Coll.	7.59
1955	Shrewsbury School	7.24
1956	Eton Coll.	7.25
1957	St. Paul's School	7.19
1958	St. Edward's School	6.59
1959	St. Edward's School	7.15

Shortened course from Remenham Barrier.

STEWARDS' CHALLENGE CUP

Instituted in 1841, the second senior Henley event, and, for four-oared crews, the counterpart of the Grand. Until 1873 contested in coxed fours, since then in coxswainless fours.

1841	Oxford Club, London (The Midge)	—
1842	Oxford Club, London (The Midge)	9.16
1843	St. George's Club, London	10.15
1844	Oxford Univ. B.C.	9.16
1845	Oxford Univ. B.C.	8.25
1846	Oxford Univ. B.C.	—
1847	Christ Church Oxf.	R.O.
1848	Christ Church Oxf.	R.O.
1849	Leander Club	—
1850	Oxford Univ. B.C.	R.O.
1851	Cambridge Univ. qualification	8.54
1852	Oxford Univ. B.C.	—
1853	Oxford Univ. B.C.	8.57
1854	Pembroke Coll. Oxf.	9.83
1855	Royal Chester R.C.	—
1856	Argonaut Club, London	—
1857	London R.C.	8.25
1858	London R.C.	R.O.
1859	Third Trinity B.C. Cam.	8.25
1860	First Trinity B.C. Cam.	9.26
1861	First Trinity B.C. Cam.	9.35
1862	Brasenose Coll. Oxf.	8.40
1863	University Coll. Oxf.	8.24
1864	London R.C.	8.45
1865	Third Trinity B.C. Cam.	8.13
1866	University Coll. Oxf.	9.28
1867	University Coll. Oxf.	8.45
1868	London R.C.	8.22
1869	London R.C.	8.36
1870	Etonian Club, Oxf.	8.5
1871	London R.C.	9.9
1872	London R.C.	9.21
1873	London R.C.	8.23
1874	London R.C.	9.0
1875	London R.C.	7.56
1876	London R.C.	8.27
1877	London R.C.	9.7
1878	London R.C.	8.37
1879	Jesus Coll. Cam.	9.37
1880	Thames R.C.	7.58
1881	Hertford Coll. Oxf.	8.15
1882	Hertford Coll. Oxf.	—
1883	Thames R.C.	—
1884	Kingston R.C.	—
1885	Trinity Hall Cam.	7.53
1886	Thames R.C.	7.39
1887	Trinity Hall Cam.	7.53
1888	Trinity Hall Cam.	8.25
1889	Thames R.C.	7.53
1890	Brasenose Coll. Oxf.	7.37
1891	Thames R.C.	7.45
1892	Royal Chester R.C.	8.38
1893	Magdalen Coll. Oxf.	7.45
1894	Thames R.C.	8.20
1895	London R.C.	7.43
1896	London R.C.	8.42
1897	Leander Club	7.30
1898	Leander Club	7.42
1899	Magdalen Coll. Oxf.	7.51
1900	Leander Club	7.55
1901	Third Trinity B.C. Cam.	7.54
1902	Third Trinity B.C. Cam.	7.45
1903	Third Trinity B.C. Cam.	8.5
1904	Third Trinity B.C. Cam.	7.30
1905	Leander Club	R.O.
1906	Leander Club	7.36
1907	Magdalen Coll. Oxf.	8.42
1908	Magdalen Coll. Oxf.	7.40
1909	Thames R.C.	7.38
1910	Winnipeg R.C., Canada	7.52
1911	Thames R.C.	7.35
1912	New Coll. Oxf.	7.36
1913	New Coll. Oxf.	—
1914	Leander Club	7.52
1920	Magdalen Coll. Oxf.	8.3
1921	Magdalen Coll. Oxf.	7.32
1922	Eton Vikings Club	8.25
1923	Third Trinity B.C. Cam.	7.30
1924	Third Trinity B.C. Cam.	8.37
1925	Third Trinity B.C. Cam.	7.27
1926	Thames R.C.	7.34
1927	Thames R.C.	8.1
1928	Thames R.C.	7.43
1929	First Trinity B.C. Cam.	7.32
1930	London R.C.	7.34
1931	London R.C.	8.45
1932	Thames R.C.	8.9
1933	Pembroke Coll. Cam.	8.16
1934	Pembroke Coll. Cam.	7.24
1935	F.C. Zurich R.C., Switzerland	7.14
1936	F.C. Zurich R.C., Switzerland	7.50
1937	Leander Club	8.52
1938	Leander Club	7.33
1939	R.C. Zurich, Switzerland	8.9
1946	Leander Club	7.48
1947	Thames R.C.	8.4
1948	Thames R.C.	7.48
1949	Trinity Coll. Oxf.	7.13
1950	Hellerup Roklub, Denmark	8.3
1951	Thames R.C.	7.53
1952	Thames R.C.	7.24
1953	Leander Club	7.25
1954	Club Krylia Sovetov, U.S.S.R.	8.26
1955	Club Krylia Sovetov, U.S.S.R.	7.40
1956	Thames R.C.	8.6
1957	Club Krylia Sovetov, U.S.S.R.	7.35
1958	National Provincial Bank R.C.	7.14
1959	St. Edmund Hall and Lincoln Coll. Oxf.	7.39

LADIES' CHALLENGE PLATE

Instituted in 1845. Eight-oar event restricted to college and non-collegiate clubs of Oxford and Cambridge Universities, public schools, Trinity College, Dublin, Royal Military Academy, Sandhurst, and R.A.F. College, Cranwell.

Winners since 1946

1946	Jesus Coll. Cam.	7.8
1947	First and Third Trinity B.C. Cam.	7.21
1948	Eton College	7.15
1949	Lady Margaret B.C. Cam.	6.50
1950	New Coll. Oxf.	7.25
1951	Pembroke Coll. Cam.	7.25
1952	Lady Margaret B.C. Cam.	6.50
1953	Jesus Coll. Cam.	7.0
1954	First and Third Trinity B.C. Cam.	7.33
1955	Queens' Coll. Cam.	7.26
1956	Peterhouse Cam.	7.41
1957	Pembroke Coll. Cam.	7.11
1958	Jesus Coll. Cam.	6.51
1959	Lady Margaret B.C. Cam.	7.13

THAMES CHALLENGE CUP

Instituted in 1868. Open eight-oar event, except that no crew may compete for the Thames Cup and the Grand, Ladies', or Princess Elizabeth Cup at the same regatta.

Winners since 1946

1946	Imperial College B.C.	7.11
1947	Kent School, U.S.A.	7.22
1948	Princeton Univ., U.S.A.	7.20
1949	Princeton Univ., U.S.A.	6.58
1950	Kent School, U.S.A.	7.34
1951	Univ. of Pennsylvania, U.S.A.	7.19
1952	Univ. of Pennsylvania, U.S.A.	7.3
1953	Royal Air Force	6.59
1954	Massachusetts Institute of Technology, U.S.A.	7.24
1955	Massachusetts Institute of Technology, U.S.A.	7.21
1956	Princeton Univ., U.S.A.	7.10
1957	Princeton Univ., U.S.A.	7.8
1958	Harvard Univ., U.S.A.	6.57
1959	Harvard Univ., U.S.A.	7.13

ROWING QUIZ

1. What is a ran-dan?

★

2. When and how did Henley become "Royal"?

★

3. There is only one case of father and son representing Great Britain in the Olympic Games Regatta. Who were they?

★

4. When, and by whom, was the verdict announced "Dead heat for Oxford by five yards"

QUIZ ANSWERS

1. Boat propelled by three persons, stroke and bow rowing with one oar each, and the middle man sculling. 2. In 1851, the year of the Great Exhibition, when H.R.H. Prince Albert became patron. 3. C. D. Burnell in the winning Leander Eight of 1908, and R. D. Burnell, winner of the Double Sculls in 1948. 4. Allegedly by "Honest" John Phelps, in the Boat Race of 1877. This was the last occasion on which a professional waterman judged the Boat Race.

THE SILVER GOBLETS AND NICKALLS CHALLENGE CUP

Instituted in 1845 for pair-oars, the trophies originally being two silver wherries. These were replaced by presentation silver goblets in 1850, the Nickalls Challenge Cup being added in 1895, presented by Mr. Tom Nickalls in commemoration of the fact that his two sons had then won the event, either together or in partnership with others, for the past five years. Open to all amateurs.

1845	G. Mann and F. M. Arnold (Caius Coll. Cam.)	—
1846	M. Haggard and W. H. Milman (Christ Church Oxf.)	—
1847	W. S. Falls and W. Coulthard (St. George's Club, London)	—
1848	M. Haggard and W. H. Milman (Christ Church Oxf.)	—
1849	E. G. Peacock and F. Playford (Thames Club, London)	—
1850	J. J. Hornby (Brasenose Coll. Oxf.) and J. W. Chitty (Balliol Coll. Oxf.)	—
1851	J. Aitken (Exeter Coll. Oxf.) and J. W. Chitty (Balliol Coll. Oxf.)	—
1852	H. R. Barker and P. H. Nind (Christ Church Oxf.)	—
1853	R. Gordon and J. B. Barlee (Christ's College Cam.)	10.0
1854	W. F. Short (New Coll. Oxf.) and E. Cadogan (Christ Church Oxf.)	9.36
1855	A. A. Casamajor and J. Nottidge (Wandle Club)	—
1856	A. A. Casamajor and J. Nottidge (Argonaut Club, London)	—
1857	E. Warre and A. P. Lonsdale (Balliol Coll. Oxf.)	9.22
1858	H. H. Playford and A. A. Casamajor (London R.C.)	—
1859	E. Warre (Balliol Coll. Oxf.) and J. Arkell (Pembroke Coll. Oxf.)	9.0
1860	A. A. Casamajor and W. Woodbridge (London R.C.)	11.50
1861	W. Champneys and W. B. Woodgate (Brasenose Coll. Oxf.)	—
1862	W. Champneys and W. B. Woodgate (Brasenose Coll. Oxf.)	9.45
1863	R. Shepherd and W. B. Woodgate (Brasenose Coll. Oxf.)	R.O.
1864	J. R. Selwyn and R. A. Kinglake (Third Trinity B.C. Cam.)	9.29
1865	J. C. F. May and F. Fenner (London R.C.)	9.7
1866	E. L. Corrie and W. B. Woodgate (Kingston R.C.)	9.23
1867	E. L. Corrie and M. M. Brown (Kingston R.C.)	9.90
1868	W. C. Crofts and W. B. Woodgate (Brasenose Coll. Oxf.)	—
1869	A. de L. Long and W. Stout (London R.C.)	9.20
1870	E. L. Corrie and E. Hall (Kingston R.C.)	—
1871	A. de L. Long and F. S. Gulston (London R.C.)	10.17
1872	A. de L. Long and F. S. Gulston (London R.C.)	—
1873	C. C. Knollys and A. Trower (Kingston R.C.)	9.22
1874	A. de L. Long and F. S. Gulston (London R.C.)	10.3
1875	W. Chillingworth and C. Herbert (Ino R.C.)	—
1876	S. Le B. Smith and F. S. Gulston (London R.C.)	8.55
1877	W. H. Eyre and J. Hastie (Thames R.C.)	—
1878	T. C. Edwards-Moss and W. A. Ellison (Etonian Club, Oxf.)	9.14
1879	R. H. Labat and F. S. Gulston (London R.C.)	11.16
1880	W. H. Eyre and J. Hastie (Thames R.C.)	8.45
1881	W. H. Eyre and J. Hastie (Thames R.C.)	9.4
1882	D. E. Brown and J. Lowndes (Hertford Coll. Oxf.)	—
1883	G. Q. Roberts and D. E. Brown (Twickenham R.C.)	9.22
1884	J. Lowndes and D. E. Brown (Twickenham R.C.)	9.1
1885	H. McLean and D. H. McLean (Etonian Club, Oxf.)	—
1886	F. E. Churchill and S. D. Muttlebury (Third Trinity B.C. Cam.)	8.40
1887	C. T. Barclay and S. D. Muttlebury (Third Trinity B.C. Cam.)	8.15
1888	N. P. Symonds (Cambridge Univ. B.C.) and E. Buck (Oxford Univ. B.C.)	—
1889	J. C. Gardner and S. D. Muttlebury (Cambridge Univ. B.C.)	8.25
1890	Lord Ampthill and G. Nickalls (Oxf. Univ. B.C.)	8.38
1891	Lord Ampthill and G. Nickalls (Leander Club)	8.36
1892	V. Nickalls and W. A. L. Fletcher (Oxf. Univ. B.C.)	9.7
1893	V. Nickalls and W. A. L. Fletcher (Oxf. Univ. B.C.)	8.44
1894	V. Nickalls and G. Nickalls (Formosa B.C.)	9.35
1895	V. Nickalls and G. Nickalls (London R.C.)	9.11
1896	V. Nickalls and G. Nickalls (London R.C.)	9.10
1897	E. R. Balfour and G. Nickalls (Leander Club)	8.59
1898	A. Bogle and W. J. Fernie (Thames R.C.)	8.41
1899	C. K. Philips and H. W. M. Willis (Leander Club)	8.49
1900	C. J. D. Goldie and G. M. Maitland (Trinity Coll. Cam.)	8.33
1901	H. J. Hale and F. W. Warre (Balliol Coll. Oxf.)	8.50
1902	W. Dudley Ward and C. W. H. Taylor (Third Trinity B.C. Cam.)	8.36
1903	L. Klaus and A. Ehrenberg (Victoria R.C., Berlin, Germany)	8.45
1904	C. J. D. Goldie and C. W. H. Taylor (Third Trinity B.C. Cam.)	8.33
1905	R. H. Nelson and P. H. Thomas (Third Trinity B.C. Cam.)	8.40
1906	B. C. Johnstone and R. V. Powell (Third Trinity B.C. Cam.)	9.15
1907	B. C. Johnstone and R. V. Powell (Leander Club)	8.52
1908	H. R. Barker and A. C. Glastone (Christ Church Oxf.)	8.26
1909	B. C. Johnstone and E. G. Williams (Leander Club)	8.30
1910	J. S. Burn and G. L. Thomson (Leander Club)	8.45
1911	J. Beresford and A. H. Cloutte (Thames R.C.)	8.15
1912	B. Logan and C. G. Rought (Thames R.C.)	8.36
1913	A. A. Swann and S. E. Swann (Trinity Hall Cam.)	8.39
1914	A. A. Swann and S. E. Swann (Trinity Hall Cam.)	9.2
1920	G. O. Nickalls and R. S. C. Lucas (Magdalen Coll. Oxf.)	8.53
1921	J. A. Campbell and H. B. Playford (Jesus Coll. Cam.)	8.52
1922	G. O. Nickalls and R. S. C. Lucas (Magdalen Coll. Oxf.)	9.19
1923	W. F. Godden and R. E. Eason (Trinity Coll. Oxf.)	8.12
1924	C. R. M. Ely and J. A. Macnabb (Third Trinity B.C. Cam.)	10.6
1925	R. E. Morrison and E. C. Hamilton-Russell (Third Trinity B.C. Cam.)	8.17
1926	H. R. Carver and E. C. Hamilton-Russell (Third Trinity B.C. Cam.)	8.36
1927	R. A. Nisbet and T. N. O'Brien (London R.C.)	9.23
1928	G. C. Killick and J. Beresford, jun. (Thames R.C.)	9.57
1929	G. C. Killick and J. Beresford, jun. (Thames R.C.)	8.32
1930	W. A. Prideaux and H. R. N. Rickett (Third Trinity B.C. Cam.)	8.42
1931	H. R. A. Edwards and L. Clive (Christ Church Oxf.)	9.57
1932	H. R. A. Edwards and L. Clive (Christ Church Oxf.)	9.5
1933	J. H. C. Powell and J. E. Gilmour (Eton Vikings Club)	9.17
1934	H. Braun and H. G. Moller (R. Wiking, Germany)	8.9
1935	T. S. Cree and D. W. Burnford (Jesus Coll. Cam.)	8.20
1936	R. E. Offer and J. S. Offer (Kingston R.C.)	9.17
1937	W. E. Wingate and W. D. Baddeley (Vesta R.C.)	9.43
1938	W. G. R. M. Laurie and J. H. T. Wilson (Leander Club)	8.8
1939	C. B. Sanford and H. Parker (Trinity Hall Cam.)	9.5
1946	J. F. Burgess and C. G. Burgess (Leander Club)	8.47
1947	J. H. Pinches and E. M. Sturges (London R.C.)	8.46
1948	W. G. R. M. Laurie and J. H. T. Wilson (Leander Club)	8.30
1949	A. S. F. Butcher and T. H. Christie (Thames R.C.)	8.20
1950	J. Rosa and C. van Antwerpen (Société Royale Nautique Anversoise, Belgium)	9.10
1951	J. G. P. Crowden (Pembroke Coll. Cam.) and C. B. M. Lloyd (Lady Margaret B.C. Cam.)	8.52
1952	H. C. I. Bywater and T. H. Christie (Westminster Hospital B.C.)	8.6
1953	R. Baetens and M. Knuysen (Antwerp S.C., Belgium)	8.10
1954	I. Buldakov and V. Ivanov (Club Khimik, U.S.S.R.)	8.44
1955	I. Buldakov and V. Ivanov (Club Khimik, U.S.S.R.)	8.30
1956	R. J. Thompson and G. M. Wolfson (Pembroke Coll. Cam.)	8.45
1957	D. A. T. Leadley and C. G. V. Davidge (Leander Club)	8.17
1958	D. A. T. Leadley and C. G. V. Davidge (Leander Club)	8.4
1959	R. B. Norton and H. H. Scurfield (Hertford Coll. Oxf.)	8.20

THE VISITORS' CHALLENGE CUP

Originally the "District Fours" for local four-oar crews. Renamed in 1847, as a four-oar event with qualifications the same as for the Ladies' Plate. Coxswainless since 1874.

Winners since 1946

1946	First and Third Trinity B.C. Cam.	7.59
1947	Trinity Hall Cam.	8.0
1948	Magdalen Coll. Oxf.	7.51
1949	Clare Coll. Cam.	7.31
1950	Lady Margaret B.C. Cam.	8.8
1951	Trinity Hall Cam.	8.9
1952	Pembroke Coll. Cam.	7.15
1953	Magdalen Coll. Oxf.	7.29
1954	First and Third Trinity B.C. Cam.	7.57
1955	Trinity Hall Cam.	7.58
1956	Merton Coll. Oxf.	7.47
1957	Pembroke Coll. Cam.	7.33
1958	Keble Coll. Oxf.	7.32
1959	Pembroke Coll. Cam.	7.50

Great Britain Coxswainless Four at Los Angeles Olympics, 1932. One of our finest-ever fours: R. D. George (bow), J. Beresford jun., H. R. A. Edwards, J. C. Badcock (stroke)

ROWING QUIZ

1. On what occasion was the Henley trophy shared by two finalists after a dead heat?

★

2. Since 1930 three men have won three events at Henley at the same regatta. Who are they?

★

3. On how many occasions has the Boat Race verdict been decided by a sinking?

★

4. What is the Philadelphia Gold Cup?

★

5. Who invented the sliding seat?

★

6. What was the occasion of the cry "The Hall, the Hall, I bawl the Hall"?

★

7. Who is the patron saint of coxswains?

QUIZ ANSWERS

1. The Centenary Double Sculls Race in 1939 resulted in a dead heat between J. Beresford Jr. and L. F. Southwood of Thames R.C., and G. Scherli and E. Broschi of Trieste, Italy, and there was no row off. 2. H. R. A. Edwards won the Grand, Stewards' and Goblets, in 1931. E. C. Hamilton-Russell and R. E. Morrison won the Stewards', Visitors' and Goblets, in 1925. 3. Twice; in 1859 "Cambridge sank"; in 1925 "Oxford sank". In 1898 Cambridge water-logged—verdict for Oxford "easily". In 1912 Cambridge sank, Oxford water-logged and emptied their boat, and the race was declared void, Oxford winning the re-row by six lengths. In 1951 Oxford sank, the race was declared void, and Cambridge won the re-row by twelve lengths. 4. To celebrate J. Kelly senior's Olympic successes the citizens of Philadelphia presented the cup for the "World's Amateur Sculling Championship". It goes automatically to the winner of the Olympic Single Sculls, who must, however, accept any challenge made within a year of his victory. 5. J. C. Babcock, Nassau Boat Club, of New York, 1857. 6. In 1895 Trinity Hall beat Cornell University in the final of the Grand, the latter being somewhat unpopular that year owing to a false start against Leander. The cry for "The Hall" was in reply to Cornell's traditional battle cry of "Cornell, Cornell, I yell Cornell". 7. St. Elmo.

B. H. T. Bushnell and R. D. Burnell (Great Britain) beating Denmark and Uruguay in the final of the Olympic Double Sculls, 1948

THE WYFOLD CHALLENGE CUP

Presented in 1847, at which time it was the custom for challengers in each event to row trial heats amongst themselves, the successful challenger contesting the final against the previous year's "holder". The Wyfold Cup was then presented to the winning challenger for the Grand.

In 1855 it was made over to a four-oar race, the qualification for which is now similar to that for the Thames Cup.

Winners since 1946

1946	King's Coll. London	7.57
1947	Quintin B.C.	8.19
1948	Victoria Lake R.C., South Africa	7.55
1949	Lensbury R.C.	7.41
1950	Royal Engineers	8.13
1951	Caius Coll. Cam.	7.55
1952	Corpus Christi Coll. Cam.	7.28
1953	Royal Air Force	7.38
1954	Royal Engineers	8.6
1955	Thames R.C.	7.51
1956	Royal Engineers	7.56
1957	National Provincial Bank R.C.	7.49
1958	Burton Leander R.C.	7.35
1959	Moseley R.C.	7.45

C. G. V. Davidge (Leander Club)　　D. A. T. Leadley (Leander Club)

DOUBLE SCULLS CHALLENGE CUP

A Double Sculls race for presentation goblets was instituted in 1939 to mark the centenary year, the Challenge Cup being added in 1946. Open to all amateurs.

1939	J. Beresford, jun., and L. F. Southwood (Thames R.C.) and G. Scherli and E. Broschi (Societa Canottieri Di Trieste, Italy), dead heat	8.35
1946	R. E. Panelo and E. D. Chafuen (Buenos Aires R.C., Argentina)	8.8
1947	W. E. C. Horwood and D. C. H. Garrod (Quintin B.C.)	8.23
1948	B. Piessens (Antwerp S.C.) and W. A. Collet (Société Royale Sport Nautique de Bruxelles) (Belgium)	8.2
1949	E. W. Parsner and A. E. Larsen (D.F.D.S. Roklub, Denmark)	7.39
1950	E. W. Parsner and A. E. Larsen (D.F.D.S. Roklub, Denmark)	8.21
1951	P. Bradley and R. D. Burnell (Leander Club)	8.41
1952	R. George (Union Nautique de Liege) and J. van Stichel (Antwerp S.C.) (Belgium)	7.37
1953	E. Schriever and P. Stebler (Seeclub, Zurich, Switzerland)	7.37
1954	E. Schriever and P. Stebler (Seeclub, Zurich, Switzerland)	8.46
1955	G. Zhilin and I. Emchuk (Club Burevestnik, U.S.S.R.)	7.55
1956	S. C. Rand and W. H. Rand (Royal Air Force R.C.)	7.47
1957	A. Berkutov and Y. Tukalov (Club Krasnoe Znamia, U.S.S.R.)	7.41
1958	A. Berkutov and Y. Tukalov (Trud Club, Leningrad, U.S.S.R.)	8.6
1959	C. G. V. Davidge and S. A. Mackenzie (Leander Club)	7.50

The reigning Olympic and European champions, A. Berkutov and Y. Tukalov (Trud Club, Leningrad), practising at Henley, 1958

J. S. Burke (Penn Athletic Club, Philadelphia) wins Diamond Sculls in 1938 in record time. Possibly the fastest sculler of all time.

ROWING QUIZ

1. Only one man has won a Boat Race five times. Who?

★

2. Which oarsman was knighted for his services to rowing?

★

3. What is the minimum weight for coxswains?

★

4. Name one Henley trophy now competed for at Marlow Regatta.

★

5. What is the Triple Crown of sculling?

★

6. What is a "button" and what purpose does it serve?

QUIZ ANSWERS

1. C. R. W. Tottenham, coxed Oxford from 1854 to 1868. 2. The late Sir Harcourt Gold, chairman of the Henley Committee of Management, was knighted in 1948. 3. 6½ stone. 4. The Public Schools Cup, transferred to Marlow in 1885. 5. National title to triple winner of Diamonds, Wingfields and London Cup (Metropolitan Regatta). Since 1920 this has been achieved only by J. Beresford jun. and T. A. Fox. 6. Raised leather collar round oar, to prevent it slipping out of rowlock.

WINGFIELD SCULLS

Instituted by Mr. Henry C. Wingfield, in 1832, as the Amateur Sculling Championship of the Thames. Original course from Westminster to Putney. In 1849 course altered to Putney to Kew, and, since 1861, from Putney to Mortlake. Open to amateur scullers of Great Britain and Northern Ireland. Also British Amateur Sculling Championship since 1952.

Winners since 1920

		Time
1920	J. Beresford, jun.	23 m. 14 s.
1921	J. Beresford, jun.	
1922	J. Beresford, jun.	22 m. 13 s.
1923	J. Beresford, jun.	24 m. 27 s.
1924	J. Beresford, jun.	24 m. 36 s.
1925	J. Beresford, jun.	23 m. 27 s.
1926	J. Beresford, jun.	won on foul
1927	T. D. A. Collet	23 m. 10 s.
1928	T. D. A. Collet	23 m. 00 s.
1929	T. D. A. Collet	21 m. 47 s.
1930	D. Guye	23 m. 50 s.
1931	D. Guye	
1932	D. Guye	21 m. 1 s.
1933	L. F. Southwood*	21 m. 11 s.
1934	C. K. Buckle*	22 m. 6 s.
1935	P. H. Jackson	22 m. 11 s.
1936	P. H. Jackson*	22 m. 31 s.
1937	R. Hope*	21 m. 44 s.
1938	P. H. Jackson*	22 m. 40 s.
1939–45	No race	
1946	R. D. Burnell*	22 m. 36 s.
1947	B. T. H. Bushnell*	22 m. 14 s.
1948	P. N. Carpmael	25 m. 45 s.
1949	P. N. Carpmael	22 m. 55 s.
1950	E. M. Sturgess*	22 m. 7 s.
1951	T. A. Fox	22 m. 14 s.
1952	T. A. Fox	24 m. 33 s.
1953	T. A. Fox	22 m. 30 s.
1954	S. C. Rand	24 m. 43 s.
1955	D. V. Melvin	22 m. 05 s.
1956	A. J. Marsden	25 m. 33 s.
1957	W. G. Beech	22 m. 57 s.
1958	D. V. Melvin*	22 m. 12 s.
1959	J. M. Russell	22 m. 37 s.

* Resigned

S. A. Mackenzie, European Single Sculls champion, three times winner of the Diamond Sculls.

THE DIAMOND CHALLENGE SCULLS

Open to all amateurs, instituted in 1884, and generally regarded as the Blue Riband of sculling.

1844	T. B. Bumpsted (London Amateur Scullers Club)	10.32
1845	S. Wallace (Leander Club)	—
1846	E. G. Moon (Magdalen Coll. Oxf.)	—
1847	W. Maule (First Trinity B.C. Cam.)	10.45
1848	W. L. Bagshawe (Third Trinity B.C. Cam.)	—
1849	T. R. Bone (London)*	—
1850	T. R. Bone (Meteor Club)	—
1851	E. G. Peacock (Thames Club)	—
1852	E. Macnaghten (First Trinity B.C. Cam.)	—
1853	S. R. Rippingall (Peterhouse Cam.)	10.2
1854	H. H. Playford (Wandle Club)	—
1855	A. A. Casamajor (Argonaut Club, London)	9.27
1856	A. A. Casamajor (Argonaut Club, London)	—
1857	A. A. Casamajor (London R.C.)	—
1858	A. A. Casamajor (London R.C.)	R.O.
1859	E. D. Brickwood (Richmond)*	10.0
1860	H. H. Playford (London R.C.)	12.8
1861	A. A. Casamajor (London R.C.)	10.4
1862	E. D. Brickwood (London R.C.)†	9.40
1863	C. B. Lawes (Third Trinity B.C. Cam.)	9.43
1864	W. B. Woodgate (Brasenose Coll. Oxf.)	10.10
1865	E. B. Michell (Magdalen Coll. Oxf.)	9.11
1866	E. B. Michell (Magdalen Coll. Oxf.)	9.55
1867	W. C. Crofts (Brasenose Coll. Oxf.)	10.2
1868	W. Stout (London R.C.)	9.6
1869	W. C. Crofts (Brasenose Coll. Oxf.)	9.56
1870	John B. Close (First Trinity B.C. Cam.)	9.43
1871	W. Fawcus (Tynemouth R.C.)	10.9
1872	C. C. Knollys (Magdalen Coll. Oxf.)	10.48
1873	A. C. Dicker (Lady Margaret B.C. Cam.)	9.50
1874	A. C. Dicker (Lady Margaret B.C. Cam.)	10.50
1875	A. C. Dicker (Lady Margaret B.C. Cam.)	9.15
1876	F. L. Playford (London R.C.)	9.28
1877	T. C. Edwards-Moss (Brasenose Coll. Oxf.)	10.20
1878	T. C. Edwards-Moss (Brasenose Coll. Oxf.)	9.37
1879	J. Lowndes (Hertford Coll. Oxf.)	12.30
1880	J. Lowndes (Derby)*	9.10
1881	J. Lowndes (Derby)*	9.28
1882	J. Lowndes (Derby)*	11.43
1883	J. Lowndes (Twickenham R.C.)	10.2
1884	W. S. Unwin (Magdalen Coll. Oxf.)	9.44
1885	W. S. Unwin (Magdalen Coll. Oxf.)	9.22
1886	F. I. Pitman (Third Trinity B.C. Cam.)	9.5
1887	J. C. Gardner (Emmanuel Coll. Cam.)	8.51
1888	G. Nickalls (Magdalen Coll. Oxf.)	8.36
1889	G. Nickalls (Magdalen Coll. Oxf.)	8.56
1890	G. Nickalls (Magdalen Coll. Oxf.)	8.57½
1891	G. Nickalls (Magdalen Coll. Oxf.)	R.O.
1892	J. J. K. Ooms (Neptunus R.C., Amsterdam, Holland)	10.9
1893	G. Nickalls (Magdalen Coll. Oxf.)	9.12
1894	G. Nickalls (Formosa B.C.)	9.32
1895	Hon. R. Guinness (Leander Club)	9.11
1896	Hon. R. Guinness (Leander Club)	9.35
1897	E. H. Ten Eyck (Wachusett B.C., Worcester, U.S.A.)	8.35
1898	B. H. Howell (Trinity Hall Cam.)	8.29
1899	B. H. Howell (Thames R.C.)	8.38
1900	E. G. Hemmerde (Univ. Coll. Oxf.)	8.42
1901	C. V. Fox (Guards Brigade R.C.)	8.52
1902	F. S. Kelly (Balliol Coll. Oxf.)	8.59
1903	F. S. Kelly (Leander Club)	8.41
1904	L. F. Scholes (Toronto R.C., Canada)	8.23
1905	F. S. Kelly (Leander Club)	8.10
1906	H. T. Blackstaffe (Vesta R.C.)	8.35
1907	Captain W. H. Darell (Household Brigade B.C.)	9.24
1908	A. McCulloch (Leander Club)	8.25
1909	A. A. Stuart (Kingston R.C.)	8.30
1910	W. D. Kinnear (Kensington R.C.)	8.51
1911	W. D. Kinnear (Kensington R.C.)	8.14
1912	E. W. Powell (Eton Vikings Club)	8.49
1913	C. McVilly (Derwent R.C., Tasmania)	8.49
1914	S. Sinigaglia (Lario Club, Como, Italy)	9.0
1920	J. Beresford, jun. (Thames R.C.)	8.57
1921	F. E. Eyken (Delft Univ. B.C., Laga, Holland)	8.26
1922	W. M. Hoover (Duluth B.C., Minnesota, U.S.A.)	9.32
1923	M. K. Morris (London R.C.)	8.23
1924	J. Beresford, jun. (Thames R.C.)	10.32
1925	J. Beresford, jun. (Thames R.C.)	8.26
1926	J. Beresford, jun. (Thames R.C.)	8.45
1927	R. T. Lee (Worcester Coll. Oxf.)	9.6
1928	J. Wright (Argonaut R.C., Canada)	8.24
1929	L. H. F. Gunther (Roei-Zeilvereening de Amstel, Holland)	8.42
1930	J. S. Guest (Don R.C., Canada)	8.29
1931	R. Pearce (Leander B.C., Hamilton, Canada)	10.3
1932	H. Buhtz (Berliner R.C., Germany)	9.15
1933	T. G. Askwith (Peter house Cam.)	9.7
1934	H. Buhtz (Berliner R.C., Germany)	8.10
1935	E. Rufli (F. C. Zurich R.C., Switzerland)	8.15
1936	E. Rufli (F. C. Zurich R.C., Switzerland)	9.22
1937	J. Hasenohrl (Ruderverein Ellida, Austria)	9.12
1938	J. W. Burk (Penn Athletic Club, U.S.A.)	8.2
1939	J. W. Burk (Penn Athletic Club, U.S.A.)	9.13
1946	J. Séphériadès (Société Nautique de la Basse Seine, France)	8.21
1947	J. B. Kelly (Univ. of Pennsylvania, U.S.A.)	8.49
1948	M. T. Wood (New South Wales Police R.C., Australia)	8.24
1949	J. B. Kelly (Univ. of Pennsylvania, U.S.A.)	8.12
1950	A. D. Rowe (Leander Club)	9.11
1951	T. A. Fox (Pembroke Coll. Cam.)	8.59
1952	M. T. Wood (Sydney R.C., Australia)	8.12
1953	T. A. Fox (London R.C.)	8.12
1954	P. Vlasic (Mornar Club, Yugoslavia)	8.42
1955	T. Kocerka (A.Z.S. Bydgoszcz, Poland)	8.33
1956	T. Kocerka (A.Z.S. Bydgoszcz, Poland)	8.37
1957	S. A. Mackenzie (Sydney R.C., Australia)	8.25
1958	S. A. Mackenzie (Sydney R.C., Australia)	8.6
1959	S. A. Mackenzie (Sydney R.C., Australia)	8.29

* These scullers would today be described as "unattached". Reference is to town of origin, not to a club.
† After a dead heat with W. B. Woodgate, in 9 min. 22 sec.

OXFORD AND CAMBRIDGE EIGHT-OARED RACE

(105 races rowed. Cambridge 58 wins, Oxford 46 wins. One dead-heat)

Year	Winner	Time	Won by
1829	Oxf.	14m 30s	easily
1836	Cam.	36m 0s	1 min
1839	Cam.	31m 0s	1m 45s
1840	Cam.	29m 30s	¾ length
*1841	Cam.	32m 30s	1m 4s
1842	Oxf.	30m 45s	13 sec
1845	Cam.	23m 30s	30 sec
†1846	Cam.	21m 5s	3 lengths
1849	Cam.	22m 0s	easily
1849	Oxf.	—	foul
1852	Oxf.	21m 36s	27 sec
1854	Oxf.	25m 29s	11 strokes
1856	Cam.	25m 50s	½ length
‡1857	Oxf.	22m 35s	35 sec
1858	Cam.	21m 23s	22 sec
1859	Oxf.	24m 40s	Cam. sank
1860	Cam.	26m 5s	1 length
1861	Oxf.	23m 30s	48 sec
1862	Oxf.	24m 41s	30 sec
1863	Oxf.	23m 6s	43 sec
1864	Oxf.	21m 40s	27 sec
1865	Oxf.	21m 24s	4 lengths
1866	Oxf.	25m 25s	15 sec
1867	Oxf.	22m 40s	½ length
1868	Oxf.	20m 56s	6 lengths
1869	Oxf.	20m 5s	3 lengths
1870	Cam.	22m 4s	1¼ lengths
1871	Cam.	23m 5s	1 lengths
1872	Cam.	21m 15s	2 lengths
§1873	Cam.	19m 35s	3¼ lengths
1874	Cam.	22m 25s	3¼ lengths
1875	Oxf.	22m 2s	10 lengths
1876	Cam.	20m 20s	easily
1877	Oxf. Cam.	24m 8s	dead heat
1878	Oxf.	22m 13s	10 lengths
1879	Cam.	21m 18s	3½ lengths
1880	Oxf.	21m 23s	3¾ lengths
1881	Oxf.	21m 51s	3 lengths
1882	Oxf.	20m 12s	7 lengths
1883	Oxf.	21m 18s	3½ lengths
1884	Cam.	21m 39s	2¼ lengths
1885	Oxf.	21m 36s	2½ lengths
1886	Cam.	22m 29s	¼ length
1887	Cam.	20m 52s	2½ lengths
1888	Cam.	20m 48s	7 lengths
1889	Cam.	20m 14s	2¾ lengths
1890	Oxf.	22m 3s	bare length
1891	Oxf.	21m 48s	½ length
1892	Oxf.	19m 21s	2¼ lengths
1893	Oxf.	18m 47s	1 length 4ft
1894	Oxf.	21m 39s	3½ lengths
1895	Oxf.	20m 50s	2¼ lengths
1896	Oxf.	20m 1s	⅖ length
1897	Oxf.	19m 12s	2½ lengths
1898	Oxf.	22m 15s	easily
1899	Cam.	21m 4s	3¼ lengths
1900	Cam.	18m 47s	20 lengths
1901	Oxf.	22m 31s	⅖ length
1902	Cam.	19m 9s	5 lengths
1903	Cam.	19m 32⅕s	6 lengths
1904	Cam.	21m 37s	4½ lengths
1905	Oxf.	20m 35s	3 lengths
1906	Cam.	19m 24s	3½ lengths
1907	Cam.	20m 26s	4½ lengths
1908	Cam.	19m 20s	2½ lengths
1909	Oxf.	19m 50s	3½ lengths
1910	Oxf.	20m 14s	3½ lengths
1911	Oxf.	18m 29s	2¾ lengths
‖1912	Oxf.	22m 5s	6 lengths
1913	Oxf.	20m 53s	3 lengths
1914	Cam.	20m 23s	4½ lengths
1920	Cam.	21m 11s	4 lengths
1921	Cam.	19m 45s	1 length
1922	Cam.	19m 27s	4½ lengths
1923	Oxf.	20m 54s	3 lengths
1924	Camb.	18m 41s	4½ lengths
1925	Cam.	21m 50s	Oxf. w'log'd
1926	Cam.	19m 25s	5 lengths
1927	Cam.	20m 14s	3 lengths
1928	Cam.	20m 25s	10 lengths
1929	Cam.	19m 24s	7 lengths
1930	Cam.	19m 9s	2 lengths
1931	Cam.	19m 26s	2½ lengths
1932	Cam.	19m 11s	5 lengths
1933	Cam.	20m 57s	2¼ lengths
1934	Cam.	18m 3s	4¼ lengths
1935	Cam.	19m 38s	4½ lengths
1936	Cam.	21m 6s	5 lengths
1937	Oxf.	22m 39s	3 lengths
1938	Oxf.	20m 30s	2 lengths
1939	Cam.	19m 3s	4 lengths
1946	Oxf.	19m 54s	3 lengths
1947	Cam.	23m 1s	10 lengths
1948	Cam.	17m 50s	5 lengths
1949	Cam.	18m 57s	¼ length
1950	Cam.	20m 15s	3½ lengths
¶1951	Cam.	20m 50s	12 lengths
1952	Oxf.	20m 23s	canvas
1953	Cam.	19m 54s	8 lengths
1954	Oxf.	20m 23s	4½ lengths
1955	Cam.	19m 10s	16 lengths
1956	Cam.	18m 36s	1¼ lengths
1957	Cam.	19m 10s	2 lengths
1958	Cam.	18m 15s	3½ lengths
1959	Oxf.	18m 52s	6 lengths

Notes on Table of Winners of Boat Race

* *Oxford used carvel built boat for first time.*
† *Outriggers first used in Boat Race.*
‡ *Keelless boat used for first time (by Oxford).*
§ *Both crews used sliding seat for first time.*
‖ *Re-row after both boats had sunk.*
¶ *Re-row after Oxford sank in first race.*

The Course

The first race, in 1829, was rowed at Henley. 1836–1842, Westminster to Putney.

In 1846, 1856 and 1863 race was rowed on ebb tide from Mortlake to Putney.

All other races rowed from Putney to Mortlake.

A famous Cambridge coach, H. R. N. Rickett, Chairman of the Henley Committee of Management

The first Oxford boat, 1829, now in the Science Museum

BOAT RACE CREWS SINCE 1950

1950

WINNERS

CAMBRIDGE (*Middlesex*)	st.	lb.
H. H. Almond, L.M.B.C. (bow)	10	6
D. M. Jennens, Clare	12	4
A. L. Macleod, L.M.B.C.	12	9
P. M. O. Massey, L.M.B.C.	13	9
W. T. Arthur, L.M.B.C.	13	0
E. A. P. Bircher, Christ's	13	6
C. B. M. Lloyd, L.M.B.C.	12	9
J. L. M. Crick, L.M.B.C. (str)	12	8
A. C. R. Armstrong-Jones, Jesus (cox)	8	8
Average	12	8½

LOSERS

OXFORD (*Surrey*)	st.	lb.
J. G. C. Blacker, Balliol (bow)	12	2
P. Gladstone, Christ Church	12	11
H. J. Renton, Magdalen	12	4
J. M. Clay, Magdalen	12	7½
G. C. Frisk, Oriel	11	10½
J. Hayes, New College	13	0
D. N. Callender, Trinity	12	4
A. J. M. Cavenagh, Magdalen (str)	11	3
J. E. C. Hinchcliffe, Trinity (cox)	8	6
Average	12	3½

1951

CAMBRIDGE (*Middlesex*)	st.	lb.
*H. H. Almond, L.M.B.C. (bow)	10	6½
D. D. Macklin, L.M.B.C.	11	11
J. G. P. Crowden, Pembroke	12	10
R. F. A. Sharpley, L.M.B.C.	13	8
E. J. Worlidge, L.M.B.C.	12	13¼
*C. B. M. Lloyd, L.M.B.C.	12	12½
W. A. D. Windham, Christ's	13	0
*D. M. Jennens, Clare (str)	12	9
J. F. K. Hinde, Pembroke (cox)	9	4
Average	12	7

OXFORD (*Surrey*)	st.	lb.
J. F. E. Smith, New College (bow)	11	11
A. J. Smith, Merton	12	11
*H. J. Renton, Magdalen	13	1½
L. A. F. Stokes, New College	13	3
M. J. Hawkes, New College	12	11½
C. G. Turner, New College	14	6
*D. N. Callender, Trinity	12	6½
C. G. V. Davidge, Trinity (str)	13	7½
G. Carver, Balliol (cox)	8	7
Average	12	13¼

1952

OXFORD (*Surrey*)	st.	lb.
N. W. Sanders, Merton (bow)	10	7
*P. Gladstone, Christ Church	12	12
C. D. Milling, Merton	12	1
*L. A. F. Stokes, New College	13	0
M. L. Thomas, Jesus	13	6
K. H. Keniston, Balliol	13	6
H. M. C. Quick, Merton	13	4
*C. G. V. Davidge, Trinity (str)	12	7
D. R. Glynne-Jones, Jesus (cox)	8	12
Average	12	9

CAMBRIDGE (*Middlesex*)	st.	lb.
E. J. N. T. Coghill, Pembroke (bow)	12	4
G. A. H. Cadbury, King's	12	2
*J. G. P. Crowden, Pembroke	12	8
G. T. Marshall, King's	13	6½
J. R. Dingle, L.M.B.C.	14	0
*R. F. A. Sharpley, L.M.B.C.	13	8
N. B. M. Clack, L.M.B.C.	12	9½
J. S. M. Jones, L.M.B.C. (str)	11	12½
*J. F. K. Hinde, Pembroke (cox)	9	3
Average	12	11½

1953

CAMBRIDGE (*Surrey*)	st.	lb.
J. A. N. Wallis, L.M.B.C. (bow)	11	12½
*J. S. M. Jones, L.M.B.C.	12	3
J. R. A. Macmillan, 1st and 3rd Trinity	13	0½
*G. T. Marshall, King's	13	5
D. A. T. Leadley, Emmanuel	13	3½
L. B. McCagg, Emmanuel	13	0
J. M. King, L.M.B.C.	12	8½
P. D. Hall, Corpus Christi (str)	12	6
B. M. Eddy, Pembroke (cox)	8	10
Average	12	10

OXFORD (*Middlesex*)	st.	lb.
R. A. Byatt, New College (bow)	12	4
*A. J. Smith, Merton	12	9
J. M. Wilson, Trinity	13	3
E. C. B. Hammond, B.N.C.	13	2
*M. L. Thomas, Jesus	13	10
D. T. H. Davenport, University	13	1
*H. M. C. Quick, Merton	13	5
J. S. Howles, University (str)	12	0
W. R. Marsh, University (cox)	8	10
Average	12	13

1954

OXFORD (*Surrey*)	st.	lb.
R. A. Wheadon, Balliol	11	13
E. V. Vine, B.N.C.	12	0
J. A. Gobbo, Magdalen	12	9
R. D. T. Raikes, Merton	12	6
*H. M. C. Quick, Merton	13	12
J. McLeod, New College	12	1
E. O. G. Pain, Lincoln	12	0
J. J. H. Harrison, Trinity (str)	11	9
*W. R. Marsh, University (cox)	8	12
Average	12	4½

CAMBRIDGE (*Middlesex*)	st.	lb.
*J. A. N. Wallis, L.M.B.C. (bow)	12	2
J. C. G. Stancliffe, Pembroke	12	3
K. D. Hill, Jesus	12	7
K. A. Masser, Trinity Hall	13	13
M. G. Baynes, Trinity Hall	13	1
C. M. Davies, Clare	13	11
J. N. Bruce, Clare	12	1
M. J. Marshall, Jesus (str)	11	9
J. W. Tanburn, Jesus (cox)	8	9
Average	12	7½

Cambridge and Yale University crews before their race in America in 1951. Cambridge won

ROWING QUIZ

1. Who were the lightest and heaviest oarsmen to race in the Boat Race?

★

2. Which has been the most popular, and which the most successful station in the Boat Race?

★

3. Identify the couplet:
"And the end of our long-boat fleet is Defiance—(to Westminster men!)."

★

4. What is a repêchage?

QUIZ ANSWERS

1. A. H. Higgins (Oxford 1882) 9 stone 6 lbs.; J. J. Toogood (Oxford 1829) 14 stone 10 lbs. 2. In 96 races from Putney to Mortlake Surrey has been chosen 54 times and Middlesex 42 times. Middlesex has won 55 times, and Surrey 42 times. (Both stations assumed to have "won" the dead heat of 1877.) 3. The closing couplet to a verse of the Eton Boating Song, written by William Cory, in 1865, music by A. H. Drummond. 4. The system of drawing, obligatory in international competitions, whereby all those beaten in qualifying heats are re-drawn, thus having a second chance of reaching the finals.

ROWING QUIZ

1. Why is the Henley course described as "about 1 mile and 550 yards"?

★

2. What were, or are, (a) The Monarch, (b) a toothpick, (c) Leviathan? (below)

3. What famous sculler was awarded the Olympic Diploma of Merit in 1949?

QUIZ ANSWERS

1. This was the length of the original course from Temple Island to Henley Bridge. Today starting and finishing posts are one mile and 570 yards apart. An average eight, 60 feet long, starting stern on, therefore rows exactly one mile 550 yards. But the distance varies for other boats according to their length. 2. (a) The Monarch is the last surviving ten-oar, now used for processional purposes at Eton. (b) after invention of out-riggers, sculling boats became extremely long and narrow, hence the nickname "toothpick". (c) Leviathan—Oxford University's sixteen-oar coaching punt. 3. J. Beresford, Jr., the only man to have represented Great Britain in five consecutive Olympiads.

DOGGETT'S COAT AND BADGE

Instituted by Thomas Doggett, in 1716, and thus the oldest annual event in the English sporting calendar, the race to be contested from London Bridge to Chelsea, by "six watermen that are out of their time (i.e. apprenticeship) within the year past . . . for ever". The organizing of the race was later vested in the Fishmongers' Company. Today the contestants are permitted to opt against accepting the money prize, and can thus retain their amateur status.

Winners since 1919

Year	Name	District
1919	Phelps, Harry T.	Putney
1920	Hayes, Harry	Deptford
1921	Briggs, Albert E.	Ratcliffe Coft
1922	Phelps, Thomas J.	Putney
1923	Phelps, R. W.	Putney
1924	Green, H. C.	Poplar 210
1925	Barry, Henry A.	Barnes Bridge
1926	Green, T. G. M.	Mortlake
1927	Barry, Louis B.	Barnes
1928	Phelps, John L.	Putney
1929	Taylor, Charles F.	Blackwall
1930	Phelps, E. A.	Putney
1931	Harding, T. J.	Putney
1932	Silvester, H. T.	Hammersmith
1933	Phelps, Eric L.	Putney
1934	Smith, Harold J.	Gravesend 220
1935	Gobbett, A. E.	Blackwall
1936	Taylor, J. A.	Gravesend
1937	Silvester, W. F.	Hammersmith
1938	Phelps, Edwin H.	Putney
1939	Thomas, D. E.	Dagenham
1940	Lupton, Eric G.	Northfleet
1941	Bowles, G. D.	Isleworth
1942	Dott, Frank	Erith
1943	McGuiness, E. F.	Greenwich
1944	Ambler, Frank E.	Twickenham230
1945	Thomas, Sidney	Dagenham
1946	Anson, Jack D.	Northfleet
1947	Palmer, James V.	Gravesend
1948	Clark, H. F.	Inford
1949	Dymott, A. H.	Gravesend
1950	Palmer, G. J.	Gravesend
1951	Martin, M. A. J.	Charlton
1952	Green, G. E.	Putney
1953	Bowles, R. A.	Brentford
1954	Everest, K. C.	Hornchurch 240
1955	Goulding, J. T.	Deptford
1956	Williams, C.	Deptford
1957	Collins, K. C.	Bermondsey
1958	Crouch, R. G.	East Greenwich
1959	G. L. Saunders	Erith

J. Beresford Jun. and E. Phelps pacing B. H. T. Bushnell when he raced in Argentina in 1947. Beresford and Phelps were respectively, and at various times, amateur and professional champions

Boat Race Crews since 1950—contd.

1955

CAMBRIDGE (Middlesex)	st.	lb.	OXFORD (Surrey)	st.	lb.
*D. K. Hill, Jesus	12	4	*J. A. Gobbo, Magdalen	12	10
P. Dubois, First and Third	13	3	*E. V. Vine, Brasenose	11	13
A. A. Mays-Smith, First and Third Trinity	14	0	J. M. Wilson, Trinity	13	5
*K. A. Masser, Trinity Hall	13	12	D. P. Wells, Magdalen	13	2
S. G. D. Tozer, First & Third	13	12	*R. D. T. Raikes, Merton	12	3
R. A. G. Monks, First & Third.	13	9	*J. McLeod, New College	12	1
J. J. Vernon, Trinity Hall	12	1	*E. O. G. Pain, Lincoln	12	0
A. R. Muirhead, L.M.B.C. (str)	12	2	G. Sorrell, Christ Church (str)	11	12
G. T. Harris, Jesus (cox)	9	4	I. Watson, Keble (cox)	9	2
Average	13	2	Average	12	6

1956

CAMBRIDGE (Surrey)	st.	lb.	OXFORD (Middlesex)	st.	lb.
J. A. L. Russell, Clare (bow)	12	2	*E. V. Vine, BNC (bow)	11	12
J. F. Hall-Craggs, L.M.B.C.	12	7	*J. G. McLeod, New College	12	0
M. J. H. Nightingale, Trinity	13	7	N. Paine, Trinity	12	0
*A. A. M. Mays-Smith, Trinity	14	6	K. L. Mason, Queens'	12	3
I. W. Welsh, Queens'	13	11	R. Barrett, Pembroke	14	3
*K. A. Masser, Trinity Hall	13	2	D. A. Cross, Balliol	13	2
M. G. Baynes, Trinity Hall	13	3	R. H. Carnegia, New College –	13	5
M. G. Delahooke, Jesus (str)	12	11	B. S. Mawer, Merton (str)	12	0
J. P. M. Denny, Jesus (cox)	10	0	B. E. B. K. Venner, St. Edmund Hall (cox)	9	11
Average	13	3	Average	12	7

1957

CAMBRIDGE (Surrey)	st.	lb.	OXFORD (Middlesex)	st.	lb.
M. H. Bartlett, Peterhouse	11	8	*G. Sorrell, Christ Church	11	2
C. J. Pumphrey, Magdalen	12	0	S. F. A. Miskin, University	12	9
J. A. Pitchford, Christ's	13	10	R. L. Howard, Worcester	13	7
T. P. A. Norman, Trinity	13	7	A. H. Stearns, Merton	13	12
J. R. Meadows, Jesus	14	0	P. F. Barnard, Christ Church.	14	6
*M. G. Delahooke, Jesus	13	1	*R. Barrett, Pembroke	14	7
R. J. Thompson, Pembroke	12	4	*R. H. Carnegie, New College.	13	12
I. C. F. S. Clayre, Queen's	12	6	*K. A. Mason, The Queen's-.	12	3
R. C. Milton, Emmanuel (cox)	9	2	A. Said, Pembroke (cox)	7	10
Average	12	12	Average	13	5

1958

CAMBRIDGE (Surrey)	st.	lb.	OXFORD (Middlesex)	st.	lb.
A. T. Denby, Radley and Magdalene (bow)	12	4	*G. Sorrell, St. Paul's and Christ Church (bow)	11	13
J. R. Giles, Winchester and Emmanual	12	7	M. J. W. Hall, Winchester and Lincoln	12	5
*J. A. Pitchford, Tonbridge and Christ's	13	10	J. H. Ducker, Monkton Combe and St. Edmund Hall	12	13
R. D. Carver, Eton and Trinity.	13	3	*S. F. A. Miskin, St. Paul's and University	12	13
R. G. Ritchie, Geelong C.S. and Corpus Christi	14	2	F. D. M. Badcock, Harrow and Christ Church	13	3
P. D. Rickett, Eton and Trinity.	13	6	R. Rubin, Yale and Merton	14	8
D. C. Christie, Eton and Pembroke	13	12	J. L. Fage, Wrekin and St. Edmund Hall	12	13
M. B. Maltby, Bedford and Pembroke (stroke)	12	9	D. C. R. Edwards, Downside and Christ Church (stroke).	13	2
J. S. Sulley, Radley and Selwyn (cox)	8	8	J. G. Rowbotham, Winchester and Hertford (cox)	9	0
Average	13	3½	Average	13	0

1959

OXFORD (Middlesex)	st.	lb.	CAMBRIDGE (Surrey)	st.	lb.
S. C. H. Douglas-Mann, Westminster and St. Edmund Hall (bow)	12	5	J. R. Owen, Bedford and L.M.B.C. (bow)	11	8
A. T. Lindsay, Eton and Magdalen	12	8	*J. R. Giles, Winchester and Emmanuel	12	9
*R. L. Howard, Shrewsbury and Worcester	13	10	T. C. Heywood-Lonsdale, Eton and Trinity	13	5
D. C. Rutherford, Rugby and Magdalen	13	0	B. M. P. Thompson-McCausland, Eton and Trinity	12	9
*J. L. Fage, Wrekin and St. Edmund Hall	13	3	G. H. Brown, Shrewsbury and Trinity Hall	13	9
*D. C. R. Edwards, Downside and Christ Church	13	2	J. Beveridge, St. Paul's and Jesus	13	1
D. W. Shaw, Shrewsbury and Keble	13	0	*D. C. Christie, Eton and Pembroke	14	2
J. R. H. Lander, Shrewsbury and Christ Church (stroke)	12	4	*M. B. Maltby, Bedford and Pembroke (stroke)	12	9
*J. G. Rowbotham, Winchester and Hertford (cox)	9	1	*J. S. Sulley, Radley and Selwyn (cox)	8	8
Average	12	12	Average	12	13½

* Old Blues.

OTHER RACES

In addition to the races here listed, Oxford and Cambridge have raced each other at Henley Regatta five times (Oxford won 3 and Cambridge 2), once at the Thames Regatta—now defunct (1844, Oxford won)—and four times in war-time races, of which each university won two. "Blues" are awarded only when a man actually races in an official inter-university boat race.

HEAD BOATS IN SUMMER EIGHTS AT OXFORD AND MAY RACES AT CAMBRIDGE

Oxford		Cambridge	
1920	Magdalen	1919	Third Trinity
1921	New	1920	Jesus
1922	New	1921	Jesus
1923	Magdalen	1922	Jesus
1924	Christ Church	1923	Pembroke
1925	Christ Church	1924	Jesus
1926	Christ Church	1925	Jesus
1927	Christ Church	1926	Lady Margaret
1928	Brasenose	1927	Jesus
1929	Brasenose	1928	First Trinity
1930	Brasenose	1929	Third Trinity
1931	Brasenose	1930	Jesus
1932	Magdalen*	1931	Pembroke
1933	Oriel	1932	Pembroke
1934	Oriel	1933	Pembroke
1935	Oriel	1934	Pembroke
1936	Oriel	1935	Jesus
1937	New College	1936	Jesus
1938	Trinity	1937	Jesus
1939	Trinity	1938	Jesus
1946	Trinity	1939	Jesus
1947	Trinity	1940	Trinity Hall
1948	Trinity	1941	Clare
1949	Trinity	1942	Clare
1950	New College	1943	Clare
1951	Merton	1944	Clare
1952	Balliol	1945	First and Third Trinity
1953	Magdalen	1946	Trinity Hall
1954	Magdalen	1947	Jesus
1955	Balliol	1948	Jesus
1956	Balliol	1949	Clare
1957	Queen's	1950	Lady Margaret
1958	Christ Church	1951	Lady Margaret
1959	St. Edmund Hall	1952	Lady Margaret
		1953	Lady Margaret
		1954	Lady Margaret
		1955	Jesus
		1956	Jesus
		1957	Jesus
		1958	Jesus
		1959	Lady Margaret

G. O. Nickalls, Chairman of the Amateur Rowing Association

HEAD OF THE RIVER

The Head of the River Race, instituted by the late Steve Fairbairn, takes place over the tideway championship course, normally from Mortlake to Putney, a week before the University Boat Race. It attracts probably the largest entry of competing oarsmen in the world. In 1959 there were 276 eights starting—that is, nearly 2,500 oarsmen and coxswains. The race is on a time basis. There are many other head-of-the-river races in different parts of the country.

1926	London R.C.
1927	London R.C. and Thames R.C.
1928	London R.C.
1929	London R.C.
1930	London R.C.
1931	London R.C.
1932	London R.C.
1933	London R.C.
1934	London R.C.
1935	London R.C.
1936	Thames R.C.
1937	No race
1938	Cam. Univ. Goldie B.C.
1939	London R.C.
1946	Imperial Coll. London B.C.
1947	Jesus Coll. Cam. B.C.
1948	Thames R.C.
1949	London R.C.
1950	London R.C.
1951	Jesus Coll. Cam. B.C.
1952	Jesus Coll. Cam. B.C.
1953	Thames R.C.
1954	Royal Air Force R.C.
1955	Thames R.C.
1956	Thames R.C.
1957	Oxf. Univ. Isis B.C.
1958	Barn Cottage
1959	Barn Cottage

Royal Tennis

INTRODUCTION

In order to distinguish it from its infant off-shoot Lawn Tennis, the game correctly called simply Tennis is now variously described as Royal Tennis, Court Tennis or Real Tennis.

The origins of Tennis lie in mediaeval times when in certain French monasteries a game called *Jeu de Paume* (literally—game of the palm of the hand) was played in the cloisters. We are continually reminded of the French origin by the special vocabulary that is still attached to Tennis.

The earliest references to the game are in the twelfth century. The playing of this game by clerics gave rise to disapproval from some quarters. The use of rackets, instead of the gloved hand, seems to have started in the fifteenth century.

The game came to the British Isles, possibly first via Scotland where the ties with France were so much closer, probably in the first half of the thirteenth century.

The origin of the word Tennis is uncertain. Of the many ingenious theories, perhaps the most feasible is that the word came from the habit of players shouting "Tenez" before serving. Just as today the word "play" is shouted by the marker in a rackets match.

The scoring of 15, 30, 40 and game probably derived from the fact that in the middle ages the number 60 was of great significance; for example 60 seconds per minute and 60 minutes per hour. Thus it would seem that "40" is a shortened version of "45". Similarly in modern practice in Lawn Tennis, when players are scoring among themselves, the call "fif" means "fifteen".

The word "love" means "nothing" in Shakespearean English—for example "neither for love nor money" or "a labour of love". There is no good reason why the same word should not have been used to mean nought or zero in tennis.

SOME TECHNICAL TERMS PECULIAR TO THE GAME OF TENNIS

Bandeau. The strip of wall immediately below a penthouse, usually made of the same material as the penthouse.

Bisque. One stroke in a set conceded to an opponent (Rule 22).

James Dear, former British and World Champion, at play.

Chase. A chase is made whenever the ball falls in the hazard court, or anywhere on the service side, or enters a gallery, except the winning gallery (Rule 9).

Dedans. The opening at the back of the service side.

Grille. The opening in the grille wall.

Side Penthouse. The penthouse above the galleries, up to its junction with the other penthouses.

Tray. The inner part of the bottom of an opening behind the ledge, usually made of wood.

Albert Johnson, 1957 World Champion, in action.

WORLD'S TENNIS CHAMPIONSHIP

c. 1740	Clerge	France
1765	Raymond Masson	France
1785	Joseph Barcellon	France
1816	Marchesio	Italy
1819	Philip Cox	G.B.
1829	J. Edmond Barre	France
1862	Edmund Tompkins	G.B.
1871	Edmund Tompkins	G.B.
1871	George Lambert	G.B.
1885	Tom Pettitt	U.S.A.
1890	Tom Pettitt	U.S.A.
1890	Tom Pettitt	U.S.A.
1890	Charles Saunders	G.B.
1895	Peter Latham	G.B.
1898	Peter Latham	G.B.
1904	Peter Latham	G.B.
1905	Cecil Fairs	G.B.
1906	Cecil Fairs	G.B.
1907	Peter Latham	G.B.
1908	Peter Latham	G.B.
1908	Cecil Fairs	G.B.
1910	Cecil Fairs	G.B.
1912	G. F. Covey	G.B.
1914	Mr. Jay Gould	U.S.A.
1916	Mr. Jay Gould	U.S.A.
1916	G. F. Covey	G.B.
1922	G. F. Covey	G.B.
1923	G. F. Covey	G.B.
1926	G. F. Covey	G.B.
1928	Pierre Etchebaster	France
1930	Pierre Etchebaster	France
1937	Pierre Etchebaster	France
1948	Pierre Etchebaster	France
1949	Pierre Etchebaster	France
1950	Pierre Etchebaster	France
1955	James Dear	G.B.
1957	Albert Johnson	G.B.
1959	Northrup R. Knox	U.S.A.

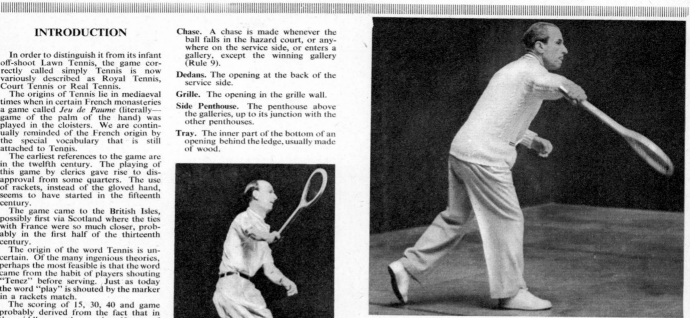

Pierre Etchebaster of France, World Champion from 1928 to 1955, playing at the Queen's Club in 1953.

AMATEUR TENNIS CHAMPIONSHIP

1888	J. M. Heathcote	
1889	Sir E. Grey	
1890	E. B. C. Curtis	
1891	Sir E. Grey	
1892	H. E. Crawley	
1893	H. E. Crawley	
1894	H. E. Crawley	
1895	Sir E. Grey	
1896	Sir E. Grey	
1897	J. B. Gribble	
1898	Sir E. Grey	
1899	E. H. Miles	
1900	E. H. Miles	
1901	E. H. Miles	
1902	E. H. Miles	
1903	E. H. Miles	
1904	V. H. Pennell	
1905	E. H. Miles	
1906	E. H. Miles	
1907	Jay Gould	U.S.A.
1908	Jay Gould	U.S.A.
1909	E. H. Miles	
1910	E. H. Miles	
1911	Hon. N. S. Lytton	
1912	E. M. Baerlein	
1913	Hon. N. S. Lytton	
1914	E. M. Baerlein	
1919	E. M. Baerlein	
1920	E. M. Baerlein	
1921	E. M. Baerlein	
1922	E. M. Baerlein	
1923	E. M. Baerlein	
1924	E. M. Baerlein	
1925	E. M. Baerlein	
1926	E. M. Baerlein	
1927	E. M. Baerlein	
1928	L. Lees	
1929	E. M. Baerlein	
1930	E. M. Baerlein	
1931	L. Lees	
1932	Lord Aberdare	
1933	L. Lees	
1934	L. Lees	
1935	L. Lees	
1936	L. Lees	
1937	L. Lees	
1938	Lord Aberdare	
1939	W. D. Macpherson	
1946	L. Lees	
1947	Lord Cullen	
1948	P. Kershaw	
1949	Ogden Phipps	U.S.A.
1950	A. B. Martin	U.S.A.
1951	P. Kershaw	
1952	Lord Cullen	
1953	Hon. M. G. L. Bruce	
1954	Hon. M. G. L. Bruce	
1955	R. C. Riseley	
1956	Hon. M. G. L. Bruce	
1957	Hon. M. G. L. Bruce	
1958	Northrup R. Knox	U.S.A.

ROYAL TENNIS QUIZ

1. The longest reign by a World Champion is 33 years by a Frenchman. Name him.

★

2. A tennis court is divided into two sides. Name them.

★

3. Who is the reigning World and Amateur Tennis Champion and what is his nationality? *(below)*

4. What restriction is there concerning the length of a racket?

★

5. How many courts are there in existence in Great Britain: (a) between 100 and 150; (b) between 40 and 50; or (c) 11?

QUIZ ANSWERS

1. Edmond Barre (France), 1829 to 1862. 2. Service side and Hazard side. 3. Northrup R. Knox; American. 4. None whatever. 5. (b).

Rugby Union

Compiled by **Ross McWhirter**

Rugby Union Correspondent:
The Star

INTRODUCTION

Rugby Union Football is an amateur 15-men-a-side team game of football in which handling is the distinctive feature. The object of the game is to score more points than the opposing side by grounding the oval-shaped ball behind the other team's "try line" and so scoring three points for a "try". If the ball is then successfully place kicked between the goal-posts but over the 10-ft. high crossbar, the try is then deemed to have been "converted" into a goal, which is worth five points. There are three other methods of scoring, each worth three points: the dropped goal (i.e. the ball is kicked on the "half volley"); the penalty goal, which may be taken either by a placed kick or by a drop kick; and the rare goal from a mark which follows a "fair catch" and may be taken by a placed kick or a drop kick.

The game is governed by a code of 37 laws (N.B. not rules) which can only be made or altered by the International Rugby Football Board, which consists of two representatives from each of the four home unions (England, Ireland, Scotland and Wales) and from the three Dominion unions (Australia, New Zealand and South Africa).

These laws also apply by choice in France and other non-Commonwealth countries.

The best short description of the game is contained in Law 13, headed "Mode of Play":

"A match is started by a kick-off, after which any player who is on-side may, at any time, kick, pick up, or run with the ball, or tackle an opponent holding the ball (except as provided for in

D. F. Allison, with J. E. Williams holding the ball, converts England's second try against Ireland during the 1956 International at Twickenham.

Laws 15 and 16). The ball may be passed or knocked from one player to another provided it is not passed, knocked or thrown forward, by hand or arm."

HISTORY

The most important dates in the history of the game are as follows:

1823 By tradition, on hearsay evidence only, a boy at Rugby School, named William Webb Ellis, is alleged to have run forwards with the ball in his arms, which was against the practice of the day.

1870 The game introduced to New Zealand.

1871 The Rugby Union was formed in London and the first-ever international match, between Scotland and England, took place at Edinburgh.

1873 The Scottish Rugby Union formed.

1876 The game was introduced in South Africa.

1877 The number of players in international matches was reduced from 20 to 15 a side.

1877 A club was formed in France.

1879 The Irish Rugby Union formed.

1880 The Welsh Rugby Union formed.

1888 A British team toured Australia and New Zealand.

1889 The South African Rugby Football Board formed.

1890 The International Board formed.

1893 The split between Rugby Union and Rugby League (then known as the Northern Union) took place over the loss of a

motion advocating the payment of compensation for wages lost by players ("broken time"). The clubs who broke away totalled 22—from Yorkshire, Lancashire and Cheshire.

1905 The present scoring values were adopted (but see 1948–9). The first All-Blacks visited the British Isles. England played France for the first time.

1906 The first Springboks visited the British Isles.

1909 Twickenham used for the first time.

1923 A centenary match was staged at Rugby School.

1925 Murrayfield opened by the Scottish Rugby Union.

1931 The Four Home Unions broke with France owing to allegations of professionalism.

1946–7 The International Championship was restarted, with France again taking part.

1948–9 The dropped goal was cut in value from four points to three points.

MOST CAPPED PLAYERS

ENGLAND

W. W. Wakefield	31
E. Evans	30
R. Cove-Smith	29
J. Butterfield	28
A. T. Voyce	27
J. S. Tucker	27
C. N. Lowe	25
J. MacG. K. Kendall-Carpenter	23
W. J. A. Davies	22
J. G. G. Birkett	21
H. G. Periton	21

RUGBY QUIZ

1. What date is given traditionally as the year in which Rugby football was "invented" at Rugby School?

   ★

2. To whom is attributed the "invention" of Rugby football?

   ★

3. In what year was the Rugby Union founded?

QUIZ ANSWERS

1. 1823. 2. The Rev. William Webb Ellis (1807–1872). 3. 1871.

J. MacG. Kendall Carpenter (England)

W. I. D. Elliot (Scotland)

N. Shehadie (Australia)

SCOTLAND

J. MacD. Bannerman	37
I. S. Smith	32
W. I. D. Elliot	29
W. M. Simmers	28
J. C. McCallum	26
G. P. S. Macpherson	26
D. Drysdale	26
W. E. Maclagan	25
J. B. Nelson	25
Mark Morrison	23
J. A. Beattie	23

IRELAND

J. W. Kyle	46
G. V. Stephenson	42
N. J. Henderson	40
E. O'D. Davy	34
G. T. Hamlet	30
W. E. Crawford	30
J. D. Clinch	30
J. L. Farrell	29
M. Sugden	28
J. S. McCarthy	28

WALES

K. J. Jones	44
R. M. Owen	35
W. J. Bancroft	33
J. R. G. Stephens	32
W. J. Trew	29
C. I. Morgan	29
A. J. Gould	27
W. C. Powell	27
M. C. Thomas	27
R. C. C. Thomas	26

M. Prat (France)

FRANCE

J. Prat	38
G. Dufau	33
A. Cassayet	32
A. Jaurreguy	28
E. Ribere	27
G. Basquet	26
R. Bienes	25
M. Prat	25
L. Mias	23
M. Celya	23

AUSTRALIA

N. Shehadie	28
C. T. Burke	26
E. T. Bonis	21
C. J. Windon	20
A. Cameron	19
K. A. Cross	17
W. H. Cerutti	17
E. Stapleton	15
A. R. Miller	15
T. Allen	14
N. V. Cottrell	14
H. J. Solomon	14

R. C. Hemi (New Zealand)

NEW ZEALAND

R. A. White	23
K. Skinner	20
R. W. H. Scott	17
R. A. Jarden	16
R. C. Hemi	16
R. R. King	14
F. Roberts	12
A. Cottrell	11
G. F. Hart	11
J. Hunter	11
C. Seeling	11

SOUTH AFRICA

J. du Rand	21
M. M. Louw	18
C. Koch	18
W. F. Bergh	17
B. L. Osler	17
D. Craven	16
P. J. Nel	16
G. H. Brand	16
H. J. Bekker	15
P. J. Mostert	14

L. P. MacLachlan (Scotland) breaks for the line, closely pursued by English forwards, during the 1954 England v. Scotland International. England beat Scotland by 13 points to 3.

ENGLAND v. SCOTLAND

England 35 wins, Scotland 27, drawn 12

1870–71	Scotland	1G, 1T to 1T
1871–72	England	2G, 2T to 1G
1872–73	Draw	No score
1873–74	England	1G to 1T
1874–75	Draw	No score
1875–76	England	1G, 1T to 0
1876–77	Scotland	1G to 0
1877–78	Draw	No score
1878–79	Draw	1G each
1879–80	England	2G, 3T to 1G
1880–81	Draw	1G, 1T each
1881–82	Scotland	2T to 0
1882–83	England	2T to 1T
1883–84	England	1G to 1T
1884–85	No match	
1885–86	Draw	No score
1886–87	Draw	1T each
1887–88 } 1888–89 }	No match	
1889–90	England	1G, 1T to 0
1890–91	Scotland	3G to 1G
1891–92	England	1G to 0
1892–93	Scotland	2DG to 0
1893–94	Scotland	2T to 0
1894–95	Scotland	1PG, 1T to 1PG
1895–96	Scotland	1G, 2T to 0
1896–97	England	1G, 1DG, 1T to 1T
1897–98	Draw	1T each
1898–99	England	1G to 0
1899–1900	Draw	No score
1900–01	Scotland	3G, 1T to 1T
1901–02	England	2T to 1T
1902–03	Scotland	1DG, 2T to 2T
1903–04	Scotland	2T to 1T
1904–05	Scotland	1G, 1T to 0
(Modern scoring values adopted)		
1905–06	England	9 pts. (3T) to 3 pts. (1T)
1906–07	Scotland	8 (1G, 1T) to 3 (1T)
1907–08	Scotland	16 (1G, 2DG, 1T) to 10 (2G)
1908–09	Scotland	18 (3G, 1T) to 8 (1G, 1T)
1909–10	England	14 (1G, 3T) to 5 (1G)

1910–11	England	13 (2G, 1T) to 8 (1G, 1T)
1911–12	Scotland	8 (1G, 1T) to 3 (1T)
1912–13	England	3 (1T) to 0
1913–14	England	16 (2G, 2T) to 15 (1G, 1DG, 2T)
1914–19	No matches	
1919–20	England	13 (2G, 1T) to 4 (1DG)
1920–21	England	18 (3G, 1T) to 0
1921–22	England	11 (1G, 2T) to 5 (1G)
1922–23	England	8 (1G, 1T) to 6 (2T)
1923–24	England	19 (3G, 1DG) to 0
1924–25	Scotland	14 (2G, 1DG) to 11 (1G, 1PG, 1T)
1925–26	Scotland	17 (2G, 1DG, 1T) to 9 (3T)
1926–27	Scotland	21 (1G, 1DG, 4T) to 13 (2G, 1PG)
1927–28	England	6 (2T) to 0
1928–29	Scotland	12 (4T) to 6 (2T)
1929–30	Draw	No score
1930–31	Scotland	28 (5G, 1T) to 19 (2G, 1PG, 2T)
1931–32	England	16 (2G, 2T) to 3 (1T)
1932–33	Scotland	3 (1T) to 0
1933–34	England	6 (2T) to 3 (1T)
1834–35	Scotland	10 (2G) to 7 (1DG, 1T)
1935–36	England	9 (3T) to 6 (1G, 1PG)
1936–37	England	6 (2T) to 3 (1PG)
1937–38	Scotland	21 (2PG, 5T) to 16 (1DG, 3PG, 1T)
1938–39	England	9 (3PG) to 6 (2T)
1939–46	No matches	
1946–47	England	24 (4G, 1DG) to 3 (1G)
1947–48	Scotland	6 (2T) to 3 (1PG)
(Dropped goal reduced to three points)		
1948–49	England	19 (2G, 3T) to 3 (1PG)
1949–50	Scotland	13 (2G, 1T) to 11 (1G, 1PG, 1T)
1950–51	England	5 (1G) to 3 (1T)
1951–52	England	19 (2G, 1DG, 2T) to 3 (1T)
1952–53	England	26 (4G, 2T) to 8 (1G, 1T)
1953–54	England	13 (2G, 1T) to 3 (1T)
1954–55	England	9 (1PG, 2T) to 6 (1PG, 1T)
1955–56	England	11 (1G, 2PG) to 6 (1PG, 1T)
1956–57	England	16 (2G, 1PG, 1T) to 3 (1PG)
1957–58	Draw	3 (1PG) to 3 (1PG)
1958–59	Draw	3 (1PG) to 3 (1PG)

G. J. Bendon (England) makes a break with the ball during the 1959 England v. Scotland match.

RUGBY QUIZ

1. In what year was the first ever Rugby international match and between which countries was it played?

★

2. How many players were there on each side in the early internationals?

★

3. When was the International Board formed?

QUIZ ANSWERS

1. In 1871 between Scotland and England at Raeburn Place, Edinburgh 2. 20 aside until 1877. 3. 1890.

257

RUGBY QUIZ

1. Which country has won the Triple Crown most often?

    ★

2. What was a "field" goal and when was it abolished?

    ★

3. In what year did the Four Home Unions break off relations with France, and when was the breach healed?

QUIZ ANSWERS

1. England. 2. A punt or fly hack that sent the ball between the goal posts and over the bar was so termed. This method of scoring was abolished in 1905. 3. 1931 to 1939, but the intervention of the war prevented an actual resumption of international matches until 1946/47.

The England v. Ireland International of 1938, played at Dublin. F. J. Reynolds, the English scrum-half, gets away from a scrum in the Irish 25. England won by 36 points to 14.

ENGLAND v. IRELAND

England 44 wins, Ireland 22, drawn 5

1874–75	England	2G, 1T to 0
1875–76	England	1G, 1T to 0
1876–77	England	2G, 2T to 0
1877–78	England	2G, 1T to 0
1878–79	England	3G, 2T to 0
1879–80	England	1G, 1T to 1T
1880–81	England	2G, 2T to 0
1881–82	Draw	2T each
1882–83	England	1G, 3T to 1T
1883–84	England	1G to 0
1884–85	England	2T to 1T
1885–86	England	1T to 0
1886–87	Ireland	2G to 0
1887–89	No match	
1889–90	England	3T to 0
1890–91	England	2G, 3T to 0
1891–92	England	1G, 1T to 0
1892–93	England	2T to 0
1893–94	Ireland	1DG, 1T to 1G
1894–95	England	2T to 1T
1895–96	Ireland	2G to 1DG
1896–97	Ireland	1G(m), 3T to 2PG, 1T
1897–98	Ireland	1PG, 2T to 1PG, 1T
1898–99	Ireland	1PG, 1T to 0
1899–1900	England	1G, 1DG, 2T to 1DG
1900–01	Ireland	2G to 1PG, 1T
1901–02	England	2T to 1T
1902–03	Ireland	1PG, 1T to 0
1903–04	England	2G, 3T to 0
1904–05	Ireland	1G, 4T to 1T
(*Modern scoring values adopted*)		
1905–06	Ireland	16 (2G, 2T) to 6 (2T)
1906–07	Ireland	17 (2G(1m), 3T) to 4 (1DG)
1907–08	England	13 (2G, 1T) to 3 (1PG)
1908–09	England	11 (1G, 2T) to 5 (1G)
1909–10	Draw	No score
1910–11	Ireland	3 (1T) to 0
1911–12	England	15 (5T) to 0
1912–13	England	15 (1PG, 4T) to 4 (1DG)
1913–14	England	17 (1G, 4T) to 12 (1G, 1DG, 1T)
1914–19	No matches	
1919–20	England	14 (1G, 3T) to 11 (1G, 1PG, 1T)
1920–21	England	15 (1G, 1DG, 2T) to 0
1921–22	England	12 (4T) to 3 (1T)
1922–23	England	23 (2G, 1DG, 3T) to 5 (1G)
1923–24	England	14 (1G, 3T) to 3 (1T)
1924–25	Draw	6 each (2T)
1925–26	Ireland	19 (2G, 1PG, 2T) to 15 (3G)
1926–27	Ireland	8 (1G, 1T) to 6 (1PG, 1T)
1927–28	England	7 (1DG, 1T) to 6 (2T)
1928–29	Ireland	6 (2T) to 5 (1G)
1929–30	Ireland	4 (1DG) to 3 (1T)
1930–31	Ireland	6 (1PG, 1T) to 5 (1G)
1931–32	England	11 (1G, 2PG) to 8 (1G, 1PG)
1932–33	England	17 (1G, 4T) to 6 (1PG, 1T)
1933–34	England	13 (2G, 1T) to 3 (1T)
1934–35	England	14 (1G, 3PG) to 3 (1T)
1935–36	Ireland	6 (2T) to 3 (1T)
1936–37	England	9 (1PG, 2T) to 8 (1G, 1T)
1937–38	England	36 (6G, 1PG, 1T) to 14 (1G, 3T)
1938–39	Ireland	5 (1G) to 0
1940–46	No matches	
1946–47	Ireland	22 (2DG, 1PG, 3T) to 0
1947–48	Ireland	11 (1G, 2T) to 10 (2G)
(*Dropped goal reduced to three points*)		
1948–49	Ireland	14 (1G, 2PG, 1T) to 5 (1G)
1949–50	England	3 (1T) to 0
1950–51	Ireland	3 (1PG) to 0
1951–52	England	3 (1T) to 0
1952–53	Draw	9 each (2PG, 1T)
1953–54	England	14 (1G, 1PG, 2T) to 3 (1PG)
1954–55	Draw	Ireland 6 (1PG, 1T); England 6 (2T)
1955–56	England	20 (1G, 3PG, 2T) to 0
1956–57	England	6 (1PG, 1T) to 0
1957–58	England	6 (2T) to 0
1958–59	England	3 (1PG) to 0

ENGLAND v. WALES

England 30 wins, Wales 26, drawn 8

1880–81	England	7G, 1DG, 6T to 0
1881–82	No match	
1882–83	England	2G, 4T, to 0
1883–84	England	1G, 2T, to 1G
1884–85	England	1G, 4T, to 1G, 1T
1885–86	England	1G, 2T to 1G
1886–87	Draw	No score

P. B. Jackson (England) kicks to touch during the 1958 International against Australia.

1887–88 and 1888–89	No matches	
1889–90	Wales	1T to 0
1890–91	England	2G, 1T to 1G
1891–92	England	3G, 1T to 0
1892–93	Wales	1G, 1PG, 2T to 1G, 3T
1893–94	England	5G (1m) to 1T
1894–95	England	1G, 3T to 2T
1895–96	England	2G, 5T to 0
1896–97	Wales	1G, 2T to 0
1897–98	England	1G, 3T to 1DG, 1T
1898–99	Wales	4G, 2T to 1T
1899–1900	Wales	2G, 1PG to 1T
1900–01	Wales	2G, 1T to 0
1901–02	Wales	1PG, 2T to 1G, 1T
1902–03	Wales	3G, 2T to 1G
1903–04	Draw	England 1G, 1PG, 2T; Wales 3G (1m)
1904–05	Wales	2G, 5T to 0
(*Modern scoring values adopted*)		
1905–06	Wales	16 (2G, 2T) to 3 (1T)
1906–07	Wales	22 (2G, 4T) to 0
1907–08	Wales	27 (3G, 1DG, 1PG, 2T) to 18 (3G, 1T)
1908–09	Wales	8 (1G, 1T) to 0
1909–10	England	11 (1G, 1PG, 1T) to 6 (2T)
1910–11	Wales	15 (1PG, 4T) to 11 (1G, 2T)
1911–12	England	8 (1G, 1T) to 0
1912–13	England	12 (1G, 1DG, 1T) to 0
1913–14	England	10 (2G) to 9 (1G, 1DG)
1914–19	No matches	
1919–20	Wales	19 (1G, 2DG, 1PG, 1T) to 5 (1G)
1920–21	England	18 (1G, 1DG, 3T) to 3 (1T)
1921–22	Wales	28 (2G, 6T) to 6 (2T)
1922–23	England	7 (1DG, 1T) to 3 (1T)
1923–24	England	17 (1G, 4T) to 9 (3T)
1924–25	England	12 (1PG, 3T) to 6 (2T)
1925–26	Draw	3 each (1T)
1926–27	England	11 (1G, 1PG, 2G (1m)) to 9 (1PG, 2T)

(*contd. p. 259, col. 1*)

. R. Kavanagh (Ireland) moving across to intercept and effectively stop an English forward during the 1958 International at Twickenham. England won by 6 points to 0.

Season	Winner	Score
1927–28	England	10 (2G) to 8 (1G, 1T)
1928–29	England	8 (1G, 1T) to 3 (1T)
1929–30	England	11 (1G, 1PG, 1T) to 6 (1PG, 1T)
1930–31	Draw	England 11 (1G, 2PG); Wales 11 (2G (1m)), (1T)
1931–32	Wales	12 (1G, 1DG, 1PG) to 5 (1G)
1932–33	Wales	7 (1DG, 1T) to 3 (1T)
1933–34	England	9 (3T) to 0
1934–35	Draw	England 3 (1PG); Wales 3 (1T)
1935–36	Draw	No score
1936–37	England	4 (1DG) to 3 (1T)
1937–38	Wales	14 (1G, 2PG, 1T) to 8 (1G, 1T)
1938–39	England	3 (1T) to 0
1940–45	No matches	
1946–47	England	9 (1G, 1DG) to 6 (2T)
1947–48	Draw	England 3 (1PG); Wales 3 (1T)

(Dropped goal reduced to three points)

Season	Winner	Score
1948–49	Wales	9 (3T) to 3 (1DG)
1949–50	Wales	11 (1G, 1PG, 1T) to 5 (1G)
1950–51	Wales	23 (4G, 1T) to 5 (1G)
1951–52	Wales	8 (1G, 1T) to 6 (2T)
1952–53	England	8 (1G, 1T) to 3 (1PG)
1953–54	England	9 (3T) to 6 (1PG, 1T)
1954–55	Wales	3 (1PG) to 0
1955–56	Wales	8 (1G, 1T) to 3 (1PG)
1956–57	England	3 (1PG) to 0
1957–58	Draw	England 3 (1T); Wales 3 (1PG)
1958–59	Wales	5 (1G) to 0

Pat Sykes (England) makes a dash for the ball against Wales at Cardiff, 1953.

ENGLAND v. FRANCE

England 24 wins, France 8, drawn 2

Season	Winner	Score
1905–06	England	35 (4G, 5T) to 8 (1G, 1T)
1906–07	England	41 (5G, 1DG, 4T) to 13 (2G, 1PG)
1907–08	England	19 (2G, 3T) to 0
1908–09	England	22 (2G, 4T) to 0
1909–10	England	11 (1G, 2T) to 3 (1T)
1910–11	England	37 (5G, 2PG, 2T) to 0
1911–12	England	18 (1G, 1DG, 3T) to 8 (1G, 1T)
1912–13	England	20 (1G, 5T) to 0
1913–14	England	39 (6G, 3T) to 13 (2G, 1T)
1915–18	No matches	
1919–20	England	8 (1G, 1PG) to 3 (1T)
1920–21	England	10 (2G) to 6 (2PG)
1921–22	Draw	England 11 (1G, 2PG); France 11 (1G, 2PG)
1922–23	England	12 (1G, 1DG, 1T) to 3 (1PG)
1923–24	England	19 (2G, 3T) to 7 (1DG, 1T)
1924–25	England	13 (3G (1m)) to 11 (1G, 2T)
1925–26	England	11 (1G, 2T) to 0
1926–27	France	3 (1T) to 0
1927–28	England	18 (3G, 1T) to 8 (1G, 1T)
1928–29	England	16 (2G, 2T) to 6 (2T)
1929–30	England	11 (1G, 2T) to 5 (1G)
1930–31	England	14 (2DG, 2T) to 13 (2G, 1T)
1932–45	No matches	
1946–47	England	6 (2T) to 3 (1PG)
1947–48	France	15 (1G, 1DG, 2T) to 0

(Dropped goal reduced to three points)

Season	Winner	Score
1948–49	England	8 (1G, 1DG) to 3 (1DG)
1949–50	France	6 (2T) to 3 (1T)
1950–51	France	11 (1G, 1DG, 1T) to 3 (1T)
1951–52	England	6 (2PG) to 3 (1T)
1952–53	England	11 (1G, 2T) to 0
1953–54	France	11 (1G, 1DG, 1T) to 3 (1T)
1954–55	France	16 (2G, 2DG) to 9 (2PG, 1T)
1955–56	France	14 (1G, 2PG, 1T) to 9 (2PG, 1T)
1956–57	England	9 (3T) to 5 (1G)
1957–58	England	6 (2T) to 0
1958–59	England	3 (1PG) to 0

M. R. Steele-Bodger clears for England versus France at Twickenham, 1948.

SCOTLAND v. IRELAND

Scotland 35 wins, Ireland 32, drawn 3

Season	Winner	Score
1876–77	Scotland	6G, 2T to 0
1877–78	No match	
1878–79	Scotland	2G, 1T to 0
1879–80	Scotland	3G, 2T to 0
1880–81	Ireland	1G to 1T
1881–82	Scotland	2T to 0

A. Ashcroft (England)   A. J. F. O'Reilly (Ireland)

Season	Winner	Score
1882–83	Scotland	1G, 1T to 0
1883–84	Scotland	2G, 2T to 1T
1884–85	Scotland	1G, 2T to 0
1885–86	Scotland	4G, 2T to 0
1886–87	Scotland	2G, 2T to 0
1887–88	Scotland	1G to 0
1888–89	Scotland	1DG to 0
1889–90	Scotland	1DG, 1T to 0
1890–91	Scotland	4G, 2T to 0
1891–92	Scotland	1T to 0
1892–93	Draw	No score
1893–94	Ireland	1G to 0
1894–95	Scotland	2T to 0
1895–96	Draw	No score
1896–97	Scotland	1G, 1PG to 1T
1897–98	Scotland	1G, 1T to 0
1898–99	Ireland	3T to 1PG
1899–1900	Draw	No score
1900–01	Scotland	3T to 1G
1901–02	Ireland	1G to 0
1902–03	Scotland	1T to 0
1903–04	Scotland	2G, 3T to 1T
1904–05	Ireland	1G, 2T to 1G

(Modern scoring values adopted)

Season	Winner	Score
1905–06	Scotland	13 (3G (1m)) to 6 (2T)
1906–07	Scotland	15 (3G) to 3 (1PG)
1907–08	Ireland	16 (2G, 2T) to 11 (1G, 1PG, 1T)
1908–09	Scotland	9 (3T) to 3 (1PG)
1909–10	Scotland	14 (1G, 3T) to 0
1910–11	Ireland	16 (2G, 2T) to 10 (1DG, 2T)
1911–12	Ireland	10 (1DG, 1PG, 1T) to 8 (1G, 1T)
1912–13	Scotland	29 (4G, 3T) to 17 (2G, 1DG, 1T)
1913–14	Ireland	6 (2T) to 0
1915–18	No matches	
1919–20	Scotland	19 (2G, 1PG, 2T) to 0
1920–21	Ireland	9 (3T) to 8 (1G, 1T)
1921–22	Scotland	6 (2T) to 3 (1T)
1922–23	Scotland	13 (2G, 1T) to 3 (1T)
1923–24	Scotland	13 (2G, 1T) to 8 (1G, 1T)
1924–25	Scotland	14 (2G, 1DG) to 8 (1G, 1PG)
1925–26	Ireland	3 (1T) to 0
1926–27	Ireland	6 (2T) to 0
1927–28	Ireland	13 (2G, 1T) to 5 (1G)
1928–29	Scotland	16 (2G, 2T) to 7 (1DG, 1T)
1929–30	Ireland	14 (1G, 3T) to 11 (1G, 2T)
1930–31	Ireland	8 (1G, 1T) to 5 (1G)
1931–32	Ireland	20 (4G) to 8 (1G, 1T)
1932–33	Scotland	8 (2DG) to 6 (2T)
1933–34	Scotland	16 (2G, 1PG, 1T) to 9 (3T)
1934–35	Ireland	12 (4T) to 5 (1G)
1935–36	Ireland	10 (1DG, 2T) to 4 (1DG)
1936–37	Ireland	11 (1G, 2T) to 4 (1DG)
1937–38	Scotland	23 (2G, 1DG, 1PG, 2T) to 14 (1G, 3T)

(contd. on p. 260, col. 1)

RUGBY QUIZ

1. The Oxford versus Cambridge match has been played at 6 venues. Where was the match played from 1888 to 1921, immediately before it was transferred to Twickenham?

★

2. If a player makes a "fair catch" he may take any of three types of kick. Name them.

★

3. Why is the Calcutta Cup, which is held by the winner of the annual England versus Scotland match, so called?

QUIZ ANSWERS

1. Queen's Club, West Kensington, London. 2. A punt, a drop kick or a place kick. But only either of the last two can score a goal. 3. It was made in India from the rupees left in the bank by the disbanded Calcutta Club in 1878.

R. W. D. Marques (England)

B. Meredith (Wales)

England v. Ireland—*contd.*

1938–39	Ireland	12 (1PG, 1G (m), 2T) to 3 (1T)
1940–45	No matches	
1946–47	Ireland	3 (1T) to 0
1947–48	Ireland	6 (2T) to 0

(Dropped goal reduced to three points)

1948–49	Ireland	13 (2G, 1PG) to 3 (1PG)
1949–50	Ireland	21 (3G, 2PG) to 0
1950–51	Ireland	6 (1DG, 1T) to 5 (1G)
1951–52	Ireland	12 (1PG, 3T) to 8 (1G, 1PG)
1952–53	Ireland	26 (4G, 2T) to 8 (1G, 1PG)
1953–54	Ireland	6 (2T) to 0
1954–55	Scotland	12 (2PG, 1DG, 1T) to 3 (1PG)
1955–56	Ireland	14 (1G, 3T) to 10 (2G)
1956–57	Ireland	5 (1G) to 3 (1PG)
1957–58	Ireland	12 (2PG, 2T) to 6 (2T)
1958–59	Ireland	8 (1G, 1PG) to 3 (1PG)

K. Mullen (Ireland)

M. C. Thomas (Wales)

H. Tanner (Wales).

Ken Jones (Wales) tussles for possession with H. F McLeod (Scotland) at Murrayfield, 1957.

SCOTLAND v. WALES

Wales 32 wins, Scotland 29, drawn 2

1882–83	Scotland	3G to 1G
1883–84	Scotland	1G, 1T to 0
1884–85	Draw	No score
1885–86	Scotland	2G, 1T to 0
1886–87	Scotland	4G, 8T to 0
1887–88	Wales	1T to 0
1888–89	Scotland	2T to 0
1889–90	Scotland	1G, 2T to 1T
1890–91	Scotland	3G, 6T to 0
1891–92	Scotland	1G, 1T to 1T
1892–93	Wales	1G, 3T to 0
1893–94	Wales	1G, 1T to 0
1894–95	Scotland	1G, to 1DG
1896–97	Wales	2T to 0

1897–98	No match	
1898–99	Scotland	1G(m), 2DG, 3T to 2G
1899–1900	Wales	4T to 1T
1900–01	Scotland	3G, 1T to 1G, 1T
1901–02	Wales	1G, 3T to 1G
1902–03	Scotland	1PG, 1T to 0
1903–04	Wales	3G, 1DG, 1T to 1T
1904–05	Wales	2T to 1T

(Modern scoring values adopted)

1905–06	Wales	9 (3T) to 5 (1G)
1906–07	Scotland	6 (2T) to 3 (1PG)
1907–08	Wales	6 (2T) to 5 (1G)
1908–09	Wales	5 (1G) to 3 (1PG)
1909–10	Wales	14 (1G, 3T) to 0
1910–11	Wales	32 (2G, 1DG, 6T) to 10 (1DG, 2T)
1911–12	Wales	21 (3G, 2DG, 1T) to 6 (2T)
1912–13	Wales	8 (1G, 1T) to 0
1913–14	Wales	24 (2G, 2DG, 1PG, 1T) to 5 (1G)
1915–18	No matches	
1919–20	Scotland	9 (2PG, 1T), to 5 (1G)
1920–21	Scotland	14 (1G, 1PG, 2T) to 8 (2DG)
1921–22	Draw	Scotland 9 (1PG, 2T); Wales 9 (1G, 1DG)
1922–23	Scotland	11 (1G, 2T) to 8 (1G, 1PG)
1923–24	Scotland	35 (4G, 1DG, 4T) to 10 (2G)
1924–25	Scotland	24 (1G, 1DG, 5T) to 14 (1G, 1PG, 2T)
1925–26	Scotland	8 (1G, 1PG) to 5 (1G)
1926–27	Scotland	5 (1G) to 0
1927–28	Wales	13 (2G, 1T) to 0
1928–29	Wales	14 (1G, 3T) to 7 (1DG, 1PG)
1929–30	Scotland	12 (1G, 1DG, 1T) to 9 (1G, 1DG)
1930–31	Wales	13 (2G, 1T to 8 (1G, 1T)
1931–32	Wales	6 (1PG, 1T) to 0
1932–33	Scotland	11 (1G, 1PG, 1T) to 3 (1T)
1933–34	Wales	13 (3G, 1T) to 6 (1 PG, 1T)
1934–35	Wales	10 (1DG, 2T) to 6 (2T)
1935–36	Wales	13 (2G, 1T) to 3 (1T)
1936–37	Scotland	13 (2G, 1T) to 6 (2T)
1937–38	Scotland	8 (1G, 1PG) to 6 2T)
1938–39	Wales	11 (1G, 1PG, 1T) to 3 (1PG)
1940–45	No matches	
1946–47	Wales	22 (2G, 1PG, 3T) to 8 (1G, 1PG)
1947–48	Wales	14 (1G, 1PG, 2T) to 0

(Dropped goal reduced to three points)

1948–49	Scotland	6 (2T) to 5 (1G)
1949–50	Wales	12 (1DG, 1PG, 2T) to 0
1950–51	Scotland	19 (2G, 1DG, 1PG, 1T) to 0
1951–52	Wales	11 (1G, 2PG) to 0
1952–53	Wales	12 (1PG, 3T) to 0
1953–54	Wales	15 (1PG, 4T) to 3 (1T)
1954–55	Scotland	14 (1G, 1DG, 1PG, 1T) to 8 (1G, 1T)
1955–56	Wales	9 (3T) to 3 (1PG)
1956–57	Scotland	9 (1DG, 1PG, 1T) to 6 (1PG, 1T)
1957–58	Wales	8 (1G, 1T) to 3 (1PG)
1958–59	Scotland	6 (1PG, 1T) to 5 (1G)

RUGBY QUIZ

1. Which seven countries today have seats on the International Board?

*

2. There has only been one change in the scoring values since the present system was introduced in 1906. Name it.

*

3. Which country do the (a) All Blacks, (b) Wallabies, (c) Springboks represent?

QUIZ ANSWERS

1. England, Ireland, Scotland, Wales (the Four Home Unions) and Australia, South Africa and New Zealand (the Dominion Unions). 2. The dropped goal was devalued from 4 points to 3 in 1948–49. 3. (a) New Zealand, (b) Australia, (c) South Africa.

M. W. Swan jumps in the line out for Scotland against Wales, Cardiff, 1958.

J. D. Brewis (S. Africa)

C. I. Morgan (Wales)

R. E. G. Jeeps (England)

M. F. Lane (Ireland)

J. Prat (France)   G. Rimmer (England)   J. Kavanagh (Ireland)

Murrayfield, 1958. A. R. Smith (Scotland) meets strong opposition from the powerful French forwards.

SCOTLAND v. FRANCE

Scotland 17 wins, France 11, drawn 1

1909–10	Scotland	27 (3G, 4T) to 0
1910–11	France	16 (2G, 2T) to 15 (1G, 1DG, 2T)
1911–12	Scotland	31 (5G, 1PG, 1T) to 3 (1T)
1912–13	Scotland	21 (3G, 2T) to 3 (1T)
1913–14	No match	
1915–18	No matches	
1919–20	Scotland	5 (1G) to 0
1920–21	France	3 (1T) to 0
1921–22	Draw	3 (1T) each
1922–23	Scotland	16 (2G, 2T) to 3 (1G(m))
1923–24	France	12 (4T) to 10 (1DG, 1PT, 1T)
1924–25	Scotland	25 (2G, 5T) to 4 (1DG)
1925–26	Scotland	20 (1G, 1PG, 4T) to 6 (1PG, 1T)
1926–27	Scotland	23 (4G, 1PG) to 6 (2T)
1927–28	Scotland	15 (5T) to 6 (2T)
1928–29	Scotland	6 (1PG, 1T) to 3 (1T)
1929–30	France	7 (1DG, 1T) to 3 (1T)
1930–31	Scotland	6 (2PG) to 4 (1DG)
1932–45	No matches	
1946–47	France	8 (1G, 1T) to 3 (1PG)
1947–48	Scotland	9 (2PG, 1T) to 8 (1G, 1PG)
(Dropped goal reduced to three points)		
1948–49	Scotland	8 (1G, 1T) to 0
1949–50	Scotland	8 (1G, 1T) to 5 (1G)
1950–51	France	14 (1G, 2PG, 1T) to 12 (2PG, 2T)
1951–52	France	13 (2G, 1PG) to 11 (1G, 2PG)
1952–53	France	11 (1G, 1DG, 1PG) to 5 (1G)
1953–54	France	3 (1T) to 0
1954–55	France	15 (1PG, 4T) to 0
1955–56	Scotland	12 (2PG, 2T) to 0
1956–57	Scotland	6 (1DG, 1PG) to 0
1957–58	Scotland	11 (1G, 1PG, 1T) to 9 (2PG, 1T)
1958–59	France	9 (2DG, 1T) to 0

IRELAND v. WALES

Wales 38 wins, Ireland 21, drawn 3

1881–82	Wales	2G, 2T to 0
1882–83	No match	
1883–84	Wales	1G, 2T to 0
1884–86	No match	
1886–87	Wales	1G to 3T
1887–88	Ireland	2G, 1T to 0
1888–89	Ireland	2T to 0
1889–90	Draw	1G each
1890–91	Wales	1G, 1DG to 1DG, 1T
1891–92	Ireland	1G, 2T to 0
1892–93	Wales	1T to 0
1893–94	Ireland	1PG to 0
1894–95	Wales	1G to 0
1895–96	Ireland	1G, 1T to 1G
1896–97	No match	
1897–98	Wales	1G, 1PG, 1T to 1PG
1898–99	Ireland	1T to 0
1899–1900	Wales	1T to 0
1900–01	Wales	2G to 3T
1901–02	Wales	1G, 1DG, 2T to 0
1902–03	Wales	6T to 0
1903–04	Ireland	1G, 3T to 4T
1904–05	Wales	2G to 1T
(Modern scoring values adopted)		
1905–06	Ireland	11 (1G, 2T) to 6 (2T)
1906–07	Wales	29 (2G, 1DG, 1PG, 4T) to 0
1907–08	Wales	11 (1G, 2T) to 5 (1G)
1908–09	Wales	18 (3G, 1T) to 5 (1G)
1909–10	Wales	19 (1DG, 5T) to 3 (1T)
1910–11	Wales	16 (2G, 1PG, 1T) to 0
1911–12	Ireland	12 (1G, 1DG, 1T) to 5 (1G)
1912–13	Wales	16 (2G, 1PG, 1T) to 13 (2G, 1PG)
1913–14	Wales	11 (1G, 2T) to 3 (1T)

1915–18	No matches	
1919–20	Wales	28 (3G, 1DG, 3T) to 4 (1DG)
1920–21	Wales	6 (1PG, 1T) to 0
1921–22	Wales	11 (1G, 2T) to 3 (1T)
1922–23	Ireland	5 (1G) to 4 (1DG)
1923–24	Ireland	13 (2G, 1T) to 10 (1DG, 2T)
1924–25	Ireland	19 (2G, 1PG, 2T) to 3 (1T)
1925–26	Wales	11 (1G, 2T) to 8 (1G, 1PG)
1926–27	Ireland	19 (2G, 1PG, 2T) to 9 (1G, 1DG)
1927–28	Ireland	13 (2G, 1T) to 10 (2G)
1928–29	Draw	5 (1G) each
1929–30	Wales	12 (1PG, 3T) to 7 (1DG, 1PG)
1930–31	Wales	15 (1G, 1DG, 2T) to 3 (1T)
1931–32	Ireland	12 (4T) to 10 (1DG, 2T)
1932–33	Ireland	10 (1DG, 1PG, 1T) to 5 (1G)
1933–34	Wales	13 (2G, 1T) to 0
1934–35	Ireland	9 (2PG, 1T) to 3 (1PG)
1935–36	Wales	3 (1PG) to 0
1936–37	Ireland	5 (1G) to 3 (1PG)
1937–38	Wales	11 (1G, 1PG, 1T) to 5 (1G)
1938–39	Wales	7 (1DG, 1T) to 0
1940–45	No matches	
1946–47	Wales	6 (1PG, 1T) to 0
1947–48	Ireland	6 (2T) to 3 (1T)
(Dropped goal reduced to three points)		
1948–49	Ireland	5 (1G) to 0
1949–50	Wales	6 (2T) to 3 (1PG)
1950–51	Draw	Wales 3 (1PG); Ireland 3 (1T)
1951–52	Wales	14 (1G, 2PG, 2T) to 3 (1PG)
1952–53	Wales	5 (1G) to 3 (1T)
1953–54	Wales	12 (1DG, 3PG) to 9 (2PG, 1T)
1954–55	Wales	21 (3G, 1PG, 1T) to 3 (1PG)
1955–56	Ireland	11 (1G, 1DG, 1PG) to 3 (1PG)
1956–57	Wales	6 (2PG) to 5 (1G)
1957–58	Wales	9 (3T) to 6 (1PG, 1T)
1958–59	Wales	8 (1G, 1T) to 6 (1PG, 1T)

W. R. Evans (Wales) dives to pass to Lloyd Williams against France at Cardiff Arms Park, 1958.

RUGBY QUIZ

1. Is it permissible if there is no score, or a draw, after 80 minutes to play extra time, provided the two captains agree?

★

2. The wind blows the ball which has crossed the touch line back into the field of play. Would you, as touch judge, be right or wrong to raise your flag?

★

3. Which Rugby club has as its motto "Rugby football is a game for gentlemen in all classes, but never for a bad sportsman in any class"?

QUIZ ANSWERS

1. In no circumstances. The captains may not opt out of the Laws. 2. Right. 3. The Barbarian R.F.C. (founded in 1890).

261

IRELAND v. FRANCE

Ireland 19 wins, France 11, drawn 1

1908–09	Ireland	19 (1PG, 2G, 2T) to 8 (1G, 1T)
1909–10	Ireland	8 (1G, 1T) to 3 (1T)
1910–11	Ireland	25 (3G, 1DG, 2T) to 5 (1G)
1911–12	Ireland	11 (1G, 2T) to 6 (2T)
1912–13	Ireland	24 (3G, 3T) to 0
1913–14	Ireland	8 (1G, 1T) to 6 (2T)
1915–18	No matches	
1919–20	France	15 (5T) to 7 (1DG, 1T)
1920–21	France	20 (4G) to 10 (2G)
1921–22	Ireland	8 (1G, 1PG) to 3 (1T)
1922–23	France	14 (1G, 3T) to 8 (1G, 1T)
1923–24	Ireland	6 (2T) to 0
1924–25	Ireland	9 (1PG, 2T) to 3 (1T)
1925–26	Ireland	11 (1G, 1PG, 1T) to 0
1926–27	Ireland	8 (1G, 1PG) to 3 (1T)
1927–28	Ireland	12 (4T) to 8 (1G, 1T)
1928–29	Ireland	6 (2T) to 0
1929–30	France	5 (1G) to 0
1930–31	France	3 (1T) to 0
1932–45	No matches	
1946–47	France	12 (4T) to 8 (1G, 1PG)
1947–48	Ireland	13 (2G, 1T) to 6 (2T)

(Dropped goal reduced to three points)

1948–49	France	16 (2G, 2PG) to 9 (3PG)
1949–50	Draw	France 3 (1DG); Ireland 3 (1PG)
1950–51	Ireland	9 (1PG, 2T) to 8 (1G, 1T)
1951–52	Ireland	11 (1G, 1PG, 1T) to 8 (1G, 1PG)
1952–53	Ireland	16 (2G, 2T) to 3 (1DG)
1953–54	France	8 (1G, 1T) to 0
1954–55	France	5 (1G) to 3 (1PG)
1955–56	France	14 (1G, 2DG, 1T) to 8 (1G, 1PG)
1956–57	Ireland	11 (1G, 1PG, 1T) to 6 (2PG)
1957–58	France	11 (1G, 1DG, 1PG) to 6 (2PG)
1958–59	Ireland	9 (1DG, 1PG, 1T) to 5 (1G)

A struggle before the line in the Irish International against France, 1928.

WALES v. FRANCE

Wales 26 wins, France 6, drawn 0

1907–08	Wales	36 (3G, 1PG, 6T) to 4 (1DG)
1908–09	Wales	47 (7G, 4T) to 5 (1G)
1909–10	Wales	49 (8G, 1PG, 2T) to 14 (1G, 2PG, 1T)
1910–11	Wales	15 (3G) to 0
1911–12	Wales	14 (1G, 3T) to 8 (1G, 1T)
1912–13	Wales	11 (1G, 2T) to 8 (1G, 1T)
1913–14	Wales	31 (5G, 2T) to 0
1915–19	No matches	
1919–20	Wales	6 (2T) to 5 (1G)
1920–21	Wales	12 (2PG, 2T) to 4 (1DG)
1921–22	Wales	11 (1G, 2T) to 3 (1T)
1922–23	Wales	16 (2G, 1PG, 1T) to 8 (1G, 1T)
1923–24	Wales	10 (1DG, 2T) to 6 (2T)
1924–25	Wales	11 (1G, 2T) to 5 (1G)
1925–26	Wales	7 (1DG, 1T) to 3 (1T)
1926–27	Wales	25 (2G, 5T) to 7 (1G, 1DG, 1T)
1927–28	France	8 (1G, 1T) to 3 (1T)
1928–29	Wales	8 (1G, 1T) to 3 (1T)
1929–30	Wales	11 (2DG, 1T) to 0
1930–31	Wales	35 (5G, 1DG, 2T) to 3 (1T)
1932–45	No matches	
1946–47	Wales	3 (1PG) to 0
1947–48	France	11 (1G, 2T) to 3 (1PG)

(Dropped goal reduced to three points)

1948–49	France	5 (1G) to 3 (1T)
1949–50	Wales	21 (3G, 1PG, 1T) to 0
1950–51	France	8 (1G, 1PG) to 3 (1T)
1951–52	Wales	9 (1DG, 2PG) to 5 (1G)
1952–53	Wales	6 (2T) to 3 (1PG)
1953–54	Wales	19 (2G, 3PG) to 13 (2G, 1PG)
1954–55	Wales	16 (2G, 2T) to 11 (1G, 1DG, 1PG)
1955–56	Wales	5 (1G) to 3 (1T)
1956–57	Wales	19 (2G, 1PG, 2T) to 13 (2G, 1T)
1957–58	France	16 (2G, 1DG, 1PG) to 8 (1G, 1T)
1958–59	France	11 (1G, 1T, 1PG) to 3 (1PG)

C. H. Davison (New Zealand)

W. C. W. Murdoch
(Scotland)

THE INTERNATIONAL CHAMPIONSHIP

The International Championship, or, as the French prefer to call it, "The Championship of the Five Nations", is an unofficial annual all play all competition between England, Ireland, Scotland, Wales and France. The scoring is 2 points for a win and 1 for a draw. France was the last country to enter in 1909–10, but fell out from 1931–32 to 1938–39.

1909–10	England
1910–11	Wales
1911–12	England / Ireland
1912–13	England
1913–14	England
1919–20	England / Scotland / Wales
1920–21	England
1921–22	Wales
1922–23	England
1923–24	England
1924–25	Scotland
1925–26	Ireland / Scotland
1926–27	Scotland / Ireland
1927–28	England
1928–29	Scotland
1929–30	England
1930–31	Wales
1931–32	England / Wales / Ireland
1932–33	Scotland
1933–34	England
1934–35	Ireland
1935–36	Wales
1936–37	England
1937–38	Scotland
1938–39	England / Wales / Ireland
1946–47	Wales / England
1947–48	Ireland
1948–49	Ireland
1949–50	Wales
1950–51	Ireland
1951–52	Wales
1952–53	England
1953–54	England / France / Wales
1954–55	Wales / France
1955–56	Wales
1956–57	England
1957–58	England
1958–59	France

H. B. Toft

RUGBY QUIZ

1. Who holds the try scoring record in the university match?

★

2. Is there any restriction on the number of forwards in a pack?

★

3. What is the tactical move known as a "Garryowen" and why is it so named?

QUIZ ANSWERS

1. The late R. W. Poulton (later Poulton-Palmer) who scored 5 tries for Oxford against Cambridge in 1909. 2. The minimum is three and the only maximum is the total number of players in a side—15. 3. It is a high punt designed to land just ahead of a charging pack of forwards. It is named after the Irish club that invented this gambit.

England v. France, 1959, at Twickenham. G. J. Bendon (England) in possession.

P. Sykes (England)

HISTORY OF SCORING IN RUGBY FOOTBALL

In the early days of Rugby Football the only way to win a match was to kick a goal. A try of itself was of no value. Thus, for example, when Oxford played Cambridge at the Oval in 1874 and scored two tries to nil, the result was recorded as a draw, because no goal was scored. However, in the next year three tries were regarded as being worth a goal. In 1887 the scoring system was that a goal was worth 3 points and a try 1 point. This scoring system was the one that had been used by Cheltenham College for some time previously.

In 1889 the Rugby Union decided to differentiate between a goal and a penalty goal. The latter was marked down to the value of 2 points.

The International Rugby Football Board, formed in 1890, decided that for the purpose of international matches, the scoring should be as follows: a goal to be worth 4 points, a dropped goal or a goal from a mark to be worth 3 points and a try 2 points.

The scoring values as we know them today were introduced for the 1905–06 season as follows: a converted goal equals 5 points, a try and a penalty goal and a goal from a mark 3 points, and a dropped goal 4 points. The last mentioned was changed in 1948–49 by being reduced to 3 points. With that one change the scoring values at Rugby Football have thus remained unchanged for over 50 years. There have been several attempts to change the laws on scoring, notably by reducing the value of the penalty goal to 2 points, but this requires a two-thirds majority at a Board Meeting and this has yet to be secured.

England v. South Africa at Twickenham, 1952. P. A. du Toit, harried by English forwards, passes out from the scrum.

Wales v. Scotland at Cardiff Arms Park in 1958. The ball goes loose as T. Weatherstone of Scotland is tackled by M. C. Thomas of Wales.

M. G. Culliton
(Ireland)

I. W. Y. Kemp
(Scotland)

L. Mias (France) leaps high to catch a loose ball during France's 16 pts. to 8 victory over Wales in 1958.

WINNERS OF THE TRIPLE CROWN

ENGLAND. 12 times. 1883–4; 1891–2; 1912–13; 1913–14; 1920–1; 1922–3; 1923–4; 1927–8; 1933–4; 1936–7; 1953–4; 1956–7.
WALES. 9 times. 1892–3; 1899–1990; 1901–2; 1904–5; 1907–8; 1908–9; 1910–11; 1949–50; 1951–2.
SCOTLAND. 8 times. 1890–1; 1894–5; 1900–1; 1902–3; 1906–7; 1924–5; 1932–3; 1937–8.
IRELAND. 4 times. 1893–4; 1898–9; 1947–8; 1948–9.

H. G. O. Owen-Smith
(England)

R. A. White
(New Zealand)

J. Buchler (South Africa)

All Blacks v. Southern Counties, 1953. R. A. White (All Blacks) jumps high for the ball.

THE HOSPITALS CUP

Champions: Guy's (27 times), St. Thomas's (14), St. Mary's (14), London (8), St. Bartholomew's (5), St. George's (3), Middlesex (1).

	Winners	Runners-up
1875	Guy's 1G, 1TD to 2TD	St. George's
1876	St. George's 5TD to 1TD	University College
1877	Guy's 6TD to 1TD	St. Thomas's

(contd. on p. 263, Col. 1)

RUGBY QUIZ

In what season was Twickenham first used?

QUIZ ANSWER
1909–10.

J. Butterfield
(England)

Prince Alex Obolensky, regarded by many as the finest wing three-quarter ever, scoring a brilliant try for Oxford in the 1937 match against Trinity College, Dublin.

Bevan slithers across the line to score a try for the All Blacks in their match against the North-West Counties at Manchester in 1954.

J. E. Woodward
(England)

D. M. Davies
(Wales)

RUGBY QUIZ

1. Who is the youngest player ever to appear in an international?

★

2. Who is the oldest player ever to appear in an international?

★

3. Are substitutes allowed to replace injured players in any circumstances?

QUIZ ANSWERS

1. C. Reid (Scotland) played in the 1881 Calcutta Cup match against England three weeks after his 17th birthday. 2. L. E. Saxby (Gloucester) was 40 when he was twice capped by England in 1932. 3. No. But in Australia and New Zealand the International Board have allowed a dispensation in certain circumstances.

Wales v. France at Cardiff Arms Park 1956. Cliff Morgan, Welsh fly half, sends out a perfect pass to his winger, Ken Jones.

1921	Guy's 3 (1T) to 0	St. Bartholomew's
1922	Guy's 42 (6G, 4T) to 3 (1PG)	London
1923	Guy's 3 (1T) to 0	St. Bartholomew's
1924	St. Bartholomew's 11 (1G, 1PG, 1T) to 3 (1T)	King's College
1925	Guy's 7 (1DG, 1T) to 0	London
1926	St. Thomas's 3 (1T) to 0	Guy's
1927	Guy's 10 (2G) to 0	King's College
1928	St. Bartholomew's 11 (1G, 1PG, 1T) to 3 (1T)	London
1929	Guy's 3 (1T) to 0	London
1930	Guy's 23 (4G, 1T) to 9 (1PG, 2T)	St. Bartholomew's
1931	St. Bartholomew's 8 (1G, 1T) to 0	St. Mary's
1932	Guy's 13 (1DG, 1PG, 1G(m) 1T) to 7 (1DG, 1T)	St. Mary's
1933	Guy's 7 (1DG, 1T) to 0	St. Bartholomew's
1934	St. Mary's 32 (4G, 1PG, 3T) to 7 (1DG, 1T)	St. Thomas's
1935	St. Mary's 14 (1G, 2PG, 1T) to 3 (1T)	King's College
1936	St. Mary's 19 (2G, 3T) to 8 (1G, 1T)	St. Thomas's
1937	St. Mary's 11 (1G, 1PG, 1T) to 4 (1DG)	Guy's
1938	St. Mary's 18 (3G, 1T) to 0	Guy's
1939	St. Mary's 5 (1G) to 3 (1T)	St. Thomas's
1946	St. Mary's 18 (3G, 1T) to 8 (1G, 1PG)	Guy's
1948	Guy's 8 (1G, 1T) to 3 (1PG) *(Dropped goal reduced to three points)*	St. Mary's
1949	St. Mary's 6 (2T) to 5 (1G)	Guy's
1950	St. Thomas's 8 (1G, 1T) to 6 (1DG, 1PG)	London
1951	St. Mary's 9 (2PG, 1T) to 8 (1G, 1PG)	London
1952	St. Mary's 13 (1G, 3T) to 9 (3T)	St. Thomas's
1953	St. Mary's 14 (1G, 1PG, 2T) to 6 (2PG)	London
1954	St. Thomas's 3 (1DG) to 0	St. Mary's
1955	London 9 (1PG, 2T) to 3 (1T)	Guy's
1956	St. Mary's 16 (2G, 1DG, 1T) to 0 after replay	Guy's
1957	London 5 (1G) to 3 (1PG) after replay	St. Bartholomew's
1958	St. Thomas's 6 (2PG) to 3 (1PG)	Guy's
1959	St. Mary's 6 (2T) to 0 after replay	St. Bartholomew's

RUGBY QUIZ

1. What nationality are the following players: A. Obolensky, G. Nepia, J. Prat and B. L. Osler?

*

2. Name the only club affiliated to two National Rugby Unions.

*

3. What is the longest time a match may be held up for injury?

*

4. What is the world record for a Rugby crowd?

*

5. What is the highest score recorded in the game?

*

QUIZ ANSWERS

1. Russian, who played for England, a Maori New Zealander, a Frenchman and a South African respectively. 2. Newport in Monmouth, England is affiliated to both the (English) Rugby Union and the Welsh Rugby Union. 3. Two minutes. 4. 95,000 at Ellis Park, Johannesburg on Aug. 6, 1955, when the British Lions beat South Africa 23–22. 5. The highest with modern scoring values is 171–0 by Queen's College, Taunton, over Huish Grammar School in 1920. All 15 members scored, of whom H. G. Reason contributed 7 tries and 10 conversions (41 points).

W. W. Wakefield   **G. P. S. MacPherson**   **Ronald Cove-Smith**

TEN INTERNATIONAL MATCHES OF THE 1959 SEASON

FRANCE v. SCOTLAND
(in Paris)

January 10—France won by 2 dropped goals, 1 try (9 points) to 0

FRANCE: P. Lacaze 6 (2DG); H. Rancoule, J. Bouquet, A. Marquesuzaa, J. Dupuy; A. Labazuy, P. Danos; A. Quaglio, R. Vigier, A. Roques, L. Mias (*Captain*), B. Mommejat, M. Celaya, J. Barthe, F. Moncla 3 (3T).

SCOTLAND: K. J. F. Scotland; A. R. Smith, T. McClung, I. H. P. Laughland, C. Elliot; G. H. Waddell, S. Coughtrie; H. F. McLeod, N. S. Bruce, I. R. Hastie, M. W. Swan, J. W. Y. Kemp, G. K. Smith, J. T. Greenwood (*Captain*), A. Robson.

WALES v. ENGLAND
(at Cardiff)

January 17—Wales won by 1 goal (5 points) to 0.

WALES: T. E. Davies, 2 (1 con.); J. Collins, H. J. Davies, M. Price, D. Bebb, 3 (1T); C. Ashton, L. Williams; R. Prosser, B. V. Meredith, D. R. Main, R. H. Williams, I. Ford, R. C. C. Thomas (*Captain*), J. Faull, J. Leleu.

ENGLAND: J. G. G. Hetherington; P. B. Jackson, M. S. Phillips, J. Butterfield (*Captain*), P. H. Thompson; A. B. W. Risman, S. R. Smith; L. H. Webb, J. A. S. Wackett, G. J. Bendon, J. D. Currie, R. W. D. Marques, R. Higgins, B. J. Wightman, A. J. Herbert.

SCOTLAND v. WALES
(at Murrayfield)

February 7—Scotland won by 1 penalty goal and 1 try (6 points) to 1 goal (5 points)

SCOTLAND: K. J. F. Scotland, 3 (1PG); A. R. Smith, T. McClung, G. D. Stevenson, T. G. Weatherstone; G. H. Waddell, S. Coughtrie; H. F. McLeod, N. S. Bruce, 3 (1T), I, R. Hastie, M. W. Swan, J. W. Y. Kemp, G. D. Smith, J. T. Greenwood (*Captain*), A. Robson.

WALES: T. E. Davies, 2 (1 con.); J. Collins, H. J. Davies, M. Price, 3 (1T)· D. Bebb; C. Ashton, L. Williams; R. Prosser, B. V. Meredith, D. R. Main· R. H. Williams, I. Ford, R. C. C. Thomas (*Captain*), J. Faull, L. Leleu.

IRELAND v. ENGLAND
(in Dublin)

February 14—England won by 1 penalty goal (3 points) to 0.

IRELAND: N. J. Henderson; N. H. Brophy, A. J. F. O'Reilly, J. F. Dooley, A. C. Pedlow; M. A. English, A. A. Mulligan; B. G. Wood, A. R. Dawson (*Captain*), S. Miller, W. A. Mulcahy, N. A. Murphy, P. J. A. O'Sullivan, R. Cavanagh.

ENGLAND: J. G. G. Hetherington; P. B. Jackson, M. S. Phillips, J. Butterfield (*Captain*), P. H. Thompson; A. B. W. Risman, 3 (1PG); R. E. G. Jeeps; L. H. Webb, J. A. S. Wackett, G. J. Bendon, J. D. Currie, R. W. D. Marques, A. J. Herbert, A. Ashcroft, J. W. Clements.

ENGLAND v. FRANCE
(at Twickenham)

February 28—A draw, each side scoring a penalty goal (3 points)

ENGLAND: J. G. G. Hetherington, 3 (1PG); P. B. Jackson, M. S. Phillips, J. Butterfield (*Captain*), P. H. Thompson; A. B. W. Risman, S. R. Smith; L. H. Webb, H. O. Godwin, G. J. Bendon, R. W. D. Marques, J. D. Currie, J. W. Clements, A. Ashcroft, A. J. Herbert.

FRANCE: P. Lacaze; C. Darrouy, A. Boniface, A. Marquesuzaa, J. Dupuy; A. Labazuy, 3 (1PG), P. Danos; A. Quaglio, R. Vigier, A. Roques, M. Celaya, B. Mommejat, M. Crauste, J. Barthe (*Captain*), F. Moncla.

SCOTLAND v. IRELAND
(at Murrayfield)

February 28—Ireland won by 1 goal and 1 penalty goal (8 points) to 1 penalty goal (3 points)

SCOTLAND: K. J. F. Scotland, 3 (1PG); A. R. Smith, T. McClung, G. D. Stevenson, T. G. Weatherstone; G. H. Waddell, S. Coughtrie; H. F. McLeod, N. S. Bruce, I. R. Hastie, M. W. Swan, J. W. Y. Kemp, G. K. Smith, J. T. Greenwood (*Captain*), A. Robson.

IRELAND: N. J. Henderson; A. J. F. O'Reilly, J. F. Dooley, D. Hewitt, 8 (1T, 1 con. 1PG), N. H. Brophy; M. A. F. English, A. A. Mulligan; B. G. M. Wood, A. R. Dawson (*Captain*), S. Millar, M. G. Culliton, W. A. Mulcahy, N. A. Murphy, P. J. A. O'Sullivan, J. R. Kavanagh.

WALES v. IRELAND
(at Cardiff)

March 14—Wales won by 1 goal, 1 try (8 points) to 1 penalty goal, 1 try (6 points)

WALES: T. E. Davies, 2 (1 con.); J. Collins, M. C. Thomas, M. Price, 3 (1T), D. I. Bebb; C. Ashton, L. Williams; R. Prosser, B. V. Meredith, D. R. Main, R. H. Williams, D. J. E. Harris, R. C. C. Thomas (*Captain*), J. Faull, H. J. Morgan.

IRELAND: N. J. Henderson; A. J. F. O'Reilly, 3 (1T), J. F. Dooley, D. Hewitt, 3 (1PG), N. J. Brophy; W. J. Hewitt, A. A. Mulligan; B. G. M. Wood, A. R. Dawson (*Captain*), S. Millar, M. C. Culliton, W. A. Mulcahy, N. A. Murphy, P. J. A. O'Sullivan, J. R. Kavanagh.

ENGLAND v. SCOTLAND
(at Twickenham)

March 21—A draw, each side scoring a penalty goal (3 points)

ENGLAND: J. G. G. Hetherington; P. B. Jackson, M. S. Phillips, J. Butterfield (*Captain*), P. H. Thompson; A. B. W. Risman, 3 (1 PG), S. R. Smith; L. H. Webb, H. O. Godwin, G. J. Bendon, R. W. D. Marques, J. D. Currie, A. J. Herbert, A. Ashcroft, J. W. Clements.

SCOTLAND: K. J. F. Scotland, 3 (1 PG); A. R. Smith, J. A. P. Shackleton, G. D. Stevenson, T. G. Weatherstone; G. H. Waddell (*Captain*), S. Coughtrie; D. M. D. Rollo, N. S. Bruce, H. F. McLeod, F. H. ten Bos, J. W. Y. Kemp, G. K. Smith, J. A. Davidson, A. Robson.

FRANCE v. WALES
(in Paris)

April 5—France won by 1 goal, 1 penalty goal and 1 try (11 points) to 1 penalty goal (3 points)

FRANCE: P. Lacaze; H. Racoule, J. Bouquet, A. Marquesuzaa, J. Dupuy; A. Labazuy, 5 (1PG, 1 con.), P. Danos; A. Roques, R. Vigier, A. Quaglio, L. Mias (*Captain*), B. Mommejat, M. Crauste, J. Barthe, F. Moncla, 6 (2T).

WALES: T. E. Davies, 3 (1PG); J. Collins, J. Hurrell, M. J. Price, D. I. Bebb; M. C. Thomas, W. Watkins; R. Prosser, B. V. Meredith, D. R. Main, R. H. Williams, D. J. E. Harris, R. C. C. Thomas (*Captain*), G. Davidge, H. J. Morgan.

IRELAND v. FRANCE
(in Dublin)

April 18—Ireland won by 1 dropped goal, 1 penalty goal and 1 try (9 points) to 1 goal (5 points)

IRELAND: N. J. Henderson; A. J. F. O'Reilly, D. Hewitt, 3 (1PG), K. Flynn, N. H. Brophy, 3 (1T); M. A. F. English, 3 (1DG), A. A. Mulligan; B. G. M. Wood, A. R. Dawson (*Captain*), S. Millar, W. A. Mulcahy, G. Culliton, N. A. Murphy, P. J. A. O'Sullivan, J. R. Kavanagh.

FRANCE: P. Lacaze, 2 (1 con.); J. Dupuy, 3 (1T), L. Cassaux, A. Bouquet, H. Rancoule; C. Mantoulan, P. Danos; A. Roques, R. Vigier, A. Quaglio, L. Mias (*Captain*), B. Mommejat, F. Moncla, M. Crauste, A. Carrere.

O   265

RUGBY QUIZ

1. Which of the English Counties (or groups of Counties) has won the Inter-County Championship (instituted in 1889) most times?

*

2. Has France, which entered the International Championship in 1909–10, ever won the Championship outright?

*

3. Do the Laws specify a maximum and minimum height for the goal posts?

*

4. Has a player ever been ordered off in an international match under the control of the International Board?

*

5. Where is the Ranfurly Shield challenged for annually, and why is it so named?

*

6. In which country is the Currie Cup contested biannually and why is it so named?

*

7. If a touch judge wilfully interferes (say for example by giving advice to players) with a match, what can be done about it?

*

8. Only one country, outside the Commonwealth, has ever received an official British tour. Name it.

*

9. Has a visiting side ever come through a tour of the British Isles without losing a match? (a) Yes. (b) No.

QUIZ ANSWERS

1. Yorkshire 10 (with Gloucestershire having 9 wins). 2. Yes. In the 1958–59 season. 3. There is no maximum, but the posts must be at least 11 feet high, i.e., 1 foot higher than the top edge of the cross bar. 4. Yes, but only once. The late Cyril Brownlie (New Zealand) was ordered off when the All Blacks played England at Twickenham in 1924. 5. New Zealand. After the former Governor General, Lord Ranfurly, its donor, in 1902. 6. South Africa. After its donor Sir Donald Currie in 1891. 7. The referee can send him off. 8. The Argentine. 9(a). The second All Blacks of 1924.

THE ENGLISH COUNTY CHAMPIONSHIPS

1889	Yorkshire	undefeated	18G, 17T to 1G, 3T
1890	Yorkshire	undefeated	10G, 16T to 2G, 4T
1891	Lancashire		
1892	Yorkshire		
1893	Yorkshire		
1894	Yorkshire		
1895	Yorkshire		

Year	Champions	Runners-up	
1896	Yorkshire	Surrey	
1897	Kent	Cumberland	
1898	Northumberland	Midlands	
1899	Devon	Northumberland	
1900	Durham	Devon	
1901	Devon	Durham	
1902	Durham	Gloucestershire	
1903	Durham	Kent	
1904	Kent	Durham	
1905	Durham	Middlesex	
1906	Devon	Durham	
1907	Devon & Durham		
1908	Cornwall	Durham	
1909	Durham	Cornwall	
1910	Gloucestershire	Yorkshire	
1911	Devon	Yorkshire	
1912	Devon	Northumberland	
1913	Gloucestershire	Cumberland	
1914	Midlands	Durham	
1915–19	No matches		
1920	Gloucestershire	Yorkshire	
1921	Gloucestershire	Leicestershire	31–4
1922	Gloucestershire	N. Midlands	19–0
1923	Somerset	Leicestershire	8–6
1924	Cumberland	Kent	14–3
1925	Leicestershire	Gloucestershire	14–6
1926	Yorkshire	Hampshire	15–14
1927	Kent	Leicestershire	22–12
1928	Yorkshire	Cornwall	12–8
1929	Middlesex	Lancashire	9–8
1930	Gloucestershire	Lancashire	13–7
1931	Gloucestershire	Warwickshire	10–9
1932	Gloucestershire	Durham	9–3
1933	Hampshire	Lancashire	18–7
1934	E. Midlands	Gloucestershire	10–0
1935	Lancashire	Somerset	14–0
1936	Hampshire	Northumberland	13–6
1937	Gloucestershire	E. Midlands	5–0
1938	Lancashire	Surrey	24–12
1939	Warwickshire	Somerset	8–3
1940–46	No matches		
1947	Lancashire	Gloucestershire	14–3
1948	Lancashire	E. Counties	5–0
1949	Lancashire	Gloucestershire	9–3
1950	Cheshire	E. Midlands	5–0
1951	E. Midlands	Middlesex	10–0
1952	Middlesex	Lancashire	9–6
1953	Yorkshire	E. Midlands	11–3
1954	Middlesex	Lancashire	24–6
1955	Lancashire	Middlesex	14–8
1956	Middlesex	Devon	13–9
1957	Devon	Yorkshire	12–3
1958	Warwickshire	Cornwall	16–8
1959	Warwickshire	Gloucestershire	14–9

NUNQUAM DORMIO

Harlequins

Boroughmuir

Cross Keys

OXFORD v. CAMBRIDGE

Season	Winner	Score
1871–72	Oxford	1G, 1T to 0
1872–73	Cambridge	1G, 2T to 0
1873–74	Drawn	1T to 1T
1874–75*	Drawn	Oxford 2T to 0

* At this date no match could be won unless a goal was scored.

Season	Winner	Score
1875–76	Oxford	1T to 0
1876–77	Cambridge	1G, 2T to 0
1877–78	Oxford	2T to 0
1878–79	Drawn	— —
1879–80	Cambridge	1G, 1DG to 1DG
1880–81	Drawn	1T to 1T
1881–82	Oxford	2G, 1T to 1G
1882–83	Oxford	1T to 0
1883–84	Oxford	3G, 4T to 1G
1884–85	Oxford	3G, 1T to 1T
1885–86	Cambridge	2T to 0
1886–87	Cambridge	3T to 0
1887–88	Cambridge	1DG, 2T to 0
1888–89	Cambridge	1G, 2T to 0
1889–90	Oxford	1G, 1T to 0
1890–91	Drawn	1G to 1G
1891–92	Cambridge	2T to 0
1892–93	Drawn	— —
1893–94	Oxford	1T to 0
1894–95	Drawn	1G to 1G
1895–96	Cambridge	1G to 0
1896–97	Oxford	1G, 1DG to 1G, 1T
1897–98	Oxford	2T to 0
1898–99	Cambridge	1G, 2T to 0
1899–1900	Cambridge	2G, 4T to 0
1900–01	Oxford	2G to 1G, 1T
1901–02	Oxford	1G, 1T to 0
1902–03	Drawn	1G, 1T to 1G, 1T
1903–04	Oxford	3G, 1T to 2G, 1T
1904–05	Cambridge	3G to 2G

(Modern scoring values adopted)

Season	Winner	Score
1905–06	Cambridge	15 (3G) to 13 (2G, 1T)
1906–07	Oxford	12 (4T) to 8 (1G, 1T)
1907–08	Oxford	17 (1G, 4T) to 0
1908–09	Drawn	5 (1G) to 5 (1G)
1909–10	Oxford	35 (4G, 5T) to 3 (1T)
1910–11	Oxford	23 (4G, 1T) to 18 (3G, 1T)
1911–12	Oxford	19 (2G, 3T) to 0
1912–13	Cambridge	10 (2G) to 3 (1T)
1913–14	Cambridge	13 (1DG, 3T) to 3 (1T)
1914–19	No matches	
1919–20	Cambridge	7 (1DG, 1PG) to 5 (1G)
1920–21	Oxford	17 (1G, 4T) to 14 (1G, 3T)
1921–22	Oxford	11 (1G, 2T) to 5 (1G)
1922–23	Cambridge	21 (3G, 2T) to 8 (1G, 1T)
1923–24	Oxford	21 (3G, 2T) to 14 (1G, 1PG, 2T)
1924–25	Oxford	11 (1G, 2T) to 6 (2T)
1925–26	Cambridge	33 (3G, 6T) to 3 (1T)
1926–27	Cambridge	30 (3G, 5T) to 5 (1G)
1927–28	Cambridge	22 (2G, 2PG, 2T) to 14 (1G, 3T)
1928–29	Cambridge	14 (1G, 3T) to 10 (1DG, 1PG, 1T)
1929–30	Oxford	9 (1G, 1DG) to 0
1930–31	Drawn	Oxford 3 (1PG); Cambridge 3 (1T)
1931–32	Oxford	10 (1DG, 2T) to 3 (1T)
1932–33	Oxford	8 (1G, 1T) to 3 (1T)
1933–34	Oxford	5 (1G) to 3 (1T)
1934–35	Cambridge	29 (2G, 1DG, 1PG, 4T) to 4 (1DG)
1935–36	Drawn	— —
1936–37	Cambridge	6 (2T) to 5 (1G)
1937–38	Oxford	17 (1G, 4T) to 4 (1DG)
1938–39	Cambridge	8 (1G, 1PG) to 6 (2PG)
1939–45	War-time series only	
1945–46	Cambridge	11 (1G, 2T) to 8 (1G, 1PG)
1946–47	Oxford	15 (1G, 1DG, 2T) to 5 (1G)
1947–48	Cambridge	6 (2PG) to 0

(Dropped goal reduced to three points)

Season	Winner	Score
1948–49	Oxford	14 (1G, 1DG, 2T) to 8 (1G, 1PG)
1949–50	Oxford	3 (1T) to 0
1950–51	Oxford	8 (1G, 1PG) to 0
1951–52	Oxford	13 (2G, 1T) to 0
1952–53	Cambridge	6 (1PG, 1T) to 5 (1G)
1953–54	Drawn	Oxford 6 (1PG, 1T) to Cambridge 6 (2PG)
1954–55	Cambridge	3 (1PG) to 0
1955–56	Oxford	9 (1PG, 2T) to 5 (1G)
1956–57	Cambridge	14 (1G, 1DG, 1PG, 1T) to 9 (2PG, 1T)
1957–58	Oxford	3 (1T) to 0
1958–59	Cambridge	17 (1G, 1PG, 3T) to 6 (1PG, 1T)

1958–59 Season

Teams:

GLOUCESTERSHIRE: W. Sheen; M. G. Ellery, L. D. Watts, J. Radford, T. W. Jones; A. Holder, M. Booth; G. W. Hastings, J. D. Thorne, R. Fowke, B. J. Green, D. W. Neate, T. E. Base, G. Cripps, R. A. M. Whyte.

WARWICKSHIRE: D. R. Cook; P. B. Jackson, G. P. D. Morris, J. A. Pargetter, R. Melville; C. A. Hewitt, G. Cole; P. E. Judd, H. O. Godwin, M. R. McLean, J. Price, T. A. Pargetter, S. J. Purdy, J. F. Gardiner, R. F. Batstone.

1958–59 Season

Teams:

OXFORD: J. S. M. Scott; T. Baxter, M. S. Phillips, L. D. Watts (1PG), J. R. C. Young (1T); A. G. R. Sheil, A. O'Connor; L. T. Lombard (*Captain*), D. M. Davies, D. Jesson, L. I. Rimmer, J. R. Montgomery, F. H. ten Bos, S. H. Wilcock, W. I. Plant.

CAMBRIDGE: K. J. F. Scotland (1PG); P. R. Mills (1T), G. Windsor Lewis (*Captain*), H. J. Davies, M. R. Wade (2T); G. H. Waddell (1T), S. R. Smith D. R. J. Bird, M. T Wetson, J. J. Rainforth, D. G. Perry, V. S. J. Harding, D. A. MacSweeney, K. R. F. Bearne (1 con), D. C. Mills.

Ken Jones

Eric Evans

J. R. Stevens

ROYAL NAVY v. THE ARMY

1906–07	Navy	3G, to 2G (1P), 2T
1907–08	Navy	3G to 0
1908–09	Navy	4G (1DG), 2T to 0
1909–10	Navy	2G, 3T to 2G
1910–11	Army	2G, 4T to 3G (1P)
1911–12	Navy	2G, 2T to 1T
1912–13	Navy	3G, 1T to 1G, 1T
1913–14	Army	4G, 2T to 1G, 3T

MATCHES IN TRIANGULAR TOURNAMENT

1919–20	Navy	3G (1PG, 1m), 4T to 1G, 2T
1920–21	Navy	2G (1PG), 1T to 1DG, 2T
1921–22	Navy	2G (1DG, 1PG) to 1T
1922–23	Navy	2G, 2T to 1G, 2T
1923–24	Army	2G, 3T to 1G
1924–25	Army	1G, 2T to 1G, 1T
1925–26	Army	4G (1PG), 2T to 1G (1DG), 2T
1926–27	Navy	2T to 1T
1927–28	Army	1G, 2T to 1G
1928–29	Army	1G, 4T to 1G, 2T
1929–30	Army	2G, 2T to 2G
1930–31	Navy	2T to 0
1931–32	Army	1G, 3T to 1G
1932–33	Army	2G, 3T to 0
1933–34	Army	2G, 2T to 1G, 1PG
1934–35	Army	1G, 1PG, 1T to 1G, 1T
1935–36	Army	4T to 1T
1936–37	Army	1G, 3T to 1T
1937–38	Navy	2G to 3T
1938–39	Drawn	Navy 2T; Army 2PG
1939–45	No matches	
1945–46	Army	1G, 2T to 2PG
1946–47	Army	2G, 2PG, 1T to 1G, 2T
1947–48	Navy	1PG, 2T to 1G, 1T
1948–49	Army	1G, 2DG, 2PG, 3T to 1PG
1949–50	Army	2G, 1PG, 1T to 2PG
1950–51	Navy	1G, 1DG, 1T to 0
1951–52	Army	1G, 2PG to 1T
1952–53	Army	3 (1PG) to 0
1953–54	Navy	8 (1G, 1T) to 6 (1DG, 1PG)
1954–55	Navy	8 (1G, 1PG) to 3 (1T)
1955–56	Army	6 (2T) to 3 (1PG)
1956–57	Army	6 (1DG, 1PG) to 3 (1T)
1957–58	Navy	14 (1G, 3PG) to 0
1958–59	Navy	6 (1DG, 1T) to 0

St. Barts. Hospital

Old Paulines

Lansdowne

TRIANGULAR TOURNAMENT CHAMPIONS

1920	Royal Navy
1921	Royal Navy
1922	Royal Navy
1923	Royal Air Force
1924	A tie
1925	The Army & R.A.F.
1926	The Army
1927	Royal Navy
1928	The Army
1929	The Army
1930	The Army
1931	Royal Navy
1932	The Army
1933	The Army
1934	The Army
1935	A tie
1936	The Army
1937	The Army
1938	Royal Navy
1939	Royal Navy
1940–45	No matches
1946	The Army
1947	Royal Air Force
1948	A tie
1949	The Army & R.A.F.
1950	The Army
1951	Royal Navy
1952	The Army
1953	The Army
1954	A tie
1955	Royal Air Force
1956	A tie
1957	The Army
1958	Royal Air Force
1959	Royal Air Force

ROYAL NAVY v. ROYAL AIR FORCE

1919–20	Navy	1PG, 3T to 1T
1920–21	Navy	5G (1DG) 3T to 1T
1921–22	Navy	3T to 1PG, 1T
1922–23	R.A.F.	1T to 0
1923–24	Navy	2G, 2T to 1PG, 2T
1924–25	R.A.F.	1PG to 0
1925–26	Navy	1G, 1T to 1T
1926–27	Navy	1G, 1T to 1T
1927–28	Navy	1G to 0
1928–29	Navy	1G, 1T to 1PG
1929–30	Navy	1G, 1T to 1T
1930–31	Navy	2G, 2T to 0
1931–32	Navy	2G, 1PG, 3T to 1G
1932–33	Navy	2G, 1DG to 1T
1933–34	Navy	4G, 1DG, 4T to 0
1934–35	Navy	1G, 1T to 1G, 1T
1935–36	R.A.F.	1T to 0
1936–37	Drawn	R.A.F. 1PG; Navy 1T
1937–38	Navy	2G to 1PG, 1T
1938–39	Navy	1G, 1T to 1PG
1939–45	No matches	
1945–46	R.A.F.	2PG, 1T to 2PG
1946–47	Drawn	1G each
1947–48	R.A.F.	1G, 2DG, 1PG to 1G, 1PG, 1T
1948–49	R.A.F.	1G, 1PG, 1T to 0
1949–50	Drawn	Navy 6 (1DG, 1PG); R.A.F. 6 (1PG, 1T)
1950–51	Navy	1PG, 1T to 1G
1951–52	Navy	2T to 0
1952–53	Drawn	3 (1T) each
1953–54	R.A.F.	12 (1PG, 3T) to 6 (1PG, 1T)
1954–55	R.A.F.	6 (1PG, 1T) to 3 (1PG)
1955–56	Navy	11 (1G, 1PG, 1T) to 9 (1PG, 2T)
1956–57	Navy	8 (1G, 1T) to 6 (1PG, 1T)
1957–58	R.A.F.	14 (1G, 2PG, 1T) to 3 (1PG)
1958–59	R.A.F.	12 (1DG, 1PG, 2T) to 9 (3PG)

THE ARMY V. ROYAL AIR FORCE

1919–20	Army	3G, 2T to 3T
1920–21	R.A.F.	5G (1PG), 1T to 1T
1921–22	Army	4G, 1T to 1G, 1T
1922–23	R.A.F.	2G, 1T to 1G
1923–24	R.A.F.	2G (1PG) to 1T
1924–25	Drawn	2T each
1925–26	Army	1G, 2T to 0
1926–27	Army	2G, 4T to 0
1927–28	Army	3G, 1T to 2T
1928–29	Army	3G, 4T to 0
1929–30	Army	1G, 3T to 1G, 1T
1930–31	R.A.F.	2G, 2T to 1G
1931–32	Army	3G, 2T to 1DG
1932–33	Army	1G, 1DG, 1T to 1T
1933–34	Army	1G, 3T to 1T
1934–35	R.A.F.	1PG, 1T to 1T
1935–36	Army	2G, 1PG, 1T to 1G
1936–37	Army	4G, 1PG, 1G(m), 1T to 3T
1937–38	Army	1G, 1DG, 1PG, 1T to 1DG, 1T
1938–39	R.A.F.	1G, 1DG, 1PG, 2T to 1PG
1939–45	No matches	
1945–46	Army	1G, 1PG, 1T to 1PG, 1T
1946–47	R.A.F.	1G, 1T to 0
1947–48	Army	1G, 1DG, 1PG, 1T to 1G, 1T
1948–49	Drawn	1PG each
1949–50	Army	1G, 2T to 1PG
1950–51	Army	1G, 1DG, 2T to 0
1951–52	Army	9 (2PG, 1T) to 6 (1DG, 1T)
1952–53	Army	11 (1G, 1DG, 1PG) to 3 (1DG)
1953–54	Army	16 (2G, 2T) to 3 (1T)
1954–55	Drawn	6 (1PG, 1T) each
1955–56	R.A.F.	26 (4G, 1PG, 1T) to 9 (1PG, 2T)
1956–57	Army	14 (1G, 1DG, 2T) to 9 (1DG, 2PG)
1957–58	Drawn	R.A.F. 3 (1DG); Army 3 (1T)
1958–59	R.A.F.	11 (1G, 1PG, 1T) to 3 (1T)

J. W. Kyle

W. I. D. Elliot

N. Henderson

RUGBY QUIZ

1. Only 8 of the original 20 clubs that were founder members of the Rugby Union still survive. Name three of them.

★

2. By what means was a Rugby football inflated before the introduction of the rubber bladder?

★

QUIZ ANSWERS

1. From: Blackheath, Civil Service, Guy's Hospital, Harlequins, King's College, Richmond, St. Paul's, Wellington College. 2. By the use of a pig's bladder.

MIDDLESEX SEVEN FINALISTS

Year	Winners	Pts.	Runners-up	Pts.
1926	Harlequins I	25	St. Mary's Hospital	3
1927	Harlequins I	28	Blackheath	6
1928	Harlequins I	19	Blackheath	8
1929	Harlequins I	16	Rosslyn Park	9
1930	London Welsh	6	Blackheath II	0
1931	London Welsh	9	Harlequins I	5
1932	Blackheath I	18	Harlequins II	10
1933	Harlequins I	23	Wasps	0
1934	Barbarians	6	Richmond I	3
1935	Harlequins I	10	London Welsh	3
1936	Sale	18	Blackheath I	6
1937	London Scots. I	19	O.M.T.'s	3
1938	Met. Police I	13	London Scots. I	3
1939	Cardiff	11	London Scots. I	6
1940	St. Mary's H. I	14	O.C.T.U. Sandhst.	10
1941	Cambridge U.	6	Welsh Guards	0
1942	St. Mary's H. I	8	R.A.F.	6
1943	St. Mary's H. I	8	Middlesex H.	3
1944	St. Mary's H. I	15	R.A.F., Jurby	5
1945	Nottingham	6	St. Mary's H. I	3
1946	St. Mary's H. I	13	Cardiff	3
1947	Rosslyn Park	12	Richmond I	6
1948	Wasps I	14	Harlequins I	5
1949	Heriot's F.P.	16	London Scottish I	6
1950	Rosslyn Park	16	Heriot's F.P.	0
1951	Richmond II	13	Wasps	10
1952	Wasps	12	St. Thomas's H. I	10
1953	Richmond I	10	London Welsh	3
1954	Rosslyn Park I	16	London Scottish I	0
1955	Richmond I	5	St. Luke's, Exeter	0
1956	London Welsh I	24	Emmanuel College, Cambridge	10
1957	St. Lukes, Exeter	18	London Welsh	5
1958	Blackheath	16	Saracens	3
1959	Loughborough College	3	London Welsh	0

Rugby League

Compiled by Stanley Chadwick
Editor: Rugby League Review

SIXTY-FOUR YEARS OF RUGBY LEAGUE FOOTBALL. OVERSEAS EXPANSION BUT HOME DOMICILE

The establishment in the rival roses counties of Lancashire and Yorkshire of the game of professional Rugby, now known as Rugby League, was principally due to the fact that the twenty clubs concerned in the "breakaway" had both long and excellent playing records, with good support in their respective neighbourhood. Indeed, during the first two seasons the Laws of Play were the same as under Rugby Union. It was claimed by the new body that it had simply "legalised openly" what many R.U. clubs had been doing surreptitiously for a long time, and thus put an end to the need for subterfuge and deception.

Representatives of twenty-one of the leading Lancashire and Yorkshire Rugby Union clubs— Lancashire 9, Yorkshire 12— assembled at the George Hotel, Huddersfield, on Thursday, August 29, 1895. Only Dewsbury decided not to resign Rugby Union membership and join in the formation of the Northern Rugby Football Union on the principle of payment of players for bona fide "broken time" in fulfilling match engagements.

While the latter was the chief bone of contention, the Northern R.U. clubs had several times requested permission to organise a League competition. The frequent investigations, unfair suspensions, and insults received at the hands of the southern representatives of the Rugby Union were bitterly resented.

Rugby League football is now played by both professionals and amateurs in Lancashire, Yorkshire, and Cumberland. Teams consist of thirteen players; there is no line-out; and a try counts three points irrespective of whether the goal is kicked. A goal, either as the result of a try being scored or awarded, and from a penalty or a dropped kick, is awarded two points.

There are several other alterations compared with the amateur code, for one of the major industries of the Rugby League over the years has been alterations to the Laws of Play. On one occasion— 1952-53—the play-the-ball Law was actually changed in mid-season, but a satisfactory method has yet to be evolved.

The thirty professional clubs comprise the Northern Rugby Football League. Public support and playing strength is best indicated by recording that on one afternoon last season there was a record attendance for a League match of 47,747, with receipts of £4,804, while not many miles away two League teams played before 751 spectators paying £63 8s. 0d.

Professional Rugby League players do not receive a wage, but only payment per match. There are no annual or weekly disbursements, or anything payable during the close season or during suspension. The amount of match payments depends upon the financial resources of the respective club, as also does cup-tie bonuses and other incentives offered for success in the League Competition. It is now possible for a player transferred to another club to receive a percentage payment based on the amount of his transfer fee.

The Rugby Football League—the name was adopted in 1922—each season organises a Challenge Cup Competition, the final of which has been played at Wembley since 1929 (except 1932 and war years). There are also County Cup Competitions at the commencement of the season.

Regular tours have been made of this country by New Zealand and Australian teams since 1907 and 1908 respectively, return visits being undertaken by English sides. Since August 7, 1947, there has been a ban on the signing of Australian R.L. players by English clubs, subsequently extended to Rugby Union players (1952). The ban on the signing of New Zealand players has been in operation since December 15, 1947.

When in August, 1907, A. H. Baskerville's team of New Zealanders called at Sydney en route to make the first tour by an overseas team of English clubs, three matches were played under Rugby Union rules. A direct result of this visit was the formation of the New South Wales Rugby League to play the thirteen-a-side code. It was these Sydney sportsmen—now called "Pioneers"—who gave the name "Rugby League" to the new game. R.L. football is also played in the State of Queensland.

The late Jean Galia, a great French Rugby Union international player, was responsible for the introduction of the game in his country in 1934. He captained the first French team which played six matches in England. This last season the Rugby Football League has encouraged a second attempt to establish R.L. in Italy to the extent of £7,635.

Rugby League football in England is, unfortunately, still confined to three counties. With the Australasian market closed, clubs have turned to South African Rugby Union personalities to supply a little of the missing glamour.

While English, Welsh, and Scottish Rugby Union players are still tempted to turn professional, there is no indication that R.L. clubs are prepared to go over to Rugby League lock, stock, and barrel, and thus supply the game with well-established and supported teams in different parts of the country. The 1895 "split" will have to be repeated on a large scale if Rugby League football is ever to become a truly national game in the land of its birth.

R.L. QUIZ

1. Which club has won the R.L. Challenge Cup most times?

★

2. Has the R.L. Challenge Cup Final ever ended in a drawn game?

★

3. How many of the present Northern Rugby League teams (professional clubs) have never reached the Final?

★

4. Who was the unlucky Welshman with four Final appearances but was on the losing side each time?

★

5. Can you name the clubs for whom the following played: (1) J. Sullivan, (2) J. Parkin, (3) Ernest Ward, (4) K. Gee, (5) A. Ellaby, (6) H. Bath?

QUIZ ANSWERS

1. Leeds. 7 times (including one replayed Final). 2. Two Finals. 1910 (Leeds v. Hull) and 1954 (Warrington v. Halifax). 3. 5 teams (Blackpool Borough, Bramley, Doncaster, Liverpool City, Whitehaven). 4. Dai Morgan Davies. 1928 and 1933 for Warrington; 1935 for Huddersfield; 1937 for Keighley. 5. (1) Wigan, (2) Wakefield T., (3) Bradford N., (4) Wigan, (5) St. Helens, (6) Warrington.

THE RUGBY LEAGUE CHALLENGE CUP COMPETITION

The Northern Union (now Rugby League) Challenge Cup Competition had its origin at a meeting held in the George Hotel, Huddersfield, on March 5th, 1896, when the members accepted the recommendation of a sub-committee that Cup-ties should be arranged during the next season on the "sudden death" principle. The first draw was made in Huddersfield on September 3rd, 1896, and on March 2nd, 1897, the design of Messrs. Fattorini and Sons, Bradford, for a Cup for annual competition was selected. The original value of the Challenge Cup was £60, while the medals for the winning team and runners-up were valued at £3 3s. 0d. and £1 10s. 0d. each respectively. All clubs in membership or honorary membership of the Rugby Football League are eligible to compete. The competition is divided into qualifying rounds and competition proper, and it is usual for the professional clubs to be exempt until the competition proper.

RESULTS AND RECORDS OF PAST FINALS

	Year	Date	Winners	G.	T.	Pts.	Runners-up	G.	T.	Pts.	Attend.	Receipts	Venue
1	1897	Apl. 24	Batley	*1	2	10	St. Helens	0	1	3	13,492	£624 17 7	Leeds

Dropped goal. Awarded 4 points under old scoring rule.

	Year	Date	Winners	G.	T.	Pts.	Runners-up	G.	T.	Pts.	Attend.	Receipts	Venue
2	1898	,, 23	Batley	2	1	7	Bradford	0	0	0	27,941	£1,586 3 0	Fallowfield Manchester
3	1899	,, 29	Oldham	5	3	19	Hunslet	3	1	9	15,762	£946 16 1	Fallowfield Manchester
4	1900	,, 28	Swinton	2	4	16	Salford	1	2	8	17,864	£1,110 1 0	Leeds
5	1901	,, 27	Batley	0	2	6	Warrington	0	0	0	29,569	£1,650 18 6	Rochdale
6	1902	,, 26	Broughton R.	5	5	25	Salford	0	0	0	15,006	£846 11 0	Leeds
7	1903	,, 25	Halifax	2	1	7	Salford	0	0	0	32,509	£1,834 16 6	Salford
8	1904	,, 30	Halifax	1	2	8	Warrington	0	1	3	17,041	£936 5 6	Leeds
9	1905	,, 29	Warrington	0	2	6	Hull K. R.	0	0	0	19,638	£1,271 18 0	Leeds
10	1906	,, 28	Bradford (Park Avenue)	1	1	5	Salford	0	0	0	15,855	£920 0 0	Broughton
11	1907	,, 27	Warrington	4	3	17	Oldham	0	1	3	18,500	£1,010 0 0	Huddersfield
12	1908	,, 25	Hunslet	4	2	14	Hull	0	0	0	18,000	£903 0 0	Leeds
13	1909	,, 24	Wakefield T.	1	5	17	Hull	2	1	7	23,587	£1,489 15 3	Huddersfield
14	1910	,, 16	Leeds	2	1	7	Hull	0	0	0	19,413	£1,102 15 6	Huddersfield
Replay		,, 18	Leeds	7	4	26	Hull	3	2	12	11,608	£657 6 6	Salford
15	1911	,, 29	Broughton R.	2	0	4	Wigan	0	0	0	8,000	£376 0 0	Leeds
16	1912	,, 27	Dewsbury	1	2	8	Oldham	1	1	5	15,371	£853 0 0	Leeds
17	1913	,, 26	Huddersfield	3	0	9	Warrington	1	1	5	22,754	£1,446 9 6	Halifax
18	1914	,, 18	Hull	1	2	6	Wakefield T.	0	0	0	19,000	£1,035 5 0	Oldham
19	1915	May 1	Huddersfield	5	9	37	St. Helens	0	1	3	8,000	£472 0 0	Oldham

1915-16, 1916-17, 1917-18, 1918-19—*Cup Competition suspended (European War).*

	Year	Date	Winners	G.	T.	Pts.	Runners-up	G.	T.	Pts.	Attend.	Receipts	Venue
20	1920	Apl. 10	Huddersfield	3	5	21	Wigan	2	2	10	14,000	£1,936 0 0	Leeds
21	1921	,, 30	Leigh	2	3	13	Halifax	0	0	0	25,000	£2,700 0 0	Broughton
22	1922	,, 29	Rochdale H.	2	2	10	Hull	0	3	9	32,596	£2,964 0 0	Leeds
23	1923	,, 28	Leeds	6	5	28	Hull	0	1	3	29,335	£2,390 0 0	Wakefield
24	1924	,, 12	Wigan	3	5	21	Oldham	2	0	4	41,831	£3,714 9 3	Rochdale
25	1925	,, 25	Oldham	2	4	16	Hull K. R.	0	1	3	28,000	£2,878 0 0	Leeds
26	1926	May 1	Swinton	3	1	9	Oldham	1	1	5	27,000	£2,551 0 0	Rochdale
27	1927	,, 7	Oldham	4	6	26	Swinton	2	1	7	33,448	£3,170 0 0	Wigan
28	1928	Apl. 14	Swinton	1	1	5	Warrington	1	0	2	33,909	£3,159 1 11	Wigan
29	1929	May 4	Wigan	2	3	13	Dewsbury	0	1	3	41,500	£5,614 4 6	Wembley
30	1930	,, 3	Widnes	2	2	10	St. Helens	0	0	0	36,544	£3,102 0 0	Wembley
31	1931	,, 2	Halifax	5	4	22	York	4	0	8	40,368	£3,909 0 0	Wembley
32	1932	Apl. 9	Leeds	4	1	11	Swinton	4	0	8	29,000	£2,479 0 0	Wigan
33	1933	May 6	Huddersfield	6	3	21	Warrington	4	3	17	41,874	£6,465 14 6	Wembley
34	1934	,, 5	Hunslet	3	2	11	Widnes	1	1	5	41,280	£4,686 8 0	Wembley
35	1935	Apl. 4	Castleford	3	2	11	Huddersfield	1	0	2	39,000	£6,000 0 0	Wembley
36	1936	May 4	Leeds	3	4	18	Warrington	1	0	2	51,250	£7,070 0 0	Wembley
37	1937	May 8	Widnes	3	4	18	Keighley	1	1	5	47,699	£6,704 0 0	Wembley
38	1938	,, 7	Salford	2	1	7	Barrow	2	0	4	51,243	£7,174 0 0	Wembley

	Year	Date	Winners	G.	T.	Pts.	Runners-up	G.	T.	Pts.	Attend.	Receipts			Venue
39	1939	May 6	Halifax	4	4	20	Salford	0	1	3	55,453	£7,813	3	0	Wembley
	1939–40—*Cup Competition suspended (War-time difficulties).*														
40	1941	May 17	Leeds..........	2	5	19	Halifax	1	0	2	29,000	£1,622	0	0	Bradford
41	1942	June 6	Leeds..........	3	3	15	Halifax	5	0	10	15,250	£1,276	0	0	Bradford
42	1943	Apl. 24	Dewsbury	2	4	16	Leeds.........	3	1	9	10,470	£820	0	0	Dewsbury
		Apl. 26	Dewsbury	0	0	0	Leeds.........	3	0	6	16,000	£1,521	0	0	Leeds
	(Dewsbury won the Cup on aggregate, 16—15.)														
43	1944	Apl. 15	Bradford N. ...	0	0	0	Wigan	0	1	3	21,500	£1,663	0	0	Wigan
		,, 22	Bradford N. ...	1	2	8	Wigan	0	0	0	30,000	£2,061	0	0	Bradford
	(Bradford Northern won the Cup on aggregate, 8—3.)														
44	1945	,, 28	Huddersfield ..	2	1	7	Bradford N. ..	2	0	4	9,041	£1,184	3	7	Huddersfield
		May 5	Huddersfield ..	0	2	6	Bradford N. ..	1	1	5	17,500	£2,050	0	0	Bradford
	(Huddersfield won the Cup on aggregate, 13—9.)														
45	1946	May 4	Wakefield T. ..	2	3	13	Wigan	0	4	12	54,730	£12,013	13	6	Wembley
46	1947	,, 3	Bradford N. ...	1	2	8	Leeds.........	2	0	4	77,605	£17,434	5	0	Wembley
47	1948	,, 1	Wigan	1	2	8	Bradford N. ..	0	1	3	†91,465	£21,121	9	9	Wembley
48	1949	,, 7	Bradford N. ...	3	2	12	Halifax	0	0	0	†95,000	£22,000	0	0	Wembley
49	1950	,, 6	Warrington ...	5	3	19	Widnes	0	0	0	†95,000	£24,723	0	0	Wembley
50	1951	,, 5	Wigan	2	2	10	Barrow	0	0	0	†94,262	£24,797	19	0	Wembley
51	1952	Apl. 19	Workington T...	3	4	18	Featherstone R.	2	2	10	*73,000	£23,000	0	0	Wembley
52	1953	,, 25	Huddersfield ..	3	3	15	St. Helens	2	2	10	89,588	£30,865	12	3	Wembley
53	1954	,, 24	Warrington ...	2	0	4	Halifax	2	0	4	81,777	£29,706	0	0	Wembley
	Replay	May 5	Warrington ...	1	2	8	Halifax	2	0	4	102,569	£18,623	0	0	Odsal Stm, Bradford
54	1955	Apl. 30	Barrow	6	3	21	Workington T..	3	2	12	67,000	£27,500	0	0	Wembley
55	1956	,, 28	St. Helens	2	3	13	Halifax	1	0	2	80,000	£29,500	0	0	Wembley
56	1957	May 11	Leeds..........	0	3	9	Barrow	2	1	7	77,000	£32,546	0	0	Wembley
57	1958	,, 10	Wigan	2	3	13	Workington T.	3	1	9	*66,000	″£31,030	0	0	Wembley
58	1959	,, 9	Wigan	6	6	30	Hull	5	1	13	*80,000	£33,000	0	0	Wembley

† *All-Ticket Match.*   * *Television of the whole match.*   ″ *Plus* £2,000 *TV fee*—£33,030.

Leeds have won the Cup seven times (one replayed final); Huddersfield six times; Wigan six times; and Halifax four times. Warrington have been finalists on ten occasions, but only won the Cup four times.

The Cup has been won on 32 *occasions by Yorkshire clubs. There have been* 29 "*Battles of the Roses*", 14 *all-Yorkshire finals,* 12 *all-Lancashire finals,* 2 *Lancashire v. Cumberland finals, and* 1 *Yorkshire v. Cumberland final.*

Highest score: 37—3 (*Huddersfield v. St. Helens,* 1915).

Attendance Record: 102,569. *Warrington v. Halifax, replayed final at Odsal Stadium, Bradford, May* 5, 1954 (*evening kick-off*).

Receipts Record: £33,000 *plus B.B.C. television rights payment, Wigan v. Hull, at Wembley, May* 9, 1959.

Twenty-four finals played at Wembley and thirteen at Headingley, Leeds. Two replayed finals.

THE NORTHERN RUGBY FOOTBALL LEAGUE CLUBS FOUNDER MEMBERS

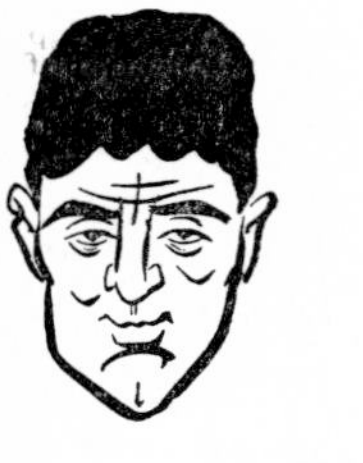

James Ledgard

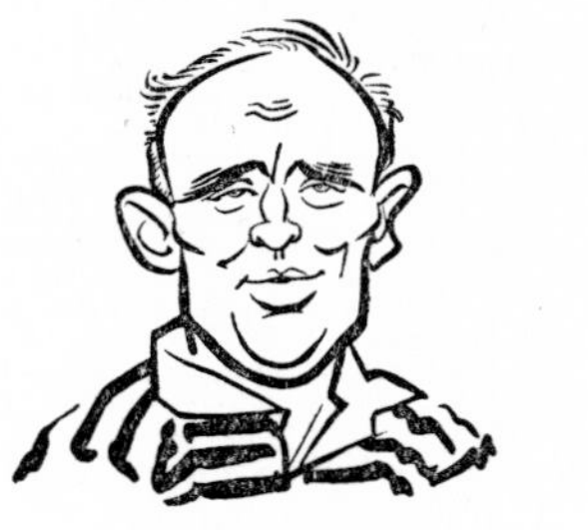

Brian Bevan

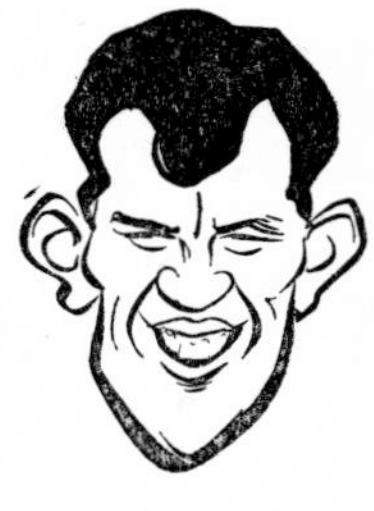

Michael Sullivan

YORKSHIRE

HUDDERSFIELD. The most famous name in Rugby League and birthplace of the game. The club is an amalgamation of the Huddersfield Athletic Club (1864) and St. John's Cricket Club (1866), with ground at "Fartown". "The Empire Team of Stars and all Talents" (1909–15) included Harold Wagstaff (local), Edgar Wrigley (New Zealand), A. A. Rosenfeld (Australia), Douglas Clark (Cumberland), Ben Gronow (Wales), T. P. Gleeson (Australia), and Johnny Rogers (Wales). Other famous wearers of the "Claret and Gold" (club colours) have been Ernest Mills and Ray Markham (both Australians), L. C. Bowkett, and Alex Fiddes. After the last war Huddersfield again looked "Down Under", and signed such stars as Lionel Cooper, Pat Devery, Johnny Hunter, and Peter Henderson. The club is now finding it hard to maintain its former playing standards.

HULL. Formed by a number of old public school boys in 1865, but for the first few seasons had difficulty in finding opponents. New ground at The Boulevard coincided with severance of relations with the Yorkshire Rugby Union and inauguration of the "Northern Union". Sensational signing of the great William Batten in 1913 for the then record sum of £600. Hull's Australian captain, H. Gilbert, was the first overseas player to have his name inscribed on the N.U. Challenge Cup (1914 Final), while Dicky Fifield is another Australian still remembered in the port. Three postwar appearances in the Northern Rugby League Championship Final, with two victories. Last season played for the first time in Wembley R.L. Challenge Cup Final.

HALIFAX. Only eight persons at first meeting in 1873, but a week later after two others made their appearance the club was launched on its career. Has played at Thrum Hall since 1886. Fine goal-kicker in Hubert Lockwood (898 goals). "All Black" Tom W. Lynch signed (1951) for £5,000, the highest fee paid to a New Zealand player by an English club. The style of play adopted by Halifax during recent seasons has been the subject of considerable controversy, culminating with a threat by the club to withdraw from the Yorkshire Challenge Cup Competition.

WAKEFIELD TRINITY. Will always be associated with the memorable deeds of "Jonty" Parkin. Incidentally, he was the last R.L. player to buy his own transfer! The club had its origin in a Young Men's Society held in connection with Holy Trinity Church, Wakefield, and at first was confined to members. Many honours but never played in Northern Rugby League Championship Final. Signed Derek Turner (Oldham) on February 28, 1959, for record fee of £8,000 by a Yorkshire R.L. club.

BATLEY. Made history by winning the first Challenge Cup Competition established by the "Northern Union" three times in five years, including the first and second years. The club's nickname of "Gallant Youths" originated with their "T'Owd Tin Pot" (Yorkshire R.U. Cup) victory in 1885. During 1880 Batley Cricket Club rented the high-altitude ground at Mount Pleasant and shortly afterwards were joined by the local Athletic club's football team.

HUNSLET. When Hunslet won all four Cups in season 1907–8, the record of their forwards earned them the title of "The Terrible Six". Albert E. Goldthorpe and his four brothers had a long and memorable association with Hunslet during the club's early years. The ground at Parkside is now being considerably extended. Last season, having finished third in the League table, in the play-off semi-final, Hunslet defeated R.L. Challenge cup finalists Wigan 22–11 points, at Central Park, only themselves to be dramatically beaten by St. Helens in a record Final score.

LEEDS. Fabulous Leeds, with its spectacular history—everything except the Northern Rugby League Championship—and galaxy of top-ranking players costing thousands of pounds, performing on the hallowed Headingley turf. Jeff Moores, Frank O'Rourke, Eric Harris, and Vic Hey were Australian captures between the two wars, together with Jim Brough. After the last war came H. E. Cook, burly New Zealand full-back and prolific goal-kicker, with Australians Arthur Clues, E. Verrenkamp, L. Kenny, Bruce Ryan (from Hull), Ken Kearney, Bob McMaster, and Keith McLellan. The signing of Lewis Jones, Llanelly R.U. international, for a fee of £6,000, was a then (1952) Rugby League record. Last season Leeds gave Springbok centre Wilf Rosenberg £4,000 and a four-year contract. Finally, record seven times winners of the R.L. Challenge Cup.

LANCASHIRE

ROCHDALE HORNETS. Will new manager-coach Jim Sullivan write a fresh page in the history of this eighty-eight-year-old club is the 64,000 dollar question in Rugby League. The Hornets almost ceased existence during April, 1939, and the League had to provide the necessary finance for the season's fixtures to be completed. Australians Cec Aynsley and Vic Armburster were two pre-war signings. Cecil Fifield, former Hull Australian player, was appointed manager-coach in 1950, and he brought over with him five young players. Wally McArthur, Australian aborigine wing three-quarter, played with the Hornets from 1953 until he went to Blackpool shortly before the close of season 1954–55.

OLDHAM. For quarter of a century Oldham's Joseph Platt was the first honorary secretary and guiding arm of the new Northern Rugby Football Union. The club was the first Lancashire side to win the N.U. Challenge Cup (1899), subsequently being finalists in four successive seasons (two victories). Watersheddings ground was used for the first time on September 28, 1889, and the G. F. Hutchins Memorial Stand was completed in 1954. World record R.L. fee of £10,650 paid for transfer of Ike Southward from Workington Town on March 11, 1959. Last season Oldham's playing terms were £12 for an away win, £10 home win, and £5 for a loss.

ST. HELENS. The "Saints" had a splendid run of successes during the seven seasons Jim Sullivan, former Wigan international full-back, was their trainer-coach. Although taking part in the first final of the N.U. Challenge Cup (1897), St. Helens had to wait fifty-nine years before winning the trophy (they had, however, been three times runners-up since the first final). In the last seven seasons the "Saints" have played in five Northern League play-off semi-finals, and twice won the Championship. South African wing three-quarter Tom Van Vollenhoven was signed at a fee of £8,000 on October 15, 1957, and in his first full season finished top English R.L. try scorer. Vollenhoven carries on the good work of former star players at Knowsley Road—Alf Ellaby, A. Frodsham, Leslie Fairclough, Jim Stott, Stan McCormick, George Langfield, and Peter Metcalfe, to mention just a few. Alan Prescott has succeeded Sullivan as trainer-coach.

WARRINGTON. The "Wire" (one of the town's chief industries is wire making). Champion losers R.L. Challenge Cup—ten times finalists but only four wins. Also Northern League Champions only in post-war seasons—three times—twice in successive years. The club, however, goes back to 1875, and had its origin in an organisation called Warrington Zingari. Former Wigan and New Zealand stand-off half-back, C. R. Mountford, has been team manager since June, 1951. The list of Warrington players will always be overshadowed by the "Don Bradman of Rugby League", Brian Bevan, but Harry Bath, Harold Palin, Albert and Danny Naughton, of recent years, with Jack Fish, Dan Frawley, W. Shankland, and Dave Brown, still remembered by an older generation, must not be overlooked.

WIDNES. A club with a tradition of local-born players. They have done battle in four Wembley Cup Finals with such sides, and won twice. The Widnes club was formed in 1875, and wearers of its black and white hooped jerseys have included Jack O'Gara (full-back), J. Hoey, Tommy McCue, and Colin Hutton. Never Northern League Champions but on four occasions in the "top four".

LEIGH. Phoenix-like the club has arisen from the ruins of its old pre-war home at Mather Lane, sold to a local brewery company because of declining support. Membership was retained of the Northern Rugby League, and the present Kirkhall Lane ground opened at the commencement of season 1947–48. Signings Jimmy Ledgard (£2,650 full-back and goal-kicker), Australians Trevor Allan (£5,000) and Rex Mossop (£4,000), together with Wigan's Joe Egan (£5,000), showed the Rugby League that Leigh had returned in a big way. The club even attempted to turn E. McDonald Bailey, amateur world sprint champion, into a R.L. player! Last season reached the semi-final of the R.L. Challenge Cup. Mr. James Hilton, the man behind the new Leigh, died at the early age of forty-seven years on April 21, 1959. Kirkhall Lane ground was renamed "Hilton Park" in his memory.

WIGAN. Jokes about Wigan Pier but never Wigan Rugby League Club. Rivals of Huddersfield in playing feats and personalities. Won more cups over and over again than any other club in the game—the actual total is forty-two. And for good measure, runners-up on twenty-eight occasions. Central Park, the team's home since 1902, had the addition of a big new stand four seasons ago. Players who have contributed to Wigan's fame include Jim Leytham, Bert Jenkins, Lance B. Todd (New Zealand), Jim Sullivan—in eighteen consecutive seasons kicked over 100 goals each season—Ken Gee, Joe Egan, Brian C. Nordgren and Cecil Mountford (both New Zealand), E. H. Ward, Billy Boston (Welsh coloured R.U. centre), Michael Sullivan—at signing, record fee of £9,500—and South African full-back, Fred Griffiths.

R.L. QUIZ

1. Who was Lance B. Todd?

*

2. How many seasons did A. J. ("Gus") Risman play (Salford, Dewsbury, Leeds, Workington T., and Batley)?

QUIZ ANSWERS

1. New Zealand "All Blacks" centre three-quarter signed by Wigan, 1908. Secretary-manager of Salford from 1929. Died in car accident returning from Oldham on November 14, 1942, aged fifty-nine years. 2. Twenty-seven seasons (aged forty-three years when retired).

THE NORTHERN RUGBY FOOTBALL LEAGUE CHAMPIONSHIP

The first and second divisions of the Northern Rugby League were merged into one competition for the 1905–06 season, the club with the best percentage of points being designated champions. For the following season (1906–07) the present method of deciding the Championship Cup and Medals was instituted: the four clubs having the highest number of points at the completion of their League fixtures to play-off for the Championship, the club finishing first in the table to play the club finishing fourth, and the club finishing second to play the club finishing third, the first and second clubs to have choice of grounds. The winners of the semi-finals decided the final on neutral ground, but in the County of the club (taking part in the final) having the highest number of points. Since season 1952–53 the Northern League Management Committee have decided the venue of the final, irrespective of the County and League position of the finalists.

RESULTS AND RECORDS OF PAST FINALS

	Year	Date		Winners	G.	T.	Pts.		Runners-up	G.	T.	Pts.	Attend.	Receipts			Venue
1	1907	Apl. 20	1	Halifax	3	4	18	2	Oldham.....	0	1	3	13,200	£772	7	0	Huddersfield
2	1908	May 2	1	Hunslet	2	1	7		Oldham.....	2	1	7	14,000	£690	0	0	Salford
	Replay	" 9	2	Hunslet	3	2	12	1	Oldham.....	1	0	2	14,054	£800	0	0	Wakefield
3	1909	" 1	1	Wigan	2	1	7	3	Oldham.....	0	1	3					Salford
4	1910	Apl. 23	3	Oldham.......	2	3	13	3	Wigan	2	1	7	14,000				Broughton
5	1911	May 6	2	Oldham.......	4	4	20	1	Wigan	2	1	7	20,000	£717	6	0	Broughton
6	1912	" 4	1	Huddersfield ..	2	3	13	2	Wigan	1	1	5	12,000	£591	0	0	Halifax
7	1913	" 3	1	Huddersfield ..	4	7	29	2	Wigan	1	0	2	17,000	£914	0	0	Wakefield
8	1914	Apl. 25	1	Salford	1	1	5	1	Huddersfield ..	0	1	3	8,091	£474	0	0	Leeds
9	1915	" 24	1	Huddersfield ..	7	7	35	3	Leeds	1	0	2	14,000	£750	0	0	Wakefield

1915–16, 1916–17, 1917–18, 1918–19—No League Championship play-off.

	Year	Date		Winners	G.	T.	Pts.		Runners-up	G.	T.	Pts.	Attend.	Receipts			Venue
10	1920	Apl. 24	1	Hull	0	1	3	1	Huddersfield ..	1	0	2	12,000	£1,615	0	0	Leeds
11	1921	May 7	1	Hull	2	4	16	1	Hull K. R. ..	4	2	14	10,000	£1,200	0	0	Leeds
12	1922	" 6	2	Wigan	5	1	13	1	Oldham.....	1	0	2	30,000				Broughton
13	1923	" 5	4	Hull K. R. ..	3	1	15	2	Huddersfield ..	1	1	5	14,000	£1,370	0	0	Leeds
14	1924	" 3	2	Batley	2	3	13	1	Wigan	2	1	7	15,000				Broughton
15	1925	" 2	1	Hull K. R. ..	3	1	9	1	Swinton	1	1	5	25,000				Rochdale
16	1926	" 8	1	Wigan	2	6	22	2	Warrington ..	2	2	10	20,000				St. Helens
17	1927	Apl. 30	2	Swinton	1	3	15	1	S. Helens R. ..	1	2	8					Warrington
18	1928	May 5	1	Swinton	1	3	11	3	F'th'stone R. ..	0	0	0					Oldham
19	1929	" 11	1	Huddersfield ..	1	0	2	3	Leeds	0	0	0	25,604	£2,028	0	0	Halifax
20	1930	" 10	1	Huddersfield ..	1	0	2	2	Leeds	0	0	0	30,350	£2,085	0	0	Wakefield
	Replay	" 12	1	Huddersfield ..	2	2	10	4	Leeds	0	0	0	18,563	£1,319	0	0	Halifax
21	1931	" 9	1	Swinton	4	2	14	2	Leeds	2	1	7	31,000	£2,100	0	0	Wigan
22	1932	" 7	2	St. Helens	3	1	9	1	Huddersfield ..	1	1	5	20,000	£980	0	0	Wakefield
23	1933	Apl. 29	1	Salford	3	1	15	2	Swinton	1	1	5	18,000				Wigan
24	1934	" 28	2	Wigan	3	1	15	4	Salford	0	1	3	31,565	£2,113	0	0	Warrington
25	1935	May 11	1	Swinton	4	2	14	2	Warrington ..	1	0	3	27,000	£1,710	0	0	Runcorn
26	1936	" 9	1	Hull	6	3	21	3	Widnes	1	0	2	17,276	£1,208	0	0	Huddersfield
27	1937	" 1	1	Salford	5	1	13	2	Warrington ..	4	1	11	32,000	£2,000	0	0	Wigan
28	1938	Apl. 30	1	Hunslet	1	2	8	2	Leeds	0	0	0	54,112	£3,572	0	0	Elland Road, Leeds
29	1939	May 13	2	Salford	1	2	8	2	Castleford...	0	2	6	69,504	£4,301	4	0	Maine Road, Manchester

1939–40, 1940–41, 1941–42, 1942–43, 1943–44, 1944–45—Emergency League Championship during war-time seasons

	Year	Date		Winners	G.	T.	Pts.		Runners-up	G.	T.	Pts.	Attend.	Receipts			Venue
30	1946	May 18	1	Wigan	2	3	13	2	Huddersfield ..	2	0	4	67,136	£8,386	13	0	Maine Road, Manchester
31	1947	June 21	1	Wigan	2	3	13	2	Dewsbury ..	2	0	4	40,599	£5,894	12	6	" "
32	1948	May 8	2	Warrington ..	3	3	15	4	Bradford N. ..	1	1	5	69,143	£9,791	12	6	" "
33	1949	" 14	3	Huddersfield ..	2	3	13	1	Warrington ..	3	2	12	75,194	£11,073	0	0	" "
34	1950	" 13	1	Wigan	4	4	20	2	Huddersfield..	1	0	2	65,065	£11,500	0	0	" "
35	1951	" 12	3	Workington T..	4	6	26	1	Warrington ..	1	3	11	61,618	£10,993	7	0	" "
36	1952	" 10	2	Wigan	2	3	13	1	Bradford N. ..	3	0	6	48,684	£8,215	6	0	Leeds Rd., Huddersfield
37	1953	" 9	1	St. Helens	3	6	24	2	Halifax	4	2	14	51,083	£11,502	16	6	Maine Road, Manchester
38	1954	" 8	2	Warrington ...	4	0	8	1	Halifax	2	1	7	36,519	£9,076	0	0	" "
39	1955	" 14	1	Warrington ...	2	1	7	2	Oldham.....	0	1	3	49,343	£11,516	0	0	" "
40	1956	" 12	4	Hull	2	2	10	2	Halifax	0	3	9	36,678	£9,179	0	0	" "
41	1957	" 18	1	Oldham.......	3	3	15	2	Hull	4	2	14	62,233	£12,054	0	0	Odsal Stdm., Bradford
42	1958	" 17	4	Hull	4	4	20	3	Workington T.	0	1	3	58,149	£11,149	0	0	" "
41	1959	" 16	1	St. Helens	5	4	22	2	Hunslet	1	3	11	52,560	£10,146	0	0	" "

NOTE:—Positions of the winners and runners-up in the final League table indicated by black prefix figures.

Wigan have won the Championship eight times; Huddersfield six times; Hull five times; and Salford and Swinton each four times.
Twenty-three of the clubs to finish at the head of the League table have won the Championship in the forty-three finals played, while fifteen occupying second place have carried off the trophy. Two clubs finishing third and three fourth respectively have been able to style themselves "Champions".
The Championship has been won on 25 occasions by Lancashire clubs. There have been 22 "Battles of the Roses", 11 all-Lancashire finals, 8 all-Yorkshire finals, 1 Cumberland v. Lancashire final, and 1 Yorkshire v. Cumberland final.
Huddersfield have been runners-up 6 times, Leeds and Oldham each 5 times and 1 replayed final, and Warrington and Wigan each 5 times. Halifax have been finalists on four occasions but only won the Cup the season the Championship play-off was inaugurated.
Highest score: 44–22 (St. Helens v. Hunslet, 1959).
Attendance Record: 75,194 Huddersfield v. Warrington, at Maine Road, Manchester, May 14, 1949.
Receipts Record: £12,054 Oldham v. Hull, at Odsal Stadium, Bradford, May 18, 1957.
Eleven finals have been played on the ground of Manchester City A.F.C. at Maine Road. There have been two replayed finals.

EMERGENCY LEAGUE CHAMPIONSHIP

	Lancashire		Yorkshire	
	Winners	Runners-up	Winners	Runners-up
1939–40	Swinton	Salford	Bradford N.	Huddersfield
1940–41	Wigan	Warrington	Bradford N.	Hull
1941–42, 1942–43, 1943–44, 1944–45—Competition Suspended.				

EMERGENCY LEAGUE CHAMPIONSHIP

Year	Date	Winners	Pts.	Runners-up	Pts.	Venue
1940†	May 18	Bradford N.	21	Swinton	13	Swinton
	" 25	Bradford N.	16	Swinton	9	Bradford
(Bradford Northern won the Championship on aggregate, 37–32)						
1941†	Apl. 12	Bradford N.	17	Wigan	6	Wigan
	" 14	Bradford N.	28	Wigan	9	Bradford
(Bradford Northern won the Championship on aggregate, 45–15)						
1942	A. 18	Dewsbury	13	Bradford N.	0	Leeds
1943	May 15	Dewsbury	11	Halifax	3	Dewsbury
	" 23	Dewsbury	22	Halifax	13	Halifax
(Dewsbury won the Championship on aggregate, 33–16, but on July 30th, 1943, the Rugby League Council declared the Championship null and void, and fined Dewsbury £100.)						
1944	May 13	Wigan	13	Dewsbury	9	Wigan
	" 20	Wigan	12	Dewsbury	5	Dewsbury
(Wigan won the Championship on aggregate, 25–14)						
1945	May 19	Bradford N.	2	Halifax	9	Halifax
	" 21	Bradford N.	24	Halifax	11	Bradford
(Bradford Northern won the Championship on aggregate, 26–20)						

† Championship Play-offs between winners of Yorkshire and Lancashire Emergency Leagues.

R.L. QUIZ

1. When and where was the Northern Rugby Football Union formed?

★

2. How many founder clubs are still members?

★

3. On what date were the opening matches played?

QUIZ ANSWERS

1. On Thursday, August 29, 1895, at a meeting in the George Hotel, Huddersfield, Yorkshire. 2. 14. 3. Saturday, September 7, 1895. All clubs' fixtures except Huddersfield and Oldham.

FOUR CUPS IN ONE SEASON

Hunslet (1907–08); Huddersfield (1914–15); Swinton (1927–28).

MOST CUPS AND FINALS

	R.L. Cup	N.L. Champ.	Lancs. Cup	Lancs. Champ.	Total
WIGAN	6	8	13	15	42
			Yorks. Cup	Yorks. Champ.	
HUDDERSFIELD	6	6	12	11	35

Runners-up: Wigan 28 times. Winners and Runners-up 70 times.
Huddersfield 22 times. Winners and Runners-up 57 times.

A. A. Rosenfeld

Jim Sullivan

Gus Risman

PLAYED IN BOTH FINALS

During the season 1953–54, for the first time in the history of both the R.L. Challenge Cup and the Northern League Championship, the same two clubs played in both Finals. Seventeen teams, however, have been one of the finalists in both Competitions during the season. Huddersfield (twice), and Hunslet, Swinton, and Warrington (once each) have won both Cups in one season.

R.L. CHALLENGE CUP

	Winners	Runners-up
1906–07	—	Oldham
1907–08	Hunslet	—
1910–11	—	Wigan
1912–13	Huddersfield	—
1914–15	Huddersfield	—
1919–20	Huddersfield	—
1923–24	Wigan	—
1924–25	—	Hull K.R.
1926–27	—	Swinton
1927–28	Swinton	—
1938–39	—	Salford
1945–46	—	Wigan
1947–48	—	Bradford N.
1952–53	—	St. Helens
1953–54	Warrington	Halifax
1955–56	—	Halifax

N.L. CHAMPIONSHIP

	Winners	Runners-up
1906–07	—	Oldham
1907–08	Hunslet	—
1910–11	—	Wigan
1912–13	Huddersfield	—
1914–15	Huddersfield	—
1919–20	—	Huddersfield
1923–24	—	Wigan
1924–25	Hull K.R.	—
1926–27	Swinton	—
1927–28	Swinton	—
1938–39	Salford	—
1945–46	Wigan	—
1947–48	—	Bradford N.
1952–53	St. Helens	—
1953–54	Warrington	Halifax
1955–56	—	Halifax

CHAMPION CLUBS

FROM THE COMMENCEMENT OF THE NORTHERN RUGBY FOOTBALL UNION TO THE INAUGURATION OF THE LEAGUE CHAMPIONSHIP PLAY-OFF.

LANCASHIRE SENIOR COMPETITION

	Winners	Runners-up
1895–96	Runcorn	Oldham

(Runcorn defeated Oldham with whom they tied in the Competition)

1896–97	Broughton R.	Oldham
1897–98	Oldham	Swinton
1898–99	Broughton R.	Oldham
1899–1900	Runcorn	Oldham
1900–01	Oldham	Swinton

YORKSHIRE SENIOR COMPETITION

	Winners	Runners-up
1895–96	Manningham	Halifax
1896–97	Brighouse R.	Manningham
1897–98	Hunslet	Bradford

(Hunslet defeated Bradford with whom they tied in the Competition).

1898–99	Batley	Hull
1899–1900	Bradford	Batley
1900–01	Bradford	Halifax

NORTHERN RUGBY LEAGUE

	Winners	Runners-up
1901–02	Broughton Rangers	Salford

First Division

	Winners	Runners-up
1902–03	Halifax	Salford
1903–04	Bradford	Salford

(Bradford defeated Salford with whom they tied in the League.)

1904–05	Oldham	Bradford

Second Division

	Winners	Runners-up
1902–03	Keighley	Leeds
1903–04	Wakefield T.	St. Helens

(St. Helens defeated Holbeck with whom they tied in the League).

1904–05	Dewsbury	Barrow

NORTHERN RUGBY FOOTBALL LEAGUE

	Winners	Runners-up
1905–06	Leigh	Hunslet

NORTHERN RUGBY FOOTBALL WAR LEAGUE

	Winners	Runners-up
1915–16	Dewsbury	Leeds
1916–17	Dewsbury	Leeds
1917–18	Barrow	Dewsbury

Lancashire Section

	Winners	Runners-up
1918–19	Barrow	Leigh

Yorkshire Section

	Winners	Runners-up
1918–19	Hull	Bramley

NORTHERN LEAGUE LEADERS

But only twenty-three (marked *) have been League Champions and five (marked †) were defeated in the Play-off Semi-Final

1906–07	*Halifax	1932–33	*Salford
1907–08	Oldham	1933–34	Salford
1908–09	*Oldham	1934–35	*Swinton
1909–10	*Oldham	1935–36	*Hull
1910–11	Wigan	1936–37	*Salford
1911–12	*Hudd.	1937–38	*Hunslet
1912–13	*Hudd.	1938–39	*Salford
1913–14	Hudd.	1945–46	*Wigan
1914–15	*Hudd.	1946–47	*Wigan
1919–20	Hudd.	1947–48	†Wigan
1920–21	Hull K.R.	1948–49	Warr.
1921–22	Oldham	1949–50	*Wigan
1922–23	†Hull	1950–51	Warr.
1923–24	Hudd.	1951–52	B'ford N.
1924–25	Swinton	1952–53	*St. Helens
1925–26	*Wigan	1953–54	Halifax
1926–27	St. Helens R.	1954–55	*Warr.
1927–28	*Swinton	1955–56	Warr.
1928–29	*Hudd.	1956–57	*Oldham
1929–30	*St. Helens	1957–58	†Oldham
1930–31	*Swinton	1958–59	*St. Helens
1931–32	Hudd.		

Wigan have finished at the top of the League during eight seasons and Huddersfield seven seasons.

Leeds have never been League leaders or won the championship.

R.L. QUIZ

1. Which prominent club has never been Northern League leaders or champions?

★

2. How many of the present thirty clubs have never won the Northern Rugby Football League Championship (top four clubs play-off)?

★

3. Which club holds the scoring record for all matches played in one season?

★

4. Did a referee make his exit from a famous R.L. ground in the uniform of a policeman?

★

5. In which match did all the Leeds players score?

★

6. Name the minister of religion who became a well-known R.L. referee?

★

7. When was Odsal Stadium opened?

★

8. Which player holds the scoring record for any tourist to Australasia?

★

9. When did the hard state of the different grounds cause the postponement for the first time of all the Northern Rugby Football League fixtures?

QUIZ ANSWERS

1. Leeds. Defeated in eight play-off semi-finals and five finals. 2. 17 clubs. 10 clubs have taken part in each season's fixtures since the Championship was inaugurated. 3. Huddersfield. Season 1914–15. 1,269 points from 47 matches. 4. Yes. Mr. E. H. Smirk, of Wigan. From Fartown ground, 1908. 5. Leeds 102 points, Coventry 0. April 12, 1913. 6. The Rev. Frank H. Chambers, O.B.E. United Methodist Church, with pastorates at Hunslet Carr, Doncaster, Hanley, Dewsbury, Huddersfield, and Westcliffe-on-Sea. Referee twelve seasons. 7. September 1, 1934. Record crowd of 20,000, with receipts £803. 8. L. Jones (Leeds). During 1954 tour in 21 matches kicked 127 goals and scored 8 tries, a total of 278 points. 9. Saturday, February 16, 1929 (thirteen matches).

ADMITTED TO MEMBERSHIP OF THE NORTHERN RUGBY LEAGUE

YORKSHIRE

BRAMLEY. June 2, 1896. Club formed eighty years ago largely through the efforts of the then vicar of the parish, the Rev. S. W. Cope, who was the first president. Jimmy Lomas, subsequently appointed captain of the first N.U. team to tour "Down Under", played a whole season with Bramley. The Barley Mow ground—named after the neighbouring hostelry—was also the scene of the debut of Huddersfield's "promising youngster" Harold Wagstaff. Bramley, dwarfed by city neighbours Leeds and Hunslet, have neither won a major R.L. trophy nor finished runners-up in any Cup or League Competition. However, the members have never lost heart and, indeed, have ambitious ground plans for the future.

HULL KINGSTON ROVERS. June 1, 1897. The players' white jerseys, with a red breast-band, is responsible for their nickname "The Robins". A R.L. record which still stands is G. H. ("Tich") West's 53 points, obtained from 11 tries and 10 goals, in a 1905 cup-tie against a Cumberland side. Craven Park, opened in 1922, was sold to a greyhound racing syndicate at the close of season 1939–40, but the club resumed activities after the war. Among the Rovers' players have been A. ("Bunker") Carmichael, South African George Van Rooyan, and Bryn Goldswain.

YORK. April 25, 1898. Club formed in 1868. One Wembley appearance—defeated by Halifax—but three Yorkshire Challenge Cup victories. Often Northern League wooden spoonists, but recently made habit of finishing just above the half-way line. Two big signings last season—Jeff Stevenson, from Leeds, for £7,500, at the time the biggest sum ever paid by a Yorkshire club, and Hugh Gillespie, South African R.U. centre, who received a signing-on fee of £2,000 spread over three years.

DEWSBURY. June 7, 1898. The Dewsbury club did not take up the place reserved for them at the inauguration of the "Northern Union", but they changed their mind after three seasons. Won the N.U. Challenge Cup in 1912, also wartime final of 1943 (aggregate score home and away games), and were Wigan's opponents in the first R.L. final played at Wembley (1929). Prominent players in J. Lyman, Joe Lyman, Frank Gallagher, and J. A. Ledgard, who was transferred to Leigh for £2,650, and after eleven seasons with the Lancashire club has returned to Crown Flatt.

KEIGHLEY. April 12, 1900. The day following a complimentary dinner celebrating their success in the No. 1 Competition of the Rugby Union, Keighley joined the professional code. Harry Myers, still regarded as the finest player who has ever worn a Keighley jersey, received a fatal injury in a match at

Dewsbury during the first half of season 1906–7. The team reached the final of the R.L. Challenge Cup during the Coronation Year of Their Majesties King George VI and Queen Elizabeth (1937). Joe Phillips, former Bradford Northern New Zealand player, set up a new club goalkicking and points scoring record in season 1957–58.

BRADFORD NORTHERN. June 25, 1907. Formed at a meeting on May 24, 1907, after the founder member Bradford club at Park Avenue had decided to embrace Soccer. The club made a wonderful ground transformation when they left Birch Lane in 1934 for the vast Odsal Stadium. After the last war the side, under the leadership of Ernest Ward, twice won the R.L. Challenge Cup and obtained other honours. George Carmichael, Eric Batten, Trevor Foster, Kenneth Traill, the late Frank Whitcombe, Jack Kitching, W. T. H. Davies, J. A. Phillips, and Jack McLean, have been some of the "Northern Lights". Odsal Stadium since the war has housed many big crowds, and at the replayed R.L. Challenge Cup Final on the evening of May 5, 1954, a world record attendance for a Rugby League match was established.

FEATHERSTONE ROVERS. June 7, 1921. The "enfant terrible" of the Rugby League. Many highly placed sides have fallen in League and Cup matches at Post Office Road ground, including League leaders St. Helens in (Contd. next page two successive seasons third round R.L. Challenge cup-ties. Astounded the whole R.L. world by reaching the final at Wembley for the first time in season 1951–52; mighty Wigan were their victims in another third-round game. Jack Hirst was for many seasons the team's centre three-quarter, and yeoman service was given to the club by Eric Batten, signed from Bradford Northern at a fee of about £500, as player-coach and later trainer.

CASTLEFORD. February 17, 1926. Castleford R.L. club not only ousted a Soccer club in public favour but secured the defunct team's ground as their home. Senior status was achieved after five seasons in the Yorkshire Senior Competition. The only club to defeat Huddersfield in the final of the R.L. Challenge Cup (1935). Arthur Atkinson, born within a stone's throw of the ground, helped to build up a good side, and others have been Jim Croston, Leslie Adams (from Leeds), Denzil Webster (transferred to York in 1956), and Ernest Ward (from Bradford N., 1953).

DONCASTER. April 30, 1951. Club formed early in 1951 with a capital of £6,000. Gareth Price, Halifax and former Leeds centre three-quarter, appointed first manager-coach, but resigned after first season. Victory over Wakefield Trinity in opening match at York Road Stadium. Present Bentley Road ground opened on August 27, 1953. Loss of £2,877 and £1,823 respectively first two seasons, with profit of £620 third campaign. Poor playing record apart from first season when placed eleventh in final League table, with twenty-one matches won and one drawn. Last three seasons bottom team, with only five, four, and three matches won each season.

LANCASHIRE

SALFORD. May 7, 1896. The "Red Devils"—all-red jerseys. Quickly made a name for themselves in the "Northern Union" with four Cup Final appearances in seven seasons (failed to score in two consecutive finals). Captain Jimmy Lomas led the first N.U. tourists "Down Under" (1910). Under managership of the late Mr. Lance B. Todd—"the Herbert Chapman of Rugby"—Salford enjoyed many triumphs. A. J. ("Gus") Risman, for long a great Salford player, is now the club's team manager-coach. Other "Reds" have been A. Edwards, Barney Hudson, E. Jenkins, W. Watkins, G. Curran, and Tom Danby—1950 Australasian tour tries record holder.

SWINTON. May 7, 1896. Third and last of the three clubs to win all four Cups in one season (1927–28). Last season's revival in playing form enabled the team to finish sixth in the Northern League. The title of "Lions" was adopted from the sign of "The White Lion", the hostelry which was the headquarters of the "Swinton and Pendlebury Club". An early "discovery" was the now legendary Jim Valentine. The present ground at Station Road, scene of many Lancashire Challenge Cup Finals and Test Matches, was opened on March 2, 1929. Prominent players have been Martin Hodgson, Jack and Bryn Evans, Chris Brockbank, F. Buckingham, and J. Blan, while the late Samuel Jones was secretary for forty-two years.

BARROW. April 20, 1897. The remote outpost of R.L. football until the advent of the first professional Cumberland club. Barrow won their first R.L. trophy when they defeated Oldham in the final of the Lancashire Challenge Cup on October 23, 1954. Before the season ended the R.L. Challenge Cup was placed alongside the first cup. The name of Willie Horne is synonymous with Barrow, but others who have given great service have been Harry Gifford, Jim Lewthwaite, Bryn Knowelden, and Roy Francis. Australian Harry Bath first played for Barrow before joining Warrington.

LIVERPOOL CITY. 1922, as Wigan Highfield. A variety of strange moves and experiences before settling down at Knotty Ash (season 1950–51). First founded as Wigan Highfield; changed name to London Highfield in 1933 and for one season played their home matches at the White City Stadium under floodlight; returned to Lancashire as Liverpool Stanley; finally, became Liverpool City from season 1951–52. Most successful season was 1935–36, when they finished second in the Northern League, and just failed to beat Widnes in the play-off semi-final by a single point (10–9). Present average home attendance around 500.

BLACKPOOL BOROUGH. May 6, 1954. "The Babes" of the Rugby League. Formed October 1, 1953, with ground at Greyhound Stadium, South Shore. Name changed to Blackpool Borough a few hours before first home match. Chris Brockbank, retired Warrington secretary-manager, accepted similar position with the new club. Players signed included Kia Rika (Halifax Maori), H. H. ("Ike") Fishwick (Warrington), Reg Stanford and Wally McArthur (Rochdale Hornets, Australians). First season finished third from bottom of the League table, with loss of £2,259. Last season seventh from bottom, winning fifteen matches.

CUMBERLAND

WORKINGTON TOWN. January 24, 1945. First senior professional Cumberland R.L. club. A. J. ("Gus") Risman player-manager until his resignation at the commencement of season 1954–55. Just failed to finish as one of the first four clubs in the Northern League at the end of their third season. However, in sixth and seventh seasons carried off the Northern League Championship (1950–51) and the R.L. Challenge Cup (1951–52), the first time both trophies taken to Cumberland. Again Wembley finalists April 30, 1955, but defeated by Barrow. Third time—1958—runners-up to Wigan. Also lost to Hull in Northern League Championship Final same season. J. W. Brough, former Leeds and England Test captain, succeeded Risman as manager. New ground at Derwent Park opened August 27, 1956. Wearers of the club's colours have been Australians John R. Mudge and Anthony H. Paskins, "Eppie" Gibson, A. Pepperell, J. H. Lawrenson, and Ike Southward (record transfer to Oldham).

WHITEHAVEN. May 13, 1948. All the original founders of this second senior professional Cumberland club were connected with Kells junior team. Jack Kitching (Bradford N.) first player-manager-coach. E. Gibson (Workington T.) appointed coach 1957. While not achieving the spectacular playing success of their near neighbours Workington Town, the club has justified its admittance to the Northern League. Great goal-kicker in J. J. McKeown (now retired), Dick Huddart (transferred to St. Helens), Sidney Lowdon (to Salford), and Springbok Anthony Forster.

FORMER NORTHERN RUGBY LEAGUE CLUBS
FOUNDER MEMBERS

TYLDESLEY (Lancashire). Last season 1899–1900.

LIVERSEDGE (Yorkshire). Last season 1901–02.

MANNINGHAM (Yorkshire). Last season 1902–03. Winners of first season's League Championship and Yorkshire Senior Competition. Played at Valley Parade and changed to Association football under title of Bradford City. (Loss on final season of £603.)

BRIGHOUSE RANGERS (Yorkshire). Last season 1905–06. Effects of club sold by auction.

BRADFORD (Yorkshire). Last season 1906–07. Previous season won N.U. Challenge Cup, but a loss of £500 was responsible for the guinea members' decision to adopt the Association game at Park Avenue, although a majority in favour of returning to Rugby Union (later declared illegal).

BROUGHTON RANGERS (Lancashire). Last season 1954–55. Founded 1869 and first played at Wheater's Field and later The Cliff, Lower Broughton. Twice winners of the N.U. Challenge Cup, and the Northern League Championship in season 1901–02 (no top four clubs play-off). Transfer to Belle Vue Zoological Gardens, Manchester, in 1933, and became Belle Vue Rangers from season 1946–47. Notice to quit Belle Vue during June, 1955, but resolved to revert to old title of Broughton Rangers and play on the Harris Stadium. Excluded from the Northern League because unable to comply with the League Management Committee's requirements. Sixty years' membership of the code.

OTHER CLUBS

STOCKPORT (Cheshire). Last season 1902–03. The first club admitted to the Northern Rugby Football Union immediately after the formation of that body on August 29, 1895.

RUNCORN (Cheshire). Last season 1917–18. "The Linnets" secured the place originally reserved for Dewsbury.

NEW CLUBS

LIVERPOOL CITY. One season, 1906–07. Played 30, Won 0. Points for 76, Against 1,398.

WELSH CLUBS. Merthyr Tydvil, four seasons, 1907–08 to 1910–11. Ebbw Vale, 1907–08 to 1911–12. Aberdare, 1908–09. Barry, 1908–09. Treherbert, 1908–09 and 1909–10. Mid Rhondda, 1908–09.

COVENTRY. Three seasons, 1910–11 to 1912–13.

ST. HELENS RECREATION. Founded in 1878 by Messrs. Pilkington Brothers, Limited. First played Rugby Union football, in season 1896–97 "Northern Union", then for a period Soccer, returning to the Northern Rugby Football Union in 1912–13. Membership of the Northern League from first post-war season (1919–20). First Lancashire Challenge Cup success in 1923. Prominent players were A. E. Fildes, Tom Dingsdale, Oliver Dolan, Frank Bowen, and Albert J. Pimblett. Resigned from the Rugby Football League at end of season 1938–39.

PONTYPRIDD (Wales). One full season (1926–27), resigning after eight matches following season.

CARLISLE CITY (Cumberland). Brief existence of less than two months in season 1928–29.

LONDON. Acton and Willesden, one season, 1935–36. Streatham and Mitcham, one season, 1935–36, resigning before end of second season.

NEWCASTLE (Newcastle upon Tyne). Seasons 1936–37 and 1937–38.

CARDIFF (Wales). Admitted to Northern League at same meeting as Doncaster (April 30, 1951). Just two days short of a year's membership the League Management Committee decided that it was not "a sound proposition" for the club to continue in senior football. Playing record—Won 5, Lost 31. Points for 342, Against 1,024. This third disastrous Welsh venture cost the League £2,324, but with the club's share of pools, etc., the loss was brought down to £866.

Note—With the clubs comprising the present Northern Rugby League (30), the total clubs listed is 53.

R.L. QUIZ

1. An Australian player after three seasons with an English club returned home and was subsequently appointed captain of an Australian team which toured England and France. Who was he?

QUIZ ANSWER

1. Kenneth Howard Kearney (hooker). Wallabies Rugby Union tour of Great Britain, 1947–48. Signed by Leeds on June 8, 1948 (£1,000 and three years' contract). Declined new contract, returned to Australia, joined St. George Club, N.S.W., selected a member of Australian team which toured England 1952–53 season, and captain of the 1956–57 Australian touring team.

THE LANCASHIRE COUNTY RUGBY FOOTBALL CHALLENGE CUP

The reconstruction of the Northern Rugby Football League which inaugurated the 1905–06 season established County Challenge Cup Competitions for the Lancashire and Yorkshire Clubs. The first round matches are played as early as the third week in the season, with the final during October.

RESULTS OF FINAL TIES

	Year	*Date*	*Winners*	*G. T. Pts.*	*Runners-up*	*G. T. Pts.*	*Attend.*	*Receipts*	*Venue*
1	1905	Dec. 2	Wigan	0	Leigh	0	—	—	Broughton
	(*replay*)	,, 11	Wigan	8	Leigh	0	—	—	Broughton
2	1906	,, 1	Broughton R.	15	Warrington	6	—	—	Wigan
3	1907	Nov. 20	Oldham	16	Broughton R.	9	—	—	Rochdale
4	1908	Dec. 19	Wigan	10	Oldham	9	—	—	Broughton
5	1909	Nov. 27	Wigan	22	Leigh	5	—	—	Broughton
6	1910	Dec. 3	Oldham	4	Swinton	3	—	—	Broughton
7	1911	,, 2	Rochdale H.	12	Oldham	5	—	—	Broughton
8	1912	,, 11	Wigan	21	Rochdale H.	5	—	—	Salford
9	1913	,, 6	Oldham	5	Wigan	0	—	—	Broughton
10	1914	,, 5	Rochdale H.	3	Wigan	2	—	—	Broughton
			1915–16, 1916–17, 1917–18—*No Cup Competition*						
11	1919	May 10	Rochdale H.	22	Oldham	0	—	—	Salford
12	1919	Dec. 6	Oldham	7	Rochdale H.	0	—	—	Salford
13	1920	,, 4	Broughton R.	6	Leigh	3	—	—	Salford
14	1921	,, 3	Warrington	7	Oldham	5	—	—	Broughton
15	1922	Nov. 25	Wigan	20	Leigh	2	—	—	Salford
16	1923	,, 24	St. Helens R.	17	Swinton	0	—	—	Wigan
17	1924	,, 22	Oldham	10	St. Helens R.	0	—	—	Salford
18	1925	Dec. 10	Swinton	15	Wigan	11	—	—	Broughton
19	1926	Nov. 20	St. Helens	10	St. Helens R.	2	—	—	Warrington
20	1927	,, 19	Swinton	5	Wigan	2	—	—	Oldham
21	1928	,, 24	Wigan	5	Widnes	4	—	—	Warrington
22	1929	,, 23	Warrington	15	Salford	2	—	—	Wigan
23	1930	,, 29	St. Helens R.	18	Wigan	3	—	—	Swinton
24	1931	,, 21	Salford	10	Swinton	8	—	—	Broughton
25	1932	,, 19	Warrington	10	St. Helens	9	—	—	Wigan
26	1933	,, 18	Oldham	12	St. Helens R.	0	—	—	Swinton
27	1934	Oct. 20	Salford	21	Wigan	12	—	—	Swinton

	Year	Date	Winners	G.	T.	Pts.	Runners-up	G.	T.	Pts.	Attend.	Receipts	Venue
28	1935	Oct. 19	Salford			15	Wigan			7	—	—	Warrington
29	1936	,, 17	Salford			5	Wigan			2	—	—	Warrington
30	1937	,, 23	Warrington			8	Barrow			4	—	—	Wigan
31	1938	,, 22	Wigan			10	Salford			7	—	—	Swinton
32	1940	Apl. 20	Swinton			5	Widnes			4	—	—	Widnes
		,, 29	Swinton			16	Widnes			11	—	—	Swinton
							(after extra time)						
							(Swinton won the Cup on aggregate, 21–15)						
1940–41, 1941–42, 1942–43, 1943–44, 1944–45—*No Cup Competition. Oldham, Wigan, St. Helens and Barrow played in the Yorkshire Challenge Cup Competition.*													
33	1945	Oct. 27	Widnes	2	1	7	Wigan	0	1	3	28,184	£2,600 0 0	Warrington
34	1946	,, 26	Wigan	3	1	9	Belle Vue R.	0	1	3	21,618	£2,658 0 0	Swinton
35	1947	Nov. 1	Wigan	2	2	10	Belle Vue R.	2	1	7	23,110	£3,043 0 0	Warrington
36	1948	,, 13	Wigan	4	2	14	Warrington	1	2	8	39,015	£5,518 0 0	Swinton
37	1949	Oct. 29	Wigan	1	6	20	Leigh	2	1	7	35,000	£4,751 0 0	Warrington
38	1950	Nov. 4	Wigan	5	6	28	Warrington	1	1	5	42,541	£6,222 0 0	Swinton
39	1951	Oct. 27	Wigan	1	4	14	Leigh	0	2	6	33,230	£5,432 0 0	Swinton
40	1952	Nov. 29	Leigh	5	4	22	St. Helens	1	1	5	34,785	£5,793 0 0	Swinton
41	1953	Oct. 24	St. Helens	5	2	16	Wigan	1	2	8	42,793	£6,790 0 0	Swinton
42	1954	,, 23	Barrow	3	2	12	Oldham	1	0	2	25,204	£4,603 0 0	Swinton
43	1955	,, 15	Leigh	7	4	26	Widnes	3	1	9	26,507	£4,090 0 0	Wigan
44	1956	,, 20	Oldham	2	2	10	St. Helens	0	1	3	39,544	£6,274 0 0	Wigan
45	1957	,, 19	Oldham	2	3	13	Wigan	1	2	8	42,497	£6,918 0 0	Swinton
46	1958	,, 25	Oldham	3	2	12	St. Helens	1	0	2	38,780	£6,933 0 0	Swinton

Wigan have won the Cup thirteen times (including six consecutive seasons) and finished runners-up on eleven occasions (twenty-four times finalists out of forty-six finals).

Oldham are next with nine victories, including the last three finals (five times runners-up). Leigh took part in the first final (1905) *but did not win the Cup until* 1952 *(fortieth final), having been six times runners-up. Barrow's success in the* 1954 *final was their first Cup in Rugby League football.*

Highest score: 28–5 (*Wigan v. Warrington*, 1950).

Attendance Record: 42,793, *St. Helens v. Wigan, at Swinton, October* 24, 1953.

Receipts Record: £6,933. *Oldham v. St. Helens, at Swinton, October* 25, 1958.

Swinton R.L. Club's Station Road ground venue of fourteen finals. First final the only match to be replayed.

THE YORKSHIRE COUNTY RUGBY FOOTBALL CHALLENGE CUP

The Yorkshire Challenge Cup, which was designed and manufactured by Messrs. Fattorini & Sons, Ltd., of Bradford, is of classic design, stands 3 ft. in height, and has a weight of 200 ounces. The Cup rests on an ebony plinth with silver shields affixed round with the winners' names. On the foot on the front is the Yorkshire Arms chased in relief, and encircled in a laurel, while on the reverse is a Yorkshire rose treated in a similar manner. A large panel on the body of the Cup contains the inscription, while at the extreme top is a lifelike figure.

RESULTS OF FINAL TIES

	Year	Date	Winners	G.	T.	Pts.	Runners-up	G.	T.	Pts.	Attend.	Receipts	Venue
1	1905	Dec. 2	Hunslet			13	Halifax			3	—	—	Park Avenue, Bradford
2	1906	,, 1	Bradford			8	Hull K.R.			5	—	—	Wakefield
3	1907	,, 21	Hunslet			17	Halifax			0	—	—	Leeds
4	1908	Nov. 28	Halifax			9	Hunslet			5	—	—	Wakefield
5	1909	,, 27	Huddersfield			21	Batley			0	—	—	Leeds
6	1910	Dec. 3	Wakefield T.			8	Huddersfield			2	—	—	Leeds
7	1911	Nov. 25	Huddersfield			22	Hull K.R.			10	—	—	Wakefield
8	1912	,, 23	Batley			17	Hull			3	—	—	Leeds
9	1913	,, 29	Huddersfield			19	Bradford N.			3	—	—	Halifax
10	1914	,, 28	Huddersfield			31	Hull			0	—	—	Leeds
1915–16, 1916–17, 1917–18—*No Cup Competition*													
11	1919	May 17	Huddersfield			14	Dewsbury			8	—	—	Leeds
12	1919	Nov. 29	Huddersfield			24	Leeds			5	—	—	Halifax
13	1920	,, 27	Hull K.R.			2	Hull			0	—	—	Leeds
14	1921	,, 26	Leeds			11	Dewsbury			3	—	—	Halifax
15	1922	Dec. 2	York			5	Batley			0	—	—	Leeds
16	1923	Nov. 24	Hull			10	Huddersfield			4	—	—	Leeds
17	1924	,, 22	Wakefield T.			9	Batley			8	—	—	Leeds
18	1925	,, 28	Dewsbury			2	Huddersfield			0	—	—	Wakefield
19	1926	Dec. 1	Huddersfield			10	Wakefield T.			3	—	—	Leeds
20	1927	Nov. 26	Dewsbury			8	Hull			2	—	—	Leeds
21	1928	,, 24	Leeds			5	Featherstone R.			0	—	—	Wakefield
22	1929	,, 30	Hull K.R.			13	Hunslet			7	—	—	Leeds
23	1930	,, 22	Leeds			10	Huddersfield			2	—	—	Halifax
24	1931	,, 21	Huddersfield			4	Hunslet			2	—	—	Leeds
25	1932	,, 19	Leeds			8	Wakefield T.			0	—	—	Huddersfield
26	1933	Nov. 25	Yorks			10	Hull K.R.			4	—	—	Leeds
27	1934	Oct. 27	Leeds			5	Wakefield T.			5	—	—	Dewsbury
	(replay)	31	Leeds			2	Wakefield T.			2	—	—	Huddersfield
	(second replay)	Nov. 7	Leeds			13	Wakefield T.			0	—	—	Hunslet
28	1935	Oct. 19	Leeds			3	York			0	—	—	Halifax
29	1936	,, 17	York			9	Wakefield T.			2	—	—	Leeds
30	1937	,, 30	Leeds			14	Huddersfield			8	—	—	Wakefield
31	1938	Oct. 22	Huddersfield			18	Hull			10	—	—	Odsal, Bradford
32	1940	June 22	Featherstone R.			12	Wakefield T.			9	—	—	Odsal, Bradford
33	1941	Apl. 5	Bradford N.			15	Dewsbury			5	—	—	Huddersfield
34	1941	Dec. 6	Bradford N.			24	Halifax			0	—	—	Huddersfield
35	1942	Nov. 28	Dewsbury			7	Huddersfield			0	—	—	Dewsbury
		Dec. 5	Dewsbury			0	Huddersfield			2	—	—	Huddersfield
							(Dewsbury won the Cup on aggregate, 7–2)						
36	1943	Nov. 27	Bradford N.			5	Keighley			2	—	—	Odsal, Bradford
		Dec. 4	Bradford N.			5	Keighley			5	—	—	Keighley
							(Bradford Northern won the Cup on aggregate, 10–7)						
37	1944	Dec. 2	Halifax			12	Hunslet			3	—	—	Hunslet
		,, 9	Halifax			2	Hunslet			0	—	—	Halifax
							(Halifax won the Cup on aggregate, 14–3)						
38	1945	Nov. 3	Bradford N.	1	1	5	Wakefield T.	1	0	2	24,252	£1,930 0 0	Halifax
39	1946	,, 2	Wakefield T.	2	2	10	Hull	0	0	0	29,000	£3,720 0 0	Leeds
40	1947	,, 1	Wakefield T.	2	1	7	Leeds	2	1	7	24,334	£3,463 0 0	Huddersfield
	(replay)	,, 5	Wakefield T.	1	2	8	Leeds	2	1	7	32,000	£3,258 0 0	Odsal, Bradford
41	1948	Oct. 30	Bradford N.	3	4	18	Castleford	3	1	9	31,393	£5,053 0 0	Leeds
42	1949	,, 29	Bradford N.	4	1	11	Huddersfield	2	0	4	36,000	£6,365 0 0	Leeds
43	1950	Nov. 4	Huddersfield	5	2	16	Castleford	0	1	3	28,610	£5,148 0 0	Leeds
44	1951	Oct. 27	Wakefield T.	4	3	17	Keighley	0	1	3	25,595	£3,347 4 0	Huddersfield
45	1952	Nov. 15	Huddersfield	3	4	18	Batley	1	2	8	15,000	£2,448 17 6	Leeds
46	1953	Oct. 31	Bradford N.	2	1	7	Hull	1	0	2	26,000	£3,843 0 0	Leeds
47	1954	,, 23	Halifax	5	4	22	Hull	4	2	14	26,000	£4,637 0 0	Leeds
48	1955	,, 22	Halifax	2	2	10	Hull	2	2	10	23,000	£4,383 0 0	Leeds
	(replay)	Nov. 2	Halifax	2	1	7	Hull	0	0	0	14,000	£2,315 0 0	Odsal, Bradford
49	1956	Oct. 20	Wakefield T.	4	5	23	Hunslet	1	1	5	31,147	£5,607 0 0	Leeds

R.L. QUIZ

1. It was once planned to construct a railway line across the centre of a R.L. ground. Where was it?

★

2. Which player made the nearest approach to A. A. Rosenfeld's record total of 80 tries in one season?

★

3. What is the highest total of goals kicked by a player in a R.L. Challenge Cup Final?

★

4. Which two clubs were "double" finalists in the R.L. Challenge Cup and Northern Rugby League Championship Finals for the first time in the history of both competitions?

★

5. Has Rugby League football been played by an American team?

★

6. What is the record profit made by a Northern Rugby League club?

★

7. When was the first Rugby League match played in France?

★

8. Has there ever been a first and second division of the Northern Rugby Football League?

★

9. When was the present title of Rugby Football League adopted by the Northern Rugby Football Union?

★

10. Has a team of local-born players won the R.L. Challenge Cup?

QUIZ ANSWERS

1. Fartown, Huddersfield. 2. L. W. Cooper (Huddersfield). 73 tries, season 1951–52. 3. W. F. Young (Leeds) kicked 7 goals in the 1910 replayed Final. Also kicked 2 goals in the drawn game. 4. Warrington and Halifax, season 1953–54. 5. The American All Stars toured Australia and New Zealand in 1953. Played 26, Won 7, Lost 17, Drawn 2. 6. £10,407 by St. Helens, season 1952–53. 7. December 31, 1933. Australia v. England, at Paris. 8. Three seasons—1902–03; 1903–04; 1904–05. 9. On June 14, 1922, at the annual meeting held in Huddersfield. The Northern Rugby Football League, which is the body responsible for the weekly fixtures of the professional clubs, remained unchanged. 10. The Widnes Cup team in the 1930 Final, except for the veteran South African forward, G. Van Rooven, who received a free transfer from Wigan. Again, in the 1937 Final, all the Widnes players were locals except one who was born in neighbouring Runcorn.

R.L. QUIZ

1. The first player transferred for a fee of £1,000 was ————?

*

2. Who was called the "Toowoomba Ghost"?

*

3. When did the "Northern Union" first impose a ban on the signing of Australian and New Zealand players by English clubs?

*

4. How many overseas players accepted contracts with English R.L. clubs from the first signing in 1908 to 1948?

*

5. On which ground was the first match played between a team from overseas and an English club?

*

6. What was the "Rorke's Drift Test"?

*

7. What was the "Odsal Battle"?

*

8. How many English R.L. teams have visited Australia?

*

9. One of the finest Australian wingmen of his day is now a Markets Superintendent. For which English club did he play seven seasons?

QUIZ ANSWERS

1. Stanley Brogden, from Bradford Northern to Huddersfield, 1929. 2. Eric V. Harris. Leeds Australian, with uncanny running power. 3. February 11, 1913. Two years' residential qualification before Australian or New Zealand player allowed to play for N.L. club. Residential qualification remained in force until 1923, but reimposed after a few weeks, continuing to June 9, 1927. Subsequently further agreements made by R.L. Council. 4. Australians 68, New Zealanders 57, South Africans 11. Total 136. 5. Bramley, October 9, 1907 (Bramley v. New Zealand). 6. Third Test Match at Sydney

The Yorkshire County Rugby Football Challenge Cup—contd.

	Year	Date	Winners	G.	T.	Pts.	Runners-up	G.	T.	Pts.	Attend.	Receipts			Venue
50	1957	Oct. 19	Huddersfield	3	3	15	York	1	2	8	23,000	£4,143	0	0	Leeds
51	1958	„ 18	Leeds	3	6	24	Wakefield T.	4	4	20	26,927	£3,831	0	0	Odsal, Bradford

Huddersfield have won the Cup twelve times, and finished runners-up on seven occasions.
Leeds, with eight Cup victories (1934 won after second replay), have been runners-up twice. Halifax have won four finals (1955 after replay), and been runners-up three times. Hull have one success and been nine times runners-up. Keighley (twice runners-up) and Castleford (once runners-up) have not yet won the Cup. Bramley never reached the final.
Highest score: 31–0 (Huddersfield v. Hull, 1914).
Attendance Record: 36,000 (Gates closed) Bradford Northern v. Huddersfield, at Headingley, Leeds, October 29, 1949.
Receipts Record: £6,365. Final as attendance.
Leeds Club's Headingley ground venue of twenty-six finals.
Three replayed finals (two Leeds v. Wakefield Trinity).

QUIZ ANSWERS—contd.

between Australia and England, on July 4, 1914. A most terrific struggle, and England finished the game with ten men owing to injuries, while for a few minutes had actually only nine players on the field. 7. Third Test Match at Odsal Stadium, Bradford, between England and Australia, on December 13, 1952. Many fights and ugly incidents. D. Hall, Australia's vice-captain, sent off by the referee in the second half. Public rumpus over the match and R.L. Council subsequently accepted report that the "unworthy interludes" occupied "about forty-five seconds". 8. 11 Touring Teams. One World Cup Team. 9. Raymond T. Markham. Huddersfield, 1932 to 1939.

COUNTY CHAMPIONSHIP WINNERS (POST-WAR SEASONS)

First County Match was played at Stockport on October 21, 1895, between Cheshire and Lancashire, the latter being winners.

	Winners	Runners-up	Bottom County
1945–46	Lancashire	Yorkshire	Cumberland
1946–47	Yorkshire	Cumberland	Lancashire
1947–48	Lancashire	Cumberland	Yorkshire
1948–49	Cumberland	Lancashire	Yorkshire
1949–50	Yorkshire	Lancashire	Cumberland
1950–51	Cumberland	Yorkshire	Lancashire
1951–52	Yorkshire	Lancashire	Cumberland
1952–53	Lancashire	Yorkshire	Cumberland
(won on points average)			
1953–54	Yorkshire	Cumberland	Lancashire
(won after play-off)			
1954–55	Yorkshire	Lancashire	Cumberland
1955–56	Lancashire	Yorkshire	Cumberland
1956–57	Lancashire	Cumberland	Yorkshire
1957–58	Yorkshire	Cumberland	Lancashire
1958–59	Yorkshire	Lancashire	Cumberland
(won after play-off)			

RUGBY LEAGUE WORLD CUP COMPETITION

The winning team holds a silver trophy costing 3,000,000 francs (£5,000) donated by M. Paul Barriere, president of the French R.L.

FIRST COMPETITION HELD IN FRANCE—1954

Date		G.	T.	Pts.		G.	T.	Pts.	Venue	Att.	Receipts.
Oct. 30	France	5	4	22	New Zealand	2	3	13	Paris	13,240	
„ 31	England	5	6	28	Australia	2	3	13	Lyons	10,250	
Nov. 7	Australia	5	8	34	New Zealand	6	1	15	Marseilles	20,000	
„ 7	England	2	3	13	France	2	3	13	Toulouse	37,471	£14,276
„ 11	France	3	3	15	Australia	1	1	5	Nantes	13,000	£6,000
„ 11	England	4	6	26	New Zealand	3	0	6	Bordeaux	14,000	£4,720
FINAL											
„ 13	England	2	4	16	France	3	2	12	Paris	30,368	£11,395
										138,329	

FINAL TABLE

		P.	W.	L.	D.	For G.	T.	Pts.	Against G.	T.	Pts.	Points Awarded
1	England	4	3	0	1	13	19	83	10	8	44	7
2	France	4	2	1	1	13	12	62	7	11	47	5
3	Australia	3	1	2	0	8	12	52	14	10	58	2
4	New Zealand	3	0	3	0	11	4	34	14	18	82	0

England won the first R.L. World Cup Competition.

SECOND COMPETITION HELD IN AUSTRALIA—1957

Date		G.	T.	Pts		G.	T.	Pts.	Venue	Att.	Receipts
June 15	England	4	5	23	France	1	1	5	Sydney	50,000	
„ 15	Australia	5	5	25	New Zealand	1	1	5	Brisbane	28,000	
„ 17	England	3	0	6	Australia	5	7	31	Sydney	58,665	£20,000
„ 17	France	4	2	14	New Zealand	2	2	10	Brisbane (floodlight)	28,000	
„ 22	Australia	7	4	26	France	3	1	9	Sydney	35,000	
„ 25	England	3	5	21	New Zealand	7	5	29	Sydney	14,263	
Non-Competitive Match											
June 29	Australia	4	4	20	The Rest (Eng., France, N.Z.)	1	3	11	Sydney	20,000	
										233,928	

FINAL TABLE

		P.	W.	L.	For G.	T.	Pts.	Against G.	T.	Pts.	Points Awarded
1	Australia	3	3	0	17	16	82	7	2	20	6
2	England	3	1	2	10	10	50	13	13	65	2
3	New Zealand	3	1	2	10	8	44	12	12	60	2
4	France	3	1	2	8	4	28	13	11	59	2

Australia won the second R.L. World Cup Competition.

TOP SCORERS IN POST-WAR SEASONS—ALL MATCHES

GOALS		TRIES		POINTS		
(Record: 224, by B. Ganley, Oldham, 1957–58)		*(Record: 80, by A. A. Rosenfeld, Hudd. 1913–14)*		*(Record—501, by L. Jones, Leeds, 1956–57)*		
1945–46 J. Bawden (*Hudd.*)	95	E. Batten (*Bradford N.*)	35	J. Bawden (*Hudd.*)	256	(goals 95, tries 22)
1946–47 F. Miller (*Hull*)	106	B. Bevan (*Warr.*)	48	J. Bawden (*Hudd.*)	244	(goals 92, tries 20)
1947–48 E. H. Ward (*Wigan*)	150	B. Bevan (*Warr.*)	67	E. H. Ward (*Wigan*)	333	(goals 150, tries 11)
1948–49 E. H. Ward (*Wigan*)	155	L. W. Cooper (*Hudd.*)	65	E. H. Ward (*Wigan*)	361	(goals 155, tries 17)
1949–50 K. Gee (*Wigan*)	147	B. C. Nordgren (*Wigan*)	64	H. Palin (*Warr.*)	319	(goals 146, tries 9)
1950–51 H. E. Cook (*Leeds*)	165	B. Bevan (*Warr.*)	69	H. E. Cook (*Leeds*)	348	(goals 165, tries 6)
1951–52 J. A. Ledgard (*Leigh*)	149	L. W. Cooper (*Hudd.*)	73	J. A. Phillips (*Bradford N.*)	314	(goals 133, tries 16)
1952–53 A. H. Bath (*Warr.*)	173	B. Bevan (*Warr.*)	72	A. H. Bath (*Warr.*)	388	(goals 173, tries 14)
1953–54 P. Metcalfe (*St. Helens*)	157	B. Bevan (*Warr.*)	70	P. Metcalfe (*St. Helens*)	377	(goals 157, tries 21)
1954–55 J. A. Ledgard (*Leigh*)	184	B. Bevan (*Warr.*)	68	J. A. Ledgard (*Leigh*)	386	(goals 184, tries 6)
1955–56 { A. H. Bath (*Warr.*)	162	J. McLean (*Bradford N.*)	64	A. H. Bath (*Warr.*)	369	(goals 162, tries 15)
1955–56 { J. A. Ledgard (*Leigh*)	162					
1956–57 L. Jones (*Leeds*)	198	W. J. Boston (*Wigan*)	60	L. Jones (*Leeds*)	501	(goals 198, tries 35)
1957–58 B. Ganley (*Oldham*)	224	M. Sullivan (*Wigan and Hudd.*)	53	B. Ganley (*Oldham*)	463	(goals 224, tries 5)
1958–59 B. Ganley (*Oldham*)	192	T. Van Vollenhoven (*St. Helens*)	62	F. Griffiths (*Wigan*)	397	(goals 176, tries 15)

B. Bevan (Warrington) top try scorer six seasons (three in succession).

NOTE: A. H. Bath, B. Bevan, and L. W. Cooper signed from Australia; H. E. Cook, J. McLean, B. C. Nordgren and J. A. Phillips signed from New Zealand.

TEST MATCHES

ENGLAND AND AUSTRALIA
Results and Records

	Year	Date		G.	T.	Pts.		G.	T.	Pts.	Attend.	Receipts	Venue
1	1909	Jan. 2	Eng.	1	4	14	Aust.	0	3	9	7,000	£248 10 6	Huddersfield
2	1909	,, 23	,,	3	3	15	,,	1	1	5		£568 0 0	Newcastle
3	1909	Feb. 15	,,	0	2	6	,,	1	1	5	22,000	£227 0 0	Birmingham
											9,000		

England won the "Ashes". Won 3.

4	1910	June 19	Eng.	3	7	27	Aust.	4	4	20	40,000		Sydney (R.A.C.)
5	1910	July 9	,,	2	3	13	,,	2	3	13			Sydney
6	1910	,, 13	,,	3	3	15	,,	7	6	32			Sydney

England won 1, Lost 1, Drawn 1.

7	1911	Nov. 8	Eng.	2	2	10	Aust.	2	5	19	7,000	£338 0 0	Newcastle
8	1911	Dec. 16	,,	1	3	11	,,	1	3	11	6,000	£336 0 0	Edinburgh
9	1912	Jan. 1	,,	1	2	8	,,	3	9	33	4,000	£213 17 3	Birmingham

Australia won the "Ashes". Won 2, Drawn 1.

10	1914	June 27	Eng.	4	5	23	Aust.	1	1	5			Sydney
11	1914	,, 29	,,	2	1	7	,,	3	2	12			Sydney (S.C.G.)
12	1914	July 4	,,	4	2	14	,,	0	2	6			Sydney

England won the "Ashes". Won 2, Lost 1.

13	1920	June 26	Eng.	2	0	4	Aust.	1	2	8			Brisbane
14	1920	July 3	,,	1	2	8	,,	3	5	21			Sydney
15	1920	,, 10	,,	4	5	23	,,	2	3	13			Sydney

Australia won the "Ashes". Won 2, Lost 1.

16	1921	Oct. 1	Eng.	0	2	6	Aust.	1	1	5	31,700	£3,891 4 6	Leeds
17	1921	Nov. 5	,,	1	0	2	,,	2	4	16	21,504	£2,924 8 0	Hull
18	1922	Jan. 14	,,	0	2	6	,,	0	0	0	22,000	£2,500 0 0	Salford

England won the "Ashes". Won 2, Lost 1.

19	1924	June 23	Eng.	5	4	22	Aust.	0	1	3		£4,500 0 0	Sydney
20	1924	,, 28	,,	1	1	5	,,	0	1	3		£2,600 0 0	Sydney
21	1924	July 12	,,	1	3	11	,,	6	3	21		£3,320 0 0	Brisbane

England won the "Ashes". Won 2, Lost 1.

22	1928	June 23	Eng.	3	3	15	Aust.	3	2	12		£4,348 0 0	Brisbane
23	1928	July 14	,,	1	2	8	,,	0	0	0		£4,298 0 0	Sydney
24	1928	,, 21	,,	4	2	14	,,	6	3	21		£3,118 0 0	Sydney

England won the "Ashes". Won 2, Lost 1.

25	1929	Oct. 5	Eng.	1	2	8	Aust.	5	7	31	20,000	£2,065 0 0	Hull
26	1929	Nov. 9	,,	3	1	9	,,	0	1	3	31,402	£3,902 0 0	Leeds
27	1930	Jan. 4	,,	0	0	0	,,	0	0	0	34,709	£4,186 11 0	Swinton
28	1930 (extra Test)		,,	0	1	3	,,	0	0	0	16,743	£2,056 0 0	Rochdale

England won the "Ashes". Won 2, Lost 1, Drawn 1.

29	1932	June 6	Eng.	1	2	8	Aust.	3	0	6	70,204	£6,513 17 9	Sydney
30	1932	,, 18	,,	0	2	6	,,	3	3	15	26,500	£3,119 0 0	Brisbane
31	1932	July 16	,,	3	4	18	,,	5	1	13		£4,252 0 0	Sydney

England won the "Ashes". Won 2, Lost 1.

32	1933	Oct. 7	Eng.	2	0	4	Aust.	0	0	0	32,500	£4,659 0 0	Belle Vue, Manchester
33	1933	Nov. 11	,,	2	1	7	,,	1	1	5	29,618	£3,873 0 0	Leeds
34	1933	Dec. 16	,,	5	3	19	,,	5	2	16	10,990	£1,515 14 0	Swinton

England won the "Ashes". Won 3.

35	1936	June 29	Eng.	1	2	8	Aust.	6	4	24	63,920	£6,116 0 0	Sydney
36	1936	July 4	,,	3	2	12	,,	2	1	7	30,000	£3,908 0 0	Brisbane
37	1936	,, 18	,,	3	2	12	,,	2	1	7	53,546	£4,299 0 0	Sydney

England won the "Ashes". Won 2, Lost 1.

38	1937	Oct. 16	Eng.	1	1	5	Aust.	2	0	4	32,000	£3,942 0 0	Leeds
39	1937	Nov. 13	,,	2	3	13	,,	0	1	3	31,724	£3,815 0 0	Swinton
40	1937	Dec. 18	,,	0	1	3	,,	2	3	13	9,000	£1,237 0 0	Huddersfield

England won the "Ashes". Won 2, Lost 1.

41	1946	June 17	Eng.	1	2	8	Aust.	1	2	8	64,527	£10,130 6 3	Sydney
42	1946	July 6	,,	1	4	14	,,	1	1	5	45,190	£5,190 0 0	Brisbane
43	1946	,, 20	,,	4	2	20	,,	2	1	7	35,294	£4,572 0 0	Sydney

England won the "Ashes". Won 2, Drawn 1.

44	1948	Oct. 9	Eng.	1	7	23	Aust.	3	5	21	36,529	£8,020 8 6	Leeds
45	1948	Nov. 6	,,	2	4	16	,,	2	1	7	37,137	£6,764 14 0	Swinton
46	1949	Jan. 29	,,	4	5	23	,,	0	3	9	43,500	£6,877 0 0	Odsal, Bradford

England won the "Ashes". Won 3.

47	1950	June 12	Eng.	0	2	6	Aust.	2	0	4	47,215	£6,769 0 0	Sydney
48	1950	July 1	,,	0	1	3	,,	3	3	15	35,000	£7,377 0 0	Brisbane
49	1950	,, 22	,,	1	0	2	,,	1	1	5	47,178	£6,117 0 0	Sydney

Australia won the "Ashes". Won 2, Lost 1.

50	1952	Oct. 4	Eng.	5	3	19	Aust.	3	0	6	34,305	£8,628 0 0	Leeds
51	1952	Nov. 8	,,	3	5	21	,,	1	1	5	32,943	£6,776 0 0	Swinton
52	1952	Dec. 13	,,	2	1	7	,,	6	5	27	30,509	£5,466 0 0	Odsal, Bradford

England won the "Ashes". Won 2, Lost 1.

53	1954	June 12	Eng.	3	2	12	Aust.	8	7	37	65,884	£16,842 6 0	Sydney
54	1954	July 3	,,	10	6	38	,,	3	5	21	45,000	£13,190 0 0	Brisbane
55	1954	,, 17	,,	2	4	16	,,	4	4	20	67,577	£17,217 10 0	Sydney

Australia won the "Ashes". Won 2, Lost 1.

56	1956	Nov. 17	Eng.	3	5	21	Aust.	2	2	10	22,473	£4,837 0 0	Wigan
57	1956	Dec. 1	,,	3	1	9	,,	5	4	22	23,364	£4,172 0 0	Odsal, Bradford
58	1956	,, 15	,,	2	5	19	,,	0	0	0	17,542	£4,225 0 0	Swinton

England won the "Ashes". Won 2, Lost 1.

59	1958	June 14	Eng.	1	2	8	Aust.	5	5	25	68,777	£29,548 0 0	Sydney
60	1958	July 5	,,	5	5	25	,,	3	4	18	32,965	£17,108 0 0	Brisbane
61	1958	,, 19	,,	8	8	40	,,	4	3	17	68,720	£29,548 0 0	Sydney

England won the "Ashes". Won 2, Lost 1.

R.L. QUIZ

1. Who were the three Cumberland brothers signed by Huddersfield?

★

2. Which player has scored most points in one season?

QUIZ ANSWERS

1. Stanley Vincent Pepperell (1934), George Russell Pepperell (1939), Albert James Pepperell (1943). 2. Lewis Jones (Leeds). Season 1956–57, 501 points (198 goals and 35 tries).

SOME RUGBY LEAGUE RECORDS

World Record Attendance. 102,569, Warrington v. Halifax, Challenge Cup Final Replay, Odsal Stadium, Bradford, May 5, 1954 (evening kick-off).

World Record Receipts. £33,000 plus B.B.C. television rights payment, Wigan v. Hull, R.L. Challenge Cup Final, Wembley, May 9, 1959.

Record Attendance Northern Rugby League Championship Final. 75,194, Huddersfield v. Warrington, Maine Road, Manchester, May 14, 1949.

Record Receipts. £12,054, Oldham v. Hull, Odsal Stadium, Bradford, May 18, 1957.

Record Attendance Test Match. 70,204 (gates closed), First Test Match, Australia v. England, Sydney, June 6, 1932.

Record Receipts Test Match. £29,548 (all-ticket), First Test Match, Australia v. England, Sydney, June 14, 1958. Receipts equalled Third Test Match, Australia v. England, Sydney, July 19, 1958.

Record Score. Huddersfield 19 goals, 27 tries—119 points; Swinton Park Rangers 1 goal—2 points. At Huddersfield, February 28, 1914, N.U. Challenge Cup, first round.

Personal Goal Kicking Record for a Single Match. 22 goals (44 points), by J. Sullivan (Wigan), Wigan v. Flimby and Fothergill (Cumb.). At Wigan, February 14, 1925, R.L. Challenge Cup, first round.

Personal Try and Points Record for a Single Match. 11 tries, 10 goals—53 points, by G. H. ("Tich") West (Hull Kingston Rovers), Hull K.R. v. Brookland Rovers (Cumb.). At Hull, March 4, 1905, N.U. Challenge Cup, first round.

Season's Scoring Record. During season 1914–15 Huddersfield played 47 matches and obtained a total of 207 goals and 285 tries—1,269 points.

Consecutive League Matches without Defeat. Huddersfield from March 30, 1912, to January 4, 1913 (both dates inclusive) played 26 successive League matches without a defeat (19 successive League matches won in season 1912–13).

Quickest Century of Goals. B. Ganley (Oldham), 103 goals kicked by November 9, 1957 (18 matches).

Record Benefit Match. The late William ("Billy") Batten, of Hull, received £1,079 13s. 8d., when Hull played York at The Boulevard on April 3, 1920.

First Television Broadcast of R.L. Match. Second Test Match, England v. New Zealand, at Station Road, Swinton, on November 10, 1951. The first Northern sporting event televised by the B.B.C., and undertaken following suggestion made by the editor of Rugby League Review.

No Two Divisions. Between March 12, 1952, and June 11, 1958, seven attempts were made at special meetings to split the Northern Rugby Football League into two divisions, with relegation and promotion for clubs at end of each season. On each occasion the requisite two-thirds majority of the clubs present and voting at the respective meetings was not obtained for the change to be made.

WORLD RECORD TRY SCORER

Brian Bevan, Warrington's Australian right wing three-quarter, at the completion of his thirteenth season with the Lancashire club, had scored a total of 727 tries in all matches (club and representative). His tries total for Warrington stands at 680.

Bevan established a new English try scoring record on February 27, 1954 (eighth season), when against St. Helens, at Wilderspool Stadium, he scored a try and made his tries total 462. The fifteen-year-old record was set up by Alf Ellaby (St. Helens and Wigan) with 461 tries, covering fourteen seasons and two Australasian tours. Bevan reached the 500th mark on September 25, 1954; completed his tenth season (1955–56) with the total at 607; and scored his 700th try against Liverpool City on December 20, 1958. His highest number of tries scored in one season was 72 during 1952–53—eight short of Rosenfeld's record of 80 tries in one season.

Brian Bevan was born at Sydney, New South Wales, on June 24, 1924. He made his debut as a Warrington player on September 14, 1946 (v. Salford), scored a try and kicked a goal. Incidentally, Bevan has kicked 36 goals, and with his 727 tries his points total is now 2,253.

The ace scoring winger has thrilled English crowds on innumerable occasions with his wizardry and electrifying runs. Throughout his career he has never been guilty of an unworthy action, and has obtained the highest honours open to a player in English Rugby League football. Unlike other Australian players Bevan did not receive a large signing-on fee, and the £300 paid by Warrington was undoubtedly the cheapest but most profitable investment ever made by a Rugby League club.

CHAMPION GOAL KICKER

James Sullivan, Wigan's great Welsh full-back, in twenty-four seasons and three Australasian tours, kicked a total of 2,959 goals and scored 96 tries—6,206 points. He played in fifteen Test Matches against Australia. Sullivan's 204 goals kicked in season 1933–34 remained a R.L. record until it was surpassed by B. Ganley (Oldham) with 224 goals in season 1957–58.

R.L. QUIZ

1. When was professionalism adopted?

★

2. Who holds the record for the number of points scored in English Rugby League football?

★

3. Name the world record R.L. try scorer.

★

4. Which player set up an individual try scoring record for one season?

★

5. When was the R.L. Challenge Cup Final first played at Wembley?

QUIZ ANSWERS

1. July 19, 1898. No player allowed to play football unless he was in full employment. Many fines and suspensions for failure to comply with this "work rule". 2. James Sullivan (Wigan). 6,206 points. 3. Brian Bevan (Warrington). 727 tries during thirteen seasons. 4. A. A. Rosenfeld (Huddersfield). Scored 80 tries in season 1913–14. 5. May 4, 1929. Wigan v. Dewsbury.

COMPLETE RECORD OF TEST MATCHES PLAYED BETWEEN ENGLAND AND AUSTRALIA

	P.	W.	L.	D.	Goals	Tries	Points
England	61	37	20	4	137	166	772
Australia	61	20	37	4	144	147	729

England won the "Ashes" 16 times. Australia won 4 times. (1910 series each country won 1 Test and drawn 1.)
England have won all three Test Matches on three occasions—1909, 1933 and 1948–49 (all played in England).
Highest Score: England 40 points, Australia 17 points, Third Test Match, at Sydney, July 19, 1958.
Attendance Record: 70,204 (gates closed). First Test Match, at Sydney, June 6, 1932.
Receipts Record: £29,548. First Test Match, at Sydney, June 14, 1958. Receipts equalled, Third Test Match, at Sydney, July 19, 1958.

ENGLAND AND NEW ZEALAND

Results and Records

	Year	Date		G.	T.	Pts.		G.	T.	Pts.	Attend.	Receipts			Venue
1	1908	Jan. 25	Eng.	1	4	14	N.Z.	0	2	6	8,000	£300	0	0	Leeds
2	1908	Feb. 8	,,	0	2	6	,,	3	4	18	13,000				Chelsea
3	1908	,, 15	,,	1	1	5	,,	1	2	8	4,000	£200	0	0	Cheltenham

New Zealand won the "Ashes". Won 2, Lost 1.

4	1910	July 30	Eng.	8	12	52	N.Z.	4	4	20	20,000				Wellington

England Won 1.

5	1914	Aug. 1	Eng.	2	4	16	N.Z.	2	3	13	22,000	£710	0	0	Auckland

England Won 1.

6	1920	July 31	Eng.	5	7	31	N.Z.	2	1	7	34,000				Auckland
7	1920	Aug. 7	,,	2	5	19	,,	0	1	3					Christchurch
8	1920	,, 14	,,	1	3	11	,,	2	2	10	5,000				Wellington

England won the "Ashes". Won 3.

9	1924	Aug. 2	Eng.	1	2	8	N.Z.	2	4	16	22,000				Auckland
10	1924	,, 6	,,	1	3	11	,,	2	3	13	6,000				Wellington
11	1924	,, 9	,,	5	7	31	,,	3	4	18	14,000				Dunedin

New Zealand won the "Ashes". Won 2, Lost 1.

12	1926	Oct. 2	Eng.	5	6	28	N.Z.	4	2	20	14,500	£1,650	0	0	Wigan
13	1926	Nov. 13	,,	3	5	21	,,	1	3	11	5,000	£592	13	6	Hull
14	1927	Jan. 15	,,	4	8	32	,,	4	3	17	6,000	£552	0	0	Leeds

England won the "Ashes". Won 3.

15	1928	Aug. 4	Eng.	2	3	13	N.Z.	4	3	17	28,000				Auckland
16	1928	,, 18	,,	2	3	13	,,	1	1	5	12,000				Dunedin
17	1928	,, 25	,,	0	2	6	,,	1	1	5	21,000				Christchurch

England won the "Ashes". Won 2, Lost 1.

18	1932	July 30	Eng.	3	6	24	N.Z.	3	1	9	25,000				Auckland
19	1932	Aug. 13	,,	5	5	25	,,	4	2	14	8,000				Christchurch
20	1932	,, 20	,,	4	4	20	,,	3	4	18	20,000				Auckland

England won the "Ashes". Won 3.

21	1936	Aug. 8	Eng.	2	2	10	N.Z.	4	0	8					Auckland
22	1936	,, 15	,,	4	5	23	,,	4	1	11	16,000				Auckland

England Won 2.

23	1946	Aug. 10	Eng.	1	2	8	N.Z.	5	1	13	10,000				Auckland

New Zealand Won 1.

24	1947	Oct. 4	Eng.	1	3	11	N.Z.	2	2	10	28,445	£5,027	18	6	Leeds
25	1947	Nov. 8	,,	2	1	7	,,	2	2	10	29,031	£4,880	0	0	Swinton
26	1947	Dec. 20	,,	5	5	25	,,	3	1	9	42,685	£5,750	0	0	Odsal, Bradford

England won the "Ashes". Won 2, Lost 1.

27	1950	July 29	Eng.	2	2	10	N.Z.	5	2	16	10,000				Christchurch
28	1950	Aug. 12	,,	2	3	13	,,	4	4	20	20,000	£3,250	0	0	Auckland

New Zealand Won 2.

29	1951	Oct. 6	Eng.	3	5	21	N.Z.	3	3	15	37,033	£5,513	0	0	Odsal, Bradford
30	1951	Nov. 10	,,	4	4	20	,,	2	5	19	28,246	£5,403	0	0	Swinton
31	1951	Dec. 15	,,	2	4	16	,,	0	4	12	18,649	£3,720	0	0	Leeds

England won the "Ashes". Won 3.

32	1954	July 24	Eng.	3	7	27	N.Z.	2	1	7	30,000				Auckland
33	1954	,, 31	,,	4	2	14	,,	7	2	20	6,000				Greymouth
34	1954	Aug. 14	,,	3	2	12	,,	3	0	6					Auckland

England won the "Ashes". Won 2, Lost 1.

35	1955	Oct. 8	Eng.	5	5	25	N.Z.	0	2	6	21,937	£4,799	0	0	Swinton
36	1955	Nov. 12	,,	3	7	27	,,	3	2	12	24,443	£3,998	0	0	Odsal, Bradford
37	1955	Dec. 17	,,	2	3	13	,,	5	6	28	11,000	£1,747	10	0	Leeds

England won the "Ashes". Won 2, Lost 1.

38	1958	July 26	Eng.	2	2	10	N.Z.	3	3	15	25,000	£7,000	0	0	Auckland
39	1958	Aug. 9	,,	7	6	32	,,	3	3	15	30,000				Auckland

England Won 1, Lost 1.

Complete Record of Test Matches Played between England and New Zealand

	P.	W.	L.	D.	Goals	Tries	Points
England	39	27	12	0	112	162	710
New Zealand	39	12	27	0	106	96	500

England won the "Ashes" 8 times. New Zealand won twice.
England have won all three Test Matches on four occasions.
Highest Score: England 52 points, New Zealand 20 points, Test Match at Wellington, July 30, 1910.
Attendance Record: 42,685. Third Test Match, at Odsal, Bradford, December 20, 1947.
Receipts Record: £7,000. First Test Match, at Auckland, July 26, 1958. (Second Test receipts not available.)

ENGLAND AND FRANCE

Official Test Matches replacing the International Tournament Championship. (Various representative matches played between the two countries in previous seasons.)

Results and Records

	Year	Date		G. T. Pts.		G. T. Pts.	Attend.	Receipts	Venue
1	1957	Jan. 26	Eng.	9 9 45	France	3 2 12	18,600	£3,028 0 0	Leeds
2	1957	Mar. 3	,,	5 3 19	,,	5 3 19			Toulouse
3	1957	Apl. 10	,,	7 5 29	,,	4 2 14	23,250	£2,650 0 0	St. Helens

England won the "Ashes". Won 2, Drawn 1.

4	1957	Nov. 3	Eng.	5 5 25	France	1 4 14			Toulouse
5	1957	,, 23	,,	10 8 44	,,	3 3 15	19,152	£2,772 0 0	Wigan
6	1958	Mar. 2	,,	4 5 23	,,	3 1 9	20,000		Grenoble

England won the "Ashes". Won 3.

7	1959	Mar. 14	Eng.	7 12 50	France	3 3 15	22,000	£3,470 0 0	Leeds
8	1959	Apl. 5	,,	3 3 15	,,	3 6 24			Grenoble

England Won 1, Lost 1.

Complete Record of Test Matches played between England and France

	P.	W.	L.	D.	Goals	Tries	Points
England	8	6	1	1	50	50	250
France	8	1	6	1	25	24	122

Highest Score: England 50 points, France 15 points, Test Match at Leeds, March 14, 1959.

TOUR RECORDS

AUSTRALIAN TEAMS IN ENGLAND

					P.	W.	L.	D.	For	Agst.
1	*1908–09	..	..	..	45	17	22	6	511	474
2	*1911–12	..	..	..	35	28	5	2	619	281
3	*1921–22	..	..	..	36	27	9	0	763	242
4	1929–30	..	..	..	35	24	9	2	708	347
5	1933–34	..	..	..	36	26	10	0	691	282
6	1937	..	..	..	25	13	11	1	293	232
7	1948–49	..	..	..	27	15	12	0	348	275
8	1952	..	..	..	27	23	3	1	816	248
9	1956	..	..	..	19	10	9	0	335	296

*1908–09 tourists included one New Zealand player; 1911–12, four New Zealanders; 1921–22, also New Zealand players.

On December 31, 1933, the Australians defeated England in the first Rugby League match played in France (at Paris). Commencing with the 1937–38 team, tours have been made of France at the conclusion of each England visit.

D. Brown kicked 114 goals and scored 19 tries, a total of 285 points, during the 1933–34 tour.

ENGLISH TEAMS IN AUSTRALIA

					P.	W.	L.	D.	For	Agst.
1	1910	..	..		14	9	4	1	340	247
2	1914	..	..		12	9	3	0	341	134
3	1920	..	..		15	12	3	0	377	230
4	1924	..	..		18	14	4	0	466	258
5	1928	..	..		16	11	4	1	324	219
6	1932	..	..		18	15	2	1	483	172
7	1936	..	..		17	14	3	0	401	204
8	1946	..	..		20	16	3	1	638	198
9	1950	..	..		19	15	4	0	603	178
10	1954	..	..		22	13	7	1	627	426

(1 match abandoned after 56 minutes because of fighting between players—referee walked off the field)

11	1958	..	..		21	19	1	1	810	378

The 1958 tour resulted in the most victories and highest points scoring total by any English team to visit Australia.

TOUR SCORING RECORDS (including N.Z. matches)

Most goals—127, by L. Jones (Leeds), 1954.
Most tries—38, by M. Sullivan (Wigan), 1958.
Most points—278, by L. Jones (Leeds), 1954.

NEW ZEALAND TEAMS IN ENGLAND

					P.	W.	L.	D.	For	Agst.
1	1907–08	..	..	..	35	19	14	2	414	294
2	1926–27	..	..	..	34	16	18	0	557	589
3	*1939	..	..	..	2	2	0	0	41	13
4	1947	..	..	..	27	16	10	1	391	240
5	1951–52	..	..	..	28	18	10	0	482	348
6	1955	..	..	..	27	14	11	2	473	433

* Tour abandoned following declaration of war.

The first New Zealand team to tour England included one Australian player—Herbert Henry Messenger ("The Master")—and he was the champion point scorer.

The last three New Zealand teams have played matches in France at the conclusion of their England tour.

ENGLISH TEAMS IN NEW ZEALAND

					P.	W.	L.	D.	For	Agst.
1	1910	.	..	..	4	4	0	0	187	47
2	1914	..	..	..	6	6	0	0	194	62
3	1920	..	..	..	10	9	1	0	361	102
4	1924	..	..	..	9	7	2	0	272	117
5	1928	..	..	..	9	7	2	0	263	99
6	1932	..	..	..	8	8	0	0	299	87
7	1936	..	..	..	8	8	0	0	210	56
8	1946	..	..	..	7	5	2	0	145	78
9	1950	..	..	..	6	4	2	0	161	88
10	1954	..	..	..	10	8	2	0	292	106
11	1958	..	..	..	9	8	1	0	386	108

277

Bernard Ganley

Billy Boston

Lewis Jones

INTERNATIONAL TOURNAMENT CHAMPIONSHIP

	Winners	Runners-up
1934–35	England	France
1935–36	Wales	England
1936–37	Wales	England
1937–38	Wales	England
1938–39	France	Wales

Tournament suspended during war-time seasons but England and Wales played matches on several occasions.

1945–46	England	France
1946–47	England	Wales
1947–48	England	France
1948–49	France	England
1949–50	England	Other Nationalities
1950–51	France	Other Nationalities
1951–52	France	England
1952–53	Other Nationalities	Wales
	(won on points average)	
1953–54	England	Other Nationalities
1954–55	No Competition	
1955–56	Other Nationalities	France

Other Nationalities team (first season 1949–50) selected from overseas and Scottish players on the registers of English Northern League clubs. During season 1955–56 Welshmen included in Other Nationalities, as Wales was not considered of sufficient strength to participate in the International Tournament Championship.

Sailing

Compiled by **Hugh Somerville**
Editor: The Yachtsman

A BRIEF HISTORY OF BRITISH YACHTING

King Charles II is always considered to have been the father of British Yachting. He was very fond of a small boat of about 20 tons, which was presented to him by the management of the East India Company. The arrival of this vessel on the Thames in 1660 encouraged Commissioner Phineas Pett to build a boat during the following winter. A third was built by Christopher Pett for the Duke of York, while another Dutch boat was also afloat on the Thames in 1661. Incidentally, it is believed that the word "yacht" is derived from the Dutch "yaghten", "to hunt".

In 1662 there was a record of the first race between the King and the Duke of York, the King winning over a course from Greenwich to Gravesend, and back. The stake was £100.

There is not much more record of any organised yachting in British waters until 1720, when the Water Club of the Harbour of Cork was formed. It consisted of not more than 25 members, who appear to have contented themselves with manœuvring in company offshore and convivial living. The club was very active until 1765, but then interest seems to have been lost until 1806, when an attempt was made to revive it. As so often happens, another club in the locality, the Little Monkstown, was formed by the survivors of the old Water Club to form the Cork Yacht Club, now the Royal Cork Y.C.

Meanwhile another club, the Lough Ree, had been formed in 1770, with a fine fleet of boats which sailed there. In 1773 a "Marine Fete" was held at Starcross in Devon, from which event the Yacht Club of that name claims its origin. In 1780 a "regatta" or "water party" was held at Bassenthwaite, organised by a Mr. Pocklington for the entertainment of tourists. There is also evidence that there was a regatta at Whitstable in 1792. However, it is doubtful if any of

these events or organisations had any influence on the general pattern of yachting in the British Isles.

It is more certain that it was the encouragement by the Duke of Cumberland of the sport of racing in small boats on the Thames, which really started the sport as we know it on the right path. This royal patronage resulted in the formation in 1775 of the Cumberland Society. There were by then a large number of small sailing vessels on the Thames; indeed, there had been a race in 1749 from Greenwich to the Nore and back for a plate presented by the Prince of Wales.

Memorials of the Royal Yacht Squadron records that "The primitive sport of yachting on the Thames was no sport of millionaires like that of Cowes to-day"—it was written in 1903—"but the relaxation of the professional man, who, when his day's work was done, stepped into his little cutter at the Temple Stairs, and of the retired City Merchant with his country house at Chelsea or Marylebone and his boat on the river as the chief solace of his leisure."

Much of this early racing took place between Blackfriars and Putney, and after it was over the competitors often repaired to the Vauxhall Gardens. Mr. Smith, the owner of the tea gardens, was the first Commodore, and many of the Society's early cups were presented by the management. Some of these can be seen in a glass case in the Royal Thames Y.C., as can the fleet flags.

Thomas Taylor, who was Commodore from 1780 to 1816, owned the centreboard cutter *Cumberland*, whose model is also in the Royal Thames Y.C., giving an idea of the type of boat in use at the time.

In 1823 the Society's name was changed to the Coronation Society to mark the coronation of King George IV. The Society was split into two over a protest in the first race held under the new name. A number of the competitors who disagreed with the committee met at the White Horse Tavern and formed the Thames Y.C., now the Royal Thames Y.C.

The Society struggled on until 1831, when it was finally dissolved, most members joining the Thames Y.C.

Turning to the south coast, it appeared that "a taste for sea bathing among English people of condition" had attracted many such people to Cowes, where there were many bathing machines on a fine beach to the west of the

Castle. The menfolk began to take an interest in sailing in the local craft. As early as 1788 there was a race round the Isle of Wight, while a naval regatta was held there in 1776.

In 1815 a number of these "people of condition" met at the Thatched House Tavern, St. James's Street, to form the Yacht Club—now the Royal Yacht Squadron.

The following clubs will have celebrated their centenary by 1960. This list gives a good idea of how the sport has spread.

Established	Club
1720	R. Cork Y.C.
1770	Lough Ree Y.C.
1773	Starcross Y.C.
1775	R. Thames Y.C.
1815	R. Dee Y.C.
1815	Royal Yacht Squadron.
1820	Lough Erne Y.C.
1824	R. Northern Y.C.
1827	R. Western Y.C. of England.
1829	R. Gibraltar Y.C.
1830	Kungl. Svenska. Segel Sallskapet (R. Swedish Y.C.O.)
1831	R. Irish Y.C.
1836	Lough Derg Y.C.
1837	R. Southern Y.C.
1838	Deben Y.C.
1838	R. Hobart Regatta Association.
1838	R. London Y.C.
1838	R. St. George Y.C.
1843	R. Harwich Y.C.
1844	New York Y.C.
1844	R. Bermuda Y.C.
1844	R. Mersey Y.C.
1845	R. Victoria Y.C.
1846	R. Bombay Y.C.
1846	R. Engineer Y.C.
1847	R.Y.C. de Ostende
1847	R. Welsh Y.C.
1847	R. Yorkshire Y.C.
1850	K. Nederlandsche Zeil en Roei-vereeniging (R. Netherlands).
1850	R. Channel Islands Y.C.
1850	Fareham Sailing and Motor Boat Club.
1851	K. Roei-en Zeilvereeniging "De Maas" (R. Maas).
1851	R.Y.C. de Belgique.
1852	R. Canadian Y.C.
1853	R.Y.C. of Victoria.
1856	R. Clyde Y.C.
1856	Associaciao Naval de Lisboa
1857	R. Temple Y.C.
1858	R. Natal Y.C.
1858	Cercle de la Voile de Paris.
1859	R. Geelong Y.C.
1859	R. Norfolk and Suffolk Y.C.
1860	Goteborgs Kungl. Segel Saltskap.
1860	R. Windermere Y.C.

The first purely inland sailing club in England was the R. Windermere Yacht Club, founded in 1860, while the pride of seniority among the sailing clubs on the upper part of the River Thames is taken by the Thames Sailing Club of Surbiton, founded in 1870.

The Yacht Racing Association was founded in 1875 with the Marquess of Exeter as President and Dixon Kemp as Secretary.

To enlarge the scope of the Y.R.A., particularly in view of the enormous increase in the popularity of yachting after the Second World War, the name was changed to Yachting Association, and subsequently with royal patronage to the Royal Yachting Association.

In America, the New York Y.C. was founded in 1844 by John C. Stevens on board his schooner *Gimcrack*. The New York Y.C. must have been one of the first to hold races for amateurs only. The model room of this famous club at 37E 44th Street, New York, has the most fabulous collection of yacht models in the world, including all the America's Cup

Challengers and Defenders side by side. Every member on election presents the Club with a half model of his yacht with the bow facing to the right.

It was of course Commodore Stevens and others who brought the Schooner *America* to British waters in 1851. They won the cup which now bears her name for a race round the Isle of Wight, westabout, on August 22nd.

About this time, yachtsmen and designers became conscious of measurement rules. By raking their sternposts, new yachts were evading the "Builders" or "Yacht" measurement rule of 1770. In 1854, some clubs, including the Royal Thames Y.C. (in 1855), adopted the formula from which is derived the Thames measurement. This is still used for estimating tonnage and quoting prices. It penalises beam and is one of the causes of the comparative narrowness of British yachts. The formula is:

$$\frac{L - B \times b \times \frac{1}{2} B}{94} = \text{tonnage}$$

where B is extreme beam and L is the length between the stern and the sternpost on deck.

In 1881 a new tonnage rule known as the "1730" rule was adopted which encouraged a most unhealthy type of vessel known as the "plank in edge"; so that this was superseded in 1886 by Dixon Kemp's Length and Sail Area rule.

$$\frac{\text{Length and Sail Area}}{6,000} = \text{rating.}$$

In this, Length was that on the waterline in feet and the sail area was in square feet. Some of the finest yachts ever to be built were under this rule including *Britannia* and many small "rater" classes. However, this tended to produce rather extreme craft, so that it was superseded by the Linear rating rule.

$$\frac{L + B + \frac{3}{4}G + \frac{1}{2}\sqrt{\text{sail area}}}{2}$$

G being girth.

In 1904 correspondence between the secretary of the Yacht Racing Association, Major Brooke Heckstall-Smith and the Y.C. de France resulted in the calling of a conference to devise an international yacht measurement rule. The result was the first meeting of what has now become the International Yacht Racing Union. Eleven countries met in 1906 to produce the "International Rule of 1906". This rule has been modified from time to time up to the present day when it is virtually obsolescent. It has, however, produced a number of fine racing yachts and the present formula should go on record because it is that to which the 17th America's Cup Challenger and Defender was designed and built: Rating in linear units, either feet or metres=

$$\frac{L + 2d + \sqrt{S - F}}{2.37}$$

where L is measured length
    d is girth difference (i.e. the difference from skin girth and chain girth)
    S is measured Sail Area, which is that of the mainsail plus 85 per cent of the fore triangle
and F is Freeboard

This rule should not be confused with the Universal Rule which was evolved in America and to which the J-class defenders and challengers were built.

This was virtually killed by rising costs as far as J-class boats were concerned and by the design of the 1937 Cup defender *Ranger*, which completely outclassed her rivals.

The latest of the I.Y.R.U. formulae is that to which the 5.5-metre class is built. This is virtually the same as was used in 1920 for the International 18-foot class to which only five were built.

YACHTING QUIZ

1. Where would you find the cranse iron?

    *

2. What are buttock lines?

QUIZ ANSWERS

1. It is the iron rigging band at the bowsprit end. 2. Curves derived from a series of longitudinal sections of a hull by vertical planes parallel to the keel and at uniform intervals from it.

This formula is:

$$9\left(\frac{L\sqrt{S}}{123\sqrt{D}}+\frac{L+\sqrt{S}}{4}\right)=5.5 \text{ metre rating}$$

where S is the *actual* measured sail area. This was aimed at eliminating the free area obtained by Genoa jibs in the International rule boats. The Genoa, incidentally, was first used by Sven Salen of Sweden in a six metre at Genoa regatta in 1927

D is displacement in cubic feet of 64 lb.

L is measured length.

However, the classes which appeared under these rules have waned in popularity, chiefly due to expense. In their place have come the dinghy classes and the offshore racers. Dinghy racing as we know it in England today appears to have started at the foundation of the International 14-ft. Class. This came about because on St. Valentine's Day 1923 the Dinghy Committee of the Y.R.A. was formed under the chairmanship of Sir John Field Beale.

A few years before a so-called national 14-ft. class had been adopted by the Y.R.A. but its rules did not quite embrace the 14-footers which had been evolved independently for many years on the Broads and by the West of England Conference. The dinghy committee altered the rules of the National 14's to incorporate these boats and this undoubtedly boosted the class considerably. There was another considerable fillip given to it by the presentation in 1927 by the then Prince of Wales of the Cup which bears his name. This was first raced for in 1927. The evolution of the class, which was given international status in 1928, is told in Uffa Fox's famous books. It was from them that many budding dinghy sailors found encouragement, so that when the war finished in 1945 the English dinghy world was ripe for development by Uffa Fox and other builders and designers, such as Jack Holt. The latter, through the *Yachting World*, has made a tremendous contribution to the growth of dinghy sailing. Perhaps as a measure of the growth of this side of the sport one can take the Royal Yachting Association fixture list for 1959. This gives the dates of principal events of the classes of which the owners' associations are recognised by the R.Y.A. There are 27 of these classes of which only seven were in existence before the war.

In 1922 the Cruising Club of America was formed to revive the races from New York to Bermuda and a couple of years later the Ocean Racing Club, soon to have the prefix Royal, was formed in England. This was founded in connection with the Fastnet Race, the first of which was held in 1925 and won by the famous *Jolie Brise*, owned by Lt. Cdr. E. G. Martin, the father of the R.O.R.C. She won it again in 1929 and 1930 under the ownership of Robert Somerset.

Such is the influence of the Royal Ocean Racing Club that its rating rule has been used for many years by designers in England as their guide. In fact very few cruising yachts in England have been built since the war without the R.O.R.G. measuring them for rating soon after they were launched.

This rating rule of 1957 as amended in 1958 is as follows:

Measured Rating

$$=.15\frac{L\sqrt{S}}{\sqrt{BD}}+.2(L+\sqrt{S})$$

When L is measured length
B is Beam
D is Depth
S is rated Sail Area.

Perhaps this brief historical note has tended to ignore cruising too much. Suffice to say that the majority of those who sail race neither inshore nor offshore. They merely enjoy pottering in boats of any shape or size. Of the clubs catering for the cruising man, the best known are the Royal Cruising Club, founded in 1880, the Cruising Association established in 1908, the Clyde Cruising Club (1909) and the Little Ship Club, which although established in 1926 has the largest membership of any in the British Isles and whose contribution to the war effort in 1939–45 by running seamanship and navigation training courses was second to none.

SEAWANHAKA CORINTHIAN YACHT CLUB INTERNATIONAL CHALLENGE CUP

Generally known as the Seawanhaka Cup, this trophy was presented by the club whose name it bears for the purpose of promoting small yacht racing and developing the Corinthian spirit among yachtsmen. Any organised yacht club of good standing of any country foreign to the country holding the Cup may challenge for it.

Matches are limited to yachts whose racing measurement shall not exceed the maximum limit of the so-called 25-foot racing length class or fall below the so-called 15-foot racing length of the Seawanhaka Club. At present sailed in the Six-metre class.

1st Match. Oyster Bay 15 ft. Class. Sept. 1895. *Ethelwynn* (U.S.A.) beat *Spruce IV* (Miniana Y.C., G.B.).

2nd Match. Oyster Bay. July 1896. *Glencairn* (R. St. Lawrence Y.C.) beat *El Heirie* (Seawanhaka C.Y.C.).

3rd Match. Lake St. Louis. August 1897. *Glencairn II* (R. St. Lawrence) beat *Momo* (Seawanhaka C.Y.C.).

4th Match. Lake St. Louis. August 1898. *Dominion* (R. St. Lawrence Y.C.) beat *Challenger* (Seawanhaka C.Y.C.).

5th Match. Lake St. Louis. August 1899. *Glencairn III* (R. St. Lawrence Y.C.) beat *Constance* (Seawanhaka C.Y.C.).

6th Match. Lake St. Louis. August 1900. *Redcoat* (R. St. Lawrence Y.C.) beat *Minnesota* (White Bear Y.C., U.S.A.).

7th Match. Lake St. Louis, July 1901. *Senneville* (R. St. Lawrence Y.C.) beat *Greyfriar* (Island S.C., G.B.).

8th Match. Lake St. Louis. August 1902. *Trident* (R. St. Lawrence Y.C.) beat *Tecumseh* (Bridgeport Y.C., U.S.A.).

9th Match. Lake St. Louis. July-Aug. 1903. *Thorella II* (R. St. Lawrence Y.C.) beat *Kolutoo* (Manchester Y.C., U.S.A.).

10th Match. Lake St. Louis. August 1904. *Noorna* (R. St. Lawrence Y.C.) beat *White Bear* (White Bear Y.C.).

11th Match. Lake St. Louis. July 1905. *Manchester* (Manchester Y.C.) beat *Alexandra*, U.S.A. (R. St. Lawrence Y.C.).

12th Match. Massachusetts Bay. July 1910. *Massachusetts* (Manchester Y.C.) beat *St. Lawrence* (R. St. Lawrence Y.C.).

13th Match Marblehead. September 1922. *Coila III* (R. Northern T.C.) beat *Sakie* (Manchester Y.C.).

14th Match. Rothesay. August 1923. *Coila III* (R. Northern Y.C.) beat *Lea* (Seawanhaka C.Y.C.).

15th Match. Rothesay. August 1924. *Coila III* (R. Northern Y.C.) beat *Unni* (K.N.S.), Norway.

16th Match. Rothesay. July 1925. *Lanai* (Seawanhaka C.Y.C.) beat *Coila III* (R. Northern Y.C.).

17th Match. Oyster Bay. September 1927 *Noreg* (K.N.S.) beat *Clytie* (Seawanhaka C.Y.C.).

18th Match. Hanko. August 1928. *Akaba* (Seawanhaka C.Y.C.) beat *Figaro V* (K.N.S.).

19th Match. Oyster Bay. September 1929. *Caryl* (R. Northern Y.C.) beat *Gypsy* (Seawanhaka C.Y.C.).

20th Match. Rothesay. June 1931. *Saskia* (R. Northern Y.C.) beat *Priscilla III* (Seawanhaka C.Y.C.).

21st Match. Rothesay. August 1932. *Jill* (Seawanhaka C.Y.C.) beat *Maida* (R. Northern Y.C.).

22nd Match. Oyster Bay. October 1934. *Bob Kat* (Seawanhaka C.Y.C.) beat *Kyla* (R. Northern Y.C.).

23rd Match. Oyster Bay. September 1935. *Challenge* (Seawanhaka C.Y.C.) beat *Norma IV* (K.N.S.).

24th Match. Oyster Bay. September 1937. *Rebel* (Seawanhaka C.Y.C.) beat *Buri* (K.N.S.).

25th Match. Oyster Bay. September 1938. *Circe* (R. Northern Y.C.) beat *Goose* (Seawanhaka C.Y.C.).

26th Match. Rothesay. August 1939. *Circe* (R. Northern Y.C.) beat *Noreg III* (K.N.S.).

27th Match. Rothesay. July 1947. *Djinn* (Seawanhaka C.Y.C.) beat *Johan* (R. Northern Y.C.).

28th Match. Oyster Bay. September 1948. *Llanoria* (Seawanhaka C.Y.C.) beat *Maybe VI* (K.S.S.S. Sweden).

29th Match. Oyster Bay. September 1953. *Llanoria* (Seawanhaka C.Y.C.) beat *Marylette* (R.Y.S., G.B.).

30th Match. Oyster Bay September 1956. *Titia* (R. Canadian Y.C.) beat *Goose* (Seawanhaka C.Y.C.).

31st Match. Toronto. August 1957. *Goose* (Seawanhaka C.Y.C.) beat *Titia* (R. Canadian Y.C.).

6 METRES BRITISH-AMERICAN CUP

The result of a desire on the part of a group of British and American yachtsmen to encourage international racing. The Cup was originally donated one half by Percy Chubb on behalf of Seawanhaka Corinthian Y.C. and the other half by the Royal Yacht Squadron, Royal Thames Y.C., Royal London Y.C. and Royal Victoria Y.C. Has always been held in the Six-metre class.

1st Match. Cowes. July 1921. Britain: 117 points to 88.

2nd Match. Oyster Bay. September 1922. America: 111 to 104.

3rd Match. Cowes. August 1923. Britain: 129 to 86.

4th Match. Oyster Bay. September 1924. Britain: 4 races to 3. (Revised conditions.)

2nd Series

A second series arranged between Seawanhaka Corinthian Y.C. and representatives of Royal Yacht Squadron, Royal Thames Y.C., Royal Victoria Y.C., Royal London Y.C., Royal Northern Y.C. and Royal Clyde Y.C.

1st Match. Hunter's Quay. July 1928. Britain: 3 races to 1.

2nd Match. Oyster Bay. September 1930. America: 4 races to 0.

3rd Match. Solent. July 1932. America: 4 to 0.

3rd Series

In 1934 a third series was organised between the previous signatory clubs. Trophy was a silver model of a Six-metre.

1st Match. Oyster Bay. September 1934. America: 3 races to 0.

2nd Match. Rothesay. July 1936. America: 4 races to 0.

3rd Match. Oyster Bay. September 1938. America: 4 races 0.

4th Match Solent. July 1949. America: 4 races to 2.

4th Series

For a Cup presented by Mrs. George Nichols. This had been given to her husband, the late George Nichols, by the City of Newport.

1st Match. Solent. July 1951. America: 4 races to 3.

2nd Match. Oyster Bay. September 1953. America: 4 races to 0.

3rd. Match. Solent. August 1955. America: 4 races to 0.

THE BRITANNIA CUP

Presented to the Royal Yachting Association by King George VI to commemorate the centenary of the race won at Cowes by the schooner *America*. At present for vessels of not less than 32 ft. waterline length.

1951	*Taiseer IV*	Group Captain R. J. F. Barton, C.B.E.
1952	*Zoraida*	Captain F. Ratsey, R.N. (Retd.)
1953	*Carina*	Richard Nye (U.S.A.)
1954	*St. Barbara*	Royal Artillery Y.C.
1955	*Carina*	Richard Nye (U.S.A.)
1956	*Taiseer V*	Group Captain R. J. F. Barton, C.B.E.
1957	*Uomie*	Selwyn B. Slater
1958	*Griffin II*	Royal Ocean Racing Club

AMERICA'S CUP

A £100 silver cup originally presented by the Royal Yacht Squadron for a race East-about round the Isle of Wight between the schooner *America* and fifteen British yachts. Won by *America* by 21 minutes (some authorities make it 18 and others 8) from the cutter *Aurora* on 22nd August, 1851.

Presented to the New York Yacht Club by the survivors of the syndicate who owned *America* on 5th July, 1857, as a perpetual challenge cup.

Subsequent challenges:

1. 8th August, 1870, Magic beat Cambria.
2. 18th–20th October, 1871, Columbia and Sappho beat Livonia 4 races to 1.
3. 11th–12th August, 1876, Madelaine beat Countess of Dufferin 2 races.
4. 9th–19th November, 1881, Mischief beat Atlanta 2 races.
5. 14th–16th. September, 1885, Puritan beat Genesta 2 races.
6. 9th–11th September, 1886, Mayflower beat Galatea 2 races.
7. 27th–30th September, 1887, Volunteer beat Thistle 2 races.
8. 7th–13th October, 1893, Vigilant beat Valkyrie II 3 races.
9. 7th–12th September, 1895, Defender beat Valkyrie III 3 races
10. 16th–20th October, 1899, Columbia beat Shamrock I 3 races.
11. 28th September–4th October, 1901, Columbia beat Shamrock II 3 races.
12. 22nd August–3rd September, 1903, Reliance beat Shamrock III 3 races.
13. 15th–27th July, 1920, Resolute beat Shamrock IV 3 races to 2.
14. 13th–18th September, 1930, Enterprise beat Shamrock V 4 races.
15. 17th–26th September, 1934, Rainbow beat Endeavour 4 races to 2.
16. 31st July–5th August, 1937, Ranger beat Endeavour II 4 races.
17. 20th–26th September, 1958, Columbia beat Sceptre 4 races.

The 14th–16th Cup races were sailed in J-class yachts and the 17th in International Twelve-metres.

YACHTING QUIZ

1. What is a Yuloh?

★

2. Where would you find the skeg of a boat?

★

3. What is Buys-Ballots Law?

★

4. What is Abaca?

5. Where would you find a Rogue's Yarn?

QUIZ ANSWERS

1. A Chinese sweep used for sculling over the stern of a boat. 2. Under the transom of a boat: it is placed there to keep it steady. 3. If the observer's back is to a wind in the northern hemisphere then the barometric pressure will be lower on his left hand than on his right. 4. A Philippine plant from which Manila hemp is made. 5. In a rope. It is the coloured thread inserted in each strand of a rope issued by H.M. Dockyards. Each dockyard has a different colour.

THE GOLD CUP

Presented in 1919 by Nylandska Yaktklubben to commemorate the adoption of its new flag. Originally competed for in 40 sq. metre Skerry Cruisers. Transferred to 6 metres 1922.

1922	IRENA V	Norway
1923	ELIZABETH IV	Norway
1924	KONKRET	Sweden
1925	ELIZABETH VI	Norway
1926	LANAI	U.S.A.
1927	MAY BE	Sweden
1928	FIGARO V	Norway
1929	INGEGARD	Sweden
1930	IAN	Sweden
1931	ABU	Norway
1932	ABU	Norway
1933	"KSSS"	Sweden
1934	WHITE LADY	Norway
1935	VIGRE	Norway
1936	INDIAN SCOUT	U.S.A.
1937	LULU	U.S.A.
1938	GOOSE	U.S.A.
1939	GOOSE	U.S.A.
1947	GOOSE	U.S.A.
1948	GOOSE	U.S.A.
1949	MAY BE VI	Sweden
1950	TRICKSON VI	Sweden
1951	ELIZABETH X	Norway
1952	LLANORIA	U.S.A.

International 5.5 metre Class
The Gold Cup. Previously raced for in 6-metres class.

1953	JAN IX	Sweden	Hanko
1954	JAN IX	Sweden	Marstrand
1955	TWINS VII	Italy	Sandhamn
1956	NORNA VIII	Norway	Genoa
1957	FLAME	U.S.A.	Hanko
1958	SABRE	U.S.A.	Houston

CLASS RACING
ONE TON CUP

Presented to Cercle de la Voile de Paris by a syndicate of members in 1898. Originally raced for in the "One Ton" Class (keel weight) then in 6.50 metres, and since 1925 in 6 metres.

1899	BELOUGA	France
1900	SIDI FEKKA	France
1901	SCOTIA	G.B.
1902	SCOTIA	G.B.
1903	CHOCOLAT	France
1906	FAY-FOLLET	France
1907	ONKEL-ADOLPH	Germany
1908	WINDSPIEL XI	Germany
1909	WINDSPIEL XII	Germany
1910	AGNES II	Sweden
1911	WINDSPIEL XIV	Germany
1912	BUNTY	G.B.
1913	CREMONA	G.B.
1920	CORDELLA	G.B.
1921	CORDELLA	G.B.
1922	CORDELLA	G.B.
1924	HOLLAND'S HOPE	Holland
1925	PRINCESS JULIANA	Holland
1926	ZENITH	G.B.
1927	PETITE AILE	France

YACHTING QUIZ

1. What are vangs?

*

2. What is the difference between a bark (or barque) and a brig?

*

3. What is meant by careening a vessel?

*

4. What is a thole pin?

*

5. What is a soldier's wind?

QUIZ ANSWERS

1. Ropes controlling the lateral movement of the after end of a sprit or gaff. 2. A bark (barque) is a vessel with three or more masts fore and aft rigged, or aftermast and square rigged on the others. A brig is a two-masted vessel, square rigged on both. 3. Heeling a vessel over in order to get at the bottom. 4. A peg fitted in a rowing boat's gunwale to act as the fulcrum for an oar. 5. A wind which allows a vessel to sail to her destination and return on one tack each way.

1928	YARA III	France
1929	BISSBI	Sweden
1930	BISSBI	Sweden
1931	BISSBI	Sweden
1932	ABU	Norway
1933	VARG V	Norway
1934	WHITE LADY	Norway
1935	IAN	Sweden
1936	TIDSFORDRIF	Sweden
1937	TIDSFORDRIF	Sweden
1938	NORNA VI	Norway
1939	NOREG III	Norway
1946	MAY BE VI	Sweden
1947	MAY BE VI	Sweden
1948	MAY BE VI	Sweden
1949	TRICKSON VI	Sweden
1950	MAY BE VI	Sweden
1951	MAY BE VI	Sweden
1952	LLANORIA	U.S.A.
1953	YLLIAM VIII	Switzerland
1954	YLLIAM IX	Switzerland
1955	YLLIAM IX	Switzerland
1956	YLLIAM IX	Switzerland
1957	LLANORIA	U.S.A.
1958	ROYAL THAMES	G.B.
1959	MAY BE VIII	Sweden

DINGHY RACING
ROYAL CANOE CLUB SAILING CHALLENGE CUP

This Challenge Cup has been raced for every year since its inception in 1875. This makes it the oldest small-boat sailing trophy in the world.

Winners

1875	NAUTILUS	W. Baden-Powell
1878	PEARL	E. B. Tredwen
1879	NAUTILUS	W. Baden-Powell
1880	PEARL	E. B. Tredwen
1881	LUSLINE	A. H. Tredwen
1882	PEARL	E. B. Tredwen
1883	PEARL	E. B. Tredwen
1884	GLADYS	T. F. Knowles
1885	NAUTILUS	W. Baden-Powell
1886	NAUTILUS	W. Baden-Powell
1887	CHARM	W. Stewart
1888	CHARM	W. Stewart
1889	CHARM	W. Stewart
1890	WHIZZ	E. R. T. Croxall
1891	STELLA	C. E. Webster
1892	BATTLEDORE	R. A. Hinckley
1893	STELLA	C. E. Webster
1894	BATTLEDORE	R. A. Hinckley
1895	VIPER	C. C. Lynam
1896	YANKEE	W. W. Howard
1897	FLOTSAM	Guy Ellington
1898	RANI	J. Pain Clark
1899	VANESSA	B. de Quincey
1900	SNARK	F. W. Hodges
1901	CHINA	Guy Ellington
1902	PORPOISE	Linton Hope
1903	NANA	O. F. Gasson
1904	JETSAM	M. E. Botting
1905	UNA	C. E. Browne
1906	GENETTA	B. de Quincey
1907	KISMET	Linton Hope
1908	HAZE	Linton Hope
1909	MAYFLY	B. de Quincey
1910	Declared void	
1911	HAZE	M. E. Botting
1912	HAZE	R. A. Smith
1913	AQUAMARINE	B. de Quincey
1914	AQUAMARINE	B. de Quincey
First World War		
1919	HAZE	R. A. Smith
1920	TRITONELLE	H. T. Camphin
1921	VENTURE	H. Carr
1922	TRITONELLE	H. T. Camphin
1923	UNA	C. E. Browne
1924	TRITONELLE	H. T. Camphin
1925	TRITONELLE	H. T. Camphin
1926	GENETTA	E. Freeman
1927	HAZE	R. A. Smith
1928	GENETTA	E. Freeman
1929	VENTURE	H. T. Camphin
1930	GENETTA	E. Freeman
1931	GENETTA	E. Freeman
1932	WANDERER	Uffa Fox
1933	VALIANT	R. de Quincey
1934	AQUAMARINE	F. C. C. Knight
1935	DEFIANT	R. de Quincey
1936	WAKE	R. de Quincey
1937	GALLANT	W. B. de Quincey
1938	RADIANT	Cyril Stollery
1939	RADIANT	Cyril Stollery
Second World War		
1947	DEFIANT	P. V. MacKinnon
1948	FLYING FISH	C. Harris St. John
1949	WAKE	F. J. Aumonier
1950	WAKE	F. J. Aumonier
1951	GALLANT	G. H. Goodson
1952	MEDERHA	R. E. Head
1953	MEDERHA	R. E. Head
1954	SPINDRIFT	J. H. Stothert
1955	SPINDRIFT	J. H. Stothert
1956	FIREBIRD	R. E. Head
1957	FIREBIRD	R. E. Head
1958	SHRIKE	A. H. Emus

THE INTERNATIONAL DRAGON CUP

Presented in 1937 by members of the Clyde Yacht Club's Conference with the intention of bringing together as many nationalities as possible for Yacht Racing in a friendly spirit.

1937	Hanko	FAFNE	Rolf Bilner	Sweden
1938	Travemunde	HEBBE III	H. Dobler	Germany
1939	Gothenburg	GEDOS	Pelle Gedda	Sweden
1947	Clyde	CERES	W. H. Barnett	N. Ireland
			Helmsman: E. Strain	
1948	Arendal	PAN	Thor Thorvaldsen	Norway
1949	Marstrand	SNAP	Erik Volkert	Denmark
			Helmsman: Ole Berntsen	
1950	Vejle	PAN	Thor Thorvaldsen	Norway
1951	Clyde	LIL	Thorkil Warrer	Denmark
1952	Hanko	JEPPE VIII	Ivind Christensen	Norway
1953	Marstrand	GUSTEL X	Theodor Thomsen	Germany
1954	Skovshoved	TOPHAT	P. Salomonsen	Denmark
			Helmsman: Ole Berntsen	
1955	Muiden	GUSTEL XI	Theodor Thomsen	Germany
1956	Clyde	LIL	Thorkil Warrer	Denmark
1957	Hanko	TIP	O. Berntsen	Denmark
1958	Marstrand	ARETUSA	Marquess Paolo Pallavicino	Italy
			Helmsman: Sergio Sorrentino	
1959		TIT	W. Dyer	Canadian

INTERNATIONAL DRAGON CLASS
EDINBURGH CUP Presented in 1949 by H.R.H. Prince Philip, Duke of Edinburgh

1949	Cowes	BLUE SKIES	F. R. Woodroffe & C. W. Lallow	G.B.
1950	Lowestoft	BLUE SKIES	F. R. Woodroffe & C. W. Lallow	G.B.
1951	Clyde	LIL	T. Warrer	Denmark
1952	Torbay	TAISEER	J. A. Day	G.B.
1953	Cultra	ASHAKA	A. F. Buckley	Eire
			(sailed Dr. A. J. Mooney)	
1954	Bembridge	VANA	W. Gordon-Smith	G.B.
1955	Lowestoft	TANIA	K. Preston & J. Raymond	G.B.
1956	Clyde	ARETUSA	Marchese Paolo Pallavicino	Italy
			(sailed S. Sorrentino)	
1957	Torbay	VIKING	P. Dyas	G.B.
1958	Cultra	NIRVANA II	A. F. Buckley	Eire
			(sailed Dr. A. J. Mooney)	
1959	Cowes	APPOLLYON	B. Banks	G.B.

INTERNATIONAL 14 FT. DINGHY CLASS
PRINCE OF WALES CUP

Presented by H.R.H. The Prince of Wales in 1927

1927	IREX	C. Atkey, Cowes
1928	AVENGER	Uffa Fox, Lowestoft
1929	DARING	Uffa Fox, Plymouth
1930	GOLDEN EYE	T. Thornycroft, Lowestoft
1931	CATHERINE	F. Morgan-Giles, Ryde
1932	R.I.P.	Stewart Morris, Torquay
1933	R.I.P.	Stewart Morris, Lowestoft
1934	LIGHTNING	J. Winter, Falmouth
1935	ALARM	Stewart Morris, Osborne Bay
1936	ALARM	Stewart Morris, Clyde
1937	THUNDER	Peter Scott, Lowestoft
1938	THUNDER AND LIGHTNING	Peter Scott and John Winter, Falmouth
1939	HAWK	G. C. Ratsey, Cowes
1946	THUNDER AND LIGHTNING	John Winter, and Peter Scott, Brixham
1947	MARTLET	Stewart Morris, Hunstanton
1948	MARTLET	Stewart Morris, Cowes
1949	MARTLET	Stewart Morris, Torquay
1950	WINDSPRITE	Bruce Banks, Hunstanton
1951	WINDSPRITE	Bruce Banks, Plymouth
1952	MORDICUS	A. M. Martin, Seaview
1953	WINDSPRITE	Bruce Banks, Lowestoft
1954	BARILEA	de Forest Trimingham, Weymouth
1955	WINDSPRITE	Bruce Banks, Seaview
1956	WILDFIRE	David Thorpe, Torquay
1957	BOLERO	Stewart Morris, Hunstanton
1958	ATAU HAU	G. Smale, Cowes
1959	HAMBLE BABY	C. Currey, Lowestoft

NATIONAL 14 FT. MERLIN-ROCKET CLASS
CHAMPIONSHIP WINNERS

1946	GENTLY	J. Holt and B. Moore, Hayling Island
1947	GENTLY	J. Holt and B. Moore, Hayling Island
1948	CLARE	R. J. Ledwith, Poole
1949	GENTLY	J. Holt and B. Moore, Cowes
1950	GENTLY	B. Moore, Burnham
1951	DALLY	K. A. Mollart, Torquay
1952	CIRRUS	I. Proctor, Poole
1953	DIABOLO	J. L. Brain, Cowes
1954	SOO FOR	M. H. R. Pruett, Falmouth
1955	MAGICIAN	J. L. Brain, Plymouth
1956	SOO ME	J. Oakeley, Whitstable
1957	CREW CUT	J. Oakeley, Torquay
1958	CREW CUT	J. Oakeley, Plymouth
1959	RESTLESS III	B. Southcott, Whitstable

12 FT. NATIONAL CLASS
SIR WILLIAM BURTON TROPHY

1936	ITCH	C. Stollery, Poole
1937	FARANDOLE	A. W. B. Macdonald, Chichester Harbour
1938	WRATH	C. R. Wyche, Harwich
1939	WESTWIND	B. Banks, Torquay
1946	LAUGHTER	J. Holt and B. Moore, Felixstowe
1947	SILHOUETTE	Howard Williams, Brixham
1948	WITCH	Dr. R. S. Steavenson, Calshot
1949	WANTON	M. Goffe, Weymouth

1950	WESTWIND	B. Banks, Falmouth
1951	YOSHIKO	G. Cowap, Hunstanton
1952	DAPHNE	A. and S. Jardine, Weymouth
1953	WITCHCRAFT	Dr. R. S. Steavenson, Torbay
1954	CHIQUITA	B. E. Perry, Westcliff-on-Sea
1955	PROGRESS	G. Keen, Plymouth
1956	CHIPS	K. Musto, Weymouth
1957	ELUSIVE	John Oakeley, Falmouth
1958	INTUITION	P. C. Nicholson, Scarborough
1959	EXTRAVAGENCE	J. Oakeley, Weymouth

12 FT. NATIONAL CLASS
Y.W. POINTS CUP

1936	ITCH,	C. Stollery
1937	FARANDOLE	A. W. B. Macdonald
1938	WRATH	C. R. Wyche
1939	HOPTURTLE	B. Moore
1946	LAUGHTER	J. Holt and B. Moore
1947	WESTWIND	B. Banks
1948	WESTWIND	B. Banks
1949	WANTON	M. Goffe
1950	WESTWIND	B. Banks
1951	ZITHER	C. Norbury
1952	DAPHNE	A. and S. Jardine
1953	MACH-ONE	R. Creagh-Osborne
1954	TERTIUM QUID	A. and S. Jardine
1955	WITCHCRAFT	Dr. R. S. Steavenson
1956	TERTIUM QUID	A. and S. Jardine
1957	ELUSIVE	John Oakeley
1958	INTUITION	P. C. Nicholson
1959	YAKOPU	B. Terry

Mr. J. M. Laing's *Vashti*.

NATIONAL FIREFLY CLASS
SIR RALPH GORE CHALLENGE CUP

1947	FOXGLOVE	A. J. Wilson, Hayling Island
1948	FINELLA	Stewart Morris, Hayling Island
1949	CHARYBDIS	Miss E. Tomlinson and I. G. Butler, Harwich
1950	FINELLA	Stewart Morris, Poole Harbour
1951	JAVELIN	S. and A. Jardine, Abersoch
1952	SABRE	Brian Southcott, Plymouth
1953	ALARM	J. Conway Jones, Hunstanton
1954	JAVELIN	S. and A Jardine, Stokes Bay
1955	FLAMING ONION	Richard Roscoe, Torquay
1956	VECTOR	Michael Cook, Benllech
1957	VECTOR	Michael Cook, Westcliff
1958	ATAXIA	S. P. Tinley, Restronguet

SIR RICHARD FAIREY POINTS CUP

1947	FOXGLOVE	A. J. Wilson
1948	WINDFLY	Bruce Banks
1949	JEANNIE	Harry Dennis
1950	JAVELIN and ELFIN II	A. and S. Jardine and R. N. Vine
1951	JAVELIN	A. and S. Jardine
1952	LUCCIOLA	John Oakeley
1953	CHAOTIC	G. A. Revett
1954	JAVELIN	S. and A. Jardine
1955	FLAMING ONION	Richard Roscoe
1956	CE	John Hooper
1957	VECTOR	Michael Cook
1958	GOBLIN	J. B. Heron

THE HORNET CLASS
CHAMPIONSHIP WINNERS

1952	JACKSTRAW	R. Pitcher
1953	FLYING CLOUD	B. Moore
1954	JACK SPRAT,	O. Lee
	FLYING CLOUD	B. Moore
1955	GHOST	M. H. Corbin
1956	SCORCHER	T. Greenslade
1957	SCORCHER	T. Greenslade
1958	TANTALUS	J. Partridge

INTERNATIONAL FLYING DUTCHMAN CLASS
WORLD CHAMPIONSHIP WINNERS

1954	FRITHJOFNA	Conrad Gulcher (Holland), Lake Geneva
1955	ISTRIA	Vittorio Porta (Italy), Muiden
1956	MACKY V	Rolf Mulka (W. Germany), Starnberg
1957	MACKY V	Rolf Mulka (W. Germany), Rimini
1958	FALCON V	Rolly Tasker (Australia)
1959	ALDEBARAN	M. Capio (Italy)

OFFSHORE RACING
FASTNET RACE

The principal event of the Royal Ocean Racing Club. Held in alternate years to the C.C.A. Bermuda Race. Course from Cowes round the Fastnet Rock to Plymouth.

1925	JOLIE BRISE	Lt. Cdr. E. G. Martin
1926	ILEX	Royal Engineer Y.C.
1927	TALLY HO	Lord Stalbridge
1928	NINA	Paul Hammond (U.S.A.)
1929	JOLIE BRISE	Robert Somerset
1930	JOLIE BRISE	Robert Somerset
1931	DORADE	R. Stephens (U.S.A.)
1933	DORADE	R. & O. J. Stephens (U.S.A)
1935	STORMY WEATHER	P. Le Boutillier (U.S.A.)
1937	ZEEAREND	C. Bruynzeel (Holland)
1939	BLOODHOUND	Isaac Bell
1947	MYTH OF MALHAM	Capt. J. H. Illingworth, R.N.
1949	MYTH OF MALHAM	Capt. J. H. Illingworth, R.N.
1951	YEOMAN	O. A. Aisher
1953	FAVONA	Sir Michael Newton
1955	CARINA	R. S. Nye (U.S.A.)
1957	CARINA	R. S. Nye (U.S.A.)
1959	ANITRA	S. Hansen (Sweden)

THE BERMUDA RACE

Originally an annual race from Gravesend Bay to Bermuda. This event was allowed to lapse between 1911 and 1923. The revival was due to the initiative of the magazine *Yachting*. Since 1926 the race has been sponsored by the Cruising Club of America in conjunction with the Royal Bermuda Y.C. Now held in alternate years to the Fastnet Race. Since 1936 the start has been at Newport R.I.

Winners

1906	TAMERLAINE	Frank Maier
1907	DERVISH	H. A. Morss
1908	VENONA	E. J. Bliss
1909	MARGARET	Geo. S. Runk
1910	VAGRANT	H. S. Vanderbilt
1923	MALABAR IV	John G. Alden
1924	MEMORY	R. N. Bavier
1926	MALABAR VII	John G. Alden
1928	RUGOSA II	Russell Grinell
1930	MALABAR X	John G. Alden
1932	MALABAR X	R. I. Gale
1934	EDLU	R. J. Schaefer
1936	KIRAWAN	R. P. Baruch
1938	BARUNA	H. C. Taylor
1946	GESTURE	A. H. Fuller
1948	BARUNA	H. C. Taylor
1950	ARGYLL	Wm. T. Moore
1952	CARINA	R. S. Nye
1954	MALAY	D. D. Strohmeier
1956	FINISTERRE	Carleton Mitchell
1958	FINISTERRE	Carleton Mitchell

The Swiss *Pousse-moi-Pas IV*, Flying Dutchman Class yacht. World championships 1959.

YACHTING QUIZ

1. Where would you expect to find a Zulu?

★

2. What is a wind sail?

★

3. What is a triatic stay?

★

4. What is a raffee?

★

5. What is the correct name for the wisps of bunting or cloth in the shrouds to indicate the direction of the wind?

QUIZ ANSWERS

1. On the east coast of Scotland. It is a fore and aft rigged fishing vessel. 2. A canvas tube used as a ventilator. 3. A stay connecting the foremast and mainmast head in a schooner. 4. A triangular sail set above a squaresail on a fore and aft rigged vessel. 5. Dog vanes.

Finale (O. J. Lee) in the Royal Corinthian Yacht Club Regatta 1957.

Carina (R. S. Nye), twice winner of the Offshore Racing Fastnet race.

Mrs. Sopwith (now Lady Sopwith), Sir Ralph and Lady Gore aboard *Endeavour II*.

A National Firefly off Phoenix Wharf, near the New Slipway, Plymouth.

1933	DORADE	Roderick Stephens, Jr.	U.S.A.
1934	MAY L.	W. B. Reese	England
1935		Charles F. Tillinghast	U.S.A.
1936	ARIELLE	Marin Marie	France
1937	DUCKLING	Charles W. Atwater	U.S.A.
Without date	IGDRASIL	Roger S. Strout	U.S.A.
1938	CAPLIN	Cdr. Robert D. Graham, R.N.	England
1939	IRIS	John Martucci	U.S.A.
1940		British Yachtsmen at Dunkerque	England

(This medal is held by the National Marine Museum at Greenwich)

1941	ORION	Robert Neilson	U.S.A.
1947	GAUCHO	Ernesto C. Uriburi	Argentina
1950	LANG SYNE	William P. and Phyllis Crowe	U.S.A.
1952	STORNOWAY	Alfred Petersen	U.S.A.
1953	OMOO	L. G. Van de Wiele	Belgium
1954	VIKING	Sten and Brita Holmdahl	Sweden
1955	WANDERER III	Eric and Susan Hiscock	England
1956	MISCHIEF	H. W. Tillman	England
Without date		Carleton Mitchell	U.S.A.
1957	LANDFALL II	Dr. William F. Holcomb	U.S.A.

THE OLYMPIC GAMES

1896. **1st Olympiad** ATHENS.

No yachting recorded.

1900. **2nd Olympiad** PARIS. Olympic regatta Le Havre.

5 nations—16 yachts.

Over 10 metre Class

1.	*Esterel*		France
2.	*Rosen*		France
3.	*Quand-Meine*		France

10 metre Class

1.	*Aschenbrödel*	M. Wiesner	Germany
2.	*Scotia*	M. M. Gretton	G.B.
3.	*Crabe II*	M. Baudrier	France

8 metre Class

1.	*Ollé*	E. Shaw	G.B.
2.	*Susse*		France

6 metre Class

1.	*Lerina*	H. de Pourtalès	Switzerland
2.		M. Wiesner	Germany

1904. **3rd Olympiad** ST. LOUIS.

No Yachting.

SYDNEY TO HOBART RACE

Organised by the Cruising Yacht Club of Australia in co-operation with the Royal Yacht Club of Tasmania. It originated when Captain J. H. Illingworth gave a lecture to the Club in 1945.

1945	RANI	Captain J. H. Illingworth
1946	CHRISTINA	J. R. Bull
1947	WESTWARD	G. D. Gibson
1948	WESTWARD	G. D. Gibson
1949	TRADE WINDS	M. E. Davey
1950	NERIDA	C. P. Haselgrove
1951	STRUEN MARIE	T. Williamson
1952	INGRID	J. S. Taylor
1953	RIPPLE	R. Hobson
1954	SOLVEIG	T. & M. Halvorsen
1955	MOONBI	H. S. Evans
1956	SOLO	V. MEYER
1957	ANITRA V	T. & M. Halvorsen
1958	SIANDRA	G. Newland

Uffa Fox

YACHTING QUIZ

1. Which yacht has won the Fastnet race three times and the Blue Water Medal twice?

*

2. What type of craft was she?

*

3. Which of the following America's Cup challengers were not built on the Clyde: (a) Shamrock I, (b) Valkyrie II, (c) Thistle, (d) Shamrock III, (e) Shamrock V, (f) Galatea?

*

4. If you see a yacht wearing a white ensign without a burgee, what is she?

*

5. Which is the "odd man out" here: The Brambles; The Shingles; The Shambles?

QUIZ ANSWERS

1. *Jolie Brise*. Fastnet 1925, 1929, 1930. Blue Water Medal 1926 and 1932. 2. Le Havre Pilot Cutter. 3. *Shamrock I* and *V* and *Galatea*. 4. She is probably one of the R.N.C. Dartmouth Seamanship Training Craft. 5. The Shambles, off Portland. The other two are in the Solent Area.

The Cruising Club of America
BLUE WATER MEDAL

Feeling that there were many noteworthy voyages made in small boats, and frequent examples of meritorious seamanship displayed by amateur sailors of all nationalities that went unrecognized, it seemed to the members of The Cruising Club of America that this organisation was the fitting one to properly record and reward such adventure upon the sea.

Therefore, at the annual meeting on February 27th, 1923, the following resolution was passed, founding a medal that, it was hoped, might prove an incentive for carrying on the spirit of adventure and upholding the best traditions of seafaring that are our heritage from the past.

"Moved and seconded that the Club found, out of funds to be sought for the purpose, a medal to be known as 'The Blue Water Medal of the Cruising Club of America', to be awarded annually, in the discretion of the Board of Governors, for the year's most meritorious example of seamanship, the recipient to be selected from among the amateurs of all the nations."

In pursuance of this resolution a suitable medal, five inches in diameter, was made, the design being by the late Arthur Sturgis Hildebrand, a member of this club and one of the crew of the yacht *Leiv Eriksson*, lost in the Arctic with all hands in September, 1924.

At the Annual Meeting held January 8th, 1931, the following resolution was unanimously carried:

"RESOLVED: That the Governing Board be and hereby is authorized to approve of the awarding of the Blue Water Medal, without date, on the recommendation of the Committee on Awards."

THE BLUE WATER MEDAL AWARDS

1923	FIRECREST	Alain J. Gerbault	France
1924	SHANGHAI	Axel Ingwersen	Denmark
1925	ISLANDER	Harry Pidgeon	U.S.A.
1926	JOLIE BRISE	E. G. Martin	England
1927	PRIMROSE IV	Frederick L. Ames	U.S.A.
1928	SEVEN BELLS	Thomas F. Cooke	U.S.A.
1929	POSTSCRIPT	F. Slade Dale	U.S.A.
1930	CARLSARK	Carl Weagant	U.S.A.
1931	SVAAP	William A. Robinson	U.S.A.
Without date	JOLIE BRISE	Robert Somerset	England

Scene at the International Burnham-on-Crouch Cadet Week 1958.

Stavros Niarchos' yacht *Creole*.

The International Dragon Class race, Burnham Sailing Week 1957.

1908. 4th Olympiad. LONDON. Olympic regatta at Ryde and on Clyde.

5 nations—20 yachts.

12 metre Class

| 1. | *Hera* | T. C. Glen-Coats and J. H. Downes } | G.B. |
| 2. | *Mouchette* | C. MacIver | G.B. |

8 metre Class

1.	*Cobweb*	Blair Cochrane	G.B.
2.	*Vinga*	C. L. Hellström	Sweden
3.	*Sorais*	Duchess of Westminster	G.B.

7 metre Class

| *Heroine* Sailed over | C. J. Rivett-Carnac | G.B. |

6 metre Class

1.	*Dormy*	G. V. Laws	G.B.
2.	*Zut*	L. Huybrechts	Belgium
3.	*Guyoni*	H. Arthus	France

Sir Malcolm Campbell in *Bluebird* 1947.

MOTOR BOATING (at 4th Olympiad).

A. Class	1. *Camille*	E. B. Thubron	France
B. Class	1. *Gyrinus*	T. Thornycroft	G.B.
C. Class	1. *Gyrinus*	T. Thornycroft	G.B.

1912. 5th Olympiad. STOCKHOLM. Olympic regatta at Sandham.

6 nations—20 yachts.

12 metre Class

1.	*Magda IX*	A. Larsen	Norway
2.	*Erne Sigae*	N. Persson	Sweden
3.	*Heatherbell*	E. Krogias	Finland

10 metre Class

1.	*Kitty*	N. Asp	Sweden
2.	*Nina*	H. Wahl	Finland
3.	*Gallia II*	A. Vishnegradsky	Russia

8 metre Class

1.	*Taifun*	T. Glad	Norway
2.	*Sans Atout*	B. Heyman	Sweden
3.	*Lucky Girl*	B. and G. Talberg	Finland

6 metre Class

1.	*Mac Miche*	O. Thubé	France
2.	*Narduig II*	O. Reeds-Thott	Denmark
3.	*Kerstin*	D. Broströn	Sweden

1916. 6th Olympiad. Not celebrated.

1920. 7th Olympiad. ANTWERP.

	12 metre Class (old type)		
Atalanta	H. Ostervold	Norway
	12 metre Class (new type)		
Heira II	J. Friele	Norway
	10 metre Class (old type)		
Eleda	E. Herselth	Norway
	10 metre Class (new type)		
Mosk II	A. Arentz	Norway

8 metre Class (old type)

| 1. | *Irene* | A. Rungvold | Norway |
| 2. | *Fornebo* | M. N. Nielson | Norway |

8 metre Class (new type)

1.	*Sildra*	M. Konow	Norway
2.	*Lynn II*	J. Salvesen	Norway
3.	*Antwerpia V*	—	Norway

7 metre Class

| *Ancora* | D. Winifred | G.B. |

6.5 metre Class

| 1. | *Oranye* | J. Carp | Netherlands |
| 2. | *Rose Pompon* | A. Weil | France |

6 metre Class (old type)

1.	*Edelweiss II*	E. Corneilla	Belgium
2.	*Marini II*	L. Ericson	Norway
3.	*Stella*	H. Agersborg	Norway

40 sq. metre Class

| 1. | *Sif* | T. Holm | Sweden |
| 2. | *Elsie* | G. Svensson | Sweden |

30 sq. metre Class

| *Kullan* | G. Lundquist | Sweden |

12 ft. C.B. boat

| *Beatriss III* | A. E. Van der Biesen | Netherlands |

18 ft. C.B. boat

| *Brat* | | Netherlands |

YACHTING QUIZ

1. In Cowes Week a yacht which is dressed overall gets under way, still dressed overall. Is this correct?

★

2. Which is the "odd man out": (a) Sirius; (b) Betelgeuse; (c) Venus; (d) Aldebaran?

★

3. What is a lazy painter?

4. In what vessels did the following make famous voyages: (a) Voss; (b) Hiscock; (c) Nye; (d) Gerbault; (e) Dwight Long; (f) Mulhauser?

★

5. What cloud formations portend (a) wind; (b) rain; (c) fine weather.

QUIZ ANSWERS

1. No. She should "undress" when she weighs anchor or lets go. 2. Venus, which is a planet. The rest are stars. 3. A rope which is the second and perhaps lighter painter in a boat. 4. (a) Tillikum; (b) Wanderer III; (c) Carina; (d) Firecrest; (e) Idle Hour; (f) Amaryllis. 5. (a) Cirrus; (b) Nimbus; (c) Cumulus.

Twelve-foot Nationals at Putney in the R.T.Y.C. Winter Trophy 1959.

Sir Malcolm prepares to attack world's water speed record on Lake Coniston 1947.

Mrs. F. G. Mitchell's *Nauta* at Burnham Yacht Week 1947.

Mr. H. R. Attwood's *Flica II* at Cowes 1957.

YACHTING QUIZ

1. What is the oldest established yacht club in the world?

★

2. If you return in your yacht to a British port from abroad, what signal should you fly?

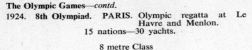

The Olympic Games—*contd.*

1924. 8th Olympiad. PARIS. Olympic regatta at Le Havre and Menlon.
15 nations—30 yachts.

8 metre Class

1. *Bera*	A. Ringvold	Norway
2. *Emity*	E. E. Jacob	G.B.
3. *Namoussa*	Brequet	France

6 metre Class

1. *Elizabeth V*	E. Lunde	Norway
2. *Bongo*	V. Vett	Denmark
3. *Willem Six*	J. R. Carp	Netherlands

12 ft. C.B. boat

1. —	Leon Huybrechts	Belgium
2. —	Henrik Robert	Norway
3. —	Hans Dittmar	Finland

1928. 9th Olympiad. AMSTERDAM.
21 nations—40 yachts.

8 metre Class

1. *Aile VI*	Mme. V. Heriot	France
2. { *Hollandia*	L. D. de Wit	Holland
{ *Sylvia*	J. Sandblom	Sweden

6 metre Class

1. *Norna*	Crown Prince Olav	Norway
2. *Hi Hi*	M. Wett	Denmark
3. *Tutti V*	A. Fable	Estonia

12 ft. Dinghy

1. —	S. Thorell	Sweden
2. —	H. Robert	Norway
3. —	B. Broman	Finland

1932. 10th Olympiad. LOS ANGELES.
11 nations—22 yachts.

8 metre Class

1. *Angelita*	O. Churchill	U.S.A.
2. *Santa Maria*	Maitland	Canada

6 metre Class

1. *Bissbi*	T. Holm	Sweden
2. *Gallant*	F. Conant	U.S.A.
3. *Caprice*	P. Rogers	Canada

Int. Star Class

1. *Jupiter*	G. Gray	U.S.A.
2. *Joy*	C. Ratsey	G.B.
3. *Swedish Star*	G. Asther	Sweden

Olympic Monotype

1. —	J. Lebrun	France
2. —	J. Maas	Holland
3. —	S. Cansino	Spain

QUIZ ANSWERS

Dizzy (H. C. Han), winner of the Thames Merlin Trophy for the National Merlin Rocket Class.

1936. 11th Olympiad. BERLIN. Olympic Regatta at Kiel.

8 metre Class

1. *Italia*	M. Reggio	Italy
2. *Silja*	O. Ditlev-Simonsen (Jun.)	Norway
3. *Gerenama III*	H. Howaldt	Germany

6 metre Class

1. *Lalage*	C. A. Boardman	G.B.
2. *Lully II*	M. Konow	Norway
3. *Maybe*	S. Salen	Sweden

Star Class

1. *Wansee*	Dr. P. Bischoff	Germany
2. *Sunshine*	A. Lauria	Sweden
3. *Bem II*	A. Maas	Netherlands

Olympic Monotype

1. —	D. Kagchelland	Netherlands
2. —	W. Krogman	Germany
3. —	P. Scott	G.B.

1940. 12th Olympiad. Not Celebrated.
1944. 13th Olympiad. Not Celebrated.

1948. 14th Olympiad. LONDON. Olympic Regatta, Torquay.
21 nations—75 yachts.

6 metres

1. *Llanoria*	H. F. Whiton	U.S.A.
2. *Djinn*	E. Sieburger	Argentina
3. *Ali Baba II*	T. Holm	Sweden

Dragons

1. *Pan*	T. Thorvaldsen	Norway
2. *Slaghoken*	F. Bohlin	Sweden
3. *Snap*	W. Berntsen	Denmark

Stars

1. *Hilarius*	H. Smart	U.S.A.
2. *Kurush III*	Dr. C. Cardenas	Cuba
3. *Starita*	A. Maas	Netherlands

Swallows

1. *Swift*	S. Morris	G.B.
2. *Symphony*	D. de Almaida-Bello	Portugal
3. *Migrant*	L. Pirie	U.S.A.

Fireflies

1. —	P. Elvström	Denmark
2. —	R. Evans	U.S.A.
3. —	J. de Jong	Netherlands

Burrasca (D. W. W. Edwards) leads from *Driftwood* (P. C. Dixon) and *Leda* (N. L. R. Bowden) in a Firefly Class race.

The *Sceptre*, 1958 challenger for the America's Cup, in training off Cowes.

A typical Hornet 500 racing during Burnham Week 1958.

1956. 16th Olympiad. MELBOURNE.

5.5 metres

1.	*Rush V*	L. Thorn	Sweden
2.	*Vision*	R. S. G. Perry	G.B.
3.	*Burraddoo*	A. Sturrock	Australia

Dragons

1.	*Slaghoken II*	F. Bohlin	Sweden
2.	*Tip*	O. Berntsen	Denmark
3.	*Bluebottle*	G. H. Mann	G.B.

Stars

1.	*Kathleen*	H. Williams	U.S.A.
2.	*Merope III*	A. Straulino	Italy
3.	*Gem IV*	D. Knowles	Bahamas

12 sq. metre Sharpies

1.	*Jest*	P. Mander	New Zealand
2.	*Falcon IV*	R. Tasker	Australia
3.	*Chuckles*	J. Blackall	G.B.

Finns

1.	—	P. Elvström	Denmark
2.	—	A. Nelis	Belgium
3.	—	J. Marvin	U.S.A.

1952. 15th Olympiad. HELSINKI.
29 nations—93 yachts.

6 metres

1.	*Llanoria*	H. F. Whiton	U.S.A.
2.	*Elizabeth X*	F. Ferner	Norway
3.	*Ralda*	E. Westerlund	Finland

5.5 metres

1.	*Complex II*	Dr. B. Chance	U.S.A.
2.	*Encore*	P. Lunde	Norway
3.	*Hojwa*	F. Wassen	Sweden

Dragons

1.	*Pan*	T. Thorvaldsen	Norway
2.	*Tornado*	P. Gedda	Sweden
3.	*Gustel X*	T. Thomsen	Germany

Stars

1.	*Merope*	A. Straulino	Italy
2.	*Comanche*	J. Reid	U.S.A.
3.	*Espadarte*	F. de Andrade	Portugal

Finns

1.	—	P. Elvström	Denmark
2.	—	C. Currey	G.B.
3.	—	R. Sarby	Sweden

Enterprise Class yachts jockeying for position at the start of a race. Burnham Week 1958.

A Shearwater catamaran lifts one hull clear in a stiff breeze during Burnham Week 1958.

YACHTING QUIZ

1. What is meant by Thames Measurement?

★

2. What does the letter U signalled in morse code mean?

★

3. What does the letter H signalled on a vessel's siren mean?

★

4. If a steamer blows three short blasts on her siren, what does it mean?

★

5. What is the deadwood of a boat?

★

6. Where would you meet a Flying Dutchman?

★

7. What is the difference between flotsam and jetsam?

★

8. How can the distance in miles to the horizon be calculated at sea?

QUIZ ANSWERS

1. An approximate representation of the internal capacity of a yacht derived from a system of measurement adopted by the Royal Thames Yacht Club in 1854. The formula is: $\frac{L-B \times b \times \frac{1}{2}B}{94}$ where L=length measured from the fore side of the stern to the after side of the sternpost on deck, and B=extreme breadth. 2. You are standing into danger. 3. Keep out of my way, I cannot keep out of yours. 4. My engines are going full speed astern. 5. Strong pieces of timber connecting the stern or sternposts to the keel. 6. Apart from the international racing class of that name, it is a phantom vessel, commanded by Vanderdecken, said to be met off Cape of Good Hope. Sighted and reported by H.M.S. *Bacchante* at 4 a.m. 11th July 1881. 7. Flotsam are goods and fittings that remain floating after a shipwreck. Jetsam are goods which have been thrown out of a ship and which have sunk. 8. Multiply the square root of the height of the eye in feet by 1.15.

285

Lt.-Col. R. S. G. Perry's *Unique* lays well over in the early stages of the 5.5 metre-International Class Cayley Cup race at Cowes 1954.

NATIONAL OUTBOARD HYDROPLANE CHAMPIONS 1952–1958

"A" CLASS

1952	H. L. G. Melly	(L.H.R.C.)
1953	A. E. Moore	(S.H.C.)
1954	H. W. Barnes-Moss	(S.O.R.C.)
1955	O. E. Moore	(S.H.C.)
1956	H. W. Barnes-Moss	(S.O.R.C.)
1957	J. Moore	(S.H.C.)
1958	J. Moore	(L.M.B.R.C.)

"B" CLASS

1952	A. Darby	(L. & O.B.M.B.C.
1953	J. Estes	(L. & O.B.M.B.C.
1954	C. Bottoms	(B.O.R.C.)
1955	C. Bottoms	(B.O.R.C.)
1956	P. Mason	(L.M.B.R.C.)
1957	F. Johnson	(B.O.R.C.)
1958	R. A. Tognola	(B.O.R.C.)

"C" CLASS

1952	R. H. Evans	(B.O.R.C.)
1953	C. E. Mayes	(L. & O.B.M.B.C.)
1954	C. E. Mayes	(L. & O.B.M.B.C.)
1955	T. E. Mansell	(B.O.R.C.)
1956	P. Mason	(L.M.B.R.C.)
1957	F. Johnson	(B.O.R.C.)

"D" CLASS

1957	J. Mountford	(B.H.R.C.)
1958	J. Mountford	(B.H.R.C.)

"X" CLASS

1952	H. L. G. Melly	(L.H.R.C.)
1953	N. Wilson-Smith	(L.H.R.C.)
1954	H. L. G. Melly	(L.H.R.C.)
1955	E. Lloyd Jones	(L.H.R.C.)
1956	H. L. G. Melly	(L.H.R.C.)
1957	H. L. G. Melly	(L.H.R.C.)
1958	H. L. G. Melly	(L.H.R.C.)

YACHTING QUIZ

1. The crew of A is holding the jib sheet outboard with his foot. The crew of B shouts that this constitutes an outrigger; and so is not allowed. Is B's crew correct?

★

2. The crew of yacht A, having been fouled by yacht B, attach a handkerchief to the shrouds. At the subsequent protest meeting the helmsman of B states that the handkerchief is not a protest flag. Is he correct?

★

3. When may a Sailing Committee disqualify a yacht without a protest or hearing?

★

4. What is meant by the Time-on-Distance method of handicapping?

QUIZ ANSWERS

1. No. No part of the body of a crew is an outrigger. 2. The R.Y.A. prescribes that: "A protest flag shall be either a flag or burgee or a rectangular piece of material, no smaller than the distinguishing flag customarily worn by the protesting yacht." Therefore, the handkerchief may well be a perfectly valid protest flag. However, in some countries abroad a special flag is specified by the National Authority. 3. If the yacht fails to cross the starting and finishing line in accordance with the racing rules and sailing instructions. 4. The actual time allowance, to be subtracted from a yacht's elapsed time to produce her corrected time, is based upon the yacht's rating and the length of the course. Time allowances of competitors can be, and usually are, published before the race so that the competitor can ascertain reasonably certainly how he has fared, if he watched the other yachts finish.

DUCHESS OF YORK TROPHY
for Outboard Dinghies

Winners:

1954	Mr. G. E. Bowell
1955	No race
1956	Mr. G. E. Bowell
1957	Mr. L. J. Derrington
1958	Mr. L. J. Derrington

LADY BRECKNOCK TROPHY
for Inboards

Winners:

1955	Mr. A. G. M. Peace
1956	No race
1957	,,
1958	Mr. A. E. Peace

MOUNTBATTEN OF BURMA TROPHY
for Inboards

(Run by Lowestoft and Oulton Broads Motor Boat Club—Headquarters at The Wherry Hotel, Oulton Broad)

Winners:

1953	C. Middleditch
1954	G. C. Wakling
1955	G. C. Wakling
1956	W. Day
1957	A. E. Peace
1958	A. G. M. Peace

Left to right: Mr. T. Sopwith's *Endeavour*, Mr. W. L. Stephenson's *Velsheda* and Mr. G. B. Lambert's *Yankee*.

Redwings beating for the first mark in the National Championships at Torbay.

BRITISH NATIONAL AND WORLD MOTOR BOAT RECORDS

(Compiled by The Marine Motoring Association Ltd.)

WORLD RECORDS

Unrestricted Water Speed Record.
"Bluebird" (Jet Boat) D. M. Campbell (1959) Speed 260.35 m.p.h.

Inboard Engined Classes.

Class	Driver		Type of Record		Speed
800 Kilogram	H. C. Notley	(1937)	Duration 6 hours		30.85 m.p.h.
800 Kilogram	H. C. Notley	(1937)	Duration 9 hours		29.65 m.p.h.
800 Kilogram	H. C. Notley	(1937)	Duration 12 hours		29.22 m.p.h.
800 Kilogram	N. H. Buckley	(1958)	Duration 1 hours		89.08 m.p.h.
1,200 Kilogram	N. H. Buckley	(1959)	Speed		120.61 m.p.h.
Unlimited (Petrol)	N. H. Buckley	(1956)	Duration 1 hour		79.66 m.p.h.
Runabout E.I.	J. J. Fenn				
	C. G. Wood				
(2,000 c.c. max)	P. G. Stanton	(1958)	Duration 3 hours		30.95 m.p.h.
,,	,,		Duration 6 hours		30.93 m.p.h.
,,	,,		Duration 9 hours		32.06 m.p.h.
,,	,,		Duration 12 hours		31.38 m.p.h.

Outboard Engined Classes.
Utility Runabout:

Class	Driver		Type of Record		Speed
BU (350 c.c. max)	L. J. Derrington	(1958)	Duration 4 hours		25.25 m.p.h.
,,	,,	(1958)	Duration 6 hours		23.72 m.p.h.

BRITISH NATIONAL RECORDS

Outboard Hydroplane.

Class	Driver		Type	Speed
A (250 c.c. max)	T. E. Mansell	(1957)	Speed	54.44 m.p.h.
B (350 c.c. max)	H. G. Lawrence	(1958)	Speed	59.03 m.p.h.
C (500 c.c. max)	A. Pemberton	(1958)	Speed	60.57 m.p.h.
D (700 c.c. max)	E. Brandon	(1958)	Speed	61.13 m.p.h.
X (1,000 c.c. max)	H. L. G. Melly	(1958)	Speed	59.83 m.p.h.

Utility Outboard Runabout.

Class	Driver		Type	Speed
BU (350 c.c. max)	L. J. Derrington	(1958)	Speed	33.10 m.p.h.
C1U (600 c.c. max)	R. Allen	(1958)	Speed	29.56 m.p.h.

H.M. the Queen and H.R.H. the Duke of Edinburgh's Dragon Class yacht *Bluebottle*.

J. Herbert Thom, winner of the Seawanhaka Cup in 1938 and 1939. Scottish Island Class champion since the war.

Sir Henry Segrave *(bottom left)* with *Miss England II*.

Mr. D. K. Luke's *Zaida* (17-foot One Design Class).

Uffa Fox (white pullover) aboard *Cowslip*, H.R.H. the Duke of Edinburgh's Flying Fifteen Class yacht.

YACHTING QUIZ

1. Can an owner sail a yacht other than his own in a race in which his own yacht competes?

★

2. What signal is made by the Sailing Committee:

    (a) To abandon a race
    (b) To postpone a race until a later date?

★

3. Under what circumstances can the Sailing Committee order a general recall.

★

4. What are the distinguishing letters on the sail of yachts of international classes from the following countries:

    (a) Austria
    (b) Spain
    (c) Australia
    (d) Chile?

★

5. At 11.30 p.m., the night before the Britannia Cup race, the crew of the Ruritanian entry is seen going on board, each with a cwt. of ballast. Is this permitted?

QUIZ ANSWERS

1. No. Unless he has had the previous consent of the Sailing Committee. 2. (a) Hoisting of the letter 'N' International Code and the firing of three guns. (b) The Answering Pendant hoisted over letter 'A' International Code. 3. "In the event of there being a number of unidentified premature starters, or an error in starting procedure, or for any other valid reason." 4. (a) OE; (b) E; (c) KA; (d) X. 5. No. No ballast, whether movable or fixed, may be shipped, unshipped or shifted after 9 p.m. of the day previous to that on which the race is sailed.

ANDRE—WORLD SPEED RECORD

Winners:

1928	Gar Wood "Miss America"	Detroit	92.862 m.p.h.
1930	Sir Henry Segrave "Miss England II"	Windermere	98.7 m.p.h.
1931	Kaye Don ,, ,,	Argentina	103.48 m.p.h.
1931		Lake Garda	110.24 m.p.h.
1932	Gar Wood "Miss America IX"	Miami	111.65 m.p.h.
1932	Kaye Don "Miss England III"	Loch Lomond	119.75 m.p.h.
1932	Gar Wood "Miss America X"	Detroit	124.86 m.p.h.
1937	Sir Malcolm Campbell "Bluebird"	Maggiore	129.5 m.p.h.
1938	,, ,, ,, ,,	Switzerland	130.94 m.p.h.
1939	,, ,, ,, ,,	Coniston	141.74 m.p.h.
1950	Stanley Sayers "Slo-mo-shun IV"	Lake Washington	160.323 m.p.h.
1952		,, ,,	178.497 m.p.h.
1955	Donald Campbell "Bluebird"	Ullswater	202.32 m.p.h.
1955	,, ,, ,, ,,	America	216.2 m.p.h.
1956	,, ,, ,, ,,	Windermere	225.63 m.p.h.
1957	,, ,, ,, ,,	Coniston	239.07 m.p.h.
1958	,, ,, ,, ,,	,,	248.62 m.p.h.
1959	,, ,, ,, ,,	,,	260.35 m.p.h.

Donald Campbell, present holder of the world water speed record.

Show Jumping

Compiled by
Capt. G. H. S. Webber
Secretary General: The British
Show Jumping Association

THE HISTORY OF SHOW JUMPING

For many centuries the horse has been the friend and servant of man. This noble animal has helped to win wars, has for many years been the most important form of transport, and has been a companion in sport, whether it be riding, driving, hunting or racing.

In the early days, whether in battle or in sport, it was not necessary that the horse should jump, except perhaps a ditch or small bank; however, in the eighteenth century, with the passing of the Enclosure Act, the situation changed. No longer was it possible to cross the country without jumping, and the rider soon realised not only how well the horse could jump, but also the thrill of this new form of horsemanship.

The birth of show jumping took place in 1866 when a class for show jumpers was arranged at a harness show in Paris. The horse and rider first appeared in the ring to parade before the public and were then sent out into the nearby country to jump some natural obstacles. This was of little interest to the spectator and, soon after, it was so organised that a few simple fences were built in the arena. Fifteen years later the sport came to England, to be known as "lepping" competitions. By 1900 "lepping" or jumping competitions took place at the more important shows, but entries were small, seldom exceeding fifteen or twenty, and ladies riding side-saddle competed in special classes.

In 1912 jumping was first included among the equestrian events of the Olympic Games, but each country had its own rules, and so the Fédération Equestre Internationale came into being, to standardise these. In Britain there were no standard rules, and each show decided how the judging should be conducted, and many of the marks were given for style. This led to dissatisfaction and confusion to the spectator, and the British Show Jumping Association was formed to standardise the judging of jumping competitions.

ADMINISTRATION

International show jumping is controlled throughout the world by the Fédération Equestre Internationale (F.E.I.) which also controls the equestrian events of the Olympic Games.

The F.E.I. is an international equestrian union of the national federations of some forty countries, each of which agrees to comply with the statutes and general regulations of the F.E.I.

The committee of the F.E.I. is made up of two representatives of each affiliated nation and meets once a year. This committee elects, by secret vote, from amongst its members a bureau of eight members who serve for four years and might be termed the board of directors. Great Britain is at present represented on the Bureau of the F.E.I.

The national federation of Great Britain is the British Horse Society, 16 Bedford Square, London, W.C.1, and they delegate the responsibility for show jumping to the British Show Jumping Association (B.S.J.A.) of the same address.

The B.S.J.A. is, therefore, the controlling body of show jumping in Great Britain, and is responsible for framing the national rules. Every show of repute that includes show-jumping classes in its schedule is now affiliated to the B.S.J.A. and holds its competitions under rules and regulations approved by this Association.

Colonel M. P. Ansell making a presentation to Lt.-Col. C. T. Walwyn, retiring President of the B.S.J.A. after 30 years in office as Chairman or President.

THE GROWTH OF SHOW JUMPING

In the years immediately following the First World War, jumping formed a small part of almost every agricultural show and was creating much interest amongst the spectators. There were no recognised rules for judging the competitions, and, from what one hears, competitors were very much at the mercy of judges and executives. A rider never knew whether the competition would be judged on one or more rounds. In fact, this depended on what suited the executive's programme best! If there was plenty of time and spectators were enjoying the jumping, it was likely that word would be sent to the judges to make them all jump again! When it came to deciding the winner it was purely the judges' opinion, and there is little

Lt. J. A. Talbot-Ponsonby, 7th Q.O. Hussars on Chelsea, King's Cup Winner at Olympia in 1930 and 1932.

doubt that some unhappy awards were made. Very early in the 'twenties some of the regular jumping competitors, civilians and regular officers, decided that an association to regulate their sport and to protect them from the whims of judges and executives was an urgent necessity. In this way the British Show Jumping Association was formed, and there are records of an annual general meeting being held at Olympia in 1923 and finally the Association was incorporated under the Companies Acts on the 31st December, 1925.

A survey of the early minute-books gives a splendid example of what can come of small beginnings if there is an earnest endeavour to attain one's objective. The goal was clearly defined—"the encouragement of show jumping"; and the efforts of the Association have always been devoted to this end. The B.S.J.A. is concerned with show jumping and show jumping only.

This newly formed Association immediately set itself to the introduction of a code of rules for the sport. In the first place, these were based mainly on the existing international rules, little known in England at that time. Not unnaturally, as a result of past experience, the emphasis of all new rules was on what jumps might or might not be used, and the Association sought to protect its members, not only by the introduction of rules for judging and a list of approved judges, but by laying down restrictions on courses and obstacles. This is very understandable, and it is only recently that the turn in the other direction in favour of variety and the minimum restriction on course builders has come. This is a result of a number of years' experience and very considerable improvement in the knowledge of what is a good test as opposed to what would be a trap.

The sincere efforts made by the early committees of the Association to improve and encourage the sport met with considerable success, and we find a small but steady increase in membership continuing for a number of years, but this advancement came to a stop just prior to the Second World War. The interest and entertainment had gone out of the jumping due to the sameness, lack of enterprise and initiative in the building of courses. For fear of transgressing the rules and incurring the disfavour of competitors, show executives put up the same few fences round the outside of the ring with a water-jump down the centre, or, in the absence of water, a triple bar. The time element did not come into it in any way, with the result that the test became one of jumping individual fences unconnected with each other, and it was only some years after the formation of the Association that a rule was introduced penalising circling between fences! Jumping at this tempo ceased to be entertaining and show executives banished

SHOW JUMPING QUIZ

1. When may a horse/pony be down-graded?

★

2. Does prize money won in sweepstake competitions count for grading?

★

3. Does prize money won in team or pair competitions count for grading?

★

4. Is the order of jumping for a competition drawn by lot?

★

5. Are there a minimum number of obstacles for adult jumping competitions?

★

6. If "cups" are used to support poles etc., how deep may they be?

QUIZ ANSWERS

1. Never. 2. Yes. 3. No. 4. Usually it is, but (except in international shows) if time may be the deciding factor the order must be drawn. 5. Yes; not less than seven, except in special competitions. 6. The depth must not exceed one third of the diameter of the element it supports.

it to the end of their programmes. This was not a happy or profitable era for the Association as individual members were dissatisfied at the relatively little interest taken in jumping and were not always backward in expressing their dissatisfaction. Affiliated shows were critical of the Association that they were not able to discipline their members, and thus a vicious circle which could have become most harmful to the B.S.J.A. was arising. The Second World War came as a severe shock to all and the plans for improvement of jumping were all of necessity postponed.

H.M. The Queen presents the Queen Elizabeth II Cup to Dawn Palethorpe (Mrs. Wofford), winner in 1955 and 1956

Capt. G. H. S. Webber making a presentation at the Horse of the Year Show, Harringay, to Miss Ann Townsend on Irish Lace.

SHOW JUMPING QUIZ

1. Is there a maximum height of obstacles for novice horses?

★

2. Is there a maximum height of obstacles for ponies?

★

3. Is there a minimum height of obstacles at shows affiliated to the B.S.J.A.?

★

4. If two obstacles appear to be rather close together how do you know whether it is a combination obstacle or two separate obstacles?

QUIZ ANSWERS

1. Yes. Grade "B" 4' 3", Grade "C" 4'. 2. Yes. Grade "J.A." 4' 3", Grade "J.C." 3' 9". Ponies not exceeding 14.2 hh. 4'. Ponies not exceeding 13.2 hh. 4'. Ponies not exceeding 12.2 hh. 3' 6". *Note.* The above do not apply in a jump-off or in championship competitions nor in junior competitions if the first prize is £15 or over, but 5' may not be exceeded under any circumstances in junior competitions. 3. No, the obstacles may be as low as the judges consider appropriate. 4. By the numbering. Combination obstacles carry only one number—e.g. 7a, 7b, 7c; if they were separate obstacles they would be numbered 7, 8, 9. *Note.* In a combination obstacle the maximum distance between any two fences must not exceed 39' 4", measured from the inside element of the two fences at ground level.

The Growth of Show Jumping—*contd.*

However, by 1945, jumping had a following, and the election of Lt.-Col. Mike Ansell as Vice-President and Chairman of the Association proved to be the turning-point in the affairs of the B.S.J.A. The Association has been well and truly served by many, but no one man has done as much for jumping as has Mike Ansell. Unable to compete himself, he brought to the sport all his knowledge and experience, together with the determination that jumping should take its rightful place among British sports. Registration and grading were introduced which could deal with the increasing amount of recording work which these innovations brought with them.

The sport had to be made attractive to the competitor to make sure that there were enough entries for all the shows, and also to the spectators to get the gate-money out of which good prize-money was to come. An immense amount of hard work was put in and rewarded by the fact that every show of any standing became affiliated to the Association, realising the value of having a body which could give valuable assistance.

Another item which had an important influence on the future of show jumping was the fact that the first post-war Olympiad was allocated to Great Britain in 1948. It was soon realised by the B.S.J.A. that somehow Great Britain, the host nation, must be adequately represented at show jumping. Strenuous training and far-seeing planning followed and finally the winning of the bronze medals at Wembley was a great achievement.

The years between the Olympiad in London and that in Helsinki in 1952 were years of triumph for British show jumping, and the sporting crowds were delighted to watch a contest in which their own country was able to resist the challenge from all comers. Finally the Olympic gold medals at Helsinki stirred the whole country, and show jumping was right on the map.

We now find that almost every show stages well-organised and well-patronised jumping competitions. Variety has been introduced in courses, fences and competitions, to the advantage of owners and spectators. The White City, which is England's official International Horse Show, draws large crowds through the turn-stiles for the cheaper seats. The Horse of the Year Show at Harringay has had "House Full" notices out, and many people have had to go home and watch the jumping on their television sets. Show jumping is a great sport today, and provided it continues to be conducted on the right lines its future should be assured. The international effort must be maintained as there can be little doubt that it is this which has provided the chief stimulus.

PRINCE OF WALES CUP
Team Competition

Won outright in 1928 by Great Britain and re-presented.

1929	Great Britain
1930	Great Britain
1931	France
1932	France
1933	No Show
1934	France
1935	Great Britain
1936	France
1937	Ireland
1938	Great Britain
1939	Great Britain
1947	France
1948	United States of America
1949	Great Britain
1950	Great Britain
1951	Great Britain
1952	Great Britain
1953	Great Britain
1954	Great Britain
1955	Italy
1956	Great Britain
1957	Great Britain
1958	United States of America
1959	United States of America

The return of the victorious gold medal winners, Olympic Games, Helsinki, 1952.

B.S.J.A. CHAMPIONSHIPS

THE ADULT NATIONAL CHAMPIONSHIP
Presented by Mrs. H. S. Lees Smith

1945	Lt.-Col. N. Kindersley's MAGUIRE ridden by the Owner
1946	R. Hall's SPARKIE ridden by the Owner
1947	Lt.-Col. N. Kindersley's MAGUIRE ridden by the Owner
1948	T. Makin's LIMERICK ridden by S. Hayes
1949	T. Makin's SHEILA ridden by S. Hayes
1950	T. Makin's SHEILA ridden by S. Hayes
1951	A. H. Payne's RED KNIGHT and RED ADMIRAL ridden by Alan Oliver
1952	A. Massarella and Sons' COSTA ridden by D. Beard
1953	Lt.-Col. H. M. Llewellyn's FOXHUNTER ridden by the Owner
1954	A. H. Payne's RED ADMIRAL ridden by Alan Oliver
1955	L. Cawthraw's LARRY and SUNDAY MORNING ridden by E. Williams
1956	L. Cawthraw's MONTANA and PEGASUS XIII ridden by E. Williams
1957	T. H. Edgar's JANE SUMMERS ridden by the Owner
1958	T. Mulholland's TIM II ridden by P. McMahon
1959	A. H. Payne's JOHN GILPIN ridden by Alan Oliver

THE LADIES CHAMPIONSHIP CUP
Presented by Mrs. G. A. Williams

1948	Lady Dudley's PRINCESS ridden by the Owner
1949	Miss A. Hinchcliffe's VICTORY BOY ridden by the Owner
1950	A. Massarella and Sons' PADDY V ridden by Mrs. A. E. Dickenson
1951	Miss P. Rose's WITHOUT RESERVE ridden by the Owner
1952	Miss P. Smythe's PRINCE HAL ridden by the Owner
1953	Miss P. Smythe's TOSCA ridden by the Owner
1954	Capt. J. Palethorpe's EARLSRATH RAMBLER ridden by Miss D. Palethorpe
1955	R. Hanson's FLANAGAN ridden by Miss P. Smythe
1956	Miss A. Morley's NUGGET ridden by the Owner
1957	Miss P. Smythe's PRINCE HAL ridden by the Owner
1958	R. Hanson's FLANAGAN ridden by Miss P. Smythe
1959	Mr. J. L. King's MR. POLLARD ridden by Miss P. Smythe

THE WALWYN CHALLENGE CUP
Presented by Lt.-Col. C. T. Walwyn, D.S.O., O.B.E., M.C.

For Adult Competitors under International Rules.

1947	A. J. Woollam's GAY LADY ridden by A. Beard
1948	Miss P. Smythe's FINALITY ridden by the Owner
1949	Mrs. and Miss P. Smythe's LEONA ridden by Miss P. Smythe
1950	W. H. White's NIZEFELA ridden by the Owner
1951	T. Makin's SNOWSTORM ridden by S. Hayes
1952	Miss P. Smythe's TOSCA ridden by the Owner
1953	W. H. White's NIZEFELA ridden by the Owner
1954	A. H. Payne's RED ADMIRAL and GALWAY BOY ridden by Alan Oliver
1955	S. W. Woodhall's RAPIER ridden by P. Woodhall
1956	A. H. Payne's RED ADMIRAL ridden by Alan Oliver
1957	Miss A. Morley's NUGGET ridden by J. Walmsley
1958	L. Carter's FACEY ridden by Miss J. Nash
1959	Mr. A. Kitson's PRINCE CHARLES ridden by Miss C. Beard

Peter Robeson on Craven "A"

Wilf White on Nizefela

Col. H. Llewellyn on Foxhunter

THE NORTHERN CHAMPIONSHIP CUP
Presented by Lt.-Col. M. P. Ansell, D.S.O.

1946 J. Woollam's BARTESTREE ridden by A. Beard
1947 R. J. O'Neill's 'ANDSOME ridden by the Owner
1948 T. Taylor's JORROCKS ridden by the Owner
1949 T. Makin's SHEILA ridden by S. Hayes
1950 T. Makin's SHEILA ridden by S. Hayes
1951 T. Makin's SHEILA ridden by S. Hayes
1952 Miss P. Smythe's TOSCA ridden by the Owner
1953 W. H. White's NIZEFELA ridden by the Owner
1954 Miss P. Smythe's TOSCA ridden by the Owner
1955 W. H. White's NIZEFELA ridden by the Owner
1956 { R. Hanson's FLANAGAN ridden by Miss P. Smythe
     { L. Cawthraw's PEGASUS XIII ridden by E. Williams
1957 L. Cawthraw's DUMBELL ridden by E. Williams
1958 J. King's MR. POLLARD ridden by Miss P. Smythe
1959 D. Massarella & Sons' DUMBELL ridden by M. Freer

THE B.S.J.A. MIDLAND CHAMPIONSHIP CUP
Presented by Lt.-Col. R. H. L. Brackenbury, O.B.E.

1946 Lt.-Col. H. M. Llewellyn's KILGEDDIN ridden by the Owner
1947 E. Williams' TIM II ridden by the Owner
1948 E. Williams' TIM II ridden by the Owner
1949 Not held
1950 E. Williams' UMBO ridden by the Owner
1951 E. Williams' UMBO ridden by the Owner
1952 Miss P. Smythe's TOSCA and PRINCE HAL ridden by the Owner
1953 T. H. Edgar's JANE SUMMERS ridden by the Owner
1954 W. H. White's NIZEFELA ridden by the Owner
1955 S. W. Woodhall's PIAVE ridden by W. Woodhall
1956 T. Mulholland's TIM II ridden by P. McMahon
1957 W. H. White's NIZEFELA ridden by the Owner
1958 Mrs. J. C. Howard's ROYAL LORD ridden by G. Hobbs
1959 { T. Mulholland's TIM II ridden by P. McMahon
     { Miss J. Harper's ROSALYN ridden by Owner

Pat Smythe

Ted Williams

THE SOUTH OF ENGLAND CHAMPIONSHIP CUP
Presented by the White City Stadium Ltd.

1946 Lt.-Col. H. M. Llewellyn's KILGEDDIN ridden by the Owner
1947 Not held
1948 G. H. Bunn's SAFETY MATCH ridden by D. Bunn
1949 Miss P. Nesfield's THOMAS ridden by the Owner
1950 T. Makin's SHEILA ridden by S. Hayes
1951 Miss J. Legg's RUFUS ridden by the Owner
1952 Miss P. Smythe's TOSCA ridden by the Owner
1953 { Lt.-Col. H. M. Llewellyn's FOXHUNTER ridden by the Owner
     { Miss M. Delfosse's FANNY ROSA ridden by the Owner
1954 A. H. Payne's RED STAR II ridden by Alan Oliver
1955 A. H. Payne's RED STAR II ridden by Alan Oliver
1956 Miss P. Smythe's PRINCE HAL ridden by the Owner
1957 { Miss M. Barnes' GALA QUEEN ridden by the Owner
     { Miss P. Smythe's CAROUSEL ridden by the Owner
     { R. Hanson's FLANAGAN ridden by Miss P. Smythe
1958 W. R. Butters' GUNGA-DIN ridden by Miss G. Butters
1959 F. M. Broome's BALLAN EXCELSIOR ridden by D. Broome

THE EASTERN COUNTIES CHAMPIONSHIP CUP
Presented by Lt.-Col. E. B. Gordon, C.M.G., D.S.O.

1949 E. Williams' UMBO ridden by the Owner
1950 E. Williams' TIM II ridden by the Owner
1951 T. Makin's SHEILA ridden by the Owner
1952 L. T. Norton's TRADESMAN ridden by E. Williams
1953 Miss V. Machin Goodall's HALCYON ridden by the Owner
1954 A. H. Payne's JOHN GILPIN ridden by Alan Oliver
1955 { E. Williams' SUNDAY MORNING ridden by the Owner
     { P. Robeson's CRAVEN "A" ridden by the Owner
1956 Mrs. Cawthraw's DUMBELL ridden by E. Williams
1957 L. Cawthraw's SUNDAY MORNING ridden by E. Williams
1958 { F. Oliver's JOHNNY's VENTURE OF NAIRDWOOD ridden by F. Welch
     { Mrs. Cawthraw's DUMBELL ridden by E. Williams
1959 { Mr. and Mrs. L. Cawthraw's YORKSHIREMAN ridden by E. Williams
     { F. D. Wright's STONE PARK ridden by B. Hales

Olympic possibles for 1960 in training at Arundel, April 1959.

THE WELSH CHAMPIONSHIP CUP
Presented by the B.S.J.A.

1949 A. H. Payne's RED STAR II ridden by Alan Oliver
1950 S. W. Woodhall's LULU ridden by W. Woodhall
1951 J. G. Jenks' PADDY XIX ridden by the Owner
1952 S. W. Woodhall's SALTY ridden by W. Woodhall
1953 Miss J. Allport's JOE ridden by the Owner
1954 S. W. Woodhall's PIAVE ridden by W. Woodhall
1955 T. G. Jenks' FINEST VIEW ridden by the Owner
1956 Miss P. Smythe's PRINCE HAL ridden by the Owner
1957 W. H. White's NIZEFELA ridden by the Owner
1958 F. Broome's WILDFIRE ridden by D. Broome
1959 T. Edgar's DISCUTIDO ridden by the Owner

THE JUNIOR NATIONAL CHAMPIONSHIP CUP
Presented by Col. F. N. Falkner, O.B.E.

1945 J. Betteridge's JOHNNIE B ridden by the Owner
1946 Miss M. Lockhart's JEAN ridden by the Owner
1947 A. H. Payne's THUMBS UP ridden by Alan Oliver
1948 J. Copley's DICKY ridden by the Owner
1949 F. R. Price's DIZZY DAISY
1950 S. Powell's SHADOW III ridden by the Owner
1951 A. Lawson's WILLY L
1952 A. Makin's BALLYDOYLE PRINCE ridden by T. Makin
1953 Miss L. Ollerton's POTHEEN ridden by the Owner
1954 P. Oliver's TONY OF NAIRDWOOD ridden by the Owner
1955 P. Oliver's LULU ridden by T. Makin
1956 { J. Mac's CAREA ridden by the Owner
     { Miss L. Martin's SHAMUS ridden by the Owner
     { P. Oliver's KANGAROO ridden by the Owner
1958 Miss J. Doney's TOMMY HAWK ridden by the Owner
     { P. Oliver's KANGAROO ridden by the Owner
1959 P. Oliver's KANGAROO ridden by the Owner

THE GRADE "C" CHAMPIONSHIP CUP
Presented by Major H. Faudel Phillips

1946 P. Banbury's CITY LIGHTS
1947 E. Bradley's TANGLE
1948 G. L. Trigg's TWILIGHT HOUR
1949 J. P. Ford's ROUND UP
1950 Miss P. Pritchard's JILLIAN II
1951 Miss P. Reeves' SMOKEY XI
1952 C. C. Miller's CULLMULLEN
1953 Miss S. Powell's EILEEN'S COTTAGE
1954 Foxhunter Stud Farms' ST. TEILO
1955 I. Rabinowitz's GREYDAWN
1956 F. Oliver's RED OXIDE, and Miss S. Ogle's FATHER MAC
1957 F. Oliver's RED LINK, and L. Vendyback's Q.C. II
1958 Grades "B" and "C" Championship Cup, Benenden Riding Establishment's BALLY HIGH
1959 V. Williams' JUDY'S GINGER

THE NATIONAL YOUNG RIDERS CHAMPIONSHIP
Presented by T. Gear, Esq.

1958 D. T. Wright's GREY MORNING ridden by D. Wright
1959 Mrs. C. White's RED SOCKS ridden by the Owner

SHOW JUMPING QUIZ

1. What is the age limit for junior members?

    ★

2. What is the maximum height for ponies?

    ★

3. Can one lease a horse/pony for show jumping?

    ★

4. Can one change a horse/pony's name once it has been registered?

    ★

5. What grades are used in show jumping?

    ★

6. May a horse/pony compete in a competition for horses/ponies in a higher grade?

QUIZ ANSWERS

1. Under 16 on the 1st day of January of the current year. 2. Not exceeding 14.2 hh. (½ inch allowed for shoes). 3. Yes, for any period not less than three months. 4. Yes, on payment of a fee of £5. 5. Horses/ponies are graded on total winnings. Adult competitions: Grade "A" £150 and over. Grade "B" £30 to under £150, Grade "C" nil to under £30. Junior Competitions: Grade "J.A." £50 and over, Grade "J.C." nil to under £50. 6. No, the competition is confined to horses/ponies in the grade or grades named.

THE LONSDALE CHAMPIONSHIP
Test Competition

1947	Chev. de Selliers de Moranville	(Belgium)	SEA PRINCE
1948	Col. A. A. Frierson	(U.S.A.)	RASCAL
1949	Mr. W. H. White	(G.B.)	TAILSMAN
1950	Lt.-Col. H. M. Llewellyn	(G.B.)	FOXHUNTER
1951	Cmdt. J. Garcia Cruz	(Spain)	QUONIAM
1952	Mr. T. Makin	(G.B.)	SHEILA
1953	Lt.-Col. H. M. Llewellyn	(G.B.)	FOXHUNTER
	Mr. A. H. Payne	(G.B.)	GALWAY BOY
	C.O.N.I.	(Italy)	URUGUAY
1954	Mr. P. Robeson	(G.B.)	CRAVEN "A"
1955	Lt. P. d'Inzeo	(Italy)	URUGUAY
1956	Lt.-Col. H. M. Llewellyn	(G.B.)	FOXHUNTER
1957	Capt. P. d'Inzeo	(Italy)	THE ROCK
1958	Capt. P. d'Inzeo	(Italy)	THE ROCK
1959	Miss A. Townsend	(G.B.)	BANDIT IV
	Mrs. W. Wofford	(G.B.)	HOLLANDIA

THE DAILY MAIL CUP
Individual Championship

1934	Lt. Y. Bizard	(France)	
1935	Department for Defence	(Ireland)	ARACHON
1936	Maj. J. H. Dudgeon	(G.B.)	LIMERICK LACE
1937	Equitation School, Weedon	(G.B.)	GOBLET
1938	Capt. Y. Bizard	(France)	SAMMY
1939	Lt.-Col. Allexandro Bettoni	(Italy)	GOBE MOUCHE
1947	Mr. B. Butler	(G.B.)	ADIGRAT
1948	M. d'Orgeix	(France)	TANKARD
1949	Maj. D. N. Stewart	(G.B.)	SUCRE DE POMME
1950	Mr. S. Hayes	(G.B.)	KILGEDDIN
1951	Lt.-Col. H. M. Llewellyn	(G.B.)	TANKARD
1952	Mr. B. Butler	(G.B.)	FOXHUNTER
1953	Lt. R. d'Inzeo	(Italy)	TANKARD
1954	Mr. P. Robeson	(G.B.)	MERANO
1955	Miss P. Smythe	(G.B.)	CRAVEN "A"
1956	Mr. A. H. Payne	(G.B.)	PRINCE HAL
1957	Miss P. Smythe	(G.B.)	GALWAY BOY
1958	Capt. P. d'Inzeo	(Italy)	PRINCE HAL
1959	Mr. H. Wiley	(U.S.A.)	URUGUAY
			NAUTICAL

SHOW JUMPING QUIZ

1. If a horse/pony knocks down the water-jump obstacle and lands in the water, what faults are incurred?

★

2. Does time count in competitions under B.S.J.A. rules?

★

3. May time be used to decide a competition under B.S.J.A. rules?

★

4. What is the present high-jump record for a horse?

★

5. What is the present long-jump record for a horse?

QUIZ ANSWERS

1. Four faults. 2. Yes. A "time allowed", based on 300 yards per minute, according to the length of the course, is included. Exceeding the "time allowed" is penalised by ¼ fault for every second or part of a second. The "time limit" is always twice the "time allowed". Exceeding the "time limit" incurs elimination. 3. No, except special competitions with their own specific rules for judging. 4. 2 metres 47—approximately 8' 2". The British record is 7' 6¼" by the late Mr. F. W. Foster's "Swank" ridden by D. Beard at the International Horse Show, Olympia, London, in 1937. 5. 8 metres 30—approximately 27'.

THE SUNDAY GRAPHIC CUP
Victor Ludorum

1950	Lt.-Col. H. M. Llewellyn	FOXHUNTER	
1951	Miss M. McDowell (Ireland)	HACK ON	Col. J. Lewis
1952	Mr. G. B. Robeson	CRAVEN "A"	P. Robeson
1953	Miss P. Smythe	TOSCA	
1954	Miss P. Smythe	PRINCE HAL	
1955	Capt. J. Palethorpe	EARLSRATH RAMBLER	Miss D. Palethorpe
1956	Capt P. d'Inzeo (Italy)	CELEBRATION	
1957	Mr. W. H. White	NIZEFELA	
1958	Miss A. Morley	NUGGET	J. Walmsley

Alan Oliver on Red Admiral

Elizabeth Anderson and Sunsalve

THE SUNDAY TIMES CUP
Adult Inter-County Teams

1953	Yorkshire
1954	Shropshire
1955	Yorkshire
1956	Buckinghamshire
1957	Derbyshire
1958	Cheshire

THE EAGLE TROPHY
Junior Inter-County Teams

1956	Sussex
1957	Dorset
1958	Yorkshire

HORSE OF THE YEAR SHOW

THE LEADING SHOW JUMPER OF THE YEAR

1949	Mr. J. Snodgrass	FINALITY	Miss P. Smythe
1950	Mr. T. Makin	SHEILA	S. Hayes
1951	Hon. Dorothy Paget	EFOREGIOT	A. Beard
1952	Mr. R. Hanson	SNOWSTORM	W. Hanson
1953	Mr. A. H. Payne	RED ADMIRAL	A. Oliver
1954	Capt. J. Palethorpe	EARLSRATH RAMBLER	Miss D. Palethorpe
1955	Mrs. N. Cawthraw	SUNDAY MORNING	E. Williams
1956	Mrs. N. Cawthraw	DUMBELL	E. Williams
1957	Mr. L. Cawthraw	PEGASUS XIII	E. Williams
1958	Mr. J. King, M.F.H.	MR. POLLARD	Miss P. Smythe
	Mr. T. H. Edgar	JANE SUMMERS	T. Edgar

THE LEADING JUNIOR SHOW JUMPER OF THE YEAR

1949	Miss Y. Fossey	VINTAGE
1950	Miss P. Moss	BRANDY OF WHITE CLOUD
1951	A. Watkins	TONY
1952	T. Barnes	MUNDEN MAGPIE
1953	R. J. Howle	LUCKY STRIKE
	A. Makin	SPRINGBOK
1954	A. Makin	BALLYDOYLE PRINCE
	Miss M. Barnes	MUNDEN MAGPIE
1955	Miss V. Wood	CARREG GUEST
1956	J. James	CHERRY
1957	Miss B. Vincent	LULU II
1958	Miss S. Barnes	BACCARAT
	Miss D. C. Anholm	PAUL V

THE DAILY EXPRESS FOXHUNTER CHAMPIONSHIP

1954	Miss F. Stanbury	DREAMBOAT	
1955	Miss B. P. Rose	ROYAL LORD	
1956	Mr. C. H. Van Raalte	ANDREW COBB, ESQ., M.F.H.	J. Weaver
1957	Miss A. Barker	LUCKY SAM	
1958	Mr. T. G. Thomas	RAMBLER IV	A. John

ROYAL INTERNATIONAL HORSE SHOW

THE QUEEN ELIZABETH II CUP

1949	Miss Iris Kellett	(Ireland)	RUSTY	
1950	Miss Jill Palethorpe	(G.B.)	SILVER CLOUD	
1951	Miss Iris Kellett	(Ireland)	RUSTY	
1952	Mrs. G. Rich	(G.B.)	QUICKSILVER III	
1953	Miss Marie Delfosse	(G.B.)	FANNY ROSA	
1954	Mlle J. Bonnaud	(France)	CHARLESTON	
1955	Capt. J. Palethorpe	(G.B.)	EARLSRATH RAMBLER	Miss D. Palethorpe
1956	Capt. J. Palethorpe	(G.B.)	EARLSRATH RAMBLER	Miss D. Palethorpe
1957	Miss E. Anderson	(G.B.)	SUNSALVE	
1958	Mr. John King, M.F.H.	(G.B.)	MR. POLLARD	Miss P. Smythe
1959	Miss A. Clement	(Germany)	NICO	

THE KING GEORGE V GOLD CUP

*1934	Lt. J. A. Talbot-Ponsonby	(G.B.)	BEST GIRL
1935	Capt. J. J. Lewis	(Ireland)	TRAMORE BAY
1936	Cmdt. J. G. O'Dwyer	(Ireland)	LIMERICK LACE
1937	Capt. Y. Bizard	(France)	HONDURAS
1938	Maj. J. C. Friedberger	(G.B.)	DEREK
1939	Lt. Allexandro Bettoni	(Italy)	ADIGRAT
1947	M. Jonqueres d'Oriola	(France)	MARQUIS III
1948	Lt.-Col. H. M. Llewellyn	(G.B.)	FOXHUNTER
1949	Mr. B. Butler	(G.B.)	TANKARD
1950	Lt.-Col. H. M. Llewellyn	(G.B.)	FOXHUNTER
1951	Capt. K. Barry	(Ireland)	BALLYNEETY
1952	Sen. don Carlos Figueroa	(Spain)	GRACIEUX
1953	Lt.-Col. H. M. Llewellyn	(G.B.)	FOXHUNTER
1954	Fr. Thiedemann	(Germany)	METEOR
1955	Lt.-Col. Cartasegna	(Italy)	BRANDO
1956	Mr. W. Steinkraus	(U.S.A.)	FIRST BOY
1957	Capt. P. d'Inzeo	(Italy)	URUGUAY
1958	Mr. H. Wiley	(U.S.A.)	MASTER WILLIAM
1959	Mr. H. Wiley	(U.S.A.)	NAUTICAL

* Won outright.

Skating

Compiled by **Howard Bass**
Editor: The Skater and Skier

ICE SKATING QUIZ

1. Which famous skater's maiden name was Jepson-Turner?

★

2. In figure skating competitions the judges display two separate sets of marks. What is each set for?

★

3. Who has skated the 10,000 metres in the fastest time?

★

4. What limitation on spins is imposed in ice dance championships?

QUIZ ANSWERS

1. Belita, the film star. 2. One for contents of programme, the other for manner of performance. 3. Norway's Hjalmar Andersen, whose record time of 16 minutes 32.6 seconds was set up at Hamar in 1952. 4. Spins must not exceed one and a half revolutions.

National Skating Association

NOTES ON THE HISTORY OF ICE SKATING

In some of the world's museums there still exist examples of bone skates believed to be at least twenty centuries old. Originally they were made from shank or rib bones of the elk, ox, reindeer and other animals long before the discovery of iron. Skating in a primitive form almost certainly originated in Scandinavia before the birth of Christ and is mentioned in early Scandinavian literature of the second century.

Since the Middle Ages the sport has thrived on the canals of Holland, and a Dutch wood-carving printed in 1498 portrays St. Lydwina of Schiedam who broke a rib while skating and is now known as the patron saint of skaters.

The sport is mentioned by Samuel Pepys, who described in his diary how, in 1662 on the canal in St. James's Park, London, "It being a great Frost, did see people with their skeetes, which is a very pretty art."

The world's first skating club was formed at Edinburgh in 1742. About a century later the sport was introduced into North America by British soldiers and the first American club was founded in 1849. The first all-iron skate was invented the following year by E. W. Bushnell of Philadelphia.

The birth of mechanically refrigerated ice rinks dates from 1876, when John Gamgee built a small one near King's Road, Chelsea. Another opened in Manchester the next year and they have since multiplied throughout the world, including such climatically unnatural territories as Australia and South Africa, so that today the existence of hundreds of artificially frozen rinks makes participation possible in all seasons.

Two and a half million pairs of skates are retailed each year now in North America alone, where the number of rinks has more than doubled since 1947 to nearly 400. There are about 250 in Canada. England has 14 and Scotland 10.

The sport's first federation, the National Skating Association of Great Britain, was instituted in 1879. The United States Figure Skating Association was inaugurated in 1886 and that of the Canadians in 1888. Other countries followed suit and these national associations collaborated in 1892 to found the International Skating Union, the world's governing administrative body which has since supervised and standardised ice figure, ice dance and ice speed skating regulations.

Carol Heiss

Championships and competitions comprise four major variations of the sport—solo figure skating, pair skating, ice dancing and speed skating.

Speed skating, the oldest branch of the sport, remains to this day the more widely practised in Scandinavian countries, particularly Norway. International championships are decided over four distances—500, 1,500, 5,000 and 10,000 metres—and the first world championship was staged at Amsterdam in 1893 and won by J. Eden of Holland.

Speed skaters are said to be the fastest *self-propelled* humans in the world, averaging some twenty miles an hour over the shorter distances. Over a mile the speed skater is in fact more than a minute faster than the runner.

Britain's oldest speed skating club is Aldwych, founded in 1896 and won by with headquarters and home rink now at Richmond. Other prominent clubs in Britain have been Birmingham Mohawks, Bournemouth, Brighton, Crossmyloof, Durham, Nottingham, Southampton and, especially before the war, Streatham.

Paul and Ria Falk

The first world championship in ice figure skating was staged at St. Petersburg (now Leningrad) in 1896 and won by Dr. Gilbert Fuchs of Munich. It is interesting to note that the third contest was held at the old National Skating Palace in London's Argyll Street on the site now occupied by the Palladium Theatre.

A separate women's championship began in 1906 and interest heightened when, in 1927, Norway's Sonja Henie at the age of thirteen won the first of ten consecutive victories. The tremendous increase in enthusiasm for skating during the last two decades is, to some extent, attributed to the public imagination and interest captured by Sonja Henie's skating films in the 'thirties.

Modern British successes in figure skating by world champions like Jeannette Altwegg, Cecilia Colledge, Megan Taylor and Graham Sharp may have been due largely to the thoroughness in practice and execution of the "school" figures, and the national characteristic of calm temperament may have been an asset.

An American ascendancy has made itself felt, however, particularly in free-skating and more noticeably among the men, since Dick Button in 1948 introduced a more athletic style with marked progress in elevation of jumps, originality and manner of artistic presentation.

Men's and women's figure skating championships are divided into two parts, the first comprising compulsory figures. From the internationally recognised schedule of forty-one different figures six are normally selected in senior contests and, for the skating of these, two-thirds of the total marks are awarded.

The second part, for the remaining third of the marks, is free-skating, in which competitors are able to perform as they like and are marked for (a) manner and (b) contents of performance. In major championships the men are each required to free-skate for five minutes and the women for four minutes, each entrant supplying his or her own chosen recording of musical accompaniment. Pair skating competitions comprise free-skating only, each pair skating for five minutes in a senior championship.

The newest of the competitive skating sports is ice dancing and, although there is evidence of the waltz being skated on ice at Halifax, Nova Scotia, in 1885, this branch did not really come into its own until between the wars. The first world ice dance championship was held as recently as 1950, when Michael McGean and Lois Waring (U.S.A.) were the victors in London. Each year since, the title has been monopolised by British dancers who have led the way in developing what is now the most popular public participant branch of skating.

A senior international championship requires each couple to skate four selected compulsory dances and also a free-dancing programme of three minutes' duration, the purpose of the latter being to test the competitors' general dancing knowledge, ability and inventiveness.

John and Jennifer Nicks

The basic difference between ice dancing and pair skating is that, in dancing, certain limitations are imposed on the separations of partners, duration of spins and certain tests of physical prowess and skating skill which do not form part of the dance sequence. In pair skating a greater impression of unison and harmonious composition is required.

Championship results in ice figure, pair and dance events are determined by a panel of, usually, seven, nine or more judges. The complicated, systematic marking is so arranged that the skaters' final placings are decided by the judges' *majority* decision, thus minimising any effect on the result by an unduly biased official.

Ice figure skating was first included in the Olympic Games in 1908 and it was not until 1924 that speed skating was added and the first separate Winter Olympic Games organised at Chamonix. Ice dancing has yet to win Olympic admission.

The 1928 Olympic programme was memorable as the occasion on which Gilles Grafström, of Sweden, won his third consecutive gold medal in the men's figure skating, while, in the women's, Sonja Henie at the age of fourteen won the first of her three, repeating the feat in 1932 at Lake Placid and again in 1936 at Garmisch-Partenkirchen.

When the 1952 Games were held in Oslo the Norwegian authorities announced that 130,000 people assembled to watch the four speed skating events, three of which were won by Norway's Hjalmar Andersen. The women's free-skating packed Bislett Stadium to capacity, 28,000, and at this meeting Jeannette Altwegg became the first British skater ever to win an Olympic title, for which she was later rewarded with the M.B.E.

The 1956 Games at Cortina d'Ampezzo marked in particular a Russian domination in the speed contests, winning three of the four races. On the superbly prepared, frozen surface of the Misurina Lake all four Olympic speed records were beaten that year and two new world's best times were achieved, one with an incredible dead-heat by two Russians, Eugenij Grischin and Yurij Mikailov, in the 1,500 metres.

Bibliography: *This Skating Age* (Howard Bass), *Wings On My Feet* (Sonja Henie), *Dick Button On Skates* (Dick Button), *Skate With Me* (Barbara Ann Scott), *Thin Ice* (Jacqueline du Bief), *N.S.A. Handbook*, *The Skater and Skier* magazine.

WORLD MEN'S FIGURE CHAMPIONS

Year	Name	Country	Venue
1896	G. Fuchs	(Germany)	St. Petersburg
1897	G. Hügel	(Austria)	Stockholm
1898	H. Grenander	(Sweden)	London
1899	G. Hügel	(Austria)	Davos
1900	G. Hügel	(Austria)	Davos
1901	U. Salchow	(Sweden)	Stockholm
1902	U. Salchow	(Sweden)	London
1903	U. Salchow	(Sweden)	St. Petersburg
1904	U. Salchow	(Sweden)	Berlin
1905	U. Salchow	(Sweden)	Stockholm
1906	G. Fuchs	(Germany)	Munich
1907	U. Salchow	(Sweden)	Vienna
1908	U. Salchow	(Sweden)	Troppau
1909	U. Salchow	(Sweden)	Stockholm
1910	U. Salchow	(Sweden)	Davos
1911	U. Salchow	(Sweden)	Berlin
1912	F. Kachler	(Austria)	Manchester
1913	F. Kachler	(Austria)	Vienna
1914	G. Sandahl	(Sweden)	Helsingfors
1922	G. Grafström	(Sweden)	Stockholm
1923	F. Kachler	(Austria)	Vienna
1924	G. Grafström	(Sweden)	Manchester
1925	W. Böckl	(Austria)	Vienna
1926	W. Böckl	(Austria)	Berlin
1927	W. Böckl	(Austria)	Davos
1928	W. Böckl	(Austria)	Berlin
1929	G. Grafström	(Sweden)	London
1930	K. Schäfer	(Austria)	New York
1931	K. Schäfer	(Austria)	Berlin
1932	K. Schäfer	(Austria)	Montreal
1933	K. Schäfer	(Austria)	Zürich
1934	K. Schäfer	(Austria)	Stockholm
1935	K. Schäfer	(Austria)	Budapest
1936	K. Schäfer	(Austria)	Paris
1937	F. Kaspar	(Austria)	Vienna
1938	F. Kaspar	(Austria)	Berlin
1939	G. Sharp	(Great Britain)	Budapest
1947	H. Gerschwiler	(Switzerland)	Stockholm
1948	R. Button	(U.S.A.)	Davos
1949	R. Button	(U.S.A.)	Paris
1950	R. Button	(U.S.A.)	London
1951	R. Button	(U.S.A.)	Milan
1952	R. Button	(U.S.A.)	Paris
1953	H. Jenkins	(U.S.A.)	Davos
1954	H. Jenkins	(U.S.A.)	Oslo
1955	H Jenkins	(U.S.A.)	Vienna
1956	H. Jenkins	(U.S.A.)	Garmisch-Partenkirchen
1957	D. Jenkins	(U.S.A.)	Colorado Springs
1958	D. Jenkins	(U.S.A.)	Paris
1959	D. Jenkins	(U.S.A.)	Colorado Springs

WORLD LADIES' FIGURE CHAMPIONS

Year	Name	Country	Venue
1906	M. Syers	(Great Britain)	Davos
1907	M. Syers	(Great Britain)	Vienna
1908	L. Kronberger	(Hungary)	Troppau
1909	L. Kronberger	(Hungary)	Budapest
1910	L. Kronberger	(Hungary)	Berlin
1911	L. Kronberger	(Hungary)	Vienna
1912	M. Horvath	(Hungary)	Davos
1913	M. Horvath	(Hungary)	Stockholm
1914	M. Horvath	(Hungary)	St. Moritz
1922	H. Plank	(Austria)	Stockholm
1923	H. Plank	(Austria)	Vienna
1924	H. Plank	(Austria)	Christiania
1925	J. Szabo	(Austria)	Davos
1926	J. Szabo	(Austria)	Stockholm
1927	S. Henie	(Norway)	Oslo
1928	S. Henie	(Norway)	London
1929	S. Henie	(Norway)	Budapest
1930	S. Henie	(Norway)	New York
1931	S. Henie	(Norway)	Berlin
1932	S. Henie	(Norway)	Montreal
1933	S. Henie	(Norway)	Stockholm
1934	S. Henie	(Norway)	Oslo
1935	S. Henie	(Norway)	Vienna
1936	S. Henie	(Norway)	Paris
1937	C. Colledge	(Great Britain)	London
1938	M. Taylor	(Great Britain)	Stockholm
1939	M. Taylor	(Great Britain)	Prague
1947	B. Scott	(Canada)	Stockholm
1948	B. Scott	(Canada)	Davos
1949	A. Vrzanova	(Czechoslovakia)	Paris
1950	A. Vrzanova	(Czechoslovakia)	London
1951	J. Altwegg	(Great Britain)	Milan
1952	J. du Bief	(France)	Paris
1953	T. Albright	(U.S.A.)	Davos
1954	G. Busch	(Germany)	Oslo
1955	T. Albright	(U.S.A.)	Vienna
1956	C. Heiss	(U.S.A.)	Garmisch-Partenkirchen
1957	C. Heiss	(U.S.A.)	Colorado Springs
1958	C. Heiss	(U.S.A.)	Paris
1959	C. Heiss	(U.S.A.)	Colorado Springs

WORLD DANCE CHAMPIONS

Year	Name	Country	Venue
1950	M. McGean and L. Waring	(U.S.A.)	London
1951	L. Demmy and J. Westwood	(Great Britain)	Milan
1952	L. Demmy and J. Westwood	(Great Britain)	Paris
1953	L. Demmy and J. Westwood	(Great Britain)	Davos
1954	L. Demmy and J. Westwood	(Great Britain)	Oslo
1955	L. Demmy and J. Westwood	(Great Britain)	Vienna
1956	P. Thomas and P. Weight	(Great Britain)	Garmisch-Partenkirchen
1957	C. Jones and J. Markham	(Great Britain)	Colorado Springs
1958	C. Jones and J. Markham	(Great Britain)	Paris
1959	C. Jones and D. Denny	(Great Britain)	Colorado Springs

Tenley Albright

Jeannette Altwegg   Erica Batchelor

Cecilia Colledge

ICE SKATING QUIZ

1. Who has been twice Olympic, three times world and seven times a national men's ice figure champion? (*Below.*)

2. Which three dances constitute the N.S.A. bronze medal test?

★

3. Who won the first world championship in ice figure skating?

★

4. Which British skater was awarded the M.B.E. after winning an Olympic gold medal?

★

5. Who invented the skating fox-trot?

QUIZ ANSWERS

1. Dick Button (U.S.A.). 2. Fourteen-step, European waltz and fox-trot. 3. Dr. Gilbert Fuchs, of Munich, in 1896 at St. Petersburg. 4. Jeannette Altwegg, women's Olympic ice figure skating champion in 1952. 5. Erik Van der Weyden and Eva Keats in London, 1933.

OLYMPIC MEN'S FIGURE CHAMPIONS

Year	Name	Country	Venue
1908	U. Salchow	(Sweden)	London
1920	G. Grafström	(Sweden)	Antwerp
1924	G. Grafström	(Sweden)	Chamonix
1928	G. Grafström	(Sweden)	St. Moritz
1932	K. Schäfer	(Austria)	Lake Placid
1936	K. Schäfer	(Austria)	Garmisch-Partenkirchen
1948	R. Button	(U.S.A.)	St. Moritz
1952	R. Button	(U.S.A.)	Oslo
1956	H. Jenkins	(U.S.A.)	Cortina d'Ampezzo

OLYMPIC LADIES' FIGURE CHAMPIONS

Year	Name	Country	Venue
1908	M. Syers	(Great Britain)	London
1920	M. Julienne	(Sweden)	Antwerp
1924	H. Plank	(Austria)	Chamonix
1928	S. Henie	(Norway)	St. Moritz
1932	S. Henie	(Norway)	Lake Placid
1936	S. Henie	(Norway)	Garmisch-Partenkirchen
1948	B. Scott	(Canada)	St. Moritz
1952	J. Altwegg	(Great Britain)	Oslo
1956	T. Albright	(U.S.A.)	Cortina d'Ampezzo

OLYMPIC PAIR CHAMPIONS

Year	Name	Country	Venue
1908	H. Burger and F. Hübler	(Germany)	London
1920	W. Jakobsson and W. Jakobsson	(Finland)	Antwerp
1924	A. Berger and H. Englemann	(Austria)	Chamonix
1928	P. Brunet and A. Joly	(France)	St. Moritz
1932	P. Brunet and A. Brunet	(France)	Lake Placid
1936	E. Baier and M. Herber	(Germany)	Garmisch-Partenkirchen
1948	P. Baugniet and M. Lannoy	(Belgium)	St. Moritz
1952	P. Falk and R. Falk	(Germany)	Oslo
1956	K. Oppelt and S. Schwarz	(Austria)	Cortina d'Ampezzo

WORLD PAIR CHAMPIONS

Year	Champions	Country	Venue
1908	H. Burger and F. Hübler	(Germany)	St. Petersburg
1909	J. Johnson and J. Johnson	(Great Britain)	Stockholm
1910	H. Burger and F. Hübler	(Germany)	Berlin
1911	W. Jakobsson and F. Eilers	(Finland)	Vienna
1912	J. Johnson and J. Johnson	(Great Britain)	Manchester
1913	K. Mejscrik and N. Engelmann	(Austria)	Stockholm
1914	W. Jakobsson and W. Jakobsson	(Finland)	St. Moritz
1922	H. Berger and N. Engelmann	(Austria)	Manchester
1923	W. Jakobsson and W. Jakobsson	(Finland)	Davos
1924	H. Berger and N. Engelmann	(Austria)	Christiania
1925	L. Wrede and J. Szabo	(Austria)	Vienna
1926	P. Brunet and A. Joly	(France)	Berlin
1927	L. Wrede and J. Szabo	(Austria)	Vienna
1928	P. Brunet and A. Joly	(France)	London
1929	O. Kaiser and L. Scholz	(Austria)	Budapest
1930	P. Brunet and A. Brunet	(France)	New York
1931	L. Szollas and B. Rotter	(Hungary)	Berlin
1932	P. Brunet and A. Brunet	(France)	Montreal
1933	L. Szollas and B. Rotter	(Hungary)	Stockholm
1934	L. Szollas and B. Rotter	(Hungary)	Helsingfors
1935	L. Szollas and B. Rotter	(Hungary)	Budapest
1936	E. Baier and M. Herber	(Germany)	Paris
1937	E. Baier and M. Herber	(Germany)	London
1938	E. Baier and M. Herber	(Germany)	Berlin
1939	E. Baier and M. Herber	(Germany)	Budapest
1947	P. Baugniet and M. Lannoy	(Belgium)	Stockholm
1948	P. Baugniet and M. Lannoy	(Belgium)	Davos
1949	E. Kiraly and A. Kekessy	(Hungary)	Paris
1950	M. Kennedy and K. Kennedy	(U.S.A.)	London
1951	P. Falk and R. Baran	(Germany)	Milan
1952	P. Falk and R. Falk	(Germany)	Paris
1953	J. Nicks and J. Nicks	(Great Britain)	Davos
1954	N. Bowden and F. Dafoe	(Canada)	Oslo
1955	N. Bowden and F. Dafoe	(Canada)	Vienna
1956	K. Oppelt and S. Schwarz	(Austria)	Garmisch-Partenkirchen
1957	R. Paul and B. Wagner	(Canada)	Colorado Springs
1958	R. Paul and B. Wagner	(Canada)	Paris
1959	R. Paul and B. Wagner	(Canada)	Colorado Springs

EUROPEAN PAIR CHAMPIONS

Year	Champions	Country	Venue
1930	S. Szálay and O. Organista	(Hungary)	Vienna
1931	S. Szálay and O. Organista	(Hungary)	St. Moritz
1932	P. Brunet and A. Brunet	(France)	Paris
1933	K. Zwack and I. Papez	(Austria)	London
1934	L. Szollas and B. Rotter	(Hungary)	Prague
1935	E. Baier and M. Herber	(Germany)	St. Moritz
1936	E. Baier and M. Herber	(Germany)	Berlin
1937	E. Baier and M. Herber	(Germany)	Prague
1938	E. Baier and M. Herber	(Germany)	Troppau
1939	E. Baier and M. Herber	(Germany)	Zakopane
1947	P. Baugniet and M. Lannoy	(Belgium)	Davos
1948	E. Kiraly and A. Kekesy	(Hungary)	Prague
1949	E. Kiraly and A. Kekesy	(Hungary)	Milan
1950	L. Nagy and M. Nagy	(Hungary)	Oslo
1951	P. Falk and R. Baran	(Germany)	Zürich
1952	P. Falk and R. Baran	(Germany)	Vienna
1953	J. Nicks and J. Nicks	(Great Britain)	Dortmund
1954	M. Grandjean and S. Grandjean	(Switzerland)	Bolzano
1955	L. Nagy and M. Nagy	(Hungary)	Budapest
1956	K. Oppelt and S. Schwarz	(Austria)	Paris
1957	Z. Dolezal and V. Suchankova	(Czechoslovakia)	Vienna
1958	Z. Dolezal and V. Suchankova	(Czechoslovakia)	Bratislava
1959	H. Baumler and M. Kilius	(Germany)	Davos

EUROPEAN DANCE CHAMPIONS

Year	Champions	Country	Venue
1954	L. Demmy and J. Westwood	(Great Britain)	Bolzano
1955	L. Demmy and J. Westwood	(Great Britain)	Budapest
1956	P. Thomas and P. Weight	(Great Britain)	Paris
1957	C. Jones and J. Markham	(Great Britain)	Vienna
1958	C. Jones and J. Markham	(Great Britain)	Bratislava
1959	C. Jones and D. Denny	(Great Britain)	Davos

BRITISH MEN'S FIGURE CHAMPIONS

Year	Champion	Venue
1903	*H. Torrome	Henglers
1904	*E. Syers	Princes
1905	H. Torrome	Princes
1906	H. Torrome	Princes
1907	J. Greig	Princes
1908	*A. March	Princes
1909	J. Greig	Princes
1910	J. Greig	Princes
1911	*A. March	Princes
1912	A. Cumming	Princes
1913	B. Williams	Princes
1914	A. Cumming	Princes
1921	*K. Beaumont	Manchester
1922	J. Page	Manchester
1923	J. Page	Manchester
1924	J. Page	Manchester
1925	J. Page	Manchester
1926	J. Page	Manchester
1927	J. Page	London I.C.
1928	J. Page	Manchester
1929	J. Page	London I.C.
1930	J. Page	Manchester
1931	J. Page	Oxford
1932	I. Bowhill	Purley
1933	J. Page	Bournemouth
1934	G. Sharp	Manchester
1935	G. Sharp	Westminster
1936	G. Sharp	Streatham
1937	G. Sharp	Harringay
†1937	G. Sharp	Wembley
1938	G. Sharp	Wembley
1946	G. Sharp	Wembley
†1946	A. Apfel	Wembley
1947	G. Sharp	Wembley
1949	M. Carrington	Empress Hall
1950	M. Carrington	Empress Hall
1952	A. Swan	Empress Hall
†1952	M. Booker	Streatham
1953	M. Booker	Streatham
1954	M. Booker	Streatham
1955	M. Booker	Streatham
1956	M. Booker	Streatham
1957	M. Booker	Streatham
1958	D. Clements	Nottingham

* Highest placed man was runner-up to a lady in event open also to ladies before separate contests were instituted in 1927. Ladies who came first in the years indicated by asterisks were M. Syers (1903 and 1904), D. Smith (1908 and 1911) and J. Johnson (1921).
† Second championship held during the same calendar year.

BRITISH LADIES' FIGURE CHAMPIONS

Year	Champion	Venue
1927	G. Shaw	London I.C.
1928	C. Wilson	Manchester
1929	G. Shaw	London I.C.
1930	G. Shaw	Manchester
1931	W. Field	Golders Green
1932	M. Taylor	Manchester
1933	M. Taylor	Park Lane

EUROPEAN MEN'S FIGURE CHAMPIONS

Year	Champion	Country	Venue
1891	O. Uhlig	(Germany)	Hamburg
1892	E. Engelmann	(Austria)	Vienna
1894	E. Engelmann	(Austria)	Vienna
1895	T. von Foldvary	(Hungary)	Budapest
1898	U. Salchow	(Sweden)	Trondhjem
1899	U. Salchow	(Sweden)	Davos
1900	U. Salchow	(Sweden)	Berlin
1901	G. Hügel	(Austria)	Vienna
1904	U. Salchow	(Sweden)	Davos
1905	M. Bohatsch	(Austria)	Bonn
1906	U. Salchow	(Sweden)	Davos
1907	U. Salchow	(Sweden)	Berlin
1908	E. Herz	(Austria)	Warsaw
1909	U. Salchow	(Sweden)	Budapest
1910	U. Salchow	(Sweden)	Berlin
1911	P. Thoren	(Sweden)	St. Petersburg
1912	G. Sandahl	(Sweden)	Stockholm
1913	U. Salchow	(Sweden)	Christiania
1914	F. Kachler	(Austria)	Vienna
1922	W. Böckl	(Austria)	Davos
1923	W. Böckl	(Austria)	Christiania
1924	F. Kachler	(Austria)	Davos
1925	W. Böckl	(Austria)	Triberg
1926	W. Böckl	(Austria)	Davos
1927	W. Böckl	(Austria)	Vienna
1928	W. Böckl	(Austria)	Troppau
1929	K. Schäfer	(Austria)	Davos
1930	K. Schäfer	(Austria)	Berlin
1931	K. Schäfer	(Austria)	Vienna
1932	K. Schäfer	(Austria)	Paris
1933	K. Schäfer	(Austria)	London
1934	K. Schäfer	(Austria)	Seefeld
1935	K. Schäfer	(Austria)	St. Moritz
1936	K. Schäfer	(Austria)	Berlin
1937	F. Kaspar	(Austria)	Prague
1938	F. Kaspar	(Austria)	St. Moritz
1939	G. Sharp	(G.B.)	Davos
1947	H. Gerschwiler	(Switzerland)	Davos
1948	*R. Button	(U.S.A.)	Prague
1949	E. Rada	(Austria)	Milan
1950	E. Kiraly	(Hungary)	Oslo
1951	H. Seibt	(Austria)	Zürich
1952	H. Seibt	(Austria)	Vienna
1953	C. Fassi	(Italy)	Dortmund
1954	C. Fassi	(Italy)	Bolzano
1955	A. Giletti	(France)	Budapest
1956	A. Giletti	(France)	Paris
1957	A. Giletti	(France)	Vienna
1958	K. Divin	(Czech.)	Bratislava
1959	K. Divin	(Czech.)	Davos

* Since 1948 only Europeans have been eligible.

EUROPEAN LADIES' FIGURE CHAMPIONS

Year	Champion	Country	Venue
1930	F. Burger	(Austria)	Vienna
1931	S. Henie	(Norway)	St.-Moritz
1932	S. Henie	(Norway)	Berlin
1933	S. Henie	(Norway)	London
1934	S. Henie	(Norway)	Prague
1935	S. Henie	(Norway)	St. Moritz
1936	S. Henie	(Norway)	Berlin
1937	C. Colledge	(G.B.)	Prague
1938	C. Colledge	(G.B.)	St. Moritz
1939	C. Colledge	(G.B.)	London
1947	*B. Scott	(Canada)	Davos
1948	*B. Scott	(Canada)	Prague
1949	E. Pawlik	(Austria)	Milan
1950	A. Vrzanova	(Czech.)	Oslo
1951	J. Altwegg	(G.B.)	Zürich
1952	J. Altwegg	(G.B.)	Vienna
1953	V. Osborn	(G.B.)	Dortmund
1954	G. Busch	(Germany)	Bolzano
1955	H. Eigel	(Austria)	Budapest
1956	I. Wendl	(Austria)	Paris
1957	H. Eigel	(Austria)	Vienna
1958	I. Wendl	(Austria)	Bratislava
1959	H. Walter	(Austria)	Davos

* Since 1948 only Europeans have been eligible.

British Ladies' Figure Champions—contd.

Year	Champion	Venue
1934	M. Taylor	Westminster
1935	C. Colledge	Streatham
1936	C. Colledge	Westminster
1937	C. Colledge	Westminster
†1937	C. Colledge	Wembley
1938	C. Colledge	Wembley
1946	C. Colledge	Wembley
†1946	D. Walker	Wembley
1947	J. Altwegg	Wembley
1948	J. Altwegg	Wembley
1949	J. Altwegg	Empress Hall
1950	J. Altwegg	Empress Hall
1952	V. Osborn	Empress Hall
†1952	V. Osborn	Streatham
1953	Y. Sugden	Streatham
1954	Y. Sugden	Streatham
1955	Y. Sugden	Streatham
1956	E. Batchelor	Streatham
1957	D. Peach	Streatham
1958	P. Pauley	Nottingham

† Second championship held during the same calendar year.

ICE SKATING QUIZ

1. Name the world's ruling authority in amateur ice skating.

*

2. Who has won the world pair skating championships both on ice and rollers?

*

3. Are there any ice rinks in South Africa?

*

4. Name the world's oldest national skating federation.

5. Who is the only British skater to have won a world ice figure title twice during the last fifty years?

QUIZ ANSWERS

1. The International Skating Union. 2. Paul and Ria Falk (Germany), on ice in 1951 and 1952 and on rollers in 1951. 3. Yes, two; at Johannesburg and Durban. 4. The National Skating Association of Great Britain, formed in 1879. 5. Megan Taylor, in 1938 and 1939.

BRITISH PAIR CHAMPIONS

		Venue
1914	J. Johnson and J. Johnson	Edinburgh
1921	K. Beaumont and K. Beaumont	Manchester
1922	K. Beaumont and K. Beaumont	Manchester
1923	J. Page and E. Muckelt	Manchester
1924	J. Page and E. Muckelt	Manchester
1925	J. Page and E. Muckelt	Manchester
1926	J. Page and E. Muckelt	Manchester
1927	J. Page and E. Muckelt	London I.C.
1928	J. Page and E. Muckelt	Manchester
1929	J. Page and E. Muckelt	London I.C.
1930	J. Page and E. Muckelt	Manchester
1931	J. Page and E. Muckelt	Oxford
1932	K. Mackenzie and K. Mackenzie	Purley
1933	R. Murdoch and M. Phillips	Bournemouth
1934	L. Cliff and V. Supple	Birmingham
1935	L. Cliff and L. Cliff	Crossmyloof
1936	L. Cliff and L. Cliff	Manchester
1937	L. Cliff and L. Cliff	Harringay
†1937	L. Cliff and L. Cliff	Wembley
1938	L. Cliff and L. Cliff	Wembley
1946	D. Silverthorne and W. Silverthorne	Wembley
†1946	D. Silverthorne and W. Silverthorne	Wembley
1947	J. Nicks and J. Nicks	Wembley
1948	J. Nicks and J. Nicks	Wembley
1949	J. Nicks and J. Nicks	Empress Hall
1950	J. Nicks and J. Nicks	Empress Hall
1952	J. Nicks and J. Nicks	Empress Hall
†1952	J. Nicks and J. Nicks	Streatham
1953	R. Hudson and J. Higson	Streatham
1954	R. Hudson and V. Higson	Streatham
1955	A. Holles and J. Coates	Streatham
1956	A. Holles and J. Coates	Streatham
1957	A. Holles and J. Coates	Streatham
1958	A. Holles and J. Coates	Nottingham

† Second championship held during the same calendar year.

BRITISH DANCE CHAMPIONS

		Venue
1937	R. Wilkie and D. Wallis	Richmond
1938	R. Wilkie and D. Wallis	Westminster
1939	R. Wilkie and D. Wallis	Westminster
1947	A. Edmonds and P. Borrajo	Wembley
1948	A. Edmonds and P. Borrajo	Wembley
1949	R. Hudson and S. Cooke	Wembley
1950	R. Hudson and S. Cooke	Wembley
1951	J. Slater and J. Dewhirst	Nottingham
1952	J. Slater and J. Dewhirst	Nottingham
1953	J. Slater and J. Dewhirst	Nottingham
1954	L. Demmy and J. Westwood	Nottingham
†1954	L. Demmy and J. Westwood	Nottingham
1955	P. Thomas and P. Weight	Nottingham
1956	C. Jones and J. Markham	Nottingham
1957	C. Jones and J. Markham	Nottingham
1958	C. Jones and D. Denny	Nottingham

† Second championship held during the same calendar year.

NORTH AMERICAN PAIR CHAMPIONS

1923	B. McLennan and D. Jenkins	(Canada)
1925	N. Niles and T. Blanchard	(U.S.A.)
1927	C. Bangs and M. McDougall	(Canada)
1929	M. Wilson and C. Wilson	(Canada)
1931	M. Wilson and C. Wilson	(Canada)
1933	M. Wilson and C. Samuel	(Canada)
1935	G. Hill and M. Vinson	(U.S.A.)
1937	R. McCreath and V. Clarke	(Canada)
1939	B. Fox and J. Tozzer	(U.S.A.)
1941	R. McCreath and E. O'Meara	(Canada)
1947	W. Diestelmeyer and S. Morrow	(Canada)
1949	P. Kennedy and K. Kennedy	(U.S.A.)
1951	P. Kennedy and K. Kennedy	(U.S.A.)
1953	N. Bowden and F. Dafoe	(Canada)
1955	N. Bowden and F. Dafoe	(Canada)
1957	R. Paul and B. Wagner	(Canada)
1959	R. Paul and B. Wagner	(Canada)

Courtney Jones and
Doreen Denny

WORLD MEN'S SPEED CHAMPIONS
Decided over four distances: 500, 1,500, 5,000 and 10,000 metres

			Venue					Venue
1893	J. Eden	(Holland)	Amsterdam		1929	C. Thunberg	(Finland)	Oslo
1895	J. Eden	(Holland)	Hamar		1930	M. Staksrud	(Norway)	Oslo
1896	J. Eden	(Holland)	St. Petersburg		1931	C. Thunberg	(Finland)	Helsingfors
1897	T. McCullock	(Canada)	Montreal		1932	I. Ballangrud	(Norway)	Lake Placid
1898	P. Oestlund	(Norway)	Davos		1933	H. Engnestangen	(Norway)	Trondhjem
1899	P. Oestlund	(Norway)	Berlin		1934	B. Evensen	(Norway)	Helsingfors
1900	E. Engelsaas	(Norway)	Christiania		1935	M. Staksrud	(Norway)	Oslo
1901	F. Wathén	(Finland)	Stockholm		1936	J. Ballangrud	(Norway)	Davos
1904	P. Sinnerud	(Norway)	Christiania		1937	M. Staksrud	(Norway)	Oslo
1905	D. Koning	(Holland)	Groningen		1938	J. Ballangrud	(Norway)	Davos
1908	O. Mathisen	(Norway)	Davos		1939	B. Wasenius	(Finland)	Helsingfors
1909	O. Mathisen	(Norway)	Christiania		1947	L. Parkkinen	(Finland)	Oslo
1910	N. Strunikoff	(Russia)	Helsingfors		1948	O. Lundberg	(Norway)	Helsinki
1911	N. Strunikoff	(Russia)	Trondhjem		1949	K. Pajor	(Hungary)	Oslo
1912	O. Mathisen	(Norway)	Christiania		1950	H. Andersen	(Norway)	Eskilstuna
1913	O. Mathisen	(Norway)	Helsingfors		1951	H. Andersen	(Norway)	Davos
1914	O. Mathisen	(Norway)	Christiania		1952	H. Andersen	(Norway)	Hamar
1922	H. Ström	(Norway)	Christiania		1953	O. Goncharenko	(Russia)	Helsinki
1923	C. Thunberg	(Finland)	Stockholm		1954	B. Schilkov	(Russia)	Sapporo
1924	R. Larsen	(Norway)	Helsingfors		1955	S. Ericsson	(Sweden)	Moscow
1925	C. Thunberg	(Finland)	Oslo		1956	O. Goncharenko	(Russia)	Oslo
1926	I. Ballangrud	(Norway)	Trondhjem		1957	K. Johannesen	(Norway)	Ostersund
1927	B. Evensen	(Norway)	Tammerfors		1958	O. Goncharenko	(Russia)	Helsinki
1928	C. Thunberg	(Finland)	Davos		1959	J. Jaervinen	(Finland)	Oslo

NORTH AMERICAN MEN'S FIGURE CHAMPIONS

1923	S. Badger	(U.S.A.)
1925	M. Rogers	(Canada)
1927	M. Rogers	(Canada)
1929	M. Wilson	(Canada)
1931	M. Wilson	(Canada)
1933	M. Wilson	(Canada)
1935	M. Wilson	(Canada)
1937	M. Wilson	(Canada)
1939	M. Wilson	(Canada)
1941	R. McGrath	(Canada)
1947	R. Button	(U.S.A.)
1949	R. Button	(U.S.A.)
1951	R. Button	(U.S.A.)
1953	H. Jenkins	(U.S.A.)
1955	H. Jenkins	(U.S.A.)
1957	D. Jenkins	(U.S.A.)
1959	D. Jackson	(Canada)

WORLD LADIES' SPEED CHAMPIONS
Decided over four distances: 500, 1,000, 3,000 and 5,000 metres

			Venue					Venue
1936	K. Klein	(U.S.A.)	Stockholm		1952	L. Selichowa	(Russia)	Kokkola
1937	L. Schou-Nilsen	(Norway)	Davos		1953	K. Schegoleeva	(Russia)	Lillehammer
1938	L. Schou-Nilsen	(Norway)	Oslo		1954	L. Selichowa	(Russia)	Ostersund
1939	V. Lesche	(Finland)	Tammerfors		1955	R. Shukowa	(Russia)	Kuopio
1947	V. Lesche	(Finland)	Drammen		1956	S. Kondakowa	(Russia)	Kvarnsveden
1948	M. Isakova	(Russia)	Turku		1957	I. Artamonova	(Russia)	Imatra
1949	M. Isakova	(Russia)	Konigsberg		1958	I. Artamonova	(Russia)	Kristinehamn
1950	M. Isakova	(Russia)	Moscow		1959	T. Rilova	(Russia)	Sverdlovsk
1951	E. Huttunen	(Finland)	Eskilstuna					

NORTH AMERICAN LADIES' FIGURE CHAMPIONS

1923	T. Blanchard	(U.S.A.)
1925	B. Loughran	(U.S.A.)
1927	B. Loughran	(U.S.A.)
1929	C. Wilson	(Canada)
1931	C. Samuel	(Canada)
1933	C. Samuel	(Canada)
1935	C. Samuel	(Canada)
1937	M. Vinson	(U.S.A.)
1939	M. Thacker	(Canada)
1941	M. Thacker	(Canada)
1945	B. Scott	(Canada)
1947	B. Scott	(Canada)
1949	Y. Sherman	(U.S.A.)
1951	S. Klopfer	(U.S.A.)
1953	T. Albright	(U.S.A.)
1955	T. Albright	(U.S.A.)
1957	C. Heiss	(U.S.A.)
1959	C. Heiss	(U.S.A.)

EUROPEAN MEN'S SPEED CHAMPIONS

			Venue					Venue
1892	F. Schilling	(Austria)	Vienna		1927	B. Evesen	(Norway)	Stockholm
1893	R. Ericson	(Sweden)	Berlin		1928	C. Thunberg	(Finland)	Oslo
1895	A. Naess	(Norway)	Budapest		1929	I. Ballangrud	(Norway)	Davos
1896	J. Seyler	(Germany)	Hamburg		1930	I. Ballangrud	(Norway)	Trondhjem
1897	J. Seyler	(Germany)	Amsterdam		1931	C. Thunberg	(Finland)	Stockholm
1898	G. Estlander	(Finland)	Helsingfors		1932	C. Thunberg	(Finland)	Davos
1899	P. Oestlund	(Norway)	Davos		1933	I. Ballangrud	(Norway)	Wiborg
1900	P. Oestlund	(Norway)	Czorba-See		1934	M. Staksrud	(Norway)	Hamar
1901	R. Gundersen	(Norway)	Trondhjem		1935	K. Wazulek	(Austria)	Helsingfors
1902	I. Schwartz	(Norway)	Davos		1936	I. Ballangrud	(Norway)	Oslo
1904	R. Gundersen	(Norway)	Davos		1937	M. Staksrud	(Norway)	Davos
1905	I. Vicander	(Finland)	Stockholm		1938	C. Mathisen	(Norway)	Oslo
1906	R. Gundersen	(Norway)	Davos		1939	A. Berzins	(Latvia)	Riga
1907	M. Oeholm	(Sweden)	Davos		1947	A. Seyffarth	(Sweden)	Stockholm
1908	M. Oeholm	(Sweden)	Klagenfurt		1948	R. Liakley	(Norway)	Hamar
1909	O. Mathisen	(Norway)	Budapest		1949	S. Farstad	(Norway)	Davos
1910	N. Strunikoff	(Russia)	Wiborg		1950	H. Andersen	(Norway)	Helsinki
1911	N. Strunikoff	(Russia)	Hamar		1951	H. Andersen	(Norway)	Oslo
1912	O. Mathisen	(Norway)	Stockholm		1952	H. Andersen	(Norway)	Ostersund
1913	W. Ipolitoff	(Russia)	St. Petersburg		1953	K. Broekman	(Holland)	Hamar
1914	O. Mathisen	(Norway)	Berlin		1954	B. Schilkov	(Russia)	Davos
1922	C. Thunberg	(Finland)	Helsingfors		1955	S. Ericsson	(Sweden)	Falun
1923	H. Ström	(Norway)	Hamar		1956	E. Grischin	(Russia)	Helsinki
1924	R. Larsen	(Norway)	Oslo		1957	O. Goncharenko	(Russia)	Oslo
1925	O. Polacsek	(Austria)	St. Moritz		1958	O. Goncharenko	(Russia)	Eskilstuna
1926	J. Skutnabb	(Norway)	Chamonix		1959	K. Johannesen	(Norway)	Gothenburg

Johnny Cronshey

ICE SKATING QUIZ

1. Who attracted world-wide interest in skating by her films after winning three Olympic and ten consecutive world titles?

*

2. How many compulsory figures are there in the internationally recognised schedule?

*

3. When was ice skating first included in the Olympic Games?

*

4. Who has won the world ice dance championship the most times?

*

5. What is the origin of the term "axel jump"?

*

6. Who is known as the patron saint of skaters?

QUIZ ANSWERS

1. Sonja Henie. 2. Forty-one. 3. In 1908, held in London. 4. Lawrence Demmy and Jean Westwood (Great Britain), five years in succession from 1951. 5. Named after its Norwegian originator, Axel Paulsen. 6. St. Lydwina of Schiedam, Holland, who sustained a broken rib while skating at the age of sixteen.

Yvonne Sugden

OLYMPIC SPEED CHAMPIONS

500 METRES

			Venue
1924	C. Jewthaw	(U.S.A.)	Chamonix
1928	G. Thunberg	(Finland)	St. Moritz
1932	J. Shea	(U.S.A.)	Lake Placid
1936	I. Ballangrud	(Norway)	Garmisch-Partenkirchen
1948	F. Helgesen	(Norway)	St. Moritz
1952	K. Henry	(U.S.A.)	Oslo
1956	E. Grischin	(Russia)	Cortina d'Ampezzo

1,500 METRES

1924	G. Thunberg	(Finland)	Chamonix
1928	G. Thunberg	(Finland)	St. Moritz
1932	J. Shea	(U.S.A.)	Lake Placid
1936	C. Mathisen	(Norway)	Garmisch-Partenkirchen
1948	F. Farstad	(Norway)	St. Moritz
1952	H. Andersen	(Norway)	Oslo
1956	E. Grischin (Russia) / J. Michailov (Russia)		Cortina d'Ampezzo

5,000 METRES

1924	C. Thunberg	(Finland)	Chamonix
1928	I. Ballangrud	(Norway)	St. Moritz
1932	I. Jaffee	(U.S.A.)	Lake Placid
1936	I. Ballangrud	(Norway)	Garmisch-Partenkirchen
1948	A. Liakley	(Norway)	St. Moritz
1952	H. Andersen	(Norway)	Oslo
1956	B. Shilkov	(Russia)	Cortina d'Ampezzo

10,000 METRES

1924	J. Skutnabb	(Finland)	Chamonix
1932	I. Jaffee	(U.S.A.)	Lake Placid
1936	I. Ballangrud	(Norway)	Garmisch-Partenkirchen
1948	A. Seyffarth	(Sweden)	St. Moritz
1952	H. Andersen	(Norway)	Oslo
1956	S. Ericsson	(Sweden)	Cortina d'Ampezzo

BRITISH NATIONAL ICE SPEED LEAGUE WINNERS

1933	Streatham	1950	Aldwych	1955	Aldwych
1934	Streatham	1951	Aldwych	1956	Nottingham
1937	Streatham	1952	Aldwych	1957	Birmingham
1938	Southampton	1953	Nottingham	1958	Birmingham
1939	Aldwych	1954	Aldwych	1959	Birmingham

WORLD MEN'S SPEED RECORDS

			Time		Venue
500 metres	E. Grischin	(Russia)	40.2 s.	1956	Misurina
1,000 metres	E. Grischin	(Russia)	1 m. 22.8 s.	1955	Alma Ata
1,500 metres	E. Grischin	(Russia)	2 m. 8.6 s.	1956	Misurina
	J. Michailov	(Russia)	2 m. 8.6 s.	1956	Misurina
3,000 metres	A. Huiskes	(Holland)	4 m. 40.2 s.	1953	Davos
5,000 metres	B. Shilkov	(Russia)	7 m. 45.6 s.	1955	Alma Ata
10,000 metres	H. Andersen	(Norway)	16 m. 32.6 s.	1952	Hamar

WORLD LADIES' SPEED RECORDS

			Time		Venue
500 metres	T. Rilova	(Russia)	45.6 s.	1955	Alma Ata
1,000 metres	T. Rilova	(Russia)	1 m. 33.4 s.	1955	Alma Ata
1,500 metres	K. Schegolewa	(Russia)	2 m. 25.5 s.	1953	Alma Ata
3,000 metres	R. Zhukova	(Russia)	5 m. 13.8 s.	1953	Alma Ata
5,000 metres	R. Zhukova	(Russia)	9 m. 1.6 s.	1953	Alma Ata

OLYMPIC SPEED RECORDS

			Time		Venue
500 metres	E. Grischin	(Russia)	40.2 s.	1956	Misurina
1,500 metres	E. Grischin	(Russia)	2 m. 8.6 s.	1956	Misurina
	J. Michailov	(Russia)	2 m. 8.6 s.	1956	Misurina
5,000 metres	B. Shilkov	(Russia)	7 m. 48.7 s.	1956	Misurina
10,000 metres	S. Ericsson	(Sweden)	16 m. 35.9 s.	1956	Misurina

BRITISH SPEED RECORDS

			Time		Venue
¼ mile	R. Wyman		35.0 s.	1933	Rickmansworth
½ mile	J. Dymock		1 m. 18.9 s.	1958	Ayr
1 mile	F. Dix		2 m. 27.2 s.	1912	Cowbit Wash
1½ miles	N. Holwell		4 m. 12.2 s.	1952	Bury Fen
3 miles	J. Hearn		8 m. 52.8 s.	1956	Ayr
500 metres	J. Cronshey		42.9 s.	1956	Misurina
1,000 metres	J. Cronshey		1 m. 35.5 s.	1947	Lillehammer
1,500 metres	J. Cronshey		2 m. 15.0 s.	1956	Misurina
3,000 metres	N. Holwell		4 m. 57.1 s.	1953	Gjovik
5,000 metres	J. Cronshey		8 m. 10.1 s.	1956	Misurina
10,000 metres	J. Cronshey		17 m. 5.6 s.	1956	Misurina

BRITISH SPEED CHAMPIONS

OUTDOOR
ONE-AND-A-HALF MILES

		Venue
1880	F. Norman	Welsh Harp
1881	F. Norman	Lingay Fen
1887	R. Wallis	Cowbit
1889	W. Loveday	Lingay Fen
1890	W. Loveday	Lingay Fen
1891	W. Housden	Swavesey
1892	J. Aveling	Lingay Fen
1895	A. Tebbit	Swavesey
1900	A. Tebbit	Littleport
1902	A. Tebbit	Lingay Fen
1905	A. Tebbit	Lingay Fen
1908	F. Dix	Lingay Fen
1909	F. Dix	Lingay Fen
1912	F. Dix	Lingay Fen
1927	C. Horn	Lingay Fen
1929	C. Horn	Swavesey
1933	C. Horn	Lingay Fen
†1933	C. Horn	Lingay Fen
1947	H. Howes	Bury Fen
1951	R. Sheer	Bury Fen
1952	N. Holwell	Bury Fen
1954	N. Holwell	Cambridge
1955	N. Holwell	Bury Fen
1956	J. Hearn	Bury Fen
1959	J. Dymock	Swavesey

†Event held twice during the same calendar year.

INDOOR ONE MILE

		Venue
1930	W. Broomhall	Richmond
1931	J. Brown	Streatham
1932	W. Wallace	Streatham
1933	R. Wyman	Streatham
1934	T. Grace	Oxford
1935	K. Kennedy	Streatham
1936	W. Fullerton	Streatham
1937	K. Kennedy	Harringay
1938	S. Rawlins	Richmond
1939	S. Rawlins	Southampton
1946	H. Howes	Richmond
1947	G. Purvis	Richmond
1948	G. Welham	Durham
1949	N. Holwell	Birmingham
1950	N. Holwell	Queen's
1951	H. Howes	Richmond
1952	T. Laming	Crossmyloof
1953	T. Laming	Richmond
1954	G. Welham	Nottingham
1955	J. Hearn	Crossmyloof
1956	A. Connell	Crossmyloof
1957	I. Luke	Ayr
1958	B. Grummitt	Nottingham
1959	J. Dymock	Nottingham

INDOOR HALF-MILE

		Venue
1932	W. Broomhall	Richmond
1933	R. Wyman	Purley
1934	T. Grace	Purley
1935	K. Kennedy	Streatham
1936	H. Tipper	Richmond
1937	K. Kennedy	Harringay
1938	S. Rawlins	Southampton
1939	S. Rawlins	Richmond
1946	H. Howes	Wembley
1947	F. Cosham	Wembley
†1947	G. Purvis	Richmond
1949	N. Holwell	Brighton
1950	H. Howes	Wembley
†1950	G. Nichol	Brighton
1952	G. Welham	Bournemouth
1953	N. Holwell	Southampton
1954	T. Malkin	Birmingham
1955	A. Connell	Crossmyloof
1956	C. Johnson	Richmond
1957	I. Luke	Crossmyloof
1958	B. Grummitt	Crossmyloof
1959	A. Hunt	Crossmyloof

†Event held twice during the same calendar year.

INDOOR QUARTER-MILE

		Venue
1947	G. Welham	Streatham
†1947	D. Blundell	Richmond
1948	F. Cosham	Richmond
1949	G. Welham	Empress Hall
1951	G. Nichol	Richmond
1952	J. Dymock	Richmond
†1952	J. Dymock	Richmond
1954	H. Howes	Southampton
1955	C. Johnson	Richmond
†1955	I. Luke	Crossmyloof
1957	I. Luke	Richmond
†1957	C. Johnson	Southampton
1959	J. Dymock	Richmond

†Event held twice during the same calendar year.

Compiled by Howard Bass
Editor: The Skater and Skier

Ski-ing

THE HISTORY OF SKI-ING

Competitive ski-ing as now practised is a modern sport, but the world's first skiers probably existed five thousand years ago. The Höting ski, the oldest to be discovered, is in fact calculated by experts to date that far back, having been preserved through the ages in a peat bog. A fragment of another, salvaged in Finland, is believed to be two thousand years old, and there is further historical evidence in a Stone Age rock carving of a man on skis found at Rödey, in Norway. There are many references in the ancient Scandinavian sagas, which describe Ullr as the god of ski-ing, and in literature of the sixth century. There seems little doubt that the sport's origin may be attributed to the Scandinavian area.

In 1206, Hakon Hakonsön, the two-year-old son of King Sverre of Norway, was saved from enemy capture by two skiers who carried the child across snow-clad mountains. These king's supporters were known as "Birch Legs" and their feat is still commemorated today by Norway's annual Birch Leg marathon ski race from Lillehammer to Rena, across the same route as that used more than 750 years previously by the young prince's liberators.

Modern ski-ing may be said to originate from the invention of ski bindings around 1880 by a Norwegian, Sondre Nordheim, often described as "the father of ski-ing". His first big demonstration to his compatriots, by ski-ing from his home in Mordegal to Oslo in 1868, inspired the Winter Olympic Games organisers to select the same course, a distance of 115 miles, over which the Olympic flame was carried by skiers in relays to Oslo in 1952.

Military ski races of a kind took place in Norway as early as 1767, but the world's first recorded civilian contest was held at Tromso, Norway, in 1843. As an organised sport ski-ing is rather less than a hundred years old and Norway's and the world's first ski club, the Trysil, was not founded until 1861.

Ski-jumping competitions originated in 1879 at Huseby, near Oslo, then called Christiania, and the pioneer skiers from this region invented the telemark and christiania turns which revolutionised early technique. Norwegian emigrants subsequently introduced ski-ing to most other countries during the late nineteenth century.

By a curious paradox the English, who have to go to other countries to find suitable terrain, played a major part in the sport's development. E. C. Richardson was the first to devise systematic proficiency tests in 1901 and, two years later, he founded the Ski Club of Great Britain which, surprisingly, was the world's first official national ski-ing administration. The National Ski Association of America was instituted in 1904, the Norwegian Ski Association in 1908 and the world governing body, the *Fédération Internationale de Ski* or F.I.S., in 1910.

Other Englishmen, Vivian Caulfeild and Arnold Lunn, were prominently active soon after this, using their influence with the pen as well as by practical demonstration. The first important British ski race was contested at Montana in 1911 for a challenge cup presented by Lord Roberts of Kandahar.

Lunn, already a pioneer of straight "downhill" racing, later invented the modern slalom race. In this, a series of pairs of flags, called "gates", are expertly positioned so that competitors, by ski-ing through them in turn, are tested more for skill in pace checking and turning technique than for sheer speed.

The first slalom race was held at Mürren in 1922 for the Alpine Ski Challenge Cup. Two years later the Kandahar Ski Club was formed and another Englishman, F. W. Edlin, founded the Parsenn Derby ski race at Davos.

In March, 1927, Lunn and a successful Austrian instructor, Hannes Schneider, met in the Austrian Arlberg and together devised the Arlberg-Kandahar ski racing competition, first held in 1928 at St. Anton and now the most important international event apart from the world and Olympic championships.

There are two distinct forms of competitive ski-ing, each requiring its own particular kind of terrain and named after the area of its development. *Alpine* events comprise downhill and slalom racing and *Nordic* events consist of ski jumping and cross-country (*langlauf*) racing.

Senior Alpine championships today usually include three events—downhill, slalom and giant slalom, and a fourth title, decided on a points basis, is awarded to the best all-round (*combined*) performer in the three—who, as such, may not necessarily win any of them.

The primary aim in a downhill race is to get from the start at the top to the finish at the bottom in the quickest possible time, choosing the most suitable course for the purpose. Speeds above fifty miles an hour are quite possible in this event.

A slalom course is appreciably shorter and less steep than the downhill. Forty gates are used in championships and any gate missed means disqualification unless the competitor retraces his steps to have another go. The minimum distance between the two flags of each gate should be ten feet. Each pair of flags is distinguished by red, yellow or blue colours. Each entrant has two runs, either over the same course or two different courses, and the times of both runs count as they are added together.

The giant slalom, not always included in the less important contests, is something of a compromise between the ordinary slalom and the downhill race. The course is longer than the ordinary slalom and has wider gates. Each contestant has only one run.

In early Alpine races competitors originally started simultaneously, but this was soon found to be impractical and the "first past the flag" principle was abolished in favour of the present system whereby racers start one at a time, at regular intervals, usually each minute.

Holding both hands on the same stick, known as "stick riding", is not allowed by the rules of ski racing. "Tobogganing" on skis or deliberately slithering downhill on part of the body are not permitted and, though one may at no time descend completely ski-less, a competitor who loses a ski during a race is permitted to finish the course on the other without being penalised.

In Nordic long-distance cross-country running the most favoured senior championship distances nowadays are 18 kilometres and 50 kilometres, approximately equivalent to eleven and thirty miles respectively. There are also Nordic relay races. Nordic courses are usually circular, starting and finishing at the same spot without involving any appreciable uphill ski-ing. These events call for a high degree of hardiness, stamina and training and are practised mostly in Scandinavian territory, which is usually more suitable and different from that used for Alpine racing. For this reason Nordic and Alpine events are not frequently held at the same venue.

The other branch of Nordic events, ski jumping, is by far the most spectacular from the onlooker's point of view. Longer, heavier and wider skis than normal are used for competitive jumping. The famous Holmenkollen Hill near Oslo is to ski jumpers what Wimbledon is to tennis players and events here annually attract crowds of more than 100,000. Ski jumping is a highly specialised art and only practised by a minority of skiers in the same way that high diving is a speciality performed by only a few swimmers. Ski jumps are judged by a panel, normally of five officials, who take style as well as the length of a jump into account.

The first world championships in Nordic events were held at Zakopane, Poland, in 1929. The most notable pre-war jumper, Birger Ruud (Norway), won three world and two Olympic titles. Finns have successfully challenged Norway more recently, winning both the 1954 world and 1956 Olympic honours, but ski jumping has remained largely a Norwegian prerogative.

An Anglo-Norwegian enterprise enabled Londoners to watch top-class ski jumping on Hampstead Heath in 1950 and 1951, when sixty tons of snow in insulated crates were specially imported from Norway.

Persistent persuasion led the F.I.S. to recognise downhill contests officially and to organise the first world championships in Alpine events at Mürren in 1931, when Walter Prager (Switzerland) and Esmé MacKinnon (Great Britain) won the men's and women's titles. Since the war the world championships, both Alpine and Nordic, have been held quadrennially.

Olympic inclusion dates from 1924, when skiers joined ice skaters, ice hockey players and bob-sledders in the first separate Winter Olympic Games at Chamonix. Norwegians were exclusively triumphant, Thorleif Haug being outstanding as winner of both the 18 kilometres and the 50 kilometres races, while Jacob Tullin-Thams was the best jumper.

In the second meeting at St. Moritz the Norwegians were again very successful, with Alf Anderson supreme in the jumping, but Per Hedlund won the 50 kilometres for Sweden.

SKI-ING QUIZ

1. What is the name given to the devices for attaching the ski boot to the ski?

⋆

2. What, in ski-ing parlance, is a "stem"?

⋆

3. Which former British ski-ing champion is the son of a well-known actor?

⋆

4. Has London ever staged official ski jumping contests?

⋆

5. Name the world controlling organisation for competitive ski-ing.

⋆

6. What do yellow flags in the snow signify?

⋆

7. How many "gates" are there usually in a senior slalom course?

⋆

8. Is a competitor disqualified if he loses a ski during a race?

⋆

9. What German word now in common use describes a forward-leaning position and also a style of ski trousers tapering down to the boot?

⋆

10. Which Alpine competition is regarded as next in international importance to the world and Olympic championships?

QUIZ ANSWERS

1. Ski bindings. 2. A braking position; the name given to a turn which is used to brake forward motion. 3. Noël Harrison, 1953 champion, the son of Rex Harrison. 4. Yes, at Hampstead Heath in 1950 and 1951 on snow specially imported in crates from Norway. 5. Fédération Internationale de Ski (F.I.S.), formed in 1910. 6. Danger, denoting that the area is unsafe for ski-ing. 7. Forty. 8. No; it is permissible to finish the course on one ski. 9. Vorlage. 10. The Arlberg-Kandahar.

SKI-ING QUIZ

1. In what year was ski-ing first incorporated in the Winter Olympic Games?

*

2. What is the ideal length of ski sticks?

*

3. Who has been British women's champion most times?

*

4. Which famous Army general gave his name to a ski-ing cup?

*

5. Why is the "christiania" turn so called?

*

6. Name the world's oldest national ski-ing administrative body.

*

7. Where and when were the first world Alpine ski racing championships held?

*

8. What is the best wood used in ski manufacturing?

*

9. Who won the first women's world Alpine ski racing championship?

*

10. Which Italian ski-ing resort has staged the Winter Olympic Games?

QUIZ ANSWERS

1. In 1924 at Chamonix. 2. Approximately equal to the height of the armpit. 3. Isobel Roe, 1938, 1939, 1948 and 1949. 4. Field Marshal Lord Montgomery of Alamein, formerly president of the Kandahar Ski Club. 5. Named after the original name for Oslo, where ski-ing pioneers first devised this turn. 6. The Ski Club of Great Britain, founded in 1903. 7. Mürren in 1931. 8. Hickory, because of its superior strength. Ash, birch and maple are also used, are lighter and less durable. 9. Esmé MacKinnon (Great Britain) at Mürren in 1931. 10. Cortina d'Ampezzo, in 1956.

The History of Ski-ing—contd.

The ski-ing honours still remained a monopoly for northern Europe in the 1932 Games at Lake Placid and for the second time Norway's versatile Johan Gröttumsbraaten was combined champion as best all-round performer.

Alpine events were added for the first time in 1936 at Garmisch-Partenkirchen, the two best performers both being Germans, Franz Pfnür (men) and Christel Cranz (women). Fraulein Cranz was thus the first women's ski-ing Olympic gold medallist.

St. Moritz was host for the first post-war "little Olympiad" in 1948, which reflected a growing Swedish strength in cross-country racing, with gold medals for Martin Lundström and Nils Karlsson. Norway's Peter Hugsted took the jumping title.

It was France's year in the Alpine disciplines, with Henri Oreiller claiming new attention as downhill and combined winner. Gretchen Fraser won America's first-ever gold ski-ing medal for coming first in the women's slalom and Trude Jochum-Beiser likewise claimed Austria's first honour as women's combined champion.

Oslo lent a new character to the 1952 meeting. Being in the first capital city to organise the Winter Olympics, there were more pleasure-seeking casual spectators to augment the enthusiasts who travel specially to a winter sports resort.

Now attracting more interest than ever before, the women's Alpine events brought success to a 19-year-old American, Andrea Mead-Lawrence, in both slalom and giant slalom, Austria's Trude Jochum-Beiser adding the downhill to her previous Olympic victory.

Zeno Colò (Italy) and Othmar Schneider (Austria) were successful in the men's downhill and slalom respectively and a historical note was added when Stein Eriksen, in the giant slalom, won Norway's only gold medal to date in Alpine ski-ing.

Although outclassed by many "all-season" skiers, the British representatives strove valiantly against overwhelming odds. Notable among the British women were Hilary Laing, Sheena Mackintosh, Fiona Campbell and Vora Mackintosh. The highest placed men were John Boyagis, Rupert de Larrinaga and Noël Harrison.

An innovation in 1952 was the first Olympic ladies' cross-country race, decided over 10 kilometres, won by Lydia Wideman of Finland. Her compatriot, Veikko Hakulinen, came first in the men's 50 kilometres and the Finns also won the men's 4 by 10 kilometres relay. Norway's Hallgeir Brenden held off three other Finns to claim the 18 kilometres.

The jumping at Holmenkollen came as a fitting, spectacular finale to these memorable Games, the local Arnfinn Bergmann winning the special jumping event and his fellow countryman, Simon Slättvik, taking the combined Nordic title. Four years later the VIIth Winter Olympic Games went to Cortina d'Ampezzo in Italy and attracted a record of 947 competitors from 32 nations. The outstanding individual was a 21-year-old Austrian from Kitzbühel, Toni Sailer, who won all three Alpine events impressively and was hailed by many as the world's supreme skier. In the women's events Switzerland gained two awards through Madeleine Berthod (downhill) and Renée Collard (slalom). The best British women were Adeline Pryor, Zandra Nowell, Susan Holmes, Jocelyn Wardrop-Moore and Jean Stanford, the men's leading performers being Charlach Mackintosh, Nigel Gardner, Noël Harrison, Peter Seilern, Sandy Whitelaw and Robin Hooper.

In their first appearance in the Games the Russians provided perhaps a foretaste of things to come, with victories in the Nordic relay race and by Ljuborj Kezyreva in the women's 10 kilometres. In the other cross-country events Sixten Jernberg of Sweden was the best performer, earning a gold medal for the 50 kilometres and two silver and one bronze besides. Finland's Antii Hyvarinen stole the jumping honours.

In recent years British interest and participation in Nordic races, hitherto very small, has increased as a result of ski training in the Services and a plucky contingent of British Army competitors entered the 1956 Olympic cross-country races, the most successful being Andrew Morgan, Maurice Gover, John Moore, James Spencer, Aubrey Fielder, Thomas Cairney, Dominik Graham and Richard Aylmer.

The extent to which Alpine racing, the "junior partner" of competitive ski-ing, has gradually superseded the longer established Nordic disciplines in general interest underlines a significant trend in progress and was aptly summed up by Sir Arnold Lunn (knighted in 1955 "for services to British ski-ing and Anglo-Swiss relations") when he wrote in *The Skater and Skier*:

"Today the Alpine forms of competition are so incomparably more popular and carry so much more prestige than the Scandinavian that countries take rank according to their prowess in the Alpine disciplines."

Bibliography: *The Magic of Ski-ing* (Howard Bass), *Ski-ing for Beginners* (F. Broderman and G. A. McPartlin), *Look and Learn* (Tomm Murstad), *A History of Ski-ing*, *The Story of Ski-ing* and *Ski-ing for Beginners* (Sir Arnold Lunn), *The Ski Runs of Switzerland* and *The Ski Runs of Austria* (James Riddell), *The British Ski Year Book*, *The Skater and Skier* magazine.

WORLD CHAMPIONS: MEN'S NORDIC EVENTS

	18 KILOMETRES	50 KILOMETRES	JUMPING	COMBINED
1929	V. Saarinen (*Finland*)	A. Knuuttlia (*Finland*)	S. Ruud (*Norway*)	H. Vinjarengen (*Norway*)
1930	A. Rustadstuen (*Norway*)	S. Utterström (*Sweden*)	G. Andersen (*Norway*)	H. Vinjarengen (*Norway*)
1931	J. Gröttumsbraaten (*Norway*)	O. Stenen (*Norway*)	B. Ruud (*Norway*)	J. Gröttumsbraaten (*Norway*)
1933	N. Englund (*Sweden*)	V. Saarinen (*Finland*)	M. Reymond (*Switzerland*)	S. Eriksson (*Sweden*)
1934	S. Nurmela (*Finland*)	E. Wiklund (*Sweden*)	K. Johanson (*Norway*)	O. Hagen (*Norway*)
1935	K. Karppinen (*Finland*)	N. Englund (*Sweden*)	B. Ruud (*Norway*)	O. Hagen (*Norway*)
1937	L. Bergendahl (*Norway*)	P. Niemi (*Finland*)	B. Ruud (*Norway*)	S. Röen (*Norway*)
1938	P. Pitkänen (*Finland*)	K. Jalkanen (*Finland*)	A. Ruud (*Norway*)	O. Hoffsbakken (*Norway*)
1939	J. Kurikkala (*Finland*)	L. Bergendahl (*Norway*)	J. Bradl (*Austria*)	G. Berauer (*Germany*)
1950	K. Aström (*Sweden*)	G. Eriksson (*Sweden*)	H. Björnstad (*Norway*)	H. Hasu (*Finland*)
1954	—	V. Kuzin (*Russia*)	M. Pietikainen (*Finland*)	S. Stenersen (*Norway*)
1958	—	S. Jernberg (*Sweden*)	—	P. Korhonen (*Finland*)

30 KILOMETRES: 1954 V. Kuzin (*Russia*)—only year contested.

15 KILOMETRES: 1954 V. Hakulinen (*Finland*)
             1958 V. Hakulinen (*Finland*)

RELAY TEAM RACE: 1937 *Norway*   1950 *Sweden*
                  1938 *Finland*   1954 *Finland*
                  1939 *Finland*   1958 *Sweden*

WORLD CHAMPIONS: LADIES' NORDIC EVENTS

10 KILOMETRES: 1954 L. Kezyreva (*Russia*)

RELAY TEAM RACE: 1954 Russia

WORLD CHAMPIONS: MEN'S ALPINE EVENTS

	DOWNHILL	SLALOM	GIANT SLALOM	COMBINED
1931	W. Prager (*Switzerland*)	—	—	—
1932	G. Lantschner (*Austria*)	F. Däuber (*Germany*)	—	O. Fuerrer (*Switzerland*)
1933	W. Prager (*Switzerland*)	A. Seelos (*Austria*)	—	A. Seelos (*Austria*)
1934	D. Zogg (*Switzerland*)	F. Pfnür (*Germany*)	—	D. Zogg (*Switzerland*)
1935	F. Zingerle (*Austria*)	A. Seelos (*Austria*)	—	A. Seelos (*Austria*)
1936	R. Rominger (*Switzerland*)	R. Matt (*Austria*)	—	R. Rominger (*Switzerland*)
1937	E. Allais (*France*)	E. Allais (*France*)	—	E. Allais (*France*)
1938	J. Couttet (*France*)	R. Rominger (*Switzerland*)	—	E. Allais (*France*)
1939	H. Lantschner (*Germany*)	R. Rominger (*Switzerland*)	—	J. Jennewein (*Germany*)
1950	Z. Colò (*Italy*)	G. Schneider (*Switzerland*)	Z. Colò (*Italy*)	—
1954	C. Pravda (*Austria*)	S. Eriksen (*Norway*)	S. Eriksen (*Norway*)	S. Eriksen (*Norway*)
1958	T. Sailer (*Austria*)	J. Rieder (*Austria*)	T. Sailer (*Austria*)	T. Sailer (*Austria*)

WORLD CHAMPIONS: LADIES' ALPINE EVENTS

	DOWNHILL	SLALOM	GIANT SLALOM	COMBINED
1931	E. MacKinnon (*Gt. Britain*)	E. MacKinnon (*Gt. Britain*)	—	—
1932	P. Wiesinger (*Italy*)	R. Streiff (*Switzerland*)	—	R. Streiff (*Switzerland*)
1933	I. Wersin-Lantschner (*Austria*)	I. Wersin-Lantschner (*Austria*)	—	I. Wersin-Lantschner (*Austria*)
1934	A. Rüegg (*Switzerland*)	C. Cranz (*Germany*)	—	C. Cranz (*Germany*)
1935	C. Cranz (*Germany*)	A. Rüegg (*Switzerland*)	—	C. Cranz (*Germany*)
1936	E. Pinching (*Gt. Britain*)	G. Paumgarten (*Austria*)	—	E. Pinching (*Gt. Britain*)
1937	C. Cranz (*Germany*)	C. Cranz (*Germany*)	—	C. Cranz (*Germany*)
1938	L. Resch (*Germany*)	C. Cranz (*Germany*)	—	C. Cranz (*Germany*)
1939	C. Cranz (*Germany*)	C. Cranz (*Germany*)	—	C. Cranz (*Germany*)
1950	T. Jochum-Beiser (*Austria*)	D. Rom (*Austria*)	D. Rom (*Austria*)	—
1954	I. Schopfer (*Switzerland*)	T. Klecker (*Austria*)	L. Schmidt (*France*)	I. Schopfer (*Switzerland*)
1958	L. Wheeler (*Canada*)	I. Bjornbakken (*Norway*)	L. Wheeler (*Canada*)	F. Danzer (*Switzerland*)

OLYMPIC CHAMPIONS: MEN'S NORDIC EVENTS

	18 KILOMETRES	50 KILOMETRES	JUMPING	COMBINED
1924	T. Haug *(Norway)*	T. Haug *(Norway)*	J. Tullin-Thams *(Norway)*	T. Haug *(Norway)*
1928	J. Gröttumsbraaten *(Norway)*	P. Hedlund *(Sweden)*	A. Andersen *(Norway)*	J. Gröttumsbraaten *(Norway)*
1932	S. Utterström *(Sweden)*	V. Saarinen *(Finland)*	B. Ruud *(Norway)*	J. Gröttumsbraaten *(Norway)*
1936	E. Larsson *(Sweden)*	E. Wiklund *(Sweden)*	B. Ruud *(Norway)*	O. Hagen *(Norway)*
1948	M. Lundström *(Sweden)*	N. Karlsson *(Sweden)*	P. Hugsted *(Norway)*	H. Hasu *(Finland)*
1952	H. Brenden *(Norway)*	V. Hakulinen *(Finland)*	A. Bergmann *(Norway)*	S. Slättvik *(Norway)*
1956	—	S. Jernberg *(Sweden)*	A. Hyvarinen *(Finland)*	S. Stenersen *(Norway)*

15 KILOMETRES: 1956 H. Brenden *(Norway)*
30 KILOMETRES: 1956 V. Hakulinen *(Finland)*
RELAY TEAM RACE: 1936 *Finland* 1952 *Finland* 1948 *Sweden* 1956 *Russia*

OLYMPIC CHAMPIONS: LADIES' NORDIC EVENTS

10 KILOMETRES: 1952 L. Wideman *(Finland)*
             1956 L. Kezyreva *(Russia)*
RELAY TEAM RACE: 1956 *Finland*

OLYMPIC CHAMPIONS: MEN'S ALPINE EVENTS

	DOWNHILL	SLALOM	GIANT SLALOM	COMBINED
1936	—	—		F. Pfnür *(Germany)*
1948	H. Oreiller *(France)*	E. Reinalter *(Switzerland)*	—	H. Oreiller *(France)*
1952	Z. Colò *(Italy)*	O. Schneider *(Austria)*	S. Eriksen *(Norway)*	—
1956	T. Sailer *(Austria)*	T. Sailer *(Austria)*	T. Sailer *(Austria)*	

OLYMPIC CHAMPIONS: LADIES' ALPINE EVENTS

	DOWNHILL	SLALOM	GIANT SLALOM	COMBINED
1936	—	—		C. Cranz *(Germany)*
1948	H. Schlunegger *(Switzerland)*	G. Frazer *(U.S.A.)*	—	T. Jochum-Beiser *(Austria)*
1952	T. Jochum-Beiser *(Austria)*	A. Mead-Lawrence *(U.S.A.)*	A. Mead-Lawrence *(U.S.A.)*	—
1956	M. Berthod *(Switzerland)*	R. Collard *(Switzerland)*	O. Reichert *(Germany)*	—

MEN'S ALPINE CHAMPIONS OF GREAT BRITAIN

1921 L. Dobbs	1931 W. Bracken	1947 C. Mackintosh	1955 N. Gardner
1922 C. Pitman	1933 C. Hudson	1948 D. Garrow	1956 G. Whitelaw
1923 L. Dodds	1934 F. Cameron	1949 D. Horsfield	1957 P. Seilern
1924 L. Dodds	1935 J. Riddell	1950 S. Parkinson	1958 P. Seilern
1926 W. Dodds	1937 L. Robinson	1951 J. Boyagis	1959 G. Pitchford
1927 B. Marden	1938 R. Gardner	1952 J. Boyagis	
1929 W. Bracken	1939 J. Palmer-Tomkinson	1953 N. Harrison	
1930 W. Bracken		1954 R. Hooper	

LADIES' ALPINE CHAMPIONS OF GREAT BRITAIN

1921 O. Major	1930 E. MacKinnon	1939 I. Roe	1954 A. Pryor
1922 M. Hollingsworth	1931 A. Sale-Barker	1947 G. Greenland	1956 S. Holmes
1923 O. Major	1933 B. Duthie	1948 I. Roe	1957 S. Holmes
1924 K. Dobbs	1934 B. Duthie	1949 I. Roe	1958 S. Holmes
1926 M. Beckton	1935 E. Pinching	1950 M. Chable	1959 C. Petre
1927 J. McConnell	1937 E. MacFie	1951 A. Mackintosh	
1929 T. Turner	1938 I. Roe	1952 A. Mackintosh	
		1953 H. Laing	

LANGLAUF CHAMPIONS OF GREAT BRITAIN

1929 C. Legard	1937 D. Kingsford	1950 H. France	1955 J. Moore
1930 H. Spence	1938 R. Readhead	1951 F. Cooke	1956 A. Morgan
1931 R. Bushell	1939 D. Bradley	1952 H. France	1957 A. Morgan
1933 F. Walter	1948 J. Nash	1953 J. Spencer	1958 K. Templer
1934 F. Walter	1949 F. Cooke	1954 T. Cairney	1959 J. Moore

SKI JUMPING RECORDS

WORLD RECORD: 71 metres, H. Kaarstein *(Norway)*, at Holmenkollen in 1947.
BRITISH RECORD: 57 metres, C. Wyatt in 1931.

Henri Oreiller

Noël Harrison

Lucille Wheeler

SKI-ING 1958-59

24th ARLBERG-KANDAHAR INTERNATIONAL COMPETITION

(Garmisch-Partenkirchen, February 6-8, 1959)

MEN'S DOWNHILL
1. K. Schranz *(Austria)* 2 m. 43.2 s.
2. R. Staub *(Switzerland)* 2 m. 44.0 s.
3. H. Lanig *(W. Germany)* 2 m. 46.2 s.

MEN'S SLALOM
1. F. Bonlieu *(France)* 120.6 s.
2. E. Hinterseer *(Austria)* 121.3 s.
3. C. Bozon *(France)* 123.9 s.

MEN'S COMBINED RESULT
1. K. Schranz *(Austria)*
2. R. Staub *(Switzerland)*
3. P. Granshammer *(Austria)*

LADIES' DOWNHILL
1. E. Netzer *(Austria)* 1 m. 54.3 s.
2. M. Chamot-Berthod *(Switzerland)* 1 m. 54.8 s.
3. A. Heggtveit *(Canada)* 1 m. 54.9 s.

LADIES' SLALOM
1. B. Snite *(U.S.A.)* 79.2 s.
2. A. Heggtveit *(Canada)* 79.3 s.
3. S. Sperl *(W. Germany)* 79.4 s.

LADIES' COMBINED RESULT
1. A. Heggtveit *(Canada)*
2. B. Snite *(U.S.A.)*
3. E. Netzer *(Austria)*

BRITISH MEN'S ALPINE CHAMPIONSHIP 1958-59

(Zermatt, January 9, 1959)

DOWNHILL—1. G. Pitchford, 2 m. 25.8 s. 2. N. Gardner, 2 m. 27.0 s. 3. C. Gladstone, 2 m. 27.9 s.
SLALOM—1. G. Pitchford, 72.5 s. 2. R. Skepper, 73.4 s. 3. Z. Kaye, 77.7 s.
COMBINED RESULT—1. G. Pitchford, 2. C. Gladstone. 3. N. Gardner.

BRITISH LADIES' ALPINE CHAMPIONSHIP 1958-59

(Wengen, January 22, 1959)

DOWNHILL—1. J. Shearing, 2 m. 32.6 s. 2. Z. Nowell, 2 m. 34.2 s. 3. J. Gibbs, 2 m. 34.8 s.
SLALOM—1. C. Petre. 2. S. Holmes. 3. T. Heald.
COMBINED RESULT—1. C. Petre. 2. Z. Nowell. 3. T. Heald.

Susan Holmes

Veikko Hakulinen

Hilary Laing

SKI-ING QUIZ

1. Who originated the Arlberg-Kandahar race?

★

2. What is the minimum distance between the two flags of a slalom "gate"?

★

3. Name the site of Norway's foremost ski jump.

★

4. Who became recognised as the world's supreme Alpine skier at Bad Gastein in 1958?

★

5. Name the venue of the 1960 Winter Olympic Games.

★

6. Who captained the British Olympic ski team in 1948?

★

7. Under what name are long-distance cross-country ski-ing and ski jumping collectively known?

★

8. Who was British men's ski-ing champion three times in succession?

★

9. Name the only Norwegian to win an Olympic gold medal for an Alpine event.

★

10. Where and when was the first Arlberg-Kandahar held?

QUIZ ANSWERS

1. Sir Arnold Lunn and Hannes Schneider. 2. Ten feet. 3. Holmenkollen Hill, on the outskirts of Oslo. 4. Toni Sailer. 5. Squaw Valley, California. 6. Jimmy Palmer-Tomkinson. 7. Nordic events. 8. Bill Bracken, from 1929 to 1931. 9. Stein Eriksen, at Oslo in 1952. 10. At St. Anton in 1928.

Snooker

Compiled by Richard Holt

Editor: The Billiard Player

SNOOKER QUIZ

1. Player nominates Green after a foul and leaves the balls as follows and in a straight line: cue-ball, Yellow, Green, Red (the ball "on"). Green (nominated ball) thus obstructs. Is this a foul (snookering with the nominated ball)?

★

2. Player picks up the cue-ball in mistake: what is the penalty?

★

3. What is the highest possible score in one stroke?

★

4. Rule 8 states "Reds are never re-spotted". Comment on this.

★

5. What professional, not English, broke the world break record in England only to find it beaten shortly afterwards? What was unusual about his cue?

★

6. What is the world amateur break record?

★

7. What should the referee do if he has not seen a stroke which a player appeals against as a foul?

★

8. How many times can Yellow be potted in succession?

★

9. What well-known snooker professional performed a notable feat in first-class cricket? What notable snooker feat did he perform?

★

10. Who was the last official professional world champion?

QUIZ ANSWERS

1. No foul. When the ball "on" is snookered by more than one ball, the effective snookering ball is the one nearest to the cue-ball. 2. 7 points. 3. 16: all Reds (15), plus a free-ball (1). 4. An error; Reds are never *spotted*. 5. George Chenier 144 (1950), beaten by Joe Davis 146; it was a two-piece cue. 6. 106 (1956). Made on officially tested standard table. 7. Consult spectators nearest to the incident. 8. Three times: (1) as Red, free ball; (2) as colour after a Red; (3) as first of the colours. 9. Albert Brown (Birmingham); playing for Warwickshire (1934), he took 6 Indian wickets of Test Match calibre. Playing Alec Brown in 1949 (*News of the World* Tournament), the latter needed two frames to win, leading 17–13 (best of 37): Albert Brown won all 7 frames of the final session. 10. Horace Lindrum (1952), after which there have been no official contests owing to a dispute.

THE DERIVATION OF SNOOKER

The game of snooker derived from Pool, Black Pool and Pyramids. Gradually it ousted these games, and a frame of snooker used to be played at professional billiards matches, in the early part of the century up to late in the twenties, if the players reached the stipulated number of points (at billiards) before the session ended. Gradually the game grew popular and acquired independent status. As in the mid-thirties professional billiard matches, of a week's or fortnight's duration, suffered a decline in popularity, due chiefly to the dominance of close-cannon play, snooker attracted more and more, and this was in a great measure due to the research into the possibilities of the game by Joe Davis, who, by emphasizing the vital importance of cue-ball control, converted snooker into a game of genuine skill.

ACHIEVEMENTS (SNOOKER)

Joe Davis made his first hundred-break at snooker in 1928: up to March 1959 he had made 645 such breaks.

In 1950 Joe Davis made 6 hundred-

Sidney Smith

Walter Lindrum   Joe Davis

breaks at snooker in one week's play against G. Chenier (Canada).

In 1937 and 1938 Joe Davis won the *Daily Mail* "Gold Cup" Tournament.

In 1950 Joe Davis made a snooker break of 146 v. G. Chenier (Canada).

In 1952, Joe Davis, playing against W. Donaldson, won 9 successive frames, scoring 966 points to 210, with an aggregate of 100 points or over in 8 of the frames, and a break of over 50 in all 9. Joe Davis has three times made 3 successive hundred-breaks at snooker; also, in 1949, v. W. Smith, in a combined billiards and snooker match, he made a break of 639 at billiards and two breaks of 106 and 115 (snooker) in one session.

Joe Davis has also cleared the table, (*a*) from the opening shot and (*b*) of all the balls, on many occasions.

George Chenier (Canada) 144 (1950), made in England; official record break but beaten by Joe Davis, 146 (1950) and later, 147 (1955).

Other breaks by professionals, although not passed as official, not having been made, or claimed as having been made, on standard tables: Rex Williams 147 (1955); C. McConachy 147 (1952); W. Donaldson 142 (1946); H. Lindrum 141 (1937); Fred Davis 140 (1952).

PROFESSIONAL MATCH-PLAY CHAMPIONSHIPS

	Winner	Runner-up
1952	Fred Davis	W. Donaldson
1953	Fred Davis	W. Donaldson
1954	Fred Davis	W. Donaldson
1955	Fred Davis	John Pulman
1956	Fred Davis	John Pulman
1957	John Pulman	Jack Rea
1958 & 1959	No contest	

RECORDS (SNOOKER)

PROFESSIONAL

World Professional Snooker Championship Record Break: Joe Davis 136 (1946).
World Record Break: Joe Davis 147 (1955).

AMATEUR

Record Break: G. H. Povall (South Africa) 106 (1956).

PROFESSIONAL SNOOKER TOURNAMENTS

"DAILY MAIL"

	Winner	Runner-up
1937	J. Davis	H. Lindrum
1938	J. Davis	W. Smith
1939	Alec Brown	S. Smith
1940	Alec Brown	S. Lee

"NEWS OF THE WORLD"

	Winner	Runner-up
1950	J. Davis	S. Smith
1951	Alec Brown	J. Pulman
1952	S. Smith	Albert Brown
1953	J. Davis	J. Rea
1954	J. Pulman	J. Davis
1955	J. Rea	J. Davis
1956	J. Davis	F. Davis
1957	J. Pulman	F. Davis
1958	F. Davis	J. Pulman
1959	F. Davis	J. Davis

ENGLISH AMATEUR SNOOKER CHAMPIONSHIP

	Winner	Runner-up	Frames
1916	C. N. Jacques	—	—
1917	C. N. Jacques	—	—
1918	"T. N. Palmer"	—	—
1919	S. H. Fry	—	—
1920	A. R. Wisdom	—	—
1921	M. J. Vaughan	S. H. Fry	—
1922	J. McGlynn	C. Cox jun.	—
1923	W. Coupe	E. Forshall	—
1924	W. Coupe	H. G. Olden	—
1925	J. McGlynn	W. L. Crompton	—
1926	W. Nash	A. W. Casey	—
1927	O. T. Jackson	F. Whitall	—
1928	P. H. Matthews	F. T. W. Leaphard	—
1929	L. Steeples	F. Whitall	—
1930	L. Steeples	F. Whitall	—
1931	P. H. Matthews	H. Kingsley	—
1932	W. E. Bach	O. T. Jackson	—
1933	E. Bedford	A. Kershaw	—
1934	C. H. Beavis	P. H. Matthews	—
1935	C. H. Beavis	D. Hindmarch	—
1936	P. H. Matthews	C. H. Beavis	—
1937	K. Kennerley	W. H. Dennis	—
1938	P. H. Matthews	K. Kennerley	—
1939	P. Bendon	K. Kennerley	—
1940	K. Kennerley	A. Brown	—
1941–5	No contests		
1946	H. J. Pulman	Albert Brown	5–3
1947	H. Morris	C. A. Kent	5–1
1948	S. Battye	T. Postlethwaite	6–4
1949	T. C. Gordon	S. Kilbank	6–4
1950	A. Nolan	Gary Owen	6–5
1951	Rex Williams	P. Bendon	6–1
1952	C. Downey	J. Allen	6–1
1953	T. C. Gordon	G. Humphries	6–5
1954	G. Thompson	C. Wilson	11–9
1955	M. Parkin	A. Nolan	11–7
1956	T. C. Gordon	R. Reardon	11–9
1957	R. Gross	S. Haslam	11–6
1958	Marcus Owen	J. T. Fitzmaurice	11–8
1959	Marcus Owen	A. Barnett	11–5

WORLD PROFESSIONAL SNOOKER CHAMPIONSHIP

	Winner	Runner-up	Frames
1927	Joe Davis	T. A. Dennis	20–11
1928	Joe Davis	F. Lawrence	16–13
1929	Joe Davis	T. A. Dennis	19–14
1930	Joe Davis	T. A. Dennis	25–12
1931	Joe Davis	T. A. Dennis	25–21
1932	Joe Davis	Clark McConachy	30–19
1933	Joe Davis	Willie Smith	25–18
1934	Joe Davis	Tom Newman	25–23
1935	Joe Davis	Willie Smith	25–20
1936	Joe Davis	Horace Lindrum	34–27
1937	Joe Davis	Horace Lindrum	32–29
1938	Joe Davis	Sidney Smith	37–24
1939	Joe Davis	Sidney Smith	43–30
1940	Joe Davis	Fred Davis	37–36
1941–45	No contests		
1946	Joe Davis	Horace Lindrum	78–67
1947	Walter Donaldson	Fred Davis	82–63
1948	Fred Davis	Walter Donaldson	84–61
1949	Fred Davis	Walter Donaldson	80–65
1950	Walter Donaldson	Fred Davis	51–46
1951	Fred Davis	Walter Donaldson	58–39
1952	*Horace Lindrum	*Clark McConachy	94–49

Record Break: Joe Davis 136 (1946).

Only entrants. The other professionals, owing to a difference about terms and conditions with the Billiards Association & Control Council, did not enter. No official championship has taken place since 1952, the professionals running their own Match-play Championship. Joe Davis retired from Championship Play in 1946.

Record Break: R. Lomas 80 (1958). Also J. Longden 78 (1950); P. Bendon 75 (1951); R. Williams 74 (1951); P. Houlihan 74 (1954).

Note: Apart from the English and other National Amateur Snooker Championships, the best amateurs, whose play in the last few years has more and more approached that of the professionals—the difference is in degree rather than in kind—have made many breaks ranging from 100 upwards. The highest of these have been: Leo Levitt (Canada) 147 (1948); Marcus Owen 142 (1959); G. Thompson 141 (1953); G. Cox 140 (1958). Such breaks, however, have, for the most part, been made in clubs, billiard halls, etc., in which the tables are scarcely ever standard, or, if, in rare cases, they have been so, have not been officially passed. They do not, therefore, qualify as records, and the 106 break of G. H. Povall (South Africa) is the present official world amateur record.

Clark McConachy

Willie Smith

Tom Newman

SNOOKER AMATEUR CHAMPIONSHIPS: EIRE, ALL-IRELAND AND NORTHERN IRELAND

Winners from 1952

	EIRE	ALL-IRELAND	N. IRELAND
1952	W. Brown	J. Stevenson	J. Stevenson
1953	S. Brooks	J. Stevenson	J. Stevenson
1954	S. Fenning	S. Fenning	W. Seeds
1955	S. Fenning	J. Stevenson	J. Stevenson
1956	W. Brown	W. Brown	S. Brooks
1957	J. Connolly	M. Gill	M. Gill
1958	G. Gibson	G. Gibson	W. Agnew
1959	*No official contest.*	*No official contest.*	W. Hanna

(1958 Open Snooker, G. Gibson)

AUSTRALIAN AMATEUR SNOOKER CHAMPIONSHIP

	Winner	*Runner-up*
1953	W. Simpson	*Robert Marshall*
1954*	W. Simpson	*F. Edwards*
1955	E. Pickett	*J. Harris*
1956	Robert Marshall	*W. Simpson*
1957*	W. Simpson	*N. Squires*
1957	W. Simpson	*Robert Marshall*
1958	Frank Harris	*K. Burles*

* open

Open Championship (1954): F. Edwards, in Australia for the Amateur World Billiards Championship, took part.

Open Championship: N. Squires is a professional.

Record Break: W. Simpson 81 (1954). Also W. Simpson 64 (1955), 62 (1957) and 61 (1956); N. Squires 66 and 60 (1957); N. Gahan 63 (1958).

INDIAN AMATEUR SNOOKER CHAMPIONSHIP

	Winner
1939	P. K. Deb
1940	P. K. Deb
1941	V. R. Freer
1942	P. K. Deb
1943–45	No contests
1946	T. A. Selvaraj
1947	Capt. T. Sadler
1948	Wilson Jones
1949	T. A. Selvaraj
1950	F. Edwards*
1951	T. A. Selvaraj
1952	Wilson Jones
1953	A. L. Driffield†
1954	Wilson Jones
1955	T. A. Selvaraj
1956	J. M. Lafir
1957	J. M. Lafir
1958	Wilson Jones
1959	J. M. Lafir

Record Break: C. Hirjee 80 (1954).
* Visiting India.
† In India for World Billiards C'ship.

SCOTTISH AMATEUR SNOOKER CHAMPIONSHIP

POST-WAR PERIOD

	Winner	*Runner-up*
1946	J. Levey	N. McGowan
1947	J. Levey	T. Gray
1948	I. Wexelstein	R. Walls
1949	W. Ramage	P. Spence
1950	W. Ramage	R. McKendrick
1951	A. Wilson	A. Wishart
1952	D. Emerson	P. Spence
1953	P. Spence	H. D. Thompson
1954	D. Edmond	P. Spence
1955	B. Demarco	P. Spence
1956	W. Barrie	R. McKendrick
1957	T. Paul	H. D. Thompson
1958	J. Phillips	J. Ferguson
1959	J. Phillips	E. Sinclair

Record Break: H. D. Thompson 59 (1956). W. Barrie 70, in Open (1955).

WOMEN'S SNOOKER CHAMPIONSHIPS

PROFESSIONAL

1934–40	Ruth Harrison
1941–47	No contests
1948	Ruth Harrison
1949	Agnes Morris
1950	Thelma Carpenter (No contests since.)

AMATEUR

1933	Margaret Quinn
1934	Ella Morris
1935	Molly Hill
1936	Vera Seals
1937	E. Morland-Smith
1938	Ella Morris
1939	Agnes Morris
1940–46	No contests
1947	M. Knight
1948	Joan Adcock
1949	Rosemary Davies
1950	Pat Holden
1951	Rosemary Davies
1952	Rosemary Davies
1953	Rita Holmes
1954	Maureen Barrett
1955	Maureen Barrett
1956	Maureen Barrett
1957	Rita Holmes
1958*	Rita Holmes

* Really 1958–59 (since 1947, 12 championships spread over 13 years).

SNOOKER QUIZ

1. Which amateur (in the Amateur Championship) made successive breaks of 62 and 68, and won the frame by 134–0 in three visits?

*

2. Mention two snooker terms which are always confused one with the other?

*

3. The following are key words in snooker technique: "head", "parallel", "through", "one". Make their meaning clear.

*

4. What snooker professional won the Boys' Billiards Championship at 15, yet dislikes billiards? What was his highest break?

*

5. What is the basis of "Black ball" play?

QUIZ ANSWERS

1. Clifford Wilson (Tredegar) in 1954. 2. "Plant" and "set". 3. Keep the head down; keep the cue parallel with the table; make a good "follow-through"; one-ball practice. 4. Walter Donaldson: 142. 5. Top-of-the-table play at billiards.

Compiled by **John Wick**
Editor: Speedway World

Speedway

HISTORY

For more than 30 years speedway racing has had a most chequered career. The first meeting in this country was held at High Beech (Epping Forest) in February, 1928. This new sport, which hailed from Australia, immediately caught the imagination of the public and it was not long before many new tracks were in operation.

In 1929 league racing commenced with eleven teams competing. The following year this number rose to twenty-six and the league was split into North and South sections.

From then on the pattern changed. A number of tracks closed down but by 1939 there were still thirteen active teams in the National League.

The sport hit a boom period after the war and at one time there were three divisions of the league in operation containing well over thirty clubs. During the past three or four years many of these tracks have closed down but today the sport has a firm footing and although the league contains only nine clubs there are at least another half-a-dozen or so open licence tracks in operation.

The sport is controlled by the Speedway Control Board, a sub-committee of the Auto Cycle Union, and is affiliated to the F.I.M., the recognised world controlling body for all motor sports.

The main competition is the Speedway Championship of the World which is held yearly at the Empire Stadium, Wembley, and has attracted crowds of over 90,000. This competition is open to all riders in the world and so far the title has been captured by Australia, New Zealand, England, America and Sweden.

Here are the records covering the major events since the sport became a competitive one in 1929:

TEST MATCHES

ENGLAND v. AUSTRALIA

1930

Wimbledon	England 17,	Australia 35
Manchester	England 56,	Australia 39
Stamford Bridge	England 49,	Australia 46
Belle Vue	England 51,	Australia 45
Wembley	England 49,	Australia 45

1931

Crystal Palace	England 55,	Australia 37
Leicester	England 46,	Australia 47
Wembley	England 53,	Australia 43
Belle Vue	England 53,	Australia 41
Stamford Bridge	England 48,	Australia 46

SPEEDWAY QUIZ

1. What famous speedway rider is now a manager?

*

2. Who was known as "Cyclone"?

*

3. What pre-war rider is now a promoter?

*

4. For whom did Gus Kuhn ride?

*

QUIZ ANSWERS

1 Squib Burton (Leicester). 2. Billy Lamont. 3. Charlie Dugard (Eastbourne). 4. Stamford Bridge.

301

Eric Chitty

Peter Craven

Ronnie Moore

SPEEDWAY QUIZ

1. Which rider who took part in the first speedway meeting ever held in this country is still competing in the sport today?

★

2. What is the record transfer fee ever paid for a rider?

★

3. Who is chairman of the Speedway Control Board?

★

4. Name the rider with most World Final appearances.

★

5. Which rider has the best record in the Brandonapolis?

★

6. Three of the present-day clubs were members of the original speedway league. Who are they?

★

7. Who holds the recognised world speedway record?

★

8. For how many English clubs has Aub Lawson ridden?

★

9. What famous brother partnerships have ridden for Harringay?

★

10. Have Wales ever had a speedway track?

★

11. Name the nationality of ex-West Ham skipper, Eric Chitty?

★

12. Who has been connected with the sport the longest?

QUIZ ANSWERS

1. Phil Bishop. 2. Harringay paid £3,000 for Split Waterman from Wembley. 3. Lt.-Col. R. V. C. Vernon Brook, O.B.E. 4. Jack Parker nine times. 5. Eddie Rigg with a first, 2 seconds and 2 thirds. 6. Southampton, Coventry and Wimbledon. 7. K. Gurtner. 8. Wembley, West Ham and Norwich. 9. Jack and Norman Parker; Vic and Ray Duggan. 10. Yes, Cardiff. 11. Canadian. 12. Johnnie S. Hoskins—promoter in Australia in 1924.

TEST MATCHES—contd.

1932		
Stamford Bridge	England 50,	Australia 41
Wembley	England 35,	Australia 59
Belle Vue	England 53,	Australia 43
Crystal Palace	England 45,	Australia 49
Wembley	England 51,	Australia 42
1933		
Wembley	England 76,	Australia 47
Belle Vue	England 61,	Australia 65
Crystal Palace	England 63½,	Australia 62½
Wimbledon	England 62,	Australia 64
West Ham	England 74,	Australia 52
1934		
Wembley	England 34,	Australia 69
New Cross	England 58,	Australia 48
Wimbledon	England 51,	Australia 54
Belle Vue	England 60½,	Australia 45½
West Ham	England 50,	Australia 57
1935		
Wembley	England 56,	Australia 52
New Cross	England 59,	Australia 46
Belle Vue	England 58,	Australia 48
West Ham	England 40,	Australia 66
Harringay	England 63,	Australia 44
1936		
Wembley	England 65,	Australia 43
New Cross	England 49,	Australia 56
Belle Vue	England 70,	Australia 38
Wimbledon	England 58,	Australia 47
West Ham	England 35,	Australia 73
1937		
Wembley	England 66,	Australia 41

Rest of series abandoned. Injuries prevented Australia fielding a full team.

1938		
Belle Vue	England 52,	Australia 56
Wembley	England 63,	Australia 44
New Cross	England 47,	Australia 61
West Ham	England 55,	Australia 51
Wimbledon	England 58,	Australia 49

Aub Lawson

1939		
New Cross	England 62,	Australia 46
Wimbledon	England 55,	Australia 53
Harringay	England 48,	Australia 58
Belle Vue	England 65,	Australia 42
Wembley	England 71,	Australia 36

1940–46 No contests.

1947		
Bradford	England 65,	Australia 43
West Ham	England 58,	Australia 50
Wembley	England 49,	Australia 57
1948		
Wimbledon	England 61,	Australia 45
Belle Vue	England 69,	Australia 39
New Cross	England 57,	Australia 51
Harringay	England 58,	Australia 50
West Ham	England 45,	Australia 63
1949		
Wembley	England 41,	Australia 67
Birmingham	England 53,	Australia 53
New Cross	England 62,	Australia 46
Harringay	England 53,	Australia 53
Bradford	England 72,	Australia 33

1950		
West Ham	England 47,	Australia 60
Belle Vue	England 58,	Australia 50
New Cross	England 63,	Australia 45
Wimbledon	England 62,	Australia 46
Wembley	England 53,	Australia 55
1951		
Harringay	England 48,	Australia 60
Bradford	England 59,	Australia 49
Wembley	England 49,	Australia 58
Birmingham	England 46,	Australia 62
West Ham	England 49,	Australia 58
1952		
Wimbledon	England 52,	Australia 56
Wembley	England 52,	Australia 56
Belle Vue	England 50,	Australia 58
New Cross	England 46,	Australia 62
Harringay	England 55,	Australia 53
1953		
Norwich	England 46,	Australia 62
Wembley	England 57,	Australia 51
Birmingham	England 61,	Australia 47

With Australia being unable to field a full representative side the series ended and was replaced the following year with an England v. Australasian series, New Zealand riders coming into the overseas' team.

1954		
West Ham	England 60,	Australasia 48
Belle Vue	England 64,	Australasia 44
Bradford	England 56,	Australasia 52
1955		
Wimbledon	England 39,	Australasia 67
Wembley	England 67,	Australasia 41
West Ham	England 42,	Australasia 66
Bradford	England 66,	Australasia 42
Birmingham	England 61,	Australasia 46
Norwich	England 57,	Australasia 51
Belle Vue	Match cancelled.	
1956		
Bradford	England 55,	Australasia 53
Birmingham	England 65,	Australasia 43
Poole	England 57,	Australasia 51

1957 No contest.

1958		
Swindon	England 51,	Australasia 57
Oxford	England 44,	Australasia 64
Coventry	England 65,	Australasia 43
Belle Vue	England 58,	Australasia 50
Southampton	England 63,	Australasia 45

1959

At Southampton, Sept. 8

England (52): R. How 16; P. Craven 11; K. McKinlay 11; I. Williams 6; M. Broadbanks 6; B. Crutcher 2; D. Bradley 0; G. White 0.

Barry Briggs

Australasia (56): P. Moore 12; A. Lawson 12; B. Briggs 11; G. Mardon 8; R. Moore 8; C. Taylor 5; B. Duckworth 0.

At Norwich, Sept. 12

England (62): P. Craven 16; R. How 16; K. McKinlay 12; M. Broadbanks 9; R. Trott 6; C. Roger 3; J. Unstead 0.

Australasia (46): A. Lawson 13; G. Mardon 9; P. Moore 4; B. Duckworth 4; C. Taylor 3; B. Briggs 0; J. Chamberlain 0.

At Swindon, Sept. 26

England (55): P. Craven 13; M. Broadbanks 11; R. How 11; I. Williams 8; G. McGregor 6; K. McKinlay 5; D. Bradley 1.

Australasia (53): B. Briggs 16; R. Moore 14; G. Mardon 7; P. Moore 6; A. Lawson 5; N. Street 3; J. Geran 2.

1956		
Wembley	England 49,	Sweden 59
Wimbledon	England 52,	Sweden 53
Norwich	England 66,	Sweden 42
Kumla	Sweden 65,	England 43
Osterholm	Sweden 71,	England 37
Stockholm	Sweden, 69	England 39

1957 No contest.

1958

At Southampton, July 1

England (59): B. Crutcher 15; D. Bradley 12; P. Craven 12; K. McKinlay 9; R. How 8; A. Forrest 1; J. Squibb 1; M. Broadbanks 1.

Sweden (49): O. Fundin 16; O. Nygren 13; R. Sormander 9; B. Forsberg 5; J. Jansson 3; P. Soederman 3; D. Forsberg 0.

At Norwich, July 2

England (50): P. Craven 13; B. Bales 11; B. Crutcher 9; K. McKinlay 6; A. Forrest 4; R. How 3; G. White 2; M. Broadbanks 2.

Sweden (58): R. Sormander 18; O. Fundin 16; O. Nygren 15; P. Soederman 5; B. Forsberg 4; D. Forsberg 0; J. Jansson 1.

At Wimbledon, July 7

England (71): P. Craven 18; R. How 15; B. Crutcher 13; K. McKinlay 11; I. Williams 7; M. Broadbanks 3; C. Brine 2; D. Bradley 0.

Sweden (37): O. Fundin 15; R. Sormander 8; O. Nygren 8; P. Soederman 3; B. Forsberg 1; D. Forsberg 1; J. Jansson 1.

At Gothenburg, September 24

Sweden (61): O. Nygren 17; O. Fundin 16; R. Sormander 14; A. Carlsson 6; P. Soederman 6; B. Neilsson 1; A. Jonsson 1.

England (46): P. Craven 13; R. How 8; M. Broadbanks 8; G. White 7; K. McKinlay 6; D. Bradley 4.

At Stockholm, September 26

Sweden (62): O. Nygren 18; R. Sormander 12; O. Fundin 12; P. Soederman 9; B. Ericsson 6; B. Neilsson 5.

England (46): P. Craven 14; K. McKinlay 12; R. How 8; G. White 6; D. Bradley 5; M. Broadbanks 1.

At Malilla, September 28

Sweden (48): R. Sormander 17; O. Fundin 11; O. Nygren 8; P. Soederman 4; T. Karlsson 4; A. Jonsson 2; O. Andersson 2.

England (60): P. Craven 19; G. White 13; K. McKinlay 9; D. Bradley 8; M. Broadbanks 6; R. How 6; B. Bales 2.

1959—No Contest.

1955		
Vaxjo	Sweden 51,	Australasia 45
Norkopping	Sweden 47,	Australasia 49
Gothenburg	Sweden 59,	Australasia 36
1956		
Vaxjo	Sweden 58,	Australasia 50
Norkopping	Sweden 52,	Australasia 52
Stockholm	Sweden 60,	Australasia 48
1957		
Vaxjo	Sweden 44,	Australasia 40
Norkopping	Sweden 54,	Australasia 40
Stockholm	Sweden 59,	Australasia 37
1958		

At Vaxjo, October 5

Sweden (56): O. Fundin 13; O. Nygren 12; P. Soederman 10; R. Sormander 9; T. Karlsson 6; L. Carlsson 6; A. Nilsson 0.

Australasia (40): R. Moore 12; B. Briggs 7; P. Moore 5; R. Johnston 5; A. Lawson 5; J. Geran 4; N. Street 2.

At Norkopping, October 7

Sweden (51): O. Nygren 15; O. Fundin 15; R. Sormander 8; B. Knutsson 3; P. Soederman 3; J. Jansson 1; B. Lindarw 1.

Australasia (45): A. Lawson 13; R. Johnston 8; P. Moore 7; R. Moore 5; B. Briggs 5; J. Geran 4; N. Street 3.

At Stockholm, October 9

Sweden (49): O. Fundin 15; P. Soederman 12; O. Nygren 11; B. Knutsson 4; R. Sormander 3; B. Nilsson 3; B. Ericsson 1.

Australasia (47): R. Johnston 11; R. Moore 10; A. Lawson 9; B. Briggs 8; J. Geran 6; N. Street 2; T. Redmond 1.

Vic Duggan

ENGLAND v. POLAND

1958

At Southampton, June 3
England (83): D. Bradley 15; P. Craven 14; R. How 13; G. Jackson 11; A. Forrest 9; G. White 9; K. McKinlay 8; I. Williams 4.
Poland (25): F. Kapala 9; J. Suchecki 6; E. Kupczynski 4; J. Maj 2; M. Kaiser 2; H. Zyto 2; S. Tkocz 0.

At Ipswich, June 5
England (77): P. Craven 18; K. McKinlay 13; D. Bradley 13; R. How 10; N. Boocock 10; G. White 10; G. Jackson 3.
Poland (30): F. Kapala 10; M. Kaiser 8; H. Zyto 7; J. Maj 2; J. Suchecki 2; E. Kupczynski 1; S. Tkocz 0.

At Leicester, June 6
England (84): K. McKinlay 15; P. Craven 15; G. White 13; R. How 12; D. Bradley 10; A. Forrest 8; G. Jackson 7; I. Williams 4.
Poland (24): M. Kaiser 10; F. Kapala 7; H. Zyto 7; E. Kupczynski 0; J. Maj 0; J. Suchecki 0.

At Warsaw, September 29
Poland (27): S. Tkocz 7; M. Polukard 7; M. Kaiser 6; S. Kwoczala 4; P. Waloszek 3; F. Kapala 0; H. Zyto 0.
England (81): P. Craven 17; G. White 14; M. Broadbanks 12; K. McKinlay 12; D. Bradley 10; R. How 10; B. Bales 6.

Brian Crutcher

At Rybnik, October 4
Poland (33): J. Maj 13; S. Tkocz 7; M. Polukard 6; E. Kupczynski 4; M. Kaiser 2; E. Ruran 1; L. Kwocstata 0.
England (75): P. Craven 18; M. Broadbanks 15; G. White 14; K. McKinlay 13; B. Bales 6; R. How 6; D. Bradley 3.

At Wroclaw, October 6
Poland (51): M. Kaiser 15; K. Pociejowicz 15; E. Kupczynski 8; M. Polukard 5; H. Zyto 2; J. Maj 2.
England (56): P. Craven 17; K. McKinlay 14; R. How 13; G. White 6; D. Bradley 2; M. Broadbanks 2; B. Bales 2.
1959—No Contest.

WORLD CHAMPIONSHIP

1936 Lionel Van Praag (Australia)
1937 Jack Milne (U.S.A.)
1938 Bluey Wilkinson (Australia)
1939 Contest cancelled at outbreak of war.
1949 Tommy Price (England)
1950 Freddie Williams (Wales)
1951 Jack Young (Australia)
1952 Jack Young (Australia)
1953 Freddie Williams (Wales)
1954 Ronnie Moore (New Zealand)
1955 Peter Craven (England)
1956 Ove Fundin (Sweden)
1957 Barry Briggs (New Zealand)
1958 Barry Briggs (New Zealand)
1959
1. Ronnie Moore (New Zealand & Wimbledon) 15 points
2. Ove Fundin (Sweden) 13
3. Barry Briggs (New Zealand & Wimbledon) 11
4. Olle Nygren (Sweden) 11
5. Aub Lawson (Australia & Norwich) 11
6. Brian Crutcher (England & Southampton) 10
7. Arne Carlsson (Sweden) 8
8. George White (England & Swindon) 7
9. Peter Craven (England & Belle Vue) 7
10. Geoff Mardon (New Zealand & Southampton) 6
11. Rune Sormander (Sweden) 6
12. Mieczyslaw Polukard (Poland) 5
13. Josef Hofmeister (Germany) 4
14. Peter Moore (Australia & Norwich) 3
15. Ron How (England & Wimbledon) 3
16. Cyril Roger (England & Norwich) 0

BRITISH CHAMPIONSHIP
(in place of World Championship)

1946 Tommy Price (England)
1947 Jack Parker (England)
1948 Vic Duggan (Australia)

LEAGUE WINNERS

Southern League
1929 Stamford Bridge
1930 Wembley
1931 Wembley
1952 Rayleigh
1953 Rayleigh & Exeter

Northern League
1930 Belle Vue
1931 Belle Vue
1946 Middlesbrough

National League
1932 Wembley
1933 Belle Vue
1934 Belle Vue
1935 Belle Vue
1936 Div. 1 – Belle Vue
     Div. 2 – Southampton
1937 Div. 1 – West Ham
     Div. 2 – Bristol
1938 Div. 1 – New Cross
     Div. 2 – Hackney Wick
1939 Div. 1 – Belle Vue
     Div. 2 – Newcastle
1940–45 No competition
1946 Div. 1 – Wembley
1947 Div. 1 – Wembley
     Div. 2 – Middlesbrough
     Div. 3 – Eastbourne
1948 Div. 1 – New Cross
     Div. 2 – Bristol
     Div. 3 – Exeter
1949 Div. 1 – Wembley
     Div. 2 – Bristol
     Div. 3 – Stoke
1950 Div. 1 – Wembley
     Div. 2 – Norwich
     Div. 3 – Oxford
1951 Div. 1 – Wembley
     Div. 2 – Norwich
     Div. 3 – Poole
1952 Div. 1 – Wembley
     Div. 2 – Poole
1953 Div. 1 – Wembley
     Div. 2 – Coventry
1954 Div. 1 – Wimbledon
     Div. 2 – Bristol
1955 Div. 1 – Wimbledon
     Div. 2 – Poole
1956 Div. 1 – Wimbledon
     Div. 2 – Swindon
1957 Div. 1 – Swindon
1958 Div. 1 – Wimbledon
1959 Div. 1 – Wimbledon

Team	P.	W.	D.	L.	Pts.
Wimbledon	16	13	0	3	26
Leicester	16	8	1	7	17
Coventry	16	8	1	7	17
Norwich	16	8	0	8	16
Southampton	16	8	0	8	16
Poole	16	8	0	8	16
Oxford	16	7	0	9	14
Swindon	16	6	0	10	12
Belle Vue	16	5	0	11	10

SOUTHERN AREA LEAGUE

1954 Rye House
1955 Rye House
1956 Rye House
1957 Rayleigh Rovers
1958 No competition
1959 Eastbourne

Team	P.	W.	D.	L.	Pts.
Eastbourne	8	5	1	2	11
Yarmouth	8	4	1	3	9
Aldershot	8	4	0	4	8
Rye House	8	3	0	5	6
Ipswich	8	3	0	5	6

LONDON RIDERS' CHAMPIONSHIP

1930 Jack Ormston (Wembley)
1931 Joe Francis (Crystal Palace)
1932 No competition
1933 No competition
1934 Tom Farndon (New Cross)
1935 Tom Farndon (New Cross)
1936 Vic Huxley (Wimbledon)
1937 Jack Milne (New Cross)
1938 Eric Chitty (West Ham)
1939 Jack Milne (New Cross)
1940–44 No competition
1945 Ron Johnson (New Cross)
1946 Ron Johnson (New Cross)
1947 Vic Duggan (Harringay)

MATCH RACE CHAMPIONSHIP

1931 Vic Huxley
1932 Jack Parker; Eric Langton
1933 Ron Johnson; Tiger Stevenson
1934 Tom Farndon
1935 Tom Farndon
1936–45 No competition
1946 Bill Kitchen; Jack Parker
1947 Jack Parker; Vic Duggan
1948 Jack Parker
1949 Jack Parker
1950 Jack Parker; Aub Lawson
1951 Aub Lawson; Jack Parker; Split Waterman
1952 Split Waterman; Jack Young
1953 Jack Young
1954 Jack Young; Ronnie Moore
1955 Jack Young; Ronnie Moore
1956 Ronnie Moore; Brian Crutcher; Peter Craven
1957 Peter Craven
1958 Peter Craven; Ove Fundin; Brian Crutcher
1959 Ove Fundin; Peter Craven

MIDLAND CUP

1951 Leicester beat Birmingham
1952 Coventry beat Birmingham
1953 Birmingham beat Coventry
1954 Birmingham beat Coventry
1955 Birmingham beat Leicester
1956–59 No competition

NATIONAL TROPHY

1931 Wembley beat Stamford Bridge
1932 Wembley beat Belle Vue
1933 Belle Vue beat Wembley
1934 Belle Vue beat Wembley
1935 Belle Vue beat Harringay
1936 Belle Vue beat Hackney Wick
1937 Belle Vue beat New Cross
1938 Wimbledon beat Wembley
1939–45 No competition
1946 Belle Vue beat Wimbledon
1947 Belle Vue beat Wembley
1948 Wembley beat New Cross
1949 Belle Vue beat West Ham
1950 Wimbledon beat Bradford
1951 Wimbledon beat Wembley
1952 Harringay beat Birmingham
1953 Wimbledon beat Wembley
1954 Wembley beat Norwich
1955 Norwich beat Wembley
1956 Wimbledon beat Belle Vue
1957 No competition
1958 Belle Vue beat Norwich
1959 Wimbledon beat Southampton

1st Round: Oxford 111, Swindon 104.
2nd Round: Norwich 127, Poole 89; Wimbledon 110, Coventry 106; Belle Vue 116, Leicester 100; Southampton 112, Oxford 104.
Semi-Finals: Wimbledon 129, Belle Vue 87; Southampton 128, Norwich 88.
Final: Wimbledon 123; Southampton 93.

BRITANNIA SHIELD

1957 Belle Vue beat Norwich
1958 Belle Vue beat Wimbledon
1959 Wimbledon beat Belle Vue

MIDLAND RIDERS' CHAMPIONSHIP

1952 Len Williams (Leicester)
1953 Graham Warren (Birmingham)
1954 Ron Mountford (Birmingham)
1955 Ken McKinlay (Leicester)
1956 Ken McKinlay (Leicester)
1957 No competition
1958 Jack Geran (Leicester)
1959 Ken McKinlay (Leicester)

SOUTHERN RIDERS' CHAMPIONSHIP

1958 Barry Briggs (Wimbledon)
1959 Ron How (Wimbledon)

S.A.L. RIDERS' CHAMPIONSHIP

1954 Alby Golden (Ringwood)
1955 Mike Broadbanks (Rye House)
1956 Leo McAuliffe (Eastbourne)
1957 Leo McAuliffe (Rayleigh)
1958 No competition
1959 Dave Hankins (Ipswich)

BRANDONAPOLIS

1949 Jack Parker (Belle Vue)
1950 Les Hewitt (Coventry)
1951 Eddie Rigg (Bradford)
1952 Ronnie Moore (Wimbledon)
1953 Jack Young (West Ham)
1954 Geoff Mardon (Wimbledon)
1955 Ken McKinlay (Leicester)
1956–59 No competition

Squash

Compiled by J. H. Horry
Secretary: The Squash Rackets Association

INTRODUCTION

Squash rackets is generally thought to have had its origin at Harrow School in the eighteen seventies when boys waiting for their turn to play rackets knocked a soft ball round some walls adjacent to the racket court. It is the ball which gives its name to the game, which thrived in country houses when in the absence of any organised rules both the court and balls were of varying sizes. The Tennis and Rackets Association finally appointed a sub-committee to frame rules and to lend some semblance of organisation to the game. It was not until 1929 that the Squash Rackets Association was formed and this body now, by means of its affiliations with national associations over all the world except America, virtually controls the game.

In the United States and Canada a slightly different version of the game is played, with a narrower court and a hard ball. The U.S.A. Squash Racquets Association was formed in 1907 and so far efforts to bring the two games together have failed. From time to time reciprocal visits are made by teams from the two countries but the lack of practice in the different conditions makes international competition not seriously practicable.

Women are taking to the game in greater numbers although it is not played in girls' schools to anything like the extent to which it is played in boys' schools. The Wolfe-Noel Cup for Women is the one international competition between the U.S.A. and Great Britain which is regularly played, and the Women's Amateur Championship was started a year before the Amateur Championship.

Throughout the season 1922–23 is indicated by the date "1922" and similarly for all seasons.

THE OPEN CHAMPIONSHIP

1930   Championship instituted. C. R. Read (Queen's Club) designated champion.
*1930   D. G. Butcher (Conservative) *beat* C. R. Read (Queen's), 9–6, 9–5, 9–5 at Queen's and 9–3, 9–5, 9–3 at the Conservative Club.
*1931   D. G. Butcher (Conservative) (holder) *beat* C. Arnold (Bath), 9–0, 9–0, 9–0 at Conservative and 9–3, 9–0, 9–5 at the Bath Club.
*1932   F. D. Amr Bey (amateur champion) *beat* D. G. Butcher (Conservative) (holder), 9–0, 9–7, 9–1 at the Conservative and 5–9, 6–9, 9–2, 9–1, 9–0 at the Bath Club.
*1934   F. D. Amr Bey (holder) *beat* D. G. Butcher (Conservative), 9–4, 8–10, 10–8, 9–0 at the Conservative and 9–6, 6–9, 9–2, 0–9, 9–5 at the Bath Club.
*1935   F. D. Amr Bey (holder) *beat* J. Dear (Prince's) (professional champion), 9–3, 6–9, 8–10, 9–2, 9–4 at the Bath Club and 9–4, 9–7, 3–9, 9–7 at the R.A.C.
*1936   F. D. Amr Bey (holder) *beat* J. Dear (Prince's) (professional champion), 9–7, 7–9, 9–7, 5–9, 9–6 at the R.A.C. and 9–7, 8–10, 9–1, 9–6 at the Bath Club.
*1937   F. D. Amr Bey (holder) *beat* J. Dear (Prince's) (professional champion), 10–8, 10–8, 4–9, 1–9, 9–4 at the R.A.C. and 9–7, 8–10, 9–6, 9–5 at the Bath Club.
*1938   J. Dear (Prince's) (professional champion) *beat* A. E. Biddle (Junior Carlton), 5–9, 9–6, 5–9, 9–6, 9–5 at the Lansdowne Club.
*1946   M. A. Karim (Gezira S.C.) *beat* J. Dear (Queen's) (holder), 9–1, 9–4, 3–9 at the Lansdowne Club and 5–9, 7–9, 9–8, 9–7, 9–4 at the R.A.C.
1947   M. A. Karim (Gezira S.C.) (holder) *beat* J. Dear (Queen's), 9–5, 9–3, 5–9, 1–9, 10–8 at the Lansdowne Club.
1948   M. A. Karim (Gezira S.C.) (holder) *beat* B. C. Phillips (amateur), 9–4, 9–2, 9–10, 9–4 at the Lansdowne Club.
1949   M. A. Karim (Gezira S.C.) (holder) *beat* A. Bari (Cricket Club of India, Bombay), 9–4, 9–2, 9–7 at the Lansdowne Club.
1950   Hashim Khan (R.P.A.F., Peshawar) *beat* M. A. Karim (Gezira S.C.) (holder), 9–5, 9–0, 9–0 at the Lansdowne Club.
1951   Hashim Khan (R.P.A.F., Peshawar) (holder) *beat* M. A. Karim (Gezira S.C.), 9–5, 9–7, 9–0 at the Lansdowne Club.
1952   Hashim Khan (R.P.A.F., Risalpur) (holder) *beat* R. B. R. Wilson (amateur), 9–2, 8–10, 9–1, 9–0 at the Lansdowne Club.
1953   Hashim Khan (R.P.A.F., Risalpur) (holder) *beat* Azam Khan (R.P.A.F., Peshawar), 6–9, 9–6, 9–6, 7–9, 9–5 at the Lansdowne Club.
1954   Hashim Khan (R.P.A.F., Risalpur) (holder) *beat* Azam Khan (R.P.A.F., Peshawar), 9–7, 7–9, 9–7, 5–9, 9–7 at the Lansdowne Club.
1955   Hashim Khan (R.P.A.F., Risalpur) (holder) *beat* Roshan Khan (R.P.N., Karachi), 9–4, 9–2, 5–9, 9–5 at the Lansdowne Club.
1956   Roshan Khan (R.P.N., Karachi) *beat* Hashim Khan (R.P.A.F., Risalpur) (holder), 6–9, 9–5, 9–2, 9–1 at the Lansdowne Club.
1957   Hashim Khan (Pakistan Air Force) *beat* Azam Khan (New Grampians S.R.C.), 9–7, 6–9, 9–6, 9–7 at the Lansdowne Club.
1958   Azam Khan (New Grampians S.R.C.) *beat* Mohibullah Khan (Pakistan Air Force), 9–5, 9–0, 9–1 at the R.A.C.

* *From its institution until the 1946–47 season the championship was played on the challenge system, with home-and-home matches and the stipulation that a third match should be played if the results of the first two were level.*

PUBLIC SCHOOLS' OLD BOYS' COMPETITION

LONDONDERRY CUP
(*Singles, five-a-side*)

	Winners	Runners-up
1934	Eton	Charterhouse
1935	Winchester	Eton
1936	Eton	Winchester
1937	Winchester	Eton
1938	Harrow	Tonbridge
1947	Harrow	Wellington
1948	Lancing	Tonbridge
1949	Tonbridge	Charterhouse
1950	Lancing	Charterhouse
1951	Haileybury	Winchester
1952	Haileybury	Rugby
1953	Lancing	Harrow
1954	Lancing	R.N.C. Dartmouth
1955	Harrow	Haileybury
1956	Lancing	Rugby
1957	Lancing	Rugby
1958	Lancing	Brentwood

THE AMATEUR CHAMPIONSHIP

Played in 1922 at Lords, from 1923 to 1938 at the Bath Club and from 1946 to 1957 at the Lansdowne Club. In 1958 it was played at the R.A.C.

1922   T. O. Jameson *beat* J. E. Palmer-Tomkinson, 17–15, 12–15, 15–0
1923   T. O. Jameson *beat* C. le C. Browning, 15–11, 16–14
1924   W. D. Macpherson *beat* J. E. Palmer-Tomkinson, 17–14, 8–15, 15–7
1925   V. A. Cazalet *beat* J. E. Palmer-Tomkinson, 15–8, 12–15, 18–17
1926   J. E. Palmer-Tomkinson *beat* V. A. Cazalet, 9–5, 9–7, 7–9, 9–6
1927   V. A. Cazalet *beat* H. W. Backhouse, 4–9, 9–6, 3–9, 10–8, 9–4
1928   W. D. Macpherson *beat* V. A. Cazalet, 9–3, 9–1, 5–9, 1–9, 9–1
1929   V. A. Cazalet *beat* W. F. Basset, 9–2, 9–5, 9–7
1930   V. A. Cazalet *beat* K. C. Gandar-Dower, 9–2, 6–9, 7–9, 9–6, 9–2
1931   F. D. Amr Bey *beat* W. D. Macpherson, 9–7, 9–6, 4–9, 5–9, 9–0
1932   F. D. Amr Bey *beat* E. Snell, 9–1, 9–0, 9–4
1933   F. D. Amr Bey *beat* G. O. M. Jameson, 9–0, 9–2, 9–4
1934   C. P. Hamilton *beat* D. M. Backhouse, 9–7, 9–0, 9–4
1935   F. D. Amr Bey *beat* E. Snell, 9–1, 9–0, 9–1
1936   F. D. Amr Bey *beat* E. Snell, 9–4, 9–0, 9–2
1937   F. D. Amr Bey *beat* J. F. Stokes, 9–3, 9–4, 9–2
1938   K. C. Gandar-Dower *beat* D. I. Burnett, 2–9, 10–8, 9–6, 10–8
1939 to 1945 } No competition
1946   N. F. Borrett *beat* J. A. Gillies, 9–3, 9–6, 9–3
1947   N. F. Borrett *beat* J. R. Thompson, 9–2, 9–4, 9–4
1948   N. F. Borrett *beat* B. C. Phillips, 9–2, 9–4, 9–2
1949   N. F. Borrett *beat* H. J. A. Dagnall, 9–4, 9–5, 10–8
1950   N. F. Borrett *beat* G. Hildick-Smith (South Africa), 9–6, 10–8, 9–1
1951   G. Hildick-Smith (South Africa) *beat* B. C. Phillips, 9–3, 9–2, 9–2
1952   A. Fairbairn *beat* R. B. R. Wilson, 9–2, 9–2, 4–9, 9–1
1953   A. Fairbairn *beat* R. B. R. Wilson, 7–9, 9–1, 9–7, 9–7
1954   R. B. R. Wilson *beat* A. Fairbairn, 9–7, 8–10, 9–6, 9–4
1955   I. Amin (Egypt) *beat* R. B. R. Wilson, 4–9, 9–7, 2–9, 9–7, 10–8
1956   R. B. R. Wilson *beat* D. Callaghan (South Africa), 7–9, 8–10, 9–1, 9–4, 9–6
1957   N. H. R. A. Broomfield *beat* I. Amin (Egypt), 9–1, 9–7, 9–4
1958   N. H. R. A. Broomfield *beat* I. Amin (Egypt), 9–2, 9–6, 1–9, 9–7

SQUASH QUIZ

1. Of the three Services which player has the most championships to his credit?

        ★

2. What nationals of which countries have won the Open Championship the greatest number of times?

        ★

3. What happens if during a rally a player drops his handkerchief on the floor?

        ★

4. Has an Englishman ever won the U.S. Amateur Championship and has an American ever won the British Amateur Championship?

        ★

QUIZ ANSWERS

1. Capt. A. A. T. Seymour-Haydon won the R.N. Championship 6 times in all. 2. Egypt and Pakistan have tied with 9 wins each. 3. If the ball in play touches the handkerchief a let may be allowed. If the opponent of the player dropping the handkerchief loses the rally he can appeal on the grounds that he was distracted; if the referee considers that the rally was so lost he can award a let. The player dropping the handkerchief cannot appeal on these grounds. 4. G. Robarts of England won the U.S. Amateur Championship in 1923. No American has won the British Amateur Championship.

THE PROFESSIONAL CHAMPIONSHIP OF THE BRITISH ISLES

This championship is open to professionals of any nationality.
†1920   C. R. Read (Queen's) *beat* A. W. B. Johnson (R.A.C.) at Queen's Club, 15–8, 15–2, 15–5 *and lost* 15–12, 9–15, 3–15, 10–15 at the Royal Automobile Club.
†1928   C. R. Read (Queen's) *beat* A. W. B. Johnson (R.A.C.) at Queen's Club, 9–1, 9–0, 9–0 *and lost* 6–9, 9–3, 8–10, 9–2, 4–9 at the Royal Automobile Club.
*1930   D. G. Butcher (Conservative) *beat* C. R. Read (Queen's) (holder), 9–6, 9–5, 9–5 at Queen's and 9–3, 9–5, 9–3 at the Conservative Club.
*1931   D. G. Butcher (Conservative) (holder) *beat* C. Arnold (Bath Club), 9–0, 9–0, 9–0 at the Conservative Club and 9–3, 9–0, 9–5 at Prince's.
*1933   D. G. Butcher (Conservative) (holder) *beat* J. P. Dear (Prince's), 9–2, 9–3, 9–5 at the Conservative Club and 9–6, 9–7, 1–9, 4–9, 10–8 at Prince's.
*1935   J. P. Dear (Prince's) *beat* D. G. Butcher (Conservative) (holder), 9–3, 9–4, 9–3 and 9–4, 9–1, 9–0 at the Lansdowne Club.
*1936   J. P. Dear (Prince's) (holder) *beat* D. G. Butcher (St. John's Wood S.R.C.), 8–10, 9–3, 9–5, 9–4 at Prince's and 9–4, 9–6, 9–0 at St. John's Wood.
*1937   J. P. Dear (Prince's) (holder) *beat* A. E. Biddle (Junior Carlton), 9–7, 4–9, 0–9, 9–5, 9–3 and 9–5, 9–3, 9–1 at the Royal Automobile Club.

*1938 J. P. Dear (Prince's) (holder) *beat* A. E. Biddle (Junior Carlton), 5–9, 9–5, 5–9, 9–6, 9–5 and 6–9, 9–1, 9–2, 9–6 at the Royal Automobile Club.
1947 L. W. R. Keeble (Lansdowne Club) *beat* A. E. Biddle (Junior Carlton), 6–9, 0–9, 9–3, 9–7, 9–4 at the Hampstead S. and R.F.C.
1948 A. E. Biddle (Junior Carlton) *beat* L. W. R. Keeble (Lansdowne), 0–9, 9–7, 9–0, 9–7 at the Lansdowne Club.
1949 J. P. Dear (Queen's Club) *beat* A. Bari (Cricket Club of India, Bombay), 9–3, 9–4, 9–0 at the Lansdowne Club.
1950 Hashim Khan (R.P.A.F., Peshawar) *beat* A. Bari (Cricket Club of India), 9–4, 9–7, 7–9, 8–10, 9–3 at the Lansdowne Club.
1951 Hashim Khan (R.P.A.F., Peshawar) *beat* L. W. R. Keeble (Lansdowne), 9–3, 9–3, 9–3 at the Lansdowne Club.
1952 Hashim Khan (R.P.A.F., Risalpur) *beat* Azam Khan (R.P.A.F., Peshawar), 9–6, 4–9, 9–7, 5–9, 9–6 at the Lansdowne Club.
1953 Hashim Khan (R.P.A.F., Risalpur) *beat* Azam Khan (R.P.A.F.), Peshawar, 5–9, 9–6, 7–9, 9–5, 9–7 at the Lansdowne Club.
1954 Hashim Khan (R.P.A.F., Risalpur) *beat* Azam Khan (R.P.A.F., Peshawar), 7–9, 9–6, 8–10, 9–5, 9–6 at the Lansdowne Club.
1955 *Not played.*
1956 Azam Khan (New Grampians S.R.C.) *beat* Roshan Khan (R.P.N., Karachi), 10–8, 9–2, 9–0 at the Lansdowne Club.
1957 *Not played.*
1958 Azam Khan (New Grampians S.R.C.) *beat* Nazrullah Khan (Junior Carlton Club) 9–4, 9–0, 9–6 at the R.A.C.

THE PROFESSIONAL CHAMPIONSHIP OF THE UNITED KINGDOM

This championship, instituted in 1954, is open only to professional members of the S.R.A. born and practising in the United Kingdom.
1954 J. H. Giles (Abbeydale Park S.R.C.) *beat* D. W. Harman (unattached), at the Hampstead S. and R.F.C., 9–1, 9–4, 9–1.
1955 J. H. Giles (Abbeydale Park S.R.C.) *beat* D. W. Harman (Ealing S.C.), at the Lansdowne Club, 1–9, 9–6, 9–7, 9–5.
1956 J. H. Giles (R.A.C.) *beat* W. J. Moss (Edgbaston L.T.C.), at the Lansdowne Club, 3–9, 9–4, 9–5, 9–2.
1957 J. H. Giles (R.A.C.) (holder) *beat* W. J. Moss (Edgbaston L.T.C.), 9–6, 9–7, 9–0 at the R.A.C., and 2–9, 1–9, 9–3, 9–5, 9–0 at Edgbaston L.T.C.
1958 J. H. Giles (R.A.C.) (holder) *beat* W. J. Moss (Edgbaston L.T.C.), 9–6, 9–7, 9–0 at the R.A.C., and 9–7, 9–7, 9–4 at Edgbaston L.T.C.

THE WOMEN'S CHAMPIONSHIP

Challenge Cup presented by The Queen's Club. Medals presented by S.R.A. to Finalists.
Played in 1922–39 at The Queen's Club; 1947–58 at The Lansdowne Club.

	Winners	*Runners-up*
1922	Miss J. Cave	Miss N. Cave
1922	Miss S. Huntsman	Miss N. Cave
1923	Miss N. Cave	Miss J. Cave
1924	Miss J. Cave	Miss N. Cave
1925	Miss C. Fenwick	Miss N. Cave
1926	Miss C. Fenwick	Miss N. Cave
1928	Miss J. Cave	Miss C. Fenwick
1929	Miss N. Cave	Miss C. Fenwick
1930	Miss N. Cave	Miss C. Fenwick
1931	Miss C. Fenwick	Miss N. Cave
1932	Miss S. Noel	Miss J. Cave
1933	Miss S. Noel	Miss S. Keith-Jones
1934	Miss S. Noel	Miss M. Lumb
1934	Miss M. Lumb	Hon. Anne Lytton-Milbanke
1936	Miss M. Lumb	Hon. Anne Lytton-Milbanke
1937	Miss M. Lumb	Mrs. I. H. McKechnie
1938	Miss M. Lumb	Mrs. I. H. McKechnie
1939	Miss M. Lumb	Miss S. Noel

1940–1946. *No Competition*

1947	Miss J. Curry *beat* Mrs. R. J. Teague	
1948	Miss J. Curry *beat* Miss J. R. M. Morgan, 9–5, 9–0, 9–10, 6–9, 10–8
1949	Miss J. Curry *beat* Miss J. R. M. Morgan, 2–9, 9–3, 10–8, 9–0
1950	Miss J. R. M. Morgan *beat* Miss J. Curry, 9–3, 9–3, 9–0
1951	Miss J. R. M. Morgan *beat* Miss J. Curry, 9–1, 2–9, 9–3, 9–4
1951	Miss J. R. M. Morgan *beat* Miss J. Curry, 9–3, 9–1, 9–5
1953	Miss J. R. M. Morgan *beat* Mrs. H. R. J. Townsend, 9–4, 9–2, 9–4
1954	Miss J. R. M. Morgan *beat* Miss S. Speight, 9–3, 9–1, 9–7
1954	Miss J. R. M. Morgan *beat* Mrs. G. R. Turner, 9–5, 9–3, 9–4
1956	Miss J. R. M. Morgan *beat* Miss Sheila Speight, 9–6, 9–4, 9–2
1957	Miss J. R. M. Morgan *beat* Miss Sheila Speight, 4–9, 9–5, 9–1, 9–6
1958	Miss J. R. M. Morgan *beat* Mrs. H. G. Macintosh, 9–2, 9–4, 9–2
1958	Miss J. R. M. Morgan *beat* Mrs. H. G. Macintosh, 9–4, 9–1, 9–5

OXFORD v. CAMBRIDGE

Played 28: Oxford won 10, Cambridge won 18.

Played from 1925 to 1931 at Queen's Club; from 1932 to 1937 at the Bath Club; in 1938 at the Junior Carlton Club; in 1945 at Trenchard House; from 1946 to 1951 at the Conservative Club; from 1952 at the Bath Club.

1925	Oxford, 4 ties to 0
1926	Oxford, 4 ties to 1
1927	Oxford, 5 ties to 0
1928	Oxford, 4 ties to 1
1929	Oxford, 4 ties to 1
1930	Cambridge, 5 ties to 0
1931	Cambridge, 5 ties to 0
1932	Cambridge, 5 ties to 0
1933	Cambridge, 3 ties to 2
1934	Cambridge, 4 ties to 1
1935	Cambridge, 4 ties to 1
1936	Cambridge, 5 ties to 0
1937	Cambridge, 3 ties to 2
1938	Cambridge, 5 ties to 0
1945	Oxford, 4 ties to 1
1946	Cambridge, 3 ties to 2
1947	Oxford, 4 ties to 1
1948	Oxford, 5 ties to 0
1949	Oxford, 4 ties to 1
1950	Oxford, 4 ties to 1
1951	Cambridge, 4 ties to 1
1952	Cambridge, 3 ties to 2
1953	Cambridge, 3 ties to 2
1954	Cambridge, 3 ties to 2
1955	Cambridge, 3 ties to 2
1956	Cambridge, 5 ties to 0
1957	Cambridge, 4 ties to 1
1958	Cambridge, 3 ties to 2

THE INTER-COUNTY CHAMPIONSHIP

1929	Yorkshire *beat* Sussex 3 ties to 2
1930	Kent *beat* Yorkshire 5 ties to 0
1931	Sussex *beat* Lancashire 5 ties to 0
1932	Sussex *beat* Lancashire 4 ties to 1
1933	Yorkshire *beat* Sussex 3 ties to 2
1934	Sussex *beat* Yorkshire 4 ties to 1
1935	Sussex *beat* Northumberland 5 ties to 0
1936	Sussex *beat* Cheshire 5 ties to 0
1937	Middlesex *beat* Yorkshire 5 ties to 0
1938	Sussex *beat* Hampshire 5 ties to 0
1946	Middlesex *beat* Warwickshire 4 ties to 1
1947	Middlesex *beat* Surrey 3 ties to 2
1948	Surrey *beat* Essex 4 ties to 1
1949	Middlesex *beat* Devon 3 ties to 2
1950	Sussex *beat* Warwickshire 4 ties to 1
1951	Sussex *beat* Middlesex 3 ties to 2
1952	Sussex *beat* Devon 3 ties to 1, 1 unplayed
1953	Sussex *beat* Surrey 3 ties to 2
1954	Surrey *beat* Yorkshire 3 ties to 2
1955	Surrey *beat* Yorkshire 4 ties to 1
1956	Surrey *beat* Sussex 3 ties to 2
1957	Surrey *beat* Yorkshire 5 ties to 0
1958	Surrey *beat* Essex 5 ties to 0

INTERNATIONAL MATCHES

GREAT BRITAIN v. CANADA
1923	Great Britain won by 4 ties to 1 at Philadelphia
1926	Great Britain won by 4 ties to 2 at Toronto

GREAT BRITAIN v. SOUTH AFRICA
1955	South Africa won by 3 matches to 1 in South Africa
1956	Great Britain won by 3 matches to 0 in Great Britain

GREAT BRITAIN v. U.S.A.
1923	U.S.A. won by 3 ties to 2 at Philadelphia
1924	Great Britain won by 5 ties to 0 at Bath Club, London
1926	Great Britain drew with U.S.A., 3 ties all, at Toronto
1928	Great Britain won by 5 ties to 0 at Bath Club, London
1935	Great Britain won by 5 ties to 0 at Bath Club, London

ENGLAND v. SCOTLAND
†1937	England won by 6 ties to 1 in London
†1938	England won by 5 ties to 2 in Edinburgh
1947	England won by 5 ties to 0 in Edinburgh
1948	England won by 5 ties to 0 in London
1949	England won by 5 ties to 0 in Edinburgh
1950	England won by 5 ties to 0 in London
1951	England won by 5 ties to 0 in Edinburgh
1952	England won by 4 ties to 1 in London
1953	England won by 5 ties to 0 in Edinburgh
1954	England won by 5 ties to 0 in London
1955	England won by 4 ties to 1 in Edinburgh
1956	England won by 5 ties to 0 in London
1957	England won by 5 ties to 0 in Edinburgh
1958	England won by 5 ties to 0 in London

†Five singles and two doubles

ENGLAND v. IRELAND
1948	England won by 5 ties to 0 in Dublin
1949	England won by 5 ties to 0 in London
1950	England won by 5 ties to 0 in Dublin
1951	England won by 5 ties to 0 in London
1952	England won by 4 ties to 1 in Dublin
1953	England won by 5 ties to 0 in London
1954	England won by 5 ties to 0 in Dublin
1955	England won by 5 ties to 0 in London
1956	England won by 5 ties to 0 in Dublin
1957	England won by 5 ties to 0 at the Wimbledon S. and B.C.
1958	England won by 5 ties to 0 in Dublin

ENGLAND v. WALES
1951	England won by 5 ties to 0 in Cardiff
1952	England won by 5 ties to 0 in London
1953	England won by 5 ties to 0 in London
1954	England won by 4 ties to 1 in Cardiff
1955	England won by 5 ties to 0 in London
1956	England won by 5 ties to 0 in Cardiff
1957	England won by 4 ties to 1 in London
1958	England won by 5 ties to 0 in Cardiff

ENGLAND v. DENMARK
1948	England won by 5 ties to 0 in Copenhagen
1949	England won by 5 ties to 0 in London

ENGLAND v. NETHERLANDS
1953	England won by 5 ties to 0 in London

ENGLAND v. SOUTH AFRICA
1956	England won by 5 ties to 0 in Birmingham

SCOTLAND v. IRELAND
1937	Scotland won by 4 ties to 1 in Edinburgh
1938	Scotland won by 4 ties to 1 in Dublin
1946	Ireland won by 5 ties to 0 in Edinburgh
1947	Ireland won by 5 ties to 0 in Dublin
1948	Ireland won by 4 ties to 1 in Edinburgh
1949	Ireland won by 3 ties to 2 in Dublin
1950	Scotland won by 3 ties to 2 in Edinburgh
1951	Scotland won by 3 ties to 2 in Dublin
1952	Scotland won by 4 ties to 1 in Edinburgh
1953	Scotland won by 5 ties to 0 in Belfast
1954	Scotland won by 5 ties to 0 in Edinburgh
1955	Scotland won by 5 ties to 0 in Dublin
1956	Scotland won by 4 ties to 1 in Edinburgh
1957	Scotland won by 5 ties to 0 in Dublin
1958	Scotland won by 5 ties to 0 in Edinburgh

SCOTLAND v. WALES
1947	Scotland won by 4 ties to 1 in Cardiff
1948	Scotland won by 4 ties to 1 in Edinburgh
1949	Wales won by 4 ties to 1 in Cardiff
1950	Scotland won by 4 ties to 1 in Edinburgh
1951	Wales won by 4 ties to 1 in Cardiff
1952	Wales won by 4 ties to 1 in Edinburgh
1953	Wales won by 3 ties to 2 in Cardiff
1954	Wales won by 3 ties to 2 in Edinburgh
1955	Wales won by 3 ties to 2 in Cardiff
1956	Scotland won by 4 ties to 1 in Edinburgh
1957	Scotland won by 4 ties to 1 in Cardiff
1958	Scotland won by 3 ties to 2 in Edinburgh

SCOTLAND v. DENMARK
1949	Scotland won by 5 ties to 0 in Edinburgh

SQUASH QUIZ

1. How many past holders of the Amateur Championship are no longer alive?

★

2. Who has been runner up in the Open Championship the most times?

★

3. How is an appeal for a let made?

★

QUIZ ANSWERS

1. I. V. A. Cazalet, C. P. Hamilton, K. C. Gander-Dower; all killed in the 1939 war. 2. J. Dear, five times. 3. By addressing to the referee or marker the words "Let, please".

IRELAND v. WALES

1947	Ireland won by 5 ties to 0 in Dublin
1948	Wales won by 3 ties to 2 in Cardiff
1949	Ireland won by 3 ties to 2 in Dublin
1950	Wales won by 3 ties to 2 in Cardiff
1951	Ireland won by 3 ties to 2 in Dublin
1952	Wales won by 3 ties to 2 in Cardiff
1953	Wales won by 4 ties to 1 in Dublin
1954	Wales won by 5 ties to 0 in Cardiff
1955	Wales won by 4 ties to 1 in Dublin
1956	Wales won by 4 ties to 1 in Cardiff
1957	Wales won by 3 ties to 2 in Dublin
1958	Wales won by 4 ties to 1 in Cardiff

IRELAND v. BELGIUM

1952	Belgium won by 4 ties to 1 in Brussels

IRELAND v. NETHERLANDS

1952	Ireland won by 5 ties to 0 at The Hague

WALES v. DENMARK

1953	Wales won by 5 ties to 0 in Stockholm

WALES v. SWEDEN

1953	Wales won by 5 ties to 0 in Stockholm

DENMARK v. SWEDEN

1939	Sweden won by 9 ties to 3 in Stockholm
1945	Sweden won by 11 ties to 1 in Stockholm
	Sweden won by 8 ties to 1 in Stockholm
1946	Sweden won by 8 ties to 4 in Copenhagen
1947	Sweden won by 9 ties to 0 in Stockholm
1948	Sweden won by 7 ties to 1 in Copenhagen
1949	Sweden won by 3 ties to 2 in Stockholm
1950	Sweden won by 5 ties to 0 in Copenhagen
1951	Sweden won by 5 ties to 0 in Stockholm
1952	Sweden won by 4 ties to 1 in Copenhagen
1953	Sweden won by 3 ties to 2 in Stockholm
1954	Sweden won by 3 ties to 2 in Copenhagen
1955	Denmark won by 4 ties to 1 in Stockholm
1956	Denmark won by 3 ties to 2 in Copenhagen
1957	Sweden won by 4 ties to 1 in Stockholm
1958	Denmark won by 5 ties to 0 in Copenhagen

CANADA v. U.S.A.

The Lapham Trophy

The Lapham Trophy was presented in the 1921–22 season by Henry G. Lapham of Massachusetts for competition between Canada and the U.S.A. In 1923 and 1926 the English touring teams were invited to take part, while in 1958 the Jesters Touring Team was similarly invited.

1921	U.S.A. 11, Canada 2
1922	U.S.A. 9, Canada 3
1923	U.S.A. 7½, England 6, Canada 1½
1924	U.S.A. 10, Canada 5
1925	U.S.A. 13, Canada 2
1926	England 17½, U.S.A. 16½, Canada 11
1927	U.S.A. 14, Canada 1
1928	Canada 8, U.S.A. 4
1929	U.S.A. 8, Canada 1
1930	Canada 6, U.S.A. 5
1931	U.S.A. 8, Canada 0
1932	Canada 11, U.S.A. 4
1933	U.S.A. 10, Canada 1
1934	U.S.A. 11, Canada 4
1935	U.S.A. 10, Canada 2
1936	Canada 8, U.S.A. 7
1937	U.S.A. 13, Canada 2
1938	Canada 11, U.S.A. 4
1939	Canada 10, U.S.A. 5
1940	U.S.A. 8, Canada 7
1941	U.S.A. 13, Canada 2
1942	Canada 8, U.S.A. 4
1943	U.S.A. 12, Canada 3
1944	Canada 12, U.S.A. 3
1945	U.S.A. 13, Canada 2
1946	Canada 9, U.S.A. 6
1947	U.S.A. 10, Canada 5
1948	Canada 7, U.S.A. 3
1949	U.S.A. 7, Canada 6
1950	U.S.A. 8, Canada 6
1951	Canada 9, U.S.A. 6
1952	U.S.A. 9, Canada 6
1953	U.S.A. 14, Canada 1
1954	Canada 7, U.S.A. 6
1955	U.S.A. 11, Canada 4
1956	Canada 11, U.S.A. 4
1957	U.S.A. 9, Canada 6
1958	Canada 30 pts., Jesters 10 pts., U.S.A. 10 pts.

BELGIUM v. NETHERLANDS

1954	Belgium won by 5 ties to 0 in The Hague
1955	Belgium won by 5 ties to 0 in Brussels
1956	Belgium won by 3 ties to 2 in The Hague
1957	Belgium won by 5 ties to 0 in Brussels

THE AMATEUR VETERANS' CHAMPIONSHIP

For those who have reached 45 years of age on January 1st. This championship is played concurrently with the Amateur Championship and was played at the Lansdowne Club from 1951 to 1957. In 1958 it was played at the R.A.C.

1951	G. O. M. Jameson *beat* W. B. Scott, 9–2, 9–1, 9–3
1952	G. O. M. Jameson *beat* I. E. Dear, 9–5, 9–5, 9–6
1953	G. O. M. Jameson *beat* W. A. J. Rushbrooke, 9–6, 5–9, 0–9, 9–6, 9–3
1954	G. O. M. Jameson *beat* Lord Ronaldshay, 9–5, 9–6, 9–7
1955	G. O. M. Jameson *beat* C. M. Carr, 9–3, 9–1, 9–6
1956	H. W. P. Whiteley (South Africa) *beat* E. J. E. Readwin, 9–5, 9–0, 9–6
1957	F. R. D. Corbett *beat* A. P. Pellew, 10–8, 9–7, 9–2
1958	F. R. D. Corbett *beat* J. B. Atkinson, 9–2, 4–9, 9–1, 9–2

Women's Squash

THE WOLFE-NOEL CUP

1933	Great Britain *beat* U.S.A., 4 ties to 1, New York
1934	Great Britain *beat* U.S.A., 5 ties to 0, London
1935	U.S.A. *beat* Great Britain, 3 ties to 2, Boston
1936	Great Britain *beat* U.S.A., 5 ties to 0, London
1937	U.S.A. *beat* Great Britain, 3 ties to 2, New York
1939	Great Britain *beat* U.S.A., 5 ties to 0, London
1949	U.S.A. *beat* Great Britain, 3 ties to 2, Philadelphia
1950	Great Britain *beat* U.S.A., 5 ties to 0, London
1952	U.S.A. *beat* Great Britain, 4 ties to 1, Boston
1953	Great Britain *beat* U.S.A., 5 ties to 0, London
1955	Great Britain *beat* U.S.A., 4 ties to 1, Philadelphia
1957	Great Britain *beat* U.S.A., 5 ties to 0, London
1959	U.S.A. *beat* Great Britain, 3 ties to 2, Philadelphia

Swimming

Compiled by **Pat Besford**

Swimming Correspondent: The Daily Mail

BRIEF HISTORY OF SWIMMING

1869 Metropolitan Swimming Association formed.

1874 This Association became the Swimming Association of Great Britain.

1878 The first national championship, 100 yards free-style for men, was promoted by the South-East London S.C. It was won by J. S. Moore with a time of 1 min. 16¼ secs.

1886 The S.A. of G.B. became The Amateur Swimming Association. Its first officers were: President, A. Clark; Hon. Secretary, W. W. Ramsden; Hon. Treasurer, C. J. Davidson.

1888 Scottish Amateur Swimming Association formed. A.S.A. Club Water Polo championship instituted, Burton S.C. beat Otter S.C., 3–0 goals, in the final.

1895 H. S. Martin won the plain diving championship, the first national diving event organised.

1896 Three swimming events for men (100 m., 500 m. and 1,200 m. free-style) were included in the first revived Olympic Games in Athens.

1900 Jack Jarvis (G.B.) won three Olympic titles in Paris.

1901 Miss H. Thorp won the first women's A.S.A. championship, 100 yards free-style, in 1 min. 30.4 secs.

1903 The A.S.A. instituted 200 yards breast-stroke and 150 yards back-stroke championships for men.

1908 The Federation International de Natation Amateur (F.I.N.A.) was formed in London on July 19 at a meeting convened by the A.S.A. at the Manchester Hotel. George Hearn, then Hon. Secretary of the A.S.A. whose idea was this Federation, became the first Hon. Secretary of F.I.N.A.

1912 Women's events included in the Olympic Games for the first time.

1914 Swimming was included in the curriculum of elementary schools.

1920 Miss Lucy Morton (Blackpool) won the new women's 200 yards breast-stroke (3 mins. 10 secs.) and 150 yards back-stroke (2 mins. 19 secs.) championships of the A.S.A.

1921 Harold Fern, for 16 years Hon. Secretary of the Southern Counties A.S.A., became Hon. Secretary of the A.S.A. He still holds this office.

1924 Miss Morton became the first British woman to win an Olympic swimming title, 200 m. breast-stroke in 3 mins. 33.2 secs., in Paris.

1926 European Swimming League formed in Budapest at the time of the first European swimming championships.

1930 Miss Joyce Cooper (Mermaid and England) won four gold medals at the first British Empire Games in Hamilton, Ontario.

1936 Butterfly, as a variation of breast-stroke, was used in the Olympic games for the first time, but the title was won by T. Hamuro (Japan) using the orthodox underwater arm recovery. The A.S.A. would not recognise this butterfly stroke. Alderman Fern was elected President of F.I.N.A., holding office until 1948.

1946 Wallasey S.C. organised open junior events in conjunction with the national swimming championships at the New Brighton pool. These were so successful that in 1947 the A.S.A. decided to organise official junior national championships. They also decided to recognise butterfly-stroke.

1952 Three Britons, Harold Fern (Hon. Treasurer), Ernest Scott (Hon. Secretary, International Water Polo Board) and Gregory Matveieff (Hon. Secretary, International Diving Committee) were elected by the F.I.N.A.; a record for one country.

1956 The A.S.A. entered into a 3-year contract with the B.B.C. for the televising of International and other swimming fixtures. Judy Grinham (Hampstead L.S.C.), age 17, won the Olympic 100 m. back-stroke title in Melbourne, the first British champion in 32 years. She was elected "Sportswoman of the Year".

1957 Diana Wilkinson (Stockport S.C.), age 13, succeeded Miss Grinham as national "Sportswoman of the Year".

(continued on page 307, col. 4)

SWIMMING QUIZ

1. What is the F.I.N.A.?

*

2. How many national swimming associations are affiliated to this federation?

*

3. What swimming events make up the official Olympic programme?

*

4. Which are the major regional games or championships in which swimming is included?

QUIZ ANSWERS

1. Federation International de Natation Amateur (International Amateur Swimming Federation), the world governing body. 2. 75. 3. Free-style: 100 m., 400 m., 1,500 m. (men only); Back-stroke: 100 m.; Breast-stroke: 200 m.; Butterfly: 200 m. (men), 100 m. (women); 4×200 m. free-style relay (men); 4×100 m. free-style relay (women) and, in the 1960 Games in Rome, 4×100 m. medley relay events. 4. European Championships; British Empire and Commonwealth Games; Pan-American Games; Central American Games; Asian Games; Mediterranean Games.

WORLD RECORD CONDITIONS: World records may be set up only in pools of 50 metres (for metric distances) or 55 yards in length. This decision was taken at the F.I.N.A. Congress held during the Olympic Games in Melbourne in 1956. An operative date of May 1st, 1957 was set for the start of this new "long course" list. Prior to this date records for distances up to and including 440 yards were able to be set up in pools of 25 yards and onwards, but all these "short course" records were wiped out on May 1st, 1957.

METRIC AND YARDS CONVERSIONS

Metres	—	Yards
100	—	109.36
200	—	218.72
400	—	437.44
800	—	874.88
1,500	—	1,640.20

Yards	—	Metres
110	—	100.58
220	—	201.17
440	—	402.34
880	—	804.67
1,650	—	1,508.70

WORLD RECORDS
MEN
(s. Salt water.   m. Mixed, salt and fresh water.)

Event	Name and Country	Time m. s.	Venue	Date	British best (long course performance) Name	Time m. s.	Year
Free-style							
100 m.	J. Devitt (Australia)	54.6	Brisbane	28.1.57	R. Roberts and	58.0	1955
110 yds.	J. Devitt (Australia)	55.1	N. Sydney m.	7.2.59	I. Black	58.0	1959
200 m.	T. Yamanaka (Japan)	2 01.5	Osaka	27.7.59	I. M. Black	2 05.6	1958
220 yds.	J. Konrads (Australia)	2 02.2	N. Sydney m.	16.1.59	I. M. Black	2 05.6	1958
400 m.	T. Yamanaka (Japan)	4 16.6	Osaka	27.7.59	I. M. Black	4 28.4	1958
440 yds.	J. Konrads (Australia)	4 19.0	N. Sydney m.	7.2.59	I. M. Black	4 28.4	1958
800 m.	J. Konrads (Australia)	8 59.6	N. Sydney m.	10.1.59	I. M. Black	9 25.5	1958
880 yds.	J. Konrads (Australia)	8 59.6	N. Sydney m.	10.1.59	I. M. Black	9 25.5	1958
1,500 m.	J. Konrads (Australia)	17 28.7	Melbourne	22.2.58	I. M. Black	18 05.8	1958
1,650 yds.	J. Konrads (Australia)	17 28.7	Melbourne	22.2.58	I. M. Black	18 06.2	1958
Back-stroke							
100 m.	J. Monckton (Australia)	1 01.5	Melbourne	15.2.58	G. Sykes	1 04.8	1958
110 yds.	J. Monckton (Australia)	1 01.5	Melbourne	15.2.58	G. Sykes	1 04.8	1958
200 m.	F. McKinney (U.S.A.)	2 17.8	Osaka	25.7.59	G. Sykes	2 23.9	1959
220 yds.	J. Monckton (Australia)	2 18.4	Melbourne	18.2.58	G. Sykes	2 27.0	1957
Breast-stroke							
100 m.	M. Suan-Su (Chin. P.R.)	1 11.1	Tokyo	18.9.59	C. Walkden	1 17.5	1957
110 yds.	T. Gathercole (Australia)	1 12.4	Townsville	28.6.58	A. Longega	1 18.1	1954
200 m.	T. Gathercole (Australia)	2 36.5	Townsville	28.6.58	C. Walkden	2 43.9	1958
220 yds.	T. Gathercole (Australia)	2 36.5	Townsville	28.6.58	C. Walkden	2 43.9	1958
Butterfly							
100 m.	T. Ishimoto (Japan)	1 00.1	Los Angeles	29.6.58	G. Symonds	1 05.3	1957
110 yds.	T. Jecko (U.S.A.)	1 03.2	New London s.	14.8.58	I. M. Black	1 06.0	1957
200 m.	M. Troy (U.S.A.)	2 16.4	Los Altos	11.7.59	I. M. Black	2 21.8	1958
220 yds.	M. Troy (U.S.A.)	2 18.6	Louisville	22.7.59	I. M. Black	2 22.6	1958
Individual Medley							
400 m.	I. M. Black (G.B.)	5 08.8	Cardiff	6.6.59	I. M. Black	5 08.8	1959
440 yds.	I. M. Black (G.B.)	5 08.8	Cardiff	6.6.59	I. M. Black	5 08.8	1959
Free-style Relays							
4 x 100 m.	National team (U.S.A.) (Follett, Larsen, Farrell, Alkire)	3 44.4	Tokyo	21.7.59	Tasker, Boyes, Rigby, McKechnie	3 59.9	1957
4 x 110 yds.	National team (Australia) (Devitt, Chapman, Shipton, Konrads)	3 47.3	Sydney s.	9.2.58	Tasker, Boyes, Rigby, McKechnie	3 59.9	1957
4 x 200 m.	National team (Japan) (Yamanaka, Fukui, Kenjo, Fujimoto)	8 18.7	Osaka	26.7.59	Williams, Roberts, McKechnie, J. Wardrop	8 39.1	1956
4 x 220 yds.	National team (Australia) (Konrads, Hamilton, Devitt, Chapman)	8 24.5	Sydney s.	5.3.58	Clarke, Black, Barnes, McKechnie	8 49.4	1958
Medley Relays							
4 x 100 m.	National team (Australia) (Monckton, Gathercole, Wilkinson, Devitt)	4 10.4	Osaka	22.8.58	Sykes, Walkden, Symonds, McKechnie	4 26.4	1958
4 x 110 yds.	National team (Australia) (Monckton, Gathercole, Wilkinson, Devitt)	4 14.2	Cardiff	25.7.58	Sykes, Walkden, Symonds, McKechnie	4 26.4	1958

WOMEN

Event	Name and Country	Time m. s.	Venue	Date	British best (long course performance) Name	Time m. s.	Year
Free-style							
100 m.	D. Fraser (Australia)	1 01.2	Schiedam	10.8.58	N. Steward	1 04.5	1959
110 yds.	D. Fraser (Australia)	1 01.4	Cardiff	27.7.58	N. Steward	1 04.8	1959
200 m.	D. Fraser (Australia)	2 14.7	Melbourne	22.2.58	N. Rae	2 25.3	1959
220 yds.	D. Fraser (Australia)	2 14.7	Melbourne	22.2.58	N. Rae	2 25.3	1959
400 m.	Vacant, basic time	4 47.2	—	—	N. Rae	5 03.2	1959
440 yds.	L. Crapp (Australia)	4 48.6	Sydney s.	20.10.56	N. Rae	5 03.2	1959
800 m.	I. Konrads (Australia)	10 11.4	Hobart	19.2.59	E. Ferguson	11 37.2	1958
880 yds.	I. Konrads (Australia)	10 11.4	Hobart	19.2.59	E. Ferguson	11 37.2	1958
1,500 m.	I. Konrads (Australia)	19 25.7	N. Sydney m.	14.1.59	No times recorded		
1,650 yds.	I. Konrads (Australia)	19 25.7	N. Sydney m.	14.1.59	No times recorded		
Back-stroke							
100 m.	C. Cone (U.S.A.)	1 11.4	Chicago	6.9.59	J. Grinham	1 11.9	1958
110 yds.	J. Grinham (G.B.)	1 11.9	Cardiff	23.7.58	J. Grinham	1 11.9	1958
200 m.	S. Tanaka (Japan)	2 37.1	Tokyo	12.7.59	M. Edwards	2 41.1s.	1957
220 yds.	C. Cone (U.S.A.)	2 37.9	Redding	17.7.59	M. Edwards	2 41.1s.	1957
Breast-stroke							
100 m.	K. Beyer (E. Germany)	1 19.6	Leipzig	12.9.58	A. Lonsbrough	1 22.0	1959
110 yds.	Vacant, basic time	1 21.6	—	—	A. Lonsbrough	1 23.0	1959
200 m.	A. Lonsbrough (G.B.)	2 50.3	Waalwijk	25.7.59	A. Lonsbrough	2 50.3	1959
220 yds.	A. den Haan (Holland)	2 52.5	Blackpool s.	18.5.57	A. Lonsbrough	2 53.0	1959
Butterfly							
100 m.	N. Ramey (U.S.A.)	1 09.1	Chicago	2.9.59	C. Gosden	1 13.0	1959
110 yds.	N. Ramey (U.S.A.)	1 09.8	Chicago	2.9.59	C. Gosden	1 13.4	1959
200 m.	B. Collins (U.S.A.)	2 37.0	Redding, Calif.	19.7.59	No British times		
220 yds.	B. Collins (U.S.A.)	2 37.0	Redding, Calif.	19.7.59	No British times		
Individual Medley							
400 m.	S. Ruuska (U.S.A.)	5 40.2	Redding, Calif.	17.7.59	C. Gosden	6 04.7	1959
440 yds.	S. Ruuska (U.S.A.)	5 40.2	Redding, Calif.	17.7.59	C. Gosden	6 04.7	1959

1958 Miss Grinham achieved an historic treble by adding the Empire and European back-stroke titles to her Olympic one. She also broke two world back-stroke records.

Swimming made a clean sweep in National sports polls. Miss Grinham again became top sportswoman; Ian Black (Aberdeen) 17, triple gold medallist at the European championships, was chosen as top sportsman by the Sports Writers' Association (the first swimmer and first Scot to be honoured), in a national poll and in two B.B.C. television polls. Diana Wilkinson was the best junior sportsgirl.

SWIMMING QUIZ
WORLD RECORDS

1. Who has broken the most individual world records since the Second World War? (below)

★

2. Who broke the most world records in one swim?

★

GENERAL

3. Can a 440 yards world record be set up in a 50 metres bath?

★

4. Can a 400 metres world record be set up in a 55 yards bath?

★

5. What is the order of swimming in a medley relay?

QUIZ ANSWERS

1. Jon Konrads (Australia), 20, between January 1958 and February 1959. 2. Arne Borg (Sweden), five, September 11th, 1925, in Stockholm: 300 yards, 300 m., 400 m., 440 yards and 500 yards free-style. Only 400 m. and 440 yards are now recognised world-record distances. 3. No. Yards records must be set up in baths 55 yards in length. 4. Yes. If the record for the yards distance (i.e. 440 yards) is better than the standing record for the shorter metric distance (i.e. 400 metres=437.44 yards), then it counts for the metric distance but only one world-record certificate is given. 5. 1. Back-stroke; 2. Breast-stroke; 3. Butterfly; 4. Free-style. In international rules "free-style" designates any style other than back-stroke, breast-stroke or butterfly.

Free-style Relays

4 x 100 m.	National team (Australia) (Fraser, Leech, Morgan, Crapp)	4	17.1	Melbourne	6.12.56	Wilkinson, Noakes, Toms, Steward	4 23.5	1959
4 x 110 yds.	National team (Australia) (Crapp, Morgan, Colquhoun, Fraser)	4	17.4	Cardiff	19.7.58	Wilkinson, Noakes, Toms, Steward	4 23.5	1959

Medley Relays

4 x 100 m.	National team (U.S.A.) (Cone, Bancroft, Collins, von Saltza)	4	44.6	Chicago	6.9.59	Edwards, Lonsbrough, Gosden, Wilkinson	4 53.6	1959
4 x 110 yds.	National team (England) (Grinham, Lonsbrough, Gosden, Wilkinson)	4	54.0	Cardiff	25.7.58	Grinham, Lonsbrough, Gosden, Wilkinson	4 54.0	1958

BRITISH RECORD HOLDERS

* Long course (55-yards bath) times

Event	MEN	m. s.	WOMEN	m. s.
FREE-STYLE:				
100 yards	N. J. McKechnie (*Wallasey*)	51.8	D. E. Wilkinson (*Stockport*)	58.7
110 yards	N. J. McKechnie (*Wallasey*)	57.8	N. Steward (*Hornchurch*)	1 04.8*
220 yards	I. M. Black (*R. Gordon College, Aberdeen*)	2 05.6*	D. E. Wilkinson (*Stockport*)	2 25.2
440 yards	I. M. Black (*R. Gordon College, Aberdeen*)	4 28.4*	N. Rae (*Motherwell*)	5 03.2*
880 yards	I. M. Black (*R. Gordon College, Aberdeen*)	9 25.5*	E. Ferguson (*York City*)	11 37.3*
One mile	I. M. Black (*R. Gordon College, Aberdeen*)	19 17.5*	E. Ferguson (*York City*)	23 31.8*
BACK-STROKE:				
100 yards	G. Sykes (*Coventry*)	57.0	J. B. Grinham (*Hampstead*)	1 04.8
110 yards	J. C. Wardrop (*Motherwell*)	1 04.2	M. Edwards (*Heston*)	1 11.7
BREAST-STROKE:				
100 yards	C. C. Walkden (*Beckenham*)	1 04.4	C. L. Gosden (*Croydon*)	1 14.7
110 yards	C. C. Walkden (*Beckenham*)	1 10.4	C. L. Gosden (*Croydon*)	1 22.4
200 yards	C. C. Walkden (*Beckenham*)	2 21.9	A. Lonsbrough (*Huddersfield*)	2 35.1
220 yards	C. C. Walkden (*Beckenham*)	2 36.3	A. Lonsbrough (*Huddersfield*)	2 53.0*
BUTTERFLY:				
100 yards	I. M. Black (*R. Gordon College, Aberdeen*)	54.8	S. Watt (*Aberdeen, Thistle*)	1 04.7
110 yards	I. M. Black (*R. Gordon College, Aberdeen*)	1 00.8	S. Watt (*Aberdeen, Thistle*)	1 12.0
200 yards	G. H. Symonds (*Coventry*)	2 06.6	No record for women	—
220 yards	G. H. Symonds (*Coventry*)	2 19.7	No record for women	—
INDIVIDUAL MEDLEY:				
440 yards	Vacant	—	Vacant	—
440 yards	I. M. Black (*R. Gordon College, Aberdeen*)	5 08.8*	C. Gosden (*Croydon*)	6 04.7*

BRITISH JUNIOR RECORD HOLDERS

Swimmers must be under 16 on the day of the performance
* Long course (55-yards bath) times

Event	BOYS	m. s.	GIRLS	m. s.
FREE-STYLE:				
100 yards	I. M. Black (*R. Gordon College, Aberdeen*)	53.2	D. E. Wilkinson (*Stockport*)	58.7
110 yards	I. M. Black (*R. Gordon College, Aberdeen*)	59.0	D. E. Wilkinson (*Stockport*)	1 05.6*
220 yards	I. M. Black (*R. Gordon College, Aberdeen*)	2 12.5	D. E. Wilkinson (*Stockport*)	2 25.2
440 yards	I. M. Black (*R. Gordon College, Aberdeen*)	4 43.2*	N. Rae (*Motherwell*)	5 03.2*
BACK-STROKE:				
100 yards	C. Bissett (*Warrender*)	1 01.4	C. Hussey (*Nottingham*)	1 06.6
110 yards	N. J. McKechnie (*Wallasey*)	1 09.2	C. Hussey (*Nottingham*)	1 13.2
BREAST-STROKE:				
100 yards	C. C. Wilkinson (*Stockport*)	1 08.5	J. Dyson (*Kingston*)	1 14.7
110 yards	C. C. Wilkinson (*Stockport*)	1 15.6	C. L. Gosden (*Croydon*)	1 24.2
200 yards	C. C. Wilkinson (*Stockport*)	2 28.7	A. M. R. Turnbull (*Galashiels*)	2 39.4
220 yards	C. C. Wilkinson (*Stockport*)	2 43.7	J. Dyson (*Kingston*)	2 58.1*
BUTTERFLY:				
100 yards	I. M. Black (*R. Gordon College, Aberdeen*)	57.3	J. Oldroyd (*Dewsbury*)	1 06.6
110 yards	I. M. Black (*R. Gordon College, Aberdeen*)	1 03.6	J. Oldroyd (*Dewsbury*)	1 13.2

EUROPEAN RECORD HOLDERS

(Long course performances only)

Event	MEN	m. s.	WOMEN	m. s.
FREE-STYLE:				
100 m.	P. Pucci (*Italy*)	56.1	C. Gastelaars (*Holland*)	1 02.9
200 m.	Vacant, basic time	2 05.2	C. Schimmel (*Holland*)	2 22.1
400 m.	I. M. Black (*G.B.*)	4 28.4	C. Schimmel (*Holland*)	4 52.4
800 m.	G. Montserret (*France*)	9 22.7	C. Schimmel (*Holland*)	10 22.3
1,500 m.	I. M. Black (*G.B.*)	18 05.8	C. Schimmel (*Holland*)	19 46.2
BACK-STROKE:				
100 m.	R. Christophe (*France*)	1 02.2	R. van Velsen (*Holland*)	1 11.7
200 m.	W. Wagner (*E. Germany*)	2 19.8	R. Dobber (*Holland*)	2 37.5
BREAST-STROKE:				
100 m.	W. Minaschkin (*U.S.S.R.*)	1 11.5	K. Beyer (*E. Germany*)	1 19.6
200 m.	K. Enke (*E. Germany*)	2 38.6	A. Lonsbrough (*G.B.*)	2 50.3
BUTTERFLY:				
100 m.	F. Dennerlein (*Italy*)	1 01.8	A. Voorbij (*Holland*)	1 10.5
200 m.	F. Dennerlein (*Italy*)	2 19.5	T. Lagerberg (*Holland*)	2 38.9
INDIVIDUAL MEDLEY:				
400 m.	I. M. Black (*G.B.*)	5 08.8	Vacant, basic time	5 49.0
FREE-STYLE RELAY:				
4 x 100 m.	National team (*U.S.S.R.*) (Morgatchev, Lujkowski, Sorokin, Polevoi)	3 47.1	National team (*Holland*) (Schimmel, Lagerberg, Kraan, Gastelaars)	4.22.9
4 x 200 m.	National team (*U.S.S.R.*) (Sorokin, Stroujanov, Nikolaev, Nikitin)	8 27.1	No record for women	

(contd. opposite)

OLYMPIC GAMES

1. Judy Grinham, who won the 100 m. back-stroke title in 1956, was the first British swimmer in how many years to win an Olympic medal? Who was the swimmer before Judy, what was the event?

＊

2. Who was the youngest person to win an Olympic championship?

＊

WORLD RECORDS

3. Which world record stood for the longest time?

＊

4. Which world record stood for the shortest time?

＊

5. Who has broken the most individual world records?

QUIZ ANSWERS

1. 32 years. Miss Lucy Morton, 200 m. breast-stroke in 1924. 2. Aileen Riggin (U.S.A.) who won the springboard diving in 1920 when she was only 13. 3. Women's 100 m. free-style, 20 years. Willy den Ouden (Holland) recorded 64.6 seconds in Amsterdam on February 27th, 1936. Dawn Fraser (Australia), with 64.5 seconds in Sydney, February 21st, 1956, was first to improve Miss den Ouden's time. 4. Women's 110 yards back-stroke, 15 minutes. Margaret Edwards (Great Britain) defeated Lenie de Nijs (Holland) in an international match at the Derby bath, Blackpool, on May 18th, 1957, in a world-record time of 1 min. 13.5 secs. Fifteen minutes later she had to turn out in the medley relay and on the first leg was beaten by Greetje Kraan (Holland) whose "split" time, 1 min. 13.2 secs., broke Margaret's new record. M. Lusien (France) and G. Kettesy (Hungary) both broke the men's 400 m. individual medley record on April 24th, 1953; Lusien in Troyes, Kettesy in Budapest. As there was no note of the exact time of the day they broke their records, both times were ratified, the slower one first. 5. Ragnhild Hveger (Denmark), 41 records between 1936 and 1942, for distances from 200 m. to 1,760 yards free-style and for 200 m. and 400 m. back-stroke.

EUROPEAN CHAMPIONS

* European championships record.
† European record.
‡ World and European record.

Men			Women		

100 METRES FREE-STYLE

	Men	m. s.		Women	m. s.
1926	I. Barany (Hungary)	1 01.0	1926		
1927	A. Borg (Sweden)	1 00.0	1927	M. Vierdag (Neth.)	1 15.0
1931	I. Barany (Hungary)	59.8	1931	Y. Goddard (France)	1 10.0
1934	F. Csik (Hungary)	59.7	1934	W. den Ouden (Neth.)	1 07.1
1938	K. Hoving (Neth.)	59.8	1938	R. Hveger (Denmark)	1 06.2
1947	A. Jany (France)	56.9	1947	F. Nathansen (Den.)	1 07.8
1950	A. Jany (France)	57.7	1950	I. Schumacher (Neth.)	1 06.4
1954	I. Nyeki (Hungary)	57.8	1954	K. Szoke (Hungary)	1 05.8
1958	P. Pucci (Italy)	56.3	1958	K. Jobson (Sweden)	1 04.7
	V. Polevoi (U.S.S.R.)	56.9		C. Gastelaars (Neth.)	1 05.0
	G. Dobai (Hungary)	57.5		J. Grinham (G.B.)	1 05.4
				Relay heat	
Heat:	P. Pucci (Italy)	56.1*†		*1st leg: Gastelaars (Neth.)*	1 03.7*†

(contd. on p. 309, col. 1)

European Record Holders—*(contd.)*

Event	MEN	m. s.	WOMEN	m. s.
MEDLEY RELAY:				
4 x 100 m.	National team (*U.S.S.R.*) (Barbier, Minaschkin, Zsenyenkov, Polevoi)	4 16.5	National team (*Holland*) (van Velsen, den Haan, Lagerberg, Gastelaars)	4 51.5

400 METRES FREE-STYLE

Year	Name	m.	s.	Year	Name	m.	s.
1926	A. Borg (Sweden)	5	14.2	1926	—		
1927	A. Borg (Sweden)	5	08.6	1927	M. Braun (Neth.)	6	11.8
1931	I. Barany (Hungary)	5	04.0	1931	M. Braun (Neth.)	5	42.0
1934	J. Taris (France)	4	55.5	1934	H. Mastenbroek (Neth.)	5	27.4
1938	B. Borg (Sweden)	4	51.6	1938	R. Hveger (Denmark)	5	09.0
1947	A. Jany (France)	4	35.2	1947	K. Harup (Denmark)	5	18.2
1950	A. Jany (France)	4	48.0	1950	G. Andersen (Den.)	5	30.9
1954	G. Csordas (Hungary)	4	38.8	1954	A. Sebo (Hungary)	5	14.4
1958	I. M. Black (G.B.)	4	31.3	1958	J. Koster (Neth.)	5	02.6*
	B. Nikitin (U.S.S.R.)	4	36.2		C. Schimmel (Neth.)	5	02.6
	P. Galetti (Italy)	4	38.1		N. Rae (G.B.)	5	07.7
	Heat: I. M. Black (G. B.)	4	29.9*				

1,500 METRES FREE-STYLE

Year	Name	m	s
1926	A. Borg (Sweden)	21	29.2
1927	A. Borg (Sweden)	19	07.2
1931	O. Halassy (Hungary)	20	49.0
1934	J. Taris (France)	20	01.5
1938	B. Borg (Sweden)	19	55.6
1947	G. Mitro (Hungary)	19	28.0
1950	H. Lehmann (W. Germany)	19	48.2
1954	G. Csordas (Hungary)	18	57.8
1958	I. M. Black (G.B.)	18	05.8*†
	J. Katona (Hungary)	18	13.0
	G. Androssov (U.S.S.R.)	18	30.2

CHAMPIONSHIP VENUES

1926	Budapest
1927	Bologna
1931	Paris
1934	Magdeburg
1938	London
1947	Monaco
1950	Vienna
1954	Turin
1958	Budapest

100 METRES BACK-STROKE

Year	Name	m.	s.	Year	Name	m.	s.
1926	G. Frohlich (Germany)	1	16.0	1926	—		
1927	E. Lundahl (Sweden)	1	17.4	1927	W. den Turk (Neth.)	1	24.6
1931	G. Deutsch (Germany)	1	14.8	1931	M. Braun (Neth.)	1	22.8

(contd. above)

Ian Black

Roy Romain

4 × 200 METRES FREE-STYLE RELAY

Year	Team	m	s
1926	Germany	9	57.2
1927	Germany	9	49.6
1931	Hungary	9	34.0
1934	Hungary	9	30.2
1938	Germany	9	17.6
1947	Sweden	9	00.5
1950	Sweden	9	06.5
1954	Hungary	8	47.8
1958	U.S.S.R. (Nikolajev, Strujanov, Luzkovskij, Nikitin)	8	33.7*
	2. Italy	8	41.2
	3. Hungary	8	45.3

4 × 100 METRES FREE-STYLE RELAY

Year	Team	m.	s.
1926	—		
1927	Great Britain	5	11.0
1931	Netherlands	4	55.0
1934	Netherlands	4	41.5
1938	Denmark	4	31.4
1947	Denmark	4	32.3
1950	Netherlands	4	33.9
1954	Hungary	4	30.6
1958	Netherlands (Schimmel, Lagerberg, Kraan, Gastelaars)	4	22.9†
	2. Great Britain (Grinham, Ferguson, Samuel, Wilkinson)	4	24.2
	3. Sweden	4	28.5

4 × 100 METRES MEDLEY RELAY

Year	Team	m.	s.
1958	U.S.S.R. (Barbier, Minaschkin, Zsenyenko, Polevoj)	4	16.5*
	2. Hungary	4	20.4
	3. Italy	4	21.9

Year	Team	m.	s.
1958	Netherlands (de Nijs, den Haan, Voorbij, Gastelaars)	4	52.9‡
	2. U.S.S.R.	4	54.2
	3. Great Britain (Grinham, Lonsbrough, Gosden, Wilkinson)	4	54.3

SPRINGBOARD DIVING

Year	Name	points	Year	Name	points
1926	A. Mundt (Ger.)	186.42	1926	—	—
1927	E. Riebschlager (Ger.)	173.86	1927	C. Barnett (Austria)	103.32
1931	E. Riebschlager (Ger.)	136.22	1931	O. Jordan (Ger.)	77.00
1934	L. Esser (Ger.)	137.74	1934	O. Jensch-Jordan (Ger.)	74.87
1938	E. Weiss (Ger.)	148.02	1938	B. Slade (G.B.)	103.60
1947	R. Heinkele (France)	126.71	1947	M. Moreau (France)	100.43
1950	H. Aderhold (W. Ger.)	183.60	1950	M. Moreau (France)	155.58
1954	R. Brener (U.S.S.R.)	153.25	1954	V. Choumitcheva (U.S.S.R.)	129.45
1958	L. Ujvari (Hungary)	141.17	1958	N. Krutova (U.S.S.R.)	124.22
	2. H. Rosenfeldt (W. Ger.)	139.77		2. C. Welsh (G.B.)	123.42
	3. R. Brener (U.S.S.R.)	139.39		3. V. Dedova (Choumitcheva) (U.S.S.R.)	122.75

HIGHBOARD DIVING

Year	Name	points	Year	Name	points
1926	H. Luber (Germany)	110.80	1926	—	
1927	H. Luber (Germany)	114.86	1927	B. White (G.B.)	36.04
1931	J. Staudinger (Austria)	111.82	1931	M. Epply (Austria)	34.28
1934	H. Stork (Germany)	98.99	1934	H. Schieche (Germany)	35.43
1938	E. Weiss (Germany)	124.67	1938	I. M. Beeken (Denmark)	37.09
1947	T. Christiansen (Denmark)	105.55	1947	N. Pelissard (France)	60.03
1950	G. Haase (W. Germany)	158.13	1950	N. Pelissard (France)	86.67
1954	R. Brener (U.S.S.R.)	144.01	1954	T. Karakachjanz (U.S.S.R.)	79.86
1958	B. Phelps (G.B.)	143.74	1958	A. Karezkaite (U.S.S.R.)	81.14
	2. M. Csacsba (U.S.S.R.)	136.87		2. R. Gorohovszkaja (U.S.S.R.)	80.93
	3. J. Marton (Hungary)	134.68		3. B. Hanson (Sweden)	80.34

Year	Name	m.	s.	Year	Name	m.	s.
1934	J. C. P. Besford (G.B.)	1	11.7	1934	H. Mastenbroek (Neth)	1	20.3
1938	H. Schlauch (Germany)	1	09.0	1938	C. Kint (Neth.)	1	15.0
1947	G. Vallerey (France)	1	07.6	1947	K. Harup (Denmark)	1	15.9
1950	G. Larsson (Sweden)	1	09.4	1950	R. v.d. Horst (Neth.)	1	17.1
1954	G. Bozon (France)	1	05.1	1954	G. Wielema (Neth.)	1	13.2
1958	R. Christophe (France)	1	03.1*	1958	J. Grinham (G.B.)	1	12.6
	L. Barbier (U.S.S.R.)	1	03.9		M. Edwards (G.B.)	1	12.9
	W. Wagner (E. Germany)	1	05.5		L. Viktorova (U.S.S.R.)	1	13.9

1st leg medley relay final:
J. Grinham (G.B.) 1 12.0*

200 METRES BREAST-STROKE

Year	Name	m.	s.	Year	Name	m.	s.
1926	E. Rademacher (Ger.)	2	52.6	1926	—		
1927	E. Rademacher (Ger.)	2	55.2	1927	H. Schrader (Ger.)	3	20.4
1931	J. Reingoldt (Finland)	2	52.2	1931	C. Wolstenholme (G.B.)	3	16.2
1934	E. Sietas (Germany)	2	49.0	1934	M. Genenger (Ger.)	3	09.1
1938	J. Balke (Germany)	2	45.8	1938	I. Sorensen (Denmark)	3	05.4
1947	R. Romain (G.B.) Bu.	2	40.1	1947	N. van Vliet (Neth.)	2	56.6
1950	H. Klein (W. Germany) Bu.	2	38.6	1950	R. Vergauwen (Belgium)	3	00.1
1954	K. Bodinger (E. Ger.)	2	40.9*	1954	U. Happe (W. Ger.)	2	54.9
1958	L. Kolesnikov (U.S.S.R.)	2	41.1	1958	A. den Haan (Neth.)	2	52.0*
	R. Lazzari (Italy)	2	41.3		A. Lonsbrough (G.B.)	2	53.5
	K. Bodinger (W. Ger.)	2	41.4		W. Urselmann (Ger.)	2	53.8

Bu=won using butterfly prior to separation of this stroke from breast-stroke in 1952.

200 METRES BUTTERFLY-STROKE

Year	Name	m.	s.
1954	G. Tumpek (Hungary)	2	32.2
1958	I. M. Black (G.B.)	2	21.9
	P. Pasdirek (Czecho.)	2	22.6
	G. Symonds (G.B.)	2	25.8
	Heat: I. M. Black (G.B.)	2	21.8*

100 METRES BUTTERFLY-STROKE

Year	Name	m.	s.
1954	J. Langenau (E. Ger.)	1	16.6
1958	T. Lagerberg (Neth.)	1	11.9*
	A. Voorbij (Neth.)	1	12.1
	M. Skupilova (Czecho.)	1	14.3

SWIMMING QUIZ

1. What is the age qualification to take part in junior A.S.A. (of England) championships?

★

2. What is the age qualification to set up a British junior swimming record?

★

3. How many time-keepers must there be for a world record?

★

4. And for British and English records?

★

5. What is the maximum height of the platform or "take off" from which a start may be made in international events?

★

6. How many district swimming associations are there in England?

QUIZ ANSWERS

1. Under 16 years on April 1st in the year of the competition. 2. Under 16 years on the date the record is made. 3. Three. When the time of two time-keepers agrees, that shall be accepted. When all three differ, the middle watch shall be accepted. 4. Senior records—as for world records; Junior records—two watches, and, when differing, the slowest to be accepted. 5. 2' 6" (or 75 centimetres) above the surface of the water. 6. Five: Midlands, North, North-East, South and West.

BRITISH EMPIRE AND COMMONWEALTH CHAMPIONS

*Empire Games record.
† World Record.
‡ World and European Record.

110 YARDS FREE-STYLE
(100 yards, 1930/34)

	Men	m.	s.		Women	m.	s.
1930	M. Bourne (Canada)		56.0	1930	J. Cooper (England)	1	07.0
1934	B. Nurleigh (Canada)		55.0	1934	P. Dewer (Canada)	1	03.0
1938	R. Pirie (Canada)		59.6	1938	E. de Lacey (Australia)	1	10.1
1950	J. Salmon (Canada)	1	00.4	1950	M. McQuade (Australia)	1	09.1
1954	J. Henricks (Australia)		56.6	1954	L. Crapp (Australia)	1	05.8
1958	J. Devitt (Australia)		56.6	1958	D. Fraser (Australia)	1	01.4†
	2. G. Chapman (Australia)		56.6		2. L. Crapp (Australia)	1	03.8
	3. G. Shipton (Australia)		57.0		3. A. Colquhoun (Australia)	1	04.0
	Heat: J. Devitt (Australia)		56.5*				

440 YARDS FREE-STYLE
(400 yards, 1930)

	Men	m.	s.		Women	m.	s.
1930	N. P. Ryan (Australia)	4	39.8	1930	J. Cooper (England)	5	25.4
1934	N. P. Ryan (Australia)	5	03.0	1934	P. Dewar (Canada)	5	45.6
1938	R. Pirie (Canada)	4	54.6	1938	D. J. Green (Australia)	5	39.9..
1954	D. G. Agnew (Australia)	4	49.4	1950	J. Harrison (S. Africa)	5	26.4
1954	G. Chapman (Australia)	4	39.8	1954	L. Crapp (Australia)	5	11.4
1958	J. Konrads (Australia)	4	25.9*	1958	I. Konrads (Australia)	4	49.4*
	2. I. M. Black (Scotland)	4	28.5		2. D. Fraser (Australia)	5	00.8
	3. G. Winram (Australia)	4	32.4		3. L. Crapp (Australia)	5	06.7

(contd. on p. 310, col. 1)

SWIMMING QUIZ

1. Who was the youngest to swim the Channel?

★

2. Who was the oldest?

★

3. Who was the first to swim both ways?

★

4. What was this person's other swimming claim to fame?

★

5. Who was the first to make a double crossing in one year?

★

6. And the youngest to make the double crossing?

★

7. What other Channel record does this swimmer hold?

★

QUIZ ANSWERS

1. Marilyn Bell of Canada who was 17 when she crossed from France to England on July 31st, 1955. 2. Dr. William Edward "Ted" Barnie, a Scottish science master, 54. 3. Edward "Ted" Temme, of Plaistow, London; France to England on August 5, 1927 and England to France August 18, 1934. 4. He was a British Olympic water polo player (1928 and 1936). 5. Dr. Barnie; England to France on July 28, 1951 and France to England on August 16, 1951. 6. Philip Mickman; as an 18-year-old Ossett, Yorks, schoolboy, he swam from France to England on August 22-23, 1949. He was a 21-year-old R.A.F. National Serviceman when he made the return journey on September 2nd, 1952. 7. He holds the "record" for the longest successful swim from France to England; 23 hours 48 minutes.

1,650 YARDS FREE-STYLE
(1,500 yards, 1930/34)

1930 N. P. Ryan (Australia)	18	55.0
1934 N. P. Ryan (Australia)	18	25.4
1938 R. Leivers (England)	19	46.4
1950 G. Johnston (S. Africa)	19	55.7
1954 G. Johnston (S. Africa)	19	01.5
1958 J. Konrads (Australia)	*17*	*45.4**
2. G. Winram (Australia)	*18*	*17.2*
3. M. McLachlan (S. Africa)	*18*	*19.1*

CHAMPIONSHIP VENUES

1930	HAMILTON
1934	LONDON
1938	SYDNEY
1950	AUCKLAND
1954	VANCOUVER
1958	CARDIFF

110 YARDS BACK-STROKE
(100 yards, 1930/34)

1930 J. W. Tripett (England)	1	05.4	1930 J. Cooper (England)	1	15.0
1934 P. Francis (Scotland)	1	05.2	1934 P. Harding (England)	1	13.8
1938 P. Oliver (Australia)	1	07.9	1938 P. Norton (Australia)	1	19.5
1950 J. C. Wild (S. Africa)	1	07.7	1950 J. J. Davies (Australia)	1	18.6
1954 W. J. Brockway (Wales)	1	06.5	1954 J. Harrison (S. Africa)	1	15.2
1958 J. Monckton (Australia)	*1*	*01.7**	*1958 J. Grinham (England)*	*1*	*11.9‡*
2. J. Hayres (Australia)	*1*	*03.5*	*2. M. Edwards (England)*	*1*	*12.6*
3. W. Wheaton (Canada)	*1*	*06.5*	*3. P. Gould (New Zealand)*	*1*	*13.7*

220 YARDS BREAST-STROKE
200 yards, 1930/1934

1930 J. Aubin (Canada)	2	35.4	1930 C. Wolstenholme (Eng.)	2	54.6
1934 N. Hamilton (Scotland)	2	41.6	1934 C. Dennis (Australia)	2	50.2
1938 J. G. Davies (England) Bu.	2	51.9	1938 D. Storey (England)	3	06.3
1950 D. Hawkins (Australia)	2	54.1	1950 H. O. Gordon (Scotland)	3	01.7
1954 J. A. Doms (N. Zealand)	2	52.6	1954 H. O. Gordon (Scotland)	2	59.2
1958 T. Gathercole (Australia)	*2*	*41.6**	*1958 A. Lonsbrough (England)*	*2*	*53.5**
2. P. Rocchi (S. Africa)	*2*	*44.9*	*2. J. Dyson (England)*	*2*	*58.2*
3. C. C. Walkden (England)	*2*	*47.3*	*3. C. Gosden (England)*	*2*	*58.4*
Bu—Butterfly before separation of stroke.					

220 YARDS BUTTERFLY

1958 I. M. Black (Scotland)	*2*	*22.6**
2. G. Symonds (England)	*2*	*25.5*
3. B. Wilkinson (Australia)	*2*	*31.0*

110 YARDS BUTTERFLY

1958 B. Bainbridge (Australia)	*1*	*13.5**
2. T. Stavely (N. Zealand)	*1*	*14.4*
3. M. Iwasaki (Canada)	*1*	*15.9*

4 × 220 YARDS FREE-STYLE RELAY
(200 yards, 1930/34)

1930 Canada	8	42.4
1934 Canada	8	40.6
1938 England	9	19.0
1950 New Zealand	9	27.7
1954 Australia	8	47.6
1958 Australia (Konrads, Wilkinson, Chapman, Devitt)	*8*	*33.4**
2. Scotland (Sreenan, Still, Leiper, Black)	*8*	*54.2*
3. Canada	*9*	*01.8*

4 × 110 YARDS FREE-STYLE RELAY
(100 yards, 1930/34)

1930 England		—
1934 Canada	4	21.8
1938 Canada	4	48.3
1950 Australia	4	44.9
1954 South Africa	4	33.9
1958 Australia (Fraser, Morgan, Crapp, Colquhoun)	*4*	*17.4†*
2. Canada	*4*	*30.0*
3. England (Grinham, Noakes, Marshall, Wilkinson)	*4*	*31.5*

4 × 110 YARDS MEDLEY RELAY
(3 × 100 yards, 1934, 3 × 110 yards, 1938/1954)

1934 Canada	3	11.2	1934 Canada	3	42.0
1938 England	3	28.2	1938 England	3	57.7
1950 England	3	26.3	1950 Australia	3	53.8
1954 Australia	3	22.0	1954 Scotland	3	51.0
1958 Australia (Monckton, Gathercole, Wilkinson, Devitt)			*1958 England (Grinham, Lonsbrough, Gosden, Wilkinson)*		
	4	*14.2†*		*4*	*54.0‡*
2. Canada	*4*	*26.3*	*2. Australia*	*4*	*55.1*
3. England (Sykes, Walkden, Symonds, McKechnie)	*4*	*26.4*	*3. Canada*	*5*	*01.6*

SPRINGBOARD DIVING

	points		points
1930 A. Phillips (Canada)		1930 D. E. Whitsett (S. Africa)	
1934 J. B. Ray (England)	117.12	1934 J. Moss (Canada)	62.27
1938 R. Masters (Australia)	126.36	1938 I. Donnett (Australia)	91.18
1950 G. Athans (Canada)	169.21	1950 E. Child (England)	126.58
1954 P. Heatly (Scotland)	146.76	1954 P. A. Long (England)	128.27
1958 K. R. Collin (England)	*126.78*	*1958 C. Welsh (England)*	*118.81*
2. W. Patrick (Canada)	*124.61*	*2. I. McDonald (Canada)*	*117.01*
3. P. D. Tarsey (England)	*118.81*	*3. E. Ferris (England)*	*113.30*

HIGHBOARD DIVING

	points		points
1930 A. Phillips (Canada)	—	1930 M. Stoneburgh (Canada)	39.30
1934 T. J. Mather (England)	83.83	1934 B. Macready (England)	30.74
1938 C. D. Tomalin (England)	108.74	1938 L. Hook (Australia)	36.47
1950 P. Heatly (Scotland)	156.07	1950 E. Child (England)	70.89
1954 W. Patrick (Canada)	142.70	1954 B. McAulay (Australia)	86.55
1958 P. Heatly (Scotland)	*147.79*	*1958 C. Welsh (England)*	*77.23*
2. B. Phelps (England)	*144.49*	*2. P. A. Long (England)*	*73.69*
3. R. Cann (England)	*138.50*	*3. M. Wieland (England)*	*65.82*

RESULTS OF INTERNATIONAL MATCHES SINCE THE WAR

Sw.—Swimming; Di.—Diving; Wp.—Water-Polo; *Salt water

Date	Result	Events	Venue	Points
1948 Oct. 2/3	G.B. beat Denmark	Sw., Di.	Copenhagen	99–87
1950 Sept. 8/9	G.B. beat Germany	Sw., Di.	Oberhausen	97–94
1951 June 17	G.B. lost to France	Sw.	Brest	52–60
1953 June 27	G.B. lost to Holland	Sw.	*Blackpool	18–30
1955 April 30	England beat France	Sw. (Women)	London	38–26
June 16/17	G.B. lost to W. Germany	Sw., Di., Wp.	Aberdeen	103–110
Aug. 7/8	England beat Denmark	Sw.	Copenhagen	72–63
1956 June 1/2	G.B. beat France	Sw.	Smethwick	86–82
Aug. 3/4	G.B. lost to Holland	Sw.	Coatbridge	72–80
Sept. 27/28	G.B. lost to Hungary	Sw.	*Blackpool	78–98
Oct. 15	England beat Denmark	Sw.	Birmingham	69–57
1957 Feb. 16/17	G.B. lost to Germany	Sw., Di.	Hildesheim	79–111
May 17/18	G.B. drew Holland	Sw.	*Blackpool	78–78
June 21/22	G.B. lost to W. Germany	Sw., Di.	Liverpool	84–102
July 16/17	G.B. beat Yugoslavia	Sw.	London	115–55
Aug. 2/3	G.B. beat Italy	Sw.	Coatbridge	50–22
Aug. 16/17	G.B. beat Sweden	Sw.	Smethwick	60–22
Aug. 17	England beat France	Di.	*Minehead	2–0ev.
Sept. 27	England beat China	Sw.	Pekin	9–3ev.
Oct. 7	England beat China	Sw.	Canton	8–3ev.
1958 April 18/19	G.B. beat W. Germany	Sw.	Cardiff	106½–63½
May 16/17	G.B. beat Holland	Sw.	*Blackpool	95–75
June 13/14	G.B. beat France	Sw.	*Blackpool	113–57
June 21/22	England drew France	Di.	Paris	1–1ev.
July 5/6	G.B. beat W. Germany	Sw., Di., Wp.	Munich	122–112
Oct. 11/12	G.B. beat Sweden	Sw., Di.	Malmo	103–93
June 28	England lost to U.S.S.R.	Di.	*Blackpool	1–3ev.
1959 May 29/30	G.B. beat E. Germany	Sw.	Smethwick	99–69
June 13/14	G.B. lost to E. Germany	Di.	Leipzig	15–29
July 25/26	G.B. lost to Holland	Sw., Wp.	Waalwijk	89–112
July 31/ Aug. 1	G.B. beat Hungary	Sw.	Cardiff	113–72
Aug. 1	England lost to E. Germany	Di.	Dawdon	20–21
Aug. 14/15	G.B. beat W. Germany	Sw., Di., Wp.	*Blackpool	141–99
Aug. 22/23	G.B. beat Sweden and Italy	Sw., Di.	Rome	170–150–138
Sept. 25/26	G.B. lost to Holland	Sw.	Coatbridge	92–93

BOLOGNA TROPHY

Bologna Trophy (Inter-Country Speed Swimming Contest—England v. Scotland v. Wales). In 1927 Great Britain won the Women's 4 × 100 metres free-style relay at the European championships in Bologna. The winning team was Joyce Cooper and Marion Laverty (England), Valerie Davies (Wales) and Ellen King (Scotland). It was decided that the trophy given to them should be competed for annually (except in Olympic year) by swimmers from the three countries.

Past Results

Year	Venue	England	Scotland	Wales
1929	Paisley	19 (1st)	17	—
1930	Nelson	34 (1st)	24	14
1931	Rhyl	36 (1st)	23	13
1933	Dunfermline	32 (1st)	27	13
1934	Hastings	28 (1st)	25	17
1935	Newport (Mon)	35 (1st)	22	14
1937	Renfrew	35 (1st)	22	15
1938	Wembley	34 (1st)	20	18
1939	Barry	36 (1st)	20	16
1947	Aberdeen	30 (1st)	28	14
1949	Birmingham	32 (1st)	25	15
1950	Aberdare	26	30 (1st)	16
1951	Kilmarnock	24	32 (1st)	16
1953	Birmingham	33 (1st)	24	15
1954	Newport (Mon)	28 (1st)	27	17
1955	Aberdeen	34 (1st)	24	14
1956*	Gateshead	40 (1st)	28	16
1957	Newport (Mon)	39 (1st)	30	15
1958	Kilmarnock	37 (1st)	25	19
1959	Liverpool	38 (1st)	29	17

* Held in Olympic Year because Games were during the winter

T. M. YEADEN MEMORIAL TROPHY

Awarded to the English swimmer whose performance is adjudged the best of the year.

938 Doris Storey (*Montague Burton S.C., Leeds*)
939 Norman Wainwright (*Hanley S.C.*)
940–1945 No award
946 Jack Hale (*Hull Kingston S.C.*)
947 Roy Romain (*Otter S.C.*)
948 Jack Hale (*Hull Kingston S.C.*)
949 Margaret Wellington (*Beckenham L.S.C.*)
950 Daphne Wilkinson (*Woolwich S.C.*)
951 Daphne Wilkinson (*Woolwich S.C.*)
952 Daphne Wilkinson (*Woolwich S.C.*)
953 Lillian Preece (*Wallasey S.C.*)
954 Pat Symons (*Northumberland A.S.C.*)
955 Graham Symonds (*Coventry S.C.*)
956 Judy Grinham (*Hampstead Ladies S.C.*)
957 Diana Wilkinson (*Stockport S.C.*)
958 Judy Grinham (*Hampstead Ladies S.C.*)

GEORGE HEARN CUP

Awarded to the English diver whose performances are adjudged the best of the year: Instituted 1954.

1954 Ann Long (*Ilford D.C.*)
1955 Charmian Welsh (*Durham City S.C.*)
1956 David Tarsey (*Ealing*)
1957 Charmian Welsh (*Durham City S.C.*)
1958 Brian Phelps (*Highgate D.C.*)

G. MELVILLE CLARK NATIONAL MEMORIAL TROPHY

Awarded to the English club whose divers are the most successful each year. Instituted 1951.

1951 *Highgate D.C.*   1956 *Highgate D.C.*
1952 *Highgate D.C.*   1957 *Highgate D.C.*
1953 *Highgate D.C.*   1958 *Highgate D.C.*
1954 *Highgate D.C.*
1955 *Highgate D.C.*

Neil McKechnie

Jack Wardrop

VENUES OF NATIONAL (A.S.A.) CHAMPIONSHIPS

Championships were held at varied venues around the country until 1934. Since then the bulk of the championships have been held at centralised venues:

	Swimming	Diving
1935	South Shore, Blackpool	New Brighton, Wallasey
1936	Empire Pool, Wembley	Empire Pool, Wembley
1937	Scarborough, Yorks.	Scarborough, Yorks.
1938	Great Yarmouth	Empire Pool, Wembley
1939	Minehead, Somerset	Minehead, Somerset
1940–45	No championships	
1946	New Brighton, Wallasey	New Brighton, Wallasey
1947	Hastings & St. Leonards	Hastings & St. Leonards
1948	Scarborough, Yorks.	Hastings & St. Leonards
1949	Queen Street, Derby	Weston-super-Mare
1950	Kingsway, Lancaster	Morecambe & Heysham
1951	Kingsway, Lancaster	New Brighton, Wallasey
1952	King Alfred, Hove	New Brighton, Wallasey
1953	Derby Bath, Blackpool	Derby Bath, Blackpool
1954	Derby Bath, Blackpool	Derby Bath, Blackpool
1955	Derby Bath, Blackpool	Derby Bath, Blackpool
1956	Derby Bath, Blackpool	Derby Bath, Blackpool
1957	Derby Bath, Blackpool	Derby Bath, Blackpool
1958	Derby Bath, Blackpool	Derby Bath, Blackpool
1959	Derby Bath, Blackpool	Derby Bath, Blackpool

NATIONAL CHAMPIONS

Championships organised by the Amateur Swimming Association (of England) but open to the World.

* Long course—55 yards or longer bath.

Men

110 YARDS FREE-STYLE

(100 yards up to 1952.) Instituted 1878

		sec.
1946	*A. Jany (France)*	52.0
1947	*P. Kendall (Sutton & Cheam)*	55.2
1948	R. Stedman (*Beckenham*)	55.0
1949	R. Stedman (*Beckenham*)	53.7
1950	P. Kendall (*Sutton & Cheam*)	54.1
1951	G. Larsson (*Sweden*)	52.1

HENRY BENJAMIN NATIONAL MEMORIAL TROPHY

Awarded to the most successful Englishmen's swimming and water-polo club. Instituted 1910.

1910	*Wigan S.C.*
1911	*Hyde Seal S.C.*
1912	*Hyde Seal and Middlesbrough*
1913	*Middlesbrough S.C.*
1914–1919	*No award*
1920	*Hammersmith S.C.*
1921	*Middlesbrough S.C.*
1922	*Penguin S.C.*
1923	*Penguin S.C.*
1924	*Penguin S.C.*
1925	*Weston-super-Mare S.C.*
1926	*Penguin S.C.*
1927	*Penguin S.C.*
1928	*South Manchester S.C.*
1929	*Oldham Police S.C.*
1930	*Oldham Police S.C.*
1931	*Plaistow United S.C.*
1932	*Plaistow United S.C.*
1933	*Otter and Plaistow United*
1934	*Oldham Police S.C.*
1935	*Otter S.C.*
1936	*Penguin S.C.*
1937	*Otter S.C.*
1938	*Otter S.C.*
1939–1945	*No award*
1946	*Otter S.C.*
1947	*Hull Kingston S.C. and Otter S.C.*
1948	*Otter S.C.*
1949	*Otter S.C.*
1950	*Otter S.C.*
1951	*Penguin S.C.*
1952	*Penguin S.C.*
1953	*Otter S.C.*
1954	*Coventry S.C.*
1955	*Otter S.C.*
1956	*Wallasey S.C.*
1957	*Wallasey S.C.*
1958	*Wallasey and Stoke Newington*

SWIMMING QUIZ

1. Who made the longest successful swim from England to France?

★

2. Who hold the Channel crossing records for (*a*) men; (*b*) women?

★

3. Who is the President of the Channel Swimming Association and why is he especially suitable to hold this office?

1952	J. C. Wardrop (*Motherwell*)		53.4
1953	*R. Roberts (*Otter*)		59.5
1954	*G. Baxter (*Gloucester City*)		60.0
1955	*R. Roberts (*Otter*)		58.5
1956	*N. J. McKechnie (*Wallasey*)		58.9
1957	*N. J. McKechnie (*Wallasey*)		59.2
1958	*I. M. Black (*Robert Gordon College, Aberdeen*)		58.3
1959	*I. M. Black (*Robert Gordon College, Aberdeen*)		58.0

Most wins: Six by J. H. Tyers (1892–1897) and J. H. Derbyshire (1898–1901 and 1903–1904).

220 YARDS FREE-STYLE

Instituted 1880

		m.	s.
1946	*A. Jany (*France*)	2	14.0
1947	*J. I. Hale (*Hull*)	2	20.1
1948	J. I. Hale (*Hull*)	2	16.4
1949	P. O. Ostrand (*Sweden*)	2	13.6
1950	J. C. Wardrop (*Motherwell*)	2	16.6
1951	G. Larsson (*Sweden*)	2	12.2
1952	J. C. Wardrop (*Motherwell*)	2	11.2
1953	*R. Roberts (*Otter*)	2	15.8
1954	*J. C. Wardrop (*Motherwell*)	2	11.7
1955	*N. J. McKechnie (*Wallasey*)	2	13.8
1956	*N. J. McKechnie (*Wallasey*)	2	11.3
1957	*N. J. McKechnie (*Wallasey*)	2	12.0
1958	*I. M. Black (*Robert Gordon College, Aberdeen*)	2	7.2
1959	*I. M. Black (*Robert Gordon College, Aberdeen*)	2	6.0

Most wins: Six by J. H. Tyers (1892–1897).

440 YARDS FREE-STYLE

Race originally promoted by Portsmouth S.C. 1884 and conducted as a salt-water championship until 1934.

		m.	s.
1946	*J. I. Hale (*Hull Kingston*)	4	56.2
1947	*J. I. Hale (*Hull Kingston*)	5	00.4
1948	J. I. Hale (*Hull Kingston*)	5	02.4
1949	P. O. Ostrand (*Sweden*)	4	47.5
1950	J. C. Wardrop (*Motherwell*)	4	54.8
1951	J. C. Wardrop (*Motherwell*)	4	49.5
1952	J. C. Wardrop (*Motherwell*)	4	47.2
1953	*R. C. Sreenan (*Whitehall, Dundee*)	4	54.4
1954	*G. H. Symonds (*Coventry*)	4	53.8
1955	*N. J. McKechnie (*Wallasey*)	4	47.0
1956	*N. J. McKechnie (*Wallase*)	4	45.8
1957	*R. C. Sreenan (*Whitehall, Dundee*)	4	53.6
1958	*I. M. Black (*Robert Gordon College, Aberdeen*)	4	28.4
1959	*I. M. Black (*Robert Gordon College, Aberdeen*)	4	32.9

Most Wins: Five by N. Wainwright (1935–1939).

HALF MILE

Originally promoted by the *Sporting Life* 1881.

		m.	s.
1946	*J. I. Hale (*Hull Kingston*)	10	27.4
1947	*J. I. Hale (*Hull Kingston*)	10	49.6
1948	*J. I. Hale (*Hull Kingston*)	10	58.6

SWIMMING QUIZ

1. Who was Edward May?

*

2. What is the approximate cost of making an attempt on the Channel?

*

3. What conditions do the Channel Swimming Association lay down to officially recognise a crossing?

QUIZ ANSWERS

1. He was a Scunthorpe man who in 1954 twice attempted to make the crossing without an accompanying boat. On the second occasion he lost his life. His body was washed ashore on the French coast some weeks later. 2. Between £70 and £80 (figures supplied by the C.S.A.): hire of boat, including services of pilot, £50; boat for training £15; Lanoline, chart, food etc. £5, and C.S.A. fees £6 6s. 0d. 3. "The aspirant must walk into the sea from the shore of departure and swim across the English Channel until he or she actually touches the shore of the mainland on the opposite coast."

Year	Name		m.	s.
1949	*J. C. Wardrop	(*Motherwell*)	10	30.3
1950	*J. C. Wardrop	(*Motherwell*)	10	29.1
1951	*D. Bland	(*Lambton*)	10	33.1
1952	*J. C. Wardrop	(*Motherwell*)	10	03.6
1953	*R. C. Sreenan	(*Whitehall, Dundee*)	10	24.6
1954	*G. H. Symonds	(*Coventry*)	10	48.4
1955	*R. C. Sreenan	(*Whitehall, Dundee*)	10	27.7
1956	*N. J. McKechnie	(*Wallasey*)	10	12.9
1957	*R. C. Sreenan	(*Whitehall, Dundee*)	10	07.8
1958	*R. C. Sreenan	(*Whitehall, Dundee*)	10	07.8
1959	*R. Campion	(*Stoke Newington*)	10	13.5

Most wins: Seven by J. G. Hatfield (1912–13, 1921–25).

MILE

Instituted 1869. Originally promoted by the Metropolitan Swimming Association. Course 1869–1872: River Thames—Putney Aqueduct to Hammersmith Bridge. Thereafter still water—long course.

Year	Name		m.	s.
1946	*J. I. Hale	(*Hull Kingston*)	21	47.2
1947	*J. I. Hale	(*Hull Kingston*)	21	33.2
1948	*J. I. Hale	(*Hull Kingston*)	21	25.2
1949	*D. Bland	(*Lambton*)	22	13.2
1950	*D. Bland	(*Lambton*)	21	54.9
1951	*D. Bland	(*Lambton*)	21	33.8
1952	*J. C. Wardrop	(*Motherwell*)	20	53.2
1953	*R. C. Sreenan	(*Whitehall, Dundee*)	21	11.4
1954	*R. C. Sreenan	(*Whitehall, Dundee*)	22	13.2
1955	*R. C. Sreenan	(*Whitehall, Dundee*)	21	16.4
1956	*R. C. Sreenan	(*Whitehall, Dundee*)	20	57.4
1957	*R. C. Sreenan	(*Whitehall, Dundee*)	21	23.2
1958	*I. M. Black	(*Robert Gordon College, Aberdeen*)	19	17.5
1959	*R. Campion	(*Stoke Newington*)	20	48.2

Most wins: Nine by J. C. Hatfield (1912–14, 1921–24, 1929–30).

LONG DISTANCE

Originally known as "Lords' and Commons' Race" (1877 to 1879), the first cup having been presented by a number of Members of Parliament. Course, River Thames until 1947 when held in The Serpentine, London (approximately 3 miles).

Year	Name		m.	s.
1947	J. I. Hale	(*Hull Kingston*)	73	30.2
	(Discontinued 1948)			

Most wins: Eight by J. A. Jarvis (1898–1904 and 1906). J. G. Hatfield won seven times between 1913 and 1931, a span of 18 years.

110 YARDS BACK-STROKE

(150 yards up to 1946, 100 yards 1947–1952). Instituted 1903.

Year	Name		m.	s.
1946	*G. Vallery	(*France*)	1	38.6
1947	*A. D. Kinnear	(*Arbroath*)	1	04.0
1948	W. J. Brockway	(*Maindee*)	1	02.6
1949	W. J. Brockway	(*Maindee*)	1	00.8
1950	W. J. Brockway	(*Maindee*)	1	01.2
1951	W. J. Brockway	(*Maindee*)		59.7
1952	R. Wardrop	(*Motherwell*)	1	00.4
1953	*W. J. Brockway	(*Maindee*)	1	08.8
1954	*W. J. Brockway	(*Maindee*)	1	07.2
1955	*W. J. Brockway	(*Maindee*)	1	08.4
1956	*G. Sykes	(*Coventry*)	1	08.2
1957	*G. Sykes	(*Coventry*)	1	06.7
1958	*G. Sykes	(*Coventry*)	1	07.4
1959	*G. Sykes	(*Coventry*)	1	05.5

Most wins: Seven by J. C. P. Besford (1927–28, 1930–32, 1935–36), W. J. Brockway (1948–51, 1953–55).

220 YARDS BREAST-STROKE

(200 yards up to 1946.) Instituted 1903.

Year	Name		m.	s.
1946	*J. G. Davies	(*Otter*)	2	39.6
1947	*R. Romain	(*Otter*)	Bu. 2	30.0
1948	R. Romain	(*Otter*)	Bu. 2	30.8
1949	R. Romain	(*Otter*)	Bu. 2	30.7
1950	P. C. Jervis	(*Retford*)	2	34.7
1951	D. Snelling	(*Darwen*)	Bu. 2	34.0
1952	P. C. Jervis	(*Retford*)	2	29.8
1953	*P. C. Jervis	(*Retford*)	2	53.0
1954	*P. C. Jervis	(*Retford*)	2	51.3
1955	*C. C. Walkden	(*Beckenham*)	2	47.3
1956	*C. A. Walkden	(*Beckenham*)	2	46.0
1957	*B. B. Day	(*Sheffield*)	2	50.3
1958	*C. C. Walkden	(*Beckenham*)	2	43.9
1959	*G. Rowlinson	(*Bolton*)	2	48.5

Most wins: Five by P. Courtman (1907–09, 1912–13).
Bu.=Championship won using butterfly prior to the separation of this stroke from breast-stroke in 1952.

---

220 YARDS BUTTERFLY

Year	Name		m.	s.
1953	*B. Barnes	(*Preston*)	2	44.2
1954	*J. I. Hale	(*Hull Kingston*)	2	39.5
1955	*G. H. Symonds	(*Coventry*)	2	36.3
1956	*D. Dickson	(*Stoke Newington*)	2	43.8
1957	*R. Campion	(*Stoke Newington*)	2	44.2
1958	*I. M. Black	(*Robert Gordon College, Aberdeen*)	2	25.2
1959	*I. M. Black	(*Robert Gordon College, Aberdeen*)	2	22.7

CLUB FREE-STYLE TEAM

Instituted 1909 for a trophy to perpetuate the memory of Captain Webb. Became a County team championship in 1946–47 then reverted to a club event 4×220 yards (or nearest distance) from 1948 to 1954. From 1955 it has been 4×110 yards free-style.

Year	Name	m.	s.
1946	*Yorkshire A.S.A. (free-style)	10	01.0
1947	*Yorkshire A.S.A. (medley)	7	57.2
1948	Otter S.C. (London)	10	54.4
1949	Otter S.C. (London)	11	05.4
1950	Blackpool S.C.	10	58.7
1951	Sparkhill S.C. (Birmingham)	10	33.6
1952	Sparkhill S.C. (Birmingham)	9	37.6
1953	*Sparkhill S.C. (Birmingham)	9	42.4
1954	*Coventry S.C.	9	38.4
1955	*Otter S.C. (London)	4	06.2
1956	*Otter S.C. (London)	4	09.2
1957	*Wallasey S.C.	4	06.1
1958	*York City B.C.	4	01.4
1959	*York City B.C.	4	02.6

Peter Heatly   Diana Wilkinson   John Brockway

CLUB MEDLEY RELAY
Instituted 1946

Various distances until 1954. From 1955 event 4×110 yards, one man each back-stroke, breast-stroke, butterfly and free-style.

Year	Name	m.	s.
1946	*Otter S.C. (London), (330 yd.)	3	46.4
1947	*Otter S.C. (London), (660 yd.)	7	51.2
1948	Otter S.C. (London), (660 yd.)	7	53.4
1949	Otter S.C. (London), (600 yd.)	6	52.2
1950	Otter S.C. (London), (600 yd.)	7	02.0
1951	Penguin S.C. (London), (600 yd.)	6	56.7
1952	Penguin S.C. (London), (660 yd.)	7	41.6
1953	*Otter S.C. (London), (660 yd.)	7	46.3
1954	Otter S.C. (London), (660 yd.)	7	32.2
1955	*Otter S.C. (London)	4	36.5
1956	*Stoke Newington S.C. (London)	4	46.8
1957	*Otter S.C. (London)	4	46.4
1958	*Stoke Newington S.C.(London)	4	44.9
1959	*Stoke Newington S.C. (London)	4	38.0

3 METRES SPRINGBOARD DIVING
Instituted 1935

Year	Name	points
1946	R. Mulinghausen (*France*)	116.30
1947	L. E. Kern (*Highgate*)	105.90
1948	P. Heatly (*Portobello*)	113.50
1949	P. Heatly (*Portobello*)	174.91
1950	P. Heatly (*Portobello*)	176.51
1951	T. A. Turner (*Highgate*)	160.67
1952	T. A. Turner (*Highgate*)	176.60
1953	T. A. Turner (*Highgate*)	135.14
1954	T. A. Turner (*Highgate*)	134.20
1955	P. D. Tarsey (*Ealing*)	133.43
1956	P. D. Tarsey (*Ealing*)	134.02
1957	P. J. Squires (*Highgate*)	125.14
1958	K. R. Collin (*Isleworth*)	135.00
1959	P. J. Squires (*Highgate*)	150.39

Most wins: Four by F. Hodges (1936–39) and T. A. Turner (1951–54).

HIGHBOARD DIVING
Instituted 1907

Year	Name	points
1946	L. W. G. Marchant (*Highgate*)	105.43
1947	L. Brunnhage (*Sweden*)	101.86
1948	G. F. Ward (*Highgate*)	87.83
1949	P. Heatly (*Portobello*)	140.23
1950	P. Heatly (*Portobello*)	147.64
1951	P. Heatly (*Portobello*)	142.18
1952	T. A. Turner (*Highgate*)	131.25
1953	P. D. Tarsey (*Ealing*)	139.59
1954	T. A. Turner (*Highgate*)	135.43
1955	P. J. Squires (*Highgate*)	135.00
1956	P. D. Tarsey (*Ealing*)	138.33
1957	P. Heatly (*Portobello*)	139.33
1958	B. E. Phelps (*Highgate*)	139.58
1959	B. E. Phelps (*Highgate*)	148.61

Most wins: Seven by C. D. Tomalin (1931, 1933–37, 1939).

PLAIN DIVING
Instituted 1895

		points
1946	L. W. G. Marchant (*Highgate*)	49.30
1947	L. W. G. Marchant (*Highgate*)	43.70
1948	L. W. G. Marchant (*Highgate*)	49.72
1949	L. W. G. Marchant (*Highgate*)	47.92
1950	L. W. G. Marchant (*Highgate*)	52.81
1951	G. J. D. Redfern (*Highgate*)	38.75
1952	G. J. D. Redfern (*Highate*)	57.28
1953	P. Elliott (*Highgate*)	47.60
1954	P. D. Tarsey (*Ealing*)	57.28
1955	P. J. Squires (*Highgate*)	59.11
1956	P. J. Squires (*Highgate*)	55.98
1957	B. E. Phelps (*Highgate*)	57.79
1958	K. R. Collin (*Isleworth*)	54.99
1959	P. J. Squires (*Highgate*)	55.98
		67.01

Most wins: Eight by L. W. G. Marchant, (1933–1935, 1946–1950), 17-years span.

1 METRE SPRINGBOARD DIVING
Instituted 1937

		points
1946	F. G. Hodges (*Highgate*)	135.85
1947	J. Webb (*Highgate*)	93.16
1948	P. Elliott (*Highgate*)	93.35
1949	P. Heatly (*Portobello*)	128.60
1950	P. Heatly (*Portobello*)	127.32
1951	P. Heatly (*Portobello*)	110.09
1952	T. A. Turner (*Highgate*)	121.94
1953	T. A. Turner (*Highgate*)	113.32
1954	T. A. Turner (*Highgate*)	102.31
1955	F. H. Mercer (*Highgate*)	110.68
1956	Y. Raanan (*Maccabi Israel*)	106.88
1957	K. R. Collin (*Isleworth*)	120.39
1958	P. J. Squires (*Highgate*)	124.57
1959	K. R. Collin (*Isleworth*)	132.53

Most wins: Three by P. Heatly (1949–1951), T. A. Turner (1952–1954).

NATIONAL CHAMPIONS
Women
110 YARDS FREE-STYLE
(100 yards up to 1952.) Instituted 1901

		m.	s.
1946	*N. Riach (*Motherwell*)	1	03.0
1947	*N. Riach (*Motherwell*)	1	02.4
1948	M. Wellington (*Beckenham*)	1	02.8
1949	E. McA. Turner (*Galashiels*)	1	02.4
1950	P. M. Linton (*Maindee*)	1	02.4
1951	P. M. Linton (*Maindee*)	1	03.5
1952	A. M. Barnwell (*Worthing*)	1	02.2
1953	*J. Botham (*South Manchester*)	1	09.7
1954	*J. Botham (*South Manchester*)	1	09.4
1955	*F. Ewart (*Hastings and St. L*)	1	08.3
1956	*V. Grant (*Toronto, Canada*)	1	07.0
1957	*D. E. Wilkinson (*Stockport*)	1	05.7
1958	*J. B. Grinham (*Hampstead*)	1	06.8
1959	*N Steward (*Hornchurch*)	1	05.2

Most wins: Six by J. Fletcher (1906–09, 1911–12), C. M. Jeans (1919–20, 1922–25).

220 YARDS FREE-STYLE
Instituted 1912

		m.	s.
1946	*N. Riach (*Motherwell*)	2	36.0
1947	*C. Gibson (*Motherwell*)	2	29.2
1948	C. Gibson (*Motherwell*)	2	32.6
1949	M. Wellington (*Beckenham*)	2	34.2
1950	P. M. Linton (*Maindee*)	2	33.1
1951	D. R. Wilkinson (*Woolwich*)	2	31.1
1952	L. Preece (*Wallasey*)	2	32.0
1953	*L. Preece (*Wallasey*)	2	33.7
1954	*J. Botham (*South Manchester*)	2	34.3
1955	*V. Grant (*Toronto, Canada*)	2	34.7
1956	*V. Grant (*Toronto, Canada*)	2	30.6
1957	*J. B. Grinham (*Hampstead*)	2	30.0
1958	*E. Ferguson (*York City*)	2	28.6
1959	*N. Steward (*Hornchurch*)	2	25.6

Most wins: Five by M. J. Cooper (1927–29, 1931–32).

440 YARDS FREE-STYLE
Instituted 1924

		m.	s.
1946	*N. Riach (*Motherwell*)	5	50.0
1947	*C. Gibson (*Motherwell*)	5	23.2
1948	C. Gibson (*Motherwell*)	5	39.8
1949	M. Wellington (*Beckenham*)	5	36.4
1950	D. R. Wilkinson (*Sparkhill*)	5	26.2
1951	D. R. Wilkinson (*Woolwich*)	5	17.6
1952	D. R. Wilkinson (*Woolwich*)	5	20.4
1953	*D. R. Wilkinson (*Woolwich*)	5	29.8
1954	*C. M. Brown (*Newcastle-u-Lyme*)	5	33.2
1955	*J. Clarke (*Isleworth*)	5	34.8
1956	*M. Girvan (*Motherwell*)	5	29.5
1957	*E. Ferguson (*York City*)	5	33.0
1958	*E. Ferguson (*York City*)	5	13.1
1959	*N. Steward (*Hornchurch*)	5	12.9

Most wins: Five by M. J. Cooper (1928–32).

110 YARDS BACK-STROKE
(150 yards up to 1946, 100 yards 1947–52.) Instituted 1920

		m.	s.
1946	*M. Berlioux (*France*)	1	52.6
1947	*C. Gibson (*Motherwell*)	1	10.4
1948	N. Lane (*New Zealand*)	1	11.8
1949	H. M. Yate (*Mermaid*)	1	10.2
1950	M. McDowall (*Kilmarnock*)	1	11.7
1951	M. McDowall (*Kilmarnock*)	1	09.2

1952	M. McDowall (*Kilmarnock*)	1	09.8
1953	*M. McDowall (*Kilmarnock*)	1	18.6
1954	*J. P. Symons (*Northumberland*)	1	16.9
1955	*J. B. Grinham (*Hampstead*)	1	15.3
1956	*J. B. Grinham (*Hampstead*)	1	14.5
1957	*J. Hoyle (*Watford*)	1	16.0
1958	*J. B. Grinham (*Hampstead*)	1	12.9
1959	*M. Edwards (*Heston*)	1	12.5

Most wins: Four by M. McDowall (1950–53).

220 YARDS BREAST-STROKE
(200 yards up to 1946.) Instituted 1920

		m.	s.
1946	*J. Caplin (*Brighton*)	3	01.2
1947	*E. Church (*Northampton*)	2	52.8
1948	E. Church (*Northampton*)	2	54.2
1949	J. Caspers (*Netherlands*)	2	47.1
1950	H. O. Gordon (*Hamilton*)	2	46.0
1951	H. O. Gordon (*Hamilton*)	2	45.5
1952	H. O. Gordon (*Hamilton*)	2	43.0
1953	*M. Grundy (*Blackpool*)	3	07.9
1954	*M. Grundy (*Blackpool*)	3	03.8
1955	*H. O. Gordon (*Hamilton*)	3	00.1
1956	*H. O. Gordon (*Hamilton*)	2	59.2
1957	*C. Gosden (*Croydon*)	2	56.5
1958	*A. Lonsbrough (*Huddersfield*)	2	55.8
1959	*A. Lonsbrough (*Huddersfield*)	2	54.0

Most wins: Five by M. Hinton (1929 and 1931–34), H. O. Gordon (1950–52 and 1955–56).

110 YARDS BUTTERFLY
Instituted 1953

		m.	s.
1953	*M. Ivinson (*Border City, Carlisle*)	1	24.2
1954	*F. Webb (*Cheam Ladies*)	1	24.0
1955	*C. Macadam (*Heston*)	1	17.7
1956	*A. Morton (*Blackpool*)	1	17.4
1957	*C. Gosden (*Croydon*)	1	16.9
1958	*S. Watt (*Thistle, Aberdeen*)	1	14.5
1959	*S. Watt (*Thistle, Aberdeen*)	1	13.9

CLUB FREE-STYLE RELAY
(4×100 yards until 1951; 4×110 yards from 1952). Instituted 1948

		m.	s.
1948	*Beckenham Ladies S.C. (Kent)*	4	38.0
1949	*Weston-super-Mare S.C. (Somerset)*	4	36.6
1950	*Croydon Ladies S.C. (Surrey)*	4	40.7
1951	*Croydon Ladies S.C. (Surrey)*	4	39.5
1952	*Mermaid S.C. (London)*	4	57.0
1953	*Mermaid S.C. (London)*	5	01.8
1954	*Mermaid S.C. (London)*	4	59.4
1955	*Leander S.C. (Surrey)*	5	02.3
1956	*Mermaid S.C. (London)*	4	53.3
1957	*Kingston Ladies S.C. (Surrey)*	4	53.0
1958	*Kingston Ladies S.C. (Surrey)*	4	49.8
1959	*Beckenham Ladies S.C. (Kent)*	4	45.3

CLUB MEDLEY RELAY

Back-stroke, breast-stroke and two free-style legs: 1935–55, butterfly substituted for first free-style leg 1955; 4×100 yards, 1935–46; 4×110 yards, 1946–8; 4×100 yards, 1949–51, 4×110 yards, 1952 on. Instituted 1935

		m.	s.
1946	*Mermaid S.C. (London)*	5	59.2
1947	*Beckenham L.S.C. (Kent)*	5	38.1
1948	*Mermaid S.C. (London)*	5	27.4

Christine Gosden   Brian Phelps

SWIMMING QUIZ
OLYMPIC GAMES

1. Who has won the most gold medals at the Olympic Games?

★

2. Who has won the most individual gold medals (excluding relay or water-polo events)?

QUIZ ANSWERS

1. Johnny Weissmuller (U.S.A.)—five: 100 m. free-style in 1924 and 1928, 400 m. free-style in 1924, member of 4×200 m. relay team in 1924 and 1928. 2. Mrs. Pat McCormick (U.S.A.)—four: highboard and springboard diving in 1952 and 1956. C. M. Daniels (U.S.A.) also won four individual gold medals between 1904 and 1908, but one of these, for 100 m. free-style, was at the Interim Games in Athens in 1906 (which took place additionally to the normal four-year span of an Olympiad).

1. Which nation resigned from the F.I.N.A. for political reasons in 1958?

*

2. Where are the A.S.A.'s advanced training courses for (a) swimming and (b) diving held?

QUIZ ANSWERS

1. The All China Athletic Federation (Red China) in protest against the affiliation of the Formosan Chinese Swimming Association. 2. (a) Loughborough, Leicester; (b) Dawdon Colliery, Durham.

*

1949	Northampton A.S.C.	4	55.2
1950	Hampstead L.S.C. (London)	4	56.9
1951	Croydon L.S.C. (Surrey)	4	56.6
1952	Mermaid S.C. (London)	5	26.4
1953	*Mermaid S.C. (London)	5	19.0
1954	*Mermaid S.C. (London)	5	22.7
1955	*Mermaid S.C. (London)	5	15.0
1956	*Leander S.C. (Surrey)	5	24.7
1957	*Heston S.C. (Middlesex)	5	21.7
1958	*Heston S.C. (Middlesex)	5	14.5
1959	*Heston S.C. (Middlesex)	5	12.4

3 METRES SPRINGBOARD DIVING
Instituted 1935

		points
1946	E. Child (Isander)	97.57
1947	P. Winterton (Isander)	89.01
1948	E. Child (Plaistow)	102.79
1949	E. Child (Plaistow)	101.15
1950	D. A. Newman (Mermaid)	106.38
1951	P. A. Long (Ilford)	107.98
1952	D. A. Drew (Heston)	120.84
1953	C. I. Welsh (Durham)	117.00
1954	C. I. Welsh (Durham)	118.39
1955	P. A. Long (Ilford)	108.31
1956	P. A. Long (Ilford)	112.61
1957	P. A. Long (Ilford)	112.20
1958	P. A. Long (Ilford)	125.40
1959	M. J. Watson (Bournemouth)	128.48

Most wins: Five by P. A. Long (1951, 1955–58).

HIGHBOARD DIVING
Instituted 1924

		points
1946	E. Child (Isander)	34.83
1947	E. Child (Isander)	52.86
1948	M. A. Hider (Isander)	61.34
1949	E. Child (Plaistow)	67.55
1950	P. A. Long (Ilford)	52.04
1951	K. R. Cuthbert (Willesden)	63.59
1952	P. A. Long (Ilford)	67.95
1953	P. A. Long (Ilford)	74.48
1954	P. A. Long (Ilford)	76.92
1955	C. I. Welsh (Durham)	69.80
1956	C. I. Welsh (Durham)	76.06
1957	C. I. Welsh (Durham)	71.06
1958	C. I. Welsh (Durham)	83.70
1959	P. A. Long (Ilford)	81.17

Most wins: Six by B. White (1924–29).

PLAIN DIVING
Instituted 1953

		points
1953	C. I. Welsh (Durham)	51.35
1954	P. A. Long (Ilford)	59.85
1955	P. A. Long (Ilford)	52.00
1956	C. I. Welsh (Durham)	54.65
1957	C. I. Welsh (Durham)	58.71
1958	P. A. Long (Ilford)	59.92
1959	E. Ferris (Mermaid)	61.13

1 METRE SPRINGBOARD DIVING
Instituted 1949

		points
1949	E. Child (Plaistow)	89.12
1950	K. R. Cuthbert (Willesden)	68.59
1951	P. A. Long (Ilford)	68.20
1952	C. I. Welsh (Durham)	82.89
1953	C. I. Welsh (Durham)	84.25
1954	C. I. Welsh (Durham)	80.71
1955	C. I. Welsh (Durham)	85.38
1956	C. I. Welsh (Durham)	80.45
1957	E. Ferris (Mermaid)	102.56
1958	C. I. Welsh (Durham)	99.58
1959	N. Thomas (Isleworth)	106.85

NATIONAL JUNIOR CHAMPIONS

Championships organised by the Amateur Swimming Association (of England) but open to the world.
A competitor must be under 16 on April 1st in the year of the championship.
*Long course—55 yards bath.

Boys
110 YARDS FREE-STYLE
(100 yards up to 1952.) Instituted 1947

		m.	s.
1947	*T. Miller (Plaistow)		58.6
1948	J. C. Wardrop (Motherwell)		57.4
1949	T. D. Welsh (Galashiels)		58.4
1950	R. Drew (Bristol)		57.6
1951	J. Whitehead (Leigh)		57.7
1952	B. Lord (Lowermoor)		55.0
1953	*W. Chapman (Eccles)	1	03.2
1954	*G. Baxter (Gloucester)	1	00.0
1955	*K. Wallwork (Swinton)	1	01.5
1956	*P. Kendrew (York City)	1	00.6
1957	*I. M. Black (Robert Gordon College, Aberdeen)	1	00.0
1958	*C. J. Hansard (Swansea)	1	01.4
1959	*C. J. Hansard (Swansea)	1	00.5

220 YARDS FREE-STYLE
Instituted 1953

		m.	s.
1953	*B. R. Jackson (Southport)	2	26.4
1954	*N. J. McKechnie (Wallasey)	2	20.2
1955	*K. Wallwork (Swinton)	2	19.1
1956	*I. M. Black (Robert Gordon College, Aberdeen)	2	19.2
1957	*I. M. Black (Robert Gordon College, Aberdeen)	2	10.0
1958	*A. C. Galbraith (Carlisle)	2	18.8
1959	*P. Hammond (Sheffield English Steel)	2	16.9

John Monckton (*Australia*)   Cathie Gibson   Ron Stedman

110 YARDS BACK-STROKE
(100 yards up to 1952.) Instituted 1947

		m.	s.
1947	*R. Wardrop (Motherwell)	1	09.0
1948	R. Wardrop (Motherwell)	1	07.2
1949	A. J. Gurr (East Ham)	1	08.5
1950	J. B. Luke (Renfrew)	1	06.1
1951	A. McK. Treen (Heath Town)	1	06.5
1952	H. Rigby (Southport)	1	03.8
1953	*D. Davies (Bristol)	1	14.6
1954	*M. Peacock (Sutton and Cheam)	1	11.9
1955	*B. Bulmer (York City)	1	11.1
1956	*P. Kendrew (York City)	1	11.9
1957	*A. Turner (Sheffield)	1	11.6
1958	*A. C. Galletly (Perth)	1	11.7
1959	*R. Thomas (Bristol City)	1	10.2

110 YARDS BREAST-STROKE
(100 yards up to 1952.) Instituted 1947

			m.	s.
1947	*R. Thomson (Motherwell)	Bu.	1	11.3
1948	R. Thomson (Motherwell)	Bu.	1	14.2
1949	J. Bailey (East Ham)	Bu.	1	10.5
1950	D. Williamson (Sunderland)	Bu.	1	13.5
1951	P. Alp (Hounslow)	Bu.	1	11.8
1952	T. Holborn (Birkenhead)	Bu.	1	06.6
1953	*H. H. Smith (Paisley)		1	21.0
1954	*A. Longega (Sutton and Cheam)		1	18.1
1955	*R. Manning (Sunderland)		1	21.3
1956	*R. Manning (Sunderland)		1	20.8
1957	*H. Bentham (Trafford Park)		1	21.1
1958	*G. B. Hill (Nottingham)		1	19.7
1959	*C. C. Wilkinson (Stockport)		1	18.2

Bu.=Championship won using butterfly prior to the separation of this stroke from breast-stroke in 1952.

110 YARDS BUTTERFLY
Instituted 1955

		m.	s.
1955	*G. Bowker (Hyde)	1	15.1
1956	*I. M. Black (Robert Gordon College, Aberdeen)	1	10.3
1957	*I. M. Black (Robert Gordon College, Aberdeen)	1	06.0
1958	*I. Blyth (Dundee)	1	08.2
1959	*T. Glenville (Hull Olympic)	1	08.3

SPRINGBOARD DIVING
Instituted 1952

		points
1952	K. R. Collin (Isleworth)	64.56
1953	R. Cann (Blackpool)	71.79
1954	J. A. Butcher (Highgate)	70.93
1955	C. Giecco (Isleworth)	71.57
1956	B. E. Phelps (Highgate)	70.54
1957	B. E. Phelps (Highgate)	81.40
1958	B. E. Phelps (Highgate)	85.89
1959	B. E. Phelps (Highgate)	89.47

NATIONAL JUNIOR CHAMPIONS

Girls

110 YARDS FREE-STYLE
(100 yards up to 1952.) Instituted 1947

		m.	s.
1947	*M. Girvan (*Motherwell*)	1	06.5
1948	D. R. Wilkinson (*Leamington*)	1	10.2
1949	A. Douglas (*Leicester*)	1	06.2
1950	J. Botham (*South Manchester*)	1	05.6
1951	A. M. Barnwell (*Worthing*)	1	02.8
1952	F. Ewart (*Hastings and St. Leonards*)	1	04.0
1953	*F. Hogben (*Abroath*)	1	12.5
1954	*M. Spooner (*Holbeck*)	1	11.4
1955	*C. Barry (*Stoke Newington*)	1	10.5
1956	*S. Grant (*Toronto, Canada*)	1	09.4
1957	*D. E. Wilkinson (*Stockport*)	1	05.7
1958	*D. E. Wilkinson (*Stockport*)	1	05.6
1959	*M. E. Toms (*Beckenham Ladies*)	1	06.5

220 YARDS FREE-STYLE
Instituted 1952

		m.	s.
1952	*V. Nares-Pillow (*Surrey L.*)	2	41.1
1953	*F. Hogben (*Abroath*)	2	44.0
1954	*B. Kingston (*Heston*)	2	44.4
1955	*C. Barry (*Stoke Newington*)	2	38.2
1956	*S. Grant (*Toronto, Canada*)	2	37.3
1957	*D. E. Wilkinson (*Stockport*)	2	28.6
1958	*D. E. Wilkinson (*Stockport*)	2	26.4
1959	*J. Samuel (*Surrey Ladies*)	2	25.9

110 YARDS BACK STROKE
(100 yards up to 1952.) Instituted 1947

		m.	s.
1947	*M. Girvan (*Motherwell*)	1	12.6
1948	M. Girvan (*Motherwell*)	1	14.4
1949	R. Markland (*Kingston*)	1	10.8
1950	M. McDowall (*Kilmarnock*)	1	10.5
1951	M. McDowall (*Kilmarnock*)	1	08.8
1952	P. Musgrove (*York City*)	1	09.6
1953	*S. Tolton (*Worthing*)	1	17.5
1954	*J. Tiso (*Sparkhill*)	1	16.8
1955	*J. Tiso (*Sparkhill*)	1	15.9

		m.	s.
1956	*V. Christie (*Hampstead*)	1	19.1
1957	*J. Edwards (*Bristol*)	1	19.1
1958	*B. Tyrer (*Mermaid, London*)	1	17.0
1959	*C. Hussey (*Nottingham*)	1	16.0

110 YARDS BREAST-STROKE
100 yards up to 1952. Instituted 1947.

			m.	s.
1947	*H. O. Gordon (*Hamilton*)		1	21.4
1948	H. O. Gordon (*Hamilton*)		1	23.2
1949	H. O. Gordon (*Hamilton*)		1	18.0
1950	J. Wrigley (*Lowermoor*)		1	19.2
1951	J. Wrigley (*Lowermoor*)		1	19.1
1952	B. Harvey (*Leander*)	*Bu.*	1	18.0
1953	*D. Taylor (*Ilford*)		1	27.8
1954	*M. Grundy (*Blackpool*)		1	26.8
1955	*C. Gosden (*Croydon*)		1	29.4
1956	*P. Powley (*Bournemouth*)		1	28.2
1957	*J. Dyson (*Kingston*)		1	26.1
1958	*J. Dyson (*Kingston*)		1	25.3
1959	*C. Barber (*Heston*)		1	24.8

Bu.—Championship won using butterfly prior to the separation of this stroke from breast-stroke in 1952.

110 YARDS BUTTERFLY
Instituted 1955

		m.	s.
1955	*C. Gosden (*Croydon*)	1	24.6
1956	*S. Grant (*Toronto, Canada*)	1	23.4
1957	*J. Dyson (*Kingston*)	1	22.4
1958	*J. Oldroyd (*Dewsbury*)	1	16.0
1959	*P. Baines (*Ilford*)	1	17.6

SPRINGBOARD DIVING
Instituted 1952

		points
1952	C. I. Welsh (*Durham*	71.95
1953	C. I. Welsh (*Durham*)	74.15
1954	A. Woods (*Isleworth*)	69.33
1955	J. Gill (*Hammersmith*)	63.52
1956	E. Nicholson (*Fulham*)	71.87
1957	V. A. Borton (*Isander*)	60.00
1958	M. J. Watson (*Bournemouth*)	69.73
1959	M. J. Watson (*Bournemouth*)	82.87

SUCCESSFUL CHANNEL SWIMS

* Officially approved by the Channel Swimming Association (but other crossings have been properly and honestly performed).

England to France

	Year	Hours	Time mins
*Matthew Webb (*Britain*)	1875	21	45
*Thomas Burgess (*Britain*)	1911	22	35
*Henry Sullivan (*U.S.A.*)	1923	26	50
Edward "Ted" Temme (*G.B.*)	1934	14	29
Tom Blower (*G.B.*)	1948	15	31
Hassan Abd El Rehim (*Egypt*)	1949	15	46
*W. Edward "Ned" Barnie (*G.B.*)	1951	19	2
*Florence Chadwick (*U.S.A.*)	1951	16	19
Tom Blower (*G.B.*)	1951	18	42
Saied El Arabi (*Egypt*)	1952	17	42
*Philip Rising (*G.B.*)	1952	18	38
*Philip Mickman (*G.B.*)	1952	18	44
Abdel Latif Abdu Heif (*Egypt*)	1953	13	45
*Florence Chadwick (*U.S.A.*)	1953	14	42
*William Pickering (*G.B.*)	1955	14	6
*Florence Chadwick (*U.S.A.*)	1955	13	55
*Gerald Forsberg (*G.B.*)	1957	13	33
*Mihir Sen (*India*)	1958	14	45
*Paul Herron (*U.S.A.*)	1959	15	0
*Abilio Couto (*Brazil*)	1959	12	49
*Brojen Das (*Pakistan*)	1959	13	26

France to England

	Year	Hours	mins
*Enrico Tiraboschi (*Italy*)	1923	16	33
*Charles Toth (*U.S.A.*)	1923	16	58
*Gertrude Ederle (*U.S.A.*)	1926	14	39
*Millie Corson (*U.S.A.*)	1926	15	29
*Arnst Vierkotter (*Germany*)	1926	12	40
Georges Michel (*France*)	1926	11	5
Norman Derham (*G.B.*)	1926	13	57
*Edward "Ted" Temme (*G.B.*)	1927	14	29
*Mercedes Gleitze (*G.B.*)	1927	15	15
Ivy Gill (*G.B.*)	1927	15	9
*Ivy Hawke (*G.B.*)	1928	19	16
*Hilda "Laddie" Sharp (*G.B.*)	1928	14	58
*Ishak Helmy (*Egypt*)	1928	23	40
*Margaret "Peggy" Duncan (*South Africa*)	1930	16	17
*Ethel "Sunny" Lowry (*G.B.*)	1933	15	45
Emma Faber (*Austria*)	1934	14	30

(*exact time doubtful—claimed women's record*)

	Year	Hours	mins
Haydn Taylor (*G.B.*)	1935	14	38
Tom Blower (*G.B.*)	1937	13	31½
Bruna Wendel Piarre (*Germany*)	1938	15	33
Fernley Wheatcroft (*G.B.*)	1938	13	45
Sally Bauer (*Sweden*)	1939	15	22
Daniel Carpie (*Peru*)	1947	14	46
Giovanni Gambi (*Italy*)	1948	11	36

(*Found exhausted on beach near Shakespeare Colliery*)

	Year	Hours	mins
Hassan Abd el Rehim (*Egypt*)	1948	17	38
*Philip Mickman (*G.B.*)	1949	23	48
Gernand du Moulin (*Belgium*)	1949	21	59
Mahri Hassan Hamad (*Egypt*)	1949	15	22
Zasson Zirganos (*Greece*)	1949	18	45
Florence Chadwick (*U.S.A.*)	1950	13	20

Daphne Wilkinson   Charmian Welsh

*Hassan Abd el Rehim (*Egypt*)	1950	10	50
Roger le Morvan (*France*)	1950	11	2
Mahri Hassan Hamad (*Egypt*)	1950	12	10
*Walter "Sam" Rockett (*G.B.*)	1950	14	17
*W. Edward "Ned" Barnie (*G.B.*)	1950	14	50
*Eileen Fenton (*G.B.*)	1950	15	31
Zasson Zirganos (*Greece*)	1950	16	19
Antonio Abertondo (*Argentina*)	1950	16	25
Jenny Kammersgaard (*Denmark*)	1950	16	30

(*The nine successes from el Rehim to Kammersgaard were achieved on one day, August 22, in the first post-war Channel race—organised by the* Daily Mail.)

Abdel Latif Abdu Heif (*Egypt*)	1951	15	43
*Philip Rising (*G.B.*)	1951	15	55
Mahri Hassan Hamad (*Egypt*)	1951	12	12
Roger le Morvan (*France*)	1951	12	13
Hassan Abd el Rehim (*Egypt*)	1951	12	25
Saled el Arabi (*Egypt*)	1951	12	42
*Brenda Fisher (*G.B.*)	1951	12	43
Godfrey Chapman (*G.B.*)	1951	12	56
Winnie Roach (*Canada*)	1951	13	25
Enrique Duarte (*Argentina*)	1951	13	26
Lars-Bertil Warle (*Sweden*)	1951	13	28
Raphael Morand (*France*)	1951	13	45
Daniel Carpio (*Peru*)	1951	13	50
*Jenny James (*G.B.*)	1951	13	55
Zasson Zirganos (*Greece*)	1951	14	10
Antonio Abertondo (*Argentina*)	1951	14	14
Jan van Hemsbergen (*Holland*)	1951	14	30
Sally Bauer (*Sweden*)	1951	14	40
*W. Edward "Ned" Barnie (*G.B.*)	1951	15	1
Jenny Kammersgaard (*Denmark*)	1951	15	38

(*The eighteen swimmers from Hamad to Kammersgaard were successful in the second* Daily Mail *Channel race on August 16.*)

*Victor Birkett (*G.B.*)	1952	15	36
*Kathleen Mayoh (*G.B.*)	1952	16	35
Bakr Hussein (*Egypt*)	1952	18	12

(contd. on p. 316 col. 1)

SWIMMING QUIZ

OLYMPIC GAMES

1. Has a competitor ever represented different countries at the Olympic Games?

★

2. Can *anyone* who has changed his or her nationality represent different countries at the Olympic Games?

★

3. Name the husband and wife who both won gold medals at the same Games.

★

QUIZ ANSWERS

1. Birte Christoffersen-Hanson. As Miss Christoffersen she won a bronze medal for Denmark in the highboard diving in 1948. As Mrs. Hanson she represented Sweden in the highboard diving (8th) and springboard diving (9th) in the 1956 Games. 2. No. Only under certain conditions: (a) if the former country has been incorporated into another State; (b) if the first appearance in the Games was for a country which had, at that time, no national Olympic committee (viz. was not eligible to take part); or (c), in the case of a woman, when she has taken new nationality by marriage. Mrs. Hanson qualified under (c). 3. Deszo Gyarmati and Eva Szekely-Gyarmati. They competed together for Hungary in the 1948 Olympics (before they were married) and in the 1952 and 1956 Olympic Games. Deszo, one of the world's greatest water-polo players, won a silver medal in 1948 and gold medals in 1952 and 1956. Eva, a finalist in the 200 m. breast-stroke event in 1948, became Olympic champion for this event in 1952 (swimming butterfly) and 2nd (swimming breast-stroke) in 1956.

SWIMMING QUIZ

1. Who was taken ill during an Olympic event, yet went on to win a silver medal? Give the name, the year, the event.

*

2. What did this swimmer become famous for later?

*

QUIZ ANSWERS

1. Greta Andersen of Denmark in 1948. She collapsed during a heat of the 400 metres free-style and was lifted unconscious from the bath while the race was in progress. Two days later she helped Denmark to second place in the 4 × 100 m. relay. Two days before her collapse Miss Andersen had won the 100 m. free-style title. 2. Swimming the English Channel and other long-distance swimming feats. Now married to an American, Miss Andersen holds the women's record for the crossing, Cap Gris Nez to St. Margaret's Bay: 11 hours 1 minute, set up on August 24th, 1958. This is only 9 minutes outside the men's record.

Dawn Fraser (Australia)

Lorraine Crapp (Australia)

Successful Channel Swims—contd.

Abdel Moneim Abdu (*Egypt*)	1952	17	30
Damian Piza Beltran (*Mexico*)	1953	15	23
*Toufic A. Bleik (*Lebanon*)	1953	16	5
*Murat Guler (*Turkey*)	1954	16	50
Baptista Pereira (*Portugal*)	1954	12	25
Mahri Hassan Hamad (*Egypt*)	1954	12	49
*Brenda Fisher (*G.B.*)	1954	14	36
Margaret Feather (*G.B.*)	1954	16	23
Zasson Zirganos (*Greece*)	1954	16	23
Antonio Abertondo (*Argentina*)	1954	16	53
Mohammed el Soussi (*Syria*)	1954	17	55

(The seven swimmers from Pereira were successful in the Butlin's international Channel Race on August 21.)

*Marilyn Bell (*Canada*)	1955	14	36
Abdel Latif Abdu Heif (*Egypt*)	1955	11	44
Thomas L. Park (*U.S.A.*)	1955	12	2
Syder Guiscardo (*Argentina*)	1955	14	33
Damian P. Beltran (*Mexico*)	1955	15	8

(The four swimmers from Heif were successful in the 2nd Butlin's Channel Race on August 15.)

*Frederick Oldman (*G.B.*)	1955	14	31
*Jacques Amyet (*Canada*)	1956	13	2
*Greta Andersen (*Denmark*)	1957	13	53
*Kenneth Wray (*G.B.*)	1957	16	00

(Andersen and Wray were the only two successful swimmers in Butlin's 3rd Channel Race on August 21.)

*Abilio Couto (*Brazil*)	1958	12	45
*Bert Thomas (*U.S.A.*)	1958	19	31
*Greta Andersen (*U.S.A.*)	1958	11	1
*Brojen Das (*Pakistan*)	1958	14	52
Ronald Tarr (*G.B.*)	1958	15	12
Raphael Morand (*France*)	1958	16	22
*Ramon Ocana (*Mexico*)	1958	17	5

(Andersen, Das, Tarr, Morand and Ocana were the successful swimmers in Butlin's 4th Channel Race on August 23.)

*Montserrat Tresseras (*Spain*)	1958	14	14
*Jose Vitos (*Spain*)	1958	15	11
*June Gilbert (*G.B.*)	1958	16	52
*Paul Herron (*U.S.A.*)	1958	12	00
*Georges Pourcelle (*France*)	1958	13	1

1959

*Alfredo Camarero (*Argentina*)	11	43
*Herman Willemse (*Holland*)	12	49
Baptiste Perreira (*Portugal*)	13	12
*Helge Jensen (*Denmark*)	13	17
*Brojen Das (*Pakistan*)	13	53
*El Nawab (*Irak*)	15	12
*Greta Andersen (*U.S.A.*)	15	25
*Myrna Thompson (*U.S.A.*)	15	35
*William Bristow (*G.B.*)	18	1

(The nine swimmers from Camarero were

successful in Butlin's 5th Channel Race on August 27.)

*Denis Pearson (*Rhodesia*)	15	36
*Osman Ghandour (*Lebanon*)	12	5
*Bimal Chundra (*India*)	13	50
*Rodolfo Rodriquez (*Spain*)	12	53
*Niko Nestor (*Yugoslavia*)	12	6
*Miguel Gonzalez (*Mexico*)	14	44
*Gordon Hill (*G.B.*)	12	48

OLYMPIC CHAMPIONS
100 METRES FREE-STYLE

Year	Men	m.	s.	Women	m.	s.
1896	A. Hajos (*Hungary*)	1	22.2	—		
1900	J. A. Jarvis (*G.B.*)	1	16.4	—		
1904	Z. de Halmay (*Hungary*)	1	02.8	—		
1908	C. M. Daniels (*U.S.A.*)	1	05.6	—		
1912	D. Kahanamoku (*U.S.A.*)	1	03.4	F. Durack (*Australia*)	1	22.2
1920	D. Kahanamoku (*U.S.A.*)	1	00.4	E. Bleibtrey (*U.S.A.*)	1	13.6
1924	J. Weissmuller (*U.S.A.*)		59.0	E. Lackie (*U.S.A.*)	1	12.4
1928	J. Weissmuller (*U.S.A.*)		58.6	A. Osipowich (*U.S.A.*)	1	11.0
1932	Y. Miyazaki (*Japan*)		58.2	H. Madison (*U.S.A.*)	1	06.8
1936	F. Czik (*Hungary*)		57.6	H. Mastenbroek (*Neth.*)	1	05.9
1948	W. Ris (*U.S.A.*)		57.3	G. Anderson (*Denmark*)	1	06.3
1952	C. Scholes (*U.S.A.*)		57.4	K. Szoke (*Hungary*)	1	06.8
1956	J. Henricks (*Australia*)		55.4	D. Fraser (*Australia*)	1	02.0

400 METRES FREE-STYLE

Year	Men	m.	s.	Women	m.	s.
1896	*P. Neumann (*Austria*)	8	12.6	—		
1900	J. A. Jarvis (*G.B.*)	No time		—		
1904	†C. M. Daniels (*U.S.A.*)	6	16.2	—		
1908	H. Taylor (*G.B.*)	5	36.8	—		
1912	G. R. Hodgson (*Canada*)	5	24.4	—		
1920	N. Ross (*U.S.A.*)	5	26.8	E. Bleibtrey (*U.S.A.*)	‡4	34.0
1924	J. Weissmuller (*U.S.A.*)	5	04.2	M. Norelius (*U.S.A.*)	6	02.2
1928	A. Zorilla (*Argentina*)	5	01.6	M. Norelius (*U.S.A.*)	5	42.8
1932	C. Crabbe (*U.S.A.*)	4	48.4	H. Madison (*U.S.A.*)	5	28.5
1936	J. Medica (*U.S.A.*)	4	44.5	H. Mastenbroek (*Neth.*)	5	26.4
1948	W. Smith (*U.S.A.*)	4	41.0	A. Curtis (*U.S.A.*)	5	17.8
1952	J. Boiteux (*France*)	4	30.7	V. Gyenge (*Hungary*)	5	12.1
1956	M. Rose (*Australia*)	4	27.3	L. Crapp (*Australia*)	4	54.6

* 500 metres.   † 440 yards (402.34 m.).   ‡ 300 metres.

1,500 METRES FREE-STYLE

1896	*A. Hajos (*Hungary*)	18	22.2
1900	†J. A. Jarvis (*G.B.*)	13	40.0
1904	‡E. Rausch (*Germany*)	27	18.2
1908	H. Taylor (*G.B.*)	22	48.4
1912	G. R. Hodgson (*Canada*)	22	00.0
1920	N. Ross (*U.S.A.*)	22	23.2
1924	A. M. Charlton (*Australia*)	20	06.6
1928	A. Borg (*Sweden*)	19	51.8
1932	K. Kitamura (*Japan*)	19	12.4
1936	N. Terada (*Japan*)	19	13.7
1948	J. McLane (*U.S.A.*)	19	18.5
1952	F. Konno (*U.S.A.*)	18	30.0
1956	M. Rose (*Australia*)	17	58.9

* 1,200 metres.
† 1,000 metres.
‡ 1,760 yards (1609.35 metres).

> **Odd events at early Olympic Games (MEN)**
>
> | | m. | s. |
> |---|---|---|
> | 50 YARDS FREE-STYLE: | | |
> | 1904 Z. de Halmay (*Hungary*) | | 28.0 |
> | 200 METRES FREE-STYLE: | | |
> | 1900 G. C. Lane (*Australia*) | 2 | 25.2 |
> | 220 YARDS FREE-STYLE: | | |
> | 1904 C. M. Daniels (*U.S.A.*) | 2 | 44.2 |
> | 880 YARDS FREE-STYLE: | | |
> | 1904 E. Rausch (*Germany*) | 13 | 11.4 |
> | 400 METRES BREAST-STROKE: | | |
> | 1904 G. Zacharias (*Germany*) | 7 | 23.6 |
> | 1912 W. Bathe (*Germany*) | 6 | 29.6 |
> | 1920 H. Malmroth (*Sweden*) | 6 | 31.8 |
> | SWIMMING UNDER WATER: | | |
> | 1900 M. Devendeville (*France*) | | 60 metres |
> | PLUNGING FOR DISTANCE: | | |
> | 1904 W. E. Dickey (*U.S.A.*) 62 ft. 6 in. | | |

100 METRES BACK-STROKE

Year	Men	m.	s.	Women	m.	s.
1900	*W. Hoppenberg (*Germany*)	2	47.0	—		
1904	†W. Brack (*Germany*)	1	16.8	—		
1908	A. Bieberstein (*Germany*)	1	24.6	—		
1912	H. Hebner (*U.S.A.*)	1	21.2	—		
1920	W. Kealoha (*U.S.A.*)	1	15.2	—		
1924	W. Kealoha (*U.S.A.*)	1	13.2	S. Bauer (*U.S.A.*)	1	23.2
1928	G. Kojac (*U.S.A.*)	1	08.2	M. Braun (*Neth.*)	1	22.0
1932	M. Kiyokawa (*Japan*)	1	08.6	E. Holm (*U.S.A.*)	1	19.4
1936	A. Kiefer (*U.S.A.*)	1	05.9	D. Senff (*Neth.*)	1	18.9
1948	A. Stack (*U.S.A.*)	1	06.4	K. M. Harup (*Denmark*)	1	14.4
1952	Y. Oyakawa (*U.S.A.*)	1	05.7	J. C. Harrison (*South Africa*)	1	14.3
1956	D. Theile (*Australia*)	1	02.2	J. Grinham (*Great Britain*)	1	12.9

* 200 metres.   † 100 yards.

200 METRES BREAST-STROKE

		m.	s.		m.	s.
A.						
1908	F. Holman (*G.B.*)	3	09.2	—		
1912	W. Bathe (*Germany*)	3	01.8	—		
1920	R. Malmroth (*Sweden*)	3	04.4	—		
1924	R. D. Skelton (*U.S.A.*)	2	56.6	L. Morton (*G.B.*)	3	33.2
1928	Y. Tsuruta (*Japan*)	2	48.8	H. Schrader (*Germany*)	3	12.6
1932	Y. Tsuruta (*Japan*)	2	45.4	C. Denis (*Australia*)	3	06.3
B.						
1936	T. Hamuro (*Japan*) (Br.)	2	42.5	H. Mayehata (*Japan*) (Br.)	3	03.6
1948	J. Verdeur (*U.S.A.*) (Bu.)	2	39.3	N. van Vliet (*Holland*) (Br.)	2	57.2
1952	J. G. Davies (*Austrl.*) (Bu.)	2	34.4	E. Szekely (*Hungary*) (Bu.)	2	51.7
C.						
1956	M. Furukawa (*Japan*)	2	34.7	U. Happe (*Germany*)	2	53.1

A. Before butterfly had been invented.
B. When breast-stroke (under-water recovery) or butterfly (over-water recovery) could be swum in this event: Br.—won on breast-stroke. Bu.—won on butterfly.
C. After butterfly had been separated from breast-stroke and there was a different championship for the new stroke.

Graham Sykes

Judy Grinham

Chris C. Walkden

Margaret Edwards

200 METRES BUTTERFLY
Men

		m.	s.
1956	W. Yorzyk (*U.S.A.*)	2	19.3

100 METRES BUTTERFLY
Women

		m.	s.
	S. Mann (*U.S.A.*)	1	11.0

4 x 200 METRES FREE-STYLE RELAY / 4 x 100 METRES FREE-STYLE RELAY

Year		m. s.		m. s.
1900	Germany (5 x 40 m.)	No time	—	
1904	U.S.A. (4 x 50 yards)	2 04.6	—	
1908	Great Britain	10 55.6	—	
1912	Australia	10 11.6	Great Britain	5 52.8
1920	U.S.A.	10 04.4	U.S.A.	5 11.6
1924	U.S.A.	9 53.4	U.S.A.	4 58.8
1928	U.S.A.	9 36.2	U.S.A.	4 47.3
1932	Japan	8 58.4	U.S.A.	4 38.0
1936	Japan	8 51.5	Netherlands	4 36.0
1948	U.S.A.	8 46.0	U.S.A.	4 29.2
1952	U.S.A.	8 31.1	Hungary	4 24.4
1956	Australia (O'Halloran, Devitt, Rose, Henricks)	8 23.6	Australia (Fraser, Leech, Morgan, Crapp)	4 17.1

WATER-POLO Men

	Winners	Runners-up
1900	G.B.	Belgium
1904	U.S.A. (New York)	U.S.A. (Chicago)
1908	G.B.	Belgium
1912	G.B.	Sweden
1920	G.B.	Belgium
1924	France	Belgium
1928	Germany	Hungary
1932	Hungary	Germany
1936	Hungary	Germany
1948	Italy	Hungary
1952	Hungary	Yugoslavia
1956	Hungary	Yugoslavia

SPRINGBOARD DIVING

Year	Men	points	Women	points
1904	G. E. Sheldon (*U.S.A.*)	12.66	—	
1908	A. Zuerner (*Germany*)	85.50	—	

Winners at the 1906 Interim Games (Athens)
MEN

100 m. free-style: C. M. Daniels (*U.S.A.*) 1 13.0
400 m. free-style: O. Scheff (*Austria*) 6 23.8
1,600 m. free-style: H. Taylor (*G.B.*) 28 28.0
4 x 250 m. relay: *Hungary* 17 16.2
Springboard diving: G. Walz (*Germany*)

SWIMMING QUIZ

1. Who has won the most gold medals at one Olympic Games?

★

2. Who improved his final placing at three successive Games—and won a medal each time?

★

3. What Olympic title did film-star Esther Williams win?

QUIZ ANSWERS

1. Three swimmers each won three: Jack Jarvis (G.B.), in 1900 (100, 1,000 and 4,000 metres free-style); Johnny Weissmuller (U.S.A.), in 1924 (100, 400 metres free-style and 4×200 m. relay); Murray Rose (Australia) 1956 (400 and 1,500 metres free-style and 4×200 m. relay). 2. Joaquim Capilla (Mexico) who won these places in the highboard diving event; 1948 (3rd), 1952 (2nd) and 1956 (1st). 3. She never swam in the Olympics. She was 100 m. free-style champion of the United States in 1939 with a time of 69 seconds.

1912	P. Guenther (*Germany*)	79.23		
1920	L. Kuehn (*U.S.A.*)	675.00	A. Riggin (*U.S.A.*)	9.00
1924	A. C. White (*U.S.A.*)	696.40	E. Becker (*U.S.A.*)	474.50
1928	P. Desjardins (*U.S.A.*)	185.40	H. Meany (*U.S.A.*)	78.62
1932	M. Galitzen (*U.S.A.*)	161.38	G. Coleman (*U.S.A.*)	87.52
1936	R. Degener (*U.S.A.*)	163.57	M. Gestring (*U.S.A.*)	89.27
1948	B. Harlan (*U.S.A.*)	163.64	V. M. Draves (*U.S.A.*)	108.74
1952	D. G. Browning (*U.S.A.*)	205.29	P. McCormick (*U.S.A.*)	147.30
1956	B. Clotworthy (*U.S.A.*)	159.56	P. McCormick (*U.S.A.*)	142.36

HIGHBOARD DIVING

1912	E. Adlerz (*Sweden*)	73.94		
1920	C. Pinksten (*U.S.A.*)	100.67	—	
1924	A. C. White (*U.S.A.*)	487.30	—	
1928	P. Desjardins (*U.S.A.*)	98.74	E. Becker-Pinkston (*U.S.A.*)	31.60
1932	H. Smith (*U.S.A.*)	124.80	D. Poynton (*U.S.A.*)	40.26
1936	M. Wayne (*U.S.A.*)	113.58	D. Poynton-Hill (*U.S.A.*)	33.93
1948	S. Lee (*U.S.A.*)	130.05	V. M. Draves (*U.S.A.*)	68.87
1952	S. Lee (*U.S.A.*)	156.28	P. McCormick (*U.S.A.*)	79.37
1956	J. Capilla (*Mexico*)	152.44	P. McCormick (*U.S.A.*)	84.85

HIGH PLAIN DIVING

1908	H. Johansson (*Sweden*)	83.75		
1912	E. Adlerz (*Sweden*)	200.00	G. Johansson (*Sweden*)	181.00
1920	A. Wallmann (*Sweden*)	183.50	S. Fryland (*Denmark*)	6.00
1924	R. Eve (*Australia*)	160.00	C. Smith (*U.S.A.*)	166.00

It is virtually impossible to compare the scores gained by the various Olympic diving champions. The tests have varied, in difficulty and numbers of dives, from Games to Games and the method of scoring has also been subject to change.

OLYMPIC RECORD HOLDERS

Event	Men	m.	s.	Women	m.	s.
100 m. free-style:	J. Henricks (*Australia*)		55.4	D. Fraser (*Australia*)	1	02.0
400 m. free-style:	M. Rose (*Australia*)	4	27.3	L. Crapp (*Australia*)	4	54.6
1,500 m. free-style:	G. Breen (*U.S.A.*)	17	52.9	No event for women		
100 m. back-stroke:	D. Theile (*Australia*)	1	02.2	J. Grinham (*G.B.*)	1	12.9
200 m. breast-stroke:	M. Furukawa (*Japan*)	2	34.7	U. Happe (*Germany*)	2	53.1
200 m. butterfly:	W. Yorzyk (*U.S.A.*)	2	18.6			
100 m. butterfly:				S. Mann (*U.S.A.*)	1	11.0
4 x 200 m. relay:	Australia	8	23.6			
4 x 100 m. relay:	—			Australia	4	17.1

SCOTTISH CHAMPIONS
Championships organised by the Scottish Amateur Swimming Association and open to natives of Scotland or persons who have resided in Scotland for six months immediately prior to the date of the championship.

100 YARDS FREE STYLE

	Instituted 1888 Men	s.	Instituted 1907 Women	m.	s.
Year					
1950	J. C. Wardrop (*Motherwell*)	53.6	M. Girvan (*Motherwell*)	1	05.4
1951	J. C. Wardrop (*Motherwell*)	52.6	C. Gibson (*Motherwell*)	1	02.8
1952	J. C. Wardrop (*Motherwell*)	52.2	D. Melville (*Aberdeen*)	1	04.2
1953	T. D. Welsh (*Galashiels*)	54.0	F. Hogben (*Arbroath*)	1	04.7
1954	I. C. Spence (*Gordonians, Aberdeen*)	55.0	C. Gibson (*Motherwell*)	1	03.6
1955	T. D. Welsh (*Galashiels*)	54.9	F. MacDonald (*Dundee*)	1	04.9
1956	R. Murphy (*Hawick*)	55.0	M. Girvan (*Motherwell*)	1	03.7
1957	J. C. M. Hill (*Warrender*)	54.7	M. Girvan (*Motherwell*)	1	02.3
1958	A. T. Still (*Gordonians, Aberdeen*)	54.8	C. R. S. Harris (*Carnegie*)	1	03.1
1959	I. M. Black (*Robert Gordon College, Aberdeen*)	52.0	N. Rae (*Motherwell*)	1	00.7

100 YARDS BACK STROKE

	Instituted 1913	m.	s.	Instituted 1924	m.	s.
1950	R. Wardrop (*Motherwell*)	1	03.4	M. McDowall (*Kilmarnock*)	1	09.2
1951	R. Wardrop (*Motherwell*)	1	03.2	M. McDowall (*Kilmarnock*)	1	08.9
1952	R. Wardrop (*Motherwell*)	1	03.6	M. McDowall (*Kilmarnock*)	1	09.4
1953	R. S. Burns (*Perth*)	1	04.2	M. McDowall (*Kilmarnock*)	1	08.3
1954	T. W. Robson (*Hawick*)	1	02.1	M. McDowall (*Kilmarnock*)	1	10.0
1955	R. S. Burns (*Perth*)	1	01.5	M. McDowall (*Kilmarnock*)	1	12.0
1956	R. S. Burns (*Perth*)	1	01.3	M. McDowall (*Kilmarnock*)	1	08.0
1957	T. W. Robson (*Hawick*)	1	03.1	M. McDowall (*Kilmarnock*)	1	08.8
1958	J. C. M. Hill (*Warrender*)	1	03.2	M. McDowall (*Kilmarnock*)	1	09.3
1959	J. C. M. Hill (*Warrender*)	1	02.4	F. Johnston (*Warrender*)	1	12.8

200 YARDS BREAST STROKE

	Instituted 1913	m.	s.	Instituted 1924	m.	s.
1950	J. B. Service (*Glasgow*)	2	42.0	H. O. Gordon (*Hamilton*)	2	50.6
1951	I. C. Spence (*Gordonians, Aberdeen*)	2	35.0	H. O. Gordon (*Hamilton*)	2	44.1
1952	I. C. Spence (*Gordonians, Aberdeen*)	2	35.4	H. O. Gordon (*Hamilton*)	2	45.3
1953	J. B. Service (*Glasgow*)	2	34.5	H. O. Gordon (*Hamilton*)	2	44.9
1954	J. B. Service (*Western B.*)	2	29.8	H. O. Gordon (*Hamilton*)	2	41.8
1955	I. C. Spence (*Gordonians, Aberdeen*)	2	37.7	H. O. Gordon (*Hamilton*)	2	46.2
1956	I. Percy-Rob (*Warrender*)	2	31.0	H. O. Gordon (*Hamilton*)	2	46.7
1957	I. Percy-Rob (*Warrender*)	2	29.6	H. O. Gordon (*Hamilton*)	2	41.2
1958	I. Percy-Rob (*Warrender*)	2	36.0	A. M. R. Turnbull (*Galashiels*)	2	51.5
1959	J. MacTaggart (*Kilmarnock*)	2	32.9	A. M. R. Turnbull (*Galashiels*)	2	48.0

220 YARDS FREE STYLE

	Instituted 1888	m.	s.	Instituted 1891 (200 yards up to 1954)	m.	s.
1950	J. C. Wardrop (*Motherwell*)	2	20.0	M. Girvan (*Motherwell*)	2	24.6
1951	J. C. Wardrop (*Motherwell*)	2	17.2	C. Gibson (*Motherwell*)	2	20.8
1952	J. C. Wardrop (*Motherwell*)	2	10.0	C. Gibson (*Motherwell*)	2	23.9
1953	R. C. Sreenan (*Whitehall, Dundee*)	2	19.4	D. Melville (*Aberdeen*)	2	24.9
1954	A. T. Still (*Gordonians, Aberdeen*)	2	16.4	M. Girvan (*Motherwell*)	2	21.2
1955	J. Baillie (*Renfrew*)	2	20.8	F. Hogben (*Arbroath*)	2	44.2
1956	J. D. Baillie (*Renfrew*)	2	18.2	M. Girvan (*Motherwell*)	2	38.6
1957	R. Murphy (*Hawick*)	2	15.0	M. Girvan (*Motherwell*)	2	36.5
1958	I. M. Black (*Robert Gordon College, Aberdeen*)	2	08.2	M. Girvan (*Motherwell*)	2	36.0
1959	I. M. Black (*Robert Gordon College, Aberdeen*)	2	07.2	N. Rae (*Motherwell*)	2	27.3

440 YARDS FREE STYLE

	Instituted 1890	m.	s.	Instituted 1931	m.	s.
1950	J. C. Wardrop (*Motherwell*)	5	07.2	M. Girvan (*Motherwell*)	5	46.3
1951	J. C. Wardrop (*Motherwell*)	4	55.9	C. Gibson (*Motherwell*)	5	38.6
1952	J. C. Wardrop (*Motherwell*)	4	41.9	D. Melville (*Aberdeen*)	5	45.7
1953	R. C. Sreenan (*Whitehall, Dundee*)	4	54.1	M. Girvan (*Motherwell*)	5	41.5
1954	R. C. Sreenan (*Whitehall, Dundee*)	4	50.8	M. Girvan (*Motherwell*)	5	31.0
1955	R. C. Sreenan (*Whitehall, Dundee*)	4	49.1	F. Hogben (*Arbroath*)	5	53.3
1956	J. Baillie (*Renfrew*)	5	05.0	F. Hogben (*Arbroath*)	5	45.7
1957	J. Baillie (*Renfrew*)	5	00.3	M. Girvan (*Motherwell*)	5	30.4
1958	I. M. Black (*Robert Gordon College, Aberdeen*)	4	37.2	N. Rae (*Motherwell*)	5	23.8
1959	I. M. Black (*Robert Gordon College, Aberdeen*)	4	50.3	N. Rae (*Motherwell*)	5	06.6

200 YARDS BUTTERFLY / 100 YARDS BUTTERFLY

	Instituted 1954	m.	s.	Instituted 1954	m.	s.
1954	H. H. Smith (*Paisley*)	2	32.5	H. R. Laird (*Belmont*)	1	24.6
1955	H. H. Smith (*Paisley*)	2	35.5	F. MacDonald (*Dundee*)	1	16.1
1956	H. H. Smith (*Paisley*)	2	32.0	F. MacDonald (*Dundee*)	1	15.7
1957	H. H. Smith (*Paisley*)	2	31.6	S. Watt (*Aberdeen*)	1	09.8
1958	I. M. Black (*Robert Gordon College, Aberdeen*)	2	09.9	S. Watt (*Aberdeen*)	1	10.1
1959	I. M. Black (*Robert Gordon College, Aberdeen*)	2	08.6	S. Watt (*Aberdeen*)	1	06.7

Table Tennis

Compiled by
W. Harrison Edwards
Editor: Table Tennis

MEN'S DOUBLES WORLD CHAMPIONSHIPS

1926–27	Dr. R. Jacobi and Dr. D. Pecsi (*Hungary*)
1927–28	A. Liebster and R. Thum (*Austria*)
1928–29	G. V. Barna and M. Szabados (*Hungary*)
1929–30	G. V. Barna and M. Szabados (*Hungary*)
1930–31	G. V. Barna and M. Szabados (*Hungary*)
1931–32	G. V. Barna and M. Szabados (*Hungary*)
1932–33	G. V. Barna and S. Glancz (*Hungary*)
1933–34	G. V. Barna and M. Szabados (*Hungary*)
1934–35	G. V. Barna and M. Szabados (*Hungary*)
1935–36	R. G. Blattner and J. H. McClure (*U.S.A.*)
1936–37	R. G. Blattner and J. H. McClure (*U.S.A.*)
1937–38	S. Schiff and J. H. McClure (*U.S.A.*)
1938–39	G. V. Barna (*Hungary*) and R. Bergmann (*Austria*)
1939–45	No championships
1946–47	B. Vana and A. Slar (*Czechoslovakia*)
1947–48	B. Vana and L. Stipek (*Czechoslovakia*)
1948–49	F. Tokar and I. Andreadis (*Czechoslovakia*)
1949–50	F. Sido and F. Soos (*Hungary*)
1950–51	B. Vana and I. Andreadis (*Czechoslovakia*)
1951–52	N. Fujii and T. Hayashi (*Japan*)
1952–53	J. Koczian and F. Sido (*Hungary*)
1953–54	V. Harangozo and Z. Dolinar (*Yugoslavia*)
1954–55	I. Andreadis and L. Stipek (*Czechoslovakia*)
1955–56	I. Ogimura and Y. Tomita (*Japan*)
1956–57	I. Andreadis and L. Stipek (*Czechoslovakia*)
1957–58	No championship
1958–59	I. Ogimura and T. Murakami (*Japan*)

WOMEN'S DOUBLES WORLD CHAMPIONSHIPS

1927–28	M. Mednyanszky (*Hungary*) and F. Flamm (*Austria*)
1928–29	E. Metzger and E. Ruester (*Germany*)
1929–30	M. Mednyanszky and A. Sipos (*Hungary*)
1930–31	M. Mednyanszky and A. Sipos (*Hungary*)
1931–32	M. Mednyanszky and A. Sipos (*Hungary*)
1932–33	M. Mednyanszky and A. Sipos (*Hungary*)
1933–34	M. Mednyanszky and A. Sipos (*Hungary*)
1934–35	M. Mednyanszky and A. Sipos (*Hungary*)
1935–36	M. Kettnerova and M. Smidova (*Czechoslovakia*)
1936–37	V. Depetrisova and V. Votrubcova (*Czechoslovakia*)
1937–38	V. Depetrisova and V. Votrubcova (*Czechoslovakia*)
1938–39	T. Pritzi and H. Bussmann (*Austria*)
1939–45	No championships
1946–47	G. Farkas (*Hungary*) and T. Pritzi (*Austria*)
1947–48	Mrs. V. Thomas and M. Franks (*England*)
1948–49	H. Elliot (*Scotland*) and G. Farkas (*Hungary*)
1949–50	D. Beregi (*England*) and H. Elliot (*Scotland*)
1950–51	D. Rowe and R. Rowe (*England*)
1951–52	S. Narahara and T. Nishimura (*Japan*)
1952–53	G. Farkas (*Hungary*) and A. Rozeanu (*Rumania*)
1953–54	D. Rowe and R. Rowe (*England*)
1954–55	A. Rozeanu and E. Zeller (*Rumania*)
1955–56	A. Rozeanu and E. Zeller (*Rumania*)
1956–57	L. Mosoczy and A. Simon (*Hungary*)
1957–58	No championship
1958–59	T. Namba and K. Yamaizumi (*Japan*)

TABLE TENNIS QUIZ

1. Two left-handers won the European team championship for England. Who were they?

2. What is the height of the playing surface from the ground?

3. Can naturalised players represent England?

4. When was the first international played in this country?

5. By what other names has table tennis been known?

6. How many net cords are allowed before the server is penalised?

7. When was the Ping Pong Association formed?

8. When was the English Table Tennis Association formed?

9. Who is the only man to have been both President and Chairman of the E.T.T.A. at the same time?

QUIZ ANSWERS

1. Ann Haydon and Diane Rowe in 1958. 2. Two feet six inches. 3. Yes. Victor Barna, Richard Bergmann and Dora Beregi (now Mrs. Devenny) are notable examples. 4. March 9, 1923, between England and Wales. 5. Gossima and Ping Pong. 6. There is no limit to the number of net cords. 7. 1902. It went out of existence shortly afterwards and was re-formed in 1921–22. 8. April 24, 1927. 9. Ivor Montagu in 1927–28 and 1928–29.

HISTORY

Table Tennis is one of the many sports of British origin, but its exact beginnings are somewhat obscure. There is an early reference to a similar type of game in 1881, but its introduction is generally credited to a Mr. James Gibb in 1899 under the name of "Gossima".

A year later the name was changed to "Ping Pong", derived from the sound of the ball hitting the bat, and in 1902 the Ping Pong Association was formed to organise championships.

It was only a temporary craze and the Association collapsed, to be resuscitated in 1921, from which date come the first records of national championships—A. Donaldson, of Durham, and Mrs. Scott, of London, being the first men's and women's singles champions.

Difficulties arose when it was discovered that "Ping Pong" was a registered trade name. The Association was accordingly dissolved and re-formed as "The Table Tennis Association", being changed again to its existing title of "The English Table Tennis Association" in 1927.

Meanwhile, the game was growing in popularity on the Continent and in January 1926 the foundations to the International Table Tennis Federation were laid following a meeting in Berlin, called by Dr. Olaf Lehmann, of Germany, and attended by representatives of Austria, England, Germany and Hungary and subsequently Czechoslovakia and Sweden.

They entrusted England with holding a European Championship in London the following December, at the conclusion of which the International Federation was formed. The championships were immediately given a "World" recognition, and the first singles champions were the Hungarians Dr. Roland Jacobi and Miss Maria Mednyanszky.

Synonymous with the organisation of both the English and international game is the Hon. Ivor Montagu. He was in at the resuscitation of the Ping Pong Association, became President of the English Association in 1927, and has also been Chairman and subsequently President of the International Federation since its formation.

Equipment has undergone many changes. Early bats were vellum-covered frames, followed by wooden rackets, later to be covered by cork, pimpled rubber and in recent years sponge, which has brought a major crisis to the sport, with some countries, including England, wanting this surface banned.

There is a record of a small india-rubber ball being used in the earliest stages, but this was replaced by the introduction of the celluloid ball at the beginning of the century.

Battles have also raged over the method of scoring, with arguments for one game of 50-up, and also the Lawn Tennis system, before the existing method of best of three (or five) games of 21-up was adopted.

So vast has become the organisation of world championships, with more than 70 nations affiliated to the International Federation, that these are now held biennially.

MEN'S SINGLES WORLD CHAMPIONSHIPS

1926–27	Dr. R. Jacobi (*Hungary*)
1927–28	Z. Mechlovits (*Hungary*)
1928–29	F. J. Perry (*England*)
1929–30	G. V. Barna (*Hungary*)
1930–31	M. Szabados (*Hungary*)
1931–32	G. V. Barna (*Hungary*)
1932–33	G. V. Barna (*Hungary*)
1933–34	G. V. Barna (*Hungary*)
1934–35	G. V. Barna (*Hungary*)
1935–36	S. Kolar (*Czechoslovakia*)
1936–37	R. Bergmann (*Austria*)
1937–38	B. Vana (*Czechoslovakia*)
1938–39	R. Bergman (*Austria*)
1939–45	No championships
1946–47	B. Vana (*Czechoslovakia*)
1947–48	R. Bergmann (*England*)
1948–49	J. Leach (*England*)
1949–50	R. Bergmann (*England*)
1950–51	J. Leach (*England*)
1951–52	H. Satoh (*Japan*)
1952–53	F. Sido (*Hungary*)
1953–54	I. Ogimura (*Japan*)
1954–55	T. Tanaka (*Japan*)
1955–56	I. Ogimura (*Japan*)
1956–57	T. Tanaka (*Japan*)
1957–58	No championship
1958–59	Jung Kuo-Tuan (*China*)

WOMEN'S SINGLES WORLD CHAMPIONSHIPS

1926–27	M. Mednyanszky (*Hungary*)
1927–28	M. Mednyanszky (*Hungary*)
1928–29	M. Mednyanszky (*Hungary*)
1929–30	M. Mednyanszky (*Hungary*)
1930–31	M. Mednyanszky (*Hungary*)
1931–32	A. Sipos (*Hungary*)
1932–33	A. Sipos (*Hungary*)
1933–34	M. Kettnerova (*Czechoslovakia*)
1934–35	M. Kettnerova (*Czechoslovakia*)
1935–36	R. H. Aarons (*U.S.A.*)
1936–37	Title vacant—finalists R. H. Aarons (*U.S.A.*) and T. Pritzi (*Austria*)
1937–38	T. Pritzi (*Austria*)
1938–39	V. Depetrisova (*Czechoslovakia*)
1939–45	No championships
1946–47	G. Farkas (*Hungary*)
1947–48	G. Farkas (*Hungary*)
1948–49	G. Farkas (*Hungary*)
1949–50	A. Rozeanu (*Rumania*)
1950–51	A. Rozeanu (*Rumania*)
1951–52	A. Rozeanu (*Rumania*)
1952–53	A. Rozeanu (*Rumania*)
1953–54	A. Rozeanu (*Rumania*)
1954–55	A. Rozeanu (*Rumania*)
1955–56	T. Okawa (*Japan*)
1956–57	F. Eguchi (*Japan*)
1957–58	No championship
1958–59	K. Matsuzaki (*Japan*)

MIXED DOUBLES WORLD CHAMPIONSHIPS

1926–27	Z. Mechlovits and Mrs. M. Mednyanszky (*Hungary*)
1927–28	Z. Mechlovits and Mrs. M. Mednyanszky (*Hungary*)
1928–29	I. Kelen and Miss A. Sipos (*Hungary*)
1929–30	M. Szabados and Mrs. M. Mednyanszky (*Hungary*)
1930–31	M. Szabados and Mrs. M. Mednyanszky (*Hungary*)
1931–32	G. V. Barna and Miss A. Sipos (*Hungary*)
1932–33	I. Kelen and Mrs. M. Mednyanszky (*Hungary*)
1933–34	M. Szabados and Mrs. M. Mednyanszky (*Hungary*)
1934–35	G. V. Barna and Miss A. Sipos (*Hungary*)
1935–36	M. Hamr and Miss G. Kleinova (*Czechoslovakia*)
1936–37	B. Vana and Miss V. Votrubcova (*Czechoslovakia*)
1937–38	L. Bellak (*Hungary*) and Miss W. Woodhead (*England*)
1938–39	B. Vana and Miss V. Votrubcova (*Czechoslovakia*)
1939–45	No championships
1946–47	F. Soos and Miss G. Farkas (*Hungary*)
1947–48	R. Miles and Miss T. Thall (*U.S.A.*)
1948–49	F. Sido and Miss G. Farkas (*Hungary*)
1949–50	F. Sido and Miss G. Farkas (*Hungary*)
1950–51	B. Vana (*Czechoslovakia*) and Miss A. Rozeanu (*Rumania*)
1951–52	F. Sido (*Hungary*) and Miss A. Rozeanu (*Rumania*)
1952–53	F. Sido (*Hungary*) and Miss A. Rozeanu (*Rumania*)
1953–54	I. Andreadis (*Czechoslovakia*) and Miss G. Farkas (*Hungary*)
1954–55	K. Szepesi and Miss E. Koczian (*Hungary*)
1955–56	E. Klein and Mrs. L. Neuberger (*U.S.A.*)
1956–57	I. Ogimura and Miss F. Eguchi (*Japan*)
1957–58	No championship
1958–59	I. Ogimura and F. Eguchi (*Japan*)

Miss A. Rozeanu   T. Tanaka   Miss G. Farkas

SWAYTHLING CUP
(Men's Team World Championship)

1926–27	Hungary
1927–28	Hungary
1928–29	Hungary
1929–30	Hungary
1930–31	Hungary
1931–32	Czechoslovakia
1932–33	Hungary
1933–34	Hungary
1934–35	Hungary
1935–36	Austria
1936–37	U.S.A.
1937–38	Hungary
1938–39	Czechoslovakia
1939–45	No championship
1946–47	Czechoslovakia
1947–48	Czechoslovakia
1948–49	Hungary
1949–50	Czechoslovakia
1950–51	Czechoslovakia
1951–52	Hungary
1952–53	England (*R. Bergmann, J. Leach, A. Simons, B. Kennedy*)
1953–54	Japan
1954–55	Japan
1955–56	Japan
1956–57	Japan
1957–58	No championship
1958–59	Japan

MARCEL CORBILLON CUP
(Women's Team World Championship)

1933–34	Germany
1934–35	Czechoslovakia
1935–36	Czechoslovakia
1936–37	U.S.A.
1937–38	Czechoslovakia
1938–39	Germany
1939–45	No championship
1946–47	England (*E. Blackbourn, V. Dace, M. Franks*)
1947–48	England (*D. Beregi, M. Franks, V. (Dace) Thomas*)
1948–49	U.S.A.
1949–50	Rumania
1950–51	Rumania
1951–52	Japan
1952–53	Rumania
1953–54	Japan
1954–55	Rumania
1955–56	Rumania
1956–57	Japan
1957–58	No championship
1958–59	Japan

VENUES OF PAST WORLD CHAMPIONSHIPS

1926–27	London
1927–28	Stockholm
1928–29	Budapest
1929–30	Berlin
1930–31	Budapest
1931–32	Prague
1932–33	Baden (Nr. Vienna)
1933–34	Paris
1934–35	London
1935–36	Prague
1936–37	Baden (Nr. Vienna)
1937–38	London
1938–39	Cairo
1946–47	Paris
1947–48	London
1948–49	Stockholm
1949–50	Budapest
1950–51	Vienna
1951–52	Bombay
1952–53	Bucharest
1953–54	London
1954–55	Utrecht
1955–56	Tokyo
1956–57	Stockholm
1958–59	Dortmund

ENGLAND'S SWAYTHLING CUP RECORD SINCE 1926-27

v. Austria.	Won 7, lost 11
v. Belgium.	Won 5
v. Brazil.	Won 4
v. Cambodia.	Won 1
v. China.	Won 2
v. Czechoslovakia.	Won 4, lost 15
v. Denmark.	Won 1
v. Egypt.	Won 3
v. France.	Won 6, lost 3
v. Germany.	Won 11, lost 1
v. Greece.	Won 2
v. Hungary.	Won 3, lost 12
v. India.	Won 10, lost 2
v. Iran.	Won 1
v. Ireland.	Won 3
v. Israel.	Won 1
v. Italy.	Won 3
v. Japan.	Won 1, lost 1
v. Jersey.	Won 1
v. Latvia.	Won 5, lost 3
v. Lebanon.	Won 3
v. Lithuania.	Won 6
v. Luxembourg.	Won 2
v. Malta.	Won 1
v. Netherlands.	Won 5
v. New Zealand.	Won 1

v. Pakistan.	Won 2
v. Palestine.	Won 1
v. Poland.	Won 2, lost 3
v. Portugal.	Won 2
v. Rumania.	Won 5
v. Saarland.	Won 1
v. Scotland.	Won 1
v. South Korea.	Won 1
v. South Vietnam.	Lost 1
v. Spain.	Won 3
v. Sweden.	Won 7, lost 1
v. Switzerland.	Won 6
v. U.S.A.	Won 2, lost 6
v. Vietnam.	Won 1
v. Wales.	Won 14
v. Yugoslavia.	Won 6, lost 5

ENGLAND'S CORBILLON CUP RECORD SINCE 1933-34

v. Austria.	Won 3, lost 4
v. China.	Won 2, lost 2
v. Belgium.	Won 6
v. Czechoslovakia.	Won 3, lost 4
v. Denmark.	Won 2
v. East Germany.	Won 1
v. Finland.	Won 1
v. France.	Won 7, lost 1
v. Germany.	Won 3, lost 4
v. Holland.	Won 1
v. Hong Kong.	Won 1
v Hungary.	Won 7, lost 4
v. India.	Won 2
v. Ireland.	Won 2
v. Italy.	Won 4
v. Japan.	Won 2, lost 2
v. Jersey.	Won 1
v. Lithuania.	Won 1
v. Netherlands.	Won 6
v. Norway.	Won 1
v. Portugal.	Won 1
v. Rumania.	Won 3, lost 4
v. Scotland.	Won 3
v. South Korea.	Won 1
v. Spain.	Won 1
v. Sweden.	Won 5
v. Switzerland.	Won 6
v. U.S.A.	Won 10, lost 2
v. Wales.	Won 8
v. Yugoslavia.	Won 1

ENGLISH OPEN CHAMPIONSHIPS MEN'S SINGLES

1921–22	A. Donaldson (*Durham*)
1922–23	M. Cohen (*London*)
1923–24	P. Bromfield (*Kent*)
1924–25	P. N. Nanda (*India*)
1925–26	R. G. Suppiah (*India*)
1926–27	R. G. Suppiah (*India*)
1927–28	Dr. D. Pecsi (*Hungary*)
1928–29	A. Malecek (*Czechoslovakia*)
1929–30	S. Glancz (*Hungary*)
1930–31	M. Szabados (*Hungary*)
1931–32	M. Szabados (*Hungary*)
1932–33	G. V. Barna (*Hungary*)
1933–34	G. V. Barna (*Hungary*)
1934–35	G. V. Barna (*Hungary*)
1935–36	A. Ehrlich (*Poland*)
1936–37	G. V. Barna (*Hungary*)
1937–38	G. V. Barna (*Hungary*)
1938–39	R. Bergmann (*London*)
1939–40	R. Bergmann (*London*)
1940–45	No championships
1945–46	B. Vana (*Czechoslovakia*)
1946–47	V. Tereba (*Czechoslovakia*)
1947–48	R. Bergmann (*London*)
1948–49	M. Reisman (*U.S.A.*)
1949–50	R. Bergmann (*London*)
1950–51	A. Ehrlich (*France*)
1951–52	R. Bergmann (*London*)
1952–53	M. Haguenauer (*France*)
1953–54	R. Bergmann (*London*)
1954–55	Z. Dolinar (*Yugoslavia*)
1955–56	E. Gyetvai (*Hungary*)
1956–57	Z. Berczik (*Hungary*)
1957–58	F. Sido (*Hungary*)
1958–59	I. Ogimura (*Japan*)

ENGLISH OPEN CHAMPIONSHIPS WOMEN'S SINGLES

1921–22	Mrs. Scott
1922–23	Miss K. M. Berry (*Surrey*)
1923–24	Miss K. M. Berry (*Surrey*)
1924–25	Miss K. M. Berry (*Surrey*)
1925–26	Miss G. Vasey (*Whitby*)
1926–27	Miss D. Gubbins (*Wales*)
1927–28	Miss Erika Metzger (*Germany*)
1928–29	Miss M. Smidova (*Czechoslovakia*)
1929–30	Miss D. Gubbins (*Wales*)
1930–31	Miss V. Bromfield (*London*)
1931–32	Mrs. M. Mednyanszky (*Hungary*)
1932–33	Miss D. M. Emdin (*St. Albans*)
1933–34	Miss M. Osborne (*Birmingham*)
1934–35	Miss M. Osborne (*Birmingham*)
1935–36	Miss M. Kettnerova (*Czechoslovakia*)
1936–37	Miss R. H. Aarons (*U.S.A.*)
1937–38	Miss D. Beregi (*Hungary*)
1938–39	Miss J. Nicoll (*Wembley*)
1939–40	Miss V. Dace (*London*)
1940–45	No championships
1945–46	Miss D. Beregi (*Exeter*)
1946–47	Miss G. Farkas (*Hungary*)
1947–48	Miss G. Farkas (*Hungary*)
1948–49	Miss P. McLean (*U.S.A.*)
1949–50	Miss M. Shahian (*U.S.A.*)
1950–51	Miss T. Pritzi (*Austria*)
1951–52	Miss L. Wertl (*Austria*)
1952–53	Miss R. Rowe (*Middlesex*)
1953–54	Miss L. Wertl (*Austria*)
1954–55	Miss R. Rowe (*Middlesex*)
1955–56	Miss G. Farkas (*Hungary*)
1956–57	Miss F. Eguchi (*Japan*)
1957–58	Miss A. Simon (*Netherlands*)
1958–59	Miss F. Eguchi (*Japan*)

TABLE TENNIS QUIZ

1. When is the time limit invoked and what is the length of subsequent games?

*

2. Who has won the most singles titles in the world championships?

*

3. Can a player who has dropped his racket return the ball with an empty hand?

*

4. How many players competed in the singles events at the 1926 world championships?

*

5. Who were England's representatives in the first world championships?

*

6. How is it possible to tell the difference between the Rowe twins?

*

7. Is it true that Middlesex have won the Premier Division of the National County Championship since its inauguration in 1947?

*

8. What is the Victor Barna Award and who has won it most times?

QUIZ ANSWERS

1. When a game is unfinished after 20 minutes' play it is awarded to the player who is ahead. If they are level they are given five minutes more to decide the next point. Subsequent games will be of ten minutes' duration. 2. Angelica Rozeanu (Rumania) with six. 1950, 51, 52, 53, 54, 55. 3. No. 4. Eighty. 64 in the men's singles and 16 in the women's singles. 5. P. Bromfield (Captain), C. W. Allwright, J. Thompson, B. Bernstein, F. J. Burles. 6. Diane Rowe is left-handed; Rosalind Rowe right-handed. 7. No. Surrey were champions in 1956 and again in 1959. 8. A trophy presented each season for the most notable performance by an English player. Both Ann Haydon and Diane Rowe have won it three times.

ENGLISH OPEN CHAMPIONSHIPS
MEN'S DOUBLES

1926–27	P. Bromfield (*Kent*) and L. S. E. Farris (*London*)
1927–28	C. H. Bull (*Kent*) and F. J. Perry (*Ealing*)
1928–29	C. H. Bull (*Kent*) and F. J. Perry (*Ealing*)
1929–30	C. H. Bull (*Kent*) and F. J. Perry (*Ealing*)
1930–31	M. Szabados and G. V. Barna (*Hungary*)
1931–32	H. Kolar and A. Malecek (*Czechoslovakia*)
1932–33	G. V. Barna and S. Glancz (*Hungary*)
1933–34	G. V. Barna (*Hungary*) and T. E. Sears (*London*)
1934–35	G. V. Barna (*Hungary*) and T. E. Sears (*London*)
1935–36	L. Bellak and M. Szabados (*Hungary*)
1936–37	S. Schiff and A. Berenbaum (*U.S.A.*)
1937–38	G. V. Barna and L. Bellak (*Hungary*)
1938–39	G. V. Barna and L. Bellak (*Hungary*)
1939–40	R. Bergmann (*London*) and A. Liebster (*London*)
1940–45	No championships
1945–46	B. Vana and A. Slar (*Czechoslovakia*)
1946–47	B. Vana and A. Slar (*Czechoslovakia*)
1947–48	R. Bergmann (*London*) and T. Flisberg (*Sweden*)
1948–49	R. Bergmann (*London*) and G. V. Barna (*Middlesex*)
1949–50	Z. Dolinar and V. Harangozo (*Yugoslavia*)
1950–51	J. Leach (*Essex*) and J. Carrington (*Surrey*)
1951–52	Z. Dolinar and V. Harangozo (*Yugoslavia*)
1952–53	R. Bergmann (*London*) and J. Leach (*Essex*)
1953–54	B. Kennedy (*Yorkshire*) and A. Simons (*Gloucestershire*)
1954–55	I. Andreadis and L. Stipek (*Czechoslovakia*)
1955–56	K. Szepesi and E. Gyetvai (*Hungary*)
1956–57	I. Ogimura and T. Tanaka (*Japan*)
1957–58	Z. Berczik and F. Sido (*Hungary*)
1958–59	T. Murakami and I. Ogimura (*Japan*)

ENGLISH OPEN CHAMPIONSHIPS
MIXED DOUBLES

1926–27	L. S. E. Farris and Miss J. Ingram (*London*)
1927–28	Dr. D. Pecsi (*Hungary*) and Miss Metzger (*Germany*)
1928–29	F. J. Perry (*Ealing*) and Miss W. H. Land (*London*)
1929–30	S. Glancz (*Hungary*) and Miss M. Gal (*Hungary*)
1930–31	S. Glancz (*Hungary*) and Miss V. Bromfield (*London*)
1931–32	M. Szabados and Mrs. M. Mednyanszky (*Hungary*)
1932–33	G. V. Barna (*Hungary*) and Miss D. M. Emdin (*St. Albans*)
1933–34	G. V. Barna (*Hungary*) and Miss D. M. Emdin (*St. Albans*)
1934–35	G. V. Barna (*Hungary*) and Miss M. Osborne (*Birmingham*)
1935–36	G. V. Barna (*Hungary*) and Miss M. Osborne (*Birmingham*)
1936–37	R. G. Blattner and Miss R. H. Aarons (*U.S.A.*)
1937–38	G. V. Barna (*Hungary*) and Miss M. Osborne (*Birmingham*)
1938–39	B. Vana and Miss V. Votrubcova (*Czechoslovakia*)
1939–40	G. V. Barna (*Hungary*) and Miss M. Osborne (*Birmingham*)
1940–45	No championships
1945–46	E. J. Filby (*Plymouth*) and Miss D. Beregi (*Exeter*)
1946–47	B. Vana and Miss V. Votrubcova (*Czechoslovakia*)
1947–48	F. Sido and Miss G. Farkas (*Hungary*)
1948–49	R. Miles and Miss T. Thall (*U.S.A.*)
1949–50	J. Leach and Miss M. Franks (*Essex*)
1950–51	G. V. Barna (*Middlesex*) and Miss H. Elliot (*Scotland*)
1951–52	J. Leach (*Essex*) and Miss D. Rowe (*Middlesex*)
1952–53	G. V. Barna and Miss R. Rowe (*Middlesex*)
1953–54	J. Leach (*Essex*) and Miss D. Rowe (*Middlesex*)
1954–55	A. W. C. Simons (*Gloucestershire*) and Miss H. Elliot (*Scotland*)
1955–56	J. Leach (*Essex*) and Miss D. Rowe (*Middlesex*)
1956–57	K. Tsunoda and Miss T. Namba (*Japan*)
1957–58	F. Sido and Miss E. Koczian (*Hungary*)
1958–59	T. Murakami and Miss K. Matsuzaki (*Japan*)

R. Miles

Miss L. Wertl

I. Ogimura

TABLE TENNIS QUIZ

1. Has table tennis ever been included in the Olympic Games?

*

2. When is the ball classed as in play?

*

3. How many world championship titles has Victor Barna won?

*

4. Who has won most world championship titles?

*

5. What is the correct height of the top of a table tennis net above the playing surface?

*

6. How many countries entered the first world championships in 1926?

*

7. What is a "paddle"?

QUIZ ANSWERS

1. No. 2. Immediately it leaves the server's hand. 3. Fifteen. Five singles, eight men's doubles and two mixed doubles. 4. Maria Mednyanszky (Hungary) with 18. Five singles, seven women's doubles and six mixed doubles. 5. Six inches. 6. Seven. Austria, Czechoslovakia, England, Germany, Hungary, India, Wales. 7. An American term for a table tennis bat.

ENGLISH OPEN CHAMPIONSHIPS
JUNIOR SINGLES (BOYS)

1932–33	C. W. Davies (*Manchester*)
1933–34	M. B. W. Bergl (*Harrow*)
1934–35	H. Lurie (*Manchester*)
1935–36	G. B. Sellman (*Ealing*)
1936–37	K. Stanley (*Manchester*)
1937–38	K. Stanley (*Manchester*)
1938–39	K. Stanley (*Manchester*)
1939–40	J. P. Bermingham (*Wembley*)
1940–45	No championships
1945–46	D. A. Miller (*London*)
1946–47	W. Rowe (*Torquay*)
1947–48	M. Thornhill (*Middlesex*)
1948–49	D. G. Ellison (*Lancashire*)
1949–50	J. Lowe (*Middlesex*)
1950–51	B. Malmquist (*Sweden*)
1951–52	K. Freundorfer (*Germany*)
1952–53	K. Freundorfer (*Germany*)
1953–54	K. Freundorfer (*Germany*)
1954–55	B. Onnes (*Netherlands*)
1955–56	I. Harrison (*Gloucester*)
1956–57	P. Czichowski (*Germany*)
1957–58	C. Gosling (*Middlesex*)
1958–59	M. Ness (*West Germany*)

ENGLISH OPEN CHAMPIONSHIPS
JUNIOR SINGLES (GIRLS)

1939–40	Miss E. Blackbourn (*Exeter*)
1940–45	No championships
1945–46	Miss J. Mackay (*Birmingham*)
1946–47	No championship
1947–48	Miss A. Wood (*Lancashire*)
1948–49	Miss A. Wood (*Lancashire*)
1949–50	Miss R. Rowe (*Middlesex*)
1950–51	Miss D. Munnings (*Lincolnshire*)
1951–52	Miss J. Rook (*Surrey*)
1952–53	Miss A. Haydon (*Warwickshire*)
1953–54	Miss J. Rook (*Surrey*)
1954–55	Miss A. Haydon (*Warwickshire*)
1955–56	Miss A. Haydon (*Warwickshire*)
1956–57	Miss H. Dauphin (*Germany*)
1957–58	Miss J. Harrower (*Middlesex*)
1958–59	Miss Y. J. Hwang (*Korea*)

ENGLISH OPEN CHAMPIONSHIPS
WOMEN'S DOUBLES

1926–27	Miss D. Gubbins (*Wales*) and Miss J. Ingram (*London*)
1927–28	Miss W. H. Land and Miss B. Somerville (*London*)
1928–29	Miss M. Smidova (*Czechoslovakia*) and Miss P. Moser (*London*)
1929–30	Miss W. H. Land (*London*) and Miss M. Gal (*Hungary*)
1930–31	Mrs. L. M. Holt (*London*) and Miss N. Wood (*St. Albans*)
1931–32	Mrs. M. Mednyanszky (*Hungary*) and Mrs. Martin (*London*)
1932–33	Miss N. Wood (*St. Albans*) and Miss W. Woodhead (*Amersham*)
1933–34	Miss D. M. Emdin (*St. Albans*) and Miss P. Moser (*London*)
1934–35	Miss M. Osborne (*Birmingham*) and Miss W. Woodhead (*Amersham*)
1935–36	Miss Krebsbach (*Germany*) and Miss D. M. Emdin (*St. Albans*)
1936–37	Miss M. Osborne (*Birmingham*) and Miss W. Woodhead (*Amersham*)
1937–38	Miss M. Osborne (*Birmingham*) and Miss W. Woodhead (*Amersham*)
1938–39	Miss V. Depetrisova and Miss V. Votrubcova (*Czechoslovakia*)
1939–40	Miss J. Nicoll (*Wembley*) and Miss D. Beregi (*Hungary*)
1940–45	No championships
1945–46	Miss D. Beregi (*Exeter*) and Miss V. Dace (*London*)
1946–47	Miss V. Dace (*London*) and Miss E. Blackbourn (*Exeter*)
1947–48	Miss G. Farkas (*Hungary*) and Miss L. R. Barnes (*Surrey*)
1948–49	Miss P. McLean and Miss T. Thall (*U.S.A.*)
1949–50	Miss D. Rowe and Miss R. Rowe (*Middlesex*)
1950–51	Miss D. Rowe and Miss R. Rowe (*Middlesex*)
1951–52	Miss D. Rowe and Miss R. Rowe (*Middlesex*)
1952–53	Miss D. Rowe and Miss R. Rowe (*Middlesex*)
1953–54	Miss D. Rowe and Miss R. Rowe (*Middlesex*)
1954–55	Miss D. Rowe and Miss R. Rowe (*Middlesex*)
1955–56	Miss D. Rowe (*Middlesex*) and Miss A. Haydon (*Warwickshire*)
1956–57	Miss T. Okawa and Miss T. Namba (*Japan*)
1957–58	Miss A. Haydon and Miss P. Mortimer (*Warwickshire*)
1958–59	Miss F. Eguchi and Miss K. Matsuzaki (*Japan*)

J. Leach

Miss M. Franks

G. V. Barna

ENGLISH OPEN CHAMPIONSHIPS
JUNIOR DOUBLES (BOYS)

1949–50	J. Lowe (*Middlesex*) and P. Smith (*Essex*)
1950–51	B. Malmquist and L. Pettersson (*Sweden*)
1951–52	A. Danton and D. M. Eagles (*Kent*)
1952–53	A. Danton (*Kent*) and R. Dorking (*Essex*)
1953–54	R. Dorking (*Essex*) and M. G. MacLaren (*Surrey*)
1954–55	E. Klein (*U.S.A.*) and B. Onnes (*Netherlands*)
1955–56	K. D. Edwards and I. Harrison (*Gloucestershire*)
1956–57	P. Czichowski and W. Prandke (*Germany*)
1957–58	I. Barclay (*Scotland*) and H-J. Fromm (*East Germany*)
1958–59	M. Ness and P. Russ (*West Germany*)

ENGLISH OPEN CHAMPIONSHIPS
JUNIOR DOUBLES (GIRLS)

1949–50	Miss D. Rowe and Miss R. Rowe (*Middlesex*)
1950–51	Miss D. Munnings (*Lincolnshire*) and Miss J. Titterington (*Lancashire*)
1951–52	Miss U. Paulsen and Miss H. Walz (*Germany*)
1952–53	Miss A. Haydon (*Warwickshire*) and Miss J. Rook (*Surrey*)
1953–54	Miss A. Haydon (*Warwickshire*) and Miss J. Rook (*Surrey*)
1954–55	Miss J. Fielder (*Kent*) and Miss A. Haydon (*Warwickshire*)
1955–56	Miss A. Haydon (*Warwickshire*) and Miss D. Worrall (*Staffordshire*)
1956–57	Miss H. Dauphin and Miss L. Muser (*Germany*)
1957–58	Miss C. Bannach and Miss I. Woschee (*East Germany*)
1958–59	Miss J. Fischer and Miss H. Scheithe (*West Germany*)

ENGLISH OPEN CHAMPIONSHIPS
JUNIOR MIXED DOUBLES

1949–50	P. Smith (*Essex*) and Miss R. Rowe (*Middlesex*)
1950–51	L. Pettersson (*Sweden*) and Miss D. Spooner (*Middlesex*)
1951–52	K. Freundorfer and Miss U. Paulsen (*Germany*)
1952–53	D. Phillips (*Wales*) and Miss F. Lauber (*Austria*)
1953–54	R. Dorking (*Essex*) and Miss A. Haydon (*Warwickshire*)
1954–55	E. Klein (*U.S.A.*) and Miss W. Bates (*Sussex*)
1955–56	L. F. Landry (*Middlesex*) and Miss A. Haydon (*Warwickshire*)
1956–57	P. Czichowski and Miss H. Dauphin (*Germany*)
1957–58	D. W. Grant (*Hampshire*) and Miss S. M. Hession (*Essex*)
1958–59	P. Racey (*Beds*) and Miss Y. J. Hwang (*Korea*)

ENGLISH OPEN CHAMPIONSHIPS
MEN'S VETERAN SINGLES

1932–33	Z. Mechlovits (*Hungary*)
1933–34	J. Thompson (*Bristol*)
1934–35	A. J. Wilmott (*London*)
1935–36	E. C. Gunn (*Plymouth*)
1936–37	A. Melnick (*London*)
1937–38	H. Knibbs (*Liverpool*)
1938–39	Z. Mechlovits (*Hungary*)
1939–40	A. J. Wilmott (*London*)
1940–45	No championships
1945–46	R. V. Bryant (*Salisbury*)
1946–47	J. Taylor (*London*)
1947–48	E. Reay (*Durham*)
1948–49	S. Sugarhood (*Essex*)
1949–50	S. Sugarhood (*Essex*)
1950–51	L. Thompson (*Buckinghamshire*)
1951–52	A. D. Brook (*Sussex*)
1952–53	L. C. Kerslake (*Devon*)
1953–54	L. C. Kerslake (*Devon*)
1954–55	A. D. Brook (*Sussex*)
1955–56	H. G. Spiers (*Warwickshire*)
1956–57	L. C. Kerslake (*Devon*)
1957–58	R. L. Sharman (*Middlesex*)
1958–59	R. L. Sharman (*Middlesex*)

ENGLISH OPEN CHAMPIONSHIPS
WOMEN'S VETERAN SINGLES

1949–50	Mrs. H. Roy Evans (*Wales*)
1950–51	Mrs. S. Betling (*France*)
1951–52	Mrs. S. Betling (*France*)
1952–53	Mrs. I. B. Bell (*Essex*)
1953–54	Mrs. C. Cook (*Yorkshire*)
1954–55	Mrs. I. B. Hunter (*Devon*)
1955–56	Mrs. G. Davies (*Lancashire*)
1956–57	Mrs. I. B. Bell (*Essex*)
1957–58	Mrs. V. F. Cherriman (*Middlesex*)
1958–59	Mrs. I. B. Bell (*Essex*)

Miss A. Haydon

WELSH OPEN CHAMPIONSHIPS
WOMEN'S SINGLES

1927–28	Miss D. E. Gubbins (*Wales*)
1928–29	Miss D. E. Gubbins (*Wales*)
1929–36	No championships
1936–37	Mrs. H. Roy Evans (*Wales*)
1937–38	Mrs. B. Morgan (*Wales*)
1938–39	Miss D. M. Emdin (*England*)
1939–45	No championships
1945–46	Miss A. Bates (*Wales*)
1946–47	Miss M. Franks (*England*)
1947–48	Miss D. Beregi (*England*)
1948–49	Miss T. Pritzi (*Austria*)
1949–50	Miss M. Franks (*England*)
1950–51	Miss R. Rowe (*England*)
1951–52	Miss H. Elliot (*Scotland*)
1952–53	Miss R. Rowe (*England*)
1953–54	Miss R. Rowe (*England*)
1954–55	Miss A. Haydon (*England*)
1955–56	Miss A. Haydon (*England*)
1956–57	No championship
1957–58	Miss K. Best (*England*)
1958–59	Miss P. Mortimer (*England*)

WELSH OPEN CHAMPIONSHIPS
MEN'S SINGLES

1927–28	H. E. T. Coles (*Wales*)
1928–29	H. E. T. Coles (*Wales*)
1929–36	No championships
1936–37	A. D. Brook (*England*)
1937–38	E. Bubley (*England*)
1938–39	J. K. Hyde (*England*)
1939–45	No championships
1945–46	G. R. Harrower (*England*)
1946–47	J. Leach (*England*)
1947–48	R. Bergmann (*England*)
1948–49	R. Bergmann (*England*)
1949–50	A. Simons (*England*)
1950–51	J. Leach (*England*)
1951–52	G. Amouretti (*France*)
1952–53	R. Bergmann (*England*)
1953–54	H. Venner (*England*)
1954–55	B. Kennedy (*England*)
1955–56	B. Kennedy (*England*)
1956–57	No championship
1957–58	A. Rhodes (*England*)
1958–59	K. Craigie (*England*)

WELSH OPEN CHAMPIONSHIPS
MEN'S DOUBLES

1927–28	S. Glancz and L. Bellak
1928–29	F. H. D. Wilde and A. E. Dupe
1929–36	No championships
1936–37	R. Baglow and T. Lisle
1937–38	S. Proffitt and H. Lurie
1938–39	J. K. Hyde and H. Lurie
1939–45	No championships
1945–46	R. Baglow and R. Hammett
1946–47	G. V. Barna and G. Harrower
1947–48	J. Leach and J. Carrington
1948–49	H. Bednar and H. Just
1949–50	J. Leach and J. Carrington
1950–51	J. Leach and A. Simons
1951–52	A. Simons and B. Kennedy
1952–53	R. Bergmann and J. Leach
1953–54	K. Craigie and A. Rhodes
1954–55	A. Simons and B. Kennedy
1955–56	A. Simons and B. Kennedy
1956–57	No championship
1957–58	K. Craigie and L. Adams
1958–59	R. Stevens and R. Raybould

EUROPEAN CHAMPIONSHIPS
(inaugurated 1957–58)

1957–58 FINAL RESULTS

Men's Singles
Z. Berczik (Hungary) beat E. Gyetvai (Hungary) 21–19, 21–16, 23–21.

Women's Singles
E. Koczian (Hungary) beat A. Haydon (England) 21–15, 14–21, 24–22, 17–21, 21–16.

Men's Doubles
L. Stipek and L. Vyhnanovsky (Czechoslovakia) beat T. Reiter and O. Bottner (Rumania) 21–11, 21–13, 21–17.

Women's Doubles
A. Rozeanu and E. Zeller (Rumania) beat E. Koczian and L. Mosoczy (Hungary) 18–21, 21–15, 21–17, 21–19.

Mixed Doubles
Z. Berczik and Miss G. Farkas (Hungary) beat F. Sido and Miss E. Koczian (Hungary) 21–14, 21–13, 11–21, 21–12.

Men's Team Championship: Final
HUNGARY beat Czechoslovakia, 5–2.

England's record (B. Kennedy, I. Harrison, B. Merrett, A. Rhodes): beat France, 5–1; beat East Germany, 5–0; beat Switzerland, 5–0; beat Greece, 5–0; lost to Hungary, 1–5; lost to Rumania, 1–5; lost to Russia, 2–5.

Women's Team Championship: Final
ENGLAND beat Rumania, 3–1.

England's record (A. Haydon, D. Rowe): beat Hungary, 3–0; beat Belgium, 3–0; beat Poland, 3–0; beat France, 3–0; beat East Germany, 3–0; beat Switzerland, 3–0; beat Austria, 3–0.

TABLE TENNIS QUIZ

1. What is the Swaythling Cup, by whom was it presented and when?

★

2. How many Englishmen have won the world singles title?

★

3. Who was the last home-born player to win the men's singles at the English "Open"?

★

4. Helen Elliot, of Scotland, won the world's women's doubles in two successive years with different partners. Who were they?

QUIZ ANSWERS

1. The trophy for the men's world team championship, donated by the Dowager Lady Swaythling in 1926. 2. Two. Fred Perry in 1928–29 and Johnny Leach in 1948–49, 1950–51. 3. P. Bromfield (Kent) in season 1923–24. 4. Gizi Farkas (Hungary) in 1948–49, and Dora Beregi (England) in 1949–50.

WELSH OPEN CHAMPIONSHIPS
WOMEN'S DOUBLES

1927–28	Mrs. G. D. Horspool and Miss M. Mossford
1928–36	No championships
1936–37	Mrs. E. H. Evans and Mrs. B. Morgan
1937–38	Mrs. E. H. Evans and Mrs. B. Morgan
1938–39	Mrs. D. Day and Miss D. Emdin
1939–45	No championships
1945–46	Miss A. Bates and Miss G. Thomas
1946–47	Miss M. Franks and Miss V. Patterson
1947–48	Miss D. Beregi and Miss P. Barnes
1948–49	Miss M. Franks and Miss A. Wood
1949–50	Miss E. M. Steventon and Miss A. Bates
1950–51	Madam Roland and Miss M. Franks
1951–52	Miss D. Rowe and Miss R. Rowe
1952–53	Miss D. Rowe and Miss R. Rowe
1953–54	Miss D. Rowe and Miss R. Rowe
1954–55	Miss A. Haydon and Miss K. Best
1955–56	Mrs. R. Cornett and Miss D. Rowe
1956–57	No championship
1957–58	Miss K. Best and Miss P. Mortimer
1958–59	Miss D. Rowe and Miss P. Mortimer

WELSH OPEN CHAMPIONSHIPS
MIXED DOUBLES

1927–28	L. Bellak and Mrs. P. Chamberlain
1928–36	No championships
1936–37	A. D. Brook and Mrs. Hutchings
1937–38	T. Lisle and Mrs. E. H. Evans
1938–39	A. Liebster and Mrs. D. Day
1939–47	No championships
1947–48	R. Bergmann and Miss D. Beregi
1948–49	O. Eckl and Miss T. Pritzi
1949–50	J. Leach and Miss M. Franks
1950–51	Title vacant
1951–52	Title vacant
1952–53	B. Kennedy and Miss R. Rowe
1953–54	G. V. Barna and Miss R. Rowe
1954–55	I. Jones and Miss S. Jones
1955–56	B. Kennedy and Mrs. R. Cornett
1956–57	No championship
1957–58	R. Raybould and Miss S. Jones
1958–59	R. Stevens and Miss D. Rowe

Miss D. Rowe

R. Bergmann

VICTOR BARNA AWARD
(Presented each season for the most notable performance by an English player.)

1952–53	A. W. C. Simons (*Gloucestershire*)
1953–54	Miss D. Rowe and Miss R. Rowe (*Middlesex*)
1954–55	Miss D. Rowe (*Middlesex*)
1955–56	Miss A. Haydon (*Warwickshire*)
1956–57	Miss A. Haydon (*Warwickshire*)
1957–58	Miss A. Haydon (*Warwickshire*) and Miss D. Rowe (*Middlesex*)
1958–59	J. Leach (*Essex*)

TABLE TENNIS QUIZ

1. Which player won a world singles championship at table tennis and later a Wimbledon lawn tennis singles titles?

*

2. How many countries took part in the inaugural National County Championship in season 1947–48 and who were the winners?

*

3. Have the county champions ever beaten the Rest of England in the annual challenge match?

*

4. Ann Haydon established a record when, in 1954 at the age of 15, she became the youngest player to have represented England in the world championships. Who was the previous youngest?

QUIZ ANSWERS

1. Fred Perry, who won the world championship in 1929 and the Wimbledon title in 1934, 35 and 36. 2. Fifteen counties represented by 19 teams playing in three divisions. Middlesex won the Premier Division, Hampshire the Southern Division, and Lancashire the Northern Division, 3. Yes. Middlesex beat the Rest 6–4 in 1955. 4. Her father, Adrian Haydon, who was 16.

WELSH
OPEN CHAMPIONSHIPS
BOYS' SINGLES

1945–46	D. Black
1946–47	G. Morgan
1947–48	N. Parker
1948–49	L. Devereux
1949–50	S. Jackson
1950–51	K. Pittard
1951–52	B. Merrett
1952–53	D. Phillips
1953–54	R. Dorking
1954–55	D. Norris
1955–56	L. Landry
1956–57	No championship
1957–58	D. Parry
1958–59	M. Ellis

WELSH
OPEN CHAMPIONSHIPS
GIRLS' SINGLES

1949–50	Miss A. Howell
1950–51	Miss D. Spooner
1951–52	Miss S. Jones
1952–53	Miss S. Jones
1953–54	Miss A. Haydon
1954–55	Miss M. Thomas
1955–56	Miss M. McMeekin
1956–57	No championship
1957–58	Miss S. Morgan
1958–59	Miss S. Morgan

POST-WAR
INTERNATIONALS
Number of appearances in brackets.

ADAMS, L.G. (Mddx) 1954 (3).
ALLCOCK, R. (Lancs) 1950–58 (5).
BAKER, R. (Lancs) 1952 (1)
BAKER, Miss Y. (Essex) 1954 (2).
BARNA, G. V. (Mddx) 1948–56 (23); *Swaythling Cup 1948–9–50.*
BARNES, Miss L. R. M. (Surrey) 1946–50 (11); *Corbillon Cup 1949–50.*
BEREGI, Miss D. (Devon) 1946–50 (16); *Corbillon Cup 1948, 1950.*

BERGMANN, R. (Mddx) 1948–57 (79); *Swaythling Cup 1948–9–50, 1952–3–4–5–6–7.*
BEST, Miss C. K. (Yorks) 1952–59 (26); *Corbillon Cup 1952–3–4, 59.*
BIRD, Mrs. B., see Isaacs, Miss B.
BLACKBOURN, Miss E. (Devon) 1946–47 (15); *Corbillon Cup 1947.*
BRUMWELL, F. B. (Essex) 1950 (1).
BUBLEY, E. (Mddx) 1947–48 (12); *Swaythling Cup 1947–8.*
BURRIDGE, D. (Mddx) 1955–59 (8).
CARRINGTON, J. H. (Essex) 1946–48 (10).
CASOFSKY, B. (Lancs) 1946–49 (10); *Swaythling Cup 1947.*
COHEN, L. (Lancs) 1946 (1).
COLLINS, Mrs. D., see Rowe, Miss D.
CORNETT, Miss R., see Rowe, Miss R.
CRAIGIE, K. R. (Surrey) 1949–55 (14); *Swaythling Cup 1954.*
CRAYDEN, R. J. (Surrey) 1949–51 (9); *Swaythling Cup 1951.*
CROSBY, Mrs. J. (Devon) 1949–50 (7); *Corbillon Cup 1949.*
CROUCH, B. E. (Mddx) 1950 (4); *Swaythling Cup 1950.*
CUMBERBATCH, Mrs. M. (Warwicks) 1954 (1).
DACE, Miss V. S. (Surrey) 1946–50 (25); *Corbillon Cup 1947–8, 1950.*
DAVIES, C. W. (Lancs) 1946 (1).
DENSHAM, T. (Herts) 1959 (1).
DEVENNY, Mrs. D. (Devon), see Beregi, Miss D.
DEVEREUX, L. (Devon) 1950 (1).
FIELDER, Miss J. (Kent) 1957–59 (9); *Corbillon Cup 1957.*
FILBY, E. J. (Surrey) 1947–49 (7); *Corbillon Cup 1947.*
FRANKS, Miss M. (Essex) 1946–52 (37); *Corbillon Cup 1947–8–9–50–1–2.*
FRY, Miss M. (Mddx) 1952–57 (2).
GOODMAN, E. (Lancs) 1946–47 (8); *Swaythling Cup 1947.*
GRIFFIN, R. (Gloucs) 1957 (1).
HARRISON, I. (Gloucs) 1956–59 (31); *Swaythling Cup 1957, 59.*
HARROWER, G. R. (Mddx) 1946–48 (6).
HARROWER, Miss J. (Mddx) 1959 (1).
HAYDON, A. A. (Warwicks) 1947–52 (2); *Swaythling Cup 1952.*
HAYDON, Miss A. (Warwicks) 1954–59 (63); *Corbillon Cup 1954–5–6–7, 59.*
HEAD, J. E. (Surrey) 1952 (1).
HINCHLIFF, R. (Yorks) 1954–57 (4).
HODSON, E. (Mddx) 1956–59 (5).
HOOK, Mrs. M. E. (Essex), see Miss M. E. Franks.
HOUSE, D. A. (Somerset) 1958 (2).
HURLOCK, K. (Surrey) 1951 (1)
INGBER, J. (Lancs) 1958–59 (10). *Swaythling Cup 1959.*
ISAACS, Miss B. (Surrey) 1955–59 (7).
JONES, Miss M. (Gloucs) 1947–50 (4).
KENNEDY, B. (Yorks) 1948–59 (74); *Swaythling Cup 1951, 1953, 1955–6–7–9*
KNOTT, Mrs. M. (Warwicks), see Miss M. Osborne.
LANDRY, L. F. (Mddx) 1956–59 (4).
LEACH, J. A. (Essex) 1946–59 (150); *Swaythling Cup 1947–8–9–50–1–2–3–4, 5–6–7–9*
LENTLE, Mrs. I. (Mddx) 1949 (1).
LITTON, R. F. (Devon) 1947–48 (2).
LOWE, J. (Mddx) 1956 (1).
LURIE, H. (Lancs) 1948 (1).
MERRETT, B. (Gloucs) 1952–59 (34); *Swaythling Cup 1955.*
MERRETT, K. A. (Surrey) 1946–47 (2).
MILBANK, Miss B. (Essex) 1954–55 (3).
MILES, Mrs. C. (Mddx) 1946 (1).
MILLER, D. A. (Mddx) 1948–50 (4).
MILLER, Mrs. J. (Mddx) 1950–53 (7); *Corbillon Cup 1951.*
MORTIMER, Miss P. (Warwicks) 1955–59 (13); *Corbillon Cup 1959.*
OSBORNE, Miss M. (Warwicks) 1947 (1); *Corbillon Cup 1947.*
PATTERSON, Miss V. M. (Essex) 1947 (1).
PIPER, Miss M. (Surrey) 1954–59 (2).
POOLE, W. (Warwicks) 1950 (2).
RAYBOULD, R. (Essex) 1959 (2).
RHODES, A. (Mddx) 1953–59 (26); *Swaythling Cup 1955, 1957.*
ROBERTS, Miss J. (Mddx), see Mrs. J. Miller.
ROOK, Miss J. (Surrey) 1954–59 (15); *Corbillon Cup 1957.*
ROWE, Miss D. (Mddx) 1950–59 (111); *Corbillon Cup 1951–2–3–4–5–6–7–9.*
ROWE, Miss R. (Mddx) 1950–56 (59); *Corbillon Cup 1951–2–3–4–5.*
RUMJAHN, R. (Lancs) 1947 (1).
SEAMAN, Miss Y. J. (Mddx) 1954 (1).
SHARMAN, R. (Surrey) 1947–49 (10); *Swaythling Cup 1949.*
SHEAD, P. (Sussex) 1954–55 (2).
SHEPHERD, A. (Lancs) 1949 (1).
SIMONS, A. W. C. (Gloucs) 1947–58 (77); *Swaythling Cup 1949–50–1–2–3–4.*
STANLEY, K. (Lancs) 1947–52 (7).

STEVENS, R. J. (Essex) 1958–59 (5).
STEVENTON, Miss B. (Notts) 1946–49 (6); *Corbillon Cup 1948.*
THOMAS, Mrs. V. S. (Surrey), see Miss V. S. Dace.
THOMPSON, Mrs. C. K., see Best, Miss C. K.
THORNHILL, M. H. (Mddx) 1950–59 (22); *Swaythling Cup 1951, 59.*
TODD, Mrs. V. M. (Essex), see Miss V. M. Patterson.
VENNER, H. T. (Surrey) 1950–59 (24); *Swaythling Cup 1950, 1952, 1954.*
WINN, Miss J. (Surrey) 1954–55 (5); *Corbillon Cup 1955.*
WOOD, Miss A. (Lancs) 1949–51 (7); *Corbillon Cup 1949.*

POST-WAR
JUNIOR INTERNATIONALS
Number of appearances in brackets.

BAKER, R. (Lancs) 1949 (1).
BACKHOUSE, D. (Staffs) 1954–55 (7).
BARR, B. (Lancs) 1954 (1).
BATES, Miss W. (Sussex) 1955 (3).
BEAMISH, K. H. (Essex) 1948 (1).
BLOY, D. (Kent) 1957 (1).
BOOTH, C. (Lancs) 1951–53 (7).
BOWN, Miss L. (Cheshire) 1957 (1).
BROCKLEBANK, S. (Kent) 1950 (1).
BURRIDGE, D. (Mddx) 1950–54 (4).
BUTCHER, Miss J. (Mddx) 1958 (1).
COLE, P. (Suffolk) 1957 (4).
COLLINS, J. (Suffolk) 1956 (1).
CORNELL, A. (Essex) 1955 (1).
DEATON, C. (Derby) 1957 (1).
DENSHAM, T. (Surrey) 1954–55 (7).
DEVEREUX, L. (Devon) 1948–49 (3).
DORKING, R. (Essex) 1953–54 (4).
EAGLES, D. M. (Kent) 1950 (1).
ELLISON, D. (Lancs) 1949 (2).
ENGLAND, W. (Notts) 1952 (1).
FIELDER, Miss J. (Kent) 1955 (3).
GLADWISH, G. (Sussex) 1956 (1).

GOSLING, C. (Mddx) 1958–59 (6).
GRANT, D. (Hants) 1957–59 (2).
HAMILL, B. (Mddx) 1958 (1).
HARRISON, I. (Gloucs) 1955–56 (3).
HARROWER, Miss J. (Mddx) 1957–59 (10).
HAYDON, Miss A. (Warwicks) 1953–54 (4).
HEPPELL, Miss P. (Northumberland) 1952 (1).
HESSION, Miss S. (Essex) 1957–58 (5).
HICKS, Miss M. (Mddx) 1958 (1).
HODSON, E. (Mddx) 1955–56 (3).
HOUSE, D. A. (Somerset) 1952–53 (2).
HUNT, J. (Herts) 1951 (2).
INGBER, J. (Lancs) 1951–52 (3).
JACKSON, R. (Yorks) 1954 (1).
JACOBS, A. (Kent) 1957 (1).
JONES, I. D. (Mddx) 1952 (1).
KENNEDY, B. (Yorks) 1948 (2).
KNIGHT, W. A. (Northants) 1952 (1).
LANDRY, L. F. (Mddx) 1955–56 (6).
LIVESEY, G. (Lancs) 1958–59 (4).
LOWE, J. (Mddx) 1950 (2).
LUMSDEN, G. (Durham) 1954 (1).
MACLAREN, M. (Surrey) 1954 (3).
MERRETT, B. (Gloucs) 1951–52 (5).
MORLEY, R. (Gloucs) 1953 (1).
PIDDOCK, A. (Kent) 1957 (3).
PIERCE, W. (Lancs) 1949 (2).
PULLAR, G. (Lancs) 1953 (2).
RACEY, P. (Beds) 1959 (4).
ROOK, Miss J. (Surrey) 1952–54 (6).
SHANNON, Miss M. (Surrey) 1958–59 (6).
SMITH, P. F. (Essex) 1950 (2).
SPOONER, Miss D. E. (Mddx) 1952 (2).
TARLING, K. (Gloucs) 1956 (1).
TAYLOR, E. (Durham) 1958 (2).
THOMPSON, R. (Yorks) 1948 (1).
THORNHILL, M. H. (Mddx) 1948 (2).
TINDALE, P. (Northumberland) 1956 (1).
WOODFORDE, J. G. (Somerset) 1957 (1).
WRIGHT, Miss D. (Cheshire) 1959 (2).
WRIGHT, Miss F. (Yorks) 1955 (2).

NATIONAL COUNTY CHAMPIONSHIPS WINNERS

Premier Division

1947–48	Middlesex		1954–55	Hampshire
1948–49	Middlesex		1955–56	Berkshire
1949–50	Middlesex		1956–57	Buckinghamshire
1950–51	Middlesex		1957–58	Kent
1951–52	Middlesex		1958–59	Bedfordshire
1952–53	Middlesex			
1953–54	Middlesex		*Northern Division*	
1954–55	Middlesex		1947–48	Lancashire
1955–56	Surrey		1948–49	Cheshire
1956–57	Middlesex		1949–50	Northumberland
1957–58	Middlesex		1950–51	Yorkshire
1958–59	Surrey		1951–52	Yorkshire
			1952–53	Yorkshire

Second Division South

1951–52	Middlesex		*Midland Division*	
1952–53	Middlesex		1951–52	Warwickshire
1953–54	Surrey		1952–53	Staffordshire
1954–55	Middlesex		1953–54	Staffordshire
1955–56	Middlesex		1954–55	Worcestershire
1956–57	Surrey		1955–56	Warwickshire
1957–58	Kent		1956–57	Warwickshire
1958–59	Hertfordshire		1957–58	Warwickshire
			1958–59	Leicestershire

Second Division North

1951–52	Lancashire		*Eastern Division*	
1952–53	Lancashire		1951–52	Buckinghamshire
1953–54	Cheshire		1952–53	Bedfordshire
1954–55	Warwickshire		1953–54	Hertfordshire
1955–56	Cheshire		1954–55	Bedfordshire
1956–57	Lincolnshire		1955–56	Suffolk
1957–58	Cheshire			
1958–59	Lincolnshire		*Junior Division (South)*	
			1949–50	Middlesex

Second Division West

1955–56	Devon		1950–51	Glamorgan
1956–57	Glamorgan		1951–52	Kent
1957–58	Staffordshire		1952–53	Sussex
1958–59	Glamorgan		1953–54	Surrey
			1954–55	Sussex
Southern Division			1955–56	Middlesex
1947–48	Hampshire		1956–57	Middlesex
1948–49	Hampshire		1957–58	Middlesex
1949–50	Devon		1958–59	Middlesex
1950–51	Surrey			
1951–52	Sussex		*Junior Division (North)*	
1952–53	Kent		1955–56	Cheshire
1953–54	Berkshire		1956–57	Yorkshire
			1957–58	Lancashire
			1958–59	Lancashire

THE CHAMPION COUNTY v. THE REST OF ENGLAND

1948	Champion County (Middlesex)	4	The Rest	5
1949	Champion County (Middlesex)	4	The Rest	5
1950	Champion County (Middlesex)	4	The Rest	5
1951	Champion County (Middlesex)	4	The Rest	6
1952	Champion County (Middlesex)	5	The Rest	5
1953	Champion County (Middlesex)	3	The Rest	7
1954	Champion County (Middlesex)	4	The Rest	6
1955	Champion County (Middlesex)	6	The Rest	4
1956	Champion County (Surrey)	4	The Rest	6
1957	Champion County (Middlesex)	4	The Rest	4
1958	Champion County (Middlesex)	1	The Rest	6

Compiled by **Pat Besford**
Swimming Correspondent
The Daily Mail

Water-Polo

INTRODUCTION

Great Britain, the "father" of Association Football, was also the pioneer of water-polo. Leading nation in the world from the turn of the century until the early twenties, Great Britain won the Olympic water-polo tournaments of 1900, 1908, 1912 and 1920.

There have been many changes in the rules of water-polo over the years; probably the most important being the decision in 1950 to allow free movement after a foul. The consequent elimination of the "static" forward and "stopper" back did much to clean up and speed up this often called "dirtiest team game".

Present-day water-polo is dominated by the Iron Curtain countries: Hungary (Olympic champions in 1932, '36, '52 and '56), Jugoslavia and the Soviet Union. Only they are able to spend the huge amount of time and money necessary to build a champion team under modern water-polo conditions. However, a Briton, Mr. E. J. Scott, is the Hon. Secretary of the International Water Polo Board.

INTERNATIONAL WATER-POLO MATCHES

England v. Scotland

	Winner	Venue	Score
1890	Scotland	London	4–0
1891	Scotland	Glasgow	2–0
1892	England	Liverpool	4–0
1893	England	Glasgow	3–0
1894	England	Nottingham	4–1
1895	England	Edinburgh	3–0
1896	England	London	4–2
1897	Scotland	Edinburgh	2–1
1898	England	Liverpool	8–3
1899	England	Aberdeen	5–1
1900	England	Leicester	5–0
1901	England	Glasgow	7–0
1906	England	Glasgow	5–1
1908	England	Bradford	9–0
1910	England	Hamilton	3–1
1912	England	Weston-s-Mare	4–0
1920	England	Paisley	7–3
1922	England	Blackburn	12–1
1924	England	Glasgow	5–4
1926	England	Birmingham	7–3
1928	England	Dundee	6–1
1930	England	Gt. Yarmouth	9–0
1932	England	Prestwick	5–1
1934	England	Hastings	6–0
1936	England	Portobello	8–1
1938	England	Leeds	6–2
No matches during the war			
1948	England	Aberdeen	6–2
1950	England	Exmouth	10–0
1952	England	Kilmarnock	6–3
1954	England	Morecambe	7–2
1956	England	Coatbridge	9–2
1958	England	Morecambe	7–2

England v. Ireland

	Winner	Venue	Score
1895	England	London	12–0
1898	England	Dublin	7–0
1899	England	London	12–0
1900	England	Belfast	5–0
1901	England	Radcliffe	8–0
1902	England	Dublin	6–1
1903	England	Swindon	6–0
1904	England	Belfast	10–1
1906	England	Leicester	2–1
1908	England	Cork	10–0
1910	England	Weston-s-Mare	7–1
1912	England	Belfast	6–4
1920	England	Newcastle	11–0
1922	England	Belfast	6–4
1924	England	Cheltenham	8–2
1926	England	Dublin	9–3
1928	England	Birmingham	7–0
1930	England	Dublin	6–3
1932	England	Coventry	11–1
1934	England	Bangor, Co. D.	7–2
1936	England	Uxbridge	11–1
1938	England	Dublin	6–1
No matches during the war			
1948	England	Skegness	9–3
1950	England	Dublin	19–3
1952	England	Tynemouth	13–1
1954	England	Cork	9–1
1956	England	Morecambe	6–0
1958	England	Bangor, Co. D.	10–5

England v. Wales

	Winner	Venue	Score
1898	England	Newport	4–0
1899	England	Warrington	8–1
1900	England	Penarth	7–3
1901	England	Leicester	7–0
1902	England	Newport	8–0
1903	England	Weston-s-Mare	10–1
1904	England	Penarth	5–2
1905	Draw	Bradford	3–3
1907	England	Swansea	7–1
1909	England	Ilfracombe	16–0
1911	England	Penarth	9–1
1913	England	Brighton	8–1
1921	England	Newport	12–3
1923	England	Gt. Yarmouth	4–1
1925	England	Penarth	9–3
1927	England	Croydon	6–3
1929	England	Newport	8–0
1931	England	Barking	14–2
1933	England	Newport	9–2
1935	England	Luton	6–0
1937	England	Cardiff	13–3
No matches during the war			
1947	England	Wallasey	4–1
1949	England	Barry	4–1
1951	England	Exmouth	13–3
1953	England	Barry	11–1
1955	England	Morecambe	10–1
1957	England	Newport	6–3
1959	England	Morecambe	16–2

CLUB WATER-POLO CHAMPIONSHIP

Instituted 1888

	Winners	Runners-up	Score
1888	Burton	Otter	3–0
1889	Burton	Amateur	2–0
1890	Hanley	Burton	6–0
1891	Burton	Nautilus	3–2
1892	Nautilus	Hanley	3–2
1893	Tunbridge W.	Hanley	3–1
1894	Osborne	Leicester	8–2
1895	Osborne	Leicester	8–1
1896	Osborne	Leicester	3–0
1897	Osborne	People's Pal.	9–2
1898	Osborne	People's Pal.	3–2
1899	Osborne	St. Helens	5–1
1900	Leicester	Hyde Seal	2–1
1901	Osborne	Worthing	6–2
1902	Wigan	Leicester	5–2
1903	Hyde Seal	St. Helens	4–2
1904	Hyde Seal	Wigan	4–2
1905	Hyde Seal	Weston-s-M.	4–0
1906	Weston-s-M.	Polytechnic	6–4
1907	Weston-s-M.	Wigan	3–2
1908	Hyde Seal	Polytechnic	5–2
1909	Wigan	Polytechnic	4–3
1910	Wigan	Polytechnic	5–4
1911	Hyde Seal	Wigan	7–6
1912	Hyde Seal	Hornsey	8–2
1913	Hyde Seal	Wigan	4–1
1914	Weston-s-Mare & Sheffield, Hyde Seal & Burslem: Semi-finalists*		
1920	Hyde Seal	Hammersmith	10–1
1921	Weston-s-M.	Hyde Seal	11–10
1922	Walsall	Weston-s-M.	6–5
1923	Blackburn	Avondale	8–1
1924	Hyde Seal	Weston-s-M.	7–5
1925	Weston-s-M.	Hyde Seal	6–1
1926	Penguin	Weston-s-M.	4–2
1927	Penguin	Harpurhey	4–3
1928	Plaistow U.	Walsall	5–3
1929	Plaistow U.	Harpurhey	4–3
1930	Plaistow U.	Harpurhey	8–2
1931	Plaistow U.	L'pool Police	7–3
1932	Penguin	Coventry	5–4
1933	Coventry	Cheltenham	6–5
1934	Oldham Pol.	Plaistow U.	5–4
1935	Plaistow U.	Hyde Seal	5–2
1936	Plaistow U.	Oldham Pol.	4–0
1937	Plaistow U.	Polytechnic	5–2
1938	Plaistow U.	Otter	5–1
1947	Avondale	Bradford Dol.	8–5
1948	Penguin	Otter	2–1
1949	Plaistow U.	Bradford Dol.	9–6
1950	Motherwell	Bradford Dol.	8–3
1951	Motherwell	Plaistow U.	7–6
1952	Penguin	Cheltenham	7–5
1953	Plaistow U.	Motherwell	7–2
1954	Plaistow U.	Cheltenham	6–5
1955	Cheltenham	Plaistow U.	7–2
1956	Polytechnic	Cheltenham	9–5
1957	Polytechnic	Cheltenham	5–3
1958	Cheltenham	Polytechnic	7–5

* Championship abandoned in 1914 owing to war. No matches until 1920.

COUNTY WATER-POLO CHAMPIONSHIP

Instituted 1896

	Winners	Runners-up	Score
1896	Lancashire	Middlesex	4–1
1897	Lancashire	Staffordshire	9–2
1898	Lancashire	Leicestershire	3–2
1899	Lancashire	Middlesex	4–2
1900	Lancashire	Middlesex	3–1
1901	Lancashire	Surrey*	2–2
1902	Lancashire	Surrey	6–2
1903	Lancashire	Middlesex	7–1
1904	Middlesex	Lancashire	3–2
1905	Cheshire	Middlesex	5–1
1906	Lancashire	Middlesex	11–7
1907	Lancashire	Somerset	4–2
1908	Middlesex	Lancashire	7–5
1909	Lancashire	Somerset	6–1
1910	Lancashire	Somerset	6–3
1911	Middlesex	Cheshire	5–4
1912	Lancashire	Middlesex	1–0
1913	Cheshire	Middlesex	5–4
1914	Cheshire and Surrey (Finalists)†		
1920	Lancashire	Surrey	4–1
1921	Surrey	Lancashire	7–1
1922	Cheshire	Somerset	7–3
1923	Middlesex	Lancashire	4–2
1924	Staffordshire	Somerset	5–1
1925	Lancashire	Middlesex	8–3
1926	Lancashire	Middlesex	9–5
1927	Middlesex	Lancashire	5–4
1928	Lancashire	Essex	2–1
1929	Middlesex	Lancashire	6–3
1930	Middlesex	Lancashire	8–4
1931	Essex	Warwickshire	9–1
1932	Middlesex	Yorkshire	6–2
1933	Essex	Gloucestershire	4–2
1934	Essex	Cheshire	9–2
1935	Essex	Lancashire	5–0
1936	Essex	Lancashire	2–1
1937	Essex	Yorkshire	9–5
1938	Essex	Gloucestershire	8–1
1946	Somerset	Yorkshire	6–5
1947	Middlesex	Yorkshire	7–6
1948	Surrey	Lancashire	4–3
1949	Surrey	Lancashire	6–5
1950	Lancashire	Glamorgan	5–4
1951	Lancashire	Essex	5–4
1952	Gloucs.	Middlesex	7–6
1953	Essex	Gloucestershire	8–7
1954	Cheshire	Gloucestershire	9–5
1955	Gloucs.	Cheshire	7–4
1956	Middlesex	Gloucestershire	7–5
1957	Middlesex	Gloucestershire	6–5
1958	Gloucs.	Middlesex	5–4
1959	Gloucs.	Cheshire	8–5

* Surrey withdrew after a draw.
† Championship abandoned in 1914 owing to the war.

MINOR COUNTIES WATER-POLO CHAMPIONSHIP

Instituted 1954

	Winners	Runners-up	Score
1954	Hampshire	Notts.	9–5
1955	Sussex	Cambridgeshire	7–3
1956	Hampshire	Notts.	3–2
1957	Sussex	Lincolnshire	10–2
1958	Hampshire	Suffolk	7–4

JUNIOR

A junior must be under 18 on January 1st in the year of the championship.

JUNIOR COUNTY WATER-POLO CHAMPIONSHIP

(Junior Inter-District until 1952).

Instituted 1949

1949	South	West	5–3
1950	South	North-East	8–6
1951	South	West	8–2
1952	South	North	7–4
1953	Lancashire	Surrey	9–8
1954	Cheshire	Surrey	3–2
1955	Cheshire	Warwickshire	10–3
1956	Cheshire	Middlesex	6–3
1957	Middlesex	Lancashire	8–3
1958	Surrey	Lancashire	7–6
1959	Gloucs.	Surrey	12–8

JUNIOR CLUB WATER-POLO CHAMPIONSHIP

Instituted 1947

1947	Plaistow U.	Cheltenham	7–4
1948	Plaistow U.	Leeds Leander	9–4

1949	Cheltenham	Stafford E.E.	8–3
1950	Plaistow U.	Cheltenham	6–5
1951	Birkenhead	Middlesbrough	6–4
1952	Plaistow U.	Birkenhead	6–4
1953	Birkenhead	Cheltenham	7–6
1954	Avondale	Birkenhead	5–4
1955	Sutton & Cheam	Birkenhead	5–1
1956	Shiverers (Hove)	Wallasey	6–0
1957	Sutton & Cheam	Cheltenham	9–1
1958	Sutton & Cheam	Bootle	5–2

Water Ski-ing

The art of travelling competitively on water skis in the wake of, and while holding a rope from, a towing motor launch is rapidly becoming a popular summer sport.

Since the inaugural meeting of the national administrative organisation, The British Water Ski Federation, took place in the offices of the Central Council of Physical Recreation in October, 1951, the competitive element in Britain has accelerated to such an extent that British participants usually are well to the fore in the international championships organised by the World Water Ski Union.

The two leading clubs in London are Princes and Ruislip, the latter having contributed the greater number of international performers so far. In world championships a national team comprises four men and two women.

The skis used are specially made for the water sport, being appreciably wider than those used on snow. Snow skiers find it comparatively easy to adapt their technique, one of the most successful in this respect being Alan Crompton.

The sport's origin is believed to date back to 1920, when successful experiments were carried out on the Lake of Annecy, in France. Major competitions have since been contested in three parts—free-style, slalom and jumping, with a combined award to the best all-round performer, but the free-style is sometimes regarded as too much trick ski-ing and is not always included in leading events.

Recent television commentaries by Jack May, himself a well known British exponent, have greatly increased public interest in this very modern sport, considered by some to be still very much in its infancy.

BRITISH CHAMPIONSHIPS

Men's Overall Champions

1952	Eddy Arida
1953	David Nations
1954	David Nations
1955	David Nations
1956	David Nations
1957	David Nations
1958	Peter Felix
1959	Lance Callingham

Women's Overall Champions

1957	Joan Anderson
1958	Anna Gerber
1959	Maureen Lynn-Taylor

JUMPING RECORDS

World Men—Mike Osborn (U.S.) 140 ft.
  „ *Women*—Nancy Rideout (U.S.) 76 ft.
British Men—Lance Callingham 92 ft.
  „ *Women*—Jillian Rowe 57¾ ft.

WORLD CHAMPIONSHIPS

Men's Overall Champions

1949	C. Jourdain (France) } tie Guy de Clerq (Belgium)
1950	Dick Pope Jnr. (U.S.)
1953	Alfredo Mendoza (U.S.)
1955	Alfredo Mendoza (U.S.)
1957	Joe Cash (U.S.)
1959	Chuck Stearns (U.S.)

Women's Overall Champions

1949	Willa Worthington (U.S.)
1950	Willa Worthington McGuire (U.S.)
1953	Leah Maria Rawls (U.S.)
1955	Willa Worthington McGuire (U.S.)
1957	Marina Doria (Switzerland)
1959	Vickie Van Hook (U.S.)

Weightlifting

Compiled by **Oscar State**
Hon. Secretary: British Empire and Commonwealth Weightlifting Council

HISTORICAL NOTES AND COMPETITION LIFTS

Weightlifting has undoubtedly been practised in some form or other since early times. "Modern" weightlifting with barbells and dumb-bells began to grow really popular towards the end of the 19th century and the first championship open to the world was held in 1891 at the Café Monico, Piccadilly, London, the winner being Lawrence Levy of England. The first Olympic Games of modern times in 1896 also featured weightlifting, but at one bodyweight only.

Most countries had conflicting rules and techniques and disagreed about the lifts to be used in competition. These differences were finally resolved in 1920 by the formation of the International Weightlifting Federation. The founder, Jules Rosset of France, formulated an agreed set of rules which were used for the 1920 Olympic Games in Antwerp and this federation has controlled world weightlifting ever since.

In 1928, at the demand of the International Olympic Committee, the competition lifts were fixed at Two Hands Clean and Press, Two Hands Snatch, Two Hands Clean and Jerk. These three lifts are now used for all national, world and Olympic championships and for international contests. The seven bodyweights now recognised are —Bantam (123¾ lbs. 56 kg.), Feather (132¼ lb. 60 kg.), Light (148¾ lb. 67.5 kg.), Middle (165¼ lb. 75 kg.), Light heavy (181⅞ lb. 82.5 kg.), Middle heavy (198⅜ lb. 90 kg.), Heavy (Over 198⅜ lb. 90 kg.). The address of the international federation is E. Gouleau, Secretaire-general F.I.H.C., 9 Avenue des Gobelins, Paris 5e, France.

The British Amateur Weight-Lifters' Association was founded in 1911 and the present secretary is H. C. Franklin-Crate, 58 Toronto Road, Leytonstone, London E.11.

The British Empire and Commonwealth Weightlifting Council was founded in 1948 on the occasion of the Olympic Games in London. The present secretary is Oscar State, 4 Godfrey Avenue, Twickenham, Middlesex.

WEIGHTLIFTING QUIZ

1. Which lifter has held world records in four different bodyweight classes?

★

2. Which British lightweight lifter holds Empire and British lightweight records but has never won a British lightweight title?

★

3. Which lifter has held Empire records in three different bodyweight classes?

★

4. Who was the first lifter to total 1,000 lbs.?

★

5. Who was the first lifter to total 500 kilogrammes (1,102 lbs.)? ★

6. Who has cleaned and jerked the greatest weight in relation to his own bodyweight?

★

7. What is the greatest weight lifted overhead with one hand?

8. What is the greatest weight lifted overhead with two hands?

★

9. What is the greatest weight lifted by one man without the aid of special harness?

★

10. Name the first British lifter to raise double bodyweight overhead with two hands.

QUIZ ANSWERS

1. Tommy Kono in lightweight, middleweight, light-heavyweight and middleheavyweight classes. 2. Jim Halliday. 3. Gerry Gratton, Canada, in middleweight, light-heavyweight and middleheavyweight classes; Ken McDonald, Australia, in light-heavyweight, middleheavyweight and heavyweight classes. 4. Steve Stanko, U.S.A., on 19th April 1941 at York, U.S.A. (actual total 1,002 lbs.). 5. Paul Anderson, U.S.A., on 16th April 1955 at High Point, North Carolina, U.S.A. (actual total 1,142½ lbs.). 6. Chen Ching-kai, China, at a bodyweight of 127 lbs. jerked 326¼ lbs., which is 72¼ lbs. more than double bodyweight. 7. A Bent Press of 386 lbs. by Arthur Saxon, Germany, in England during 1906. 8. Paul Anderson, U.S.A., jerked 500 lbs. after taking it from stands. 9. A Back Lift of 5,700 lbs. by Paul Anderson, U.S.A. 10. W. A. Pullum.

OLYMPIC GAMES WEIGHTLIFTING RESULTS

1948—LONDON

Bantamweight class	J. N. De Pietro	U.S.A.	231¼	198¼	248	677½
Featherweight class	M. S. I. Fayad	Egypt	203¼	231¼	297½	732¼
Lightweight class	I. Shams	Egypt	214¼	253¼	325	793½
Middleweight class	F. I. Spellman	U.S.A.	259	264½	336	859½
Light heavyweight class	S. A. Stanczyk	U.S.A.	286½	286½	347	920
Heavyweight class	J. Davis	U.S.A.	303	303	391½	997½

1952—HELSINKI

Bantamweight class	I. Udodov	U.S.S.R.	198½	214½	281	694
Featherweight class	R. Chimishkian	U.S.S.R.	214½	231½	297½	743½
Lightweight class	T. Kono	U.S.A.	231½	259	308½	798½
Middleweight class	P. George	U.S.A.	253½	281	347	881½
Light heavyweight class	T. Lomakin	U.S.S.R.	275½	281	363½	920¼
Middle heavyweight class	N. Schemansky	U.S.A.	281	308½	391½	980½
Heavyweight class	J. Davis	U.S.A.	330½	319½	363½	1,013½

1956—MELBOURNE

Bantamweight class	C. Vinci	U.S.A.	231½	231½	292	754½
Featherweight class	I. Berger	U.S.A.	236½	236½	303	776½
Lightweight class	I. Ryibak	U.S.S.R.	242½	264½	330½	837½
Middleweight class	F. Bogdanovsky	U.S.S.R.	292	270	363½	925½
Light heavyweight class	T. Kono	U.S.A.	308½	292	385½	986½
Middle heavyweight class	A. Vorobyev	U.S.S.R.	325	303	391½	1,019½
Heavyweight class	P. Anderson	U.S.A.	369½	319½	413½	1,102

EMPIRE GAMES WEIGHTLIFTING RESULTS

1950—AUCKLAND, NEW ZEALAND

Bantamweight class	Tho Fook Hung	Malaya	210	190	250	655
Featherweight class	Koh Eng Tong	Malaya	205	215	270	685
Lightweight class	J. Halliday	England	205	245	310	760
Middleweight class	G. A. Gratton	Canada	260	230	300	795
Light heavyweight class	J. Varaleau	Canada	250	250	315	815
Heavyweight class	R. H. Cleghorn	New Zealand	285	275	345	900

1954—VANCOUVER, CANADA

Bantamweight class	M. Megennis	England	190	190	240	620
Featherweight class	R. Wilkes	Trinidad	200	215	275	690
Lightweight class	V. Barberis	Australia	230	235	300	765
Middleweight class	J. Halliday	England	225	250	325	800
Light heavyweight class	G. A. Gratton	Canada	275	275	340	890
Middle heavyweight class	K. Daly	Canada	275	275	330	880
Heavyweight class	D. Hepburn	Canada	370	300	370	1,040

1958—CARDIFF, WALES

Bantamweight class	R. J. Gaffley	South Africa	205	195	260	660
Featherweight class	Tan Ser Cher	Singapore	215	195	275	685
Lightweight class	Tan Howe Liang	Singapore	235	225	330	790
Middleweight class	B. Blenman	Barbados	235	240	320	795
Light heavyweight class	P. Caira	Scotland	280	265	330	875
Middle heavyweight class	M. Santos	Australia	290	260	340	890
Heavyweight class	K. A. McDonald	England	300	305	400	1,005

WORLD CHAMPIONSHIPS

1946—PARIS, FRANCE

Featherweight class	A. Anderson	Sweden	198¼	220½	286½	705
Lightweight class	S. Stanczyk	U.S.A.	231¼	253½	325	809¾
Middleweight class	K. Touni	Egypt	253½	248	330½	832
Light heavyweight class	G. Novak	U.S.S.R.	308½	286½	341½	936½
Heavyweight class	J. Davis	U.S.A.	297½	303	358	958½

1947—PHILADELPHIA, U.S.A.

Bantamweight class	J. N. De Pietro	U.S.A.	225¾	192¾	242½	661
Featherweight class	R. Higgins	U.S.A.	231¼	198¼	253½	683
Lightweight class	P. George	U.S.A.	214¾	242½	319½	776¾
Middleweight class	S. Stanczyk	U.S.A.	259	281	352½	892½
Light heavyweight class	J. Terpak	U.S.A.	253½	264½	336	854
Heavyweight class	J. Davis	U.S.A.	308½	308½	385¾	1,002¾

1949—THE HAGUE, HOLLAND

Bantamweight class	M. Namdjou	Iran	198¼	214¾	275½	688½
Featherweight class	M. S. I. Fayad	Egypt	203¾	231¼	297½	732½
Lightweight class	I. Shams	Egypt	214¾	248	314	776¾
Middleweight class	K. Touni	Egypt	264½	264½	347	876
Light heavyweight class	S. Stanczyk	U.S.A.	286½	281	341½	909
Heavyweight class	J. Davis	U.S.A.	303	308½	363¾	975¼

1950—PARIS, FRANCE

Bantamweight class	M. Namdjou	Iran	198¼	209¼	275½	683
Featherweight class	M. S. I. Fayad	Egypt	203¾	225¾	292	721½
Lightweight class	J. Pitman	U.S.A.	231¼	236¾	308½	776½
Middleweight class	K. Touni	Egypt	275½	270	336	881½
Light heavyweight class	S. Stanczyk	U.S.A.	275½	286½	363¾	925¾
Heavyweight class	J. Davis	U.S.A.	319½	325	374¾	1,019¼

1951—MILAN, ITALY

Bantamweight class	M. Namdjou	Iran	198¼	214¾	286½	699½
Featherweight class	S. K. Gouda	Egypt	198¼	214¾	270	683
Lightweight class	I. Shams	Egypt	214¾	242½	297½	754¾
Middleweight class	P. George	U.S.A.	248	275½	347	870½
Light heavyweight class	S. Stanczyk	U.S.A.	281	270	336	887
Middle heavyweight class	N. Schemansky	U.S.A.	275½	292	374¾	942¼
Heavyweight class	J. Davis	U.S.A.	314	286½	352½	953

1953—STOCKHOLM, SWEDEN

Bantamweight class	I. Udodov	U.S.S.R.	203¾	214¾	275½	694
Featherweight class	N. Saksonov	U.S.S.R.	209¼	231¼	303	743½
Lightweight class	P. George	U.S.A.	231¼	253½	330½	815¼
Middleweight class	T. Kono	U.S.A.	264½	264½	369¼	898¼
Light heavyweight class	A. Vorobyev	U.S.S.R.	281	297½	369¼	947¾
Middle heavyweight class	N. Schemansky	U.S.A.	281	297½	396¾	975¼
Heavyweight class	D. Hepburn	Canada	369¼	297½	363¾	1,030½

1954—VIENNA, AUSTRIA

Bantamweight class	B. Farkhutdinov	U.S.S.R.	220½	209¼	264½	694
Featherweight class	R. Chimishkian	U.S.S.R.	231¼	236¾	303	771
Lightweight class	D. Ivanov	U.S.S.R.	242½	253½	314	810
Middleweight class	P. George	U.S.A.	259	281	352½	892½
Light heavyweight class	T. Kono	U.S.A.	308½	270	380¼	958¾
Middle heavyweight class	A. Vorobyev	U.S.S.R.	314	314	385¾	1,013¾
Heavyweight class	N. Schemansky	U.S.A.	330½	330½	413¼	1,074¼

1955—MUNICH, GERMANY

Bantamweight class	V. Stogov	U.S.S.R.	231¼	220½	286½	738
Featherweight class	R. Chimishkian	U.S.S.R.	225¾	236¾	308½	771
Lightweight class	N. Kostilev	U.S.S.R.	248	275½	319½	843
Middleweight class	P. George	U.S.A.	264½	281	347	892½
Light heavyweight class	T. Kono	U.S.A.	314	281	363¾	958¾
Middle heavyweight class	A. Vorobyev	U.S.S.R.	319½	308½	374¾	1,002¾
Heavyweight class	P. Anderson	U.S.A.	407¾	319½	402¼	1,129½

1957—TEHERAN, IRAN

Bantamweight class	V. Stogov	U.S.S.R.	236¾	231¼	292	760
Featherweight class	E. Minaev	U.S.S.R.	259	231¼	308½	798¾
Lightweight class	V. Bushuev	U.S.S.R.	264½	259	314	837½
Middleweight class	T. Kono	U.S.A.	297½	270	358	925½
Light heavyweight class	T. Lomakin	U.S.S.R.	314	292	385¾	991¾
Middle heavyweight class	A. Vorobyev	U.S.S.R.	325	314	396¾	1,035¾
Heavyweight class	A. Medvedev	U.S.S.R.	363¾	325	413¼	1,102

1958—STOCKHOLM, SWEDEN

Bantamweight class	V. Stogov	U.S.S.R.	236¾	231¼	286½	754½
Featherweight class	I. Berger	U.S.A.	253½	242½	325	821
Lightweight class	V. Bushuev	U.S.S.R.	275½	259	325	859½
Middleweight class	T. Kono	U.S.A.	297½	286½	363¾	947¾
Light heavyweight class	T. Lomakin	U.S.S.R.	308½	286½	374¾	969¾
Middle heavyweight class	A. Vorobyev	U.S.S.R.	330½	314	380¼	1,024¾
Heavyweight class	A. Medvedev	U.S.S.R.	352½	319½	396¾	1,068¾

WEIGHTLIFTING QUIZ

1. Which lifters have won successive world titles in three different bodyweight classes?

★

2. Which lifters have won two Olympic Games titles?

★

3. Which lifters have won two Empire Games titles?

QUIZ ANSWERS

1. Stanley Stanczyk, U.S.A.—world lightweight champion 1946, world middleweight champion 1947, Olympic light-heavyweight champion 1948; Tommy Kono, U.S.A.—Olympic lightweight champion 1952, world middleweight champion 1953, world light-heavyweight champion 1954. 2. Louis Hostin, France—1932, 1936; John Davis, U.S.A.—1948, 1952; Tommy Kono, U.S.A.—1952,1956. 3. Jim Halliday, England—1950, 1954; Gerry Gratton, Canada—1950, 1954.

BRITISH CHAMPIONSHIPS

1945

Bantamweight class	W. McConnell	155	180	230	565
Featherweight class	J. Creus	180	190	250	620
Lightweight class	G. Espeut	200	205	260	665
Middleweight class	E. Peppiatt	210	220	280	710
Light heavyweight class	E. Roe	220	230	270	720

1946

Bantamweight class	W. McConnell	160	180	220	560
Featherweight class	J. Creus	180	195	255	630
Lightweight class	G. Espeut	210	200	270	680
Middleweight class	W. Watson	190	230	280	700
Light heavyweight class	E. Roe	215	230	300	745
Heavyweight class	R. Martin	230	235	290	755

1947

Bantamweight class	W. McConnell	160	170	220	550
Featherweight class	J. Creus	185	205	265	655
Lightweight class	G. Espeut	215	210	285	710
Middleweight class	W. Watson	210	240	305	755
Light heavyweight class	M. Barnett	235	235	315	785
Heavyweight class	A. Knight	250	255	300	805

1948

Bantamweight class	A. Greenhalgh	192¾	170¾	225¾	589¼
Featherweight class	J. Creus	181¾	214¾	270	666½
Lightweight class	R. Eland	203¾	203¾	264½	672
Middleweight class	J. Halliday	214¾	242½	303	760¼
Light heavyweight class	E. Roe	225¾	236¾	303	765½
Heavyweight class	A. Knight	253½	253½	330	837

1949

Bantamweight class	M. Megennis	170	175	230	575
Featherweight class	J. Creus	185	210	255	650
Lightweight class	H. Goodman	205	200	260	665
Middleweight class	J. Halliday	210	250	315	775
Light heavyweight class	E. Roe	240	245	310	795
Heavyweight class	M. Barnett	264½	253½	319½	837½

1950

Bantamweight class	M. Megennis	175	180	245	600
Featherweight class	J. Creus		Walkover		
Lightweight class	Y. Evans	195	215	280	690
Middleweight class	J. Halliday	220	230	305	755
Light heavyweight class	E. Roe	245	245	310	800
Heavyweight class	M. Barnett	270	255	340	865

1951

Bantamweight class	M. Megennis	180	185	240	605
Featherweight class	J. Creus	180	210	260	650
Lightweight class	J. Elliott	190	195	250	635
Middleweight class	E. Peppiatt	220	225	290	735
Light heavyweight class	E. Roe	235	230	295	760
Middle heavyweight class	S. Harrington	220	245	330	795
Heavyweight class	G. Brooks	225	235	305	765

1952

Bantamweight class	M. Megennis	185	185	240	610
Featherweight class	J. Creus	180	210	260	650
Lightweight class	Y. Evans	205	215	275	695
Middleweight class	J. Halliday	210	250	310	770
Light heavyweight class	P. Caira	250	235	285	770

1953

Bantamweight class	F. Cope	180	180	245	605
Featherweight class	J. Creus	185	220	275	680
Lightweight class	J. McIntosh	200	210	280	690
Middleweight class	F. Williamson	205	240	300	745
Light heavyweight class	L. Willoughby	240	230	320	790
Middle heavyweight class	M. Barnett	270	235	300	805
Heavyweight class	T. Griffiths	270	245	300	815

1954

Bantamweight class	M. Megennis	195	195	260	650
Featherweight class	R. Jenkins	175	180	250	605
Lightweight class	F. Williamson	185	225	285	695
Middleweight class	J. Halliday	215	240	310	765
Light heavyweight class	P. Caira	255	230	305	790
Middle heavyweight class	M. Barnett	270	250	330	850
Heavvweight class	T. Griffiths	260	245	315	820

1955

Bantamweight class	F. Cope	175	175	240	590
Featherweight class	M. Megennis	200	200	260	660
Lightweight class	B. Helfgott	220	215	275	710
Middleweight class	F. Williamson	210	240	305	755
Light heavyweight class	P. Caira	265	235	320	820
Middle heavyweight class	M. Barnett	275	250	330	855
Heavyweight class	D. Hillman	280	230	305	815

British Championships—*cont.*

1956					
Bantamweight class	R. Brownbill	180	185	235	600
Featherweight class	J. Creus	195	220	270	685
Lightweight class	B. Helfgott	235	210	280	725
Middleweight class	F. Williamson	210	245	290	745
Light heavyweight class	P. Caira	280	260	310	760
Middle heavyweight class	S. Harrington	240	260	335	835
Heavyweight class	E. Morton	260	255	320	835
1957					
Bantamweight class	R. Brownbill	185	190	240	615
Featherweight class	C. Robertson	210	175	250	635
Lightweight class	A. Carroll	240	190	275	705
Middleweight class	H. Hartley	215	230	295	740
Light heavyweight class	P. Caira	290	260	330	880
Middle heavyweight class	S. Harrington	240	240	320	800
Heavyweight class	K. McDonald	285	275	390	950
1958					
Bantamweight class	R. Brownbill	190	190	245	625
Featherweight class	A. Robinson	185	190	260	635
Lightweight class	B. Helfgott	235	220	290	745
Middleweight class	L. Levine	240	215	295	750
Light heavyweight class	P. Caira	280	245	325	850
Middle heavyweight class	R. Gore	260	255	320	835
Heavyweight class	K. McDonald	295	285	380	960
1959					
Bantamweight c'ass	R. Brownbill	190	190	240	620
Featherweight class	H. Norville	200	190	260	650
Lightweight class	C. Goring	235	220	265	720
Middleweight class	F. Williamson	215	245	305	765
Light heavyweight class	P. Caira	290	260	315	865
Middle heavyweight class	L. Martin	300	280	350	930
Heavyweight class	K. McDonald	290	260	365	915

WEIGHTLIFTING QUIZ

1. When and where were the first world weightlifting championships held?

★

2. Who was the first world champion weightlifter?

★

3. What were the lifts used in the first world championship?

★

4. Who was the only British lifter to win an Olympic gold medal?

★

5. Which British lifters have won three British titles in one day?

★

6. What are the lifts used in present-day world championships?

★

7. Which lifter has won most world titles and how many?

★

8. Which British lifter has won most titles? (Even stone championships excluded as not being under international rules.)

QUIZ ANSWERS

1. 28th March 1891 at the Café Monico, Piccadilly, London. 2. Lawrence Levy, England. 3. There were ten lifts, consisting mainly of repetition or alternate pressing with 56 lbs. or 84 lbs. in each hand. 4. Launceston Elliott at the 1896 Olympic Games in Athens with a Right Hand Lift of 156½ lbs. 5. G. Butler won the 11 stone, 12 stone (a walkover) and heavyweight classes in 1903. W. A. Pullum won the 9 stone, 10 stone and 11 stone classes in 1913. 6. Two Hands Clean and Press, Two Hands Snatch, Two Hands Clean and Jerk—all with barbell. 7. John Davis, U.S.A.—Olympic heavyweight champion 1948, 1952; world light-heavyweight champion 1938; world heavyweight champion 1946, 1947, 1949, 1950, 1951—eight in all. 8. Julian Creus, British featherweight champion 1945, 1946, 1947, 1948, 1949, 1950, 1951, 1952, 1953, 1956—ten in all.

WORLD RECORDS

Bantamweight class			
Press	D. Moyer	U.S.A.	241¼
Snatch	V. Stogov	U.S.S.R.	231¼
Jerk	Chen Ching-kai	China	307½
Total	V. Stogov	U.S.S.R.	760
Featherweight class			
Press	V. Korzh	U.S.S.R.	261
Snatch	M. Zielinski	Poland	248
Jerk	I. Berger	U.S.A.	325
Total	I. Berger	U.S.A.	821
Lightweight class			
Press	F. Nikitin	U.S.S.R.	287½
Snatch	N. Kostilev	U.S.S.R.	275½
Jerk	Tan Howe Liang	Singapore	347
Total	V. Bushuev	U.S.S.R.	859½
Middleweight class			
Press	V. Timoshenko	U.S.S.R.	308½
Snatch	T. Kono	U.S.A.	294¼
Jerk	A. Kurinov	U.S.S.R.	373½
Total	T. Kono	U.S.A.	947¾
Light heavyweight class			
Press	M. Paterni	France	331¾
Snatch	R. Plyukfelder	U.S.S.R.	307½
Jerk	V. Pegov	U.S.S.R.	390
Total	T. Lomakin	U.S.S.R.	991¾
Middle heavyweight class			
Press	A. Zhitetsky	U.S.S.R.	338¼
Snatch	F. Osipa	U.S.S.R.	321¾
Jerk	C. Emrich	U.S.A.	407¾
Total	A. Vorobyev	U.S.S.R.	1,035¾
Heavyweight class			
Press	P. Anderson	U.S.A.	408¾
Snatch	Y. Vlasov	U.S.S.R.	333¾
Jerk	Y. Vlasov	U.S.S.R.	435¼
Total	P. Anderson	U.S.A.	1,129½

BRITISH RECORDS

Bantamweight class			
Press	J. Cannon	....	196¾
Snatch	J. Creus	....	201
Jerk	J. Creus	....	260½
Total	J. Creus	....	655½
Featherweight class			
Press	G. Robertson	....	209¾
Snatch	J. Creus	....	221½
Jerk	J. Creus	....	276¾
Total	J. Creus	....	695
Lightweight class			
Press	A. Carroll	....	241
Snatch	J. Halliday	....	246¼
Jerk	J. Halliday	....	310¼
Total	J. Halliday	....	760
Middleweight class			
Press	L. Levine	....	251
Snatch	J. Halliday	....	260¾
Jerk	G. Fairclough	....	331¼
Total	J. Halliday	....	800
Light heavyweight class			
Press	P. Caira	....	301
Snatch	J. Halliday	....	260¾
Jerk	S. Harrington	....	341
Total	P. Caira	....	892½
Middle heavyweight class			
Press	L. Martin	....	306¼
Snatch	L. Martin	....	290¾
Jerk	L. Martin	....	370¼
Total	L. Martin	....	965
Heavyweight class			
Press	D. Hillman	....	316¼
Snatch	K. McDonald	....	306¾
Jerk	K. McDonald	....	402½
Total	K. McDonald	....	1,005

EMPIRE RECORDS

Bantamweight class			
Press	R. Gaffley	South Africa	215
Snatch	C. Henderson	Australia	203
Jerk	G. Gaffney	South Africa	270
Total	R. Gaffley	South Africa	695
Featherweight class			
Press	M. King	St Vincent	242
Snatch	J. Creus	England	221½
Jerk	R. Wilkes	Trinidad	286½
Total	M. King	St. Vincent	730
Lightweight class			
Press	Tan Howe Liang	Singapore	267½
Snatch	Tan Howe Liang	Singapore	248
Jerk	Tan Howe Liang	Singapore	347
Total	Tan Howe Liang	Singapore	830
Middleweight class			
Press	G. Gratton	Canada	270
Snatch	G. Gratton	Canada	266
Jerk	G. Fairclough	England	331¼
Total	G. Gratton	Canada	860
Light heavyweight class			
Press	P. Caira	Scotland	301
Snatch	G. Gratton	Canada	283
Jerk	G. Gratton	Canada	351¼
Total	G. Gratton	Canada	910
Middle heavyweight class			
Press	L. Martin	Jamaica	306¼
Snatch	L. Martin	Jamaica	290¾
Jerk	L. Martin	Jamaica	370¼
Total	L. Martin	Jamaica	965
Heavyweight class			
Press	D. Hepburn	Canada	381
Snatch	K. McDonald	England	306¾
Jerk	K. McDonald	England	402½
Total	D. Hepburn	Canada	1,040

OLYMPIC RECORDS

Bantamweight class			
Press	J. de Pietro	U.S.A.	231½
Snatch	C. Vinci	U.S.A.	231¼
Jerk	Yu In Ho	Korea	297½
Total	C. Vinci	U.S.A.	754½
Featherweight class			
Press	E. Minaev	U.S.S.R.	253½
Snatch	I. Berger	U.S.A.	236¾
Jerk	I. Berger	U.S.A.	303
Total	I. Berger	U.S.A.	776½
Lightweight class			
Press	R. Khabutdinov	U.S.S.R.	275½
Snatch	I. Ryibak	U.S.S.R.	264½
Jerk	I. Ryibak	U.S.S.R.	330½
Total	I. Ryibak	U.S.S.R.	837½
Middleweight class			
Press	F. Bogdanovsky	U.S.S.R.	292
Snatch	P. George	U.S.A.	281
Jerk	F. Bogdanovsky	U.S.S.R.	363¾
Total	F. Bogdanovsky	U.S.S.R.	925¾
Light heavyweight class			
Press	T. Kono	U.S.A.	308½
Snatch	T. Kono	U.S.A.	292
Jerk	T. Kono	U.S.A.	385¾
Total	T. Kono	U.S.A.	986¼
Middle heavyweight class			
Press	A. Vorobyev	U.S.S.R.	325
Snatch	N. Schemansky	U.S.A.	308½
Jerk	N. Schemansky	U.S.A.	391¼
Total	A. Vorobyev	U.S.S.R.	1,019¼
Heavyweight class			
Press	H. Selvetti	Argentine	385¾
Snatch	J. Davis	U.S.A.	319½
Jerk	P. Anderson	U.S.A.	413¼
Total	P. Anderson	U.S.A.	1,102

Wrestling

THE BRITISH AMATEUR WRESTLING ASSOCIATION

The Association was formed in 1904 with the title of National Amateur Wrestling Association, which was changed in 1944 to the British Amateur Wrestling Association.

The Association have three Counties Associations affiliated to them: the Eastern and Midland Counties Association, Northern Counties Association, Southern Counties Association.

The Association is managed by a Council which is constituted of Hon. Secretary, Assistant Hon. Secretary, Treasurer, Chairman, Vice Chairman, Trustee, and nine members elected annually from affiliated clubs, and a representative from each Counties Association. The Council meet every three months.

An Executive Committee consisting of the officers of the Association and the representatives from each Counties Association meet as and when required to deal with urgent matters between Council meetings.

A Technical Committee consisting of seven members is elected at the Annual General Meeting to deal with matters of a technical nature—rules, etc.

The Association is affiliated to the International Amateur Wrestling Federation.

The aim of the Association is for the furtherance of Amateur Wrestling as a recreational sport.

WINNERS OF OLYMPIC TITLES (GRECO-ROMAN STYLE)

Flyweight

1948	P. Lombardie	Italy
1952	B. Gourevitch	U.S.S.R.
1956	N. Soloviev	U.S.S.R.

Bantamweight

1924	E. Putsep	Estonia
1928	K. Leucht	Germany
1932	J. Brendel	Germany
1936	M. Lorinez	Hungary
1948	K. Pettersen	Sweden
1952	I. Hodos	Hungary
1956	K. Vyroupaev	U.S.S.R.

Featherweight

1912	K. Koskela	Finland
1920	O. Friman	Finland
1924	K. Antila	Finland
1928	W. Vali	Estonia
1932	G. Gozzie	Italy
1936	Y. Erkan	Turkey
1948	M. Oktav	Turkey
1952	J. Pounkine	U.S.S.R.
1956	R. A. Makinen	Finland

Lightweight

1908	E. Porro	Italy
1912	E. Ware	Finland
1920	E. Ware	Finland
1924	O. Friman	Finland
1928	L. Keresztes	Hungary
1932	E. Malmberg	Sweden
1936	L. Koskila	Finland
1948	K. Freij	Sweden
1952	C. Saffine	U.S.S.R.
1956	K. E. Lehtonen	Finland

Welterweight

1932	I. Johansson	Sweden
1936	R. Svedberg	Sweden
1948	E. G. Andersson	Sweden
1952	M. Szilvasi	Hungary
1956	M. Bayrak	Turkey

Middleweight

1908	F. Martensson	Sweden
1912	C. Johansson	Sweden
1920	C. Westergren	Sweden
1924	E. Westerlund	Finland
1928	V. A. Kokkinen	Finland
1932	V. A. Kokkinen	Finland
1936	I. Johansson	Sweden
1948	R. Gronberg	Sweden
1952	R. Gronberg	Sweden
1956	G. Kartosa	U.S.S.R.

Light Heavyweight

1908	W. Weckman	Finland
1912	A. Ahlgren	Sweden
	J. Bohling	Finland

No decision after nine hours' wrestling

1920	C. Johansson	Sweden
1924	C. O. Westergren	Sweden
1928	I. Moustafa	Egypt
1932	R. Svensson	Sweden
1936	A. Cadier	Sweden
1948	K. Nilsson	Sweden
1952	K. Grondahl	Sweden
1956	V. Nikolaev	U.S.S.R.

Heavyweight

1908	R. Weiss	Germany
1912	Y. Saarela	Finland
1920	A. Lindfors	Finland
1924	H. Deglane	France
1928	J. R. Svensson	Sweden
1932	C. Westergren	Sweden
1936	K. Palusala	Estonia
1948	A. Kirecci	Turkey
1952	I. Kotkas	U.S.S.R.
1956	A. Parfenov	U.S.S.R.

WINNERS OF OLYMPIC TITLES (FREE STYLE)

Flyweight

1948	V. Vitala	Finland
1952	H. Gemici	Turkey
1956	N. Tzalkalamanidze	U.S.S.R.

Bantamweight

1908	G. Mehnert	U.S.A.
1924	K. Pihlajanaki	Finland
1928	K. Makinen	Finland
1932	R. E. Pearce	U.S.A.
1936	O. Zombori	Hungary
1948	N. Akar	Turkey
1952	S. Ishii	Japan
1956	M. Dagistanli	Turkey

Featherweight

1908	G. Dole	U.S.A.
1924	R. Reed	U.S.A.
1928	A. R. Morrison	U.S.A.
1932	H. Pihlajamaki	Finland
1936	K. Pihlajamaki	Finland
1948	G. Bilge	Turkey
1952	B. Sit	Turkey
1956	S. Sasahara	Japan

Lightweight

1908	G. de Relwyskow	G. Britain
1920	K. Antila	Finland
1924	R. Vis	U.S.A.
1928	O. Kapp	Estonia
1932	C. Pacome	France
1936	H. Karpati	Hungary
1948	C. Atik	Turkey
1952	O. Anderberg	Sweden
1956	E. Habibi	Iran

Welterweight

1924	H. Gehri	Switzerland
1928	A. Haavisto	Finland
1932	F. van Bebber	U.S.A.
1936	F. W. Lewis	U.S.A.
1948	Y. Dogu	Turkey
1952	W. Smith	U.S.A.
1956	M. Ikeza	Japan

Middleweight

1908	S. V. Bacon	G. Britain

1920	F. Leino	Finland
1924	F. Haggmann	Switzerland
1928	E. Kyburg	Switzerland
1932	I. Johansson	Sweden
1936	E. Poilve	France
1948	G. Brand	U.S.A.
1952	D. Cimakuridze	U.S.S.R.
1956	N. S. Nikolov	Bulgaria

Light Heavyweight

1920	A. Larsson	Sweden
1924	J. Spellman	U.S.A.
1928	T. Sjosteat	Sweden
1932	P. J. Mehringer	U.S.A.
1936	K. Fredell	Sweden
1948	H. Wittenberg	U.S.A.
1952	B. Palm	Sweden
1956	G. R. Takhti	Iran

Heavyweight

1908	G. C. Okelly	G. Britain
1920	R. Roth	Switzerland
1924	H. Steele	U.S.A.
1928	J. Richtoff	Sweden
1932	J. Richtoff	Sweden
1936	K. Palusalu	Estonia
1948	G. Bobis	Hungary
1952	A. Mekokishvili	U.S.S.R.
1956	H. Kaplan	Turkey

WINNERS OF BRITISH EMPIRE WRESTLING TITLES (FREE STYLE)

Flyweight

1950	A. Harris	Australia
1954	L. Baise	South Africa
1958	I. R. Epton	South Africa

Bantamweight

1930	J. Trifinov	Canada
1934	E. Melrose	Scotland
1938	E. Purcell	Australia
1950	D. Mudgway	New Zealand
1954	G. Jameson	Australia
1958	M. Akhtar	Pakistan

Featherweight

1930	C. Chillcott	Canada
1934	R. McNab	Canada
1938	R. Purchase	Australia
1950	J. C. Armitt	New Zealand
1954	A. Geldenhuys	South Africa
1958	A. Geldenhuys	South Africa

Lightweight

1930	H. Thomas	Canada
1934	R. E. Garrard	Australia
1938	R. E. Garrard	Australia
1950	R. E. Garrard	Australia
1954	G. Pienaar	South Africa
1958	M. Ashraf	Pakistan

Welterweight

1930	R. Priestley	Canada
1934	J. Schlemier	Canada
1938	J. Trevaskis	Australia
1950	H. Hudson	Canada
1954	N. Loubser	South Africa
1958	M. Bashir	Pakistan

Middleweight

1930	M. Chepwick	Canada
1934	T. Evans	Canada
1938	T. Evans	Canada
1950	J. Vachon	Canada
1954	H. van Zyl	South Africa
1958	H. van Zyl	South Africa

Light Heavyweight

1930	L. McIntyre	Canada
1934	W. H. Cubbin	South Africa
1938	E. R. Scarf	Australia
1950	P. Morton	South Africa
1954	J. Theron	South Africa
1958	J. Theron	South Africa

Heavyweight

1930	E. McCready	Canada
1934	J. Knight	Australia
1938	J. Knight	Australia
1950	J. Armstrong	Australia
1954	K. Richmond	England
1958	Lila Ram	India

BRITISH FLYWEIGHT CHAMPIONS

1948	H. Parker	Yorkshire
1949	W. McGuffie	Lancashire
1950	R. Petersen	Denmark
1951	R. Petersen	Denmark
1952	W. Pilling	Yorkshire
1953	W. Pilling	Yorkshire
1954	A. Leyland	Lancashire
1955	A. Leyland	Lancashire
1956	A. Leyland	Lancashire
1957	W. Garrick	Middlesex
1958	P. Christie	Middlesex
1959	J. Bews	Scotland

BRITISH BANTAMWEIGHT CHAMPIONS

1948	R. Cazaux	Yorkshire
1949	K. Irvine	Middlesex
1950	R. Gilderdale	Yorkshire
1951	L. Cheetham	Lancashire
1952	K. Irvine	Middlesex
1953	K. Irvine	Middlesex
1954	W. Parker	Middlesex
1955	V. Benbridge	Buckinghamshire
1956	W. Parker	Middlesex
1957	W. Pilling	Yorkshire
1958	J. Turnbull	Scotland
1959	W. Pilling	Yorkshire

BRITISH FEATHERWEIGHT CHAMPIONS

1948	A. Parsons	Middlesex
1949	R. Cazaux	Yorkshire
1950	R. Cazaux	Yorkshire
1951	R. Cazaux	Yorkshire
1952	H. Hall	Lancashire
1953	H. Hall	Lancashire
1954	H. Hall	Lancashire
1955	H. Hall	Lancashire
1956	H. Hall	Lancashire
1957	H. Hall	Lancashire
1958	A. Aspen	Lancashire
1959	D. Allpress	Middlesex

WRESTLING QUIZ

Can you name the wrestlers who have held the British championships titles the most times in the following weights?

★

1. Bantamweight.

★

2. Featherweight.

★

3. Lightweight.

★

4. Welterweight.

★

5. Middleweight.

★

6. Light-heavyweight.

★

7. Heavyweight.

QUIZ ANSWERS

1. Joe Reid, Lancashire, six times, 1930–35. 2. Herbert Hall, Oldham, six times, 1952–57. 3. Arthur Thompson, Yorkshire, eight times, 1933–40. 4. Don Irvine, London, five times, 1947–50, 1952. 5. Tom Baldwin, London, eight times, 1941–42, 1944–46, 1948, 1951–52. 6. John Sullivan, London, four times, 1945–48. 7. Fred Oberlander, London, eight times, 1939–45, 1948. Ken Richmond, London, nine times, 1949–50, 1952–56, 1958, 1959.

BRITISH LIGHTWEIGHT CHAMPIONS

1948	P. Luck	Essex
1949	J. Vard	Ireland
1950	E. Ostrand	Denmark
1951	J. Vard	Ireland
1952	R. Myland	Hertfordshire
1953	D. Ickringill	Lancashire
1954	T. Zacharek	Gloucestershire
1955	P. Luck	Essex
1956	J. Taylor	Yorkshire
1957	G. McKenzie	Scotland
1958	H. Hall	Lancashire
1959	H. Hall	Lancashire

WRESTLING QUIZ

1. Can you name the British wrestlers who have won a first prize in the Olympic Games?

*

2. Under international rules, if a man is in danger of a fall at the end of six minutes, what should the referee do?

*

3. Can you name five of the illegal holds in amateur wrestling?

QUIZ ANSWERS

1. Lightweight, G. de Relwskow. Middleweight, S. V. Bacon. Heavyweight, G. C. O. Kelly, in 1908. 2. Allow the bout to continue until a fall is obtained or until the dangerous situation has passed, then stop bout for judges' decisions. 3. Strangle or half-strangle. Flying mare with palm uppermost. Toe-hold with a twist. Scissors on head or body. Hammerlock.

BRITISH WELTERWEIGHT CHAMPIONS

1948	D. Irvine	Middlesex
1949	D. Irvine	Middlesex
1950	D. Irvine	Middlesex
1951	R. Myland	Hertfordshire
1952	D. Irvine	Middlesex
1953	G. Farquhar	Scotland
1954	J. Stephens	Middlesex
1955	D. Ickringill	Lancashire
1956	M. Pretorius	Middlesex
1957	J. Feeney	Ireland
1958	J. Feeney	Ireland
1959	J. Feeney	Ireland

BRITISH MIDDLEWEIGHT CHAMPIONS

1948	T. Baldwin	Middlesex
1949	D. Irvine	Middlesex
1950	C. Schadd	Switzerland
1951	T. Baldwin	Middlesex
1952	T. Baldwin	Middlesex
1953	H. Kendall	Middlesex
1954	H. Kendall	Middlesex
1955	G. Farquhar	Scotland
1956	G. Farquhar	Scotland
1957	G. Farquhar	Scotland
1958	R. Myland	Hertfordshire
1959	F. Lee	Warwickshire

BRITISH LIGHT HEAVYWEIGHT CHAMPIONS

1948	J. Sullivan	Middlesex
1949	L. Pidduck	Middlesex
1950	K. Richmond	Middlesex
1951	D. Irvine	Middlesex
1952	I. Bankier	Middlesex
1953	I. Bankier	Middlesex
1954	H. Hall	Lancashire
1955	D. Eichenberger	Switzerland
1956	G. Martina	Ireland
1957	W. Robinson	Lancashire
1958	H. Kendall	Middlesex
1959	H. T. Hall	Lancashire

BRITISH HEAVYWEIGHT CHAMPIONS

1948	F. Overlander	Middlesex
1949	K. Richmond	Middlesex
1950	K. Richmond	Middlesex
1951	L. Pidduck	Middlesex
1952	K. Richmond	Middlesex
1953	K. Richmond	Middlesex
1954	K. Richmond	Middlesex
1955	K. Richmond	Middlesex
1956	K. Richmond	Middlesex
1957	A. Buck	Lancashire
1958	K. Richmond	Middlesex
1959	K. Richmond	Middlesex

WINNERS OF WORLD CHAMPIONSHIP TITLES (FREE STYLE)

Helsinki 1951

Flyweight	A. Yucel	Turkey
Bantamweight	N. Akar	Turkey
Featherweight	N. Zafar	Turkey
Lightweight	O. Anderberg	Sweden
Welterweight	C. Atik	Turkey
Middleweight	H. Zafer	Turkey
Light Heavyweight	Y. Dogu	Turkey
Heavyweight	B. Antonsson	Sweden

Tokio 1954

Flyweight	F. Abas	Turkey
Bantamweight	D. Dagistanly	Turkey
Featherweight	F. Sasakara	Japan
Lightweight	L. Tovfighe	Iran
Welterweight	I. Baldoadze	U.S.S.R.
Middleweight	M. Zandi	Iran
Light Heavyweight	A. Inglas	U.S.S.R.
Heavyweight	A. Mekokishvili	U.S.S.R.

Istanbul 1957

Flyweight	M. Kartel	Turkey
Bantamweight	U. Akbas	Turkey
Featherweight	M. Dagistanly	Turkey
Lightweight	A. Bestaev	U.S.S.R.
Welterweight	B. Wachtany	U.S.S.R.
Middleweight	N. Sorubi	Iran
Light Heavyweight	S. Petkop	Bulgaria
Heavyweight	H. Kaplan	Turkey

WINNERS OF WORLD CHAMPIONSHIP TITLES (GRECO-ROMAN STYLE)

Naples 1953

Flyweight	Gourevitch	U.S.S.R.
Bantamweight	Terjan	U.S.S.R.
Featherweight	Anderberg	Sweden
Lightweight	Freij	Sweden
Welterweight	Chatvorjan	U.S.S.R.
Middleweight	Kartozija	U.S.S.R.
Light Heavyweight	Englas	U.S.S.R.
Heavyweight	Antonnsson	Sweden

Karlsruhe 1955

Flyweight	I. Fraba	Italy
Bantamweight	V. Stachkevitch	U.S.S.R.
Featherweight	J. Polyak	Hungary
Lightweight	G. Gamarnik	U.S.S.R.
Welterweight	V. Maneev	U.S.S.R.
Middleweight	G. Kortosia	U.S.S.R.
Light Heavyweight	V. Nikolnev	U.S.S.R.
Heavyweight	A. Masur	U.S.S.R.

Budapest 1958

Flyweight	B. Gourevitch	U.S.S.R.
Bantamweight	O. Karavaev	U.S.S.R.
Featherweight	I. Polyak	Hungary
Lightweight	R. Dogan	Turkey
Welterweight	K. Aylvaz	Turkey
Middleweight	C. Kartosia	U.S.S.R.
Light Heavyweight	R. Abachidze	U.S.S.R.
Heavyweight	I. Bozdane	U.S.S.R.

WINNERS OF WORLD CUP COMPETITIONS (FREE STYLE)

Istanbul 1956

Flyweight	H. Akbas	Turkey
Bantamweight	M. Dagistanly	Turkey
Featherweight	S. Shoze	Japan
Lightweight	B. Alinberg	U.S.S.R.
Welterweight	I. Zengin	Turkey
Middleweight	I. Atlar	Turkey
Light Heavyweight	A. Atlan	Turkey
Heavyweight	H. Kaplan	Turkey

Holder of Cup	Turkey	Points	44
	U.S.S.R.	,,	31.5
	Bulgaria	,,	25.5
	Iran	,,	18.5
	Japan	,,	18

Eleven nations competed.

Sofia 1958

Flyweight	Sayadov	U.S.S.R.
Bantamweight	U. Akbas	Turkey
Featherweight	Meghouguian	U.S.S.R.
Lightweight	Siniavski	U.S.S.R.
Welterweight	Ogan	Turkey
Middleweight	Gungor	Turkey
Light Heavyweight	Alboul	U.S.S.R.
Heavyweight	Ahmedov	Bulgaria

Holders of Cup	U.S.S.R.	Points	38
	Turkey	,,	34.5
	Bulgaria	,,	30
	Iran	,,	24.5
	Italy	,,	10.5

Eleven nations competed.

The Publishers gratefully acknowledge the generous help of the following individuals and organisations:

Sporting Governing Bodies. All England Netball Association, All England Women's Hockey Association, Amateur Athletic Association, Amateur Basketball Association, Amateur Boxing Association, Amateur Fencing Association, Amateur Gymnastic Association, Amateur Rowing Association, Amateur Swimming Association, Auto Cycle Union, The Badminton Association of England, The Billiards Association and Control Council, The British Amateur Wrestling Association, British Canoe Union, The British Chess Federation, British Empire and Commonwealth Games Federation, The British Horse Society, The British Ice Hockey Association, The British Judo Association, The British Olympic Association, The British Show Jumping Association, British Water Ski Federation, The Croquet Association, English Table Tennis Association, English Bridge Union, The Eton Fives Association, The Football Association, The Football Association of Wales, Gaelic Athletic Association, The Grand National Archery Society, The Hockey Association, Hurlingham Polo Association, The Irish Football Association, The Lawn Tennis Association, Marylebone Cricket Club, National Rifle Association, National Roller Hockey Association, National Skating Association of Great Britain, The National Small-Bore Rifle Association, The Royal Automobile Club, The Royal Yachting Association, Rugby Fives Association, The Ski Club of Great Britain, The Scottish Football Association, The Squash Rackets Association, Tennis and Rackets Association, Women's Amateur Rowing Association, British Crown Grcen Amateur Bowling Association.

Illustrators. *Caricatures:* Spark of the *Evening News. Jacket:* C. Johnstone, W. H. Wiggins. *Colour Badges:* J. Lewsley, Edgar Sears.

Photos. THE SPORT AND GENERAL PRESS AGENCY LTD., ANGLING TIMES, BOXING NEWS, JUDO, THE YACHTSMAN, THE GREYHOUND RACING ASSOCIATION, MARYLEBONE CRICKET CLUB, HYLTON CLEAVER ESQ., THE SCIENCE MUSEUM, AUTOCAR, THE MOTOR, THE ASSOCIATED PRESS LTD., THE CENTRAL PRESS PHOTOS LTD., P.A.–REUTERS PHOTOS LTD., MIRRORPIC, RADIO TIMES PICTURE LIBRARY, FOX PHOTOS LTD., THE TIMES, MONTY, W. W. ROUCH & CO. LTD., KEMSLEY PICTURE SERVICE, BARRATTS PHOTO PRESS, TOPICAL PRESS AGENCY, BRITISH AUTOMOBILE RACING CLUB, WORLD BOWLS, NEWS CHRONICLE, EILEEN RAMSEY, G. BUSHELL AND SON, STEARN AND SONS LTD.

Made and printed in Great Britain by Purnell and Sons Ltd. (Paulton), Somerset and London.

THE BRITISH OLYMPIC
ASSOCIATION

BE&CG

BRITISH EMPIRE
AND COMMONWEALTH GAMES
FEDERATION

AMATEUR
FENCING
ASSOCI-
ATION

THE BRITISH
CANOE UNION

THE
FOOTBALL
ASSOCIATION

AUTO-CYCLE UNION

THE
LAWN
TENNIS
ASSOCI-
ATION

ALL ENGLAND
NETBALL
ASSOCI-
ATION

AENA

AMATEUR ATHLETIC
ASSOCIATION

THE
SKI CLUB
OF GREAT
BRITAIN

BIHA

THE
BILLIARDS ASSOCIATION
& CONTROL COUNCIL

AMATEUR BOXING
ASSOCIATION

EBA

ENGLISH BOWLING
ASSOCIATION

THE SCOTTISH FOOTBALL
ASSOCIATION LIMITED

THE
BRITISH
ICE
HOCKEY
ASSOCIATION

MARYLEBONE
CRICKET CLUB

TENNIS
AND RACKETS
ASSOCIATION

ARA

AMATEUR
ROWING
ASSOCIATION